WHO'S WHO IN SCOTLAND 2002

Who's Who
in
Scotland
2002

Carrick Media

Published by Carrick Media
1/4 Galt House, 31 Bank Street, Irvine KA12 0LL
01294 311322

Copyright 2002 Carrick Media

Printed in England by Bookcraft Limited

British Library Cataloguing-in-Publication Data
A catalogue record for this book is available from the British Library

ISBN 0 946724 50 4

Preface

Welcome to the twelfth edition of Who's Who in Scotland, now firmly established as the dictionary of national biography.

We have compared Who's Who in Scotland to a wee Scottish burgh. Pursuing that metaphor a little further, we seem to be bucking the general trend of declining population. The number of people included in this edition has never been higher: it stands at 4,828.

There are more than 500 new entries. Most are people who have recently been appointed to the sorts of public offices and academic posts that guarantee an invitation to appear in the book. Taking a closer look at these new kids on the block, we discover that only 20% are women. Should Who's Who in Scotland be blamed for this? Sections of the press appear to think so. This is illogical. We cannot be held responsible for the recruitment policies of Scottish institutions. We merely reflect the reality of the situation.

We referred in last year's preface to the establishment of a new national organisation, the Institute of Contemporary Scotland, which came into being largely as a result of the philanthropy of Who's Who in Scotland biographees. We are delighted to report that the Institute is increasingly recognised as an intellectual force in the land – as the *Herald* called it "a thorn in the flesh of all those in charge of dumbing down our society".

Finally, a word of thanks to the 4,800 individuals who have responded to our requests for information, without whose co-operation there would be no book.

The Editor
Irvine, Ayrshire
April 2002

THE DIRECTORY

Alphabetical index to advertisers starts on page 580.

AGRICULTURE AND HORTICULTURE

SAC (THE SCOTTISH AGRICULTURAL COLLEGE)
West Mains Road, Edinburgh EH9 3JG
Tel: 0131 535 4185 Fax: 0131 535 4332
e-mail: j.elder@ed.sac.ac.uk
Contact: Dr Michael Smith, Manager of Research and Development, 0131 535 4074, m.l.smith@ed.sac.ac.uk; Dr David West, Manager of Education and Training, 01292 525356, d.i.west@au.sac.ac.uk; Mr Don Stevenson, Manager Advisory and Consultancy Services, 01292 525121, d.stevenson@au.sac.ac.uk
Working within the broad areas of agriculture, food and environmental science, and rural business management, SAC provides a wide range of teaching and training courses, and research and development, and consultancy services. With its three Centres of Study at Aberdeen, Ayr, and Edinburgh, and 23 local offices, eight veterinary centres and seven research and development farms located throughout Scotland, SAC has a strong Scottish base. However, it draws both its students and its clients from all parts of the UK and overseas.

SCOTTISH AGRICULTURAL SCIENCE AGENCY
82 Craigs Road, East Craigs, Edinburgh EH12 8NJ
Tel: 0131 244 8890 Fax: 0131 244 8940
e-mail: library@sasa.gsi.gov.uk
web: www.sasa.gov.uk
Contact: Dr. R.K.M. Hay, Director, 0131 244 8843; Mrs L. Clark, Librarian, 0131 244 8826, Lynda.Clark@sasa.gsi.gov.uk; S. Cooper, Deputy Director, 0131 244 8932, Simon.Cooper@sasa.gsi.gov.uk
The purpose of SASA is: to provide government with scientific information and advice on agricultural and horticultural crops, and aspects of the environment; to perform statutory and regulatory work in relation to national, European Union (EU) and other international legislation and agreements on plant health, bee health, plant variety registration, crop improvement, genetic resources, the protection of crops, food and the environment; to conduct research and development in support of statutory work undertaken above

SCOTTISH CROP RESEARCH INSTITUTE
Invergowrie, Dundee DD2 5DA
Tel: 01382 562731 Fax: 01382 562426
e-mail: wmacfa@scri.sari.ac.uk
Contact: Professor J.R. Hillman, Director; Mr D. Watt, Secretary; Mr. T.D. Heilbronn, Scientific Liaison Officer.
The Institute is financed principally by the Scottish Executive Environment and Rural Affairs Department and external contracts (c. £13m. per annum). It undertakes research to advance knowledge in the biological sciences, to improve the quality of crops, and to control losses due to pests and diseases with due regard to the environment. It is the lead centre in the UK for research on potatoes and soft fruit, and has major inputs into barley and brassicas, and other temperate, tropical and subtropical crops.

ANIMALS AND WILDLIFE

DEER COMMISSION FOR SCOTLAND
"Knowsley", 82 Fairfield Road, Inverness IV3 5LH
Tel: 01463 231751 Fax: 01463 712931
e-mail: deercom@aol.com
web: www.dcs.gov.uk
Contact: Andrew Raven, Chairman; Nick Reiter, Director; David Balharry, Technical Director.
The Deer Commission for Scotland is the non departmental public body charged with furthering the conservation, control and sustainable management of all species of wild deer in Scotland, and keeping under review all matters, including welfare, relating to deer.

NORTH ATLANTIC SALMON CONSERVATION ORGANIZATION (NASCO)
11 Rutland Square, Edinburgh EH1 2AS
Tel: 0131 228 2551 Fax: 0131 228 4384
e-mail: hq@nasco.int
web: www.nasco.int
Contact: Dr. Malcolm L. Windsor.
NASCO is an international, inter-governmental, treaty organization. It is the only inter-governmental organization with its headquarters in Scotland. NASCO is dedicated to the conservation, restoration, enhancement and rational management of wild Atlantic salmon stocks. NASCO has as its member parties: Canada, Denmark (in respect of the Faroe Islands and Greenland), the European Union, Iceland, Norway, the Russian Federation, and the United States of America. All international negotiations on any aspect of the conservation of wild Atlantic salmon in the North Atlantic area are now organised through Scotland.

PET FOSTERING SERVICE SCOTLAND (PFSS)
PO Box 6, Callander, Perthshire FK17 8ZU
Tel: 01877 331496
Contact: Anne Docherty, Chair, 01877 330996; Pamela Hunter, National Co-ordinator, 01383 730005.
PFSS provides emergency care for the pets of owners in a crisis who cannot make alternative arrangements for their care, and who cannot afford commercial kennel/cattery etc fees. Priority is given to elderly owners. Volunteers care for the pets in their (volunteers') homes until pets can be returned to owners. (NB It is not for holidays, nor re-homing of animals).

SCOTTISH SOCIETY FOR THE PREVENTION OF CRUELTY TO ANIMALS
Company Limited by Guarantee No.: 201401
Scottish Charity No.: SCO06467
Braehead Mains, 603 Queensferry Road, Edinburgh EH4 6EA
Tel: 0131 339 0222 Fax: 0131 339 4777
web: www.scottishspca.org
Contact: Ian Gardiner, Chief Executive; Kathleen Bunyon, Support Services Director.
The Scottish SPCA works to prevent cruelty to animals and to promote kindness and humanity in their treatment, including: (a) the Inspectorate acting to enforce animal welfare legislation, rescue animals in distress and provide advice and guidance to those in charge of animals; (b) Animal Welfare Centres caring for and rehabilitating injured, abused and abandoned pets, farm animals and wildlife; (c) a School education programme and information for the public; (d) campaigns for improved animal welfare legislation and husbandry system.

SCOTTISH WILDLIFE TRUST (SWT)
Cramond House, Kirk Cramond, Cramond Glebe Road, Edinburgh EH4 6NS
Tel: 0131 312 7765 Fax: 0131 312 8705
e-mail: enquiries@swt.org.uk web: www.swt.org.uk
Contact: Steve Sankey, Chief Executive, 0131 312 7765, Ext. 4702, e-mail: enquiries@swt.org.uk
Established in 1964, the Scottish Wildlife Trust is the leading voluntary body protecting all forms of Scottish wildlife and Scotland's natural environment. The SWT owns and manages 126 wildlife reserves, has identified over 3,000 wildlife sites, trains 120 individuals in practical conservation work each year and runs high-profile campaigns on a wide variety of environmental issues. The SWT has a network of offices, staff, conservation teams and local member centres throughout Scotland – details available. Current membership is 20,000.

ARTISTIC AND CULTURAL

BORDERLINE THEATRE COMPANY LTD
North Harbour Street, Ayr KA8 8AA
Tel: 01292 281010 Fax: 01292 263825
e-mail: enquiries@borderlinetheatre.co.uk
web: www.borderlinetheatre.co.uk

Contact: Eddie Jackson, Producer, eddie@borderlinetheatre.co.uk
One of Scotland's leading touring theatre companies, producing exciting, accessible and challenging theatre touring all over Scotland. Company also has an extensive education and outreach programme of work in schools, with youth groups, adult groups and audiences.

BRITISH COUNCIL SCOTLAND
The Tun (3rd Floor), 4 Jackson's Entry, Holyrood Road, Edinburgh EH8 8PJ
Tel: 0131 524 5700 Fax: 0131 524 5701
web: www.britishcouncil.org/scotland
The British Council connects people worldwide with learning opportunities and creative ideas from the UK and builds lasting relationships between the UK and other countries. It has offices in 109 countries and 7,300 staff worldwide. The British Council enhances Scotland's international reputation and contributes to an international, outward-looking Scotland. It offers its partners in Scotland a gateway to its global networks, and provides its audiences worldwide with a window on Scotland.

BT SCOTTISH ENSEMBLE
Centre for Contemporary Arts, 350 Sauchiehall Street, Glasgow G2 3JD
Tel: 0141 332 4747 Fax: 0141 332 3555
e-mail: office@btscottishensemble.co.uk
web: www.btscottishensemble.co.uk
Contact: Heather Duncan, General Manager, heather.duncan@btscottishensemble.co.uk; Freya Mitchell, Events Manager, freya.mitchell@btscottishensemble.co.uk; Claire Durham, Marketing Manager, claire.durham@btscottishensemble.co.uk
A dynamic group of 12 string players directed from the violin by its outstanding Artistic Director, Clio Gould. Originally formed in 1969 as the Scottish Baroque Ensemble by violinist Leonard Friedman, it boasts an extensive repertoire spanning from the Baroque to the present day. New commissions and world-class soloists feature regularly at some 75 concerts and BBC recordings each year. Offers a diverse education programme including workshops and children's concerts.

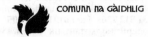

ROYAL FINE ART COMMISSION FOR SCOTLAND
Bakehouse Close, 146 Canongate, Edinburgh EH8 8DD
Tel: 0131 556 6699 Fax: 0131 556 6633
e-mail: plan@RoyfinartcomforSco.gov.uk
web: www.RoyfinartcomforSco.gov.uk

Contact: Charles Prosser, Secretary.
The Commission, established in 1927, advises government on the visual impact and quality of design of construction projects. It reports its views to the Scottish Executive and local authorities and may recommend that planning applications be called in by Scottish Ministers for determination. It publicises its work in various ways including exhibitions and publications. Although the government finances it, the Commission remains totally independent and gives its opinions impartially.

ROYAL LYCEUM THEATRE COMPANY
30b Grindlay Street, Edinburgh EH3 9AX
Tel: 0131 248 4800 Fax: 0131 228 3955
Contact: Dr Michael Shea, Chairman; Mr Kenny Ireland, Chief Executive and Artistic Director; Ms Sadie McKinlay, Administration Director.
Established in 1965, the Royal Lyceum Theatre has a reputation for excellence in classical and contemporary work. We are Scotland's leading and most successful producing drama company, committed to developing our theatrical talents while presenting the best of international drama. We: attract a wide audience; tour at home and abroad; have a vibrant youth theatre and education programme; implement innovative access policies with signed and audio described performances; and are a key part of the community.

THE ROYAL SCOTTISH ACADEMY
17 Waterloo Place, Edinburgh EH1 3BG
Tel: 0131 558 7097 Fax: 0131 557 6417
web: www.royalscottishacademy.org
Contact: Dr. Ian McKenzie Smith, OBE, PRSA, PPRSW, FRSA, LLD, President, 0131 558 7097; Bruce Laidlaw, Administrative Secretary, 0131 558 7097; Wendy Jones, Public Relations Officer, 0131 552 8789.
The aim of the Royal Scottish Academy – a body of 39 Academicians and 46 Associates founded in 1826 – is to present Scotland's rich variety of art, through its Annual Exhibition featuring works by members and non-members. The RSA also gives financial and material encouragement to young artists, through the unique Students' Art Exhibition and the valued Kinross and Salvesen Scholarships. For dates and venues contact 0131 558 7097.

ROYAL SCOTTISH NATIONAL ORCHESTRA
73 Claremont Street, Glasgow G3 7JB
Tel: 0141 226 3868 Fax: 0141 221 4317
e-mail: admin@rsno.org.uk

R S N O
ROYAL SCOTTISH
NATIONAL ORCHESTRA

Contact: Simon Crookall, Chief Executive; James Miller, CBE, Chairman; Alexander Lazarev, Principal Conductor.
The Royal Scottish National Orchestra is Scotland's national symphony orchestra performing a wide range of world-class standard music, supported by innovative community and education work, throughout Scotland and beyond.

Scottish **Book** Trust

SCOTTISH BOOK TRUST
137 Dundee Street, Edinburgh EH11 1BG
Tel: 0131 229 3663 Fax: 0131 228 4293
e-mail: info@scottishbooktrust.com
web: www.scottishbooktrust.com

SBT promotes a love of reading and a knowledge of books, writers and writing to people of all ages and backgrounds throughout Scotland. It has a particularly strong reputation for its work in children's books and reading, including the Scottish Friendly-sponsored mobile project, Words on Wheels. It also publishes a wide range of resources, undertakes training and administers the Scottish Arts Council-funded Writers in Scotland Scheme.

web: www.spl.org.uk
Contact: Robyn Marsack, Director; Iain Young, Librarian.
A free reference and lending library for Scotland's poetry in its three languages throughout the centuries and up-to-date, and for British and international poetry. Stock includes books, audio and video tapes, CDs, magazines and newscuttings. Children's collection and Young People's service. Online computer catalogue, INSPIRE. Lending is free to the public; also by post, and from travelling van and branches. The Library has charitable status: membership £20 (organisations £30) for reading room, newsletter and to support the work.

THE SCOTTISH TARTANS SOCIETY
The Scottish Tartans Museum, The Institute Hall, 138 Mid Street, Keith, Banffshire
Tel: 01542 888419 Fax: 01542 886900
e-mail: stsmuseum@plus.net
Museum Liaison Officer: Mrs Linda J. Gorn; Honorary Secretary: Mr Robert McBain.
An Incorporation Noble in the Noblesse of Scotland Inaugurated on 13th May 1963 by Sir Thomas Innes of Learney, GCVO, Lord Lyon King of Arms 1945–1969. The Scottish Tartans Society is a long established worldwide authority on Scottish tartans and dress. The Society maintains two museums, one in Keith (Mid Street) and one in Franklin, North Carolina, USA, comprising unique collections of tartan and tartan-related artefacts. The Society has an extensive library and artefacts and provides advice and information on all tartan-related subjects including clans and families. The Society also publishes the journal, *Tartans*. Membership is welcome by application to: The Membership Secretary, c/o The Scottish Tartans Museum, The Institute Hall, 138 Mid Street, Keith, Banffshire.

SOCIETY OF ANTIQUARIES OF SCOTLAND
Royal Museum, Chambers Street, Edinburgh EH1 1JF
Tel: 0131 247 4115/4133 Fax: 0131 247 4163
e-mail: f.ashmore@nms.ac.uk
Contact: Fionna Ashmore, Director.
The Society, founded in 1780, is the second oldest antiquarian society in Britain; an active body, it organises lectures, conferences, seminars and excursions, publishes an annual *Proceedings*, a twice-yearly Newsletter and a Monograph series. It plays an important role in the cultural life and heritage of Scotland, sponsoring all aspects of archaeological and historical research. Drawing on its wide range of available expertise, it provides an impartial and independent voice on heritage matters and is represented on many committees and councils.

THEATRE ROYAL, GLASGOW
Hope Street, Glasgow
Tel: 0141 332 3321
web: www.theatreroyalglasgow.com
Contact: Martin Ritchie, Theatre Manager.
One of Glasgow's premier lyric theatres, the Theatre Royal is owned by Scottish Opera and is managed by the company. The Theatre Royal stages world-class opera, is the Glasgow base for Scottish Ballet, and presents international drama, dance and children's shows.

TOSG THEATRE COMPANY
Sabhal Mor Ostaig, Sleat, Isle of Skye IV44 8RQ
Tel: 01471 888542 Fax: 01471 888541
e-mail: adminstrator@tosg.org
web: www.tosg.org
Contact: Simon Mackenzie, Director; Janet Ward, Administrator.
Scotland's only professional Gaelic theatre company. Mainly touring productions, with an emphasis on new writing. The company has a support and advice system for new Gaelic writers.

BUSINESS

BARR HOLDINGS LIMITED
Heathfield, Ayr KA8 9SL
Tel: 01292 281311 Fax: 01292 618678
Contact: W.J. Barr, OBE, CEng, FICE, FCIOB, FIMgt, Executive Chairman.
Construction, development, steelwork, quarries, homes, precast concrete, ready mix concrete, ports, joinery, cranes, waste management, facilities management, plant and transport.

FEDERATION OF SMALL BUSINESSES
74 Berkeley Street, Glasgow G3 7DS
Tel: 0141 221 0775 Fax: 0141 221 5954
e-mail: scotland.policy@fsb.org.uk
web: www.fsb.org.uk
Contact: Jim Torrance, Scottish Policy Convenor; John Downie, Scottish Parliamentary Officer.
A non-party political campaigning pressure group which exists to promote and protect the interests of all who are either self employed or who run their own businesses; the Federation is funded by members' subscriptions. Formed in 1974, it is the UK's largest business organisation with 120,000 members (12,500 in Scotland) in over 300 branches in Britain, and has strong links with organisations representing 31 million businesses throughout the European community.

GREATER GLASGOW AND CLYDE VALLEY TOURIST BOARD
11 George Square, Glasgow G2 1DY
Tel: 0141 204 4480 Fax: 0141 204 4772
e-mail: corporate@seeglasgow.com
web: www.seeglasgow.com
Contact: Professor Eddie Friel, Chief Executive, eddie.friel@seeglasgow.com; Scott Taylor, Director, Marketing, scott.taylor@seeglasgow.com; Ms Moira Dyer, Manager, Public Relations, moira.dyer@seeglasgow.com
The official destination marketing organisation of the Greater Glasgow and Clyde Valley area. The primary function is to increase the number of leisure tourists and convention delegates to the area and provide quality visitor servicing through a network of Tourist Information Centres that are linked to the national network operated by the 14 Area Tourist Boards. Our Ambassador programme is designed to provide support to local people in membership of national and international associations in attracting conferences to the destination.

SCOTTISH BUSINESS IN THE COMMUNITY
PO Box 408, Bankhead Avenue, Edinburgh EH11 4HE
Tel: 0131 442 2020 Fax: 0131 442 3555
e-mail: info@sbcscot.com
web: www.sbcscot.com

Contact: Samantha Barber, Chief Executive; George Borthwick, CBE, Chairman.
SBC's aim is to promote corporate social responsibility and involve businesses in supporting the economic and social regeneration of communities across Scotland. This is achieved through: Business Support Groups – channelling private sector support through community focused business groupings; Professional Firms Network – administering a pool of pro bono services offered by participating companies; Development Assignment Programme – arranging employee secondments into community initiatives; Partners in Leadership – linking senior managers with head teachers for mutual exchange of management and leadership skills; Senior Executive Programme – co-ordinating the provision of in-kind professional support by retired managers.

THE SCOTTISH CHAMBERS OF COMMERCE
12 Broughton Place, Edinburgh EH1 3RX
Tel: 0131 557 9500 Fax: 0131 558 3257
e-mail: mail@scottishchambers.org.uk
web: www.scottishchambers.org.uk
Contact: Mr Lex Gold, CBE, Director.
The Scottish Chambers of Commerce (SCC) is the most extensive business support organisation in Scotland. Collectively the member Chambers employ over 170 executive staff, have a turnover of about £7.3m., and have over 9,000 member companies who, in turn, employ more than 50 per cent of the Scottish workforce. SCC co-ordinates member Chamber activities at national and international level. It encourages development of Chamber services such as Export Support and Training and Education. It is the authentic national voice of the business community and plays a major role in influencing Government policy and decisions at all levels.

CHARITABLE AND VOLUNTARY

AGE CONCERN SCOTLAND
Leonard Small House, 113 Rose Street, Edinburgh EH2 3DT
Tel: 0131 220 3345 Fax: 0131 220 2779
e-mail: enquiries@acscot.org.uk
web: www.ageconcernscotland.org.uk

Contact: Mrs Betty Bridgeford, Chairman; Maureen O'Neill, Director, 0131 625 9317; Jess Barrow, Head of Policy and Public Affairs, 0131 625 9327.
Age Concern Scotland is a national voluntary organisation with the primary aim of improving the quality of life for older people in Scotland. Age Concern Scotland is committed to working throughout Scotland to ensure that all older people have their rights upheld, their voices heard and have choice and control over all aspects of their lives. We provide a comprehensive information service on all issues affecting older people. Age Concern Scotland has over 250 local groups in membership, who provide practical services including day care, lunch clubs and information and advice as well as social activities.

ALZHEIMER SCOTLAND – ACTION ON DEMENTIA
22 Drumsheugh Gardens, Edinburgh EH3 7RN
Tel: 0131 243 1453 Fax: 0131 243 1450
e-mail: alzscot@alzscot.org

Contact: James H. Jackson, OBE, Chief Executive; Paul Mooney, Quality and Service Development Director; Jan Killeen, Public Policy Director; Stephen Balmer, Finance Director.
Alzheimer Scotland
Action on Dementia
A membership organisation which represents the interests of people with dementia and their carers to policy makers. Provides direct services, including carer support/education, 24-hour freephone helpline – 0808 808 3000 – and information service. Other activities: conferences, publications, campaigns, research, fundraising, public awareness.

APEX SCOTLAND
9 Great Stuart Street, Edinburgh EH3 7TP
Tel: 0131 220 0130 Fax: 0131 220 6796
e-mail: admin@apexscotland.org.uk
web: www.apexscotland.org.uk
Contact: Bernadette Monaghan, Director; Philip Dunion, Depute Director; Aidan McCorry, Depute Director.
By addressing the employability needs of offenders, ex-offenders and young people at risk, Apex Scotland will improve the employment prospects of clients, therefore reducing offending and contributing to safer communities.

web: www.rnli.org.uk
Registered Charity No. 209603.
Contact: Mrs Maren Caldwell, LLB, MICFM, National Organiser, Scotland; Mr John Caldwell, Inspector of Lifeboats, Scotland
The RNLI is a voluntary organisation that relies entirely on public donations. It exists solely to save lives at sea. The RNLI has given a commitment to the British and Irish governments to provide cover to 50 miles offshore; this is achieved with a modern fleet of 311 fast lifeboats. The crews are all highly trained local volunteers, who will turn out 24 hours a day, 365 days a year – no matter what the weather! Some 50 lifeboats are based in Scotland which on average launch over 900 times annually and save 100 lives.

ROYAL SCOTTISH AGRICULTURAL BENEVOLENT INSTITUTION
Ingliston, Edinburgh EH28 8NB
Tel: 0131 333 1023 Fax: 0131 333 1027
e-mail: rsabi@rsabi.org.uk
web: www.rsabi.org.uk
Contact: Ian Purves-Hume, Director; Elizabeth Brash, Welfare Secretary.
Exists to provide financial and in-kind help, welfare advice and support to any person in difficulty who is or has been in farming, forestry, horticulture, fish farming, and rural estate work in Scotland, and their dependants. Supported entirely by voluntary donation. Enquiries in complete confidence to the above address by FREEPOST, telephone, fax or e-mail.

THE ROYAL SOCIETY FOR THE RELIEF OF INDIGENT GENTLEWOMEN OF SCOTLAND
14 Rutland Square, Edinburgh EH1 2BD
Tel: 0131 229 2308 Fax: 0131 229 0956
Contact: Mr W.F. MacTaggart, Chairman; Mr George F. Goddard, Secretary and Cashier; Miss Mabel M. Douglas, Caseworker.
The Society originated in 1847 to assist ladies of Scottish birth or education with professional or business backgrounds who exist on low incomes with limited capital. Applications are considered from spinsters, widows and divorcees aged 50 and over, who qualify by birth or education and are daughters or widows of professional or business men. Ladies who have attained this status by their own endeavours or were prevented from doing so by devoting their lives to the care of relatives are also considered. The Society makes a regular charitable grant to ladies admitted to the roll and other grants are made for specific needs. Regular visiting and counselling is undertaken by the Society's caseworkers and representatives.

ST. ANDREW'S AMBULANCE ASSOCIATION
48 Milton Street, Glasgow G4 0HR
Tel: 0141 332 4031 Fax: 0141 332 6582
e-mail: firstaid@staaa.demon.co.uk
web: www.firstaid.org.uk
Contact: Mr Brendan Healy, Chief Executive; Mrs Christine Cuthbertson, Marketing and Fundraising Manager.
St. Andrew's Ambulance Association, a Scottish registered charity, was established in 1881. Every year we teach over 20,000 people vital lifesaving skills. Over 2,000 voluntary members of St. Andrew's Ambulance Corps give their personal time to help others by providing First Aid cover at public events throughout Scotland. The Association is committed to making Scotland a safer place to live by ensuring as many people as possible receive first aid training.

THE SCOTTISH GENEALOGY SOCIETY
Library and Family History Centre, 15 Victoria Terrace, Edinburgh EH1 2JL
Tel: 0131 220 3677 Fax: 0131 220 3677
e-mail: info@scotsgenealogy.com
web: www.scotsgenealogy.com
Contact: Dr. J. Cranstoun, Honorary Librarian; Miss J.P.S. Ferguson, Honorary Secretary; Sales Secretary.
The aims are to promote research into Scottish family history and to collect, exchange and publish material relating to genealogy, but the Society does not engage in professional research. *The Scottish Genealogist* is published quarterly and lectures are held monthly from September until April. The library holds books, periodicals, microfilm and microfiche. Publications include transcriptions of gravestones which are a valuable adjunct to pre-1855 records.

SCOTTISH NATIONAL WAR MEMORIAL
The Castle, Edinburgh EH1 2YT
Tel: 0131 226 7393 Fax: 0131 225 8920
Contact: Lieutenant Colonel I. Shepherd, Secretary to the Trustees; Mrs Janey Whitson, Administrative Assistant.
Maintains and amends the Rolls of Honour of Scots who fell in the two World Wars and Campaigns after 1945. Administers the memorial building in Edinburgh Castle.

SENSE SCOTLAND
5th Floor, 45 Finnieston Street, Glasgow G3 8JU
Tel: 0141 564 2444 Fax: 0141 564 2443
e-mail: info@sensescotland.org.uk
web: www.sensescotland.org.uk
Sense Scotland works with deafblind and multi-sensory impaired children, adults and their families. We provide a range of services including support to families and carers, respite support for children and adults, community living and day support, holidays, health support and a wide variety of art activities. Sense Scotland also works with other voluntary organisations to influence and inform policy at Scottish Executive and local authority level.

STRESSWATCH SCOTLAND
23 Campbell Street, Kilmarnock KA1 4HL
Tel: 01563 570886 Fax: 01563 570886
e-mail: office@stresswatchscotland.com
web: www.stresswatchscotland.com
Contact: Margaret Macbrayne, National Co-ordinator, 01369 701362; Rosalina Rowan, Chairperson; Annette Smith, Administrator, 01563 570886, office@stresswatchscotland.com
Aims: to provide support, information and advice to those who suffer from stress, anxiety, phobias and panic attacks; to guide, encourage and assist volunteers to set up local self-help groups in Scotland; to promote a better understanding and to encourage further research into anxiety, phobias and panic. Stresswatch Scotland has self help groups throughout Scotland, telephone recovery programme and telephone helpline (01563 574144). A range of reasonably priced cassettes, booklets and leaflets is available by post.

TURNING POINT SCOTLAND
54 Govan Road, Glasgow G51 1JL
Tel: 0141 427 8200 Fax: 0141 427 8201
e-mail: info@turningpointscotland.com
web: www.turningpointscotland.com

Contact: Netta Maciver, OBE, Chief Executive; Kenny Crawford, Finance and Systems Manager; Ken Blackie, Fundraising Co-ordinator.

Turning Point Scotland is a charity registered in Scotland. It tackles social exclusion by developing customised community care packages for people with problems arising from their mental health, drug or alcohol misuse or their learning disability.We manage 23 projects throughout Scotland with a further three in development. Our aim is to provide a quality service that is flexible and which meets the varying needs of everyone who uses our services.

VOLUNTEER DEVELOPMENT SCOTLAND
Stirling Enterprise Park, Springbank Road, Stirling FK7 7RP
Tel: 01786 479593 Fax: 01786 449285
e-mail: vds@vds.org.uk
web: www.vds.org.uk
Contact: Shirley Bwye, Information Officer, shirley.bwye@vds.org.uk
Volunteer Development Scotland is Scotland's national centre for volunteering and community involvement. We are committed to extending the range and effectiveness of voluntary work by giving volunteering a voice, promoting good practice and developing new initiatives. We work across all sectors and through national and local networks. Our services include the provision of specialist training, information, advice on policy development, consultancy, publications and development projects with specific groups such as volunteering in the health service, employer-supported volunteering and black and ethnic minority volunteering. The Active Communities Development Unit has recently been established within VDS. web: www.vds.org.uk

CHILDREN

CHILDREN IN SCOTLAND
Princes House, 5 Shandwick Place, Edinburgh EH2 4RG
Tel: 0131 228 8484 Fax: 0131 228 8585
e-mail: info@childreninscotland.org.uk
Contact: Dr Bronwen Cohen, Chief Executive.
Children in Scotland is an independent agency representing over 300 voluntary, statutory and professional organisations and individuals. It works with its members to identify and promote the interests of children and their families. Its activities include information, training, policy, practice development and research, and it produces a monthly subscription magazine. Specific development areas include early years (including rural childcare), disability/special needs, HIV/AIDS and parenting. Based within Children in Scotland are two specialist groups: Enquire (0131 222 2400), the independent information service on special educational needs; and The Scottish Parenting Forum, which provides information, advice and research to parents and those working with parents. Web: http://www.childreninscotland.org.uk

ST. ANDREW'S CHILDREN'S SOCIETY
Gillis Centre, 113 Whitehouse Loan, Edinburgh EH9 1BB
Tel: 0131 452 8248 Fax: 0131 452 8248
e-mail: info@standrews-children.org.uk
Contact: Stephen Small, Director, ssmall@standrews-children.org.uk; Claire McMahon, Administrator, cmcmahon@standrews-children.org.uk; Maureen McEvoy, Chairperson.
Has been in existence since 1922. Offers support, advice and assistance to pregnant women considering adoption for their children. We now offer adoption and foster care to children from 0-18 years as well as a counselling service to adopted adults and birth family members.

SAVE THE CHILDREN
7th floor, Haymarket House, 8 Clifton Terrace, Edinburgh EH12 5DR
Tel: 0131 527 8200 Fax: 0131 527 8201
e-mail: scotland@scfuk.org.uk
Contact: Alison Davies, OBE, Programme Director; Mary Cresswell, Corporate Fundraising Executive; Joyce Sperber, Information Officer.
Save The Children's work in Scotland, based on the UN Convention on the Rights of the Child, has three interconnected aims: building a movement for children's rights in Scotland; promoting the interests of the most marginalised children; developing the role of children and young people as community activists in their own communities. By encouraging children and young people to express their views, to take part in research, development and running of initiatives to address issues that concern them, we aim to give children and young people in Scotland the chance to take part in society, to contribute and grow.

SCOTTISH CHILD LAW CENTRE
54 East Crosscauseway, Edinburgh EH8 9HD
Tel: 0131 667 6333 Fax: 0131 662 1713
web: www.sclc.org.uk
Contact: Alison Cleland, Convenor, a.cleland@napier.ac.uk; Katy Macfarlane, 0131 667 6333.
Exist to promote knowledge and the use of children's rights and welfare for the benefit of under 18s in Scotland. Free telephone helpline for under 18s: 0800 3288970.

CONSERVATION

THE ARCHITECTURAL HERITAGE SOCIETY OF SCOTLAND
The Glasite Meeting House, 33 Barony Street, Edinburgh EH3 6NX
Tel: 0131 557 0019 Fax: 0131 557 0049
e-mail: administrator@ahss.org.uk
web: www.ahss.org.uk
Contact: Dr Seán O'Reilly, Director; Mrs Pauline Robinson, Administrator.
The AHSS, Scotland's national amenity body dedicated to the study and protection of historic buildings and places, has a network of panels that monitor planning applications. Benefits of membership include the society's publications, illustrated talks and lectures on architecture, day trips and weekend tours. Each year there is a conference and study tour and regular smaller local conferences and seminars.

EDINBURGH WORLD HERITAGE TRUST
5 Charlotte Square, Edinburgh EH2 4DR
Tel: 0131 220 7720 Fax: 0131 220 7730
e-mail: info@ewht.org.uk
web: www.ewht.org.uk
Contact: Richard Griffith, MA(Cantab), Dip Arch(Cantab), RIAS, Director.
Established 1 April 1999 (replacing the Edinburgh New Town Conservation Committee, est. 1970, and the Edinburgh Old Town Renewal Trust, est. 1985). Funded by Scottish Executive (Historic Scotland) and City of Edinburgh Council. Main functions: to award grants for appropriate external repairs, advise central and local government as a formal consultee on major policy and development issues, and monitor and promote the World Heritage Site. Board representation: City of Edinburgh Council; Historic Buildings Council for Scotland; Scottish Civic Trust; Cockburn Association; Architectural Heritage Society of Scotland; local residents and business interests.

of trees and woodlands for the benefit of all. By publishing the journal *Scottish Forestry*, the Society seeks to disseminate original research and technical innovation that will enhance the creation of diverse woodlands, their multipurpose management and the wide enjoyment of the woodland environment by all. The Society also seeks to encourage the use of wood in new and innovative ways.

THE SCOTTISH CIVIC TRUST
The Tobacco Merchants House, 42 Miller Street, Glasgow G1 1DT
Tel: 0141 221 1466 Fax: 0141 248 6952
e-mail: sct@scotnet.co.uk
web: www.scotnet.co.uk/sct
Contact: John N.P. Ford, Director; Terrence Levinthal, Technical Director; Jane M. Nelson, Buildings at Risk.
The Scottish Civic Trust is a national charity concerned with improving the quality of Scotland's built environment. It encourages high quality in planning, the conservation and, where necessary, adaptation for re-use of older buildings of distinction or historic interest. It publishes, on behalf of Historic Scotland, *The Buildings at Risk Bulletin*, illustrating a wide variety of all kinds of buildings in need of rescue and re-use. It co-ordinates Doors Open Day in September, when interesting buildings not normally open, give free access to the public. The Trust is the umbrella organisation for local civic and amenity groups.

SCOTTISH ENVIRONMENT PROTECTION AGENCY
Erskine Court, Castle Business Park, Stirling FK9 4TR
Tel: 01786 457700 Fax: 01786 446885
e-mail info@ sepa.org.uk
web: www.sepa.org.uk
Contact: Ken Collins, Chairman, 01786 457700; M. Patricia Henton, Chief Executive, 01786 457700; Monica Straughan, Public Relations Manager, 01786 457723.
The Scottish Environment Protection Agency (SEPA) has a wide range of environmental protection responsibilities covering discharges to the aquatic environment, emissions to air, the regulation of waste management and the control of radioactive substances. In addition to specific statutory powers to issue, monitor and enforce environmental licences, SEPA has more general duties to protect and improve Scotland's environment.

ECONOMIC DEVELOPMENT AND PLANNING

THE PLANNING EXCHANGE
Tontine House, 8 Gordon Street, Glasgow G1 3PL
Tel: 0141 248 8541 Fax: 0141 248 8277
e-mail: info@planex.co.uk
Contact: Tony Burton, OBE, Managing Director, tony.burton@planex.co.uk; Connie Young, Marketing and Membership Director, connie.young@planex.co.uk; Christine Johnston, Head of Information Service, christine.johnston@planex.co.uk
The Planning Exchange provides an information service on all aspects of local development including economic development, planning, housing, social services, education, skills and training, transport and infrastructure. A weekly current awareness service is included as well as telephone and electronic access to the database. Local and central government, government agencies, consultants, regeneration partnerships and private firms throughout the UK use the service. It also produces a number of publications and organises training and other events. Full details are on the web site at www.planex.co.uk

SCOTTISH ENTERPRISE
150 Broomielaw, Atlantic Quay, Glasgow G2 8LU
Tel: 0141 248 2700 Fax: 0141 221 3217
e-mail: network.helpline@scotent.co.uk
web: www.scottish-enterprise.com

Scottish Enterprise
Network

Chairman: Sir Ian Robinson; Chief Executive; Dr Robert M. Crawford.
Scottish Enterprise is the main economic development agency for Scotland covering 93 per cent of the population from Grampian to the Borders. The Scottish Enterprise Network consists of Scottish Enterprise and 12 local enterprise companies. Working in partnership with the private and public sectors, the Network aims to build more and better businesses, to develop the skills and knowledge of Scottish people, and to encourage innovation to make Scottish business internationally competitive. The agency was set up in 1991 under the Enterprise and New Towns Scotland Act and reports to the Scottish Executive. To find out more information please visit the Scottish Enterprise website at www.scottish-enterprise.com or call our network helpline on 0845 6078787.

SCOTTISH ENTERPRISE EDINBURGH AND LOTHIAN
Apex House, 99 Haymarket Terrace, Edinburgh EH12 5HD
Tel: 0131 313 4000 Fax: 0131 313 4231
Contact: David Crichton, Chief Executive; Professor John Archer, Chairman.
Scottish Enterprise Edinburgh and Lothian is the local enterprise company serving Edinburgh and Lothian. Across a range of activities, Scottish Enterprise Edinburgh and Lothian contributes to the economic well-being of the whole community and focuses on growing existing and new businesses, attracting new investment, improving skills and developing a modern infrastructure and environment.

SCOTTISH ENTERPRISE GLASGOW
Atrium Court, 50 Waterloo Street, Glasgow G2 6HQ
Tel: 0141 204 1111 Fax: 0141 248 1600
Contact: Tom O'Neill, Chairman; Ron Culley, Chief Executive; Gordon Kennedy, Deputy Chief Executive.
Glasgow is the largest city in Scotland in terms of population, jobs, companies and investment. Its sphere of influence affects almost half of the Scottish population. Within the Scottish Enterprise network, Scottish Enterprise Glasgow's task of delivering economic development in Glasgow is unique, since it is the only Local Enterprise Company to serve an exclusively city area. Glasgow's urban context and scale presents a special set of challenges and problems, as well as genuine advantages and opportunities.

SCOTTISH ENTERPRISE LANARKSHIRE
New Lanarkshire House, Strathclyde Business Park, Bellshill ML4 3AD
Tel: 01698 745454 Fax: 01698 842211
e-mail: selenquiry@scotent.co.uk
web: www.scottish-enterprise.com/lanarkshire
Contact: David Ennis, OBE, Chairman.
Scottish Enterprise Lanarkshire is part of the Scottish Enterprise Network and is the principal economic development body in Lanarkshire. Working with a range of partners, SE Lanarkshire is active in areas such as e-commerce, local company development, new business creation, exporting, product development, inward investment, social inclusion and property development. SE Lanarkshire is also part of a Lanarkshire network of local public bodies which is committed to "Changing Gear", a 10-year economic strategy which provides a framework for building a dynamic, healthier and more prosperous Lanarkshire.

EDUCATION
(see also SCHOOLS)

ASSOCIATION OF SCOTTISH COLLEGES
Argyll Court, The Castle Business Park, Stirling FK9 4TY
Tel: 01786 892100 Fax: 01786 892109
e-mail: enquiries@ascol.org.uk
Contact: Tom Kelly, Chief Executive; Jane Polglase, Policy Manager.
The Association of Scottish Colleges (ASC) represents Further Education colleges throughout Scotland. ASC is the policy and representative voice for the work of Scottish FE and fulfils this role by: informing and advising Government and senior politicians about the work of FE and responding to government consultations; making sure that the FE sector is involved in policy and decision making in Scotland; consulting with members on key policy issues and developing a sense of collective purpose.

CARDONALD COLLEGE
690 Mosspark Drive, Glasgow G52 3AY
Tel: 0141 272 3333 Fax: 0141 272 3444
e-mail: enquiries@cardonald.ac.uk
web: www.cardonald.ac.uk
Contact: Ros Micklem, Principal, 0141 272 3201; Eleanor Harris, Depute Principal, 0141 272 3240; David Baillie, Secretary to Board of Management, 0141 272 3208.
The College's mission is "to meet the aspirations of each student or client by providing a valuable and enjoyable learning experience". It provides a wide variety of courses at both non-advanced and advanced levels in a range of disciplines, from holistic therapies to electronic engineering. There is increasing emphasis on community outreach and open learning. Most subjects are available on a full-time or part-time basis and a business development unit keeps the College close to market realities.

CENTRE FOR EDUCATION FOR RACIAL EQUALITY IN SCOTLAND
Room 2.5, Charteris Building, Faculty of Education, University of
Edinburgh, Holyrood Road, Edinburgh EH8 8AQ
Tel: 0131 651 6371 Fax: 0131 651 6511
e-mail: ceres@ed.ac.uk
Contact: Rowena Arshad, OBE, Director, 0131 651 6371, rowena.arshad@ed.ac.uk; Edna Sommerville, Senior Adminstrator, 0131 651 6371, edna.sommerville@ed.ac.uk; Rana Syed, Research/Information Officer, 0131 651 6371, rana.syed@ed.ac.uk
CERES is a Scottish Executive funded initiative. Its main aim is the promotion of multicultural and anti-racist education in Scottish education. It provides consultancy and public development advice for mainstreaming racial equality into institutional processes and curricular development. It houses one of the most extensive libraries on academic multicultural publications which can be accessed by people interested in race equality and education issues. CERES also runs national and regional conferences and seminars, engages in research and works directly with parents who are interested in racial equality issues. web: http://dns1.mhie.ac.uk/~ceres/

COMMUNITY LEARNING SCOTLAND
Rosebery House, 9 Haymarket Terrace, Edinburgh EH12 5EZ
Tel: 0131 313 2488 Fax: 0131 313 6800
e-mail: info@cls.dircon.co.uk
web: www.communitylearning.org
Contact: Charlie McConnell, Chief Executive; Fiona Black, Deputy Chief Executive; Linda McTavish, Chair.

CLS is the national community education agency, acting as a focus and source of advice on community learning and youth issues. Our key functions are: to be a national resource centre; to advise policy and decision makers; to promote and support best practice. CLS is a non-departmental public body.

DUMFRIES AND GALLOWAY COLLEGE
Heathhall, Dumfries DG1 3QZ
Tel: 01387 261261 Fax: 01387 250006
e-mail: info@dumgal.ac.uk
web: www.dumgal.ac.uk
Contact: Mr T. Jakimciw, Principal, 01387 243808; Mrs A.C. Sinyard, Depute Principal, 01387 243808; Mr I. Beach, Assistant Principal; Mr J.C. Crooks, Assistant Principal.
We pride ourselves on our friendly atmosphere and excellent facilities. We are able to offer courses and training in a wide variety of occupational areas, so whatever your chosen career path or your personal development needs, there is something on offer for everyone at Dumfries and Galloway College. We have student support services, student accommodation, a mobile learning resource, childcare facilities and a wide range of opportunities for adults. Dumfries and Galloway College: Welcome to your Future.

DYSLEXIA INSTITUTE SCOTLAND
74 Victoria Crescent Road, Dowanhill, Glasgow G12 9JN
Tel: 0141 334 4549 Fax: 0141 339 8879
e-mail: glasgow@dyslexia-inst.org.uk
web: www.dyslexia-inst.org.uk
Contact: Mrs Elizabeth Mackenzie, Principal; Elizabeth Robin, Administrator; Morven McKenna, Administrator.
The Dyslexia Institute wants to see all dyslexic people identified and taught so that they are able to reach their full potential and make their maximum contribution to society.

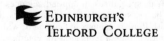

THE UNIVERSITY OF EDINBURGH
Old College, South Bridge, Edinburgh EH8 9YL
Tel: 0131 650 1000 Fax: 0131 650 2147
Contact: Lord Sutherland of Houndwood, Principal, 0131 650 2150; Melvyn Cornish, Secretary, 0131 650 2139, M.Cornish@ed.ac.uk; Stephanie Noblett, Media Officer, 0131 650 2246, Stephanie.Noblett@ed.ac.uk
The University of Edinburgh, with some 20,500 students and over 3,400 academic and research staff, is one of Europe's leading centres of higher education, devoted to excellence in teaching and research across a broad range of disciplines and professions. It especially values its intellectual and economic relationship with the Scottish community that forms its base and provides a wide range of research, educational, commercial and cultural services for its client groups.

EDINBURGH'S TELFORD COLLEGE
Crewe Toll, Edinburgh EH4 2NZ
Tel: 0131 332 2491 Fax: 0131 343 1218
e-mail: @ed.coll.ac.uk
web: www.ed-coll.ac.uk

EDINBURGH'S TELFORD COLLEGE

Contact: Dr. Ray Harris, Principal and Chief Executive, Ext. 7201, ray.harris@ed-coll.ac.uk; Mr Gregor Irving, Depute Principal, Ext. 7315, gregi@ed-coll.ac.uk; Mr Jim Haluch, Head of Marketing, Ext. 7478, jimh@ed-coll.ac.uk
The College mission is "to be accessible, responsive and flexible, and to achieve excellence". It aims to meet the educational and training needs of individuals, industry and the wider community. In pursuit of these goals, it works in partnership with a wide range of local, national and international organisations. The number of students enrolled with the College in 2000-2001 exceeded 20,000, many of them studying part-time and by distance learning.

UNIVERSITY
of
GLASGOW

UNIVERSITY OF GLASGOW
University Avenue, Glasgow G12 8QQ
Tel: 0141 339 8855
web: www.gla.ac.uk

Contact: Professor Sir Graeme Davies, Principal and Vice-Chancellor; Professor Malcolm D. McLeod, Vice-Principal (External Relations and Marketing), 0141 330 4285; Mr Mike Brown, Director of Publicity Services, 0141 330 4919.
The University of Glasgow (founded 1451, annual turnover £232m.) has over 16,500 full-time students, and more students in science-based courses than any UK university outside London. It has one of the largest medical schools in Europe. One of Britain's top research universities, Glasgow's earnings from research grants and contracts in 1999-2000 exceeded £60m. Employing over 5,500 staff, the University makes a substantial contribution to the local community and Scottish culture.

GLENROTHES COLLEGE
Stenton Road, Glenrothes, Fife KY6 2RA
Tel: 01592 772233 Fax: 01592 568182
e-mail: college@glenrothes.ac.uk
web: www.glenrothes-college.ac.uk

Contact: Dr Craig Thomson, Principal.
Glenrothes College strives to provide high quality, accessible learning opportunities that are relevant to the individuals, communities and organisations which we serve. We offer programmes, via full-time and part-time attendance and a flexible provision including distance and on-line learning, work based and community based learning. Non advanced, advanced and post experience programmes are available in: Administration, Business and Management; Creative Skills including Media, Design; Catering, Hospitality, Sport and Tourism; Engineering and Computing; Health and Social Care.

HEADTEACHERS' ASSOCIATION OF SCOTLAND
University of Strathclyde, Jordanhill Campus, Southbrae Drive,
Glasgow G13 1PP
Tel: 0141 950 3298 Fax: 0141 950 3434
e-mail: head.teachers@strath.ac.uk
Contact: George Ross, General Secretary; Lyn Honnan, Admin and Finance Officer.
Professional support to head teachers, depute head teachers and assistant head teachers in Scottish secondary schools and the enrichment of education in Scotland.

HERIOT-WATT UNIVERSITY, EDINBURGH
Edinburgh EH14 4AS
Tel: 0131 451 3444 Fax: 0131 451 3441
web: www.hw.ac.uk
Contact: Professor John S. Archer, Principal and Vice Chancellor; Mairi Thornton, Director of Corporate Communications, m.s.m.thornton@hw.ac.uk; Gillian McFadzean, Director of Technology and Research Services, g.mcfadzean@hw.ac.uk
Heriot-Watt specialises in applied sciences and mathematics, engineering and design, textiles, business management and languages. There are 6,000 students in Edinburgh and at its Scottish Borders campus in Galashiels, with a further 9,000 distance learning students in 140 countries. With a reputation for enterprise, innovative education and leading edge but practical research, Heriot-Watt is one of the top UK universities for income from business and industry. It also has one of the highest graduate employment rates in the country. The Edinburgh Conference Centre at Heriot-Watt is a leading conference venue.

JAMES WATT COLLEGE OF FURTHER AND HIGHER EDUCATION
Finnart Street, Greenock PA16 8HF
Tel: 01475 724433 Fax: 01475 888079
Contact: Professor Bill Wardle.

A multi-campus college which includes the main campus, the Waterfront Business and Management Centre and the new North Ayrshire Campus based at Kilwinning in North Ayrshire, making it the largest college in Scotland. Total enrolments: 23,000.

JEWEL & ESK VALLEY COLLEGE
24 Milton Road East, Edinburgh EH15 2PP
Tel: 0131 660 1010 Fax: 0131 657 2276
e-mail: info@jevc.ac.uk
web: www.jevc.ac.uk
Contact: H McKenzie, Principal, 0131 657 7274; Information Office, 0131 657 5204, info@jevc.ac.uk; J. Coyne, Marketing Manager, 0131 657 7271, jcoyne@jevc.ac.uk
College of further education with three main campuses in Edinburgh, East Lothian and Midlothian, plus many satellite centres throughout the region. Provider of further and higher education courses, both vocational and recreational, by full-time, part-time, evening classes and flexible learning.

LEAD SCOTLAND – LINKING EDUCATION AND DISABILITY
Queen Margaret University College, Clerwood Terrace, Edinburgh EH12 8TS
Tel: 0131 317 3439 Fax: 0131 339 7198
e-mail: enquiries@lead.org.uk
web: www.lead.org.uk
Contact: Rona Connolly, Director.
Lead Scotland empowers and enables physically and/or sensory impaired adults in Scotland to access education and lifelong learning opportunities. In many areas of Scotland, organisers work with individuals to provide guidance and support into education. Volunteers are involved in many ways, supporting students and organisers. Nationally, we promote equal opportunities for disabled people in education, and develop innovative ways of using ICT to assist the learning process.

LEARNING AND TEACHING SCOTLAND (LT SCOTLAND)
Gardyne Road, Dundee DD5 1NY
Tel: 01382 443600 Fax: 01382 443645/46
and at
74 Victoria Crescent Road, Glasgow G12 9JN
Tel: 0141 337 5000 Fax: 0141 337 5050
e-mail: enquiries@LTScotland.com (for both offices)
web: www.LTScotland.com

Contact: Mike Baughan, Chief Executive; Professor Tom Wilson, Chairman.
Learning and Teaching Scotland (LT Scotland) is a national public body sponsored by the Scottish Executive Education Department. LT Scotland's remit is to provide advice, support, resources and staff development which enhance the quality of educational experiences in Scotland, with a view to improving attainment and achievement and promoting lifelong learning. It combines expertise on the school and pre-school curriculum and on the use of information and communications technology (ICT) in education and lifelong learning. LT Scotland is actively involved in software and internet development and multimedia production of educational resources.

MOTHERWELL COLLEGE
Dalzell Drive, Motherwell ML1 2DD
Tel: 01698 232323 Fax: 01698 232527
e-mail:rmillham@motherwell.co.uk
web: www.motherwell.ac.uk
Contact: Richard Millham, Principal and Chief Executive.
Motherwell College will develop its role as a key provider of local, national and international learning opportunities, making a full contribution to the economic, social and cultural life of the local community and meeting the needs of individual learners.

REID KERR COLLEGE
Renfrew Road, Paisley, Renfrewshire PA3 4DR
Tel: 0141 581 2222
web: www.reidkerr.ac.uk

Contact: Joe Mooney, Principal, 0141 581 2201, jmooney@reidkerr.ac.uk; John Doyle, Director of Curriculum, 0141 581 2215, jdoyle@reidkerr.ac.uk; Douglas Paxton, Director of Finance and Corporate Services, 0141 581 2214, djpaxton@reidkerr.ac.uk; Judith McClarty, Director of Human Resources, 0141 581 2213, jmcclarty@reidkerr.ac.uk

Reid Kerr College, Paisley, is one of Scotland's leading colleges of further and higher education and with over 16,000 students and 600 courses, serves the education and training needs of Renfrewshire and its surrounding areas. Courses are offered on a full-time, part-time, and distance learning basis in a wide variety of areas including built environment; business & management; computing & e-commerce; engineering; hospitality; hairdressing & beauty; science; sport; health & care; support for learning; communication & languages; and creative arts.

THE ROBERT GORDON UNIVERSITY
Schoolhill, Aberdeen AB10 1FR
Tel: 01224 262000 Fax: 01224 263000
e-mail: i.centre@rgu.ac.uk
web: www.rgu.ac.uk

Contact: Professor William Stevely, Principal; Dr Adrian Graves, University Secretary; Jonathan Shackleton, Public Affairs, 01224 262031.

The Robert Gordon University is one of the oldest technology institutes in the UK, with a reputation for excellence in providing highly relevant vocational education. It delivers more than 300 courses to approximately 10,000 students in the arts, management, engineering, pharmacy, health and the sciences. It currently has the best graduate employment record of all Scottish universities with only 1.2 per cent of first degree graduates classified as unemployed in January 2001.

SCOTTISH COUNCIL FOR RESEARCH IN EDUCATION
15 St. John Street, Edinburgh EH8 8JR
Tel: 0131 557 2944 Fax: 0131 556 9454
e-mail: scre@scre.ac.uk

Contact: Dr Valerie Wilson, Director, valerie.wilson@scre.ac.uk

SCRE's mission is to conduct research for the benefit of education in Scotland and elsewhere. It also supports research through disseminating its own and others' research by conventional and electronic publications and conferences. It supplies information and consultancy to help others conduct and disseminate research and provides training in research methods through workshops and seminars. web: http://www.scre.ac.uk

SCOTTISH FURTHER EDUCATION UNIT
Argyll Court, Castle Business Park, Stirling FK9 4TY
Tel: 01786 892000 (switchboard) Fax: 01786 892001
e-mail: sfeu@sfeu.ac.uk
web: www.sfeu.ac.uk

SFEU
SCOTTISH FURTHER
EDUCATION UNIT

Contact: Alison Reid, Chief Executive, 01786 892030; John Laird, Director, 01786 892004; John Young, Director, 01786 892051; Brian Wright, Director, 01786 892003.

SFEU is the primary agency whose purpose is to contribute to the development of learning provision within FE colleges through the support of staff and the curriculum. Working in partnership with all colleges in Scotland, as well as other key national agencies, we hold a unique position within FE, providing a strong understanding of the development issues within post-school education. Our commitment is to build on these strengths to maintain our leading edge position and thereby contribute to the advancement of further education in Scotland. SFEU's dynamic portfolio is tailored through a continuing process of close collaboration with colleges and other partners to ensure that developmental and support needs are identified and addressed.

SCOTTISH QUALIFICATIONS AUTHORITY
Hanover House, 24 Douglas Street, Glasgow G2 7NQ
Tel: 0845 279 1000 Fax: 0141 242 2244
e-mail: helpdesk@sqa.org.uk
web: www.sqa.org.uk
Contact: Bill Morton, Interim Chief Executive; Professor John Ward, Chairman.
The Scottish Qualifications Authority (SQA) develops and awards most of the qualifications on offer in Scotland's schools, colleges, workplaces, and education centres. The SQA works in partnership with education, business, and industry to develop qualifications which meet the needs of individuals, society and the economy. The qualifications system in Scotland is based on three main qualification "types" – most of which are made up of units. These range from National Qualifications taken at school and college, to Higher National Certificates (HNCs) and Higher National Diplomas (HNDs) taken at college, and Scottish Vocational Qualifications (SVQs) which are designed for the workplace.

SCOTTISH SECONDARY TEACHERS' ASSOCIATION
15 Dundas Street, Edinburgh EH3 6QG
Tel: 0131 556 5919 Fax: 0131 556 1419
e-mail: info@ssta.org.uk
Contact: David H. Eaglesham, BEd, General Secretary.
The Association was founded to advance education in Scotland and to safeguard and promote the interests of Scottish secondary teachers especially regarding salaries and conditions of service. We represent members within schools, at local authority levels, and nationally through bodies such as the SNCT and GTC. This representation is carried out for individuals as well as the whole membership, and involves shaping the future of education in Scotland as well as offering a comprehensive range of services to members.

THE SCOTTISH UNIVERSITY FOR INDUSTRY
The Europa Building, 450 Argyle Street, Glasgow G2 8LG
Tel: 0141 285 6000 Fax: 0141 285 6001
e-mail: martino@scottishufi.com
web: www.scottishufi.com   www.learndirectscotland.com
Contact: Frank Pignatelli, Chief Executive, 0141 285 6010, annc@scottishufi.com; Martin Osler, PR Manager, 0141 285 6042, martino@scottishufi.com
The Scottish University for Industry was set up to promote lifelong learning for all throughout Scotland. It does this through its learndirect Scotland brand that includes freephone helpline 0808 100 9000. Callers are directed to learning opportunities across Scotland. Also gives quality assurance branding to learning centres (301 branded to date). Website: www.learndirectscotland.com

SSERC LIMITED (TRADING AS SSERC AND STS SUPPORT SERVICES)
St. Mary's Building, 23 Holyrood Road, Edinburgh EH8 8AE
Tel: 0131 558 8180 Fax: 0131 558 8191
e-mail: sts@sserc.org.uk
web: www.sserc.org.uk
Contact: John Richardson, Executive Director.
Technical resource support for education. Advisory, information, consultancy, testing and training services on anything connected with the purchase, use (including health and safety), maintenance and repair of equipment and materials for education. Health and safety, management training and consultancy. Publishers of electronic, interactive reference materials.

UNIVERSITIES SCOTLAND
53 Hanover Street, Edinburgh EH2 2PJ
Tel: 0131 226 1111 Fax: 0131 226 1100
e-mail: contact@universities-scotland.ac.uk
web: www.universities-scotland.ac.uk

Contact: Mr David Caldwell, Director; Robin McAlpine, Public Affairs Officer.
"The most effective regional organisation of its kind in the UK" (Commission on Scottish Education). Universities Scotland is the official voice of the Scottish universities and higher education colleges. The Convener (2000–2002) is Lord Sutherland of Houndwood, Principal and Vice-Chancellor, University of Edinburgh. The Convener (2002-2004) is Professor Bill Stevely, Principal and Vice-Chancellor, The Robert Gordon University.

ENERGY

BRITISH ENERGY plc
3 Redwood Crescent, Peel Park, East Kilbride G74 5PR
Tel: 01355 262000 Fax: 01355 262626
web: www.british-energy.com
Contact: Dr Robin Jeffrey, Executive Chairman; David Gilchrist, Managing Director, Generation; Doug McRoberts, Public Relations Director.
British Energy, one of the UK's largest electricity generators with around one fifth of the market, owns and operates the UK's eight modern nuclear power stations. Two are based in Scotland at Hunterston B in Ayrshire and Torness in East Lothian. The company also acquired the coal-fired power station, Eggborough, to provide more flexible generating plant in England and Wales under the New Electricity Trading Arrangements, which came into force in March 2001. The company has overseas interests, most notably in Canada and the United States. The Bruce Power partnership, formed between British Energy and Cameco Corporation, is involved with the Bruce nuclear power station in South-Western Ontario. AmerGen, a joint venture between British Energy and Exleon Corporation, has acquired a portfolio of three nuclear generating plants in the US. British Energy employs around 5,000 people in the UK and has an annual turnover of around £2bn.

ENERGY ACTION SCOTLAND (EAS)
Suite 4A, Ingram House, 227 Ingram Street, Glasgow G1 1DA
Tel: 0141 226 3064 Fax: 0141 221 2788
e-mail: eas@eas.org.uk
web: www.eas.org.uk
Contact: Ann Loughrey, Director; Norman Kerr, Development Officer.
Energy Action Scotland is the national charity which aims to eliminate fuel poverty by: raising awareness of fuel poverty, particularly as it affects low income households, and working towards affordable warmth for all; identifying effective solutions which can transform cold, damp houses into warm, dry homes; securing public and private investment in domestic energy efficiency initiatives. Current publications include *Energy Review* (quarterly journal), *Fuel Poverty Now, Scottish Fuel Poverty Update.*

SCOTTISH GAS
Granton House, 4 Marine Drive, Edinburgh EH5 1YB
Tel: 0131 559 5000 Fax: 0131 559 5011
e-mail: elizabeth.orrock@centrica.co.uk
Contact: Tom Laidlaw, Director; Hamish McPherson, Corporate Affairs; Steve Gorry, General Manager.
Scottish Gas aims to be the first choice for energy and services to homes and businesses. The company is focused on developing a range of products and services to make life easier for customers. Energy supply is a key component of the current range, which also includes home services such as telecommunications, installation and servicing of domestic heating, home security, electrical repairs and plumbing, in addition to a growing financial services business. Scottish Gas has a substantial programme of community relations work and employs around 2,500 staff across Scotland.

EUROPEAN COMMISSION

EUROPEAN COMMISSION – REPRESENTATION IN SCOTLAND
9 Alva Street, Edinburgh EH2 4PH
Tel: 0131 225 2058 Fax: 0131 226 4105
Contact: Elizabeth Holt, Head of Representation and Spokesman in Scotland; Diana Hart,
PA and Administration; Janet Williamson, Information Officer.
The Representation and its staff keep the European Commission in touch with developments
and thinking in Scotland, with an emphasis on political reporting, Scottish media coverage of
the EU and the provision of information to the public through the Scottish European
Resources Network. It liaises with Scottish government, the Scottish Parliament and other
bodies with an interest in the European Union. For further information, see our websites
www.cec.org.uk or www.europe.org.uk

FINANCIAL

ADAM & COMPANY GROUP plc
22 Charlotte Square, Edinburgh EH2 4DF
Tel: 0131 225 8484 Fax: 0131 225 5136

Contact: Ray Entwistle, Group Managing Director; Mark Hedderwick, Managing Director,
Adam & Company Investment Management Limited; Douglas Corner, Director (Glasgow).
Adam & Company is a private bank that effectively combines banking with investment
management – providing a full asset and liability management service. As well as all the
normal facilities expected from a bank, Adam holds in great store the old-fashioned
courtesies that were a hallmark of banking in bygone days and endeavours to provide
guidance in most aspects of the financial life of their clients.

AEGON ASSET MANAGEMENT
AEGON House, 3 Lochside Avenue, Edinburgh Park, Edinburgh EH12 9SA
Tel: 0131 339 9191 Fax: 0131 339 9567
e-mail: seam@scoteq.co.uk
Contact: Russell Hogan, Managing Director; Colin McLatchie, Chief Operating Officer;
Colin Black, Executive Director.
AEGON Asset Management (formerly Scottish Equitable Asset Management), the asset
management arm of AEGON UK, currently manages funds in excess of £34 billion. The
fund management team of over 60 dedicated investment professionals covers 9
specialist/regional teams, providing an enviable track record. It is a fundamentally driven
research-oriented investment organisation using a broad range of tools on the qualitative and
quantitative spectrum to produce consistently excellent results.

AEGON UK
AEGON House, 3 Lochside Avenue, Edinburgh EH12 9XX
Tel: 0131 339 9191 Fax: 0131 339 9567
Contact: Scott White, Group PR Manager; Shona Johnstone, Head of Group
Communications.
AEGON UK group companies include Scottish Equitable plc, AEGON Asset Management,
Scottish Equitable International Holdings, Guardian Financial Services, AEGON Individual
Protection, HS Administrative Services. AEGON UK, through the Scottish Equitable brand,
is one of the UK's leading providers of pensions and investment products and services and

currently manages funds in excess of £34bn. AEGON UK is part of the multinational AEGON Group which is one of the largest insurers in the world and currently manages world-wide assets in excess of £175bn.

AUDITOR GENERAL FOR SCOTLAND
ACCOUNTS COMMISSION FOR SCOTLAND
AUDIT SCOTLAND
110 George Street, Edinburgh EH2 4LH
Tel: 0131 477 1234 Fax: 0131 477 4567
web: www.audit-scotland.gov.uk
The **Auditor General** holds the Scottish Executive and other public spending bodies (except local authorities) to account for the proper efficient and effective use of public funds. The Auditor General is Robert W. Black. The **Accounts Commission** ensures that local authorities, fire and police boards, spend £9bn. of public money properly and wisely. **Audit Scotland** provides services to the Auditor General and Accounts Commission.

BANK OF ENGLAND
Agency for Scotland, 19 St. Vincent Place, Glasgow G1 2DT
Tel: 0141 221 7972
e-mail: scotland@bankofengland.co.uk
web: www.bankofengland.co.uk
Contact: Janet Bulloch, Agent for Scotland.
Reports to the Monetary Policy Committee on business conditions in Scotland, as well as representing the Bank of England in Scotland.

THE CHARTERED INSTITUTE OF BANKERS IN SCOTLAND
Drumsheugh House, 38b Drumsheugh Gardens, Edinburgh EH3 7SW
Tel: 0131 473 7777 Fax: 0131 473 7788
e-mail: info@ciobs.org.uk
Contact: Professor Charles W. Munn, Chief Executive; Colin A. Morrison, Director of Education; Derek J. Langley, Director of Business Development.
The Chartered Institute of Bankers in Scotland is the professional and educational body for the Scottish Financial Services Industry. The main aims of the Institute are to: encourage the highest standards of professionalism and conduct amongst its members; improve and extend the knowledge and expertise of those engaged in the financial services industry; conduct examinations and promote the continued study of financial services; establish links, co-operate with other professional or educational bodies and represent the financial services industry both nationally and internationally. web: http://www.ciobs.org.uk

CIPFA (THE CHARTERED INSTITUTE OF PUBLIC FINANCE & ACCOUNTANCY)
8 North West Circus Place, Edinburgh EH3 6ST
Tel: 0131 220 4316 Fax: 0131 220 4305
e-mail: cipfa.scotland@cipfa.org
web: www.cipfascotland.org.uk

CIPFA

Contact: Ian Doig, Director, CIPFA in Scotland, ian.doig@cipfa.org; Angela Scott, Senior Manager (Policy and Technical Services), CIPFA in Scotland, angela.scott@cipfa.org; Fraser MacPherson, Senior Manager (Events and Support Services), CIPFA in Scotland, fraser.macpherson@cipfa.org
CIPFA (The Chartered Institute of Public Finance and Accountancy) is one of the leading professional accountancy bodies in the UK and the only one which specialises in the public services. It is responsible for the education and training of professional accountants. CIPFA's members work in public service bodies, in the national audit agencies and major accountancy firms. They are respected throughout for their high technical and ethical standards and professional integrity. As such, CIPFA is the leading independent commentator on managing and accounting for public money.

THE COMMITTEE OF SCOTTISH CLEARING BANKERS
Drumsheugh House, 38 Drumsheugh Gardens, Edinburgh EH3 7SW
Tel: 0131 473 7700 Fax: 0131 473 7799
e-mail: info@scotbanks.co.uk
Contact: Mrs Susan Rice, Chairman; Mr George Mitchell, Deputy Chairman; Mr Gordon P. Fenton, Secretary.
The Committee is the trade association of the four Scottish clearing banks (Bank of Scotland, The Royal Bank of Scotland plc, Clydesdale Bank PLC and Lloyds TSB Scotland plc) and represents the industry in the financial structure of Scotland. Contact is maintained with the Scottish Executive, Bank of England, Financial Services Authority and other appropriate professional and economic development organisations. The Committee addresses issues which are of specific relevance to Scotland and which are non-competitive, providing a forum in which such matters can be debated.

MONEY ADVICE SCOTLAND
Suite 306, Pentagon Centre, 36 Washington Street, Glasgow G3 8AZ
Tel: 0141 572 0237 Fax: 0141 572 0517
e-mail: moneyadv@globalnet.co.uk
web: www.moneyadvicescotland.org.uk
Contact: Yvonne Gallacher, OBE, Chief Executive; Keith Hudson, Office and Accounts Manager.
Money Advice Scotland (MAS) aims to: promote the development of free, independent, confidential, impartial money advice; represent the views of its members on policy issues to government; promote and provide training, standards and Scottish Vocational Qualifications in money advice; promote and provide a channel of communication for the exchange of information and views of money advisors; produce research in money advice and related matters. MAS is committed to: the establishment of efficient, co-ordinated and effective support mechanisms; developing further the existing links with Europe; the establishment of standards and quality service.

 **THE ROYAL BANK OF SCOTLAND GROUP**
PO Box 31, 42 St Andrew Square, Edinburgh EH2 2YE
Tel: 0131 556 8555 Fax: 0131 557 6565 Telex: 72230 RBSCOT
web: www.rbs.co.uk
Sir George Ross Mathewson, CBE, DUniv, LLD, FRSE, FCIBS, Chairman; Frederick Anderson Goodwin, DUniv, FCIBS, FCIB, Group Chief Executive.
The Royal Bank of Scotland Group, headquartered in Edinburgh, provides high quality banking, insurance and related financial services. The Royal Bank of Scotland was founded in 1727 and is one of the UK's top 10 companies with share listings in London and New York. Its core market is the United Kingdom and it is active in Europe to serve and develop its UK banking customer base, and in the north-east USA to diversify its earnings. The Royal Bank's aim is to be recognised as the best performing financial services group in the United Kingdom while remaining mindful of its responsibilities to shareholders, customers, employees and the communities in which it operates. Through organic growth and acquisitions it is one of the UK's fastest growing financial groups. It is currently the second largest bank in the UK and in Europe.

SCOTTISH EQUITABLE PLC
Scottish Equitable House, Edinburgh Park, Edinburgh EH12 9SE
Tel: 0131 339 9191 Fax: 0131 339 9567
Contact: Graham Dumble, Managing Director; Jayne Ponzio, Head of Corporate Communications; Louise McVicker, Public Affairs Manager.
One of the UK's leading providers of insured pension, personal investment, employee benefits and protection products for the corporate and personal markets. Scottish Equitable distributes its range of products and services via a dedicated, well trained sales force and focuses its attention on the IFA distribution channel. The company has one of the highest ratings of financial strength by leading ratings agency Standard & Poors.

SCOTTISH MUTUAL ASSURANCE PLC
Abbey National House, 301 St Vincent Street, Glasgow G2 5HN
Tel: 0141 248 6321 Fax: 0141 275 9230
web: www.scottishmutual.co.uk

Contact: Graham Pottinger, Chief Executive.
Since its acquisition by Abbey National plc in 1992, Scottish Mutual has flourished apace and now ranks amongst the pre-eminent providers of long term savings and life assurance products. Scottish Mutual's year on year business growth is driven by innovative and competitive products backed by a commitment to the IFA distribution channel.

GEOLOGY

BRITISH GEOLOGICAL SURVEY, SCOTLAND
Murchison House, West Mains Road, Edinburgh EH9 3LA
Tel: 0131 667 1000 Fax: 0131 667 1877
e-mail: c.browitt@bgs.ac.uk

Contact: Dr. Chris W.A. Browitt, Director, BGS Scotland, c.browitt@bgs.ac.uk; Dr David J. Kerridge, Global Seismology and Geomagnetism Group, d.kerridge@bgs.ac.uk; Dr Nigel T. Fannin, Petroleum Geology and Offshore Surveys, n.fannin@bgs.ac.uk
BGS Scotland conducts the national geological survey for Northern Britain on land, and for the whole of the UK Continental Shelf. It builds databases for environmental surveys and research through its geochemical and groundwater divisions and is the authority for the national earthquake and geomagnetic monitoring programmes. Leading-edge research in petroleum geology and reservoir engineering supports the Scottish oil industry.

HEALTH

ARTHRITIS CARE IN SCOTLAND
Phoenix House, 7 South Avenue, Clydebank Business Park, Clydebank G81 2LG
Tel: 0141 952 5433 Fax: 0141 952 5433
e-mail: scotlandoffice@arthritiscare.org.uk
web: www.arthritiscare.org.uk/scotland
Contact: Gill Watt, Director, Scotland; Katy Green, Administrator, Scotland.
Arthritis Care has been working with and for people with arthritis for more than 50 years. In Scotland, 100 branches, self-help groups and Young Arthritis Care groups provide social, educational, therapeutic and recreational activities locally. Information and advice is available from a range of booklets and leaflets, and from a freephone helpline. Empowerment training is available to enable people of all ages to take control of their arthritis and their lives.

BRITISH MEDICAL ASSOCIATION
Scottish Office, 14 Queen Street, Edinburgh EH2 1LL
Tel: 0131 247 3000 Fax: 0131 247 3001
e-mail: info.edinburgh@bma.org.uk
Contact: Dr Bill O'Neill, Scottish Secretary; Members' Enquiries: 0131 247 3000; Public/Press Enquiries: 0131 247 3050/3052.
The British Medical Association in Scotland represents doctors from all branches of medicine. It is a voluntary professional association, independent trade union, scientific and educational body and a publishing house. The BMA and the BMJ Publishing Group, which is one of the most influential medical publishers in the world, produce a wide range of journals, reports and medical books. With a UK membership of 120,000, and 13,000 in Scotland, the BMA is regarded as the voice of the medical profession.

CHEST, HEART AND STROKE SCOTLAND

65 North Castle Street, Edinburgh EH2 3LT
Tel: 0131 225 6963 Fax: 0131 220 6313
e-mail: admin@chss.org.uk
web: www.chss.org.uk

Contact: Mr David H. Clark, Chief Executive; Professor Charles Forbes, FRCP, FRSEd; Chairman; Mrs Janet Buncle, Director of Public Relations.

Chest, Heart and Stroke Scotland aims to improve the quality of life for people in Scotland affected by chest, heart and stroke illness, through medical research, advice and information, and support in the community. CHSS funds research into all aspects of the prevention, treatment and social impact of chest, heart and stroke disease, and provides a network of support services for patients and carers throughout Scotland.

COMMON SERVICES AGENCY for NHSScotland

Trinity Park House, South Trinity Road, Edinburgh EH5 3SE
Tel: 0131 552 6255 Fax: 0131 552 8651
web: www.show.scot.nhs.uk/csa

Contact: Mr Graeme Millar, Chairman, 0131 551 8148; Mr Stuart Bain, Chief Executive, 0131 551 8148; Mrs Ruth Wallace, Executive Co-ordinator, 0131 551 8869.

The Common Services Agency plays an active role in NHSScotland by providing clinical support and advice for Scotland's health and patient care. This national co-ordination and concentration of knowledge is central to healthcare planning. It develops specialised expertise within Scotland, and generates substantial savings for NHSScotland through purchasing and administrative economies of scale.

EPILEPSY ACTION SCOTLAND (EAS)

48 Govan Road, Glasgow G51 1JL
Tel: 0141 427 4911 Helpline: 0141 427 5225 Fax: 0141 419 1709
e-mail: enquiries@epilepsyscotland.org.uk
web: www.epilepsyscotland.org.uk

Contact: Hilary Mounfield, Chief Executive, 0141 427 4911; Allana Parker, Public Relations Officer, 0141 419 1701.

Epilepsy Action Scotland works to enable people with epilepsy to maximise their choices in life. EAS lobbies for better policies and services to meet local needs and campaigns against the stigma of epilepsy by raising public awareness. It provides relevant literature, information and an interactive website. Its helpline offers advice to people with epilepsy and their families. EAS is a training provider. It also runs a community support service for adults with learning disabilities. There is a network of support groups and branches.

ERSKINE HOSPITAL

Bishopton, Renfrewshire PA7 5PU
Tel: 0141 812 1100 Fax: 0141 812 3733
web: www.erskine.org.uk

Contact: Colonel M.F. Gibson, OBE, DL, Chief Executive.

Erskine Hospital is the leading Scottish charity caring for ex-Service men and women. Founded in 1916, it has cared through both World Wars and the many modern day conflicts. Today, it provides unrivaled nursing, dementia, residential and respite care for young and elderly ex-Service personnel in homes at Bishopton and Erskine, near Glasgow, and at Gilmerton, Edinburgh. It also cares across Scotland through Partnership (bursary) Schemes with other quality care providers. A holiday home in Dunoon, supported workshops providing employment for disabled people, a training and conference centre, and 55 cottages for war pensioners complete the Erskine community.

HEALTH EDUCATION BOARD FOR SCOTLAND
Woodburn House, Canaan Lane, Edinburgh EH10 4SG
Tel: 0131 536 5500 Fax: 0131 536 5501
web: www.hebs.com
Contact: Martin Raymond, Deputy Director of Programmes and Communications/Head of Public Affairs; Graham Robertson, Acting Chief Executive.
The Health Education Board for Scotland gives leadership to the health education effort in Scotland. Its aim is to promote good health through the empowerment of individuals, groups and communities. HEBS is committed to the development, implementation and support of effective, efficient and ethical health education, responsive to the needs and priorities of the population and its sub-groups. As well as providing programmes of health education at the national level, the Board facilitates the development and co-ordination of complementary initiatives sub-nationally across Scotland. It contributes to the education and training of relevant professionals and others, reviews, undertakes and commissions relevant research, and gives advice on policies which affect health. The Board's tasks involve communication and collaboration with a wide range of partners, in Scotland and beyond.

HIGH BLOOD PRESSURE FOUNDATION
Dept. of Medical Sciences, Western General Hospital, Edinburgh EH9 1JN
Tel: 0131 332 9211 Fax: 0131 537 1012
e-mail: hbpf@hbpf.org.uk
www.hbpf.org.uk
Registered charity SCO 22286
Contact: Rosalind Newton, Director; Mrs B.L. Rennie, WS, Chairman.
The High Blood Pressure Foundation is dedicated to improving the basic understanding, assessment, treatment and public awareness of high blood pressure, and, in so doing, help promote the welfare of people with high blood pressure.

LEUKAEMIA RESEARCH FUND
43 Westbourne Gardens, Glasgow G12 9XQ
Tel: 0141 339 0690 Fax: 0141 339 0690
Contact: Mrs Mae Naddell, Scottish Secretary, 0141 639 4949; Mrs Loraine Hutton, Chairman, Glasgow, 0141 561 8134; Mrs Claire Mulholland, Secretary, Glasgow, 0141 339 0690.
Founded in 1960, we want to improve treatments, find cures and prevent all forms of leukaemia and related cancers including Hodgkin's disease and other lymphomas, myeloma, the myelodysplasias, myeloproliferative disorders and aplastic anaemia. We are committed to nationally organised research of the highest calibre, guided by strict impartial expert advice, and to international collaboration. We aim to co-ordinate fundraising throughout the UK towards these ends. Our administration costs are five per cent.

PAIN ASSOCIATION SCOTLAND
Head Office, Cramond House, Cramond Glebe Road, Edinburgh EH4 6NS
Tel: 0131 312 7955 Fax: 0131 312 6007
e-mail: pain_association_scotland@compuserve.com
web: www.painassociation.com
Contact: Mr David Falconer, National Organiser; Mr Rory McPherson, Chairman.
Through a network of local peer support groups the Association offers training, education, information and a community-based pain management programme. The organisation provides support and understanding for people with chronic pain and their carers. Information, training and advice is available for health and social welfare professionals who are interested and working with people in chronic pain.

SCOTTISH HEART AND ARTERIAL RISK PREVENTION (SHARP)
University Department of Medicine, Ninewells Hospital and Medical
School, Dundee DD1 9SY
Tel: 01382 660111 (Ext. 33124) Fax: 01382 660675
e-mail: s.r.mcewan@dundee.ac.uk

*Contact: Dr Shirley R. McEwan, MBE, FRCPEdin, Hon Secretary and Medical
Administrator, e-mail: s.r.mcewan@dundee.ac.uk; Mrs Doreen Howley, Business
Administrator.*

SHARP is a Scottish medical charity founded and run by clinicians, whose aim is to reduce
the incidence of premature diseases of the heart and arteries, which lead to heart attacks,
strokes and gangrene. The aims of the organisation are pursued through research, the
identification through screening of high risk individuals, the education of health
professionals at scientific meetings, and the raising of awareness in the public of the need for
a healthy lifestyle, through the production of educational materials.

HOUSING

BIELD HOUSING ASSOCIATION LIMITED
22 Windsor Street, Edinburgh EH7 5JR
Tel: 0131 273 4000 Fax: 0131 557 6327
e-mail: info@bield.co.uk

*Contact: Alister M. Green, Chief Executive; Alister McDonald, Director of Corporate
Services; James H. Thomson, Director of Housing and Community Services; Glen Waddell,
Director of Financial Services; Sheila McKenzie, Director of Human Resources; Stewart
Clark, Director of Property Services.*

Bield's primary objective is to be a leading and innovative provider of high quality housing,
care and community services for older people in need or at risk. We are a non-profit making
organisation with charitable status, governed by legislation promoting and regulating
registered housing associations. We provide supported housing and community alarm, day
and home care services to about 12,000 older people in the Borders, Lothian, Fife, Tayside,
Forth Valley and Strathclyde.

SCOTTISH FEDERATION OF HOUSING ASSOCIATIONS
38 York Place, Edinburgh EH1 3HU
Tel: 0131 556 5777 Fax: 0131 557 6028
e-mail: sfha@sfha.co.uk
web: www.sfa.co.uk

*Contact: David Orr, Director, dorr@sfha.co.uk; Dave Alexander, Deputy Director,
dalexander@sfha.co.uk; Jimmy Black, Communications Officer, jblack@sfha.co.uk.*

The SFHA aims to contribute to the provision of high quality, affordable housing and
housing related services, and to the creation of sustainable communities, by promoting,
representing and providing services to Registered Social Landlords in Scotland, and by
campaigning on their behalf.

LAND

THE CROWN ESTATE
10 Charlotte Square, Edinburgh EH2 4DR
Tel: 0131 226 7241 Fax: 0131 220 1366
e-mail: cescotland@crownestate.co.uk
web: www.crownestate.co.uk

Contact: Michael Cunliffe, Head of Scottish Estates; Ian Grant, Scottish Commissioner.

The Crown Estate manages substantial property holdings held "in the right of the Crown". In

Scotland, this includes urban commercial properties, rural estates, half of the foreshore and almost all of the seabed out to the 12 mile territorial limit. The Estate is managed under the provisions of the Crown Estate Act 1961. The entire net surplus from the Estate is paid to the Treasury.

THE MACAULAY LAND USE RESEARCH INSTITUTE
Craigiebuckler, Aberdeen AB15 8QH
Tel: 01224 498200 Fax: 01224 311556
e-mail: enq@macaulay.ac.uk
web: www.macaulay.ac.uk

Contact: Public Relations Manager
We are an international leader in research on the use of rural land resources for the benefit of people and the environment. Specifically we assess the opportunities for integrating new land uses with traditional land use and we develop our understanding of the impact of land use on the soils and waters of river catchments and of the ecology of soils, trees, plants and grazing animals and their inter-relationships. Our reputation is built on relevance and excellence.

SCOTTISH LANDOWNERS' FEDERATION
Stuart House, Eskmills Business Park, Musselburgh EH21 7PB
Tel: 0131 653 5400 Fax: 0131 653 5401
e-mail: slfinfo@slf.org.uk
Contact: Robert W. Balfour, FRICS, Convener; Maurice S. Hankey, BSc, PhD, Director.
Represents the whole spectrum of landowners in Scotland. There are approximately 3,500 members. Aims to promote high standards of management and use of land; to ensure proper communication between its members, other organisations and the wider public on matters relating to the ownership of land; and to ensure that legislation and policies affecting landownership and use are prepared with proper consideration for the responsibilities and rights of landowners, in addition to the well-being of rural communities, the environment, and the wider public interest.

LAW
(see also LAW FIRMS under "PROFESSIONAL SERVICES")

COUNCIL ON TRIBUNALS, SCOTTISH COMMITTEE
44 Palmerston Place, Edinburgh EH12 5BJ
Tel: 0131 220 1236 Fax: 0131 225 4271
e-mail: sccot@gtnet.gov.uk
web: www.council-on-tribunals.gov.uk
Contact: R. John Elliot, DKS, Chairman; Mrs Marjorie Macrae, Secretary.
Independent body established in 1958 now operating under the Tribunals and Inquiries Act 1992. Principal statutory function to review the constitution and working of a wide range of specified tribunals. Members sit in on selected tribunal hearings. The Council must be consulted before procedural rules are made for the tribunals listed in the Act and before rules are made by the Lord Chancellor or Scottish Ministers which relate to statutory inquiries. Annual Report published each December.

THE LAW SOCIETY OF SCOTLAND
26 Drumsheugh Gardens, Edinburgh EH3 7YR
Tel: 0131 226 7411 Fax: 0131 225 2934
e-mail: lawscot@lawscot.org.uk
Contact: David M. Preston, President; Douglas R. Mill, Chief Executive.
The Law Society of Scotland is the membership body of the Scottish legal profession. The Society promotes the interests of solicitors and the public in relation to the

Scottish solicitors profession. It regulates its members, arranges the master insurance policy for all practising solicitors and administers the Scottish Solicitors Guarantee Fund. It provides services including: continuing legal education; advice on professional practice, European law, mediation, a solicitor referral service; and Dial-A-Law, an information and referral service. The Society promotes law reforms and undertakes legal research. Web: http://www.lawscot.org.uk

THE LEGAL DEFENCE UNION LIMITED
274 Sauchiehall Street, Glasgow G2 3EH
Tel: 0141 307 5000 Fax: 0141 307 5005
web: www.bakertilly.co.uk

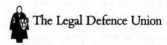 The Legal Defence Union

Contact: Christopher Alexander Craig, Accounts Controller; Walter Hecht, Partner.
The Legal Defence Union was founded in November 1987 to offer Scottish solicitors insurance cover for the cost of legal representation in regard to: complaints, disciplinary hearings, certain criminal and civil proceedings, employment disputes and industrial tribunal appearances. The directors are also committed to offering prompt, courteous and expert guidance and advice on professional problems of all kinds. The formation of the Union was sponsored by the Scottish Law Agents Society and the Glasgow Bar Association. The President of the Scottish Law Agents Society together with the President of the Glasgow Bar Association or their nominees are entitled to attend as ex-officio directors of the company. Telephone requests for urgent professional guidance or assistance may be made direct to the Chairman or any of the members of the board and will be treated with complete confidentiality. Details of contact numbers for our telephone advice line are published in the Blue Book and the White Book. For enquiries of an administrative nature regarding LDU membership, or claims under the policy, telephone Marsh UK Ltd, 0131 311 4200.

THE SCOTTISH LEGAL HISTORY GROUP
c/o The Secretary, Stair Building, University of Glasgow, Glasgow G12 8QQ
Tel: 0141 330 5537 Fax: 0141 330 4900.
e-mail: j.finlay@law.gla.ac.uk

Contact: Dr John Finlay, Secretary, 0141 330 5537, j.finlay@law.gla.ac.uk
Founded in 1981 to encourage the study of, promote interest in, and further the knowledge of Scottish legal history, the Group holds an annual conference, normally each October. Since 1983, this has been held in the Advocate's Library, Edinburgh. The membership includes, but is by no means restricted to, academic lawyers, historians and members of the legal profession. For further details, contact the Secretary, as above.

SCOTTISH SOCIETY FOR COMPUTERS & LAW
Morison Bishop, Erskine House, 68 Queen Street, Edinburgh EH2 4NN
Tel: 0131 226 6541 Fax: 0131 226 3156
e-mail: marion.menzies@morisonbishop.co.uk

Contact: Janice Webster, Chairman, secretary@slas.co.uk; Iain Mitchell, QC, Vice-Chairman, igmitchell@easynet.co.uk; Brandon Malone, Meetings Convenor, b.malone@bellscott.co.uk.
The Scottish Society is a devolved body linked to the parent Society of Computers and Law based in Bristol. Its mission is to carry out the charitable aims and objectives set out in its Memorandum and Articles of Association and, in particular, within Scotland to seek, wherever possible, the fullest participation in and discussion of developments in the field of law and information technology, both of which affect and benefit the legal profession as well as the wider community. This is done by a programme of events throughout the year, including lectures, seminars and conferences as well as articles in the magazine of the parent Society and our own newsletter and website. The Society monitors new and proposed legislation on all aspects of IT and "e-Commerce" and the practical application of IT to the legal profession, clients and the courts. For further information contact the Company Secretary at the Morison Bishop address.

LOCAL GOVERNMENT

ANGUS COUNCIL
The Cross, Forfar DD8 1BX
Tel: 01307 461460 Fax: 01307 461874
web: www.angus.gov.uk
Contact: Mr A.B. Watson, Chief Executive, 01307 473023.
Scottish local authority providing full range of services, with the following key themes: to promote the identity of and represent the interests of Angus locally, nationally and internationally; to aim to provide excellent public services, maximising the use of available resources to meet local needs; to improve economic prosperity in Angus; to improve the environment and the quality of life in Angus, with an emphasis on sustainability; to promote equal opportunities/reduce inequalities in Angus; to value staff as the Council's most important asset, and seek to ensure long-term employment prospects for a locally based and directly employed workforce; to develop partnerships.

COMMISSIONER FOR LOCAL ADMINISTRATION IN SCOTLAND
(LOCAL GOVERNMENT OMBUDSMAN)
23 Walker Street, Edinburgh EH3 7HX
Tel: 0131 225 5300 Fax: 0131 225 9495
Contact: Ian F Smith, Commissioner.
The Commissioner (Local Government Ombudsman) investigates complaints of injustice against local authorities and others arising from maladministration. The Ombudsman will not normally accept a complaint unless it has first been raised formally with the authority. The service is independent and impartial and there is no charge. Information, leaflets and complaint forms are available on application. A new Public Service Ombudsman for Scotland will take over the Commissioner's functions during 2002.

COSLA (CONVENTION OF SCOTTISH LOCAL AUTHORITIES)
Rosebery House, 9 Haymarket Terrace, Edinburgh EH12 5XZ
Tel: 0131 474 9200 Fax: 0131 474 9292
e-mail: enquiries@cosla.gov.uk
web: www.cosla.gov.uk
Contact: Oonagh Aitken, Chief Executive.
Local government in Scotland is represented collectively by COSLA (Convention of Scottish Local Authorities). COSLA exists to promote and protect the interests of councils in Scotland by providing a forum for discussion on matters of common concern. COSLA ascertains the views of member councils and communicates these to central government, other bodies and the public.

EAST AYRSHIRE COUNCIL
Council Headquarters, London Road, Kilmarnock KA3 7BU
Tel: 01563 576000 Fax: 01563 576500
Contact: John Clayton, Head of Corporate Development and Communication, 01563 576195, john.clayton@east-ayrshire.gov.uk; David Montgomery, Chief Executive; Councillor Drew McIntyre, Leader of the Council.
Built on the four core values of quality, equality, access and partnership, the Council delivers local government services within East Ayrshire including the communities of: Kilmarnock, Stewarton, Kilmaurs, Dunlop, Crosshouse, Fenwick, Galston, Darvel, Newmilns, Mauchline, Auchinleck, Sorn, Cumnock, Muirkirk, Lugar, Logan, New Cumnock, Dalmellington, Drongan, Patna, Ochiltree, Catrine, Stair, Rankinston.

GLASGOW CITY COUNCIL
City Chambers, George Square, Glasgow G2 1DU
Tel: 0141 287 2000 Fax: 0141 287 5666
web: www.glasgow.gov.uk

Contact: James Andrews, Chief Executive; John Brown, Head of Public Relations and Marketing.
Scotland's largest "unitary" council serving City of Glasgow. Population 609,000. Budget 2002/3 over £2bn. (gross). Main services – education, social work, housing, environmental health, local roads, parks and recreation, planning, licensing, economic development, museums and art galleries and libraries.

MIDLOTHIAN COUNCIL
Midlothian House, Buccleuch Street, Dalkeith, Midlothian EH22 1DJ
Tel: 0131 270 7500 Fax: 0131 271 3050
web: www.midlothian.gov.uk
Contact: Susan Whiteford, Communications Manager.
Midlothian is situated to the south of Scotland's capital city of Edinburgh. Midlothian Council serves a population of 82,000, covering a geographical area of 35,527 hectares, incorporating the main towns of Penicuik, Bonnyrigg, Dalkeith, Mayfield and Easthouses, Loanhead and Gorebridge. The Council employs over 4,000 people.

MAPS

ORDNANCE SURVEY
Grayfield House, 5 Bankhead Avenue, Edinburgh EH11 4AE
Tel: 0131 442 2590 Fax: 0131 453 3021
Contact: Graham E. Little, Operations Manager Scotland.
Ordnance Survey is Great Britain's national mapping agency, responsible for the official definitive topographic mapping of the country. Ordnance Survey provides a wide range of products to meet customer and national interest needs, ranging from walking maps through to large scale digital data. We also provide national and international consultancy. Map update in Scotland is undertaken from a network of six offices and managed from a head office in Edinburgh. For general enquiries, please ring our customer information helpline: 0845 605 0505. Additional information is available at http://www.ordnancesurvey.co.uk

MARINE AND COASTAL

NORTHERN LIGHTHOUSE BOARD
84 George Street, Edinburgh EH2 3DA
Tel: 0131 473 3100 Fax: 0131 220 2093
e-mail: enquiries@nlb.org.uk
web: www.nlb.org.uk
Contact: James Taylor, Chief Executive; Lorna Hunter, Public Relations and Information Officer. Chairman: The Lord Joseph Maclay.
The Board provides marine aids to navigation – lighthouses, buoys, beacons and a precision satellite navigation system in Scotland and the Isle of Man. It receives no public monies and is funded entirely by light dues paid by merchant shipping and fishing vessels.

SCOTTISH ASSOCIATION FOR MARINE SCIENCE
Dunstaffnage Marine Laboratory, Oban, Argyll PA37 1QA.
Tel: 01631 559000 Fax: 01631 559001
e-mail: mail@dml.ac.uk
web: www.sams.ac.uk
Contact: Professor Graham B. Shimmield, FIBiol, FRSE, Director; Dr Anuschka Miller Activities Manager.
The Scottish Association for Marine Science (SAMS) is based at Dunstaffnage Marine

Laboratory (DML). SAMS promotes education and research in marine science, and scientists from SAMS play a major role in many national and international scientific programmes. The Laboratory operates two research vessels with state-of-the-art navigation, remote sensing and marine sampling equipment. SAMS is an academic partner in the UHI Millennium Institute and runs an undergraduate degree course in marine science.

MEDIA

GRAMPIAN TELEVISION
Queen's Cross, Aberdeen AB15 4XJ
Tel: 01224 846846 Fax: 01224 846800
e-mail: gtv@grampiantv.co.uk
web: www.grampiantv.co.uk
Contact: Derrick Thomson, Managing Director, derrick.thomson@smg.plc.uk; Bert Ovenstone, Head of Public Relations, bert.ovenstone@grampiantv.co.uk; Hilary Buchan, Press and PR Officer, hilary.buchan@grampiantv.co.uk
Grampian Television, which serves the largest transmission area in the UK, celebrated its 40th Anniversary in September 2001. Grampian has ensured that its viewers enjoy a service that meets its distinctive regional requirements, including Gaelic. North Scotland's favourite channel has had its licence for a 10-year period renewed by the Independent Television Commission.

INDEPENDENT TELEVISION COMMISSION
123 Blythswood Street, Glasgow G2 4AN
Tel: 0141 226 4436 Fax: 0141 226 4682
web: www.itc.org.uk
Contact: Alan Stewart, Head of ITC, Scotland; Claire Mack, National Programmes Manager, ITC, Scotland; Kirstin Elsby, Media and PR Officer, ITC, Scotland.
The Independent Television Commission (ITC) is the public body responsible for licensing and regulating all non-BBC television services operating in or for the UK. These include ITV, Channel 4, Channel 5, digital services, a range of cable, satellite, text and data services. The National Office in Scotland has a particular responsibility to liaise with the licensees in Scotland and to promote awareness and understanding of the ITC's functions.

NORTHSOUND RADIO LIMITED
45 King's Gate, Aberdeen AB15 4EL
Tel: 01224 337000 Fax: 01224 400003
e-mail: adam.findlay@srh.co.uk
Contact: Adam Findlay, Managing Director; Fiona Stalker, Head of News.
Commercial radio station serving NE Scotland, broadcasting local and national news and weather, local information. Split into two services, Northsound One on FM, and Northsound Two on AM, the station provides entertainment and information as the top-rated broadcaster in national research.

SCOTTISH SCREEN
249 West George Street, Glasgow G2 4QE
Tel: 0141 302 1700 Fax: 0141 302 1711
e-mail: info@scottishscreen.com
web: www.scottishscreen.com
Contact: John Archer, Chief Executive, 0141 302 1700, john.archer@scottishscreen.com; Alison Maxwell, Head of Training and Education, 0141 302 1761, alison.maxwell@scottishscreen.com; Steve McIntyre, Head of Production Development, 0141 302 1752, steve.mcintyre@scottishscreen.com

Scottish Screen is responsible to the Scottish Parliament for developing all aspects of screen industry and culture in Scotland through script and company development, short film production, distribution of National Lottery film production finance, training, education, exhibition funding, the Film Commission locations support and the Scottish Screen archive.

SMG (formerly Scottish Media Group)
200 Renfield Street, Glasgow G2 3PR
Tel: 0141 300 3000 e-mail: corporateaffairs@smg.plc.uk web: www.smg.plc.uk
Contact: Andrew Flanagan, Chief Executive; George Watt, Group Finance Director; Callum Spreng, Director, Corporate Affairs.
SMG is Scotland's largest media group. It has a number of divisions. Grampian Television and Scottish Television are the ITV licence holders for most of Scotland. In addition to The Herald, Evening Times and Sunday Herald, the group also publishes a number of nationally circulating consumer and trade magazines. The outdoor advertising business, Primesight, and well-known cinema advertising company, Pearl and Dean, comprise the group's Out of Home division. In March 2000, Virgin Radio joined the group as part of SMG's acquisition of Ginger Media Group. The addition, also, of Ginger Television to sit alongside SMG TV Productions makes SMG the sixth largest television programme producer in the UK. The company's s1 suite of websites includes s1jobs.com – Scotland's top recruitment site and s1play.com – the Scottish listings site.

PROFESSIONAL SERVICES

1. ACCOUNTANTS

FINDLAY & COMPANY
11 Dudhope Terrace, Dundee DD3 6TS
Tel: 01382 221511 Fax: 01382 322299
e-mail: mail@findlay-ca.co.uk
web: www.findlay-ca.co.uk
Contact: Colin Walker, Managing Partner, colin@findlay-ca.co.uk; Euan Webster, Partner, euan@findlay-ca.co.uk; Hugh Grant, Partner, hugh@findlay-ca.co.uk
Findlay & Company has six Principal Partners and one Associate with a diverse client base ranging from sole traders through partnerships, small and medium family companies to government funded organisations and large conglomerates. Operating in the service, manufacturing, building, financial, retail and agricultural sectors of industry, each receiving the same high quality consultancy and personal service, earning Findlay & Company the reputation as one of Tayside's foremost accountancy firms.

GERBER LANDA & GEE, CHARTERED ACCOUNTANTS
11/12 Newton Terrace, Glasgow G3 7PJ
Tel: 0141 221 7446 Fax: 0141 248 2469
e-mail: mail@gerberlandagee.co.uk
web: www.gerberlandagee.co.uk

Gerber
&Landa
Gee
CHARTERED ACCOUNTANTS

Contact: Thomas Hughes, LLB, CA, ATII; Charles Martin, CA, ATII; James Murphy, CA; Harry Seddon, FCCA; Ann McLaren, BA, CA.
Gerber Landa & Gee was formed in 1968 by an amalgamation of three practices. Since then the firm has developed a leading reputation as advisors to family business. We have assisted many businesses through their formative years and are experienced in advising the more established business to assist growth and meet the changing economic environment. Our aim is to provide a quality service to clients supported by confidentiality and integrity.

McCABES
56 Palmerston Place, Edinburgh EH12 5AY
Tel: 0131 225 6366 Fax: 0131 220 1041
Contact: Jeffrey A.C. Meek, Managing Partner, e-mail: jeff@mccp.co.uk;
Barry W. Laurie, Head of Tax Consultancy, e-mail: barry@mccp.co.uk;
Robert M.W. Clark, Compliance Partner, e-mail: robert@mccp.co.uk
One of Scotland's foremost firms of chartered accountants with clients throughout the UK. Focussed on consultancy services that help businesses to set and attain their goals. Key growth services, strategic planning, business finance and tax consultancy and accountancy. Key markets: hospitality and leisure, technology and media, property, wealth preservation.

2. ARCHITECTS

IAN BURKE ASSOCIATES
10 Belford Road, Edinburgh EH4 3BL
Tel: 0131 225 2958 Fax: 0131 226 3716
e-mail: iba@ianburke.co.uk

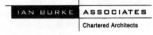

Contact: Mr Lindsay Manson, lindsay.manson@ianburke.co.uk; Mr David Pollard,
david.pollard@ianburke.co.uk; Mr Allan Munro, allan.munro@ianburke.co.uk
Ian Burke Associates were established in 1969 and have successfully grown to become one of the most respected and distinguished architectural practices in Scotland. We have built up a considerable portfolio which has resulted in repeat business from existing clients and enticed new customers to utilise our services. Our ethos is to be innovative and provide an overall vision which our clients and end-users can benefit from. We strive to be efficient and to focus on delivering the optimum solution which our colleagues can understand and implement. Ian Burke Associates have offices in Edinburgh and Dundee and have recently developed associate offices in London and Kiev.

RICHARD MURPHY ARCHITECTS
The Breakfast Mission, 4 Old Fishmarket Close, Edinburgh EH1 1RW.
Tel: 0131 220 6125 Fax: 0131 220 6781
e-mail: mail@richardmurphyarchitects.com
web: www.richardmurphyarchitects.com
Contact: Richard Murphy, Principal; Bill Black, Senior Associate.
Richard Murphy received his diploma in Architecture from Edinburgh University and later lectured there. Richard has also lectured in Europe, North America and Asia. Now celebrating its 10th anniversary, Richard Murphy Architects has established itself as one of the country's leading design practices, having received numerous awards for its work in the arts, education, and housing. Some highlights of its work include Dundee Contemporary Arts, Harmeny School, Dublin Street Lane housing, and the Stirling Tolbooth.

SIMPSON & BROWN ARCHITECTS
St Ninian's Manse, Quayside Street, Edinburgh EH6 6EJ
Tel: 0131 555 4678 Fax: 0131 553 4576
e-mail: admin@simpsonandbrown.co.uk
web: www.simpsonandbrown.co.uk
Contact: James Simpson, BArch, FRIAS, RIBA, FSA Scot; A Stewart Brown, BArch(Hons),
ARIAS, RIBA.
The practice is proud of its reputation for scholarly and conscientious conservation, for green and beautiful buildings, and for caring for the needs and interests of its clients.

3. CHARTERED SURVEYORS

DM HALL
36 Melville Street, Edinburgh EH3 7HA
Tel: 0131 477 6000 Fax: 0131 477 6016
e-mail: enquiries@dmhall.co.uk
web: www.dmhall.co.uk

Contact: Douglas Sutherland, Partner; Max Mendelssohn, Commercial Partner; Michael Ramsay, Residential Partner.
DM Hall Chartered Surveyors has over 100 years experience in general practice surveying work and 28 offices throughout Scotland. The firm has a wide portfolio including specialist commercial advice in rating, property valuation, agency, business sales, property management and all aspects of country property. This service is provided across Scotland to all the major lenders, solicitors, brokers and agents, currently active in the various market sectors

STRUTT & PARKER
28 Walker Street, Edinburgh EH3 7HR
Tel: 0131 226 2500 Fax: 0131 226 2508
e-mail: andrew.rettie@struttandparker.co.uk
web: www.struttandparker.com
Contact: Andrew Rettie, FRICS.
One of the leading firms of national estate agents, chartered surveyors, and sporting letting agents. A partnership, established in 1885, of experienced property professionals who act for landowners, city institutions, farmers, and investors throughout the UK. For a highly personal service, contact Andrew Rettie, FRICS.

4. LAW FIRMS

BIGGART BAILLIE
Dalmore House, 310 St. Vincent Street, Glasgow G2 5QR
Tel: 0141 228 8000 Fax: 0141 228 8310
7 Castle Street, Edinburgh EH2 3AP
Tel: 0131 226 5541 Fax: 0131 226 2278
e-mail: info@biggartbaillie.co.uk
web: www.biggartbaillie.co.uk

Contact: Campbell Smith, Managing Partner.
Biggart Baillie provide practical commercial and corporate legal advice that counts. Areas of law that we have particular recognised in-depth expertise in include corporate finance, banking, pensions, energy and utilities, IT and intellectual property, construction, commercial litigation, employment and commercial property.

BOYDS
146 West Regent Street, Glasgow G2 2RZ
Tel: 0141 221 8251 Fax: 0141 226 4799
e-mail: mail@boydslaw.com
web: www.boydslaw.com
Contact: Robert Gall, Managing Partner, e-mail: rgall@boydslaw.com; Martin Street, Marketing Director, mstreet@boydslaw.com
We are a client focused organisation, always aiming to achieve the commercial objectives of our clients by providing practical solutions. We are also an accredited Investor in People organisation committed to the development of good client relationships and staff alike.

BURNETT & REID
15 Golden Square, Aberdeen AB10 1WF
Tel: 01224 644333 Fax: 01224 632173
e-mail: mail@burnett-reid.co.uk
Contact: Michael D. McMillan, Managing Partner; Alastair O. Robertson, Senior Partner;
Angus M. Matheson, Commercial Partner.
Aberdeen's longest established legal firm can trace its roots back to 1754. The firm
traditionally specialised in agriculture. It now covers most fields of law. The firm is
mentioned in Chambers Guide as having special expertise in acting for working farmers,
large estates and in acquisitions and sales. The court department specialises in family law
and in child law. The firm also provides services for private client, property and corporate
work.

FYFE IRELAND WS
Orchard Brae House, 30 Queensferry Road, Edinburgh
EH4 2HG
Tel: 0131 343 2500 Fax: 0131 343 3166
e-mail: mail@fyfeireland.com
web: www.fyfeireland.com

FYFE IRELAND
ws
S O L I C I T O R S

Contact: David Lindgren, Head of Corporate, dlindgren@fyfeireland.com; Greig
Honeyman, Head of Private Client Services, ghoneyman@fyfeireland.com; James Roscoe,
Head of Commercial Property, jroscoe@fyfeireland.com
Based in Edinburgh, this well regarded firm is also represented in London. Fyfe Ireland
operates primarily in the "business to business" sector but also undertakes private client
work. Although the firm's history dates back to 1830, the firm with its 13 partners is very
forward looking and is often referred to as "punching above its weight".

GOLDS SOLICITORS
8 Newton Terrace, Glasgow G3 7PJ
Tel: 0141 300 4300. Fax: 0141 300 4350
G O L D S **e-mail: golds@golds.co.uk**
solicitors **web: www.golds.co.uk**
Contact: Stephen H. Gold, Senior Partner, shg@golds.co.uk; Jonathan Edwards, Managing
Partner, je@golds.co.uk; Louise Rutherford, Client Services Manager, lr@golds.co.uk
Having won *Professional Services Company of the Year* at the National Business Awards of
Scotland 2000, Golds is now firmly placed as one of Scotland's top corporate and
commercial law firms. The firm's 11 partners and over 100 staff provide a full range of
services including: banking and building society work; commercial litigation; commercial
property; corporate and commercial; information technology and intellectual property; debt
recovery; housing association work; and employment and human rights services.

THE KELLAS PARTNERSHIP
2-6 High Street, Inverurie, Aberdeenshire AB51 3XQ
Tel: 01467 627300 Fax: 01467 622030
e-mail: info@kellas.biz
web: www.kellas.biz
Contact: Stephen J. Dowds, LLB, NP, sjd@kellas.biz; Hamish M. Duthie, LLB, NP,
hmd@kellas.biz; Louise E. Robertson, LLB, NP, ler@kellas.biz
The Kellas Partnership (formerly Stronachs Inverurie) has offices in Inverurie and Kemnay
and is one of the longest established firms in the area. Equipped to provide a wide range of
expert, specialised legal services to meet today's needs and demands, the firm offers a
friendly and helpful approach to all clients. Comprehensive range of services including
estate agency, conveyancing, executries, court work (civil and criminal, including
representation at Inverurie District Court) and legal aid.

LEDINGHAM CHALMERS
5 Melville Crescent, Edinburgh EH3 7JA
Tel: 0131 200 1000 Fax: 0131 200 1080
e-mail: mail@ledinghamchalmers.com
web: www.ledinghamchalmers.com

LEDINGHAM
CHALMERS

Contact: David K. Laing, Senior Partner; Brian Hay, Director of Finance; Dorothy Miller, Director of Human Resources.
Providing legal services from a unique network of offices in Edinburgh (contact: Gavin Farquhar, 0131 200 1030), Aberdeen (contact: Malcolm Laing, 01224 408511) and Inverness (contact: Fiona Neilson, 01463 667400) and in three key overseas locations: Istanbul, Turkey; Baku, Azerbaijan; and Stanley, Falkland Islands.

MacROBERTS SOLICITORS
152 Bath Street, Glasgow G2 4TB
Tel: 0141 332 9988 Fax: 0141 332 8886
Excel House, 30 Semple Street, Edinburgh EH3 8BL
Tel: 0131 229 5046 Fax: 0131 229 0849
e-mail: maildesk@macroberts.com
web: www.macroberts.com

Contact: John E.N. Macmillan, Managing Partner.
As one of Scotland's leading commercial law firms, MacRoberts offers a comprehensive range of legal services to corporate, commercial, public sector and private clients. The firm prides itself on being highly attuned to clients' needs and through offices in Glasgow and Edinburgh, provides quality legal services in a prompt, efficient and friendly manner. Practice groups: banking; construction; corporate; corporate tax; employment; environmental and planning; IP/IT; litigation; pensions; projects; property; private client.

MURRAY BEITH MURRAY WS
39 Castle Street, Edinburgh EH2 3BH
Tel: 0131 225 1200 Fax: 0131 225 4412
e-mail: mbm@murraybeith.co.uk
web: www.murraybeith.co.uk www.eLaw.co.uk
Contact: John Scott Moncrieff, Managing Partner; Sandy Finlayson, Head of Commercial; Hugh Younger, Head of Private Client; Ruthven Gemmell, Head of Asset Management.
Murray Beith Murray is a progressive Edinburgh-based practice, which offers an extensive range of services to private and business clients. The firm's core business is private client work and the firm is regarded as one of Scotland's leading firms in this field. The Legal Services department also offers commercial advice to assist companies from start-up, through the early years, to flotation and beyond. An efficient and personal service is combined with excellent financial contacts and deal-making skills. The firm's award-winning Asset Management department offers a full financial planning service, including a comprehensive, independent overview of a client's investment and financial needs. Established in 1949, Murray Beith Murray actively seeks to combine its traditional strength of a dedicated client service with modern management and innovative use of technology.

TODS MURRAY WS
66 Queen Street, Edinburgh EH2 4NE
Tel: 0131 226 4771 Fax: 0131 225 3676
33 Bothwell Street, Glasgow G2 6NL
Tel: 0141 275 4771 Fax: 0141 275 4781
TODS MURRAY WS
SOLICITORS
e-mail: maildesk@todsmurray.com
web: www.todsmurray.com
Contact: Peter Misselbrook, Chairman; John Biggar, Managing Partner.
Tods Murray is one of Scotland's leading all-service law firms with offices in Edinburgh and Glasgow, providing specialist advice in corporate, banking, commercial and employment law, capital projects and commercial property law, construction law and commercial

litigation, private clients, agriculture and estate law, investment funds and corporate financial services, e-commerce, IT and IP, media and entertainment law, leisure and timeshare.

TURCAN CONNELL
Princes Exchange, 1 Earl Grey Street,
Edinburgh EH3 9EE
Tel: 0131 228 8111 Fax: 0131 228 8118
e-mail: enquiries@turcanconnell.com
web: www.turcanconnell.com

TURCAN CONNELL
SOLICITORS

Contact: Douglas A. Connell, dac@turcanconnell.com; Simon A Mackintosh, sam@turcanconnell.com; Ian R. Clark, irc@turcanconnell.com
Turcan Connell focuses exclusively on private clients, trusts and charities. Fifteen Partners and a staff of over 190 bring together a combination of skills and expertise unique in Scotland. These cover asset protection, land and property, succession, taxation, family law, investment management and pensions, trusts and charities. The firm offers full discretionary investment management services to private individuals, trusts, charities and pension funds. Advice on pensions planning is provided by in-house actuaries and the firm's lawyers.

TURNER MACFARLANE GREEN
RWF House, 5 Renfield Street, Glasgow G2 5EZ
Tel: 0141 204 1777 Fax: 0141 204 1771
Contact: John Woods; Mark Wilson; Sheena Savage.
Turner Macfarlane Green is a firm specialising in work for banks, building societies and finance houses. Its services cover a wide range from secured lending to debt recovery and litigation.

5. REPUTATION MANAGEMENT

GREAT CIRCLE COMMUNICATIONS LIMITED
8 Doune Terrace, Edinburgh EH3 6DY
Tel: 0131 225 4646 Fax: 0131 225 5555
e-mail: frontdesk@greatcircle.co.uk
web: www.greatcircle.co.uk
Contact: Rachel Jones; Michael Groves.
Great Circle provides brand management, strategic marketing and PR support. Our team is highly skilled, experienced and passionate and we take pride in developing innovative campaigns which deliver measurable results. One particular area of expertise is corporate social responsibility.

PROFESSIONAL AND TRADE ORGANISATIONS

INSTITUTE OF CHARTERED FORESTERS
7A St. Colme Street, Edinburgh EH3 6AA
Tel: 0131 225 2705 Fax: 0131 220 6128
e-mail: icf@charteredforesters.org
Contact: Mr T.J.D. Rollinson, BSc, FICFor, President; Mr M.T. Gale, BSc, FICFor, Vice President; Mrs M.W. Dick, OBE, FRSA, Executive Director.
Founded at Aberdeen in 1926 and incorporated by Royal Charter in 1982. The Institute is the professional body for forestry and arboriculture throughout the UK and has as its main objective the maintenance and improvement of professional standards of practice of all

aspects of forestry and arboriculture. A code of ethics and professional conduct is backed by a formal professional complaints procedure. Chartered Foresters are employed in every branch of the profession and industry, local and national government, conservation bodies, universities and colleges, research institutes. The Chartered Forester brings a vital contribution to the conservation and productivity of natural resources.

SCOTTISH DAIRY ASSOCIATION
4A Torphichen Street, Edinburgh EH3 8JQ
Tel: 0131 221 0109 Fax: 0131 221 0220
e-mail: sda@scotdairy.org.uk
Contact: K.J. Hunter, Secretary.
Representing the interests of dairy companies active in the Scottish market.

INSTITUTE OF DIRECTORS

SCOTTISH DIRECTOR DEVELOPMENT CENTRE
c/o Institute of Directors, 29 Abercromby Place, Edinburgh EH3 6QE
Tel: 0131 524 9890 Fax: 0131 524 9899
Contact: Michael Fass, Programme Director.
The Centre provides personal and professional development facilities and services for members and non-members to acquire more skills and knowledge about being a company director and fulfilling their corporate governance responsibilities. A wide variety of programmes, courses and workshops are organised all year round, including: Diploma and Chartered Director, Director Networks, Executive Coaching, The Professional Director Series, and Board Consultancy.

THE SCOTTISH PHARMACEUTICAL FEDERATION
135 Wellington Street, Glasgow G2 2XD
Tel: 0141 221 1235 Fax: 0141 248 5892, 0141 226 5047
e-mail: spf@npanet.co.uk
Contact: F.E.J. McCrossin, Secretary/Treasurer; I.J. Johnstone, Chairman; A.J. Taylor, Vice Chairman; B. Cuddihy, Public Affairs Executive.
The SPF represents owners of community pharmacies in Scotland, looking after the interests of some 500 members who own approximately 1,050 pharmacies. In conjunction with the National Pharmaceutical Association, to which it is affiliated, it provides members with professional indemnity cover, business and financial services, commercial insurance, information and guidance on pharmaceutical and business matters. The SPF is run by an Executive Council of 16 members from all parts of Scotland.

RELIGIOUS

THE CHURCH OF SCOTLAND
121 George Street, Edinburgh EH2 4YN
Tel: 0131 225 5722 Fax: 0131 220 3113
web: www.cofscotland.org.uk
Contact: Rev. Dr. Finlay A.J. Macdonald, Principal Clerk of the General Assembly.
The Church of Scotland, part of the one Holy, Catholic and Apostolic Church, is the national church in Scotland, recognised by the State but independent in spiritual matters. Trinitarian in doctrine, Reformed in tradition and Presbyterian in polity, it exists to glorify God, to work for the advancement of Christ's kingdom throughout the world and to provide religious services for the people in Scotland, through parish ministry. It co-operates with other churches in various ecumenical bodies in Scotland and beyond.

CHURCH OF SCOTLAND BOARD OF SOCIAL RESPONSIBILITY
Charis House, 47 Milton Road East, Edinburgh EH15 2SR
Tel: 0131 657 2000 Fax: 0131 657 5000
e-mail: info@charis.org.uk
Contact: Ian Baillie, CBE, Director of Social Work, ibaillie@charis.org.uk; Hugh Brown,
Communications Officer (Media), hbrown@charis.org.uk
The Board of Social Responsibility is the social care arm of the Church of Scotland, with
over 80 homes and projects. It employs 1,600 staff, has an annual expenditure of £39.2m.
and has been caring "in Christ's name" since 1869. Every day of the year 4,000 people across
Scotland are cared for or offered assistance by Board staff.

CHURCH OF SCOTLAND GUILD
121 George Street, Edinburgh EH2 4YN
Tel: 0131 225 5722 Fax: 0131 220 3113
e-mail: guild@cofscotland.org.uk
Contact: Alison Twaddle, General Secretary, Ext. 218,
atwaddle@cofscotland.org.uk; Fiona Lange, Information Officer, Ext. 332,
flange@cofscotland.org.uk
The Guild is a movement within the Church of Scotland whose aim is "to invite and
encourage all women to commit their lives to Jesus Christ and to enable them to express
their faith in worship, prayer, and action". With around 1,400 groups across Scotland, the
Guild has raised over £750,000 in the past five years for projects at home and abroad. The
Guild is represented on other church boards as well as other ecumenical, national and
international bodies.

FREE PRESBYTERIAN CHURCH OF SCOTLAND
133 Woodlands Road, Glasgow G3 6LE
Tel: 0141 332 9283 Fax: 0141 332 4271
e-mail: fpcofsoffice@cs.com web: www.fpchurch.org.uk
Contact: Rev. J. MacLeod, MA, Clerk of Synod, 16 Matheson Road, Stornoway, Isle of Lewis
HS1 2LA, Tel: 01851 702755. Fax: 01851 702919, e-mail: synodclerk@fpchurch.org.uk; Mr
R.A. Campbell, General Treasurer, as above; Moderator of Synod, 2001–02: Rev. D.J.
MacDonald, Free Presbyterian Manse, Evelix, Dornoch, Sutherland IV25 3RD.
The Free Presbyterian Church of Scotland exists to promote the biblical doctrines of the
Christian faith in the UK and abroad by preaching the Gospel, administering the Sacraments
and exercising ecclesiastical discipline, and by publishing and selling Christian literature and
providing educational and medical facilities, along with care for the elderly and for orphans.

THE SALVATION ARMY
East Scotland Division: 5 East Adam Street, Edinburgh EH8 9TF
Tel: 0131 662 3301 Fax: 0131 662 3311
e-mail: robert.mcintyre@salvationarmy.org.uk
Contact: Major Robert McIntyre
**West Scotland Division: 4 Buchanan Court, Cumbernauld Road, Stepps,
Glasgow G33 6HZ**
Tel: 0141 559 5001 Fax: 0141 779 5011
Contact: Lt. Col. Hugh Rae
North Scotland Division: Deer Road, Woodside, Aberdeen AB24 2BL
Tel: 01224 496001 Fax: 01224 496011
Contact: Major David Hinton.
The Salvation Army is an integral part of the universal Christian church. Its message is
based on the Bible, its motivation is the love of God as revealed in Jesus Christ. Its mission
is to proclaim his Gospel, to persuade men and women to become his disciples and to engage
in a programme of practical concern for the needs of humanity. Its ministry is offered to all,
regardless of race, creed, colour or sex.

SCHOOLS

ALBYN SCHOOL FOR GIRLS
17-23 Queen's Road, Aberdeen AB15 4PB
Tel: 01224 322408 Fax: 01224 209173
e-mail: information@albynschool.co.uk
web: www.albynschool.co.uk

Contact: Miss Jennifer S. Leslie, Headmistress; Mrs Louie Parker, Head of Lower School.

Albyn School provides a caring, supportive and happy atmosphere where girls are enabled to achieve excellence in academic subjects and participate in a wide range of extra-curricular activities. There is a high staff-pupil ratio from totally committed teachers meeting the needs of individual pupils. Girls leaving Albyn have confidence, poise and high regard of their personal worth to equip them for the modern world. Albyn School for Girls exists to provide education on a non-profit making basis.

BELMONT HOUSE SCHOOL
Sandringham Avenue, Newton Mearns, Glasgow G77 5DU
Tel: 0141 639 2922 Fax: 0141 639 9860
e-mail: headmaster@belmontschool.co.uk
Contact: Stuart McCulloch, Headmaster.

The school aims to: cultivate an environment that allows and encourages all pupils to develop personal excellence; promote a flexible educational experience in which the individual is of paramount importance; foster an atmosphere of diligence, tolerance, mutual respect and concern for others; sustain a safe, supportive and welcoming environment; encourage a dynamic partnership between all members of the school community.

FETTES COLLEGE
Carrington Road, Edinburgh EH4 1QX
Tel: 0131 311 6701 Fax: 0131 311 6714
Contact: Mr Michael Spens, Headmaster.

The purpose of the school is to provide an education based on Christian principles which will enable each pupil to develop his or her own individual talents to the full. Particular emphasis is placed on academic excellence, good personal relationships and strong pastoral care. Thriving artistic, dramatic and musical traditions coupled with a wide range of sporting activities exist. The school is coeducational with 580 pupils aged between 8 and 18.

HIGH SCHOOL OF DUNDEE
Euclid Crescent, Dundee DD1 1HU
Tel: 01382 202921 Fax: 01382 229822
e-mail: admissions@hsd.dundeecity.sch.uk
web: www.hsd.dundeecity.sch.uk
Contact: Mr A. Michael Duncan, MA, BPhil, DipEd, Rector.

A fully co-educational independent school of 1,080 pupils (junior school 350 pupils) offering all through education for pupils from 5 to 18. Emphasis is placed upon the needs and welfare of the individual. Pupils are prepared for SQA examinations with over 90 per cent of final leavers entering university. There is an extensive range of sporting, cultural and social activities with games, music, drama and debating particularly strong.

HUTCHESONS' GRAMMAR SCHOOL
21 Beaton Road, Glasgow G41 4NW
Tel: 0141 423 2933 Fax: 0141 424 0251
e-mail: rector@hutchesons.org
Contact: Mr John Knowles, Rector.

The new millennium sees Hutchesons' enter its fifth century of existence, with a reputation for academic excellence to match its longevity. Co-educational and non-denominational, we accept pupils from age five to 18 years, offering unparalleled opportunities for educational achievement, sporting participation, creative expression and community involvement. Our traditional ethos is allied to impressive facilities – a new infant building, science block, sports hall and library and information centre – with exciting plans for an adjacent ICT and music centre about to be realised. In August 2001, we merged with Laurel Park School, establishing in the west end of Glasgow a second Hutchesons' primary school.

KELVINSIDE ACADEMY
33 Kirklee Road, Glasgow G12 0SW
Tel: 0141 357 3376 Fax: 0141 357 5401
e-mail: rector@kelvinsideacademy.gla.sch.uk

Kelvinside Academy *Contact: J.L. Broadfoot, Rector; Mrs T. Littlefield, Head of Lower School; Mrs J. Monks, Head of Nursery.*

A leading independent day school for boys and girls aged three to 18. Our aim is to encourage each pupil to achieve his or her fullest potential in all academic, sporting and cultural fields, in what is a friendly but disciplined environment. Small classes and individual attention are main features. A rich and rounded education produces confident and articulate young people ready and skilled for Higher Education and the world of work.

LOMOND SCHOOL
10 Stafford Street, Helensburgh, Argyll & Bute G84 9JX
Tel: 01436 672476 Fax: 01436 678320
e-mail: admin@lomond-school.demon.co.uk
web: www.lomond-school.org
Contact: Mr A. Macdonald; Mr W. MacKenzie; Mr I. McKellar.

An independent co-educational day and boarding school with a strong academic reputation and commitment to developing the whole person. Brand new facilities. An excellent school in an ideal setting.

ST. COLUMBA'S SCHOOL, KILMACOLM
Duchal Road, Kilmacolm, Renfrewshire PA13 4AU
Tel: 01505 872238 Fax: 01505 873995
e-mail: stcolumba@rmplc.co.uk
web: www.stcolumbas.renfrew.sch.uk
Contact: Mr A.H. Livingstone, Rector.

Founded in 1897, St. Columba's is one of Scotland's foremost schools with a roll of 690 students. The school is non-denominational and has equal numbers of boys and girls at all stages. It has an excellent academic reputation and, in addition, is strong musically, on the sporting front and in its participation in the Duke of Edinburgh Awards' Scheme. The aim of St Columba's is to produce mannerly, mature and successful young people who have, at the same time, a care and concern for others.

ST GEORGE'S SCHOOL FOR GIRLS
Garscube Terrace, Edinburgh EH12 6BG
Tel: 0131 332 4575 Fax: 0131 313 2976
e-mail: office@st-georges.edin.sch.uk
web: www.st-georges.edin.sch.uk
Contact: Headmistress: Dr Judith McClure, MA, DPhil, FRSA, FSAScot, head@stgeorges.edin.sch.uk

St George's provides a caring, stimulating and challenging environment for our 970 students. Our aim is to promote women of independent mind. Emphasis is placed on personal achievement and responsibility. Sixty boarders live on campus in Houldsworth House. St

George's examination results are outstanding. Almost all our leavers go on to universities and colleges. Students enter the school from Early Years and thereafter there is a structured progression to Sixth Form. We welcome enquiries throughout the year.

ST. LEONARDS (incorporating St. Leonards Junior School and St. Leonards Sixth Form College)
St. Andrews, Fife KY16 9QJ
Tel: 01334 472126 Fax: 01334 476152
e-mail: info@stleonards-fife.org
web: www.stleonards-fife.org
Contact: Mrs Wendy A. Bellars, Principal; Mrs Jennifer B. Wylie, Registrar.

St. Leonards, set in the medieval university town of St. Andrews, comprising St. Leonards Junior School (ages 3 to 8), St. Leonards Middle School (8 to 12), St. Leonards Senior School (12 to 16) and St. Leonards Sixth Form College (16 to 19), provides first class boarding and day education for boys and girls. Our aim is to encourage the best in each of our students, academically, in sport, music and drama; indeed in whatever field they choose to explore. Public examinations taken are GCSEs and A Levels. In a relaxed and friendly yet purposeful atmosphere, students will be made ready to move to the next stage of their lives.

ST. MARGARET'S SCHOOL FOR GIRLS
17 Albyn Place, Aberdeen AB10 1RU
Tel: 01224 584466 Fax: 01224 585600
e-mail: info@stmargaret.aberdeen.sch.uk
web: www.stmargaret.aberdeen.sch.uk
Contact: Mrs Lyn McKay, Headmistress.

St. Margaret's School for Girls in Aberdeen (age range 3 to 18 years) is one of the leading girls' schools in Scotland. We aim to make the education of pupils a happy and rewarding experience, where talents are encouraged and goals are set. We pride ourselves on working in partnership with parents and the community. Our academic results are excellent. A thoroughly modern curriculum is delivered, using up-to-date methodology and resources. We educate for life with a wide extra-curricular and personal development programme.

ST. MARY'S MUSIC SCHOOL
Coates Hall, 25 Grosvenor Crescent, Edinburgh EH12 5EL
Tel: 0131 538 7766 Fax: 0131 467 7289
e-mail: info@st-marys-music-school.co.uk
web: www.st-marys-music-school.co.uk
Contact: Mrs Jennifer Rimer, Headteacher; Mr John Grundy, Director of Music.

Independent specialist music school, day and boarding, offering integrated music and academic education to instrumental pupils and the choristers of St. Mary's Cathedral. Sixty-five pupils, age nine to 19, supported by the Aided Places scheme or by scholarships. Entry by audition at any stage, including 6th year. Prospectus available. Also runs Saturday morning community classes.

STEWART'S MELVILLE COLLEGE AND THE MARY ERKSINE SCHOOL
Queensferry Road, Edinburgh EH4 3EZ
Tel: 0131 332 7925 Fax: 0131 343 2432
e-mail: principal@esmgc.com
web: www.stewartsmelville.edin.sch.uk
Contact: David Gray, Principal; Bryan Lewis, Headmaster of the Junior School, Ext. 4244; Ian McGregor, Bursar, Ext. 3150.

Two single-sex schools, each combining academic excellence with a very wide range of extra-curricular activity, share a single co-educational Junior School, a fully twinned Sixth Form and management by one Principal and Governing Council. Through a unique structure, our schools seek to achieve the "best of both worlds". This large operation (over 2,600 boys and girls) prides itself on the personal and social development of every individual. Facilities are superb. The schools' reputations in music, drama and sport are exceptional.

SCIENCE

SCOTTISH SCIENCE TRUST
12 Queen Street, Edinburgh EH2 1JE
Tel: 0131 226 3481 Fax: 0131 226 3482
e-mail: trust@sst.org.uk
web: www.sst.org.uk
Contact: Dr Chris Brittain, Executive Director, 0131 226 3481, chris.brittain@sst.org.uk;
Fiona Curle, Administrator, 0131 226 0240, fiona.curle@sst.org.uk
The Scottish Science Trust aims to engage the public in issues relating to science, engineering, technology and medicine in Scotland. It facilitates the development of existing science centres, the creation of new ones, and the integration of outreach projects to form a coherent network throughout Scotland for the 21st century. Through the network the Trust will help visitors, and those living and working in Scotland to understand the opportunities and rewards of, as well as the dilemmas created by science.

SPORT

sportscotland
Caledonia House, South Gyle, Edinburgh EH12 9DQ
Tel: 0131 317 7200 Fax: 0131 317 7202   **sport**scotland
e-mail: library@sportscotland.org.uk
web: www.sportscotland.org.uk
Contact: Ian Robson, Chief Executive; Kate Vincent, Director of Corporate Strategy
sportscotland is the national agency dedicated to promoting sporting opportunities for all Scots at all levels, whatever their interest and ability. Everything we do is driven by three visions: widening opportunities – creating a country where sport is more widely available to all; developing potential – creating a country where sporting talent is recognised and nurtured; achieving excellence – creating a country achieving and sustaining world class performances in sport.

TENNIS SCOTLAND
177 Colinton Road, Edinburgh EH14 1BZ
Tel: 0131 444 1984 Fax: 0131 444 1973
e-mail: gloria.duncan@tennisscotland.org
web: www.tennisscotland.org
Contact: Gloria Duncan, Secretary and Director of Administration, 0131 443 8952,
gloria.duncan@tennisscotland.org; Matthew J. Hulbert, Director of Tennis, 0131 443 8954,
matthew.hulbert@tennisscotland.org
Governing Body for tennis in Scotland.

TOURISM

VISITSCOTLAND
23 Ravelston Terrace, Edinburgh EH4 3TP
Tel: 0131 332 2433
web: www.visitscotland.com
VisitScotland *Contact: Peter Lederer, Chairman; Philip Riddle, CEO; Press Office, 0131*
472 2211.
VisitScotland is the national agency for the development of tourism in Scotland. VisitScotland aims to help maximise the economic benefit of tourism throughout the country by: leading the industry and providing strategic guidance, increasing visitor expenditure, increasing the seasonal spread of expenditure, developing tourism outwith main areas, increasing competitiveness by promoting quality and value for money.

TRANSPORT

FIRSTGROUP PLC
395 King Street, Aberdeen AB24 5RP
Tel: 01224 650102 Fax: 01224 650149
e-mail moir.lockhead@firstgroup.com
web: www.firstgroup.com

Contact: Moir Lockhead, OBE, Chief Executive, 01224 650102; Robbie Duncan, Business Change Director, 01224 650114; Lois Brown, PA to Chief Executive, 01224 650102, loisbrown@firstgroup.com; Iain Lanaghan, Group Finance Director.

First is a leading UK-based international passenger operator with an annual turnover of £2bn and a workforce of over 50,000. First has three core operations which comprise UK buses, UK passenger rail franchises and US school buses and transit management. With a fleet of some 10,000 vehicles and over 23% market share of the UK bus market, the Group is the UK's largest bus operator. Through First Great Eastern, First Great Western and First North West Trains, the company is now one of the UK's largest train operators, operating inner-city, regional and commuter trains, delivering train services across some 2,320 route miles and to more than 380 stations. First is all about quality. Our aim is to provide a superior quality of service for all our customers, and a high-quality return on our shareholders' investment.

RAIL PASSENGER COMMITTEE SCOTLAND
CALEDONIAN MACBRAYNE USERS' COMMITTEE
5th Floor, Corunna House, 29 Cadogan Street, Glasgow G2 7AB
Tel: 0141 221 7760 Fax: 0141 221 3393
e-mail: scottishrailusers@supanet.com

Contact: Mike Lunan, Convener; Bill Ure, Secretary; Robert Samson, Deputy Secretary.

Statutory body which exists to represent rail and ferry users' interests; to monitor quality of service provided by train operating companies and Caledonian MacBrayne; to undertake investigation into rail quality of service matters as directed by the Strategic Rail Authority and Rail Regulator; to act as "Court of Appeal" for passengers who are dissatisfied with how their complaints are handled by train operators. Holds four public meetings each year to question senior railway managers on quality of service matters. Reports annually to the First Minister and Minister of Transport on rail and ferry matters.

RAILTRACK plc
Buchanan House, 58 Port Dundas Street, Glasgow G4 0LQ
Tel: 0141 335 2424 Fax: 0141 335 2070
Contact: Janette Anderson, Director (Scotland).

As the owner/operator of Britain's rail infrastructure of track, stations, signals, structures and overhead equipment, it is Railtrack's mission to work with our industry partners to create a safe, reliable and efficient rail network of world standard, and which forms the heart of Britain's 21st century transport system.

SCOTRAIL
Caledonian Chambers, 87 Union Street, Glasgow G1 3TA
Tel: 0141 335 4787 Fax: 0141 335 4791
e-mail: enquiries@scotrail.co.uk
Contact: Alastair McPherson, Managing Director, 0141 335 4500; John Boyle, Corporate Affairs Director, 0141 335 4447; Kenny McPhail, Finance Director, 0141 335 4136.

ScotRail is Scotland's national rail passenger operator, providing suburban, interurban and rural services within Scotland and also the Caledonian Sleepers linking Scotland with London. We run two thousand trains daily which in 2001 carried 63.2 million passengers. The routes supported by Strathclyde Passenger Transport comprise the biggest suburban network in Britain outside London.

STRATHCLYDE PASSENGER TRANSPORT
Consort House, 12 West George Street, Glasgow G2 1HN
Tel: 0141 332 6811 Fax: 0141 332 3076
web: www.spt.co.uk
Contact: Dr Malcolm Reed, Director General; Douglas Ferguson, Director of Operations; Iain Wylie, Director of Corporate Services.
SPT is Scotland's only passenger transport authority and executive, investing in rail, bus, Underground and ferry services for 42 per cent of Scotland's population. We finance ScotRail passenger services in the west of Scotland and set train fares and timetables. We run the SPT Underground and Renfrew-Yoker Ferry. SPT currently subsidises about 150 bus services in areas where local communities are not already served by commercial operators. We also subsidise a number of local ferry services.

UNIONS

AMICUS (MSF Section)
John Smith House, 145-165 West Regent Street, Glasgow G2 4RZ
Tel: 0141 229 6100 Fax: 0141 229 6102
e-mail: glasgow@msf.org.uk
web: www.msf.org.uk
Contact: John Wall, National Secretary; Lee Whitehill, Policy and Communications Officer, whitehill@msf.org.uk; Roger Lyons, General Secretary.
AMICUS is the new union created from the merger between AEEU and MSF. With 1.2 million members AMICUS is the largest private sector union in the UK and Scotland and is the largest affiliate to the Labour Party.

PROSPECT SCOTLAND
18 Melville Terrace, Stirling FK8 2NQ
Tel: 01786 465999 Fax: 01786 465516
e-mail: scotland@prospect.org.uk
web: www.prospect.org.uk
Contact: Alan Denney.

Prospect is a new union representing engineers, scientists, professionals and managers. Combining the former IPMS and EMA, we now have a separate Prospect (EMA) Scottish and North-Eastern office at 30 New Street, Musselburgh, East Lothian EH21 6JP, Telephone: 0131 665 4487, Fax: 0131 665 4487. Prospect provides the UK's largest collective voice for professionals at work. Our members are in transport, defence, environment, agriculture, energy, health and safety and heritage.

SCOTTISH TRADES UNION CONGRESS
333 Woodlands Road, Glasgow G3 6NG
Tel: 0141 337 8100 Fax: 0141 337 8101
e-mail: info@stuc.org.uk
Contact: Bill Speirs, General Secretary.
The STUC first convened in Glasgow in 1897. It is completely independent (not a Scottish regional organisation of the TUC, and not affiliated to any political party) and is financed from the subscriptions of its affiliated unions, who represent over 630,000 Scottish workers. Hours and conditions of work have remained a central preoccupation, but it plays a wider role in campaigning for equality and social justice, both in Scotland and internationally.

UNIFI
146 Argyle Street, Glasgow G2 8BL
Tel: 0141 221 6475 Fax: 0141 204 3315
web: www.unifi.org.uk
Contact: Sandy Boyle, Deputy General Secretary.

The largest financial services union in Europe with a membership of 155,000, with sole recognition in HBOS, Clydesdale Bank, Royal Bank of Scotland Group (including NatWest), Barclays and HSBC and membership in Lloyds TSB Scotland.

UNISON, SCOTLAND
14 West Campbell Street, Glasgow G2 6RX
Tel: 0141 332 0006 Fax: 0141 331 1203
e-mail: matt.smith@unison.co.uk
web: www.unison-scotland.org.uk
Contact: Matt Smith.

UNISON is the largest trade union in the country, representing a range of members across the public services – local government, the National Health Service, higher and further education, the electricity, gas, water and transport industries and a range of public and voluntary organisations. UNISON provides a range of membership services in addition to its professional negotiation and representation role. It has offices in Glasgow, Edinburgh, Aberdeen and Inverness. UNISON is committed to campaigning actively in support of public services in Scotland.

WHISKY

THE SCOTCH MALT WHISKY SOCIETY
The Vaults, 87 Giles Street, Edinburgh EH6 6BZ
Tel: 0131 554 3451 Fax: 0131 553 1003
e-mail: enquiries@smws.com
web: www.smws.com
Contact: Richard Gordon, Managing Director; Willie Phillips, Chairman.

The Scotch Malt Whisky Society is a private club for anyone who enjoys a good dram of malt whisky. Services to members include being able to order the Society's exclusive single cask bottlings with delivery to your door, visiting the Members' Rooms and bars in London, Edinburgh and Switzerland, and attending Society tastings which are held countrywide. Flats are available at the Edinburgh Rooms and all Members' Rooms offer fine dining and room hire facilities. The Society can also accommodate corporate events, offering whisky tastings, dinners and room hire.

YOUTH

THE BOYS' BRIGADE
Scottish Headquarters, Carronvale House, Carronvale Road, Larbert, Stirlingshire FK5 3LH
Tel: 01324 562008 Fax: 01324 552323
e-mail: carronvale@boys-brigade.org.uk
web: www.boys-brigade.org.uk
Contact: Mr Tom Boyle, Director, Scotland, Scottish Headquarters; Brigade Secretary; BB UK Headquarters, 01442 231681, e-mail: felden@boys-brigade.org.uk

The Boys' Brigade is a national voluntary youth organisation committed to the personal and social development of approximately 24,000 children and young people in Scotland. As part of the community education provision, promoting the concept of life-long learning, the organisation seeks to serve local churches in most communities in Scotland by offering a range of informal educational programmes which are led by over 4,000 voluntary youth workers operating in 568 local units throughout the country.

THE PRINCE'S TRUST – SCOTLAND
1st Floor, The Guildhall, 57 Queen Street, Glasgow G1 3EN
Tel: 0141 204 4409 Fax: 0141 221 8221
web: www.princes-trust.org.uk
Contact: Euan Davidson, Director – Scotland.
The Prince's Trust Scotland supports socially and economically excluded young people aged 14–25 years to realise their full potential. In particular, it supports young people in their move towards education, training, and employment. It does this through a combination of research and development, influencing policy, programme delivery and intensive support.

YOUTHLINK SCOTLAND
Rosebery House, 9 Haymarket Terrace, Edinburgh EH12 5EX
Tel: 0131 313 2488 Fax: 0131 313 6800
e-mail: info@youthlink.co.uk
web: www.youthlink.co.uk
Contact: Simon Jaquet, Chief Executive, sjaquet@youthlink.co.uk
Youthlink Scotland is the intermediary body for the voluntary youth work sector in Scotland. It exists to support and promote the work and collective aspirations of the voluntary youth sector in the interests of young people. With 50 member organisations, Youthlink's main functions are networking, co-ordination and sharing of resources; providing youth work information; developing projects; specialist training.

YWCA OF GREAT BRITAIN, SCOTTISH NATIONAL COUNCIL
7b Randolph Crescent, Edinburgh EH3 7TH
Tel: 0131 225 7592 Fax: 0131 467 7008
e-mail: info@ywcascotland.org
web: www.ywcascotland.org

YWCA of Great Britain
Scottish National Council

Contact: Joan Bree, Communications Officer; Elaine Samson, Chief Executive.
The YWCA enables women to develop their full potential in mind, body and spirit and to participate at all levels of society. We are unique in being part of a national and international organisation which delivers services locally, with a single gender focus, mainly in disadvantaged communities. Our values are social justice and inclusion, equality of opportunity, openess, and respect for self, others, our Christian basis and for the whole person.

Biographies

An A to Z of prominent people in Scotland

A

Abercrombie, Ian R., QC, LLB (Hons); b. 7.7.55, Bulawayo. Educ. Milton High School; Edinburgh University. Recreations: travelling; walking. Address: (h.) 7 Lauder Road, Edinburgh EH9 2EW; T.-0131-668 2489.

Aberdeen and Temair, June Marchioness of, CBE, DL, GCStJ, FRCM, FRSE. Musical Director and Conductor, Haddo House Choral and Operatic Society, since 1945. Educ. Southlands School, Harrow; Royal College of Music. Chairman: Scottish Children's League, 1969-84, NE Scotland Music School, since 1975, Advisory Council, Scottish Opera, 1979-90. Address: Haddo House, Aberdeen AB41 7EQ; T.-01651 851216.

Abernethy, Hon. Lord (John Alastair Cameron). Senator, College of Justice, since 1992; b. 1.2.38, Newcastle-upon-Tyne; m., Elspeth Mary Dunlop Miller; 3 s. Educ. St. Mary's School, Melrose; Glenalmond College, Perth; Pembroke College, Oxford. National Service, 2nd Lt., RASC, Aldershot and Malta, 1956-58. Called to the Bar, Inner Temple, 1963; admitted Member, Faculty of Advocates, 1966; Advocate-Depute, 1972-75; Standing Junior Counsel to Department of Energy, 1976-79, Scottish Development Department, 1978-79; QC (Scotland), 1979; Vice-Dean, Faculty of Advocates, 1983-92; President, Pensions Appeal Tribunals for Scotland, 1985-92 (Legal Chairman, 1979-85); Chairman, Faculty Services Ltd., 1983-89 (Director, 1979-83); Hon. Fellow, Pembroke College, Oxford, 1993; International Bar Association: Vice Chairman, 1993-94, Chairman, Judges' Forum, 1994-98, Member, Council, Section on Legal Practice, since 1998, and Member, Council, Human Rights Institute, 1998-2000; Member, Executive Committee, Society for the Welfare and Teaching of the Blind (Edinburgh and South East Scotland), 1979-92; Trustee, Arthur Smith Memorial Trust, since 1975, Chairman, since 1990; President, Scottish Medico-Legal Society, 1996-2000; Governor, St. Mary's School, Melrose, since 1998. Publications: Medical Negligence: an introduction, 1983; Reproductive Medicine and the Law (Contributor). Recreations: travel; sport; nature conservation; Africana. Address: (b.) Court of Session, Parliament House, Edinburgh EH1 1RQ; T.-0131-225 2595.

Abram, Henry Charles, LLB, WS. Solicitor, Tods Murray WS, since 1973; b. 11.8.51, Glasgow; m., Leslie Anne Hamilton; 2 s.; 1 d. Educ. Merchiston Castle School; Aberdeen University. Articled Tods Murray WS; qualified, 1976; Partner, 1978; Chairman, Management Board, 1994-97; Chairman, 1998. Member, Council, Law Society of Scotland, 1983-86; Chairman of Governors, Merchiston Castle School; Member, High Constables and Guard of Honour of Holyrood House; Director, The Crimson Edge Ltd.; Director, Colinton Castle Sports Club Ltd. Recreations: shooting; stalking; golf; skiing; running. Address: (b.) 66 Queen Street, Edinburgh EH2 4NE; T.-0131-226 4771; e-mail: charles.abram@todsmurray.com

Adam, Brian James, BSc, MSc. MSP (SNP), North East Scotland, since 1999; b. 10.6.48, Newmill; m., Dorothy Mann; 4 s.; 1 d. Educ. Keith Grammar School; Aberdeen University. Former Principal Biochemist, Aberdeen Royal Infirmary; Aberdeen City Councillor, 1988-99. Address: (b.) 70 Rosemount Place, Aberdeen AB25 2XJ.

Adam, James Seymour, FIOD. Author, broadcaster and poet; b. 4.12.07, Dundee; m., Flora MacDonell; 1 s.; 1 d. Educ. Dens Road School, Dundee; Hyndland Academy, Glasgow; School of Accountancy, Glasgow. Advertisement department, Scottish Daily Express; advertising agency Account Executive; Staff Captain, War Office; Features Editor, Glasgow Evening News then Daily Record; Assistant Editor, Evening Times; Editor, Weekly Scotsman; General Manager, Scotsman Publications; Managing Director, Chester Chronicle Newspapers; Managing Director, Middlesbrough Evening Gazette. Produced Claymore with Sir Alastair Dunnett in 1933, an adventure magazine for boys which led him to make first solo crossing of the Minch by kayak; organiser of first ever International Gathering of the Clans, 1977. Publications: Declaration of Arbroath; New Verses for an Auld Sang; Laughter in the Kirk; More Laughter in the Kirk; Gaelic Scots Wordbook; Business Diaries of Sir Alexander Grant; A Fell Fine Baker; Over the Minch; You'll Never Make a Bloody Officer; poetry in Scots and Gaelic. Address: 4 Southlawn Court, Easter Park Drive, Edinburgh EH4 6SJ; T.-0131-312 8445.

Adams, Professor Carol Alison, BA, MSc, PhD, CA. Professor of Accounting, University of Glasgow, since 1998 (Head, Department of Accounting and Finance, since 2001); b. 11.9.59, Driffield; m., Adrian; 1 s.; 1 d. Educ. Queen Elizabeth Grammar School, Hexham, Northumberland; University of Stirling; London School of Economics. KPMG, 1981-85 (qualified CA, 1984); Financial Controller, Company Secretary, John Graham Shoes Ltd., 1985-86; Supervising Senior, KPMG, 1986-87; Senior Lecturer, Polytechnic of West London, 1987-91; University of Glasgow: Lecturer, 1992-95, Senior Lecturer, 1995-98. Council Member, Institute of Social and Ethical Accountability, since 1998. Recreations: running; swimming. Address: (b.) Stair Building, 5–9 The Square, Glasgow G12 8QQ; T.-0141-330 6855; e-mail: c.adams@accfin.gla.ac.uk

Adams, Professor (Charles) David, MA, MCD, PhD, FRTPI, MRICS, FRSA. Professor and Head of Department of Land Economy, University of Aberdeen, since 1997; b. 10.9.54, Menston, England; m., Judith Banks; 1 s.; 1 d. Educ. Rossall School; University of Cambridge; University of Liverpool. Planning Assistant, Leeds City Council, 1978-83; Research Assistant, University of Reading, 1983-84; Lecturer, University of Manchester, 1984-93; University of Aberdeen: Senior Lecturer, 1993-95, Reader, 1995-97. Publications: Urban Planning and the Development Process, 1994; Land for Industrial Development (Co-author). Recreations: walking; listening to classical music. Address: (b.) University of Aberdeen, St. Mary's, King's College, Old Aberdeen AB24 3UF; T.-01224 273692.

Adams, Irene, JP. MP (Labour), Paisley North, since 1990; b. 1947; m., Allen Adams (deceased); 1 s.; 2 d. Former local councillor. Address: House of Commons, London SW1A 0AA.

Adams, James Gordon Leitch, MA, PhD, FTS. Economic Consultant; b. 17.10.40, Glasgow; m., Rowan Hopwood (deceased); 1 s.; 1 d. Educ. Dundee High School; St Andrews University; Queen's University, Canada; McGill University. Economist, Canadian Federal Government, 1966-68; Secretary, Canada-Newfoundland Joint Planning Committee, 1968-70; Regional Economist, Highlands and Islands Development Board, 1970-75; Lecturer, Glasgow University, 1975-82; Director of Planning and Development, Scottish Tourist Board, 1983-99. International Executive Service Corps Volunteer (USA), since 2000; Tourism Adviser, Government of Armenia, 2000, Government of Kyrgyzstan, 2001, Eurasia Foundation, 2001; Member, Board of Management, Stevenson College, since 1991; Visiting Scholar, Napier University, since 1999; Visiting Lecturer, Oskar Lange Institute, Poland, 1978, Jawaharlal Nehru University, India, 1981. Recreations: mountaineering; golf. Address: (h.) 5 Corrennie Drive, Edinburgh; T.-0131-447 8073; e-mail: jgladams@hotmail.com

Adams, Ralph Gange, LLB, CA. Global Leader, Financial Advisory Services, Deloitte Touche Tohmatsu, since 1999; b. 30.10.55, Calcutta; m., Kirstine Mary Park; 2 s.; 2 d. Educ. Trinity College, Glenalmond; University of Dundee. Deloitte & Touche: indentured student, 1976-79; qualified as CA, 1979; seconded to Melbourne Office, 1980; seconded to Bank of Scotland, Glasgow and Edinburgh, 1984; Partner, 1986; Partner in Charge, Edinburgh Office, 1990-93, Scottish Offices, 1993-99. Recreations: tennis; golf; music; theatre. Address: (b.) Deloitte & Touche, 39 George Street, Edinburgh EH2 2HZ; T.-0131-225 6834.

Adams, Robert William, OBE, FCMA, FCCA, JDipMA. Chairman, Hanover Housing Association, 1995-98; Honorary President, Scottish Furniture Manufacturers Association; b. 27.9.22, Glasgow; m., Mary Ann Ritchie; 2 s.; 1 d. Educ. Shawlands Academy, Glasgow. H.C. Stewart & Co., CA, Glasgow; Lieutenant, Parachute Regiment; South of Scotland Electricity Board; James Colledge (Cocoa) Ltd., West Africa; Highland Home Industries Ltd.; Managing Director, A.H. McIntosh & Co. Ltd., until 1982. Member, Glenrothes Development Corporation, 1976-84; former Member: Scottish Sports Council; Council, Institute of Cost and Management Accountants; Scottish Sports Council; former Convenor, Scottish Athletic Coaching Committee; former Scottish Chairman, Writers' Guild. Publication: Coming Apart (play). Recreations: tennis; golf. Address: (h.) Achray, Shore Road, Aberdour, Fife; T.-01383 860269.

Adams, Sheenagh, MA (Hons), MCIH. Head, Voluntary Issues Unit, Scottish Executive, since 1999; b. 31.8.57, Dundee; m., Peter Craig; 2 d. Educ. Harris Academy, Dundee; St. Andrews University. Welfare Rights Officer, Strathclyde Regional Council, 1979-82; Tenant Participation Officer, Clydebank Council and TPAS, 1982-85; Principal Management Officer, Falkirk District Council, 1985-90; Principal, Scottish Office, 1990-99; Secretary, Historic Buildings Council for Scotland, 1995-99; Head, Heritage Policy, Historic Scotland, 1995-99. Address: (b.) 3-H78, Victoria Quay, Edinburgh EH6 6QQ; e-mail: sheenagh.adams@scotland.gsi.gov.uk

Adamson, James G., CBE, FRSA. Chairman, AMF Insight Ltd., Edinburgh; b. 25.5.41, Rosyth; m., Ann May; 2 s.; 2 d. Educ. Heriot-Watt University. MoD (Navy), Rosyth; Honeywell Computer Systems; ITT; Marconi Space & Defence; NCR, AT&T (now NCR). President, Fife Society for the Blind; Chairman, Home Media Networks; NE Chairman, Spektra Systems Ltd. Recreations: sailing; singing. Address: (b.) 20 Stafford Street, Edinburgh EH3 7BD; e-mail: jgadamson@amfinsight.co.uk

Adamson, Rev. Sidney, MA, BD. Minister, Church of Scotland; b. 3.8.11, Arbroath; m., Margaret T. Sharpe, JP; 1 s. Educ. Dumbarton Academy; Glasgow University and Trinity College; Royal Scottish Academy of Music and Drama. Ministries: St Ninian's, Sanquhar, 1937-47 (including war service), Trinity Church, Renfrew, 1947-54, High Kirk of Rothesay, 1954-59, St Michael's Inveresk, Musselburgh, 1959-85. Moderator of Presbytery: Dumfries, 1939, Dunoon, 1958, Dalkeith, 1964 and 1965; former Moderator, Synod of Lothian and Tweeddale; Army Chaplain, India, 1944-47; Territorial Army Chaplain, 1952-66; Chaplain, Royal British Legion (Scotland), Paisley, Renfrew, Rothesay, Musselburgh, and Honorary Vice President, Edinburgh & Lothian Area Council, 1973; Industrial Chaplain, Babcock & Wilcox Ltd., Renfrew, 1948-54; Chaplain, British Sailors' Society, 1955-85; Editor, Homeward Bound (Forces magazine, India), 1946-47. Publications: Two Centuries of Service (history of Sanquhar congregation), 1941; St Michael's Kirk at Inveresk (four editions between 1963 and 1984). Recreations: (at suitable periods) ballroom dancing; shooting; swimming; (always) reading; theatre; freelance journalism; ex-service welfare. Address: 48 Hailes Gardens, Colinton, Edinburgh EH13 0JH; T.-0131-441 2471.

Addison, Alexander, MBE, MB, ChB, FRCGP, DObstRCOG. Senior Partner, Addison, Scott, Kane & Ferguson, 1978-95; Chairman, Lanarkshire LMC, 1989-95; Member, Scottish Committee, BMA, since 1984, and Fellow, BMA, since 1993; Member, RCCC Council, 1996-2000; Medical Officer and Anti-Drugs Officer, RCCC; b. 23.8.30, Kerala; m., Joan Wood; 3 s. Educ. Keith Grammar School; Aberdeen Grammar School; Aberdeen University. House Surgeon and Physician, Woodend General Hospital, Aberdeen, 1954-55; Captain, RAMC; Junior Medical Specialist, Cowglen MH, 1955-58; SHO, Bellshill MH, 1958-59; GP in Douglas and Physician to Lady Home Hospital, 1959-95; Member, West of Scotland Faculty of GP College, 1967-79 and of Scottish Council, 1976-78; Member, Lanarkshire LMC, since 1972, and of AMAC, since 1975; Chairman, Lanarkshire AMAC, 1982-86; Chairman, Scottish Association of General Practitioner Hospitals, 1985-87; Member, Scottish Committee of Medical Commission on Accident Prevention, 1976-98; Member, National Medical Consultative Committee, 1977-83; Honorary Surgeon, St. Andrews Ambulance Association, 1959-89. Recreations: curling; golf; reading. Address: (h.) 7 Addison Drive, Douglas, Lanarkshire ML11 0PZ; T.-01555 851302.

Adiceam, Ashok, PhD. Director, French Institute of Scotland, since 2001; Cultural Attaché, since 2001; b. 18.12.70, New Delhi, India. Educ. Institute of Political Sciences, Paris. Head of Resource Centre, European Commission Social Plan Office, Paris, 1993; Cultural Attaché and Director, Alliance Francaise, Nigeria, 1994-96; Festival Organiser (World Music), Maison des Cultures du Monde, Paris, 1996-97; Director, Alliance Française, Kerala, India, 1997-2000; Head of Exchange Programme, Ministry of Culture, Paris, 2000-01. Publication: Cultural Policy in France, 2001. Recreations: reading; theatre; music. Address: (b.) 13 Randolph Crescent, Edinburgh EH3 7TT; T.-0131-225 5366; e-mail: director@ifecosse.org.uk

Ager, Professor Alastair Kenneth St. Clair, BA, PhD, MSc, CPsychol. Director, Centre for International Health Studies, Queen Margaret University College Edinburgh, since 1997; Professor of Applied Psychology, Queen Margaret College Edinburgh, since 1992; Research Associate, Queen Elizabeth House, University of Oxford, since, 1996; b. 24.6.56, Birmingham; m., Wendy; 1 s.; 1 d. Educ. Coleshill Grammar School; University of Keele; University of Wales, Cardiff; University of Birmingham. Posts in clinical and applied psychology; Lecturer in Clinical Psychology, University of Leicester, 1985; Senior Lecturer and Head of Psychology, University of Malawi, 1988; Head, Department of Management and Social Sciences, Queen Margaret College, 1992. British Psychological Society: Member, Professional Affairs Board, 1994-96, Member, Division of Clinical Psychology – Scottish Branch, 1994-97. Publications: The Life Experiences Checklist, 1990; Microcomputers and Clinical Psychology, 1991; Refugees: Perspectives on the Experience of Forced Migration, 1999. Recreations: music; golf; skiing; church affairs. Address: Queen Margaret University College Edinburgh, Clerwood Terrace, Edinburgh EH12 8TS; T.-0131-317 3491.

Agnew of Lochnaw, Sir Crispin Hamlyn. 11th Baronet (created 1629); Chief of the Agnews; Advocate 1982; Queen's Counsel (1995); Unicorn Pursuivant of Arms, 1981-86, Rothesay Herald of Arms, since 1986; Trustee, John Muir Trust; Chairman, Crofting Law Group; b. 13.5.44, Edinburgh; m., Susan Rachel Strang Steel; 1 s.; 3 d. Educ. Uppingham School; Royal Military Academy, Sandhurst. Commissioned Royal Highland Fusiliers, 1964, as 2nd Lieutenant; Major, 1977; Retired, 1981. Member:

Royal Navy Expedition to East Greenland, 1966; Joint Services Expedition to Elephant Island, Antarctica, 1970-71; Army Nuptse Himal Expedition, 1975; Army Everest Expedition, 1976; Leader: Army East Greenland Expedition, 1968; Joint Services Expedition to Chilean Patagonia, 1972-73; Army Api Himal Expedition, 1980. Publications: Licensing (Scotland) Act 1976 (4th edition) (Co-author); Agricultural Law in Scotland, 1996; Connell on the Agricultural Holdings (Scotland) Acts (Co-author) 1996; Land Obligations, 1999; Crofting Law, 2000; articles in various newspapers and journals. Recreations: mountaineering; sailing. Address: 6 Palmerston Road, Edinburgh EH9 1TN; T.-0131-668 3792.

Agnew, Ian, MA (Hons) (Cantab). Rector, Perth High School, 1975-92; b. 10.5.32, Newcastle-upon-Tyne; m., Gladys Agnes Heatherill; 1 d. Educ. King's College School, London; Pembroke College, Cambridge. Assistant Teacher of Modern Languages, Melville College, Edinburgh, 1958-63; Assistant Teacher of Modern Languages, then Principal Teacher of Russian, George Heriot's School, Edinburgh, 1964-70; Housemaster, Craigmount Secondary School, Edinburgh, 1970-73; Deputy, Liberton High School, Edinburgh, 1973-75. Non-Executive Director, Perth and Kinross Healthcare NHS Trust; Minute Secretary, Headteachers Association of Scotland, 1979-81; Committee Member, SCCORE; President: Perthshire Musical Festival, 1978-88, Perth Chamber Music Society, 1982-89; Past President, Rotary Club of Perth St. John's; Past Chairman: Barnton and Cramond Conservative Association and West Edinburgh Conservative and Unionist Association; Serving Officer (OStJ), Priory of Scotland of the Most Venerable Order of St. John; Member, Society of High Constables, City of Perth; Governor: Balnacraig School, Perth, since 1981, Kilgraston School, 1990-99, Convent of the Sacred Heart, Bridge of Earn; Secretary, Friends of Perth Festival of the Arts, 1996-99; Member, Advisory Group, Perth College Development Trust; Chairman, Friends of St. John's Kirk, Perth. Recreations: music (opera); reading; tennis; gardening. Address: (h.) Northwood, Heughfield Road, Bridge of Earn, Perthshire PH2 9BH; T.-01738 81 2273.

Ailsa, 8th Marquess of (Archibald Angus Charles Kennedy); b. 13.9.56; 2 d. Address: Cassillis House, Maybole KA19 7JN.

Ainsley, Sam, BA (Hons). Senior Lecturer and Head, Master of Fine Art Programme, Glasgow School of Art, since 1991; Member, Scottish Arts Council, since 1998, and Chair, Visual Art Committee, since 1998; b. 27.3.50, North Shields; m., Brian David Smillie; 1 s. Educ. Tynemouth Grammar School; Jacob Kramer College, Leeds; University of Northumbria; Edinburgh College of Art. Lecturer, Edinburgh College of Art (part-time), 1978-81; Lecturer, Glasgow School of Art, 1981-89; Lecturer, MFA Glasgow and Environmental Art Department, Glasgow School of Art, 1989-91; as artist, represented in major group shows, numerous one person and group exhibitions since 1978. Chair, International Curatorium, Tramway; selector, numerous art awards, residencies, commissions etc.; Trustee, Arts Trust of Scotland; external examiner for art schools; Chair of Fine Art, Glasgow School of Art, 1996-98; Fulbright Exchange Lecturer, 1988-89. Recreations: travel; literature; film. Address: (b.) 167 Renfrew Street, Glasgow G3 6RQ; T.-0141-353 4726.

Ainslie, Allan, BSc (Hons), FRICS. Chief Valuer Scotland, since 1998; b. 16.2.51, Edinburgh; m., Jennifer Anne Park; 1 s.; 1 d. Educ. Broxburn Academy; Napier College; Edinburgh University. Valuer, Valuation Office, Inland Revenue, 1976-79; Senior Valuer, 1980-85; Principal Valuer, 1986-90; First Class Valuer, 1991-92; District Valuer (Fife and Central), 1992-95; District Valuer

Scotland South East, 1996-97. Recreations: tennis; badminton; gardening. Address: (b.) 50 Frederick Street, Edinburgh EH2 1NG; T.-0131-465 0700.

Airlie, 13th Earl of (David George Coke Patrick Ogilvy), KT, GCVO, PC, KStJ, Royal Victorian Chain, JP. Former Lord Chamberlain of Queen's Household; Chancellor, University of Abertay, Dundee, since 1994; Director, Baring Stratton Investment Trust plc, since 1986; President, National Trust for Scotland, since 1997; Hon. President, Scottish Council, The Scout Association; Chairman, Historic Royal Palaces, since 1998; b. 17.5.26, London; m., Virginia Fortune Ryan; 3 s.; 3 d. Educ. Eton College. Lieutenant, Scots Guards, 1944; serving 2nd Bn., Germany, 1945; Captain, ADC to High Commissioner and C-in-C Austria, 1947-48; Malaya, 1948-49; resigned commission, 1950; Chairman, Ashdown Investment Trust Ltd., 1968-82; Director, J. Henry Schroder Wagg & Co. Ltd., 1961-84 (Chairman, 1973-77); Chairman, Schroders plc, 1977-84; Scottish and Newcastle Breweries plc, until 1983; Director, Royal Bank of Scotland Group, 1983-93; Director, Royal Bank of Scotland plc, 1991-93; Chairman, General Accident Fire & Life Assurance Corporation plc, 1987-97; Chancellor of the Royal Victorian Order, 1984-97; Trustee, Royal Collection Trust, 1993; Ensign, Queen's Body Guard for Scotland (Royal Company of Archers) (President, Council, since 2001). Address: (h.) Cortachy Castle, Kirriemuir, Angus.

Airlie, Countess of (Virginia Fortune Ryan), DCVO. Lady in Waiting to HM The Queen, since 1973; Chairman, National Galleries of Scotland, 1997-2000 (Trustee since 1995); President, Angus Red Cross, since 1988; b. 9.2.33, London; 3 s.; 3 d. Educ. Brearley School, New York City. Commissioner, Royal Fine Arts Commission; Trustee, Tate Gallery, 1983-95; Trustee, National Gallery, London, 1989-95; Member, Industrial Design Panel, British Rail, 1974-91; Trustee, American Museum in Britain, since 1985 (Chairman, since 2001); Founder/Governor, Cobham School. Address: (b.) Cortachy Castle, Kirriemuir, Angus; T.-01575 540231.

Aitchison, James Douglas, MA (Hons), MEd (Hons). Head Teacher, Boclair Academy, Bearsden, since 1991 (Head Teacher, Gleniffer High School, Paisley, 1984-91); b. 2.7.47, Glasgow. Educ. High School of Glasgow; Glasgow University; University of Marburg. Teacher, Lycee Faidherbe, Lille; Principal Teacher, Bearsden Academy; Assistant Head Teacher, Gryffe High School, Houston. Recreations: curling; walking; travel. Address: (h.) 44 Keystone Road, Milngavie, Glasgow G62 6QG; T.-0141-956 6693.

Aitchison, Thomas Nisbet, MA, MSc. Chief Executive, City of Edinburgh Council, since 1995; Chairman, SOLACE Scotland; b. 24.2.51, Edinburgh; m., Kathleen Sadler; 1 s.; 2 d. Educ. Glasgow University; Heriot-Watt University. Lothian Regional Council: Department of Manpower Services, 1982-85, Department of Management and Information Services, 1985-87, Corporate Planning Manager and Depute Director, 1987-91, Depute Chief Executive, 1991-94, Chief Executive, 1994-95. Honorary Secretary, Council, Edinburgh International Festival; Member, Court, Napier University. Recreations: hillwalking; football; music. Address: (b.) Council Headquarters, Wellington Court, 10 Waterloo Place, Edinburgh EH1 3EG.

Aitken, Professor Alastair, BSc, MSc, PhD. Professor of Protein Biochemistry, University of Edinburgh, since 1999; b. 16.4.47, Dundee; m., Michele Learmonth; 3 s.; 1 d. Educ. Grove Academy, Broughty Ferry; Heriot-Watt University; Newcastle University; Edinburgh University. Royal Society European Exchange Fellow, Microbial Physiology, Institut Pasteur, Paris, 1975-77, Chargé de Recherche, Department of Virology, 1977-78; MRC Postdoctoral Research Fellow,

Department of Biochemistry, University of Dundee, 1978-83; Lecturer, Department of Pharmaceutical Chemistry, University of London, 1983-86; member, scientific staff, Laboratory of Protein Structure, National Institute for Medical Research, Mill Hill, 1986-88. Deputy Chairman, Editorial Board, Biochemical Journal, 1995-99; Member, Medical Research Council Grant Advisory Board, since 1998. Recreations: hillwalking; bird watching in South America/Asia. Address: (b.) Division of Biomedical and Clinical Laboratory Sciences, University of Edinburgh, Hugh Robson Building, George Square, Edinburgh EH8 9XD; T.-0131-650 3721; e-mail: alastair.aitken@ed.ac.uk

Aitken, Rev. Ewan, BA (Hons), BD (Hons). Parish Minister, St. Margaret's Church of Scotland, Edinburgh, since 1995; Member, City of Edinburgh Council (Executive Member Education); b., 27.4.62, Paisley; m., Hilary Brown; 1 s. Educ. Woodmill High School, Dunfermline; University of Sussex; University of Edinburgh. Youth Worker, Ruchill Parish Church, 1980-81; Vice President (sabbatical), University of Sussex Union, 1982-83; Regional Secretary, Student Christian Movement, 1985-87; Pastor, West Avenue Presbyterian Church, Buffalo, NY, 1990-91; Assistant Minister, South Leith Parish Church, Edinburgh, 1991-93; Staff Member, St. Andrews Church of Scotland, Tiberias, Israel, 1993-94; Locum Minister, St. Andrews, Gisborne, New Zealand, 1994-95. Recreations: following Dunfermline Athletic F.C.; vegetarian cookery; laughter; collecting earrings. Address: (b.) 176 Restalrig Road South, Edinburgh EH7 6EA; T.-0131-554 7400.

Aitken, Joan Nicol, JP, SSC. Solicitor; Scottish Prisons Complaints Commissioner, since 1999; Mediator; b. 26.2.53, Glasgow; m., Alistair Bruce Dodds; 1 d. Educ. James Gillespie's High School for Girls; Dundee University. Local goverment and private practice. Council Member, Law Society of Scotland, 1988-91; Editor, Journal of Law Society of Scotland, 1991-98; former Part-time Chairman: Employment Tribunals (Scotland), Disability Appeal Tribunals, Child Support Appeal Tribunals; Member, Scottish Consumer Council, 1987-93; Member, General Dental Council; was first woman member, Society of Solicitors in the Supreme Courts of Scotland; Scottish Labour Party candidate, Inverness East Nairn and Lochaber, Scottish Parliament election, 1999. Address: (b.) Saughton House, Broomhouse Drive, Edinburgh EH11 3XA; T.-0131-244 8423; e-mail: joan.aitken@scotland.gsi.gov.uk

Aitken, Keith, MA (Hons). Freelance Journalist and Broadcaster, since 1995; b. 31.10.57, Edinburgh; m., Christine Willett; 1 d. Educ. George Watson's College, Edinburgh; University of Edinburgh. The Scotsman: graduate trainee, 1979-82, Parliamentary Correspondent, 1982-85, Labour Correspondent, 1985-88, Industrial Editor, 1988-92, Economics Editor and Chief Leader Writer, 1992-95; former Columnist: The Scotsman, The Herald; Columnist, The Scottish Daily Express, Scotland on Sunday; Writer and Presenter, discussion programmes and documentaries, BBC Radio Scotland, World Service and Radio 4. Former Member, Court, Napier University. Awards include Business and Industry Writer of the Year, Scottish Press Awards, 1986 and 1987. Publications: The Bairns o' Adam, 1997; How Scotland's Parliament Will Work, 1999; Understanding Scotland's Parliament, 1999. Recreations: walking; cycling; gardening; reading; deplorable blues guitar. Address: 25 Bridge Road, Colinton Village, Edinburgh EH13 0LH; T.-0131-441 7982; e-mail: keith@kaitken.fsnet.co.uk

Aitken, Professor Robert Cairns Brown, CBE, MB, ChB, DPM, MD, DSc (Hon), FRCPEdin, FRCPsych. Medical, Royal Infirmary of Edinburgh NHS Trust, 1994-97; Professor of Rehabilitation Studies, Edinburgh University, 1974-94 (Dean, Faculty of Medicine, 1990-91, Vice-Principal, 1991-94); Honorary Consultant in Rehabilitation Medicine, Lothian Health Board, 1974-94; b. 20.12.33,

Dunoon; m., Audrey May Lunn; 1 s.; 1 d. Educ. Dunoon Grammar School; Cargilfield School, Edinburgh; Sedbergh School, Yorkshire; Glasgow University. Institute of Aviation Medicine, RAF, 1959-62; Orpington and Maudsley Hospitals, 1962-66; Senior Lecturer/Consultant Psychiatrist, Royal Infirmary and Royal Edinburgh Hospital, 1967-74. President, International College of Psychosomatic Medicine, 1985-87; Chairman, Napier Polytechnic of Edinburgh Governors, 1983-90; Member, Council for Professions Supplementary to Medicine, 1983-90; Member, General Medical Council, 1991-96; Director, Lothian Health Board, 1991-93; Editor, Journal of Psychosomatic Research, 1979-85; occasional WHO consultant; Foundation Secretary, then President, Society for Research in Rehabilitation, 1981-83; Member, Human Genetics Advisory Commission, 1996-99. Publications: papers on measurement of mood; flying phobia; management of disability. Recreations: people, places and pleasures of Edinburgh, Scotland and beyond. Address: (h.) 11 Succoth Place, Edinburgh EH12 6BJ; T.-0131-337 1550.

Aitken, William Mackie. JP, DL, ACII. MSP (Conservative), Glasgow, since 1999 (Vice Convener, Justice 2 Committee; Deputy Conservative Parliamentary Business Manager); b. 15.4.47, Glasgow. Educ. Allan Glen's School, Glasgow. Chairman, Scottish Young Conservatives, 1975-77; Councillor, City of Glasgow, 1976-99: Convenor, City Licensing Committee and Vice-Convenor, Personnel Committee, 1977-79, Leader of the Opposition, City Council, 1980-84 and 1992-96, Bailie of the City, 1980-84, 1988-92, 1996-99. Recreations: football; reading; foreign travel. Address: (h.) 35 Overnewton Square, Glasgow G3 8RW; T.-0141-357 1284.

Aitkin, John, TD, CA, MBE. Retired Chartered Accountant; b. 10.9.33, Denholm; m., Elizabeth Charlotte Fraser; 1 s.; 1 s. (deceased); 1 d. Educ. Hawick High School. Qualified as a CA, 1956; National Service (commissioned 2nd Lt.), 1956-58; joined John J. Welch & Co., CA, Hawick, 1958, Partner, 1961-97; served in TA, 1958-73; Committee of Management, Royal British Legion Housing Association Ltd., 1978-91 (Chairman, 1986-91); National Chairman, Royal British Legion Scotland, 1995-98 (Hon. Treasurer, 1985-90); Earl Haig Fund Scotland: Member, Executive Committee, 1992-99, Director, since 1999; Regimental Trustee, King's Own Scottish Borderers, since 1980; Member, Management Committee, Ex-Services Mental Welfare Society, since 1998; Member, Central Advisory Committee on War Pensions, 1995-98; Committee Member, British Commonwealth Ex-Services League, since 1998; President, Hawick Callants Club, 1991; Member, East Scotland War Pensions Committee, since 2001; Director, Scottish Borders Housing Association Ltd., since 2001. Recreations: gardening; reading; walking. Address: (h) Appletreehall House, Hawick TD9 8PW; T.-01450 372424.

Akintoye, Professor Akintola, BSc (Hons), MSc, PhD, MCIOB, MRICS, ANIQS. Professor of Construction Economics and Management, Glasgow Caledonian University, since 1999 (Director of Research, School of the Built and Natural Environment, since 2001); b. 8.12.57, Nigeria; m., Bolajoko Akintoye. Educ. University of Salford. Quantity Surveyor; Lecturer in Quantity Surveying, University of Ife, Nigeria, eight years; Lecturer in Building, Salford College of Technology, one year; Lecturer, then senior Lecturer, then Reader, Glasgow Caledonian University. Chairman, Association of Researchers in Construction Management; Co-Editor, Journal of Financial Management of Property and Construction; Visiting Professor, Asian Institute of Technology and Hong Kong Polytechnic University; member, two working commissions, International Council for Research and Innovation in Building and Construction, Netherlands. Recreation: badminton. Address: (b.) School of the Built and Natural Environment, Glasgow Caledonian University, Cowcaddens Road, Glasgow G4 0BA; T.-0141-331 3626; e-mail: akin@gcal.ac.uk

Alba, Carlos, BA (Hons), DipJour. Deputy Editor, Sunday Times Scotland, since 2001; b. 28.8.65, Glasgow; m., Hilary; 1 d. Educ. High School of Glasgow; University of Strathclyde. Reporter: Dumfries and Galloway Standard, 1990-92, Press and Journal, 1992-95; Chief Reporter, Edinburgh Evening News, 1995-96; Education Correspondent, The Herald, 1996-98; Scottish Political Editor, Daily Record, 1998-2000; Deputy News Editor, Sunday Times Scotland, 2000-01. Publication: Keep the Faith (Co-Author), 2001. Recreation: shouting at Celtic defenders. Address: (b.) 124 Portman Street, Glasgow G41 1EJ; T.-0141-420 5274; e-mail: Carlos.Alba@sunday-times.co.uk

Alcock, Stephen Robert, MB, ChB, PhD. Head, Department of Clinical Microbiology, Western Infirmary, Glasgow, since 1993; b. 24.6.45, Sutton Coldfield; m., Jean Margaret Dzack; 1s.; 1d. Educ. Aberdeen Academy; Bearsden Academy; Aberdeen University. House Officer, Aberdeen Royal Infirmary, 1969-70; Lecturer, Bacteriology, Aberdeen University, 1970-81; Senior Lecturer, Bacteriology, Glasgow University since 1981; Hon. Consultant, Bacteriology, Greater Glasgow Health Board, since 1981. Recreations: books; Roman history; angling. Address: (h.) 2 Midlothian Drive, Shawlands, Glasgow, G41 3NE; T.-0141-647 1521.

Alder, Professor Elizabeth, BSc, PhD, CPsychol, FBPsS. Professor and Director of Research, Faculty of Health and Life Sciences, Napier University, since 2000; b. 2.11.44, St. Andrews; m., Dr. George Alder; 3 d. Educ. Edgbaston High School, Birmingham; Aberdeen University; Edinburgh University. Lecturer, Napier College, Edinburgh, 1971-75; Senior Research Officer, MRC Reproductive Biology Unit, Edinburgh, 1975-87; Senior Lecturer, Queen Margaret College, Edinburgh, 1987-95; Senior Lecturer, Dundee University, 1995-2000. President Elect, International Society for Psychosomatic Obstetrics and Gynaecology. Publication: The Psychology of Health, 1999. Recreations: hillwalking; skiing; gardening. Address: (b.) Faculty of Health and Life Sciences, Napier University, 74 Canaan Lane, Edinburgh EH9 2TB; T.-0131-536 5672; e-mail: e.m.alder@napier.ac.uk

Alexander, Professor Alan, MA. Chairman-Designate, Scottish Water, since 2001; Chairman, West of Scotland Water Authority, since 1999; Professor of Local and Public Management, Strathclyde University, 1993-2000, now Emeritus Professor (Head, Department of Human Resource Management, 1993-96, Professor of Local Government, 1987-93); b. 13.12.43, Glasgow; m., Morag MacInnes (Morag Alexander, qv); 1 s.; 1 d. Educ. Possil Secondary School, Glasgow; Albert Secondary School, Glasgow; Glasgow University. Lecturer/Assistant Professor, Political Science, Lakehead University, Ontario, 1966-71; Lecturer in Politics, Reading University, 1971-87. Member of Board, Housing Corporation, 1977-80; Member, Standing Research Committee on Local and Central Government Relations, Joseph Rowntree Memorial Trust, 1988-92; conducted inquiry into relations between Western Isles Islands Council and BCCI, 1991; Director, Scottish Local Authorities Management Centre, 1987-93; Member, Commission on Local Government and the Scottish Parliament, 1998-99; Chair, Glasgow Regeneration Fund, 1998-2001; Trustee, Quarriers, 1995-2000. Publications: Local Government in Britain since Reorganisation, 1982; The Politics of Local Government in the UK, 1982; L'amministrazione locale in Gran Bretagna, 1984; Borough Government and Politics: Reading, 1835-1985, 1985; Managing the Fragmented Authority, 1994; The Future of DLOs/DSOs in Scotland, 1998. Recreations: theatre;

cinema; hill-walking; avoiding gardening. Address: A'Chomraich, Dull, Aberfeldy PH15 2JQ; T.-01887 820726; e-mail: alan.alexander@dial.pipex.com

Alexander, Professor David Alan, MA (Hons), CPsychol, FBPS, PhD. Professor of Mental Health, University of Aberdeen, since 1994 (Director, Centre for Trauma Research, since 1999); Hon. Consultant, Police and Fire Services, since 1989; b. 28.8.43, Ellon. Educ. George Watson's College, Edinburgh; Morgan Academy, Dundee; University of St. Andrews; University of Dundee. MRC Research Scholar; Lecturer then Senior Lecturer in Mental Health; Visiting Lecturer, FBI Academy, Virginia, USA; Visiting Professor to universities in USA, Russia, Croatia, Spain and West Indies. Publications: co-author of three books; numerous professional articles. Recreations: badminton; squash; hill-walking. Address: (b.) Medical School, Foresterhill, Aberdeen AB25 2ZD; T.-01224 681818.

Alexander, Major-General David Crichton, CB. Commandant, Scottish Police College, 1979-87; b. 28.11.26, Aberdour; m., 1, Diana Joyce (Jane) Fisher (deceased); 2, Elizabeth Patricia Fleming; 1 s.; 1 step-s.; 2 d. Educ. Edinburgh Academy; Staff College, Camberley; Royal College of Defence Studies. Royal Marines, 1944-77 (2nd Lieutenant to Major-General, including Equerry and Acting Treasurer to Duke of Edinburgh); Director-General, English Speaking Union, 1977-79. President, Corps of Commissionaires, 1994-97; Member, Civil Service Final Selection Board, 1978-88; Chairman, Edinburgh Academy, 1985-90; Freeman, City of London; Liveryman, Painter Stainers' Company; Member, Transport Users Consultative Committee for Scotland, 1989-93; President, SSAFA Fife, 1990-94. Recreations: fishing; golf; gardening. Address: (h.) Baldinnie, Park Place, Elie KY9 1DH; T.-01333 330882.

Alexander, Douglas, MA (Hons), LLB, DipLP. MP (Labour), Paisley South, since 1997; Minister of State, Department of Trade and Industry, e-Commerce and Competitiveness, since 2001; b. 26.10.67, Glasgow; m., Jacqui Christian. Educ. Park Mains High School, Erskine; University of Edinburgh; University of Pennsylvania. Speechwriter for Dr. Gordon Brown, MP, 1990; Brodies WS, Edinburgh, 1994-96; Solicitor, Digby Brown, Edinburgh, 1996-97. Publication: New Scotland, New Britain, 1999. Recreations: running; angling. Address: House of Commons, Westminster, London SW1A 0AA; T.-020 7219 3000.

Alexander, Douglas Gavin. MP (Labour), Paisley South, since 1997; b. 26.10.67. Educ. University of Edinburgh; University of Pennsylvania. Admitted, Solicitor, 1995. Address: House of Commons, London SW1A 0AA.

Alexander, Rev. Douglas Niven, MA, BD. Minister, Erskine Parish Church, Bishopton, 1970-99, retired; b. 8.4.35, Eaglesham; m., Dr. Joyce O. Garven; 1 s.; 2 d. Educ. Hutchesons' Boys' Grammar School, Glasgow; Glasgow University (President, SRC, 1958); Union Theological Seminary, New York. Assistant Minister, St. Ninian's Church, Greenock, 1961-62; Warden, Iona Community House, Glasgow, 1963-70. Secretary, Scottish Union of Students, 1958; Assessor to Lord Rector, Glasgow University, 1969-71; Chaplain to Erskine Hospital, since 1970; Moderator, Paisley Presbytery, 1984; Mair Memorial Lecturer, Glasgow University, 1987; Chairman, British Churches Committee for Channel 4 TV, 1986-88; Convener, Church of Scotland Board of Communication, 1987-91; Member: Scottish Committee, IBA, 1988-90; National Religious Advisory Committee, IBA, 1988-90; Central Religious Advisory Committee, 1988-92; National Religious Advisory Committee, ITC, 1991-92; Scottish Viewers Consultative Committee, ITC, 1991-92; Member, Church of Scotland Board of Social Responsibility, since

1997. Recreation: researching ways of salmon poachers! Address: West Morningside, Main Road, Langbank PA14 6XP; T.-01475 540249; e-mail: Douglas.Alexander2@btinternet.com

Alexander, Professor Michael Joseph, BA, MA (Oxon), FEA. Berry Professor of English Literature, St. Andrews University, since 1985; b. 21.5.41, Wigan; m., 1, Eileen Mary McCall (deceased); 2, Mary Cecilia Sheahan; 1 s.; 2 d. Educ. Downside School; Trinity College, Oxford; Perugia University; Princeton University. Editor, William Collins, London, 1963-65; Lecturer, University of California, 1966-67; Editor, Andre Deutsch, London, 1967-68; Lecturer: East Anglia University, 1968-69, Stirling University, 1969; Senior Lecturer, 1977; Reader, 1985. Represents Scotland on Round Britain Quiz. Publications: Earliest English Poems (Translator), 1966; Beowulf (Translator), 1973; Twelve Poems, 1978; The Poetic Achievement of Ezra Pound, 1979; History of Old English Literature, 1983; Macmillan Anthology of English Literature, 1989; Beowulf (Editor), 1995; Sons of Ezra (Editor), 1995; Beowulf and Grendel (Translator), 1995; The Canterbury Tales – The First Fragment (Editor), 1996; The Canterbury Tales : Illustrated Prologue (Editor), 1996; A History of English Literature, 2000. Address: (b.) School of English, St. Andrews University, St. Andrews KY16 9AL; T.-01334 462666; e-mail: mja4@st-and.ac.uk

Alexander, Morag, BA (Hons), OBE. Convener, Scottish Social Services Council, since 2001; Director, Equal Opportunities Commission, Scotland, 1992-2001; b. 10.10.43, Kilwinning; m., Professor Alan Alexander (qv); 1 s.; 1 d. Educ. Lourdes Secondary School, Glasgow; Glasgow University; Lakehead University, Ontario. Research Assistant, ASTMS, 1971-73; Editor and Researcher, RIPA, 1973-82; freelance journalist and consultant, 1982-90; Founding Editor, Women in Europe, 1985-89, and UK Correspondent, Women of Europe, 1987-92; Founding Director, Training 2000 (Scotland) Ltd., Scottish Alliance for Women's Training, 1990-92; Member, Policy Committee, Children in Scotland, Chair, Early Years Advisory Group, since 1995; Board Member, Turning Point Scotland; Member, Board, Partnership for a Parliament, 1997; Member, Scottish Senate, the Windsor Meetings, 1997-2000; Member, Expert Panel on Procedures and Standing Orders, Scottish Parliament, 1997-98; Member, Committee of Inquiry into Student Finance, since 1999; Member, Governing Body, Queen Margaret University College. Recreations: music; opera; visiting art galleries and museums; hill-walking. Address: A'Chomraich, Dull, Aberfeldy PH15 2JQ; T.-01887 820726; e-mail: morag.alexander@dial.pipex.com

Alexander, Samuel, BL. Honorary Sheriff, Dumbarton, since 1983; b. Glasgow; m., Isabella Kerr Ligertwood; 2 s. Educ. Govan High School; Glasgow University. Formerly Consultant and Senior Partner, Keyden Strang & Co., Solicitors, Glasgow. Recreations: golf; reading. Address: (h.) 1 Hillneuk Avenue, Bearsden, Glasgow G61 3PY; T.-0141-942 4674.

Alexander, Walter Ronald, CBE. Chairman, Walter Alexander plc, 1979-90 (Managing Director, 1973-79); Company Director; b. 6.4.31; m., 1, Rosemary Anne Sleigh (m. diss.); 2 s.; 2 d.; 2, Mrs Lorna Elwes. Educ. Loretto School; Cambridge University (MA Hons). Chairman and Managing Director, Tayforth Ltd., 1961-71; Chairman, Scottish Automobile Company Ltd., 1971-73; Director: Scotcros plc, 1965-82 (Chairman, 1972-82); Investors Capital Trust plc, 1967-99; Clydesdale Bank plc, 1970-96; RIT and Northern plc, 1973-84; Dawson International plc, 1979-96; Chairman, Scottish Appeals Committee, Police Dependants' Trust, 1974-81; President, Public Schools Golfing Society, 1973-79; Chairman: PGA, 1982-85; Royal and Ancient Golf Club of St. Andrews Trust, since 1987; Governor, Loretto School, 1961-89; Comr., Queen Victoria

School, 1987-92; Scottish Free Enterprise Award, 1977. Recreation: golf. Address: Moonzie Mill, Balmullo, St. Andrews KY16 0AH; T.-01334 870990.

Alexander, Wendy, MA (Hons), MA (Econ), MBA. MSP (Labour), Paisley North, since 1999; Minister for Enterprise, Transport and Lifelong Learning; Minister for Communities, 1999-2000; b. 27.6.63, Glasgow. Educ. Park Mains School, Erskine; Pearson College, Canada; Glasgow University; Warwick University; INSEAD, France. Research Officer, Scottish Labour Party, 1988-92; Senior Associate, Booz Allen & Hamilton Int., 1994-97; Special Adviser to Secretary of State for Scotland, 1997-98. Address: (b.) Scottish Parliament, Edinburgh EH99 1SP.

Allan, Angus, BSc (Hons). Principal, Oatridge Agricultural College, since 2001; b. 28.3.60, Glasgow; m., Sandra; 3 s. Educ. Larkhall Academy; Edinburgh University. Lecturer in Agriculture, Kirkley College, Northumberland, 1982-85; farming, Ross-shire, 1985-88; Elmwood College, Cupar, 1988-2001 (latterly as Assistant Principal). Church of Scotland Elder. Recreation: sailing. Address: Craigmore, The Barony, Cupar; e-mail: angusallan@hotmail.com

Allan, Charles Maitland, MA, MUniv (Aberdeen). Journalist, Economist and Farmer; b. 19.8.39, Stirling; m., Fiona Vine; 2 s.; 2 d. Educ. Dartington Hall; Aberdeen University. Lecturer in Economic History, Glasgow University, 1962-63; Lecturer in Economics, St. Andrews University, 1963-65; Lecturer and Senior Lecturer, Strathclyde University, 1965-74; Producer/Presenter, BBC, 1982-86; Editorial Adviser, Leopard Magazine; Managing Editor, Ardo Publishing Co. Publications: Theory of Taxation; Death of a Papermill; Farmer's Diary I, II, III, IV, V; Neeps and Strae. Recreation: cycling; World Caber Tossing Champion, 1972. Address: (h.) Whinhill of Ardo, Methlick, Ellon, Aberdeenshire; T.-01651 806 218; e-mail: chas@charlieallan.com

Allan, Eric, MA (Hons). Head Teacher, St. Michael's Academy, Kilwinning, since 1994; b. 6.9.55, Inverness; m., Elaine; 2 d. Educ. Dingwall Academy; Glasgow University; Jordanhill College. Teacher: St. Andrew's Academy, Saltcoats, St. Brendan's High School, Linwood (Principal Teacher, Geography); Assistant Head Teacher, St. Brendan's, 1987-92; Depute Head Teacher, Trinity High School, Renfrew, 1992-94. Recreations: golf; supporting Kilmarnock FC; reading; music. Address: (h.) 3 Holmes Crescent, Kilmarnock; T.-01563 524199.

Allan, Gary James Graham, LLB (Hons). Advocate, since 1994; b. 21.1.58, Aberdeen; m., Margaret Muriel Glass; 1 s.; 1 d. Educ. Aberdeen Grammar School; University of Aberdeen. Legal apprenticeship, McGrigor Donald & Co., Solicitors, Glasgow and Edinburgh; qualified as Solicitor, 1982; Hughes Dowdall, Solicitors, Glasgow: joined as Assistant Solicitor, 1982, Partner, 1986-93; sometime Advocate Depute ad hoc, since 2001. Executive Member, Glasgow Bar Association, 1983-93; Local Parliamentary Liaison Officer, Law Society of Scotland, 1986-88; Rector's Warden and Vestry Member, St. Margaret's Episcopal Church, Newlands, Glasgow; Director, Hillhead High School War Memorial Trust, since 2000. Recreations: family; watching sport; reading; music; friends. Address: (b.) Advocates Library, Parliament House, Parliament Square, Edinburgh EH1 1RF; T.-0131-226 5071; e-mail: gallanpleader@hotmail.com

Allan, George Alexander, MA (Hons). Headmaster, Robert Gordon's College, Aberdeen, 1978-96; b. 3.2.36, Edinburgh; m., Anne Violet Veevers; 2 s. Educ. Daniel Stewart's College, Edinburgh; Edinburgh University. Teacher of Classics, Glasgow Academy, 1958-60; Daniel Stewart's College: Teacher of Classics, 1960-63, Head of Classics, 1963-73 (appointed Housemaster, 1967); Schoolmaster Fellow Commoner, Corpus Christi College,

Cambridge, 1972; Deputy Headmaster, Robert Gordon's College, 1973-77. Former Chairman and former Secretary, Headmasters' Conference (Scottish Division) (Member, National Committee, 1982 and 1983); Governor, Welbeck College, 1980-89; Council Member, Scottish Council of Independent Schools, 1988-96 and since 1997; Director, Edinburgh Academy, since 1996. Recreations: gardening; golf; music. Address: 5 Abbey View, Kelso, Roxburghshire TD5 8HX.

Allan, James Morrison, FRICS, ACIArb, MIPS. Chartered Surveyor; b. 1.10.43, Edinburgh; m., Elizabeth Howie Sneddon Jack; 2 s. Educ. George Watson's College; Heriot Watt College. Joined Phillips Knox & Arthur as Apprentice Quantity Surveyor, 1960; qualified ARICS, 1965; FRICS, 1975; RICS: Chairman, National Junior Organisation, 1975-76; Chairman, Quantity Surveyors Committee in Scotland, 1988-89; Chairman, RICS in Scotland, 1991-92; Member, RICS Management Board, 1992-95; Chairman, RICS Business Services Ltd.; Member, RICS Strategy and Resources Board. Recreations: family; caravanning and motoring; golf. Address: (h.) 4 Stevenson Way, Longniddry, East Lothian EH32 0PF; T.-01875 852377.

Allan, Sheriff John Douglas, BL, DMS. Sheriff of Lothian and Borders at Edinburgh, since 2000; President, Sheriffs' Association, since 2000 (Secretary, 1991-97, Vice-President, 1997-2000); b. 2.10.41, Edinburgh; m., Helen E.J. Aiton; 1 s.; 1 d. Educ. George Watson's College, Edinburgh; Edinburgh University. Solicitor in private practice, Edinburgh, 1963-67; Procurator Fiscal Depute, Edinburgh, 1967-71; Solicitor, Crown Office, Edinburgh, 1971-76; Assistant Procurator Fiscal, then Senior Assistant Procurator Fiscal. Glasgow, 1976-79; Solicitor, Crown Office, Edinburgh, 1979-83; Procurator Fiscal for Edinburgh and Regional Procurator Fiscal for Lothians and Borders, 1983-88; Sheriff of Lanark, 1988-2000. Part-time Lecturer in Law, Napier College, Edinburgh, 1963-66; Chairman, Judicial Commission, General Assembly of the Church of Scotland, since 1998; Member, Board, Scottish Children's Reporter Administration, since 1995; Council Member, Commonwealth Magistrates' and Judges' Association, since 2000. Holder, Scout "Medal of Merit". Recreations: Scouts; youth leadership; walking; Church. Address: (b.) Sheriff Court House, 27 Chambers Street, Edinburgh EH1 1LB; T.-0131-225 2525; e-mail: Sheriff.JDAllan@scotcourts.gov.uk

Allan, Richard James Paul, BSc, PhD, FSA (Scot). Chairman, Executive Committee, Royal Zoological Society of Scotland, 1995-2000; Hon. Vice President: Shetland Sheep Breeders Group, since 1992, Eriskay Pony Society, since 1997; b. 26.5.30, Glasgow; m., Norma Adam Dick; 3 s. Educ. High School of Glasgow; University of Glasgow; Royal Technical College, Glasgow. Technical service with ICI Fibres Division in man-made fibres and development of commercial computing; left industry to develop countryside and wildlife interests and farming; fronted development of rare breeds in Scotland, assisted by Royal Zoological Society of Scotland. Founder Chairman, Border Country Life Association; Member, Scottish Borders Council Heritage Steering Group (preparing series of booklets on Borders history and archaeology). Publications: The Scottish Borderland (Co-Editor, Contributor), 1988; Wool Quality (Co-Author), 1992; many articles on rare breeds. Recreations: photography; gardening; walking; reading; classical music. Address: (h.) Buskinburn House, Coldingham, Eyemouth, Berwickshire TD14 5UA; T.-018907 71215.

Alldridge, Alasdair, BArch (Hons), DipUD, FRIAS, RIBA, MAPM. Director, Wittets Ltd., Chartered Architects, since 1985; b. 14.1.50, Glasgow; m., Jenny Small; 2 s.; 1 d. Educ. Loretto School; Heriot-Watt University; Edinburgh College of Art. Assistant Architect: Borders Regional Council, 1975-77, J & W Wittets, 1982-85. Vice-President,

RIAS, 1991-93, Incorporation Representative, 1993-95; Chairman, Skye and Lochalsh Education Business Partnership, 1990-95; Lay Member, HMI Schools Inspectorate, 1996-2000; Convenor, AHSS Cases Panel, 1990-2001; Director, An Tuireann Arts Centre, since 2000. Recreations: reading; language; collecting foreign names of rainbows. Address: (h.) Kinloch, Isle Ornsay, Isle of Skye IV43 8QY; T.-01471 822 434; e-mail: alldridgeskye@lineone.net

Allen, Professor John Walter, MA, FSAS, FRSE. Professor of Solid State Physics, St. Andrews University, since 1980; b. 7.3.28, Birmingham. Educ. King Edward's High School, Birmingham; Sidney Sussex College, Cambridge. RAF, 1949-51; Staff Scientist, Ericsson Telephones Ltd., 1951-56; Services Electronics Research Laboratory, 1956-68; Visiting Associate Professor, Stanford University, 1964-66; joined Department of Physics, St. Andrews University, 1968. Recreations: archaeology; country dancing. Address: (b.) Department of Physics and Astronomy, St. Andrews University, North Haugh, St. Andrews, Fife KY16 9SS; T.-01334 463331.

Allison, Professor Arthur Compton, BSc, DipNumMath, PhD, FBCS. Former Vice Principal and Professor of Computing Science, Glasgow University, now Honorary Research Fellow; b. 24.3.41, Belfast; m., Dr. Joyce Allison; 3 d. Educ. Queen's University, Belfast; Glasgow University. Glasgow University, 1962-67; Smithsonian Institution, Boston, 1967-73; Glasgow University, 1973-83; Northeastern University, Boston, 1983-84; Glasgow University, since 1984. Elder, Church of Scotland. Recreations: running; curling. Address: (b.) Glasgow University, Glasgow G12 8QQ; T.-0141-330 4453.

Allison, Charles William, MBChB, FRCA. Consultant Anaesthetist, Stracathro Hospital, Brechin, since 1982; Consultant, Ninewells Hospital, Dundee; Honorary Senior Lecturer, Dundee University; b. 1.7.52, Newport on Tay; m., Elspeth Stratton; 2 d. Educ. Madras College, St. Andrews; Dundee University. Training grades in anaesthesia, Dundee, 1976-81; Clinical Research Fellow, Hospital for Sick Children, Toronto, 1982. Editor, Annals of the Scottish Society of Anaesthetists, since 1999. Publications: papers and book chapter. Recreations: golf; photography. Address: Summerbank House, Brechin, Angus DD9 6HL; T.-01356 623624; e-mail: charlie@cwallison.fsnet.co.uk

Allison, John Andrew, MA, LLB. Honorary Sheriff, Cupar, since 1986; Solicitor (retired 1993); b. 10.5.36, Glasgow; m., Elizabeth; 2 s.; 1 d. Educ. Paisley Grammar School; Glasgow University. Legal apprenticeship, McGrigor, Donald and Co., Glasgow; Legal Assistant, Glenrothes Development Corporation; Partner, Pagan Osborne and Grace, WS, Fife; Member, Council, Law Society of Scotland; Dean, Society of Solicitors for Eastern District of Fife. Past President, Glenrothes Rotary Club. Recreations: oil painting; hillwalking; Rotary. Address: (h.) Craigrothie House, by Cupar, Fife; T.-01334 828606.

Allsop, Rev. Thomas Douglas, MA, BD. Minister, Beechgrove Church, Aberdeen, 1977-99; b. 2.3.34, Kilmaurs; m., Marion Morrison Urie; 2 s.; 1 d. Educ. Kilmarnock Academy; Glasgow University and Trinity College. Assistant Minister, St. Marnock's, Kilmarnock; Minister: Kirriemuir South (after a union called Kirriemuir St. Andrew's), 1959-65; Minister, Knightswood St. Margaret's, Glasgow, 1965-77. Founder Chairman, Kirriemuir Round Table; Moderator, Dumbarton Presbytery, 1975, Aberdeen Presbytery, 1994-95; Burgess, City of Aberdeen. Recreations: photography; golf; musical appreciation. Address: 2 Carnegie Gardens, Aberdeen AB15 4AW; T.-01224 318474.

Almaini, Professor A.E.A., BSc(Eng), MSc, PhD, CEng, FIEE. Professor, School of Engineering, Napier University, since 1991; b. 1.7.45, Baghdad; m., Shirley May; 2 s.; 1 d. Educ. London University; Salford University; Loughborough University. Research Scientist, Scientific Research Foundation, 1970-79; Lecturer, then Senior Lecturer, Napier University, 1980-91. Publication: Electronic Logic Systems (book); many papers published. Recreation: gardening. Address: (b.) School of Engineering, Merchiston Campus, Edinburgh EH10 5DT; T.-0131-455 2325.

Alston, Robin Peter, MD, FRCA. Consultant, Department of Anaesthesia, Critical and Pain Medicine, Royal Infirmary of Edinburgh, since 1993; Senior Lecturer, University of Edinburgh, since 1994; b. 2.5.54, Glasgow; m., Linda. Educ. Leith Academy; Glasgow University. Registrar, Department of Anaesthesia, Aukland Hospital, New Zealand; Lecturer, Department of Anaesthesia, University of Glasgow, 1985-90; Assistant Professor, Department of Anaesthesiology, University of Washington, Seattle, USA. Member, Scottish Standing Committee, Association of Anaesthetists of Great Britain and Ireland. Advisory Editor, Perfusion. Recreations: skiing; travel. Address: Department of Anaesthesia, Royal Infirmary, Lauriston Place, Edinburgh EH10 5AU; T.-0131-229 6437; e-mail: p.alston@ed.ac.uk

Alstead, Brigadier (Francis) Allan (Littlejohns), CBE, DL, MPhil, FCIT, FIMgt, FIPD, FInstAM, FRSA, FInstD, FBISA. Director, Alstead Consulting, since 2000; Chief Executive, sportscotland (formerly Scottish Sports Council), 1990-2000; Chef de Mission for Scottish Team, Commonwealth Games 2002; b. 19.6.35, Glasgow; m., Joy Veronica Edwards; 2 s. Educ. Glasgow Academy; Royal Military Academy, Sandhurst; Royal Naval Staff College; Joint Services Staff College; Edinburgh University; University of Wales, Aberystwyth. Commissioned into King's Own Scottish Borderers, 1955; commanded 1st Bn., KOSB, 1974-76 (Mention in Despatches); Military Assistant to Quarter-Master-General,, 1976-79; Instructor, Army Staff College, Camberley, 1979-81; Assistant Chief of Staff, BAOR, 1981-84 (Colonel); Commander, 51st Highland Brigade, 1984-87 (Brigadier); NATO Research Fellow, Edinburgh University, 1987-88; NATO Reinforcement Co-ordinator, 1988-90. Member, Royal Company of Archers (Queen's Bodyguard in Scotland); Deputy Lieutenant, City of Edinburgh; Regimental Trustee, KOSB; Trustee, Youth Sport Trust, 1992-99; Deputy Hon. Colonel, City of Edinburgh Universities OTC, 1990-99; Governor: Moray House College, 1991-97, Glasgow Academy, 1995-2001; Member, Executive, Scottish Council, Development and Industry, 1995-2000; Member, Lowland TAVRA; Chairman, Mercy Corps Scotland; Board Member, Mercy Corps International, USA; Director and Trustee, Seagull Trust; Non-Executive Director, JRG Ltd; Member, General Council, Erskine Hospital; Member, Council, National Playing Fields Association; President, SSAFA, Edinburgh and Midlothian, 1990-98. Publications: Ten in Ten; The Reinforcement of Europe in Crisis and War. Recreations: running; swimming; tennis. Address: (b.) 9 Inverleith Row, Edinburgh EH3 5LS; T.-(b.) 0131-467 0168; (h.) 0131-556 5599; e-mail: allan@alstead.com

Amyes, Professor Sebastian Giles Becket, BSc, MSc, PhD, DSc, FRCPath, FIBiol. Professor of Microbial Chemotherapy and Head of Medical Microbiology Department, Edinburgh University; b. 6.5.49, Stockton Heath; 1 s.; 1 d. Educ. Cranleigh School; University College, London. Edinburgh University, since 1977; Reader, 1988; Professor, 1992, Head of Medical Microbiology Department, 1997. Royal Pharmaceutical Society annual conference award, 1984; C.L. Oakley lectureship, Pathological Society, 1987. Recreations: fishing; opera; golf; exploring parts of the world that the tour companies have not yet found. Address: (b.) Department of Medical Microbiology, Medical School, Teviot Place, Edinburgh EH8 9AG; T.-0131-650 3163.

Ancram, Earl of (Rt. Hon. Michael Andrew Foster Jude Kerr), PC, DL, QC. Advocate; MP (Conservative), Devizes, since 1992; Deputy Leader of the Opposition and Shadow Foreign Seretary, since 2001; former Chairman, Conservative Party; b. 7.7.45; m.; 2 d. Educ. Ampleforth; Christ Church, Oxford; Edinburgh University. MP: Berwickshire and East Lothian, 1974, Edinburgh South, 1979-87; Parliamentary Under Secretary of State, Scottish Office, 1993-94; Minister of State, Northern Ireland Office, 1994-97; Chairman, Conservative Party in Scotland, 1980-83. DL, Roxburgh District.

Anderson, Alex, DipTP, MRTPI. Director of Planning and Transport, Angus Council, since 1995; b. 21.3.47, Dundee; m., Maureen; 2 s. Educ. Grove Academy, Dundee; Duncan of Jordanstone College. Address: (b.) Department of Planning and Transport, St. James House, St. James Road, Forfar DD8 2ZP; T.-01307 473405.

Anderson, Andrew Duncan, MA, LLB. Senior Partner, James Guthrie and Co., Solicitors, Kilmarnock, since 1996; President, Scottish Law Agents Society, since 2001; b. 23.12.41, Kilmarnock; m., Eveline; 3 s. Educ. Kilmarnock Academy; Glasgow University. Joined James Guthrie and Co., 1967 (Partner, since 1971). Council Member, Scottish Law Agents Society, since 1992. Chairman (part-time), Tribunals, Appeals Service; Dean, Kilmarnock Faculty of Solicitors, 1992. Recreations: golf; bridge; gardening. Address: (b.) 3 Portland Road, Kilmarnock KA1 2AN; T.-01563 525155.

Anderson, Professor Annie S., BSc, PhD, SRD. Research Professor of Food Choice, Department of Medicine, University of Dundee, Director, Centre for Public Health Nutrition Research, since 1996; b. 24.12.57, Torphins; m., Professor Mike Lean; 1 s.; 2 d. Educ. Cults Academy, Aberdeen; RGIT; University of Aberdeen. Dietitian, Cambridge Area Health Authority, 1979-81; Research Assistant, Medical School, University of Cambridge, 1982-84; Research Dietitian, Grampian Health Board, 1985-86; Postgraduate Research Student, Department of Obstetrics, University of Aberdeen, 1987-91; Research Fellow (Human Nutrition), University of Glasgow, 1991-96; Member, Dundee University Court, 1999-2001; Editor, Journal of Human Nutrition and Dietetics; Member, Scientific Advisory Committee on Nutrition, 2001-04. Recreation: genealogy. Address: Hatton Castle, Newtyle, Blairgowrie PH12 8UN; T.-01382 496442.

Anderson, Arthur Andrew, MBE, FRAgS, FGAJ. Chairman, Royal Scottish Agricultural Benevolent Institution; Owner, Denmill Production Company; b. 21.11.44, Dumfries; m., Andrea Jane MacKenzie; 2 s.; 2 d. Educ. Barnard Castle School. Copy Boy, The Scotsman, 1961-64; Reporter, Scottish Farmer, 1964-65; Sub-Editor, Glasgow Herald, 1965-66; Agricultural Reporter, The Scotsman, 1967-69; Scottish Correspondent, Farmers Weekly, 1970-73; News/Farming Producer and Reporter, BBC Radio Carlisle, 1973-75; General Programme Producer, BBC Radio Scotland, 1975-77; joined BBC TV, Aberdeen, 1977, former Head of Production, BBC Aberdeen; Producer, Landward, BBC Scotland, 1979-2001. Winner RICS TV Award, John Deere Journalism Award, Norsk Hydro TV Award, One World Broadcasting Trust Prize, Netherthorpe Award; Member, Aberdeen Children's Panel, 1982-89; Chairman, Guild of Agricultural Journalists, 1997-99. Recreation: hill-walking. Address: (h.) Denmill Cottage, Burnett Street, Auchenblae AB30 1WP; T.-01561 320248; e-mail: Arthur-Anderson@ukgateway.net

Anderson, David Alexander, BA (Hons), MEd, FCIPD, FRSA. Chief Executive, Scottish Enterprise Dunbartonshire, since 1998; b. 2.12.54, Perth; m., Tricia; 3 s.; 1 d. Educ. Arbroath High School; University of Stirling; University of Newcastle; University of Sheffield. Graduate Management Trainee, Department of Employment; Local Office Manager, Newcastle, Department of Employment, 1980-84; Manpower Services Commission: Programme Development Manager, Newcastle, 1984-86, Policy Manager, Head Office, Sheffield, 1986-90; Operations Manager, Training Agency, Ayrshire, 1990-91; Director of Skills Development, Enterprise Ayrshire, 1991-97. Director: The Keynote Trust, Strathclyde European Partnership; Member, Institute of Directors. Recreations: golf; music. Address: (b.) Spectrum House, Clydebank Business Park, Clydebank G81 2DR; T.-0141-951 2121;e-mail: david.a.anderson@scotent.co.uk

Anderson, David Rae, MA (Hons), LLB, LLM, WS, NP. Solicitor, since 1961 (Senior Partner, Allan Grant Solicitors); part-time Legal Chairman, Employment (formerly Industrial) Tribunals, since 1971; Honorary Sheriff, since 1981; accredited solicitor-mediator; b. 27.1.36, Stonehaven; m., Jean Strachan (deceased). Educ. Mackie Academy, Stonehaven; Aberdeen University; Edinburgh University; Australian National University, Canberra. Barrister and Solicitor of Supreme Court of Victoria, Australia, 1962; Legal Officer, Attorney-General's Department, Canberra, 1962-65; part-time research student, Law Faculty, Australian National University, Canberra, and part-time Lecturer in Legal History, 1962-65; returned to Scotland, 1965, in private legal practice, Edinburgh, 1965-67, Alloa and Central Scotland, since 1967; Interim Town Clerk, Burgh of Alva, 1973; former part-time Reporter to Secretary of State for Scotland for public enquiries; twice Dean, Society of Solicitors of Clackmannanshire; Member, Council, Law Society of Scotland, 1984-2000; Council Member, Scottish Universities Law Institute; Council Member, Commonwealth Lawyers Association; former Member, UK Delegation, Council of the Bars and Law Societies of the European Community; Member, Stirling University Conference; Elder, Church of Scotland; Parliamentary candidate, 1970 and 1971; formerly served, RNVR; Past President, Alloa Rotary Club. Recreations: climbing and hill-walking; reading, especially historical biography and English literature; music, especially opera; interested in current affairs, architecture, stately homes and travel. Address: (h.) 3 Smithfield Loan, Alloa FK10 1NJ; T.-01259 213096; (b.) 8 Shillinghill, Alloa FK10 1JT; T.-01259 723201.

Anderson, Donald Craig. Leader, City of Edinburgh Council, since 1999; b. 27.7.62, Edinburgh; m., Kirsty; 1 s.; 1 d. Educ. Liberton High School, Edinburgh; Napier College, Edinburgh. Medical Laboratory Scientific Officer, Scottish Blood Transfusion Service, until 1998; Lothian Regional Councillor, 1986-96, Chair, Economic Development Committee, 1992-96; City of Edinburgh Councillor, since 1995, Convener, Economic Development Committee, 1996-99; Board Member: Scottish Tourist Board, Edinburgh International Festival, Edinburgh Fringe Festival. Address: (b.) City Chambers, High Street, Edinburgh; T.-0131-529 3261.

Anderson, Dorothy Elizabeth, BSc (Hons), MB, ChB, MRCP(UK), DMRD, FRCR, FRCP(Glas). Consultant Radiologist, Glasgow Royal Infirmary, since 1981; Honorary Clinical Lecturer, then Senior Lecturer, Glasgow University, since 1982; b. 26.9.50, Glasgow; m., David Anderson; 1 s.; 1 d. Educ. Glasgow High School for Girls; Glasgow University. Pre-registration posts, Stobhill Hospital and Glasgow Royal Infirmary; post-registration year, Respiratory Unit, Knightswood Hospital; trained in radiology, Western Infirmary, Glasgow (Registrar, then Senior Registrar). Recreation: choral singing; walking; reading; history. Address: (h.) 18 Milverton Avenue, Bearsden, Glasgow G61 4BE; T.-0141-942 7510; e-mail: Dorothy.Anderson@northglasgow.scot.nhs.uk

Anderson, Douglas Kinloch, OBE, MA. Chairman, Kinloch Anderson (Holdings) Ltd., Edinburgh, since 1975; Director: Martin Currie Portfolio Investment Trust PLC; Fidelity Special Values PLC; Martin Currie Capital Return Trust PLC; b. 19.2.39, Edinburgh; m., Deirdre Anne; 2 s.; 1 d. Educ. George Watson's Boys College; St. Andrews University. Joined Kinloch Anderson Ltd., 1962 (fifth generation in family business); Assistant on Master's Court, Edinburgh Merchant Company, 1976-79; elected Honorary Member, St. Andrew's Society of Washington DC, 1985; Board Member, Scottish Tourist Board, 1986-92; Member, Edinburgh Festival Council, 1988-90; President, Edinburgh Royal Warrant Holders Association, 1987-88; former Member, Scottish Committee, Institute of Directors; President, Edinburgh Chamber of Commerce, 1988-90; Master, Edinburgh Merchant Company, 1990-92; Deputy Chairman, Edinburgh Marketing Ltd., 1990-92; Director, Lothian and Edinburgh Enterprise Ltd., 1990-95; elected Leith High Constable, 1993; Freeman, City of London. Recreations: golf; fishing; watching rugby; travel (non-business). Address: (b.) Commercial Street/Dock Street, Leith, Edinburgh EH6 6EY; T.-0131-555 1355.

Anderson, Gordon Alexander, CBE, CA, FCMA. Chartered Accountant; b. 9.8.31, Glasgow; m., Eirene Cochrane Howie Douglas; 2 s.; 1 d. Educ. High School of Glasgow. Apprentice CA, Moores Carson & Watson, Glasgow, 1949-54; qualified CA, 1955; National Service, Royal Navy, 1955-57 (Sub Lieutenant); Partner, Moores Carson & Watson, 1958 (firm name changed to McClelland Moores, 1958, Arthur Young McClelland Moores, 1968, Arthur Young, 1985, Ernst & Young, 1989); Chairman, Arthur Young, 1987-89; Deputy Senior Partner, Ernst & Young, 1989-90; Director: Lloyds TSB Group plc, 1993-99, TSB Bank Scotland plc, 1991-99 (Chairman, 1994-99), High School of Glasgow Ltd., 1975-81 and since 1990 (Chairman of Governors, since 1992), Merchants House of Glasgow, since 1996; Member, Council on Tribunals and its Scottish Committee, 1990-96; Chairman, Bitmac Ltd., 1990-96; Director: Douglas Firebrick Co. Ltd., 1960-70; Member, Scottish Milk Marketing Board, 1979-85; Institute of Chartered Accountants of Scotland: Member, Council, 1980-84, Vice President, 1984-86, President, 1986-87. Recreations: golf; gardening. Address: (h.) Ardwell, 41 Manse Road, Bearsden, Glasgow G61 3PN; T.-0141-942 2803.

Anderson, Rev. Professor Hugh, MA, BD, PhD, DD, FRSE. Professor of New Testament Language, Literature and Theology, Edinburgh University, 1966-85; b. 18.5.20, Galston, Ayrshire; m., Jean Goldie Torbit; 1 s.; 1 s. (deceased); 1 d. Educ. Kilmarnock Academy; Glasgow University. Chaplaincy work, Egypt and Palestine, 1945-46; Lecturer in Old Testament, Glasgow University, 1946-51; Minister, Trinity Church, Pollokshields, Glasgow, 1951-57; Professor of Biblical Criticism, Duke University, North Carolina, 1957-66; special appointments including A.B. Bruce Lecturer in New Testament, Glasgow University, 1954-57; Katharine McBride Visiting Professor, Bryn Mawr College, Pennsylvania, 1972-73; Kenan Distinguished Visiting Professor, Meredith College, North Carolina, 1982-83; Pendergrass Visiting Professor, Florida Southern College, 1985-86, 1987-88. Awarded Schweitzer Medal from North Carolina History and Science Foundation. Publications: Psalms 1-45; Historians of Israel; The New Testament in Historical and Contemporary Perspective (Editor with W. Barclay); Jesus and Christian Origins; Jesus; The Gospel of Mark: Commentary; 3 and 4 Maccabees (Commentary). Recreations: golf; gardening; music. Address: (h.) Morningside Way, 23/13 Maxwell Street, Edinburgh EH10 5HT.

Anderson, Iain Buchanan, MA, DipEd, LGSM. Music Presenter/Sports Commentator, BBC, since 1985; m., Marion Elizabeth; 3 s.; 1 d. Educ. Bellahouston Academy, Glasgow; Glasgow University; Guildhall School. Lecturer in Speech and Drama, Jordanhill College, 1967; Arts Editor/Presenter, Radio Clyde, 1974. Former Rugby Correspondent, Scotland on Sunday. Address: (h.) Elmhurst, Station Road, Langbank PA14 6YA; T.-0147 554 0733.

Anderson, Ian Wilson Russell, MBChB, FRCS (Glasgow), FRCS (England), FRCS (Edinburgh), FFAEM. Consultant, Accident and Emergency, Victoria Infirmary, Glasgow; Honorary Clinical Senior Lecturer, University of Edinburgh; b. 4.5.51, Prestwick. Educ. Ayr Academy; University of Glasgow. House Officer posts, Glasgow; completed general professional training in surgery, 1980; completed specialist training in accident and emergency medicine and surgery, 1984; main interest in initial assessment and resuscitation of trauma. Member, Council, Medical and Dental Defence Union of Scotland; President, Faculty of Accident and Emergency Medicine; Member, Council, Royal College of Physicians and Surgeons of Glasgow. Recreations: travel; golf; motoring. Address: Accident and Emergency Department, Victoria Infirmary, Glasgow G42 9TY; T.-0141-201 5305.

Anderson, James A., MA, MEd, MBA, DipEd. Director of Education, Angus Council, since 1995; b. 21.8.49, Aberdeen; m., Linda; 1 s.; 1 d. Educ. Aberdeen Grammar School; Aberdeen University; Edinburgh University; Stirling University. Teacher, Assistant Principal Teacher, Principal Teacher of Mathematics, 1973-84; Tayside Regional Council: Assistant Director of Education, 1984-87, Area Education Officer, 1987-91, Senior Assistant Director of Education, 1991-95, Director of Education, 1995-96. Recreations: golf; bridge. Address: (b.) Angus Council, County Buildings, Market Street, Forfar DD8 3WE; T.-01307 473235.

Anderson, James Killoch, OBE, MB, ChB, FFCM, FCR, JP. Former Unit Medical Officer, Glasgow Royal Infirmary and Royal Maternity Hospital, Glasgow (retired, 1988); b. 3.2.23, Johnstone; m., Irene Webster Wilson; 1 s.; 2 d. Educ. High School of Glasgow; Glasgow University. Deputy Medical Superintendent, Glasgow Royal Infirmary and Associated Hospitals, 1954; appointed Medical Superintendent, 1957; District Medical Officer, Eastern District, Greater Glasgow Health Board, 1974; Unit Medical Officer, Unit East 1, Greater Glasgow Health Board, 1984. Corps Commandant and Council Member, St. Andrew's Ambulance Association, 1957-82; Member of Committee, Scottish Ambulance Service, 1957-74; Director, North Parish, Washing Green Society, Glasgow, since 1957; Member, Scottish Technical Education Council, since 1974; Member, Science Development Team, 16-18s Action Plan, Scottish Education Department. Recreations: gardening; golf. Address: (h.) 15 Kenilworth Avenue, Helensburgh G84 7JR; T.-01436 3739.

Anderson, Janette, BAcc, CA. Director Scotland, Railtrack; b. 16.4.64, Glasgow; m., Brian Anderson; 1 d. Arthur Andersen and Co., 1984-88; Digital Equipment Scotland, 1988-90; Price Waterhouse, 1990-92; Chief Accountant, ScotRail, 1992-93; Railtrack: Financial Controller, 1993-97, Business Development Manager, 1997; Governor, Glasgow School of Art, since 2000. Recreations: jazz; travel. Address: (b.) Buchanan House, 58 Port Dundas Road, Glasgow G4 0LQ; T.-0141-335 3555.

Anderson, Kenneth, MBChB, MD, FRCP (Glas & Edin). Consultant Physician with special interest in respiratory medicine; b. Glasgow; m., M. Ruth Adamson. Educ. Allan Glen's School; Glasgow University. Visiting Physician, University of Colorado Hospitals, Denver. Honorary Senior Lecturer, Medicine, University of Glasgow; Honorary

Lecturer, Environmental Health, University of Strathclyde; Chairman, British Lung Foundation Scotland; Member, Scottish, British and American Thoracic Societies. Recreations: rugby; golf; tennis; gardens. Address: (b.) Crosshouse Hospital, Kilmarnock KA1 0BE; T.-01563 521133; (h.) Fairhaven, 14 Sarazen Drive, Troon KA10 6JP.

Anderson, Professor Michael, OBE, MA, PhD, FBA, FRSE. Professor of Economic History, University of Edinburgh, since 1979; b. 21.2.42, Woking; m., Rosemary Elizabeth Kitching; 1 s.; 1 d. Educ. Kingston Grammar School; Queens' College, Cambridge. University of Edinburgh: Assistant Lecturer, 1967-69, Lecturer, 1969-75, Reader, 1975-79, Dean of Faculty of Social Sciences, 1985-89, Vice-Principal, 1989-93, and 1997-2000, Acting Principal, 1994, Senior Vice-Principal, since 2000. Member: Scottish Records Advisory Council, 1984-93, Economic and Social Research Council, 1990-94, Follett Committee on Libraries and Follett Implementation Group, 1993-97, British Library Board, since 1994, Council of British Academy, 1995-98; Curator, Royal Society of Edinburgh, 1997-99; Trustee, National Library of Scotland, since 1998, Chairman, since 2000; Chairman, Research Support Libraries Programme, since 1998. Publications: Family Structure in Nineteenth Century Lancashire, 1971; Approaches to the History of the Western Family, 1981; Population Change in North-Western Europe 1750-1850; many papers on family sociology and history and historical demography. Recreations: natural history; gardening; study of ancient civilisations. Address: (b.) Department of Economic and Social History, University of Edinburgh, William Robertson Building, George Square, Edinburgh EH8 9JY; T.-0131-650 3844.

Anderson, Moira, OBE. Singer; b. Kirkintilloch; m., Dr. Stuart Macdonald. Educ. Ayr Academy; Royal Scottish Academy of Music, Glasgow. Began with Kirkintilloch Junior Choir, aged six; made first radio broadcast for BBC in Scotland, aged eight; was Teacher of Music in Ayr before becoming professional singer; made first professional broadcast, White Heather Club, 1960; has toured overseas, had her own radio and TV series; has introduced Stars on Sunday, ITV; appeared in summer shows, cabaret, pantomime and numerous other stage shows; several Royal Variety performances.

Anderson, Peter David, MA, PhD, FSA Scot, FRHistS, FRSA. Deputy Keeper, National Archives of Scotland (formerly Scottish Record Office), since 1993; b. 10.3.47, Greenock; m., Jean Johnstone Smith; 1 s.; 1 d. Educ. Hutchesons' Grammar School, Glasgow; St. Andrews University; Edinburgh University. Teacher of History, Cranhill Secondary School, Glasgow, 1972-73; Research Assistant, Scottish Record Office, 1974-80; Registrar, National Register of Archives (Scotland), 1980-83; Secretary, NRA(S), 1984-85; Conservation Officer, 1985-89; Head, Records Liaison Branch, 1989-93. Member, International Council on Archives Committee on Electronic Records; Convener, Society of Archivists Legislation Panel, since 1996; Chair, International Council on Archives Committee on Archive Buildings and Equipment, since 1996; Secretary, Scottish Oral History Group, 1984-88, Deputy Convener, since 1988; Chair, Linlithgow Players, 1994-97. Publications: Robert Stewart, Earl of Orkney, Lord of Shetland, 1533-93, 1982; Black Patie, 1993. Recreations: drawing and painting; drama. Address: (b.) National Archives of Scotland, HM General Register House, Edinburgh EH1 3YY; T.-0131-535 1406.

Anderson, Robert Alexander, LLB, DipLP, NP. Solicitor, since 1983; Partner, Lindsay & Kirk, Aberdeen, since 1988; President, Aberdeen Bar Association,1996-98; b. 31.5.60, Nairn; m., Nicola Mary; 1 s.; 1 d. Educ. Nairn Academy; University of Glasgow. Trained at J.A. McGoogan & Co., Coatbridge, 1981-83, Legal Assistant, 1983-85; Legal

Assistant, Lindsay & Kirk, Aberdeen, 1985-88. Involved on voluntary basis with Aberdeen Women's Aid; Tutor in Criminal Court Practice, Aberdeen University. Recreation: orienteering. Address: (b.) 39 Huntly Street, Aberdeen AB10 1TJ; T.-01224 641402.

Anderson, Professor Robert David, MA, DPhil. Professor of Modern History, Edinburgh University, since 1994; b. 11.7.42, Cardiff. Educ. Taunton School, Somerset; Queen's and St. Antony's Colleges, Oxford. Assistant Lecturer, Glasgow University, 1967-69; Lecturer, then Senior Lecturer and Reader, Edinburgh University, 1969-94. Publications: Education in France 1848-1870, 1975; France 1870-1914: Politics and Society, 1977; Education and Opportunity in Victorian Scotland, 1983 (winner, Scottish Arts Council Literary Award, 1984); The Student Community at Aberdeen 1860-1939 (1988); Universities and Elites in Britain since 1800, 1992; Education and the Scottish People 1750-1918, 1995. Address: (b.) Department of History, Edinburgh University, Edinburgh; T.-0131-650 3786; e-mail: r.d.anderson@ed.ac.uk

Anderson, Rev. Robert Scott, MA, BD (Hons). Chief Executive, Scottish Churches World Exchange, since 1986; Principal, St. Colm's International House; b. 11.11.57, Glasgow; m., Jennifer Jane Paterson; 1 s.; 2 d. Educ. Hutchesons' Boys' Grammar School; Glasgow University. Assistant Manager, Glen Dairy Co. Ltd.; Assistant Minister, St. John's Renfield Church. Member: Glasgow Eastern Merchants and Tradesmen's Society, Incorporation of Tailors of Rutherglen, Community Action Network, SENSCOT; Trustee, The Starfish Initiative; Trustee, Barataria Foundation. Recreations: skiing; walking; orchid growing; reading poetry; literature. Address: St. Colm's International House, 23 Inverleith Terrace, Edinburgh; e-mail: we@stcolms.org

Anderson, Ruth. Chief Executive, Barataria Foundation, since 1999; b. 14.10.54, Glasgow; widow; 1s.; 1d. Began career as local authority education officer especially in economic development and rural issues; Director, RTS (Education and Training); Head of Department, Rural Forum Scotland; Founder member, Sustainable Economics Network; Founder, Scotbarter. Publications: Economy Systems in Rural Scotland; Financial Instruments; Working Together. Recreations: gardening; travel; reading very bad novels. Address: (h.) Keepers Cottage, Pitlardie, Perth, PH1 3H2; T.-01738 582232.

Anderson, EurIng Professor Thomas Alfred, CEng, FICE, FCIWEM, FIHT, FIOSH, FIMgt. Chairman, NHS Complaints Procedures, Lanarkshire Health Board; Member: Engineering Professional Board, Business and Science Board, Professional Review Management Board, and Technical Board, Chartered Institution of Water and Environmental Management; Director: Scottish Greenbelt Foundation, Land Trust Co. Ltd.; Public Sector Management Consultant, Joint Board for Engineering Management; Visiting Professor, Department of Civil, Structural and Environmental Engineering and Department of Biology, Paisley University, since 1992; Member and West Area Chairman, Scottish Water and Sewerage Customers' Council; Independent Adviser to Secretary of State on appointments to executive Non-Departmental Public Bodies, 1995-2000; b. 9.11.34, Glasgow; m., Margaret; 3 d. Educ. Strathbungo Senior Secondary School; Royal Technical College, Glasgow; Paisley College of Technology. City Engineer's Department, Corporation of the City of Glasgow: Senior Civil Engineer, 1964-68, Assistant Chief Civil Engineer, 1968-75; Strathclyde Regional Council: Assistant Director of Sewerage, 1975-81, Depute Director of Sewerage, 1981-91, Director of Sewerage, 1991-94. Institution of Municipal Engineers National Medal and Prize Winner, 1980; Examiner/Reviewer, Institution of Civil Engineers, since

1977; Freeman, City of London; Liveryman, Company of Water Conservators; Member, Industrial Advisory Committee/ Specialist Visiting Lecturer, Glasgow Caledonian University; Elder, Church of Scotland. Publications: technical papers. Recreations: gardening; golf; cricket. Address: (h.) Craigela, Ryefield Avenue, Drumpellier, Coatbridge ML5 1LG; T.-01236 424146.

Anderson, Very Rev. Canon William Rutherfoord Turnbull, MA, FTCL. Parish Priest, St. Francis R.C. Church, Aberdeen, previously Administrator, St. Mary's R.C. Cathedral, Aberdeen; b. 7.1.31, Glasgow. Educ. George Watson's College, Edinburgh; University of Edinburgh; Sidney Sussex College, Cambridge. Curate, St. David's, Dalkeith, 1960-61; staff, St. Mary's College, Blairs, Aberdeen, 1961-69; Producer, BBC Scotland Religious Department, 1969-77; Spiritual Director, Pontifical Scots College, Rome, 1977-85; staff, St. Mary's College, Blairs, Aberdeen, 1985-86; R.C. Chaplain, University of Aberdeen 1986-93. Canon, R.C. Diocese of Aberdeen; former Major Scholar, Sidney Sussex College, Cambridge; Poetry Society Gold Medal for verse-speaking, 1980; Preacher of the Year, The Times and College of Preachers, 1996; Warrack Lecturer, Aberdeen University, 1998. Recreations: walking; music and poetry; speech and drama adjudication; contributing to Press and Journal. Address: (b.) 231 Deeside Gardens, Aberdeen AB15 7PR; T.-01224 315893.

Andrew, Hugh, BA (Oxon), FSA Scot. Managing Director, Birlinn Ltd (incorporating John Donald); Managing Director, Seol Ltd.; Director, Compass Independent Book Sales Ltd.; b. 8.4.62. Educ. Glasgow Academy; Magdalen College, Oxford. Set up own publishing company, Birlinn Ltd., 1992; Joint Managing Director, Canongate Books, 1994-99. Recreations: reading; music; travel; archaeology; history; islands. Address: (b.) West Newington House, 10 Newington Road, Edinburgh EH9 1QS; T.-0131-668 4371; e-mail: hugh@birlinn.co.uk

Andrew, John Anthony, MA, FRICS. Chief Estates Adviser, Scottish Executive (previously Scottish Office), since 1996; b. 10.10.52, Ormskirk; m., Mary MacLeod MacKay; 3 s. Educ. Ormskirk Grammar School; Heanor Grammar School; Downing College, University of Cambridge. Valuation Office, Inland Revenue, Cleveland North, 1976-78; Lecturer in Land Economy, University of Aberdeen, 1978-81; Valuation Office, Inland Revenue, Aberdeen and Dumfries, 1981-89; Principal Estates Surveyor, Scottish Office, 1989-92 and 1994-96; Principal, Scottish Office Agriculture and Fisheries Department, Land Use and Conservation Division, 1992-94. Member: RICS Scottish Council, Castle Rock Housing Association Ltd. Management Committee, Napier University Building Department IPAC; External Examiner, Heriot-Watt University; Member, Editorial Advisory Board, Journal of Facilities Management. Address: Scottish Executive Land and Property Division, X Spur, Saughton House, Broomhouse Road, Edinburgh EH11 3XD; T.-0131-244 4521; e-mail: anthony.andrew@scotland.gsi.gov.uk

Andrews, June, RMN, RGN, MA(Hons). Director of Nursing, Forth Valley Acute Hospitals NHS Trust; nurse, since 1980; b. Kilwinning. Educ. Ardrossan Academy; Glasgow University; Nottingham University. NHS nursing and management posts, Nottingham and London; Royal College of Nursing: adviser on ethics and Aids, Assistant Director Policy and Research, Scottish Board Secretary. Regular contributor to nursing press. Address: (b.) Forth Valley Acute Hospitals NHS Trust, Westburn Avenue, Falkirk FK1 5ST; e-mail: jandrews@sri.scot.nhs.uk

Angiolini, Elish Frances, LLB (Hons), DipLP. Solicitor General for Scotland, since 2002; b. 24.6.60; m.; 2 c. Educ. Notre Dame High School, Glasgow; Strathclyde University. Traineeship, Crown Office, 1983-84; Procurator Fiscal Depute, South Strathclyde, 1984-90;

Crown Office: Senior Legal Assistant, Law Officers' Secretariat, 1990-92; Senior Depute Procurator Fiscal, Management Services Group, 1992-94; Senior Depute Procurator Fiscal, Solemn Unit, Procurator Fiscal's Office, Glasgow, 1994-95; Assistant Procurator Fiscal, Glasgow, 1995-97; Head, Crown Office and Procurator Fiscal Service Policy Group, 1997-2000; Regional Procurator Fiscal, Grampian, Highland and Islands, 2000-2002. Address: (b.) 25 Chambers Street, Edinburgh EH1 1LA.

Angus, Rev. James Alexander Keith, LVO, TD, MA. Extra Chaplain to HM The Queen, since 1996; b. 16.4.29, Aberdeen; m., Alison Jane Daly; 1 s.; 1 d. Educ. High School of Dundee; St. Andrews University. Assistant Minister, Glasgow Cathedral, 1955-56; Minister: Hoddam Parish Church, 1956-67, Gourock Old Parish Church, 1967-79; Minister, Braemar and Crathie Parish Churches, 1979-95. TA: Captain, Royal Artillery, 1950-56, Chaplain, 1957-77; Convener, Committee of Chaplains to HM Forces, General Assembly, 1981-85; LVO, 1990; Domestic Chaplain to HM The Queen in Scotland, 1979-96. Recreations: hill-walking; fishing; golf. Address: (h.) Darroch Den, Hawthorn Place, Ballater, Aberdeenshire AB35 5QH; T.-013397 56260.

Angus, Rae, MA (Hons), MLitt, FRSA, MCIPD. Principal, Aberdeen College, since 1993; b. 1947, Ellon; m., Alison Hay; 2 d. Educ. Peterhead Academy; Aberdeen University. Further Education Lecturer, 1975; Research Fellow, Aberdeen University, 1978-80; Aberdeen College of Commerce, 1981-90, latterly as Depute Principal; Depute Principal, Aberdeen College of Further Education, 1991-93. Recreations: reading; walking; computing. Address: (b.) Gallowgate, Aberdeen AB25 1BN; T.-01224 612000.

Annand, David Andrew, DA, ARBS, JP. Sculptor; b. 30.1.48, Insch, Aberdeenshire; m., Jean; 1 s.; 1 d. Educ. Perth Academy; Duncan of Jordanstone College of Art, Dundee. Lecturer, Sculpture Department, Duncan of Jordanstone College of Art, Dundee, 1972-74; Art Department, St. Saviour's High School, Dundee, 1975-88; full-time sculptor, since 1988; RSA Latimer Award, 1976; RSA Benno Schotz Award, 1978; RSA Ireland Alloys Award, 1982; Scottish Development Agency Dundee Technology Park Competition, 1986, "Deer Leap", Sir Otto Beit Medal, 1986; Royal Botanic Garden, Edinburgh "Ardea Cinerea", 1987; Winner, Almswall Road Sculpture Competition, Irvine Development Corporation, "The Ring", 1989; Winner, Perth High Street Sculpture Competition, Perth Partnership "Nae Day Sae Dark", 1989; Baxters of Speyside "Royal Stag" cast by Powderhall Bronze, 1993; Tranent Massacre Memorial bronze casting by Powderhall Bronze, 1995; Winner, competition to design sculpture for Lord Street, Wrexham, 1995, "Y Bwa" Civic Society Award, 1995; Winner, competition to design sculpture, Ashworth Roundabout, Blackpool, "Helter-skelter", 1995; Strathcarron Hospice composition, 1996; British High Commission, Hong Kong, "Three Cranes in Flight", 1997; Hamilton Town Square "Strongman", 1998; Aberdeen Angus Bull, Alford, 2001; The Declaration of Arbroath, Arbroath, 2001; Civic Pride, Barnet, London, 2001; other commissions completed in 2001 for BT Brentwood and Maidstone Borough Council. Recreations: music; bird watching; wine and food. Address: Pigscrave Cottage, The Wynd, Kilmany, Cupar, Fife KY15 4PT; T.-01382 330 714.

Annand, Louise Gibson, MBE, MA (Hons), AMA, DU. Artist; b. 27.5.15, Uddingston; m., 1, Alistair Matheson (deceased); 2, Roderick MacFarquhar (deceased). Educ. Hamilton Academy; Glasgow University. Teacher, primary and secondary schools, Glasgow, 1939-49; Assistant, Schools Museum Service, 1949-70; Museums Education Officer, 1970-80. Past Chairman: Scottish Educational Film Association (Glasgow Production Group); Glasgow Lady Artists Club Trust; National Vice-Chairman, Scottish

Educational Media Association, 1979-84; President: Society of Scottish Women Artists, 1963-66 and 1980-85; Member, Royal Fine Art Commission for Scotland, 1979-86; President, Glasgow Society of Women Artists, 1977-79, 1988-91; Visiting Lecturer in Scottish Art, Regina University, 1982; Chairman, J.D. Fergusson Foundation, since 1982 (Trustee, since 1983); Member, Business Committee, General Council, University of Glasgow, 1981-85, 1988-91; Honorary Member, Saltire Society, since 1993; DUniv, Glasgow University, 1994; exhibited widely since 1945; produced numerous 16mm films, including the first on Charles Rennie Mackintosh, 1966. Recreations: mountaineering (Ladies Scottish Climbing Club). Address: (h.) 22 Kingsborough Gardens, Glasgow G12 9NJ; T.-0141-339 8956.

Annandale and Hartfell, 11th Earl of (Patrick Andrew Wentworth Hope Johnstone of Annandale and of That Ilk). Chief, Clan Johnstone; Baron of the Barony of the Lands of the Earldom of Annandale and Hartfell, and of the Lordship of Johnstone; Hereditary Steward, Stewartry of Annandale; Hereditary Keeper, Keys of Lochmaben Castle; Deputy Lieutenant, Dumfriesshire, 1987-92, Vice-Lieutenant, since 1992; b. 19.4.41, Auldgirth, Dumfriesshire; m., Susan Josephine; 1 s.; 1 d. Educ. Stowe School; Royal Agricultural College, Cirencester. Member: Dumfriesshire County Council, 1970-75, Dumfries and Galloway Regional Council, 1975-85, Scottish Valuation Advisory Council, 1982, Solway River Purification Board, 1973-85; Underwriter, Lloyds, London, 1976. Address: (b.) Annandale Estates Office, St. Anns, Lockerbie DG11 1HQ.

Anstruther, Sir Ralph (Hugo), of that Ilk, 7th Bt. of Balcaskie and 12th of Anstruther, GCVO, MC, DL, BA. Equerry to the Queen Mother, since 1959, and Treasurer since 1961; b. 13.6.21. Educ. Eton; Magdalene College, Cambridge. Major (ret.), Coldstream Guards. Member, Queen's Bodyguard for Scotland (Royal Company of Archers); DL, Fife, 1960; DL, Caithness-shire, 1965. Address: Balcaskie, Pittenweem, Fife; Watten, Caithness.

Anton, Alexander Elder, CBE, MA, LLB, LLD (Hon), FBA; b. 1922; m., Doris May Lawrence; 1 s. Educ. Aberdeen University. Solicitor, 1949; Lecturer, Aberdeen, 1953-59; Professor of Jurisprudence, Glasgow University, 1959-73; Honorary Professor, 1984, Aberdeen University; Member, Scottish Law Commission, 1966-82; UK Delegate to Hague Conference on Private International Law, 1964-82; Chairman, Scottish Rights of Way Society, 1988-92. Publications: Private International Law, 1967 and 1990; Civil Jurisdiction in Scotland, 1984. Recreation: hill-walking. Address: (h.) 5 Seafield Drive West, Aberdeen AB15 7XA.

Antoni, Ferenc András, MD, PhD, FRSE. Senior Non-Clinical Scientist, University of Edinburgh, since 1997; b. 13.6.55, Budapest, Hungary; m., Dr. Megan C. Holmes; 3 s. Educ. schools in Budapest; Semmelweis Medical University, Budapest. Demonstrator, Department of Physiology, Semmelweis Medical University, Budapest; Research Associate then Researcher, Institute of Experimental Medicine, Hungarian Academy of Sciences; part-time Lecturer, Semmelweis Medical University, 1980-83; Physician on call, St. John's Hospital, Budapest, 1980-83; National Institute of Mental Health, Bethesda, USA: Visiting Associate, Laboratory of Cell Biology, 1983-85, Guest Scientist, Endocrinology and Reproduction Research Branch, National Institute of Child Health and Development, 1984-85; University of Oxford: Demonstrator, Department of Human Anatomy, 1985-89, Stipendiary Lecturer, Wadham and Hertford colleges, 1987-88; University of Edinburgh: Research Scientist then Senior Non-Clinical Scientist, MRC Brain Metabolism Unit, 1989-99, Honorary Fellow, Department of Pharmacology, then Neuroscience, since 1990; Member, MRC External Scientific Staff, Department of Neuroscience, since 1999.

Mortyn Jones Memorial Lecture, British Neuroendocrine Group, 1995. Recreations: skiing; tennis; concerts; hillwalking. Address: (b.) Department of Neuroscience, University of Edinburgh, Edinburgh EH8 9JZ; T.-0131-651 1884; e-mail: ferenc.antoni@ed.ac.uk

Anwar, Aamer, MA (Hons), DipRCmR, LLB, DipLP, FCS. Lawyer, since 2000; consultant trainer and guest university lecturer, since 1997; b. Manchester. Educ. Liverpool College; University of Glasgow; University of Liverpool; Strathclyde University; Glasgow Graduate School of Law. Scottish Organiser, Anti-Nazi League, 1992-94; Organiser, Coalition Against Criminal Justice Bill, 1992-93; freelance journalist, 1994-95; Racial Equality Officer, 1995-97; Law School Tutor and Guest Lecturer, 1999-2002; Consultant and Trainer to Crown Office and Procurator Fiscal Service, 2000-01. Spokesperson, Chhokar Family Justice Campaign; Director, Scottish Legal Action Group; Director, Positive Action in Housing; Member, Editorial Board, Scottish Left Review; Member, Justice Minister's Stephen Lawrence Steering Committee; recently voted one of Scotland's top 20 eligible bachelors. Recreations: haute cuisine cook; public speaking; fighting the establishment; demonstrations; spending time with his niece Raabiah; literature and journalism. Address: (b.) c/o Scottish Fire Brigades Union, 4th Floor, 52 St. Enoch Square, Glasgow G1 4AA; e-mail: aamer@lawyer.com

Arbuthnott, 16th Viscount of (John Campbell Arbuthnott), KT, CBE, DSC, FRSE, FRSA, BGCOStJ, LLD. Lord Lieutenant, Kincardineshire, 1977-99; b. 26.10.24; m.; 1 s.; 1 d. Educ. Fettes College; Gonville and Caius College, Cambridge. Served RNVR (Fleet Air Arm), 1942-46. Member, Countryside Commission for Scotland, 1967-71; Chairman, Red Deer Commission, 1969-75; Member, Aberdeen University Court, 1978-84; President, Scottish Landowners Federation, 1974-79; President, Royal Scottish Geographical Society, 1984-87; Chairman, Scottish Widows' Fund and Life Assurance Society, 1984-87; Lord High Commissioner to the General Assembly of the Church of Scotland, 1986, 1987; President, Royal Zoological Society of Scotland, 1976-96; President, Scottish Agricultural Organisation Society, 1980-83; President, Federation of Agricultural Cooperatives (UK), 1983-87; Deputy Chairman, Nature Conservancy Council, 1980-85, and Chairman, Scottish Committee, NCC; Chairman, Aberdeen and Northern Marts Ltd., 1986-91, Director, 1973-91; Director, Clydesdale Bank PLC, 1989-92 (Northern Area, 1975-85); Director, Britoil, 1988-90; Prior of Scotland, The Order of St. John, 1983-95; Member, Royal Commission on Historical Manuscripts, 1988-95; Member, BP Scottish Advisory Board, 1990-97; Hon. Air Commodore, No. 612 (County of Aberdeen) Squadron, Royal Aux. Air Force, Leuchars. Address: (h.) Arbuthnott House, by Laurencekirk, Kincardineshire AB30 1PA.

Arbuthnott, Professor Sir John Peebles, PhD, ScD, FIBiol, HonFTCD, FRSE, FIIB, FRCPath, HonFRCPSGlasg. Principal and Vice Chancellor, Strathclyde University, 1991-2000; b. 8.4.39; m., Elinor Rutherford Smillie; 1 s.; 2 d. Educ. Glasgow University; Trinity College, Dublin. Assistant Lecturer, then Lecturer, Department of Bacteriology, Glasgow University, 1960-67; Research Fellow of the Royal Society, 1968-72; Senior Lecturer, Department of Microbiology, then Senior Lecturer, Department of Bacteriology, Glasgow University, 1972-75; Professor of Micriobiology, Trinity College, Dublin, 1976-88; Professor of Microbiology, Nottingham University, 1988-91. Secretary/Treasurer, Carnegie Trust for the Universities of Scotland, since 2000; Member, Board, Food Standards Agency; Chairman, Scottish Food Advisory Committee, since 2000; Chairman, National Review of Allocation of Health Resources in Scotland, 1997-99; Chairman, Standing Committee on Resource Allocation to NHS in Scotland, since 2001; Director, Scottish Science Trust. DSc: University Lodz, Poland,

University Teknologi, Malaysia, Glasgow University, Glasgow Caledonian University; LLD: Queens University, Belfast, Aberdeen University; DEd, Queen Margaret University College; DUniv, Strathclyde University; Distinguished Fellowship, International Medical University, Malaysia. Recreations: bird-watching; photography; golf. Address: (h.) 93 Kelvin Court, Great Western Road, Glasgow G12 0AH.

Archer, Gilbert Baird, DL. Chairman, Tods of Orkney Ltd, since 1970; former Chairman, John Dickson & Sons Ltd; b. 24.8.42, Edinburgh; m., Irene Conn; 2 d. Educ. Melville College. Vice Convenor, George Watson's College, 1978-80; Governor, Fettes College, 1986-90; Director, Scottish Council of Independent Schools, 1988-91; Council Member, Governing Bodies Association of Independent Schools, 1988-91; Governor, Napier University, 1991-97; Chairman, St. Columba's Hospice; Past President, Edinburgh Chamber of Commerce & Manufactures; Past Chairman, Scottish Chambers of Commerce; former Deputy President, Association of British Chambers of Commerce; Chairman, Edinburgh Common Purpose, 1991-94; Past Moderator, High Constabulary of the Port of Leith; Liveryman, Worshipful Company of Gunmakers, London; Past Master, The Company of Merchants of the City of Edinburgh. Recreations: fishing; shooting. Address: (b.) 12 Broughton Place, Edinburgh EH1 3RX; T.-0131-556 4518.

Archer, Professor John Stuart, BSc, PhD, FRSE, FREng. Principal and Vice-Chancellor, Heriot-Watt University, since 1997; b. 15.6.43, London; m., Lesley; 1 s.; 1 d. Educ. County Grammar School, Chiswick; City University, London; Imperial College of Science, Technology and Medicine. Trainee, ICI (Mond Division); Senior Research Engineer, Imperial Oil (Esso Canada), Calgary; Senior Petroleum Engineer, British Gas Corporation (Exploration Division); Manager Reservoir Studies, D and S Petroleum Consultants, London and Calgary; Director and Co-founder, ERC Energy Resources Consultants Ltd., London; Professor of Petroleum Engineering, Imperial College, London University; Pro Rector (Resources) and Deputy Rector, Imperial College of Science, Technology and Medicine. Director, Centre for Marine and Petroleum Technology; Advisory Editor, Kluwer and Elsevier; Non-Executive Director, LEEL (Lothian and Edinburgh Enterprise Ltd); Fellow, City and Guilds Institute; Distinguished Faculty Award, Society of Petroleum Engineers; Lubbock-Sambrook Award, Institute of Energy. Recreations: music; art; theatre; golf. Address: (b.) Heriot-Watt University, Riccarton, Edinburgh EH14 4AS; T.-0131-451 3360.

Archer, John William, BA (Hons). Independent film and television producer; b. 19.9.53, Evesham; 3 s. Educ. Dean Close School, Cheltenham; University of Birmingham; University College, Cardiff. Researcher, Nationwide, 1975-77; Director, BBC TV, London: Writers and Places, Global Report, Omnibus; Producer, The Book Programme, Did You See...?; Editor, Saturday Review, A Week of British Art; Head of Music and Arts, BBC Scotland, 1989, including editing Edinburgh Nights; Executive Producer, The Bigger Picture, Billy Connolly's World Tour of Scotland/Australia; producing and directing Stevenson's Travels; BAFTA Award, best programme/ series without a category for Did You See...?, 1983; Chief Executive, Scottish Screen, 1996-2001. Member, British Screen Advisory Council. Recreations: walking; tree planting; mountain biking; necessary gardening; novels. Address: (h.) Southernwood, Drymen, Glasgow G63 0BG; e-mail: archers@clara.co.uk

Ardrey, Adam, LLB (Hons). Advocate, since 1990; b. 21.4.55, Bellshill; m., Dorothy-Anne; 1 s.; 2 d. Educ. Coatbridge High School; Glasgow University. Solicitor, 1979-89; Chairman, Social Security Appeal Tribunals and Disability Appeal Tribunals; Presenter, Open to Question and Talking Point, Lanarkshire TV; SNP candidate, Hamilton South, Scottish Parliamentary Elections, 1999; Chairman, Moira Anderson Foundation, since 2000. Recreations: family; friends; reading. Address: (b.) Advocates' Library, Parliament House, Edinburgh.

Argent, Graham Charles George, BSc, PhD. Head, Tropical Section, Royal Botanic Garden, since 1999; President, Botanical Society of Scotland; b. 15.5.41, Berkhamstead, Herts; m., Susan Margaret; 2s.; 1d. Educ. Dartford Technical School; University of Leicester. Research Assistant Demonstrator, University College, North Wales, Bangor, 1963-69; Research Fellow, New Guinea Biological Foundation, 1969-73; Research Staff, Royal Botanic Garden, Edinburgh, since 1974. Royal Horticultural Society Loder Cup for major contribution to rhododendron research; Member, Committee, Flora of Thailand. Address: (b.) Royal Botanic Garden, Inverleith Row, Edinburgh, EH3 5LR; T.-0131-248 2929; e-mail: g.argent@rbge.org.uk

Armour, Professor Sir James, CBE, PhD, Dr hc Utrecht, Hon. DVM&S (Edin), Hon.DU (Glasgow), HonFIBiol, FRCVS, FRSE, FMedSci. Emeritus Professor of Veterinary Parasitology, Glasgow University; Vice-Principal (Planning - External Relations), 1991-95; Dean, Faculty of Veterinary Medicine, 1986-91; Chairman, Glasgow Dental Hospital and School NHS Trust, 1995-99; Vice-President, Royal Society of Edinburgh, 1998-2000; b. 17.9.29, Basra, Iraq; m., 1, Irene Morris (deceased); 2, Christine Strickland; 2 s.; 2 d. Educ. Marr College, Troon; Glasgow University. Colonial veterinary service, Nigeria, 1953-60; Research Scientist, Wellcome Ltd., 1960-63; Glasgow University: Research Fellow, 1963-67, Lecturer/Senior Lecturer, 1967-73, Reader, 1973-76. Chairman, Government Committee on Animal Medicines, 1987-95; Chairman, Editorial Board, In Practice (veterinary journal), 1980-90; Chairman, Governing Body, Institute of Animal Health, 1989-97; Member, Governing Body: Moredun Research Institute, Edinburgh, since 1997, Institute of Aquaculture, Stirling, since 1997; Member, Hannah Foundation Board, since 1998; Trustee, Scottish Science Trust, 1999-2001; Chairman: Moredun Foundation for Animal Health and Welfare, since 2000, Higher Education Funding Council Research Assessment Panels for Agriculture, Food Science and Veterinary Science, 1999-2001. Awards: RCVS John Henry Steel Medal, Royal Agricultural Society Bledisloe Award, BVA Wooldridge Medal, Pfizer WAAVP Award, BVA Chiron Award. Publications: joint author of textbook on veterinary parasitology; editor, two books; 150 scientific articles. Recreation: golf. Address: (h.) Mokoia, 11 Crosbie Road, Troon, Ayrshire; T.-01292 314068; e-mail: jarmour@amserve.net

Armour, Robert Malcolm, MBA, LLB (Hons), DipLP, WS, NP. Company Secretary, British Energy plc, since 1995, and Director, Corporate Affairs, since 1999; Director: British Nuclear Industry Forum, Quality Scotland Foundation, Electricity Association Limited, British Energy International Limited, Eggborough Power Limited; b. 25.9.59, Edinburgh; m., Anne Ogilvie White. Educ. Daniel Stewart's and Melville College, Edinburgh; Edinburgh University. Solicitor, Haldanes McLaren and Scott, WS, Edinburgh, 1983-86; Partner, Wright, Johnston and MacKenzie, Edinburgh, 1986-90; Scottish Nuclear Limited: Company Secretary, 1990-95, Director, Performance Development, 1993-95. Recreations: golf; curling. Address: British Energy plc, 3 Redwood Crescent, Peel Park, East Kilbride G74 5PR.

Armstrong, Dr Ernest McAlpine, FRCSEd, FRCPGlas, FRCPEd, FRCGP, FFPHM. Chief Medical Officer, Scottish Executive Health Department, since 2001; b. 3.6.45, Motherwell; m., Dr Katherine Mary Dickson Armstrong; 2 s. Educ. Hamilton Academy; Glasgow University. Junior posts, medicine and surgery, Glasgow Royal and Western Infirmaries; Lecturer in Pathology, Glasgow University, 1971-74; General Practitioner, Connel, 1975-93; Secretary, British Medical Association, London, 1993-2000. Recreations: music; hill-walking; sailing. Address: (b.) Scottish Executive Health Department, St Andrew's House, Edinburgh; T.-0131-244 2264.

Armstrong, Robert Douglas. Advocate, since 1990; m., Sally Grossart; 1 d. Address: (b.) Advocates' Library, Parliament House, Edinburgh EH1 1RF.

Arnold, Andy, MA (Hons), DipEd. Founder and Artistic Director, The Arches, Glasgow, since 1991; Theatre Director, since 1980; Community Artist and Cartoonist, since 1974; b. Southend-on-Sea. Artistic Director, Theatre Workshop, Edinburgh, 1980-85; Director, Bloomsbury Theatre, London, 1986-89; directing credits include: Metropolis: The Theatre Cut, Caligari, The Devils, The Crucible, Sexual Perversity in Chicago, I Licked a Slag's Deodorant, The Caretaker, A Midsummer Night's Dream, Jund and the Paycock, Playboy of the Western World; Freelance Director, The Battle of Stirling Bridge, Stirling Castle, 1997. Two Paper Boat awards; Spirit of Mayfest Award; only Scottish-based artist shortlisted for 1999 Creative Briton Award. Recreations: holidays; five-a-side football; Hibernian F.C. Address: (b.) The Arches, 253 Argyle Street, Glasgow G2 8DL; T.-0141-565 1002; e-mail: andy@thearches.co.uk

Arnold, James Edward, MBE, MA (Hon), MUniv, BA, CertEd, FRSA. Director, New Lanark Conservation Trust, since 1974; b. 16.3.45, Glasgow; m., Rose. Educ. Caludon Castle Comprehensive School; York University; London University. Recreations: New Lanark and life. Address: (b.) Mill Number Three, New Lanark, Lanark; T.-01555 661345.

Arnott, Ian Emslie, DA, DipTP, ARSA, RIBA, ARIAS. Consultant Architect, since 1994; Chairman, Saltire Society; b. 7.5.29, Galashiels. Educ. Galashiels Academy; Edinburgh College of Art. Flying Officer, RAF, 1955-57; Founding Partner, then Chairman, Campbell and Arnott, 1962-94; External Examiner, Dundee University, 1989-93. RSA Gold Medal for Architecture, 1981; nine Civic Trust Awards; one RIBA Award; two EAA Awards. Recreations: music; painting; reading; swimming; resting. Address: The Rink, Gifford, East Lothian EH41 4JD; T.-01620 810278.

Arnott, James Mackay, TD, BL, WS, SSC. Solicitor; Consultant, MacRoberts Solicitors; Visiting Professor, University of Strathclyde and Joint Director, LLM in Construction Law; b. 22.3.35, Blackford, Perthshire; m., Jean Barbara Allan; 3 s. Educ. Merchiston Castle School, Edinburgh; Edinburgh University. National Service, RAF, 1957-60; TA, 1961-77. Council Member, Law Society of Scotland, 1983-85 (Convenor, Law Reform Committee); Secretary, Scottish Building Contract Committee; Director and Secretary, Scottish Council for International Arbitration. Recreation: cricket. Address: (b.) 152 Bath Street, Glasgow G2 4TB; T.-0141-332 9988; Excel House, 30 Semple Street, Edinburgh EH3 8BL; T.-0131-229 5046; e-mail:jim.arnott@macroberts.co.uk

Arnott, John Michael Stewart, BA. Chairman, Scottish Wildlife Trust, since 1999 (Member, Council, since 1995); b. 12.6.33; m., Lynne Gladstone-Millar; 1 s.; 1 d. Educ. Peterhouse, Cambridge. Pilot, RAF, 1952-54; Announcer, Producer, Editor Talks and Features, Edinburgh Manager, BBC Scotland, 1960-90; Member, 1982-92, Vice-Chairman, 1986-92, Countryside Commission for Scotland; Chairman, Isle of May Bird Observatory, 1980-85; Chairman, Fair Isle Bird Observatory Trust, 1983-85; Member: Committee for Scotland, Nature Conservancy

Council, 1986-91, NCC Advisory Committee on Birds, 1990-91; Chairman, CCS Advisory Panel on Management of Mountain Areas, 1989-90; Member, National Parks of England and Wales Review Panel, 1990; President, Scottish Ornithologists' Club, 1984-87; Member: South East Regional Board, Scottish Natural Heritage, 1992-95, Board, Edinburgh Green Belt Trust, 1992-97; President, Scottish Arctic Club, 1995-98; Vice-Chairman, Royal Society for Nature Conservation, since 2001. Sony Award for Radio Feature, 1985. Recreations: ornithology; hill-walking. Address: (h.) East Redford House, 133 Redford Road, Edinburgh EH13 0AS; T.-0131-441 3567.

Arnott, Kate, FCIPD. Human Resource Consultant; Lay Member, Employment Tribunal Service (Scotland); b. 13.1.43, Galashiels; m., Bert Arnott; 3 s.; 2 d. Educ. St. George's School for Girls, Edinburgh. Worked for Marks and Spencer and Harrods; Senior Personnel Officer, Ferranti (Scotland), 1966-69 and 1979-88. Chairman, Complaints Review Panel, Lothian Health Board; former Chairman, Edinburgh's Telford College Board of Management (Member, since 1995). Recreations: music; reading; arts and crafts; trying to keep fit. Address: 14 West Savile Road, Edinburgh EH16 5NQ; T.-0131-667 6874.

Arshad, Rowena, MEd (Community Education), OBE. Director, Centre for Education for Racial Equality in Scotland (CERES), since 1994; Lecturer in Equity and Rights, since 1991; Equal Opportunities Commissioner for Scotland; Member (first ever black woman Member), Scottish Trades Union Congress General Council, since 1997; b. 27.4.60, Brunei Town, Brunei; m., Malcolm Quarrie Parnell; 1 s.; 1 d. Educ. Methodist Girls School, Penang, West Malaysia; Moray House Institute of Education; Edinburgh University. Education and Campaigns Organiser, Scottish Education and Action for Development, 1985-88; Director, Edinburgh Multicultural Education Centre, 1988-90. Convenor, Educational Institute of Scotland Anti-Racist Committee; Member, Editorial Board, Scottish Affairs journal; Member, Advisory Committee, Centre for Scottish Public Policy; Member, Scottish Higher Education Funding Council; Member, Independent Committee of Inquiry into Student Finance; Member, Working Party on Guidelines in Sex Education in Scottish Schools (Section 2A); Member, Scottish Executive Race Equality Advisory Forum. Author of numerous contributions to publications on equality. Recreations: keen reader of Scottish Highland history; active trade unionist; dogs and animal issues. Address: (b.) CERES, Moray House, Charteris Building, Room 5, Floor 2, Holyrood Road, Edinburgh EH8 8AQ; T.-0131-651 6371.

Arthur, Adrian, BL. Editor, The Courier, Dundee, since 1993; b. 28.9.37, Kirkcaldy; m., Patricia Mill; 1 s.; 2 d. Educ. Harris Academy, Dundee; St. Andrews University. Joined staff of People's Journal; through the editorial ranks of The Courier (Deputy Editor, 1978-93). Recreations: golf; travel; Rotary. Address: (b.) 80 Kingsway East, Dundee DD4 8SL; T.-01382 223131.

Arthur, Lt. General Sir Norman, KCB (1985); Lord Lieutenant, Stewartry of Kirkcudbright, Dumfries and Galloway Region; b. 6.3.31, London (but brought up in Ayrshire, of Scottish parents); m., Theresa Mary Hopkinson; 1 s.; 1 d.; 1 s. (deceased). Educ. Eton College; Royal Military Academy, Sandhurst. Commissioned Royal Scots Greys, 1951; commanded Royal Scots Dragoon Guards, 1972-74, 7th Armoured Brigade, 1976-77, 3rd Armoured Division, 1980-82; Director, Personal Services (Army), 1983-85; commanded Army in Scotland, and Governor of Edinburgh Castle, 1985-88; retired, 1988; Honorary Colonel, Royal Scots Dragoon Guards, 1984-92; Col. Comdt. Military Provost Staff Corps, 1983-88; Honorary Colonel, 205 (Scottish) General Hospital, Territorial Army, 1988-93; Colonel, The Scottish Yeomanry, 1992-97; mentioned in Despatches, 1974.

Officer, Royal Company of Archers; President, Scottish Conservation Projects Trust, 1989-93; Vice President, Riding for the Disabled Association, Edinburgh and the Borders, 1988-94; Chairman: Army Benevolent Fund, Scotland, 1988-2000, Leonard Cheshire Foundation, SW Scotland, 1994-2000; Member, Committee, Automobile Association, 1990-98; humanitarian aid work, Croatia and Bosnia, since 1992; President, Reserve Forces and Cadet Association, Lowlands, since 2000; Member, British Olympic equestrian team (three-day event), 1960. Recreations: riding; country sports; country life; reading. Address: (h.) Newbarns, Dalbeattie, Kirkcudbrightshire DG5 4PY; T.-01556 630227.

Arthurson, Paul Andrew, LLB (Hons), DipLP, DipLaw. Advocate, since 1991; b. 16.12.64, London; m., Dr. Sharon E. McAuslane; 1 d. Educ. Daniel Stewart's and Melville College, Edinburgh; Edinburgh University; Worcester College, Oxford University. Called to Scottish Bar, 1991; Temporary Sheriff, 1998. Recreations: hillwalking; family life. Address: (b.) Advocates' Library, Parliament House, Edinburgh EH1 1RF; T.-0131-226 5071.

Artis, Iain N.J., LLB, MBA. Advocate, since 1999; b. 23.1.55, Falkirk; m., Heather; 1 d. Educ. Falkirk High School; Edinburgh University; Strathclyde University. Contracts Executive, Ferranti Plc, 1977; Legal/Commercial Manager, James Howden & Co. Ltd., 1985; Administration Manager, Long John International Ltd., 1987; Company Secretary, Allied Distillers Ltd., 1990; Secretary, Allied Domecq Spirits and Wine, 1995. Recreations: reading; woodwork; garden; clay target shooting. Address: (b.) 10 Park Avenue, Stirling FK8 2QR; T.-01786 461626.

Ashcroft, Professor Brian Kemp, BA (Hons), MA. Policy Director, Fraser of Allander Institute, Strathclyde University, since 1999; Adviser on Budget Process to Finance Committee, Scottish Parliament; Member, Scottish Executive's Economic Consultants Group, since 2000; Member, Scottish Executive's Economic Statistics Consultants' Group, since 2000; Member, Northern Ireland Economic Council, since 1995; b. 5.3.47, Stockton-on-Tees; widower; 1 s.; 2 d. Educ. Stockton Grammar School; Lancaster University. Rock musician, 1962-65; Construction Industry: labourer, clerk, office manager, 1965-70; Lecturer, Glasgow Polytechnic, 1974-76; Strathclyde University: Lecturer/Senior Lecturer, 1976-89, Research Director, 1989 then Director, 1989-99, Fraser of Allander Institute. Publications: over 30 academic papers/books. Recreations: photography; jogging; trying to hide his English origins. Address: (b.) 100 Cathedral Street, Glasgow G4 0LN; T.-0141-552 4400.

Asher, Catherine Archibald, OBE, BA, RGN, SCM, RNT, DUniv. Chairman, National Board for Nursing, Midwifery and Health Visiting for Scotland, 1982-95; b. 6.7.33, Edinburgh. Educ. Woodside School, Glasgow; Edinburgh University; Open University. Ward Sister, Glasgow Royal Infirmary, 1956-61; Nurse Teacher, Senior Tutor, Principal Nursing Officer (Teaching), Glasgow Royal Infirmary School of Nursing, 1963-74; Director of Nurse Education, Glasgow Eastern College of Nursing and Midwifery, 1974-91; Acting Principal, Glasgow College of Nursing and Midwifery, 1991-95; Governor, University of Paisley, since 1996. Recreations: golf; swimming. Address: (h.) 73 Roman Court, Roman Road, Bearsden, Glasgow G61 2NW.

Asher, Professor R. E., BA, PhD, DLitt, FRSE, FRAS. Professor of Linguistics, Edinburgh University, 1977-93, Professor Emeritus and Honorary Fellow, Faculty of Arts, since 1993; b. 23.7.26, Gringley-on-the-Hill, Nottinghamshire. Educ. King Edward VI Grammar School, Retford; University College London. Assistant, Department of French, University College, London, 1951-53; Lecturer in Linguistics, then Lecturer in Tamil, School of Oriental and African Studies, London, 1953-65; joined Department of Linguistics, Edinburgh University, 1965; Dean, Faculty of Arts, 1986-89; Member, University Court, 1989-92; Vice-Principal, 1990-93; Curator of Patronage, 1991-93; Director, Centre for Speech Technology Research, 1994. Visiting appointments: Visiting Professor of Linguistics, University of Illinois, Urbana-Champaign, 1967; Visiting Professor of Tamil and Malayalam, Michigan State University, 1968; Visiting Professor of Linguistics, University of Minnesota, 1969; Chaire des Professeurs Etrangers, Collège de France, 1970; Subrahmaniya Bharati Fellow, Tamil University, Thanjavur, 1984-85; Visiting Professor, International Christian University, Tokyo, 1994-95; first occupant of Vaikom Muhammed Basheer Chair, Mahatma Gandhi University, Kottayam, Kerala, 1995-96. Medal, Collège de France, Paris, 1970; Gold Medal, Kerala Sahitya Akademi, India, 1983. Publications: A Tamil Prose Reader, 1971; Some Landmarks in the History of Tamil Prose, 1973; Me Grandad 'ad an Elephant! (translation), 1980; Towards a History of Phonetics (Co-Editor), 1981; Tamil, 1982; Studies on Malayalam Language and Literature, 1989; National Myths in Renaissance France: Francus, Samothes and the Druids, 1993; Scavenger's Son (translation), 1993; Atlas of the World's Languages (Co-Editor), 1994; Encyclopedia of Language and Linguistics (Editor-in-Chief), 1994; Concise History of the Language Sciences: from the Sumerians to the Cognitivists (Co-Editor), 1995; Malayalam, 1997; Basheer, Stories of the Freedom Struggle (Editor), 1998; The Novels and Stories of Vaikom Muhammed Basheer, 1999. Address: (b.) Department of Theoretical and Applied Linguistics, University of Edinburgh, Adam Ferguson Building, Edinburgh EH8 9LL; T.-0131-650 3484.

Ashmore, Fionna Margaret, BA (Hons), FSA, FSAScot. Director, Society of Antiquaries of Scotland, since 1992; b. 21.5.50, London; m., P.J. Ashmore; 2 s.; 1 d. Educ. Oporto British School, Portugal; Convent of the Sacred Heart, Tunbridge Wells; University College, Cardiff; Glasgow University. Research on Portuguese Iron Age; archaeological indexer; Assistant Editor, Proceedings of the Society of Antiquaries of Scotland, 1978-90; Assistant Secretary, Cockburn Association, 1990-92. Recreations: reading; cinema; eating out; visiting buildings and archaeological sites. Address: (b.) Royal Museum of Scotland, Chambers Street, Edinburgh EH1 1JF; T.-0131-247 4115; e-mail: f.ashmore@nms.ac.uk

Ashworth, Bryan, MA, PhD, MD, FRCP(Lond), FRCP(Edin), FRSA. Honorary Senior Lecturer (Medical History), St Andrews University, since 1997; Associate Lecturer, Society of Apothecaries (London), since 1998; Honorary Librarian, Royal College of Physicians of Edinburgh, 1982-91; Consultant Neurologist, Royal Infirmary and Western General Hospital, Edinburgh, and Senior Lecturer in Medical Neurology, Edinburgh University, 1971-92; b. 5.5.29, Oundle, Northants. Educ. Laxton School; Oundle School; St. Andrews University. National Service, Captain RAMC, Northern Nigeria, 1953-55; junior hospital posts, Manchester and Bristol; Wellcome-Swedish Travelling Research Fellow, Karolinska Hospital, Stockholm, 1965-66; Lecturer in Clinical Neurology, Manchester University, and Honorary Consultant Physician, Manchester Royal Infirmary, 1967-71; Chairman and Director (non-executive), Robert Bailey and Son, PLC, Stockport, 1978-2000. Publications: Clinical Neuro-ophthalmology, 2nd edition, 1981; Management of Neurological Disorders, 2nd edition, 1985; The Bramwells of Edinburgh, 1986. Recreations: writing; walking. Address: (h.) 13/5 Eildon Terrace, Edinburgh EH3 5NL; T.-0131-556 0547.

Aspden, Professor Richard Malcolm, PhD, DSc, FIPEM. Professor of Orthopaedic Surgery, Aberdeen University, since 2000; b. 23.9.55, Malta; m., Anne

Maclean; 3 s.; 2 d. Educ. Bosworth College, Desford; University of York; University of Manchester (postgraduate). Research Associate, University of Manchester; Wellcome Research Fellow: University of Lund, University of Manchester, University of Aberdeen. Hon. Treasurer, Haddo Children's Theatre; European Editor, Journal of Back and Musculoskeletal Research. Publications: 2 books; 70 research papers. Recreations: woodworking; music; hill-walking. Address: (b.) University of Aberdeen, Department of Orthopaedics, Polwarth Building, Foresterhill, Aberdeen AB25 2ZD; T.-01224 552767.

Aspinall, Professor Peter Alan, MSc PhD. Professor of Environmental Studies, Department of the Built Environment, Heriot-Watt University, since 2000; b. 31.10.40, Wigan; m., Anne Patricia; 2d. Educ. Clitheroe Royal Grammar School; Edinburgh University. Ross Foundation Research Fellow (colour vision); Lecturer, Architecture; Professor, Environmental Studies and Research Director, Edinburgh College of Art. Hon. Fellow Ophthalmology Department, Edinburgh University, since 1974; Member: Colour Group; Ergonomic Group; European Personal Construction Association; Scientific Committee, Architectural School, Florence. Recreations: golf; tennis; piano. Address: (b.) Building Department, Heriot Watt University, Edinburgh; T.-0131-556 7641; e-mail: p.aspinall@hw.ac.uk

Atholl, 11th Duke of (John Murray); b. 19.1.29; m.; 2 s. 1 d. Succeeded to the title, 1996; lives in South Africa.

Atkinson, Professor David, BSc, PhD, FIBiol, CBiol, MIEEM, FRSA, MISoilSci. Vice Principal (Research and Education), Scottish Agricultural College; b. 12.9.44, Blyth; m., Elisabeth Ann Cocks; 1 s.; 2 d. Educ. Newlands County Secondary Modern School; Hull University; Newcastle-upon-Tyne University. East Malling Research Station, Maidstone, 1969-85; Macaulay Institute for Soil Research, 1985-87; Macaulay Land Use Research Institute, 1987-88; Professor of Agriculture, Aberdeen University, and Head, Land Resources Department, Scottish Agricultural College, 1988-93; former Deputy Principal (R. &D.) and Dean, Edinburgh Centre, Scottish Agricultural College. Member, BCPC Council, since 1994. Recreations: music; reading thrillers; quotations. Address: (b.) SAC, West Mains Road, Edinburgh EH9 3JG; e-mail: datkinson@ed.sac.ac.uk

Atkinson, Kate. Author; b. York; 2 children. Winner of several prizes for short stories, including Ian St. James Award; Winner, 1995 Whitbread First Novel Award for Behind the Scenes at the Museum; other novels: Emotionally Weird; Human Croquet; play: Abandonment; lives in Edinburgh.

Atkinson, Norman Keir, DipEd, FMA, AMA, FSA(Scot). Chairman, Angus Museums and Heritage Forum; Acting Director, Cultural Services, Angus Council, 1999 (Head of Support Services, Cultural Services,1996-99); Vice President, Pictish Arts Society; b. 8.1.50, Arbroath; m., Noreen; 1 s; 1 d. Educ. Arbroath High; Dundee College of Education; Leicester University. Teacher, Angus County Council, 1972-75; Assistant Keeper, then Acting Keeper, Extension Services, Dundee Museum, 1975-77; District Curator, Angus District Council, 1977-96. Past President, Scottish Museums Federation; former Vice-Chairman, Scottish Museums Council. Recreations: football; archaeology; wildlife. Address: (b.) County Buildings, Forfar DD8 3WF; T.-01307 461460.

Atkinson, Valerie, MA (Hons). Deputy Head, News and Current Affairs, BBC Scotland, since 1997; b. 28.12.44, Glasgow; m., Ian Atkinson; 1 s.; 1 d. Educ. Hillhead High School, Glasgow; University of Glasgow. Awards: BAFTA Scotland, 1993, ISDD National Television Award, 1993,

Industrial Society, 1994, Commission for Racial Equality Race in the Media Award, 1998. Trustee, National Galleries of Scotland, since 1998. Address: (b.) BBC Current Affairs, Queen Margaret Drive, Glasgow G12 8DG.

Attwooll, Elspeth, LLB, MA. Member of the European Parliament (Liberal Democrat), since 1999; b. 1.2.43; m. Educ. St Andrews University. Recreations: reading, especially legal theory; detective fiction. Address: 2a Whitton Street, Glasgow G20 0AN; T.-0141-946 1370.

Atwell, Brian Harvey. Convenor, Sutherland Trust, since 2001 (Trustee, since 1997); Trustee, Dumfries and Galloway Care Trust, since 2001; b. 19.9.39, Glasgow; m., Ann Ramsay; 2 d. Educ. Trinity Academy, Edinburgh. Career civil servant, 1958-94; Industrial Counsellor, Forestry Commission, 1981-89; Couple Counsellor, since 1977; Trainer, Scottish Association of Counselling, 1979-83; Member, Civil Service Training Advisory Committee, 1982-88; Chair, Marriage Counselling Scotland, 1994-98; a Director, Confederation of Scottish Counselling Agencies, 1995-2000; Vice Convenor, Marriage Counselling Dumfries and Galloway, 1996-99. Recreations: jazz music; fly fishing; sailing. Address: (h.) Lattimer House, Dalbeattie DG5 4EW.

Audain, Irene, MA (Hons), DipInfoScience. Director, Scottish Out of School Care Network, since 1993; b. 10.7.56, Glasgow. Educ. University of Glasgow; University of Strathclyde. Has worked in voluntary sector developing childcare, community development, campaigning on women's issues, children's rights, housing and peace education. Recreation: travel. Address: (b.) Floor 9, Fleming House, 134 Renfrew Street, Glasgow G3 6ST; T.-0141-331 1301.

Auld, Professor Alan Graeme, MA, BD, PhD, DLitt, FSA Scot. Professor of Hebrew Bible, Edinburgh University, since 1995; b. 14.8.41, Aberdeen; m., Dr Sylvia Joyce Auld; 2 s.; 1 d. Educ. Robert Gordon's College, Aberdeen; Aberdeen University; Edinburgh University. Assistant Director, British School of Archaeology in Jerusalem, 1969-72; Lecturer, then Senior Lecturer, in Hebrew and Old Testament Studies, Edinburgh University, 1972-95. Publications: Joshua, Moses and the Land; Amos; Kings Without Privilege; Joshua Retold. Recreations: walking; gardening; travel. Address: (b.) New College, Mound Place, Edinburgh EH1 2LX; T.-0131-650 7992.

Austin, Professor Brian, BSc, PhD, DSc, FRSA. Professor, Department of Biological Sciences, Heriot-Watt University; b. 5.8.51, Barnet; m., Dawn Amy; 1 d. Educ. Mount Grace School, Potters Bar; University of Newcastle-upon-Tyne. Research Associate, 1977-78; Senior Scientific Officer, 1978-84; Lecturer, 1984-89; Reader, 1989-92. Recreations: reading; writing; walking. Address: (b.) Heriot-Watt University, Riccarton, Edinburgh EH14 4AS; T.-0131-451 3452.

Austin, Juliet Leathes, BA (Hons). Headmistress, Kilgraston School, since 1993; b. 22.4.44, Reading; m., Anthony James Kirkpatrick Austin; 1 d. Educ. Downe House; Birmingham University. Downe House School, 1972-82, latterly as Head of English and Housemistress; Headmistress, Combe Bank School, 1982-93. Recreations: sailing; walking; writing. Address: (b.) Kilgraston School, Bridge of Earn, Perth PH2 9BQ; T.-01738 812257.

Axford, Nicola Dawn, BA (Hons). General Manager, Pitlochry Festival Theatre; Drama Officer, Scottish Arts Council, 2000-01; Arts Consultant; b. 17.10.60, London; m., Prof. Ian Brown. Educ. Bradford University. Director, Big Bird Music Theatre, 1982-86; Administrator, Major Road Theatre Company, 1986-87; Drama Finance Officer, Arts Council of Great Britain, 1987-91; Business Manager, PW Productions Ltd., 1991-92; Administrator, Manchester City of Drama 1994 Ltd., 1993-94; General Manager, Royal Lyceum Theatre Company, 1994-98. Director, Major Road Theatre Company. Address: (h.) 30 Haddington Place, Edinburgh EH7 4AG; T.-0131-556 3987; e-mail: nikki.axford@pitlochry.org.uk

Azmy, Amir Fouad, FRCS(Lond), FRCS(Glas), FRCS(Edin). Consultant Paediatric Surgeon, Royal Hospital for Sick Children, Glasgow, since 1980; Clinical Senior Lecturer, Glasgow University, since 1980; b. 1.11.39, Egypt; m., Dr F.S. Mohsen; 1 s.; 1 d. Registrar, Paediatric Surgery, RHSC, Glasgow, and Westminster Children's Hospital, London; Senior Registrar, Royal Hospital for Sick Children, Great Ormond Street, London. Member, Executive, BAPS . Publications: Surgical Emergency in Children, 1994; Surgery of Childhood Tumours, 1999. Address: (b.) Royal Hospital for Sick Children, Yorkhill, Glasgow G3 8SJ; T.-0141-201 0000.

B

Bader, Douglas, MA, FRSA, FIL. Rector, Perth Grammar School, since 1985; b. 22.11.41, Stirling; m., May Heather; 3 s. Educ. Larbert High School. Teacher of Modern Languages, High School of Glasgow, 1965-69; Principal Assistant, then Principal Teacher, Alloa Academy, 1969-74; Assistant Rector, Forfar Academy, 1974-79; Depute Rector, Montrose Academy, 1979-85. Member, Headteachers' Association of Scotland. Recreations: singing; basketball; canoeing. Address: (b.) Perth Grammar School, Gowans Terrace, Perth PH1 5AZ; T.-01738 620071.

Bagnall, John Michael, MA (Cantab), DipLib, MIInfSci. University Librarian, Dundee University, since 1987; b. 22.4.45, South Yorkshire. Educ. Mexborough Grammar School; Sidney Sussex College, Cambridge. Diploma in Librarianship, University College, London; Assistant Librarian and Sub-Librarian, Newcastle upon Tyne University. Recreations: music; bird-watching; languages. Address: University Library, Dundee DD1 4HN; T.-01382 344082.

Baikie, Fiona M., BA (Hons), FRSA, MIM. Principal and Chief Executive, Edinburgh's Telford College, since 1996; b. 15.11.44, Leicester; m., Jim (musician). Educ. John Neilson Institute, Paisley; Strathclyde University; Open University. Advertising and publishing assistant, 1965-69; Lecturer, then Senior Lecturer, Telford College, 1969-80; Head, Department of Commerce, Ayr College, 1980-82, Head, Department of Business Studies, 1982-88; Edinburgh's Telford College: Assistant Principal 1988-94, Vice Principal, 1994-96. Board Member, Association of Scottish Colleges, Edinburgh Compact, City of Edinburgh Lifelong Learning Partnership, CITB; Member, National Art Collections Fund. Recreations: languages and travel; collecting first editions; art. Address: (b.) Crewe Toll, Edinburgh EH4 2NZ; T.-0131-332 2491.

Baikie, Professor Iain, PhD, BSc (Hons), FInstP. Professor of Physics, Robert Gordon University, since 1992; Visiting Scientist, Brown University, USA, since 1997; b. 15.8.60, Wick; m., Elana Koponen-Baikie; 2 s. Educ. Wick High School; Heriot-Watt University; Twente University. Lecturer in Physics, University of Twente, 1987-88; Rotary International Scholar, Brown University, 1989-90; secondment to Marine Biological Laboratory, Mass., USA, 1997; secondment to Kelvin Research Center, ERI, Thurso, 2000. Recreations: sea kayaking; squash; volleyball. Address: 32 Thurso Road, Wick, Caithness; T.-01955 602773.

Bailey, Captain Ronald Richard. Master Mariner; Harbour Master, Clydeport, since 1997; b. 22.4.54, Guildford; 2 s. Educ. London Nautical School. Merchant Navy Officer, Mobil Shipping Company and Maersk Line, 1971-84; Assistant Harbour Master, then Harbour Master, Manchester Ship Canal, 1984-96. Former Director, Walk the Plank Charity. Recreations: golf; skiing; walking; travel. Address: (b.) Clydeport Operations Limited, Estuary Control, Campbell Street, Greenock PA16 8AW; T.-01475 726221.

Baillie, Ian David Hunter, CBE, CQSW. Director of Social Work, Church of Scotland Board of Social Responsibility, since 1990; Director, Social Care Association (Education), since 1987; Auxiliary Minister, United Reformed Church; b. 18.12.40, Dundee; m., Margaret MacCallum McFarlane; 3 d. Educ. Hutchesons Boys Grammar School. Eight years in life assurance; 30 years, to date, in social work; Member, Executive, International Christian Federation for Prevention of Alcoholism and Drug Addiction. Recreations: sport (watching); reading. Address: (b.) Charis House, 47 Milton Road East, Edinburgh EH15 2SR; T.-0131-657 2000.

Baillie, Jackie. MSP (Labour), Dumbarton, since 1999; Minister for Social Justice, since 2000; Deputy Minister for Communities, 1999-2000; b. 15.1.64, Hong Kong; m., Stephen; 1 d. Educ. Glasgow University (part-time: to be completed). Co-ordinator, Gorbals Unemployed Workers Centre, 1987-90; Resource Centre Manager, Strathkelvin District Council, 1990-96; Community Economic Development Manager, East Dunbartonshire Council, 1996-99. Board Member, Volunteer Development Scotland, 1997-99; Chairperson, Scottish Labour Party, 1997-98. Address: (b.) Dumbarton Constituency Office, 125 College Street, Dumbarton G82 1NH; T.-01389 734214.

Baillie, Professor John, MA, CA. Visiting Professor of Accountancy: Heriot-Watt University, Edinburgh, since 1989, University of Glasgow, since 1996; Johnstone-Smith Professor of Accountancy, Glasgow University, 1983-88; Partner, Scott-Moncrieff, since 1993; Partner, KPMG, 1978-92; b. 7.10.44; m., Annette Alexander; 1 s.; 1 d. Educ. Whitehill School. Institute of Chartered Accountants of Scotland: Convenor, Research Committee, 1994-99, member, various technical and professional affairs committees. Recreations: keeping fit; reading; music; golf. Address: (h.) The Glen, Glencairn Road, Kilmacolm, Renfrewshire; T.-Kilmacolm 3254.

Baillie, William James Laidlaw, CBE, P/PRSA, HRA, PPRSW, RGI, HRHA, HRWA, HFRBS, HBWS, HSSA, DAEdin, DLitt. President, Royal Scottish Academy, 1990-98; professional painter, since 1950; b. 19.4.23, Edinburgh; m. Helen Gillon; 1 s.; 2 d. Educ. Dunfermline High School; Edinburgh College of Art. Army Service (mainly Far East) 1942-47; Lecturer/Senior Lecturer in Drawing and Painting, Edinburgh College of Art, 1960-88; President, Royal Scottish Society of Painters in Water Colours, 1974-88; Royal Scottish Academy: Associate, 1968, Academician, 1979, Treasurer, 1980-90; 26 solo exhibitions in UK and abroad. Awards: 1980 EIS Award RSA, Cargill Award RGI, 1989 May Marshall Brown Award RSW, Sir William Gillies Award RSW; DLitt, Heriot Watt University, 1997. Recreations: music; travel. Address: 6A Esslemont Road, Edinburgh EH16 5PX; T.-0131-667 1538.

Bain, Aly. Fiddler; b. 1945, Lerwick. Co-founder, Boys of the Lough, 1972; Soloist; TV and radio anchorman.

Bain, Professor Andrew David, OBE, FRSE. Chairman of Trustees, Scottish Enterprise Pension Scheme, since 1995; Member, Appeal Panel, Competition Commission, since 2000; b. 21.3.36, Glasgow; m., Eleanor Riches; 3 s. Educ. Glasgow Academy; Cambridge University. Various posts, Cambridge University, 1959-67; Professor of Economics: Stirling University, 1967-77, Strathclyde University, 1977-84; Group Economic Advisor, Midland Bank, 1984-90. Member: Committee to Review the Functioning of Financial Institutions, 1977-80, Monopolies and Mergers Commission, 1980-81; Visiting Professor, Glasgow University, 1991-97; Board Member, Scottish Enterprise, 1991-97; Member, TEC National Council, 1994-97. Publications: The Control of the Money Supply, 1970; The Economics of the Financial System (2nd Edition), 1992. Address: (b.) Department of Economics, Glasgow University, Glasgow G12 8RT; T.-0141-330 6866.

Bain, Iain Andrew, MA. Editor and Proprietor, The Nairnshire Telegraph, since 1987; b. 25.2.49, Nairn; m., Maureen Beattie; 3 d. Educ. Nairn Academy; Aberdeen University. Joined The Geographical Magazine, 1974, Editor, 1981-87. Chairman, Trustees, Nairn Museum. Recreations: reading; writing; photography; golf. Address: (b.) 10 Leopold Street, Nairn IV12 4BG; T.-01667 453258.

Bain, Professor John, MD, FRCGP. Professor of General Practice, University of Dundee, since 1992; b. 18.8.40, Aberdeen. Educ. Inverurie Academy; University of Aberdeen. Principal in General Practice, Livingston; Professor of Primary Medical Care, University of Southampton. Recreations: golf; hill-walking; photography. Address: (b.) Tayside Centre for General Practice, Kirsty Semple Way, Dundee DD2 4AD; T.-01382 632771.

Bain, Simon. Business Writer and Money Editor, The Herald, since 1997; b. 20.8.51, London; m., Norma; 1 s.; 1 d. Educ. St Paul's School; Christ's College, Cambridge. Reporter, The Scotsman, 1981-88; Business Editor, Scotland on Sunday, 1988-96. British Press Award winner, 1981; Scottish Press Award winner, 1986, 1992, 1998, 2000, Journalist of the Year 2000; Industrial Society Award winner, 1999; B & B Personal Finance Award winner, 1994, 1998. Address: (h.) 32 Craigleith Drive, Edinburgh; T.-0131-200 8158.

Baird, Alex James, MBA, FRICS, MBIFM, LicIPD. Chairman, Royal Institution of Chartered Surveyors, Scotland, 2000-2001; Head of Special Projects, Housing and Technical Resources, South Lanarkshire Council, since 1995; b. 20.7.48, Kirkmichael, Banffshire; m., Doreen; 1 s.; 1 d. Educ. Dalziel High School, Motherwell; Open University; College of Estate Management, Reading University. Valuer, Valuation Office, 1970-75; Strathclyde Regional Council: Estates Surveyor leading to Depute Director of Estates, 1975-95; Assessor, Investors in People. Address: (b.) Council Offices, Almada Street, Hamilton, NL3 OAA; T.-01698 454787; e-mail: alex.baird@southlanarkshire.gov.uk

Baird, Professor David Tennent, CBE, BA (Cantab), MB, ChB, DSc, FRCP, FRCOG, FRS(Ed), M.Acad.Med.Sci. Emeritus Professor of Reproductive Endocrinology, Edinburgh University, since 2000; b. 13.3.35, Glasgow; m. 1, Frances Lichtveld (m. dissolved); 2 s.; m. 2, Anna Frances Glasier. Educ. Aberdeen Grammar School; Aberdeen University; Trinity College, Cambridge; Edinburgh University. After clinical training in endocrinology as well as obstetrics, spent three years (1965-68) as an MRC travelling Research Fellow at Worcester Foundation for Experimental Biology, Shrewsbury, Mass., USA, conducting research on reproductive endocrinology; Deputy Director, MRC Unit of Reproductive Biology, Edinburgh, 1972-77; Professor of Obstetrics and Gynaecology, Edinburgh University, 1977-85; Medical Research Council Professor of Reproductive Endocrinology, Edinburgh University, 1985-2000; served on a number of national and international committees. Publications: four books on reproduction. Recreations: ski mountaineering; music; sport. Address: (b.) Edinburgh University, Centre for Reproductive Biology, 37 Chalmers Street, Edinburgh EH3 9EW; T.-0131-229 2575.

Baird, Professor James Ireland, BSc(Hons), PhD, MICE, CEng, MInstW. Professor of Environment, Glasgow Caledonian University, since 1994; b. 31.10.58, Patna, Ayrshire; m., Janice McLauchlan; 1 s.; 1 d. Educ. James Hamilton Academy, Kilmarnock; University of Glasgow. Research Engineer, British Hydromechanics Research Association; Research and Development Manager, Water Research Centre, Medmenham, Bucks. General Councillor, Institute of Wastes Management. Recreation: hillwalking. Address: (h.) 3 Lashley Grove, Overtown, Wishaw ML2 0PR; T.-01698 360684; e-mail: j.baird@gcal.ac.uk

Baird, John Alexander, MD, FRCPsych, DCH. Consultant Forensic Psychiatrist, Glasgow, since 1993; b. 28.8.47, Edinburgh; m., Ann Easson; 3 s. Educ. Daniel Stewart's College, Edinburgh; Edinburgh University. Consultant Psychiatrist, State Hospital, Carstairs, 1981-85, Physician Superintendent, 1985-92. Standing Committee on Difficult Prisoners: Member, 1985-88, Chairman, 1988-91; Member,

Parole Board for Scotland, 1992-94, and since 1998; Member, Advisory Committee on Prisoner Management, 1993-98; Secretary, Forensic Faculty, Royal College of Psychiatrists, since 2000. Recreation: hill walking. Address: (b.) Leverndale Hospital, 510 Crookston Road, Glasgow G53 7TU.

Baker, Frances J.T., MBE, MSc, BA, RGN, OHNC, Cert Ed. Lecturer in Homeopathy and Nursing, Napier University; Past President, Federation of Occupational Health Nurses in the EU (FOHNEU); b. 29.4.34, Ayr; m., Alan; 1 s.; 1 d. Educ. Ayr Academy; London University (External); Manchester University. Casualty Staff Nurse, Ayr County Hospital; Sister, NCB, North Staffs; Lecturer, Senior Lecturer, Head of Health and Nursing Studies, Stoke on Trent Cauldon College, 1975-82; Senior Nursing Officer, British Gas Scotland, 1982-95. Member, National Board for Nursing, Midwifery and Health Visiting for Scotland, 1988-93. Publications: Role of Occupational Health Nurse in the Care of the Pregnant Woman at Work; Counselling Role of the Occupational Health Nurse; Homeopathy in the Workplace. Recreations: opera and classical music; theatre; swimming; reading. Address: (b.) Pardovan House, Linlithgow EH49 7RU.

Baker, Professor Michael John, TD, BA, BSc (Econ), DipM, CertITP (Harvard), DBA (Harvard), LLD, FCIM, F.SCOTVEC, FCAM, FRSA, FRSE, FAM, FSQA. Professor of Marketing, Strathclyde University, 1971-99, Emeritus Professor, since 1999 (Deputy Principal, 1984-91); b. 5.11.35, Debden; m., Sheila; 1 s.; 2 d. Educ. Worksop College; Bede, Gosforth and Harvey Grammar Schools; Durham University; London University; Harvard University. Royal Artillery, 1956 (2nd Lt.); Richard Thomas & Baldwins (Sales) Ltd., 1958-64; Lecturer: Medway College of Technology, 1964-66, Hull College of Technology, 1966-68; FME Fellow, Harvard Business School, 1968-71; Member, Vice-Chairman and Chairman, SCOTBEC, 1973-85; Member, SSRC Management Committee, 1976-80; Dean, Strathclyde Business School, 1978-84; Marketing Education Group: Chairman, 1974-87, President, since 1987; Chairman, Institute of Marketing, 1987; Member: SHERT, 1983-96, UGC Business and Management Sub-Committee, 1986-89, Chief Scientist's Committee, 1985-96, ESRC Research Resources Board, 1994-96; Governor, CAM; Visiting Professor: Glasgow Caledonian University, Surrey University; Special Professor, Nottingham University; Honorary Professor, Aberystwyth University; Distinguished Visiting Professor, Monash University, Australia; Chairman: Westburn Publishers Ltd, Scottish Management Projects Ltd. Publications: Marketing New Industrial Products; Market Development; Marketing (6th edition, 1996); The Marketing Book (Editor, 4th edition, 1999); The Role of Design in International Competitiveness; Marketing and Competitive Success; Dictionary of Marketing & Advertising (3rd edition, 1998); Research for Marketing; Perspectives on Marketing Management (Editor); Marketing: Theory & Practice (Editor, 3rd edition, 1996); Marketing Strategy and Management (3nd edition, 2000); Companion Encyclopedia of Marketing (2nd edition, 1999); The Marketing Manual, 1998; Product Strategy and Management, 1998; Marketing: Critical Perspectives (five volumes), 2001. Recreations: sailing; gardening; travel. Address: (b.) Strathclyde University, 173 Cathedral Street, Glasgow G4 ORQ; T.-0141-552 4400; e-mail: mjb@westburn.co.uk

Baker, Professor Michael John, BSc (Eng), ACGI, DIC, MICE, MIStructE, FSaRS. Professor of Safety Engineering, Aberdeen University, since 1991; b. 20.10.40, Oxford; m., Margaret Eleanor Lucas; 1 s.; 1 d. Educ. Leighton Park School, Reading; Imperial College of Science, Technology and Medicine, London. Civil Engineer, N.C.B., 1962-65; Research Assistant/Fellow, Imperial College, London, 1966-77; Lecturer in Structural Engineering, 1978-86,

Reader in Structural Reliability, 1986-91. Member of the Plenum, International Joint Committee on Structural Safety; Member, Research Strategy Board, Offshore Safety Division, Health and Safety Executive. Recreations: mountaineering; gardening. Address: (h.) 2 Thornton Place, Watson Street, Banchory, Kincardineshire AB31 5UB; T.-01330 825495.

Baker, Professor Thomas Neville, BMet, PhD, DMet (Sheffield), DSc (Strathclyde), FIM, FInstP, CEng, CPhys. Professor, Department of Mechanical Engineering – Metallurgy and Engineering Materials Group, Strathclyde University; b. 11.1.34, Southport; m., Eileen May Allison. Educ. King George V School, Southport; Sheffield University. National Service, Royal Corps of Signals; Research Metallurgist, Nelson Research Laboratories, English Electric Co., Stafford, 1958-60; Scientist, Project Leader, Tube Investments Research Laboratories, Hinxton Hall, Cambridge, 1961-64; Department of Metallurgy, Strathclyde University: SRC Research Fellow, 1965, Lecturer, 1966, Senior Lecturer, 1976, Reader, 1983, Professor, 1990, Professor of Metallurgy (1886 Chair), 1992, Vice Dean, School of Chemical and Materials Science, 1979-82, Head, Department of Metallurgy, 1986-87, Head, Division of Metallurgy and Engineering Materials, 1988-90; Committee Member, Institute of Metals, Metal Science Committee, 1980-94, Materials Technology Committee, since 1994, Process Science and Technology Committee since 1996; Chairman, Annual Conference on Metals and Materials, 1982-92; Member, Council, Scottish Association for Metals, 1975-79 and since 1997, Vice-President, 1999-2000, President, 2001. Publications: Yield, Flow and Fracture in Polycrystals (Editor), 1983; Titanium Technology in Microalloyed Steels (Editor), 1997; over 160 learned society publications. Recreations: music; literature; creating a garden. Address: (b.) Department of Mechanical Engineering, Strathclyde University, Glasgow; T.-0141-548 3101.

Baldwin, Professor Norma, BA (Hons), DipSocAdmin, MPhil. Professor of Child Care and Protection, University of Dundee, since 1995 (Associate Dean, Faculty of Education and Social Work, Member, University Court); b. 21.5.39, Hull; 2 s. Educ. Malet Lambert, Hull; University of Manchester; London School of Economics; University of Warwick. Probation Officer, then Senior Probation Officer, Greater Manchester; Principal Officer, Warwickshire Social Services Department; Lecturer, Senior Research Fellow, Senior Lecturer, University of Warwick. Publications: The Power to Care in Children's Homes, 1990; Residents' Rights (Co-Author), 1993; Developing Neighbourhood Support and Child Protection Strategies (Co-author), 1998; Protecting Children: Promoting their Rights (Editor), 2000. Recreations: walking; gardening; theatre; music. Address: (b.) Department of Social Work, University of Dundee, Dundee DD5 1NY; T.-01382 464229; e-mail: n.baldwin@dundee.ac.uk

Balfour, 4th Earl of (Gerald Arthur James Balfour), JP; b. 23.12.25; m. Educ. Eton; HMS Conway. Member, East Lothian County Council, 1960-75; farmer. Address: (h.) The Tower, Whittingehame, Haddington EH41 4QA; T.-01368 850208.

Balfour of Burleigh, Lord (Robert Bruce), CEng, FIEE, FRSE, Hon. D Litt (Robert Gordon), Hon. DUniv (Stirling), Hon. FRIAS. Vice Lord-Lieutenant, Clackmannan, since 1995; Chairman, Capella Nova; Chancellor, Stirling University, 1988-98; b. 6.1.27, London. Educ. Westminster School, London. Graduate Apprentice, English Electric Company, 1951; various positions in manufacturing mangement; started English Electric's manufacturing operations in India as General Manager of new company in Madras, 1957-64; returned to Liverpool as General Manager; appointed General Manager, D. Napier & Son, before leaving the company in 1968; joined Bank of Scotland as a Director, 1968; Deputy Governor, Bank of Scotland, 1977-91. Forestry Commissioner, 1971-74; Chairman: Scottish Arts Council, 1971-80, Federation of Scottish Bank Employers, 1977-86, The Turing Institute, 1983-92, Scottish Committee, ABSA, 1988-94, United Artists Communications (Scotland) Ltd., until 1996; Director: Scottish Investment Trust plc, 1971-96, Tarmac plc, 1981-90, William Lawson Distillers Ltd., 1984-96, Television Educational Network, 1990-96, Edinburgh Book Festival, 1981-96 (Chairman, 1981-87); Member, British Railways (Scottish) Board, 1982-92; Treasurer: Royal Society of Edinburgh, 1989-94, Royal Scottish Corporation; President, Friends of Vellore; President, Franco-Scottish Society, 1985-96; Life Member and Trustee, 1990-96, John Muir Trust. Address: House of Lords, London SW1A 0PW.

Balfour of Burleigh, Lady (Janet Morgan), MA, DPhil, FRSAS, Hon LLD (Strathclyde), Hon DLitt (Napier), FRSE. Writer; Company Director; b. 5.12.45, Montreal; m., Lord Balfour of Burleigh. Educ. Newbury County Girls' Grammar School; Oxford University; Sussex University; Harvard University. Member: Central Policy Review Staff, Cabinet Office, 1978-81, Board, British Council, 1989-99; Special Adviser to Director-General, BBC, 1983-86; Chairman, Cable & Wireless Flexible Resource Ltd., 1993-97; Non-Executive Director: Cable & Wireless, W.H. Smith, 1989-95, Midlands Electricity, 1990-96, Scottish American Investment Co., since 1991, Scottish Oriental Smaller Companies Investment Trust, since 1994, The Scottish Life Assurance Company, 1995-2001, Nuclear Generation Decommissioning Fund Ltd, since 1996, New Medical Technologies plc, since 1997, BPB plc, since 2000, Stagecoach plc, since 2001, Scottish Medical Research Fund, 1992-94; Member: Scottish Museums Council Development Resource, 1988-97, Ancient Monuments Board for Scotland, 1990-97, Book Trust Scotland, 1992-99, Scottish Economic Council, 1993-95, Scottish Hospitals Endowment Research Trust, 1992-98, Dorothy Burns Charity, since 1994; Chairman, Scotland's Book Campaign, 1994-96, Scottish Cultural Resources Access Network, since 1995, Scottish Museum of the Year Award, since 1999; Trustee, Carnegie Endowment for the Universities of Scotland, since 1993. Publications: Diaries of a Cabinet Minister 1964-70 by Richard Crossman (4 volumes) (Editor); The Future of Broadcasting, (Co-Editor), 1982); Agatha Christie: a biography, 1984; Edwina Mountbatten: a life of her own, 1991. Recreations: music of Handel; sea bathing; pruning; ice skating out of doors.

Balfour, Alastair. Businessman; Private Investor; Writer; b. 15.6.47, Edinburgh; m., Anne Johnstone (second marriage); 2 s.; 3 d. Educ. Royal High School, Edinburgh. Trained as journalist with The Scotsman, 1966-68; became Industrial Reporter in Glasgow, 1974-78; joined Daily Record as Economics Correspondent, 1978-81; Business Editor, Sunday Standard, 1981-83; co-launched Scottish Business Insider, 1984; Editor, 1986-90; Editorial Director, until 1993; Managing Director, The Insider Group, 1993-99. Member, Strathclyde Graduate Business School Council; Member, Scottish Advisory Board, Xansa Plc; Director, The Entrepreneurial Exchange; Chairman, Company Creators Ltd.; Director, Vestech PLC; Director, Scottish Community Foundation. Recreations: family; sailing. Address: Kessogbank, 60 Glasgow Road, Blanefield, Stirlingshire G63 9BP; T.-01360 770750.

Balfour, Ian Leslie Shaw, MA, LLB, BD, PhD, SSC, NP. Solicitor (Consultant, Balfour & Manson) since 1955; b. 16.6.32, Edinburgh; m., Joyce Margaret Ross Pryde; 3 s.; 1 d. Educ. Edinburgh Academy; Edinburgh University. Qualified as Solicitor, 1955; commissioned, RASC, 1955-57; 1959-97: Partner, then Senior Partner, Balfour & Manson; Secretary, Oliver & Son Ltd., 1959-89; Fiscal to Law Society of Scotland, 1981-2000. Baptist Union of Scotland: President, 1976-77, Law Agent, 1964-97, Secretary, Charlotte Baptist Chapel, Edinburgh, 1980-2000,

Secretary, Scottish Baptist College, since 1983; Secretary, Elba Housing Society Ltd., 1969-92; Council, Society for Computers and Law, 1988-92; Director, Edinburgh Medical Missionary Society; Honorary Vice-President, Lawyers Christian Fellowship, since 1997. Recreations: gardening; home computing; lay preaching. Address: (h.) 38 Murrayfield Road, Edinburgh; T.-0131-337 2880; e-mail: I_Balfour@email.msn.co

Balfour, Peter Edward Gerald, CBE. President, Scottish Council (Development and Industry), 1985-92 (Chairman, 1978-85); Director, Royal Bank of Scotland, 1972-90; Chairman, Charterhouse plc, 1985-91; b. 9.7.21, Woking; m., 1, Grizelda Ogilvy, 2, Diana Wainman; 3 s.; 2 d. Educ. Eton College. Served Scots Guards, 1940-54; joined William McEwan & Co., brewers, 1954; appointed Director, 1958; Director, Scottish Brewers, 1959; Scottish and Newcastle Breweries, 1961 (Chairman and Managing Director, 1970-83); Director and Vice Chairman, RBS Group, 1978. Recreations: farming; forestry. Address: (h.) Scadlaw House, Humbie, East Lothian; T.-01875 833252.

Balfour, Robert William, DL, BSc, FRICS. Managing Partner, Balbirnie Home Farms, since 1991; Convenor, Scottish Landowners Federation, since 1999; b. 25.3.52, Edinburgh; m., Jessica McCrindle; 4 s. (1 deceased). Educ. Eton; Edinburgh University. Management trainee, Ocean Group, 1974-78; Surveyor, Bell-Ingram, Perth, 1978-88; Bidwells Chartered Surveyors, Perth, 1988-94, Associate Partner, 1991; Director, Tayforth Marketing Group, since 1998; Member, Beef Assurance Scheme Membership Panel, since 1999; Chairman, RICS RPD (Scotland), 1990-91; Member, Board of Management, Elmwood College, 2000; DL (Fife), 1994; Elder, Markinch Parish Church; Member, Royal Company of Archers. Recreations: golf; skiing; music; arts; shooting. Address: (b.) Pitillock Farm, Freuchie KY15 7JQ; T.-01337 857437; e-mail: balfour-balbirnie@msn.com

Balfour, William Harold St. Clair. Solicitor (retired); b. 29.8.34, Edinburgh; m., 1, Patricia Waite (m. dissolved); 1 s.; 2 d.; 2, Alice Ingsay McFarlane; 2 step. d. Educ. Hillfield, Ontario; Edinburgh Academy; Edinburgh University. Partner, Balfour & Manson, 1962-98; Clerk to Admission of Notaries Public, 1971-92; Prison Visiting Committee, 1965-70; Chairman, Basic Space Dance Theatre, 1980-86; Friends of Talbot Rice Art Centre, 1982-97, Garvald Trustees, since 1980, Wellspring Management, 1990-97. Recreations: sailing; walking; wine. Address: (h.) 11 Nelson Street, Edinburgh EH3 6LF; T.-0131-556 7298.

Ball, Geoffrey A., FCA. Executive Chairman, CALA Group Limited (Group Managing Director, since 1974); Chairman, Intelli plc; b. 4.8.43, Bristol; m., Mary Elizabeth; 3 s.; 1 d. Educ. Cotham Grammar School, Bristol. Former Managing Director, Greencoat Properties Ltd.; non-executive Director, Scottish Mortgage & Trust p.l.c. Recreations: golf; music. Address: 26 Hermitage Drive, Edinburgh EH10 5BT; T.-0131-535 5200.

Ball, Graham Edmund, BDS, FDS RCS (Eng), FDS RCS (Edin), MHSM. Consultant in Dental Public Health, Fife, Borders and Lothian Health Boards, since 1995; Chairman, Scottish Consultants in Dental Public Health, since 1998; Honorary Senior Lecturer in Dental Public Health, University of Edinburgh; Honorary Senior Lecturer, School of Biomedical Sciences, St Andrews University; b. 14.12.53; m., Carolyn Bowyer; 1 s.; 2 d. Educ. King Edward VI School, Southampton; Welsh National School of Medicine. Registrar, Oral and Maxillofacial Surgery, Portsmouth hospitals, 1979-81; Associate Specialist (part-time), Oral Surgery, Wessex Cardiothoracic Unit, 1982-84; general dental practice, 1984-88; Clinical Community Dental Officer, Orkney Health Board, 1988-91; Chief

Administrative Dental Officer, Orkney Health Board, 1991-95. Recreations: sailing; walking. Address: (b.) Fife Health Board, Springfield House, Cupar, Fife; T.-01334 421095.

Ball, William Ian, DipCE, MEd, MCIPD, FRSA. Head, Department of Community Education, University of Dundee, since 1996 (Associate Dean, Faculty of Education and Social Work, since 2001); Chair, Board of Directors, Volunteer Development Scotland, since 2000; b. 4.9.53, Arbroath; m., Lorna; 1 s.; 1 d. Educ. Arbroath Academy; Dundee College of Education; Open University. Youth and Community Worker: Angus County Council, 1974-75; Tayside Regional Council, 1975-79; Youth Work Training Organiser, Scottish Association of Youth Clubs, 1979-81; Assistant Regional Community Education Officer, Highland Regional Council, 1981-85; Lecturer in Community Education, Dundee College of Education, 1985-97; Head, School of Community Education and Social Work Education, Northern College, since 1997. Member, Board, Youth Link Scotland. Recreations: long distance running; reading; family. Address: (b.) University of Dundee, Gardyne Road Campus, Broughty Ferry, Dundee; T.-01382 464389; e-mail: w.i.ball@norcol.ac.uk

Ballantyne, Professor Colin Kerr, MA, MSc, PhD, DSc, FRSE, FRSA. Professor in Physical Geography, St. Andrews University, since 1994; b. 7.6.51, Glasgow; m., Rebecca Trengove; 1 s.; 1 d. Educ. Hutchesons' Grammar School; Glasgow University; McMaster University; Edinburgh University. Lecturer in Geography, St. Andrews University, 1980-89, Senior Lecturer in Geography and Geology, 1989-94. Gordon Warwick Award, 1987; Presidents' Medal, Royal Scottish Geographical Society, 1991; Newbigin Prize, Royal Scottish Geographical Society, 1992; Scottish Science Award, Saltire Society, 1996; Wiley Award, British Geomorphological Research Group, 1999. Publications: The Quaternary of the Isle of Skye, 1991; The Periglaciation of Great Britain, 1994. Recreations: music; travel; mountaineering; skiing; writing. Address: (h.) Birchwood, Blebo Craigs, Fife KY15 5UF; T.-01334 850567; e-mail: ckb@st-and.ac.uk

Ballantyne, Fiona Catherine, MA, MCIM. Director, 4Consulting Ltd., since 2001; Member, Board, Queen Margaret University College, Edinburgh, since 1995; Director, Edinburgh Audience Development Initiative Ltd., since 1998; Member, Scottish Committee, Institute of Directors, since 1996; Member, Audit Committee, Scottish Further Education Funding Council; b. 9.7.50, Bristol; m., A. Neil Ballantyne. Educ. Marr College, Troon; Edinburgh University. Former Market Researcher and Market Research Manager; Research and Planning Manager, Thistle Hotels Ltd., 1975-77; Assistant Marketing Manager, Lloyds & Scottish Finance Group, 1977-79; Scottish Development Agency: Marketing Manager, Small Business Division, 1979-84, Head of Small Business Services, 1984-88, Director, Tayside and Fife, 1988-90; Managing Director, Ballantyne Mackay Consultants, since 1990; Vice-Chair: BBC Broadcasting Council for Scotland, 1991-96, Duncan of Jordanstone College of Art, 1988-94; Director, Edinburgh Healthcare Trust, 1994-96; Director, The Essentia Group (formerly Network Scotland Ltd.), 1991-2000, Chairman, 1997-2001; Member, Board, Scottish Campaign for Learning, 1997-98. Recreations: walking; swimming; tapestry; painting. Address: (b.) 2-8 Millar Crescent, Edinburgh EH10 5HW; T.-0131-447 9700.

Band, Thomas Mollison. Chairman: Perth Theatre Ltd., since 1995 (Director, since 1994), Edinburgh Europa Ltd., 1994-98, Select Line Breaks Ltd., 1995-98; Governor: Edinburgh Telford College, 1990-98, Queen Margaret College, since 1995; b. 28.3.34, Aberdeen; m., Jean McKenzie Brien; 1 s.; 2 d. Educ. Perth Academy. Principal, Tariff Division, Board of Trade, London, 1969-73; Director (Location of Industry), Department of Industry, Glasgow, 1973-76; Assistant Secretary: (Industrial Policy), Scottish

Economic Planning Department, 1976-78, (Housing), Scottish Development Department, 1978-82, (Finance), Scottish Office, 1982-84; Director, Historic Buildings and Monuments, Scottish Development Department, 1984-87; Chief Executive, Scottish Tourist Board, 1987-94; Member, Board of Management, Perth Housing Association, since 1993, Vice Chairman, since 1998; Chairman, Andersons Enterprises Ltd., 1994-99. Recreations: gardening; skiing; shooting. Address: (h.) Heathfield, Pitcairngreen, Perthshire; T.-01738 583 403.

Banfill, Professor Phillip Frank Gower, BSc, PhD, CChem, FRSC. Professor of Construction Materials, Heriot-Watt University, since 1995; b. 20.3.52, Worthing; m., Patricia; 1 s.; 1 d. Educ. Lancing College; Southampton University; Liverpool University. Former Lecturer, Liverpool University. Publications: three books; 85 papers. Recreations: sailing; choral singing; bee-keeping. Address: (b.) Department of Building Engineering and Surveying, Heriot-Watt University, Riccarton, Edinburgh EH14 4AS; T.-0131-449 5111; e-mail: P.F.G.Banfill@hw.ac.uk

Bankowski, Professor Zenon Krzysztof, LLB. Professor of Legal Theory, University of Edinburgh, since 1993; b. 9.10.46, Germany. Educ. Becket School, Nottingham; Dundee University. Lecturer in Law, University College, Cardiff; successively Lecturer, Senior Lecturer, Reader, Edinburgh University. Recreation: athletics. Address: (h.) 76 Thirlestane Road, Edinburgh; T.-0131-447 4365; e-mail: Z.Bankowski@ed.ac.uk

Banks, Iain M. Novelist; b. 1954. Educ. schools in North Queensferry, Gourock, Greenock; Stirling University. Hitch-hiked through Europe, Scandinavia, Morocco, 1975, later worked for British Steel and IBM, and as a costings clerk in London. Books: The Wasp Factory, 1984; Walking on Glass, 1985; The Bridge, 1986; Consider Phlebas, 1987; Espedair Street, 1987; The Player of Games, 1988; Canal Dreams, 1989; Use of Weapons, 1990; The State of the Art, 1991; The Crow Road, 1992; Against a Dark Background, 1993; Complicity, 1993 (No. 1 bestseller in paperback); Feersum Endjinn, 1994; Whit, 1995; Excession, 1996; Song of Stone, 1997; Inversions, 1998.

Banks, Professor William McKerrell, BSc, MSc, PhD, CEng, FIMechE, FIM, FREng, FRSA. Professor of Advanced Materials, Strathclyde University, since 1991 (Director, Centre for Advanced Structural Materials); Co-Director, Scottish Polymer Technology Network; Vice President, IMechE; b. 28.3.43, Irvine; m., Martha Ruthven Hair; 3 s. Educ. Irvine Royal Academy; Strathclyde University. Senior Research Engineer, G. & J. Weir Ltd., 1966-70; Lecturer, Senior Lecturer, Reader, Professor, Strathclyde University, since 1970. Recreations: family; Bible teaching; gardening; travel. Address: (h.) 19 Dunure Drive, Hamilton ML3 9EY; T.-01698 823730.

Bannister, John Roy, National (GB) Compliance Director, Traffic Area Network; Clerk to the Scottish Traffic Commissioner, 1987-2000; b. 3.11.46, London; m., Jan; 1 s., 1 d. Educ. Edmonton County Grammar School. Department of Transport: London, 1965-72, 1984-87, Newcastle upon Tyne, 1972-83; Manager, International Road Freight Office, Newcastle upon Tyne, 1983-84. Recreations: home brewing/wine; foreign travel; railways. Address: (h.) 13 Warrender Court, North Berwick, East Lothian; T.-01620 894683; e-mail: jbnberwick@aol.com

Barbenel, Professor Joseph Cyril, BDS, BSc, MSc, PhD, LDS RCS(Eng), CBiol, FIBiol, CPhys, FInstP, CEng, FIPEM, FRSE. Professor, Strathclyde University, since 1982; Head, Tissue Mechanics Division, since 1970; Vice-Dean (Research), Faculty of Engineering; b. 2.1.37, London; m., Lesley Mary Hyde Jowett; 2 s.; 1 d. Educ. Hackney Downs Grammar School, London; London Hospital Medical College; Queen's College, Dundee (St.

Andrews University); Strathclyde University. Dental House Surgeon, London Hospital, 1960; National Service, RADC, 1960-61 (Lieutenant, 1960, Captain, 1961); general dental practice, London, 1963; student, 1963-67; Lecturer, Department of Dental Prosthetics, Dental School, Dundee, 1967-69; Senior Lecturer, Strathclyde University, 1970-82. Member, Administrative Committee, International Federation for Medical and Biological Engineering; Vice President (International Affairs), Institute of Physics and Engineering in Medicine. Recreations: music; art; theatre. Address: (b.) University of Strathclyde, Bioengineering Unit, 106 Rottenrow, Glasgow G4 ONW; T.-0141-552 4400.

Barber, Samantha, BA. Chief Executive, Scottish Business in the Community, since 2000; b. 16.10.69, Dunfermline. Educ. High School of Dundee; University of Northumbria; University of Orleans; University of Dijon; University of Nancy. Policy Advisor, European Parliament, 1994-98; Director, Business for Scotland, 1998-2000; Director, Right Track; Member, Glasgow Alliance Director's Group, Member, Advisory Council for the Millennium Forest for Scotland Trust. Recreations: reading; cooking; ballet; hill walking. Address: (b.) 10 Bankhead Crossway South, Edinburgh, EH11 4EX; T.-0131-442 2020; Fax.-0131-442 3555.

Barbour, John, BL. Consultant, Wright and Crawford Solicitors, Paisley (former Senior Partner); b. 22.9.29, Barrhead; m., Martha Wallace; 1 d. Educ. Camphill School, Paisley; Glasgow University. Qualified as Solicitor, 1952; Partner, Wright and Crawford, 1960-2000. Honorary Sheriff, Paisley; Elder, Bourock Church, Barrhead; Past Dean, Faculty of Procurators, Paisley; Past Chairman, Accord Hospice, Paisley; Past President, Paisley Burns Club; Past President, Paisley Rotary Club. Recreations: reading; walking; bowling. Address: (h.) 104 Paisley Road, Barrhead G78 1NW; T.-0141-881 3083.

Barbour, Very Rev. Robert Alexander Stewart, KCVO, MC, MA, BD, STM, DD, DipEd. Minister, Church of Scotland, since 1954; Chaplain, then Extra Chaplain to the Queen in Scotland, since 1976; b. 11.5.21, Edinburgh; m., Margaret Pigot; 3 s.; 1 d. Educ. Rugby School; Balliol College, Oxford; St. Mary's College, St. Andrews. Army (Scottish Horse), 1940-45, Territorial Army, 1947-54; Editorial Assistant, Thomas Nelson & Sons, 1948-49; Secretary, Edinburgh Christian Council for Overseas Students, 1953-55; Lecturer and Senior Lecturer in New Testament Language, Literature and Theology, New College, Edinburgh University, 1955-71; Professor of New Testament Exegesis, Aberdeen University, 1971-86; Master, Christ's College, Aberdeen, 1977-82; Prelate, Priory of Scotland, Order of St. John, 1977-93; Moderator, General Assembly of the Church of Scotland, 1979-80; Dean, Chapel Royal in Scotland, 1981-91;Honorary Secretary, Novi Testamenti Societas, 1970-77. Recreations: music; forestry; walking. Address: (h.) Old Fincastle, Pitlochry PH16 5RJ; T.-01796 473209; e-mail: rasbarbour@netscapeonline.co.uk

Barker, Alan. Music Director, The Scottish Ballet, since 1992; b. Australia. Educ. Melbourne University. Former Musical Director, New Zealand Ballet, and Artistic Director, New Zealand Opera; former Resident Conductor, Australian Ballet; joined American Ballet Theatre, 1978, as Associate Conductor, promoted to Principal Conductor, 1980; Music Director, Sacramento Ballet, 1987-90; Music Director, Pittsburgh Ballet Theatre, 1988-90; has conducted Royal Swedish Ballet, Royal Danish Ballet, National Ballet of Canada, Gothenburg Opera Ballet, and Birmingham Royal Ballet. Address: (b.) Scottish Ballet, 261 West Princes Street, Glasgow G4 9EE; T.-0141-331 2931.

Barker, Professor John Reginald, BSc, MSc, PhD, FBIS, FRAS, FRSE. Professor of Electronics, Department of Electronics and Electrical Engineering, University of Glasgow, since 1985; b. 11.11.42, Stockport; m., Elizabeth Carol; 2 s.; 1 d. Educ. New Mills Grammar School; University of Edinburgh; University of Durham; University of Warwick. University of Warwick: SRC Personal Research Fellowship, 1969-70, Lecturer in Physics, 1970-84, Senior Lecturer, 1984-85; Affiliate Professor, Colorado State University, 1979-83; Distinguished Science Lecturer, Yale University, 1992; Irvine Lectures in Chemistry, St. Andrews, 1994; broadcasting: History of the Microchip, 1982; The Magic Micro Mission, 1983. Member, various SERC/DTI committees, 1987-93: Devices Committee, Electronic Materials Committee, National Committee for Superconductivity, Materials Commission, Molecular Electronics Committee (Chairman, 1990-93). Publications: over 215 scientific papers; Physics of Non-Linear Transport in Semi-conductors (Co-Author), 1979; Granular Nanoelectronics (Co-Author), 1991. Recreations: hill-walking; astronomy; reading; cooking. Address: (b.) Nanoelectronics Research Centre, Department of Electronics and Electrical Engineering, University of Glasgow, Glasgow G12 8QQ; T.-0141-330 5221.

Barker, Ralph Fraser, MA (Hons), DipEd. Rector, Alloa Academy, since 1995; b. 10.7.51, Edinburgh; m., Suzanne; 2 s.; 1 d. Educ. Royal High School, Edinburgh; Edinburgh University. Teacher of Mathematics, then Assistant Principal Teacher, Royal High School, 1974-81; Principal Teacher, Knox Academy, 1981-84; Assistant Head Teacher, then Depute Head Teacher, Queensferry High School, 1984-94. Recreation: public transport, especially buses. Address: (b.) Claremont, Alloa FK10 2EQ; T.-01259 214979; e-mail: rbarker@clacks.gov.uk

Barlow, Nevile Robert Disney, OBE, DL, FRICS. Chartered Surveyor and Farmer; Chairman, Scottish Borders Valuation Appeal Panel, since 1995; b. 3.2.41, Bagshott, Surrey; m., Myfanwy Louise Kerr-Wilson; 3 s. Educ. Winchester College; Royal Agricultural College, Cirencester. Assistant Agent, Bathurst Estate, Cirencester, 1963-95; Resident Sub-Agent, Bletchingdon Park, 1966-67; Head Factor, National Trust for Scotland, 1986-91; Vice-President, Scottish Landowners' Federation, (Convener, 1991-94); Member, Board, East of Scotland Water, 1995-99; Member, East Region Board, Scottish Environmental Protection Agency, 1996-2000. Recreations: shooting; fishing; sailing; rowing. Address: The Park, Earlston TD4 6AB; T.-01896 849267.

Barltrop, Professor Nigel Douglas Philip, BSc, CEng, FICE, FRINA, MSNAME. Director of Research, Department of Naval Architecture and Marine Engineering, Glasgow and Strathclyde Universities, since 2001; b. 10.2.52, London; m., Suzanne Joyce; 1 s.; 2 d. Educ. Southgate County Grammar School; Southampton University. Joined Freeman Fox and Partners, 1973; W.S. Atkins: joined 1977, Chief Engineer, 1984, Technical Director, 1988; moved to Glasgow University, 1995, as Head of Department and John Elder Chair; Research Director of first joint department of Glasgow and Strathclyde Universities, since 2001. Member, Board of Management, Glasgow College of Nautical Studies; Member, Offshore Structures Committees, International Standards Organisation; Member, Collision and Grounding Committee, International Ship Structures Congress. Recreations: mountain walking; Scottish country dancing. Address: (b.) NA-ME, Universities of Glasgow and Strathclyde, 100 Montrose Street, Glasgow G4 0LZ; T.-0141-548 3315.

Barnard, Professor Alan John, BA, MA, PhD, FSAScot. Professor of the Anthropology of Southern Africa, Edinburgh University, since 2001; b. 22.2.49, Baton Rouge, USA; m., Dr Joy E. Barnard. Educ. New Providence High School; George Washington University; McMaster University; University College London. Junior Lecturer in Social Anthropology, University of Cape Town, 1972-73; Field Research with Bushmen in Botswana, 1974-75 and later; Lecturer in Social Anthropology, University College London, 1976-78; Lecturer in Social Anthropology, 1978-90, Senior Lecturer, 1990-94, Reader, 1994-2001, Edinburgh University. Hon. Secretary, Association of Social Anthropologists, 1985-89. Publications include: Hunters and Herders of Southern Africa, 1992; Kalahari Bushmen (children's book), 1993; Encyclopaedia of Social and Cultural Anthropology (Co-Editor), 1996; History and Theory in Anthropology, 2000; Social Anthropology, 2000; The Hunter-Gatherer Peoples, 2001; Africa's Indigenous Peoples (Co-Editor), 2001; Self- and Other Images of Hunter-Gatherers (Co-Editor), 2002. Recreations: walking; cooking; watercolour painting. Address: (b.) School of Social and Political Studies, Edinburgh University, Adam Ferguson Building, George Square, Edinburgh EH8 9LL; T.-0131-650 3938.

Barnes, James David Kentish. Director, Dobbie Garden Centres PLC, since 1969; Director, National Trust for Scotland Trading Company, since 1998; b. 18.4.30, Chester; m., Susan Mary Harter; 1 s.; 1 d. Educ. Eton College; Royal Military Academy Sandhurst. Army 1948-57 (served Korea, Middle East and Germany); joined John Waterer Sons and Crisp (horticulture), 1957, Managing Director 1968-84; Owner and Managing Director, Dobbie and Co. Edinburgh, 1968-94. National Trust for Scotland: Member, Council, Convener, Gardens Committee, 1996-2000. Address: (h.) Biggar Park, Biggar, Lanarkshire ML12 6JS; T.-01899 220185.

Barnet, James Paul, MA, LLB. Former Partner, Macbeth Currie & Co., Solicitors, now Consultant; Honorary Sheriff, Tayside Central and Fife, at Dunfermline; former Dean, Dunfermline District Society of Solicitors; b. 20.7.37, Darlington; m., Margaret Smart; 4 s. Educ. Dunfermline High School; Edinburgh University. Admitted as Solicitor, 1961. Council Member, Law Society of Scotland, 1985-88; Captain, Scottish Universities Golfing Society, 1980-81; President, Dunfermline Rotary Club, 1985-86. Recreations: golf; reading; quoting Dr. Johnson. Address: (h.) 33 Drumsheugh Gardens, Edinburgh EH3 7RN.

Barnicoat, Martin Kevin, ACIB. Scotland Director, Barclays Bank PLC, since 1998; b. 29.5.52, Truro, Cornwall; 1 d. Educ. Falmouth Grammar School; Bath University. Barclays Bank PLC: Credit Risk Assistant Director, 1989-91, Head of Pricing for UK Large Corporates, 1991-93, Credit Director for North and Central Wales, Shropshire and Hereford, 1993-95, Area Director for West Midlands, 1995-97. Recreations: golf; rugby; walking; music. Address: (h.) 1 Belhaven Place, Mearns Craig, Newton Mearns, Glasgow; T. (b.)-0141-207 3088.

Barr, David George Dryburgh, MB, ChB, FRCPEd, DCH, FRCPCH. Consultant Paediatrician, Lothian Health Board, since 1971; part-time Senior Lecturer, Department of Child Life and Health, Edinburgh University, since 1977; Clinical Director for Medicine, Royal Hospital for Sick Children, Edinburgh, 1994-97; b. 14.2.36, Edinburgh; m., Anna Blair; 2 s.; 1 d. Educ. Daniel Stewart's College, Edinburgh; Edinburgh University. Senior Registrar, Royal Hospital for Sick Children, Edinburgh, 1965-69; Research Fellow, children's hospital, Zurich, Switzerland, 1969-70; Consultant Paediatrician, Edinburgh Northern and West Fife Hospitals, 1971-77; seconded to Ministry of Health and University of Riyadh, Saudi Arabia, 1980-83. Address: (b.) Royal Hospital for Sick Children, Sciennes Road, Edinburgh.

Barr, Sheriff Kenneth Glen, MA, LLB. Sheriff of South Strathclyde, Dumfries and Galloway, at Dumfries, since 1976; b. 20.1.41, Glasgow. Educ. Royal High School; Edinburgh University. Admitted Faculty of Advocates, 1964. Address: (b.) Sheriff's Chambers, Sheriff Court House, Dumfries DG1 2AN.

Barr, Professor William James, OBE, CEng, FICE, FCIOB, FIMgt. Chairman and Chief Executive, Barr Holdings Limited (which includes Barr Limited, W. & J. Barr and Sons (Scotland) Limited, Alpha Crane Limited, Alpha Services Limited, Alpha Access Limited, Econospace Limited, Barr Quarries Limited, Barmix Concrete, Barr Construction, Barr Steel, Solway Precast, Solway Crane, Barr Homes, Barr Environmental, Barr Technical Services, Barr Construction Services); Chairman and Managing Director, Barr Leisure Limited; Chairman and Managing Director, Ice Hockey Services Ltd.; b. 12.3.39, Ayr; m., Marlean Ramage; 2 s.; 1 d. Educ. Girvan High School; Glasgow University; Paisley University. Chairman, Freeport (Scotland) Ltd; Chairman, Thomas Telford Ltd.; Member, Council and Executive, Institution of Civil Engineers; former Chairman, Glasgow and West of Scotland Association, Institution of Civil Engineers; Visiting Professor, Strathclyde University; former Chairman, Craigie College of Education; Chairman, Ayr College Board; Member, Court, Paisley University; former Chairman, Ayrshire Hospice; Founder Chairman, Laigh Milton Viaduct Conservation Project; former Vice-Chairman, Enterprise Ayrshire; Past President, Ayr Chamber of Commerce; former Board Member, Ayrshire Chamber of Commerce and Industry; Past President, Association for Science and Education; Board Member, Ice Hockey Superleague; Member, AME Board. Recreations: the works of Robert Burns and Thomas Telford; walking; reading. Address: (h.) Harkieston, Maybole, Ayrshire, KA19 7LP; T.-01655 883123; (b.) Heathfield, Ayr KA8 9SL; T.-01292 281311.

Barraclough, David Rex, BSc, DSc, MInstP, CPhys. Chairperson, Enable (formerly Scottish Society for the Mentally Handicapped), 1998-2001; b. 7.3.40, Halifax; m., Christine; 1 s.; 1 d. Educ. Crossley and Porter Boys' School, Halifax; Imperial College, London University. Research Physicist, AEI Ltd., 1962-64; Research Assistant, Bradford University, 1964-68; Geophysicist, British Geological Survey, 1969-2000. Vice-President, Royal Astronomical Society, 1999-2000. Recreations: walking; reading; listening to music. Address: (h.) 49 Liberton Drive, Edinburgh.

Barrett, Professor Ann, MB, BS, FRCR, FRCP, MD. Professor of Radiation Oncology, Glasgow University, since 1986; Consultant, Royal Hospital for Sick Children, since 1986; b. 27.2.43, London; m., Adrian Bell; 1 s.; 2 d. Educ. Queen Elizabeth's Grammar School; St. Bartholomew's Hospital. Formerly Consultant in Radiotherapy and Oncology, Royal Marsden Hospital; Director, Beatson Oncology Centre, Glasgow, 1986-91; President, Scottish Radiological Society, 1995-97; Scottish College of Radiologists: Chairman, Scottish Standing Committee, 1994-97, Registrar and Dean Elect, 2000-02; President, European Society for Therapeutic Radiation Oncology, 1997-99; former Member, MRC Molecular and Cell Medicine Board; Associate Editor, Medical and Paediatric Oncology. Publications: Cancer in Childhood (Co-editor); Practical Radiotherapy Planning (Co-author). Recreations: walking; music; novels. Address: (b.) Beatson Oncology Centre, Western Infirmary, Glasgow; T.-0141-211 2123.

Barrett, John Andrew. MP (Liberal Democrat), Edinburgh West, since 2001; b. 11.2.54, Hobart, Australia; m., Carol; 1 d. Educ. Forrester High School; Telford College; Napier Polytechnic. Company Director, ABC Productions, 1985-2001; Member, City of Edinburgh Council, 1995-2001; Director, The EDI Group, 1995-99; Board Member, Edinburgh International Film Festival, 1995-2001; Board Member, Lothian and Borders Screen Industry Office, 1998-2001; Member, Edinburgh Filmhouse Board, 1999-2001. Scottish Liberal Democrat Westminster Spokesman on Transportation; Vice-President, Scottish Liberal Club. Recreations: cinema; travel; music. Address: (b.) House of Commons, London SW1A 0AA; T.-020 7219 8224; e-mail: barrettj@parliament.uk

Barrie, Scott, MA, CQSW. MSP (Labour), Dunfermline West, since 1999; b. 10.3.62, St Andrews. Educ. Auchmuty High School, Glenrothes; Edinburgh University; Stirling University. Fife Regional Council: Social Worker, 1986-90, Senior Social Worker, 1990-91,Team Manager, 1991-96; Team Leader, Fife Council, 1996-99. Recreations: football; hill-walking; CAMRA. Address: (b.) Unit 3, Albany Business Centre, Gardeners Street, Dunfermline KY12 0RN; T.-01383 731885.

Barron, Christopher, BA (Hons). Chief Executive, Scottish Ballet/Scottish Opera since 2000; b. 17.11.49, Uxbridge; m., Julia. Educ. Cheltenham Grammar School; University of Wales, Swansea; Central School of Speech and Drama. 69 Theatre Company, Manchester (now Royal Exchange), 1969-71; Stage Manager: Glyndebourne Festival Opera, 1970-71; Glyndebourne Touring Opera, 1970-72; Wexford Festival Opera, 1970-72; Donovan Maule Theatre, Nairobi, 1971-72; Production Manager, Palace Theatre, Watford, 1972-74; Company Manager, Musica Nel Chiostro, Batignano, Italy, 1974-79; General Manager: Palace Theatre, Wexford, 1978-81; Buxton Festival and Opera House, 1981-84; Edinburgh International Festival, 1984-89; Associate Festival Director, Edinburgh International Festival, 1989 -92; Director, Manchester City of Drama, 1992-94; Artistic Director and Chief Executive, Brighton Festival and Dome, 1995-99; Member, Arts Council Touring Panel; Board Member: Musica Nel Chiostro; Dance Umbrella; National Opera Studio. Recreations: walking. Address: (h.) 39 Elmbank Crescent, Glasgow, G2 4PT; T.-0141-248 4567.

Barron, Professor Laurence David, DPhil, BSc, MInstP, FRSE. Gardiner Professor of Chemistry, Glasgow University; b. 12.2.44, Southampton; m., Sharon Aviva Wolf; 1 s.; 1 d. Educ. King Edward VI Grammar School, Southampton; Northern Polytechnic, London; Lincoln College, Oxford. Post-doctoral research, Cambridge University, 1969-75; Ramsay Memorial Fellow, 1974-75; Glasgow University: Lecturer in Chemistry, 1975-80, Reader, 1980-84, Professor since 1984. Corday-Morgan Medal, Chemical Society, 1977; G.M.J. Schmidt Memorial Lecturer, Weizmann Institute of Science, 1984; F.L. Conover Memorial Lecturer, Vanderbilt University, 1987; Sir Harold Thompson Award, 1992; EPSRC Senior Fellow, 1995-2000. Publication: Molecular Light Scattering and Optical Activity, 1982. Recreations: water-colour painting; walking; music; radio-controlled model aircraft. Address: (b.) Chemistry Department, The University, Glasgow G12 8QQ; T.-0141-339 8855.

Barrow, Professor Geoffrey Wallis Steuart, MA (Hons), BLitt, DLitt, FBA, FRSE, FSA, FSA Scot, FRHistS, Hon. DLitt (Glasgow and Newcastle upon Tyne). Sir William Fraser Professor of Scottish History and Palaeography, Edinburgh University, 1979-92; b. 28.11.24, Headingley, Leeds; m., Heather Elizabeth Agnes Lownie; 1 s.; 1 d. Educ. St. Edward's School, Oxford; Inverness Royal Academy; St. Andrews University; Pembroke College, Oxford. Royal Navy and RNVR (Sub-Lieutenant), 1943-46; Lecturer in History, University College, London, 1950-61; Professor of Medieval History, Newcastle-upon-Tyne University, 1961-74; Professor of Scottish History, St. Andrews University, 1974-79. Member, Royal Commission on Historical Manuscripts, 1984-90; Royal Historical Society, Council, 1963-74; Joint Literary Director, 1964-74; Vice President, 1982-86; former Chairman: Council, Scottish History Society (President, 1973-77); President: Saltire Society, 1987-90, Scottish Record Society, 1993-97; Vice-President, Commission Internationale de Diplomatique. Publications: Feudal Britain, 1956; Acts of Malcolm IV, 1960; Robert Bruce, 1965 and 1988; Acts of William I, 1971; The Kingdom of the Scots, 1973; The Scottish Tradition (Editor), 1974; The Anglo-Norman Era in Scottish History, 1980; Kingship and Unity: Scotland 1000-1306, 1981; Scotland and its neighbours, 1992; Charters of King David I, 1999. Recreations: hill-walking; visiting graveyards; travel. Address: (h.) 12A Lauder Road, Edinburgh EH9 2EL; T.-0131-668 2173.

Barry, Professor (David) Andrew. Chair of Environmental Engineering, University of Edinburgh, since 1998 (Head, School of Civil and Environmental Engineering, since 2000); Director, Contaminated Land Assessment and Remediation Research Centre, University of Edinburgh; b. 19.4.58; m., Suellen Jill de Waard; 2 s.; 1 d. Educ. University of Queensland; Griffith University, Australia; Royal Melbourne Institute of Technology. Research Associate, Center for Environmental and Hazardous Materials Studies, Virginia Polytechnic Institute and State University, 1985-86; Postgraduate Research Soil Scientist, University of California, 1986-88; University of Western Australia: Lecturer in Subsurface Hydrology, Centre for Water Research, 1989-91, Senior Lecturer and Hydrology Group Leader, Department of Environmental Engineering, 1991-93, Associate Professor, Department of Environmental Engineering, 1994-98. Visiting Associate Professor, University of North Carolina, Chapel Hill, 1994; Visiting Scientist, Massachusetts Institute of Technology, 1996; Honorary Fellow, University of Western Australia, 1998-99. Address: (b.) School of Civil and Environmental Engineering, University of Edinburgh, Edinburgh EH9 3JN; T.-0131-650 7204; e-mail: a.barry@ed.ac.uk

Bartlett, Professor Christopher John, BA, PhD, FRHistS, FRSE. Emeritus Professor of International History, Dundee University (Head of Modern History Department, 1983-88); Member, Scottish Examination Board; b. 12.10.31, Bournemouth; m., Shirley Maureen Briggs; 3 s. Educ. Queen Elizabeth's Grammar School, Wimborne; University College, Exeter; London School of Economics. Assistant Lecturer, Edinburgh University, 1957-59; Lecturer, University of the West Indies, Jamaica, 1959-62; Lecturer, Queen's College, Dundee, 1962-68; Reader, Dundee University, 1968-78. Publications: Great Britain and Sea Power 1815-53; Castlereagh; The Long Retreat; The Rise and Fall of the Pax Americana; A History of Postwar Britain 1945-74; The Global Conflict 1880-1990; British Foreign Policy in the Twentieth Century; The Special Relationship since 1945; Defence and Diplomacy 1815-1914; The Annual Register 1987-97 (UK and Scotland chapters); Peace, War and the European Great Powers, 1814-1914. Address: (b.) Department of History, The University, Dundee.

Bartlett, Professor Robert John, MA, DPhil, FRHS, FBA, FSA, FRSE. Professor of Mediaeval History, St. Andrews University, since 1992; b. 27.11.50, London; m., Honora Hickey; 1 s.; 1 d. Educ. Battersea Grammar School; Peterhouse, Cambridge; St. John's College, Oxford. Lecturer in History, Edinburgh University, 1980-86; Professor of Medieval History, University of Chicago, 1986-92. Publications: Gerald of Wales 1146-1223, 1982; Trial by Fire and Water: the medieval judicial ordeal, 1986; The Making of Europe, 1993; England under the Norman and Angevin Kings, 2000. Recreations: walking; squash. Address: (b.) Department of Mediaeval History, St. Andrews University, St. Andrews KY16 9AL; T.-01334 463308.

Barton, John M, WS. President, Rent Assessment Panel for Scotland, since 1997; Solicitor, since 1960. Address: (b.) 48 Manor Place, Edinburgh.

Bartos, Professor Peter J.M., MSc(Eng), MSc(Econ), PhD, CEng, MICE, MIStructE, FCS. Director of Advanced Concrete and Masonry Centre, since 1997; Professor of Civil Engineering, Paisley University, since 1992; b. 25.11.39, Czech Republic; m., Helena Bartos; 2 s. Educ. Neruda Grammar School, Prague; Czech Technical University; Southampton University. Lecturer, Reader, Professor, Glasgow College, until 1979, then Paisley University. President, UK Concrete Society, 1977-78; Chairman, Scottish Region, Concrete Society, 1990-91; Member, Board of Directors, RILEM. Publications: four books. Address: (h.) 4 Craigmillar Avenue, Milngavie, Glasgow G62 8AU; T.-0141-956 1706.

Baster, Jeremy, BA, MPhil, MBA, MRTPI. Director of Development and Planning, Orkney Islands Council, since 1996; b. 5.2.47, New York; m., Miriam Landor; 2 s.; 1 d. Educ. Leighton Park School, Reading; St. John's College, Oxford; University College, London. Early career in consultancy; Economist, Scottish Council (Development and Industry), 1975-80; Economist, Orkney Islands Council, 1980-85; Director of Economic Development, Orkney Islands Council, 1985-96. Director, Soulisquoy Printmakers Ltd. Address: (b.) Council Offices, School Place, Kirkwall KW15 1NY; T.-01856 873535.

Batchelor, Louise Mary, BA (Hons). Environment Correspondent, BBC Scotland, since 1994; b. 23.2.53, Swanage; m., David Batchelor; 2 s. Educ. Dorchester Grammar School; Reading University. Milton Keynes Gazette, 1974; Oxford Mail, 1977; BBC Radio Scotland, 1978; Presenter/Reporter, Reporting Scotland, 1980; Presenter, Newsnight, 1981-82; Presenter, Breakfast News (Scotland), 1982-83; presenter, various programmes, including Voyager, Fringes of Faith; Presenter, Newsroom South East, 1989. Media Natura Award, 1996, for environment reporting; Director, Fair Isle Bird Observatory Trust; Member, Steering Group, Portmoak Community Woodlands. Recreations: walking; bird watching; playing cello. Address: (h.) The Old Manse, Scotlandwell, Kinross KY13 9HY; T.-01592 840233.

Bateman, Derek Walls. Presenter, BBC Scotland, since 1995; b. 10.5.51, Selkirk; m., Alison Edgar (deceased); 2 d. Educ. Selkirk High School; Edinburgh College of Commerce. Scotsman Publications; Glasgow Herald; BBC Scotland; Scotland on Sunday; freelance (Sunday Times, STV); BBC Scotland (Presenter, Good Morning Scotland). Publication: Unfriendly Games (Co-Author), 1986. Recreation: wine. Address: (b.) BBC Scotland, Queen Margaret Drive, Glasgow G12 8DG; T.-0141 338 2676; e-mail: derekbateman@yahoo.com

Bateman, Meg (Vivienne Margaret), MA (Hons), PhD. Gaelic poet; b. 13.4.59, Edinburgh; 1 s. Educ. Mary Erskine School, Edinburgh; University of Aberdeen. Poetry collections: Orain Ghaoil (1990); Aotromachd is Dàin Eile (Lightness and Other Poems), (1997) shortlisted for Stakis Prize); translations of Gaelic poetry published in An Anthology of Scottish Women Poets, Gàir nan Clàrsach (The Harps' Cry). Address: (b.) Sabhal Mòr Ostaig, Sleat, Isle of Skye IV44 8RQ; T.-01471 888310; e-mail: sm00meg@groupwise.uhi.ac.uk

Bates, Professor David Richard, BA, PhD, Docteur Honoris Causa, FRHistS, FSA, FFCS. Edwards Professor of Medieval History, University of Glasgow, since 1994; b. 30.4.45, Coventry; m., Helen Mary; 1 s.; 1 d. Educ. King Edward VI Grammar School, Nuneaton; University of Exeter. Research Assistant, Documents Section, Imperial War Museum, 1969-71; Fellow, University College,

Cardiff, 1971-73; Lecturer, Senior Lecturer, Reader in History, 1973-94, Head of History and Welsh History, 1988-92, University of Wales, Cardiff; Head, Department of History, University of Glasgow, 1997-2001. Visiting Professor, Ecole Nationale des Chartes, Paris, 1999; British Academy Marc Fitch Research Reader, 2001-03. Publications: Normandy Before 1066, 1982; A Bibliography of Domesday Book, 1986; William the Conqueror, 1989; Bishop Remigius of Lincoln 1067-1092, 1992; England and Normandy in the Middle Ages (Co-Editor), 1994; Contributor, The History Today Companion to British History; Conflict and Co-existence: Nationalism and Democracy in Modern Europe: Essays in Honour of Harry Hearder (Co-Editor), 1997; Regesta Regum Anglo-Normannorum: The Acta of William I 1066-1087, 1998; General Editor: The Medieval World series. Recreations: walking; music; reading; watching sport. Address: (b.) Department of History (Medieval History), University of Glasgow, Glasgow G12 8QQ; T.-0141-330 4511; e-mail: D.Bates@medhist.arts.gla.ac.uk

Bates, Peter James, CertSocAdmin, DipSocWk. Chairperson, NHS Tayside, since 2001; Lay Member, HMI, since 2000; b. 6.5.45, Birmingham; m., Ann; 1 s.; 3 d. Educ. St Augustine's, Handsworth; Birmingham University. Social Worker; Depute Director of Social Work, Strathclyde University; Director of Social Work: Tayside, Dundee, Highland; Director of Social Work and Housing, Stirling; management consultant. Recreations: music; reading; sport. Address: (h.) 3 James Place, Broughty Ferry, Dundee DD5 1EE; T.-01382 424026.

Bath, Professor Michael, BA, MA, PhD, FSAS. Professor of Renaissance Studies, Strathclyde University, since 2000; b. 25.12.42, Barnet; m., Penelope; 2 s.; 1 d. Educ. Poole Grammar School; Keble College, Oxford. Lecturer, then Reader, then Professor, Department of English Studies, Strathclyde University, since 1968. Chairman, International Society for Emblem Studies. Publications: The Image of the Stag in Western Art, 1992; Speaking Pictures, 1994; Reading Poetry, 1996; Renaissance Decorative Painting in Scotland, 2001. Address: (b.) Department of English Studies, Strathclyde University, Livingstone Tower, 26 Richmond Street, Glasgow G1 1XH; T.-0141-548 3632.

Batho, Mark Thomas Scott, MA (Hons). Head, Social Justice Group, Scottish Executive, since 2000; b. 10.6.56, Ashtead, Surrey; m., Vivienne Ann; 2 s.; 1 d. Educ. Glyn Grammar School, Epsom; St Andrews University. Joined Scottish Office as Administration Trainee, 1979. Non-Executive Board Member, Community Enterprise, Strathclyde. Address: (b.) Scottish Executive, Victoria Quay, Edinburgh EH6 6QQ; T.-0131-244 7114.

Bauckham, Professor Richard John, MA, PhD, FBA. Professor of New Testament Studies, St. Andrews University, since 1992, and Bishop Wardlaw Professor, since 2000; b. 22.9.46, London. Educ. Enfield Grammar School; Clare College, Cambridge. Fellow, St. John's College, Cambridge, 1972-75; Lecturer in Theology, Leeds University, 1976-77; Lecturer in the History of Christian Thought, Manchester University, 1977-87, Reader, 1987-92; Fellow of the British Academy, 1998. Publications: Tudor Apocalypse; Jude, 2 Peter; Moltmann: Messianic Theology in the Making; The Bible in Politics; Jude and the Relatives of Jesus in the Early Church; The Theology of the Book of Revelation; The Climax of Prophecy; The Theology of Jurgen Moltmann; James; The Fate of the Dead. Recreations: walking; novels; poetry; gardening; sleeping. Address: (b.) St. Mary's College, St. Andrews KY16 9JU; T.-01334 462830; e-mail: rjb@st-andrews.ac.uk

Baughan, Mike, BEd, FRSA. Chief Executive, Learning and Teaching Scotland (formerly Scottish Consultative Council on the Curriculum); b. 11.6.44, Dumfries; m., Anna; 1 s.; 1 d. Educ. St. Joseph's College, Dumfries; Dundee University; Dundee College of Education. RAF; brief career in industrial banking; English Teacher, secondary schools, Dundee, 1971-75; Principal Teacher of Guidance then Assistant Rector, St. Saviour's High, Dundee, 1975-82; Churchill Fellow, 1977; Adviser in Education, Tayside Regional Council, 1982-87; Rector, Webster's High School, Kirriemuir, 1987-97; Scottish Consultative Council on the Curriculum: Development Fellow, 1997-98, appointed Chief Executive, 1998. Member, Ancient Monuments Board for Scotland; Member, Board, SCRAN; Member, Board, Young Enterprise Scotland; Member, various national education committees. Recreations: hillwalking; fishing; theatre; travel. Address: (b.) Gardyne Road, Broughty Ferry, Dundee DD5 1NY; T.-01382 443600.

Baum, Professor Thomas George (Tom), BA, MA, MPhil, PhD, FTS. Professor of International Hospitality Management, Scottish Hotel School, Strathclyde University, since 1996; Head of Department, Scottish Hotel School, since 1998; b. 20.12.52, Aberdeen; m., Brelda; 1 s. Educ. Wynstones Rudolf Steiner School, Gloucester; University of Wales Aberystwyth; Nottingham Trent University; Strathclyde University. Researcher, Nottingham Trent University, 1976-79; Lecturer, University of Ulster, 1979-82; Manager/Consultant, CERT, Dublin, 1982-90; Senior Lecturer, then Professor, University of Buckingham, 1990-96. Publications: six books; 75 scientific papers. Recreations: travel; golf; DIY; supporting Southampton and Hampshire (cricket). Address: (b.) Scottish Hotel School, Strathclyde University, 94 Cathedral Street, Glasgow G4 0LG; T.-0141-548 3954.

Baxby, Keith, BSc, MB, BS, FRCS. Consultant Urological Surgeon, Tayside Health Board, since 1977; Honorary Senior Lecturer, Dundee University, since 1977; Editor, Urology News; b. 17.4.44, Sheffield. Educ. King Edward VII School, Sheffield; Durham University. House Officer, Royal Victoria Infirmary, Newcastle-upon-Tyne, 1968-69; Surgical Registrar, Newcastle University Hospitals, 1969-73; Northern Counties Kidney Fund Research Fellow, 1973-74; Senior Urological Registrar, Newcastle General Hospital, 1974-77; Visiting Professor of Urology, Louisiana State University, 1981; WHO Fellow in Clinical Urodynamics, 1984. Recreations: deer-stalking; cycling. Address: (b.) Department of Urology, Ninewells Hospital, Dundee; T.-01382 660111.

Baxter, Audrey Caroline, BA, DipACC. Managing Director, Baxters of Speyside Ltd.; b. 25.5.61; m., Colin McNiven. Educ. St. Leonard's School; Heriot-Watt University. International banking, Kleinwort Benson Ltd, London, 1983-87; Director, Corporate Planning, Baxters of Speyside, 1988-90. Address: (b.) W.A. Baxter and Sons Ltd, Fochabers, Moray.

Baxter, Brian Newland, BSc, MSc, PhD, CEng, FRINA, FIES. Visiting Professor, Department of Ship and Marine Technology, Strathclyde University, since 1980; b. London; m., Nadina McLeod; 2 d. Educ. King's College, Newcastle; Durham University. Scientific Officer, Royal Naval Scientific Service, 1948-50; Lecturer in Naval Architecture, King's College, Newcastle, 1950-57; Chief Representative, Bureau Veritas in the UK, 1957-62; Director, Yarrow & Co., Glasgow, 1962-79; Deputy Managing Director, Yarrow Shipbuilders, Glasgow, 1967-81; Director, British Shipbuilders Training and Education Co., 1981-84. President, Institution of Engineers and Shipbuilders in Scotland, 1979-81; Trustee: Seagull Trust, since 1984, Scottish Maritime Museum, since 1986, Clyde Maritime

Trust, 1993. Recreations: reading; writing. Address: (h.) Dunelm, Kilmacolm, RenfrewshirePA13 4DQ; T.-0150 587 2092.

Baxter, Mary Ross, MBE, MA, LRAM; b. 23.9.27, Glasgow. Educ. Park School, Glasgow; Glasgow University. John Smith & Son, Booksellers, Glasgow, 1952-56; British European Airways, Glasgow Office, 1956-60; Director, National Book League Scotland (now known as Scottish Book Trust), 1960-89; former President, International PEN Scottish Centre; Trustee, The Pushkin Prizes in Scotland. Honorary Member, Scottish Library Association. Recreations: music; books; home-decorating; cooking; gardening. Address: (h.) 18 Crown Terrace, Glasgow G12 9ES; T.-0141-357 0327; e-mail: marybaxglasgow@cs.com

Baxter, Peter R., DHE. Curator, Benmore Botanic Garden, since 1995; b. 30.6.58, Irvine; m.; 1 s.; 1 d. Address: (b.) Benmore Botanic Garden, Benmore, Dunoon PA23 8QU; e-mail: p.baxter@rbge.org.uk

Baxter, (William) Gordon, OBE, LLD, DBA. President: W.A. Baxter & Sons Ltd., since 1994 (Chairman, 1970-94); b. 8.2.18, Fochabers, Moray; m., Ena E. Robertson; 2 s.; 1 d. Educ. Ashville College, Harrogate; Aberdeen University. ICI Explosives Ltd., 1940-45 (Research and Development Manager, various military projects); joined family business, 1946; Managing Director, 1947-71; Member, British Export Council Committee for Exports to USA, 1964-72; Member, North American Advisory Group, DTI, 1979-89; former Director, Grampian Regional Board, Bank of Scotland; President, Chartered Institute of Marketing: Northern Branch; Member of Council, Royal Warrant Holders Association, London; Honorary Fellow, Chartered Institute of Marketing; President, Scotland International; Honorary Member, Institute of Home Economics. Recreations: fishing; tennis; cricket. Address: (h.) Speybank House, Fochabers, Moray; T.-01343 821234.

Baynham, John William, CBE, Doctor (honoris causa) (Edinburgh), Doctor (honoris causa) (Queen Margaret University College, BSc, PhD, DIC. Chairman, Lothian Health Board, 1990-97; Chairman, Scottish Health Board Chairmen's Group, 1995-97; b. 20.1.29, Blantyre; m., Marie B. Friel; 1 d. Educ. Bathgate Academy; Aberdeen University; Imperial College, London. Scottish Agricultural Industries PLC, 1955-87, latterly as Agribusiness Director. Member, Lothian Health Board, 1987-90; Chairman, Board of Governors, Moray House Institute of Education, Heriot Watt University, 1991-95; Governor, Queen Margaret College, 1995-99; Chairman, Salaries Committee, Conference of Scottish Centrally Funded Colleges, 1995-99. Recreations: Rotary; golf; grandchildren. Address: (h.) 2/18 Succoth Court, Succoth Park, Edinburgh EH12 6BZ; T.-0131-337 2813.

Bealey, Professor Frank William, BSc (Econ), DSc (Econ). Professor of Politics, Aberdeen University, 1964-90; b. 31.8.22, Bilston, Staffordshire; m., Sheila Hurst; 1 s.; 2 d. Educ. King Edward VI Grammar School, Stourbridge; London School of Economics. Seaman, Royal Navy, 1941-46; Extra-Mural Lecturer, Manchester University, 1951-52; Lecturer, Keele University, 1952-64; Temporary Lecturer, Birmingham University, 1958-59. Treasurer and founder Member, Society for the Study of Labour History, 1960-63; Convener, Committee for Social Science, Aberdeen University, 1970-74 and 1986-89; Fellow, Royal Historical Society, 1971; Editorial Board, Political Studies, 1975-83; Visiting Fellow, Yale University, 1980; Organiser, Parliamentary All-Party Group, Social Science and Policy, 1984-89; Trustee, Jan Hus Educational Foundation, since 1981; Co-ordinator: EC Tempus Project (Political Science, Czechoslovakia), 1990-93. Publications: Labour and Politics 1900-1906 (Co-author); Constituency Politics (Co-

author); The Social and Political Thought of the British Labour Party; The Post Office Engineering Union; The Politics of Independence (Co-author); Democracy in the Contemporary State; Elements in Political Science (Co-author); A Dictionary of Political Science; Power in Business and the State. Recreations: reading poetry; darts; eating and drinking; watching football and cricket. Address: (h.) 11 Viewforth Terrace, Edinburgh EH10 4LH.

Bean, Paul. General Manager, Marriott Dalmahoy, since 2000; Regional Director for Scotland, Whitbread PLC, since 2000; b. 22.2.64, Liverpool; m., Lorna; 2 d. Educ. Ruffwood Comprehensive School, Kirkby; Cassio College, Watford. General Manager, Jarvis Hotels, 1990-93; General Manager, then Regional General Manager, Hilton Hotels, 1994-98; Director of Operations, Hilton International, Brussels, 1998-2000. Committee Member: CBI, BUA; Member, Tourism Forum; Trustee, HIT Scotland. Recreations: golf; music; cooking. Address: (b.) Marriott Dalmahoy Hotel and Country Club, Kirknewton, near Edinburgh EH27 8EB.

Beastall, Graham Hedley, BSc, PhD, EurClinChem, FRCPath. Top Grade Biochemist (Endocrinology), Glasgow Royal Infirmary, since 1981; Honorary Senior Lecturer, Glasgow University, since 1983; b. 11.12.47, Liverpool; m., Judith; 2 s. Educ. Liverpool Institute High School for Boys; Liverpool University. Lecturer in Biochemistry, Liverpool University, 1971-72; Lecturer in Steroid Biochemistry, Glasgow University, 1972-76; Senior Biochemist (Endocrinology), then Principal Biochemist (Endocrinology), Glasgow Royal Infirmary, 1976-81.Chairman, Association of Clinical Biochemists, 1994-97; Chairman, Conference of Clinical Scientists Organisations, 1996-98; Chairman, Scottish Affairs Committee, Royal College of Pathologists, 2000-02; Secretary, European Communities Confederation of Clinical Chemistry, 1996-2002. Recreations: Scouting; gardening. Address: (b.) Department of Clinical Biochemistry, Royal Infirmary, Glasgow G4 OSF; T.-0141-211 4632.

Beat, Janet Eveline, BMus, MA. Composer; Lecturer, Glasgow University since 1996; Artistic Director and Founder, Soundstrata (electro-acoustic ensemble); Honorary Research Fellow, Music Department, Glasgow University; b. 17.12.37, Streetly. Educ. High School for Girls, Sutton Coldfield; Birmingham University. Freelance Orchestral Player, 1960s; Lecturer: Madeley College of Education, 1965-67, Worcester College of Education, 1967-71, Royal Scottish Academy of Music and Drama, 1972-96; founder Member and former Council Member, Scottish Society of Composers; a Director, Scottish Electro-Acoustic Music Association; wrote musical criticism for The Scotsman; G.D. Cunningham Award, 1962; her works have been performed throughout Scotland as well as in Switzerland, Germany, Poland, North America, South America, Greece, Australia, and Japan. Recreations: travel; reading; photography. Address: c/o Scottish Music Information Centre, 1 Bowmont Gardens, Glasgow, G12 9LR; T.-0141-334 6393.

Beath, Professor John Arnott, MA, MPhil. Professor of Economics, St. Andrews University, since 1991 (Head, School of Social Sciences, 1991-98); b. 15.6.44, Thurso; m., Dr. Monika Schroder. Educ. Hillhead High School; St. Andrews, London, Pennsylvania and Cambridge Universities. Research Officer, Department of Applied Economics, Cambridge University; Fellow, Downing College, Cambridge; Lecturer, then Senior Lecturer in Economics, Bristol University. Member, Research Priorities Board, Economic and Social Research Council, 1996-2000; Chair, Conference of Heads of University Departments of Economics, since 1997; Member, Council and Executive Committee, Royal Economic Society; RAE Panellist, 1996, 2001. Publication: The Economic Theory of Product

Differentiation. Recreations: gardening; golf; music. Address: (h.) Simonden, Ceres, Cupar KY15 5PP; T.-01334 858920.

Beattie, Alistair Duncan, MD (Hons), FRCPGlas, FRCPLond. Consultant Physician, Southern General Hospital, Glasgow, since 1976; Honorary Clinical Lecturer, Glasgow University, since 1977; b. 4.4.42, Laurencekirk; m., Gillian Margaret McCutcheon; 3 s.; 2 d. Educ. Paisley Grammar School; Glasgow University. Junior hospital appointments, Royal Infirmary and Western Infirmary, Glasgow, 1965-69; Department of Materia Medica, Glasgow University: Research Fellow, 1969-73, Lecturer, 1973-74; MRC Research Fellow, Royal Free Hospital, London, 1974-75. Honorary Treasurer, Medical and Dental Defence Union of Scotland. Recreations: golf; music. Address: (h.) Flat 3/2 Lauderdale Mansions, 47 Novar Drive, Glasgow G12 9UB; T.-0141-334 0101.

Beattie, Andrew Watt, LLB (Hons), DipLP, NP. Assistant Scottish Parliamentary Counsel, since 1999; b. 16.11.72, Aberdeen; m., Claire Louise. Educ. Elgin Academy; Edinburgh University. Solicitor, Corporate, Shepherd & Wedderburn, WS, 1995-99. Recreations: hillock-walking; softball; football. Address: (b.) Office of the Scottish Parliamentary Counsel, Victoria Quay, Edinburgh EH6 6QQ; T.-0131-244 1665.

Beattie, Bryan William, JP, BA, FRSA. Chairman, Board of Governors, Eden Court Theatre, since 1996; Board Member, Scottish Screen, since 1998; b. 3.5.60, Dundee; m., Emer Leavy; 1 d. Educ. High School of Dundee; Stirling University. Director, Stirling Festival, 1984-86; established Stirling Writers Group, Stirling Youth Theatre; Arts Development Officer for Scotland, Scottish Council on Disability, 1986-87; Principal, Creative Services (arts consultancy), since 1992; Chairman, Scottish Youth Theatre, 1993-99; Councillor, Highland Regional Council, 1994-96, and Highland Council, 1995-99 (Chairman, Cultural and Leisure Services Committee, 1995-99); Board Member, Ross and Cromarty Enterprise, since 1996, Vice-Chairman, since 1999; Member, University of Highlands and Islands Foundation, 1996-99; Founder Member, Highlands and Islands Alliance, 1998; author of plays for radio and theatre; broadcaster; columnist, Press and Journal; occasional acting. Recreations: music; books; sport; regular breathing; remembering family and friends' names. Address: (h.) Drumderfit, North Kessock, by Inverness, IV1 3ZF; T.-01463 731596; e-mail: bryan@cali.co.uk

Beattie, Johnny. Comedian and entertainer; b. 1926, Glasgow. Established his career as principal comic in Robert Wilson's touring revue. Has appeared frequently in pantomime and in summer seasons at the Gaiety, Ayr.

Beattie, Robert Barrowman, MBE, FRSA. Community Investment Co-ordinator, IBM, since 1989; President, Volunteer Development Scotland, since 2000; b. 22.4.48, Douglas; m., Isobel Elizabeth Fitzsimmons; 1 s.; 1 d. Educ. Carrick Academy, Maybole. Midland Bank Group, 1966-76; Regional Manager, Scotland and Northern Ireland, Alex Lawrie Factors, 1976-77; sales, marketing and strategic planning, IBM, 1977-89. Vice-Convenor, Advisory Committee, Scottish Science Library, 1989-2001; Founder and Convenor, Scottish Mental Health Working Group, 1992-94; Non-Executive Director: Scottish Council for Voluntary Organisations, 1989-98, Volunteer Development Scotland, 1991-98, Edinburgh Health Care NHS Trust, 1992-98, Centre for Scottish Public Policy, 1998; Member: Steering Committee, EdStart, 1990-98, Steering Group, Lothian Employers Network on Disabilities, 1991-98, Scottish Community Involvement Practitioners Forum, since 1993, Advisory Group, Edinburgh Common Purpose, since 1993, Steering Group, Fairbairn Fellow, 1994-97, Board of Management, Stevenson College, 1997-98, Advisory Group, SELLIC, 1997-98, Expert Panel on Information and Communications Technology for the Scottish Parliament, 1998-99, Advisory Group, Healthy Research Initiative, Edinburgh University, 1998-2000, Scottish Charities Appeals Advisory Committee, BBC Scotland, since 1998, National Action Group, Beattie Committee Report, since 2000; Chairman: Scottish Corporate/Voluntary Sector Think Tank, 1993-96, Edinburgh Telematics Partnership, since 1995, John Wheatley Centre's Telematics Advisory Committee for a Scottish Parliament, 1996-97, Scottish Development Centre for Mental Health, since 1997, The Beattie Committee, 1998-99, Scottish Further Education Funding Council, 1998-2001; Trustee, The Albion Trust, since 1994; Honorary Patron, Dynamic Earth Appeal, 1996-98; Vice Chairman, AGENDA: Social Responsibility in Scotland, since 2001. Address: (b.) IBM United Kingdom, Buchan House, 21 St. Andrew Square, Edinburgh EH2 1AY; T.-0131-558 4376; e-mail: robert_beattie@uk.ibm.com

Beattie, Professor Vivien Ann, MA (Hons), PhD, CA. Professor of Accountancy, University of Stirling, since 1997; Director of Research, Institute of Chartered Accountants of Scotland, since 1998; b. 9.5.58, Renfrew; m., John Stewart Beattie; 1 s. Educ. Renfrew High School; St. Andrews University. Student CA, Mann Judd Gordon, Chartered Accountants, Glasgow, 1980-83; Lecturer then Senior Lecturer, Portsmouth Polytechnic, 1983-86; Lecturer, Southampton University, 1987-93; Senior Lecturer then Reader, Stirling University, 1993-97. Recreations: hillwalking; tapestry; dogs. Address: (h.) 43 Menteith View, Dunblane FK15 0PD; T.-01786 825687; e-mail: V.A.Beattie@stirling.ac.uk

Beaumont, Professor Paul Reid, LLB, LLM. Professor of European Union and Private International Law, University of Aberdeen, since 1995 (Head, Law School, since 2000); b. 27.10.60, Hamilton; m., Marion; 1 s.; 1 d. Educ. Claremont High School, East Kilbride; Glasgow University; Dalhousie University, Canada. University of Aberdeen: Lecturer in Public Law, 1983-91, Senior Lecturer in Public Law, 1992-95. Academic Co-ordinator, Lawyers Christian Fellowship. Author and editor of several books. Recreations: golf; stamp collecting. Address: School of Law, University of Aberdeen, Aberdeen AB24 3UB; T.-01224 272439; e-mail: p.beaumont@abdn.ac.uk

Beaumont, Professor Phillip Barrington, BEcon (Hons), MEcon, PhD. Professor, Department of Management Studies, Glasgow University, since 1990; b. 13.10.49, Melbourne, Australia; m., Patricia Mary Ann McKinlay; 2 children. Educ. Camberwell High School, Melbourne; Monash University, Melbourne; Glasgow University. Glasgow University: Research Fellow, Lecturer, 1976-84; Senior Lecturer, 1984-86; Reader, 1986-90. Visiting Professor: Massachusetts Institute of Technology, Boston, 1982, McMaster University, 1986, Case Western Reserve University, 1988, Cornell University, 1990. Publications: Bargaining in the Public Sector, 1978; Safety at Work and the Trade Unions, 1981; Job Satisfaction in Public Administration, 1983; The Decline of Trade Union Organization, 1987; Change in Industrial Relations, 1990; Public Sector Industrial Relations, 1991; Human Resource Management, 1993; The Future of Employment Management, 1995. Recreations: tennis; badminton; cricket; shooting; fishing. Address: (b.) The University, Glasgow G12 8QQ; T.-0141-339 8855.

Beaumont, Professor Steven Peter, MA, PhD, FRSE, CEng, MIEE, MIEEE. Director, Institute for System Level Integration; Chief Executive, System Level Integration Ltd.; Professor of Nanoelectronics, Department of Electronics and Electrical Engineering, Glasgow University; b. 20.2.52, Norwich; m., Joanne Mary; 1 s.; 2 d. Educ. Norwich School; Corpus Christi College, Cambridge University. Research Fellow, Glasgow University, 1978-83; Barr and Stroud Lecturer in Electronics, Glasgow University, 1983-

86, Senior Lecturer, 1986-89; Director: Intellemetrics Ltd., 1982-90, Scot-Flow Dynamics Ltd; Electronics Scotland; CST Ltd. Recreations: walking; crofting. Address: (h.) 13 Kelvinside Terrace South, Glasgow G20 6DW; T.-0141-330 5380.

Bechhofer, Professor Frank, MA. University Fellow, Edinburgh University; b. 10.10.35, Nurnberg, Germany; m., Jean Barbara Conochie; 1 s.; 1 d. Educ. Nottingham High School; Queens' College, Cambridge. Junior Research Officer, Department of Applied Economics, Cambridge University, 1962-65; Edinburgh University: Lecturer in Sociology, 1965-71, Reader in Sociology, 1971-87, Director, Research Centre for Social Sciences, 1984-97, Professor of Social Research, 1988-97. Address: (h.) 51 Barnton Park View, Edinburgh EH4 6HH; T.-0131-339 4083; e-mail: frank@bechhofer.demon.co.uk

Beck, Professor Matthias Peter, MUP, MArch, PhD, FRSA. Professor of Risk Management, Glasgow Caledonian University, since 1999; b. 17.2.64, West Germany. Educ. Theodor Heuss Gymnasium; Universitat Stuttgart; University of Kansas; Massachusetts Institute of Technology. Lecturer in Economics and Economic History, Glasgow University, 1994-95; Lecturer in Economics, St Andrews University, 1995-98; Executive Co-Director, European Centre for Occupational Health Safety and the Environment, since 2000. Phi Kappa Phi (Honour Society), 1989; Vorhees Scholarship, 1990. Recreations: antique collecting and restoring. Address: (b.) Division of Risk, Glasgow Caledonian University, Cowcaddens Road, Glasgow G4 0BA; T.-0141-331 3152.

Beckett, Rev. David Mackay, BA, BD. Minister, Greyfriars Tolbooth and Highland Kirk, Edinburgh, since 1983; Moderator, Presbytery of Edinburgh, 1999-2000; b. 22.3.37, Glasgow; m., Rosalie Frances Neal; 2 s. Educ. Glenalmond; Trinity Hall, Cambridge; St. Andrews University. Assistant Minister, Dundee Parish Church (St. Mary's), 1963-66; Minister, Clark Memorial Church, Largs, 1966-83. Convener, Committee on Public Worship and Aids to Devotion, General Assembly, 1978-82; President, Church Service Society, 1986-88; Secretary, General Assembly Panel on Doctrine, 1987-95. Publication: The Lord's Supper, 1984. Address: (h.) 12 Tantallon Place, Edinburgh EH9 1NZ; T.-0131-667 8671.

Bedford, Professor Tim, BSc(Hons), MSc, PhD. Professor of Decision Making and Risk Analysis, Strathclyde University, since 2001; b. 14.4.60, London. Educ. Oulder Hill, Rochdale; Warwick University. Fellow, Kings College, Cambridge, 1984-87; Lecturer in Probability, Delft University of Technology, Netherlands, 1987-94; Senior Lecturer in Applications of Decision Theory, Delft University of Technology, 1994-2000. Publication; Probabilistic Risk Analysis: Foundations and Methods. Recreations: music; walking; family. Address: (b.) Department of Management Science, 40 George Street, Glasgow; T.-0141-548 2394.

Bedi, Tarlochan Singh, JP, MB, BS, FRCPsych, DPM. Consultant Psychiatrist and Honorary Clinical Senior Lecturer, Southern General Hospital, Glasgow, since 1980; b. India; m., Dr. T.H. Ratani; 1 s. Educ. Poona University, India. Junior House Officer, Aga Khan Hospital, Nairobi; Senior House Officer, Glenside and Barrow Hospital, Bristol; Registrar, Coneyhill Hospital, Gloucester; Senior Registrar, Gartnavel and Southern General Hospital, Glasgow; Consultant Psychiatrist, Woodilee Hospital, Lenzie. Past President: Scottish Asian Action Committee, Glasgow; Indian Social and Cultural Association, Glasgow; Indian Graduates Society, Glasgow. Recreations: music; photography; culinary arts. Address: 156 Prestonfield, Milngavie G62 7QA; T.-0141-570 0734.

Beevers, Professor Clifford, BSc, PhD, MILT. Professor of Mathematics, Heriot Watt University, since 1993; b. 4.9.44, Castleford; m., Elizabeth Ann; 2 d. Educ. Castleford Grammar School; Manchester University. Senior Lecturer, 1985; Director, CALM, 1985. Past Chairman, Edinburgh Branch, British Retinitis Pigmentosa Society. Recreations: walking; jogging; music; theatre. Address: (b.) Department of Mathematics, Heriot Watt University, Riccarton, Edinburgh EH14 4AS; T.-0131-451 3233; e-mail: C.E.Beevers@hw.ac.uk

Begg, Anne, MA. MP (Labour), Aberdeen South, since 1997; b. 6.12.55, Forfar. Educ. Brechin High School; University of Aberdeen; Aberdeen College of Education. Teacher of English and History, Webster's High, Kirriemuir, 1978-88; Assistant Principal Teacher, then Principal Teacher of English, Arbroath Academy, 1988-97. Disabled Scot of the Year, 1988. Recreations: cinema; theatre; reading; public speaking. Address: (b.) House of Commons, London SW1A 0AA; T.-0171-219 2140.

Begg, David, BA (Hons). Chairman, UK Commission of Integrated Transport; Professor of Transport, Robert Gordon University; Non-Executive Director, Shadow Strategic Authority; Member, Government Advisory Panel on Transport White Paper; Member, Northern Ireland Panel of Transport Experts; Board Member, Transport for London; b. 12.6.56, Edinburgh. Educ. Portobello High School. Management employee, BR, 1979-81; Lecturer in Economics, Napier University, 1981-91. Publications: articles on transport economics and local government finance. Recreations: golf; watching Hibernian F.C. Address: (b.) 5th Floor, Romney House, Tufton Street, London SW1P 3RA; e-mail: adrienne.tear@dtlr.gsi.gov.uk

Begg, Professor Hugh MacKemmie, MA, MA, PhD, DipTP, FRTPI. Consultant Economist and Chartered Planner; part-time Reporter, Scottish Executive Inquiry Reporters Unit; External Adjudicator, Scottish Enterprise; Visiting Professor, University of Abertay, Dundee; Member, Local Government Boundary Commission for Scotland; Member, Private Legislation Procedure (Scotland) Extra-Parliamentary Panel; Consultant, United Nations Development Project; b. 25.10.41, Glasgow; m., Jane Elizabeth Harrison; 2 d. Educ. High School of Glasgow; St. Andrews University; University of British Columbia. Lecturer in Political Economy, St. Andrews University; Research Fellow, Tayside Study; Lecturer in Economics, Dundee University; Assistant Director of Planning, Tayside Regional Council; Visiting Professor, Technical University of Nova Scotia; Consultant, UN Regional Development Project, Egypt and Saudi Arabia; Consultant, Scottish Office Industry Department, Scottish Office Agriculture and Forestry Department; Head, School of Town and Regional Planning, Dundee University. Recreations: local history; hill walking; rugby. Address: (h.) 4 Esplanade, Broughty Ferry, Dundee; T.-01382 779642.

Begg, Ian McKerron, DA, FRIAS, FSA Scot, FFCS. Architect (own practice), since 1983; b. 23.6.25, Kirkcaldy; 3 d. Educ. Kirkcaldy High School; Edinburgh College of Art. Partner, Robert Hurd & Partners, 1951-83; Interim Director, Edinburgh New Town Conservation Committee; Interim Director, Edinburgh Old Town Committee for Conservation and Renewal. Honorary Member, Saltire Society. Recreations: travel, particularly to Paris; supporting Scotland's identity. Address: Ravens'Craig, Plockton, Ross-shire IV52 8UB; T.-01599 544 265; e-mail: ian.begg@btinternet.com

Begg, William Kirkwood, OBE. Chairman and Managing Director, Begg, Cousland Holdings Ltd.; Chairman, Begg Cousland & Co. Ltd.; b. 5.2.34; m., Thia St Clair; 2 s.; 1 d. Educ. Glenalmond College. Former Chairman, Scottish Advisory Committee on Telecommunications; former Member, CBI SME Council; former Privy Council

Nominee to General Convocation, Strathclyde University; Director, Weavers' Society of Anderston; Founder Trustee, Dallas Benevolent Fund; Trustee, James Paterson Trust; Director (former Vice Chairman), The Wise Group; Director, Commercially Wise Ltd.; Director, Merchants' House of Glasgow; former Member, Scottish Industrial Development Advisory Board; former Member, CBI Council for Scotland. Recreations: sailing; shooting; DIY. Address: (h.) 3 Mirrlees Drive, Glasgow G12 0SH.

Beggs, Professor Jean Duthie, PhD, BSc, FRS, FRSE. Professor of Molecular Biology, Edinburgh University, since 1999; b. 16.4.50, Glasgow; m., Dr Ian Beggs; 2s. Educ. Glasgow High School for Girls; Glasgow University. Post-doctoral Fellow, University of Edinburgh, 1974-77; Post-doctoral Fellow, ARC Plant Breeding Institute, Cambridge, 1977-79; Lecturer, Department of Biochemistry, Imperial College of Science and Technology, London, 1979-85; Royal Society University Research Fellow, Edinburgh University, 1985-89; Royal Society Cephalosporin Fund Senior Research Fellow, University of Edinburgh. 1989-99; Edinburgh University Professorial Research Fellow, 1994-99; Beit Memorial Fellowship, 1976-79; Elected Member, EMBO, 1991; Member various committees of Royal Society (London and Edinburgh), Biochemical Society, RNA Society. Recreations: walking; skiing; scuba diving. Address: (b.) Institute of Cell and Molecular Biology, Edinburgh University, King's Buildings, Mayfield Road, Edinburgh, EH9 3JR; T.-0131-650 5351.

Belch, Professor Jill J. F., MB, ChB, FRCP, MD (Hons). Professor of Vascular Medicine and Biology, Dundee University, since 1993; Chairman, UK Forum on Angiology, since 1995; b. 22.10.52, Glasgow; m., Tom van der Ham; 1 s.; 3 d. Educ. Morrison's Academy, Crieff; University of Glasgow. University of Glasgow and Royal Infirmary: Research Fellow, 1980, Lecturer, 1984; University of Dundee and Ninewells Hospital: Senior Lecturer, 1987, Reader, 1990. Medical Adviser, Raynaud's and Scleroderma Association. Publications: over 200 peer-reviewed articles in scientific journals. Recreations: family; skiing. Address: (b.) University Department of Medicine, Ninewells Hospital, Dundee DD1 9SY; T.-01382 632457.

Belcher, Professor (Claire) Alice, BSocSc, MPhil, PhD, FCA. Professor of Law, Dundee University, since 2000; b. 11.12.59, Stoke-on-Trent; m., Peter; 3 s.; 3 d. Educ. Congleton County Grammar School for Girls; Keele University; Cambridge University; Manchester University. Trained as CA with Peat, Marwick, Mitchell & Co.; Lecturer in Accounting, then Lecturer in Law, Keele University, 1987-95; Senior Lecturer in Law, Dundee University, 1996-99. Publication: Corporate Rescue. Recreation: gardening. Address: (b.) Department of Law, Dundee University, Dundee DD1 4HN; T.-01382 344607.

Belcher, Ormonde Philip Paul Rashleigh, MB, BS, MD, FRCS. Consultant Cardiac Surgeon, since 1995; Senior Lecturer, Department of Cardiac Surgery, Glasgow University, since 1995; b. 28.4.49, London; m., Eleanor Susan Walsh; 1 s.; 2 d. Educ. Rugby School; Middlesex Hospital Medical School. Senior Registrar, National Heart and Chest Hospitals; Research Fellows, Medical College of Wisconsin; Research Fellow, Charing Cross and Westminster Medical School. Publications: papers in scientific and professional journals. Recreations: music; carpentry. Address: (h.) 23 Ledcameroch Crescent, Bearsden, Glasgow G61 4AD; T.-0141-931 5408.

Belfall, David J., BA (Hons). Head, Housing and Area Regeneration Group, Scottish Executive; b. 26.4.47, Colchester; m., Lorna McLaughlan; 1 s.; 1 d. Educ.

Colchester Royal Grammar School; St. John's College, Cambridge. Home Office, 1969-88 (Private Secretary to Permanent Under Secretary of State, 1973-74); Scottish Office, 1988-99: Under Secretary, Police and Emergency Services, 1988-91, Health Policy and Public Health, 1991-95; Head, Housing and Area Regeneration Group, 1995-99. Address: (b.) Scottish Executive, Victoria Quay, Edinburgh EH6 6QQ.

Belhaven and Stenton, 13rd Lord (Robert Anthony Carmichael Hamilton); b. 27.2.27. Succeeded to title, 1961.

Bell, Sheriff Andrew Montgomery, BL. Sheriff of Lothian and Borders, at Edinburgh, since 1990 (Sheriff of Glasgow and Strathkelvin, at Glasgow, 1984-90); b. 21.2.40, Edinburgh; m., Ann Margaret Robinson; 1 s.; 1 d. Educ. Royal High School, Edinburgh; Edinburgh University. Solicitor, 1961-74; called to Bar, 1975; Sheriff of South Strathclyde, Dumfries and Galloway, at Hamilton, 1979-84. Address: (h.) 5 York Road, Edinburgh EH5 3EJ; T.-0131-552 3859.

Bell, Arthur J.A., CBE, BSc, FRSA, FIDM. Writer and Lecturer; Marketing Consultant; former Chairman, Scotland Direct (Holdings) Ltd., and subsidiaries; b. 6.10.46, Brechin; m., G. Susan Bell; 4 c. Educ. Royal High School, Edinburgh; Edinburgh University. Chair, New Lanark Housing Association, 1979-99; Vice Chair, New Lanark Conservation Trust; Chairman, Food Trust of Scotland; former Editor, Small Business News; Editor, History of British Direct Marketing Association; three times parliamentary candidate. Publication: Complete Edinburgh Pub Guide/A Flavour of Edinburgh (Co-author). Address: (h.) Culter House, Biggar ML12 6PZ; 3 Chemin de la Serre, Haute Ville, Camares, Aveyron, France.

Bell, Professor Colin, BA, MSc, FRSE, FRSA, AcSS. Principal and Vice-Chancellor, University of Stirling, since 2001; b. 1.3.42, Enfield; m., Dr. Janette Webb; 1 s.; 3 d. Educ. Judd School, Tonbridge; Keele University; University College, Swansea. University of Essex, 1968-75; Professor of Sociology: University of New South Wales, 1975-80, University of Aston, 1980-84; Professor of Sociology and Vice Principal, University of Edinburgh, 1988-98; Vice-Chancellor, University of Bradford, 1998-2001. Publications: Middle Class Families, 1968; Community Studies (jointly), 1971; The Sociology of Community, 1974; Property, Paternalism and Power, 1978; Doing Sociological Research, 1978. Recreations: jazz; blues; domesticity. Address: (b.) Principal's Office, University of Stirling, Stirling FK9 4LA; T.-01786 467011; e-mail: principal@stirling.ac.uk

Bell, Colin John, MA (Hons), HonLLD (Aberdeen). Broadcaster; Journalist; Author; b. 1.4.38, London; m., Caroline Rose Bell; 1 s.; 3 d. Educ. St. Paul's School; King's College, Cambridge. Journalist, The Scotsman, 1960-62 and 1975-78; Journalist/Contributor, London Life, Sunday Times, Sunday Telegraph, Daily Mirror, Sunday Mail, etc.; Lecturer, Morley College, 1965-68; College Supervisor, King's College, Cambridge, 1968-75; Parliamentary candidate (SNP), West Edinburgh, 1979; European Parliamentary candidate (SNP), North East Scotland, 1979; Vice-Chairman, SNP, 1978-84; Campaign Director, Euro Election, 1984; a Senior Fellow, the 21st Century Trust, 1990; Rector, Aberdeen University, 1991-93. Publications: City Fathers, 1969; Boswell's Johnson, 1971; Scotch Whisky, 1985; Radical Alternative (Contributor), 1978; The Times Reports (Series) (Editor); Scotland's Century, 1999. Recreations: jazz; Scottish history. Address: (h.) Cockburnhill, Balerno, Midlothian.

Bell, Professor David Nevin Fraser, MA, MSc, PhD. Professor of Economics, Stirling University, since 1990; Co-Director, Scottish Economic Policy Network, since

2000; b. 16.12.51, Inverness; 1 s.; 1 d. Educ. Dornoch Academy; Aberdeen University; London School of Economics. Lecturer in Economics, St Andrews University, 1974-75; Research Fellow, Fraser of Allander Institute, Strathclyde University, 1975-83; Research Fellow, Macromodelling Bureau, 1983-85; Lecturer in Economics, Glasgow University, 1985-90. Member, Care Development Group, Scotstat. Recreations: golf; walking; bird-watching; photography. Address: (b.) Department of Economics, Stirling University, Stirling FK9 4LA; T.-01786 467486.

Bell, Donald Atkinson, MSc, BSc, PhD, FIMechE, CEng, MIEE, FBCS. Director, Marchland Consulting Ltd., since 1990 (Director, National Engineering Laboratory, 1983-90); b. 28.5.41, Belfast; m., Joyce Louisa Godber; 2 s. Educ. Royal Belfast Academical Institution; Queen's University, Belfast; Southampton University; Glasgow University. National Physical Laboratory, Teddington, 1966-77; Electronics Applications Division, Department of Industry, 1978-82. Address: (b.) Marchland Consulting Ltd., 108 East Kilbride Road, Glasgow G76 8JF; T.-0141-644 2000.

Bell, George Armour, OBE, JP, BSc, MB, ChB, FFCS. Former Chairman, Monklands and Bellshill Hospitals NHS Trust; Vice President, Tenovus-Scotland; b. 8.7.20, Bellshill; m., Elizabeth Davidson Porteous (deceased); 2 s. Educ. Bellshill Academy; Glasgow University. War Service, 609 Squadron – Normandy to Germany, SMO Prestwick, SMO Brize Norton, RAF. Retired General Practitioner, Bellshill; former Member, Lanarkshire Health Board; founder Chairman, Crime Prevention Panel, Bellshill and District; former Red Cross Detachment Medical Officer, Bellshill; founder Chairman, Community Council for Mossend; Honorary Member, Rotary; Life Member, BMA; Life Member, RAF Association. Publication: To Live Among Heroes, 2001. Address: (h.) 16 Imlach Place, Parkside Gardens, Motherwell ML1 3FD.

Bell, Graham, MBChB, FRCS, ChM. Consultant Surgeon, Inverclyde Royal Hospital, since 1973; b. 9.8.36, Glasgow; 4 s. Educ. Kelvinside Academy; Glasgow University. Lecturer in Surgery, Department of Surgery, Glasgow Royal Infirmary, 1963-73. Recreations: golfing; fishing. Address: (h.) 11 Dalziel Drive, Glasgow G41 4JA; T.-0141-427 0233.

Bell, G. Susan, ACIS, FSA (Scot), MIDM; b. 31.8.46; m., Arthur J.A. Bell, CBE; 2 s.; 2 d. Educ. College of Commerce, Glasgow. Investment Analyst, Edinburgh, 1970-74; Conservative Parliamentary candidate: Motherwell, 1970, Caithness & Sutherland, February 1974; Chairman, Conservative Candidates Association, 1971-74; joined Liberal Democrats, 1997; Member, Council, CBI Scotland, 1986-93; Board Member: Scottish Tourist Board, 1983-88, SCOTVEC, 1987-95, Southern General Hospital Trust, 1993-95; Member, Council, National Trust for Scotland, 1983-88; former Chair, Women into Business; Board Member, FEDMA (European Direct Marketing Association). Recreations: garden; reading. Address: (h.) Culter House, Coulter, Biggar; T.-01899 220064; 3 Chemin de la Serre, 12360 Camarès, France 12.

Bell, Robin, MA, MSc. Poet and Broadcaster; b. 4.1.45, Dundee; 2 d. Educ. Morrison's Academy, Crieff; St. Andrews University; Perugia University, Italy; Union College, New York; Columbia University, New York. Formerly: Director of Information, City University of New York, Regional Opportunity Program; Assistant Professor, John Jay College of Criminal Justice, City University of New York; Member, US Office of Education Task Force in Educational Technology; Audio-Visual Editor, Oxford University Press; Editor, Guidebook series to Ancient Monuments of Scotland; Secretary, Poetry Association of Scotland. Scottish Radio and Television Industries Award for Best Radio Feature, 1984; Sony Award, Best British Radio Documentary, 1985. Publications: The Invisible Mirror; Culdee, Culdee; Sawing Logs; Strathinver: A Portrait Album 1945-53; Collected Poems of James Graham, Marquis of Montrose (Editor); Radio Poems; The Best of Scottish Poetry; Bittersweet Within My Heart: collected poems of Mary Queen of Scots (Translator/Editor); Scanning the Forth Bridge; Le Château des Enfants. Address: (h.) The Orchard, Muirton, Auchterarder PH3 1ND.

Bellany, Dr John, CBE (1994), RA; b. June, 1942, Port Seton; m., 1, Helen Margaret Percy; 2, Juliet Gray Lister (deceased); 3, for second time, Helen Margaret Bellany; 2 s.; 1 d. Educ. Cockenzie Public School; Preston Lodge, Prestonpans; Edinburgh College of Art; Royal College of Art, London. Lecturer in Fine Art, Winchester School of Art, 1969-73; Head, Faculty of Painting, Croydon College of Art, 1973-78; Visiting Lecturer in Painting, R.C.A., 1975-85; Lecturer in Fine Art, Goldsmiths College, London University, 1978-84; elected Fellow Commoner, Trinity Hall, Cambridge, 1988; lived and painted in Mexico, 1996; one-man exhibitions include: Arts Council touring show; Rosa Esman Gallery, New York; Christine Abrahams Gallery, Melbourne; Ikon Gallery, Birmingham; Walker Art Gallery, Liverpool; Roslyn Oxley Gallery, Sydney; National Portrait Gallery, London; Galerie Krikhar, Amsterdam; Fischer Fine Art, London; retrospective — Scottish National Gallery of Modern Art; Serpentine Gallery, London; Kimsthalle, Hamburg; Museum Ostral, Dortmund; Ruth Siegel Gallery, New York; Raab Gallery, Berlin; Fitzwilliam Museum, Cambridge; Kelvingrove Museum and Art Gallery (50th birthday tribute); Beaux Arts Gallery, Berkeley Square Gallery, London; Edinburgh Festival, 1997; elected ARA, 1987; RA, 1992; Hon. RSA, 1987; elected Senior Fellow, Royal College of Art, London, 1999; joint 1st prize, Athena International Award, 1985; honorary doctorates, Edinburgh University, 1996, Heriot-Watt University, 1998. Recreation: motoring around Europe in search of beauty.

Bellars, Wendy Ann, MA (Hons), Dip Ed, PGCE. Principal, St. Leonards School, St Andrews, since 2001; b. 25.12.60, Glasgow; m., Bryan Perrey Bellars. Educ. Hillhead High School, Glasgow, Glasgow University; Jordanhill College, Glasgow. Assistant Teacher: Renfrew High School, 1983-85; Gordonstoun School, Moray, 1985-88; King's School Chester: Assistant Teacher; Head of English, 1988-95; Deputy Head, Bishop's Stortford College, Hertfordshire, 1995-2000; HMC/ISI Inspector, since 1994. Recreations: reading; theatre; playing and listening to music; walking the dogs; being with friends. Address (b.) St. Leonards House, St Andrews, Fife, KY16 9QJ; T.-01334 472126; e-mail: wab@stleonards-fife.org

Belton, Professor Valerie, PhD, MA, BSc (Hons). Professor of Management Science, University of Strathclyde, since 1999 (Vice-Dean Academic, Strathclyde Business School, since 2001); b. 9.8.56, Rotherham. Educ. Wath upon Dearne School; Durham University; Lancaster University, Cambridge University. Operational Research Analyst, Civil Aviation Authority; Academic, University of Kent, 1984-88; Academic, University of Strathclyde, since 1988. Chair, International Society of Multicriteria Decision Making; Editor, Journal of Multicriteria Decision Analysis; author of a book and many academic articles. Recreations: orienteering; mountain biking. Address: (b.) University of Strathclyde, Management Science, 40 George Street, Glasgow G1 1QE; T.-0141-548 3615; e-mail: val@mansci.strath.ac.uk

Beltrami, Joseph, SSC, BL, NP. Solicitor/Advocate (Beltrami & Co.); b. 15.5.32, Rutherglen; m., Brigid D.; 3 s. Educ. St. Aloysius College, Glasgow; Glasgow University. Intelligence Corps, 1954-56 (Sgt.); qualified as Solicitor, 1956; specialised in criminal law; has instructed in more than 500 murder cases; closely associated with two cases of Royal Pardon; in first batch of Solicitor/Advocates to have rights of audience in High Court and Court of Criminal Appeal. Chairman, soccer testimonials: Jim Johnstone and Bobby Lennox, 1976; Danny McGrain, 1980. Publications: The Defender, 1980; Glasgow - A Celebration (Contributor), 1984; Tales of the Suspected, 1988; A Deadly Innocence, 1989; A Scottish Childhood (Contributor), 1998. Recreations: bowls; soccer; snooker; writing; boxing. Address: (h.) 12 Valence Tower, Regents Gate, Bothwell, Lanarkshire; T.-01698 817841.

Bendall, Ian, BA, PGCE, MA. Rector and Principal, Morrison's Academy, since 2001; b. 14.11.58, Portsmouth.; m., Kathryn; 3 s.; 1 d. Educ. Crypt Grammar School, Gloucester; University of Reading. Career: King William's College, Isle of Man, 1981-86; Head of Geography and Boarding Housemaster, Reading Blue Coat School, 1986-96; Deputy Headmaster, Queen Elizabeth's Hospital, Bristol, 1996-2001. Recreations: rugby (now spectator); sailing; hillwalking; landscape photography. Address: (b.) Morrison's Academy, Ferntower Road, Crieff, Perthshire PH7 3AN; T.-01764 653885; e-mail: principal@morrisons.pkc.sch.uk

Benedetti, Giovanni. Chairman: Benedetti International Plc, Pendigo Ltd., Wallace Cameron & Co. Ltd., Wrap Film Systems Ltd., GB Consulting and Management Services Ltd., KSS Supplies; Director, Prince's Scottish Youth Business Trust; b. 6.3.43, Italy; m., Francesca; 2 d. Arrived in Britain aged 11; worked in uncle's cafe until age of 19; started his own business with two dry-cleaning shops; opened his first factory in Ardrossan, 1970; company bought by BET, 1989. Recreations: skiing; sailing.

Bennet, George Charters, BSc, MBChB, FRCS. Consultant Orthopaedic Surgeon, Royal Hospital for Sick Children, Glasgow, since 1982; President, British Society for Children's Orthopaedic Surgery; b. 8.8.46, Edinburgh; m., Louise Spilsbury; 3 s. Educ. Holy Cross Academy; University of Edinburgh. Junior surgical posts, Edinburgh, Sheffield, London; orthopaedic training, Southampton, London, Oxford, Toronto. Honorary Consultant in paediatric orthopaedic surgery to Army; Member, Council, Medical and Dental Defence Union of Scotland. Books, chapters and scientific papers published on orthopaedic surgery and trauma in childhood. Recreations: rugby union; fishing; reading. Address: Department of Orthopaedic Surgery, Royal Hospital for Sick Children, Glasgow G3 8SJ; T.-0141-201 0275.

Bennett, David Andrew, MA, LLB, WS, NP. Partner, Bennett & Robertson, Solicitors, Edinburgh, since 1964; b. 27.3.38, Edinburgh; m., Marion Miller Park; 2 d. Educ. Melville College, Edinburgh; Fettes College, Edinburgh; Edinburgh University. Director, Jordans (Scotland) Ltd.; Member, Council, Law Society of Scotland, 1984-90. Session Clerk, Liberton Kirk, since 1975; Scottish Editor, Palmer's Company Law, since 1970, and Gore-Browne on Companies, since 1975. Recreations: most sports and arts. Address: (b.) 16 Walker Street, Edinburgh EH3 7NN; T.-0131-225 4001; e-mail:David-Bennett@benrob.co.uk

Bennett, Helen Margaret, PhD, FSA Scot. Crafts Director, Scottish Arts Council, since 1993; Group Director, Creative Arts, 1996-2001; Vice-President, World Crafts Council – Europe, since 2000; b. 25.6.48, Newark; m., Philip Edwin Bennett; 1 d. Educ. Lilley and Stone High School for Girls, Newark; Exeter University; Edinburgh University. Edinburgh Common Purpose Graduate, 1996. Assistant Curator, Borough of Weston-super-Mare, 1969-71; Curator of Agricultural and Social History, Bristol City Museums, 1971-72; Research Assistant, Costume and Textiles, National Museum of Antiquities of Scotland, 1974-81; freelance arts administrator, 1984-88; Head of Crafts Division, Scottish Development Agency, 1989-91;

freelance cultural consultant, 1991-93. Governor, Edinburgh College of Art, 1992-2000. Recreations: walking; gardening; textile crafts. Address: (b.) 12 Manor Place, Edinburgh EH3 7DD; T.-0131-226 6051; e-mail: helen.bennett@scottisharts.org.uk

Bennett, Robin Alexander George, MA, LLB, MSI. Solicitor, Bennetts, Cupar, since 1992; b. 6.6.40, Edinburgh; m., Mary Funk; 2 d. Educ. Hillhead High School, Glasgow; Glasgow University. Assistant: Harrisons and Crosfield, Malaysia and Brunei, 1965-78, Drummond Johnstone and Grosset, Cupar, 1978-80; Solicitor (Partner): Drummond Cook and Mackintosh, Cupar, 1980-90, Wallace and Bennett, 1990-92. Chairman, Tranquilliser Addiction Solicitors Group, 1988-90; Founder/Secretary, Scottish TSB Depositors Association, 1986; Chairman, Ceres and District Community Council, 1980-82 and 1993-98; Vice Convener, Scottish Legal Action Group, 1989-95; Honorary Sheriff, Cupar, since 1991. Recreations: hillwalking; water gardening. Address: (h.) Sandakan, Curling Pond Road, Ceres, Fife KY15 5NB; T.-01334 828452.

Bennett, Sigurdur Arthur, LLB(Hons). Advocate, since 1982; b. 21.9.57, Edinburgh. Educ. Edinburgh Academy; Edinburgh University. Standing Junior Counsel, Ministry of Defence (RAF), 1991-97. Muirhead Prize for Civil Law, 1976; Member, Faculty Council, 1992-96. Publications: Divorce in the Sheriff Court; Personal Injury Damages in Scotland; Style Writs for the Sheriff Court. Address: 3 Royal Circus, Edinburgh EH3 6TL; T.-0131-225 9904; e-mail: sigbennett@aol.com

Bennett, William Walter, BSc, BPhil. Director, Edinburgh Association of Mental Health, since 2000; b. 19.11.44; m., Christine; 1 s.; 2 d. Educ. Ashton-under-Lyne Grammar School; Edinburgh University. Social Worker and Team Leader, 1970-83; Adviser (Social Work), Scottish Office, 1983-88; Director, NCH in Scotland, 1988-91; Director of Social Work, Shetland, 1991-99; Interim Chief Executive, Shetland Islands Council, 1999. Recreations: walking; fitness training; drama and shows; reading; wine. Address: (h.) 1 St. Fillan's Terrace, Edinburgh EH10 5NH; T.-0131-447 8755; e-mail: banska.bill@virgin.net

Bennie, Norma, DipCOT, MBE. Vice Chairman, Mental Welfare Commission (Commissioner, since 1994); has worked in healthcare management, Renfrewshire and Inverclyde Primary Care Trust, since 1993; b. 11.11.46, Beith; m., Ernest H. Bennie; 2 s.; 1 d. Educ. Spier's School, Beith; Glasgow School of Occupational Therapy. Occupational Therapist, 1968-93. Recreations: walking; sailing; reading. Address: (b.) Merchiston Hospital, Brookfield, By Johnstone PA5 8TY; T.-01505 384010.

Bennison, Dr Jennifer Marion, MA, MBBChir, MRCGP. General Practitioner; GP Principal, Rose Garden Medical Centre, Edinburgh, since 1998; Honorary Secretary, Scottish Council, Royal College of General Practitioners; b. Essex; m., Dr Seth Armitage; 1 s.; 2 d. Educ. Hertfordshire and Essex High School for Girls; Corpus Christi College, Cambridge; Royal Free Hospital School of Medicine, London. GP Principal, Leith Walk Surgery, Edinburgh, 1993-98; Director, Phased Evaluation Programme, RCGP Scotland, since 1999. Committee Member, Edinburgh Bach Society Choir. Recreations: walking; singing. Address: (b.) Rose Garden Medical Centre, 4 Mill Lane, Leith, Edinburgh EH6 6TZ; T.-0131-554 1274.

Bentley, Professor Michael, BA, PhD, FRHistS. Professor of Modern History, St Andrews University, since 1995; b. 12.8.48, Rotherham; 1 s.; 1 d. Educ. Oakwood School, Rotherham; Sheffield University; St John's College, Cambridge. Lecturer in History,

Sheffield University, 1971-95. Publications: The Liberal Mind; Politics without Democracy; Climax of Liberal Politics; Companion to Historiography; Lord Salisbury's World. Recreations: reading; golf. Address: (b.) Department of Modern History, St Andrews University, St Andrews KY16 9AL; T.-01334 462895.

Benton, David Charles, RGN, RMN, BSc, MPhil. Chief Executive, National Board for Nursing, Midwifery and Health Visiting for Scotland, since 1998; b. 29.10.57, Torphins; m., (Elizabeth) Denise MacRae; 2 s.; 1 d. Educ. Elgin Academy; Robert Gordon's Institute of Technology; Dundee Institute of Technology; Highland College of Nursing and Midwifery. Staff Nurse then Charge Nurse (acute psychiatry and drug abuse services), Craig Duncan Hospital, Inverness; District Research Nurse, North East Essex Health Authority; Director of Quality and Nurse Advisor, Tower Hamlets Health Authority, subsequently East London and the City Health Authority, 1992-95; Regional Nurse Director, NHS Executive (Northern and Yorkshire), 1995-98. Visiting Professor of Nursing Policy, University of Northumbria, 1996; Member, ETA IOTA Chapter, Sigma Theta Tau. Dr George MacKenzie Award, 1983; Nursing Standard Leadership Award, 1993; Nursing Times 3M Award, 1994; Nuffield Travelling Fellow, 1999; Fellow, Florence Nightingale Foundation, 2001. Recreations: walking; taekwon-do. Address: (h.) 35 Whitehaugh Park, Peebles EH45 9DB; T.-0172 172 2735.

Bermudez, Professor Jose Luis, MA (Cantab), PhD (Cantab). Professor of Philosophy, Stirling University, since 2001; b. 17.2.67, Bogota, Colombia. Educ. St Paul's School, London; King's College, Cambridge. British Academy postdoctoral research, 1993-96; Fellow, Cambridge University, 1996-99; Lecturer, Stirling University, 1999-2000. Publications: The Body and The Self (Co-Editor); The Paradox of Self-Consciousness; Reason and Nature; Thinking Without Words. Recreations: climbing; aviation. Address: (b.) Department of Philosophy, Stirling University, Stirling FK9 4LA.

Berry, Professor Christopher Jon, BA, PhD. Professor of Political Theory, University of Glasgow, since 1995 (Head, Department of Politics, since 1998); b. 19.6.46, St. Helens; m., Christine Emma, 2 s. Educ. Upholland Grammar School; Nottingham University; London School of Economics. Lecturer, then Senior Lecturer, then Reader, Department of Politics, University of Glasgow. Publications: five books, many articles. Recreations: reading contemporary literature; walking. Address: (b.) Adam Smith Building, University of Glasgow, Glasgow G12 8RT; T.-0141-330 5064; e-mail: c.j.berry@socsci.gla.ac.uk

Berry, Graham, CA. Director, Scottish Arts Council, since 2002; b. 12.1.45, Edinburgh; 1 s.; 1 d. Educ. Royal High School, Edinburgh; CA Apprentice, Edinburgh, 1963-68; CA, Price Waterhouse, London, 1968-70; Divisional Chief Accountant, Trust House Forte, London, 1970-74; Company Secretary, 1974-86: Scottish Film Council, Scottish Council for Educational Technology; Glasgow Film Theatre, Filmhouse Ltd., Scetlander Ltd.; Finance Officer, Stirling University, 1986-89; Depute Director and Head of Funding and Resources, Scottish Arts Council, 1989-2002. Recreations: mountaineering; photography. Address: (b.) Scottish Arts Council, 12 Manor Place, Edinburgh EH3 7DD; T.-0131-226 6051; e-mail: graham.berry@scottisharts.org.uk

Berry, John, CBE (1968), DL (Fife) (1969), BA (Cantab), MA (Cantab), PhD (St. Andrews) Hon. LLD Dundee (1970), HonDSc St. Andrews (1991), FRSE (1936). Adviser and Consultant on environmental and wildlife conservation (retired); b. 5.8.07, Edinburgh; m., Hon. Bride Fremantle; 2 s.; 1 d. Educ. Ardvreck School, Crieff; Eton College; Trinity College, Cambridge. Salmon Research Officer, Fishery Board for Scotland, 1930-31; Biological Research Station, University College, Southampton: Research Officer, 1932-36; Director, 1936-39; Chief Press Censor for Scotland, 1940-44; Biologist and Information Officer, North of Scotland Hydro-Electric Board, 1944-49; Environment Conservation Adviser, 1944-89 (to South of Scotland Electricity Board, 1969-89, to Scottish Landowners Federation, 1984-87); Director of Nature Conservation in Scotland, 1949-67; consultancy work 1968-90. Honorary Life Member, Swiss League for Protection of Nature, 1946; founder Member (1948), International Union for Conservation of Natural Resources and first President, International Union Commission on Ecology; Member, Executive Board, International Waterfowl Research Bureau, 1963-72; Honorary Corresponding Member, Danish Natural History Society, since 1957; Vice-President and Honorary Life Fellow, Royal Zoological Society of Scotland, since 1959; Honorary Life Fellow: Wildfowl Trust, 1983; Glasgow Natural History Society, 1951; Member, Dundee University Court, 1970-78; Director, British Pavilion, Expo 71, Budapest; Member, Scottish Marine Biological Association, 1947-71 (Council, 1947-54 and 1957-66). Recreations: natural history (especially insects, water birds and fish); music. Address: (h.) The Garden House, Tayfield, Newport-on-Tay, Fife DD6 8HA; T.-01382 543118.

Berry, William, MA, LLB, WS, NP. Chairman, Murray Beith Murray, WS, Edinburgh; Chairman, Inchcape Family Investments Ltd.; Director: Scottish American Investment Co. Plc, Fleming Continental European Investment Trust Plc, Alliance Trust plc, Dawnfresh Seafoods Ltd., Inchcape Family Investments Ltd., and other companies; formerly Director (Chairman, 1993-99), Scottish Life Assurance Co.; b. 26.9.39, Newport-on-Tay; m., Elizabeth Margery Warner; 2 s. Educ. Ardvreck, Crieff; Eton College; St. Andrews University; Edinburgh University. Interests in farming, forestry, etc. Depute Chairman, Edinburgh Festival Society, 1985-89; Member Council/Board, New Town Concerts Society Ltd.; Member, St. Andrews University Court. Performer in three records of Scottish country dance music. Recreations: music; shooting; forestry; conservation. Address: (b.) 39 Castle Street, Edinburgh EH2 3BH; T.-0131-225 1200.

Betts, Michael William, CBE, FCIT, FILT. Traffic Commissioner for Scotland, since 1992; Senior Traffic Commissioner, Great Britain, since 1996; b. 3.3.38, Bournemouth; m., Margaret Irene Lussi; 2 d. Educ. Hardye's School, Dorchester; Royal Military Academy, Sandhurst. Commissioned Royal Army Service Corps, 1957; Brigadier Logistics, British Army of the Rhine, 1987-90; Director of Movements (Army), Ministry of Defence, 1991-92; ADC to HM The Queen, 1990-92. Freeman, City of London, 1993; Freeman and Liveryman, Worshipful Company of Carmen, 1993; Member, National Transport Forum for Scotland; Leader, Edinburgh Members Group, RSPB. Recreations: sailing; skiing; bird-watching. Address: (b.) Scottish Traffic Area Office, Floor J, Argyle House, 3 Lady Lawson Street, Edinburgh EH3 9SE; T.-0131-200 4905.

Bevan, John Stuart, BSc (Hons), MBChB (Hons), MD, FRCP (Edin). Consultant Physician and Endocrinologist, Aberdeen Royal Infirmary, since 1991; Honorary Senior Clinical Lecturer, Aberdeen University, since 1991; Secretary, Clinical Committee, Society for Endocrinology, 1997-2000; Visiting Endocrinologist to Orkney Islands, since 1994; b. 18.9.53, Portsmouth; m., Sheena Mary; 2 s.; 2 d. Educ. Portsmouth Northern Grammar School; Dunfermline High School; Edinburgh University. Registrar in Endocrinology, Radcliffe Infirmary, Oxford, 1981-83; Medical Research Council Training Fellow in Endocrinology, Oxford, 1984-86; Senior Registrar in Medicine and Endocrinology, University Hospital of Wales, Cardiff, 1987-90; Associate Editor, Clinical Endocrinology, since 1994; Member, Specialist Advisory Committee for Endocrinology and Diabetes, since 1998. Publications: papers on clinical neuroendocrinology, particularly the treatment of human pituitary tumours. Recreations: cricket; guitar; ornithology. Address: (b.) Department of Endocrinology, Aberdeen Royal Infirmary, Wards 27/28, Foresterhill, Aberdeen AB25 2ZN; T.-01224 554437; e-mail: j.s.bevan@arh.grampian.scot.nhs.uk

Beveridge, John Mackenzie, BSc (Hons), FREHIS. Director of Public Affairs and Corporate Communications, Scottish Environment Protection Agency, since 2001; b. 27.2.53, Glasgow; m., Donna; 2 d. Educ. Camphill High School, Paisley; University of Strathclyde. Depute Director, Environmental Services, Argyll and Bute District Council, 1987-90; Director of Environmental Protection and Leisure Services, Dumbarton District Council, 1990-95; Director, West Region, Scottish Environment Protection Agency, 1995-2001. Royal Environmental Health Institute of Scotland: President, 1994-95, Member, Executive Council, since 1985. Director, Loch Lomond Steamship Company. Address: (b.) SEPA, Erskine Court, Castle Business Park, Stirling FK9 4TR; T.-01786 457700.

Beveridge, Stuart Gordon Nicholas, LLB (Hons), DipLP, NP. Partner, Grant Smith Law Practice, since 2001; b. 19.3.68, Edinburgh. Educ. George Heriot's School; Daniel Stewart's and Melville College; Edinburgh University. Campbell Smith and Co., Solicitors, Edinburgh; Legal Adviser, Citizen's Advice Bureau, Edinburgh; Aberdein Considine and Co., Aberdeen (Partner, since 1998). President, Aberdeen Bar Association, 2001-02 (Committee Member, since 1995). Recreations: wine; cooking; cinema; motorcycles. Address: (b.) 7 Waverly Place, Aberdeen AB10 1XK; T.-01224 621620.

Bewsher, Colonel Harold Frederick, LVO, OBE. Chairman, The Atlantic Salmon Trust, since 1995; Member, Executive Committee, Association of Deer Management Groups in Scotland, since 1998; Chairman, The Airborne Initiative (Scotland) Ltd., 1995-98; Brigadier, The Queen's Bodyguard for Scotland, since 1996 (Secretary, 1982-94); b. 13.1.29, Glasgow; m., Susan Elizabeth Cruickshank; 2 s. Educ. Merchiston Castle School; Royal Technical College; Glasgow University; Royal Military Academy, Sandhurst. Regular Army, The Royal Scots, 1949-72; Director-General, Scotch Whisky Association, 1973-94. Chairman: New Club, Edinburgh, 1981-82, Scottish Society for the Employment of Ex-Regular Soldiers, Sailors and Airmen, 1973-83; Freeman, City of London, 1992; Liveryman, Worshipful Company of Distillers, 1993. Recreations: outdoors — salmon fishing, field sports. Address: (b.) 3 Blacket Place, Edinburgh EH9 1RJ; T.-0131-667 4600.

Bhopal, Professor Raj Singh, CBE, BSc, MBChB, MD, MPH, FFPHM, FRCP (Edin). Bruce and John Usher Chair of Public Health, University of Edinburgh, since 1999 (Head, Department of Community Health Sciences); Honorary Consultant in Public Health Medicine, Lothian Health Board, since 1999; b. 10.4.53, Moga, Punjab, India; m., Roma; 4 s. Educ. University of Edinburgh; University of Glasgow. House Officer/Senior House Officer, medicine and surgery, 1978-82; Trainee GP, 1980; Registrar/Senior Registrar/Lecturer in Public Health Medicine, 1983-88; Senior Lecturer/Honorary Consultant in Public Health Medicine, 1988-91; Professor of Epidemiology and Public Health, University of Newcastle upon Tyne, 1991-99 (Head, Department of Epidemiology and Public Health); Non-Executive Director (Vice-Chairman), Newcastle and North Tyneside Health Authority, 1992-96; Non-Executive Director, Health Education Authority, 1998-99. Publications: over 100 papers in journals and chapters in books on Legionnaires' disease, environmental epidemiology, primary care, ethnicity and health, application of epidemiology in public health and health care. Recreations: chess; hill climbing; photography; travel;

music; reading. Address: (b.) Public Health Sciences, University of Edinburgh, Medical School, Teviot Place, Edinburgh EH8 9AG; T.-0131-650 3216.

Biddulph, 5th Lord (Anthony Nicholas Colin). Interior Designer and Sporting Manager; b. 8.4.59; m., Hon. Sian Gibson-Watt; 2 s. Educ. Cheltenham; RAC, Cirencester. Recreations: shooting; design; fishing; skiing. Address: Address: (h.) Makerstoun, Kelso TD5 7PA; T.-01573 460 234; 8 Orbel Street, London SW11 3NZ; T.-020 7228 9865.

Biggart, Thomas Norman, CBE (1984), WS, MA, LLB. Partner, Biggart Baillie & Gifford, Solicitors, Glasgow and Edinburgh, 1959-95; b. 24.1.30; m., Eileen Jean Anne Gemmell; 1 s.; 1 d. Educ. Morrison's Academy, Crieff; Glasgow University. Royal Navy, 1954-56 (Sub-Lt., RNVR). Law Society of Scotland: Council Member, 1977-86; Vice-President, 1981-82; President, 1982-83; President, Business Archives Council, Scotland, 1977-86; Member, Executive, Scottish Council (Development and Industry), 1984-94; Member: Scottish Tertiary Education Advisory Council, 1984-87, Scottish Records Advisory Council, 1985-91; Director: Clydesdale Bank, 1985-97; Independent Insurance Group, 1986-2000 (Chairman, 1989-93); Chairman, Beechwood, Glasgow, 1989-97; Trustee, Scottish Civic Trust, 1989-97; Member, Council on Tribunals (Chairman, Scottish Committee), 1990-98; Honorary Member, American Bar Association, 1982; OStJ, 1968. Recreations: golf; hill-walking. Address: (h.) Gailes, Kilmacolm, Renfrewshire PA13 4LZ; T.-0150 587 2645.

Bills, David James, CBE, FICF, MIFA, BSc(For). Director General and Deputy Chairman, Forestry Commission, since 1995; b. 9.2.48, Australia; m., Michele Hartam-Ellis; 1 s.; 2 d. Educ. University of Tasmania; Australian National University. Research Scientist, Forest Research Institute (Australia); Department of Agriculture, Australian Government; various forestry positions, Associated Pulp and Paper Mills, becoming General Manager, North Forest Products (North Ltd.). Past President, National Association of Forest Industries, Australia; former Vice-President, Australian Forest Development Institute. Recreations: sailing; ski-ing; classic cars; music. Address: (h.) 17 Lansdowne Crescent, Edinburgh EH12 5EH; T.-0131-538 4926.

Binnie, Frank Hugh. Chairman, ScotiX, The Scottish Internet Exchange, since 1999; Chief Executive Officer, Scotlandis; Executive Chair, Scotnom Ltd., since 2000; Senior Executives Career and Training Consultant, since 1997; former Chief Executive, The Caledonian Foundation; b. 1.3.50, Edinburgh; m., Fiona Margaret McLean Nicolson (née Hart); m., 1 d. Educ. Loughborough Grammar; De Montfort University. Design Management Trainee, Corahs Textiles, Leicester, 1970-73; Manufacturing Manager, Floreal Knitwear, Mauritius, 1973-76; Sales Manager, Kemptons Knitwear, Leicester, 1976-79; General Manager Design, Texport Unilever, 1979-82; Manufacturing Manager, Kilspindie Knitwear, 1982-85; Director and Company Secretary, Midlothian Enterprise, 1985-88; Managing Director, Perkins, Hodgkinson and Gillibrand (Coxmore plc), 1988-90; Chief Executive, Scottish Design (formerly Director, The Design Council Scotland), 1990-96. External Assessor, MBA, University of Westminster; Assessor, Management Course, De Montfort University; Member: Licensing Executive, Coutts Scottish Advisory Committee, Institute of Directors, Scottish Council Development and Industry, Guid Club; Visiting Professor in Engineering Design, Strathclyde University; Fellow, Chartered Society of Designers; Fellow, Royal Society of Arts, Design and Manufacturing; Chairman, Textile Institute Fashion, Product Design and Marketing Group. Recreations: yachting; chess; classic cars; internet. Address: (b.) Binnie International, 80 Berkeley Street, Glasgow G3 7DS; T.-0141-572 1098.

Birchall, Rosalind Mary. Trustee for Scotland, British Red Cross, since 2001; Chairman, Scottish Council, British Red Cross, since 1998; b. 25.8.41, Edinburgh; m., Julian D. Birchall; 1s.; 1d. Educ. St Mary's School. Calne, Wiltshire; studied history of Art and French in France. Personal Assistant, Courtauld Institute of Art, London, 1966-69; British Red Cross: joined Tweeddale Branch, 1983; President, Tweeddale Branch, 1992- 97; Borders Representative, Scottish Central Council, Glasgow, 1995-97; voluntary service: Riding for the Disabled Association (Borders Chairman); Royal Edinburgh Repository and Self Aid Society. Recreations: country pursuits; gardening; riding; tennis; travel. Address: (h.) The Old Manse, Drumelzier, Biggar, Lanarkshire; T.-01899 830319.

Bird, Professor Colin C., CBE, MBChB, PhD, FRCPath, FRCPE, FRCSE, FRSE, FAMS. Dean, Faculty of Medicine, Edinburgh University, since 1995; b. 5.3.38, Kirkintilloch; m., Ailsa M. Ross; 2 s.; 1 d. Educ. Lenzie Academy; Glasgow University. McGhie Cancer Research Scholar, Glasgow Royal Infirmary, 1962-64; Lecturer in Pathology: Glasgow University, 1964-67, Aberdeen University, 1967-72; MRC Goldsmiths Travelling Fellow, Chicago, 1970-71; Senior Lecturer in Pathology, Edinburgh University, 1972-75; Professor and Head, Department of Pathology, Leeds University, 1975-86; Professor of Pathology and Head, Department of Pathology, Edinburgh University, 1986-95. Recreations: golf; hill walking; music. Address: (h.) 45 Ann Street, Edinburgh, EH4 1PL.

Bird, Jackie. Journalist; b. 31.7.62, Bellshill; 1 s.; 1 d. Educ. Earnock High School. Music/Film/Television Editor, Jackie Magazine; Radio News Reporter and Presenter, Radio Clyde; Reporter, Evening Times; Reporter, Sun; Reporter/Presenter, TVS; Presenter, Reporting Scotland. Patron, Glasgow Cat and Dog Home. Recreations: swimming; aerobics; running; music; animal welfare. Address; (b.) BBC, Queen Margaret Drive, Glasgow.

Bird, Michael George, MA, OBE. Director, The British Council, Scotland, since 2001; b. 5.1.60; m., Simone Lees. Educ. Bedales School; Cambridge University; Voronezh University; Harvard University. Teacher, Vienna, Austria, 1983-85; British Council: London, 1985-87; Assistant Director (Education and Training) Moscow, 1987-91; European Liaison Officer, Brussels, 1991-93; Director, St Petersburg, 1993-97; Director, Ukraine, 1997-2000. Recreations: music; travel; mountain walking. Address: (b.) 3 Bruntsfield Crescent, Edinburgh, EH10 4HD; T.-0131-446 3020.

Birley, Tim(othy) Grahame, BSc(Eng), MSc, ACGI, FRTPI, FRICS, FRSA. Independent adviser on sustainable development and public policy, since 1995; b. 13.3.47, Kent; m., Catherine Anne; 1 s.; 2 d. Educ. Sir Roger Manwood's Grammar School; Imperial College, London University; Edinburgh University. Local government, 1965-71; academic appointments, 1973-81; Director, Energy and Environment Research, 1982-85; Scottish Office: Inquiry Reporter, 1985-87, Principal Inquiry Reporter, 1987-88, Deputy Director of Building, 1988-90, Head, Rural Affairs Division, 1990-95. Non-Executive Director, RPT (Scotland), 1989-91; Central Scotland Woodlands, 1991-92; Director, Centre for Human Ecology, Edinburgh University, 1995-96; Chair, Project Selection Panel, Millennium Forest for Scotland Trust, 1996-97; Board Member: Forward Scotland, Landwise, 1996-2000; Vice-President, APRS. Recreation: family outings. Address: (b.) 6 Malta Terrace, Edinburgh EH4 1HR; T.-0131-332 3499.

Birss, Rev. Alan David, MA (Hons), BD (Hons). Minister, Paisley Abbey, since 1988; b. 5.6.53, Ellon; m., Carol Margaret Pearson. Educ. Glenrothes High School; St. Andrews University; Edinburgh University. Assistant Minister, Dundee Parish Church (St. Mary's), 1978-80; Minister, Inverkeithing Parish Church of St. Peter, 1982-88. Member, Council, Church Service Society and Scottish Church Society. Address: The Manse of Paisley Abbey, 15 Main Road, Castlehead, Paisley PA2 6AJ; T.-0141-889 3587.

Bisset, David W., ALA, MIInfSc, FSA (Scot), DEAB. Secretary, Scottish Esperanto Association, since 1997; Vice Chairman, Architectural Heritage Society of Scotland (Strathclyde); Vice President, Esperanto Society of Britain; Chairman, Esperanto Publicity Commission, since 1997; b. 8.8.38, Motherwell; m., Jean; 1 s.; 1 d. Educ. Dalziel High, Motherwell; University of Strathclyde. Librarian, Coatbridge Technical College, 1962-72; Head of Library Services, Bell College of Technology, Hamilton, 1972-95. Various positions within the Esperanto Movement in Scotland and Britain; Hon. Vice-President, Hamilton Civic Society. Recreations: cultural tourism; town walking; architectural history. Address: (h.) 47 Airbles Crescent, Motherwell ML1 3AP; T.-01698 263199; e-mail: david@bisset100.freeserve.co.uk

Bisset, Raymond George, OBE. Convener, Aberdeenshire Council, since 1999; Chairman, Scotland's Fisheries Development Department, since 2000; b. 16.8.42, Ellon; m., Heather Bisset. Educ. Inverurie Academy; Aberdeen University; College of Education. Chemistry/Physics Teacher, Ellon Academy, 1963-64; Maths/General Science Teacher, Insch School, 1965-74; Head Teacher: Keithall Primary School, 1975-76; Kintore Primary and Secondary School, 1977-81; Kintore Primary School, 1981-94. Provost, Gordon District Council, 1992-96; Member, North of Scotland Water Board, 1995-99; Chairman, Gordon Area Tourist Board, 1986-89, 1991-96; Hon. President, University for Children and Communities; former Chairman, Inverurie and District Round Table; Founder Chairman, North East Scotland Anglers' Federation; Hon. President, Inverurie Arthritis Society. Recreations: angling; golf; hill walking; reading; amateur writing. Address: (h.) The Schoolhouse, Keithhall, Inverurie, Aberdeenshire, AB51 0LX; T.-01467 621015.

Bisset, Dr (William) Michael, BSc, MBChB, DCH, MSc, MD, FRCP, FRCPCH. Consultant Paediatric Gastroenterologist, since 1992; b. 17.2.56, Edinburgh; m., Amanda Bisset. Educ. George Watson's College, Edinburgh; Edinburgh University; London University. Lecturer n Paediatric Gastroenterology, 1986-92. Croom Lecturer, RCPEd, 1993. Address: (b.) Royal Aberdeen Children's Hospital, Cornhill Road, Aberdeen; T.-01224 554715.

Black, Rev. Archibald Tearlach, BSc. Chairman of Council, The Saltire Society, 1997-2001; retired Church of Scotland minister; b. 10.6.37, Edinburgh; m., Bridget Mary Baddeley; 2 s.; 1 d. Educ. Merchiston School; St. Andrews University; New College, Edinburgh. St. Andrew's Church, Calcutta, 1964-66; St. Columba's, Pont Street, London, 1966-68 (Assistant); Carstairs with Carstairs Junction, 1969-74; Chaplain, The State Hospital; Ness Bank Church, Inverness, 1974-97. Elected Member of Council, National Trust for Scotland, 1991-96, re-elected, 1997. Recreations: photography; the arts; the conservation and enrichment of all aspects of Scotland's natural and cultural heritage. Address: (h.) 16 Elm Park, Inverness IV2 4WN; T.-01463 230588; e-mail: archieblack@inbhirnis.fsnet.co.uk

Black, Elspeth Catherine, LLB, NP. Solicitor, since 1973; Honorary Sheriff, Dunoon, since 1997; b. 25.10.50, Kilmarnock; m., James Anthony Black; 1 s.; 1 d. Educ. Kilmarnock Academy; Glasgow University. Apprentice, then Assistant, Wright, Johnston and McKenzie, Glasgow, 1971-74; Assistant, Messers Wm. J. Cuthbert and Hogg, Fort William, 1974-75; Assistant, then Partner, Kenneth W. Pendreich and Co. Dunoon, 1975-87; Partner, Elspeth C.

Black and Co., Dunoon and Anderson Banks and Co., Oban, Fort William and Balivanich, 1987-98; Partner, Corngall Black, Dunoon, since 1998; accredited Child Law Specialist. Honorary Solicitor to Scottish Amateur Swimming Association. Recreations: swimming coaching (Assistant Coach, Dunoon ASC); running/fitness training. Address: (b.) 20 John Street, Dunoon; T.-01369 704777.

Black, Sir James (Whyte), Kt, FRCP, FRS. Chancellor, Dundee University, since 1992; b. 14.6.24; m., Rona McLeod Mackie. Educ. Beath High School, Cowdenbeath; St Andrews University. Assistant Lecturer in Physiology, St Andrews University, 1946; Lecturer in Physiology, University of Malaya, 1947-50; Senior Lecturer, Glasgow University Veterinary School, 1950-58; ICI Pharmaceuticals Ltd., 1958-64; Head of Biological Research and Deputy Research Director, Smith, Kline and French, Welwyn Garden City, 1964-73; Professor and Head, Department of Pharmacology, University College, London, 1973-77; Director of Therapeutic Research, Wellcome Research Laboratories, 1978-84; Professor of Analytical Pharmacology, King's College Hospital Medical School, London University, 1984-93, now Emeritus. Joointly won Nobel Prize for Physiology or Medicine, 1988.

Black, Laurie, FRSA. Executive Chairman, Taste of Scotland (Chairman, since 1994); Chairman, Taste of Burns Country, since 1995; Joint Partner, Fouters Bistro, Ayr, since 1973; Vice-Chairman, Ayrshire and Arran Tourism Industry Forum, since 2000; b. 10.7.48, West Germany; m., Fran; 1 s.; 1 d. Educ. Horley Secondary School; Bournemouth Technical College. Former policeman; left police, 1973, to open restaurant in Ayr. Member, Scottish Tourist Board working party on natural cooking of Scotland; Director: Taste of Scotland, since 1993, Ayrshire and Arran Tourist Board. Recreations: cooking; travel; walking; music; computing; wine; golf. Address: (b.) 2A Academy Street, Ayr; T.-01292 261391.

Black, Professor Robert, QC, LLB (Hons), LLM, FRSA, FRSE, FFCS. Professor of Scots Law, Edinburgh University, since 1981; Temporary Sheriff, 1981-94; b. 12.6.47, Lockerbie. Educ. Lockerbie Academy; Dumfries Academy; Edinburgh University; McGill University, Montreal. Advocate, 1972; Lecturer in Scots Law, Edinburgh University, 1972-75; Senior Legal Officer, Scottish Law Commission, 1975-78; practised at Scottish bar, 1978-81; QC, 1987; General Editor, The Laws of Scotland: Stair Memorial Encyclopaedia, 1988-96 (formerly Deputy and Joint General Editor). Publications: An Introduction to Written Pleading, 1982; Civil Jurisdiction: The New Rules, 1983; various articles on the Lockerbie disaster. Recreations: beer and books, not necessarily in that order. Address: (h.) 6/4 Glenogle Road, Edinburgh EH3 5HW; T.-0131-557 3571; e-mail: Robert.Black@ed.ac.uk

Black, Robert William, MA (Hons, Econ), MSc (Town Planning), MSc (Public Policy). Auditor General for Scotland, since 2000; b. 6.11.46, Banff; m., Doreen Mary Riach; 3 s.; 1 d. Educ. Robert Gordon's College, Aberdeen; Aberdeen University; Heriot-Watt University; Strathclyde University. Nottinghamshire County Council, 1971-73; City of Glasgow Corporation, 1973-75; Strathclyde Regional Council, 1975-85; Chief Executive: Stirling District Council, 1985-90, Tayside Regional Council, 1990-95; Controller of Audit, Accounts Commission for Scotland, 1995-99. Fellow, Royal Statistical Society. Recreations: the outdoors and the arts. Address: (b.) 110 George Street, Edinburgh EH2 4LH.

Black, Rev. William Broad, MA, BD. Minister, Stornoway High Church of Scotland, since 1998; b. 7.4.46, Edinburgh; m., Kathleen Clarkson; 3 d. Educ. Kelso High School; Aberdeen University; Edinburgh University. Minister, Kinlochbervie and Durness, 1970-

80; Missionary, Overseas Missionary Fellowship in Korea, 1981-97. Publications: various books in Korean. Recreations: music; theatre; reading. Address: (h.) 1 Goathill Road, Stornoway HS1 2NJ; T.-01851 703106.

Black, Willliam Scott, FCIBS, MBA. Director, Account Management Operations, Royal Bank of Scotland plc; President, The Chartered Institute of Bankers in Scotland; b. 8.3.48; m., Margaret Aitken; 1 s.; 1 d. Educ. Kelso High School; Strathclyde University Business School. Joined Royal Bank of Scotland plc, 1964; Treasurer, John Menzies plc, 1981-82; rejoined Royal Bank of Scotland plc, 1982; General Manager (Development), Royal Scottish Assurance, 1990-91; Assistant Director, Network, Royal Bank of Scotland plc, 1991-93. Recreations: golf; gardening; reading; keep fit. Address: (b.) Younger Building, 3 Redheughs Avenue, Edinburgh EH12 9RB; e-mail: Bill.Black@rbs.co.uk

Blackadder, Elizabeth, OBE, RA, RSA. Artist; Her Majesty's Painter and Limner in Scotland; b. 24.9.31, Falkirk. Educ. Falkirk High School; Edinburgh University; Edinburgh College of Art. Lecturer, School of Drawing and Painting, Edinburgh College of Art, 1962-66; first Scottish woman painter elected full member, Royal Academy and Royal Scottish Academy.

Blackie, Alan John, BA, DipYCS. Director of Education and Community Services, East Lothian, since 1995; b. 6.6.48, Haddington; 2 d. Educ. Knox Academy, Haddington; Jordanhill College, Glasgow; Open University. Community Education Service, Dunbarton County Council/Strathclyde Regional Council, 1971-79; Community Education Officer, Castlebrae High School, Edinburgh, 1979-87; Education Officer, then Assistant Director of Education, Lothian, 1987-95. Member, ADES. Recreations: hill-walking; golf; skiing. Address: (h.) Byre Court, East Saltoun, EH34 5ED; T.-01875 340083.

Blackie, Professor John Walter Graham, BA (Cantab), LLB (Edin). Professor of Law, Strathclyde University, since 1991; Advocate, since 1974; b. 2.10.46, Glasgow; m., Jane Ashman. Educ. Uppingham School; Peterhouse, Cambridge; Harvard; Merton College, Oxford; Edinburgh University. Open Exhibitioner, Peterhouse, Cambridge, 1965-68; St. Andrews Society of New York Scholar, Harvard, 1968-69; practised at Scottish bar, 1974-75; Edinburgh University: Lecturer, 1975-88, Senior Lecturer in Scots Law, 1988-91. Director, Blackie & Son Ltd., publishers, 1970-93. Recreations: music; sailing. Address: (h.) The Old Coach House, 23a Russell Place, Edinburgh EH5 3HW.

Blackmore, Professor Stephen, BSc, PhD, FRSE, FLS, FIBiol. Regius Keeper, Royal Botanic Garden Edinburgh, since 1999; Visiting Professor, Glasgow University, since 1999; Visiting Professor, Reading University; b. 30.7.52, Stoke on Trent; m., Patricia Jane Melrose; 1 s.; 1 d. Educ. St George's School, Hong Kong; Reading University. Royal Society Aldabra Research Station, Seychelles, 1976; Lecturer and Head of National Herbarium, University of Malawi, 1977; Palynologist, British Museum (Natural History), 1980; Keeper of Botany, Natural History Museum, 1990. Publications: author of numerous research papers on plant taxonomy and palynology. Recreations: photography; hill-walking; blues guitar music. Address: (b.) Royal Botanic Garden, 20A Inverleith Row, Edinburgh EH3 5LR; T.-0131-248 2930; e-mail: S.Blackmore@rbge.org.uk

Blackshaw, Alan, OBE, VRD. Management Consultant; Member, Cairngorms Partnership Advisory Panel, since 1998 (Chair, Recreation Forum, since 1998); Adviser on public access to land: Scottish Environment Link, since 1994, Central Council of Physical Recreation, since 1997;

Academic Adviser, Highlands and Islands University Project, since 1998 (Chair, Tourism, Hospitality and Leisure Group, 1988-99, Member, Environment and Natural Sciences Faculty Board, since 2000); President, The Alpine Club, since 2001; b. 7.4.33; m., 1, Jane Elizabeth Turner (m. dissolved); 1 d.; 2, Dr. Elspeth Paterson Martin; 1 s.; 2 d. Educ. Merchant Taylors' School, Crosby; Wadham College, Oxford (MA). Royal Marines (commissioned), 1954-56, and RM Reserve, 1956-76. Entered Home Civil Service, Ministry of Power, 1956; Principal Private Secretary to Minister of Power, 1967-69; Department of Energy: Under Secretary, 1974, Offshore Supplies Office, 1974-78 (Director-General, 1977-78), Coal Division, 1978-79; Consultant, N.C.B., 1979-86; Consultant Director, Strategy International, 1980-91; Member: Scottish Council Development and Industry, 1974-78, Scottish Sports Council, 1990-96, Scottish Natural Heritage, 1992-97 (Chairman: Task Force on Access, 1992-94, Audit Committee, 1995-97); Vice-Chair, UN Inter-Governmental Conference on Sustainable Mountain Development, Trento, Italy, 1996; Member, Adventure Activities Licensing Authority, since 1996; Director, Moray Badenoch and Strathspey Enterprise, 1998-2000; Patron, British Mountaineering Council, since 1979 (President, 1973-76); Chairman: Standing Advisory Committee on Mountain Training Policy, 1980-86, Sports Council's National Mountain Centre, Plas y Brenin, 1986-95, Mountaineering Commission, UIAA, (Berne, Switzerland), 1990-2001, Access and Conservation Working Group, UIAA, 1995-98, UK Mountain Training Board, 1991-94; President, Snowsport Scotland, 1994-2000; Honorary Adviser, Mountaineering Council of Scotland, since 1995; Director, Paths for All Partnership, 1996-97; President, Ski Club of Great Britain, since 1997; Council Member, Mountain Forum, Katmandu, since 1999; UIAA Special Representative, UN Year of the Mountains, since 2000; International Olympic Committee, Lausanne, Award for voluntary service to sport and Olympism, 2001; Freeman, City of London; FRGS; FInstPet. Publication: Mountaineering, 1965. Recreations: mountaineering; sailing; skiing. Address: (h.) Rhu Grianach, Kingussie Road, Newtonmore PH20 1AY; T.-01540 673239.

Blaikie, Professor Andrew, MA, PhD. Professor of Historical Sociology, University of Aberdeen, since 1999 (Director of Research in Social Sciences and Law, since 1999); b. 30.11.56, St. Anne's. Educ. Kirkham Grammar School; Downing College, Cambridge; Queen Mary College, London. University of London: Research Officer, Bedford College, 1985-87, Lecturer, Birkbeck College, 1986-91; Department of Sociology, University of Aberdeen: Lecturer, 1991, Senior Lecturer, 1995. Nuffield Foundation Research Fellow, 1998; Member, Executive Committee, British Sociological Association, 1997-2001; Secretary, Economic and Social History Society of Scotland, 1994-99. Publications: Illegitimacy, Sex and Society, 1993; Ageing and Popular Culture, 1999. Recreations: swimming; hillwalking. Address: (h.) 5 Pilot Square, Aberdeen AB11 5DS; T.-01224 588313; e-mail: a.blaikie@abdn.ac.uk

Blair, (Ann) Kay, MA (Hons), FCS, MCIM. Managing Director, Business Perceptions; business journalist; Board Member, Scottish Legal Aid Board, since 1994; Non-Executive Director, Scottish Ambulance Service, since 1999; b. 12.4.53, Edinburgh; m., William; 1 s.; 2 d. Educ. James Gillespie's High School for Girls; St. Andrews University; School of Slavonic and Eastern European Studies, London University. Journalist/ Researcher on Eastern Europe and Manager, Business Information Service, Financial Times, 1977-80; Marketing Information Manager, Scottish Development Agency, 1980-81; formerly: Marketing Columnist, The Scotsman, Non-Executive Director, Edinburgh Sick Children's NHS Trust.

Recreations: skiing; cinema; travel. Address: (b.) 8 Winton Terrace, Edinburgh EH10 7AP; T.-0131-477 7477; e-mail: busper@lineone.net

Blair, Anna Dempster, DPE. Writer and Lecturer; b. 12.2.27, Glasgow; m., Matthew Blair; 1 s.; 1 d. Educ. Hutchesons' Girls Grammar School, Glasgow; Dunfermline College. Novels: A Tree in the West; The Rowan on the Ridge; Short Stories: Tales of Ayrshire; Scottish Tales; The Goose Girl of Eriska; Seed Corn; social history: Tea at Miss Cranston's; Croft and Creel; More Tea at Miss Cranston's. Recreations: film-making; travel; reading; friendship. Address: (h.) 20 Barrland Drive, Giffnock, Glasgow G46 7QD; T.-0141-638 0676.

Blair, Frank. Director Scotland, Advisory Conciliation and Arbitration Service, since 1995; b. 18.4.48, Wishaw; m.; 2 s.; 1 d. Various posts, Department of Employment/ Employment Service, 1967-82; ACAS Conciliator, 1982-91; Deputy Director Scotland, 1991-95. Mediator, Drumcree Parade Dispute, 1999. Recreation: golf. Address: (b.) 123 Bothwell Street, Glasgow; T.-0141-242 1700.

Blair, John Samuel Greene, OBE (Mil), TD, KStJ, BA, Hon. DLitt (St. Andrews), ChM, FRCSEdin, FRCP, FICS, D(Obst)RCOG, FSAScot, FRHistS. Vice-President, International Society for the History of Medicine, since 2000; Honorary Reader, History of Medicine and Apothecaries Lecturer, St. Andrews University, since 1997 (Senior Lecturer, 1993-97); Honorary Senior Lecturer in Surgery, Dundee University, 1967-90; Member, Editorial Board, Vesalius, since 1994; b. 31.12.28, Wormit, Fife; m., Ailsa Jean Bowes, MBE; 2 s.; 1 d. Educ. Dundee High School; St. Andrews University (Harkness Scholar, 1946-50). National Service, RAMC, 1952-55; Tutor, Department of Anatomy, St. Salvator's College, St. Andrews, 1955; surgical and research training, Manchester, Dundee, Cambridge, London, 1957-65; Member, Court of Examiners, Royal College of Surgeons of Edinburgh, 1964-93; Consultant Surgeon, Perth Royal Infirmary, 1965-90; postgraduate Clinical Tutor, Perth, 1966-74; first North American Travelling Fellow, St. Andrews/Dundee Universities, 1971; Secretary, Tayside Area Medical Advisory Committee, 1974-83; Member, Education Advisory Committee, Association of Surgeons, 1984-88; Secretary, Perth and Kinross Division, British Medical Association, 1982-90; Member, Scottish Council and Chairman's Sub-Committee, BMA, 1985-89; Fellow of the BMA, 1990; Chairman, Armed Forces Committee, BMA, 1992-98; President: British Society for the History of Medicine, 1993-95, Scottish Society for the History of Medicine, 1990-93; British National Delegate, International Society for the History of Medicine, 1999-2001; Honorary Colonel (TA), RAMC; Member, Principal's Council, St Andrews University, 1989-99; Elder, Church of Scotland; Hospitaller, Priory of Scotland, Order of St. John of Jerusalem; Mitchiner Lecturer, Army Medical Services, 1994; Haldane Tait Memorial Lecturer, 1998; Osler Club Lecturer, 1998; Birmingham Medical History Society Lecturer, 1998; Douglas Guthrie Memorial Lecturer, 1998; Brigadier Ian Haywood Lecturer, 1999; Haywood Society Lecturer, 1999; Pybus Society Lecturer, 2001. Publications: books on medical history and anatomy including the history of medicine at St. Andrews University, 1987, the centenary history of the RAMC, 1998, and The Conscript Doctors – Memories of National Service, 2001. Recreations: golf; travel; bridge. Address: (h.) 143 Glasgow Road, Perth; T.-Perth 623739.

Blair, Robin Leitch, MB, ChB, FRCSEdin, FRCS(C), FACS. Head, Department of Otolaryngology, Ninewells Hospital and Medical School, Dundee, since 1984; Consultant Otolaryngologist, Tayside University Hospitals Trust; b. 28.11.45, Gourock; m., Elizabeth Anne Manson; 2 d. Educ. Greenock Academy; Edinburgh University; University of Toronto. House Surgeon, Royal Infirmary,

Edinburgh; Lecturer, Department of Anatomy, Glasgow University; Assistant Professor, Department of Otolaryngology, University of Toronto. President, Section of Laryngology and Rhinology, Royal Society of Medicine; Chairman, SAC in Otolaryngology. Address: (b.) Department of Otolaryngology, Ninewells Hospital and Medical School, Dundee DD1 9SY; T.-01382 632162; e-mail: robinlblair@hotmail.com

Blair, Robin Orr, LVO, MA, LLB, WS. Lord Lyon King of Arms and Secretary, Order of the Thistle, since 2000. Educ. Rugby School; St. Andrews University; Edinburgh University. Partner, Dundas & Wilson, 1967-97 (Managing Partner, 1976-83 and 1988-91); Partner, Turcan Connell WS, 1997-2000. Purse Bearer to the Lord High Commissioner to General Assembly of Church of Scotland. Address: Court of the Lord Lyon, HM New Register House, Edinburgh EH1 3YT; T.-0131-556 7255.

Blake, Professor Christopher, CBE, FRSE, MA, PhD. Chairman, Glenrothes Development Corporation, 1987-96; b. 28.4.26; m.; 2 s.; 2 d. Educ. Dollar Academy; St. Andrews University. Royal Navy, 1944-47; teaching posts, 1951-53; Assistant, Edinburgh University, 1953-55; Stewarts & Lloyds Ltd., 1955-60; Lecturer, then Senior Lecturer, St Andrews University, 1960-67; Dundee University: Senior Lecturer, then Professor of Economics, 1967-74; Bonar Professor of Applied Economics, 1974-88; Director, Alliance Trust plc, 1974-94; Director, William Low & Co. plc, 1980-90 (Chairman, 1985-90). Recreation: golf. Address: (h.) Westlea, 14 Wardlaw Gardens, St. Andrews, Fife, KY16 9DW.

Blakey, Rev. Ronald Stanton, MA, BD, MTh. Editor, Church of Scotland Year Book, since 2000; b. 3.7.38, Glasgow; m., Kathleen Dunbar; 1 s. Educ. Hutchesons' Boys' Grammar School, Glasgow; Glasgow University. Minister: St. Mark's, Kirkconnel, 1963-67; Bellshill West, 1967-72; Jedburgh Old Parish with Edgerston and Ancrum, 1972-81. Member, Roxburgh District Council, 1974-80 (Chairman of Council, 1977-80); Religious Adviser, Border Television, 1973-81; Member, Borders Region Children's Panel, 1974-80; JP, 1974-80; Church of Scotland: Deputy Secretary, Department of Education, 1981-88; Secretary, Assembly Council, 1988-98; Israel Project Secretary, Board of World Mission, 1998-2000. Publication: The Man in the Manse, 1978. Recreation: collecting antiquarian books on Scotland. Address: (h.) 61 Orchard Brae Avenue, Edinburgh EH4.

Blanchflower, Brian William, BSc (Hons), PGCSE (Distinction). Rector, Lochgelly High School, Fife, since 1996; b. 8.1.56, Belfast; m., Karen Ann Simpson; 1 s.; 1 d. Educ. Dunfermline High School; University of Edinburgh; Moray House College of Education. Teacher of Mathematics and Geography, Inverkeithing High School, 1979-83; Assistant Principal Teacher of Geography, Buckhaven High School, 1983-84; Principal Teacher of Geography, Beath High School, 1984-87; Assistant Rector, 1987-90, Depute Rector, 1990-96, Lochgelly High School. Recreations: rugby; hill-walking. Address: (b.) Lochgelly High School, Station Road, Lochgelly, Fife KY5 8LZ; T.-01592 418000; e-mail: blancb@lochgelly.fife.sch.uk

Blaxter, Professor John Harry Savage, MA (Oxon), DSc (Oxon), HonDUniv(Stirling), FIBiol, FRSE. Hon. Professor, Stirling University; Hon. Research Fellow, Scottish Association for Marine Science; b. 6.1.29, London; m., Valerie Ann McElligott; 1 s.; 1 d. Educ. Berkhamsted School; Brasenose College, Oxford. SO, then SSO, Marine Laboratory, Aberdeen, 1952-64; Lecturer, Zoology Department, Aberdeen University, 1964-69; PSO, 1969, SPSO, 1974, DCSO, 1985-91, Scottish Marine Biological Association, Oban; Hon. Professor, St. Andrews University, 1990-99; President, Fisheries Society of the British Isles, 1992-97 (Beverton Medal, 1998); Individual Achievement

Award, American Institute of Fisheries Research Biologists, 1998; Editor, Advances in Marine Biology, 1980-97; Editor, ICES Journal of Marine Science, 1991-97; Member, Editorial Board, Encyclopaedia of Ocean Sciences, 1998-2001; Trustee, Argyll Fisheries Trust, since 1999. Recreations:golf; gardening. Address: (h.) Dems Lodge, Barcaldine, Oban PA37 1SF.

Bleiman, David, MA, MBA, FCIPD. Assistant General Secretary (Scotland), Association of University Teachers, since 1982; President, STUC, 2001-02, Member, General Council, since 1990; Member, East of Scotland Water Authority, since 1998; b. 7.8.53, Cape Town; m., Maureen McGibbon; 1 s.; 1 d. Educ. Haberdashers' Aske's School; Christ's College and King's College, Cambridge. W.E.A. Tutor, 1978; General Secretary, Scottish Further Education Association, 1979-82. Member, Independent Committee of Inquiry into Student Finance, 1999. Publication: Labour and Scottish Nationalism (Co-author), 1980. Recreation: collecting 78rpm records and wind-up gramophones. Address: (b.) 6 Castle Street, Edinburgh EH2 3AT; T.-0131-226 6694.

Bloomer, Keir, BA. Chief Executive, Clackmannanshire, since 2000; b. 1.7.47, Glasgow; m., Jacquetta Megarry; 1 s.; 1 d. Educ. Greenock Academy; Cambridge University. Teacher, 1969-81; Depute General Secretary, Educational Institute of Scotland, 1981-84; Education Officer, then Depute Director of Education, Strathclyde Regional Council, 1984-95; Executive Director, Education and Community Services, Clackmannanshire, 1995-2000. Address: Greenfield, Alloa FK10 2AD; T.-01259 452002.

Bloxwich, Janet Elizabeth. Principal Bassoon, Orchestra of Scottish Opera, since 1980; b. 11.4.56, Brentwood; m., Alan J. Warhurst. Educ. Belfairs High School; Southend Technical College; Royal College of Music, London. Two years freelancing in London; on staff at Royal Scottish Academy, since 1997. Recreations: hillwalking; woodturning; instrument repairs; cooking. Address: 91 Fotheringay Road, Pollokshields, Glasgow G41 4LH; T.-0141-423 2303.

Bluck, Professor Brian John, BSc, PhD, DSc, FRSE, FGS. Emeritus Professor of Tectonics and Sedimentation, University of Glasgow; b. 29.8.35, Bridgend, S. Wales; m., Barbara Mary; 1 s.; 1 d. Educ. Bridgend County Grammar; University College, Wales, Swansea. Visiting Research Scholar, University of Illinois, USA, 1961; NATO Research Fellow, 1962; Assistant Lecturer, 1962, Reader, 1981, University of Glasgow. Awarded Keith Medal, Royal Society of Edinburgh, 1981; Lyell Fund, Geological Society of London, 1981; Saltire/Royal Bank of Scotland Award for contributions to geology in Scotland, 1991; Clough Medal, Geological Society of Edinburgh, 2000. Recreations: hillwalking; music; theatre. Address: (b.) Division of Earth Science, University of Glasgow, Glasgow G12 8QQ; T.-0141-330 5447.

Blyth, Professor Thomas Scott, BSc, DesSc, DSc, CMath, FIMA, FRSE, Corr. Member, Soc.Roy.Sc. Liege. Professor of Pure Mathematics, St Andrews University, since 1977; b. 3.7.38, Newburgh; m., Jane Ellen Christine Pairman; 1 d. Educ. Bell-Baxter High School, Cupar; St Andrews University. NATO Research Scholar, Sorbonne, 1960-63; St Andrews University: Lecturer in Mathematics, 1963-72, Senior Lecturer, 1972-73, Reader, 1973-77; Dean, Faculty of Science, 1994-98; Chairman, British Mathematical Colloquium, 1987; President, Edinburgh Mathematical Society, 1979-80. Publications: more than 100 research papers and eight books. Address (b.) Mathematical Institute, North Haugh, St Andrews KY16 9SS; T.-01334 463720; e-mail: tsb@st-and.ac.uk

Bolland, Alexander, QC (Scot),. BD, LLB; b. 21.11.50, Kilmarnock; m., Agnes Hunter Pate Moffat; 1 s.; 2 d. Educ. Kilmarnock Academy; St. Andrews University; Glasgow University. Admitted Faculty of Advocates, 1978; Captain, Army Legal Services, 1978-80; Standing Junior Counsel to Department of Employment in Scotland, 1988-92; QC (Scot), since 1992; Temporary Sheriff, 1988-99; part-time Chairman, Industrial Tribunals, since 1992. Recreations: Hellenistics; walking; reading. Address: (h.) 60 North Street, St. Andrews, Fife; T.-01334 474599.

Bolland, Mike. Head of Comedy and Entertainment, BBC Scotland; b. 27.2.47, Glasgow; m., Katie Lander; 2 s.; 3 d. Educ. Hillhead High School. Office Boy, BBC Scotland, 1963-65; Film Editor, BBC Scotland, 1965-73; Senior Producer, Community Programmes, BBC Television, 1973-81; Commissioning Editor, Youth Programmes, Channel 4 Television, 1981-83; Senior Commissioning Editor, Entertainment, Channel 4 Television, 1983-86; Head of Arts and Entertainment, Channel 4 Television, 1986-88; Controller Arts and Entertainment/Deputy Director of Programmes, Channel 4 Television, 1988-90; Managing Director, Channel X Communications, 1990-96. Various awards including Golden Rose of Montreux for The Comic Strip. Recreations: music; motoring; mountains; mirth. Address: (b.) BBC Scotland, Queen Margaret Drive, Glasgow, G12 8DG; T.- 0141 338 2370.

Bomont, Robert George, DUniv, BSc (Econ), IPFA, JP. University Secretary, Stirling University, 1973-95; General Commissioner of Income Tax, since 1977; b. 6.5.35, Preston; m., Marian; 1 s.; 2 d. Educ. Preston Grammar School; London University. Trainee and qualified accountant, Lancashire County Council, 1951-64; Assistant Finance Officer, Lancaster University, 1964-66; Accountant, then Accountant and Deputy Secretary, Stirling University, 1966-73. Member, Council of Management, Strathcarron Hospice. Recreations: golf; gardening; DIY. Address: (h.) Wester Ardoch, Feddal Road, Braco, by Dunblane, Perthshire.

Bond, Professor Sir Michael R., MD, PhD, FRSE, FRCSEdin, FRCA (Hon), FRCPsych, FRCPSGlas, DPM, DSc (Leics, Hon). Emeritus Professor of Psychological Medicine, Glasgow University; President Elect, International Association for the Study of Pain; b. 15.4.36, Balderton, Nottinghamshire; m., Jane; 1 s.; 1 d. Educ. Magnus Grammar School, Newark; Sheffield University. Professor of Psychological Medicine, Glasgow University, 1973-98 (former Vice-Principal, Glasgow University; former Administrative Dean, Faculty of Medicine). Former Director (former Chairman), Head Injuries Trust for Scotland; former Member, Council, St. Andrews Ambulance Association; Past President, Pain Society; Director, Prince and Princess of Wales Hospice, Glasgow. Governor (Deputy Chairman), Glasgow High School; Trustee, Lloyds TSB Foundation; Fellow, Royal Society of Arts; Knight Bachelor, 1995. Recreations: reading; music; painting. Address: (b.) No. 2 The Square, University of Glasgow, University Avenue, Glasgow G12 8QQ; T.-0141-330 3692; e-mail: m.bond@admin.gla.ac.uk

Bone, Professor (James) Drummond, MA. Vice-Chancellor, University of Liverpool, since 2002; b. 11.7.47, Ayr; m., Vivian. Educ. Ayr Academy; Glasgow University; Balliol College, Oxford. Lecturer in English and Comparative Literary Studies, Warwick University; Lecturer and Senior Lecturer, English Literature, Glasgow University (Vice-Principal, 1995-99); Principal, Royal Holloway, University of London, 2000-02. Academic Editor and Advisory Editor, The Byron Journal; Co-Editor, Romanticism. Recreations: music; skiing; Maseratis. Address: (h.) The Old Manse, Bow of Fife, Cupar, Fife.

Bone, Professor Thomas R., CBE, MA, MEd, PhD, FCCEA, FRSGS. Professor and Deputy Principal, Strathclyde University, until 1996; b. 2.1.35, Port Glasgow; m., Elizabeth Stewart; 1 s.; 1 d. Educ. Port Glasgow High School; Greenock High School; Glasgow University; Jordanhill College. Teacher of English, Paisley Grammar School, 1957-62; Lecturer in Education: Jordanhill College, 1962-63, Glasgow University, 1963-67; Jordanhill College: Head of Education Department, 1967-71, Principal, 1972-92. Member, Dunning Committee, 1975-77; Chairman, Educational Advisory Council, IBA, 1985-88; Vice-Chairman: Scottish Examination Board, 1977-84; Scottish Tertiary Education Advisory Council, 1984-87; Chairman: Scottish Council for Educational Technology, 1981-87, Standing Conference on Studies in Education, 1982-84, Council for National Academic Awards Board for Organisation and Management, 1983-87, Council for National Academic Awards Committee for Teacher Education, 1987-89, General Teaching Council for Scotland, 1990-91; Member, Complaints Committee, Law Society of Scotland, 1996-2000. Publication: School Inspection in Scotland, 1968; articles in journals. Recreation: golf. Address: (h.) 7 Marchbank Gardens, Ralston, Paisley.

Bonnar, Anne Elizabeth, MA. Director, Bonnar Keenlyside; Arts Management Consultant; Trustee, National Galleries of Scotland; b. 9.10.55, St. Andrews; m., Fernley Thompson; 2 s.; 2 d. Educ. Dumbarton Academy; Glasgow University; City University, London; Jordanhill College of Education. Publicity Officer, Citizens' Theatre, Glasgow, 1981-85; General Manager, Traverse Theatre, 1986-91. Address: (b.) Grange Distillery House, Burntisland, Fife KY3 0AA; T.-01592 874478; e-mail: anne@b-k.co.uk

Bonnar, David James, OBE, FRSA. Independent Arts Adviser; Crafts Galleries Operator (artisanat); Director (National Lottery), Scottish Arts Council, 1994-99; b. 20.10.50, Dunfermline; m., Sally Elizabeth Armour; 2 s. Educ. Dunfermline High School. Royal Bank of Scotland, 1968-73; Theatre Royal, Glasgow, 1975-80; Theatre Royal, Newcastle upon Tyne, 1980-84; General Manager, Perth Repertory Theatre, 1984-94. Recreations: singing; gardening; opera; architecture. Address: (h.) 12 Queen Street, Perth PH2 0EQ; T.-01738 633424.

Bonney, Professor Norman Leonard, BSc (Econ) (Hons), MA, PhD. Research Professor, Robert Gordon University, since 2000; b. 4.3.44, Great Yarmouth; 3 s. Educ. Great Yarmouth Grammar School; London School of Economics; University of Chicago. Lecturer, Senior Lecturer, Department of Sociology, Aberdeen University, 1971-96; Professor and Head, Department of Psychology and Sociology, Napier University, 1996-2000. Councillor, Aberdeen City Council, 1974-88 (Convener, Town Planning Committee, 1981-85; Convener, Industrial Development, 1974-80). Recreations: walking; swimming; tennis. Address: Schoolhill, Aberdeen, AB10 1FR; e-mail: n.bonney@rgu.ac.uk

Bonnington, Alistair James, LLB (Hons), DipBusAdmin. Solicitor, BBC Scotland, since 1992; Honorary Professor, University of Glasgow; part-time Lecturer, University of Strathclyde; b. 28.5.52, Glasgow; m., Alison Margaret (deceased); 2 s.; 1 d. Educ. Hillhead High School, Glasgow; University of Glasgow; Bradford University. Apprentice, Biggart, Baillie and Gifford, Solicitors, Glasgow; pursued career in private practice, specialising in court work and media law. Secretary, Scottish Media Lawyers' Society. Publication: Scots Law for Journalists (Co-Author). Recreation: golf. Address: (b.) Broadcasting House, Queen Margaret Drive, Glasgow G12 8DG; T.-0141-338 2352.

Bonomy, Hon. Lord (Iain Bonomy). Senator of the College of Justice, since 1997; b. 15.1.46, Motherwell; m., Jan; 2 d. Educ. Dalziel High School; University of Glasgow. Apprentice Solicitor, East Kilbride Town Council, 1968-70; Solicitor, Ballantyne & Copland, 1970-83; Advocate, 1984-93; Queen's Counsel, 1993-96; Advocate Depute, 1990-93; Home Advocate Depute, 1993-96. Surveillance Commissioner, since 1998. Address: (b.) Parliament House, Edinburgh; T.-0131-225 2595.

Boon, Nicholas, MA, BChir, MD, FRCPE. Consultant Cardiologist, Royal Infirmary of Edinburgh, since 1986; Honorary Senior Lecturer, University of Edinburgh, since 1986; b. 31.12.50, London; m., Anne Robertson; 2 d. Educ. Canford School, Dorset; Gonville and Caius College, Cambridge University; Middlesex Hospital Medical School, London. Lecturer and Senior Registrar in Cardiovascular Medicine, John Radcliffe Hospital, Oxford, 1983-86; Clinical Director, Royal Infirmary, Edinburgh, since 1996. Member: Council, British Cardiac Society, since 1994, Council, British Heart Foundation, since 1997. Author of scientific papers on heart disease; Co-Editor, Davidson's Principles and Practice of Medicine, 18th Edition. Recreations: golf; skiing. Address: Department of Cardiology, Royal Infirmary of Edinburgh, Edinburgh EH3 9YW; T.-0131-536 2004/6.

Boreham, Professor Nicholas Charles, MA, PhD, CPsychol. Professor of Education and Employment, Stirling University, since 2001; b. 27.5.45, Wimbledon; m., Elizabeth Horton; 2 d. Educ. Nottingham University. Educational Researcher, Schools Council, East Anglian Examinations Board and Joint Board of Clinical Nursing Studies, 1971-76; Lecturer and Senior Lecturer in Higher Education, Manchester University, 1976-93; Professor of Education, Manchester University, 1993-2001. Address: (b.) Institute of Education, Stirling University, Stirling FK9 4LA; T.-01786 467617.

Borley, Lester, CBE, DLitt, FRSGS, FTS. Chairman: Icomos (UK), Cultural Tourism Committee; Council Member, Europa Nostra; b. 7.4.31, Pontardawe, S. Wales; m., Mary Alison Pearce; 3 d. Educ. Dover County Grammar School; Queen Mary College, University of London. Joined British Travel Association, London, 1955: Assistant to General Manager (USA), New York, 1956-61, Manager, Midwestern States (USA), Chicago, 1961-64, Manager, Australia, 1964-67, Manager, West Germany, Frankfurt, 1967-70; Chief Executive, Scottish Tourist Board, 1970-75; Chief Executive, English Tourist Board, 1975-83; Director, National Trust for Scotland, 1983-93; Secretary General, Europa Nostra, The Hague, 1992-96; Visiting Lecturer: Academia Istropolitana, Slovakia, International Cultural Centre, Cracow; Adviser, World Monuments Fund, New York; Vice President, Edinburgh Film House; Trustee: Hopetoun House Trust, Cromarty Arts Trust. Recreations: gardening; visiting museums and galleries; reading social history; music. Address: (h.) 4 Belford Place, Edinburgh EH4 3DH; T.-0131-332 2364.

Borthwick of that Ilk, Lord (John Hugh Borthwick), DL. 24th Lord Borthwick; Hereditary Falconer of Scotland to The Queen; b. 14.11.40; m. Adelaide; 2 d. Educ. Gordonstoun; Edinburgh School of Agriculture. Address: (h.) Crookston, Heriot, Midlothian EH38 5YS.

Borthwick, Alan Charles, LLB, NP. Partner, Brechin Tindal Oatts, Solicitors, Glasgow and Edinburgh, since 1983; b. 25.4.57, Glasgow; m., Sheila; 1 d. Educ. Glasgow Academy; Glasgow University. Brechin Robb, Solicitors, 1977-81; joined Tindal Oatts & Rodger, 1981. Member, Council, Law Society of Scotland, 1995-98; Board Member, Children's Hospice Association Scotland; a Trustee, Parents Oncology Support, Yorkhill. Recreations:

golf; skiing; garden; family. Address: (b.) 48 St. Vincent Street, Glasgow G2 5HS; T.-0141-221 8012; e-mail: acb@bto.co.uk

Boswell, Sir Alexander, KCB, CBE, DL. Chairman, Scottish Veterans' Residences; b. 3.8.28, Malaya (of Scottish parents); m., Jocelyn Pomfret; 5 s. Educ. Merchiston Castle School; RMA, Sandhurst. Enlisted in Army, 1947; commissioned Argyll & Sutherland Highlanders, 1948; regimental appointments, 1949-58; Staff College, Camberley, 1959; Military Assistant (GSO 2) to GOC Berlin, 1960-62; Company Commander, then Second in Command 1 A & SH, Malaya and Borneo, 1963-65; Directing Staff, Staff College, Camberley, 1965-68; Commanding Officer, 1 A & SH, 1968-71; Colonel GS Army Strategic Command, 1971; Brigadier Commanding 39 Infantry Brigade, 1972-74; Chief of Staff, 1st British Corps, 1974-76; National Defence College, Canada, 1976-77; GOC 2nd Armoured Division, 1978-80; Director, Territorial Army and Cadets, 1980-82; GOC Scotland and Governor of Edinburgh Castle, 1982-85; Lieutenant Governor and Commander in Chief, Bailiwick of Guernsey, 1985-90. Address: c/o Bank of Scotland, 52 Shandwick Place, Edinburgh EH2 4SB.

Bouchier, Professor Ian Arthur Dennis, CBE, MB, ChB, MD, FRCP, FRCPEdin, FFPHM, Hon. FCP (SAf), FIBiol, FMedSci, MD h.c., FRSE, FRSA. Professor of Medicine, Edinburgh University, 1986-97 (now Emeritus Professor); b. 7.9.32, Cape Town, South Africa; m., Patricia Norma Henshilwood; 2 s. Educ. Rondebosch Boys High School; Cape Town University. Instructor in Medicine, School of Medicine, Boston University, 1964; London University: Senior Lecturer in Medicine, 1965; Reader in Medicine, 1970; Professor of Medicine, Dundee University, 1973-86. Member: Court, Dundee University, Council, Royal Society, Edinburgh, Medical Research Council; former Chief Scientist, Scotland; Past President, World Organization of Gastroenterology; former Dean, Faculty of Medicine and Dentistry, Dundee University; Past President, British Society of Gastroenterology. Publications: Clinical Skills (2nd edition), 1982; Gastroenterology (3rd edition), 1982; Gastroenterology: clinical science and practice (2nd edition), 1993. Recreations: music; history of whaling; cooking. Address: (h.) 8A Merchiston Park, Edinburgh EH10 4PN.

Boulton, Professor Geoffrey Stewart, OBE, FRS, FRSE, BSc, PhD, DSc, FGS. Regius Professor of Geology and Mineralogy, Edinburgh University, since 1986 (Vice-Principal, Edinburgh University, since 1999, Provost and Dean, Faculty of Science and Engineering, 1994-99); b. 28.11.40, Stoke-on-Trent; m., Denise Bryers; 2 d. Educ. Longton High School; Birmingham University. Geological Survey of GB, 1962-64; University of Keele, 1964-65; Birmingham University, 1965-67; Water Supply Department, Kenya, 1968; University of East Anglia, 1968-81; Extraordinary Professor, University of Amsterdam, 1981-86. Kirk Bryan Award of the Geological Society of America, 1976; President, Quaternary Research Association, 1991-94; President, British Glaciological Society, 1989-91; President, Geological Society of Edinburgh, 1991-94; Member: Nature Conservancy Council for Scotland Science Board, 1991-92, Natural Environmental Research Council, 1993-98 (Chair, Earth Science and Technology Board, 1993-98), Royal Commission on Environmental Pollution, Scottish Higher Education Funding Council, since 1997, Scottish Association for Marine Science Council, since 1998, Royal Society Council, since 1997. Seligman Crystal, International Glaciological Society, 2001. Recreations: violin; sailing; mountaineering. Address: (b.) Department of Geology and Geophysics, University of Edinburgh, Grant Institute, Kings Buildings, West Mains Road, Edinburgh EH9 3JW; e-mail: g.boulton@ed.ac.uk

Bovey, Keith S., BL. Solicitor, since 1951; President, Scottish CND; b. 31.7.27, Renfrew; m., Helen Cameron; 1 s.; 1 d. Educ. Paisley Grammar School; Glasgow University. Army, 1944-48. Publication: Misuse of Drugs, A Handbook for Lawyers. Address: (b.) 13A Pentland Terrace, Edinburgh EH10 6EY; T.-0131-452 8822.

Bowden, Frederick A.W. Chief Executive, Tullis Russell Group, since 1991; b. 20.1.47, Aberdeen; m., Sheila; 2 s.; 1 d. Educ. Robert Gordon's Institute of Technology. Production Management Trainee, Inverness Paper Company, 1964-68; held several management positions, Arzo Wiggins Appleton, 1968-91; Operations Director/Managing Director/Chief Executive, Tullis Russell Group, since 1991. Chairman, River Leven Trust; Non-Executive Director, Scottish Enterprise Fife, Scottish National Training Organisations. Address: (b.) Markinch, Glenrothes KY7 6PB.

Bowdler, Timothy John, BSc, MBA. Chief Executive, Johnston Press plc; b. 16.5.47, Wolverhampton; m., Margaretha Eklund; 2 d. Educ. Wrekin College; Birmingham University; London Business School. Recreations: golf; tennis; skiing. Address: (b.) 53 Manor Place, Edinburgh EH3 7EG; T.-0131-225 3361; tbowdler@johnstonpress.co.uk

Bowen, Sheriff Principal Edward Farquharson, TD, QC, LLB. Advocate; Sheriff Principal, Glasgow and Strathkelvin, since 1997; Temporary Judge of the Court of Session, since 2000; Visiting Professor of Law, University of Strathclyde, since 1999; b. 1.5.45, Edinburgh; m., Patricia Margaret Brown; 2 s.; 2 d. Educ. Melville College, Edinburgh; Edinburgh University. Admitted Solicitor, 1968; Advocate, 1970; Standing Junior Counsel, Scottish Education Department, 1976; Advocate Depute, 1979-83; Sheriff of Tayside, Central and Fife, at Dundee, 1983-90; Partner, Thorntons WS, 1990-91; resumed practice at Scottish Bar; QC, 1992; Chairman (Part-time) Industrial Tribunals, 1995-97; Member, Criminal Injuries Compensation Board, 1996-97; Governor, Dundee Institute of Technology, 1987-90. Served RAOC TA/TAVR, 1964-80. Recreation: golf. Address: (b.) Sheriff's Chambers, Sheriff Court, 1 Carlton Place, Glasgow G5 9DA.

Bower, Professor Daphne Jane, BSc, PhD, MBA, MA/FPM, IMC. Professor of Entrepreneurship, Glasgow Caledonian University, since 1999; b. 7.9.45, Dunfermline; m., Dr Kenneth Lyall; 1 s.; 3 d. Educ. Dunfermline High School; Edinburgh University; Lancaster University; Ecole Suprieure de Commerce de Lyon. Awarded Royal Society Senior Research Fellowship, 1989; since 1990 involved in research, consultancy and teaching of innovation management; Member, RSA Scottish Committee; Member, Scottish Higher Education Funding Council; Member, Scottish Hospitals Endowments Trust. Recreations: hill-walking; gardening. Address: (b.) Department of Economics and Enterprise, Glasgow Caledonian University, 70 Cowcaddens Road, Glasgow G4 0BA.

Bowler, David P., BA, MPhil, FSA Scot. Director, SUAT Ltd., since 1993; b. 9.12.55, Southampton. Educ. McGill University, Montreal; Lincoln College, Oxford. Address: (b.) 55 South Methven Street, Perth PH1 5NX; T.-01738 622393; e-mail: director@suat.demon.co.uk

Bowler, Professor Kenneth Charles, BSc, ARCS, DPhil, CPhys, FInstP. Professor of Computational Particle Physics, Edinburgh University, since 1999; b. 4.10.43, Luton; Beds; m., Christine Mary Bowler; 2d. Educ. Luton Grammar School; Imperial College, London; Sussex University. Edinburgh University: Lecturer in Mathematical Physics, 1968; Senior Lecturer, Physics, 1986; Reader, Physics, 1994. Publications: numerous papers on theoretical and computational particle physics in European and US scientific journals. Recreations: hill walking; cycling; tennis; classical music. Address: (b.) Department of Physics and Astronomy, Edinburgh University, The King's Buildings, Edinburgh, EH9 3JZ; T.-0131-650 5239.

Bowman, Professor Adrian William, BSc (Hons), DipMathStat, PhD, FRSE. Professor of Statistics, University of Glasgow, since 1995; b. 3.1.55, Ayr; m., Janet Edith Forster; 2 s.; 1 d. Educ. Prestwick Academy; Ayr Academy; University of Glasgow; University of Cambridge. Lecturer in Mathematical Statistics, University of Manchester, 1981-86; University of Glasgow: Lecturer in Statistics, 1986-90, Senior Lecturer in Statistics, 1990-92, Reader in Statistics, 1992-95. Publications: Applied Smoothing Techniques for Data Analysis, (Co-author), 1997; Statistics and Problem Solving (Co-editor), 1999. Recreations: music, particularly singing. Address: (b.) Department of Statistics, University of Glasgow, Glasgow G12 8QQ; T.-0141-330 4046; e-mail: adrian@stats.gla.ac.uk

Bowman, (Bernard) Neil, LLB, NP. Consultant, formerly Senior Partner, Bowman Scottish Lawyers, Solicitors, Dundee and Forfar, 1984-98; b. 11.11.43, Dundee; m., Pamela Margaret Munro Wright; 2 d. Educ. High School of Dundee; Edinburgh University; St. Andrews University. Apprenticeship, Sturrock Morrison & Gilruth, Solicitors, Dundee, 1967-69; admitted Solicitor, 1969; Notary Public, 1970; assumed Partner, Gray Robertson & Wilkie 1970 (subsequently Bowman Gray Robertson and Wilkie, now Bowman) 1971. Secretary: Dundee Institute of Architects, 1970-96, Dundee Building Trades (Employers) Association, 1970-89, Dundee Construction Industry Group Training Association, 1970-93, Tayside Construction Safety Association, 1975-89; Joint Secretary, Local Joint Council for Building Industry, 1970-89, and Local Joint Apprenticeship Committee for the Building Industry, 1970-89; Clerk, Three United Trades of Dundee and to Mason Trade, Wright Trade and Slater Trade of Dundee, 1970-2000; Lord Dean of Guild of Guildry Incorporation of Dundee, 1987-90; first Lord President, Court of Deans of Guild of Scotland, 1989; Director, High School of Dundee, 1980-90; Chairman, High School of Dundee Scholarship Fund, 1987-90; Co-opted Member, Law Society of Scotland Committees — Public Relations and Conference, 1982-90, Complaints, 1987-90; Member: Working Party on "Corporate Conveyancing," 1989, School Age Team Sports Enquiry, 1989; Committee Member and National Selector, Scottish Cricket Union, 1974-83; Selector, 1990; President: Scottish Counties Cricket Board, 1981, Scottish Cricket Union, 1989. Recreations: cricketophile; travel; golf. Address: (b.) 37 E. High Street, Forfar; T.-01307 468868; e-mail: bnb@ecosse.net

Bowman, Sheriff Pamela Margaret Munro, LLB, NP. Sheriff of Grampian, Highland and Islands at Aberdeen; formerly Sheriff in Glasgow; Partner, Bowman, Solicitors, Dundee and Forfar, 1980-97; b. 1.8.44, Stirling; m., (Bernard) Neil Bowman; 2 d. Educ. Beacon School, Bridge of Allan, Stirling High School; Queens College, Dundee, St. Andrews University. Admitted Solicitor and Notary Public, 1967; Member, Scottish Legal Aid Board, 1994-97; Non-Executive Director, Angus NHS Trust, 1994-97. Recreation: theatre.

Bowman, Professor Emeritus William Cameron, BPharm, PhD, DSc, FIBiol, FRSE, FRSA, FRPharmS, HonFFARCS. Head, Department of Physiology and Pharmacology, Strathclyde University, 1966-87 and 1990-94; b. 26.4.30; m., Anne Wyllie Stafford; 1 s.; 1 d. Educ. London University. RAF (commissioned officer), 1955-57; Lecturer, then Reader in Pharmacology, London University, 1952-66. Dean, School of Pharmaceutical Sciences, Strathclyde University, 1974-77; Vice Principal,

Strathclyde University, 1986-90; Visiting Professor: McGill University, Montreal; Cornell University, New York; Ohio Medical College. Member: Nomenclature Committee, BP Commission, 1964-67; Biology Committee, MOD, 1966-75; TCT and SEAR Sub-Committees, CSM, 1972-83; Biomedical Research Committee, SHHD, 1980-85; Chairman, Committee: British Pharmacological Society, 1981-84 (Foreign Secretary 1992-97), Heads of UK Pharmacology Departments, 1990-94; Member: Executive Committee, European Federation of Pharmacologists, 1991-96, Scottish Hospital Endowments Research Trust, since 1996; Secretary General, International Union of Pharmacology, 1994-98; Director, IUPHAR Media since 1997; Chairman, Science Advisory Board, Medpharma plc, since 1999. Publications: Textbook of Pharmacology, 1968, 1980; Pharmacology of Neuromuscular Function, 1980, 1990; Dictionary of Pharmacology, 1986; many research articles in scientific journals. Address: Department of Physiology and Pharmacology, Strathclyde University, Glasgow G4 0NR; T.-0141-552 4400.

Bownes, Professor Mary, BSc, DPhil, FIBiol, CBiol, FRES. Personal Chair of Developmental Biology, Edinburgh University, since 1994; b. 14.11.48, Drewsteignton; m., Michael J. Greaves; 1 d. Educ. Maldon Grammar School; Sussex University. Lecturer, Essex University; Lecturer, Senior Lecturer, Reader, Convener, Senate's Postgraduate Studies Committee, Edinburgh University. Publications: 100 research articles and reviews. Address: (b.) Institute of Cell and Molecular Biology, Edinburgh University, Darwin Building, Mayfield Road, Edinburgh EH9 3JR; T.-0131-650 5369; e-mail: Mary.Bownes@ed.ac.uk.

Bowser of Argaty and the King's Lundies, David Stewart, JP, BA (Agric). Trustee, Scottish Forestry Trust, 1983-89 (Chairman, 1987); Member, Queen's Bodyguard for Scotland (Royal Company of Archers); Chairman, Dunblane Museum Trust, since 1992; b. 11.3.26; m.; 1 s.; 4 d. Educ. Harrow; Trinity College, Cambridge. Captain, Scots Guards, 1944-47. Member, Perth County Council, 1954-61; President, Highland Cattle Society, 1970-72; Forestry Commissioner, 1974-82; Chairman, Scottish Council, British Deer Society, 1988-94. Address: Auchlyne, Killin, Perthshire FK21 8RG.

Boxer, Professor David Howell, BSc, PhD. Professor of Biochemistry, Dundee University, since 1991, Head, Biochemistry Department, 1988-93, Dean, Science and Engineering Faculty, 1994-99, Deputy Principal, since 2000; m., Dr. Maureen Boxer; 1 s.; 2 d. Educ. Aberdare Boys' Grammar School; Bristol University. Dundee University: Lecturer in Biochemistry, 1976, Senior Lecturer, 1985. Nuffield Research Fellow, 1983-84; Chairman, Biochemistry Biophysics Sub-Commitee, SERC, 1990-92. Recreations: travelling; skiing. Address: (b.) MSI/WTB Complex, School of Life Sciences, Dundee University, Dundee DD1 5EH.

Boyack, Sarah. MSP (Labour), Edinburgh Central, since 1999; Minister for Transport and Environment, 1999-2000, Minister for Transport and Planning, 2000-0001. Former lecturer in planning. Address: (b.) Scottish Parliament, Edinburgh EH99 1SP; T.-0131-348 5751.

Boyd, Alan Robb, LLB, BA, NP. Director, Public Law, McGrigor Donald, since 1997; b. 30.7.53, Glasgow; m., Frances Helen; 2 d. Educ. Irvine Royal Academy; Dundee University. Principal Solicitor, Shetland Islands Council, 1979-81; Principal Solicitor, Glenrothes Development Corporation, 1981-84; Legal Advisor, Irvine Development Corporation, 1984-87. Law Society of Scotland: Member, Council, 1985-97, Convener, Finance Committee, 1992-94, Vice-President, 1994-95, President, 1995-96; President, European Company Lawyers' Association, 1992-94;

Convenor, Association for Scottish Public Affairs, 1998-2000. Recreations: golf; skiing; music. Address: (h.) 45 Craigholm Road, Ayr KA7 3LJ; T.-01292 262542.

Boyd, Rt Hon Colin David, PC, QC, BA (Econ), LLB, FRSA. Lord Advocate, since 2000; Solicitor General for Scotland, 1997-2000; Member of the Scottish Executive, since 1999; b. 7.6.53, Falkirk; m., Fiona Margaret MacLeod; 2 s.; 1 d. Educ. Wick High School; George Watson's College, Edinburgh; University of Manchester; University of Edinburgh. Solicitor, 1978-82; called to Bar, 1983; Advocate Depute, 1993-95; took Silk, 1995. Legal Associate, Royal Town Planning Institute. Publication: The Legal Aspects of Devolution (Contributor), 1997. Recreations: hill-walking; reading. Address: (b.) Crown Office, 25 Chambers Street, Edinburgh EH1 1LA; T.-0131-226 2626.

Boyd, Rev. Dr. Donald MacLeod, MB, ChB, DipTheol, FCS. Minister, Inverness Free Presbyterian Church of Scotland, 1989-2000 (Clerk, Northern Presbytery, 1991-2000); Church Tutor in Systematic Theology, 1995-2000; b. Glasgow; m., Elizabeth Schouten; 1 s.; 3 d. Educ. Glasgow Academy; Glasgow University. Southern General Hospital, 1978; Stobhill General Hospital, 1979; Vale of Leven Hospital, 1979; ordained Free Presbyterian Church of Scotland, 1983; Clerk of Religion and Morals Committee, 1984-92 and Convener, 1992-94; Deputy to Australia and New Zealand, 1988; Member, Churches Liaison Committee on AIDS, Highland Health Board, 1992-94; Member, Highland Regional Council Education Committee, 1994-96; Moderator of Synod of Free Presbyterian Church of Scotland, 1997-98. Publication: Popular History of the Origins of the Free Presbyterian Church of Scotland, 1987. Recreations: reading; writing; gardening; walking; photography; British Sign Language; historical research; advanced driving. Address: Ebenezer, Westhill, Inverness IV2 5JY.

Boyd, Professor Ian L., BSc, PhD, DSc. Professor in Biology, St Andrews University, since 2001; Director, Sea Mammal Research Unit, since 2001; b. 9.2.57, Kilmarnock; m., Sheila M.E. Aitken; 1 s.; 2 d. Educ. George Heriot's School, Edinburgh; Aberdeen University; Cambridge University. Churchill Fellow, 1980; Institute of Terrestrial Ecology, Monks Wood, 1982-87; British Antarctic Survey, 1987-2001; Antarctic Service Medal of the United States, 1995; Bruce Medal, Royal Society of Edinburgh, 1995; Honorary Professor, Birmingham University, 1997; Scientific Medal, Zoological Society of London, 1998; Editor, Journal of Zoology, 1999. Member, Council, Hebridean Trust and Seamark Trust. Publications: six books; 100 papers. Recreations: rugby referee; walking; photography. Address: (b.) Gatty Marine Laboratory, St Andrews University, St Andrews KY16 8LB; T.-01334 462630.

Boyd, Ian Mair, MSc, CA. Group Finance Director, The Weir Group PLC, since 1981; Director, Glasgow Income Trust plc, since 1990; b. 4.9.44, Ayr; m., Theodora; 2 s.; 1 d. Educ. Ayr Academy; London Business School. The Weir Group PLC: Financial Controller International Division, 1975-78, Group Chief Accountant, 1978-81. Director, Inveresk PLC, 1993-2001; Council Member, Institute of Chartered Accountants of Scotland, 1987-93; Chairman, Group of Scottish Finance Directors, 1990-91. Recreations: golf; hill-walking; fishing. Address: (b.) The Weir Group PLC, Cathcart, Glasgow G44 4EX; T.-0141-637 7111; e-mail: im.boyd@wg.weir.co.uk

Boyd, Joe, BSc (Hons), DipEd, MEd. Headteacher, St. David's High, Dalkeith, since 1997; Author, since 1989; b. 10.11.53, Ayr; m., Moira McCabe; 1 s.; 2 d. Educ. St. David's High, Dalkeith; University of St. Andrews; Moray House; University of Edinburgh. President, Students' Union, University of St. Andrews, 1975-76; teaching, various Lothian schools, including Beeslack High School, St. Augustine's High School, St. David's High School, 1977-97. Member, National Joint Working Party (Revised Higher Chemistry), 1987-90; seconded to SOEID, to work with HM Inspectorate, 1996-97; led Inservice workshops for teachers, 1983-97. Publications: co-author of 27 titles, including Understanding Science series, and Scottish Science 5-14. Recreations: cycling; hill-walking; football; sailing; skiing; reading. Address: (b.) St. David's High School, Abbey Road, Dalkeith, Midlothian; T.-0131-663 1961.

Boyle, Rt. Rev. Mgr. Hugh Noonan, PhL, STL, FSA Scot. Canon, Chapter of Metropolitan Cathedral Church of St. Andrew, Glasgow, since 1984; Chapter Secretary, since 1991; Prelate of Honour, since 1987; Archivist, Archdiocese of Glasgow, since 1973; b. 14.1.35, Glasgow. Educ. St. Aioysius' College, Glasgow; Glasgow University; Pontifical Scots College and Pontifical Gregorian University, Rome, 1956-63. National Service, RAF, 1954-56; ordained priest, Rome, 1962; Assistant Priest: St. Philomena's, Glasgow, 1963-66, St. Eunan's, Clydebank, 1966-76; Administrator, Metropolitan Cathedral Church of St. Andrew, Glasgow, 1983-92; Parish Priest, St. Leo's, Dumbreck, 1992-93; Chaplain, Bon Secours Convent Hospital, Glasgow, 1995-2000; Assistant Catholic Chaplain, Victoria Infirmary, Glasgow, 1995-98; Archdiocese of Glasgow: Assistant Archivist, 1967-73; Chancellor, 1976-83. Editor, Catholic Directory for Scotland and Western Catholic Calendar, since issues of 1975; Member: Scottish Catholic Communications Commission, 1979-87; Scottish Catholic Heritage Commission, since 1981; Patron, Hutchesons' Hospital, since 1983. Recreations: music (listening); walking. Address: 10 Braehead Quadrant, Neilston, Glasgow G78 3EL.

Boyle, Iain Thomson, BSc (Hons), MB, ChB, FRCP, FRCP (London and Glasgow), FSA (Scot), DUniv (Strathclyde). Honorary Librarian, Royal College of Physicians and Surgeons of Glasgow; b. 7.10.35, Glasgow; m., Elizabeth Johnston Carmichael; 1 s.; 2 d. Educ. Paisley Grammar School; Glasgow University. Lecturer in Medicine, Glasgow University and Glasgow Royal Infirmary, 1964-70; Hartenstein Research Fellow, Wisconsin University, 1970-72; Senior Lecturer in Medicine, Glasgow University and Glasgow Royal Infirmary, 1973-84; Reader in Medicine, Glasgow University and Glasgow Royal Infirmary, 1984-96. Chairman, Board of Management, Scottish Medical Journal, 1987-96; President, Bone and Tooth Society, 1994-96; Editor, Scottish Medical Journal, 1978-83; Co-Editor, Bone, 1983-97; Council Member, Royal College of Physicians and Surgeons, 1984-88; Secretary: Scottish Society for Experimental Medicine, 1984-88, Scottish Society of Physicians, 1984-88; President: Caledonian Philatelic Society, 1983-84, Association of Scottish Philatelic Societies, 1995-96, Harveian Society of Edinburgh, 1991; Medical Advisor, University of Strathclyde, 1991-2000; Visiting Professor in Physiology/Pharmacology, University of Strathclyde, 1994-2000; Vice President (Medical), Royal College of Physicians and Surgeons of Glasgow, 1992-94; Chairman, National Scientific Advisory Committee, Tenovus-Scotland, 1997-99; Senior Vice President, Scottish Postal History Society, 2000-02; Fletcher Prize, Royal College of Physicians and Surgeons of Glasgow, 1973. Recreations: philately; Scottish social history; France and the French; angling; gardening; golf. Address: (h.) 7 Lochbrae Drive, High Burnside, Rutherglen, Glasgow G73 5QL.

Boyle, James. Chairman, Scottish Arts Council, since 2001. Former Controller, BBC Radio Scotland; former Controller, BBC Radio 4. Address: (b.) 12 Manor Place, Edinburgh, EH3 7DD; T.-0131-226 6051.

Boyle, John Stirling, MA, DPA, FRSA. Director, Corporate Affairs, ScotRail, since 1994; b. 17.9.39, Paisley; m., Helen Dickson; 2 s.; 1 d. Educ. Camphill School, Paisley; Glasgow University. School Teacher, 1960-61; Reporter, Sunday Post, 1961-62; Technical Writer, Harland Engineering Company, 1962-64; Health Education Officer, Stirling County, 1964-66; Public Relations Officer, Heriot-Watt University, 1966-73; Director, External Relations, Scottish Council (Development and Industry), 1973-83; Director of Public Affairs (Scotland), British Rail, 1983-92; Director, Corporate Affairs (Scotland), British Railways Board, 1992-94. Recreation: motor cycling. Address (b.) Caledonian Chambers, 87 Union Street, Glasgow G1 3TA; T.-0141-335 4447.

Boyle, Sandy, DGA. Deputy General Secretary, UNIFI; Member, STUC General Council, since 1992; President, UNI Europa Banking Committee; b. 23.12.45, Falkirk; m., Elizabeth Ross Cockrill; 1 s.; 1 d. Educ. Falkirk High School. Civil Servant, 1964-92. Vice-President, Society of Civil and Public Servants; Deputy President, National Union of Civil and Public Servants (President, NUCPS, 1989-92); Member: STUC Executive, War on Want Council of Management, ACTSA Scottish Executive, Central Arbitration Committee. Recreations: trade union badge collector; music; reading; bridge; watching Falkirk F.C. Address: (b.) 146 Argyle Street, Glasgow G2 8BL; T.-0141-221 6475.

Bradford, Nicola Barbara, DL, LTCL. Partner, Kincardine House, since 1986; Suzuki Piano Teacher, since 1996; Vice Chairman, Children 1st, since 1997; b. 12.9.57, Prestwick; m., Andrew E. H. Bradford; 2 s.; 1 d. Educ. West Heath School, Kent; College of Occupational Therapy, Edinburgh. Occupational Therapist, Aberdeen, 1978-80. Board Member, North East Scotland Music School; Deputy Lieutenant, County of Aberdeenshire. Recreations: playing the piano; sailing; walking; gardening; charitable fundraising; Cocker spaniels. Address: Kincardine, Kincardine O'Neil, Aberdeenshire AB34 5AE; T.-013398 84225.

Bradley, Professor David Allan, BTech, PhD, CEng, FIEE. Professor of Mechatronic Systems, University of Abertay Dundee, since 1998; Visiting Professor, Lancaster University, since 2000; b. 22.4.46. South Shields. Educ. Ermysteds Grammar School, Skipton; Bradford University. Lecturer/Senior Lecturer, Lancaster University, 1972-95; Research Engineer, New Zealand Electricity, 1982-83; Visiting Professor, Technical University of Denmark, 1992; Professor of Computer Systems, University of Wales, Bangor, 1995-98. Recreations: military history; reading; photography; travel; cricket. Address: (b.) School of Science and Engineering, University of Abertay, Dundee, Bell Street, Dundee, DD1 1HG; T.-01382 308234.

Bradley, Rev. Dr. Ian Campbell, MA, BD, DPhil. Writer and Broadcaster; Reader in Practical Theology, St Andrews University; Member, Committee to Revise the Church Hymnary; b. 28.5.50, Berkhamsted; m., Lucy Patricia; 1 s.; 1 d. Educ. Tonbridge School, Kent; New College, Oxford; St. Andrews University. Research Fellow, New College, Oxford, 1971-75; Staff Journalist, The Times, 1976-82; ordained into Church of Scotland, 1990; Head, Religious Broadcasting, BBC Scotland, 1990-91. Publications: The Call to Seriousness, 1974; William Morris and his World, 1975; The Optimists, 1976; The Penguin Annotated Gilbert & Sullivan, 1980; The Strange Rebirth of Liberal Britain, 1982; Enlightened Entrepreneurs, 1986; The Penguin Book of Hymns, 1989; God is Green, 1990; O Love That Wilt Not Let Me Go, 1990; Marching to the Promised Land, 1992; The Celtic Way, 1993; The Power of Sacrifice, 1995; The Complete Annotated Gilbert and Sullivan, 1996; Columba, Pilgrim and Penitent, 1996; Abide with Me – the World of the Victorian Hymn, 1997; Celtic Christianity:

Making Myths and Chasing Dreams, 1999; The Penguin Book of Carols, 1999; Colonies of Heaven: Celtic Models for Today's Church, 2000; God Save the Queen – The Spiritual Dimension of Monarchy, 2002. Recreations: music; walking; family; spas. Address: (b.) St Mary's College, South Street, St Andrews KY16 9JU; T.-01334 462840.

Bradley, John Russell, MA, LLB, DipLP, NP. Solicitor, DLA, Edinburgh (formerly Bird Semple) since 1989; b. 20.11.62, Glasgow; 3 s. Educ. Eastbank Academy, Glasgow; Glasgow University. Trainee, Wright & Crawford, Paisley, 1987-89; Bird Semple: Assistant, 1989-94, Associate, 1994-97; Partner, since 1997. Recreations: hockey (not often enough); golf (mostly in the rough). Address: (b.) 27 Thistle Street, Edinburgh EH2 1BS; T.-08700 111 111.

Bradley, Professor Robert Harold, BSc (Hons), PhD. Professor of Materials, Robert Gordon University, Aberdeen, since 1997; b. 3.5.55, Wolverhampton; m., Sara Louise Bradley; 1 s. Educ. Sheffield University. Department of Physics, Loughborough University, 1987-97. Publications: 150 in scientific journals, conference proceedings, book chapters. Recreations: fishing; shooting; rock climbing; walking; music; antiques; wine. Address: (h.) Viewbank House, Brechin DD9 7AP; T.-01356 626145.

Brady, Adrian J.B, BSc, MB, ChB, MD, FRCP (Glasg), FRCPE. Consultant Cardiologist, Glasgow Royal Infirmary, since 1996; b. 27.5.61, Edinburgh; m., Lucy; 1 s.; 2 d. Educ. Edinburgh Academy; Scotus Academy; Edinburgh University. Trained in Cardiology at Hammersmith Hospital and National Heart and Lung Institute, London; Winner, American Heart Association Young Investigator Award, 1993; Winner, British Cardiac Society Young Investigator Award, 1993; Chairman, Hypertension Research Group, 1992-96; Member, Committee for the British Society of Cardiovascular Research, since 1998; Faculty Member, American Heart Association. Recreations: skiing; golf; roller blading. Address: (b.) Cardiology Department, Queen Elizabeth Building, Glasgow Royal Infirmary, Glasgow, G31 2ER; T.-0141-211 4727.

Brady, Paul A., BSc (Hons), PhD. Head of Fisheries Group, Scottish Executive Environment and Rural Affairs Department, since 1999; b. 28.7.49, Glasgow; 2 s.; 1 d. Educ. St. Mungo's Academy, Glasgow; University of Glasgow. Joined Scottish Office, 1974; posts in Industry, Police, and Energy areas, 1974-88; headed team advising on electricity privatisation, 1988-90; led on Higher Education reforms, 1991-92; Director of Policy, Scottish Higher Education Funding Council, 1992-93; Head, Finance Division (industry, transport and agriculture), Scottish Office, 1993-94; Director of Finance and Planning, Scottish Enterprise, 1994-98; Director of Finance, National Health Service in Scotland Management Executive, 1998-99. Recreations: walking; music; family. Address: (b.) SEERAD, Pentland House, 47 Robb's Loan, Edinburgh EH14 1TY; T.-0131-244 6034; e-mail: paul.brady@scotland.gsi.gov.uk

Braid, Sheriff Peter John, LLB (Hons), WS. Partner, Morton Fraser, Solicitors, since 1985; Solicitor Advocate, since 1995; Part-time Sheriff, since 2001; b. 6.3.58, Edinburgh; m., Heather McIntosh; 2 s. Educ. George Watson's College, Edinburgh; University of Edinburgh. Apprentice, 1980-82; has specialised in litigation since 1982, now concentrates on commercial litigation. Publications: articles on enforcement of judgements, food safety, the millennium bug. Recreations: golf; bridge. Address: (b.) 30/31 Queen Street, Edinburgh EH2 1JX; T.-0131-247 1000.

Brailsford, Sidney Neil, QC, BA, LLB; b. 15.8.54, Edinburgh; m., Elaine Nicola Robbie; 3 s. Educ. Daniel Stewart's College, Edinburgh; Stirling University; Edinburgh University. Admitted Scottish Bar, 1981, English Bar, 1990; Standing Junior Counsel, Department of Agriculture and Fisheries, 1987-92; QC, 1994; Advocate Depute, 1999-2000. Treasurer, Faculty of Advocates, 2000; Member, Court, Stirling University, 2001. Recreations: food; wine; travel; reading; American history and politics; baseball; supporting Heart of Midlothian Football Club. Address: (b.) Advocates Library, Parliament House, Edinburgh EH1 1RF; T.-0131-226 5071; e-mail: neil.brailsford@advocates.org.uk

Braithwaite, Robert Barclay, BSc, CEng, FICE, MASCE. General Manager, Aberdeen Harbour Board, since 1990; b. 17.2.48, Glasgow; m., Christine Isobel Ross; 2 s. Educ. Hutchesons' Boys' Grammar School; Strathclyde University. Graduate/Assistant Engineer, Rendel Palmer & Tritton, Consulting Civil Engineers, London, 1969-74; Aberdeen Harbour Board: Deputy Harbour Engineer, 1974-75, Harbour Engineer, 1976-86, Assistant, then Deputy General Manager and Harbour Engineer, 1986-89. Council Member, Aberdeen Chamber of Commerce; Chairman, British Ports Association, 1998-2000; Chairman, Aberdeen Safer Community Trust. Recreations: hill running; cycling; reading. Address: (b.) Harbour Office, 16 Regent Quay, Aberdeen AB11 5SS; T.-01224 597000.

Bramley, John Stuart, BSc (Hons), PhD. Dean of Science, Strathclyde University since 1996; b. 8.12.43, Nottingham; m., Christabel; 1s.; 2d. Educ. Long Eaton Grammar School, Derbyshire; Leeds University. Strathclyde University: Lecturer; Senior Lecturer. Recreations:gardening; family history. Address: (b.) Strathclyde University, Glasgow, G1 1XQ; T.-0141-552 4400.

Brand, David Allan, LLB (Hons), WS, NP. Solicitor; Senior Lecturer in Law, University of Dundee (Director of Studies, Diploma in Legal Practice; Associate Dean, Faculty of Law and Accountancy); b. 4.3.50, Dundee; 1 d. Educ. Grove Academy, Broughty Ferry; Dundee University. Former Partner, Thorntons WS, Dundee. Former Member of Council, Law Society of Scotland; former Dean, Faculty of Procurators and Solicitors in Dundee. Recreations: all types of music; amateur operatics; theatre. Address: (b.) Department of Law, University of Dundee, Dundee DD1 4HN; T.-01382 223181.

Brand, Janet Mary Valentine, BA (Hons), DipTP, MRTPI. Senior Lecturer, Strathclyde University, since 1973 (Member of Senate, 1984-91 and since 1992; Member of Court, 1989-91; Convener, Programme of Opportunities for Women Committee, 1990-93); b. 19.4.44, Bath; 2 d. Educ. County High School for Girls, Brentwood; Exeter University. Local authority appointments in Departments of Planning, Essex County Council, London Borough of Barking and City of London, 1965-70; Senior Lecturer, South Bank Polytechnic, 1970-73. Specialist Assessor in Town and Country Planning and Landscape, HEFCE, since 1996. Recreations: the environment; gardening; family pursuits; travelling. Address: (b.) Department of Environmental Planning, Strathclyde University, 50 Richmond Street, Glasgow; T.-0141-548 3905; e-mail: j.m.v.brand@strath.ac.uk

Brankin, Rhona. MSP (Labour), Midlothian, since 1999; Educ. Aberdeen University. Former teacher and lecturer on special educational needs; Deputy Minister for: Culture and Sport, 1999-2000, for Environment and Rural Development, 2000-01; former Chair, Scottish Labour Party. Address: (b.) Scottish Parliament, Edinburgh EH9 1SP; T.-0131-348 5838.

Brannan, Micheline H., MA. Head, Civil and Criminal Law Group, Scottish Executive Justice Department, since 2001; b. 23.10.54, Glasgow; m., Michael N. Brannan; 2 s. Educ. Hutchesons' Grammar School; St. Hilda's College, Oxford. Scottish Office: joined as administrative trainee, 1976, promoted to Principal, 1982, Industry Department for Scotland, 1982-84, Scottish Education Department, 1985-88, Home and Health Department Criminal Justice Group, 1989-95; Head, Civil Law Division, Scottish Office Home Department, 1995-2001 (latterly Scottish Executive Justice Department). Recreations: cycling; Jewish cultural activities. Address: (b.) Saughton House, Broomhouse Drive, Edinburgh; T.-0131-244 2131.

Breaks, Michael Lenox, BA, DipLib. University Librarian, Heriot-Watt University, since 1985; b. 12.1.45, Plymouth; m., Barbara Lawson; 1 s.; 1 d. Educ. St. George's College, Weybridge; Leeds University. Assistant Librarian: University College, Swansea, York University; Social Sciences Librarian, University College, Cardiff, 1977-81; Deputy Librarian, University College, Dublin, 1981-85. Chairman, JANET National User Group, 1991-93; Non-Executive Director, UKERNA, 1994-97; Member: SCONUL Executive Board, 1991-96, SLIC Management Committee, Board of Trustees, EduServ, JISC Committee on Electronic Information; President, IATUL; Editor, New Review of Information Networking. Recreations: gardening; sailing; walking. Address: (h.) 2 Corrennie Gardens, Edinburgh EH10 6DG; T.-0131-451 3570; e-mail: m.l.breaks@hw.ac.uk

Brebner, Professor Gordon John, BSc, PhD. Professor of Computer Systems, Edinburgh University, since 1999; b. 27.7.57, Edinburgh; m., Rosemary Brebner. Educ. George Heriot's School, Edinburgh; Edinburgh University. Department of Computer Science, Edinburgh University: Demonstrator; Lecturer; Senior Lecturer, 1981- 99; Director, Institute for Computing Systems Architecture, Edinburgh University, since 1999; Hon. Senior Research Fellow, Glasgow University, since 2000. Publications: Hon. Editor, IEE Proceedings; Computers in Communication, 1997. Recreations: recreational cricket; dry humour. Address: (b.) James Clerk Maxwell Building, Edinburgh University, The King's Buildings, Mayfield Road, Edinburgh, EH9 3JZ; T.-0131-650 5180; e-mail: G.Brebner@ed.ac.uk

Breeze, David John, BA, PhD, FSA, PPSA Scot, FRSE, FRSA, MIFA. Chief Inspector of Ancient Monuments, Scotland, since 1989; Visiting Professor, Department of Archaeology, Durham University, since 1993; Honorary Professor, Edinburgh University, since 1996; b. 25.7.44, Blackpool; m., Pamela Diane Silvester; 2 s. Educ. Blackpool Grammar School; Durham University. Inspector of Ancient Monuments, Scotland, 1969-88; Principal Inspector of Ancient Monuments, Scotland, 1988-89. Member: International Committee of the Congress of Roman Frontier Studies, since 1983, International Committee on Archaeological Heritage Management, since 1997, Council, Society of Antiquaries of London, 1984-86, Council, Royal Society of Edinburgh, 1997-2000; Trustee, Senhouse Roman Museum, since 1985; Chairman: 1989 and 1999 Hadrian's Wall Pilgrimages, British Archaeological Awards, since 1993; President: South Shields Archaeological and Historical Society, 1983-85, Society of Antiquaries of Scotland, 1987-90; Corresponding Member, German Archaeological Institute. Publications: The Building of Hadrian's Wall, The Army of Hadrian's Wall, Hadrian's Wall, and Roman Officers and Frontiers (all Co-author); Roman Scotland: a guide to the visible remains; Roman Scotland: some recent excavations (Editor); The Romans in Scotland (Co-author); The Northern Frontiers of Roman Britain; Roman Forts in Britain; Studies in Scottish Antiquity (Editor); Hadrian's Wall, a souvenir guide; A Queen's Progress, an introduction to the buildings associated with Mary Queen of Scots in Scotland; The Second Augustan Legion in North Britain; Service in the Roman Army (Co-editor); Invaders of Scotland (Co-author); Roman Scotland: Frontier Country; The Stone of Destiny: Symbol of Nationhood (Co-author); Historic Scotland, 5000 Years of Scotland's Heritage. Recreations: reading; walking; travel. Address: (b.) Historic Scotland, Longmore House, Salisbury Place, Edinburgh, EH9 1SH; T.-0131-668 8724; e-mail: david.breeze@scotland.gov.uk

Bremner, Douglas, BSc (Hons); b. 18.9.38, Glasgow; m., Vivien; 3 s. Educ. Aberdeen Grammar School; Aberdeen University. Whaling Inspector, Crown Agents, South Georgia; Warden, Malham Tarn Field Centre, Field Studies Council; National Trust for Scotland: Principal/Chief Ranger, Culzean Country Park, Chief Ranger, Scotland, Head of Interpretation/Presentation, Regional Director, Lothians, Borders, Dumfries and Galloway Region. Publication: For the Benefit of the Nation, The National Trust for Scotland, The First Seventy Years, 2001. Recreations: natural history; walking; gardening; painting; sound recording. Address: (h.) 3 Bonaly Terrace, Colinton, Edinburgh EH13 0EL; T.-0131-441 4966.

Bremner, Mairi, JP. Councillor, Comhairle Nan Eilean Siar, since 1980; Chair, Comunn na Gaidhlig, since 1997; b. 14.9.45, South Uist; m., Robert George Stewart Bremner; 3 s. Educ. Lochaber High School; Notre Dame College of Education. Schoolteacher, 1966-69; business partner in hotel and retail with husband, 1969-90; Member, European Bureau of Lesser Used Languages (Chair, Scottish Centre); Director, Uist Building Preservation Trust; Director, Proiseact Uibhist 2000; Board Member, TOSG Theatre Group. Recreations: reading; walking; cooking; music; Gaidhlig culturre. Address: Carnan House, Iochdar, South Uist HS8 5RH; T.-01870 610 270.

Brett, Timothy Edward William, BSc (Hons), FHSM, DipHSM, GradIPM. Chief Executive, Tayside Health Board; b. 28.3.49, Gravesend; m., Barbara Jane; 2 s.; 1 d. Educ. Gravesend Grammar School for Boys; Bristol University. Unit Administrator, Plymouth General Hospital, 1981-85; Dundee General Hospitals Unit: Unit Administrator, 1985-87, Unit General Manager, 1987-93; Chief Executive, Dundee Teaching Hospitals, 1993-97; General Manager, Tayside Health Board. Recreations: hill-walking; squash; swimming; theatre; church activities. Address: (h.) Woodend Cottage, Hazelton Walls, Cupar KY15 4QL; T.-01382 632598; e-mail: tewbrett@btinternet.com

Brett Young, Michael Jonathan, DL. Manager, East Sutherland Village Advisory Service, 1986-99; Director: Voluntary Groups, East Sutherland, 1996-99, and since 2001, Highland Advice and Information Network Ltd., 1994-99; Deputy Lieutenant, Sutherland, since 1995; b. 18.10.37, Salisbury; m., Helen Dorothy Anne Barker; 2 s. Educ. Dartmouth. Royal Australian Navy, 1956-69; Sales and Marketing Manager, 1969-79; Senior Account Manager, 1979-84. Chairman, PR Committee, Retread Manufacturers Association, 1975-79; Executive Member, Community Organisations Group, Scotland, 1990-93; Chairman: East Sutherland Council of Social Service, 1991-94, East Sutherland Local Community Care Forum, 1993-99; Executive Member, SSAFA, Sutherland; Chairman, Dornoch Cricket Club, since 1991. Recreations: cricket; naval history; music. Address: (h.) West Shinness Lodge, Lairg, Sutherland; T.-01549 402495.

Brettle, Raymond Patrick, BSc, MBChB, MD, FRCPEd. Consultant Physician, Regional Infectious Disease Unit, Western General Hospital, Edinburgh, since 1998; Reader in Medicine, University of Edinburgh, since 1995; b. 20.3.49, Halesowen; m., Helene Ferrier; 1 s.; 3 d. Educ. Halesowen Grammar School; Edinburgh University.

Registrar, Hammersmith Hospital, London, 1977-79; Senior Registrar, City Hospital, Edinburgh, 1979-83; Fellow, Bowman Gray School of Medicine, Winston Salem, N. Carolina, 1982-83; Consultant, Regional Infectious Disease Unit, City Hospital, Edinburgh, 1983-98; Senior Lecturer, University of Edinburgh, 1983-95. Chairman, Medical Advisory Committee, Milestone House; Founder Member, British HIV Association. Recreations: computing; walking; DIY. Address: RIDU, Western General Hospital, Edinburgh, EH4 2XU; T.-0131-537 2841; e-mail: raybrettle@hotmail.com

Brew, David Allan, BA, MSc. Chief Executive, Institute of Chartered Accountants of Scotland; b. 19.2.53, Kettering. Educ. Kettering Grammar School; Heriot-Watt University; Strathclyde University; European University Institute, Florence. Administration Trainee and HEO(D), Scottish Office, 1979-81; Administrator, DGV, Commission of the EC, 1981-84; Principal, Scottish Office, Glasgow, 1984-88, Edinburgh, 1988-90; Head: Electricity Privatisation Division, 1990-91, European Funds and Co-ordination Division, 1991-95, Sea Fisheries Division,1995-98; Cabinet Office, Constitution Secretariat, 1998-99. Member, Court, Heriot-Watt University, 1985-91, and since 2000. Recreations: languages; music; film; gastronomy. Address (h.) 1 Dundas Street, Edinburgh, EH3 6QG; T.-0131-556 4692.

Bridges, Professor Roy Charles, BA, PhD, FRGS, FRHistS, FFCS. Emeritus Professor of History, Aberdeen University; b. 26.9.32, Aylesbury; m., Jill Margaret Bridges; 2 s.; 2 d. Educ. Harrow Weald County Grammar School; Keele University; London University. Lecturer in History, Makerere University, Uganda, 1960-64; joined Aberdeen University, 1964, becoming Head, History Department, Chairman, African Studies Group. Council Member: Royal Historical Society, 1995-98, Hakluyt Society, 1991-95, 1998-2001 (Vice-President, 2001); Treasurer, Scottish Institute of Missionary Studies; Chairman, Garioch Area, Aberdeenshire Forum of Community Councils, since 1999. Publications: Africa in Times Atlas of World Exploration; Compassing the Vaste Globe of the Earth (Co-editor), 1996; Imperialism, Decolonization and Africa, 1999. Recreations: cricket; geology; gardening. Address: (h.) Newmachar House, Newmachar AB21 0RD; T.-01651 863046.

Brining, James Edward; MA (Cantab) (Hons). Artistic Director, TAG Theatre Co., since 1997; b. 10.6.68, Leeds. Educ. Leeds Grammar School; Girton College, Cambridge University. Formed Rendezvous Theatre Company 1989; Proteus Theatre Co.: Administrative Director, 1990, Artistic Director, 1992; Community Director, Orange Tree Theatre, Richmond, 1995; Vice-Chair, Federation of Scottish Theatre. Recreations: films, music, football (playing, and watching Leeds United). Address: (b.) TAG Theatre Co., 18 Albion Street, Glasgow G1 1LH.

Brittain, Christopher Neil, MBA, MBChB, MRCGP, DRCOG, DFFP, DipIMC, RCS(Edin.), FRSocMed, FFCS, MInstD. Executive Director, Scottish Science Trust, since 1999; b. 3.3.49, Birmingham; m., Rosemary; 1 s.; 1 d. Educ. Bishop Vesey's Grammar School, Sutton Coldfield; St. Andrews University; Dundee University; Heriot Watt University. Senior Partner, Anstruther Medical Practice, 1978-97; Co-ordinator for Scotland, Sargent Cancer Care for Children, 1997-99. Chairman, British Association of Immediate Care, 1994-97; Director, Resuscitation Council UK, 1995-1997. Recreations: music; walking. Address: (h.) The White House, Smithy Brae, Kilrenny, Anstruther, Fife KY10 3JN; T.-01333 310191.

Britton, Professor Celia Margaret, MA (Cantab), PhD, FBA. Carnegie Professor of French and Director, Centre for Francophone Studies, Aberdeen University, since 1991; b. 20.3.46, Stanmore, Middx. Educ. North London Collegiate

School; New Hall, Cambridge. Temporary Lecturer in French, Kings College, London, 1972-74; Lecturer in French Studies, Reading University, 1974-91. Publications: Claude Simon: Writing The Visible, 1987; The Nouveau Roman: fiction, theory and politics, 1992; Claude Simon (Editor), 1993; Edouard Glissant and Postcolonial Theory, 1999; articles on French literature and cinema, French Caribbean literature. Address: (b.) Department of French, Aberdeen University, Old Aberdeen, AB9 2UB; T.-01224 272163; e-mail: c.britton@abdn.ac.uk

Broadfoot, John, CBE, BCom, CPFA, FRSA. Depute Chairman, Scottish Children's Reporter Administration, 1995-2001; b. 4.10.34; m., Joan McGregor Hardie; 1 s. Educ. Royal High School, Edinburgh; Edinburgh University. Early career with City Chamberlain, Edinburgh, and Stirling County Council, 1952-75; Director of Finance, Central Regional Council, 1975-87; Chief Executive, Central Regional Council, 1987-89; Controller of Audit, The Accounts Commission, 1989-94. Chairman, CIPFA Directors of Finance in Scotland, 1978-79; Chairman, Scottish Branch, CIPFA, 1979-80; Chairman, Local Authorities (Scotland) Accounts Advisory Committee, 1982-87; Commissioner, Public Works Loan Board, 1985-89; Board Member, East of Scotland Water, since 1998; Chairman, Strathcarron Hospice, since 1999; Chairman, RSA in Scotland, since 1999. Recreations: reading; music; cutting grass. Address: (h.) 65 Laburnum Grove, Stirling, FK8 2PR; T.-01786 475602.

Broadfoot, John Ledingham, BA, MEd. Rector, Kelvinside Academy, since 1998; b. 16.12.48, Glasgow; m., Cecilia; 1 s.; 2 d. Educ. Merchiston Castle School; Leeds University; Stirling University. Teacher of English, Kingston College, Jamaica, 1971-73; Assistant Principal Teacher, then Principal Teacher of English, Penicuik High School, 1973-78; Principal Teacher of English, Preston Lodge High School, East Lothian, 1978-87; Head of English, then Director of Studies, Strathallan School, Perthshire, 1987-98. Recreations: Scottish literature; theatre; mountaineering; sailing. Address: Kelvinside Academy, 33 Kirklee Road, Glasgow G12 OSW; T.-0141-357 3376.

Broadie, Professor Alexander, MA, PhD, DLitt, FRSE. Professor of Logic and Rhetoric, Glasgow University. Educ. Royal High School, Edinburgh; Edinburgh University; Balliol College, Oxford. Henry Duncan Prize Lecturer in Scottish Studies, Royal Society of Edinburgh, 1990-93; Gifford Lecturer, Aberdeen University, 1994. Publications: A Samaritan Philosophy, 1981; George Lokert: Late-Scholastic Logician, 1983; The Circle of John Mair, 1985; Introduction to Medieval Logic, 1987; Notion and Object, 1989; The Tradition of Scottish Philosophy, 1990; Paul of Venice: Logica Magna, 1990; Robert Kilwardby O.P.: on time and imagination, 1993; Introduction to Medieval Logic (2nd edition), 1993; The Shadow of Scotus, 1995; The Scottish Enlightenment: an anthology, 1997; Why Scottish Philosophy Matters, 2000; The Scottish Enlightenment: The Historical Age of the Historical Nation, 2001. Address: (b.) Philosophy Department, The University, Glasgow G12 8QQ; T.-0141-330 5692.

Brock, Professor David John Henry, BA (Oxon), PhD, FRCPath, FRSE, FRCPE. Professor of Human Genetics, Edinburgh University, 1985-98; Director, Human Genetics Unit, Edinburgh University, 1983-98; Chairman, Department of Medicine, Western General Hospital, 1994-97; b. 5.6.36, London; 4 s. Educ. Diocesan College, Cape Town; Cape Town University; Oxford University. Postdoctoral Fellow: Massachusetts Institute of Technology, 1962-63; Harvard University, 1963-66; Oxford University, 1966-67; Senior Scientific Officer, ARC Animal Breeding Research Organisation, 1967-68; joined Edinburgh University as Lecturer in Human Genetics, 1968;

appointed Reader, 1978. Address: (h.) Craigden, Glenfoot, Perthshire; T.-01738 850333; e-mail: david@brock9894.freeserve.co.uk

Brockie, Rev. Colin Glynn Frederick, BSc (Eng), BD. Minister, Kilmarnock: Grange, since 1978; Clerk to Presbytery of Irvine and Kilmarnock, since 1992; Hon. Chaplain, 327 (Kilmarnock) Squadron, Air Training Corps, since 1978; b. 17.7.42, Westcliff on Sea; m., Barbara Katherine Gordon; 2 s.; 1 d. Educ. Musselburgh Grammar School; Aberdeen Grammar School; University of Aberdeen. Probationary year, Aberdeen: Mastrick, 1967-68; Minister, St. Martin's, Edinburgh, 1968-78. Recreations: billiards; photography; computing. Address: Grange Manse, 51 Portland Road, Kilmarnock, Ayrshire KA1 2EQ; T.-01563 525311.

Brockington, Professor John Leonard, MA, DPhil. Professor of Sanskrit, University of Edinburgh, since 1998 (Head, School of Asian Studies, 1998-99); Secretary General, International Association of Sanskrit Studies; b. 5.12.40, Oxford; m., Mary Fairweather; 1 s.; 1 d. Educ. Mill Hill School; Corpus Christi College, Oxford. Lecturer in Sanskrit, 1965-82, Head, Department of Sanskrit, 1975-98, Senior Lecturer, 1982-89, Reader, 1989-98. Publications: The Sacred Thread, 1981; Righteous Rama, 1984; Hinduism and Christianity, 1992; The Sanskrit Epics, 1998; Epic Threads, 2000. Recreation: gardening. Address: (b.) School of Asian Studies, 7 Buccleuch Place, Edinburgh EH8 9LW; T.-0131-650 4174; e-mail: J.L.Brockington@ed.ac.uk

Brocklebank, Ted. TV Producer; Managing Director, Greyfriars Productions; b. 24.9.42, St. Andrews; 2 s. Educ. Madras College, St. Andrews. D.C. Thomson, Dundee, 1960-63; Freelance Journalist, 1963-65; Scottish TV, 1965-70; Grampian Television: Reporter, 1970-76, Head of News and Current Affairs, 1977-85, Head of Documentaries and Features, 1985-95. BAFTA Award for What Price Oil?; Radio Industries Club of Scotland Special Award (Documentary) for Tale of Two Cities; Norwegian Amanda award for Oil, eight-part series on world oil business, networked on Channel 4 and throughout USA on PBS; BMA Award for Scotland the Grave. Recreations: Trustee, St Andrews Preservation Trust; Board Member, Byre Theatre, St Andrews; Committee Member, Scottish Cancer Research Campaign. Address: (b.) Greyfriars Productions, 6 Alexandra Place, St. Andrews KY16 9XD.

Brodie of Lethen, Ewen John. Lord Lieutenant of Nairnshire, since 1999; b. 16.12.42, Inverness; m., Mariota Menzies; 3 d. Educ. Harrow School. Lt., Grenadier Guards, 1961-64; IBM (UK) Ltd., 1965-74; estate management, since 1975; Director, John Gordon & Son Ltd., since 1992. Recreation: countryside sports. Address: (h.) Lethen House, Nairn IV12 5PR; T.-01667 452079.

Brodie, James, FFCS. National Chairman, Victim Support Scotland, since 1998; Director, The Ayrshire Hospice, since 1987; b. 29.4.38, Elderslie; m., Anne Tweedie; 1 s. Educ. Ayr Academy. Joined Ayrshire Constabulary, 1955, and retired as Superintendent; during career was: Chairman, West of Scotland Security Association; Chairman, Ayrshire and Arran Review Committee on Child Abuse; National Secretary, SASD; Director, Strathclyde Police Crime Prevention courses; Member, National Council, SACRO; Member, Home Office Working Party on vandalism caused by fires; Member, Secretary of State's Working Party on Police Community courses; Member, Executive Committee, Strathclyde Federation of Boys' Clubs. Elder, St Columba Church; Chairman, Appeals Committee, The Ayrshire Hospice; Member, Management Committee, Victim Support South Ayrshire; Co-Chairman, Joint Management Committee, 1st Ayr Company, BB.

Recreations: reading; music; gardening. Address: (h.) 3 Portmark Avenue, Doonbank, Ayr KA7 4DD; T.-01292 443553.

Brodie, Robert, CB, MA, LLB. Part-time Sheriff, since 2000; Part-time Chairman, Employment Tribunals in Scotland, since 2000; b. 9.4.38, Dundee; m., Jean Margaret McDonald; 2 s.; 2 d. Educ. Morgan Academy, Dundee; St. Andrews University; Queen's College, Dundee. Scottish Office: Legal Assistant, 1965; Senior Legal Assistant, 1970; Deputy Director, Scottish Courts Administration, 1975; Assistant Solicitor, Scottish Office, 1982; Deputy Solicitor to Secretary of State for Scotland, 1984-87; Solicitor to Secretary of State for Scotland, 1987-98. Chairman, Scottish Tourette Syndrome Support Group, 1993-98; Chair, Scottish Association of Citizens Advice Bureaux, 1999; Temporary Sheriff, 1999-2000; President, Edinburgh Bach Society, since 2000. Recreations: music; hill-walking. Address: (h.) 8 York Road, Edinburgh; T.-0131-552 2028.

Brodie, William, BSc, CBiol, MIBiol. Rector, Wallace High School, Stirling, since 1984; b. 16.9.37, Hamilton; m., Helen Bland; 1 s.; 1 d. Educ. Hamilton Academy; Glasgow University; Paisiey College of Technology. Teacher, Wishaw High School, 1965-67; Principal Teacher of Biology, Hutchesons' Grammar School, Glasgow, 1967-74; Assistant Rector, Graeme High School, Falkirk, 1974-79; Depute Rector, Kirkintilloch High School, 1979-81; Rector, Balfron High School, 1981-84. Chair, British Heart Foundation, Falkirk and District Branch, since 1997; Director, Glenbervie Golf Club, Larbert. Recreations: golf; tennis; gardening. Address: (b.) Wallace High School, Dumyat Road, Stirling FK9 5HW; T.-01786 462166.

Broni, David Alexander Thomas, MBA. Senior Executive, Scottish Development International (formerly Locate in Scotland), since 1995; b. 25.10.57, Glasgow; m., Ann Frances; 1 s.; 1 d. Educ. St. Mungo's Academy. Joined civil service, 1975; Manpower Services Commission, 12 years, Training Agency, 2 years, Scottish Office Industry Department, 2 years; Head of Secretariat, Scottish Enterprise, 4 years. Recreations: adventure racing; swimming; rugby; opera. Address: (b.) Atlantic Quay, 150 Broomielaw, Glasgow G2 8LU; T.-0141-228 2854; e-mail: david.broni@scotent.co.uk

Brooke, (Alexander) Keith, FRAgS. Member, Panel of Agricultural Arbiters appointed by Secretary of State for Scotland; b. 11.2.46, Minnigaff; m., Dilys K. Littlejohn; 1 s.; 3 d. Educ. George Watson's College, Edinburgh. President, Blackface Sheep Breeders Association, 1985-86, Hon. President, 1989-90; Director: Royal Highland and Agricultural Society of Scotland, 1986-93 and since 1994 (Convener, Public Relations and Education Committee, Chairman, Royal Highland Education Trust, 1998-2001, currently Chief Steward, Press Radio and Television), Animal Diseases Research Association, now Moredun Foundation for Animal Health and Welfare, 1981-96, Wallets Marts PLC, 1989-91, Scottish, English and Welsh Wool Growers Ltd., 1988-95, Wigtownshire Quality Lamb Ltd., 1991-96; Chairman, Blackface Sheep Breeders' Development Board, 1996-99; Member: Council of Awards of Royal Agricultural Societies, since 1997, Council, British Rouge de l'Ouest Sheep Society,1986-97 (Chairman, 1990-92, Treasurer, 1994-97). Address: (h.) Carscreugh, Glenluce, Newton Stewart, DG8 0NU; T.-01581 300334.

Brooke, Hazel, MBE, MA. Executive Director, Scottish Cot Death Trust, since 1988; Non Executive Trustee, Yorkhill NHS Trust, since 1998; b. 31.7.45, Forfar; m., Anthony Brooke; 2d. Educ. Inverness Royal Academy; Edinburgh University; Strathclyde University. Unilever, London; The Rank Organisation, London; Scottish Council, Development and Industry, Edinburgh; Glasgow University; Director, Yorkhill Family Bereavement Service; Member, Merchant's House,

Glasgow. Recreations: reading; wine appreciation; swimming. Address: (h.) 9 Campbell Drive, Glasgow; T.-0141-942 7492.

Brookes, Tommy, JP. Provost of Stirling, since 1999; b. 1.3.40, Plean, Stirling; m., Thelma; 1 s.; 2 d. Educ. East Plean. District Councillor, Sauchenford Ward, Stirling Council, since 1984; appointed Justice of the Peace, 1968; Member, Edinburgh Direct Aid. Recreations: life long supporter of Falkirk F.C. Address: (b.) Stirling Council, Viewforth, Stirling; T.-01786 443138; e-mail: brookest@stirling.gov.uk

Brooks, James, DSc, PhD, MPhil, BTech, FRSC, CChem, FGS, CGeol. Senior Partner, Brooks Associates Glasgow, since 1986; President-elect, Baptist Union of Scotland, 2002; b. 11.10.38, Co. Durham; m., Jan Slack; 1 s.; 1 d. Educ. Salt Grammar School, Yorkshire; University of Bradford. Research Scientist, British Petroleum, 1969-75; Senior Research Fellow, Bradford University, 1975-77; Research Associate/Senior Scientist, British National Oil Corporation/Britoil PLC, 1977-86. Visiting Lecturer, Glasgow University, 1978-98; Chairman/Director, Petroleum Geology '86 Limited, 1985-99; Geological Society: Vice President, 1984-87, Secretary, 1987-90; Founder, The Petroleum Group; AAPG Distinguished Achievement Award for service to petroleum geology and human need, 1993; AAPG Distinguished Lecturer to North America, 1989-90; Geological Society Distinguished Service Award, 1999; Honorary Life Member, AAPG; Church Secretary, Queen's Park Baptist Church, Glasgow. Publications: 18 books; 85 research papers. Recreations: travel; reading; writing; sport (English soccer!); Christian work. Address: (h.) 10 Langside Drive, Newlands, Glasgow G43 2EE; T.-0141-632 3068.

Brooks, Patrick William, BSc, MB, ChB, DPM, FRCPsych. Former Senior Medical Officer, Scottish Office Department of Health; b. 17.5.38, Hereford. Educ. Hereford High School; Bishop Vesey's Grammar School, Sutton Coldfield; Edinburgh University. Royal Edinburgh and associated hospitals, including State Hospital, Carstairs, and Western General Hospital, Edinburgh: Senior House Officer, 1964-66; Registrar, 1966-69; Senior Registrar, 1969-74; Medical Officer, Scottish Home and Health Department, 1974-81. A founder Member, Edinburgh Festival Fringe Society, 1959 (Vice-Chairman, 1964-71); Chairman, Edinburgh Playhouse Society, 1975-81; Secretary, Lothian Playhouse Trust, 1981-83; former Chairman, The Scottish Arts Lobby (SALVO); Chairman, The Friends of Paintings in Hospitals, Scotland; Chairman, Friends of The Talbot Rice Art Gallery. Recreations: opera; ballet; music; theatre; cinema; modern Scottish art; travel. Address: (h.) 11 Thirlestane Road, Edinburgh EH9 1AL.

Broster, Rev. David, BA, DipTh, CPS, FFCS. Minister, Kilbirnie: St. Columba's, since 1983; Clerk, Ardrossan Presbytery, since 1989; b. 14.3.44, Liverpool; m., Margaret Ann Mercer; 2 d. Educ. Liverpool Institute High School; United Theological College, University of Wales; Open University. Ordained by Presbyterian Church of Wales, 1969; Minister, Park Place, Tredegar, Gwent, 1969-78; Clubmoor Presbyterian Church of Wales, Liverpool, 1978-83; Clerk, Association in East, Presbyterian Church of Wales, 1981-83; Moderator, Synod of Ayr, 1991-92; Secretary, Nan Stevenson Charitable Trust, since 1989. Chairman, Moorpark School Board; Past Chairman, Garnock Valley Crime Prevention Panel; Past President, Garnock Valley Rotary. Recreations: computing; advanced driving; gardening; curling. Address: St. Columba's Manse, Kilbirnie, Ayrshire; T.-01505 683342; e-mail: david@broster.org

Broun, Janice Anne, BA. Freelance journalist and author; b. 24.3.34, Tipton; m., Canon Claud Broun; 2 s.; 1 d. Educ. Dudley Girls High School; St. Anne's College, Oxford.

Publications: Conscience and Captivity: Religion in Eastern Europe, 1988; Prague Winter, 1988; Albania: Religion in a Fortress State, 1989; Bulgaria: Religion Denied, 1989; Romania: Religion in a Hardline State, 1989; six entries in Censorship: A World Encyclopedia, 2001; frequent contributions to Keston Institute publications. Recreations: swimming; cycling; music; art history; travel. Address: Martin Lodge, Ardross Place, Alness, Ross-shire, IV17 0PX; T.-01349 882442.

Browitt, Chris W.A., PhD, FRSE. Director, British Geological Survey Scotland, since 1994; President, European Meditteranean Seismological Centre, since 1994; b. 3.9.43, Darlington. Educ. Darlington Grammar School; Durham University. Honorary Fellow, Edinburgh University; since 1971, has developed the UK seismic monitoring and information service and led the UK's efforts in earthquake risk reduction worldwide; Member, UK National Committee for Disaster Reduction; Member, Executive Committee, International Seismological Centre. Recreations: swimming and cycling. Address: (b.) British Geological Survey, Murchison House, W. Mains Road, Edinburgh.

Brown, Alan. Chairman, Scottish Road Safety Campaign, since 1995; Head of Road Safety Branch, Scottish Executive, (formerly Scottish Office), since 1995; b. 9.5.47, Methil; m., Marion Dougal; 1 s.; 1 d. Educ. Buckhaven High School. Joined Scottish Office, 1965: posts in Education, Social Work Services, Transport, Local Government, and Criminal Justice. County Bird Recorder for East Lothian, 1983-89; Member: Lothian Birds Record Committee, 1983-96 and since 1998, Scottish Birds Record Committee, 1984-94 (Secretary, 1984-86), Council, Scottish Ornithologists Club, 1986-90, British Birds Rarities Committee, 1987-95. Recreations: birdwatching in the world's remote places (the ecstasy); supporting Hibernian FC (the agony); rock music; motor-cycling. Address: (b.) The Scottish Executive, Victoria Quay, Edinburgh EH6 6QQ; T.-0131-244 0836.

Brown, Professor Alice, MA, PhD. Professor of Politics, University of Edinburgh, since 1997 (Vice Principal, since 1999); Co-Director, Institute of Governance, since 1998; b. 30.9.46, Edinburgh; m., Alan James Brown; 2 d. Educ. Boroughmuir High School, Edinburgh; Stevenson College, Edinburgh; University of Edinburgh. Lecturer in Economics, University of Stirling, 1984; University of Edinburgh: Lecturer, Departments of Economics, Continuing Education and Politics, 1985-92, Senior Lecturer in Politics, 1992-97, appointed Head of Politics Department, 1995, appointed Head, Planning Unit, 1996, Personal Chair, 1997. Currently: Member, Wicks Committee on Standards in Public Life; Council Member, Scottish Higher Education Funding Council; Chair, Community Planning Task Force, Scottish Executive; Member, Advisory Group to Equal Opportunities Commission; Board and Executive Member, Centre for Scottish Public Policy; Member, Scottish Committee, British Council; Member, Hansard Society Scotland Working Group; Assistant Editor, Scottish Affairs journal; Member, Editorial Board, Talking Politics; founder Member, Scottish Gender Equality Research Network; Member, CBI Scotland Working Group on Business Awareness for Members of the Scottish Parliament. Publications: A Major Crisis? (Joint Author), 1996; Gender Equality in Scotland (Joint Author), 1997; Politics and Society in Scotland (Joint Author), 1996; The Scottish Electorate (Joint Author), 1999; New Scotland, New Politics (Joint Author), 2001. Recreations: reading; music; cooking. Address: Institute of Governance, Chisholm House, High School Yards, Edinburgh EH1 1LZ; T.-0131-650 2459.

Brown, Professor Alistair J.P., BSc, PhD. Professor of Molecular and Cell Biology, Aberdeen University, since 1998; b. 5.2.55; m., Carolyn Michie; 2 s. Educ. George Watson's College, Edinburgh; University of Aberdeen. Biotechnology Lecturer, Glasgow University, 1983-89; Aberdeen University: Biotechnology Lecturer, 1989-91, Senior Lecturer, 1992-96, Reader, 1996-98. Recreation: watching his sons, Myles and Cameron play football and rugby. Address: (b.) Institute of Medical Sciences, Foresterhill, Aberdeen AB25 2ZD; T.-01224 273183.

Brown, Allan, MA (Hons). Chief Writer, Scotland on Sunday, since 2001; b. 12.1.67, Glasgow. Educ. Claremont High School, East Kilbride; University of Glasgow; University of Strathclyde. Press Officer, Glasgow 1990: Year of Culture, 1990; freelance work, 1990-93; News Sub-Editor, Scottish Sun, 1995; Sunday Times Scotland: Sub-Editor, 1996, Deputy Editor, Features, 1998, Chief Writer, 1999, Columnist. Bank of Scotland Feature Writer of the Year, 1998-99, 2000-01; Scottish Journalist of the Year, 1998-99. Publications: Inside The Wicker Man – The Morbid Ingenuities, 2000; The Downs (novel), 2002. Recreation: humbly seeking the truth. Address: (b.) Barclay House, Holyrood Road, Edinburgh; T.-07970 958048.

Brown, Andrew Gibson, QPM. Chief Constable, Grampian Police, since 1998; b. 11.4.45, Kelso; m., Fiona; 1 s.; 1 d. Lothian and Borders Police: Detective Chief Superintendent, 1992-93, Assistant Chief Constable, 1993-98. Address: (b.) Police HQ, Queen Street, Aberdeen AB10 1ZA; T.-01224 386000.

Brown, Rev. Colin Campbell, BD. Minister, Darnley United Free Church, Glasgow, since 1979; Teacher (part-time) of Religious Education, Williamwood High School, Glasgow, since 1987; b. 30.8.54, Perth; m., Joyce; 1 s. Educ. Perth High School; University of Edinburgh; Moray House College of Education. Convener, United Free Church Youth Committee, 1985-89; Moderator, Presbytery of Glasgow and the West, 1990-91; Convener, Action of Churches Together in Scotland Education Group, 1992-94; Convener, United Free Church Ministry and Home Affairs Committee, since 1997; part-time Religious Education Teacher, Renfrew High School, 1980-87. Address: 2 Waukglen Drive, Southpark, Darnley, Glasgow G53 7UG; T.-0141-638 6101.

Brown, Douglas Carl Jessen, DA (Edin), DMS, MPhil, FRSA, MSDC, MIMGT, AIST, ASIC. Honorary Secretary, Commonwealth Games Council for Scotland, since 1999; Member, Board of Management, Scottish Amateur Swimming Association, since 1995; b. 2.10.40, Edinburgh; m., Noreen Simpson; 2 s.; 2 d. Educ. High School of Dundee; Edinburgh College of Art; Edinburgh College of Commerce; Open University. Lecturer, then Depute Head, School of Design, Edinburgh College of Art, 1964-86; Director, School of Design, Edinburgh College of Art/Heriot-Watt University, 1986-95 (retired); professional practice in design and making, silversmith and jeweller; Member, Senate, Heriot-Watt University, 1986-95; Secretary, Association of Scottish Schools of Design, 1988-90; Member, Board of Governors, Edinburgh College of Art, 1974-79, 1988-89; teaching and competitive swimming at club and district levels, 1977-89; Administrative Co-ordinator for all aquatic events, Commonwealth Games, 1986; Chairman, Organising Committee, European Swimming Cup, 1988; Technical Co-ordinator, European Junior Swimming and Diving Championships, 1997; Member, Amateur Swimming Federation of Great Britain Committee, 1995-2001. Recreations: reading; photography; travel; boating; fishing. Address: (h.) 29 Hartington Place, Edinburgh EH10 4LF; T.-0131-229 6924.

Brown, Professor Ewan, CBE, MA, LLB, CA, FRSE, FCIBS. Merchant Banker; Executive Director: Noble Grossart Ltd., since 1971; Chairman: Scottish Knowledge Plc, Lloyds TSB Scotland Plc; Director: Lloyds TSB Group Plc, John Wood Group Plc; Noble Grossart Investments Ltd.; Stagecoach Holdings Plc; James Walker (Leith) Ltd.; b. 23.3.42, Perth; m., Christine; 1 s.; 1 d. Educ. Perth Academy; St. Andrews University. CA apprentice with Peat Marwick Mitchell, 1964-67. Honorary Professor in Finance, Heriot Watt University; Trustee, Carnegie Trust for the Universities of Scotland; Chairman, University Court, Heriot-Watt University; Master, The Company of Merchants of the City of Edinburgh, 1994-95; Lord Dean of Guild, City of Edinburgh, 1995-97; Council Member: Institute of Chartered Accountants of Scotland, 1988-91, Scottish Business School, 1974-80; Previous directorships: Scottish Transport Group, 1983-88, Scottish Development Finance, 1983-93, Pict Petroleum plc, 1973-95, Scottish Widows Bank plc, 1994-97; Chairman, Dunedin Income Growth Investment Trust Plc, 1996-2001; Governor, Edinburgh College of Art, 1986-89; Session Clerk, Mayfield Church, 1983-88. Recreations: family; golf; skiing; Scottish watercolours; Mah Jongg. Address: (b.) 48 Queen Street, Edinburgh; T.-0131-226 7011.

Brown, Francis Henry, BA (Hons), MHSM, DipHSM. Director of Operations, Tayside Primary Care NHS Trust, since 1999; b. 17.4.47, Falkirk; m., Marion Muir Crawford; 2 s. Educ. Falkirk High School; Strathclyde University. Joined NHS as graduate trainee, 1975; various management/senior management posts, Borders Health Board, Ayrshire and Arran Health Board, and within Tayside, 1977-99. Recreations: music; swimming; cycling; gentle jogging. Address: (b.) Royal Dundee Liff Hospital, Dundee DD2 5NF; T.-01382 423115; e-mail: frank.brown@tpct.scot.nhs.uk

Brown, Hamish Macmillan, MBE, D.Litt, FRSGS. Author, Lecturer, Photographer and Mountaineer; b. 13.8.34, Colombo, Sri Lanka. Educ. several schools abroad; Dollar Academy. National Service, RAF, Middle East/East Africa; Assistant, Martyrs' Memorial Church, Paisley; first-ever full-time appointment in outdoor education (Braehead School, Fife; served many years on Scottish Mountain Leadership Board; has led expeditions world-wide for mountaineering, skiing, trekking, canoeing, etc. Publications: Hamish's Mountain Walk, 1979 (SAC award); Hamish's Groats End Walk, 1981 (Smith's Travel Prize shortlist); Time Gentlemen, Some Collected Poems, 1983; Eye to the Hills, 1982; Five Bird Stories, 1984; Poems of the Scottish Hills (Editor), 1982; Speak to the Hills (Co-Editor), 1985; Travels, 1986; The Great Walking Adventure, 1986; Hamish Brown's Scotland, 1988; Climbing the Corbetts, 1988; Great Walks Scotland (Co-author), 1989; Scotland Coast to Coast, 1990; Walking the Summits of Somerset and Avon, 1991; From the Pennines to the Highlands, 1992; The Bothy Brew & Other Stories, 1993; The Fife Coast, The Last Hundred, 1994; 25 Walks – Fife, 1995; Fort William and Glen Coe Walks, 1996; Exploring the Edinburgh to Glasgow Canal, 1997; Compendium: Hamish's Mountain Walks/Climbing the Corbetts, 1997; Fife in Focus, Photographs of the Fife Coast; 25 Walks, Skye and Kintail, 2000. Recreations: books; music; Morocco. Address: 26 Kirkcaldy Road, Burntisland, Fife, KY3 9HQ; T.-01592 873546.

Brown, Hilary Neilson, DipDomSc, DipEd. Chef/Proprietrix, La Potiniere, since 1975; b. 6.6.52, Glasgow; m., David Richard Brown. Educ. Hutcheson' Girls' Grammar School; Glasgow and West of Scotland College of Domestic Science; Jordanhill College of Education. Teacher, Bellarmine Secondary School, 1973-75. Michelin Star, since 1991; Egon Ronay Star, since 1985; AA Rosettes, since 1977. Publication: La Potiniere and Friends, 1990. Recreations: health and fitness; cinema; France. Address: (b.) La Potiniere, Gullane, East Lothian; T.-01620 843214.

Brown, Professor Ian James Morris, MA (Hons), MLitt, PhD, DipEd, FRSA, FFCS. Playwright, since 1969; Professor of Drama, Queen Margaret University College, Edinburgh, since 1995 (Dean, Arts Faculty, since 1999, Head, Drama Department, 1996-99, Reader, 1994-95); Director, Scottish Centre for Cultural Management and Policy, since 1996; b. 28.2.45, Barnet; m., 1, Judith Sidaway; 2, Nicola Axford; 1 s.; 1 d. Educ. Dollar Academy; Edinburgh University; Crewe and Alsager College. Schoolteacher, 1967-69, 1970-71; Lecturer in Drama, Dunfermline College, 1971-76; British Council: Assistant Representative, Scotland, 1976-77, Assistant Regional Director, Istanbul, 1977-78; various posts, Crewe and Alsager College, 1978-86, latterly Leader, BA (Hons) Drama Studies; Programme Director, Alsager Arts Centre, 1980-86; Drama Director, Arts Council of Great Britain, 1986-94. British Theatre Institute: Vice Chairman, 1983-85, Chairman, 1985-87; Member, International Advisory Committee, O'Neill Theatre Center, since 1994; Chair, Scottish Society of Playwrights, 1973-75, 1984-87, 1997-99; plays include Mother Earth, The Bacchae, Carnegie, The Knife, The Fork, New Reekie, Mary, Runners, Mary Queen and the Loch Tower, Joker in the Pack, Beatrice, First Strike, The Scotch Play, Bacchai, Wasting Reality, Margaret, A Great Reckonin. Recreations: theatre; sport; travel; cooking. Address: (b.) Queen Margaret University College, Clerwood Terrace, Edinburgh EH12 8TS.

Brown, J. Craig, CBE, DUniv, BA, DipPE. Director of Football Development, Scottish Football Association (International Team Manager, 1993-2001); b. 1.7.40, Glasgow; 2 s.; 1 d. Educ. Hamilton Academy. Professional footballer: Rangers F.C., 1958-60, Dundee F.C., 1960-66, Falkirk F.C., 1966-68; Assistant Manager, Motherwell F.C., 1975-77; Manager, Clyde F.C., 1977-86; Assistant National Coach and Under-21 Coach, 1986-93; Vice President, Union of European Football Trainers; FIFA Instructor; Hon. Lecturer, Paisley University; Sports Photographers' Personality of the Year, 1989, 1996; City of Glasgow Sportsperson of the Year, 1997; Bells Manager of the Month, five occasions. Teacher of primary school subjects, Deputy Headteacher, Headteacher and Lecturer in Primary Education, 1963-86. Publications: Activity Methods in the Middle Years, 1975; Craig Brown, The Autobiography, 1998. Recreation: golf. Address: (b.) Scottish Football Association, Hampden Park, Glasgow G42 9AY; T.-0141-616 6074.

Brown, James Armour, OBE, RD, BL. Partner, Kerr Barrie & Duncan (formerly Kerr, Barrie & Goss), Solicitors, Glasgow, 1957-91 (Consultant, 1991-93); b. 20.7.30, Rutherglen; m., Alexina Mary Robertson McArthur; 1 s. Educ. Rutherglen Academy; Glasgow University. National Service, Royal Navy, 1951-53; commissioned RNVR, 1952; served with Clyde Division, RNVR/RNR, 1953-72; Captain, 1972; Senior Reserve Supply Officer on staff of Admiral Commanding Reserves, 1973-76; Naval ADC to The Queen, 1975-76; Member, Suite of Lord High Commissioner to General Assembly of Church of Scotland, 1961-63; Session Clerk, Stonelaw Parish Church, Rutherglen, 1964-81; Member, Church of Scotland Committee on Chaplains to HM Forces, 1975-82 (Vice-Convener, 1979-82); Clerk, Incorporation of Bakers of Glasgow, 1964-89; Deacon, Society of Deacons and Free Preseses of Glasgow, 1978-80; Member, Glasgow Committee, Order of St. John of Jerusalem, since 1961 (Chairman, 1982-93, Honorary President, since 1995); Member, Chapter of the Priory of Scotland of the Order of St. John, 1970-99 and since 2000; KStJ, 1975; GCStJ, 2000; Preceptor of Torphichen, Priory of Scotland, 1984-92, and 1998-99; Chancellor, Priory of Scotland, 1992-97; Hon. Chairman, Orders and Medals Research Society (Scottish Branch), 1987- 91. Recreations: music; historical research. Address: (h.) 6 Arran Way, Bothwell, Glasgow G71 8TR; T.-01698 854226.

Brown, Rt. Hon. (James) Gordon. PC, MA, PhD, MP. Chancellor of the Exchequer, since 1997; MP (Labour), Dunfermline East, since 1983; b. 20.2.51; m. Educ. Kirkcaldy High School; Edinburgh University. Rector, Edinburgh University, 1972-75; Temporary Lecturer, Edinburgh University, 1976; Lecturer, Glasgow College of Technology, 1976-80; Journalist and Current Affairs Editor, Scottish Television, 1980-83. Contested (Labour) South Edinburgh, 1979; Chairman, Labour Party Scottish Council, 1983-84; Opposition Chief Secretary to the Treasury, 1987; Shadow Minister for Trade and Industry, 1989. Publications: The Red Paper on Scotland (Editor), 1975; The Politics of Nationalism and Devolution (Co-Editor), 1980; Scotland: The Real Divide, 1983; Maxton, 1986; Where There is Greed, 1989. Recreations: reading and writing; football; golf; tennis. Address: 21 Ferryhills Road, North Queensferry, Fife.

Brown, Jenny, MA (Hons). Head of Literature, Scottish Arts Council; b. 13.5.58, Manchester; m., Alexander Richardson; 4 s. Educ. George Watson's College; Aberdeen University. Assistant Administrator, Edinburgh Festival Fringe Society, 1980-82; Director, Edinburgh Book Festival, 1983-91; Presenter, Scottish Television book programmes, 1989-94; National Co-ordinator, Readiscovery Campaign, 1994-95; Commissioner, Press Complaints Commission, 1993-97; Non-Executive Director, Scottish Television (Regional) Ltd., since 1998; Governor, George Watson's College. Address: (b.) Scottish Arts Council, 12 Manor Place, Edinburgh EH3 7DD.

Brown, John Caldwell, DA, RSW. Painter; Member, Board, Leith School of Art, since 1991; b. 19.10.45, Irvine; m., Elizabeth Ann (deceased); 3 s. Educ. Ardrossan Academy; Glasgow School of Art. RSA Carnegie Travelling Scholarship and GSA Cargill Travelling Scholarship, 1968; Director of Art, Fettes College, 1971-86; Director of Art, Malvern College, 1986-88; Head of Art, Edinburgh Academy, 1988-97; former Lecturer (part-time): Edinburgh College of Art, Leith School of Art; solo exhibitions: GSA, 1970, Moray House, 1989, Torrance Gallery, 1992, Open Eye Gallery, 1996, 1998 and 2000, Duncan Miller Fine Art London, 1996, 1997, 1999, 2000. James Torrance Award, RGI, 1970; Scottish Arts Club Award SAAC, 1993; Scottish Provident Award, 1993; Heinzel Gallery Award SAAC, 1994. Address: (h.) 92 Trinity Road, Edinburgh EH5 3JU; T.-0131-552 8676.

Brown, Professor John Campbell, BSc, PhD, DSc, FRAS, FRSE, FInstP. Astronomer Royal for Scotland, since 1995; Professor of Astrophysics, Glasgow University, 1984-96, Regius Chair of Astronomy, since 1996; Honorary Professor, Edinburgh University, since 1996, Aberdeen University, since 1997; b. 4.2.47, Dumbarton; m., Dr. Margaret I. Brown; 1 s.; 1 d. Educ. Dumbarton Academy; Glasgow University. Glasgow University Astronomy Department: Research Assistant, 1968-70, Lecturer, 1970-78, Senior Lecturer, 1978-80, Reader, 1980-84; Nuffield Fellow, 1983-84; Kelvin Medallist, 1983-86; Armagh Robinson Medallist, 1998; DAAD Fellow, Tubingen University, 1971-72; ESRO/GROC Fellow, Space Research Laboratory, Utrecht, 1973-74; Visitor: Australian National University, 1975, High Altitude Observatory, Colorado, 1977; NASA Associate Professor, Maryland University, 1980; NSF Fellow, University of California at San Diego, 1984; Brittingham Professor, University of Wisconsin, 1987; Visiting Professor: University of Amsterdam, 1999, ETH Zurich, 1999, NASA Goddard SFC, 1999, CNRS Meudan, 1999. Member: SERC Solar System Committee, 1980-83, Council, Royal Astronomical Society, 1984-87, 1990-93 (Vice-President, 1986-87), Council, Royal Society of Edinburgh, 1997-2000, International Astronomical Union, since 1976; President, BAAS Physics Section, since

2001. Recreations: cycling; walking; painting; lapidary; conjuring; photography; woodwork. Address: (b.) Department of Physics and Astronomy, Glasgow University, Glasgow G12 8QW; T.-0141-330 5182.

Brown, John Souter, MA (Hons), MIPR. Head of Public Relations and Marketing, Glasgow City Council, since 1996; b. 15.10.48, Glasgow; m., Angela McGinn; 1 s.; 1 d. Educ. Kirkcaldy High School; Edinburgh University. Statistics and Information Officer, Lanark County Council, 1970-72; Senior Officer (Research, Planning Publicity), Manchester City Social Services Department, 1972-75; Press Officer, Strathclyde Regional Council, 1975-80; Journalist and Presenter, Scottish Television, 1980-82; Editor, What's Your Problem?, 1982-84; Ways and Means, 1984-86; Senior Producer (Politics), Scottish Television, 1986-91; North of Scotland TV Franchise Team, 1991; Managing Director, Lomond Television, 1992-93; Head of Public Relations, Strathclyde Regional Council, 1993-96; Chair, Volunteer Centre, Glasgow, 1996-98; Director, Scottish Foundation, since 1990. Address: (b.) Public Relations and Marketing, City Chambers, George Square, Glasgow G2 1DU; T.-0141-287 0901; e-mail: pr@glasgow.gov.uk

Brown, Keith James, MA (Hons). Leader, Clackmannanshire Council, since 1999; b. 20.12.61, Edinburgh; m., Tammy; 2 s.; 1 d. Educ. Tynecastle High School; Dundee University. Royal Marines, 1980-83; local government administrative officer, since 1988. Elected Member, SNP National Council; Member, European Committee of the Regions; Member, Association of Electoral Administrators. Recreations: astronomy; hill-walking; football. Address: (b.) Clackmannanshire Council, Greenfield, Alloa FK10 2AD.

Brown, Professor Kenneth Alexander, BSc, MSc, PhD, FRSE. Professor of Mathematics, Glasgow University; Vice-President, London Mathematical Society, 1997-99; b. 19.4.51, Ayr; m., Irene M.; 2 s. Educ. Ayr Academy; Glasgow University; Warwick University. Recreations: reading; running. Address: (b.) Mathematics Department, Glasgow University, Glasgow G12 8QW; T.-0141-330 5180; e-mail: kab@maths.gla.ac.uk

Brown, Professor Kenneth J., BSc, PhD, FRSE. Professor in Mathematics, Heriot-Watt University, since 1993; b. 20.12.45, Torphins; m., Elizabeth Lobban; 1 s.; 2 d. Educ. Banchory Academy; Robert Gordon's College; Aberdeen University; Dundee University. Lecturer in Mathematics, Heriot Watt University, 1970-81, Senior Lecturer, 1981-91, Reader, 1991-93. Publications: 45 papers. Recreations: theatre; reading. Address: (h.) 3 Highlea Grove, Balerno, Edinburgh EH14 7HQ; T.-0131-449 5314.

Brown, R. Iain F, MBE, MA, MEd, ABPsS, ChPsychol. Honorary Senior Research Fellow, Department of Psychology, Glasgow University, since 1968; b. 16.1.35, Dundee; m., Catherine G.; 2 d. Educ. Daniel Stewart's College, Edinburgh; St. Andrews University; Edinburgh University; Glasgow University. Education Department, Corporation of Glasgow; Department of Psychological Medicine, Glasgow University. National Training Adviser, Scottish Council on Alcohol, 1979-94; Member, Executive, Scottish Council on Alcohol, 1980-94 and Alcohol Focus Scotland, since 1998; Chairman: Society for the Study of Gambling, London, 1987-92, European Association for the Study of Gambling, 1992-95, Glasgow Council on Alcohol, since 1985, Confederation of Scottish Counselling Agencies, 1989-93. Various publications, mainly on addictions, in scientific books and journals. Recreations: travel; music. Address: (h.) 13 Kirklee Terrace, Glasgow G12 0TH; T.-0141-339 7095.

Brown, Robert, LLB (Hons). MSP (Liberal Democrat), Glasgow, since 1999; b. 1947, Newcastle upon Tyne; m.; 1 s.; 1 d. Educ. Gordon Schools, Huntly; Aberdeen University. Solicitor; former Senior Civil Partner, Ross Harper and Murphy; former Glasgow District Councillor (Leader, Lib Dem Group, 1977-92). Address: (b.) Olympic House, Suite 1, 2nd Floor; 142 Queen Street, Glasgow G1 3BU; T.-0141-243 2421; Scottish Parliament, Edinburgh EH99 1SP; T.-0131-348 5792; e-mail: robert.brown.msp.@scottish.parliament.uk

Brown, Russell Leslie. MP (Labour), Dumfries, since 1997; b. 17.9.51, Annan; m., Christine Margaret Calvert; 2 d. Educ. Annan Academy. Employed by ICI for 23 years in variety of positions; Local Councillor, since 1986. Recreations: walking; sport, especially football. Address: 5 Friars Vennel, Dumfries DG1 2RQ; T.-01387 247902.

Brown, Professor Sally, BSc, MA, PhD, FSCRE, FEIS, FRSA, FRSE. Professor of Education, Stirling University, 1990-2001, now Emeritus Professor (Deputy Principal, 1996-2001); b. 15.12.35, London; m., Professor Charles Brown (deceased); 2 s. Educ. Bromley High School GPDST; University College, London; Smith College, Massachusetts; Stirling University. Lecturer in College of Education, London, and College of Technology, Nigeria; University Lecturer, Nigeria; School Science Teacher, Helensburgh; University Researcher, Stirling; Research Adviser to Scottish Education Department; Director, Scottish Council for Research in Education, 1986-90. Former President, British Educational Research Association; former Chair, Central Region Child Protection Committee; Governor, Queen Margaret University College; Chair, Education Panel, UK Research Assessment Exercise 2001 (RAE2001); Deputy Chair, Economic and Social Research Council Teaching and Learning Programme; Chair, Board of Advisers to Research Centre for Gaelic Leirsinn; Trustee, Teacher Support Scotland. Publications: 130 (articles, monographs, books) on educational research and education generally. Recreations: golf; reading; music. Address: (b.) Department of Education, Stirling University, Stirling FK9 4LA.

Brown, Samuel Jeffrey, BA (Hons). Rector, Moffat Academy, since 1990; b. 10.4.51, Airdrie; m., Elizabeth Scobbie Hamilton; 2 d. Educ. Airdrie Academy; Strathclyde University. Teacher of History/Modern Studies/Economics, Lockerbie Academy, 1974-78; Assistant Principal Teacher of Guidance, Lockerbie Academy, 1978-80; Principal Teacher of History, Dumfries High School, 1980-83; Assistant Rector with responsibility for lower school and educational needs, Stranraer Academy, 1983-88; Depute Rector, Moffat Academy, 1988-90. Reader, Church of Scotland, since 1985; Associate Assessor, HMI Schools, since 2000; Trustee, Moffat Museum. Recreations: hill-walking; canoeing; gardening; theatre; films; music of all types; reading. Address: (b.) Moffat Academy, Moffat, DG10 9DA; T.-01683 220114.

Brown, Steven, LLB (Hons). Solicitor; Partner, McClure Naismith, since 1986; b. 20.11.56, Irvine; m., Carol Anne; 1 s. Educ. Irvine Royal Academy; University of Edinburgh. Trained with Kilgour McNeil & Syme, 1978-80; Assistant Solicitor, J&F Anderson, 1980-85. Recreations: family; computers; music; golf. Address: (b.) 49 Queen Street, Edinburgh EH2 3NH; T.-0131-220 1002.

Brown, Professor Stewart J., BA, MA, PhD, FRHistS. Professor of Ecclesiastical History, Edinburgh University, since 1988; Dean, Faculty of Divinity, since 2000; b. 8.7.51, Illinois; m., Teri B. Hopkins-Brown; 1 s.; 1 d. Educ. University of Illinois; University of Chicago. Fulbright Scholar, Edinburgh University, 1976-78; Whiting Fellow in the Humanities, University of Chicago, 1979-80; Assistant to the Dean, College of Arts & Sciences, and Lecturer in

History, Northwestern University, 1980-82; Associate Professor and Assistant Head, Department of History, University of Georgia, 1982-88; Visiting Lecturer, Department of Irish History, University College, Cork, 1986; Editor, Scottish Historical Review, 1993-99. Publications: Thomas Chalmers and the Godly Commonwealth in Scotland, 1982 (awarded Agnes Mure Mackenzie Prize from Saltire Society); Scotland in the Age of the Disruption (Co-author), 1993; William Robertson and the Expansion of Empire (Editor), 1997; Piety and Power in Ireland 1760-1960 (Co-editor), 2000; Scottish Christianity in the Modern World (Co-editor), 2000; The National Churches of England, Ireland and Scotland, 1801-1846, 2001. Recreations: swimming; hill-walking. Address: (h.) 160 Craigleith Hill Avenue, Edinburgh EH4 2NB; T.-0131-343 1712.

Brown, Professor (Susanne) Moira, BSc, PhD, FRCPath, FRSE. Professor of Neurovirology, Glasgow University, since 1995; Chief Executive, Chief Scientist and Director, Crusade Laboratories Ltd., since 1999; b. 21.3.46, Greenock; m., Alasdair Macdougall Brown. Educ. Greenock Academy; Strathearn School, Belfast; Queen's University, Belfast; Glasgow University. MRC Virology Unit, Glasgow, 1971-95; Wistar Institute, Philadelphia, 1977-80. Chairperson, Scottish Hospital Endowments Research Trust. Recreations: walking; travel; dogs; Christian faith. Address: (h.) 5 Bellshaugh Road, Glasgow G12 0SN; T.-0141-357 2239.

Brown, William Alan, Master Mariner; Marine Superintendent, Scottish Fisheries Protection Agency, since 1997; b. 4.10.49, Edinburgh; m., Elizabeth Ann Connell; 1 s.; 1 d. Educ. Boroughmuir Secondary School; Leith Nautical College. Cadet to Second Officer, British and Commonwealth Shipping, 1967-77; Second Officer to Chief Officer, Fred. Olsen Lines, 1977-80; Scottish Fisheries Protection Agency (formerly DAFS), since 1980: Second Officer, then First Officer, then Commander. Address: (b.) Pentland House, 47 Robb's Loan, Edinburgh EH14 1TY.

Brown, Rev. William David, BD, CQSW. Chairman, Children 1st, since 2000; Minister, Murrayfield Parish Church, Edinburgh, since 2001; b.21.8.48. Edinburgh; m., Shirley; 1s.; 1d. Educ. Forrester High School; Edinburgh University; Moray House College. Scottish Office, 1964-70; Royal Scottish Society for the Protection of Cruelty to Children (now Children 1st): Inspector and Project Officer, 1970-78; Development Officer, Scotland. 1978-83; New College studying for BD, 1983-87; Church of Scotland Minister, Carlisle and Longtown, 1987-2001; Chairman, Carlisle One World Centre, 1995-2001; Chairman, Churches Together, Carlisle. Recreations: reading; walking. Address: (h.) 45 Murrayfield Gardens, Edinburgh. EH12 6DH; T.-0131-337 5431.

Browne, Desmond, MP, LLB (Hons). Labour MP, Kilmarnock and Loudoun, since 1997; Under Secretary of State, Northern Ireland Office, since 2001; b. 22.3.52; m., Maura; 2 s. Educ. St Michael's Academy, Kilwinning; Glasgow University. Partner, Ross Harper and Murphy, 1980-85; Senior Partner, McCluskey Browne, Kilmarnock, 1985-92; called to the Bar, 1993; Member, Council, Law Society of Scotland, 1988-91; Chair, Children's Rights Group, 1981-86; Member, Sheriff Court Rules Council, 1990-92; Member, Dean's Council, Faculty of Advocates, 1994-97. Recreations: football; swimming; reading. Address: (b.) House of Commons, Westminster, London SW1A 0AA.

Browning, Professor George Gordon, MD, ChB, FRCS(Ed.), FRCPS(Glas). Professor of Otolaryngology, Head and Neck Surgery, University of Glasgow, since 1991; Honorary Consultant Otolaryngologist, Glasgow Royal Infirmary, since 1978; Senior Consultant Otologist to British MRC Institute of Hearing Research, since 1992; b. 10.1.41, Glasgow; m., Annette; 1 s.; 2 d. Educ. Kelvinside Academy; University of Glasgow. Resident House Surgeon, Western Infirmary, Glasgow, 1964-65; West of Scotland General Surgical Training Scheme, 1965-70; West of Scotland Otorhinolaryngological Training Scheme, 1970-76; MRC Wernher-Piggot Travelling Fellow, Harvard University, 1976-77. President, Otorhinolaryngological Research Society UK, 1992-94; Chairman, British Society of Academics in Otolaryngology, UK, 1995-99; Vice-Chairman, Specialist Advisory Committee in Otolaryngology, 1997-99; President, Section of Otology, Royal Society of Medicine, 1999-2000; Chairman, Academic Board, Royal Society of Medicine, since 2001 (Vice-Chairman, 2000-01); Member, Post-Graduate Examining Boards, FRCS Edinburgh, since 1997, and FRCPS Glasgow, since 1987. Publications: Updated ENT (3rd Edition), 1994; Picture Tests in Otolaryngology (Co-Author), 1998; Clinical Otology and Audiology (2nd Edition), 1998; Otoscopy – A Structured Approach (Co-Author), 1995; over 80 scientific articles. Recreations: silversmithing; skiing; swimming. Address: (b.) Department of Otolaryngology, Glasgow Royal Infirmary University NHS Trust, 16 Alexandra Parade, Glasgow G31 2ER; T.-0141-211 4695.

Brownlie, Alistair Rutherford, OBE, MA, LLB, SSC, FFCS; b. 5.4.24, Edinburgh; m., Martha Barron Mounsey. Educ. George Watson's; Edinburgh University. Served as radio operator in 658 Air O.P. Squadron RAF, Europe and India; apprenticed to J. & R.A. Robertson, WS; qualified Solicitor, 1950; in private practice; Member, Committee on Blood Grouping (House of Lords); Solicitor for the poor, 1955-64, in High Court of Justiciary; Secretary, SSC Society, 1970-95, now Archivist; former Member, Council, Law Society of Scotland; Legal Aid Central Committee; Chairman, Legal Aid Committee, Scottish Legal Aid Board, 1986-90; founder Member, Past President, now Hon. Member, Forensic Science Society; Member, Vice-Chairman, Scottish Council of Law Reporting, 1975-97; Chairman, Edinburgh Western Diabetes Research Trust; Fellow, RSA; Elder, Church of Scotland and United Reformed Church. Publications: The Universities and Scottish Legal Education; Drink, Drugs and Driving (Co-author); Crime Investigation: art or science (Editor); various papers on forensic science, criminal law and legal aid. Recreations: the pen, the spade, and the saw. Address: (h.) 8 Braid Mount, Edinburgh; T.-0131-447 4255.

Bruce, Alistair James, LLB, NP. Solicitor; Partner, Lows Orkney, Solicitors, Kirkwall, since 1985; b. 4.12.58, Perth; m., Jane; 2 s. Educ. Perth Academy; University of Dundee. Apprenticeship with A.C. Morrison and Richards, Advocates, Aberdeen, 1980-82; Assistant Solicitor, T.P. and J.L. Low, Kirkwall, 1982-85. Member, Council, Law Society of Scotland, 1996-98. Past President, Rotary Club of Kirkwall; Secretary; Orkney Arts Theatre, J.P. Advisory Committee for Orkney; Past Chairman, Family Mediation, Orkney. Recreations: golf; drama; St. Magnus Cathedral Choir. Address: (b.) 5 Broad Street, Kirkwall, Orkney; T.-01856 873151; e-mail: alistairb@lowsorkney.co.uk

Bruce, David, MA, Chevalier de L'Ordre des Arts et des Lettres. Writer and Consultant; Director, Scottish Film Council, 1986-94; b. 10.6.39, Dundee; m., Barbara; 1 s.; 1 d. Educ. Dundee High School; Aberdeen Grammar School; Edinburgh University. Freelance (film), 1963; Assistant Director, Films of Scotland, 1964-66; Director, Edinburgh International Film Festival, 1965-66; Promotions Manager, Mermaid Theatre, London, 1966-67; Executive Officer, British Universities Film Council, 1967-69; joined Scottish Film Council as Assistant Director, 1969; Depute Director, SFC and Scottish Council for Educational Technology, 1977-86. Chairman, Mental Health Film Council, 1982-84; Chairman, Scottish Society for History of Photography,

1983-86; Chairman, Association of European Film Institutes, 1990-94. Various publications, including Scotland–the movie, 1996. Recreations: movies; music; photo-history. Address: (h.) Rosebank, 150 West Princes Street, Helensburgh G84 8BH; e-mail: David.Bruce@btinternet.com

Bruce, Fraser Finlayson, RD, MA (Hons), LLB, FSA(Scot). Regional Chairman, Industrial Tribunals for Scotland 1993-97 (Permanent Chairman, 1982-93); Solicitor, since 1956; b. 10.10.31, Kirkcaldy; m., Joan Gwendolen Hunter (deceased); 2 step-s. Educ. St. Andrews University. National Service, Royal Navy, 1956-58, commissioned Sub-Lieutenant, RNVR; Legal Assistant: Lanark County Council, 1958-60, Inverness County Council, 1960-66; Depute County Clerk: Argyll County Council, 1966-70, Inverness County Council, 1970-72; County Clerk, Inverness County Council, 1972-75; Joint Director of Law and Administration, Highland Regional Council, 1975-82; Temporary Sheriff, 1984-92. Served RNVR, 1956-76, retiring as Lieutenant-Commander RNR. Recreations: hill walking; Gaelic language; reading (in philosophy and naval/military history). Address: (h.) Drumdunan House, by Grantown-on-Spey PH26 3LG;T.- 01479 873969.

Bruce, George, OBE, MA, DLitt, DLitt. Poet/Critic/Lecturer; b. 10.3.09, Fraserburgh; m., Elizabeth Duncan; 1 s.; 1 d. Educ. Fraserburgh Academy; Aberdeen University. Teacher, English Department, Dundee High School, 1935-46; BBC Producer, Aberdeen, 1946-56; BBC Talks (Documentary) Producer, Edinburgh, with special responsibility for arts programmes, 1956-70; first Fellow in Creative Writing, Glasgow University, 1971-73; Visiting Professor, Union Theological Seminary, Richmond, Virginia, and Writer in Residence, Prescott College, Arizona, 1974; Visiting Professor of English, College of Wooster, Ohio, 1976-77; Scottish-Australian Writing Fellow, 1982; E. Hervey Evans Distinguished Fellow, St. Andrews Presbyterian College, North Carolina, 1985; Vice-Chairman, Council, Saltire Society; Council Member, Advisory Council of the Arts in Scotland; Extra-Mural Lecturer, Glasgow, St. Andrews and Edinburgh Universities; Executive Editor, The Scottish Review, 1975-76; Honorary President, Scottish Poetry Library. Publications: Sea Talk, 1944; Selected Poems, 1947; Landscapes and Figures, 1967; Collected Poems, 1970; The Red Sky, 1985; Perspectives: Poems 1970-86, 1987; Scottish Sculpture Today (Co-author), 1947; Neil M. Gunn, 1971; Anne Redpath, 1974; The City of Edinburgh, 1974; Festival in the North, 1975; Some Practical Good, 1975; William Soutar 1898-1943, The Man and Poet, 1978; A Scottish Postbag (Co-author), 1986; To Foster and Enrich – The First Fifty Years of the Saltire Society, 1986; The Scottish Literary Revival, 1962 (Editor); Scottish Poetry Anthologies 1-6 (Co-Editor), 1966-72; The Land Out There, anthology (Editor), 1991; Pursuit – Poems 1986-1998, 1999; Today Tomorrow – Collected Poems, 1933-2000, 2001; Woman of the North Sea (art/poetry collaboration with John Bellany), 2001. Recreation: visiting friends. Address: 25 Warriston Crescent, Edinburgh EH3 5LB; T.-0131-556 3848.

Bruce, Malcolm Gray, MA, MSc. MP (Liberal Democrat, formerly Liberal), Gordon, since 1983; President, Scottish Liberal Democrats, since 2000; Liberal Democrat Shadow Secretary of State for the Department of the Environment, Food and Rural Affairs, since 2001; Chairman, Liberal Democrat Parliamentary Party, 1999-2001; b. 17.11.44, Birkenhead; m. 2, Rosemary Vetterlein; 1 s.; 2 d. Educ. Wrekin College; St. Andrews University; Strathclyde University. Trainee Journalist, Liverpool Daily Post & Echo, 1966-67; Section Buyer, Boots the Chemist, 1968-69; Fashion Retailing Executive, A. Goldberg & Sons, 1969-70; Research and Information Officer, NESDA, 1971-75; Marketing Director, Noroil Publishing, 1975-81; Director,

Aberdeen Petroleum Publishing; Editor/Publisher, Aberdeen Petroleum Report, 1981-83; Co-Editor, Scottish Petroleum Annual, 1st and 2nd editions; Called to the Bar (Gray's Inn), 1995. Vice Chairman, Political, Scottish Liberal Party, 1975-84; Rector, Dundee University, 1986-89. Recreations: reading; music; theatre; hill-walking; cycling; travel. Address: (b.) House of Commons, London, SW1A 0AA.

Bruce, Roderick Lawrence, LLB (Hons). Partner, Dickson Minto WS, since 1986; b. 8.3.48, Edinburgh; m., Jane; 1 s.; 3 d. Educ. Boroughmuir School; Edinburgh University. Partner, Dundas and Wilson CS, 1977-86. Recreations: golf; squash; skiing; theatre. Address: (b.) 11 Walker Street, Edinburgh EH3 7NE. T.-0131-225 4455; e-mail: roderick.bruce@dmws.com

Bruce, Professor Steve, BA, PhD. Professor of Sociology, Aberdeen University, since 1991; b. 1.4.54, Edinburgh; m., Elizabeth S. Duff; 1 s.; 2 d. Educ. Queen Victoria School, Dunblane; Stirling University. Variously Lecturer, Reader and Professor of Sociology, Queen's University of Belfast, 1978-91. Publications: author of numerous books on religion, and on the Northern Ireland conflict. Recreation: playing Scottish country dance music. Address: (b.) Department of Sociology, Aberdeen University, Aberdeen AB24 3QY; T.-01224 272761.

Bruce, Professor Victoria Geraldine, OBE, BA, MA, PhD, CPsychol, FBPsS, FRSE, FBA. Professor of Psychology, Stirling University, since 1992; Deputy Principal (Research), Stirling University, 1995-2000 and since 2001; b. 4.1.53; m., Professor A.M. Burton. Educ. Newcastle-upon-Tyne Church High School for Girls; Newnham College, Cambridge. Lecturer, then Reader, then Professor of Psychology, Nottingham University, 1978-92. Member, Economic and Social Research Council, 1992-96, and Chair, Research Programmes Board, 1992-96; Chair, SHEFC Research Policy Advisory Group, since 1998 President, European Society for Cognitive Psychology, 1996-98; Editor, British Journal of Psychology, 1995-2000; Chair, Psychology Panel for 1996 and 2001 RAE, University Funding Councils' Research Assessment Exercise; Member, Scottish Higher Education Funding Council, 1995-2001; Member, Broadcasting Council for Scotland, 1999-2001; Member, Council for Science and Technology, since 2000; Member, Council, British Academy, since 2000; President, British Psychological Society, 2001-02. Publications: numerous papers and several books on visual perception and cognition. Recreations: dogs; walking; games. Address: (h.) The Mill House, Fintry, Stirlingshire G63 0YD; T.-01360 860 342.

Brunt, Professor Peter William, CVO, OBE, MD, FRCP(Lond), FRCP(Edin). Consultant Physician, Aberdeen Royal Infirmary, 1970-2001; Clinical Professor of Medicine, Aberdeen University, 1996-2001; Physician to The Queen in Scotland, 1983-2001; non-stipendiary Minister in Episcopal Church of Scotland; b. 18.1.36, Prestatyn; m., Marina Evelyn Anne Lewis; 3 d. Educ. Manchester Grammar School; King George V School; Liverpool University. Recreations: mountaineering; music. Address: (h.) 17 Kingshill Road, Aberdeen AB15 5JY; T.-Aberdeen 314204.

Bruntisfield, 2nd Baron (John Robert Warrender); b. 7.2.21; succeeded to title, 1993. Educ. Eton; Royal Military Academy, Sandhurst.

Brunton, Rodger James Horne, DipArch, RIBA, FRIAS, MaPS. Principal, Brunton Design Studio, since 1999; b. 11.7.51, Dundee; m., Sheila; 1 s.; 1 d. Educ. Morgan Academy, Dundee; School of Architecture, Duncan of Jordanstone College of Art. Dundee District Council, 1975-80; Robbie and Wellwood Architects, 1980-85; Brunton Voigt Partnership, 1985-99. Past President, Dundee

Institute of Architects; Secretary, Dundee Institute of Architecture; Secretary, Morgan Academy Former Pupils Association; Past Chairman, School Board, Carnoustie High School. Recreations: after-dinner speaking; amateur operatics; keep fit. Address: (b.) 95 Dundee Street, Carnoustie DD7 7EW; T.-01241 858153; e-mail: architects.bds@virgin.net

Bryan, Katharine Ann, BSc, MSc. Chief Executive, North of Scotland Water Authority, since 2000; b. 25.11.52, Salford; m., Michael Bryan; 2d. Educ. Marple Hall Grammar School; University of Durham; University of Aston, Birmingham. Various scientific posts, Severn Trent Water Authority, 1976-1988; Regional Manager, Fisheries Conservation Recreation, National Rivers Authority, 1988-92; Regional General Manager, National Rivers Authority, Wessex Region, 1992-93; Regional General Manager, National Rivers Authority, South Western Region, 1993-95; Regional Director, Environment Agency, South West, 1995-2000; Liveryman of the Worshipful Company of Water Conservators; Vice-Chairman and Director, Sustainability Southwest, 1998-2000. Recreations: natural history; gardening; walking; antique collection and restoration. Address: (b.) North of Scotland Water Authority, Cairngorm House, Beechwood Park North, Inverness, IV2 3ED; T.-01463 245423.

Bryan, Pauline Christina. Director, Employee Counselling Service, since 1989; b. 3.1.50, London; partner Vincent Mills. Educ. St. Edward the Confessor School; Open University. Messenger, Daily Mirror; Secretary, National Labour Press, 11 years; Development Officer, Fabian Society, 1981-86; Secretary, Local Health Council, 1986-89. Publication: Winning Women's Votes, (Fabian Tract) 1985. Recreations: politics; music. Address: 120 Bath Street, Glasgow G2 2EN; T.-0141-332 9833.

Bryce, Professor Charles F.A., BSc, PhD, DipEdTech, EurBiol, CBiol, FIBiol, CChem, FRSC. Professor and Head, School of Life Sciences, Napier University, since 1983; b. 5.9.47, Lennoxtown; m., Maureen; 2 s. Educ. Lenzie Academy; Shawlands Academy; Glasgow University; Max Planck Institute, Berlin. Former Executive Editor, Computer Applications in the Biosciences; Member, EFB Task Group on Public Perceptions of Biotechnology; Chairman, EFB Working Party on Education and Member, EFB Executive Board; Adviser to the Committee on Science and Technology in Developing Countries (India); former Chairman, UK Deans of Science Committee; Vice President, European Association for Higher Education in Biotechnology; actively involved in quality audit and quality assessment in biomedical sciences in UK, Bangladesh and Zambia. Recreations: competitive bridge; collecting wine. Address: (b.) Napier University, 10 Colinton Road, Edinburgh EH10 5DT; T.-0131-455 2525.

Bryce, Colin Maxwell, DA (Edin), CertEd, FCSD, FRSA. Dean, Faculty of Arts and Social Science, Napier University, since 1997; b. 14.9.45, Edinburgh; m., Caroline Joy; 2 s. Educ. Royal High School, Edinburgh; Edinburgh College of Art; Moray House College of Education. Art and Design Teacher, Portobello High School, 1968-75; Head of Art and Design, Wester Hailes Education Centre, 1975-85; Education Advisory Officer/Senior Education Officer/Director, The Design Council Scotland, 1985-90; Managing Director, Quorum Graphic Design, 1990-91; Principal, Hunter Maxwell Associates, 1991-92; Head, Department of Design, Napier University, 1992-97. Board Member: Craigmillar Opportunity Trust, Newbattle Abbey College. Recreations: looking, listening, and talking. Address: (b.) Napier University, Craighouse Campus, Craighouse Road, Edinburgh, EH10 5LG; T.-0131-455 6368; e-mail: cm.bryce@napier.ac.uk

Bryce, Professor Tom G.K., BSc, MEd, PhD, CPsychol. Professor, Department of Educational Studies, Faculty of Education, Strathclyde University, Jordanhill Campus, since 1993; Vice-Dean (Research), since 1997; b. 27.1.46, Glasgow; m., Karen Douglas Stewart; 1 s.; 1 d. Educ. King's Park Secondary School, Glasgow; Glasgow University. Teacher of Physics, Jordanhill College School, 1968-71; P.T. of Physics, King's Park Secondary School, 1971-73; part-time Lecturer in Psychology, Glasgow University, 1972-75; Open University Tutor, 1979-84; Lecturer, 1973, Head of Psychology, 1983, Head, Division of Education and Psychology, 1987-93, Jordanhill College of Education; Head, Department of Educational Studies, University of Strathclyde, 1993-94. Chairman, Editorial Board, Scottish Educational Review. Publications include: Scottish Education (Co-Editor), 1999. Recreations: moutaineering (Munro completer); badminton. Address: (b.) Jordanhill Campus, Southbrae Drive, Glasgow, G13 1PP; T.-0141-950 3220.

Bryden, Professor Ian Gordon, BSc, PhD, CEng, CPhys, FIMechE, FIMarE, MInstP. Professor and Associate Dean, Faculty of Design and Technology, Robert Gordon University, since 1996; b. 12.9.58, Dumfries; 2 s.; 1 d. Educ. Lockerbie Academy; University of Edinburgh. Research Assistant, Heriot-Watt University; Research Engineer, BMT Ltd.; Lecturer, Heriot-Watt University; Senior Engineer, ICIT/IOE. Recreations: reading; cycling; music. Address: (b.) The Robert Gordon University, Schoolhill, Aberdeen AB10 1FR; T.-01224-262 301.

Bryden, Professor John Marshall, BSc (Hons), PhD, FRSA. Chair of Human Geography and Joint Director, Arkleton Centre for Rural Development Research, since 1995; Programme Director, Arkleton Trust, since 1980; Member, Scottish Land Fund, since 1999; b. 18.12.41, Perth; m., Elspeth Anderson Mowat (divorced); 2 s.; 2 d. Educ. Edinburgh Academy; Glasgow Academy; Wrekin College; University of Glasgow; University of the West Indies; University of East Anglia. Economist, Economic Planning Staff, Ministry of Overseas Development, 1965-67; Lecturer, Overseas Development Group, University of East Anglia, 1967-72; Regional Economic Adviser, Commonwealth Caribbean, 1968-70; Head, Land Development Division, Highlands and Islands Development Board, 1972-79; Research Director, Arkleton Trust (Research) Ltd., 1985-95. Visiting Professor, University of Guelph, Canada, 1994; Member, Land Reform Policy Group and Rural Affairs Group, Scottish Office, 1997-99; Member, Policy Advisory Committee, Foundation for the Development of Polish Agriculture, since 1998; Member, International Advisory Board, Polson Institute, Cornell University, since 2001; Deputy Chairman, Leirsinn Research Centre for Gaelic, Sabhal Mor Ostaig, since 2001. Publications: Tourism and Development, 1973; Agrarian Change in the Scottish Highlands (Co-author), 1976; Towards Sustainable Rural Communities, 1994; Rural Employment – An International Perspective (Co-author), 1997. Recreations: folk music; jazz; hillwalking; sailing. Address: University of Aberdeen, St. Mary's, Kings College, Aberdeen AB24 3UF; T.-01224 272352.

Buccleuch, 9th Duke of, and Queensberry, 11th Duke of (Walter Francis John Montagu Douglas Scott), KT (1978), VRD, JP. Hon. Captain, RNR; Captain and President of the Council, Queen's Bodyguard for Scotland (Royal Company of Archers), 1996-2001; Lord Lieutenant of Roxburgh, 1974-98, and of Ettrick and Lauderdale, 1975-98; b. 28.9.23, London; m., Jane McNeill, daughter of John McNeill, QC, Appin, Argyll; 3 s.; 1 d. Educ. Eton; Christ Church, Oxford. Served World War II, RNVR; MP (Conservative), Edinburgh North, 1960-73; PPS to the Scottish Office, 1961-64; Chairman, Royal Association for Disability and Rehabilitation, since 1978, and President, 1993-2000; President: Royal Highland and Agricultural Society of Scotland, 1969, St. Andrew's Ambulance

Association, Royal Scottish Agricultural Benevolent Institution, Scottish National Institution for War Blinded, Royal Blind Asylum and School, Galloway Cattle Society, East of England Agricultural Society, 1976, Commonwealth Forestry Association, 1979-99, Royal Scottish Forestry Society, 1994-96; Chairman: Living Landscape Trust, since 1985, Buccleuch Heritage Trust, since 1986; Vice-President: Children First, International Spinal Research Trust, Disablement Income Group Scotland, Disabled Drivers Motor Club, Spinal Injuries Association; Honorary President: Moredun Foundation for Animal Health, Scottish Agricultural Organisation Society; DL: Selkirk, 1955, Midlothian, 1960, Roxburgh, 1962, Dumfries, 1974; FRAGS, 1995; Hon. MSc, University College, Northampton, 2000; Chancellor, Most Ancient & Most Noble Order of the Thistle, since 1992; Chairman, Association of Lord Lieutenants, 1990-98. Recreations: travel; country sports; painting; photography; classical music. Address: Bowhill, Selkirk; T.-Selkirk 20732; and Drumlanrig Castle, Thornhill; T.-Thornhill 30248.

Buchan, 17th Earl of (Malcolm Harry Erskine); b. 4.7.30. Educ. Eton. Succeeded to title, 1984.

Buchan, Alexander Stewart, MB, ChB, FRCA. Consultant in charge of Obstetric Anaesthesia, Simpson Memorial Maternity Pavilion, Edinburgh, since 1988; b. 7.9.42, Aberdeen; m., Henrietta Young Dalrymple; 1 s. Educ. Loretto School; Edinburgh University. Anaesthetic training in Edinburgh, apart from work in Holland, 1972; appointed Consultant in NHS, 1975; Royal Infirmary, Edinburgh, Royal Hospital for Sick Children, and Princess Margaret Rose Orthopaedic Hospital. Publication: Handbook of Obstetric Anaesthesia, 1991; Simpson Handbook of Obstetric Anaesthesia, 2000. Recreations: sailing; fishing; golf. Address: (h.) 21 Chalmers Crescent, Edinburgh EH9 1TS; T.-0131-667 1127.

Buchan of Auchmacoy, Captain David William Sinclair, JP, KStJ. Chief of the Name of Buchan; b. 18.9.29; m., The Hon. Susan Blanche Fionodbhar Scott-Ellis; 4 s.; 1 d. Educ. Eton; Royal Military Academy, Sandhurst. Commissioned Gordon Highlanders, 1949; served Berlin, BAOR and Malaya; ADC to GOC-in-C, Singapore, 1951-53; retired 1955. Member, London Stock Exchange; Senior Partner, Messrs Gow and Parsons, 1963-72. Changed name from Trevor through Court of Lord Lyon King of Arms, 1949, succeeding 18th Earl of Caithness as Chief of Buchan Clan. Member: Queen's Body Guard for Scotland (Royal Company of Archers); The Pilgrims; Friends of Malta GC; Council, St. John's Ambulance, London; Vice-President, Bucks CCC; Member, Council for London, Order of St. John; Master, Worshipful Company of Borderers, 1992; President, Ellon Cricket Club. Address: Auchmacoy House, Ellon, Aberdeenshire AB41 8RB.

Buchanan, Rev. Fergus Cameron, MA (Hons), BD (Hons). Minister, Milngavie: St Paul's, since 1988; b. 26.9.54, Glasgow; m., Gabrielle; 3 s. Educ. Crookston Castle Secondary School; Glasgow University. Assistant Minister, Glasgow Cathedral, 1981-83; Minister, Ardeer Parish Church, Stevenston, 1983-88. Moderator, Presbytery of Dumbarton, 1996. Major Maxwell Forsyth Fellowship, 1981; John Hope Prize, 1981; Member, Board of Social Responsibility, 1990-98; Member, Board of Ministry, since 1999. Recreations: searching for the perfect read; yearning for the perfect weight; dreaming of the perfect team. Address: (h.) 8 Buchanan Street, Milngavie G62 8DD; T.-0141-956 1043; e-mail: f.c.buchanan@btinternet.com

Buchanan, Hugh Ross, BA. Artist; b. 29.5.58; m., Ann de Rohan; 3 d. Educ. Wellington College; Edinburgh College of Art. Architectural painter, since 1981; commissioned by Prince of Wales, House of Commons, National Trust, Bank of Scotland, etc.; part-time lecturer, Edinburgh College of Art; Board Member, Buchanan

Society; formerly: part-time Lecturer, University of Malta summer school, Member, Council, National Trust for Scotland, Member, Conservative Arts and Heritage Committee; former Board Member: Dundee Printmakers, DCAC Ltd., Scottish Arts Council. Publication: The Eloquence of Shadows (Co-author). Recreation: motorcycle maintenance. Address: (h.) Woodhall, Pencaitland, East Lothian EH34 5DH; T.-01875 341326.

Buchan, William Menzies, DA. Head of Fine Art, 1977-90, Acting Director, 1990-91, Deputy Director, 1991-92, Glasgow School of Art; b. 7.10.32, Caroni Estate, Trinidad, West Indies. Educ. Glasgow School of Art. Art Teacher, Glasgow, 1956-61; Exhibitions Officer, then Art Director, Scottish Arts Council, 1961-77. Chairman, Stills Gallery, Edinburgh, 1987-92; Member, Fine Art Board, Council for National Academic Awards, 1978-81. Publications: Scottish Art Review, 1965, 1967, 1973; Seven Scottish Painters catalogue, IBM New York, 1965; The Glasgow Boys catalogue, 1968; Joan Eardley, 1976; Mr Henry and Mr Hornel Visit Japan catalogue, 1978; Japonisme in Art (Contributor), 1980; A Companion to Scottish Culture (Contributor), 1981; The Stormy Blast catalogue, Stirling University, 1981; The Golden Age of British Photography (Contributor), 1984; The Photographic Collector (Contributor), 1985; Willie Rodger: A Retrospective (Contributor to catalogue), 1986; Scottish Photography Bulletin (Contributor), 1988; History of Photography (Contributor), 1989; Mackintosh's Masterwork (Editor), 1989; British Photography in the 19th Century (Contributor), 1989; The Art of the Photographer J. Craig Annan, 1992; Photography 1900 (Contributor), 1993; J. Craig Annan: selected texts and bibliography, 1994; The Dictionary of Art (Contributor), 1995; Woven Image: Contemporary British Tapestry Catalogue (Contributor), 1996; Studies in Photography (Contributor), 1996; Charles Rennie Mackintosh: Art, Architecture and Design (CD Rom, General Editor), 1997; The Dictionary of Women Artists (Contributor), 1997; Studies in Photography (Contributor), 1997. Recreations: gardening; cooking. Address: (h.) Allan Water School House, by Skelfhill, Hawick TD9 0PH; T.-01450 850311.

Buchanan-Jardine, Sir Andrew Rupert John, MC. Landowner; Deputy Lieutenant; b. 2.2.23, London; 1 s.; 1 d. Educ. Harrow; Royal Agricultural College. Joined Royal Horse Guards, 1941; served NW Europe; retired as Major, 1949. Joint Master, Dumfriesshire Foxhounds, 1950; JP. Recreation: country pursuits. Address: (h.) Dixons, Lockerbie, Dumfriesshire; T.-01576 202508.

Buchanan-Smith, Robin D., BA, ThM; b. 1.2.36, Currie, Midlothian; m., Sheena Mary Edwards; 2 s. Educ. Edinburgh Academy; Glenalmond; Cambridge University; Edinburgh University; Princeton Theological Seminary. Minister, Christ's Church, Dunollie, Oban, 1962-66; Chaplain: St. Andrews University, 1966-73, 8th Argylls, 1962-66, Highland Volunteer, 1967-69; British Council of Churches Preacher to USA, 1968; Commodore, Royal Highland Yacht Club, 1977-81; Member, Board of Directors, Scottish Television, 1982-96 (Chairman, Staff Trust, since 1993); Chancellor's Assessor, St. Andrews University, 1981-85; Chairman: Scotland's Heritage Hotels, 1988-91, Cross Trust, since 1989; Trustee: Carnegie Trust for the Universities of Scotland, since 1986, Scottish Orthopaedic Research Trust into Trauma, since 1992. Recreations: sailing; Scotland. Address: Isle of Eriska, Ledaig, Argyll PA37 1SD; T.-01631 720371.

Buck, Andrew Robin, BCom, CA. Managing Director, Abuckus Ltd., Dumfries, since 1979; b. 6.2.44, Carlisle; m., Rowena Rosemary Morewood; 2 d. Educ. Bradfield College, Berkshire; Edinburgh University. Qualified CA with Wallace and Somerville, CA, Edinburgh 1967; Shell International Group, Philippines and Nigeria, 1967-73;

Edward Bates Ltd., Edinburgh, 1974; Peat Marwick Mitchell & Co., Hong Kong, 1976-79. Member, Council, Institute of Chartered Accountants of Scotland, 1989-95 and 1997-2003 (Chairman, South West Area, 1991-95); Partner, DG Format, Dumfries, 1985-2000; Chairman, Corporate Presentation Systems Ltd., 1989-94; Lecturer, University of Northumbria, Carlisle, 1995-2000; Volunteer Member, BESO. Recreations: skiing; sailing. Address: Blackhall Wood, Carlisle.

Buckland, Professor Stephen T., BSc, MSc, PhD, CStat. Professor of Statistics, St. Andrews University, since 1993 (Director, Centre for Research into Ecological and Environmental Modelling, since 1999); b. 28.7.55, Dorchester; m., Patricia A. Peters; 1 d. Educ. Foster's School, Sherborne; Southampton University; Edinburgh University; Aberdeen University. Lecturer in Statistics, Aberdeen University, 1977-85; Senior Scientist, Tuna/Dolphin Program, Inter-American Tropical Tuna Commission, San Diego, 1985-87; Senior Consultant Statistician, Scottish Agricultural Statistics Service, 1988-93, Head, Environmental Modelling Unit, 1991-93. Publications: The Birds of North-East Scotland (Co-editor), 1990; Distance Sampling: estimating abundance of biological populations (Co-author), 1993; Introduction to Distance Sampling (Co-Author), 2001. Recreations: natural history; walking; reading. Address: (b.) School of Mathematics and Statistics, St. Andrews University, North Haugh, St. Andrews KY16 9SS; T.-01334 463787.

Buckley, Ernest Graham, MD, FRCPE, FRCGP, FRCSE. Chief Executive, Scottish Council for Postgraduate Medical and Dental Education, since 1993; b. 16.10.45, Oldham; m., Dr. Felicity Buckley; 2 s.; 1 d. Educ. Manchester Grammar School; Edinburgh University. General Practitioner, Livingston, 1974-93; Editor: British Journal of General Practice, 1982-90, Medical Education. Secretary, Association for the Study of Medical Education, 1991-98. Recreations: gardening; history; upholstery. Address: (b.) 2nd Floor, Hanover Buildings, 66 Rose Street, Edinburgh EH2 2NN; T.-0131-225 4365.

Buckley, Michael Sydney, MA. Scottish Parliamentary Commissioner for Administration (also for UK), since 1999; Health Service Commissioner for Scotland (also for England and for Wales); b. 20.6.39, Beckenham; m., 1, Shirley Stordy (deceased); 2, Judith Cartmell Cobb; 1 s.; 1 d.; 2 step s.; 1 step d. Educ. Eltham College; Christ Church, Oxford. Treasury, 1962-68, 1971-77, 1980-82; Civil Service Department, 1968-71; Department of Trade and Industry, 1977-80; Cabinet Office, 1982-85; Department of Energy, 1985-91; Chairman, Dartford and Gravesham NHS Trust, 1995-96. Recreations: reading; gardening; listening to music. Address: (b.) 28 Thistle Street, Edinburgh EH2 1EN; T.-0131-225 7465.

Buddle, (Elizabeth) Anne. Head of Exhibitions and Collections Management, National Galleries of Scotland, since 2000 (Registrar, 1993-2000); b. 4.5.51, Chatham, Kent; m., A.V.B. Norman (deceased); 1 s. (from husband's pr. m.). Educ. Christ's Hospital, Hertford. Placers Department, British Museum, 1971; Victoria and Albert Museum, 1972-93: Public Relations, 1972-73, Indian Section, 1973-78, Department of Prints, Drawings and Paintings, 1978-88, Loans Officer, 1988-89, Registrar, 1989-93. Publications: papers and exhibition catalogues. Recreations: choral singing; study of church monuments; gardening; countryside; 18th-century South India. Address: (b.) National Galleries of Scotland, Belford Road, Edinburgh EH4 3DR; T.-0131-624 6315; e-mail: anne.buddle@natgalscot.ac.uk

Bulfield, Professor Grahame, CBE, PhD, Hon. DSc, FIBiol, FRASE, FRSE. Director and Chief Executive, Roslin Institute (Edinburgh), since 1993; b. 12.6.41. Educ. Kings School, Macclesfield; Leeds University; Edinburgh

University. Fullbright Fellow and NIH Postdoctoral Fellow, Department of Genetics, University of California, Berkeley, 1968-70; SRC Resettlement Fellow, 1970-71, and Research Associate, 1971-76, Institute of Animal Genetics, Edinburgh University; Lecturer and Convenor of Medical Genetics, Department of Genetics, Medical School and School of Biological Sciences, Leicester University, 1976-81; Head of Genetics Group, AFRC Poultry Research Centre, Roslin, 1981-86; Head of Gene Expression Group, 1986-88, and Head of Station and Associate Director, 1988-93, Edinburgh Research Station, Institute of Animal Physiology and Genetic Research. Hon. Fellow, 1981-90, and Hon. Professor, since 1990, Division of Biological Sciences, Edinburgh University; Non-Executive Director, Rosgen Ltd., since 1997; Chairman: Roslin Nutrition Ltd., since 1997, Roslin Biotechnology Centre, since 1998. Recreations: fell-walking; cricket. Address: (b.) Roslin Institute, Roslin, Midlothian EH25 9PS; T.-0131-527 4457.

Bulloch, Janet, MA. Bank of England Agent for Scotland, since 1998. Educ. St. Andrews University. Career Bank of England official. Director: Right Track (Scotland) Ltd., Glasgow Chamber of Commerce. Address: (b.) Bank of England, Agency for Scotland, 19 St. Vincent Place, Glasgow G1 2DT; T.-0141-221 7972; e-mail: scotland@bankofengland.co.uk

Bunch, Antonia Janette, OBE, MA, FLA, FIInfSc, FSA Scot, FRSA. Freelance writer, editor, researcher; b. 13.2.37, Croydon. Educ. Notting Hill and Ealing High School; Strathclyde University. Assistant Librarian, Scottish Office; Librarian, Scottish Health Service Centre; Lecturer, Strathclyde University; Director, Scottish Science Library. Founding Chairman, Association of Scottish Health Sciences Librarians; Member: Standing Committee on Science and Technology Libraries, IFLA, 1987-91, Advisory Committee, British Library Science Reference and Information Service, 1987-96, Advisory Committee on Telematics for the Scottish Parliament, 1996-97; Chairman: Friends of St. Cecilia's Hall and the Russell Collection of Early Keyboard Instruments, since 1997, Trustee, Scottish Homeopathic Research and Education Trust, since 1998. Publications: Libraries in Hospitals (Co-author), 1969; Hospital and Medical Libraries in Scotland: an Historical and Sociological Study, 1975; Health Care Administration: an Information Sourcebook, 1979. Recreations: gardening; music; travelling in Italy. Address: Dove Cottage, Garvald, Haddington, East Lothian EH41 4LL.

Buncle, Tom, BA, MA. Managing Director, Yellow Railroad International Tourism Consultancy; b. 25.6.53, Arbroath; m., Janet; 2 s. Educ. Trinity College, Glenalmond; Exeter University; Sheffield University. Various overseas posts (North America, Europe, Asia), British Tourist Authority, 1978-91; International Marketing Director, then Chief Executive, Scottish Tourist Board. Recreations: wind-surfing; scuba diving; cycling; sailing; hill-walking, tennis. Address: (b.) 73 Morningside Park, Edinburgh EH10 5EZ; T.-0131-447 1712; e-mail: tom@yellowrailroad.com

Burchell, Professor Ann, BSc, PhD. Professor of Molecular Medicine, Dundee University, since 2000; b. 23.2.51, Sunderland; m., Professor Brian Burchell; 1 s.; 1 d. Educ. Harrogate Convent; Dundee University. Dundee University: Research Fellow, 1983; New Blood Lecturer, Department of Medicine, 1985-89; Senior Lecturer in Molecular Medicine, Department of Obstetrics and Gynaecology, 1989-92; Lister Institute Research Fellow, 1989-94; Reader in Molecular Medicine, 1992-2000. Member, Lister Institute of Preventative Medicine; Member, Scientific Advisory Committee, Association for Glycogen Storage Disease. Publications: 137 papers. Recreations: golf; reading. Address: (b.) Department of Obstetrics and

Gynaecology, Tayside Institute of Child Health, Level 4, Ninewells Hospital, Dundee DD1 9SY; T.-01382 632445.

Burgess, William George, MA, PhD. Private Secretary to Deputy First Minister, Scottish Executive, since 2000; b. 8.5.70, Aberdeen; m., Adrienne Kirk. Educ. Keith Grammar School; Churchill College, Cambridge University. Social Work Services Group, Scottish Office, 1994-96; Finance Group, Scottish Office, 1996-97; Referendum Bill Team, Scotland Bill Team, Scotland Act Implementation, 1997-2000. Scottish Young Scientist of the Year, 1988; CEGB Prize, Cambridge University, 1991; Treasurer, Edinburgh Royal Choral Union, 1998-2000. Recreations: choral music; historical research. Address: (b.) St Andrew's House, Edinburgh EH1 3DG; T.-0131-244 5227.

Burgon, Robert Douglas, BA, MLitt, APMI. Director and Secretary, Scottish & Northern Ireland Plumbing Employers' Federation, since 1988; Secretary and Pensions Manager, Plumbing Pensions (UK) Ltd., since 1988; b. 3.8.55, Haddington; m., Sheila Georgina Bryson. Educ. North Berwick High School; Heriot Watt University. SNIPEF: Assistant Industrial Relations Officer, 1978, Assistant to the Director, 1979, Secretary, 1983. Recreation: music (church organist). Address: (b.) 2 Walker Street, Edinburgh EH3 7LB; T.-0131-225 2255.

Burley, Elayne Mary, BA (Hons). Head of Business Development, Napier University; b. 17.10.44, Cheshire; 2 s.; 1 d. Educ. Astley Grammar School for Girls; Leeds University. Leeds Polytechnic, 1966-68; Lecturer, Gordon Institute of Technology, Victoria, Australia, 1970-72; Lecturer, Open University in Scotland, 1972-84; Head of Training, Scottish Council for Voluntary Organisations, 1984-91. Recreations: golf; bridge; performing arts; walking on the beach; collecting blue and white china. Address: (b.) 74 Canaan Lane, Edinburgh; T.-0131-536 5686.

Burley, Lindsay, MB, ChB, FRCPE, FRCGP, FRSA, MHSM. Chief Executive, NHS Borders; b. 2.10.50, Blackpool; m., Robin Burley. Educ. Queen Mary School, Lytham; University of Edinburgh. Lothian Health Board: Consultant Physician, Unit General Manager, Director of Planning and Development. Address: (b.) Newstead, Melrose, Roxburghshire TD6 9DB; T.-01896 825515; e-mail: lindsay.burley@borders.scot.nhs.uk

Burnet, George Wardlaw, LVO, BA, LLB, WS, KStJ, JP. Lord Lieutenant, Midlothian, since 1992; b. 26.12.27, Edinburgh; m., Jane Elena Moncrieff; 2 s.; 1 d. Educ. Edinburgh Academy; Lincoln College, Oxford; Edinburgh University. Senior Partner, Murray Beith & Murray, WS, 1983-91; Chairman, Life Association of Scotland Ltd., 1985-93; Chairman, Caledonian Research Foundation, 1988-99. Brigadier, Queen's Bodyguard for Scotland (Royal Company of Archers); former Midlothian County Councillor; Convenor, Church of Scotland Finance Committee, 1980-83; Hon. Fellow, Royal Incorporation of Architects in Scotland. Address: (h.) Rose Court, Inveresk, Midlothian EH21 7TD.

Burnett, Charles John, KStJ, DA, AMA, FSAScot, FHSS, MLitt. Ross Herald of Arms; Chamberlain, Duff House, Banff, since 1997; Curator of Fine Art, Scottish United Services Museum, Edinburgh Castle, 1985-96; Vice-President, Heraldry Society of Scotland, since 1986; Vice-Patron, Genealogical Society of Queensland, since 1986; b. 6.11.40, Sandhaven, by Fraserburgh; m., Aileen E. McIntyre; 2 s.; 1 d. Educ. Fraserburgh Academy; Gray's School of Art, Aberdeen; Aberdeen College of Education. Advertising Department, House of Fraser, Aberdeen, 1963-64; Exhibitions Division, Central Office of Information, 1964-68 (on team which planned British pavilion for World

Fair, Montreal, 1967); Assistant Curator, Letchworth Museum and Art Gallery, 1968-71; Head, Design Department, National Museum of Antiquities of Scotland, 1971-85. Heraldic Adviser, Girl Guide Association in Scotland, since 1978; Librarian, Priory of the Order of St. John in Scotland, 1987-99; Vice President, Society of Antiquaries of Scotland, 1992-95; Honorary Citizen of Oklahoma, 1989; Chevalier, Orders of St. Maurice and St. Lazarus, 1999. Recreations: reading; visiting places of historic interest. Address: (h.) Seaview House, Portsoy, Banffshire, AB45 2RS; T.-01261 843378.

Burnett, David Anderson, DA(Edin), RIBA, FRIAS. Partner, Burnett Pollock Associates, Architects, since 1974; b. 9.6.44, Edinburgh; m., Rosemary; 3 s. Educ. George Watson's College, Edinburgh; Edinburgh College of Art; Heriot-Watt University. Graduate Architect, Chamberlin Powell and Bon, London, 1968-70; Project Architect, Casson Conder and Partners, London, 1970-72; Group Leader, Sir Basil Spence Glover and Ferguson, Edinburgh, 1973-74. Recreations: golf; writing; travel. Address: Burnett Pollock Associates, 17B Graham Street, Edinburgh EH6 5QN; T.-0131-555 3338; e-mail: dburnett@burnettpollock.co.uk

Burnett, Robert Gemmill, LLB, SSC, NP. Solicitor, since 1972; b. 18.1.49, Kilmarnock; m., Patricia Margaret Masson; 1 s.; 2 d. Educ. George Heriot's School, Edinburgh; Edinburgh University. Apprentice, then Assistant, then Partner, Drummond Miller WS; Partner, Burnett Christie. Solicitor to General Teaching Council. Recreations: golf; gardening. Address: (b.) 53 George IV Bridge, Edinburgh; T.-031-225 3456.

Burnett, Rodney Alister, MB, ChB, FRCP, FRIPHH, FRCPath. Lead Clinician in Pathology, University Department of Pathology, Western Infirmary, Glasgow, since 1985; b. 6.6.47, Congleton; m., Maureen Elizabeth Dunn; 2 d. Educ. Sandbach School; St. Andrews University. Lecturer in Pathology, Glasgow University, 1974-79; Consultant in administrative charge, Department of Pathology, Stobhill Hospital, Glasgow, 1979-85. Specialist Adviser, Royal Institute for Public Health and Hygiene, and Chairman, Board of Education and Examination for Anatomical Pathology Technology. Address: (h.) 134 Brownside Road, Cambuslang, Glasgow G72; T.-0141-641 3036.

Burnett, Rosemary King, BA (Hons). Scottish Development Manager, Amnesty International, since 1995; b. 15.11.48, Rio de Janeiro; m., David Burnett; 3 s. Edud. St Monica's School; London University. ActionAid Week Co-ordinator, ActionAid, 1985-89; Press/Appeals Officer, Citizens Advice Scotland, 1989-95. Chair, Friends of the Earth Scotland, 1993-96; Chair, National Consumer Congress, 1994-95; Member, Scottish Consumer Council, 1993-94; Member, Council, Scottish Civic Forum; Treasurer, Scottish Development Education Centre. Recreations: tennis; reading; conversation. Address: (b.) 6 Castle Street, Edinburgh EH2 3AT; T.-0131-466 6202; e-mail: Rosemary.Burnett@amnesty.org.uk

Burnett, Rupert Gavin, BCom, CA, FCMA; b. 6.11.39, India; m., Elspeth Maclean; 2 s.; 1 d. Educ. George Watson's College; Edinburgh University; Harvard Business School. Procter & Gamble Ltd., 1963-65; Management Consultant, McLintock, Moores and Murray, 1965-68; Chartered Accountant, Arthur Young (latterly Ernst & Young), 1968-91, Partner, 1970; Honorary Professor, Stirling University, 1991-2000; Member, Council, Institute of Chartered Accountants of Scotland, 1990-96; Chairman, Glasgow Area Committee, 1992-95; CCAB Audit Practices Committee, 1986-91; Chairman, Church of Scotland Investors Trust, 1996-2000; General Trustee, Church of Scotland, since 1995 (Chairman, Finance Committee);

various non-executive directorships. Recreations: watching amateur rugby; brown trout fishing; croft; family. Address: (h.) Littleward Wester, by Thornhill, Stirling.

Burnett-Stuart of Crichie, George Slessor. Farmer and Landowner, since 1969; b. 3.1.48, Cobham; m., Patricia De Lavenne; 2 d. Educ. Winchester College; Bordeaux University. Elected Member, Council and Executive, National Trust for Scotland; President, Stewart Society; Member, Council, Scottish Agricultural College; Past Chairman, Grampian Farming Forestry Wildlife Group;Treasurer, Friends of Grampian Stones. Recreations: kite-flying; travelling; tree-planting. Address: Crichie House, Stuartfield, Peterhead AB4 8DY; T.-01771 24202.

Burnie, Joan Bryson. Associate Editor, Daily Record, since 2001, and Columnist, since 1987; b. 19.12.41, Glasgow; 1 s.; 1 d. Educ. Hutchesons' Girls' Grammar School. Filed pix, Herald; married; had children; freelanced; Contributing Editor, Cosmopolitan, 1977-81; You (Mail on Sunday), 1984-90; "Just Joan", Daily Record, since 1979; hacks around the air waves for BBC Radio 5 and BBC Scotland. Publications: Scotland The Worst; Post Bus Country. Recreations: lunch; walking dogs; gardening.

Burns, Rt. Rev. John Joseph, PhL, STh. Vicar General, Diocese of Motherwell, since 1992; Parish Priest, St. Bride's, Bothwell, since 1992; Vicar General for Pastoral Care and Planning, since 1992; b. 19.2.32, Rutherglen. Educ. Our Lady's High, Motherwell; St. Joseph's College, Dumfries; Gregorian University, Rome; Scots College, Rome. Assistant Priest, Motherwell Cathedral, 1956-65; Full-time Chaplain, Our Lady's High School, Motherwell, 1965-78; Resident at St. Brendan's, Motherwell, 1971-78; Diocesan Master of Ceremonies, 1956-81; Director of Religious Education, Diocese of Motherwell, 1978-85; Resident at Diocesan Centre, Motherwell, 1978-85; Parish Priest, St. Aidan's, Wishaw, 1983-92. Publications: series of Religious Education books for pupils and teachers, S1-S5, 1979-82. Recreations: general reading; walking; watching football. Address: St. Bride's, Fallside Road, Bothwell, Lanarkshire; T.-01698 852710.

Burnside, David Melville, LLB, NP. Senior Partner, Burnside Kemp Fraser, Solicitors, since 1989; b. 5.3.43, Dumfries; m., Gill; 3 s.; 2 d. Educ. Dumfries Academy; University of Edinburgh. Apprentice Solicitor, Melville & Lindesay W.S., Edinburgh, 1964-67; Assistant Solicitor: National Coal Board Legal Department, 1967-70, Clark & Wallace, Advocates, Aberdeen, 1970-71 (Partner, 1971-89); formed Burnside Advocates (later Burnside Kemp Fraser), 1989; acted for families in Chinook, Brent Spar and Cormorant Alpha helicopter crashes and Piper Alpha explosion (joint lead negotiator for Piper Alpha settlement); Member, Personal Injury Panel; Member, Executive Committee, and Scottish Convenor, Association of Personal Injury Lawyers, 1990-96; certified by Law Society of Scotland as an employment law specialist; Treasurer, Employment Law Group; Past President: Aberdeen Bar Association, Junior Chamber, Aberdeen; Member, Board of Directors, Legal Defence Union; President, Society of Advocates in Aberdeen, 2000-01 (Treasurer, 1999-2000); Member, Edinburgh Town Council, 1967-70; Chairman, Board of Governors, Albyn School for Girls, since 2001. Recreations: family; music; theatre; tennis; skiing; following the Dons. Address: (b.) 48 Queen's Road, Aberdeen AB15 4YE; T.-01224 327500.

Burnside, John. Writer; b. 19.3.55, Dunfermline. Scottish Arts Council Book Award, 1988, 1991, 1995; shortlisted for Forward Prize, 1992; Geoffrey Faber Memorial Prize, 1994; shortlisted for T.S. Eliot Prize, 1994; selected for New Generation Poets, 1994. Publications: poetry: The hoop, 1988; Common Knowledge, 1991; Feast Days, 1992; The myth of the twin, 1994; Swimming in the flood, 1995; A Normal Skin, 1997; The Asylum Dance, 2000; fiction: The

Dumb House, 1997; The Mercy Boys, 1999; Burning Elvis, 2000. Address: (b.) c/o Jonathan Cape, Random House, 20 Vauxhall Bridge Road, London SW1V 2SA.

Burrows, Professor Noreen, LLB, PhD, FRSA. Jean Monnet Professor of European Law, Glasgow University, since 1990; b. 22.1.51, Preston; m., Alastair Swanson; 1 s. Educ. Notre Dame High School, St Helens; Edinburgh University. Lecturer in Law, Leicester University, 1977-79; Lecturer in Law, then Senior Lecturer, 1979-90; Head, School of Law, 1990-94; Trustee, Caledonian Research Foundation; Member, Board, Scotland in Europe; Chair, Glasgow University Equal Opportunities Committee. Selector, VSO; Trustee and Secretary, Dunbartonshire Wind Ensemble. Publications include: Devolution; European Social Law. Recreations: walking; family life. Address: (b.) School of Law, Glasgow University, Glasgow G12 8QQ; T.-0141-330 4172.

Burt, Gillian Robertson, MA (Hons), FRSA. Headmistress, Craigholme School, Glasgow, since 1991; b. 7.2.44, Edinburgh; m., Andrew Wallace Burt; 1 s.; 1 d. Educ. Mary Erskine School; Edinburgh University; Moray House College of Education. Teacher of Geography, Tabeetha Church of Scotland School, Jaffa, Israel, 1966-67; Teacher of Geography, Boroughmuir Secondary School, 1967-70; Head of Geography, St. Hilary's School, Edinburgh, 1970-71, 1976-86, Head of Careers, 1986-91 (merged with St. Margaret's School, 1983); Member, Governing Board, SCIS and of its Management Committee; Member, ISCO Scottish Council. Recreations: music; theatre; walking; cooking; foreign travel. Address: (b.) Craigholme School, 72 St Andrews Drive, Glasgow G41 4HS; T.-0141-427 0375.

Burt, John Clark, MA (Hons), CertEd. Principal, Angus College, since 1996; b. 25.4.51, Dunfermline; m., Dory; 1 s.; 1 d. Educ. Dunfermline High School; Edinburgh University; Moray House College. Marketing Economist, Lloyds and Scottish Finance, 1974-76; Lecturer/Senior Lelcturer in Economics and Marketing, Fife College, 1976-96. Chair, Association of Scotland Principals' Forum; Chair, Tayside Careers Ltd.; Member, Scottish Welfare to Work Advisory Task Force; Membewr, East of Scotland European Partnership. Recreations: golf;' hill-walking; running; Italian language. Address: (b.) Keptie Road, Arbroath DD11 3EA; T.-01241 432600.

Burt, Peter Alexander, MA, MBA, FCIBS. Deputy Chairman, HBOS, since 2001; Group Chief Executive, Bank of Scotland, 1996-2001; b. 6.3.44, Nairobi; m., 3 s. Educ. Merchiston Castle School, Edinburgh; St Andrews University; University of Pennsylvania; Wharton School of Finance and Commerce. Joined Hewlett Packard Company, Palo Alto, 1968, as an Information Systems Analyst; joined Conversational Software Ltd., Edinburgh, as Marketing Director, 1970, and progressed to be Managing Director; Edward Bates & Sons Ltd., merchant bank, 1974-75; joined Bank of Scotland, 1975, as Executive Assistant, Special Duties; Assistant General Manager, 1979; Divisional General Manager, 1984; Joint General Manager and Head, International Division, 1985; Treasurer and Chief General Manager, 1988; appointed to Board, 1995; Director, Bank of Western Australia, 1995-2000; Director, Bank of Wales PLC, since 1996. Address: (b.) The Mound, Edinburgh EH1 1YZ.

Burt, Professor Steven Leslie, BA, PhD, FRSA. Professor of Retail Marketing, University of Stirling, since 1998 (Head, Department of Marketing, since 2000); Director, Institute for Retail Studies, University of Stirling, since 1999; b. 23.3.60, Chorley, Lancashire; m., Wendy Hayes; 2 s. Educ. Bolton School; Queen's College, Oxford University; University of Wales; University of Stirling.

University of Stirling: Research Fellow then Lecturer then Senior Lecturer, 1984-98, Head, Department of Marketing, 1993-95, Acting Director, Institute for Retail Studies, 1993-96. President, European Association for Education and Research in Commercial Distribution. Recreation: watching Stirling Albion Football Club. Address: (b.) Department of Marketing, University of Stirling, Stirling FK9 4LA; T.-01786 467399.

Burton, Lord (Michael Evan Victor Baillie). Landowner and Farmer; b. 27.6.24, Burton-on-Trent; m., 1, Elizabeth Ursula Foster Wise (m. diss., deceased); 2, Coralie Denise Cliffe; 2 s.; 3 d. (1 d. deceased). Educ. Eton; Army. Scots Guards, 1942 (Lt., 1943); Lovat Scouts, 1948; Member, Inverness County Council, 1948-75; JP, 1961-75; Deputy Lieutenant, Inverness, 1963-65; Executive Member, Scottish Landowners Federation, 1963-92; has served on numerous committees. Recreations: shooting, fishing and hunting (not much time); looking after the estate. Address: Dochgarroch Lodge, Inverness IV3 8JG; T.-01463 861252/861377.

Burton, Anthony Winston, OBE, BA (Hons). Managing Director, The Planning Exchange; b. 14.10.40, Leicester; 2 s.; 1 d. Educ. Wyggeston; Keele University. Vice Chairman, Strategic Planning Society; Director (Non-Executive): Consumers' Association, Scottish Greenbelt Company. Recreations: cooking; sailing. Address: (h.) 9 Marchmont Terrace, Glasgow G12 9LS; T.-0141-334 7697.

Busby, John Philip, NDD, DA (Edin), RSW, ARSA, PPSSA; b. 2.2.28, Bradford; m., Joan; 1 s.; 2 d. Educ. Ilkley Grammar School; Leeds College of Art; Edinburgh College of Art. Lecturer in Drawing and Painting, Edinburgh College of Art, 1956-88; Founder Member, Society of Wildlife Artists; illustrated 30 books on natural history; author and illustrator: Birds in Mallorca, Drawing Birds, John Busby Nature Drawings, The Living Birds of Eric Ennion. Recreations: music; bird-watching; travel. Address: (h.) Easter Haining, Ormiston Hall, East Lothian EH35 5NJ; T.-01875 340512; e-mail: jj.busby@lineone.net

Bush, Paul Anthony, BEd, DipSC, FISC. Chief Executive, Scottish Swimming, since 1998; b. 11.6.57, Leicester; m., Katriona Christine. Educ. Gateway Sixth Form College, Leicester; Borough Road College; Moray House College. Professional Swimming Coach, Bradford and Leicester; Sports/Swimming Development Officer, Leeds City Council; Technical Director, Amateur Swimming Association; Assistant Head of Development, English Sports Council; Director, Sporting Initiatives Sports Marketing and Media Consultancy. Leicestershire County Swimming Coach; Swimming Team Manager, Olympic, World, European, Commonwealth Games; Chef de Mission, BOA, European Youth Olympics; General Team Manager, Scottish Commonwealth Games Council, Manchester, 2002; Fellow, BISA; General Secretary, British Swimming Coaches Association; Member, English Sports Council Task Force – Young People and Sport; Event Director, World Cyclo Cross Championships, Leeds; school governor. Recreations: golf; walking the dogs; sport in general; travel. Address: (b.) Scottish Swimming, National Swimming Academy, University of Stirling, Stirling FK9 4LA.

Bushe, Frederick, OBE, RSA (1987), DA, DAE. Sculptor, since 1956; Founder Director, Scottish Sculpture Workshop, 1979-96; b. 1.3.31, Coatbridge; m., Fiona M.S. Marr; 1 d.; 3 s., 1 d. by pr. m. Educ. Our Lady's High School, Motherwell; Glasgow School of Art. Lecturer in Sculpture: Liverpool College of Education, 1962-69, Aberdeen College of Education, 1969-79; full-time Artist since 1979; established Scottish Sculpture Workshop and Scottish Sculpture Open Exhibition; exhibited in numerous one man and group exhibitions, since 1962. Recreations: music; cooking. Address: (h.) Rose Cottage, Lumsden, Huntly, Aberdeenshire AB54 4JJ; T.-01464 861394.

Busuttil, Professor Anthony, OBE, MOM, MD, FRCPath, FRCP(Glasg), FRCPE, DMJ(Path). Regius Professor of Forensic Medicine, Edinburgh University, since 1987; Past Chairman, European Council for Legal Medicine; Honorary Consultant Pathologist, Edinburgh Universities NHS Trust, since 1976; Police Surgeon, Lothian and Borders Police Force, since 1980; b. 30.12.45, Rabat, Malta; m., Angela; 3 s. Educ. St. Aloysius' College, Malta; Royal University of Malta. Junior posts, Western Infirmary, Glasgow; Lecturer in Pathology, Glasgow University. Address: (h.) 78 Hillpark Avenue, Edinburgh EH4 7AL; T.-0131-336 3241.

Bute, 7th Marquess of (John Colum Crichton-Stuart); b. 26.4.58; m.; 1 s.; 3 d. British Formula Three Champion, 1984; Formula One Ferrari Test Driver, 1985; JPS Lotus Grand Prix Driver, 1986; Works Driver for World Champion Sports Prototype Team Silk Cut Jaguar, 1988 (Joint Winner, Le Mans, 1988); Lead Driver for Toyota GB, World Sports Prototype Championship, 1989, 1990.

Butler, Bill, MSP. MSP (Labour), Glasgow Anniesland, since 2000; m., Patricia Ferguson (qv). Educ. Stirling University; Notre Dame College of Education. English teacher, 20 years; elected Glasgow City Councillor, 1987 (Convener, Policy and Resources (e-Glasgow) Working Group; Vice-Convener, Policy and Resources Committee; Secretary, Labour Group). Address: (b.) Constituency Advice Office, 129 Dalsetter Avenue, Glasgow G15 8SZ; e-mail: bill.butler.msp@scottish.parliament.uk

Butler, Vincent Frederick, RSA, RGI. Sculptor; b. 27.10.33, Manchester; m., Camilla Meazza; 2 s. Educ. Edinburgh College of Art; Accademia di Belle Arti, Milan. Tutor in English Language, British School, Milan, 1957-60; Head, Department of Sculpture, Ahmadu Bello University, Nigeria, 1960-63; Lecturer, Edinburgh College of Art, 1960-89. Recreations: travel; languages. Address: (h.) 17 Dean Park Crescent, Edinburgh EH4 1PH; T.-0131-332 5884.

Butlin, Ron, MA, DipAECD. Poet, Novelist, Journalist; b. 17.11.49, Edinburgh. Educ. Dumfries Academy; Edinburgh University. Writer in Residence, Lothian Region Education Authority, 1979, Edinburgh University, 1981, 1984-85; Scottish/Canadian Writing Exchange Fellow, University of New Brunswick, 1983-84; Writer in Residence for Midlothian, 1989-90; Writer in Residence, Craigmillar Literacy Trust; Novelist in Residence, St. Andrews University, 1998-99. Publications: poetry: Stretto, 1976; Creatures Tamed by Cruelty, 1979; The Exquisite Instrument, 1982 (Scottish Arts Council Book Award); Ragtime in Unfamiliar Bars, 1985 (SAC Book Award, Poetry Book Society recommendation); Histories of Desire 1995; prose: The Tilting Room (short stories), 1983 (SAC Book Award); The Sound of My Voice (novel), 1987; Blending In (play), 1989; Mauritian Voices (Editor), 1996; Night Visits (novel), 1997; When We Jump We Jump High!, 1998; Faraway Pictures (opera), 2000. Recreations: music; travel. Address: (h.) 7 West Newington Place, Edinburgh EH9 1QT; T.-0131-667 0394.

Butter, Sir David Henry, KCVO, MC. Lord Lieutenant, Perth and Kinross, 1975-95; Landowner and Company Director; b. 18.3.20, London; m., Myra Alice Wernher; 1 s.; 4 d. Educ. Eton College; Oxford University. Served in World War II, 2nd Lt., Scots Guards, 1940; served in Western Desert, North Africa, Sicily and Italy (ADC to GOC 8th Army, 1944); Temporary Major, 1946; retired, 1948; Captain, Queen's Bodyguard for Scotland (Royal

Company of Archers); President, Highland TAVR, 1979-84; Member, Perth County Council, 1955-74; Deputy Lieutenant, Perthshire, 1956; Vice Lieutenant, Perthshire, 1960-71; Lord Lieutenant of County of Perth, 1971-75, of Kinross, 1974-75; Governor, Gordonstoun School, 1954-86. Recreations: golf; skiing; travel; shooting. Address: Cluniemore, Pitlochry, Perthshire.

Butterworth, Neil, MA, HonFLCM. Chairman, Scottish Society of Composers, since 1991; Broadcaster; b. 4.9.34, Streatham, London; m., Anna Mary Barnes; 3 d. Educ. Rutlish School, Surrey; Nottingham University; London University; Guildhall School of Music, London. Lecturer, Kingston College of Technology, 1960-68; Head, Music Department, Napier College, Edinburgh, 1968-87; Music Critic, Times Educational Supplement, 1983-97. Conductor: Sutton Symphony Orchestra, 1960-64, Glasgow Orchestral Society, 1975-83 and since 1989; Chairman: Incorporated Society of Musicians, Edinburgh Centre, 1981-86, Inveresk Preservation Society, 1988-95; Churchill Fellowship, 1975. Publications: Haydn, 1976; Dvorak, 1980; Dictionary of American Composers, 1983; Aaron Copland, 1984; Vaughan Williams, 1989; Neglected Music, 1991; Samuel Barber, 1996; The American Symphony, 1998; Film Music, 2002; over 300 compositions. Recreations: autographs; collecting books and records; giant jigsaw puzzles. Address: (h.) 1 Roderick Place, West Linton, Peeblesshire EH46 7ES; T.-01968 661112.

Byers, Eric George, MA, DipTRP, FIMgt, MRTPI. Strategic Manager, Fife Council, since 2000; b. 29.1.51, Aberdeen; m., Nicky; 1 s. Educ. Aberdeen Grammar School; University of Aberdeen; University of Glasgow. Central Regional Council, 1975-80; Borders Regional Council, 1980-85; Fife Regional Council, 1985-95; Head, Economic Development Service, Fife Council, 1995-2000. Address: (b.) Fife House, North Street, Glenrothes; T.-01592 413883; e-mail: eric.byiers@fife.gov.uk

Byng, Jamie. Publisher, Canongate Books, since 1994; b. 27.6.69, Winchester; m., Whitney Osborn McVeigh; 1 s.; 1 d. Educ. Winchester College; Edinburgh University. Recreations: tennis; cooking; deejaying; reading; drinking. Address: (b.) 14 High Street, Edinburgh EH1 1TE; T.-0131-557 5111.

Byrne, John. Dramatist and stage designer; b. 1940, Paisley. Plays include: The Slab Boys, Cuttin' A Rug, Still Life (trilogy); Normal Service; Cara Coco; television series: Tutti Frutti; Your Cheatin' Heart.

C

Cackette, Paul, LLB (Hons), DipLP, NP. Divisional Solicitor, Office of Solicitor, Scottish Executive, since 2000; b. 26.3.60, Edinburgh; m., Helen Thomson; 1 s.; 2 d. Educ. George Heriot's School, Edinburgh; Edinburgh University. Admitted as a Solicitor, 1985; Solicitor, Kirkcaldy District Council, 1985-88; joined Office of Solicitor to Secretary of State for Scotland, 1988-99. Recreations: literature; athletics. Address: (b.) Victoria Quay, Edinburgh EH6 6QQ; T.-0131-244 0507.

Cadell, Patrick Moubray, CBE, BA, FSA (Scot). Keeper of the Records of Scotland, 1991-2000; b. 17.3.41, Linlithgow; m., Sarah King (d. 1996); 2 s.; 1 d. Educ. Merchiston Castle School, Edinburgh; Cambridge University; Toulouse University. Information Officer, British Museum; Assistant Keeper, Department of MSS, British Museum; Keeper of Manuscripts, National Library of Scotland, 1983-90. Bailie, Abbey Court of Holyrood; Past President, West Lothian History and Amenity Society. Recreations: walking; the French language. Address: 27 Ellen's Glen Road, Edinburgh EH17 7QL.

Cadell of Grange, William Archibald, DL, MA (Cantab), FRIAS, RIBA. Vice Lieutenant, West Lothian, since 2001; b. 9.3.33; m., Mary-Jean Carmichael; 3 s. Educ. Merchiston Castle; Trinity College, Cambridge; Regent Street Polytechnic. Founded William A. Cadell, Architects, 1968, retired 1995; Manager, Grange Estate, 1971-2000; Chairman, Drum Housing Development, since 1991; Commissioner, Royal Fine Art Commission for Scotland, 1992-2000; Trustee, Architectural Heritage Fund, since 1997. Recreations: gardening; forestry; the arts. Address: Grange, Linlithgow, West Lothian; T.-01506 842946.

Caddy, Professor Brian, BSc, PhD, CChem, MRSC. Professor of Forensic Science, Strathclyde University, 1992-99, now Emeritus Professor; b. 26.3.37, Burslem, Stoke-on-Trent; m., Beryl Ashworth; 1 s.; 1 d. Educ. Longton High School, Stoke-on-Trent; Sheffield University. MRC Research Fellow, 1963-66; Strathclyde University: Lecturer in Forensic Science, 1966-77, Senior Lecturer in Forensic Science, 1977-92. Founder Member, European Network of Forensic Science Institutes; President, Forensic Science Society, 1999; Member, Executive Committee, Council for the Registration of Forensic Practitioners, 1999. Publications: two books; over 90 papers/articles. Editor, Science and Justice (Forensic Science Society journal), 1993-1999. Recreations: reading; painting; walking the dog; dining with friends; good food and wine. Address: (h.) 5 Kings Park, Torrance, Glasgow G64 4DX; T.-01360 622 358; e-mail: B.Caddy@strath.ac.uk

Caie, Professor Graham Douglas, MA, PhD, FEA, FRSA. Professor of English Language, Glasgow University, since 1990; Senate Assessor, Glasgow University Court; b. 3.2.45, Aberdeen; m., Ann Pringle Abbott; 1 s.; 1 d. Educ. Aberdeen Grammar School; Aberdeen University; McMaster University, Canada. Teaching Assistant, McMaster University, 1968-72; Amanuensis and Lektor, Copenhagen University, 1972-90. Chairman, Medieval Centre, Copenhagen University, 1985-90; Visiting Professor: McMaster University, 1985-86, Guelph University, 1989; Associate Fellow, Clare Hall, Cambridge, 1977-78; Member, English Panel: SQA, UCAS, Research Assessment Exercise; Vice-President, Scottish Texts Society; Secretary, European Society for the Study of English; Trustee, National Library of Scotland; Member, Council, Dictionary of Older Scottish Tongue; Convener, Friends of Glasgow University Library. Publications: Judgement Day II edition, The Theme of Doomsday in Old English Poetry; Beowulf; Bibliography of Junius XI MS; numerous articles. Address: (h.) 12B Upper Glenburn Road, Bearsden, Glasgow G61 4BW; T.-0141-943 1192; e-mail: G.Caie@englang.arts.gla.ac.uk

Caimbeul, Aonghas Phàdraig, MA. Sgrìobhadair; Fearnaidheachd (òraidiche agus craoladair); r. Uibhist-a-Deas; p., Liondsaidh; 4 n. Foghlam: Ard-Sgoil an Obain; Oilthaigh Dhùn Eideann. Treis aig: A' Phàipear Bheag, BBC Rèidio, Grampian Telebhisean; Sgrìobhaiche an t-Sabhail Mhòir, 1990-92; Oraidiche an sin on uairsin; Crìosdaidh; ag obair air nobhal mòr an-dràsda. Air foillseachadh: 2 leabhar bàrdachd; nobhal dheugairean; dà nobhal eile tighinn a-mach am bliadhna. Cuir-seachad: bhith ris an teaghlach agus leughadh Tolstoy. Seòladh: Sabhal Mòr Ostaig, An Teanga, Slèite, an t-Eilein Sgitheanach; F.-01471 844373.

Cairns, David, MP. Labour MP, Greenock and Inverclyde, since 2001. Educ. Gregorian University, Rome; Franciscan Study Centre. Priest, 1991-94; Director, Christian Socialist Movement, 1994-97; researcher for MP, 1997-2001. Address: (b.) House of Commons, London SW1A 0AA.

Cairns, Very Rev. John Ballantyne, LTh, LLB. Parish Minister, Aberlady and Gullane, since 2001; Chaplain to the Queen, since 1997; Chaplain to the Lieutenancy of Dumbarton, since 1997; Moderator, General Assembly of the Church of Scotland, 1999-2000; General Trustee of Church of Scotland, since 1995; b. 15.3.42, London; m., Dr. Elizabeth Emma Bradley; 3 s. Educ. Sutton Valence School, Kent; Bristol University; Edinburgh University. Messrs Richards, Butler & Co., Solicitors, City of London, 1964-68; Administrative Assistant, East Lothian County Council, 1968-69; Assistant Minister, St. Giles, Elgin, 1973-75; Minister, Langholm, Ewes and Westerkirk Parish Churches, 1975-85, also linked with Canonbie, 1981-85; Clerk, Presbytery of Annandale and Eskdale, 1980-82; Minister, Riverside Church, Dumbarton, 1985-2001; Convener, Maintenance of the Ministry Committee and Joint Convener, Board of Ministry and Mission, Church of Scotland, 1984-88; Chairman, Judicial Commission of General Assembly, 1993-98; Convener, General Assembly Committee on Chaplains to Her Majesty's Forces, 1993-98; Moderator, Presbytery of Dumbarton, 1993-94; Chaplain to Moderator of General Assembly, 1995; Divisional Chaplain, Strathclyde Police, 1997-2001. Publications: Keeping Fit for Ministry, 1988; Democracy and Unwritten Constitutions, 1989. Recreations: golf; gardening; music; Robert Burns. Address: The Manse, Hummel Road, Gullane, East Lothian EH31 2BG.

Cairns, Professor John William, LLB, PhD. Professor of Legal History, University of Edinburgh, since 2000; b. 17.8.55, Crieff. Educ. Hutchesons' Boys' Grammar School; University of Edinburgh. Lecturer in Jurisprudence, Queen's University of Belfast; Lecturer, Senior Lecturer, Reader, University of Edinburgh; Visiting Professor: Southern Methodist University, Dallas, 1986, Miami, 1988, 1991, 1995. Chairman, Council, The Stair Society; Member, Editorial Committee, Journal of Legal History. Recreations: cooking; reading; cinema. Address: (b.) University of Edinburgh, Faculty of Law, Old College, South Bridge, Edinburgh EH8 9YL; T.-0131-650 1000; e-mail: john.cairns@ed.ac.uk

Cairns, Michael Francis, BSc (Hons), CQSW, DMS. Director, RNIB Scotland, since 2000; b. 30.10.48, Dumbarton; m., Krystina Anna Cairns; 2 s.; 1 d. Educ. St Johns College, Southsea; Bedford and Goldsmiths Colleges, London University. Various posts in social work and management in England and Scotland; Director, Age Concern, Scotland, 1989-93. Recreations:

golf; music; gardener's labourer. Address: (b.) Dunedin House, 25 Ravelston Terrace, Edinburgh, EH4 3TP; T.-0131-311 8500.

Cairns, Robert, MA, DipEd. Chairman, East of Scotland Water, since 1998; Member, City of Edinburgh Council, since 1995 (Convener, Planning Committee, since 1995); b. 16.7.47, Dundee; 2 s. Educ. Morgan Academy; Edinburgh University; Moray House College of Education. Assistant Editor, Scottish National Dictionary, 1969-74; Parliamentary candidate (Labour), North Edinburgh, 1973, February 1974; Teacher, James Gillespie's High School, 1975-96; Member, City of Edinburgh District Council, 1974-95 (Convener, Planning and Development Committee, 1986-95); Board Member: Edinburgh World Heritage Trust, Old Town Community Development Project; Queen's Hall; Canongate Youth Project; Member, Historic Buildings Council. Recreations: gardening; theatre. Address: (h.) 70 Ratcliffe Terrace, Edinburgh; T.-0131-667 1741.

Cairns, Professor Robert Alan, BSc, PhD, FInstP, FRSE. Professor, School of Mathematical and Computational Sciences, St. Andrews University, since 1991 (Reader, 1985-91); b. 12.3.45, Glasgow; m., Ann E. Mackay. Educ. Allan Glen's School, Glasgow; Glasgow University. Lecturer in Applied Mathematics, St. Andrews University, 1970-83; Senior Lecturer, 1983-85; Consultant, UKAEA Culham Laboratory, since 1984. Member, SERC Laser Committee, 1990-93; Member, SERC Atomic and Molecular Physics Sub-Committee, 1990-93; Chairman, Plasma Physics Group, Institute of Physics, 1999-2001 (Committee Member, 1981-84); Member, Editorial Board, Plasma Physics, 1983-85; Editor, Journal of Plasma Physics, since 1995. Publications: Plasma Physics, 1985; Radiofrequency heating of plasmas, 1991. Recreations: music (listening to and playing recorder and baroque flute); golf; hill-walking. Address: (b.) School of Mathematical and Computational Sciences, St. Andrews University, North Haugh, St. Andrews, Fife KY16 9SS; T.-01334 463707.

Caithness, 20th Earl of (Malcolm Ian Sinclair), PC; b. 3.11.48; m.; 1 s.; 1 d. Educ. Marlborough; Royal Agricultural College, Cirencester. Succeeded to title, 1965; Paymaster General and Minister of State, HM Treasury, 1989-90; Minister of State, Foreign and Commonwealth Office, 1990-92; Department of Transport, 1992-94; Chief Executive, Clan Sinclair Trust, since 1999; elected Member, House of Lords, since 1999.

Calder, Professor Andrew Alexander, MD, FRCS (Edin), FRCP (Glas), FRCP (Edin), FRCOG. Professor of Obstetrics and Gynaecology, University of Edinburgh, since 1987 (Vice Dean of Medicine, since 1997); b. 17.1.45, Aberdeen; m., Valerie Anne Dugard; 1 s.; 2 d. Educ. Glasgow Academy; Glasgow University. Clinical training posts, Glasgow, 1968-72; Research Fellow, Nuffield Department of Obstetrics and Gynaecology, University of Oxford, 1972-75; Lecturer/Senior Lecturer, Obstetrics and Gynaecology, University of Glasgow, 1975-86; Consultant Obstetrician and Gynaecologist: Glasgow Royal Infirmary and Royal Maternity Hospital, 1978-86, Royal Infirmary of Edinburgh and Simpson Memorial Maternity Pavilion, since 1987; British Exchange Professor, University of California, Los Angeles, 1992. Blair Bell Memorial Lecturer, RCOG, 1977; WHO Travelling Fellow, Uruguay, 1985. Recreations: music; golf; curling; history of medicine. Address: Department of Obstetrics and Gynaecology, Royal Infirmary of Edinburgh, Little France, Edinburgh; e-mail: andrew.calder@ed.ac.uk

Calder, Angus Lindsay, MA, DPhil. Writer; b. 5.2.42, Sutton, Surrey; m., 1, Jennifer Daiches; 1 s.; 2 d.; 2, Catherine Kyle; 1 s. Educ. Wallington County Grammar School; Kings College, Cambridge. Lecturer in Literature, Nairobi University, 1968-71; Visiting Lecturer, Chancellor College, Malawi University, 1978; Reader and Staff Tutor in Arts, Open University in Scotland, 1979-93; Visiting Professor of English, University of Zimbabwe, 1993; Distinguished Visiting Scholar, University of Waikato, 1995; Member, Board of Directors, Royal Lyceum Theatre Company, 1984-96; Editorial Board, Wasafiri; Member, Panel of Judges, Saltire Society Scottish Book of the Year Award, 1983-97; Member, Board, 2000 + 3 Estaitis, since 1998; Eric Gregory Award for Poetry, 1967. Publications: The People's War: Britain 1939-1945, 1969 (John Llewellyn Rhys Memorial Prize); Revolutionary Empire, 1981 (Scottish Arts Council Book Award); The Myth of the Blitz, 1991; Revolving Culture: notes from the Scottish Republic, 1994 (SAC Book Award); Waking in Waikato (poems), 1997; Wars (anthology), 1999; Horace in Tollcross (poems), 2000. Recreations: curling; cricket. Address: (h.) 15 Spittal Street, Edinburgh EH3 9DY; T.-0131-229 8196.

Calder, Finlay, OBE. Grain Exporter; b. 20.8.57, Haddington; m., Elizabeth; 1 s.; 1 d. Educ. Daniel Stewart's and Melville College. Played rugby for Scotland, 1986-90; captained Scotland, 1989; captained British Isles, 1989.

Calder, George, BA (Hons) (Cantab), LLB, MIPD. Head, Scottish Executive EU Office, since 1999; b. 20.12.47; m., Kathleen; 2 d. Educ. George Watson's College, Edinburgh; Cambridge University; Edinburgh University. Joined Civil Service (Department of Employment), 1971; worked in European Commission (cabinet of George Thomson), 1977-79; Treasury, 1979-87; Manpower Services Commission, 1987-99, with posts in Edinburgh, Glasgow and Newcastle; Scottish Office/Scottish Executive (Head of European Fund and Co-ordination Division, Head of Personnel, Head of Water Services Unit), from 1999. Recreations: football; book collecting; hill-walking; country. Address: (b.) Scottish Executive EU Office, 6 Rond Point Schuman, 104C Brussels, Belgium.

Calder, Jenni, BA, MPhil. Freelance Writer; Head of Museum of Scotland International, National Museums of Scotland, Edinburgh, since 1998; b. 3.12.41, Chicago, Illinois; 1 s.; 2 d. Educ. Perse School for Girls, Cambridge; Cambridge University; London University. Freelance writer, 1966-78; taught and lectured in Scotland, England, Kenya and USA; Lecturer in English, Nairobi University, 1968-69; joined Royal Scottish Museum, 1978. Publications: Chronicles of Conscience: a study of George Orwell and Arthur Koestler, 1968; Scott (with Angus Calder), 1969; There Must be a Lone Ranger: the Myth and Reality of the American West, 1974; Women and Marriage in Victorian Fiction, 1976; Brave New World and Nineteen Eighty Four, 1976; Heroes: from Byron to Guevara, 1977; The Victorian Home, 1977; The Victorian Home from Old Photographs, 1979; RLS, A Life Study, 1980; The Robert Louis Stevenson Companion (Editor), 1980; Robert Louis Stevenson and Victorian Scotland (Editor), 1981; The Strange Case of Dr Jekyll and Mr Hyde (Editor), 1979; Kidnapped (Editor), 1981; Catriona (Editor), 1981; The Enterprising Scot (Editor), 1986; Island Landfalls (Editor), 1987; Bonny Fighters: The Story of the Scottish Soldier, 1987; Open Guide to Animal Farm and Nineteen Eighty Four, 1987; The Wealth of a Nation (Editor), 1989; St. Ives, a new ending, 1990; Scotland in Trust, 1990; Treasure Islands (Editor), 1994; Mediterranean (poems, as Jenni Daiches), 1995; Tales of the South Seas (Editor), 1996; The Nine Lives of Naomi Mitchison, 1997; Everyman's Poetry: Robert Louis Stevenson (Editor), 1997; Present Poets anthology, Editor), 1998; Translated Kingdoms (anthology, Editor), 1999; A Beleaguered City and Other Tales of the Seen and the Unseen (Editor), 2000. Recreations: music; films; walking the dog. Address: (h.) 31 Station Road, South Queensferry, West Lothian; T.-0131-331 1287.

Calder, Professor Muffy, BSc, PhD. Professor of Formal Methods (Computer Science), Glasgow University, since 1999; b. 21.5.58, Shawinigan, Quebec, Canada; m., David Calder. Educ. Stirling University; St Andrews University. Research Fellow, Edinburgh University and Stirling University, 1983-87; Lecturer/Senior Lecturer, Computing Science, Glasgow University, 1988-99. Recreations: road running; hillrunning. Address: (b.) Department of Computer Science, Glasgow University. T.-0141-330 4969.

Calder, Robert Russell, MA. Critic, Philosophical Writer, Historian of Ideas, Poet, Freelance Journalist, Book Reviewer, Performer and Singer; b. 22.4.50, Burnbank. Educ. Hamilton Academy; Glasgow University; Edinburgh University. Co-Editor, Chapman, 1974-76 and since 1988; Editor, Lines Review, 1976-77; Theatre Critic and Feature Writer, Scot, 1983-86; books: A School of Thinking, 1995; Narcissism, Nihilism, Simplicity (Editor), 1992; poetry: Il Re Giovane, 1976, Ettrick & Annan, 1981; Serapion, 1996. Recreations: music - opera singing; jazz piano. Address: (h.) 23 Glenlee Street, Burnbank, Hamilton ML3 9JB; T.-01698 824244.

Calderwood, Sir Robert, Kt. Chairman, Greater Glasgow Health Board, 1993-97; Chief Executive, Strathclyde Regional Council, 1980-92; b. 1.3.32; m., Meryl Anne; 3 s.; 1 d. Educ. William Hulme's School, Manchester; Manchester University (LLB Hons). Town Clerk: Salford, 1966-69, Bolton, 1969-73, Manchester, 1973-79. Director, Glasgow Garden Festival 1988 Ltd., 1985-88; Chairman, Strathclyde Buses Ltd., 1989-93; Member: Parole Board for England and Wales, 1971-73, Society of Local Authority Chief Executives, 1974-92 (President, 1989-90), Scottish Consultative Committee, Commission for Racial Equality, 1981-88; Director, European Summer Special Olympic Games 1990 (Strathclyde) Ltd., 1989-90; Member, Council, Industrial Society, 1983-92; Director: GEC (Scotland) Ltd., 1991-99, Scottish Opera, 1991-96 (Deputy Chairman, 1991-96); Member: Employers' Panel, Industrial Tribunals in Scotland, 1992-98, Local and Central Government Relations Research Committee, Joseph Rowntree Foundation, 1992-97; Director, Quality Scotland Foundation, 1991-92; Honorary Patron, Scottish Overseas Aid, 1993-98; Honorary Member, The Incorporation of Coopers, Trades House of Glasgow, since 1994; Member, Court of Governors, Glasgow Caledonian University, 1994-96. Hon. Fellow, IWEM, 1992. Recreations: theatre; watching rugby; interested in United Nations activities. Address:(h.) 6 Mosspark Avenue, Milngavie, Glasgow G62 8NL.

Caldwell, David Cleland, SHNC, MA, BPhil. Director, Universities Scotland, since 2000; b. 25.2.44, Glasgow; m., Ann Scott Macrae; 1 s.; 1 d. Educ. George Watson's College, Edinburgh; St. Andrews University; Glasgow University. Warwick University: Lecturer in Politics, 1969-76, Administrative Assistant, 1976-77, Assistant Registrar, 1977-80; Registry Officer, Aberdeen University, 1980-84; Secretary, The Robert Gordon University, 1984-2000. Member: Warwick District Council, 1979-80, Grampian Regional Council, 1983-84; Parliamentary candidate (Labour), North East Fife, 1983; Member, Aberdeen Grammar School Council, 1983-88 (Chairman, 1985-88); Member, St. Andrews University Court, 1986-94 (Convener, Audit Commitee, 1990-94); Member, Board of Management, Moray College, 1995-2001; Director, Viscom (Aberdeen) Ltd., 1992-97 (Chairman, 1994-95); Director, RGIT Ltd., 1997-99. Address: (b.) Universities Scotland, 53 Hanover Street, Edinburgh EH2 2PJ; T.-0131-226 1111.

Caldwell, David Hepburn, MA, PhD, FSA, FSAScot. Keeper of History and Applied Art and Director, Finlaggan Archaeological Project, National Museums of Scotland; b. 15.12.51, Kilwinning, Ayrshire; m., Margaret Anne McGovern; 1 s.; 2 d. Educ. Ardrossan Academy; Edinburgh University. Joined staff, National Museum of Antiquities, 1973. Publications: The Scottish Armoury, 1979; Scottish Weapons and Fortifications, 1981; Scotland's Wars and Warriors, 1998; Islay, Jura and Colonsay, A Historical Guide, 2001. Recreation: travelling. Address: (h.) 3 James Park, Burntisland, Fife KY3 9EW; T.-872175.

Caldwell, Maren L., LLB, MICFM. National Organiser, Scotland, RNLI; b. 20.4.47, Glasgow; m., John Caldwell; 2 s. Educ. Glasgow High School for Girls; Glasgow University. Appeal Director, Strathcarron Hospice, 1989-92; Director of Fundraising, Scottish Medical Research Fund, 1992-94; Administrator, Scottish Hospital Endowments Research Trust, 1993-94; Depute Campaign Director, Children 1st, 1994-96. Member, Business Committee, General Council, Glasgow University, 1982-92, and Convenor, Social Affairs Committee of the Business Committee, 1988-92; Trustee, University of Glasgow Trust, 1989-97. Recreations: watching rugby; gardening; opera; being a motorbike passenger; sailing. Address: Unit 3, Ruthvenfield Grove, Inveralmond Industrial Estate, Perth PH1 3GL.

Caldwell, Miller H., MA, CQSW, DipSocWk, DipRS, FFCS. Dumfries and Galloway Authority Reporter, since 1996; b. 6.10.50, Glasgow; m., Jocelyn M. France; 2d. Educ. Glasgow Academy; London University; Moray House College; Jordanhill College. Fraternal Worker, Ghana, West Africa, Overseas Council, Church of Scotland, 1972-78; Postgraduate student, 1978-80; School Social Worker, Central Regional Council, 1980-83; Kilmarnock and Loudon Reporter, 1983-88; Area Reporter, Kyle and Carrick, Cumnock and Doon Valley, 1988-92; Principal Reporter, Dumfries and Galloway, 1992-95; Regional Reporter, 1995. President, Dumfries and Galloway Burns Club, 2000-01 (direct descendent of Robert Burns); Chairman, Dumfries Branch SASD; South West contact for Ghanaians in need. Recreations: all things West African; dog walking; piano and oboe. Address: (h.) Netherholm, Edinburgh Road, Dumfries; T.-01387 263998; e-mail: miller.caldwell@btinternet.com

Caldwell, Sheila Marion, BA (Hons), ARSGS. Member, Council, Royal Scottish Geographical Society; b. England; m., Major Robert Caldwell, TD. Educ. Tunbridge Wells Grammar School; University College, London. Founder/Principal, Yejide Girls' Grammar School, Ibadan, Nigeria; first Principal, Girls' Secondary (Government) School, Lilongwe, Malawi; Depute Head, Mills Grammar School, Framlingham, Suffolk; Head, St. Columba's School, Kilmacolm, 1976-87; Treasurer, Secondary Heads' Association, Scotland, 1984-87; Public Affairs Liaison, Glasgow Association of Women Graduates. Recreations: travel; art history and architecture; music, opera and ballet; cooking. Address: (h.) 27 Oxford Road, Renfrew PA4 0SJ; T.-0141-886 2296.

Callander, Alex James, MA, FSIP. Joint Senior Partner, Baillie Gifford & Co., since 2001; b. 1.4.60, Dundee; m., Rhona; 1 s.; 1 d. Educ. Glenalmond College; St John's College, Cambridge. Baillie Gifford & Co: joined 1982; Trainee Fund Manager; Fund Manager; Client Services Manager/Director; Manager/Head, Institutional Clients' Department. Chairman, Institute of Investment Management and Research, 1997-99. Recreations: hiking; travelling. Address: (b.) 1 Rutland Court, Edinburgh; T.-0131-222 4000.

Callander, Alexander Dougal, BA (Oxon), LLB, WS. Solicitor (retired); Honorary Sheriff at Stirling, 1991; b. 10.3.26, Doncaster; m., Mona Patricia Meldrum; 1 s.; 2 d. Educ. Winchester College; Magdalen College, Oxford University; Edinburgh University. Director, James Dougall and Sons (refactories industry), 1952-62; Mathie Macluckie and Lupton, Solicitors, Stirling: Assistant, 1962, Partner,

1963, retired 1994. Recreations: hillwalking; fishing; golf. Address: (h.) Coldon, Port of Menteith, Stirling FK8 3RD; T.-01877 385275.

Calman, Professor Sir Kenneth Charles, KCB 1996, MD, PhD, FRCP, FRCS, FRSE. Vice-Chancellor and Warden, Durham University, since 1998; b. 25.12.41, Glasgow; m., Ann; 1 s.; 2 d. Educ. Allan Glen's School, Glasgow; Glasgow University. Lecturer in Surgery, Western Infirmary, Glasgow, 1968-72; MRC Clinical Research Fellow, London, 1972-73; Professor of Oncology, Glasgow University, 1974-84; Dean of Postgraduate Medicine, 1984-89; Chief Medical Officer, Scottish Home and Health Department, 1989-91; Chief Medical Officer, Department of Health, 1991-98. Recreations: golf; jogging; gardening; cartoons; sundials. Address: (h.) 585 Anniesland Road, Glasgow; T.-0141-954 9423.

Cameron of Lochbroom, Rt. Hon. Lord (Kenneth John Cameron), Life Baron (1984), PC (1984), MA (Oxon), LLB, QC, FRSE, Hon. FRIAS. Senator of the College of Justice, since 1989; Chairman, Royal Fine Art Commission for Scotland; b. 11.6.31, Edinburgh; m., Jean Pamela Murray; 2 d. Educ. Edinburgh Academy; Corpus Christi College, Oxford; Edinburgh University. Advocate, 1958; Queen's Counsel, 1972; President, Pensions Appeal Tribunal for Scotland, 1976; Chairman, Committee of Investigation Under Agricultural Marketing Act 1958, 1980; Advocate Depute, 1981; Lord Advocate, 1984; Hon. Bencher, Lincoln's Inn; Hon. Fellow, Corpus Christi College, Oxford. Recreations: fishing; sailing. Address: (h.) Stoneyhill House, Musselburgh.

Cameron, Alasdair, FSA Scot. Farmer and Crofter; b. 12.6.44, Dingwall; m., Jeannette Benzie; 2 d. Educ. Dingwall Academy. Hon. President, Black Isle Farmers Society; Chairman, Northern Counties Valuators Association; former Vice-Chairman, Crofters Commission; Member: Royal Highland Education Trust, Highlands and Islands Forum, Scottish Agricultural Arbiters Association, Scottish Vernacular Buildings Working Group, Historic Farm Buildings UK; Past Chairman: Highland Farming and Forestry Advisory Group, Dingwall Round Table. Recreations: photography; industrial archaeology; local history; the countryside. Address: Wellhouse Farm, Black Isle, Muir of Ord, Ross-shire IV6 7SF; T.-01463 870416.

Cameron, Alastair Ian. Co-ordinator, Scottish Churches Housing Agency, since 1994; b. 3.4.53, Dundee; m., Mary Jane Elton; 2 s.; 1 d. Educ. Glasgow Academy; Lenana School, Nairobi; University of Kent at Canterbury. Neighbourhood Worker, Rochdale Metropolitan Council, 1980-85; Development Worker, Edinburgh Council for the Single Homeless, 1985-92; Housing Strategy Manager, Wester Hailes Partnership, 1992-94. Trustee, EverGreen, Portobello; Board Member, Rural Housing Service; Board Member, National Rent Deposit Forum; Member, Religious Society of Friends. Recreations: raising children; traditional music; cycling; allotment gardening. Address: 3 Esplanade Terrace, Edinburgh EH15 2ES; e-mail: cameron@care4free.net

Cameron, Allan John, MBE, DL, JP. Farmer and Landowner, since 1947; b. 25.3.17, Edinburgh; m., Elizabeth Vaughan-Lee; 2 s.; 2 d. Educ. Harrow; Royal Military College. Regular officer, Queen's Own Cameron Highlanders, 1936-47 (ret. Major); Member: Ross and Cromarty County Council, 1955-75 (Chairman, Education Committee, 1962-75), Ross and Cromarty District Council, since 1975 (Convener, since 1991); former Commissioner: Red Deer Commission, Countryside Commission for Scotland; former Member, BBC Council for Scotland; President: Royal Caledonian Curling Club, 1963,

International Curling Federation, 1965-69. Recreations: curling; golf; shooting; fishing; gardening. Address: (h.) Allangrange, Munlochy, Ross and Cromarty IV8 8NZ; T.-014638 11249.

Cameron, Most Rev. Andrew Bruce. Primus of the Scottish Episcopal Church, since 2000; Bishop of Aberdeen and Orkney, Scottish Episcopal Church, since 1992; b. 2.5.41, Glasgow; m., Elaine Cameron; 2 s. Educ. Eastwood Secondary School; Edinburgh Theological College. Curate, Helensburgh and Edinburgh, 1964-70; Chaplain, St. Mary's Cathedral, Edinburgh, 1970-75; Diocesan and Provincial Youth Chaplain, 1969-75; Rector, St. Mary's Church, Dalmahoy, and Anglican Chaplain, Heriot Watt University, 1975-82; Churches Development Officer, Livingston Ecumenical Parish, 1982-88; Rector, St. John's Episcopal Church, Perth, 1988-92; Convener, Mission Board, Scottish Episcopal Church, 1988-92. Recreations: music; theatre; various sports; gardening. Address: (b.) Diocesan Office, 39 Kings Crescent, Aberdeen AB24 3HP; T.-01224 636653; (h.) Bishop's House, Ashley House, Ashley Gardens, Aberdeen, AB10 6RQ; T.-01224 208142; e-mail: bishop@aberdeen.anglican.org

Cameron, Colin. Head of Network Programmes, BBC Scotland, since 2000; b. 30.3.50; m., Christine Main; 2 s. Educ. Glasgow Academy; Duke of York School, Nairobi; Polytechnic of Central London. Journalist, Current Affairs, BBC Scotland, 1973-76; Film Director, That's Life, 1976-77; Producer/Director, Everyman and Heart of the Matter, 1977-85; Editor, Brass Tacks, BBC North, 1985-88; Head of Documentary Features, BBC Television, 1988-91; BBC Scotland: Head of Television, 1991-96, Head of Production, 1997-2000. Advisor, Glasgow Common Purpose; Director, The Research Centre; RTS International Current Affairs Award, 1984; UN Association Media Peace Prize, 1984. Recreations: dinghy sailing; cycling; hillwalking; cinema; Scottish art. Address: (b.) BBC Scotland, Queen Margaret Drive, Glasgow, G12 8DG; T.-0141-338 2424.

Cameron, David Roderick Simpson, RIBA, ARIAS, MRTPI, FSA Scot, FFCS. Artist; retired Architect/Planner; President, Clan Cameron Association Scotland, since 1999; b. 2.6.41, Inverness; m., Filitsa Boulton; 1 s.; 2 d. Educ. Angusfield and George Watson's College; Edinburgh College of Art; Newcastle University. Architect, Rowand Anderson, Kininmonth and Paul, 1968-71; Conservation Officer, Edinburgh Corporation and Edinburgh District Council, 1971-83; Depute Executive Director of Planning, City of Edinburgh District Council, 1983-96; European Union, ECOS Project Manager (Edinburgh and Berlin team) for revival of Kazimierz quarter of Krakow, Poland, 1993-95; Principal, Chambers Design, 1996-97; Consultant, Broad and Hughes Architects, 1997-99; Director, AUi Ltd., 1998-2001. Chairman: The Saltire Society, 1990-95, Sir Patrick Geddes Memorial Trust, 1991-99; Convener: Saltire Performing Arts Committee, 1991-94, Historic Burghs Association of Scotland, 1993-99, Charles Cameron Conservation Campaign, 1994-96; Saltire Planning and Environment Committee, 1993-98, Scottish Environment and Amenity Link, 1996-97; Secretary: Saltire Arts and Crafts in Architecture Award Panel, 1987-94, Saltire Housing Award Panel, 1974-83, and Panel Member since 1998; Hon. Secretary, Edinburgh Architectural Association, 1972-75, and Editor, EAA Review, 1980-84; Member: International Society of City and Regional Planners, 1987-2001, Executive Committee, Scottish Society of Directors of Planning, 1988-96, Council, National Trust for Scotland, 1994-99, Grants Council, Scottish Community Foundation, since 1996, Scottish Homes Advisory Group on Physical Quality, 1996-98; Member, European Association of Historic Towns and Regions, 1999-2001; Freedom, Bergues, France, 1998. Recreations: art; fishing; forestry; Hillman Imp car; Scottish and Greek heritage. Address: (b.) Impart Enterprises, 4 Dovecot Road, Edinburgh EH12 7LE; T.-0131-539 2745.

Cameron, Younger of Lochiel, Donald Angus, MA, FCA, DL. Director, J. Henry Schroder & Co. Limited, 1984-99; President, Highland Society of London, 1994-97; b. 2.8.46, London; m., Lady Cecil Kerr; 1 s. 3 d. Educ. Harrow; Christ Church, Oxford. 2nd Lieutenant, Queen's Own Cameron Highlanders (TA), 1966-68; Chartered Accountant, 1971. Vice-Lieutenant, Lochaber, Inverness, Badenoch and Strathspey. Address: (h.) Achnacarry, Spean Bridge, Inverness-shire.

Cameron of Lochiel, Colonel Sir Donald (Hamish), KT (1973), CVO, TD, JP. 26th Chief of the Clan Cameron; Lord Lieutenant, County of Inverness, 1971-86; Chartered Accountant; b. 12.9.10; m., Margaret Gathorne-Hardy; 2 s. 2 d. Educ. Harrow; Balliol College, Oxford. Lt.-Col. commanding: Lovat Scouts, 1944-45; 4/5th Bn. (TA), Queen's Own Cameron Highlanders, 1955-57; Colonel, 1957 (TARO); Vice-Chairman, Royal Bank of Scotland, 1969-80; Chairman: Culter Guard Bridge Holdings Ltd., 1970-76, Scottish Widows Life Assurance Society, 1964-67; President: Scottish Landowners Federation, 1979-84, Royal Highland and Agricultural Society of Scotland, 1971, 1979, 1987; Member, Scottish Railways Board (Chairman, 1959-64). Address: (h.) Achnacarry, Spean Bridge, Inverness-shire.

Cameron, Rt. Rev. Douglas M. Bishop of Argyll and the Isles, since 1993; b. 23.3.35, Natal; m., Anne Patricia Purnell; 2 d. Educ. Eastwood Grammar School; Edinburgh Theological College; University of the South, Sewanee, Tennessee. Curate, Christ Church, Falkirk, 1962-65; Priest, Papua New Guinea, 1965-74, Archdeacon, 1972-74; Rector: St. Fillan's and St. Hilda's, Edinburgh, 1974-88, St. Mary's, Dalkeith, and St. Leonard's, Lasswade, 1988-92; Canon and Synod Clerk, Diocese of Edinburgh, 1990-92; Dean of Edinburgh, 1991-92. Recreations: hill-walking; music; cooking. Address: (b.) The Pines, Ardconnel Road, Oban PA34 5DR; T.-01631 566912.

Cameron, Professor Dugald, OBE, DA, FCSD, FRSA. Director, Glasgow School of Art, 1991-99; Visiting Professor, University of Strathclyde, since 1999; Visiting Professor, Department of Aerospace Engineering, University of Glasgow, since 2000; Companion, Royal Aeronautical Society, 1996; Industrial Design Consultant, since 1965; b. 4.10.39, Glasgow; m., Nancy Inglis. Educ. Glasgow High School; Glasgow School of Art. Industrial Designer, Hard Aluminium Surfaces Ltd., 1962-65; Visiting Lecturer, Glasgow School of Art, 1963-70; Head of Product Design, Glasgow School of Art, 1970-82; Head of Design, 1982-91. Hon. Professor, Glasgow University, 1993-99; Director, Squadron Prints, 1977-2000; Member: Engineering Advisory Committee, Scottish Committee, Council of Industrial Design, since 1966, Industrial Design (Engineering) Panel and 3D Design Board, CNAA, since 1978, Scottish Committee of Higher Education, Design Council; commission RAFVR (T), 1974. Publications: Glasgow's Own (a history of 602 City of Glasgow Squadron, Royal Auxiliary Air Force), 1987; Glasgow's Airport, 1990. Recreations: railways; flying (lapsed private pilot); aviation history (particularly Scottish). Address: (h.) Achnacraig, Skelmorlie, Ayrshire.

Cameron, Duncan Inglis, OBE, JP, BL, DUniv, CA, FRSGS. Director of Administration and Secretary, Heriot-Watt University, 1965-90; b. 26.8.27, Glasgow; m., Elizabeth Pearl Heron (deceased); 2 s.; 1 d. Educ. Glasgow High School; Glasgow University. RAF, 1945-48; CA apprentice, Alfred Tongue & Co., 1948-51; Qualified Assistant, Cooper Brothers & Co., 1951-52; Assistant Accountant, Edinburgh University, 1952-65; Commonwealth Universities Administrative Fellow, 1972. President, Edinburgh Junior Chamber of Commerce, 1962-63; Governor, Keil School, Dumbarton, 1967-85; Chairman of Council, Royal Scottish Geographical Society, 1983-88 (Trustee, since 1973); Governor, Scottish College of

Textiles, 1991-98; Chairman, Bioscot Ltd., 1983-84; Chairman, Edinburgh Conference Centre Ltd., 1987-90; Director, Heriot-Watt Computer Application Services Ltd., 1987-90; Chairman, SCOT Innovation and Development Ltd., 1991-98; Member: Universities Central Council on Admissions, 1967-90, Directing Group, Programme on Institutional Management in Higher Education, OECD, Paris, 1986-90, Executive Committee, Federated Superannuation System for Universities, since 1988, Executive Committee, Scottish Norwegian Business Forum, 1991-96, Board of Management, Petroleum Science and Technology Institute, 1989-93, Board of Directors, Leith School of Art, 1995-99; Chairman, Edinburgh Society of Glasgow University Graduates, 1984-85; Session Clerk, St. Ninian's Church, Corstorphine, 1969-96; Convener, Finance Committee, Action of Churches Together in Scotland, 1993-96; Vice-Convener, Personnel Committee, Church of Scotland, 1996-99; Honorary Fellow, Royal Scottish Geographical Society, 1989; Honorary Doctor, Heriot-Watt University, 1991; Officer of the Royal Norwegian Order of St. Olav, 1979. Recreations: travel; photography. Address: (h.) 11 The Hermitage, 1 Kinellan Road, Edinburgh EH12 6ES; T.-0131 346 4454.

Cameron, Brigadier Ewen Duncan, OBE. Deputy Director, National Trust for Scotland, 1998-2000; b. 10.2.35, Bournemouth; m., Joanna Margaret Hay; 2 d. Educ. Wellington College; Royal Military Academy, Sandhurst. Commissioned The Black Watch, 1955; DS, The Staff College, 1972-75; Commanding Officer, 1st Bn., The Black Watch, 1975-78; Commander, Royal Brunei Armed Forces, 1980-82; Indian College of Defence Studies, Delhi, 1983; Divisional Brigadier, Scottish Division, 1984-86; Director of Administration and Personnel, National Trust for Scotland, 1986-98. Member, Queen's Bodyguard for Scotland (Royal Company of Archers). Recreations: opera; bridge; bird-watching; travel; gardening. Address: (h.) The Old Manse, Arngask, Glenfarg, Perthshire PH2 9QA; T.-01577 830394.

Cameron, Sheriff Ian Alexander, MA, LLB. Sheriff of Grampian, Highland and Islands, at Elgin, since 2001; b. 5.11.38, Elgin; m., Dr. Margaret Anne Innes; 1 s. Educ. Elgin Academy; Edinburgh University; Aberdeen University. Partner, Stewart and McIsaac, Solicitors, Elgin, 1962-86; Sheriff at Edinburgh, 1987-93, at Wick, Dornoch and Stornoway, 1993-2001. Recreation: travel. Address: Braemoray, Elgin, IV30 4NJ; T.-01343 542731; 19/4 Damside, Dean Village, Edinburgh, EH4 3BB; T.-0131-220 1548.

Cameron, James, BSc (Hons), PhD. Head Teacher, Kilchuimen Academy, Fort Augustus, since 1992; b. 29.1.47, Fraserburgh; m., Jo; 2 s.; 2 d. Educ. Peterhead Academy; University of Aberdeen; Aberdeen College of Education. Research Chemist, Courtaulds Ltd., Coventry, 1972-76; Teacher: Robert Gordon's College, Aberdeen, 1977-79, Peterhead Academy, 1979-83; Principal Teacher (Chemistry), Dyce Academy, Aberdeen, 1983-89; Assistant Head Teacher, Northfield Academy, Aberdeen, 1989-92. Recreations: walking; DIY; caravanning; reading. Address: Kilchuimen Academy, Station Road, Fort Augustus; T.-01320 366296.

Cameron, Professor Rev. James Kerr, MA, BD, PhD, FRHistS. Professor of Ecclesiastical History, St. Andrews University, 1970-89; b. 5.3.24, Methven; m., Emma Leslie Birse; 1 s. Educ. Oban High School; St. Andrews University; Hartford Theological Seminary, Hartford, Connecticut. Ordained as Assistant Minister, Church of the Holy Rude, Stirling, 1952; appointed Lecturer in Church History, Aberdeen University, 1955; Lecturer, then Senior Lecturer in Ecclesiastical History, St. Andrews University, 1956-70; Dean, Faculty of Divinity, 1978-83. President: Ecclesiastical History Society, 1976-77, British Sub-Commission, Commission Internationale d'Histoire

Ecclesiastique Comparee, 1979-92; Vice-President, International Association for Neo-Latin Studies, 1979-81; Honorary Fellow, Ecclesiastical History Society, 2000; Co-Editor and Contributor, Theologische Realenzyklopädie (Vol. 17 onwards). Publications: Letters of John Johnston and Robert Howie, 1963; First Book of Discipline, 1972; Contributor to: Acta Conventus Neo-Latini Amstelodamensis, 1973; Advocates of Reform, 1953; The Scottish Tradition, 1974; Renaissance and Renewal in Christian History, 1977; Reform and Reformation: England and the Continent, 1979; Origins and Nature of the Scottish Enlightenment, 1982; A Companion to Scottish Culture, 1981; Humanism in Renaissance Scotland, 1990; The Impact of Humanism on Western Europe, 1990; A History of Religion in Britain, 1994; The Universities of Aberdeen and Europe, The First Three Centuries, 1995; Scotland and the Low Countries 1124-1994, 1996. Recreation: gardening. Address: (h.) Priorscroft, 71 Hepburn Gardens, St. Andrews KY16 9LS; T.-01334 473996; e-mail: jkc6@st-andrews.ac.uk

Cameron, J. Gordon, MA, LLB, DipLP, WS, NP. Partner, Stuart & Stuart WS, since 1987; b. 15.11.57, Edinburgh; m., Deborah Jane; 1 s.; 1 d. Educ. George Watson's College; Aberdeen University. Joined Stuart & Stuart WS as assistant, 1985. Hon. Secretary and Treasurer, Royal Celtic Society. Recreations: hill-walking; cycling; keep-fit; hill-running; photography; foreign travel. Address: (b.) 23 Rutland Street, Edinburgh EH1 2RN; T.-0131-228 6449.; e-mail: gcameron@stuartandstuart.co.uk

Cameron, John Bell, CBE, FRAgricS, AIAgricE. Director, South West Trains, since 1995; Chairman, Scottish Beef Council, since 1997; Farmer, since 1961; b. 14.6.39, Edinburgh; m., Margaret Clapperton. Educ. Dollar Academy. Vice President, National Farmers' Union, 1976-79, President, 1979-84; Member, Agricultural Praesidium of EEC, 1979-84; Chairman, EEC Advisory Committee for Sheepmeat, 1982-90; Chairman, World Meats Group, (IFAP), since 1983; Chairman, Board of Governors, Dollar Academy, since 1985; Chairman, United Auctions Ltd., since 1985; Member, Board of Governors, Macaulay Land Use Research Institute, since 1987; Chairman, British Railways (Scottish) Board, 1988-93 (Member, 1988-94); honorary doctorate of technology, Napier University, 1998. Long Service Award, Royal Observer Corps. Recreations: flying; shooting; travelling. Address: (h.) Balbuthie Farm, by Leven, Fife; T.-01333 730210.

Cameron, (John Roderick) Hector, LLB, NP. Solicitor; Director, Telecom Service Centres Ltd.; b. 11.6.47, Glasgow; m., Rosemary Brownlee; 1 s.; 1 d. Educ. High School of Glasgow; Friends School, Wigton; St. Andrews University. Admitted Solicitor, 1971; Partner, Bishop, Milne Boyd & Co., 1973; Chairman, Glasgow Junior Chamber of Commerce, 1981; Managing Partner, Bishop & Co., 1985; Partner, Dorman Jeffrey & Co., 1990; Director, Merchants House of Glasgow, 1986; Director, Glasgow Chamber of Commerce, 1987. Recreations: reading; sailing; golf. Address: (h.) 2 Lancaster Crescent, Glasgow G12 0RR.

Cameron. Rev. Dr. John Urquhart, BA, BSc, PhD, BD, ThD. Minister, Parish of Broughty Ferry, since 1974; b. 10.6.43, Dundee; m., Jill Sjoberg; 1 s.; 1 d. Educ. Falkirk High School; St. Andrews University; Edinburgh University; University of Southern California. Marketing Executive, Beechams, London, 1969-73; Assistant Minister, Wellington Church, Glasgow, 1973-74; Chaplain, Royal Naval Reserve, 1976-81; Marketing Consultant, Pergamon Press, Oxford, 1977-81; Religious Education Department, Dundee High School, 1980-87; Sports Journalist and Travel Writer, Hill Publications, Surrey, since 1981; Physics Department, Dundee College of Further Education, 1987-95; Moderator, Presbytery of Dundee, 1993-94; Chaplain, Royal Caledonian Curling Club, 1980-95; Chaplain, Black

Watch ACF, 1994-99. National and international honours in both summer and winter sports, 1960-85; sports scholarship, University of Southern California, 1962-64. Recreations: golf; skiing; curling. Address: St. Stephen's Manse, 33 Camperdown Street, Broughty Ferry; T.-01382 477403.

Cameron, Sheriff Lewis, MA, LLB. Solicitor, since 1962; Sheriff of South Strathclyde Dumfries and Galloway at Hamilton, since 1994, at Dumfries, 1988-94; b. 12.8.35, Glasgow; m., Sheila Colette Gallacher; 2 s.; 2 d. Educ. St. Aloysius College; Blairs College; St. Sulpice, Paris; Glasgow University. RAF, 1954-56; admitted Solicitor, 1962. Member, Legal Aid Central Committee, 1970-80; Legal Aid Secretary, Airdrie, 1978-87; Chairman, Social Security Appeal Tribunals, 1983-88; Dean, Airdrie Society of Solicitors, 1984-85; Tutor, Strathclyde University, 1981-88; Treasurer, Monklands Victim Support Scheme, 1983-88; Chairman: Dumfries and Galloway Family Conciliation Service, 1988-92, Dumfries and Galloway, Scottish Association for the Study of Delinquency, 1988-92; Member, Scotland Committee, National Children's Homes; Trustee, Oscar Marzaroli Trust; Chairman, PHEW, 1994-2000. Address: (b.) Sheriff Court House, Beckford Street, Hamilton.

Cameron, Sir Roy, QPM, BA, MPhil. HM Chief Inspector of Constabulary for Scotland, since 2002; Chief Constable, Lothian and Borders Police, 1996-2002; m., Margaret; 2 s. Dunbartonshire Constabulary, 1966; Assistant Chief Constable, Strathclyde Police,1990; Chief Constable, Dumfries and Galloway Constabulary, 1994. Recreations: walking; swimming; music; reading.

Cameron, Sandy, MA (Hons), MBA. Head of Environment Strategy, Scottish Executive, since 1999; b. 20.7.52, Hawick; m., Alyson Oglesby; 2 s. Educ. Inverness Royal Academy; Edinburgh University. Joined Scottish Office, 1975; posts including Head of NHS Financial Management, 1985-88, Director (Asia), Locate in Scotland; based in Tokyo, 1988-93; Head, Forestry Review Group, 1993-96; Head of Environmental Special Projects, 1996-99. Member of Council, Japan Society of Scotland, since 1995, Chair, since 2000; elected Member, General Executive Committee, Scottish Executive Group, Public and Commercial Services Union, since 1998. Recreations: running; reading; films; things Japanese. Address: (b.) 1-H Victoria Quay, Edinburgh EH6 6QQ; T.-0131-244 7700.

Cameron, Thomas Anthony (Tony). Chief Executive, Scottish Prison Service, since 1999; b. 3.2.47; m., Elizabeth Christine Sutherland; 2 s. Educ. Stranraer High School. Department of Agriculture and Fisheries for Scotland, 1966; Private Secretary to Deputy Under Secretary of State, Scottish Office, 1972, to Permanent Under Secretary of State, 1973-74; HEO(D), DAFS, 1974-77; Principal, DAFS, 1977-82; Assistant Secretary, DAFS, 1982-87; Scottish Office Finance Division, 1987-92; Head of Food and Agriculture, Scottish Office, 1992-99. Member, Duke of Edinburgh's Sixth Commonwealth Study Conference, Australia. Recreations: reading; mountaineering; cycling. Address: (b.) Calton House, 5 Redheughs Rigg, Edinburgh EH12 9HW; T.-0131-244 8745.

Cameron-Jones, Professor Margot, MA, MEd. Professor of Teacher Education, Edinburgh University, since 1990; b. 11.1.39, Isle of Man; m., Richard John; 1 s. Educ. St. Winifred's School, Llanfairfechan; University of Edinburgh. Address: (b.) Faculty of Education, Edinburgh University, Holyrood Road, Edinburgh EH8 8AQ; T.-0131-651 6160.

Campbell of Croy, Baron (Gordon Thomas Calthrop Campbell), PC (1970), MC and Bar. Consultant, oil industry, 1975-94; Director, Alliance and Leicester

Building Society and Chairman of its Scottish Board, 1975-94; Chairman, Stoic Insurance Services, 1979-93; b. 8.6.21; m.; 2 s.; 1 d. Educ. Wellington. Commissioned, Regular Army, 1939 RA; Major, 15th Scottish Division, 1942; wounded and disabled, 1945; entered HM Foreign Service, 1946 and served in the Foreign Office, at the UN, in the Cabinet Office (Private Secretary to the Secretary of the Cabinet) and in the Embassy in Vienna; MP (Conservative), Moray and Nairn, 1959-74; Government Whip, 1961-62; Lord Commissioner of the Treasury and Scottish Whip, 1962-63; Parliamentary Under-Secretary of State, Scottish Office, 1963-64; Opposition Spokesman on Defence, 1967-68; Shadow Cabinet, 1969-70; Secretary of State for Scotland, 1970-74; Chairman, Scottish Committee, International Year of Disabled, 1981; Partner, Holme Rose Estate and Farms; Trustee, Thomson Foundation, since 1980; Chairman; Advisory Committee on Pollution of the Sea, 1987-89, Scottish Council of Independent Schools, 1976-80; Vice Lord Lieutenant of Nairnshire, 1988-99; President, Anglo-Austrian Society, 1991-99. Address: (h.) Holme Rose, Cawdor, Nairnshire.

Campbell, Alan Grant, LLB. Chief Executive, Aberdeenshire Council, since 1995; b. 4.12.46, Aberdeen; m., Susan Black; 1 s.; 2 d. Educ. Aberdeen Grammar School; Aberdeen University. Admitted Solicitor, Scotland, 1970; various legal appointments, Aberdeen County Council, 1968-75; Grampian Regional Council: Assistant Director of Law and Administration, 1975-79, Depute Director, 1979-84, Director of Law and Administration, 1984-91, Chief Executive, 1991-95. Chairman, SOLACE (Scotland), 1997-99. Recreations: competitive cycling and following the Tour de France; photography; the enjoyment of red wine; gardening. Address: Woodhill House, Westburn Road, Aberdeen AB16 5GB; T.-01224 665400.

Campbell, Alastair James, LLB. Partner, Mitchells Roberton, Solicitors, since 1985; b. 29.12.48, Glasgow; m., Pamela Crichton; 3 s. Educ. Merchiston Castle School, Edinburgh; University of Strathclyde. Qualified as Solicitor, 1972; Partner, Mackenzie Roberton & Co. (later Mitchells Roberton), 1975. Secretary, National Burns Homes, Mauchline, Ayrshire, since 1976. Recreations: golf; tennis; curling. Address: (b.) George House, 36 North Hanover Street, Glasgow G1 2AD; T.-0141-552 3422.

Campbell of Airds, Alastair Lorne, OStJ. Chief Executive, Clan Campbell, since 1984; Archivist, Inveraray Castle, since 1984; H.M. Unicorn Pursuivant of Arms, Court of the Lord Lyon, since 1987; b. 11.7.37, London; m., Mary-Ann Campbell-Preston; 3 s.; 1 d. Educ. Eton; R.M.A., Sandhurst. Regular Army, 1955-63 (commissioned Argyll and Sutherland Highlanders); Reid Pye and Campbell, 1963-71 (Managing Director, 1970-71); Waverley Vintners Ltd., 1972-83 (Marketing Director, 1972, Managing Director, 1977). Member: Queen's Bodyguard for Scotland (Royal Company of Archers), Chapter of Scottish Priory, Order of St John; FSA Scot; Patron, Armorial and Heraldry Society of Australasia; Chairman, Advisory Committee on Tartan to the Lord Lyon; Member, Council, National Trust for Scotland, 1996-2001; Honorary Research Fellowship, University of Aberdeen, 1996-2001. Publications: Two Hundred Years — The Highland Society of London; The Life and Troubled Times of Sir Donald Campbell of Ardnamurchan; The History of Clan Campbell – Vol. I. Recreations: painting; fishing; walking. Address: (h.) Inverawe Barn, Taynuilt, Argyll PA35 1HU; T.-01866 822207.

Campbell, Alison Rigg, MA. Scotland Adviser, Esmée Fairbairn Foundation; freelance fundraiser; b. 20.8.50, Paisley; m., Niall; 3 s. Educ. Cumnock Academy; University of St. Andrews. Scottish Office, 1972-77; Action on Smoking and Health, 1987-91; Director, Lintel Trust, 1992-2000. Secretary, Church and Nation Committee, Church of Scotland, 1991-96; Committee Member, Scottish

Refugee Council; Director, Edinburgh Academy. Recreations: walking; talking. Address: 15 Warriston Crescent, Edinburgh EH3 5LA; T.-0131 556 2895.

Campbell, Alistair Bromley, OBE. Farmer; Agricultural Consultant and Valuer; b. 23.6.27, Charing, Kent; m., Rosemary Pullar (deceased); 1 s.; 2 d. Educ. Tonbridge School. Training in agriculture, 1944-47; self-employed Farmer, 1948-81; Agricultural Consultant, Arbiter, Valuer, 1968-81; Agricultural Adviser and Valuer, South of Scotland Electricity Board, 1972-81; Vice-Chairman, Countryside Commission for Scotland, 1972-81 (Member from 1969); Member: Secretary of State's Panel of Agricultural Arbiters, 1968-81, Scottish Land Court, 1981-92; Chairman, Executive Committee of Council of Management, Strathcarron Hospice, Denny; former Council Member, British Trust for Conservation Volunteers (Chairman, Scottish Regional Committee, 1975-84); Chairman of Council, Scottish Conservation Projects Trust, 1984-97; Church Warden, St. Mary's Episcopal Church, Dunblane, since 1960; Honorary Vice-President and a Director, Doune and Dunblane Agricultural Society; former Convener, Legal Committee, NFU of Scotland; General Commissioner of Income Tax, since 1971; Chairman, Scottish Executive Committee, Association of Agriculture, 1980-86. Address: (h.) Grainston Farm, Kilbryde, Dunblane, Perthshire FK15 9NF; T.-01786 823304.

Campbell, Andrew Robertson, OBE, JP, DL. Convener, Dumfries and Galloway Council, since 1999; b. 18.06.44, Castle Douglas; m., Maureen; 1s.; 1d. Educ. Loretto School. Farmer in partnership with wife and son; Director, Royal Highland Agricultural Show; Scottish Director, NFU Mutual Insurance Society; Past President, Castle Douglas Rotary; Board Member: Residual Scottish Milk Marketing Board; Scottish Agricultural College; Scottish Enterprise Dumfries and Galloway; Councillor, since 1995. Recreations: rugby supporter and past player; country sports. Address: (h.) Cuil, Castle Douglas, DG7 1QB; T.-01556 502172.

Campbell, Andy, DipID. Managing Director, Red Lemon Studios Ltd, since 1996; b. 18.5.72, Paisley; m., Claire Campbell; 1s.; 1d. Educ. Sacred Heart High School, Paisley; Glasgow College of Building and Printing. Director, Young Enterprise; Past Chairman, Scottish Games Alliance; Finalist, Entrepreneur of the Year. Address: (b.) 175 West George Street, Glasgow, G2 2LB.

Campbell, Cairns. Director, The Big Idea, Irvine, 1997-2000; Director and Trustee, Baxi Partnership since 1984; b. 9.10.44, Paisley; m., Isabel; 1s. Educ. John Neilson Institution. Various management posts in engineering and electronics; Director, Employee Ownership Scotland; Chief Executive, Asset Trust Ltd; Director, Nobel Exhibition Trust; Premier Prize, Institute of Social Invention, 1986; Honorary Doctorate, Middlesex University, 2000. Recreations: sailing. Address: (h.) Knockandon, East Bennan, Isle of Arran KA27 8SH; T.-01770 820630.

Campbell, Catherine, JP, BSc, BA (Hons), MSc. Educational Psychologist; Member, Scottish Milk Marketing Board, 1981-92; Chairman, Cumbernauld "I" Tech, 1984-88; b. 10.1.40, Glasgow; m., John Campbell; 2 s.; 1 d. Educ. Notre Dame High School; Glasgow University; Open University; Strathclyde University. Teacher of Mathematics, 1962-68; Member: Cumbernauld and Kilsyth District Council, 1969-78, Cumbernauld Development Corporation, 1975-84. Jubilee Medal, 1977; CACDP (stage 3 sign language). Recreations: promotion of equal opportunities for deaf people; cooking; homecrafts. Address: (h.) 10 Westray Road, Cumbernauld G67 1NN; T.-0123 67 24834.

Campbell, Christopher Robert James, LLB (Hons). Managing Partner, Dundas and Wilson, since 1996; b. Edinburgh; m., Kay; 1 s.; 1 d. Educ. Daniel Stewart's and Melville College; University of Edinburgh. Joined Dundas and Wilson, 1980: Assistant Solicitor, 1982, Partner, 1987, Partner in Charge of Glasgow Office, 1991, Deputy Managing Partner, 1995. Honorary Professor of Commercial Law, University of Glasgow. Recreations: golf; music; football. Address: (b.) Saltire Court, 20 Castle Terrace, Edinburgh EH1 2EN; T.-0131-228 8000.

Campbell, Colin MacIver, MA (Hons). MSP (SNP), West of Scotland, since 1999; National Secretary, Scottish National Party, 1997-99 (Defence Spokesman, since 1995); b. 31.8.38, Ralston, Paisley; m., Evelyn; 3 s. Educ. Paisley Grammar School; Glasgow University; Jordanhill College of Education. Teacher: Hillhead High School, 1961-63, Paisley Grammar School, 1963-67; Principal Teacher, Greenock Academy, 1967-73; Depute Head Teacher, Merksworth High, 1973-77; Head Teacher, Westwood Secondary, 1977-89; Tutor (part-time), Strathclyde University Senior Studies Institute, 1995-98. Member, Renfrewshire Council, 1995-99; General Election Candidate: 1987, 1992, 1997; Euro Candidate: 1989, 1994. Elder, Church of Scotland; Former Chairman, Kilbarchan Civic Society and Kilbarchan Community Council; Convener, Kilbarchan SNP; Past Convener, Renfrew West SNP. Recreation: military history. Address: (h.) Braeside, Shuttle Street, Kilbarchan PA10 2PR.

Campbell, David Ross, CBE, CMIM, FInstD. Chairman, Health Education Board for Scotland, since 1995; Scotland Board Member, New Opportunities Fund; Chairman and Director of a number of private companies; b. 27.9.43, Glasgow; m., Moira. Educ. Whitehill Senior Secondary School, Glasgow; James Watt Memorial College, Greenock. Officer, Merchant Navy, 1961-68; Sales Executive, 1968-69; various management positions, George Outram & Co. Ltd., 1969-73; Managing Director, Scottish & Universal Newspapers Ltd., 1974-84; Executive Director, Scottish & Universal Investments Ltd.; Chief Executive, Clyde Cablevision Ltd., 1982-84; Chairman and Chief Executive, West Independent Newspapers Ltd., 1984-94; Chairman, Saltire Holdings Ltd., 1991-93. Past President: Scottish Newspaper Proprietors Association, Glasgow Chamber of Commerce; Liveryman and Freeman, City of London; Regional Chairman, PSYBT. Recreations: golf; theatre; reading. Address: (h.) Summerlea, Summerlea Road, Seamill KA23 9HP.

Campbell, Donald. Writer; b. 25.2.40, Wick; m., Jean Fairgrieve; 1 s. Educ. Boroughmuir High School, Edinburgh. Playwright, essayist, lyricist and poet; stage plays include: The Jesuit, 1976; The Widows of Clyth, 1979; Blackfriars Wynd, 1980; Till All The Seas Run Dry, 1981; Howard's Revenge, 1985; Victorian Values, 1986; The Fisher Boy and the Honest Lass, 1990; The Ould Fella, 1993, Nancy Sleekit, 1994, Glorious Hearts, 1999; also active as writer and director in a number of community projects; script co-ordinator, The Dundee Mysteries, Dundee Rep; poetry includes: Rhymes 'n Reasons, 1972; Blether, 1979; Selected Poems: 1970-1990, 1990; other work includes: A Brighter Sunshine (theatre history), 1983, Playing for Scotland (theatre history), 1996, four television plays, 50 radio programmes; Fellow in Creative Writing, Dundee University, 1987-89; William Soutar Fellow, Perth, 1991-93; Royal Literary Fund Fellow, Napier University, 2000-01; awards include: three Fringe Firsts; Silver Medal, 1983 New York Radio Festival for A Clydebuilt Man; Radio Industries Club Award for The Miller's Reel, 1987. Address: (h.) 85 Spottiswoode Street, Edinburgh EH9 1BZ; T.-0131-447 2305.

Campbell, Donald McKechnie, MA (Hons), BA. Headteacher, Islay High School, since 1997; Member, West of Scotland Water Authority; Company Secretary, Islay Development Company; Crofter; b. 3.8.55, Glasgow; m., Fiona; 1 s.; 1 d. Educ. Clydebank High School; University of Glasgow; Open University. Assistant Teacher, Bearsden Academy, 1978-82; Tiree High School: Principal Teacher, 1982-93, Depute Head Teacher, 1993-97; Member, Argyll and Bute District Council, 1988-94; Member, BBC Scotland Gaelic Advisory Committee, 1995-2001; Member, West Region Board, Scottish Environment Protection Agency, 1996-99. Recreations: cinema; theatre; keeping fit. Address: (h.) Schoolhouse, Lennox Street, Port Ellen, Isle of Islay, Argyll PA42 7BW; T.-01496 302579.

Campbell, Professor Donald Murray, BSc, PhD, FInstP. Professor of Musical Acoustics, Edinburgh University, since 2000; b. 20.10.42, Inverness; m., Dr Jean Patricia Campbell; 2 s. Educ. Dingwall Academy; Edinburgh University. Demonstrator, Department of Natural Philosophy, Edinburgh University, 1968-73; Lecturer, then Senior Lecturer, Department of Physics, Edinburgh University, 1973-2000. Publication: The Musician's Guide to Acoustics (Co-author), 1987. Recreations: music-making. Address: (b.) Department of Physics and Astronomy, Edinburgh University, Edinburgh EH9 3JZ; T.-0131-650 5262.

Campbell, Doreen Ann, MB, ChB, MFPHM, MHSM. Senior Medical Officer, Scottish Executive, since 1996; b. 1.2.55, Bearsden; m., Dr Gordon G. Birnie; 1 s.; 2 d. Educ. St Leonard's School, St Andrews; Glasgow University. Recreations: skiing; tennis. Address: (b.) Health Department, Scottish Executive, St Andrew's House, Edinburgh.

Campbell, Doris Margaret, MD, FRCOG. Reader, Obstetrics and Gynaecology and Reproductive Physiology, Aberdeen University; b. 24.1.42, Aberdeen; m., Alasdair James Campbell; 1 s.; 1 d. Educ. Aberdeen High School for Girls; Aberdeen University. Resident house officer posts, Aberdeen, 1967-69; Research Fellow, Aberdeen University, 1969-73; Registrar in Obstetrics and Gynaecology, Aberdeen Hospitals, 1973-74; Lecturer in Obstetrics and Gynaecology and Physiology, Aberdeen University, 1974-84. Former Member, Scottish Women's Hockey Council. Recreations: bridge; badminton; guiding. Address: (h.) 77 Blenheim Place, Aberdeen; T.-01224 639984; e-mail: d.m.campbell@abdn.ac.uk

Campbell, Wing Commander George, MBE, SBStJ, DL, MIMgt; b. 24.11.22, Renton; m., Marion T.H. Halliday; 1 s.; 1 d. Educ. Vale of Leven Academy. Joined RAF, 1941; served in UK, India, Burma, Malaya, Singapore; demobilised, 1946, and continued in Royal Air Force Voluntary Reserve (Training Branch), serving with Air Training Corps; formed 2319 (Vale of Leven) Squadron, 1956; appointed to Wing Staff, Glasgow, and Western Wing, 1973; promoted to Wing Commander, 1978; retired, 1983; attended Bisley as competitor, coach, and team captain for 48 years; Vice Chairman, 602 City of Glasgow Squadron, Royal Auxiliary Air Force Squadron Museum; Chairman: 912 Squadron ATC, Duke of Edinburgh Award (County Co-ordinating Committee); Elder, Church of Scotland; County Representative, Royal Air Forces Benevolent Fund; Director, Dumbartonshire Branch, British Red Cross, 1983-92; Past President, Dumbarton Rotary Club; Past Chairman, RNLI, Dumbarton Branch. Address: (h.) Valeview, Comley Bank, Oxhill, Dumbarton; T.-Dumbarton 763700.

Campbell, Hugh Hall, QC, BA (Hons), MA (Oxon), LLB (Hons), FCIArb. Queen's Counsel, since 1983; b. 18.2.44, Glasgow; m., Eleanor Jane Kerr; 3 s. Educ. Glasgow Academy; Trinity College, Glenalmond; Exeter College, Oxford; Edinburgh University. Called to Scottish Bar, 1969; Standing Junior Counsel to Admiralty, 1976. Recreations: carnival, wine, music. Address: (h.) 12 Ainslie Place, Edinburgh EH3 6AS; T.-0131-225 2067.

Campbell, Rev. Iain Donald, MA, BD, MTh. Minister, Back Free Church of Scotland, Isle of Lewis, since 1995; b. 20.9.63, Stornoway; m., Anne M. Davidson; 2 s.; 1 d. Educ. Nicolson Institute, Stornoway; University of Glasgow; Free Church College. Minister, Snizort Free Church, Isle of Skye, 1988-95; Editor, The Instructor (Free Church of Scotland youth magazine), 1990-96; Editor, The Monthly Record of the Free Church of Scotland, 1996-2000. Publications: In Thy Likeness, 1990; Heart of the Gospel (Editor), 1995; The Doctrine of Sin, 1999. Recreations: reading; walking. Address: Free Church Manse, Vatisker, Isle of Lewis HS2 0LN; T.-01851 820317; e-mail: iaind@backfreechurch.co.uk

Campbell, Professor Ian, MA, PhD. Professor of Scottish and Victorian Literature, Edinburgh University, since 1992; b. 25.8.42. Lausanne, Switzerland. Educ. Lausanne; Findochty; Buckie; Mackie Academy, Stonehaven; Aberdeen University; Edinburgh University. Joined staff, English Department, Edinburgh University, 1967; Visiting Professor, Guelph, Duke, UCLA; Europa Professor, Maine; Visiting Lecturer, United States, Canada, France, Switzerland, Italy, Japan. Publications: editorial team of Carlyle Letters, numerous books and articles on Scottish and Victorian Literature. Recreations: music; sport. Address: (b.) Department of English, Edinburgh University, David Hume Tower, George Square, Edinburgh, EH8 9JX; T.-0131-650 4284.

Campbell, Sir Ian, CBE, OStJ, VRD, JP. Deputy Chairman, Heath (Scotland) Ltd., 1987-95; Chairman, Select Assured Properties PLC, 1989-96; Director, Hermiston Securities, since 1990; b. 3.2.23, Edinburgh; m., Marion Kirkhope Shiel; 1 d. Educ. Daniel Stewart's College, Edinburgh. Royal Navy, 1942-46; Royal Naval Reserve, 1946-64 (retired with rank of Commander); John Line & Sons, 1948-61 (Area Manager, West of England); Managing Director, MacGregor Wallcoverings Ltd., 1965-77; Finance Director, Scottish Conservative Party, 1977-89. Director, Travel System Ltd., 1987-90; Councillor, City of Edinburgh, 1984-88; Member, Transport Users Consultative Committee for Scotland, 1981-87; Freeman, City of Glasgow, 1991. Recreations: golf; vintage cars; water colour painting. Address: (h.) Merleton, 10 Boswall Road, Edinburgh EH5 3RH; T.-0131-552 4825.

Campbell, Sir Ilay Mark, Bt, MA (Oxon). Director, High Craigton Farming Co.; b. 29.5.27, Edinburgh; m., Margaret Minette Rohais Anderson; 2 d. Educ. Eton; Christ Church, Oxford. Christie's: Scottish Agent, 1968, Joint Scottish Agent, 1973-92, Chairman, 1978-96; Honorary Vice-President, Scotland's Garden Scheme; Trustee: Crarae Gardens Charitable Trust, since 1978, Tree Register of the British Isles, since 1988; Chairman, Church Buildings Renewal Trust, 1993-98 (Trustee, 1993-2001); Past President, Association for the Protection of Rural Scotland; former Convener, Church of Scotland Committee on Artistic Matters; Member, Historic Buildings Council for Scotland, 1989-98; Member, Gardens Committee, National Trust for Scotland, 1995-2001; former Scottish Representative, National Arts Collection Fund. Recreations: heraldry; genealogy; collecting heraldic bookplates. Address: (h.) Crarae Lodge, Inveraray, Argyll PA32 8YA; T.-01546 86274/370.

Campbell, James Hugh, BL. Senior Partner, Bird Semple Fyfe Ireland, WS, 1987-91, Consultant until 1993; b. 13.11.26, Old Kilpatrick; m., Iris Burnside Hercus; 2 s.; 1 d. Educ. Bearsden Academy; Glasgow University. Bird Son & Semple: Partner, 1952-65, then Senior Partner, 1965-73; Senior Partner, Bird Semple Crawford Herron, 1973-87. Member, Council, Law Society of Scotland, 1986-95 (President, 1991-92); President, Glasgow Juridical Society, 1952; Deacon, Incorporation of Wrights in Glasgow, 1980-81; Honorary Member, Royal Faculty of Procurators,

Glasgow. Recreations: music; reading; golf. Address: (h.) 24 Woodvale Avenue, Giffnock, Glasgow G46 6RQ; T.-0141-638 2630.

Campbell, John David, QC, LLB, FCIArb. Queen's Counsel, since 1998; Advocate since 1981; b. 4.5.49, Inverness; m., Marion J. Foy; 2s.; 3d. Educ. Gordonstoun; Edinburgh University. Solicitor, 1972-78; Assistant Director of Legal Aid, Hong Kong, 1978-81; Magistrate, Hong Kong, 1978-81; Chairman, Executive Board, Chartered Institute of Arbitrators, since 2001. Publication: Scottish Planning Encyclopaedia (Contributor), 2001. Recreations: music; tennis; golf. Address: (b.) Advocates' Library, Parliament House, Edinburgh, EH1 1RF; T.-0131-226 5071; e-mail: jcampbellqc@ednet.co.uk

Campbell, John Ivor, FCCA. Director of Corporate Resources, Scottish Borders Council, since 2001; b. 23.8.51, Galashiels; m., Sheila; 2 d. Educ. Kelso High School. Roxburgh County Council, 1970-75; Borders Regional Council, 1975-84; Chief Accountant, Fife Regional Council, 1984-86; Depute Director of Finance, Glenrothes Development Corporation, 1986-88; Director of Finance, Roxburgh District Council, 1988-96; Director of Financial Services, Scottish Borders Council, 1995-2001. Past President, Scottish Branch, Association of Chartered Certified Accountants; Member, ACCA International Assembly, 1997-2000; Chairman, CIPFA Scottish Branch Directors of Finance Section, 2000-01; Treasurer, Scottish Borders Tourist Board, since 1989. Address: (b.) Council Headquarters, Newtown St. Boswells, Melrose, TD6 0SA; T.-01835 824000.

Campbell, Kenneth Lindsay, MBChB, FRCS (Edin), MD. Consultant Colorectal Surgeon, Ninewells Hospital and Medical School and Fernbrae Hospital, Dundee; b. 27.6.62, Aberdeen. Educ. Royal High School, Edinburgh; University of Aberdeen; Harvard University. Lecturer in Surgery, University of Aberdeen; Surgical Fellow, Ninewells Hospital and Medical School, Dundee. Address: (b.) Ward 8, Ninewells Hospital and Medical School, Dundee, DD1 9SY; T.-01382 633886.

Campbell, Rev. M. Douglas, BA, MDiv. Executive Director, Scottish Bible Society, since 2001; b. 30.5.69, Detroit; m., Emily Riley. Educ. Greenhills School, Ann Arbor, Michigan; Kenyon College and Princeton Theological Seminary. Assistant Director, Alumni Affairs, Kenyon College, 1991-93; Assistant Minister, New Kilpatrick Parish Church, Bearsden, Glasgow, 1995-96; Associate Minister, New Kilpatrick, 1997-99; Field Development Officer, Scottish Bible Society, 1999-2001. Recreations: founder of cappella singing ensemble. Address: (b.) 7 Hampton Terrace, Edinburgh EH12 5XU; T.-0131-337 9701.

Campbell, Mary Theresa MacLeod, BA, CA. Founding Director, British Linen Advisers Ltd., since 1999; Council Member, Institute of Chartered Accountants, since 2000; b. 24.2.59, Glasgow; m., John Alexander Campbell; 2 s.; 2 d. Educ. Lochaber High School; University of Stirling. Ernst and Young, Glasgow, Inverness and London, 1980-86; Noble Group Limited, 1986-98 (Director, 1990, CEO, Noble Strategic Advisers Ltd., 1997); Director, British Linen Bank Ltd., 1998-99. Chair, Fundraising Committee, Gateway Theatre; Member, Taigh na Gaidhlig. Recreations: Gaelic culture and language; theatre; opera; Barra. Address: (b.) 12 Melville Street, Edinburgh EH3 7NS; T.-0131-243 8323; e-mail: mary.campbell@britishlinen.co.uk

Campbell, Melfort Andrew, FRSA. Chief Executive Officer, IMES Group Ltd., since 1997; b. 6.6.56, Exeter; m., Lucy Nickson; 3 d. Educ. Ampleforth College, York. Managing Director: Water Weights Ltd., 1985, Industrial and Marine Engineering SUCS Ltd., 1995. Director,

Scottish Enterprise Grampian; Chairman, CBI Scotland Smaller Firms. Recreations: fishing; shooting; rugby; tennis. Address: (b.) Tern Place, Denmore Road, Bridge of Don, Aberdeen AB23 8JX; T.-01224 705777; e-mail: melfort.campbell@imes-group.com

Campbell, Professor Michael, BSc, PhD, CPhys, FInstP, FInstMC. Professor of Physics and Optical Engineering, Glasgow Caledonian University, since 1996; b. 8.1.47; m., Imelda Anne Keating. Educ. Holyrood Senior Secondary School, Glasgow; University of Paisley; University of Glasgow. Research Fellow, University of Glasgow, 1975-77; Senior Research Physicist, GMI Ltd., Inchinnan, 1977-79; Physics Master, High School of Stirling, 1980-86; Lecturer, Senior Lecturer, Reader, Professor, Glasgow Caledonian University, since 1986; Tutor (part-time), Open University, 1976-86. Scientific Adviser, Central Regional Council, 1981-86; National Examiner, SCOTVEC HND, 1988-92; Member, Committee of Scottish Professors of Physics, since 1996; Chairman, ScotSense, since 1992; Glasgow Ambassador Award, 1998; EPSRC Peer Review College Member, since 1997; Institute of Physics Committees: Member, Instrumentation Science and Technology Group, since 1994, Applied Optics Division, since 1997, Optics Group, since 1999; Vice President, Royal Philosophical Society of Glasgow, 1997-99. Publications: Sensor Systems for Environmental Monitoring, Volumes I and II (Editor). Recreations: travelling; gardening; model engineering. Address: (b.) School of Engineering, Science and Design, Glasgow Caledonian University, Cowcaddens Road, Glasgow G4 0BA; T.-0141-331 3658; e-mail: m.campbell@gcal.ac.uk

Campbell, Neil Martin, MA, BSc, RMN, RGN, DPSN. Chief Executive, NHS Grampian; b. 9.11.57; m., Debra Ann; 3 s.; 2 d. Educ. St. Dominic's Comprehensive School; De La Salle Grammar School; Liverpool John Moores University; University of Manchester; University of Lancaster. Divisional Manager, Liverpool Priority Services Unit, 1987-89; Director of Operations, North Mersey Community NHS Trust, 1989-91; Co-ordinator for Priority Services, Mersey Regional Health Authority, 1991-93; Director for Service Development and Commissioning, South Cheshire Health Authority, 1993-96; Board General Manager (Chief Executive), Dumfries and Galloway Health Board. Member: Board, Dumfries and Galloway Enterprise Company, Advisory Board, Scottish Development Centre for Mental Health, Board, Strathclyde University National Centre for Training and Education in Prosthetics and Orthotics. Address: (b.) Summerfield House, 2 Eday Road, Aberdeen AB15 6RE.

Campbell, Niall Gordon, BA. Under Secretary, Civil and Criminal Law Group, Scottish Executive Justice Department, (formerly Scottish Office Home Department) since 1997; b. 9.11.41, Peebles; m., Alison M. Rigg; 3 s. Educ. Edinburgh Academy; Merton College, Oxford. Entered Scottish Office 1964; Assistant Secretary, 1978; various posts in Scottish Education Department and Scottish Development Department; Under Secretary, Social Work Services Group, 1989-97. Address (h.) 15 Warriston Crescent, Edinburgh.

Campbell, Robert Craig, BSc, MCIM. Senior Policy Adviser, NFU Scotland, since 1999 (Policy Director, 1996-99); b. 29.4.47, Glasgow; m., Elizabeth Helen C.; 2 d. Educ. Glasgow Academy; St. Andrews University. Scottish Council (Development and Industry): Research Executive, 1970-77, Research Director, 1977-84, Director, Overseas Projects Unit, 1984-86, Policy Research Director, 1986-88, Chief Economist, 1988-96. Recreation: angling. Address: (b.) The Rural Centre, West Mains, Ingliston, Newbridge EH28 8LT.

Campbell, (Robert) Mungo (McCready), BA, MPhil, FRSA. Deputy Director, Hunterian Art Gallery, University of Glasgow, since 1997; b. 8.10.59, Newcastle upon Tyne; m., Teresa Margaret Green; 1 s. Educ. Royal Grammar School, Newcastle upon Tyne; University of Durham; University of Glasgow. Assistant Keeper, National Gallery of Scotland, Edinburgh, 1987-97; Member, Scottish Arts Council Visual Arts Committee. Recreations: walking with my son and his dog; cooking good food; eating good food. Address: (b.) Hunterian Art Gallery, 82 Hillhead Street, Glasgow G12 8QQ; T.-0141-330 4735.

Campbell, Rev. Roderick D.M., TD, BD, FSA Scot. Minister, Mearns Parish Church, 1979-97; Vice Chairman, Greater Glasgow Health Board, 1994-96 (Member, 1989-96); Chairman: Greater Glasgow Drug Action Team, 1995-97, Victoria Infirmary NHS Trust, 1997-99; Chaplain, 3rd (Volunteer) Battalion The Royal Highland Fusiliers; Staff Chaplain, TA Army HQ, Scotland, since 1997; Locum Minister, Ruchazie Parish Church, since 1997; b. 1.8.43, Glasgow; m., Susan Norman; 2 d. Educ. Daniel Stewart's College, Edinburgh; Arbroath High School; Jordanhill College of Education; New College, Edinburgh University. Teacher, Technical Subjects, Glasgow, Tanzania and London, 1967-70; Associate Minister, St. Andrew's, Nairobi, 1975-78; Chieftain, Caledonian Society of Kenya, 1978; founder Member, Ndugu Society of Kenya, 1975; Chairman, Institute of Advanced Motorists (Kenya), 1977-78. Convener, Lodging House Mission, Glasgow Presbytery, 1981-86; Convener, National Church Extension Committee, Church of Scotland, 1987-89; Deacon, Incorporation of Barbers, Trades House, Glasgow, 1992-93. Recreations: swimming; horse-riding; hill-walking; fishing. Address: 22 Greenlaw Road, Newton Mearns, Glasgow G77 6ND; T.-0141 639 7328.

Campbell, Rt. Hon. (Walter) Menzies, CBE (1987), PC, QC, MA, LLB. MP (Liberal Democrat), North East Fife, since 1987; Advocate, since 1968; Queen's Counsel, since 1982; Liberal Democrat Shadow Foreign Secretary, since 2001; Member, Parliamentary Assembly of OSCE, 1992-1997, and since 1999; Member, North Atlantic Assembly, since 1989; b. 22.5.41, Glasgow; m., Elspeth Mary Urquhart. Educ. Hillhead High School, Glasgow; Glasgow University; Stanford University, California. President, Glasgow University Union, 1964-65; took part in Olympic Games, Tokyo, 1964; AAA 220-yards champion, 1964, 1967; Captain, UK athletics team, 1965, 1966; 1966 Commonwealth Games, Jamaica; UK 100-metres record holder, 1967-74. Advocate Depute, 1977-80; Standing Junior Counsel to the Army in Scotland, 1980-82. Parliamentary candidate (Liberal): Greenock and Port Glasgow, February, 1974, and October, 1974, East Fife, 1979, North East Fife, 1983; Chairman, Scottish Liberal Party, 1975-77; Member, Select Committee on Defence, 1992-99; Party Spokesman on Defence, Foreign Affairs and Sport, until 1997, Foreign Affairs and Defence, 1997-2001; Member: UK Sports Council, 1965-68; Scottish Sports Council, 1971-81; Chairman, Royal Lyceum Theatre, Edinburgh, 1984-87; Member, Broadcasting Council for Scotland, 1984-87. Recreations: all sports; music; theatre. Address: (b.) House of Commons, London SW1A 0AA; T.-0171-219 4446.

Campbell, William Kilpatrick, MA (Hons). Director, Mainstream Publishing, since 1978; Director, Edinburgh Book Festival, since 1992; b. 1.3.51, Glasgow; 2 d. Educ. Kilmarnock Academy; Edinburgh University. Postgraduate research, Universities of Edinburgh and California; world travel, 1975; Publications Manager, Edinburgh University Student Publications, 1976-78. Publications: Alternative Edinburgh (Co-Editor), 1972; Another Edinburgh, 1976. Recreations: soccer; tennis; rugby; wine; books; people. Address: (b.) 7 Albany Street, Edinburgh EH1 3UG; T.-0131-557 2959; e-mail: bill.campbell@mainstreampublishing.com

Campbell-Gibson, Lt.Comdr. R.N. (Ret.) Hugh Desmond; b. 18.8.24; m., Deirdre Wilson; 2 s.; 1 d. Educ. Royal Naval College, Dartmouth. Naval cadet, 1937-41; served Royal Navy, 1941-60; war service convoy duties, Atlantic and Mediterranean; farmed Glenlussa, by Campbeltown, 1960-68; farmed and ran hotel, Dunmor, Seil, Argyll, 1969-83; now manages family woodlands at Melfort. Recreations: gardening; fishing. Address: (h.) Tighnamara, Melfort, Kilmelford, Argyll; T.-Kilmelford 224.

Campsie, Alistair Keith, SDA. Author, Journalist and Piper; b. 27.1.29, Inverness; m., Robbie Anderson; 2 s.; 1 d. Educ. West Sussex High School; Lanark Grammar School; West of Scotland College of Agriculture. Inspector of Agriculture, Sudan Government Service, 1949; Cocoa Survey Officer, Nigeria, 1951; experimental staff, National Institute of Agricultural Engineering (Scotland), 1953; Country Editor, Weekly Scotsman, 1954; Sub-Editor, Verse Writer, Scottish Daily Mail, 1955; Founder Editor, East African Farmer and Planter, 1956; Chief Sub-Editor, Weekly Scotsman, 1957; designed and appointed first Editor, Geneva Weekly Tribune, 1958; Chief Feature Writer, Scottish Daily Mail, 1959; Columnist, Science Correspondent and Senior Writer, Scottish Daily Express, 1962-73; founded The Piper's Press, 1988; two Scottish Arts Council writer's bursaries; two SAC publisher's awards. Publications: Poems and a Pibroch (with Hugh MacDiarmid), 1972; By Law Protected, 1976; The MacCrimmon Legend or The Madness of Angus Mackay, 1980; We Bought a County Pub (under pen-name Alan Mackinnon), 1984; Perfect Poison, 1985; Pibroch: the tangled Web (radio series), 1985; Dundas or How They Murdered Robert Burns (play), 1987; The Clarinda Conspiracy, 1989; The True Story of the Ball of Kirriemuir, 1989; Cary Grant Stopped Me Smoking, 1991; Hunt Down a Prince, 1994; Burns, The Political Prisoner (in press); The MacCrimmon Scam (in press). Recreations: bagpipes (playing and composing); good whisky; self-important people. Address: No. 1 Netherwood Stow Cottages, St. Cyrus, DD10 0DG; T.-01674 850838.

Canavan, Dennis, BSc (Hons), DipEd. MSP, Falkirk West, since 1999; b. 8.8.42, Cowdenbeath. Educ. St. Bride's and St. Columba's Schools, Cowdenbeath; Edinburgh University. Principal Teacher of Mathematics, St. Modan's High School, Stirling, 1970-74; Assistant Head, Holyrood High School, Edinburgh, 1974; Leader, Labour Group, Stirling District Council, 1974; MP, West Stirlingshire, 1974-83; MP, Falkirk West, 1983-2001; Chair: Scottish Parliamentary Labour Group, 1980-81, PLP Northern Ireland Committee, 1989-97; Member: Foreign Affairs Select Committee, 1982-97, British–Irish Inter-Parliamentary Body, since 1992, International Development Select Committee, 1997-99; Scottish Parliament European Committee, since 1999; Convener, All-Party Sports Group, Scottish Parliament, since 1999. Honorary President, Milton Amateurs Football Club. Recreations: marathon running; hill-walking; fishing; swimming; football (former Scottish Universities football internationalist). Address: (b.) Constituency Office, 37 Church Walk, Denny FK6 6DF; T.-01324 825922.

Candlish, Kenneth Henry, BL, JP, DL. Retired Solicitor; Deputy Lieutenant, Berwickshire; b. 22.8.24, Edinburgh; m., Isobel Robertson-Brown; 2 d. Educ. George Watson's; Edinburgh University. Depute County Clerk, West Lothian, 1951-64; County Clerk, Berwickshire, 1964-75. Recreations: photography; wine-making; music. Address: (h.) The Elms, Duns, Berwickshire; T.-Duns 883298.

Canning, Very Rev. Bernard John Canon, FSA Scot. Parish Priest, St. Thomas', Neilston, Glasgow, since 1999; Paisley Diocesan Archivist, since 1983; b. 30.3.32, Derry. Educ. St. Eugene's Boys' School, Derry; St. Columb's College, Derry; St. Kieran's College, Kilkenny. Ordained Priest for the Diocese of Paisley, 1956; Assistant: St. James's, Renfrew, 1956-68, St Fergus', Paisley, 1968-74, St Laurence's, Greenock, 1974-87; Parish Priest: Christ the King, Howwood, and Our Lady of Fatima, Lochwinnoch, 1987-95, St James's, Paisley, 1995-96, St. John the Baptist's, Port Glasgow, 1996-99. Hon. Canon, Paisley Cathedral Chapter, 1989, full Member, 2001; Member, Editorial Board, The Parish Magazine & Journal, Glasgow, 1962-74; first Press Officer, Paisley Diocese, 1964-88; Member, Board of Governors, National Catholic Press Office, 1968-87. Publications include: Joy and Hope: St. Fergus', Paisley, 1971; A Building from God: St James's, Renfrew 1877-1977, 1977; Padraig H. Pearse and Scotland, 1979; Irish-born Secular Priests in Scotland 1829-1979, 1979; Adventure in Faith: St Ninian's, Gourock 1880-1980, 1980; The Living Stone: St Aloysius', Springburn 1882-1982, 1982; Instruments of His Work : Little Sisters of the Poor, Greenock 1884-1984, 1984; St. Mungo's, Ladyburn, Greenock 1935-1985, 1985; The Charleston Story: St Charles', Paisley, 1986; Bishops of Ireland 1870-1987, 1989; St. Fillan's, Houston 1841-1991, 1991; St. Mary's, Paisley 1891-1991, 1991; The Poor Sisters of Nazareth & Derry 1892-1992, 1992; St Colm's Church, Kilmacolm, 1992; Bishop Neil Farren, Bishop of Derry 1893-1980, 1993; St John the Baptist Parish, Port Glasgow, 1846-1996, 1996. Recreation: historical research. Address: (b.) 70 Main Street, Neilston, Glasgow G78 3NJ.

Cannon, Steven, MA (Hons). Secretary, Aberdeen University, since 1998; b. 19.12.57, Keighley; m., Joyce. Educ. St. Bedes Grammar School, Bradford; Dundee University. Administrative Assistant, then Admissions Officer, Warwick University, 1983-86; Financial and Administration Manager, Warwick University Science Park, 1986-88; Financial Manager, Ninewells Hospital and Medical School, Dundee, 1988-93; College Secretary, Duncan of Jordanstone College of Art, 1993-94; Deputy Secretary, Dundee University, 1994-96; Secretary to the Council and Director of Finance and Central Services, Scottish Higher Education Funding Council, 1996-98. Recreations: family interests; golf; cricket; music. Address: (b.) Kings College, University of Aberdeen, Aberdeen AB24 3FX

Cantlay, Michael Brian, BA, MBA. Chairman and Managing Director, Highland Industries Ltd, since 1993; Deputy Chairman, VisitScotland, since 2000; Chair, Local Enterprise Company Chairmen, since 2000; b. 2.2.64, Galashiels; m., Linda. Educ. McLaren High School, Callander; Strathclyde University. Managing Director, Glencarn Holdings since 1982; Managing Director, William Glen and Son Ltd, since 1983; Partner, Glens of Callander, since 1985; Managing Director, Strathlomond Ltd., since 1988; Director, Stirling District Trossachs Ltd, 1989-94; Managing Director, Hector Russell Ltd. since 1993; Managing Director, R. G. Lawrie, since 1993; Managing Director, R.S. MacDonald Ltd, since 1993; Managing Director, Deeside Handloom Weavers, since 1993; President, Hector Russell Inc., since 1995; President, Hector Russell (Canada) Inc., since 1998; Executive Committee Member, Argyll, the Isles, Loch Lomond, Stirling and Trossachs Tourist Board, 1991-95, Non Executive Director, since 1995; Governor, Scottish Tartans Authority, since 1994; Board Member, Scottish Tourist Board, since 1998; Member, Loch Lomond and Trossachs Interim Committee, since 1999; Chairman, Scottish Enterprise Forth Valley, 1995-2001; Advisory Member, Scottish Enterprise Board, since 2000; Councillor, Callander Community Council, 1989-92; Chairman: Callander Community Council, 1992-93, Rural Stirling Economic Partnership, 1988-90, McLaren Leisure Centre, 1999-2000, Trossachs Tourist Association, 1991-93; Board Member, Callander Primary School, 1990-91; Young Manager of the Year,

1992, Scottish Thistle Tourist Awards. Address: (h.) Callandrade Pines, Invertrossachs Road, Callander, FK17 8HW.

Cantley, Maurice, OBE, BSc, PhD. Innovations Advisor, Innovators Counselling and Advisory Service for Scotland; Director, Inverness Medical Ltd.; b. 6.6.37, Cambuslang; m., Rosalind Diana Jones; 2 d. Educ. Bedford Modern and Bristol Grammar; Bristol University. Unilever Ltd., 1961-67; McCann Erickson Advertising, London, 1967-76; Director of Recreation and Tourism, Tayside Regional Council, 1976-82; Head of Tourism, HIDB, 1982-85; Marketing Director, Highlands and Islands Development Board, 1985-91. Director, Highlands and Islands Enterprise, 1991-99; Hon. Education Officer, Society of Cosmetic Chemists of GB, 1963-66; Chairman, Association of Directors of Recreation, Leisure and Tourism, 1980-82. Recreations: driving north of Ullapool; natural history; off-road biking. Address: (h.) Oldshorebeg, Kinlochbervie, Sutherland IV27 4RS; T.-01971 521257; e-mail: mauricecan@cali.co.uk

Caplan, Lady (Joyce Caplan), DipEd. Chairman, Couple Counselling Scotland, since 1997; Chairman, Children's Classic Concerts (Edinburgh), since 1999; Lecturer, Continuing Education, Edinburgh University, since 1980; b. 21.2.46; m., Lord Caplan; 1 d. Educ. Dale School, Nottingham; Clifton College, Nottingham. Primary School Teacher/Assistant Head, 1967-75; Member of Children's Panel, 1978-81; Governor, Lomond School, Helensburgh, 1985-89; Chairman, Play in Scottish Hospitals, 1990-96; Chairman, Smiths Place Group, 1992-95; Chairman, Scottish Play Council, 1992-95; Member, Friends of Queens Hall Committee, Edinburgh, 1995-98; Committee, Friends of University Library, Edinburgh, since 1999; Membership Secretary, Poetry Association of Scotland, since 1997; Chairman, various Book Festival events, 1997-2000; Chairman, Arvon Foundation, since 1999. Recreations; books; music; friends; paintings; poetry; malt whisky. Address: (h.) Nether Liberton House, Old Mill Lane, Edinburgh EH16 5TZ.

Caplan, Hon. Lord (Philip Isaac Caplan), MA, LLB, LLD(Hon), QC. Senator of the College of Justice, 1989-2000; b. 24.2.29, Glasgow; m., Joyce Stone (2nd m.); 2 s.; 2 d. Educ. Eastwood School; Glasgow University. Solicitor, 1952-56; called to Bar, 1957; Standing Junior Counsel to Accountant of Court, 1964-70; Chairman, Plant Varieties and Seeds Tribunal, Scotland, 1977-79; Sheriff of Lothian and Borders, at Edinburgh, 1979-83; Sheriff Principal of North Strathclyde, 1983-88; Member, Sheriff Courts Rules Council, 1984-88; Commissioner, Northern Lighthouse Board, 1983-88; Chairman, Scottish Association for the Study of Delinquency, 1985-89, Hon. Vice President, 1990; Member, Advisory Council on Messengers at Arms and Sheriff Officers, 1987-88; Chairman, Scottish Association of Family Conciliation Services, 1989-94, Honorary President, since 1994; Chairman, James Powell UK Trust. FRPS (1988), AFIAP (1985). Recreations: photography; bridge; music; reading. Address: (b.) Court of Session, Parliament House, Edinburgh.

Carbery, Emeritus Professor Thomas Francis, OBE, KSG, FRSA, MSc, PhD, DPA. Former Professor, Strathclyde Business School, Strathclyde University; Member, Board of Directors, Energy Action Scotland, since 1996; b. 18.1.25, Glasgow; m., Ellen Donnelly; 1 s.; 2 d. Educ. St. Aloysius' College, Glasgow; Glasgow University; Scottish College of Commerce. Cadet navigator/meteorologist, RAF, 1943-47; civil servant, 1947-61; Lecturer, then Senior Lecturer, Scottish College of Commerce, 1961-64; Strathclyde University: Senior Lecturer in Government-Business Relations, 1964-75, Head, Department of Office Organisation, 1975-79, Professor of Office Organisation, 1979-85, Professor of

Business Information, 1985-88; part-time Professor of Marketing, 1988-90. Member: Independent Broadcasting Authority, 1970-79, Broadcasting Complaints Commission, 1981-86, Royal Commission on Gambling, 1975-77, Transport Users Consultative Committee (Chairman, Scottish TUCC), 1975-81, Scottish Consumer Council (latterly Vice-Chairman), 1976-84, Scottish Legal Aid Board, 1986-92, Data Protection Tribunal, 1985-99, Church of Scotland Committee on Higher Education, 1986-87, Press Council, 1987-90; Chairman, Scottish Transport Research Group, 1983-87; Chairman, South of Scotland Consumers Committee/Office of Electricity Regulation, 1990-95; Chairman, Strathclyde University Inter-denominational Chaplaincy Committee, 1981-87; Joint Editor, Bulletin of Society for Co-operative Studies, 1967-95; Member (former Chairman), Scottish Catholic Communications Commission; Member, Scottish Catholic Education Commission, 1980-93. Recreations: conversation; watching television; spectating at association football. Address: (h.) 24 Fairfax Avenue, Glasgow, G44 5AL; T.-0141-637 0514.

Cardownie, Steve. Member, Edinburgh City Council (Executive Member for Leisure and Culture); Director, Scot-Slav Ltd.; b. 1.6.53, Leith; m.; 2 s. Educ. Leith Academy; Telford College. Civil service; National Executive Committee Member, CPSA, five years; Employment Tribunal Member, 19 years; Councillor, Edinburgh, 12 years; Director: Edinburgh International Festival Council, Festival City Theatres, Royal Lyceum Theatre, Traverse Theatre, Edinburgh Audience Development Initiative, Scottish International Children's Festival; Scot-Slav Ltd., SPLITS Technologies Ltd. Recreations: hill-walking; running; Heart of Midlothian FC; theatre; reading; fine wines and ale sampling. Address: (b.) City Chambers, High Street, Edinburgh; T.-0131-529 3266; e-mail: steve.cardownie@edinburgh.gov.uk

Carey, Frank A., BSc, MD, FRCPath. Consultant Pathologist, since 1995; Clinical Leader, Tayside University Hospitals, since 2000; b. 5.7.61, Cork, Ireland; m., Dr Julie Curran; 1 s.; 1 d. Educ. University College, Cork. Senior House Officer, Cork University Hospital, 1986-87; Registrar in Pathology, Royal Infirmary of Edinburgh, 1987-89; Senior Registrar, Royal Infirmary of Edinburgh, 1989-95; Consultant, Tayside University Hospitals, since 1995. Member, Scottish Council, Royal College of Pathologists. Address: (b.) Department of Pathology, Ninewells Hospital and Medical School, Dundee DD1 9SY; T.-01382 632548.

Cargill, Kenneth George, MA, LLB. Project Executive, Pacific Quay Project, BBC Scotland, since 1999; Visiting Professor in Journalism, University of Strathclyde; Honorary Professor, Politics Department, University of Glasgow; b. 17.2.47, Arbroath; m., Una Gallacher. Educ. Arbroath High School; Edinburgh University. BBC TV Scotland: Researcher, Current Affairs, 1972; Reporter, Current Account, 1973; Film Director, Public Account, 1978; Producer, Current Account, 1979, Agenda, 1981, People and Power (London), 1983; Editor of the day, Reporting Scotland, 1983; Editor, Scotland 2000, 1986-87; Deputy Editor, News and Current Affairs, Television, 1984-88; Head of TV News, Current Affairs and Sport, 1988-94; Head of News and Current Affairs, 1994-99. Publication: Scotland 2000 (Editor), 1987. Recreations: passive gardening; active consumption of Havana cigars, malt whisky; reading about UK and US politics and journalism. Address: (b.) Broadcasting House, Queen Margaret Drive, Glasgow G12 8DG; T.-0141-338 2250.

Carlisle, Elva A.M., MA. National Convener, Church of Scotland Guild, 2000-01; b. 27.5.35, Linlithgow; m., Dr J.M. Carlisle (deceased); 2 s. Educ. Marr College, Troon; Glasgow University. Teacher in Ayrshire and

Glasgow until early retirement, 1992; Elder, Church of Scotland; Member, Church of Scotland Board of Parish Education. Recreations: reading; doing crosswords; opera; visiting other countries. Address: (h.) 117 Fotheringay Road, Glasgow G41 4LG; T.-0141-423 4554.

Carloway, Hon. Lord (Colin John MacLean Sutherland). Senator of the College of Justice, since 2000; b. 20.5.54; m., Jane Alexander Turnbull; 2 s. Educ. Edinburgh Academy; Edinburgh University (LLB Hons). Advocate, 1977; Advocate Depute, 1986-89; QC (Scot), 1990. Treasurer, Faculty of Advocates, 1994-2000. Address: (b.) Parliament House, Edinburgh, EH1 1RQ.

Carlyle, Robert, OBE. Actor and Director; b. 14.4.61; m., Anastasia Shirley. Trained, RSAMD; Duncan Macrae Memorial Prize for Scots verse. Credits include: (film) The Full Monty, Carla's Song, Trainspotting, Riff Raff (European film of the year), Priest, Plunkett and MacLeane, Ravenous, The Beach, Angela's Ashes, The World Is Not Enough, There's Only One Jimmy Grimble, To End All Wars, 51st State; (television) Hamish Macbeth (title role); (theatre) Twelfth Night, Cuttin' A Rug, Othello; (television and theatre) Go Now, Face; as Director of Rain Dog Theatre Company: Wasted, One Flew Over the Cuckoo's Nest (Paper Boat Award), Conquest of the South Pole, Macbeth (Paper Boat Award); Best Actor: Evening Standard Film Awards, 1998; Film Critics' Circle Awards, 1998, Bowmore Whisky/Scottish Screen Awards, 2001, Michael Elliott Awards, 2001; David Puttnam Patrons Award. Address: c/o ICM, Oxford House, 76 Oxford Street, London W1N 0AX.

Carmichael, Alexander Morrison (Alistair), MP. Liberal Democrat MP, Orkney and Shetland, since 2001; b. 15.7.65; m., Kathryn Jane; 2 s. Educ. Islay High School; Aberdeen University. Hotel manager, 1984-89; Procurator Fiscal Depute, Crown Office, Edinburgh and Aberdeen, 1993-96; solicitor in private practice, 1996-2001. Address: (b.) House of Commons, London SW1A 0AA.

Carmichael, Elizabeth Young, MA (Hons), DipLib. Head, Community Services Division, Justice Department, Scottish Executive, since 1999; b. 6.10.47, Edinburgh; 1 s.; 1 d. Educ. Lasswade High School; Edinburgh University. Librarian, Scottish Office, 1972; Historic Buildings Council for Scotland, 1981; Scottish Office, since 1982 (Education Department, Health Department, Finance Group, Voluntary Issues Unit). Member, Management Committee, Midlothian Befriending. Recreations: travel; food; gardens; writing; teenage psychology. Address: (b.) F Spur, Saughton House, Edinburgh EH11 3EX; T.-0131-244 5434.

Carmichael, Ian Henry Buist, MA (Hons), LLB. Advocate, since 1973; b. 17.5.25, Dundee; m., Jean; 2 d. Educ. High School of Dundee; Edinburgh University. Solicitor, Dundee, 1951-57; Advocate, 1957-60; Solicitor, Glasgow, 1960-64; Procurator Fiscal Depute, latterly Senior Depute, Glasgow, 1964-85; readmitted, Faculty of Advocates, 1973; Senior Depute in change of Deaths Unit, Glasgow, 1982-85; Advocate in private practice, since 1985. Publication: Sudden Deaths and Fatal Accident Inquiries, 1993. Recreations: music; photography. Address: (h.) 4 Fleurs Avenue, Glasgow G41 5BE.

Carmichael of Carmichael (Richard John). 26th Baron of Carmichael, since 1980; 30th Chief of Name and Arms of Carmichael, since 1981; Chartered Accountant; Farmer; b. 1.12.48, Stamford; m., Patricia Margaret Branson; 1 s.; 2 d. Educ. Hyton Hill Preparatory School; Kimbolton School; Coventry College of Technology. Audit Senior, Coopers and Lybrand, Tanzania, 1972; Audit Manager, Granger

Craig Tunnicliffe, Tauranga, New Zealand, 1974; ACA, 1971; FCA, 1976; Factor/Owner, Carmichael Estate, 1980; Director: Carmichael Heritage Leisure Ltd., Clan Chiefs Ltd., Royal Highland and Agricultural Society of Scotland; claims family titles: Earldom of Hyndford, Viscountcies of Inglisberry and Nemphlar, and Lordship Carmichael of Carmichael. Member, Standing Council of Scottish Chiefs; Chairman, Clyde Valley Tourism Group; New Zealand Orienteering Champion, 1977; International Controller, International Orienteering Federation, 1994. Recreations: orienteering; skiing; Clan Carmichael Association. Address: Carmichael House, Carmichael, by Biggar, Lanarkshire ML12 6PG; T.-01899 308336.

Carnegy of Lour, Baroness (Elizabeth Patricia), DL. Life Peer, since 1982; Member, Delegated Powers and Regulatory Reform Committee, House of Lords, since 2001; b. 28.4.25. Educ. Downham School. Cavendish Laboratory, Cambridge, 1943-46; Girl Guides Association: Training Adviser for Scotland, 1958-62 and for Commonwealth HQ, 1963-65; co-opted Angus County Council Education Committee, 1967-75; Councillor, Tayside Regional Council, 1974-82; Chairman, Education Committee, 1976-82; Chairman, Working Party on Professional Training in Community Education Scotland, 1975-77; Commissioner, Manpower Services Commission, 1979-82, and Chairman, Committee for Scotland, 1980-83; Member, Scottish Economic Council, 1980-92; President for Scotland, Girl Guides Association, 1979-89; Member, Scottish Council for Tertiary Education, 1979-84; Chairman, Scottish Council for Community Education, 1980-88; Member, Council and Finance Committee, Open University, 1984-96; Member, Court, St. Andrews University, 1991-96; Honorary Sheriff, 1969-84; Deputy Lieutenant, 1988-2001; Fellow, Royal Society of Arts, 1987; Honorary LLD: Dundee University, 1991, University of St. Andrews, 1997; Honorary DUniv, Open University, 1998. Address: (h.) Lour, Forfar, Angus DD8 2LR; T.-01307 82 237.

Carnegy-Arbuthnott, David, TD, DL, LLD, CA. Landowner; b. 17.7.25, London; m., Helen Adamson Lyell (deceased); 2 s.; 2 d. Educ. Stowe. Emergency commission, The Black Watch, 1944-47; Chartered Accountant, 1953; in practice, Dundee, 1956-86; TA, 1955-69; Brevet Colonel, 1969; Hon. Colonel, 1st Bn., 51st Highland Volunteers (TA), 1980-89; Deputy Lieutenant, County of City of Dundee, 1973-89, Angus, 1989-2001; Member, Queen's Bodyguard for Scotland (Royal Company of Archers), since 1959; Governor: Dundee College of Education, 1985-87, Northern College of Education, 1987-91; President, Dundee Chamber of Commerce, 1971-72; Member of Court, Dundee University, 1977-85; Convener, Standing Committee, Scottish Episcopal Church, 1987-92; Trustee, Scottish Episcopal Church, since 1992. Recreations: shooting; country pursuits. Address: (h.) Meadowburn, Balnamoon, Brechin, Angus DD9 7RH; T.-01356 660273.

Carr, Professor Chris, MA, PhD, DMS, ACMA, CEng, MIMechE. Professor of Corporate Strategy, Edinburgh University, since 1999; b.13.8.51, Brentwood; m., Jennifer Munro; 1s.; 1d. Educ. Harrow; Trinity Hall, University of Cambridge; Warwick University. Early career in industry with British Aerospace, GKN; Lecturer: Buckingham University; Warwick University; Bath University; Senior Lecturer/Associate Research Director, Manchester Business School; Visiting Professor, International Business, Witten-Herdecke University, Germany; teaching posts: HEC, France; University of Carlos III, Spain; overseas teaching experience in USA, India, China, Turkey, Russia. Publications: Britain's Competitiveness, 1990; Strategic Investment Decisions, 1994; numerous articles in academic journals including the Strategic Management

Journal. Recreations: politics; tennis; sailing; golf. Address: (b.) Edinburgh University Management School, William Robertson Building, 50 George Square, Edinburgh EH8 9JY; T.-0131-650 6307; e-mail: Chris.Carr@ed.ac.uk

Carr, John Roger, CBE, JP, FRICS. Chairman, Countryside Commission for Scotland, 1985-92 (Member, since 1979); b. 18.1.27, Ackworth, Yorkshire; m., Cathrine Elise Dickson Smith; 2 s. Educ. Ackworth & Ayton (Quaker) School. Royal Marines, 1944-47; Gordon Highlanders TA, 1950-55; Factor, Walker Scottish Estates Co., Ballater; Factor, subsequently Director and General Manager, Moray Estates Development Co., Forres; former Convenor, Scottish Recreational Land Association; former Council Member, Scottish Landowners Federation; former District Councillor, Moray; Chairman, Scottish Committee, European Year of Environment, 1986-88 (and Member, UK Committee); Member, Macaulay Land Use Research Institute, 1987-97; Director, UK 2000 Scotland, 1990-92; Chairman, Countryside Around Towns Forum, 1991-95; Vice President, FWAG Scotland, 1993-98. Recreations: most country pursuits. Address: (b.) Goosehill, Invererne Road, Forres, Moray IV36 1DZ; T.-01309 671320.

Carr Smart, Isabel Anne, BA. Proprietor, Smart Solutions; Scottish Director, YWCA, 1992-2000; b. 23.6.54, Gifford. Educ. Berwickshire High School, Duns; Edinburgh University; Jordanhill College of Education. Rhodesia Ministry of Education, 1976; Lothian Regional Council Community Education, 1978-80; Church of Scotland Board of World Mission and Unity, Pakistan, 1981-85; Area Secretary, South Scotland, Christian Aid, 1985-92. Address: (h./b.) 47 Duncanson Drive, Burntisland, Fife KY3 9JS; T.-01592 873929; e-mail: icsmart@fish.co.uk

Carradice, Professor Ian, BA, PhD, FSA, FSA Scot. Professor, School of Art History, St Andrews University, since 1989; Keeper of Museum Collections, St Andrews University, since 1989; b. 10.7.53, Kendal; m., Maria Ines Urioste; 3 d. Educ. Quarry Bank High School, Liverpool; Liverpool University; St Andrews University. Curator, British Museum, London, 1977-89 (Department of Coins and Medals); Chairman, Sylloge Nummorum Graecorum, since 1994; University Director, Scottish Museums Council, 1994-2001; Convener, University Museums in Scotland, since 1999. Publications (books) include: Coinage and Finances in the Reign of Domitian; Coinage in the Greek World (Co-author); Greek Coins; Roman Provincial Coinage Vol. II (Co-author). Recreations: golf; fly fishing. Address: (b.) School of Art History, St Andrews University, St Andrews KY16 9AD; T.-01334 462402.

Carrie, Professor Allan Stewart, PhD, MSc, BSc (Eng), FIEE, SMIEEE, FIOM, CEng. Professor of Manufacturing Systems, Department of Design, Manufacture and Engineering Management, University of Strathclyde, since 1987; b. 7.5.42, Glasgow; m., Marie; 2 s. Educ. Fettes College, Edinburgh; Paisley College of Technology (University of London external degree); University of Birmingham. Babcock & Wilcox, Renfrew: Student Apprentice, 1960-63, Graduate Engineer, 1963-64, Methods Engineer, 1964-65; Industrial Engineer, Northern Electric, Montreal, 1966-67; University of Strathclyde: Lecturer, 1968-79, Senior Lecturer, 1979-85, Reader, 1985-87. Recreation: Scottish country dancing. Address: (b.) University of Strathclyde, 75 Montrose Street, Glasgow G1 1XJ; T.-0141-548 2894.

Carrigan, Daniel, BA (Hons). Scottish Regional Secretary, AEEU, since 1997; b. 5.4.48, Glasgow; m., Ruth; 3s. Educ. St Thomas Aquinas, Glasgow; Strathclyde University. Electrician, Clydeside, 1965-76; mature student, 1976-80; Trades Union Officer, EETPU, 1980-94; National Officer, AEEU, since 1987.

Recreations: reading; football; politics. Address: (b.) 145-165 West Regent Street, Glasgow, G2 4RZ; T.-0141-248 7131; e-mail: D.Carrigan@aeeu.org.uk

Carson, James Grant, MA, DipEd, FSAScot. Chairman, Scottish National Committee, English-Speaking Union in Scotland, since 1996; b. Isle of Fetlar, Shetland; m., Catherine Nisbet; 1 s.; 1 d. Educ. John Watson's; Fettes College, Edinburgh; Trinity College, University of Cambridge. Former Depute Rector, Jordanhill School. Leader, ESU Pupil Exchanges to USA, 1975-94; ESU Debates Convenor; Member, Chorus: Edinburgh Festival, Scottish Opera; Director of plays and operas; Hon. President, Greenock Burns Club, 1986. Recreations: gardening; bridge; reading; travel; food; wine. Address: 23 Atholl Crescent, Edinburgh EH3 8HQ; T.-0131-229 1528.

Carswell, William Steven, MA, LLB. Chairman, General Trustees of the Church of Scotland, since 1999; b. 13.7.29, Manchester; m., Jean Lang Sharpe; 2 s. Educ. Hutchesons' Boys' Grammar School; Glasgow University. Legal Assistant, Dunbarton County Council, 1953-56; Legal Assistant, Stirling County Council, 1956-59; Partner, McGrigor Donald, 1960-89. Recreations: golf; walking; cycling. Address:(h.) 13 Stratton Drive, Giffnock, Glasgow G46 7AB; T.-0141-638 1286; e-mail: wscarswell@aol.com

Carter, Christopher John, BA (Hons), PhD, MRTPI (Rtd). Higher Education Consultant; b. 5.2.41, Capel, Surrey; m., Ann Fisher Prince; 1 s.; 1 d. Educ. Ottershaw School, Chertsey, Surrey; Birmingham University; Glasgow University. Town Planning Assistant, Cumbernauld Development Corporation, 1963-64 and 1967-68; Visiting Lecturer in Geography, Brock University, St. Catharines, Ontario, 1968-69; Lecturer/Senior Lecturer in Planning, Glasgow School of Art, 1969-76; Principal Lecturer in Planning, Coventry (Lanchester) Polytechnic, 1976-78; Senior Lecturer/Head, Department of Town and Regional Planning, Duncan of Jordanstone College of Art, 1978-81; Vice Principal, Duncan of Jordanstone College of Art, 1981-93, Acting Principal, 1993-94; Director, Duncan of Jordanstone College and Deputy Principal, Dundee University, 1994-97. Winner, RTPI Prize, 1970. Member: Board of Governors, Dundee Institute of Technology, 1989-91; Scottish Committee, Universities Funding Council, 1989-92; Scottish Higher Education Funding Council, 1992-93; Member: Board of Governors, Northern College, 1994-95, Board of Management, Elmwood College, since 1997. Publications: Innovations in Planning Thought and Practice at Cumbernauld New Town 1956-62; The Designation of Cumbernauld New Town (case study) (Co-author); A Future for Higher Education in Scotland (Contributor), 1997; Quality Assurance in Higher Education – An International Perspective (Contributor), 1998. Recreations: skiing; running; photography; music. Address: (h.) Etchachan, 12A Deshar Road, Boat of Garten, Inverness-shire PH24 3BN; T.-01479 831732; e-mail: cjcarter-uodfdp@mail.u-net.com

Carter, Professor Sir David Craig, MB, ChB, MD, FRCSEdin, FRCPEdin, FRCSIre (Hon), FACS (Hon), FRACS (Hon), LLD (Hon), FRSEd, FRCGP (Hon), FAcadMedSci, FFPHM, DSc (Hon), LLD (Hon). Vice Principal, Edinburgh University, since 2000; Chairman, Scientific Advisory Committee, Cancer Research Campaign, since 2000; President, British Medical Association, since 2001; Chief Medical Officer (Scotland), 1996-2000; Surgeon to the Queen in Scotland, 1993-97; b. 1.9.40, Penrith; m., Ilske; 2 s. Educ. St. Andrews University. Lecturer in Clinical Surgery, Edinburgh University, 1969-74; 12-month secondment as Lecturer in Surgery, Makerere University, Kampala, Uganda, 1972; Senior Lecturer in Surgery, Edinburgh University, 1974-79;12-month secondment as Associate Professor of Surgery, University of California, 1976; St. Mungo

Professor of Surgery, Glasgow University, 1979-88; Honorary Consultant, Glasgow Royal Infirmary, 1979-88; Regius Professor of Surgery, Edinburgh University, 1988-96; Honorary Clinical Consultant, Edinburgh Royal Infirmary, 1988-96. Former Council Member, Royal College of Surgeons of Edinburgh; former Member, Broadcasting Council for Scotland; former Chairman, Scottish Council for Postgraduate Medical and Dental Education; former Co-editor, British Journal of Surgery; Member, Medical Advisory Committee, Higher Education Funding Council, 1994-97; Non-executive Director, Lothian Health Board, 1994-96; President, Surgical Research Society, Association of Surgeons (Great Britain and Ireland), 1996-97; Vice President, Royal Society of Edinburgh, since 2000; Moynihan Prize, 1973; James IV Association of Surgeons Travelling Fellow, 1975. Recreations: golf; music. Address: (b.) University Department of Surgery, Royal Infirmary, Edinburgh EH3 9YW; T.-0131-536 3812.

Carter, Roger, MBE, BSc, PhD, FTS, MTMI. Managing Partner, Tourism Enterprise and Management; b. 8.12.45, Dorking; m., Dee; 3 s. Educ. Dorking County Grammar School; Birmingham University; Strathclyde University. Transport Development Unit, Strathclyde University, 1970; Leader, Research Unit, Greater London and SE Sports Council, 1970-71; Director of Research and Planning, Scottish Tourist Board, 1971-82; Director, Heart of England Tourist Board, 1982-90; Chief Executive, Edinburgh Tourist Board, 1990-96. Recreations: travel; reading. Address: (b.) TEAM, 1/1 Liddesdale Place, Edinburgh EH3 5JW; T.-0131-557 5867.

Cartmell, Professor Mathew Phillip, BSc (Hons), PhD, CEng, FIMechE, MASME, MAIAA. Professor of Applied Dynamics, Glasgow University, since 1998; b. 17.6.58, Altrincham, Manchester; m., Fiona C. Cartmell; 2 d. Educ. Hulme Grammar School, Oldham; Edinburgh University. Research and Development Engineer, Ferranti Ltd, 1980-81; Research Fellow, Edinburgh University, 1984-85; Lecturer, Robert Gordon Institute of Technology, Aberdeen, 1985-87; Lecturer, Aberdeen University, 1987-91; Lecturer, University of Wales, Swansea, 1991-94; Senior Lecturer, Edinburgh University, 1994-98; R.A.H. Mayers Award for Outstanding Achievement; Committee Member, IMechE, IOP. Publications: one book, invited chapters, over 100 research papers. Recreations: vintage vehicles; music; walking. Address: (b.) Department of Mechanical Engineering, James Watt Building, Glasgow University, Glasgow, G12 8QQ. T.-0141-330 4337.

Carty, Matthew John, MB, ChB, FRCSEdin, FRCPSGlas, FRCOG. Consultant Obstetrician and Gynaecologist, Southern General Hospital, Glasgow, since 1977; b. 8.3.42, Hamilton; m., Caroline Martin; 2 s.; 2 d. Educ. St. Aloysius College, Glasgow; Glasgow University. Lecturer in Midwifery, Nairobi University, Kenya, 1970-71; Lecturer in Midwifery, Glasgow University, 1972-77. Recreation: golf. Address: (h.) 31 Monreith Road, Newlands, Glasgow; T.-0141-632 1033.

Casely, (Frederick) Gordon (Polson), OStJ, FRSA, FSAScot. Hon. Vice-President, Lonach Highland and Friendly Society, since 1990; b. 29.6.43, Glasgow; m., Valerie Ann Thomas; 1 s. Educ. Hutchesons' Boys Grammar School. Reporter, D.C. Thomson & Co. Ltd., Dundee, Aberdeen and Elgin, 1966-68; Feature Writer, Evening Express, Aberdeen, 1968-73; PRO, Greater Glasgow Passenger Transport Executive, 1973-78; public affairs posts in banking, offshore and energy industries, 1978-95 (Assistant Director, CBI Scotland, 1988-91); Head of Communications, Aberdeenshire Council, 1995-98. Director, Herald Strategy Ltd.; Founder Member, Heraldry Society of Scotland, 1977; Press Officer, Commonwealth Games Council for Scotland, 1989-93; Member: Scottish Commonwealth Games Team, Auckland, 1990, Guild Burgess of Aberdeen, 1992; President, Aberdeen Welsh Society, 1997-98. Recreations: cycling; veteran athletics; promoting heraldry; heritage issues. Address: (h.) 45 Beaconsfield Place, Aberdeen AB15 4AB; T.-01224 647927; gcasely@herald-strategy.co.uk

Cash, John David, CBE, BSc, MB, ChB, PhD, FRCPath, FRCPGlas, FRCPE, FRCSEdin, FRCP, FFCS. National Medical and Scientific Director, Scottish National Blood Transfusion Service, 1979-96; Honorary Professor, Department of Medicine, Edinburgh University, 1987-96; Non-Executive Director, National Institute of Biological Standards and Control, since 1996; b. 3.4.36, Reading; m., Angela Mary Thomson; 1 s.; 1 d. Educ. Ashville College, Harrogate; Edinburgh University. Edinburgh and South East Scotland Blood Transfusion Service: Deputy Director, 1969, Regional Director, 1974. President, Royal College of Physicians of Edinburgh, 1994-98; Adviser in Blood Transfusion, WHO; Governor, Fettes College. Recreations: fishing; gardening. Address: 1 Otterburn Park, Edinburgh EH14 1JX.

Caskie, Rev. J. Colin, BA, BD. Minister at Carnoustie, since 1983; b. 17.8.47, Glasgow; m., Alison McDougall; 2 s.; 1 d. Educ. Knightswood Secondary School; Strathclyde University; Glasgow University. Minister, Penilee: St Andrew, 1977-83; Moderator, Presbytery of Angus, 1995; Chairman, The Duncan Trust, since 1992; Vice-Convenor, General Assembly's Board of Stewardship and Finance, 1998-2001, Convenor, since 2001. Recreations: stamp collecting; gardening. Address: (h.) 11 Ardenconnel Way, Rhu, Helensburgh G84 8LX.

Cassidy, Professor James, MB, ChB, MSc, MD, FRCP (Glasgow, Edinburgh). Professor of Oncology, University of Aberdeen, since 1994; Consultant Oncologist, Aberdeen Royal Hospital NHS Trust, since 1994; b. 28.8.58, Lennoxtown; divorced; 2 s.; 1 d. Educ. St. Mirin's Academy, Paisley; University of Glasgow. General Training, Wales and Scotland MRCP (UK), 1985; Lecturer in Oncology, University of Edinburgh. Member, Board of Governors, ICRF. Recreations: soccer; cycling; music. Address: (b.) Institute of Medical Sciences, Foresterhill, Aberdeen; T.-01224 681818, Ext. 53019.

Cassidy, Peter D., MA, CQSW, DipSW, MBA. Independent Social Affairs Adviser and Management Consultant; Adviser to Scottish Parliament Health and Community Care Committee; Social Affairs Expert, Grampian Television; Visiting Research Fellow, Robert Gordon University, Aberdeen; Consultant, Scottish Institute for Residential Child Care; Member, Board, Scottish Commission for the Regulation of Care; television presenter/interviewer; b. 14.12.48, Dundee; m., Patricia; 3 d. Educ. Lawside Academy, Dundee; Edinburgh University; Dundee University. Lothian Region: Social Worker, Edinburgh, 1974-77, Senior Social Worker, Midlothian, 1977-82, Area Manager, West Lothian, 1982-88; Depute Director then Senior Depute Director, Fife Region, 1988-95; Director of Social Work Services, Aberdeen City Council, 1995-2000. President, Association of Directors of Social Work, 1998; Convener, Directors of Social Work, 1997-99; Chair, British Agencies for Adoption and Fostering, 1997-2001. Recreations: family; film; football; music; pursuing Dalmation on walks. Address: (b.) Heathpark, Arbeadie Road, Banchory AB31 5XA; T.-01330 820278.

Castillo, Professor Susan, BA, MPhil, PhD. John Nichol Professor of American Literature, University of Glasgow, since 2001 (Head of English Literature, since 1999); b. 15.3.48, Jackson, Mississippi, USA; 1 s.; 1 d. Educ. Randolph-Macon Woman's College; Oporio University, Portugal. Lecturer, Oporto University, 1978-94; Vice-Principal for International Relations, Fernando Pessoa

University, 1994-96; Department of English Literature, University of Glasgow: Lecturer, 1996-99, Reader, 1999-2001. Robert E. McNair Visiting Professor in Southern Studies, University of South Carolina, 1993; External Examiner: in English Literature, Sheffield University, in American Studies, Brunel University. Associate Editor, Journal of American Studies, since 2001; Editor, American Studies in Britain, 1997-2000. Publications: Native American Women in Literature and Culture (Editor), 1997; Pos-Colonialismo e Identidade (Editor), 1997; Engendering Identities (Editor), 1996; The Literatures of Colonial America – An Anthology, (Contributor), 2000; many journal articles; translator of several books into English. Recreations: collecting antique maps; blues singing. Address: (b.) Department of English Literature, University of Glasgow, Glasgow G12 8QQ; T.-0141-330 5296.

Cates, Professor Michael Elmhirst, MA, PhD. Professor of Natural Philosophy, University of Edinburgh, since 1995; b. 5.5.61, Bristol. Educ. Clifton College; Trinity College, University of Cambridge. Research Fellow, Trinity College, University of Cambridge, 1985-89; Cavendish Laboratory, Cambridge: Royal Society University Research Fellow, 1988-89, University Assistant Lecturer, 1989-92, University Lecturer, 1992-94. Maxwell Medal and Prize, Institute of Physics, 1991; Prix Franco-Britannique de l'Academie des Sciences, Paris, 1994. Publications: 150 publications in scientific journals. Recreations: hill-walking; painting. Address: (b.) Department of Physics and Astronomy, University of Edinburgh, Kings Buildings, Edinburgh EH9 3JZ; T.-0131-650 5296.

Catto, Professor Graeme R.D., MB, ChB (Hons), MD (Hons), DSc, FRCP, FRCPE, FRCPGlas, FRCGP (Hon), FRSE, FRSA, FMedSci. Vice-Principal, King's College London, and Dean, Guy's, King's and St. Thomas' Hospitals Medical and Dental Schools, since 2000; Chief Scientist, NHS in Scotland, 1997-2000; Vice-Principal 1995-2000, Professor in Medicine and Therapeutics 1988-2000, Aberdeen University; Honorary Consultant Physician/Nephrologist, 1977-2000; Chairman, Robert Gordon's College; b. 24.4.45, Aberdeen; m., Joan Sievewright; 1 s.; 1 d. Educ. Robert Gordon's College; Aberdeen University. Research Fellow/ Lecturer/Senior Lecturer/Reader in Medicine, Aberdeen University, 1970-88; Harkness Fellow of Commonwealth Fund of New York, 1975-77 (Fellow in Medicine, Harvard Medical School and Peter Bent Brigham Hospital, Boston); Dean, Faculty of Clinical Medicine, Aberdeen University, 1992-98; Vice Chairman, Aberdeen Royal Hospitals NHS Trust, 1992-99; Member, Scottish Higher Education Funding Council, since 1996; Member, General Medical Council, Education and Standards Committee, since 1994 (Chairman, since 1999); Treasurer, Academy of Medical Sciences, since 1998; Governor, PPP Medical Foundation, since 2000; Member, Lambeth, Southwark and Lewisham Health Authority, since 2000. Recreations: hills and glens. Address: Maryfield, Glenbuchat, Strathdon, Aberdeenshire AB36 8TS; T.-0197 56 41317.

Cawdor, 7th Earl of (Colin Robert Vaughan Campbell); b. 30.6.62; m., Lady Isabella Stanhope; 1 s.; 1 d. Succeeded to title, 1993. Educ. Eton; St. Peter's College, Oxford.

Cawthra, David Wilkinson, CBE, BSc, FREng, FICE, FInstCES. Principal, Cawthra & Co; b. 5.3.43, Halifax; m., Maureen Mabel Williamson; 1 s.; 1 d. Educ. Heath Grammar School, Halifax; Birmingham University. Mitchell Construction Company Ltd., 1964-73; Tarmac Construction Ltd., 1973-79; Balfour Beatty Ltd., 1979-91; Chief Executive, The Miller Group Limited, 1992-94. Member, NEDO Construction Industry Sector Group, 1990-92; Vice-President, Institution of Civil Engineers, 1996-99. Recreations: hill-walking; American history. Address: (b.) 68 Ravelston Dykes, Edinburgh EH12 6HF; T.-0131-337 2155; e-mail: cawthraco@msn.com

Chalmers, David James, BA, MA, DipEd. Headteacher, Biggar High School, since 1995; b. 17.12.50, Falkirk; m., Isobel. Educ. Falkirk High School; Stirling University; Lancaster University; Edinburgh University. Entered teaching, 1974; taught in West Lothian, Midlothian, Tayside and South Lanarkshire; seconded to Understanding British Industry, early 1980s; actively involved in outdoor education. Former Vice-Convener, Scottish Parent Teacher Council. Recreations: walking; cycling; skiing. Address: (b.) Biggar High School, John's Loan, Biggar ML12 6AG; T.-01899 220144.

Chalmers, David Watson Penn. Director and Deputy Chief Executive, Dunfermline Building Society, since 1995; b. 28.4.46, Dundee; m., Jacky; 1 d. Educ. Harris Academy, Dundee. Joined Dunfermline Building Society, 1968. Deputy Chairman, CML Scotland; Member, Committee of Management, Kingdom Housing Association Ltd.; Chairman, Kingdom Initiatives Housing Association Ltd.; Member, Mortgage Practitioners Panel and Social Housing Panel, Council of Mortgage Lenders; Chairman, Dundee Employment and Aftercare Project Ltd.; Trustee, Lintel Trust; Chairman, Business Enterprise Scotland. Recreations: golf; chess; hill-walking; running. Address: (b.) Caledonia House, Carnegie Avenue, Dunfermline KY11 8PJ; T.-01383 627727.

Chalmers, Rev. John Pearson, BD. Depute General Secretary, Department of Ministry, Church of Scotland, since 1995; Convenor, Board of Governors, Donaldson's College, since 1999; b. 5.6.52, Bothwell; m., Elizabeth; 2 s.; 1 d. Educ. Marr College; Strathclyde University; Glasgow University. Minister, Renton Trinity, 1979-86; Clerk, Dumbarton Presbytery, 1982-86; Minister, Palmerston Place, Edinburgh, 1986-95. Recreations: golf; bee-keeping. Address: (b.) 121 George Street, Edinburgh EH2 4YN; T.-0131-225 5722.

Chamberlain, April, Joint Managing Director, The Comedy Unit, since 1996; b. 21.4.59, London; m., Paul Bassett; 2 s.; 2 d. Educ. Addey and Stanhope Grammar School. Joined BBC Scotland as Business Manager, Comedy Department, 1993; The Comedy Unit, since 1996. Address: (b.) The Comedy Unit Ltd., Glasgow TV and Film Studio, Craigmont Street, Glasgow; T.-0141-305 6666; Fax: 0141-305 6600; e-mail: aprilchamberlain @comedyunit.co.uk

Chamberlain, Rt. Rev. Canon Neville, BA, MA. Episcopal Bishop of Brechin, since 1997; b. 1939. Educ. Nottingham University; Oxford University. Deacon, 1963; ordained Priest, 1964; Curate, St. Paul's, Birmingham, 1963-64; Priest-in-Charge, St. Michael's, Birmingham, 1964-69; Rector, Deer Creek Parish, USA, 1967-68; Vicar, St. Michael's Anglican Methodist Church, 1969-72; Executive Secretary, Lincoln Social Responsibility Committee, 1974-82; Canon and Prebend, Lincoln Cathedral, 1979; Rector, St. John the Evangelist, Edinburgh, 1982-97. Address: (b.) Diocesan Centre, Pine Grove, 334 Perth Road, Dundee DD2 1EQ; T.-01382 640007; e-mail: office@brechin.anglican.org

Chambers, Fergus Allan, FHCIMA. Director, Direct and Care Services (formerly Catering and Domestic Care Services), Glasgow City Council, since 1995; b. 20.1.56, Glasgow; m., Ruth Elizabeth; 1 s.; 1 d. Educ. Uddingston Grammar School; Glasgow College of Food Technology. Various posts, commercial catering group, 1977-82; Business Development Manager, Sutcliffe Catering, 1982-86; General Manager, Moccomat UK, 1986-88; Depute Director, Strathclyde Regional Council/Catering Direct, 1988-95. Chairman, Springboard Scotland; Trustee and Honorary Secretary, Hospitality Industry Trust of Scotland; Chairman, Industry Dinner Committee; Member, Executive Committee, Association of Civic Hosts; Winner: Cost

Sector Catering Education Award, 1999, Catering Forum Award for Excellence, 1999, Foodservice Caterer of the Year, 1999. Recreations: golf; DIY. Address: (h.) 24 Clydeford Drive, Kylepark, Uddingston, Glasgow G71 7DJ; T.-01698 813814; (b.) 0141-353 9130.

Chambers, Professor Helen Elizabeth, MA, PhD. Professor of German, St Andrews University, since 1999; b. 4.3.47, Glasgow; m., Hugh Rorrison; 2 s. Educ. Hutchesons' Girls' Grammar School, Glasgow; Glasgow University; Freiburg University. Lecturer, then Senior Lecturer in German, Leeds University, 1972-99; Visiting Lecturer in German, Melbourne University, 1998. Publications: Supernatural and Irrational Elements in the Works of Theodor Fontane, 1980; Co-existent Contradictions: Joseph Roth in Retrospect (Editor), 1991; Theodor Fontane: The London Symposium (Co-Editor), 1995; T. Fontane, Effi Briest (Co-Translator), 1995; The Changing Image of Theodor Fontane, 1997; Theodor Fontane and the European Context (Co-Editor), 2001. Recreations: theatre; film; travel. Address: (b.) School of Modern Languages, St Andrews University, St Andrews KY16 9PH; T.: 01334 463655.

Chaplain, Professor Mark Andrew Joseph, BSc (Hons), PhD. Professor of Mathematical Biology, Dundee University, since 2000; b. 1.5.64, Dundee; m., Fiona; 3 s. Educ. St John's RC High School, Dundee; Dundee University. Lecturer, School of Mathematical Sciences, Bath University, 1990-96; Senior Lecturer, Department of Maths, Dundee University, 1996-98; Reader in Mathematical Biology, Dundee University, 1998-2000. Whitehead Prize, London Mathematical Society, 2000. Publication: On Growth and Form: Spatio-Temporal Pattern Formation in Biology. Recreations: children; golf; squash; badminton; tennis. Address: (b.) Department of Mathematics, Dundee University, Dundee DD1 4HN; T.-01382 345369.

Chapman, Francis Ian, CBE, FRSA, CIMgt, DLitt (Hon). President, Scottish Radio Holdings PLC, 1996-2001 (Chairman, 1972-96); Chairman: Media and Income Trust PLC, 2000-01, Media Zeros PLC, 2000-01, National Academy of Writing, since 2000, Radio Trust PLC, 1997-2000; b. 26.10.25, St. Fergus, Aberdeenshire; m., Marjory Stewart Swinton; 1 s.; 1 d. Educ. Shawlands Academy, Glasgow; Ommer School of Music. War Service: RAF air crew cadet, 1943-44; National Service coal mines, 1945-47. William Collins: trainee, 1947, Sales Representative, New York Branch, 1951, General Sales Manager, London, 1955, appointed to main operating Board as Group Sales Director, 1960; appointed to Board, William Collins (Holdings) Ltd. as Joint Managing Director, 1967; Deputy Chairman, William Collins (Holdings) Ltd., 1976; Chairman, William Collins Publishers Ltd., 1979; Chairman and Chief Executive, William Collins PLC, 1981-89; Chairman, Hatchards Ltd., 1976-89; Pan Books Ltd.: Board Member, 1962-84, Chairman, 1971-73; Chairman, Harvill Press Ltd., 1976-89; Board Member, Book Tokens Ltd., 1981-95; Member, Governing Council, SCOTBIC, since 1983; Board Member, IRN Ltd., 1983-85; President, Publishers Association, 1979-81; Trustee, Book Trade Benevolent Society, since 1982; Board Member, Scottish Opera Theatre Royal Ltd., 1974-79; Director, Stanley Botes Ltd., 1985-89; Non-Executive Director, Guinness PLC, 1986-91; Joint Chairman and Chief Executive, Harper and Row, New York, 1987-89; Director, United Distillers PLC, 1988-93; Chairman and Managing Director, Chapmans Publishers Ltd., 1989-94; Chairman, Guinness Publishing, 1991-96 (Deputy Chairman, 1997-99); Deputy Chairman, Orion Publishing Group, 1993-94; President, SAS Guinness Media, Paris, 1996-99. Scottish Free Enterprise Award, 1985; Hon. DLitt, Strathclyde, 1990. Recreations: reading;

golf; swimming; music; grandchildren. Address: Kenmore, 46 The Avenue, Cheam, Surrey SM2 7QE.

Chapman, Professor John N., MA, PhD, FInstP, FRSE. Professor, Physics and Astronomy, Glasgow University, since 1988; b. 21.11.47, Sheffield; m., Judith M.; 1 s.; 1 d. Educ. King Edward VII School, Sheffield; St. John's College and Fitzwilliam College, Cambridge. Research Fellow, Fitzwilliam College, Cambridge; Lecturer, Glasgow University. Publication: Quantitative Electron Microscopy (Co-Editor). Recreations: photography; walking; squash. Address: (b.) Department of Physics and Astronomy, Glasgow University, Glasgow G12 8QQ; T.-0141-330 4462; e-mail: j.chapman@physics.gla.ac.uk

Chapman, Professor Robert, BSc, PhD, CPhys, FInstP. Professor of Physics since 1993, and Head, School of Information and Communication Technologies, since 2000, University of Paisley; b. 10.8.41, Holytown; m., Norma Gilchrist Hope; 3 d. Educ. Bellshill Academy; University of Glasgow. UKAEA Research Fellow, AWRE, Aldermaston, and AERE, Harwell, 1966-70; University of Manchester: Lecturer, 1970-75, Senior Lecturer, 1975-87, Reader in Physics, 1987-93; University of Paisley: Head, Department of Physics, 1993-96, Head, Department of Electronic Engineering and Physics, 1996-2000. Recreations: walking; gardening; listening to music. Address: (b.) School of Information and Communication Technologies, University of Paisley, Paisley PA1 2BE; T.-0141-848 3600.

Chapman, Robert Sutherland, MB, ChB (Hons), FRCP(Glas), FRCP(Edin), FRCP(Lond). Consultant Dermatologist, Stobhill NHS Trust and Greater Glasgow Health Board; Clinical Senior Lecturer, Glasgow University, since 1973; b. 4.6.38, Cults, Aberdeenshire; m. 1, Dr. Rosalind S. Slater (deceased); 2 s.; 1 d.; m. 2, Gladys Jean. Educ. Turriff Academy; Aberdeen University. House Officer, Aberdeen Royal Infirmary; Research Fellow, Department of Materia Medica and Therapeutics, Aberdeen University; Registrar and Senior Registrar in Dermatology, Aberdeen Hospitals; Senior Registrar in Dermatology, Middlesex Hospital and St. John's Hospital for Diseases of the Skin, London. Recreations: gardening; hill-walking. Address: (h.) 10 Douglas Muir Place, Milngavie, Glasgow G62 7RS; T.-0141-955 0171.

Charlesworth, Professor Brian, BA, PhD, FRS, FRSE. Royal Society Research Professor, Edinburgh University, since 1997; b. 29.4.45, Brighton; m., Deborah Maltby; 1 d. Educ. Haberdasher's Aske's Elstree School; Queens' College, Cambridge. Post-doctoral Fellow, University of Chicago, 1969-71; Lecturer, Genetics, University of Liverpool, 1971-74; Lecturer, Biology, Sussex University, 1974-82; Reader in Biology, Sussex University, 1982-84; Professor of Biology, University of Chicago, 1985-92; G.W. Beadle Distinguished Service Professor of Ecology and Evolution, University of Chicago, 1992-97; Darwin Medal, The Royal Society, 2000. Publications: Evolution in Age-structured Populations, 1994. Recreations: walking; listening to classical music. Address: (b.) ICAPB, Edinburgh University, The King's Buildings, Edinburgh, EH9 3JT; T.-0131-650 5750.

Chart, Helga, RSW, DA. Artist; b. 31.8.44, Edinburgh; m., Bert Robertson; 1 s. Educ. Trinity Academy, Edinburgh; Edinburgh College of Art. Art Teacher, Craigmount High School, Edinburgh, 1971-79; Lecturer in Art and Design, Edinburgh's Telford College, 1983-96. Council Member, Royal Scottish Society of Painters in Watercolours; Council Member, Scottish Artists and Artist Craftsmen, 1998-2000. RSA Stuart Award, 1967; RSA City of Edinburgh Award, 1985; SSA IBM Award, 1985; RSW Council Award, 1998; Duff Memorial Award, 1999. Recreations: gardening; birdwatching. Address: (h.) 19 Dalrymple Crescent, The Grange, Edinburgh EH9 2NX; T.-0131-667 1150.

Chatterji, Professor Monojit, BA, MA, PhD. Bonar Professor of Applied Economics, Dundee University, since 1989 (Head, Department of Economic Studies, 1993-97); Member, Advisory Group, BBC World Service; b. 15.1.51, Bombay; m., Anjum Rahmatulla; 1 s.; 2 d. Educ. Cathedral School, Bombay; St. Columba's, Delhi; Elphinstone College, Bombay; Christ's College, Cambridge. Winner, LTSN Annual Prize. Recreations: tennis; cinema; history; theology. Address: (b.) Department of Economics, Dundee University, Dundee; T.-01382 344371.

Cheape, Ronald David, FRICS. Chairman, Ogilvie Group Ltd, since 1995; b. 4.8.36, Larbert; m., Catherine; 3 d. Educ. Royal Technical College, Glasgow; Heriot Watt College, Edinburgh. Apprenticeship and Quantity Surveyor, Stirling County Council, 1953-60; Quantity Surveyor, British Rail (Scottish region), 1960-64; Senior Contracts Officer, East African Railways and Harbours, Nairobi, Kenya, 1964-69; Area Supervisor/Chief Surveyor/Technical Manager, Weir Construction, Coatbridge, 1969 -74; Ogilvie Builders, Stirling: Chief Surveyor, 1974-84; Surveying Director, 1984- 88; Managing Director, 1988-97; President, Scottish Building Employers' Federation, 2000; Chairman, Lochgoilhead Centre Board, Scout Association. Recreations: golf; hill walking; reading; Scout Association. Address: (b.) Ogilvie Group Ltd, PO Box 7, Stirling, FK7 8ES; T.-01786 812273 (h.) 01324 554951; e-mail: ronnie.cheape@ogilvie.co.uk

Cheetham, Professor Juliet, OBE, MA. Social Work Commissioner, Mental Welfare Commission for Scotland, since 1998; National Co-ordinator, SHEFC Contract Research Staff Initiative, 1996-97; Professor and Director, Social Work Research Centre, Stirling University, 1986-95; b. 12.10.39, Jerusalem; m., Christopher Paul Cheetham; 1 s.; 2 d. Educ. St. Andrews University; Oxford University. Probation Officer, Inner London, 1959-65; Lecturer in Applied Social Studies and Fellow of Green College, Oxford University, 1965-86. Member: Committee of Enquiry into Working of the Abortion Act; Northern Ireland Human Rights Commission; Commission of Racial Equality; Social Security Advisory Committee; Council for National Academic Awards; Economic and Social Research Council. Recreation: canal boats. Address: (b.) Peffermill House, 91 Peffermill Road, Edinburgh EH16 5UX.

Chester, Richard Waugh, MBE, ARAM, GRSM, ARCM, FRSA. Director, National Youth Orchestras of Scotland, since 1987; b. 19.4.43, Hutton Rudby; m., Sarah Chapman-Mortimer; 1 s.; 2 d. Educ. The Friends' School, Great Ayton; Huddersfield University; Royal Academy of Music. Flautist: BBC Northern Ireland, 1965, Royal Scottish National Orchestra, 1967; Conductor; Teacher; Examiner. Chairman, Glasgow Festival Strings; Member, Scottish Arts Council; President, European Federation of National Youth Orchestras; Member, Board, World Youth Orchestras Conference and World Federation of Amateur Orchestras; Chairman, Governors, St. Mary's Music School, Edinburgh; Director: National Youth Choir of Scotland, Concerto Caledonia; Trustee: Lochaber Music School, Acting for Charities Trust, Scottish Schools Orchestra Trust. Recreations: tennis; swimming; good food. Address: (h.) Milton of Cardross, Port of Menteith, Stirling FK8 3JY; T.-01877 385634; (b.) National Youth Orchestras of Scotland, 13 Somerset Place, Glasgow G3 7JT; T.-0141-332 8311; e-mail: richardchester@nyos.co.uk

Chesworth, Air Vice Marshal George Arthur, CB, OBE, DFC. Lord-Lieutenant of Moray, since 1994; b. 4.6.30; m.; 1 s. (deceased); 2 d. RAF, 1948-84; Chief Executive, Glasgow Garden Festival, 1985-98.

Cheyne, Rev. Professor Alexander Campbell, MA (Hons), BLitt, BD, HonDLitt (Memorial University, Newfoundland). Professor of Ecclesiastical History,

Edinburgh University, 1964-86; Principal, New College, Edinburgh, 1984-86; Moderator, Edinburgh Presbytery, Church of Scotland, 1987-88; Hon. President, Scottish Church History Society, since 1998; b. 1.6.24, Errol, Perthshire. Educ. Kirkcaldy High School; Edinburgh University; Oriel College, Oxford; New College, Edinburgh; Basel University, Switzerland. National Service (Instructor, Army School of Education), 1946-48; Glasgow University: Assistant Lecturer, 1950-51, Lecturer in History, 1951-53; Lecturer in Ecclesiastical History, Edinburgh University, 1958-64. Carnegie Scholar, 1948-50; Aitken Fellow, 1956-57; Visiting Professor, Wooster College, Ohio, 1973; Chalmers Lecturer (Trinity College, Glasgow, and Christ's College, Aberdeen), 1976-80; Visiting Fellow, Wolfson College, Cambridge, 1979; Burns Lecturer, Knox College, Dunedin, New Zealand, 1980; Lee Lecturer, 1993; President, Scottish Church History Society, 1986-89. Publications: The Transforming of the Kirk: Victorian Scotland's Religious Revolution, 1983; The Practical and the Pious: Essays on Thomas Chalmers 1780-1847 (Editor), 1985; The Ten Years' Conflict and the Disruption, 1993; Studies in Scottish Church History, 1999; contributions to: Reformation and Revolution: Essays presented to Hugh Watt, 1967; introduction to Movements of Religious Thought in Britain during the Nineteenth Century, 1971; The Westminster Confession in the Church Today, 1982; The Bible in Scottish Life and Literature, 1988; In Divers Manners, 1990; Christ, Church and Society: essays, 1993; Dictionary of Scottish Church History and Theology, 1993; William Robertson Smith: Essays in Reassessment, 1995; From Disruption to Diversity: Edinburgh Divinity 1846-1996, 1996; Oxford Dictionary of the Christian Church, 1997; recipient of festschrift, Scottish Christianity in the Modern World, 2000. Recreation: classical music. Address: (h.) 12 Crossland Crescent, Peebles EH45 8LF; T.-01721 722288.

Chezeaud, Jacques-Marcel, BA (Hons). Rector, St. Joseph's College, Dumfries, since 1994; b. 16.8.52, Bourges, France; m., Joan I. Campbell; 1 s.; 1 d. Educ. Lycee Alain Fournier, France; Orleans University; Stirling University. Foreign language assistant, Wallace Hall and Sanquhar Academies, 1974-75; manager, wine trade, 1979-80; Teacher, English/French, Biggar High School and St. Mary's Academy, Bathgate, 1980-82; Principal Teacher, Modern Languages, Our Lady's High School, Broxburn, 1982-85; Depute Rector, St. Columba's High School, Perth, 1985-91; Depute Head, St. David's High School, Dalkeith, 1991-94. Member, Executive Committee, Scottish Association for Language Teaching. Recreations: long-distance running; reading; good food and wines. Address: (b.) St. Joseph's College, Craigs Road, Dumfries DG1 4UU; T.-01387 252893.

Chick, Jonathan Dale, MA (Cantab), MB, ChB, MPhil, FRCPE, FRCPsych. Consultant Psychiatrist, Royal Edinburgh Hospital, since 1979; part-time Senior Lecturer, Edinburgh University, since 1979; b. 23.4.45, Wallasey; m., Josephine Anna; 2 s. Educ. Queen Elizabeth Grammar School, Darlington; Corpus Christi College, Cambridge; Edinburgh University. Posts in Edinburgh teaching hospitals, 1971-76; scientific staff, MRC Unit for Epidemiological Studies in Psychiatry, 1976-79. Adviser, WHO, Department of Transport; awarded Royal College of Psychiatrists Research Medal and Prize. Publication: Drinking Problems (Co-author). Recreations: wheels, reels, spiels and stichomythia.

Child, Maureen, BSc (Hons), PhD. Executive Member for Finance, City of Edinburgh Council, since 2000; Member, UK Commission on Sustainable Development, since 2000; b. 9.8.50; 2 s. Educ. Morrison's Academy for Girls, Crieff; Edinburgh University. Editor, The Portobello Reporter, 1983-90; Sessional Tutor, Adult Basic Education Unit, 1992-95; Councillor, City of Edinburgh Council, since 1995. Recreations: family;

friends; environmental and community activism. Address: (b.) City Chambers, High Street, Edinburgh EH1 1YJ; T.-0131-529 3268.

Chirnside, Peter Huett, BSc (Hons). National Co-ordinator, Tear Fund, since 1979; b. 27.12.49, Lancaster; m., Fiona; 1 s.; 1 d. Educ. Silcoates School, Wakefield; University of Dundee. Teacher of Biology, Mackie Academy, 1973-79. Chairman, Scottish Mission Secretaries Fellowship, 1984-98; Member, Scottish Lausanne Committee, since 1995. Address: (b.) Challenge House, 29 Canal Street, Glasgow G4 0HD; e-mail: peter.chirnside@tearfund.org

Chisholm, Professor Derrick Mackenzie, BDS, PhD, FDSRCPS(Glas), FDSRCS(Edin), FFDRCS(Ire), FRCPath. Boyd Professor of Dental Surgery, University of Dundee, since 1978; Honorary Consultant in Oral Medicine and Pathology, since 1978; b. 27.3.40, Glasgow; m., June Romayne Race; 1 step-s.; 1 step-d. Educ. Hillhead High School; University of Glasgow. Clinical Research Assistant in Oral Medicine, 1966-68; University of Glasgow: Lecturer in Oral Medicine and Pathology, 1968-76, Senior Lecturer in Oral Medicine and Pathology, 1976-78; University of Dundee: Dean of Dentistry, 1982-89, Deputy Principal, 1989-91; Vice-Principal, 1991-92. Visiting Professor of Oral Pathology, University of Illinois, USA, 1970-72; Grantholder, Dental Health Services Research Unit, SHHD, 1982-92; Member, General Dental Council, 1982-94; President, British Society for Oral Pathology, 1985; Member, Dental Committee, Medical Research Council, 1989-94; Chairman, National Dental Advisory Committee, 1990-94; Member, Board of Governors, Duncan of Jordanstone College of Art, 1993-94. Publications: Salivary Glands in Health and Disease, 1975; Introduction to Oral Medicine, 1978. Recreations: gardening; reading; music. Address: Bruckley House, St. Andrews, Fife KY16 9YF; T.-01334 838375.

Chisholm, Duncan Douglas, MB, ChB, FRCPsych, DPM, DPsychother. Consultant Child and Adolescent Psychiatrist, Department of Child and Family Psychiatry, Royal Aberdeen Children's Hospital, since 1975; Clinical Senior Lecturer, Department of Mental Health, Aberdeen University, since 1975; Honorary Reader, The Robert Gordon University; b. 8.10.41, Grantown-on-Spey; m., Rosemary Galloway Doyle; 2 d. Educ. Grantown Grammar School; Aberdeen University. Pre-registration House Officer, Aberdeen, 1965-66; post-registration Senior House Officer/Registrar, Royal Cornhill Hospital and Ross Clinic, Aberdeen, 1966-70; Senior Registrar in Child and Adolescent Psychiatry, 1970-75 (including one-year sabbatical, Clarke Institute of Psychiatry, Toronto, 1973-74). Academic Secretary, Scottish Child and Adolescent Section, Royal College of Psychiatrists, 1994-97. Recreations: reading; chess; crosswords; literature, history and culture of Scotland and Scottish Highlands; golf. Address: (h.) Figurettes, 6 Crombie Road, Westhill, Aberdeenshire AB32 6PN; T.-01224 749197.

Chisholm, Duncan Fraser, JP. Former Managing Director, Duncan Chisholm & Sons Ltd., Inverness; Chairman, The Kiltmakers Association of Scotland Ltd., since 2000; b. 14.4.41, Inverness; m., Mary Rebecca MacRae; 1 s.; 1 d. Educ. Inverness High School. Member, Inverness District Council, 1984-92; Member, Board of Governors, Eden Court Theatre, Inverness, 1984-88; President, Inverness and Highland Chamber of Commerce, 1983-84 (Vice-President, 1982-83); Member, Highland TAVRA Committee, 1988-92; Vice-Chairman, Inverness, Loch Ness and Nairn Tourist Board, 1988-96; President, Clan Chisholm Society, 1978-89; Chairman, Inverness Town Twinning Committee, 1992-98; Member, Management Committee: Highland Export Club, since 1998, Inverness Town Management, since 1997; GSL, Scout Association, since 1969 (Scout Leader, 1960-69); Session Clerk, St. Columba High Church,

Inverness. Recreations: swimming; music; painting. Address: (b.) 47-51 Castle Street, Inverness; T.-01463 234599.

Chisholm, Duncan John, FRICS, IRRV. Assessor and Electoral Registration Officer for Fife (previously for Fife Regional Council), since 1990; b. 22.1.53, Musselburgh; m., Ann Thomson; 1 s.; 1 d. Educ. Trinity Academy, Edinburgh. Apprentice Surveyor, Midlothian County Assessor, 1970-74; Valuer, Midlothian County Assessor, 1974-75; Valuer, Senior Valuer, Divisional Assessor, Lothian Regional Assessor, 1975-89. President, Scottish Assessors' Association, 1997-2000. Recreations: golf; music; eating; real ale. Address (b.) Fife House (03), North Street, Glenrothes, Fife; T.-Glenrothes 414141.

Chisholm, Malcolm. MP (Labour), Edinburgh North and Leith (formerly Edinburgh Leith), since 1992; MSP, (Labour), Edinburgh North and Leith, since 1999 (Minister for Health and Community Care, Scottish Executive); b. 7.3.49; m.; 2 s.; 1 d. Former teacher. Parliamentary Under-Secretary of State, Scottish Office (Minister for Local Government, Housing and Transport) 1997 (resigned over cuts). Address: (b.) House of Commons, London, SW1A 0AA; Scottish Parliament, Edinburgh EH99 1SP.

Chiswick, Derek, MB, ChB, MPhil, FRCPsych. Honorary Senior Lecturer in Forensic Psychiatry, Edinburgh University; Consultant Forensic Psychiatrist, Lothian Primary Care NHS Trust; b. 7.1.45, Hampton, Middlesex; m., Ann Williams; 3 d. Educ. Preston Manor County School, Wembley; Liverpool University. Member, Home Office Advisory Board on Restricted Patients, 1991-97; Member, MacLean Committee on Serious Violent and Sexual Offenders, 1999. Recreation: relaxing with family. Address: (h.) 6 St. Catherine's Place, Edinburgh EH9 1NU; T.-0131-667 2444.

Chitnis, Paul Bernard, BA (Hons). Chief Executive, Scottish Catholic International Aid Fund, since 1996; b. 29.11.60, Birmingham; m., Tracey; 2 s.; 1 d. Educ. Stonyhurst College; Nottingham University. Appeal Director and Communications Director, Handicapped Children's Pilgrimage Trust, 1986-89; Appeals Director, Sick Children's Trust, 1989-90; Head of Appeals, Christian Aid, 1990-94; Head of Fundraising, Crossroads, 1994-95. Founder and Chairman of Trustees, The Newman Trust, 1981-90; Chair, Network of International Development Organisations in Scotland; Secretary, Scottish Cross-Party Parliamentary Group on Development. Address: (b.) 19 Park Circus, Glasgow G3 6BE; T.-0141-354 5555; e-mail: pchitnis@sciaf.org.uk

Christian, Professor Reginald Frank, MA (Hons) (Oxon). Professor of Russian and Head of Department, St. Andrews University, 1966-92, now Emeritus Professor; b. 9.8.24, Liverpool; m., Rosalind Iris Napier; 1 s.; 1 d. Educ. Liverpool Institute High School; Queen's College, Oxford. RAF, 1943-46 (aircrew), flying on 231 Sqdn. and 6 Atlantic Ferry Unit (Pilot Officer, 1944); Foreign Office (British Embassy, Moscow), 1949-50; Lecturer and Head of Russian Department, Liverpool University, 1950-55; Senior Lecturer, then Professor of Russian and Head of Department, Birmingham University, 1955-66; Visiting Professor: McGill University, Montreal, 1961-62, Institute of Foreign Languages, Moscow, 1964-65; Dean, Faculty of Arts, St. Andrews University, 1975-78; Member, University Court, 1971-73, 1981-85. President, British Universities Association of Slavists, 1967-70; Member, International Committee of Slavists, 1970-75; Honorary Vice-President, Association of Teachers of Russian; Member, UGC Arts Sub-Committee on Russian Studies. Publications: Russian Syntax (with F.M. Borras), 1959 and 1971; Korolenko's Siberia, 1954; Tolstoy's War and Peace: A Study, 1962; Russian Prose Composition (with F.M. Borras), 1964 and 1974; Tolstoy: A Critical Introduction, 1969; Tolstoy's

Letters, edited, translated and annotated, 1978; Tolstoy's Diaries, edited, translated and annotated, 1985 and 1994; Alexis Aladin – The Tragedy of Exile, 1999. Recreations: violin; fell-walking; formerly association football. Address: (h.) Culgrianach, 48 Lade Braes, St. Andrews, Fife; T.- 01334 474407; Scioncroft, Knockard Road, Pitlochry; T.- 01796 472993.

Christie, Campbell, CBE, DLitt. Convener, Management Board, Scottish Civic Forum; General Secretary, Scottish Trades Union Congress, 1986-98; Visiting Professor, Glasgow Caledonian University; Honorary Professor, Glasgow University; b. 23.8.37, Carsluith, Kirkcudbrightshire; m., Elizabeth Brown Cameron; 2 s. Educ. Albert Senior Secondary School, Glasgow; Woolwich Polytechnic, London. Civil Servant, Department of Health and Social Security, 1954-72; National Officer, then Deputy General Secretary, Society of Civil and Public Servants, 1972-86.

Christie, John, MTheol, DipEd. Director of Lifelong Learning, Scottish Borders Council, since 2001 (Director of Education, 1995-2001); Non-Executive Director, Learning and Teaching Scotland, 2000-04; b. 25.12.53, Edinburgh; m., Katherine; 2 d. Educ. Daniel Stewart's College; St. Andrews University; Edinburgh University; Moray House College of Education. Teacher, 1977-83; Principal Assistant, Stockport MBC, 1983-85; Assistant Director of Education, then Depute Director of Education, Tayside Regional Council, 1985-95. Hon. Treasurer, Association of Directors of Education in Scotland, since 1995; Member: Health Education Board for Scotland, 1991-97, Advisory Committee on Scottish Qualification for Headship, since 1999, Scotland Against Drugs Primary School Initiative, COSLA/SEED Group on Value-Added in Schools; Non-Executive Director, Scottish Consultative Council on the Curriculum, 1995-2000. Recreation: house-building. Address: (b.) Council HQ, Newtown St. Boswells TD6 0SA; T.-01835 825095.

Chrystie, Kenneth, LLB (Hons), PhD. Senior Partner, McClure Naismith; Chairman, Hugh Fraser Foundation, 1988; President, Royal Glasgow Institute of the Fine Arts, since 1997; b. 24.11.46, Glasgow; m., Mary; 1 s.; 2 d. Educ. Duncanrig Senior Secondary; University of Glasgow; University of Virginia. Joined McClure Naismith, 1968. Founder Member and Director, Intellectual Property Lawyers Organisation; Member, DTI Committees, Arbitration Law Reform. Publications: contributor to Encyclopedia of Scots Law, Labour Law Handbook and other legal publications. Recreations: golf; curling; tennis. Address: (b.) 292 St. Vincent Street, Glasgow G2 5TQ; T.- 0141-204 2700; e-mail: kchrystie@mcclurenaismith.com

Clapham, David Charles, LLB, SSC. Solicitor (Principal, private practice, since 1984); Part-time Immigration Adjudicator, since 2001; Temporary Sheriff, 1998-99; Secretary, Glasgow, Argyll and Bute and Dunbartonshire Local Valuation Panel, since 1996; part-time Chairman, Social Security Appeal Tribunals, since 1992, and Disability Appeal Tribunals, since 2000; Director, Legal Defence Union; b. 16.10.58, Giffnock; m., Debra Harriet Clapham; 1 s.; 2 d. Educ. Hutchesons' Boys' Grammar School, Glasgow; Strathclyde University. Legal apprenticeship, 1979-81; admitted Solicitor, 1981; admitted Notary Public, 1982; founded own legal practice, 1984; Tutor, Strathclyde University, 1984-92; part-time Lecturer, Glasgow University, 1991-94; Secretary, Strathclyde Region Local Valuation Panel, 1988-96; Glasgow Bar Association: Secretary, 1987-91, Vice President, 1991-92, President, 1992-93; Secretary, Scottish Law Agents Society, 1994-97; Council Member, Royal Faculty of Procurators in Glasgow, 1996-99; Governor, Belmont House School. Recreations: reading; collecting books. Address: (b.) 79 West Regent Street, Glasgow G2 2AW; T.- 0141-332 5537.

Clark, Alastair Trevor, CBE (1976), LVO (1974), MA (Oxon), AMA, FSA Scot, FRSSA. Barrister (Middle Temple); Member, Race Relations Assessors Panel, Scottish Sheriff Courts, since 1983; b. 10.6.23, Glasgow; m., Hilary Agnes Mackenzie Anderson. Educ. Giffnock Academy; Glasgow Academy; Edinburgh Academy; Magdalen College, Oxford; Inns of Court (Middle Temple); Ashridge Management College. War service, Queen's Own Cameron Highlanders and Royal West African Frontier Force, Nigeria, India and Burma, 1942-46; Administrative Branch, HM Colonial Service (later HMOCS): Nigeria, 1949-59 (Secretary to Cabinet, Northern Region; Senior District Officer), Hong Kong, 1960-72 (Director of Social Welfare; Deputy and Acting Director of Urban Services; Acting Chairman Urban Council; Clerk of Councils; Principal Assistant Colonial Secretary, etc.), Western Pacific, 1972-77 (Chief Secretary Western Pacific High Commission; Deputy and Acting Governor, Solomon Islands); retired, 1977; Vice-President, Hong Kong Scout Association, 1965-72; Joint Founder, HK Outward Bound School; Honorary Secretary, St. John's Cathedral Council, 1963-72; USA State Department Country Leader Fellowship to USA, 1972; Selector, Voluntary Service Overseas, 1978-80; Leverhulme Trust Grant, 1979-81; Chairman, Scottish Museums Council, 1981-84 and 1987-90; Member, Council, National Trust for Scotland, 1981-84 and 1987-90; Member, Museums Association Council, 1983-86 and 1990-94; Member, Edinburgh International Festival Council, 1980-86 and 1990-94; Vice-Chairman, Committee of Area Museum Councils, 1983-84; Member, Secretary of State's Museums Advisory Board, 1983-85; Trustee, National Museums of Scotland, 1985-87; a Director, Royal Lyceum Theatre Company, 1982-84; Member: Lothian Health Board, 1981-89, City of Edinburgh District Council, 1980-88, Court of Directors, Edinburgh Academy, 1979-84; a Governor, Edinburgh Filmhouse, 1980-84 and since 1987; Member, National Museums of Scotland Charitable Trust, since 1987; Member, Almond Valley Heritage Trust, since 1990 (Vice Chairman, since 1993); Trustee, Stirling Smith Art Gallery and Museum, since 1993; Volunteer Guide, National Museums of Scotland, since 1993; Council Member, Royal Scottish Society of Arts (Science and Technology), since 1998. Publication: A Right Honourable Gentleman — Abubakar from the Black Rock, 1991. Recreations: music; books; theatre; netsuke; cartophily. Address: (h.) 11 Ramsay Garden, Edinburgh EH1 2NA; T.-0131-225 8070.

Clark, Alex. Member, Board of Directors, Arran Theatre and Arts Trust; Trustee: James Milne Memorial Trust, Hugh MacDiarmid Memorial Trust, Scottish Working People's History Trust; b. 2.1.22, Larkhall; m., Jessie Beveridge McCulloch; 1 s.; 1 d. Educ. Larkhall Academy. Grain miller, 1936-39; coal miner, 1939-53; political organiser, 1953-69; Scottish and Northern Ireland Secretary, British Actors Equity Association, 1969-84; created the post of STUC Arts Officer, 1985-87; founder Member, Boards, Scottish Youth Theatre, Scottish Theatre Company, Royal Lyceum Theatre Company; Glasgow Jazz Festival, Mayfest (Founder); also served on Boards of Pitlochry Festival Theatre and Cumbernauld Theatre Company, Scottish Ballet, Scottish Opera, Glasgow Film Theatre; Member: Scottish Arts Council's Review Committee on Scottish Theatre Company, 1987, Working Party on a National Theatre for Scotland, 1987, STUC Entertainment and Arts Committee, 1975-94. Lord Provost's Award for services to the city of Glasgow, 1987; Winner, ABSA-Goodman & Reed Elsevier Award for Services to the Arts, 1994. Recreations: reading; music; theatre; walking; gardening. Address: (h.) Ponfeigh, 8 Strathwhillan, Brodick, Isle of Arran.

Clark, Alistair Campbell, MA, LLB, WS. Formerly Senior Partner, Blackadder, Reid, Johnston (formerly Reid, Johnston, Bell & Henderson), Solicitors, Dundee; Honorary Sheriff, Tayside Central & Fife, since 1986; Director,

Dovetail Enterprises; Trustee, Dundee Disabled Children's Association, since 1993; Chairman, Scottish Conveyancing and Executry Services Board, since 1996; Member, Nominations Committee, Scottish Enterprise Tayside, since 1998; b. 4.3.33, Dundee; m., Evelyn M. Clark; 3 s. Educ. Grove Academy, Broughty Ferry; St. Andrews University. Dean, Faculty of Procurators and Solicitors in Dundee, 1979-81, Hon. Life Member, since 1991; President, Law Society of Scotland, 1989-90 (Council Member, since 1982); founder Chairman, Broughty Ferry Round Table; Founder President, Claverhouse Rotary Club, Dundee. Recreations: family; travel; erratic golf. Address: (h.) Blythehill, 16 Balmyle Road, West Ferry, Dundee DD51JJ; T.-01382 477989.

Clark, Amanda Jane, SHND, Communication Studies. Chief Executive, Taste of Scotland, since 1994; b. 15.9.62, Hong Kong; m., Thomas Brander; 1s.; 2d. Educ. Craigholme School, Glasgow; Napier Polytechnic, Edinburgh. Director, Sales and Marketing, George Intercontinental Hotel, Edinburgh; Sales Manager Howard Hotel, Edinburgh. Recreations: swimming; walking; reading. Address: (b.) 33 Melville Street, Edinburgh; e-mail: tastescotland@sol.co.uk

Clark, Barbara E., MA, DipG. Assistant General Secretary, Scottish Secondary Teachers' Association, since 1997; b. 13.3.46, Stirling; m., John; 1 s.; 1 d. Educ. St. Modan's High School; University of Glasgow; Notre Dame College; Moray House. Alva Academy: Teacher of English, 1968-69 and 1979-85, A.P.T. Guidance, 1969-70 and 1985-90, P.T. Guidance, 1970-73; Guidance Development Officer, Central Region, 1990-93; P.T. Guidance, Bo'ness Academy, 1993-97; Education Liaison Officer, Children's Panel, 1995-96. Member, General Teaching Council, 1992-97; Vice-President then President, S.S.T.A., 1993-97. Recreations: reading; theatre; music; walking; art; travel. Address: (h.) 16 Lothian Crescent, Causewayhead, Stirling FK9 5SB; T.-01786 462968.

Clark, David Findlay, OBE, DL, MA, PhD, CPsychol, FBPsS, ARPS. Deputy Lieutenant, Banffshire, since 1992; Consulting Clinical Psychologist; former Director, Area Clinical Psychology Services, Grampian Health Board; Clinical Senior Lecturer, Department of Mental Health, Aberdeen University; b. 30.5.30, Aberdeen; m., Janet Ann Stephen; 2 d. Educ. Banff Academy; Aberdeen University. Flying Officer, RAF, 1951-53; Psychologist, Leicester Industrial Rehabilitation Unit, 1953-56; Senior, then Principal Clinical Psychologist, Leicester Area Clinical Psychology Service, and part-time Lecturer, Leicester University and Technical College, 1956-66; WHO short-term Consultant, Sri Lanka, 1977; various lecturing commitments in Canada and USA, since 1968. Honorary Sheriff, Grampian and Highlands; former Governor, Aberdeen College of Education; Member, Grampian Children's Panel, 1970-85; Safeguarder (Social Work Scotland Act, 1969 and Children (Scotland) Act, 1995), 1985-2000; Past Chairman, Clinical Division, British Psychological Society. Publications: Help, Hospitals and the Handicapped, 1984; One Boy's War, 1997; Stand By Your Beds!, 2001; book chapters and technical and magazine articles. Recreations: photography; sailing; writing; chess; guitar playing; painting and drawing; golf; hill-walking. Address: (h.) Glendeveron, 8 Deveron Terrace, Banff AB45 1BB; T.-01261 812624; e-mail: drdavidfindlayclark@lineone.net

Clark, David McNair, MA, BD. Minister, The Steeple, Dundee, since 2000; b. 26.2.48, Glasgow. Educ. Hutchesons' Grammar School; University of Glasgow. Principal Teacher of Geography, Kelso, 1975; Church of Scotland Minister, Airdrie, 1989; General Director, Scripture Union Scotland, 1996-2000. Recreations: outdoor pursuits – cycling and running. Address: 128 Arbroath Road, Dundee DD4 7HR; T.-01382 455411; e-mail: david_clark@bun.com

Clark, Derek John, BMus (Hons), DipMusEd (Hons), DRSAMD. Head of Music, Scottish Opera, since 1997; b. 22.8.55, Glasgow; m., Heather Fryer; 1 d. Educ. Dumbarton Academy; Royal Scottish Academy of Music and Drama; University of Durham; London Opera Centre. Debut as professional accompanist, 1976; joined music staff, Welsh National Opera, 1977, conducting debut 1982; Guest Conductor, Mid Wales Opera, 1989-92; Guest Coach and Conductor, Welsh College of Music, 1990-97; Conductor, South Wales Opera, 1994-96; Guest Coach, RSAMD, since 1997; arranger/composer since late 1980s including work for radio and television; musicals for young people; choral music. Silver Medallist, Worshipful Company of Musicians, 1976. Recreation: reading. Address: (b.) Scottish Opera, 39 Elmbank Crescent, Glasgow G2 4PT; T.-0141-248 4567.

Clark, Professor Frank, CBE, MHSM, DipHSM. Director, Strathcarron Hospice, since 1996; Chairman, Forth Valley NHS Board, since 2001; Honorary Professor, University of Stirling, since 1997; Visiting Professor, Glasgow Caledonian University, since 1993; b. 17.10.46, Aberdeen; m., Linda Margaret; 2 d. Educ. Aberdeen Academy. Greater Glasgow Health Board: Assistant District Administrator, 1977-81, District General Administrator, 1981-83; Lanarkshire Health Board: Director of Administrative Services, 1983-84, Secretary, 1984-85; General Manager, Lanarkshire Health Board, 1985-96; Chairman, Scottish Health Board General Managers Group, 1993-95 (Vice-Chairman, 1995-97); Non-Executive Director, VAMW Homes Ltd. and VAMW Training, since 1997; Board Member, New Lanarkshire Ltd., 1994-98; Member, Council of Management, Scottish Partnership Agency, 1998-2001 (Deputy Chairman, 1999-2001); Chairman, Scottish Hospices since 1998-2001; Member, Help the Hospices IHRC, since 1998; Chairman: Central Scotland Healthcare NHS Trust, 1999, Forth Valley Primary Care NHS Trust, 1999; Member, Forth Valley Health Board, 1999; President, Rotary Club of Cumbernauld, 2000. Recreations: reading; music; gardening; driving; swimming; DIY; poetry. Address: (b.) Strathcarron Hospice, Randolph Hill, Denny FK6 5HJ; T.-1324 826222.

Clark, Graham M. BSc, PhD, CChem, FRSC, FIMgt, FRSA. Principal, Inverness College, since 1999; b. 2.8.41, Dumfries; m., Linda A.; 3 d. Educ. George Watson's College, Edinburgh; Edinburgh University. Research Fellow, Hull University, 1966-67; Lecturer, Huddersfield Polytechnic, 1967-79; Head of Applied Science, North East Surrey College of Technology, 1980-85; Deputy Director, Nene College, Northampton, 1986-89; Principal: Angus College of Further Education, 1990-92, Falkirk College of Further and Higher Education, 1992-99. Editor, Thermal Analysis Reviews and Abstracts, 1986-93. Recreations: golf; hill walking; UK philately. Address: (b.) Inverness College, Longman Road, Inverness IV1 1SA; T.-01463 273203.

Clark, Gregor Munro, LLB. Scottish Parliamentary Counsel, Scottish Executive, since 1999; b. 18.4.46, Glasgow; m., 1, Jane Maralyn Palmer (deceased); 2, Alexandra Groves Miller or Plumtree; 1 s.; 2 d. Educ. Queen's Park Senior Secondary School, Glasgow; Queen's College, St Andrews University. Admitted Faculty of Advocates, 1972; Lord Advocate's Department, 1974-99 (Assistant Parliamentary Draftsman, then Deputy Parliamentary Draftsman, then Parliamentary Draftsman); Counsel to the Scottish Law Commission, 1995-2000. Recreation: piano. Address: (b.) Office of the Scottish Parliamentary Counsel, Victoria Quay, Edinburgh EH6 6QQ; T.-0131-244 1671.

Clark, Guy Wyndham Nial Hamilton, MSi, JP, DL, MFH. Deputy Lieutenant, Renfrewshire, since 1987; Director, Aberdeen Asset Managers, since 2001; b. 28.3.44; m., Brighid Lovell Greene; 2 s.; 1 d. Educ. Eton. Commd. Coldstream Guards, 1962-67; Investment Manager, Murray Johnstone Ltd., Glasgow, 1973-77; Partner, R.C. Greig & Co. (Stockbrokers), Glasgow, 1977-86; Director, Greig, Middleton & Co. Ltd., 1986-97; Managing Director, Murray Johnstone Private Investors Ltd., 1997-2001. Chairman, JP Advisory Committee, since 1991; Joint Master, Lanarkshire and Renfrewshire Foxhounds, since 1999. Recreations: field sports. Address: (h.) Braeton, Inverkip PA16 0DU; T.-01475 520 619; e-mail: guy.clark@aberdeen_asset.com

Clark, M. Lynda, QC. Advocate-General for Scotland; MP (Labour), Edinburgh Pentlands, since 1997. Admitted Advocate, 1977; called to English Bar, 1988; contested Fife North East (Labour), 1992. Address: (b.) House of Commons, London, SW1A 0AA.

Clark, Professor Norman George, BSc, MA, PhD, FWAAS. Professor of Environmental Studies, Strathclyde University, since 1996; Director, Graduate School of Environmental Studies, since 1996; b. 18.5.42, Buchlyvie; m., Brenda; 2 d. Educ. George Watson's College; Edinburgh University. Previously held academic posts, Glasgow University and Sussex University; Founding Director, Graduate Studies, Science Policy Research Unit, Sussex University; Founding Director, Technology Planning and Development Unit, University of Ife, Nigeria; Visiting Professor, Institute for Advanced Studies, University of Sao Paulo; Consultant to Forth Estuary Forum, 1999-2000; Fellow, World Academy of Arts and Sciences, since 1990. Recreations: sailing; golf; reading. Address: (b.) Wolfson Centre, Strathclyde University, Glasgow G4 0NW; T.-0141-548 4078.

Clark, Pamela Ann Dean, LLB (Hons). Head of Policy, The Highland Council; b. 18.10.60, Inverness. Educ. Lossiemouth High School; Edinburgh University; Aberdeen College of Education. Welfare Benefits Adviser, Central Regional Council; Legal Services Adviser, Citizens Advice Scotland; Director, Tenant Participation Advisory Service; Executive Director, Highland Community Care Forum. Former Member: Scottish Homes Board, Scottish Homes Advisory Committee on Housing Information and Advice, Commission on the Future of the Voluntary Sector in Scotland; Member, Scottish Consumer Council. Recreations: swimming; cinema. Address: (h.) Bridge House, Resaurie, Inverness.

Clark, Susan Agnes, BA, CQSW. Member, Fife Council, since 1995; Senior Social Worker (part time), Dundee City Council, since 1999; Member, Main Board, Scottish Environmental Protection Agency, since 1999 (Chair, National Health and Safety Committee, since 2001); b. 14.11.55, Glasgow. Educ. Marr College, Troon; Glasgow College of Technology; Dundee University. Social Worker/Manager, Strathclyde Regional Council, Northamptonshire County Council, Fife Regional Council, National Foster Care Association; former Councillor, North-East Fife District Council; former Chair, East Area Community Services Committee, Fife Council; Opposition Spokesperson for Social Strategy. Elder, Cupar Old and St Michael of Tarvit Parish Church. Recreations: travelling in Europe; skiing; reading; music, especially opera and classical. Address: (h.) 16 Well Street, Cupar KY15 4AX; T.-01334 655592.

Clarke, (Christopher) Michael, BA (Hons), FRSA. Director, National Gallery of Scotland, since 2001; b. 29.8.52, York; m., Deborah Clare Cowling; 2 s.; 1 d. Educ. Felsted School, Essex; Manchester University. Art Assistant, York City Art Gallery, 1973-76; Research Assistant, British Museum, 1976-78; Assistant Keeper in charge of prints, Whitworth Art Gallery, Manchester, 1978-84; Assistant Keeper, National Gallery of Scotland, 1984-87, Keeper, 1987-2001. Visiting Fellow, Yale Center for British Art, 1985. Publications include: The Tempting Prospect; A Social History of English Watercolours; The Arrogant Connoisseur (Co-Editor); Richard Payne Knight; Lighting Up the Landscape – French Impressionism and its Origins; Corot and the Art of Landscape; Eyewitness Art – Watercolours; Corot, Courbet und die Maler von Barbizon (Co-Editor); Oxford Concise Dictionary of Art Terms. Recreations: listening to music; tennis; golf. Address: (b.) National Gallery of Scotland, The Mound, Edinburgh EH2 2EL; T.-0131-624 6511.

Clarke, Eric Lionel. MP (Labour), Midlothian, 1992-2001; b. 9.4.33, Edinburgh; m., June; 2 s.; 1 d. Educ. Holy Cross Academy; W.M. Ramsey Technical College; Esk Valley Technical College. Coal miner, 1949-77; General Secretary, NUM Scottish Area, 1977-89; County Councillor, Midlothian, 1962-74; Regional Councillor, Lothian, 1974-78. Recreations: fly fishing; gardening; carpentry. Address: (h.) 32 Mortonhall Park Crescent, Edinburgh; T.-0131-654 1585.

Clarke, Kevin John, BA. Secretary, University of Stirling, since 1995; b. 8.3.52, Reading; m., Linda Susan Stewart; 2 d. Educ. Presentation College, Reading; University of Stirling. Scientific Officer, British Library Lending Division, 1975-77; Administrative Assistant, Loughborough University, 1977-83; Assistant Registrar, University of Newcastle upon Tyne, 1983-85; Clerk to the Senatus Academicus, 1985-89, Deputy Secretary, 1989-95, University of Aberdeen. Recreations: music; hill-walking; gardening. Address: (b.) University of Stirling, Stirling FK9 4LA; T.-01786 467018; e-mail: p.l.norman@stir.ac.uk

Clarke, Hon. Lord (Matthew Gerard Clarke). Senator of the College of Justice, since 2000. Educ. Holy Cross High School, Hamilton; Glasgow University (MA, LLB). Solicitor, 1972; Lecturer, Depatment of Scots Law, Edinburgh University, 1972-78; admitted, Faculty of Advocates, 1978; QC (Scot), 1989; a Judge, Courts of Appeal of Jersey and Guernsey, 1995-2000; Leader, UK Delegation, Council of the Bars and Law Societies of EC, 1992-96; Hon. Fellow, Europa Institute, Edinburgh University, since 1995.

Clarke, Owen J., CBE. Chairman, Scottish Ambulance Service, since 1997; b. 15.3.37, Edinburgh; m., Elizabeth; 2 s.; 1 d. Educ. Portobello High School, Edinburgh. Head of Inland Revenue, North of England, 1988-90; Head of Inland Revenue, Scotland, 1990-97. Director, Friends of Craigmillar, 1994-2001. Recreations: jogging; golf; hill-walking. Address: (h.) Dyngarth, Redholm Park, North Berwick EH39 4RA; T.-01620 892623.

Clarke, Peter, CBE, BSc, PhD, LLD (Hon), CChem, FRSC, DEd(Hon), FInstPet. b. 18.3.22, Mansfield; m., Ethel (deceased); 2 s. Educ. Queen Elizabeth's Grammar School, Mansfield; University College, Nottingham. Principal, Robert Gordon's Institute of Technology, Aberdeen, 1970-85. Chairman: Scottish Vocational Education Council, 1985-91, Aberdeen Enterprise Trust, 1984-92, Industrial Training Centre, Aberdeen, 1989-95; President: Association of Principals of Colleges, 1980-81, Association for Educational and Training Technology, 1993-95; Member, Science and Engineering Research Council, 1978-82; Trustee, Gordon Cook Foundation, since 1988. Recreation: walking. Address: (h.) 108 Whinhill Gate, Aberdeen AB11 7WF; T.-01224 587477.

Clarke, Professor Roger John, ALCM, BA, BTech, MSc, PhD, CEng, MIEE, MIEEE. Professor of Electronic Engineering, Heriot Watt University, since 1989; b.

1.10.40, Ewell, Surrey; m., Yvonne Clarke; 1 s. Educ. Gravesend Grammar School; Loughborough University. Development Engineer, STC Ltd., Woolwich, 1962-64; Research Associate, then Lecturer in Electrical Engineering, Loughborough University, 1964-86; Reader in Electrical Engineering, Heriot Watt University, 1986-89. Recreations: gardening; playing the cello; Shakespeare. Address: (b.) Department of Computing and Electrical Engineering, Heriot Watt University, Riccarton, Edinburgh EH14 4AS; T.-0131-451 3323.

Clarke, Rt. Hon. Thomas, CBE, JP. MP (Labour), Coatbridge and Chryston (formerly Monklands West); Shadow Secretary of State for Scotland, 1992-93; b. 10.1.41, Coatbridge. Educ. Columba High School, Coatbridge; Scottish College of Commerce. Former Assistant Director, Scottish Council for Educational Technology; Provost of Monklands, 1975-82; Past President, Convention of Scottish Local Authorities; MP, Coatbridge and Airdrie, 1982-83; author, Disabled Persons (Services Consultation and Representation) Act, 1986; elected four times to Shadow Cabinet; director, amateur film, Give Us a Goal. Recreations: films; walking; reading. Address: (h.) 37 Blairhill Street, Coatbridge ML5 1PG; T.-01236 600800.

Clarkson, Professor Euan Neilson Kerr, MA, PhD, DSc, FRSE. Professor of Palaeontology, University of Edinburgh, since 1998 (Reader, 1981-98); b. 9.5.37; m., Cynthia; 4 s. Educ. Shrewsbury School; Emmanuel College, University of Cambridge. University of Edinburgh: Assistant Lecturer, 1963-65, Lecturer, 1965-78, Senior Lecturer, 1978-81, Director of Studies, 1967-73 and 1995-2001, Associate Dean, Science Faculty, 1978-81; many university committees. Trustee, Natural History Museum, 1987-92. President: Edinburgh Geological Society, 1983-87, Palaeontological Association, since 1998; Clough Medal, 1993; Keith Medal, 1994. Publications: Invertebrate Palaeontology and Evolution; 80 scientific articles. Recreations: classical music; hillwalking; writing; painting; wine. Address: (b.) Department of Geology and Geophysics, University of Edinburgh, West Mains Road, Edinburgh EH9 3JW.

Clarkson, Graeme Andrew Telford, LLB. Senior Partner, Baird & Company, Solicitors, Kirkcaldy, since 1990; b. 6.9.53, Fraserburgh; m., Moira; 3 s. Educ. High School of Dundee; Aberdeen University. Law Apprentice, Allan MacDougall & Co., Edinburgh; Assistant, Ranken & Reid, Edinburgh; Assistant, then Partner, Baird & Company. Past Chairman, Kirkcaldy Round Table; former Council Member, Law Society of Scotland. Address: (b.) 2 Park Place, Kirkcaldy Fife; T.-01592 268608.

Cleland, Ronald John, BA. Chairman, North Glasgow University Hospitals NHS Trust, since 1998; Board Member, NHS Greater Glasgow, since 1999; b. 29.5.46, Glasgow; m., Sheena; 2 s.; 2 d. Educ. Allan Glen's School; Strathclyde University. Director and Partner, Thomson Partners Ltd., since 1987. Recreations: sporting interests, both actively and as spectator. Address: (b.) 14 Sandyford Place, Glasgow G3 7NB; T.-0141-248 3666.

Clements, Professor John Barklie, BSc, PhD, FRSE. Professor of Virology, Glasgow University, since 1995; b. 14.3.46, Belfast. Educ. Belfast Royal Academy; Queen's University, Belfast. Research Fellow, California Institute of Technology, 1971-73; joined Institute of Virology, Glasgow University, 1973; Cancer Research Campaign Travelling Fellow, Department of Biochemistry and Molecular Biology, Harvard University, 1983; Council Member, Society for General Microbiology, 1984-88; Member, MRC Physiological Systems and Disorders Board, 1990-94; Chairman, Grants Committee B, PMIB, 1992-94; Member, Clinical and Biomedical Research Committee, Scottish Home and Health Department, 1990-93. Recreations: walking; golf; music. Address: (b.) Institute of Virology, Glasgow University, Glasgow; T.-0141-330 4027.

Clerk of Penicuik, Sir John Dutton, 10th Bt, CBE (1966), VRD, FRSE, JP. Lord Lieutenant of Midlothian, 1972-92; Commodore RNR (Retd); b. 30.1.17; m.; 2 s.; 2 d. Educ. Stowe. Former Lieutenant, Queen's Bodyguard for Scotland (Royal Company of Archers). Address: (h.) Penicuik House, Penicuik, Midlothian EH26 9LA.

Clifford, Sir Timothy Peter Plint, BA, AMA, LLD, DLitt, FRSE, FRSA, FSAScot. Director-General, National Galleries of Scotland, since 2001, Director, 1984-2001; b. 26.1.46; m., Jane Olivia Paterson; 1 d. Educ. Sherborne; Perugia University; Courtauld Institute, London University. Manchester City Art Galleries: Assistant Keeper, Department of Paintings, 1968-72, Acting Keeper, 1972; Assistant Keeper, Department of Ceramics, Victoria and Albert Museum, London, 1972-76; Assistant Keeper, British Art, Department of Prints and Drawings, British Museum, London, 1976-78; Director, Manchester City Art Galleries, 1978-84. Chairman, International Committee for Museums of Fine Art (ICOM), 1980-83; Member, Museums and Galleries Commission, 1983-88; Member, Board, British Council, 1987-92; Member, Executive Committee, Scottish Museums Council; Vice President, Turner Society, 1984-86 and since 1989; Vice-President, Frigate Unicorn Preservation Society, since 1987; British Institute of Management's Special Award, 1991; Member, Ateneo Veneto (Italy), since 1997. Commendatore all'Ordine del Merito della Repubblica Italiana, 1988 (Cavaliere, since 1988); Member, Advisory Council, Friends of Courtauld Institute, since 1990; President, NADFAS, since 1996 (Vice-President, 1990-96); Trustee, the former Royal Yacht Britannia, since 1998. Recreations: bird-watching; entomology. Address: (b.) National Galleries of Scotland, The Mound, Edinburgh, EH2 2EL.

Clift, Benedict, BMSc (Hons), MBChB, FRCSEd, FRCSOrth. Consultant Orthopaedic and Trauma Surgeon, Ninewells Hospital, Dundee, since 1995; Clinical Director of Musculoskeletal and A. & E. Services; Honorary Senior Lecturer, Dundee University; m., 22.7.62, Manchester; m., Alison; 1 s.; 2 d. Educ. Cardinal Langley Grammar School; Dundee University. Recreations: jazz; trees; Dante. Address: (b.) Department of Orthopaedic and Trauma Surgery, Ninewells Hospital, Dundee DD1 9SY; T.-01382 660111.

Clive, Eric McCredie, CBE, MA, LLB, LLM, SJD, FRSE. Visiting Professor, Faculty of Law, Edinburgh University, since 1999; b. 24.7.38, Stranraer; m., Kay McLeman; 1 s.; 2 d. Educ. Stranraer Academy; Stranraer High School; Universities of Edinburgh, Michigan, Virginia. Lecturer, Senior Lecturer, Reader, Professor of Scots Law, Faculty of Law, Edinburgh University, 1962-81; Commissioner, Scottish Law Commission, 1981-99. Publications: The Law of Husband and Wife in Scotland (4th edition), 1997; legal articles. Address: (h.) 14 York Road, Edinburgh EH5 3EH; T.-0131-552 2875.

Closier, Michael John. Group Chief Executive, Scottish Exhibition and Conference Centre, since 1992; Director and Depute Chairman, Exhibition Venues Association; Non Executive Director, Greater Glasgow and Clyde Valley Tourist Board, since 1993; b. 15.2.47, London; m., Anne-Marie; 1 s. 1 step-d. Educ. Lanchester Polytechnic. Managing Director, Compuser Ltd.; Technical Director, Centronics Ltd.; Managing Director, Bix Ltd.; Director, Peerless Control Systems. Member: IoD, CBI, ICCA, Advisory Committee, Glasgow Common Purpose; Past Chair, NAEH. Recreations: fell walking; gardening; opera; cooking. Address: SECC, Glasgow G3 8YW; T.-0141-275 6210.

Clouting, David Wallis, BDS, MSc, LDSRCS (Eng), DDPH. Specialist in dental public health; Clinical Director of Community Dental Services, Borders Primary Care NHS Trust, since 2000 (Dental Services Manager, 1999-2000); b. 29.3.53, London; m.; Dr. Margaret M.C. Bacon; 3 s.; 1 d. Educ. Leyton County High School for Boys; University College Hospital Dental School, London; Institute of Dental Surgery, London; Joint Department of Dental Public Health, London Hospital Medical College and University College. Senior Dental Officer for Special Needs, East and North Hertfordshire Health Authorities, 1983-90; Chief Administrative Dental Officer, Borders Health Board, 1990-95; Community Dental Services Manager, Borders Community Health Services NHS Trust, 1995-99. Recreations: amateur radio; DIY; swimming; hill walking; sailing. Address: (b.) Borders Primary Care NHS Trust, Dental Department, 2/3 Dingleton Cottages, Dingleton Road, Melrose TD6 9HR.

Clow, Robert George Menzies. Former Chairman, John Smith & Son (Glasgow) Ltd. (Managing Director (1969-94); b. 27.1.34, Sian, Shensi, North China; m., Katrina M. Watson. Educ. Eltham College, London. Interned by Japanese as a child; National Service, RAF; trained as a bookseller, Bumpus London; worked in Geneva; joined John Smith & Son (Glasgow), 1960. Founded, with others, The New Glasgow Society, 1965 (Chairman 1967, 1968); worked for 12 years in rehabilitating St. Vincent Crescent, Glasgow, as founder member, St. Vincent Crescent Area Association; Secretary, First Glasgow Housing Association, since 1978; Chairman, St. Vincent Crescent Buildings Preservation Trust; restored Aiket Castle, 1976-79 (winner of an Europa Nostra Merit Award, 1989; National Trust for Scotland: Member, Council 1978 and 1991, Member, Executive, 1980-90; Executive Member, Committee, Strathclyde Building Preservation Trust, 1986; appointed to Architectural Heritage Fund Executive, 1989. Recreations: farming; bee keeping; opera; restoring old houses; swimming; skiing; reading on holiday. Address: Aiket Castle, Dunlop, Ayrshire; T.-(b.) 015604 84643.

Clyde, The Rt. Hon. The Lord (James John Clyde), PC, Baron (Life Peer), DUniv (Edin), DUniv (Heriot-Watt), DLitt (Napier), BA (Oxon), LLB. Lord of Appeal in Ordinary, 1996-2001; Senator of the College of Justice, 1985-96; b. 29.1.32, Edinburgh; m., Ann Clunie Hoblyn; 2 s. Educ. Edinburgh Academy; Corpus Christi College, Oxford; Edinburgh University. Called to Scottish Bar, 1959; QC, 1971; Advocate Depute, 1973-74; Chancellor to Bishop of Argyll and the Isles, 1972-85; a Judge of the Courts of Appeal of Jersey and Guernsey, 1979-85; Chairman: Medical Appeal Tribunal, 1974-85, Committee of Investigation for Scotland on Agricultural Marketing, 1984-85, Scottish Valuation Advisory Council, 1987-96 (Member, since 1972); Member, UK Delegation to CCBE, 1978-84 (Leader, 1981-84); Chairman of the Inquiry into the removal of children from Orkney, 1991-92. Trustee and Manager, St. Mary's Music School, 1976-93; Trustee, National Library of Scotland, 1978-94; Director, Edinburgh Academy, 1979-88; Vice-President, Royal Blind Asylum and School, since 1987; President, Scottish Young Lawyers' Association, 1988-97; Chairman, St. George's School for Girls, 1989-97; Governor, Napier Polytechnic for Edinburgh, 1989-93; Chancellor's Assessor and Vice Chairman, Court, Edinburgh University, 1993-97. Recreations: music; gardening. Address: (h.) 12 Dublin Street, Edinburgh, EH1 3PP.

Clydesmuir, 3rd Baron (David Ronald Colville); b. 8.4.49; m.; 2 s.; 2 d. Educ. Charterhouse. Succeeded to title, 1996.

Clyne, Rev. Douglas Roy, BD. Minister, Old Parish Church, Fraserburgh, since 1973; b. 9.11.41, Inverness; m., Annette Taylor; 1 s. Educ. Inverness High School; Aberdeen University. Accountancy, Inverness County

Council and Highland Printers Ltd.; studied for ministry; Assistant Minister, Mastrick Parish Church, Aberdeen. Address: (b.) Old Parish Church Manse, 97 Saltoun Place, Fraserburgh AB43 9RY; T.-01346 518536; e-mail: manse1@supanet.com

Coats, Sir William David, Kt, DL, HonLLD (Strathclyde), 1977. Chairman, Coats Patons PLC, 1981-86; Deputy Chairman, Clydesdale Bank PLC, 1985-93; b. 25.7.24, Glasgow; m., The Hon. Elizabeth L.G. MacAndrew; 2 s.; 1 d. Educ. Eton College. Joined J. & P. Coats Ltd., 1948, as management trainee; held various appointments and became a Director, 1957; appointed Director, Coats Patons PLC, on its formation, 1960; Deputy Chairman, 1979. Recreations: golf; shooting. Address: (h.) The Cottage, Symington, Ayrshire KA1 5QG.

Cobbe, Professor Stuart Malcolm, MA, MD, FRCP. Professor of Medical Cardiology, Glasgow University, since 1985; b. 25.48, Watford; m., Patricia Frances; 3 d. Educ. Royal Grammar School, Guildford; Cambridge University. Training in medicine, Cambridge and St. Thomas Hospital, London; qualified, 1972; specialist training in cardiology, National Heart Hospital, London, and John Radcliffe Hospital, Oxford; research work, University of Heidelberg, 1981; Consultant Cardiologist and Senior Lecturer, Oxford, 1982-85. Recreation: walking. Address: (b.) Department of Medical Cardiology, Queen Elizabeth Building, Royal Infirmary, Glasgow G31 2ER; T.-0141-211 4722.

Cochran, Hugh Douglas, BA (Oxon), LLB. Advocate in Aberdeen, since 1958; b. 26.4.32, Aberdeen; m., Sarah Beverly Sissons; 4 s.; 2 d. Educ. Loretto; Trinity College, Oxford; Edinburgh University. Partner: Cochran & Macpherson, 1958-80, Adam, Cochran, 1980-93; Member, Grampian Health Board, 1980-88; Chairman, Castlehill Housing Association, 1974-83. Secretary, Aberdeen Association for the Prevention of Cruelty to Animals, 1972-96; Registrar, Diocese of Aberdeen and Orkney, 1984-98. Recreations: cycling; collecting stamps; archaeology. Address: 16 Huntly Mews, Aboyne AB34 5QP.

Cochrane, Keith Robertson, BAcc (Hons), CA. Group Chief Executive, Stagecoach Group plc, since 2000; b. 11.2.65, Edinburgh; m., Fiona Margaret; 1 s.; 1 d. Educ. Dunblane High School; Glasgow University. Audit Manager Arthur Andersen, 1990 -93; Financial Consultant/Company Secretary, Stagecoach Holdings, 1993-96; Group Finance Director, Stagecoach Holdings, 1996-2000. Recreations: golf; music; travel; reading. Address: (b.) Stagecoach Group plc, 10 Dunkeld Road, Perth, PH1 5TW; T.-01738 442111; e-mail: kcochrane@stagecoachgroup.com

Cochrane of Cults, 4th Baron (Ralph Henry Vere Cochrane), DL; b. 20.9.26; m.; 2 s.; succeeded to title, 1990. Educ. Eton; King's College, Cambridge.

Cockburn, David William, LLB, WS, NP. Senior Partner, Archibald Campbell and Harley WS, since 1970; b. 4.2.43, Peebles; m., Evelyn; 1 d. Educ. Peebles High School; Edinburgh University. Apprentice, Glasgow Corporation, 1964-66; Assistant: Breeze Paterson and Chapman, Glasgow, 1966-69, Archibald Campbell and Harley, WS, 1969-70; lectures widely on commercial property and planning law. Recreations: sports; hillwalking. Address: (b.) 37 Queen Street, Edinburgh EH2 1JX; T.-0131-220 3000.

Cockburn, Professor Forrester, CBE, FRSE, MD, FRCPGlas, FRCPEdin, FRCPCH (Hon), FRCSEd (Hon), DCH. Past Chairman, Yorkhill NHS Trust; Emeritus Professor and Senior Research Fellow, Department of Child Health, Royal Hospital for Sick Children, Yorkhill, Glasgow; formerly Samson Gemmell Professor of Child Health, Glasgow University; b. 13.10.34, Edinburgh; m.,

Alison Fisher Grieve; 2 s. Educ. Leith Academy; Edinburgh University. Early medical training, Edinburgh Royal Infirmary, Royal Hospital for Sick Children, Edinburgh, and Simpson Memorial Maternity Pavilion, Edinburgh; Research Fellow in Paediatric Metabolic Disease, Boston University; Visiting Professor, San Juan University, Puerto Rico; Nuffield Fellow, Institute for Medical Research, Oxford University; Wellcome Senior Research Fellow, then Senior Lecturer, Department of Child Life and Health, Edinburgh University. Publications: a number of textbooks on paediatric medicine, neonatal medicine, nutrition and metabolic diseases. Recreation: sailing. Address: (b.) University Department of Child Health, Royal Hospital for Sick Children, Yorkhill Glasgow, G3 8SJ; T.-0141-201 0236.

Cocker, Douglas, DA, ARSA. Sculptor; b. 23.3.45, Alyth, Perthshire; m., Elizabeth Filshie; 2 s.; 1 d. Educ. Blairgowrie High School; Duncan of Jordanstone College of Art, Dundee. SED Travelling Scholar, Italy and Greece, 1966; RSA Andrew Carnegie Travelling Scholar, 1967; RSA Benno Schotz Award, 1967; Greenshields Foundation (Montreal) Fellowship, 1968-69 (studies in New York and Greece); RSA Latimer Award, 1970; Arts Council of GB Award, 1977; East Midlands Arts Award, 1979; Scottish Arts Council Major Bursary, 1989; Lecturer in Sculpture, Grays School of Art, Aberdeen, 1982-90; Essex Fine Art Fellowship, 1991-92; Visiting Artist: Newcastle Polytechnic, Duncan of Jordanstone College of Art, Edinburgh College of Art, Glasgow Art College and Tyler University, Philadelphia. Numerous solo and group exhibitions; various major public commissions. Recreations: reading; travel; sport. Address: (h.) Lundie Mill, Lundie, Angus DD2 5NW.

Cockhead, Peter, BSc (Econ), MA, MSc, MRTPI. Director of Planning and Strategic Development, Aberdeen City Council, since 1995; b. 1.12.46, Beckenham; m., Diana Douglas; 2 s.; 1 d. Educ. Beckenham Grammar School; London School of Economics; University of Witwatersrand, South Africa; University of Edinburgh. Lecturer: University of Witwatersrand, 1970-71, University of Edinburgh, 1973-74; Consultant: OECD, Paris, 1974, Percy Johnson-Marshall and Associates, Edinburgh, 1974-75; Grampian Regional Council: Assistant Director of Planning, 1975-83, Depute Director of Planning, 1983-90, Regional Planning Manager, 1990-95. Chairman, Scottish Society of Directors of Planning, 1997-98; Chairman, Scottish Planning Education Forum, 1999-2000; Executive Secretary, North Sea Commission, 1992-95. Recreations: hillwalking; swimming; music; family. Address: (h.) 158 Midstocket Road, Aberdeen AB15 5HT; T.-01224 522270.

Coffey, Daniel, JP. Councillor, East Ayrshire; Provost, Kilmarnock and Loudoun District, 1992-96; b. 19.7.54, Kilmarnock. Educ. St. Joseph's, Kilmarnock. SNP Group Leader: Kilmarnock and Loudoun District, 1988-92, Strathclyde Regional Council, 1986-90; SNP Group Leader and Leader of the Opposition: Strathclyde Regional Council, 1994-96, East Ayrshire Council, 1995-99; Member, Justices Committee, East Ayrshire; Convener, East Ayrshire Liaison Committee, 1999-2000; Member, European Committee of the Regions, 1994-98; Bureau Member and Treasurer, European Alliance Group; Convener, Convention of Scottish Local Authorities SNP Group, 1992-96; Member, SNP National Executive, National Council and National Assembly; former SNP Depute Spokesperson, Europe, Foreign Affairs, and Local Government; former Treasurer and Convener, Association of Nationalist Councillors; Treasurer: Kilmarnock FC Supporters Association, Kilmarnock FC Supporters Travel Club; Hon. President: Burns Federation, Kilmarnock Amateur Operatic Society. Recreations: football supporter; marathon runner; Burns. Address: (h.) 7 Craufurdland

Road, Kilmarnock, KA3 2HT; T.-01563 531916; (b.) East Ayrshire Council, London Road Centre, London Road, Kilmarnock KA3 7BU; T.-01563 576055.

Cogdell, Professor Richard John, BSc, PhD, FRSE. Hooker Professor of Botany, Glasgow University, since 1993; b. 4.2.49, Guildford; m., Barbara; 1 s.; 1 d. Educ. Royal Grammar School, Guildford; Bristol University. Post-doctoral research, USA, 1973-75; Botany Department, Glasgow University, 1975-94, now Institute of Biomedical and Life Sciences. Member, Board of Governors, Scottish Crop Research Institute. Recreations: cricket; aerobics; Scottish dancing; theatre. Address: (b.) Division of Biochemistry and Molecular Biology, Glasgow University, Glasgow G12 8QQ; T.-0141-330 4232; e-mail: R.Cogdell@bio.gla.ac.uk

Coggins, Professor John Richard, MA, PhD, FRSE. Professor of Enzymology and Director/Dean, Institute of Biomedical and Life Sciences, Glasgow University, since 2000; b. 15.1.44, Bristol; m., Dr. Lesley F. Watson; 1 s.; 1 d. Educ. Bristol Grammar School; Queen's College, Oxford; Ottawa University. Post-doctoral Fellow: Biology Department, Brookhaven National Laboratory, New York, 1970-72, Biochemistry Department, Cambridge University, 1972-74; Glasgow University: Lecturer/Senior Lecturer/ Professor, Biochemistry Department, 1974-95, Director, Graduate School of Biomedical and Life Sciences, 1995-97, Head, Division of Biochemistry and Molecular Biology, 1997-98, Research Director, Institute of Biomedical and Life Sciences, 1998-2000. Chairman: Molecular Enzymology Group, Biochemical Society, 1982-85, Biophysics and Biochemistry Committee, SERC, 1985-88; Managing Director, Biomac Ltd., 1988-94; Member, DTI-Research Councils Biotechnology Joint Advisory Board, 1989-94; Member of Council, AFRC, 1991-94; Biochemistry Adviser to UFC, 1989-92; Member of Council, Hannah Research Institute, since 1994; Governing Member, Caledonian Research Foundation, since 1994; Chairman, HEFC Research Assessment Panel for Biochemistry, 1995-96; Research Awards Convener, Royal Society of Edinburgh, since 1999. Recreations: sailing; travelling. Address: (b.) Planning Office, IBLS, West Medical Building, Glasgow University, Glasgow G12 8QQ; T.-0141-330 3524; e-mail: j.coggins@bio.gla.ac.uk

Cohen, Professor Anthony Paul, BA, MSc (SocSc), PhD, FRSE. Professor of Social Anthropology, Edinburgh University, since 1989; Provost of Law and Social Sciences, Dean, Social Sciences, Edinburgh University, since 1997; Convener, Scottish Forum for Graduate Education, 1996-98; b. 3.8.46, London; m., Dr. Bronwen J. Cohen; 3 s. Educ. Whittingehame College, Brighton; Southampton University. Research Fellow, Memorial University of Newfoundland, 1968-70; Assistant Professor, Queen's University, Kingston, Ontario, 1970-71; Lecturer/Senior Lecturer in Social Anthropology, Manchester University, 1971-89. Publications: The Management of Myths; The Symbolic Construction of Community; Whalsay: Symbol, Segment and Boundary in a Shetland Island Community; Self Consciousness: an alternative anthropology of identity; Belonging (Editor); Symbolising Boundaries (Editor); Humanising the City? (Co-Editor); Questions of Consciousness (Co-Editor); Signifying Identities (Editor). Recreations: occasional thinking; music; novels. Address: (b.) 55 George Square, Edinburgh EH8 9JH; T.-0131-650 4089.

Cohen, Cyril, OBE, JP, FRCPEdin, FRCPGlas. Honorary Fellow, Dundee University; retired Consultant Physician, Geriatric Medicine, and Hon. Senior Lecturer, Geriatric Medicine, Dundee University; Chairman, Angus Community Care Forum; b. 2.11.25, Manchester; m., Dr. Sarah E. Nixon; 2 s. Educ. Manchester Central High School; Victoria University, Manchester. Embarked on career in geriatric medicine, 1952. Past President,

Forfarshire Medical Association; former Chairman, Advisory Group on Health Education for Elderly People, Health Education Board for Scotland; former Member/Chairman, Angus District and Tayside Area Medical Committees; Secretary/Chairman, Tayside Area Hospital Medical Services Committee; Member, Scottish and UK Central Committee, Hospital Medical Services, and Chairman, Geriatric Medicine Sub-committee; Past Chairman, Scottish Branch, British Geriatric Society (former Council Member); Member, Panel on Nutrition of the Elderly, COMA; Honorary Vice-President, Dundee and District Branch, British Diabetic Association; Life Member, Manchester Medical Society; former Member, Chief Scientist's Committee for Research on Equipment for the Disabled and Health Services Research Committee; former Chairman, Angus Access Panel; Director, Angus Community Care Charitable Trust; Director, Angus Care and Repair; Member, Angus Joint Planning Group, Care in the Community; Member, Angus SVQ Management Committee; Honorary President, Radio North Angus (Hospital Radio); former Member, Brechin and Forfar School Councils, Forfar Academy School Board and Central Committee on Primary Education; Secretary, Aberlemno Community Council; former Vice-Chairman, Angus Association of Voluntary Organisations and Member, Brechin Day Care Centre Committee; former Director, Scottish Hospital Advisory Service; Past President, Montrose Burns Club and Brechin Arts Guild; Member, League of Friends, Forfar Hospitals; Past Chairman, Angus Care of the Elderly Group; Member, Age Concern Angus Executive. Publications: many on geriatric medicine and care of the elderly. Recreations: photography; short walks; being at home. Address: (h.) Mansefield, Aberlemno, Forfar DD8 3PD; T.-0130-783 259.

Cohen, Lady Patricia Townsend Wade, BSc, PhD. Professor of Molecular Biology, Dundee University, since 2001; Head of Molecular Biology and Special Appointments Scientist, Medical Research Council Protein Phosphorylation Unit, Department of Biochemistry, Dundee University; b. 3.5.44, Worsley, Lancashire; m., Professor Sir Philip Cohen (qv); 1 s.; 1 d. Educ. Bolton School; University College, London. Postdoctoral Research Fellow, Department of Medical Genetics, Washington University, Seattle, USA, 1969-71; Department of Biochemistry, Dundee University: Science Research Council Fellowship, 1971-72, Research/Teaching Fellow (part-time), 1972-83, Lecturer (part-time), 1983-90, Senior Lecturer, 1990-91, Reader, 1995. Publications: 120 papers and reviews in scientific journals. Recreations: reading; skiing; golf. Address: (h.) Inverbay II, Invergowrie, Dundee DD2 5DQ; T.-01382 562328; e-mail: p.t.w.cohen@dundee.ac.uk

Cohen, Professor Sir Philip, BSc, PhD, FRS, FRSE, FRSA. Royal Society Research Professor, University of Dundee, since 1984 and Director, Wellcome Trust Biocentre, since 1997; Honorary Director, Medical Research Council Protein Phosphorylation Unit, since 1990; b. 22.7.45, London; m., Patricia Townsend Wade (qv); 1 s.; 1 d. Educ. Hendon County Grammar School; University College, London. Science Research Council/NATO postdoctoral Fellow, Department of Biochemistry, University of Washington, 1969-71; Dundee University: Lecturer in Biochemistry, 1971-78, Reader in Biochemistry, 1978-81, Professor of Enzymology, 1981-84. Publications: 400 papers and reviews, one book. Recreations: bridge; golf; natural history. Address: (h.) Inverbay II, Invergowrie, Dundee; T.-01382 562328.

Cohn, Professor Samuel Kline, MA, PhD, FRHistS. Professor of History, Glasgow University, since 1995; b. 1949, Birmingham, Alabama; m., Genevieve Warwick; 2 s. Educ. Indian Springs School; Harvard University. Assistant Professor, Wesleyan University, Connecticut, 1978-79; Assistant Professor, Brandeis University, 1979-86; Associate Professor of History, Brandeis University,

1986-89; Visiting Professor, Brown University, 1990-91; Professor of History, Brandeis University, 1989-95. Publications include: Women in the Streets: Essays on Sex and Power in the Italian Renaissance, 1996; The Cult of Remembrance and the Black Death: Six Renaissance Cities in Central Italy, 1997; The Black Death and the Transformation of the West (Co-author), 1997; Creating the Florentine State: Peasants and Rebellion, 1348-1434, 1999; The Black Death Transformed: Disease and Culture in Early Renaissance Europe, 2002. Recreation: hill-running. Address: (h.) 14 Hamilton Drive, Glasgow; T.-0141-330 4369.

Cole-Hamilton, Professor David John, BSc, PhD, CChem, FRSC, FRSE. Irvine Professor of Chemistry, St. Andrews University, since 1985; b. 22.5.48, Bovey Tracey; m., Elizabeth Ann Brown; 2 s.; 2 d. Educ. Haileybury and ISC; Hertford; Edinburgh University. Research Assistant, Temporary Lecturer, Imperial College, 1974-78; Lecturer, Senior Lecturer, Liverpool University, 1978-85. Sir Edward Frankland Fellow, Royal Society of Chemistry, 1984-85; Corday Morgan Medallist, 1983; President: Chemistry Section, British Association for the Advancement of Science, 1995, Chemistry Sectional Committee, Royal Society of Edinburgh, 1993-95; Vice President, Royal Society of Chemistry, Dalton Council, 1996-99. Museums and Galleries Commission Award for Innovation in Conservation, 1995 (runner-up); Royal Society of Chemistry Award for Organometallic Chemists, 1998; Tilden Lecturer, Royal Society of Chemistry, 2000-2001; Scientific Editor, Journal of the Chemical Society, Dalton Transactions, since 2000. Address: (b.) Department of Chemistry, The Purdie Building, St. Andrews, Fife KY16 9ST; T.-01334 463805.

Collingham, Lynne, LLB (Hons), DipLP. Associate Solicitor, Goldsmith and Hughes, Solicitors, East Kilbride; Secretary/Treasurer, Scottish Sunday School Union for Christian Education, since 1993; b. 1.4.67, Glasgow; m., Douglas; 2 s. Educ. Woodfarm High School; University of Glasgow. AJ&A Graham Solicitors, Glasgow, 1990-92; Associate Solicitor, Andrew MacAllan and Son, Glasgow, 1992-99. Address: (b.) 51 Strathmore House, Princes Square, East Kilbride; (h.) 2 Fraser Avenue, Newton Mearns, Glasgow G77 6HW; T.-0141-571 7359.

Collings, Peter, PhD. Principal Finance Officer, Scottish Executive; m.; 2 c. Educ. Cambridge University; Sheffield University. Joined Civil Service, 1975; joined Scottish Office, 1977: posts held include Director of Finance, NHS Management Executive, Principal Finance Officer, Head of Finance. Address: Victoria Quay, Edinburgh EH6 6QQ.

Collins, Professor David John, BEd, MSc, AdDipCouns, PhD. Chair of Physical Education and Sport Performance, and Head, Department of Physical Education, Sport and Leisure, University of Edinburgh, since 1998; accredited sport psychologist working with athletes, since 1984; b. 31.12.53, Forest of Dean, Gloucester; divorced; 1 s.; 2 d. Educ. Royal Liberty School, Romford, Essex; Borough Road College, University of London. Officer, Royal Marines; Teacher of PE and Mathematics, public, state and special schools; Senior Lecturer in Movement Studies, St. Mary's College, Twickenham; Visiting Professor, Pennsylvania State University; Senior Lecturer then Reader then Professor, Manchester Metropolitan University. Member, British Olympic Association's Psychology Steering Group. Publications: five books; over 70 scientific publications. Recreations: outdoor pursuits; martial arts; training; curry. Address: University of Edinburgh, Holyrood Road, Edinburgh EH8 8AQ; T.-0131-651 6522.

Collins, Dennis Ferguson, MA, LLB, WS, FRPSL. Senior Partner, Carlton Gilruth, Solicitors, Dundee, 1976-93; Honorary Sheriff; b. 26.3.30, Dundee; m., Elspeth Margaret Nicoll; 1 s.; 1 d. Educ. High School of Dundee; St.

Andrews University. Part-time Lecturer in Scots Law, St. Andrews University, then Dundee University, 1960-79; Agent Consulaire for France in Dundee, 1976-96; Hon. Secretary, Dundee Society for Prevention of Cruelty to Children, 1962-90; Treasurer, Dundee Congregational Church, since 1966; Past President, Dundee and District Philatelic Society; Past President, Association of Scottish Philatelic Societies; Dean, Faculty of Procurators and Solicitors in Dundee, 1987-89. Recreations: Chinese postal history; gardening; Sherlock Holmes pursuits; travelling in France. Address: (h.) Stirling House, Craigiebarn Road, Dundee DD4 7PL; T.-01382 458070.

Collins, Kenneth Darlington, BSc (Hons), MSc. Chairman, Scottish Environment Protection Agency, since 1999; Member (Labour), European Parliament, 1979-99; b. 12.8.39, Hamilton; m., Georgina Frances Pollard; 1 s.; 1 d. Educ. St. John's Grammar School; Hamilton Academy; Glasgow University; Strathclyde University. Steelworks apprentice, 1956-59; University, 1960-65; Planning Officer, 1965-66; WEA Tutor, 1966-67; Lecturer: Glasgow College of Building, 1967-69, Paisley College of Technology, 1969-79; Member: East Kilbride Town and District Council, 1973-79, Lanark County Council, 1973-75, East Kilbride Development Corporation, 1976-79; Chairman, NE Glasgow Children's Panel, 1974-76; European Parliament: Deputy Leader, Labour Group, 1979-84, Chairman, Environment Committee, 1979-84 and 1989-99 (Vice-Chairman, 1984-87), Socialist Spokesman on Environment, Public Health and Consumer Protection, 1984-89; Fellow, Royal Scottish Geographical Society; Hon. Fellow, Chartered Institute of Water and Environment Management; Hon. Fellow, Institute of Waste Management; Board Member, Institute for European Environmental Policy, London; Fellow, Industry and Parliament Trust; Board Member, Energy Action Scotland; Member, British Waterways Scotland Group; Chairman, Central Scotland Countryside Trust, 1998-2001; Chairman, Tak Tent Cancer Support, since 1999. Recreations: music; boxer dogs; gardening; occasional golf. Address: (b.) 11 Stuarton Park, East Kilbride G74 4LA; T.-013552 37282; e-mail: kencollins@kcollins.fsbusiness.co.uk

Collins, Kenneth E., MPhil, PhD, MRCGP. Hon. Vice-President, Glasgow Jewish Representative Council, since 2001 (Hon. President, 1998-2001, President, 1995-98); Chairman, Scottish Council of Jewish Communities; b. 23.12.47, Glasgow; m., Irene Taylor; 1 s.; 3 d. Educ. High School of Glasgow; Glasgow University. General medical practitioner in Glasgow, since 1976; Medical Officer, Newark Lodge, Glasgow, since 1978; Research Associate, Wellcome Unit for the History of Medicine, Glasgow University. Past Chairman, Glasgow Board of Jewish Education. Publications: Aspects of Scottish Jewry, 1987; Go and Learn: International Story of the Jews and Medicine in Scotland, 1988; Second City Jewry, 1990. Address: (h.) 3 Glenburn Road, Giffnock, Glasgow G46 6RE.

Coltrane, Robbie, DA. Actor/Director; b. 31.3.50, Glasgow. Educ. Trinity College, Glenalmond; Glasgow School of Art. Film credits: Subway Riders, 1979, Balham Gateway to the South, 1980, Britannia Hospital, 1981, Scrubbers, 1982, Krull, 1982, Ghost Dance, 1983, Chinese Boxes, 1984, The Supergrass, 1984, Defense of the Realm, 1985, Revolution, 1985, Caravaggio, 1985, Absolute Beginners, 1985, Mona Lisa, 1985, Eat the Rich, 1987, The Fruit Machine, 1987, Slipstream, 1988, Bert Rigby, You're a Fool, 1988, Danny Champion of the World, 1988, Let It Ride, 1988, Henry V, 1988, Nuns on the Run, 1989, Perfectly Normal, 1989, Pope Must Die, 1990, Oh What A Night, 1991, Adventures of Huck Finn, 1992, Goldeneye, 1995, Buddy, 1996, Montana, 1997, Frogs for Snakes, 1997, Message in a Bottle, 1998, The World Is Not Enough, 1999, From Hell, 2000, Harry Potter and the Philosopher's Stone, 2001; theatre credits: The Bug, 1976, Mr Joyce is Leaving, 1978, The Slab Boys, 1978, The Transfiguration

of Benno Blimpie, 1978, The Loveliest Night of the Year, 1979-80, Dick Whittington, 1979, Snobs and Yobs, 1980, Yr Obedient Servant (one-man show), 1987, Mistero Buffo (one-man show), 1990; television credits include: roles in several The Comic Strip Presents productions, lead role in Tutti Frutti (BBC Scotland), Alive and Kicking, 1991, Coltrane in a Cadillac, 1992, Cracker, 1993, 1994, 1995, Ebbtide, 1996, Coltrane's Planes and Automobiles, 1997, Alice in Wonderland, 1998. Recreations: vintage cars; sailing; painting; reading; movies. Address: c/o CDA, 19 Sydney Mews, London SW3 6HL.

Colville of Culross, 4th Viscount (John Mark Alexander Colville, QC); b. 19.7.33; m.; 1 s.; 4 s. by pr. m. Educ. Rugby; New College, Oxford. Barrister; Minister of State, Home Office, 1972-74; Director, Securities and Futures Authority, 1987-93; Chairman: Mental Health Act Commission, 1983-88, Alcohol Education and Research Council, 1984-90, Parole Board, 1988-92; UK Representative, UN Human Rights Commission, 1980-83; Member, UN Working Group on Disappeared Persons, 1980-84 (Chairman, 1981-84); Special Rapporteur on Human Rights in Guatemala, 1983-86; Member, UN Human Rights Committee, since 1996; reports on Prevention of Terrorism Act and Northern Ireland Emergency Powers Act, 1986-93; Circuit Judge, 1995-99, Assistant Surveillance Commissioner, since 2001.

Colvin, Professor Calum Munro, OBE, DA, MA (RCA). Professor of Fine Art Photography, Dundee University, since 2001; artist, since 1985; b. 26.10.61, Glasgow; m., Shirley Jean; 2 s.; 1 d. Educ. North Berwick High School; Duncan of Jordanstone College of Art and Design; Royal College of Art, London. Lecturer in Fine Art, Duncan of Jordanstone, Dundee University, from 1993; Research Fellow in Digital Imaging, University of Northumbria, 1995-96; 13th Higashikawa Overseas Photographer Prize, 1997; has exhibited work internationally since 1986 with work in many collections; recent solo exhibitions include Scottish National Gallery of Modern Art, 1998, University of Salamanca, 1998; Kawasaki City Museum, 1998.Address: (h.) 25 Marlborough Street, Edinburgh EH15 2BD; T.-0131-669 0218.

Colvin, David, CBE, DUniv (Stirling). Chair, SACRO; Governor, St Columba's Hospice; Scottish Correspondent, Action on Child Exploitation; Chair, Exhibiting Societies of Scotland Association; Vice Chair, Scottish Consortium on Crime and Criminal Justice; b. 31.1.31, Glasgow; m., Elma; 2 s.; 3 d. Educ. Whitehill School, Glasgow; Glasgow University; Edinburgh University. Probation Officer, Glasgow, 1955-60; Psychiatric Social Worker, Scottish Prison Service, 1960-61; Crichton Royal Hospital, Dumfries, 1961-65; Family Service Unit, Paisley, 1965-66; Adviser in Social Work, then Chief Adviser in Social Work, Scottish Office, 1966-91; Director of Social Work, Shetland, 1991. Former Chair, Dumfries Constituency Labour Party; former Chair, Scottish Marriage Council; Governor, National Institute for Social Work, 1981-91; Scottish Secretary, British Association of Social Workers, 1992-96; Scottish Chair, NCH Action for Children, 1992-97; Trustee, Scottish Disability Foundation, since 1999. Recreations: mountaineering; encouragement of fine and applied arts. Address: (h.) The Studio, 53 Windsor Place, Edinburgh EH15 2AF; T.-0131-468 0087.

Comerford, Michael Brendan, BSc (Hons), CEng, MRINA. Regional Manager, Scotland and N. Ireland, Maritime and Coastguard Agency, since 1999; b. 16.3.61, Rawtenstall; m., Caroline Dorothee Searle; 2 s.; 1 d. Educ. St Bede's College, Manchester; Southampton University. Surveyor, Lloyd's Register of Shipping; manufacturing executive, Procter and Gamble; Surveyor, SW England and Wales, Bureau Veritas; Centre Manager Aberdeen, Chief of District NE Scotland, nominated Senior Executive BVQI Scotland, Bureau Veritas; Managing Director, Marine Division, Lithgows Ltd.; Managing Director: Buckie Shipyard Ltd., Campbeltown Shipyard Ltd., Malakoff and Wm. Moore Ltd., J. Fleming Engineering Ltd. Management Committee Member, Milltown Community; School Board Member; Parochial Council Member. Recreations: music (contemporary folk and classical guitar); outdoor sports; photography. Address: (b.) Marine House, Blaikies Quay, Aberdeen AB11 5EZ; T.-01224 574122.

Comins, David, MA, PGCE. Rector, The Glasgow Academy, since 1994; b. 1.3.48, Scarborough; m., (Christine) Anne Speak; 1 s.; 2 d. Educ. Scarborough Boys' High School; Downing College, Cambridge. Assistant Maths Teacher: Mill Hill School, 1971-75, Strathallan School, 1975-76, Glenalmond College, 1976-80; Head of Maths, then Director of Studies, Glenalmond College, 1980-89; Deputy Head, Queen's College, Taunton, 1989-94. Winston Churchill Fellow, 1981. Recreations: mountaineering; ballet; crosswords; music. Address: (h.) 11 Kirklee Terrace, Glasgow G12 OTH; T.-0141-357 1776; e-mail: rector@theglasgowacademy.org.uk

Comley, David John, BSc, PhD, FIH. Director of Housing Services, Glasgow City Council, since 1988; b. 25.4.50, Carshalton. Educ. Ashlyns School, Berkhamsted; Birmingham University. Housing Management Trainee, then District Housing Manager, Dudley Metropolitan Borough, 1976-80; District Housing Manager, then Assistant Director, then Depute Director, Glasgow City Council. Chair, Scottish Asylum Seekers Consortium, since 2000. Recreations: jazz; classical music; hill-walking; literature; cinema; theatre. Address: (b.) Wheatley House, 25 Cochrane Street, Glasgow, G1 1HZ; e-mail: david.comley@gch.glasgow.gov.uk

Conn, Stewart. Poet and playwright; b. 1936, Glasgow, brought up Kilmarnock. Educ. Glasgow University. Author of numerous stage plays, including The Burning, Herman, The Aquarium, By the Pool, Clay Bull; television work includes The Kite, Bloodhunt; recent poetry includes In the Kibble Palace, The Luncheon of the Boating Party, At the Aviary, In the Blood; Stolen Light; Distances: a personal evocation of people and places; his production of Carver (by John Purser) won Gold Medal Award, International Radio Festival, 1991; left BBC, 1992; e-mail: stewart@jsconn.freeserve.co.uk

Connaghan, John, BA, MBA. Chief Executive, Fife Acute Hospitals, since 1998; Director, National Waiting Times Unit, since 2002; b. 2.9.54, Glasgow; 3 s.; 1 d. Educ. St Mungo's Academy; Strathclyde University. General Manager, Chas Letts (Scotland) Ltd., 1980; General Manager, South Glasgow, NHS, 1987; Chief Executive, Western General, Edinburgh, 1992. Director, OPEX Ltd., since 1998; Director, MKJCCT, since 1998; Board Member, CRAG, since 1999. Recreations: fine wine; golf. T.-07836 704107.

Connal, Robert Craig, LLB(Hons). Solicitor, since 1977; Partner, McGrigor Donald, since 1980; Solicitor Advocate, since 1996; b. 7.7.54, Brentwood; m., Mary Ferguson Bowie; 2 d. Educ. Hamilton Academy; University of Glasgow. Apprentice, Brown, Mair, Gemmill & Hislop, 1975-77; Assistant, McGrigor Donald, 1977-1980. Council Member, Royal Faculty of Procurators in Glasgow, 1995-98; Member, Thorntonhall Community Council (Chairman, Planning Committee), 1997-99. Publications: Contributor, Stair Memorial Encyclopedia; many articles in press and professional journals. Recreations: rugby referee; gardens (but not gardening). Address: (b.) Pacific House, 70 Wellington Street, Glasgow G2 6SB; T.-0141-248 6677; e-mail: craig.connal@mcgrigors.com

Connarty, Michael, BA, DCE. MP (Labour), Falkirk East, since 1992; Secretary, All-Party Group for Chemical Industries; Member, House of Commons Information Select Committee; Board Member, Parliamentary Office of Science and Technology; Member, European Scrutiny Select Committee, since 1998; Secretary, Parliamentary Offshore Oil and Gas Group; Chair, Parliamentary Jazz Appreciation Group, since 1999; b. 3.9.47, Coatbridge; m., Margaret Doran; 1 s.; 1 d. Educ. Stirling University; Jordanhill College of Education; Glasgow University. Member, Scottish Executive, Labour Party, 1981-92; Chair, Labour Party Scottish Local Government Committee, 1988-90; Chairman, Scottish Parliamentary Labour Party Group, 1998-99; Member: Convention of Scottish Local Authorities, 1980-90 (Depute Labour Leader, 1988-90), Stirling District Council, 1977-90 (Council Leader, 1980-90); Vice-Chair, Socialist Educational Association, 1983-85; Council Member, Educational Institute of Scotland, 1984-85; Founding Secretary, Labour Coordinating Committee (Scotland); Vice-Chairman, Scottish MAP, 1988-95; Scottish Task Force Leader on Skills and Training in Scotland and Youth and Students, 1995-97; Member, Select Committee on the Parliamentary Commissioner for Administration, 1995-97; Chair, Economy, Industry and Energy Committee, Scottish PLP Group, 1993-97; Scottish Co-ordinator, Labour Crime and Drugs Campaign, 1993-97; PPS to Tom Clarke, MP, 1987-88; Secretary, PLP Science and Technology Comittee, 1992-97; Member, European Directives Committee on Agriculture, Environment and Health and Safety, 1993-96. Recreations: family; hill-walking; reading; music; Falkirk FC; Bo'ness United FC. Address: (b.) 5 Kerse Road, Grangemouth FK3 8HQ; T.-01324 474832.

Connell, Douglas Andrew, LLB, NP, WS, FRSA. Joint Senior Partner, Turcan Connell; b. 18.5.54, Callander; m., Marjorie Elizabeth; 2 s. Educ. McLaren High School; Edinburgh University. Qualified as a solicitor, 1976; admitted as a Writer to the Signet, 1976; President, Scottish Young Lawyers Association, 1975-76; Tutor in Scots Law, Edinburgh University, 1974-76; Partner, Dundas and Wilson, 1979-97. Member, Revenue Committee, Law Society of Scotland, 1979-92; Scottish Arts Council: Member, 1994-97, Chairman, Lottery Committee, 1994-97; Member, Edinburgh Festival Council, 1997-2001; Trustee: Pushkin Prizes in Scotland, Art Galleries of Scotland Foundation, Usher Hall Conservation Trust, Historic Scotland Foundation; Patron, National Galleries of Scotland; Fellow, Royal Society of Arts; Chairman, Edinburgh Book Festival, 1991-95. Recreations: books; travel; good food. Address: (b.) Princes Exchange, 1 Earl Grey Street, Edinburgh EH3 9EE; T.-0131-228 8111; e-mail: dac@turcanconnell.com

Connell, Professor John Muir Cochrane, MBChB, MD, FRCP, FAHA, FMedSci. Professor of Endocrinology, Glasgow University, since 1996; Honorary Consultant Physician, Western Infirmary, Glasgow, since 1987; b. 10.10.54; m., Dr Lesley Connell; 3 s.; 1 d. Educ. Hutchesons' Grammar School; Glasgow University. Research Fellow, MRC Blood Pressure Unit, Western Infirmary, Glasgow; MRC Travelling Fellow, Howard Florey Institute, Melbourne, 1986-87; Senior Clinical Scientist and Hon. Consultant Phsyician, MRC Blood Pressure Unit, 1987-94; Professor in Medicine, Department of Medicine and Therapeutics, Western Infirmary, 1994-96. Honorary Secretary, Association of Physicians of Gt. Britain and Ireland; Member, grant-awarding committees, British Heart Foundation, etc. Recreations: family; golf. Address: (b.) Department of Medicine and Therapeutics, Western Infirmary, Glasgow G11 6NT; T.-0141-211 2108.

Connelly, David, MA (Oxon), FSAScot. Trustee and Secretary, Buildings of Scotland Trust, since 1990; b. 23.2.30, Halifax; m., Audrey Grace Salter; 1 s.; 1 d. Educ. Heath Grammar School, Halifax; Queen's College, Oxford. Colonial Administrative Service, Tanganyika, 1954-62; Assistant Secretary, St. Andrews University, 1962-63; Principal, Commonwealth Relations Office, 1963-64; First Secretary, British High Commission, New Delhi, 1964-66; Principal, Scottish Office, 1966-73; Assistant Secretary, 1973-87; Director, Historic Buildings and Monuments, Scotland, 1987-90; Chairman, Cockburn Conservation Trust, Edinburgh, 1990-96. Recreations: opera; literature; history; architecture; walking the hills; country life. Address: c/o Royal Bank of Scotland plc, 36 St. Andrew Square, Edinburgh EH2 2YB.

Connolly, Billy. Stand-up comedian; actor; television presenter; b. 24.11.42; m. 1., Iris (m. dissolved) 1 s.; 1 d.; 2, Pamela Stephenson; 3 d. Welder, Clyde shipyards; began showbusiness career with Gerry Rafferty as The Humblebums; first solo concert, 1971; has toured throughout the world with stand-up comedy shows; television: Androcles and the Lion, Head of the Class (USA), Billy (USA), Billy Connolly's World Tour of Scotland (Scottish BAFTA: Best Entertainment Programme), Down Among the Big Boys (Scottish BAFTA: Best Drama), The Bigger Picture (Scottish BAFTA: Best Arts Programme), The Life and Crimes of Deacon Brodie, Billy Connolly's World Tour of Australia, Return to Nose and Beak (Comic Relief special), Billy Connolly: A Scot in the Arctic; Gentleman's Relish; films: Absolution, Bullshot, Water, The Big Man, Treasure Island (Muppet movie), Mrs Brown, Still Crazy, The Changeling, PAWS, The Debt Collector, The Boon Dock Saints, The Imposters, Beautiful Joe; An Everlasting Piece; Cletis Tour; Gabriel and Me; appeared with Scottish Opera in Die Fledermaus; theatre: wrote The Red Runner, performed in The Beastly Beatitudes of Blathazar B; videos: Live at Hammersmith, Bite Your Bum (Music Week and Record Business Award, 1981), Hand-picked By Billy Connolly, 25 BC, Billy and Albert, An Audience with Billy Connolly, Billy Connolly Live, Live '94, World Tour of Scotland (Two Bites of), World Tour of Australia, Two Night Stand; tribute television programme and video: Erect for 30 Years; gold disc for album Pick of Billy Connolly, 1982; UK No. 1 hit with D.I.V.O.R.C.E.; books: Gullible's Travels, 1982, Billy Connolly's World Tour of Australia, 1996. Address: c/o Tickety-boo, The Boat House, Crabtree Lane, London SW6 6TY.

Connolly, Liz, BA (Hons), MBA. Chief Executive, Scottish Enterprise, Lanarkshire; b. 21.11.58, Glasgow. Educ. Our Lady and St. Francis School, Glasgow; Strathclyde University. Media Planner, J.F. Green Associates, 1981-83; Marketing and Economic Research, SDA, 1983-91; Planning Executive in Policy Planning Unit, S.E. National, 1991-92; Head of Strategy then Director of Strategy, LDA, 1992-98; Chief Executive, Enterprise Ayrshire, 1999-2000. Member: Board, Bell College, Board, Strathclyde European Partnership. Recreations: music; theatre; keep fit; socialising. Address: (b.) New Lanarkshire House, Strathclyde Business Park, Bellshill ML4.

Connon, Joyce Blair. Scottish Secretary, Workers Educational Association, since 1992; b. 11.6.47, Edinburgh; m., Neil Connon; 1 s.; 1 d. W.E.A. Tutor Organiser, Lothian, 1988; District Secretary, South-East Scotland, 1989. Chair, Learning Link Scotland; Member, Scottish European Social Fund Objective Three Programme Monitoring Committee; Director, Edinburgh's Lifelong Learning Partnership. Recreations: reading; theatre; walking. Address: (b.) W.E.A., Riddle's Court, 322 Lawnmarket, Edinburgh EH1 2PG; T.-0131-226 3456.

Connor, Professor James Michael, MD, DSc, BSc (Hons), MB, ChB (Hons), FRCP. Professor of Medical Genetics and Director, West of Scotland Regional Genetics Service, since 1987 (Wellcome Trust Senior Lecturer and Honorary Consultant in Medical Genetics, Glasgow University, 1984-87); b. 18.6.51, Grappenhall, England; m., Dr. Rachel A.C. Educ. Lymm Grammar School, Cheshire; Liverpool University. House Officer, Liverpool Royal Infirmary; Resident in Internal Medicine, Johns Hopkins Hospital, USA; University Research Fellow, Liverpool University; Instructor in Internal Medicine, Johns Hopkins Hospital, USA; Consultant in Medical Genetics, Institute of Medical Genetics, Yorkhill, Glasgow. Publications: Essential Medical Genetics (Co-author), 1984 (5th edition, 1997); Principles and Practice of Medical Genetics (Co-Editor), (4th edition, 2002); various articles on aspects of medical genetics. Recreations: windsurfing; white water kayaking. Address: (h.) East Collarie Farm, by Fenwick, Ayrshire.

Considine, John, MA, MEd. Rector, Inverness Royal Academy, since 1993; Director, HI Arts (Chairman, since 1998); b. 26.11.50, Glasgow; m., Hellen L. Campbell; 1 s.; 2 d. Educ. St. Aloysius College; Glasgow University. Teacher: St. Margaret Mary's, Glasgow, 1973, Inverness High, 1974, Millburn Academy, Inverness, 1976; Principal Teacher, then Assistant Rector, Charleston Academy, Inverness, 1978-88; Depute Rector, Woodmill High, Dunfermline, 1988-93. Member, Inverness College Board of Management, and Chair, College Personnel Sub-Committee, 1995-99; President, Highland Secondary Headteachers Association, 1997-98. Recreations: hill-walking; running; squash. Address: (b.) Inverness Royal Academy, Culduthel Road, Inverness; T.-01463 222884.

Constanda, Professor Christian, MSc, PhD, DSc. Professor of Mathematics, Strathclyde University, since 2000; b. 1.1.44, Romania; m., Lia; 1 s. Educ. University of Iasi. Research Fellow, Romanian Academy of Science, 1966; Lecturer, then Senior Lecturer, then Reader, Strathclyde University, 1976-2000; Visiting Professor, Univesity of Tulsa, since 1986; Chairman, International Consortium on Integral Methods in Science and Engineering; Member, Board of Directors, International Society for Analysis, Its Applications and Computation. Publications: four books authored, six edited, two translated; 80 papers. Recreations: reading; music; travel. Address: (b.) Department of Mathematics, Strathclyde University, Livingstone Tower, 26 Richmond Street, Glasgow G1 1XH; T.-0141-548 3714.

Conti, Most Rev. Mario Joseph, STL, PhL, DD, FRSE. Archbishop of Glasgow, since 2002; Bishop of Aberdeen, 1977-2002; Member, Pontifical Council for the Promotion of Christian Unity, Rome, since 1984; Member, Historic Buildings Council of Scotland, since 2000; b. 20.3.34, Elgin. Educ. St. Marie's Convent; Springfield School, Elgin; Blairs College, Aberdeen; Scots College, Pontifical Gregorian University, Rome. Ordained priest, Rome, 1958; Curate, St. Mary's Cathedral, Aberdeen, 1959-62; Parish Priest, St. Joachim's, Wick and St. Anne's, Thurso, 1962-77. Commendatore, Order of Merit, Italian Republic; President-Treasurer, SCIAF, 1977-85; President, National Liturgy Commission, 1981-85; Member, International Commission for English in the Liturgy, 1978-87; Chairman, Scottish Catholic Heritage Commission; President, Commission for Christian Doctrine and Unity, since 1986; first Convener, Central Council, ACTS, 1990; Co-Moderator, Joint Working Group of the World Council of Churches and the Roman Catholic Church, since 1996; Head of Catholic Delegation to 8th General Assembly, World Council of Churches, Harare, 1998; a President, Churches Together in Britain and Ireland, since 1999; Member, Pontifical Commission for the Cultural Heritage of the Church, since 1994; Knight Commander of the Holy Sepulchre, 1989; Conventual Chaplain Ad Honorem, 1991,

Principal Chaplain to British Association of the Sovereign Military Order of Malta, 1995-2000. Recreations: music; art. Address: Bishop's House, 3 Queen's Cross, Aberdeen AB15 4XU; T.-01224 319154.

Convery, Francis, ARSA. Head of Painting, Grays School of Art, Aberdeen, since 1997; b. 12.2.56, Paisley; 3 d. Educ. St. Mirin's Academy, Paisley; Edinburgh College of Art. Part-time Lecturer, Edinburgh College of Art, 1984-86. Solo exhibitions: Edinburgh University Festival Hall, 1984, Mercury Gallery, Edinburgh, 1984, Andrew Grant Gallery, Edinburgh College of Art, 1988; The Scottish Gallery, Edinburgh, 1991 and 1995, Art Wise, British Airways, Aberdeen Airport, 1998-99; exhibited in numerous group exhibitions, Britain and internationally; work in public collections; President, Aberdeen Artists Society, 1996; Member, Selection and Arrangements Committee, Royal Scottish Academy, 1998; Consultant and Adviser, Art Wise, 1997. Address: Davo House, Fordoun, by Laurencekirk, Aberdeenshire AB30 1JL; T.-01561 320920.

Cook, Rev. James Stanley Stephen Ronald Tweedie, BD, DipPSS. Minister, Hamilton West Parish Church, 1974-2001; b. 18.8.35, Tullibody; m., Jean Douglas Maclachlan; 2 s.; 1 d. Educ. Whitehill Senior Secondary School, Glasgow; St Andrews University. Apprentice quantity surveyor, Glasgow, 1953-54; regular soldier, REME, 1954-57; Assistant Preventive Officer, Waterguard Department, HM Customs and Excise, 1957-61; Officer, HM Customs and Excise, 1961-69; studied for the ministry, 1969-74. Chairman, Cruse (Lanarkshire), 1983-93, 1994-99; Chairman, Cruse – Scotland, 1991-95, Convener, since 1999; Member, Council, Cruse UK, 1988-94; Member, National Training Group, Cruse, 1987-94; Member, Action Research for Crippled Child Committee, 1977-94; Substitute Provincial Grand Master, Lanarkshire (Middle Ward), 1983-88; Honorary Provincial Grand Chaplain, since 1989; founder Member, Wishaw Victim Support Scheme, 1985; President, Hamilton Rotary Club, 1994-95; Member, Hamilton Crime Prevention Panel, 1976-2000, Chairman, 1986-87; Moderator, Presbytery of Hamilton, 1999-2000. Recreations: music; photography; DIY; computer work. Address: Mansend, 137a Old Manse Road, Netherton, Wishaw ML2 0EW.

Cook, Rev. John Weir, MA, BD. Minister, St Philip's Church, Edinburgh, since 1988; b. 10.2.37, Greenock; m., Elizabeth Anne Gifford; 1 s.; 2 d. Educ. Greenock Academy; High School of Glasgow; Glasgow University. Princeton Seminary. Minister: St Andrew's Church, Calcutta, 1962-69; Minister, Henderson Church, Kilmarnock, 1970-88. Recreations: sport; reading; theatre and cinema; travel. Address: (h.) 6 St Mary's Place, Edinburgh; T.-0131-669 2410; e-mail: jwc@freeuk.com

Cook, Lis, BA (Hons), RN, RM, DN. Nurse Director, Queen's Nursing Institute, Edinburgh, since 1995; b. 9.7.58, Prestwich; m., Robert Cook; 1 s.; 2 d. Educ. Canon Slade Grammar School, Bolton; Robert Gordon University, Aberdeen. Nurse and Midwife, Bolton; Island Nurse, Fair Isle; District Nurse, Shetland; Community Nursing Education Officer, Royal College of Nursing, Scotland, 1995- 98; Non-Executive Director, Lanarkshire Primary Care Trust, since 1999; Director, QNIS Millennium Award Scheme, since 1999; Chair, NNMHVAC. Chairman, Biggar High School Board. Publications: A Celebration of Practice Nursing (co-author). Recreations: cycling; reading; films. Address: (b.) 31 Castle Terrace, Edinburgh, EH1 2EL; T.-0131-229 2333; e-mail: qnis@aol.com

Cook, Rt. Hon. Robin, PC. MP (Labour), Livingston, since 1983 (Edinburgh Central, 1974-83); Leader of the House of Commons, since 2001; b. 28.2.46. Formerly Opposition Spokesman on: Trade and Industry, Health and Social Security, Foreign and Commonwealth Affairs; Secretary of State for Foreign and Commonwealth Affairs, 1999-2001. Address: (b.) House of Commons, London, SW1A 0AA.

Cooke, Professor David John, BSc, MSc, PhD, CPsych, FBPsS. Professor of Forensic Clinical Psychology, Glasgow Caledonian University, since 1992; Head of Forensic Clinical Psychology, Greater Glasgow Community and Mental Health Services NHS Trust, since 1984; Glasgow University: Honorary Lecturer, since 1984, Honorary Senior Research Fellow, since 1989, Visiting Professor, since 1997; b. 13.7.52, Glasgow; m., Janet Ruth Salter; 2 d. Educ. Larbert High School; St. Andrews University; Newcastle-upon-Tyne University; Glasgow University. Clinical Psychologist, Gartnavel Royal Hospital, 1976-83; Cropwood Fellow, Institute of Criminology, Cambridge University, 1986. Recreations: sailing; opera; cooking. Address: (b.) Douglas Inch Centre, 2 Woodside Terrace, Glasgow G3 7UY; T.-0141-211 8016.

Cooke, Nicholas Huxley, MA (Oxon), FRSA, FFCS. Director, CLEAR Services, since 2000; b. 6.5.44, Godalming, Surrey; m., Anne Landon; 2 s.; 3 d. Educ. Charterhouse School; Worcester College, Oxford. Retail management, London, 1967; chartered accountancy training, London, 1968-71; British International Paper, London, 1972-78; Director (Scotland), British Trust for Conservation Volunteers, 1978-84; Director, Scottish Conservation Projects Trust, 1984-98. Member, Policy Committee, SCVO; Member, Committee, Scottish Employer Supported Volunteering Group; Chair, Scottish Committee, Voluntary Sector NTO; Chair, Gowanbank Historic Village; Secretary, Scottish Senior Alliance for Volunteering in the Environment (SSAVE); Trustee, Callander Youth Project Trust; Board Member: Youthlink Scotland, Dundee Waste and Environment Trust, Falkirk Environment Trust, 1997-99; Member, Scottish Committee, European Year of the Environment, 1987-88. Recreations: fishing; walking; marginal gardening; outdoor conservation work. Address: (b.)Easter Stonefield, Port of Menteith, Stirling FK8 3RD; T.-01877 382926; e-mail: Nhcooke@aol.com

Cooney, Paul Francis. Managing Director, Radio Clyde, since 2000; b. 3.12.56, Blantyre, Scotland; m., Annette; 1 s.; 2 d. Educ. Holy Cross High School, Hamilton; Blairs College, Aberdeen. News Trainee, Radio Clyde, 1976-77; News Reporter/Sports Editor/News Editor, 1978-87; PR Manager, Celtic Football Club, 1987; PR Manager, Radio Clyde, 1987-91; Programme Controller, Century Radio, Dublin, 1991-92; Sports Presenter, Scottish Television, 1992-95; Director of PR, Radio Clyde, 1995-96; Managing Director, West Sound FM Ltd, 1996-2000. TRICS News/Sport Radio Journalist of the Year, 1985; New York Radio Award for Sports Programming; Sony Silver and Bronze Awards, 1986-91 and 1997. Address: (b.) Radio Clyde, Clydebank Business Park, Clydebank, Glasgow G81 2RX.

Cooper, Alexander (Sandy), FRIAS, RIBA. Senior Partner, Cooper Cromar architects, since 1984; b. 1.8.52, Glasgow; m., Janice; 3 s. Educ. Eastwood High School; Glasgow School of Art. Qualified, 1983; set up own practice; projects include substantial commissions throughout Glasgow and elsewhere. Saltire Society Award, 1992; Civic Trust Award, 1993; Scottish Property Award, 2000; Member, GIA Council, 1994-98. Recreations: sailing; golf; time with family and friends. Address: (h.) 1 Capelrig Lane, Newton Mearns, Glasgow G77 6XZ; T.-0141-332 2570.

Cooper, Professor Christine, BA, MSc, PhD. Professor of Accounting, Strathclyde University, since 1999; b. 16.3.56, London; 1 d. Educ. Crown Woods, Eltham, London; Greenwich University; London School of Economics. Senior Lecturer in Accounting, Strathclyde

University, 1995-99. Trustee, Association for Accountancy and Business Affairs. Address: (b.) Department of Accounting and Finance, Strathclyde University, Glasgow, G4 0LN; T.-0141-357 4318.

Cooper, Rev. David, BA, MPhil. Superintendent Minister, Edinburgh and Forth Circuit, since 1992; Secretary to Synod of Methodist Church in Scotland, since 1995; b. 6.11.49, Seaham; m., Veronica; 3 s.; 1 d. Educ. Bede Grammar School for Boys, Sunderland; University of Manchester; Hartley Victoria Methodist College. Minister: Morpeth Circuit, Newcastle District, 1977, Lerwick, North Roe and North Isles Circuit, Shetland District, 1980, Witney and Faringdon Circuit, Oxford and Leicester District, 1985. World Council of Churches Scholarship, University of Ghana, 1976-77. Recreation: music. Address: (b.) Central Hall, Tollcross, Edinburgh EH3 9BP; T.-0131-221 9029.

Cooper, Dr Kevin Gary, MBChB, MSc, MD, MRCOG. Consultant Gynaecologist, since 1998; b. 9.1.63, Edinburgh; m., Valerie Nelson; 2 s. Educ. Balfron High School; Edinburgh University. Two years' clinical research funded by Chief Scientist Office into management of menstrual disorders; trained in advanced minimal access surgery; completed specialist training, 1998, and took up consultant post, Aberdeen Royal Infirmary, 1998; pioneered microwave treatment for heavy periods. Recreations: golf; fishing. Address: (h.) 27 Abbotshall Road, Cults, Aberdeen AB15 9JX; T.-01224 861244.

Cooper, Professor Sally-Ann, BSc, MB, BS, MD, FRCPsych. Professor of Learning Disabilities, Department of Psychological Medicine, Glasgow University, since 1999; Honorary Consultant in Learning Disabilities Psychiatry, Greater Glasgow Primary Care NHS Trust, since 1999; b. 28.4.61, Lincoln; m., Mark Guy Venner Anderson. Educ. Medical College of St Bartholomew's Hospital, London. Address: (b.) Department of Psychological Medicine, Glasgow University, Academic Centre, Gartnavel Royal Hospital, 1055 Great Western Road, Glasgow G12 0XH; T.-0141-211 3701.

Copland, Rt. Rev. Mgr. John Forbes. Prelate of Honour to His Holiness the Pope; Vicar General R.C. Diocese of Aberdeen, 1979-2000; Provost of Cathedral Chapter, since 1996; Parish Priest, St. Thomas', Keith, since 1974; b. 26.12.20, Glenlivet. Educ. Tombae R.C. School; Blairs College Junior Seminary; Gregorian University, Rome; St. Peter's, Glasgow; St Joseph's, London. Ordained Priest, 1946; Curate: St. Peter's, Aberdeen, 1946, St Mary's Cathedral, Aberdeen, 1948; Parish Priest: Church of Annuniciation, Portsoy, 1951, St Andrew's, Braemar, 1964, St Joseph's, Woodside, Aberdeen, 1968. Chairman, Portsoy Improvement Association, 1954-64; Group Scoutmaster, Portsoy, 1952-64; Area Chairman, O.A.P.'s Association, 1958-64; Member: Aberdeenshire Education Committee, 1964-74, Grampian Education Committee, 1974-86; Chairman and Founder Member, Braemar Mountain Rescue Association, 1965-66; Founder Member, Aberdeen Cyrenians, 1970; President, Keith Initiative, since 1990. Recreations: hill-walking; stone polishing; photography. Address: (h.) St. Thomas' Rectory, Chapel Street, Keith, Banffshire AB55 5AL; T.-01542 882352.

Corbett, Gavin. Convenor, Executive, Scottish Green Party, since 1998; Head of Campaigns, Shelter Scotland, since 2001; b. 9.10.65, Cumnock; partner, Karen Robertson. Educ. Cumnock Academy; Glasgow University. Joined Shelter Scotland as campaign worker, 1993-2000; Policy Officer, Institute of Housing, 2000-2001. Recreations: climbing hills; cycling; campaigning. Address: (h.) 28 Briarbank Terrace, Edinburgh EH11 1SU; T.-0131-337 5227.

Cormack, John James Callender, LVO, MD, FRCGP. General Medical Practitioner; Apothecary to HM Household at the Palace of Holyroodhouse, 1991-2001; Chairman, Corstorphine Trust, since 1995; b. 21.2.34, Edinburgh; m., Joy Mackenzie Gourlay; 1 s.; 2 d. Educ. Edinburgh Academy; Edinburgh University. House Officer, Grenfell Mission, Canada, 1960-61; Medical Officer, CCAP Mission Hospital, Nyasaland, 1961-62; Principal in general practice, Corstorphine, 1964-2000; part-time Lecturer, Department of General Practice, Edinburgh University, 1966-76; Member, Panel of Examiners, Royal College of General Practitioners, 1971-82. Elder (former Joint Session Clerk), Corstorphine Old Parish Church; Hon. Librarian and Trustee, Royal Medical Society; Governor, St. Columba's Hospice. Publications: Practice – Clinical Management in General Practice (Co-editor); Teaching General Practice (Co-editor). Recreations: cycling; walking; painting; Scottish history. Address: (b.) 5 Gordon Road, Edinburgh EH12 6NB; T.-0131-334 3266.

Corner, David John, BA (Oxon), FRHS. Secretary and Registrar, St. Andrews University, since 1991; Honorary Lecturer, Department of Mediaeval History, St. Andrews University, since 1991; b. 24.10.47, Birmingham; m., Carol Ann; 2 s. Educ. King Edward VI Grammar School, Aston, Birmingham; Worcester College, Oxford. Prize Fellow, Magdalen College, Oxford, 1972-75; Lecturer, Department of Mediaeval History, St. Andrews University, 1975-91. Governor, Newbattle Abbey College, since 1991; President, St. Andrews Association of University Teachers, 1985-88. Recreations: cinema; sport. Address: St. Andrews University, College Gate, North Street, St. Andrews KY16 9AJ; T.-01334 462549.

Corner, Douglas Robertson, FCIBS. Director, Adam and Company PLC, since 1997; b. 19.5.44, Glasgow; m., Alice Cairns; 1 s.; 1 d. Educ. Duncanrig Secondary School, East Kilbride. Clydesdale Bank PLC (latterly as General Manager, Banking), 1969-95; Head of Human Resources and Consultant to Venture Capital Division, Murray Johnstone Ltd., 1995-97. Director: Quarriers, Glasgow International Jazz Festival (Chairman, Management Committee), Chorus Trust, Forth Valley Acute Hospitals NHS Trust. Recreations: golf; collecting Scottish contemporary paintings. Address: (b.) 238 West George Street, Glasgow G2 4DY; T.-0141-226 4848.

Cornish, Melvyn David, BSc, PGCE. Deputy Secretary, Edinburgh University, since 1991; b. 29.6.48, Leighton Buzzard; m., Eileen Joyce Easterbrook; 1 s.; 1 d. Educ. Cedars Grammar School, Leighton Buzzard; Leicester University. Chemistry Teacher, Jamaica and Cumbria, 1970-73; Administrator, Leicester Polytechnic, 1973-78; Senior Administrative Officer, Assistant Secretary, Director of Planning, Edinburgh University, 1978-91. Recreations: hill-walking; photography; travel. Address: (b.) Old College, South Bridge, Edinburgh; T.-0131-650 2136; e-mail: m.d.cornish@ed.ac.uk

Cornwell, Professor John Francis, PhD, BSc, DIC, ARCS, FRSE. Professor of Theoretical Physics, St. Andrews University, since 1979 (Chairman, Physics Department, 1984-85); b. 28.1.37, London; m., Elizabeth Margaret Burfitt; 2 d. Educ. Ealing Grammar School; Imperial College, London. Lecturer in Applied Mathematics, Leeds University, 1961-67; St. Andrews University: Lecturer in Theoretical Physics, 1967-73, Reader, 1973-79. Publications: Group Theory in Physics, three volumes, 1984, 1989; Group Theory and Electronic Energy Bands in Solids, 1969. Recreations: sailing; hill-walking; tennis; badminton; golf. Address: (b.) Department of Physics and Astronomy, St. Andrews University, North Haugh, St. Andrews, Fife KY16 9SS; T.-01334 476161.

Cornwell, Professor Keith, BSc, PhD, DEng, FIMechE. Professor, Department of Mechanical and Chemical Engineering and Director of Quality, Heriot-Watt University; b. 4.4.42, Abingdon; m., Sheila Joan Mott; 1 s.; 1 d. Educ. City University, London. Research Fellow, then Lecturer, Middlesex Polytechnic; Lecturer, Head of Department, Dean of Engineering, Heriot-Watt University. Secretary, UK Committee on Heat Transfer. Publications: The Flow of Heat; numerous journal papers. Recreations: classic cars; hillwalking. Address: (h.) Strathview, Templar Place, Gullane EH39 2AH.

Corrie, John Alexander. Member (Conservative), European Parliament for West Midlands Region, since 1999 (for Worcestershire and South Warwickshire, 1994-99); Co-ordinator, Development Committee, since 1999; Member, Budgets Committee, since 1999; Co-President, ACP/EU Joint Parliamentary Assembly; farms family farm in Galloway; b. 1935; m.; 1 s.; 2 d. Educ. Kirkcudbright Academy; George Watson's College, Edinburgh; Lincoln Agricultural College, New Zealand. Nuffield Farming Scholar, 1972; National Chairman, Scottish Young Conservatives, 1964; MP (Conservative): Bute and North Ayrshire, 1974-83, Cunninghame North, 1983-87; PPS to Secretary of State for Scotland, 1979-81; introduced Private Member's Bill to reduce upper limit on abortion, 1979; Member: European Assembly, 1975-76 and 1977-79, Council of Europe, 1983-87, Western European Union (Defence Committee), 1983-87; Chief Whip, Conservatives in Europe, 1997-99; Senior Instructor, British Wool Board, Agricultural Training Board, 1970-74; elected to Council, Belted Galloway Cattle Society, 1978; Chairman, Scottish Transport Users Consultative Committee, 1988-94; Vice Chairman, Central Transport Consultative Committee, 1988-94; Council Member, Royal Agricultural Society of England, 1992-2000; Industrial Fellowship with Conoco and Du Pont, USA, 1987; awarded Wilberforce Plaque for Humane Work, 1981. Publications: Forestry in Europe; Fish Farming in Europe; The Importance of Forestry in the World Today; Towards a Community Rural Policy (Co-author). Address: (h.) Park of Tongland, Kirkcudbright DG6 4NE.

Corsar, Charles Herbert Kenneth, LVO, OBE, TD, JP, DL, MA. Farmer, since 1953; Secretary for Scotland, Duke of Edinburgh's Award, 1966-87; b. 13.5.26, Edinburgh; m., The Honourable Dame Mary Corsar, DBE, FRSE (qv) ; 2 s.; 2 d. Educ. Merchiston Castle; King's College, Cambridge. Commissioned, The Royal Scots TA, 1948; commanded 8/9 Bn.,The Royal Scots TA, 1964-67; Edinburgh and Heriot-Watt Universities OTC, 1967-72; TA Colonel, 1972-75; Hon. ADC to The Queen, 1977-81; Honorary Colonel, 1/52 Lowland Volunteers, 1975-87; Chairman, Lowland TA and VR Association, 1984-87; Zone Commissioner, Home Defence, East of Scotland; County Councillor, Midlothian, 1958-67; Deputy-Lieutenant, Midlothian; Vice President, The Boys Brigade, 1970-91 and President, Edinburgh Bn., Boys Brigade, 1969-87 (Hon. President, Edinburgh Bn.,1987-98); Chairman, Scottish Standing Conference of Voluntary Youth Organisations, 1973-78; Governor: Merchiston Castle School, Clifton Hall School; Chairman: Wellington List D School, 1978-84, Earl Haig Fund Scotland, 1984-90; Secretary, Royal Jubilee and Princes' Trusts (Lothian and Borders); Member, Scottish Sports Council, 1972-75; Elder, Church of Scotland, since 1956. Recreations: gardening; bee-keeping; shooting. Address: (h.) Burg, Torloisk, Ulva Ferry, Isle of Mull PA74 6NH; T.-01688 500289; 11 Ainslie Place, Edinburgh EH3 6AS; T.-0131-225 6318.

Corsar, Kenneth, MA (Hons), MEd (Hons), FRSA. Director of Education, Glasgow City Council, since 1995; b. 16.7.46, Clackmannan; m., Mary Massie; 2 s. Educ. Alloa Academy; St. Andrews University; Glasgow University. Teacher, Principal Teacher of Classics, 1970-75; Education Officer, Senior Education Officer, Divisional Education Officer, Strathclyde Regional Council, 1975-90; Divisional Education Officer, Depute Director of Education, Strathclyde Regional Council, 1990-95. Vice-President, Association of Directors of Education in Scotland, 1992-93, President, 1993-94. Recreations: golf; calligraphy. Address: (b.) India Street, Glasgow; T.-0141-287 6710; (h.) 9 Eaglesfield Crescent, Strathaven, Lanarkshire; T.-01357 520817; e-mail: kenneth.corsar@glasgow.gov.uk

Corsar, The Hon. Dame Mary Drummond, DBE (1993), FRSE, MA; b. 8.7.27, Edinburgh; m., Colonel Charles H.K. Corsar (qv); 2 s.; 2 d. Educ. Westbourne, Glasgow; St. Denis, Edinburgh; Edinburgh University. Chairman, Women's Royal Voluntary Service, 1988-93; Chairman, Scotland, WRVS, 1981-88; Midlothian Girl Guides: Secretary, 1951-66, County Commissioner, 1966-72; Deputy Chief Commissioner, Girl Guides Scotland, 1972-77; Member: Parole Board for Scotland, 1982-89, Executive Committee, Trefoil Centre, since 1975, Visiting Committee, Glenochil Detention Centre, 1976-94; Management Committee, Church of Scotland Youth Centre, Carberry, 1976-82; Chairman, Lloyds TSB Foundation Scotland, 1994-97. Recreations: countryside; reading; handicrafts. Address: (h.) Burg, Torloisk, Ulva Ferry, Isle of Mull PA74 6NH; T.-0168 8500289.

Cosgrove, Hon. Lady (Hazel Josephine Aronson), QC, LLB, LLD. Senator of the College of Justice in Scotland, since 1996; b. 12.1.46, Glasgow; m., John A. Cosgrove; 1 s.; 1 d. Educ. Glasgow High School for Girls; Glasgow University. Advocate at Scottish Bar, 1968-79; Sheriff: Glasgow and Strathkelvin at Glasgow, 1979-83, Lothian and Borders at Edinburgh, 1983-96; Temporary Judge, Court of Session and High Court, 1992-96; Past Chairman, Mental Welfare Commission for Scotland; Past Chairman, Expert Panel on Sex Offending; Depute Chairman, Boundaries Commission for Scotland. Recreations: swimming; walking; opera; foreign travel. Address: (b.) Parliament House, Edinburgh EH1 1RQ; T.-0131-225 2595.

Cosgrove, Stuart, PhD. Head of Programmes (Scotland, Wales and Northern Ireland), Channel Four Television, since 1997; b. Perth. Educ. Hull University. Lecturer, film and television; cultural critic; Media Editor, NME; contributor, The Face, The Guardian, The Observer, Arena; regular presenter, The Late Show, BBC TV; joined Channel Four after period as independent producer; appointed Senior Commissioning Editor, then Controller of Arts and Entertainment, before returning to Scotland. Recreation: supporter of St Johnstone F.C. Address: (b.) 227 West George Street, Glasgow G2 2ND; T.-0141-568 7100.

Costelloe Baker, Linda, MBA. Scottish Legal Services Ombudsman, since 2000. Educ. Manchester Business School. Management Consultant; Member, Parole Board for Scotland, 1995-2000; Chairman, South Lanarkshire Children's Panel Advisory Committee, 1996-2000; Member, Criminal Injuries Compensation Appeals Panel, 1996-2000. Address: (b.) 17 Waterloo Place, Edinburgh, EH1 3DL; T.-0131-244 3055; e-mail: ombudsman@slso.org.uk

Cotter, Elizabeth Faith, MBE, LLB. Solicitor; Partner, Stewarts and Murdochs, since 1997; b. 1.9.43, Motherwell; m., James Logan Millar Cotter; 2 s.; 1 d. Educ. Westbourne School; Glasgow University. Stewarts Nicol McCormick, 1966-68; Motherwell and Wishaw District Council, 1968-69; Director, Motherwell Times Ltd., 1966-84; Partner, Bellshill Speaker, 1966-84; Partner, Stewarts Nicol D. & J. Hill, 1984-97. Part-time Commissioner, Mental Welfare Commission for Scotland; Director, Scottish Association for Mental Health. Recreations: reading; gardening; fishing; antiques. Address: (b.) 1 Royal Bank Place, Buchanan Street, Glasgow G1 3AA; T.-0141-248 8810.

Coulsfield, Rt. Hon. Lord (John Taylor Cameron), QC, BA, LLB. Senator of the College of Justice, since 1987; b. 24.4.34, Dundee; m., Bridget Deirdre Sloan. Educ. Fettes College; Corpus Christi College, Oxford; Edinburgh University. Admitted to Faculty of Advocates, 1960; Queen's Counsel, 1973; Lecturer in Public Law, Edinburgh University, 1960-64; Advocate Depute, 1977-80; Keeper of the Advocates Library, 1977-87; Chairman, Medical Appeal Tribunals, 1985-87; Judge of the Appeal Courts of Jersey and Guernsey, 1986-87; Scottish Judge, Employment Appeal Tribunal, 1992-96; Chairman, Joint Standing Committee on Legal Education, since 1997; Trustee, National Library of Scotland, since 2000.

Coulthard, Charles Hugh, BA. Managing Director, Scotland, Ofgem, since 1999; b. 14.9.42, Barry, South Wales; m., Irene Russell Hamilton; 2 s. Educ. Barry Grammar School; Strathclyde University. Joined HM Customs and Excise, 1963; Scottish Office, 1974; seconded to Office of Electricity Regulation, 1990; seconded to Office of Electricity Regulation for Northern Ireland, 1992, as Deputy Director General. Recreations: fishing; music. Address: Ofgem Scotland, Regent Court, 70 West Regent Street, Glasgow G2 2QZ; T.-0141-331 1772.

Coulthard, William George, LLB. Solicitor, since 1971; Honorary Sheriff, since 1988; b. 13.3.48, Whitehaven; m., Fiona Jane McQueen; 1 s.; 2 d. Educ. Glasgow Academy; Glasgow University. Partner in legal firm, since 1974; Dean, Faculty of Procurators, Stewartry of Kirkcudbright, 1986-88; Chairman, Castle Douglas High School Board, 1990-94; President, Castle Douglas Rotary Club, 1995. Recreations: golf; jogging. Address: (h.) Netherby, Castle Douglas DG7 1BA; T.-01556 502965.

Couper, Jean, BSc, MIMgt. Chairman, Scottish Legal Aid Board, since 1998 (Member, since 1994); Member, Police Advisory Board for Scotland; Director, Catalyst Consulting, since 1995; b. 31.8.53, Kilmarnock; m., John Anderson Couper; 1 s.; 1 d. Educ. Kilmarnock Academy; University of Glasgow. Production Engineer and Foundry Manager, Glacier Metal Co. 1974-79; Materials Manager, Levi Strauss, 1979-81; Management Consultant: Arthur Young, 1982-87, Price Waterhouse, 1987-95; Vice-Chairman, Wise Group, 1988-96; Vice Chairman, Heatwise Glasgow Ltd., 1988-96; Deputy Chairman, Health Education Board for Scotland, 2000-01 (Member, 1994-2001); National President, Junior Chamber Scotland, 1983; Senator, Junior Chamber International. Recreations: gardening; skiing. Address: Lismore House, 36 Sherbrooke Avenue, Pollokshields, Glasgow G41 4EP; T.-0141-427 3416.

Courtney, Professor James McNiven, BSc, PhD, Dr sc nat, ARCST, EurChem, CChem, FRSC, FIM. Professor, Bioengineering Unit, Strathclyde University, since 1989; Tenured Professor, International Faculty for Artificial Organs, since 1992; Visiting Professor, Danube University, Austria, since 1999; b. 25.3.40, Glasgow; m., Ellen Miller Courtney; 2 s.; 1 d. Educ. Whitehill Senior Secondary School; Royal College of Science and Technology; Strathclyde University. Rubber technologist: MacLellan Rubber Ltd., Glasgow, 1962-65; Uniroyal Ltd., Dumfries, 1965-66; Bioengineering Unit, Strathclyde University: Lecturer, 1969-81, Senior Lecturer, 1981-86, Reader, 1986-89. Recreation: football supporter (Glasgow Rangers). Address: (b.) Strathclyde University, Bioengineering Unit, 106 Rottenrow, Glasgow G4 0NW; T.-0141-548 3349.

Cousin, David Alastair Henry, BVMS, MRCVS, DBR, JP. Partner, veterinary practice, Kintyre, since 1972; Honorary Sheriff, Campbeltown Sheriff Court, since 1990; b. 19.4.44, Kincardine on Forth; m., Anne Macleod; 1 s.; 1 d. Educ. Balfron High School; Glasgow University. Liverpool University. Veterinary practice, Campbeltown: Veterinary Assistant, 1966, Junior Partner, 1972, Senior Partner, 1982. Former Commodore, Campbeltown Sailing Club, 1995; Honorary Treasurer, Kintyre Piping Society; Chairman, Argyll Veterinary Clinical Club. Recreations: sailing; shooting; gardening; music. Address: (h.) Southpark, Kilkerran Road, Campbeltown; T.-01586 553108.

Coutts, Alister William, DQS, BA (Hons), MBA (Dist), MSc, PhD, FRICS, FCIOB, FIMgt. Director of Property and Architectural Services, The Highland Council, since 1998; Tutor, Open University, since 1992; b. 21.12.50, Aberdeen; m., Sheelagh Anne; 1 s.; 2 d. Educ. Robert Gordon's College, Aberdeen; University of Abertay, Dundee; Open University; University of Hong Kong; Heriot-Watt University. Armour and Partners, Chartered Quantity Surveyors: Assistant Quantity Surveyor, 1969-71, Quantity Surveyor, 1975-76; Senior Quantity Surveyor, Anderson Morgan Associates, Chartered Surveyors, 1976-78; Professional Officer, Public Works Department, Hong Kong Government, 1978-81; Lecturer, University of Hong Kong, 1978-80; Project Co-ordinator, Hong Kong Mass Transit Railway Corporation, 1981-89; Lecturer, Hong Kong Polytechnic University, 1984-89; Project Management and Development Director, DCI (Holdings) Ltd., 1989-93; Lecturer, University of Dundee, 1991-92; Director of Operations, Fife Healthcare NHS Trust, 1993-98. President, Scottish Football Association Referees (Angus and Perthshire), 1994-96. Recreations: soccer referee; hillwalking. Address: (h.) Mo Tien, 29 Lady Nairne Drive, Perth PH1 1RF; T.-01738 634330.

Coutts, Rev. Fred, MA, BD. Hospital Chaplain, Grampian University Hospitals NHS Trust (based at Aberdeen Royal Infirmary); Moderator, Presbytery of Aberdeen, 2000-01; Healthcare Chaplaincy Training Officer (Scotland), 1997-2001; b. 13.1.47, Forfar; m., Mary Lawson Fraser Gill; 2 s.; 1 d. Educ. Brechin High School; Dollar Academy; St. Andrews University; Edinburgh University. Assistant Minister, Linwood Parish Church, 1972-74; Minister: Buckie North, 1974-84, Mastrick, Aberdeen, 1984-89. Chairman: Buckie Community Council, 1981-83, Moray Firth Community Radio Association, 1982-83. Recreations: music; photography; computing. Address: 9A Millburn Street, Aberdeen, AB11 6SS; T.-01224 583805; e-mail: fred.coutts@btinternet.com

Coutts, Herbert, SBStJ, AMA, FMA, FFCS, FSAScot. Director of Recreation, Edinburgh City Council, since 1998; City Curator, Edinburgh City Museums and Art Galleries, 1973-96, Head of Museums and Galleries, 1996-97, Head of Heritage and Arts, 1997-98; b. 9.3.44, Dundee; m., Angela E.M. Smith; 1 s.; 3 d. Educ. Morgan Academy, Dundee. Assistant Keeper of Antiquities and Bygones, Dundee City Museums, 1965-68; Keeper, 1968-71; Superintendent, Edinburgh City Museums, 1971-73; Vice-President, Museum Assistants Group, 1969-70; Member: Government Committee on future of Scotland's National Museums and Galleries, 1979-80; Council, Museums Association, 1977-78, 1987-88; Council, Society of Antiquaries of Scotland, 1981-82; Board, Scottish Museums Council, 1985-88; Museums Adviser, COSLA, 1985-90; Member, Paxton House Trust, since 1988; Member, East Lothian Community Development Trust, since 1989; External Examiner, St. Andrews University, 1994-97. Member, Board, Museums Training Institute, since 1995; Contested Angus South (Lab), 1970; major projects include: City of Edinburgh Art Centre, Museum of Childhood extension, People's Story Museum, City Art Centre extension, Usher Hall restoration. Publications: Ancient Monuments of Tayside; Tayside Before History; Edinburgh: an illustrated history; Huntly House; Lady Stair's House; The Pharaoh's Gold Mask; Gold of the Pharaohs (Editor); Dinosaurs Alive! (Editor); Sweat of the Sun — Gold of Peru (Editor); Golden Warriors of the Ukrainian Steppes (Editor); StarTrek – the exhibition (Editor); Quest for a Pirate (Editor); Gateway to the Silk

Road – Relics from the Han to the Tang Dynasties from Xi'an, China (Editor); Faster, Higher, Stronger – The Story of the Olympic Movement (Editor). Recreations: family; gardening; opera; writing; reading; walking. Address: (h.) Kirkhill House, Queen's Road, Dunbar EH42 1LN; T.- 01368 63113.

Coutts, T(homas) Gordon, MA, LLB, QC, FCIArb. Queen's Counsel, since 1973; b. 5.7.33, Aberdeen; m., Winifred K. Scott; 1 s.; 1 d. Educ. Aberdeen Grammar School; Aberdeen University. Advocate, 1959; Chairman, Industrial Tribunals, 1972; Chairman, Medical Appeal Tribunals, 1984; Vice President (Scotland), VAT and Duties Tribunals, 1996; Temporary Judge, Court of Session, 1991; Special Commissioner, Income Tax, 1996; Chairman, Financial Services and Markets Tribunal, 2001; Chartered Arbitrator Recreations: travel; stamp collecting. Address: (h.) 6 Heriot Row, Edinburgh.

Cowan, Sheriff Annella Marie, LLB (Hons), MSc. Sheriff of Grampian Highland and Islands at Aberdeen since 1997; b. 14.11.53, Sheffield; m., James Temple Cowan (marriage dissolved). Educ. Elgin Academy; University of Edinburgh. Admitted Solicitor, 1978; Procurator Fiscal Depute, 1978-86; seconded to Scottish Law Commission, 1984-86; admitted Faculty of Advocates, 1987; Sheriff, Tayside Central and Fife at Stirling, 1993. Recreation: equestrianism. Address: Sheriff's Chambers, Sheriff Court, Aberdeen AB10 1WP; T.-01224 648316.

Cowan, Brigadier Colin Hunter, CBE, MA, FRSA, CEng, MICE. Chief Executive, Cumbernauld Development Corporation, 1970-85; b. 16.10.20, Edinburgh; m., 1, Elizabeth Williamson (deceased); 1 s. (deceased); 1 s.; 1 d.; 2, Mrs Janet Burnett. Educ. Wellington College; Trinity College, Cambridge. Commissioned, Royal Engineers, 1940; service in India and Burma, Royal Bombay Sappers and Miners, 1942-46; staff and regimental appointments, UK and Malta, 1951-60; commanded Field Engineer Regiment, Germany, 1960-63; Defence Adviser, UK Mission to UNO, New York, 1964-66; Chief Staff Officer to Engineer-in-Chief (Army), Ministry of Defence, 1966-68; Brigadier, Engineer Plans (Army), Ministry of Defence, 1968-70. Recreations: hill-walking; photography; music. Address: (h.) Flat 11, Varrich House, 7 Church Hill, Edinburgh EH10 4BG; T.-0131-447 9768.

Cowan, David Lockhart, MB, ChB, FRCSEdin. Consultant Otolaryngologist, City Hospital, Royal Hospital for Sick Children and Western General Hospital, Edinburgh, since 1974; Honorary Senior Lecturer, Edinburgh University; b. 30.6.41, Edinburgh; m., Eileen M. Masterton; 3 s.; 1 d. Educ. George Watson's College, Edinburgh; Trinity College, Glenalmond; Edinburgh University. Scottish Representative, Council, British Association of Otolaryngologists. Publications: Logan Turner's Diseases of the Ear, Nose and Throat (Co-author); Paediatric Otolaryngology (Co-author). Recreations: golf; all sport. Address: (h.) Kellerstane House, Gogar Station Road, Edinburgh EH12 9BS; T.-0131-339 0293.

Cowan, Professor Edward James, MA. Professor of Scottish History, Glasgow University, since 1993; b. 15.2.44, Edinburgh; widower; 1 s.; 2 d. Educ. Dumfries Academy; Edinburgh University. Lecturer in Scottish History, Edinburgh University, 1967-79; Professor of History and Chair of Scottish Studies, University of Guelph, Ontario, 1979-93. Recreations: hill-walking; Scottish folk music. Address: (b.) 9 University Gardens, Glasgow G12 8QH.

Cowan, Rev. Gordon Leith. Former Moderator, United Free Church of Scotland; Minister, Leith: Ebenezer UF Church of Scotland, since 1987; Presbytery Clerk, since 1992; b. 2.8.39, Glasgow; m., Agnes Allan Copeland; 2 s.; 2 d. Educ. Whitehill Senior Secondary School, Glasgow;

Glasgow University; UF Congregational College, Edinburgh. Former Apprentice CA and book-keeper; Minister: Cumnock St. Andrews UF Church, 1968-76, Glasgow Wynd, 1976-87. Children's Panel Member, 1972-87. Recreations: genealogy; Scotland; watching athletics. Address: (h.) 14 Wardie Crescent, Edinburgh EH5 1AG; T.-0131-552 2349.

Cowan, John Mervyn, TD, MCIBS. Lt. Col. (Retd), RA/TA; Chairman: Royal Artillery Association Scottish Region, since 1991, The Sandilands Trust, since 1994, SSAFA West Lothian, since 2001, Earl Haig Fund (Scotland), 1993-99, b. 13.2.30, Oban; m., Marion Neilson Kidd; 1 s.; 2 d. Educ. Oban High School. National Bank of Scotland, National Commercial Bank of Scotland, Royal Bank of Scotland, 1946-90 (retired); TA commission, 1963; commanded 207 (Scottish) Battery RA(V), 1980-82; J.S.L.O., HQ Scotland, 1982-90; Member, RA Council for Scotland; Trustee, 445 and City of Edinburgh RA Regimental Trusts. Recreations: travel; charitable works; sport. Address: (h.) 43 Hunter Grove, Bathgate EH48 1NN; T.-01506 655784.

Cowan, Margaret Morton (Lady Cowan), MA, JP. Member, Council, National Trust for Scotland (Member, Executive Committee, 1990-2000, Member, Highland Committee, 1996-2000); b. 4.11.33, Newmilns; m., Sir Robert Cowan ; 2 d. Educ. St. George's School for Girls, Edinburgh; Edinburgh University. British Petroleum Company, 1955-59; Teacher, West Midlands Education Authority, 1965-76; Consultant and Lecturer in Use of Language, Hong Kong, 1976-81; Member, Justice of the Peace Committee, Inverness, 1985-2000; Member, Scottish Committee, British Council, 1991-2000; Convener, Highland Festival, 1992-97. Address: (h.) 1 Eyre Crescent, Edinburgh EH3 5ET; T.-0131-556 3379.

Cowe, Alan Wilson, MA, LLB. Secretary and Clerk, Church of Scotland General Trustees, since 1964; b. 9.8.38, Kelso; m., Agnes Cunningham Dick. Educ. Dunfermline High School; Edinburgh University. Law apprentice, Simpson Kinmont & Maxwell, WS, Edinburgh; Assistant to Secretary, Church of Scotland General Trustees, 1963-64. Recreations: running; hill-walking; theatre; jazz. Address: (b.) 121 George Street, Edinburgh EH2 4YR; T.-0131-225 5722; e-mail: acowe@cofscotland.org.uk

Cowie, Alan, PGCE. Freelance journalist and broadcaster; Head, Current Affairs, Grampian Television, 1998-2000; b. 28.4.48, Aberdeen; m., Evelyn; 2 d. Educ. Aberdeen Grammar School; Central College, London; Jordanhill College of Education, Glasgow. Teacher, Glasgow, 1971-72; Reporter/Presenter, Radio Scotland, 1972-75; joined Grampian Television as News Reporter, 1975; Programme Editor, 1988. Burgess, City of Aberdeen. Recreations: Scottish art; music; fishing; e-mail: alancowietv@aol.com

Cowie, Professor John McKenzie Grant, BSc, PhD, DSc, CChem, FRSC, FRSE. Professor Emeritus, Heriot-Watt University, since 1998; b. 31.5.33, Edinburgh; m., Agnes Neilson; 1 s.; 1 d. Educ. Royal High School Edinburgh; Edinburgh University. Assistant Lecturer, Edinburgh University, 1956-58; Associate Research Officer, National Research Council, Canada, 1958-67; Lecturer, Essex University, 1967-69; Senior Lecturer, Stirling University, 1969-73; Professor of Chemistry, Stirling University, 1973-88; Founding Professor of Chemistry and Materials, Heriot-Watt University, 1988-98; Hon. President, Stirling Voluntary Organisations and Stirling Council of Disabilities; Past Chairman and Vice-Chairman, Spinal Injuries, Scotland; Past Vice-Chairman, Disability Scotland; Past Chairman: Macrogroup UK; British High Polymer Forum. Publications: Polymers, Chemistry and Physics of

Modern Materials. Recreations: reading; music; painting. Address: (h.) Traquair, 50 Back Road, Dollar, Clackmannanshire, FK14 7EA; T.-01259 742031.

Cowie, Julian Martin, BA, CPFA, ACIS, IRRV. Director for Finance and Corporate Services, Dumfries and Galloway Council, since 1995; b. 5.1.52, Castlerea, Eire; m., Anne Marie; 2 s.; 1 d. Educ. St. Joseph's College, Dumfries; Heriot-Watt University. Trainee Accountant, Midlothian CC, 1973-74; Assistant Accountant, Lothian Health Board, 1974-76; Accountant, Lothian RC, 1976-77; Senior Accountant, Fife RC, 1977-79; Chief Accountant, Dumfries and Galloway RC, 1979-85; Depute Director of Finance, Nithsdale District Council, 1985-92; Director of Financial Services, Annandale and Eskdale District Council, 1992-95. Address: (b.) Carruthers House, English Street, Dumfries DG1 2HP; T.-01387 260250.

Cowie, Hon. Lord (William Lorn Kerr Cowie), MA (Cantab), LLB (Glas). Senator of the College of Justice in Scotland, 1977-94; Botswana Court of Appeal, 1995-98; b. 1.6.26, Glasgow; m., Camilla Henrietta Grizel Hoyle; 2 s.; 2 d. Educ. Fettes College, Edinburgh; Clare College, Cambridge; Glasgow University. RNVR, 1944-47 (Sub. Lt.); Member, Faculty of Advocates, 1952; QC, 1967. Scottish rugby internationalist, 1953. Recreation: fishing. Address: (h.) 20 Blacket Place, Edinburgh.

Cowley of Innerwick, Col. Victor Charles Vereker, TD, DL; b. 4.4.18, Glasgow; m., Moyra McClure; 1 s.; 2 d. Educ. St. Mary's, Melrose; Merchiston Castle School. Young master printer, 1937; commissioned, RATA, 1939; served France, North Africa, Sicily, Italy, Burma, Indo China; Col. Depute CRA 51st Highland Division; Chairman, Brownlie Scandrett and Graham Ltd. (retired 1960); Vice Convener, East Lothian County Council, 1973; Regional Councillor, Lothian, 1975; Commissioner of Income Tax, East Lothian, 1965-87. Recreations: shooting; golf. Address: Crowhill, Innerwick, Dunbar EH42 1QT; T.-01368 840279.

Cox, Derek, MBChB, MRCP(UK), MFPHM. Director of Public Health, Dumfries and Galloway Health Board, since 1999; b. 29.7.45, Glasgow. Educ. Hutchesons' Boys Grammar School; Glasgow University. Research Fellow, Cardiology, Glasgow University; Senior House Officer/Registrar in Cardiology, Glasgow Royal Infirmary; Medical Officer/Senior Medical Officer, Falkland Islands Government Medical Department; Registrar, General Surgery, Bignold Hospital, Wick; GP, Walls, Shetland; Director of Public Health, Shetland Health Board, 1990-99. Address: (h.) Aitkenmoor, Annan Water, Moffat DG10 9LS; T.-01683 220789.

Cox, Gilbert Kirkwood, MBE, JP. Lord Lieutenant of Lanarkshire, since 2000; retired General Manager Scotland, Associated Perforators & Weavers Ltd.; Director/Trustee, Airdrie Savings Bank, since 1987 (President, 1996-98); b. 24.8.35, Chapelhall, Airdrie; m., Marjory Moir Ross Taylor; 2 s.; 1 d. Educ. Airdrie Academy. National Coal Board, 1953-63; David A. McPhail & Sons Ltd., 1963-68; D.A. Monteith Holdings, 1968-71. Chair, Board of Management, Coatbridge College, 1997-2000; founder Member and Past President, Monklands Rotary Club; Member, Scottish Kidney Research Fund. Recreations: golf; gardening; walking. Address: (h.) Bedford House, Commonhead Street, Airdrie ML6 6NS; T.-01236 763331; e-mail: gibby@bedcom.freeserve.co.uk

Cox, Sheriff Principal Graham Loudon, QC, MA, LLB, Sheriff Principal of South Strathclyde Dumfries and Galloway, 1993-2000; b. 22.12.33, Newcastle-upon-Tyne; m., Jean Nelson; 3 c. by pr. m. Educ. Hamilton Academy; Grove Academy; Edinburgh University. Army 1956-61 (latterly Major, Directorate of Army Legal Services); called to the Bar, 1962; Advocate-Depute, 1966-68; Sheriff of

Tayside Central and Fife, at Dundee, 1968-93; QC, 1993; Secretary, Sheriffs' Association, 1987-91, President, 1991-93; Honorary Vice-President, Scottish Association for the Study of Delinquency, since 1996; Vice-Chairman, Northern Lighthouse Board, 1997-2000; Member, Council, Commonwealth Magistrates and Judges Association, 1991-94 and 1997-2000. Recreations: golf; restoration of decaying property. Address: (h.) Crail House, Crail, Fife, KY10 3ST; T.-01333 450270; e-mail: coxcrail@aol.com

Cox, Peter. Editor, Daily Record, since 2000; b. 4.3.50, London; m., Kay; 2 s.; 2 d. Educ. Ilford County High School; Nottingham University. Assistant Editor, The Sun; Deputy Editor, New York Post; Executive Editor, Daily Mirror; Deputy Editor, Daily Record; Editor, Sunday Mail, 1999-2000. Recreations: cooking; travel. Address; (b.) One Central Quay, Glasgow G3 8DA; T.-0141-309 3000.

Coyne, Marian, MA, PGCE, DipSW. Spokesperson, European Federation of Green Parties, since 2000; b. 12.7.52, Milngavie; 3 s. Educ. Notre Dame High School, Glasgow; Glasgow University; Edinburgh University. Teacher of primary subjects, Glasgow, Dar es Salaam and Dumfries, 1975-80; full-time childcare, 1980-85; social worker, 1987-99; former Principal Speaker, Scottish Green Party. Recreations: photography; hill-walking; writing; day-dreaming. Address: (h.) 1 Lady Nairne Place, Edinburgh EH8 7LZ.

Craig, Gordon. Chairperson, State Hospitals Board for Scotland, since 2001; management consultant, since 1998; b. 12.9.47, Huntly; m., Linda May; 2 s. Educ. Gordon Schools, Huntly. Health Service technician, 1964-70; Research Officer, Scottish Trades Union Congress, 1970-77; Trade Union Officer, 1977-86; Depute Director Personnel, Glasgow City Council, 1987-95; Depute Director, Cleansing, 1995-98. Recreations: golf; football. Address: (b.) State Hospital, Carstairs, Lanark ML11 8RP; T.-01555 841325.

Craig, Emeritus Professor Gordon Younger, BSc, PhD, CGeol, FRSE. Emeritus Professor of Geology, Edinburgh University, since 1984; Trustee, Dynamic Earth Charitable Trust, 1995-2001; b. 17.1.25, Milngavie; m., Mary Thornton; 2 s.; 2 step s.; 1 step d. Educ. Hillhead High School; Bearsden Academy; Glasgow University. Edinburgh University: Lecturer, 1947; James Hutton Professor of Geology, 1967-84; Visiting Professor, University of Colorado, 1958-59, UCLA, 1959, 1965; Leverhulme Fellow, ANU, Canberra, 1978; Distinguished Foreign Scholar, Mid-America State Universities, 1980; Green Professor, University of British Columbia, 1977, Texas Christian University, 1994; President: Edinburgh Geological Society, 1967-69, International Commission on the History of the Geological Sciences, 1984-89; Clough Medal, Edinburgh Geological Society, 1987; History of Geology Division Award, Geological Society of America, 1990. Publications: Geology of Scotland (Editor), 1991 (3rd ed.); James Hutton: The Lost Drawings (Co-author), 1977; A Geological Miscellany (Co-author), 1982. Recreations: golf; gardening. Address: (h.) 14 Kevock Road, Lasswade, Edinburgh EH18 1HT; T.-0131-663 8275.

Craig, Rev. Maxwell Davidson, MA, BD, ThM. Minister, St. Andrew's Scots Church, Jerusalem, 1999-2000; Chaplain to the Queen in Scotland, since 1986; b. 25.12.31; m., Janet Margaret Macgregor; 1 s.; 3 d. Educ. Oriel College, Oxford; Edinburgh University. National Service, 1st Bn., Argyll and Sutherland Highlanders (2nd Lt.), 1954-56. Assistant Principal, Ministry of Labour, 1957-61; Private Secretary to Parliamentary Secretary, 1959-61; left civil service for ministry of Church of Scotland, 1961; Parish Minister, Falkirk, Glasgow and Aberdeen, 1966-91; General Secretary, Action of Churches Together in Scotland, 1990-98. Convener, Church and Nation Committee, Church of Scotland, 1984-88; Chairman:

Falkirk Children's Panel, 1970-72, Hillhead Housing Association Ltd., 1975-89; Member, Strathclyde Children's Panel, 1973-86. Recreations: hill-walking; choral singing. Address: (h.) 9 Kilbryde Crescent, Dunblane, Perthshire FK15 9BA; T.-01786 823147; e-mail: maxwellcraig@hotmail.com

Craig, Robert, OBE, BA, MA, ALA. Director, Scottish Library Association, since 1984, and Scottish Library and Information Council, since 1991; b. 2.7.43, Hamilton; m., Ann Beaton; 1 s.; 1 d. Educ. Dalziel High School; Strathclyde University. Depute County Librarian, Lanark County Council, 1974-75; Principal Education Librarian, Glasgow Division, Strathclyde Regional Council, 1975-79; Lecturer, Strathclyde University, 1979-84. Publications: Scottish Libraries (Editor); Lights in the Darkness (Co-Editor); Scotland 1939 (Co-author); Scotland 1945 (Co-author). Recreations: reading; gardening; football. Address: (b.) Scottish Centre for Information and Library Services, 1 John Street, Hamilton ML3 7EU; T.-01698 458888.

Craigie, Cathie. MSP (Labour), Cumbernauld and Kilsyth, since 1999; b. 1954, Stirling; m.; 2 c. Councillor, Cumbernauld and Kilsyth District Council, 1984-96 (Council Leader, 1994-96); Member, North Lanarkshire Council, 1985-99; former Chair, Cumbernauld Housing Partnership. Address: (b.) Scottish Parliament, Edinburgh EH99 1SP.

Craigie Halkett, Hugh Dalzell. Chief Executive Officer, Vestech PLC, since 2000; Chairman, H.D. Management Ltd., since 1995; b. 28.10.68; m., Clare Anne. Educ. Harrow School. Founded H.D. Management, 1995; founded Vestech PLC, 2000; nominated for 2001 Corporate Elite Award; Conservative Parliamentary candidate, Livingston, 1997. Recreations: skiing; shooting; politics; Scottish history; bagpipes. Address: (h.) 20 Chester Street, Edinburgh EH3 7RA; T.-0131-718 6014.

Cramb, Auslan, MA (Hons). Scottish Correspondent, Daily Telegraph since 1994; b. 6.10.56, Dunoon; m., Catriona; 1 s.; 1 d. Educ. Perth Academy; Aberdeen University. Reporter, Press and Journal, 1979-82; Reporter, Press Association, Glasgow, 1982-85; The Herald, Glasgow, 1985-90; Environment Correspondent, The Scotsman, 1990-94. Scottish Specialist Writer of the Year, 1992 and 1993. Publications: Who Owns Scotland Now?, 1996; Fragile Land, 1998. Address: (b.) Daily Telegraph, 5 Coates Crescent, Edinburgh, EH3 7AL.

Cramb, Rev. Erik McLeish, LTh. National Co-ordinator, Scottish Churches Industrial Mission; Moderator, Presbytery of Dundee, 2001-02; b. 26.12.39, Glasgow; m., Elizabeth McLean; 2 s.; 3 d. Educ. Woodside Secondary School, Glasgow; Glasgow University and Trinity College. Minister: St. Thomas' Gallowgate, Glasgow, 1973-81, St. Paul's United Church, Kingston, Jamaica, 1981-84, Yoker, Glasgow, 1984-89; Organiser for Tayside, Scottish Churches International Mission, 1989-97. Socialist; Member, Iona Community; Chairman, Church Action on Poverty. Recreation: supports Partick Thistle. Address: (h.) 65 Clepington Road, Dundee DD4 7BQ; T.-01382 458764; e-mail: erikcramb@aol.com

Cramond, Ronald Duncan, CBE (1987), MA, FIMgt, FSA (Scot). Chairman, The Greenbelt Foundation, since 1999; Secretary, Intellectual Access Trust, since 1995; b. 22.3.27, Leith; m., 1, Constance MacGregor (deceased); 1 s.; 1 d; m., 2, Ann Rayner. Educ. George Heriot's School; Edinburgh University. Commissioned Royal Scots, 1950; entered War Office, 1951; Private Secretary to Parliamentary Under Secretary of State, Scottish Office, 1956; Principal, Department of Health for Scotland, 1957; Mactaggart Fellow, Glasgow University, 1962; Haldane Medallist in Public Administration, 1964; Assistant Secretary, Scottish Development Department, 1966; Under Secretary, 1973; Under Secretary, Department of Agriculture and Fisheries for Scotland, 1977. Deputy Chairman, Highlands and Islands Development Board, 1983-88; Member, Scottish Tourist Board, 1985-88; Trustee: National Museums of Scotland, 1985-96, Cromarty Arts Trust, 1988-91, Bo'ness Heritage Trust, 1989-97, Scottish Civic Trust, 1988-95; Vice President, Architectural Heritage Society of Scotland, 1989-94; Chairman, Scottish Museums Council, 1990-93; Commissioner, Countryside Commission for Scotland, 1988-92; Chairman, Scottish Greenbelt Foundation, 1992-2000. Recreations: hill-walking; testing a plastic hip. Address: (b.) The Greenbelt Foundation, 189 St. Vincent Street, Glasgow G2 5QD.

Crampsey, Robert A. McN., MA (Hons), ARCM, DUniv (Stirling). Freelance Broadcaster and Writer; b. 8.7.30, Glasgow; m., Dr. Veronica R. Carson; 4 d. Educ. Holyrood School, Glasgow; Glasgow University; London University (External). RAF, 1952-55 (demobilised in rank of Flt. Lt.); Head of History Department, St. Aloysius College, Glasgow, 1967-71; Assistant Head Teacher, Holyrood Secondary School, 1971-74; Rector, St. Ambrose High School, Coatbridge, 1974-86. Winner, Brain of Britain, BBC, 1965; Churchill Fellow, 1970; semi-finalist, Mastermind, 1972-73; BBC Sports Commentator. Publications: History of Queen's Park FC; Puerto Rico; The Manager; The Scottish Footballer; The Edinburgh Pirate (Arts Council Award); The Run Out; Mr Stein (a biography); The Young Civilian; The Glasgow Golf Club 1787-1987; The Empire Exhibition; The Somerset Cricket Quiz Book; The Surrey Cricket Quiz Book; Ranfurly Castle Golf Club — a centenary history; The Official Centenary History of the Scottish Football League; Scottish Railway Connections; The King's Grocer - a Life of Sir Thomas Lipton. Recreations: travel; things Hispanic; listening to and playing music; cricket. Address: (h.) 15 Myrtle Park, Glasgow G42; T.-0141-423 2735.

Cranstoun of That Ilk and Corehouse, David Alexander Somerville, TD, MA, MSc, PhD, DL. Cereal Specialist, SAC, since 1982; Member, Queen's Bodyguard for Scotland (Royal Company of Archers); b. 19.12.43, Washington DC; m., Dr. iur. M.M. Glättli; 2 s. Educ. Winchester College; Trinity College, Oxford. National List Trials Officer, ESCA, 1973. Director, Scottish Quality Cereals; Hon. Director, Lord Roberts Workshops (Edinburgh); Vice Chairman, SSAFA Forces Help; Commissioned Queens Own Lowland Yeomanry (TA), 1964, Lt. Col., 1982; Comd District Specialist Training Team, 1988, TA Col. Lowlands, 1990; Hon. Col. Glasgow and Lanarkshire Bn. ACF, 2001. Recreation: forestry. Address: (h.) Corehouse, Lanark ML11 9TQ.

Craven, Professor Alan James, MA, PhD, FInstP, CPhys. Professor of Physics, University of Glasgow, since 1998; b. 18.4.47, St. Helens; m., Rosalind; 1 s.; 1 d. Educ. Prescot Grammar School; Emmanuel College, Cambridge University. Cavendish Laboratory, Cambridge: Research Student, 1969-75, Post-doctoral Research Assistant, 1975-78; Department of Physics and Astronomy, University of Glasgow: Lecturer, 1978-89, Senior Lecturer, 1989-91, Reader in Physics, 1991-98. Address: Department of Physics and Astronomy, University of Glasgow, Glasgow G12 8QQ; T.-0141-330 5892.

Crawford, Allan James, MA, LLB, SSC. Solicitor, since 1971; Partner, HBM Sayers, solicitors; Solicitor Advocate, since 1994; Part-time Tutor in Civil Advocacy, University of Strathclyde, since 1990; b. 9.6.46, Glasgow; m., Patricia; 1 s.; 2 d. Educ. King's Park School, Glasgow; University of Glasgow. Law apprenticeship, Maclay, Murray, Spens, 1969-71; joined Cochran, Sayers, Cook, Solicitors, 1971. Former Temporary Sheriff. Recreations: music; opera; tennis; badminton. Address: (b.) 13 Bath Street, Glasgow G2 1HY; T.-0141-353 2121.

Crawford, Barbara Elizabeth, MA (Hons), PhD. Lecturer in Medieval History, St. Andrews University, since 1972; Member, Royal Commission on Ancient and Historical Monuments of Scotland, since 1995; Chair, Treasure Trove Advisory Panel for Scotland, since 1994; b. 5.4.40, Barnsley; m., Robert M.M. Crawford; 1 s. Educ. Queen Margaret's School; St. Andrews University. Carnegie Senior Scholarship, 1968; Temporary Lecturer, Department of History, Aberdeen University, 1969; elected Fellow, Society of Antiquaries London, 1973; Fellow Society of Antiquaries of Scotland, 1964; Member Norwegian Academy of Science and Letters, 1997; Fellow, Royal Society of Edinburgh, 2001; Leverhulme Research Fellow, 2000-01. Publications: Scandinavian Scotland, 1987; The Biggings, Papa Stour, Shetland, 1999. Recreations: exploring areas of Viking settlement in Scotland and North Atlantic. Address: (h.) Kincaple Cottage, St. Andrews KY16 9SH.

Crawford, Professor Dorothy H., MBBS, PhD, MD, DSc, FRCPath. Professor of Medical Microbiology, University of Edinburgh, since 1997; b. 13.4.45, Glasgow; m., Dr. W.D. Alexander; 2 s. Educ. St. Thomas's Hospital Medical School. Senior Lecturer then Reader, Royal Post-graduate Medical School, London, 1985-90; Professor of Medical Microbiology, London School of Hygiene and Tropical Medicine, 1990-97. Address: (b.) Division of Biomedical and Clinical Laboratory Sciences, University of Edinburgh Hugh Robson Building, George Square, Edinburgh EH8 9XD.

Crawford, Hugh William Jack, BArch, DipTP, RIBA, FRIAS, FRTPI. Principal, Sir Frank Mears Associates, since 1985; Part-time Inquiry Reporter (Local Plans), Scottish Executive, since 1982; b. 19.1.38, Dalry; m., Catherine Mary McIntyre; 1 s.; 2 d. Educ. Dalry High School; University of Strathclyde. Partner, Sir Frank Mears and Partners, 1965-85. Scottish Chairman, Royal Town Planning Institute, 1979, 1980, 1992; President, Committee of Liaison for Planning Practitioners in Member Countries of the European Union; President of Honour, European Council of Town Planners, Brussels, since 1985; former National Vice-President, Pedestrians Association; Vice President, Association of Mediators. Recreations: walking; visiting historic buildings and towns; art galleries and museums. Address: (b.) 24 Minto Street, Edinburgh EH9 1SB; T.-0131-662 9922; e-mail: h.crawford@btinternet.com

Crawford, Professor Robert, MA, DPhil, FRSE, FEA. Professor of Modern Scottish Literature, School of English, St. Andrews University, since 1995; Associate Director, St. Andrews Scottish Studies Institute, since 1993; Poet and Critic; b. 23.2.59, Bellshill; m., Alice Wales; 1 s.; 1 d. Educ. Hutchesons' Grammar School, Glasgow; Glasgow University; Balliol College, Oxford. Snell Exhibitioner & Carnegie Scholar, Balliol College, Oxford, 1981-84; Elizabeth Wordsworth Junior Research Fellow, St. Hugh's College, Oxford, 1984-87; British Academy Postdoctoral Fellow, Department of English Literature, Glasgow University, 1987-89; Lecturer in Modern Scottish Literature, School of English, St. Andrews University, 1989-95. Former Co-Editor, Verse Magazine; Co-Editor, Scottish Studies Review. Publications: The Savage and the City in the Work of T.S. Eliot, 1987; A Scottish Assembly, 1990; Sharawaggi (Co-author), 1990; About Edwin Morgan (Co-Editor), 1990; Other Tongues: young Scottish poets in English, Scots and Gaelic (Editor), 1990; The Arts of Alasdair Gray (Co-Editor), 1991; Devolving English Literature, 1992; Talkies, 1992; Reading Douglas Dunn (Co-Editor), 1992; Identifying Poets, 1993; Liz Lochhead's Voices (Co-Editor), 1993; Twentieth Century Literature of Scotland: a selected bibliography, 1995; Talking Verse (Co-Editor), 1995; Masculinity, 1996; Penguin Modern Poets 9 (Co-Author), 1996; Robert Burns and Cultural Authority (Editor), 1997; Launch-site for English Studies: Three

Centuries of Literary Studies at the University of St. Andrews (Editor), 1997; Impossibility, 1998; The Scottish Invention of English Literature (Editor), 1998; The Penguin Book of Poetry from Britain and Ireland since 1945 (Co-Editor), 1998; Spirit Machines, 1999; The New Penguin Book of Scottish Verse (Co-Editor), 2000; Scottish Religious Poetry (Co-Editor), 2000; The Modern Poet, 2001. Recreation: mischief. Address: (b.) School of English, St. Andrews University, St. Andrews, KY16 9AL; T.-01334 476161, Ext. 2666.

Crawford, 29th Earl of, and Balcarres, 12th Earl of (Robert Alexander Lindsay), KT, PC, DL. Premier Earl of Scotland; Head of House of Lindsay; b. 5.3.27; m., Ruth Beatrice Meyer; 2 s.; 2 d. Educ. Eton; Trinity College, Cambridge. Grenadier Guards, 1945-49; MP (Conservative), Hertford, 1955-74; Welwyn and Hatfield, February to September, 1974; Opposition Front Bench Spokesman on Health and Social Security, 1967-70; Minister of State for Defence, 1970-72; Minister of State for Foreign and Commonwealth Affairs, 1972-74; Chairman, Lombard North Central Bank, 1976-80; Director, National Westminster Bank, 1975-88; Director, Scottish American Investment Co., 1978-88; Vice-Chairman, Sun Alliance & London Insurance Group, 1975-91; President, Rural District Councils Association, 1959-65; Chairman, National Association of Mental Health, 1963-70; Chairman, Historic Buildings Council for Scotland, 1976-83; Chairman, Royal Commission on Ancient and Historical Monuments of Scotland, 1985-95; First Crown Estate Commissioner, 1980-85; Deputy Lieutenant, Fife; Chairman, National Library of Scotland, 1990-2000; Lord Chamberlain to HM Queen Elizabeth The Queen Mother, since 1992. Address: (h.) Balcarres, Colinsburgh, Fife KY9 1HL.

Crawford, Robert Caldwell. Composer; b. 18.4.25, Edinburgh; m., Alison Braedine Orr; 1 s.; 1 d. Educ. Melville College, Edinburgh; Keswick Grammar School; Guildhall School of Music, London. Freelance Composer and Critic until 1970; BBC Music Producer, 1970-85; Chairman, Music Advisory Committee for Sir James Caird's Travelling Scholarships Trust, 1978-93. Recreations: carpentry; hill-walking; gardening; beekeeping. Address: (h.) 12 Inverleith Terrace, Edinburgh EH3 5NS; T.-0131-556 3600.

Crawford, Robert Hardie Bruce, JP. MSP (SNP), Mid Scotland and Fife, since 1999; Shadow Minister, Environment and Energy, since 2001 (Shadow Minister, Transport and the Environment, 2000-01); Chief Whip, SNP Scottish Parliamentary Group, 1999-2000; b. 16.2.55, Perth; m., Jacqueline; 3 s. Educ. Kinross High School; Perth High School. Civil servant, Scottish Office, 1974-99; Leader, Perth and Kinross Council, 1995-99; Chairman, Kinross-shire Partnership Ltd., 1997-99; Chairman, Perth and Kinross Recreation Facilities Ltd, 1995-99; Member: Perthshire Tourist Board, Scottish Enterprise Tayside, Perth College, 1995-99. Recreations: golf; watching Dunfermline Athletic. Address: (h.) 12 Douglas Crescent, Kinross; T.-01577 863531.

Crawford, Robert MacKay, PhD, BA (Hons), FRSE. Chief Executive Scottish Enterprise, since 2000; b. 14.6.51, Scotland; 1 s.; 1 d. Educ. Glasgow University; Harvard University; Strathclyde University. Director, Locate In Scotland, 1991-94; Managing Director, Operations, Scottish Enterprise, 1994-96; World Bank Washington D.C., USA, 1996-98; Partner, Foreign Investment, Ernst and Young, 1998-2000. Recreations: running; reading, especially history and biography. Address: (b.) Scottish Enterprise, 150 Broomielaw, Atlantic Quay, Glasgow G2 8LU; T.-0141-248 2700.

Crawford, Robin, LLB, CA. Partner, KPMG, since 1979; Head of Forensic Accounting, KPMG Scotland, since 1990; b. 2.10.48, Greenock; m., Elizabeth; 1 s.; 1 d. Educ. Greenock Academy; Glasgow University. Qualified as CA, 1972; Partner, KPMG (then Peat, Marwick, Mitchell & Co.), 1979, Partner in charge Aberdeen office, 1981-84, Head of Audit, KPMG Glasgow, 1992-2001, Head of Consumer and Industrial Markets, Scotland, 1997-2001, Member, KPMG UK Board Nominations Panel. Governor, then Vice-Chairman, Laurel Bank and Laurel Park Schools, 1988-98; Member, Council, CBI Scotland (Member, Economics and Tax Committee); Member, Audit Committee, Erskine Hospital. Recreations: golf; fly fishing; hillwalking. Address: (b.) KPMG, 24 Blythswood Square, Glasgow G2 4QS; T.-0141-226 5511; e-mail: robin.crawford@kpmg.co.uk

Crawford, Ronald Lyndsay, MA, BLitt, Dr h.c., Commander of the Polish Order of Merit, 1989 (Gold Medal, 1982). Higher Education Consultant; b. 31.1.39, Paisley; m., Evelyn Ewing Knox; 2 s. Educ. Paisley Grammar School; Glasgow University; University of Freiburg. Editor, educational publishing, 1961-63; Strathclyde University: Administrative Assistant, 1963-67, Assistant, then Senior Assistant Registrar, 1967-73, Secretary to Court, 1973-81, Academic Registrar, 1981-93; Secretary, Committee of Scottish University Principals, 1988-98; Secretary, Committee of Scottish Higher Education Principals, 1993-99. Honorary Citizen, Lodz, Poland; President, Scottish-Polish Cultural Association, 1985-92. Recreations: fishing; boating; music. Address: (b.) PO Box 5497, Newton Mearns, Glasgow G77 6ZG; T.-0141-639 4273.

Crawford, Rudy, BSc (Hons), MBChB, FRCS (Glas), FFAEM. Consultant in Accident and Emergency Care, Royal Infirmary, Glasgow, since 1990; Honorary Clinical Senior Lecturer, Glasgow University, since 1991; b. 5.5.49, Glasgow; m., Jane Crawford; 1 s.; 1 d. Educ. Glasgow University. Temporary Lecturer in Anatomy, Glasgow University; general surgery training; specialist training in accident and emergency medicine and surgery, Glasgow and Aberdeen; formerly member of offshore specialist team providing medical support for North Sea oil emergencies; Member, Faculty Prehospital Care, and Examiner, Royal College of Surgeons of Edinburgh; founder Member, Scottish Trauma Audit Group; Vice Chairman, Council, St. Andrew's Ambulance Association; former Member, SCOTMEG/CRAG Working Group on Accident and Emergency Services. Publication: Authorised First Aid Manual of UK Voluntary Aid Societies (Co-Author). Recreations: karate; running; photography; travel; Rotary International. Address: (b.) Accident and Emergency Department, Royal Infirmary, Glasgow G4 0SF; T.-0141-211 5166.

Crawford, Ruth, LLB (Hons), DipLP. Advocate, since 1993; b. 17.7.65, Glasgow. Educ. Cranley School for Girls; George Heriot's School; Aberdeen University. Standing Junior Counsel to Keeper of the Registers of Scotland, since 1998. Address: Advocate's Library, Parliament House, Parliament Square, Edinburgh EH1 1RF; T.-0131-226 5071.

Crawford, Thomas, MA. Former Reader in English, Aberdeen University; b. 6.7.20, Dundee; m., Jean Rennie McBride; 1 s.; 1 d. Educ. Dunfermline High School; Edinburgh University; University of Auckland. University of Auckland: Lecturer in English, 1953-60, Senior Lecturer, 1960-62, Associate Professor, 1963-65; Lecturer in English, Edinburgh University, 1965; Commonwealth Research Fellow, Hamilton, Ontario, 1966; Senior Lecturer in English, then Reader, Aberdeen University, 1967-85; Warnock Fellow, Yale University, various times, since 1978. Past President, Association for Scottish Literary Studies; former Editor, Scottish Literary Journal.

Publications: Burns: a study of the poems and songs, 1960; Scott, 1965; Scott, selected poems (Editor), 1972; Love, Labour, and Liberty, 1976; Society and the Lyric, 1980; Boswell, Burns and the French Revolution, 1990; Correspondence of James Boswell and William Johnson Temple 1756-1795, Vol I. (Editor), 1997; Boswell in Scotland and Beyond (Editor), 1997. Recreations: walking and rambling; music. Address: (h.) 34 Summerhill Terrace, Aberdeen AB15 6HE; T.-01224 311764.

Crawley, David Jonathan, MA (Oxon). Head of Food and Agriculture Group, Scottish Executive Environment and Rural Affairs Department, since 1999; b. 6.5.51, Barnet; m., Anne Anderson; 1 s.; 2 d. Educ. Chichester High School; Christ Church, Oxford. Scottish Office, 1972-81; Department of Energy, 1981-84; Assistant Secretary, Scottish Education Department, 1984-87; Principal Private Secretary to Secretary of State for Scotland, 1987-89; Counsellor, UK Permanent Representation to European Communities, Brussels, 1990-94; Head, Private Finance Unit, Scottish Office, 1995-97; Head, Schools Group – Scottish Office Education and Industry Department, 1998-99. Recreations: family; walking; gardening. Address: (b.) Pentland House, 47 Robb's Loan, Edinburgh EH14 1TY.

Creally, Eugene P., LLB (Hons), PhD. Clerk of Faculty, Faculty of Advocates, since 1999; b. 3.2.61, Dungannon, Co. Tyrone; 1 s. Educ. St Patrick's Academy, Dungannon; Queens University, Belfast; Edinburgh University. Admitted to Faculty of Advocates, 1993. Address: (b.) Advocates Library, Parliament House, Edinburgh EH1 1RF; T.-0131-226 5071.

Crean, Gerard Patrick, PhD, FRCPE, FRCPG, FRCPI; President, Scottish Fiddle Orchestra; Former Consultant Physician, Ross Hall Hospital, Glasgow; Consultant Physician and Physician-in-charge, Gastro-Intestinal Centre, Southern General Hospital, Glasgow, 1967-92; b. 1.5.27, Courtown Harbour, County Wexford; m., Janice Dodds Mathieson; 1 s.; 2 d. Educ. Rockwell College, Cashel, County Tipperary; University College, Dublin. House appointments, Mater Misericordiae Hospital, Dublin, Western General Hospital, Edinburgh and Edinburgh Royal Infirmary; Registrar, then Senior Registrar, Western General Hospital, Edinburgh; Member, scientific staff, Medical Research Council Clinical Endocrinology Unit, Edinburgh; Honorary Lecturer, Department of Therapeutics, Edinburgh University; Visiting Professor in Physiology, Pennsylvania University. Clarke Prize, Edinburgh Pathological Club; contributed to several textbooks. Past President, British Society of Gastroenterology. Recreations: fiddle playing; traditional music; history of Antarctic exploration; golf. Address: (h.) St. Ronan's, Duchal Road, Kilmacolm PA13 4AY.

Cresswell, Lyell Richard, BMus (Hons), MusM, PhD. Composer; b. 13.10.44, Wellington, New Zealand; m., Catherine Mawson. Educ. Victoria University of Wellington; Toronto University; Aberdeen University. Music Organiser, Chapter Arts Centre, Cardiff; Forman Fellow, Edinburgh University, 1980-82; Canadian Commonwealth scholarship, 1969-70; Dutch Government bursary, 1974-75; Ian Whyte Award, 1978; APRA Silver Scroll, 1979; Cramb Fellow, Glasgow University, 1982-85; Winner, Scottish Arts Council Creative Scotland Award, 2001. Address: (h.) 4 Leslie Place, Edinburgh EH4 1NQ; T.-0131-332 9181; e-mail: lyellcresswell@talk21.com

Crichton, David, MA (Hons). Chief Executive, Scottish Enterprise Edinburgh and Lothian, since 1998; b. 14.10.55, Bridge of Allan; m., Pat; 2 s. Educ. Larbert High School; Edinburgh University. Industrial Economist, SDA, Glasgow, 1979-84; Director, Firn Crichton Roberts Ltd., 1984-89; Head of Projects, SDA, Edinburgh, 1989-91; Director of Projects, LEEL, 1991-98; Director, Alba Centre,

Livingston, 1998. Address: (b.) Scottish Enterprise Edinburgh and Lothian, Apex House, 99 Haymarket Terrace, Edinburgh EH12 5HD; T.-0131-313 4000.

Crichton, John Hugh McDiarmid, BMedSci (Hons), BMBS, PhD, MRCPsych, MILT. Consultant Forensic Psychiatrist, since 2000; Honorary Fellow in Law, since 2000; b. 8.9.66, Edinburgh; m., Dr. Anne-Marie Crichton; 1 d. Educ. Edinburgh Academy; Nottingham University; Trinity Hall, Cambridge. Nightingale Research Scholar, Institute of Criminology, Cambridge University, 1993; Lecturer in Developmental Psychiatry, Cambridge University, 1997; Lecturer in Forensic Psychiatry, Edinburgh University, 1998. Member, Department of Health Review into Homicide Inquiries. Publication: Psychiatric Patient Violence: Risk and Response, 1995. Recreation: not working. Address: (b.) Orchard Clinic, Royal Edinburgh Hospital, Edinburgh EH10 5HF; T.-0131-537 5858; e-mail: john.crichton@lpct.scot.nhs.uk

Crichton, Robin, FRAI. Film Producer and Director, since 1961; b. 14.5.40, Bournemouth; m., 1, Trish Dorrell, 2, Flora Maxwell Stuart; 3 d. Educ. Sherborne; Paris; Edinburgh. Built Scotland's first independent film studio, 1968; started film training scheme, now Napier University M.A., 1970; founded first animation studio in Scotland; managed first independent outside broadcast unit in Scotland; Founder Member: Scottish ACTT Committee, Scottish Film Archive; former UK Vice-Chair and Scottish Chair, Independent Programme Producers' Association; former Co-ordinator, Working Party, Scottish Screen; co-initiated Annual Co-production Conference; organised Scottish stand at international TV television markets; Churchill Fellowship, 1990 (to study models for Scottish Screen); Co-production Consultant to various European broadcasters and producers; former Project Leader, Eureka Audiovisual Federation; founder Director, Scottish Screen Locations; Consultant Programme Buyer, Gaelic Television Committee. Publications: Sara; The Curious Case of Santa Claus; Christmas Mouse. Recreations: dancing; gardening; DIY. Address: Keeper's House, Traquair, by Innerleithen, Peeblesshire EH44 6PP; T.-01896 831188.

Critchlow, Howard Arthur, BDS, FDSRCS(Eng), FDSRCPS(Glas). Consultant Oral Surgeon (Honorary Senior Lecturer), Glasgow Dental Hospital, Stobhill General Hospital and Royal Hospital for Sick Children, Glasgow, since 1976; b. 22.4.43, Littleborough; m., Avril; 1 s.; 1 d. Educ. Nottingham High School for Boys; Sheffield University. General dental practice, Sheffield; oral surgery training posts, Sheffield, Southampton, Odstock and Newcastle. Recreations: gardening; hill-walking; running. Address: (b.) Glasgow Dental Hospital and School, 378 Sauchiehall Street, Glasgow G2 3JZ; T.-0141-211 9600.

Croall, Alastair Menzies, LLB. Chief Executive, Scottish Borders Council, since 1995; b. 18.12.46, Kirkcaldy; m., Pauline; 3 s. Educ. Kirkcaldy High School; Edinburgh University. Worked with Roxburgh County Council, Moray and Nairn Joint County Council, Ross and Cromarty County Council; joined Borders Regional Council, 1975; appointed Depute Chief Executive and Solicitor to the Council, 1986. Recreations: walking; rugby; reading. Address: (b.) Council Headquarters, Newtown St. Boswells, Melrose, TD6 0SA; T.-01835 825055.

Croan, Sheriff Thomas Malcolm, MA, LLB. Sheriff of North Strathclyde at Kilmarnock, since 1983; b. 7.8.32, Edinburgh; m., Joan Kilpatrick Law; 1 s.; 3 d. Educ. St. Joseph's College, Dumfries; Edinburgh University. Admitted to Faculty of Advocates, 1956; Standing Junior Counsel, Scottish Development Department, 1964-65 and (for highways work), 1967-69; Advocate Depute, 1965-66; Sheriff of Grampian, Highland and Islands at Banff and Peterhead, 1969-83. Recreation: sailing. Address: (h.) Overdale, 113 Bentinck Drive, Troon.

Croft, Trevor Anthony, BSc, DipTRP, MRTPI, ARSGS, FRSA, FFCS. National heritage development consultant, since 2001; Consultant, The National Trust for Scotland, since 2001; Director, The National Trust for Scotland, 1997-2001; b. 9.6.48, Bradford; m., Janet Frances Halley; 2 d. Educ. Belle Vue Boys Grammar School, Bradford; Hull University; Sheffield University. Senior Assistant Planning Officer, N. Ireland Government, 1971-72; Assistant Planning Officer, Countryside Commission for Scotland, 1972-75; Physical Planning Officer, Office of the President, Malawi Government, 1976-78; Parks Planning Officer, Department of National Parks and Wildlife, Malawi Government, 1978-82; Planning Officer, then Head of Policy Research, then Regional Director, then Deputy Director/Director of Countryside, National Trust for Scotland, 1982-96. Member, Forestry Commission, South Conservancy Regional Advisory Committee, 1987-90; Member, Council, Royal Scottish Geographical Society, 1998-2001 (Chairman, Dunfermline Branch, 1993-96); Member, Council, Europa Nostra, 1999-2001; Treasurer, European Network of National Heritage Organisations, 2000-01. Recreations: sailing; travel; photography; equestrian vaulting; hill-walking. Address: (h.) Glenside, Tillyrie, Milnathort, Kinross KY13 0RW; T.-01577 864105.

Crofton, Sir John Wenman, KB, MA, MD, Dr h.c. Bordeaux, DSc hc, FRCP, FRCPE, Hon FRSE; b. 27.3.12, Dublin; m., Eileen Chris Mercer, MBE; 2 s.; 3 d. Educ. Tonbridge; Sidney Sussex College, Cambridge. Professor of Respiratory Diseases, Edinburgh University, 1952-77; Dean, Faculty of Medicine, 1963-66; Vice-Principal, 1969-70; President, Royal College of Physicians of Edinburgh, 1973-76; Vice-Chairman, Scottish Committee, Chest, Heart and Stroke Association, 1976-90; Chairman: Scottish Health Education Co-ordinating Committee, SHHD, 1981-86, Tobacco and Health Committee, International Union Against Tuberculosis and Lung Disease, 1984-88; Edinburgh Medal for Science and Society, 1995; Galen Medal for Therapeutics, Society of Apothecaries, 2001; DSc hc, Imperial College, London University. Recreations: history; music; reading science; mountains. Address: (h.) 13 Spylaw Bank Road, Edinburgh EH13 0JW; T.-0131-441 3730; eapretty@breathemail.net

Crofts, Roger Stanley, CBE, BA, MLitt, CertEd, FRSE, FRSGS, FRSA. Chief Executive, Scottish Natural Heritage, since 1991; Visiting Professor in Environmental Management, Royal Holloway, London University; Honorary Professor in Geography, University of Aberdeen; b. 17.1.44, Leicester; m. Lindsay Manson; 1 s.; 1 d. Educ. Hinckley Grammar School; Liverpool University; Leicester University. Research Assistant in Geography: Aberdeen University, 1966-72, University College, London, 1972-74; entered Scottish Office, 1974; Senior Research Officer, 1974-78; Principal Research Officer, 1978-84; Assistant Secretary, Highlands and Tourism Division, Industry Department, 1984-88; Assistant Secretary, Rural Affairs Division, Scottish Development Department, 1988-91. Member, Council (Chair), World Commission on Protected Areas (Europe); Member, Council: National Trust for Scotland, Scottish Association of Marine Science; Chairman, IUCN UK Committee, since 1999. Recreations: gardening; choral singing; hill-walking; wildflower photography. Address: (h.) 6 Old Church Lane, Duddingston Village, Edinburgh EH15 3PX; T.-0131-661 7858.

Cromartie, Earl of (John Ruaridh Grant Mackenzie), MIExpE. Land manager, since 1989; Executive Member, Mountaineering Council of Scotland, since 1990; Explosives Consultant, since 1979; b. 12.6.48, Inverness; m., Janet Clare Harley; 2 s. Educ. Rannoch School; Strathclyde University. Research Geologist, New Quebec, 1970s; Chief of the Clan Mackenzie and as such do (unpaid) visits to USA, Canada, Australia, as unofficial ambassador for Scotland; many articles on mountaineering; co-author of guide books on mountaineering. Recreations: mountaineering; geology; art. Address: (h.) Castle Leod, Strathpeffer IV14 9AA; T.-01997 421264.

Crompton, Professor David William Thomasson, OBE, MA. PhD, ScD, FRSE. Managing Director, St Andrew's Clinics for Children, since 1992; b. 5.12.37, Bolton; m., Effie Mary Marshall; 1 s.; 2 d. Educ. Bolton School; Sidney Sussex College, University of Cambridge; Fellow, Sidney Sussex College, Cambridge, 1964-85; Lecturer, Parasitology, Cambridge University, 1968-85; Adjunct Professor, Nutritional Sciences, Cornell University, since 1981; John Graham Kerr Professor of Zoology, Glasgow University, 1985-2000; Visiting Professor, University of Nebraska, 1982; Chairman, Company of Biologists Ltd., 1994-2000; Scientific Medal, Zoological Society of London, 1977; Member, WHO Expert Committee on Parasitology; Hon. Member, American Society of Parasitologists, 2001. Publications: author/editor,11 books; Co-editor, Parasitology, 1972- 82; author/co-editor, 250 scientific papers, Recreations: books; gardening; terriers especially bull terriers. Address: (h.) Melrose Cottage, Tyndrum, Perthshire, FK20 8SA; T.-01838 400203; e-mail: dwtc@tyndrum.demon.co.uk

Crook, Rt. Rev. John Michael, BA. Episcopal Bishop of Moray, Ross and Caithness, since 1999; b. 1940. Educ. University College St David, Lampeter; College of the Resurrection, Mirfield. Deacon, 1964, Priest, 1965; Curate, St. John's, Horninglow, 1964-66; Curate, All Saints, Bloxwich, 1966-70; Rector, St. Michael and All Angels, Inverness, 1970-74; Rector, St. John the Evangelist, with St. Michael and All Angels, Inverness, 1974-78; Chaplain, ACF, 1973-78; Editor, Northern See, 1972-78; Rector, St. Mary's Aberfoyle and St. Modoc's, Doune and St. Andrew's Callander, 1978-87; Canon, St. Ninian's Cathedral, Perth, 1985-99; Rector, St. Saviour's, Bridge of Allan, 1987-99; Synod Clerk, St. Andrews, 1997-99. Address: 11 Kenneth Street, Inverness IV3 5NR.

Crookall, Simon Philip. Chief Executive, Royal Scottish National Orchestra, since 1997; b. 1.10.60, Macclesfield. Educ. Nantwick and Acton Grammar School; King's College, Cambridge. Academic Assistant/Assistant to Principal/Front of House Manager, Royal Scottish Academy of Music and Drama, Glasgow, 1983-89; General Manager, Queen's Hall, Edinburgh, 1989-95; General Manager, Royal Scottish National Orchestra, 1995-96. Recreations: singing as soloist for Council for Music in Hospitals; Member, Order of St. John. Address: (b.) RSNO Centre, 73 Claremont Street, Glasgow G3 7JB; T.-0141-225 3550.

Crory, Peter George, BA, DMS, JP. National General Secretary, YMCA Scotland, since 2000; b. 6.4.64, Newry; m., Pauline; 1 s. 1 d. Educ. Methodist College, Belfast; Queen's University, Belfast. General Secretary, YMCA Lisburn, 1988-2000; Director, Modus Management Services, 1998-2000. Address: (b.) 11 Rutland Street, Edinburgh EH11 2AE; T.-0131-228 1464.

Crosbie, William, BSc(Hons). Headteacher, Castlebrae Community High School, since 1991; b. 14.8.50, Dumbarton; m., Rosemary; 1 s.; 1 d. Educ. Clydebank High School; University of Glasgow; Moray House College of Education. Teacher of Chemistry, Greenfaulds High School, Cumbernauld, 1973-76; Assistant Principal Teacher of Science, Holy Rood R.C. High School, Edinburgh, 1976-78; Castlebrae High School, Edinburgh: Principal Teacher of Chemistry, 1978-87, Assistant Headteacher, 1987-89, Depute Headteacher, 1989-91. Scottish Teacher of the Year, 1993; Scottish Schools Ethos Award, 1997; Standard Life Edinburgh Education Award for Raising Achievement,

2000. Recreations: golf; cinema; swimming. Address: (b.) 2a Greendykes Road, Edinburgh EH16 4DP; T.-0131-661 1282; e-mail: william.crosbie@castlebrae.edin.sch.uk

Crosby, William Scott, CBE (1982), BL. Lawyer; b. 31.7.18, Hawick; m., Margaret Elizabeth Bell; 3 s. Educ. Hawick High School; Edinburgh University. Army Service, 1939-46; Croix de Guerre, 1945; acted as Brigade Major 152 Brigade, 1945; Former Senior Partner, Storie, Cruden & Simpson, Advocates, Aberdeen; Chairman, Grampian Health Board, 1973-82; President, Society of Advocates in Aberdeen, 1984-85. Address: (h.) 2 Earls Court Gardens, Aberdeen AB15 4BU.

Crosfield, Rev. Canon George Philip Chorley, OBE, MA (Cantab). Provost, St. Mary's Cathedral, Edinburgh, 1970-90; Hon. Canon, St. Mary's Cathedral, since 1991; b. 9.9.24, London; m., Susan Mary Jullion; 1 s.; 2 d. Educ. George Watson's College, Edinburgh; Selwyn College, Cambridge. Royal Artillery, 1942-46 (Captain); Priest, 1952; Assistant Curate: St. David's, Pilton, Edinburgh, 1951-53, St. Andrew's, St. Andrews, 1953-55; Rector, St. Cuthbert's, Hawick, 1955-60; Chaplain, Gordonstoun School, 1960-68; Canon and Vice-Provost, St. Mary's Cathedral, Edinburgh, 1968-70. Recreations: gardening; walking; carpentry. Address: (h.) 21 Biggar Road, Silverburn, near Penicuik EH26 9LQ; Tel.-01968 676607.

Cross, Professor Rod, BSc(Econ), BPhil. Professor of Economics, University of Strathclyde, since 1991; b. 27.3.51, Wigan. Educ. Wigan Grammar School; London School of Economics; University of York. Research Assistant, University of Manchester, 1972-74; Temporary Lecturer, Queen Mary College, University of London, 1974-75; Lecturer, University of St. Andrews, 1975-91. Adviser to Governor, Polish National Bank, 1990-92; Occasional Member, H.M. Treasury Academic Panel. Publications: Economic Theory and Policy in the UK, 1982; Unemployment Hysteresis and the Natural Rate Hypothesis (Editor), 1988; The Natural Rate of Unemployment, 1995. Recreations: hillwalking; rugby league and union, fiction. Address: (b.) Department of Economics, University of Strathclyde, Curran Building, 100 Cathedral Street, Glasgow G4 0LN; T.-0141-548 3855/4555.

Crowe, Sheriff Frank Richard, LLB, SSC, NP. Sheriff of Tayside Central and Fife at Dundee; Solicitor Advocate; 15.3.52, Kirkcaldy; m., Alison Margaret Purdom (separated); partner, Margaret Elizabeth Scott; 2 d.; 1 s. Educ. Kirkcaldy High School; Royal High School, Edinburgh; University of Dundee. Law Apprentice, North of Scotland Hydro-Electric Board, 1973-75; Procurator Fiscal Depute: Dundee, 1975-78, Glasgow 1978-81; Senior Legal Assistant, Crown Office, 1981-83; Senior Depute Procurator Fiscal, Edinburgh 1983-87; Senior Depute i/c Crown Office Fraud Unit, 1987-88; Assistant Solicitor i/c High Court Unit, Crown Office, 1988-91; Procurator Fiscal, Kirkcaldy, 1991-96; Regional Procurator Fiscal, South Strathclyde, Dumfries and Galloway, 1996-99; Procurator Fiscal, Hamilton, 1996-99; Deputy Crown Agent, Crown Office, 1999-2001. Member: Management Committee, Lothian Victim Support Scheme, 1983-89, Training Advisory Committee, Victim Support Scotland, 1994-98, Council, Law Society of Scotland, 1996-99, Scottish Executive Stephen Lawrence Steering Group, 1999-2001. Recreations: golf; cycling; racing; music. Address: (b.) Sheriff's Chambers, Sheriff Court House, 6 West Bell Street, Dundee DD1 9AD.

Crowe, Victoria Elizabeth, MA (RCA), ARSA, RSW. Artist, Painter and Printmaker; b. 8.5.45, Kingston-on-Thames; m., Michael Walton; 1 s. (deceased); 1 d. Educ. Ursuline Convent Grammar School, London; Kingston College of Art; Royal College of Art. Part-time Lecturer, Drawing and Painting, Edinburgh College of Art, 1968-98; solo exhibitions: Scottish Gallery, Edinburgh, 1970, 1973,

1977, 1982, 1995, 1998, 2001; Thackeray Gallery, London, 1983, 1985, 1987, 1989, 1991, 1994, 1999, 2001; Bruton Gallery, Bath and Leeds, 1989, 1993, 1998; A Shepherd's Life, retrospective, Scottish National Portrait Gallery, Mercer Art Gallery, Harrogate, Inverness Art Gallery, Swanston Museum, Thurso, Hatton Art Gallery, Newcastle upon Tyne, 2000-01; exhibited throughout Europe and USA with Artists for Nature Foundation; work in public collections. Recreation: travel. Address: (h.) Bank House, Main Street, West Linton, Peeblesshire EH46 7EE.

Crowther, Professor Margaret Anne, BA, DPhil, FRHS, FRSE. Professor of Social History, University of Glasgow, since 1994; Chairman, Scottish Records Advisory Council, 1995-2001; b. 1.11.43, Adelaide, South Australia; m., John McCauley Crowther; 1 s. Educ. Walford Grammar School; Adelaide University; Oxford University. Publications: The Workhouse System, 1981; On Soul and Conscience, 1988. Recreation: gardening. Address: (b.) Centre for the History of Medicine, University of Glasgow, Glasgow G12 8QO; T.-0141-330 6071.

Cruickshank, Alastair Harvey, LLB, WS, NP, DL. Solicitor and Consultant, Condies, Solicitors, Perth, since 1967; b. 10.8.43, Perth; m., Moira E. Pollock (deceased); 2 s. Educ. Perth Academy; Edinburgh University. Apprentice, then Assistant, Shepherd & Wedderburn, WS, Edinburgh, 1964-67; Assistant, then Partner, then Consultant, Condie Mackenzie & Co. (now Condies), since 1967. Diocese of Brechin: Registrar, 1974-99, Chancellor, since 2000; Member, Perth Society of High Constables; Captain, Royal Perth Golfing Society, since 2001. Recreations: hill-walking; sailing; chamber music, opera and classical music generally. Address: (b.) 2 Tay Street, Perth PH1 5LJ; T.-01738 440088.

Cruickshank, Alistair Booth, MA, FRSGS, FRCGS; b. 3.8.31, Dumfries; m., Sheena Carlin Brown (qv); 2 s.; 1 d. Educ. High School of Stirling; Glasgow University; Georgia University. RAF, 1956-58; Glasgow University, 1958-61; Nottingham University, 1961-65; Glasgow University, 1965-86. Director, Royal Scottish Geographical Society, 1986-96; ordained Auxiliary Minister, Church of Scotland, 1991; Deputy Lieutenant, County of Clackmannan, since 1991. Recreations: fly fishing; peoples and places.

Cruickshank, Donald Gordon, MA, CA, MBA, LLD. Chairman, SMG plc, since 1999; Chairman, London Stock Exchange plc, since 2000; b. 17.9.42, Elgin; m.; 1 s.; 1 d. Educ. Fordyce Academy; Robert Gordon's College; Aberdeen University; Manchester University. Consultant, McKinsey & Co. Inc., 1972-77; Times Newspapers, 1977-80 (Commercial Director, 1977-79; General Manager, Sunday Times, 1979-80); Managing Director (Finance Administration and Planning), Information and Entertainment Division, Pearson plc, 1980-84; Managing Director, Virgin Group plc, 1984-89; Chairman, Wandsworth Health Authority, 1986-89; Chief Executive, National Health Service in Scotland, 1989-93; Non-Executive Director, Christian Salvesen plc, 1994-95; Director General, Telecommunications, 1993-98; Chairman, Action 2000 (UK Government's Millennium Bug Campaign), 1997-2000; Fellow, London School of Economics, since 1997; Chairman, Chancellor's Review of UK Banking, 1998-2000. Address: (b.) London Stock Exchange, Old Broad Street, London EC2N 1HP.

Cruickshank, Sheena Carlin, JP. Lord Lieutenant, County of Clackmannan, since 2001; b. 26.3.36, Stirling; m., Alistair Booth Cruickshank; (qv); 2 s.; 1 d. Educ. High School of Stirling. Recreation: quilting.

Crummy, Helen Murray, MBE, DLitt, DL, JP; b. 10.5.20, Edinburgh; m., Larry Crummy; 3 s. Educ. James Clark's School. Co-Founder Member and Organising Secretary, 23

years, Craigmillar Festival Society; served on Morris Committee (Housing and Social Work); former Member: Scottish Council for Community Education, Scottish Arts Council Development Committee, various Gulbenkian committees, DHSS Appeals Tribunal, Lothian Regional Council Education Advisory Committee. Recreations: writing; historical research; reading; gardening. Address: (h.) 4 Whitehill Street, Newcraighall, Musselburgh EH21 8RA; T.-0131-669 7344.

Crump, Professor John, BDS, BA, PhD. Professor, University of Stirling, since 1997; b. 2.8.44, Leeds; m., Taeko Midorikawa; 2 d. Educ. Emanuel School; London University; Sheffield University. Dental Surgeon until 1973; research at University of Tokyo, 1973-75, and University of Sheffield, 1975-78; Senior Lecturer, University of York, 1978-96. Publications include: The Origins of Socialist Thought in Japan; State Capitalism; Non-market Socialism in the 19th and 20th Centuries; Hatta Shuzo and Pure Anarchism in Japan. Recreations: walking the hills; keeping fit; revolutionary thought. Address: (b.) Scottish Centre for Japanese Studies, University of Stirling, Stirling FK9 4LA; T.-01786 466085.

Cubie, Andrew, CBE, FRSE, LLD (Glasgow), DUniv (Edinburgh), DBA (QMUC), NP, WS, FRSA. Partner, Fyfe Ireland WS, since 1994; Chairman, Bird Semple Fyfe Ireland WS, 1991-94; b. 24.8.46, Northallerton; m., Dr. Heather Ann Cubie; 1 s.; 2 d. Educ. Dollar Academy; Edinburgh University. Partner, Fyfe Ireland & Co., WS, 1971; non-executive Director: Murray VCT3 PLC, Norfrost Holdings Ltd., Kinloch Anderson Ltd., and a number of other private companies; Chairman: Quality Scotland Foundation, Napier University Court, Scottish Credit and Qualification Framework, RNLI Scotland, Scotland's Health at Work, WS Society Education and Training Committee; Vice President and Deputy Chairman, Fundraising Committee, RNLI; Vice-President and Chairman in Scotland, British Executive Service Overseas; Trustee for Scotland Common Purpose; Chairman, Independent Committee of Inquiry into Student Finance; sometime Member: Ministerial Action Group on Standards in Scottish Schools, Independent Commission on Local Government and the Scottish Parliament, Consultative Steering Group on the Scottish Parliament; former Chairman: CBI Scotland, Governing Council George Watson's College. Recreation: sailing. Address: (b.) Orchard Brae House, 30 Queensferry Road, Edinburgh EH4 2HG; T.-0131-343 2500.

Cullen, Paul B., LLB (Hons), QC. Queen's Counsel, since 1995; b. 11.3.57, Gosforth; m., Joyce Nicol; 2 s.; 1 d. Educ. St Augustine's High School, Edinburgh; Edinburgh University. Clerk, Faculty of Advocates, 1986-91; Standing Junior Counsel, Department of the Environment in Scotland, 1988-91; Advocate Depute, 1992-95; Solicitor General for Scotland, 1995-97; Consultative Steering Group on the Scottish Parliament, 1998-99; Chairman, Public Inquiry into Gilmerton Limestone Emergency, 2001. Chairman, Scottish Conservative Parliamentary Disciplinary Panel; Vice President, Edinburgh South Conservatives. Recreations: tennis; bridge. Address: (b.) Advocates' Library, Parliament House, Edinburgh EH1 1RF; T.-0131-226 5071.

Cullen, Rt. Hon. Lord (William Douglas Cullen), PC, LLD, DUniv, FRSE, HonFREng. Senator of the College of Justice, since 1986; Lord President and Lord Justice General, since 2001; b. 18.11.35, Edinburgh; m., Rosamond Mary Downer; 2 s.; 2 d. Educ. Dundee High School; St. Andrews University (MA); Edinburgh University (LLB). Called to the Scottish Bar, 1960; QC, 1973; Advocate-Depute, 1977-81; Chairman: Inquiry into the Piper Alpha Disaster, 1988-90, Inquiry into the Shootings at Dunblane Primary School, 1996, Ladbroke Grove Rail Inquiry, 1999-

2001. Member, Royal Commission on the Ancient and Historical Monuments of Scotland, 1987-97; Member, Napier University Court, since 1996; Chairman: Cockburn Association, 1984-86, Board of Governors, St. Margaret's School, Edinburgh, since 1994; Honorary President, SACRO, since 2000. Recreations: gardening; natural history. Address: (b.) Court of Session, Parliament House, Edinburgh; T.-0131-240 6732.

Culley, Ron, MSc, CQSW, CSW, DipYCS. Chief Executive, Scottish Enterprise Glasgow, since 2000; b. 2.2.50, Glasgow; m., 1, Margaret Ferguson; 2 s.; m., 2, Jean Pollock; 2 s. Educ. Craigbank Comprehensive School; Jordanhill College of Education; Moray House College of Education; Strathclyde University. Social work and social policy development posts, Strathclyde Regional Council, 1975-87; Govan Initiative Ltd: Assistant Chief Executive, 1987-88, Chief Executive, 1988-2001. Founding Board Member, Scottish Urban Regeneration Forum; Governor, Scottish Police Training College; Board Member: Police Advisory Board for Scotland, Quality Scotland, Glasgow Alliance; Friend of Govan Initiative; Secretary, Govan Honours Society; Member, Task Force on Wider Impacts, Glasgow Housing Association; Leader, Task Force on Upper Clyde Shipbuilding; Panel Member, Investors In People Scotland, 1998-2000; Candidate (Labour), Scotland SW Region, Scottish Parliamentary election, 1999; Chairman, Glasgow Local Economic Development Network, 1996-2000; Board Member, Strathclyde European Partnership, 1987-2000; Secretary, Ibrox Community Trust, 1987-2000. Publications: Merkat Forces (Co-Author), 1994; The New Guards, 1999. Recreations: family and friends; playing guitar; watching association football; fair weather golf; fair weather gardening; socialising; reading biographies; American politics; irreverence; laughing out loud. Address: (b) Atrium Court, 50 Waterloo Street, Glasgow, G2 6HQ; T.-0141-242 8213; e-mail: ron.culley@scotent.co.uk

Cumming, Lt. Col. Alaistair Michael, OBE. Regimental Secretary to The Highlanders (Seaforth, Gordons and Camerons), since 1995; b. 22.12.41, Singapore; m., Hilary Katharine Gray; 2 d. Educ. Bradfield College, Berkshire. Cadet, RMA Sandhurst, 1960-61; commissioned into The Gordon Highlanders, 1962; Lt. Col.: Commander Ground Liaison Team, Germany, 1985-88; Naval and Military Attache, British Embassy, Poland, 1989-92; Commander Support Weapons Wing, Netheravon, 1992-95. Recreations: cricket; golf; tennis; shooting; skiing. Address: (b.) RHQ, The Highlanders, Cameron Barracks, Inverness IV2 3XD.

Cumming, Alexander James, MA (Hons), CIMA, IPFA. Chief Executive, Grampian University Hospitals NHS Trust, since 1994; b. 7.3.47, Aberdeen; m., Margaret Callan; 1 s.; 2 d. Educ. Fordyce Academy; Robert Gordon's College; Aberdeen University. VSO, 1968-70; Accountant, Company Secretary, Chief Accountant, 1970-75; joined Grampian Health Board, 1975. Address: (b.) Foresterhill House, Ashgrove Road West, Aberdeen; T.-01224 681818.

Cumming, Eric Alexander, MIMgt, AInstAM, FRSA, FSA(Scot). Sheriff Clerk, Glasgow, since 2001; Head of Operations, Scottish Court Service, since 1998; b. 9.5.54, Glasgow; m., Isabel Rodger. Educ. Albert Senior Secondary School; Glasgow College of Commerce. Entered Scottish Court Service (Sheriff Clerk's Branch), 1972; posts in Glasgow, Nairn, Ayr, Dumbarton; Depute Clerk of Session and Justiciary, 1983; Sheriff Clerk, Ayr, 1990-92; Deputy Principal Clerk of Justiciary, 1992-95; Principal, Scottish Court Service HQ, 1995-2001. Recreations: Clyde steamers; reading; naval history. Address: (b.) Glasgow Sheriff Court, 1 Carlton Place, Glasgow G5 9DA; T.-0141-429 8888.

Cumming, Grant Philip, BSc (Hons), MD, MBChB, MRCOG. Consultant, Obstetrician and Gynaecologist, Dr. Grays Hospital, Elgin, since 2000; Honorary Senior Lecturer, Grampian University Hospitals NHS Trust, since 2000; b. 8.5.61, Derby; m., Fiona; 1 s.; 1 d. Educ. George Heriots School, Edinburgh; St. Andrews University; Victoria University, Manchester. Aberdeen Royal Infirmary and Maternity Hospital, 1996-2000. Medical Director, The Menopause and You (CD Rom). Recreations: golf; conjuring. Address: (b.) Dr Grays Hospital, Elgin, Moray; T.-01343 543131; e-mail: grant.cumming@arh.grampian.scot.nhs.uk

Cumming, Robert Currie, BL, FCIBS, ACIB, FRCSEdin (Hon.), FRSGS; b. 21.5.21, Strathaven; m., Mary Jean McDonald Crombie. Educ. Hutchesons' Grammar School, Glasgow; Glasgow University. Former Executive Director, Royal Bank of Scotland Group PLC and Royal Bank of Scotland PLC; Chairman, English Speaking Union — Scotland, 1984-90; Trustee, Royal Scottish Geographical Society. Recreations: fishing; golf; walking. Address: (h.) 3 Succoth Park, Edinburgh EH12 6BX; T.-0131-337 1910.

Cunliffe, Michael James Paton, BSc, MSc, MCIWEM. Head of Scottish Estates, The Crown Estate, since 1998; b. 9.3.47, Sunderland; m., Jocelyn Mary Willoughby; 1 s.; 1 d. Educ. Kendal Grammar School; Edinburgh University. Joined Scottish Office, 1971; Principal, Development and Education Departments, 1975-82; Assistant Secretary, Development, Industry and Education Departments, 1982-95; Director of Corporate Services, East of Scotland Water, 1995-98. Elder, St Andrew's and St George's Church, Edinburgh. Recreations: sailing; country walks; listening to music. Address: (b.) Crown Estate Office, 10 Charlotte Square, Edinburgh EH2 4DR; T.-0131-226 7241.

Cunningham, David Kenneth, BEd, MEd (Hons), FRSA. Head Teacher, Hillhead High School, Glasgow, since 1993; b. 19.4.48, Saltcoats; m., Marion S. Shedden; 2 d. Educ. Ardrossan Academy; Glasgow University; Jordanhill College of Education. Principal Teacher of English, North Kelvinside Secondary, 1976-80; Assistant Head Teacher, Garthamlock Secondary, 1980-82; Adviser in English, Dunbarton Division, 1982-90, Education Officer (Acting), 1989-90; Inspector, Quality Assurance Unit, Strathclyde Regional Council, 1990-93; Examiner, Setter, Principal Examiner, SEB, 1979-90; Member, Board, Glasgow Area, Young Enterprise Scotland; Headteachers Association of Scotland: Executive Member, since 1997, Vice President, 2000-01, President, 2001-02; Member, UCAS Standing Committee, since 1997; Director, Notre Dame Centre for Children, Young People and Families, since 1999; Associate Assessor, HMI; Member, New National Qualifications Steering Group, since 2001; Member, Ministerial Task Group New National Qualifications; Chair, English and Communications Higher Still Revision Group. Publications: Reading for 'S' Grade English, 1988. Recreations: various sports; reading; photography; travel; family. Address: (h.) 7 Waterfoot Road, Newton Mearns, Glasgow; T.-0141-639 3367.

Cunningham, Professor Ian M.M., CBE, FRSE, FIBiol, FRAgS, Hon. Assoc. RCVS, Bsc, PhD, FRSGS, Dr hc; b. 30.9.25, Kirknewton; m., Agnes Whitelaw Frew. Educ. Lanark Grammar School; Edinburgh University. Assistant Economist, West of Scotland Agricultural College, 1946-47; Lecturer in Agriculture, Durham School of Agriculture, 1947-50; Lecturer, then Senior Lecturer, Edinburgh University, 1950-68; Director, Hill Farming Research Organisation, 1968-80; Professor of Agriculture, Glasgow University, and Principal, West of Scotland Agricultural College, 1980-87. Member: Farm Animal Welfare Council, Hill Farming Advisory Committee, Scotland; Chairman, Board, Macaulay Land Use Research Institute, 1987-95; Chairman, National Trust for Scotland, 1998-2000; George

Hedley Memorial Award for services to the sheep industry; Massey Ferguson Award for services to British agriculture; Sir William Young Award for services to livestock production in Scotland; Hon. Assoc., RCVS. Address: (h.) 5 The Bridges, Peebles EH45 8BP.

Cunningham, Right Rev. Monsignor John, JCD. Prelate of Honour, since 1999; Parish Priest, St. Patrick's Greenock, since 1992; Chairman, Roman Catholic Scottish National Tribunal, 1986-92; Papal Chaplain, since 1994; Vicar General, Diocese of Paisley, since 1997; b. 22.2.38, Paisley. Educ. St. Mary's College, Blairs, Aberdeen; St. Peter's College, Cardross; Scots College and Gregorian University, Rome. Assistant Priest, Our Lady of Lourdes, Bishopton, 1964-69; Professor of Canon Law, St. Peter's College, Cardross and Newlands (Glasgow), 1967-81; Advocate of the Roman Catholic Scottish National Tribunal, 1970-82; Assistant Priest, St. Columba's, Renfrew, 1974-86; Vice-President, RC Scottish National Tribunal, 1982-86. Address: 5 Orangefield Place, Greenock PA15 1YX; T.-01475 720223.

Cunningham, Robert Ritchie, MA (Hons). Rector, Inverness High School, since 1991; b. 22.5.53, Stirling; m., Linda; 2s. Educ. Friends Grammar School, Lisburn, Northern Ireland; Lenzie Academy; Glasgow University. Teacher, Geography/Economics/Geology, Cumbernauld High School, 1977-80; Principal Teacher, Geography, John Nelson High School, Paisley, 1989-84; Field Development Officer, Scottish Examinations Board, 1984-86; Adviser, Social Studies, Highland Council, 1986-91; Director, Inverness and Nairn Enterprise, since 1998. Publications: co-author of over 20 publications including 4 textbooks. Recreations: golf; salsa; Rotary. Address: (b.) Inverness High School, Montague Row, Inverness, IV3 5DZ; T.-01463 233586.

Cunningham, Roseanna. MSP (SNP), Perth, since 1999 (SNP Deputy Leader, since 2000; Shadow Minister for Justice and Convener, Justice and Home Affairs Committee, 1999-2000); MP (SNP), Perth, 1995-2001; b. 27.7.51, Glasgow. Educ. University of Western Australia. SNP Research Department, 1977-79; law degree, Edinburgh University; Trainee Solicitor, Dumbarton District Council, 1983-84; Solicitor, Dumbarton, 1984-86; Solicitor, Glasgow, 1986-89; called to the Scottish Bar, 1990. Recreations: folk festivals; reading; cinema; cats; novice hill-walker. Address: (b.) Scottish Parliament, Edinburgh EH99 1SP.

Cunningham, Very Rev Thomas James Canon, STL, PhL. Parish Priest, St. Cadoc's RC Church, Newton Mearns, since 1990; Canon, RC Paisley Diocesan Chapter, since 1999; b. 22.11.31, Orange, New Jersey, USA. Educ. St. Mary's College, Blairs, Aberdeen; Universita Gregoriana; Pontifico Collegio Scozzese, Rome. Assistant: St. Joseph's, Clarkston, 1956, St. Charles', Paisley, 1956-57, St. Mungo's, Greenock, 1957-60, St. Joseph's, Clarkston, 1960-66, St. Cadoc's, Newton Mearns, 1966-71, St. James' Renfrew, 1971-75, St. Peter's, Paisley, 1975-86; Parish Priest, St. Anthony's, Johnstone, 1986-90. Member, Editorial Staff, Catholic Parish Magazine and Journal, 1969-76; Secretary, Property Committee, Paisley Diocese, 1970-2000; First Secretary, Paisley Diocesan Priests' Council, 1971-77; Pailsey Diocesan Chaplain, Union of Catholic Mothers, 1978-2000; Chaplain, Sanctuary Alcoholic Rehabilitation Centre, Paisley, 1983-89; Representative: Paisley Gleniffer School Council, 1978-86, East Renfrewshire Education Committee, 1995-2001. President: Renfrew Rotary Club, 1974-75, Paisley Rotary Club, 1980-81. Recreations: sailing; writing. Address: St. Cadoc's, 24 Fruin Avenue, Newton Mearns, Glasgow G77 6HA; T.-0141-639 1073.

Cunningham, Wylie. Executive Secretary, Scotland, The Institution of Civil Engineers, since 2000; b. 4.4.45, Kilmarnock; m., Margot Smith. Educ. Irvine Royal Academy. Journalism, Glasgow Herald, 1963-68; political representation, NFU, 1968-76; public affairs and relations, Charles Barker, 1976-82; Director, St Andrew's Ambulance Association, 1982-88; public affairs, Urban Regeneration Partnership, 1988-94; Scottish Director, Road Haulage Association, 1994-98; Scottish Head, Association of Chartered Certified Accountants, 1998-2000. Has written several works of children's fiction. Recreations: charity work; writing; cooking; walking; good wine; silly films; professional and political irreverence. Address: (b.) 105 West George Street, Glasgow; T.-0141-221 3181.

Cunningham-Jardine, Ronald Charles. Lord Lieutenant, Dumfries, since 1991; Farmer; b. 19.9.31, Edinburgh; m., Constance Mary Teresa Inglis; 1 s.; 1 d. Educ. Ludgrove; Eton; Royal Military Academy, Sandhurst. Royal Scots Greys (retired as Captain), 1950-58. Recreations: all country sports. Address: (h.) Fourmerkland, Lockerbie, Dumfriesshire DG11 1EH; T.-01387 810226.

Curran, Margaret. MSP (Labour), Glasgow Baillieston, since 1999; Deputy Minister for Social Justice, Scottish Executive, since 2001. Educ. Glasgow University. Former Lecturer in Community Education. Address: (b.) Scottish Parliament, Edinburgh EH99 1SP; T.-0131-348 5842.

Currie, Eleanor Jean, MA, DipSecEd. Director of Education, East Renfrewshire Council, 1995-2001; b. 1.6.50, Ayr; m., Robert L. Currie. Educ. Cumnock Academy; Glasgow University; Jordanhill College. Teacher/Principal Teacher of Modern Studies; seconded to Consultative Committee on the Curriculum; Principal Office (Staffing), then Education Officer (Renfrew Division), then Senior Education Officer (Dumbarton Division), then Divisional Assistant Director of Education (Dumbarton Division), Strathclyde Regional Council. Recreations: keep fit exercising; walking; travel.

Currie, Rev. Ian Samuel, MBE, BD. Minister, Oakshaw Trinity Church, Paisley, since 1991; b. 14.8.43, Glasgow; m., Jennifer; 1 s.; 1 d. Educ. Bellahouston Academy; Trinity College; University of Glasgow; Minister: Blairhill Dundyvan Church, Coatbridge, 1975-80, St John's Church, Paisley, 1980-91. Chair, Victim Support Scotland, 1993-98; Director, Wynd Centre, Paisley. Recreation: chess. Address: (b.) Oakshaw Trinity Church Office, 6 School Wynd, Paisley PA1 2DB; T.-0141-887 4647.

Currie, Ken. Painter; b. 1960, North Shields. Educ. Paisley College; Glasgow School of Art. Worked on two films about Glasgow and Clyde shipbuilding, 1983-85; specialises in political realism, including a series of murals for the People's Palace Museum, Glasgow, on the socialist history of the city.

Curtice, Professor John Kevin, MA (Oxon). Professor of Politics, Strathclyde University, since 1998; Head of Research, National Centre for Social Research Scotland, since 2001; b. 10.12.53, Redruth; m., Lisa; 1 d. Educ. Truro School; Magdalen and Nuffield Colleges, Oxford. Research Fellow, Nuffield College, Oxford; Lecturer in Politics, Liverpool University; Fellow, Netherlands Institute for Advanced Study, 1988-89; Senior Lecturer in Politics, Strathclyde University, 1989-96; Reader in Politics, Strathclyde University, 1997-98. FRSA. Publications include: How Britain Votes; Understanding Political Change; Labour's Last Chance; On Message; New Scotland, New Politics; The Rise of New Labour; New Scotland, New Society; British Social Attitudes. Recreations: music; gardening. Address: (b.) Department of Government, Strathclyde University, 16 Richmond Street, Glasgow G1 1XQ; T.-0141-548 4223.

Curtis, Professor Adam Sebastian Genevieve, MA, PhD. Professor of Cell Biology, Glasgow University, since 1967; Director, Centre for Cell Engineering, since 1996; President, Tissue and Cell Engineering Society, 2001-03; b. 3.1.34, London; m., Ann Park; 2 d. Educ. Aldenham School; Kings College, Cambridge. University College, London: Honorary Research Assistant, 1957-62, Lecturer in Zoology, 1962-67. Director, Company of Biologists Ltd., 1961-99; Governor, Westbourne School, 1985-90; Council Member, Royal Society of Edinburgh, 1983-86; President, Society of Experimental Biology, 1991-93; Editor, Scottish Diver magazine, 1978-91, and 1994-97; President, Scottish Sub-Aqua Club, 1972-76. Recreations: sports diving; gardening. Address: (h.) 2 Kirklee Circus, Glasgow G12 0TW; T.-0141-339 2152.

Cuschieri, Professor Sir Alfred, MD, ChM, FRCSEd, FRCSEng, FIBiol, MD Liverpool Univ (Hon), FRCSI (Hon), FRCPSGlas (Hon), FRSE. Professor and Head, Department of Surgery and Molecular Oncology, Dundee University, since 1976; b. 30.9.38, Malta; m., Dr. M.P. Holley; 3 d. Educ. St. Aloysius College; Royal University of Malta; Liverpool University. Lecturer/Senior Lecturer/Reader in Surgery, then Professor of Surgery, Liverpool University. Recreations: fishing; music. Address: (h.) Denbrae Mill, Strathkinness Low Road, St Andrews, Fife KY16 9TY.

Cusine, Sheriff Douglas James, LLB, FRSA. Sheriff, Grampian, Highland and Islands at Aberdeen, since 2001; All-Scotland Floating Sheriff based at Peterhead, 2000-01; b. 2.9.46, Glasgow; m., Marilyn Calvert Ramsay; 1 s.; 1 d. Educ. Hutchesons' Boys' Grammar School; Glasgow University. Solicitor, 1971, Lecturer in Private Law, Glasgow University, 1974-76; Aberdeen University: Lecturer in Private Law, 1977-82, Senior Lecturer, 1982-90, Professor, Department of Conveyancing and Professional Practice of Law, 1990-2000. Member: Council, Law Society of Scotland, 1988-97, Lord President's Advisory Council on Messengers-at-Arms and Sheriff Officers, 1989-97; Member, UK Delegation to CCBE, 1997-2000. Publications: Marine Pollution: Law and Practice (Co-Editor), 1980; Cases and Materials in Commercial Law (Co-Editor), 1987; A Scots Conveyancing Miscellany (Editor), 1987; New Reproductive Techniques: A Legal Perspective, 1988; Law and Practice of Diligence (Co-Author), 1989; Reproductive Medicine and the Law (Co-Editor), 1990; Standard Securities, 1990; Missives (Co-Author), 1993; Requirements of Writing (Co-Author), 1995; various articles on medico-legal issues and conveyancing. Recreations: swimming; walking; bird-watching. Address: Sheriff Court House, Castle Street, Aberdeen AB10 1WP.

Cuthbertson, Iain, MA (Hons), FRSAMD. Actor; b. 4.1.30. Educ. Glasgow Academy; Aberdeen Grammar School; Aberdeen University. General Manager/Director of Productions, Citizens' Theatre, Glasgow, 1962-65; Associate Director, Royal Court Theatre, London, 1965; Director, Perth Theatre, 1967-68; sometime Administrator, Playhouse Theatre, Nottingham; stage performances include title roles in Armstrong's Last Goodnight (Citizens'), The Wallace (Edinburgh Festival), Serjeant Musgrave's Dance (Royal Court), Sutherland's Law (TV series); 1,500 broadcasts; TV work includes Budgie, Charles Endell Esq.; premiere of A Drunk Man Looks at the Thistle, set to music and dance; Hon. LLD, Aberdeen University; former Board Member, Scottish Theatre Company; former Hon. President, SCDA; Visiting Stage Director and Tutor, Royal Scottish Academy of Music and Drama. Recreations: countryside; sailing. Address: (b.) Janet Welch, Personal Management, 46 The Vineyard, Richmond, Surrey TW10 6AN.

Cuthbertson, Ian Jardine, LLB, NP, FIPA, FABRP, FInstD. Solicitor, Notary Public and Licensed Insolvency Practitioner; Partner, Dundas & Wilson, Solicitors, Glasgow and Edinburgh, since 1979; b. 8.5.51, Glasgow; m., Sally Jane; 1 s.; 2 d. Educ. Jordanhill College School, Glasgow; Glasgow University. Apprenticeship, Messrs Boyds; admitted as Solicitor, 1974; Partner, Messrs Boyds, 1978; jointly founded firm of Dorman Jeffrey & Co., 1979, merged with Dundas & Wilson, 1997. Recreations: watching football and rugby. Address: (b.) 191 West George Street, Glasgow; T.-0141-222 2200; Saltire Court, Castle Terrace, Edinburgh; T.-0131-228 8000.

Cuthbertson, Rev. Malcolm, BA, BD (Hons). Minister, Easterhouse: St. George's and St. Peter's Church of Scotland, since 1984; b. 3.4.56, Glasgow; m., Rena Fennel; 1 s.; 2 d. Educ. Grangemouth High School; Stirling University; Aberdeen University. Probationer Assistant, Crown Court Church, London, 1983-84. Recreations: eating out; reading theology. Address: 3 Barony Gardens, Glasgow G69 6TS; T.-0141-573 8200; e-mail: malcuth@aol.com

Cuthell, Rev. Thomas Cuthbertson, MA, BD. Minister, St. Cuthbert's Parish Church, Edinburgh, since 1976; b. 18.2.41, Falkirk. Educ. Bo'ness Academy; University of Edinburgh. Assistant Minister, St. Giles Cathedral, Edinburgh; Minister, North Church, Uphall. Recreations: travel; music; sailing. Address: St. Cuthbert's Parish Church, 5 Lothian Road, Edinburgh EH1 2EP; T.-0131-229 1142.

Cutler, Timothy Robert (Robin), CBE, BSc, DSc. Forestry Consultant; b. 24.7.34, India; m., Ishbel W.M.; 1 s.; 1 d. Educ. Banff Academy; Aberdeen University. Colonial Forest Service, Kenya, 1958-64; New Zealand Government Forestry, 1964-90, latterly Chief Executive, New Zealand Ministry of Forestry; Director General, Forestry Commission, 1990-95. Recreations: tennis; golf; travel. Address: 14 Swanston Road, Edinburgh EH10 7BB; T.-0131-445 5437.

Czerkawska, Catherine Lucy, MA (Hons); MA (postgraduate). Novelist and Playwright; b. 3.12.50, Leeds; m., Alan Lees; 1 s. Educ. Queen Margaret's Academy, Ayr; St. Michael's Academy, Kilwinning; Edinburgh University; Leeds University. Wrote and published two books of poetry (White Boats and a Book of Men); taught EFL in Finland and Poland; Community Writer in Fife; thereafter, full-time freelance writer working on novels (The Golden Apple, Shadow of the Stone), radio, television and stage plays; Pye Award for Best Radio Play of 1980, O Flower of Scotland; Scottish Radio Industries Club Award, 1983, for Bonnie Blue Hen; Wormwood, and Quartz produced Traverse Theatre, Edinburgh, 1997 and 2000. Recreations: antique textiles; local history; gardening. Address: 38 Patna Road, Kirkmichael KA19 7PJ; T.-01655 750386; e-mail: catherine@czerkawska.fsnet.co.uk

D

Daiches, Professor David, CBE, MA (Edin), DPhil (Oxon), Hon. DLitt (Edinburgh, Glasgow, Sussex, Brown, Guelph), Docteur de l'Universite (Sorbonne), DUniv (Stirling), Dottore in Lettere (Bologna). Writer; b. 2.9.12, Sunderland; m., Isobel J. Mackay (deceased); 1 s.; 2 d. Educ. George Watson's College, Edinburgh; Edinburgh University; Balliol College, Oxford. Professor of English, Cornell University, 1946-51; University Lecturer in English and Fellow of Jesus College, Cambridge, 1951-61; Professor of English, Sussex University, 1961-77; Director, Institute for Advanced Studies in the Humanities, Edinburgh University, 1980-86. President, Saltire Society, 1981-87, now Hon. President; Past President, Association for Scottish Literary Studies. Publications: numerous works of criticism and biography, including A Critical History of English Literature; Robert Burns; Sir Walter Scott and His World; The Paradox of Scottish Culture; God and the Poets (Gifford Lectures, 1983); A Weekly Scotsman and Other Poems. Recreations: music; talking. Address: (h.) 22 Belgrave Crescent, Edinburgh EH4 3AL.

Dair, Thomas Morrison. Convener, Fife Council, since 2001; Non-Executive Director, East of Scotland Water; Member, St Andrews University Court; Member, St Andrews Links Trust; b. 13.3.35, Cowdenbeath; m., Helen; 1 s.; 1 d. Educ. Beath High School; Lauder College, Dunfermline. Member, Cowdenbeath Burgh Council, 1972-75; Fife County Council, 1972-75; Fife Regional Council, 1975-96 (Education Convener, 1978-94; Vice-Convener, 1994-96); Vice-Convener, Fife Council, 1999-2001. JP. Recreations: golf; gardening; reading. Address: (h.) 5 Barclay Street, Cowdenbeath K14 9SY; T.-01383 510434.

Dalby, Martin, BMus, ARCM. Composer; freelance music/recording producer; Chairman, Composers' Guild of Great Britain; b. 25.4.42, Aberdeen; m., Hilary. Educ. Aberdeen Grammar School; Royal College of Music. Music Producer, BBC Radio 3, 1965-71; Cramb Research Fellow in Composition, Glasgow University, 1971-72; Head of Music, BBC Scotland, 1972-91; Executive Music Producer, BBC Scotland, 1991-93. Recreations: flying; railways; bird-watching; hill-walking. Address: (h.) 23 Muirpark Way, Drymen, near Glasgow G63 ODX; T.-01360 660427; e-mail: martin.dalby@euphony.net

Dale, Brian Graeme, LLB, WS, NP. Partner, Brooke & Brown, WS, Dunbar, since 1974; b. 20.11.46, London; m., Judith Gail de Beaufort Franklin; 4 s.; 2 d. Educ. Bristol Grammar School; Aberdeen University. Diocese of Edinburgh, Scottish Episcopal Church: Treasurer, 1971-2000, Secretary, 1974-90, Registrar, 1974-2001, Chancellor, since 2001; Honorary Secretary, Abbeyfield Society (Dunbar) Ltd. Recreations: music; bridge; singing; family life. Address: (h.) 5 The Doon, Spott, Dunbar, East Lothian; T.-Dunbar 862059.

Dale, Professor John Egerton, BSc, PhD, FRSE, FIBiol. Emeritus Professor of Plant Physiology, Edinburgh University, since 1993; b. 13.2.32, London; m., Jacqueline Joyce Benstock; 1 s.; 2 d. Educ. City of London School; Kings College, London. Plant Physiologist, Empire Cotton Growing Corporation, Uganda, 1956-61; Edinburgh University: Lecturer in Botany, then Reader, 1961-85, Professor of Plant Physiology, 1985-93, Head, Division of Biological Sciences, 1990-93. Secretary, Society for Experimental Biology, 1974-79; Secretary General, Federation of European Societies of Plant Physiology, 1978-84; Trustee, Peter Potter Gallery, 1994-99; Institute of Biology: Chairman, Scottish Branch, since 1999, Member, Council, since 2000; Scottish Wildlife Trust: Vice-

Chairman, since 1999, Convener, Conservation Stategy Committee. Publications: 100 papers on growth of leaves and related topics. Recreations: the arts; travel; gardening. Address: (h.) The Old Bothy, Drem, North Berwick, EH39 5AP; T.-01620 850394.

Dalhousie, Earl of (James Hubert Ramsay), DL, OStJ. Chairman: Jamestown Investments Ltd., Scottish Woodlands Ltd., Dunedin Smaller Companies Investment Trust plc, Brechin Castle Centre Ltd.; President: Caledonian Club, British Deer Society; Vice-Chairman, Game Conservancy Trust; b. 17.1.48, London; m.; 1 s.; 2 d. Educ. Ampleforth College. Commissioned, Coldstream Guards, 1968-71; investment banker. Governor, London Goodenough Trust for Overseas Graduates; Trustee, Mental Health Foundation. Address: (b.) Dalhousie Estates Office, Brechin DD9 6SG; .-01356 624566.

Dalkeith, Earl of (Richard Walter John Montagu Douglas Scott). Member, National Heritage Memorial Fund, since 2000; President, Royal Scottish Geographical Society, since 1999; Regimental Trustee, King's Own Scottish Borderers; Member, Millennium Commission, since 1994; b. 14.2.54; m., Lady Elizabeth Kerr; 2 s.; 2 d. Son and heir of 9th Duke of Buccleuch (qv). Deputy Chairman, Independent Television Commission, 1996-98. Address: (h.) Dabton, Thornhill, Dumfriesshire.

Dallas, Garry, BA (Hons), DipTP, MSc, MRTPI. Director, Development and Environmental Services, Clackmannanshire Council, since 2001; b. 15.8.59, Kirkcaldy; m., Ruth. Educ. Glenrothes High School; Strathclyde University; Heriot-Watt University. Planning Officer, Principal Planner, Planning Manager, Property Development Manager, Head of Planning and Property Development, Clackmannan District Council, 1983-95; Executive Director, Development Services, Clackmannanshire Council, 1995-2001. Founding Director, Alloa Tower Building Preservation Trust. Recreations: motor sports; swimming; golf. Address: (b.) Clackmannanshire Council, Greenfield, Alloa FK10 2AD; T.-01259 452180.

Dalrymple, Sir Hew (Fleetwood) Hamilton-, 10th Bt (created 1697), GCVO, 2001 (KCVO, 1985, CVO, 1974). Lord Lieutenant, East Lothian, 1987-2001; Captain General, Queen's Bodyguard for Scotland (Royal Company of Archers); Gold Stick for Scotland, since 1996; b. 9.4.26; m., Lady Anne-Louise Mary Keppel; 4 s. Educ. Ampleforth; Staff College, Camberley, 1957. Commissioned Grenadier Guards, 1944; DAAG HQ 3rd Division, 1958-60; Regimental Adjt., Grenadier Guards, 1960-62; retired, 1962; Vice-Chairman, Scottish & Newcastle Breweries, 1983-86 (Director, 1967-86); Chairman, Scottish American Investment Co., 1985-91 (Director, 1967-94); DL, East Lothian, 1964; JP, 1987. Address: Leuchie, North Berwick, East Lothian; T.-North Berwick 2903.

Dalrymple-Hamilton, Christian Margaret, MBE, DL; b. 20.9.19, Devon. Former President: Wigtownshire Girl Guides, Wigtownshire Branch British Red Cross Society. Address: (h.) Cladyhouse, Cairnryan, Stranraer, Wigtownshire.

Dalrymple Hamilton, North John Frederick, OBE, TD, MA (Hons), DL. Farmer and Estate Manager; b. 7.5.50, Edinburgh; m., Sally Anne How; 2 s.; 1 d. Educ. Eton College; Aberdeen University. Scottish and Newcastle Breweries, 1972-82; certificate of farming practice, East of Scotland College of Agriculture, 1982-84; farming of Bargany Estate, since 1984. TA Commission, 1967-95; Member, Queen's Bodyguard for Scotland; Deputy

Lieutenant for Ayrshire; President, RBL(S), Maybole Branch. Address: (h.) Lovestone, Girvan, Ayrshire KA26 9RF.

Dalyell, Kathleen Mary, DL, MA, FRSAS. Chairman, Royal Commission on Ancient and Historical Monuments of Scotland, since 2000; Administrator, The Binns; Director, Heritage Education Trust, since 1987; Director, Weslo Housing Association, since 1994; Director, Carmont Settlement Trust, since 1997; Deputy Lieutenant, West Lothian; b. 17.11.37, Edinburgh; m., Tam Dalyell; 1 s.; 1 d. Educ. Convent of Sacred Heart, Aberdeen; Edinburgh University; Craiglochart Teacher Training College. Teacher of History, St. Augustine's Secondary School, Glasgow, 1961-62; James Gillespie's High School for Girls, Edinburgh, 1962-63; Member, Historic Buildings Council for Scotland, 1975-87; Member, Lady Provost of Edinburgh's Delegation to China, 1987; Member, National Committee of Architectural Heritage Society for Scotland, 1983-89 (Vice-Chair, 1986-89); Chairman, Bo'ness Heritage Trust, 1988-93; Trustee, Paxton Trust, 1988-92; Member, Ancient Monuments Board for Scotland, 1989-2000; Member, Royal Fine Art Commission for Scotland, 1992-2000. Recreations: reading; travel; hillwalking; chess. Address: The Binns, Linlithgow EH49 7NA; T.-01506 83 4255.

Dalyell, Tam. MP (Labour), Linlithgow (formerly West Lothian), since 1962; Father of House of Commons, since 2001; Weekly Columnist, New Scientist, since 1967; Chairman, All-Party Latin America Group, since 1998; b. 9.8.32, Edinburgh; m., Kathleen Wheatley; 1 s.; 1 d. Educ. Edinburgh Academy; Harecroft; Eton; King's College, Cambridge; Moray House, Edinburgh. National Service, Scots Greys; Teacher, Bo'ness Academy, 1957-61; Deputy Director of Studies, Ship-School Dunera, 1961-62; Member, Public Accounts Committee, 1962-66; PPS to R.H.S. Crossman, 1964-70; Vice-Chairman, Parliamentary Labour Party, 1974-76; Member, European Parliament, 1975-78; Member: National Executive Committee, Labour Party, 1986-87, Advisory Council on Biological Sciences, Edinburgh University; a Vice-President, Research Defence Society; led Parliamentary Delegation to: Bolivia, 2000, Peru, 1999. Hon. Doctor of Science, Edinburgh University, 1994; Hon. Doctor, City University, London, 1998. Publications: Case for Ship Schools, 1959; Ship-School Dunera, 1961; Devolution: the end of Britain?, 1978; A Science Policy for Britain, 1983; One Man's Falklands, 1983; Misrule, 1987; Dick Crossman: a portrait, 1989. Address: (h.) The Binns, Linlithgow EH49 7NA; T.-01506-834255.

Dalziel, Graeme Davies, BA, CA. Chief Executive, Dunfermline Building Society, since 2001; b. 25.11.54, Glasgow; m., Anne; 2 s.; 1 d. Educ. Eastwood High School; University of Strathclyde. Qualified as CA with Thornton Baker, Chartered Accountants, Glasgow, 1977-81; Scottish Equitable Life Assurance Society, 1981-94: Group Chief Accountant, Director, Scottish Equitable Fund Managers Ltd.; Scottish Widows, 1994-98: Head of Finance, Director, Scottish Widows Fund Management, Scottish Widows Property Management, Pensions Management (SWF) Ltd.; Finance Director, Dunfermline Building Society, 1998-2001. Finance Director of the Year, 2001; Member, Board of Management, Lauder College; Director, Enterprise Lauder Ltd. Recreations: golf; gardening; family. Address: (b.) Caledonia House, Carnegie Avenue, Dunfermline KY11 8PJ; T.-01383 627727; e-mail: graeme.dalziel@dunfermline-bs.co.uk

Dane, Graham Charles, BSc, BA, MEd, MIL, MInstP, CPhys. Principal Teacher of Physics, St. Augustine's High School, Edinburgh, since 1983; b. 19.7.50; m., Margaret Coupar; 1 s.; 1 d. Educ. St. Andrews University. Teacher of Science, Merksworth High School, Paisley, 1973-75; Information Scientist, The Electricity Council, London,

1975-77; Teacher of Physics, Forrester High School, Edinburgh, 1978-80; Assistant Principal Teacher of Science, Deans Community High School, Livingston, 1980-83. Elected Member, General Teaching Council for Scotland (Convener, Committee on Exceptional Admission to the Register), 1995-2001; holder of numerous trade union positions over the years, mainly in the EIS (Member, Executive Council, EIS); Member, Board, SCRE, 1992-98; Chair, Currie Community Council; Vice-Chair, Socialist Educational Association Scotland; Governor, Donaldson's College (Convener, Education Committee). Recreations: learning new things; meeting people he likes; enjoying the arts. Address: (h.) 25 Thomson Road, Edinburgh EH14 5HT.

Daniels, Peter William, MA. Chief Executive, East Renfrewshire Council, since 1995; b. 8.6.49, Wishaw; m., Anne M.S. Smith; 3 s.; 1 d. Educ. Brandon High School, Motherwell; Dalziel High School, Motherwell; Glasgow University; Jordanhill College of Education, Glasgow. Lecturer in Public Administration, Bell College of Technology, Hamilton, 1972-75; Personal Assistant to Chief Executive, Renfrew District Council, 1975-81; Assistant Chief Executive, Leicester City Council, 1981-83; Chief Executive, Clydesdale District Council, 1983-95. Member, East Kilbride District Council, 1979-81; Member, Scottish Records Advisory Council, since 1998. Recreations: Motherwell Football Club; classical music; playing clarinet. Address: (b.) East Renfrewshire Council, Eastwood Park, Rouken Glen Road, Giffnock, East Renfrewshire G46 6UG; T.-0141-577 3010.

Dareau, Margaret Grace, MA. Senior Editor, Scottish National Dictionary Association, since 2001; Senior Editor and Editorial Director, Dictionary of the Older Scottish Tongue, 1984-2001; b. 11.3.44, Dumfries; m., Michel Dareau; 1 s.; 2 d. Educ. Annan Academy; Edinburgh University. Research Assistant on Linguistic Atlas of Late Middle English, 1967; Kennedy Scholarship to study linguistics, MIT, 1967; began work at Dictionary of Older Scottish Tongue, 1968; Editor, Concise Scots Dictionary, 1976-77, 1980-84; Glossary Editor, Edinburgh Encyclopedia of Language and Linguistics. Recreation: painting; horse riding. Address: (h.) The Old Manse, Howgate, Penicuik EH26 8QB; T.-01968 673028.

Darling, Alistair Maclean, LLB. MP (Labour), Edinburgh Central, since 1987; Secretary of State for Work and Pensions, since 2001; Member, Faculty of Advocates, since 1984; b. 28.11.53, London; m., Margaret Vaughan; 1 s.; 1 d. Educ. Loretto School; Aberdeen University. Solicitor, 1978-83; Advocate, since 1984; Member: Lothian Regional Council, 1982-87, Lothian and Borders Police Board, 1982-87; Governor, Napier College, 1985-87; Chief Secretary to the Treasury, 1997-98; Secretary of State for Social Security, 1998-2001. Address: (b.) 15A Stafford Street, Edinburgh EH3 7BU; T.-0131-476 2552.

Darling, Ian Marshall, FRICS. Director, Chesterton Scotland, since 1996; Board Member, British Waterways; b. 16.4.45, Perth; m., Kate; 1 s.; 1 d. Educ. Perth Academy; London University (College of Estate Management and Wye College). Qualified as a Chartered Surveyor, 1968; Partner, Bell Ingram, 1974; Managing Partner, 1987-96. Chairman, Royal Institution of Chartered Surveyors in Scotland, 1997-98; Master, Company of Merchants of the City of Edinburgh; Member, Council, RSPB. Recreations: nature conservation; ornithology. Address: (b.) 36 Castle Street, Edinburgh EH2 3HT; T.-0131-226 4791.

Darwent, Rt. Rev. Frederick Charles, LTh (Hon), JP. Bishop of Aberdeen and Orkney, 1978-92; b. 20.4.27, Liverpool; m., 1, Edna Lilian Waugh (deceased); 2 d.; 2, Roma Evelyn Fraser. Educ. Warbreck School, Liverpool; Ormskirk Grammar School; Wells Theological College, Somerset. Followed a banking career, 1943-61; War

Service, Far East, 1945-48; ordained Deacon, 1963, Priest, 1964, Diocese of Liverpool; Curate, Pemberton, Wigan, 1963-65; Rector: Strichen, 1965-71, New Pitsligo, 1965-78, Fraserburgh, 1971-78; Canon, St. Andrew's Cathedral, Aberdeen, 1971; Dean of Aberdeen and Orkney, 1973-78. Recreations: amateur stage (acting and production); calligraphy; music. Address: (h.) 107 Osborne Place, Aberdeen AB25 2DD; T.-01224 646497.

Das, Sachinandan, MB, BS, FRCR, DMRT. Head, Department of Radiotherapy and Oncology, Dundee University, 1987-2000; Chairman, Tayside Oncology Research Committee, since 1987; b. 1.8.44, Cuttack, India; m., Dr. Subhalaxmi; 1 s.; 1 d. Educ. Ravenshaw Collegiate School; SCB Medical College, Cuttack, India; Utkal University. Senior House Officer in Radiotherapy, Plymouth General Hospital, 1969-70; Registrar in Radiotherapy and Oncology, then Senior Registrar, Mersey Regional Centre for Radiotherapy, Liverpool, 1970-77; Consultant in administrative charge, Ninewells Hospital, Dundee, 1987-91, Clinical Director, 1991-98; Regional Postgraduate Education Advisor in Radiotherapy and Oncology, since 1987. Member: Standing Scottish Committee, National Medical Consultative Committee, Scottish Paediatric Oncology Group, Joint Radiological Safety Committee, Radiation Hazards Sub-Committee, Unit Medical and Dental Advisory Committee; Council Member, Scottish Radiological Society, 1987-93. Recreations: hill-walking; table tennis; reading. Address: (h.) Grapevine, 42 Menzieshill Road, Dundee DD2 1PU; T.-Dundee 642915.

Datta, Dipankar, MBBS, FRCPGlas, FRCPLond. Consultant Physician (with special interest in gastroenterology), 1975-97; former Honorary Senior Clinical Lecturer and Clinical Sub-Dean, Glasgow University; Founder Director, Scottish Overseas Aid; b. 30.1.33, Chittagong, India; m., Dr. J.B. Datta; 1 s.; 1 d. Educ. Calcutta University. Former Vice Chairman, UN Association, Glasgow; former Chairman, Overseas Doctors' Association, Scottish Division; former Chairman, British Medical Association, Lanarkshire; former Member, Central Executive Committee, Scottish Council, United Nations Association; former Member, Lanarkshire Health Board; former Member, Scottish Council, British Medical Association; former Member, Executive Committee, Scottish Council, Royal Commonwealth Society for the Blind; former Member, Senate, Glasgow University; former Member, General Medical Council; Chairman, South Asia Voluntary Enterprise; former Chairman, Scottish India Forum. Recreations: reading - history, economics and international politics. Address: (h.) 9 Kirkvale Crescent, Newton Mearns, Glasgow G77 5HB; T.-0141-639 1515; e-mail: dipankardatta@hotmail.com

Datta, Pradip Kumar, MS, FRCS(Edin), FRCS(Eng), FRCS(Ire), FRCS(Glas). Consultant Surgeon, Caithness General Hospital, since 1980; b. 14.5.40, Calcutta, India; m., Swati; 1 s. Educ. St. Aloysius High School, Visakhapatnam, India; Andhra University, Visakhapatnam, India. Surgical Registrar: Hope Hospital, Salford, Poole General Hospital, Plymouth General Hospital, Royal Cornwall Hospital, Truro; Senior Surgical Registrar, Whittington Hospital, London; Member, Council, and Surgical Tutor, Royal College of Surgeons of Edinburgh. Visiting Lecturer: University Sains Malaysia, National University of Singapore. Recreations: playing squash; fly-fishing. Address: (h.) Garvyk, 17 Newton Avenue, Wick KW1 5LJ; T.-01955 605050.

Davenport, Dr Richard John, DM, MRCP(UK), BMBS (Hons), BMedSci. Consultant Neurologist, Western General Hospital, Edinburgh, since 1999, Royal Infirmary, Edinburgh, since 1999; b. 22.9.63, Chester; m., Meryl Peat. Educ. King's College, Wimbledon; Nottingham University Medical School. Nottingham University Medical School, 1982-87; House Officer,

Queen's Medical Centre, Nottingham, 1987-88; Senior House Officer and Registrar, Stoke-on-Trent, 1988-91; Registrar, then Research Registrar, Edinburgh, 1992-96; Advanced Neurological Trainee, Perth, Australia, 1997-98; Senior Registrar, Edinburgh, 1998. Recreations: cooking; travel; walking the dog. Address: (h.) 25 Granby Road, Edinburgh EH16 5NP; T.-0131-537 2072.

Davidson, Hon. Lord (Charles Kemp Davidson), MA, LLB, FRSE. Chairman, Scottish Law Commission, 1988-96; Senator of the College of Justice, 1983-96; Deputy Chairman, Boundaries Commission for Scotland, 1985-96; b. 13.4.29, Edinburgh; m., Mary Mactaggart; 1 s.; 2 d. Educ. Fettes College, Edinburgh; Oxford University; Edinburgh University. Advocate, 1956; QC (Scot), 1969; Keeper, The Advocates Library, 1972-77; Vice Dean, Faculty of Advocates, 1977-79; Dean, 1979-83; Procurator to the General Assembly of the Church of Scotland, 1972-83; Chairman, National Health Service Tribunal for Scotland, 1970-83. Address: (h.) 22 Dublin Street, Edinburgh EH1 3PP; T.-0131-556 2168.

Davidson, Professor Colin William, BSc, DipER, PhD, CEng, HonFIEE. Consulting Engineer; b. 18.9.34, Edinburgh; m., Ranee M.N. Cleland; 2 d. Educ. George Heriot's School; Edinburgh University. Lecturer, Edinburgh University, 1956-61; Electronics Engineer, Nuclear Enterprises (GB) Ltd., 1961-64; Lecturer, Heriot-Watt College/University, 1964-67; Associate Professor, Chulalongkorn University, Bangkok, 1967-68; Heriot-Watt University: Senior Lecturer, 1968-85, Professor of Electrical Engineering, 1985-88, Dean of Engineering, 1976-79 and 1984-87, Head of Department, 1979-87. Member, Lothian Regional Council, 1990-94; Vice-President, Institution of Electrical Engineers, 1990-93, 1995-98, Honorary Treasurer, 1999-2001; Member, Engineering Council Senate and Board for Engineers' Regulation, 1996-98; Freeman, City of London; Liveryman, Worshipful Company of Engineers. Recreation: sailing (Royal Highland Yacht Club). Address: (h.) 6/14 Succoth Court, Succoth Park, Edinburgh EH12 6BY; T.-0131-337 6310.

Davidson, David. MSP (Conservative), North East Scotland, since 1999; Conservative Spokesperson on Finance and Tourism; b. 1943, Edinburgh; m.; 3 s.; 2 d. Educ. Trinity Academy, Edinburgh; Heriot-Watt University; Manchester Business School. Registered pharmacist; former proprietor and director of a group of community pharmacies in North of England; former Director, Unichem Ltd.; founder Chairman, Association of Scottish Community Councils; Managing Director, family farming business; former Member, Pharmaceutical Advisory Committees, Scottish Office. Address: (b.) Scottish Parliament, Edinburgh EH99 1SP; T.-0131-348 5653; e-mail: David.Davidson.msp@scottish.parliament.uk

Davidson, Professor Donald Allen, BSc, PhD, FRSE. Professor of Environmental Science, Stirling University, since 1991; b. 27.4.45, Lumphanan; m., Caroline E. Brown; 1 s.; 2 d. Educ. Robert Gordon's College, Aberdeen; Aberdeen University; Sheffield University. Lecturer, St. David's University College, Wales, 1971-76; Lecturer, Senior Lecturer, Reader, Strathclyde University, 1976-86; Reader, Stirling University, 1986-91. Member, Soil Biodiversity Steering Committee, Natural Environmental Research Council. Publications include: The Evaluation of Land Resources, 1992; many papers. Recreations: exploring the countryside; real ale. Address: (b.) Department of Environmental Science, Stirling University, Stirling FK9 4LA; T.-01786 467840.

Davidson, Duncan Lewis Watt, BSc (Hons), MB, ChB, FRCPEdin. Consultant Neurologist, Tayside Health Board, since 1976; Honorary Senior Lecturer in Medicine, Dundee University, since 1976; b. 16.5.40, Kingston, Jamaica; m.,

Dr. Anne V.M. Maiden; 4 s.; 1 d. Educ. Knox College, Jamaica; Edinburgh University. House Officer, Senior House Officer, Registrar and Senior Registrar posts in medicine and neurology, Edinburgh, 1966-75; Peel Travelling Fellowship, Montreal, 1973-74; MRC clinical scientific staff, MRC Brain Metabolism Unit, Edinburgh, 1975-76. Recreations: gardening; photography. Address: (h.) Brooksby, Queens Terrace, St. Andrews, Fife KY16 9ER; T.-01334 76108.

Davidson, Euan, LLB(Hons). Director-Scotland, The Prince's Trust, since 2000; b. 8.7.58, Bellshill; m., 1, Elspeth Robertson (divorced); 2, Dawn Gaw; 1 s.; 1 d. Educ. Hutchesons' Grammar School, Glasgow; University of Glasgow. Wright, Johnston and Mackenzie, Solicitors, Glasgow: Apprentice, 1979, Solicitor, 1981, Partner, 1985, Managing Partner, 1991-94; Clydeport plc: Director and Secretary, 1994, Corporate Services Director, 1996, Operations Director, 1997; Commercial Director, 1999-2000. Member of Council, British Ports Association, 1997-2000; Member, Scottish National Transport Forum, 1998-2000; Session Clerk, Cairngryffe Parish Church. Recreations: hillwalking; gardening. Address: (b.) 57 Queen Street, Glasgow G1 3EN; T.-0141-204 4409; e-mail: euandavi@princes-trust.org.uk

Davidson, Ian Graham, MA (Hons). MP (Labour and Co-op), Glasgow Pollok, since 1997 (Glasgow Govan 1992-97);b. 8.9.50, Jedburgh; m., Morag Mackinnon; 1 s.; 1 d. Educ. Jedburgh Grammar School; Galashiels Academy; Edinburgh University; Jordanhill College of Education. Project Manager, Community Service Volunteers, 1985-92; Councillor, Strathclyde Regional Council, 1978-92 (Chair, Education Committee, 1986-92); Member, Public Accounts Select Committee, since 1997, Member, Committee of Selection, 1997-99; Secretary: Trade Union Group of Labour MPs, Tribune Group of MPs. Address: House of Commons, London SW1A 0AA.

Davidson, Rev. Ian Murray Pollock, MBE, MA, BD. Minister, Allan Park South Church and Church of the Holy Rude, Stirling, 1985-94; Chairman, General Trustees, Church of Scotland, 1994-99; b. 14.3.28, Kirriemuir; m., Isla; 2 s. Educ. Montrose Academy; St. Andrews University. National Service, 1949-51; Minister: Crieff North and West Church (St. Andrew's), 1955-61, Grange Church, Kilmarnock, 1961-67, Cambuslang Old Church, 1967-85; Convener, Maintenance of the Ministry Committee and Board, Church and Ministry Department, 1981-84; General Trustee, since 1975. Publications: At the Sign of the Fish (history of Cambuslang Old Parish Church), 1975; A Guide to the Church of the Holy Rude. Recreations: travel; photography; reading; writing. Address: (h.) 13/8 Craigend Park, Edinburgh EH16 5XX; T.-0131-664 0074.

Davidson, John F., MB, ChB, FRCPEdin, FRCPath. Consultant Haematologist, Glasgow Royal Infirmary, 1969-98; b. 11.1.34, Lumphanan; m., Laura G. Middleton; 1 s.; 1 d. Educ. Robert Gordon's College, Aberdeen; Aberdeen University. Surgeon Lt., RN; Registrar in Medicine, Aberdeen Royal Infirmary; Research Registrar in Medicine, then Senior Registrar in Haematology, Glasgow Royal Infirmary; Honorary Clinical Senior Lecturer, Glasgow University; Honorary Consultant Haematologist, Strathclyde University. Secretary, British Society for Haematalogy, 1983-86; President, British Society for Haematology, 1990-91; Chairman: BCSH Haemostasis and Thrombosis Task Force, 1986-91, Steering Committee NEQAS in blood coagulation, 1986-91; Member, Council, Royal College of Pathologists, two terms; Secretary, Joint Committee on Haematology, Royal College of Pathologists and Royal College of Physicians; Chairman, UK Joint Working Group on Quality Assurance. Editor, Progress in Fibrinolysis, Volumes I to VII; Chairman, International Committee on Fibrinolysis, 1976-84; Co-Editor in Chief,

Fibrinolysis, 1986-96. Recreation: gardening. Address: (h.) Craigiebank, 20 Roman Road, Bearsden, Glasgow; T.-0141-942 3356.

Davidson, John Knight, OBE, MD, FRCP (Edin), FRCP (Glas), FRCR, (Hon) FACR, (Hon) FRACR. Consultant Radiologist; expert adviser on bone disease in compressed air and diving medicine; b. 17.8.25, Edinburgh; m., Edith E. McKelvie; 2 s.; 1 d. Educ. George Watson's Boys College, Edinburgh; Edinburgh University. Adviser in Bone Disease in Divers MRC, Aberdeen, US Navy, 1970-92; Non Executive Director, Yorkhill NHS Trust, 1993-95; Member, Council, Medical and Dental Defence Union, 1971-95; Chairman, Health Policy, Council, Scottish Conservative and Unionist Association, 1991-95; Member, BBC Medical Advisory Group, 1988-95; Consultant Radiologist in Administrative Charge, Western Infirmary and Gartnavel General, Glasgow, 1967-90; Royal College of Radiologists: Member, Council, 1984-87, Chairman, Examining Board, 1976-79, Scottish Committee, 1985-89; Member, Council, Royal Glasgow Institute of Fine Arts, 1978-88; Deputy President, Glasgow and Renfrewshire, British Red Cross Society, 1988-93; Honorary Fellow: Royal Australian College of Radiology, 1981, Scottish Radiological Society, 1990, American College of Radiology, 1992, Medical and Dental Defence Union, Scotland, 1995; Honorary Fellow and Medallist, International Skeletal Society, 1995; Rohan Williams Professor, Australasia, 1977; Aggarwal Memorial Oration, India, 1988. Editor, Aseptic Necrosis of Bone and numerous publications. Recreations: golf; painting; bridge; meeting people; skiing. Address: (h.) 15 Beechlands Avenue, Netherlee, Glasgow G44 3YT; T.-0141-637 0290.

Davidson, Julie Wilson. Writer and Broadcaster; freelance contributor to radio, television, books, newspapers and magazines, since 1981, now specialising in travel writing; b. 11.5.43, Motherwell; m., Harry Reid (qv); 1 d. Educ. Aberdeen High School for Girls. Trainee Journalist, D.C. Thomson Ltd., Dundee, 1961-64; Feature Writer and Sub-Editor, Aberdeen Press & Journal, 1964-67; The Scotsman: Feature Writer, 1967-77, Columnist, 1977-81; Columnist, The Herald, 1995-97; Television Critic, The Herald, 1981-95. Columnist/Critic of the Year, Scottish Press Awards, 1985; Critic of the Year, Scottish Press Awards, 1988-89-92-94-95; Canada Travel Award, 1992; Travelex Travel Writers Award, 1999; Scottish Thistle Travel Media Award, 1999. Recreations: reading; walking; travelling; lunching; e-mail: julied@features.sagehost.co.uk

Davidson, Neil Forbes, QC, BA, MSc, LLB, LLM. Solicitor General for Scotland, since 2000; b. 13.9.50; m. Educ. Stirling University; Bradford University; Edinburgh University. Admitted, Faculty of Advocates, 1979; Standing Junior Counsel to Registrar General, 1982, to Department of Health and Social Security, 1988; called to the Bar, Inner Temple, 1990. Address: Crown Office, 25 Chambers Street, Edinburgh EH1 1LA; T.-0131- 226 2626.

Davidson, Professor Peter Robert Keith Andrew, BA, MA, PhD (Cantab), MA, FSAS. Chalmers Regius Professor of English, Aberdeen University, since 2000; b. 14.5.57, Glasgow; m., Jane Barbara Stevenson. Educ. Clare College, Cambridge; York University. Lecturer, St Andrews University, 1989-90; Universiteit Leiden, 1990-92; Lecturer, Warwick University, 1992-2000 (Senior Lecturer, 1995, Reader, 1998). Publications: Poems and Translations of Sir Richard Fanshawe; Poetry and Revolution. Recreation: casuistry. Address: (b.) King's College, Aberdeen AB24 2UB.

Davidson, Sheriff Richard Alexander, LLB, NP. Sheriff of Tayside Central and Fife at Dundee, since 1994; b. 3.11.47, Lennoxtown; m., Shirley Margaret Thomson; 1 s.; 1 d. Educ. Oban High School; Glasgow University.

Apprentice Solicitor, 1969-72; Assistant Solicitor, 1972-76; Partner, Tindal Oatts, 1976-94. Member, Glasgow and North Argyll Legal Aid Committee, 1984-89. Address: (b.) Sheriff Courthouse, West Bell Street, Dundee.

Davidson, Professor Robert, MA, BD, DD, FRSE. Moderator, General Assembly of the Church of Scotland, 1990-91; Professor of Old Testament Language and Literature, Glasgow University, 1972-91; Principal, Trinity College, Glasgow, 1981-91; b. 30.3.27, Markinch, Fife; m., Elizabeth May Robertson; 4 s.; 4 d. Educ. Bell-Baxter School, Cupar; St. Andrews University. Lecturer in Biblical Studies, Aberdeen University, 1953-60; Lecturer in Hebrew and Old Testament Studies, St. Andrews University, 1960-66; Lecturer/Senior Lecturer in Old Testament, Edinburgh University, 1966-72. Publications: The Bible Speaks, 1959; The Old Testament, 1964; Genesis 1 - 11, 1973; Genesis 12 - 50, 1979; The Bible in Religious Education, 1979; The Courage to Doubt, 1983; Jeremiah Volume 1, 1983; Jeremiah Volume 2, Lamentations, 1985; Ecclesiastes, Song of Songs, 1986; Wisdom and Worship, 1990; A Beginner's Guide to the Old Testament, 1992; Go by the Book, 1996; The Vitality of Worship, 1998. Recreations: music; gardening. Address: (h.) 30 Dumgoyne Drive, Bearsden, Glasgow G61 3AP; T.-0141-942 1810.

Davie, George Elder. Philosopher; b. 1912, Dundee; m., Elspeth Davie (deceased). Educ. Edinburgh University. Taught at Edinburgh University until 1939 and at Queen's University, Belfast, 1945-59, before returning to Edinburgh; leading scholar of the Scottish Enlightenment; books include: The Democratic Intellect, 1961, and The Crisis of the Democratic Intellect, 1986.

Davie, Ivor Turnbull, MB, ChB, FRCA, FRCPE, HonFCPS. Consultant Anaesthetist, Western General Hospital, Edinburgh, 1971-98; Honorary Senior Lecturer, Edinburgh University, 1979-97; Lecturer, Central Midwives Board (Scotland), 1974-97; b. 23.2.35, Edinburgh; m., Jane Elizabeth Fleischmann; 1 s.; 1 d. Educ. Royal High School, Edinburgh; Edinburgh University. Member, Board of Examiners, Faculty of Anaesthetists, Royal College of Surgeons of England and Royal College of Anaesthetists, 1978-91; President, Edinburgh and East of Scotland Society of Anaesthetists, 1990-91; Tutor, Faculty of Anaesthetists, 1979-87; Regional Educational Adviser, Royal College of Anaesthetists, 1988-95; Member, Editorial Board, British Journal of Obstetrics and Gynaecology, 1980-84; Visiting Medical Officer, Westmead Centre, Sydney, NSW, 1983. Address: (h.) 26 Kingsburgh Road, Edinburgh EH12 6PZ; T.-0131-337 1117.

Davies, Alan Graham, LLB(Hons), Dip. Legal Practice. Solicitor in private practice since 1983, Partner, since 1987; Council Member, Law Society of Scotland, since 1996; b. 4.2.59, Perth; m., Fiona; 2 s.; 1 d. Educ. Perth Grammar School; University of Edinburgh. Accredited family law mediator. Recreations: squash; golf; football (President, Methven Amateur F.C.). Address: (b.) 25 South Methven Street, Perth; T.-01738 620451.

Davies, Professor Sir Graeme John, Kt, BE, MA, PhD, ScD, FREng, FRSE. Principal and Vice-Chancellor, Glasgow University, since 1995; b. 7.4.37, New Zealand; m., Florence; 2 d. Educ. Mt. Albert Grammar School, Auckland; University of Auckland; Cambridge University. Junior Lecturer, University of Auckland, 1960-62; Lecturer, Cambridge University, 1962-77; Professor of Metallurgy, Sheffield University, 1978-86; Vice-Chancellor, Liverpool University, 1986-91; Chief Executive: Universities Funding Council, 1991-93, Higher Education Funding Council for England, 1992-95. Chairman, USS Ltd., since 1996. Hon. LLD, Liverpool, 1991; Hon. FRSNZ, 1993; Hon. DMet, Sheffield, 1995; Hon. DSc, Nottingham, 1995; Hon. FTCL, 1995; Hon. LLD, Strathclyde, 2000; FIMechE; FIM; FRSA; CBIM; DL, Merseyside, 1989-93; Hon. DEng, Manchester

Metropolitan University, 1996. Recreations: bird-watching; golf; The Times crossword. Address: (b.) Glasgow University, Glasgow G12 8QQ; T.-0141-330 5995.

Davies (a.k.a. Glasse-Davies), Professor R. Wayne, MA, PhD, ScD. Robertson Professor of Biotechnology, Glasgow University, since 1989; b. 10.6.44, Cardiff; m., Victoria Glasse; 3 s.; 2 d. Educ. Queen Elizabeth's Hospital, Bristol; St. John's College, Cambridge. Research Fellow, University of Wisconsin, 1968-71; H3 Professor, Universität zu Köln, FRG, 1971-77; Lecturer, University of Essex, 1977-81; Senior Lecturer, UMIST, 1981-83; Vice-President, Scientific and Research Director, Allelix Biopharmaceuticals, Toronto, 1983-89; Neuropa Ltd.: Founding Director, 1996, CEO, 1997-2000; Founder, NIM Ltd., 2000. Recreations: poetry and literature; cello; skiing. Address: (b.) Robertson Laboratory of Biotechnology, Institute of Biomedical and Life Sciences, Glasgow University, 54 Dumbarton Road, Glasgow G11 6NU.

Davies, Trevor John, BA. Independent Television Producer, since 1981; b. 23.1.44, London; lives with Elaine Pidgeon; 1 step-s.; 1 step-d. Educ. University of Leicester. General Secretary, Scottish Union of Students, 1968; Secretary, Open University in Scotland, 1969-74; Assistant Director, Scottish Council of Social Service, 1974-78; Freelance Journalist and Broadcaster, 1978-85; credits include: Producer, The Big Day, Glasgow, 1990; Executive Producer, Hamish MacBeth; Producer, Bombay Blue. Councillor, Edinburgh Town Council, 1971-75; Parliamentary Candidate, 1974; Councillor, Lothian Region Council, 1974-78; Chair: Scottish Volleyball Association, 1979-83, Edinburgh Central Citizens' Advice Bureau, 1980-84; Vice-Chair, Edinburgh Council of Social Service, 1982-84; Director and Vice-Chair, Wester Hailes Community Enterprises, 1983-91; Scottish Convener and UK Council Member, Independent Programme Producers Association, 1988-91; Governor, Scottish Film Council, 1990-95; Chair, Scottish Screen Industry Project, 1991-94; Candidate, elections to Scottish Parliament, 1999; Member, City of Edinburgh Council, since 2001. Recreations: jazz; gardening. Address: (b.) 10 Scotland Street, Edinburgh EH3 6PS; T.-0131-557 4580; e-mail: trevor@skyline.uk.com

Davis, Carl, MB, MCh, FRCS(I), FRCS(Glas), FRCS(Paed). Consultant Paediatric Surgeon, since 1992; b. 7.10.56, Cork; m., Sheila; 2 s.; 2 d. Educ. University College, Cork. Started ECMO (Extracorporeal membrane oxygenation) service for Scotland, 1992. Hon. Clinical Lecturer, Glasgow University. Address: (b.) Department of Paediatric Surgery, Royal Hospital for Sick Children, Yorkhill, Glasgow G3 8SJ; T.-0141-201 0000.

Davis, Christine A.M., CBE, MA, DipEd. Chairman, Scottish Agricultural Wages Board, since 1995 (Member, since 1990); Member, Scottish Panel on Public Appointments; Member, Court, University of St. Andrews, since 2000; Chairman, Scottish Legal Aid Board, 1991-98; b. 5.3.44, Salisbury; m., Robin John Davis; 2 d. Educ. Perth Academy; Ayr Academy; St. Andrews University; Aberdeen University; Aberdeen College of Education. Teacher of History and Modern Studies, Cumbernauld High School and High School of Stirling, 1967-69; joined Dunblane Town Council and Perth and Kinross Joint County Council, 1972; undertook research in Canada on Ontario Hydro and small claims in Ontario courts, 1977-78; Chairman, Electricity Consultative Council for North of Scotland, 1980-90; Member: North of Scotland Hydro Electric Board, 1980-90, Scottish Economic Council, 1987-95, Scottish Committee of the Council on Tribunals, 1989-95; Clerk, Britain Yearly Meeting, Society of Friends (Quakers), 1991-95; a President, Council of Churches for Britain and Ireland, 1990-92; Trustee, Joseph Rowntree

Charitable Trust. Recreations: embroidery; bird-watching; walking. Address: (h.) 24 Newton Crescent, Dunblane, Perthshire FK15 ODZ; T.-Dunblane 823226.

Davis, Dennis Tyrone, OBE, OStJ, QFSM, CEng, CIMgt, FIFireE (Life), MinstE. Her Majesty's Chief Inspector of Fire Services for Scotland, since 1999; b. 10.2.47; m., Maureen; 2 s. Educ. Queen Mary's Grammar School, Walsall. Joined Walsall Fire Brigade, 1965; Cheshire Fire Brigade, 1971; Assistant Chief Fire Officer, 1983; Deputy Chief Fire Officer, 1984; Chief Fire Officer, Cheshire Fire Brigade, 1986. Chairman, Management Committee, Institution of Fire Engineers; Chairman, Fire Conferences and Exhibitions Ltd.; Past President, Institution of Fire Engineers; Past President, Chief and Assistant Chief Fire Officers' Association. Recreation: sailing. Address: (b.) HM Fire Service Inspectorate, Scottish Executive, Saughton House, Broomhouse Drive, Edinburgh EH11 3XD; T.-0131-244 2342; e-mail: dennis.davis@scotland.gsi.gov.uk

Davis, Gerry. Journalist/Public Relations Consultant, since 1970; TV Producer and Presenter, since 1989; Media Training Provider, since 1991; b. 7.10.35, Glasgow; m., June Imray; 1 s.; 1 d. Educ. Shawlands Academy, Glasgow; Strathclyde University. Trainee analytical chemist, ICI; pharmaceutical chemist; actor; television continuity announcer/programme presenter/reporter, BBC Radio Scotland. Former Radio Reporter of the Year/Presenter of the Year. Recreation: holidaying. Address: (b.) Davis Media, 10 Wellwood Terrace, Cults, Aberdeen AB15 9JA; T.-01224 862330; e-mail: gd@davismedia.co.uk

Davis, Margaret Thomson. Novelist; b. Bathgate; 2 s. Educ. Albert Secondary School. Worked as children's nurse; Red Cross nurse; short story writer; novelist; author of autobiography, The Making of a Novelist; novels include The Breadmakers, A Baby Might Be Crying, A Sort of Peace, The Prisoner, The Prince and the Tobacco Lords, Roots of Bondage, Scorpion in the Fire, The Dark Side of Pleasure, A Very Civilised Man, Light and Dark, Rag Woman Rich Woman, Daughters and Mothers, Wounds of War, A Woman of Property, A Sense of Belonging, Hold Me Forever, Kiss Me No More,A Kind of Immortality, Burning Ambition. Committee Member: International PEN (Scottish Branch); Society of Authors; Lecturer in Creative Writing; Honorary President, Strathkelvin Writers Club. Recreations: reading; travelling; being with friends.

Davis, Ray, DipArch, MSc, DipUD, RIBA, FRIAS. Managing Director, Davis Duncan Architects, since 1981; b. 11.2.48, Glasgow; m., Ruth; 3 d. Educ. Aberdeen Grammar School; Robert Gordon University; Heriot Watt University. Alison and Hutcheson and Partners: Architect, Edinburgh Office, 1973-79, Senior Architect and Office Manager, Glasgow, 1979-81; Visiting Lecturer, Planning Department, Mackintosh School, 1979-81; formed Ray Davis Architects and Urban Design Consultants, 1981; part-time Design Tutor, Department of Architecture, Strathclyde University, 1981-86; formed current practice, 1982. Convenor, Baptist Union Property Group, 1997. Recreations: golf; sketching; skiing; church. Address: North Elgin, 6 Balfleurs Street, Milngavie, Glasgow; T.-0141-956 1458; e-mail: rdavis@davisduncan.co.uk

Davison, Timothy Paul, BA (Hons), MHSM, DipHSM, MBA, MPH. Chief Executive, Greater Glasgow Primary Care NHS Trust, since 1999; b. 4.6.61, Newcastle upon Tyne; m., Hilary Williamson; 1 s. Educ. Kenton School, Newcastle upon Tyne; Stirling University; Glasgow University. Appointments in Stirling Royal Infirmary, Royal Edinburgh Hospital, Glasgow Royal Infirmary, 1984-90; Sector General Manager, Gartnavel Royal Hospital, 1990-91; Unit General Manager, Mental Health Unit, Glasgow, 1991-92, Community and Mental Health Unit, Glasgow, 1992-94; Chief Executive, Greater Glasgow

Community and Mental Health Services NHS Trust, 1994-99. Non-Executive Director, Clinical Standards Board for Scotland. Recreations: tennis; military and political history. Address: (b.) Gartnavel Royal Hospital, 1055 Great Western Road, Glasgow G12 0XH; T.-0141-211 3782.

Dawe, Jennifer Ann (Jenny), MA, PhD. Leader, Liberal Democrat Group, City of Edinburgh Council, since 1999; Senior Welfare Rights Officer, Welfare Rights Team, East Lothian Council, since 1996; b. 27.4.45, Edinburgh; 4 s. Educ. Trinity Academy; Aberdeen University; Edinburgh University. Former Librarian; Tutor, American and Commonwealth History Department, Edinburgh University, 1985-87; Admin and Information Officer, Lothian Community Relations Council, 1988-90; Welfare Rights Officer, Lothian Regional Council, 1990-96. Elected to City of Edinburgh Council, 1997. Recreations: travel; reading; rediscovering gardening since recent house move; Hearts supporter. Address: (b.) City Chambers, High Street, Edinburgh; T.-0131-529 4987.

Dawson, Professor John Alan, BSc, MPhil, PhD, FILT. Professor of Marketing, Edinburgh University, since 1990; Visiting Professor, Escuela Superior de Administración y Dirección de Empresas (ESADE), Barcelona; b. 19.8.44, Hyde; m., Jocelyn Barker; 1 s.; 1 d. Educ. Lady Manners School, Bakewell; University College, London; Nottingham University. Lecturer, Nottingham University; Lecturer, Senior Lecturer, Reader, St. David's University College, Wales; Fraser of Allander Professor of Distributive Studies, Stirling University; Visiting Lecturer, University of Western Australia; Visiting Research Fellow, Australian National University; Visiting Professor: Florida State University, Chuo University, University of South Africa, University of Marketing and Distribution Sciences, Kobe, Baconni University, Milan. Chairman, National Museums of Scotland Retailing Ltd. Publications: Evaluating the Human Environment, 1973; Man and His World, 1975; Computing for Geographers, 1976; Small-Scale Retailing in the UK, 1979; Marketing Environment, 1979; Retail Geography, 1980; Commercial Distribution in Europe, 1982; Teach Yourself Geography, 1983; Shopping Centre Development, 1983; Computer Methods for Geographers, 1985; Retailing in Scoland 2005, 1988; Evolution of European Retailing, 1988; Retailing Environments in Developing Countries, 1990; Competition and Markets, 1992; European Cases in Retailing, 1999. Recreations: sport; writing. Address:(b.) Edinburgh University, 50 George Square, Edinburgh; T.-0131-650 3827.

Dawson, Peter, MA. Secretary, Royal and Ancient Golf Club of St Andrews, since 1999; b. 28.5.48, Aberdeen. Educ. Corpus Christi College, Cambridge. Address: (b.) Royal and Ancient Golf Club of St Andrews, Fife KY16 9JD.

Dawson, Hon. Lord (Thomas Cordner Dawson), QC (Scot), LLB. Senator of the College of Justice in Scotland, since 1995; b. 14.11.48; m., 2 s. Educ. Royal High School of Edinburgh; Edinburgh University. Advocate, 1973; QC, 1986; Lecturer, Dundee University, 1971-74; Advocate Depute, 1983-87; Solicitor-General for Scotland, 1992-95. Address: Court of Session, Parliament House, Parliament Square, Edinburgh, EH1 1RQ.

Dawson Scott, Robert, MA, MLitt. Head of Content, scotsman.com; b. 24.7.56, London; 3 d. Educ. Oxford University; Strathclyde University. Recreations: skiing; hill-walking. Address: (b.) 6 Westercraigs, Glasgow G31 2HZ; T.-0141-554 7106.

Deacon, Susan, MA (Hons). MSP (Labour), Edinburgh East and Musselburgh, since 1999; Minister for Health and Community Care; b. Musselburgh; 1 d. Educ. Musselburgh Grammar School; Edinburgh University. Research Officer,

West Lothian District Council; various senior management positions, East Lothian District Council; MBA, Edinburgh University, 1992; worked as senior training consultant, then as Director of MBA programmes, Edinburgh Business School, Heriot-Watt University. Address: (b.) Scottish Parliament, Edinburgh EH99 1SP; T.-0131-348 5753.

Deakins, Professor David Arthur, BSc(Econ.), BA(Bus. Studs.), MA(Bus. Econ.), FRSA. Associate Dean (Research) and Professor of Enterprise Development, University of Paisley, since 1994; b. 5.1.50, Cheshire; m., June Patricia Eglen; 1 s.; 2 d. Educ. Sutton Secondary Modern Boys' School; University of London (External Degree); University of Essex. Lecturer: Rothenham College of Technology, 1975-81, Chelmsford College of Further Education, 1981-88, University of Central England, Birmingham, 1988-94. President, Institute for Small Business Affairs. Publications: Entrepreneurship and Small Firms, 1999; Entrepreneurship in the Nineties, 1997. Recreations: cycling; walking; mountain biking. Address: (b.) Paisley Enterprise Research Centre, Paisley Business School, University of Paisley, Paisley PA1 2BE; T.-0141-848 3933.

Dean, (Catherine) Margaret, MA, JP. Lord Lieutenant of Fife, since 1999; b. 16.11.39, Edinburgh; m., Brian Dean; 3 d. Educ. George Watson's Ladies' College; Edinburgh University. Teacher of English; Past Chairman, Dunfermline Heritage Trust; Member, Crossford School Board. Recreations: bridge; theatre; family (grandchildren); walking. Address: (h.) Viewforth, 121 Rose Street, Dunfermline KY12 0QT; T.-01383 722488.

Deane, Robert Fletcher, MB, ChB, MSc, FRCSEdin, FRCSGlas. Consultant Urological Surgeon, since 1971; b. 25.3.38, Glasgow; m., Sylvia Alison Yuill; 3 s. Educ. Hillhead High School, Glasgow; Glasgow University. Consultant Urologist, Western Infirmary, Glasgow, since 1971; Senior Consultant Surgeon to Family Planning Association, Glasgow; Member, Specialist Advisory Committee (Urology); Founder, Board of Intercollegiate Specialty Board in Urology; President, British Association of Urological Surgeons, 1998-2000. Publication: Urology Illustrated. Recreations: golf; music. Address: (h.) 27 Bellshaugh Lane, Glasgow G12 0PE; T.-0141-334 8102.

Deans, Rev. Graham Douglas Sutherland, MA, BD(Hons), MTh (Oxon). Parish Minister, St. Mary's Parish Church, Dumfries, since 1987; b. 15.8.53, Aberdeen; m., Marina Punler. Educ. Mackie Academy, Stonehaven; University of Aberdeen; Westminster College, Oxford. Assistant Minister, Craigsbank Parish Church, Corstorphine, 1977-78; Parish Minister, Denbeath with Methilhill, 1978-87. Depute Clerk and Treasurer, Presbytery of Kirkcaldy, 1981-87; Chaplain, Randolph Wemyss Memorial Hospital, 1980-87; Moderator, Presbytery of Dumfries and Kirkcudbright, 1994-95; Convener: Committee on Glebes, 1991-92, Committee on Music and Worship, 1993-96, Committee on the Maintenance of the Ministry, 1997-2000 (Member, since 1991, Vice-Convener, 1991-96), Committee on Ministry, since 2000; Member: Assembly Committee on Probationers, 1991-97, Maintenance of the Ministry Committee, 1991-98, Board of Ministry, since 1998, Ministry Support Committee, 1998-2001, Ministry Development Committee, since 2001; Trustee, Housing and Loan Fund, since 1999; Member, Executive Committee, Hymn Society of Great Britain and Ireland, 1998-2001. Publications: A History of Denbeath Church, 1980; Children's Addresses in the Expository Times, 1983, 1987 and 1988; Presbyterian Praise, 1999; contributions to Bulletin of the Hymn Society. Recreation: music. Address: (h.) 47 Moffat Road, Dumfries DG1 1NN; T.-01387 254873.

Deans, Joyce Blair, CBE, DUniv, BArch, PPRIAS, RIBA, ACIArb, FRSA. Architect; President, Royal Incorporation of Architects in Scotland, 1991-93 (first woman President); b. 29.1.27, Glasgow; m., John Albert Gibson Deans; 2 s.; 2 d. Educ. Laurel Bank School for Girls; University of Strathclyde. Re-entered profession as Assistant, private practice, 1968; appointed Associate, 1972; established own practice, 1981; elected Member, Council: Glasgow Institute of Architects, 1975-90 (first woman President, 1986-88), Royal Incorporation of Architects, 1979-95; first female Vice President, Royal Incorporation of Architects in Scotland, 1986-88; Member, Building Standards Advisory Committee, 1987-96; Chairman, BSAC (Research), 1988-96; (first woman) Chairman, Scottish Construction Industry Group, 1996-2001 (Member, since 1991); Director: Cairn Housing Association, 1988-99, Glasgow West Conservation Trust, 1987-2000; Governor: Laurel Bank School for Girls 1981-99, Glasgow School of Art, 1986-98; Vice Chairman, Court, Strathclyde University, 2000-02 (Member, since 1992), Deputy Chairman of Court (Estates), since 1993; elected Vice President, Royal Institute of British Architects, 1993-95, and 1999-2001; Member: RIBA Council, 1991-2001, Patrick Geddes Award Panel, since 1993; Industrial Assessor (Architecture), SHEFC, 1994-95; External Examiner, Part 3, since 1994; Member, Professors' Advisory Team, University of Strathclyde, since 1993; Member, MSc Management Advisory Board, University of Northumbria at Newcastle, since 1997. Hon. DUniv (University of Strathclyde), 1996; MBE, 1989. Recreations: gardening; golf; walking; reading; theatre. Address: 11 South Erskine Park, Bearsden, Glasgow G61 4NA; T.-0141-942 6795.

Deans, Mungo Effingham, BSc(Econ), LLB. Regional Adjudicator, Immigration Appellate Authority, since 1996; part-time Legal Member, Immigration Appeal Tribunal; b. 25.5.56, Lytham St. Annes; m., Kathryn Atkinson; 3 s. Educ. Fettes College, Edinburgh; London School of Economics; University of Edinburgh. Admitted as Solicitor, 1981; Lecturer, Department of Law: Napier University, 1981-82, Dundee University, 1983-96; Chairman: Social Security Appeal Tribunals, 1989-99, Disability Appeal Tribunals, 1992-99; Immigration Adjudicator, 1994. Publication: Scots Public Law, 1995. Recreations: Scottish history; fine art. Address: (b.) Immigration Appellate Authority, 5th Floor, Eagle Building, 215 Bothwell Street, Glasgow G2 7EZ; T.-0141-242 7553.

Deary, Professor Ian John, BSc, PhD, MBChB, FRCPE, AFBPsS, CPsychol, MRCPsych. Professor of Differential Psychology, University of Edinburgh, since 1995; b. 17.5.54, Carluke; m., Ann Marie Barclay; 1 s.; 2 d. Educ. Hamilton Academy; University of Edinburgh. House Officer, Royal Infirmary of Edinburgh, 1983-84; Senior House Officer in Psychiatry, Maudsley Hospital, London, 1984-85; Department of Psychology, University of Edinburgh: Lecturer, 1985-90, Senior Lecturer, 1990-92, Reader, 1992-95. Past President, International Society for the Study of Individual Differences. Publications: Looking Down on Human Intelligence; Intelligence – A Very Short Introduction; Personality Traits (Co-author); editor of two books on personality; over 100 refereed scientific papers, principally on human cognitive ability and personality. Recreations: saxophone; lyric-writing; late Victorian novels; English Romantic composers; cycling; Motherwell F.C. Address: (b.) Department of Psychology, University of Edinburgh, 7 George Square, Edinburgh EH8 9JZ; T.-0131-650 3452.

Delahunt, Jim, BA. Presenter, Scotsport, Monday Night Live, Scottish Television, since 1998; Columnist, Sunday Herald, since 1999; Columnist, The Scottish Farmer, since 1983; b. 10.5.62, Irvine. Educ. St. Andrews Academy, Saltcoats; Glasgow Caledonian University. Reporter, Kilmarnock Free Press; Reporter, West Sound; Editor, Daily Winner; Night News Editor, Radio Clyde; Sub-

Editor, The Sunday Times; Sub-Editor, Reporter then Presenter, Scottish Television, 1990-98. Recreations: horse-racing; ex-amateur jockey. Address: Scottish Television, Cowcaddens, Glasgow; T.-0131-300 3734.

Della Sala, Professor Sergio F., MD, PhD. Chair of Psychology, Aberdeen; b. 23.9.55, Milan. Senior Neurologist, Milan teaching hospital; Head, Neuropsychology Unit, Veruno, Italy. Address: (b.) King's College, Aberdeen University, Aberdeen.

Demarco, Professor Richard, OBE, RSW, SSA, Hon. FRIAS, FRSA, DA, Hon. DFA, ACA, Hon. LLD (Dundee). Artist and Writer; Director, Richard Demarco Gallery, since 1966; b. 9.7.30, Edinburgh; m., Anne Muckle. Educ. Holy Cross Academy, Edinburgh; Edinburgh College of Art. National Service, KOSB, 1954-56; Art Master, Duns Scotus Academy, Edinburgh, 1957-67; Vice-Chairman, Board, Traverse Theatre Club, 1963-67; Director, Sean Connery's Scottish International Education Trust, 1972-73; Member: Board of Governors, Carlisle School of Art, 1970-74, Edinburgh Festival Society, 1971-86; Contributing Editor, Studio International, 1982-84; External Assessor, Stourbridge College of Art, 1988-90; Artistic Director, European Youth Parliament, since 1993; Professor of European Cultural Studies, Kingston University, since 1993; Director, Demarco European Art Foundation, since 1993; Trustee, Kingston-Demarco European Cultural Foundation, since 1993; Honorary Member, Scottish Arts Club; Elected Member, L'Association International des Critiques D'Art (AICA), 1994. Awards: Gold Order of Merit, Polish People's Republic; Chevalier de L'Ordre Des Arts Et Des Lettres; Order of Cavaliere Della Republica d'Italia; Scottish Arts Council Award for services to Scotland's visual arts, 1975; Medal, International Theatre Institutes of Great Britain and Poland, 1992; Honorary Doctorate, Atlanta College of Art, 1993; Arts Medal, Royal Philosophical Society of Glasgow, 1995; appointed Commander, Military and Hospitaller Order of St. Lazarus of Jerusalem, 1996. Publications: The Road to Meikle Seggie; The Artist as Explorer; A Life in Pictures; Kunst=Kapital: The Adam Smith Lecture, 1995; Honouring Colmcille, 1997. Recreation: walking "The Road to Meikle Seggie".

Dempster, Alastair Cox, FCIBS. Chairman, Scottish Community Foundation, since 1996; Chairman, sportscotland, since 1999; b. 22.6.40, Glasgow; m., Kathryn; 2 s. Educ. Paisley Grammar School. Royal Bank of Scotland, 1955-62; various managerial appointments, Scotland, Hong Kong, New York, 1962-81; AGM, International Division, Royal Bank of Scotland, 1981-86; Director of Commercial Banking and International/ Executive Director, TSB Scotland plc, 1986-91; TSB Bank Channel Islands Ltd.: Chief Executive, 1991-92; Deputy Chairman, 1992-96; Chief Executive, Lloyds TSB Bank Scotland, 1992-98. Chairman, Committee of Scottish Clearing Bankers, 1993-95; President, Chartered Institute of Bankers in Scotland, 1995-97; Member, Scottish Council Development and Industry and Executive Committee, 1992-98; Convener, Heriot Watt Audit Committee; Member, Heriot Watt University Court, 1993-99; Director, Scottish Homes, 1994-98; Director, Office of the Banking Ombudsman; Director, Scottish Financial Enterprise, 1994-98; Director, Aberforth Split Level Trust plc; Vice Chairman, Board of Governors, Edinburgh College of Art; Member, Scottish Hospital Endowment Research Trust; Director, Waddies Print Group; Director, Scottish Equity Partnership; Member, UK Sports Council, since 1999. Recreations: golf; tennis; bridge. Address: (h.) Dalshian, 8 Harelaw Road, Edinburgh EH13 0DR; T.-0131-441 5202.

Dempster, Harriet, MA (Hons), MSc, Dip. Social Work. Director of Social Work, Highland Council, since 1999; b. 31.3.52, Sheffield; m., Ian Dempster; 1 s.; 1 d. Educ. McLaren High, Callander; Edinburgh University; Dundee University; Stirling University. Researcher, Tayside Health Board, 1987-90; Principal Officer, Tayside Region, 1990-92; Assistant Chief Inspector, Scottish Office Social Work Services Inspectorate, 1992-96; Head of Children's Services, Dundee City Council, 1996-99. Associate Editor, Child Abuse Review, 1990-99; Honorary Professor, Social Work Research Centre, Stirling University; Chair, Association of Directors of Social Work Children and Families Committee. Recreations: keep-fit; films; art. Address: (b.) The Highland Council, Glenurquhart Road, Inverness IV3 5NX.

Denholm, Alastair Kennedy, DUniv, FUniv, FCIBS, FInstP; SBStJ; b. 27.9.36, Glasgow; m., Rosalind Murray Hamilton. Educ. Hutchesons' (Boys) Grammar School. Clydesdale Bank PLC, 1953-91; Managing Director, Quality Management Advisers (Scotland), 1992-98; Director, The Prince's Scottish Youth Business Trust, since 1985; Member, Board, Central College of Commerce, since 1991; Governor, Hutchesons' Grammar School, since 1996; Lord Dean of Guild, Merchants House of Glasgow, since 2001; Lay Member, Audit Registration Committee, Institute of Chartered Accountants of Scotland, since 1995; Director, Glasgow Bute Benevolent Society, since 1980; Director, Glasgow Native Benevolent Society, since 1991; Governor, Glasgow Caledonian University (including its founding organisation), 1978-95; Deacon, Incorporation of Hammermen, 1988-89; Chairman, Glasgow Junior Chamber of Commerce, 1976-77; Treasurer, Action for Disaster, 1973-95; Chairman, Chartered Institute of Bankers in Scotland, Glasgow, 1987-88; Director, Glasgow Chamber of Commerce, 1994-97; Treasurer and Elder, Williamwood Parish Church of Scotland, since 1962; District Governor, Rotary International District 1230, 1999-2000; HOEC Treasurer, Rotary International World Conference 1997, 1996-98. Recreations: golf; curling; Rotary. Address: (h.) Whitley, 28 Milverton Road, Whitecraigs, Glasgow G46 7JN; T.-0141-638 2939.

Denholm, James Allan, CBE, CA, FRSA. Director, William Grant & Sons Ltd., 1975-96; Director, Scottish Mutual Assurance Society, since 1987 (Deputy Chairman, since 1992); Director, Scottish Cremation Society Limited, since 1980; Director, Abbey National plc, 1992-97; Director, Abbey National Life plc, since 1994; b. 27.9.36, Glasgow; m., Elizabeth Avril McLachlan, CA; 1 s.; 1 d. Educ. Hutchesons Boys Grammar School, Glasgow; Institute of Chartered Accountants of Scotland. Apprenticed, McFarlane Hutton & Patrick, CA, Glasgow (Sir William McLintock prizeman); Chief Accountant, A. & W. Smith & Co. Ltd., Glasgow, 1960-66; Secretary, William Grant & Sons Ltd., 1968-96; Chairman, East Kilbride Development Corporation, 1983-94 (Member, since 1979). Council Member, Institute of Chartered Accountants of Scotland, 1978-83, 1989-93 (President, 1992-93); Director and Treasurer, Glasgow YMCA, 1966-79; Chairman, Glasgow Junior Chamber of Commerce, 1972-73; Elder, New Kilpatrick Parish Church, since 1971; Visitor of the Incorporation of Maltmen in Glasgow, 1980-81; President, The Deacons' Association of Glasgow, 1994-95; Preses, The Weavers' Society of Anderston, 1994-95; Deacon, Society of Deacons and Free Preseses of Glasgow, 1999-00; Patron, Royal Incorporation of Hutchesons Hospital, since 1998; President, 49 Wine and Spirit Club of Scotland, 1983-84; Trustee, Scottish Cot Death Trust; Director, Association for the Relief of Incurables, West of Scotland, since 1999; President, The Nomads Club, 1998-99; Fellow, Society of Antiquaries of Scotland, since 1987; Deacon Convener, The Trades House of Glasgow, 1998-99. Recreations: shooting; golf. Address: (h.) Greencroft, 19 Colquhoun Drive, Bearsden, Glasgow G61 4NQ; T.-0141-942 1773.

Denney, Alan Alexander, National Officer Scotland, Institution of Professionals, Managers and Specialists (IPMS), since 1990; b. 25.1.57, Stirling; m., Jacqueline May; 2 s.; 1 d. Educ. Plaistow Grammar School; East Ham College of Technology. Civil Service (Department of Trade), 1975-78; Institution of Professionals, Managers and Specialists (formerly IPCS), since 1979. Address: (b.) 18 Melville Terrace, Stirling FK8 2NQ; T.-01786 465999; e-mail: denneya@ipms.org.uk

Dennis, Mark D., BA, LLB (Cantab), JD, FSA Scot. Advocate, since 1997; Immigration Appeals Adjudicator, since 2001; b. 22.1.50, California, USA; m., Rona R. Ramsay; 3 s.; 1 d. Educ. Sonoma Valley High School; University of California; California Western School of Law; Cambridge University. International Legal Consultant, London, 1977-78; Attorney at Law, 1979-95; part-time Lecturer in Law, Sonoma State University, 1979-94. Publications: Scottish Heraldry: An Invitation; Scotland's Heraldic Heritage: The Lion Rejoicing. Recreation: painting. Address: (b.) Advocates' Library, Parliament House, Edinburgh, EH1 1RF; T.-0131-260 5607.

Dennis, Richard Benson, PhD, BSc. Managing Director, Edinburgh Instruments Ltd.; Director, Edinburgh Sensors Ltd.; Founder, Mütek GmbH, West Germany; b. 15.7.45, Weymouth; m., Beate Stamm; 2 d. Educ. Weymouth Grammar School; Reading University. SRC Postdoctoral Fellow, Reading; Guest Fellow, Freiburg University, 1968-70; Lecturer/Senior Lecturer, Heriot-Watt University, 1970-91; Alexander von Humboldt Fellow, Munich University, 1976-78; Treasurer: UK Laser and Electro-Optic Trade Association, UK Consortium of Photonics and Optics; Council Member, Scottish Consultative Committee on the Curriculum, 1991-94; Chairman, Balerno High School Board, 1990-94; Joint Winner, Department of Industry EPIC Award (Education in Partnership with Industry and Commerce), 1982. Recreations: bridge; sport. Address: (b.) Edinburgh Instruments Ltd., 2 Bain Square, Kirkton Campus, Livingston; T.-01506 425300.

Dennis, Roy, MBE. Wildlife Consultant/Ornithologist; Specialist, species recovery projects, UK and overseas; Director, Highland Foundation for Wildlife, since 1996; crofter, since 1985; b. 4.5.40; m., Marina MacDonell; 2 s.; 1 d. Educ. Price's School. Migration Research Assistant, UK Bird Observatories, 1958-59; Warden, Lochgarten Osprey Reserve, 1960-63; Warden, Fair Isle Bird Observatory, 1963-70; Highland Officer, RSPB, 1971-87, Regional Officer (North Scotland), 1987-91; Main Board Member, Scottish Natural Heritage, 1992-97; Director, Cairngorms Partnership, 1995-97; Member, Deer Commission for Scotland, since 1999. Publications: Ospreys and Speyside Wildlife; Birds of Badenoch and Strathspey; Puffins; Ospreys; Peregrine Falcons; Divers; The Loch; Golden Eagles. Recreations: travel; photography; cross-country skiing; bird-watching. Address: Inchdryne, Nethybridge, Invernessshire PH25 3EF; T.-01479 831 384.

Denniston, Rev. David William, BD, DipMin, FCS. Minister, North Church, Perth, since 1996; b. 23.4.56, Glasgow; m., Jane Ross; 2 s.; 1 d. Educ. Hutchesons' Boys Grammar School, Glasgow; University of Glasgow. Minister: Ruchazie Parish Church, Glasgow, 1981-86, Kennoway, Fife, 1986-96. Recreations: hill-walking; fishing; music. Address: (h.) 127 Glasgow Road, Perth PH2 0LU; T.-01738 625728; e-mail: david.denniston@blueyonder.co.uk

Dent, John Anthony, MMedEd, MD, FRCS (Edin). Senior Lecturer and Honorary Consultant, Orthopaedic and Trauma Surgery, University of Dundee, since 1990; Director, Clinical Skills Centre, University of Dundee, since 2001; b. 4.3.53, Kendal; m., Frances Jane Wyllie; 1 s.; 1 d. Educ. Haversham Grammar School, Cumbria; University of Dundee. Hand Research Fellow, Princess Margaret Rose Orthopaedic Hospital, Edinburgh; Christine Kleinert Hand Fellow, University of Louisville, Kentucky, USA; co-established Dundee Hand Surgery Service, Ninewells Hospital, Dundee; undergraduate teaching, Clinical Skills Centre, since 1997; has worked in curriculum development and implementation, University of Dundee Medical School, since 1997; External Examiner: University of Brighton, 1995-98, University of Sunderland, 1998-2001. Member, Examinations Committee, Royal College of Surgeons of Edinburgh, since 1997; Member, National Panel of Specialists for Training in Orthopaedic and Trauma Surgery, 1993-2000; Guest Lecturer: University of Gezira, Sudan, 1996, and to Association of Surgeons of India, Bombay, 1996. Publications: papers on upper limb surgery and medical education; The Musculoskeletal System: Core Topics in the New Curriculum (Co-Author/Editor), 1997; Churchill's Mastery of Medicine: Surgery 2 (Co-Author/Editor), 1997; A Practical Guide for Medical Teachers (Co-Editor), 2001. Recreations: heraldry; history; gardens. Address: (b.) Clinical Skills Centre, Ninewells Hospital and Medical School, Dundee DD1 9SY; T.-01382 633937; e-mail: j.a.dent@dundee.ac.uk

Deregowski, Professor Jan Bronislaw, BSc, BA, PhD, DSc, FBPsS, FRSE. Professor of Psychology, Aberdeen University, since 1986 (Reader, 1981-86); b. 1.3.33, Pinsk, Poland; m., Eva Loft Nielsen; 2 s.; 1 d. Educ. London University. Lecturer, then Senior Lecturer, Aberdeen University, 1969-81. Publications: Illusions, Patterns and Pictures: a cross-cultural perspective; Distortion in Art; Perception and Artistic Style (Co-author). Address: (b.) Department of Psychology, King's College, Old Aberdeen AB24 2UB; T.-Aberdeen 272246; e-mail: j.b.deregowski@abdn.ac.uk

Dervaird, Hon. Lord (John Murray), MA (Oxon), LLB (Edin), FCIArb. Professor Emeritus, Edinburgh University, since 1999; Dickson Minto Professor of Company Law, Edinburgh University, 1990-99 (Dean, Faculty of Law, 1994-96); b. 8.7.35, Stranraer; m., Bridget Jane Godfrey; 3 s. Educ. Stranraer schools; Edinburgh Academy; Corpus Christi College, Oxford; Edinburgh University. Advocate, 1962; QC, 1974; Law Commissioner (part-time), 1979-88; Senator of the College of Justice, 1988-89; Chairman, Scottish Council for International Arbitration, since 1989; Member, London Court of International Arbitration, since 1990; Trustee, David Hume Institute, since 1992; Member, ICC Committee on Business Law, Paris, since 1992; Chairman, BT Scottish Ensemble, 1988-99; Member: City Disputes Panel, since 1994, Panel of Arbitrators, International Centre for Settlement of Investment Disputes, since 1998, Advisory Board International Arbitration, Paris, since 2000; Hon. President, Advocates' Business Law Group, since 1988; Chairman, Edinburgh Wigtownshire Association, since 1997; Hon. Vice President, Advanced Technology Arbitration, Paris, since 2000. Publications: Stair Encyclopaedia of Scots Law (Contributor); articles on legal and ornithological subjects. Recreations: farming; gardening; bird-watching; music; curling. Address: (h.) Auchenmalg House, Auchenmalg, Glenluce, Wigtownshire.

Devereux, Alan Robert, CBE, DL, CEng, MIEE, CBIM. Chairman, Scottish Ambulance Service NHS Trust, 1995-97; Founder, Quality Scotland Foundation; International Director, Gleneagles PLC, since 1990; Director, Scottish Mutual Assurance Society, since 1976; Director, Abbey National Life, since 1999; b. 18.4.33, Frinton-on-Sea; m., 1, Gloria Alma Hair (deceased); 1 s.; 2, Elizabeth Tormey Docherty. Educ. Colchester School; Clacton County High School; Mid Essex Technical College. Marconi's Wireless Telegraph Company: apprentice, 1950-55, Standards Engineer, 1955-56; Technical Production Manager, Halex Division, British Xylonite Company, 1956-58; Technical Sales Manager, SPA Division, Sanitas Trust, 1958-65; General Manager, Dobar Engineering, 1965-67; various managerial posts, Norcros Ltd., 1967-69; Group Managing Director, Scotcros Ltd., 1969-78; Deputy Chairman, Scotcros Ltd., 1978-80. CBI: Chairman, Scotland, 1977-79 (Deputy Chairman, 1975-77), Council Member, 1972-84, Member, President's Advisory Committee, 1979; UK Regional Chairman, 1979; Chairman, Small Industries Council for Rural Areas of Scotland, 1975-77; Member, Scottish Development Agency, 1977-83; Chairman, Scottish Tourist Board, 1980-90; Director, Children's Hospice Association for Scotland; Scottish Free Enterprise Award, 1978; Deputy Lieutenant, Renfrewshire, since 1985. Recreations: walking; charities; reading. Address: (h.) South Fell, 24 Kirkhouse Road, Blanefield, Glasgow G63 9BX; T.-0360 770464.

Devine, John, FRICS, IRRV. Member, Lands Tribunal for Scotland, 1991-2001; b. 23.10.29, Glasgow; m., Agnes Susan McLaughlin; 2 s.; 1 d. Educ. St. Mary's College, Blairs, Aberdeen; Glasgow College of Technology; College of Estate Management. Apprentice and qualified assistant, Thomas Binnie & Hendry, Chartered Valuation Surveyors, 1947-57; Senior Valuer, Fife County Council's Assessor's Department, 1957-62; Partner, then Senior Partner, Graham & Sibbald, Chartered Surveyors, 1962-91. Member: Board of Management, Fife College of Further and Higher Education, 1992-98, Scottish Valuation and Rating Council, 1996-2000. Recreation: golf. Address: (h.) 80 Milton Road, Kirkcaldy KY1 1TP; T.-01592 264806.

Devine, Rt. Rev. Joseph, PhD. Bishop of Motherwell, since 1983; b. 7.8.37, Glasgow. Educ. St. Mary's College, Blairs, Aberdeen; St. Peter's College, Cardross; Pontifical Scots College, Rome. Ordained Priest, Glasgow, 1960; Private Secretary to Archbishop of Glasgow, 1964-65; Assistant Priest, St. Robert Bellarmine, Glasgow, 1965-67; St. Joseph's, Helensburgh, 1967-72; on staff, St. Peter's College, Cardross, 1967-74; Assistant Chaplain, Catholic Chaplaincy, Glasgow University, 1974-77; nominated Titular Bishop of Voli, and Auxiliary Bishop to Archbishop of Glasgow, 1977. President, Catholic Communications Commission. Recreations: reading; watching sport. Address: (b.) Diocesan Centre, Coursington Road, Motherwell ML1 1PW; T.-01698 269114.

Devine, Professor Thomas Martin, BA, PhD, DLitt (Queen's Belfast and Abertay, Dundee), FRHistS, FRSE, HonMRIA, FBA. University Research Professor in Scottish History and Director, Research Institute of Irish and Scottish Studies, Aberdeen University, since 1998; Director, Arts and Humanities Research Board, Centre for Irish and Scottish Studies, since 2001; b. 30.10.46, Motherwell; m., Catherine Mary Lynas; 2 s. of whom 1 deceased; 3 d. Educ. Our Lady's RC High School, Motherwell; Strathclyde University. Strathclyde University: Lecturer, then Senior Lecturer and Reader, Department of History, 1969-88 (Head of Department, 1990-92), Dean, Faculty of Arts and Social Sciences, 1993-94, Deputy Principal, 1994-97, Professor of Scottish History, 1988-98, Director of Research Centre in Scottish History, 1994-98; Visiting Professor, University of Guelph, Canada, 1983 and 1988 (Adjunct Professor in History, since 1988); Adjunct Professor in History, University of North Carolina; Governor, St. Andrews College of Education, 1990-94. Joint Founding Editor, Scottish Economic and Social History, 1980-84. British Academy/Leverhulme Trust Senior Research Fellow, 1992-93; Trustee, National Museums of Scotland, since 1995; Member, RAE Panel in History, 1992, 1996; Member, Council, British Academy, 1999-2001; Convener, Irish-Scottish Academic Initiative, since 1998; Chair, Joint Working Party, NMS and NTS, Museum of Scottish Country Life; Member, Advisory Group, Glasgow City of Architecture and Design, 1999; Winner: Senior Hume Brown Prize, 1977, Agnes Mure MacKenzie Prize for Scottish Historical Research, Saltire Society, 1992, Henry Duncan Prize, Royal Society of Edinburgh, 1995; Royal Gold Medal, Royal Society of Edinburgh, 2001. Publications: The Tobacco Lords, 1975; Lairds and Improvement in Enlightenment Scotland, 1979; Ireland and Scotland 1600-1850 (Co-Editor), 1983; Farm Servants and Labour in Lowland Scotland 1770-1914, 1984; A Scottish Firm in Virginia 1767-77, 1984; People and Society in Scotland 1760-1830 (Co-Editor), 1988; The Great Highland Famine, 1988; Improvement and Enlightenment (Editor), 1989; Conflict and Stability in Scottish Sociey (Editor), 1990; Irish Immigrants and Scottish Society in the Eighteenth and Nineteenth Centuries (Editor), 1991; Scottish Emigration and Scottish Society, 1992; Scottish Elites, 1993; The Transformation of Rural Scotland, 1994; Clanship to Crofters' War, 1994; Industry, Business and Society in Scotland since 1700 (Co-Editor), 1994; Glasgow: I, Beginnings to 1830, 1995; St. Mary's, Hamilton: a social history; Exploring the Scottish Past, 1995; Scotland in the Twentieth Century (Co-Editor), 1996; Eighteenth Century Scotland: New Perspectives (Co-Editor), 1998; The Scottish Nation, 1700–2000, 1999; Celebrating Columba – Irish–Scottish Connections 597–1997 (Co-Editor), 1999; Scotland's Shame? – Bigotry and Sectarianism in Modern Scotland, 2000. Recreations: walking and exploring the Hebrides; watching skilful football; travelling in Italy. Address: (b.) Research Institute of Irish and Scottish Studies, Aberdeen University, King's College, 19 College Bounds, Old Aberdeen AB24 3UG.

de Vink, Peter Henry John, BComm. Managing Director, Edinburgh Financial and General Holdings Ltd., since 1978; b. 9.10.40, Amsterdam; m., Julia Christine (Krista) Quarles van Ufford; 1 s.; 1 d. Educ. Edinburgh University. National Service, Dutch Army, 1961-63; Edinburgh University, 1963-66; Ivory and Sime Investment Managers, 1966-78, latterly as Director. Address: (b.) 7 Howe Street, Edinburgh EH3 6TE; T.-0131-225 6661; (h.) Huntly Cot, Temple, Midlothian EH23 4TS; T.-01875 830345.

Dewar, Douglas, MA (Hons), CA. Finance Director, Scottish Airports Ltd., since 1992; b. 18.6.47, Glasgow; m., Nancy; 1 s.; 1 d. Educ. High School of Glasgow; Glasgow University. Arthur Young McClelland Moores; Scotish Co-ordinated Investments Ltd.; Scottish Express Ltd. (Finance Director); Stansted Airport Ltd. (Finance Director). Address: (b.) Scottish Airports Ltd., St. Andrews Drive, Glasgow Airport, Glasgow PA3 2SW; T.-0141-848 4298.

Dewar, Ian McGregor, CA. Vice Chairman, St. Johnstone Football Club Ltd.; b. 21.8.46, Helensburgh; m., Avril; 2 s. Educ. Hutchesons' Grammar School, Glasgow. Qualified as CA, 1969; joined Price Waterhouse (later PricewaterhouseCoopers) Glasgow, 1969, Partner, 1979, Senior Partner, Edinburgh, 1995-2001. Past President, Junior Chamber, Scotland. Recreations: golf; gardening; soccer. Address: Croit En Deoir, 12 Comley Park, Dunfermline KY12 7HU; T.-01383 625031.

Dewar-Durie, Andrew Maule, CBE. Deputy Chairman, Sea Fish Industry Authority, since 2000; b. 13.11.39, Bath; m., Marguerite Kottulinsky; 2 s.; 1 d. Educ. Wellington College. Regular soldier, Argyll and Sutherland Highlanders, 1958-68, retiring with rank of Captain; Export Representative to Senior Export Director, White Horse Distillers, 1968-83; International Sales Director, Long John International, 1983-87; James Burrough Distillers: International Sales Director, 1987-89, Managing Director, 1990; Chief Executive Officer, James Burrough Ltd., 1990-91, Managing Director, 1991-92; Allied Distillers Ltd.: Managing Director, 1992-97, Chairman, 1997-99. Deputy Lieutenant, Dunbartonshire, since 1996; CBI Scotland: Council Member, 1993, Vice Chairman, 1996, Chairman, 1997-99; Non-Executive Director, Dumyat Investment Trust PLC, 1995-2000; Non-Executive Director, Britannia Asset Management, since 2001; Director, Scotch Whisky Association, 1992-99; Keeper of the Quaich, since 1989, Master, since 1992; Liveryman, Worshipful Company of Distillers, since 1986; Council Member, Gin and Vodka

Association of GB, 1997-99; President, Edinburgh Royal Warrant Holders Association, 1999-2000; Director, Edinburgh Military Tattoo, since 2000. Recreations: tennis; rough shooting; sailing; theatre; cinema. Address: Finnich Malise, Croftamie, West Stirlingshire G63 0HA; T.-0136 066 0257.

Dewhurst, Professor John Hugh Llewellyn, MA, PhD, CStat. Professor of Regional Economics, University of Dundee; b. 7.3.47, Marlow; m., Wendy Jane; 1 s.; 1 d. Educ. Sir William Borlase School; Sidney Sussex College, Cambridge; University of Kent. Lecturer in Economic and Social Statistics, University of Dundee, 1969-92; Principal Research Fellow, University of Queensland, 1988-89; Senior Lecturer in Economic and Social Statistics, University of Dundee, 1992-99. Past Chairman, British and Irish Section, Regional Science Association International. Recreations: amateur dramatics; arboriculture. Address: (h.) 12 West Hemming Street, Letham, Forfar, Angus DD8 2PU; T.-01307 818306; e-mail: j.h.l.dewhurst@dundee.ac.uk

Dewing, Irene Isabel Joan, DL; b. 21.9.36, Inverness; m., William Beresford Dewing; 2 d. Educ. Heatherley, Inverness. Deputy Lieutenant. Address: (h.) The Hollies, Kildary, Rossshire; T.-01862 842204.

Di Rollo, Simon Ronald, LLB (Hons). Advocate, since 1987; b. 28.10.61, Edinburgh; m., Alison Margaret; 1 s.; 1 d. Educ. Holy Cross Academy; Scotus Academy; Edinburgh University. Admitted to Faculty of Advocates, 1987; Advocate Depute, 1997-2000. Recreations: Italian; cooking; walking; golf. Address: (b.) Advocates' Library, Parliament House, Edinburgh EH1 1RF.

Dick, Alan. Provost of South Lanarkshire, since 1999. b. 20.5.44. Glasgow; m., Barbara; 2 step s.; 2 d. Educ. Lennoxtown Secondary School; Cambuslang School of Building; Glasgow College of Building and Printing. Career in a number of operational management posts in the gas industry, 1959- 94; Member, Labour Party, since 1967; Member, Children's Panel, Glasgow, 1971-80; Councillor, since 1980 (East Kilbride District Council/South Lanarkshire Council); Founder, East Kilbride Arts Council, 1980; Chair, Education, 1995-99; Life Member, Unison, since 1994; Justice of the Peace, 1980-96; Recreations: bowling; fishing; walking; reading; the arts. Address: (h.) 26 Jamieson Drive, Calderwood, East Kilbride, G74 3EA; T.-01355 239633.

Dick, David, OBE, DIC, CEng, FIEE. Managing Director, Clerkington Publishing Co. Ltd., since 1998; b. 20.3.29, Edinburgh; m., Muriel Elsie Margaret Buchanan; 5 d. Educ. Boroughmuir School, Edinburgh; Heriot-Watt College, Edinburgh; Imperial College, London. Electrical Engineer, North of Scotland Hydro-Electric Board, 1951-54; Lecturer, Dundee College of Technology, 1954-60; Head, Department of Electrical Engineering, Coatbridge Technical College, 1960-64; Depute Principal, Napier College of Science and Technology, Edinburgh, 1964-69; Principal, Stevenson College of Further Education, Edinburgh, 1969-87. Manpower Services Commission: Chairman, Lothian District Manpower Committee, 1981-82, Member, Lothian and Borders Area Manpower Board, 1982-85; Member and Chairman, various committees: Scottish Technical Education Council, Scottish Business Education Council, 1969-87; Member and Chairman, Fire Services Examination Board (Scotland), 1968-86; Member, Construction Industry Training Board, 1976-85; Member: Electrical Engineering Services Committee, CITB, 1976-88, General Convocation, Heriot-Watt University, Edinburgh, 1970-73; Past Chairman, Scottish Committee, Institution of Electronic and Radio Engineers; former Honorary President, Edinburgh and District Spastics Association; Lay Inspector of Fire Services for Scotland, 1994-99.

Publications: Capital Walks in Edinburgh – The New Town, 1994; Street Biographies of the Royal Burgh of Haddington, 1997; Who was Who on the Royal Mile, Edinburgh, 1997; Who was Who in Durban Street Names, 1998; A Scottish Electrical Enlightenment (Editor), 2000; A Millennium of Fame of East Lothian, 2000. Recreations: music (flute); gardening; writing historical biographies. Address: (h.) West Lodge, Clerkington, near Haddington, East Lothian.

Dick, Rev. John Hunter Addison, MA, MSc, BD. Parish Minister, Aberdeen: Ferryhill, since 1982; b. 27.12.45, Dunfermline; 3 s. Educ. Dunfermline High School; Edinburgh University. Research Assistant, Department of Geography, Edinburgh University, 1967-70; Senior Tutor, Department of Geography, Queensland University, 1970-78; student of divinity, 1978-81; Assistant Minister, Edinburgh: Fairmilehead, 1981-82. Governor, Robert Gordon's College; Trustee, Aberdeen Endowments Trust. Recreations: music. Address: Ferryhill Manse, 54 Polmuir Road, Aberdeen AB11 7RT; T.-01224 586933.

Dickinson, Professor Harry Thomas, BA, DipEd, MA, PhD, DLitt, FRHistS, FRSE. Professor of British History, Edinburgh University, since 1980; Professor of British History, Nanjing University, since 1987; b. 9.3.39, Gateshead; m., Jennifer Elizabeth Galtry; 1 s.; 1 d. Educ. Gateshead Grammar School; Durham University; Newcastle University. Teacher of History, Washington Grammar School, 1961-64; Earl Grey Fellow, Newcastle University, 1964-66; History Department, Edinburgh University: Assistant Lecturer, 1966-68, Lecturer, 1968-73, Reader, 1973-80; Associate Dean (Postgraduate), 1992-96; Convener, Senatus PGS Committee, 1998-2001; Visiting Professor, Nanjing University, China, 1980, 1983, 1985, 1987, 1994; Fulbright Scholar, 1973; Huntington Library Fellowship, 1973; Folger Shakespeare Library Fellowship, 1973; Winston Churchill Fellow, 1980; Leverhulme Award, 1986-87; Ahmanson Fellowship, UCLA, 1987; Anstey Lecturer, University of Kent, 1989; Douglas Southall Freeman Professor, University of Richmond, Virginia, 1987; Chairman, Publications Committee, Historical Association, 1991-94; Vice-President: Royal Historical Society, 1991-95, Historical Association, 1995-97 (Deputy President, 1997-98); Member, Humanities Committee, CNAA, 1991-93; National Auditor, Higher Education Quality Council, 1993-95; Team Assessor, History, TQA, SHEFC, 1995-96; Member, Marshall Aid Commonwealth Commission, 1987-96; Member, QAA History Subject Benchmarking Committee, 1998-99; Academic Auditor, QAA, since 1997; Academic Reviewer, QAA, since 1998; Editor, History, 1993-2000. Publications: Bolingbroke; Walpole and the Whig Supremacy; Liberty and Property; British Radicals and the French Revolution; The Correspondence of Sir James Clavering; Politics and Literature in the 18th Century; The Political Works of Thomas Spence; Caricatures and the Constitution 1760-1832; Britain and the French Revolution; The Politics of the People in Eighteenth-century Britain; Britain and the American Revolution; The Challenge to Westminster (Co-Author); many pamphlets, essays and reviews. Recreations: reading; films. Address: (h.) 44 Viewforth Terrace, Edinburgh EH10 4LJ; T.-0131-229 1379.

Dickinson, Professor Keith William, BSc, MEng, PhD, CEng, MICE, FIHT. Assistant Principal, Academic Development, Napier University, since 1997; b. 17.9.48, Liverpool; m., Dorothy Mills; 1 s.; 1 d. Educ. Ormskirk Secondary School; Sheffield Polytechnic; University of Sheffield. Senior Lecturer and Director, Transport Engineering Research Unit, Napier Polytechnic, 1986-90; Napier University: Head, Civil & Transportation Engineering, 1990-94, Dean, Faculty of Engineering, 1994-97. Recreations: walking; travelling; fishing; drawing.

Address: (b.) Napier University, Craighouse Campus, Craighouse Road, Edinburgh EH10 5LG; T.-0131-455 6001; e-mail: k.dickinson@napier.co.uk

Dickson, Alan David James. Chief Executive, Capability Scotland, since 1997; b. 26.3.50, Leicester; m., Janet; 1 d. Educ. Worksop College Public School. Management training, Steetley Manufacturing; Divisional Manager, Help the Aged; Scottish Organiser, LEPRA; Assistant Director, then Depute Director, Scottish Council for Spastics. Vice-President, Cerebral Palsy International Sports and Recreation Association; Convener, Community Care Providers Scotland; Chairman, Disability Agenda Scotland. Recreations: golf; squash; tennis. Address: (b.) 22 Corstorphine Road, Edinburgh EH12 6HP; T.-0131-337 9876.

Dickson, Alastair Ronald. Senior Partner, Dickson Minto WS, since 1985; b. 16.1.51, Glasgow; 2 s.; 1 d. Educ. Glenalmond College; Edinburgh University. Trained, Dundas & Wilson, 1971-73; Maclay, Murray & Spens, 1973-76; Dundas & Wilson, 1976-85 (Partner, from 1978); Founding Partner, Dickson Minto WS, 1985. Recreations: golf; squash; hill-walking; skiing. Address: (b.) 11 Walker Street, Edinburgh EH3 7NE; T.-0131-225 4455.

Dickson, Andrew Gauld, MA, PhD. Head of Countryside and Natural Heritage Unit, Scottish Executive Environment and Rural Affairs Department, since 1999; b. 30.11.49, Dumfries; m., Wilma Ann Frame; 1 s.; 1 d. Educ. George Watson's College, Edinburgh; Edinburgh University. Lecteur D'Anglais: Universite de Caen, 1971-72, Universite de Metz, 1973-74; Civil Servant, Scottish Office, then Scottish Executive, since 1976. Recreations: reading; playing music badly; dilettantism; Francophilia. Address: (b.) 1-J, Victoria Quay, Edinburgh EH6 6QQ; T.-0131-244 6416; e-mail: andrew.dickson@scotland.gov.uk

Dickson, Professor James Holms, BSc, MA, PhD, FLS, FRSE. Professor of Archaeobotany and Plant Systematics, Glasgow University, since 1998 (Reader in Botany, 1993-98); b. 29.4.37, Glasgow; m. Camilla A. Lambert, 1 s.; 1 d. Educ. Bellahouston Academy; University of Glasgow; University of Cambridge. Fellow, Clare College, University of Cambridge, 1963-70; Lecturer then Senior Lecturer in Botany, University of Glasgow, 1970-93. Leader, Trades House of Glasgow Expedition to Papua, New Guinea, 1987; Consultant, Britoil, Glasgow Garden Festival, 1988; currently working on plant remains found with 5,300 year old Tyrolean Iceman, and with 550 year old British Columbian iceman. Neill Medallist, Royal Society of Edinburgh, 1996; twice Past President, Glasgow Natural History Society; Past President, Botanical Society of Scotland. Publications: five books, including The Changing Flora of Glasgow, and Plants and People in Ancient Scotland; many papers on Scottish flora, Ice Age plants, archaeobotany, the Tyrolean Iceman. Address: (b.) Graham Kerr Building, Glasgow University; T.-0141-330 4364.

Dickson, John (Iain) Anderson, BSc, DipArch, MaPS, RIBA, PPRIAS. Architect; President, Royal Incorporation of Architects in Scotland, 1999-2001; Partner, George Watt & Stewart, Aberdeen, since 1980; b. 28.5.51, Hamilton. Educ. Aberdeen Grammar School; Scott Sutherland School of Architecture, Robert Gordon's Institute of Technology, Aberdeen. Architectural Assistant: Department of Housing and Construction, Darwin, Australia, 1973-74, W.G. Crerar & Partners, Inverness, 1976-77; Architect, George Watt & Stewart, Aberdeen, 1977-80. Chairman, Kincardine and Deeside Area, British Field Sports Soicety, 1995-98; Chairman, RIAS Practice Board, 1995-99; Member, RIBA Council, 1999-2001; Director, Aberdeenshire Housing Partnership, since 1999; Member, Scottish Construction Industry Group, 1999-2001; Member,

Leadership Group, Scottish Enterprise Forestry Cluster, 2000; Member, Sounding Board, Scottish Executive Review of Scotland's Cities, 2001. Recreations: field sports; fishing; shooting; good food. Address: (b.) 24 North Silver Street, Aberdeen AB10 1RL; T.-01224 639232.

Dickson, Leonard Elliot, CBE, MC, TD, DL, BA (Cantab), LLB. Retired Solicitor; b. 17.3.15, Edinburgh; m., Mary Elisabeth Cuthbertson; 1 s.; 1 d. Educ. Uppingham; Magdalene College, Cambridge; Glasgow University. 1st Bn., Glasgow Highlanders HLI, 1939-46; former Senior Partner, Dickson, Haddow & Co., Solicitors, Glasgow (retired, 1985); Clerk, Clyde Lighthouses Trust, 1953-65; Secretary, Glasgow Society of Sons of Clergy, 1953-83; serving Officer, TA, 1939-55 (Lt. Col. commanding 1st Bn., Glasgow Highlanders, 1952-55); Chairman, Lowland TAVR, 1968-70; Member, Glasgow Executive Council, NHS, 1956-74 (Vice Chairman, 1970-74). Recreations: travel; gardening. Address: (h.) Bridge End, Gartmore, Stirling FK8 3RR; T.-01877 382 220.

Dickson, Sheriff Robert Hamish, LLB, WS. Sheriff of South Strathclyde, Dumfries & Galloway at Airdrie, since 1988; b. 19.10.45, Glasgow; m., Janet Laird Campbell; 1 s. Educ. Glasgow Academy; Drumtochty Castle; Glenalmond; Glasgow University. Solicitor, Edinburgh, 1969-71, and Glasgow, 1971-86; Partner, Brown Mair Gemmill & Hislop, Solicitors, Glasgow, 1973-86; appointed floating Sheriff of South Strathclyde, Dumfries & Galloway at Hamilton, 1986. Publication: Medical and Dental Negligence, 1997. Recreations: golf; music; reading. Address: (b.) Airdrie Sheriff Court, Airdrie; T.-Airdrie 751121.

Diggle, Professor Jeremy, BA (Hons) MA, MEd, PGCE. Professor, Head of Gray's School of Art, Aberdeen since 1999; b. 17.2.55, Welwyn Garden City; m., Valerie Diggle, 1s.; 2d. Educ. Richard Hind Secondary Technical School; St Martins School of Art; Royal College of Art. Artist in experimental media, since 1981; teaching in higher education, since 1986; Head of visual research, Exeter College of Art, University of Plymouth; exhibited internationally; Board member, ELIA. Recreations: stargazing. Address: (h.) Smiddy Park, Kineff, Angus.

Dillon, J. Shaun H., DRSAM (Comp), FSA Scot. Professional Musician; Composer, Oboist and Teacher of Woodwind; b. 30.12.44, Sutton Coldfield. Educ. Berwickshire High School; Fettes College; Royal Scottish Academy of Music; Guildhall School of Music. Studied composition with Frank Spedding and Edmund Rubbra; awarded prize for composition for Leicestershire Schools Orchestra, 1965; commissions from various bodies, including Scottish Amateur Music Association; Instructor of Woodwind: Edinburgh Corporation, 1967-72, Aberdeen Corporation (latterly Grampian Region), 1972-81; Freelance Musician, since 1981; sometime Director of Music, St. Mary's Cathedral, Aberdeen; two suites of Airs and Graces for strings published; Secretary, Association of Instrumental and Vocal Specialists, 1975-78. Recreations: reading, especially history, literature; crosswords; playing flute (badly) in ceilidh bands. Address: (b.) 34 Richmond Street, Aberdeen AB25 4TR; T.-01224 630954.

Dixon, Professor Geoffrey Richard, BSc, PhD, FIHort, FIBiol, CBiol. Professor of Horticulture, University of Strathclyde; Managing Director, GreenGene International; formerly Head of Horticulture, Director, Scottish Horticultural Advisory Service, SAC; b. 13.6.42, London; m., Kathleen Hilda Edwards; 1 s.; 1 d. Educ. Pewley County School, Guildford; Wye College, University of London. Plant Pathologist, National Institute of Agricultural Botany, Cambridge, 1968-78; Head, Horticulture Division and Chairman, Crop Production and Protection Group, and

Senior University Lecturer, Aberdeen School of Agriculture, 1978-87; Chairman, Education and Research Commission, International Society for Horticultural Science; Chairman, International Clubroot Working Group; Visiting Professor, Mansourah University, Egypt; Honorary Professor, Von Humboldt University, Berlin; Senior Research Scholar, University of Wisconsin; Visiting Lecturer, University of Horticulture, Budapest; Vice-Chairman, Education and Training Committee; President-Elect, Institute of Horticulture (former Chairman, Scottish Branch); Member, Examinations Board, Royal Horticultural Society; created Freeman Citizen of Glasgow and Late-Collector, Incorporation of Gardeners of Glasgow; Member of the Master Court; Liveryman, Worshipful Company of Fruiterers of the City of London; Chairman, Agricultural Sciences Committee, and Member, Science Policy Board, Institute of Biology. Wain Fellowship, BBSRC; Nuffield Foundation Fellowship, European Community Erasmus Programme Co-ordinator. Publications: Vegetable Crop Diseases; Plant Pathogens and their control in Horticulture; 200 scientific papers. Recreations: gardening; photography; travel; hill-walking. Address: (h.) Helenton Mote, Symington, by Ayr KA1 5PP; T.-01563 830251.

Dixon-Carter, Clare, OBE. President, Highland and Western Isles Branch, British Red Cross; Director, Glenurquhart Care Project; b. 18.9.38, London. Educ. Moira House School, Eastbourne. Technical staff, EMI; hotel management, 1959-65; Assistant Regional Organiser for Scotland, World Worldlife Fund, 1969-77; joined Invernessshire Branch, British Red Cross, 1965; Branch Director, 1979-86; awarded Voluntary Medical Service Medal, 1983; BRCS Badge of Honour for distinguished service and life membership of society, 1986; Scottish Central Council Branch: Vice-Chairman, 1986-90, Chairman, 1990-97; Vice-Chairman, British Red Cross 1996-2000. Recreations: photography; travel; music; theatre. Address: (h.) Easter Balnabaan, Drumnadrochit, Invernessshire IV63 6UX; T.-01456 450310.

Dobie, Margaret G.C., OBE, MA, DipSocStud, FFCS. Hon. Vice President, Scottish Association for the Study of Delinquency; Chair, Dumfries & Galloway Valuation Appeal Panel, since 1987; b. Galloway; m., James T.J. Dobie; 3 s. Educ. Benedictine Convent, Dumfries; Dumfries Academy; Edinburgh University. Medical Social Worker; Chair, Dumfries and Galloway Regional Children's Panel, 1971-77; Social Worker, Child Guidance Service, Dumfries; Secretary, Scottish Association for the Study of Delinquency, 1982-87; Member, Broadcasting Council for Scotland, 1987-91; Chair, Dumfries and Galloway Children's Panel Advisory Committee, 1982-89; Chair, Children's Panel Advisory Group, 1985-88; Member, Polmont Young Offenders' Institution Visiting Committee, 1992-99. Recreations:travel; tennis; reading. Address: (h.) 8 New Abbey Road, Dumfries DG2 7ND; T.-01387-254 595.

Dobie, Rev. Rachel Jean Wayland, LTh. Minister, Broughton, Glenholm, Kilbucho linked with Skirling, linked with Stobo, Drumelzier linked with Tweedsmuir; b. 17.8.42, Forres; m., Kirkpatrick H. Dobie; 1 s.; 1 d. Educ. Dumfries Academy; Jordanhill College; Edinburgh University. Primary schoolteacher, 1963-80; Auxiliary Minister, Dalbeattie with Urr, 1990-93; Church of Scotland Sunday School Adviser, 1976-86; Reader, 1982-90; Chair, Marriage Guidance, Dumfries, 1984-86; Member, General Assembly Youth Education Committee, 1985-93; Vice-Convener, General Assembly Board of Parish Education 1993-97; Hon. Secretary, Church Service Society; Contributor to BBC religious broadcasting. Publication: Time Together, 1981. Recreations: music; fine arts. Address: (h.) The Manse, Broughton, Biggar ML12 6HQ; T.-01899 830331.

Dobson, Professor Alan Peter, BA, PGCE, MSc, PhD, FRHistSoc. Professor of Politics, Dundee University,

since 1999; b. 5.1.51, Withnell, Lancs; m., Beverly Jane; 3 d. Educ. Chorley Grammar School; Durham University; Southampton University; Durham University. Department of Political Theory and Government, 1978-99; Senior Research Fellow, Norwegian Nobel Institute, 1997. Publications: (most recent) US Economic Statecraft for Survival, 1933-99. Recreations: walking; cooking; singing; gardening. Address: (b.) Department of Politics, Dundee University, Perth Road, Dundee DD1 4HN; T.-01382 344588.

Docherty, Anne, MA, DipEd, DipAdEd. Director, Society for Companion Animal Studies, since 1988; Chair, Pet Fostering Service Scotland; b. 5.10.36, Kirkcaldy; m., David Docherty. Educ. Beath High School, Cowdenbeath; St Andrews University; Edinburgh University. School teacher, 1957-67; College lecturer, 1967-80; Assistant Director, Scottish Institute of Adult Education, 1980-87; Chair, 1985-88, General Secretary, 1988-97, National Association of Educational Guidance for Adults. Recreations: music; literature; gardens; animals. Address: (h.) 10(B) Leny Road, Callander FK17 8BA; T.-01877 330996.

Docherty, Michael. Chief Executive, South Lanarkshire Council; b. 12.1.52, Glasgow; m., Linda; 2 s.; 1 d. Educ. St. Mungo's Academy, Glasgow. Trainee Accountant, Electricity Board, 1971-74; Accountancy Assistant, Coatbridge Town Council, 1974-75; Accountant, Monklands District Council, 1975-77, Stirling District Council, 1977-79; Senior Accountant, Monklands District Council, 1979-82; Principal Accountant, Renfrew District Council, 1982-84; Depute Director of Finance, Motherwell District Council, 1984-91; Director of Finance, Hamilton District Council, 1991-92; Chief Executive, Hamilton District Council, 1992-96. Recreations: running; reading; hill-walking. Address: (b.) Council Offices, Almada Street, Hamilton ML3 0AA.

Docker, Chris. Director, Exit, since 1992; Founder, International Drugs Consensus Working Party, 1993; Director, Living Will and Values History Project, since 1996; b. 29.1.53, Birmingham. Educ. Bishop Veseys Grammar School; Glasgow University (Masters in Law and Ethics in Medicine). Worked in publishing (human rights) and marketing before embarking on campaigning career. National Member Officer, British Mensa, since 2001; Award Winner, Natural Death Centre, 1996. Publications: Departing Drugs; Beyond Final Exit; and contributions to other books. Address: (b.) 17 Hart Street, Edinburgh EH1 3 RN; T.-0131-556 4404; e-mail: aez61@dial.pipex.com

Dodd, Raymond Henry, PhD, MA, BMus, ARAM. Cellist and Composer; b. 31.3.29; m., Doreen Joyce; 1 s.; 1 d. Educ. Bryanston School; Royal Academy of Music; Worcester College, Oxford. Music Master, Sedbergh School, 1951-55; Aberdeen University: Lecturer in Music, 1956, Senior Lecturer in Music, 1971-91, Head of Department, 1981-88; Visiting Professor of Music, Wilson College, USA, 1972-73. Various orchestral, vocal and chamber music compositions; awarded Szymanowski Medal, Polish Ministry of Art and Culture, 1982. Address: (h.) 14 Giffordgate, Haddington, East Lothian EH41 4AS; T.-01620 824618.

Dodds, Alistair Bruce, MA (Hons), MBA, FIPD. Director of Corporate Services and Depute Chief Executive, The Highland Council; Company Secretary, Eden Court Theatre; b. 23.8.53, Kelso; m., Joan N. Aitken; 1 d. Educ. Glenrothes High School; Edinburgh University; Strathclyde University; Dundee University. Assistant Director of Personnel, Fife Regional Council, 1988; Depute Director of Manpower Services, Highland Regional Council, 1991;

Director of Personnel Services, The Highland Council, 1995. Recreations: Scottish contemporary art; watching rugby; golf; walking dogs. Address: Highland Council, Glenurquhart Road, Inverness IV3 5NX; T.-01463 702845.

Doherty, Elizabeth, MA. Head Teacher, St Columba's High School, Gourock, since 1998; b. 5.7.45, Derry; m., James Doherty; 2 s.; 2 d. Educ. St Columba's High School, Greenock; Glasgow University. Teacher, St Columba's High School, 1967-68; St Stephen's Junior Secondary School, 1968-70 (became St Stephen's High School); career break, 1973-82; Teacher of English, Sacred Heart High School, Paisley, 1982-84; Assistant Principal Teacher of Guidance, St Cuthbert's High School, 1984-87; Principal Teacher/Assistant Head Teacher, St Stephen's High School, 1987-96; Depute Head, St Columba's High School, 1996-98. Recreations: reading; travelling; eating out. Address: (b.) St Columba's High School, Burnside Road, Gourock PA19 1XX; T.-01475 715250.

Doherty, (Joseph) Raymond, QC, LLB (Edinburgh), BCL (Oxon), LLM (Harvard). Advocate, since 1984; QC, since 1997; b. 30.1.58, Stirling; m., Arlene Donaghy; 1 s.; 2 d. Educ. St Joseph's College, Dumfries. Standing Junior Counsel to Ministry of Defence (Army), 1990-91; Standing Junior Counsel to Scottish Office Industry Department, 1992-97; Advocate Depute, 1998-2001. Clerk, Faculty of Advocates, 1990-95; Joint Editor, Valuation for Rating, since 1990; Contributor, Stair Memorial Encyclopaedia of the Laws of Scotland. Recreations: skiing; theatre. Address: (b.) Advocates' Library, Parliament House, Edinburgh EH1 1RF; T.-0131-226 5071.

Doherty, Una, LLB. Advocate, since 1999; b. Stirling; m., Douglas Fairley. Educ. High School of Stirling; Edinburgh University. Solicitor, 1988-98; Litigation Partner, Balfour and Manson, 1993-98. Address: (b.) Advocates' Library, Parliament House, Edinburgh EH1 1RF; T.-0131-226 5071.

Doig, Barbara Dalrymple, BSc (Hons). Head, External Relations Division, Scottish Executive, since 2000; b. 29.9.47, Dunfermline; m., Ian; 1 d. Educ. Bo'ness Academy; Alloa Academy; University of Glasgow. Scottish Development Department: Research Officer, Population, 1969-74, Research Secretary, 1974-75, Senior and Principal Research Officer, Civil Law, 1976-84; Principal Research Officer, Local Government Finance, 1985-88; Depute Director, Central Research Unit, 1989-93; Project Sponsor, Victoria Quay, 1993-95; Head, Accommodation and Parliament Accommodation Divisions, 1995-99; Holyrood Project Sponsor and Scottish Parliament Director, 1999-2000. Member, Scottish Advisory Committee, British Council. Recreations: walking; theatre; design. Address: (b.) 2-02 W. St. Andrew's House, Regent Road, Edinburgh; T.-0131-244 7944; e-mail: barbara.doig@scotland.gov.uk

Doig, Ian, CPFA, FCCA. Director, CIPFA in Scotland (Chartered Institute of Public Finance and Accountancy); Secretary, Local Authority (Scotland) Accounts Advisory Committee, since 1986; Director, FSF LTD.; b. 25.11.45, Glasgow; m., Barbara; 1 d. Educ. Alva and Alloa Academies; Strathclyde University. Address: (b.) CIPFA in Scotland, 8 North West Circus Place, Edinburgh EH3 6ST; T.-0131-220 4316; e-mail: cipfa.scotland@cipfa.org

Doig, P. Michael R., MA (Hons), FRSA. Head Teacher, Bearsden Academy, since 2001; b. 2.5.48, Glasgow; m., Catherine; 2 s. Educ. High School of Glasgow; Glasgow University. Teacher/Assistant Principal Teacher/Principal Teacher of Modern Languages, 1972-81; Assistant Head Teacher, Hermitage Academy, Helensburgh, 1981-85; Depute Head Teacher, Kirkintilloch High School, 1985-92; Head Teacher, Cumbernauld High School, 1992-2000.

Member, National Executive, Headteachers' Association of Scotland. Recreations: music; golf; current affairs. Address: (b.) Bearsden Academy, Morven Road, Bearsden, Glasgow G61 3SU; T.-0141-942 2449.

Dominiczak, Professor Anna F., MD, FRCP, FMedSci. British Heart Foundation Chair of Cardiovascular Medicine, University of Glasgow, since 1997; Honorary Consultant Physician and Endocrinologist, since 1993; b. 26.8.54, Gdansk, Poland; m., Dr. Marek Dominiczak; 1 s. Educ. Copernicus High School, Gdansk; Medical School, Gdansk. Junior House Officer, Glasgow Royal Infirmary, 1982; Senior House Officer (and Registrar) in Medicine, Royal Alexandra Hospital, Paisley, 1983-86; MRC Clinical Scientist and Honorary Registrar (and Senior Registrar), Western Infirmary, Glasgow, 1986-92; British-American Research Fellow and Associate Professor, University of Michigan, Ann Arbor, USA, 1990-91; University of Glasgow: Clinical Lecturer and Honorary Senior Registrar in Medicine and Endocrinology, 1992-93, British Heart Foundation Senior Research Fellow, Senior Lecturer then Reader in Medicine, 1993-97. Member, MRC Physiological Medicine Board, 2000-04; Member, British Heart Foundation Project Grant Committee, 2000-03. Recreation: modern literature. Address: (b.) Department of Medicine and Therapeutics, Western Infirmary, Dumbarton Road, Glasgow G11 6NT; T.-0141-211 2688; e-mail: ad7e@clinmed.gla.ac.uk

Donachie, Professor William David, BSc, PhD, MAcadEurop, FAmerAcadMicrobiol, FRSE. Professor of Bacterial Genetics, Edinburgh University, 1993-2000, now Professor Emeritus; b. 27.4.35, Edinburgh; m.,Millicent Masters, BS, MS, PhD; 1 s. Educ. Dunfermline High School; Edinburgh University. Assistant Lecturer in Genetics, Edinburgh University, 1958-62; Research Associate in Biochemical Sciences, Princeton University, 1962-63; Lecturer in Genetics, Edinburgh University, 1963-65; Scientific Staff, MRC Molecular Genetics Unit, London and Edinburgh, 1965-74; Senior Lecturer/Reader in Molecular Biology, Edinburgh University, 1974-93. Publications: 91 research papers. Recreations: drawing; natural history; T'ai Chi. Address: (b.) Institute of Cell and Molecular Biology, Edinburgh University, Darwin Building, King's Buildings, Mayfield Road, Edinburgh EH9 3JR; T.-0131-650 5354; e-mail: William.Donachie@ed.ac.uk

Donald, Sheriff Brian George, LLB. Sheriff at Kirkcaldy, since 1999; b. 11.7.44, Dundee. Educ. Lawside Academy, Dundee; St Andrews University. Postgraduate legal apprenticeship, Edinburgh, 1965-67; Assistant Solicitor, A.C. White, Ayr, 1967-69; taught English, Shenker Institute, Rome, 1970 and 1971; Partner, J. & A. Hastie, SSC, Edinburgh, 1972-97; Consultant, Gillam Mackie, SSC, and Fyfe Ireland, WS, Edinburgh, 1997-99; Member, Government Committee (on alternatives to prosecution), 1978-83; taught civil advocacy and course administrator, Edinburgh University, 1981-91; Founder Member, Scottish Legal Aid Board, 1986-91. Recreations: theatre; music; travel; foreign languages (French, Italian and German). Address: (h.) 20 Howe Street, Edinburgh; T.-0131-225 8755.

Donald, Colin Dunlop, BA (Cantab), LLB, DUniv, FRSA, DL; b. 24.7.34, Strathaven; m., Theresa Ann Gilliland; 2 s.; 1 d. Educ. Cargilfield; Rugby; Gonville and Caius College, Cambridge; Glasgow University. National Service, 1953-55, 2nd Lt., The Cameronians (Scottish Rifles); Partner and latterly Consultant, McGrigor Donald, Solicitors, Glasgow, 1966-94; Vice-President, National Trust for Scotland; Deputy Chairman, Universities Superannuation Scheme Ltd.; Trustee: Lloyds, TSB Foundation for Scotland, 1994-2000; Director, Lloyds TSB Scotland plc, 1998-2000; a

Deputy Lieutenant of Stirling and Falkirk. Recreations: golf and other outdoor sports. Address: (h.) 33 Park Terrace, Stirling FK8 2JS; T.-01786 473565.

Donald, George Malcolm, RSA, RSW, DA, ATC, MEd. Lecturer, Edinburgh College of Art; Director, Centre for Continuing Studies, ECA; b. 12.9.43, Ootacamund, South India; 1 s.; 1 d. Educ. Robert Gordon's College; Aberdeen Academy; Edinburgh College of Art; Hornsey College of Art; Edinburgh University. Joined Edinburgh College of Art as Lecturer, 1969; Visiting Lecturer, five Faculties of Art in India, 1979; Visiting Professor: University of Central Florida (Art, 1981, Drawing and Anatomy, 1985), Strasbourg, 1986, Belgrade, 1987, Sechuan Fine Art Institute, China, 1989, Chinese Academy of Fine Art, 1994, Osaka and Kyoto Universities, Japan, 1999; Latimer Award, RSA, 1970; Guthrie Award, RSA, 1973; Scottish Arts Council Bursary, 1973; RSA Gillies Bequest Travel Award to India, 1978; SAC Travel and Study Award, Indiana, 1981; RSA Gillies Prize, 1982; RSW Mary Marshall Brown Award, 1983; RGI Cargill Award, 1987; former Council Member, Printmakers Workshop (Edinburgh); one man shows: Florida, 1985, Helsinki, 1985, Edinburgh Festival, 1985, Belgrade, 1987, Florida, 1987, Edinburgh, 1988, 1990, London, 1992-94, Edinburgh 1993, 1994, 1995, 1998, 1999, 2002. Address: (h.) Bankhead, by Duns, Berwickshire TD11 3QJ; T.-01361 883014; e-mail: g.donald@eca.ac.uk

Donald, Hugh R. OBE, LLB (Hons), WS. Partner, Shepherd and Wedderburn (Chief Executive, 1994-1999); b. 5.11.51, Edinburgh; m., M. Grace Donald; 1 s.; 1 d. Educ. Melville College, Edinburgh; Edinburgh University. Shepherd and Wedderburn: legal training, 1973-75, Assistant Solicitor, 1975-77, Partner, since 1977. Chairman, Family Mediation Scotland. Recreations: family; church; gardening. Address: Saltire Court, 20 Castle Terrace, Edinburgh EH1 2ET; T.-0131-228 9900.

Donald, Marion Coats, DipArch, MPhil, RIBA, FRIAS. Principal, John and Marion Donald, Chartered Architects, since 1976; part-time Lecturer, Scott Sutherland School, Robert Gordon University, since 1988; Partner, Castlegate Design Group; b. 15.5.47, Aberdeen; m., John Donald; 1 s.; 1 d. Educ. Aberdeen High School for Girls; Colchester County High School for Girls; Scott Sutherland School of Architecture, RGIT; Scott Sutherland School, Robert Gordon University. Student architect, Sir Basil Spence Glover and Ferguson, 1972; Architectural Assistant, SSHA, 1973-74; Architect, Jenkins and Marr, 1974-76. Former Chairman, Aberdeen Soroptimist Housing Society Ltd; Elder and Session Clerk, Queen's Cross Church. RIBA Award, 1998; Aberdeenshire 2000 Award; Association for Preservation of Scotland Award, 1995; Aberdeen Civic Society Award, 1984. Recreations: family; gardening; music; art and architecture. Address: 177b Queen's Road, Aberdeen AB15 8BS; T.-01224 313014.

Donald, Rev. Peter Harry, MA, PhD, BD. Minister, Crown Church, Inverness, since 1998; b. 3.2.62, Edinburgh; m., Brigid Mary McNeill; 1 s.; 1 d. Educ. George Watson's College; Gonville and Caius College, University of Cambridge; University of Edinburgh. Scouloudi Research Fellow, Institute of Historical Research, University of London, 1986-87; Probationer Assistant, St. Michael's Church, Edinburgh, 1990-91; Minister, Leith St. Serf's Parish Church, 1991-98. Hon. Secretary, Scottish Church History Society; Member, Faith and Order Commission. Publication: An Uncounselled King: Charles I and the Scottish Troubles 1637-1641, 1990. Recreations: golf; swimming; racquet sports; piano; singing; walking; family. Address: 39 Southside Road, Inverness IV2 4XA; T.-01463 231140.

Donald, Susan, MA (Hons). Editor, Planning, BBC Scotland; Educ. George Watson's Ladies' College, Edinburgh; Edinburgh University. Daily Mirror Trainee, 1979-81; Journalist, Daily Mirror/Sunday Mirror Manchester, 1982-83; Journalist, BBC, 1983 -87; News Editor, BBC, London, 1987-88; Deputy News Editor, Daily Express, 1989; News Editor, Independent Television News, 1989-93; Reporter, Frontline Scotland, BBC Scotland, 1994-99. Royal Television Society's Regional Documentary Award for Open to Abuse, 1997. Recreations: squash; swimming; skiing. Address: (b.) BBC Scotland, Broadcasting House, Queen Margaret Drive, Glasgow, G12 8DG.

Donaldson, Professor Gordon Bryce, MA, PhD, FInstP, FRSE. Professor of Applied Physics, Strathclyde University (Head of Department, 1993-98); Honorary Editor, Superconductor Science and Technology, since 1998; Treasurer, European Society for Applied Superconductivity, since 2001; b. 10.8.41, Edinburgh; m., Christina Martin; 1 s.; 1 d. Educ. Glasgow Academy; Christ's College, Cambridge. Cavendish Laboratory, Cambridge, 1962-65; Lecturer in Physics, Lancaster University, 1966-75; Strathclyde University: Lecturer, 1976, Senior Lecturer, 1978, Professor, 1985; Visiting Scientist and Fulbright Scholar, University of California, 1975; Visiting Professor, University of Virginia, 1981; Chairman, Institute of Physics Low Temperature Group, 1990-93; DTI/SERC Coordinator for National Superconductivity Programme, 1990-93; 1999-2000 Honorary Fellow, Commonwealth Scientific and Industrial Research Organisation, Australia. Address: (b.) Department of Physics and Applied Physics, Strathclyde University, Glasgow G4 ONG.

Donaldson, Graham H.C., MA, MEd. HM Depute Senior Chief Inspector of Education, since 1996; b. 11.12.46, Glasgow; m., Dilys; 2 s.; 1 d. Educ. High School of Glasgow; Glasgow University. Teacher, Craigbank Secondary School, Glasgow; Principal Teacher, Dunbartonshire Council; Lecturer, Jordanhill College; Curriculum Evaluator, Consultative Committee on the Curriculum; HM Inspector of Schools; HM Chief Inspector of Schools. Publication: James IV – A Renaissance King. Recreations: golf; reading. Address: (b.) HM Inspectorate of Education, G Spur, Saughton House, Broomhouse Drive, Edinburgh EH11 3XD; T.-0131-244 7120.

Donaldson, Professor Iain Malcolm Lane, BSc, MB, ChB, MA, FRCPE, MRCP. Professor of Neurophysiology, Edinburgh University, since 1987; b. 22.10.37; m.; 1 s. Educ. Edinburgh University. House Physician and Surgeon, Research Fellow, Honorary Lecturer, Honorary Senior Registrar, Departments of Medicine and Surgical Neurology, Edinburgh University, 1962-69; Anglo-French Research Scholarship, University of Paris, 1969-70; Research Officer, University Laboratory of Physiology, Oxford, 1970-79; Fellow and Tutor in Medicine, St. Edmund Hall, Oxford, 1973-79; Professor of Zoology, Hull University, 1979-87; Emeritus Fellow, St. Edmund Hall, Oxford, since 1979. Recreation: studying the past. Address: (b.) Department of Neuroscience, Edinburgh University, Appleton Tower, Crichton Street, Edinburgh EH8 9LE.

Donaldson, James Andrew, BDS, BA, DFM. Principal in general dental practice; b. 28.2.57, Glasgow; m., Patricia H. Winter; 1 s.; 3 d. Educ. Coatbridge High School; Dundee University; Open University; Glasgow University. Dental Adviser, British Antarctic Survey, 1986-97; Member: National Council, General Dental Practitioners Association, since 1989, Scottish General Dental Services Committee, 1991-93, Aberdeen District Council, 1984-86, Grampian Regional Council, 1986-88; Director, "Open Wide" Dental Courses; contested (Liberal Democrat) Aberdeen North, elections to Scottish Parliament, 1999, Westminster election, 2001. Recreations: golf; skiing; football. Address: (h.) Ellon Castle, Ellon, AB41 9QN; T.-01358 721865.

Donaldson, Marion. Fashion Designer; b. 1944, Glasgow. Trained as primary school-teacher; with husband, founded fashion company, mid-1960s.

Donaldson, William, MA, PhD. Writer, Researcher, Traditional Musician; b. 19.7.44, Fraserburgh. Educ. Fraserburgh Academy; Aberdeen University. Publications: Popular Literature in Victorian Scotland, 1986; The Jacobite Song, 1988; The Language of the People, 1989; The Highland Pipe and Scottish Society 1750–1950, 2000. Recreation: piobaireachd. Address: (b.) 13 Mile End Avenue, Aberdeen.

Donegan, Kate, BA. Governor, HMP and YOI, Glenochil, since 2001; b. 21.4.53, Newport on Tay; m., Chris Donegan; 2 s. Educ. Kirkcaldy High School; Stirling University. Assistant Governor: Cornton Vale, 1977-84, Barlinnie Prison, 1984-87; Deputy Governor: Reading Prison, 1987-89; Deputy Governor, Perth Prison, 1989-91; Head, Operational Manpower, Planning Unit, 1991-93; seconded to Staffing Structure Review Team, 1993-94; Deputy Governor, Barlinnie Prison, 1994-95; Deputy Chief Inspector of Prisons, 1995-96; Governor, HM Prison and Institution, Cornton Vale, 1996-2001. Recreations: gardening; reading; computing. Address: (b.) HM Prison and YOI, Glenochil, Tullibody, Clackmannanshire FK10 3AD; T.-01259 767203; e-mail: kathleen.donegan@sps.gov.uk

Donnachie, Ian, MA, MLitt, PhD, FRHistS, FSA (Scot). Senior Lecturer in History, since 1985, Staff Tutor, since 1970, Director, Centre for Scottish Studies, Open University in Scotland; b. 18.6.44, Lanark. Educ. Lanark Grammar School; Glasgow University; Strathclyde University. Research Assistant, Galloway Project, Strathclyde University, 1967-68; Lecturer in Social Studies: Napier Polytechnic, 1968-70, Deakin University, Victoria, 1982; Visiting Fellow: Deakin University, Victoria and Sydney University, NSW, 1985; Hon. Lecturer, Dundee University, since 1998; Vice-Chairman, Friends of New Lanark; Consultant: SHEFC, HEFCE, QAA; Member: Universities Association for Continuing Education (Scotland); Member, Council, Economic and Social History Society of Scotland; Trustee, Scottish Brewing Archive. Publications include: A History of the Brewing Industry in Scotland; Industrial Archaeology in the British Isles (jointly); Scottish History 1560-1980 (jointly); That Land of Exiles: Scots in Australia (jointly); Forward! Labour Politics in Scotland 1888-1988 (Co-Editor); A Companion to Scottish History from the Reformation to the Present (jointly); The Manufacture of Scottish History (Co-editor); Historic New Lanark: the Dale and Owen Industrial Community since 1785 (Co-author); Studying Scottish History, Literature and Culture; Modern Scottish History: 1707 to the present (Co-Editor); Robert Owen, Owen of New Lanark and New Harmony; Dictionary of Scottish History (jointly). Recreations: walking; cycling; countryside. Address: (b.) 10 Drumsheugh Gardens, Edinburgh EH3 7QJ; T.-0131-226 3851; e-mail: i.donnachie@open.ac.uk

Donnelly, Dougie, LLB. Broadcaster; sports video writer and director; b. 7.6.53, Glasgow; m., Linda; 3 d. Educ. Hamilton Academy; Strathclyde University. Presenter, BBC Television Sport, since 1978: Grandstand, World Championship snooker, Olympic Games (summer and winter), World Cup, Commonwealth Games, Ryder Cup, golf, Sportscene, Match of the Day; Mid-Morning Show, Album Show, Radio Clyde, 1976-92; Columnist, Evening Times; after-dinner speaker, conference and seminar host. Recreations: sport; travel; reading; good food and wine. Address: (b.) David John Associates, 6 Victoria Crescent Road, Glasgow G12 9DB; T.-0141-357 0532.

Donnison, Professor David. Honorary Research Fellow, Glasgow University; Visiting Professor, Warwick University; b. 19.1.26. Lecturer: Manchester University, 1950-53, Toronto University, 1953-55; London School of Economics and Political Science: Reader, 1956-61, Professor, 1961-69; Director, Centre for Environmental Studies, London, 1969-75; Chairman, Supplementary Benefits Commission, 1975-80; Professor of Town and Regional Planning, Glasgow University, 1980-90. Address: (b.) Glasgow University, Glasgow G12 8RT.

Donohoe, Brian H. MP (Labour), Cunninghame South, since 1992; b. 10.9.48, Kilmarnock; m., Christine; 2 s. Educ. Irvine Royal Academy; Kilmarnock Technical College. Secretary, Irvine and District Trades Council, 1973-81; Chair: North Ayrshire and Arran LHC, 1977-79, Cunninghame Industrial Development Committee, 1975-79; former full-time trade union official (NALGO). Recreation: gardening. Address: (h.) 5 Greenfield Drive, Irvine, Ayrshire; T.-01294 274419.

Donovan, Professor Robert John, BSc, PhD, CChem, FRSC, FRSE. Professor of Chemistry, Edinburgh University, since 1979; b. 13.7.41, Nantwich; m., Marion Jacubeit; 1 d. Educ. Sandbach School; University College of Wales, Aberystwyth; Cambridge University. Research Fellow, Gonville and Caius College, 1966-70; Edinburgh University: Lecturer in Physical Chemistry, 1970-74, Reader in Chemistry, 1974-79. Member: Physical Chemistry Panel, Science & Engineering Research Council, 1977-80, Management Committee, SERC Synchrotron Radiation Source, Daresbury, 1977-80, SERC Synchrotron Radiation Facility Committee, 1979-84; Chairman, SERC Laser Facility Committee, 1989-92; Member, SERC Science Board, 1989-92; Chairman, Facilities Commission, SERC, 1993-94; awarded Corday-Morgan Medal and Prize, Royal Society of Chemistry, 1975; Member: Faraday Council, Royal Society of Chemistry, 1981-83, 1991-93; Vice President, Royal Society of Edinburgh, 1998-2001 (Member, Council, since 1996); Tilden Prize, Royal Society of Chemistry, 1995. Recreations: hill-walking; skiing; sail-boarding; cross-country riding. Address: (b.) Department of Chemistry, Edinburgh University, West Mains Road, Edinburgh EH9 3JJ; T.-0131-650 4722; e-mail: R.Donovan@ed.ac.uk

Doohan, John Patrick, BA, CQSW, LLB, DipLP. Advocate; b. 13.6.53, Glasgow; m., Elizabeth; 2 s.; 2 d. Educ. Glasgow University; Aberdeen University. Social work, 1975-82; law trainee, 1985-88; devil, 1988-89; called to Bar, 1989. Recreations: football; reading. Address: (b.) Faculty of Advocates, Parliament House, Edinburgh.

Doran, Frank, LLB(Hons). MP (Labour), Aberdeen Central, since 1997; b. 13.4.49; 2 s. Educ. Leith Academy; University of Dundee. Solicitor, 1977-87; MP (Labour), Aberdeen South, 1987-92; Co-ordinator, National Trade Union Political Fund Ballot Campaign, 1993-96. Address: (b.) House of Commons, London SW1A 0AA; T.-0171-219 3000.

Dorman, Arthur Brian, LLB, FIMgt. Solicitor; Partner, Brian Dorman, Solicitors; Director: Rita Rusk International Ltd., Marblehead Brand Development Limited; b. 21.6.45, Glasgow; 1 s.; 1 d. Educ. Hillhead High School; Glasgow University. Recreation: occasional golf. Address: Shawhill House, Hurlford, Ayrshire KA1 5HZ; T.-01563 525590.

Dorward, David Campbell, MA, ARAM. Composer, since 1944; Music Producer, BBC, 1962-91; b. 7.8.33, Dundee; m., Janet Offord; 1 s.; 2 d. Educ. Morgan Academy, Dundee; St. Andrews University; Royal Academy of Music. Teaching, 1960-61; Freelance, 1961-62. Arts Adviser, Lamp of Lothian Collegiate Trust, since 1967; Member, Scottish Arts Council, 1972-78; Consultant Director,

Performing Right Society, 1985-90; Patron's Fund Award, 1958; Royal Philharmonic Prizewinner, 1958; compositions include four string quartets, two symphonies, four concertos, Tonight Mrs Morrison (one-act opera), A Christmas Carol (musical), and incidental music for TV, radio, film and stage. Recreations: photography; computers; walking in the country. Address: (h.) Dovecot House, Preston Road, Prestonpans EH32 9JZ; T.-01875 810 512.

Dorward, David Philip, MA (Hons), LLB; b. 10.4.31, Dundee; m., Joy Stewart; 2 s. Educ. Dundee High School; St. Andrews University. Joined St. Andrews University as Administrative Assistant, 1959; successively Assistant Secretary, Deputy Secretary, Secretary; retired; Honorary Sheriff, Tayside, Central and Fife at Cupar, since 1995. Publications: Scottish Surnames; Scotland's Place-Names; Dundee, Names, People and Places; The Glens of Angus. Recreations: music; golf; gardening; walking; European travel. Address: (h.) 7 Drumcarrow Crescent, Strathkinness, Fife KY16 9XT; T.-0133 485630.

Dougall, Rev. Neil James, BD, DipMin. Minister, St David's Broomhouse Church,, Edinburgh, since 1991; Chair, Scripture Union Scotland, since 1999; b. 8.2.63, Nairobi, Kenya; m., Helen; 2 d. Educ. George Heriots School, Edinburgh; Aberdeen University; Glasgow University. Ordained, Edinburgh Presbytery, 1991. Recreations: cycling; reading. Address: (b.) Scripture Union Scotland, 9 Canal Street, Glasgow, G4 0AB.

Douglas, Alan. Journalist and Broadcaster; b. 16.10.51, Dundee; m., Viv Lumsden (qv); 2 d. Educ. Forfar Academy. Local newspapers, 1970-74; BBC Local Radio Reporter and Producer, 1974-78; Reporter/Presenter, BBC TV Scotland, 1978-89; freelance broadcaster and journalist, BBC TV and Radio, corporate and Scottish TV; Partner, The Broadcasting Business (media consultancy); Motoring Columnist, Glasgow Evening Times, Scottish Field. Former Guild of Motoring Writers' Regional Journalist of the Year. Recreations: cars; walking; eating; drinking. Address: (b.) Broadcasting Business, 9 Lethington Road, Glasgow G46 6TA; e-mail: alan@broadcastingbusiness.co.uk

Douglas, Allan Fraser, BSc (Hons), PGDip. Rector, Wallace Hall Academy, since 1996; b. 9.11.46, Aberdeen; m., Isabel Gordon Pearson; 2 s.; 1 d. Educ. Aberdeen Academy; Strathclyde University. Research Chemist, 1969-71; Teacher of Chemistry, Annan Academy, 1972-73, Lockerbie Academy, 1973-79; Research Chemist, St Andrews University, 1979-82; Teacher of Chemistry, Dumfries Academy, 1982-88, Assistant Head Teacher/Depute Rector, 1988-96. Recreations: dinghy sailing; gardening; hill-walking. Address: (b.) Wallace Hall Academy, Station Road, Thornhill, Dumfries and Galloway DG3 5DS; T.-01848 330294.

Douglas, Rev. Andrew Morrison, MA. Clerk to the Presbytery of Aberdeen, since 1995; b. 23.2.30; b. Orange, Australia; m., Margaret Rennie; 2 s.; 2 d. Educ. Robert Gordons College, Aberdeen; University of Aberdeen. Minister: Lochcraig, Fife, 1957-62, Bon Accord St Paul's, Aberdeen, 1963-72, Southesk, Brechin, 1972-77, High Church Hilton, Aberdeen, 1977-95. Recreations: golf; gardening; choral singing. Address: (b.) Aberdeen Presbytery Office, c/o Mastrick Parish Church, Greenfern Road, Aberdeen AB16 6TR; T.-01224 690494.

Douglas, Gavin Stuart, RD, QC, MA, LLB; b. 12.6.32. Educ. South Morningside School; George Heriot's School; Edinburgh University. Qualified as Solicitor, 1955; National Service, Royal Navy; admitted to Faculty of Advocates, 1958; Sub-editor (part-time), The Scotsman, 1957-61; Member, Lord Advocate's Department in London, (as Parliamentary Draftsman) 1961-64; returned to practice at Scots Bar, 1964; Junior Counsel to Board of Trade, 1965-71; Counsel to Scottish Law Commission, 1965-96; Hon. Sheriff, 1965-71; a Chairman of Industrial Tribunals, 1966-78; Counsel to Secretary of State for Scotland under Private Legislation Procedure (Scotland) Act 1936, 1969-1975, Senior Counsel under that Act since 1975; Member, Lothian Health Board, 1981-85; Member, Board, Leith Nautical College, 1981-84; Editor, Session Cases, seven volumes, 1976-82; Temporary Sheriff, 1990-99; President, Temporary Sheriffs' Association, 1998-99. Recreations: golf; skiing. Address: (b.) Parliament House, Parliament Square, Edinburgh EH1 1RF.

Douglas, Hector, MBA, FCCA, DipComm. Head, Aberdeen Business School, since 1998; b. 30.3.50, Inverness; m., Dr Anne M.S. Douglas; 1s. Educ. Inverness Royal Academy; Robert Gordon's Institute of Technology. HM Customs, 1971-80; Lecturer, Robert Gordon University, 1980. Recreations: family; music; cooking. Address: (h.) Kintore Cottage, Banchory-Devenick, Aberdeen; T.-01224 869802.

Douglas, Professor Neil James, MD, FRCP, FRCPE. Professor of Respiratory and Sleep Medicine, Edinburgh University; Director, Scottish National Sleep Laboratory; Vice-President, Royal College of Physicians of Edinburgh; Consultant Physician, since 1983; b. 28.5.49, Edinburgh; m., Dr. Sue Galloway; 1 s.; 1 d. Educ. Dundee High School; Trinity College, Glenalmond; St. Andrews University; Edinburgh University. Lecturer in Medicine, Edinburgh University, 1974-83; MRC Travelling Fellow, University of Colorado, 1980-81. Recreations: fishing; gardening; eating. Address: (b.) Respiratory Medicine Unit, Department of Medicine, Royal Infirmary, Lauriston Place, Edinburgh EH3 9YW; T.-0131 536 3252.

Douglas, Sadie Naomi, MBE. Administrative Director, Scottish Civic Trust, 1983-93; b. Huddersfield; m., Alexander Douglas (deceased); 1 s. Educ. Longley Hall, Huddersfield; Huddersfield Technical College. Worked with Oxfam, 1966-70; Organising Secretary, Facelift Glasgow, 1970-73; Trust Secretary, Scottish Civic Trust, 1973-83. Member, Countrywide Holiday Association (Past President, Glasgow CHA Club); Chairman, West Kilbride Amenity Society. Recreation: voluntary work. Address: (h.) Hillhouse, Ardneil Avenue, West Kilbride, Ayrshire KA23; T.-01294 822465.

Douglas-Home, Lady (Lavinia) Caroline, DL, FSA Scot. Estate Factor, Douglas and Angus Estates, 1960-95; Trustee, National Museum of Antiquities of Scotland, 1982-85; Deputy Lieutenant, Berwickshire, since 1983; b. 11.10.37 (daughter of Baron Home of the Hirsel, KT, PC). Educ. privately. Woman of the Bedchamber (Temporary) to Queen Elizabeth the Queen Mother, 1963-65; Lady-In-Waiting (Temporary) to HRH Duchess of Kent, 1966-67; President, Borders Branch, British Red Cross, since 1998. Recreations: fishing; gardening; reading; antiquities. Address: (h.) Heaton Mill House, Cornhill-on-Tweed, Northumberland; T.-01890 882303.

Douglas Home, Mark. Editor, The Herald, since 2000; b. 31.8.51, Galashiels; m., Colette; 1 s.; 1 d. Educ. Eton; University of the Witwatersrand, Johannesburg. Scottish Correspondent, The Independent, 1986-90; News Editor, The Scotsman, 1990-93; Assistant Editor, The Scotsman, 1993-94; Deputy Editor, Scotland on Sunday, 1994-98; Editor, Sunday Times Scotland, 1999-2000. Address: (b.) 200 Renfield Street, Glasgow; T.-0141-302 7000.

Douglas Miller, Andrew, BA. Joint Managing Director Jenners Princes Street Edinburgh Ltd., since 2001 (Managing Director, since 1996); b. 29.9.63, Edinburgh; m., Helen Bateman; 2 s. Educ. Harrow School; City of London Polytechnic. Jenners Princes Street Edinburgh Ltd.: General Manager, 1993, Merchandise Director, 1994. Address: 48 Princes Street, Edinburgh EH2 2YJ.

Dover, Sir Kenneth James, MA, DLitt, Hon.LLD (St. Andrews, Birmingham), Hon.LittD (St. Andrews, Bristol, London, Liverpool, Durham), Hon.DHL (Oglethorpe), FRSE, FBA. Chancellor, St. Andrews University, since 1981; b. 11.3.20, Croydon; m., Audrey Ruth Latimer; 1 s.; 1 d. Educ. St. Paul's School, London; Balliol College, Oxford; Merton College, Oxford. Fellow and Tutor, Balliol College, Oxford, 1948-55; Professor of Greek, St. Andrews, 1955-76; President, Corpus Christi College, Oxford, 1976-86. Served in Royal Artillery, 1940-45; President, Hellenic Society, 1971-74; President, Classical Association, 1975; President, British Academy, 1978-81; Foreign Honorary Member, American Academy of Arts and Sciences, since 1979; Foreign Member, Royal Netherlands Academy, since 1979; Honorary Fellow, Balliol, Corpus Christi and Merton Colleges, Oxford. Recreations: gardening; historical linguistics. Address: (h.) 49 Hepburn Gardens, St. Andrews, Fife KY16 9LS; T.-01334 473589.

Dow, Professor Alexander Carmichael, MA, PhD. Professor of Scottish Economy, Division of Economics and Enterprise, Glasgow Caledonian University; b. 28.8.46; m., Sheila Christine; 2 d. Educ. Perth Academy; St. Andrews University; Simon Fraser University; University of Manitoba. Research Officer, Commonwealth Secretariat; Lecturer and Assistant Professor, University of Toronto; Lecturer, Stirling University; Head, Department of Economics, Glasgow Caledonian University, 1989-99. Recreations: curling; travel. Address: (b.) Division of Economics and Enterprise, Glasgow Caledonian University, Cowcaddens Road, Glasgow G4 0BA; T.-0141-331 3309; e-mail: acdo@gcal.ac.uk

Dow, Rear-Admiral Douglas Morrison, CB, DL. Director, The National Trust for Scotland, 1992-97; b. 1.7.35; m., Felicity Margaret Mona Napier; 2 s.; Educ. George Heriot's School; BRNC Dartmouth. Joined RN, 1952; served Staff of C-in-C Plymouth, 1959-61; HMS Plymouth, 1961-63; RN Supply Sch., 1963-65; Staff of Comdr FEF, 1965-67; HMS Endurance, 1968-70; BRNC Dartmouth, 1970-72; Cdr 1972; Assistant Director, Officer Appointments (S), 1972-74; Sec to Comdr British Navy Staff, Washington, 1974-76; HMS Tiger, 1977-78; NDC Latimer, 1978-79; Captain 1979; CSO(A) to Flag Officer Portsmouth, 1979; Sec to Controller of Navy, 1981; Captain, HMS Cochrane, 1983; Commodore, HMS Centurion, 1985; RCDS, 1988; Rear Admiral, 1989; Director General, Naval Personal Services, 1989-92. Vice-Chairman, George Heriot's Trust, since 1996. Recreations: rugby union; fly fishing; shooting; golf; gardening. Address: (h.) Tor Lodge, 1 Eskbank Terrace, Dalkeith, Midlothian EH22 3DE.

Dow, Dr Frances, MA (Hons) DPhil, FRHistS. Provost, Faculty Group of Arts, Divinity and Music, Edinburgh University, since 1997; Dean of Arts, since 1997; Senior Lecturer, History, Edinburgh University, since 1988; b. 2.9.47. Edinburgh. Educ. John Watsons School, Edinburgh; Edinburgh University; York University. Research Fellow, Birmingham University, 1972-74; Lecturer, History, Edinburgh University, 1974-88; Assistant Principal, Edinburgh University, 1995-97.Governor, Newbattle Abbey College, 1989-97; Member, Marshall Aid Commemoration Commission, since 1998; Trustee, Scotland Inheritance Fund, since 1995; Member, Lothian Health Board Research Ethics sub-committee, since 1999. Publications: Cromwellian Scotland, 1979; Radicalism in the English Revolution, 1640-1660, 1985. Address: (h.) 7 Douglas Crescent, Edinburgh, EH12 5BB; T.-0131-337 0132.

Dow, Professor Sheila Christine, MA (Hons), PhD. Professor in Economics, Stirling University, since 1996 (Head of Department, since 2002); Chair, International Network for Economic Method, since 2001; b. 16.4.49, Dumfries; m., Professor Alexander Dow; 2 d. Educ. Hawick

High School; St. Andrews University; University of Manitoba; McMaster University; Glasgow University. Overseas Office, Bank of England, 1970-72; Economist, then Senior Economist, Department of Finance, Government of Manitoba, 1973-77; Lecturer, then Reader, Department of Economics, Stirling University, 1979-96. Publications: Macroeconomic Thought, 1985; Financial Markets and Regional Economic Development, 1990; Money Matters (Co-author), 1982; Money and the Economic Process, 1993; The Methodology of Macroeconomic Thought, 1996; Economic Methodology: An Inquiry, 2002. Recreations: travel; various sports. Address: (b.) Department of Economics, Stirling University, Stirling FK9 4LA; T.-01786 467474.

Dowds, Donal, BSc, MBA, MICE. Managing Director, Scottish Airports Limited, since 1999; b. 3.5.53, Ireland; m., Jane Marie; 2 s.; 1 d. Educ. Paisley College of Technology; Glasgow University. Scottish Airports: Project Engineer, 1979, Planning Manager, 1981; Traffic and Commercial Manager, Aberdeen Airport, 1984; Terminal Development Manager, Gatwick, 1987; Operations Director, Glasgow Airport, 1988; Managing Director, Glasgow Airport, 1992; Managing Director, Edinburgh Airport, 1996. Director: AOA, since 1999, Glasgow Chamber of Commerce, since 1999, Scottish Enterprise Renfrewshire, since 2000; Member: CBI Transport Committee, since 1999, SCDI Executive Committee, since 1999, Board, VisitScotland, since 2000. Recreations: travel; reading; clay pigeon shooting; golf. Address: (b.) St Andrew's Drive, Glasgow Airport, Paisley PA3 2SW; T.-0141-848 4583.

Downes, Bob, DipTP, BPhil. National Manager, BT Scotland, since 2001; b. 10.8.51, Belfast; 2 s. Educ. Portora Royal School, Enniskillen; Dundee University; Duncan of Jordanstone College of Art, Dundee. Local government, 1976-82; Dundee Project, 1982-84; SDA, 1984-87; Director: North East, SDA, 1987-90, Conran Roche Planning, London, 1990-92; independent consultant, 1992-93; Chief Executive, Dumfries and Galloway Enterprise, 1993-94; Director, Scottish Enterprise, 1994-99; BT Scotland: Director, Economic Development, 1999-2000; Director, e-business Development, 2000-01. Advisor, Flax Trust, Belfast, since 1994; Director: Wise Group, Glasgow, since 1997, Emerging Business Trust, Belfast, since 1996, Businesslab, since 1999; Member, President's Executive Committee, National Council for Urban Economic Development, Washington D.C., since 1996; Member, Advisory Board, The Competitiveness Institute, Barcelona, 1998-99. Recreations: running; cycling; live music; travelling; films; pub crack; Jim Thompson novels; journalists' biographies; Kelvin walkway. Address: (h.) 21 Cleveden Road, Kelvinside, Glasgow G12 0PQ.

Downes, Professor Charles Peter, MIBiol, PhD, FRSE. Head, School of Life Sciences, Dundee University, since 2000; Professor of Biochemistry, since 1989; b. 15.10.53, Manchester; m., Dr Elizabeth Naomi; 1 s.; 1 d. Educ. Kings School, Macclesfield; Stockport College of Technology; Birmingham University. Experimental Officer, ICI Pharmaceuticals, 1973-78; MRC Training Fellow, Cambridge, 1981-83; Research Group Leader, ICI Pharmaceuticals, 1983-85; Cellular Pharmacologist/Senior Cellular Pharmacologist, Smith Kline and French/Smith Kline Beecham, 1985-89. Chairman, The Biochemical Society, 2000-2004. Recreations: golf; previously playing, now spectating, football. Address: (b.) School of Life Sciences, WTB/MSI Complex, Dundee University, Dow Street, Dundee DD1 5EH; T.-01382 345156.

Downie, Professor Robert S., MA, BPhil, FRSE, FRSA. Professor of Moral Philosophy, Glasgow University, since 1969 (Stevenson Lecturer in Medical Ethics, 1984-88); b. 19.4.33, Glasgow; m., Eileen Dorothea Flynn; 3 d. Educ.

High School of Glasgow; Glasgow University; Queen's College, Oxford. Tutor, Worcester College, Oxford, 1958-59; Glasgow University: Lecturer in Moral Philosophy, 1959-68, Senior Lecturer, 1968-69; Visiting Professor: Syracuse University, New York, 1963-64, Dalhousie University, Nova Scotia, 1976. Publications: Government Action and Morality, 1964; Respect for Persons, 1969; Roles and Values, 1971; Education and Personal Relationships, 1974; Caring and Curing, 1980; Healthy Respect, 1987; Health Promotion: models and values, 1990; The Making of a Doctor, 1992; Francis Hutcheson, 1994; The Healing Arts: an Oxford illustrated anthology, 1994; Palliative Care Ethics, 1996; Medical Ethics, 1996; Clinical Judgement – Evidence in Practice, 2000. Recreation: music. Address: (b.) Department of Philosophy, Glasgow University G12 8QQ; T.-0141-339 8855.

Dowse, Pauline Hazel, GMusRNCM, PPRNCM, PGDipRNCM. Principal Cellist, Royal Scottish National Orchestra, since 1989; b. 10.3.63, Chelmsford; m., Dr. Peter Argondizza; 2 c. Educ. Chelmer Valley High School; Colchester Institute; Royal Northern College of Music, Banff School of Fine Arts, Banff, Alberta, Canada. Co-Principal Cellist, English National Opera Orchestra, 1988. Address: (h.) 38 Hallydown Drive, Jordanhill, Glasgow G13 1UF; T.-0141-954 9346.

Doyle, Professor Christopher John, BA, MSc. Head: Management Division, since 1997, Applied Economics and Agricultural Systems Department, since 1989, Scottish Agricultural College, Auchincruive; Adjunct Professor of Agricultural Economics, Glasgow University, since 1989; Vice Dean (Education), 1991-94, and Professor of Agricultural Economics, since 1994, Scottish Agricultural College, Auchincruive; b. 21.8.48, Sale, Cheshire; m., Alice; 1. d. Educ. St. Ambrose College, Cheshire; Keele University; Newcastle upon Tyne University. Departmental Demonstrator in Agricultural Economics, Oxford University, 1972-76; Research Officer, Centre for Agricultural Strategy, Reading University, 1976-79; Principal Scientific Officer, Institute for Grassland and Animal Production, 1979-86; Senior Economist, Ruakura Research Centre, MAF, New Zealand, 1987; Principal Scientific Officer, Institute for Grassland and Animal Production, 1988-89. Publications: 130 scientific papers and publications. Recreations: languages; foreign travel; modern history; theatre. Address: (b.) Scottish Agricultural College, Auchincruive, Ayr KA6 5HW; T.-01292 525053.

Doyle, Rev. David Wallace, MA(Hons), BD(Hons). Minister, St. Mary's Parish Church, Motherwell, since 1987; b. 12.4.48, Glasgow; m., Alison W. Britton; 1 s.; 1 d. Educ. High School of Glasgow; University of Glasgow; Corpus Christi, University of Cambridge. Assistant Minister, East Kilbride Old Parish Church, 1973-74; Minister, Tulliallan and Kincardine Parish Church, Fife, 1977-87. Recreations: music, gardening. Address: (h.) Manse of St. Mary's, 19 Orchard Street, Motherwell ML1 3JE; T.-01698 263472.

Doyle, Roberta, BA. Director of Public Affairs, National Galleries of Scotland, since 2000; b. 5.1.60, Glasgow; m., Mahmut Cemal Öztürk. Educ. Notre Dame High School, Glasgow; University of Strathclyde. Marketing Manager, Citizens' Theatre, 1986; Director of Marketing and Press, Scottish Ballet, 1990; Director of Marketing and Press, Scottish Opera, 1992. Chair, Clyde Unity Theatre Co.; Board Director, Anatomy Performance Co; Vice-Chair, Theatrical Management Association Marketing Committee. Recreations: theatre; film; travel; riding. Address: (b.) National Galleries of Scotland, The Mound, Edinburgh EH2 2EL; T.-0131-624 6200.

Draper, Professor Paul Richard, BA, MA, PhD. Walter Scott and Partners Professor of Finance, University of Edinburgh, since 1997; b. 28.12.46, Hayes; m., Janet Margaret; 1 s.; 1 d. Educ. Exeter, Reading and Stirling Universities. Lecturer: St. Andrews and Edinburgh Universities; Professor of Finance, Strathclyde University, 1986-97 (Head, Department of Accounting and Finance, 1990-95, Vice Dean, Strathclyde Business School, 1993-97). Member, Research Assessment Panel for Accounting and Finance 2001. Publication: Scottish Financial Sector (Co-Author), 1988; Investment Trust Industry in the UK, 1989; The Cost of Equity Capital (Co-Author), 1999. Recreations: renovating country cottages; home computing. Address: (h.) 19 Upper Gray Street, Newington, Edinburgh; T.-0131-667 4087.

Drewry, James Michael, FITSA, DCA. Director of Environmental and Consumer Services, City of Edinburgh Council, since 1996; b. Hexham. Trained, Northumberland County Council; Inspector of Weights and Measures, Cheshire County Council; Senior Assistant Chief Trading Standards Officer, Humberside County Council, 1976-79; County Consumer Protection Officer, Durham County Council, 1980-89; Director of Trading Standards, Lothian Regional Council, 1989-96. Past Chairman, Institute of Trading Standards Administration; Chairman, Prosafe (Product Safety Enforcement Forum of Europe); President, European Consumer Product Safety Association; Adviser, Convention of Scottish Local Authorities. Recreations: squash; golf; travel. Address: (b.) Chesser House, 500 Gorgie Road, Edinburgh EH11 3YJ; T.-0131-469 5454; e-mail: mike.drewry@edinburgh.gov.uk

Driscoll, Morag Catherine, BA (Hons), MA, MPhil, LLB, DipLP, NP, WS. Solicitor (Court Partner), Doughtys, since 1998; b. Dorking, Surrey. Educ. Convent of the Sacred Heart, Winnipeg, Canada; Manitoba University; Winnipeg University; St. Andrews University; Edinburgh University. Varied previous career including Tutor in History, Canada. Member, Council, Law Society of Scotland, since 2000 (and Member: Professional Practice Committee, Legal Aid Committee, Education and Training Committee). Recreations: horses; pottery; gardening. Address: (b.) Doughtys WS, Ayton, Berwickshire TD14 5QH; T.-01890 81209; e-mail: moraglaw@aol.com

Drummond, Humphrey, MC. Writer and Farmer; Proprietor and Managing Director, The Historical Press; b. 18.9.22, Old Buckenham, Norfolk; m., Cherry Drummond, 16th Baroness Strange; 3 s.; 3 d. Educ. Eton; Trinity College, Cambridge. Captain, 1st Mountain Regiment; former General Secretary, Council for Preservation of Rural Wales; Welsh Representative, National Trust; Chairman, Society of Authors (Scotland), 1976-82. Publications: Our Man in Scotland; The Queen's Man; The King's Enemy; Falconry For You; Falconry; Balkan Assault; Nazi Gold. Recreations: mechanical musical instruments; pre-Raphaelitism. Address: Megginch Castle, Errol, Perthshire; T.-01821 642 222.

Drummond, Rev. John Whiteford, MA, BD. Minister, Rutherglen West Parish Church, since 1986; b. 27.6.46, Glasgow; m., Barbara S. Grant; 1 s.; 3 d. Educ. Bearsden Academy; University of Glasgow. Probationer Assistant, St. Francis-in-the-East Church, Bridgeton, 1970-71; Ordained Assistant, King's Park Parish Church, Glasgow, 1971-73; Minister, Linwood Parish Church, 1973-86. Recreations: reading; television; family. Address: (h.) 12 Albert Drive, Rutherglen G73 3RT; T.-0141-569 8547.

Drummond, Lorna Allison, LLB, MPhil, DipLP. Advocate, since 1998; b. 19.12.67, Edinburgh; m., Derrick Guild; 1 d. Educ. Hutchesons' Grammar School; Glasgow University; Cambridge University; Edinburgh University. Trainee Solicitor, Scottish Executive; Assistant Legal Secretary to Scottish Law Officers and Assistant Scottish Parliamentary Counsel. Address: (b.) Faculty of Advocates, Parliament House, Parliament Square, Edinburgh EH1 1RF; T.-0131-226 5071.

Drummond, Rev. Norman Walker, MA, BD. Chairman, Drummond International, since 1999; Founder and Chairman, Columba 1400, Community and International Leadership Centre, Isle of Skye, since 1997; Director, The Change Partnership Scotland, since 1999; Chairman, Community Action Network Scotland, since 2000; b. 1.4.52, Greenock; m., Lady Elizabeth Kennedy; 3 s.; 2 d. Educ. Merchiston Castle School; Fitzwilliam College, Cambridge; New College, Edinburgh. Chaplain to the Forces, 1976-82; Depot, The Parachute Regiment and Airborne Forces, 1977-78; 1st Bn., The Black Watch (Royal Highland Regiment), 1978-82; Chaplain, Fettes College, 1982-84; Headmaster, Loretto School, 1984-95; Minister, Kilmuir and Stenscholl, Isle of Skye, 1996-98; BBC National Governor and Chairman, Broadcasting Council for Scotland, 1994-99; former Chairman, BBC Children in Need Board of Trustees; Member, Queen's Bodyguard for Scotland (Royal Company of Archers); Past President: Victoria League for Overseas Students in Scotland, Edinburgh Bn., Boys' Brigade; former Governor, Gordonstoun School; Chairman, Aiglon College, Switzerland; former Member, Scottish Committee for Imperial Cancer Research; Trustee, Foundation for Skin Research; former Member, Scottish Committee, Duke of Edinburgh's Award Scheme; former Member, Court, Heriot-Watt University; former Chairman, Musselburgh and District Council of Social Services. Publications: The First Twenty Five Years (the official history of the Black Watch Kirk Session); Mother's Hands. Recreations: rugby football; cricket; golf; curling; traditional jazz. Address: Drummond International, 10a Drummond Place, Edinburgh EH3 6PH.

Drummond, Sheriff Thomas Anthony Kevin, LLB, QC. Sheriff, Lothian and Borders at Jedburgh, Selkirk and Duns, since 2000; b. 3.11.43, Howwood, Renfrewshire; m., Margaret Evelyn Broadley; 1 d. (1 d. deceased). Educ. St. Mirin's Academy, Paisley; Blairs College, Aberdeen; Edinburgh University. Admitted, Faculty of Advocates, 1974; Advocate Depute, 1985-90; Member, Firearms Consultative Committee, 1989-97; Member, Criminal Injuries Compensation Board, 1990-96; Home Advocate Depute, 1996-97; Sheriff, Glasgow and Strathkelvin, 1997-2000. Joint Chairman, Institute of Chartered Accountants of Scotland, 1993-2000. Publications (legal cartoons): The Law at Work; The Law at Play; Great Defences of Our Time. Recreations: fishing; shooting. Address: (h.) Pomathorn House, Penicuik, Midlothian; T.-01968 674064; e-mail: kdrummondqc@aol.com

Drummond Young, Hon. Lord (James Edward Drummond Young), QC. Senator of the College of Justice in Scotland; b. 1950; m.; 1 d. Educ. Cambridge University; Harvard University; Edinburgh University. Admitted, Faculty of Advocates, 1976. Address: Parliament House, Parliament Square, Edinburgh EH1 1RQ.

Drury, John Kenneth, MBChB, PhD, FRCS. Consultant, General Surgeon, Victoria Infirmary NHS Trust, since 1996 (Clinical Director, General Surgery, 1993-99); b. 23.1.47; m., Gillian Gilmore; 1 s.; 1 d. Educ. Paisley Grammar School; University of Glasgow. Research Fellow, Department of Physiology, University of Glasgow, 1973-76; West of Scotland Surgical Training Scheme, 1976-86. Committee Member, RNLI; Member: Vascular Society of Great Britain, European Society for Vascular and Endovascular Surgery. Recreations: sailing; golf; local art. Address: (b.) Department of Surgery, South Glasgow University Hospitals NHS Trust – Victoria Infirmary, Glasgow G42 9TY; T.-0141-201 5464; e-mail: jkd.alba@dial.pipex.com

Dry, Philip John Seaton, LLB. Partner, Biggart Baillie, Solicitors, since 1972; President, Law Society of Scotland, 1998-99; b. 21.4.45, Lincolnshire; m., Joyce Christine Hall; 1 s.; 1 d. Educ George Watson's College; Greenock Academy; Glasgow University. Apprenticeship with Biggart Lumsden & Co., 1966-68; Assistant Solicitor, 1968-70; Council Member, Law Society of Scotland, 1991-2001; Member, Post Office Users' Council for Scotland, 1995-98; Director, Glasgow Renfrewshire Society. Recreations: sailing; the garden; opera; swimming; travel. Address: (b.) Dalmore House, 310 St. Vincent Street, Glasgow G2 5QR; T.-0141-228 8000.

Drysdale, Professor David Douglas (Dougal), BSc, PhD, FIFireE, CEng. Professor of Fire Safety Engineering, Edinburgh University, since 1998; b. 30.9.39, Dunfermline; m., Judith McIntyre; 3 s. Educ. Edinburgh Academy; Edinburgh University; Cambridge University. Post-doctoral Fellow, University of Toronto, 1966-67; Research Lecturer, Leeds University, 1967-74; Lecturer, Fire Engineering, Edinburgh University, 1974-92; Visiting Professor, Centre for Fire Safety Studies, Worcester Polytechnic Institute, Mass., USA, 1982; Reader, Fire Safety Engineering, Edinburgh University, 1990-98; SFPE Man of the Year (USA), 1983; Fire Research Lecture, 1995; SFPE Arthur B. Guise Medal for eminent achievement advancing the Science of Fire Protection Engineering, 1995. Publications: Introduction to Fire Dynamics, 1998; Handbook of Fire Protection Engineering (co-ed.), 1995; Fire Safety Journal (ed.), since 1988. Recreations: music; hill walking; coarse golf. Address: (b.) School of Civil and Environmental Engineering, Edinburgh University, King's Buildings, Edinburgh, EH9 3JN; T.-0131-650 5724.

Dudley Edwards, Owen, BA, FRHistS, FSA (Scot). Reader in History, Edinburgh University; b. 27.3.38, Dublin; m., Barbara Balbirnie Lee; 1 s.; 2 d. Educ. Belvedere College, Dublin; University College, Dublin; Johns Hopkins University, Baltimore. Visiting Lecturer in History, University of Oregon, 1963-65; Assistant Lecturer in History, Aberdeen University, 1966-68; Lecturer in History, Edinburgh University, 1968-79; Visiting Lecturer, California State University of San Francisco, 1972-73; Visiting Associate Professor, University of South Carolina, 1973; Sir David Owen Evans Lecturer, University College of Wales, Aberystwyth, 1987; Journalist and Broadcaster, notably for Irish Times, 1959-95, and BBC, since 1969; contributor to various journals, especially The Scotsman, Scottish Affairs; Life Member: American Historical Association, Organisation of American Historians, Royal Medical Society (Edinburgh University), Royal Lyceum Theatre Club; External Examiner: Queen's University, Belfast, Bradford University, Manchester University, Sorbonne, University College Cardiff, Oxford University, National University of Ireland, Galway; Chair, Edinburgh University Settlement, 1996-99; Member, Editorial Board, Journal of American Studies, since 1995; Chair, Council, Roman Catholic Parish of St Albert the Great, Edinburgh, 1986-89, 1995-98; Hon. Vice-President, Scottish Homosexual Rights Association (and successor organisation), 1977-97. Publications: Celtic Nationalism (with Gwynfor Evans, Ioan Rhys and Hugh MacDiarmid), 1968; The Sins of Our Fathers - Roots of Conflict in Northern Ireland, 1970; The Mind of an Activist - James Connolly, 1971; P.G. Wodehouse - a Critical and Historical Essay, 1977; Burke and Hare, 1980; The Quest for Sherlock Holmes: a Biographical Study of Arthur Conan Doyle, 1982; Eamon de Valera, 1987; Macaulay (Historians on Historians), 1988; The Edinburgh Festival, 1990; City of 1000 Worlds — Edinburgh in Festival, 1991; as Editor/Contributor: 1916 - The Easter Rising (with Fergus Pyle), 1968; Conor Cruise O'Brien Introduces Ireland, 1969; James Connolly: Selected Political Writings (with Bernard C. Ransom), 1973; Scotland, Europe and the American Revolution (with George Shepperson), 1976; Christmas Observed (with Graham Richardson), 1981; Edinburgh (with Graham Richardson), 1983; A Claim of Right for Scotland, 1989; The Fireworks of Oscar Wilde, 1989; A. Conan Doyle: The Exploits of Brigadier Gerard,

1991; The Oxford Sherlock Holmes (General Editor), 1993; The Complete Brigadier Gerard, 1995. Address: (b.) Department of History, Edinburgh University, 50 George Square, Edinburgh, EH8 9JY.

Duff, Professor (Robin) Antony, BA, FRSE. Professor, Department of Philosophy, Stirling University, since 1990; b. 9.3.45, Fareham. Educ. Sedbergh School; Christ Church, Oxford. Visiting Lecturer, University of Washington, Seattle, 1968-69; Department of Philosophy, Stirling University, since 1970. British Academy Research Readership, 1989-91; Leverhulme Major Research Fellowship, 2000-2005. Publications: Trial and Punishment; Intention, Agency and Criminal Liability; Criminal Attempts; Punishment, Communication and Community. Address: (b.) Department of Philosophy, Stirling University, Stirling FK9 4LA; T.-01786 467556.

Duffin, Brian James, MA, FFA, CIMgt. Chief Executive, Scottish Life, since 1999; Director, Heart of Midlothian Plc, since 1997; b. 20.1.55, Enniskillen, Co Fermanagh, Northern Ireland; m., Joan M. Baird; 3s. Educ. Methodist College, Belfast; St Catharine's College, Cambridge. Scottish Life: Actuarial Trainee; Fellow, Faculty of Actuaries, 1979; Assistant Investment Manager, 1983; General Manager Marketing, 1988; General Manager Administration, 1995; Member, Council, Faculty of Actuaries, 1991-96. Recreations: golf; football; rugby; gardening; Irish literature. Address: (b.) 8 Craigleith View, Edinburgh, EH4 3JZ; T.-0131-456 7500.

Duffin, Stuart, DA, RE, ARSA. Studio Workshop Manager, Glasgow Print Studio, since 1989; b. 13.6.59. Educ. Gray's School of Art, Aberdeen. Member of staff, Glasgow Print Studio, 1984; SAC award to study and travel in Italy, 1987; exchange visit to Senej Print Workshop, Moscow, 1992; solo exhibitions: Glasgow Print Studio, 1995, 2001, Gallery of Jerusalem Print Workshop, 1998. Arts Adviser, Moor Fire Productions. Address: (b.) Glasgow Print Studio, 22 King Street, Glasgow G1 5QP; T.-0141-552 0704; e-mail: gallery@gpsart.co.uk

Duffty, Paul, MB, ChB, FRCP, FRCPE, FRCPCH, LMCC. Consultant Paediatrician, since 1982; Senior Lecturer in Child Health, Aberdeen University, since 1982; b. 1.9.46, Leeds; m., Lesley Marjory Macdonald; 2 d. Educ. Leeds Central High School; Aberdeen University. Lecturer in Child Health, Aberdeen University, 1972-75; Trainee in General Practice, Aberdeen, 1975-76; Lecturer in Child Health, Aberdeen University, 1976-78; Fellow in Neonatology, Toronto University, 1978-80; Staff Paediatrician, Hospital for Sick Children, Toronto, and Assistant Professor, Toronto University, 1980-82. Recreations: hill-walking; cross-country skiing; philately. Address: (h.) 13 Louisville Avenue, Aberdeen; T.-01224 317072.

Duffus, Professor Carol Margaret, BSc, MS, PhD, DIC, DSc, FRSA, FRSE. Director Management Development, Scottish Agricultural College and Professor, Crop Science and Technology, 1997-2000, Emeritus Professor, Crop Science, since 2000; b. Belfast; m., John Henderson Duffus; 2 d. Educ. Victoria College, Belfast; Queens's University, Belfast; University of Michigan, Ann Arbor, USA; Imperial College, London; University of Edinburgh. Lecturer in Biochemistry, School of Molecular Sciences, University of Warwick, 1966; Lecturer, University of Edinburgh and East of Scotland College of Agriculture, 1968; Scottish Agricultural College: Head, Agricultural Biochemistry Department, 1987, Head, Crop Sciences Division, 1990. Member: Scottish Natural Heritage, South East Regional Board, Scientific Advisory Committee, 1990-97, Law Society of Scotland Complaints Committee, 1993-95, Scientific Advisory Committee, Scottish Science Trust,

since 1999; President, Association of Applied Biologists, 1999-2000. Publications: Carbohydrate Metabolism in Plants (Co-Author), 1984; Toxic Substances in Crop Plants (Co-Author), 1991. Recreations: gardening; chamber music; golf. Address: (b.) Scottish Agricultural College, King's Buildings, West Mains Road, Edinburgh EH9 3JG; T.-0131-535 4060.

Duffus, John Henderson, BSc, PhD, DSc, CBiol, MIBiol, CChem, FRSC. Director, Edinburgh Centre for Toxicology (EdinTox). Educ. Arbroath High School; Edinburgh University; Heriot-Watt University. Research Fellow: Warwick University, 1965-67, Edinburgh University, 1967-70; Lecturer, Heriot-Watt University, 1970-80; Senior Lecturer in Environmental Toxicology, Heriot-Watt University, 1980-97; Hon. Fellow in Public Health Sciences, Edinburgh University, since 1997; WHO Consultant, Toxicology and Chemical Safety, since 1981; Member, UK Department of the Environment Advisory Committee on Hazardous Substances, 1991-99; Titular Member, IUPAC Commission on Toxicology, 1991-2001, Chair, 1997-2001; Titular Member, IUPAC Committee on the Teaching of Chemistry, 1999-2001; Member, RSC Committee on Environment, Health and Safety; Member, UK HSE Biocides Consultative Committee. Publications: Environmental Toxicology, 1980; Environmental Toxicology and Ecotoxicology, 1986; Magnesium in Mitosis and the Cell Cycle (Co-Author), 1987; Yeast: A Practical Approach (Co-Editor), 1988; The Toxicology of Chemicals, Series 1, Carcinogenicity, Vol III, Vol IV (Co-Editor/Author), 1991-93; Toxic Substances in Crop Plants (Co-Editor/Author), 1991; Cancer and Workplace Chemicals, 1995; Carcinogenicity of Inorganic Substances (Chief Editor/Author), 1997; Chemical Risk Assessment (Co-Author), 1999; Risk Assessment and Elemental Speciation, 2001. Address: (b.) Edinburgh Centre for Toxicology, 43 Mansionhouse Road, Edinburgh EH9 2JD.

Duffy, Graham Woodburn, FRSA. Managing Director, Graphic Partners Ltd., since 2000; b. 19.6.42, Edinburgh; m., Rosemary Jean; 1 s.; 1 d. Educ. Royal High School, Edinburgh; Heriot Watt College/Edinburgh College of Art. Andrew Grant Scholar, Edinburgh College of Art, 1961-63; Graphic Designer, Pillans and Wilson, 1963-67; Graphic Designer/ Typographer, Forth Studios, 1967-68; self-employed Design Consultant, 1969-71; Partner, Graphic Partners Design Consultants, 1971-2000. Director: Edinburgh Chamber of Commerce, since 1992, Scottish Design, 1994-99. Recreations: masters rowing; skiing; English literature; music; theatre; film. Address: (b.) 179 Canongate, Edinburgh EH8 8BN; T.-0131-557 3558.

Duffy, Professor Jean Henderson, MA, DPhil. Professor of French, Edinburgh University, since 1999; b. 27.8.55, Dunoon; m., George Paul Marshall. Educ. Gourock High School; Greenock High School; Glasgow University; Oxford University. Kathleen Bourne Research Fellow, St. Anne's College, Oxford University, 1981-83; Sheffield University: Lecturer, French, 1983-91; Senior Lecturer, French, 1992-94; Reader, French, 1994-96; Professor of French, 1996-99. Publications: Reading Between the Lines: Claude Simon and the Visual Arts, 1988; Butor: La Modification, 1990; Structuralism, 1992; Colette, Le Ble en Herbe, 1989; Using French Vocabulary, 1999. Recreations: reading; cinema; walking. Address: (b.) SELC, Edinburgh University, 59-60 George Square, Edinburgh; T.-0131-650-8410.

Duffy, Professor John Alastair, BSc, PhD, DSc, CChem, FRSC. Professor of Chemistry, Aberdeen University, since 1996; Quality Assessor for Scottish Higher Education Funding Council, 1993-94; b. 24.9.32, Birmingham; m., Muriel F.L. Ramsay; 1 s.; 1 d. Educ. Solihull School, Warwickshire; Sheffield University. Research Chemist, Albright & Wilson, Oldbury, 1958-59; Lecturer in

Inorganic Chemistry, Wolverhampton Polytechnic, 1959-61; Senior Lecturer in Inorganic Chemistry, NE Wales Institute, 1961-65; Lecturer, Senior Lecturer, Reader in Chemistry, Aberdeen University, 1966-96; Assessor in Inorganic Chemistry for Ordinary and Higher National Certificates and Diplomas in Scotland, 1971-82; Consultant to Schott Glaswerke, Mainz, West Germany, 1984-86; Past Chairman, NE Scotland Section, Royal Society of Chemistry. Blackwell Prize, University of Aberdeen, 1995. Publications: General Inorganic Chemistry, 1966; Bonding Energy Levels and Bands in Inorganic Solids, 1990; 150 scientific publications. Recreations: 20th-century opera; music. Address: (h.) 35 Beechgrove Terrace, Aberdeen AB15 5DR; T.-01224 641752; e-mail: j.a.duffy@abdn.ac.uk

Duffy, Sheila Sinclair, MA. Freelance researcher, journalist and genealogist; b. 6.8.46, Cumberland; m., Paul Young; 2 d. Educ. St. Joseph's, Nicosia; Boroughmuir School, Edinburgh; Edinburgh University. Auxiliary nurse, Edinburgh Royal Infirmary, 1965-66; croupier, Edinburgh night club, 1966-67; graduate trainee, Scottish Television, 1967-68, then Reporter and Interviewer; Women's Editor, Radio Clyde, 1973-99; former Columnist, Weekly News, Scottish Field, Evening Times. Vice-Chairman, Visiting Committee, Glenochil Young Offenders Institution. Glenfiddich Food Writer Award, 1986. Address: c/o Sinclair Ancestral Research, 9 Woodside Crescent, Glasgow G3 7UL; e-mail: editorgwsfhs@hotmail.com

Dukes, Professor Paul, BA (Cantab), MA, PhD. Professor of History, Aberdeen University, 1988-99, Emeritus Professor, since 1999; b. 5.4.34, Wallington; 1 s.; 1 d. Educ. Wallington County Grammar School; Cambridge University. Advisory Editor, History Today. Publications: several books on aspects of Russian, American, European and world history. Recreations: hill-walking; travel. Address: (b.) History Department, Aberdeen University, Aberdeen; T.-01224 272465.

Dumble, Graham, FRSA. Managing Director, Scottish Equitable plc, since 1999; b. 27.1.59, Galashiels; m., Ailsa; 1 s.; 1 d. Educ. Galashiels Academy. Joined Scottish Equitable on leaving school, 1977, management posts, primarily in customer service, then: Marketing Director, 1992, Operations Director, 1997; Member, Executive Board, Aegon UK, since 1999. Scottish Marketeer of the Year, 1994. Recreations: most sports (especially Rugby Union) as spectator; contemporary music (well, it was contemporary once). Address: (b.) Scottish Equitable House, Edinburgh Park, Edinburgh EH12 9SE; T.-0131-549 3905; e-mail: gwdumble@scoteq.co.uk

Dunbar, Sir Archibald Ranulph, MA, DipAgric (Cantab), DTA (Trin). Retired; b. 8.8.27, London; m., Amelia M.S. Davidson; 1 s.; 2 d. Educ. Wellington College; Pembroke College, Cambridge. Military Service, Cameron Highlanders (attached Gordon Highlanders), 1945-48; Imperial College of Tropical Agriculture, Trinidad, 1952-53; Agricultural Officer, Colonial Service, Uganda (later Overseas Civil Service, Uganda) 1953-70; Landowner, Duffus Estate, Elgin, since 1970. Honorary Sheriff, Sheriff Court District of Moray, since 1989; Knight of Honour and Devotion, Sovereign Military Order of Malta, 1989. Recreations: swimming; railways; model railways; military models. Address: (h.) The Old Manse, Duffus, Elgin, Moray; T.-01343 830270.

Dunbar, Sheriff Ian Duncan, LLB. Resident Sheriff, Dundee, since 2000, Floating Sheriff, Dundee, 1998-2000; Partner, Miller Hendry, Solicitors, 1990-98; b. 31.10.48, Dundee; m., Susan Young. Educ. Lawside Academy, Dundee; Queens College, Dundee/St. Andrews University. Law apprentice, Soutar Reid & Mill, Dundee, 1969-71; Assistant Solicitor, Sneddon Campbell & Munro, Perth, 1971-72, Partner, 1972-85; merged to form Miller Sneddon,

1985, Partner, 1985-90; merged to form Miller Hendry, 1990. President, Law Society of Scotland, 1993-94. Recreations: golf; rugby; cooking; wine. Address: (h.) Craigrownie, Forgandenny Road, Bridge of Earn, Perth PH2 9HA.

Dunbar, John Greenwell, OBE, MA, FSA, FSA Scot, HonFRIAS. Architectural historian; Secretary, Royal Commission on the Ancient and Historical Monuments of Scotland, 1978-90; b. 1.3.30, London; m., Elizabeth Mill Blyth. Educ. University College School, London; Balliol College, Oxford. joined staff, Royal Commission on the Ancient and Historical Monuments of Scotland, 1953. Publications: The Historic Architecture of Scotland, 1966; Accounts of the Masters of Works, Volume 2 (1616-1649), (Joint Editor), 1982; Sir William Burrell's Northern Tour, 1997; Scottish Royal Palaces, 1999. Address: (h.) Paties Mill, Carlops, by Penicuik, Midlothian EH26 9NF; T.-01968 660250.

Dunbar, Lennox Robert, DA, ARSA. Head of Printmaking, Grays School of Art, since 1987; Painter and Printmaker; b. 17.5.52, Aberdeen; m., Jan Storie; 2 s.; 1 d. Educ. Aberdeen Grammar School; Grays School of Art. Part-time Lecturer, 1975-82; Etching Technician, Peacock Printmakers, 1978-82; Education Officer, Peacock Printmakers, 1982-86; appointed Lecturer in Painting and Printmaking, Grays School of Art, 1986; Visiting Lecturer, Duncan of Jordanstone College of Art, Dundee, and Newcastle University; Visiting Artist/Tutor, Louisiana State University; participated in many group and one-man exhibitions; numerous awards including Latimer Award, 1978, Guthrie Award, 1984, Shell Expro Premier Award, 1991 and 1993; work in many private and public collections.

Dunbar, Morrison Alexander Rankin, CBE, KCSJ, FCIOB, FFB, FIMgt, FRSAMD, FRSA. Chairman: Royal Scottish Academy of Music and Drama Trust, since 1992, Westbourne Music, since 1998; b. 27.4.29, Glasgow; m., Sally Joan Sutherland; 2 s.; 1 d. Educ. Belmont House; Gresham House. Managing Director, Morrison Dunbar Ltd. Builders, 1957-81. President: Scottish Building Contractors Association, 1968, Scottish Building Employers Federation, 1975, Building Employers Confederation, 1980, Builders Benevolent Institution, 1987; Lord Dean of Guild, Merchants House of Glasgow, 1991-93; Chairman: Epilepsy Association of Scotland, 1990-93, Royal Scottish Academy of Music and Drama, 1987-91, Royal Scottish National Orchestra, 1993-97; Member, Trades House of Glasgow. Recreations: music; art galleries; golf. Address: (h.) 18 Devonshire Terrace Lane, Glasgow G12 9XT; T.-0141-357 1289.

Dunbar-Nasmith, Professor Emeritus Sir James Duncan, CBE, BA, DA, RIBA, PPRIAS, FRSA, FRSE. Chairman, Scottish Civic Trust; Vice-President, Europa Nostra; Trustee, Edinburgh World Heritage Trust; Partner, Law and Dunbar-Nasmith, Architects, Edinburgh and Forres 1957-99; b. 15.3.27, Dartmouth. Educ. Lockers Park; Winchester College; Trinity College, Cambridge; Edinburgh College of Art. Lt., Scots Guards, 1945-48; ARIBA, 1954; President: Edinburgh Architectural Association, 1967-69, Royal Incorporation of Architects in Scotland, 1971-73; Member, RIBA Council, 1967-73 (Vice-President and Chairman, Board of Architectural Education, 1972-73); Council, ARCUK, 1976-84, Board of Education, 1976-88 (Vice Chairman, 1977); Professor and Head, Department of Architecture, Heriot-Watt University and Edinburgh College of Art, 1978-88; Member: Royal Commission on Ancient and Historical Monuments of Scotland, 1972-96, Ancient Monuments Board for Scotland, 1969-82 (interim Chairman, 1972-73), Historic Buildings Council for Scotland, 1966-93; Trustee, Architectural Heritage Fund, Theatres Trust, 1983-95; Deputy Chairman, Edinburgh Festival Society, 1981-85. Recreations: music;

theatre; skiing; sailing. Address: (b.) 4 Blackie House, Lady Stair's Close, Edinburgh EH1 2NY; T.-0131-225 4236; e-mail: jd.nasmith@virgin.net

Duncan, (Alan) Michael, MA, BPhil, DipEd. Rector, High School of Dundee, since 1997; b. 13.8.48, Glasgow. Educ. Grove Academy; St Andrews University. Morgan Academy, Dundee: Teacher of English, 1972-74, Assistant Principal Teacher of English, 1974-78; Robert Gordon's College, Aberdeen: Head of English, 1978-85, Assistant Headmaster, 1985-93, Deputy Headmaster, 1993-97. Member, Governing Board, Scottish Council for Independent Schools; Member, Scottish Committee, Independent Schools Careers Organisation. Recreations: reading; gardening. Address: (b.) High School of Dundee, Euclid Crescent, Dundee DD1 1HU; T.-01382 202921; e-mail: amduncan@hsd.dundeecity.sch.uk

Duncan, Professor Archibald Alexander McBeth, MA, FBA, FRSE, FRHistS. Professor of Scottish History, Glasgow University, 1962-93, Emeritus Professor, since 1993, currently Honorary Research Fellow; b. 17.10.26, Pitlochry; m., Ann Hayes Sawyer; 2 s.; 1 d. Educ. George Heriot's School, Edinburgh; Edinburgh University; Balliol College, Oxford. Lecturer: Balliol College, 1950-51, Queen's University, Belfast, 1951-53, Edinburgh University, 1953-61; Leverhulme Fellow, 1961-62; Clerk of Senate, Glasgow University, 1978-83; Dean of Faculties, Glasgow University, 1998-2000. Publications: Scotland, The Making of the Kingdom; revised 3rd edition of W.C. Dickinson's Scotland from Earliest Times to 1603; Regesta Regum Scottorum, v., The Acts of Robert I 1306-29, 1988; edition of John Barbour's The Bruce, 1997. Recreation: swimming. Address: (h.) 17 Campbell Drive, Bearsden, Glasgow G61 4NF; T.-0141-942 5023; e-mail: aamduncan@aol.com

Duncan, Atholl Scott. Executive Editor, News, BBC Scotland, since 1996; b. 27.5.63, Edinburgh. Educ. George Watson's College, Edinburgh; Napier College, Edinburgh. Reporter, DC Thomson, 1982-85; joined BBC, 1985; Researcher, BBC Scotland News, 1985-86; Assistant Producer, Newsnight, London, 1987; Producer, 1988, then Editor, 1995, Reporting Scotland. Member, Board, sportscotland, since 2001. Recreations: football; rugby; running; watching Scottish sports teams' glorious failures across the globe. Address: (b.) BBC Scotland, Queen Margaret Drive, Glasgow G12 8DG; T.-0141-338 2632; e-mail: atholl.duncan@bbc.co.uk

Duncan, Geoffrey Cheyne Calderhead, BL. Lord Dean of Guild, Merchants House of Glasgow, 1993-95; b. 6.10.29, Whitecraigs, Glasgow; m., Lorna Dowling (deceased); 1 s.; 1 d. Educ. Belmont House School; Glasgow Academy; Glasgow University. Solicitor in private practice, 1951-91; Partner, Aitken, Hamilton & Duncan, 1951-70; Partner, Kerr, Barrie & Duncan, 1970-91; Chairman, Glasgow Junior Chamber of Commerce, 1963-64; Director, The Girls' School Company Ltd., 1964-90 (Chairman, 1977-90); Chairman, St. Columba's School, 1972-83; Director, The West of Scotland School Company Ltd., 1972-92 (Chairman, 1989-92); Member: Board of Management, Glasgow South Western Hospitals, 1964-69, Clyde River Purification Board, 1969-75; Director, Glasgow Chamber of Commerce, 1972-92; Chairman, Glasgow Post Office Advisory Committee, 1974-84; Member, Post Office Users' National Council, 1974-87; Chairman, Post Office Users' Council for Scotland, 1984-87; Chairman, Advisory Committee on Telecommunications for Scotland, 1984-87; Director, The Merchants' House of Glasgow, since 1982; Trustee, Ferguson Bequest Fund, 1987-97; Member: Executive Committee, Abbeyfield Quarrier's Society (now Abbeyfield Strathgryffe Society), 1981-97 (Chairman, 1988-96), Council of Management, Quarrier's Homes, 1985-93; Director, The Scottish Cremation Society Ltd.,

since 1978 (Chairman, 1993-2001); Member, Iona Cathedral Management Board, 1990-93; Director, Iona Abbey Ltd., 1993-96; Chairman, Renfrewshire Valuation Appeal Panel, 1993-99; General Commissioner for Income Tax, since 1994; Patron, Royal Incorporation of Hutcheson's Hospital, since 1995; Director, City of Glasgow Native Benevolent Association, since 1998; Patron, 2001 Campaign, University of Glasgow, 1999. Recreations: gardening; photography. Address: (h.) Mid Clevans, Bridge of Weir, Renfrewshire PA11 3HP; T.-01505 612566.

Duncan, Heather Margaret, MusB. General Manager, BT Scottish Ensemble, since 1998; b. 26.1.61, Stafford. Educ. Walton High School; Manchester University; Royal Academy of Music, London. Cellist, 1984-87; Administrator, Projects Co-ordinator, Acting General Manager, Monteverdi Choir and Orchestra Ltd., 1987-98. Recreations: cello playing; fitness training; gardening. Address: (b.) CCA 350 Sauchiehall Street, Glasgow G2 3JD; T.-0141-332 4747.

Duncan, James Wann, MBE, Hon. LLD, JP, MIMFT. Rector's Assessor, University of Dundee, 1992-98; former Vice-Chairman, Tayside Health Board (Convener, General Purposes Committee); Convener, Personnel and Accommodation Sub-Committee, Management Committee, Common Services Agency for the Scottish Health Service; retired Senior Chief Maxillofacial Technician, Dundee Royal Infirmary; b. 14.7.25, Dundee; m., Hilda Mackenzie Gray; 3 d. Educ. Stobswell Secondary School; Dundee College of Technology. Former Convener, Property Equipment Supplies Committee, General Board of Management, Dundee General Hospitals; former Vice-Convener, General Purposes Committee, General Board of Management, Dundee Northern Hospitals; former Member, Dundee Town Council (Senior Magistrate); former Convener: Dundee Art Galleries and Museums Committee, Further Education Committee, Dundee Police Committee; former Member, Board of Governors, Scottish Police College; Member, Dundee District Council, 1974-77 (Convener, Planning and Development Committee); Chairman, Dundee City Labour Party, 1960-62; former Member, Scottish Council, SDP; former Scottish Representative, National Committee for Dental Technicians, USDAW; former Member, STUC Health and Social Services Committee; former Member, University of Dundee Court. Recreations: golf; gardening; DIY. Address: (h.) 13 Clive Road, Downfield, Dundee DD3 8LP; T.-01382 825488.

Duncan, Peter, BCom (Hons). Conservative MP, Galloway and Upper Nithsdale, since 2001; b. 10.7.65, Kilwinning; m., Lorna; 1 s.; 1 d. Educ. Ardrossan Academy; Birmingham University. Project Manager, Mackays Stores Ltd., 1985-88; Managing Director, John Duncan and Son, 1988-2000. Member, Scottish Affairs Select Committee, since 2001. Recreations: Scottish rugby; English cricket. Address: (b.) House of Commons, London SW1A 0AA; T.-0207 219 8235.

Duncan, Robert Alexander, BCom, CA. Director UK Bus, Firstgroup PLC, since 1997; b. 31.5.50, Aberdeen; m., Gail; 2 d. Educ. Robert Gordon's College, Aberdeen; Edinburgh University. Qualified CA, Coopers and Lybrand, Glasgow; Audit Manager, Brussels, four years; various finance positions; Finance Director, Grampian Transport; Managing Director GRT Bus Group; Regional Director North, First Group PLC. Director, Auris Limited. Recreations: golf; fishing; cycling; art and antique hunting. Address: 395 King Street, Aberdeen; T.-01224 650114.

Duncan, William, BSc (Hons), GradCIPD, PhD. Executive Secretary, Royal Society of Edinburgh, since 1985; Executive Secretary, RSE Scotland Foundation, since 1996; Secretary to Trustees, Scottish Science Trust, 1997-98; b.

6.12.50, Edinburgh. Educ. Linlithgow Academy; Edinburgh University. Greater London Council, 1975-78; Lothian Regional Council, 1978-85. Recreations: contemporary music; opera. Address: (b.) 22/26 George Street, Edinburgh EH2 2PQ; T.-0131-240 5000.

Duncan Millar, James, LVO, psc. Managing Partner, A&J Duncan Millar, Remony Estate, since 1986; Commissioner, Deer Commission for Scotland, since 1996; b. 5.4.48, Aberfeldy; m., Susan Ferrier Marshall; 1 s.; 1 d. Educ. Loretto School; RMA Sandhurst. Commissioned, The Black Watch, 1968-86; Army Staff College, Camberley, 1982. Chair, Kenmore and District Community Council; Member, Highland Perthshire Communities Partnership. Recreation: downhill skiing. Address: Remony, Aberfeldy, Perthshire PH15 2HR; e-mail: remony@btinternet.com

Dundas-Bekker, Althea Enid Philippa, DL. Deputy Lieutenant, Midlothian, since 1991; b. 4.11.39, Gorebridge; m., Aedrian Ruprecht Bekker (deceased); 2 d. Secretarial work abroad, in London, and with the National Trust for Scotland; inherited Arniston House, 1970, and restoring ever since. Member, National Trust for Scotland Curatorial Committee; Commissioner, Royal Commission on Historical Manuscripts; Trustee: Arniston Village Improvement Trust, Scottish Businessman's Achievement Award Trust; Member, Church of Scotland Committee on Artistic Matters. Recreation: Scottish history; Scottish songs; walking dogs. Address: (h.) Arniston House, Gorebridge, Midlothian EH23 4RY; T.-01875 830238; e-mail: email@dundasbekker.fsnet.co.uk

Dundee, 12th Earl of (Alexander Henry Scrymgeour). Hereditary Royal Standard-Bearer for Scotland; b. 5.6.49; m.; 1 s.; 3 d. Educ. Eton; St. Andrews University. Address: Farm Office, Birkhill, Cupar, Fife.

Dundonald, 15th Earl of (Iain Alexander Douglas Blair); b. 17.2.61; m., Marie Beatrice Louise Russo; 2 s.; 1 d. Educ. Wellington College; Royal Agricultural College, Cirencester. Company Director; Hon. Chilean Consul to Scotland. Recreations: marine and rural environment; rural housing; Scottish affairs. Address: Lochnell Castle, Ledaig, Argyll.

Dunion, Kevin Harry, OBE, MA (Hons), MSc, FRSA. Chief Executive, Friends of the Earth Scotland, since 1991; Honorary Senior Research Fellow, University of Strathclyde; b. 20.12.55, Bridge of Allan; m., Linda Dunion (qv); 2 s. Educ. St. Andrew's High School, Kirkcaldy; St. Andrews University; Edinburgh University. HM Inspector of Taxes, 1978-80; Administrator, Edinburgh University Students Association, 1980-84; Scottish Campaigns Manager, Oxfam, 1984-91. Editor, Radical Scotland, 1982-85; Chair: Scottish Education and Action for Development, 1990-92, Friends of the Earth International, 1996-99 (Treasurer, 1993-96); Member: Secretary of State's Advisory Group on Sustainable Development, 1996-99, Lord Provost's Commission on Sustainable Development for Edinburgh, 1997-98, Scottish Council for Voluntary Organisations Policy Committee, 1999-2001, Scottish Power Environmental Forum, Scottish Executive Ministerial Group on Sustainable Scotland, Board, Scottish Natural Heritage, United Nations Environment and Development International Advisory Board. Publication: Living in the Real World: An International Role for Scotland's Parliament. Address: (b.) Bonnington Mill, 72 Newhaven Road, Edinburgh EH6 5QG; T.-0131-554 9977; e-mail: kdunion@foe-scotland.org.uk

Dunion, Linda M., BSc (Soc Sci). Head of Public Affairs, BMA Scotland; b. 15.9.56, Perth; m., Kevin Dunion (qv). Educ. Morrisons Academy Girls' School, Crieff; Edinburgh University. Formerly: Councillor, Edinburgh District

Council, Director, SEAD (Scottish Education and Action for Development), Director, Scottish Down's Syndrome Association, Assistant Director, Age Concern Scotland. Address: 39B John Street, Cellardyke, Fife KY10 3BA.

Dunlop, Sheriff Principal Alastair, QC, LLB. Sheriff Principal, Tayside Central and Fife, since 2000; b. 30.6.51, London; m., Evelyn T. Barr; 1 s.; 2 d. Educ. Glenalmond; Dundee University. Admitted Solicitor, 1976; Advocate, 1978; QC, 1990; Advocate Depute, 1985-88; Standing Junior Counsel, Department of Transport, 1988-90; part-time Chairman, Pensions Appeal Tribunal, 1991-2000; Procurator to General Assembly, Church of Scotland, 1991-2000; part-time Chairman, Employment Tribunals, 1998-2000. Recreations: golf; sailing; skiing; music. Address: (h.) 5 Temple Village, Gorebridge, Midlothian; T.-01875 830344.

Dunlop, Alastair Barr, OBE (1989), FRICS. Deputy Chairman, Lothians Ethics of Medical Research Committee, since 1984; General Commissioner for Income Tax, since 1991; Member, NHS Complaints Panel; b. 27.12.33, Calcutta; m., Catriona C.L.H. MacLaurin; 1 s.; 1 d. Educ. Radley. Member, British Schools Exploring Society Expedition, Arctic Norway, 1950. National Service, 1952-54 (active service, Malaya: 2nd Lt., 1st Bn., RWK); commerce, City of London, 1954-58; agricultural student, 1959-61; Land Agent, Inverness, 1962-71 (Partner, Bingham Hughes & Macpherson); Joint Founding Director, Martin Paterson Associates Ltd., 1971; ecology studies, Edinburgh University, 1973-74. Member, Lothian Health Board, 1983-91 (Vice-Chairman, 1989-91); Scottish Member, RICS Committee for Wilson Report on Financial Institutions, 1973-74; Chairman: Edinburgh and Borders Branch, RICS, 1977, Paintings in Hospitals Scotland; Life Member, Institute of Directors; President and Past President, Edinburgh South Conservative Association; Chairman: South Edinburgh Conservative Association, 1980-84 and 1992-00, Central and South, Scottish Conservative and Unionist Association, 1985-88, Edinburgh Branch, World Wildlife Fund, 1982-96; elected Member, Council, National Trust for Scotland, 1992-97. Recreations: golf; skiing; fine arts. Address: 46 Dick Place, Edinburgh EH9 2JB; T.-0131-667 5343.

Dunlop, Eileen. Children's Writer; b. 13.10.38, Alloa; m., Antony Kamm (qv). Educ. Alloa Academy; Moray House College. Publications: Robinsheugh, 1975; A Flute in Mayferry Street, 1976; Fox Farm, 1978; The Maze Stone, 1982 (SAC Book Award); Clementina, 1985 (SAC Book Award); The House on the Hill, 1987 (commended, Carnegie Medal); The Valley of Deer, 1989; Finn's Island, 1991; Tales of St. Columba, 1992; Green Willow's Secret, 1993; Finn's Roman Fort, 1994; Tales of St. Patrick, 1995; Castle Gryffe, 1995; Waters of Life, 1996; The Ghost by the Sea, 1997; Warrior's Bride, 1998; A Royal Ring of Gold, 1999; Ghoul's Den, 1999; The Haunting of Alice Fairlie, 2001; Co-author, with Antony Kamm: Scottish Verse to 1800, 1985; A Book of Old Edinburgh, 1983. Recreations: reading; gardening; theatre. Address: (h.) 46 Tarmangie Drive, Dollar FK14 7BP; T.-01259 742007.

Dunlop, Ian Hunter. Chief Executive, Aberdeen and Grampian Tourist Board, since 2001; b. 15.10.51, Aldershot; m., Jacqueline; 3 s. Educ. Sunderland College of Education; Durham University. Park Barn School, Guildford, 1974-82; Highland Wildlife Park, Kincraig, 1983-87; Highlands and Islands Development Board, 1987-91; Highlands and Islands Enterprise, 1991-94; Scottish Tourist Board, 1994-2001. Chairman: Cairngorm Ski Club. Recreations: British Association of Snowsport Instructors – international ski teacher diploma; golf; cycling; Scottish history. Address: (b.) 27 Albyn Place, Aberdeen AB10 1YL; T.-01224 288826.

Dunlop, Sheriff William, LLB. Sheriff of North Strathclyde, since 1995; b. 7.3.44, Glasgow; m., Janina Marthe; 1 s.; 2 d. Educ. High School of Glasgow; Glasgow University. Solicitor, 1968-84; called to Scottish Bar, 1985. Governor, The High School of Glasgow, 1999; Member, Council, Sheriffs' Association, since 2001; International Rugby Board Match Commissioner for European Cup and Six Nations matches, 1999; Chairman, Scottish Rugby Union Championship Appeals Panel, 2000. Address: (b.) Sheriff Court, Castlehill, Campbeltown, PA28 6AN; T.- 01586 552503.

Dunmore, 12th Earl of (Malcolm Kenneth Murray); b. 17.9.46; m.; 1 s.; 1 d. Succeeded to title, 1995; lives in Australia.

Dunn, Bill, BA. Chief Executive, Ayr Locality Enterprise Resource Trust (ALERT), since 1988; b. 26.2.48, Ayr; m., Sheila; 2 s.; 2 d. Educ. Ayr Academy; Strathclyde University. Transport Manager, National Freight Corporation/British (later Scottish) Road Services, 1970-73; Administrator, Ayrshire Joint Police Committee, 1973; Internal Audit Department, British Steel Corporation, Glasgow, 1973-81; Garnock Valley Task Force: Project Co-ordinator, 1981-83, Business Development Consultant, 1983-84; Managing Director, Development Executive, 1984-88. Recreations: family; golf; football; music; DIY; model railways. Address: (b.) 16 Smith Street, Ayr KA7 1TD; T.-01292 264181.

Dunn, Professor Douglas Eaglesham, BA, FRSL, Hon.LLD (Dundee, 1987), Hon.DLitt (Hull, 1995). Professor, School of English, St. Andrews University, since 1991 (Head of School, 1994-99), and Director, St. Andrews Scottish Studies Institute, since 1993; b. 23.10.42, Inchinnan. Educ. Renfrew High School; Camphill Senior Secondary School, Paisley; Hull University. Books of poems: Terry Street, 1969, The Happier Life, 1972, Love or Nothing, 1974, Barbarians, 1979, St. Kilda's Parliament, 1981, Elegies, 1985, Selected Poems, 1986, Northlight, 1988, Dante's Drum-Kit, 1993, The Donkey's Ears, 2000, The Year's Afternoon, 2000; Secret Villages (short stories), 1985; Boyfriends and Girlfriends (short stories), 1995; Andromache (translation), 1990; Poll Tax: The Fiscal Fake, 1990; Editor: Choice of Lord Byron's Verse, 1974, The Poetry of Scotland, 1979, A Rumoured City: New Poets from Hull, 1982; Two Decades of Irish Writing: a Critical Survey, 1975; The Essential Browning, 1990; Scotland: an anthology, 1991; Faber Book of Twentieth Century Scottish Poetry, 1992; Oxford Book of Scottish Short Stories, 1995; 20th Century Scottish Poems, 2000; author of plays, and TV films using commentaries in verse. Gregory Award, 1968; Somerset Maugham Award, 1972; Geoffrey Faber Memorial Prize, 1975; Hawthornden Prize, 1982; Whitbread Award for Poetry and Whitbread Book of the Year Award, 1985; Cholmondeley Award, 1989. Honorary Visiting Professor, Dundee University, 1987; Fellow in Creative Writing, St. Andrews University, 1989-91; Honorary Fellow, Humberside College, 1987. Address (b.) School of English, St. Andrews University, St. Andrews KY16 9AL.

Dunn, James Clark. Motoring Correspondent, The Scotsman, since 1986; b. 11.7.51, Dunfermline; m., Margaret; 1 s.; 1 d. Educ. Dunfermline High School; Napier University. Alloa Advertiser, 1970-74; Home Counties Newspapers, 1974-75; PR, SSEB, 1975-84. UK Motoring Writer of the Year, 1990. Publications: David Coulthard the Flying Scot; David Coulthard In the Wheeltracks of Legends. Recreations: sailing; fishing; classic cars. Address: (h.) 3 Thorniewood Gardens, Uddingston G71 6NQ; T.-0131-620 8513.

Dunnett, Dorothy, OBE. Writer, since 1960; Portrait Painter, since 1950; b. 25.8.23, Dunfermline; m., Sir Alastair M. Dunnett; 2 s. Civil Service: Assistant Press Officer, Scottish Government Departments, Edinburgh, 1940-46, Executive Officer, Board of Trade, Glasgow, 1946-55; Trustee for the Secretary of State for Scotland, Scottish National War Memorial, 1962-96; Non-Executive Director, Scottish Television p.l.c., 1979-92; Fellow, Royal Society of Arts, since 1986; Trustee, National Library of Scotland, since 1986; Board, Edinburgh Book Festival, 1988-95. Publications (novels): Game of Kings, 1961; Queens' Play, 1964; The Disorderly Knights, 1966; Dolly and the Singing Bird, 1968; Pawn in Frankincense, 1969; Dolly and the Cookie Bird, 1970; The Ringed Castle, 1971; Dolly and the Doctor Bird, 1971; Dolly and the Starry Bird, 1973; Checkmate, 1975; Dolly and the Nanny Bird, 1976; King Hereafter, 1982; Dolly and the Bird of Paradise, 1983; Niccolo Rising, 1986; The Spring of the Ram, 1987; The Scottish Highlands (Co-author), 1988; Race of Scorpions, 1989; Moroccan Traffic, 1991; Scales of Gold, 1991; The Unicorn Hunt, 1993; To Lie with Lions, 1995; Caprice and Rondo, 1997; Gemini, 2000; Contributor, Scottish Short Stories, anthology, 1973, and A Scottish Childhood, anthology, 1998. Recreations: travel; medieval history; opera; orchestral music; ballet. Address (h.) 87 Colinton Road, Edinburgh EH10 5DF; T.-0131-337 2107.

Dunnett, Major Graham Thomas, TD, JP. Lord Lieutenant of Caithness, since 1995; b. 8.3.29, Wick; m., Catherine Elizabeth Sinclair; 3 s. Educ. Wick High School; Archbishop Holgates Grammar School, York. 1st Seaforth Highlanders, Malaya, 1948-51; 11th Seaforth Highlanders, Caithness, 1951-71; became 2nd Lieutenant, 1950, Lieut., 1952, Captain, 1956, Major and Coy. Comdr., 1964; Deputy Lieutenant of Caithness, 1975; Vice Lieutenant, 1986. Recreations: gardening; walking; country dancing. Address: Cathel Sheiling, Loch Calder, Thurso KW14 7YH; T.-01847 871220.

Durie, Roy Ross, FRICS, MIMgt. Senior Partner, Ryden, Edinburgh; b. 11.5.48, Edinburgh; m., Dorothy; 1 s.; 3 d. Educ. Edinburgh Academy; Britannia Royal Naval College, Dartmouth. Royal Navy Officer (Lt. R.N.), 1966-72; joined Ryden, 1973. Chairman, Chamber Developments Ltd.; Director, Edinburgh Chamber of Commerce; Chairman, Merchant Company Finance and Property Committee; Elder, St. Giles, Edinburgh; Past Chairman, ISVA, Scotland. Recreations: walking; swimming; sailing; skiing; golf; rugby. Address: (b.) Ryden, 46 Castle Street, Edinburgh EH2 3BN; T.-0131-225 6612; e-mail: roy.durie@ryden.co.uk

Durrani, Professor Tariq Salim, BSc (Hons), MSc, PhD, FIEE, FREng, FIEEE, FRSE. Professor, Department of Electronic and Electrical Engineering, Strathclyde University, since 1986; b. 27.10.43, Amraoti, India; m., Clare Elizabeth; 1 s.; 2 d. Educ. Marie Colaco High School, Karachi; Engineering University, Dacca; Southampton University. Research Fellow, Southampton University, 1970-76; joined academic staff, Strathclyde University, 1976, Chairman, Department of Electronic and Electrical Engineering, 1986-90, Deputy Principal, 1990-91, and since 2000; Director, Scottish Electronics Technology Group, since 1983; President, IEEE Signal Processing Society, 1993-94; Chair: IEEE Periodicals Council, 1996-98, Management Committee, IT Associate Companies Scheme (ITACS). Publications: six books; over 290 technical research papers. Recreation: playing occasional golf badly. Address: (b.) Department of Electronic and Electrical Engineering, Strathclyde University, Glasgow; T.-0141-548 2883.

Durward, William Farquharson, MB, ChB, FRCP(Edin), FRCP(Glas). Consultant Neurologist, Greater Glasgow and Lanarkshire Health Boards, since 1977; Honorary Clinical Senior Lecturer in Neurology, Glasgow University, since 1978; Director, Cloburn Quarry Co. Ltd.; b. 16.9.44, Kilmarnock; m., Ann Roy Paterson; 1 s.; 1 d. Educ. Kilmarnock Academy; Glasgow University; Boston

University. Employed by NHS, since 1968; specialist training grades, 1969-77. Recreations: walking; reading; railway conservation. Address: (h.) Overdale, 20 South Erskine Park, Bearsden, Glasgow G61 4NA; T.-0141-942 3143.

Duthie, Sir Robert (Robin) Grieve, CBE (1978), CA, LLD, CBIM, FRSA, FRIAS, DTech (Napier). Chairman, RG Duthie & Co. Ltd., since 1984; Director, Devol Engineering Ltd., since 1993; Vice Chairman, BP Advisory Board Scotland, since 1990; b. 2.10.28, Greenock; m., Violetta Noel Maclean; 2 s.; 1 d. Educ. Greenock Academy. Apprentice Chartered Accountant, Thomson Jackson Gourlay and Taylor, CA, 1946-51; joined Blacks of Greenock, 1952; appointed Managing Director, 1962; Chairman, Black & Edgington, 1972-83. Chairman, Inverkip Society, 1966; Director, Greenock Chamber of Commerce, 1966; Member, Clyde Port Authority, 1971-83 (Chairman, 1977-80); Director, Royal Bank of Scotland plc, 1978-98; Director, British Assets Trust plc, 1977-98; Chairman, Scottish Development Agency, 1979-88; Chairman, Britoil PLC, 1988-90; Chairman, Neill Clerk Group plc, 1993-98; Director, Greenock Provident Bank, 1969-75 (Chairman, 1975); Member, Scottish Telecommunications Board, 1972-77; Council Member, Institute of Chartered Accountants of Scotland, 1973-78; Member: East Kilbride Development Corporation, 1976-78, Strathclyde Region Local Valuation Appeal Panel, 1976-83; CBI Tax Liaison Officer for Scotland, 1976-79; Chairman, Made Up Textile Association of Great Britain, 1972; Member: British Institute of Management Scottish Committee, 1976, Glasgow and West of Scotland Committee, Scottish Council (Development and Industry), 1975-79; Chairman, Greenock Club, 1972; Captain, Greenock Cricket Club, 1960-61; Commissioner, Queen Victoria School, Dunblane, 1972-89; Commissioner, Scottish Congregational Ministers Pension Fund, since 1973; Member, Scottish Economic Council, 1980-96; Member of Council, Royal Caledonian Curling Club, 1984-88; Treasurer, Nelson Street EU Congregational Church, Greenock, since 1970. Awarded Honorary Degree of Doctor of Laws, Strathclyde University, 1984. Recreations: curling; golf. Address: (h.) Fairhaven, 181 Finnart Street, Greenock, PA16 8JA; T.-01475 722642.

Du Vivier, Paul Eastwood, FIMgt, Captain RN (Rtd.). Chief Executive, Scottish Fisheries Protection Agency, since 1995; b. 24.5.45, Bath; m., Diana Rochsoles Robertson; 1 s.; 2 d. Educ. Malvern College; Britannia Royal Naval College, Dartmouth. Service at sea, 1965-88; in command, HMS Maxton, 1974-76, HMS Achilles, 1980-81; service in MoD Naval Secretary's Department, 1977-79, Naval Plans, 1981-84; BRNC Dartmouth, 1984-86; HMS Dryad, 1989-91; Board President, Admiralty Interview Board, 1991; Director, Joint Maritime Operational Training Staff, 1991-94; Chief of Staff to Flag Officer Scotland, Northern England and Northern Ireland, 1994-95; Member, Institute of Directors; Selected Naval Member, Lowland RFCA; Member, Scottish Council, KGFS. Address: (b.) Pentland House, 47 Robb's Loan, Edinburgh EH14 1TY; T.-0131-244 6059.

Duxbury, Professor Geoffrey, BSc, PhD, CPhys, FInstP, FRSE. Professor, Chemical Physics, Strathclyde University; b. 6.11.42, Blackburn; m., Mary R.; 1 s.; 1 d. Educ. Cheadle Hulme School; Sheffield University. Junior Research Fellow, National Physical Laboratory, 1967-69; Research Assistant, Research Associate, Lecturer in Chemical Physics, Bristol University, 1970-80; Senior Lecturer/Reader, Strathclyde University, 1981-86. Marlow Medal, Faraday Division, Royal Society of Chemistry, 1975. Publication: Infrared Vibration-Rotation Spectroscopy: From Free Radicals to the Infrared Sky, 2000. Address: (b.) Department of Physics and Applied Physics, Strathclyde University, Glasgow, G4 0NG; T.-0141-548 3271.

Dyer, James A.T., MB, ChB (Hons), FRCPsych, FFCS. Medical Commissioner, Mental Welfare Commission for Scotland, since 1991, and Director, since 1993; b. 31.12.46, Arbroath; m., Suzanne Whitaker; 2 s.; 1 d.; 1 step-s.; 2 step d. Educ. Bo'ness Academy; Robert Gordon's College, Aberdeen; Aberdeen University. Trainee General Practitioner, Skene, Aberdeenshire, 1971-72; junior clinical appointments, then Senior Registrar in Psychiatry, Royal Edinburgh Hospital, 1972-77; Scientific Officer, MRC Unit for Epidemiological Studies in Psychiatry, Edinburgh, 1977-80; Consultant Psychiatrist, Royal Edinburgh Hospital, 1981-91; Treasurer, Scottish Division, Royal College of Psychiatrists; FRSA; Member, Medical Action for Global Security. Recreations: walking; reading; family. Address: (b.) 1 Frankscroft, Peebles EH45 9DX; T.-01721 724729.

E

Eadie, Helen. MSP (Labour), Dunfermline East, since 1999; b. Stenhousemuir; m.; 2 d. Educ. Larbert High School; Falkirk Technical College; London School of Economics. Former Chair, STUC Youth Advisory Committee; former full-time Administrator, GMB, Glasgow; former Equal Opportunities and Political Officer, GMB, London; former Assistant to Harry Ewing MP and Alex Eadie MP (father-in-law); served in local government, 1986-99; former Vice-President, North Sea Commission; former Vice-Chair, South East Scotland Partnership in Transport. Address: (b.) Scottish Parliament, Edinburgh EH99 1SP; T.-0131-348 5749; e-mail: helen.eadie.msp@scottish.parliament.uk

Eagles, Henry Allan, MA (Hons). Head of News and Current Affairs, Grampian Television, since 2000; b. 17.4.49, Cheltenham. Educ. High School of Glasgow; Dundee University. The Scotsman, 1975-80; Scottish Television, 1981-91; freelance television producer, 1992-99. Address: (b.) Grampian Television, Queen's Cross, Aberdeen AB15 4XJ; T.-01224 846846.

Eagles, John Mortimer, MBChB, MPhil, FRCPsych. Consultant Psychiatrist, Royal Cornhill Hospital, Aberdeen, since 1985; Honorary Reader in Mental Health, Aberdeen University, 1985-2000; b. 21.10.52, Newport-on-Tay; m., Janette Isobel Rorke; 2 d. Educ. Bell-Baxter High School, Cupar; Aberdeen University; Edinburgh University. Resident House Officer posts, Aberdeen, 1977-78; Senior House Officer/Registrar in Psychiatry, Royal Edinburgh Hospital, 1978-82; Lecturer, Department of Mental Health, Aberdeen University, 1982-85; Psychiatric Tutor for trainee psychiatrists, Aberdeen, 1987-92. Chairman, North-East Regional Postgraduate Medical Education Committee, 1990-95; Secretary, Scottish Division, Royal College of Psychiatrists Research Advisory Group, since 1998. Recreations: cricket; golf; travel; reading. Address: (h.) 41 Binghill Park, Milltimber, Aberdeenshire AB13 0EE; T.-01224 732434.

Eaglesham, David Hillhouse, BEd. General Secretary, Scottish Secondary Teachers Association, since 1996; b. 7.9.50, Glasgow; m., Doreen; 1 s.; 2 d. Educ. Victoria Drive Secondary School, Glasgow; Glasgow University; Jordanhill College. Teacher, Govan High School, 1973-77; Departmental Manager, Marks and Spencer, 1977-78; Teacher/Assistant Principal Teacher, Mearns Castle High School, 1978-82; Principal Teacher of Modern Studies, Cathkin High School, 1982-84; Assistant General Secretary, SSTA, 1994-96. Recreations: golf; gardening. Address: (b.) 15 Dundas Street, Edinburgh EH3 6QG; T.-0131-556 5919.

Eardley, Catherine Elizabeth, MA (Cantab). Head of Investor Services, Representative Office, J P Morgan Plc, since 2000; b. 22.12.62, Colne, Lancashire. Educ. Buchan School, Isle of Man; Trinity Hall, Cambridge. Morgan Stanley, 1984-88; Paribas Capital Markets Ltd, 1988-92; Senior Sales Executive, Chase Manhattan Plc, 1992-2000; British Horse Society Intermediate Teacher. Recreations: dressage; horse breeding; hill walking. Address: (b.) 91 George Street, Edinburgh, EH2 3ES; T.-0131-225 7776; e-mail: Catherine.Eardley@Chase.com

Early, Andrew John, QFSM, BSc, MIFireE, MIOSH. Firemaster, Central Scotland Fire Brigade; b. 1946; m., Maureen. Firefighter, South Western Area, 1965; Leading Firefighter, South Western Area, 1970; Sub Officer, South Western Area, 1971; Assistant Divisional Fire Officer, Central Region Fire Brigade, 1975; Divisional Officer (Course Director), Fire Service Technical College, 1978; Third Officer (Divisional Officer) Central Scotland Fire Brigade, 1984; Assistant Firemaster, Central Scotland Fire Brigade, 1996. Recreations: keep fit. Address: (b.) Main Street, Maddiston, Falkirk, FK2 0LG; e-mail: csfb1@globalnet.co.uk

Eason, Iain Walter, BArch (Hons), RIBA, FRIAS. Managing Director, Covell Matthews Architects Ltd., since 1999; Managing Director, Covell Matthews Haines Ltd., since 2000; b. 11.5.46, Glasgow; m., Dr. Patricia J. Eason. Educ. High School of Glasgow; University of Strathclyde. Architectural Assistant: Department of Highways, Toronto and George Robb Architect, Tornoto, 1969, Vogul and Strunk, New York, 1970; Covell Matthews: Architect, 1971-78, Associate, 1978-87, Director, since 1987, Finance Director, 1992-2001. Former Treasurer, West Edinburgh Liberal Association; Committee Member, Scottish Liberal Club. Winner, Times Conservation Award. Recreations: golf; gardening; building conservation. Address: (b.) 6 Manor Place, Edinburgh EH3 7DD; T.-0131-226 3366; e-mail: admin@covellmatthews-edin.co.uk

Eassie, Hon. Lord (Ronald Mackay). Senator of the College of Justice, since 1997; b. 1945; m.; 1 s. Educ. Berwickshire High School; St. Andrews University; Edinburgh University. Admitted, Faculty of Advocates, 1972; QC, 1986. Address: Parliament House, Parliament Square, Edinburgh EH1 1RQ.

Eastmond, Clifford John, BSc, MD, FRCP, FRCPE. Associate Medical Director, since 1999 and Consultant Rheumatologist, since 1979, Aberdeen Royal Hospitals NHS Trust (Clinical Director of Medicine, 1995-99); Clinical Senior Lecturer, Aberdeen University, since 1979; b. 19.1.45, Ashton-under-Lyne; m., Margaret Wadsworth; 2 s.; 1 d. Educ. Audenshaw Grammar School; Edinburgh University. House Officer posts, Edinburgh, one year; moved to Liverpool for further training, subsequently to Rheumatism Unit, Leeds. Elder, Church of Scotland. Recreations: skiing; hill-walking; music; shooting. Address: (h.) The Rowans, Skene, Aberdeenshire AD32 6YP; T.-01224 790370.

Easton, Sir Robert William Simpson, CBE (1980), DUniv, CEng, FIMechE, FIMarE, FRINA. Chairman, Clydeport Pension Trust; Chancellor, University of Paisley, since 1993; b. 30.10.22, Glasgow; m., Jean Fraser; 1 s.; 1 d. Educ. Govan High School, Glasgow; Royal Technical College, Glasgow. Apprentice, Marine Engineer, 1939-51; Manager, Yarrow & Co. Ltd., 1951-65; Yarrow Shipbuilders Ltd.: Director, 1965-70, Deputy Managing Director, 1970-77, Managing Director, 1977-91; Main Board Director, Yarrow & Co. Ltd., 1971-77; Chairman: Yarrow Shipbuilders Ltd., 1979-94, Clyde Port Authority, 1983-93, GEC Scotland, 1990-99, GEC Naval Systems, 1991-94; Director: Supermarine Consortium Ltd., 1986-94, Glasgow Development Agency, 1990-94, West of Scotland Water Board, 1993-95, Caledonian MacBrayne Ltd., 1997-2000; Vice-President, Clyde Shipbuilders Association, 1972-79; Freeman, City of London, 1982; Honorary Vice-President, RINA; Trustee, Seagull Trust, 1984; Director, Merchant House of Glasgow, 1994; Member, Incorporation of Hammermen, 1989; Past President, Institute of Welding; Past President, Institute of Engineers and Shipbuilders, Scotland. Recreations: golf; walking; family. Address: (h.) Springfield, Stuckenduff Road, Shandon, Argyllshire G84 8NW; T.-01436 820 677.

Easton, Robin Gardner, OBE, MA, DUniv, DipEd. Rector, The High School of Glasgow, since 1983; b. 6.10.43, Glasgow; m., Eleanor Mary McIlroy; 1 s.; 1 d. Educ. Kelvinside Academy; Sedbergh School; Christ's College, Cambridge; Wadham College, Oxford. Teacher of French and German, Melville College, Edinburgh, 1966-72; Housemaster and Deputy Head, French Department, Daniel

Stewart's and Melville College, 1972-78; Head, Modern Languages, George Watson's College, 1979-83. Elder, Church of Scotland. Recreations: watching rugby; tennis; hill-walking; visiting ancient monuments. Address: (h.) 21 Stirling Drive, Bearsden, Glasgow G61 4NU; T.-0141-943 0368.

Eastwood, Martin Anthony, MB, MSc, FRCPE. Retired Gastroenterologist; Honorary Librarian, Royal College of Physicians of Edinburgh, 1995-2000; b. 7.8.35, Hull; m., Jenny; 3 s.; 1 d. Educ. Minster Grammar School, Southwell; Edinburgh University. Publications: papers on physiology of the colon and nutrition; History of Western General Hospital Edinburgh (Co-Author), 1995; Principles of Human Nutrition, 1996; E.B. Jamieson Anatomist and Shetlander, 1999. Address: (h.) Hill House, North Queensferry KY11 1JJ.

Eccles, Alexander Charles William Anderson, RD—, BA, LLB, WS. Temporary Sheriff, since 1984; part-time Chairman, Social Security Appeals Tribunals, since 1985, and Rent Assessment Committee, since 1975; part-time Chairman, Industrial Tribunals, since 1991; b. 8.1.33, Newcastle upon Tyne; m., Judith Margaret Hardy; 2 s.; 2 d. Educ. Loretto; Gonville and Caius College, Cambridge; Edinburgh University. National Service, 1951-53 (commissioned HLI); TA, Royal Scots, 1953-59; qualified Solicitor and WS, 1960; Assistant with various firms and local authorities, 1960-68; Partner, J.L. Anderson & Co., Solicitors, Cupar, Kinross, Glenrothes and Cowdenbeath, 1968-84. Lt. Cdr., RNR, 1966-85; Rugby Blue, Edinburgh University (played for Scottish Universities and Durham County). Recreations: rugby; squash; reading military history. Address: (h.) Fernbank, Bridgend, Ceres, Fife KY15 5LS.

Eckford, James Millar, OBE, FCIS, FHSM, FIM, FCS, FRSA. Health Management Consultant; Chairman: Ayrshire Careers Partnership Ltd., Dalmellington and District Conservation Trust, Ayrshire Adult Guidance Network; Member, Board, Ayr College (Chairman, Audit Committee); Assistant Governor, Rotary District 1230; b. 8.7.36, Leith; m., Joan Miller. Educ. George Heriot's School, Edinburgh. District Administrator, East Fife District, Fife Health Board, 1974-79; Board Secretary, Forth Valley Health Board, 1979-85; Board General Manager, Ayrshire and Arran Health Board, 1985-95. Recreations: Rotary; bowling. Address: (h.) 22 Abbots Way, Doonfoot, Ayr KA7 4EY; T.-01292 442323.

Eddie, Rev. Duncan Campbell, MA (Hons), BD (Hons). Minister, Holburn West, Aberdeen, since 1999; b. 17.2.63, Fraserburgh; m., Dr. Carol Buchanan; 2 s. Educ. Mackie Academy, Stonehaven; Aberdeen University; Edinburgh University. Assistant Minister, Edinburgh, 1990-91; Minister, Old Cumnock: Crichton West linked with St. Ninian's, 1992-99. Recreations: music; reading. Address: 31 Cranford Road, Aberdeen AB10 7NJ; e-mail: holburnwest@ashleypark.fsnet.co.uk

Eden, Professor Colin, BSc, PhD. Professor of Management Science, University of Strathclyde, since 1987 (Director, Graduate School of Business, since 1999); b. 24.12.43, Birmingham; m., Christine. Educ. Moseley Grammar School, Birmingham; University of Leicester; University of Southampton. Operational Researcher; Operational Research Manager; Management Consultant; Lecturer, then Senior Lecturer, then Reader, University of Bath School of Management. Publications: six books, most recently Making Strategy: The Journey of Strategic Management. Recreations: sailing; skiing. Address: (b.) 199 Cathedral Street, Glasgow G4 0QU; T.-0141-553 6155; e-mail: colin@gsb.strath.ac.uk

Edge, David Owen, BA, MA, PhD, FRSE, FRAS, FRSA. Reader Emeritus in Science Studies, since 1992, Edinburgh University; b. 4.9.32, High Wycombe; m., Barbara Corsie; 2 s.; 1 d. Educ. Aberdeen Grammar School; Leys School, Cambridge; Gonville and Caius College, Cambridge. Assistant Physics Master, Perse School, Cambridge; Producer, Science Unit, Talks Department, BBC Radio, London, 1959-66; Senior Fellow, Society for the Humanities, and Senior Research Associate, Science, Technology and Society Program, Cornell University, 1973; Reader in Science Studies, Edinburgh University, 1979-92. Scottish HQ Adviser for Students, Scout Association, 1966-85; President (Past Chairman), Scout & Guide Graduate Association; Circuit Steward, Methodist Church, Edinburgh and Forth Circuit, 1983-86; Editor, Social Studies of Science, 1971-2002; Member: various CNAA panels and committees, since 1972, Edinburgh University Court, 1983-86, DQA Auditing Team, HEQC, 1991-97, ABRC Working Party on Peer Review, 1990-91; QAA Auditor, 1997-2001; Chair, Board of Science Policy Support Group, 1989-93; President, Society for Social Studies of Science (4S), 1985-87. John Desmond Bernal Prize, 1993; Fellow, American Association for the Advancement of Science, 1989; Fellow, Royal Society of Edinburgh, 1992. Publications: Astronomy Transformed (Co-author), 1976; Science in Context (Co-Editor), 1982. Recreations: hill-walking; music; watching sport - especially soccer and baseball. Address: (h.) 25 Gilmour Road, Edinburgh EH16 5NS; T.-0131-667 3497.

Edgeler, Ian George, MIMgt. Director of Corporate Services, Scottish Natural Heritage, since 1999; b. 2.12.49, Gravesend; m., Jane; 4 s. Educ. Springhead School; Britannia Royal Naval College, Dartmouth. Joined Royal Navy as Cadet Seaman Officer, 1968; specialised as aircrew (Observer), 1976; flying and specialist operations posts; promoted to Commander, 1988; retired from Royal Navy, 1993; Director of Corporate Services, Royal Botanic Garden Edinburgh, 1993-99. Recreations: amateur gardener and exhibitor; travel; family pursuits. Address: (b.) 12 Hope Terrace, Edinburgh EH9 2AS; T.-0131-446 2222.

Edward, Judge David Alexander Ogilvy, CMG, QC, MA, LLD, FRSE. Judge of the Court of Justice of the European Communities, since 1992 (Judge of the Court of First Instance, 1989-92); Advocate, since 1962; b. 14.11.34, Perth; m., Elizabeth Young McSherry; 2 s.; 2 d. Educ. Sedbergh School; University College, Oxford (Hon. Fellow, 1995); Edinburgh University. National Service, RNVR, 1956-57 (Sub-Lt.); Clerk, Faculty of Advocates, 1967-70, Treasurer, 1970-77; President, Consultative Committee, Bars and Law Societies of the European Community, 1978-80; Salvesen Professor of European Institutions, Edinburgh University, 1985-89 (Hon. Professor, since 1990); Member: Law Advisory Committee, British Council, 1974-88, Panel of Arbitrators, International Centre for Settlement of Investment Disputes, 1981-89; Chairman, Continental Assets Trust plc, 1986-89; Director, Adam & Company plc, 1984-89; Director, Harris Tweed Association Ltd., 1985-89; Specialist Adviser to House of Lords Select Committee on the European Communities, 1985-88; Trustee: National Library of Scotland, 1966-95, Industry and Parliament Trust, since 1995, Carnegie Trust for the Universities of Scotland, since 1995, Hopetoun Foundation (Chairman, Hopetoun House Preservation Trust, 1988-92); President, Franco-Scottish Society, since 1996; Hon. President, Scottish Council for International Arbitration; President, Johnson Society, 1995-96; President, Edinburgh Sir Walter Scott Club, 2001-02. Hon. Bencher, Gray's Inn, 1992; Hon. LLD: Edinburgh University, 1993, Aberdeen University, 1997, Napier University, 1998; Dr. h.c.: Universität des Saarlandes, 2001, Westfälische Wilhelms-Universität Münster, 2001. Address: (h.) 32 Heriot Row, Edinburgh EH3 6ES; (b.) EC Court of Justice, L-2925 Luxembourg; T.-00-352-43032203; e-mail: david.edward@curia.eu.int

Edward, Ian, MA, LLB. Solicitor (retired); b. 3.9.35, Aberdeen; m., 1, Marguerite Anne Leiper (deceased); m., 2, Gudrun Clapier; 2 s.; 1 d. Educ. Robert Gordon's College, Aberdeen; University of Aberdeen; Fitzwilliam College, University of Cambridge. HM Colonial Service (District Officer, Northern Rhodesia), 1959-63; C. & P. H. Chalmers, Solicitors, Aberdeen (now Ledingham Chalmers): Legal Assistant, Partner, Senior Partner, Consultant, 1963-2000. Part-time Chairman of Employment Tribunals, since 1997; Historian, Royal Aberdeen Golf Club. Recreations: golf; gardening; hill-walking. Address: (h.) 23 St. Fillan's Terrace, Edinburgh EH10 5PJ; T.-0131-447 8353.

Edwards, Frederick Edward, LVO, RD, DUniv, MUniv, FIMgt. President, Volunteer Development Scotland, since 1993; b. 9.4.31, Liverpool; 2 s.; 1 d. Educ. St. Edward's College, Liverpool; Glasgow University. Midshipman to Second Officer, Alfred Holt & Co., 1948-57; awarded Perm. Commn. RNR, 1953; Lt.-Cmdr., 1963; Reserve Decoration, 1972; Clasp, 1982; Management Trainee, Morgan Crucible Group, 1957-60; Probation Service, Liverpool, 1960-69; Director of Social Work: Joint County Council of Moray and Nairn, 1969-75, Grampian Region, 1975-76, Strathclyde Regional Council, 1976-93; Visiting Professor of Social Administration and Social Work, Glasgow University, 1988-93; Trustee, New Lanark Conservation Trust, since 1993; President, Disability Scotland, 1995-99; Chairman, Capability Scotland, 1997-2001. Member: Council, Scottish Wildlife Trust, 1994, Board, Scottish Environment Agency, since 1999. Awarded Hon. Doctorate, Paisley University, 1993. Recreations: hill-walking; natural history; Scottish country dancing. Address: (h.) Gardenfield, Ninemileburn, by Penicuik EH26 9LT; T.-01968 674566.

Edwards, Gareth Huw, MA (Oxon), PGCE. Principal, George Watson's College, Edinburgh, since 2001; b. 9.4.58, Swansea; m., Jane; 1 d. Educ. Tudor Grange Grammar School; Solihull Sixth Form College; Exeter College, Oxford; Bristol University. Assistant Master, King Edward School, Birmingham, 1981-85; Head of Classics, Bolton School, Boys Division, 1985-90; Vice Principal, Newcastle under Lyme School, 1990-96; Rector, Morrison's Academy, Crieff, 1996-2001. Recreations: singing; squash; modern Greek. Address: (b.) George Watson's College, Colinton Road, Edinburgh EH10 5EG; T.-0131-447 7931.

Edwards, George Lowden, CEng, MIMechE, MIEE, FIMgt, FInstPet, FRSA, FSAScot, FFCS. Chairman Scotland, GPC International; Director: SSK Conferences and Events, Essentia Group Ltd., NMS Hospitality and Events; Trustee, Scottish Civic Trust; Chairman, Association of Professional Political Consultants in Scotland; b. 6.2.39, Kirriemuir; m., Sylvia Izatt; 1 d. Educ. Webster's Seminary, Kirriemuir; Dundee Institute of Technology. Production Engineer, Burroughs Machines Ltd., Cumbernauld, 1961-64; Development Division, Scottish Council (Development and Industry), Edinburgh, 1964-67; General Manager, GR Designs Ltd., Perth, 1967-68; London Director, Scottish Council (Development and Industry), 1968-78; Manager, Public Affairs Scotland, Conoco (UK) Ltd., Aberdeen, 1978-83; Manager, Public Affairs, Conoco (UK) Ltd., London, 1983-85; Head of Corporate Affairs, Clydesdale Bank PLC, 1988-96. Honorary Fellow, University of Abertay, Dundee. Recreations: music; travel; food and wine. Address: (h.) 1 Back Dean, Edinburgh EH4 3UA; e-mail: georgedwards@sol.co.uk

Edwards, Gordon, MA, CPFA. Director of Finance, Aberdeen City Council, since 1996; b. 1.4.56, Aberdeen; m., Diane; 2 d. Educ. Aberdeen Grammar School. Assistant Director of Finance, Grampian Regional Council, 1991-96. Address: (b.) Town House, Broad Street, Aberdeen AB10 1AH.

Edwards, Kevin John, MA, PhD, FSA, FSAScot. Professor in Physical Geography, University of Aberdeen, since 2000; b. 18.9.49, Dartford; m., Rachel Ann Regan; 2 s. Educ. Northfleet Boys' School; Gravesend Grammar School; St. Andrews University; Aberdeen University. Tutorial Fellow in Geography, University of Aberdeen, 1972-75; Lecturer in Environmental Reconstruction and Research Member, Palaeoecology Centre, Queen's University of Belfast, 1975-80; University of Birmingham: Lecturer in Biogeography, 1980-90, Senior Lecturer in Geography, 1990-92, Reader in Palaeoecology, 1992-94; Honorary Research Fellow, Limnological Research Center, University of Minnesota, 1983; Professor of Palaeoecology, Department of Archaeology and Prehistory, University of Sheffield, 1994-2000 (Head of Department, 1996-99). Member, NERC Radiocarbon Dating Laboratory Committees, since 1995; Chairman, Oxford University Radiocarbon Accelerator Unit Users' Committee, 1995-2000; Deputy Chairman, SCAPE Trust, since 2001. Publications: Quaternary History of Ireland (Co-Editor), 1985; Scotland: Environment and Archaeology 8000BC-AD1000 (Co-Editor), 1997; Holocene Environments of Prehistoric Britain (Co-Editor), 1999; numerous articles in geography, archaeology, botany and quaternary science. Recreations: reading; archaeology. Address: (b.) Department of Geography and Environment, University of Aberdeen, Elphinstone Road, Aberdeen AB24 3UF; T.-01224 272346; e-mail: kevin.edwards@abdn.ac.uk

Edwards, Neil, DMS, DCA, MTSI. Head of Trading Standards, Fife Council, since 1996; b. 6.10.45, Wrexham, N. Wales. Educ. Yale High School, Wrexham; Liverpool Polytechnic. Inspector of Weights and Measures, Denbighshire CC, 1967-74; Area Officer, Department of Trading Standards, Clywd CC, 1974-78; retail management, Italy, 1978-81; Trading Standards Officer, Durham CC, 1981-83; Principal Trading Standards Officer, West Midlands CC, 1983-86; Depute Director of Trading Standards, Dumfries and Galloway RC, 1986-88; Director of Trading Standards and Consumer Protection, Fife Regional Council, 1988-96. Recreation: sport. Address: (b.) Fife House (03), North Street, Glenrothes, Fife KY7 5LT; T.-01592 416353; e-mail: neil.edwards@fife.gov.uk

Edwards, Rob (Robert Philip), MA. Environment Editor, Sunday Herald, since 1999; Consultant, New Scientist, since 1994; Freelance Journalist, since 1980; Television Producer, since 1990; b. 13.10.53, Liverpool; m., Fiona Grant Riddoch; 2 d. Educ. Watford Boys Grammar School; Jesus College, University of Cambridge. Organiser, Scottish Campaign to Resist the Atomic Menace, 1977-78; Campaigns Organiser, Shelter (Scotland), 1978-80; Research Assistant to Robin Cook M.P., 1980-83; Freelance Journalist, writing for Social Work Today, The Scotsman, New Statesman, 1980-89; Environment Editor, Scotland on Sunday, 1989-94; Correspondent, The Guardian and Columnist, Edinburgh Evening News, 1989-94; Freelance Journalist, writing for New Scientist, The Sunday Herald, The Observer etc., since 1994; various media awards. Publications: Co-author of three books, including Still Fighting for Gemma, 1995. Recreations: music; opera; mountains. Address: 53 Nile Grove, Edinburgh EH10 4RE; T.-0131-447 2796; e-mail: robed@madasafish.com

Egan, Professor Vincent, BSc (Hons), PhD, DClinPsy, CPsychol. Director, Postgraduate courses in Forensic Psychology, Glasgow Caledonian University, since 2001; Clinical and Forensic Psychologist, since 1996; b. 13.1.61, London; m., Judith Claire; 2 s.; 3 s. Educ. Cardinal Newman School, Hove; Goldsmiths College, London; Edinburgh University; Leicester University. Research Associate, Royal Edinburgh Hospital, 1987-93;

Clinical Psychologist, Trent Regional Health Authority, 1993-96; Clinical-Forensic Psychologist, Arnold Lodge RSU, Leicester, 1996-2000. Recreations: good food; good wine; good books; good conversation. Address: (b.) Department of Psychology, Glasgow Caledonian University, Cowcaddens Road, Glasgow G4 0BA; T.-0141-331 3037.

Eglinton and Winton, Earl of. Chairman, Edinburgh Investment Trust, since 1994. Grieveson Grant, 1957-72 (Partner, from 1964); Gerrard & National, 1972-92 (Managing Director, from 1972, Deputy Chairman, from 1980); Chairman, Gerrard Vivian Gray, 1989-95. Address: (h.) Balhomie, Cargill, Perth PH2 6DS; T.-01250 883222.

Eilbeck, Professor John Christopher, BA, PhD, FIMA, FRSE. Professor, Department of Mathematics, Heriot-Watt University, since 1986 (Head of Department, 1984-89, Dean of Science, 1998-2001); b. 8.4.45, Whitehaven; 3 s. Educ. Whitehaven Grammar School; Queen's College, Oxford; Lancaster University. Royal Society European Fellow, ICTP, Trieste, 1969-70; Research Assistant, Department of Mathematics, UMIST, Manchester, 1970-73; Heriot-Watt University: Lecturer, Department of Mathematics, 1973-80, Senior Lecturer, 1980-85, Reader, 1985-86; Long-term Visiting Fellow, Center for Nonlinear Studies, Los Alamos National Laboratory, New Mexico, 1983-84; Visiting Fellow, Corpus Christi College, Cambridge, 2001. Publications: Rock Climbing in the Lake District (Co-author), 1975; Solitons and Nonlinear Wave Equations (Co-author), 1982. Recreation: mountaineering. Address: (b.) Department of Mathematics, Heriot-Watt University, Riccarton, Edinburgh EH14 4AS; T.-0131-451 3220.

Elder, Derek Ian, BSc, CEng, MICE, FRSA. Director, Townhouse Public Affairs and Company Secretary, Business Locums Ltd., since 2000; Member, Board of Management, Glasgow College of Nautical Studies; Secretary, Castlemilk Business, Environment, Training and Audit (C-BETA), since 2001; b. 11.7.54, Lennoxtown; divorced; 1 s.; remarried; 1 d. Educ. Allan Glen's School, Glasgow; Paisley College of Technology. Apprentice, Crouch and Hogg Consulting Engineers, Glasgow, 1972-75; Strathclyde Regional Council, 1975-78; Scottish Development Agency, 1981-90; Dumbartonshire Enterprise, 1991-94; Director, Strathkelvin Development Company, 1991-94; Assistant Director, CBI Scotland, 1994-97; Deputy Chief Executive, Scottish Financial Enterprise, 1996-99. Member, Board, Scottish Environment Protection Agency, West Region, 1997-2000. Recreations: old computers; old cars; bad guitar. Address: (h.) 51 Orchard Brae Avenue, Edinburgh EH4 2HR; e-mail: derekelder@hotmail.com

Elder, Dorothy-Grace. MSP (SNP), Glasgow, since 1999; former columnist, Scotland on Sunday, Scottish Daily Express, and Daily Express; Television Scriptwriter and Producer; m., George Welsh; 1 s.; 2 d. D.C. Thomson newspapers; Glasgow Herald as reporter, investigation writer, news feature writer, leader writer; TV and radio news, BBC Scotland; feature writer and columnist, Scottish Daily News Co-operative; feature writer and columnist, Sunday Mail; productions for Scotland and the network, BBC and Scottish TV. Trustee, Yorkhill Children's Fund, Royal Hospital for Sick Children; Member, ACHE UK Committee (opposing child pornography); Honorary President, Glasgow NE Multiple Sclerosis Society; Honorary President, No Panic; Oliver Award winning columnist, 1995-96; British Reporter of the Year, UK Press Awards, 1996-97; citation, Humanitarian Aid Work, City of Pushkin, Russia, 1998, 1999; Convenor: Scottish Parliament's cross-party CND group, Scottish Parliament's cross-party group on chronic pain. Address: Room 2.21, Scottish Parliament HQ, George IV Bridge, Edinburgh.

Elders, Rev. (Iain) Alasdair, MA, BD. Minister, Broughton St. Mary's Parish Church, Edinburgh, since 1992; b. 17.4.39, Sunderland; m., Hazel Stewart Steven; 1 s.; 1 d. Educ. Daniel Stewart's College, Edinburgh; Edinburgh University. Assistant Minister: Edinburgh: St. Andrew's, 1961-63, Edinburgh: High (St. Giles Cathedral), 1963-65; Minister, Cumbernauld: Abronhill (church extension charge), 1965-73; Minister, Edinburgh: Broughton McDonald, 1973-92; Secretary, Cumbernauld Council of Churches, 1971-72; Chairman: Council of East End Churches of Edinburgh, 1978-82, New Town, Broughton and Pilrig Community Council, 1986-89 and since 1992; Scout Commissioner, 1966-90; Secretary, East End Churches Together, since 1989; Vice-Chairman, Edinburgh and East of Scotland Society for the Deaf, 1978-97; Moderator, Edinburgh Presbytery, 1994. Address: Broughton St. Mary's Manse, 103 East Claremont Street, Edinburgh EH7 4JA; T.-0131-556 7313; e-mail: alelders@hotmail.com

Elgin, 11th Earl of, and Kincardine, 15th Earl of, (Andrew Douglas Alexander Thomas Bruce), KT (1981), DL, JP; 37th Chief of the Name of Bruce; Captain, Queen's Bodyguard for Scotland (Royal Company of Archers); President, Royal Scottish Automobile Club; b. 17.2.24; m., Victoria Usher; 3 s.; 2 d. Educ. Eton; Balliol College, Oxford. Lord Lieutenant of Fife, 1987-99; President, Scottish Amicable Life Assurance Society, 1975-94; Chairman, National Savings Committee for Scotland, 1972-78; Member, Scottish Postal Board, 1980-96; Lord High Commissioner, General Assembly, Church of Scotland, 1980-81; Grand Master Mason of Scotland, 1961-65; President, Royal Caledonian Curling Club, 1968-69; President, Boys Brigade (UK), 1963-85; Hon. LLD, Dundee, 1977, Glasgow, 1983. Address: (h.) Broomhall, Dunfermline KY11 3DU.

Eliott of Redheugh, Margaret Frances Boswell. Chief of Clan Elliot; Chairman, Elliot Clan Society and Sir Arthur Eliott Memorial Trust; b. 13.11.48; m., 1, Anthony Vaughan-Arbuckle (deceased); 1 s.; 1 d.; 2, Christopher Powell Wilkins. Educ. Hatherop Castle School. Address: Redheugh, Newcastleton, Roxburghshire.

Ellington, Marc Floyd, DL. Baron of Towie Barclay; Laird of Gardenstown and Crovie; Deputy Lieutenant, Aberdeenshire, since 1984; b. 16.12.45; m., Karen Leigh; 2 d. Member: British Heritage Commission (representing Scottish Tourist Board), Heritage Lottery Fund Committee for Scotland; Vice-President, Buchan Heritage Society; Chairman: Grampian Regional Council Tourism Task Force, 1992-96, Heritage Press (Scotland), Soundcraft Audio; Director: Gardenstown Estates Ltd., Heritage Sound Recordings; Director, Grampian Enterprise Ltd., 1992-96; Member, Historic Buildings Council for Scotland, 1980-98; Communications, Tourism and Heritage Consultant. Saltire Award, 1973; Civic Trust Award, 1975; European Architectural Heritage Award, 1975; SBStJ; FSA. Recreations: sailing; historic architecture; art collecting; music. Address: Towie Barclay Castle, Auchterless, Turriff, Aberdeenshire AB53 8EP; T.-01888 511347.

Elliot, Alison Janet, MA, MSc, PhD. Associate Director, Centre for Theology and Public Issues, University of Edinburgh; Member, Central Committee and Church and Society Commission, Conference of European Churches; b. 27.11.48, Edinburgh; m., John Christian Elliot; 1 s.; 1 d. Educ. Bathgate Academy; Edinburgh University; Sussex University. Research Associate, Department of Linguistics, Edinburgh University, 1973-74; Lecturer in Psychology, Lancaster University, 1974-76, Edinburgh University, 1977-85; Convener, Church and Nation Committee, Church of Scotland, 1996-2000; Session Clerk, Greyfriars Kirk, Edinburgh. Publication: Child Language, 1981.

Recreations: music; cookery. Address: (b.) CTPI, New College, Mound Place, Edinburgh EH1 2LX; T.-0131-650 8943; e-mail: elliot@div.ed.ac.uk

Elliot, Frances Mary, MB, ChB, MBA, MRCGP. Medical Director, Fife Primary Care NHS Trust; Non-executive Member, Board, HEBS, since 1996; Principal in general practice, 1987-98; b. 13.4.60, Edinburgh; m., John Gordon Elliot. Educ. St. Columba's High School, Dunfermline; Glasgow University; Stirling University. Recreations: hill-walking; cycling; photography; bird watching. Address: (h.) Moruisg, Kinaldy Meadows, by St. Andrews KY16 8NA; T.-01334 478881.

Elliot, Sir Gerald Henry; b. 24.12.23, Edinburgh; m., Margaret Ruth Whale; 2 s.; 1 d. Educ. Marlborough College; New College, Oxford. Chairman: Christian Salvesen PLC, 1981-88, Scottish Provident Institution, 1983-89, Scottish Arts Council, 1980-86, Prince's Scottish Youth Business Trust, 1987-94; Vice Chairman, Scottish Business in the Community, 1987-89; Trustee, National Museums of Scotland, 1987-91; Member of Court, Edinburgh University, 1984-93; Chairman: Scottish Unit Managers Ltd., 1984-88, Martin Currie Unit Trusts, 1988-90; Chairman, Forth Ports Authority, 1973-79; Chairman, Scottish Opera, 1987-92; Chairman of Trustees, David Hume Institute, 1985-95; Chairman, Institute of Directors, Scottish Division, 1989-92; Trustee and Director, Edinburgh Festival Theatre, 1995-98; Member, Court of Regents, Royal College of Surgeons, 1990-99; President, UN50 Scotland, 1994-95; Fellow, Royal Society of Edinburgh, since 1977; Honorary Consul for Finland in Edinburgh and Leith, 1957-89; Hon. d.h.c., Edinburgh University, 1989; Hon. LLD, Aberdeen University, 1991. Address: (b.) 39 Inverleith Place, Edinburgh EH3 5QD; T.-0131-552 6208.

Elliot, Robert John, LLB, WS. Solicitor; Chairman, Scottish Committee, Council on Tribunals, since 1998; Deputy Keeper of W.S. Society, since 1999; b. 18.1.47, Edinburgh; m., Christine; 1 s.; 1 d. Educ. Loretto School; Edinburgh University. Partner, Lindsays WS, since 1973; President, Law Society of Scotland, 1997-98. Recreations: golf; Scottish country dancing; detective novels; argument. Address: (b.) 11 Atholl Crescent, Edinburgh EH3 8HE; T.-0131-229 1212.

Elliott, Professor Richard Michael, BSc, DPhil, FRSE. Professor of Molecular Virology, Glasgow University, since 1995; Joint Head, Division of Virology, Glasgow University, since 1998; b. 2.2.54, Freetown, Sierra Leone; m., Margaret Gibson (dec.); 2 d. Educ. Royal Grammar School, Guildford, Surrey; University of Surrey; Oxford University. Post-doctoral Fellow, Mount Sinai Medical Centre, New York, USA, 1979-81; Post-doctoral Fellow, MRC Virology Unit, Glasgow University, 1981-86; MRC Senior Fellow, Glasgow University, 1986-95. Publications: editor of 2 books, author of over 70 publications. Recreations; fly fishing; art deco ceramics. Address: (b.) Institute of Virology, Church Street, Glasgow University, Glasgow, G11 5JR; T.-0141-330 4024.

Elliott, Professor Robert F., BA (Oxon), MA, FRSE. Professor of Economics, Aberdeen University, since 1990; b. 15.6.47, Thurlow, Suffolk; m., Susan Elliott Gutteridge; 1 s. Educ. Haverhill Secondary Modern School, Suffolk; Ruskin College and Balliol College, Oxford; Leeds University. Joined Aberdeen University, 1973, as Research Fellow, then Lecturer; Director, Scottish Doctoral Programme in Economics, 1989-99; Member, Training Board, ESRC, 1995-99; Chair of Reviews for, and Consultant to, many public and private sector organisations, including Megaw Committee of Inquiry into Civil Service Pay, the EEC Commission, HM Treasury OECD, HIDB, DETR, and McCrone Committee, Scottish Executive.

Publications: books on Pay in the Public Sector, 1981; Incomes Policies, Inflation and Relative Pay, 1981; Incomes Policy, 1981; Unemployment and Labour Market Efficiency, 1989; Labour Market Analysis, 1990; Public Sector Pay in the EU, 1999. Recreations: music; reading; hill-walking; golf. Address: (h.) 11 Richmondhill Place, Aberdeen AB15 5EN; T.-01224 314901.

Elliott, Hon. Lord (Walter Archibald Elliott), QC, MC, BL. President, Lands Tribunal for Scotland, 1971-92; Chairman, Scottish Land Court, 1978-92; Ensign, Queen's Bodyguard for Scotland (Royal Company of Archers); b. 6.9.22, London; m., Susan Isobel MacKenzie Ross; 2 s. Educ. Eton College; Edinburgh University. 2nd Bn., Scots Guards, 1943-45 (Staff Captain, 1947); Advocate and at the Inner Temple, Barrister-at-Law, 1950; QC (Scotland), 1963; conducted Edinburgh ring road inquiry, 1967. Publications: Us and Them: a study of group consciousness, 1986; Esprit de Corps, 1995. Recreation: gardening. Address: (h.) Morton House, 19 Winton Loan, Edinburgh EH10 7AW; T.-0131-445 2548.

Ellison, Rosemary E. H., LRAM, DipRAM. Member, Scottish Chamber Orchestra, since 1982; Violin Teacher: Royal Scottish Academy of Music Junior School, since 1993, St. Mary's Music School, Edinburgh, since 1996; b. 29.7.40, Sherborne, Dorset. Educ. Sherborne School for Girls, Dorset; Royal Academy of Music, London. Bath Festival/Menuhin Festival Orchestra, 1966-76; staff, Yehudi Menuhin School, 1964-72; Academy of St. Martin in the Fields, 1972-82. Director: Scottish Chamber Orchestra, since 1985, Queens Hall Co. Edinburgh, since 1985. Recreations: skiing; hillwalking; gardening. Address: 12 St. Bernard's Row, Edinburgh EH4 1HW.

Elphinstone, 19th Lord (Alexander Mountstuart Elphinstone); b. 15.4.80. Succeeded to title, 1994.

Elson, Stephen, BA, AMA, FMA, FSA Scot. Head of Technical Services, National Museums of Scotland, since 1990; b. 7.5.49, Burton on Trent; m., Nicola Eddy; 1 s.; 1 d. Educ. Burton on Trent Grammar School; University of Leeds. Museum Curator, University of Strathclyde, 1973-75; Depute Keeper of Decorative Art, Glasgow Museums and Art Galleries, 1975-79; Director, Scottish Craft Centre, 1979-81; Director, North of England Museums Service, 1981-90. Recreations: music; painting; reading. Address (b.) Chambers Street, Edinburgh EH1 1JF; T.-0131-247 4152.

Elvidge, John William, BA. Head, Scottish Executive Education Department, since 1999; b. 9.2.51, London. Educ. Sir George Monoux School; St Catherine's College, Oxford. Scottish Office, 1973-88; Director of Implementation, Scottish Homes, 1988-89; Scottish Office, 1989-98, latterly as Head of Economic Infrastructure Group, Scottish Office Development Department; Cabinet Office, 1998-99 (Deputy Head of Economic and Domestic Secretariat). Recreations: reading; theatre; music; film; painting; food; wine; sport; walking. Address: (b.) 3-D93, Victoria Quay, Edinburgh EH6 6QQ; T.-0131-244 1481.

Emberson, Eleanor Avril, BSc, PhD. Head of New Educational Developments Division, Scottish Executive Education Department, since 2001; b. 14.9.67, Irvine; m., Matthew Emberson. Educ. Arran High School; St Andrews University. Senior Assistant Statistician, Retail Prices Index, Central Statistical Office, 1993-95; Head, GES Data Unit, HM Treasury, 1995-98; Finance Co-ordinaton Team Leader, Scottish Executive Finance, 1998-99; Head of Curriculum, International and Information Technology Division, Scottish Executive Education Department, 1999-2001. Address: (b.) Scottish Executive Education Department, Victoria Quay, Edinburgh EH6 6QQ; T.-0131-244 0983.

Emerson, Richard Martyn, BA, FSA, FSA(Scot), FRSA, IHBC. Chief Inspector of Historic Buildings, Historic Scotland, since 1999; b. 19.12.49, Munster, Germany; m., 1, Vanessa Leadam Andrews (m. dissolved); 2 s.; 1 d.; 2, Anne Grenfell Macdonald; 1 s.; 1 d. Educ. Wellington College; Courtauld Institute of Art, London University. Deputy Conway Librarian, Courtauld Institute of Art, 1971-73; Research Assistant, National Monuments Record for Scotland, Royal Commission on the Ancient and Historical Monuments of Scotland, 1973-78; Principal Inspector of Historic Buildings, Historic Scotland, 1978-99. Assessor: Royal Fine Art Commission for Scotland, Historic Buildings Council for Scotland. Address: (b.) Longmore House, Salisbury Place, Edinburgh EH9 1SH; T.-0131-668 8745.

Emmanuel, Professor Clive Robert, BSc (Econ), MA, PhD, ACIS. Professor of Accounting and Director of CIFA; Adjunct Professor, Deakin University, Australia, since 1997; b. 23.5.47; m.; 1 s.; 2 d. Educ. UWIST; Lancaster University; UCW, Aberystwyth. Steel Company of Wales, Port Talbot, 1964-68; Lecturer, Lancaster University, 1974-78; Senior Lecturer, then Reader, UCW, Aberystwyth, 1978-87; Associate Professor, University of Kansas, 1980-82. Address: (b.) Department of Accounting and Finance, Glasgow University, Glasgow.

Emslie, Rt. Hon. Lord (George Carlyle), MBE, PC, LLD, FRSE. Lord Justice General of Scotland, 1972-89; Lord President of the Court of Session, 1972-89; b. 6.12.19, Glasgow; m., Lilias Ann Mailer Hannington (deceased); 3 s. Educ. High School of Glasgow; Glasgow University. Commissioned A. & S.H., 1940; served War of 1939-45 (Despatches), North Africa, Italy, Greece, Austria, 1942-46; p.s.c. Haifa, 1944; Brigade Major (Infantry), 1944-46; Advocate, 1948; Advocate-Depute (Sheriff Courts), 1955; QC (Scotland), 1957; Sheriff of Perth and Angus, 1963-66; Dean, Faculty of Advocates, 1965-70; Senator of the College of Justice, 1970-72; Chairman, Scottish Agricultural Wages Board, 1969-73; Member, Council on Tribunals (Scottish Committee), 1962-70; Hon. Bencher, Inner Temple, 1974, and Inn of Court of N. Ireland, 1981; PC, 1972; Baron (Life Peer), created 1980. Recreation: golf. Address: (h.) 47 Heriot Row, Edinburgh EH3 6EX; T.-0131-225 3657.

Emslie, Hon. Lord; Hon. (George) Nigel (Hannington) Emslie. Senator of the College of Justice in Scotland, since 2001; b. 17.4.47. Admitted, Faculty of Advocates, 1972; QC (Scotland), 1986; Dean, Faculty of Advocates, 1997-2001. Address: (b.) Parliament House, Edinburgh EH1 1RQ; T.-0131-225 2595.

Emslie, Donald Gordon. Chief Executive, SMG Television, since 1999; Managing Director, Broadcasting, Scottish Television since 1997; b. 8.5.57; m., Sarah; 2 d. Appointed to SMG plc Board, 1999; Director, GMTV Ltd.; Director, ITV Ltd. Director, Scottish Screen. Address: (b.) 200 Renfield Street, Glasgow G2 3PR; T.-0141-300 3780.

Engeset, Jetmund, FRCSE, FRCSG. Consultant surgeon, Grampian Health Board, since 1987; Surgeon to the Queen in Scotland, since 1985; b. 22.7.38; m., Anne Robertson; 2 d. Educ. Oslo University; Aberdeen University.

English, William John, OBE, CPFA. Council Member, Scottish Arts Council; Board Member, Glasgow School of Art, Arches Theatre, House for an Art Lover; General Commissioner of Taxes; b. 14.8.34, Glasgow; m., Mary; 2 s.; 1 d. Educ. St Mungo's Academy, Glasgow. Director of Finance, Glasgow City Council, 1974-94. Address: (h.) 64 Dumgoyne Drive, Bearsden, Glasgow G61 3AW; T.-0141-942 6431.

Ennis, David, OBE. Chairman, Scottish Enterprise Lanarkshire, since 2000; Senior Director, Oki (UK) Ltd., since 1987; b. 10.8.47, Paisley; 2 s. Educ. St Mirin's Academy, Paisley; Glasgow College of Technology. Personnel Manager, Philips Electric; Personnel Director, Oki (Uk) Ltd. Former Member, Advisory Committee, Scottish University for Industry; former Chairman, Scottish Electronics Forum Skills Group; former Chairman, Advisory Group, Education for Work and Enterprise. Recreations: golf; magic; badminton. Address: (b.) Oki (UK) Ltd., 3 Castlecary Road, Cumbernauld, Glasgow; T.-01236 502559.

Entwistle, Raymond Marvin, FCIB, FCIBS. Managing Director, Adam & Company Group Plc, since 1993; b. 12.6.44, Croydon; m., Barbara Joan Hennessy; 2 s.; 1 d. Educ. John Ruskin Grammar School. Several managerial appointments with Lloyds Bank. Governor, Edinburgh College of Art, 1989-99; Chairman, Fruit Market Gallery, Edinburgh, 1988-2000; Non-executive Director: John Davidson (Holdings) Ltd, 1992-96, JW International Plc., 1995-96, Dunedin Smaller Companies Investment Trust PLC, since 1998. Recreations: golf; shooting; fishing; antiques. Address: (b.) 22 Charlotte Square, Edinburgh EH2 4DF; T.-0131-225 8484.

Erdal, David Edward, MA, MBA, PhD. Director, Tullis Russell & Co. Ltd. (Chairman, 1985-96); Director, Job Ownership Ltd.; Chairman, Tayburn Ltd.; Director, China Heartland Fund; Executive Director, Baxi Partnership Ltd. (Chairman, 1994-99); b. 29.3.48, Umtali, Zimbabwe; 1 s.; 1 d. Educ. Glenalmond; Brasenose College, Oxford; Harvard Business School; University of St. Andrews. English Language Teacher, London, 1972-74; Tianjin Foreign Language Institute, People's Republic of China, 1974-76; joined Tullis Russell, 1977. Trustee, Baxi Partnership; Fellow, Royal Society of Arts. Recreations: sailing; skiing; reading. Address: (h.) West Court, Hepburn Gardens, St Andrews KY16 9LN; T.-01334 473724.

Erickson, Professor John, MA, FRSE, FBA, FRSA. Honorary Fellow, Centre for Defence Studies, and Professor Emeritus, Edinburgh University; b. 17.4.29, South Shields; m., Ljubica; 1 s.; 1 d. Educ. South Shields High School; St. John's College, Cambridge. Research Fellow, St. Antony's College, Oxford; Lecturer, Department of History, St. Andrews University; Lecturer/Reader, Department of Government, Manchester University; Reader/Professor, Defence Studies, Edinburgh University. President, Association of Civil Defence and Emergency Planning Officers, until 1984; Visiting Professor, Yale University, 1987; Hon. Fellow, Aerospace Academy of Ukraine, 1995. Publications: The Soviet High Command, 1962; The Road to Stalingrad, 1975; The Road to Berlin, 1984; Soviet Ground Forces, An Operational Assessment, 1986; Barbarossa, The Axis and the Allies (Editor and Contributor), 1994; The Soviet Armed Forces, 1918–1992: Research Guide to Soviet Forces (jointly), 1996; The Russian Front 1941-45 (jointly), 1999; The Russian General Staff 1716-1999, forthcoming. Recreation: model-making. Address: (b.) 13 Ravelston House Road, Edinburgh EH4 3LP; T.-0131-332 1787.

Eriksen, Gunn; b. 28.12.56, Grimstad, Norway; m., Fred Brown. Educ. Grimstad, Norway; tutored in ceramics by Rolf Tiemroth. Worked as ceramicist in Norway and Scotland; exhibited ceramics and weaving in Norway; since 1980 has run Altnaharrie Inn with Fred Brown; various awards, including maximum ratings in Good Food Guide, AA Restaurant Guide, Egon Ronay etc. Recreations: reading; sailing; skiing; design. Address: (b.) Altnaharrie Inn, Ullapool IV26 2SS; T.-01854 633230.

Erroch, Bruce Alasdair, LLB (Hons), DipLP. Advocate, since 1998; b. 7.5.68, Elderslie. Educ. Paisley Grammar School; Wm. B. Barbour Academy; University of Glasgow.

Solicitor, Glasgow and Lanarkshire, 1990-97; devilling at Scottish Bar, 1997-98. Publication: Product Liability (Contributor), 1993. Recreations: lunching; contemplating cigarettes; defending civilisation in the face of barbarity. Address: Advocates' Library, Parliament House, Edinburgh EH1 1 RF; T.-0131-226 5071.

Erroll, 24th Earl of (Merlin Sereld Victor Gilbert Hay). Hereditary Lord High Constable of Scotland; b. 20.4.48; m.; 2 s.; 2 d. Educ. Eton; Trinity College, Cambridge. Succeeded to title, 1978.

Erskine, Donald Seymour, DL, FRICS. Factor and Director of Estates, National Trust for Scotland, 1961-89; b. 28.5.25, London; m., Catharine Annandale McLelland; 1 s. 4 d. Educ. Wellington College. RA (Airborne), 1943-47 (Captain); Pupil, Drumlanrig Estate, 1947-49; Factor, Country Gentlemen's Association, Edinburgh, 1950-55; Factor to Mr A.L.P.F. Wallace, 1955-61. Member, Queen's Bodyguard for Scotland (Royal Company of Archers); Deputy Lieutenant, Perth and Kinross; General Trustee, Church of Scotland, 1989-2000. Recreations: golf; shooting; singing. Address: (h.) Cleish House, Cleish, Kinrossshire KY13 0LR; T.-01577 850232.

Esler, Professor Philip Francis, BA (Hons), LLB, LLM, DPhil. Vice-Principal for Research and Provost, St Andrews University, 1998-2001; Professor of Biblical Criticism, since 1995; b. 27.8.52, Sydney, Australia; m., Patricia Kathryn Curran; 2 s.; 1 d. Educ. Marist Bros High School, Eastwood, Sydney; Sydney University; Oxford University (Magdalen). Solicitor, NSW Supreme Court, 1979-81 and 1984-86; Barrister, NSW Supreme Court, 1986-92; Reader in New Testament, St Andrews University, 1992-95. Member, Board, Scottish Enterprise Fife. Publications: Community and Gospel in Luke-Acts, 1987; The First Christians in their Social Worlds, 1994; Galatians, 1998. Recreations: walking; tennis; reading. Address: Kilninian House, Kemback, Fife, KY15 5TS; T.-01334 462851; e-mail: pfe@st-andrews.ac.uk

Espley, Arthur James, MBChB, DRCOG, FRCS(Edin). Consultant Orthopaedic Surgeon, Perth Royal Infirmary, since 1981; Honorary Senior Lecturer, Department of Traumatic Orthopaedic Surgery, University of Dundee, since 1981; b. 19.2.44, Southend; m., Erica Strang; 1 s.; 2 d. Educ. Belfast Royal Academy; Edinburgh University Medical School. Governor, Craigclowan Preparatory School, Perth, 1995-2001; Honorary President, Arthritis Care, Perth, 1996-2001. Recreations: golf; gardening. Address: (h.) Couttie Bridge Cottage, Coupar Angus, Blairgowrie PH13 9HF; T.-01828 627301; e-mail: arthur.espley@tuht.scot.nhs.uk

Evans, Alan Thomson, BMedBiol, MD, FRCPath. Consultant and Honorary Senior Lecturer in Pathology, since 1993; b. 20.9.62, Buckhaven; m., Caroline; 1 s.; 1 d. Educ. Buckhaven High School; University of Aberdeen. House Officer, Aberdeen Royal Infirmary 1986-87; Senior House Officer in Pathology, Ninewells Hospital, Dundee, 1987-88; Lecturer in Pathology, University of Dundee, 1988-90; Senior Registrar in Pathology, Ninewells Hospital, Dundee, 1990-93. Chairman, Pathology Division, Scottish Melanoma Group; Examiner in Dermatopathology, Royal College of Pathologists. Recreations: gardening; architectural history; opera. Address: Department of Pathology, Ninewells Hospital and Medical School, Dundee DD1 9SY; T.-01382 632548; e-mail: alan.t.evans@tuht.scot.nhs.uk

Evans, David Pugh, ARCA, RSA, RSW; paints in Edinburgh; b. 20.11.42, Gwent. Educ. Newbridge Grammar School; Newport College of Art; Royal College of Art. Lecturer, Edinburgh College of Art, 1965-68; Fine Art Fellow, York University, 1968-69; Lecturer, Edinburgh

College of Art, 1969-2000; travelled and painted throughout USA, 1975; solo exhibitions: Marjorie Parr Gallery, London; Mercury Gallery, London; York University; Fruitmarket Gallery, Edinburgh; Open Eye Gallery, Edinburgh; Gilbert Parr Gallery, London. Address: (h.) 17 Inverleith Gardens, Edinburgh EH3 5PS; T.-0131-552 2329.

Evans, James, MBE, RD, DL, BSc, CEng, FRINA, MIMechE. Managing Director: Thomas Evans (Berwick) Ltd.; Consultant Naval Architect, since 1990; b. 9.5.33, South Shields; m., Patricia Alexena Kerr; 1 s.; 2 d. Educ. Merchiston Castle School; Kings College, Durham. Apprenticeship, 1950-56; Royal Navy, 1956-58; YARD, 1958-63; UKAEA, 1963-68; RNR, 1956-80 (retired as Captain (E) RNR); Member, Eyemouth Burgh Council, 1972-75; Berwickshire County Council; Chairman, Berwickshire District Council; Managing Director, Eyemouth Boat Building Co. Ltd., 1988-90; Deputy Lieutenant, Berwickshire, since 1978; Chairman: Berwick Freemen's Guild, since 1975, Fishing Boat Builders Association, 1979-90, Berwickshire District Council, 1980-96; Technical Adviser, Scottish Fishermen's Federation, since 1993; Lord President, Court of Deans of Guild Scotland, 1994-95; Secretary, Eyemouth Port Association, since 1996. Awarded Silver Medal, Nuclear Engineering Society, 1962; Gold Cross of Merit (Poland), 1999; Hon ADC, The Queen, 1979-80. Address: (h.) Makore, Northburn View, Eyemouth, Berwickshire; T.-Eyemouth 50231; e-mail: jevans@makore.freeserve.co.uk

Eveling, Stanley, BA, BPhil. Playwright; b. 4.8.25, Newcastle upon Tyne; m., Kate Howell; 2 s.; 2 d. Educ. King's College, Durham University; Lincoln College, Oxford. Recreations: golf; tennis; going abroad. Address: (b.) 30 Comely Bank, Edinburgh EH4 1AJ.

Everett, Peter, BSc (Hons), SPMB. Director: Edinburgh Java Trust plc, since 1995, Ramco Energy Ltd., since 1993; b. 24.9.31, London; m., Annette Patricia Hyde; 3 s.; 1 d. Educ. George Watson's College; Edinburgh University. Royal Engineers, 1953-55 (2nd Lt.); joined Shell International Petroleum Company, 1955; Managing Director: Brunei Shell Petroleum Co. Ltd., 1979-84, Shell UK Exploration and Production, 1985-89; retired, 1989. Honorary Professor, Heriot Watt University, 1989. Recreation: golf. Address: (h.) Cluain, Castleton Road, Auchterarder, Perthshire PH3 1JW.

Ewing of Kirkford, Lord (Harry Ewing), DL. Deputy Lord Lieutenant, Fife, since 1995; b. 20.1.31; m., Margaret; 1 s.; 1 d. MP (Labour), Stirling and Falkirk Burghs, 1971-74, Stirling, Falkirk and Grangemouth, 1974-83, Falkirk East, 1983-92; Under Secretary of State for Scotland, 1974-79; Opposition Spokesman on Scottish Affairs, 1979-83, UK Trade and Industry, 1983-84, Scottish Affairs, 1984-87; Joint Chair, Scottish Constitutional Convention, 1987-96; Chairman, Ewing Inquiry into availability of housing for wheelchair disabled, since 1993; Chairman, Scottish Disability Foundation, since 1994; Member, Council of Europe, 1987-92; Opposition Spokesman on Transport and Scottish Affairs, House of Lords, since 1992; Hon. Doctorate, Stirling University, 1998. Address: (h.) Gowanbank, 45 Glenlyon Road, Leven KY8 4AA.

Ewing, Annabelle Janet, MP. SNP MP, Perth, since 2001; b. 20.8.60. Educ. Craigholme School; Glasgow University; Johns Hopkins University; Europa Institute, Amsterdam University. Admitted Solicitor, 1986; Legal Service, EC, 1987; worked for law firms in Brussels, 1987-96; lawyer, EC, 1997; Partner, Ewing & Co., Solicitors, since 1998. Address: (b.) House of Commons, London SW1A 0AA.

Ewing, Fergus. MSP (SNP), Inverness East, Nairn and Lochaber, since 1999; b. 20.9.57; m., Margaret Ewing, MP. Educ. Loretto School, Edinburgh; Glasgow University. Self-employed Solicitor; Member, SNP National Executive, National Council. Recreations: piano; reading; running; hill-walking; former member of local mountain rescue team. Address: (b.) Scottish Parliament, Edinburgh EH99 1SP; T.-0131-348 5731.

Ewing, Margaret Anne, MA, BA (Hons). MP (Moray), since 1987 (Parliamentary Leader, SNP, 1987-99); MSP (SNP), Moray, since 1999 (Leader, SNP Group, since 1999); b. 1.9.45, Lanark; m., Fergus Stewart Ewing. Educ. Biggar High School; Glasgow University; Strathclyde University; Jordanhill College. Schoolteacher, 1968-74 (Principal Teacher of Remedial Education, St. Modan's, Stirling, 1972-74); SNP MP (East Dunbartonshire), 1974-79; Freelance Journalist, 1979-81; Co-ordinator, West of Scotland CSS Scheme, 1981-87. Recreations: gardening; reading; arts in general. Address: (h.) Burns Cottage, Tulloch's Lane, Tulloch's Brae, Lossiemouth, Moray IV31 6QY; T.-0134381 3218/2222.

Ewing, Winifred Margaret, MA, LLB, NP. MSP (SNP), Highlands and Islands, since 1999; President, Scottish National Party; b. 10.7.29, Glasgow; m., Stewart Martin Ewing; 2 s.; 1 d. Educ. Queen's Park School; Glasgow University. Solicitor, since 1952; former Secretary and President, Glasgow Bar Association; President, Soroptimist Club (Glasgow), 1966; MP (SNP), Hamilton, 1967-70, Moray and Nairn, 1974-79; Member, European Parliament, 1975-99. Doctor, Open University; Doctor of Laws, Glasgow University; Freeman of Avignon; Comptroller of Scottish Privileges of Veere (Zeeland). Recreations: walking; reading; painting; swimming. Address: (h.) Goodwill, Miltonduff, Elgin IV30 8TL.

F

Fabiani, Linda. MSP (SNP), Central Scotland, since 1999; b. 14.12.56, Glasgow. Educ. Hyndland School, Glasgow; Napier College, Edinburgh; Glasgow University. Various Housing Association posts, 1982-99. Recreations: music; literature; friends. Address: (b.) Scottish Parliament, Edinburgh EH99 1SP.

Fagan, Anne Maria, CBE, BA, FRSA. Head Teacher, John Ogilvie High School, Hamilton, since 1991; Chair/President, Catholic Head Teachers' Association of Scotland, 2000-02; b. 17.12.47, Airdrie; m., Bernard Fagan; 2s. Educ. St Patrick's High School, Coatbridge; Strathclyde University. Teacher, Business Education, Columba High School, Coatbridge; Principal Teacher, Cardinal Newman High School, Bellshill; Member, South Lanarkshire Orchestral Society. Recreations: singing; fitness training; piano playing. Address: (b.) John Ogilvie High School, Farm Road, Hamilton, MK3 9LA; T.-01698 820811; e-mail: afagan@johnogilvie.s-lanark.sch.uk

Fagan, Bernard, BSc, FRSA. Head Teacher, St Ambrose High School, since 1986; b. 16.4.47, Coatbridge; m., Anne Marie; 2 s. Educ. St Patrick's High School, Coatbridge; Glasgow University. Assistant Head Teacher, Our Lady's High School, Motherwell; Depute Head Teacher, Taylor High School, New Stevenston. Member, Board of Management, Coatbridge College, St Philip's School. Recreations: reading; running; sports; travel. Address: (b.) St Ambrose High School, Blair Road, Coatbridge ML5 2EW; T.-01236 427671.

Fair, James Stuart, CBE, LLD, MA, LLB, MSc, WS. Solicitor; formerly Senior Partner, Thorntons, WS, Dundee; Honorary Sheriff; b. 30.9.30, Perth; m., Anne Lesley Cameron; 2 s.; 1 d. Educ. Perth Academy; St. Andrews University; Edinburgh University; Napier University. Past Chairman: University Court, Dundee, Review Committee, Perth Prison, Dundee Port Authority, Dundee Teaching Hospitals NHS Trust; former Dean, Faculty of Procurators and Solicitors, Dundee; Past President: Dundee and Tayside Chamber of Commerce & Industry, Dundee Choral Union; former Member, Scottish Solicitors' Discipline Tribunal; former Member, Committee on Medical Ethics, Ninewells Hospital and Medical School, Dundee; former Clerk, Commissioners of Inland Revenue (Dundee District); Trustee, Sir James Caird's Travelling Scholarship Trust; Chairman, Dundee Incubator Company; Trustee, Dundee Heritage Trust; Member, Development Board, National Museums of Scotland. Hon. Doctor of Laws, Dundee University. Address: (h.) Beechgrove House, 474 Perth Road, Dundee DD2 1LL.

Fairbairn, The Hon. Mrs Elizabeth, MBE. Chairman: Lothian Housing Association, Live Music Now! Scotland; Vice-Chairman, Edinburgh World Heritage Trust; Trustee, Scottish National War Memorial; Council Member, The Cockburn Association; President, Clan Mackay Society; b. 21.6.38; 3 d. Address: 38 Moray Place, Edinburgh EH3 6BT; T.-0131-225 2724.

Fairgrieve, Brian David, OBE, DL, MB, ChB, FRCSEd. Deputy Lieutenant, Falkirk and Stirling Districts; General Surgeon, Falkirk Royal Infirmary, 1960-87; b. 21.2.27, Glasgow. Educ. Glasgow Academy; Glasgow University. RMO, 2/6th Gurkha Rifles, 1952-54; initial medical training, Western Infirmary, Glasgow, Stobhill General Hospital, Killearn Hospital; Area Scout Commissioner, 21 years; President, Forth Valley Area Scout Council; Past President, Rotary Club of Falkirk; Lecturer and Examiner, Scotish Police College; Member, Council, St. Andrew's Ambulance Association; former Director, Incorporated Glasgow Stirlingshire & Sons of the Rock Society; Hon. Vice President, Grangemouth Rugby Club; awarded Silver Wolf, 1983, and OBE, 1986, for services to International Scouting. Recreations: photography; travel. Address: (h.) 19 Lyall Crescent, Polmont, Falkirk FK2 0PL; T.-01324 715449.

Fairgrieve, James Hanratty, DA, ARSA, RSW. Painter; b. 17.6.44, Prestonpans; m., Margaret D. Ross; 2 s.; 1 d. Educ. Preston Lodge Senior Secondary School; Edinburgh College of Art. Postgraduate study, 1966-67; Travelling Scholarship, Italy, 1968; Senior Lecturer in Drawing and Painting, Edinburgh College of Art, 1968-98; President, SSA, 1978-82; exhibited in Britain and Europe, since 1966. Recreation: angling. Address: (h.) Burnbrae, Gordon, Berwickshire.

Fairhead, Nigel Derek, FCA. Director of Finance, National Trust for Scotland, since 1991; b. 17.10.52, Malaya; m., Morag McGregor; 1 s.; 1 d. Educ. Brighton College; Hendon College. Trained with Spain Brothers & Co., Kent; qualified as a chartered accountant, 1976; Price Waterhouse, Paris, 1978-79; Marcus Hazelwood, Cheltenham, 1979-81; joined National Trust for Scotland, 1981; Member, Standard Life Ethical Unit Trust Committee. Address: (b.) 28 Charlotte Square, Edinburgh EH2 4ET; T.-0131-243 9300.

Fairley, Douglas, LLB. Advocate, since 1999; b. 20.2.68, Glasgow; m., Una Doherty. Educ. Hutchesons' Grammar School; University of Glasgow. Solicitor, Maclay Murray and Spens, 1992-98. Member, Council, National Youth Orchestra of Scotland. Publication: Contempt of Court in Scotland (Co-Author). Recreations: music; tennis; skiing; curling. Address: (b.) Advocates' Library, Parliament House, Edinburgh EH1 1RF; T.-0131-226 5071.

Fairley, Janet Christine, PhD, MPhil, BA (Hons). Elected Fellow, Institute of Popular Music, Liverpool University, 1998; b. Birkenhead; 1 s.; 2 d. Taught, Catholic University, Temuco, Chile, 1971-73; Hon. Fellow, Institute of Latin American Studies, 1989-97; Leverhulme Research Fellow, 1992; British Council-Andes Foundation Visiting Professor in Musicology, University of Chile, 1994; Director, Edinburgh Book Festival, 1995-97; AHRB Research Grant 2000; Editorial Board, Popular Music Journal, Cambridge University Press, since 1988; Editorial team, New Grove Dictionary of Music and Musicians, 1998; freelance journalist since late 1980s; freelance broadcaster, since 1989, producing arts programmes (Presenter, Earthbeat, 1989-93); world music critic, Folk Roots, Classic CD, Gramophone, Songlines; numerous academic publications; contributor, Rough Guide to World Music; UK Chair, International Vice-Chair, International Association for the Study of Popular Music, 1985-92. Recreations: yoga; Latin, salsa, tango and flamenco dancing; tennis; swimming; reading; singing; music; theatre; film. Address: (h.) 7A Cluny Gardens, Edinburgh EH10 6BE.

Fairweather, Clive Bruce, OBE. HM Chief Inspector of Prisons for Scotland, since 1994; b. 21.5.44, Edinburgh; m., Ann; 1 s.; 1 d. Commanding Officer: Scottish Division Depot, 1984-87, 1st Bn., King's Own Scottish Borderers, 1987-89; Divisional Colonel, The Scottish Division, 1991-94. Address: (b.) Scottish Executive, Broomhouse Drive, Edinburgh.

Fairweather, Rev. Ian C.M., MA (Hons), BD. Associate Minister, Glasgow Cathedral, 1985-90; b. 7.3.20, Glasgow; m., Joan Margaret Dickinson. Educ. Hutchesons' Boys' Grammar School, Glasgow (Dux); Glasgow University. Professor of Philosophy, Scottish Church College, Calcutta, and Murray College, Sialkot, 1945-47; Minister, Perceton & Dreghorn Parish Church, 1948-63; Lecturer in Religious Studies and Religious Education, Jordanhill College of Education, 1964-82. Church of Scotland Representative,

General Teaching Council for Scotland, 1983-91; Hon. Fellow, New College, Edinburgh, 1984-85. Publications: The Quest for Christian Ethics: an inquiry into ethics and Christian ethics (Co-author); Religious Education (Co-author). Recreation: reading. Address: (h.) 86 Whittingehame Court, 1300 Great Western Road, Glasgow G12 0BH.

Falconer, David. President, GMB, Scotland, since 1992; National Vice-President, GMB, since 1997; b. 13.11.38, Dundee; m., Rose; 2s.; 3d. Educ. Logie Secondary School, Dundee. Apprentice Welder, 1955-60; since 1960 employed in shipyards throughout Britain and also in the oil construction industry, also on the construction of Tay Road Bridge; President, Engineering section, GMB, since 1990; Member, General Council, STUC. Recreations: golf; walking; reading. Address: (b.) Kimberley Buildings, 38 Whitehall Street, Dundee; T.- 01382 225491.

Falconer, Professor Kenneth John, MA, PhD (Cantab), FRSE. Professor in Pure Mathematics, St. Andrews University, since 1993; b. 25.1.52, Middlesex; m., Isobel Jessie Nye; 1 s.; 1 d. Educ. Kingston Grammar School; Corpus Christi College, Cambridge. Research Fellow, Corpus Christi College, Cambridge, 1977-80; Lecturer, then Reader, Bristol University, 1980-93; Visiting Professor: Oregon State University, 1985-86, Isaac Newton Institute, Cambridge, 1999. Publications: The Geometry of Fractal Sets; Fractal Geometry — Mathematical Foundations and Applications; Techniques in Fractal Geometry; Unsolved Problems in Geometry (Co-author); 75 papers. Recreations: hill-walking and long distance walking (Chair, Long Distance Walkers Association, formerly Editor of its magazine Strider). Address: (h.) Lumbo Farmhouse, St. Andrews, Fife; T.-01334 478507.

Falkland, 15th Viscount (Lucius Edward William Plantagenet Cary). Premier Viscount of Scotland on the Roll; b. 8.5.35, London; 2 s.; 3 d. (1 deceased). Educ. Wellington College; Alliance Francaise, Paris. Formerly journalist, theatrical agent, chief executive of international trading company; entered Parliament, 1984 (SDP), 1987 (Liberal Democrats); Deputy Chief Whip, House of Lords, for Liberal Democrats, since 1987; Culture, Media, Sport and Tourism Spokesman, since 1994; elected Member, House of Lords, since 1999. Recreations: racing; golf; motor-cycling; cinema. Address: (b.) House of Lords, London SW1.

Fallick, Professor Anthony Edward, BSc, PhD, FRSE, FRSA. Professor of Isotope Geosciences, University of Glasgow, since 1996; Director, Scottish Universities Environmental Research Centre, since 1998; Head of Isotope Geosciences Unit, Scottish Universities Research and Reactor Centre, East Kilbride, 1986-99; b. 21.4.50, Chatham; Educ. St. Columba's High School, Greenock; University of Glasgow. Research Fellow: McMaster University, Canada, 1975-78, University of Cambridge, 1978-80; Research Fellow, Lecturer, Reader, Professor, Scottish Universities Research and Reactor Centre, East Kilbride, since 1980; 1997 Schlumberger Medallist, Mineralogical Society of Great Britain and Ireland; 2001 Richard A. Glenn Award, American Chemical Society. Address: (b.) S.U.R.R.C., Rankine Avenue, East Kilbride, Glasgow G75 0QF; T.-013552 23332; e-mail: t.fallick@suerc.gla.ac.uk

Fallon, Edward Brian. Executive Member for the Environment, City of Edinburgh Council (Member, City of Edinburgh Council, since 1995, Deputy Chairman, Labour Group, 1995-99, former Convener, General Purposes and Consumer Services Committee); b. 10.11.47, Edinburgh; divorced; 1 s.; 1 d. Educ. St. Anthony's School, Edinburgh; Napier College; Edinburgh School of Building and Crafts. Elected, Lothian Regional Council, 1982, Deputy Leader,

1990-96, and Chair, General Purposes Committee, 1986-96; Convener, Protective Services Committee, COSLA, 1990-96; Chairman, Lothian Valuation Joint Board, 1995-99; Vice-President, ECOSA; Hon. Vice-President, ITSA; Chairman, LACOTS, 1997-99. Recreations: golf; football; rugby; reading; swimming. Address: (b.) City Chambers, High Street, Edinburgh, EH1 1YJ; T.-0131-529 3271.

Fannin, A. Lorraine, BA (Hons), DipEd. Director, Scottish Publishers Association, since 1987; Director and Company Secretary, Scottish Book Source; Member, British Council Publishers Advisory Committee; Trustee, National Library of Scotland; b. Belfast; m., Dr. Nigel Fannin; 2 s.; 1 d. Educ. Victoria College, Belfast; Queen's University, Belfast; Reading University. Teacher of modern languages; radio broadcaster; journalist; owned children's bookshop, 1979-89. Recreations: gardens; galleries; books and friends and relaxing in Fife with both. Address: (b.) 137 Dundee Street, Edinburgh EH11 1BG; T.-0131-228 6866.

Farley-Sutton, Captain Colin David, RN, CEng, FIMechE, DL. Independent Consulting Engineer, retired; Deputy Lieutenant, Caithness, since 1986; b. 20.12.31, Rugby; m., Sheila Wilson Baldwin; 2 s.; 2 d. Educ. Rugby College of Technology and Arts; RN Engineering College, Plymouth; RN College, Greenwich. Royal Navy, 1950-82 (Captain Superintendent, HMS Vulcan, Dounreay, 1980-82). President, Caithness Branch, Red Cross, 1991-97. Address: (h.) Shepherd's Cottage, Lynegar, Watten, Caithness KW1 5YJ; T.-01955 621697.

Farmer, Sir Tom, CBE, KCSG. Chairman and Chief Executive, Kwik-Fit Holdings PLC, since 1984; b. 10.7.40, Edinburgh; m., Anne Drury Scott; 1 s.; 1 d. Educ. Holy Cross Academy. Address: (b.) 17 Corstorphine Road, Edinburgh; T.-0131-337 9200.

Farquhar, Caroline McAra Barclay Murray, MBE, MBA. Chief Executive, Right Track, since 1984; b. 10.12.54, Airdrie; m., James. Educ. Coatbridge High School; Strathclyde University. Civil Servant, DHSS, 1972-75; Scheme Consultant, Community Industry, 1975-77; Detached Youth Worker, Torran Road Project, 1977-79; Project Manager, Project Fullemploy, 1979-84. Chair, STAG (Support Training Action Group); Director, Careers Partnership; Executive Member, Education Business Partnership; Member, Glasgow Learning Alliance; Member, Scottish Office Beattie Committee; Member, European Parliament Social Inclusion Commission. Publication: Altered Perspectives – A Review of Special Needs Training in Scotland. Recreations: walking; painting watercolours; tapestry; cross stitch; eating out. Address: (b.) 3rd Floor, Brook Street Studios, 60 Brook Street, Glasgow G40 2AB; T.-0141-556 1991.

Farquhar, Charles Don Petrie, OBE, JP, DL. Member, Dundee City Council (Depute Lord Provost, 2001, Chairman, Leisure Services Committee); b. 4.8.37, Dundee; 2 d. Educ. Stobswell Secondary School; Dundee Trades College; NCLC. Time-served engineer; elected Dundee Corporation, 1965; former Magistrate and Chairman of various Committees; served Royal Engineers (TRG NCO); Supervisory Staff, Plant Engineering Division, NCR; elected Dundee District Council, 1974; Lord Provost and Lord Lieutenant, City of Dundee District, 1975-77; Past Chairman, Tayside and Fife Committee for Employment of Disabled People. Recreations: numismatics; DIY; pool; bowls. Address: (h.) 2 Killin Avenue, Dundee DD3 6EB.

Farquhar, William John, OBE, MA, DSA, FHSM. Secretary, Clinical Resource and Audit Group, NHS in Scotland, 1989-98; b. 29.5.35, Maud, Aberdeenshire; m., Isabel Henderson Rusk; 4 s. Educ. Peterhead Academy; Aberdeen University; Manchester University. National Administrative Trainee, Scottish Health Service; Hospital Secretary, Whitehaven Hospital, Cumberland; Deputy

Secretary and Treasurer, West Cumberland Hospital Management Committee; Regional Staff Officer, South-Eastern Regional Hospital Board; Deputy Secretary, Eastern Regional Hospital Board; Lothian Health Board: District Administrator, South Lothian District, then Administrator, Operational Services. Secretary, Scottish Health Service Planning Council, 1985-89; Director, Planning Unit, Scottish Home and Health Department, 1987-90; Secretary, Scottish Health Service Advisory Council, 1989-93; Council of Europe Medical Fellowship, 1988; Elder, Colinton Parish Church; Vice-Convener, Church of Scotland Board of National Mission, 1991-94; Convener, Health Care Advisory Group, Board of World Mission, 1991-99, Honorary Secretary, since 1999; Secretary, Morningside Justice and Peace Group, since 2000; Member, Executive Committee, Crossroads, Edinburgh. Recreations: gardening; walking. Address: (h.) Craigengar, 7 Harelaw Road, Colinton, Edinburgh EH13 0DR; T.-0131-441 2169.

Farquharson, Angus Durie Miller, OBE, MA, FRICS, JP. Lord Lieutenant of Aberdeenshire, since 1998; Vice Lord Lieutenant, 1987-98 (DL, 1984); b. 27.3.35, Haydon Bridge; m., Alison Mary Farquharson of Finzean; 2 s.; 1 d. Educ. Trinity College, Glenalmond; Downing College, Cambridge. Chartered Surveyor, Estate Factor, Farmer and Forester; Council Member, Scottish Landowners Federation, 1980-88; Member: Regional Advisory Committee, Forestry Commission, 1980-94; Red Deer Commission, 1986-92; Nature Conservancy Committee for Scotland, 1986-91; NE Committee, SNH, 1991-94; Scottish Council, Guides Association; Hon. President, Kincardine/ Deeside Scouts; Elder and General Trustee, Church of Scotland; Patron and Founder, Birse Community Trust. Recreations: gardening; shooting; walking; local history; nature conservation. Address: (h.) Finzean House, Finzean, Banchory, Aberdeenshire, AB31 6NZ; T.-01330850 229.

Farquharson, Captain Colin Andrew, JP, DL, FRICS. Lord Lieutenant of Aberdeenshire, 1987-98; Chartered Surveyor and Land Agent, since 1953; b. 9.8.23; m., 1, Jean Sybil Mary Hamilton (deceased, 1985); 2 d.; 1 d. deceased; 2, Clodagh, JP, DL, widow of Major Ian Houldsworth of Dallas, Morayshire; 3 step s.; 2 step d. Educ. Rugby. Grenadier Guards, 1942-48; ADC to Field Marshal Sir Harald Alexander (Earl Alexander of Tunis), 1945; Member, Board of Management, Royal Cornhill Hospitals, 1962-74; Director, MacRobert Farms (Douneside), 1971-87; Chairman, Gordon Local Health Council, 1975-81; Member, Grampian Health Board, 1981-89; DL, Aberdeenshire, 1966; Vice Lord Lieutenant, Aberdeenshire, 1983-87; Member, Queen's Bodyguard for Scotland (Royal Company of Archers), since 1964. Recreations: shooting; fishing; farming. Address: Whitehouse, Alford, Aberdeenshire AB33 8DP.

Farquharson, Kenneth James (Kenny), MA (Hons), DipJour. Scottish Political Editor, The Sunday Times, since 1998; b. 8.5.62, Dundee; m., Caron Stoker; 2 s. Educ. Lawside R.C. Academy, Dundee; University of Aberdeen; University College, Cardiff. Industry Reporter, Coventry Evening Telegraph, 1985-88; Scotland on Sunday: Investigative Reporter, 1989-93, Political Editor, 1993-97; Political Editor, Daily Record, 1997-98. Director, Scottish European Aid, 1993-94; Convenor, Scottish Parliamentary Journalists' Association, 1997-2000. Political Journalist of the Year, 2001, Scottish Press Awards. Publication: Restless Nation (Co-author), 1996. Recreations: cooking; architecture; Scottish writing and Scottish painting. Address: (b.) 124 Portman Street, Glasgow G41 1EJ; T.-0141-420 1000.

Farrar, Bill, BSc (Hons). Managing Director, Highland Distillers, since 2000; b. 3.4.58; m., Julie Ann; 1 s.; 2 d. Educ. Magdalen College School, Oxford; Manchester University. Brand Manager to Marketing Manager, J. & B. Whisky, 1985-89; Marketing Manager, The Famous Grouse, 1989-93; Marketing Director, then Commercial Director, Highland Distillers, 1994-2000. Recreations: hockey; golf; tennis. Address: (b.) West Kinfauns, Perth PH12 7XZ; T.-01738 44 0000.

Farrell, Sheriff James Aloysius, MA, LLB. Sheriff of Lothian and Borders, since 1986; b. 14.5.43, Glasgow; m., 1, Jacqueline Allen (divorced); 2 d.; m., 2, Patricia McLaren. Educ. St. Aloysius College; Glasgow University; Dundee University. Admitted to Faculty of Advocates, 1974; Advocate-Depute, 1979-83; Sheriff: Glasgow and Strathkelvin, 1984-85, South Strathclyde, Dumfries and Galloway, 1985-86. Recreations: sailing; cycling; hill-walking. Address: (b.) Sheriff's Chambers, Edinburgh; T.-0131-225 2525.

Farrington, Dennis Joseph, BSc, DPhil, LLM, FRSA. Deputy Secretary, Stirling University, since 1986; b. 13.8.47, Ellesmere Port; m., Julia Baverstock; 1 s.; 1 d. Educ. Ellesmere Port County Grammar School; University of Kent; University of Ulster. Civil Service, 1972-81: Customs and Excise, 1972-73, Northern Ireland Office, 1973-78, HM Stationery Office, 1978-81; Personnel Officer, Hull University, 1981, Administrative Secretary, 1986; Deputy Secretary and Registrar, Stirling University, 1986-95. Secretary, Conference of University Administrators, 1982-88; Chairman, Cancer Research Campaign, Stirling, 1987-91. Publications: Universities and the Law (Co-author), 1990; The Law of Higher Education, 1994, 2nd edition, 1998; Going to University, 1996. Recreations: DIY; home computing. Address: (b.) Stirling University, Stirling FK9 4LA; T.-01786 467017.

Fass, Rev. Michael J., MA. Director, Partners in Economic Development Ltd., since 1992; b. 22.6.44, Sonning, Berks; m., Iola Mary Ashton; 1 s.; 2 d. Educ. Eton College; Trinity College, Cambridge; IMD, Lausanne. Served C Squadron (Berkshire Yeomanry) Berkshire and Westminster Dragoons (TA), 1963-68; worked in industry at Hays Wharf, Miles Druce-GKN, and DTI's Small Firms Service; Director, West Lothian Enterprise Ltd., 1983-92. Director, Prince's Scottish Youth Business Trust, 1989-97; NSM Priest in Charge, Collegiate Church of St. Matthew, Rosslyn Chapel, Roslin (Scottish Episcopal Church), since 1997; Chairman, Industrial Christian Fellowship and Late Moderator, Christians in Secular Ministry. Publication: The Vital Economy, Integrating Training and Enterprise (Co-Author). Address: 60 Braid Road, Edinburgh EH10 6AL.

Faulkner, Professor Douglas, WhSch, PhD, DSc, RCNC, FREng, FRINA, FIStructE, FSNAME. President, Institution of Engineers and Shipbuilders in Scotland, 1995-97; Head, Department of Naval Architecture and Ocean Engineering, Glasgow University, 1973-95, now Emeritus Professor; b. 29.12.29, Gibraltar; m., Isobel Parker Campbell; 3 d. Educ. Sutton High School, Plymouth; HM Dockyard Technical College, Devonport; Royal Naval College, Greenwich. Aircraft carrier design, 1955-57; production engineering, 1957-59; structural research, NCRE Dunfermline, 1959-63; Assistant Professor of Naval Construction, RNC, Greenwich, 1963-66; Structural Adviser to Ship Department, Bath, 1966-68; Naval Construction Officer attached to British Embassy, Washington DC, 1968-70; Member, Ship Research Committee, National Academy of Sciences, 1968-71; Research Associate and Defence Fellow, MIT, 1970-71; Structural Adviser, Ship Department, Bath, and Merrison Box Girder Bridge Committee, 1971-73; UK Representative, Standing Committee, International Ship Structures Congress, 1973-85; Member, Marine Technology Board, Defence Scientific Advisory Council; Expert Assessor: Lord Donaldson's Assessment (Derbyshire), 1995, Department of Transport (re. Derbyshire survey), 1996. Awarded: David W. Taylor Medal; William Froude Medal; Peter the Great Medal.

Recreations: hill-walking; music; croquet; GO. Address: (h.) 4 Murdoch Drive, Milngavie, Glasgow G62 6QZ; T.-0141-956 5071.

Fawkes, Robert, BSc, BA (Hons), Headteacher, Park Mains High School, Erskine, since 1995; b. 17.7.50; m., Margaret Ann; 2 s. Educ. Knightswood Secondary School; Glasgow University. Teacher, North Kelvinside; Principal Teacher of Guidance, Cranhill Secondary School; Principal Teacher of Mathematics, Waverley Secondary School; Assistant Headteacher, Cathkin High School; Depute Headteacher, Waverley Secondary School; Headteacher, Blantyre High School. Recreations: squash; hillwalking. Address: (b.) Park Mains High School, Barrhill Road, Erskine PA8 6EY; T.-0141-812 2801.

Fearn, Professor David Ross, BSc, PhD, FRSE. Professor of Applied Mathematics, University of Glasgow, since 1993 (Head, Department of Mathematics, since 1997); b. 11.2.54, Dundee; m., Elvira D'Annunzio; 1 s.; 1 d. Educ. Grove Academy, Dundee; University of St. Andrews; University of Newcastle upon Tyne. Research Associate: Florida State University, 1979-80, University of Cambridge, 1980-85; University of Glasgow: Lecturer, 1985-90, Senior Lecturer, 1990-92, Reader, 1992-93. Member, Board of Governors, Morrison's Academy, Crieff. Recreations: walking; gardening; DIY. Address: (b.) University Gardens, Glasgow G12 8QW; T.-0141-330 5417.

Fee, Kenneth, MA, FRCS. Editor, Scots Independent, since 1985; b. 14.7.31, Glasgow; m., Margery Anne Dougan; 3 s.; 1 d. Educ. Gourock High School; Hamilton Academy; Glasgow University. President, Glasgow University SRC and Scottish Union of Students; Editor, Gum, Ygorra and GU Guardian; sometime in military intelligence; Sub-Editor, Glasgow Herald; former Managing Director, Strathclyde Publishing Group; itinerant teaching; Member, Scottish Executive, NASUWT, 1983-98; various SNP branch, constituency and national offices, since 1973. Publication: How to Grow Fat and Free. Recreations: chess; gastronomy; campaigning. Address: (h.) 157 Urrdale Road, Dumbreck G41 5DG; T.-0141-427 0117.

Fenton, Professor Emeritus Alexander, CBE, MA, BA, DLitt, HonDLitt (Aberdeen), FRSE, FSA, FRSGS, HRSA, FSA Scot. Director, European Ethnological Research Centre, since 1989; Honorary Professor of Antiquities to Royal Scottish Academy, since 1996; b. 26.6.29, Shotts; m., Evelyn Elizabeth Hunter; 2 d. Educ. Turriff Academy; Aberdeen University; Cambridge University. Senior Assistant Editor, Scottish National Dictionary, 1955-59; part-time Lecturer, English as a Foreign Language, Edinburgh University, 1958-60; National Museum of Antiquities of Scotland: Assistant Keeper, 1959-75, Deputy Keeper, 1975-78, Director, 1978-85; part-time Lecturer, Department of Scottish History, Edinburgh University, 1974-80; Research Director, National Museums of Scotland, 1985-89; Chair of Scottish Ethnology and Director, School of Scottish Studies, Edinburgh University, 1990-94; Honorary Fellow, School of Scottish Studies, since 1969; Foreign Member: Royal Gustav Adolf Academy, Sweden, since 1978, Royal Danish Academy of Sciences and Letters, since 1979; Honorary Member: Volkskundliche Kommission fur Westfalen, since 1980, Hungarian Ethnographical Society, since 1983, Kungl. Humanistiska Vetenskapsfundet i Lund, Sweden, since 1998; Jury Member, Europa Prize for Folk Art, 1975-95; President, Permanent International Committee, International Secretariat for Research on the History of Agricultural Implements; Honorary President, Scottish Vernacular Buildings Working Group; Honorary President, Scottish Country Life Museums Trust; Secretary and Trustee, Friends of the Dictionary of the Older Scottish Tongue; Secretary and Trustee, Scotland Inheritance Fund; Co-Editor: Tools and Tillage, since 1968, The Review of Scottish Culture, since 1984. Publications: The Various Names of Shetland, 1973, 1977; Scottish Country Life, 1976, 1999 (Scottish Arts Council Book Award); The Diary of a Parish Clerk (translation from Danish), 1976; The Island Blackhouse, A Guide to the Blackhouse at 42 Arnol, Lewis, 1978 (re-issued, 1989); A Farming Township, A Guide to Auchindrain, the Museum of Argyll Farming Life, 1978; The Northern Isles, Orkney and Shetland, 1978, 1997 (Dag Stromback Award); The Rural Architecture of Scotland (Co-author), 1981; The Shape of the Past 1, 1985; If All The World Were a Blackbird (translation from Hungarian), 1985; The Shape of the Past II, 1986; 'Wirds an' Wark 'e Seasons Roon on an Aberdeenshire Farm, 1987; Country Life in Scotland, Our Rural Past, 1987; Scottish Country Life, 1989; The Turra Coo, 1989; Craiters...or Twenty Buchan Tales, 1995. Recreation: languages. Address: (b.) European Ethnological Research Centre, National Museums of Scotland, Chambers Street, Edinburgh, EH1 1JF; T.-0131-247 4086.

Fenton, Gordon Perring, MCIBS. Secretary, Committee of Scottish Clearing Bankers, since 1998; b. 18.1.48, Perth; m., Margaret Elizabeth; 2 s.; 1 d. Educ. Perth High School. Royal Bank of Scotland, 1965-98: Dundee; Perth; London; Houston, Texas; Head Office, Edinburgh, latterly Head of Sponsorship and Community Programme. Scottish Committee Member, Arts and Business; Executive Committee Member, Scottish Council Development and Industry. Recreations: reading; foreign travel; tennis. Address: Drumsheugh House, 38 Drumsheugh Gardens, Edinburgh EH3 7SN; T.-0131-473 7770.

Fenwick, Dorothy, MIPR. Head of Corporate Affairs, Railtrack Scotland, since 1999; b. Lanarkshire; m., Andrew Fenwick. Journalist, Scottish weekly newspapers, 1978-87; Press and PR Executive, Scottish Development Agency, 1987-90; Communications Manager, Scottish Homes, 1990-98; Advisor, Lothian Health Board, 1998-99. Chairman, Institute of Public Relations, 1999-2000. Recreations: Scottish arts; home affairs. Address: (b.) Buchanan House, 58 Port Dundas Road, Glasgow G4 0LQ; T.-0141-335 2061.

Fenwick, Hubert Walter Wandesford. Architectural Historian and Lecturer; Chairman, Royal Martyr Church Union; b. 17.7.16, Glasgow. Educ. Huntley School, New Zealand; Royal Grammar School, Newcastle-upon-Tyne. Architectural student; qualified, 1950; office of Ian G. Lindsay, then Lorimer & Matthew, Edinburgh; gave up architectural career, 1958; RIBA Examiner for Scotland in History of Architecture, until post abolished; Assistant Secretary and PRO, Scottish Georgian Society, 1960-65; Council Member, Cockburn Association, 1966; Scottish Editor, Church Illustrated, 1959-64; Editor and Manager, Edinburgh Tatler and Glasgow Illustrated, 1966-67; regular contributor to Scots Magazine, 25 years, and other journals. Publications: Architect Royal; Auld Alliance; Scotland's Historic Buildings; Scotland's Castles; Chateaux of France; Scotland's Abbeys and Cathedrals; View of the Lowlands; Scottish Baronial Houses. Recreations: foreign travel; architectural history; sketching and photography (for own books and articles); gardening. Address: The Priory, Pittenweem, Fife KY10 2LJ; T.-013333 311 453.

Ferguson, Professor Allister Ian, BSc, MA, PhD, FInstP, CPhys, FFCS. Professor of Photonics, Strathclyde University, since 1989; Technical Director, Institute of Photonics, University of Strathclyde, since 1996; Director, Coherent Scotland Ltd.; b. 10.12.51, Aberdeen; m., Kathleen Ann Challenger. Educ. Aberdeen Academy; St. Andrews University. Lindemann Fellow, Stanford University, 1977-79; SERC Research Fellow, St. Andrews, 1979-81; SERC Advanced Fellow, Oxford, 1981-83; Junior Research Fellow, Merton College, Oxford, 1981-83; Lecturer, then Senior Lecturer, Southampton University, 1983-89. Fellow: Royal Society of Edinburgh, since 1993, Institute of Physics, Optical Society of America, Institution of Electrical and Electronics Engineers. Address: (b.) Department of Physics and Applied Physics, Strathclyde University, Glasgow, G4 0NG; T.-0141-548 3359.

Ferguson, David Joseph. Board Secretary, National Board for Nursing, Midwifery and Health Visiting for Scotland, since 1993; b. 7.8.55, Edinburgh; 1 s.; 2 d. Educ. George Watson's College, Edinburgh. Executive Officer, The Scottish Office, 1974-81; Senior Administrator, National Board for Nursing, Midwifery and Health Visiting for Scotland, 1982-92. Recreations: music; reading; cinema; football; walking; spending time with family. Address: (b.) 22 Queen Street, Edinburgh EH2 1NT; T.-0131-247 6619; e-mail: david.ferguson@nbs.org.uk

Ferguson, Douglas, MA, MIMgt, MCIT, FIHT. Director of Operations, Strathclyde Passenger Transport Executive, since 1997; b. 21.5.52, Glasgow; m., Margaret; 2 s.; 3 d. Educ. Allan Glen's School; Glasgow University. Strathclyde Regional Council, 1975-79; joined Strathclyde Passenger Transport Executive, 1979. Recreation: cycling. Address: (b.) Consort House, 12 West George Street, Glasgow G2 1HN; T.-0141-333 3244.

Ferguson, Iain William Findlay, QC, LLB (Hons), DipLP. Queen's Counsel, since 2000; b. 31.7.61, Edinburgh; m., Valerie Laplanche; 2 s. Educ. Firrhill High School, Edinburgh; Dundee University. Advocate, 1987; Standing Junior Counsel to Ministry of Defence (Army), 1991-98, and to Scottish Development Department (Planning matters), 1998-2000. Recreations: cooking; rugby; cycling. Address: (h.) 16 McLaren Road, Edinburgh EH9 2BN; T.-0131-667 1751.

Ferguson, Joan P.S., MBE, MA, ALA, FRCPEdin. Hon. Secretary, Scottish Genealogy Society, since 1960; b. 15.9.29, Edinburgh. Educ. George Watson's Ladies College; Edinburgh University. Scottish Central Library, 1952-66; Librarian, Royal College of Physicians of Edinburgh, 1966-94. Member, Scottish Records Advisory Council, 1987-93; Compiler: Scottish Newspapers, Scottish Family Histories; Contributor, Companion and New Companion to Scottish Culture. Recreations: genealogy; gardening; reading. Address: (h.) 21 Howard Place, Edinburgh EH3 5JY; T.-0131-556 3844.

Ferguson, Professor Pamela Ruth, LLB (Hons), DipLP, PhD. Professor of Scots Law, University of Dundee, since 2000; b. 7.4.63, Glasgow; m., Dr. Euan W. Macdonald; 1 s. Educ. Bearsden Academy; Glasgow University; Dundee University. Procurator Fiscal Depute/Trainee Solicitor, Crown Office, Edinburgh and Procurator Fiscal's Office, Kirkcaldy, 1986-89; Lecturer, 1989-95; Senior Lecturer, 1995-99. Winner, Dr. John McCormick Prize (jointly), Most Distinguished Law Graduate, 1985; awarded Royal Society of Edinburgh Research Fellowship, 1997. Address: (b.) Department of Law, University of Dundee, Dundee DD1 4HN; T.-01382 345189; e-mail: p.r.ferguson@dundee.ac.uk

Ferguson, Patricia. MSP (Labour), Glasgow Maryhill, since 1999; Minister for Parliamentary Business; former Deputy Presiding Officer; b. 1958, Glasgow; m., William G. Butler. Educ. Gartnethill Convent Secondary School, Glasgow. Address: (b.) Unit 1A, Firhill House, 55 Firhill Road, Glasgow G20 7SD.

Ferguson, Rev. Ronald, MA, BD, ThM. Freelance journalist and author; Minister, St. Magnus Cathedral, Orkney, 1990-2001; Columnist, The Herald, since 1997; b. 27.10.39, Dunfermline; m., Cristine Jane Walker; 2 s.; 1 d. Educ. Beath High School, Cowdenbeath; St. Andrews University; Edinburgh University; Duke University. Journalist, Fife and Edinburgh, 1956-63; University, 1963-71; ordained Minister, Church of Scotland, 1972; Minister,

Easterhouse, Glasgow, 1971-79; exchange year with United Church of Canada, 1979-80; Deputy Warden, Iona Abbey, 1980-81; Leader, Iona Community, 1981-88. Publications: Geoff: A Life of Geoffrey M. Shaw, 1979; Grace and Dysentery, 1986; Chasing the Wild Goose, 1988; The Whole Earth Shall Cry Glory (Co-Editor), 1985; George MacLeod, 1990; Daily Readings by George MacLeod (Editor), 1991; Black Diamonds and the Blue Brazil, 1993; Technology at the Crossroads, 1994; Love Your Crooked Neighbour, 1998; Donald Dewar Ate My Hamster, 1999; Hitler Was A Vegetarian, 2001; plays: Every Blessed Thing, 1993, Orkneyinga, 1997; poetry: Pushing the Boat Out (Contributor), 1997. Recreation: supporting Cowdenbeath Football Club. Address: (h.) Vinbrek, Orphir, Orkney KW17 2RE; T.-01856 811378; e-mail: ronferguson@clara.co.uk

Ferguson, William, MCIBS. Chief Executive, Aberdeen Enterprise Trust, since 1996; b. 18.8.46, Stranraer; m., Matti; 1 s.; 1 d. Educ. George Watson's College, Edinburgh. Employed by Clydesdale Bank PLC, retiring as District Manager North. Member, Membership Committee, Royal Northern Club. Recreations: golf; rugby spectating; curling. Address: (b.) 27 Albyn Place, Aberdeen; T.-01224 252168.

Ferguson, William James, OBE, FRAgS. Farmer, since 1954; Director, Hannah Research Institute, since 1995; Vice Lord Lieutenant, Aberdeenshire; Honorary Fellow, SAC, since 1999; b. 3.4.33, Aberdeen; m., Carroll Isobella Milne; 1 s.; 3 d. Educ. Turriff Academy; North of Scotland College of Agriculture. National Service, 1st Bn., Gordon Highlanders, 1952-54, serving in Malaya during the emergency. Former Director, Rowett Research Institute, Aberdeen; former Chairman, Aberdeen Milk Company; former Chairman, North of Scotland College of Agriculture; former Member, Scottish Country Life Museums Trust Ltd.; former Vice Chairman, SAC. Recreations: golf; field sports. Address: Rothiebrisbane, Fyvie, Turriff, Aberdeenshire AB53 8LE; T.-01651 891 213.

Fergusson of Kilkerran, Sir Charles, 9th Bt; b. 10.5.31; m., Hon. Amanda Mary Noel-Paton; 2 s.

Fergusson, Alexander Charles Onslow, DL. MSP (Conservative), South of Scotland, since 1999; b. 8.4.49, Leswalt; m., Jane Merryn Barthold; 3 s. Educ. Eton; West of Scotland Agricultural College. Farm management adviser, 1970-71; farmer, 1971-99; restaurateur, 1981-86. Community Councillor; JP, 1998-99; Deputy Lieutenant of Ayrshire, 1998-99. Recreations: curling; rugby (spectator); cricket. Address: (h.) Grennan, Dalry, Kirkcudbright DG7 3PL; T.-01644 430250.

Fergusson, Professor David Alexander Syme. MA, BD, DPhil. Professor of Divinity, Edinburgh University, since 2000; b. 3.8.56, Glasgow; m., Margot McIndoe; 2 s. Educ. Kelvinside Academy; Glasgow University; Edinburgh University; Oxford University. Assistant Minister, St. Nicholas Church, Lanark, 1983-84; Associate Minister, St. Mungo's Church, Cumbernauld, 1984-86; Lecturer, Edinburgh University, 1986-90; Professor of Systematic Theology, Aberdeen University, 1990-2000. Chaplain to Moderator of the General Assembly, 1989-90; President, Society for the Study of Theology, 2000-02. Publications: Bultmann, 1992; Christ, Church and Society, 1993; The Cosmos and the Creator, 1998; Community, Liberalism and Christian Ethics, 1998. Recreations: football; golf; jogging. Address: 23 Riselaw Crescent, Edinburgh EH10 6HN; T.-0131-447 4022; e-mail: David.Fergusson@ed.ac.uk

Ferrier, Professor Robert Patton, MA (Cantab), BSc, PhD, FInstP, FRSE. Professor of Natural Philosophy, Glasgow University, since 1973; b. 4.1.34, Dundee; m., Valerie Jane Duncan; 2 s.; 1 d. Educ. Morgan Academy,

Dundee; Queen's College, Dundee, St. Andrews University. Scientific Officer, AERE Harwell, 1959-61; Research Associate, Massachusetts Institute of Technology, 1961-62; Senior Research Assistant, Cavendish Laboratory, Cambridge, 1962-65; Fellow, Fitzwilliam College, Cambridge, 1964-73; Assistant Director of Research, Cavendish Laboratory, Cambridge, 1965-71; Lecturer in Physics, Cambridge University, 1971-73; Guest Scientist, IBM Research Division, California, 1972-73. Member, Physics Committee, SERC, 1979-82 (Chairman, Semiconductor and Surface Physics Sub-Committee, 1979-82). Recreations: tennis; reading crime novels; garden and house maintenance. Address: Department of Physics and Astronomy, The University, Glasgow G12 8QQ; T.-0141-330 5388.

Fewson, Emeritus Professor Charles Arthur, OBE, BSc, PhD, FRSE, FIBiol, FRSA. Emeritus Professor, Glasgow University (Director, Institute of Biomedical and Life Sciences, 1994-2000); b. 8.9.37, Selby, Yorkshire; m., Margaret C.R. Moir; 2 d. Educ. Hymers College, Hull; Nottingham University; Bristol University. Research Fellow, Cornell University, New York, 1961-63; Department of Biochemistry, Glasgow University: Assistant Lecturer, 1963-64, Lecturer, 1964-68, Senior Lecturer, 1968-79, Reader, 1979-82; Professor, 1982-94. Address: (h.) Branxholm, Trinity Lane, Innellan, Dunoon PA23 7SP; T.-01369 830059.

Field, Christopher David Steadman, MA, DPhil, ARCM. Hon. Fellow, Faculty of Music, Edinburgh University; b. 27.4.38, Frimley; m., Elizabeth Ann. Educ. Winchester College Choir School; Radley College; New College, Oxford. Lecturer in Music, St. Andrews University, 1974-76, Senior Lecturer, 1976-87; Senior Lecturer in Music, Edinburgh University, 1987-95, Dean, Faculty of Music, 1993-95; Associate Director, Scottish Early Music Consort, 1979-98; Member, Governing Board, RSAMD, 1973-82; Hon. Music Adviser, Scottish Arts Council, since 1996. Recreation: gardening. Address: (h.) 2 Maynard Road, St. Andrews KY16 8RX.

Fife, 3rd Duke of (James George Alexander Bannerman Carnegie); b. 23.9.29; m., Hon. Caroline Cecily Dewar (m. diss.); 1 s.; 1 d. Educ. Gordonstoun. National Service, Scots Guards, Malaya, 1948-50; Royal Agricultural College; Clothworkers' Company and Freeman, City of London; President, ABA, 1959-73; Vice Patron, ABA, 1973-94; Ships President, HMS Fife, 1964-87; a Vice-Patron, Braemar Royal Highland Society; a Vice-President, British Olympic Association. Address: Elsick House, Stonehaven, Kincardineshire AB39 3NT.

Findlay, David J., BSc (Hons), MB, ChB, FRCPsych. Consultant Psychiatrist, Tayside Primary Care NHS Trust, since 1991; part-time Policy Adviser, Care of the Elderly, Scottish Executive Health Department, 1998-2001, Departmental Specialty Adviser in Psychiatry (Old Age), since 2001; Honorary Senior Lecturer, Department of Psychiatry, Dundee University, since 1991; b. 2.6.54, Duns; m., Patricia; 1 s.; 3 d. Educ. Ayr Academy; Glasgow University. Junior House Officer, 1979-80; Gartnavel Royal Hospital Training Scheme, 1980-83; Lecturer in Psychiatry, Dundee University, 1984-87; Consultant Psychiatrist and Clinical Tutor, Gartnavel Royal Hospital, 1987-91; Royal Dundee Liff Hospital: Service Manager, Old Age Psychiatry, 1993-1996, Clinical Director, Elderly Services, 1996-99, Secretary, Old Age Section, RCPsych Scottish Division, since 1998. Recreations: chess; reading; films. Address: (b.) Gowrie House, Royal Dundee Liff Hospital, Dundee DD2 5NF; T.-01382 423105; e-mail: david.findlay@tpct.scot.nhs.uk

Findlay, Donald Russell, QC, LLB (Hons), MPhil, FRSA. Advocate, since 1975; former Lord Rector, St. Andrews University; b. 17.3.51, Cowdenbeath; m., Jennifer E.

Borrowman. Educ. Harris Academy, Dundee; Dundee University; Glasgow University. Sometime Lecturer in Commercial Law, Heriot-Watt University. Recreations: Glasgow Rangers FC; Egyptology; archaeology; wine; ethics; travelling first class. Address: (b.) Advocates Library, Parliament House, Parliament Square, Edinburgh EH1 1RF; T.-0131-226 2881; e-mail: donaldrfin@aol.com

Findlay, Johan, JP. Honorary Sheriff, since 1995; Member, Parole Board for Scotland; b. 30.9.52, Ayr; m., David Gibson Findlay; 2 s.; 2 d. Educ. St. Joseph's Convent, Girvan. Chairman: Nithsdale Justices Committee, 1991-98, Dumfries Branch, Scottish Association for the Study of Delinquency, 1993-2000, Training Committee of the District Courts Association, 1995-96, Dumfries and Galloway Justices Committee, 1997-98; President, Lockerbie Little Theatre, 1990-96. Publication: All Manner of People (history of the JP in Scotland). Recreations: books; theatre. Address: (h.) The Birks, Watchhill Road, Lochmaben, Dumfries DG11 1RX; T.-01387 810911.

Findlay, Richard. Group Chief Executive, Scottish Radio Holdings Plc; b. 5.11.43; m., Elspeth; 2 s.; 1 d. Educ. Royal Scottish Academy of Music and Drama. Broadcasting Service of Saudi Arabia; Central Office of Information; Capital Radio; Radio Forth Ltd; Scottish Radio Holdings Plc. Recreations: music; golf; boating. Address: (b.) Scottish Radio Holdings Plc, Clydebank Business Park, Clydebank, Glasgow, G81 2RX; T.-0141 565 2202.

Findlay, Richard Martin, LLB, NP. Entertainment and Media Law Partner, Tods Murray WS, Edinburgh, since 1990; b. 18.12.51, Aberdeen. Educ. Gordon Schools, Huntly; Aberdeen University. Trained, Wilsone & Duffus, Advocates, Aberdeen; Legal Assistant, Commercial Department, Maclay Murray & Spens, Glasgow and Edinburgh, 1975-78; Partner, Ranken & Reid SSC, Edinburgh, 1979-90. Member: International Association of Entertainment Lawyers, International Entertainment and Multimedia Law and Business Network, The Writers' Guild, Scottish Media Lawyers Society, Business in the Arts Placement Scheme, Theatrical Management Association, BAFTA Scotland Committe; Trustee, Peter Darrell Trust; former Managing Editor, i2i (The Business Journal of the International Film Industry); Company Secretary: Gay Men's Health Ltd., Edinburgh International Jazz and Blues Festival, Moonstone International Ltd.; Director: Royal Lyceum Theatre Company Ltd., Lothian Gay and Lesbian Switchboard Ltd., Audio Description Film Fund Ltd. Recreations: music; theatre; opera; cinema. Address: (b.) 66 Queen Street, Edinburgh EH2 4NE; T.-0131-226 4771.

Finlay, Robert Derek, BA, MA, FInstD, FRSA, MCIM. Chairman, Dawson International PLC, 1995-98; b. 16.5.32, London; m., Una Ann Grant; 2 s.; 1 d. Educ. Kingston Grammar School; Emmanuel College, Cambridge. Lt., Gordon Highlanders, 1950-52; Mobil Oil Co. UK, 1953-61; Associate, Principal, Director, McKinsey & Co., 1961-79; Managing Director, H.J. Heinz Co. Ltd., 1979-81; Senior Vice-President, World HQ, H.J. Heinz Co., 1981-93. Member, London Committee, Scottish Council Development and Industry, since 1975; Member: Board, US China Business Council, 1983-93, Board, Pittsburgh Public Theatre, 1986-93, US Korea Business Council, 1986-92, Board, Pittsburgh Symphony Society, 1989-93; Vice Chairman, World Affairs Council of Pittsburgh, 1986-93; Chairman, Board, Visitors Center for International Studies, University of Pittsburgh, 1989-93. Recreations: tennis; rowing; music; theatre. Address: (h.) Grantully Castle, by Aberfeldy, PH15 2EG.

Finlayson, Niall Diarmid Campbell, OBE, MBChB, PhD, FRCP, FRCPE, FRCSE. Consultant Physician, Royal Infirmary of Edinburgh, since 1973; President, Royal College of Physicians of Edinburgh, since 2001 (Vice-

President, 1999-2000); b. 21.4.39, Georgetown, Guyana; m., Dale Kristin Anderson; 1 s.; 1 d. Educ. Loretto School, Musselburgh; Edinburgh University. Lecturer in Therapeutics, Edinburgh University, 1966-69; Assistant Professor of Medicine, Cornell University Medical College, New York Hospital, USA, 1970-72. Recreations: history; music. Address: (b.) Royal College of Physicians of Edinburgh, 9 Queen Street, Edinburgh; T.-0131-247 3638; e-mail: n.finlayson.rcpe.ac.uk

Finn, Anthony, MA (Hons), FEIS (1997). Rector, St. Andrew's High School, Kirkcaldy, since 1988; b. 4.6.51, Irvine; m., Margaret Caldwell. Educ. St. Joseph's Academy, Kilmarnock; Glasgow University. Teacher, Principal Teacher, Assistant Head Teacher, Depute Head Teacher, Acting Head Teacher, St. Andrew's Academy, Saltcoats, 1975-88. Member: General Teaching Council (Convener, Education Committee); Chair, SEED Memorandum Committee, 1991-2001; Member, Advisory Committee, Scottish Qualification for Headship; formerly: Member, Catholic Education Commission for Scotland, Teachers' Representative, National Committee for the Staff Development of Teachers, Governor, Moray House Institute of Education, Assessor, Teacher Education, Scottish Higher Education Funding Council, former Chair, Fife Secondary Head Teachers Association. Recreations: sport; travel; literature; current affairs. Address: (h.) 1 Blair Place, Kirkcaldy KY2 5SQ; T.-01592 640109.

Finnie, James Ross, CA. MSP (Liberal Democrat), West of Scotland, since 1999; Minister for Environment and Rural Development, Scottish Executive, since 2000 (Minister for Rural Affairs, 1999-2000); b. 11.2.47, Greenock; m., Phyllis Sinclair; 1 s.; 1 d. Educ. Greenock Academy. Member, Executive Committee, Scottish Council (Development and Industry), 1976-87; Chairman: Scottish Liberal Party, 1982-86, Scottish Liberal Democrats General Election Campaign, 1997; Member: Inverclyde District Council, 1977-97, Inverclyde Council, 1995-99. Address: (h.) 91 Octavia Terrace, Greenock PA16 7PY; T.-01475 631495.

Firth, Professor William James, BSc, PhD, CPhys, FInstP, FRSE. Freeland Professor of Natural Philosophy Strathclyde University (Head, Department of Physics and Applied Physics, since 2001); b. 23.2.45, Holm, Orkney; m., Mary MacDonald Anderson; 2 s. Educ. Perth Academy; Edinburgh University; Heriot-Watt University. Lecturer to Reader, Physics, Heriot-Watt University, 1967-85. Fellow, Optical Society of America. Recreation: sports (Edinburgh University Hockey Blue, 1967-68). Address: (b.) John Anderson Building, 107 Rottenrow, Glasgow G4 0NG.

Fisher, Archie. Folk singer, guitarist, composer, broadcaster; b. 1939, Glasgow. First solo album, 1966; presenter, Travelling Folk, BBC Radio; Artistic Director, Edinburgh International Folk Festival, 1988-92.

Fisher, Gregor. Actor (television, theatre, film). Credits include (BBC TV): Rab C. Nesbitt series (leading role), Naked Video series, Scotch and Wry, Para Handy. Best Actor award, Toronto Festival, for One, Two, Three.

Fisher, Kenneth Holmes, BA, ACIS, MCIM, DipABCC. Depute Principal, North Glasgow College, since 1987; b. 19.3.41, Glasgow. Educ. Hillhead High School, Glasgow. Administrative appointments, Colvilles Ltd., 1957-67; Lecturer and Senior Lecturer, Anniesland College, Glasgow, 1967-75; Head: Department of Business Studies, Cumbernauld College, 1975-80, Department of Commerce, Anniesland College, Glasgow, 1980-86. Address: (b.) 110 Flemington Street, Glasgow G21 4BX; T.-0141-558 9001.

Fisher, Mark, BA. Editor, The List, since 2000; b. 13.7.64, Bromborough; m., Jane Ellis; 1 s.; 1 d. Educ. Wirral Grammar School; University of Kent at Canterbury. Joined The List as Production Co-ordinator,

1987; Managing Editor and Founder, Theatre Scotland, 1992-95; Chief Theatre Critic, The Herald, 1996-2000. Publication: Made in Scotland, play anthology (Editor), 1995. Address: (b.) 14 High Street, Edinburgh EH1 1TE; T.-0131-550 3071.

Fitton, Professor John Godfrey, BSc, PhD, FGS, FRSE. Professor of Igneous Petrology, Edinburgh University, since, 1999; b. 1.10.46, Rochdale; m., Dr Christine Ann Fitton; 2 s.; 1 d. Educ. Bury Grammar School; Durham University. Turner and Newall Research Fellow, Manchester University, 1971-72; Edinburgh University: Lecturer, 1972-89; Senior Lecturer, 1989-94; Reader, 1994-99; served on NERC, Research Grants and ODP Committees; Co-Chief Scientist, Ocean Drilling Programme Leg 192, 2000. Publications: Alkaline Igneous Rocks (ed. with B.G.J. Upton). Recreations: house restoration; walking; wine; old maps. Address: (b.) Department of Geology and Geophysics, Edinburgh University, West Mains Road, Edinburgh, EH9 3JW; T.-0131-650 8529; e-mail: Godfrey.Fitton@glg.ed.ac.uk

Fitzgerald, Professor Alexander Grant, BSc, PhD, DSc, CPhys, FInstP, FRSE. Head, Department of Electronic Engineering and Physics, and Harris Professor of Physics, Dundee University, since 1992; b. 12.10.39, Dundee; m., June; 1 s.; 2 d. Educ. Perth Academy; Harris Academy; St. Andrews University; Cambridge University. Research Fellow, Lawrence Berkeley Laboratory, University of California; Lecturer, Senior Lecturer, Reader, Professor, Dundee University. Publications: 160 conference and journal papers; book: Quantitative Microbeam Analysis (Co-editor). Recreations: swimming; golf. Address: (b.) Department of Electronic Engineering and Physics, Dundee University, Dundee, DD1 4HN; T.-01382 344553; e-mail: a.g.fitzgerald@dundee.ac.uk

Fitzpatrick, Brian, MSP. Labour MSP, Strathkelvin and Bearsden, since 2001; b. 9.6.61; m., Marie Macdonald; 1 s.; 2 d. Educ. Glasgow University. Called to Scottish Bar, 1993; Solicitor, Glasgow, Edinburgh and London, 1984-92; Head of Policy, First Minister's Policy Unit, Scottish Parliament, 1999-2000. Address: (b.) Scottish Parliament, Edinburgh EH99 1SP.

FitzRoy, Professor Felix R., BSc, MSc, PhD. Professor of Economics, St Andrews University; Member, Editorial Boards, Small Business Economics, Economic Analysis; b. 17.8.38, London; m., Renate; 1 s.; 1 d. Educ. University College, London; Aberdeen University. Lecturer, Economics Department, Heidelberg University; Research Fellow, Science Centre, Berlin; Visiting Professor, European University Institute, Florence. Publication (book): Management and Economics of Organization (Co-author), 1998. Recreations: cycling; philosophy; ecology; cosmology. Address: (b.) Department of Economics, St Andrews University, St Andrews KY16 9AL; T.-01334 462437; e-mail: frf@st-andrews.ac.uk

Fladmark, Professor Emeritus, (Jahn) Magnus, DA(Edin), DipTP, CertHort, HonFRIAS. Professor Emeritus, Robert Gordon University, since 2002; Founding Executive Director and Trustee, The Heyerdahl Institute, Norway; b. 12.2.37, Romsdal, Norway; m., Caroline Ashton Miller; 1 s.; 3 d. Educ. Gjermundnes Agricultural College; Ulvestad Commercial College; Hamar Cathedral School; Military College; Edinburgh College of Art. Press Photographer, 1953-55; National Service, Norwegian Army, 1957-58; PSV Conductor, Scottish Omnibuses, 1959-61; Architect, Moira and Moira, 1964-66; Research Fellow, Edinburgh College of Art, 1966-67; Planning Officer, Scottish Office, 1967-70; Lecturer and ODA Programme Director, Edinburgh University, 1970-76; Head of Research and Development, Countryside Commission for Scotland, 1976-92; Director, Robert Gordon University

Heritage Unit, 1992-2002, Professor in Heritage Management, 1994. Chairman, Royal Town Planning Institute (Scotland), 1981-82; Governor, Edinburgh College of Art, 1982-88; Council Member, Saltire Society, 1984-88; Chairman, Scottish Interagency Liaison Group, 1987-90; Founding Chairman, Countryside Around Towns Forum, 1989-91; Convener, Scottish Forum on the Environment, 1989-92; MOD UK Committee on Environmental Matters, 1989-92; Assessor, Loch Lomond Park Authority, Scottish Wildlife Trust and Central Scotland Countryside Trust, 1990-92; Trustee, Sir Patrick Geddes Memorial Trust, since 1991; Visiting Lecturer, Chinese Society of Rural Development Planning, Taichung, Taiwan, 1994; External Examiner, Plymouth University, since 2001; Glenfiddich Living Scotland Award, 1986; Fladmark of Fladmark, since 1981. Publications: The Countryside Around Towns, 1988; The Mountain Areas of Scotland: Conservation and Management (Co-Author), 1990; Tomorrow's Architectural Heritage: Landscape and Buildings in the Countryside (Co-Author), 1991; Heritage: Conservation, Interpretation and Enterprise (Editor), 1993; The SYHA Environmental Chapter: Enjoying the Great Outdoors and the Cultural Riches of Scotland (Co-Author), 1994; The Wealth of a Nation: Heritage as a Cultural and Competitive Asset, 1994; Cultural Tourism (Editor), 1994; Sharing the Earth: Local Identity in Global Culture (Editor), 1995; In Search of Heritage as Pilgrim or Tourist? (Editor), 1998; Heritage and Museums: Shaping National Identity (Editor), 2000; Heritage and Identity: Shaping the Nations of the North (Editor), 2002. Recreations: Norse history; architecture as a cultural phenomenon; fighting personal ignorance. Address: (b.) Scott Sutherland School, Robert Gordon University, Aberdeen AB10 7QB; T.-01224 263700; e-mail: mfladmark@hotmail.com

Flanagan, Andrew, BAcc, CA. Chief Executive, SMG plc, since 1997; b. 15.3.56, Glasgow; m., Virginia; 2 s.; 1 d. Educ. Hillhead High School; Glasgow University. Trainee Accountant, Touche Ross, 1976-79; Senior Auditor, Price Waterhouse, Brussels, 1979-81; Manager of Financial Control, ITT Inc., Brussels, 1981-86; Finance Director, PA Consulting, London, 1987-91; Group Finance Director, BIS Group, London, 1991-93; Group Finance Director, then Managing Director, Scottish Television, 1993-97. Recreations: golf; skiing. Address: (b.) 200 Renfield Street, Glasgow G2 3PR; T.-0141-300 3089.

Flanagan, Caroline Jane, LLB, DipLP, NP. Partner, Ross & Connel, Solicitors, Dunfermline, since 1990; Member, Council, Law Society of Scotland, since 1998; b. 12.1.61, Bridge of Allan; m., Roy Flanagan; 1 s.; 1 d. Educ. Dollar Academy; Edinburgh University. Trainee, then Assistant Solicitor, Edinburgh, 1982-87; Assistant, then Partner, Ross and Connel, since 1988; accredited as specialist in family law, since 1996; Dean, local Faculty of Solicitors, 1998-2000. Address: (b.) 10 Viewfield Terrace, Dunfermline, KY12 7JH; T.-01383 721156.

Fleck, Professor James, MA, BSc, MSc. Chair of Organisation of Industry and Commerce, University of Edinburgh, since 1996 (Director, University of Edinburgh Management School, 1996-99); b. 18.7.51, Kano, Nigeria; m., Heather Anne Morrison; 2 s.; 3 d. Educ. Perth Academy; University of Edinburgh; Manchester University. Engineer, MK-Shand, Invergordon, 1974-75; Computer Programmer, CAP Limited, London, 1976; Research Fellow and Lecturer, Technology Policy Unit, University of Aston, 1980-85; Lecturer in Operations Management, Heriot-Watt University, 1985-86; Lecturer, then Senior Lecturer, Department of Business Studies, University of Edinburgh, 1986-96. Joseph Lister Lecturer for the Social Sciences, British Association for the Advancement of Science, 1995-96. Publications: Expertise and Innovation – Information Technology Strategies in the Financial Services Sector (Joint Author), 1994; Exploring Expertise (Joint Editor), 1998. Recreations: reading; DIY; windsurfing;

eating out. Address: (h.) Grange Park House, 38 Dick Place, Edinburgh EH9 2JB; T.-0131-667 3176.

Fleetwood, Gordon, LLB, NP, WS. Partner, Fleetwood & Robb, Solicitors, since 1986; Solicitor-Advocate, since 1994; b. 3.10.51, Elgin; m., Jean Arthur; 2 d. Educ. Elgin Academy; University of Edinburgh. Recreations: fishing; curling. Address: (b.) 11 Queensgate, Inverness IV1 1DF; T.-01463 226232.

Fleming, Archibald Macdonald, KSJ, MA, BCom, PhD, FRSA. Director of Lifelong Learning, Strathclyde University, since 1987 (Director, Management Development Programmes, Strathclyde Business School, 1984-87); Lecturer, Department of Information Science, Strathclyde University, since 1968; Consultant on Management Training and Development, since 1970; b. 19.6.36, Glasgow; m., Joan Moore; 1 s.; 1 d. Educ. Langholm Academy; Dumfries Academy; Edinburgh University. W. & T. Avery, 1961-63; IBM (UK) Ltd., 1963-64; Sumlock Comptometer Ltd., 1964-68; Consultancies: Scottish Co-operative Wholesale Society, 1969, Hotel and Catering Industry Training Board, 1971, Scottish Engineering Employers Association, 1973. Member: Strathclyde Children's Panel, Committee on Food Processing Opportunities in Scotland, Scottish Council (Development and Industry), Vice-President, Royal Philosophical Society of Glasgow, since 1998, International Vocational Education and Training Association, Church of Scotland Education Committee, American Association of Adult and Continuing Education; Vice-Chairman, Universities Council for Adult and Continuing Education (Scotland), since 1990. Publication: Collins Business Dictionary (with B. McKenna). Recreation: reading, observing and talking on Scotland and the Scots. Address: (b.) 40 George Street, Glasgow G1 1QE; e-mail: a.m.fleming@strath.ac.uk

Fleming, Professor George, BSc, PhD, FREng, FRSE, FICE, FASCE. Professor of Civil Engineering, Strathclyde University, since 1985, and Managing Director of Envirocentre, since 1995; Non-Executive Director, WRAP; b. 16.8.44, Glasgow; m., Irene Fleming; 2 s.; 1 d. Educ. Knightswood Secondary School, Glasgow; Strathclyde University; Stanford University, California. Research Assistant, Strathclyde University, 1966-69; Stanford University, 1967; Senior Research Hydrologist, Hydrocomp International, California, 1969-70; Research Associate, Stanford University, 1969-70; Director and Vice President, Hydrocomp International, Palo Alto and Glasgow, 1970-79; Lecturer, then Senior Lecturer, then Reader in Civil Engineering, Strathclyde University, 1971-85; Visiting Professor, University of Padova, Italy, since 1980; Vice Dean, Engineering Faculty, Strathclyde University, 1984-87. President, Institution of Civil Engineers, 1999-00; Member, Scottish Exports Forum. Publications: Computer Simulation in Hydrology, 1975; The Sediment Problem, 1977; Deterministic Models in Hydrology, 1979. Recreations: farming; fishing; food. Address: (b.) John Anderson Building, 107 Rottenrow, Glasgow G4 0NG; T.-0141-553 4169; e-mail: g.fleming@strath.ac.uk

Fleming, Maurice. Editor, The Scots Magazine, 1974-91; b. Blairgowrie; m., Nanette Dalgleish; 2 s.; 1 d. Educ. Blairgowrie High School. Trained in hotel management before entering journalism; worked on various magazines; has had five full-length plays performed professionally, as well as one-act plays by amateurs; founder Member: Traditional Music and Song Association of Scotland, Scottish Poetry Library; Past Chairman, Blairgowrie, Rattray and District Civic Trust; Past Chairman, Blair in Bloom. Publications: The Scots Magazine — A Celebration of 250 Years (Co-Editor); The Ghost O' Mause and Other Tales and Traditions of East Perthshire; Old Blairgowrie and Rattray; The Real Macbeth and Other Stories from Scottish History; The Sidlaws: Tales, Traditions and

Ballads. Recreations: walking; reading; bird-watching; enjoying the countryside; folksong and folklore. Address: (h.) Craigard, Perth Road, Blairgowrie; T.-Blairgowrie 873633.

Fleming, Tom, CVO, OBE. Actor and Director; b. 29.6.27, Edinburgh. Professional theatre debut, 1945, in company led by Edith Evans; Co-Founder, Edinburgh Gateway Company, 1953; joined Royal Shakespeare Company at Stratford upon Avon, 1962, and played several classical roles, including Prospero, Brutus, Cymbeline, Buckingham and Kent; toured with RSC in USSR, USA and Europe, 1964; Director and Founder, Royal Lyceum Theatre Company, 1965; there played title role in Galileo; Director, Scottish Theatre Company, 1982-87; awarded Roman Szlydowski Prize for his production of The Thrie Estaites, Warsaw, 1986; TV work includes portrayals of Robert Burns, William Wallace, Jesus of Nazareth, Henry IV, Weir of Hermiston, and Sir John Reith; films include Mary, Queen of Scots, King Lear, Meetings with Remarkable Men; Radio and television commentator, including Coronation, Silver Jubilee celebrations, Cenotaph service 1965-99, VE and VJ Day 50th anniversaries, ten royal and state funerals including that of Diana, Princess of Wales, Edinburgh Military Tattoo, since 1966; Hon. Member, Saltire Society, Royal Scottish Pipers' Society, Scottish Arts Club. Andrew Fletcher of Saltoun Award for Services to Scotland, 2000. Publications: So That Was Spring; Miracle at Midnight; Voices Out of the Air (Editor); It's My Belief; BBC Book of Memories; A Scottish Childhood, Volume II (Contributor). D.Univ (Heriot-Watt); D.Litt (Queen Margaret University College); FRSAMD.

Fletcher, Sheriff Michael John, LLB. Sheriff of Tayside Central and Fife at Perth, since 2000; b. 5.12.45, Dundee; m., Kathryn Mary; 2 s. Educ. High School of Dundee; St. Andrews University. Partner, Ross Strachan & Co., 1970-88; Partner, Miller Hendry (Hendry and Fenton), 1988-94; Part-time Lecturer in Civil and Criminal Procedure, University of Dundee, 1974-94; Legal Aid Reporter, 1978-94; Temporary Sheriff, 1991-94; Sheriff of South Strathclyde Dumfries & Galloway at Dumfries, 1994-99; Sheriff of Lothian and Borders at Edinburgh, 1999-2000; Editor, Scottish Civil Law Reports, since 1999. Publication: Delictual Damages (Co-Author). Recreations: golf; gardening.

Fletcher, Professor Roger, MA, PhD, FIMA, FRSE. Professor of Optimization, Department of Mathematics, Dundee University, since 1984; b. 29.1.39, Huddersfield; m., Mary Marjorie Taylor; 2 d. Educ. Huddersfield College; Cambridge University; Leeds University. Lecturer, Leeds University, 1963-69; Principal Research Fellow, then Principal Scientific Officer, AERE Harwell, 1969-73; Senior Research Fellow, then Senior Lecturer, then Reader, Dundee University, 1973-84. Publications: Practical Methods of Optimization, 2nd edition, 1987. numerous others. Recreations: hill-walking; music; bridge. Address: (h.) 43 Errol Road, Invergowrie, Dundee DD2 5BX; T.-01382 562452.

Flett, Ian Stark, CBE (1984), MA, MEd, ABPS; b. 26.1.20, Aberdeen; m., Moyra. Educ. Aberdeen Grammar School; Aberdeen University; Aberdeen College of Education. RAF, Signals and Intelligence Branch, 1940-46; Teacher, Aberdeen, 1947-49; Adviser, Durham, 1949-54; Assistant Education Officer, Preston, 1954-59; Deputy Education Officer, Southport, 1959-63; Deputy Education Officer, City of Hull, 1963-66; Member, Dalegacy Institute of Education, Hull University, 1963-66; Director of Education, Fife, 1966-85; General Secretary, Association of Directors of Education in Scotland, 1975-85; President, 1979-80; Adviser to Association of County Councils, 1970-74; Principal Adviser, Convention of Scottish Local Authorities, 1975-84; Member: Consultative Committee on the Curriculum, 1977-87, General Teaching Council, 1976-

84; Governor, Craiglockhart College of Education, 1977-83; Chairman: Scottish Association of Educational Management and Administration, 1981-84, Scottish Centre for Tuition of the Disabled, 1980-89, National Association for Gifted Children Scotland, 1985-93. Publication: The Years of Growth 1945-75, 1989. Recreations: music; gardening. Address: (h.) 5 Townsend Place, Kirkcaldy, Fife KY1 1HB; T.-01592 260279.

Flint, Professor David, TD, MA, BL, CA. Professor of Accountancy, Glasgow University, 1964-85 (Vice-Principal, 1981-85); b. 24.2.19, Glasgow; m., Dorothy Mary Maclachlan Jardine; 2 s.; 1 d. Educ. High School of Glasgow; Glasgow University. Royal Signals, 1939-46 (Major; mentioned in Despatches); Partner, Mann Judd Gordon & Company, Chartered Accountants, Glasgow, 1951-71; Lecturer (part-time), Glasgow University, 1950-60; Dean, Faculty of Law, 1971-73. Council Member, Scottish Business School, 1971-77; Institute of Chartered Accountants of Scotland: President, 1975-76, Vice-President, 1973-75, Convener, Research Advisory Committee, 1974-75 and 1977-84, Convener, Working Party on Future Policy, 1976-79, Convener, Public Sector Committee, 1987-89, Convener, Taxation Review and Research Sub-Committee, 1960-64; Trustee, Scottish Chartered Accountants Trust for Education, 1981-87; Member: Management Training and Development Committee, Central Training Council, 1966-70, Management and Industrial Relations Committee, Social Science Research Council, 1970-72 and 1978-80, Social Sciences Panel, Scottish Universities Council on Entrance, 1968-72; Chairman, Association of University Teachers of Accounting, 1969; Member, Company Law Committee, Law Society of Scotland, 1976-85; Scottish Economic Society: Treasurer, 1954-62, Vice-President, 1977-88, Hon. Vice-President, 1988-99; Member, Commission for Local Authority Accounts in Scotland, 1978-80; President, European Accounting Association, 1983-84. Publication: Philosophy and Principles of Auditing, 1988. Recreation: golf. Address: (h.) 16 Grampian Avenue, Auchterarder, Perthshire PH3 1NY; T.-01764 663978.

Flockhart, (David) Ross, OBE, BA, BD, D.Univ; b. 20.3.27, Newcastle, NSW, Australia; m., Pamela Ellison Macartney; 3 s.; 1 d.; 1 d. (deceased). Educ. Knox Grammar School, Sydney; Sydney University; Edinburgh University. Royal Australian Engineers, 1945-46; Chaplain to Overseas Students, Edinburgh, 1955-58; Parish Minister (Church of Scotland), Northfield, Aberdeen, 1958-63; Warden, Carberry Tower, Musselburgh, 1963-66; Lecturer and Senior Lecturer, School of Community Studies, Moray House College of Education, 1966-72; Director, Scottish Council for Voluntary Organisations, 1972-91. Member: Scottish Arts Council, 1976-82, Court, Stirling University, 1989-98, Council, National Trust for Scotland, 1995-2000; former Trustee and Vice-Chairman, Community Development Foundation. Recreations: gardening; sailing. Address: (h.) Longwood, Humbie, East Lothian EH36 5PN; T.-01875 833208; e-mail: rossflock@ednet.co.uk

Flowerdew, Stuart Alan, LLB(Hons), DipLP, NP. Solicitor; Partner, Flowerdew Allan, solicitors, Peterhead, since 1999; Secretary and Treasurer, Faculty of Solicitors in Peterhead and Fraserburgh, since 1993; Chairman, Victim Support, Aberdeenshire, since 2000; b. 5.2.67, Kings Lynn; m., Natalie Anne Lamb. Educ. Forres Academy; University of Dundee. Trainee/Assistant, Miller Hendry, Perth, 1989-92; Assistant: Stewart and Watson, Peterhead, 1992-94, Masson & Glennie, Peterhead, 1994-96; Associate, John MacRitchie & Co., SSC, Peterhead, 1997-1999. Recreation: cricket. Address: (b.) 2 Kirk Street, Peterhead; T.-01779 481717; (h.) Kildare, 114 Queen Street, Peterhead; T.-01779 473117.

Flyn, Derek, LLB, NP, FSAScot. Solicitor in private practice, since 1977; Partner, Macleod and MacCallum, since 1978; b. 22.8.45, Edinburgh; m., Fiona Mairi

Macmillan; 2 s.; 1 d. Educ. Broughton School, Edinburgh; Dundee University. Scottish Court Service, 1962-72 (Sheriff Clerk Depute at Portree, 1967-70); accredited by Law Society of Scotland as specialist in crofting law since 1993; Council Member, Scottish Law Agents Society, since 1993 (President, 1999-2000); Vice-Chairman, Crofting Law Group, since 1994. Publications: Crofting Law (Co-author), 1990; Green's Annotated Crofters Act (Co-author), 1993. Recreations: music; walking; reading; writing. Address: (b.) 28 Queensgate, Inverness IV1 1YN; T.-01463 239393.

Follett, Professor Georgina Louise Patricia, MDes, FRSA, FCSD. Dean, Duncan of Jordanstone College (formerly Head, School of Design); b. 16.7.49, London; m., Adrian Franklin; 1 s.; 1 d. Educ. Channing School; Royal College of Art. Course Leader, Sir John Cass College, 1979-88; Acting Head, Grays School of Art, 1988-93; Jeweller (exhibitions include one woman show, Jewellery Gallery, Victoria and Albert Museum). Recreations: gardening; drawing; reading. Address: Duncan of Jordanstone College, Perth Road, Dundee DD1 4HT; T.-01382 345289.

Foot, Professor Hugh Corrie, BA, PhD, FBPsS. Professor of Psychology, Strathclyde University, since 1992, Vice-Dean (Research), Faculty of Arts and Social Sciences; b. 7.6.41, Northwood, Middx; m., Daryl M.; 1 s.; 1 d. Educ. Durham University; Queen's College, Dundee. Research Fellow, Dundee University, 1965-68; University of Wales Institute of Science and Technology: Lecturer, 1968-77, Senior Lecturer, 1977-88; Reader, University of Wales College of Cardiff, 1989-91. Recreations: tennis; hill walking. Address: Department of Psychology, Strathclyde University, 40 George Street, Glasgow, G1 1QE; T.-0141-552 4400, Ext. 2580; e-mail: h.foot@strath.ac.uk

Forbes, 22nd Lord (Nigel Ivan Forbes), KBE (1960), JP, DL. Premier Lord of Scotland; b. 19.2.18; m., Hon. Rosemary Katharine Hamilton-Russell; 2 s.; 1 d. Educ. Harrow; Sandhurst. Retired Major, Grenadier Guards; Military Assistant High Commissioner, Palestine, 1947-48; Representative Peer for Scotland, 1955-63; Minister of State, Scottish Office, 1958-59. Member: Scottish Committee, Nature Conservancy, 1961-67, Aberdeen and District Milk Marketing Board, 1962-72, Sports Council for Scotland, 1966-71; Chairman: River Don District Board, 1962-73, Scottish Branch, National Playing Fields Association, 1965-80, Rolawn Ltd., 1975-98, Alford Car Transport Service, since 2000; President: Royal Highland and Agricultural Society of Scotland, 1958-59, Scottish Scout Association, 1970-88; Deputy Chairman, Tennant Caledonian Breweries Ltd., 1964-74; Director: Grampian Television Ltd., 1960-88, Blenheim Travel Ltd., 1981-88. Address: (h.) Balforbes, Alford, Aberdeenshire AB33 8DR; T.-019755 62516.

Forbes, Alexander Douglas, MA, LLB. Chairman, Scottish Friendly Assurance Society Ltd., since 1996; Consultant (formerly Partner), Robertson Paul (Solicitors), Glasgow; b. 18.2.37, Glasgow; m., Rachel Mary; 1 s.; 2 d. Educ. High School of Glasgow; Glasgow University. Solicitor, since 1961. Recreations: curling; angling; walking. Address: (h.) 29 Tannoch Drive, Milngavie, Glasgow G62 8AR; T.-0141-956 3561; e-mail: dforbes358@aol.com

Forbes, Professor Charles Douglas, DSc, MD, MB, ChB, FRCP, FRCPGlas, FRCPEdin, FRSA, FRSE. Professor of Medicine, Dundee University, and Honorary Consultant Physician, Dundee Teaching Hospitals NHS Trust, since 1987; b. 9.10.38, Glasgow; m., Janette MacDonald Robertson; 2 s. Educ. High School of Glasgow; Glasgow University. Assistant Lecturer in Materia Medica, Glasgow University; Lecturer in Medicine, Makerere, Uganda; Registrar in Medicine, Glasgow Royal Infirmary; Reader in Medicine, Glasgow University; Fellow, American Heart Association; Fullbright Fellow; Director, Regional Haemophilia Centre, Glasgow. Recreation: gardening. Address: (h.) East Chattan, 108 Hepburn Gardens, St. Andrews KY16 9LT; T.-01334 472428.

Forbes, David Fraser, LLB (Hons). Regional Officer, Scottish Health Visitors' Association/UNISON; b. 11.4.56, Glasgow; m., Isabel Hamilton; 3 d. Educ. Greenock Academy; Edinburgh University. Porter, Royal Edinburgh Hospital, and Senior Shop Steward, NUPE, 1978-87; Diploma in Accountancy, Stirling University, 1987-88. Address: (b.) Douglas House, 60 Belford Road, Edinburgh, EH4 3UQ.

Forbes, Ronald Douglas, ARSA. Artist; Head of Painting, Duncan of Jordanstone College of Art, 1995-2001; b. 22.3.47, Braco; m., Sheena Henderson Bell; 1 s.; 2 d. Educ. Morrison's Academy, Crieff; Edinburgh College of Art. Leverhulme Senior Art Fellow, Strathclyde University, 1973-74; Head of Painting, Crawford School of Art, Cork, Ireland, 1974-78; Artist in Residence, Livingston, 1978-80; Scottish Arts Council Studio Residence Bursary, Amsterdam, 1980; Lecturer, Glasgow School of Art, 1979-83; Director, Master Fine Art postgraduate studies, Duncan of Jordanstone College of Art, University of Dundee, 1983-95; Artist in Residence, University of Tasmania Hobart Centre for the Arts. First Prize, first Scottish Young Contemporary Exhibition, 1967; BBC Scope Film Prize, 1975; RSA Guthrie Award, 1979; Scottish Arts Council Award for Film-making, 1979; Highland Society of London Award, Royal Scottish Academy, 1996. Recreations: cinema; theatre; gardening. Address: (h.) 13 Fort Street, Dundee DD2 1BS; T.-01382 641498.

Ford, Carole Louise, BSc, MSc, DipAdEduc. Head Teacher, Kilmarnock Academy, since 1997; b. Glasgow; m., Ian Ford; 1 s. Educ. Eastwood High School; Glasgow University; University of Wisconsin-Madison; Jordanhill College of Education. Mathematics Teacher until 1983; Principal Teacher, Mathematics, 1983-90; Assistant Head Teacher, Clydebank High School, 1990-94; Depute Head Teacher, Coatbridge High School, 1994-97; Chair, Scottish Secondary Mathematics Group, since 1997. Publications: Heinemann Higher Mathematics (co-author); Heinemann Mathematics for S1 to S4 Pupils (co-author). Recreations: knitting; reading; travel. Address: (b.) Kilmarnock Academy, Elmbank Drive, Kilmarnock; T.-01563 525509.

Ford, Gordon J.W., BA, DipEd. Principal, Inveralmond Community High School, Livingston, since 2001; b. 1.5.52, Inverkeithing; m., Audrey; 1 s.; 2 d. Educ. Kirkcaldy High School; Knox Academy; Stirling University. Teacher of History, Modern Studies, 1974-87; Assistant Headteacher, Greenhall High School, 1987-89; Depute Headteacher: Ainslie Park High School, 1989-91, Armadale Academy, 1991-93; Headmaster, Broughton High School, 1993-2001. Publication: Timetabling Explained. Recreations: coaching rugby; tennis; music; tai chi. Address: (b.) Inveralmond Community High School, Willowbank, Ladywell, Livingston EH54 6HN; T.-01506 438093; e-mail: Gordon.Ford@westlothian.org.uk

Ford, Professor Ian, BSc, PhD, FRCP (Glas), FRSE. Professor of Biostatistics and Director, Robertson Centre for Biostatistics, Glasgow University, since 1991, Dean, Faculty of Computing Science, Mathematics and Statistics, since 2000; b. 4.2.51, Glasgow; m., Carole Louise Ford; 1 s. Educ. Hamilton Academy; Glasgow University. Visiting Lecturer, University of Wisconsin, Madison, 1976-77; Lecturer, then Senior Lecturer, Reader, Personal Professor and Professor, Glasgow University, since 1977. Publications: 110 papers. Recreations: gardening; travel. Address: (b.) Robertson Centre for Biostatistics, Boyd Orr Building, Glasgow University, Glasgow; T.-0141-330 4744.

Ford, James Allan, CB, MC. Author; b. 10.6.20, Auchtermuchty; m., Isobel Dunnett; 1 s.; 1 d. Educ. Royal High School, Edinburgh; Edinburgh University. Employment Clerk, Ministry of Labour, 1938-39; Executive Officer, Inland Revenue, 1939-40; Captain, The Royal Scots, 1940-46 (POW, Far East, 1941-45); Executive Officer, Inland Revenue, 1946-47; Department of Agriculture for Scotland, 1947-66 (Assistant Secretary, 1958); Registrar General for Scotland, 1966-69; Under Secretary, Scottish Office, 1969-79. Trustee, National Library of Scotland, 1981-91. Publications (novels): The Brave White Flag, 1961; Season of Escape, 1963; A Statue for a Public Place, 1965; A Judge of Men, 1968; The Mouth of Truth, 1972. Recreation: gardening. Address: (h.) 6 Hillpark Court, Edinburgh EH4 7BE; T.-0131 336 5398.

Ford, John Noel Patrick, CStJ, FInstD. Director, Scottish Civic Trust; Chairman, Glasgow Committee, Order of St. John, since 1993; Trustee, New Lanark Conservation Trust, since 1994; Member, Council, Europa Nostra; Representative Member, Council, National Trust for Scotland; b. 18.12.35, Surbiton; m., Roslyn Madeleine Penfold; 2 s.; 2 d. Educ. Tiffin School, Kingston on Thames. Retired, 1992, as Chairman, Scotland and Northern Ireland, and Marketing Director, OCS Group Ltd. Deacon, Incorporation of Masons of Glasgow, 1985-86; Deacon Convener, Trades House of Glasgow, 1991-92; Regional Chairman, Glasgow, Princes Scottish Youth Business Trust, 1993-2001; Governor, Hutchesons' Educational Trust, 1986-2001; General Commissioner of Inland Revenue, Glasgow North. Recreations: golf and sport in general; gardening. Address: (b.) 42 Miller Street, Glasgow G1 1DT; T.-0141 221 1466.

Forrest, Professor Sir (Andrew) Patrick (McEwen), Kt (1986), BSc, MD, ChM, FRCS, FRCSEdin, FRCSGlas, FRCPEd, DSc (Hon), LLD (Hon), FACS (Hon), FRACS (Hon), FRCSCan (Hon), FRCR (Hon), FFPHM (Hon), FIBiol, FRSE. Professor Emeritus, Edinburgh University; Chairman, Scottish Cancer Foundation; b. 25.3.23, Mount Vernon, Lanarkshire; m., 1. Margaret Beryl Hall (deceased); 1s.; 1d.; 2. Margaret Anne Steward; 1 d. Educ. Dundee High School; St. Andrews University. House Surgeon, Dundee Royal Infirmary; Surgeon Lieutenant, RNVR; Mayo Foundation Fellow; Lecturer and Senior Lecturer, Glasgow University; Professor of Surgery, Welsh National School of Medicine; Regius Professor of Clinical Surgery, Edinburgh University; Visiting Scientist, National Cancer Institute, USA; Associate Dean of Clinical Studies, International Medical College, Malaysia; Chief Scientist (part-time), Scottish Home and Health Department, 1981-87; Chairman, Working Group, Breast Cancer Screening, 1985-86; President: Surgical Research Society, 1974-76, Association of Surgeons of Great Britain and Ireland, 1988-89; Lister Medal, Royal College of Surgeons of England, 1987; Member, Kirk Session, St. Giles Cathedral. Publications: Prognostic Factors in Breast Cancer (Co-author), 1968; Principles and Practice of Surgery (Co-author), 1985; Breast Cancer: the decision to screen, 1990. Recreations: sailing; golf. Address: (h.) 19 St. Thomas Road, Edinburgh EH9 2LR; T.-0131-667 3203.

Forrest, Robert Jack, OBE, FRAgS, DL. Chairman, Royal Scottish Agricultural Benevolent Institution, since 1996; Director, Scottish Agricultural College, since 1996; b. 4.1.39, Duns; m., Jennifer McCreath; 2 s.; 1 d. Educ. Loretto School; East of Scotland College of Agriculture. Director, Royal Highland & Agricultural Society of Scotland, 1979-95 (Hon. Treasurer, 1985-88, Chairman, 1989-90, Hon. Secretary 1991-95); President, British Simmental Cattle Society, 1983-84; President, Scottish Agricultural Arbiters Association, 1993-94; Director, Scottish Borders Enterprise, 1994-98; Director, Scottish SPCA, since 1998; Elder, Bonkyl Church. Address: (h.) Scotston Park, Hardens Road, Duns, Berwickshire.

Forrester, Rev. Professor Duncan Baillie, MA (Hons), BD, DPhil, HonDTheol (Iceland), HonDD (Glasgow and St. Andrews). Dean, Faculty of Divinity, New College, Edinburgh, 1996-00 (Principal, 1986-96), Professor of Christian Ethics and Practical Theology, 1978-2001, Director, Centre for Theology and Public Issues, 1984-2000; Church of Scotland Minister; b. 10.11.33, Edinburgh; m., Rev. Margaret McDonald; 1 s.; 1 d. Educ. Madras College, St. Andrews; St. Andrews University; Chicago University; Edinburgh University. Part-time Assistant in Politics, Edinburgh University, 1957-58; Assistant Minister, Hillside Church, Edinburgh, and Leader of St. James Mission, 1960-61; as Church of Scotland Missionary, Lecturer and then Professor of Politics, Madras Christian College, Tambaram, South India, 1962-70; ordained Presbyter, Church of South India, 1962; part-time Lecturer in Politics, Edinburgh University, 1966-67; Chaplain and Lecturer in Politics, Sussex University. Member, WCC Faith and Order Commission, 1983-96; President: Society for Study of Theology, 1991-93, Society for Study of Christian Ethics, 1991-94, Church Service Society, 1999-2001; Templeton UK Award, 1999. Publications: Caste & Christianity, 1980; Encounter with God (Co-author), 1983; Studies in the History of Worship in Scotland (Co-Editor), 1984; Christianity and the Future of Welfare, 1985; Theology and Politics, 1988; Just Sharing (Co-author), 1988; Beliefs, Values and Policies, 1989; Worship Now Book II (Co-editor), 1989; Theology and Practice (Editor), 1990; The True Church and Morality, 1997; Christian Justice and Public Policy, 1997; Truthful Action: Explorations in Practical Theology, 2000; On Human Worth: A Christian Vindication of Equality, 2001. Recreations: hill-walking; reading; listening to music. Address: (h.) 25 Kingsburgh Road, Edinburgh, EH12 6DZ; T.-0131-337 5646; e-mail: d.forrester@ed.ac.uk

Forrester, Frederick Lindsay, MA (Hons), DipEd, FEIS. Educational journalist and consultant; Depute General Secretary, Educational Institute of Scotland, 1992-2000; b. 10.2.35, Glasgow; 1 s.; 1 d. Educ. Victoria Drive Senior Secondary School, Glasgow; Glasgow University; Jordanhill College of Education. Teacher of English, Glasgow secondary schools, 1962-64; Teacher of English and General Studies, Coatbridge Technical College, 1964-67; Assistant Secretary, Educational Institute of Scotland, 1967-75, Organising Secretary, 1975-92. Recreations: walking; cycling; swimming; foreign travel. Address: (h.) 31 Glenbervie Grove, Dunfermline KY11 8TH; T.-01383 739013.

Forrester, Ian Stewart, QC, MA, LLB, MCL. Honorary Visiting Professor in European Law, Glasgow University, since 1991; Member, European Advisory Board, Tulane University Law School, since 1992; b. 13.1.45, Glasgow; m., Sandra Anne Therese Keegan; 2 s. Educ. Kelvinside Academy, Glasgow; Glasgow University; Tulane University of Louisiana. Admitted to Faculty of Advocates, 1972; admitted to Bar of State of NY, 1977; Queen's Counsel (Scotland), 1988; called to Bar, Middle Temple, 1996. Maclay, Murray & Spens, 1968-69; Davis Polk & Wardwell, 1969-72; Cleary Gottlieb Steen & Hamilton, 1972-81; established independent chambers, Brussels, 1981; Co-Founder, Forrester & Norall, 1981 (Forrester Norall & Sutton, 1989; White & Case/Forrester Norall & Sutton, 1998), practising before European Commission and Courts; Member, Blackstone Chambers, Temple, London. Chairman, British Conservative Association, Belgium, 1982-86; author of numerous papers on European law; Elder, St. Andrew's Church of Scotland, Brussels. Recreations: politics; wine; cooking; restoring old houses.

Forrester, Professor John V., MD (Hons), FRCS(Ed), FRCOphth, FRCS(G). Cockburn Professor of Ophthalmology, since 1984; Editor, British Journal of Ophthalmology, 1992-2000; b. 11.9.46, Glasgow; m., Anne Gray; 2 s.; 2 d. Educ. St. Aloysius College, Glasgow;

Glasgow University. Various hospital appointments, Glasgow, 1971-78; MRC Travelling Fellow, Columbia University, New York, 1976-77; Consultant Ophthalmologist, Southern General Hospital, 1979-83; Spinoza Professor, University of Amsterdam, 1997. Recreation: family. Address: (b.) Department of Ophthalmology, Aberdeen University, Aberdeen AB25 2ZD; T.-01224 553782.

Forrester, Rev. Margaret Rae, MA, BD. Minister, St. Michael's, Edinburgh, since 1980; b. 23.11.37, Edinburgh; m., Duncan B. Forrester; 1 s.; 1 d. Educ. George Watson's Ladies' College; Edinburgh University and New College. Assistant Pastor, Tambaram, Madras; Minister, Telscombe Cliffs URC, Sussex; Assistant Minister, St. George's West, Edinburgh; Chaplain, Napier College, Edinburgh. Convener, Board of World Mission and Unity, Church of Scotland, 1992-96; Moderator, Presbytery of Edinburgh, 2000-01. Recreation: gardening. Address: 25 Kingsburgh Road, Edinburgh EH12 6DZ; T.-0131-337 5646.

Forsyth of Drumlean, Rt. Hon. Lord (Michael Bruce Forsyth), PC, Kt, MA. MP (Conservative), Stirling, 1983-97; Secretary of State for Scotland, 1995-97; Vice Chairman, Investment Banking Europe, J.P. Morgan & Co., since 2000; b. 16.10.54, Montrose; m., Susan Jane; 1 s.; 2 d. Educ. Arbroath High School; St. Andrews University. National Chairman, Federation of Conservative Students, 1976; Member, Westminster City Council, 1978-83; Member, Select Committee on Scottish Affairs; Parliamentary Private Secretary to the Foreign Secretary, 1986-87; Chairman, Scottish Conservative Party, 1989-90; Parliamentary Under Secretary of State and Minister of State, Scottish Office, 1987-92; Minister of State, Department of Employment, 1992-94; Minister of State, Home Office, 1994-95. Director, Robert Fleming International Ltd., 1997-2000; Chairman, Aberfoyle Angling Protection Association; Member, Development Board, National Portrait Gallery; Member, Select Committee on Monetary Policy; Member, Scottish Advisory Network, Imperial Cancer Research Fund, 2000-01; Patron, Craighalbert Centre. Recreations: fishing; mountaineering; astronomy; gardening; art. Address: House of Lords, London SW1A 3PW.

Forsyth of That Ilk, Alistair Charles William, JP, KHS, FSCA, FSA Scot, FInstPet, CStJ. Baron of Ethie; Chief of the Name and Clan of Forsyth; b. 7.12.29; m., Ann Hughes; 4 s. Educ. St. Paul's School; Queen Mary College, London. Company Director; CStJ, 1982; KHS, 1992; Freeman of the City of London; Liveryman of the Scriveners Company. Recreations: Scottish antiquities. Address: (h.) Dundrennan, Falkland, Fife.

Forsyth, Alistair James Menteith, OStJ, MTheol, LLB, DipLP, FSAScot. Advocate, since 1995; b. 21.12.60, Calcutta; m., Isabelle Richer. Educ. Fettes College; St. Andrews University; Buckingham University; Edinburgh University; Inns of Court School of Law. Executive, publishing and insurance, 1983-86; called to English Bar, Inner Temple, 1990, Member, Lincolns Inn, 1991; employed Lindsays WS, 1992-94; qualified as Solicitor and Notary Public, 1993. Lt., Ayrshire (Earl of Carrick's Own) Yeomanry Sqn., Queen's Own Yeomanry, 1983-88, Inns of Court and City Yeomanry, 1988-90; Member, Committee, Heraldry Society of Scotland, 1983-86; Secretary, Angus Branch, Order of St. John, 1983-86. Recreations: heraldry; genealogy; history; wine. Address: Dundrennan, Horsemarket, Falkland, Fife KY15 7BG; T.-01337 858735.

Forsyth, Bill. Film Director and Script Writer; b. 1947, Glasgow. Films include: Gregory's Girl, 1981, Local Hero, 1983, Comfort and Joy, 1984, Housekeeping, 1988, Breaking In, 1990, Being Human, 1993; Gregory's Two Girls, 1999. BAFTA Awards: Best Screenplay, 1982, Best Director, 1983.

Forsyth, Janice, MA (Hons). Broadcaster; b. Glasgow. Educ. Glasgow High School for Girls; Glasgow University. Presenter, Janice Forsyth Show, Working Lives (Radio Scotland), Artists' Question Time (Radio 3); TV includes: Filmnight (C4), Don't Look Down, NB and Festival Cinema (all Scottish); Columnist; Scotsman/Scotland on Sunday. Board Member, Giant Productions. Recreations: cinema; travel; theatre.

Forsyth, Roderick Hugh (Roddy). Journalist; b. 22.9.53, Lennoxtown; m., Marian Charlotte Reilly; 2 d. Educ. Allan Glen's School, Glasgow. Journalist, D.C. Thomson & Co., 1972-74; Scottish Daily News, 1975; Editor, Carnoustie Times, 1976-77; Editor, What's On in Glasgow, 1978-79; Editor, Clyde Guide, 1979-80; Journalist, Glasgow Herald, 1980-81; Sunday Standard, 1982-83; freelance, since 1983; Scottish Football Correspondent: The Times, 1988-93, Daily and Sunday Telegraph, since 1993, BBC Radio Sport, since 1983, RTE Ireland, since 1988, Ireland on Sunday, since 1996. Publications: The Only Game, 1990; Fields of Green, 1996; Blue and True, 1996.

Forte, Professor A.D.M., LLB, MA. Professor of Commercial Law, Aberdeen University, since 1993; b. 9.5.49, Lower Largo; m.; 1 d. Educ. St Joseph's College, Dumfries; Edinburgh University. Lecturer, Glasgow University, 1977-80, Dundee University, 1981-84; Senior Lecturer, Edinburgh University, 1985-92. Recreations: fishing; sailing; coastal walking; reading. Address: (b.) School of Law, Aberdeen University, Aberdeen AB24 3UB; T.-01224 272414.

Forteath, John Wyllie. Leader, Dumfries and Galloway Council, since 1999; b. 7.10.48, Dumfries. Educ. Dumfries High School. Process worker, 1965-98; Councillor, since 1986; Provost of Dumfries, 1996-99; involved in various charitable and voluntary organisations; active trade unionist and Labour Party member. Recreations; fishing; reading. Address: (b.) 11 Parkhead Drive, Stoop, Dumfries, DG1 3BY; T.-01387 263659.

Forteviot, 4th Baron (John James Evelyn Dewar). Member, Queen's Bodyguard for Scotland (Royal Company of Archers); b. 5.4.38. Educ. Eton. Black Watch (RHR), 1956-58.

Forty, Professor Arthur John, CBE, BSc, PhD, DSc, LLD, DUniv, FRSE. Principal and Vice-Chancellor, Stirling University, 1986-94; b. 4.11.28, Shrivenham; m., Alicia Blanche Hart Gough; 1 s. Educ. Headlands School, Swindon; Bristol University. RAF, 1953-56; Senior Scientist, Tube Investments Ltd., 1956-58; Lecturer, Bristol University, 1958-64; founding Professor of Physics, Warwick University, 1964-86; Pro-Vice-Chancellor, Warwick Univ., 1970-86; Member, Physics and Materials Science Committees, SERC, 1970-74; Member: UGC, 1982-86 (Vice-Chairman, 1985-86), Computer Board, Universities and Research Councils, 1982-85 (Chairman, 1988-91); Chairman, Committee of Scottish University Principals, 1990-92; Member, British Library Board, 1987-94; Chairman, Information Systems Committee, UFC, 1991-92; Hon. Fellow and Chairman, EPCC, Edinburgh University, 1994-97; Member, Board of Trustees, National Library of Scotland, 1995-2001; Member, Academic Advisory Board, University of the Highlands and Islands, since 1999; author of "Forty Report" on future facilities for advanced research computing. Recreations: dinghy sailing; gardening. Address: (h.) Port Mor, St. Fillans, Perthshire PH6 2NF.

Foster, Elizabeth. BA, MSc, MBA, FRSA. Director, Family Mediation Scotland, since 1997; b. Glasgow; 1 d. Educ. Albert Secondary School, Glasgow; Strathclyde University; Glasgow University. Research Officer, National Children's Bureau, 1979-83; Projects Manager, Aberlour

Child Care Trust, 1983-86; Assistant Divisional Director, Save the Children, 1986-96. Recreations: walking; skiing; sailing; reading; music; films. Address: (b.) 18 York Place, Edinburgh EH1 3EP; T.-0131-558 9898; e-mail: efoster.fms@btconnect.com

Foster, John, CBE, FRICS, FRTPI, RIBA, ARIAS, FRSA; b. 13.8.20, Glasgow; m., Daphne Househam; 1 s.; 1 d. Educ. Whitehill School, Glasgow; Royal Technical College, Glasgow. Surveyor with private firm in Glasgow, 1937; Air Ministry during War; Assistant Planning Officer: Kirkcudbright County Council, 1945-47, Holland Joint Planning Committee, Lincolnshire, 1947-48; Deputy County Planning Officer, Holland County Council, 1948-52; Deputy Planning Officer, Peak Park Planning Board, 1952-54; Director: Peak District National Park Board, 1954-68, Countryside Commission for Scotland, 1968-85. Hon. Vice-President, Ramblers Association Scotland (President, 1994-2000); Hon. Vice-President, Countrywide Holidays Association; Hon. Fellow, Royal Scottish Geographical Society; Patron, Scottish Council for National Parks; Hon. Member and Past Vice Chairman, Commission on National Parks and Protected Areas, World Conservation Union; Hon. Member, European Federation of Nature and National Parks; Vice-Chairman, Heritage Unit Advisory Board, Robert Gordon University, Aberdeen; Life Member, National Trust for Scotland; George Waterston Memorial Award, 1991; Hon. Fellow, Robert Gordon University. Recreations: walking; swimming; photography; philately; reading; travel. Address: (h.) Birchover, Ferntower Road, Crieff PH7 3DH; T.-01764 652336.

Foster, Professor John Odell, MA, PhD. Professor of Social Sciences, Paisley University, since 1981; b. 21.10.40, Hertford; m., Renee Prendergast; 1 d. Educ. Guildford Grammar School; St. Catherine's College, Cambridge. Postdoctoral Research Fellow, St. Catherine's College, Cambridge, 1965-68; Lecturer in Politics, Strathclyde University, 1966-81. Chair, Scottish Committee, Communist Party of Britain, (Secretary, 1988-2000). Publications: Class Struggle and the Industrial Revolution, 1974; Politics of the UCS Work-In, 1986; Track Record: the Caterpillar Occupation, 1988; Paying for the Piper (Co-author), 1996. Recreation: hill-walking. Address: (h.) 845 Govan Road, Glasgow G51.

Foster, Kate, BA (Hons), PGDip Journalism. Health Correspondent, The Scotsman, since 2001; b. 8.11.74, Christchurch, England; m., Darren Robertson. Educ. Forrester High School, Edinburgh; Stirling University. Freelance journalist, 1998-99; News Reporter, Scottish News Agency, 1999-2000; General News Reporter, The Scotsman, 2000-01. Recreations: tennis; scuba diving; jet skiing; dinner parties. Address: (b.) Scotsman Publications, 108 Holyrood Road, Edinburgh EH8 8AS; T.-0131-620 8516; e-mail: kfoster@scotsman.com

Foubister, Graeme Craigie, BSc, MBChB, FRCSEd (Orth). Consultant Trauma and Orthopaedic Surgeon, Tayside University Hospital NHS Trust, since 1994; b. 12.6.56, Edinburgh; m., Elizabeth; 2 d. Educ. Daniel Stewart's and Melville College; Edinburgh University. Surgical Registrar: Royal Infirmary, Edinburgh, St. James' University Hospital, Leeds. Recreations: gardening; hillwalking. Address: (h.) Newton Bank House, Abernyte, Perth PH14 9SY; T.-01828 686584; e-mail: graeme.foubister@btinternet.com

Foulds, Emeritus Professor Wallace Stewart, CBE, MD, ChM, FRCS, FRCSGlas, DO, Hon. FRCOphth, Hon. DSc (Strathclyde), Hon. FRACO, Hon. FCMSA. Emeritus Professor of Ophthalmology, Glasgow University; Visiting Professor, National University of Singapore and Singapore National Eye Centre; Co-Director, Singapore Eye Research Institute; b. 26.4.24, London; m., Margaret Holmes Walls; 1 s.; 2 d. Educ. George Watson's Boys College, Edinburgh;

Paisley Grammar School; Glasgow University. RAF Medical Branch, 1946-49; training posts, Moorfields Eye Hospital, London, 1952-54; Research Fellow, Institute of Ophthalmology, London University, and Senior Registrar, University College Hospital, London, 1954-58; Consultant Ophthalmologist, Addenbrookes Hospital, Cambridge, 1958-64; Tennent Professor, Glasgow University, 1964-89; Honorary Lecturer, Cambridge University and Research Fellow, London University, 1958-64; Past President: Ophthalmological Society of UK, Faculty of Ophthalmologists; Past Chairman, Association for Eye Research; Founder President, Royal College of Ophthalmologists. Recreations: sailing; diving; DIY; natural history. Address: Kinnoul Place, 68 Dowanside Road, Glasgow G12 9DL; T.-0141-334 2463.

Foulis, Alan Keith, BSc, MD, MRCPath, FRCP(Ed). Consultant Pathologist, Royal Infirmary, Glasgow, since 1983; b. 25.5.50, Glasgow; m., Anne Don Martin; 1 s.; 1 d. Educ. Glasgow Academy; Glasgow University. Trained in pathology, Western Infirmary, Glasgow, following brief flirtation with surgery at Aberdeen Royal Infirmary; C.L. Oakley Lecturer, Pathological Society, Oxford, 1987; Bellahouston Medal, Glasgow University, 1987; R.D. Lawrence Lecturer, British Diabetic Association, Manchester, 1989. Publications: research papers on diseases of the pancreas. Recreations: choral and Leider singing; walking; cycling; arctophilia; natural history. Address: (h.) 32 Tannoch Drive, Milngavie, Glasgow; T.-0141-956 3092.

Foulkes, George, JP, BSc. MP (Labour and Co-operative), Carrick, Cumnock and Doon Valley, since 1979; Minister of State for Scotland, since 2001; b. 21.1.42, Oswestry; m., Elizabeth Anna; 2 s.; 1 d. Educ. Keith Grammar School; Haberdashers' Aske's School; Edinburgh University. Opposition Spokesman on Foreign Affairs, 1984-92, Defence, 1992-93, Overseas Development, 1994-97; Parliamentary Under-Secretary of State, Department for International Development; 1997-2001. President, Scottish Union of Students, 1964-66; Director: European League for Economic Co-operation, 1967-68, Enterprise Youth, 1968-73, Age Concern Scotland, 1973-79; Chairman: Lothian Region Education Committee, 1974-79, Education Committee, COSLA, 1975-79; Rector's Assessor, Edinburgh University, 1968-71; Treasurer, Parliamentarians for Global Action. Recreations: boating; watching football (Heart of Midlothian and Ayr United). Address: (h.) 18A Ewenfield Road, Ayr KA7 2QB; T.-01292 265776.

Fowkes, Professor Francis Gerald Reid, MB, ChB, PhD, FRCPE, FFPHM. Professor of Epidemiology, Edinburgh University, since 1994; Director, Wolfson Unit for Prevention of Peripheral Vascular Diseases, since 1989; Hon. Consultant Public Health Medicine, since 1985; b. 9.5.46, Falkirk; 1.s.; 1 d. Educ. George Watson's College, Edinburgh; Edinburgh University. Senior Lecturer, University of Wales, 1980-85; Reader/Professor, Edinburgh University, since 1985. Address: (b.) Department of Public Health Sciences, Edinburgh University, Teviot Place, Edinburgh EH8 9AG; T.-0131-650 3220.

Fowler, Agnes Isobel, BSc, FRSAMD, FRSA, FFCS. Director of Finance and Administration, Royal Scottish Academy of Music and Drama; b. 13.2.42, Glasgow; m., William M. Fowler; 2 s.; 1 d. Educ. Dumbarton College School; Glasgow University. Governor, Associated Board, Royal Schools of Music; Member, Merchants House of Glasgow. Recreations: hill-walking; swimming; gardening; Church. Address: (h.) Hillside, 7 Main Street, Drymen, Glasgow; T.-01360 660009; e-mail: i.fowler@rsamd.ac.uk

Fowlie, Hector Chalmers, OBE, MB, ChB, FRCPEdin, FRCPsych, DPM. Retired Consultant Psychiatrist; b. 21.6.29, Dundee; m., Christina N.M. Walker; 2 s.; 1 d. Educ. Harris Academy, Dundee; St. Andrews University. House Officer, Maryfield Hospital, Dundee, and Perth

Royal Infirmary; Registrar, Dundee Royal Mental Hospital; Lecturer, Department of Psychiatry, Medical School, Dundee University; Consultant Psychiatrist and Deputy Physician Superintendent, Gartnavel Royal Hospital, Glasgow; Physician Superintendent, Royal Dundee Liff and Strathmartine Hospitals; Consultant Psychiatrist, Tayside Health Board. Vice-Chairman, Mental Welfare Commission for Scotland, 1984-89; sometime Vice-Chairman, Parole Board for Scotland; Member, Tayside Health Board; Council of Europe Scholar; Consultant, WHO; Past Chairman: Dundee Association for Mental Health, Dundee Healthcare NHS Trust; President, Rotary Club of Claverhouse, 1999-00; formerly Member of Court, Abertay University, Dundee. Recreations: reading; bowling. Address: (h.) 21 Clepington Road, Dundee; T.-01382 456926.

Fowlis, Angela, DCE. Director, Scottish Pre-Retirement Council, since 2000; b. 1.1.48, Dunfermline. Educ. Kings Park Secondary, Glasgow; Jordanhill College of Education. Primary/nursery Teacher, 1968-76; Lecturer, Langside College, 1976-95; Head of Department, Langside College, 1995-98. Recreations: singing; gardening; golf; badminton. Address: (b.) Alexandra House, 204 Bath Street, Glasgow, G2 4HL; T.-0141-332 9427.

Fox, Andrew John Arthur, MA. Manager, Scottish Fisheries Museum Trust Ltd; b. 1.5.53, Bristol; m., Lyubov Mikhailovna Yampolskaya; 1 s. Educ. Dundee High School; University of Aberdeen; University of St. Andrews. Assistant Collector of Taxes, Dundee and London, 1977-78; Teacher of English, Invergordon Academy, 1979-80; Information Worker, Dundee Association for Social Services, 1985-86; H.M. Frigate Unicorn: Curator, 1987-90, Project Supervisor, 1992-94, General Manager, 1995-99. Publications: three books of poetry. Recreations: writing; reading; swimming. Address: (b.) St. Ayles, Harbourhead, Anstruther KY10 3AB; T.-01333 310628.

Fox, Professor Keith Alexander Arthur, BSc (Hons), MB, ChB, FRCP. Duke of Edinburgh Professor of Cardiology, Edinburgh University, since 1989; Honorary Consultant Cardiologist, Royal Infirmary of Edinburgh; b. 27.8.49, Salisbury, Rhodesia; m., Aileen E.M.; 1 s.; 1 d. Educ. Falcon College; Edinburgh University. Assistant Professor of Medicine, Washington University School of Medicine, 1980-85; Senior Lecturer in Cardiology and Consultant Cardiologist, University Hospital of Wales College of Medicine, 1985-89. Address: (b.) Department of Cardiology, Royal Infirmary of Edinburgh, Lauriston Place, Edinburgh EH3 9YW; T.-0131 536 2743.

Fraile, Emeritus Professor Medardo, PhD. Writer; Emeritus Professor in Spanish, Strathclyde University, since 1985; b. 21.3.25, Madrid; m., Janet H. Gallagher; 1 d. Educ. Madrid University. Teacher of Spanish language and literature, Ramiro de Maeztu Secondary School, Madrid, 1956-64; Assistant in Spanish, Southampton University, 1964-67; Strathclyde University: Assistant Lecturer in Spanish, 1967-68, Lecturer, 1968-79, Reader, 1979-83, Personal Professor, 1983-85. Travelling Scholarship for authors, 1956; Premio Sesamo for short story writing, 1956; literary grant, Juan March Foundation, 1960; Book of the Year award, 1965; La Estafeta Literaria Prize for short stories, 1970; Hucha de Oro Prize for short stories, 1971; research grant, Carnegie Trust, 1975; Ibanez Fantoni Prize for journalism, 1988; Encomienda con Placa de la Orden Civil de Alfonso X El Sabio, 1999. Publications: El Weir de Hermiston by R.L. Stevenson (Translator), 1995; short stories translated into eight languages (Complete Short Stories, Madrid, 1991); five books for children; a novel; books of essays and literary criticism; contributor to periodicals in many countries. Recreations: swimming; walking. Address: (h.) 24 Etive Crescent, Bishopbriggs, Glasgow G64 1ES; T.-0141-772 4421.

Frain-Bell, William John, MA, LLB, DipLP. Advocate, since 1999; Editor-in-Chief, Firm Publications, since 1999; b. 18.5.71, Dumfries; m., Joanna Michie. Educ. Loretto School; University of St. Andrews; University of Aberdeen. Trainee Solicitor, Tods Murray WS, 1996-98; Barrister, Middle Temple, since 2000. Conservative Parliamentary Candidate: Banff and Buchan, 1997, Hamilton North, 2000. Recreations: sailing; skiing; travel; golf. Address: (h.) 33 Moray Place, Edinburgh EH3 6BX; T.-0131 225 6931; e-mail: bill@firmmagazine.com

France, Anthony James, MA, MB, BChir, FRCP. Consultant Physician, Dundee Teaching Hospitals, since 1989; Honorary Senior Lecturer, Dundee University, since 1989; b. 5.4.54, London; m., Rosemary; 1 s.; 2 d. Educ. Perse School, Cambridge; Magdalene College, Cambridge; St. Thomas' Hospital, London. Qualified 1978; specialises in management of HIV infection, communicable diseases and respiratory medicine. Recreations: photography; gardening; decorating an old house. Address: (b.) Ninewells Hospital, Dundee DD1 9SY; T.-01382 660111.

France, Professor (Emeritus) Peter, MA, PhD, FBA. Professor of French, Edinburgh University, 1980-90, Endowment Fellow, 1990-2000; b. 19.10.35, Londonderry; m., Siân Reynolds; 3 d. Educ. Bradford Grammar School; Magdalen College, Oxford. Fellow, Magdalen College, Oxford, 1960-63; Lecturer, then Reader in French, Sussex University, 1963-80; French Editor, Modern Language Review, 1979-85; President: British Comparative Literature Association, 1992-98, International Society for the History of Rhetoric, 1993-95. Publications: Racine's Rhetoric, 1965; Rhetoric and Truth in France, 1972; Poets of Modern Russia, 1982; Diderot, 1982; Rousseau: Confessions, 1987; Politeness and its Discontents, 1992; New Oxford Companion to Literature in French, 1995; Translator: An Anthology of Chuvash Poetry, 1991, Gennady Aygi: Selected Poems, 1997; Oxford Guide to Literature in English Translation, 2000. Address: (b.) 60 George Square, Edinburgh EH8 9JU; T.-0131-650 8417.

Franceschild, Donna, BA. TV Scriptwriter, since 1990; playwright, since 1979; b. 22.11.53, Illinois; partner, Richard Golding; 1 s. Educ. University of California, Los Angeles. TV credits include: Eureka Street, A Mug's Game, Takin' Over the Asylum, And the Cow Jumped Over the Moon, Bobbin' and Weavin', The Necklace; theatre credits include: And the Cow Jumped Over the Moon, The Sunshine Cafe, Rebel!,, Songs for Stray Cats and Other Living Creatures; Tap Dance on a Telephone Line; Mutiny on the M1, Diaries, The Soap Opera, The Cleaning Lady; film credit: Donovan Quick. Creative Writing Fellow, Universities of Glasgow and Strathclyde. Recreation: hill-walking. Address: (b.) Making Waves Film and TV, Suite 116, 211 Piccadilly, London W1V 9LD; T.-0207 917 2871.

Franchi, (Sarah) Jane. Reporter/Presenter, BBC Scotland, since 1979; b. 15.10.50, Calcutta; m., Alan Franchi. Educ. Benenden School; Edinburgh College of Commerce. Reporter, Aberdeen Journals, 1970; Press and Publicity Officer, Grampian TV, 1971-79. Trustee, Aberdeen Football Club Supporters Trust. Recreations: swimming; football (spectating!); embroidery; theatre. Address: (b.) BBC Scotland, Queen Margaret Drive, Glasgow G12 8DG; T.-0141-338 3440.

Francis, John Michael, BSc, ARCS, PhD, DIC, FRSGS, FRSE, FRZSS. Chair, UK National Commission for UNESCO, since 2000; Honorary Fellow, University of Edinburgh, since 2000; b. 1.5.39, London; m., Eileen; 2 d. Educ. Gowerton Grammar School, near Swansea; Imperial College of Science and Technology, London University. CEGB Berkeley Nuclear Laboratories, 1963-70; Director, Society, Religion and Technology Project, Church of Scotland, 1970-74; Senior Research Fellow, Heriot-Watt

University, 1974-76; Principal, Scottish Development Department, 1976-81; Assistant Secretary, Scottish Office, 1981-84, and 1992-95; Director – Scotland, Nature Conservancy Council, 1984-91, then Chief Executive, Nature Conservancy Council for Scotland; Senior Policy Adviser, Home Department, Scottish Office, 1995-99. Consultant, World Council of Churches, 1971-83; Chairman, SRT Project, Church of Scotland, 1979-94; Member: Oil Development Council for Scotland, 1973-76, Advisory Committee for Scotland, Nature Conservancy Council, 1973-76, Council, National Trust for Scotland, 1984-92; Chairman, Edinburgh Forum, 1986-92; Professional Member, World Future Society, Washington DC, since 1992; Member: John Muir Trust, since 1994, British Association for the Advancement of Science; UK Representative, Millennium Project, United Nations University; Trustee, Society, Religion and Technology Project Trust, since 1998; Member, SUPRA, since 1999; Chairman, Sector Committee, Sustainable Development, Peace and Human Rights, UK Commission for UNESCO, since 1999. Publications: Scotland in Turmoil, 1972; Changing Directions, 1973; Facing Up to Nuclear Power, 1976; The Future as an Academic Discipline, 1975; The Future of Scotland, 1977; North Sea Oil and the Environment (Jointly), 1992; contributions to scientific journals. Recreations: theatre; hill-walking; ecumenical travels. Address: (h.) 49 Gilmour Road, Newington, Edinburgh EH16 5NU; T.-0131-667 3996.

Franklin, Ian Maxwell, BSc, MB, ChB, FRCP (Lond, Glasg, Edin), FRCPath, PhD. Professor of Transfusion Medicine, Glasgow University, since 1996; National Medical and Scientific Director, Scottish National Blood Transfusion Service, since 1997; Honorary Consultant, Bone Marrow Transplant Unit, Glasgow Royal Infirmary; b. 6.9.49, London; m., Dr. Anne Christine Bush; 1 s.; 1 d. Educ. Owen's Boys School, Islington; Leeds University; University College London Medical School. MRC Research Training Fellow, University College London Medical School, 1977-80; Consultant Haematologist, Queen Elizabeth Hospital, Birmingham, 1982-92; Director of Haematology, Central Birmingham Health Authority, 1989-91; Director, Glasgow and West of Scotland Blood Transfusion Service, 1996-97; Consultant-in-Administrative Charge, Bone Marrow Transplant Unit, Glasgow Royal Infirmary, 1992-97. Scientific Secretary, British Society for Haematology, 1995-98; Chairman, Working Party on Relationship Between Blood Banks and Bone Marrow Transplant Units, Council of Europe, 1995-96; author of various papers. Recreations: sailing; cycling; eating and drinking; music. Address: (b.) Department of Medicine, Glasgow University, Royal Infirmary, 10 Alexandra Parade, Glasgow; T.-0141-211 1202.

Franks, Peter, AGSM. Principal Trumpet, Scottish Chamber Orchestra, since 1984; Trumpet Teacher, Royal Scottish Academy of Music and Drama, since 1989; b. 22.4.58, Aylesbury; m., Maureen Hilary Rutter; 1 s.; 1 d. Educ. Aylesbury Grammar School; Guildhall School of Music and Drama. Sub-principal Trumpet, Scottish Chamber Orchestra, 1981-84. Address: 29 West Bankton Place, Murieston West, Livingston EH54 9ED; T.-01506 415514.

Fransman, Professor Martin, BA, MA, PhD. Professor of Economics, University of Edinburgh, since 1996; Director, Institute for Japanese-European Technology Studies, since 1988; b. 17.4.48, Johannesburg; m., Tamar Ludwin; 1 s.; 2 d. Educ. University of the Witwatersrand; University of Sussex. Lecturer: University of Swaziland, 1971-77, University of London, 1977-78; University of Edinburgh: Lecturer, 1978-86, Reader, 1987-96. Publications: The Market and Beyond, 1990 (Masayoshi Ohira Prize, 1991); Japan's Computer and Communications Industry, 1995; Visions of Innovation, 1999. Recreations: hill-walking; foreign travel; music; cinema. Address: (b.) Institute for Japanese-European Technology Studies, University of Edinburgh, 25 Buccleuch Place, Edinburgh EH8 9LN; T.-0131-650 4060; e-mail: M.Fransman@ed.ac.uk

Franz, Rev. Kevin Gerhard, MA, BD, PhD. General Secretary, Action of Churches Together in Scotland, since 1999; Chairman, Perth and Kinross Association of Voluntary Service, 1995-2000; b. 16.6.53, St. Andrews; m., Veda; 1 s.; 1 d. Educ. Bell-Baxter High School, Cupar; University of Edinburgh. Assistant Curate, St. Martin and St. Luke, Edinburgh, 1979-83; Rector, St. John, Selkirk, 1983-90; St. Ninian's Cathedral, Perth: Provost, 1990-99, Canon, 1999. Recreations: travel in Eastern Europe; watching rugby. Address: (b.) Scottish Churches House, Kirk Street, Dunblane FK15 0AJ; T.-01786 823588.

Fraser of Carmyllie, Lord (Peter Fraser), PC, QC. Minister of State, Department of Trade and Industry, 1995-97; b. 29.5.45; m., 1 s.; 2 d. MP (Conservative), Angus South, 1979-83, Angus East, 1983-87; Solicitor-General for Scotland, 1982-89; Lord Advocate, 1989-92; Minister of State, Scottish Office, 1992-95.

Fraser, Alan Alexander, BSc (Hons), MBChB, MRCPsych. Consultant Psychiatrist, Southern General Hospital, Glasgow, since 1987; Honorary Clinical Senior Lecturer in Psychiatry, Glasgow University, since 1988; Visiting Consultant: Priory Hospital, Glasgow; b. 17.10.55, Kilbirnie. Educ. Spier's School, Beith; Glasgow University. Address: (h.) 65 Dowanside Road, Glasgow G12 9DL; T.-0141-357 2283.

Fraser, Alan William, MA (Hons). Head of 21st Century Government Unit, Scottish Executive, since 2001; b. 17.12.51, Lennoxtown; m., Joan; 2 s.; 1 d. Educ. Daniel Stewart's College; Banff Academy; Aberdeen University. Entered Scottish Office, 1973; Assistant Secretary to Inquiry into UK Prison Services, 1978-79; Private Secretary to Minister of State, 1979-81; secondment to Aberdeen District Council, 1981-82; Head, New Towns Branch, IDS, 1982-85; Manager, Scottish Office Efficiency Unit, 1985-88; Head, Industrial Policy and Technology Division, SOID, 1988-91; Principal Private Secretary to Secretary of State for Scotland, 1991-93; Head, Enterprise and Tourism Division, Scottish Office Education and Industry Department, 1993-99; Director of Personnel, Scottish Executive, 1999-2000; Director for Civil Service Reform, 2000-01. Recreations: hill-walking; skiing; wind-surfing. Address; (b.) Victoria Quay, Leith, Edinburgh EH6 6QQ; T.-0131-244 7833.

Fraser, Andrew Kerr, MB, ChB, MPH, FRCP, FFPHM. Deputy Chief Medical Officer, Scottish Executive, since 1997; b. 10.12.58, Edinburgh; m., Geraldine M.; 3 s.; 1 d. Educ. George Watson's College; Aberdeen University; Glasgow University. Medical Director, National Services Division, NHS in Scotland; Director of Public Health, Highland Health Board. Recreations: music; mountain walking. Address: (b.) St Andrew's House, Edinburgh EH1 3DG; e-mail: andrew.fraser@scotland.gsi.gov.uk

Fraser, Callum George, BSc, PhD, FAACB. Clinical Leader, Biochemical Medicine, Ninewells Hospital and Medical School, since 1983; Honorary Senior Lecturer, Dundee University; b. 3.1.45, Dundee; m., Stella Sim; 2 d. Educ. Dunfermline High School; Perth Academy; Aberdeen University. Postdoctoral Fellow, National Research Council of Canada, 1969-70; Lecturer in Chemical Pathology, Aberdeen University, and Honorary Biochemist, Grampian Health Board, 1970-75; Chief Clinical Biochemist, Flinders Medical Centre, South Australia, 1975-83; Honorary Senior Lecturer, then Honorary Associate Professor, Flinders University of South Australia, 1975-83; Honorary Senior Lecturer, St. Andrews University, 1988-2000. Former Chairman, Education

Division, International Federation of Clinical Chemistry; former Member, Commission on Teaching of Clinical Chemistry, International Union of Pure and Applied Chemistry. Recreations: sailing; reading; travel. Address: (b.) Biochemical Medicine, Ninewells Hospital, Dundee DD1 9SY; T.-01382 632512; e-mail: callum.fraser@tuht.scot.nhs.uk

Fraser, Sir Campbell, FRSE, BCom, DUniv, DL, LLD, CBIM. Chairman, Tandem Computers Ltd., 1987-97; Non-Executive Director, Bridgewater Paper Ltd., 1985-99; Chairman, Riversoft Ltd., 1997-99; b. 2.5.23, Dunblane; m., Myar McLaren (deceased); 2 d. Educ. McLaren High School, Callander; Dundee School of Economics; University of Glasgow; McMaster University. Economist, Raw Cotton Commission; Staff, Economist Intelligence Unit; many positions with Dunlop Holdings (Chairman, 1978-83); Non-Executive Director, Morgan Crucible; Chairman, Scottish Television, 1975-91; Non-Executive Director, 3 i's; Non-Executive Director, B.A.T. Industries Ltd.; Non-Executive Director, British Petroleum PLC and associated companies; Past President, Confederation of British Industry; Chairman: Wells Fargo's International Advisory Council, Barkers (Scotland) Ltd., Tandem Inc. International Advisory Council (Director, Tandem Inc.); Trustee: The Economist, Institute of Hepatology; Governor, N.I.E.S.R.; Visiting Professor: University of Stirling, University of Strathclyde; Chairman, Business School, Strathclyde University. Recreations: reading history; writing; supporting Dundee FC. Address: c/o The Caledonian Club, 9 Halkin Street, London SW1X 7DR.

Fraser, Sir Charles Annand, KCVO, WS, DL. Partner, W. & J. Burness, 1956-92 (retired); former Chairman, Adam and Company PLC; former Director: British Assets Trust PLC, Scottish Television PLC, Scottish Business in the Community, Stakis PLC; b. 16.10.28, Humbie, East Lothian; m., Ann Scott-Kerr; 4 s. Educ. Hamilton Academy; Edinburgh University. Purse Bearer to Lord High Commissioner to General Assembly of Church of Scotland, 1969-88; served on Court, Heriot-Watt University, 1972-78; Council Member, Law Society of Scotland, 1966-72; Chairman, Lothian & Edinburgh Enterprise, 1991-94. Recreations: gardening; skiing; piping. Address: (h.) Shepherd House, Inveresk, Midlothian; T.-0131-665 2570.

Fraser, David James, MA, MHSM, MIPD. Chief Executive, Scottish Qualifications Authority, since 2002; b. 1.7.52, Fraserburgh; m., Anne; 1 s. Educ. Peterhead Academy; Aberdeen University. Peat Marwick Mitchell & Co., City of London, 1974-75; Scottish Health Service Management Training Scheme, 1975-77; Lothian Health Board, 1977-93; Chief Executive, North Ayrshire and Arran NHS Trust, 1993-99; Chief Executive, Dumfries and Galloway Primary Care Trust, 1999-01. Recreations: gardens; photography; opera. Address: (b.) Ironmills Road, Dalkeith EH22 1LE; T.-0131-561 6867.

Fraser, Hugh Donald George, MBE, QPM, DipSM, OStJ, FBIM, MIPM, MIIRSM. Councillor, City of Edinburgh Council, for Balerno ward, since 1996; Honorary Secretary, Scottish Chamber of Safety, since 1979; former Senior Assistant Secretary, Heriot-Watt University; b. Edinburgh; m., Margaret Jane Stothard; 1 s.; 2 d. War Service, RAF Aircrew, 1939-45 (Pilot); Edinburgh City Police, 1941-71; Chief Superintendent, Research and Planning Branch, Home Office, London, 1966-68; Deputy Commandant, Scottish Police College, 1968-71. Honorary Secretary, Edinburgh and District Spastic Association, 14 years; Member: Edinburgh Accident Prevention Council, Lothian Retirement Committee; Member, Lothian Regional Council, 1982-96. Recreations: Burns' enthusiast; work with senior citizens; jogging; the theatre. Address: (h.) 181 Braid Road, Edinburgh EH10 6JA; T.-0131-447 1270.

Fraser, James Edward, CB, MA (Aberdeen), BA (Cantab), FSA (Scot). Assistant Local Government Boundary Commissioner for Scotland, since 1997; Secretary of Commissions for Scotland, 1992-94; b. 16.12.31, Aberdeen; m., Patricia Louise Stewart; 2 s. Educ. Aberdeen Grammar School; Aberdeen University; Christ's College, Cambridge. Royal Artillery, 1953-55 (Staff Captain, "Q", Tel-El-Kebir, 1954-55); Assistant Principal, Scottish Home Department, 1957-60; Private Secretary to Permanent Under-Secretary of State, Scottish Office, 1960-62; Private Secretary to Parliamentary Under-Secretary of State, Scottish Office, 1962; Principal, 1962-69: SHHD, 1962-64, Cabinet Office, 1964-66, HM Treasury, 1966-68, SHHD, 1968-69; Assistant Secretary: SHHD, 1970-76, Scottish Office Finance Division, 1976; Under Secretary, Local Government Finance Group, Scottish Office, 1976-81, Scottish Home and Health Department, 1981-91. President: Scottish Hellenic Society, Edinburgh and Eastern Scotland, 1987-93, Aberdeen Grammar School Former Pupils' Club, 1997-98 (Hon. Vice-President, since 1998). Recreations: reading; music; walking; Greece, ancient and modern; DIY. Address: (h.) 59 Murrayfield Gardens, Edinburgh EH12 6DH; T.-0131-337 2274.

Fraser, Jeremy William, LLB (Hons), DipLP, NP. Solicitor; Legal Adviser and Company Secretary, Lloyds TSB Scotland plc, since 1990; b. 2.5.62, Inverness; m., Claudia Bölling; 4 children. Educ. Alloa Academy; Edinburgh University. Lindsay Duncan & Black WS; Lloyds Bowmaker Ltd. Recreations: hockey; squash; golf; hill-walking. Address: (b.) 120 George Street, Edinburgh; T.-0131-225 4555; e-mail: Jeremy.Fraser@lloydstsb.co.uk

Fraser, John A., DipEd, DipPhysEd. Head Teacher, Craigmount High School, since 1999; b. 3.6.52, Inverness; 3 s.; 1 d. Educ. Kingussie High School; Jordanhill College of Education. P.E. Teacher, Northfield Academy; Principal Teacher of Guidance, Northfield Academy; Assistant Head Teacher, Hazlehead Academy; Depute Rector, then Rector, Mearns Academy. Recreation: sport. Address: (b.) Craigs Road, Edinburgh EH12 8NH.

Fraser, John A.W., MA, FEIS, JP, DL. Deputy Lieutenant for Shetland, since 1985; b. 9.11.28, Lerwick; m., Jane Ann Jamieson; 2 s. Educ. Anderson Educational Institute; Edinburgh University; Moray House College of Education. Education Officer, RAF, 1950-52; Teacher, Baltasound Junior Secondary School, 1952-54; Head Teacher: Haroldswick Primary School, 1954-59, Aith Junior High School, 1959-66, Scalloway Junior High School, 1966-88. Former Member, National Council, EIS; Member, Scalloway Waterfront Trust; General Commissioner of Income Tax; Honorary Librarian, Shetland Family History Society; Honorary Researcher, Shetland Bus Friendship Society. Recreations: genealogy; travel; gardening. Address: (h.) Broadwinds, Castle Street, Scalloway, Shetland; T.-01595 880644.

Fraser, Kit, BA. Presenter, Good Morning Scotland, BBC Radio Scotland; b. 3.12.51, Giffnock; m., Fiona Morrison; 2 s. Educ. Kingussie High School; University of Stirling. Entered journalism with D.C. Thomson (worked on The People's Journal, Sunday Post, Dundee Courier); joined BBC on setting up of BBC Highland, Inverness; Radio Scotland: Producer, 1978-88, Reporter, 1988-97, Presenter, Newsdrive, Politics Tonight. Publications: Christie Boy, father's autobiography (Editor). Recreations: five-a-side football; golf; real ale. Address: c/o Newsroom, BBC Scotland, Queen Margaret Drive, Glasgow G12 8DG.

Fraser, Lindsey M., BA (Hons), PGCE. Executive Director, Scottish Book Trust, since 1991; b. 15.8.61, Edinburgh. Educ. George Watson's College; York University; Froebel Institute, London. Manager, Heffers Children's Bookshop, Cambridge, 1986-91. Sir Stanley Unwin Travelling Fellowship, 1989. Publications: Points

North (Editor), 2000; Telling Tales: Theresa Breslin, 1999; Telling Tales: J.K. Rowling, 2000; Stories from Scotland (Co-Editor). Address: (b.) Scottish Book Trust, Scottish Book Centre, 137 Dundee Street, Edinburgh EH11 1BG; T.-0131-229 3663.

Fraser, Lady Marion Anne, LT, MA, LRAM, ARCM, LLD, DUniv (Stirling). Honorary President, Scottish International Piano Competition, since 1999 (Chairman, 1995-99); Chair, Scottish Association of Mental Health, 1995-99; b. 17.10.32, Glasgow; m., Sir William Kerr Fraser; 3 s.; 1 d. Educ. Hutchesons' Girls' Grammar School; University of Glasgow; RSAMD. Lord High Commissioner to General Assembly of the Church of Scotland, 1994; Her Majesty's High Commissioner to the General Assembly of the Church of Scotland, 1995. Formerly Director: RGI, Scottish Opera, Laurel Bank School; Founder Chairman, Friends of the RSA; Director, St. Mary's Music School; Chair: Board, Christian Aid, 1990-97; Trustee, Scottish Churches Architectural Heritage Trust; President, Scotland's Churches' Scheme, 1997; Member, Sponsoring Group, Churches' Enquiry into Unemployment and the Future of Work, 1995-97; Trustee, Lamp of Lothian Collegiate Trust, since 1996. Recreations: family and friends; people and places. Address: (h.) Broadwood, Edinburgh Road, Gifford, East Lothian EH41 4JE; T.-01620 810 319.

Fraser, Professor Patricia, MA, PhD. Aberdeen Asset Management Professor of Finance and Investment Management, University of Aberdeen, since 1995; b. 30.6.43, Arbroath; m., Finlay McRae Fraser; 3 s. Educ. Arbroath High School; University of Dundee. Lecturer in Financial Economics, Dundee University, 1989-94; Senior Lecturer in Finance, University of Stirling, 1994-95; Houblon-Norman Fellow, Bank of England, 1992. Visiting Professor: University of Tasmania, University of Western Australia, Curtin University. Recreations: reading; travel; walking; conversation with friends. Address: (b.) Department of Accountancy and Finance, University of Aberdeen, Dunbar Street, Aberdeen AB24 3QY; T.-01224 272210.

Fraser, Professor Robert, BSc, MSc, PhD, DSc, FRSE, FIBiol. Senior Nonclinical Scientist, MRC, since 1967; Honorary Professor, Glasgow University, since 1994; b. 25.8.36, Barnet; m., Patricia Fraser; 2 d. Educ. East Barnet Grammar School; Nottingham University. Postgraduate Medical School, London, 1958-59; Inner London Education Authority, 1959-64; St Mary's Hospital Medical School, 1964-67; MRC Blood Pressure Unit, Glasgow, 1967-94; Honorary Lecturer/Senior Lecturer, 1967-94; MRC Blood Pressure Group, Glasgow, since 1994. Recreations: music; history; gardening; sport. Address: (b.) MRC Blood Pressure Group, Western Infirmary, Glasgow G11 6NT; T.-0141-211 2109.

Fraser, Robert Dunbar, MA (Hons), MIMgt. Rector, Kirkcaldy High School, since 1989; b. 30.11.45, Dingwall; m., Annice; 2 s.; 2 d. Educ. Dingwall Academy; Aberdeen University. Depute Rector, Culloden Academy, 1979-84; Rector, Keith Grammar School, 1984-89. Recreations: sports; golf; DIY; being with family. Address: (h.) Elphinstone Lodge, 77 Hepburn Gardens, St. Andrews, Fife.

Fraser, Sheriff Simon William Hetherington, LLB, NP. Sheriff of North Strathclyde at Dumbarton, since 1989; b. 2.4.51, Carlisle; m., Sheena Janet; 1 d. Educ. Glasgow Academy; Glasgow University. Solicitor, 1973; Partner, Flowers & Co., Solicitors, Glasgow, 1976-89; Temporary Sheriff, 1987-89. Glasgow Bar Association: Secretary, 1977-79, President, 1981-82. Recreations: flying; watching cricket, and Partick Thistle. Address: (b.) Sheriff Court, Church Street, Dumbarton; T.-01389 763266.

Fraser, Professor William Douglas, BSc, MSc, PhD, FRICS. Professor, Division of Land Economics and Law, Paisley University, since 1986; b. 3.1.40, Edinburgh. Educ. Edinburgh Academy; London University; Strathclyde University. Partner, Bingham, Hughes and Macpherson, Chartered Surveyors, Inverness, 1970-72; Lecturer: Department of Land Economics, Paisley College, 1972-83, Centre for Property Valuation and Management, City University, London, 1983-86. Publication: Principles of Property Investment and Pricing, 1984. Recreations: climbing; gardening. Address: (b.) Division of Land Economics and Law, Paisley University, Paisley PA1 2BE; T.-0141-848 3450; e-mail: william.fraser@paisley.ac.uk

Fraser, Professor William Hamish, MA, DPhil, FRHistS. Professor of History, Strathclyde University (Dean, Faculty of Arts and Social Studies, 1987-93); b. 30.6.41, Keith; m., Helen Tuach; 1 d. Educ. Keith Grammar School; Aberdeen University; Sussex University. Lecturer in History, Strathclyde University, 1966-77. Chair, Economic and Social History Society of Scotland; Chair, Scottish Working People's History Trust. Publications: Trade Unions and Society 1850-1880, 1973; Workers and Employers, 1981; The Coming of the Mass Market, 1982; Conflict and Class: Scottish Workers 1700–1838, 1988; People and Society in Scotland 1830–1914, 1990; Glasgow 1830–1914 (Co-author), 1996; Alexander Campbell and the Search for Socialism, 1996; A History of British Trade Unionism, 1700-1998, 1999; Scottish Popular Politics, 2000; Aberdeen: A New History (Co-Editor), 2000. Recreations: hill-walking; skiing. Address: (h.) 112 High Station Road, Falkirk FK1 5LN; T.-01324 622868.

Fraser, Sir William Kerr, GCB (1984), LLD, FRSE. Chancellor, Glasgow University, since 1996; b. 18.3.29; m., Lady Marion Fraser, LT (qv); 3 s.; 1 d. Educ. Eastwood Secondary School; Glasgow University. RAF, 1952-55; various posts in Scottish Office, 1955-88, including Permanent Under Secretary of State, Scottish Office, 1978-88; Principal and Vice Chancellor, Glasgow University, 1988-95. Chairman, Royal Commission on the Ancient and Historical Monuments of Scotland, 1995-2000; Chairman, Scotland Inheritance Fund. Address: (h.) Broadwood, Edinburgh Road, Gifford, East Lothian EH41 4JE; T.-01620 810 319.

Frater, John W.B., MA. Chief Executive, Royal Environmental Health Institute of Scotland, since 1994; b. 12.5.58, Irvine; m., Caroline E. Mackenzie. Educ. Loudoun Academy; Dundee University. Recreations: reading; wine; pottering around locomotive sheds. Address: (b.) 3 Manor Place, Edinburgh; T.-0131-225 6999.

Frazer, Rev. Richard Ernest, BA, BD, DMin(Prin), SubChStJ. Minister, St. Machar's Cathedral, Old Aberdeen, since 1993; b. 20.11.57, Stirling; m., Katherine Tullis Sinclair; 2 s.; 1 d. Educ. Doncaster Grammar School; University of Newcastle upon Tyne; University of Edinburgh. Assistant Minister, St. Giles Cathedral, Edinburgh, 1985-87; Minister, Schoharie, Breakabeen, N. Bleheim, New York, USA, 1987-88; Minister, Cargill-Burrelton with Collace, 1988-93. Publication: A Collace Miscellany: a History of the Parish of Collace (Co-Editor and Contributor), 1992. Recreations: family; walking; squash; timber construction. Address: (b.) St. Machar's Cathedral, The Chanonry, Old Aberdeen AB24 1RQ; T.-01224 485988.

French, William Allan, DL, BSc, MSc, CEng, FIM, FIEE, FIBF. Depute Lieutenant, Stirling and Falkirk Districts, since 1994; b. 30.12.41, Falkirk; m., Joyce; 2 d. Educ. George Watson's College, Edinburgh; Strathclyde University. Scientific Officer, UKAEA, Dounreay; Production Manager, British Aluminium Co. Ltd., Falkirk; Lecturer, Napier College, Edinburgh; Head, Department of

Industrial Engineering, Falkirk College of Technology; Associate Principal, Falkirk College of Further and Higher Education, 1986-99. Director, Careers Central Ltd., 1995-99; Secretary, Forth Valley Area Scout Association; District Scout Commissioner; founder Area Chairman, Central Scotland Round Table; Past President, Larbert Rotary Club. Recreations: golf; bridge; bowling; scouting; rotary; music. Address: (h.) 26 Broomhill Avenue, Larbert FK5 3EH; T.-01324 556850.

Frew, Rev. Michael William, BSc, BD. Parish Minister, Carluke: St. John's, since 1991; b. 16.5.51, Edinburgh; m., Margaret; 3 s.; 1 d. Educ. Broughton Senior Secondary; University of Edinburgh. Parish Minister: Alloa West; Organiser for Evangelism, Church of Scotland Department of National Mission. Recreations: cycling; walking; football. Address: 18 Old Bridgend, Carluke, Lanarkshire ML8 4HN; T.-01555 772259.

Friel, Professor Edward J. Chief Executive, Greater Glasgow and Clyde Valley Tourist Board, since 1997; Broadcaster and Writer; President, Glasgow Chamber of Commerce; b. 20.9.41, Londonderry; m., Eleanor; 3 s. Educ. Northern Ireland. Northern Ireland Tourist Board: Director, North America, Chief Executive, 1991; Director, Marketing and Public Relations, Scottish Opera; Proprietor, Eddie Friel Associates, since 1992; Chief Executive, Greater Glasgow Tourist Board and Convention Bureau, 1983-97; a Director: Scottish National Youth Orchestra, Glasgow Centre for Contemporary Arts; Visiting Professor, Scottish Hotel School, Strathclyde University; Governor, Glasgow Caledonian University; Fellow, Royal Society of Arts; Fellow, Tourism Society; Hon.DUniv., Glasgow University. Recreations: golf; music; theatre; opera. Address: (b.) 11 George Square, Glasgow G2 1DY; T.-0141-566 4001.

Friel, Sheriff James D., PhL, LLB. Sheriff, Glasgow and Strathkelvin, since 1998; b. 9.11.43, Croy; m., Anne Currie; 3 s.; 1 d. Educ. Blairs College, Aberdeen; Gregorian University, Rome; Glasgow University. Procurator Fiscal Depute, Dundee, 1970, Glasgow, 1971; Senior Depute Procurator Fiscal, Glasgow, 1978; Assistant Solicitor, Crown Office, Edinburgh, 1983; Senior Assistant Procurator Fiscal, Glasgow, 1988; Regional Procurator Fiscal, North Strathclyde, 1991-98. Recreations: sports, especially football; music; reading. Address: (b.) Glasgow Sheriff Court, 1 Carlton Place, Glasgow G5 9DA; T.-0141-418 5258.

Frier, Brian Murray, BSc (Hons), MD, FRCP (Edin), FRCP (Glas). Consultant Physician, Royal Infirmary, Edinburgh, since 1987; Honorary Professor of Diabetes, Edinburgh University, since 2001; b. 28.7.47, Edinburgh; m., Dr. Isobel M. Wilson; 1 d. Educ. George Heriot's School, Edinburgh; Edinburgh University. Research Fellow in Diabetes and Metabolism, Cornell University Medical Centre, The New York Hospital, 1976-77; Senior Medical Registrar, Royal Infirmary, Edinburgh, 1978-82; Consultant Physician, Western Infirmary and Gartnavel General Hospital, Glasgow, 1982-87. Chairman, Honorary Advisory Panel for Driving and Diabetes to Secretary of State for Transport, since 2001; R.D. Lawrence Lecturer, British Diabetic Association, 1986; Governor, George Heriot's Trust, Edinburgh, 1987-94. Publications: Hypoglycaemia and Diabetes: clinical and physiological aspects, 1993; Hypoglycaemia in Clinical Diabetes, 1999; publications on diabetes and hypoglycaemia. Recreations: appreciation of the arts; ancient and modern history. Address: (h.) 100 Morningside Drive, Edinburgh EH10 5NT; T.-0131-447 1653; e-mail: brian_frier@hotmail.com

Frith, Professor Simon, BA, MA, PhD, FRSA. Professor of Film and Media, Stirling University, since 1999; Director, ESRC Media Economics and Media Culture Programme, 1995-2000; b. 25.6.46, England. Educ. Leys School, Cambridge; Balliol College, University of Oxford; University of California, Berkeley. Lecturer, then Senior Lecturer in Sociology, University of Warwick, 1972-87; Director, John Logie Baird Centre, 1987-99, and Professor of English Studies, 1988-99, University of Strathclyde; Rock Critic, Sunday Times, 1982-86; Pop Critic, Observer, 1987-91; Chair of Judges, Mercury Music Prize. Publications: Sound Effects, 1981; Art into Pop, 1987; Music for Pleasure, 1988; Performing Rites, 1996. Recreations: music; reading; walking. Address: (b.) Department of Film and Media Studies, Stirling University, Stirling FK9 4LA; T.-01786 467520.

Frizzell, Edward W. CB, MA (Hons). Head, Scottish Executive Enterprise and Lifelong Learning Department, since 1999; b. 4.5.46, Paisley; m., Moira Calderwood; 2 s.; 1 d. Educ. Paisley Grammar School; Glasgow University. Scottish Milk Marketing Board, 1968-73; Scottish Council (Development and Industry), 1973-76; DAFS, Scottish Office, 1976-78; First Secretary, Fisheries, Office of the UK Permanent Representative to European Communities, Brussels (Foreign and Commonwealth Office), 1978-82; Assistant Secretary (Grade 5), Scottish Education Department, Higher Education Division, 1982-86; Scottish Office Finance Division, 1986-89; Director, Locate in Scotland, Scottish Office Industry Department (Grade 4), 1989-91; Chief Executive, Scottish Prison Service (Grade 3), 1991-99. Address: (b.) Meridian Court, Cadogan Street, Glasgow G2 6AT.

Frow, Professor John, BA, MA, PhD, FAHA. Regius Professor of Rhetoric and English Literature, Edinburgh University, since 2000; b. 13.11.48, New South Wales; m., Christine Alavi; 1 d. Educ. Wagga High School; Australian National University; Cornell University. Lecturer/Senior Lecturer, Murdoch University, 1975-88; Visiting Professor, University of Minnesota, 1988; Darnell Professor of English, University of Queensland, 1989-99. Publications: Marxism and Literary History, 1986; Cultural Studies and Cultural Value, 1995; Time and Commodity Culture, 1997; Accounting for Tastes, 1999. Address: (b.) Department of English Literature, Edinburgh University, Edinburgh EH8 9JX; T.-0131-650 6856; e-mail: j.frow@ed.ac.uk

Frutin, Bernard Derek, MBE, FRSA, MInstPkg. Inventor; Executive Chairman, Rocep Group of Companies; b. 7.2.44, Glasgow; m., 1, Victoria Dykes (divorced); m., 2, Karen Smith; 1 s.; 3 d. Educ. Kelvinside Academy, Glasgow. Winner of nine international innovator awards since 1989, including John Logie Baird and British Institute of Packaging Environmental Awards; Innovator of the Year, 1989 (Institute of Packaging); Finalist, 1992 Prince of Wales Award; Institute of Packaging Starpack Award for TEC Innovation, 2001. Recreations: sailing; skiing; fine food; listening to music. Address: (b.) Rocep Lusol Holdings Ltd., Rocep Business Park, Rocep Drive, Renfrew PA4 8XY; T.-0141-885 2222.

Fry, Dominic Lawrence Charlesworth. Group Director, Corporate Communications, Scottish Power Plc, since 2000; b. 28.8.59, London; m., Ann-Marie Finn; 1 s. Educ. Christ's Hospital; University of North Carolina, USA; Universite Paul Valery III, Montpelier, France. Communications consultancies, 1980-90; Communications Director, AT & T UK Ltd., 1990-95; Communications Director, Eurotunnel Plc, 1995-96; Communications Director, J. Sainsbury, Plc, 1996-2000; Director, Almeida Theatre; Communications Advisor: Royal Shakespeare Company, Environment Task Force, CBI Scotland; Prince's Youth Business Trust Advisor. Recreations: tennis; rugby union; reading. Address: (b.) Scottish Power Plc, 1 Atlantic Quay, Glasgow, G2 8SP; T.-0141-636 4560.

Fry, Professor Stephen C., BSc, PhD, FRSE. Professor of Plant Biochemistry, Edinburgh University, since 1995; b. 26.11.53, Sheffield; m., Verena Ryffel; 3 d. Educ. Thornbridge School, Sheffield; Leicester University. Postdoctoral Research Fellow, Cambridge University, 1978-79; Royal Society Rosenheim Research Fellow, Cambridge University, 1979-82; Senior Research Associate, University of Colorado, 1982-83; Lecturer in Botany, then Reader in Plant Biochemistry, Edinburgh University, 1983-95. President's Medal, Society for Experimental Biology, 1988. Publication: The Growing Plant Cell Wall: Chemical and Metabolic Analysis, 1988. Recreations: hill-walking; paper chromatography. Address: (b.) The Edinburgh Cell Wall Group, Institute of Cell and Molecular Biology, Edinburgh University, King's Buildings, Mayfield Road, Edinburgh EH9 3JH; T.-0131-650 5320; e-mail: S.Fry@ed.ac.uk

Fulton, Rev. John Oswald, BSc, BD. General Secretary, United Free Church of Scotland, since 1994; Moderator, General Assembly, United Free Church, 2000-01; b. 9.7.53, Glasgow; m., Margaret P.; 1 d. Educ. Clydebank High School; Glasgow University. Ordained as minister, 1977; Minister, Croftfoot U.F. Church, Glasgow, 1977-94. Recreations: reading; gardening; photography. Address: (b.) 11 Newton Place, Glasgow G3 7PR; T.-0141-332 3435; e-mail: ufcos@charis.co.uk

Fulton, Rikki, OBE, DLitt, DArts. Actor; b. 15.4.24, Glasgow; m., Kate Matheson. Educ. Whitehill Secondary School. Invalided out of RNVR as Sub-Lt., 1945; began professional career broadcasting with BBC in Glasgow; Presenter, BBC Showband, London, 1951-55; appeared in numerous pantomimes and revues with Howard & Wyndham from 1955, including Five Past Eight shows; television work including Scotch & Wry (creator, Rev. I.M. Jolly) and starring roles in The Miser and A Winter's Tale; films including The Dollar Bottom, Gorky Park, Local Hero, Comfort and Joy and The Girl in the Picture. Scottish TV Personality of the Year, 1963 and 1979; Best Light Entertainment Performance of the Year, 1969 and 1983; President's Award, Television and Radio Industries Club, 1988; Lifetime Achievement Award, BAFTA Scotland, 1993. Recreations: bridge; chess; reading; music (listening and piano); writing; painting.

Furley, Professor Peter Anthony, MA, DPhil. Professor of Biogeography, University of Edinburgh, since 1997; b. 5.8.35, Gravesend; m., Margaret Brenda Dunlop; 1 s.; 3 d. Educ. Gravesend Grammar School; Brasenose College, Oxford University. Tutor, Oxford; University of Edinburgh: Lecturer, 1962, Senior Lecturer, 1975; Professor of Ecology, University of Brasilia, Brazil, 1976; Reader in Tropical Biogeography and Soils, 1989. Publications: Geography of the Biosphere, 1983; Nature and Dynamics of Forest–Savanna Boundaries, 1992; The Forest Frontier – Brazilian Roraima, 1994; Ecological and Environmental Research in Belize (three volumes), 2001. Recreations: travel; hillwalking. Address: Department of Geography, University of Edinburgh, Drummond Street, Edinburgh EH8 9XP; T.-0131-650 2517/2523.

Furnell, Professor James R.G., MA (Hons), DCP, PhD, LLB, FBPsS, DipLP. Consultant Clinical Psychologist (Child Health), Forth Valley Health Board, 1980-98; Advocate (called to Scottish Bar, 1993); Chartered Clinical and Forensic Psychologist; Honorary Fellow, Edinburgh University, since 1987; b. 20.2.46, London; m., Lesley Anne Ross; 1 s.; 1 d. Educ. Leighton Park Society of Friends School, Reading; Aberdeen University; Glasgow University; Stirling University; Dundee University. Clinical Psychologist, Royal Hospital for Sick Children, Glasgow, 1970-72; Senior Clinical Psychologist, Forth Valley Health Board, 1972-80. Member: National Consultative Committee of Scientists in Professions Allied to Medicine, 1984-87 (Secretary, Clinical Psychology Sub-Committee), Forth Valley Health Board, 1984-87; Chairman, Division of Clinical Psychology, British Psychological Society, 1988-89; Visiting Professor, Caledonian University, since 1996. Recreations: flying; cross-country skiing. Address: (b.) Glensherup House, Glendevon, by Dollar, Perthshire FK14 7JY; T.-01259 781234.

Furness, Professor Raymond Stephen, BA, MA, PhD. Formerly Professor of German, St. Andrews University, now Emeritus Professor; b. 25.10.33, Builth Wells; m., Janice Fairey; 1 s.; 2 d. Educ. Welwyn Garden City Grammar School; University College, Swansea. Modern Languages Department, University of Manchester Institute of Science and Technology; Department of German, Manchester University. Publications: Expressionism; Literary History of Germany 1890-1945; Wagner and Literature; A Companion to Twentieth Century German Literature; An Introduction to German Literature 1871-1990 (Co-Author); The Dedalus Book of German Decadence; Zarathustra's Children. Recreation: claret. Address: (h.) The Dirdale, Boarhills, St. Andrews KY16 8PP; T.-01334 880469.

Furness, Col. Simon John, DL. Landowner; Vice Lord Lieutenant, Berwickshire, since 1990; b. 18.8.36, Ayton. Educ. Charterhouse; RMA, Sandhurst. Commissioned Durham Light Infantry, 1956, 2nd Lt.; served Far East, UK, Germany; active service, Borneo, Northern Ireland; retired, 1978; Deputy Colonel (Durham) The Light Infantry, 1989-93. Member, Executive, National Trust for Scotland, 1986-96; Chairman: Berwickshire Civic Society, since 1996, Eyemouth Museum Trust, since 1981. Recreations: field sports; gardening. Address: The Garden House, Netherbyres, Eyemouth, Berwickshire TD14 5SE; T.-01890 750337.

Furness, William Arthur, BA, MSc. Chief Executive, Edinburgh Chamber of Commerce; Chair, Scottish Council for Research in Education; b. 6.9.45, London. Educ. St. Benedict's Abbey School, Ealing; Exeter University; London University. Various posts within BT. Director, Edinburgh Science Festival; Director, Scottish Council Development and Industry; Board Member, Scottish Environment Protection Agency. Recreations: travel; dogs; reading; art. Address: (b.) 152 Morrison Street, Edinburgh EH3 8EB.

Fyfe, Andrew, MA (Hons). Executive Director, Glasgow Alliance, since 1998; b. 26.6.54, Glasgow; m., Louise Drummond; 2 d. Educ. Hutchesons', Glasgow; Glasgow University. Research Assistant, Strathclyde University, 1975-78; Senior Development Officer, Govanhill Housing Association, 1978-81; Director, Shettleston Housing Association, Glasgow, 1982-89; Scottish Homes: Director Strategic Development, 1989-92, Director Operations, 1992-97; Managing Director, Glasgow and North Clyde, 1997-98; Member, Glasgow 1999 Festival Company; Chairman, Scottish Federation of Housing Associations, 1987-89. Address: (b.) 39 St Vincent Place, Glasgow G1 2ER; T.-0141-572 1300; e-mail: fyfea@glasgowalliance.co.uk

Fyfe, Maria, BA (Hons). MP, Glasgow Maryhill, 1987-2001; Chair, Labour Departmental Committee on International Development, 1997-2001; Member, Council of Europe, 1997-2001; Member, British-Irish Parliamentary Body, 1997-2001; b. 25.11.38, Glasgow; m., James (deceased); 2 s. Educ. Notre Dame High School, Glasgow; Strathclyde University. Glasgow District Councillor, 1980-87; Senior Lecturer, Central College of Commerce, 1977-87; Member, Scottish Executive Committee, Labour Party, 1981-87; Opposition Spokesperson on Women, 1988-91; Scottish Affairs Spokesperson, 1992-95; Chair, Scottish All-Party Parliamentary Group on Children, 1996-99. Address: 10 Ascot Avenue, Glasgow G12 0AX.

G

Gabbitas, Peter, BA, DipIHSM, MBA. Chief Executive, East and Midlothian NHS Trust; b. 15.8.61, Leeds; m., Karen; 1 d. Educ. St Thomas Aquinas Grammar School; Durham University; Warwick University. Hospital Director, then Director of Operations, Dudley Group of Hospitals. Member, Scottish Partnership Forum; Member, Whitley Council. Recreations: golf; gardening; stained glass. Address: (b.) St John's Hospital, Howden, Livingston EH54 6PP; T.- 01506 419666.

Gage, Simon Martin, BSc, MSc, PhD. Research Physicist, University of Edinburgh, since 1985; Events Manager, since 1990, and Director, since 1994, Edinburgh International Science Festival; b. 18.5.62, London; m., Sarah Price; 1 d. Educ. Ivybridge Comprehensive School; University of Bristol; University of Dundee; University of Edinburgh. Publications: author of science books for children, including Light and Illusion Activity Pack. Recreations: cycle touring; classical music; walking on hot coals and other demonstrations of unusual scientific principles. Address: (b.) Edinburgh International Science Festival, Roxburgh's Court, off 323 High Street, Edinburgh EH1 1PW.

Galbraith, Professor Roderick Allister McDonald, BSc, PhD (Cantab), CEng, MRAeS. Shoda Professor of Aerospace Engineering, Glasgow University; b. 4.8.47, Lowmoor, England; m., Lynn Margaret Fraser. Educ. Greenock High School; James Watt Memorial College; Paisley College of Technology; Cambridge University. Apprentice Draughtsman/Engineer, Scott's Shipbuilding & Engineering Co. Ltd., 1964-72; Department of Aerospace Engineering, Glasgow University: joined 1975; Reader, 1989, Professor, 1992. Publications: over 100 reports and publications on aerodynamics. Recreations: sailing; walking. Address: (b.) Department of Aerospace Engineering, Glasgow University, Glasgow G12 8QQ; T.- 0141-330 5295.

Galbraith, Samuel Laird, BSc, MBChB, MD, FRCSGlas. MSP (Labour), Strathkelvin and Bearsden, 1999-2001; Minister for Environment, Sport and Culture, 2000-01; MP (Labour), Strathkelvin and Bearsden, 1987-2001; Neurosurgeon; b. 18.10.45. Minister for Children and Education, 1999-2000.

Galea, Paul, MD (Malta), DCH, FRCP(Glas), FRCPCH. Consultant Paediatrician, Royal Hospital for Sick Children, Yorkhill, Glasgow; previously Consultant Neonatologist, Royal Maternity Hospital, Glasgow; b. 8.10.50, Rabat, Malta; m., Irene. Educ. Royal University of Malta. Recreations: gardening; DIY, classical music. Address: (h.) 30 Garngaber Avenue, Lenzie, Glasgow G66 4LL; T.-0141-776 6031; e-mail: paul.galea@yorkhill.nhs.scot.uk

Gallacher, Yvonne Jean, DPA, DCA, DTM. Chief Executive, Money Advice Scotland, since 1997; b. 11.3.58, Glasgow; m., J. Michael Gallacher. Educ. Woodside Senior Secondary School; Glasgow Caledonian University; Stow College; Central College of Commerce. Local government service, 1975-87; trading standards, 1987-97. Convenor, Money Advice Scotland, 1994-97; Member, Scottish Consumer Council; Member, Financial Services Authority Independent Consumer Panel and Consumer Education Forum; Member, Scottish Qualifications Authority Care Advisory Group; Member, UK Money Advice Trust Advisory Committee; Member, Cross Party Working Group on Poinding and Warrant Sales. Publications: A Guide to Money Advice in Scotland (Co-Author); Managing Debt. Recreations: opera; swimming; entertaining; gardening.

Address: (b.) Suite 306, The Pentagon Centre, 36 Washington Street, Glasgow G3 8AZ; T.-0141-572 0238; e-mail: y.gallacher@ntlworld.com

Gallagher, Frank, MA, LLB, DipLP. Advocate, since 1990; b. 22.2.60, Glasgow; m., Louise; 3 s.; 1 d. Educ. Glasgow University. Solicitor, 1985-90; called to Bar, 1990; Advocate Depute, since 2001. Address: (h.) 98 Fernlea, Bearsden, Glasgow; T.-0141-584 9946.

Gallagher, Jim. Head, Scottish Executive Justice Department, since 2000. Educ. Glasgow University; Edinburgh University. Joined Scottish Office, 1976; worked in Home and Development Departments, Central Service Finance; Private Secretary to Minister for Home Affairs, 1979-80, and to successive Secretaries of State for Scotland, 1989-91; worked on criminal justice issues, 1980s; Director of Human Resources, Scottish Prison Service, 1991-96; seconded to UK Cabinet Secretariat, 1999; Member, Prime Minister's Policy Unit, 1999-2000. Address: (b.) Saughton House, Broomhouse Drive, Edinburgh, EH11 3XD; T.-0131-556 8400.

Gallagher, Sister Maire T., CBE, MA (Hons), MEd, FScotVec, DCE, FSQA. Retired Headteacher; Sister of Notre Dame Religious Congregation, since 1959; b. 27.5.33, Glasgow. Educ. Notre Dame High School, Glasgow; Glasgow University; Notre Dame College of Education. Principal Teacher of History, Notre Dame High School, Glasgow; Lecturer in Secondary Education, Notre Dame College of Education; Headteacher, Notre Dame High School, Dumbarton, 1974-87; Chairman, Scottish Consultative Council on the Curriculum, 1987-91 (Member, Consultative Committee on the Curriculum, since 1976). Member, Executive, Secondary Heads Association (Scottish Branch), 1976-83; Coordinator, Christian Life Movement Groups, West of Scotland; Member, Action of Churches Together in Scotland, since 1999 (Member, Central Council, 1990-99); Fellow, Scottish Qualifications Authority, 1997. Recreations: reading; dress-making; bird-watching. Address: (h.) Sisters of Notre Dame, 67 Moorpark Avenue, Penilee, Glasgow G52 4ET; T.-0141 810 4214.

Gallhofer, Profesor Sonja, MagPhil, MA (Econ), MSc(Econ), DrPhil. Professor of Critical Accounting, Glasgow Caledonian University, since 1999; b. Graz, Austria; m., Professor Jim Haslam. Educ. Karl-Franzens Universitat; Manchester University; London School of Economics.Lecturer in Accounting, UMIST, 1988-89, Essex University, 1989-94; Associate Professor of Accounting, University of Waikato, New Zealand, 1995-98; Senior Research Fellow, Glasgow Caledonian University, 1998-99. Recreations: music; theatre; walking. Address: (b.) Division of Accounting and Finance, Caledonian Business School, Glasgow Caledonian University, Cowcaddens Road, Glasgow G4 0BA; T.-0141-331 3709.

Gallie, Philip Roy, TEng, MIPlantE. MSP (Conservative), South of Scotland, since 1999; Conservative Spokesman on Constitutional Affairs (previously on Justice and Home Affairs); b. 3.6.39, Portsmouth; m., Marion Wands. Educ. Dunfermline High School; Kirkcaldy Technical College. Apprenticeship, H.M. Dockyard, Rosyth, 1955-60; Merchant Navy, 1960-64; electricity industry, 1964-92; MP (Conservative), Ayr, 1992-97; Vice-Chairman, Scottish Conservative and Unionist Party, 1995-97. Recreations: sports; politics. Address: (b.) 1 Wellington Square, Ayr KA7 1EN; T.-01292 283439.

Galloway, David J., MB, ChB, MD, FRCS. Consultant Surgeon, since 1989; Honorary Treasurer, Royal College of Physicians and Surgeons of Glasgow; b. 17.2.55, Dumbarton; m., Christine; 2 d. Educ. Dumbarton Academy; Glasgow University. Surgical training,

Western Infirmary, Glasgow, 1978-81; Lecturer in Surgery, Western Infirmary, Glasgow, 1982-87; Fellow in Surgical Oncology, Memorial Sloan Kettering Cancer Center, New York, 1987-88. Chair, Spectrum Trust. Recreations: tennis; computing; video editing. Address: (h.) 19 Kilmahew Avenue, Cardross, Argyll and Bute G82 5NG; T.-07768 517233.

Galloway, George. MP, Glasgow Kelvin, since 1997; MP, Glasgow Hillhead, 1987-97; Senior Vice-Chair, Parliamentary Labour Party Foreign Affairs Committee; b. 16.8.54, Dundee; 1 d. Educ. Harris Academy, Dundee. Production Worker, Michelin Tyres, 1974; Dundee Labour Party Organiser, 1977; General Secretary, War on Want, 1983. Chairman, Scottish Labour Party, 1981-82; Member, Scottish Labour Party Executive Committee, 1974-84; Founder and first General Secretary, Trade Union Friends of Palestine, 1979. Recreations: football; music; films. Address: (b.) House of Commons, Westminster, London; T.-0171-219 6940.

Galloway, Janice. Writer; b. 2.12.56, Saltcoats. Educ. Ardrossan Academy; Glasgow University. Variety of paid and unpaid work, including 10 years' teaching English in Ayrshire; music criticism for Glasgow Herald, The Observer, Scotland on Sunday; fiction writing, including collections of short stories and novels; Co-Editor, New Writing Scotland, 1990-92; Times Literary Supplement Research Fellow to the British Library, 1999. Publications: The Trick Is To Keep Breathing, 1990; Blood, 1991; Foreign Parts, 1994; Where You Find It, 1996; Pipelines (Co-Author), 2000; Clara, 2002. Staged work: The Trick is to Keep Breathing; Fall. Song cycle: Clara (Co-Writer); Monster, for orchestra and voices (Co-Writer). Opera: Monster (Co-Writer).

Galloway, Michael Peter, BSc (Hons), MA, MRTPI, MCIT, MILT. Director of Planning and Transportation, Dundee City Council, since 1997; b. 12.5.57, Aberfeldy; m., Joyce; 1 d. Educ. Perth Academy; Dundee University; Oxford Brookes University. Glasgow District Council: Planning Assistant, 1980-82, Planning Officer, 1982-84; Principal Planning Officer: London Borough of Lewisham, 1984-88, Manchester City Council, 1988-89; Assistant Chief Planning Officer, Glasgow City Council, 1989-91; Director, Crown Street Regeneration Project, 1991-97. Recreations: painting; travel; sailing; scuba diving. Address: (b.) Tayside House, Crichton Street, Dundee DD1 3RB; T.-01382 433610.

Galloway, 13th Earl of (Randolph Keith Reginald Stewart); b. 14.10.28; m.; succeeded to title, 1978. Educ. Harrow. Address: Senwick House, Brighouse Bay, Borgue, Kirkcudbrightshire, DG6 4TP.

Galt, Rose, MA (Hons), FEIS. President, Institute of Contemporary Scotland; b. 19.3.37, Glasgow; m., William Galt (deceased); 1 d. Educ. Possil Secondary School, Glasgow; Glasgow University; Jordanhill College of Education. President, Educational Institute of Scotland, 1979-80; General Teaching Council for Scotland: Convener, 1987-89, Depute Registrar (Education), 1990-95. Recreations: reading; cinema; crosswords; bridge. Address: 38 Meadow View, Cumbernauld, Glasgow G67 2BZ; e-mail: rose@kildrum.demon.co.uk

Gamble, Alan James, LLB(Hons), LLM, Advocate. District Chairman, The Appeals Service (formerly Independent Tribunal Service), Glasgow, since 1993; Deputy Social Security and Child Support Commissioner, Edinburgh, since 1994; b. 29.4.51, Glasgow; m., Elizabeth Waugh; 2 s.; 1 d. Educ. High School of Glasgow; University of Glasgow; Harvard Law School, USA. Law Apprentice, 1974-76; admitted to Faculty of Advocates, 1978; Lecturer, then Senior Lecturer in Law, University of

Glasgow, 1976-93. Bible Teacher, Christian Brethren Assemblies; Trustee, Interlink, and other charitable trusts; Dr J. McCormick Prize, 1972; Harkness Fellow, 1972-74. Publications: Contributor, Stair Memorial Encyclopedia; articles in legal journals and Christian periodicals. Recreations: reading; hill-walking. Address: (b.) Wellington House, 134-136 Wellington Street, Glasgow G2 2XL; T.-0141-354 8443.

Gamble, Kevin George Alfred, BEng. Executive Director, Weir Group PLC, since 1995; b. 1.9.47, Liverpool; m., Marie-Luise Paganetty; 2 s.; 1 d. Educ. Liverpool College; University of Liverpool. Stewarts & Lloyds, Bilston, Staffs, 1965-1970; Stone Manganese Marine Ltd., 1970-82; G.E.C. Turbine Generators Ltd., Rugby, 1982-88; Managing Director, Express Lift Co. Ltd., Northampton, 1988-92; Executive Director, Senior Engineering Group plc, 1992-95. Director, Northamptonshire Training and Enterprise Council, 1989-94. Recreations: tennis; family; garden. Address: (b.) Weir Group plc, 149 Newlands Road, Cathcart, Glasgow G44 4EX; T.-0141-308 3713.

Gammie, Professor Elizabeth, DipM, BA, CA, PhD. Professor of Accountancy, Robert Gordon University, since 2000; b. 20.12.61, Dundee; m., Robert Peter; 1 s.; 1 d. Educ. High School of Dundee; Robert Gordon University. Qualified as CA, 1986, with Ernst and Whinney; became a Lecturer, 1989. Member, Education Committee, Institute of Chartered Accountants of Scotland. Recreation: equestrianism. Address: (h.) Bogfon Cottage, Maryculter, Aberdeen AB12 5GR; T.-01224 735403.

Gane, Professor Christopher H.W., LLB. Professor of Scots Law, University of Aberdeen, since 1994 (Dean, Faculty of Law, since 1995); b. 1.12.49, Jedburgh; m., Christine Mary; 2 s. Educ. Jedburgh Grammar School; Hawick High School; Edinburgh University; Université d' Aix en Provence. Lecturer in Law, University of Reading, 1974-77; Lecturer in Scots Law, University of Edinburgh, 1977-80; University of Lancaster: Lecturer in Law, 1980-87, Senior Lecturer in Law, 1987-90; University of Sussex: Senior Lecturer in Law, 1990-92, Professor of Law, 1992-94. Visiting Professor in Criminal Law, University of Antwerp, 1991-92; University of Notre Dame: Associate Professor of Law (Adjunct), 1987-92, Professor of Law (Adjunct), 1992-94; Honorary Sheriff of Grampian, Highland and Islands. Publications: A Casebook on Scottish Criminal Law (Co-author), 1980; Criminal Procedure in Scotland – Cases and Materials (Co-author), 1983; Sexual Offences, 1992; Criminal Procedure Systems in the European Community (Joint Author), 1993; Human Rights and the Administration of Justice (Co-author), 1997; contributor of numerous chapters and articles. Recreations: reading; music; cinema; playing guitar. Address: (b.) School of Law, University of Aberdeen, Aberdeen AB24 3UB; T.-01224 273689.

Garbutt, David Charles Gemmell, QPM, LLD, GradIPD. Director, Scottish Police College, since 1998; HM Assistant Inspector of Constabulary for Scotland, Edinburgh, 1997; b. 16.8.45, Harthill; m., Moira Murdoch; 1 s.; 1 d. Educ. College of Commerce, Hull; Napier, Edinburgh. Joined Edinburgh City Police, 1964; transferred to Kingston upon Hull, 1967; returned to Edinburgh, 1970; promoted Chief Superintendent, 1987, as Divisional Commander, West Lothian; promoted Assistant Chief Constable, Lothian and Borders Police, 1991; appointed Deputy Chief Constable, Grampian Police, 1992. Recreations: hill-walking; cycling; curling. Address: (b.) Tulliallan Castle, Kincardine, Alloa FK10 4BE; T.-01259 732000.

Garden, Neville Abbot. Broadcaster; Writer and Lecturer on musical and media matters; b. 13.2.36, Dalbeattie; m., Jane Fowler; 1 s., 1 d.; 3 d. by pr. m. Educ. George Watson's College, Edinburgh. Reporter, Sub-Editor,

Feature Writer, Evening Dispatch, 1953-63; Daily Columnist and Music Critic, Edinburgh Evening News, 1963-64; Senior Feature Writer, Scottish Daily Express, 1964-78; Presenter, Good Morning Scotland, BBC Radio Scotland, 1978-90, Queen Street Garden, 1990-93; Music Critic and Columnist, Sunday Standard, 1981-83; Music Writer, Scotland on Sunday, since 1988; Conductor: Edinburgh Grand Opera, seven years; Edinburgh Ballet Theatre, nine years. Publication: Bloomsbury Good Music Guide.

Garden, Ralph, MA, FFA. Chief Executive, Scottish Office Pensions Agency, since 1998; b. 21.4.50, Aberchirder; 2 s.; 1 d. Educ. Robert Gordon's College; Aberdeen University. Scottish Widows, 1972-96 (various posts, finally as Executive Director, Client Services); Government Actuary's Department, 1997-98. Honorary Secretary, Faculty of Actuaries; Chairman, Education and CPD Board, Faculty and Institute of Actuaries. Recreations: golf; curling; hillwalking; tennis. Address: (b.) St. Margaret's House, 151 London Road, Edinburgh; T.-0131-244 3211.

Gardiner, Iain Derek, FRICS. Chartered Surveyor, since 1957; Senior Partner, Souter & Jaffrey, Chartered Surveyors, 1986-95; b. 22.12.33, Glasgow; m., Kathleen Elizabeth Johnson; 2 s.; 1 d. Educ. Hutcheson's Grammar School, Glasgow; Royal Technical College, Glasgow. Trainee and Assistant Quantity Surveyor, John H. Allan & Sons, Glasgow, 1950-57; National Service, Royal Engineers, 1957-59; Souter & Jaffrey, Inverness: Quantity Surveyor, 1959-63, Partner, 1963-86. Past Chairman, Royal Institution of Chartered Surveyors in Scotland; Chairman: Inverness Area, RICS in Scotland, 1969-70, Quantity Surveyors Committee, RICS in Scotland, 1989-90, Friends of Eden Court Theatre, 1981-82, Inverness Area Scout Council. Recreations: swimming; travel; cookery; Scouting. Address: (h.) 77 Stratherrick Road, Inverness IV2 4LL; T.-01463 235607.

Gardiner, Ian Ritchie. Chief Executive, Scottish Society for the Prevention of Cruelty to Animals, since 2001; b. 8.2.50, Irvine; m., Louise Elisabeth Leverkuehn; 1 s.; 1 d. Educ. Fettes College. Commissioned, Royal Marines, 1968; Sultan of Oman's Armed Forces, 1973-75; 45 Commando RM, 1980-83; Army Staff College, 1984; Ministry of Defence and Equerry to HRH Duke of Edinburgh, 1985-87; Instructor, RN Staff College, 1987-90; Commanding Officer, RM School of Music, 1990-92; Commanding Officer, 40 Commando RM, 1994-96; Member, Royal College of Defence Studies, 1997; Secretary to NATO Military Committee, Brussels, 1998-2001, as Brigadier RM. Distinguished Service Medal for Gallantry (Oman). Publication: Above All, Courage (Contributor), 1985; International Encyclopedia of Public Policy and Administration (Contributor), 1997. Recreations: exploring battlefields; sitting down and eating with friends. Address: (b.) Scottish SPCA, Braehead Mains, 603 Queensferry Road, Edinburgh EH4 6EA; T.-0131-339 0222; e-mail: IGardiner@scottishspca.org

Gardiner, John Ronald, BL, WS, NP. Consultant, Brodies W.S, Solicitors, since 2001 (Senior Partner, 1992-2001, Partner, 1964-2001); b. 25.10.38, Rangoon; m., Aileen Mary Montgomery; 1 s.; 1 s. (deceased); 1 d. Educ. Fettes College; University of Edinburgh. Admitted Solicitor, 1963; admitted Writer to the Signet, 1964; Partner, Brodie Cuthbertson & Watson W.S. (now Brodies W.S.), 1964; Notary Public, 1966. Governor, Fettes Trust, 1986-96; Member, Rent Assessment Panel for Scotland, 1973-97; Hon. Secretary: Standing Council of Scottish Chiefs, 1970-72, Salmon and Trout Association (Scottish Branch), 1971-84. Recreations: fishing; shooting; golf; gardening. Address: (b.) 15 Atholl Crescent, Edinburgh EH3 8HA; T.-0131-228 3777.

Gardner, Angela Joy, BSc (Hons). Independent Public Affairs Consultant, AJ Enterprises, since 1994; b. 16.9.62, Wolverhampton; m., Andrew Ronald Gardner; 2 d. Educ. Codsall High School; UMIST. BP Chemicals Ltd., South Wales and Grangemouth, 1984-90; BP Schools Link Officer, 1985-90; Senior Public Affairs Officer, BP, 1990-94. Member, General Teaching Council for Scotland, 1990-98; Member, Scottish Examination Board, 1991-94; Honorary Member, The IDES Network; Member, Scottish Qualifications Authority Engineering Advisory Group, since 1999. Address: (h.) 72 Craigcrook Road, Edinburgh EH4 3PN; T.-0131-336 5164.

Gardner, James, BSc. Headteacher, Dunblane High School, since 1989; b. 3.2.41, Glasgow; m., Margaret Catherine; 1 s.; 1 d. Educ. Allan Glen's School, Glasgow; Glasgow University; Strathclyde University. Teacher of Mathematics, Allan Glen's School, 1968-76; Principal Teacher of Mathematics, Cranhill Secondary, Glasgow, 1976-80; Assistant Head Teacher, Dunoon Grammar School, 1980-84; Depute Rector, Wallace High School, Stirling, 1984-89. Member, British Antarctic Survey, 1963-66. Recreations: climbing; skiing; orienteering; chess; golf. Address: (b.) Dunblane High School, Highfields, Dunblane; T.-01786 823823.

Garland, Harry Mitchell, MBE, CQSW, FBIM. Chairman, Secretary of State's Advisory Committee on Scotland's Travelling People, since 1987; b. 7.7.28, Aberdeen; m., Phyllis Sandison; 1 s.; 1 d. Educ. Rockwell Academy, Dundee; Robert Gordon's College, Aberdeen; Moray House College, Edinburgh; Edinburgh University. Probation Officer/Senior Probation Officer/Principal Probation Officer, 1958-69; Depute Director of Social Work, Aberdeen and Kincardine Counties, 1969-73; Director of Social Work: Paisley Burgh, 1973-74, Western Isles, 1974-78, Central Region, 1978-86. Chairman, National Association of Probation Officers in Scotland, 1968-69; President, Association of Directors of Social Work, 1983; Member, Forth Valley Health Board, 1986-90. Recreations: voluntary work; church; golf; walking. Address: (h.) 7 Cromarty View, Nairn IV12 4HX; T.-01667 453684.

Garner, John Angus McVicar, MB, ChB, DRCOG, DCH, FRCGP. Principal in general practice, since 1980; British Medical Association: Chairman, Scottish Council, Member, Council; Vice Chairman, Medical and Dental Defence Union of Scotland; Director, Professional Affinity Group Services; b. 4.9.50, London; m., Catherine Lizbeth; 1 s.; 1 d. Educ. Eltham College; Edinburgh University. Lothian Local Medical Committee: Secretary, 1986-89, Chairman, 1991-92; Member: General Medical Services Committee, since 1989, National Medical Advisory Committee, 1989-95; Past Chairman, Scottish General Medical Services Committee; former Treasurer, General Medical Services Defence Fund Ltd. Recreations: amphibians and photographing fungi. Address: (h.) 8 Hope Street, Edinburgh EH2 4DB; T.-0131-226 2880; e-mail: johngarne@aol.com

Garrick, Sir Ronald, FEng, FRSE. Chairman (former Chief Executive), The Weir Group Plc, b. 21.8.40; m.; 2 s.; 1 d. Non-Executive Director: Bank of Scotland, 2000-01, HBOS, since 2001. Address: (b.) Weir Group PLC, 149 Newlands Road, Glasgow, G44 4EX.

Garrioch, Magnus Allan, MB, ChB, FRCA. Consultant in Anaesthesia and Intensive Care, South Glasgow University NHS Trust, since 1994; Part-time Senior Lecturer, Anaesthesia, Glasgow University, since 1999; b. 30.5.61, Stockport. Educ. New Mills School, Derbyshire; Birmingham University. Junior House Officer: Birmingham General; Royal Shrewsbury Hospital; Senior House Officer/Registrar, Glasgow Royal Infirmary; Clinical Fellow in Shock Trauma,

Washington Hospital Centre, USA; Senior Registrar, Lothian Health Board. Address: (h.) 44 Hamilton Avenue, Pollockshields, Glasgow, G41 4JD; T.- 0141-201 1658.

Garrod, Professor Neil, BSc (Hons), PhD, ACIS. Professor of Financial Analysis and Dean, Faculty of Law and Financial Studies, Glasgow University, since 1993; b. 7.6.54; m., Sonja Gortnar; 1 s.; 1 d. Educ. Guthlaxton Upper School, Wigston; Manchester Institute of Science and Technology. Lecturer in Business Finance, University College of Wales, Aberystwyth, 1979-87; Associate Professor, Graduate Management Institute, Union College, New York, 1987-89; Senior Lecturer in Accounting and Finance, University of Wales, Bangor, 1989-90, Royal Insurance Professor of Finance and Accounting, 1990-93. Recreation: running. Address: (b.) Department of Accounting and Finance, Glasgow University, Glasgow G12 8LE; T.-0141-330 5426.

Garrod, Professor Simon Christopher, MA, PhD, FRSE. Professor of Cognitive Psychology, Glasgow University, since 1990; b. 19.11.47, London; 1 s.; 1 d. Educ. Bradfield College, Berks; Oxford University; Princeton University. Lecturer, Senior Lecturer, Reader in Psychology, Glasgow University, 1975-90; Visiting Research Fellow, Max Plank Institute, 1980; Residential Fellow, Netherlands Institute for Advanced Study, 1988. Publications: Understanding Written Language; Language Processing. Recreations: fishing; hill-walking. Address: (b.) Department of Psychology, Glasgow University, 58 Hillhead Street, Glasgow G12 8QT; T.-0141-330 5033.

Gartland, Professor Kevan Michael Andrew, BSc (Hons), PhD. Professor of Biological Sciences, University of Abertay Dundee, since 1999; b. 15.10.60, Birmingham; m., Jill Susan Gartland; 1 d. Educ. St Phillip's Grammar School, Edgbaston; Leeds University; Nottingham University. Research Assistant, Plant Genetic Manipulation Group, Nottingham University, 1982-85; British Technology Research Fellow, Plant Genetic Manipulation Group, 1985-86; Lecturer, Plant Molecular Biology, De Montfort University, Leicester, 1986-92; Special Lecturer, Biotechnology, Open Learning, Greenwich University, 1992-96; University of Abertay Dundee: Senior Lecturer, Plant Biotechnology, 1992-95; Leader, Biological Sciences Division, 1995 - 98; Associate Head, Molecular and Life Sciences, 1996-98; Division Leader, Molecular and Life Sciences, School of Science and Engineering, since 1998. Member: Heads of University Biological Sciences Executive Committee, Biochemical Society Education Group Committee, Biochemical Society Professional Education Committee, UK Tree Biotechnology Group Committee. Recreations; country living; gentle walking; visiting interesting places. Address: (b.) Molecular and Life Sciences Division, School of Science and Engineering, University of Abertay, Dundee, DD1 1HG; T.-01382 308000; e-mail: k.gartland@abertay.ac.uk

Gaskin, Professor Maxwell, DFC (and bar), MA. Jaffrey Professor of Political Economy, Aberdeen University, 1965-85; b. 18.11.21, Liverpool; m., Brenda Stewart; 1 s.; 3 d. Educ. Quarry Bank School, Liverpool; Liverpool University. War Service, RAF, 1941-46; Lecturer and Senior Lecturer in Economics, Glasgow University, 1951-65; Head, Department of Political Economy, Aberdeen University, 1965-81; Economic Consultant to Secretary of State for Scotland, 1965-87; Member, Scottish Agricultural Wages Board, 1972-90; Chairman: Foresterhill and Associated Hospitals Board, 1972-74, Flax and Hemp and Retail Bespoke Tailoring Wages Councils, 1978-93; Member, Civil Engineering EDC, 1978-84; Chairman, Section F, British Association, 1978-79; President, Scottish Economic Society, 1981-84; Fellow, Royal Economic Society. Publications: The Scottish Banks: A Modern Survey, 1965; North East Scotland: A Survey of its Development Potential (Co-author), 1969; Economic Impact of North Sea Oil on Scotland (Co-author), 1978; Employment in Insurance, Banking and Finance in Scotland, 1980; The Political Economy of Tolerable Survival (Editor), 1981. Recreations: music; gardening. Address: (h.) Westfield, Ancrum, Roxburghshire TD8 6XA; T.-018353 830237.

Gaston, Rev. Arthur Raymond Charles, MA, BD. Minister, St. Athernase Parish, Leuchars, since 1998; b. 25.5.36, Atherstone; m., Evelyn Wilson Mather; 1 s.; 2 d. Educ. The Gordon Schools, Huntly; Aberdeen University. Teacher of Mathematics, 1961-62; Principal of theological college in Madagascar, 1962-67; Missionary with London Missionary Society, 1967-69; Minister, Sauchie Parish Church, 1969-75, Dollar with Muckhart with Glendevon, 1975-89, Scottish Church, Knox's Chapel, Geneva, 1989-93; Secretary for Staffing, Board of World Mission, Church of Scotland, 1993-98; Secretary, Presbytery of Europe, since 1997. Recreations: water colour painting; walking; choral singing; wildlife. Address: (h.) The Manse, 7 David Wilson Park, Balmullo, Fife KY16 0NP; T.-01334 870038.

Gavin, Anthony John, CBE, BSc, DipEd, FRSA. Head Teacher, St. Margaret's Academy, Livingston, since 1993; b. 11.10.41, Perth; m., Charlotte Duffy; 2 d. Educ. Perth Academy; St. Andrews University. Teacher, St. Andrew's High School, Kirkcaldy, 1964-71; Principal Teacher/Assistant Headteacher, St. David's High School, Dalkeith, 1971-77; Depute Headteacher, St. Augustine's High School, Edinburgh, 1977-79; Headteacher, St. Saviour's High School, Dundee, 1979-93; TVEI Adviser Scotland, 1986-90. Member, Scottish Community Education Council, 1993-96; Chair, Catholic Headteachers' Association of Scotland, 1994-96; Member, Strategy Group, Higher Still Development Programme Scotland, 1996-2000; Member, Court, Edinburgh University; Member, Board of Catholic Education, Glasgow University, 1999; Director, St. Mary's Music School, Edinburgh. Recreations: music; golf. Address: (h.) 5 Colinton Court, Glenrothes KY6 3PE; T.-01592 743462.

Gavin, Derek, FRICS, IRRV, DipLED. Chartered Surveyor, since 1971; Executive Director, Stirling Enterprise Park and Stirling Enterprise, since 1984; b. 12.12.46, Perth; m., Terry; 1 s. Educ. Perth Academy; College of Estate Management. Trainee Surveyor, Bell Ingram, Perth, 1964-69; Management Surveyor, Scottish Industrial Estates Corporation, Glasgow, 1969-72; Valuation Surveyor, Bell Ingram, Perth, 1972-77; Estates Property Manager, Central Regional Council, 1977-84. Recreations: curling; golf; keep fit. Address: (b.) John Player Building, Players Road, Stirling; T.-01786 463416; e-mail: dgavin@stirling-enterprise.co.uk

Gawthrop, Professor Peter John, MA, DPhil, FIEE, FIMechE, FRSA, CEng, EurIng. Wylie Professor of Mechanical Engineering, Glasgow University, since 1987; b. 10.3.52, Seascale; 2 d. Educ. Whitehaven Grammar School; Queen's College, Oxford. W.W. Spooner Research Fellow, New College, Oxford; Lecturer, then Reader, Sussex University. Recreation: hill-walking. Address: (b.) Department of Mechanical Engineering, James Watt Building, Glasgow University, Glasgow G12 8QQ; T.-0141-339 8855.

Gebbie, George C., LLB (Hons). Advocate, since 1987; b. 27.1.58, Motherwell; m., Anne Gebbie-Oiben; 1 s.; 1 d. Educ. Dalziel High School, Motherwell; Aberdeen University. Legal apprentice to Crown Agent, 1979-81; Procurator Fiscal Depute, Glasgow, 1981-83; Solicitor in private practice, Glasgow, 1983-87. SNP candidate, East Kilbride, 1997 General Election. Recreation: socialising with friends. Address: (b.) Advocates' Library, Edinburgh, EH1 1RF; T.-0131-226 5071.

Geddes, Keith, CBE. Policy Director, Pagoda Public Relations, since 1999; b. 8.8.52, Selkirk. Educ. Galashiels Academy; Edinburgh University; Heriot Watt University. Housing Rights Worker, Shelter, 1977-84; Chair, Lothian Region Education Committee, 1987-90; Leader, Lothian Regional Council, 1990-96; Leader, City of Edinburgh Council, 1996-99. Board Member, Scottish Natural Heritage; Board Member, Accounts Commission; Chair, Young People Speak Out. Recreations: golf; cricket; hill-walking; watching Gala Rugby Football Club. Address: (h.) 7 Howard Street, Edinburgh EH3 5JP; T.-0131-624 2365.

Gemmell, Professor Curtis Glen, BSc, PhD, MIBiol, FRCPath. Professor of Bacterial Infection and Epidemiology, and Depute Head of Academic Department of Immunology and Bacteriology, Glasgow University; Visiting Professor, University of Strathclyde; Honorary Bacteriologist, Greater Glasgow Health Board; Director, Scottish MRSA Reference Laboratory; b. 26.8.41, Beith, Ayrshire; m., Anne Margaret; 2 d. Educ. Speir's School, Beith; Glasgow University. Glasgow University: Assistant Lecturer, 1966-68, Lecturer, 1968-69; Paisley College of Technology: Lecturer, 1969-71, Senior Lecturer, 1971-76; Glasgow University: Senior Lecturer, 1976-90, Reader, 1990-2000; Visiting Associate Professor, University of Minnesota, Minneapolis, 1979-80. Recreations: gardening; golf. Address: (h.) Sunninghill, 19 Lawmarnock Crescent, Bridge of Weir PA11 3AS; T.-Bridge of Weir 613350.

Gemmell, Gavin John Norman, CBE, CA. Senior Partner, Baillie, Gifford & Co., 1989-2001 (Partner, 1967-2001); Deputy Chairman, Scottish Widows Fund & Life Assurance Society, since 1995; Director: SEEL, since 1995, SFE, since 1998; b. 7.9.41, Edinburgh; m., Kathleen Fiona Drysdale; 1 s.; 2 d. Educ. George Watson's College. Qualified CA, 1964; joined Baillie, Gifford & Co., 1964; Chairman, Standing Committee, Scottish Episcopal Church, since 1997; Trustee, National Galleries of Scotland, since 1999; Member, Court, Heriot Watt University, since 2001. Recreations: golf; foreign travel. Address: (h.) 14 Midmar Gardens, Edinburgh EH10 6DZ; T.-0131-447 8135; e-mail: gavingemmell@blueyonder.co.uk

Gemmell, William Ruthven, LLB, WS. Partner, Murray Beith Murray WS, since 1987; Director, Inchcape Family Investments Ltd., Lawshare Ltd. and other companies; b. 4.4.57; m., Fiona Elizabeth Watson; 1 s.; 1 d. Educ. Loretto; Edinburgh University; Aberdeen University. Apprentice at Law, Brodies WS, 1979-82; Trainee Accountant, Arthur Young CA, 1983-85; Solicitor, Murray Beith Murray WS, 1985-87. Law Society of Scotland: Chairman, Investor Protection Committee, since 1992, Council Member, since 1993; Member: Financial Services Tribunal, 1993-2001, Financial Services Authority Small Business Panel, since 1999, Financial Services and Markets Tribunal, since 2001. Address: (b.) 39 Castle Street, Edinburgh EH2 3BH; T.-0131-225 1200.

Gemmill, Robert, MA, DUniv(Glas), FIMC, CMC. Member, Business Committee, General Council, Glasgow University, 1987-98, Assessor of the General Council on the University Court, 1990-98, and Co-opted Court Member, since 1998; b. 20.2.30; m., 1, Anne MacMurchy Gow (deceased); 2, Elisabeth Mary MacLennan; 2 s.; 1 d. Educ. High School of Glasgow; Glasgow University. Manufacturing management, Procter & Gamble Ltd., 1953-56; Management Consultant, PA Management Consultants Ltd., 1956-85. Played rugby football for Glasgow High School FP, Northumberland, Cheshire, Barbarians and Scotland (1950 and 1951). Recreations: golf; travel; music. Address: (h.) 123 Fotheringay Road, Glasgow G41 4LG; T.-0141-423 1860.

Gennard, Professor John, BA (Econ), MA (Econ), FIPM. Professor of Human Resource Management, Strathclyde University, since 1981; b. 26.4.44, Manchester; m., Florence Anne Russell; 1 s.; 1 d. Educ. Hulme Grammar School for Boys; Sheffield University; Manchester University. Research Officer, Industrial Relations Department, then Lecturer in Industrial Relations, London School of Economics, 1968-81. Publications: The Reluctant Militants (Co-author), 1972; Financing Strikers, 1978; Industrial Relations and Job Security, 1979; The Closed Shop in British Industry, 1984; A History of the National Graphical Association, 1990; A History of the Society of Graphical and Allied Trades, 1995; Employee Relations, 1997. Recreations: football; swimming; politics; trade unions; food and drink. Address: (h.) 4 South Avenue, Carluke, Lanarkshire; T.-01555 51361.

Gent, William, OBE. H.M. Commissioner (part-time), Mental Welfare Commission for Scotland, since 1996; b. 3.3.44, Crawcrook, Co. Durham; m., Audrey Charlton; 1 s.; 1 d. Educ. Hookergate Grammar School. Staff Nurse/Deputy Charge Nurse, Prudhoe Hospital, 1965-66; Charge Nurse, Balderton Hospital, 1966-69; Nursing Officer, Earls House Hospital, 1969-73; Royal Scottish National Hospital: Senior Nursing Officer, 1973-85, Director of Nursing, 1985-93; Director of Nursing and Quality and Executive Board Member, 1993-94; Clinical Director, Central Scotland Health Care Trust, 1994-99. Member, NBS, 1983-93, UKCC, 1988-93. Recreations: reading; walking; DIY; caravanning; golf. Address: (h.) 4 Glenearn Park, Forgandenny, Perth.

Gentleman, Douglas, BSc, MBChB, FRCS(Eng), FRCS(Glas). Consultant, Centre for Brain Injury Rehabilitation, Dundee, since 1997; Honorary Consultant Neurosurgeon, Ninewells Hospital, Dundee, since 1992; b. 2.1.54, Glasgow; m., Marjorie Armstrong; 1 s.; 1 d. Educ. Hutchesons' Grammar School, Glasgow; University of Glasgow. Hospital training posts, Glasgow, Manchester, Southampton, 1978-92. Member, General Medical Council, since 1984 (Chairman, Scottish Council, 1993-99, Chairman, Fitness to Practise Policy Committee, since 2001). Address: 49 Cleppington Road, Dundee DD4 7EL; T.-01382 423196 (b.); e-mail: douglas.gentleman@tpct.scot.nhs.uk

George, John Charles Grossmith, FHS. Linlithgow Pursuivant of Arms Extraordinary, since 2001; Kintyre Pursuivant of Arms, 1986-2000; b. 15.12.30, London; m., Margaret Mary Maria Mercedes Weld. Educ. Ampleforth. Lt., Hertfordshire Yeomanry, 1951-54; films and television advertising, 1952-62; College of Arms, 1962-72; Earl Marshal's Liaison Officer with the Churchill family, 1965; Green Staff Officer, Prince of Wales's Investiture, 1969; Garioch Pursuivant, 1976. Chairman, Philbeach Light Opera Society, 1961-63; Vice President, BBC "Mastermind" Club, 1979-81; Knight in Obedience, Sov. Mil. Ord. of Malta; Commander, Ord. Pro Merito Melitense; Knight Constantinian Order of St. George. Publications: The Puffin Book of Flags, 1975; The French Heralds (paper), 1985; numerous historical articles. Recreations: English light opera and musical comedies; hagiographies; sports. Address: (h.) Flat 15, 1 New Cut Rigg, Craighall Road, Edinburgh EH6 4QR; T.-0131-551 3900.

George, Professor Judith Wordsworth, MA (Oxon), PhD. Deputy Scottish Director, The Open University, since 1984; Professor in Educational Research and Development; b. 26.8.40, Bradford; 2 d. Educ. Heath Grammar School, Halifax; Somerville College, Oxford. Tutor in Philosophy, St. Andrews University; Lecturer in History of Fine Art, Manchester University; Tutor in Classics, Open University; Senior Counsellor, Open University in Scotland.

Recreations: gardening; classical music; hill-walking. Address: (b.) 10 Drumsheugh Gardens, Edinburgh EH3 7QJ; T.-0131-549 7130.

George, Professor William David, MB, BS, FRCS, MS. Regius Professor of Surgery, Glasgow University, since 1981; b. 22.3.43, Reading; 1 s.; 3 d. Educ. Henley Grammar School; London University. Lecturer in Surgery, Manchester University, 1973-77; Senior Lecturer in Surgery, Liverpool University, 1977-81. Member, National Committees, British Association of Surgical Oncology and Surgical Research Society. Recreations: veteran rowing; golf. Address: (b.) University Department of Surgery, Western Infirmary, Glasgow G11 6NT; T.-0141-211 2166.

Gerber, Pat, MA (Hons). Author and Lecturer; b. 17.3.34, Glasgow; m., Cyril Gerber; 3 s.; 2 d. Educ. St. Leonard's School; Glasgow University. Publications: The Ghost of Glenmellish; Stranger on the River; The Stone of Destiny; Maiden Voyage; Outdoors Scotland; several plays. Recreations: reading; travel; swimming; tennis; hill-walking; sailing; cars; sewing; music. Address: (h.) 6 Golf Road, Clarkston, Glasgow G76 7LZ; T.-0141-638 2269; e-mail: patriciagerber@aol.com

Gerson, Jack Barton. Dramatist and Novelist; b. 31.7.28, Glasgow; 1 d. Educ. Hillhead High School, Glasgow. RAF, two years; worked in advertising and cinema distribution, 1949-59; writing full-time since 1959; won BBC Television Play Competition, 1959, for Three Ring Circus; has written more than 100 hours of television drama; created two series, The Regiment and The Omega Factor; 14 radio plays; novels include Whitehall Sanction, Assassination Run, Treachery Game, The Back of the Tiger, Deaths Head Berlin, The Evil Thereof, The Fetch. Recreations: cinema; reading; swimming; Caribbean Islands; sleeping in front of television set. Address: (b.) The Agency, 24 Pottery Lane, Holland Park, London W11 4LZ.

Gerstenberg, Frank Eric, MA (Cantab), PGCE, FRSA. Principal, George Watson's College, Edinburgh, 1985-2001; b. 23.2.41, Balfron; m., Valerie MacLellan; 1 s.; 2 d. Educ. Trinity College, Glenalmond; Clare College, Cambridge; London University. Assistant Master, Kelly College, Tavistock, 1963-67; Housemaster and Head of History, Millfield School, 1967-74; Headmaster, Oswestry School, 1974-85. Recreations: skiing; sailing; travelling; music. Address: (h.) Sylvan House, Goose Green, Gullane EH31 2AT; T.-01620 842805; e-mail: f.e.g@btinternet.com

Gibb, Alexander Russell. Service Delivery Director, Royal Mail, North of UK, since 1999; Director and General Manager, Royal Mail Scotland and Northern Ireland, 1996-99; b. 19.9.46, Motherwell; m., Elizabeth Ann Watney. Educ. Wishaw High School. Management Trainee, Post Office, 1965; Assistant Controller, Royal Mail, 1968; Assistant Head Postmaster, Oxford, 1976; Head Postmaster, Aberdeen, 1984; Operations Controller, Scotland, Royal Mail, 1986; Operations Director, Scotland, Royal Mail, 1992. Director, Quality Scotland Foundation. Recreations: sport; walking; family; travel. Address: (b.) 102 West Port, Edinburgh EH3 9HS; T.-0131-228 7400.

Gibb, George Frederick Cullen, MA, LLB. Consultant to Messrs Marshall Wilson, Solicitors, Falkirk, since 1997; Honorary Sheriff at Falkirk, since 1987; b. 19.3.33, Edinburgh; m., Inga Mary Grieve; 1 s.; 2 d. Educ. George Heriot's School, Edinburgh; Edinburgh University. Messrs Marshall Wilson, Solicitors: Partner, 1964, Senior Partner, 1990. Recreations: golf; music; bowls; reading. Address: (h.) 85 Muirhead Road, Larbert, Stirlingshire; T.-01324 562713.

Gibb, Peter Robertson, BSc (Hons), DipAdArchStd, ARC. Executive Director, Land Reform Scotland, since 1999; b. 22.9.62, Aberdeen. Educ. Hazlehead Academy,

Aberdeen; Scott Sutherland School of Architecture; RGIT, Aberdeen. Principal, Peter Robertson Gibb Architect, 1991-96; Co-ordinator, Scottish Ogilvie Society, 1994-97; Co-ordinator, Land Reform Scotland, 1997-99. Executive Member, Scottish Land Reform Convention; Editor, William Ogilvie's Birthright in Land, 1997. Recreation: gardening. Address: (b.) Land Reform Scotland, The Chalmer, Mill of Towie, Cullen, Buckie AB56 4TA; T.-01542 841 842.

Gibbs, Lavinia. Trustee, National Galleries of Scotland, 1986-98; Member: Brodick Country Park Committee, since 1980, Ayrshire and Arran Health Council, since 1994; b. 7.6.39, London; m., Stephen Gibbs; 2 s.; 1 d. Educ. Heathfield, Ascot; Ipswich Civic College. Librarian, Courtauld Institute of Art, London, 1960-66; Child Care Officer/Social Worker, Royal Borough of Kensington and Chelsea, 1968-73; Representative for Norfolk, National Art Collections Fund, 1968-73; Member, Council, National Trust for Scotland, 1975-80, and Curatorial Committee, 1982-92. Recreation: gardening. Address: (h.) Dougarie Lodge, Isle of Arran KA27 8EB.

Gibbs, Ronald Percy, OBE. President, Phab Scotland, since 1992 (Chairman, 1984-92); a Director, Handicabs (Lothian), since 1985; Convener, History Section, The Cramond Association, since 1983; b. 1.6.21, London; m., Margaret Eleanor Dean; 3 s.; 1 d. Educ. Owen's School, Islington. Ministry (later Department) of Transport, 1938-81; set up the Ports Office for Scotland in Edinburgh, 1973, and remained Head of that Office until retiral in 1981. Recreations: transport and communications; music; Scottish and industrial history; photography. Address: (h.) 13 Inveralmond Drive, Edinburgh EH4 6JX; T.-0131-312 6034.

Gibbs, Stephen Cokayne, OBE; b. 18.7.29, Hertingfordbury, England; m., Lavinia Bacon; 2 s.; 1 d. Educ. Eton College. Served with KRRC (60th Rifles), 1947-49; TA, service with QVR (TA), 1951-63: Lt., 1951, Captain, 1956, Major, 1958; Port Line Ltd., 1949-62: Assistant Manager, 1957, London Manager, 1959; Charles Barker PLC, 1962-87: Director, 1962, Deputy Chairman, 1982-87. Non-Executive Director, Swallow Group PLC, 1970-99; National Trust for Scotland: Member, Executive, 1986-2000 and Council, 1991-96; Member: TUCC for Scotland, 1992-97, Deer Commission for Scotland, 1993-2000; Chairman: Association of Deer Management Groups, since 1994, Isle of Arran District Salmon Fishery Board, since 1990. Recreations: shooting; fishing. Address: The Estate Office, Dougarie, Isle of Arran KA27 8EB; T.-01770 840259.

Gibson, Edgar Matheson, MBE, TD, DL, DA. Deputy Lieutenant, Orkney, since 1976; Honorary Sheriff, Grampian, Highlands and Islands, since 1992; full-time professional artist since 1990; b. 1.11.34, Kirkwall; m., Jean McCarrick; 2 s.; 2 d. Educ. Kirkwall Grammar School; Gray's College of Art, Aberdeen. National Service, 1958-60; TA and TAVR service to 1985 with Lovat Scouts, reaching Lt. Col.; Battalion Second in Command, 2/51 Highland Volunteers, 1973-76; Joint Services Liaison Officer for Orkney, 1980-85; Cadet Commandant, Orkney Lovat Scouts ACF, 1979-86, Honorary Colonel, since 1986; Member, Orkney Health Board, 1991-99; Vice Chairman, Italian Chapel Preservation Committee, since 1994; Hon. President: Society of Friends of St. Magnus Cathedral, since 1994, Orkney Craftsmen's Guild, since 1997 (Chairman, 1962-82); President, Orkney Branch, SSFA and FHS, since 1997 (Chairman, 1990-97); Chairman: St. Magnus Cathedral Fair Committee, since 1982, Northern Area, Highland TA&VR Association, 1987-93. Recreation: whisky tasting. Address: (h.) Transcona, New Scapa Road, Kirkwall, Orkney; T.-0856 2849.

Gibson, Ian Ford, BSc, BA, MEd. Head Teacher, Woodfarm High School, Glasgow, since 1995; b. 16.4.49, Girvan; m., Marion Kennedy; 1 s.; 1 d. Educ. Hamilton Academy; Glasgow University; The Open University; Strathclyde University. Mathematics Teacher, Hamilton Academy, 1972-74; Assistant Principal Teacher, Mathematics, Earnock High, 1974-80; Principal Teacher, Mathematics/Assistant Head Teacher/Deputy Head Teacher, Barrhead High, 1980-95. Recreations: bowling; following junior football. Address: (b.) Woodfarm High School, Robslee Road, Thornliebank, Glasgow; T.-0141-577 2600.

Gibson, Ian Robert Lusk, MA, DipHSM. Director for Scotland and Northern Ireland, Macmillan Cancer Relief, since 1996; b. 15.5.53, Kilmarnock; m., Rosemary Margaret Copland. Educ. Dollar Academy; Edinburgh University. Various NHS management posts, 1976-86; Assistant General Manager, Royal Infirmary of Edinburgh, 1986-89; Civil Servant, 1989-90; Operations Director, Mediguard Services, 1990-92; Regional Director, Scottish Ambulance Service, 1992-96. Trustee, Edinburgh Cyrenians, since 1993. Recreations: golf; tennis; skiing; hill-walking; politics; gardening; foreign languages. Address: (b.) 9 Castle Terrace, Edinburgh; T.-0131-229 3276.

Gibson, J.N. Alastair, MD, FRCS(Edin), FRCS(Orth). Consultant Spinal Surgeon, Lothian University Hospitals, since 1993; Senior Lecturer (part-time), University of Edinburgh, since 1993; b. 21.10.54, Bellshill; m., Laurie-Ann; 2 s.; 1 d. Educ. King Edward VII Grammar School, Sheffield; Royal London Hospital Medical College, London. House Surgeon, London Hospital, 1978-79; Surgical Registrar, Ninewells Hospital, Dundee, 1981-83; Clinical Research Fellow, University of Dundee, 1984-86; University of Edinburgh: Lecturer, 1986-91, Senior Lecturer, 1993-97; Spinal Fellow, Royal North Shore Hospital, Sydney, 1992; Visiting Scholar, University of Sydney, 1992; Orthopaedic Consultant, The Thistle Foundation, since 1995; Visiting Surgeon, BUPA Murrayfield Hospital, Edinburgh, since 1998. Publications: contributor to books and professional journals. Recreation: golf. Address: Department of Orthopaedic Surgery, The New Royal Infirmary of Edinburgh, Little France, Edinburgh; T.-0131-536 4600; e-mail: j.n.a.gibson@ed.ac.uk

Gibson, John Alan, MB, ChB, MD, FRCGP, FRSMed, DObstRCOG, CBiol, FIBiol, FLS, FZS, FRGS, FRMS, FGS, FSA (Scot). Senior Honorary Secretary, British Medical Association, since 1979; Chairman, Scottish Natural History Library, since 1974; Editor, the Scottish Naturalist, since 1972; b. 15.5.26, Kilbarchan; m., Dr. Mary M. Baxter; 1 d. Educ. Lindisfarne School; Paisley Grammar School; Glasgow University. Family doctor, village of Kilbarchan; Hon. Secretary, Renfrewshire Division, BMA, 1957-2001; last Secretary, Renfrewshire Local Medical Committee; first Secretary, Argyll and Clyde Area Medical Committee; Member, Central Council, Central Ethical Committee, Scottish Council and Scottish GMS Committee, BMA; Past President, West of Scotland Branch, BMA; Hon. President, Renfrewshire Division, BMA; Fellow, Royal Society of Medicine; Life Fellow, Royal College of General Practitioners; Life Fellow, BMA; Scottish Representative and Vice-President, Society for the Bibliography of Natural History; Scientific Meetings Secretary, Vice-President and Hon. Member, Society for the History of Natural History; Chairman: Friends of Glasgow University Library, Scottish Natural History Trust; former Chairman, Clyde Area Branch, Scottish Wildlife Trust; Chairman, Clyde Area Biological Records Centre; President, Renfrewshire Natural History Society; Secretary and Honorary Life Member, Scottish Society for the Protection of Birds; Scientific Fellow, Zoological Society of London; Life Fellow: RSPB, Royal Zoological Society of Scotland, Royal Geographical Society; Chairman: Clyde

Bird Club, Clyde Mammal Group, Clyde Reptile and Amphibian Group; Honorary President, Kintyre Bird Club; Honorary Secretary and Life Fellow, Royal Physical Society of Edinburgh; Gold Medal, Scottish Society for the Protection of Birds, 1967; Queen's Silver Jubilee Medal, 1977; Fellowship, BMA, 1982. Publications: Mammals of West of Scotland; Birds of Clyde Area; Atlas of Clyde Vertebrates; Regional Bibliography of West of Scotland Vertebrates; Bibliography of Scottish Vertebrate Zoology; 300 scientific papers, books and reports on Scottish natural history, 1939-2001. Recreations: natural history; golf (Royal Troon). Address: (h.) Foremount House, Kilbarchan PA10 2EZ; T.-01505 702419.

Gibson, Kenneth James, BA (Econ). MSP (SNP), Glasgow, since 1999; Shadow Minister for Social Justice, Housing and Urban Regeneration, since 2001; Deputy Convenor, Social Justice Committee, since 2001; b. 8.9.61; m., Lynda Dorothy Payne; 2 s.; 1 d. Educ. Bellahouston Academy, Glasgow; Stirling University. Sales Representative and Trainer, pharmaceutical industry, 1988-99; Product Development Adviser, Glasgow Garden Festival, 1987-88; Systems Development Officer, British Steel, 1982-86. Leader of the Opposition, Glasgow City Council, 1998-99. Shadow Local Government Minister, 1999-2001; SNP Local Government Spokesperson, since 1997. Recreations: swimming; reading; theatre; cinema. Address: (b.) Scottish Parliament, Edinburgh EH99 1SP; T.-0131-348 5924.

Gibson, Martin Francis, OBE. Chief Executive, Erskine Hospital, since 1995; b. 21.10.46, Edinburgh; m., Lesley; 1 s.; 1 d. Educ. Fettes College; Royal Military Academy, Sandhurst. Address: (b.) Erskine Hospital, Bishopton PA7 5PU; T.-0141-814 4508.

Gibson, Sheriff William Erle, BA, LLB. Sheriff, since 1989; b. 30.8.34, Glasgow; m., Anne; 1 s.; 2 d. Educ. Dollar Academy; Trinity Hall, Cambridge; Glasgow University. Solicitor in Glasgow, 1961-89; Clerk to General Commissioners of Taxes, City of Glasgow, 1968-89; Clerk to General Council, Glasgow University, 1976-86. Recreations: golf; fishing; piping; hill-walking; the family. Address: (h.) 7A Briarwell Road, Milngavie, Glasgow; T.-0141-956 2770.

Gifford, Professor Paul Peerless Dennis, MA, DesL. Buchanan Professor of French, St Andrews University, since 1987; b. 23.4.44; m., Irma Cynthia Mary Warwick; 1 s.; 2 d. Educ. Wolverhampton Grammar School; King Edward VI School, Norwich; Trinity Hall, Cambridge. University of Toulouse, 1968-72 and 1983-85; University of Ulster, 1972-83 and 1985-87. Publications: Paul Valery: Le Dialogue des Choses Divines, 1989; Reading Paul Valery: Universe in Mind, 1999; Faith, Identity and the Common Era, 2001. Recreations: skiing; sailing; wine-tasting. Address: (h.) 51 Radernie Place, St Andrews KY16 8QR; T.-01334 477243.

Gifford, Professor Thomas Douglas MacPharlain, MA, PhD, FRSE. Head, Department of Scottish Literature, University of Glasgow, since 1994; Honorary Librarian of Abbotsford (Walter Scott's Library), since 1993; b. 14.7.40; m., Anne Tait Gifford; 3 d. Educ. Hillhead High School; University of Glasgow; Baliol College, University of Oxford. Lecturer then Senior Lecturer, University of Strathclyde, 1967-86; University of Glasgow: Senior Lecturer, 1986, Reader, 1990, Professor and Chair of Scottish Literature, 1995. Publications: James Hogg; Neil Gunn and Lewis Grassic Gibbon; History of Scottish Literature - The Nineteenth Century (Editor), 1988; History of Scottish Women's Writing (Co-editor) 1998. Address: (h.) 9 Shielhill, Ayr KA7 4SY; T.-01292 443360.

Gilbert, Colin, BA (Hons). Joint Managing Director, The Comedy Unit, since 1996 (Producer/Director, Chewin' The Fat); b. 3.4.52, Glasgow; m., Joanna; 1 s.; 1 d. Educ. St. Paul's School, Barnes; University of York. BBC Scotland: Assistant Floor Manager, 1975-79, Production Manager, 1979-80; Script Editor, Not The Nine O'Clock News, 1980-82; Head of Comedy, BBC Scotland, 1983-95; credits as Producer/Director include: Naked Video, Rab C. Nesbitt, City Lights. RTS Reith Award for Services to Broadcasting; BAFTA Scotland Award for Outstanding Contribution to Film and TV Production; RTS Best Sit-Com Award (Rab C. Nesbitt). Address: The Comedy Unit, The Glasgow TV and Film Studio, Craigmont Street, Glasgow G20 9BT; T.-0141-305 6666; e-mail: colingilbert@comedyunit.co.uk

Gilbert, George, DA, RSW. Painter; Partner, Courtyard Gallery, since 1994; b. 12.9.39, Glasgow; m., Lesley Johnston; 3 s. Educ. Victoria Drive Secondary School, Glasgow; Glasgow School of Art. Teacher of Art, Aberdeenshire, Glasgow, Fife, 1963-89; painter (exhibited widely), since 1963. Elected: RSW, 1973 (Council Member, 1994-98); SAAC, 1991, PAI, 1992. Artstore Award, 1992; Gillies Award (RSW), 1993. Recreations: walking; reading; music; the arts. Address: 44 Marketgate South, Crail, Fife KY10 3TL; T.-01333 450797.

Gilchrist, June Margaret. Advocate; b. 28.6.42, Edinburgh; m., James Gilchrist; 1 s.; 2 d. Educ. Edinburgh University. Solicitor, Ranken and Reid, Edinburgh; Procurator Fiscal Depute, Edinburgh; called to the Bar, 1993. Recreation: travel. Address: (h.) 21 Heriot Row, Edinburgh, EH3 6EN; T.-0131-226 2160.

Gilchrist, Stewart Kerr, BSc (Hons), DMS, MIMgt, MIMBM. Executive Director (Housing and Technical Resources), South Lanarkshire Council, since 1997; b. 17.2.49, Glasgow; m., Jean; 1 s.; 1 d. Educ. Renfrew High School; Camphill Secondary School, Paisley; Heriot-Watt University; Glasgow College of Technology. Lanarkshire County Council: Management Trainee, 1971, Maintenance Co-ordinator, 1973; Strathclyde Regional Council: Co-ordination and Development Manager, 1975, Assistant Head of Building and Works, 1980, Depute Director, Building and Works, 1986, Senior Depute Director, Building and Works, 1988, Director of Building and Works, 1994; Director of Technical Services, South Lanarkshire Council, 1995. Scottish Secretary, Association for Public Service Excellence. Recreations: family; church; gardening. Address: (b.) Council Offices, Almada Street, Hamilton ML3 0AA'; T.-01698 454406.

Gildea, John, LLB, DipLP, MSc. Advocate; b. 9.1.69, Airdrie; m., Tanya Kirkpatrick. Educ. St Aloysius College; Strathclyde University. Recreations: rowing (blue at university; coach, Strathclyde University Rowing Club); golf. Address: 114 Hill Street, Glasgow G3 6UA.

Giles, Cecilia Elspeth, CBE, MA. Member, Rail Users Consultative Committee for Scotland, 1989-97; b. Dumfries. Educ. Queen Margaret's School, Yorkshire; Edinburgh University. Administrative staff, Khartoum University, 1956-57; joined Administrative staff, Edinburgh University, 1957; Assistant Secretary, Edinburgh University, 1972-87; Committee of Vice-Chancellors and Principals' Administrative Training Officer (seconded part-time), 1983-85. President, Edinburgh University Graduates' Association, 1989-91, Member, Executive Committee and Editorial Committee, since 1987; Member, Business Committee, General Council, Edinburgh University, 1988-93, Convener, Constitutional Sub-Committee, 1991-93; Member, Church of Scotland Board of Stewardship and Finance, 1986-93, Vice Convener 1990-93; Member, Church of Scotland Assembly Council, 1993-96. Publication: Scotland for the Tourist (Co-author).

Recreations: entertaining friends, family and godchildren; theatre. Address: (b.) Graduates' Association, 5 Buccleuch Place, Edinburgh EH8 9LW.

Gilhooly, Professor Mary Lynn Martin, BSc, MEd, MPhil, PhD, CPsychol. Professor of Health Studies and Director, Centre of Gerontology and Health Studies, Paisley University, since 1994; b. 22.1.47, Washington, USA; m., Professor Kenneth Gilhooly; 1 s. Educ. Universities of Oregon, Aberdeen and Glasgow. Research Assistant, Department of Psychology, Aberdeen University; Research Fellow, University of Southern California; Research Officer, MRC Medical Sociology Unit, Aberdeen; Lecturer, Behavioural Sciences Group, Faculty of Medicine, Glasgow University. President, British Society of Gerontology. Address: (b.) Centre of Gerontology and Health Studies, Paisley University, Paisley PA1 2BE; T.-0141-848 3771.

Gill, Rt. Hon. Lord (Brian Gill), MA, LLB, PhD, Hon. LLD (Glas). Senator of the College of Justice in Scotland, since 1994; Lord Justice Clerk, since 2001; Chairman, Scottish Law Commission; Chairman, Royal Scottish Academy of Music and Drama; b. 25.2.42; m.; 5 s.; 1 d. Educ. St. Aloysius College; Glasgow University; Edinburgh University. Advocate, 1967; Advocate-Depute, 1977-79; Standing Junior Counsel: Foreign and Commonwealth Office (Scotland), 1974-77, Home Office (Scotland), 1979-81, Scottish Education Department, 1979-81; QC, 1981; called to the Bar, Lincoln's Inn, 1991; Keeper, Advocates' Library, 1987-94. Address: (b.) Court of Session, Parliament House, Parliament Square, Edinburgh, EH1 1RQ.

Gill, Professor Evelyn Margaret, BSc, PhD, BA. Director, Macaulay Land Use Research Institute, Aberdeen, since 2000; b. 10.1.51, Edinburgh. Educ. Mary Erskine School for Girls; Edinburgh University; Massey University, New Zealand; Open University. Researcher, Forage Intake, AFRC Grassland Research Institute, 1976-89; Overseas Development Administration, 1979-81; Natural Resources Institute, Kent, 1989-96; Chief Executive, Natural Resources International Ltd., 1996-2000; Visiting Professor: Greenwich University; Leeds University; Honorary Professor, University of Aberdeen; Trustee, International Livestock Research Institute. Recreations: hill walking; skiing; reading. Address: (b.) Macaulay Land Use Research Institute, Aberdeen, AB15 8QH; T.-01224 318611.

Gill, Kerry James Graham. Journalist; b. 29.4.47, Newcastle; m., Andrea Kevan; 2 d. Educ. Durham School; Warwick University. Westminster Press, 1969-71; Evening Post, 1971-72; The Journal, 1972-77; The Scotsman, 1977-87 (Reporter and Glasgow Editor); The Observer, 1979-87; The Times, 1987-93; Daily Record, 1994; Scottish Daily Express, since 1996 (Assistant Editor, Executive Editor, Editor, Editor Politics Policy and Comment). Recreations: modern French history; gardening; reading. Address: (h.) Spout Burn, Main Street, Fintry, Stirlingshire; T.-01360 860427.

Gill, Professor Roger William Thomas, BA (Hons), BPhil, MA, PhD, AFBPsS, FIPD, FIMgt, FRSA, CPsychol. Director, Research Centre for Leadership Studies, The Leadership Trust, and Visiting Professor of Business Administration (Human Resource Management), Strathclyde University Graduate School of Business, since 1992; b. 3.10.45, Cumbria; 1 s.; 1 d. Educ. Merchant Taylors' School, Crosby; St. Peter's College, Oxford; Liverpool University; Bradford University. English Electric, 1967-68; Inbucon/AIC Management Consultants, 1969-71; Personnel Manager, De La Rue, 1971-72; Manpower Manager, Associated Weavers, 1972-74; Lecturer, Bradford University Management Centre, 1974-

78; Assistant Professor, State University of New York at Binghamton, 1979-82; Managing Director, Roger Gill & Associates, Singapore, 1982-90; Regional Manager (Asia), PA Consulting Group, Singapore, 1990-91. Publications: numerous articles and research reports. Recreations: music; theatre; food and wine; reading; doing nothing. Address: (h.) Craigmarloch Cottage, Kilmacolm PA13 4SE; T.-01505 874386.

Gillespie, Professor Thomas Alastair, BA, PhD, FRSE. Professor of Mathematical Analysis, University of Edinburgh, since 1997; b. 15.2.45, Torrance; m., Judith Anne Nelmes; 2 s.; 1 d. Educ. Glasgow Academy; University of Cambridge; University of Edinburgh. Lecturer, 1968-87, Senior Lecturer, 1987-92, Reader in Mathematics, 1992-97, University of Edinburgh; Visiting Professor, Indiana University, 1973-74, 1983-84. Recreations: gardening; making music; jogging. Address: (b.) Department of Mathematics and Statistics, James Clerk Maxwell Building, Edinburgh EH9 3JZ; T.-0131-650 5081.

Gillies, Anne Lorne, MA, PhD, PGCE, LRAM, Drhc. Singer and Writer, since 1962; b. 21.10.44, Stirling; 1 s.; 2 d. Educ. Oban High School; Edinburgh University; London University; Jordanhill College of Education; Glasgow University. Singer: TV, radio, concert, recital, theatre, recording; writer: scripts, children's books, novels, articles, autobiography, songs; education/ community development: teacher, resource development; National Education Officer, Comunn na Gaidhlig, 1988-90, Arts Development Officer, Govan Initiative Ltd., 1991-93; Producer and Writer, Scottish Television 1993-95; Lecturer in Gaelic, University of Strathclyde, 1995-98. Recreation: married bliss. Address: (h.) 33 Stewarton Road, Dunlop, Ayrshire KA3 4DQ.

Gillies, Norman Neil Nicolson, BA, Dr.hc (Aberdeen), MIMgt, FRSA. Director, Sabhal Mor Ostaig, since 1988; b. 1.3.47, Flodigarry, Isle of Skye; m., Jean Brown Nixon; 1 s.; 2 d. Educ. Portree High School; Strathclyde University; Open University. College Secretary, Sabhal Mor Ostaig, 1983-88; Director: Skye and Lochalsh Enterprise Ltd., 1990-99, Sabhal Mor Ostaig (Developments) Ltd., Canan Ltd., Ionad Chaluim Chille, Ile; Member: Barail (Centre for Highlands and Islands Policy Studies); Leirsinn Research Centre; University of the Highlands and Islands Academic Council (Chair, Academic Standards Committee, Chair, Linguistic and Cultural Identity Forum); Gaelic Television Training Trust; Chair, Columba Initiative Council. Recreations: reading; broadcasting; family. Address: (h.) Innis Ard, Ardvasar, Isle of Skye IV45 8RU; T.-01471 844 281.

Gillies, Rev. Dr. Robert Arthur, BD, PhD. Rector, St. Andrew's Episcopal Church, St. Andrews, since 1991; b. 21.10.51, Cleethorpes; m., Elizabeth; 3 s. Educ. Barton-upon-Humber Grammar School; Edinburgh University; St. Andrews University. Medical Laboratory Technician, 1968-72; Curate: Christ Church, Falkirk, 1977-80, Christ Church Morningside, and Chaplain, Napier College, 1980-84; Chaplain, Dundee University, 1984-90. Hon. Lecturer, Department of Philosophy, Dundee University, 1985-95. Publications: A Way for Healing, 1995; Informing Faith, 1996; Healing: Broader and Deeper, 1998; New Language of Faith, 2001. Recreations: Scotland's mountains and England's canals. Address: St. Andrew's Rectory, Queen's Terrace, St. Andrews, Fife KY16 9QF; T.-01334 473344.

Gillies, Valerie, MA, MLitt, FSAScot. Poet; b. 4.6.48, Edmonton, Canada; m., William Gillies; 1 s.; 2 d. Educ. Edinburgh University; University of Mysore, S. India. Writer to the School, Boroughmuir High School and Edinburgh Academy; Radio and Television Scriptwriter; Poet to Borders Festival; Writer in Residence, Duncan of Jordanstone College of Art and Dundee District Libraries; Writer in Residence, East Lothian and Midlothian District Libraries; Writer in Residence, Edinburgh University;

Senior Arts Worker (Hospital Arts), Artlink. Publications: Each Bright Eye; Bed of Stone; Tweed Journey; The Chanter's Tune; The Ringing Rock; St. Kilda Song; Men and Beasts. Recreations: whippet-racing; field-walking; tai chi; swimming. Address: (h.) 67 Braid Avenue, Edinburgh EH10 6ED; T.-0131-447 2876.

Gillies, Professor William, MA (Edin), MA (Oxon). Professor of Celtic, Edinburgh University, since 1979; b. 15.9.42, Stirling; m., Valerie; 1 s.; 2 d. Educ. Oban High School; Edinburgh University; Corpus Christi College, Oxford; Dublin University. Dublin Institute for Advanced Studies, 1969-70; Lecturer, Edinburgh University, 1970-79; Fellow, Royal Society of Edinburgh, 1990. Director, SNDA Ltd. Recreations: walking; gardening; music; Taoist tai chi. Address: (h.) 67 Braid Avenue, Edinburgh EH10 6ED.

Gillingham, Professor John, CBE, MBE(Mil), FRSE, FRCSEng, FRCSEdin, FRCPEdin, MD(Hon), Thessaloniki, FRACS(Hon), FRCSI(Hon), FCMSA(Hon), FRCPGlas (Hon), FRSA. Member, Court of Regents, Royal College of Surgeons of Edinburgh; Professor Emeritus, Department of Surgical Neurology University of Edinburgh; Foundation Professor of Surgical Neurology, Kind Saud University, Saudi Arabia, 1983-85; Honorary Consultant Neurosurgeon, St. Bartholomew's Hospital, since 1980; b. 15.3.16, Dorchester, Dorset; m., Judy; 4 s. Educ. Hardy's School, Dorset; St. Bartholomew's Hospital Medical College, London University. House Officer posts, St. Bartholomew's; Lieutenant, RAMC, Military Hospital for Head Injuries, Oxford, 1940-41; Surgeon (later o/c Major), No. 4 Mobile Neurosurgery Unit, North African Desert and Italy, 1942-45; St. Bartholomew's Hospital: Senior Registrar, 1946-47, Senior Registrar, Neurosurgery Unit, 1957; Senior Lecturer, then Reader, then Professor of Surgical Neurology, Edinburgh University, 1950-79; Consultant Neurosurgeon, Royal Infirmary of Edinburgh and Western General Hospital, Edinburgh; Consultant Neurosurgeon to the Army in Scotland, 1970-83, and to the Armed Forces of Saudi Arabia, 1979-83; Hon. President, World Federation of Neurosurgical Societies, 1979; President, Royal College of Surgeons of Edinburgh, 1979-82. Publications: Head Injuries (Editor); Stereotactic Surgery; 84 papers on stereotactic surgery, head and spinal injuries, epilepsy, cerebro-vascular surgery, postgraduate training and education. Recreations: sailing; landscape gardening (cactus). Address: Easter Park House, Easter Park Drive, Barnton Avenue, Edinburgh EH4 6SN; T.-0131-336 3528.

Gillon, Karen Macdonald. MSP (Labour), Clydesdale, since 1999; b. 18.8.67, Edinburgh; m., James Gillon; 1 s. Educ. Jedburgh Grammar School; Birmingham University. Youth Worker, Terminal One Youth Centre, Blantyre, 1991-94; Community Education Worker, North Lanarkshire Council, 1994-97; PA to Rt. Hon. Helen Liddell, MP, 1997-99. Recreations: sport; music; flower arranging; reading; cooking. Address: (b.) 11 Wellgate, Lanark ML11 9DS; T.-01555 660526; e-mail: karen.gillon.msp@scottish.parliament.uk

Gilloran, Professor Alan James, MA PhD. Dean, Faculty of Social Sciences and Health Care, Queen Margaret University College, Edinburgh since 1996; Sociologist; b. 7.6.56, Edinburgh; m., Barbara; 1 s.; 1 d. Educ. Daniel Stewart's College, Edinburgh; University of Edinburgh. Researcher, Wester Hailes Representative Council; Research Assistant, Moray House; Research Fellow, University of Edinburgh; Lecturer in Sociology and Social Policy, University of Stirling. Chair, South East Scotland Wider Access Regional Forum; Member, Care Development Group on Free Personal Care for Elderly People. Publications: academic articles; book chapters; five funded research reports into dementia and mental health. Recreations: badminton; wine; travel. Address: (b.) Queen

Margaret University College, Clerwood Terrace, Edinburgh EH12 8TS; T.-0131-317 3700; e-mail: agilloran@qmuc.ac.uk

Gilmore, Professor William C., LLB, LLM, MA, PhD. Professor, International Criminal Law, Edinburgh University, since 1996; b. 31.3.51, Nassau, Bahamas; m., Dr Patricia Shepherd; 1 s.; 1 d. Educ. St Joseph's College, Dumfries; Edinburgh University; University of London; Carlton University. Lecturer, Law, University of West Indies, Barbados, 1973-75; Commonwealth Projects Officer, IILED, Washington D.C., 1977-79; Lecturer/Senior Lecturer/Reader, Faculty of Law, Edinburgh University, 1979-96; Assistant Director, Legal Division/Head, Commercial Crime Unit, Commonwealth Secretariat, Marlborough House, London, 1991-93. Publications include: Dirty Money, 1995; Newfoundland and Dominion Status, 1988; The Grenada Intervention, 1984. Recreations: travel; fishing. Address: (b.) Old College, South Bridge, Edinburgh, EH8 9YL.

Gilmour, Colonel Sir Allan Macdonald, KCVO, OBE, MC (and Bar), DSC (USA); b. 23.11.16, Edinburgh; m., Jean Wood; 3 s.; 1 d. Educ. Cargilfield, Edinburgh; Winchester College; Trinity College, Oxford. Commissioned Seaforth Highlanders, 1939; served War in Middle East, Sicily and NW Europe; Regimental and Staff appointments, 1945-69, including Instructor, Staff College, Quetta, and Chief of Staff, Ghana Armed Forces; Member, Sutherland County Council, 1970; Member, Highland Health Board, 1974 (Chairman, 1982-84); DL, Sutherland, 1969; Lord Lieutenant of Sutherland, 1972-96; Member, Highlands and Islands Development Consultative Council, 1980-88; Chairman: Sutherland District Council, 1974-78, East Sutherland Council of Social Service, 1972-76; Member: Board, Scottish National Orchestra Society, 1976-86, Highland Regional Council, 1976-96; President, Highland Territorial & Auxiliary Reserve Association, 1988-91; Chairman, Highland River Purification Board, 1994-96. Recreation: fishing. Address: (h.) Invernauld, Rosehall, Lairg, Sutherland; T.-0154 984 204.

Gilmour, Andrew Parr, BSc (Hons). Rector, Rothesay Academy, since 1983; b. 26.4.46, Glasgow; m., Elizabeth Morrison MacPherson; 1 s.; 2 d. Educ. Allan Glen's School, Glasgow; Glasgow University. Teacher of Chemistry, Allan Glen's School, 1969; Dunoon Grammar School: Principal Teacher of Chemistry, 1972, Assistant Rector, 1975; Depute Head Teacher, Mearns Castle High School, 1981. Recreations: golf; badminton; rugby (spectating nowadays); swimming; cycling; windsurfing; gardening. Address: (h.) Millford, 34 Mount Stuart Road, Rothesay, Isle of Bute; T.-01700 503336.

Gilmour, Douglas Graham, BSc (Hons), MB, ChB, MD, FRCS. Consultant Vascular Surgeon, Glasgow Royal Infirmary, since 1983; b. 15.4.47, Glasgow; m., Evelyn Jean; 2 s.; 2 d. Educ. Kelvinside Academy, Glasgow; Glasgow University. House Surgeon/Physician, then Senior House Officer/Registrar in Surgery, Western Infirmary, Glasgow, 1971-77; Glasgow Royal Infirmary: Senior Registrar in Surgery, 1977-80, Senior Lecturer (Honorary Consultant) in Surgery, 1980-83. Recreations: family; golf; skiing; sailing; flying. Address: (b.) Vascular Surgery Department, Royal Infirmary, Glasgow; T.-0141-211 4772.

Gilmour, John, DL, MFH. Farmer; b. 15.7.44, Edinburgh; m., Valerie Jardine Russell; 2 s.; 2 d. Educ. Eton; Aberdeen College. Captain, FFY/SH (TA); Member, Queen's Bodyguard for Scotland (Royal Company of Archers); Hon. Col. FFY/SH (TA); Trustee and Director, The Moredun Foundation; Chairman, Scottish Farm Venison. Recreations: fishing; reading. Address: Balcormo Mains, Leven, Fife; T.-01333 360229.

Gilmour, John. Head of Sports Policy Unit, Scottish Executive Education Department, since 1998; b. 20.11.50, Dunfermline; m., Ann C. Educ. Dunfermline High School. Various posts, Scottish Office, since joining Civil Service, 1970. Recreations: sport; reading. Address: (b.) Sports Policy Unit, Scottish Executive Education Department, Victoria Quay, Edinburgh EH6 6QQ; T.-0131-244 0993.

Gilmour, John Andrew George, MA, LLB, NP. Solicitor; Marketing Consultant; Honorary Sheriff at Dumbarton, since 1991; b. 17.11.37, Balloch; m., Roma Aileen; 3 d. Educ. Morrison's Academy, Crieff; Edinburgh University. Consultant, McArthur Stanton; President, Strathclyde Junior Chamber of Commerce, 1973; Director, Dumbarton Enterprise Trust, 1985-2000; Dean, Faculty of Dunbartonshire Solicitors, 1988-90; Law Society accredited Liquor Licensing Specialist, 1993. Recreations: sport; music; gastronomy. Address: (h.) Cramond Cottage, 19 East Lennox Drive, Helensburgh; T.-01436 675057.

Gilmour, Col. Sir John Edward, 3rd Bt, DSO, TD, JP, BA. Lord Lieutenant of Fife, 1980-87; b. 24.10.12, Edinburgh; m., Ursula Mabyn Wills; 2 s. Educ. Eton College; Trinity Hall, Cambridge; Dundee School of Economics. Served with Fife and Forfar Yeomanry, 1939-45; served on Fife County Council, 1951-61; MP (Conservative), East Fife, 1961-79; Chairman, Conservative Party in Scotland, 1965-67; Lord High Commissioner, General Assembly, Church of Scotland, 1982, 1983. Recreation: gardening. Address: (h.) Montrave, Leven, Fife, KY8 5NY; T.-Leven 426159.

Gilmour, John Scott, CA, ATII, CIArb, TEP. Partner, Hardie Caldwell, CA, Glasgow, since 1989; b. 9.8.44, Glasgow; m., Susan. Educ. Glasgow Academy. Chartered Accountant, since 1968. Member, Council, Institute of Chartered Accountants of Scotland, since 1997. Director, Glasgow Opportunities; Director, Merchants House of Glasgow. Recreation: water skiing; skiing; walking. Address: (b.) Savoy Tower, 77 Renfrew Street, Glasgow G2 3BY; T.-0141-333 9770; e-mail: jsgilmour@hardiecaldwell.co.uk

Gilmour, William McIntosh, OStJ, BL. Honorary Sheriff, Dumbarton; Lawyer; b. 9.3.23, Newcastle-upon-Tyne; m., Elinor Adams. Educ. Hillhead High School; Cally House, Gatehouse of Fleet; Glasgow University. Early experience with legal firms in Glasgow; became Partner, latterly Senior Partner, in firm in Dunbartonshire; now retired; former Dean, Faculty of Solicitors in Dunbartonshire; founder Member and Past President, Clydebank Rotary Club; Past Deacon, Society of Deacons and Free Presces; former Chairman for Dunbartonshire, Order of St. John; Member, Incorporation of Gardeners (Glasgow Trades House). Recreations: dog-walking (formerly, motor sport). Address: (h.) 65 Killermont Road, Bearsden, Glasgow; T.-0141-942 0498.

Gimblett, Sheriff Margaret, MA. Sheriff at Dunoon, since 1999; b. 24.9.39, Perth; m., Iain; 1 s.; 1 d. Educ. St. Leonards, St. Andrews; University of Edinburgh; University of Glasgow. Retail Management, John Lewis Partnership, London, until 1970; Partner, Russel and Aitken, Solicitors, 1972-95; Temporary Sheriff, 1994-95; Sheriff, Glasgow and Strathkelvin, 1995-99; Churchill Fellow. Recreations: gardening; tourism. Address: (b.) Dunoon Sheriff Court, George Street, Dunoon PA23 8BQ; T.-01369 704166.

Gimingham, Professor Charles Henry, OBE, BA, PhD, ScD, FRSE, FIBiol, FFCS. Regius Professor of Botany, Aberdeen University, 1981-88; b. 28.4.23, Leamington; m., Elizabeth Caroline Baird; 3 d. Educ. Gresham's School, Holt, Norfolk; Emmanuel College, Cambridge. Research Assistant, Imperial College, London, 1944-45; Department of Botany, Aberdeen University: Assistant, 1946-48, Lecturer, 1948-61, Senior Lecturer, 1961-64, Reader, 1964-69, Professor, since 1969, Head of Department, 1981-88; Member: Scottish Committee of Nature Conservancy, 1966-69, Scottish Advisory Committee, Nature Conservancy Council, 1970-80, Countryside Commission for Scotland, 1980-92; President, Botanical Society of Edinburgh, 1982-84; Vice-Chairman, NE Regional Board, Nature Conservancy Council for Scotland, 1991-92; Member: NE Regional Board, SNH, 1992-96, Science Advisory Committee, SNH, 1996-99, Board of Management, Hill Farming Research Organisation, 1981-87, Governing Body, Aberdeen College of Education, 1981-87, Council of Management, Macaulay Institute for Soil Research, 1983-87, Board of Management, Macaulay Land Use Research Institute, 1987- 90; British Ecological Society: Joint Secretary, 1956-61, Vice-President, 1962-64, Joint Editor, Journal of Ecology, 1975-78, President, 1986-87; Patron, Institute of Ecology and Environmental Management, 2000. Publications: Ecology of Heathlands, 1972; Introduction to Heathland Ecology, 1975; Lowland Heathland Management Handbook, 1992. Recreations: hill-walking; photography; history and culture of Japan. Address: (h.) 4 Gowanbrae Road, Bieldside, Aberdeen.

Gimson, George Stanley, QC (Scot); b. 1915. Educ. High School of Glasgow; Glasgow University. Advocate, 1949; QC, 1961; Sheriff Principal: Aberdeen, Kincardine and Banff, 1972-74, Grampian, Highland and Islands, 1975-82; Member, Edinburgh Central Hospitals Board, 1960-70 (Chairman, 1964-70); Director, SNO Society Ltd., 1962-80; Trustee, National Library of Scotland, 1963-76; Chairman: Pensions Appeals Tribunals, Scotland, 1971-95, RSSPCC, Edinburgh, 1972-76, Scottish Far-East P.O.W. Association, since 1996; Hon. LLD, Aberdeen, 1981. Address: (h.) 16 Royal Circus, Edinburgh EH3 6SS.

Girdwood, Professor Ronald Haxton, CBE, MB, ChB (Hons), MD, PhD, FRCPEd, FRCP, FRCPI, FRCPath, Hon. FACP, Hon. FRACP, FRSE. President, Royal College of Physicians of Edinburgh, 1982-85; Chairman, Scottish National Blood Transfusion Association, 1980-95; b. 19.3.17, Arbroath; m., Mary Elizabeth Williams; 1 s.; 1 d. Educ. Daniel Stewart's College, Edinburgh; Edinburgh University; Michigan University. Army service, RAMC, UK and India, 1942-46, successively as Lt., Captain, Major and Lt.-Col. (when posted to Burma); Lecturer, then Senior Lecturer, Reader in Medicine, Edinburgh University, 1946-62; Research Fellow, Michigan University, 1948-49; Consultant Physician, Edinburgh Royal Infirmary, 1950-82; Professor of Therapeutics and Clinical Pharmacology, Edinburgh University, 1962-82 (Dean, Faculty of Medicine, 1975-79); President, Edinburgh University Church of Scotland Society, 1938-39; Elder, Kirk of the Greyfriars, since 1955; Chairman, Scottish Group, Nutrition Society, 1961-62; President, British Society for Haematology, 1963-64; Chairman, Executive Committee, Edinburgh and SE Scotland Blood Transfusion Association, 1970-95; Member, UK Committee on Safety of Medicines, 1972-83; Chairman, Medico-Pharmaceutical Forum, 1985-87; President, University of Edinburgh Graduates' Association, 1991-92; Member, Board of Governors, St. Columba's Hospice, 1985-97; Suniti Panja Gold Medal, Calcutta School of Tropical Medicine, 1980; given the Freedom of Sirajgunj, Bangladesh, 1984; Oliver Memorial Award for services to blood transfusion, 1991. Publications: Travels with a Stethoscope, 1991; editor of four medical books and more than 300 medical papers. Recreations: writing; photography. Address: (h.) 2 Hermitage Drive, Edinburgh EH10 6DD; T.-0131-447 5137.

Girvin, Professor Brian, BA, MA, PhD. Professor of Comparative Politics, University of Glasgow, since 2000; b. 16.7.50, Cork; partner, Rona Fitzgerald; 1 s. Educ. Sullivan's Quay CBS, Cork; University College, Cork. Temporary Lecturer, National Institute for Higher Education, Limerick, 1978-82; University College, Cork: Temporary Teaching Assistant, 1983-86, Director of European Studies, 1986-88, Lecturer in Modern History, 1986-95; Senior Lecturer in Politics, University of Glasgow, 1995-2000. Publications: Politics and Society in Contemporary Ireland (Co-Editor), 1986; The Transformation of Contemporary Conservatism (Editor), 1988; Between Two Worlds: Politics and Economy in Independent Ireland, 1989; The Right in the Twentieth Century: Conservatism and Democracy, 1994; The Green Pool Negotiations and the Origins of the Common Agricultural Policy (Co-Editor), 1995; Ireland and the Second World War: Politics, Society and Remembrance (Co-Editor), 2000; From Union to Union: Nationalism, Democracy and Religion in Ireland since 1800, 2002. Recreation: mountaineering; cooking; arguing; film; music; books. Address: Department of Politics, University of Glasgow G12 8RT; T.-0141-330 5353; e-mail: b.girvin@socsci.gla.ac.uk

Given-Wilson, Professor Christopher John, MA, PhD, FRHistS. Professor of Late Mediaeval History, St Andrews University, since 1998; b. 27.2.49, Singapore; m., Alice Freda Curteis; 2 d. Educ. Downside School; St Andrews University. Lecturer in Mediaeval History, St Andrews University, 1978-98. Alexander Prize, Royal Historical Society, 1986. Publications: seven books on late mediaeval British history. Recreations: golf; reading; travel; walking. Address: (b.) Department of Mediaeval History, The University, St Andrews KY16 9AJ; T.-01334 463318.

Glasby, Michael Arthur, BM, BCh, MA, MSc (Oxon), MA (Cantab), CBiol, MIBiol, FICS, FRCS (Edin), FRCS (Eng). Reader in Experimental Neurology and Honorary Consultant, Edinburgh University, since 1997; b. 29.10.48, Nottingham; m., Celia M.E. Robinson. Educ. High Pavement Grammar School, Nottingham; Christ Church, Oxford; Oxford Medical School. Senior Scholar and Assistant Tutor in Physiology, Christ Church, Oxford, 1971-76; Surgeon, Harefield Hospital Transplant Trust, 1981-83; Fellow and Lecturer in Anatomy, New Hall, Cambridge, 1983-87; Lecturer in Anatomy, Royal College of Surgeons of England, 1984-87; joined Edinburgh University as Lecturer, 1987; Reader in Anatomy, 1992-97. Editor, anatomy textbook for surgeons and physiology textbook for surgeons; numerous articles. Recreations: golf; Latin and Greek literature; music; beekeeping; wine. Address: (b.) Department of Clinical Neurosciences, Edinburgh University, Western General Hospital, Crewe Road, Edinburgh EH4 2XU; T.-0131-537 2905.

Glasgow, 10th Earl of (Patrick Robin Archibald Boyle), DL. Television Director/Producer; b. 30.7.39; m., Isabel Mary James; 1 s.; 1 d. Educ. Eton; Paris University. Sub.-Lt., RNR, 1959-60; Producer/Director, Yorkshire TV, 1968-70; freelance Film Producer, since 1971; created Kelburn Country Centre (leisure park), 1977, and now manages this and Kelburn Estate; Deputy Lieutenant, Ayrshire. Address (b.) Kelburn Castle, Fairlie, Ayrshire KA29 0BE; T.-01475 568685.

Glasier, Anna, MB, ChB, BSc, FRCOG, MD. Director, Lothian Primary Care NHS Trust Family Planning and Well Woman Services, since 1990; Senior Lecturer, Department of Obstetrics and Gynaecology, Edinburgh University, since 1990; Consultant Gynaecologist, Lothian Health Board, since 1989; b. 16.4.50, Salisbury; m., Dr. David T. Baird. Educ. Lord Digby's School, Sherborne. Clinical Research Scientist, Medical Research Council Centre for Reproductive Biology, Edinburgh, 1989-90. Recreations: ski mountaineering; sailing. Address: (b.) 18 Dean Terrace, Edinburgh EH4 1NL; T.-0131-332 7941.

Glass, Alexander, OBE, MA, DipEd. Rector, Dingwall Academy, 1977-97; b. 1.6.32, Dunbar; m., Edith Margaret Duncan Baxter; 3 d. Educ. Dunbar Grammar School; Edinburgh University; Heidelberg University; University of Aix-en-Provence. Teacher of Modern Languages, Montrose Academy, 1958-60; Special Assistant Teacher of Modern Languages, Oban High School, 1960-62; Principal Teacher of Modern Languages, Nairn Academy, 1962-65; Principal Teacher of French and Assistant Rector, Perth Academy, 1965-72; Rector, Milne's High School, Fochabers, 1972-77. Chairman, COSPEN; former President, Highland Secondary Headteachers' Association; former Chairman, Highland Region Working Party for Modern Languages; former Chairman, Children's Panel Chairmen's Group; former Chairman, Highland Children's Panel; Chairman, Highland Children's Panel Advisory Committee's Monitoring Sub-Committee; Reader, Church of Scotland; Auxiliary Minister, Presbytery of Ross; Scottish Community Drama Association: Divisional Secretary/Festival Organiser, Highland Division, Member, General Council; former Chairman and Secretary, Scottish Secondary Schools' Travel Trust; Member, Highland Health Council; Member, Church of Scotland Board of Social Responsibility; Church of Scotland Representative, Highland Education Committee. Churchill Fellow, 1991. Recreations: amateur drama; foreign travel; Rotary. Address: (h.) Craigton, Tulloch Avenue, Dingwall IV15 9TU; T.-01349 863258.

Glass, Douglas James Allan, LVO, MB, ChB. General Practitioner, Ballater, since 1987; Apothecary to HM Household, Balmoral, since 1988; Partner in farm (D.L. Glass), since 1982; b. 8.10.53, Dinnet, Aboyne; m., Suzanne; 1 s.; 4 d. Educ. Aboyne Academy; Banchory Academy; Aberdeen University. Junior House Officer, 1977-78; Senior House Officer, 1978-79; General Practitioner Trainee, 1979-80; General Practice, Australia and New Zealand, 1980-81; General Practice Principal, Peterhead, 1981-87. Church Elder. Recreations: dry stane dyking; golf; snooker; football. Address: (h.) Deecastle, Dinnet, Aboyne, Aberdeenshire; T.-013397 55686.

Glasser, Lesley Scott Dent, MBE, BA (Cantab), PhD, DSc, CChem, FInstP, CPhys, FRSC, FRSE, DSc (Hon, RGU); b. 19.5.32, Grimsby; m., Professor Fredrik Paul Glasser; 1 s.; 2 d. Educ. Wintringham Grammar School; Newnham College, Cambridge; Aberdeen University. Research Fellow, Lecturer, Senior Lecturer, Reader, Aberdeen University Department of Chemistry, 1958-85. Member, Board of Directors, Satrosphere (former Managing Director); President, ASE Scotland, 1996; Secretary, UK Crystallographic Council, 1978-82; Trustee, National Museums of Scotland; Trustee, Scottish Mining Museum; Member, Council, Royal Society of Edinburgh, and Convenor, Links with Young People Committee; Member, Council, British Association for the Advancement of Science; Chairman, Scottish Branch, Institute of Physics, 1995-97; Kelvin Medal and Prize, Institute of Physics, 1998. Recreation: gardening. Address: (b.) Satrosphere, The Tramsheds, 179 Constitution Street, Aberdeen AB24 5TU; e-mail: glasser@ifb.co.uk

Gleeson, Steven, LLB, DipLP, NP. Solicitor/Partner, Gleeson McCafferty, since 2001; b. 8.6.58, Edinburgh; 1 s.; 1 d. Educ. Royal High School, Edinburgh; Dundee University. Allan McDougall & Co., Edinburgh, 1983-86; Rollo Davidson and McFarlane, Cupar, 1986-96; Partner, Spence Gleeson, Glenrothes, 1996-2001. Former Dean, Kirkcaldy Law Society; Vice-Convener, CALM Scotland, 1994-95; Member, Law Society of Scotland Legal Aid Committee, since 1999. Recreations: rugby (coach); travel. Address: (b.) 4 Acorn Court, Glenrothes, Fife; T.-01592 611660.

Glen, Duncan Munro. Writer and Lecturer; Sole Owner, Akros Publications, since 1960; b. 11.1.33, Cambuslang; m., Margaret Eadie; 1 s.; 1 d. Educ. West Coats, Cambuslang; Edinburgh College of Art. Book Designer, London; Lecturer in Typography; Editor, Robert Gibson & Co. Ltd.; Lecturer, then Senior Lecturer, then Head of Graphic Design, Lancashire Polytechnic; Professor and Head, Department of Visual Communication, Nottingham Trent University (Emeritus Professor); Member, Council for Academic Awards, 1979-89; Editor: Akros, poetry magazine, 1-51, ZED 2 0, 1-15, Scottish Poetry Library Newsletter; special personal award, Scottish Arts Council (for services to literature), 1975; Howard Sergeant Memorial Award, 1991; honorary doctorate, Paisley University, 2000. Author and editor of many books including Hugh MacDiarmid and The Scottish Renaissance, Selected Essays of Hugh MacDiarmid, In Appearances: Poems, The Autobiography of a Poet, Makars' Walk, The Poetry of the Scots, Selected Poems 1965-1990, Hugh MacDiarmid: Out of Langholm and Into the World; A Nation in a Parish; Four Scottish Poets; Splendid Lanarkshire; New Selected Poems, 1987-96; Illustrious Fife: literary, historical and architectural pathways and walks; A New History of Cambuslang; Scottish Literature: a new history from 1299 to 1999; Selected Scottish and Other Essays; Printing Type Designs: a new history from Gutenberg to 2000; John Atman and Other Poems, 2001; Three/tritto translators of poems by Duncan Glen – Nat Scammacca, Enzo Bonventre, Marco Scalabrino, 2001. Recreation: walking. Address: (h.) 33 Lady Nairn Avenue, Kirkcaldy, Fife KY1 2AW; T.-01592 651522.

Glen, Eric Stanger, MB, ChB, FRCSGlas, FRCSEdin. Consultant Urological Surgeon, Walton Urological Teaching and Research Centre, Southern General Hospital, Glasgow, 1972-99; b. 20.10.34, Glasgow; m., Dr. Patricia. Educ. Glasgow University. Pre-Consultant posts, Western and Victoria Infirmaries, Glasgow; Ship Surgeon, Royal Fleet Auxiliary. Formerly Medical Director, Continence Resource Centre and Helpline for Scotland; Past Chairman, Area Medical Committee; Founder and former Secretary, International Continence Society; former Honorary Clinical Senior Lecturer, Glasgow University; former Member, Surgical Examination Panel, Royal College of Physicians and Surgeons of Glasgow; Founder, Urological Computing Society. Publications: chapters in books; papers on urodynamics, urology and computing. Recreations: travel; writing; computer applications. Address: (h.) 9 St. John's Road, Pollokshields, Glasgow G41 5RJ; T.-0141-423 0759; e-mail: eric@pollokshields.fsnet.co.uk

Glen, William Hamish. Artistic Director, Dundee Rep, since 1992; Chair, Federation of Scottish Theatre; b. 20.12.57, Edinburgh; m., Denise Maria Winford. Educ. Edinburgh Academy. ASM, Traverse Theatre, 1979-81; Trainee Director, Tron Theatre, 1986-87, Associate Director, 1988-89; Artistic Director, Winged Horse, 1990-92; worked as freelance director in Lithuania and Finland. Address: (b.) Tay Square, Dundee; T.-01382 227684.

Glenarthur, 4th Baron (Simon Mark Arthur), Bt, DL, FCIT, FRAeS. DL, Aberdeenshire, since 1987; Director: Millennium Chemicals Inc., since 1996, Whirly Bird Services Ltd., since 1995; a Governor, Nuffield Hospitals, since 2000; b. 7.10.44; m.; 1 s.; 1 d. Educ. Eton. Retired Major, 10th Royal Hussars (PWO); Helicopter Captain, British Airways, 1976-82; a Lord in Waiting 1982-83; Parliamentary Under Secretary of State: Department of Health and Social Security, 1983-85, Home Office, 1985-86; Minister of State: Scottish Office, 1986-87, Foreign and Commonwealth Office, 1987-89; Consultant: British Aerospace PLC, 1989-99, Hanson PLC, 1989-99, Imperial Tobacco Ltd., 1996-98; Deputy Chairman, Hanson Pacific Ltd., 1994-97; Chairman, St. Mary's Hospital, Paddington, NHS Trust, 1991-98, British Helicopter Advisory Board, since 1992, European Helicopter Association, since 1996;

President, National Council for Civil Protection, since 1991; Member (Brigadier), Queen's Bodyguard for Scotland (Royal Company of Archers); Scottish Patron, The Butler Trust, since 1994; a Commissioner, Royal Hospital Chelsea, since 2001. Address: (b.) PO Box 11012, Banchory AB31 6JZ; T.-01330 844467.

Glennie, John Ellis, FCCA, CIPFA, IHEEM. Chief Executive, Borders General Hospital NHS Trust, since 1995; b. 28.9.48, Keith; 2 s; 1 d. Educ. Keith Grammar School. Joined NHS as a trainee accountant, Aberdeen, 1966, and progressed through a number of posts to become Director of Finance, Darlington Health Authority, 1982; Director of Finance, Information and Computing, Central Manchester Health Authority, 1985-91; Director of Finance, then Deputy Chief Executive/Director of Operations, Central Manchester Healthcare NHS Trust, 1992-95. National Treasurer, Healthcare Financial Management Association; Chairman, Property and Environment Forum. Address: (b.) Borders General Hospital NHS Trust, Melrose TD6 9BS; T.-01896 826000.

Glennie, Robert. Senior Partner, McGrigor Donald, since 2000; b. 4.4.51, Glasgow. Educ. Jordanhill College School, Glasgow; Strathclyde University. Qualified, 1978; assumed as Partner, McGrigor Donald, 1980; Managing Partner, London Office, 1989. Recreations: hill-walking; cinema; tropical fruit farming. Address: (b.) Pacific House, 70 Wellington Street, Glasgow G2 6SB.

Gloag, Ann. Director, Stagecoach Holdings plc, since 1986 (Managing Director, 1986-94, Executive Director, 1986-2000); b. 10.12.42. Educ. Perth High School. Nursing, 1960-80; Founding Partner, Stagecoach, 1980. Address: (b.) Stagecoach Group, 10 Dunkeld Road, Perth PH1 5TW.

Glover, Rev. Robert Lindsay, BMus, BD, ARCO. Minister, Chalmers Memorial, Cockenzie and Port Seton, since 1997; b. 21.7.45, Watford; m., Elizabeth Mary Brown; 2 s.; 2 d. Educ. Langholm Academy; Dumfries Academy; Glasgow University. Minister: Newton Parish, near Dalkeith, 1971-76, St. Vigeans Parish, Arbroath, 1976-85, Knox's, Arbroath, 1982-85, St. George's West, Edinburgh, 1985-97. Recreations: music; reading; travel. Address: Braemar Villa, 2 Links Road, Port Seton, Prestonpans, East Lothian EH32 0HA; e-mail: rlglover@btinternet.com

Glover, Sue, MA. Writer; b. 1.3.43, Edinburgh; m., John Glover; 2 s. Educ. St. George's School, Edinburgh; Montpellier University; Edinburgh University. Original drama and other scriptwriting for radio, television and theatre; theatre productions include: The Seal Wife, Edinburgh Festival, 1980; An Island in Largo, Byre Theatre, 1981; The Bubble Boy, Glasgow Tron, 1981; The Straw Chair, Traverse Theatre, 1988; Bondagers, Traverse Theatre, 1991 (winner, 1990 LWT Plays on Stage Award); Sacred Hearts, 1994; Artist Unknown, 1996; Shetland Saga, Traverse Theatre, 2000; television work includes: The Spaver Connection; Mme Montand and Mrs Miller; Dear Life; televised version of The Bubble Boy won a silver medal, New York Film and Television Festival, and a merit, Chicago International Film Festival, 1983. Publications: The Bubble Boy: You Don't Know You're Born, 1991; Bondagers (Made in Scotland), 1995; Bondagers and The Straw Chair, 1997; Shetland Saga, 2000. Recreations: house and garden. Address: 8 Water Wynd, Pittenweem, Fife.

Godden, Tony Richard Hillier, CB, BSc (Econ); b. 13.11.27, Barnstaple; m., Marjorie Florence Snell; 1 s.; 2 d. Educ. Barnstaple Grammar School; London School of Economics. Commissioned, RAF Education Branch, 1950; entered Civil Service, 1951; first appointed to Colonial Office; Private Secretary to Parliamentary Under Secretary of State, 1954-55; seconded to Cabinet Office, 1957-59; joined Scottish Home Department, 1961; Assistant

Secretary, Scottish Development Department, 1964; Under Secretary, 1969; Secretary, Scottish Economic Planning Development, 1973-80; Secretary, Scottish Development Department, 1980-87. Member: The Council on Tribunals and its Scottish Committee, 1988-94, Advisory Board on Ancient Monuments, 1990-95; Secretary, Friends of the Royal Scottish Academy, 1988-2000. Address: 9 Ross Road, Edinburgh EH16 5QN.

Godfrey, Professor Alan Dearn, BA (Hons), CPFA, FCCA. Professor of Accounting and Head, Division of Accounting and Finance, Caledonian Business School, Glasgow Caledonian University; b. 12.5.46, Falkirk; 1 s.; 1 d. Educ. Falkirk High School; Strathclyde University. Financial Consultant, Engineering Services Ltd., 1972-76; Lecturer, then Senior Lecturer, Glasgow College, 1976-88; Depute Head of Department, then Acting Head of Department, Glasgow Polytechnic, 1988-93. Recreations: music; golf. Address: (b.) Division of Accounting and Finance, Glasgow Caledonian University, Glasgow G4 0BA; T.-0141-331 3361.

Godfrey, Andrew Paul, CA. Regional Managing Partner, Scottish Region, Grant Thornton, since 1998; b. 12.8.53, Edinburgh; m., Irene; 2 s. Educ. Morrison's Academy; Edinburgh University. Joined Grant Thornton Glasgow Office, 1982; Scottish Managing Partner, 1998; Head of Grant Thornton International and European Services. Recreation: keen member of Dunblane and Gleneagles Golf Clubs. Address: (b.) 114 West George Street, Glasgow G2 1QF.

Godman, Norman. MP (Labour), Greenock and Inverclyde (formerly Greenock and Port Glasgow) 1983-2000; b. 11.4.38; m. Educ. Hull University; Heriot-Watt University. Former teacher.

Godman, Trish. MSP (Labour), West Renfrewshire, since 1999; Convener, Local Government Committee; b. 1939; m.; 3 s. Educ. St Gerard's Senior Secondary School; Jordanhill College. Former Regional Councillor; former Member, Glasgow City Council. Recreations: music; dancing; reading; cinema; learning to be a grandmother. Address: (b.) Scottish Parliament, Edinburgh EH99 1SP; T.-0131-348 5837.

Gold, Lex, CBE. Director, Scottish Chambers of Commerce; Chairman, Scottish Premier League; Director, Caledonian MacBrayne; Director, Scotlander Ltd; Director, NorthLink Orkney and Shetland Ferries Ltd.; b. 14.12.40, Rigside; m., Eleanor; 1 s.; 1 d. Educ. Lanark Grammar School. Sub-Editor, Daily Record; professional footballer; joined Civil Service, Glasgow, 1960; Inland Revenue, two years, Civil Service Department, four years, Home Office, 21 years, Training Agency, three years; former Managing Director, Scottish Enterprise; former Director, CBI Scotland; former Chairman, Hibernian Football Club Ltd. Address: (b.) 12 Broughton Place, Edinburgh EH1 3RX.

Gold, Stephen H., LLB, NP. Senior Partner, Golds Solicitors, Glasgow; b. 14.4.49, Glasgow; m., Ruth Copland; 1 s.; 1 d. Educ. Eastwood High School, Strathclyde University;. Member, Marketing Committee, and former Member of Council, Law Society of Scotland. Recreations: modern jazz; theatre and cinema; football; good conversation. Address: (b.) 8 Newton Terrace, Glasgow G3 7PJ; T.-0141-300 4300.

Goldberg, Professor Sir Abraham, KB, MD, DSc, FRCP, FRCPEdin, FRCPGlas, FRSE. Regius Professor of the Practice of Medicine, Glasgow University, 1978-89; Founder President, Faculty of Pharmaceutical Medicine of Royal Colleges of Physicians of UK, 1989; b. 7.12.23, Edinburgh; m., Clarice Cussin; 2 s.; 1 d. Educ. Sciennes School, Edinburgh; George Heriot's School, Edinburgh; Edinburgh University. House Physician, Royal Hospital for

Sick Children, Edinburgh, 1946-47; RAMC, 1947-49 (granted rank of honorary Major on discharge); Nuffield Research Fellow, UCH Medical School, London, 1952-54; Eli Lilly Travelling Fellow in Medicine (MRC), Department of Medicine, Utah University, 1954-56; Glasgow University: Lecturer in Medicine, 1956-59, Titular Professor of Medicine, 1967-70, Regius Professor of Materia Medica, 1970-78. Chairman, Grants Committee 1, Clinical Research Board, MRC, 1973-77; Member, Chief Scientist's Committee, SHHD, 1977-83; Chairman, Biomedical Research Committee, SHHD, 1977-83; Editor, Scottish Medical Journal, 1962-63; Chairman, Committee on Safety of Medicines, 1980-86; Fitzpatrick Lecturer, Royal College of Physicians, London, 1988; Goodall Memorial Lecturer, Royal College of Physicians and Surgeons of Glasgow, 1989; City of Glasgow Lord Provost's Award, 1988. Publications: Disorders of Porphyrin Metabolism (Co-Author), 1987; Recent Advances in Haematology (Joint Editor), 1971; Clinics in Haematology "The Porphyrias" (Co-Author), 1980. Recreations: medical history; literature; writing; walking; swimming. Address: (h.) 16 Birnam Crescent, Bearsden, Glasgow G61 2AU.

Goldie, Annabel MacNicoll, DL, LLB, NP. MSP (Conservative), West of Scotland, since 1999, Deputy Convener, Enterprise and Lifelong Learning Committee; Deputy Lord Lieutenant, Renfrewshire, since 1993; Director, Prince's Scottish Youth Business Trust, since 1994; b. 27.2.50, Glasgow. Educ. Greenock Academy; Strathclyde University. Solicitor in private practice, since 1978; Scottish Conservative Party: Deputy Chairman, 1995-97, Chairman, March-July 1997, Deputy Chairman, 1997-98, Deputy Leader, since 1998; Elder, Church of Scotland; Member, West of Scotland Advisory Board, Salvation Army; Member, Strathclyde University Court. Recreations: weeding; walking dog; cycling. Address: (b.) Scottish Parliament, Edinburgh EH1 1SP; T.-0131-348 5663.

Gomatam, Professor Jagannathan, BSc, MSc, PhD. Professor of Applied Mathematics, Glasgow Caledonian University, since 1990; b. 20.8.40, India; m., Jean McGregor. Educ. University of Madras; Syracuse University. Research Assistant, Physics Department, then Instructor, Mathematics Department, Syracuse University, 1966-70; Post-Doctoral Research Fellow, Physics Department, Syracuse University, 1970-71; Research Scholar, School of Theoretical Physics, Dublin Institute for Advanced Studies, 1971-73; Lecturer/Reader, Glasgow Caledonian University, 1973-90. Senior Visitor, Mathematical Institute, Oxford University, 1986-87; elected to Peer Review College, EPSRC, 2000. Address; (b.) Department of Mathematics, Glasgow Caledonian University, 70 Cowcaddens Road, Glasgow G4 0BA.

Good, Anne, SRN. Founder, Action Against Allergy in Scotland; retired Nursing Officer; b. 27.12.19, Stornoway; m., Dr. Rankine Good (deceased). Educ. Stornoway School, Isle of Lewis. Trained as Pyschiatric Nurse, 1938-41; trained as Registered General Nurse, Eastern District Hospitals, Glasgow, 1942-45; trained as Certificated Midwife, Lennox Castle Maternity Hospital; Departmental Sister, Hartwood Psychiatric Hospital, 1947-48; theatre work, Edinburgh Royal Neurosurgical Unit; lived abroad for over 11 years. Director, Schizophrenia Association in Scotland; has had an interest in schizophrenia for 72 years, and in food in relation to mental health. Address: (h.) 59 Barrington Drive, Glasgow G4 9ES; T.-0141-339 3705.

Gooday, Professor Graham W., BSc, PhD, FRSE, FIBiol. Professor of Microbiology, Aberdeen University, since 1984; b. 19.2.42, Colchester; m., Margaret A. Mealing; 1 s.; 2 d. Educ. Hove Grammar School for Boys; Bristol University. VSO, Sierra Leone, 1964; Research Fellowships: Leeds University, 1967, Glasgow and Oxford

Universities, 1969; Lecturer, Senior Lecturer, Reader, Aberdeen University, 1972-84; Honorary Professorial Fellow, Rowett Research Institute, 1992; Member: Aquatic Life Sciences Committee, NERC, 1984-87, Council, Society for General Microbiology, 1976-80; British Mycological Society: Member, Council, 1974-77, President, 1993, Centenary Fellow, 1996; awarded first Fleming Lectureship, Society for General Microbiology, 1976. Recreation: open countryside. Address: (b.) Department of Molecular and Cell Biology, Institute of Medical Sciences, University of Aberdeen, Aberdeen AB25 2ZD; T.-01224 273147; e-mail: g.w.gooday@abdn.ac.uk

Goodlad, Professor Robina, MA (Hons), MPhil, MCIH. Professor of Housing and Urban Studies, University of Glasgow, since 1998; b. 16.8.50, Lerwick; m., Peter D. Taylor; 2 d. Educ. Anderson Educational Institute, Lerwick; Aberdeen University; Glasgow University. Worked for Planning Exchange; Director, Tenant Participation Advisory Service, 1980-84; Lecturer then Senior Lecturer, University of Glasgow, 1984-98. Labour Candidate, Orkney and Shetland, 1979 and 1983. Publications: three books; many articles and book chapters. Address: (b.) Department of Urban Studies, University of Glasgow, 25 Bute Gardens, Glasgow; T.-0141-330 4516; e-mail: R.Goodlad@socsci.gla.ac.uk

Goodman, Professor Anthony Eric, MA (Oxon), BLitt (Oxon), FRHistS. Professor of Medieval and Renaissance History, Edinburgh University, 1993-2001, Professor Emeritus, since 2001; b. 21.7.36, London; m., Jacqueline; 1 d. Educ. Selhurst Grammar School, Croydon; Magdalen College, Oxford. Joined staff, Edinburgh University, 1961. Secretary, Edinburgh Branch, Historical Association, since 1975. Publications: The Loyal Conspiracy, 1971; A History of England from Edward II to James I, 1977; The Wars of the Roses, 1981; A Traveller's Guide to Medieval Britain (Co-author), 1986; The New Monarchy, 1471-1534, 1988; John of Gaunt, 1992. Address: (h.) 23 Kirkhill Gardens, Edinburgh EH16 5DF; T.-0131-667 5988.

Goodman, Professor Timothy Nicholas Trewin, BA, MSc, DPhil, FRSE. Professor of Applied Physics, Dundee University, since 1994; b. 29.4.47; m., Chootin; 3 d. Educ. Judd School, Tonbridge; St John's College, Cambridge; Warwick University; Sussex University. Teacher in Malaysia under VSO scheme, 1973; Teacher in Singapore, 1974-75; Lecturer in Malaysia, 1975-79; Lecturer, Dundee University, 1979-90; Professor in Texas, USA, 1990-91; Reader, Dundee University, 1992-94. Elder, Steeple Church, Dundee. Recreations: hill-walking; Scottish country dancing. Address: (b.) Department of Mathematics, Dundee University, Dundee DD1 4HN; T.-01382 344488.

Goodsman, James Melville, CBE. Consultant, Democracy International Ltd.; Director, Capitalize Ltd.; b. 6.2.47, St. Andrews; m., Victoria Smitherman. Educ. Elgin Academy. Conservative Party Agent, 1968-80; Deputy Central Office Agent, North West Area, 1980-84; Assistant Director (Community Affairs), CCO, 1984-89; Head, Community and Legal Department, CCO, 1989-90; Director, Conservative Party in Scotland, 1990-93; Chairman, Edinburgh Morayshire Club, 1996-97. Recreations: golf; Church music; gardening. Address: (b.) The Old Schoolhouse, Collessie, Fife KY15 7UU; T.-01337 810745.

Goodwin, Frederick Anderson, DUniv, LLB, CA, FCIBS. Group Chief Executive, Royal Bank of Scotland Plc, since 2000; b. 17.8.58, Paisley; m., Joyce. Educ. Glasgow University. Touche Ross: joined, 1979; Partner, 1988; Executive Director, Short Brothers Plc, Belfast, 1989-90; Chief Operating Officer, BCCI Worldwide Liquidation, 1992-95; Deputy Chief Executive, Clydesdale Bank Plc, 1995; Chief Executive/Director, Clydesdale Bank, 1996; Chief Executive/Director,

Clydesdale Bank and Yorkshire Bank Plc, 1997-98; Deputy Chief Executive, Royal Bank of Scotland, Plc, 1998-2000; Chairman, The Prince's Trust, Scotland; Director, Scottish Financial Enterprise. Recreations; golf; cars. Address: (b.) 42 St Andrew Square, Edinburgh, EH2 2YE; T.-0131 523 2033.

Goodwin, Michael David, OBE, FIMgt. Managing Director, Electrical Contractors' Association of Scotland (SELECT) since 1991; The Director, Scottish Joint Industry Board, since 1993; Director: Scottish Electrical Contractors' Insurance, since 1991, Electrical Engineering Training Foundation, National Electrotechnical Training, Aspect Ltd., National Inspection Council for Electrical Installation Contracting; Trustee, Scottish Electrical Training Trust, since 1991; b. 18.1.40, Colombo; m., Anne Dundas, nee Finlay; 2 s.; 2 d. Educ. Stowe School; Britannia Royal Naval College, Dartmouth. Graduated as full career commission officer, Royal Navy, 1960; NATO appointments, 1980-86; retired as Commander, 1988; Assistant Director, Administration, Information and Settlement Division, International Stock Exchange, 1988-91. Recreations: tennis; theatre; music; reading; clay shooting; swimming. Address: (b.) Bush House, Bush Estate, Midlothian EH26 0SB; T.-0131-445 5577.

Gordon of Strathblane, Lord (James Stuart Gordon), CBE, DLitt., DUniv, MA (Hons). Chairman, Scottish Radio Holdings, since 1996; Director, Johnston Press plc, since 1996, The AIM Trust plc, since 1996; Member, BP Scottish Advisory Board, since 1990; Trustee, National Galleries of Scotland, since 1998; b. 17.5.36, Glasgow; m., Anne Stevenson; 2 s.; 1 d. Educ. St. Aloysius College, Glasgow; Glasgow University (President of the Union, 1958-59). Political Editor, STV, 1965-73; Managing Director, Radio Clyde, 1973-96; Chief Executive, Scottish Radio Holdings, 1991-96; Member, Court, Glasgow University, 1984-97; Chairman, Advisory Group on Listed Sports Events on Television, 1997-98; Chairman, Scottish Tourist Board, 1998-2001; Member, Review Panel on the Future Funding of the BBC; Winner, Observer Mace Debating Tournament, 1957; Sony Special Award for Services to Radio, 1984. Chairman, Scottish Exhibition Centre, 1983-89; Member, Scottish Development Agency, 1981-90. Recreations: his children; genealogy; golf. Address: (b.) Scottish Radio Holdings, Clydebank Business Park, Clydebank, Glasgow G81 2RX; T.-0141-565 2202.

Gordon, Alexander Crawford, LLB (Hons), Dip LP. Assistant Scottish Parliamentary Counsel, since 1999; Solicitor, since 1991; b. 29.2.68, Paisley. Educ. Eastwood High School; Glasgow University. Procurator Fiscal Service: Crown Office, Linlithgow, Kilmarnock, Glasgow, 1990-97; Assistant Legal Secretary to the Lord Advocate and Assistant Scottish Parliamentary Counsel (London), 1997-99. Recreations: cinema; theatre; eating and drinking; travel; Rangers FC. Address: (b.) Office of the Scottish Parliamentary Counsel, Victoria Quay, Edinburgh EH6 6QQ.

Gordon, Charles, FFCS. Leader, Glasgow City Council, since 1999; Non-Executive Member, SECC Ltd., since 1997; Non-Executive Director: Hampden Park Ltd.; Chair, Strathclyde Concessionary Travel Joint Committee; Member, BAFTA Scottish Committee; b. 28.10.51, Glasgow; 2 s. Educ. St Mungo's Academy, Glasgow. Member, Strathclyde Regional Council, 1987-96 (Vice-Chair, Roads/Transport Committee, 1990-94, Chair, 1994-96); elected to City of Glasgow Council, 1995 (Chair, Roads Committee, 1995-96); Chair, Strathclyde Passenger Transport Authority, 1996-99; President, Glasgow Trades Council, 1985-90. Recreations: reading; conversation; football. Address: (b.) City Chambers, Glasgow G2 1DU; T.-0141-287 4100.

Gordon, Donald Neil, MA, LLB, WS, NP, MSI, TEP. Partner, Blackadders (formerly Carltons) Solicitors, since 1979; Senior Tutor, Diploma in Legal Practice, University of Dundee, since 1994; Dean, Faculty of Procurators and Solicitors in Dundee, 1999-2001; b. 30.3.51, Aberdeen; m., Alison Mary Whyte; 1 s.; 1 d. Educ. Robert Gordon's College, Aberdeen; University of Aberdeen; University of Edinburgh. Law Apprenticeship, Edinburgh, 1973-75; Assistant Solicitor, Carlton & Reid, Dundee, 1975-79. WS, 1975; Notary Public, 1975; Chairman, Dundee Citizens Advice Bureau, 1996-2001; Honorary French Consul, Dundee, since 1996; President, Abertay Rotary Club; Treasurer, Dundee Orchestral Society, 1978-2001; Past Chairman, High School of Dundee Parents Association. Recreations: music; gardening; Rotary. Address: (b.) 34 Reform Street, Dundee DD1 1RJ; T.-01382 229222.

Gordon, Professor George, MA (Hons), PhD, FRGS. Director of Academic Practice, Strathclyde University, since 1987; b. 14.11.39, Edinburgh; m., Jane Taylor Collins; 2 d. Educ. George Heriot's School; Edinburgh University. Edinburgh University: Vans Dunlop Scholar, 1962-64, Demonstrator, 1964-65; Strathclyde University: Assistant Lecturer, 1965-66, Lecturer, 1966-80, Dean, Faculty of Arts and Social Studies, 1984-87; served on SUCE and SCE Geography Panels, SCOVACT, and General Teaching Council for Scotland; Chairman, Council, Royal Scottish Geographical Society, since 1999; Vice President, British Association for the Advancement of Science, 1991-97; former Member, General Assembly of Open University; Member, Senate and Court, Strathclyde University; Governor, Jordanhill College of Education, 1982-93 (Chairman, 1987-93). Publications: Regional Cities of the UK 1890-1980 (Editor), 1986; Perspectives of the Scottish City (Editor), 1985; The Making of Scottish Geography (Co-Author), 1984; Settlement Geography, 1983; Urban Geography (Co-Author), 1981; Scottish Urban History (Co-Editor), 1983; Settlement Geography (Co-Author), 1983. Recreations: theatre-going; watching sport. Address: (b.) Centre for Academic Practice, Strathclyde University, 50 George Street, Glasgow; T.-0141-548 2637.

Gordon, Sheriff Gerald Henry, CBE, QC, MA, LLB, PhD, LLD. Sheriff of Glasgow and Strathkelvin, 1978-99; Temporary Judge, Court of Session and High Court of Justiciary, since 1992; b. 17.6.29, Glasgow; m., Marjorie Joseph; 1 s.; 2 d. Educ. Queen's Park Senior Secondary School; Glasgow University. Advocate, 1953; Procurator Fiscal Depute, Edinburgh, 1960-65; Edinburgh University: Head, Department of Criminal Law and Criminology, 1965-72, Personal Professor of Criminal Law, 1969-72, Dean, Faculty of Law, 1970-73, Professor of Scots Law, 1972-76; Sheriff of South Strathclyde, Dumfries and Galloway, at Hamilton, 1976-77; Member: Interdepartmental Committee on Scottish Criminal Procedure, 1970-77, Committee on Criminal Appeals and Miscarriages of Justice, 1995-96, Scottish Criminal Cases Review Commission, since 1999. Publications: Criminal Law of Scotland, 1967, 1978; Renton & Brown's Criminal Procedure (Editor), 1972, 1983, 1996. Recreations: Jewish studies; coffee conversation; crosswords.

Gordon, Giles Alexander Esme, FRSL. Director, Curtis Brown Ltd., Literary Agents, since 1995; b. 23.5.40, Edinburgh; m., 1, Margaret Anna Eastoe (deceased); 1 s.; 1 s. (deceased); 1 d.; 2, Maggie McKernan; 1 s.; 2 d. Educ. Edinburgh Academy; Edinburgh College of Art. Trainee Publisher, Oliver & Boyd, Edinburgh, 1959-63; Advertising Manager, Secker & Warburg, 1963-64; Editor, Hutchinson, 1964-66; Plays Editor, Penguin Books, 1966-67; Editorial Director, Victor Gollancz, 1967-73; Literary Agent, Anthony Sheil Associates, later Sheil Land Associates, 1973-95. C. Day Lewis Fellow in Writing, KCL, 1974-75; Secretary and Chairman, Society of Young Publishers; Member: Literature Panel, Arts Council, 1968-72; Committee of Management, Society of Authors;

Committee, Association of Authors' Agents; Council, RSL, 1992-94; Committee, Authors Club, since 1992; Lecturer: Tufts University in London, 1970-74, Hollins College, London, 1983-86; Theatre Critic: Spectator, London Daily News, Drama; Books Columnist, The Times, 1993-95; Columnist, Edinburgh Evening News, 1999-2001; Restaurant Critic, Caledonia, 1999-2001; Editor, Drama; Editor, Bloomsbury Classics Short Stories, since 1995, Clarion Tales, 1996-99; Member, Committee, Society of Authors in Scotland, 1997-99. Publications: Pictures from an Exhibition, 1970; The Umbrella Man, 1971; About a Marriage, 1972; Girl with Red Hair, 1974; Factions (Co-Editor), 1974; Walter and the Balloon (Co-Author), 1974; Beyond the Words (Editor), 1975; Farewell, Fond Dreams, 1975; Prevailing Spirits (Editor), 1976; 100 Scenes from Married Life, 1976; Members of the Jury (Co-Editor), 1976; You Always Remember the First Time (Co-Editor), 1976; A Book of Contemporary Nightmares (Editor), 1977; Enemies, 1977; The Illusionist, 1978; Modern Scottish Short Stories (Co-Editor), 1978; Ambrose's Vision, 1980; Shakespeare Stories (Editor), 1982; English Short Stories 1940-80 (Editor), 1982; Best Short Stories (Co-Editor, annually), 1986-95; English Short Stories: 1900 to the present (Editor), 1988; The Twentieth Century Short Story in English: a bibliography (Editor), 1989; Aren't We Due a Koyalty Statement?, 1993; The Best of Best Short Stories 1986-95 (Co-Editor), 1995; Scotland from the Air, 1996. Recreations: theatre; opera; walking; travelling; eating; drinking; book collecting. Address: Curtis Brown, 37 Queensferry Street, Edinburgh EH2 4DS; T.-0131-225 1290.

Gordon, Ian. Head of Department, Scotland Office, since 1999; b. 27.12.52; m., Alison Margaret Bunting; 2 s. Department of Energy, 1975-81; Scottish Office, 1981-99: Industry Department, 1981-85, Education Department, 1985-90, Agriculture and Fisheries Department, 1990-99, latterly as Fisheries Secretary. Address: (b.) Dover House, Whitehall, London SW1A 2AU; T.-0207-270 6769.

Gordon, Major General Robert Duncan Seaton, CBE, MA. GOC 2nd Division/ Governor, Edinburgh Castle, since 2000; GOC, 2nd Division, York, since 1999; b. 23.11.50, Yorkshire; m., Virginia (Gina) Ruth; 2 s. Educ. Wellington College; St Catharine's College, Cambridge. Commissioned, 17th/21st Lancers, 1970; Served at regimental duty, Germany, UK, Northern Ireland, Cyprus, Canada; Royal Military College of Science, 1981; Staff College, Camberley, 1982; Chief of Staff, 4th Armoured Brigade, 1982-84; Military Assistant, CINC BAOR/COMNORTHAG, 1987-90; Commanding Officer (Lt. Col.), 17th/21st Lancers, 1990-92; Secretary, Chiefs of Staff Committee, (Colonel) Ministry of Defence, 1992-94; Brigade Commander, 19 Mech Bde, Catterick and Bosnia, 1994-96; Higher Command and Staff course, 1994; Royal College of Defence Studies, 1996; Director Public Relations (Army), 1996-99; Military Adviser, Edinburgh Tattoo; Trustee, Scottish National War Memorial Commission; Trustee, Queen Victoria School, Dunblane; Hon. Vice President, Royal British Legion, Scotland; Vice President, Earl Haig Fund, Scotland. Recreations: reading; off shore sailing; moving house; country pursuits; golf. Address: (b.) HQ 2 Div., Craigie Hall, South Queensferry, West Lothian; T.-0131-310 2061.

Gordon, Robert Smith Benzie, CB, MA. Head, Finance and Central Services Department, Scottish Executive, since 2001; b. 7.11.50, Aberdeen; m., Joyce Cordiner; 2 s.; 2 d. Educ. Gordon Schools, Huntly; Aberdeen University. Joined Scottish Office, 1973; Principal, Scottish Development Department, 1979-85; Principal Private Secretary to Secretary of State for Scotland, 1985-87; Assistant Secretary: Department of Agriculture and Fisheries, 1988-90, Management, Organisation and Industrial Relations Division, Scottish Office, 1990-91; Director, Administrative Services, 1991-97; Head, Constitution Group, 1997-99; Head, Executive Secretariat, Scottish Executive, 1999-2001. Address: (b.) St. Andrew's House, Edinburgh EH1 3DG; T.-0131-244 7937.

Gordon, Professor William Morrison, MA, LLB, PhD, FRSE. Douglas Professor of Civil Law, Glasgow University, 1969-99; Professorial Research Fellow, 1999-2001; Solicitor (non-practising), since 1956; b. 3.3.33, Inverurie; m., Isabella Evelyn Melitta Robertson; 2 s.; 2 d. Educ. Inverurie Academy; Robert Gordon's College, Aberdeen; Aberdeen University. National Service, Royal Navy, 1955-57; Assistant in Jurisprudence, Aberdeen University, 1957-60; Glasgow University: Lecturer in Civil Law, 1960-65, Senior Lecturer in Law, 1965-69 (and Sub-Dean of Faculty); Dean of Faculty, 1974-76. Elder and, until 1998, Session Clerk, Jordanhill Parish Church; Literary Director, The Stair Society, 1985-98. Publications: Studies in Transfer of Property by Traditio, 1970; Scottish Land Law, (2nd Ed.), 1999; Stair Society Miscellany III, 1992; European Legal History (3rd Ed.), (with others), 2000. Recreation: golf. Address: 26 Southbrae Drive, Glasgow G13 1PY; T.-0141-954 9037.

Gordon-Gillies (nee McCall-Smith), Anne Bethea, MA, LLB. Advocate; Honorary Sheriff of South Strathclyde, Dumfries and Galloway, at Lanark, since 1960; b. 12.4.22, Lochgilphead, Argyll; m., Sheriff Principal M.G. Gillies, T.D., Q.C. (d. 1997). Educ. Sherborne School for Girls, Dorset; Edinburgh University. Served in WAAF, until 1946; called to Scottish Bar, 1951; married, 1954. Member, Valuation Appeal Panel, Strathclyde, 1974-88. Recreations: gardening; cats. Address: (h.) The Coach House, Broadgait, Gullane, East Lothian EH31 2DH; T.-01620 842971.

Goring, Rev. Iain McCormick, BSc, BD. Minister, Callander Kirk, since 1985; b. 22.7.50, Edinburgh; m., Janet Page; 2 s.; 1 d. Educ. Dunfermline High School; University of Edinburgh. Minister, Lochwood Parish Church, Easterhouse, Glasgow, 1977-85. Address: (h.) The Manse, Aveland Park Road, Callander, Perthshire FK17 8FD; T.-01877 330097.

Gorman, Brian, MA. Vice President, Commonwealth Youth Exchange Council, since 1999; Board Member, Suspect Culture Theatre Co., since 1998; b. 31.10.51, Wishaw. Educ. Our Lady's High School, Motherwell; University of Glasgow; Jordanhill College. Teacher, Columba High School, Coatbridge, 1974-76; Principal Teacher of Modern Studies, St. John's High, Dundee, 1976-78; Group Travel Manager, Cotter Tours, Glasgow, 1978-84; Director, English-Speaking Union (Scotland), 1984-93; Chairman, Suspect Culture Theatre Co., 1994-98. Recreations: theatre; debating. Address: (h.) 15/3 Easter Dalry Road, Edinburgh EH11 2TR; T.-0131-346 1327.

Gorman, Christopher Simon. Entrepreneur; Director, Reality Group, since 1998; b. 25.12.66, Hartlepool; m., Mary; 3 s. Educ. English Martyrs Secondary and Sixth Form College. Corporate Account Manager: Quadrant Group PLC, 1987-89, Racal-Vodac PLC, 1989-90; Business Development Manager, Securicor Cellular Services, 1990-93; Director and Shareholder, DX Communications, 1993-98. Director, Entrepreneurial Exchange; Chairman, Hillington Park Innovation Centre; Director, Save the Children; Scottish Entrepreneur of the Year, 2000; UK E-Business Entrepreneur of the Year, 2000. Recreations: travel; music; films. Address: (b.) Team Advisors Ltd., PO Box 5551, Glasgow G52 4YU; T.-0870 6006662.

Gorrie, Donald Cameron Easterbrook, OBE, DL, MA, JP. MSP (Liberal Democrat), Central Scotland, since 1999, Spokesperson on Finance and Procedures; Backbencher of the Year, 1999; b. 2.4.33, India; m., Astrid Salvesen; 2 s.

Educ. Hurst Grange, Stirling; Oundle School; Corpus Christi College, Oxford. Schoolmaster: Gordonstoun School, 1957-60, Marlborough College, 1960-66; Scottish Liberal Party: Director of Research, 1969-71, Director of Administration, 1971-75; Member, Edinburgh Town Council, 1971-75; Leader, Liberal Democrat Group: Lothian Regional Council, 1974-96, City of Edinburgh District Council, 1980-96, City of Edinburgh Council, 1995-97; MP (Liberal Democrat), Edinburgh West, 1997-2001. Director, 'Edinburgh Translations'; Chairman, Edinburgh Youth Orchestra; Member, Board, Queens Hall; President, Corstorphine AAC; former Member, Board: Lothian Association of Youth Clubs, Edinburgh Youth Cafe, Diverse Attractions, Castle Rock and Lothian Housing Associations, Edinburgh Festival, Scottish Chamber Orchestra, Royal Lyceum Theatre Company; former Scottish native record holder, 880 yards. **Address:** (h.) 9 Garscube Terrace, Edinburgh EH12 6BW; T.-0131-337 2077.

Gossip, Michael A.J., OBE, JP, BL. Honorary Sheriff, Dunoon, since 1989, and Campbeltown, since 1997; Clerk, Presbytery of South Argyll, since 1996; b. 27.4.33, Edinburgh; m., Margaret; 1 s.; 2 d. **Educ.** George Watson's Boys' College, Edinburgh; Edinburgh University. Legal Assistant, Midlothian County Council, 1955-57; Dumfries County Council: Senior Legal Assistant, 1957-60, Depute County Clerk, 1960-71; Argyll County Council: Depute County Clerk, 1971-72, County Clerk, 1972-75; Chief Executive, Argyll and Bute District Council, 1974-96. Recreations: bowls; gardening. **Address:** (h.) Tigh-na-Coille, Ardrishaig, Argyll PA30 8EP; T.-01546 603454; e-mail: gossip@dial.pipex.com

Gotts, Iain McEwan, DipLE, DipTP, FRICS, MRTPI. Director, DTZ Pieda Consulting, since 1997; b. 26.2.47, Glasgow; m., Pamela; 1 s.; 2 d. **Educ.** Jordanhill College School, Glasgow; Paisley College of Technology; Heriot-Watt University/Edinburgh College of Art. Trainee Surveyor, British Rail Property Department, Glasgow, 1965-68; further education, 1968-72; Surveyor/Land Economist, Wright & Partners, Edinburgh, 1972-76; Chief Executive, Pieda plc, 1976-97. Chairman, Erskine Stewart's Melville Governing Council, since 1999. Recreations: music; golf; rugby. **Address:** (b.) 28 Drumsheugh Gardens, Edinburgh EH3 7RN; T.-0131-225 5737.

Goudie, Andrew William, PhD, MA, BA(Econ), BA. Chief Economic Adviser, Scottish Executive, since 1999; Head, Analytical Services Group, Scottish Executive; b. 3.3.55, London; m., Christine Goudie; 2 s.; 2 d. **Educ.** Haberdashers' Aske's School, Elstree; Queens' College, University of Cambridge. University of Cambridge, 1978-85: Research Officer, Department of Applied Economics, Research Fellow, Queens' College, Fellow and Director of Studies, Robinson College; Senior Economist, The World Bank, Washington DC, 1985-90; Senior Economic Adviser, Scottish Office, 1990-95; Principal Economist, OECD, Paris, 1995-96; Chief Economist, DFID (formerly ODA), London, 1996-99. Publications: articles in learned journals. **Address:** (b.) St. Andrews House, Regent Road, Edinburgh EH1 3DG; T.-0131-244 3430; e-mail: andrew.goudie@scotland.gsi.gov.uk

Gow, Sir (James) Michael, GCB, DL (Edinburgh), FSAScot. President, Royal British Legion Scotland, 1986-96; President, Earl Haig Fund (Scotland), 1986-96, Vice-President, since 1996; Vice-President, Officers' Association Scotland, since 1986 (President, 1985-86); b. 3.6.24; m., Jane Emily Scott; 1 s.; 4 d. **Educ.** Winchester College. Enlisted, Scots Guards, 1942; commissioned, 1943; served NW Europe 1944-45; Malayan Emergency, 1949; Equerry to the late HRH Duke of Gloucester, 1952-53; Brigade Major, 1955-57; Regimental Adjutant, Scots Guards, 1957-60; Instructor, Army Staff College, 1962-64; Command, 2nd Bn Scots Guards, Kenya and England, 1964-66; GSO1,

HQ London District, 1966-67; Command, 4th Guards Brigade, 1968-69; Imperial Defence College, 1970; Brigadier General Staff (Int.) HQ, BAOR and Assistant Chief of Staff, G2 HQ, Northag, 1971-73; GOC 4th Div., BAOR, 1973-75; Director of Army Training, 1975-78; General Officer Commanding, Scotland, Governor of Edinburgh Castle, 1979-80; Commander-in-Chief, BAOR and Commander, Northern Army Group, 1980-83 (awarded die Plakette des deutschen Heeres); ADC Gen. to the Queen, 1981-84; Commandant, Royal College of Defence Studies, 1984-86. Colonel Commandant: Intelligence Corps, 1973-86, Scottish Division, 1979-80. Chairman: Scottish Ex-Services Charitable Organisation, 1989-96, Scots at War Trust, since 1992, Ludus Baroque, since 1999; Patron, Disabled Income Group Scotland, since 1993; Vice-President: Scottish National Institution for the War Blinded, 1995, Royal Caledonian Schools Education Trust, 1996-2000; Lieutenant, Queen's Body Guard for Scotland, (Royal Company of Archers); UK Member, Eurogroup US Tour, 1983; UK Kermit Roosevelt Lecturer, USA, 1984; Vice President: Queen Victoria School, Dunblane, 1979-80, Royal Caledonian Schools, Bushey, 1980-99; County Commissioner, British Scouts, W. Europe, 1980-83 (Silver Acorn); Elder, Canongate Kirk, since 1988; President, National Association of Sheltered Employment, 1993-2000; Freeman: City of London, 1980, State of Kansas, USA, 1984; Freeman and Liveryman, Painters' and Stainers' Company, 1980. Publications: Trooping the Colour: A History of the Sovereign's Birthday Parade by the Household Troops, 1989; Jottings in a General's Notebook, 1989; General Reflections, 1991. Recreations: sailing; music; travel; reading. **Address:** (h.) 18 Ann Street, Edinburgh EH4 1PJ; T.-0131-332 4752.

Gow, Sheriff Neil, QC (Scot). Sheriff of South Strathclyde at Ayr, since 1976; b. 24.4.32; m., Joanna; 1 s. **Educ.** Merchiston Castle School, Edinburgh; Glasgow University; Edinburgh University. Advocate, 1957-76.

Grace, Professor John, BSc, PhD, FIBiol, FRSE. Professor of Environmental Biology, Edinburgh University, since 1992; Head, Institute of Ecology and Resource Management, since 2000; b. 19.9.45, Northampton; m., Elizabeth Ashworth; 2 s.; 1 d. **Educ.** Bletchley Grammar School; Sheffield University. Lecturer, then Reader in Ecology, Edinburgh University, 1970-92. Co-Editor, Functional Ecology, 1986-99; Technical Editor, International Society for Biometeorology, 1983-98; Member, Terrestrial Life Sciences Committee, Natural Environment Research Council, 1986-89; Council Member, British Ecological Society, since 1983, President-Elect, 2001. Publications: Plant Response to Wind, 1977; Plants and their Atmospheric Environment (Co-Editor), 1981; Plant-atmosphere Relationships, 1983. Recreations: hill-walking; cycling; fishing; bridge. **Address:** (h.) 25 Craiglea Drive, Edinburgh EH10 5PB; T.-0131-447 3030; e-mail: jgrace@ed.ac.uk

Grace, Paul Henry, BSc, FFA. Director, Scottish Equitable Policyholders Trust Ltd., since 1998; Director and Honorary Treasurer, Victim Support Scotland Ltd., since 1998; Director, Student Loan Company Ltd., since 1999; Chairman, National Provident Life Fund Supervisory Board, since 2000; Member, Scottish Life Fund Supervisory Committee, since 2001; b. 25.9.38, Bletchley; m., Aileen Anderson; 1 d. **Educ.** Bedford Modern School; St. Andrews University. Joined Scottish Equitable as Actuarial Trainee, 1960; joined Zurich Life Assurance Co. as Actuary and Life Manager, 1965; rejoined Scottish Equitable, 1980; Managing Director and Actuary, Scottish Equitable Policyholders Trust Ltd., 1994-98. President, Faculty of Actuaries, 1996-98. Publication: Introduction to Life Assurance, 1988. Recreations: golf; gardening. **Address:** 16 Succoth Avenue, Edinburgh EH12 6BU; T.-0131-337 5079.

Graham, Rev. A. David M., BA, BD. Minister, Rosemount Parish Church, Aberdeen, since 1990; b. 17.7.40, Tralee; m., Mary A. Taylor; 2 s.; 1 d. Educ. Wesley College, Dublin; Methodist College, Belfast; Queen's University, Belfast; Glasgow University. Assistant, South Leith Parish; Secretary for Christian Education, Scottish National Council of YMCAs; Minister, Anderston Parish, Glasgow; Warden, Iona Abbey; Minister, Rosemount Parish, Aberdeen. Recreations: jogging; climbing. Address: 22 Osborne Place, Aberdeen AB25 2DA; T.-01224 648041.

Graham. Rev. Alasdair Giffen, BD, Dip. Ministry. Minister, Arbroath West Kirk, since 1990; Part-time Chaplain, Arbroath Infirmary; b. 20.4.54, Lanark; m., Joan Janet Forsyth; 1 d. Educ. Gordon Schools, Huntly; Kirkcaldy High School; University of Glasgow. Probationary Assistant, Mastrick Church, Aberdeen, 1980-81; Minister, Redgorton and Stanley Churches, Perthshire, 1981-86; Chaplain, HM Prison, Perth; Minister, St Margaret's Church, Arbroath, 1986-90. District Scout Chaplain; Chaplain, Angus Training Group. Recreations: time with family; badminton; swimming. Address: (h.) 1 Charles Avenue, Arbroath DD11 2EY; T.-01241 872244.

Graham, Professor David I., MB, ChB, PhD, FRCPath, FRCPS, FRSE. Professor of Neuropathology, Glasgow University, since 1983; b. 20.7.39, Glasgow; m., Joyce; 1 s.; 1 d. Educ. Penarth County Grammar School; Welsh National School of Medicine, Cardiff. Registrar, Western Infirmary, Glasgow, 1965-68; Lecturer, Department of Neuropathology, Glasgow, 1968-72; Fogarty Fellow, Laboratory of Neuropathology, Philadelphia, 1972-74; Senior Lecturer, Glasgow, 1974-83. Publications: several books; 300 papers. Recreations: hill-walking; music. Address: (b.) Department of Neuropathology, Institute of Neurological Sciences, Southern General Hospital, Govan Road, Glasgow G51 4TF; T.-0141-201 2113.

Graham, Elspeth Forbes, MA, PhD. Senior Lecturer in Geography, St. Andrews University, since 1997; Member, Local Government Boundary Commission for Scotland, since 1994; Member, Parliamentary Boundary Commission for Scotland, since 1999; b. 7.2.50, Edinburgh; 1 s.; 1 d. Educ. George Watson's Ladies College, Edinburgh; St. Andrews University; Durham University. Visiting Lecturer, University of Minnesota, 1979-80. Publications: Postmodernism and the Social Sciences (Co-editor), 1992; research papers on population policies and issues. Recreations: Celtic music and literature; local history. Address: (b.) Department of Geography, St. Andrews University, St. Andrews KY16 9ST; T.-01334 463908.

Graham, Professor Gordon, MA, MA, PhD. Regius Professor of Moral Philosophy, University of Aberdeen, since 1996; b. 15.7.49, Belfast; 1 s.; 1 d. Educ. Methodist College, Belfast; University of St. Andrews; University of Durham. Lecturer in Moral Philosophy, University of St. Andrews, 1975-95; Director, St. Andrews University Music Centre, 1991-95. Publications: Historical Explanation Reconsidered, 1983; Politics in its Place – A Study of Six Ideologies, 1986; Contemporary Social Philosophy, 1988; Living the Good Life – An Introduction to Moral Philosophy, 1990; The Idea of Christian Charity – A Critique of Some Contemporary Conceptions, 1990; With Strings and Pipe – Essays in Church Music (Editor), 1994; Ethics and International Relations, 1996; The Shape of the Past – A Philosophical Approach to History, 1997; Philosophy of the Arts – An Introduction to Aesthetics, (2nd Ed.), 2000; The Internet – A Philosophical Inquiry, 1999; Evil and Christian Ethics, 2001. Recreation: hillwalking. Address: (b.) Department of Philosophy, University of Aberdeen, Aberdeen AB24 3UB; T.-01224 272372.

Graham, Ian, BSc(Econ) (Hons), DipEdTech (CNAA). Principal, John Wheatley College, Glasgow, since 1992; b. 26.6.51, Devizes. Educ. Queen Victoria School, Dunblane. Lecturer/Senior Lecturer, Reid Kerr College, Paisley, 1975-86; Head of Department, Clydebank College, 1986-88; Further Education Officer, Strathclyde Regional Council, 1988-89; HM Inspector of Schools, 1989-90; Assistant Director of Education (FE), Strathclyde Region, 1990-92. Fellow, Royal Society of Arts; Fellow, Institute of Personnel and Development; Member, Board, Association of Scottish Colleges; Member, Board, West of Scotland Colleges' European Partnership. Recreations: reading; cinema; foreign travel; admiring Burmese cats. Address: (b.) 1346 Shettleston Road, Glasgow G32 9AT; T.-0141-778 2426.

Graham, John James, OBE, MA, MUniv (Aberdeen), FEIS. Joint Editor, The New Shetlander, 1956-98; b. 12.7.21, Lerwick; m., Beryl Smith; 3 s.; 2 d. Educ. Lerwick Central Secondary School; Edinburgh University. RAF Training Command, 1941-44; Bomber Command, 1944-46; Principal Teacher of English, Anderson Educational Institute, Lerwick, 1950-66; Headmaster: Lerwick Central Secondary School, 1966-70, Anderson High School, Lerwick, 1970-82; Member: Consultative Committee on the Curriculum, 1976-80, Broadcasting Council for Scotland, 1981-84; President, Shetland Folk Society. Publications: A Grammar and Usage of the Shetland Dialect (Co-author); Northern Lights (Joint Editor); The Shetland Dictionary; Shadowed Valley (novel); Strife in the Valley (novel); Four Centuries of Education in Shetland; A Shetland Anthology (Co-Editor). Recreations: local history; golf. Address: (h.) 10 Reform Lane, Lerwick, Shetland; 01595 693425.

Graham, John Michael Denning, LLB (Hons), NP, FRSA. Solicitor and Notary Public, since 1970; Director, Business Law, MacRoberts, Solicitors, Glasgow and Edinburgh; Lecturer in Law, Glasgow Graduate Law School; Honorary Fellow, Glasgow Caledonian University; Director, John Smith & Son (Glasgow) Ltd.; Part-time Chairman, Appeals Service, since 1995; Vice Chairman, Pharmaceutical Lists National Appeal Tribunal; Chairman, Scottish Society of Epicureans; b. 7.9.44, Kirkintilloch; m., Christina Jeanne Sinclair; 2 s. Educ. Royal Belfast Academical Institution; Queen's University, Belfast. Senior and Founding Partner, Messrs. Paterson Robertson & Graham, Solicitors, 1971-99; Head of Business Law, Golds, Solicitors, Glasgow, 1999-2001. Former Member, Court, Glasgow Caledonian University; former (founding) Director, Glasgow Solicitors Property Centre; former Director, West Glasgow NHS Trust. Recreations: tennis; golf; hang-gliding. Address: (b.)152 Bath Street, Glasgow; T.-0141-332 9988.

Graham, John Murdo, DipCom, FEIS. Retired Schoolmaster; Honorary Sheriff of Grampian, Highland and Islands at Stornoway; b. 1.5.36, Coll, near Stornoway; m., Murdina Macdonald; 3 s.; 1 d. Educ. Nicolson Institute, Stornoway; Scottish College of Commerce; Jordanhill College of Education. Nicolson Institute, Stornoway: Assistant Teacher, 1959-68, Principal Teacher of Business Studies and Economics, 1968-72, Assistant Rector, 1972-88. Member, North of Scotland Electricity Consumers' Committee, 1992-2000; Member, Social Security Appeal Tribunals, 1982-99; Member, New Appeals Service, Social Security Act, 1998; Member, Council, Educational Institute of Scotland, 1975-85; Elder and Honorary Congregational Treasurer, Stornoway Free Church; General Trustee and Member, Finance, Law and Advisory Committee, Free Church of Scotland. Recreations: current affairs; world stock markets; walking; angling; gardening. Address: (h.) 25 Goathill Road, Stornoway, Isle of Lewis HS1 2NL; T.-01851 703469.

Graham, John Strathie, BA. Head, Scottish Executive Environment and Rural Affairs Department (formerly Scottish Office Agriculture, Environment and Fisheries Department), since 1998; b. 27.5.50, Edinburgh; m., Anne Graham; 2 s.; 1 d. Educ. Edinburgh Academy; Corpus Christi College, Oxford. Joined Scottish Office, 1972; Principal, Scottish Economic Planning Department, 1976; Assistant Secretary, Industry Department for Scotland, 1982; Private Secretary to Secretary of State, 1983; Assistant Secretary: Planning Division, Scottish Development Department, 1985, Finance Division 1, 1990; Under Secretary, Local Government Group, 1991; Principal Finance Officer, 1996. Recreations: exploring Scotland; listening to music. Address: (b.) Pentland House, Edinburgh EH14 1TY.

Graham, Keith H.R., LLB, WS. Principal Clerk, Scottish Land Court, since 1982; b. 29.5.47, Edinburgh; m., Patricia; 2 d. Educ. George Watson's College; Edinburgh University. Apprenticeship, Davidson & Syme, WS, 1968-70; private practice, 1970-72; Legal Assessor, Scottish Land Court, 1972-82. Publication: The Scottish Land Court: Practice and Procedure. Address: (b.) 1 Grosvenor Crescent, Edinburgh EH12 5ER; T.-0131-225 3595.

Graham, (Lord) Donald, BSc, MBA. Director of Information Technology, Adam & Company plc, since 1991; Director: Fruit Market Gallery, since 1992, KDCL Ltd., Property Developers, since 1992, Children's Music Foundation, since 1995; b. 28.10.56, Salisbury, Southern Rhodesia; m., Bridie; 1 s.; 3 d. Educ. St. Andrews College, South Africa; St. Andrews University; INSEAD. Recreations: piping; music; golf. Address: (b.) Adam & Company plc, 22 Charlotte Square, Edinburgh EH2 4DF; T.-0131-225 8484.

Graham, Professor Neil Bonnette, BSc, PhD, CChem, FRSC, FIM, FRSE. Professor in Chemical Technology, Strathclyde University, 1973-97; Emeritus Professor in Chemistry, since 1997; b. 23.5.33, Liverpool; 1 s.; 3 d. Educ. Alsop High School, Liverpool; Liverpool University. Research Chemist, Research Scientist, Canadian Industries Ltd., MacMasterville PQ, Canada, 1956-67; Assistant Group Head, then Group Head, Polymer Chemistry, ICI, Runcorn, Cheshire. Member: Advisory Committee on Dental and Surgical Materials, 1980-86; Expert Advisor to the Secretary of State on Active Medical Implants, since 1993; sometime member of various committees, Society of Chemical Industry, Royal Society of Chemistry and Plastics and Rubber Institute; Founder and Technical Director, Polysystems Ltd., 1980-90; Founder and Chairman: Smart Tech Ltd., since 2000, Ocutec Ltd., since 2001; Trustee, James Clerk Maxwell Trust; Director, Mission Aviation Fellowship (Scotland), 1999; Trustee, MacKinnon McNeill Trust. Recreations: music; walking. Address: (b.) Strathclyde University, Department of Pure and Applied Chemistry, Thomas Graham Building, 295 Cathedral Street, Glasgow G1 1XL; T.-0141-548 2133.

Graham, Sir Norman William, Kt (1971), CB (1961), MA, DLitt (Heriot-Watt), DUniv (Stirling), FRSE; b. 11.10.13, Dundee; m., Catherine Mary Strathie; 2 s.; 1 d. Educ. High School of Glasgow; Glasgow University. Assistant Principal, Department of Health for Scotland, 1936; Principal, Ministry of Aircraft Production, 1941; Principal Private Secretary to Minister, 1944; Assistant Secretary, Department of Health for Scotland, 1945; Under Secretary, 1956; Secretary, Scottish Education Department, 1964-73.

Graham, Lieutenant General Sir Peter, KCB, CBE, DLitt. Chairman, Regimental Trust Fund, The Gordon Highlanders, since 1986; Chairman, The Gordon Highlanders Museum Management Committee, since 1994; b. 14.3.37; m., Dr Alison Mary Morren; 3 s. Educ. Fyvie Village School, Aberdeenshire; Hall School, Hampstead;

St. Paul's School, London; RMA Sandhurst. Commissioned The Gordon Highlanders, 1956; regimental appointments, Dover, Germany, Scotland, Kenya, 1957-62; HQ Highland Brigade, 1962-63; Adjutant 1 Gordons, Kenya, Edinburgh, Borneo (Despatches), 1963-66; Staff Captain, HQ 1 Br Corps, 1966-67; Australian Staff College, 1968; Company Commander, 1 Gordons, Germany, 1969-70; Brigade Maj., HQ 39 Brigade, Northern Ireland, 1970-72; 2nd i/c, 1 Gordons, Ulster, Singapore, 1972-74; Military Assistant to Adjutant General MoD, 1974-75; CO, 1 Gordons, Scotland, Ulster, 1976-78; COS, HQ 3 Armoured Division, Germany, 1978-82; Comd UDR, Ulster (Despatches), 1982-84; Canadian National Defence College, Ontario, 1984-85; Deputy Military Secretary, MoD, 1985-87; GOC Eastern District, 1987-89; Commandant RMA, Sandhurst, 1989-91; GOC Army in Scotland and Governor, Edinburgh Castle, 1991-93. Colonel, The Gordon Highlanders, 1986-94; Member, Royal Company of Archers, since 1985. Publications: The Gordon Highlanders Pipe Music Collection (Co-author), 1983 and 1985; DLitt, Robert Gordon University, 1996. Recreations: stalking; hill-walking; shooting; reading; pipe music; gardening under my wife's directions. Address: (b.) The Gordon Highlanders Museum, Viewfield Road, Aberdeen AB15 7XH; T.-01224 311200.

Graham, Riddell, BSc, FTS. Chief Executive, Scottish Borders Tourist Board, since 1996, Director, 1990-96; b. 13.2.54, Galashiels; m., Sandra; 1 s. Educ. Galashiels Academy; Edinburgh University. Borders Regional Council, 1976-83, latterly as Assistant Tourist Officer; joined Scottish Borders Tourist Board, 1983, as Assistant Director of Tourism. Recreations: mountain biking; watching rugby. Address: (b.) Shepherds Mill, Whinfield Road, Selkirk; T.-01750 20555; e-mail: rgraham@scot-borders.co.uk

Graham, Rev. William Peter, MA, BD. Clerk, Edinburgh Presbytery, since 1993; b. 24.11.43, Edinburgh; m., Isabel Arnot Brown; 2 s. Educ. George Watson's College, Edinburgh; Edinburgh University. Assistant Minister, Dundee (St. Mary's) Parish Church, 1966-68; Minister, Chirnside Parish Church, 1968-93, Bonkyl & Preston, 1973-93, Edrom-Allanton, 1978-93; Clerk, Duns Presbytery, 1982-93; Convener, General Assembly's Nomination Committee, 1990-93; Vice-Convener: Committee on Education for Ministry, 1996-98, Board of Ministry, 1998-99, Board of Communication, since 1999; Governor, George Watson's College, since 1998. Recreations: golf; theatre; reading. Address: (b.) 10 Palmerston Place, Edinburgh EH12 5AA; T.-0131-225 9137.

Grahame, Christine, MA, LLB, DipEd, DipLLP. MSP (SNP), South of Scotland, since 1999 (Convener, Justice Committee); b. 9.9.44, Burton-on-Trent; 2 s. Educ. Boroughmuir School; Edinburgh University. Secondary teacher, 1966-82; solicitor, 1987-99. Recreations: gardening; drinking malt whisky; cats. Address: Scottish Parliament, Edinburgh EH99 1SP; T.-0131-348 5000; e-mail: christine.grahame.msp@scottish.parliament.uk

Grahame, David Currie, MA (Hons). Executive Director, LINC Scotland, since 1993; b. 10.12.53, Hawick. Educ. Langholm Academy; Lockerbie Academy; St. Andrews University. Hotelier and company director, 1980-87; Small Business Consultant, 1987-90; Area Manager, Princes Scottish Youth Business Trust, 1990-91; Head of Business Development, Glasgow Opportunities Enterprise Trust, 1991-93; Founding Director, LINC Scotland; Member, Rating Valuation Appeals Panel; Member, Scottish Hospital Endowments Research Trust; Member, Executive Board, EBAN, Brussels. Recreations: music; classic cinema; food and wine. Address: (b.) Queens House, 19 St. Vincent Place, Glasgow G1 2DT.

Grainger, John McGregor Leighton, MBE, FTS. Chief Executive, Perthshire Tourist Board, since 1982; b. 3.9.43, Aberdeen; m., Kathleen; 1 s. (deceased); 2 d. Assistant Tourist Officer, Aberdeen Town Council, 1959-67; Tourism Manager, Dunbar Town Council, 1967-69, Director of Tourism, Perth Tourist Association, 1969-74; Senior Tourist Officer, Tayside Regional Council, 1974-82. Recreations: fishing; hill-walking. Address: (b.) Lower City Mills, West Mill Street, Perth PH1 5QP; T.-01738 627958.

Grains, Florence Barbara, OBE, FFCS, JP. Member, Shetland Islands Council, since 1986 (Chairman, Planning Board); Director, Shetland Careers Service; b. 2.11.32, Shetland; m., Alistair M. Grains (deceased); 4 s. Educ. Whiteness School, Shetland; Lerwick FE Centre. Retired Sub-postmaster, Whiteness, Shetland. Former Chairman, Shetland Health Board; Chairman, Alting Debating Society; Chairman, Shetland Amenity Trust; Chairman, Postwatch Shetland; Member, Postwatch Scotland; Trustee, Walls and District Agricultural Society; GCSL, 1st Whiteness/Weisdale; Chairman, Foula Electricity Trust; Member, Aith Lifeboat Branch Committee; Trustee, Scottish National War Memorial; Chairman, Visiting Committee, Legalised Police Cells. Address: (h.) Hoove, Whiteness, Shetland ZE2 9LL; T.-01595 84 0243.

Grant, Donald Blane, CBE, TD, LLD, CA; b. 8.10.21, Dundee; m., Lavinia Margaret Ruth Ritchie; 3 d. Educ. Dundee High School. Royal Artillery, 1939-46 (retired as Major); Partner, Thomson, McLintock & Co., 1950-86. Chairman, Tayside Health Board, 1984-91; Chairman: Scottish Legal Aid Board, 1986-91, Mathew Trust, Caird Travelling Scholarships Trust. Recreations: golf; fishing; shooting; gardening. Address: (h.) 24 Albany Road, Broughty Ferry, Dundee DD5 1NT.

Grant, Dr. Douglas, TD, FRSE, FSA Scot; b. 6.1.18; m., Enid Whitsey; 3 s. Educ. George Watson's College; University of St. Andrews. Lt.-Col., RA (served W. Africa and staff), 1939-46; Scottish Widows Fund, 1936-39; Director: Oliver and Boyd Ltd., 1947-67, Edinburgh C. of C., 1952-56, New Education Ltd., 1962-66, Bracken House Publications Ltd., 1963-67, Sprint Productions Ltd., 1963-80, E. & S. Livingston Ltd., 1963-67, Darien Press Ltd., 1963-68, R. & R. Clark Ltd., 1963-80, Port Seton Offset Printers Ltd., 1965-75, T. & A. Constable Ltd., 1965-75, British Journal of Educational Psychology, 1970-91, Pindar (Scot) Ltd., 1986-89, Macdonald Lindsay (Printers) Ltd., 1978-89; Chairman: Scottish Journal of Theology Ltd., 1948-91, Robert Cunningham & Sons Ltd., 1952-76, Hunter and Foulis Ltd., 1963-75, Port Seton Offset Printers Ltd., 1965-75, Multi Media (AU) Services Ltd., 1967-75, Church of Scotland Publications Committee, 1971-76, Scottish Academic Press Ltd., 1969-91, Scottish International Review Ltd., 1970-75, Handsel Press Ltd., 1975-91, Scottish Academic Press (Journals) Ltd., 1976-91, Clark Constable Printers Ltd., 1978-89; Consultant Editor: Scottish Academic Press, 1991-99, Dunedin Academic Press, since 2000. Trustee: The Lodge Trust (Natural History), 1949-85, Darling (Ogilby) Investment Trust, 1955-78, Kilwarlin Trust, since 1964, Esdaile Trust, since 1975 (Chairman), Society for the Benefit of Sons and Daughters of the Clergy of the Church of Scotland, since 1990 (Chairman); Committee Member: Scottish Council of Law Reporting, 1947-93 (Consultant, since 1993), Police Dependents' Trust (Lothian and Borders Police), since 1956, NEDO, 1968-75, New College University of Edinburgh Finance Board, since 1970, University of Edinburgh Court, 1972-84, Scottish Arts Council, 1975-79; President: Edinburgh Master Printers' Association, 1962-64, Edinburgh Booksellers' Society, 1977-80, Edinburgh Amateur Angling Club, 1978-80; Honorary Fellow, Edinburgh Geological Society, 1992; Hon. DLitt, University of St. Andrews, 1986. Address: 2G East Road, North Berwick, East Lothian EH39 4HN; T.-01620 894972.

Grant, (Helen) Rae. Party Administrator, Scottish Liberal Democrats, since 1989; b. 17.12.40, Edinburgh; m., James Sturrock Grant; 2 d. Educ. Boroughmuir High School; Torphichen Commercial College. Party Secretary, 1974-89. Recreations: reading; swimming; walking. Address: (b.) 4 Clifton Terrace, Edinburgh EH12 5DR; T.-0131-337 2314.

Grant, Ian David, CBE, FRAgS. Scottish Crown Estate Commissioner, since 1996; Deputy Chairman, Scottish and Southern Energy PLC, since 2000; b. 28.7.43, Dundee; m., Eileen May Louisa Yule; 3 d. Educ. Strathallan School; East of Scotland College of Agriculture. Chairman, EEC Cereals Working Party, 1982-88 and International Federation of Agricultural Producers, Grains Committee, 1984-90; President, NFU of Scotland, 1984-90; Director: East of Scotland Farmers Ltd., NFU Mutual Insurance Society Ltd., Clydesdale Bank PLC, 1989-97, Scottish Exhibition Centre; Member: Scottish Council, CBI, 1984-96, Board, British Tourist Authority, 1990-98, Scottish Economic Council, 1993-97; Chairman: Scottish Tourist Board, 1990-98 (Member, 1988-90), Cairngorms Partnership, since 1998; Vice President, Royal Smithfield Club; Honorary Doctorate, Business Administration, Napier University. Recreations: travel; swimming; music. Address: (h.) Leal House, Alyth PH11 8JQ. Tel.: 01828 632695.

Grant, Major James MacAlpine Gregor, TD, NDA, MRAC. Landowner and Farmer, since 1961; b. 18.2.38, Nakuru, Kenya; m., Sara Marjory, DL; 3 d. Educ. Eton; Royal Agricultural College, Cirencester. National Service, Queen's Own Cameron Highlanders, 1957-58; TA with 4/5th Queen's Own Cameron Highlanders; Volunteers with 51st Highland Volunteers. Address: Roskill House, Munlochy, Rossshire IV8 8PA; T.-01463 811207.

Grant, Very Rev. Malcolm Etheridge, BSc (Hons), BD (Hons). Provost and Rector, Cathedral Church of S. Andrew, Inverness; b. 6.8.44, Maidstone; m., Katrina Russell Nuttall; 1 s.; 1 d. Educ. Dunfermline High School; Edinburgh University; Edinburgh Theological College. Assistant Curate: S. Mary's Cathedral, Glasgow, 1969-72, Grantham Parish Church, in charge of Church of the Epiphany, Earlesfield, 1972; Team Vicar, Earlesfield, Grantham Team Ministry, 1972-78; Priest-in-charge, S. Ninian's, Invergordon, 1978-81; Examining Chaplain to Bishop of Moray, Ross and Caithness, 1979-81; Member, Highland Region Education Committee, 1979-81; Provost and Rector, Cathedral Church of S. Mary the Virgin, Glasgow, 1981-91; Rector, S Paul's, Strathnairn, and Priest-in-charge, S Mary's-in-the-Fields, Culloden, 1991-97. Address: 15 Ardross Street, Inverness IV3 5NS; T.-01463 233535.

Grant, Professor Peter Mitchell, PhD, FIEE, FIEEE, FRSE, FREng. Professor of Electronic Signal Processing, Edinburgh University, since 1987 (Head, Department of Electronics and Electrical Engineering, since 1999); b. 20.6.44, St. Andrews; m., Marjory Renz; 2 d. Educ. Strathallan School; Heriot-Watt University; Edinburgh University. Publications: Digital Communications (Co-Author), 1997; Digital Signal Processing (Co-Author), 1998. Address: (b.) Department of Electronics and Electrical Engineering, Edinburgh University, Edinburgh EH9 3JL; T.-0131-650 5569.

Grant, Rhoda, BSc. MSP (Labour), Highlands and Islands, since 1999; b. 26.6.63, Stornoway; m., Christopher Mark Grant. Educ. Plockton High School; Inverness College; Open University. Administrative and clerical posts, private sector; administration and accounts, Highland Regional Council; Office Manager, UNISON; Labour Party posts include: Secretary, Inverness East Branch, Secretary, Local Government Committee. Address: (b.) Scottish Parliament, Edinburgh EH99 1SP; T.-0131-348 5766.

Grant, Richard Anthony, BSocSc, MSc. Head of Housing Division 2, Scottish Executive Development Department, since 1997; Head of Division, Land Use and Crofting, Scottish Office Agriculture and Fisheries Department, 1991-97; b. 12.6.48, Leicester; m., Jacqueline Claire; 1 s.; 1 d. Educ. Loughborough College School; Birmingham University; Strathclyde University. Research Officer/Senior Research Officer, Scottish Education Department and Scottish Development Department, 1969-75; Principal Research Officer, Housing Research Unit, Scottish Development Department, 1975-77; Principal, Sports Policy Branch, Scottish Education Department, 1977-79; Principal Research Officer, Housing and Urban Renewal Research Unit, Scottish Development Department, 1979-85; Principal: Land Use and Conservation Branch, Department of Agriculture and Fisheries, 1986-89, NHS Management Executive, 1989-91. Recreations: cycling; hill-walking; cross-country skiing. Address: (b.) RG1/73, Victoria Quay, Leith, Edinburgh; T.-0131-224 5511.

Grant of Dalvey, Sir Patrick Alexander Benedict, 14th Bt, FSA Scot, LLB. Chieftain of Clan Donnachy; Company Director; b. 5.2.53; m.; 2 s. Educ. Glasgow University. Former deerstalker and inshore fisherman.

Grant of Rothiemurchus, John Peter, DL. Landowner; b. 22.10.46, Rothiemurchus; m., Philippa; 1 s.; 2 d. Educ. Gordonstoun. Chairman and Director, Scot Trout Limited, 1989-95; Past Chairman, Highland Region, Forestry, Farming and Wildlife Advisory Group; Patron, Highland Hospice; Vice-President, Scottish Landowners' Federation, since 1991; Deputy Lieutenant, Districts of Lochaber, Inverness, Badenoch and Strathspey, 1986-2001; Member: Council, National Trust for Scotland, 1990-95, Native Woodlands Advisory Panel to the Forestry Commission, 1993-97, National Access Forum, 1993-99, Cairngorm Partnership, since 1995; Chairman, Tourism and Enivronment Task Force, 1995-98; President, Royal Zoological Society of Scotland, since 1996. Recreations: skiing; shooting. Address: (b.) Doune of Rothiemurchus, by Aviemore; T.-01479 810647; e-mail: rothie@enterprise.net

Grant Peterkin, Major General Anthony Peter, OBE, BA. Army Officer, since 1967; Military Secretary and Chief Executive, Army Personnel Centre, Glasgow, since 2000; Landowner; b. 6.7.47, London; m., Joanna Young; 1 s.; 1 d. Educ. Ampleforth College; University of Durham; University of Madras. Commissioned into Queen's Own Highlanders, 1967: service in Middle East, Germany, Northern Ireland, Belize, Hong Kong and India; ADC to CGS; Command of 1st Bn. Queen's Own Highlanders, Belize and Germany, 1987-89; Higher Command and Staff Course, Camberley, 1991; Military Adviser to UN Mission, Iraq and Kuwait, 1991; Commander, 24 Airmobile Brigade, 1993-94; Royal College of Defence Studies, 1995; Army Director of Manning and Career Management, 1996-98; Managing Director, OSCE Mission in Kosovo, 1999; GOC, 5 Division, 2000. Recreation: travelling off the beaten track in Indochina. Address: (h.) Grange Hall, Forres, Morayshire; T.-01309 672742.

Gratwick, Professor Adrian Stuart, MA (Cantab), Dphil (Oxon). Professor of Classical Philology, St Andrews University, since 1997; b. 31.3.43, Stanmore, Middlesex; m., Jennifer Rosemary Clark; 2 s.; 1 d. Educ. St Brendan's College, Bristol; St John's College, Cambridge; Balliol College, Oxford. St Andrews University: Assistant Lecturer in Humanity, 1967, Lecturer, 1970, Reader, 1983; Visiting Professor of the Classics, Harvard University, 1995. Publications: Cambridge History of Classical Literature (Contributor). Recreation: woodwork. Address: (b.) School of Greek, Latin and Ancient History, St Andrews University, St Andrews, Fife.

Gray, Lord (Angus Diarmid Ian Campbell-Gray); b. 3.7.31, Kilconquhar; m., 1, Patricia Margaret Alexander (deceased); 2, Cecilia Wilfrida Williams (née Dimsdale); 1 s.; 3 d. Educ. Eton. Address: (h.) Airds Bay, Taynuilt, Argyll.

Gray of Contin, Lord (Hamish Gray), PC, DL. Business and Parliamentary Consultant, since 1986; b. 28.6.27, Inverness; m., Judith W. Brydon; 2 s.; 1 d. Educ. Inverness Royal Academy. Queen's Own Cameron Highlanders, 1945-48; Director, family and other private companies, 1949-70; MP, Ross and Cromarty, 1970-83; Government Whip, 1971-74; Opposition Spokesman on Energy, 1975-79; Minister of State for Energy, 1979-83; Minister of State for Scotland, 1983-86; Spokesman for Government in Lords for Scotland, Employment and Energy, 1983-86. Non-Executive Director, Allied Deals Capital Ltd.; Vice President: Neighbourhood Energy Action (President, Energy Action Scotland), 1987-98, Scottish Association of Youth Clubs, 1987-98; Lord Lieutenant, Invernessshire, since 1996. Recreations: golf; cricket; hill-walking; reading. Address: (h.) Achneim House, Flichity, Invernessshire IV2 6XE.

Gray, Adam, OBE, NDA, NDD, FRAgS. Farmer; b. 6.8.29, Borgue, Kirkcudbright; m., Elaine West Russell; 3 s. Educ. George Watson's Boys College; West of Scotland Agricultural College. Nuffield Scholar, 1955; Past President, Stewartry NFU; Member, NFU Council; Director: Royal Highland & Agricultural Society (Honorary Vice-President, 1994-95), Scottish Milk Marketing Board, 1981-94; former Council Member, British Simmental Cattle Society; former Chairman: SW Scotland Grassland Society, Kirkcudbright District Council, UK Milk Publicity Council; Past President, Scottish Agricultural Arbiters Association; former Director, Scottish Pride Ltd.; Honorary President, Stewartry Agricultural Society; Governor, West of Scotland Agricultural College, 1980-86; Governor, Hannah Research Institute; Secretary, Kirkcudbright Burns Club; Past President: Kirkcudbright Rotary Club. Awarded OBE, 1994, FRAgS, 1997. Publications: Borgue Academy; White Gold?; A Scots Agricultural Glossary; Borgue: The Land and the People. Recreations: rugby; local history. Address: (h.) Ingleneuk, Borgue, Kirkcudbright; T.-01557 870 250.

Gray, Alasdair. Artist and Writer; b. 28.12.34, Glasgow; m., Morag McAlpine; 1 s. Educ. Whitehill Senior Secondary School; Glasgow Art School. Part-time Art Teacher, 1958-62; Scene Painter, 1963-64; has since lived by drawing, painting, writing; Associate Professor of Creative Writing: Glasgow University, Strathclyde University; Glasgow People's Palace and The Collins Gallery, Strathclyde University have collections of his paintings; extant murals: Palacerigg nature reserve, Cumbernauld; Ubiquitous Chip restaurant, Glasgow; Abbots House local history museum, Dunfermline. Publications: novels: Lanark; 1982 Janine; The Fall of Kelvin Walker; Something Leather; McGrotty and Ludmilla; A History Maker; Poor Things; Mavis Belfrage; other books: Old Negatives (a life in four verse sequences); short story collections: Unlikely Stories, Mostly; Lean Tales (this last also containing work by Jim Kelman and Agnes Owens); Ten Tales Tall and True; Five Glasgow Artists (an exhibition catalogue); Saltire Self-Portrait No. 4; Why Scots Should Rule Scotland (1992 and 1997), Working Legs, a play for people without them; The Book of Prefaces, 2000; Sixteen Occasional Poems; Scottish National Library has a collection of his unpublished plays and other material. Recreations: reading; talking to friends; drinking; walking.

Gray, Alistair B., BA, CA. Managing Director, Ortak Jewellery Limited, since 1990; Board Member, Highlands and Islands Enterprise, since 1997; b. 14.6.58, Kirkwall,

Orkney; m., Linda; 3 s.; 1 d. Educ. Kirkwall Grammar School; Heriot-Watt University. Chartered Accountant, Arthur Young, Edinburgh, 1979-84. Address: Hatston, Kirkwall, Orkney KW15 1RW; T.-01856 872224.

Gray, Charles Ireland, CBE, FRSA, JP. Chair, Education, North Lanark Council; b. 25.1.29, Gartcosh; m., Catherine; 3 s.; 2 d. Educ. Coatbridge High School. Local government, since 1958; Leader, Strathclyde Regional Council, 1986-92 (Depute Leader, 1978-86); former Director, Scottish Exhibition and Conference Centre; former Member: Scottish Enterprise Board, East Kilbride Development Corporation, Scottish Development Agency, Clyde Port Authority; former Vice-Chairman, Planning Exchange; former UK Vice-President, European Committee of Regions. Recreations: music; reading; local government. Address: (b.) Civic Centre, Motherwell ML1 1TW.

Gray, Ethel Marian, CBE, JP, MA, LLD, DUniv, FEIS. Patron, LEAD (Scotland), since 1997 (Board Member, and Chairman, Advisory Committee, 1987-95); b. 19.4.23, Glasgow; m., George Deans Gray (deceased). Educ. Hutchesons' Girls Grammar School; Paisley Grammar School; Glasgow University. Teacher of English, 1946-52; Lecturer in English and Drama, Jordanhill College, 1952-63; Founding Principal, Craigie College of Education, Ayr, 1963-75; Director, Scottish Adult Literacy Agency, 1976-79; Chairman, National Book League Scotland, 1977-81; Convener, Adult Access to Education, Scottish Institute of Adult and Continuing Education, 1988-89 (President of Institute, 1984-87); Vice-Chairman, Board of Governors, The Queen's College, Glasgow, 1980-88; Chairman, Education Project for Older People, Age Concern Scotland, 1982-85; Member of Court, Chairman of Staffing Committee and Joint Faculty Staff Review Board, Heriot-Watt University, 1979-84; Adviser in Adult Education, IBA, 1983-88; Member: Scottish Tertiary Education Advisory Council, 1984-87, Scottish Advisory Committee, British Council, 1968-89, STV Education Advisory Committee, 1981-92, Scottish Community Education Council, 1979-85 (Chairman, Communications and Technology Group and Chairman, Management Committee, Micro-Electronics Project), Crawford Commission on Radio and Television Coverage, 1973-75, Committee of Enquiry on the Police, 1977-79, Consultative Committee on the Curriculum, 1965-71. Honorary Fellow, Institute of Contemporary Scotland, since 2001. Recreations: reading; travelling; theatre. Address: (h.) Flat 5, Varrich House, 7 Church Hill, Edinburgh EH10 4BG; T.-0131-447 5403.

Gray, George Bovill Rennie, OBE. Farmer; Chairman, G.B.R. Gray Ltd.; Trustee, Scottish Society for Crop Research, Invergowrie; a Director, Cruden Foundation; b. 5.3.20, Edinburgh; m., Anne Constance Dale; 4 s.; 2 d. Educ. Clayesmore, Dorset; Edinburgh and East of Scotland College of Agriculture. A Director, West Cumberland Farmers, 1955-85; Member, Moredun Foundation, 1958-97; Member, Pig Industry Development Authority, 1958-68; Chairman, Oxford Farming Conference, 1972; Member, Agricultural and Veterinary Sub-Committee, UGC, 1972-82; Lothian Regional Councilor, 1974-82. Address: Smeaton-Hepburn, East Linton EH40 3DT; T.-01620 860275.

Gray, Iain Cumming, BSc (Hons), CertEd. MSP (Labour), Edinburgh Pentlands, since 1999; Minister for Social Justice, Scottish Executive; b. 7.6.57, Edinburgh; m., Gil; 1 d.; 2 step d. Educ. Inverness Royal Academy; Edinburgh University; Moray House College. Physics/maths teacher, 1978-86; Campaign Manager, Oxfam in Scotland, 1986-99. Deputy Minister for Community Care, Scottish Executive, 1999-2000. Recreations: Hibs; running; bonsai; reading; music; hill-walking. Address: (b.) 78 Colinton Mains Drive, Edinburgh EH13 9BJ; T.-0131-477 4511; e-mail: iain.gray.msp@scottish.parliament.uk

Gray, James Allan, MB, ChB, FRCPEdin. Principal Medical Officer, Scottish Widows' Fund, Edinburgh, 1990-97; President, British Society for the Study of Infection, 1989-91; b. 24.3.35, Bristol; m., Jennifer Margaret Newton Hunter; 1 s. (deceased); 2 d. Educ. St. Paul's School, London; Edinburgh University. House Surgeon and Physician posts, Edinburgh and Middlesbrough; Short Service Commission, RAF Medical Branch, 1960-63; Senior House Officer, Research Fellow and Registrar posts, Edinburgh, 1965-67; Registrar, Bristol Royal Infirmary, 1967-68; Senior Registrar, Royal Free Hospital (Department of Infectious Diseases), London, 1968-69; Consultant in Communicable Diseases, City Hospital, Edinburgh, 1969-95; Assistant Director of Studies (Medicine), Edinburgh Post-Graduate Board, 1976-84; Honorary Senior Lecturer, Department of Medicine, Edinburgh University, 1992-95; Fellow, Royal Medical Society (Senior President, 1958-59); Founder Editor, Res Medica, 1957-58; Assistant Editor, Journal of Infection, 1979-86. Publications: Antibacterial Drugs Today (Co-author), 1983; Infectious Diseases (Co-author), 1984, 1992, new edition 1998; Edinburgh City Hospital, 1999. Recreations: hill-walking; pottery collecting; photography. Address: (h.) St. Andrews Cottage, 15 Lauder Road, Edinburgh EH9 2EN; T.-0131-667 4124.

Gray, Professor James Robertson, OBE, BSc, FRSGS, DipActMaths, FFA, FIMA, CMath, FSS. Professor and Head, Department of Actuarial Mathematics and Statistics, Heriot-Watt University, 1971-89 (now Emeritus); b. 21.2.26, Dundee; m., Catherine McAulay Towner. Educ. High School of Dundee; Edinburgh University. Actuarial Trainee, Scottish Life Assurance Company, 1947-49; St. Andrews University: Lecturer in Mathematics, 1949-50, Lecturer in Statistics, 1950-62, Senior Lecturer in Statistics (also Head of Department), 1962-71; Heriot-Watt University: established first Department of Actuarial Science in UK; Dean, Faculty of Science, 1978-81; Council Member, Faculty of Actuaries, 1969-87 (Vice President, 1983-87); Vice-Chairman, Scottish Examination Board, 1984-90 (Convener of Examinations Committee, 1982-90); former Member, Council, Royal Scottish Geographical Society and former Convener, Lecture Committee; former Vice-Chairman, Scottish Universities Council on Entrance; Past Chairman: Scottish Branch, Institute of Mathematics and Its Applications, Edinburgh Branch, Royal Statistical Society. Recreations: golf; hill-walking; bridge; music; Probus. Address: (h.) Green Gables, 9 Cammo Gardens, Edinburgh EH4 8EJ; T.-0131-339 3330.

Gray, Muriel, BA (Hons). Broadcaster; Joint Managing Director, Ideal World Productions; b. Glasgow. Educ. Glasgow School of Art. Worked as an illustrator; then as a designer with National Museum of Antiquities; was member of rock band, The Family Von Trapp; had own show with Radio Forth; was frequent presenter on Radio 1; co-presented The Tube, Channel 4; had own arts programme, The Works, Tyne Tees; own music programme, Studio 1, Border TV; presented Casebook Scotland, BBC Scotland; Frocks on the Box, Thames TV; Acropolis Now, ITV; presented The Media Show, Channel 4; Co-Producer and Presenter, Walkie Talkie, Channel 4; first woman Rector, Edinburgh University; Producer/Presenter/Director, The Munro Show, Scottish TV; Producer/Presenter, Art is Dead...Long Live TV!, Channel Four; The Golden Cagoule, BBC; Ride On. Publications: The First Fifty; The Trickster (novel); Furnace (novel). Recreation: being in the Scottish Highlands — gets grumpy and miserable if can't be up a mountain every few weeks. Address: (b.) St. Georges Studios, 93-97 St. Georges Road, Glasgow G3 6JA.

Gray, Professor Peter Michael David, MA, DPhil, FBCS. Professor, Department of Computing Science, Aberdeen University, since 1989; b. 11.2.40, Abingdon; m., Doreen F. Ross; 1 s.; 1 d. Educ. Abingdon School; Queens' College,

Cambridge; Jesus College, Oxford. Systems Analyst, Plessey Co., Poole, 1966-68; Research Fellow, Computer Research Group, Aberdeen University, 1968-72; Lecturer in Computing Science, Aberdeen University, 1972-84; Visiting Associate Professor, University of Western Ontario, 1985; Senior Lecturer, 1985-89. Reader, Church of Scotland. Publication: Logic, Algebra and Databases. Recreation: croquet. Address: (b.) Department of Computing Science, King's College, Aberdeen, AB24 3UE; T.-01224 272292; e-mail: pgray@csd.abdn.ac.uk

Gray, Professor Robert Hugh, BSc (Econ), MA (Econ), FCA, FCCA, FRSA. Professor of Accounting, Glasgow University, since 2000; b. 1.4.52, Manchester; 2 s. Educ. De La Salle College, Salford; Hull University; Manchester University. Qualified as accountant with KPMG Peat Marwick, 1976; Lecturer, Lancashire Polytechnic, UCNW Bangor, University of East Anglia; Mathew Professor of Accounting and Information Systems, Dundee University, 1990-2000; Editor, Social and Environmental Accounting; Director, Centre for Social and Environmental Accounting Research. Publications: over 200 articles; various books including Accounting for the Environment; The Greening of Accountancy; Accounting and Accountability. Recreations: golf; sailing; rock music. Address: (b.) Department of Accounting, University of Glasgow, 73 Southpark Avenue, Glasgow G12 8LE; T.-0141-330 6315.

Green, David Russell, MA (Hons). Convener, Highland Council, since 1999; Crofters Commissioner, since 1998; b. 13.6.51, Aberdeen; m., Sheila; 1 s.; 3 d. Educ. Glasgow University. Marketing consultant; trainee chartered accountant; hotelier; snowplough driver; Highland Councillor; fully diversified crofter. Address: (b.) Stac Pollaidh Self Catering, Achnahaird, Achiltibuie, Ullapool IV26 2YT; T.-01854 622340.

Green, Geoffrey, MA, PhD. Managing Director, T. & T. Clark Ltd., Professional and Academic Publishers, since 1821; b. 22.8.47, Bradford; m., Ellen Hughes; 1 s.; 1 d. Educ. Bootham School, York; University of Edinburgh. Director, T. & T. Clark Ltd., 1975 (Managing Director, 1987). Address: (b.) 59 George Street, Edinburgh EH2 2LQ; T.-0131-225 4703; e-mail: ggreen@tandtclark.co.uk

Green, Malcolm Robert, MA, DPhil. Member, Glasgow City Council (Business Manager, Member, Cultural and Leisure Services Committee and Education Services Committee); Member, Scottish Qualifications Authority, since 1997; b. 4.1.43, Leicester; m., Mary Margaret Pratley; 1 s.; 2 d. Educ. Wyggeston Grammar School, Leicester; Magdalen College, Oxford. Lecturer in Roman History, Glasgow University, 1967-98; former Member, Strathclyde Regional Council: Chairman, Environment Committee; Chairman, Education Committee, 1982-90; Convener, Education Committee, City of Glasgow Council, 1995-99; Chairman, Education Committee, Convention of Scottish Local Authorities, 1978-90. Address: (b.) City Chambers, George Square, Glasgow G2 1DU.

Green, Professor Roger Philip Hywel, MA, BLitt. Professor of Humanity (Latin), since 1995, and Head, Department of Classics, since 1997, University of Glasgow; b. 14.6.43, High Wycombe; m., Anne Mary Perry; 1 s.; 1 d. Educ. Royal Grammar School, High Wycombe; Balliol College, University of Oxford. University of St. Andrews: Assistant Lecturer, 1967-70, Lecturer, 1970-92, Senior Lecturer, 1992-94, Reader, 1994-95. Former Secretary, International Association of Neo-Latin Studies. Publications include: The Works of Ausonius, 1991; Augustine on Christian Teaching, 1997. Recreations: walking; cycling; rail travel; birdwatching; gardening; music; architecture. Address: (b.) Department of Classics, University of Glasgow, Glasgow G12 8QQ; T.-0141-330 4276.

Greene, John Gerald, MA, PhD, FBPsS. Registrar, Board of Examiners in Clinical Psychology, British Psychological Society; Clinical Lecturer, Glasgow University; b. 10.3.38, Glasgow; m., Dr. Elisabeth Rose Hamil; 2 s.; 2 d. Educ. St. Aloysius College, Glasgow; Glasgow University. Clinical Tutor, Glasgow University Master of Applied Science degree in Clinical Psychology, 1976-95; Chairman, National (Scotland) Scientific Consultative Committee on Clinical Psychological Services, 1985-87; Treasurer, International Menopause Society, 1996-99. Publications: The Social and Psychological Origins of the Climacteric Syndrome, 1984; Clinical Psychology in the Scottish Health Service (Co-author), 1984. Recreations: music; tennis; skiing. Address: (b.) The Medical Centre, 1 High Street, Neilston, Glasgow G78 3HJ.

Greene, John Henderson, MA, LLB. Former Partner, MacRoberts, Solicitors, Glasgow and Edinburgh; b. 2.6.32, Kilmarnock; m., Catriona McGillivray Scott; 1 s. Educ. Merchiston Castle School, Edinburgh; Edinburgh University. Assistant: Joseph Kirkland & Son, Solicitors, Saltcoats, 1958-60, MacRoberts, Solicitors, 1960 (appointed Partner, 1961); Law Society of Scotland: former Vice-Convener, Company Law Committee, former Member, Bankruptcy and Liquidation Committee; former Council Member, Royal Faculty of Procurators, Glasgow; founder Chairman, Troon Round Table, 1964; Captain, Royal Troon Golf Club, 1989-90; Elder, Portland Church, Troon; President, Glasgow Ayrshire Society, 1985-86, 1993-94, 1998-99; Vice-Chairman, Ayrshire and Arran Health Board, 1993-2001. Publication: Law and Practice of Receivership in Scotland (Co-Author). Recreations: golf; gardening. Address: (h.) Silvertrees, 7 Lady Margaret Drive, Troon KA10 7AL; T.-Troon 312482.

Greening, Andrew Peter, BSc, MBChB, FRCPE. Consultant Physician, Western General Hospital, Edinburgh, since 1984; part-time Reader, University of Edinburgh; b. 10.10.48, London; m., Rosemary Jean Renwick; 2 s. Educ. George Watson's College, Edinburgh; University of Edinburgh. House Officer and Senior House Officer posts, Edinburgh, 1973-75; Registrar, Senior Registrar, MRC Training Fellow posts, St. Bartholomew's and Hammersmith Hospitals and Royal Postgraduate Medical School, London, 1975-82. Director, Scottish Adult Cystic Fibrosis Service, Western General Hospital, Edinburgh, since 1992; Associate Editor, Thorax and Respiratory Medicine; Member, Grants Committees: Chest, Heart and Stroke Association, British Lung Foundation (Chair), Cystic Fibrosis Trust. International Lecturer on asthma and cystic fibrosis; Member, Scottish, British, European and American Thoracic Societies. Address: (b.) Western General Hospital, Edinburgh EH4 2XU.

Greenman, Professor Jonathan Vaughan, BA, MA, PhD. Professor of Mathematics and Its Applications, Stirling University, since 1990; b. 3.3.39, Cardiff; m., Barbara Phyllis; 2 s. Educ. Kingston Grammar School; Cambridge University. Harkness Scholar, University of California, Berkeley; Department of Physics, MIT; Stanford Research Institute, California; Department of Mathematics, Essex University; Tutor, Open University; Senior Analyst, Corporate Planning, British Petroleum plc; Industry Analyst, Centre for Global Energy Studies. Recreations: cinema; walking; travel. Address: (b.) Department of Mathematics, Stirling University, Stirling, FK9 4LA; T.-01786 467460.

Greenshields, David, MA, DipEd. Headteacher, Uddingston Grammar School, since 1997; b. 24.7.49, Thankerton; m., Megan Bond; 2 d. Educ. Biggar High School; University of Edinburgh; Moray House College. History Teacher, Lanark Grammar, 1971; Assistant Principal Teacher, Social Subjects, Auchmuty High, Fife, 1973; Assistant Principal Teacher, Guidance, Lanark Grammar, 1974; various posts, Uddingston Grammar

School, since 1978. Recreation: supporter of Heart of Midlothian F.C. Address: (b.) Uddingston Grammar School, Station Road, Uddingston G71 7BS; T.-01698 327400; (h.) Stonebyres, Lanark.

Greenwood, Professor Justin, BA (Hons), PhD. Professor of European Public Policy, Robert Gordon University, Aberdeen, since 1996; b. 17.5.60, Windlesham. Educ. Newton Abbot Grammar School; Nottingham University. Acting Head, School of Public Administration and Law, Robert Gordon University, Aberdeen; Chair: International Political Science Association Research Committee on Politics and Business; European Consortium for Political Research; Vice-President, European Thematic Network on Public Administration; Member: Research Board, European Centre for Public Affairs; Advisory Board, United Business Institute; External Examiner, Durham University; Limerick University. Publications: Editor: Current Politics and Economics of Europe; Member, Editorial Advisory Board, Business and Politics; Journal of Public Affairs. Publications: Inside the EU Business Associations, 2002; The Effectiveness of EU Business Associations (Editor), 2001; Representing Interests in the European Union, 1997; Organised Interests in the New Global Order (Co-Editor) 1999; Collective Action in the European Union: Interest and the New Politics of Associability (Co-Editor) 1997; European Casebook on Business Alliances (Editor) 1995; Organised Interests and the European Community, (jointly), 1992; Social Partnership in the European Union (Co-Editor), 2001. Address; (b.) School of Public Administration and Law, Robert Gordon University, Garthdee Road, Aberdeen, AB10 7QE; T.-01224 263406.

Greer, Professor Ian Andrew, MB, ChB, MD (Glas), MRCP(UK), FRCP(Glas), FRCP(Ed), FRCP(London), MFFP, FRCOG, MAE. Professor and Head, Department of Obstetrics and Gynaecology, Glasgow University, since 1991; Regius Professor, since 2000; Honorary Consultant Obstetrician and Gynaecologist, Glasgow Royal Infirmary and Glasgow Royal Maternity Hospital, since 1991; b. 16.4.58, Glasgow. Educ. Allan Glen's School, Glasgow; Glasgow University. Registrar in General Medicine, Glasgow Royal Infirmary; Registrar in Obstetrics and Gynaecology, Glasgow Royal Maternity Hospital and Glasgow Royal Infirmary; Lecturer in Obstetrics and Gynaecology, Edinburgh University; Clinical Research Scientist/Consultant Obstetrician and Gynaecologist, MRC Reproductive Biology Unit, Edinburgh. MRCOG Gold Medal; Blair-Bell Lectureship, Royal College of Obstetricians and Gynaecologists 1989; Travelling Fellowship, RCOG, 1989; Watson Prize Lecture, Royal College of Physicians and Surgeons of Glasgow, 1990. Address: (b.) Department of Obstetrics and Gynaecology, Glasgow University, Glasgow Royal Infirmary, Glasgow G31 2ER; T.-0141-211 4703.

Gregory, David Richard Monro, MBE, LLB. Chairman, Highland Housing and Community Care Trust; b. 31.8.39, Bournemouth; m., Jill Alison Mimpriss; 1 s.; 2 d. Educ. Marlborough College; University of Aberdeen. Royal Navy, 1957-72 (Fighter Pilot, invalided following flying accident); legal apprenticeship/Solicitor, Burnett and Reid, Aberdeen and W. & J. Burness, Edinburgh, 1975-78; Director, Margaret Blackwood Housing Association, 1978-99; Director, Scottish Trust for the Physically Disabled, 1978-99; Member, Boards of Management: Disability Scotland, Lothian Centre for Integrated Living, Disabled Persons Housing Services (Lothian), Ownership Options (Scotland). Recreations: sea canoeing; photography. Address: (h.) 32 Midmar Gardens, Edinburgh EH10 6DZ; 178 Strathan Skerray, Sutherland KW14 7TJ.

Greig, Rev. Alan, BSc, BD. Minister, Kintore Parish Church, since 1992 (Vice Convener, Board of World Mission); b. 19.11.51, Helensburgh; m., Ruth D. Evans; 2 s. Educ. Coatbridge High School; University of Strathclyde; University of Edinburgh. Probationer Minister, Northfield Parish, Aberdeen, 1976-77; Minister, Hurlford Reid Memorial Church, Ayrshire, 1977-83; Church of Scotland Missionary working with United Church of Zambia, 1983-92. Recreations: swimming; cycling; walking. Address: 6 Forest Road, Kintore, Inverurie AB51 0XG; T.-01467 632219; e-mail: greig@kincarr.free-online.co.uk

Greig, Alastair, BVM&S, FRCVS. Head of Veterinary Science Division, SAC, since 1999; b. 18.5.44, Aberdeen; m., Margaret; 1 d. Educ. Robert Gordon's College, Aberdeen; Royal (Dick) School of Veterinary Studies, Edinburgh University. Assistant in veterinary practice, Kippen, 1967-68; Veterinary Research Officer, Animal Virus Research Institute, Pirbright, 1968-73; Assistant Veterinary Investigation Officer, Dumfries Veterinary Investigation Centre, 1973-78; Assistant Veterinary Investigation Officer, St Boswells, 1978-83; Veterinary Investigation Officer, Edinburgh, 1983-91; Assistant Director, SAC Veterinary Science Division, 1991-99. Past President, BVA Scottish Branch, and BVA Scottish Metropolitan Division; Director, Vet Trust. Recreations: small-holding; gardening; walking. Address: (b.) SAC Advisory Offices, Oakbank Road, Perth, PH1 1HF; T.-01738 620042.

Greig, Christopher George, BSc, PhD. Non-Executive Chairman: William Grant & Sons Ltd., PPL Therapeutics plc, Belhaven Brewery Group plc; m., Anne; 1 s.; 2 d. Educ. Harris Academy; St. Andrews University; London University. Invergordon Distillers Group PLC, 1966-94 (Managing Director, 1983-94); Director (Non-Executive): Simpsons Malt Ltd., Edinburgh Green Belt Trust, Scottish Quality Cereals, Heriot Watt Trading, The Airborne Initiative (Scotland) Ltd.; Director: Scotch Whisky Association, C.G. (Farms) Ltd., Mosszone Ltd; Trustee, Scottish Civic Trust. Address: (h.) North Mains, Ormiston, East Lothian EH35 5NG; T.-01875 613721.

Greig, G. Andrew, MA. Author; b. 23.9.51, Bannockburn. Educ. Waid Academy, Anstruther; Edinburgh University. Full-time writer, since 1979; Writer-in-Residence, Glasgow University, 1979-81; Scottish-Canadian Exchange Fellow, 1981-82; Writer-in-Residence, Edinburgh University, 1993-94; climbed on Himalayan expeditions. Publications: six volumes of poetry including Men on Ice, Surviving Passages, The Order of the Day, Western Swing; two mountaineering books; novels: Electric Brae, Return of John Macnab; When They Lay Bare; That Summer. Recreations: climbing; fishing; music. Address: 1 Melvin Place, Stromness, Orkney KY16 3DD.

Grice, Paul Edward, BSc. Clerk and Chief Executive, Scottish Parliament, since 1999; b. 13.10.61; m.; 2 d. Department of Transport, 1985-87; Department of Environment, 1987-92; joined Scottish Office, 1992 (latterly Head of Division, Constitution Group: Referendum, Scotland Bill, then Director of Implementation). Address: Scottish Parliament, Edinburgh EH99 1SP.

Grier, Arnold Macfarlane, MB, ChB, FRCSEdin. Consultant Ear, Nose and Throat Surgeon, Highland Health Board, since 1962; National Vice-President, Scottish Council on Deafness; b. 5.9.21, Musselburgh; m., Elisabeth J. Kluten; 2 s.; 1 d. Educ. Musselburgh Grammar School; Edinburgh University. Recreations: gardening; aviculture; painting. Address: (h.) Elmbank, 68 Culduthel Road, Inverness; T.-Inverness 234682.

Grier, Scott, OBE, MA, CA, FCIT. Chairman: Loganair Limited, Scottish Tanning Industries Limited; b. 7.3.41, Kilmacolm; m., Frieda Gardiner; 2 s. Educ. Greenock High School; Glasgow University. Apprenticed, Grahams Rintoul & Co., 1962-66; Accountant, Ardrossan Harbour Company Ltd./Clydeport, from 1967; various posts, Loganair, since 1976; Director: Glasgow Chamber of Commerce, 1990-98, Caledonian MacBrayne Limited, since 1996; Chairman: Bridge of Weir Leather Co. Ltd., Andrew Muirhead & Son Ltd., W. J. & W. Lang Ltd., NCT Leather Ltd., since 1997, Garston Leather Ltd., since 1998; Governor, Scottish Sports Aid Foundation, since 1993; Member, Scottish Tourist Board, 1992-98; Recreations: golf; philately. Address: (h.) Lagavulin, 15 Corsehill Drive, West Kilbride, KA23 9HU; T.-01294 823138.

Grieve, Hon. Lord (William Robertson Grieve), VRD (1958), QC (Scot), MA, LLB. Senator of the College of Justice in Scotland, 1972-88; b. 21.10.17, Glasgow; m., Lorna St. John Benn (deceased); 1 s.; 1 d. Educ. Glasgow Academy; Sedbergh School; Glasgow University. Served with Royal Navy as an RNVR officer, 1939-45; Advocate, Scots Bar, 1947; QC, 1957; Sheriff Principal, Renfrew and Argyll, 1964-72; Judge of Appeal, Jersey and Guernsey, 1971-72; Procurator, Church of Scotland, 1968-72; Chairman, Governors, Fettes Trust, 1978-86. President, Glasgow University Union, 1938. Chairman, Board of Governors, St. Columba's Hospice, 1983-99. Recreations: golf; painting. Address: (h.) 20 Belgrave Crescent, Edinburgh EH4 3AJ; T.-0131-332 7500.

Grieve, Professor Andrew Robert, OBE, DDS, BDS, FDS RCSEd. Professor of Conservative Dentistry, 1980-99, Dean of Dentistry, 1993-97, Dundee University; Consultant in Restorative Dentistry, since 1980; b. 23.5.39, Stirling; m., Frances M. Ritchie; 2 d. Educ. Perth Academy; St. Andrews University. Junior hospital appointments and general dental practice, 1961-63; Lecturer in Operative Dental Surgery and Dental Therapeutics, St. Andrews University, 1963-65; Lecturer in Conservative Dentistry, Birmingham University, 1965; appointed Senior Lecturer and Consultant in Restorative Dentistry, Birmingham Area Health Authority (Teaching), 1975. Member, Dental Council, Royal College of Surgeons of Edinburgh, 1983-88; President: British Society for Restorative Dentistry, 1986-87 (Honorary Fellow, 2000), Royal Odonto-Chirurgical Society of Scotland, 1994-95 (Council Member, 1985-88); Chairman, Tayside Area Dental Advisory Committee, 1987-90; Member, General Dental Council, 1989-99 (Chairman, Legislation Committee, 1994-99). Recreations: woodwork; hill-walking; travel in France and study of French language and culture. Address: (h.) Ravensfield, 20 Albany Road, West Ferry, Dundee.

Grieve, John. Actor; b. 14.6.24, Glasgow. Trained, Royal Scottish Academy of Music and Drama (James Bridie Gold Medallist), followed by five full seasons, Citizens' Theatre, Glasgow; also appeared in Guthrie's production of The Anatomist, Citizens', 1968; numerous other performances on the Scottish stage, including leading roles in The Bevellers, The Flouers o' Edinburgh, The Good Soldier Schweik, Twelfth Night; television work includes The Vital Spark, Oh Brother, Doctor at Sea, New Year shows; numerous appearances in pantomime; appeared with Scottish Theatre Company in Waiting for Godot and The Thrie Estaites.

Grieve, Professor Robert, MA, PhD, CPsych, FBPsS. Professor of Psychology, Edinburgh University, since 1987; b. 2.8.44, Bathgate; m., Anne; 1 s.; 2 d. Educ. Edinburgh University. Lecturer in Psychology, St. Andrews University; Senior Lecturer in Psychology, then Associate Professor of Psychology, University of Western Australia. Address: (b.) Department of Psychology, Edinburgh University, 7 George Square, Edinburgh EH8 9JZ; T.-0131-650 3441.

Griffith, Richard Jeremy, MA (Cantab), DipArch (Cantab), RIAS. Director, Edinburgh World Heritage Trust, since 1999; b. 18.3.47, London. Educ. Malvern Boys College; St. John's College, Cambridge. Choral Scholar, 1966-69; RIBA, 1974; International Centre for Conservation and Restoration of Monuments, Rome, 1977; Listed Buildings Case Officer, Greater London Council's Historic Buildings Division, 1979-86; Senior Statutory Officer, English Heritage, London Region, 1986-94; Director, Edinburgh New Town Conservation Committee, 1994-99. Member, Council, Cockburn Association. Recreations: travel; music; skiing. Address: (b.) 5 Charlotte Square, Edinburgh EH2 4DR; T.-0131-220 7720.

Griffiths, Nigel. MP (Labour), Edinburgh South, since 1987; Parliamentary Under-Secretary of State (Minister for Small Business), Department of Trade and Industry, since 2001; Minister for Competition and Consumer Affairs, 1997-98; Vice President, Institute of Trading Standards Administration, since 1994; Chair, HEAT (Home Energy Action Team), since 1999; Chair, Scottish Charities Kosovo Appeal, since 1999; b. 20.5.55; m., Sally McLaughlin. Educ. Hawick High School; Edinburgh University; Moray House College of Education. Secretary, Lothian Devolution Campaign, 1978; Rights Adviser, Mental Handicap Pressure Group, 1979-87; City of Edinburgh District Councillor, 1980-87 (Chairperson, Housing Committee); Member: Edinburgh Festival Council, 1984-87, Edinburgh Health Council, 1982-87; Executive Member, Edinburgh Council of Social Service, 1984-87; Member, Wester Hailes School Council, 1981; Executive Member, Scottish Constitutional Convention (Chair, Finance Committee); Opposition Spokesman on Consumer Affairs, 1989-97. Recreations: travel; scuba diving; live entertainment; badminton; hill-walking; rock-climbing; architecture; reading; politics. Address: (h.) 31 Minto Street, Edinburgh EH9 2BT; T.-0131-662 4520.

Griffiths, Professor Peter Denham, CBE, BSc, MD, LRCP, MRCS, FRCPath, FRCP(Edin), FIMgt, FRSA. Emeritus Professor of Biochemical Medicine, Dundee University (Vice-Principal, 1979-85, Dean of Medicine and Dentistry, 1985-89); Director and Trustee, Scottish Hospitals Endowment Research Trust, 1994-98; b. 16.6.27, Southampton; m., Joy Burgess; 3 s.; 1 d. Educ. King Edward VI School, Southampton; Guy's Hospital, London University. House appointments, Guy's Hospital, 1956-57; Junior Lecturer in Physiology, Guy's Hospital, 1957-58; Registrar and Senior Registrar, Guy's and Lewisham Hospitals, 1958-64; Consultant Pathologist, Harlow Hospitals Group, 1964-66; Senior Lecturer in Clinical Chemistry/Honorary Consultant, St. Andrews University, then Dundee University, 1966-68. Member, General Medical Council, 1986-93; President, 1987-89, and sometime Chairman of Council, Association of Clinical Biochemists; Tayside Health Board: Honorary Consultant, 1966-89, Member, 1977-85; former Director, Dundee Repertory Theatre. Recreations: music; domestic activities. Address: (h.) 52 Albany Road, West Ferry, Dundee DD5 1NW; T.-01382 776772.

Grimble, Professor Michael John, BSc, MSc, PhD, DSc, BA, CEng, FIEE, FInstMC, FIMA, FIEEE, FRSE. Professor of Industrial Systems, University of Strathclyde, since 1981; Technical Director, ISC, since 1988; b. 30.10.43, Grimsby; m., Wendy; 1 s.; 1 d. Educ. Armstrong Street School, Grimsby; University of Birmingham. Design Engineer, GEC Electrical Projects, and seconded, Imperial College of Science and Technology, 1971-74; Senior Design Engineer, GEC Electrical Projects Limited, 1974-75; Senior Lecturer then Reader in Control Systems, Sheffield City Polytechnic, 1975-81. Awarded IEE Heaviside Premium, 1978, Coopers Hill War Memorial Prize Medal, 1979, Honeywell International Medal, 1991. Recreations: theatre; reading; family; travel and sightseeing; eating out. Address: (b.) University of Strathclyde, ICC,

Graham Hills Building, 50 George Street, Glasgow G1 1QE; T.-0141-548 2378; e-mail: m.grimble@eee.strath.ac.uk

Grimmond, Iain William, BAcc (Hons), CA. Director of Finance, Erskine Hospital for Disabled Ex-Servicemen and Women, since 1981; b. 8.8.55, Girvan; m., Marjory Anne Gordon Chisholm; 1 s.; 2 d. Educ. Hutchesons' Boys Grammar School; Glasgow University. Trainee CA, Ernst & Whinney, Glasgow, 1976-79; Assistant Treasurer, Erskine Hospital, 1979-81. Elder, Giffnock South Parish Church. Recreations: golf; football; reading. Address: (h.) 9 Wemyss Avenue, Crookfur, Newton Mearns, Glasgow G77 6AR; T.-0141-639 4894.

Grimmond, Steve, MA, MBA. Director, Leisure and Arts, Dundee City Council, since 2001; b. 12.6.63, Dundee; m., Audrey Krawec; 1 s.; 1 d. Educ. Craigie High School, Dundee; Dundee University. Dundee District Council: Special Projects Officer, Housing Department; Principal Officer, Area Renewal, Housing Department; Corporate Planning Officer, Chief Executive's Department; Policy Planning Manager, Chief Executive's Department, Dundee City Council; Area Manager, Aberdeenshire Council; Director: Dundee Contemporary Arts; Dundee Industrial Heritage; Dundee Rep; Sensation Science Centre; Dundee Cultural Quarter Developments Ltd. Recreations: Dundee Football Club; Global Cowboys Football Club; contemporary cinema; artist; printmaker; shopping at Safeway. Address: (b.) DCA, 152 Nethergate, Dundee;T.-01382 432321.

Grimson, Dermot, FRSA. Scottish Affairs Manager, Shell International, since 1999; b. 22.5.52, Glasgow. Educ. Kelvinside Academy; Glasgow School of Art. Planner, Renfrew District Council; Planner, Banff and Buchan District Council; Director, Rural Forum. Address: Shell UK, 1 Altens Farm Road, Aberdeen AB12 3FY; T.-01224 884035.

Grinyer, Professor John Raymond, MSc, FCA. Professor of Accountancy and Business Finance, Dundee University, since 1976 (Deputy Principal, 1997-2000), Dean, Faculty of Law, 1984-85, 1991-1993, Head, Department of Accountancy and Business Finance, 1976-90); b. 3.3.35, London; m., Shirley Florence Marshall; 1 s.; 2 d. Educ. Central Park Secondary Modern School, London; London School of Economics. London Electricity Board, 1950-53; National Service, RAMC, 1953-55; Halifax Building Society, 1955-56; Martin Redhead & Co., Accountants, 1956-60; Hope Agar & Co., Chartered Accountants, 1960-62; Kemp Chatteris & Co., Chartered Accountants, 1962-63; Lecturer, Harlow Technical College, 1963-66; City of London Polytechnic, 1966-71; Cranfield School of Management, 1971-76; Chairman, British Accounting Association, 1980-81 and 1990, and Scottish Representative, 1984-93. Recreations: golf; dinghy sailing; Member, Royal Tay Yacht Club. Address: (b.) The University, Dundee DD1 4HN; T.-Dundee 344192; e-mail: j.r.grinyer@dundee.ac.uk

Grinyer, Professor Peter Hugh, MA (Oxon), PhD. Emeritus Professor, St. Andrews University, since 1993; b. 3.3.35, London; m., Sylvia Joyce Boraston; 2 s. Educ. Balliol College, Oxford; London School of Economics. Senior Managerial Trainee, Unilever Ltd., 1957-59; Personal Assistant to Managing Director, E.R. Holloway Ltd., 1959-61; Lecturer and Senior Lecturer, Hendon College of Technology, 1961-64; Lecturer, The City University, London, 1965-69; The City University Business School: Senior Lecturer and Co-ordinator of Research, 1969-72, Reader, 1972-74, Professor of Business Strategy, 1974-79; Esmee Fairbairn Professor of Economics (Finance and Investment), St. Andrews University, 1979-93; Chairman, Department of Economics, 1979-85; Vice-

Principal, 1985-87 (Acting Principal, 1986); Chairman, Department of Management, 1987-89; Chairman: St. Andrews Management Institute, 1989-96, St. Andrews Strategic Management Ltd.; Member, Sub-Committee on Management and Business Studies, University Grants Committee, 1979-85; Consultant to NEDO on Sharpbenders Project, 1984-86; Visiting Professor, New York University; Non-Executive Director: Glenrothes Enterprise Trust, 1983-86, John Brown plc, 1984-86, Don Bros. Buist plc (now Don and Low (Holdings) Ltd.) 1985-91, Ellis and Goldstein plc, 1987-88; Chairman (non-executive), McIlroy Coates, 1991-95; Member, Scottish Legal Aid Board, 1992-2000; Member, Appeal Panel, Competition Commission, 2000-04; Erskine Fellow, University of Canterbury, New Zealand, 1994. Recreations: mountain walking; golf; listening to music. Address: (b.) University of St. Andrews, Department of Management, St Katherine's West, The Scores, St. Andrews KY16 9AL; T.-01334 462871.

Grossart, Sir Angus McFarlane McLeod, CBE, LLD, FRSE, DL, MA, CA. Advocate; Merchant Banker; Vice Chairman, Royal Bank of Scotland, since 1996; Chairman, Scottish Daily Record and Sunday Mail, since 1998; Director: Edinburgh US Tracker Trust, Edinburgh Fund Managers PLC, since 1983 (Deputy Chairman), Trinity Mirror Group PLC, since 1999, Scottish and Newcastle PLC, since 1998, Noble Grossart Limited, since 1969 (Chairman), The Scottish Investment Trust PLC, since 1973 (Chairman); b. 6.4.37, Glasgow; m., Gay Kerr Dodd; 1 d. Educ. Glasgow Academy; Glasgow University. CA, 1962; Advocate, Scottish Bar, 1963-69; Managing Director, Noble Grossart Ltd., since 1969; Chairman of the Trustees, National Galleries of Scotland, 1988-97; Trustee and Deputy Chairman, National Heritage Memorial Fund, since 1999; former Scottish Editor, British Tax Encyclopaedia and British Tax Review. Recreations: golf; decorative arts. Address: (b.) 48 Queen Street, Edinburgh EH2 3NR; T.-0131-226 7011.

Grosset, Alan George, MA, LLB, WS, NP. Partner, Morison Bishop, Solicitors; b. 18.1.42, Edinburgh; 1 s.; 1 d. Educ. Royal High School, Edinburgh; Edinburgh University. Law Society of Scotland "Troubleshooter" from inception of scheme, until 1987; Member, e-commerce Committee, Law Society of Scotland; Council Member, W.S. Society, 1998-2000; President, Scottish Lawn Tennis Association, 1983-84; Council Member, Lawn Tennis Association, 1980-89; first Chairman, Scottish Sports Association, 1984-90; Vice-Chairman, Scottish Sports Council, since 1994 (Member since 1984); Captain, Duddingston Golf Club, 1992-94; Founder Member, Scottish Branch, Society for Computers and Law; first Secretary, British Sports Forum, 1991-95; Vice Chairman, Confederation of British Sport; Vice Chairman, Sports Dispute Resolution Panel Ltd. Recreations: golf; tennis. Address: (b.) 68 Queen Street, Edinburgh; T.-0131-226 6541.

Grosz, David Peter, BA (Hons). Vice President, Ramblers' Association Scottish Council, since 2000; b. 2.4.39, London. Educ. Wyggeston Boys' Grammar School, Leicester; Nottingham University; School of Education, Leicester University. School Teacher, Leicester, 1962-78, West Lothian, 1978-84. Member: Ramblers' Association Executive Committee 1983-99 (Vice Chairman, 1995-98, Chairman, 1998-99), Board of Directors, Scottish Rights of Way Society, 1984-92, Council, National Trust for Scotland, 1989-94, Board of Directors, Paths for All Partnership, since 2000; Chairman: Friends of New Lanark, 1985-89, Ramblers' Association Scottish Council, 1985-96; Founding Member and Committee Member, Scottish Council for National Parks, 1991-95, and since 2000. Recreations: walking; reading; campaigning with passion for public access and countryside conservation. Address: (h.) 57 Harburn Avenue, Deans, Livingston EH54 8NH; T.-01506 410493.

Grotrian, Sarah. Secretary for Scotland, Marie Curie Cancer Care, since 1999; Scottish Fund-raising Manager, MCCC, since 1988; b. 3.11.47, Lincoln; 1 s.; 2 d. Educ. Godolphin School, Salisbury. Worked for George Neilson, antique dealer, 1969-73; Strasbourg, 1974-84; collaborated with George Neilson, research into Scottish glass, 1984-86; fund-raised for Penicuik House Trust, 1986-88; established fund-raising department for Marie Curie Scotland, 1988. Member, Board, BT Scottish Ensemble. Publications: Help for Au Pairs, 1971; Art Nouveau Architecture in Strasbourg, 1978. Address: (b.) Marie Curie House, 29a Albany Street, Edinburgh EH1 3QN.

Groves, C. Arthur, JP. Chairman: Borders Region Valuation Panel, 1991-94, Justices Committee, Ettrick and Lauderdale, 1984-94, General Inland Revenue Commissioners, since 1983; b. 28.11.24, London. Educ. Raine's Foundation, London. Selkirk Town Council, 1961-75 (Hon. Treasurer); former Selkirk County Councillor (Chairman, Finance Committee). Recreation: equestrian activities. Address: (h.) 24 Hillview Crescent, Selkirk TD7 4AZ; T.-01750 21126.

Guild, Ivor Reginald, CBE, FRSE, MA, LLB, WS; b. 2.4.24, Dundee. Educ. Cargilfield; Rugby; New College, Oxford; Edinburgh University. Director: Fulcrum Investment Trust, Scottish Oriental Smaller Companies Trust PLC; former Partner, Shepherd & Wedderburn, WS; former Procurator Fiscal to the Lyon Court. Recreations: golf; genealogy. Address: New Club, 86 Princes Street, Edinburgh EH2 2BB; T.-0131-220 1085.

Gunn, Alexander MacLean, MA, BD. Minister, Aberfeldy with Amulree and Strathbraan with Dull and Weem, since 1986; b. 26.2.43, Inverness; m., Ruth T.S.; 1 s.; 1 d. Educ. Edinburgh Academy; Beauly; Dingwall Academy; Edinburgh University and New College. Parish Minister: Wick St. Andrews and Thrumster, 1967-73; Member, Caithness Education Committee, 1968-73; Parish Minister, Glasgow St. David's Knightswood, 1973-86; Convener: Church of Scotland Rural Working Group, 1988-90, General Assembly's Presbytery Development Committee, 1990-92, General Assembly's Mission and Evangelism Resource Committee, 1992-95; Interim Convener, Board of National Mission, 1996. Chairman, Breadalbane Academy School Board, 1989-92 and since 1996. Address: The Manse, Taybridge Terrace, Aberfeldy PH15 2BS; T.-01887 820656; e-mail: amg@aberfeldypc.co.uk

Gusterson, Professor Barry Austin, PhD, FRCPath. Professor of Pathology, Glasgow University, since 2000; b. 24.10.46, Colchester; m., Ann Josephine Davies; 1 s.; 2 d. Educ. St Bartholomew's Hospital, London. Senior Clinical Scientist and Consultant, Ludwig Institute of Cancer Research, London, 1983-86; Consultant in Histopathology, Royal Marsden Hospital, 1984; Professor of Histopathology and Chairman, Section on Cell Biology and Experimental Pathology, Institute of Cancer Research, London University, 1986-2000; Founding Director, Tony Robins Breast Cancer Research Centre, London, 1998. Director, Pathology, International Breast Cancer Study Group, Berne, 1995; Oakley Lecturer, Pathological Society of Great Britain and Ireland, 1986; Chairman, Pathology Group, Organisation of European Cancer Institutes, Geneva, 1992-96. Recreations: antique English glass and furniture; gardening; walking; reading. Address: (b.) Department of Pathology, Western Infirmary, Glasgow, G11 6NT; T.-0141-211 2233.

Guy, Professor John Alexander, MA, PhD, FRHistS. Professor of Modern History, St. Andrews University, since 1991; b. 16.1.49, Australia; 1 s.; 1 d. Educ. King Edward VII School, Lytham; Clare College, Cambridge. Research Fellow, Selwyn College, Cambridge, 1970-73; Assistant Keeper of Public Records, Public Record Office, London, 1973-78; Visiting Lecturer in British History, University of California, Berkeley, 1977; History Department, Bristol University, 1978-90; British Academy Marc Fitch Research Reader, 1987-89; John Hinkley (Visiting) Professor, Johns Hopkins University, Baltimore, 1990; Richard L. Turner Professor of Humanities, and Professor of History, University of Rochester, 1990-91. St. Andrews University: Head, School of History and International Relations, 1992-94, Provost, 1994-97, Vice-Principal, 1996-97. Publications: The Cardinal's Court; The Public Career of Sir Thomas More; Law and Social Change in British History (Co-Editor); The Court of Star Chamber and its Records to the Reign of Elizabeth I; Christopher St. German on Chancery and Statute; Reassessing the Henrician Age (Co-Author); The Complete Works of Thomas More, Vol. X (Co-Editor); Tudor England; The Tudors and Stuarts (Co-Author); The Reign of Elizabeth I; The Tudor Monarchy; Thomas More; Politics, Law and Counsel in Tudor and Stuart England; The Tudors: A Very Short Introduction. Address: School of History, St. Andrews University, College Gate, St. Andrews KY16 9AJ.

Guy, Roger Robert, MSc, PhD, CEng, MICE. Director for Environment and Infrastructure, Dumfries and Galloway Council, since 1995; b. 8.8.47. Educ. Westminster City School; Imperial College, London University; Manchester University. Research Fellow, Edinburgh University, 1972; South West of Scotland Water Board, 1973; Dumfries County Council, 1974; Dumfries and Galloway Regional Council, 1975: Assistant Director (Transportation), 1987, Director Roads and Transportation, 1991. Henrici Medal, 1967; Unwin Medal, 1968. Recreation: outdoor pursuits. Address: (b.) Militia House, Council Offices, Dumfries DG1 2HR; T.-01387 260100.

Gwilt, George David, MA, FFA, FBCS. Director: European Assets Trust NV, 1979-2000, Scottish Mortgage & Trust plc, 1983-98, Hodgson Martin Ltd., 1989-2000, Edinburgh Festival Society Ltd., 1989-95; b. 11.11.27, Edinburgh; m., Ann Sylvester; 3 s. Educ. Sedbergh; St. John's College, Cambridge. Standard Life, 1949-88, latterly as Managing Director; President, Faculty of Actuaries, 1981-83; Trustee, South of Scotland TSB, 1966-83; Member: Younger Committee on Privacy, 1970-72, Monopolies and Mergers Commission, 1983-87; Convener, Scottish Poetry Library, 1988-2000. Recreations: flute playing; squash. Address: (h.) 39 Oxgangs Road, Edinburgh EH10 7BE; T.-0131-445 1266.

H

Hadden, William A., BSc, BAO, BCh, MB, FRCSEd and Orth. Consultant Orthopaedic Surgeon, since 1984; b. 23.5.46, Northern Ireland; 3 s. Educ. Methodist College, Belfast; Portadown College, Co. Armagh; Queen's University, Belfast. Surgical training, Northern Ireland, Edinburgh, Dundee, Christchurch (New Zealand). Recreations: golf; squash. Address: (b.) Perth Royal Infirmary, Perth PH1 1NX; T.-01738 473698.

Haddington, 13th Earl of (John George Baillie-Hamilton); b. 21.12.41; m.; 1 s.; 2 d. Succeeded to title, 1986. Educ. Ampleforth. Address: Mellerstain, Gordon, Berwickshire, TD3 6LG.

Haddock, Graham, MBChB, MD, FRCSGlas, FRCSEdin, FRCS(Paed). Consultant Paediatric Surgeon, since 1995; Clinical Director of Surgery, since 2000; b. 7.8.60, Greenock. Educ. Notre Dame High School, Greenock; Glasgow University. Trained in adult general surgery, Glasgow and Edinburgh, in paediatric surgery, Royal Hospital for Sick Children, Yorkhill, Royal Hospital for Sick Children, Edinburgh, and Hospital for Sick Children, Toronto. Honorary Clinical Senior Lecturer, Glasgow University; Secretary, Scottish Colleges Committee, Children's Surgical Services. Recreation: National (UK) Commissioner for Exploring Scouts (The Scout Association). Address: (b.) Department of Paediatric Surgery, Royal Hospital for Sick Children, Yorkhill, Glasgow G3 8SJ; T.-0141-201 0289.

Haddow, Christopher, QC, LLB (Hons); b. 15.5.47, Edinburgh; m., Kathleen; 3 s. Educ. George Watson's College; Edinburgh University. Admitted to Faculty of Advocates, 1971; Queen's Counsel, 1985. Former Member, Secretary of State's Valuation Advisory Council and of Scottish Valuation and Rating Council; Joint Editor, Armour on Valuation for Rating, since 1990. Recreations: hockey; walking; classic cars. Address: (h.) Abbot's Craft House, North Berwick EH39 5NG.

Hadley, Geoffrey, MBE, BSc (Hons), PhD. Honorary Senior Lecturer, Aberdeen University, since 1985; Consultant Microbiologist, since 1985; b. 7.2.32, Stoke-on-Trent; m., Margaret Murison; 3 d. by pr. m. Educ. Longton High School; Birmingham University. Research Fellow, Nottingham University, 1956-58; Lecturer, Glasgow University, 1958-60; Lecturer, then Senior Lecturer, Aberdeen University, 1960-85; seconded to University of Malaya, 1967-68; Member, Aberdeen County Council, 1973-75, Grampian Regional Council, 1974-94; Convener, Grampian Regional Council, 1986-90; British Mycological Society: Chairman of Publications, since 1985, Editor, Mycologist, Vice-President, 1987; Chairman, Aberdeen Civic Society, 1994-2000; Chairman, Grampian Heart Campaign, 1991-96; Member, Management Committee, Hanover (Scotland) Housing Association. Recreations: classical music; home brewing and wine-making; cricket; DIY. Address: (h.) Crannies, 74 Don Street, Old Aberdeen, Aberdeen AB24 1UU; T.-01224 494472.

Hadley, Ruth, MCGB. Chef; b., 18.4.49, Liverpool; m., Anthony; 1 s.; 1 d. Educ. Holly Lodge High School for Girls, Liverpool. Taste of Scotland Restaurant of the Year, 1989; Macallan Scottish Restaurant of the Year, 1993. Address: The Cross, Kingussie; T.-01540 661166; e-mail: relax@thecross.co.uk

Hagart-Alexander of Ballochmyle, Sir Claud, Bt, DL, JP, BA, CEng, MInstMC. Vice Lord-Lieutenant, Ayrshire and Arran, 1983-98; b. 6.1.27, Peking; m., Hilda Etain Acheson; 2 s.; 2 d. Educ. Sherborne; Corpus Christi College, Cambridge. Address: (h.) Kingencleugh House, Mauchline, Ayrshire KA5 5JL; T.-01290 550217.

Haggart, David Ballantine, JP, MA. Writer and Broadcaster; b. 15.3.34, Dundee; m., Gwendolen Hall; 3 s. Educ. Aberdeen Grammar School; Aberdeen University. National Service, Band of Royal Corps of Signals, 1956-58; Teacher, Perth and Kinross County Council, 1958-59; Youth Employment Officer, City of Aberdeen, 1959-63; Head of Careers Service, Aberdeen University, 1963-92; Member: Justices' Committee, Aberdeen, since 1976, Justice of the Peace Advisory Committee, since 1991; Chairman: Ferryhill Community Council, 1976-82, Castlehill Housing Association, 1991-94, Aberdeen and NE Scotland Music Festival, 1982-84; Writer and Producer, educational television programmes, including The Interview (Royal Television Society award); Editor, Current Vacancies, 1986-93; Columnist, Prospects Today, Evening Express; regular radio broadcasts, mainly on religious programmes; Presenter, Sunday Best, Northsound Radio, since 1981, Producer, since 1988. Publication: Showers of Blessings, 2000. Recreations: music; motoring; local history. Address: (h.) 24 Polmuir Road, Aberdeen AB11 7SY; T.-01224 584176.

Haggart, Mary Elizabeth, OBE; b. 8.4.24, Leicester; m., Rt. Rev. A.I.M. Haggart (deceased). Educ. Wyggeston Grammar School for Girls, Leicester; Leicester Royal Infirmary and Children's Hospital. Leicester Royal Infirmary: Staff Nurse, 1947-48, Night Sister, 1948-50, Ward Sister, 1950-56, Night Superintendent, 1956-58, Assistant Matron, 1958-61; Assistant Matron, Brook General Hospital, London, 1962-64; Matron, Dundee Royal Infirmary and Matron Designate, Ninewells Hospital, Dundee, 1964-68; Chief Nursing Officer, Board of Managements, Dundee General Hospitals and Ninewells Hospital, 1968-73; Chief Area Nursing Officer, Tayside Health Board, 1974-82; President, Scottish Association of Nurse Administrators, 1972-77; Member: Scottish Board, Royal College of Nursing, 1965-70, General Nursing Council for Scotland, 1965-70 and 1978-82; Chairman, Scottish Board of Nursing Midwifery and Health Visiting, 1980-83; Member: Standing Nursing and Midwifery Committee, 1971-74 (Vice Chairman, 1973-74), Action on Smoking and Health Scotland, 1978-82 (Chairman, Working Party, Smoking and Nurses); Governor, Dundee College of Technology, 1978-82; Honorary Lecturer, Department of Community Medicine, Dundee University and Medical School, 1980-82; Member: Management Committee, Carstairs State Hospital, 1982-92, United Kingdom Central Council for Nursing Midwifery and Health Visiting, 1980-82, Scottish Hospital Endowments Research Trust, 1986-96. Recreations: walking; music; travel. Address: (h.) 14/2 St. Margaret's Place, Edinburgh EH9 1AY.

Haggarty, William McLaughlan, TD, BL. Solicitor, since 1950; Consultant (former Senior Partner) Mathie-Morton Black & Buchanan, Ayr; Honorary Sheriff, South Strathclyde, Dumfries and Galloway; b. 22.2.26, Glasgow; m., Olive Dorothy Mary Speirs; 1 s.; 1 d. Educ. High School of Glasgow; Glasgow University. War Service, Merchant Navy, 1943-47; Chairman, National Insurance Tribunal, North and South Ayrshire, 1963-88; Lt. Col. Commanding 264 (Scottish) Regiment, Royal Corps of Transport (TA), 1966; Dean, Ayr Faculty of Solicitors, 1982; Governor, Craigie College of Education, Ayr, 1983-91. Recreations: golf; travel; gardening. Address: (b.) 4 Alloway Place, Ayr; T.-01292 263549.

Haig of Bemersyde, The Earl (George Alexander Eugene Douglas), OBE, DL, MA, ARSA, KStJ. Painter; b. 15.3.18, London; 1 s.; 2 d. Educ. Cargilfield; Stowe School; Christ Church, Oxford. 2nd Lt., Royal Scots Greys, 1938; retired on account of disability, 1951 (rank of Captain); attended Camberwell School of Arts and Crafts; paintings in many public and private collections; served Second World War; taken prisoner, 1942; Member, Royal Fine Art Commission for Scotland, 1958-61; Chairman, SE South East Scotland Disablement Advisory Committee, 1960-73; Trustee, Scottish National War Memorial, 1961-96; Trustee, National Galleries of Scotland, 1962-72; Member, Scottish Arts Council, 1968-74; Past Chairman, Royal British Legion Scotland; President: Earl Haig Fund Scotland/Royal British Legion Scotland, 1980-86, Scottish Branch, Officers Association, 1978-95, Scottish Craft Centre, 1952-73; Vice President, Scottish National Institution for War Blinded and of Royal Blind Asylum, since 1960; President, National Ex-Prisoners of War Association, 1999. Recreations: fishing; shooting. Address: (h.) Bemersyde, Melrose TD6 9DP; T.-01835 822762.

Hair, Professor Graham Barry, MMus, PhD. Composer; Professor of Music, Glasgow University, since 1990; b. 27.2.43, Geelong, Australia; m., Dr Greta Mary Hair. Educ. Geelong College, Australia; Melbourne University; Sheffield University. Senior Lecturer, Latrobe University, 1975-80; Head, School of Composition, Sydney Conservatorium of Music, 1980-90; has had many commissions, performances, CD recordings, broadcasts and musical works published. Address: (h.) 45 St. Vincent Crescent, Glasgow G3 8NG; T.-0141-221 4933; e-mail: graham.hair@virgin.net

Hajducki, Andrew Michael, QC, MA, FSA(Scot). Queen's Counsel, since 1994; b. 12.11.52, London; 2 s. (and 1 s. deceased); 1 d. Educ. Dulwich College; Cambridge University. Called to Bar of England and Wales (Gray's Inn), 1976; Advocate, 1979; QC, 1994; Temporary Sheriff, 1987-99; Safeguarder, Lothian Children's Panel, 1987-97; Tutor, Edinburgh University, 1978-80; Arbiter (Scotland), MIB Uninsured Drivers Scheme, since 2000; candidate, Scottish Liberal Party, 1978, 1980. Recreations: reading; travelling; running marathons. Address: (b.) Advocates Library, Parliament House, Edinburgh EH1 1RF; T.-0131-226 5071.

Hajivassiliou, Constantinos, BSc (Hons), MBChB, FRCS(Edin), FRCS(Glas), FRCS(Paed), MD. Consultant Paediatric/Neonatal Surgeon, Royal Hospital for Sick Children, Glasgow, since 1998; Wellcome Trust Senior Lecturer, Glasgow University, since 1999; b. 27.4.61, Nicosia; m., Eva; 2 d. Educ. Edinburgh University. House Officer, then Senior House Officer, 1986-89; Registrar, West of Scotland Rotation, 1989-92; Senior Registrar/Lecturer, Yorkhill and Glasgow University, 1992-98. Lord Moynihan Prize, Association of Surgeons of Great Britain and Ireland, 1995; many other prizes. Recreations: radio amateur; diving; flying; fishing; cooking. Address: (b.) Department of Paediatric Surgery, Royal Hospital for Sick Children, Yorkhill, Glasgow G3 8SJ; T.-0141-201 0170.

Hajto, Professor Janos Peter, PhD, DSc, FInstP. Professor of Physical Electronics, Napier University, since 1994; b. 17.4.48, Eger, Hungary; m., Eva Maria Hajto; 2 d. Educ. Kossuth Lajos University, Hungary. Rersearch Scientist, Central Research Institute of Physics, Hungarian Academy of Sciences, Budapest, 1972-82; Senior Research Fellow and Lecturer, Edinburgh University, 1982-84. Recreations: hill-walking; playing music. Address: (b.) School of Engineering, Napier University, 10 Colinton Road, Edinburgh, EH10 5DT.

Haldane of Gleneagles, James Martin, MA, CA, FRSA. 28th Laird of Gleneagles; Director: Investors Capital Trust PLC, since 1995, Stace Barr Angerstein PLC, Shires Income plc, since 1996; former Chairman, Chiene & Tait, CA (Partner, 1989-2001); former Deputy Chairman, Scottish Life Assurance Co. (Director, 1990-2001); Chairman, Queen's Hall (Edinburgh) Ltd., 1987-2001; b. 18.9.41, Edinburgh; m., Petronella Victoria Scarlett; 1 s.; 2 d. Educ. Winchester College; Magdalen College, Oxford. Partner, Arthur Young, 1970-89. Chairman, Scottish Chamber Orchestra, 1978-85; Chairman, Craighead Investments PLC, 1982-90; Trustee, D'Oyly Carte Opera Trust, 1985-92; Treasurer, Queen's Bodyguard for Scotland (Royal Company of Archers), 1992-2001; Member: Council, Edinburgh Festival Society, 1985-89, Northern and Scottish Board, Legal and General Assurance Co., 1984-87, Council, National Trust for Scotland, 1992-97, Court, Stirling University, since 1997; Chairman of Governors, Innerpeffray Library, since 1994. Recreations: music; golf. Address: (h.) Gleneagles, Auchterarder PH3 1PJ; T.-01764 682 388; (b.) 01764 682535; e-mail: haldane@gleneagles.org

Haldane, Professor John Joseph, BA, PGCE, BA, PhD, Hon LLD, FRSA, FRSE. Professor of Philosophy, St. Andrews University, since 1994; Senior Fellow, Centre for Ethics, Philosophy and Public Affairs (Director, 1988-2000); b. 19.2.54, London; m., Hilda Marie Budas; 2 s.; 2 d. Educ. St. Aloysius College, Glasgow; Wimbledon School of Art; London University. Art Master, St. Joseph's Grammar School, Abbey Wood, 1976-79; Lecturer in Moral Philosophy, St. Andrews University, 1983-90; Reader, 1990-94; Stanton Lecturer, University of Cambridge, 1999-2002; Royden Davis Professor of Humanities, Georgetown University, 2001-02. Member, Editorial Board: American Journal of Jurisprudence, Cambridge Studies in Philosophy, Ethical Perspectives, Journal of Philosophy of Education, Philosophical Explorations, Philosophical Quarterly; Contributor: The Herald, The Scotsman, The Tablet, Modern Painters. Address: (b.) Department of Moral Philosophy, St. Andrews University, St. Andrews KY16 9AL; T.-01334 462488; e-mail: jjh1@st-and.ac.uk

Hale, Professor Bob, BA, BPhil, FRSE. Professor of Metaphysical Philosophy, University of Glasgow, since 1995; British Academy Research Reader, 1997-99; b. 4.5.45, Aldershot; m., Maggie; 2 s.; 1 d. Educ. Woking County Grammar School for Boys; University of Bristol; University of Oxford. Part-time Lecturer in Philosophy, University of Nottingham; Lecturer in Philosophy, University of Lancaster; Lecturer then Reader in Logic and Metaphysics, University of St. Andrews. Publications: Abstract Objects, 1987; Reading Putnam, 1994; Blackwell Companion to Philosophy of Language (Co-Author), 1997; The Reason's Proper Study (Co-Author), 2001. Recreations: film; theatre; music; reading; hill-walking. Address: (b.) Department of Philosophy, University of Glasgow, Glasgow G12 8QQ; T.-0141-330 5173.

Haley, Christopher Simon, BSc, PhD. Head, Division of Genetics and Biometry, Roslin Institute, since 1995; b. 3.5.55, Rickmansworth; m., Sara Knott; 2 s.; 1 d. Educ. Royal Grammar School, Guildford; University of Birmingham. Post-doctoral Scientist, University of Birmingham, 1980-84; Senior Scientific Officer, Animal Breeding Research Organisation, then Institute of Animal Physiology and Genetics Research, Edinburgh, 1984-91; Principal Scientific Officer, Institute of Animal Physiology and Genetics Research, then Roslin Institute, 1991-95. Recreations: children; cooking; eating; gardening; walking; Morgan sports cars. Address: (b.) Roslin Institute, Roslin, Midlothian EH25 9PS; T.-0131-527 4200.

Halford-MacLeod, Ret. Lt. Col. Aubrey Philip Lydiat, MA (Hons), late Black Watch (RHR); retired Army Officer, Schools Liaison Officer (Scotland), Recruiting and Liaison, Scotland; Director, Round Tower Ltd., since 1993; b. 28.4.42, Bagdad; m., Alison Fiona Brown; 2 s.; 1 d. Educ. Winchester College; RMA Sandhurst; Magdalen College, Oxford. Commissioned into Black Watch, 1962; Lt., 1964; Capt., 1968; Maj., 1975; Lt. Col., 1985; appointed Commanding Officer, Glasgow and Strathclyde Universities OTC, 1985; Chief of Staff, The Scottish Division, 1988; UK Liaison Officer (as Colonel), US European Command Stuttgart, 1991; SO1 G1 Action and Support Team (Demob Cell), Army HQ Scotland, 1992; Commandant, The Black Watch ACF Battalion, 1993, as a Colonel, 2000; reverted to Lieutenant to carry out other duties. Recreations: walking the dogs; shooting; fishing; opera; model soldiers; curling; country dancing. Address: (b.) Craigiehall, Edinburgh EH30 9TN; T.-0131-310 2190; (h.) The Old Manse, 28 Skene Street, Strathmiglo KY14 7QL; T.-01337 860715/868930.

Hall, Professor Christopher, MA, DPhil, DSc, CEng, FRSC, FIM. Professor of Materials, Edinburgh University, since 1999; Director, Centre for Materials Science and Engineering, Edinburgh University, since 1999; b. 31.12.44, Henley-on-Thames; m., Sheila McKelvey; 1s.; 1d. Educ. Royal Belfast Academical Institution; Trinity College, Oxford. Lecturer, Building Engineering, UMIST, 1972- 83; Head, Rock and Fluid Physics, Schlumberger Cambridge Research, 1983-88; Head, Chemical Technology, Dowell Schlumberger, St Etienne, France, 1988-99; Scientific Advisor, Schlumberger Cambridge Research, 1990-99; Visiting Fellow, Princeton Materials Institute, Princeton University, USA, 1998; Visiting Professor, Civil and Construction Engineering, UMIST; Visiting Scientific Advisor, Schlumberger Cambridge Research, Senior Member, Robinson College, Cambridge. Address: (h.) 36 Mayfield Terrace, Edinburgh, EH9 1RZ; T.-0131-662 9285; e-mail: ChristopherHall@ed.ac.uk

Hall, Professor Denis, BSc, MPhil, PhD, MBA, FInstP, FIEE, FOSA, FRSE, CEng. Professor of Photonics, Department of Physics, Heriot-Watt University, since 1987, and Assistant Principal (Research), since 1998; b. 1.8.42, Cardiff; m., Pauline; 2 c. Educ. Manchester University; St Bartholomew's Hospital Medical College. Senior Research Scientist, Avco Everett Research Laboratory, Boston, 1972-74; Principal Scientific Officer, Royal Signals and Radar Establishment, 1974-79; Senior Lecturer/Reader in Applied Laser Physics, Hull University, 1979-87. Chairman, Quantum Electronics Group Committee, Institute of Physics, 1991-94; Chairman, Quantum Electronics and Optics Division, European Physical Society, 1998-2000. Publications: 100 in journals; 150 papers at conferences. Address: (b.) Department of Physics, Heriot-Warr University, Riccarton, Edinburgh EH14 4AS; T.-0131-451 3081.

Hall, Professor Graham Stanley, BSc, PhD, FRSE. Professor of Mathematics, University of Aberdeen, since 1996; b. 5.9.46, Warrington; 1 s.; 1 d. Educ. Boteler Grammar School, Warrington; University of Newcastle upon Tyne (Earl Grey Memorial Fellow, 1971-73); Lecturer in Mathematics, University of Aberdeen, since 1973 (Senior Lecturer, 1982, Reader, 1990, Head of Department, 1992-95). Publications: over 100 articles in research journals; General Relativity (Co-Editor), 1996. Recreation: music (piano); reading; sport. Address: (b.) Department of Mathematical Sciences, University of Aberdeen, Meston AB24 3UE; T.-01224 272748; e-mail: g.hall@maths.abdn.ac.uk

Hall, James Firth, Comendador O.M. (Portugal), Medhalha de Vasco da Gama (Portugal), OStJ. Honorary Consul of Portugal (Scotland), 1973-2000; retired Chartered Surveyor; b. 1.12.27, Edinburgh; m., Helen Davidson Smith. Educ. George Watson's Boys College. Senior Partner, D.M. Hall & Son, 1966-88; former Member, Valuation Appeal Committee; Fellow, Royal Institution of Chartered Surveyors; Member, Institute of Revenues, Ratings and Valuation; Member, International Real Estate Federation. Recreations: golf; sailing; shooting. Address: The Quik Huik, 38 Barnton Avenue, Edinburgh EH4 6JL.

Hall, Rev. Keith Ferrier, BD(Hons). Minister, Dundee Parish Church (St. Mary's), since 1994; Chaplain, Dundee High School, since 1994; b. 20.10.55, Arbroath; m., Amilia Elaine Donaldson; 2 s.; 1 d. Educ. Arbroath High School; University of St. Andrews. Minister: Blairgowrie, St. Mary's South, 1981-87, Alloa Parish, St. Mungo's, 1987-94. Recreations: family; gardening; theatre. Address: (b.) Dundee Parish Church (St. Mary's), Nethergate, Dundee DD1 4DG; T.-01382 226271; e-mail: office@dundeestmarys.co.uk

Hall, William, CBE, DFC, FRICS. Honorary Sheriff, Paisley, since 1974; b. 25.7.19, Paisley; m., Margaret Semple Gibson; 1 s.; 3 d. Educ. Paisley Grammar School. Pilot, RAFVR, 1939-45 (Despatches); Senior Partner, R. & W. Hall, Chartered Surveyors, Paisley, 1949-79; Chairman, Royal Institution of Chartered Surveyors in Scotland, 1971; Member: Valuation Advisory Council, 1970-80, Lands Tribunal for Scotland, 1971-91, Lands Tribunal for England and Wales, 1979-91; Executive Member, Erskine Hospital, 1976-99. Recreation: golf. Address: (h.) Windyridge, Brediland Road, Paisley PA2 9HF.

Hall, (William) Douglas, OBE (1985), BA, FMA; b. 9.10.26, London; m., 1, Helen Elizabeth Ellis (m. diss.); 1 s.; 1 d.; 2, Matilda Mary Mitchell. Educ. University College School, Hampstead; University College and Courtauld Institute of Art, London University, 1948-52. Intelligence Corps, 1945-48 (Middle East); Manchester City Art Galleries: Keeper, Rutherston Collection, 1953-58, Keeper, City Art Gallery, 1958-59, Deputy Director, 1959-61; Keeper, Scottish National Gallery of Modern Art, 1961-86. Recreations: music; gardening. Address: (h.) Wellgate, Morebattle, Roxburghshire TD5 8QN; T.-01573 440687.

Hallett, Professor Christine, MA (Cantab), PhD. Deputy Principal, Stirling University, since 2000, and Professor of Social Policy, since 1995; b. 4.5.49, Barnet. Educ. Queen Elizabeth's Grammar School for Girls, Barnet; Newnham College, Cambridge. Civil Servant, Department of Health and Social Security; Research officer, Oxford University, Keele University; Lecturer in Social Policy, Keele University; Senior Lecturer in Social Policy, University of West Australia; Lecturer, University of Leicester; Reader/Professor, Stirling University. Recreations: golf; tennis; sailing; hill-walking. Address: (b.) Stirling University, Stirling, FK9 4LA.

Halliburton, Ian Scott. Director, Bell Lawrie Investment Management, 1978-2001 (retired); b. 30.1.43, Huddersfield; m., Anne Whitaker; 1 s.; 1 d. Educ. Royal High School, Edinburgh; Royal Scottish Academy of Music and Drama. General banking training, Royal Bank of Scotland, 1961-63; RSAMD, 1963-66; professional actor, 1967-70; sales consultant, 1970-71; insurance broker, 1971-78. Trustee, Institute of Contemporary Scotland, since 2000. Recreations: hill-walking; listening to music; supporting the arts. Address: (h.) 259 Garrioch Road, Glasgow G20 8QZ; T.-0141-946 5426.

Halliday, James, MA, MLitt, JP. Chairman, Scots Independent Newspapers; b. 27.2.27, Wemyss Bay; m., Olive Campbell; 2 s. Educ. Greenock High School;

Glasgow University. Teacher: Ardeer FE Centre, 1953; Kildonan Secondary School, Coatbridge, 1954-56; Uddingston Grammar School, 1956-58, Dunfermline High School, 1958-67; Lecturer in History, Dundee College of Education, 1967-79; Principal Lecturer in History, 1979-87. Chairman, Scottish National Party, 1956-60; Parliamentary candidate: Stirling and Falkirk Burghs, 1955 and 1959, West Fife, 1970. Publications: World in Transformation — America; Scotland The Separate; A Concise History of Scotland; 1820: The Radical War; Story of Scotland (Co-author). Recreations: reading; folk music; football spectating. Address: (h.) 72 Fintry Place, Broughty Ferry, Dundee DD5 3BH.

Halliday, Rt. Rev. Robert Taylor, MA, BD. Bishop of Brechin, 1990-96; b. 7.5.32, Glasgow; m., Dr. Gena M. Chadwin; 1 d. Educ. High School of Glasgow; Glasgow University; Trinity College, Glasgow; Episcopal Theological College, Edinburgh. Deacon, 1957; Priest, 1958; Assistant Curate, St. Andrew's, St. Andrews, 1957-60, St. Margaret's, Newlands, Glasgow, 1960-63; Rector, Holy Cross, Davidson's Mains, Edinburgh, 1963-83; External Lecturer in New Testament, Episcopal Theological College, Edinburgh, 1963-74; Canon, St. Mary's Cathedral, Edinburgh, 1973-83; Rector, St. Andrew's, St. Andrews, 1983-90; Tutor in Biblical Studies, St. Andrews University, 1984-90. Recreations: walking; reading; gardening. Address: 28 Forbes Road, Edinburgh EH10 4ED; T.-0131-221 1490.

Halling, Professor Peter James, BA, PhD, FRSE. Robertson Professor of Bioprocess Technology, Strathclyde University, since 1996; b. 30.3.51, London. Educ. Calday Grammar School; Churchill College, Cambridge; Bristol University. Postdoctoral Fellow, University College, London, 1975-78; Research Scientist, Unilever Research, Bedford, 1978-83; Professor of Biocatalyst Science, Strathclyde University, 1990-96. Recreation: orienteering. Address: (h.) 34 Montague Street, Glasgow G4 9HX; T.-0141-552 4400.

Halliwell, Professor Francis Stephen, MA, DPhil(Oxon). Professor of Greek, University of St. Andrews, since 1995; b. 18.10.53, Wigan; m., Helen Ruth Gainford; 2 s. Educ. St. Francis Xavier's, Liverpool; Worcester College, University of Oxford. Lecturer in Classics and Drama, Westfield College, London, 1980-82; Fellow in Classics, Corpus Christi College, University of Cambridge, 1982-84; Lecturer, Senior Lecturer, Reader in Classics, University of Birmingham, 1984-95; Visiting Professor in Classics, University of Chicago, 1990; Visiting Faculty Fellow, University of California at Riverside, 1993; Visiting Professor, University of Rome, 1998. Publications: various books on Greek literature and philosophy, including Aristophanes, Plato and Aristotle. Recreations: music; golf. Address: (b.) Department of Greek, Swallowgate, University of St. Andrews, St. Andrews KY16 9AL; T.-01334 462617; e-mail: fsh@st-and.ac.uk

Halls, Michael, FREHIS, FRSH, MInstWM. Hon. Secretary, International Federation of Environmental Health (President, 1996-98); b. 6.12.39, Galashiels; m., Sheila; 1 s.; 1 d. Educ. Galashiels Academy; Heriot-Watt. Trainee Burgh Surveyor, Galashiels Town Council, 1959-63; Additional Public Health Inspector, Thame Urban District Council, 1963-64; Galashiels Town Council: Assistant Burgh Surveyor and Sanitary Inspector, 1964-68, Depute Burgh Surveyor, 1968-71, Burgh Surveyor, 1971-75; Director of Environmental Services, Ettrick and Lauderdale District Council, 1975-96. Last Honorary Secretary, Scottish Institute of Environmental Health, 1978-83; President, Royal Environmental Health Institute of Scotland, 1984-85. Recreation: golf; philately; wine drinking; music; eating; photography. Address: (h.) Eastfield, 16 Abbotsford Road, Galashiels TD1 3DS; T.- 01896 752624.

Hallsworth, Frederick Stanislavs, BAcc, CA. Senior Partner Scotland, Arthur Andersen, since 1998; b. 3.5.53, Paisley; 2 s.; 1 d. Educ. St Mirin's Academy; Glasgow University. Arthur Andersen: joined Glasgow Office, 1977; joined Brussels Office, 1981-82; Cambridge Office: Head of Corporate Finance Practice, 1988-95; Head of Assurance and Business Advisory Practice, 1991-93; Managing Partner, 1995-98. Member: Board Scottish Institute for Enterprise, since 1999, CBI Scotland Council, since 1999, Development Advisory Board, Scottish Opera and Ballet, Scottish Advisory Network, Imperial Cancer Research Fund, CBI Council Eastern Region, 1994-98, Bank of England Regional Economic Panel, East of England, 1998; Co-founder/Director, The Cambridge Network, since 1998; Hon. Treasurer and Trustee, The Cambridge Foundation, since 1996. Recreations: squash; tennis; gym. Address (b.) 191 West George Street, Glasgow, G2 2LB; T.- 0141-300 6510.

Hamblen, Professor David Lawrence, CBE, MB, BS, PhD, FRCS, FRCSEdin, FRCSGlas. Chairman, Greater Glasgow NHS Board, since 1997; Emeritus Professor of Orthopaedic Surgery, Glasgow University; Hon. Consultant Orthopaedic Surgeon to Army in Scotland; b. 31.8.34, London; m., Gillian; 1 s.; 2 d. Educ. Roan School, Greenwich; London University. The London Hospital, 1963-66; Teaching Fellow in Orthopaedics, Harvard Medical School/Massachusetts General Hospital, 1966-67; Lecturer in Orthopaedics, Nuffield Orthopaedic Centre, Oxford, 1967-68; Senior Lecturer in Orthopaedics/ Honorary Consultant, Edinburgh University/South East Regional Hospital Board, 1968-72; Professor of Orthopaedic Surgery, Glasgow University; 1972-99. Honorary Consultant in Orthopaedic Surgery, Greater Glasgow Health Board, 1972-99; Visiting Professor to National Centre for Training and Education in Prosthetics and Orthotics, Strathclyde University, 1981-2000; Member, Chief Scientist Committee and Chairman, Committee for Research on Equipment for Disabled, 1983-90; Chairman, Journal of Bone and Joint Surgery, since 1995 (Member, Editorial Board, 1978-82 and 1985-89); Secretary and Treasurer, JBJS Council of Management, 1992-95; Member, Physiological Systems Board, Medical Research Council, 1983-88; President, British Orthopaedic Association, 1990-91 (Chairman, Education Sub-Committee, 1986-89); Non-Executive Director, West Glasgow Hospitals University NHS Trust, 1994-97. Publications: Outline of Fractures (Co-Author), (11th edition, 1999); Outline of Orthopaedics (Co-Author), (13th edition, 2001). Recreations: golf; curling. Address: (h.) 3 Russell Drive, Bearsden, Glasgow G61 3BB.

Hamblin, Janet, BSc, CA. Partner, HLB Kidsons, since 1996; b. Edinburgh. Educ. St. Hilary's School, Edinburgh; Edinburgh University; Heriot Watt University. Coopers and Lybrand: from Trainee (qualified as Chartered Accountant, 1984) to Group Senior Manager. Member, Board, Scottish Business in the Community. Recreations: golf; curling; theatre. Address: HLB Kidsons, 23 Queen Street, Edinburgh EH2 1JX; T.-0131-225 6424; e-mail: jhamblin@kiedin.hlbkidsons.co.uk

Hamilton, 15th Duke of, (Angus Alan Douglas Douglas-Hamilton), MA, CEng, MIMechE, FBIS. Premier Peer of Scotland; Hereditary Keeper of Palace of Holyroodhouse; b. 13.9.38; m. Sarah Scott (deceased); 2 s.; 2 d.; m., Kay Carmichael. Educ. Eton; Balliol College, Oxford. Joined RAF, 1956; Flt.-Lt., 1963; flying instructor, 1965; Instrument Rating Examiner, 1966; invalided, 1967; Senior Commercial Pilot, 1968; Test Pilot, Scottish Aviation, 1971-72; Knight of St. John, 1974, Prior for Scotland, 1975-82; Patron, British Airways Pipe Band, 1977; Member: European Community Sub-Committee on Energy and Transport, 1975-77, Queen's Bodyguard for Scotland (Royal Company of Archers), since 1976, Royal Scottish

Pipers Society, 1977, Piobaireachd Society, 1979, Honorary Air Commodore, No. 2 (City of Edinburgh) Maritime Headquarters Unit, R.Aux.AF, 1982-93. Publication: MARIA R, 1991. Address: (b.) Lennoxlove, Haddington, East Lothian, EH41 4NZ; T.-0162 082 3720; (h.) Archerfield, by Dirleton, East Lothian EH39 5HQ; T.-0162 085 0298.

Hamilton, Rt. Hon. Lord (Arthur Campbell Hamilton), BA (Oxon), LLB (Edin). Senator of the College of Justice, since 1995; b. 10.6.42, Glasgow; m., Christine Ann; 1 d. Educ. High School of Glasgow; Glasgow University; Worcester College, Oxford; Edinburgh University. Advocate, 1968; Standing Junior Counsel to Scottish Development Department, 1975-78, Inland Revenue (Scotland), 1978-82; Queen's Counsel, 1982; Advocate Depute, 1982-85; Judge of the Courts of Appeal of Jersey and of Guernsey, 1988-95; President, Pensions Appeal Tribunals for Scotland, 1992-95. Recreations: hill-walking; music; history. Address: (b.) Parliament House, Edinburgh EH1 1RQ; T.-0131-225 2595.

Hamilton, Alex. Writer of fiction; b. 14.4.49, Glasgow. Publications: Three Glasgow Writers, 1976; Gallus, Did You Say?, 1982; Abdul the Tobacco Curer, forthcoming; The Formulae, forthcoming; many articles, songs, stories, reviews, broadcasts, audio and videotapes. Recreations: language; literature; music; theatre. Address: (h.) 12 Woodlands Drive, Glasgow G4 9EH; T.-0141-339 2258.

Hamilton, Alexander Macdonald, CBE, JP, MA, LLB. Former Vice Chairman: Royal Bank of Scotland Group plc, Royal Bank of Scotland plc; b. 11.5.25, Motherwell; m., Catherine; 2 s.; 1 d. Educ. Hamilton Academy; Glasgow University. Former Senior Partner, subsequently Consultant, McGrigor Donald, Solicitors, Glasgow; former Member, Council, Law Society of Scotland, now Convener, Diligence Committee; President of the Society, 1977-78; former Member, Court House Committee, Royal Faculty of Procurators of Glasgow; Past President, Glasgow Juridical Society; former Chairman, Scottish Committee, The Scout Association; Secretary, Cambuslang Old Parish Church; former Vice-Chairman and Legal Adviser, Cambuslang Community Council. Recreations: sailing; golf. Address: (h.) 30 Wellshot Drive, Cambuslang; T.-0141-641 1445.

Hamilton, Christine M., MA. Director, Centre for Cultural Policy Research, University of Glasgow; b. 9.8.54, Hamilton. Educ. Kirkcaldy High School; Harris Academy, Dundee; Glasgow University; City University, London (Diploma, Arts Administration). House Manager, Citizens' Theatre, Glasgow; Administrator: 7:84 Theatre Company, Tag Theatre Company; Arts Officer, Scottish Trades Union Congress; Depute Director and Director, Planning and Development, Scottish Arts Council; Depute Director, Cultural and Leisure Services, Glasgow City Council. Recreations: arts; hill-walking; swimming. Address: (b.) Gilmorehill Centre, University of Glasgow G12 8QQ; e-mail: c.hamilton.@arts.gla.ac.uk

Hamilton, David, MP. Labour MP, Midlothian, since 2001; b. 24.10.50, Dalkeith; m., Jean; 2 d. Educ. Dalkeith High School. Former coal miner, landscape gardener, training officer, training manager, chief executive, and local councillor. Recreations: films; three grandchildren. Address: (b.) 95 High Street, Dalkeith, Midlothian EH22 1AX; T.-0131-654 1585.

Hamilton, Duncan, MA, LLB. MSP (SNP), Highlands and Islands, since 1999; b. 3.10.73, Troon. Educ. Bearsden Academy; Glasgow University; Edinburgh University. Kennedy Scholar, Kennedy School of Government, Harvard University, 1997-98; Assistant to Chief Executive, Scottish National Party, 1998-99. Recreations: socialising; all sports. Address: (b.) Scottish Parliament, Edinburgh EH99 1SP; T.-0131-348 5700.

Hamilton, Gordon MacMillan, MB, ChB, DFM, MPhil, CLEM, FFCS. Medical Director, Glasgow University Health Service, since 1989; Hon. Senior Lecturer, Glasgow University, since 1989; Branch Medical Officer and Council Member, Glasgow and Renfrewshire Branch, British Red Cross, since 1992; b. 6.2.54, Motherwell. Educ. Glasgow University. Various hospital appointments, 1977-89. Past Chairman, Friends of the S.N.O.; Member, Glasgow Art Club. Recreations: tennis: squash; keep-fit; art; antiques; music. Address: (b.) University Health Service, Glasgow University, 63 Oakfield Avenue, Glasgow G12 8LP; T.-0141-330 4538; e-mail: G.Hamilton@admin.gla.ac.uk

Hamilton, Ian Robertson, QC (Scot), BL, LLD (Hon); b. 13.9.25, Paisley; m., Jeannette Patricia Mairi Stewart; 1 s.; 1 s., 2 d. by pr. m. Educ. John Neilson School, Paisley; Allan Glen's School, Glasgow; Glasgow University; Edinburgh University. RAFVR, 1944-48; called to Scottish Bar, 1954, and to Albertan Bar, 1982; Founder, Castle Wynd Printers, Edinburgh, 1955; Advocate Depute, 1962; Director of Civil Litigation, Republic of Zambia, 1964-66; Hon. Sheriff of Lanarkshire, 1967; retired from practice to work for National Trust for Scotland and later to farm in Argyll, 1969; returned to practice, 1974; Sheriff of Glasgow and Strathkelvin, May-December, 1984; returned to practice. Chief Pilot, Scottish Parachute Club, 1979-90; Student President, Heriot-Watt University, 1990-96; Rector, Aberdeen University, 1994-96; Honorary Member, Sir William Wallace Free Colliers of Scotland, 1997. University of Aberdeen, 1997: LLD (Hon), Hon Research Fellow. Publications: No Stone Unturned, 1952; The Tinkers of the World, 1957 (Foyle award-winning play); A Touch of Treason, 1990; The Taking of the Stone of Destiny, 1991; A Touch More Treason, 1993. Recreation: motor-biking. Address: (h.) Lochnaheithe, North Connel, Argyll PA37 1QX; T.-01631 710 427.

Hamilton, Rev. Ian William Finlay, BD, LTH, ALCM, AVCM. Minister, Nairn Old Parish Church, since 1986; b. 29.11.46, Glasgow; m., Margaret McLaren Moss; 1 s.; 2 d. Educ. Victoria Drive Senior Secondary School, Glasgow; University of Glasgow and Trinity College. Employed in banking, then music publishing; ordained, Alloa North Parish Church, 1978. Moderator, Presbytery of Inverness, 1990-91; Member: General Assembly Parish Re-appraisal Committee, 1994-97, General Assembly Maintenance of the Ministry Committee, since 1995; has participated in seven pulpit exchanges, Reformed Church, New Jersey, USA; Presenter, Reflections (Grampian TV), Crossfire (Moray Firth Radio). Publications: Reflections from the Manse Window; Second Thoughts; They're Playing My Song; Take Four!; I'm Trying to Connect You!; A Century of Christian Witness; several children's talks published in The Expository Times; regular contributor to Manse Window page in People's Friend. Recreations: music (piano and organ); writing; broadcasting on radio and television. Address: (h.) Nairn Old Parish Manse, 3 Manse Road, Nairn IV12 4RN; T.-01667 452203.

Hamilton, John, MA, BSc. Head Teacher, Boroughmuir High School, Edinburgh, since 2000; b. 10.1.51, Edinburgh. Educ. Trinity Academy, Edinburgh; Edinburgh University. Tynecastle High School: Teacher, History/Geography/Modern Studies, 1975-77; Teacher, Social Subjects, 1977-82; Principal Teacher Guidance, 1982-89; Assistant Head Teacher, 1989-92; Depute Head Teacher, James Gillespie's High School, 1992-99. Recreations: rugby; cricket; golf; music; travel. Address: (b.) Boroughmuir High School, Viewforth, Edinburgh; T.-0131-229 9703.

Hamilton, John Fleming, LLB, NP. Senior Partner, Maclean and Lowson, Solicitors, since 1992; b. 4.3.57, Forfar; m., Lindsey; 1 s.; 2 d. Educ. Websters High School, Kirriemuir; University of Dundee. Legal Assistant, Clark and Wallace, Solicitors, Aberdeen; Legal Assistant then Partner, Maclean and Lowson , Solicitors, Forfar and Kirriemuir. Member, Council, Law Society of Scotland (Member, Client Care, Client Relations Committee C, Competence, Guarantee Fund, and Professional Practice committees). Recreations: walking; travel; Rotary Club. Address: (b.) 94 East High Street, Forfar, Angus DD8 2ET; T.-01307 462103; e-mail: jfhamilton@ macleanandlowson.co.uk

Hamilton, Loudon Pearson, CB (1987), MA (Hons). Chairman: Scottish Agricultural and Rural Development Centre, since 1992, Hanover (Scotland) Housing Association, since 1998; b. 12.1.32, Glasgow; m., 1, Anna Mackinnon Young (deceased); 2, Rosemary Hutton; 2 s. Educ. Hutchesons Grammar School, Glasgow; Glasgow University. National Service, RA, 1953-55 (2nd Lt.); Inspector of Taxes, Inland Revenue, 1956-60; entered Scottish Office, 1960; Principal Establishment Officer, Scottish Office, 1979-84; Secretary, Scottish Office Agriculture and Fisheries Department, 1984-92. Address: (h.) Old Lyne Station, nr Peebles EH45 8NP; T.-01721 740393; e-mail: loudonhamilton@aol.com

Hamilton, Dr Mark Patrick Rogers, MBChB, MD, FRCOG. Consultant Gynaecologist, Aberdeen Maternity Hospital; Honorary Senior Lecturer, Aberdeen University; b. 24.4.55, Glasgow; m., Susan Elizabeth Duckworth; 1 s.; 1 d. Educ. High School of Glasgow; Glasgow University. Lecturer, National University of Singapore, 1985-87; Senior Registrar, Glasgow Royal Infirmary, 1987-90. Member, British Fertility Society Committee, since 1995 (Treasurer, since 2001). Address: (b.) Aberdeen Maternity Hospital, Foresterhill, Aberdeen AB25 2ZD; T.-01224 553504.

Hamilton, Robert, JP, NP. Stipendiary Magistrate, since 1984; b. 18.9.42, Falkirk; m., J. Margaret; 1 s.; 2 d. Educ. Falkirk High School. Worked as office boy, junior clerk and clerk in legal offices in Falkirk and Edinburgh; qualified as Solicitor, 1976; Legal Assistant and then Partner in Edinburgh and Leith, until 1979; became a Procurator Fiscal Depute. Recreations: football; rugby; horse racing. Address: (b.) 21 St Andrew's Street, Glasgow G1 5PW; T.-0141-287 5424.

Hamilton, Sue, BSc, MBA. Chair, Association for the Protection of Rural Scotland; b. 11.1.46; m., Malcolm. Educ. Llangefni, Anglesey; Sussex University. Various part-time teaching posts in sciences and learning support; Executive Member, Association for the Protection of Rural Scotland; Community Council Secretary; undertakes a range of activities associated with Fair Trade; Traidcraft representative. Recreations: upholstery; organic gardening; crosswords. Address: (h.) 3 Charles Court, Limekilns, Fife, KY11 3LG; T.-01383 872947.

Hamilton-Grierson, Philip John, OBE, MA. Chairman, A1 Welders Ltd.; Director: University of Highlands and Islands, Millennium Institute, Made in Scotland Ltd.; Chairman, Board, Inverness College; b. 10.10.32, Inveresk; m., Pleasaunce Jill Cardew; 1 s.; 2 d. Educ. Rugby School; Corpus Christi College, Oxford. Contracts Manager, Bristol Aircraft Ltd.; Economic Adviser, Joseph Lucas Industries Ltd.; Secretary to Liberal Parliamentary Party; Director, Gallaher Ltd.; former Deputy Chairman, Highlands and Islands Development Board; former Chairman: State Hospital, Raigmore NHS Trust, Northern College. Fellow, Royal Society of Arts. Recreations: hill-walking; tennis; music. Address: Pitlundie, North Kessock, Rossshire IV1 3XG; T.-01463 731392.

Hammerton, Professor Desmond, OBE, BSc, CBiol, FIBiol, FIWEM, FIMgt, FRSE. Visiting Professor, Department of Biology, Paisley University; b. 17.11.29,

Wakefield, Yorkshire; m., Jean Taylor; 2 s.; 2 d. Educ. Harrow Weald County School; Birkbeck College, London University. Assistant Biologist, Metropolitan Water Board, 1953-55; Research Biologist, Bristol Waterworks, 1955-58; Principal Assistant, Lothians River Purification Board, 1958-62; Director, Hydrobiological Research Unit, Khartoum University, 1962-71; Deputy Director, Clyde River Purification Board, 1971-74, Director, 1975-94; Consultant, World Health Organisation, 1977-90; Member: Aquatic Life Sciences Grants Committee, Natural Environment Research Council, 1975-79, Marine Pollution Monitoring Management Group and its Steering Committee, 1974-91, Steering Committee for the Development of Environmental Quality Objectives and Standards, Department of Environment, 1981-94, Scottish Council, Institute of Biology, 1973-76; elected to Committee of Environment Division, Institute of Biology, 1977 (Chairman, Environment Division, 1980-82), Terrestrial and Freshwater Sciences Committee, Natural Environment Research Council, 1985-89, Governor and Member, Court, University of Paisley, 1987-99, Advisory Committee on Sites of Special Scientific Interest, 1995-98, Board, Institute of Offshore Engineering, Heriot-Watt University, 1995-97, West Regional Board, Scottish Environmental Protection Agency, 1996-2000; Chairman, Scottish Council, Institute of Biology, 1995-97; Chair and Secretary, Callander Group, Scottish Wildlife Trust. Recreations: chess; tennis; hill-walking. Address: (h.) Mansefield Lodge, Ancaster Square, Callander, Stirling FK17 8BL; T.-01877 330105; e-mail: dh@enviroscot.fsworld.co.uk

Hamnett, Professor Andrew, MA, DPhil. Principal and Vice-Chancellor, Strathclyde University, since 2001. Educ. Oxford University. Research and academic posts, University of British Columbia, Oxford University, Newcastle University; Pro Vice-Chancellor, 1993-97, Deputy Vice-Chancellor, 1997-2000, Professor of Physical Chemistry, Newcastle University; physical chemist; 200 publications in books and scientific journals, covering spectroscopy, quantum theory and electrochemistry; former Chairman, Physical Chemistry sub-committee, UK Engineering and Physical Sciences Research Council; Member, Technical Opportunities Panel, EPSRC; Trustee, Westlakes Research Institute. Address: (b.) 16 Richmond Street, Glasgow, G1 1XQ; T.-0141-552 4400; e-mail: principal@strath.ac.uk

Hampson, Stephen F., MA, BPhil. Head, Enterprise and Industrial Affairs Group, Scottish Executive, since 2000; b. 27.10.45, Grimsby; m., Gunilla Brunk; 1 s.; 1 d. Educ. The Leys School, Cambridge; University College, Oxford. Lecturer, Department of Political Economy, Aberdeen University, 1969-71; Economist, National Economic Development Office, 1971-75; Economic Adviser, Scottish Office, 1975-78 and 1982-84; First Secretary, British High Commission, New Delhi, 1978-81; Assistant Secretary, Scottish Office, 1984-93; Under Secretary, Scottish Office, 1993-98; Head, Environment Group, Scottish Executive, 1998-2000. Honorary Fellow, Chartered Institution of Water and Environmental Management. Recreations: hill-walking; theatre. Address: (h.) Glenelg, Park Road, Kilmacolm, Renfrewshire; T.-Kilmacolm 872615.

Hankey, Maurice S., BSc, PhD. Director, Scottish Landowners Federation, since 1996; b. 3.7.54, Newcastle upon Tyne; m., Catherine; 1 s.; 1 d. Educ. Royal Grammar School, Newcastle upon Tyne; Wye College, London; Newcastle upon Tyne University. Specialist Adviser, East of Scotland College of Agriculture, 1978-80; Lecturer, Newcastle upon Tyne University, 1980-83; farming, 1983-90; Land Use Specialist, Scottish Landowners Federation, 1992-96. Member: Scottish Agricultural Wages Board, Board of Governors, Macaulay Land Use Research Institute. Recreations: landscape gardening; computing;

rural interests. Address: (b.) Stuart House, Eskmills Business Park, Musselburgh EH21 7PB; T.-0131-653 5400; e-mail: slfinfo@slf.org.uk

Hanlon, Professor Philip, BSc, MBChB, MRCGP, FRCP, FFPHM, MPH. Professor of Public Health, Glasgow University, since 1999; Director, Public Health Institute of Scotland, since 2001; b. 24.6.54, British North Borneo; m., Lesley; 1 s.; 1 d. Educ. Uddingston Grammar School; Glasgow University. Research Scientist, Medical Research Council, The Gamba, 1984-87; Consultant in Public Health Medicine and Director of Health Promotion, Greater Glasgow Health Board, 1988-93; Medical Director, Royal Alexandra Hospital, Paisley, 1993-94; Senior Lecturer in Public Health, Glasgow University, since 1999. Recreations: cycling; walking; reading; spending time with family. Address: (b.) Clifton House, Clifton Place, Glasgow G3 7LS; T.-0141-300 1012.

Hanna, Ronald George, CA. Chief Executive, Bett Brothers Plc, since 1992; b. 13.7.42, Glasgow; m., Ann; 2 s. Educ. High School of Glasgow; Glasgow University. Chairman, Glasgow Income Trust Plc, since 1997; Director, Edinburgh High Income Trust Plc, since 1999. Recreations: golf; skiing; sailing. Address: (b.) Argyll Court, Castle Business Park, Stirling, FK9 4TT; T.-01786 477777.

Hannaford, Professor Philip Christopher, MD, MBChB, FRCGP, MFPHM, MFFP, DRCOG, DCH. Grampian Health Board Professor of Primary Care, since 1997; Director, RCGP Centre for Primary Care Research and Epidemiology, since 1997; b. 1.7.58, London; m., Dr. Anne Carol Gilchrist; 1 s.; 1 d. Educ. Aberdeen Grammar School; Aberdeen University. GP training, Sheffield, 1982-85; research training posts, RCGP Manchester Research Unit, 1986-94; Principal, general practice, Manchester, 1986-92; Director, RCGP Manchester Research Unit, 1994-97. Publications: Evidence Guided Prescribing of the Pill (Co-editor); over 100 contributions on contraception, cardiovascular disease, HRT in scientific journals. Recreations: family; walking; music. Address: (b.) Department of General Practice and Primary Care, Foresterhill Health Centre, Westburn Road, Aberdeen; T.-01224 551278.

Hannay of Kirkdale and That Ilk, Ramsay William Rainsford., BA (Hons); b. 15.6.11, India; m., Margaret Wiseman (deceased); 1 s.; 1 d. Educ. Winchester College; Trinity College, Cambridge (Hons. degree in Law). Called to the English Bar and practised in the Bankruptcy Court; called up for service in the Forces, 1939; commissioned, HLI; served throughout the War in Europe, with a short spell in USA and Canada; demobilised with rank of Major; Legal Assistant, then Assistant Solicitor, Board of Trade, 1946-64; Honorary Sheriff, Stewartry of Kirkcudbright; Member, Queen's Bodyguard for Scotland (Royal Company of Archers); President, Dumfries and Galloway Boy Scouts Association; Chief of the Clan Hannay; Past President, Drystane Walling Association of Great Britain. Recreations: sailing; shooting; fishing. Address: (h.) Cardoness Cottage, Gatehouse-of-Fleet, Kirkcudbrightshire; T.-01557 840286.

Hanson, Professor William Stewart, BA, PhD, FSA, FSA Scot. Professor of Roman Archaeology, Glasgow University, since 2000 (Head, Department of Archaeology, since 1999); b. 22.1.50, Doncaster; m., Lesley Macinnes; 1 d. Educ. Gravesend Grammar School; Manchester University. Glasgow University: Lecturer in Archaeology, 1975; Senior Lecturer in Archaeology, 1990-2000. Chairman: Scottish Field School of Archaeology, 1982-89; Scottish Archaeological Link, 1990-96; Council for British Archaeology: Member, Executive Committee, 1989-98, Vice-President, 1995-98; President, Council for Scottish Archaeology, 1989-96; Director, large-scale archaeological excavations at several sites in Scotland and northern England, including complete excavation of the Roman Fort at Elginhaugh, Dalkeith; recipient, Glenfiddich Living Scotland Award, 1987. Publications include: Agricola and the conquest of the north; Rome's north-west frontier: the Antonine Wall (Co-Author); Scottish archaeology: new perceptions (Co-Editor); papers and articles. Recreations: tennis; film. Address: (h.) 4 Victoria Road, Stirling FK8 2RH; T.-01786 465506.

Happs, John Henderson, MA (Hons). Head Teacher, Mainholm Academy, Ayr, since 1994; b. 1.9.47, Irvine; m., Jean; 4 s.; 1 d. Educ. Irvine Royal Academy; Glasgow University; Jordanhill College. Teacher of English/Principal Teacher of English, Ravenspark Academy, 1970-80; Assistant Head Teacher/Depute Head Teacher/Acting Head Teacher, Kilwinning Academy, 1980-94. Recreations: caravanning; music; reading; computing; playing with grand-daughter. Address: (b.) Mainholm Academy, Mainholm Road, Ayr KA8 0QQ; T.-01292 267300; e-mail: john.happs@mainholmacademy.south-ayrshire.gov.uk

Hardcastle, Professor William John, BA, MA, PhD, FRSA, FIOA. Dean of Health Sciences, Queen Margaret University College, since 1999; Dean of Research, since 1999; Professor of Speech Sciences, since 1993; b. 28.9.43, Brisbane; m., Francesca; 2 s.; 1 d. Educ. Brisbane Grammar School; University of Queensland; Edinburgh University. Lecturer, Institut fur Phonetik, Universitat Kiel, 1973-74; Lecturer, then Reader, then Professor, Department of Linguistic Science, Reading University, 1974-93; Director, Scottish Centre for Research into Speech Disability, since 1997. President, International Clinical Phonetics and Linguistics Association, 1991-2000; Convenor, Scottish Universities Research Policy Consortium, since 2001. Publications include: Physiology of Speech Production; Disorders of Fluency and their Effects on Communication (Co-Author); Speech Production and Speech Modelling (Co-Editor); Handbook of Phonetic Sciences (Co-Editor); Co-articulation: Theory, Data and Techniques (Co-Editor). Recreations: hill-walking; badminton; gardening. Address: (b.) Faculty of Health Sciences, Queen Margaret University College, Clerwood Terrace, Edinburgh EH12 8TS; T.-0131-317 3680.

Hardie, Rt. Hon The Lord (Andrew Rutherford Hardie), PC, QC (Scot). Senator of the College of Justice, since 2000; b. 8.1.46, Alloa; m., Catherine Storrar Elgin; 2 s.; 1 d. Educ. St. Modan's High School, Stirling; Edinburgh University. Enrolled Solicitor, 1971; Member, Faculty of Advocates, 1973; Advocate Depute, 1979-83; Dean, Faculty of Advocates, 1994-97; Lord Advocate, 1997-2000; created Life Peer, 1997. Address: (b.) Court of Session, Parliament House, Parliament Square, Edinburgh EH1 1RF.

Hardie, Professor David Grahame, MA, PhD, FRSE. Professor of Cellular Signalling, Dundee University, since 1994; b. 25.4.50, Liverpool; m., Linda Margaret; 4 s. Educ. Merchant Taylors' School, Crosby; Cambridge University; Heriot-Watt University. Lecturer, then Senior Lecturer, then Reader, Dundee University, 1977-94. Member, Molecular and Cell Panel, Wellcome Trust, since 2001. Address: (b.) School of Life Sciences, Dundee University, Wellcome Trust Biocentre, Dundee DD1 5EH.

Hardie, Donald Graeme, KStJ, TD, JP, FIM. Director, Hardie Polymers Ltd., 1976-2001; b. 23.1.36, Glasgow; m. 1, Rosalind Allan Ker (divorced); 2 s.; m. 2, Sheena. Educ. Blairmore and Merchiston Castle. Commissioned 41st Field Regiment RA, 1955; Battery Commander 277 (Argyll & Sutherland Highlanders) Regiment RA (TA), 1966; Commanding Officer GSVOTC, 1973; TA Col. Lowlands, 1976; TA Col. DES, 1980; TA Col. Scotland, 1985; ACF

Brigadier Scotland, 1987. UTR Management Trainee, 1956-59; F.W. Allan & Ker, Shipbrokers, 1960-61; J. & G. Hardie & Co. Ltd., 1961-2001 (former Chairman); Director, Gilbert Plastics Ltd., 1973-76; Director, Ronaash Ltd., 1988-99. Lord Lieutenant, Dunbartonshire, since 1990; Hon. Col. 105 Regiment RA(V), 1992-99; Hon. Col. Glasgow & Lanarkshire ACF, 1991-2000; Keeper, Dumbarton Castle, since 1996; Chairman, RA Council of Scotland, 1993-2000; Chieftain, Balloch Games; President, SSAFA, Dunbartonshire; President, Scout Council, Dunbartonshire Area; President, Girl Guides of Dumbarton; President, Argyll and Lennox Boys Brigade; Chairman, Duke of Edinburgh Co-ordinating Committee; Trustee, Tullochan Trust; Patron, Cornerstone. Recreations: skiing; sailing; shooting; fishing. Address: (h.) Boturich Castle, Alexandria, Dunbartonshire G83 8LX.

Hardie, Sir Douglas Fleming, CBE, LLD, Hon. FRIAS. Non-Executive Chairman, DDS Medicines Research Ltd. (Contract Clinical Research), since 1997; b. 26.5.23, Dundee; m., Dorothy Alice Warner; 2 s.; 1 d. Educ. Trinity College, Glenalmond. Trooper, 58 Training Regt., RAC, 1941; commissioned RMA Sandhurst, 1942, 1 Fife & Forfar Yeomanry Flamethrowing Tank Regt., NW Europe, 1942-46 (Despatches), Major. Director, Dayco Rubber (UK) Ltd., 1956-86; Chairman, CBI Scotland, 1976-78; Director: Clydesdale Bank plc, 1981-92, The Alliance Trust plc, 1982-93, The Second Alliance Trust plc, 1982-93, Alliance Trust (Finance) Ltd., 1982-93, SECDEE Leasing, 1982-93, Alliance Trust (Nominees) Ltd., 1982-93; Chairman, A.G. Scott Textiles, 1985-87; Deputy Chairman, Scottish Development Agency, 1978-91; Chairman, Grampian Television PLC, 1989-93; Member: CBI Grand Council, London, 1976-85, Scottish Economic Council, 1977-91; Councillor, Winston Churchill Memorial Trust, 1985-98; Vice Chairman, Prince's Scottish Youth Business Trust, 1987; Past President, Dundee Rotary Club; Vice-President, Fife & Forfar Yeomanry Regimental Association; Deacon Convener, Nine Incorporated Trades of Dundee, 1951-54; Elder, Dundee Parish Church (St. Mary's). Recreations: golf; fishing. Address: (h.) The Anchorage, 8 Bingham Terrace, Dundee DD4 7HH.

Hardie, William Dunbar, MBE, MA, BA, MUniv. Writer and Entertainer; b. 4.1.31, Aberdeen; m., Margaret Elizabeth Simpson; 1 s.; 1 d. Educ. Robert Gordon's College, Aberdeen; Aberdeen University; Sidney Sussex College, Cambridge. Administrative Assistant, then Assistant Secretary, NE Regional Hospital Board; District Administrator, North District, Grampian Health Board; Secretary, Grampian Health Board, 1976-83. Co-Writer and performer, Scotland The What? (comedy revue); Writer, Dod'N'Bunty column, Aberdeen Evening Express. Recreations: reading; TV-watching; film and theatre-going; sport; avid and totally biased follower of Aberdeen's football team, Scotland's rugby team, and England's cricket team. Address: (h.) 50 Gray Street, Aberdeen AB10 6JE; T.-01224 310591.

Harding, Professor Dennis William, MA, DPhil, FRSE. Abercromby Professor of Archaeology, University of Edinburgh, since 1977; b. 11.4.40. Educ. Keble College, University of Oxford. Assistant Keeper, Department of Antiquities, Ashmolean Museum, University of Oxford, 1965; Lecturer in Celtic Archaeology, University of Durham, 1966 (Senior Lecturer, 1975); Dean, Faculty of Arts, 1983-86, Vice-Principal, 1988-91, University of Edinburgh. Member, S.A.A.S. Studentships Committee, since 1982 (Chairman, since 1997). Address: (h.) Department of Archaeology, The Old High School, Infirmary Street, Edinburgh EH1 1LT; T.-0131-650 2364.

Harding, Keith. MSP (Conservative), Mid Scotland and Fife, since 1999; Conservative Spokesperson on Local Government and Planning; m.; 2 c. Former banker and newsagent; JP; Councillor (Leader, Conservative Group,

Stirling Council); member, Forth Valley Health Board. Address: (b.) Scottish Parliament, Edinburgh EH99 1SP; T.-0131-348 5643.

Hare Duke, Rt. Rev. Michael Geoffrey, BA, MA, DD. Bishop of St. Andrews, Dunkeld and Dunblane, 1969-94 (retired); Chair, RSVP Scottish Forum on Older Volunteering, since 2001; b. 28.11.25, Calcutta; m., Grace Lydia Frances Dodd; 1 s.; 3 d. Educ. Bradfield College; Trinity College, Oxford; Westcott House, Cambridge. Sub-Lt., RNVR, 1944-46; Deacon, 1952; Priest, 1953; Curate, 1952-56; Vicar, Bury, 1956-62; Pastoral Director, Clinical Theology Association, 1962-64; Vicar, St. Paul's Daybrook and Officiating Chaplain, E. Midlands District HQ, 1964-69. Chairman, Scottish Association for Mental Health; Member, Anglican Communion Peace and Justice Network, Convener, 1992-94; Chairman, Age Concern Scotland, 1994-00. Publications: The Caring Church (Co-author); First Aid in Counselling (Co-author); Understanding the Adolescent; The Break of Glory; Freud; Good News; Stories Signs and Sacraments of the Emerging Church; Praying for Peace, reflections on the Gulf crisis; Hearing the Stranger; One Foot in Heaven, growing older and living to the full. Recreations: walking; writing; broadcasting. Address: (h.) 2 Balhousie Avenue, Perth PH1 5HN; T.-01738 622642; e-mail:BishMick@aol.com

Hargreave, Timothy Bruce, MB, MS, FRCSEdin, FRCS, FEB (Urol), FRCP(Ed). Consultant Urological Surgeon, Western General Hospital, Edinburgh, since 1978; b. 23.3.44, Lytham; m., Molly; 2 d. Educ. Harrow; University College Hospital, London University. Senior Registrar: Western Infirmary, Glasgow, University College Hospital, London; Medical Officer, Paray Mission Hospital, Lesotho. Publications: Diagnosis and Management of Renal and Urinary Disease; Male Infertility (Editor); Practical Urological Endoscopy; The Management of Male Infertility. Recreation: skiing. Address: (h.) 20 Cumin Place, Edinburgh.

Hargreaves, Jonathan, BSc, PhD. Chief Executive, East of Scotland Water, since 2000; b. 10.3.50; m., Hilary; 2 d. Educ. St Bees, Cumbria; Hatfield Polytechnic; Durham University. Business Development Manager, Northumbrian Water Group, 1990-91; Managing Director, Entec Europe Ltd., 1991-92; Managing Director, Northumbrian Water Ltd, 1993; Managing Director, Northumbrian Lyonnaise International, 1996. Recreations: gardening; skiing; DIY. Address: (b.) 55 Buckstone Terrace, Edinburgh EH10 6XH; T.-0131-445 6756.

Harkess, Ronald Dobson, OBE, BSc, MS, PhD, NDA, CBiol, MIBiol, FRAgS, FRSA. Emeritus Fellow, Scottish Agricultural College; Agricultural Scientist and Consultant; b. 11.7.33, Edinburgh; m., Jean Cuthbert Drennan (deceased); 2 d. Educ. Royal High School, Edinburgh; Edinburgh University; Cornell University. Senior Fison Research Fellow, Nottingham University, 1959-62; Assistant Grassland Adviser, West of Scotland Agricultural College, Ayr, 1962-72; Senior Agronomist, 1972-86; Technical Secretary, Council, Scottish Agricultural Colleges, 1986-90, Company Secretary, 1987-90; Company Secretary, Scottish Agricultural College, 1990-91; Assistant Principal, Scottish Agricultural College, 1991-93. Member, Earn Community Council, since 1997; Chairman, Friends of Perth Festival of the Arts, since 1997; President, Perth Philatelic Society, since 1997; President, Tay Probus, since 2001. Recreations: amateur radio; philately; gardening. Address: (h.) Friarton Bank, Rhynd Road, Perth PH2 8PT; T.-01738 643435.

Harkins, Jim. Leader of Renfrewshire Council, since 1999 (Member, since 1996); b. 17.12.41; m., Margaret; 3 d. Renfrew District Councillor, 1984-96 (Convener of Housing, four years, Chair of Finance); Community

Worker, 1982-96. Recreation: athletics. Address: (b.) North Building, Cotton Street, Paisley; T.-0141-840 3491.

Harkiss, Professor Gordon David, BSc, PhD. Professor of Veterinary Immunopathology, Edinburgh University, since 2000; Director, Wellcome Trust Laboratory for Research in Comparative Respiratory Medicine, since 1998; b. 3.8.47, Glasgow; m., Helen Diana Jane Harkiss; 1 s.; 1 d. Educ. Vale of Leven Academy; Edinburgh University. Research Officer, Tissue Physiology Department, Strangeways Research Laboratory, Cambridge, 1974-76; Scientific Officer/Senior Scientific Officer/Principal Scientific Officer, Department of Clinical Immunology, Addenbrooke's Hospital, Cambridge, 1976-83; New Blood Lecturer/Senior Lecturer/Reader, Department of Veterinary Pathology, Edinburgh University, 1998-2000. Recreations: music; reading; hill walking. Address: (b.) Department of Veterinary Pathology, Edinburgh University, Easter Bush Veterinary Centre, Easter Bush, Midlothian, EH25 9RG; T.-0131-650 8802.

Harkness, Very Rev. James, CB, OBE, MA, DD, FRSA, ChStJ. Dean of the Chapel Royal in Scotland, since 1996; Chaplain to The Queen; Moderator, General Assembly of the Church of Scotland, 1995-96; President: Royal British Legion, Scotland, since 2001, Earl Haig Fund Scotland, since 2001, The Officers' Association, Scotland, since 2001; Member, Board, Mercy Corps Scotland, since 2001; b. 20.10.35, Thornhill; m., Elizabeth Anne; 1 s.; 1 d. Educ. Dumfries Academy; Edinburgh University. Assistant Minister, North Morningside Parish Church, 1959-61; Chaplain: KOSB, 1961-65, Queen's Own Highlanders, 1965-69; Singapore, 1969-70; Deputy Warden, RAChD, 1970-74; Senior Chaplain, Northern Ireland, 1974-75; 4th Division, 1975-78; Staff Chaplain, HQ BAOR, 1978-80; Assistant Chaplain, Scotland, 1980-81; Senior Chaplain, 1st British Corps, 1981-82; BAOR, 1982-84; Deputy Chaplain General, 1985-86; Chaplain General to the Forces, 1987-95. QHC, 1982-95; General Trustee, Church of Scotland, since 1996; Chairman, Carberry Board, 1997-2000; Member, Committee on Chaplains to HM Forces, since 1997; Member, Board of World Mission, 1997-2000; President, Army Cadet Force Association Scotland; President, Society of Friends of St. Andrew's, Jerusalem. Hon. Chaplain to BLESMA, Royal British Legion Scotland, 1996-2001; Patron, St. Mary's Music School, Edinburgh; Governor, Fettes College. Recreations: walking; reading; watching sport. Address: (h.) 13 Saxe-Coburg Place, Edinburgh EH3 5BR; T.-0131-343 1297.

Harkness, John Diamond, MA, LLB. First Scottish Parliamentary Counsel to the United Kingdom, since 2000; b. 14.7.44, Glasgow. Educ. High School of Glasgow; Glasgow University. Legal Assistant, then Senior Legal Assistant, Office of the Solicitor to the Secretary of State for Scotland, 1971-79; Assistant Scottish Parliamentary Counsel, 1979-83; Depute Scottish Parliamentary Counsel, 1983-2000. Recreations: reading; opera; theatre. Address: (b.) 36 Whitehall, London SW1Y 5AA; T.-020 7210 2581.

Harlen, Professor Wynne, OBE, MA (Oxon), MA (Bristol), PhD, FRSA. Director, Scottish Council for Research in Education, 1990-99; Visiting Professor: Liverpool University, since 1990, University of Bristol, since 1999; Visiting Scholar, Exploratorium, San Francisco, since 1999; b. 12.1.37, Swindon; 1 s.; 1 d. Educ. Pate's Grammar School for Girls, Cheltenham; St. Hilda's College, Oxford; Bristol University. Teacher/Lecturer, 1958-66; Research Associate, Bristol University School of Education, 1966-73; Research Fellow, Project Director, Reading University, 1973-77; Research Fellow, Centre for Science Education, King's College, London, 1977-84; Sidney Jones Professor of Science Education, Liverpool University, 1985-90. Chair, Children in Scotland Early Years Forum, 1991-95; Member, Secretary of State's Working Party on the Development of the National Curriculum in Science, 1987-88; President, British Educational Research Association, 1993-94; Chair, OECD Science Expert Group, since 1997. Publications: 33 books, and contributions to 39 others; 136 papers. Recreations: concerts; opera; hill-walking. Address: Haymount, Bridgend, Duns, Berwickshire TD11 3DJ; T.-01361 884710; wynne@torphin.freeserve.co.uk

Harley, Professor Simon Leigh, BSc (Hons), MA (Oxon) PhD, FRSE. Professor of Lower Crustal Processes, Edinburgh University, since 1997; b. 2.7.56, Sydney, Australia; m., Anne Elizabeth; 3 s.; 1 d. Educ. Punchbowl Boys' High School; University of New South Wales; University of Tasmania. Post-doctoral Research Assistant, ETH-Zentrum, Zurich, 1981-83; Lecturer: Oxford University/Fellow St Edmund Hall, 1983-88; Edinburgh University, 1988-92; Reader, Edinburgh University, 1992-97; FRSE, 1998; Member: Sciennes School Board, 1992-96; Australian National Antarctic Research Expeditions (ANARE), 1979-80, 1982-83, 1987-88 and 1992-93. Recreations: hill walking; skiing; hockey; various racquet sports; Antarctic Society. Address: (h.) 39 Mayfield Road, Newington, Edinburgh, EH9 2NQ; T.-0131-662 4954; e-mail: sharley@glg.ed.ac.uk

Harper, Professor Alexander Murray, MB, ChB, MD (Hons). Emeritus Professor of Surgical Research, Honorary Senior Research Fellow, 1996-2000, Glasgow University; b. 31.5.33, Glasgow; m., Charlotte Maria Fossleitner; 2 s.; 1 d. Educ. Hutchesons' Grammar School; Glasgow University. House Physician and Surgeon, Southern General Hospital and Glasgow Royal Infirmary, 1957-58; McIntyre Research Scholar in Clinical Surgery, Glasgow Royal Infirmary, 1958-60; Scientific Assistant, Medical Research Council, 1960-63; Wellcome Senior Research Fellow in Clinical Science and Honorary Lecturer in Surgery, Glasgow University, 1963-68; Glasgow University: Senior Lecturer in Surgery and Surgical Physiology, 1968-69, Reader, 1969-81; Professor of Surgical Research, 1981-96. Honorary Consultant Clinical Physiologist, Greater Glasgow Health Board, 1970-96; Editor in Chief, Journal of Cerebral Blood Flow and Metabolism, 1981-89; Editor, Cerebrovascular and Brain Metabolism Reviews, 1989-96; David Patey Prize, Surgical Research Society, 1966; H.G. Wolff Award, American Association for Study of Headache, 1968; Gold Medal, British Migraine Association, 1976; Honorary Fellow, American Heart Association (Stroke Council), 1980. Recreations: fishing; contract bridge; gardening. Address: (b.) Wellcome Surgical Institute, Glasgow University, Garscube Estate, Bearsden Road, Glasgow G61 1QH; T.-0141-330 5826.

Harper, Anne Courage. Business Consultant, since 1992; Director, Mid-Deeside Ltd., since 2001; Chairman, Deeside Community Transport Group, since 2001; b. 17.9.50, Kumasi, Ghana; m., H.W. (Harry) Bawden (deceased); 2 step-s.; 1 step-d. Educ. Aberdeen High School for Girls; University of Aberdeen; University College London. Manager, British Petroleum, 1974-92; Manager, External Affairs, BP in Scotland, 1991-92. Director, Art in Partnership, 1991-2001; Lay Member, H.M. Inspectorate of Schools, since 1993; Member, Scottish Churches Industrial Mission, since 1993; Member, General Teaching Council for Scotland, 1995-2000; President, Scottish Oil Club, 1996-98; Vice Chairman, Conservative Group for Europe, 1998-2000; Member, Court, University of Aberdeen, since 2000. Recreations: gardening; politics; hillwalking. Address: (h.) 2F1, 5 Randolph Place, Edinburgh EH3 7TQ; T.-0131-226 6475.

Harper, Rev. Anne J. McInroy, BD, STM, MTh, Cert.Soc.Psych. Chaplain, Glasgow Royal Infirmary North Glasgow University Hospitals NHS Trust, since 1990; President, Scottish Association of Chaplains in Health Care; b. 31.10.49, Glasgow. Educ. Camphill Senior Secondary School, Paisley; Glasgow University; Union Theological Seminary, New York. Graduate Fellow, Union Theological Seminary, and Assistant Minister, 2nd Presbyterian Church, New York City, 1974-75; research, Church history and liturgics, Glasgow University, 1975-78; Assistant Minister, Abronhill Church, Cumbernauld, 1978-79; Christian Education Field Officer, Church of Scotland Department of Education, 1979-84; Minister, Linthouse St. Kenneth's Parish Church, 1984-90. Holder (first woman), The Scots Fellowship awarded by Union Theological Seminary, New York, 1974. Address: The Chaplain's Office, Glasgow Royal Infirmary, Glasgow G4 0SF; T.-0141-211 4000.

Harper, Rev. David Little, BSc, BD (Hons). Minister, St. Meddan's Church, Troon, since 1979; b. 31.10.47, Moffat; m., Janis Mary Clark; 2 s. Educ. Morton Academy, Thornhill; Dumfries Academy; Edinburgh University. Assistant Minister, Cumbernauld St. Mungo's, 1971-72; first Minister, New Erskine Parish Church, 1972-79. Moderator, Presbytery of Ayr, 1991-92; Member, Scottish Advisory Committee, Independent Broadcasting Authority, 1974-79; Scottish Member, Religious Advisory Panel, IBA, 1978-79. Recreations: golf; hill-walking; swimming. Address: St. Meddan's Manse, 27 Bentinck Drive, Troon, Ayrshire KA10 6HX; T.-01292 311784; e-mail: d.l.harper@btinternet.com

Harper, Douglas Ross, BSc, MD, FRCSEdin, FRCSEng, FRCSGlas. Consultant Surgeon and Director of Day Surgery, Aberdeen Royal Infirmary, since 1999; Examiner: Royal College of Surgeons of Edinburgh, since 1979, Royal College of Surgeons of Glasgow, since 1987; Honorary Senior Lecturer, Department of Clinical Surgery, Edinburgh University, since 1976; b. 16.2.40, Aberdeen; m., Dorothy Constance Wisely; 1 s.; 3 d. Educ. Aberdeen Grammar School; Aberdeen University. House Officer, Registrar and Fellow in Vascular Surgery, Aberdeen Royal Infirmary, 1967-73; Senior Registrar, Edinburgh Royal Infirmary, 1973-76; Consultant Surgeon, 1976-99, Medical Director, 1994-99, Falkirk and District Royal Infirmary NHS Trust. Elder, Bridge of Allan Chalmers Church of Scotland. Recreations: hill-walking; geology; woodwork. Address: Day Surgery Unit, Ward 7, Aberdeen Royal Infirmary, Foresterhill, Aberdeen AB25 2ZN.

Harper, Edward James, MA, BMus, ARCM, LRAM. Composer, since 1957; Reader in Music, Edinburgh University, since 1990; Director, New Music Group of Scotland, 1973-91; b. 17.3.41, Taunton; m., Dorothy Caroline Shanks. Educ. King Edward VI School, Guildford; Royal College of Music, London; Christ Church, Oxford. Main works as a Composer: Piano Concerto, 1971; Bartok Games, 1972; Ricercari in Memoriam Luigi Dallapiccola, 1975; Fanny Robin (chamber opera), Chester Mass, 1979; Clarinet Concerto, 1981; Hedda Gabler (opera, commissioned for Scottish Opera), 1985; Fantasia V (for chamber orchestra), 1985; The Mellstock Quire (chamber opera), 1987; Homage to Thomas Hardy (baritone and orchestra), 1990; The Fiddler of the Reels (str. orch.), 1993; And Winds Austere and Pure (choir and piano duet), 1993; Psalm 150 (unacc. choir), 1996; Trio (cl., cello, piano), 1997; Etude for Orchestra, 1999 (commissioned by National Youth Orchestra of Scotland); Lochinvar (opera for schools), 2000. Address: (h.) 7 Morningside Park, Edinburgh EH10 5HD; T.-0131-447 5366.

Harper, George, MA, DipTP, MRTPI. Director of Development and Environment Services, Argyll and Bute Council, since 1996; b. 21.3.51, Perth; m., Katherine; 1 s.; 1 d. Educ. Perth Academy; Aberdeen University; Heriot-Watt University (Diploma, Town and Country Planning). Planner, Dundee Corporation, 1972-75; Planner/Senior Planner, Tayside Regional Council, 1975-88; Depute Director of Planning, Argyll and Bute District Council, 1988-90; Director of Planning, Development and Tourism, Argyll and Bute District Council, 1990-96. Director, Strathclyde Building Preservation Trust. Recreations: hill-walking; football; golf; gardening; family. Address: (b.) Kilmory Castle, Lochgilphead, Argyll; T.-01546 604225; e-mail: georgeharper@argyll-bute.gov.uk

Harper, John Ross, CBE, MA, LLB. Consultant and Founder, Harper Macleod, Solicitors; b. Glasgow; m., Ursula; 2 s.; 1 d. Educ. Hutchesons' Boys' Grammar School; Glasgow University. Parliamentary Commissioner; Emeritus Professor of Law, Strathclyde University; Past President: Law Society of Scotland, Scottish Conservative & Unionist Association, International Bar Association; former Chairman, Society of Scottish Conservative Lawyers; former Parliamentary candidate (Conservative), Hamilton and West Renfrewshire; Chairman: Mining (Scotland) Ltd., The Scottish Coal Company Ltd., Alarm Protection Ltd., Scottish Coal (Deep Mine) Ltd., Africa Holdings (SA) Proprietory Ltd. Publications: Glasgow Rape Case; My Client My Lord; A Practitioner's Guide to the Criminal Courts; Fingertip Criminal Law; Rates Revaluation; Devolution; New Unionism; Scotland '97; Referendums are Dangerous; Global Law in Practice. Recreations: angling; bridge. Address: (b.) The Ca'd'oro, 45 Gordon Street, Glasgow, G1 3PE; T.-0141-221 8888; (h.) 23 Clabon Mews, Cadogan Square, London SW1X 0EG.

Harper, Robin C. M., MA, DipGC, FRSA, FEIS. MSP (Green), Lothians, since 1999; Speaker, formerly Convenor, Scottish Green Party, since 1995; Teacher, since 1962; b. 4.8.40, Thurso; m., Jenny Helen Carter Brown. Educ. St. Marylebone Grammar School; Elgin Academy; Aberdeen University. Teacher Braehead School, Fife, 1964-68; Education Officer, Kenya, 1968-70; Musician/Actor, 1971; Assistant Principal Teacher, Boroughmuir High School, 1972-99; Musical Director, Theatre Workshop, Edinburgh, 1972-75; President, Edinburgh Classical Guitar Society, 1980-90; Member, Lothian Children's Panel, 1985-88; Member, Lothian Health Council, 1993-97; President, EIS Edinburgh Local Association, 1990-91; elected Rector, University of Edinburgh, 2000-03; Member, Board, Traverse Theatre, since 2001, 3 Estaites Theatre Company, since 2000; Patron, FTC Theatre, SOS Theatre, 2001. Recreations: music; walking; photography; travel; theatre. Address: 11 Greenbank Terrace, Edinburgh EH10 6ER; T.-0131-447 1843.

Harper Gow, Maxwell Eric, CA. Acting Chief Executive, Common Services Agency for NHSScotland, since 2000; b. 1.8.45, Brighton; m., Celia Macleod; 1 s.; 2 d. Educ. Rugby School. CA Apprentice, Graham, Smart and Auman, Chartered Accountants, 1964-69; Cooper Brothers, Chartered Accountants, London, 1970-73; The EMI Group of Companies, London and Edinburgh, 1973-81; Company Secretary, A.H. McIntosh Limited, Kirkcaldy, 1981-82; Coopers and Lybrand, Edinburgh and Aberdeen, 1982-95; Director of Finance, Common Services Agency for NHSScotland, 1995-2000. Honorary Treasurer, Royal Zoological Society of Scotland. Recreations: sailing; skiing; more sailing. Address: (b.) Trinity Park House, South Trinity Road, Edinburgh EH5 3SE; T.-0131-552 6255; e-mail: harpergow@aol.com

Harries, Professor Jill Diana, MA, DPhil, FRHistS. Professor of Ancient History, St Andrews University, since 1997 (Head of School, Greek, Latin and Ancient History, since 2000); b. 20.5.50, London. Educ. Bromley High School GPDST; Somerville College, Oxford. Kennedy Scholar, 1973-74; Lecturer in Ancient History, St Andrews University, 1976-95; Senior Lecturer, 1995-97; Visiting Fellow, All Souls College, Oxford, 1996-97; Leverhulme

Fellow, 1996-97. Member of Council, St Leonard's School, St Andrews, 1998-2000. Publications: Religious Conflict in Fourth Century Rome, 1983; The Theodusian Code (Editor), 1993; Sidonius Apollinaris and the Fall of Rome, 1994; Law and Empire in Late Antiquity, 1998. Recreations: politics; walking. Address: (b.) Department of Ancient History, St Salvator's College, St Andrews KY16 9AL; T.-01334 462600.

Harris, Rev. John William Forsyth, MA. Minister, Bearsden South Church, since 1987; b. 10.3.42, Hampshire; m., Ellen Lesley Kirkpatrick Lamont; 1 s.; 2 d. Educ. Merchant Taylors' School, London; St. Andrews University; New College, Edinburgh. Ordained Assistant, St. Mary's, Haddington, 1967-70; Minister: St. Andrew's, Irvine, 1970-77, St. Mary's, Motherwell, 1977-87. Convener: Scottish Churches' Christian Aid Committee, 1986-90, Scottish Christian Aid Committee, 1990-98, Scottish Television's Religious Advisory Committee, 1990-98, Jubilee Scotland, since 2001; Vice-Convener, Board of World Mission, 1996-99; Member: Jubilee 2000 Scottish Coalition Steering Group, 1997-2000, Board of Christian Aid, 1990-98, Executive, Church and Nation Committee, 1985-91, Executive, Scottish Churches Council, 1986-90; Moderator, Dumbarton Presbytery, 1994-95. Fencing Blue, St. Andrews and Edinburgh; Scottish Fencing Team, 1963-66. Recreations: enjoying grandchildren, Cruban walking and holiday home in Kintyre. Address: 61 Drymen Road, Bearsden, Glasgow G61 2SU; T.-0141-942 0507; e-mail: jwfh@globalnet.co.uk

Harris, Marshall James, DPA. Former Director, Scottish Educational Trust for United Nations and International Affairs; Consultant, North Lanarkshire Education; b. 14.3.28, Edinburgh; m., Matilda Currie Main; 2 s.; 1 d. Educ. Armadale Secondary; Glasgow University. Accountancy, pre-1958; Scottish National Officer, UN Association, 1958-86; Secretary, Scottish Standing Committee for Voluntary International Aid. Former Liberal and Alliance candidate. Recreations: reading; member of Probus. Address: (h.) Hopetoun, Charlotte Street, Brightons, Falkirk; T.-01324 715203.

Harris, Paul Anthony, MA(Hons). Writer, since 1967; b. 22.7.48, Dartford. Educ. Bradford Grammar School; Elgin Academy; University of Aberdeen. Pirate Radio, 1969-71; Publisher, 1967-85; Publishing Consultant, 1985-2001; Journalist (Foreign Correspondent), 1990-2001. Lecturer, Cunard World University Programme; British Press Award (Bosnia), 1992. Publications: 35 books including: When Pirates Ruled the Waves, 1968, The Garvie Trial, 1969, Dictionary of Scottish Painters, 1990, Somebody Else's War, 1992, Cry Bosnia, 1995; Scotland's Century – 100 Years of Photographs, 1999; Fractured Paradise: Images of Sri Lanka, 2001. Recreations: photography; travel. Address: (h.) Whittingehame House, Haddington EH41 4QA; T.-01368 850369; e-mail: polaris@conflictanalysis.com

Harris, Raymond Richard, BSc, PhD, CStat, ARCS. Principal, Stevenson College, Edinburgh, since 2000; b. 9.5.48, Carshalton, Surrey. Educ. Raine's Foundation; Imperial College, London; Fitzwilliam College, Cambridge. Lecturer, Mathematical Statistics, Exeter University; Principal Lecturer, Applied Statistics, Sheffield City Polytechnic; Professor of Applied Statistics, University of Central Lancashire; Assistant Principal, University of Abertay Dundee; Depute Principal, Perth College; Board Member: Learning and Teaching Scotland, Colleges Open Learning Exchange Group (COLEG). Address: (b.) Stevenson College, Bankhead Avenue, Edinburgh, EH11 4DE; T.-0131-535 4628; e-mail: rharris@stevenson.ac.uk

Harris, Tom. Labour MP, Glasgow Cathcart, since 2001; b. 20.2.64, Irvine; m., Carolyn; 1 s. Educ. Garnock Academy; Napier College. Reporter, East Kilbride News/Paisley Daily Express, 1986-90; Press Officer, Labour Party in Scotland, 1990-92; Press Officer, Strathclyde Regional Council, 1993-96; Senior Media Officer, Glasgow City Council, 1996; Public Relations Manager, East Ayrshire Council, 1996-98; Chief Public Relations Officer, SPTE, 1998-2001. Recreations: badminton; astronomy; cinema; hill-walking. Address: (b.) House of Commons, Westminster, London SW1A 0AA; T.-020 7219 8237.

Harrison, Professor Andrew, BA, MA, DPhil (Oxon), CChem, MRSC. Professor of Solid State Chemistry, Edinburgh University, since 1999; b. 3.10.59, Oxford; m., Alison Ironside-Smith. Educ. Newcastle-under-Lyme High School; St John's College, Oxford. Fereday Fellow, St John's College, Oxford, 1985-88; Research Fellow, McMaster University, Canada, 1988-89; Royal Society University Research Fellow, 1990-92; Reader, Department of Chemistry, Edinburgh University, 1996; Nuffield Research Fellow, 1997-98; Eminent Visiting Professor, Riken, Japan, since 2000; Director, Centre for Science at Extreme Conditions, University of Edinburgh, since 2001. Recreations: hill walking; running; cycling; eating and drinking. Address: (b.) Department of Chemistry, Edinburgh University, Joseph Black Building, West Mains Road, Edinburgh; T.-0131-650 4745; e-mail: a.harrison@ed.ac.uk

Harrison, Professor Bryan Desmond, CBE, BSc, PhD, Hon. DAgricFor, FRS, FRSE. Emeritus Professor of Plant Virology, Dundee University, since 1997 (Professor of Plant Virology, 1991-96); b. 16.6.31, Purley, Surrey; m., Elizabeth Ann Latham-Warde; 2 s.; 1 d. Educ. Whitgift School, Croydon; Reading University. Agricultural Research Council Postgraduate Research Student, 1952-54; Scientific Officer, Scottish Horticultural Research Institute, 1954-57; Senior and Principal Scientific Officer, Rothamsted Experimental Station, 1957-66; Scottish Horticultural Research Institute/Scottish Crop Research Institute: Principal Scientific Officer, 1966, Senior Principal Scientific Officer (Individual Merit), 1969, Deputy Chief Scientific Officer (Individual Merit), 1981; Head, Virology Department, 1966-91; Foreign Associate, US National Academy of Sciences; Honorary Professor, Department of Biochemistry and Microbiology, St. Andrews University, since 1987; Honorary Research Professor, Scottish Crop Research Institute, since 1991; Honorary Visiting Professor, Dundee University, 1987-91; Honorary Visiting Professor, Zhejiang University, China, since 2001; Past President, Association of Applied Biologists; Honorary Member: Association of Applied Biologists, Phytopathological Society of Japan, Society for General Microbiology. Recreation: gardening. Address: (b.) Scottish Crop Research Institute, Invergowrie, Dundee DD2 5DA; e-mail: bharri@scri.sari.ac.uk

Hart, Rt. Rev. Monsignor Daniel J., PhL, STL, MA(Hons), Dip Ed. Parish Priest, St. Helen's Langside, Glasgow, since 1984; Domestic Prelate to His Holiness The Pope; b. 29.5.32, Shenfield. Educ. St. Patrick's High School, Dumbarton; Blairs College, Aberdeen; Pontifical Gregorian University, Rome; University of Glasgow. Principal Teacher of History, Blairs College, Aberdeen, 1961-69; Notre Dame College of Education, 1969-81: Lecturer in Religious Education, Lecturer, In-Service Department, Director, Postgraduate Secondary Course; Director, Papal Visit to Scotland, 1981-82; Director, Religious Education Centre, Archdiocese of Glasgow, 1981-83; Catholic Church Representative, Strathclyde Regional Education Committee, 1983-84; Chairman, Children's Panel Advisory Committee for Strathclyde, 1977-84 (Vice-Chairman, 1977-84); Judge, Collegiate Court, Scottish Catholic National Marriage Tribunal, since 1989; Member, Archdiocese of Glasgow Finance Council, 1986-90; Vice-Chairman, Archdiocesan Council of Priests, 1982-84 and 1998-2000; Member, Board of Governors, St.

Andrew's College of Education, 1991-99; Member, Merger Committee, St. Andrew's College of Education and University of Glasgow, 1997-99. Recreations: golf; photography; gardening; swimming; travel. Address: St. Helen's, 165 Camphill Avenue, Glasgow G41 3DR.

Hart, Morag Mary, JP, DL, RGN, RSCN. Deputy Lieutenant, Dunbartonshire, since 1989; Director, Scotsell Ltd., since 1982; b. 19.4.39, Glasgow; m., Tom Hart; 1 s.; 1 d. Educ. Westbourne School for Girls, Glasgow. Sick Children's Hospital, Glasgow, 1956-59; Western General Hospital, Edinburgh, 1960-62. County Commissioner, Dunbartonshire Girl Guides, 1982-90; Chairman, Dunbartonshire Area Scouts, since 1994; Member, The Guide Association Council for Scotland, 1982-2000. Recreations: reading; gardening; walking. Address: (h.) 18 Campbell Drive, Bearsden, Glasgow G61 4NE; T.-0141-942 1216.

Hart, Professor Robert Albert, BA (Hons), MA. Professor of Economics, Stirling University, since 1986; b. 7.1.46, Hartlepool; m., Shirley; 3 d. Educ. Hartlepool Grammar School; Liverpool University. Economics Lecturer, Aberdeen University, 1969-73, Leeds University, 1974-75; Senior Lecturer, Strathclyde University, 1976-80; Senior Research Fellow, Science Centre, Berlin, 1980-86; Head, School of Management, Stirling University, 1991-94. Recreations: walking; reading; drinking beer. Address: (b.) Department of Economics, Stirling University, Stirling FK9 4LA; T.-01786 467471.

Hart, Professor Susan Jane Ritchie, BA (Hons), PhD, DipMRS. Professor of Marketing, Strathclyde University, since 1996; Vice Dean, Strathclyde Business School, since 1999; b. 18.7.60, Edinburgh; 1 s.; 1 d. Educ. Bearsden Academy; Strathclyde University. Universite de Technologie de Compiegne, 1982-83; Procter and Gamble PLC, 1983-84; Research Assistant/Lecturer/Senior Lecturer, Department of Marketing, Strathclyde University, 1984-93; Professor of Marketing, Heriot-Watt University, 1993-95; Professor of Marketing, Stirling University, 1995-98. Editor, Journal of Marketing Management. Publications: Marketing and Competitive Success (Co-Author); New Product Development, 1996; Project Strategy and Management, 1999. Recreations: hill-walking; skiing. Address: (b.) Department of Marketing, Strathclyde University, Glasgow; T.-0141-548 4927.

Hart, Thomas, MA, LLB. Chair, Scottish Transport Studies Group, since 1994; Editor, Scottish Transport Review, since 1998; Vice President, Scottish Association for Public Transport, since 1976; Lecturer, Department of Economic and Social History, Glasgow University, 1965-98, Honorary Research Fellow, since 1998; b. 15.11.39, Kilmarnock; m., Ellen Elizabeth Jones; 2 s. Educ. Spiers School, Beith; Glasgow University. Consultant on transport and environmental issues; Founder Member and Secretary, Scottish Transport Studies Group; Founder Member, Scottish Railway Development Association (Secretary, 1962-67, Vice Chairman, 1967-72); Chairman, Scottish Association for Public Transport, 1972-76; Member, Board, TRANS*form* Scotland, since 1997. Recreations: walking; travel; gardening. Address: (h.) Birchfield, Kings Road, Beith, Ayrshire KA15 2BN; T.-01505 502164; e-mail: thstsg@aol.com

Harte, Professor Ben, BA, MA, PhD(Cantab), FRSE. Professor of Metamorphism, Edinburgh University, since 1991; b. 30.5.41, Blackpool; m., Angela Elizabeth; 1 s.; 2 d. Educ. Salford Grammar School; Trinity College, Cambridge University. Lecturer/Reader, Edinburgh University, 1965-91; Guest Research Investigator, Carnegie Institution of Washington, 1974-75; Visiting Associate

Professor, Yale University, 1982; Visiting Research Fellow, University of Cape Town, 1990; JSPS Research Fellow, Ehime University, Japan, 1999. Address: (b.) Department of Geology and Geophysics, King's Buildings, Edinburgh EH9 3JW; T.-0131-650 8528; e-mail: ben.harte@glg.ed.ac.uk

Hartley, Graeme Edward, BA, MCIArb. Deputy Director, Royal Institution of Chartered Surveyors in Scotland, since 1990; b. 9.4.61, Edinburgh; m., Lee Adams Rankine; 1 s. Educ. Perth High School; Napier University. Dundee Chamber of Commerce, 1983-85; Electrical Contractors' Association of Scotland, 1985-90. Member, Scottish Building Contract Committee, since 1986; Member, Scottish Construction Industry Group. Recreations: golf; running: X-C skiing. Address: (b.) 9 Manor Place, Edinburgh EH3 7DN; T.-0131-225 7078; e-mail: ghartley@rics.org.uk

Hartley, Keith Scott, BA, MA. Chief Curator, Scottish National Gallery of Modern Art; b. 27.1.49, Evesham. Educ. Prince Henry's Grammar School, Evesham; St. Catherine's College, University of Oxford; Courtauld Institute, University of London; Freie Universität, W. Berlin. Curator of numerous exhibitions, and author of corresponding catalogues, including: Scottish Art Since 1900, 1989, Otto Dix, Tate Gallery, 1992, The Romantic Spirit in German Art 1790-1990, 1994. A Director, Art in Partnership (Scotland). Recreations: travel; reading. Address: (b.) Scottish National Gallery of Modern Art, Belford Road, Edinburgh EH4 3DR; T.-0131-624 6251.

Harvey, Professor Alan L., BSc, PhD, MBA, CBiol, FIBiol. Director, Strathclyde Institute for Drug Research, since 1988; Professor in Physiology and Pharmacology, Strathclyde University, since 1986; b. 23.6.50, Glasgow. Educ. Hutchesons', Glasgow; Strathclyde University. Lecturer in Physiology and Pharmacology, Strathclyde University, 1974-83; Senior Lecturer, 1983-86. British Pharmacological Society Sandoz Prize, 1983; Redi Award, International Society on Toxicology, 2000; British Pharmaceutical Conference Science Award, 1983. Publications: Toxicon (Editor); Advances in Drug Discovery Techniques, 1998; Natural Product Pharmaceuticals, 2001. Address: (b.) Department of Physiology and Pharmacology, Strathclyde University, Glasgow, G4 0NR; T.-0141-553 4155.

Harvey, Melanie, BA (Hons). Editor, PA Scotland, since 2000; b. 9.7.72, Liverpool; m., Jonathan Whelan. Educ. St. Bede's RC High School, Ormskirk; University of Glasgow. Liverpool Daily Post and Echo: graduate trainee, 1995, staff job, 1996; PA News: North West Reporter, 1997, Chief Scottish Reporter, 1999; Daily Mail, 1999-2000; Scottish News Editor, PA Scotland, 2000. Recreations: watching football; gym member. Address: (b.) 124 Portman Street, Kinning Park, Glasgow G41 1EJ; T.-0141-429 0037; e-mail: melanie.harvey@pa.press.net

Harvey, Rev. William John, BA (Hons), BD (Hons). Interim Minister, Church of Scotland Board of Ministry; Moderator, Glasgow Presbytery, 1998-99; b. 17.5.37, Glasgow; m., Isabel Mary Douglas; 2 s.; 2 d. Educ. Fettes College, Edinburgh; Oxford University; Glasgow University. National Service, Argyll & Sutherland Highlanders, 1956-58; Ordained Assistant, Govan Old Parish Church, 1964-66; Member, Gorbals Group Ministry, 1963-71; Minister, Laurieston-Renwick Parish Church, Glasgow, 1968-71; Warden, Iona Abbey, 1971-76; Minister: Raploch Parish Church, Stirling, 1976-81, Govan Old Parish Church, 1981-88; Leader, The Iona Community, 1988-95. Member, Church of Scotland Committee on Church and Nation, 1978-86; Kerr Lecturer, Glasgow University, 1987. Recreations: reading; history; bread and wine-making; sea-bird watching. Address: (h.) 501 Shields Road, Glasgow G41 2RF; T.-0141-429 3774; e-mail: jonmol@care4free.net

Harvey-Jamieson, Rodger Ridout, TD, LLB, MBA, WS. Partner, Murray Beith Murray WS, since 1973; b. 30.6.47, Edinburgh; m., Alison; 1 s.; 1 d. Educ. Edinburgh Academy; Edinburgh University. Trustee, Seagull Trust; Director, Fruitmarket Gallery; Member, Queen's Bodyguard for Scotland (Royal Company of Archers). Recreations: sailing; scuba diving; archery. Address: (b.) 39 Castle Street, Edinburgh EH2 3BH.

Harwood, Professor Robert Spencer, BSc, DIC, PhD, FRMetS. Professor of Atmospheric Science, Edinburgh University, since 1997; b. 7.4.42, Stoke-on-Trent; m., Bronwyn A. Harwood; 1 s.; 2 d. Educ. Longton High School; Imperial College, London. Assistant Lecturer, Imperial College, London, 1967-68; Senior Research Officer, Oxford University, 1969-76; Lecturer, Edinburgh University, 1976-97; Member of various research councils and peer review committees. Recreations: making music; piano. Address: (b.) Institute for Meteorology, Kings Buildings, Edinburgh, EHP 3JZ; T.-0131-650 5095.

Haslam, Professor Jim, BA (Hons), ACA, CA (NZ), PhD. Professor of Accountancy, Heriot-Watt University, since 1998 (Head, Division of Accountancy and Finance); b. 22.4.60, Bolton; m., Professor Sonja Gallhofer. Educ. Smithills Grammar School, Bolton; University of Sheffield; University of Essex. Ernst and Whinney, Chartered Accountants, Manchester, 1981-84 (qualified ACA, 1984); Lecturer in Accounting, University of Aston, 1984-85; Lecturer in Accounting and Finance: University College North Wales, 1985-87, London School of Economics, 1987-90; Senior Lecturer in Accounting and Finance, University of Essex, 1990-94; Professor, University of Waikato, New Zealand, 1995-98. Visiting positions: University of Dundee, 1987, University of South Australia, 1986; International Associate, Centre for Social and Environmental Accounting Research, 1996-98; Joint Editor, Pacific Accounting Review, 1996-97; Member, various editorial boards. Publications: author of numerous articles. Recreations: theatre; concerts; walking; sport. Address: (b.) Division of Accountancy and Finance, School of Management, Heriot-Watt University, Edinburgh EH14 4AS; T.-0131-451 3716; e-mail: j.haslam@hw.ac.uk

Hassan, Gerrard Lewis, MA (Hons). Director and Co-Founder, Big Thinking, since 2001; b. 21.3.64, Dundee; m., Rosemary Catherine Ilett. Educ. Rockwell High School, Dundee; Glasgow University. Writer, researcher, consultant on Scottish and UK politics and policy; former Director, Centre for Scottish Public Policy; former Parliamentary Researcher to Mike Watson, MP. Publications: The Blair Agenda (Contributor); The Moderniser's Dilemma (Contributor); The New Scotland; Scotland's Parliament: Lessons for Northern Ireland; A Guide to the Scottish Parliament; A Different Future: A Moderniser's Guide to Scotland (Co-Editor); The New Scottish Politics (Co-Editor); The Almanac of Scottish Politics (Co-author); Tomorrow's Scotland (Co-Editor). Recreations: being positive about Scotland and life; listening to Frank Sinatra records. Address: (h.) 29 Moray Place, Strathbungo, Glasgow G41 2BL; T.-0141-423 3114.

Hastings, Gavin, OBE, DUniv (Paisley). Former rugby player; Managing Director, Hastings International; b. 1962, Edinburgh. Educ. George Watson's College, Edinburgh; Paisley University; Cambridge University. 61 Scotland Caps, 1986-95 (20 as Captain); 3 World Cups, 1987, 1991, 1995; 2 British Lions Tours: 1989, Australia, 3 Tests, 1993, New Zealand (Captain), 3 Tests; Marketing Consultant, Hastings International. e-mail: hi@hastings.uk.com

Hathorn, (Alexander) Michael, CA, CPFA. Managing Partner, Scott-Moncrieff, since 1990; Chairman, Moore Stephens (UK), Ltd., since 1991; Chairman, Baillie Gifford Shin Nippon plc; b. 5.6.48, Peterborough; m., Deborah Christian; 2 s.; 1 d. Educ. Stranraer High School; Sedbergh. Joined Scott-Moncrieff Thomson-Shiells, CA (later Scott-Moncrieff), 1967: qualified 1972, Partner, 1974. Financial Advisor, Edinburgh International Festival; Trustee and Treasurer, Age Concern Scotland. Recreations: art; music. Address: (b.) 17 Melville Street, Edinburgh EH3 7PH; T.-0131-473 3500.

Hatwell, Anthony, DFA(Lond). Sculptor; Head, School of Sculpture, Edinburgh College of Art, 1969-90; b. 21.6.31, London; m., Elizabeth; 2 d. Educ. Dartford Grammar School; Slade School of Fine Art; Borough Polytechnic; Bromley College of Art. Some exhibitions: Scottish Arts Council Edinburgh Festival Exhibition, 1978; British Sculpture in the 20th Century, Whitechapel Gallery, 1981; Built in Scotland exhibition in Edinburgh, Glasgow, and London, 1983; Slade Postgraduate Scholarship, 1956; Boise Travelling Scholarship, 1957; Assistant to Henry Moore, 1958; Member, London Group, 1959-69 (Vice-President, 1961-63); works in collections of Scottish National Gallery of Modern Art, Arts Council of GB, Scottish Arts Council, Edinburgh City Art Centre, Dundee University and private collections. Address: (h.) 4 North Street, Belhaven, Dunbar, East Lothian.

Havergal, Giles Pollock, OBE, MA, DLitt (Glasgow, Strathclyde), DDra, FRSE. Director, Citizens Theatre, Glasgow, since 1969; b. 9.6.38, Edinburgh. Educ. Harrow; University of Oxford. Director, Palace Theatre, Watford, 1964-69. Awarded St. Mungo Prize, Glasgow, 1995. Address: (b.) Citizens Theatre, Gorbals, Glasgow G5 9DS; T.-0141-429 5561.

Hawkins, Anthony Donald, CBE, BSc, PhD, FSA Scot, FRSE. Director of Fisheries Research for Scotland, since 1987; Honorary Professor, Aberdeen University; b. 25.3.42, Dorset; m., Susan Mary; 1 s. Educ. Poole Grammar School; Bristol University. Entered Scottish Office as Scientific Officer, Marine Laboratory, Aberdeen, 1965; Senior Scientific Officer, 1969, Principal Scientific Officer, 1972, Senior Principal Scientific Officer, 1978, Deputy Chief Scientific Officer, 1983; Deputy Director of Fisheries Research for Scotland, 1983; conducts research into behaviour and physiology of fish; awarded A.B. Wood Medal, Institute of Acoustics, 1978; Chairman, The Green Wedge. Publications: books on fish physiology and aquarium systems. Recreations: reading; angling; soccer; breeding whippets. Address: (b.) Marine Laboratory, PO Box 101, Victoria Road, Torry, Aberdeen; T.-01224 876544; e-mail: hawkinsad@marlab.ac.uk

Hawkins, Nigel, FRSA. Director and Chief Executive, John Muir Trust, since 1996; Chairman, Prospect PR, since 1985; b. 12.9.46, Dundee. Educ. Madras College, St Andrews. Principal Founder, John Muir Trust, 1982 (Trustee, 1982-96, Director, since 1996); Creator, Dundee City of Discovery Campaign, 1985; Founder, Prospect PR Ltd, 1985; Co-Founder, The Knoydart Foundation, 1983 (Director, since 1998); Director, Knoydart Trading Ltd., since 2000; Deputy Chairman and Director, Dundee Science Centre Trust, since 1998; Director, Sensation Ltd., since 1999; Fellow, University of Abertay Dundee, 1998; President, Dundee and Tayside Chamber of Commerce and Industry, 1997-98; Board Member, North of Scotland Water Authority, since 1998. Recreations: mountaineering; cycling; running; good food. Address: (b.) 1 Auchterhouse Park, Auchterhouse, by Dundee; T.-01382 320252; e-mail: nigelhawkins@jmt.org

Hawkins, Peter, MA, PhD. Secretary CTC, Scotland, since 1997; Board Member, Transform Scotland, 1998-2001; b. 24.8.40, Heanor, Derbyshire; m., Valerie; 3s. Educ. Nottingham High School; Sidney Sussex College, Cambridge. Lecturer, Phonetics and Linguistics, Queen Margaret College, Edinburgh (retired). Volunteer youth hostel warden. Publications: Tweed Cycleway Guide; Cycling in Edinburgh and South East Scotland; Cycle Maps of Lothians. Recreations: cycling; choral singing; walking. Address: (h.) 118/1 Stenhouse Crescent, Edinburgh; T.-0131-443 6712.

Hay, Alison. Member, Argyll and Bute Council (Leader, 1999-2001); b. 5.3.52; m., John Hay; 2s. Educ. Invergordon Academy. Liberal Democrat Councillor, Argyll and Bute District Council, 1988-94; elected Strathclyde Regional Council, 1994; elected, Argyll and Bute Council, 1995; Leader of the Opposition, 1995-99 and since 2001; Member: Programme Monitoring Committee, Argyll and the Isles Enterprise Board; COSLA Strategy Forum; Scottish Low Pay Unit; Highlands and Islands Film Commission; Auchedrain Museum Trust; Mid Argyll Partnership; Mid Argyll Locality Planning Group; Chair: Group for Recycling in Argyll and Bute, Kilmartin Glen Steering Group. Recreations: walking; reading. Address: (b.) Argyll and Bute Council, Kilmory, Lochgilphead, Argyll, PA31 8RT; T.-01546 604305.

Hay, Francis (Frank) Walker Christie, OBE, DL, MA (Hons). Deputy Lieutenant, Banffshire, since 1988; Honorary Sheriff, Banff, since 1992; Honorary Vice-President, Aberdeen, Banff and Kincardine Area, Royal British Legion Scotland; b. 20.3.23, Aberdeen; m., Margaret Anne Castel; 2 s.; 1 d. Educ. Robert Gordon's College, Aberdeen; Aberdeen University. Commissioned into Reconnaissance Corps, 1943; gazetted Captain, 1947; Teacher of History, 1950-58; Special Assistant, Turriff Academy, 1958-63; Principal Teacher of History, Breadalbane Academy, Banff Academy, 1963-74; Assistant Rector, Banff Academy, 1974-88; Member, Banffshire Education Committee, 1961-75. Recreations: furniture making; Deveron Singers. Address: (h.) 11 Fife Street, Banff AB45 1JB; T.-01261 812285.

Hay, Ian, OBE, FCIBS, FFCS, FRSA, FIAM, FHS. Chairman: Scottish Association of Master Bakers, Scottish Bakery Training Council, Food Trade Association Management, Scottish Council of National Training Organisations; Director, Bakery Training Council; Member: Low Pay Commission, Board of Management, Scottish Qualifications Authority, Careers Scotland, Employment Tribunal Panel; b. 31.8.39, Aberdeen; m., Amelia Robertson; 3 s.; 1 d. Educ. Ellon Academy. Recreations: golf; football; reading; complementary medicine. Address: (b.) 4 Torphichen Street, Edinburgh EH3 8JQ; T.-0131-229 1401; e-mail: charterhall@blueyonder.co.uk

Hay, J. Iain, FRICS, IRRV. J. Iain Hay, Chartered Surveyors, since 1992; Director, KDCL Ltd., since 1992; b. 17.7.44, Ayr; m., Elizabeth; 2 d. Educ. Kelvinside Academy. Thomas Binnie & Hendry, Chartered Surveyors, 1962-66; Dunbarton County Assessors Office, 1966-69; Bovis Homes, 1969-70; Senior Surveyor, Millar Macrae and Stewart, 1970-72, Partner, 1972-86; Partner, Knight Frank & Rutley, 1986-91 (Consultant, 1991-93); Director, Montrose Estates (1982) Ltd., 1986-93; Chairman, Royal Institution of Chartered Surveyors in Scotland, 1993-94; Past President, Property Agents International; Vice President, Rent Assessment Panel for Scotland, since 1999. Recreations: golf; gardening. Address: (h.) Castle House, Drymen, Glasgow; T.-01360 660550.

Hay, James Taylor Cantlay, MBE, BSc (Hons), DTech, FInstPet, SPE, AAPG. Oil and Gas Consultant; Chairman, Scottish Sub-sea Technology Group, since 1991; Director,

Melrose Resources plc, since 1999; b. 13.6.35, Huntly; m., Mary Gordon Davidson; 1 s.; 2 d. Educ. Banchory Academy; Aberdeen University. Geologist, Iraq Petroleum Co. Ltd., Iraq, 1958-66; Head of Geology, Abu Dhabi Petroleum Co. Ltd., Abu Dhabi, 1967-71; Lecturer in Geology, Aberdeen University, 1971-74; Senior Production Geologist, Burmah Oil, London, 1974-76; various management roles, BNOC, Aberdeen and Glasgow, 1977-80; General Manager: BNOC/Britoil, Aberdeen, 1980-87, BP Exploration, Aberdeen, 1988-91. Recreations: golf; shooting. Address: (h.) 67 Fountainhall Road, Aberdeen; T.-01224 645955.

Hay, Michael James, BSc (Hons), DipEd. Head Teacher, Tynecastle High School, since 1987; b. 8.3.47, Newport Pagnell; m., Rosalind Margaret Gibling; 1 s.; 1 d. Educ. Perth Academy; Edinburgh University. Teacher of Mathematics, Royal High School, 1968-71; Principal Teacher of Mathematics: John Watson's School, 1971-73, Leith Academy, 1973-79; Assistant Head Teacher, Penicuik High School, 1979-83; Depute Head Teacher, Tynecastle High School, 1983-87. Neighbourhood Liaison Officer, City of Edinburgh Council, since 2001. Recreations: music (organist and choirmaster); hill-walking; recreational computing. Address: (b.) Tynecastle High School, McLeod Street, Edinburgh EH11 2NJ; T.-0131-337 3488.

Hay, Sheriff Robert Colquhoun, CBE, MA, LLB, WS. Sheriff Principal of North Strathclyde, 1989-98; b. 22.9.33, Glasgow; m., Olive Black; 2 s.; 2 d. Educ. Edinburgh University. Chairman, Industrial Tribunals (Scotland), 1976-81, President, 1981-89; Commissioner of Northern Lights, 1989-98, Chairman, 1992-93; Member, Sheriff Court Rules Council, 1990-95, Chairman, 1993-95; Commissioner for Clan Hay, since 1995. Address: (h.) Rocklee, Cove, Argyll G84 0NN.

Hay, Robert King Miller, BSc, MSc, PhD, FIBiol. Director, Scottish Agricultural Science Agency, since 1990; b. 19.8.46, Edinburgh; m., Dorothea Harden Vinycomb; 2 s.; 1 d. Educ. Forres Academy, Moray; Aberdeen University; University of East Anglia. AFRC Research Fellow, Edinburgh University, 1971-74; Lecturer in Crop Production: University of Malawi, 1974-76, Edinburgh University, 1976-77; Lecturer in Environmental Sciences, Lancaster University, 1977-82; Leverhulme European Fellow, Agricultural University of Norway, 1981; Head of Plant Sciences, Scottish Agricultural College, Ayr, 1982-90; British Council Research Fellow, University of Western Australia, 1989; Visiting Scientist, McGill University, Montreal, 1997. Publications: Environmental Physiology of Plants; Chemistry for Agriculture and Ecology; Introduction to the Physiology of Crop Yield; Volatile Oil Crops (Editor); Science Policies in Europe: Unity and Diversity (Editor); Science and the Scottish Parliament (Editor); Crop Production in the East of Scotland; Annals of Botany (Editor); 60 scientific papers. Recreations: walking; Nordic skiing; Lismore; music; 18th century Scotland. Address: (h.) 16 Polton Road, Lasswade EH18 1AA.

Hayes, Professor John, PhD, BSc. Professor of Molecular Carcinogenesis, Dundee University, since 1997; b. 24.12.53, Hamilton; m., Shona Isabel; 2 s. Educ. Royal High School, Edinburgh; Edinburgh University. Lecturer, then Reader, in Clinical Chemistry, Edinburgh University, 1981-92; Deputy Director, Biomedical Research Centre, Dundee University, 1992-96; Honorary Non-Clinical Scientist, Imperial Cancer Research Fund, since 2000. Member, ARA Research Grants Committee, since 1998. Recreations: salmon fishing; mountain biking; hi-fi music; church. Address: (b.) Biomedical Research Centre, Ninewells Hospital and Medical School, Dundee University, Dundee DD1 9SY; T.-01382 632788.

Hayes, Professor Peter Clive, BMSc, MBChB, MD, PhD, FRCPE. Professor of Hepatology, Edinburgh Royal Infirmary, since 1998; Director, Wellcome Trust Clinical Research Facility, since 1999; b. 19.1.57, Cheshire; m., Sharon; 2 s.; 1 d. Educ. Royal High School, Edinburgh; Dundee University. Research Fellow and Honorary Lecturer, Liver Unit, King's College Hospital, London; Lecturer in Gastroenterology and Medicine, then Senior Lecturer in Hepatology, Edinburgh Royal Infirmary. Recreations: cricket; salmon fishing. Address: (b.) Department of Internal Medicine, Royal Infirmary, Edinburgh; T.-0131-536 2236.

Hazel, Professor George McLean, BSc, MSc, PhD, CEng, MICE, FCIT, FIHT. Managing Director, McLean Hazel Ltd., since 2001; Professor of Transport Policy, Robert Gordon University, 1999-2001; b. 27.1.49, Dunfermline; m., Fiona Isabella Gault; 1 s.; 2 d. Educ. Dunfermline High School; Heriot-Watt University; Cranfield Institute of Technology. Transportation Engineer: City of Edinburgh Corporation, five years, Lothian Regional Council, four years; Lecturer, Senior Lecturer, Head of Department and Professor, Napier College/Polytechnic/University, 11 years; Director, Oscar Faber TPA, three years; Director of Transportation, Lothian Regional Council, three years; Director of City Development, City of Edinburgh Council, 1996-99. Member, Secretary of State for Scotland's Advisory Group on Sustainable Development; Chairman, Edinburgh and East of Scotland Association, Institution of Civil Engineers; Vice-President, Institution of Highways and Transportation. Recreations: golf; gardening; music; vintage cars. Address: (h.) 7 Glenlockhart Valley, Edinburgh EH14 1DE; e-mail: georgehazel@mcleanhazel.com

Heading, Robert Campbell, BSc, MD, FRCPE, FRCP. Consultant Physician, Edinburgh Royal Infirmary, since 1975; Reader in Medicine, Edinburgh University, since 1992; b. 3.7.41, Stepps, Lanarkshire; m., Patricia Mary Goldie; 2 s.; 1 d. Educ. Birkenhead School; King Edward's School, Birmingham; Edinburgh University. Address: (h.) 20 Frogston Road West, Edinburgh EH10 7AR; T.-0131-445 1552.

Heald, Professor David Albert, BA, ACMA. Professor of Accountancy, Aberdeen University, since 1990; Specialist Adviser: Treasury and Civil Service Committee, House of Commons, since 1989, Scottish Affairs Committee, House of Commons, 1980-81, 1983, 1993-96; b. 25.9.47, York; m., Yvonne Duncan. Educ. Nunthorpe Grammar School, York; Leicester University; Jordanhill College. Accountant, Raleigh Industries, 1969-70, British Steel Corporation, 1971-72; Lecturer in Economics, Glasgow College of Technology, 1972-78; Lecturer in Economics, later in Management Studies, Glasgow University, 1978-90. Labour Parliamentary candidate, Roxburgh, Selkirk and Peebles, 1979. Publications: several books, including: Making Devolution Work; Financing Devolution within the UK: a study of the lessons from failure; Public Expenditure: its defence and reform; Financing a Scottish Parliament: options for debate; and numerous articles on topics such as public expenditure, government accounting, privatisation and the Private Finance Initiative. Recreations: theatre; cinema; everything French; boating on the Moray Firth. Address: (b.) Department of Accountancy and Finance, Aberdeen University, Edward Wright Building, Aberdeen, AB24 3QY; T.-01224 272213.

Hearne, John Michael, BMus, MMus. Publisher (Longship Music); Freelance Composer and Professional Singer; Conductor and Copyist; b. 19.9.37, Reading; m., Margaret Gillespie Jarvie. Educ. Torquay Grammar School; St. Luke's College, Exeter; University College of Wales, Aberystwyth. Teaching, Rugeley, Staffordshire, 1959-60; Warehouseman/ Driver, Torquay, 1961-64; Teaching: Tonlistarskoli Borgarfjardar, Iceland, 1968-69, UCW Aberystwyth, 1969-70; Lecturer, Aberdeen College of Education, 1970-87. Composer, vocal, instrumental and incidental music: BBC commission for BBCSSO, 1990 (trumpet concerto); McEwen Commission, Glasgow University, 1979; A Legend of Margaret, commissioned to celebrate 150th anniversary of St. Margaret's School, Aberdeen, 1996; Into Unchartered Seas, commissioned to commemorate centenary of launch of Discovery on Antarctic expedition; The Ben – a Cantata for Bennachie, commissioned by Gordon Forum for the Arts, 2001; Member, John Currie Singers; Awarded Radio Forth Trophy, 1985, for most outstanding work on Edinburgh Festival Fringe; joint winner, Gregynog Composers' Award for Wales, 1992. Chorus Manager, Aberdeen International Youth Festival, since 1978; Chairman: Scottish Music Advisory Committee, BBC, 1986-90, Gordon Forum for the Arts, 1991-94; Conductor, Stonehaven and District Choral Society; Past Chairman, Scottish Society of Composers; Member, Board, National Youth Choir of Scotland; Winner, Gregynog Composers' Award for Wales, 1998; Conductor, Inverurie Choral Society; Warden, Performers and Composers Section, Incorporated Society of Musicians, 1999. Recreations: motoring and travel (1954 Daimler Roadster). Address: (h.) Smidskot, Fawells, Keith-Hall, Inverurie AB51 OLN; T.-01651 882 274.

Heatly, Sir Peter, CBE, DL, BSc, CEng, FICE. Chairman, Peter Heatly & Co. Ltd., 1958-96; b. 9.6.24, Edinburgh; m., Mae Calder Cochrane. Educ. Leith Academy; Edinburgh University. Structural Designer, Redpath Brown & Co. Ltd., 1946; Lecturer in Civil Engineering, Edinburgh University, 1948. Chairman: Scottish Sports Council, 1975-87, Commonwealth Games Federation, 1982-90, International Diving Committee, 1984-88; Master, Edinburgh Merchant Company, 1988-90; awarded Honorary Doctorate, Edinburgh University, 1992, Queen Margaret College, 1994; Honorary Doctorate, Stirling University, 1998. Recreations: swimming; gardening; travel. Address: (h.) Lanrig, Balerno, Edinburgh EH14 7AJ; T.-0131-449 3998.

Hedderwick, Alexander Mark. Managing Director, Adam & Company Investment Management, since 1989; Director, Adam & Company Group PLC, since 1992; b. 13.12.48. Hedderwick Borthwick, Stockbrokers, 1969-73; Langton Underwriting Agents, Lloyds, 1973-84. Recreations: family; gardening; bee-keeping. Address: (b.) 22 Charlotte Square, Edinburgh EH2 4DF; T.-0131-225 8484.

Hedderwick, Mairi Crawford, DA (Edin). Illustrator, Writer and Public Speaker; b. 2.5.39, Gourock; 1 s.; 1 d. Educ. St. Columba's School, Kilmacolm; Edinburgh College of Art; Jordanhill College of Education. Publications: for children: Katie Morag series, Peedie Peebles series, Carpenter MacPheigh; for adults: An Eye on the Hebrides, Highland Journey; Sea Change. Recreations: a day outside ending round a table with friends, food and wine.

Heggie, Professor Douglas Cameron, MA, PhD, FRAS, FRSE. Professor of Mathematical Astronomy, Edinburgh University, since 1994; b. 7.2.47, Edinburgh; m., Linda Jane Tennent; 2 d. Educ. George Heriot's School, Edinburgh; Trinity College, Cambridge. Research Fellow, Trinity College, Cambridge, 1972-76; Lecturer in Mathematics, Edinburgh University, 1975-85, Reader, 1985-94; Council Member, Royal Astronomical Society, 1982-85; President, Commission 37, International Astronomical Union, 1985-88; Member, Board of Editors, Monthly Notices of the RAS, since 1994. Publications: Megalithic Science; scientific papers on dynamical astronomy. Recreations: family life; walking; music. Address: (b.) Edinburgh University, Department of Mathematics and Statistics, King's Buildings, Edinburgh EH9 3JZ; T.-0131-650 5035; e-mail: d.c.heggie@ed.ac.uk

Heller, Martin Fuller Vernon, FRSAMD. Actor, since 1947; b. 20.2.27, Manchester; m., Joyce Allan; 2 s.; 4 d. Educ. Rondebosch Boys High School, Cape Town; Central School of Speech Training and Dramatic Art, London. Compass Players, 1948-52; repertory seasons and/or individual productions at following Scottish theatres: St. Andrews Byre, Edinburgh Gateway, Glasgow Citizens' (eight seasons), Edinburgh Royal Lyceum, Edinburgh Traverse, Dundee Repertory, Perth Repertory, Pitlochry Festival; Founder/Artistic Director, Prime Productions; extensive television and radio work; Member: Scottish Arts Council, 1975-82 (latterly Chairman, Drama Committee), Board, Pitlochry Festival Theatre; Governor, Royal Scottish Academy of Music and Drama, 1982-94. Recreations: politics; history; listening to music. Address: (h.) 54 Hermiston, Currie, Midlothian EH14 4AQ; T.-0131-449 4055.

Helms, Professor Peter Joseph, MB, BS, PhD, FRCP, FRCPCH. Professor of Child Health, Aberdeen University, since 1991; Consultant Paediatrician, since 1982; b. 26.6.47, Melbourne; m., Kathleen Mary; 1 s.; 3 d. Educ. Wimbledon College; Royal Free Hospital School of Medicine; London University. SHO, Hospital for Sick Children, Great Ormond Street, 1976; Lecturer in Paediatrics, Charing Cross Hospital Medical School, 1977-78; Research Fellow, Institute of Child Health, London, 1978-81, National Heart and Lung Institute, London, 1981-82; Senior Lecturer, Institute of Child Health, 1982-91; Honorary Consultant Paediatrician, Hospital for Sick Children, Great Ormond Street, 1982-91. Recreations: music; hill-walking; European history. Address: (b.) Department of Child Health, Foresterhill, Aberdeen, AB25 2ZD; T.-01224 552471.

Henderson, Andrew Kerr, MBE, MB, ChB, FRCP (Glas and Edin). Consultant Physician, Lorn and the Islands District General Hospital, Oban; Honorary Clinical Senior Lecturer, Glasgow University; b. 1.3.46, Hawick; m., Doreen Innes Wilkinson; 1 s.; 2 d. Educ. Glasgow Academy; Glasgow University. Medical Registrar, Western Infirmary, Glasgow; Medical Registrar/Senior Registrar, Glasgow Royal Infirmary. Recreations: gardening; hill-walking. Address: (h.) Birkmoss, North Connel, Argyll; T.-01631 710379; e-mail: andrewkhenderson@hemscott.net

Henderson, David A., FCCA. Group Chief Executive, Aegon UK, since 1998; Chairman, Scottish Equitable PLC, since 1999; b. 16.9.44, Edinburgh; m., Constance Mary; 1 s.; 1 d. Educ. Broughton High School. Joined Scottish Equitable, 1971; appointed to Executive, 1982; Managing Director, Life and Pensions, 1991; Managing Director, UK Operations, 1993; Managing Director, Scottish Equitable plc and Deputy Chief Excutive, 1995; Chief Executive, 1997. Member, Association of British Insurers Life Insurance Council; Member, General Purpose Council, Associated Scottish Life Offices; Chairman, Pension Advisers Support System Ltd. Recreations: walking; golf; watching soccer; reading.

Henderson, Douglas Mackay, CBE, BSc, FLS, FRSE, VMH. Queen's Botanist in Scotland, since 1987; b. 30.8.27, Blairgowrie; m., Julia Margaret Brown; 1 s.; 2 d. Educ. Blairgowrie High School; Edinburgh University. Scientific Officer, Department of Agriculture, Scotland, 1948-50; Research Botanist, Royal Botanic Garden, Edinburgh, 1950-70; Nuffield Fellow, 1967; Curator, Royal Society of Edinburgh, 1978-87; Secretary, International Association of Botanical Gardens, 1969-81; Regius Keeper, Royal Botanic Garden, Edinburgh, 1970-87; Honorary Professor, Edinburgh University, since 1982; Administrator, Inverewe Garden, National Trust for Scotland, 1987-92; Council Member, National Trust for Scotland, since 1993; Secretary, Help the Aged Highland Committee.

Recreations: natural history; painting; sailing; cooking. Address: (h.) Larachan, 54 Lonemore, Gairloch, Ross-shire IV21 2DB; T.-01445 2391.

Henderson, Fiona, BA. Presenter/Reporter, BBC Reporting Scotland, since 1992; b. 26.6.63, Londonderry; m., David Nisbet; 1 s.; 1 d. Educ. Foyle College, N. Ireland; Stirling University. Radio Reporter/Producer, BBC N. Ireland, 1986-87; Researcher, TV News and Current Affairs, BBC Scotland, 1987-88; Presenter, BBC TV News, BBC Scotland, 1988-90; Presenter/Reporter, Inside Ulster, BBC N. Ireland, 1988-90; News and Current Affairs, BBC Scotland since 1991. Recreations: her family; architecture; Edinburgh; riding; reading; making sticky buns. Address: Newsroom, BBC Scotland, Queen Margaret Drive, Glasgow; e-mail: fiona.henderson.01@bbc.co.uk

Henderson, James. Registrar of Companies for Scotland, since 1992; b. 22.11.48, Kilmarnock; m., Patricia Mazs; 2 d. Educ. Kilmarnock Academy. Joined the Queen's and Lord Treasurer's Remembrancer, 1967; Department of Trade and Industry, 1981; became Companies House DTI's first agency, 1988. Recreations: bowls; rugby (spectating); reading; gardening. Address: (b.) 37 Castle Terrace, Edinburgh EH1 2EB; T.-0131-535 5855.

Henderson, John, BSc (Hons) Agric, CBiol, MIBiol. Assistant Chief Agricultural Officer, Scottish Executive Environment and Rural Affairs Department, since 1996; b. 9.4.47, Seaham Harbour; m., Alma; 1 step-s.; 2 d. Educ. Grangefield Grammar School, Stockton-on-Tees; Leeds University. Assistant Lands Officer, DAFS, Glasgow, 1970-75; Lands Officer, Crofters Commission, Inverness, 1975-80; Senior Lands Officer, DAFS, Ayr, 1980-84; Principal Agricultural Officer, SOAEFD, Kirkwall, Edinburgh, Galashiels, 1984-96. Chairman, Scottish Biodiversity Agriculture Working Group. Recreations: sporting related; gardening; wildlife. Address: (h.) Jeansburn House, Ettrickbridge, Selkirk TD7 5JN; T.-01750 52335.

Henderson, John Gunn, BA, FRSA. Project Director, EURO 2008 Bid, Scottish Football Association (on secondment from the Scottish Executive), since 2001; b. 29.5.53, Edinburgh; m., Caroline; 1 s.; 2 d. Educ. Broughton Secondary, Edinburgh; Open University. Scottish Development Department, 1970-78; Department of Agriculture and Fisheries for Scotland, 1978-85; Scottish Development Department, Trunk Roads Division, 1985-88; Scottish Office Education and Industry Department, 1988-97 (Head, Further Education Funding Unit, 1992-97); Assistant Director of Finance and Head, Private Finance Unit, 1997-2001. Recreations: reading; gardening; beachcombing. Address: (b.) Scottish Football Association, Hampden Park, Glasgow G42 9AY; T.-0141-616 6090; e-mail: John.Henderson@scottishfa.co.uk

Henderson, Meg. Author, Journalist and Scriptwriter; b. 1948, Glasgow; m., Rab; 1 s.; 2 d. Educ. Garnethill Convent Secondary School (reluctantly). Chief Cardiology Technician, Western Infirmary and Royal Infirmary, Glasgow; VSO, India; spent years fostering children; has worked for the broadsheets, Daily Mail, BBC, Channel 4. Publications: Finding Peggy, 1994; The Holy City, 1997; Bloody Mary, 1998; Chasing Angels, 2000; The Last Wanderer, 2002. Recreations: reading, history, walking, radio, peace and quiet, golf, tennis, F1 racing (without having the slightest aptitude for any of them); shouting at politicians on television (or wherever encountered). Address: c/o Karen Duffy, Flamingo Publicity, HarperCollins Publishers, 77-85 Fulham Palace Road, London W6 8JB.

Henderson, Major Richard Yates, TD, JP, BA (Oxon), LLB. Lord Lieutenant, Ayrshire and Arran, since 1991; b. 7.7.31, Nitshill; m., Frances Elizabeth Chrystal; 3 s. (inc. 1 s. dec.); 1 d. Educ. Rugby; Hertford College, Oxford;

Glasgow University. Royal Scots Greys, 1950-52; TA Ayrshire (ECO) Yeomanry, 1953-69 (Major); Deputy Lieutenant, Ayrshire and Arran, 1970-90; Partner, Mitchells Roberton, Solicitors, 1958-90, Consultant, 1991-92. Brigadier, Queen's Bodyguard for Scotland (Royal Company of Archers); President, Lowland TAVRA, 1996-2000; Hon. Colonel, Ayrshire Yeomanry Sqn., Scottish Yeomanry, 1992-97; Honorary Sheriff, South Strathclyde Dumfries and Galloway at Ayr, since 1997. Recreations: shooting; tennis; golf. Address: (h.) Blairston, by Ayr; T.-01292 441601.

Henderson, Robert Ewart, QC, LLB. Queen's Counsel, since 1982; b. 29.3.37, Glasgow; m., Carolyn Gell; 2 s.; 3 d. Educ. Larchfield School, Helensburgh; Morrison's Academy, Crieff; Glasgow University. National Service, 1956-58 (2nd Lt., RA); admitted, Faculty of Advocates, 1963; Honorary Sheriff-Substitute, Stirling, Dumbarton and Clackmannan, 1968; Standing Junior Counsel in Scotland, Department of Trade and Industry, 1970-74, Department of Trade, 1974-77; Temporary Sheriff, 1978; Chairman, Medical Appeal Tribunal, 1985-95; Chairman, War Pensions Appeal Tribunal, since 1985. Conservative Parliamentary Candidate, Invernesshire, February and October, 1974. Recreations: golf; fishing. Address: The Old Schoolhouse, East Links Road, Gullane, East Lothian EH31 2AF; T.-01620 842012; e-mail: hendersonqc@hotmail.com

Henderson-Howat, David Barclay, BSc, MA, MBA. Chief Conservator, Forestry Commission, Scotland, since 1996; b. 23.1.54, Trinidad; m., Jean Buchanan-Smith; 1 s.; 3 d. Educ. Abingdon School; University of Edinburgh; Magdalene College, University of Cambridge; University of Strathclyde. Scottish Office, 1976-79; Personal Assistant to Chief Executive, Scottish Development Agency, 1979-80; Harvesting and Marketing Manager, Thetford Forest, 1980-84; Forest Manager, Shiselweni Forest, Swaziland, 1984-86; Forest District Manager, Aberfoyle, Perthshire, 1986-90; Forestry Commission Headquarters, 1990-96. Member, Lamancha, Newlands and Kirkurd Community Council, 1992-95, and since 2000. Recreations: walking; sailing. Address: (b.) Forestry Commission, 231 Corstorphine Road, Edinburgh EH12 7AR; T.-0131-314 6162.

Hendry, Alan. Editor: John O'Groat Journal, since 1988, Caithness Courier, since 1988; b. 26.3.62, Wick; m., Yvonne; 2 s. Educ. Wick High School; Aberdeen College of Commerce. Address: (b.) 42 Union Street, Wick, Caithness KW1 5ED; T.-01955 602424; e-mail: editor@nosn.co.uk

Hendry, Professor Alan, BSc (Hons), PhD, CEng, FIM, MInstP, CPhys, FRSA. Dean, Faculty of Engineering, Strathclyde University; b. 29.1.47, Ochiltree; m., Jean Carey Kerr; 1 s.; 1 d. Educ. Cumnock Academy; Strathclyde University. Postdoctoral Research Associate, Newcastle University, 1971-75; Research Officer, Midlands Region, CEGB, 1975-76; Lecturer in Metallurgy and Assistant Director, Wolfson Research Group for High Strength Materials, Newcastle University, 1976-85; Strathclyde University: Reader in Ceramics, 1985-88, Professor of Metallurgy and Engineering Materials, since 1988, Head of Department of Metallurgy and Engineering Materials, 1990-96; Vice-Dean (Engineering), 1996-97. President, Scottish Association for Metals, 1990-92; Member, Materials Commission, SERC, 1989-92, Materials College, EPSRC, since 1994; Chairman, Engineering Education Association; Member, International Academy of Ceramics; Allan B. Dove Medal, Wire Assoc. Int., 1993. Address: (h.) Ardleven, 23 Campbell Drive, Bearsden, Glasgow G61 4NF; T.-0141-942 3169.

Hendry, Professor Arnold William, BSc, PhD, DSc, FICE, FIStructE, FRSE. Professor Emeritus, University of Edinburgh, since 1988; President, Scottish Association for Public Transport; b. 10.9.21, Buckie; m., 1, Sheila Mary

Cameron Roberts (deceased); 2, Elizabeth Lois Alice Inglis; 1 s.; 1 s. deceased; 1 d. Educ. Buckie High School; Aberdeen University. Civil Engineer, Sir Wm. Arrol & Co. Ltd., Glasgow, 1941-43; Lecturer, University of Aberdeen, 1943-49; Reader, King's College, University of London, 1949-51; Professor of Civil Engineering and Dean, Faculty of Engineering, University of Khartoum, 1951-57; Professor of Building Science, University of Liverpool, 1957-63; Professor of Civil Engineering, University of Edinburgh, 1964-88. Member, Transport Committee, Cockburn Association. Publications: nine books; over 150 papers on structural engineering. Recreations: walking; reading; travel. Address: (h.) 146/6 Whitehouse Loan, Edinburgh EH9 2AN; T.-0131-447 0368; e-mail: awhendry@waitrose.com

Hendry, Joy McLaggan, MA (Hons), DipEd. Editor, Chapman Magazine, since 1972; Writer; b. 3.2.53, Perth; m., Ian Montgomery. Educ. Perth Academy; Edinburgh University. Former teacher; Co-Editor, Chapman, 1972-76, Sole Editor, since 1976; Deputy Convener, Scottish Poetry Library Association, 1983-88; Convener, Committee for the Advancement of Scottish Literature in Schools; Member AdCas; Scottish National Theatre Steering Committee; Campaign for a Scottish Assembly; Member, Drama Committee, Scottish Arts Council; Chair, Scottish Actors Studio, 1993-2000; Member, Literature Forum for Scotland; Member, Scottish Parliament Scots Language Cross-Party Group; Lecturer (drama), Queen Margaret University College; poet and playwright; gives lectures and talks and performances of poetry and song; radio critic, The Scotsman, 1988-97; theatre reviewer; Writer-in-Residence, Stirling District Council, 1991-93. Publications: Scots: The Way Forward; Poems and Pictures by Wendy Wood (Editor); The Land for the People (Co-Editor); Critical Essays on Sorley MacLean (Co-Editor); Critical Essays on Norman MacCaig (Co-Editor); Gang Doun wi a Sang (play); radio: The Wa' at the World's End, Radio 3 (play); A Many-Faceted Thing (Memory), Radio 4 (major 4-part series). Recreations: going to theatre; cinema; reading. Address: 4 Broughton Place, Edinburgh EH1 3RX; T.-0131-557 2207.

Hendry, Professor Leo Brough, MSc, MEd, PhD, DLitt, FBPS, FECSS. Professor of Education, Aberdeen University, 1989-2001, Emeritus Professor, since 2001; Professor, Norwegian Centre for Child Research, and the Psychology Institute, Norwegian University of Science and Technology, Trondheim; b. 12.11.35, Glasgow; m., Philomena Walsh; 2 d. Educ. Hermitage Academy, Helensburgh; Jordanhill College of Education, Glasgow; Bradford University; Leicester University; Aberdeen University. School Teacher in Scottish and English schools, including two posts as Head of Department, 1957-64; Lecturer in Education and Physical Education, College of St. Mark and St. John's, Chelsea, London University Institute, 1964-66; Head of Human Movement Studies, Trinity and All Saints' Colleges, Leeds University Institute, 1966-71; Lecturer in Education, then Senior Lecturer, Aberdeen University, 1971-88; Head, Education Department, 1988-94; Member, Scottish Council for Research in Education, 1983-86. Publications: School, Sport, Leisure: three dimensions of adolescence, 1978; Adolescents and Leisure, 1981; Growing Up and Going Out, 1983; Personality and Performance in Physical Education and Sport (Co-Author), 1974; Physical Education in England (Co-Author), 1976; Towards Community Education (Co-Author), 1980; The Nature of Adolescence (Co-Author), 1990; Young People's Leisure and Lifestyles (Co-Author), 1993; Educating for Health (Co-Author), 1995; New Perspectives on Youth Disaffection (Co-Author), 1997; Growing Up, Speaking Out (Co-Author), 1998; Lifespan Development: Resources, Challenges and Risks (Co-Author), 2002; book chapters; research articles. Recreations: golf; writing; broadcasting; presenting papers at international conferences. Address: (b.) Centre for Educational Research, Department of Sociology, Aberdeen University, Aberdeen AB24 3QY; T.-01224 272731.

Hendry, Stephen, MBE. Professional snooker player; b. 13.1.69; m., Mandy. Youngest-ever Scottish Amateur Champion (aged 15); has won 72 major titles worldwide; youngest player to attain No. 1 ranking; youngest player to win World Championship, 1990; World Champion seven times; UK Champion, five times; Masters Champion, six times. Address: (b.) 110 Sport Ltd., Kerse Road, Stirling, FK7 7SG; T.-01786 462634.

Henley, Professor John Sebastian, BSc(Eng), PhD, FRSA. Professor of International Management, University of Edinburgh Management School; b. 5.4.43, Malvern; m., Sarah J. Sieley; 2 d. Educ. King Edward's School, Birmingham; University College, London; London School of Economics. Personnel Officer, Glaxo Laboratories, 1966-68; Lecturer, Industrial Relations Department, London School of Economics, 1968-72; Lecturer, Faculty of Commerce, University of Nairobi, 1972-75; joined Department of Business Studies, University of Edinburgh, 1975. Publications: co-author of three books; editor of two books; author of over 50 academic papers. Recreations: gardening; theatre; opera; sailing. Address: (b.) University of Edinburgh Management School, 50 George Square, Edinburgh EH8 9JY; T.-0131-650 3814; e-mail: J.Henley@ed.ac.uk

Henley, Rt. Rev. Michael Harry George, CB, LTh. Episcopal Bishop of St. Andrews, Dunkeld and Dunblane, since 1995; b. 16.1.38; m.; 2 d. Educ. University of London St. John's Hall. Deacon, 1961; Priest, 1962; Curate, St. Marylebone, London, 1960-64; Anglican Chaplain, St. Andrews University, 1968-72; Chaplain, RN, 1964-68 and 1972-89; Chaplain of Fleet, DG, Naval Chaplaincy, Archdeacon for RN, 1989-93; Archdeacon Emeritus of the Fleet, 1994; Locum, Diocese of St. Andrews, 1993-94. Address: 28a Balhousie Street, Perth PH1 5HJ; T.-01738 643000.

Henry, Hugh. MSP (Labour), Paisley South, since 1999; Deputy Minister for Health and Community Care; former Convener, European Committee; b. 1952, Glasgow; m.; 1 s.; 2 d. Leader, West Renfrewshire Council, 1995-99. Address: (b.) Scottish Parliament, Edinburgh EH99 1SP; T.-0131-348 5928.

Henry, Captain Michael Charles, RN (Rtd.), DL. Deputy Lieutenant, Dunbartonshire, since 1989; Director, Merchants House of Glasgow, 1990-96, and since 2000; b. 4.6.28, London; m., Nancie Elma Nicol; 2 s.; 3 d. Educ. Royal Naval College, Dartmouth. Naval career, Cadet to Captain, 1942-78; submarine specialist; commanded HM Submarines Seraph, Trump and Resolution, Britain's first Polaris submarine; fired first British missile, Cape Canaveral, and conducted first deterrent patrol, 1968; commanded 10th (Polaris) Submarine Squadron, Faslane, and Queen's Harbour Master, Clyde, 1972-74; commanded HMS Hampshire, 1975-76; Director of Naval Operations and Trade, 1976-78; Marine Manager, British National Oil Corporation, Aberdeen, 1978-80; Naval Regional Officer Scotland and Northern Ireland, Glasgow, 1980-90. Recreation: sailing. Address: (h.) Aldavhu, Garelochhead, Helensburgh G84 0EL; T.-01436 810533.

Henshelwood, James, SBStJ, JP, FISMM, MCIM, MInstM, AMNI, FFCS. Director, Glasgow Building Preservation Trust, since 1982; Member, St. John Association of Scotland; Member, Central Advisory Committee on Justices of the Peace; b. 18.2.22, Glasgow; m., Mavis Irene Watson (deceased); 3 s.; 2 d. Educ. Allan Glen's School; Whitehill Senior Secondary School; Royal Technical College, Glasgow. Joined Merchant Navy as cadet, 1938, and "swallowed the anchor" in 1953 as Master

Mariner; Special Services, RNR; Independent Councillor, Johnstone, 1966-69 (Burgh Treasurer); President, Chartered Institute of Marketing, West of Scotland Branch; Past Chairman, Nautical Institute, West of Scotland; Governor, RNLI; Chairman, Scottish Pre-Retirement Council; Past President, Glasgow Bute Benevolent Society; former Director, Glasgow Chamber of Commerce; former Captain, Bute Golf Club. Recreations: golf; sailing; walking. Address: (h.) 72 Globe Court, Calderwood, East Kilbride, Glasgow G74 3QZ; T.-013552 38851.

Henton, Margaret Patricia, BSc, CGeol, PPCIWEM, MInstWM, FGS. Chief Executive, Scottish Environment Protection Agency, since 2000; b. 30.10.49, Edinburgh; m., Richard Henton; 1 s.; 1 d. Educ. George Watson's College, Edinburgh; Manchester University. Geologist, Blue Circle Cement, 1970-71; Hydrogeologist, Clyde River Purification Board, 1972-75; Geologist, National Coal Board, 1975; Hydrologist, Forth River Purification Board, 1975-83; Regional Manager, Aspinwall & Co., 1983-89; Director Scotland and N. Ireland, Aspinwall & Co., 1989-95; Director of Environmental Strategy, Scottish Environment Protection Agency, 1995-2000. President, Chartered Institution of Water and Environmental Management, 1996-97; Council Member, Natural Environment Research Council, 1998-2001; Member, Water Panel, Competition Commission, 1998-2000. Recreations: travel; hill-walking; ornithology. Address: (b.) Erskine House, Castle Business Park, Stirling FK9 4TR; T.-01786 457700.

Herald, Sheriff John Pearson, LLB, NP, SSC. Sheriff of North Strathclyde at Greenock and Rothesay, since 1992; b. 12.7.46, Glasgow; m., Catriona; 1 d. Educ. Hillhead High School, Glasgow; Glasgow University. Partner, Carlton Gilruth, Solicitors, Dundee, 1970-91; Depute Town Clerk, Newport-on-Tay, 1970-75; Member, Angus Legal Aid Committee, 1970-79, Secretary, 1979-87; Member, Legal Aid Central Committee, 1981-87; Temporary Sheriff, 1984-91; part-time Chairman, Industrial Tribunals, 1984-91. Chairman, Dundee Citizens Advice Bureau, 1972-79 and 1982-91; President, Rotary Club of North Fife, 1989. Recreations: football; golf; reading. Address: (b.) Sheriff Court House, Nelson Street, Greenock; T.-01475 787073.

Herbert, Professor Rodney Andrew, BSc, PhD, CBiol, FIBiol, FRSE. Professor of Microbiology, Dundee University, since 1992; b. 27.6.44, York; m., Helen Joyce Macpherson Millard; 2 s. Educ. Archbishop Holgate's Grammar School, York; Bradford University; Aberdeen University. Research Fellow, Edinburgh University, 1970-71; Lecturer/Reader in Microbiology, Dundee University, 1971-92. General Secretary, Society for General Microbiology, 1989-94; President, Society for Applied Microbiology, 1997-99; Senior Visiting Scientist: British Antarctic Survey, 1976-77, Ross Sea, Antarctica, 1982-83. Recreations: music; walking; gardening. Address: (b.) Division of Environmental and Applied Biology, Biological Sciences Institue, Dundee University, Dundee DD1 4HN; T.-Dundee 23181, Ext. 4262.

Herd, Dr Robert Montgomery, MSc, MD, FRCP(Edin). Consultant Dermatologist, Western Infirmary, Glasgow, since 1999; b. 10.4.53, Glasgow; 1 d. Educ. Linlithgow Academy; Edinburgh University. Fellowship, Harvard University, in Lasers and Skin Surgery, 1996-97. Recreations: golf; skiing. Address: (h.) Bennan Farm, Loganswell, Glasgow G77 6SB; T.-01355 500278.

Herdman, John Macmillan, MA (Hons), PhD (Cantab), DipTh. Writer, since 1963; b. 20.7.41, Edinburgh. Educ. Merchiston Castle School, Edinburgh; Magdalene College, Cambridge. Creative Writing Fellow, Edinburgh University, 1977-79; Scottish Arts Council bursaries, 1976, 1982, 1998; Scottish Arts Council Book Awards, 1978 and 1993;

Hawthornden Writer's Fellowship, 1989 and 1995; William Soutar Fellowship, 1990-91. Publications: Descent, 1968; A Truth Lover, 1973; Memoirs of My Aunt Minnie/ Clapperton, 1974; Pagan's Pilgrimage, 1978; Stories Short and Tall, 1979; Voice Without Restraint: Bob Dylan's Lyrics and Their Background, 1982; Three Novellas, 1987; The Double in Nineteenth Century Fiction, 1990; Imelda and Other Stories, 1993; Ghostwriting, 1996; Cruising (play), 1997; Poets, Pubs, Polls and Pillar Boxes, 1999; Four Tales, 2000; The Sinister Cabaret, 2001. Recreations: reading; walking; listening to music. Address: (h.) Roselea, Bridge of Tilt, Blair Atholl, Perthshire; T.-01796 481437.

Heron, Garth McAllen Drennan, BA, FIPM, FRSA. Managing Partner, Garth Heron Search and Consultancy, since 1995; b. 21.5.49, Belfast; m., Louise Dick; 1 s.; 1 d. Educ. Friend's School, Lisburn; Queen's University, Belfast; Strathclyde University. Personnel Officer, United Dominions Trust Ltd., 1971-73; Personnel Manager: Alcan Aluminium Ltd., 1973-76, Bourns Ltd., Fife, 1976-78; Personnel Director, Honeywell Ltd., Bracknell, 1978-87; General Manager, Personnel Division, Clydesdale Bank, 1987-93; Personnel Director, United Distillers, 1993-95. Governor, Merchiston Castle School, Edinburgh; Elder, Cramond Kirk. Recreations: family; church; sports; cinema. Address: (b.) 4 Wemyss Place, Edinburgh EH3 6DH.

Herron, Very. Rev. Andrew, ATCL, MA, BD, LLB, DD, LLD. Moderator, General Assembly of Church of Scotland, 1971; b. 29.9.09, Glasgow; m., Joanna Fraser Neill; 4 d. Educ. Strathbungo H.G. School; Albert Road Academy; Glasgow University and Trinity College. Minister: Linwood, 1936-40, Houston and Killellan, 1940-59; Clerk, Glasgow Presbytery, 1959-81. Baird Lecturer, 1985; William Barclay Lecturer, 1989. Publications: Record Apart, 1972; Guide to the General Assembly, 1976; Guide to Congregational Affairs, 1979; Guide to the Presbytery, 1982; Kirk by Divine Right, 1985; Guide to the Ministry, 1987; Guide to Ministerial Income, 1987; The Law and Practice of the Kirk, 1950; Minority Report, 1990; Inter Alia, 1995.

Hewitt, Professor David S., MA, PhD, FEA, FRSE. Professor in Scottish Literature, Aberdeen University, since 1994 (Reader, 1991-94); b. 22.4.42, Hawick; m., Angela Catherine Williams; 1 s.; 1 d. Educ. Melrose Grammar School; George Watson's College, Edinburgh; Edinburgh University; Aberdeen University. Aberdeen University: Assistant Lecturer in English, 1964, Lecturer, 1968, Senior Lecturer, 1982; Treasurer, Association for Scottish Literary Studies, 1973-96; Editor-in-Chief, Edinburgh Edition of the Waverley Novels, 1984; President, Edinburgh Sir Walter Scott Club, 1988-89; Honorary Member, Association for Scottish Literary Studies, 1996; Elder, Cathedral Church of St. Machar, Old Aberdeen; Managing Editor, New Writing Scotland, 1983-86. Publications: Scott on Himself (Editor), 1982; Literature of the North, 1983; Scott and His Influence, 1984; Longer Scottish Poems, Vol. 2 1650-1830, 1987; Scott in Carnival, 1993; The Antiquary, 1995; Northern Visions, 1996; The Edinburgh Edition of the Waverley Novels: A Guide for Editors, 1996; Redgauntlet, 1997; The Heart of Mid-Lothian, 2002. Address: (b.) Department of English, Aberdeen University, Aberdeen AB24 3UB; T.-01224 273777; e-mail: d.s.hewitt@abdn.ac.uk

Heys, Professor Steven Darryll, BMedBiol, MB, ChB, MD, PhD, FRCS(Glas), FRCS(Ed), FRCS(Eng). Professor of Surgical Oncology, University of Aberdeen, since 1999; Director, Surgical Nutrition and Metabolism Unit, University of Aberdeen, since 1995; Consultant Surgeon, Aberdeen Royal Infirmary, since 1992; Honorary Research Fellow, Rowett Research Institute, since 1992; b. 5.7.56, Accrington; m., Margaret Susan Proctor; 2 s.; 1 d. Educ. St. Mary's College, Blackburn; Aberdeen University Medical School. House Officer/SHO, Surgery, Aberdeen Royal Infirmary, 1981-84; Registrar, Grampian Health Board, 1984-87; Wellcome Research Training Fellow, Rowett Research Institute, 1987-89; Lecturer in Surgery, Aberdeen University, 1989-92; Senior Lecturer, 1992-96, Reader, 1996-99. Examiner in Surgery, Royal College of Surgeons of Glasgow; External Examiner in Surgery, Royal College of Surgeons of England. Publications: numerous scientific papers on aspects of breast cancer, oncology, nutrition and metabolism; book chapters on nutrition, metabolism, oncology. Recreations: karate; hill-walking; golf. Address: (b.) University Medical Buildings, Foresterhill, Aberdeen AB9 2ZD.

Heywood, Barry Keith, MA, LLB. Regional Procurator Fiscal, Dundee, since 1991; b. 24.7.46, Oldham; m., Mary A.; 1 s.; 1 d. Educ. Kirkcaldy High School; Edinburgh University. Procurator Fiscal Depute, Ayr, 1971-77, Glasgow, 1977-78; Procurator Fiscal, Wick, 1978-83; Assistant Procurator Fiscal, Glasgow, 1983-86; Procurator Fiscal, Inverness, 1986-91. Recreations: walking; Roman and Byzantine history; "railway buff". Address: (b.) Caledonian House, Greenmarket, Dundee DD1 1QX.

Heywood, Peter. Director, The Living Tradition Ltd., publisher, since 1993; Director, National Folk Festival, Scotland, since 2001; b. 4.10.49, Manchester; m., Heather; 3 d. Educ. Heywood Grammar School. Long involvement with traditional music; founded The Tradition Bearers, recording traditional musicians, 1999; founded Common Ground on the Hill, Scotland, 2001. Recreations: traditional music; hill-walking. Address: (b.) The Living Tradition, PO Box 1026, Kilmarnock KA2 0LG; T.-01563 571220.

Hickman, Richard Michael, BA (Hons), MA, DipTP, MRTPI. Chief Inquiry Reporter, since 1997; b. 30.4.42, Beckenham; m., Sandie Randall; 3 s.; 1 d. Educ. Kingswood School, Bath; London School of Economics; University of British Columbia. Work in town and country planning for London County Council, Greater London Council, Lower Mainland Regional Planning Board (British Columbia), Scottish Development Department; Scottish Office Inquiry Reporters Unit, since 1979. Recreations: walking; cycling; sailing. Address: (b.) 2 Greenside Lane, Edinburgh EH1 3AG; T.-0131-244 5644.

Higgins, Sheriff Colin Kirk, LLB. Sheriff of North Strathclyde at Paisley, since 1990; b. 9.11.45, Slough; m., Anne Marie McMahon; 1 s.; 2 d. Educ. St. Patrick's High School, Coatbridge; Glasgow University. Law Apprentice, Coatbridge, 1967-69; Legal Assistant, Coatbridge, 1969-70; Legal Assistant, James Bell & Sons, 1970-73; Partner, Bell, Russell & Co., 1973-90. Dean, Airdrie Society of Solicitors, 1989-90. Recreations: reading; travel; tennis; theatre. Address (b.) Court House, St. James' Street, Paisley; T.-041-887 5291.

Higgins, Roisin Anne, LLB (Hons). Advocate, since 2000; b. 13.5.72, Bellshill. Educ. Fernhill School, Rutherglen; St Aloysius' College, Glasgow; Glasgow University. Trainee Solicitor, Maclay Murray and Spens, Edinburgh, 1995-97; Solicitor, McGrigor Donald, Edinburgh, 1997-99; devil, 1999-2000. Member, European Committee, Faculty of Advocates; Member, Commercial Law Group Committee. Address: (b.) Advocates' Library, Parliament House, Parliament Square, Edinburgh EH1 1RF; T.-0131-226 5071.

Higgs, Professor Peter Ware, BSc, MSc, PhD, FRS, FRSE, HonFInstP, DSc (Hon). Professor of Theoretical Physics, Edinburgh University, 1980-96; b. 29.5.29, Newcastle-upon-Tyne; m., Jo Ann Williamson; 2 s. Educ. Cotham Grammar School, Bristol; King's College, London. Postdoctoral Fellow, Edinburgh University, 1954-56, and London University, 1956-58; Lecturer in Mathematics, University College, London, 1958-60; Lecturer in

Mathematical Physics, then Reader, Edinburgh University, 1960-80. Hughes Medal, Royal Society, 1981; Rutherford Medal, Institute of Physics, 1984; James Scott Prize, Royal Society of Edinburgh, 1993; Paul Dirac Medal and Prize, Institute of Physics, 1997; High Energy and Particle Physics Prize, European Physical Society, 1997; Royal Medal, Royal Society of Edinburgh, 2000. Recreations: music; walking; swimming. Address: (h.) 2 Darnaway Street, Edinburgh EH3 6BG; T.-0131-225 7060.

Higham, Professor Des, BSc (Hons), MSc, PhD. Professor of Mathematics, Strathclyde University, since 1999; b. 17.2.64, Salford; m., Catherine; 1 s.; 1 d. Educ. Manchester University. Member, Grove Park Feuer's Association. Address: (b.) Strathclyde University, Livingstone Tower, 26 Richmond Tower, Glasgow G1 1XH.

Hill, Andrew. Leader, South Ayrshire Council, since 2000; Board Member, Ayr Town Centre Management Initiative, since 1999; Board Member, Scottish Enterprise Ayrshire, since 2000; Board Member, Ayr Locality Enterprise Resources Trust Ltd., since 1999; b. 17.4.37; m., Helen; 1 s.; 1 d. Educ. Lambhill Street Secondary School; Stow College, Glasgow. Vice-President, NUPE, 1987-88; Strathclyde Regional Councillor, 1990-96; South Ayrshire Councillor, since 1996. Recreations: bowls; golf; football. Address: (b.) South Ayrshire Council, County Buildings, Wellington Square, Ayr; T.-01292 612390.

Hill, Professor Malcolm, PhD. Professor for the Child and Family (formerly Professor of Social Work), University of Glasgow; Director, Centre for the Child and Society, since 1995; b. 18.9.46, London; m., Dr. Wan Ying Hill; 1 s.; 1 d. Educ. Latymer Upper School, Hammersmith; St. Edmund Hall, Oxford; University of London; University of Edinburgh. Social Worker, 1968-79; Researcher, 1979-84; Lecturer, 1985-93; Senior Lecturer, 1993-96. Publications: books on adoption, child care, family support, teenagers, middle childhood, children and society. Recreations: bridge; gardening; swimming. Address: (b.) Lilybank House, Bute Gardens, Glasgow G12 8RT; T.-0141-330 4056.

Hill, Professor Nicholas A., BSc, ARCS, MSc, PhD, DIC. Simson Professor of Mathematics, Glasgow University, since 2001; b. 10.1.59, Walsall; m., Dr Xiaoyu Luo. Educ. St Austell College; Imperial College, London; University of East Anglia. Lecturer, then Senior Lecturer, Department of Applied Mathematics, Leeds University, 1989-2001. Address: (b.) Department of Mathematics, Glasgow University, University Gardens, Glasgow G12 8QW; T.-0141-330 5176.

Hill, Professor William George, BSc, MS, PhD, DSc, FRSE, FRS. Professor of Animal Genetics, Edinburgh University, since 1983; Dean and Provost, Faculty of Science and Engineering, since 1999; b. 7.8.40, Hemel Hempstead; m., C. Rosemary Austin; 1 s.; 2 d. Educ. St. Albans School; London University; University of California; Iowa State University; Edinburgh University. Edinburgh University: Assistant Lecturer, 1965-67, Lecturer, 1967-74, Reader, 1974-83, Head, Department of Genetics, 1989-90, Institute of Cell, Animal and Population Biology, 1990-93, and Division of Biological Sciences, 1993-98; Visiting Research Associate, Iowa State University, 1967-68-69-72; Visiting Professor: University of Minnesota, 1966, Iowa State University, 1978, North Carolina State University, 1979, since 1985; Consultant Geneticist: Cotswold Pig Development Co., 1965-99, Holstein Friesian Society, 1978-98; Editor, Genetical Research, since 1996; Member: AFRC Animals Research Grant Board, 1986-92, Director's Advisory Group, AFRC Animal Breeding Research Organisation, 1982-86, AFRC Institute of Animal Physiology and Genetics Research, 1986-93, Governing Council, Roslin Institute, since 1994,

Council, Royal Society, 1993-94, Commonwealth Scholarships Commission, since 1998, RAE Panel, 2001 (Chairman); British Society of Animal Science: Vice-President, 1997-99, President, 1999-00. Recreations: farming; bridge. Address: (h.) 4 Gordon Terrace, Edinburgh EH16 5QH; T.-0131-667 3680.

Hillan, Professor Edith Margaret, PhD, MSc, MPhil, DipLSc, RGN, RSCN, RM. Professor of Midwifery, University of Glasgow, since 1998; b. 26.6.58, Johnstone; m., Professor J. Stewart Aitchison; 2 s. Educ. Paisley Grammar School; Queen Margaret College; University of Strathclyde; University of Glasgow. Sister, Midwifery/Research, Royal Maternity Hospital, Glasgow, 1980-83; University of Glasgow: SODoH Research Fellow, Department of Nursing Studies, 1983-86, Lecturer, Department of Nursing Studies, 1986-92, Senior Lecturer, Nursing and Midwifery Studies, 1992-98. Member, Council, Royal College of Midwives, since 1998; Chair, Board of Trustees, Iolanthe Midwifery Research Trust. Recreations: good wine, food and conversation. Address: Nursing and Midwifery School, University of Glasgow, Glasgow G12 8QQ; T.-0141-330 4053; e-mail: E.M.Hillan@clinmed.gla.ac.uk

Hillhouse, Sir (Robert) Russell, KCB, FRSE. Governor, Royal Scottish Academy of Music and Drama, since 2000; Chairman, Upper Deeside Access Trust, since 1998; Chairman, Hebrides Ensemble, since 2000); b. 23.4.38, Glasgow; m., Alison Fraser; 2 d. Educ. Hutchesons' Grammar School, Glasgow; Glasgow University. Entered Home Civil Service as Assistant Principal, Scottish Education Department, 1962; Principal, 1966; HM Treasury, 1971; Assistant Secretary, Scottish Office, 1974; Scottish Home and Health Department, 1977; Principal Finance Officer, Scottish Office, 1980; Under-Secretary, Scottish Education Department, 1985; Secretary, 1987; Permanent Under-Secretary of State, Scottish Office, 1988-98. Director: Bank of Scotland, 1998-2001, Scottish Provident Institution, 1999-2001. Recreation: making music. Address: 19 Regent Terrace, Edinburgh EH7 5BS; e-mail: rhillhouse@blueyonder.co.uk

Hillier, Professor Stephen Gilbert, BSc, MSc, PhD, DSc, FRCPath. Professor, Department of Reproductive and Developmental Sciences, Edinburgh University, since 1994, Director, Reproductive Medicine Laboratory, since 1985 and Director, Graduate School of Life Sciences, since 1997; Editor-in-Chief, Journal of Endocrinology, since 2000; b. 16.1.49, Hillingdon; m., Haideh; 2 d. Educ. Hayes County Grammar School; Leeds University; Welsh National School of Medicine. Postdoctoral Research Fellow, National Institutes of Health, USA, 1976-78; Research Scientist, University of Leiden, 1978-82; Senior Lecturer: Reproductive Biochemistry, RPMS, London University, 1982-85, Department of Obstetrics and Gynaecology, Edinburgh University, 1985-94. Member: Interim Licensing Authority for Human Fertilisation and Embryology, 1987-91, Human Fertilisation and Embryology Authority, 1990-96; 1991 Society for Endocrinology Medal. Publications: Ovarian Endocrinology, 1991; Scientific Essentials of Reproductive Medicine, 1996. Recreations: fly-fishing; walking. Address: (b.) Edinburgh University Centre for Reproductive Biology, 37 Chalmers Street, Edinburgh EH3 9EW; T.-0131-229 2575.

Hillis, Professor William Stewart, MBChB, FRCP, DipSportsMed, FRCS. Professor of Cardiovascular and Exercise Medicine, Glasgow University, since 1997; Consultant Cardiologist, since 1977; b. 28.9.43, Elderslie; m., Anne Marshall Craigie; 3 s.; 1 d. Educ. Clydebank High School; Glasgow University. Research Fellow in Cardiology, Vanderbilt University, 1973-74; Physician to SFA, since 1977; Vice-Chairman, UEFA Medical Committee, eight years. Publications: 200 academic papers; Treatment of Cardiovascular Disease (book) (Co-author). Recreations: running; gardening; football. Address: (b.) Department of Medicine and Therapeutics, Gardiner Institute, Western Infirmary, Dumbarton Road, Glasgow G11 6NT; T.-0141-211 2897.

Hillman, John Richard, BSc, PhD, HonDSc, CBiol, FIBiol, FLS, FIM, FIHort, FRSA, FRSE. Director, Scottish Crop Research Institute, since 1986; Visiting Professor, Dundee University, Edinburgh University and Glasgow University; Deputy Chairman, Mylnefield Research Services Ltd.; Director, Mylnefield Trust and Mylnefield Holdings Ltd.; b. 21.7.44, Farnborough, Kent; m., Sandra Kathleen Palmer; 2 s. Educ. Chislehurst and Sidcup Grammar School; University of Wales. Assistant Lecturer, 1968, and Lecturer, 1969, Physiology and Environmental Studies, Nottingham University; Lecturer, 1971, Senior Lecturer, 1977, Reader, 1980, Professor of Botany, 1982, Glasgow University; Chairman, Agriculture, Natural Resources and Environment Sector Panel, UK Technology Foresight Programme, 1994-95, Agriculture, Horticulture and Forestry Sector Panel, 1995-97; Member, Court, University of Abertay, Dundee; Member, Board, BioIndustry Association; Bawden Jubilee Lecturer, 1993; British Potato Industry Award, 1999; World Potato Congress 2000 Industry Award. Recreations: landscaping; building renovations; horology; reading. Address: (b.) Scottish Crop Research Institute, Invergowrie, Dundee DD2 5DA; T.-01382 562731.

Hills, Professor Sir Graham (John), PhD, DSc, FRSE, Hon DSc (Lodz, Southampton, Lisbon), Hon. LLD (Glasgow, Waterloo and Strathclyde), DUniv (Paisley). Principal and Vice-Chancellor, Strathclyde University, 1980-91; b. 9.4.26, Leigh-on-Sea; m., 1, Brenda Stubbington; 2, Mary Jane McNaughton; 1 s.; 3 d. Educ. Westcliff High School for Boys; Birkbeck College and Imperial College, London University. Lecturer in Physical Chemistry, Imperial College, 1949-62; Professor of Physical Chemistry, Southampton University, 1962-80. Visiting Professor, University of Western Ontario, 1968; Visiting Professor and National Science Foundation Fellow, Case-Western Reserve University, Ohio, 1968-69; Visiting Professor, Buenos Aires University, 1976; Member, Advisory Council on Science and Technology, 1987-93; (Non-Executive) Member, Scottish Post Office Board, 1986-2000; Non-Executive Director, Scottish Enterprise, 1988-94; National Governor for Scotland, BBC, 1989-94; Fellow, Birkbeck College; Fellow, Royal Scottish Academy of Music and Drama; Fellow, Royal College of Physicians and Surgeons of Glasgow; Honorary Fellow, Chartered Society of Designers, 1996; Fellow, University of East London; Director, Glasgow Chamber of Commerce, since 1981; President: Friends of Glasgow Cathedral, 1987-95, Society of Chemical Industry, 1991-93; Chairman, Quarriers Homes, 1992-97; Commander Insignia: Order of Merit of Polish People's Republic, Royal Norwegian Order of Merit. Publications: Reference Electrodes, 1961; Polarography, 1964. Recreations: music; crofting; European politics. Address: (h.) The Coach House, 2B Strathearn Road, Edinburgh EH9 2AH.

Hind, Archie. Novelist and Playwright; b. 1928. Author, The Dear Green Place, 1966.

Hinds, Lesley. Chair, Health Education Board for Scotland, since 2001; Convener, Lothian and Borders Police Board, since 1999; b. 3.8.56, Dundee; m., Martin; 1 s.; 2 d. Educ. Kirkton High School, Dundee; Dundee College of Education. Primary school teacher; councillor, since 1984 (Leader, Edinburgh District Council); Chair, Edinburgh International Conference Centre. Chair, North Edinburgh Area Renewal; Chair,

Edinburgh MIELA; Board Member, Waterfront Edinburgh. Recreations: theatre; dance; swimming; travel. Address: (h.) 4 Easter Drylaw Place, Edinburgh EH4 2QD; T.-0131-539 4499.

Hine, Professor Harry Morrison, MA, DPhil (Oxon). Scotstarvit Professor of Humanity, St. Andrews University, since 1985; b. 19.6.48, Portsmouth; m., Rosalind Mary Ford; 1 s.; 1 d. Educ. King Edward's School, Birmingham; Corpus Christi College, Oxford. P.S. Allen Junior Research Fellow, Corpus Christi College, 1972-75; Lecturer in Humanity, Edinburgh University, 1975-85. Editor (Joint), The Classical Review, 1987-93. Publications: An Edition with Commentary of Seneca, Natural Questions, Book Two, 1981; Studies in the Text of Seneca's Naturales Quaestiones, 1996; L. Annaei Senecae Naturales Quaestiones (Editor), 1996; Seneca, Medea, Translation and commentary. Recreations: walking; reading. Address: (h.) 33 Drumcarrow Road, St. Andrews, Fife KY16 8SE; T.-01334 474459; e-mail: hmh@st-and.ac.uk

Hinstridge, David Robert, BSc. Director, Inland Revenue Scotland, since 2001; b. 20.4.53, Carrickfergus; m., Margaret; 2 s. Educ. Limavady Grammar School; Edinburgh University. Training and development posts, Inland Revenue, 1975-81; District Inspector, Morpeth Tax Office, 1981-83; Officer in Charge, Inland Revenue Claims Branch, Edinburgh, 1983-89; Group Leader, Inland Revenue Special Office, Edinburgh, 1989-92; Deputy Director, Inland Revenue Scotland, 1992-98; Director, Inland Revenue Northern Ireland, 1998-2001; Director, Inland Revenue Accounts Office, 2001. Recreations: travel; military and Irish history; cooking. Address: (b.) 114 George Street, Edinburgh EH2 4LN; T.-0131-473 4100.

Hipwell, John Charles Buchanan, LLB. Advocate, since 1994; Member, Fife Council, since 2001; b. 30.10.47, Hanley Swan, England; m., Mary Elizabeth McIlroy Hipwell; 2 s.; 1 d. Educ. Gordonstoun School, Elgin; Edinburgh University. Solicitor, 1977-94. Recreations: gardening; mediaeval architecture; history. Address: (h.) Dove Cottage, 62 Main Street, Aberdour; T.-01383 860122.

Hirst, Sir Michael William, LLB, CA, FRSA. Chairman, Scottish Conservative and Unionist Party, 1993-97; b. 2.1.46, Glasgow; m., Naomi Ferguson Wilson; 1 s.; 2 d. Educ. Glasgow Academy; Glasgow University. Partner, Peat Marwick Mitchell & Co., Chartered Accountants, until 1983; Director of and Consultant to various companies; contested: Central Dunbartonshire, February and October, 1974, East Dunbartonshire, 1979; MP (Conservative), Strathkelvin and Bearsden, 1983-87; Member, Select Committee on Scottish Affairs, 1983-87; Parliamentary Private Secretary, Department of Energy, 1985-87; Vice-Chairman, Scottish Conservative Party, 1987-89; Chairman, Scottish Conservative Candidates Association, 1978-81; Member, Court, Glasgow Caledonian University, 1992-98; President, Scottish Conservative and Unionist Association; Vice Chairman, Diabetes UK; Chairman, The Park School Educational Trust; Director, Children's Hospice Association Scotland; Member, Executive Committee, Princess Louise Scottish Hospital, Erskine; Elder, Kippen Parish Church. Recreations: golf; hill-walking; skiing. Address: (h.) Glentirran, Kippen, Stirlingshire FK8 3JA; e-mail: michael.hirst@pagodapr.com

Hislop, William Stuart, BSc, MBChB, FRCP, FACG. Consultant Physician, Royal Alexandra Hospital, Paisley, since 1982; b. 27.2.48, Edinburgh; m., Dr. Linda J. Hislop; 1 s.; 3 d. Educ. Dundee High School; Kilmarnock Academy; Glasgow University. Junior House Officer, Stobhill Hospital and Southern General Hospital, 1973-74; Western Infirmary, Glasgow: Senior House Officer, 1974-76, Medical Registrar, 1976-77; Senior Registrar, Ninewells Hospital, Dundee, 1977-82. Recreations: walking; cycling;

gardening; cricket; music (country and western). Address: (b.) Ross Hall Hospital, 221 Crookston Road, Glasgow G52 3NQ; T.-0141-810 3151.

Hitchman, Professor Michael L., BSc, DPhil, CChem, FRSC, FRSA, FRSE. Young Professor of Chemistry, Strathclyde University, since 1984; b. 17.8.41, Woburn, Bedfordshire; 1 s.; 2 d. Educ. Stratton Grammar School, Biggleswade; Queen Mary College and King's College, London University; University College, Oxford. Assistant Lecturer in Chemistry, Leicester Regional College of Technology, 1963-65; Junior Research Fellow, Wolfson College, Oxford, 1968-70; ICI Postdoctoral Research Fellow, Physical Chemistry Laboratory, Oxford University, 1968-70; Chief Scientist, Orbisphere Corporation, Geneva, 1970-73; Staff Scientist, Laboratories RCA Ltd., Zurich, 1973-79; Lecturer, then Senior Lecturer, Salford University, 1979-84; Strathclyde University: Chairman, Department of Pure and Applied Chemistry, 1986-89, Vice-Dean, Faculty of Science, 1989-92; Honorary Professor, Taiyuan University of Technology, China, since 1994; Editor, Advanced Materials CVD, since 1995. Royal Society of Chemistry: Chairman, Electro-analytical Group, 1985-88, Treasurer, Electrochemistry Group, 1984-90; Member, Chemistry and Semiconductor Committees, Science and Engineering Research Council; Member, since 1985, Chairman, 1989-92, International Advisory Board, EUROCVD; Director, MATS UK Ltd.; Director, Thin Film Innovations Ltd.; Medal and Prize, British Vacuum Council, 1993. Editor, Advanced Materials Chemical Vapor Deposition, since 1995. Publications: Ring-disk Electrodes (Co-Author), 1971; Measurement of Dissolved Oxygen, 1978; Chemical Vapor Deposition (Co-Editor), 1993. Recreations: humour; cooking; eating; rambling; losing weight. Address: (b.) Department of Pure and Applied Chemistry, Strathclyde University, 295 Cathedral Street, Glasgow G1 1XL; T.-0141-548 2793.

Hobbett, Alan George, BSc (Hons), Dip. Housing. Chief Executive, Scottish Community Foundation, since 1998; b. 18.4.63, Luton; m., Joanne; 1 s.; 1 d. Educ. Denbigh Road Comprehensive School; University of Wales, Cardiff. Housing Manager, Livingston Development Corporation, 1987-89; Researcher/Lecturer, Heriot Watt University, 1989-90; Special Projects Director, Environ, Leicester, 1992-94; Director, Albion Trust, Edinburgh, 1994-98. Chair, Scottish Medical Aid for Cuba. Recreations: current affairs; bee-keeping; cycling; walking. Address: (h.) The Beach House, Luchies Road, Burntisland; T.-01592 872020; e-mail: alan@thebeachhouse.org.uk

Hobsbaum, Professsor Philip Dennis, MA, PhD, DLitt, LRAM, LGSM. Poet and Critic; Professor of English Literature, Glasgow University, 1985-97, and Honorary Professorial Research Fellow, since 1997; b. 29.6.32, London; m., Rosemary Phillips. Educ. Belle Vue Grammar School, Bradford; Downing College, Cambridge; Sheffield University. Lecturer in English, Queen's University, Belfast, 1962-66; Lecturer, Senior Lecturer, Reader in English Literature, Glasgow University, 1966-85; Chairman of writers' groups in London, 1955-59, Belfast, 1962-66, Glasgow, 1966-75. Publications: A Group Anthology (Co-Editor), 1963; The Place's Fault, 1964; In Retreat, 1966; Coming Out Fighting, 1969; Ten Elizabethan Poets (Editor), 1969; A Theory of Communication, 1970; A Reader's Guide to Charles Dickens, 1972; Women and Animals, 1972; Tradition and Experiment in English Poetry, 1979; A Reader's Guide to D.H. Lawrence, 1981; Essentials of Literary Criticism, 1983; A Reader's Guide to Robert Lowell, 1988; Wordsworth: Selected Poetry and Prose (Editor), 1989; Channels of Communication (Co-editor), 1992; Metre, Rhythm and Verse Form, 1996; over 100 articles in learned journals; over 1,000 book reviews. Recreations: walking the dog; surfing the Internet. Address: (h.) 10 Oban Drive, Glasgow G20 6AF; T.-0141 946 6653.

Hodge, Robin Mackenzie, BA (Hons). Publisher, The List magazine, since 1985; b. Edinburgh. Educ. Edinburgh Academy; Clifton College, Bristol; Durham University. Certificat Europeen en Administration de Projects Culturels (Bruxelles). Director, Canongate Publishing Ltd., 1981-84; restoration of 16th-century buildings around Tweeddale Court, Edinburgh Old Town, 1981-88; founded The List, 1985. Address: (b.) 14 High Street, Edinburgh EH1 1TE; T.-0131-558 1191.

Hogg of Cumbernauld, Lord (Norman). MP, Cumbernauld and Kilsyth, 1983-97 (MP, East Dunbartonshire, 1979-83); Lord High Commissioner, General Assembly of the Church of Scotland, 1998, 1999; Hon. President, YMCA Scotland, since 1998; Member, House of Lords Delegated Powers and Deregulation Committee, 1999; Vice-Chairman, Scottish Peers Association, since 2000; b. 12.3.38, Aberdeen; m., Elizabeth M. Christie. Educ. Ruthrieston Secondary School, Aberdeen. Local Government Officer, Aberdeen Town Council, 1953-67; District Officer, NALGO, 1967-79; Member: Transport Users Consultative Committee for Scotland, 1977-79, Select Committee on Scottish Affairs, 1979-82; Scottish Labour Whip, 1982-83; Chairman, Scottish Parliamentary Labour Group, 1981-82; Deputy Chief Opposition Whip, 1983-87; Scottish Affairs Spokesman, 1987-88; Member, Public Accounts Committee, 1991-92. Chairman, Bus Appeals Body, since 2000; Patron, Scottish Centre for Children with Motor Impairments, since 1997; Hon.LLD, University of Aberdeen, 1999. Recreation: music. Address: House of Lords, Westminster, London SW1A 0PW; T.020 7219 3000.

Hogg, Lt. Col. Colin Grant Ogilvie, DL. King's Own Scottish Borderers (KOSB), since 1962; Regimental Secretary, since 1991; b. 6.12.43, Glasgow; m., Cynthia Rose Mackenzie; 2 d. Educ. St. Mary's Preparatory School; Merchiston Castle School. Commissioned into KOSB, 1965; service with 1st Battalion in Aden, Hong Kong, Borneo, BAOR, Berlin, Northern Ireland; Deputy Assistant Adjutant General, HQ of 1st Armoured Division, Germany, 1981-83; on directing staff, Royal Military Academy, Sandhurst, 1983-84; Commanding Officer, 2nd Battalion, 52 Lowland Volunteers, 1985-88; SOI, Foot Guards and Infantry Manning and Records Office, 1988-91; retired from active list, 1991; Honorary Colonel of the Lothian and Border Army Cadet Force, since 1997. Member: Queen's Bodyguard for Scotland, since 1986, Ancient Order of Mosstroopers; Chairman, Borders Branch, SSAFA Forces Help, since 1993, Member, National Council, since 2000; Member, Board, South of Scotland Youth Awards Scheme, since 1994; Chairman, Roxburgh and Berwickshire Conservative and Unionist Association, 1995-98; Governor: Oxenfoord Castle School, 1986-93, St. Mary's School, Melrose, 1994-98; Vice President, Jedburgh Branch, Royal British Legion Scotland, since 1994; Member, National Council, Royal British Legion Scotland, since 1998; Board Member, Earl Haig Fund, since 2000; Honorary Director, Lord Roberts Workshops; Deputy Lieutenant, Roxburgh, Ettrick and Lauderdale, since 1995. Recreations: foxhunting; shooting; all equestrian events. Address: (h.) Mounthooly, Jedburgh TD8 6TJ; T.-01835 863368.

Hogg, Ian Alisdair Lawrence, MA, CA. Secretary, Scottish Rugby Union, since 1983; b. 13.6.40, Edinburgh; m., Louise; 1 s.; 1 d. Educ. George Watson's College; Edinburgh University. Chartered Accountant, 1961-78; Treasurer, Scottish Rugby Union, 1978-83. Recreations: rugby; cricket. Address: (b.) Scottish Rugby Union, Murrayfield, Edinburgh EH12 5PJ; T.-0131-346 5000.

Holloway, James Essex, BA (Hons), FSA Scot. Director, Scottish National Portrait Gallery, since 1997; b. 24.11.48, London. Educ. Marlborough College; Courtauld Institute, London University. Assistant

Keeper, National Gallery of Scotland; Assistant Keeper, National Museum of Wales; Deputy Keeper, Scottish National Portrait Gallery. Trustee, Scottish Sculpture Trust; Committee Member, Scottish Indian Arts Forum; Member, Curatorial Committee, National Trust for Scotland. Recreations: India; motorbikes. Address: (b.) 1 Queen Street, Edinburgh EH2 1JD; T.-0131-624 6401.

Holloway, Rt. Rev. Richard Frederick, BD, STM, DUniv (Strathclyde), DD (Aberdeen), DLitt (Napier), FRSE. Gresham Professor of Divinity, 1997-2001; Bishop of Edinburgh, 1986-2000; Primus of the Scottish Episcopal Church, 1992-2000; b. 26.11.33; m., Jean Elizabeth Kennedy; 1 s.; 2 d. Educ. Kelham Theological College; Edinburgh Theological College; Union Theological Seminary, New York. Curate, St. Ninian's, Glasgow, 1959-63; Priest-in-charge, St. Margaret and St. Mungo's, Glasgow, 1963-68; Rector, Old St. Paul's, Edinburgh, 1968-80; Rector, Church of the Advent, Boston, Mass, 1980-84; Vicar, St. Mary Magdalen's, Oxford, 1984-86. Recreations: long-distance walking; reading; going to the cinema; listening to music. Address: (h.) 6 Blantyre Terrace, Edinburgh EH10 5AE.

Holmes, George Dennis, CB (1979), FRSE, FICfor. Forestry Consultant, since 1987; b. 9.11.26, Conwy; m., Sheila Rosemary; 3 d. Educ. John Bright's School, Llandudno; University of Wales, Bangor. Forestry Commission, 1948-86 (Director General, 1976-86). Recreations: fishing; golf. Address: (h.) 7 Cammo Road, Barnton, Edinburgh EH4 8EF; T.-0131-339 7474.

Holmes, Dr Megan Christine, BSc, PhD. Lecturer, Department of Clinical Neurosciences, Edinburgh University, since 1998; m., Dr Ferenc A. Antoni; 3 s. Educ. Stourbridge Girls' High School; London University. Exchange Fellow, Royal Society, London, and Hungarian Academy of Sciences, Budapest, at Institute of Experimental Medicine, Budapest, 1982-83; Fogarty Visiting Fellow, Endocrinology and Reproduction Research Branch, National Institute of Child Health, Bethesda, 1983-85; Department of Medicine, Western General Hospital, Edinburgh: Wellcome Postdoctoral Fellowship, 1992-94, Wellcome Career Development Fellowship, 1995-98. Recreation: hill-walking. Address: (b.) Molecular Medicine Centre, Western General Hospital, Edinburgh EH4 2XU; T.-0131-651 1033.

Holmes, Professor Peter Henry, BVMS, PhD, MRCVS, FRSE. Professor of Veterinary Physiology, University of Glasgow, since 1982; Vice-Principal (Research), since 1997; b. 6.6.42, Cottingham, Yorkshire; m., Ruth Helen; 2 d. Educ. Beverley Grammar School, Yorkshire; University of Glasgow. Joined staff of University of Glasgow Veterinary School, Department of Veterinary Physiology, 1966. Member, Court, University of Glasgow, 1991-95; served on committees of ODA (DfID), BVA, UFAW; Chairman, International Programme Against African Trypanosomiasis. Recreations: hillwalking; tennis; cycling. Address: (b.) Research and Enterprise, No. 10 The Square, University of Glasgow, Glasgow G12 8QQ; T.-0141-330 3836.

Holroyd, Nicholas Weddall, BCL (Oxon), LLB, FSA (Scot). Advocate, since 1992; b. 11.3.64, Edinburgh. Educ. Christ Church, Oxford University; University of Edinburgh. Trainee, Dundas and Wilson, CS, 1989-91; "devilling" for the Bar, 1991-92; part-time Tutor, Edinburgh University, 1993-2001; Clerk to Faculty of Advocates Law Reform Committee, 1996; Contributor, Greens' Litigation Styles, since 1996; Chairman, New Town Branch, Edinburgh North and Leith Conservative Association, 2000-01. Recreation: golf. Address: Advocates Library, Old Parliament House, Edinburgh EH1 1RF; T.-0131-226 5071.

Holt, Elizabeth Katherine, MA (Oxon). Head of European Commission Representation in Scotland, since 1999; b. 6.12.47, Harrow; m., Richard Holt; 1d. Educ. North London Collegiate School; Lady Margaret Hall, Oxford. Scottish Office, 1975-81; European Commission Official in Employment and Social Affairs, 1981-99. Address: (b.) 9 Alva Street, Edinburgh, EH2 4PH; T.-0131-225 2058.

Home, Earl of (David Alexander Cospatrick Douglas-Home), CVO, CBE. Chairman, Coutts & Co., since 1999; b. 20.11.43, Coldstream; m., Jane Margaret Williams-Wynne; 1 s.; 2 d. Educ. Eton; Christ College, Oxford. Joined Morgan Grenfell & Co. Limited, 1966; appointed Director, 1974 (resigned, 1999); Chairman, Morgan Grenfell (Scotland) Ltd., 1986 (resigned 1999); ECGD: Member, Export Advisory Council, 1988-93, Member, Projects Committee, 1989-93; Member, Advisory Board, National Forest, 1991-94; Chairman, CEGELEC Controls Ltd., 1991-94; Council Member, Glenalmond School, since 1995; Conservative Front-Bench Spokesman on Trade, Industry and Finance, 1997-98; appointed Director, Coutts & Co., 1999; Trustee, The Grosvenor Estate, since 1993; Chairman, MAN Ltd., since 2000. Recreations: outdoor sports. Address: (b.) Coutts & Co., 440 Strand, London WC2R 0QS; T.-0171-753 1000.

Home Robertson, John David. MSP (Labour), East Lothian, since 1999 (Convenor, Holyrood Progress Group, since 2000, Scottish Executive Depute Minister for Rural Affairs, 1999-2000); MP (Labour), East Lothian, 1983-2001 (Berwick & East Lothian, 1978-83); b. 5.12.48, Edinburgh; m., Catherine Brewster; 2 s. Educ. Ampleforth College; West of Scotland Agricultural College. Farmer; Member: Berwickshire District Council, 1974-78, Borders Health Board, 1975-78; Chairman, Eastern Borders Citizens' Advice Bureau, 1976-78; Member, Select Committee on Scottish Affairs, 1979-83; Chairman, Scottish Group of Labour MPs, 1983; Scottish Labour Whip, 1983-84; Opposition Front Bench Spokesman on Agriculture, 1984-87, on Scotland, 1987-88, on Agriculture, 1988-90; Member, Select Committee on Defence, 1990-97; Member, British-Irish Parliamentary Body, 1993-99; Parliamentary Private Secretary to Dr Jack Cunningham, 1997-99; established Paxton Trust, 1988; Edinburgh Direct Aid convoys to Bosnia, 1994 and 1995 (HGV driver); Observer, elections in Sarajevo, 1996. Address: (b.) Scottish Parliament, Edinburgh EH99 1SP.

Hood, James. MP (Labour), Clydesdale, since 1987; b. 16.5.48, Lesmahagow; m., Marion; 1 s.; 1 d. Educ. Lesmahagow High School; Nottingham University. Local councillor, 1973-87; official of NUM, 1973-87; Leader, Nottingham striking miners, 1984-85; Chairman, Miners' Parliamentary Group, 1991-92; former Chairman, All-Party Group on ME; Chairman, European Scrutiny Select Committee; Member, Speaker's Panel of Chairmen; former Convenor, Scottish Labour Group of MPs Home Affairs Committee; sponsor of three Private Members' Bills on under-age drinking, Bill on ME, and Bill on school transport safety. Address: (b.) House of Commons, London SW1A 0AA; T.020 7219 4585; 01555 673177.

Hood, Professor Neil, CBE, FRSE, MA, MLitt. Professor of Business Policy, Department of Marketing, Strathclyde University, since 1979; Director, Strathclyde International Business Unit, since 1992; Deputy Chairman, Scottish Enterprise, since 2001; b. 10.8.43, Wishaw; m., Anna Watson Clark; 1 s.; 1 d. Educ. Wishaw High School; Glasgow University. Research Fellow, Scottish College of Textiles, 1966-68; Lecturer/Senior Lecturer, Paisley College of Technology, 1968-78; Economic Adviser, Scottish Economic Planning Department, 1979; Director: Locate in Scotland, 1987-89, Employment and Special Initiatives, SDA, 1989-90; Visiting Professor: International

Business, University of Texas, Dallas, 1981, Institute of International Business, Stockholm School of Economics, since 1982; Director, Euroscot Meat Exports Ltd., 1981-85; Economic Consultant to Secretary of State for Scotland, 1980-87; Director, Scottish Development Finance Ltd., 1984-90 and 1993-96; Chairman, Scottish Equity Partnership Ltd., since 2000; Chairman, Scottish Technology Fund, 1997-2000; Investment Adviser, Castleforth Fund Managers, 1984-87; Director, LIFE Ltd., 1984-86; Board Member, Irvine Development Corporation, 1985-87; Director: Prestwick Holdings PLC, 1986-87, Lamberton (Holdings) Ltd., 1989-92, GA (Holdings) Ltd., 1990-92, Shanks and McEwan PLC, 1990-94, I & S UK Smaller Companies Trust plc, 1993-98, I & S Trustlink Ltd., 1994-97, Kwik-Fit plc, since 1991, Grampian Holdings plc, since 1993, First Banking Systems Ltd., since 1996; Corporate Adviser, Scottish Power, since 1989; Chairman, John Dickie Group Ltd., 1995-2000; Director, Xansa plc (formerly FI Group plc), since 1997; Deputy Chairman, British Polythene Industries plc, since 1998; President, European International Business Association, 1985-86. Publications: Industrial Marketing — A Study of Textiles (Co-Author), 1970; Chrysler UK: A Corporation in Transition (Co-Author), 1977; The Economics of Multinational Enterprise (Co-Author), 1979; European Development Strategies of US Multinationals Located in Scotland (Co-Author), 1980; Multinationals in Retreat: The Scottish Experience (Co-Author), 1982; Multinational Investment Strategies in the British Isles (Co-Author), 1983; Industry, Policy and the Scottish Economy (Co-Editor), 1984; Transnational Corporations in the Textile Industry (Co-Author), 1984; Foreign Multinationals and the British Economy (Co-Author), 1987; Strategies in Global Competition (Co-Editor), 1987; Scottish Financial Sector (Co-Author), 1988; Marketing in Evolution (Co-Editor), 1996; Transition in Baltic States: Microlevel Studies (Co-Editor), 1997; Multinational Corporate Evolution and Subsidiary Development (Co-Editor), 1998; The Globalisation of Multinational Enterprise Activity and Economic Development (Co-Editor), 1999. Recreations: swimming; reading; gardening. Address: (h.) 95 Mote Hill, Hamilton ML3 6EA; T.-01698 424870.

Hook, Professor Andrew Dunnet, MA, PhD, FRSE. Bradley Professor of English Literature, Glasgow University, 1979-98; b. 21.12.32, Wick; m., Judith Ann (deceased); 2 s.; 1 d. (deceased). Educ. Wick High School; Daniel Stewart's College, Edinburgh; Edinburgh University; Manchester University; Princeton University. Edinburgh University: Assistant Lecturer in English Literature, 1961-63, Lecturer in American Literature, 1963-70; Senior Lecturer in English, Aberdeen University, 1970-79; Chairman, Committee for Humanities and Member, Committee for Academic Affairs, CNAA, 1987-92; Chairman: Scottish Universities Council on Entrance English Panel, 1986-92, Universities and Colleges Admissions Service English Panel, since 1995; Member: Scottish Examination Board, 1984-92, Scottish Qualifications Authority English Panel, 1996-99; President, Eighteenth-Century Scottish Studies Society, 1990-92. Publications: Scotland and America 1750-1835, 1975; American Literature in Context 1865-1900, 1983; Scott's Waverley (Editor), 1971; Charlotte Brontë's Shirley (Editor, with Judith Hook), 1974; Dos Passos: A Collection of Critical Essays (Editor), 1974; The History of Scottish Literature II, 1660-1800 (Editor), 1987; Scott Fitzgerald, 1992; The Glasgow Enlightenment (Co-Editor), 1995; From Goosecreek to Gandercleugh, 1999; Scott's The Fair Maid of Perth (Co-Editor). Recreations: theatre; opera; catching up on reading. Address: (b.) Department of English Literature, Glasgow University, Glasgow G12 8QQ.

Hooper, Ian Ross, BA. Head of Economy and Industry Division, Scotland Office, since 1999; b. 26.5.49, Edinburgh; m., Julie Ellen Vaughan; 1 s.; 1 d. Educ. Hornchurch Grammar School; University of East Anglia.

Department of the Environment, 1973-89; seconded to English Heritage, 1984-85; Depute Director (Resources) and Director, Museum of Scotland Project, National Museums of Scotland, 1989-99. Recreations: historic buildings; hill-walking; golf. Address: (b.) Scotland Office, Meridian Court, Glasgow G2 6AT; T.-0141-242 5965.

Hooper, Professor Martin Leslie, MA, PhD, FRCPE, FRSE. Professor of Molecular Pathology, University of Edinburgh, since 1996; b. 1.3.47, Walsall. Educ. Queen Mary's School, Walsall; University of Cambridge. MRC Research Scholar, MRC Laboratory of Molecular Biology, University of Cambridge, 1968-71; EMBO Research Fellow, Centre de Génétique Moléculaire, Gif-sur-Yvette, 1972-73; Research Fellow, Institute of Genetics, Glasgow, 1973-80; University of Edinburgh: Senior Lecturer in Experimental Pathology, 1980-90, Reader, Department of Pathology, 1990-96. Co-recipient, Margaret MacLellan Award, Tenovus Scotland, 1996. Recreations: walking; watching cricket; opera. Address: (b.) Sir Alastair Currie CRC Laboratories, Molecular Medicine Centre, Western General Hospital, Edinburgh EH4 2XU; T.-0131-651 1071.

Hope of Craighead, Rt. Hon. Lord (James Arthur David Hope), PC. A Lord of Appeal in Ordinary, since 1996; Chancellor, Strathclyde University, since 1998; b. 27.6.38, Edinburgh; m., Katharine Mary Kerr; 2 (twin) s.; 1 d. Educ. Edinburgh Academy; Rugby School; St. John's College, Cambridge (BA); Edinburgh University (LLB); Hon. LLD, Aberdeen (1991), Strathclyde (1993), Edinburgh (1995); Fellow, Strathclyde, 2000. National Service, Seaforth Highlanders, 1957-59; admitted Faculty of Advocates, 1965; Standing Junior Counsel to Inland Revenue, 1974-78; QC, 1978; Advocate Depute, 1978-82; Chairman, Medical Appeal Tribunal, 1985-86; Legal Chairman, Pensions Appeal Tribunal, 1985-86; Dean, Faculty of Advocates, 1986-89; A Senator of the College of Justice, Lord Justice General of Scotland, and Lord President of the Court of Session, 1989-96. President, The Stair Society, 1993; Hon. Professor of Law, Aberdeen, 1994; Baron (Life Peer), 1995. Publications: Gloag and Henderson's Introduction to Scots Law (Joint Editor, 7th edition, Assistant Editor, 8th and 9th editions); Armour on Valuation for Rating (Joint Editor, 4th and 5th editions); (Contributor) Stair Memorial Encyclopaedia of Scots Law. Address: (h.) 34 India Street, Edinburgh EH3 6HB; T.-0131-225 8245; e-mail: hopejad@parliament.uk

Hope, Colin John Filshill, OStJ, BA, FCII, FCIS, FCIT, FBIM, MCIM, DipM. Director, Merchants House of Glasgow, 1981-87, 1988-94, 1995-2001; Governor, Glasgow Educational and Marshall Trust, since 1986; b. 24.6.24, Dullatur; m., Jean Calder Douglas; 1 s.; 2 d. Educ. Glasgow High School; Glasgow Academy; Open University. RAF, 1942-47; joined Stenhouse & Partners, 1947; appointed Director, 1949; served in many capacities, including Managing Director, Stenhouse International; joined Norman Frizzell Scotland Ltd. as Managing Director, 1974; additionally Director, Norman Frizzell UK Ltd., 1976-81; Director, G.T. Senior, 1981-83 (Consultant, 1983-85); a Director, Glasgow Chamber of Commerce, 1979-88. Member: Scottish Consumer Council, 1979-85, Electricity Consultative Council for Scotland, 1979-87, General Convocation, Strathclyde University, 1980-90, Council, Insurance Ombudsman Bureau, 1981-94, Glasgow Airport Consultative Committee, since 1984; Governor, Keil School, 1986-91; former Chairman, Scottish Transport Users Consultative Committee; Member: Air Transport Committee, Association of British Chambers of Commerce, 1986-90, South of Scotland Electricity Consultative Committee, 1990-91; Director, Glasgow Native Benevolent Association, 1988-91, 1992-98 (Chairman, 1997-98); Member, Dumbartonshire Committee, Order of St. John, 1987-93. Address: (h.) 15 Chapelacre Grove, Helensburgh G84 7SH; T.-01436 673091.

Hope, William, MA. Rector, Elgin High School, since 1978; b. 26.9.43, Scotland; m., Patricia Miller. Educ. Dalbeattie High School; Kirkcudbright Academy; Edinburgh University; Jordanhill College of Education. Alloa Academy: Assistant Teacher, Principal Teacher of Guidance; Assistant Rector, Lochaber High School. Chairman, Moray Branch, UNICEF; Vice Chairman, Elgin and District Branch, Macmillan Cancer Relief; President, Forres St. Lawrence Cricket Club; Director: Moray Education Business Partnership, Moray Learning Alliance. Recreations: umpiring hockey and cricket; fishing; public speaking. Address: (b.) Elgin High School, High School Drive, Elgin, Moray; T.-01343 545181.

Horden, Professor John Robert Backhouse, MA, MLitt, DHL, FSA, FSA Scot, FRSL. Professor Emeritus of Bibliographical Studies, Stirling University; b. Warwickshire; m., Aileen Mary Douglas (deceased); 1 s. Educ. Oxford University; Cambridge University; Heidelberg University; Sorbonne; Lincoln's Inn. Former Director: Centre for Bibliographical Studies, Stirling University, Institute of Bibliography and Textual Criticism, Leeds University; former Tutor and Lecturer in English Literature, Christ Church, Oxford; Visiting Professorial appointments, Universities of Pennsylvania State, Saskatchewan, Erlangen-Nurnberg, Texas at Austin, Munster; Editor, Dictionary of Scottish Biography, since 1982; Cecil Oldman Memorial Lecturer, 1971; Marc Fitch Prize for Bibliography, 1979. Publications: Francis Quarles: A Bibliography of his Work to 1800, 1953; Francis Quarles' Hosanna and Threnodes (Editor), 1960; John Quarles: an analytical bibliography, 1960; Arthur Warwick's Spare Minutes (1634): an analytical bibliography, 1965; Annual Bibliography of English Language and Literature (Editor), 1967-75; English and Continental Emblem Books (22 vols.) (Editor), 1968-76; Art of the Drama, 1969; George Wither's Collection of Emblemes (Editor), 1973; Dictionary of Concealed Authorship, Vol. 1 (Editor), 1980; initiator and first editor, Index of English Literary Manuscripts, 11 volumes, 1980-97; Everyday Life in Seventeenth-Century England, 1974; Techniques of Bibliography, 1977; John Freeth: Political Ballad Writer and Inn Keeper, 1985; Bibliographia (Editor), 1992; Francis Quarles' Emblemes and Hieroglyphikes (Co-Editor), 1993. Recreations: golf (represented England, Warwickshire, Oxford, Cambridge); music; painting. Address: (b.) Department of English Studies, Stirling University, Stirling FK9 4LA.

Horne, Rev. Archibald Sinclair. Secretary and Lecturer, Scottish Reformation Society, since 1964; b. 9.3.27, Port Seton; m., Margaret Robertson Paterson; 2 s.; 1 d. Educ. Preston Lodge Secondary; London Bible College (External Student); New College, University of Edinburgh. Publications: Torchbearers of the Truth, 1966; In the Steps of the Covenanters, 1974. Recreations: golf; gardening; photography; producing video films. Address: (b.) Magdalene Chapel, 41 Cowgate, Edinburgh EH1 1EE; T.-0131-220 1450.

Horner, Professor Robert Malcolm Wigglesworth, CEng, BSc, PhD, MICE, MIMgt. Professor of Engineering Management, since 1986 and Director, Enterprise Management, since 2000, Dundee University (Chair, School of Engineering and Physical Sciences, 1997-99); b. 27.7.42, Bury; m., Beverley Anne Wesley; 1 s.; 1 d. Educ. The Bolton School; University College, London. Civil Engineer, Taylor Woodrow Construction Ltd., 1966-77; Lecturer, Senior Lecturer, Head, Department of Civil Engineering, Dundee University, 1977-91; Managing Director, International Maintenance Management, 1996-97. Founder Chairman, Dundee Branch, Opening Windows on Engineering; Winner, CIOB Ian Murray Leslie Award, 1980 and 1984; Atlantic Power and Gas Ltd.: Non-executive Director, 1991-97, Director, Research and Development, 1993-97; Chairman, Winton Caledonian Ltd.,

1995-97; Director, Dundee Rep., since 1991; Member, Council, National Conference of University Professors, 1989-93; Director, Scottish International Resource Project, 1994-95; Member: Technology Foresight Construction Sector Panel, since 1994, British Council Advisory Committee on Science and Engineering, since 1994; Chairman, Friends of St. Paul's Cathedral, 1993-95. Recreations: squash; gardening. Address: (h.) Westfield Cottage, 11 Westfield Place, Dundee DD1 4JU; T.-01382 225933.

Horobin, John Charles, BSc, PhD. Head of Conference and Group Services, St. Andrews University, since 1989; Director, University Hospitality Services Ltd.; b. 13.2.45, Long Eaton; m.; 2 s.; 2 d. Educ. Long Eaton Grammar School; King's College, London University; Durham University. Tutor-Organiser, WEA, Plymouth and West Devon, 1971-74; Assistant Director of Adult Education, St. Andrews University, 1974-89. Address: (b.) Residence and Business Services, St. Andrews University, 79 North Street, St. Andrews KY16 9AJ; T.-01334 462520.

Hounsell, Professor Dai (David John), BA, PhD. Professor of Higher Education, University of Edinburgh, since 2000; b. 5.7.47, Southampton; m., Jenny; 2 s. Educ. City of Bath Boys' Grammar School; Poole Grammar School; Portsmouth Polytechnic; University of Lancaster. Research Assistant, Portsmouth Polytechnic and North-East London Polytechnic, 1969-72; Information and Research Officer/Senior Research Officer, Institute for Research and Development in Post-Compulsory Education, University of Lancaster, 1972-85; Visiting Research Fellow, University of Gothenburg, 1981-82; Director/Co-Director, Centre for Teaching, Learning and Assessment, University of Edinburgh, 1985-98 (Head, Department of Higher and Further Education, 1988-2001). Editor, Higher Education, since 1988. Publications: How Students Learn (Co-Author), 1976; The Experience of Learning (Joint Author), 1984; Essay Writing for Active Learning, 1996; The ASSHE Inventory: Changing Assessment Practices in Scottish Higher Education (Joint Author), 1996; Reviewing Your Teaching (Joint Author), 1998. Recreations: hillwalking; light joinery; reading contemporary fiction. Address: (b.) Department of Higher and Community Education, University of Edinburgh, Paterson's Land, Holyrood Road, Edinburgh EH8 8AQ; T.-0131-651 6667; e-mail: dai.hounsell@ed.ac.uk

Housden, Stuart David, BSc (Hons) (Zoology). Director, RSPB Scotland, since 1993; b. 24.6.53, Croydon; m., Catherine Juliet Wilkin; 3 d. Educ. Selhurst Grammar School; Royal Holloway College, London University. Freshwater biologist, Thames Water, 1976; RSPB: Species Investigation Officer, 1977-79, Parliamentary Officer, 1979-82, Manager — Government Unit, 1982-85, Head, Conservation Planning Department, 1985-90, Head, Conservation Planning, 1990-93. Member, Cairngorms Partnership Board, 1995-97; Member, ScottishPower Environment Forum, since 1999; Churchill Fellow, 1992. Publications: Important Bird Areas in the UK (Co-Editor); numerous articles. Recreations: ornithology; travel; rugby football; politics; work. Address: (b.) Dunedin House, 25 Ravelston Terrace, Edinburgh EH4 3TP.

Houslay, Professor Miles Douglas, BSc, PhD, FRSE, FRSA, FIBiol, CBiol. Gardiner Professor of Biochemistry, Glasgow University, since 1984; b. 25.6.50, Wolverhampton; m., Rhian Mair; 2 s.; 1 d. Educ. Grammar School, Brewood, Stafford; University College, Cardiff; King's College, Cambridge; Cambridge University. ICI Research Fellow and Fellow, Queens' College, Cambridge, 1974-76; Lecturer, then Reader in Biochemistry, UMIST, 1976-82; Selby Fellow, Australian Academy of Science, 1984; Colworth Medal, Biochemical Society of Great Britain, 1984; Honorary Research Fellow, California Metabolic Research Foundation, since 1981; Editor in

Chief, Cellular Signalling; Deputy Chairman, Biochemical Journal, 1984-89; Editorial Board, Biochimica Biophysica Acta; Member: Committee, Biochemical Society, 1982-85, Research Committee, British Diabetic Association, 1986-91; Chairman, Grant Committee A, Cell and Disorders Board, Medical Research Council, 1989-92; Member: Scientific and Medical Grant Committee, Scottish Home and Health Department, 1991-94, Advisory Board for External Appointments, London University, 1990-92, HEFC RAE Basic Medical and Dental Sciences Panel, since 1996, Wellcome Trust BMB Grant Panel, 1996-2000; Chairman, British Heart Foundation Project Grant Panel; Member, British Heart Foundation Chairs and Programme Grant Panel, 1997-2000; Trustee, British Heart Foundation, since 1997; Burroughs-Wellcome Visiting Professor, USA, 2001. Publication: Dynamics of Biological Membranes; over 400 scientific papers. Address: (b.) Department of Biochemistry, Glasgow University, Glasgow G12 8QQ; T.-0141-330 5903.

Housley, Edward, MB, ChB, FRCPEdin, FRCP. Medical Specialist, Armed Forces Scotland, since 1975; Consultant Physician to the Army in Scotland, since 1998; retired Consultant Physician, Edinburgh Royal Infirmary; b. 10.1.34, Chester, USA; 1 d. Educ. Mundella Grammar School, Nottingham; Birmingham University. Postgraduate training, Department of Medicine, Birmingham University and McGill University, Montreal; former Honorary Senior Lecturer, Department of Medicine, Edinburgh University. Recreation: crossword puzzles. Address: (h.) 6 Kew Terrace, Edinburgh, EH12 5JE; e-mail: ehousley@doctors.org.uk

Houston, Anne C., CQSW. Director, ChildLine Scotland, since 1994; b. 28.8.54, Glasgow. Educ. Bishopbriggs High School; Strathclyde University. Social Worker, Intermediate Treatment Officer, Team Leader, Southampton Social Services Department, 1980-86; Project Manager/Tutor, Richmond Fellowship, Glasgow, 1986-90; Counselling Manager, Childline Scotland, 1990-94. Council Member, Stepfamily Scotland; Vice Chair and Board Member, Scottish Alliance for Children's Rights; Treasurer, Association of Chief Officers of Scottish Voluntary Organisations; Board Member, Scottish Pre-school Play Association. Recreations: reading; music; swimming; gardening; animals. Address: (b.) 18 Albion Street, Glasgow G1 1LH; T.-0141-552 1123.

Houston, Major General David, CBE. Lord Lieutenant of Sutherland, since 1991; b. 24.2.29; m.; 2 s. Educ. Latymer Upper School. Military Attaché and Commander, British Army Staff, Washington, 1977-79; HQ UKLF, 1979-80; President, Regular Commissions Board, 1980-83.

Houston, John, OBE, RSA, RSW, RGI. Artist; b. 1.4.30, Buckhaven; m., Elizabeth V. Blackadder. Educ. Buckhaven High School; Edinburgh College of Art. Travelling scholarship to Italy, 1953-54; started teaching, Edinburgh College of Art, 1955; elected: Associate, Royal Scottish Academy, 1964, Academician, 1972; Depute Head, School of Drawing and Painting, Edinburgh College of Art, 1982-89. Guthrie Award, RSA, 1964; Cargill Prize, Royal Glasgow Institute of Fine Arts, 1965, 1988; Lothians Award, RSA, 1982; Sir William Gillies Prize, RSW, 1990. Recreations: golf; fishing; travel. Address: (h.) 57 Fountainhall Road, Edinburgh EH9 2LH; T.-0131-667 3687.

Houston, Professor Robert Allan, MA (Hons). Professor of Early Modern History, St Andrews University, since 1995; b. 27.8.54, Hamilton; m., Dr Veronica A. O'Halloran. Educ. Edinburgh Academy; St Andrews University; Cambridge University. Research Fellow, Clare College, Cambridge, 1981-83; Lecturer, then Reader, in Modern History, St Andrews University, 1983-95; Visiting Professor, Erasmus University,

Rotterdam, 1994; Leverhulme Research Fellowship, 1996-97; Distinguished Visiting Scholar, Department of History, Adelaide University, 1996; FRS; Fellow, Acadamia Europaea, since 2001. Recent publications include: Conflict and identity in the history of Scotland and Ireland from the seventeenth to the twentieth century (Co-Editor), 1995; Social change in the age of Enlightenment: Edinburgh 1660-1760, 1994; Madness and society in eighteenth-century Scotland, 2000; Autism in history: The case of Hugh Blair of Borgue (Co-Author), 2000; The New Penguin History of Scotland (Co-Editor), 2001. Recreations: cinema; swimming; scuba diving; antiques; upholstering; food and drink. Address: (b.) Department of Modern History, St Andrews University, St Andrews KY16 9AL; T.-01334 462901.

Houston, Vicky, BA (Hons), PhD. Head, School of Hotel, Tourism and Retail Management, Robert Gordon University, since 1997; b. 21.4.59, Glasgow; 1 d. Educ. Bannerman High School; Glasgow Caledonian University. Researcher, 1989-92; Lecturer in Psychology, Queen's College, Glasgow, 1992-95; Senior Lecturer, then Head of Department, Queen Margaret's College, Edinburgh, 1995-97. Recreations: sailing; skiing; gourmet cooking. Address: (b.) Robert Gordon University, Kepplestone, Aberdeen; T.-0771 2005821.

Houstoun, Andrew Beatty, OBE, MC, JP, DL. Vice President, Scottish Landowners Federation, 1984-98; b. 15.10.22, Cranleigh; m., Mary Elizabeth Spencer-Nairn; 4 s. Educ. Harrow. Regular Army, 1941-56; retired as Major, 1st The Royal Dragoons; farming, Angus and Perthshire, since 1956; commanded Fife and Forfar Yeomanry/Scottish Horse (TA), 1962-65; retired Brevet Col. and Lt. Col, 1965; Angus County Councillor, 1966-75 (Vice Chairman, Education Committee); Convener, Scottish Landowners Federation, 1979-82; Chancellor's Assessor, Dundee University Court, 1981-92; Vice Lord Lieutenant, Angus, 1986-2001. Address: Kirkhill, Lintrathen, Kirriemuir, Angus DD8 5JH; T.-01575 560228.

Howard, Professor Ian, MA (Hons), RSA. Principal, Edinburgh College of Art, since 2001; b. 5.11.52, Aberdeen; m., Ruth D'Arcy; 2 d. Educ. Aberdeen Grammar School; Edinburgh College of Art; Edinburgh University. Travelling scholarship to Italy, 1976; part-time Lecturer in Painting, Gray's School of Art, Aberdeen, 1977 (appointed full-time, 1980); Dean of Faculty, Duncan of Jordanstone College of Art, University of Dundee, 1999-2001. Scottish Arts Council Award, 1979, Bursary, 1985-86; Chicago Prize, 2000; numerous one-man and group exhibitions; appointed to Faculty of Fine Art, British School at Rome, 1996. Recreations: reading; music; cooking. Address: (b.) Principal's Office, Edinburgh College of Art, Lauriston Place, Edinburgh; T.-0131-221 6060.

Howard, Philip, MA (Hons) (Cantab), MLitt. Artistic Director, Traverse Theatre, Edinburgh, since 1996; b. 27.5.63, York. Educ. Ampleforth College, York; Girton College, Cambridge; St. Andrews University. Assistant Director, Royal Court Theatre, London, 1988-90; Director, National Gaelic Youth Theatre, Isle of Benbecula, 1989-92. Director, Tosg Gaelic Theatre Company, since 1996. Address: (b.) Traverse Theatre, Cambridge Street, Edinburgh, EH1 2ED; T.-0131-228 3223.

Howat, Rev. Angus John, MA. Minister, Campbeltown, Tarbert and Islay Free Church, since 1996; Assistant Clerk, General Assembly, Free Church of Scotland, since 1998; b. 5.8.44, Monifieth; m., Irene Agnes Gardner Bickerton; 3 d. Educ. Daniel Stewart's College, Edinburgh; Edinburgh University; Strathclyde University; Free Church College. Assistant Librarian, Ayr Public Library, 1966-71; Depute County Librarian, Moray and Nairn, 1971-75; Principal Librarian, Moray District Council at Elgin, 1975-85;

Temporary Assistant Librarian, Free Church College, 1988-90; Minister, Campbeltown Free Church, 1990-96. Publication: Churches of Moray (Joint Author). Recreations: family history; walking. Address: Free Church Manse, Kilberry Road, Tarbert PA29 6XX; T.-01880 820134.

Howatson, William, MA (Hons), JP. Freelance journalist and columnist, since 1996; b. 22.1.53, Dumfries; m., Hazel Symington Paton; 2 d. Educ. Lockerbie Academy; Edinburgh University. Press and Journal: Agricultural Editor, 1984-96, Leader Writer, 1990-96. Chairman, Guild of Agricultural Journalists, 1995; Member, Scottish Water and Sewerage Customers Council, since 1995; Member, Angus College Board of Management, since 1996; Member, Health Education Board for Scotland, since 1997; Member, East Areas Board, Scottish Natural Heritage, since 1997 (Deputy Chairman, since 2000); Non Executive Director, Angus NHS Trust, 1998; Governor, Macaulay Land Use Research Institute, since 1998; Member, Aberdeenshire Council, since 1999; Board Member, Scottish Environment Protection Agency, since 1999; Member, Rail Passenger Committee for Scotland, since 2001; Columnist of the Year, Bank of Scotland Press Awards, 1992; Associate, Royal Agricultural Societies. Publication: Farm Servants and Labour in Lowland Scotland, 1770-1914 (Contributor). Recreations: gardening; hillwalking; reading; Scottish history. Address: (h.) Stone of Morphie, Hillside, Montrose; T.-01674 830746; e-mail: billhowatson@aol.com

Howe, Professor Christine Joyce, BA, PhD, CPsychol, AFBPS. Professor of Psychology, Strathclyde University, since 1998 (Head, Psychology Department, since 1997); b. 21.11.48, Birmingham; m., William Robertson; 1 s.; 1 d. Educ. King Edward VI Camp Hill School for Girls; Sussex University; Cambridge University. Career in teaching and research since 1976. Publications: Learning Language in a Conversational Context, 1983; Language Learning, 1993; Group and Interactive Learning, 1994; Conceptual Structure in Childhood and Adolescence, 1998; Gender and Classroom Interaction, 1997. Recreations: bridge; tennis; cycling; hillwalking; theatre; film; politics. Address: (b.) Department of Psychology, Strathclyde University, 40 George Street, Glasgow G1 1QE; T.-0141-548 2575; e-mail: c.j.howe@strath.ac.uk

Howe, Andrew Law, CBE, FRAgrS. Chairman: Howie Animal Feeds Ltd., since 2001, Robert Howie & Sons, 1982-2001, Scottish Milk Ltd., 1994-95; b. 14.4.24, Dunlop; m., Joan Duncan; 2 s.; 2 d. Educ. Glasgow Academy. Joined Robert Howie & Sons, 1941; War Service, RN; became Director, 1965; President, Scottish Compound Feed Manufacturers, 1968-70 and 1983-85; President, Compound Animal Feed Manufacturers National Association, 1971-72; Director, Scottish Corn Trade, 1976-78; Vice-President/Feed, UK Agricultural Supply Trade Association, 1980-81; Chairman, Scottish Council, UKASTA, 1985-87; Director, Scottish Milk Marketing Board, 1980-94 (Chairman, 1982-94); Member, CBI Scottish Council, 1989-95. Recreations: golf; gardening; wood-turning. Address: (h.) Newmill House, Dunlop, Kilmarnock KA3 4BQ; T.-01560 484936.

Howie, Professor John Garvie Robertson, CBE, MD, PhD, FRCPE, FRCGP, FMedSci. Professor of General Practice, Edinburgh University, 1980-2000; b. 23.1.37, Glasgow; m., Elizabeth Margaret Donald; 2 s.; 1 d. Educ. High School of Glasgow; Glasgow University. Registrar, Laboratory Medicine, Western Infirmary, Glasgow, 1962-66; General Practitioner, Glasgow, 1966-70; Lecturer/Senior Lecturer in General Practice, Aberdeen University, 1970-80; Member: Biomedical Research Committee, SHHD, 1977-81, Health Services Research Committee, SHHD, 1982-86, Chief Scientist Committeee, SHHD, 1987-97, Committee on the Review of Medicines,

1986-91. Publications: Research in General Practice; A Day in the Life of Academic General Practice. Recreations: golf; gardening; music. Address: (h.) 4 Ravelrig Park, Balerno, Midlothian EH14 7DL; T.-0131-449 6305.

Howie, Professor John Mackintosh, CBE, MA, DPhil, DSc, HonDUniv, FRSE. Regius Professor of Mathematics, St. Andrews University, 1970-97; b. 23.5.36, Chryston, Lanarkshire; m., Dorothy Joyce Miller; 2 d. Educ. Robert Gordon's College, Aberdeen; Aberdeen University. Assistant in Mathematics, Aberdeen University, 1958-59; Assistant, then Lecturer in Mathematics, Glasgow University, 1961-67; Senior Lecturer in Mathematics, Stirling University, 1967-70; visiting appointments:Tulane University, 1964-65, State University of New York at Buffalo, 1969-70, University of Western Australia, 1968, Monash University, 1979, Northern Illinois University, 1988, University of Lisbon, 1996; Dean of Science, St. Andrews University, 1976-79. President, Edinburgh Mathematical Society, 1972-73; Vice-President, London Mathematical Society, 1984-86 and 1990-92; Convener, SCEEB Mathematics Panel, 1970-73; Chairman, Scottish Central Committee on Mathematics, 1975-81; Member, Committee to Review Examinations (Dunning Committee), 1975-77; Chairman, Governors, Dundee College of Education, 1983-87; Keith Prize, Royal Society of Edinburgh, 1979-81; Chairman, Committee to review Fifth and Sixth Years (Howie Committee), 1990-92. Publications: An Introduction to Semigroup Theory, 1976; Automata and Languages, 1991; Fundamentals of Semigroup Theory, 1995; Real Analysis, 2001; papers in mathematical journals. Recreations: music; gardening. Address: (b.) Mathematical Institute, St. Andrews University, North Haugh, St. Andrews, KY16 9SS; T.-01334 463746; e-mail: jmh@st-and.ac.uk

Howie, Professor Peter William, MD, FRCOG, FRSE, FRCP (Glas). Professor of Obstetrics and Gynaecology, Dundee University, 1981-2001 (Deputy Principal, Dundee University, 1996-2001, Dean, Medicine and Dentistry, 1990-93); Chairman, Scottish Council for Postgraduate Medical and Dental Education, 1996-2002; b. 21.11.39, Aberdeen; m., Anne Jardine Quigg; 1 s.; 1 d. Educ. High School of Glasgow; Glasgow University. Astor Foundation Research Fellow, Royal College of Pathologists, 1970-71; Lecturer, then Senior Lecturer, Department of Obstetrics and Gynaecology, Glasgow University, 1971-78; Clinical Consultant, Medical Research Council Reproductive Biology Unit, Edinburgh, 1978-81. Recreations: golf; music. Address: (h.) 8 Travebank Gardens, Monifieth, Angus DD5 4ET; T.-01382 534802.

Howieson, John Gray, MA, DipEdTech. Head Teacher, Portree High School, since 1998; b. 4.8.53, Dumfries. Educ. Dumfries Academy; Edinburgh University; Moray House College of Education. Teacher, English and Latin, Leith Academy, 1976-81, Assistant Principal Teacher, Resources, Tynecastle High School, 1981-83; Principal Teacher, English, Whitburn Academy, 1983-87; Assistant Rector, Whitburn Academy, 1987-94; Depute Rector, Dunbar Grammar School, 1994- 98. Recreations: traditional music; reading; jogging. Address: (b.) Portree High School, Viewfield Road, Portree, Isle of Skye, IV51 9ET; T.-01478 612030; e-mail: john.howieson@highland.gov.uk

Howison, John Andrew, FRSA, BSc, MSc, CEng, MICE, MCIArb. Chief Road Engineer, Scottish Executive Development Department, since 1999; b. 12.8.46, Ruislip; m., Teresa Maria; 2 s.; 2 d. Educ. Surbiton Grammar School; Edinburgh University; Heriot Watt University. Edinburgh Corporation, 1968-70; Livingston Development Corporation, 1970-73; Department of Environment/

Department of Transport/Scottish Office, 1973-99 (Deputy Chief Engineer, Roads Directorate, Scottish Office Industry Department, 1992-99). Address: (b.) Victoria Quay, Edinburgh; T.-0131-244 7204.

Howson, Peter. Painter; b. 1958, London. Moved to Glasgow, 1962; attended Glasgow School of Art, 1975-77; spent a short period in the Scottish infantry, travelling in Europe; returned to Glasgow School of Art, 1979-81, studying under Sandy Moffat; Artist in Residence, St Andrews and part-time Tutor, Glasgow School of Art, 1985; commissioned by Imperial War Museum to visit Bosnia as war artist, 1993.

Ho-Yen, Darrel Orlando, BMSc (Hons), MBChB, MD, FRCPath, DSc. Consultant Microbiologist, Raigmore Hospital, Inverness, since 1987; Director, Scottish Toxoplasma Reference Laboratory, since 1987; Honorary Clinical Senior Lecturer, Aberdeen University, since 1987; b. 1.5.48; m., Jennifer Nicholls; 2 s. Educ. Dundee University. Ninewells Hospital and Medical School, Dundee, 1974-83; Regional Virus Laboratory, Ruchill Hospital, Glasgow, 1983-87. Publications: Better Recovery from Viral Illnesses; Diseases of Infection (Co-Author); Unwind; Human Toxoplasmosis (Co-Author); Climbing Out; Ticks (Co-author). Address: (b.) Microbiology Department, Raigmore Hospital, Inverness IV2 3UJ; T.-01463 704206.

Hubbuck, Professor John Reginald, BA (Cantab), MA, DPhil (Oxon), FRSE, FRSA, CMath, FIMA. Professor of Mathematics, Aberdeen University, since 1978; b. 3.5.41, Girvan; m., Anne Neilson; 1 s.; 1 d. Educ. Manchester Grammar School; Queens' College, Cambridge; Pembroke College, Oxford. Fellow: Gonville and Caius College, Cambridge, 1970-72, Magdalen College, Oxford, 1972-78; President, Edinburgh Mathematical Society, 1985-86. Recreation: hill-walking. Address: (h.) 8 Fonthill Terrace, Aberdeen AB11 7UR; T.-01224 588738.

Hudghton, Ian. Member of the European Parliament (SNP), since 1998; m., Lily; 1 s.; 1 d. Ran family home decorating business, 20 years; former Member, EU's Committee of the Regions; elected to Angus District Council, 1986 (Housing Convener, eight years); Depute SNP Group Leader and Property Convener, Tayside Regional Council, 1994-96; elected to Angus Council, 1995 (Leader, 1996-98); Member, SNP National Executive Committee. Address: (b.) 8 Old Glamis Road, Dundee DD3 8HP.

Hudson, Barbara Jean, BA (Hons). Dip. App.Soc.Studies. Director BAAF (Adoption and Fostering) Scotland, since 1998; b. Scunthorpe. Educ. King Edward VI Grammar School, Louth; Manchester University; Leeds University. VSO, Nigeria, 1972; Social Work Department, Norwich hospitals, 1973-75; Leeds Social Services Department, 1976-86; Bradford Social Services, 1986-98. Recreations: walking; opera; theatre; friends. Address: (b.) 40 Shandwick Place, Edinburgh EH6 4BY; T.-0131-220 4749; e-mail: scotland@baaf.org.uk

Hudson, Rev. Eric Vallance, LTh. Minister, Westerton Fairlie Memorial Church, since 1990; b. 22.2.42, Glasgow; m., Lorna Mary Miller; 1 s.; 1 d. Educ. Paisley Grammar School; Wollongong High School, NSW; Christ's College, Aberdeen and Aberdeen University. Sub-Editor, D.C. Thomson & Co. Ltd., Dundee, 1961-66; Student Assistant, West Kirk of St. Nicholas, Aberdeen, 1966-69; Senior Assistant Minister, New Kilpatrick Parish Church, Bearsden, 1971-73; Minister, Kintore Parish Church, 1973-78; Religious Programmes Officer, Scottish Television, 1978-89; Convener, Association of Bearsden Churches, 1997-99; Member: Religious Advisory Committee, Radio Clyde, Church of Scotland Board of Social Responsibility,

since 1997; Moderator, Dumbarton Presbytery, 1998-99. Address: 3 Canniesburn Road, Bearsden, Glasgow G61 1PW.

Huggins, Geoffrey L., LLB, MSSc. Head of Housing 3, Scottish Executive, since 2000; b. 24.9.65, Newtownards, N. Ireland. Educ. Bangor Grammar School; Queen's University, Belfast; Edinburgh University. Northern Ireland Office: constitutional and political development, 1991-92, security policy and operations, 1992-93, prisons policy, 1993-98; Education Department, Scottish Executive, 1998-2000. Recreations: hillwalking; cinema; travel; reading. Address: (b.) Victoria Quay, Edinburgh EH6 6QQ; e-mail: geoffhuggins@hotmail.com

Huggins, Martin, MA, FRSA. Co-Founder, Edinburgh School of English (Principal, 1969-2001); Director, Hawthorn Edinburgh Ltd., since 2001; b. 11.4.39, Edinburgh; m., 1, Astrid Chalmers Watson (m. diss.); 2 d.; 2, Margot Learmond. Educ. George Watson's College; Edinburgh University. Chairman, Scottish Craftsmanship Association, 1977-84; Governor, Edinburgh College of Art, 1980-92; Director, Edinburgh Chamber of Commerce, 1982-86; Chairman, ARELS, 1984-86; Member, British Council Recognition Advisory Committee, 1984-86; Chairman, Board of Governors, Edinburgh College of Art, 1990-92; President, Scottish Arts Club, 1990-92; Assistant, Masters Court, Edinburgh Merchant Company, 1992-95; Trustee, Hospitalfield Trust, 1994-99; Trustee, Melville Trust, since 2000. Recreations: music; travel; painting; lunching at the Arts Club. Address: (h.) 13 Ainslie Place, Edinburgh EH3 6AS; T.-0131-226 1246.

Hughes of Woodside, Lord (Robert Hughes). Life Peer; MP (Labour), Aberdeen North, 1970-97; b. 3.1.32; m.; 2 s.; 3 d. Educ. Powis Secondary School, Aberdeen; Robert Gordon's College, Aberdeen; Benoni High School, Transvaal; Pietermaritzburg Technical College, Natal. Engineering apprenticeship, South African Rubber Company, Natal, 1949-54; draughtsman, C.F. Wilson & Co., Aberdeen, 1954-70; Member, Aberdeen City Council, 1962-71; Chairman, Aberdeen City Labour Party, 1961-69; Member, Select Committee on Scottish Affairs, 1971; Opposition Junior Spokesman on Scottish Affairs, 1972-74; Parliamentary Under Secretary of State, Scottish Office, 1974-75; Chairman, Select Committee on Scottish Affairs, 1981; Opposition Junior Spokesman on Transport, 1981-83; Opposition Principal Spokesman on Agriculture, 1984-85, on Transport, 1985-87; Member, General Medical Council, 1976-79; Chairman: Anti Apartheid Movement, 1976-94, Action for Southern Africa (ACTSA), 1994-99 (Honorary President, since 1990); Vice-Convenor, Scottish Group, Labour MPs, 1989; Convenor, Scottish Group of Labour MPs, 1990-91; Member, Select Committee on Scottish Affairs, 1992-97. Address: (b.) House of Lords, London.

Hughes, Rev. Clifford Eryl, MA, BD, CertEd. Minister, St. Mary's Parish Church, Haddington, 1993-2001; b. 16.12.36, Newport, S. Wales; m., Kathleen Mackenzie Craig; 1 s.; 1 d. Educ. Dulwich College, London; King's College, University of Cambridge; New College, University of Edinburgh. Teacher, Hurst Grange School, Stirling; Headmaster, Beaconhurst School, Bridge of Allan; Headmaster, Loretto Junior School. Professional singer (opera, concert hall, radio and television performances). Recreations: listening to and reviewing music. Address: Pavilion Cottage, Briglands, Rumbling Bridge, Kinross KY13 0PS; T.-01577 840506.

Hughes, Dale William Alexander, LLB (Hons), DipLP. Advocate, since 1993; b. 21.1.67, Glasgow. Educ. George Watson's College, Edinburgh; Aberdeen University; Edinburgh University. Solicitor, since 1990-93. Tutor, University of Edinburgh. Recreations: hillwalking; theatre; opera. Address: (h.) 18 Marchall Crescent, Edinburgh EH16 5HL; (b.) Advocates Library, Edinburgh EH1; T.-0131-664 2473.

Hughes, Janis. MSP (Labour), Glasgow Rutherglen, since 1999; b. 1.5.58, Glasgow; 1 s. Educ. Queens Park School, Glasgow; Glasgow Western Nursing College. Nurse, 1980-86; Health Service administrator, 1986-99. Recreations: reading; cinema. Address: (b.) 51 Stonelaw Road, Rutherglen, Glasgow G73 3TN; T.-0141-647 0707.

Hughes, Professor John, OBE, BSc, CEng, FIMechE, Hon.FISPO. Professor and Director, National Centre for Prosthetics and Orthotics, Strathclyde University, 1972-99, Emeritus Professor, 1999; b. 20.4.34, Renfrew; m., Margaret Scoular Crichton; 2 d. Educ. Camphill School; Strathclyde University. Worked in shipbuilding and engineering, 1950-63; Strathclyde University: Lecturer in Mechanical Engineering Design, 1963-67, Senior Lecturer, Bioengineering Unit, 1967-72; Past President, International Society for Prosthetics and Orthotics. Recreations: golf; gardening. Address: (b.) Strathclyde University, Curran Building, 131 St. James' Road, Glasgow G4 OLS; T.-0141-552 4049.

Hughes, Professor Michael David. Professor of Management, University of Stirling, since 1989; b. 8.2.47, London; m., Ewa Maria Helinska-Hughes; 1 s.; 2 d. Educ. Farnborough Grammar School; Brunel University. Address: (b.) Department of Management and Organization, University of Stirling, Stirling FK9 4LA; T.-01786 467309.

Hughes, Peter Travers, OBE, FREng, FIM, FRSA, MBA, FIMgt. Chief Executive, Scottish Engineering, since 1998; b. 24.12.46, Bellshill. Educ. Wishaw High School; Technical College, Coatbridge; Strathclyde University; Dundee University. Foundry Metallurgist, Clyde Alloy, 1965-68; Foundry Metallurgist/ Chief Metallurgist/Foundry Manager, North British Steel Group, Armadale and Bathgate, 1968-76; Director and General Manager, Lake and Elliot Steelfounders and Engineers, 1976-80; Managing Director, National Steel Foundry (1914) Ltd., 1980-83; Chairman and Managing Director, Glencast Ltd, 1983-98; Member: Cabinet Office Better Regulation Taskforce, Clyde Shipyards Task Force, Scottish Manufacturing Strategy Group for Scottish Parliament, Engineering and Marine Training Authority Advisory Committee, Scottish Qualifications Authority Advisory Group, EEF Executive Board, EEF Economic Policy Committee; Vice-Convenor, West of Scotland Teaching Company Scheme. Recreations: tennis; football; golf; folksinging; after dinner speaking. Address: (b.) 105 West George Street, Glasgow, G2 1QL; T.-0141-221 3181; e-mail: peterhughes@scottishengineering.org.uk

Hughes, Roger Llewellyn, MD, FRCP (Glas), FRCA. Consultant in Anaesthesia and Intensive Care, since 1980; Honorary Senior Lecturer, since 1985; b. 2.6.47, Douglas, Isle of Man; m., Pamela Jane Finlayson; 4 d. Educ. High School of Glasgow; Glasgow University. SHO and Registrar in Anaesthesia, Glasgow Royal Infirmary; Senior Registrar then Lecturer in Anaesthesia, University of Glasgow. Chairman, Greater Glasgow Area Clinical Forum; Chairman, Area Medical Committee; Member, Greater Glasgow Unified Health Board. Recreations: reading; walking; foreign travel. Address: 7 Ballaig Avenue, Bearsden, Glasgow G61 4HA; T.-0141-942 5626; e-mail: roger@saintronans.freeserve.co.uk

Hughes Hallett, Professor Andrew Jonathan, BA (Hons), MSc (Econ), DPhil, FRSA, FRSE. Professor of Economics, Strathclyde University, since 1989; Research Fellow, Centre for Economic Policy Research, since 1985; Consultant to World Bank, European Commission, UN, IMF, since 1986; Director and Fulbright Fellow, Princeton University, 1992-94; Jean Monet Professor, since 1996; b. 1.11.47, London; m., Claudia; 2 s.; 1 d. Educ. Radley College; Warwick University; LSE; Oxford University.

Lecturer in Economics, Bristol University, 1973-77; Associate Professor, Erasmus University, Rotterdam, 1977-85; David Dale Professor, Newcastle University, 1985-89. Publications: six books; 200 papers. Address: (b.) 100 Cathedral Street, Glasgow G4 OLN; T.-0141-548 3581; e-mail: a.hughes-hallett@strath.ac.uk

Hughes Hallett, David John, FRICS. Consultant; Director, Scottish Wildlife Trust, 1989-98; Main Board Member, Scottish Environment Protection Agency, since 1995; b. 19.6.47, Dunfermline; m., Anne Mary Wright; 2 s.; 1 d. Educ. Fettes College; Reading University. Chartered Surveyor, rural practice, 1966-76; Land Use Adviser, then Director, Scottish Landowners' Federation, 1976-89. Chairman, Royal Institution of Chartered Surveyors in Scotland, 1988-89; Member, Policy Committee, Scottish Council for Voluntary Organisations. Recreations: sailing; cycling; singing. Address: (h.) 8 Crosswood Crescent, Balerno, Edinburgh EH14 7HS; T.-0131-449 2244; e-mail: hugheshallett@lineone.net

Hughson, A.V. Mark, MD, MB, ChB, FRCPsych, DPM. Consultant Psychiatrist, Leverndale Hospital, Glasgow, since 1990; Honorary Clinical Senior Lecturer, Glasgow University, since 1991; b. 12.3.47, Edinburgh; m., Joan Scally; 2 s. Educ. George Watson's College, Edinburgh; Glasgow University. Recreations: playing the organ (not too badly); skiing (badly). Address: (h.) 1 Cleveden Gardens, Glasgow G12 OPU; T.-0141-334 2473.

Huhtaniemi, Professor Ilpo Tapani, MD, PhD. Professor of Reproductive Biology, University of Aberdeen, since 2000; b. 22.5.47, Finland; 1 s.; 1 d. Educ. Vaasan Yhteiskouly, Vaasa, Finland; University of Helsinki, Finland. Associate Professor of Chemical Pathology, University of Helsinki, 1982-85; Professor and Chair of Physiology, University of Turku, Finland, 1986-2000. Address: (b.) Department of Obstetrics and Gynaecology, University of Aberdeen AB25 2ZD; T.-01224 559483; e-mail: ilpo.huhtaniemi@utu.fi

Hukins, Professor David William Laurence, PhD, DSc, CPhys, FInstP, FIPEM, FRSE. MacRobert Professor of Physics, University of Aberdeen, since 1994; Honorary Medical Physicist, Aberdeen Royal Hospitals NHS Trust, since 1994; Managing Director, Aubec R&D Ltd., since 1998; Honorary Research Affiliate, Forsyth Dental Center, Boston, MA, USA, since 1990; b. 3.2.47; Ashford; m., Celia Elizabeth; 2 s. Educ. Ashford Grammar School; Queen Mary College, University of London; King's College, University of London. Research Associate, Purdue University, IN, USA, 1971-73; Research Assistant, University of Oxford, 1973-74; University of Manchester, Department of Medical Biophysics: Lecturer, 1974-80, Senior Lecturer, 1980-91, Reader, 1991-94; Graduate Education Co-ordinator, Faculty of Medicine, University of Manchester, 1993-94. Volvo Prize, International Society for the Study of the Lumbar Spine, 1979; Thomas Stephen Prize, Medical Engineering Division, Institution of Mechanical Engineers, 1998; Member, Scientific Sub-committee, Arthritis Research Campaign, since 1998; Honorary Scientific Advisor, Manchester and Salford Back Pain Centre, 1993-96. Publications: X-Ray Diffraction by Disordered and Ordered Systems, 1981; Editor/Co-editor of five books on connective tissues, calcified tissues and back pain. Recreations: hillwalking; gardening; skiing. Address: (b.) Department of Bio-medical Physics and Bio-Engineering, University of Aberdeen, Foresterhill, Aberdeen AB25 2ZD; T.-01224 553495; e-mail: d.hukins@biomed.abdn.ac.uk.

Hulse, Martin David, BSc (Hons). Director, The Cockburn Association, since 1999; b. 3.10.73, Chorley; m., Sarah Frances. Educ. St. Michael's CE High School; Heriot-Watt University. GVA Grimley Property Surveyors, 1996-97. Director, Edinburgh Environment Partnership Grants

Scheme; Member, Development Committee, Edinburgh World Heritage Trust. Recreations: classic cars; hillwalking; cooking. Address: (b.) Trunks Close. 55 High Street, Edinburgh EH1 1SR; T.-0131-557 8686; e-mail: cockburn.association@btinternet.com

Hume, Sir Alan (Blyth), Kt, CB, MA; b. 5.1.13, Broxburn; m., Marion Morton Garrett; 1 s.; 1 d. Educ. George Heriot's School, Edinburgh; Edinburgh University. Scottish Office: entered, 1936, Under Secretary, Scottish Home Department, 1957-59, Assistant Under Secretary of State, 1959-62, Under Secretary, Ministry of Public Building and Works, 1963-64, Secretary, Scottish Development Department, 1965-73. Chairman: Ancient Monuments Board for Scotland, 1973-81, Edinburgh New Town Conservation Committee, 1975-90. Recreations: golf; fishing. Address: (h.) 12 Oswald Road, Edinburgh EH9 2HJ; T.-0131-667 2440.

Hume, David, BSc, MSc, MBA, ARSGS. Chief Executive, Scottish Borders Council, since 2001; b. Edinburgh; m., Ann Crawford; 3 d. Educ. George Heriot's School, Edinburgh; St Andrews University; University of Wales; Edinburgh University. Researcher, University of Wales Institute of Science and Technology, 1978-80; Senior Research Officer, Strathclyde Regional Council, 1980-86; Lothian Regional Council: Senior Principal Officer, Management and Information Services, 1986-90, Depute Director Corporate Services, 1990-96; City of Edinburgh Council: Director Strategic Policy, 1996-98, Director of Corporate Services, 1998-2001. Recreations: squash; cycling; motor-cycling; jazz. Address: (b.) Council HQ, Newtown St. Boswells, Melrose TD6 0SA.

Hume, John Robert, OBE, BSc, ARCST, FSA, FSA Scot, Hon FRIAS. Honorary Professor: Faculty of Arts, University of Glasgow, since 1998, School of History, University of St. Andrews, since 1999; Member, Industrial Archaeology Sub-Committee, English Heritage, since 1985; Honorary Life President, Seagull Trust, since 1994 (Chairman, 1978-93); Honorary Vice-President, Association for Industrial Archaeology; Honorary Vice-President, Scottish Railway Preservation Society, since 2000 (Chairman, 1967-76); b. 26.2.39, Glasgow; m., Catherine Hope Macnab; 4 s. Educ. Hutchesons' Boys' Grammar School; Glasgow University; Royal College of Science and Technology. Assistant Lecturer, Lecturer, Senior Lecturer in Economic History, Strathclyde University, 1964-91; Chief Inspector of Historic Buildings, Historic Scotland, 1993-99. Member, Inland Waterways Amenity Advisory Council, 1974-2001; Director, Scottish Industrial Archaeology Survey, 1978-84; Member, Ancient Monuments Board for Scotland, 1981-84; Member, Committee on Artistic Matters, Church of Scotland; Trustee: Scottish Maritime Museum, 1983-98, The Waterways Trust, since 2000, Scotland's Churches Scheme, since 2000. Publications: The Industrial Archaeology of Glasgow; The Industrial Archaeology of Scotland; as Co-Author: Workshop of the British Empire: Engineering and Shipbuilding in the West of Scotland; Beardmore: the History of a Scottish Industrial Giant; The Making of Scotch Whisky; A Bed of Nails: a History of P. MacCallum & Sons Ltd.; Shipbuilders to the World: a History of Harland and Wolff; Steam Entertainment; Historic Industrial Scenes: Scotland; Industrial History in Pictures: Scotland; Glasgow's Railway Stations; Dumfries and Galloway, an illustrated architectural guide. Recreations: photography; reading. Address: (h.) 28 Partickhill Road, Glasgow G11 5BP.

Hume, Krystyna D., BSc. Head Teacher, St. Serf's School, Edinburgh, since 1992; b. 2.10.43, Edinburgh; m., Bill Hume; 2 s. Educ. James Gillespie's High School for Girls; Edinburgh University. Teacher of Mathematics: Portobello Secondary School, 1966-74 (Housemistress, 1970-74), St.

Serf's School, 1981-92. Recreations: reading; going to the theatre and concerts; listening to music. Address: (b.) St. Serf's School, 5 Wester Coates Gardens, Edinburgh EH12 5LT; T.-0131-337 1015.

Hume, Professor Robert, BSc, MBChB, PhD, FRCP(Edin), FRCPCH. Professor of Developmental Medicine, Dundee University; Consultant Paediatrician and Honorary Consultant in Biochemical Medicine, Dundee Teaching Hospitals NHS Trust; b. 5.4.47, Edinburgh; m., Shaena Finlayson Blair; 2 d. Educ. Dalkeith High School; Edinburgh University. MRC Fellow, Department of Biochemistry, Edinburgh University, 1975-78; Lecturer, Department of Child Life and Health, Edinburgh University, 1978-80; Senior Lecturer, Department of Child Life and Health, Edinburgh University, 1980-92. Medical and Dental Defence Union of Scotland Specialist Advisor. Address: (b.) Tayside Institute of Child Health, Department of Child Health, Ninewells Hospital and Medical School, Dundee DD1 9SY; T.-01382 660111.

Humes, Professor Walter Malcolm, MA, MEd, PhD, FRSA, FCS. Professor of Education, University of Strathclyde, since 2001; b. 10.12.45, Newton Mearns. Educ. Eastwood Senior Secondary School; University of Aberdeen; University of Dundee; University of Glasgow. Teacher of English, London and Renfrewshire, 1968-74; Lecturer in English, Notre Dame College, Glasgow, 1974-76; Lecturer in Education, University of Glasgow, 1976-94; Director of Professional Studies, St. Andrew's College, 1994-99; Head of Educational Studies, University of Glasgow, 1999-2001. Editor, Scottish Educational Review, 1990-94. Publications: Scottish Culture and Scottish Education 1800-1980 (Co-Editor), 1983; The Leadership Class in Scottish Education, 1986; The Management of Educational Policy: Scottish Perspectives (Co-Editor), 1994; Scottish Education (Co-Editor), 1999; chapters in books and articles in journals on a wide range of educational topics. Recreations: literature; music; swimming. Address: (b.) Department of Educational Studies, University of Strathclyde, Jordanhill Campus, Glasgow G13 1PP; T.-0141-950 3416; e-mail: walter.humes@strath.ac.uk

Humfrey, Professor Peter Brian, BA, MA, PhD, FRSE. Professor of Art History, University of St. Andrews, since 1995; b. 9.4.47, Cyprus; m., Margaret Zarina; 2 s. Educ. Cranleigh School, Surrey; Trinity College, Dublin; Courtauld Institute of Art, London. Lecturer in Art History, University of St. Andrews, 1977; Senior Visiting Fellow, Center for Advanced Studies in the Visual Arts, National Gallery of Art, Washington D.C., 1986; Fellow, Harvard Center for Italian Renaissance Studies, Villa I Tatti, Florence, 1987, 1991; Member, Institute for Advanced Study, Princeton, 1988. Publications: Cima da Conegliano, 1983; The Altarpiece in Renaissance Venice, 1993; Painting in Renaissance Venice, 1995; Lorenzo Lotto, 1997; Dosso Dossi (Co-Author), 1998. Address: (b.) School of Art History, University of St. Andrews, St. Andrews KY16 9AL; T.-01334 462400.

Humphrey, James Malcolm Marcus, CBE, DL, OStJ, MA, FRICS. Member, Aberdeenshire Council, since 1995 (Member, Grampian Regional Council, 1974-94); Deputy Lieutenant, Aberdeenshire, since 1989; Alternate Member, European Committee of the Regions; b. 1.5.38, Montreal, Canada; m., Sabrina Margaret Pooley; 2 s.; 2 d. Educ. Eton College; Oxford University. Conservative Parliamentary candidate, North Aberdeen, 1966, Kincardine and Deeside, 1991; Council Member, National Farmers Union of Scotland, 1968-73; Member, Aberdeen County Council, 1970-75 (Chairman of Finance, 1973-75); Grampian Regional Council, 1974-78: Leader of the Council, Chairman of Finance, Leader, Conservative Group; Grand Master Mason of Scotland, 1983-88; former Chairman, Clinterty Agricultural College Council; Member, Queen's

Bodyguard for Scotland (Royal Company of Archers); Chairman, North of Scotland Board, Eagle Star Group, 1973-91; Non-Executive Director, Grampian Healthcare NHS Trust, 1993-99. Recreations: shooting; fishing; photography. Address: (h.) Dinnet, Aboyne, Aberdeenshire.

Hunt, Professor Sheila Catherine, PhD, MBA, MSc (Econ), ILTM, RGN, RM. Professor of Nursing and Midwifery and Dean, School of Nursing and Midwifery, University of Dundee, since 2000; b. 16.12.50, Southport; m., David James Hunt; 1 s; 1 d. Student Nurse, Cardiff Royal Infirmary, 1969-72; Staff Nurse, University Hospital of Wales, 1972-73; Student Midwife, South Glamorgan Health Authority, 1973-74; Staff Midwife, University Hospital of Wales, 1974-75; Midwifery Sister/Obstetric Nurse Teacher, 1975-76; Night Sister, Medical Unit, University Hospital of Wales, 1976-77; Ward Sister, Elderly Care Unit, Llandough Hospital, Cardiff, 1977-78; Student Teacher, 1978-79; Nurse Teacher, University Hospital of Wales, 1979-80; Midwifery Sister, Caerphilly Miner's Hospital, Mid Glamorgan, 1980-84; Midwifery Clinical Teacher, Mid Glamorgan Health Authority, 1984-88; Senior Midwife Teacher, Continuing Education, West Glamorgan Health Authority, 1988-91; Programme Manager/Head of Midwifery Education, Department of Nursing, Midwifery and Health Care, University of Wales, Swansea, 1991-96; Professor of Midwifery and Head, School of Women's Health Studies, Birmingham Women's NHS Trust and University of Central England, Birmingham, 1996-2000. Publications: The Social Meaning of Midwifery (Co-Author), 1995; The Midwife and Society – Perspectives, Policies and Practice (Co-Author), 1996; Challenges in Midwifery Care (Co-Editor), 1997; Pregnant Women – Violent Men: What Do Midwives Need to Know? (Co-Author), 2000. Address: (h.) 2 St. Andrews Road, Pitscottie, Fife KY15 5TF; T.-01334 828898; e-mail: sch1612@aol.com

Hunter, A. Colin J., BA. Head Teacher, Tiree High School, since 1985; b. 26.9.47, Falkirk; m., June Sinclair Stark; 2 s.; 1 d. Educ. Falkirk High School; Stirling University. Entered teaching, 1972; Teacher, Falkirk High School and Forres Academy; Principal Teacher of Biology, Whitfield High School, Dundee; Depute Head Teacher, Auchtercairn Secondary School, Gairloch. Recreations: gardening; golf; walking. Address: (h.) Cornaigmore Schoolhouse, Isle of Tiree, Argyll PA77 6XA; T.-01879 220556.

Hunter, Andrew Reid, BA (Hons), PGCE. Headmaster, Merchiston Castle School, Edinburgh, since 1998; b. 28.9.58, Nairobi, Kenya; m., Barbara G.; 2 s.; 1 d. Educ. Kenton College, Nairobi; Aldenham School, Elstree; University of Manchester; St. Luke's College, Exeter. Westbrook Hay Preparatory School, 1978-79; Worksop College, 1983-91 (Housemaster, 1987-91); Bradfield College, 1991-98 (Housemaster, 1992-98). Former Chairman, Public Schools Hockey Festival, Oxford; Committee Member, Public Schools Lawn Tennis Association. Recreations: reading; attending theatre; former men's county player, tennis, squash and hockey. Address: Castle Gates, Merchiston Castle School, Colinton, Edinburgh EH13 0PU; T.-0131-312 2202.

Hunter, Archibald Sinclair, DL, CA. Non Executive Director, Macfarlane Group PLC, Clydeport plc; Trustee, Sargent Cancer Care for Children; Governor, The Beatson Institute; Senior Partner, Scotland, KPMG, 1992-99; b. 20.8.43, Glasgow; m., Pat; 2 s.; 1 d. Educ. Queen's Park School, Glasgow. Trained with Mackie & Clark, CA, Glasgow; qualified as CA, 1966; joined Thomson McLintock, 1966; Partner, 1974; UK Board, 1992-96; Latin American Board, 1995-99; President, Institute of Chartered Accountants of Scotland, 1997-98; Chairman Elect, Strathclyde University Court. Recreations: golf; swimming; walking. Address: (b.) 24 Blythswood Square, Glasgow G2 4QS; T.-0141-226 5511.

Hunter, Christopher G.W., MA, FNI, MRIN. Principal, Glasgow College of Nautical Studies, since 1991; b. 8.10.42, Bristol; m., Irene Mary; 3 d. Educ. Pangbourne College. Seafaring career, Deck Officer to Master, 1960-77; Fleet Training Manager/Deputy Personnel Manager, Cunard Shipping Services Ltd., 1977-84; Principal, National Sea Training College, Kent, 1984-91. Vice-Chairman, Merchant Navy Training Board; Chairman, Thistle Education and Consultancy Ltd.; Chairman, Adelphi Management Company Ltd.; Chairman, Central and West of Scotland Ports Welfare Committee; Chairman, The Gorbals Initiative; Chairman, Scottish Further Education Unit; Chairman, Education and Training Committee, Nautical Institute; Governor, Training Division, Baltic and International Maritime Council. Recreation: family. Address: (b.) 21 Thistle Street, Glasgow G5 9XB; T.-0141-565 2550.

Hunter, Colin M., OBE, MB, ChB, FRCP(Ed), FRCGP, FIHM(Hon). National GP Co-ordinator Primary Care, Scottish Council for Postgraduate Medical and Dental Education, since 1999; Chairman, Primary Care Reference Group, Clinical Standards Board for Scotland, since 1999; Chairman, Clinical Effectiveness Programme in Primary Care, since 1999; Hon. Fellow, Institute of Healthcare Management, since 1996; b. 28.4.58, Stirling. Educ. High School of Stirling; Aberdeen University. Principal in general practice, Skene Medical Group, 1986; Honorary Senior Lecturer, Aberdeen University, 1988; Hon. Secretary, N.E. Scotland Faculty, RCGP, 1989-96; first member, RCGP in Scotland, to attain Fellowship of Royal College by Assessment, 1993; Sally Irvine Lecture, Glasgow, 1996; Chairman, Scottish Council, Royal College of General Practitioners, 1996-2000. Recreations: hill-walking; singing. Address: The Langdales, 1 Craigston Gardens, Westhill, Aberdeen AB32 6NL; T.-01224 742594; e-mail: colin.hunter@scpmde.scot.nhs.uk

Hunter, George Alexander, OBE (1980), KStJ. Secretary, Commonwealth Games Council for Scotland, 1978-99; Founder Governor, Scottish Sports Aid Foundation, since 1980; Member, Edinburgh City Council, since 1992; b. 24.2.26, Edinburgh; m., Eileen Elizabeth. Educ. George Watson's College, Edinburgh. Served with Cameronians, seconded to 17th Dogara Regiment, Indian Army, 1944-47 (Captain); Lawson Donaldson Seeds Ltd., 1942-82 (Director, 15 years); Honorary Consul for Malta; Secretary, Scottish Amateur Rowing Association, 1948-78 (President, 1978-84); Adviser, Sports Aid Foundation, since 1979; Treasurer, Commonwealth Games Council for Scotland, 1962-78; Member, Scottish Sports Council, 1976-84 (Chairman, Games and Sports Committee, 1976-84); Chairman, Scottish Standing Conference for Sport, 1977-84. Address: (h.) 1 Craiglockhart Crescent, Edinburgh EH14 1EZ; T.-0131-443 2533.

Hunter, James, CBE, MA (Hons), PhD. Writer and Historian; Chairman, Highlands and Islands Enterprise; Member, Broadcasting Council for Scotland; b. 22.5.48, Duror, Argyll; m., Evelyn; 1 s.; 1 d. Educ. Oban High School; Aberdeen University; Edinburgh University. Former Director, Scottish Crofters Union; former Chairman, Skye and Lochalsh Enterprise. Publications: The Making of the Crofting Community, 1976; Skye: The Island, 1986; The Claim of Crofting, 1991; Scottish Highlanders: A People and their Place, 1992; A Dance Called America: The Scottish Highlands, the United States and Canada, 1994; On the Other Side of Sorrow: Nature and People in the Scottish Highlands, 1995; Glencoe and the Indians, 1996; Last of the Free: A Millennial History of the Highlands and Islands of Scotland, 1999; Culloden and the Last Clansman, 2001. Address: (b.) Rowanbrae, Kiltarlity, Beauly IV4 7HT; T.-01463 741644.

Hunter, Professor John Angus Alexander, OBE, BA, MD, FRCPEdin. Grant Professor of Dermatology, Edinburgh University, 1981-99; b. 16.6.39, Edinburgh; m., Ruth Mary Farrow; 1 s.; 2 d. Educ. Loretto School; Pembroke College, Cambridge; Edinburgh University. Research Fellow, Institute of Dermatology, London, 1967; Registrar, Department of Dermatology, Edinburgh Royal Infirmary, 1968-70; Exchange Research Fellow, Department of Dermatology, Minnesota University, 1968; Lecturer, Department of Dermatology, Edinburgh University, 1970-74; Consultant Dermatologist, Lothian Health Board, 1974-80; Member: Executive Committee of Investigative Group, British Association of Dermatologists, 1974-76; Executive Committee, British Association of Dermatologists, 1977-79; SEC, Scottish Dermatological Society, 1980-82; Specialist Advisory Committee, (Dermatology), Joint Committee on Higher Medical Training, 1980-87 (Chairman, 1986-90); Medical Appeal Tribunal, 1981-99; Scottish Committee for Hospital Medical Services, 1983-85; President: Section of Dermatology, Royal Society of Medicine, 1993-94, Scottish Dermatological Society, 1994-97, British Association of Detmatologists, 1998-99. Publications: Common Diseases of the Skin (Co-author); Clinical Dermatology (Co-author); Skin Signs in Clinical Medicine (Co-author); Davidson's Principles and Practice of Medicine (Co-author). Recreations: music; gardening; tropical fish; golf. Address: (h.) Leewood, Rosslyn Castle, Roslin, Midlothian EH25 9PZ; T.-0131-440 2181.

Hunter, Kirk John, MA (Hons), ACIS. Chief Executive, Scottish Association of Master Bakers, since 2001; Secretary, Scottish Dairy Association, since 1989; b. 1.12.54, Glasgow; m., June Wilson. Educ. George Heriots School; Dundee University. Graduate Trainee, SSEB, 1977-79; Trade Association Executive, Thomson McLintock, Glasgow, 1980-83; Commercial Officer, Metal Trades Confederation, London and Glasgow, 1983-86; Peat Marwick McLintock, Glasgow, 1986-89. Recreations: golf; gardening; cycling. Address: (h.) 18 Ravelston Road, Bearsden, Glasgow G61 1AW; T.-0141-942 3799.

Hunter, Sir Laurence Colvin, Kt, MA, DPhil, FRSE, DUniv (Paisley). Professor of Applied Economics, Glasgow University, since 1970; b. 8.8.34, Glasgow; m., Evelyn Margaret Green; 3 s.; 1 d. Educ. Hillhead High School, Glasgow; Glasgow University; University College, Oxford. Assistant Lecturer, Manchester University, 1958-59; 2nd Lt., RAEC, 1959-61; Walgreen Postdoctoral Fellow, University of Chicago, 1961-62; joined Glasgow University as Lecturer, 1962; Vice-Principal, 1982-86; Director: External Relations, 1987-90, Business School 1996-99. Council Member, ACAS, 1974-86; Chairman, Police Negotiating Board, 1986-2000; Council Member, Economic and Social Research Council, 1989-92; Editor, Scottish Journal of Political Economy, 1966-97; President, Scottish Economic Society, 1993-96; Treasurer, Royal Society of Edinburgh, since 1999. Recreations: golf; painting; curling. Address: (h.) 23 Boclair Road, Bearsden, Glasgow G61 2AF; T.-0141-563 7135.

Hunter, Lucy, MA. Head of Higher Education, Science and Student Support Division, Scottish Executive, since 2000; b. 7.8.66, St. Andrews. Educ. Ysgol Friars, Bangor, Gwynedd; Oxford University; York University. Policy Officer, Association of County Councils, 1990-97 (seconded to Scottish Office, 1995-97); joined Scottish Office, 1997: Principal, Local Government Finance Distribution, 1995-98, Head, Constitutional Policy Branch,

1998-99; government research fellowship, 1999-2000. Publication: Managing Conflicts After Devolution: A Toolkit for Civil Servants, 2000. Address: (b.) Europa Building, 450 Argyle Street, Glasgow G2 8LG.

Hunter, Mollie. Writer; b. 30.6.22, Longniddry; m., Thomas McIlwraith; 2 s. Educ. Preston Lodge School. Freelance Journalist, until 1960; Past Chairman, Society of Authors in Scotland; writer of various types of fiction (fantasy, historical novels, "realism") for children of varying age groups; 30 titles published, including Talent Is Not Enough, on the craft of writing for children; travelled extensively (Australia, New Zealand, Canada, USA); Lecturer on writing for children; Writer-in-Residence, Dalhousie University, Halifax, Canada, on two occasions; awarded Arbuthnot Lectureship, 1975, and Carnegie Medal, 1975; Phoenix Award, 1992. Recreations: reading; gardening; music. Address: Rose Cottage, 7 Mary Ann Court, Inverness IV3 5BZ; T.-01463 713914.

Hunter, Peter Matheson, BSc, MPhil, LLB. Legal Officer, UNISON Scotland; Member, Equal Opportunities Commission Equal Pay Advisory Panel; Lay Member, Employment Appeal Tribunal, since 2000; b. 11.12.65, Aberdeen. Educ. Cults Academy; Edinburgh University; Glasgow University; Strathclyde University. Hotel worker and shop steward, 1987-90; Edinburgh Employment Rights Campaign, 1990-91; Citizens' Rights Office, 1989-92; joined Scottish Low Pay Unit, 1992, Director, 1999-2001. Lay Member, Employment Tribunal, 1995-2000; founder Member and Parliamentary Candidate for Cairdeas, The Highland and Islands Alliance. Recreations: cycling; Aberdeen FC. Address: (b.) 14 West Campbell Street, Glasgow G2 6RX; T.-0141-332 0006.

Hunter, Richard J. A., BA, CA. Group Finance Director, The Edrington Group Ltd., since 1994; Finance Director, Robertson and Baxter, since 1985; b. 11.5.55, Glasgow; m., Christine; 1 s.; 2d. Educ. Kelvinside Academy; Glenalmond College; Strathclyde University. Qualified CA, Arthur Young McClelland Moores, 1978; joined Edrington Group, 1981. Member, Council, Institute of Chartered Accountants of Scotland, since 1998. Recreations: sailing; fishing; golf. Address: (b.) 2500 Great Western Road, Glasgow G15 6RW.

Hunter, Russell. Actor; b. 18.2.25, Glasgow. Former shipyard worker; began acting as an amateur; made professional debut with Glasgow Unity Theatre, 1947; appeared in repertory with Edinburgh Gateway, Edinburgh Traverse and Glasgow Citizens'; acted with the RSC, Bristol Old Vic and at the Old Vic, London; played title role in The Servant o' Twa Maisters, 1965, opening production of Edinburgh Civic Theatre Company; played The Pope in Galileo, also at Royal Lyceum; played The Gravedigger in Hamlet, Assembly Hall, Edinburgh Festival; took title role in Cocky, one-man play, 1969; played Jock, solo play, 1972.

Hunter, Thomas Blane, BA. Chief Executive Officer, Sports Division, 1984-98; b. 6.5.61, Irvine. Educ. Cumnock Academy; University of Strathclyde.

Hunter, William, MA. Columnist, The Herald, retired 1996; b. 16.8.31, Paisley; m., Mo (deceased); 1 s.; 1 d. Educ. Paisley Grammar School; Glasgow University. Publications: The Saints; Bell the Cage!; Dear Happy Ghosts. Recreation: weeding. Address: (h.) 233 Fenwick Road, Glasgow; T.-0141-638 1323.

Hunter, William Hill, CBE, CA, JP, DL. Partner, McLay, McAlister & McGibbon, CA, 1946-91, Consultant, since 1991; Director, J. & G. Grant, Glenfarclas Distillery, 1966-92; b. 5.11.16, Cumnock; m., Kathleen Cole; 2 s. (1 s. deceased). Educ. Cumnock Academy. Enlisted as private,

RASC, 1940; commissioned Royal Artillery, 1941; Staff Captain, Middle East, 1944-46; Director: Abbey National Building Society (Scottish Advisory Board), 1966-86, City of Glasgow Friendly Society, 1966-88 (President, 1980-88); Member: CBI Scottish Council, 1978-84, Institute of Directors West of Scotland Committee, 1980-91; President: Renfrew West and Inverclyde Conservative and Unionist Association, 1972-99, Scottish Young Unionist Association, 1958-60, Scottish Unionist Association, 1964-65; contested (Unionist), South Ayrshire, 1959 and 1964; Hon. Treasurer, Quarrier's Homes, 1972-94 (Chairman, 1991-94); Member, Council of Management, Erskine Hospital, since 1998 (Hon. Financial Advisor, 1981-98); Session Clerk, Kilmacolm Old Kirk, 1972-77; Chairman: Salvation Army Advisory Board in Strathclyde, 1982-93, Salvation Army Housing Association Scotland Ltd., 1986-91; admitted to Distinguished Order of Auxiliary Service of Salvation Army, 1981; Deacon Convener, Trades House of Glasgow, 1986-87; Honorary Vice President, Royal Scottish Agricultural Benevolent Institution, since 1994; Honorary President, Friends of Glasgow Botanic Gardens, since 1994. Recreations: gardening; golf; swimming; music. Address: (h.) Armitage, Kilmacolm PA13 4PH; T.-0150587 2444.

Hunter-Blair, Sir Edward Thomas, Bart, BA (Oxon); b. 15.12.20, Ayr; m., Norma Harris; 1 s. Educ. Balliol College, Oxford; University of Paris (Diploma, French language and literature). Temporary Civil Servant, 1941-43; Journalist (Assistant Foreign Editor), London, 1944-49; Partner in business in Yorkshire, 1950-63; Member, Kirkcudbright County Council, 1970-71; Estate Owner and Forester, 1964-99; Committee Member, Scottish Association for Public Transport; Council Member, Wyndham Trust, London. Publications include: Our Troubled Future, 1994. Recreations: gardening; hill-walking (formerly). Address: Parton House, Castle Douglas DG7 3NB; T.-01644 470 234.

Hunter Blair, James, DL. Landowner and Forester; b. 18.3.26, Ayr. Educ. Eton; Oxford. Scots Guards, 1944-48; University, 1948-50; merchant bank, London, 1951-53; managed family estate, since 1953. Past President, Royal Scottish Forestry Society; former Vice-President, Royal Highland Society; Past Chairman, Historic Houses Association for Scotland. Recreations: shooting; fishing; going to the opera. Address: Blairquhan, Maybole, Ayrshire; T.-01655 770239.

Huntley, Professor Aristotle Kapranos ("John"), LLB, LLM. Professor of Law and Head, Division of Law, Glasgow Caledonian University, since 1999; b. 20.6.48, Athens; m., Christine Taylor; 2 s.; 1 d. Educ. South Shields Grammar and Technical School for Boys; University of Birmingham. Lecturer, Bristol Polytechnic, 1971-73; Sunderland Polytechnic, 1973-79; Heriot-Watt University, 1979-83; University of Strathclyde: Lecturer/Senior Lecturer, Law School, 1973-98, Vice-Dean, Business School, 1990-94; Professor of Law, Middlesex University, 1998-99. Chairman, Bearsden Choir, since 2001. Publications: Contract: Cases and Materials, 1995; contributions to Stair Memorial Encyclopaedia of Scots Law and to legal journals. Recreations: singing; reading; gardening; all things Hellenic. Address: (b.) Division of Law, Glasgow Caledonian University, Cowcaddens Road, Glasgow G4 0BA; (h.) 21 Rubislaw Drive, Bearsden, Glasgow G61 1PS; T.-0141-331 3430; e-mail: j.huntley@gcal.ac.uk

Huntly, Marquess of (Granville Charles Gomer). President: Institute of Financial Accountants, since 1989, Institute of Commercial Management, since 1988; Chief, House of Gordon, since 1988; b. 4.2.44, Aberdeen; m. 1, Jane Gibb; m. 2, Catheryn Kindersley; 1 s.; 3 d. Educ. Gordonstoun School; Institute of Commercial Management. Chairman: Hintlesham Holdings Ltd., Cock O' The North Liqueur Co. Ltd.; Director, Ampton

Investments Ltd. Chief, Aboyne Highland Games. Recreations: country sports; France. Address: Aboyne Castle, Aberdeenshire AB34 5JP; T.-01339 887 778.

Huq, Mohammed Mozammel, BA(Hons), MA, MLitt, PhD. Senior Lecturer in Economics, since 1990, and Associate Director, Developing Countries Research Unit, since 1989, University of Strathclyde; b. 29.11.40, Kakina, Bangladesh; m., Kumkum; 1 s.; 1 d. Educ. Kakina M.R.M. High School; Carmichael College, Rangpur; University of Rajshahi, Bangladesh; University of Glasgow. Lecturer in Economics, Rajshahi College (University of Rajshahi), then Associate Professor of Economics, M.C. College (University of Chittagong), Bangladesh; postgraduate research, University of Glasgow; returned to Bangladesh, 1974, as Researcher; Researcher, David Livingstone Institute of Overseas Development Studies, University of Strathclyde, 1976-87; Senior Research Fellow (on secondment), Centre for Development Studies, University of Ghana, 1982-84; Lecturer in Economics, University of Strathclyde, 1987. President, North Bengal College, Bangladesh; Chairman, Third World Science, Technology and Development Forum UK; Senior Vice President, Scottish Asian Action Committee. Publications: author and editor of several books. Recreations: tennis; bridge. Address: (b.) Department of Economics, University of Strathclyde, Glasgow G4 0LN; T.-0141-548 3863.

Hurford, Professor James Raymond, BA, PhD. Professor of General Linguistics, Edinburgh University, since 1979; b. 16.7.41, Reading; m., Sue Ann Davis; 2 d. Educ. Exeter School; St. John's College, Cambridge; University College, London. Assistant Professor, Department of English, University of California, Davis, 1968-71; Lecturer, then Senior Lecturer, Department of Linguistics, Lancaster University, 1972-79. Publications: Language and Number: the emergence of a cognitive system; Semantics: a coursebook (Co-author); The Linguistic Theory of Numerals; Grammar: a student's guide. Address: (b.) Edinburgh University, Edinburgh EH8 9YL.

Hurman, David Charles, MBChB, DTM&H, DMRT, FRCR, HonMD (Manitoba). Consultant in Clinical Oncology, Aberdeen Royal Infirmary, Grampian University Hospitals NHS Trust; Visiting Consultant, Shetland Health Board, since 1988; Clinical Senior Lecturer, Aberdeen University, since 1988; Clinical Group Co-ordinator, Anchor Unit; Macmillan Lead Cancer Clinician; b. 9.2.52, London; 1 s.; 1 d. Educ. Ashford County Grammar School; Liverpool University. Pre-registration and junior medical posts, Southport General Infirmary and Christiana Hartley Maternity Hospital, 1975-77; Medical Officer, Trans-Borneo Expedition, 1978; Mersey Regional Centre for Radiotherapy and Oncology, Clatterbridge Hospital, Bebington, 1979-86; Clinical Research Fellow, Cross Cancer Institute and University of Alberta, 1986-87; Senior Medical Officer, International Scientific Support Trust Expedition to Java and Kalimantan, 1994; Expert Adviser and Honorary Consultant, Bhaktapur Cancer Care Centre, Kathmandu, Nepal, since 1995. Recreations: foreign travel; football; cricket; hills and mountains; rock music. Address: (h.) 1 Pinecrest Walk, Bieldside, Aberdeen AB15 9FH.

Hurst, Professor Andrew, CGeol, FGS. Professor of Production Geoscience, Aberdeen University, since 1992; b. 5.9.53, Stoke-on-Trent; m., Liv Christiansen; 1 s.; 1 d. Educ. Cheadle Grammar School; Aberdeen University; Reading University. Geologist, Norway, 1981-82; Senior Geologist, Norway, 1982-90; Senior Geologist, Unocal UK, 1990-91; Advising Geologist, Unocal UK, 1991-92. William Smith Fund Award, Geological Society of London, 1993; Founding Editor, Petroleum Geoscience; Technical Programme Officer (Petroleum), European Association of Geoscientists and Engineers; editor of five books.

Recreations: squash; music; natural history. Address: (b.) Department of Geology and Petroleum Geology, King's College, Aberdeen AB24 3UE; T.-01224 273713.

Hurst, Nigel Peter, BSc, MBBS, FRCP (Edin), PhD. Consultant Rheumatologist, since 1989; Senior Lecturer, University of Edinburgh, since 1990; b. 29.4.46, London; m., Susan F. Hurst; 2 s.; 2 d. Educ. Eastbourne College; Bristol University; St. Mary's Hospital Medical School, London. Professional training in London, University Hospital of Wales and Edinburgh; research and clinical posts in Edinburgh and Adelaide; Consultant Rheumatologist and Clinical Senior Lecturer, Adelaide, 1983-89. Publications in fields of cell biochemistry and pharmacology, rheumatology and health economics. Recreations: occasional sailor, hillwalker, flyer and dilettante. Address: (h.) Fairnielaw House, Athelstaneford; T.-01620 880607/0131-537 1806.

Hurtado, Professor Larry Weir, BA, MA, PhD. Professor of New Testament Language, Literature and Theology, Faculty of Divinity, Edinburgh University, since 1996; b. 29.12.43, Kansas City; m., Shannon Hunter; 1 s.; 2 d. Educ. Case Western Reserve University. Pastor, North Shore Assembly of God, Illinois, 1971-75; Assistant Professor of New Testament, Regent College, Vancouver BC, 1975-78; Professor of Religion, University of Manitoba, Winnipeg, 1978-96. Address: (b.) New College, Mound Place, Edinburgh EH1 2LX; T.-0131-650 8920.

Hutcheson, Rev. Norman McKenzie, MA, BD, BA. Minister, Dalbeattie and Urr Parish Churches; Convener, Europe Committee, Board of World Mission, Church of Scotland, since 1998; b. 11.10.48, Leven; m., Elizabeth; 2 d. Educ. Hillhead High School, Glasgow; Glasgow University; Edinburgh University; Open University. Minister, St. Andrews, Kirkcaldy, 1973-88. Recreations: photography; travel; reading. Address: (h.) 36 Mill Street, Dalbeattiew DG5 4HE; T.-01556 610029; e-mail: norman.hutcheson@virgin.net

Hutchins, Michael John Patrick, FCIB. Managing Director, NatWest Retail Banking, Royal Bank of Scotland Group, since 2001; b. 19.4.44, Sale; m., Rosemary Isabelle; 1 s.; 2 d. Educ. Burnage Grammar School, Manchester. Career banker with William Deacon's Bank, Williams & Glyns Bank and Royal Bank of Scotland; Manager of a group of bank branches in Sheffield and Nottingham; a senior manager, International Division, running North of England and Midlands area; a branch area manager covering Cheshire and Derbyshire; Local Director, Yorkshire and North East of England; ran all branch banking operations in North of England and Midlands from Manchester, as Director; moved to Edinburgh in 1995. Director: Royal Scottish Assurance, NatWest Life Assurance, Royal Exchange Theatre (Manchester). Recreations: all sports; theatre. Address: (b.) Royal Bank of Scotland, The Younger Building, 3 Redheughs Avenue, Edinburgh; T.-0131-556 8555.

Hutchinson, Peter, PhD, FIFM. Assistant Secretary, North Atlantic Salmon Conservation Organization, since 1986 (Chairman, Scientific Committee, since 1992); b. 26.5.56, Glasgow; m., Jane MacKellaig; 1 s.; 1 d. Educ. Queen Elizabeth's Grammar School, Blackburn; Edinburgh University. Project Co-ordinator, Surface Water Acidification; Research Biologist: Institute of Terrestrial Ecology, Edinburgh University; Member, Consular Corps in Edinburgh and Leith, since 1991. Recreations: golf; squash; rugby union; angling. Address: (h.) 3 St. Ronan's Terrace, Morningside, Edinburgh.

Hutchison, David, MA, MLitt. Senior Lecturer in Media Studies, Glasgow Caledonian University, since 1975; b. 24.9.44, West Kilbride; m., Pauleen Frew; 2 d. Educ. Ardrossan Academy; Glasgow University. Tutor/Organiser, WEA (West of Scotland), 1966-69; Teacher, Reid Kerr College, Paisley, 1969-71; Lecturer in Communication Studies, Glasgow College of Technology, 1971-75; Member, West Kilbride District Council, 1970-75 (Chairman, 1972-75); Governor, Scottish Film Council, 1987-95; Member, General Advisory Council, BBC, 1988-96; author of play, Deadline, Pitlochry Festival Theatre, 1980. Publications: The Modern Scottish Theatre, 1977; Headlines: the Media in Scotland (Editor), 1978; Media Policy, 1998; various articles/chapters. Recreations: walking; sitting in cafés dreaming; the arts. Address: (b.) Department of Language and Media, Caledonian University, Cowcaddens Road, Glasgow G4 OBA; T.-0141-331 3255; dhu@gcal.ac.uk

Hutchison, Ian Somerville, OBE, JP. Member, East Renfrewshire Council; Member: Executive Committee, National Trust for Scotland, Council, Strathclyde Building Preservation Trust; Delegate to COSLA, since 1975 (Vice-President, 1979-82); b. 10.4.28, Glasgow; m., Aileen Wallace; 2 s.; 2 d. Educ. Hutchesons' Boys' Grammar School. Managing Director, Timbertection Ltd., 1973-98; former Member: Eastwood District Council, Renfrew County Council, First (Eastwood) District Council, Scottish Valuation Advisory Council, Historic Buildings Council for Scotland, Renfrewshire Valuation Appeals Committee. Recreations: gardening; fishing. Address: (h.) 39 Hazelwood Avenue, Newton Mearns, Glasgow G77 5QT; T.-0141-639 2186.

Hutchison, John Charles, JP, BSc, CEng, FICE, FIHT, FIES. Lochaber Area Manager, The Highland Council, since 1995; b. 23.7.47, Edinburgh; m., Christine Laidlaw; 1 s.; 2 d. Educ. Leith Academy; Heriot-Watt University. Student Apprentice, Redpath Brown and Co., Edinburgh, 1965-69; Graduate Engineer, Redpath Dorman Long, Bedford, 1969-71; Inverness County Council, Skye: Assistant Engineer, 1971-72, Senior Resident Engineer, 1972-75; Highland Regional Council, Lochaber: Sub-Divisional Engineer, 1975-78, Divisional Engineer, 1978-96. Honorary Sheriff, since 1994. Recreations: singing; walking; reading; Scottish culture; Europe; land. Address: (b.) Lochaber House, High Street, Fort William PH33 6EL; T.-01397 703881.

Hutchison, Sir Peter Craft, Bt, CBE, FRSE. Chairman, Forestry Commission, 1994-2001; formerly Chairman, Hutchison & Craft Ltd., Insurance Brokers; b. 5.6.35, London; m., Virginia Colville; 1 s. Educ. Eton; Magdalene College, Cambridge. National Service, Royal Scots Greys (2nd Lt.); Northern Assurance Co. (London); Director of various companies; Past Chairman, Ailsa Shipbuilding Co. Ltd.; Director, Stakis plc, 1979-91; Board Member, Scottish Tourist Board, 1981-87; Vice Chairman, British Waterways Board, 1988-97; Chairman, Board of Trustees, Royal Botanic Garden, Edinburgh, 1985-94; Chairman, Loch Lomond and Trossachs Working Party, 1991-93; Deacon, Incorporation of Hammermen of Glasgow, 1984-85. Recreations: plant hunting; gardening; calligraphy. Address: (h.) Broich, Kippen, Stirlingshire FK8 3EN; T.-01786 870317.

Hutton, Alasdair Henry, OBE, TD. Writer and Narrator, Edinburgh Military Tattoo and other public events, videos and audio guides; Senior Consultant, Career Associates; Director, Impact Weather Services; Director, European Editions Ltd.; Scottish Trustee, Community Service Volunteers; Chairman, Disease Prevention Organisation; Member, Kelso and Jedburgh Advisory Committee, Scottish Borders Enterprise; Company Secretary, Institute of Contemporary Scotland, since 2001; b. 19.5.40, London; m., Deirdre Mary Cassels (see Deirdre Mary Hutton); 2 s. Educ. Dollar Academy; Brisbane State High School. Journalist, The Age, Melbourne, 1959-61, Aberdeen Journals, 1962-64; Broadcaster, BBC, 1964-79; Member, European Parliament, 1979-89. Member, Queen's

Bodyguard for Scotland (Royal Company of Archers); Former 2ic, 15th (Scottish Volunteer) Bn., The Parachute Regiment; President, Kelso Branch, Royal British Legion; Elder, Kelso North Church of Scotland; Patron ROKPA; Chairman and Life Member, John Buchan Society; Life Member, Edinburgh Sir Walter Scott Club; Fellow, Industry and Parliament Trust; Patron, Kelso Laddies' Association; Member, Ancient Order of Mosstroopers; Honorary Chairman, Hawick Conservative Club; European Adviser, Isle of Man Parliament; Committee Member, Borders Talking Newspaper; Chairman, Kelso Millennium Trust. Address: (b.) Rosebank, Shedden Park Road, Kelso, TD5 7PX; T.-01573 224369; e-mail: AlasdairHutton@compuserve.com

Hutton, Deirdre Mary, CBE. Chairman, National Consumer Council, since 2001; Chairman, Food Chain Centre, since 2002; Vice Chairman, Scottish Environment Protection Agency, since 1999; Member, Sustainable Development Commission, since 2000; Non-Executive Director, Financial Services Authority, since 1998; Member, Better Regulation Task Force, since 1998; b. 15.3.49, Haddington; m., Alasdair Hutton (qv); 2 s. Educ. Sherborne School for Girls; secretarial college. Research Assistant, Glasgow Chamber of Commerce, 1976-81; seconded to Scotland is British Campaign and Scotland Says No Campaign during devolution referendum, 1979; formerly Member, Consultative Steering Group on Scottish Parliament; Founder Chairman, Enterprise Music Scotland Ltd.; Member, Personal Investment Authority Consumer Panel, 1994-98; Non-Executive Director: Borders Health Board, 1997-2001, Edinburgh Theatres Ltd., 1997-99; Member: Secretary of State for Trade and Industry's Competitiveness Council, 1999-2001; Chairman: Scottish Consumer Council, 1991-99, Personal Investment Authority Ombudsman Council, 1997-2000, Foresight Panel on Food Chain and Crops for Industry, 1999-2001; Member, Policy Commission on Farming and Food, 2001-2002. Honorary Doctorate, Stirling University, 2000. Recreations: music; reading; hillwalking. Address: (h.) Rosebank, Shedden Park Road, Kelso TD5 7PX; T.-01573 224368.

Hutton, William Riddell, BDS. Dentist, since 1961; Honorary Sheriff, since 1996; b. 22.10.38, Glasgow; m., Patricia Margaret Burns; 1 s.; 1 d. Educ. Hamilton Academy; Glasgow University Dental School. International Grenfell Association, Newfoundland and Labrador, 1961-64; General Practice, Lanark, 1967-2001; Member, Secretary and Chairman, Lanarkshire Local Dental Committee, 1964-94; Member and Chairman, Lanarkshire Area Dental Committee, 1975-94. Recreations: music; golf; hillwalking; travel. Address: (h.) St. Anthony, 9 Braedale Road, Lanark ML11 7AW; T.-01555 662927; e-mail: hutts.brae@virgin.com

Huxham, Professor Chris, DPhil, MSc, BSc. Professor of Management, and Director of Research, Graduate School of Business, University of Strathclyde, since 1997; b. 18.3.54, Felixstowe. Educ. South Wiltshire Grammar School; Sussex University. Lecturer, University of Aston Management Centre, 1979-84; Lecturer/Senior Lecturer in Management Science, University of Strathclyde, 1984-97. Member, Scottish Executive Task Force on Community Planning. Academy of Management Awards (USA), 1997, 2001. Publication: Creating Collaborative Advantage (Editor), 1996. Address: (b.) University of Strathclyde, Graduate School of Business, 199 Cathedral Street, Glasgow G4 0QU; T.-0141-553 6113; e-mail: chris@gsb.strath.ac.uk

Hyslop, A. Graeme, BA (Hons), MSc, TQ(FE), FRSA. Principal, Langside College, Glasgow, since 1999; b. 23.3.53, Glasgow; m., Aileen; 1 d. Educ. High School of Glasgow; Glasgow Caledonian University; Glasgow University; Strathclyde University. Car Park Attendant, 1979-80; College Lecturer, 1980-88; Further Education Officer, Strathclyde Regional Council, 1988-91; Depute Principal, Langside College, Glasgow, 1991-98. Board Member: Castlemilk Economic Development Agency, Continuing Education Gateway, West of Scotland Colleges Partnership, Glasgow Colleges Group. Recreations: sport (football, squash, golf); reading; cinema. Address: (b.) 50 Prospecthill Road, Glasgow G42 9LB; T.-0141-649 4991.

Hyslop, Fiona J., MA (Hons). MSP (SNP), Lothian, since 1999; b. 1.8.64, Irvine; m.; 1 s.; 1 d. Educ. Ayr Academy; Glasgow University. Standard Life, 1986-99, various sales and marketing positions, latterly Marketing Manager. Recreations: swimming; cinema. Address: (b.) Scottish Parliament, Edinburgh EH99 1SP; T.-0131-348 5000.

I

Bank of Scotland, 1997-2001. Recreations: golf; walking. Address: (h.) 10 Brechin Drive, Polmont, Falkirk FK2 0YH; T.-01324 713775.

Ibbett, Professor Roland Norman, BSc, MSc, PhD, FRSE, CEng, FBCS. Professor of Computer Science, Edinburgh University, since 1985, Vice-Principal, 1994-2000; b. 21.6.41, Burton upon Trent; m., Janet; 3 s.; 3 d. Educ. Burton upon Trent Grammar School. Lecturer in Computer Science, Manchester University, 1967-75, Senior Lecturer, 1975-82, Reader, 1982-85. Chairman, Conference of Professors and Heads of Computing, 1993-95. Board Member, Scottish Institute for Enterprise; Director, SLI Ltd. Publications: two books; 50 papers. Recreations: gardening; DIY; listening to music. Address: (b.) Division of Informatics, Edinburgh University, King's Buildings, Edinburgh EH9 3JZ; T.-0131-650 5119; e-mail: R.N.Ibbett@ed.ac.uk

Ibbotson, Sally Helen, BSc (Hons), MD, MBChB (Hons), FRCP (Edin). Clinical Senior Lecturer in Photobiology, Honorary Consultant Dermatologist, University of Dundee, Ninewells Hospital and Medical School, since 1998; b. 18.2.62, Newcastle upon Tyne. Educ. Central Newcastle High School for Girls; University of Leeds. House Physician and House Surgeon, Leeds General Infirmary and St. James' University Hospital, 1986-87; Teaching Fellow in Medicine, Leeds General Infirmary, 1987-89; Research Fellow, University of Leeds, 1989-92; Royal Victoria Infirmary, Newcastle upon Tyne: Registrar in Dermatology, 1992-94, Senior Registrar in Dermatology, 1994-98; Research Fellow, Harvard University, Boston, USA, 1996-97. Address: (b.) Photobiology Unit, Dermatology Department, University of Dundee, Ninewells Hospital and Medical School, Dundee DD1 9SY; T.-01382 425717; e-mail: s.h.ibbotson@dundee.ac.uk

Idiens, Dale, BA, DipEd. Depute Director, National Museums of Scotland; b. 13.5.42, Prestatyn. Educ. Wycombe High School, High Wycombe; Leicester University. Royal Scottish Museum, Department of Art and Archaeology: Assistant Keeper in Charge of Ethnography, 1964, Deputy Keeper, 1979, Keeper, Department of History and Applied Art, 1983-2001. Address: (b.) Royal Museum, Chambers Street, Edinburgh; T.-0131-225 7534; e-mail: d.idiens@nms.ac.uk

Ingle, Professor Stephen James, BA, MA (Econ), DipEd, PhD. Professor of Politics (and Head, Politics Department), Stirling University; b. 6.11.40, Ripon; m., Margaret Anne; 2 s.; 1 d. Educ. The Roan School, London; Sheffield University; Wellington University, NZ. Commonwealth Scholar, 1964-67; Lecturer in Politics, Hull University, 1967-80; Senior Lecturer, 1980-91; Head of Department, 1985-90. Secretary, Political Studies Association, 1988-89; Member, East Yorkshire Health Authority, 1985-90; Visiting Research Fellow, Victoria University of Wellington, 1993. Publications: Socialist Thought in Imaginative Literature, 1979; Parliament and Health Policy, 1981; British Party System, 1987, 1989, 1999; George Orwell: a political life, 1993. Recreations: reading; music; hill-walking. Address: (b.) Department of Politics, Stirling University, Stirling FK9 4LA; T.-01786 467593.

Inglis, Ian Brownlie, LLB, FCIBS, FRSA, WS. Director: Ivory & Sime UK Smaller Companies Trust plc, since 1992, The Edinburgh Investment Trust plc, since 1997, Murray Ventures Investment Trust PLC, since 1998; b. 6.2.41, Carluke; m., Eleanor McLuckie Taylor; 2 d. Educ. Lanark Grammar School; University of Edinburgh. Apprentice Clerk, Clerk, Apprentice Solicitor, Royal Bank of Scotland, 1957-66; Shepherd & Wedderburn WS: Apprentice Solicitor, 1966-67, Assistant Solicitor, 1967-68, Partner, 1968-98. Member, Scottish Regional Advisory Group, London Stock Exchange, 1994-2001; Director,

Inglis, Professor Emeritus James Alistair Macfarlane, CBE (1984), MA, LLB. Emeritus Professor, Glasgow University; Professor of Conveyancing, Glasgow University, 1979-93; Professor of Professional Legal Practice, Glasgow University, 1984-93; Partner, McClure, Naismith, Anderson & Gardiner, Solicitors, Glasgow, 1956-93; Honorary Member, Court of Patrons, Royal College of Physicians and Surgeons of Glasgow, since 1995; b. 24.12.28, Kilmarnock; m., Mary Elizabeth Howie; 2 s.; 3 d. Educ. Kilmarnock Academy; Fettes College; St. Andrews University; Glasgow University. Qualified as Solicitor, 1952; Member: Board of Management, Victoria and Leverndale Hospitals, 1964-74, Greater Glasgow Health Board, 1975-83; President, Rent Assessment Panel for Scotland, 1976-87; Chairman, Glasgow Hospitals Auxiliary Association, 1985-2001; Dean, Royal Faculty of Procurators in Glasgow, 1989-92; Convener, Ad Hoc Committee, Church of Scotland, into Legal Services of Church, 1978-79; Session Clerk, Caldwell Parish Church, since 1963; General Trustee, Church of Scotland, since 1994. Address: (h.) Crioch, Uplawmoor, Glasgow; T.-01505 850315.

Inglis, John, RSW, FSA(Scot), DA. Painter and Lecturer; b. 27.7.53, Glasgow; m., Heather; 2 s.; 2 d. Educ. Hillhead High School; Gray's School of Art. Travelling scholarships to Italy, 1976; Member, Dundee Group, 1979-84; one-man exhibitions: Aberdeen, 1976 and 1977; Glasgow, 1980; Skipton, 1981; Aberdeen Hospitals, 1989; Alloa Museum, 1989; Smith Art Gallery, Stirling, 1993; Illinois, USA, 1997. Scottish Arts Council Award, 1981; RSA Keith Prize, 1975; SAC Bursary, 1982; RSA Meyer Oppenheim Prize, 1982; RSW EIS Award, 1987; SAC Grant, 1988; May Marshall Brown Award, 1994, 2000. Address: (h.) 84 Burnhead Road, Larbert.

Ingold, Professor Timothy, PhD, FBA, FRSE. Professor of Social Anthropology, University of Aberdeen, since 1999; b. 1.11.48, Sevenoaks; m., Anna Kaarina; 3 s.; 1 d. Educ. Leighton Park School; Churchill College, Cambridge University. University of Manchester: Lecturer, Department of Social Anthropology, 1974-85, Senior Lecturer, 1985-90, Professor, 1990-95, Max Gluckman Professor of Social Anthropology, 1995-99; Visiting Professor: University of Helsinki, 1986, University of Tromsø, 1996-2000. Royal Anthropological Institute Rivers Memorial Medal, 1989; Award of Jean-Marie Delwart Foundation, Belgian Academy of Sciences, 1994. Publications: The Skolt Lapps Today, 1976; Hunters, Pastoralists and Ranchers, 1980; Evolution and Social Life, 1986; What Is An Animal? (Editor), 1988; Tools, Language and Cognition in Human Evolution (Co-Editor), 1993; Companion Encyclopedia of Anthropology: humanity, culture and social life (Editor), 1994; Key Debates in Anthropology, 1988-93, 1996; The Perception of the Environment, 2000. Recreation: music. Address: (b.) Department of Sociology and Anthropology, University of Aberdeen, Aberdeen AB24 3QY; T.-01224 274350; e-mail: tim.ingold@abdn.ac.uk

Ingram, Rt. Hon. Adam. MP (Labour), East Kilbride, since 1987; Minister of State for the Armed Forces, since 2001; b. 1.2.47, Glasgow; m., Maureen McMahon. Educ. Cranhill Senior Secondary School. Programmer/analyst, 1965-1970; systems analyst, 1970-77; full-time union official, 1977-87; Councillor, East Kilbride District Council, 1980-87 (Leader of the Council, 1984-87); PPS to Neil Kinnock, Leader of the Opposition, 1988-92; Labour Opposition Spokesperson on Social Security, 1993-95, Science and Technology, 1995-97; Minister of State for Northern Ireland, 1997-2001; JP. Recreations: fishing; cooking; reading. Address: (b.) House of Commons, London SW1A 0AA; T.-020 7219 4093.

Ingram, Adam Hamilton, BA (Hons). MSP (SNP), South of Scotland, since 1999; b. 1.5.51, Kilmarnock; m., Gerry; 3 s.; 1 d. Educ. Kilmarnock Academy; Paisley College. Manager, A.H. Ingram & Son, Bakers, 1971-76; Senior Economic Assistant, Manpower Services Commission, 1985-86; Researcher and Lecturer, Paisley College, 1987-88; economic development consultant, 1989-99. Recreation: golf. Address: Scottish Parliament, Edinburgh EH99 1SP; T.-0131-348 5720.

Ingram, Professor David Stanley, OBE, BSc, PhD, MA, ScD, HonDUniv (Open), FLS, FIBiol, FIHort, FRSGS (Hon), FRCPEd, FRSE. Honorary Professor and Adviser on Public Understanding of Science, University of Edinburgh, since 1991; Visiting Professor in Botany, Glasgow University, since 1991; Visiting Professor of Horticulture and Environmental Biology, Napier University, since 1998; Master, St. Catharine's College, Cambridge, since 2000; Honorary Fellow, Royal Botanic Garden Edinburgh, since 1998; Honorary Fellow, Downing College, Cambridge, since 2000; Honorary Fellow, Myerscough College, since 2001; b. 10.10.41, Birmingham; m., Alison W.; 2 s. Educ. Yardley Grammar School, Birmingham; Hull University; Cambridge University. Research Fellow, Glasgow University, 1966-68, Cambridge University, 1968-69; Senior Scientific Officer, Unit of Developmental Botany, Cambridge, 1969-74; Lecturer, then Reader in Plant Pathology, Botany Department, Cambridge University, 1974-90; Fellow (also Tutor, Dean and Director of Studies in Biology), Downing College, Cambridge, 1974-90; Regius Keeper (Director), Royal Botanic Garden, Edinburgh, 1990-98. Honorary Professor of Horticulture, Royal Horticultural Society, 1995-2000; former President, International Congress of Plant Pathology; President, British Society for Plant Pathology, 1998; Advisor to University of Edinburgh on the Public Understanding of Science, since 1998; Chairman, Advisory Committee to the Darwin Initiative for the Survival of the Species, since 1999; Member, Board, Scottish Natural Heritage, 1999-2000; author of several books and many papers in learned journals. Recreations: gardening; literature; film; theatre; music; travel. Address: St. Catharine's College, Cambridge CB2 1RL.

Ingram, Greig Webster, MA. Rector, High School of Stirling, since 1994; b. 20.11.47, Burnhervie; m., Patricia Annette Miller. Educ. Mackie Academy, Stonehaven; Aberdeen University; Aberdeen College of Education. Teacher of Modern Studies and History, 1970-74; Principal Teacher of Modern Studies, St. Margaret Mary's Secondary, Glasgow, 1974-84; Assistant Head Teacher, Eastbank Academy, Glasgow, 1984-89, Depute Head Teacher, 1989-94. Recreations: reading; music; travel; running; soccer. Address: (b.) Ogilvie Road, Stirling FK8 2PA; T.-01786 472451; e-mail: ingramg@stirling.gov.uk

Ingram, Hugh Albert Pugh, BA (Cantab), PhD (Dunelm). Scottish Trustee, Royal Society for Nature Conservation, since 2000; b. 29.4.37, Rugby; m., Dr. Ruth Hunter; 1 s.; 1 d. Educ. Lawrence Sheriff School, Rugby; Rugby School; Emmanuel College, Cambridge; Hatfield College, Durham. Demonstrator in Botany, University College of North Wales, Bangor, 1963-64; Staff Tutor in Natural Science, Department of Extra-Mural Studies, Bristol University, 1964-65; Lecturer, then Senior Lecturer in Botany (Ecology), Dundee University, 1966-97; Editor, Journal of Applied Ecology, 1991-97; Member: Executive Committee, Scottish Field Studies Association, 1989-99, Museums and Galleries Commission Working Party on the non-national museums of Scotland, 1984-86; Trustee, National Museums of Scotland, 1987-94; Chairman, Council, Scottish Wildlife Trust, 1996-99 (Vice-Chairman, Conservation and Science, 1982-87). Publications: numerous scientific research papers on hydrological aspects of the ecology of peat bogs and

other mires. Recreations: music (clarinet, piano); literature; rural history; hill-walking. Address: Johnstonfield, Dunbog, Cupar, Fife KY14 6JG; e-mail: h.a.p.ingram@dundee.ac.uk

Ingram, Professor Malcolm David, BSc, PhD, DSc, CChem, FRSC. Professor of Chemistry, Aberdeen University, since 1993; b. 18.1.39, Wallasey; m., Lorna Hardman; 1 s.; 1 d. Educ. Oldershaw Grammar School; Liverpool University. Aberdeen University: Lecturer in Physical Chemistry, 1965-78, Senior Lecturer in Chemistry, 1978-90, Reader, 1990-93. Chairman, Aberdeen and North of Scotland Section, Royal Society of Chemistry, 1990-93; Publications: 170 in scientific journals. Recreations: gardening; foreign travel. Address: (b.) Department of Chemistry, Aberdeen University, Aberdeen AB9 2UE; T.-01224 272905.

Innes, Andrew, MBChB, MD, MRCP, FRCP(Glas), FRCP(Edin). Consultant Physician/Nephrologist, Crosshouse Hospital, Kilmarnock, since 1994; b. 29.7.56, Inverness; m., Nora; 1 s.; 2 d. Educ. Dingwall Academy; University of Aberdeen. Medical Registrar, Aberdeen teaching hospitals; Senior Medical Registrar, City Hospital, Nottingham; Clinical Research Fellow, Centre de Rein Artificiel, Tassin, France. Address: (b.) Crosshouse Hospital, Kilmarnock KA2 0BE; T.-01563 577358.

Innes, Professor John, BCom, PhD, CA, FCMA. Professor of Accountancy, University of Dundee, since 1991; b. 11.7.50, Edinburgh; m., Ina. Educ. George Watson's College; University of Edinburgh. Student Accountant and Staff Auditor, KPMG, 1972-75; International Operational Auditor, Uniroyal Inc., 1975-78; Lecturer and Senior Lecturer in Accounting, University of Edinburgh, 1978-91; Canon Foundation Visiting Research Fellow, 1992-93; Visiting Professor, University of Nantes, 1997-99. Publication: various books including Handbook of Management Accounting, 1998. Recreation: tennis. Address: Department of Accountancy and Business Finance, University of Dundee, Dundee DD1 4HN; T.-01382 344197; e-mail: j.innes@dundee.ac.uk

Innes of Edingight, Sir Malcolm Rognvald, KCVO, MA, LLB, WS, KStJ. Lord Lyon King of Arms and Secretary to Order of the Thistle, 1981-2001; b. 25.5.38, Edinburgh; m., Joan Hay; 3 s. Educ. Edinburgh Academy; Edinburgh University. Carrick Pursuivant, 1958; Marchmont Herald, 1971; Lyon Clerk and Keeper of the Record, 1966; Member, Queen's Bodyguard for Scotland (Royal Company of Archers); President, Scottish Heraldry Society. Recreation: shooting. Address: Castleton of Kinnairdy, Bridge of Marnoch, Huntly, Aberdeenshire AB54 7RT; T.-01466 780866.

Innes, Norman Lindsay, OBE, BSc, PhD, DSc, FIBiol, FRSE. Agricultural Research Consultant; b. 3.5.34, Kirriemuir; m., Marjory Niven Farquhar; 1 s.; 1 d. Educ. Websters High School, Kirriemuir; Aberdeen University; Cambridge University. Senior Cotton Breeder: Sudan, 1958-66, Uganda, 1966-71; Head, Cotton Research Unit, Uganda, 1972; National Vegetable Research Station, Wellesbourne: Head, Plant Breeding Section, 1973-84, Deputy Director, 1977-84; Scottish Crop Research Institute: Deputy Director, 1986-94, Head, Plant Breeding Division, 1984-89; Honorary Lecturer, then Honorary Professor, Birmingham University, 1973-84; Governing Board Member, International Crops Research Institute for Semi-Arid Tropics, India, 1982-88; Honorary Professor, Dundee University, 1988-95; Honorary Research Professor, Scottish Crop Research Institute, since 1994; Governing Board Member, International Potato Centre, Peru, 1988-95, Chairman, 1991-95; Vice-President, Association of Applied Biologists, 1990-92, President, 1993-94; Governing Council Member, 1996-2001, Chairman, 1997-2000, International Centre of Insect Physiology and Ecology, Kenya; Member, Board of Trustees, West Africa Rice Development

Association, Côte d' Ivoire, since 1998, Chairman, since 2000; Member, Oxfam Council of Trustees, 1982-85. Recreations: photography; travel. Address: (b.) Scottish Crop Research Institute, Invergowrie, Dundee DD2 5DA; T.-01382 562731; e-mail: n.l.innes@scri.sari.ac.uk

Inverarity, James Alexander (Sandy), CBE, FRSA, FRAgS, CA. Farmer and Landowner; Chairman: Scottish Agricultural College, 1990-98, Scottish Agricultural Securities Corporation, plc, since 1987; President, Scottish Farm and Countryside Educational Trust, 1990-98; b. 17.9.35; m., Jean; 1 s.; 2 d. Educ. Loretto School. President, National Farmers Union of Scotland, 1970-71; Member: Eggs Authority, 1971-74, Farm Animal Welfare Council, 1978-88, Panel of Agricultural Arbiters, since 1983, Governing Body, Scottish Crop Research Institute, 1984-97, Dairy Produce Quota Tribunal for Scotland, 1984-85; Director, United Oilseed Producers Ltd., 1985-97 (Chairman, 1987-97). Recreations: shooting; curling. Address: Cransley, Fowlis, Dundee DD2 5NP; T.-01382 580327.

Ireland, Kenny. Artistic Director and Chief Executive, Royal Lyceum Theatre Company, since 1993; b. 7.8.45, Paisley; m., Meg; 1 d. Educ. Paisley Grammar School; Royal Scottish Academy of Music and Drama. Actor and Director. e-mail: scilla@irelandg.demon.co.uk

Ireland, Sheriff Ronald David, QC, HonLLD. Sheriff Principal, Grampian, Highland and Islands, 1988-93; b. 13.3.25, Edinburgh. Educ. George Watson's College, Edinburgh; Balliol College, Oxford (Scholar); Edinburgh University. Advocate, 1952; Clerk, Faculty of Advocates, 1957-58; Professor of Scots Law, Aberdeen University, 1958-71; QC, 1964; Dean, Faculty of Law, Aberdeen University, 1964-67; Chairman, Board of Management, Aberdeen General Hospitals, 1964-71; Sheriff, Lothian and Borders at Edinburgh, 1972-88; Director, Scottish Courts Administration, 1975-78. Address: (h.) 6A Greenhill Gardens, Edinburgh EH10 4BW.

Irons, Norman MacFarlane, CBE, DL, DLitt, DUniv, Hon. FRCSE, CEng, MIMechE, MCIBSE, JP. Lord Provost and Lord Lieutenant of the City of Edinburgh, 1992-96; Partner, Building Services Consulting Engineers, since 1993; Royal Danish Consul, Edinburgh and Leith, since 2000; b. 4.1.41, Glasgow; m., Anne Buckley; 1 s.; 1 d. Held various posts as Consulting Engineer; founded own practice, 1983. SNP Member, City of Edinburgh District Council, 1976-96; President, Edinburgh Leith and District Battalion, Boys' Brigade, since 1998. Recreation: rugby football. Address: (h.) 141 Saughtonhall Drive, Edinburgh EH12 5TS; T.-0131-337 6154; e-mail: mail@ironsfoulner.co.uk

Ironside, Leonard, JP. Member, Aberdeen City Council, since 1995, Council Leader, since 1999 (Convener, Social Work Committee); Chairman: Aberdeen International Youth Festival, since 1996, Horizon Rehabilitation Centre, since 1997; Director, Grampian Food Resource Centre Ltd; Patron, Grampian Special Olympics for Handicapped; Commonwealth Professional Wrestling Champion, since 1981; Athletics Coach, Bon Accord (Special Needs); Member, Board, Robert Gordon University; National Minimum Wage Compliance Officer, since 1999; part-time Feature Writer, Aberdeen Independent Newspapers; b. Aberdeen; m., Wendy; 2 d. Educ. Hilton Academy, Aberdeen. Member, Grampian Regional Council, 1982-96; Inspector, contributions agency, DHSS, since 1990; formerly Chairman and Founder Member, Grampian Initiative; won Commonwealth Professional Wrestling Championship at Middleweight, 1979; lost Championship, 1981; regained title, 1981; gained European Lightweight title, 1985, relinquished title, 1989; Grampian Ambassador for services to industry, 1996; awarded Scottish Sports Council Rosebowl for services to disabled sports; former

Director: Grampian Enterprise Ltd., Scottish Sub-Sea Technology Group; Member: Grampian Racial Equality Commission, Aberdeen Sports Council; former Director, Voluntary Service, Aberdeen; part-time welfare visitor, Parkinson's Disease Society, since 2001. Recreations: yoga teacher; also plays tennis, squash, badminton; cycling. Address: (h.) 42 Hillside Terrace, Portlethen, Kincardineshire; T.-Aberdeen 780929; e-mail: ironside@ifb.co.uk

Irvine of Lairg, Baron (Alexander Andrew Mackay Irvine), PC. Lord High Chancellor of Great Britain, since 1997; b. 23.6.40; m.; 2 s. Educ. Inverness Academy; Hutchesons' Boys' Grammar School, Glasgow; Glasgow University; Christ's College, Cambridge. Called to the Bar, Inner Temple, 1967; QC, 1978; a Recorder, 1985-88; Deputy High Court Judge, 1987-97.

Irvine, Joseph Andrew, BSc. Head Teacher, Brae High School, since 1988; b. 18.6.44, Lerwick; m., Ishbel; 2 s. Educ. Anderson Educational Institute, Lerwick; Aberdeen University. Teacher of Maths/Science, Lerwick Central School, 1967-68; Teacher of Maths, Assistant Principal Teacher, Principal Teacher, Anderson High School, 1968-84; Field Officer, Shetland Islands Council, 1984-88. Chairman: Northern Sports Development Trust, Shetland Recreational Trust. Recreations: sailing; photography. Address: (b.) Brae High School, Brae, Shetland ZE2 9QG; T.-01806 522 370; e-mail: joe-irvine@brae.shetland.sch.uk

Irvine-Fortescue, James William, MA (Hons), CA, JP, DL, KLJ, FSA Scot; b. 7.6.17, Wilmslow; m., Margaret Guise Yates; 3 s.; 1 d. Educ. Aberdeen Grammar School; Edinburgh Academy; Aberdeen University. War Service: Royal Army Pay Corps, 1940-46, service in India and Ceylon, 1942-46 (Major and Staff Paymaster); JP and Magistrate, Kincardineshire, 1957; Member, Kincardine County Council, 1952-73; Commissioner of Income Tax, County of Kincardine, 1957-92; Chairman: Lower Deeside District Council, 1964-73, Grampian Region Valuation Appeal Committee, 1975-90. President, Deeside Field Club, 1981-86; a Vice President, Royal Society for Asian Affairs, 1983-88; Past President, Auchinleck Boswell Society; Past Chairman, Aberdeen Music Festival. Recreations: family history research; foreign travel. Address: (h.) Kingcausie, Maryculter, Kincardineshire AB12 5FR; T.-01224 732224.

Irving, Gordon, MA (Hons). Writer, Journalist and Broadcaster; b. 4.12.18, Annan; m., Elizabeth Dickie (deceased). Educ. Dumfries Academy; Edinburgh University. Staff Journalist, Daily Record, Edinburgh and Glasgow; Reuters' News Agency, London; TV Guide, Scotland; The Viewer, Scotland; Freelance Writer/Journalist, since 1964; Travel Correspondent, UK and overseas media; Scotland Correspondent, Variety, New York. Honorary Vice-President, Scottish Music Hall Society. Publications: Great Scot! (biography of Sir Harry Lauder); The Good Auld Days; The Solway Smugglers; The Wit of the Scots; The Wit of Robert Burns; The Devil on Wheels; Brush Up Your Scotland; Annie Laurie; Take No Notice and Take No More Notice! (World's Funniest Signs); The First 200 Years (Story of Dumfries and Galloway Royal Infirmary); 90 Glorious Years (Story of the King's Theatre, Glasgow); television script: Standing Room Only (The Scottish Music Hall). Recreations: making video films of personal travels; collecting trivia; researching Scottish music-hall history; fighting bumbling bureaucrats; reading all the Sunday broadsheets; surfing the World Wide Web on Internet. Address: (h.) 36 Whittingehame Court, Glasgow G12 OBG; T.-0141-357 2265; e-mail: gordirving@aol.com

Irving, Margaret Anne, MB, ChB, FRIPH, FRCPCH. Consultant Paediatrician, Child Health, Dumfries and Galloway Primary Care Trust; b. 28.4.43, Glasgow; m., Dr John Bruce Irving; 2 s.; 1 d. Educ. Bathgate Academy;

Glasgow University. Registrar in Bacteriology, Western Infirmary, Glasgow; Principal in general practice, Ayrshire; CMO in Child Health, Salford Health Authority; Senior Clinical Medical Officer in Child Health, Dumfries & Galloway Health Board; Medical Adviser to Regional Adoption and Fostering Panel; Chairman, Scottish Medical Group, British Agencies for Adoption and Fostering, 1990-93. Recreations: gardening; opera. Address: (h.) Bonshaw Tower, Kirtlebridge, Lockerbie, Dumfriesshire DG11 3LY; T.-01461 500256.

Irwin, Professor David George, MA, PhD, FSA, FRSA. Professor Emeritus, History of Art, Aberdeen University (Professor and Head of Department, 1970-96); b. 24.6.33, London; m., Francina Sorabji; 1 s.; 1 d. Educ. Holgate Grammar School, Barnsley; Queen's College, Oxford (Exhibitioner); Courtauld Institute of Art, London University. Lecturer in History of Fine Art, Glasgow University, 1959-70; Past President, British Society for 18th Century Studies; former Council Member, Walpole Society; former Member, Art Panel, Scottish Arts Council; Member, Editorial Board, British Journal of 18th Century Studies; Committee Member: Aberdeen Art Gallery, Architectural Heritage Society of Scotland; elected Member, International Association of Art Critics; won Laurence Binyon Prize, Oxford, 1956. Publications: English Neoclassical Art; Paul Klee; Visual Arts, Taste and Criticism; Designs and Ornaments of Empire Style; Winckelmann, Writings on Art; John Flaxman, Sculptor, Illustrator, Designer; Neoclassicism; Scottish Painters, At Home and Abroad, 1700 to 1900 (with Francina Irwin). Recreations: travel; painting. Address: Balmichel Bridge Cottage, Shiskine, Isle of Arran KA27 8DT; T.-01770 860408.

Isaacs, Professor Neil William, BSc, PhD, FRSE. Joseph Black Professor of Protein Crystallography, University of Glasgow, since 1989; b. 11.6.45, Brisbane, Australia; m., Margaret; 3 d. Educ. St. Patrick's College, Brisbane; University of Queensland. Research Assistant, University Chemical Laboratories, Cambridge, 1969-72; IBM Research Fellow, University of Oxford, 1972-75; IBM World Trade Research Fellow, IBM T.J. Watson Research Center, New York, 1976; Research Fellow, University of York, 1977-78; NH and MRC Senior Research Fellow, St. Vincent's Institute of Medical Research, Melbourne, 1978-88. Publications: over 100 in scientific literature on molecular structures. Recreations: walking; gardening; reading. Address: (h.) Eastwood, Shore Road, Cove, Helensburgh G84 0NA; T.-01436 842901.

Ivory, Brian Gammell, CBE, MA (Cantab), CA, FRSA, FRSE. Chairman, The National Galleries of Scotland, since 2000; Chairman, The Scottish American Investment Company PLC, since 2001 (Director, since 2000); b. 10.4.49, Edinburgh; m., Oona Mairi MacPhie Bell-Macdonald (see Oona Mairi MacPhie Ivory); 1 s.; 1 d. Educ. Eton College; Magdalene College, Cambridge. CA apprentice, Thomson McLintock, 1971-75; joined Highland Distillers, 1976, became Director, 1978, Managing Director, 1988, Group Chief Executive, 1997-99; Chairman, Macallan Distillers Ltd., 1997-99; Director, Orpar SA, 1990-99; Director, Remy Cointreau SA, since 1991; Director, Bank of Scotland, since 1998; Director, HBOS plc, since 2001; Member, Scottish Arts Council, 1983-92 (Vice-Chairman, 1988-92); Member, Arts Council of GB, 1988-92; Chairman, The Piping Centre, since 1996; CIMgt, 1997; Member, Queen's Bodyguard for Scotland (Royal Company of Archers). Recreations: the arts; farming; hill-walking. Address: (h.) 12 Ann Street, Edinburgh, EH4 1PJ.

Ivory, Oona Mairi MacPhie, DL, MA (Cantab), ARCM, FRSA. Professional Musician; former Chairman, Scottish Ballet; Governor, Royal Scottish Academy of Music and Drama; Trustee, The Piping Trust; Founder Director, The National Piping Centre; Deputy Lieutenant, City of Edinburgh; b. 21.7.54, Ayr; m., Brian Gammell Ivory (qv);

1 s.; 1 d. Educ. King's College, Cambridge; Royal Scottish Academy of Music and Drama; Royal Academy of Music. Recreations: visual and performing arts; wild places; sailing. Address: (h.) 12 Ann Street, Edinburgh EH4 1PJ.

Izat, Alexander John Rennie, MA, FRAgS, FRSA, FFCS. Chairman: Moredun Research Institute, since 1995, Shires Income Trust, since 1996; Partner, John Izat & Partners (Farmers), since 1975; Director: Glasgow Investment Managers, since 1990, Moredun Foundation, since 1992, Shires Smaller Companies Trust, since 1997, Pentlands Science Park Ltd., U.A. Group plc (Chairman, 1992-2000); b. 14.7.32, London; m., Frederica Ann McNiel; 1 s.; 2 d. Educ. Glenalmond; Oriel College, Oxford. Partner, Williams de Broe & Co., Stockbrokers, 1955-75; farming at Balliliesk and Naemoor, 1975-87; farming at High Cocklaw, since 1987; former Member, Council, Scottish NFU; Director, Moredun Scientific Ltd., 1992-97; Past President, Fife and Kinross NFU and Kinross Agricultural Association; Director, Royal Highland Agricultural Society, 1985-97 (Hon. Treasurer, 1992-96); Member, Council, Glenalmond College, 1975-95 (Chairman, Committee of Council, 1989-95); President, Northern Area, Suffolk Sheep Society, 1989-91. Address: (b.) High Cocklaw, Berwick-upon-Tweed TD15 1UZ; T.-01289 86591.

Izod, Professor (Kenneth) John, BA (Hons), PhD, FRSA. Professor of Screen Analysis, Stirling University, since 1998 (Dean, Faculty of Arts, 1995-98; Senior Lecturer, Department of Film and Media Studies, 1978-98); b. 4.3.40, Shepperton; m., Irene Chew Geok Keng (divorced 1994); 1 s.; 1 d. Educ. Prince Edward School, Harare City, Zimbabwe; Leeds University. Clerk articled to Chartered Accountant, 1958-63; Projectionist, mobile cinema unit, 1963; Lecturer in English, New University of Ulster, 1969-78; former Governor, Scottish Film Council; Chairman, Stirling Film Theatre, 1982-89 and 1991-92; Member, National Film and Video Forum, since 1994. Publications: Reading the Screen, 1984; Hollywood and the Box Office 1895-1986, 1988; The Films of Nicolas Roeg, 1991; Introduction to Television Documentary (Co-Author); Myth, Mind and the Screen, 2001. Address: (b.) Film and Media Studies, University, Stirling FK9 4LA; T.-01786 473171; e-mail: k-j-izod@stir.ac.uk

J

Jack, Alister William. Vice Chairman, Scottish Conservative and Unionist Party, since 1997 (Scottish Conservative Party Spokesman on Industry and Economic Affairs, 1996-99); Managing Director, Aardvark Self Storage Limited, since 1995; b. 7.7.63, Dumfries; m., Ann Hodgson; 1 s.; 2 d. Educ. Trinity College, Glenalmond. Knight Frank, 1983-86; Director, Field and Lawn (Marquees) Ltd., since 1986. Member, Executive Board, Scottish Conservative Party; Parliamentary Candidate, Tweeddale, Ettrick and Lauderdale, 1997 General Election. Winner, Leith Enterprise Award, 1989; Finalist, The New Venturers 1990. Recreations: field sports; golf; sailing; skiing. Address: (b.) 30 Bankhead Drive, Sighthill, Edinburgh EH11 4EQ; T.-0131-458 1900.

Jack, George William, MA (Hons). Rector, Selkirk High School, since 1981; b. 24.7.42, Leith; m., Avril; 2 s.; 1 d. Educ. Leith Academy; Edinburgh University; Moray House College. Teacher, George Heriot's School, 1967; Principal Teacher, Mathematics, Liberton High School, 1970; Assistant Headteacher, Penicuik High School, 1975; Depute Headteacher, Craigshill High School, 1978. Edinburgh Representative, Scottish Rugby Union. Recreations: golf; beekeeping; rugby (spectating). Address: (b.) Selkirk High School, Hillside Terrace, Selkirk TD7 4EW; T.-01750 20246; e-mail: gjack@scotborders.gov.uk

Jack, Lorna Burn, MA, CA. Chief Executive, Scottish Enterprise Forth Valley, since 2000; b. 20.8.62, Fraserburgh. Educ. Fraserburgh Academy; Aberdeen University. Audit Senior, Arthur Anderson, 1982-85; Finance Manager/Company Secretary, Aberdeen Cable Services Ltd, 1985-89; Scottish Development Agency, 1989-90; Grampian Enterprise, 1990-94; Scottish Enterprise National, 1994-98; Forth Valley Enterprise, 1998-2000. Recreations: travel; reading; music; fitness; socialising. Address: (b.) Laurel House, Laurelhill Business Park, Stirling, FK7 9JQ; T.-01786 451919.

Jack, Professor Robert Barr, CBE, MA, LLB, HonDUniv (Glasgow). Senior Partner, McGrigor Donald, Solicitors, Glasgow, Edinburgh and London, 1990-93 (Partner, 1957-93); Professor of Mercantile Law, Glasgow University, 1978-93; b. 18.3.28; m., Anna Thorburn Thomson; 2 s. Educ. Kilsyth Academy; High School of Glasgow; Glasgow University. Admitted a Solicitor in Scotland, 1951; Member, Scottish Law Commission, 1974-77; Scottish Observer, Department of Trade's Insolvency Law Review Committee, 1977-82; Member, Council for the Securities Industry, 1983-85; Lay Member, Council of the Stock Exchange, 1984-86; Independent Member, Board, Securities and Futures Authority (formerly Securities Association), 1986-94; Board Member, Securities and Investments Board, 1994-97; Chairman, Review Committee on Banking Services Law, 1987-89; Member: Panel on Takeovers and Mergers, 1992-2001, Financial Law Panel, since 1993; Chairman: Brownlee plc, Timber Merchants, Glasgow, 1984-86 (Director, 1974-86); Joseph Dunn (Bottlers) Ltd., Soft Drink Manufacturers, Glasgow, since 1983; Director: Bank of Scotland, 1985-96, Scottish Metropolitan Property plc, 1980-98 (Deputy Chairman, 1991-98), Scottish Mutual Assurance plc, 1987-98 (Chairman, 1992-98), Clyde Football Club Ltd., 1980-96, Gartmore Scotland Investment Trust PLC, 1991-2001, Glasgow Development Agency, 1992-97; President, Scottish National Council of YMCAs, 1983-98 (Chairman, 1966-73); Governor, Hutchesons' Educational Trust, Glasgow, 1978-87 (Chairman, 1980-87); Chairman, The Turnberry Trust, since 1983; Member, Scottish Higher Education Funding Council, 1992-96; Governor, Beatson Institute for Cancer Research, since 1989; Trustee, Football Trust, 1998-2000; Member, West of Scotland Advisory Board, The Salvation Army, since 1995; Member, Committee of Management, Malin Housing Association, Turnberry, since 1973. Publications: lectures and articles on various aspects of company law, the statutory regulation and self-regulation of the City, and banking and insolvency law. Recreations: golf; music; hopeful supporter of one of Scotland's less fashionable football teams; a dedicated lover of the Isle of Arran. Address: (h.) 50 Lanton Road, Lanton Park, Newlands, Glasgow G43 2SR; T.-0141-637 7302; e-mail: robertjack@talk21.com

Jack, Professor Ronald Dyce Sadler, MA, PhD, DLitt, FEA, FRSE, FFCS. Professor of Scottish and Medieval Literature, Edinburgh University, since 1987; b. 3.4.41, Ayr; m., Kirsty; 2 d. Educ. Ayr Academy; Glasgow University; Edinburgh University. Department of English Literature: Assistant Lecturer, 1965, Lecturer, 1968, Reader, 1978, Associate Dean, Faculty of Arts, 1971-73; Visiting Professor, Virginia University, 1973-74; Director, Universities Central Council on Admissions, 1988-94 (Member, 1973-76); Pierpont Morgan Scholar, British Academy, 1976; Advising Editor: Scotia, 1980-96, Scottish Literary Journal, 1996-2000, Scottish Studies Review, since 2000; Member, Scottish Universities Council on Entrance, since 1981; Governor, Newbattle Abbey College, 1984-89; Beinecke Fellow, Yale, 1992; Visiting Professor, Strathclyde University, 1993; Lynn Woods Neag Distinguished Visiting Professor of British Literature, University of Connecticut, 1998; Joint Director, Bibliography of Scottish Literature in Translation, since 2000. Publications: Robert MacLellan's Jamie the Saxt (Co-Editor), 1970; Scottish Prose 1550-1700, 1972; The Italian Influence on Scottish Literature, 1972; A Choice of Scottish Verse 1560-1660, 1978; The Art of Robert Burns (Co-Author), 1982; Sir Thomas Urquhart, The Jewel (Co-Author), 1984; Alexander Montgomerie, 1985; Scottish Literature's Debt to Italy, 1986; The History of Scottish Literature, Volume 1, 1988; Patterns of Divine Comedy, 1989; The Road to the Never Land, 1991; Of Lion and of Unicorn, 1993; The Poems of William Dunbar, 1997; The Mercat Anthology of Early Scottish Literature (Co-Editor). Address: (b.) Department of English Literature, Edinburgh University, David Hume Tower, George Square, Edinburgh EH8 9JX.

Jackson, Eileen. Author; b. 18.4.26, Bristol; m., John Tunnard Jackson; 3 d. Short story/article writer, 1935-74; novels, since 1974; first novel, published USA, 1976, UK, 1978; 21 novels in over 65 editions and 10 languages; pseudonyms: Helen May, Linda Comer, Elizabeth Warne; also publishes as Eileen Jackson; Lecturer. Recreations: reading; book collecting; swimming; golf; travel. Address: (h.) Girvan Lodge, Blairquhan, Maybole, Ayrshire KA19 7QP; T.-01655 770639; e-mail: jejackson@ntlworld.com

Jackson, Gordon, QC, LLB. MSP (Labour), Glasgow Govan, since 1999; b. 1948, Saltcoats; m.; 1 s.; 2 d. Former Advocate Depute. Address: (b.) Scottish Parliament, Edinburgh EH99 1SP; T.-0131-348 5898.

Jackson, Jack, BSc (Hons), PhD, FIBiol, CIBiol. HM Staff Inspector of Schools with responsibility for science subjects; b. 31.5.44, Ayr; m., Sheilah Margaret Fulton; 1 s.; 3 d. Educ. Ayr Academy; Glasgow University; Jordanhill College of Education. Demonstrator, Zoology Department, Glasgow University, 1966-69; Lecturer in Zoology, West of Scotland Agricultural College, 1969-72; Assistant Teacher of Biology, Cathkin High School, 1972-73; Principal Teacher of Biology, Ayr Academy, 1973-83. Senior Examiner and Setter, Scottish Examination Board, 1978-83; Director, Board, Scottish Youth Theatre, 1979-82; Member: Scottish Council, Institute of Biology, 1980-83, School Board, Balerno High School, since 1989. Recreations: family life; gardening; hill-walking; conservation. Address:

(b.) HM Inspector of Schools' Office, Saughton House, Broomhouse Drive, Edinburgh EH11 3XD; T.-0131-244 8324.

Jackson, Jim, OBE, BA. Chief Executive, Alzheimer Scotland – Action on Dementia, since 1994; b. 10.2.47, Bradford; m., Jennifer; 1 s.; 1 d. Educ. Stand Grammar School; West Ham College of Technology; Open University. Playleader, 1969-72; Community Development Worker, 1972-77; Principal Assistant, Community Services and Development. Wirral, 1977-81; Consultant, Home Office Voluntary Services Unit, 1981-84; Assistant Director, Scottish Council for Voluntary Organisations, 1984-93; Director, Alzheimer's Scotland, 1993-94. Recreations: hill-walking; modern jazz. Address: (b.) 22 Drumsheugh Gardens, Edinburgh, EH3 7RN; T.-0131-243 1453; e-mail: jjackson@alzscot.org

Jackson, Professor Michael Herbert, BA, PhD, CBiol, FIBiol, FRCPath, FRSH, FRSA, MREHIS, MIEH. Professor of Environmental Health, Strathclyde University; b. 17.7.40, Hornchurch; m., Diana Evans; 2 d. Educ. Nantwich and Acton Grammar School; Open University; Strathclyde University. Lecturer, Senior Lecturer, Reader in Environmental Health, Strathclyde University, 1977-93; previously public health inspector and environmental health officer; Editor-in-Chief, International Journal of Environmental Health Research; Member, Commission on Environment and Health, 1996-97. Recreations: gardening; reading; holidaying. Address: (b.) Department of Civil Engineering, Strathclyde University, John Anderson Building, Glasgow G4 0NG; T.-0141-548 3437.

Jackson, Philip, LLB. Human Rights Adviser, Scottish Children's Reporter Administration, since 2000; Reporter Manager for West Scotland, 1996-2000; b. 3.12.50, Glasgow; m., Miriam E. Levy; 1 s.; 2 d. Educ. Allan Glen's School, Glasgow; University of Glasgow. Assistant Reporter, Glasgow Corporation, 1974; Area Reporter: Strathclyde Region (Hamilton), 1976, Glasgow South West, 1988; Divisional Reporter, Strathclyde South, 1994. Recreations: cinema; calligraphy; history. Address: (b.) Ochil House, Springkerse Business Park, Stirling; T.-01786 459500.

Jackson, Robert Penman, MIBM. Director, Dundee Contract Services, Dundee City Council, since 1996; b. 2.4.47, Dunfermline; m., Helen Paxton; 1 s.; 1 d. Educ. Beath Senior High School, Cowdenbeath; Napier College of Science and Technology, Edinburgh. RSAS Diploma. Burgh Surveyor and Sanitary Inspector, Lochgelly Town Council, 1971-75; Assistant Director of Technical Services, Dunfermline District Council, 1975-84; Director of Public Works, City of Dundee District Council, 1984-96. Recreation:golf. Address: (b.) 353 Clepington Road, Dundee; T.-Dundee 434729.

Jackson, Dr Sylvia. MSP (Labour), Stirling, since 1999. Educ. Hull University. Chemistry teacher for a number of years, then worked in educational research; former Advisor in Education to Lothian Regional Council and Edinburgh District Council; Lecturer, Moray House College. Address: (b.) Scottish Parliament, Edinburgh EH99 1SP; T.-0131-348 5742.

Jackson, Tessa, BA, MA. Former Director, Scottish Arts Council; b. 5.11.55. Educ. University of East Anglia; Manchester University; Bristol University. Art Editor, OUP, 1979-80; Exhibitions Organiser, SPAB, 1981-82; Curator, Eyemouth Museum, 1982; Curator, Collins Gallery, Strathclyde University, 1982-88; Visual Arts Officer, Glasgow 1990 (European City of Culture), 1988-91; Director, Arnolfini, Bristol, 1991-99.

Jacques, Alan, BSc, MB, FRCPsych. Consultant Psychiatrist, Royal Edinburgh Hospital, since 1999; Consultant, Dementia Services Development Centre, Stirling, since 1999; b. 20.7.45, Ballymoney, Northern Ireland. Educ. Royal Belfast Academical Institution; Queen's University, Belfast. Psychiatric training, Royal Edinburgh Hospital; Consultant Psychiatrist, Royal Victoria Hospital, 1977-94; Mental Welfare Commissioner, 1994-99; Convener, Alzheimer Scotland Action on Dementia, since 1999; Member: Management Group, Edinburgh and Leith Age Concern. Recreations: music; regular concerts at Edinburgh Festival Fringe. Address: (h.) 27 Rutland Street, Edinburgh, EH1 2AE.

James, David Nicholas Henderson, MA (Cantab). Chairman, State Hospitals Board for Scotland, 1997-2001; b. 30.12.32, Simla, India; m., Beverly Ann Catherine Hodgson (deceased); 2 s.; 1 d. Educ. Ardvreck and Loretto Schools; Peterhouse, Cambridge University. Director, Ciba-Geigy PLC, 1972-92; General Manager, St. Andrews Links Trust, 1992-97. Recreation: golf; fishing; skiing; shooting. Address: Lynedale House, West Linton, Peeblesshire EH46 7HB; T.-01968 660440.

James, Professor Keith, BSc, PhD, DSc, FIBiol, FRCPath, FRSE. Former Professor of Immunology, Edinburgh University; b. 15.3.38, Cumbria; m., Valerie Spencer Jubb; 3 s. Educ. Whitehaven Grammar School; Birmingham University. Research Fellow, Birmingham University, 1962-64; Research Assistant, University of California, 1964-65; Senior Lecturer, Edinburgh University, 1965-77, Reader, 1977-91; Past Chairman, Treasurer, Education Secretary and Trustee, British Society for Immunology; Secretary General, International Union of Immunological Societies, 1992-98; serves on the editorial board of a number of journals. Publications: Introducing Immunology (Co-Author); numerous scientific papers. Recreations: hill-walking; photography. Address: (h.) 23 Crosswood Crescent, Balerno, Edinburgh EH14 7LX; T.-0131-449 5583.

James, Mary Charlotte, BA (Hons), FFCS; b. 2.4.44; m., Lawrence Edwin James; 2 s. Educ. St. Leonards School; York University; St. Anne's College, Oxford. Headmistress, Queen Ethelburga's School, Harrogate, 1984-88; Headmistress, St. Leonards School, St. Andrews, 1988-2000. Member: Scottish Council, ISCO, 1988-99, Scottish ISIS, 1988-2000, Board, SCIS Council, 1996-99; Chairman, Demarco European Cultural Initiative; Governor, King William's College, Isle of Man; Trustee, Bishop Barrow's Charity. Recreations: reading; cooking; walking; sleeping. Address: Priorwell, Balmerino, Fife DD6 8SE; T.-01382 330 888.

James, Ron (Ronald), PhD, BSc. Managing Director, PPC Therapeutics Plc, since 1989; b. 21.8.40, Ruislip; m. Educ. Bishops Halt Grammar; Birkbeck College, London University; Imperial College, London University. Glaxo Laboratories, 1959 -63; Wilkinson Sword Plc, 1966-84; Initial Plc, 1985; Prudential Ventures Managers Ltd, 1985-89. Recreations; sailing (racing); skiing. Address: (b.) PPL Therapeutics Plc, Roslin, Midlothian, EH25 9PP; T.-0131-440 4777.

James, Stuart, BA, FLA, MIInfSc, FRSA. Librarian, Paisley University, since 1989; b. 17.3.44, Borehamwood; m., Gillian Margaret Buckman; 1 s.; 1 d. Educ. Bushey Grammar School; Birmingham University. Leeds City Libraries, 1965-69; Northampton Development Corporation, 1970-71; Irvine Development Corporation (Librarian/ Information Specialist), 1971-78; Depute Librarian, Paisley College, 1978-89. Editor, Library Review; Editor, Reference Reviews; Convenor, Scottish Academic Libraries Co-operative Training Group, 1987-92; Honorary Secretary, Library Association Cataloguing and Indexing Group, 1992-97; Chairman, Cataloguing and

Indexing Group in Scotland, 1990-97; Chairman, Information for Scotland Conference Steering Group, since 1993; Member, British Library National Bibliographic Service Advisory Board, 1995-97; Scottish Library Association: Vice-President, 1999-2000, President, 2001; Chairman, Ayrshire Libraries Forum, since 1998; Vice-Chairman, Scottish Confederation of University and Research Libraries, since 2001. Recreations: history of aviation; reading; book collecting. Address: (b.) Library, Paisley University, High Street, Paisley PA1 2BE; T.-0141-848 3750.

Jameson, Brigadier Melville Stewart, CBE. Producer, Edinburgh Military Tattoo, since 1995, Chief Executive, since 1998; b. 17.7.44, Clunie; m., Sarah Amy Walker Munro; 2 s. Educ. Glenalmond; RMA, Sandhurst. Commissioned into Royal Scots Greys, 1965; served with regiment in Germany, Northern Ireland, Cyprus, Middle East and Edinburgh (where, in 1971, regiment amalgamated with 3rd Carbiniers to form Royal Scots Dragoon Guards); following tour as Chief of Staff 52 Lowland Brigade, commanded Royal Scots Dragoon Guards, 1986-88, at Tidworth; posted as Instructor to Joint Service Defence College Greenwich; Colonel PB17 on Military Secretary's staff, Ministry of Defence; Command, 51 Highland Brigade, 1994-96 based in Perth. Member, Royal Company of Archers; Honorary Colonel, Aberdeen University OTC. Recreations: shooting; gardening; polo; music (Highland bagpipes). Address: (b.) Tattoo Office, 32 Market Street, Edinburgh EH1 1QB; T.-0131-225 4783.

Jamie, Kathleen, MA. Writer; b. 13.5.62, Johnstone. Educ. Currie High School; Edinburgh University. Publications: The Way We Live; The Autonomous Region; The Queen of Sheba; The Golden Peak.

Jamieson, Cathy, BA (Hons), CQSW. MSP (Labour and Co-operative), Carrick, Cumnock and Doon Valley, since 1999; Minister for Education and Young People, Scottish Executive, since 2001; b. 3.11.56, Kilmarnock; m., Ian Sharpe; 1 s. Educ. James Hamilton Academy, Kilmarnock; Glasgow Art School; Glasgow University; Goldsmiths College, London; Caledonian University. Professional qualification in art therapy; later trained in social work; Senior IT Worker, Strathclyde Region; Principal Officer, Who Cares? Scotland, developing policy and legislation for young people in care; Member, inquiry team which investigated child abuse in Edinburgh children's homes. Recreation: football (Kilmarnock supporter). Address: (b.) Parliamentary Information Centre, Skerrington House, Glaisnock Road, Cumnock; T.-0845 458 1800.

Jamieson, David, BSc (Hons), MSc, DipTP, MIEEM, MRTPI. Director, BTCV Scotland, since 2000; b. 28.1.66, Bridlington, East Yorkshire; m., Deana Marie; 2 s. Educ. Headlands School, Bridlington; Stirling University; Heriot-Watt University; Huddersfield University. Nature Conservation Officer, Edinburgh District Council; Senior Planner, City of Edinburgh Council. Director, Falkirk Environment Trust; Council Member, Institute of Ecology and Environmental Management; Representative Member, National Trust for Scotland. Recreations: cricket; hillwalking; nature conservation. Address: (b.) Balallan House, 24 Allan Park, Stirling FK8 2QG; T.-01786 479697; e-mail: d.jamieson@btcv.org.uk

Jamieson, Eric, BSc. Member, Historic Buildings Council for Scotland, since 1999; Vice President, Cramond Association, since 1997; b. 1.8.23, Edinburgh; m., Marianne Rona Spence; 3 s.; 1 d. Educ. Broughton School; Edinburgh University. Government research, Telecommunications Research Establishment, 1943-46; development engineering management, Ferranti Ltd., 1948-88; Director, Telewest Communication Scotland Ltd., 1985-98. Publication: Island Treasure (children's

book). Recreations: reading; writing; travel; restored 14th-century tower house. Address: (h.) Cramond Tower, Kirk Cramond, Edinburgh EH4 6HZ; T.-0131-312 8724.

Jamieson, George, LLB (Hons), DipLP. Solicitor, since 1985; Examiner, Society of Messengers-at-Arms and Sheriff Officers, since 1995; b. 21.8.61, Paisley. Educ. Paisley Grammar School; Strathclyde University. Trainee Solicitor, Hart, Abercrombie, Caldwell and Co., Paisley, 1984-86; Walker Laird, Paisley: Assistant Solicitor, 1986-89, Partner, 1990-2001; Consultant, Pattison and Son, Paisley, since 2001. Council Member, Paisley Sheriff Court District, Law Society of Scotland, since 1997. Publications: Parental Responsibilities and Rights, 1995; Summary Applications and Suspensions, 2000. Address: (b.) 19 Glasgow Road, Paisley PA1 3QX; T.-0141-889 3296; e-mail: georgegjst@aol.com

Jamieson, Rev. Gordon David, MA, BD. Director of Stewardship, Church of Scotland, since 2000; b. 1.3.49, Glasgow; m., Annette; 1 s.; 1 d. Educ. Hamilton Academy; Edinburgh University. Assistant Minister, Tron Moredun, Edinburgh, 1973-74; Minister: Schaw Kirk, Drongan, 1974-79, Elie Parish Church, linked with Kilconquhar and Colinsburgh Parish Church, 1979-86, Barnhill St. Margaret's Parish Church, Dundee, 1986-2000. Address: (b.) 121 George Street, Edinburgh EH2 4YN; T.-0131-225 5722; (h.) 41 Goldpark Place, Livingston EH54 6LW; T.-01506 412020.

Jamieson, Margaret. MSP (Labour), Kilmarnock and Loudoun, since 1999; b. 1953, Kilmarnock; m.; 1 d. Educ. Grange Academy; Ayr College. Worked in public sector catering; first female full-time officer, National Union of Public Employees, 1979; Member, Board, East Ayrshire Employment Initiative. Address: (b.) Scottish Parliament, Edinburgh EH99 1SP; T.-0131-348 5774.

Jamieson, William, BA (Econ), FRSA. Executive Editor, The Scotsman, since 2000; Director, Policy Institute, since 2000; b. 9.6.45, Newmilns; m., Elaine Margaret Muller; 1 s. Educ. Hurst Grange School, Stirling; Sedbergh School, Yorkshire; Manchester University. Reporter, Merthyr Express, 1969-71; Sub-Editor, Western Mail, 1971-73; Economics Correspondent, Thomson Regionals, 1973-77; City Reporter, Daily Express, 1978; City Editor, Thomson Regionals, 1979-86; Deputy City Editor, Today, 1986; Sunday Telegraph: Deputy City Editor, 1986-95, Economics Editor, 1995-2000. Publications: Goldstrike, 1989; Britain Beyond Europe, 1994; UBS Guide to Emerging Markets (Editor), 1996; Illustrated Guide to the British Economy, 1998; Illustrated Guide to the Scottish Economy (Editor), 1999. Recreation: reading other people's newspapers. Address: (h.) Flat 3, 138 Calton Road, Edinburgh EH8 8DP; (b.) The Scotsman, 108 Holyrood Road, Edinburgh EH8 8AS; T.-0131-620 8361; e-mail: bjamieson@scotsman.com

Janes, Derek Charles, MA, AMA. Acting Head of Heritage and Arts, City of Edinburgh Council Recreation Department, since 1999; with Edinburgh City Museums, since 1985; b. 24.3.48, Bristol; m., Diane; 1 s.; 1 d. Educ. Bristol Grammar School; George Watson's College; Edinburgh University. Lancaster City Museum, 1969-71; Assistant Curator, Bury County Borough Museum and Art Gallery, 1972-74; Keeper of Social History, Bury Metropolitan Borough Museum, 1974-76; Senior Keeper, Social History, Coventry City Council Herbert Art Gallery, 1976-84. Publication: Lancaster. Recreations: garden; house; music; towns; reading. Address: (b.) Department of Recreation, 23/25 Waterloo Place, Edinburgh EH1 3BH.

Jaquet, Simon Philip, MA (Hons). Chief Executive, Youthlink Scotland, since 2001; b. 20.12.54, Kent; m., Caroline; 1 s.; 1 d. Educ. Cranbrook School, Kent;

Edinburgh University. Child care assistant, Berlin, 1973; English Language Assistant, Lycee Technique, Forbach, France, 1975-76; Intermediate Treatment Officer, Canongate Youth Project, Edinburgh, 1977-81; Festival Co-ordinator, Westerhailes Festival Association, Edinburgh, 1981-82; freelance community arts worker, 1982-84; Youth and Community Worker, Jwaneng Town Council, Botswana, 1984-86; Director, Fast Forward Positive Lifestyles Ltd., 1987-2001. Member: Ministerial Working Group on Community Education, Board, Scottish Youth Issues Journal, Nicolson Committee Reviewing Liquor Licensing Laws in Scotland. Publications: It's My Life; Big Picture (Co-Author/Editor). Recreations: playing music; cycling; reading; swimming; photography; toy making. Address: (b.) Youthlink Scotland, Central Hall, West Tollcross, Edinburgh EH3 9BP; T.-0131-229 0339; e-mail: info@youthlink.co.uk

Jardine, Ian William, BSc, PhD. Director of Strategy and Operations (East), Scottish Natural Heritage; b. 22.5.59, Edinburgh; m., Anne Daniel; 3 s. Educ. Royal High School, Edinburgh; Durham University; Leeds University. Joined Scottish Office, 1984; worked in various departments, including Scottish Development and Industry Departments; Private Secretary to Ian Lang MP; involved in setting-up of urban partnership initiatives and management of Castlemilk Partnership; joined Scottish Natural Heritage, 1992. Recreations: acting; gardening; natural history. Address: (b.) Battleby, Redgorton, Perth PH1 3EW; T.-01738 444177.

Jardine, Leslie Thomas, LLB. Director for Community Resources, Dumfries and Galloway Council, since 1995; b. 4.6.49, Dumfries; m., Angela; 1 s. Educ. Dumfries Academy; Glasgow University. Law apprentice, then Legal Assistant, Dumfries County Council, 1972-75; Policy Planning Assistant, then Regional Public Relations Officer, then Director of Economic Development, Dumfries and Galloway Regional Council, 1985-96. Solicitor. Recreation: riding. Address: (b.) 118 English Street, Dumfries; T.-01387 260070.

Jarnecki, Liam, BSc (Hons). Director, National Union of Students Scotland, since 1998; b. 10.7.68, Taplow. Educ. Desborough School; North East London Polytechnic. North East London Polytechnic Student Union President, 1991-92; Member, National Executive Committee, National Union of Students, 1992-93; freelance researcher/journalist, 1993-95; Development and Training Officer, National Union of Students Scotland, 1995-98. Recreations: football; promotion of European music and culture. Address: (b.) 29 Forth Street, Edinburgh EH1 3LE; T.-0131-556 6598; e-mail: liam@nus_scotland.org.uk

Jarrett, Professor James Oswald, PhD, BVMS, MRCVS, FRSE. Professor of Comparative Virology, University of Glasgow, since 1995; b. 19.3.40, Glasgow; m., Angela Marie Pacitti; 3 s. Educ. Lenzie Academy; University of Glasgow. Glasgow University: Research Fellow, Department of Experimental Veterinary Medicine, 1965-73, Lecturer/Senior Lecturer, Department of Veterinary Pathology, 1973-79, Professor, since 1980. Visiting Scientist, Scripps Institute, San Diego, 1980; Director, Moredun Research Institute; Chairman, The Cat Group; John Henry Steele Memorial Medal, Royal College of Veterinary Surgeons, 2000. Publications: over 200 scientific publications. Recreations: sailing; skiing. Address: (b.) University of Glasgow, Institute of Comparative Medicine, Faculty of Veterinary Medicine, Bearsden G61 1QH; T.-0141-330 5773; e-mail: o.jarrett@vet.gla.ac.uk

Jarvie, Professor Grant, BEd, MA, PhD. Chair of Sports Studies, University of Stirling, since 1997; b. 7.11.55, Motherwell. Educ. John Watson's School, Edinburgh; University of Exeter; Queen's University; University of Leicester. Secondary School Teacher, 1979-81;

Lecturer/Senior Lecturer, Leeds Polytechnic, 1982-86; Lecturer/Senior Lecturer, University of Warwick (Director, Warwick Centre for the Study of Sport, Chairman, Physical Education Department), 1986-95; Chair/Head of Sport and Leisure Studies, Moray House Institute, Heriot-Watt University, 1995-97. President, British Society of Sports History, 1996-2001. Publications: Class, Race and Sport in South Africa's Political Economy, 1985; Highland Games: The Making of the Myth, 1991; Sport, Racism and Ethnicity (Editor), 1991; Scottish Sport in the Making of the Nation: Ninety-Minute Patriots? (Co-editor), 1994; Sport and Leisure in Social Thought, Revised 1st Ed., 1995 and Revised 2nd Ed., 1999 (Co-author); Sporting Worlds: A Critical Perspective (Co-author), 1999; Sport, Scotland and the Scots (Co-editor), 2000; Sport in the Making of Celtic Cultures (Editor), 1999; The Encyclopedia of British Sport (Co-Editor), 2000; numerous book chapters and journal articles. Recreations: squash; hillwalking. Address: Department of Sports Studies, University of Stirling, Stirling FK9 4LA; T.-01786 466490.

Jarvie, Sheriff (Marie-Lesley) Elizabeth, QC, MA (Hons), LLB. Sheriff of Lothian and Borders at Edinburgh, since 1997; b. 22.1.52, Falkirk; m., John Jarvie; 1 s.; 4 d. Educ. Larbert High School; Edinburgh University. Admitted, Scottish Bar, 1981; Crown Counsel, 1989-92; QC, 1994. Recreations: skiing; current affairs.

Jarvis, Geoffrey, FRIAS. Architectural Consultant; b. 9.1.28, London; m., Rosalind Bailey; 2 s.; 2 d. Educ. Glasgow School of Architecture. Worked for two years in Philadelphia and New York (Marcel Breuer); returned to Glasgow, setting up in private practice; Consultant to National Trust for Scotland, 1972-87; principal works include Culzean Country Park Centre; Clan Donald Centre, Skye; Chatelherault, Hamilton; Edinburgh Castle Visitor Reception Feasibility Study; Founder, New Glasgow Society; Co-Founder, Clyde Fair International, 1972-73; Co-founder, Clydebuilt, 1991; Founder, Clyde Festival Gardens 1999 Ltd.; RIBA national award, Regenerating Scotland Award, three Europa Nostra Diplomas of Merit; two Civic Trust Awards; Founder, Clyde Heritage Trust. Recreation: sight-seeing. Address: (b./h.) Manse Brae, Baldernock, Milngavie G62 6HA; T.-0141-956 3899.

Jarvis, Professor Paul Gordon, PhD, Fil dr, FRS (London), FRSE, FRS (Uppsala), FIBiol, FIChFor. Professor of Forestry and Natural Resources, Edinburgh University, 1975-2001, Emeritus Professor, since 2001; b. 23.5.35, Tunbridge Wells; m., Margaret Susan Gostelow; 1 s.; 2 d. Educ. Sir Anthony Brown's School, Brentwood; Oriel College, Oxford. PhD study, Sheffield University, 1957-60; Postdoctoral Fellow, NATO, Institute of Plant Physiology, Uppsala University, 1960-62; Fil dr, Uppsala University, 1963; Senior Lecturer in Plant Physiology, Royal College of Agriculture, Uppsala; Aberdeen University: Lecturer in Botany, 1966-72, Senior Lecturer, 1972-75. Council Member, Society for Experimental Biology, 1977-80, President, 1993-95; Commissioner, Countryside Commission for Scotland, 1976-78; Council Member, National Trust for Scotland, since 1987; Trustee, John Muir Trust, 1989-2002; Member, Governing Body, Scottish Crops Research Institute, 1977-86; Co-Founder and Sectional Editor, Plant, Cell and Environment; present interests: environmental change, biodiversity, forest ecology and carbon sequestration; serves on various editorial and review boards. Recreations: hill-walking; gardening; growing trees. Address: (h.) Duireaskin, by Aberfeldy, Perthshire PH15 2ED; T.-01887 820988.

Jaspan, Andrew, BA (Hons). Editor, Sunday Herald, since 1999; b. 20.4.53, Manchester; m.; 2 s. Educ. Beverley Grammar School; Manchester University. Founder Editor, New Manchester Review, 1977-80; Sub-Editor, Daily Telegraph and Daily Mirror, Manchester, 1980; Journalists in Europe Fellowship, Paris, 1981; Late News Editor,

Times (London), 1982-85; Assistant News Editor, Sunday Times (London), 1985-88; Editor, Sunday Times Scotland, 1988-89; Editor, Scotland on Sunday, 1989-94; Editor, The Scotsman, 1994-95; Editor, The Observer, 1995-96; Publisher and Managing Director, The Big Issue, 1996-98. Address: (b.) 200 Renfield Street, Glasgow G2 3PR.

Jasper, Professor David, MA (Cantab), MA (Oxon), BD, PhD. Dean of Divinity and Professor of Literature and Theology, University of Glasgow, since 1998; b. 1.8.51, Stockton; m., Alison Elizabeth Collins; 3 d. Educ. Dulwich College; Jesus College, Cambridge; St. Stephen's House, Oxford; Durham University. Curate of Buckingham (Anglican), 1976-79; Chaplain and Fellow, Hatfield College, Durham, 1979-87; Principal, St. Chad's College, Durham, 1988-91; Senior Lecturer then Reader, University of Glasgow, 1991-98; Director, Centre for Literature and Theology, University of Glasgow, 1991-99. Publications: six books, most recently The Sacred and Secular Canon in Romanticism, 1999. Recreations: reading; photography; walking. Address: Department of Theology and Religious Studies, University of Glasgow, Glasgow G12 8QQ; T.-0141-330 4405.

Jauhar, Pramod, MBBS, DPM, FRCPsych. Consultant Psychiatrist, since 1981; HM Medical Commissioner (part-time), since 1998; b. 15.3.48, Agra, India; m., Pamela; 2 s.; 1 d. Educ. St. Xavier School, Jaipur, India; Armed Forces Medical College, Pune, India. General professional training in psychiatry, St. Bernard's Hospital and Charing Cross Hospital, London, 1974-77; higher professional training, St. Thomas' Hospital, 1977-80; Consultant Psychiatrist, St. Brendan's Hospital, Bermuda, 1980-81; Consultant Psychiatrist and Honorary Clinical Senior Lecturer, 1981; Clinical Director, Alcohol and Drug Directorate, 1985. Member, Executive Committee, Medical Council for Alcohol, 1999; President, Rotary Club, Queen's Park, Glasgow, 2000. Recreations: golf; travel. Address: (b.) Parkhead Hospital, 81 Salamanca Street, Glasgow G31 5ES; T.-0141-211 8300; e-mail: pramodjauhar@hotmail.com

Jauncey of Tullichettle, Lord (Charles Eliot Jauncey), PC. Lord of Appeal in Ordinary, 1988-96; Senator of the College of Justice in Scotland, 1979-88; b. 8.5.25; m. 1, Jean Cunningham Graham; 2 s.; 1 d; m. 2, Sarah Camilla Cathcart; 1 d. Educ. Radley; Christ Church, Oxford; Glasgow University. Advocate, 1949; Kintyre Pursuivant of Arms, 1955; QC, 1963; Sheriff Principal of Fife and Kinross, 1971. Member, Historic Buildings Council for Scotland, 1971-92. Recreations: fishing; bicycling; genealogy. Address: (h.) Tullichettle, Comrie, Perthshire PH6 2HU; T.-01764 670349.

Jeeves, Professor Malcolm Alexander, CBE, MA, PhD (Cantab), Hon. DSc (Edin), Hon. DSc (St. And.), Hon. DUniv (Stir.), FBPsS, FMedSci, FRSE. Professor of Psychology, St. Andrews University, 1969-93, Emeritus Professor, since 1993; President, Royal Society of Edinburgh, 1996-99 (Vice-President, 1990-93); b. 16.11.26, Stamford, England; m., Ruth Elisabeth Hartridge; 2 d. Educ. Stamford School; St. John's College, Cambridge University. Lt., 1st Bn., Sherwood Foresters, BAOR, 1945-48; Exhibitioner, St. John's College, Cambridge, 1948-52; research and teaching, Cambridge and Harvard Universities, 1952-56; Lecturer, Leeds University, 1956-59; Professor and Head, Department of Psychology, Adelaide University, 1959-69 (Dean, Faculty of Arts, 1963-64); Member: Council, SERC, 1985-89, Neuroscience and Mental Health Board, MRC, 1985-89, Council, Royal Society of Edinburgh, 1985-88 (Vice President, 1990-93); Director, Medical Research Council Cognitive Neuroscience Research Group, 1983-88; Vice-Principal, St. Andrews University, 1981-85; Chairman, Executive Committee, International Neuropsychological Symposium, 1986-91; Editor-in-Chief, Neuropsychologia, 1990-93; Cairns

Memorial Lecturer, Australia, 1986; New College Lecturer, University of NSW, 1987. Honorary Sheriff, Fife, since 1986. Publications: Analysis of Structural Learning (Co-Author); Psychology Survey No. 3 (Editor); Experimental Psychology: An introduction for biologists; The Effects of Structural Relations upon Transfer (Co-Author); Thinking in Structures (Co-Author); Behavioural Science and Christianity (Editor); Free to be Different (Co-Author); Psychology and Christianity: The View Both Ways; The Scientific Enterprise and Christian Faith; Psychology: Through the eyes of faith (Co-Author); Mind Fields; Human Nature at the Millennium; Science, Life and Christian Belief (Co-author). Recreations: walking; music; fishing. Address: (b.) School of Psychology, St. Andrews University, St. Andrews KY16 9JU; T.-01334 462072.

Jeffares, Professor Alexander Norman Derry, AM, MA, PhD, DPhil, Ddel'U, DLitt, FAHA, FRSE, FRSL, FRSA. Professor of English Studies, Stirling University, 1974-86; Honorary Professor, since 1987; Managing Director, Academic Advisory Services Ltd.; Director, Colin Smythe Ltd.; b. 11.8.20, Dublin; m., Jeanne Agnes Calembert; 1 d. Educ. The High School, Dublin; Trinity College, Dublin; Oriel College, Oxford. Lecturer in Classics, Trinity College, Dublin, 1943-45; Lector in English, Groningen University, 1946-48; Lecturer in English Literature, Edinburgh University, 1949-51; Professor of English Language and Literature, Adelaide, 1951-56; Professor of English Literature, Leeds, 1957-74. Secretary, Australian Humanities Research Council, 1954-57; Honorary Fellow, Australian Academy of Humanities; Founding Chairman, Association for Commonwealth Literary and Language Studies, 1966-68 (Honorary Life Fellow); Founding Chairman, International Association for Study of Anglo-Irish Literature, 1968-70 (Honorary Life President, since 1973); Member, Scottish Arts Council (Chairman, Literature Committee, 1977-83, Vice Chairman, 1980-84); Member, Arts Council of GB, 1980-84; Chairman, Scottish Book League Scotland, 1985-87, Book Trust Scotland, 1987-89; Board Member, Book Trust, 1987-89; President, International PEN, Scottish Centre, 1986-89; Vice-President, Royal Society of Edinburgh, 1988-89; Vice-Chairman, Muckhart Community Council, 1979-86; Chairman of Judges, McVitie Prize, 1988-91. Publications: Yeats: Man and Poet; Seven Centuries of Poetry; The Scientific Background (Co-Author); A Commentary on the Poems of Yeats; A Commentary on the Plays of Yeats (Co-Author); History of Anglo-Irish Literature; Restoration Drama; New Commentary on Poems of Yeats; Brought up in Dublin (poems); Brought up to Leave (poems); An Irish Childhood (Co-Editor); A Jewish Childhood (Co-Editor); Yeats: a new biography; Yeats's Poems; Yeats's Vision; Yeats: the love poems; Always Your Friend (Co-Editor); Swift, the selected poems; Joycechoyce (Co-Editor); Ireland's Women (Co-Editor); Collins Dictionary of Quotations (Co-Editor); Images of Imagination (essays); Victorian Love Poems; Pocket History of Irish Literature; Irish Love Poems; The Irish Literary Movement; The Shadowy Rose; Oliver St. John Gogarty: Poems and Plays; Ireland's Love Poems: Wonder and a Wild Desire. Recreations: drawing; painting; restoring old houses. Address: (h.) Craighead Cottage, Fife Ness, Crail, Fife; T.-01333 450898.

Jeffcoat, Marilyn Annette, BCom, FCCA. Managing Director, D.M. Vaughan & Co. Ltd., Accountants; b. 7.4.47, Birmingham; m., 1, David Jeffcoat (marriage dissolved); 5 s.; 1 d.; m., 2, Donald Leach (qv). Educ. Erdington Grammar School, Birmingham; Edinburgh University. Worked in investment management, tax accountancy and audit with Baillie Gifford, Ivory & Sime, and Coopers & Lybrand until 1978, qualifying as a certified accountant in 1976; public practice since 1979. Member of Court, Napier University, 1990-2001 (Chairman, Audit Committee, 1994-2001); Commissioner, Mental Welfare Commission, 1992-98; Convener, One Parent Families, Scotland, 1994-99;

Director, St. Mary's Cathedral Workshop Ltd.; Treasurer: Society of Scottish Artists, 1978-93, St. Mary's Episcopal Cathedral, Edinburgh, Royal Scottish Country Dance Society; Organiser, Mendelssohn on Mull Festival; Chairman, Internet Society of Scotland; Finance Director, Spanoptic Ltd. and Director, number of other companies. Recreation: seeing the world. Address: (b.) 10 Gloucester Place, Edinburgh EH3 6EF; T.-0131-225 8282.

Jeffreys-Jones, Professor Rhodri, BA (Wales), PhD (Cantab), FRHistS. Professor of American History, Edinburgh University, since 1997 (Chair of History Department, since 2001); b. 28.7.42, Carmarthen; m., Mary Fenton; 2 d. by pr. m. Educ. Ysgol Ardudwy; University of Wales; Cambridge University; Michigan University; Harvard University. Tutor: Harvard, 1965-66, Fitzwilliam College, Cambridge, 1966-67; Assistant Lecturer, Lecturer, Senior Lecturer, Reader, Edinburgh University, 1967-97; Fellow, Charles Warren Center for the Study of American History, Harvard, 1971-72; Canadian Commonwealth Visiting Fellow and Visiting Professor, University of Toronto, 1993; Arts and Humanities Research Board Award, 2000; Chair, Scottish Association for the Study of America, since 1998. Publications: Violence and Reform in American History; American Espionage: From Secret Service to CIA; Eagle Against Empire: American Opposition to European Imperialism 1914-82 (Editor); The Growth of Federal Power in American History (Joint Editor); The CIA and American Democracy; North American Spies (Joint Editor); Changing Differences: Women and the Shaping of American Foreign Policy, 1917-1994; Eternal Vigilance? – 50 years of the CIA (Joint Editor); Peace Now! American Society and the Ending of the Vietnam War; American-British-Canadian Intelligence Relations 1939-2000 (Joint Editor). Recreations: snooker; vegetable gardening. Address: (b.) Department of History, Edinburgh University, William Robertson Building, George Square, Edinburgh EH8 9JY; T.-0131-650 3773/3780; e-mail: Jeffreys-Jones.Rhodri@ed.ac.uk

Jenkins, Archibald Ian, MA (Hons), DipEd. MSP (Liberal Democrat), Tweeddale, Ettrick and Lauderdale, since 1999; b. 18.3.41, Rothesay; m., Margery MacKay. Educ. Rothesay Academy; Glasgow University. Teacher of English, Clydebank High School, 1964-70; Principal Teacher of English, Peebles High School, 1970-99. Recreations: reading; listening to music; watching rugby. Address: (b.) Scottish Parliament, Edinburgh EH99 1SP; T.-0131-348 5802.

Jenkins, Blair, MA (Hons). Head of News and Current Affairs, BBC Scotland, since 2000; b. 8.1.57, Elgin; 3 d. Educ. Elgin Academy; Edinburgh University. Reporter, Aberdeen Evening Express, 1974-76; student, 1976-80; Producer, BBC Television News, London, 1981-84; Producer, Reporting Scotland, BBC Scotland, 1984-86; Scottish Television: Producer, Scotland Today, 1986-90, Head of News, 1990-93, Head of Regional Broadcasting, 1993-94, Director of Broadcasting, 1994-97; Media Consultant, 1998-2000. Young Journalist of the Year, Scottish Press Awards, 1977; Chairman, BAFTA Scotland, since 1998. Address: (b.) BBC Scotland, Queen Margaret Drive, Glasgow G12 8DG; T.-0141-338 2450; e-mail: blair.jenkins@bbc.co.uk

Jenkins, Robin, OBE, MA. Novelist; b. 11.9.12. Author of: So Gaily Sings the Lark, Happy for the Child, The Thistle and the Grail, The Cone-Gatherers, Guests of War, The Missionaries, The Changeling, Some Kind of Grace, Dust on the Paw, The Tiger of Gold, A Love of Innocence, The Sardana Dancers, A Very Scotch Affair, The Holy Tree, The Expatriates, A Toast to the Lord, A Far Cry from Bowmore, A Figure of Fun, A Would-be Saint, Fergus Lamont, The Awakening of George Darroch, Just Duffy, Poverty Castle, Willie Hogg, Leila, Lunderston Tales, Matthew and Sheila, Poor Angus, Childish Things. Address: (h.) Fairhaven, Toward, Dunoon PA23 7UE.

Jennett, Professor Bryan, MD, FRCS, DSc(Hon). Professor of Neurosurgery, Glasgow University, 1968-91 (Dean, Faculty of Medicine, 1981-86); Member, Court, Glasgow University, 1987-91; b. 1.3.26, Twickenham, Middlesex; m., Professor Sheila Jennett; 3 s.; 1 d. Educ. King's College, Wimbledon; King George V School, Southport; Liverpool University. Lecturer in Neurosurgery, Manchester University; Rockefeller Travelling Fellow, University of California; Hunterian Professor, Royal College of Surgeons of England. Member: Medical Research Council, 1979-83, Chief Scientist Committee, Scotland; Rock Carling Fellow. Publications: Epilepsy After Non-Missile Head Injuries; Introduction to Neurosurgery; High Technology Medicine - Benefits and Burdens; The Vegetative State – Medical Facts, Ethical and Legal Dilemmas. Recreations: writing; cruising under sail. Address: (h.) 83 Hughenden Lane, Glasgow G12 9XN.

Jennings, James, OBE, JP. Member, North Ayrshire Council, since 1996 (Chair, Social Work Committee); Former Convener, Strathclyde Regional Council; Honorary Sheriff, Kilmarnock, since 1991; Chairman, Police Negotiating Board, since 1990; b. 18.2.25; m., 1, Margaret Cook Barclay (deceased); 3 s.; 2 d.; 2, Margaret Mary Hughes, JP; 2 d. Educ. St. Palladius School, Dalry; St. Michael's College, Irvine. Steel industry, 1946-79. Member: Ayr County Council, 1958, Strathclyde Regional Council, 1974 (Vice-Convener, 1982-86); Chairman: Ayr CC Police and Law Committee, 1964-70, Ayrshire Joint Police Committee, 1970-75, North Ayrshire Crime Prevention Panel, 1970-82, Police and Fire Committee, Strathclyde Regional Council, 1978-82; contested Perth and East Perthshire, 1966; Honorary Vice-President, Royal British Legion Scotland (Dalry and District Branch); JP, Cunninghame, 1969 (Chairman, Cunninghame Justices Committee, 1974-95); Vice-Chairman, Official Side, Police Negotiating Board, 1984-86, Chairman, 1986-88; Chairman, Garnock Valley Development Executive, since 1988; Freeman of North Ayrshire, since 1997. Recreation: local community involvement. Address: (h.) 4 Place View, Kilbirnie KA25 6BG; T.-Kilbirnie 3339.

Jennings, Kevin, MB, FRCP. Consultant Cardiologist, Aberdeen Royal Infirmary, since 1983; b. 9.3.47, Charleville, Eire; m., Heather; 2 s.; 1 d. Educ. Downside; St. Bartholomew's Hospital, London. Registrar: King's College Hospital, London, London Chest Hospital; Senior Registrar, Freeman Hospital, Newcastle-upon-Tyne. Recreations: theatre; ballet; golf; windsurfing. Publication: Acute Cardiac Care. Address: 58 Rubislaw Den South, Aberdeen AB15 4AY; T.-Aberdeen 311466.

Jensen-Butler, Professor Christopher Nigel, BA, PhD. Professor, Department of Economics, University of St. Andrews, since 1996; b. 5.6.45, Derby. Educ. Bemrose School, Derby; University College, University of Durham. University of Aarhus, Denmark: Assistant Professor, 1969-72, Associate Professor, 1972-87, Department of Geography, Associate Professor, Department of Mathematics, 1987-91, Associate Professor, Department of Political Science, 1991-95; Professor of Urban and Regional Planning, Department of Geography, University of St. Andrews, 1995-96; Guest Professor, University of Lisbon, 1987; Professor, University of Copenhagen, 1999-2000. Publication: European Cities in Competition (Co-Editor), 1997. Recreations: sailing; hill-walking; classical music. Address: (b.) Department of Economics, University of St. Andrews, Castlecliffe, The Scores, St. Andrews, Fife KY16 9AL; T.-01334 462442.

Jessamine, Rev. Alistair Lindsay, MA, BD. Minister of Dunfermline Abbey, since 1991; b. 17.6.49, Hill of Beath; m., Eleanor Moore. Educ. Beath High School, Cowdenbeath; University of Edinburgh. Assistant Minister, Newlands South Parish Church, Glasgow, 1978-79; Minister, Rankin Parish Church, Strathaven linked with Chapelton, 1979-91; Chaplain: HM Prison, Dungavel, 1979-91, RAF Pitreavie Castle, 1991-95; Moderator, Presbytery of Dunfermline, 1993-94. Recreations: travel; cooking; golf. Address: Abbey Manse, 12 Garvock Hill, Dunfermline, Fife KY12 7UU; T.-01383 721022.

Jessop, Sheriff Alexander Smethurst, MA, LLB. Sheriff at Aberdeen, since 1990; b. 17.5.43, Montrose; m., Joyce Isobel Duncan; 2 s.; 1 d. Educ. Montrose Academy; Fettes College; Aberdeen University. Partner, Campbell, Middleton, Burness and Dickson, Montrose; Procurator Fiscal Depute, Perth, 1976-78; Assistant Solicitor, Crown Office, 1978-80; Senior Assistant Procurator Fiscal, Glasgow, 1980-84; Regional Procurator Fiscal, Aberdeen, 1984-87, Glasgow, 1987-90. Member, Scottish Legal Aid Board; External Examiner, Aberdeen University. Recreation: golf (Captain, Royal Montrose Golf Club). Address: (b.) Sheriff Court House, Aberdeen AB9 1AP; T.-01224 648316; e-mail: sheriff.ajessop@scotcourts.gov.uk

Jiwa, Shainool, PhD. Research Associate and Project Manager, Institute of Ismaili Studies, London, since 1999; Commissioner, Mental Welfare Commission for Scotland, since 1998; Deputy Chief Examiner, International Baccalaureate Organization, since 2000; b. 29.3.58, Shahnavaz Jiwa; 1 s.; 1 d. Educ. McGill University, Montreal (MA); Edinburgh University (PhD). Began career as part-time Lecturer in Islamic History, Edinburgh University, 1989-91; embarked on career in community development, training and practising as a counsellor; leading role in setting up a range of community-based services for minority ethnic women in Edinburgh, 1991-99; volunteer counsellor, Edinburgh Association for Mental Health, 1996-98; voluntary involvement with Ismaili Muslim community in UK. Recreations: swimming; reading; walks. Address: (h.) 9 Silverknowes Loan, Edinburgh EH4 5HS; T.-0131-539 4977.

Jobson, Roy, BEd, DPA, MEd, FRSA. Director of Education, City of Edinburgh, since 1998; b. 2.6.47, Corbridge, Northumberland; m., Maureen; 1 s.; 2 d. Educ. Bedlington Grammar School; Durham University. Assistant Teacher, The King's Grammar, Tynemouth; Head of Department, Norham High School, North Tyneside; Assistant Secretary, East Midland Exam Board; Assistant Director of Education, Gateshead Metropolitan Borough Council; Deputy Chief Education Officer, Manchester City Council; Chief Education Officer, Manchester City Council. Recreations: church; music; gardening; reading; walking. Address: (b.) Education Department, Wellington Court, Waterloo Place, Edinburgh; T.-0131 469 3322.

Johnson, Professor Christopher William, MA, MSc, DPhil, CEng, FBCS. Personal Chair in Computing Science, Glasgow University, since 1997; b. 15.4.65, Edinburgh; m., Fionnuala Muireann; 4 s. Educ. Verulam School, St. Albans; Trinity College, Cambridge. Lecturer in Computing Science, University of York, 1991-94; Senior Lecturer in Computing Science, University of Glasgow, 1994-97. Chair, IFIP Working Group 13.5 (Human Error and Systems Development). Publications: over 100 papers and articles. Winner, 1998 Systems Safety Award. Recreation: running. Address: (b.) Department of Computing Science, University of Glasgow, Glasgow G12 8QQ; T.-0141-330 6053.

Johnson, David (Charles), MA, BA, PhD. Composer; Musicologist; Publisher; 27.10.42, Edinburgh; 1 s. Educ. Aberdeen University; St. John's College, Cambridge.

Cellist, McGibbon Ensemble, 1980-96; Tutor, Edinburgh University Music Faculty, 1988-94; compositions include five operas, an orchestral suite, chamber music, songs, a piano concerto, church music, Robert Burns cantata, God, Man and the Animals, cantata. Publications: Music and Society in Lowland Scotland, 1972; Scottish Fiddle Music in the 18th Century, 1984; The Scots Cello Book, 1990; Stepping Northward, 1990; 12 Preludes and Fugues, 1996; Chamber Music of 18th Century Scotland, 2000; contributions to New Grove Dictionary of Music, 2001. Address: (h.) 8 Shandon Crescent, Edinburgh EH11 1QE. T.-0131-337 4621.

Johnson, Professor Gerry, BA, PhD. Professor of Strategic Management, Strathclyde Graduate School of Business, since 2000; Author and Consultant, since 1980; b. 15.8.45, Leicester; m., Phyllis; 3 d. Educ. City of Leicester Boys School; University College, London. Unilever/Birds Eye Foods, 1968-72; Reed International, 1972-74; Management Consultant, 1974-76; Lecturer: Hull College of Higher Education, 1976-79, Aston University, 1979-85; Senior Fellow, Manchester Business School, 1985-88; Professor, Cranfield School of Management, 1988-2000. Publication: Exploring Corporate Strategy (Co-Author), 2001. Recreations: tennis; dog walking; music. Address: (b.) University of Strathclyde Graduate School of Business, 199 Cathedral Street, Glasgow G4 0QU; T.-0141-553 6199; e-mail: gerry@gsb.strath.ac.uk

Johnson, Ian M., BA, FLA, MIInfSc, MIMgt. Head, School of Information and Media, Robert Gordon University, Aberdeen, since 1989; Chairman: Heads of Schools and Departments Committee, British Association for Information and Library Education and Research, 1997-2000; b. 17.3.45, Sheffield; m., Jean Trevena. Educ. King Edward VII School, Sheffield; Liverpool College of Commerce; Leeds Polytechnic. Sheffield City Libraries, 1962-74; Department of Education and Science (Office of Arts and Libraries), 1970-72 (on secondment); Rotherham M.B. Council, 1974-78; College of Librarianship Wales, 1978-89. Chairman, Professional Board, International Federation of Library Associations and Institutions, 1993-95; Chairman, Library Association Personnel Training and Education Group, 1994-95; Member, Library Association Council, 1996-2000; Chairman, EUCLID, 1998-2001. Recreations: theatre; cinema; travel. Address: (b.) Garthdee Road, Aberdeen AB10 7QE.

Johnson, Professor Keith Jack, BSc, PhD, FRCPath. Professor of Genetics, University of Glasgow, since 1995; b. 17.5.55, Dorset; m., Margot Ross; 1 s.; 1 d. Educ. Brockenhurst Grammar School, Hants; University of Dundee. Charing Cross and Westminster Medical School: Lecturer, 1989-93, Senior Lecturer, 1993-95. Recreations: golf; crosswords. Address: (b.) Division of Molecular Genetics, Anderson College, 56 Dumbarton Road, Glasgow; T.-0141-330 5101.

Johnston, Hon. Lord (Alan Charles Macpherson), BA (Hons) (Cantab), LLB, DUniv (Heriot Watt). Senator of the College of Justice, since 1994; Queen's Counsel (1980); b. 13.1.42, Stirling; m., Anthea Jean Blackburn; 3 s. Educ. Edinburgh Academy; Loretto School; Jesus College, Cambridge; Edinburgh University. Advocate, 1967; Standing Junior Counsel, Scottish Home and Health Department, 1972; Advocate Depute, 1978-82; Chairman: Industrial Tribunal, 1982-85, Medical Appeal Tribunal, 1985-89; Treasurer, Faculty of Advocates, 1977-89, Dean, Faculty of Advocates, 1989-93. Publication: Introduction to Law of Scotland 7th Edition (Joint Editor). Address: (h.) 3 Circus Gardens, Edinburgh; T.-0131-225 1862.

Johnston, Bruce William McLaren, CA. Chairman, The Alliance Trust plc, since 1996; Chairman, The Second Alliance Trust plc, since 1996; b. 7.2.39, Alyth. Educ. Morgan Academy, Dundee. Partner, Arthur Young (now

Ernst and Young), 1970-86; City Centre Restaurants plc: Director, 1986-88, Executive Chairman, 1988-96. Member, Court, University of Dundee. Recreation: hillwalking. Address: (b.) 64 Reform Street, Dundee; T.-01382 201700.

Johnston, Frederick Patrick Mair, CBE, FRSA, MA. Chairman, Johnston Press plc (formerly F. Johnston & Co. Ltd.), 1973-2001, Non-Executive Director, since 2001; Director, Lloyds TSB Scotland plc, since 1996; b. 15.9.35, Edinburgh; m., Elizabeth Ann Jones; 2 s. Educ. Morrison's Academy, Crieff; Lancing College, Sussex; New College, Oxford. Editorial Department, Liverpool Daily Post and Echo, 1959; Assistant Secretary, The Times Publishing Co. Ltd., 1960; Company Secretary, F. Johnston & Co. Ltd., 1969. Chairman, Central Scotland Manpower Committee, 1976-83; Member, Press Council, 1974-88; President, Scottish Newspaper Proprietors' Association, 1976-78; Treasurer, Society of Master Printers of Scotland, 1981-86; President, The Newspaper Society, 1989-90; Director, Scottish Mortgage & Trust plc, since 1991; Chairman, Edinburgh International Book Festival, 1996-2001; Director, Press Association Ltd., 1997-2001. Recreations: reading; travelling. Address: (b.) 53 Manor Place, Edinburgh EH3 7EG; T.-0131-225 3361.

Johnston, Geoffrey Edward Forshaw, LLB, CA. Managing Director, Arbuckle, Smith and Company, 1972-99; Chairman, Scottish Chambers of Commerce, 1996-2000; Non Executive Director: Scottish Friendly Assurance Society Ltd., Lamellar Therapeutics Ltd.; b. 20.6.40, Burton-Wirral, England; m., Elizabeth Anne Lockhart; 2 d. Educ. Loretto School, Musselburgh; University of St. Andrews. Wilson Stirling & Co. CA, 1959-65; Arbuckle Smith Group, since 1965: Director, 1968, management buy-out, 1984. Honorary Consul for Belgium, Scotland West and Northern Islands, 1989-95; National Chairman, British International Freight Association, 1990-91; President, Glasgow Chamber of Commerce, 1994-95; Member, Scottish Valuation and Rating Council, 1981-2001; Chairman, Central College of Commerce. Recreations: sailing; skiing; hillwalking; golf. Address: (h.) Upper Dunard, Station Road, Rhu, Dunbartonshire G84 8LW; T.-01436 820563.

Johnston, George Bonar, DA, RSW. Artist; b. 14.6.33, Edinburgh; m., Margaret (deceased); 1 s.; 1 d. Educ. Bathgate Academy; Edinburgh College of Art. Teacher, 1955-56; Army Officer, 1956-58; Teacher, 1958-59; Lecturer, 1959-66; Art Adviser, Tayside Region, 1966-91. Paintings in private and public collections in Scotland, England, France, North America, Canada. Recreations: fly fishing; reading. Address: 10 Collingwood Crescent, Barnhill, Dundee DD5 2SX; T.-01382 779857.

Johnston, Grenville Shaw, OBE, TD, KCSG, DL, CA. Chartered Accountant, since 1968; President, Institute of Chartered Accountants of Scotland, 2000-01; Vice Lord Lieutenant of Moray, since 1996; Territorial Army Officer, 1964-89 (Lt. Col.); b. 28.1.45, Nairn; m., Marylyn Jean Picken; 2 d. Educ. Blairmore School; Fettes College. Qualified in Edinburgh with Scott Moncrieff Thomson & Sheills; Thomson McLintock & Co., Glasgow, 1968-70; joined family firm, W.D. Johnston & Carmichael, Elgin, 1970; Senior Partner, 1975-2001. Commanding Officer, 2nd 51st Highland Volunteers, 1983-86; Hon. Col., 3rd Highland Volunteers, 1997-99; Knight Commander, Order of St. Gregory, 1982, for work for Pluscarden Abbey; OBE for services to Territorial Army; Chairman, Grampian Committee, Royal Jubilee Trusts, 1982-91; Member, Cairngorm Recreation Trust Ltd.; Trustee and Council Member: Queens Own Highlanders, The Highlanders; Trustee, National Museums of Scotland, since 1998; Director: Cairngorms Mountain Ltd., since 1999, Highlands and Islands Airports Ltd., since 2001. Recreations:

shooting; fishing; hockey; golf; skiing; singing (tenor). Address: (h.) Spynie Kirk House, Spynie, By Elgin, Moray IV30 3XJ.

Johnston, Ian Alistair, CB, PhD, BSc, CIMgt, FIPD, FRSA. Principal, Glasgow Caledonian University, since 1998; Honorary Treasurer, Industrial Society, since 1990; Board Member, University for Industry, since 1998; Director, Qualifications for Industry, 1996-99; b. 2.5.44, Watlington, Oxford; m., Mary Bridget Lube; 1 s.; 1 d. Educ. High Wycombe Royal Grammar School; Birmingham University. Department of Employment: Assistant Principal, 1969, Principal, 1974; First Secretary (Labour Attaché), British Embassy, Brussels, 1975-77; Director, Advisory Conciliation Arbitration Service, 1978-82; Finance Director (Under Secretary) then Chief Executive/Director General (Deputy Secretary), Manpower Services Commission, 1983-95; Deputy Principal, Sheffield Hallam University, 1995-98. Member, High Level Expert Advisory Group on Education and Training Strategy, European Commission; Assessor, National Advisory Council on Education and Training Targets, 1992-95; writes on public sector management and applying IT to learning. Recreations: bird watching; travel; tennis; armchair rugby. Address: (b.) Glasgow Caledonian University, Cowcaddens Road, Glasgow G4 0BA; T.-0141-331 3113.

Johnston, Professor Ian Alistair, BSc, PhD, FRSE. Chandos Professor of Physiology, Director, Gatty Marine Laboratory, since 1985, and Head, Division of Environmental and Evolutionary Biology, St. Andrews University, since 1997; b. 13.4.49, Barking, Essex. Educ. Addey and Stanhope Grammar School, London; Hull University. NERC Postdoctoral Research Fellow, Bristol University, 1973-75; Lecturer in Physiology, St. Andrews University, 1976-84; Reader, 1984-85; Visiting Senior Lecturer, Department of Veterinary Physiology, Nairobi University, 1981; Visiting Scientist, British Antarctic Survey base, Signy Island, South Orkneys, 1983-84; Council Member, NERC, 1995-2000; Chairman, NERC Marine Science and Technology Board; awarded Scientific Medal, Zoological Society of London. Recreations: photography; walking; reading. Address: (b.) Division of Environmental and Evolutionary Biology, St. Andrews University, St. Andrews KY16 8LB; T.-01334 463440.

Johnston, James George, BSc (Hons), AdvDip Ed, FRSA, MIM. Head Teacher, Symbister House Junior High, Shetland, since 1996; b. 1.5.54, Glasgow; m., Marilyn; 1 s. Educ. Cumbernauld High School; Glasgow University. Teacher, Greenfaulds High, 1977-80; Head of Department, Oxenford, 1980-83; Assistant Head Teacher, Oxenford, 1983-84; Head Teacher, Leverhulme Memorial School, 1984-96. Recreations: DIY. art; golf; cooking. Address: (h.) Laarsund, Hillswick, Shetland, ZE2 9RW; T.-01806 503342.

Johnston, Jim A., MA. Headteacher, Farr High School, since 1991; b. 11.9.50, Lerwick; m., Jenny Mackay; 1 d. Educ. Anderson Educational Institute; Aberdeen University; Aberdeen College of Education. Farr High School: Assistant Teacher of English, 1973-75, Principal Teacher of English, 1975-77, Depute Head, 1977-91. Chairman, Bettyhill, Strathnaver and Altnaharra Community Council, 1977-88; Company Secretary, Tongue and Farr Sports Association Ltd., since 1991; founding Chairman, Scottish Peat and Land Development Association (Caithness Branch); Chairman, Project Area Advisory Group, Duthchas Community Regeneration Project. Publications: A Future for Peat, 1981; Tongue and Farr, 1984, Gleannan am Fraoch, 1988; The Best of the Bard (Editor), 1987; Recreations: journalism; photography; crofting; reading; hillwalking. Address: (h.) Vaila, Bettyhill, by Thurso, Caithness KW14 7SS; T.-01641 521302.

Johnston, Joyce Sara Ramsay, BA, MEd. Principal, Fife College of Further and Higher Education, Kirkcaldy, since 1996; b. Brisbane, Australia. Educ. Knightswood School, Glasgow; University of Strathclyde; University of Edinburgh. Tourism Research, Australia, 1970-80; Education Administration, Dundee College, 1980-83; Depute Principal, Glenrothes College, 1983-89; Principal, Anniesland College, Glasgow, 1989-92; H.M.I., Scottish Office Education and Industry Department, 1992-96. Member, Scottish Further Education Funding Council; Board Member, Association of Scottish Colleges; Vice-Chair, Scottish Management and Enterprise Council. Recreations: reading; gardening; cinema. Address: (b.) St. Brycedale Avenue, Kirkaldy KY1 1EX; T.-01592 268591.

Johnston, Professor Marie, BSc, PhD, DipClinPsych, FBPsS, CPsychol, FRSE, FMedSci, ACSS. Professor in Psychology, St. Andrews University, since 1992; b. 6.7.44, Aberdeen; m., Derek Johnston. Educ. High School for Girls, Aberdeen; Aberdeen University; Hull University. Research Officer, Oxford University, 1971-77; Lecturer, Senior Lecturer, Reader, Royal Free Hospital School of Medicine, 1977-90; Reader, Professor of Psychology, St. Andrews University, since 1990; Honorary Clinical Psychologist, Tayside and Fife Health Boards, since 1991; first Chair, Section of Health Psychology, British Psychological Society; Past President, European Health Psychology Society. Recreation: gardening. Address: (b.) School of Psychology, St. Andrews University, St. Andrews KY16 9JU; T.-01334 62060.

Johnston, Nick. MSP (Conservative), Mid-Scotland and Fife, since 1999-2001; b. 1948, Filey; m.; 3 s.; 2 d. Educ. Robert Pathson Grammar School, Lincoln. Joined Royal Engineers; studied at Royal Military Academy, Sandhurst; left Army to study as an actuary; Group Operations Director, Eastern Western Motor Group. Recreations: cooking; hill-walking; reading; gardening; occasional sailing.

Johnston, Robin Alexander, BSc, MB, BCh, BAO, MD, FRCSEd, FRCSGlas. Consultant Neurosurgeon, since 1985 (of Queen Elizabeth National Spinal Injury Unit, since 1992); Honorary Clinical Senior Lecturer, Glasgow University, since 1990; b. 30.3.49, Belfast; m., Ann. Educ. Belfast Royal Academy; Queens University, Belfast. Various surgical posts, UK, 1974-77; neurosurgical training, Belfast, Dallas, Glasgow, 1977-85. Address: (b.) Institute of Neurological Sciences, Southern General Hospital, Glasgow; T.-0141-201 2021.

Johnston, Thomas Lothian, MA, PhD, DL, FRSA, FRSE, CIMgt, FIPD, DrHC, DEd, LLD, DUniv, DLitt, FEIS. President, Royal Society of Edinburgh, 1993-96; Chairman, Scottish Committee, Royal Society of Arts, 1991-95; b. 9.3.27, Whitburn; m., Joan Fahmy; 2 s.; 3 d. Educ. Hawick High School; Edinburgh University; Stockholm University. Served RNVR (Sub. Lieut.), 1944-47; Lecturer in Political Economy, Edinburgh University, 1953-65; Professor of Economics, Heriot-Watt University, 1966-76; Vice-Chancellor, Heriot-Watt University, 1981-88; industrial relations arbitrator and mediator; Chairman, Manpower Services Committee for Scotland, 1977-80; Member, Scottish Economic Council, 1977-91; Chairman, Enquiry into Staff Representation, London Clearing Banks, 1978-79; Member, Review Committee, New Zealand Universities, 1987; Scottish Chairman, Industry Year, 1986, and Industry Matters, 1987-89; Trustee, National Galleries of Scotland, 1989-95; academic appointments in other countries: University of Illinois, 1957, 1962-63, Queen's University, Canada, 1965, Western Australian Institute of Technology, 1979, Visiting Professor, International Institute for Labour Studies, Geneva, 1973. Publications: Collective Bargaining in Sweden, 1962; Economic Expansion and Structural Change, 1963; The Structure and Growth of the Scottish Economy (Co-Author), 1971; Introduction to Industrial Relations, 1981; translations from Swedish. Recreations: gardening; walking. Address: (h.) 14 Mansionhouse Road, Edinburgh EH9 1TZ; T.-031-667 1439.

Johnston, Very Rev. William Bryce, MA, BD, DD, DLitt. Minister, Colinton Parish Church, 1964-91; Chaplain to The Queen in Scotland, 1981-91, Extra Chaplain, since 1991; b. 16.9.21, Edinburgh; m., Ruth Margaret Cowley; 1 s.; 2 d. Educ. George Watson's College, Edinburgh; Edinburgh University. Chaplain to the Forces, 1945-49; Minister: St. Andrew's Church, Bo'ness, 1949-55, St. George's Church, Greenock, 1955-64; Chaplain, HM Prison, Greenock, 1959-64; Convener, General Assembly Committees: Adult Christian Education, 1970-72, Church and Nation, 1972-76, Inter-Church Relations, 1979-81, Judicial Commission, 1986-91; Moderator of the General Assembly, 1980; Cunningham Lecturer, New College, 1968-71; Visiting Lecturer in Social Ethics, Heriot-Watt University, 1966- 88; Member, Broadcasting Council for Scotland, 1983-87. Publications: translations of Karl Barth and John Calvin; Ethics and Defence (Contributor). Recreations: organ music; bowls. Address: (h.) 15 Elliot Road, Edinburgh EH14 1DU; T.-0131-441 3387.

Johnston, William John, BSc (Hons), DipEd(Tech). Rector, Aberdeen Grammar School, since 1987; b. 17.8.47, Kilmarnock; m., Katie Mary Maclean; 3 d. Educ. Spier's School, Beith; Glasgow University. Marketing Assistant, ICI Silicones, 1969-70; Teacher: Cranhill Secondary, 1971-73, Perth High School, 1973-75; Assistant Principal Teacher, Glenrothes High School, 1975-78; Principal Teacher, Millburn Academy, 1978-81; Assistant Rector, Kingussie High School, 1981-84; Depute Rector, Culloden Academy, 1984-87. Address: (b.) Aberdeen Grammar School, Skene Street, Aberdeen; T.-01224 642299; e-mail: wjohnston@grammar.org.uk

Johnstone, Alex. MSP (Conservative), North East Scotland, since 1999; Chief Whip and Business Manager; m.; 2 c. Dairy and arable farmer. Address: (b.) Scottish Parliament, Edinburgh EH99 1SP; T.-0131-348 5649.

Johnstone, Professor Eve Cordelia, MB, ChB, MD, FRCP, FRCPsych, FMedSci, DPM. Professor of Psychiatry and Head, Department of Psychiatry, University of Edinburgh, since 1989; b. 1.9.44, Glasgow. Educ. Park School, Glasgow; University of Glasgow. Junior posts in Glasgow hospitals; Lecturer in Psychological Medicine, University of Glasgow, 1972-74; Member of Scientific Staff, Medical Research Council, Clinical Research Centre, Northwick Park, 1974-89. Member of Council, Medical Research Council; Chairman, MRC Neurosciences Board. Publications: five books on psychiatric illness; over 200 papers on biological psychiatry. Address: (b.) Royal Edinburgh Hospital, Morningside Park, Edinburgh.

Johnstone, Sir Raymond, CBE, BA, CA. Director, RJ KILN PLC, since 1995; Chairman, Atrium Underwriting PLC (formerly Lomond Underwriting plc), since 1993; Chairman: Historic Buildings Council for Scotland, since 1995, The Nuclear Generation Decommissioning Fund Limited, since 1996, The Nuclear Trust, since 1996; b. 27.10.29, London; m., Susan Sara; 5 step s.; 2 step d. Educ. Eton; Trinity College, Cambridge. Investment Analyst, Robert Fleming & Co. Ltd., London, 1955-60; Partner (CA), Brown, Fleming & Murray (later Whinney Murray & Co.), 1960-68; Director: Scottish Amicable Life Assurance Society, 1971-97 (Chairman, 1983-85); Dominion Insurance Co. Ltd., 1973-95 (Chairman, 1978-95); Scottish Financial Enterprise, 1986-91 (Chairman, 1989-91); Summit Group PLC (Chairman, 1989-98); Murray Income PLC, 1989-99; Murray International PLC, since 1989; Murray Global Markets PLC, 1989-2000; Murray Ventures PLC, 1984-99; Murray Enterprise PLC, 1989-00; Chairman, Murray Johnstone Ltd., 1984-91 (Managing Director, 1968-88); Chairman, Forestry Commission, 1989-

94; Chairman, Murray Split Capital Trust PLC, 1991-98; Chairman, 1982-86, Hon. President, 1986-97, Scottish Opera; Chairman, Patrons of the National Galleries of Scotland, 1995-99. Recreations: fishing; shooting; opera; farming. Address: (h.) Wards, Gartocharn, Dunbartonshire G83 85B.

Johnstone, Professor William, BD, MA (Hons), DLitt. Professor of Hebrew and Semitic Languages, Aberdeen University, 1980-2001, Emeritus Professor, since 2001; Minister, Church of Scotland, since 1963; b. 6.5.36, Glasgow; m., Elizabeth M. Ward; 1 s.; 1 d. Educ. Hamilton Academy; Glasgow University; Marburg University. Lecturer in Hebrew and Semitic Languages, Aberdeen University, 1962-72, Senior Lecturer, 1972-80, Dean, Faculty of Divinity, 1983-87; President, Society for Old Testament Study, 1990. Recreation: alternative work. Address: (h.) 37 Rubislaw Den South, Aberdeen AB15 4BD; T.-Aberdeen 316022.

Jolliffe, Professor Ian, BSc, DPhil. Professor of Statistics, Aberdeen University, since 1992; b. 22.12.45, Isle of Wight; m., Jean Peddar; 1 s.; 1 d. Educ. Sandown Grammar School; Sussex University. Lecturer, then Senior Lecturer, Kent University; visiting positions, Dalhousie University, University of Guelph. Recreations: running; traditional music. Address: (b.) Department of Mathematical Sciences, Aberdeen University, King's College, Aberdeen, AB24 3UE; T.-01224 272611.

Jones, Professor Charles, MA, BLitt, DLitt, FRSA, FRSE. Forbes Professor of English Language, Edinburgh University, since 1990; b. 24.12.39, Glasgow; m., Isla Shennan. Educ. St. Aloysius College, Glasgow; Glasgow University. Lecturer in Linguistics, Hull University, 1964-67; Lecturer, Department of English Language, Edinburgh University, 1977-78; Professor of English Language, Durham University, 1978-90. Convenor, Scots Language Resource Centre Association, 1993-95; former Council Member, Saltire Society (Convenor, Education Committee); Member, Edinburgh University Court, 1993-96. Publications: An Introduction to Middle English; Phonological Structure and the History of English; Grammatical Gender in English; A History of English Phonology; A Treatise on the Provincial Dialect of Scotland (Editor); Historical Linguistics (Editor); A Language Suppressed; The Edinburgh History of the Scots Language (Editor). Recreation: breeding Soay sheep. Address: (h.) Laggan Cottage, Faladam, Midlothian, EH37 5SU; T.-01875 833 652.

Jones, Professor Colin Anthony, BA (Hons), MA. Professor of Estate Management, Heriot-Watt University, since 1998; b. 13.1.49, Wallasey; m., Fiona Jones; 2 d. Educ. Price's School, Fareham, Hants; Wallasey Grammar School; York University; Manchester University. Research student, Manchester University; Lecturer, Applied Economics, Glasgow University, 1975-80; joined Department of Land Economics, Paisley University, 1980-98; Member, UK Board, Shelter, 1978-84, and since 1990. Publications: Health of Scottish Housing (Editor). Address: (b.) Department of Building, Engineering and Surveying, Heriot-Watt University, Riccarton, Edinburgh, EH14 4AS; T.-0131-499 5111.

Jones, David, BA, CertEd. Director of Services to People (Education, Social Services, Housing, Leisure), Clackmannanshire Council, since 2001; b. 18.10.49, South Shields; m., Barbara; 2 d. Educ. Didsbury College; Open University. Mathematics Teacher: Hytton Red House School, Sunderland, 1971-75, West Southwick School, Sunderland, 1975-76, Houghton School, Sunderland, 1976-80, Biddick School, Sunderland, 1980-87; Deputy Head, Bede School, Sunderland, 1987-90; Headteacher, Washington School, Sunderland, 1991-99; Assistant

Director of Education, Sunderland, 2000-01. Recreations: MENSA; bird watching; caravaning; motoring. Address: Lime Tree House, Castle Street, Alloa FK10 1EX; T.-01259 452374.

Jones, Emeritus Professor Douglas Samuel, MBE, MA, DSc, FIMA, CMath, FRSE, CEng, FIEE, FRS. Ivory Professor of Mathematics, University of Dundee, 1965-92, now Emeritus Professor; b. 10.1.22; m., Ivy Stiles; 1 s.; 1 d. Educ. Wolverhampton Grammar School; Corpus Christi College, Oxford. Assistant Lecturer in Mathematics, University of Manchester, 1948-51; New York University: Lecturer, 1951-54, Research Professor, 1955; Senior Lecturer in Mathematics, University of Manchester, 1955-57; Professor of Mathematics, University of Keele, 1957-64. Visiting Professor, Courant Institute, 1962-63. Hon.DSc, Strathclyde, 1975; Keith Prize, RSE, 1974; van der Pol Gold Medal, International Union of Radio Science, 1981; Naylor Prize, London Mathematical Society, 1987. Trustee, Quarterly Journal of Mechanics and Applied Mathematics, 1980-92; Associate Editor: IMA Journal, since 1964, Mathematical Methods in the Applied Sciences, since 1977, Methods and Applications of Analysis, since 1992, Journal of Engineering Mathematics, since 1992; Communications in Applied Analysis, since 1997. Publications: Electrical and Mechanical Oscillations, 1961; Theory of Electromagnetism, 1964; Generalised Functions, 1966; Introductory Analysis, Vol. I, 1969, Vol. II, 1970; Methods in Electromagnetic Wave Propagation, 1979; Elementary Information Theory, 1979; The Theory of Generalised Functions, 1982; Differential Equations and Mathematical Biology, 1983; Acoustic and Electromagnetic Waves, 1986; Assembly Programming and the 8086 Microprocessor, 1988; 80X86 Assembly Programming, 1991; Introduction to Asymptotics, 1997. Recreations: golf; walking; photography. Address: 1 The Nurseries, St. Madoes, Glencarse, Perth PH2 7NX.

Jones, Professor Hamlyn Gordon, MA (Cantab), PhD, FIHort. Professor of Plant Ecology, University of Dundee, since 1997; Honorary Research Professor, Scottish Crop Research Institute, Dundee, since 1998; b. 7.12.47, Kuala Lumpur, Malaysia; m., Amanda Jane Corry; 2 d. Educ. St. Lawrence College, Ramsgate; St. John's College, University of Cambridge; Australian National University, Canberra. Research Fellow, St. John's College, Cambridge, 1973-76; Researcher, Plant Breeding Institute, Cambridge, 1972-76; Lecturer in Ecology, University of Glasgow, 1977-78; Leader of Stress Physiology Group, East Malling Research Station, Kent, 1978-88; Director, Crop Science Research and Head of Station, Horticulture Research International, Wellesbourne, Warwick, 1988-97; Special Professor, University of Nottingham, 1991-97; Honorary Professor, University of Birmingham, 1995-98. Publications: Plants and Microclimate, 1983/1992; joint editor of five other books; on editorial board of six scientific journals. Recreations: squash; tennis; mountains; lounging. Address: (b.) Biological Sciences Institute, School of Life Sciences, University of Dundee, Dundee DD1 4HN; T.-01382 344720.

Jones, Professor Huw, BA, MA. Professor of Geography and Dean, Faculty of Arts and Social Sciences, Dundee University; b. Llanidloes; 2 s. Educ. Newtown Boys Grammar School, Powys; University College of Wales, Aberystwyth. Editor, International Journal of Population Geography. Address: (b.) Department of Geography, Dundee University, Dundee DD1 4HN; T.-01382-344 427; e-mail: h.r.jones@dundee.ac.uk

Jones, Rt. Rev. Idris, BA, DMin. Episcopal Bishop of Glasgow and Galloway, since 1998; b. 1943. Educ. University College St. David, Lampeter; New College, Edinburgh; Edinburgh Theological College. Deacon, 1967; Priest, 1968; Curate, St. Mary's, Stafford, 1967-70; Precentor, St. Paul's Cathedral, Dundee, 1970-73; Priest-in-

Charge, St. Hugh's, Gosforth, Newcastle, 1973-80; Chaplain, St. Nicholas Hospital, 1975-80; Rector, St. Mary's and St. Peter's, Montrose with St. David's, Inverbervie, 1980-89; Anglican Chaplain, Dundee University and Priest-in-Charge, All Souls, Invergowrie, 1989-92; Canon, St. Paul's Cathedral, Dundee, 1984-92; Rector, Holy Trinity, Ayr, 1992-98; Director, Pastoral Studies, TISEC, 1995-99. Address: Diocesan Centre, 5 St. Vincent Place, Glasgow G1 2DH.

Jones, Keith Greig, LLB. Head of Law and Administration (North Division), Aberdeenshire Council, since 1996; b. 10.9.48, Edinburgh; m., Margaret. Educ. Aberdeen Grammar School; Aberdeen University. Various appointments in private legal practice, 1969-75; joined Law and Administration Department, Kincardine and Deeside District Council, 1975: Director of Legal Services and Depute Chief Executive, 1985-96. Trustee: Grampian Transport Museum Trust, Kinneff Old Church Preservation Trust; Member, Scottish Charity Law Review Commission, 2000-01. Address: (b.) St. Leonard's, Sandyhills Road, Banff.

Jones, Professor Peter (Howard), MA, FRSE, FRSA, FSA Scot. Director, Foundation for Advanced Studies in the Humanities, since 1997; Member, Spoliation Advisory Panel, since 2000; Professor of Philosophy, University of Edinburgh, 1984-98, Professor Emeritus, since 1998; Director, Institute for Advanced Studies in the Humanities, 1986-2000; b. 18.12.35, London; m., Elizabeth Jean Roberton; 2 d. Educ. Highgate School; Queens' College, Cambridge. Regional Officer, The British Council, London, 1960-61; Research Scholar, University of Cambridge, 1961-63; Assistant Lecturer in Philosophy, Nottingham University, 1963-64; University of Edinburgh: Lecturer in Philosophy, 1964-77, Reader, 1977-84; Visiting Professor of Philosophy: University of Rochester, New York, 1969-70, Dartmouth College, New Hampshire, 1973, 1983, Carleton College, Minnesota, 1974, Oklahoma University, 1978, Baylor University, 1978, University of Malta, 1993; Distinguished Foreign Scholar, Mid-America State Universities, 1978; Visiting Fellow, Humanities Research Centre, Australian National University, 1984; Calgary Institute for the Humanities, 1992; Lothian Lecturer, 1993; Gifford Lecturer, University of Aberdeen, 1994-95; Loemker Lecturer, Emory University, 1996; Trustee: National Museums of Scotland, 1987-99 (Chairman, Museum of Scotland Client Committee, 1991-99), University of Edinburgh Development Trust, 1990-98, Morrison's Academy, Crieff, 1984-98, Fettes College, Scots at War Trust; Member: Court, University of Edinburgh, 1987-90, Council, Royal Society of Edinburgh, 1992-95, UNESCO forum on Tolerance, Tblisi, 1995, UNESCO dialogue on Europe and Islam, since 1997; Founder Member, The Hume Society, 1974. Publications: Philosophy and the Novel, 1975; Hume's Sentiments, 1982; A Hotbed of Genius, 1986; Philosophy and Science in the Scottish Enlightenment, 1988; The Science of Man in the Scottish Enlightenment, 1989; Adam Smith Reviewed, 1992. Recreations: opera; chamber music; the arts; architecture. Address: (b.) Foundation for Advanced Studies in the Humanities, 6 Greenhill Terrace, Edinburgh EH8 9NN; T.-0131-447 6344.

Jones, Philip Neville, MSc, MMS(Dip), EuroIE, MIMgt. Chief Executive, Dumfries and Galloway Council, since 1998; b. 8.6.51; m., Jacqueline Fiona; 3 s. Educ. Kelsterton College, Deeside. Productivity Services Officer, Unilever, Port Sunlight, 1976-80; Dumfries and Galloway Regional Council: Assistant Regional Management Services Officer, 1980-86, Assistant Director Information Technology, 1986-89, Corporate Business Manager, 1989-96; Dumfries and Galloway Council: Head of Corporate Business, 1995-99, Council Monitoring Officer, 1997-99, Depute Chief Executive, 1995-98. Recreations: golf; gardening; walking.

Address: Council Offices, English Street, Dumfries DG1 2DD; e-mail: chief.executive@dumgal.gov.uk

Jones, Raymond J. Chief Executive, Royal Highland and Agricultural Society of Scotland, since 1998; b. 30.9.47, Birmingham; 2 s.; 1 d. Educ. Lordswood; Harper Adams Agricultural College. Alfa-Laval; Unilever; Managing Director, LI Ireland, 1990-92; Regional Managing Director, Diverseylever, 1992-98. Recreations: walking; sailing. Address: (b.) Royal Highland Centre, Ingliston, Edinburgh EH28 8NF; T.-0131-335 6200.

Jones, Sue, BA (Hons), PGCE, MICFM(Cert). General Secretary, Abbeyfield Society for Scotland, since 1999; b. 3.1.47, Manchester; m., Dr Roger Jones; 2 s. Educ. Orme Girls' School, Newcastle, Staffs; Birmingham University. Translator (own business), 1971-88; Collections Manager, Help the Aged, 1988-91; Appeals Manager, NCH Action for Children, 1991-95; Regional Fundraising Manager, British Diabetic Association, 1995-99. Chair, Institute of Charity Fundraising Managers (Scotland); Board Member, Volunteer Development Scotland. Recreations: walking; garden design; patchwork quilt design. Address: (b.) 15 West Maitland Street, Edinburgh EH12 5EA; T.-0131-225 7801; e-mail: abbeyfieldscotland@quista.net

Jones, Trevor, CPFA, FCCA, ACIS, MIMgt. Head, Scottish Executive Health Department and Chief Executive, NHS in Scotland, since 2000; b. 23.12.50, Penshaw, Co. Durham; m., Hazel Oliver. Entered NHS, 1978; Northern Regional Health Authority; South Manchester Health Authority; Waltham Forest Health Authority; Chief Executive, Forest Healthcare NHS Trust, 1991-95; Chief Executive, Lothian Health Board, 1995-2000. Recreations: golf; squash; Durham CCC; Sunderland AFC. Address: (b.) St. Andrew's House, Regent Road, Edinburgh EH1 3DS; T.-0131- 244 2410.

Jones, Rev. William Gerald, MA, BD, ThM. Minister, Kirkmichael with Straiton St. Cuthbert's, since 1985; Moderator, Presbytery of Ayr, 1997-98; b. 2.11.56, Irvine; m., Janet Blackstock. Educ. Dalry High School; Garnock Academy, Kilbirnie; Glasgow University; St. Andrews University; Princeton Theological Seminary, Princeton, New Jersey. Assistant Minister, Glasgow Cathedral, 1983-85. Freeman Citizen of Glasgow, 1984; Member, Incorporation of Gardeners of Glasgow, 1984; Convener, Administration Committee, Presbytery of Ayr, 1988-91; Member, Presbytery of Ayr ad hoc Committee on Doctrine and Worship, since 1998, and ad hoc Committee on Church Unity, since 1999; Member: General Assembly Panel on Worship, 1987-91, Council, Church Service Society, 1986-98, Committee to Nominate the Moderator of the General Assembly, 1988-92 and since 1998, Committee on Artistic Matters, 2000-01; Societas Liturgica, since 1989; AssChLJ (Assistant Chaplain, Order of St. Lazarus of Jerusalem), 1995; Member: Society for Liturgical Study, since 1995, Society for the Study of Theology, since 2000, Council, Scottish Church Society, since 2000; Honorary Chaplain, York Minster, 2001. Publications: Prayers for the Chapel Royal in Scotland, 1989; Worshipping Together (Contributor), 1991; Common Order (Contributor), 1994; The Times Book of Prayers (Contributor), 1997. Recreations: music; liturgies; reading; writing. Address: The Manse, Kirkmichael, Maybole, Ayrshire KA19 7PJ; T.-01655 750286; e-mail: revgerald@jonesg99.freeserve.co.uk

Jordan, Professor James Redmon, DipEE, DIC, MSc, PhD, FRSA, FIEE, FInstMC, CEng. Professor of Electronic Instrumentation, Department of Electronics and Electrical Engineering, University of Edinburgh, since 1992; b. 5.6.38, Isleworth, Middlesex; m., Dr. Elizabeth Jordan; 2 d. Educ. Twickenham College of Technology; Imperial College; University of Surrey; University of Bradford. Student apprenticeship, EMI Electronics Ltd.; early experience of machine tool control and analogue computers; Lecturer, Senior Lecturer, then Head of Department, Department of Electrical Engineering, University of Edinburgh; EPSRC Information Technology Senior Research Fellow. Director, Edinburgh Research and Innovation Ltd.; Convenor, Edinburgh University Research Committee. Recreations: appreciating the visual arts; studying natural systems; reading poetry; playing classical and jazz piano. Address: (b.) The King's Buildings, Edinburgh EH9 3JL; T.-0131-650 5595.

Joseph, Professor John E., BA, MA, PhD, FRSA. Professor of Applied Linguistics, University of Edinburgh, since 1997; b. 30.10.56, Monroe, Michigan, USA; m., Jeannette; 2 s.; 1 d. Educ. Monroe High School, Michigan; University of Michigan, Ann Arbor. Lecturer in Linguistics, Université Paul Valéry, Montpellier, France, 1980-81; Assistant then Associate Professor of French and Italian, Oklahoma State University, 1981-85; Visiting Associate Professor of French, University of Maine, 1986; Assistant, then Associate Professor of French and English Linguistics, University of Maryland at College Park, 1986-93; University Fellow, National Endowment for the Humanities, 1993; Camargo Foundation Fellow, Cassis, France, 1993; Professor of English Language and Linguistics and Head, Department of English, University of Hong Kong, 1993-96. Publications: Eloquence and Power, 1987; Ideologies of Language (Co-Author), 1990; Limiting the Arbitrary, 2000; Landmarks in Linguistic Thought II (Co-Author), 2001. Recreations: playing piano; reading literature and philosophy; theatre; concerts; swimming. Address: (b.) Department of Theoretical and Applied Linguistics, University of Edinburgh, Edinburgh EH8; T.-0131-650 3497.

Jowitt, Professor Paul William, PhD, DIC, BSc(Eng), ACGI, CEng, FICE, FICE, FRSA. Professor of Civil Engineering Systems, Heriot-Watt University, since 1987; Editor, Civil Engineering Systems, since 1985; b. 3.8.50, Doncaster. Educ. Maltby Grammar School; Imperial College. Lecturer in Civil Engineering, Imperial College 1974-86 (Warden, Falmouth Hall, 1980-86); Director, Tynemarch Systems Engineering Ltd., 1984-91 (Chairman, 1984-86); Head, Civil Engineering Department, Heriot-Watt University, 1989-91, Head, Civil and Offshore Engineering, 1991-99. Director, Scottish Institute of Sustainable Technology, since 1999; Member, East of Scotland Water Authority, since 1999. Recreations: painting; Morgan 3-wheelers; restoring old houses. Address: (h.) 14 Belford Mews, Edinburgh EH4 3BT; T.-0131-225 7583; e-mail: p.w.jowitt@hw.ac.uk

Joyce, Eric. MP, BA, MA, MBA, PGCE. MP (Labour), Falkirk West, since 2000; b. 13.10.60, Perth; m. 1, Christine Louise Guest (m. dis.); m. 2, Rosemary Anne Jones. Soldier, Black Watch, 1978-81; Officer, Adjutant General's Corps, 1987-99; Public Affairs Officer, Commission for Racial Equality, 1999-2000. Executive Member, Fabian Society; Secretary, Tamfourhill Tenants and Residents Association; Secretary, Central Scotland Racial Equality Council; former Scottish judo champion (captain, Scottish University team). Address: (b.) House of Commons, London, SW1A 0AA.

Judge, Professor David, BA, PhD, FRSA. Professor of Politics, University of Strathclyde, since 1994; b. 22.5.50, Sheffield; m., Lorraine; 1 s.; 1 d. Educ. Westfield School; Exeter University; Sheffield University. Lecturer, Paisley College, 1974-88; University of Strathclyde: Lecturer, 1988-90, Senior Lecturer, 1990-91, Reader, 1991-94; Fulbright Fellow and Visiting Professor, University of Houston, USA, 1993-94. Publications: Backbench Specialisation in the House of Commons, 1981; The Politics of Parliamentary Reform (Editor), 1983; The Politics of Industrial Closure (Joint Editor), 1987; Parliament and Industry, 1990; A Green Dimension for the European Community (Editor), 1993; The Parliamentary State, 1993; Theories of Urban Politics (Co-Editor), 1995; Representation: Theory and Practice in Britain, 1999. Recreation: breathing. Address: (b.) Department of Government, University of Strathclyde, Glasgow G1 1XQ; T.-0141-548 2365; e-mail: d.judge@strath.ac.uk

Judge, Professor Ken, MA, PhD (Cantab). Professor of Health Promotion Policy, Glasgow University, since 2000; b. 1.1.48, Lincoln; 1 s.; 1 d. Educ. Sidney Sussex College, Cambridge. Lecturer in Social Policy, Bristol University, 1974-79; Deputy Direcfor, PSSRU, Kent University, 1980-85; Director, King's Fund Policy Institute, 1986-97; Director, PSSRU, Kent University, 1997-2000. Publications include: Rationing Social Services; Charging for Social Care; Community Care: The First Steps; Tackling Inequalities in Health; Caring for Older People. Recreations: golf; tennis; cycling; hillwalking. Address: (h.) 38 Cleveden Drive, Glasgow G12 0RY; T.-0141-330 5008.

Jung, Roland Tadeusz, BA, MA, MB, BChir, MD, MRCS, LRCP, MRCP, FRCPEdin, FRCPLond. Consultant Physician (Specialist in Endocrinology and Diabetes), since 1982; Chief Scientist, Scottish Executive Health Department, since 2001; Honorary Professor, Dundee University; Chairman, Scottish Hospital Endowments Research Trust, since 2000; b. 8.2.48, Glasgow; m., Felicity King; 1 d. Educ. St. Anselm's College, Wirral; Pembroke College, Cambridge; St. Thomas Hospital and Medical School, London. MRC Clinical Scientific Officer, Dunn Nutrition Unit, Cambridge, and Honorary Senior Registrar, Addenbrooke's Hospital, Cambridge, 1977-79; Senior Registrar in Endocrinology and Diabetes, Royal Postgraduate Medical School, Hammersmith Hospital, London, 1980-82; Clinical Director of General Medicine, Dundee Teaching Hospitals Trust, 1991-94; Director of R and D, Tayside NHS Consortium, 1997-2001. Publication: Endocrine Problems in Oncology (Co-Editor), 1984; Colour Atlas of Obesity, 1990. Recreation: gardening. Address: (b.) Diabetes Centre, Ninewells Hospital and Medical School, Dundee; T.-Dundee 660111.

Junor, Gordon James, LLB (Hons), MCIArb. Advocate, since 1993; b. 18.1.56, Stannington, Northumberland. Educ. King Edward VI Grammar School, Morpeth; Edinburgh University; Northumberland University. Solicitor, local government, 1982-92. Secretary, Abbeyfield (Selkirk) Society Ltd.; Consulting Editor, Reparation Bulletin. Publication: Scottish Older Client Law Service (Housing). Recreation: hillwalking. Address: Freelands, 9 Taits Hill, Selkirk TD7 4LZ; T.-01750 22121.

Justice, David Brian, MBE, BSc. Chief Executive Officer, Quality Scotland Foundation, since 1990; b. 1.7.35, Tain; m., Marion; 2 s. Educ. Boroughmuir Senior Secondary School; Edinburgh University. General Manager, Rank Hovis McDougal, 1959; IBM Scotland, 1962-71; General Manager, IBM Banking Systems, London, 1971-73; Manager IBM Scottish Branch, 1973-76; Industry Systems, IBM Europe Headquarters, 1976-80; Regional Operations Manager, IBM London, 1980-85; Public Sector Manager, IBM Scotland, 1985-90. Recreations: golf; wine. Address: 11 AbercrombyPlace, Edinburgh EH3 6LB; T.-0131-556 2333.

K

Kamm, Antony, MA. Author; b. 2.3.31, London; m., Eileen Dunlop (qv). Educ. Charterhouse; Worcester College, Oxford. Editorial Director, Brockhampton Press, 1960-72; Senior Education Officer, Commonwealth Secretariat, 1972-74; Managing Editor (Children's Books), Oxford University Press, 1977-79; Consultant to UNESCO and other international organisations, 1963-76; part-time Lecturer in Publishing Studies, Stirling University, 1988-95; Chairman, Children's Book Group, The Publishers Association, 1963-67, and of Children's Book Circle, 1963-64; played cricket for Middlesex, 1952. Publications include: Collins Biographical Dictionary of English Literature, 1993; The Romans: an Introduction, 1995; Wallace, Bruce, and the War of Independence, 1996; Scotland in Roman Times, 1998; The Israelites: an Introduction, 1999; several anthologies. Address: (h.) 46 Tarmangie Drive, Dollar FK14 7BP; T.-01259 742007.

Kane, Patrick Mark, MA (Hons). Writer and Broadcaster; b. 10.3.64, Glasgow; m., Joan McAlpine; 1 d. Educ. St. Ambrose RC Secondary, Coatbridge; Glasgow University. Worked in London as a freelance writer; returned to Scotland to start professional music career with brother Gregory; achieved Top 10 and Top 20 singles and albums successes with Hue and Cry, 1987-89; TV arts presenter; former Rector, Glasgow University. Recreations: being with family; listening to music; reading abstruse social theory.

Kay, Professor Christian Janet, MA, AM, DipGenLing. Professor of English Language, Glasgow University, since 1996; b. 4.4.40, Edinburgh. Educ. Mary Erskine School; Edinburgh University; Mount Holyoke College. Lecturer, Glasgow University, 1979-89; Senior Lecturer, Glasgow University, 1989-96. Publications: A Thesaurus of Old English (with Jane Roberts), 1995. Recreations: music. Address: (b.) Glasgow University, Glasgow, G12 8QQ.

Kay, Stefan George, OBE, BSc, CEng, FIMechE, CIMgmt, FRSA. Group Managing Director, Inveresk PLC, 1989-2000; Non-Executive Director: Dunedin Enterprise Investment Trust PLC, since 1995, Bio-Regional Minimills Ltd., since 2001, Georgia Pacific Britain Corp., since 1996; b. 25.7.44, Peebles; m., Helen Eugenia; 2 d. Educ. Holy Cross Academy; Heriot-Watt University. Graduate Trainee, Production Superintendent, Chief Chemist, Thames Board Ltd., 1967-73; Production Manager, Dexter Ltd., Berwickshire, 1973-78; Mill MD, St. Regis Paper Co. Ltd., Berkshire and Devon, 1979-88. Past President, Paper Federation of Great Britain; awarded paper industry Gold Medal, 1996; Chairman, Environment Committee, Confederation of European Paper Industries, 1998-2000, Chairman, Eco-Label Working Party, Member, Environmental Policy Task Force; Member, Court, Heriot-Watt University; Board Member, Edinburgh Business School; Liveryman and Member of Trade and Industry Forum, Worshipful Company of Stationers and Newspaper Makers. Recreations: steam railways; classical music; science fiction and historical literature. Address: (h.) 7 King's Cramond, Edinburgh EH4 6RL; T.-0131-336 5506; e-mail: sgk@stefankay.abelgratis.co.uk

Kay, William (Billy), MA. Freelance Broadcaster/Writer/ Producer; Director, Odyssey Productions; b. 24.9.51, Galston, Ayrshire; m., Maria João de Almeida da Cruz Dinis; 1 s.; 2 d. Educ. Galston High School; Kilmarnock Academy; Edinburgh University. Producer, Odyssey series, Radio Scotland; produced about 40 documentaries on diverse aspects of working-class oral history; Writer/Presenter, TV documentaries, including Miners, BBC Scotland; Presenter, Kay's Originals, Scottish TV.

Commandeur d'Honneur, Commanderie du Bontemps de Medoc et des Graves; won Australasian Academy of Broadcast Arts and Sciences Pater award, 1987, 1988; Medallist, International Radio Festival of New York, 1990-92; Sloan Prize for writing in Scots, 1992; Wine Guild of UK 1994 Houghton Award, for Fresche Fragrant Clairettis; Winner: Heritage Society Award, 1995, Wines of France Award, 1996. Publications: Odyssey: Voices from Scotland's Recent Past (Editor); Odyssey: The Second Collection (Editor); Knee Deep in Claret: A Celebration of Wine and Scotland (Co-author); Made in Scotland (poetry); Jute (play for radio); Scots — The Mither Tongue; They Fairly Mak Ye Work (for Dundee Repertory Theatre); Lucky's Strike (play for radio); The Dundee Book. Recreations: the weans; languages; films; Dundee United. Address: (h.) 72 Tay Street, Newport on Tay, Fife DD6 8AP; e-mail: billykay@sol.co.uk

Kayne, Steven Barry, PhD, MBA, LLM, BSc, FRPharmS, FCPP, DAgVetPharm, FFHom(Hon), MPS(NZ), FNZCP. Consultant Homoeopathic and Veterinary Pharmacist; medical journalist; b. 8.6.44, Cheltenham Spa; m., Sorelle; 2 s. Educ. Westcliff High School; Aston University; Strathclyde University; Glasgow University; University of Wales. Lecturer; Visiting Lecturer, University of Strathclyde School of Pharmacy; Honorary Consultant Pharmacist, Glasgow Homeopathic Hospital; Pharmacy Dean to UK Faculty of Homoeopathy; Member: Scottish Executive, Royal Pharmaceutical Society of Great Britain; Academic Board, UK Faculty of Homoeopathy; Council, British Homoeopathic Association; Government Advisory Board on Homoeopathic Registration; UK Government Expert Advisory Panels, Committee on Safety of Medicines and Medicines Control Agency; Governor, College of Pharmacy Practice; Chairman, College of Pharmacy Practice in Scotland. Publication: Homoeopathic Pharmacy, 1997; People are Pets (Co-author), 1998; Complementary Therapies for Pharmacists, 2001; 300 papers and articles. Recreations: walking in Spey Valley; watching rugby; photography. Address: (b.) 20 Main Street, Busby, Glasgow G76 8DU; T.-07788 150345; e-mail: SKayne9665@aol.com

Kean, Jon. News Editor, Scottish Television, since 1986; b. 5.12.53, Lennoxtown by Glasgow; m., Janette; 1 d. Educ. Clifton High School, Coatbridge; Napier College. Copy Boy, Glasgow Herald/Evening Times; Reporter, Wishaw Press; Chief Reporter/Sports Editor, Airdrie and Coatbridge Advertiser; news/sport freelance, various daily/Sunday papers; TV Sub-editor, BBC Scotland, television and radio; Chief News Assistant, BBC Scotland. Best Regional News Programme, Royal Television Society, 2000; Chairman, ITV News Editor's Group. Recreations: gundog breeding/training; hunting and shooting; Kennel Club judge (field trials and shows). Address: (b.) Scottish Television, 200 Renfield Street, Glasgow G2 3PR; T.-0141 300 3360/3165; e-mail: jon.keen@smg.plc.uk

Keane, Sheriff Francis Joseph, PhL, LLB. Sheriff of Tayside, Central and Fife, at Kirkcaldy, since 1998; b. 5.1.36, Broxburn; m., Lucia Corio Morrison; 2 s.; 1 d. Educ. Blairs College, Aberdeen; Gregorian University, Rome; Edinburgh University. Partner, McCluskey, Keane & Co., 1959; Procurator Fiscal Depute, Perth, 1961, Edinburgh, 1963; Senior PF Depute, Edinburgh, 1971; Senior Legal Assistant, Crown Office, Edinburgh, 1972; Procurator Fiscal, Airdrie, 1976; Regional Procurator Fiscal, South Strathclyde, Dumfries and Galloway, 1980; Sheriff of Glasgow and Strathkelvin, 1984-93; Sheriff of Lothians and Borders, 1993-98; President, Procurators Fiscal Society, 1982-84. Recreations: music; tennis; walking; painting. Address: (b.) Sheriff Court House, Whytescauseway, Kirkcaldy KY1 1XQ; T.-01592 260171.

Kearns, Professor Ade J., BA (Hons). Professor of Urban Studies, University of Glasgow, since 2000 (Head, Department of Urban Studies, since 1996); Co-Director, ESRC Centre for Neighbourhood Research, since 2001; b. 11.10.59, Luton; m., Susan Joan; 1 s.; 1 d. Educ. Cardinal Newman RC Secondary, Luton; Sidney Sussex College, Cambridge University. Research, Shelter; Senior Housing Investment Analyst, Housing Corporation; University of Glasgow: Research Fellow, Lecturer, Senior Lecturer; Deputy Director, ESRC Centre for Housing Research and Urban Studies; Acting Director, ESRC Cities Research Programme. Member, Scottish Homes/Communities Scotland Research Advisory Panel; Member, Scottish Executive Transport and Travel Statistics Advisory Committee; Editor, two special issues, Urban Studies journal. Recreations: reading contemporary fiction; listening to music, especially pop and jazz; collecting antique furniture, metalwork and art of the Arts and Crafts movement; country walking; visiting landmark modern buildings. Address: Department of Urban Studies, 25-29 Bute Gardens, University of Glasgow, Glasgow G12 8RS; T.-0141-330 5049; e-mail: a.j.kearns@socsci.gla.ac.uk

Kearns, Mary Elizabeth, LLB(Hons), DipLP, DipTA. Consultant, Brodies W.S., Solicitors, 1997-2000 (Partner, 1995-97); Solicitor Advocate, since 1995; b. 25.4.61, London; m., Dr. Patrick Kearns; 3 s.; 2 d. Educ. St. Georges School, Harpenden; University of Edinburgh. Trainee Solicitor, W. & J. Burness W.S., Edinburgh, 1986-88; Brodies W.S., Edinburgh: Assistant Solicitor, 1988-93, Associate, 1993-95. Nominated by Secretary of State for Scotland to General Teaching Council for Scotland, 1995-99; Chairman, Scottish Council on Human Bioethics. Recreations: hill-walking; violin. Address: (b.) 2 Royal Exchange Square, Glasgow G1 3AB; T.-0131-319 2030; e-mail: marykearns@aol.com

Keating, Professor Michael James, MA, PhD. Professor of Scottish Politics, Aberdeen University, since 1999; Professor of Regional Studies, European University Institute, since 2000; b. 2.2.50, Hartlepool; m., Patricia Ann; 1 s. Educ. St Aidan's Grammar School, Sunderland; Oxford University; Glasgow College of Technology. Part-time Lecturer, Glasgow College of Technology, 1972-75; Senior Research Officer, Essex University, 1975-76; Lecturer, North Staffs Polytechnic, 1976-79; Lecturer/Senior Lecturer, Strathclyde University, 1979-88; Professor of Political Science, University of Western Ontario, 1988-99. Recreations: sailing; hill-walking; traditional music; reading. Address: (h.) Todlachie Cottage, Monymusk, Aberdeenshire AB51 7SS.

Kee, Professor A. Alistair, MA, BD, STM, PhD, DLitt. Professor of Religious Studies, Edinburgh University; b. 17.4.37, Alexandria; m., Anne Paterson; 1 s.; 1 d. Educ. Clydebank High School; Glasgow University; Union Theological Seminary, New York. Lecturer: University College of Rhodesia, 1964-67, Hull University, 1967-76; Glasgow University: Senior Lecturer, then Reader (Head, Department of Religious Studies, 1976-88); Visiting Professor: Augusta College, Georgia, 1982-83, Dartmouth College, New Hampshire, 1990,1995; delivered Jaspers Lectures, Ripon Hall, Oxford, 1975; Ferguson Lectures, Manchester University, 1986. Publications: The Way of Transcendence; A Reader in Political Theology; Constantine Versus Christ; Being and Truth; Domination or Liberation; The Roots of Christian Freedom; Marx and the Failure of Liberation Theology; From Bad Faith to Good News; Nietzsche against the Crucified. Address: (b.) Department of Theology and Religious Studies, Edinburgh University, New College, Mound Place, Edinburgh EH1 2LX; T.-0131-650 8953; e-mail: Alistair.Kee@ed.ac.uk

Keeble, Professor Neil Howard, BA, DPhil, DLitt, FRSE, FRHistS, FEA, FRSA. Professor of English, Stirling University, since 1995; Deputy Principal, since 2001; Head, Department of English Studies, 1997-2000; b. 7.8.44, London; m., Jenny Bowers; 2 s.; 1 d. Educ. Bancroft's School, Woodford Green; St. David's College, Lampeter; Pembroke College, Oxford. Foreign Lektor, Department of English, University of Aarhus, Denmark, 1969-72; Lecturer in English, Aarhus, 1972-74; Lecturer in English, Stirling University, 1974-88; Reader in English, Stirling University, 1988-95. Honorary Fellow, University of Wales, Lampeter, 2000. Publications: Richard Baxter: Puritan Man of Letters; The Literary Culture of Nonconformity in later seventeenth-century England; The Autobiography of Richard Baxter (Editor); The Pilgrim's Progress (Editor); John Bunyan: Conventicle and Parnassus (Editor); A Handbook of English and Celtic Studies in the United Kingdom and the Republic of Ireland (Editor); The Cultural Identity of Seventeenth-Century Woman (Editor); Lucy Hutchinson, Memoirs of the Life of Colonel Hutchinson (Editor); Cambridge Companion to Writing of the English Revolution (Editor); John Bunyan: Reading Dissenting Writing (Editor); Calendar of the Correspondence of Richard Baxter (Co-Compiler). Recreations: books and book-collecting; films; the Midi; gardening. Address: Duncraggan House, Airthrey Road, Stirling FK9 5JS; T.-01786 473758; e-mail: n.h.keeble@stir.ac.uk

Keegan, James Douglas, LLB, MPhil, DFM, SSC, FCIARB, FRSA, NP. Solicitor Advocate; b. Glasgow; m., Karen Keegan; 3 d. Educ. Our Lady's High School, Motherwell; Strathclyde University; Glasgow University. Solicitor, 1975; Solicitor in Supreme Court, 1976; Fellowship in Arbitration, 1994; Member, Council, Law Society of Scotland, since 1993; Member, Scottish Criminal Rules Council; Convener, Human Rights Committee, Law Society of Scotland. Recreations: football; reading; music. Address: (b.) Lomond House, Livingston, West Lothian; T.-01506 497500.

Keel, Aileen, MB, ChB, FRCP(G), FRCPath. Deputy Chief Medical Officer, Scottish Executive Health Department, since 1999; Honorary Consultant Haematologist, Edinburgh Royal Infirmary, since 1995; b. 23.8.52, Glasgow; m., Paul Dwyer; 1 s. Educ. Notre Dame High School; Glasgow University. Postgraduate training in general medicine and haematology, 1976-87; practised haematology at consultant level in both NHS and private sector in London, 1987-92, including period as Director of Pathology, Cromwell Hospital; Senior Medical Officer, Scottish Office Department of Health, 1992-98; Principal Medical Officer, 1999. Member of a number of medical advisory committees in Scotland and UK; various medical papers published. Recreations: arts in general; music in particular, especially opera; keeping fit; current affairs. Address: (b.) St. Andrew's House, Edinburgh EH1 3DG.

Keenan, Thomas Gibson. Director, Social Work and Housing Services, Inverclyde Council, since 1998; b. 18.11.54; m., Carol Keenan. Educ. Holy Cross High School; Strathclyde University; Bell College of Technology. Clerical Officer, Strathclyde Regional Council, 1975; Lanarkshire Health Board, 1978-81; Motherwell District Council, 1981-88; Kyle and Carrick District Council: Depute Director of Housing, 1988, Head of Housing, 1991; Director of Housing and Customer Services, Inverclyde Council, 1996. Chair, Association of Chief Housing Officers. Recreations: football; golf; reading current affairs. Address: (b.) Social Work and Housing Services, 195 Dalrymple Street, Greenock PA15 1LD; e-mail: Tom.Keenan@inverclyde.gov.uk

Keenan, Tom, MCC, CQSW, CSWM. HM Commissioner (part-time), Mental Welfare Commission, since 1998; social worker (freelance), since 1984; b. 13.4.52, Hamilton; partner, Margaret Macqueen; 2 d. Educ. St. Martin's Secondary School; Jordanhill College; Glasgow University. Social Worker: SRC Glasgow South West District, 1984, SRC Glasgow North East District, 1984-88; Senior Social Worker, SRC Glasgow North East District, 1988-89; Assistant District Officer, SRC Motherwell/Clydesdale, 1989-90; Senior Social Worker, SRC Glasgow North East District, 1990; District Co-ordinator/ADO (Health), SRC Glasgow South West District, 1990-91; Senior Social Worker, SRC Glasgow South East District, 1991; District Co-ordinator (Health Services), SRC Motherwell/ Clydesdale District, 1991-96; Health Social Work Manager, North Lanarkshire Council, 1996-2001. Convenor, National Mental Health Officer Steering Group; Member, British Association of Social Workers Health and Community Care Standing Committee. Recreations: playing fiddle and guitar; writing plays; hillwalking. Address (h./b.): 9 Lawrence Street, Partick, Glasgow G11 5HH; T.-0141-337 2454; e-mail: KnnTom@aol.com.uk

Keighley, Brian Douglas, MB, ChB, FRCGP. General Practitioner Principal, Balfron, since 1975; Chairman, Scottish General Medical Services Committee (BMA), 1995-98; Chairman, Joint Committee on Postgraduate Training for General Practice, 1997-2000; b. 21.5.48, Glasgow; m., Ruth Patricia Maguire; 2 s. Educ. Glasgow Academy; Glasgow University. House Officer, Law Hospital, Stobhill Hospital, 1972-73; SHO, Robroyston Hospital, 1973; SHO, Falkirk Royal Infirmary, 1974; Trainee GP, Balfron, 1974. Member: GMSC (UK) since 1992, General Medical Council, since 1994, BMA Scottish Council, BMA Council, Clinical Standards Board for Scotland, since 1999; Vice Chairman, Scottish Council for Postgraduate Medical and Dental Education (Chairman, Audit Committee). Publication: Guide to Postgraduate Medical Education, 1996. Recreations: reading; politics; angling; jogging; squash. Address: (h.) Hector Cottage, Banker's Brae, Balfron G63 0PY; T.-01360 440520; e-mail: Bkeighley@aol.com

Keiller, Mike, CA. Chief Executive, Morrison Bowmore Distillers, since 2000; b. 14.8.54, Perth; m., Helen; 1 s.; 1 d. Educ. Perth Academy; Dundee University. Guinness/UD, 1987-95; Director of Financial Planning and Control, British Telecom, 1998-2000. Recreations: hockey; golf; gardening. Address: (b.) Springburn Bond, Carlisle Street, Glasgow G21 1EQ; T.-0141-588 9011.

Keir, Professor Hamish Macdonald, BSc, PhD, DSc, CBiol, FIBiol, CChem, FRSC, FRSE. Professor of Biochemistry, Aberdeen University, 1968-96 (Vice-Principal, 1982-84); b. 5.9.31, Moffat; m., 1, Eleanor Campbell; 1 s.; 2 d.; 2, Linda Gerrie; 2 d. Educ. Ayr Academy; Glasgow University; Yale University. Hon. Secretary, The Biochemical Society, 1970-77, Chairman, 1986-89; Member, Cell Board, Medical Research Council, 1970-74; Scottish Home and Health Department, BRC, 1974-78; Ethical and Research Committees, Grampian Health Board; Science and Engineering Research Council (Biology), 1980-84; University Grants Committee (Biology), 1984-90; Royal Society — British National Committee for Biochemistry, 1986-90; Board of Governors: North of Scotland College of Agriculture, 1976-91, Longridge Towers School, since 1988; Tenovus — Scotland, Grampian Region, 1980-86; Committees of the International Union of Biochemistry, 1974-82; Chairman: Natural Environment Research Council, Institute of Marine Biochemistry, 1969-84, Universities of Scotland Purchasing Consortium, 1988-96, Board of Governors, Rowett Research Institute, 1989-93; Vice-Chairman, Governors, Macaulay Land Use Research Institute, 1987-98; President, European Union of Societies for Experimental Biology, 1989-96; European Science Foundation, 1989-99;

President, Council, Federation of European Biochemical Societies, 1980-83; Member, Executive, Ross, Skye and Inverness West Conservative and Unionist Association, since 1996. Recreations: piano; politics; travel. Address: (h.) Dundalachie, Fortrose, The Black Isle, Ross and Cromarty IV10 8TB; T.-01381 621239; e-mail: harrkeir@btinternet.com

Kellas, Professor James Grant, MA, PhD, FRHistS. Professor of Politics, Glasgow University, 1984-2001; b. 16.5.36, Aberdeen; m., Norma Rennie Craig; 2 s.; 1 d. Educ. Aberdeen Grammar School; Aberdeen University; London University. Tutorial Fellow in History, Bedford College, London University, 1961-62; Assistant in History, Aberdeen University, 1962-64; Glasgow University: Lecturer in Politics, 1964-73; Senior Lecturer, 1973-77, Reader, 1977-84. Member, Study of Parliament Group. Publications: Modern Scotland, 1968, 1980; The Scottish Political System, 1973, 1975, 1984, 1989; The Politics of Nationalism and Ethnicity, 1991, 1998. Recreations: mountaineering; music. Address: (h.) 178 Southbrae Drive, Glasgow G13 1TX; T.-0141-959 5566.

Kelly, Barbara Mary, CBE, DL, LLD, DipEd. Member, Broadcasting Council for Scotland; Member, Scottish Advisory Board, BP plc; Chairman, Architects' Registration Board; Director, Scottish Post Office Board; Convener, Millennium Forest for Scotland Trust; Trustee, Scottish Community Foundation; Partner in farming enterprise; b. 27.2.40, Dalbeattie; m., Kenneth A. Kelly; 1 s.; 2 d. Educ. Dalbeattie High School; Kirkcudbright Academy; Moray House College. Past Chairman, Scottish Consumer Council; former Member: Scottish Economic Council, National Consumer Council, Scottish Enterprise Board, Scottish Tourist Board, Priorities Board, MAFF, Board, Scottish Natural Heritage (and former Chair, West Areas Board); former Vice-Chairman, SWRI; Duke of Edinburgh's Award: former Chairman, Scottish Advisory Committee and former Member, UK Advisory Panel; former EOC Commissioner for Scotland; Past Chairman, Dumfries and Galloway Area Manpower Board, Manpower Services Commission; former Director, Clydesdale Bank plc; Past President, Rural Forum. Recreations: painting; music. Address: (h.) Barncleugh, Irongray, Dumfries DG2 9SE; T.-01387 730210.

Kelly, Daniel, LLB (Hons). Advocate, since 1991; b. 22.1.58, Dunfermline; m., Christine Marie MacLeod; 3 s.; 1 d. Educ. Edinburgh University; College of Europe, Bruges. Apprenticeship, Dundas and Wilson CS, 1979-81; Solicitor, Brodies WS, and Tutor in European Institutions, Edinburgh University, 1982-83; Solicitor, Community Law Office, Brussels, 1983-84; Procurator Fiscal Depute, 1984-90; Temporary Sheriff, 1998-99. Editor, Scots Law Times, since 1992; Editor, Sheriff Court Reports, since 1992. Recreations: swimming; cycling; golf. Address: (b.) Advocates Library, Parliament House, Edinburgh EH1 1RF.

Kelly, Professor John Shearer, BSc, MB ChB, PhD, MA, FRSE, FRCPE; FMedSci. Professor of Pharmacology, University of Edinburgh, since 1985; Director, Fujisawa Institute of Neuroscience, since 1992; b. 3.3.37, Edinburgh; m., E. Anne Wilkin; 1 s.; 1 d. Educ. George Heriot's School, Edinburgh; University of Edinburgh. House Physician, Western General Hospital, Edinburgh, 1962; House Surgeon, Royal Hospital for Sick Children, Edinburgh, 1963; University of Edinburgh, Department of Pharmacology: Assistant Lecturer, 1963-65, Lecturer, 1965-68; McGill University, Canada: Wellcome Post-doctoral Fellow, Department of Research in Anaesthesia, 1967-68, Canadian Medical Research Council Scholar and Assistant Professor, Departments of Research in Anaesthesia and Physiology, 1968-71; IBRO Research Fellow, University of Geneva, 1970; MRC Scientific Staff, Department of Pharmacology, Cambridge, 1971-79; Fellow of King's

College, Cambridge and Lecturer in Pharmacology and Neurobiology, 1976-79; Professor and Chairman, Pharmacology, St. George's Hospital Medical School, London, 1979-85. Publications: 121 papers on neuroscience; 59 book chapters; 207 abstracts. Recreations: Japan; classical music; Scottish restaurants; sailing; Scottish outdoors. Address: (b.) Department of Neuroscience, 1 George Square, Edinburgh EH8 9JZ; T.-0131-650 3519.

Kelly, Michael, CBE (1983), OStJ, JP, BSc(Econ), PhD, LLD, DL, FCIM. Public Relations Consultant, since 1984; Honorary Vice-President, Children 1st, since 1996 (Chairman, Royal Scottish Society for the Prevention of Cruelty to Children, 1987-96); Columnist: Scotsman, Evening Times; Broadcaster, Radio Clyde; Member, Economic and Social Research Council's Advisory Committee, since 2000; b. 1.11.40, Glasgow; m., Zita Harkins; 1 s.; 2 d. Educ. St. Joseph's College, Dumfries. Assistant Lecturer in Economics, Aberdeen University, 1965-67; Lecturer in Economics, Strathclyde University, 1967-80; Lord Provost of Glasgow, 1980-84; Rector, Glasgow University, 1984-87; Member, National Arts Collection Fund, 1990-96; Secretary, Scottish Industry Forum, 1995-2000; British Tourist Authority Medal for services to tourism, 1984; Robert Burns Award from University of Old Dominion, Virginia, for services to Scottish culture, 1984; Scot of the Year, 1983; Radio Scotland News Quiz Champion, 1986, 1987; Radio Scotland Christmas Quiz Champion, 1987; Honorary Mayor of Tombstone, Arizona; Kentucky Colonel, 1983. Publications: Paradise Lost: the struggle for Celtic's soul, 1994; London Lines: the capital by underground, 1996. Recreations: philately; golf; skiing. Address: (b.) 50 Aytoun Road, Pollokshields, Glasgow G41 5HE.

Kelly, Tom. Chief Executive, Association of Scottish Colleges, since 1996; b. 4.5.49, Loughborough. Educ. Hinckley Grammar School; Clare College, Cambridge. Home Civil Service, 1970-96; Head, Higher Education Division, Scottish Office, 1992-96. Address: (b.) Argyll Court, Castle Business Park, Stirling FK9 4TY; T.-01786 892100; e-mail: tom.kelly@ascol.org.uk

Kelman, James. Novelist; b. 1946, Glasgow. Works include: The Busconductor Hines; A Chancer; Greyhound for Breakfast; A Disaffection; How Late It Was How Late (Booker Prize, 1994).

Kelnar, Christopher J.H., MA, MD, FRCP, FRCPCH, DCH. Consultant Paediatric Endocrinologist, Royal Hospital for Sick Children, Edinburgh, since 1983; Reader, Department of Child Life and Health, Edinburgh University, since 1983; b. 22.12.47, London; m., Alison; 1 s.; 2 d. Educ. Highgate School, London; Trinity College, Cambridge; St. Bartholomew's Hospital, London. Research Fellow, Paediatric Endocrinology, Middlesex Hospital, London, 1979-81; Senior Registrar, Hospital for Sick Children, Great Ormond Street, London, and Tutor, Institute of Child Health, London, 1981-83. Publications: The Sick Newborn Baby, 1981 (3rd edition, 1995); Childhood and Adolescent Diabetes, 1995; Growth Disorders, 1998; chapters and papers on paediatric endocrinology. Recreations: music; gardening. Address: (b.) Royal Hospital for Sick Children, Sciennes Road, Edinburgh EH9 1LF; T.-0131-536 0000.

Kemp, Professor Peter Anthony, BSc(Hons), MPhil, DPhil. Professor of Housing and Social Policy, University of Glasgow, since 1996; b. 25.12.55, Romford; 2 d. Educ. University of Southampton; University of Glasgow; University of Sussex. Researcher, SHAC (London Housing Aid Centre), 1983-85; Research Fellow, ESRC Centre for Housing Research, University of Glasgow, 1985-87; Lecturer in Housing Studies, University of Salford, 1987-90; Joseph Rowntree Professor of Housing Policy and Director, Centre for Housing Policy, University of York,

1990-95. Publications include: The Private Provision of Rented Housing, 1988; Tax Incentives and the Revival of Private Renting, 1991; Housing and Social Policy, 1990; Single Homeless People, 1993; Managing Social Housing, 1993; Housing Benefit: an appraisal, 1992; A Comparative Study of Housing Allowances, 1997. Recreation: cycling. Address: (b.) Department of Urban Studies, University of Glasgow, 25 Bute Gardens, Glasgow G12 8RS; T.-0141-330 3665.

Kempton, Rodney Alistair, MA, BPhil, CStat, FRSE. Director, Biomathematics and Statistics Scotland (formerly Scottish Agricultural Statistics Service), since 1986; b. 2.7.46, London; m., Annelise; 2 s.; 1 d. Educ. Chislehurst and Sidcup Grammar School; Wadham College, Oxford. Rothamsted Experimental Station, Harpenden, 1970-76; Head, Statistics Department, Plant Breeding Institute, Cambridge, 1976-86. President, British Region, International Biometric Society, 1994-96. Recreations: hill-walking; cycling. Address: (b.) BioSS, The King's Buildings, Edinburgh EH9 3JZ; T.-0131-650 4902; e-mail: rob@bioss.ac.uk

Kendell, Robert Evan, CBE, MD, FRCP, FRCPsych. President, Royal College of Psychiatrists, 1996-99; Chief Medical Officer, Scottish Office Home and Health Department, 1991-96; b. 28.3.35, Rotherham; m., Ann Whitfield; 2 s.; 2 d. Educ. Mill Hill School; Cambridge University; King's College Hospital Medical School. Visiting Professor, University of Vermont College of Medicine, 1969-70; Reader in Psychiatry, Institute of Psychiatry, London University, 1970-74; Professor of Psychiatry, Edinburgh University, 1974-91, and Dean, Faculty of Medicine, 1986-90. Gaskell Medal, Royal College of Psychiatrists, 1967; Paul Hoch Medal, American Psychopathological Association, 1988; Marcé Society Medal, 1994; Fellow, Royal Society of Edinburgh, 1993; Fellow, Academy of Medical Sciences, 1998; Honorary Fellow: Royal College of Surgeons of Edinburgh, since 1995, Royal College of Physicians and Surgeons of Glasgow, since 1995. Publications: The Classification of Depressive Illnesses, 1968; The Role of Diagnosis in Psychiatry, 1975; Companion to Psychiatric Studies (Editor), 1983, 1988, 1993. Recreations: hill climbing; eating. Address: (h.) 3 West Castle Road, Edinburgh EH10 5AT.

Kennedy, Alison Louise, BA (Hons). Writer; b. 22.10.65, Dundee. Educ. High School of Dundee; Warwick University. Community Arts Worker, 1988-89; Writer in Residence, Project Ability, 1989-94; Writer in Residence, Hamilton/East Kilbride Social Work Department, 1990-92; fiction critic for Scotsman, etc.; Booker Prize Judge, 1996; five S.A.C. book awards; Saltire Best First Book Award; Saltire Best Book Award; John Llewellyn Rees/Mail on Sunday Prize; listed, Granta/Sunday Times Best of Young British Novelists; Encore Award; Festival Fringe First; Social Work Today Award. Publications: Night Geometry and the Garscadden Trains; Looking for the Possible Dance; Now That You're Back; So I Am Glad; Original Bliss; The Life and Death of Colonel Blimp (essay); Everything you Need; On Bull Fighting (non-fiction); The Audition (play); Stella Does Tricks (film); Delicate (performance piece); True (performance piece). Recreations: cinema; clarinet; fencing.

Kennedy, (Alistair James) Spencer, MA, LLB, SSC, NP. Partner, Balfour & Manson, since 1991; b. 3.5.45, Dumfries; m., Joan Margaret Whitelaw. Educ. Royal High School of Edinburgh; Edinburgh University. Estate Duty Office, 1965-68; Connell & Connell, 1968-70; Nightingale & Bell, SSC, 1970-90; Past President, Society of Solicitors in the Supreme Courts of Scotland. Recreations: hill-walking; horticulture. Address: (b.) 58 Frederick Street, Edinburgh EH2 1LS; T.-0131-200 1240.

Kennedy, Professor Angus Johnston, MA, PhD, Officier dans l'Ordre des Palmes Academiques. Stevenson Professor of French Language and Literature, Glasgow University; b. 9.8.40, Port Charlotte; m., Marjory McCulloch Shearer; 2 d. Educ. Bearsden Academy; Glasgow University. Glasgow University: Assistant Lecturer in French, 1965, then Lecturer, Senior Lecturer, Reader; former Secretary, British Branch, International Arthurian Society. Publications: books on Christine de Pizan. Address: (b.) French Department, Glasgow University, Glasgow; T.-0141-339 8855; e-mail: A.Kennedy@french.arts.gla.ac.uk

Kennedy, Professor Arthur Colville, CBE, MD, FRCP(Lond), FRCPE, FRCP(Glas), FRCPI, FRSE, FACP(Hon.), FRACP (Hon.). Consultant Physician, Royal Infirmary, Glasgow, 1959-88; Muirhead Professor of Medicine, Glasgow University, 1978-88; President, Royal College of Physicians and Surgeons of Glasgow, 1986-88; b. 22.10.22, Edinburgh; m., Agnes White Taylor; 1 s. (deceased); 2 d. Educ. Whitehill School, Glasgow; Glasgow University. Medical Officer, RAFVR, 1946-48; junior NHS posts, 1948-57; Lecturer in Medicine, Glasgow University, 1957; Senior Lecturer, 1961; Reader, 1966; Titular Professor, 1969; responsible for establishment of Kidney Unit, Glasgow Royal Infirmary, 1959; Chairman, MRC Working Party in Glomerulonephritis, 1976-88; Member, Executive Committee, National Kidney Research Fund, 1976-83; Expert Adviser to WHO on Renal Disease; Adviser to EEC on Nephrology in Developing Countries; Chairman, Professional and Linguistic Assessments Board (PLAB), GMC, 1987-89; President: Royal Medico-Chirurgical Society of Glasgow, 1971-72, European Dialysis and Transplant Association, 1972-75, Scottish Society of Physicians, 1983-84, Harveian Society of Edinburgh, 1985; Member: Greater Glasgow Health Board, 1985-89, General Medical Council, 1989-92; President, British Medical Association, 1991-92. Recreations: gardening; walking; reading; photography. Address: (h.) 16 Boclair Crescent, Bearsden, Glasgow G61 2AG; T.-0141-942 5326.

Kennedy, Charles Peter, MA (Hons). MP (SLD, formerly SDP), Ross, Cromarty and Skye, since 1983, Ross, Skye and Inverness West, since 1997; Leader, Liberal Democrats, since 1999; b. 25.11.59, Inverness. Educ. Lochaber High School, Fort William; Glasgow University; Indiana University. President, Glasgow University Union, 1980-81; Winner, British Observer Mace for Student Debating, 1982; Journalist, BBC Highland, Inverness, 1982; Fulbright Scholar, Indiana University (Bloomington Campus), 1982-83. Chairman, SDP Council for Scotland, 1986-88; SDP Spokesman on Health and Social Services, and Scotland, 1983-87; Alliance Election Spokesman, Social Security, Jan.-June, 1987; Member, Select Committee on Social Services, 1985-87; SLD Interim Joint Spokesman, Social Security, 1988; SLD Spokesman, Trade and Industry, 1988-89; President, Liberal Democrats, 1989-94; Liberal Democrat Spokesman: Health, 1989-92, Europe, 1992-97, Agriculture and Rural Affairs, 1997-99; Member: Select Committee on House of Commons Televising, 1988, Standards and Privileges Committee, 1997-99. Recreations: reading; writing. Address: (b.) House of Commons, London SW1A 0AA; T.-020 7219 6226.

Kennedy, Professor Gavin, BA, MSc, PhD, FCIM. Professor, Edinburgh Business School, Heriot-Watt University; Managing Director, Negotiate Ltd., Edinburgh; b. 20.2.40, Collingham, Yorkshire; m., Patricia Anne; 1 s.; 2 d. Educ. London Nautical School; Strathclyde University. Lecturer: Danbury Management Centre, NE London Polytechnic, 1969-71, Brunel University, 1971-73. Lecturer, National Defence College, Latimer, 1972-74; Senior Lecturer in Economics, Strathclyde University, 1973-83; Professor, Defence Finance, Heriot-Watt University, 1983-86. Publications: Military in the Third World, 1974; Economics of Defence, 1975; Bligh, 1978

(Yorkshire Post Book of the Year, 1979); Death of Captain Cook, 1978; Burden Sharing in NATO, 1979; Mathematics for Innumerate Economists, 1982; Defence Economics, 1983; Invitation to Statistics, 1983; Everything is Negotiable, 1984; Negotiate Anywhere, 1985; Macro Economics, 1985; Superdeal, 1985; The Economist Pocket Negotiator, 1987; Captain Bligh: the man and his mutinies, 1988; Do We Have A Deal?, 1991; Simulations for Training Negotiators, 1993; The Perfect Negotiation, 1993; Negotiation, 1994; Local Pay Bargaining, 1995; The Negotiate Trainer's Manual, 1996; Kennedy on Negotiation, 1997; The New Negotiating Edge, 1998; Profitable Negotiation, 1999; Influencing, 1999. Recreation: reading. Address: (h.) 99 Caiyside, Edinburgh; T.-0131-445 7778; e-mail: gavin@negweb.com

Kennedy, Rev. Gordon, BSc, BD. Church of Scotland Minister, Portpatrick linked with Stranraer St. Ninian's, since 2000; b. 15.9.63, England. Educ. Crookston Castle Secondary; University of Strathclyde; University of Glasgow. Graduate Civil Engineer, Strathclyde Regional Council, 1985-89; Probationer Assistant, Bearsden North Parish Church, 1992-93; Minister, New Cumnock Parish Church, Ayrshire, 1993-2000. Address: 2 Albert Terrace, London Road, Stranraer DG9 8AB; T.-01776 702443; e-mail: gordon.kennedy1@btinternet.com

Kennedy, Gordon Philip, MA (Hons), MPhil, MBA, MRTPI, MIED. Deputy Chief Executive, Scottish Enterprise Glasgow, since 2001; b. 30.5.57, Glasgow. Educ. St. Mungo's Academy; Glasgow University; Strathclyde University. Planning Assistant, Clydebank District Council, 1982-85; Industrial Economist, Scottish Development Agency, 1985-91; Glasgow Development Agency: Head of Strategic Projects, 1991, Head of Corporate Strategy, 1991-93; Director, Corporate Development, Glasgow Development Agency, 1993-99; Director, Group Operations, Scottish Enterprise Glasgow, 1999-2001. Member, Board, Bulkhead Ltd. Recreations: cinema; theatre; eating out. Address: (b.) Atrium Court, 50 Waterloo Street, Glasgow G2; T.-0141-204 1111.

Kennedy, Professor Hugh Nigel, PhD, FRSE. Professor of Middle Eastern History, St Andrews University, since 1998; b. 22.10.47, Hythe, Kent; m., Hilary Ann Kennedy; 1 s.; 3 d. Educ. Marlborough College; Pembroke College, Cambridge. Lecturer in Mediaeval History, St Andrews University, 1972-90, Reader in Mediaeval History, 1990-98. Publications include: The Early Abbasid Caliphate, 1981; The Prophet and the Age of the Caliphates, 1986; Crusader Castles, 1994; Muslim Spain and Portugal, 1996; The Armies of the Caliphs, 2001. Recreations: archaeology; architectural history. Address: (b.) Department of Mediaeval History, St Andrews University, St Andrews KY16 9AL; T.-01334 463316; e-mail: hnk@st-and.ac.uk

Kennedy, James, RGN, RMN, MA, DIPN, FCIPD. Scottish Secretary, Royal College of Nursing, since 2000; b. 24.9.57, Tipperary, Ireland. Educ. Christian Brothers School, Nenagh, Co. Tipperary; North London School of Nursing. Accident and emergency nurse, Whittington Hospital, London, 1979; RMN, St. Lukes Woodside Hospital, London, 1980-82; Community Charge Nurse/SNR Nurse/Clinical Teacher, Bloomsbury Health Authority, 1982-86; Islington Health Authority: Assistant Unit General Manager, 1987-91, Head of Nursing, 1991-92; Forth Valley Health Board: Chief Nursing Advisor and Director of Quality, 1992-94, Director of Strategic Planning, 1994-2000. Chair, Community Council. Publications: Drug and Alcohol Dependency Nursing (co-author). Address: (b.) RCN, 42 South Oswald Road Edinburgh, EH9 2HH; T.-0131-662 1010; e-mail: james.kennedy@rcn.org.uk

Kennedy, Norman Stewart Joseph, BSc, PhD, FIPEM. Head of Nuclear Medicine, Ninewells Hospital, Dundee, since 1989; b. 5.3.51, Edinburgh; m., Patricia Meadowcroft; 3 s.; 1 d. Educ. Broxburn Academy; Edinburgh University. Research Medical Physicist, Western General Hospital, Edinburgh, 1978-82; Senior Medical Physicist, Ninewells Hospital, Dundee 1982-89. Publications: 52 papers. Recreations: badminton; bridge. Address: (h.) St. Mary's Drive, Kinnoull Hill, Perth PH2 7BY; T.-01738 632282; e-mail: nsjkennedy@tuht.scot.nhs.uk

Kennedy, Professor Peter Graham Edward, MB, BS, MPhil, MLitt, PhD, MD, DSc, FRCPath, FRCPLond, FRCPGlas, FRSE, FMedSci. Burton Professor of Neurology and Head of Department, Glasgow University, since 1987; Consultant Neurologist, Institute of Neurological Sciences, Southern General Hospital, Glasgow, since 1986; b. 28.3.51, London; m., Catherine Ann; 1 s.; 1 d. Educ. University College School, London; University College, London; University College Medical School. Medical Registrar, University College Hospital, 1977-81; Hon. Research Assistant, MRC Neuroimmunology Project, University College, London, 1978-80; Research Fellow, Institute of Virology, Glasgow University, 1981; Registrar and Senior Registrar, National Hospital for Nervous Diseases, London, 1981-84; Assistant Professor of Neurology, Johns Hopkins University School of Medicine, 1985; "New Blood" Senior Lecturer in Neurology and Virology, Glasgow University, 1986-87. BUPA Medical Foundation "Doctor of the Year" Research Award, 1990; Linacre Medal and Lectureship, Royal College of Physicians of London, 1991; T.S. Srinivasan Endowment Lecturer and Gold Medal, 1993; Fogarty International Scholar, NIH, USA, 1993-94; Associate Editor, Journal of Neurovirology; Member: Medical Research Advisory Committee, Multiple Sclerosis Society, 1987-98, Association of Physicians Great Britain and Ireland, Association of British Neurologists; Fellow of the Academy of Medical Sciences; Secretary, International Society for Neurovirology, since 2000. Publications: Infectious Diseases of the Nervous System (Co-Editor), 2000; numerous papers on neurology, neurovirology and neurobiology. Recreations: reading and writing; music; astronomy; tennis; walking in the country; philosophy. Address: (b.) Institute of Neurological Sciences, Southern General Hospital, Glasgow G51; T.-0141-201 2474.

Kennedy, Professor Robert Alan, BA, PhD, FBPsS, FRSE. Professor of Psychology, University of Dundee, since 1972; b. 1.10.39, Stourbridge; m., Elizabeth Wanda; 1 d. Educ. King Edward VI Grammar School, Stourbridge. Senior Tutor then Lecturer in Psychology, University of Melbourne, 1963-65; Lecturer in Psychology: Queen's College, University of St. Andrews, University of Dundee, 1965-72; Senior Lecturer in Psychology, University of Dundee, 1972. Member, Psychology Committee, Social Science Research Council (UK), 1980-82; Committee Member, Experimental Psychology Society, 1984-88; Member, Scientific Affairs Board, British Psychological Society, 1986-88; Member, MRC Neuropsychology Sub-committee, 1982-89; Editorial Board: Acta Psychologica, 1980-88, Psychological Research, 1978-88; Founder Member, European Conference on Eye Movements, since 1980; Convener, Scottish Group of Professors of Psychology, 1985-91; Governor, Dundee College of Education, 1974-78; Member of Court, University of Dundee, 1976-80 and 1990-99; Convener, University Research Committee, 1994-97; Member, Council, Royal Society of Edinburgh, 1999-2001. Publications: Studies in Long-Term Memory (Co-author); The Psychology of Reading; Reading as a Perceptual Process (Editor). Recreations: hill-walking; playing the piano. Address: (b.) Psychology Department, University of Dundee, Dundee DD1 4HN; T.-01382 344622.

Kennedy, William Michael Clifford, BA, CA. Company Director; Chairman, Adam & Company PLC, since 1999; Chairman, Havelock Europea PLC, since 1998; b. 29.10.35, Edinburgh; m., Judith Victoria Gibb; 1 s.; 1 d. Educ. Edinburgh Academy; Rugby School; Merton College, Oxford. Kleinwort Benson, London, 1963-64; Partner, Martin Currie & Co., 1965-85; Director, Martin Currie Ltd., 1985, Chief Executive, 1991, Chairman and Chief Executive, 1992-96; Director, Scottish Life Assurance Co., 1976-2001; Director, Royal Infirmary of Edinburgh NHS Trust, 1993-99; Director, Fleming Income and Growth Investment Trust PLC, since 1996; Financial Adviser to Royal Scottish Academy, 1976-96. Chairman, Foundation for Skin Research. Recreations: fishing; shooting; golf; tennis; music. Address: (h.) Oak Lodge, Inveresk, Midlothian EH21 7TE; T.-0131-665 8822.

Kenway, Professor Richard Donovan, FRSE, BSc, DPhil, CPhys, MInstP. Tait Professor of Mathematical Physics, Edinburgh University, since 1994; b. 8.5.54, Cardiff; m., Anna Kenway; 1 s.; 2 d. Educ. Stanwell School, Penarth; Exeter University; Oxford University. Research Associate, Brown University, 1978-80; Post-doctoral Fellow, Los Alamos National Laboratory, 1980-82; Edinburgh University: Post-doctoral Fellow, 1982-83; Lecturer, 1983-90; Reader, 1990-94; Director of Edinburgh Parallel Computing Centre, 1993-97; Head, Department of Physics and Astronomy, 1997-2000; Chairman, Edinburgh Parallel Computing Centre, since 1997; Member, National and International Peer Review and Research Strategy Committees. Publications: co-authored one book; co-edited two books; 96 papers on theoretical particle physics and high performance computing. Recreations: munroing; running. Address: (b.) Department of Physics and Astronomy, Edinburgh University, The King's Buildings, Edinburgh, EH9 3JZ; T.-0131-650 5245; e-mail: r.d.kenway@ed.ac.uk

Kerby, Nigel Wells, BSc, PhD, CBiol, FIBiol. Managing Director, Mylnefield Research Services Ltd., since 1993; b. 5.4.53, Anglesey; m., Marigold; 1 s. Educ. Sedburgh School; United World College of the Atlantic; Leeds University. SERC Fellowship, Leeds University, 1979-82; AFRC Fellowship, Dundee University, 1982-90; Lecturer in Microbiology, Dundee University, 1990-93. Member, Institute of Directors, Institute of Advanced Motorists. Recreations: gardening; travel; golf. Address: (b.) Mylnefield Research Services Ltd., Invergowrie, Dundee, DD2 5DA; T.-01382 568568; e-mail: n.kerby@mrsltd.com

Kerevan, George, MA (Hons). Associate Editor, The Scotsman, since 2000; Chief Executive, What If Productions (Television) Ltd., since 2000; b. 28.9.49, Glasgow. Educ. Kingsridge Secondary School, Drumchapel; Glasgow University. Academic posts, Napier University, 1975-2000; freelance journalist and broadcaster, since 1980; TV director, producer and script writer, Lamancha Productions Ltd., 1989-2000; Chair, Edinburgh Technology Transfer Centre, 1985-92; Board, Edinburgh Co-operative Development Agency, 1987-92; Chair, EDI Ltd., 1988-95; Board, Edinburgh Venture Trust, 1988-93; Board, Capital Enterprise Trust, 1993-94; Chairman, New Edinburgh Ltd., 1989-95; Board, Lothian and Edinburgh Enterprise Trust, 1989-96; Chair, Edinburgh and Lothians Tourist Board, 1992-95; Board, Traverse Theatre, 1980-84; Council, Edinburgh International Festival, 1984-92; Board, Assembly Productions, 1984-88; Board, Royal Lyceum Theatre, 1984-88; Board, Edinburgh Old Town Trust, 1984-90; Board, 7:84 Theatre Company, 1986-88; Board, Edinburgh International Film Festival, 1988-94; Chair, Edinburgh International Science Festival, 1989-95; Chair, Edinburgh Film House, 1989-94; Board, Boxcar Films, 1993; Chair, Manifesto International Festival of Architecture, 1995; elected Member, Edinburgh District

Council, 1984-96 (Convenor, Economic Development Committee, 1986-95); Vice-Convenor, Economic Affairs Committee, COSLA, 1988-90; Board, John Wheatley Centre for Public Policy Research, 1988-93; SNP National Council, 1996-98; SNP environment spokesperson, 1996-98. Recreations: cooking; cats; cinema. Address: (h.) Brunstane House (South Wing), Brunstane Road South, Edinburgh EH15 2NQ; T.-0131-669 8234.

Kernohan, Robert Deans, OBE, MA, FFCS. Journalist, Writer and occasional Broadcaster; b. 9.1.31, Mount Vernon, Lanarkshire; m., Margaret Buchanan Bannerman; 4 s. Educ. Whitehill School, Glasgow; Glasgow University; Balliol College, Oxford. RAF, 1955-57; Editorial Staff, Glasgow Herald, 1957-67 (Assistant Editor, 1965-66, London Editor, 1966-67); Director-General, Scottish Conservative Central Office, 1967-71; Freelance Journalist and Broadcaster, 1972; Editor, Life and Work, The Record of the Church of Scotland, 1972-90. Chairman, Federation of Conservative Students, 1954-55; Conservative Parliamentary candidate, 1955, 1959, 1964; Member: Newspaper Panel, Monopolies and Mergers Commission (subsequently Competition Commission), 1987-99, Ancient Monuments Board for Scotland, 1990-97, Broadcasting Standards Council, 1994-97, Broadcasting Standards Commission, 1997-99; Chairman, Scottish Christian Conservative Forum, 1991; HM Inspector of Constabulary for Scotland (Lay Inspector), 1992-95; Director, Handsel Press Ltd; Trustee, Carberry Tower; Elder, Cramond Kirk, Edinburgh. Publications: Scotland's Life and Work, 1979; William Barclay, The Plain Uncommon Man, 1980; Thoughts through the Year, 1985; Our Church, 1985; The Protestant Future, 1991; The Road to Zion, 1995; The Realm of Reform (Editor), 1999; John Buchan in a Nutshell, 2000. Recreations: rugby-watching; travel; pontification. Address: (h.) 5/1 Rocheid Park, Edinburgh EH4 1RP; T.-0131-332 7851.

Kerr, Andrew Palmer. MSP (Labour), East Kilbride, since 1999; Minister for Finance and Public Services, Scottish Executive; b. 17.3.62, East Kilbride; m., Susan; 3 d. Educ. Claremont High School; Glasgow College. Research Officer, Strathkelvin District Council, 1987-90; Achieving Quality Consultancy, 1990-93; Glasgow City Council, 1993-99. Address: (b.) Civic Centre, East Kilbride; T.-01355 806223.

Kerr, Sheriff Principal Bruce Alexander, QC. Sheriff Principal of North Strathclyde, since 1999; b. 28.4.46. Admitted, Faculty of Advocates, 1973; QC, 1986; Standing Junior Counsel to Home Office, 1982-85; Advocate Depute, 1986-89; Temporary Sheriff, 1991; Permanent Sheriff, since 1994. Address: (b.) Sheriff Court House, St James Street, Paisley PA3 2HW; T.-0141-887 5291.

Kerr, David Alexander, MC, TD, JP, DL; b. 30.9.16, Inverkip; m., Elizabeth Phoebe Coxwell Cresswell; 1 s.; 1 d. Educ. Canford School. Joined Westburn Sugar Refineries Ltd., Greenock, 1936; joined 5/6 Bn., Argyll & Sutherland Highlanders, 1936; mobilised, 1939, serving in France, Belgium, North Africa, Italy, Palestine and Syria; MC, 1945; mentioned in Despatches; Territorial Decoration, 1948; returned to Westburn, 1946; Technical Director, 1949; Refinery Director, 1955; Joint Managing Director, 1960; Managing Director, 1967; Chairman, 1972; Director, The Sankey Sugar Company Ltd., 1965; Managing Director, Maubre Sugars Ltd., 1972; Director, Tate & Lyle Refineries Ltd., 1976-79; retired, 1979. County Commissioner, County of Renfrew Scout Association, 1964-70, County Chairman, 1971-73; Area President, 1976-93; Chief Commissioner for Scotland, 1977-81; Honorary Vice President, since 1981; a County Vice President,

Renfrewshire Guide Association. Recreations: garden; philately; photography. Address: (h.) Whitefarland, 88 Octavia Terrace, Greenock PA16 7PY; T.-01475 631980.

Kerr, Douglas J., JP. Convenor, Edinburgh City Council Licensing Board, since 1996, and of City Licensing Committee, 1995-97; b. 9.1.57, Perth. Educ. Perth High School. Vice-Chair, Edinburgh District Council Planning Committee, 1990-96. Recreations: cricket; golf; football; skiing. Address: (b.) City Chambers, High Street, Edinburgh EH1 1YJ; T.-0131-529 3279.

Kerr, Finlay, MB, ChB, DObsRCOG, FRCPEdin, FRCPGlas. Consultant Physician, Raigmore Hospital, Inverness, since 1976, Clinical Director, 1998-2001; Honorary Senior Lecturer, Aberdeen University, since 1976; Non-Executive Director, NHS Highland Board, since 2001; Member, Council, Royal College of Physicians of Edinburgh, since 1994; President, Scottish Cardiac Society, 2001-03; Deputy Lieutenant, Inverness, since 2000; b. 8.8.41, Edinburgh; m., Margaret Ann Carnegie Allan; 1 s.; 2 d. Educ. Keil School; Glasgow University. House Physician and Surgeon, Western Infirmary, Glasgow; House Physician, Ruchill Hospital, Glasgow; House Surgeon, Queen Mother's Hospital, Glasgow; Senior House Officer, Western Infirmary, Glasgow; Fellow, University of Southern California; Lecturer in Medicine, then Senior Registrar in Medicine, Edinburgh Royal Infirmary. Board Director, Highland Hospice, 1985-90 (Chairman, Board of Directors, 1985-87); Chairman, Area Medical Committee, 1993-96; President, Highland Medical Society, 1997-98. Recreations: sailing; windsurfing; skiing; golf. Address: (h.) The Birks, 2 Drummond Place, Inverness.

Kerr, Rev. Mgr. Philip John, PhB, STL. Parish Priest, St. Francis Xavier, Falkirk and Vicar General, Archdiocese of St. Andrews and Edinburgh, since 1999; b. 23.4.56, Edinburgh. Educ. Holy Cross Academy; St. Augustine's High School, Edinburgh; Scots College and Gregorian University, Rome. Assistant Priest, St. Francis Xavier's, Falkirk, 1980-82; Lecturer in Systematic Theology, St. Andrew's College, Drygrange, 1982-86; Vice-Rector and Lecturer in Systematic Theology, Gillis College, Edinburgh, 1986-93; Lecturer in Systematic Theology, Scotus College, Bearsden, 1993-96; R.C. Chaplain, Stirling University, 1993-99; Parish Priest: Sacred Heart, Cowie, 1993-99, Our Lady and St. Ninian, Bannockburn, 1996-99. Recreations: classical music; walking. Address: St. Francis Xavier, Hope Street, Falkirk FK1 5AT; T.-01324 623567.

Kerr, Robert James, MA (Hons), PhD. Rector, Peebles High School, since 1986; b. 14.6.47, Jedburgh; m., Isobel Grace Atkinson; 2 s.; 1 d. Educ. Kelso High School; Edinburgh University. Assistant Teacher, Lochaber High School, 1973-75; Assistant Principal Teacher of Geography, Forrester High School, 1976-77; Principal Teacher of Geography, Douglas Ewart High School, 1977-82; Assistant Rector, Elgin High School, 1982-85; Depute Rector, Forres Academy, 1985-86. Chairman, "Higher Still" Specialist Group in PSE, 1994-97. Recreations: fishing; rugby supporter; hill-walking/mountaineering; mountain biking; ornithology; skiing; travel. Address: (h.) Enniskerry, Eshiels, Peebles EH45 8NA; T.-01721 722131; e-mail: robkerr@beeb.net

Kerr, Professor William John Stanton, BDS, FDS, RCSEdin, MDS, FFD, RCSIrel, DOrthRCS, FDS RCPS Glas, DDS. Professor of Orthodontics, Glasgow Dental Hospital and School, since 1993; Honorary Consultant in Orthodontics, since 1978; b. 12.7.41, Belfast; m., Marie-Francoise; 1 d. Educ. Campbell College, Belfast; Queen's University, Belfast. Address: (b.) Glasgow Dental Hospital and School, 378 Sauchiehall Street, Glasgow G2 3JZ; T.-0141-211 9665.

Kerr, William Revill, PhD, FCIS, FCIM, MHCIMA, MBA, MSc. Chairman, Scottish Enterprise Ayrshire, since 2000; Secretary, Malin Housing Association, since 1988; b. 26.4.48, East Kilbride; m., Maria. Educ. Duncanrig Senior Secondary School, East Kilbride; Glasgow University; Strathclyde University; Glasgow Caledonian University. Former hotelier. Chairman, Ayrshire Economic Forum; Member, Advisory Board, Scottish Enterprise; PSYBT Ambassador. Recreations: sport; writing; chess; old books. Address: (b.) Malin Court, Turnberry, Ayrshire KA26 9PB; (h.) 20 Burness Avenue, Alloway, Ayr KA7 4QB; T.-01655 331457; e-mail: bill@caringmalin.org.uk

Kerrigan, Herbert Aird, QC, MA, LLB (Hons); b. 2.8.45, Glasgow; 1 s. Educ. Whitehill School, Glasgow; Aberdeen University; Keele University; Hague Academy. Admitted to Faculty of Advocates, 1970; Lecturer in Criminal Law and Criminology, Edinburgh University, 1969-73; Lecturer in Scots Law, Edinburgh University, 1973-74; Member, Longford Commission, 1972; Church of Scotland: Elder, 1967 (now at Greyfriars Tolbooth and Highland Kirk), Reader, 1969, elected Member, Assembly Council, 1981-85, Senior Chaplain to Rt. Rev. John Cairns, Moderator of the General Assembly of the Church of Scotland, 1999-00; called to the English Bar (Middle Temple), 1990; joined Chambers of Edmund Lawson, QC, 1991; appointed QC in Scotland, 1992; President, Edinburgh Royal Infirmary Samaritan Society, since 1992; Vice Convener, General Assembly of the Church of Scotland's Committee on Chaplains to Her Majesty's Forces, since 1999. Publications: An Introduction to Criminal Procedure in Scotland, 1970; Ministers for the 1980s (Contributor), 1979; The Law of Contempt (Contributing Editor), 1982; The Law of Sport (2nd edition) (Contributor), 1995. Recreation: travel. Address: (h.) 20 Edinburgh Road, Dalkeith, Midlothian EH22 1JY; T.-0131-660 3007.

Kettle, Ann Julia, MA, FSA, FRHistS, FRSA, FFCS. Senior Lecturer, Mediaeval History, University of St. Andrews, since 1964; b. 2.8.39, Orpington. Educ. Lewes Grammar School; St. Hugh's College, Oxford. University of St. Andrews: Hebdomadar, 1991-94, Dean of Arts, since 1998; President, Association of University Teachers (Scotland), 1994-96; Member, Scottish (Garrick) Committee of National (Dearing) Committee of Inquiry into Higher Education, 1996-97; Member, Scottish Higher Education Funding Council, 1997-2000. Address: (b.) Department of Mediaeval History, University of St. Andrews, St. Andrews KY16 9AL; T.-01334 463317; e-mail: ajk@st-and.ac.uk

Khan, Anvar (nee Anwar Begum Khan). Writer; Journalist; Broadcaster; Voiceover Artist; b. 13.7.67, Glasgow. Educ. Laurel Bank School, Glasgow. Editor, The Herald Diary, Fashion, Style and Beauty, The Herald, 1993-96; Feature Writer: Daily Mail, 1993-96, The Herald, 1996-2001, News of the World, 2001-02; Columnist: The Scotsman, 1997, The Herald, 1998-2001, News of the World, 2001-02; Radio Presenter: BBC Radio 4, 1997, BBC Radio Scotland, 1999-2001; Television Presenter: Citizen Khan, Scottish Television, 1997, Scottish Reporters, Scottish Television, 1999, Bravehearts and Bhangra, BBC2 East series, 1999, Made in Britain, Channel 4, 2002. Trained singer. UK Press Gazette Feature Writer of the Year, 1994. Address: e-mail: anvar.khan@ntlworld.com

Kidd, Professor Cecil, BSc, PhD, FIBiol, FRSA. Professor of Physiology (part-time), Aberdeen University, 1997-2000; Regius Professor of Physiology, 1984-97; Professor Emeritus, since 2000; b. 28.4.33, Shotley Bridge, Co. Durham; m., Margaret Winifred; 3 s. Educ. Queen Elizabeth Grammar School, Darlington; King's College, Newcastle-upon-Tyne; Durham University. Demonstrator in Physiology, King's College, Newcastle-upon-Tyne; Lecturer/Senior Lecturer/Reader in Physiology, Senior Research Associate in Cardiovascular Studies, Leeds University. Recreations: golf; opera; gardening. Address: (b.) Department of Biomedical Sciences, Medical School, Foresterhill Campus, Aberdeen University, Aberdeen AB25 2ZD; T.-01224 273004; e-mail: c.kidd@abdn.ac.uk

Kidd, David Hamilton, LLB, LLM, WS, NP. Partner, Biggart Baillie, since 1978; Solicitor Advocate, since 1994; b. 21.9.49, Edinburgh. Educ. Edinburgh Academy; Edinburgh University. Recreations: cycling; skiing; hill-walking. Address: (b.) 7 Castle Street, Edinburgh EH2 3AP; T.-0131-226 5541; e-mail: dkidd@biggartbaillie.co.uk

Kidd, James Cameron, LLB (Hons). District Chairman, The Appeals Service, since 1995; b. 17.4.48, Glasgow; m., Eileen Theresa McGinlay; 1 s.; 1 d. Educ. Hillhead High School, Glasgow; University of Glasgow. Apprentice, Bishop Milne Boyd and Co., Solicitors, Glasgow, 1971-73; Partner: Macdonalds, Solicitors, Glasgow, 1973-90, Macpherson Gibb Maguire Cook, Solicitors, Glasgow, 1990-95. Recreations: golf; opera; crosswords. Address: (h.) 8 Manor Road, Jordanhill, Glasgow G14 9LG; T.-0141-959 2592; e-mail: jimkidd17@hotmail.com

Kidd, Mary Helen (May), JP, MA. Member, Advisory Board and Council, Scottish Agricultural College, since 1991; Area President (Europe and the Mediterranean), Associated Countrywomen of the World, 2001-04; National Chairman, Scottish Women's Rural Institutes, 1993-96; m., Neil M.L. Kidd; 2 s. Educ. Brechin High School; Edinburgh University. Partner in family farming business; former Member: MAFF Consumer Panel, Scottish Consumer Council, Women's National Commission. Recreations: playing piano and organ; creative writing. Address: (h.) Holemill of Kirkbuddo, Forfar, Angus DD8 2NQ; T.-01307 820 318.

Kilbey, Professor Brian John, BSc, PhD, DSc, FRSE. Professor Emeritus, University of Edinburgh, formerly Professor of Molecular Parasitology, University of Edinburgh; b. 1.3.36, London; m., Sarah; 1 s.; 3 d. Educ. Tottenham Grammar School; University College London. Reader, Genetics, University of Edinburgh, 1975-98. Visiting Professor, University of Rochester, NY, USA, 1987-88. Address: (b.) Institute of Cell and Molecular Biology, Darwin Building, King's Buildings, Edinburgh EH9 3JY.

Killham, Professor Kenneth Stuart, BSc, PhD, FRSE, FAAM. Established Chair of Soil Science, Aberdeen University, since 1995 (Head, Department of Plant and Soil Science, 1996-2000); President, British Society of Soil Science, since 2000; Vice-Chairman, Remedios Ltd., since 1999; b. 1.3.57, Formby; m., Pauline. Educ. Merchant Taylors School, Crosby; Sheffield University. Visiting Scientist, University of California, Berkeley, 1981-83; Lecturer in Soil Microbiology, Aberdeen University, 1983-90; Reader in Soil Microbiology, Aberdeen University, 1990-93. Chairman, UK Soil Science Advisory Committee, 1997-2000. Publications: Soil Ecology; Soil Chemistry – Theory and Applications. Recreation: sailing. Address: (b.) Cruickshank Building, University of Aberdeen, St. Machar Drive, Aberdeen AB24 3UU; T.-01224 272260.

Kilpatrick, Lord (Robert Kilpatrick), MD, FRCP(Edin), FRCP, FRCPS(Glas), HonFRCS, HonFRCP(Dub), HonFRCS(Edin), FRSE. Chairman, Scottish Hospital Endowment Research Trust, 1996-2000; b. 29.7.26, Wemyss; m., Elizabeth Forbes; 2 s.; 1 d. Educ. Buckhaven High School; Edinburgh University. House Officer, Senior House Officer, Registrar, Edinburgh, 1949-54; Lecturer and Senior Lecturer, Sheffield University, 1955-66; Professor of Clinical Pharmacology, Sheffield University, 1966-75; Professor of Clinical Pharmacology and Medicine, Leicester University, 1975-89; President, General Medical Council, 1989-95; President, British Medical Association, 1997-98; Hon. Degrees: DrHc (Edin), LLD (Dundee), DSc

(Hull), DSc (Leics), LLD (Sheff). Recreation: golf. Address: (h.) 12 Wester Coates Gardens, Edinburgh EH12 5LT; T.-0131-337 7304.

Kilshaw, David Andrew George, OBE. Solicitor, since 1979; Chairman, Borders Health Board, 1993-2001; b. 18.3.53, Glencoe; 3 s. Educ. Keil School, Dumbarton. Traineeship, Brunton Miller, Solicitors, Glasgow, 1975-80; Solicitor, Borders Regional Council, 1980-83; Partner, Cullen Kilshaw Solicitors, Galashiels, Melrose and Peebles, since 1983. Recreations: golf; fishing. Address: (b.) 23 Northgate, Peebles; T.-01721 723999.

Kimbell, Professor David Rodney Bertram, MA, DPhil, LRAM, FRSA. Professor of Music, Edinburgh University, since 1987; b. 26.6.39, Gillingham, Kent; m., Ingrid Else Emilie Lübbe; 1 s.; 2 d. Educ. Dartford Grammar School; Kent College, Canterbury; Worcester College, Oxford. Lecturer in Music, Edinburgh University, 1965-78; Professor of Music, St. Andrews University, 1979-87. Publication: Verdi in the Age of Italian Romanticism, 1981; Italian Opera, 1991. Address: (h.) 3 Bellevue Crescent, Edinburgh EH3 6ND; T.-0131-556 5480.

Kincraig, Hon. Lord (Robert Smith Johnston), QC (Scot), BA (Hons), LLB. Senator of the College of Justice in Scotland, 1972-88; Chairman, Parole Review Body for Scotland; b. 10.10.18, Glasgow; m., Margaret Joan Graham (deceased); 1 s.; 1 d. Educ. Strathallan; St. John's College, Cambridge; Glasgow University. Member, Faculty of Advocates, 1942; Advocate-Depute, 1953-55; QC (Scot), 1955; contested (Unionist), Stirling and Falkirk Burghs, General Election, 1959; Home Advocate Depute, 1959-62; Sheriff of Roxburgh, Berwick and Selkirk, 1964-70; Dean, Faculty of Advocates, 1970-72. Recreations: gardening; golf. Address: (h.) Westwood Cottage, Southfield Farm, Longniddry EH32 0PL; T.-01875 853583; e-mail: rkincraig@compuserve.com

Kindley, Dr Angus David, MBChB, DCH, FRCP(Lond), FRCPEdin, FRCPH. Director, Raeden Regional Child Development Centre, Aberdeen, since 1991; Consultant, Royal Aberdeen Children's Hospital, since 1991; b. 26.4.49, Newcastle upon Tyne; m., Ceri; 1 s.; 1 d. Educ. Royal Grammar School, Newcastle upon Tyne; Leeds University. Senior Registrar, Paediatric Neurology, Alder Hey Children's Hospital; Consultant Paediatrician, Bury; Hon. Clinical Senior Lecturer, Aberdeen University. Trustee, Aberdeen Gomel Trust; Past President, Aberdeen Philatelic Society. Recreations: philately; postal history; fishing; falconry. Address: (b.) Raeden Centre, Midstocket Road, Aberdeen AB15 5TD; T.-01224 321381.

King, Professor Bernard, MSc, PhD, CIMgt, FIWSc, CBiol, FIBiol. Principal and Vice-Chancellor, University of Abertay, Dundee, since 1992; b. 4.5.46, Dublin; m., Maura Antoinette Collinge; 2 d. Educ. Synge St. Christian Brothers School, Dublin; College of Technology, Dublin; University of Aston in Birmingham. Research Fellow, University of Aston, 1972-76; Dundee Institute of Technology, 1976-91: Lecturer, Senior Lecturer, Head, Department of Molecular and Life Sciences, Dean, Faculty of Science; Assistant Principal, Robert Gordon Institute of Technology/Robert Gordon University, 1991-92. Member, Board, Scottish Enterprise Tayside; Director, Scottish Crop Research Institute; Governor, Board, Unicorn Preservation Society; Board Member, Scottish Knowledge; Board Member, Institute for Learning and Teaching. Recreations: reading; music; sailing. Address: (h.) 11 Dalhousie Place, Arbroath, DD11 2BT; T.-01382 308012.

King, Elspeth Russell, MA, FMA.Director, Smith Art Gallery and Museum, Stirling, since 1994; b. 29.3.49, Lochore, Fife. Educ. Beath High School; St. Andrews University; Leicester University. Curator, People's Palace,

Glasgow, 1974-91, with responsibility for building up the social history collections for the city of Glasgow; Director, Dunfermline Heritage Trust, 1991-94; responsible for restoration of, and new displays in, Abbot House. Publications include: The Thenew Factor: the hidden history of women in Glasgow, 1993; Blind Harry's Wallace by Hamilton of Gilbertfield (Editor), 1998; Address: (b.) Smith Art Gallery and Museum, Dumbarton Road, Stirling FK8 2RQ; T.-01786 471917; e-mail: museum@smithartgallery.demon.co.uk

King, Steve. Composer/Music Educationalist; Musician in Residence, Heriot-Watt University, since 1998; Viola Player, Scottish Chamber Orchestra, since 1984; b. 4.12.56, Waltham Cross; 2 s. Educ. Queen Eleanor Grammar School; Royal Northern College of Music. Co-Principal, Icelandic Symphony Orchestra, 1979-82. Address: (h.) 8 Hopeward Mews, Dalgety Bay KY11 9TB; T.-01383 821187.

Kingarth, Hon. Lord (Hon. Derek Emslie). Senator of the College of Justice, since 1997; b. 21.6.49. Educ. Cambridge University; Edinburgh University. Advocate, 1974; Advocate Depute 1985-1988. Address: Parliament Square, Edinburgh EH1 1RQ.

Kinnaird, Alison, MBE, MA, FGE. Glass Engraver and Artist; Clarsach Player; b. 30.4.49, Edinburgh; m., Robin Morton; 1 s.; 1 d. Educ. George Watson's Ladies College; Edinburgh University. Freelance glass artist, since 1971; exhibitions in Edinburgh, 1978, 1981, 1985, in London, 1988, 1995; work in many public and private collections; professional musician, since 1970; has produced three LPs as well as film and TV music; served on Council, Scottish Craft Centre, 1974-76; Council, SSWA, 1975-76; Member: BBC Scottish Music Advisory Committee, 1981-84, BBC Broadcasting Council for Scotland, 1984-88, SAC Crafts Commitee, 1993-96; awarded: SDA/CCC Craft Fellowship, 1980, Glass-Sellers of London Award, 1987, MBE, for services to music and art, 1997. Recreations: children; cooking; garden. Address: (h.) Shillinghill, Temple, Midlothian EH23 4SH; T.-01875 830328.

Kinnis, William Kay Brewster, PhD, FRSA. Retired Solicitor and Notary Public; b. 5.1.33, St. Andrews; m., Agnes Inglis Erskine, MA; 2 d. d. Educ. Hamilton Academy; Glasgow University; London University (External). Partner: MacArthur Stewart & Orr, Solicitors, Oban and Lochgilphead, 1959-62; Town Clerk and Burgh Chamberlain, Lochgilphead, 1960-62; Partner, Murdoch Jackson, Solicitors, Glasgow, 1963-92; Senior Partner: Miller Jackson, Solicitors, Lenzie, 1982-92, Cannon, Orpin & Murdochs, 1992-95; Consultant Lawyer, Stewarts & Murdochs, Solicitors, Glasgow, 1995-2000. Council Member, Member, Royal Faculty of Procurators, 1980-83; Governor, Baillie's Institution, 1983-94. Choral Scholar, Glasgow University, 1954-58; Choirmaster, Lochgilphead Parish Church, 1959-62; Reader, Church of Scotland, since 1960; Member, Church of Scotland Board of Practice and Procedure (Vice-Convener) and Law Committee (Convener), 1990-99; Lay Member, school inspection teams, since 1995. Recreations: choral singing; swimming; reading; travel. Address: (b.) 4 Dempster Court, St. Andrews KY16 9EU; T.-01334 476959; e-mail: mail@bkinnis.fsnet.co.uk

Kinnoull, 15th Earl of (Arthur William George Patrick Hay); b. 26.3.35; m.; 1 s.; 3 d. Educ. Eton. Chartered Land Agent; succeeded to title, 1938; former Conservative Spokesman on Aviation, House of Lords; Past President, National Council on Inland Transport.

Kinross, Lord (Christopher Patrick Balfour), LLB, WS. Solicitor, since 1975; b. 1.10.49, Edinburgh; m., Susan Jane Pitman (separated); 2 s. Educ. Eton College; Edinburgh University. Member, Royal Company of Archers, Queen's

Bodyguard for Scotland; James IV Association of Surgeons; The Military and Hospitaller Order of St. Lazarus of Jerusalem. Recreations: off-road motorsport; shooting. Address: (b.) Taylor Kinross Legal Partnership, 27 Stafford Street, Edinburgh; T.-0131-623 1997.

Kinsman, Stewart Hayes, BSc, FRICS. Chief Executive, Hanover (Scotland) Housing Association Ltd., since 1979; Chairman, Edinburgh Flood Prevention Group, since 2000; b. 18.9.43, Burntisland, Fife; 1 s.; 1 d. Educ. Kirkcaldy High School; Heriot-Watt University. Chartered Surveyor, 1966-71; Estates and Buildings Officer, Stirling University, 1971-76; Regional Manager, Hanover Housing Association (GB), 1976-79. Chairman, Scottish Federation of Housing Associations, 1998-2001; Trustee, LintelTrust. Recreations: sailing; wines; natural history. Address: (b.) 36 Albany Street, Edinburgh EH1 3QH; T.-0131-557 0598; e-mail: skinsman@hsha.org.uk

Kintore, 13th Earl of (Michael Canning William John Keith); b. 22.2.39; m.; 1 s.; 1 d. Educ. Eton; Royal Military Academy, Sandhurst.

Kirk, David, MA, BM, BCh, DM, FRCS (Eng), FRCS-RCPS (Glas), FRCS Edin). Consultant Urological Surgeon, Greater Glasgow Health Board, since 1982; Honorary Professor, Glasgow University, since 1995; b. 26.5.43, Bradford; m., Gillian Mary Wroot; 1 s.; 2 d. Educ. King Edwards School, Birmingham; Balliol College, Oxford; Oxford University Clinical Medical School. Resident House Physician and House Surgeon, Radcliffe Infirmary, Oxford; University Demonstrator, Oxford; clinical surgical posts, Oxford and Bristol; Arris and Gale Lecturer, Royal College of Surgeons (England), 1980-81; rotating surgical Registrar appointment, Sheffield; academic surgical research, Sheffield University; Senior Registrar in General Surgery, then in Urology, Bristol; Honorary Clinical Lecturer, Glasgow University, 1984-95. Secretary/Treasurer, 1983-85, Chairman, 1985-88, Scottish Urological Oncology Group; Council Member: Urology Section, Royal Society of Medicine, 1984-87, British Association of Urological Surgeons, 1988-91; Chairman: Prostate Forum, 1991-94, Intercollegiate Board in Urology, 1994-97; Specialist Adviser in Urology, National Medical Advisory Committee (Scottish Executive); Member, Specialist Advisory Committee in Urology, Joint Committee on Higher Surgical Training. Recreations: skiing; hill-walking; classical music. Address: (h.) Woodend, Prospect Road, Dullatur, Glasgow G68 0AN; T.-01236 720778; e-mail: dkirk70683@aol.com

Kirk, Professor David, BSc (Hons), MPhil, FIFST, FHCIMA. Dean, Faculty of Business and Consumer Studies, Queen Margaret University College, since 1991; b. 30.7.45, Stockport; m., Helen Kathleen; 2 s. Educ. New Mills Grammar School; University of Reading; University of Surrey. Food Technologist, International Stores; Research Fellow, University of Surrey; Lecturer, Polytechnic of the South Bank; Senior/Principal Lecturer, Sheffield City Polytechnic. Publications: Environmental Management for Hotels; Kitchen Planning and Management; The Design and Operation of Catering Equipment. Recreations: music; gardening. Address: (b.) Clerwood Terrace, Edinburgh EH12 8TS; T.-0131-317 3000; e-mail: dkirk@qmuc.ac.uk

Kirk, Professor Gordon, MA, MEd, PhD, FRSA. Dean, Faculty of Education, University of Edinburgh, since 1998; Principal, Moray House Institute of Education, 1981-98; Vice-Convener, General Teaching Council, since 1992; b. 8.5.38, Dunfermline; m., Jane D. Murdoch; 1 s.; 1 d. Educ. Camphill Secondary School, Paisley; Glasgow University. Lecturer in Education, Aberdeen University, 1965-74; Head, Education Department, Jordanhill College of Education, 1974-81; Member, Munn Committee on the Curriculum of the Secondary School, 1974-77; Chairman: Educational Broadcasting Council, Scotland, 1985-91,

Scottish Council for Research in Education, 1984-92; Member: General Teaching Council for Scotland, since 1984, Consultative Committee on the Curriculum, 1984-91, Council for National Academic Awards, 1979-93; Vice-Convener, Committee of Scottish Higher Principals, 1993-94. Publications: Scottish Education Looks Ahead (Assistant Editor), 1969; Curriculum and Assessment in the Scottish Secondary School, 1982; Moray House and Professional Education (Editor), 1985; The Core Curriculum, 1986; Teacher Education and Professional Development, 1988; Handbook of Educational Ideas and Practices (Associate Editor), 1990; Scottish Education and the European Community (Editor), 1992; 5-14: Scotland's National Curriculum (Editor), 1994; Moray House and Change in Higher Education (Editor), 1995; Professional Issues in Education series (Co-Editor); Enhancing Quality in Teacher Education, 2000. Recreations: baseball; walking; bridge. Address: (h.) Craigroyston, Broadgait, Gullane, East Lothian; T.-01620 843299.

Kirk, Professor James, MA, PhD, DLitt, FRHistS, FRSE. Professor of Scottish History, Glasgow University, since 1999; b. 18.10.44, Falkirk; m., Dr. Daphne Waters. Educ. Stirling High School; Edinburgh University. Lecturer in Scottish History, Glasgow University, 1972-89, Senior Lecturer, 1989-90, Reader, 1990-99. David Berry Prize, Royal Historical Society, 1973; Wolfson Award, 1977; Hume Brown Senior Prize in Scottish History, 1977; British Academy Major Research Awards, 1989-96; ESRC Research Award, 1993-95. President, Scottish Church History Society, 1989-92; Hon. Secretary: Scottish Record Society, since 1973, Scottish Society for Reformation History, 1980-90; Scottish Section Editor, Royal Historical Society, Annual Bibliography of British and Irish History; an Associate Editor, The New Dictionary of National Biography, 1998. Publications: The University of Glasgow 1451-1577, 1977; Records of the Synod of Lothian and Tweeddale, 1977; The Second Book of Discipline, 1980; Stirling Presbytery Records, 1981; Visitation of the Diocese of Dunblane, 1984; Patterns of Reform, 1989; Humanism and Reform, 1991; The Books of Assumption of the Thirds of Benefices: Scottish Ecclesiastical Rentals at the Reformation, 1995; Scotland's History (Editor), 1995; The Medieval Church in Scotland (Editor), 1995; Her Majesty's Historiographer, 1996; Calendar of Scottish Supplications to Rome 1447-1471, vol. 5 (Editor), 1997; The Church in the Highlands (Editor), 1998; The Scottish Churches, Politics and the Union Parliament (Editor), 2001; Contributor to: The Renaissance and Reformation in Scotland, 1983; Voluntary Religion, 1986; The Seventeenth Century in the Highlands, 1986; Scotland Revisited, 1991; Encyclopedia of the Reformed Faith, 1992, Dictionary of Scottish Church History and Theology, 1993, The Oxford Encyclopedia of the Reformation, 1996; John Knox and the British Reformations, 1999. Recreations: living in Wester Ross; viticulture. Address: (h.) Woodlea, Dunmore, Stirlingshire FK2 8LY; T.-01324 831240; e-mail: james@kirk11.fsnet.co.uk

Kirkhill, Lord (John Farquharson Smith); b. 7.5.30; m.; 1 step d. Lord Provost of Aberdeen, 1971-75; Minister of State, Scottish Office, 1975-78; Chairman, North of Scotland Hydro-Electric Board, 1979-82; Delegate, Parliamentary Assembly, Council of Europe, and W.E.U., since 1987.

Kirkness, Professor Colin Mainland, BMedBiol, MBChB, FRCS(Edin), FRCS (Glas), FRCOphth. Tennent Professor of Ophthalmology, Glasgow University, since 1991; President, European Board of Ophthalmology; Secretary, EUPO; b. 4.5.49, Kirkwall. Educ. Fraserburgh Academy; Aberdeen University. Resident Surgical Officer and Senior Resident, Moorfields Eye Hospital, London, 1980; Lecturer, 1983, Senior Lecturer and Director, 1989, Pocklington Eye Transplant Unit, Institute of Ophthalmology, London; Honorary Consultant, Moorfields

Eye Hospital, 1987. Vice-President, Royal College of Ophthalmologists, 1996-2000. Publications: books on ophthalmology; papers. Address: (b.) Tennent Institute, Upper Ground Floor, Gartnavel Hospital, Glasgow G12 0YN; T.-0141-211 2000, Ext. 2640.

Kirkpatrick, William, BSc. Rector, Blairgowrie High School, since 1995; b. 5.8.46, Kirkcaldy; m., Jenifer; 1 s. Educ. Kirkcaldy High; University of Edinburgh. Teacher of Physics, Kirkcaldy High School; Principal Teacher of Physics: Kirkland High School, Kirkcaldy High School; Assistant Head Teacher, Auchmuty High; TVEI Co-ordinator then Senior Adviser, Fife Region; Depute Rector, Auchmuty High. Address: (b.) Beeches Road, Blairgowrie PH10 6PW; T.-01250 873445.

Kirkwood, Rt. Hon. Lord (Ian Candlish Kirkwood), PC. Senator of the College of Justice, since 1987; b. 8.6.32. Advocate, 1957; QC, 1970. Address: (b.) Court of Session, Parliament House, Edinburgh, EH1 1RQ.

Kirkwood, Archy, BSc. MP (Liberal Democrat), Roxburgh and Berwickshire, since 1983; Chairman, Work and Pensions Select Committee, since 2001; Commissioner, House of Commons; b. 22.4.46, Glasgow; m., Rosemary Chester; 1 s.; 1 d. Educ. Cranhill School; Heriot-Watt University. Solicitor, Notary Public; Aide to Sir David Steel, 1971-75, 1977-78; Liberal Spokesman on Health and Social Services, and on Social Security, 1985-87; Alliance Spokesman on Overseas Development, 1987; Liberal Scottish Whip, 1987-88; Social and Liberal Democrat Convener on Welfare, Health and Education, 1988-89; Liberal Democrat Deputy Chief Whip, and Spokesman on Welfare and Social Security, 1989-92, Community Care, 1994-97; Chief Whip, 1993-97. Chairman, Joseph Rowntree Reform Trust (Trustee, since 1985); Governor, Westminster Foundation for Democracy. Recreations: music; photography. Address: (b.) House of Commons, London SW1A 0AA; e-mail: kirkwooda@parliament.uk

Kirkwood, Susan, BSc, MSc, MBA. Chairman, National Schizophrenia Fellowship (Scotland), since 1998; President, Scottish Culture and Traditions Association, since 1997; Treasurer, European Federation of Associations of Families of Mentally Ill People, since 1998; b. 18.5.50, Edinburgh. Educ. James Gillespie's High School, Edinburgh; Edinburgh University; Durham University; INSEAD. Exploration Geophysicist, 1973-83; Business Analyst, 1985-94; Company Director, since 1994. JP. Address: (h.) 78 Cairnfield Place, Aberdeen; T.-01224 630979.

Kirwan, Frank, BA, MA. Chairman: Crystal Media Group, KAL Ltd., Stroll Ltd; Visiting Professor, University of Edinburgh; Member, Accounts Commission, since 1995; Director: Underwriter Insurance, since 1998, Ferrograph Ltd., since 1999; Member, East Lothian Children's Panel; Honorary Treasurer, Oxfam UK; b. 16.7.52, Dublin; m., Moira; 1 s.; 1 d. Educ. Colaiste Mhuire, Dublin; Trinity College, University College, Dublin. Economic and Social Research Institute, 1974-76; Strathclyde University, 1976-81; Lund University, 1981-82; Fraser of Allander Institute, 1983-84; Scottish Development Agency, 1984-88; Royal Bank of Scotland, 1988-97. Recreation: gardening. Address: (h.) Gateside House, Hill Road, Gullane EH31 2BE.

Kitchen, John Philip, MA, BMus, PhD (Cantab), FRCO, LRAM. Senior Lecturer in Music, Edinburgh University, since 1987; Concert Organist, Harpsichordist, Pianist; b. 27.10.50, Airdrie. Educ. Coatbridge High School; Glasgow University; Cambridge University. Lecturer in Music, St. Andrews University, 1976-87; Harpsichordist/Organist, Scottish Early Music Consort, 1977-98; BBC and commercial recordings; music reviewer; Organist, Old St. Paul's Episcopal Church, Edinburgh. Recreations: more

music; entertaining. Address: (b.) Faculty of Music, Alison House, 12 Nicolson Square, Edinburgh EH8 9DF; T.-0131-650 2432; e-mail: J.Kitchen@music.ed.ac.uk

Klein, Bernat, CBE, FCSD, Hon. FRIAS; b. 6.11.22, Senta, Yugoslavia; m., Margaret Soper; 1 s.; 2 d. Educ. Senta, Yugoslavia; Bezalel School of Arts and Crafts, Jerusalem; Leeds University. Designer: Tootal, Broadhurst, Lee, 1948-49, Munrospun, Edinburgh, 1949-51; Chairman and Managing Director, Colourcraft, 1952-62; Managing Director, Bernat Klein Ltd., 1962-66; Chairman and Managing Director: Bernat Klein Design Ltd., 1966-81, Bernat Klein Ltd., 1982-92. Member: Design Council, 1962-68, Royal Fine Art Commission for Scotland, 1981-87. Publications: Eye for Colour, 1965; Design Matters, 1975. Recreations: tennis; reading. Address: High Sunderland, Galashiels; T.-01750 20730.

Knight, Alanna, FSA Scot. Novelist; b. Co. Durham; m., Alistair Knight; 2 s. Educ. Jesmond High School. Writing career began, 1965; novels: Legend of the Loch, 1969 (RNA First Novel Award), The October Witch, 1971, This Outward Angel, 1971, Castle Clodha, 1972, Lament for Lost Lovers, 1972, The White Rose, 1974, A Stranger Came By, 1974, The Wicked Wynsleys, 1977; historical novels: The Passionate Kindness, 1974, A Drink for the Bridge, 1976, The Black Duchess, 1980, Castle of Foxes, 1981, Colla's Children, 1982, The Clan, 1985; Estella, 1986; detective novels: Enter Second Murderer, 1988, Blood Line, 1989, Deadly Beloved, 1989, Killing Cousins, 1990, A Quiet Death, 1991, To Kill A Queen, 1992; The Evil that Men Do, 1993, The Missing Duchess, 1994, Inspector Faro and the Edinburgh Mysteries, 1994, The Bull Slayers, 1995; Murder by Appointment, 1996; Inspector Faro's Second Casebook, 1996; The Coffin Lane Murders, 1998; The Final Enemy, 2002; crime novels: the Sweet Cheat Gone, 1992, This Outward Angel, 1994; Angel Eyes, 1997; The Royal Park Murder, 1998; The Monster in the Loch, 1998; Dead Beckoning, 1999; The Inspector's Daughter, 2000; The Dagger in the Crown, 2001; Dangerous Pursuits, 2002; plays: The Private Life of R.L.S., 1973, Girl on an Empty Swing, 1977; Inspector Faro Investigates, 2001; non-fiction: The Robert Louis Stevenson Treasury, 1985; RLS in the South Seas, 1986, Bright Ring of Words (Co-Editor), 1994; radio short stories, plays and documentaries. Recreations: walking; reading; painting. Address: (h.) 24 March Hall Crescent, Edinburgh EH16 5HL; T.-0131-667 5230.

Knops, Professor Robin John, BSc, PhD, Hon.DSc, FRSE. Emeritus Professor of Mathematics, Heriot-Watt University; b. 30.12.32, London; m., Margaret; 4 s.; 2 d. Educ. Nottingham University. Nottingham University: Assistant Lecturer in Mathematics, 1956-59, Lecturer in Mathematics, 1959-62; Newcastle-upon-Tyne University: Lecturer in Applied Mathematics, 1962-68, Reader in Continuum Mechanics, 1968-71; Professor of Mathematics, Heriot-Watt University, Edinburgh, 1971-98 (Head, Department of Mathematics, 1971-83; Dean of Science, 1984-87; Vice Principal, 1988-95; Special Adviser to the Principal, 1995-97). Visiting Professor: Cornell University, 1967 and 1968; University of California, Berkeley, 1968; Pisa University, 1974; Ecole Polytechnique Federale Lausanne, Switzerland, 1980; Royal Society of Edinburgh: Council Member, 1982-92, Executive Committee Member, 1982-92, Meetings Secretary, 1982-87, Chief Executive Editor, Proceedings A, 1982-87, Curator, 1987-92; President: Edinburgh Mathematical Society, 1974-75, International Society for the Interaction of Mechanics and Mathematics, 1991-95 (Vice-President, 1995-99); Editor, Applied Mathematics and Mathematical Computation, since 1990; Convener, Executive Committee, International Centre for Mathematical Sciences, Edinburgh, 1996-99. Publications: Uniqueness Theories in Linear Elasticity (Co-author), 1971; Theory of Elastic Stability (Co-author),

1973. Recreations: walking; reading. Address: (b.) Lord Balerno Building, Heriot-Watt University, Edinburgh EH14 4AS; T.-0131-451 3363; e-mail: r.j.knops@hw.ac.uk

Knowles, Rev. John Geoffrey, BSc (Hons), MSc, PGCE, FRSA. Rector, Hutchesons' Grammar School, Glasgow, since 1999; b. 12.6.48, Loughborough; m., Roey; 3 d. Educ. St Bees School; Manchester University; Worcester College, Oxford; London University; Queen's College, Birmingham. Assistant Physics Teacher, Mill Hill School, 1970-75; Wellington College, 1975-76; Head of Physics, Watford Grammar School, 1976-84; Vice Master, Queen Elizabeth's Grammar School, Blackburn, 1984-90; Headmaster, King Edward VI Five Ways School, Birmingham, 1990-99. Former Chairman, Association of Heads of Grant Maintained Schools; former Chief Examiner, Nuffield Physics A-Level; former Vice Chairman, The Elgar Society; ordained, Church of England, 1998. Publication: Elgar's Interpreters on Record, 1985. Recreations: music; church activities. Address: (b.) Hutchesons' Grammar School, 21 Beaton Road, Glasgow G41 4NW; T.-0141-423 2933; e-mail: rector@hutchesons.org

Knox, Col. Sir Bryce Muir, KCVO, MC (and Bar), CStJ, TD, BA (Cantab); b. 4.4.16, Edinburgh; m., Patricia Mary Dunsmuir; 1 s.; 1 d. Educ. Stowe; Trinity College, Cambridge. County of Ayr: Deputy Lieutenant, 1953, Vice Lieutenant, 1970-74, Ayrshire and Arran Lord Lieutenant, 1974-91; Chairman, W. & J. Knox Ltd., Kilbirnie, 1970-78; Vice-Chairman, Lindustries Ltd., 1979 (Director, 1953-79); served with Ayrshire (ECO) Yeomanry, 1939-45, North Africa and Italy (CO, 1953-56, Hon. Col., 1960-71); Honorary Colonel, Ayrshire Yeomanry Squadron, Queen's Own Yeomanry, 1971-77; Member, Queen's Bodyguard for Scotland (Royal Company of Archers), since 1974; President, Royal Highland Agricultural Society of Scotland, 1990-91. Publications: brief historical notes of the Ayrshire Yeomanry; History of the Eglinton Hunt. Recreation: country sports. Address: (h.) Martnaham Lodge, by Ayr KA6 6ES; T.-01292 560204.

Knox, Jack, RSA, RGI, RSW, HonFRIAS. Painter; b. 16.12.36, Kirkintilloch; m., Margaret K. Sutherland; 1 s.; 1 d. Educ. Lenzie Academy; Glasgow School of Art; André Lhôte Atelier, Paris. Lecturer in Drawing and Painting, Duncan of Jordanstone College of Art, 1965-81; Head of Painting Studios, Glasgow School of Art, 1981-92. Solo exhibitions: Scottish Gallery, Edinburgh; Richard Demarco Gallery, Edinburgh; Serpentine Gallery, London; Buckingham Gallery, London; Civic Arts Centre, Aberdeen; retrospective – Fruit Market Gallery, Edinburgh, Third Eye Centre, Glasgow, touring to Aberdeen, Inverness Dundee; Kelvingrove Art Gallery and Museum, Glasgow; Open Eye Gallery, Edinburgh; many mixed exhibitions internationally; work in numerous private and public collections. Member, Scottish Arts Council, 1974-79; Member, Trustees Committee, Scottish National Gallery of Modern Art, 1975-82; Trustee, National Galleries of Scotland, 1982-87; Secretary, Royal Scottish Academy, 1990-91; Many awards, most recently, Maude Gemmell Hutchison Prize, RSA, 1998. Books illustrated: The Scottish Bestiary, by George Mackay Brown, 1986; La Pontinière, by David and Hilary Brown. Address: 31 North Erskine Park, Bearsden, Glasgow G61 4LY; T.-0141-942 6629.

Knox, William James. Member, Council, Scottish Bowling Association, since 1995; UK Employment Spokesman, Federation of Small Businesses, 1978-81, 1996-99, and since 2001; Member, Council, ACAS, 1992-2000; b. 4.8.44, Glasgow; m., Ann May; 1 d. Educ. Greenock High School; Reid Kerr College, Paisley. Partner, A.F. McPherson & Co., Builders and Merchants, since 1962; Board Member, Scottish National Federation of Building Trade Employers, 1970-79; Member, Social Security Tribunal, 1978-84;

Director, Morton Football and Athletic Club, 1986-89; Chairman, Morton Development Club, 1986-89; Member: Executive, Scottish Constitutional Convention, 1989-90, Board of Directors, Greenock Arts Guild, since 1993, Executive, Scottish Council Development and Industry, 1995-97; Chairman: UK Federation of Small Businesses, 1989-92, Inverclyde Megawatt Festival, 1994-95; President, Rotary Club of Greenock, 1995-96; Chairman, World Bowls 2004 Organising Committee, 1999-2000. Recreations: football; bowling; photography; canals. Address: (h.) 3 Moorfield Road, Gourock PA19 1DD; T.-01475 633327; e-mail: bbillknox@aol.com

Kocovsky, Professor Pavel, PhD, DSc, FRSC. Sir William Ramsay Professor of Chemistry, University of Glasgow, since 1999; b. 7.1.51, Rychnov, Czech Republic; m., Eva Sramkova; 2 d. Educ. Technical University, Prague; Czech Academy of Sciences, Prague. Lecturer, Chemistry, Institute of Organic Chemistry and Biochemistry, Czechoslovak Academy of Sciences, Prague, 1977-91; Research Associate, Cornell University, Ithaca, NY, USA, 1983-84; Visiting Professor, University of Uppsala, Sweden, 1989-90; Reader, Organic Chemistry, University of Leicester, 1991-99. Publications: over 150 research papers in chemistry journals; Synthesis of Natural Products, 1986. Recreations: photography; travel; classical music. Address: (b.) Department of Chemistry, University of Glasgow, Glasgow, G12 8QQ; T.-0141-330 4199; e-mail: P.Kocovsky@chem.gla.ac.uk

Kubie, Professor Jorge, BSc (Eng), PhD, DSc(Eng), CEng, FIMechE. Professor of Mechanical Engineering, Napier University, Edinburgh, since 1997; Head, School of Engineering, Napier University, since 1998; b. 13.6.47, Prague; m., Amanda Jane Kubie; 1s.; 4d. Educ. Prague Tertiary College; University College London; Aston University. Research and technical posts in the electricity supply industry, 1974-90; Professor, Mechanical Engineering, Middlesex University, London, 1990-97; Member, Board of Management, Borders College, since 2000. Address: (b.) School of Engineering, Napier University, Edinburgh, EH10 5DT; T.-0131-455 2595.

Kuenssberg, Nicholas Christopher, BA (Hons) (Oxon), FCIS, FInstD, CIMgt, FRSA. Chairman: iomart Group plc, since 2000, Canmore Partnership, since 1999, GAP Group Ltd., since 1996, Stac Affinity Services plc, since 2001, The Mindwarp Pavilion Ltd., since 2001, ScotlandIS, since 2001, Scottish International Resource Programme, since 2000; Non-executive Director: Sanmex International plc, since 1998, Chamberlin and Hill plc, since 1999; Member: Scottish Legal Aid Board, since 1996, Scottish Environment Protection Agency, since 1999; b. 28.10.42, Edinburgh; m., Sally Robertson; 1 s.; 2 d. Educ. Edinburgh Academy; Wadham College, Oxford. Director, J. & P. Coats Ltd., 1978-91; Chairman, Dynacast International Ltd, 1978-91; Director, Coats Patons plc, 1985-91; Director, Coats Viyella plc, 1986-91; Managing Director, Dawson International plc, 1994-95 (Managing Director, Premier Brands, 1991-94); Non-executive Director: Bank of Scotland West of Scotland Board, 1984-88, ScottishPower plc, 1984-97, Standard Life Assurance Company, 1988-99, Baxi Partnership Ltd., 1996-99; Chairman: Stoddard International PLC, 1997-2000, David A. Hall Ltd., 1997-98, Institute of Directors, Scotland, 1997-99, Association for Management Education and Training in Scotland, 1996-98; Visiting Professor, Strathclyde Business School, 1988-91; Member, Advisory Group to Secretary of State on Sustainable Development, 1996-99; Member, British Council, Scottish Committee, since 1999; Board Member: Citizens Theatre, Glasgow, since 2000, Glasgow School of Art, since 2001. Recreations: languages; opera; travel; sport. Address: (b.) 6 Cleveden Drive, Glasgow, G12 0SE; e-mail: horizon@sol.co.uk

Kuenssberg, Sally, CBE, BA, DipAdEd, FRSA. Chairman, Scottish Children's Reporter Administration, since 1995; Chairman, Yorkhill NHS Trust, since 2001; b. 30.7.43, Edinburgh; m., Nicholas; 1 s.; 2 d. Educ. St Leonard's School; University of Oxford. Language Teaching, Europe and South America, 1966-78; Partner, Heatherbank Press, Milngavie, 1981-90; Children's Panel Training Organiser, Department of Adult and Continuing Education, University of Glasgow, 1990-95. Adult Literacy Tutor, 1979-83; Member, Children's Panel, Glasgow, 1984-90. Address: (b.) SCRA, Ochil House, Springkerse Business Park, Stirling FK7 7XE.

Kyle, David Justice. Director, Board, British Deer Society, since 1997 (Vice-Chairman, Scottish Council, Director, BDS Sales and Services, since 2000, Chairman, N.E. Scotland Branch, 1995-2001); Quality Assurance Manager, Rowett Research Institute, since 2000; b. 12.2.58, St. Andrews; m., Carol Elizabeth. Educ. Bell Baxter School, Cupar. Scientific Officer, Scottish Office Agriculture and Fisheries Department, Rowett Research Institute, Aberdeen, 1981-89; Red Deer Research Unit, Macaulay Land Use Research Organisation, Glensaugh Research Station, Kincardineshire, 1989-91; Higher Scientific Officer, International Feed Resources Unit, Rowett Research Institute, 1991-2000. Member, British Association of Research Quality Assurance; Member, Institute of Clinical Research; Churchill Fellow, 1997. Recreations: deer welfare; politics; theatre; classical music. Address: Skene Croft, Glenfarquhar, Auchinblae, Aberdeenshire AB30 1TS; T.-01561 320665; e-mail: d.j.kyle@btinternet.com

Kyle, James, CBE, DSc, MCh, FRCS. Chairman, Raigmore Hospital NHS Trust, Inverness, 1993-97; b. 26.3.25, Ballymena, Northern Ireland; m., Dorothy Elizabeth Galbraith; 2 d. Educ. Ballymena Academy; Queen's University, Belfast. Scholarship to Mayo Clinic, USA, 1950; Tutor in Surgery, Royal Victoria Hospital, Belfast, 1952; Lecturer in Surgery, Liverpool University, 1957; Senior Lecturer in Surgery, Aberdeen University, 1959-60, and Surgeon, Aberdeen Royal Infirmary, 1959-89. Member, Grampian Health Board, 1973-77, Chairman, 1989-93; Chairman, Scottish Committee for Hospital Medical Services, 1976-79; elected Member, General Medical Council, 1979-94; Chairman: Scottish Joint Consultants Committee, 1984-89, Representative Body, British Medical Association, 1984-87; President, Aberdeen Medico-Chirurgical Society, 1989-90; Examiner: Belfast, Dublin, Dundee, Edinburgh, Sydney, University of West Indies; Burgess of Aberdeen. Publications: Peptic Ulcer; Pye's Surgical Handicraft; Crohn's Disease; Scientific Foundations of Surgery. Recreations: Fellow, Royal Philatelic Society, London; licensed radio amateur, GM4 CHX. Address: (h.) 7 Fasaich, Gairloch IV21 2DB; T.-01445 712398.

Kyle, Peter McLeod, MBChB, FRCS(Edin), FRCS(Glas), FRCOphth. Consultant Ophthalmologist, Southern General Hospital NHS Trust, since 1982 (Clinical Director of Ophthalmology, since 1995); Honorary Clinical Senior Lecturer, Glasgow University, since 1985; Member, Medical Appeal Tribunals, Scotland, since 1986; Member, General Optical Council; b. 19.8.51, Rutherglen; m., Valerie Anne Steele; 1 s.; 2 d. Educ. High School of Glasgow; Glasgow University. Lecturer in Ophthalmology, Glasgow University, 1980-84. Convener, Ophthalmology Sub-committee, Royal College of Physicians and Surgeons of Glasgow; Member, Opthalmology Specialist Advisory Board, Royal College of Surgeons of Edinburgh; Deacon, Incorporation of Barbers of Glasgow, 1998-99. Recreations: walking; skiing. Address: (h.) 36 Sutherland Avenue, Glasgow; T.-0141-427 4400; The Stables, Earlsferry, Fife; T.-01333 330647.

Kynoch, George Alexander Bryson, BSc. Non-Executive Chairman: London Marine Group Ltd., Muir Matheson Ltd., Benson Group Ltd. Jetcam International Holdings Ltd., The TEP Exchange Group PLC; Non-Executive Director, Premisys Technologies PLC; MP (Conservative), Kincardine and Deeside, 1992-97; Parliamentary Under Secretary of State for Scotland – Minister for Industry and Local Government, 1995-97; b. 7.10.46, Keith; m., Dr. Rosslyn Margaret McDevitt; 1 s.; 1 d. Educ. Cargilfield School, Edinburgh; Glenalmond College, Perth; Bristol University. Plant Engineer, ICI Ltd., Nobel Division, 1968-71; G. and G. Kynoch PLC, 1971-92, latterly as Group Executive Director; Non-Executive Director: Kynoch Group PLC, Aardvark Clear Mine Ltd., 1992-95, PSL Holdings Ltd., 1998, Silvertech International plc, 1997-2000, Midmar Energy Ltd., 1998-99; Member, Aberdeen and District Milk Marketing Board, 1988-92; Director, Moray Badenoch and Strathspey Local Enterprise Co. Ltd., 1991-92; Chairman, Scottish Woollen Publicity Council, 1983-90; President, Scottish Woollen Industry, 1990-91; Vice Chairman, Northern Area, Scottish Conservative and Unionist Association, 1991-92. Recreations: golf; skiing; travel. Address: (h.) Newton of Drumduan, Dess, Aboyne, Aberdeenshire AB34 5BD.

L

Lacy, Rev. David William, BA, BD. Minister, Henderson Parish Church, Kilmarnock, since 1989; Convener, General Assembly Board of Practice and Procedure and Business Committee; Member, Judicial Commission of General Assembly; b. 26.4.52, Inverness; m., Joan Stewart Roberston; 1 s.; 1 d. Educ. Aberdeen Grammar School; High School of Glasgow; University of Strathclyde; University of Glasgow and Trinity College. Assistant Minister, St. George's West, Edinburgh, 1975-77; Minister, Knightswood: St. Margaret's, Glasgow, 1977-89. Recreations: sailing; snooker; choral singing. Address: 52 London Road, Kilmarnock, Ayrshire KA3 7AJ; T.-01563 523113.

Laidlaw, Bruce, ACIS. Administrative Secretary, Royal Scottish Academy, since 1995; b. 11.7.45, Edinburgh; m., Sandra; 1 s.; 1 d. Educ. Royal High School; Napier College, Edinburgh. Assistant Secretary, Cranston London Hotels Co. Ltd., 1963-65; public service, Edinburgh City, 1966-74; Elections Officer, Lothian Regional Council, 1975-79; public service, Lothian Regional Council, 1980-95. Chairman, MS Therapy Centre, Lothian. Recreations: fishing; skiing. Address: (b.) Royal Scottish Academy, 17 Waterloo Place, Edinburgh EH1 3BG; e-mail: info@royalscottishacademy.org

Laidlaw, Professor Emeritus James Cameron, MA, PhD. Emeritus Professor of French, Aberdeen University (Professor of French, 1975-92); Honorary Fellow, Arts Faculty, Edinburgh University; b. 3.3.37, Ecclefechan; m., Elizabeth Fernie Bosomworth; 1 s.; 2 d. Educ. George Watson's College, Edinburgh; Edinburgh University; Trinity Hall, Cambridge. Research Fellow, Trinity Hall, Cambridge, 1961-63; Lecturer in Medieval French, Queen's University, Belfast, 1963-65; University Assistant Lecturer (from 1969 University Lecturer) in French, and Fellow, Trinity Hall, Cambridge, 1965-74; Visiting Fellow, Gonville and Caius College, Cambridge, 1986-87; Visiting Professor, Victoria University of Wellington, New Zealand, 1990-91; Vice-Principal, Aberdeen University, 1984-86. Member Arts Sub-Committee, University Grants Committee, 1980-89; Adviser in Modern Languages, Universities Funding Council, 1989-91; Honorary Secretary, Modern Humanities Research Association, 1961-67; Chevalier des palmes académiques. Publications: The Future of the Modern Humanities (Editor), 1969; The Poetical Works of Alain Chartier, 1974; Alain Chartier: Poèmes, 1988; Christine de Pizan Database, 2000. Recreations: walking; cycling. Address: (h.) Orchard Walls, Traquair, Innerleithen EH44 6PU; T.-01896 831227.

Laing, Alasdair North Grant, MRICS. Director, Scottish Agricultural College, since 1995; Vice Convenor, Scottish Landowners Federation, since 2000; b. 30.12.49, Forres; m., Lucy Ann Anthea Low; 2 s.; 1 d. Educ. Belhaven Hill; Eton College; Royal Agricultural Collge, Cirencester. Recreations: skiing; fishing; stalking. Address: (b.) Logie Estate Office, Forres, Moray IV36 2QN; T.-01667 658900.

Laing, Anne Katherine, LLB, NP. Solicitor (sole practitioner, since 1999); b. 18.1.54, Galashiels. Educ. Grangemouth High School; University of Dundee. Peter Young, Bo'ness: Apprenticeship, Partner, 1980, took over business in 1983, sole practitioner until 1990; Senior Partner, P.H. Young & Co., Solicitors, 1990-99; Honorary Sheriff, Tayside Central and Fife; former Director (Past President), Central Scotland Chamber of Commerce; Board Member, Scottish Enterprise Forth Valley, 1993-2000; Director, Careers Central Limited, since 1995 (Chair, since 1997). Recreations: gym; gardening; travel; food and wine. Address: (b.) 54 South Street, Bo'ness EH51 826166; e-mail: anne@phyoung.co.uk

Laing, David Kemlo, LLB. Senior Partner, Ledingham Chalmers, since 1996; b. 17.6.53, Aberdeen; m., Marina Maclean; 2 d. Educ. Robert Gordon's College, Aberdeen; University of Edinburgh. Clark and Wallace, Aberdeen, 1974-76; C. & P. H. Chalmers, Aberdeen, 1976-78, Partner, 1978-90; Partner, Ledingham Chalmers, 1991. Recreations: music; outdoors; local church. Address: (b.) 5 Melville Crescent, Edinburgh EH3 7JA; T.-0131-200 1032.

Laing, Gerald (Ogilvie-Laing of Kinkell, Gerald), NDD, FRBS. Sculptor; b. 11.2.36; 4 s.; 1 d. Educ. Berkhamsted School; RMA, Sandhurst. Commissioned Fifth Fusiliers, 1955-60; resigned commission and attended St. Martin's School of Art, 1960-64; lived in New York, 1964-69; Artist in Residence, Aspen Institute for Humanistic Studies, Colorado, 1966; moved to north of Scotland, 1969, and restored ruins of Kinkell Castle; Civic Trust Award, 1971; established a tapestry workshop in north of Scotland; Visiting Professor, University of New Mexico, 1976-77; set up bronze foundry, Kinkell Castle, to produce own work; Member, Art Committee, Scottish Arts Council, 1978-80; Professor of Sculpture, Columbia University, New York, 1986-87; Commissioner, Royal Fine Art Commission for Scotland, 1987-95; public sculpture includes Callanish, Strathclyde University, 1971; Frieze of the Wise and Foolish Virgins, Edinburgh, 1980; Fountain of Sabrina, Bristol, 1982; Conan Doyle Memorial, 1991, Edinburgh; Axis Mundi, 1991; Bank Underground Station Dragons, London, 1995; St. George and Dragon Series, Harrow, 1996; Four Rugby Players, Twickenham, 1996; portrait bust, Sir Paul Getty, National Gallery, London, 1997; Cricketer, Wormsley Cricket Ground, Bucks, 1999; Glass Wise and Foolish Virgins, Edinburgh, 1999; The Batsman, MCC, Lord's Ground, London. Address: (h.) Kinkell Castle, Dingwall IV7 8AT; T.-01349 861485; e-mail: kinkell@btinternet.com

Laing, The Hon. Mark Hector, MA. Managing Director, Simmers of Edinburgh, since 1996; Director, Scottish Business in the Community; Director, Tomorrow's Company in Scotland; Chairman, Friends of Craigmillar; b. 22.2.51, London; m., Susanna Crawford; 1 s.; 2 d. Educ. Eton College; Cambridge University. United Biscuits p.l.c., 1972-96: Factory Director, Glasgow, 1985; Production Director, McVities, 1988; Managing Director, Simmers Biscuits, 1990. Recreations: walking; gardening; fishing; shooting. Address: (b.) Simmers of Edinburgh Ltd., 90 Peffermill Road, Edinburgh EH16 5UU; T.-0131-620 7000.

Laird, Gordon, BA. Artistic Director, 7:84 Theatre Company Scotland, since 2000; b. 4.4.76, Peebles. Educ. Peebles High School; Royal Scottish Academy of Music and Drama. Assistant Director, 7:84, 1998-2000. Recreations: music; theatre; film; sport (fitness). Address: (b.) 333 Woodlands Road, Glasgow, G3 6NG; T.-0141-334 6686.

Lally, Patrick James, JP, DL, LLD, KLJ, HRGI, FRSA. Rt. Hon. Lord Provost of the City of Glasgow and Lord Lieutenant, City of Glasgow, 1996-1999; Deputy Lieutenant, Glasgow; Commandeur, Ordre National du Merite (France); Chairman, Greater Glasgow and Clyde Valley Tourist Board, 1996-99; Director, Glasgow Cultural Enterprises, 1998-99; b. Glasgow; m., Margaret Beckett McGuire; 2 s. Elected, Corporation of Glasgow, 1966-75 (Deputy Leader, 1972-75); elected City of Glasgow Council, 1975-77, and 1980-96; City Treasurer, 1984-86; Leader, City of Glasgow District Council, 1986-92 and 1994-96; Chairman, Greater Glasgow Tourist Board, 1989-96; Director, Glasgow International Jazz Festival; Hon. Director, Chinese Peoples Association for Friendship with Foreign Countries; Hon. Member, Royal Glasgow Institute of Fine Arts; Hon. Member, Rotary International; Hon. Citizen, Dalian, China; Hon. Member, Royal Faculty of Procurators in Glasgow; Knight, Order of St. Lazarus; Member, Merchants House of Glasgow; Member, Incorporation of Tailors, Glasgow; Member, Incorporation of Gardeners, Glasgow; awarded Scottish Tourist Board Silver Thistle Award, 1999. Recreations: enjoying the arts; reading; watching TV; football. Address: 2 Tamera Avenue, Glasgow G44 5BU.

Lamb, Professor Joseph Fairweather, MB, ChB, BSc, PhD, FRCPEdin, FRSE. Emeritus Professor; Chandos Professor of Physiology, St. Andrews University, 1969-93; Chairman, Save British Science Society, 1986-97; b. 18.7.28, Brechin; m., 1, Olivia Jane Horne; 3 s.; 1 d.; 2, Bridget Cecilia Cook; 2 s. Educ. Brechin High School; Edinburgh University. National Service, 1947-49; House Surgeon, Dumfries Royal Infirmary, 1955-56; House Physician, Eastern General Hospital, Edinburgh, 1956; Research Scholar, then Lecturer, Edinburgh University, 1957-61; Lecturer, then Senior Lecturer, Glasgow University, 1961-69; Editor, Journal of Physiology, 1968-74; Senior Secretary, Physiological Society, 1982-85; Chairman, Gas Greed campaign, 1994-95; Governor, Rowett Research Institute, since 1998; Chairman and Founder, Save British Science, 1986-97; Member, Appeals Panels, DHSS, 1995-2001. Publication: Essentials of Physiology, 1980. Recreations: boat-building; sailing; amateur radio. Address: (h.) Kenbrae, 23 Millbank, Cupar KY15 5DP.

Lambert, Roderick Stewart, LLB (Hons), LLM (Cantab), DipLP. Partner, Eversheds Litigation, since 2000 (Joint Head of Antitrust Litigation, since 2001); Advocate, Scottish Bar, since 1991; b. 17.8.65, St. Andrews; m., Elaine; 1 d. Educ. Madras College, St. Andrews; University of Edinburgh; Trinity Hall, Cambridge. Called to Bar, 1991; admitted as Barrister and Solicitor, High Court of New Zealand, 1995; admitted as Solicitor, England and Wales, 2000; Legal 500 expert in contentious competition law; occasional lecturer, Edinburgh University, Liverpool University, Wellington University. Recreations: climbing; viticulture. Address: (h.) Oak Farm, Wistow, Selby YO8 3UW; Ardormie, Dalrigh, Tyndrum, Perthshire; T.-0113 200 4585; e-mail: rodlambert@eversheds.com

Lambie, David, BSc (Hons), DipEd, FEIS. Chairman, Development Committee and Member, Management Committee, Cunninghame Housing Association, since 1992; Member, Board, Galloway Training Association Ltd., since 1997; MP (Labour), Cunninghame South, 1970-92; b. 13.7.25, Saltcoats; m., Netta Merrie; 1 s.; 4 d. Educ. Ardrossan Academy; Glasgow University; Geneva University. Teacher, Glagow Corporation, 1950-70. Secretary, All Party Committee for Energy Studies, 1980-92; chaired Select Committee on Scottish Affairs, 1981-87; UK Member, Council of Europe and Western European Union, 1987-92; Chairman, PLP Aviation Committee, 1988-92; Chairman, Saltcoats Labour Party, 1992-96. Recreation: watching junior football. Address: (h.) 11 Ivanhoe Drive, Saltcoats, Ayrshire KA21 6LS; T.-01294 464843.

Lamond, June Rose. Convenor, Community Services, Aberdeen City Council, since 2000; b. 6.12.33, Aberdeen; m., James Alexander Lamond; 3 d. Educ. Demonstration School; Commercial College. Regional and City Councillor, 27 years; Chairperson Aberdeen Women's Aid, 1976-86; Member, Grampian Health Board, 1975-87; Committee Member, Grampian Society for the Blind, since 1998; Committee, Voluntary Services, since 2000. Recreations: walking; travelling; reading. Address: (b.) Aberdeen City Council, Town House, Broad Street, Aberdeen.

Lamont, Johann, MA (Hons). MSP (Labour), Glasgow Pollok, since 1999; Convener, Social Justice Committee (former Deputy Convener, Local Government Committee); b. 1957, Glasgow; m.; 1 s.; 1 d. Educ. Woodside Secondary School; Glasgow University; Jordanhill College of Education; Strathclyde University. Former teacher. Address: (b.) Scottish Parliament, Edinburgh EH99 1SP; T.-0131-348 5846.

Lamont, Rev. Stewart Jackson, BSc, BD. Minister, Church of Scotland, since 1972; Freelance Journalist and Broadcaster, since 1980; Columnist, The Scotsman, since 2001; b. 8.1.47, Broughty Ferry; m., Larisa V. Gaidakova. Educ. Grove Academy, Broughty Ferry; St. Andrews University. General Council Assessor, St. Andrews University Court, 1970-82; Producer, BBC Religious Department, 1972-80; Freelance Radio and Television Presenter and Producer, 1980-91; part-time Minister, Abernyte, 1980-82; Parish Minister, Kinning Park, Glasgow, 1991-99; Executive Secretary (Brussels), Conference of European Churches, 1999-2002; Columnist, The Herald, 1981-2001. Publications: The Third Angle, 1978; Is Anybody There?, 1980; Religion and the Supernatural (Co-Author), 1985; Religion Inc. (Scientology), 1986; Scotland 2000 (BBC TV, 1987; Church and State, 1989; In Good Faith, 1989; The Swordbearer: John Knox, 1991; Glasgow Herald Book of Glasgow (Contributor); St. Andrews Rock, 1993; Life of St. Andrew, 1997. Winner, Scottish Schools Debating Competition, 1965; President of the Union, St. Andrews, 1969. Recreations: cooking; music; foreign travel. Address: La Poujade, 82160 Caylus, France.

Lamont, William David Dawson, CA, IRRV. Head of Revenues, Finance Service, The Highland Council, since 1996; b. 14.11.49, Irvine; m., Eleanor; 1 s.; 1 d. Educ. Irvine Royal Academy; Institute of Chartered Accountants of Scotland (Glasgow University). Alexander Sloan & Company, Glasgow, 1966-73; Depute Burgh Chamberlain, Royal Burgh of Irvine, 1973-75; Depute Director of Finance, Argyll & Bute District Council, 1975-90; Director of Finance, Argyll & Bute District Council, 1990-96. Recreations: family; travel; music; Rotary. Address: (b.) The Highland Council, Glenurquhart Road, Inverness IV3 5NX; T.-01463 702404.

Lamont-Brown, Raymond, JP, MA, AMIET, MJS, FSA (Scot). Author and Broadcaster; Lecturer, Centre for External Services, St. Andrews University, 1978-98, Centre for Continuing Education, Dundee University, 1988-98; Founder, Japan Research Projects, since 1965; b. 20.9.39, Horsforth, Leeds; m., Dr. Elizabeth Moira McGregor. Educ. Wheelwright Grammar School, Dewsbury; Bradford Technical College; SOAS; Nihon Daigaku, Japan. Honorary Secretary/Treasurer, Society of Authors in Scotland, 1982-89; Past President, St. Andrews Rotary Club; Vice-Chairman, St. Andrews Community Council, 1988-91; Chairman, Arthritis Care Liaison Committee (Central, Fife and Tayside), 1991-97; Member, Council, Arthritis Care, 1991-97. Publications: 50 published books, including Discovering Fife; Phantoms of the Sea; The Life and Times of Berwick-upon-Tweed; The Life and Times of St. Andrews; Royal Murder Mysteries; Scottish Epitaphs; Scottish Superstitions; Scottish Traditions and Festivals; Famous Scots; Scottish Witchcraft; Around St. Andrews; Scottish Folklore; Kamikaze: Japan's Suicide Samurai; Scotland of 100 Years Ago; Kempeitai: Japan's Dreaded Military Police; Edward VII's Last Loves; Tutor to the Dragon Emperor; John Brown; Royal Poxes and Potions. Address: (h.) 11 Seabourne Gardens, Broughty Ferry, Dundee DD5 2RT; T.-01382 732032.

Landale, Sir David William Neil, KCVO, DL. Convenor, Crichton Foundation, since 2001; b. 27.5.34, London; m., (Norah) Melanie Roper; 3 s. Educ. Eton College; Balliol College, Oxford (MA). Black Watch, Royal Highland

Regiment, 1952-54; Jardine Matheson & Co. Ltd., 1958-75, served in Hong Kong, Thailand, Taiwan and Japan (Director, 1967-75); Director, Matheson & Co. Ltd., 1975-86; Secretary and Keeper of the Records, Duchy of Cornwall, 1987-93; Director, Duchy Originals, 1989-94; Chairman, Timber Growers, 1983-86; Chairman for Scotland, Malcolm Sargent Fund, 1996-99; Member, Royal Company of Archers, Queen's Bodyguard for Scotland, since 1966; DUniv (Paisley). Recreations: all countryside pursuits; theatre; reading (history). Address: (h.) Dalswinton, Dumfries; T.-01387 740 208/279.

Lander, Ronald, OBE, BSc, Comp. IEE, FScotvec, FSQA. Chairman and Managing Director: Scotlander plc, since 1985, Scetlander Ltd., since 1986; Director: Picardy Media Group Plc, since 1998, Logical Innovations Ltd., since 2001, Pyramid Research and Development Ltd., since 2000, Young Enterprise Scotland, 1998-2001; b. 5.8.42, Glasgow; m., Elizabeth Stirling; 2 s. Educ. Allan Glen's School; Glasgow University. Chairman and Managing Director, Lander Grayburn & Co. Limited, 1970-83; Deputy Managing Director, Lander Alarm Company (Scotland) Limited, 1975-79; Managing Director, Lander Alarms Limited and Lander Alarms (Scotland) Limited, 1979-85; Chairman, Lander & Jess Limited, 1983-87; Director, Centre for Entrepreneurial Development, Glasgow University, 1985-88; Chairman, Newstel Information Ltd., 1998-99; Member, CBI Scottish Council, 1977-83, 1984-90 and since 1992; (founding) Chairman, CBI Scotland's Smaller Firms' Working Group, 1977-80; founding Chairman, Entrepreneurial Exchange, 1995-96; founder Member, CBI Industrial Policy Committee, London, 1978-86; Chairman, CBI Scotland Smaller Firms' Committee, 1993-95; Chairman, Scottish Fire Prevention Council, 1979-80; Member, Glasgow University Appointments Committee, since 1979; CBI Representative, Home Office/CBI/TUC Joint Committee on Prison Industries, 1980-87; Industrial Member, Understanding British Industry, Scotland, 1981-89; Member, Council, Scottish Business School, 1982-87; Director, British Security Industry Association Council, 1984-85; Governor, Scottish Sports Aid Foundation, 1985-88; Vice-Chairman, CBI Scotland Education and Training Committee, 1986-87; Member: Kincraig Committee (review of parole system and related matters), 1987-89, Manpower Services Committee for Scotland (later the Training Agency), 1987-88; founder Chairman, Local Employer Network (LENS) Scottish Co-ordinating Committee, 1987; Chairman, CBI Scotland Education and Training Committee, 1987-89; Director, SCOTVEC, 1987-93; Member, CBI Business/Education Task Force (the Cadbury Report), 1988; Member, Scottish Consultative Council on the Curriculum, 1988-91; Vice-Convener, Scottish Education/Industry Committee, 1988-91; founder Member, Glasgow Action, 1985; Member, Secretary of State for Scotland's Crime Prevention Committee, 1984-87; Companion IEE, 1986; Board Member, Glasgow Development Agency, 1991-99; Visiting/Honorary Professor, Glasgow University, since 1991; National Judge, National Training Awards, 1989-92; Board Member, Glasgow Science Centre, since 1999. Address: (b.) Scotlander plc, PO Box 9219, Kilmacolm PA13 4YL; T.-01505 874480.

Landsburgh, David Scott, MA. Chief Executive, Scottish Grocers Federation, since 2000; b. 19.11.55, Dundee; m., Jacqui; 2 s. Educ. High School of Dundee; Dundee University. Assistant Hospital Director: Harley Street Clinic, London 1979-83, Ross Hall Hospital, Glasgow, 1983-84; Director, Landsburgh Brothers Ltd., Dundee, 1984-93; Managing Director, DS Landsburgh Retailing Ltd., 1993-2000. President, Dundee High School Old Boys Club, 2000-01; Past President, Scottish Grocers Federation, 1994-96. Recreations: golf; wine; reading; skiing. Address: (b.) 222-224 Queensferry Road, Edinburgh EH4 2BN; T.-0131-343 3300; e-mail: dslandsburgh@hotmail.com

Lane, Professor David Michael, BSc, PhD, CEng, MIEE, MIEEE. Professor of Ocean and Systems Engineering, Heriot-Watt University, since 1998; b. 7.6.58, Isle of Man; m., Elaine Girvan Lane; 1s. Educ. Kingswood School, Bath; Heriot-Watt University. Technician, Ferranti Plc, 1977; diver/maintainer British Oceanics Ltd., 1979; Development Engineer, Ferranti Plc, 1980; Heriot-Watt University: Research Associate, 1983; Lecturer, 1986; Senior Lecturer, 1994; Director, Oceans Systems Laboratory; Visiting Professor, Florida Atlantic University, USA, since 1999; Co-founder, See-Byte Ltd, since 1999; EPSRC Peer Review College Member; EU Framework V Reviewer; Co-founder: Society for Underwater Technology (SUT) Underwater Robotics Group; Chairman, SUT Unmanned Underwater Vehicle Showcase, 2000; Associate Editor, International Journal of Systems Science; Former RAF Voluntary Reserve; Former Directing Staff, Operation Raleigh International Expedition. Recreations: family; fitness; swimming; UK private pilot's licence; British sub-aqua club advanced instructor. Address: (b.) Ocean Systems Laboratory, Department of Computing and Electrical Engineering, Heriot-Watt University, Edinburgh, EH14 4AS; T.-0131-451 3350; e-mail: dml@cee.hw.ac.uk

Lane, Professor Sir David Philip, BSc, PhD, FRS, FRSE, FRCPath, FRCS(Edin.), FMedSci. Professor of Molecular Oncology, Department of Surgery and Molecular Oncology, Dundee University, since 2000; Director, Cancer Research Campaign Cell Transformation Group, since 1990; Gibb Fellow, Cancer Research Campaign, since 1990; Founder and Chief Scientific Officer, Cyclacel Ltd., since 1996; b. 1.7.52, London; m., Professor Ellen Birgitte Lane (qv); 1 s.; 1 d. Educ. John Fisher School, Purley; University College, London. Lecturer in Zoology, then Lecturer in Biochemistry, Imperial College, London; Principal Scientist, Imperial Cancer Research Fund, South Mimms. Publications: (book) Antibodies, a laboratory manual; 230 articles. Recreations: walking; tennis; motor bikes. Address: (b.) University of Dundee, Department of Surgery and Molecular Oncology, Ninewells Hospital and Medical School, Dundee DD1 9SY; T.-01382 496362.

Lane, Professor Ellen Birgitte, BSc, PhD, FRSE, FMedSci. Cox Professor of Anatomy and Cell Biology, Dundee University, since 1991; Director, Cancer Research Campaign Cell Structure Research Group, since 1990; b. 24.12.50, Welwyn Garden City; m., David Philip Lane (qv); 1 s.; 1 d. Educ. Withington Girls' School, Manchester; University College, London. Imperial College of Science and Technology, 1975-77, University College, 1977-78, Cold Spring Harbor Laboratories, New York, 1978-80; Imperial Cancer Research Fund, 1980-90; ICRF Clare Hall Laboratories, 1985-90. Publications: scientific papers in cell biology and cancer research. Address: (b.) CRC Laboratories, School of Life Sciences, MSI/WTB Complex, Dundee University, Dundee DD1 5EH; T.-01382 344883; e-mail: e.b.lane@dundee.ac.uk

Lang of Monkton, Baron (Ian Bruce Lang), DL, PC, OStJ, BA. President of the Board of Trade, 1995-97; Life Peer; Deputy Lieutenant, Ayrshire and Arran, since 1998; Company Directorships including: Marsh & McLennan Inc., Murray tmt plc, Second Scottish National Trust plc, BFS US Special Opportunities Trust plc, Lithgows Ltd.; Chairman, Patrons of the National Galleries of Scotland, since 1999; b. 27.6.40, Glasgow; m., Sandra Caroline Montgomerie; 2 d. Educ. Lathallan School; Rugby School; Sidney Sussex College, Cambridge. MP (Conservative) Galloway and Upper Nithsdale, 1983-97 (Galloway, 1979-83); Member, Select Committee on Scottish Affairs, 1979-81; Trustee, Glasgow Savings Bank and West of Scotland TSB, 1969-82; Lord Commissioner of HM Treasury, 1983-86; Scottish Whip, 1981-83; Vice-Chairman, Scottish Conservative Party, 1983-87; Parliamentary Under Secretary of State, Scottish Office, 1986-87, and at

Department of Employment, 1986; Minister of State, Scottish Office, 1987-90; Secretary of State for Scotland, 1990-95. Member, Queen's Bodyguard for Scotland (Royal Company of Archers), since 1974; Governor, Rugby School, since 1997; President, Association for the Protection of Rural Scotland, 1998-2001; President, St. Columba's School, Kilmacolm, since 1999. Address (b.) House of Lords, Westminster, London SW1A OPW.

Lang, Professor Bernhard, Drtheol, Drtheol.habil, Eleve titulaire de l'Ecole biblique. Professor of Old Testament and Religious Studies, St Andrews University, since 1999; Editorial Director, International Review of Biblical Studies, since 1980; b. 12.7.46, Stuttgart. Educ. University of Tuebingen, Germany; Ecole biblique, Jerusalem; London School of Economics. Professor of Ancient Judaism, Tuebingen, 1977-82; Professor of Old Testament, Mainz, 1982-85; Professor of Religion, Paderborn, since 1985. Publications include: Heaven, A History, 1988; Sacred Games: A History of Christian Worship, 1997; The Hebrew God, 2002. Recreations: reading; book collecting. Address: (b.) St Mary's College, St Andrews KY16 9JU; e-mail: alang1@hrz.uni-paderborn.de

Lang, Dr Brian Andrew, MA. PhD. Principal and Vice-Chancellor, St Andrews University, since 2001; b. 2.12.45; 2 s.; 1 d. Educ. Royal High School, Edinburgh; Edinburgh University. Social anthropology research, Kenya, 1969-70; Lecturer, Social Anthropology, Aarhus University, 1971-75; Scientific Staff, SSRC, 1976-79; Historic Buildings Council for Scotland, 1979-80; National Heritage Memorial Fund, 1980-87; Director, Public Affairs, National Trust, 1987-91; Chief Executive and Deputy Chairman, British Library, 1991-2000; Chairman, European National Libraries Forum, 1993-2000; Member: Library and Information Services Council (England), 1991-94; Library and Information Commission, 1995-2000; Visiting Professor, Napier University, Edinburgh, since 1999; Visiting Scholar, Getty Institute, Los Angeles, California, 2000; Pforzheimer Lecture, University of Texas, 1998; Trustee: 21st Century Learning Initiative, 1995-99, Hopetoun House Preservation Trust, since 2001; President, Institute of Information Scientists, 1993-94 (Hon. Fellow, 1994); Hon. FLA, 1997. Publications: numerous articles and contributions to professional journals. Recreations: music; museums and galleries; tennis. Address: (b.) Office of the Principal, College Gate, St Andrews University, North Street, St Andrews, Fife, KY16 9AJ; T.-01334 462545.

Lang, Professor Margaret Frances, MA, PhD, M-ès-L, DipAppLing, Chevalier dans L'Ordre des Palmes Académiques. Professor, Head of Languages, Heriot-Watt University, since 1998; b. 24.1.40, Aberdeen; m., Dr Andrew Lang. Educ. High School for Girls, Aberdeen; Aberdeen University; Rennes University; Edinburgh University. Lecturer, Heriot-Watt University, 1971-87; Senior Lecturer, 1987-97; Reader in French, 1997-98; academic career interspersed with frequent consultancy work abroad, until 1997. Publications: numerous books and articles on French language and interpreting. Recreations: writing; travel. Address: (b.) School of Languages, Heriot-Watt University, Riccarton, Edinburgh, EH14 4AS; T.-0131-449 5111.

Lang, Stephen, MBChB, FRCPath. Consultant Histopathologist, Ninewells Hospital, Dundee, since 1990; Honorary Senior Lecturer in Histopathology, University of Dundee, since 1990; b. 19.9.58, Glasgow; separated; 2 s.; 1 d. Educ. Holy Cross High School, Hamilton; Glasgow University. RAF Medical Officer, 1982-87 (RAF Leuchars, 1982-83, RAF Halton, 1983-87); Lecturer/Honorary Senior Registrar in Histopathology, St. Bartholomew's Hospital and The Hospital for Sick Children, Great Ormond Street, London, 1987-90. Recreations: football; golf; cinema;

theatre. Address: 56 Wyvis Road, Broughty Ferry, Dundee DD5 3SU; T.-01382 800886; e-mail: stephen.lang@tuht.scot.nhs.uk

Langford, Professor David Anthony, FCIOB, MSc, MPhil, MIMgt, FRSA. Barr Professor of Construction, Strathclyde University, since 1991; b. 6.5.50, Notingham; m., Victoria; 1 d. Educ. Barstable School, Basildon; Bristol Polytechnic; Aston University; Cranfield School of Management. MSc Course Director, Department of Building Technology, Brunel University, 1975; Director of Postgraduate Studies, Bath University, 1987. Address: (b.) Department of Civil Engineering, Strathclyde University, Glasgow G4 0NG; T.-0141-552 4400.

Langlands, Sir (Robert) Alan, KT, BSc, MIHM, DUniv(Glas), FRCP, FRCS(Edin), Hon.FRCGP, FFPHM, FIA, FCGI, CIMgt. Principal and Vice-Chancellor, Dundee University, since 2000; b. 29.5.52; m., Elizabeth McDonald; 1s.; 1d. Educ. Allan Glen's School; Glasgow University. Graduate Trainee, NHS Scotland, 1974- 76; Argyll and Clyde Health Board, 1976-78; Simpson Memorial Maternity Pavilion, Elsie Inglis Hospital, 1978-81; Unit Administrator, Middlesex and University College Hospitals and Hospital for Women, Soho, 1981-85; District General Manager, Harrow Health Authority, 1985-89; Practice Leader, Health Care, Towers Perrin, 1989-91; General Manager, NW Thames Regional Health Authority, 1991-92; Deputy Chief Executive, 1993-94, Chief Executive, 1994 - 2000, NHS Executive; Member: Central R&D Committee, NHS, 1991-92; National Forum R&D, 1994-99; Health Sector Group BTI, 1998-2000; Hon. Professor, 1996-2001; Board Member, Warwick University Business School, 1999-2000; Member: Council and Court York University, 1998-2000, External Advisory Board, RCP, National Board for Bioethics, Institute, Johns Hopkins University, Advisory Board (Health), INSEAD. Recreations: living and walking in Scotland and Yorkshire. Address: (b.) Dundee University, DD1 4HN.

Langley, Crawford James, LLB (Hons), DPA, ACIS, NP. Director of Legal and Corporate Services, Aberdeen City Council, since 1995; Advocate in Aberdeen; b. 21.11.51, Glasgow; m., Janette Law Hamilton (deceased). Educ. Bellahouston Academy, Glasgow; Glasgow University. Legal apprentice, Corporation of Glasgow, 1973-75; various legal posts, Strathclyde Regional Council, 1975-89, Principal Solicitor, 1984-89; Depute Director of Law and Administration, Tayside Regional Council, 1989-91; Director of Law and Administration, Tayside Regional Council, 1991-95. Assistant Area Commissioner, Scout Association. Recreations: travel; gardening. Address: (h.) Canouan, Eassie, Angus DD8 1SG.

Langton, Professor Rae, BA (Hons), PhD. Professor of Moral Philosophy, Edinburgh University, since 1999; b. 14.2.61, Ludhiana, India; m., Dr Richard Holton. Educ. Hebron School, India; Sydney University; Princeton University. Lecturer/Senior Lecturer, Monash University, Melbourne, 1990-98; Lecturer, Sheffield University, 1998-99. Publications: numerous articles in moral and political philosophy; history of philosophy, and feminist philosophy; Kantian Humility, 1998. Address: (b.) Department of Philosophy, Edinburgh University, George Square, Edinburgh, EH8 9JX.

Larkin, Professor Maurice John Milner, MA, PhD. Professor of Modern European History, Edinburgh University, 1976-99, Emeritus Professor, since 1999; b. 12.8.32, Harrow on the Hill; m., Enid Thelma Lowe; 1 s.; 1 d. Educ. St. Philip's Grammar School, Birmingham; Trinity College, Cambridge. Assistant Lecturer, then Lecturer, Glasgow University, 1958-65; Lecturer, then Senior Lecturer, then Reader, Kent University, 1965-76.

Publications: Gathering Pace: Continental Europe 1870-1945, 1969; Church and State after the Dreyfus Affair, 1974; Man and Society in Nineteenth-Century Realism, 1977; France since the Popular Front, 1988; Religion, politics and preferment in France since 1890, 1995. Recreations: bird-watching; music; films. Address: (h.) 5 St. Baldred's Crescent, North Berwick, East Lothian EH39 4PZ; T.-01620 892777.

Last, Professor Frederick Thomas, OBE, DSc, ARCS, SHM, VMM, FRSE. Applied Biologist; Honorary Professor, Institute of Ecology and Resource Management, Edinburgh University, since 1972; Vice Chairman, Scottish Wildlife Trust, since 1995; President, Royal Caledonian Horticultural Society, since 1999; Chairman, Gardening Scotland, since 1999; b. 5.2.28, Wembley; m., Pauline Mary Cope; 2 s. Educ. Haberdashers' Aske's Hampstead School; Imperial College of Science and Technology, London. Rothamsted Experimental Station, Herts, 1950-61; Chief Plant Pathologist to Government of Sudan, 1956-58; Head, Mycology and Bacteriology, Glasshouse Crops Research Institute, Sussex, 1961-69; Visiting Professor, Pennsylvania State University, 1969-70; Member of Directorate, Institute of Terrestrial Ecology, Midlothian, 1970-86; President, Association of Applied Biologists, 1977-78; Commissioner, Red Deer Commission, 1981-86; Visiting Professor, Agriculture and Environmental Science, Newcastle upon Tyne University, 1986-94; Chairman, Advisory Committee on Sites of Special Scientific Interest, 1992-96; Trustee, Tree Advice Trust, since 1993 (Founder Chairman, 1993-98); Advisor, Chongqing Institute of Environmental Science, since 1993; Hon. Programme Convener, Royal Society of Edinburgh, 1993-98; Founder President, Dunbar's John Muir Association, 1994-97 (Patron, since 1999); Board Member, Scottish Natural Heritage, 1996-99 (Member, Scientific Advisory Committee, since 1996); Member, Joint Nature Conservation Committee, 1996-99. Publications: Tree Physiology and Yield Improvement (Joint Editor), 1976; Land and its Uses, Actual and Potential: An Environmental Appraisal (Joint Editor), 1986; Acidic Deposition, Its Nature and Impacts (Joint Editor), 1991; Tree Crop Ecosystems, 2001. Recreations: gardening; philately; travelling. Address: (h.) Furuly, Seton Mains, Longniddry, East Lothian EH32 0PG; T.-01875 852102.

Lathe, Professor Richard Frank, BSc, Dr. ès Sci. Professorial Fellow, Edinburgh University, since 1989; b. 23.4.52, London; Educ. Edinburgh University; Universite Libre de Bruxelles. Assistant Scientific Director, Transgene SA, Strasbourg; Principal Scientific Officer, ABRO, Edinburgh; Professor of Genetics/Genetic Engineering, University of Strasbourg; Director/Scientific Director, Ecole Superieure de Biotechnologie de Strasbourg. Publications: more than 100 scientific papers. Recreations: guitar; squash. Address: (b.) King's Buildings, West Mains Road, Edinburgh EH9 3JQ; T.-0131-650 5890.

Latimer, Ian James, MA. Chief Constable, Northern Constabulary, since 2001; b. 19.3.56, Carlisle; m., Margaret; 3 c. Educ. Carlisle Grammar School; Manchester University; Fitzwilliam College, Cambridge University. Joined Merseyside Police, 1981; appointed Assistant Chief Constable, Devon and Cornwall Constabulary, 1999. Address: (b.) Police Headquarters, Inverness IV2 3SY; T.-01463 715555.

Lauderdale, 17th Earl of (Patrick Francis Maitland), BA (Hons) (Oxon). Former Elf oil company Director; b. 17.3.11, Walsall; m., Stanka Lozanitch; 2 s.; 2 d. Educ. Lancing College; Brasenose College, Oxford. Journalist, Fleet Street, 1934-39; War Correspondent, Poland, 1939; Balkans/Danubian Correspondent, The Times, 1939-41; War Correspondent, with US Forces in the Pacific, News Chronicle, 1941-43; Foreign Office, 1943-45; Editor, The Fleet Street Letter Service, 1939-51; MP (Conservative),

Lanark, 1951-59; Peer, 1968-99 ("culled with other hereditary peers"); Chairman, Sub Committee B, Lords EEC Scrutiny Committee, 1974-79; Founder, Parliamentary Group for Energy Studies, since 1983; Guardian, Shrine of Our Lady of Walsingham, since 1955 (now Emeritus); Chairman, Parliamentary 'Church in Danger' Group, 1988-95; Hereditary Bearer of the National Flag of Scotland. Recreations: reading; travel; pilgrimages to St. Mary's, Haddington.

Laughlin, Patrick D., MA (Hons). Chief Executive, Kingdom of Fife Tourist Board, since 1998; b. 23.4.61, Edinburgh; m., Alison; 1 d. Educ. Perth High School; University of Edinburgh. Tourist Officer, Crieff and District Tourist Association, 1983-86; Depute Director, Perthshire Tourist Board, 1986-97. Chairman, Scottish Association of Tourist Officers, 1997-2000. Recreations: road running; travel. Address: (b.) Haig House, Balgonie Road, Markinch KY7 6AQ; T.-01592 750066.

Laurenson, James Tait, FCA. Chairman, Hopetoun House Preservation Trust; Non-Executive Director: I & S UK Smaller Companies Trust plc, since 1983, Hiscox Investment Management Ltd., since 1995, Frizzell Bank, Ltd., since 1996, Fidelity Special Values plc, since 1994; Chairman, Govett European Enhanced Investment Trust plc, since 1999; b. 15.3.41, Farnborough; m., Hilary Josephine; 1 s.; 3 d. Educ. Eton College; Magdalene College, Cambridge. Ivory & Sime PLC: joined 1968; Partner, 1970; Director, 1975; left 1983; Managing Director, Tayburn Design Group Limited, 1983-84 (Chairman, 1984-88); Managing Director, Adam & Company Group plc, 1984-93. Recreations: spending time with the family; gardening. Address: (h.) Hill House, Kirknewton, Midlothian EH27 8DR; T.-01506 881990.

Laurie, Thomas, OBE, FRICS. Senior Partner, Laurie Consultancy Group; Chairman, St. Andrews in the Square Trust; Trustee, Scottish Civic Trust; b. 11.11.38, Wishaw; m., Jennifer Rose Dunthorne; 1 s.; 2 d. Educ. Hamilton Academy; Glasgow Technical College. Partner, Robert H. Soper & Co., Cumbernauld, 1964-77; Sole Principal, Thomas Laurie Associates, Cumbernauld and Glasgow, 1977-90; Senior Partner, Keillor Laurie Martin Partnership, 1990-2000. Founder Member, Cumbernauld Theatre Group, 1961; Board Member: Cottage Theatre, Cumbernauld, 1964-72, Traverse Theatre, 1972-76 (Chairman); Chairman, WASPS; Member: Drama Panel, Scottish Arts Council, 1973-82, SAC, 1976-82. Recreations: traditional singing; all forms of art appreciation; hill-walking. Address: (h.) 21 Dunglass Avenue, Glasgow G14 9ED; T.-0141-959 4025.

Laverock, Edward, MA, LLB. Retired Solicitor; b. 21.10.19, Dunlop; m., Helen Moffat Harriet Mackison; 1 s.; 1 d. Educ. Hutchesons' Grammar School, Glasgow; Glasgow University. Partner, J. & W. Buchan, Peebles, 1945-86 (Senior Partner, 1954-86); Town Clerk, Peebles, 1948-75; Procurator Fiscal, Peeblesshire, 1949-76. Honorary Sheriff, since 1983. Address: (h.) 4 Edderston Ridge Lane, Peebles; T.-01721 720314.

Law, Professor Derek, MA, DUniv, FLA, FIInfSc, FKC, FRSE. Librarian and Head of Information Resource Directorate, University of Strathclyde, since 1998; b. 19.6.47, Arbroath; m., Jacqueline Anne; 2 d. Educ. Arbroath High School, George Watson's College, Edinburgh; University of Glasgow. Assistant Librarian, St. Andrews University, 1970-77; Sub Librarian, Edinburgh University, 1977-81; Librarian, Erskine Medical Library, 1981-83; Director of Automation, Edinburgh University Library, 1983-84; King's College, London: Librarian, 1984-93, Director of Information Services, 1993-98. Trustee, National Library of Scotland; Treasurer, International Federation of Library Associations. Barnard Prize for Informatics, 1993. Hon. Doctorate, University of Paris. Publications: Royal Navy in World War Two; The Battle of the Atlantic; Networking and the Future of Libraries. Address: (b.) Alexander Turnbull Building, 155 George Street, Glasgow G1 1RD; T.-0141-548 4585; e-mail: d.law@strath.ac.uk

Law, Jack, BA (Hons). Chief Executive, Alcohol Focus Scotland, since 2000; b. 31.10.48, Clydebank; 2 s. Educ. Clydebank High School; Open University; Jordanhill College of Education. Former professional musician, trainee manager with Building Society, sales representative and lorry driver; worked for Social Work Department, Strathclyde Regional Council and Glasgow City Council. Recreations: music; cinema; sport; hillwalking; reading. Address: (b.) Alcohol Focus Scotland, 166 Buchanan Street, Glasgow G1 2LW; T.-0141-572 6700.

Law, Professor Robin C. C., BA, PhD, FRHS, FBA. Professor of African History, University of Stirling, since 1993; b. 7.8.44, Chester. Educ. Southend-on-Sea High School; Balliol College, University of Oxford; Centre of West African Studies, Birmingham. Research Assistant in African History, University of Lagos, Nigeria, 1966-69; Research Fellow in West African History, University of Birmingham, 1970-72; University of Stirling: Lecturer in History, 1972-78, Senior Lecturer, 1978-83, Reader, 1983-93. Editor, Journal of African History, 1974-82, 1991-95; Series Editor, Hakluyt Society, since 1998. Publications: The Oyo Empire c.1600-c.1836, 1977; The Horse in West African History, 1980; The Slave Coast of West Africa, 1550-1750, 1991; The Kingdom of Allada, 1997. Address: (b.) Department of History, University of Stirling, Stirling FK9 4LA; T.-01786 467583; e-mail: r.c.c.law@stir.ac.uk

Lawrence, Professor Andrew, BSc, PhD, FRAS. Regius Professor of Astronomy, Edinburgh University, since 1994; b. 23.4.54, Margate; partner, Debbie Ann Capel; 3 s.; 1 d. Educ. Chatham House Grammar School, Ramsgate; Edinburgh University; Leicester University. Exchange Scientist, Massachusetts Institute of Technology, 1980-81; Senior Research Fellow, Royal Greenwich Observatory, 1981-84; Research Assistant, then SERC Advanced Fellow, School of Mathematical Sciences, Queen Mary College, London, 1984-89; Lecturer, Physics Department, Queen Mary and Westfield College, London, 1989-94. Publications: over 60 in learned journals. Recreations: painting electrons and teasing publishers; acting. Address: (b.) Institute for Astronomy, Edinburgh University, Royal Observatory, Blackford Hill, Edinburgh.

Lawrie, Frank James. IHBC, FRSA, FSA Scot. Director of Heritage Policy, Historic Scotland, since 1991; Member, Board of Management, Buildings of Scotland Trust; Trustee, Rainbow Sports Trust; Assessor, Railway Heritage Trust; Assessor, The Waterways Trust; Partner, The Rainbow Consultancy; b. 30.10.45, Edinburgh; m., Ann Macamon Kerr; 2 s.; 1 d. Educ. Royal High School, Edinburgh. Executive Officer, Department of Agriculture and Fisheries for Scotland, 1964-70; Higher Executive Officer, Scottish Office Finance Division, 1970-78; Senior Executive Officer, 1978-81; Principal, Department of Agriculture and Fisheries for Scotland, 1981-88; Deputy Director, Historic Buildings and Monuments, Scotland, 1988-91. Recreations: railway and canal archaeology; cricket; golf. Address: (b.) Longmore House, Salisbury Place, Edinburgh EH9 1SH; T.-0131 668 8727.

Lawrie, Nigel Gilbert, BSc, PhD. Head Teacher, Port Glasgow High School, since 1985; b. 2.6.47, Edinburgh; m., Janet Clark Warnock; 1 d. Educ. Bearsden Academy; Strathclyde University. Chemistry Teacher, Hermitage Academy, Helensburgh, 1972-75; Principal Teacher of Chemistry, Dunoon Grammar School, 1975-81; Assistant Head Teacher, Garnock Academy, 1981-84; Depute Head Teacher, Castlehead High School, Paisley, 1984-85. President, Headteachers' Association of Scotland, 1998-99;

Member: Scottish Examination Board, 1994-97, Board, SCOTVEC, 1995-97, Board, SQA, 1997-99. Recreations: reading; gardening; football; golf. Address: (b.) Port Glasgow High School, Marloch Avenue, Port Glasgow; T.-01475 715200.

Lawrie, Paul, MBE. Professional golfer; b.1.1.69, Aberdeen; m., Marian; 2 s. Assistant, Banchory; turned professional, 1986; Winner, UAP Under 25s Championship, 1992; Winner, Open Golf Championship, 1999. Honorary law doctorate, Robert Gordon University; Honorary Life Member, European Tour. Recreations: snooker; Aberdeen Football Club; cars. Attached to Meldrum House Golf Club.

Lawson, Peter John, LLB, NP. Solicitor; Partner, Hill Brown, Glasgow, since 1990; b. 25.3.58, Visakapatnam, India. Educ. Zimbabwe; Marr College, Troon; Glasgow University. Partner, McSherry Halliday, 1983-90. Chairman, Tron Theatre, Glasgow; Chairman, Raindog Theatre, Glasgow; Committee Member, BAFTA Scotland. Recreations: theatre; travel. Address: (b.) 3 Newton Place, Glasgow G3 7PU; T.-0141-332 3265; e-mail: plawson@hillbrown.co.uk

Lawson, Alexander Adamson Hutt, MD, FRCPEdin. Consultant Physician, Fife Health Board, 1969-95; Honorary Senior Lecturer, Edinburgh University, 1979-95; Medical Member and Chairman, War Pensions Appeal Tribunal, Scotland, since 1979; b. 30.7.37, Dunfermline; m., Barbara Helen Donnet; 3 s.; 1 d. Educ. Dunfermline High School; Edinburgh University. Consultant Member, Clinical Teaching Staff, Faculty of Medicine, Edinburgh University, 1971-95; Postgraduate Tutor in Medicine, West Fife, 1973-81; Medical Assessor, General Medical Council, since 1982; Member, Fife Health Board, 1981-91 (Vice-Chairman, 1989-91); President: Scottish Society of Physicians, 1989-90, West Fife Medical Society, 1982-83; Life Trustee: Carnegie Dunfermline Trust and Carnegie United Kingdom Hero Fund, since 1980 (Vice Chairman, 1995-98, Chairman, since 1998), Carnegie United Kingdom Trust, since 1983 (Vice Chairman, 2000-02), Barbara Stewart Scottish Laser Centre Trust for Cancer, since 1999; Member: Committee of Safety, Efficacy and Adverse Reactions of Drugs (Committee, Safety of Medicines, DHSS, London), 1982-84, Specialist Advisory Committee (UK) HCMT - General (Internal) Medicine, 1984-88; UK Representative to European Union of Medical Specialties, Monospecialty Committee for General Medicine, 1986-95. Publications: Common Acute Poisonings; Acute Poisoning in Principles and Practice of Medicine; Toxicology and Drug Monitoring in Chemical Diagnosis of Disease; scientific papers. Address: (h.) 12 The Heathery, Dunfermline, Fife KY11 8TS; T.-Dunfermline 622742.

Lawson, Isobel. Director/Company Secretary, Stepping Stones for Families, since 1988; Chair, Board, Childcare First Paisley Partnership; Chair, South Ayrshire Local Childcare Partnership; b. Paisley; 2 d. Training and consultancy, voluntary sector childcare/education development. Director, Scottish Council for Voluntary Organisations. Address: (b.) 55 Renfrew Street, Glasgow G2 3BD; T.-0141-331 2828.

Lawson, John Philip, BSc, FEIS. Honorary President, Scottish Youth Hostels Association, since 2001 (Chairman, 1980-2001); Headteacher, St. Joseph's School, Linlithgow, 1974-94; b. 19.8.37, Bathgate; m., Diana Mary Neal. Educ. St. Mary's Academy, Bathgate; Edinburgh University; Moray House College of Education. Teacher, West Lothian, 1962-94; held various offices in the Educational Institute of Scotland, including President, West Lothian Local Association and Chairman, Lothian Regional Executive; Member, West Lothian Children's Panel, 1972-81; Member, SYHA National Executive, since 1966; Vice-Chairman, SYHA, 1975-80; awarded: Richard Schirrmann Medal by German Youth Hostels Association, 1988, Gezel van de Rugzak, Flemish Youth Hostels Association, 1993; a Director, Scottish Rights of Way Society Ltd., since 1979; a Director, Gatliff Hebridean Hostels Trust, since 1988; President, West Lothian Headteachers Association, 1986-88; President, Federation of Youth Hostels Associations in the European Community, 1990-2001; Vice-President, International Youth Hostel Federation, 1994-98, and since 2000. Recreations: hill-walking; music; reading. Address: (h.) Ledmore, Carnbee, Anstruther KY10 2RU; T.-01333 720312.

Lawson, Lilian Keddie, BSc (Hons), MBA. Director, Scottish Council on Deafness, since 2000; b. 23.2.49, Pittenweem; m., John McDonald Young, OBE; 2 d. Educ. Donaldson's School, Edinburgh; Mary Hare Grammar School, Newbury; Edinburgh University; Strathclyde University. Administrative Assistant, progressing to Head of Administration, British Deaf Association, 1981-92; Manager, Sign Language Interpreting Services, Strathclyde Regional Council, 1992-93; Director, RNID Scotland, 1993-2000. Publication: Words in Hand (Co-Author), 1984. Recreations: gardening; her children. Address: (b.) Clerwood House, 96 Clermiston Road, Edinburgh EH12 6UT; T.-0131-314 6075.

Laybourn, Professor Peter John Robert, MA (Cantab), PhD, FIEE, FRSE. Professor of Electronic Engineering, Glasgow University, since 1985; b. 30.7.42, London; m., Ann Elizabeth Chandler; 2 d. Educ. William Hulme's Grammar School; Bristol Grammar School; Clare College, Cambridge. Research Assistant, Leeds University, 1963-66; Research Fellow, Southampton University, 1966-71; Lecturer, then Senior Lecturer, then Reader, Glasgow University, 1971-85; Honorary Editor, IEE Proceedings: Optoelectronics. Recreations: sailing; boat-building; plant collecting. Address: (h.) Ashgrove, Waterfoot Row, Thorntonhall, Glasgow; T.-0141-644 3992.

Layden, Patrick John, QC, LLB (Hons). Legal Secretary to the Lord Advocate, since 1999; b. 27.6.49, Edinburgh; m., Patricia Mary Bonnar; 3 s.; 1 d. Educ. Holy Cross Academy, Edinburgh; University of Edinburgh. Scottish Bar, 1975-77; Junior Legal Secretary/Assistant Parliamentary Counsel, Lord Advocate's Department, 1977-83; Assistant Legal Secretary and Scottish Parliamentary Counsel, 1983-99. Recreations: walking; reading. Address: (b.) 25 Chambers Street, Edinburgh EH1 1LA; T.-0131-247 2665; e-mail: patrick.layden@scotland.gsi.gov.uk

Lazarowicz, Mark, MA, LLB, DipLP. MP, Edinburgh North and Leith, since 2001 (Member, Select Committee on Scottish Affairs); Advocate; b. 8.8.53. Educ. St. Andrews University; Edinburgh University. Member, Edinburgh District Council, 1980-96: Leader of the Council, 1986-93, Chairperson, Labour Group, 1993-94; Member, City of Edinburgh Council, 1999-2001 (Executive Member for Transport, 2000-01, Convenor, Transportation Committee, 1999-2000); Deputy Leader, COSLA Labour Group, 1990-93; Vice-Chairperson, 1988-89, Chairperson, 1989-90, Scottish Labour Party; Founder Member and Board Member, Centre for Scottish Public Policy, since 1990; Chairperson, Edinburgh International Conference Centre Ltd., 1992-93; Chairperson, Edinburgh Tourist Board, 1993-94. Address: (h.) 17 Bellevue Place, Edinburgh.

Leach, Professor Donald, CBE, BSc, CMath, FIMA, CPhys, MInstP, CEng, MBCS, FRSA; Principal, Queen Margaret College, Edinburgh, 1985-96; Chairman, D.M. Vaughan and Co. Ltd., since 1998; b. 24.6.31, Croydon; m., 1, June Valentine Reid (deceased); 2 s.; 1 d.; m., 2, Marilyn Annette Jeffcoat (qv). Educ. John Ruskin Grammar School, Croydon; London University (External). Pilot Officer, Navigator, RAF, 1951-53; Physicist, British Jute Trade Research Association, Dundee, 1955-65; Technical Director, A.R. Bolton & Co. Ltd., Edinburgh, 1965-66; Napier College: Lecturer and Senior Lecturer in Mathematics, 1966-68, Head, Department of Mathematics and Computing, 1968-74, Assistant Principal/Dean, Faculty of Science, 1974-85. Member, South-Eastern Regional Hospital Board, 1969-74, and Lothian Health Board, 1977-81; Member: Scottish Health Service Information Processing and Computer Systems Advisory Group, 1979-86, Computer Steering Committee (Chairman), 1981-86; Institute of Mathematics: Council Member, 1978-81, Chairman, Scottish Branch, 1980-83, Member, Joint IMA-Royal Society of London Mathematical Education Committee, 1981-84; Council for National Academic Awards: Member, various boards, 1975-79, Science Technology and Society Board, 1979-82 (Chairman, 1981-82), Committee for Scotland, 1987-92; Chairman: Science Technology and Society Association, 1982-85, Hon. Secretary, Committee of Principals and Directors of Scottish Central Institutions (COPADOCI), 1985-88, Chairman, 1988-92; Member: Council for Professions Supplementary to Medicine, 1985-97, Council, World Association for Cooperative Education, 1991-97, Board of Directors, Higher Education Quality Council, 1992-96; President, Leith Chamber of Commerce, 1994-96; President, Edinburgh Chamber of Commerce, 1996-98; Interim Chief Executive, Edinburgh's Lifelong Learning Partnership, 1998; Honorary Fellow, Society of Chiropodists and Podiatrists, 1991; Liberal candidate, West Edinburgh, 1959, East Fife, 1961; Labour candidate, West Perthshire, 1970. Recreations: walking; cooking. Address: (h.) 18 Rothesay Terrace, Edinburgh EH3 7RY; T.-0131-226 7166; e-mail: leach@ravelston.u-net.com

Leake, Professor Robin, MA, DPhil. Vice-Principal (Estates), Glasgow University, since 2001; Professor of Endocrine Oncology, since 1998; b. 16.8.43, Tettenhall. Educ. Lancaster Royal Grammar School; St Peter's and Wolfson Colleges, Oxford. Population Council Fellow, University of Illinois; Lecturer/Senior Lecturer/Reader, Glasgow University; Past President, British Gynaecological Cancer Society; Past Secretary, British Breast Group. Chair, Kelvinside Community Council. Recreations: cricket; golf; tennis; hill-walking. Address: (b.) Room 243, Gilbert Scott Building, Glasgow University, Glasgow; T.-0141-330 5206.

Learmont, Alastair Murray, BA (Hons), DipLP. Advocate, since 1993; b. 25.10.64, Bearsted. Educ. Edinburgh Academy; Bristol University; City University; Edinburgh University. Trainee Solicitor, Anderson Strathern WS, 1991-93; Commissioning Editor, Butterworths (Scotland), 1998-99. President, Bristol University Classical Society, 1984-85; part-time Tutor, Edinburgh University, 1994-95; Tour Leader, Alternative Travel Group, Oxford, since 2000. Recreations: playing the flute; chamber music; the outdoors; exploring Italy on foot. Address: (h.) 48/2 Candlemaker Row, Edinburgh EH1 2QE; T.-0131-225 9018.

Lederer, Peter J, OBE. Managing Director, Gleneagles Hotels plc, since 1987; General Manager, The Gleneagles Hotel, since 1983; Director, Guinness Enterprises, since 1987; Chairman, VisitScotland; Board Member, Consignia Advisory Board for Scotland; b. 30.11.50; m., Marilyn Ruth MacPhail. Four Seasons Hotels, Canada, 1972-79; Vice President, Wood Wilkings Ltd., Toronto, 1979-81; General Manager, Plaza Group of Hotels, Toronto, 1981-83. Chairman: Hospitality Industry Trust Scotland, Tourism People; Trustee, Tourism and Hospitality Education Trust; Freeman, City of London; FHCIMA; Master Innholder; Liveryman, Worshipful Company of Innholders. Recreations: Matthew and Mark; TVR. Address: (b.) The Gleneagles Hotel, Auchterarder, Perthshire PH3 1NF; T.-01764 662231.

Ledger, Sir Philip Stevens, CBE, FRSE, HonLLD (Strathclyde), MA, MusB, FRCM, HonRAM, FRNCM, HonGSM, FRCO, DUniv (Birmingham). Principal, Royal Scottish Academy of Music and Drama, 1982-2001; b. 12.12.37, Bexhill-on-Sea; 1 s.; 1 d. Educ. Bexhill Grammar School; King's College, Cambridge. Master of the Music, Chelmsford Cathedral, 1962-65; East Anglia University: Director of Music, 1965-73, Dean, School of Fine Arts and Music, 1968-71; Conductor, Cambridge University Musical Society, 1973-82; Director of Music and Organist, King's College, Cambridge, 1974-82; President: Royal College of Organists, 1992-94, Incorporated Society of Musicians, 1994-95; Chairman, Committee of Principals of Conservatoires, 1994-98; Editor, Anthems for Choirs 2 and 3; Composer/Editor, Six Carols with Descants. Publication: The Oxford Book of English Madrigals (Editor). Recreations: swimming; theatre. Address: (b.) Royal Scottish Academy of Music and Drama, 100 Renfrew Street, Glasgow G2 3DB; T.-0141-332 4101.

Ledingham, Professor Iain McAllan, MD(Hons), FRCS(Ed), FRCP(Ed, Glas), FInstBiol, FCCM, FRSE. Professor Emeritus of Medical Education, University of Dundee; Fellow in Surgical Education, Royal College of Surgeons of Edinburgh, since 1999; b. 26.2.35, Glasgow; m., Eileen; 3 s. Educ. King's Park Senior Secondary, Glasgow; Central School, Aberdeen; University of Glasgow. Early training in surgery/trauma/intensive care; MRC Senior Research Fellow in hyperbaric medicine; first UK Professor of Intensive Care Medicine, University of Glasgow, 1980; Chair, Intensive Therapy Unit, Western Infirmary, Glasgow, 1985; Foundation Chair, Department of Emergency and Critical Care Medicine, Faculty of Medicine and Health Sciences, United Arab Emirates University, 1988 (Dean, FMHS, 1989). First Chair, Intensive Care Society, UK; President: European Shock Society, European Society of Intensive Care Medicine; Bellahouston Medal, University of Glasgow; La Médaille de la Ville de Paris. Recreations: jogging; hill-walking; gardening; music; reading; woodworking; occasional bad golf. Address: Kir Royale, Westown, by Errol, Perthshire PH2 7SU; T.-01821 670210.

Lee, Professor Clive Howard, MA, MLitt (Cantab). Professor of Historical Economics, Aberdeen University, since 1991; b. 21.4.42, Leeds; m., Christine Ann. Educ. West Leeds High School; Fitzwilliam College, Cambridge. Assistant Lecturer to Professor, Aberdeen University, since 1966. Publications include: The British Economy since 1700: A Macroeconomic Perspective, 1986; British Regional Employment Statistics 1841-1971, 1979; Scotland and the United Kingdom: The Economy and the Union in the Twentieth Century, 1995; Aberdeen 1800-2000: A New History (Co-Editor), 2000. Address: (b.) Department of Economics, Aberdeen University, Regent Walk, Aberdeen; T.-01224 272198.

Lee, Laura Elizabeth, RGN, MSC, DipN. Chief Executive, Maggie's Cancer Caring Centres, since 1996; b. 15.10.66, Whitbank, South Africa; m., Hani Gabra; 1 s.; 1 d. Educ. Peterhead Academy; Birmingham University. Qualified RGN, 1987; various posts in nursing in cancer care in Edinburgh and London, 1987-91; clinical nurse specialist, Edinburgh Breast Unit, 1991-96; founded Maggie's Cancer Caring Centres, 1996. Recreations: reading; swimming. Address: (b.) The Stables, Western General Hospital, Crewe Road, Edinburgh, EH4 2XG; T.-0131-537 3131.

Lee, Professor Michael Radcliffe, MA, DM, DPhil (Oxon), FRCP, FRCPE, FRSE. Emeritus Professor of Clinical Pharmacology, Edinburgh University; b. 21.11.34, Manchester; m., Judith Ann Horrocks; 1 s.; 1 d. Educ. Manchester Grammar School; Brasenose College, Oxford. Beit Memorial Fellow for Medical Research; Lecturer in Medicine, Oxford University; Lecturer in Medicine, St.

Thomas's Hospital Medical School; Medical Director, then Managing Director, Weddel Pharmaceuticals Ltd.; Senior Lecturer in Clinical Pharmacology, Leeds University. Publications: books on medicine and hypertension. Recreations: gardening; walking; old trains; old books. Address: (h.) 112 Polwarth Terrace, Edinburgh EH11 1NN; T.-0131-337 7386.

Lees, James George Grahame, MA, LLB, NP. Partner, McLean & Stewart, Solicitors, Dunblane, since 1974; Vice Chairman, Judicial Commission, Church of Scotland; b. 22.6.46, Perth; m., Hazel Margaret Raffan; 1 s.; 2 d. Educ. Dundee High School; St. Andrews University; Edinburgh University. Solicitor, J. & F. Anderson, WS, Edinburgh, 1969-72; Solicitor, McLean & Stewart, Solicitors, Dunblane, since 1972. Elder, Dunblane Cathedral Church of Scotland. Recreations: walking; photography; fishing. Address: (h.) Northbank, St. Margaret's Drive, Dunblane, FK15 ODP; T.-Dunblane 822928.

Lees, Martin McArthur, MD, FRCP(Edin), FRCS(Ed), FRCOG. Retired Consultant Obstetrician and Gynaecologist, Royal Infirmary of Edinburgh, and Senior Lecturer and Director of Studies, University of Edinburgh; b. 24.4.35; m., Maureen Yetton. Educ. Aberdeen Grammar School; University of Aberdeen. Research Fellow, University of Edinburgh; lately Regional Adviser in Obstetrics and Gynaecology, Royal College of Obstetricians and Gynaecologists; lately Regional Adviser in Gynaecology, Royal College of Surgeons of Edinburgh; Member, Board of Management and Council, Medical and Dental Defence Union of Scotland; Inspector, Human Fertilisation and Embryology Authority; Social Convener and Member of Council, Royal College of Physicians of Edinburgh; National Adviser, National Counselling Service for Sick Doctors; Past President: Edinburgh Obstetrical Society, Harveian Society of Edinburgh. Recreations: music; ornithology; reading. Address: Royal College of Physicians of Edinburgh, 9 Queen Street, Edinburgh EH2 1JQ; T.-0131-225 7324.

Lefevre, Frank Hartley, MA, LLB, NP. Solicitor and Advocate in Aberdeen, since 1959; Consultant, Lefevre Litigation; Chairman, Quantum Claims Compensation Specialists Ltd., since 1988; b. 4.12.34, Aberdeen; m., Hazel Gray; 1 s.; 2 d. Educ. Robert Gordon's College, Aberdeen; Aberdeen University. Commenced legal practice, 1959; set up, 1988, Britain's first no-win no-fee professional compensation company. Treasurer, Aberdeen Society of Advocates, 1994, President 1995; Past President, Grampian Squash Racquets Association (now Honorary President); accredited by the Law Society of Scotland as specialist in employment law, 1993, and as solicitor/ mediator, 1995; part-time Chairman, Industrial Tribunals (Scotland), 1996-99; Associate Member, Society of Advanced Legal Studies, 1998; Council Member, Law Society of Scotland, since 2000; Member, Council, Royal Aberdeen Golf Club, 1993-95. Recreations: squash; golf; music. Address: (h.) Braco Lodge, 11 Rubislaw Den North, Aberdeen; T.-01224 317170.

Leiper, Joseph, MA, DipEd. Rector, Oldmachar Academy, since 1984; b. 13.8.41, Aberdeen; m., Moira Taylor; 2d. Educ. Aberdeen Grammar School; Aberdeen University. English Teacher: Robert Gordon's College, 1972-73; Bankhead Academy, 1973-75; Principal Teacher, English, Bankhead Academy, 1975-80; Assistant Rector, 1980-82; Depute Rector, Ellon Academy, 1982-84; Chairman, Aberdeen University Business Committee, General Council, since 2000; appointed to Court, Aberdeen University, General Council Court Assessor, 2000; HMI Associate Inspector of Schools, since 2000. Recreations: sailing; reading; walking. Address: (b.) Oldmachar Academy, Jesmond Drive, Bridge of Don, Aberdeen, AB22 8UR; T.-01224 820887.

Leishman, Brian Archibald Scott, MBE. Consultant, European Liaison The International Ticketing Association (New York); Business Manager, Edinburgh Military Tattoo 1978-97; b. 16.9.36; 1 s.; 1 d. Educ. Fettes College, Edinburgh. Retired Regular Army Officer; commissioned The Cameronians (Scottish Rifles); re-badged King's Own Scottish Borderers; service in the Arabian Gulf, East Africa and Europe; Italian Staff College, 1971-73; Assistant Defence Attache, British Embassy, Rome, 1974-76; Ticketing Consultant, XIII Commonwealth Games in Edinburgh, 1986. Recreations: music; photography. Address: (h.) 61 Northumberland Street, Edinburgh EH3 6JQ; T.-0131-557 0187.

Leishman, Marista Muriel, MA. Senior Partner, The Insite Consultancy for Management and Training; b. 10.4.32, Beaconsfield; m., Murray Leishman; 1 s.; 3 d. Educ. St. George's School, Ascot; St. Andrews University. First Head of Education, National Trust for Scotland, 1979-86; two National Training Awards recognising Insite's innovatory training programmes and disabled access initiatives; writer: occasional pieces published; memoir of Sir Jamie Stormonth Darling, etc. Recreations: music; painting; writing; hill-walking. Address: 9/23 St. Leonard's Crag, Edinburgh EH8 9SP; T.-0131-662 4660.

Leishman, Mark Murray. Secretary and Head of Public Policy, BBC Scotland; b. 4.3.62, Perth. Educ. Firrhill High School, Edinburgh; Napier College, Edinburgh. Press and PR, National Trust for Scotland, 1979-81; Reporter, United News Service, 1982-84; Reporter, Fife Free Press, Kirkcaldy, 1986-87; Chief Reporter, Radio Forth/Tay, 1987-88; Reporter, Radio Clyde, 1988-90; Reporter, Political Correspondent, Sunday Times, 1990-93; Presenter, Good Morning Scotland, BBC Scotland, 1993-95. Recreations: fishing; running; golf; gym work; reading; cinema; music. Address: (b.) BBC Scotland, Queen Margaret Drive, Glasgow G12 8DG.

Leitch, Alexander Park (Sandy). Chief Executive, Zurich Financial Services (UK, Ireland, Southern Africa and Asia Pacific regions), since 1998; Trustee, National Galleries of Scotland, since 1999; b. 20.10.47, Dunfermline; divorced; 3 d. Educ. Dunfermline High School. Chief Systems Designer, National Mutual Life, 1969; Hambro Life, 1971 (Board of Directors, 1981); Allied Dunbar plc: Managing Director, 1988; Deputy Chairman, 1990; Chief Executive, 1993-96, Chairman, 1996-2001; Chief Executive, British American Financial Services (UK and International) Ltd., 1996-98; Chairman: Eagle Star Holdings Plc, since 1996, Threadneedle Asset Management, since 1996, ABI, 1998-2000 (Member, Board, since 1996, Deputy Chairman, 1997-98); Director, BAT Industries PLC, 1997-98. Chairman, SANE, 1999-2000; Deputy Chairman, Business in the Community; Chairman, Cares Incorporated; Winner, Prince of Wales Ambassador's Award, 1999. Recreations: tennis; football; antiquarian books. Address: (b.) Zurich Financial Services Ltd., 22 Arlington Street, London SW1A 1RW; T.-020 7495 5571.

Leitch, Donald H., DMS, MHCIMA, FCFA. Principal, Glasgow College of Food Technology, since 1998 (Depute Principal, 1991-98); b. 2.4.48, Glasgow; m., Mary B.; 2 s. Educ. Hyndland Senior Secondary School; Langside College, Glasgow; Glasgow College of Technology. Catering management, Health Service, 1967-70; Depute Catering Officer, Glasgow University, 1970-74; Lecturer then Senior Lecturer, Glasgow College of Food Technology, 1974-85; Head of Department, Cambuslang College, Glasgow, 1985-91. Past Chairman, Scottish Division, Cookery and Food Association. Recreations: hill-walking; gardening. Address: (b.) 230 Cathedral Street, Glasgow G1 2TG; T.-0141-552 3751.

Leitch, Iain Douglas Cameron Muil, JP, BSc, MRCVS. Honorary Sheriff, since 1997; b. 28.3.32, Glasgow; m., Kathleen Mae Nicholson; 1 s.; 2 d. Educ. Hillhead High School, Glasgow; Edinburgh University; Royal (Dick) School of Veterinary Studies. Partner, general veterinary practice, 1956-92. Former Council Member, British Veterinary Association; former Senior Baillie, Laurencekirk Town Council. Recreations: gardening; hillwalking; DIY; golf; curling; swimming; wood carving; painting; bowling; kirk session. Address: (h.) Caline, Haulkerton Wood, Laurencekirk AB30 1DZ; T.-01561 377287.

Lenman, Professor Bruce Philip, MA (Aberdeen), MLitt, LittD (Cantab), FRHistSoc. Professor of Modern History, St. Andrews University, since 1992 (formerly Reader in Modern History); b. 9.4.38, Aberdeen. Educ. Aberdeen Grammar School; Aberdeen University; St. John's College, Cambridge. Assistant Professor, Victoria University, Canada, 1963; Lecturer in Imperial and Commonwealth History, Queen's College, Dundee (St. Andrews University), 1963-67; Lecturer, Dundee University, 1967-72; United College, St. Andrews: Lecturer, Department of Modern History, 1972-78, Senior Lecturer, 1978-83; British Academy Fellow, Newberry Library, Chicago, 1982; John Carter Brown Library Fellow, Brown University, Providence, RI, 1984; Harrison Professor, College of William & Mary, VA, 1988-89; Mayers Fellow, Huntington Library, CA, 1997; Bird Professor, Emory University, Atlanta, GA, 1998. Publications: Esk to Tweed, 1975; An Economic History of Modern Scotland 1660-1976, 1977 (Scottish Arts Council Award); The Jacobite Risings in Britain 1689-1746, 1980 (Scottish Arts Council Award); Scotland 1746-1832, 1981; The Jacobite Clans of the Great Glen 1650-1784, 1984; The Jacobite Cause, 1986; The Jacobite Threat (Co-Author); 1990; The Eclipse of Parliament, 1992; England's Colonial Wars, 2000; Britain's Colonial Wars, 2001; Editor, Chambers Dictionary of World History, 1993. Recreations: golf; badminton; Scottish country dancing. Address: (b.) Department of Modern History, St. Andrews University, St. Andrews KY16 9AL; T.-01334 476161.

Lennon, Francis P, MA, MPhil. Head Teacher, St. Modan's High School, Stirling, since 1996; b. 18.6.52, Glasgow; m., Marie Lennon; 1 s.; 4 d. Educ. Salesian College, Cheshire; Holy Cross High, Hamilton. Teaching career: St Gerard's Secondary, Govan, 1975-78; Columba of Iona Secondary, Glasgow, 1978-81; Holyrood Secondary, Glasgow, 1981-84; Holy Cross High School, Hamilton, 1984-90; St Patrick's High School, Coatbridge, 1990-93; St Andrew's Secondary, Glasgow, 1993-96. Recreations: football; American football; theatre. Address: (b.) Barnsdale Road, Stirling; T.-01786 470962.

Lennon, Margaret (Maggie) Mitchell, MA, FFCS. Programme and Fellowship Director, Institute of Contemporary Scotland, since 2002 (Executive Director, 2001-02, Member, Board of Trustees, since 2001); b. 21.8.60, Dundee; m., Jim Lennon (m. dis.); 1 d. Educ. Menzieshill High School, Dundee; Edinburgh University. Waterstone and Co. Booksellers: Buyer/Assistant Manager/Manager, 1985-94; Editor, Weekend Scotsman, 1994-96; Managing Director, European Editions Ltd, 1996-99; Editor, Europe Quarterly, 1997-99; Director of Development, Dundee and Tayside Chamber of Commerce and Industry, 1999-2001; Director, Dundee Cultural Quarter Developments Ltd., 2000-01; Member, Dundee Cultural Quarter Steering Group, 2000-01; Director, ICS Events Ltd., since 2001. Recreations: reading; gardening; eating out; travel; swimming; family. Address: (b.) Institute of Contemporary Scotland, 2nd Floor, House 6, 94 Elmbank Street, Glasgow, G2 4PF; T.-0141-204 2848; e-mail: maggielennon@contemporaryscotland.com

Leslie, John, MRPharmS. Chairman, Orkney Health Board, 1991-2001; b. 1.1.35, Kirkwall; m., Evelyn MacGillivray; 1 s. Educ. Kirkwall Grammar School; Robert Gordon's Institute of Technology, Aberdeen. Member, NHS Executive Council for Orkney, 1968-74; Chairman, Kirkwall Chamber of Commerce, 1973-74; Member, Orkney Health Board, 1979-85 and since 1987. Past President, Kirkwall Rotary Club. Recreations: participating in amateur music and drama groups; simple electronics/computing. Address: (h.) Failte, Bignold Park Road, Kirkwall, Orkney; T.-01856 874002.

Leslie, Martin Rowley Melville, CVO, FRICS. Chartered Surveyor (semi-retired); Factor to Her Majesty Queen Elizabeth the Queen Mother, since 1975; Honorary Secretary and Factor to Queen Elizabeth Castle of Mey Trust, since 1996; President, Aberdeen Angus Cattle Society of Great Britain and Ireland, 1999-2000; b. 12.8.32, Malawi, Central Africa; m., Catriona Bridget Macdonald; 1 s.; 2 d. Educ. King's School, Canterbury; Royal Dick Veterinary College, Edinburgh University; College of Estate Management (correspondence course). National Service, Seaforth Highlanders and Argyll and Sutherland Highlanders (2nd Lt.), 1951-53; TA, 11th Bn., Seaforth Highlanders (retired as Captain), 1953-67; Pupil Factor, Moray Estates Development Company, Forres, 1959-60; Assistant Factor, Fairburn Estates, Conan and Gairloch Estates, Ross-shire, 1960-62; 1962-79: Factor to Welbeck Estates Company, Langwell and Braemore, Caithness and Ross-shire, Factor to Achentoul Estate Company, Achentoul, Sutherland and Ross-shire; Factor to Her Majesty the Queen, Balmoral Estates, Aberdeenshire, 1979-95. Field Trial Panel Judge for Hunt, Point and Retrieve Breeds (dogs), since 1972; Member, Deer Committee, Highland Committee of Scottish Land Owners Federation, 1972-92; Dee District Salmon Fisheries Board: Member, 1980-89, Representative on Association of Scottish District Salmon Fisheries Boards, 1981-88; Member, Deer and Uplands Committee, Scottish Landowners' Federation, 1992-96; Aberdeen Angus Cattle Society: Member, Council, 1984-86 and 1993-95, Junior Vice President, 1997-98, Senior Vice President, 1998-99, President, 1999-00; Vice-Chairman, World Angus Secretariat, Calgary, Canada, 1999 (Leader, UK and Ireland Delegation); Member, Skye District Salmon Fisheries Board, since 1996 (Chairman, since 1998); Skye District Salmon Fisheries Board Representative on Association of Scottish District Salmon Fisheries Board, since 1997. Recreations: country sports; German shorthaired pointers; reading. Address: Redcliff, Portree, Isle of Skye IV51 9DH; T.-01478 612014.

Lessels, Norman, CBE, CA. Director, Standard Life Assurance Company (Chairman, 1988-98); Director: Robert Wiseman Dairies PLC, Cairn Energy; b. 2.9.38, Edinburgh; m., Christine Stevenson; 1 s. Educ. Edinburgh Academy. Partner, Ernst & Whinney, until 1980; Partner, Chiene & Tait, CA, until 1998; President, Institute of Chartered Accountants of Scotland, 1987-88. Recreations: golf; music; bridge. Address: (b.) 50 Lothian Road, Edinburgh EH3 9BY; T.-0131-475 3000.

Leven and Melville, Earl of (Alexander Robert Leslie Melville). Lord Lieutenant of Nairn, 1969-99; b. 13.5.24, London; m., Susan Steuart-Menzies; 2 s.; 1 d. Educ. Eton. Coldstream Guards, 1942-52 (retired as Captain); ADC to Governor General of New Zealand, 1951-52; Convener, Nairn County Council, 1970-74. Chairman of Governors, Gordonstoun School, 1971-89; President, British Ski Federation, 1981-85. Address: (h.) Raith, Old Spey Bridge, Grantown-on-Spey, Morayshire PH26 3NQ; T.-01479 872908.

Leven, Marian Forbes, DA, RSW. Artist; b. 25.3.44, Edinburgh; m., Will Maclean; 2 s.; 1 d. Educ. Bell-Baxter School, Cupar; Gray's School of Art, Aberdeen. Exhibited RSA, RSW, RGI, SSA, AAS; work in private and public collections; Winner, Noble Grossart Painting Prize, 1997. Address: (h.) Bellevue, 18 Dougall Street, Tayport, Fife DD6 9JD.

Lever, Professor Anthony Fairclough, BSc, MBBS, FRCP (London, Glasgow), FRSE. Honorary Professor and Senior Research Fellow, Department of Medicine and Therapeutics, University of Glasgow, since 1994; b. 18.3.29, Epsom, Surrey; m., Dr. Rosemary S. Lever; 1 s.; 1 d. Educ. Hurstpierpoint College, Sussex; St. Mary's Hospital Medical School, London. House Physician: Sir George Pickering, St. Mary's Hospital, RMO, National Heart Hospital, Hammersmith Hospital, 1955-57; Registrar, Research Fellow, Lecturer, Honorary Senior Lecturer, Medicine, Honorary Consultant Physician, St. Mary's Hospital, 1958-67; Director, MRC Blood Pressure Unit, Western Infirmary, Glasgow, 1967-94. Max Bonn and Cheadle Gold Medals, St. Mary's. Publications: over 400 papers and reviews in scientific and medical literature. Recreation: fishing. Address: (h.) 7 Sydenham Road, Glasgow G12 9NT; T.-0141-339 0076; e-mail: afl2h@clinmed.gla.ac.uk

Levinthal, Terrence Scott, BES, DipUD, FSAScot. Technical Director, Scottish Civic Trust, since 1999; Board Member: Cockburn Conservation Trust, Solway Heritage; Member, Council, Association for the Protection of Rural Scotland; b. 9.12.61, Winnipeg. Educ. University of Waterloo; Heriot-Watt/Edinburgh College of Art. Investigator, Royal Fine Art Commission for Scotland, 1988-92; Secretary, The Cockburn Association (Edinburgh Civic Trust), 1992-99. Recreations: hill-walking, skiing, cycling and other outdoor pursuits; the arts; woodworking. Address: (b.) Scottish Civic Trust, The Tobacco Merchant's House, 42 Miller Street, Glasgow G1 1DT; T.-0141-221 1466.

Levison, Professor David Annan, MD, FRCPath. Dean of Faculty of Medicine, Dentistry and Nursing, Dundee University, since 1997; Professor of Pathology, Dundee University, since 1995; b. 4.1.44, Perth; m., Rosie; 4 s.; 2 d. Educ. Kirkcaldy High School; St Andrews University. House Officer, Leeds General Infirmary; House Officer, Dundee Royal Infirmary; Lecturer/Hon. Senior Registrar, Dundee University; Senior Lecturer, Histopathology, St Bartholomews Hospital, London; Professor of Clinical Histopathology, Guys and St Thomas' London; Treasurer, Pathological Society of Great Britain and Ireland; Member, Chief Scientist's Committee; Chairman, CSO working group on research and development restructuring. Recreations: sailing; North West of Scotland; family. Address (h.) 8 Glamis Drive, Dundee, DD2 1QL; T.-01382 668150.

Levison, Rev. Mary Irene, BA, BD, DD. Minister of the Church of Scotland (retired); (Extra) Chaplain to the Queen in Scotland, since 1991; Vice-President, St. Leonard's School, since 1996; b. 8.1.23, Oxford; m., Rev. Frederick Levison. Educ. St. Leonard's School, St. Andrews; Oxford University; Edinburgh University. Administrative Assistant, Scottish Home Department, 1943-46; Deaconess, Church of Scotland, Musselburgh, 1954-58; Tutor, St. Colm's College, 1958-61; Assistant Chaplain, Edinburgh University, 1961-64; Assistant Minister, St. Andrew's and St. George's Church and Chaplain to the retail trade, Edinburgh, 1978-83; Moderator, Edinburgh Presbytery, 1988. Publication: Wrestling with the Church, 1992. Recreations: music; travel. Address: (h.) 2 Gillsland Road, Edinburgh EH10 5BW; T.-0131-228 3118.

Liddell, Colin. Partner, Liddell Thomson, Management Consultants; b. 28.8.47, Falkirk; m., Sheena Wood Mackay. Educ. Denny High School. Journalist, Johnston Newspaper Group, 1964-69; Editor, Linlithgow Journal & Gazette, 1968-69; Journalist, Scotsman Publications, 1969-77; Senior Press Officer, Scottish Development Agency, 1977-

82; PR Director, then Chief Executive, Charles Barker Scotland, 1982-86; Public Affairs Director, United Distillers, 1986-93; Corporate Communications Director, Scottish Power plc, 1993-95. Non-Executive Director: Falkirk F.C., Billcliffe Gallery, Scottish Enterprise Glasgow, Rona Cameron Associates, Westfield Stadium Ltd. Recreations: golf; gardening; football. Address: (b.) 225 West George Street, Glasgow G2 2ND.

Liddell, Helen Lawrie, BA. MP (Labour), Airdrie and Shotts (formerly Monklands East), since 1994; Secretary of State for Scotland, since 2001; Minister for Energy and Competitiveness in Europe, 1999-2001; b. 6.12.50, Coatbridge; m., Dr. Alistair H. Liddell; 1 s.; 1 d. Educ. St. Patrick's High School, Coatbridge; Strathclyde University. Head, Economic Department, STUC, 1971-76; Economics Correspondent, BBC, 1976-77; Scottish Secretary, Labour Party, 1977-88; Scottish Daily Record and Sunday Mail Ltd.: Director of Personnel and Public Affairs, 1988-91, Director of Corporate and Public Affairs, 1991-92; Chief Executive, Business Venture Programme, 1993-94; Labour Candidate, East Fife, 1974. Economic Secretary to the Treasury, 1997-98; Minister of State, Scottish Office, 1998-99; Minister for Transport, 1999. Publication: Elite, 1990. Address: (b.) Dover House, Whitehall, London SW1A 2AU.

Lidgate, Professor David, BEng, PhD, CEng, FIEE, FInstE. Professor and Head, Department of Electrical and Electronic Engineering, Napier University, since 1994, Head of Research, Faculty of Engineering and Computing, since 1999; b. 11.7.46, Gosforth; m., Janet; 2 d. Educ. Royal Grammar School, Newcastle upon Tyne; Liverpool University. Research Engineer, A. Reyrolle & Co. Ltd., 1965-75; Lecturer, UMIST, 1975-88; Head, School of Engineering, Greenwich University, 1988-94. Member, Electricity Consumers Committee for Southern Scotland, 1994-97. Recreations: genealogy; model railways. Address: (b.) 10 Colinton Road, Edinburgh EH10 5DT; T.-0131-455 2266.

Lilley, Professor David Malcolm James, FRSE. Professor of Molecular Biology, Dundee University, since 1989; b. 28.5.48, Colchester; m., Patricia Mary; 2 d. Educ. Gilberd School, Colchester; Durham University. Joined Biochemistry Department, Dundee University, 1981; awarded: Colworth Medal by Biochemical Society, 1982, Gold Medal of G. Mendel, Czech Academy of Sciences, 1994, Gold Medal of V. Prelog in Stereochemistry, ETH, Zurich. Publications: 240 scientific papers. Recreation: foreign languages. Address: (b.) Department of Biochemistry, Dundee University, Dundee DD1 4HN; T.-01382 344243.

Lillico, William Allan, MREHIS, MInstWM. Director of Transport and Environmental Standards, Scottish Borders Council, since 1996; b. 8.3.45, Galashiels; m., Doreen Ann; 2 d. Educ. Galashiels Academy; Napier College, Edinburgh. Burgh of Galashiels: Trainee Burgh Surveyor/Sanitary Inspector, 1964-68, Junior Assistant Burgh Surveyor/Sanitary Inspector, 1968-71, Assistant Burgh Surveyor/Sanitary Inspector, 1971-72, Depute Burgh Surveyor/Sanitary Inspector, 1972-75; Ettrick and Lauderdale District Council: Area Inspector, Technical Services Department, 1975-76, Depute Director of Environmental Services, 1976-96. Recreation: golf. Address: (b.) Transport and Environmental Standards, Council Headquarters, Newton St. Boswells TD6 0SA; T.-01835 824000.

Lindhorst, Gordon John S., LLB (Hons), DipLP, LLM. Advocate, since 1995. Educ. University of Edinburgh; University of Glasgow; Universität Heidelberg. Admitted as Solicitor, 1991; Notary Public, 1992. Scottish Parliamentary Candidate, Linlithgow, 1999; Westminster Parliamentary Candidate, Linlithgow, 2001; Honorary Treasurer,

Edinburgh Branch, Alzheimer Scotland; Legal Reporter: Scots Law Times, 1995-2000, Session Cases, since 2000. Recreation: hillwalking; cabinet making; music. Address: (b.) Parliament House, Edinburgh; EH1; T.-0131-226 5071; e-mail: glindhorst@hotmail.com

Lindsay, 16th Earl of (James Randolph Lindesay-Bethune). Chairman, Scottish Quality Salmon, since 1998; Chairman, RSPB Scotland, since 1998 (Council Member, RSPB UK); Board Member, Cairngorms Partnership, since 1998; Non-Executive Director, United Auctions (Scotland) plc, since 1998; Member, Scottish Power Environment Forum, since 1998; President, International Tree Foundation, since 1995; Chairman, Genesis Quality Assurance, since 2001; Chairman, Elmwood College, since 2001; Non-Executive Director, Mining (Scotland) Ltd., since 2001; b. 19.11.55; m., Diana Mary Chamberlayne-Macdonald. Educ. Eton; Edinburgh University; University of California, Davis. Lord in Waiting (Government Whip), 1995; Parliamentary Under Secretary of State, Scottish Office, 1995-97; Member, Secretary of State's Advisory Group on Sustainable Development, 1998-99; Member, Select Committee on European Community Affairs: Environment, Public Health and Consumer Protection Sub-Committee, 1997-99; Member, UK Round Table on Sustainable Development Sub-Group, 1998-2000; Chairman, Assured British Meat Ltd., 1997-2001; Green Ribbon political award, 1995. Address: (h.) Lahill, Upper Largo, Fife KY8 6JE.

Lindsay, Frederic, MA (Hons). Writer; b. 12.8.33, Glasgow; m., Shirley; 1 s.; 3 d. Educ. North Kelvinside Senior Secondary School; Glasgow University; Jordanhill College; Edinburgh University. Worked as library assistant, teacher, lecturer; since becoming full-time writer in 1979, has published eight novels: Brond, 1984, Jill Rips, 1987, A Charm Against Drowning, 1988, After the Stranger Came, 1992, Kissing Judas, 1997, A Kind of Dying, 1998, Idle Hands, 1999, Death Knock, 2000, Darkness in My Hand, 2001; has written plays for Scottish Youth Theatre; radio plays for children; adapted Brond as serial for Channel 4. Former Chair, Society of Authors in Scotland; former Vice-President, PEN Scotland; former Member, Scottish Arts Council, Literature Committee. Recreations: cinema; theatre; television; reading. Address: (h.) 28 The Green, Pencaitland EH34 5HE; T.-01875 340955.

Lindsay, John Maurice, CBE, TD, DLitt, HonFRIAS. Consultant, Scottish Civic Trust (Director, 1967-83); b. 21.7.18; m., Aileen Joyce Gordon; 1 s.; 3 d. Educ. Glasgow Academy; Scottish National Academy of Music. Drama Critic, Scottish Daily Mail, 1946-47; Music Critic, The Bulletin, 1946-60; Border Television: Programme Controller, 1961-62, Production Controller, 1962-64, Features Executive and Chief Interviewer, 1964-67. Atlantic-Rockefeller Award, 1946; Editor: Scots Review, 1949-50, The Scottish Review, 1975-85; Member, Historic Buildings Council for Scotland, 1976-87; Secretary-General, Europa Nostra, 1983-91; Council Member, Association of Scottish Literary Studies, 1983-94, President, 1988-90; Trustee: New Lanark Conservation Trust, 1985-94, National Heritage Memorial Fund, 1980-84; HonDLitt, Glasgow, 1982. Publications: poetry: The Advancing Day, 1940; Perhaps To-morrow, 1941; Predicament, 1942; No Crown for Laughter: Poems, 1943; The Enemies of Love: Poems 1941-45, 1946; Selected Poems, 1947; Hurlygush: Poems in Scots, 1948; At the Wood's Edge, 1950; Ode for St. Andrew's Night and Other Poems, 1951; The Exiled Heart: Poems 1941-56, 1957; Snow Warning and Other Poems, 1962; One Later Day and Other Poems, 1964; This Business of Living, 1969; Comings and Goings: Poems, 1971; Selected Poems 1942-72, 1973; The Run from Life, 1975; Walking Without an Overcoat, Poems 1972-76, 1977; Collected Poems, 1979; A Net to Catch the Winds and Other Poems, 1981; The French Mosquitoes' Woman and other diversions and poems;

Requiem for a Sexual Athlete; Collected Poems 1940-90; On the Face Of It: Collected Poems, Vol. 2; News of the World: Last Poems; Speaking Likenesses: A Postscript; prose: Worlds Apart; Pocket Guide to Scottish Culture; The Scottish Renaissance; The Lowlands of Scotland: Glasgow and the North; Robert Burns: The Man, His Work, The Legend; Dunoon: The Gem of the Clyde Coast; The Lowlands of Scotland: Edinburgh and the South; Clyde Waters: Variations and Diversions on a Theme of Pleasure; The Burns Encyclopedia; Killochan Castle; By Yon Bonnie Banks: A Gallimaufry; Environment: A Basic Human Right; Portrait of Glasgow; Robin Philipson; History of Scottish Literature; Lowland Scottish Villages; Francis George Scott and the Scottish Renaissance; The Buildings of Edinburgh (Co-Author); Thank You For Having Me: A Personal Memoir; Unknown Scotland (Co-Author); Castles of Scotland: A Constable Guide; Count All Men Mortal: The Story of the Scottish Provident Institution; Victorian and Edwardian Glasgow; An Illustrated Guide to Glasgow; The Comic Poems of William Tennant (Co-Editor); Edinburgh Past and Present (Co-Author); The Youth and Manhood of Cyril Thornton (Editor); The Scottish Dog (Co-Author); A Pleasure of Gardens (Co-Author); The Scottish Quotation Book (Co-Author); The Music Quotation Book (Co-Author); The Theatre and Opera Lover's Quotation Book (Co-Author); The Burns Quotation Book (Co-Author); The Chambers Guide to Good Scottish Gardens (Co-Author); Glasgow: Fabric of a City; A Book of Scottish Verse. Recreations: music; cooking. Address: (h.) Park House, 104 Dumbarton Road, Bowling, Dunbartonshire G60 5BB.

Lindsay, Mark Stanley Hunter, LLB (Hons), DipLP. Advocate, since 1995; Standing Counsel to Home Secretary, since 2000; b. 17.5.69, Maybole; m., Rosemary; 2 s. Educ. Carrick Academy, Maybole; University of Glasgow. Energy Consultant, Jacek Mawkowski Associates, Boston, Mass., USA; Congressional Intern, Capitol Hill, Washington DC; Articled Clerk, Macallister Mazengarb, Wellington, NZ; Trainee Solicitor, Tods Murray, WS, Edinburgh; Solicitor, Scottish Office. Recreations: hillwalking; squash; classic cars; American history. Address: Advocates' Library, Parliament House, Edinburgh EH1 1RF; T.-0131-226 5071; (h.) 0131-332 2774; e-mail: MshLindsay@aol.com

Lindsay, Ranald Bruce, LLB(Hons), DipLP, NP. Solicitor-Advocate, since 1993; Solicitor, since 1986; b. 18.3.62, Bellshill; m., Jennifer Vesey; 2 s.; 1 d. Educ. Wishaw High; University of Glasgow. Trained with Bishop & Co., Glasgow, 1984-86; qualified as first Solicitor Advocate in both civil and criminal law, 1993; established own practice, 1994. Recreations: reading; films; history; model aircraft; getting away from it all. Address: (b.) Lindsay Solicitors, 33 Buccleuch Street, Dumfries DG1 2AB; T.-01387 259236.

Lindsay, Stephen James. Regimental Secretary, The Black Watch (RHR), since 1997; b. 2.3.40, London; m., Ann Powell; 3 s.; 1 d. Educ. Eton College; Royal Military Academy, Sandhurst. Commissioned into The Black Watch, 1959; commanded Royal Guard, Balmoral, 1978; Commanding Officer, 1st Bn., 51st Highland Volunteers, 1984-86; retired in rank of Lt. Col., 1995. Recreations: piping; painting. Address: (b.) Balhousie Castle, Perth PH1 5HR; T.-0131-310 8530.

Lingard, Joan Amelia, MBE. Author; b. Edinburgh; 3 d. Educ. Bloomfield Collegiate School, Belfast; Moray House College of Education, Edinburgh. Member, Scottish Arts Council, 1980-85; Chair, Society of Authors in Scotland, 1980-84; a Director, Edinburgh Book Festival, 1994-98; first novel published, 1963; has also written plays for TV, including 18-part series, Maggie, adapted from quartet of teenage books; novels: Liam's Daughter, 1963; The Prevailing Wind, 1964; The Tide Comes In, 1966; The Headmaster, 1967; A Sort of Freedom, 1968; The Lord on our Side, 1970; The Second Flowering of Emily Mountjoy, 1979; Greenyards, 1981; Sisters By Rite, 1984; Reasonable Doubts, 1986; The Women's House, 1989; After Colette, 1993; Dreams of Love and Modest Glory, 1995; 40 children's books; Awards: ZDF Preis der Leseratten, W. Germany, for The Twelfth Day of July, 1986; Buxtehuder Bulle, W. Germany for Across the Barricades, 1987; Scottish Arts Council awards for After Colette, 1994, Tom and the Tree House, 1998; Tug of War shortlisted for 1989 Carnegie Medal, 1989 Federation of Children's Book Groups Award, 1989 Sheffield Book Award, runner-up for 1990 Lancashire Children's Book Club of the Year. Recreations: reading; walking; travelling. Address: (b.) David Higham Associates, 5-8 Lower John Street, Golden Square, London W1R 4HA.

Lingard, Robin Anthony, MA, FTS. Independent Consultant; b. 19.7.41, Enfield; m., Margaret; 2 d. Educ. Felsted School; Emmanuel College, Cambridge. Joined Ministry of Aviation, 1963; Private Secretary to Joint Parliamentary Secretary, Ministry of Technology, 1966-68; appointments, Department of Industry, DTI, etc., to 1984; Head, Enterprise Unit, Cabinet Office, 1984-85; Head, Small Firms and Tourism Division, Department of Employment, 1985-87; full-time Board Member, Highlands and Islands Development Board, 1988-91; Director of Training and Social Development, Highlands and Islands Enterprise, 1991-93; Project Director, University of the Highlands and Islands Project, 1993-97. Member, Scottish Tourist Board, 1988-92; Chairman, Prince's Trust Committee for Highlands, Western Isles and Orkney; Member, Management Board, Prince's Trust and Royal Jubilee Trusts, 1989-95; Chairman, Youth Link Scotland, 1997-2000; Chairman, BBC Scotland Children in Need and Appeals Advisory Committee; DUniv (Open), 1999. Recreations: watching birds; walking; reading; aviation history; dinghy sailing. Address: (h.) Kinnairdie House, Dingwall IV15 9LL; T.-01349 861044.

Linklater of Butterstone, Baroness (Veronica Linklater). Life Peer, since 1997; Founder and Executive Chairman, The New School, Butterstone, since 1991; President, Society of Friends of Dunkeld Cathedral, since 1989; Trustee, Esmée Fairbairn Foundation, since 1991; b. 15.4.43, Meikleour, Perthshire; m., Magnus Duncan Linklater (qv); 2 s.; 1 d. Educ. Cranborne Chase; Sorbonne; University of Sussex; University of London. Child Care Officer, London Borough of Tower Hamlets, 1967-68; Co-Founder, Visitors Centre, Pentonville Prison, 1971-77; Governor, three Islington schools, 1970-85; Prison Reform Trust Winchester Prison Project, 1981-82; Founder, Administrator, Consultant, Butler Trust, 1983-87 (Trustee, since 1987); JP, Inner London, 1985-88; Co-ordinator, Trustee, Vice Chairman, Pushkin Prizes (Scotland), since 1989; Member, Children's Panel, Edinburgh South, 1989-97; Committee Member, Gulliver Award for the Performing Arts in Scotland, 1990-96; Patron, Sutherland Trust, since 1993; Trustee, Young Musicians Trust, 1993-97; Candidate (Liberal Democrat), Perth & Kinross By-Election, 1995; Director, Maggie Keswick Jencks Cancer Caring Centres Trust, since 1997; Member, Beattie Committee on Post School Provision for Young People with Special Needs, 1998-99. Hon. Doctorate, University College, Edinburgh. Recreations: music; theatre; gardening. Address: (h.) 5 Drummond Place, Edinburgh EH3 6PH; T.-0131-557 5705; e-mail: v.linklater@talk21.com

Linklater, Professor Karl Alexander, BVM&S, PhD, CBiol, FIBiol, FRAgS, FRCVS, FRSE. Principal, Scottish Agricultural College, since 1999; Professor of Agriculture, University of Glasgow, since 1999; a Director, The Moredun Foundation, since 1991; Director, Vet CPD, 1992-98; b. 1.9.39, Stromness, Orkney; m., Margaret Carr Gibb; 1 s.; 1 d. Educ. Robert Gordon's College, Aberdeen; Edinburgh University. General veterinary practice, Tarland,

Aberdeenshire, 1962-66; North of Scotland College of Agriculture, Aberdeen, 1966-67; Royal (Dick) School of Veterinary Studies, Edinburgh University, 1967-73; East of Scotland College of Agriculture, St. Boswells, 1973-86; Director, SAC Veterinary Services, 1986-97; Vice Principal, SAC, 1997-99; Member, Veterinary Products Committee, since 1990; President: Sheep Veterinary Society, 1983-85, British Veterinary Association, 1996-97, Association of Veterinary Teachers and Research Workers (Scotland), 1988-90, Scottish Branch, British Veterinary Association, 1992-94, Scottish Metropolitan Division, BVA, 1979-80; Alan Baldry Award, 1982. Recreations: sport; gardening; sheep breeding. Address: (h.) Bridge Park, Old Bridge Road, Selkirk TD7 4LG; T.-01750 20571; e-mail: karllinklater@netscapeonline.co.uk

Linklater, Magnus Duncan. Journalist; Chairman, The Little Sparta Trust, since 2000; b. 21.2.42, Harray, Orkney; m., Veronica Lyle; 2 s.; 1 d. Educ. Eton College; Cambridge University. Reporter, Daily Express, Manchester, 1965-66; London Evening Standard: Diary Reporter, 1966-67, Editor, Londoner's Diary, 1967-69; Sunday Times: Editor, Spectrum, 1969-72, Editor, Colour Magazine, 1972-75, News Editor/Features Editor, 1975-83; Managing Editor, The Observer, 1983-86; Editor, London Daily News, 1986-87; Editor, The Scotsman, 1988-94; Chairman, Edinburgh Book Festival, 1994-96; Chairman, Scottish Arts Council, 1996-2001; Presenter, Eye to Eye, Radio Scotland, 1994-97; Columnist, The Times and Scotland on Sunday; Member, National Cultural Strategy Review Group, 1999-2000. Publications: Hoax: the Howard Hughes-Clifford Irving Affair (Co-Author); Jeremy Thorpe: A Secret Life (Co-Author); The Falklands War (with Sunday Times Insight team); Massacre — the story of Glencoe; The Fourth Reich — Klaus Barbie and the Neo-Fascist Connection (Co-Author); Not With Honour — the inside story of the Westland Affair (Co-Author); For King and Conscience — John Graham of Claverhouse, Viscount Dundee (Co-Author); Anatomy of Scotland (Co-Editor); Highland Wilderness; People in a Landscape. Honorary Doctor of Arts, Napier University; Honorary Doctor of Law, Aberdeen University; Honorary Doctor of Letters, Glasgow University. Recreations: book-collecting; fishing. Address: (h.) 5 Drummond Place, Edinburgh EH3 6PH; T.-0131-557 5705.

Linkston, Alex Millar, IPFA. Chief Executive Officer, West Lothian Council, since 1996; b. 13.12.49, Bathgate; m., Margaret Cuddihy; 2 d. Educ. Lindsay High School, Bathgate; Glasgow College of Commerce. Joined West Lothian County Council as trainee accountant, 1965. Recreations: horse riding; swimming; Rotary. Address: (b.) West Lothian Council, West Lothian House, Livingston EH54 6QG; T.-01506 777141; e-mail: alex.linkston@westlothian.gov.uk

Linlithgow, 4th Marquess of (Adrian John Charles Hope); b. 1.7.46; m.; 1 s.; 1 d.; 2 s. by pr. m.; succeeded to title, 1987. Educ. Eton. Stockbroker. Address: Hopetoun House, South Queensferry, West Lothian, EH30 9SL.

Lishman, Professor Joyce, MA (Oxon), PhD, DipSW. Head, School of Applied Social Studies, Robert Gordon University, since 1993; m., Dr. J.R. Lishman; 1 s.; 1 d. Educ. Normanton Girls High School; St. Hilda's College, Oxford University; Edinburgh University; Aberdeen University. Social Worker/Senior Social Worker, Departments of Child and Family Psychiatry, Edinburgh; Research Assistant/Research Fellow, Aberdeen University; Editor, Research Highlights Series; Malcolm Sargent Social Worker, Royal Aberdeen Children's Hospital; Lecturer/Senior Lecturer, RGIT; Lead Assessor, Quality Assessment of Social Work, 1995-96. Publications: Handbook of Theory for Practice Teachers in Social Work (Editor); Communication in Social Work; The Role of Volunteer Coordinators in the Provision of Care (Co-

Author); Evaluation and Social Work Practice (Co-Author); Research Highlights in Social Work series (General Editor). Recreations: family and friends; music; theatre; reading; cycling. Address: (b.) School of Applied Social Studies, The Robert Gordon University, Kepplestone Annexe, Queen's Road, Aberdeen AB9 2PG; T.-01224 263201; e-mail: j.lishman@rgu.ac.uk

Lister-Kaye, Sir John, 8th Bt. of Grange, DUniv. Naturalist, Author, Lecturer; Member, International Committee, World Wilderness Foundation, since 1984; Vice President, Association for the Preservation of Rural Scotland, since 1998; President, Scottish Wildlife Trust, 1996-2001; b. 8.5.46; m., 1, Lady Sorrel Deirdre Bentinck; 1 s.; 2 d.; 2, Lucinda Anne Law; 1 d. Educ. Allhallows School. Founded Field Studies Centre, Highlands, 1970; founder Director, Aigas Trust, 1979; Director, AigasQuest Ltd., 1997; Director, Ninovus Estates Ltd., 1999; Chairman, Scottish Committee, RSPB, 1985-92; Member, Committee for Scotland, NCC, 1989-90; NW Regional Chairman, Scottish Natural Heritage, 1992-96; Honorary Doctorate, University of Stirling, 1995. Publications: The White Island, 1972; Seal Cull, 1979; The Seeing Eye, 1980; One for Sorrow, 1994; Ill Fares the Land, 1995. Address: (h.) House of Aigas, Beauly, Inverness-shire IV4 7AD; e-mail: jlk@aigas.co.uk

Lithgow, Sir William (James), 2nd Bt. of Ormsary, DL, LLD, CEng, FRINA, CBIM. Industrialist; Farmer; Vice Chairman, Lithgows Limited (Director, since 1956, Chairman, 1959-84, 1988-99); b. 10.5.34; m., 1, Valerie Helen Scott (deceased); 2, Mary Claire Hill; 2 s.; 1 d. Educ. Winchester College. Chairman, Hunterston Development Company Limited, 1987 (Director, since 1971); Director: Lithgows Limited, Lithgows Pty Limited; Chairman, Scott Lithgow Drydocks Ltd., 1967-78; Vice-Chairman, Scott Lithgow Ltd., 1968-78; Chairman, Western Ferries (Argyll) Ltd., 1972-85; Director, Bank of Scotland, 1962-86. Member: British Committee, Det Norske Veritas, 1966-92, Greenock District Hospital Board, 1961-66, General Board (Royal Society Nominee), Nat. Physical Lab., 1963-66; Honorary President, Students Association, and Member, Court, Strathclyde University, 1964-69; Member: Executive Committee, Scottish Council Development and Industry, 1969-85, Scottish Regional Council, CBI, 1969-76, Clyde Port Authority, 1969-71, West Central Scotland Plan Steering Committee, 1970-74, Board, National Ports Council, 1971-78, Scottish Milk Marketing Board, 1979-83; Chairman, Iona Cathedral Trustees Management Board, 1979-83; Council Member, Winston Churchill Memorial Trust, 1979-83; Member, Queen's Body Guard for Scotland (Royal Company of Archers), 1964; Fellow, Scottish Council Development and Industry; Honorary President: West Renfrewshire Battalion Boys' Brigade, Mid-Argyll Agricultural Society. Recreations: rural life; invention; photography. Address: (b.) PO Box 7, Lochgilphead, Argyll PA31 8JH; T.-01880 770700.

Little, Graham Edgar, FRSGS. Ordnance Survey Operations Manager for Scotland, since 1998; b. 6.3.49, Leeds; m., Dr Christina Woodrow; 1 s.; 1 d. Educ. Ayr Academy. Worked for Ordnance Survey since leaving school; resurvey of the Highlands and Islands of Scotland, 1970s; managing mapping activity in Southern and Central Scotland, 1980s; Account Manager (Sales and Marketing), 1988-98. Member, Executive Board Scotland, Association of Geographic Information; President, Mountaineering Council of Scotland, 1986-89; Chairman, Scottish Mountain Safety Group, 1990-92. Recreations: mountaineering; lecturing; writing; travel; bridge. Address: (b.) Ordnance Survey, Grayfield House, 5 Bankhead Avenue, Edinburgh EH11 4AE; T.-0131-442 2590.

Littlejohn, Professor David, BSc, PhD, CChem, FRSC, FRSE. Professor of Analytical Chemistry, Strathclyde University, since 1988; b. 1.5.53, Glasgow; m., Lesley Shaw MacDonald; 1 d. Educ. Duncanrig Secondary School, East Kilbride; Strathclyde University. Technical Officer, ICI Petrochemicals Division, Wilton, Middlesborough, 1978-80; Lecturer/Senior Lecturer in Chemistry, Strathclyde University, 1981-88. Awarded 15th SAC Silver Medal by Royal Society of Chemistry, 1987; Theophilus Redwood Lectureship, 2001; joint Editor in Chief, Talanta, International Journal of Pure and Applied Analytical Chemistry, 1989-91. Publications: 155 research papers, 10 reviews, one book. Address: (b.) Department of Pure and Applied Chemistry, Strathclyde University, 295 Cathedral Street, Glasgow G1 1XL; T.-0141-548 2067; e-mail: d.littlejohn@strath.ac.uk

Littlejohn, Doris, JP, BL, DUniv, CBE. Former President, Employment Tribunals (Scotland); b. 19.3.35, Glasgow; m., Robert; 3 d. Educ. Queen's Park School, Glasgow; University of Glasgow. Solicitor in private practice in Stirling until 1977. Chairman of Court, University of Stirling; Chairman, Forth Valley Primary Care NHS Trust; Member, Lord Chancellor's Panel on Review of Tribunals; Member, Review Panel on Retention of Organs after Post Mortems; former Member: Human Genetics Advisory Commission, Broadcasting Council for Scotland, General Advisory Committee, BBC. Address: Suilven, 125 Henderson Street, Bridge of Allan FK9 4RQ; T.-01786 832032.

Littlejohn, Robert King, MA (Aberdeen), MA (Sussex), MCIPD, FFCS. Registrar, Royal College of Physicians and Surgeons of Glasgow, since 1996; b. 17.3.46, Aberdeen; m., Anna; 1 s.; 2 d. Educ. Morrison's Academy, Crieff; Aberdeen University; Moray House College; Sussex University. Administrative (Education) Officer, RAF, 1969-96 including: Directorate of Air Staff Briefing and Co-ordination, 1987-90; Officer Commanding Administration Wing, RAF Leeming, 1990-93; Head of RAF Resettlement Service, 1993-96; retired in rank of Wing Commander. Recreations: golf; hill-walking; opera; Aberdeen FC. Address: (b.) 232-242 St. Vincent Street, Glasgow G2 5RJ; T.-0141-221 6072; e-mail: registrar@rcpsglasg.ac.uk

Littlejohn, William Hunter, RSA, RSW, RGI; b. 16.4.29, Arbroath. Educ. Arbroath High School; Dundee College of Art. Art teaching in Angus schools, 1953-56; Art teaching, Arbroath High School, 1956-66; Gray's School of Art, Aberdeen: Lecturer, 1966-72, Head of Painting, then Head of Fine Art, 1972-86; retired from teaching, 1986. Address: (h.) 43 Viewfield Road, Arbroath DD11 2DW.

Livesay, Admiral Sir Michael Howard, KCB, CIMgt. President, Royal British Legion Scotland, 1996-2001; President, Earl Haig Fund Scotland, 1996-2001; Commissioner, Northern Lighthouse Board, since 1994 (Chairman, 1997-2001); b. 5.4.36, Middlesbrough; m., Sally House; 2 d. Educ. Acklam Hall Grammar School; Britannia Royal Naval College. Joined Royal Navy, 1952; Commissioned 1957; Aircraft Direction Specialist, 1959; served HM Ships: Loch Alvie, Hermes, Aisne, Victorious; in command, HMS Hubberston, 1966; promoted Commander, 1970 and in command HMS Plymouth; promoted Captain, 1975; Captain, Fishery Protection and Mine Counter Measures at South Queensferry; first Commanding Officer, HMS Invincible, 1980; Director, Naval Warfare, 1982; promoted Rear Admiral, 1984; Flag Officer, Sea Training, 1984-86; Assistant Chief of Naval Staff, 1986-89; promoted Vice Admiral, 1989; Flag Officer, Scotland and Northern Ireland, 1989-91; promoted Admiral, 1991; Second Sea Lord and Chief of Naval Personnel, 1991-93; retired from RN 1993. Member, Thistle Foundation; Non-Executive Director, Scottish Nuclear, 1993-98. Recreations: fishing; golf; gardening; reading; outdoor sports. Address: c/o Naval Secretary, Victory Building, HM Naval Base, Portsmouth PO1 3LS.

Livingstone, Andrew Hugh, BSc (Hons), DipEd. Rector, St. Columba's School, Kilmacolm, since 1987; b. 7.12.44, Campbeltown; m., 1, Christine Margaret Henderson (deceased), 2, Alison Brown Reid; 1 s.; 1 d. Educ. Campbeltown Grammar School; University of Aberdeen; University of Glasgow; Jordanhill College of Education. High School of Glasgow, 1968-70; Principal Teacher, Mathematics, Paisley Grammar School, 1970-79; Assistant Rector, Williamwood High School, 1979-83; Depute Rector, Paisley Grammar School, 1987. Recreations: golf; bridge; walking; skiing. Address: (h.) Nithsdale, Lyle Road, Kilmacolm; T.-01505 872404.

Livingstone, Bill (William). Editorial Director, Dunfermline Press Group, since 1997; Chairman, Guild of Editors (Scotland), 1994-96; Life Trustee, Carnegie Dunfermline and Hero Fund Trusts, since 1991; b. 23.7.44, Dunfermline; m., Margaret Stark; 2 s.; 2 d. Educ. Dunfermline High School. Entire career with Dunfermline Press Group: Editor, Dunfermline Press, 1984-96. Hon. Vice-President, Dunfermline and District Bn., Boys' Brigade. Address: (b.) Pitreavie Business Park, Dunfermline, Fife KY11 8QS; T.-01383 728201.

Livingstone, George, MA, DipEd, MEd, FEIS. Senior Lecturer, Faculty of Education, University of Strathclyde, since 1998 (Vice-Dean, 1995-99); b. 19.5.38, Tranent; m., Jean Laidlaw Ritchie; 2 s. Educ. Preston Lodge; Edinburgh University; Glasgow University. Teacher/Head of Department, primary and secondary schools, East Lothian and Tanzania, 1960-67; Head Teacher, Glendinning School, Galashiels, 1967-70; Hamilton College of Education: Lecturer/Research Officer, 1970-78, Head of Department, 1978-83; Jordanhill College of Education: Senior Lecturer, 1983-90, Course Director, 1990-94. Government of Ethiopia Adviser in Teacher Education, since 2000; President, Association of Lecturers in Colleges of Education in Scotland, 1982-86; Member, General Teaching Council for Scotland, 1986-98 (Convener, Supply Committee, Vice-Convener, Exceptional Admissions Committee); Chairman, S.J.N.C. (F.E.), 1988-92; Selector, Glasgow District Rugby Union, 1988-94. Publications: Co-author three series of books for children; Scotland – Still a Half-educated Nation (Co-author), 1986; Scottish Education (Contributor), 1999; academic journal papers. Recreations: rugby union; walking; literature. Address: (h.) 1 Scott Grove, Hamilton; T.-01698 429756; e-mail: geoliving@hotmail.com

Livingstone, Ian Lang, CBE, BL, NP. Chairman: Lanarkshire Health Board, since 1993, Lanarkshire Development Agency, 1991-2000, Clan FM, New Lanarkshire Ltd.; Consultant Solicitor, since 1989; b. 23.2.38, Hamilton; m., Diane; 2 s. Educ. Hamilton Academy; Glasgow University. Qualified as Solicitor, 1960; Partner, Senior Partner, Ballantyne & Copland, Solicitors, Motherwell, 1962-86; Chairman and Director, family property investment and development company, since 1987. Former Chairman, Motherwell Football Club; Chairman, Board, Motherwell College, 1989-97; Member, Dalziel High School Board; Governor, David Livingstone Memorial Trust; Elder, St. Mary's Parish Church, Motherwell. Recreations: walking; football; music. Address: (h.) 223 Manse Road, Motherwell ML1 2PY; T.-01698 253750.

Livingstone, Marilyn. MSP (Labour), Kirkcaldy, since 1999. Former Head of Business School, Fife College; Councillor. Address: (b.) Scottish Parliament, Edinburgh EH99 1SP; T.-0131-348 5744.

Llewellyn, Professor Sue, BA, MSc (Soc Sci), PhD, FRSA. Professor of Management Control, Edinburgh University, since 1999; b. Manchester; 3 s. Educ. Stretford Grammar School; Manchester University. Research Fellow, Stirling University, 1989; Lecturer/Senior Lecturer, Edinburgh University, 1991-99; visiting appointments: Australia, Canada, Sweden. Publications: 50, including journal articles, books, monographs and research reports (recipient of several awards for excellence in journal articles, 1995, 1997, 1998 and 1999). Recreations: thinking things over; novels; theatre; travel. Address: (b.) Edinburgh University Management School, George Square, Edinburgh, EH8 9JY; T.-0131-0650 8381; e-mail: S.Llewellyn@ed.ac.uk

Lloyd, Ivor Graham, BA, DipLib, MLib, ALA. Head of Information Services, University of Abertay Dundee, since 1996; b. 28.10.50, Edinburgh; m., Rosemary; 1 s.; 1 d. Educ. Ainslie Park Secondary School, Edinburgh; University of Strathclyde; University of Wales. Assistant Librarian, Kirkcaldy Technical College, 1975-76; Subject Librarian, Duncan of Jordanstone College of Art, 1976-84; Depute Chief Librarian, Dundee College of Technology, 1984-89; Chief Librarian, University of Abertay Dundee, 1989-96. Recreations: golf; gardening. Address: (b.) University of Abertay Dundee, Bell Street, Dundee; T.-01382 308866.

Lloyd-Jones, Glyn Robin, MA, BA. Author and Novelist; President, Scottish PEN International, since 1997; b. 5.10.34, London; m., Sallie Hollocombe; 1 s.; 2 d. Educ. Blundell's School, Tiverton; Selwyn College, Cambridge University; Jordanhill College of Education. Teaching in Scottish secondary schools; Director, Curriculum Development Centre, Clydebank; English-Speaking Union Thyne Travel Scholarship to America, 1974; President, Scottish Association of Writers, 1981-86; Adviser, Education Department, Dunbartonshire, 1972-89; Co-ordinator, Scottish Forum for Development Education in Schools, 1996-99; radio drama: Ice in Wonderland, 1992 (winner, Radio Times new drama script award); Rainmaker, 1995. Publications: children's: Where the Forest and the Garden Meet, 1980; novels: Lord of the Dance (Winner, BBC/Arrow First Novel Competition, 1983); The Dreamhouse, 1985; Fallen Angels, 1992; education books: Assessment: From Principles to Action, 1985; How to Produce Better Worksheets, 1985; non-fiction: Argonauts of the Western Isles, 1989. Recreations: mountaineering; sea-kayaking; photography; chess. Address: (h.) 26 East Clyde Street, Helensburgh G84 7PG; T.-01436 672010.

Lo, Professor Kwok Lun, MSc, PhD, CEng, FIEE, FRSE, FRSA. Professor of Power Systems, Strathclyde University, since 1989; Visiting and Consultant Professor to several overseas universities, since 1987; power systems consultant, since 1970; b. 23.6.43; m., Dr. K.K.N. Lo; 2 s. Educ. St. Joseph's College, Hong Kong; UMIST. Began career with South Wales Switchgear Ltd., Central Electricity Generating Board, South Wales Electricity Board; joined Department of Electrical Engineering, Paisley College of Technology, 1971; joined Strathclyde University, 1977, as Lecturer, then Senior Lecturer, then Reader; author/co-author of more than 270 technical publications. Recreations: swimming; walking. Address: (b.) Department of EEE, Royal College, 204 George Street, Strathclyde University, Glasgow; T.-0141-548 2169.

Lochhead, Liz. Poet and Playwright; b. 1947, Motherwell. Educ. Glasgow School of Art. Combined teaching art and writing for eight years; became full-time writer after selection as first holder, Scottish/Canadian Writers' Exchange Fellowship, 1978; former Writer in Residence, Tattenhall Centre, Chester. Publications include: Memo for Spring, Islands, Grimm Sisters, Dreaming of Frankenstein, True Confessions; plays include: Blood and Ice, Dracula, Same Difference, Sweet Nothings, Now and Then, True Confessions, Mary Queen of Scots Got Her Head Chopped Off, The Big Picture; Perfect Days.

Lochhead, Richard Neilson, BA (Hons). MSP (SNP). North East of Scotland, since 1999; b. 24.5.69, Paisley. Educ. Williamwood High School, Clarkston; Stirling University. Economic Development Officer, Dundee City Council, 1988-99; Office Manager for Alex Salmond, 1994-98. Recreations: squash; cinema; reading; travel; five-a-side football. Address: (b.) 70 Rosemount Place, Aberdeen AB25 2XJ; T.-01224 623150.

Locke, Alasdair James Dougall, MA. Chairman, Abbot Group PLC, since 1992; b. 29.8.53, Aldershot; m., Kathleen Anne; 2 s. Educ. Uppingham School, Rutland; Wadham College, Oxford University. Assistant Vice President: Citibank N. A., 1974-78, Oceanic Finance Corporation, 1978-81; Vice President, American Express Leasing Corporation, 1981-83; Director, Henry Ansbacher and Co., Ltd., 1983-87; Deputy Chairman, Kelt Energy PLC, 1987-91. Member, OSO Advisory Board. Recreations: shooting; golf; skiing. Address: (b.) Minto Drive, Altens, Aberdeen AB12 3LW; T.-01224 299600.

Lockhart of the Lee, Angus Hew; b. 17.8.46, Dunsyre; m., Susan Elizabeth Normand; 1 s.; 1 d. Educ. Rannoch School, Perthshire; North of Scotland College of Agriculture. Recognised as Chief of the Name Lockhart, 1957; Owner and Manager, Lee and Carnwath Estates; Member, Standing Council of Scottish Chiefs. Recreations: shooting; skiing. Address: (h.) Newholm, Dunsyre, Lanark ML11 8NQ; T.-01968 682254.

Lockhart, Sheriff Brian Alexander, BL. Sheriff, Glasgow and Strathkelvin, since 1981; b. 1.10.42, Ayr; m., Christine Ross Clark; 2 s.; 2 d. Educ. Glasgow Academy; Glasgow University. Partner, Robertson Chalmers and Auld, Solicitors, 1967-79; Sheriff, North Strathclyde, at Paisley, 1979-81; Member, Parole Board for Scotland; Secretary, Sheriffs' Association. Recreations: fishing; golf; squash; family. Address: (h.) 18 Hamilton Avenue, Glasgow G41; T.-0141-427 1921.

Lockhart, Brian Robert Watson. MA (Hons), DipEd. Headmaster, Robert Gordon's College, Aberdeen, since 1996; b. 19.7.44, Edinburgh; m., Fiona Anne Sheddon; 1 s.; 2 d. Educ. George Heriot's School, Edinburgh; Aberdeen University. Teacher of History and Economic History, George Heriot's School, 1968-72; Principal Teacher of History, 1972-81; Deputy Rector, High School of Glasgow, 1981-96. Headteachers' Association of Scotland: Member, Council, 1988-2001, Member, Executive, 1989-94; Chair, Universities and Colleges Admissions Service Scottish Standing Committee, 1998-2000; Member, Higher Still Implementation Group. Recreations: reading biographies; sport; films; politics. Address: (h.) 80 Gray Street, Aberdeen AB10 6JE; T.-01224 315776.

Lockhead, Moir, OBE, IEng, MCIT, MIRTE. Deputy Chairman and Chief Executive, FirstGroup plc; b. 25.4.45, Sedgefield; m., Audrey; 3 s.; 1 d. Educ. West Cornforth Secondary School; Darlington Technical College; Middlesborough Polytechnic. Former Head of Engineering, Strathclyde Passenger Transport Executive; joined Grampian Regional Transport as General Manager, 1985; Executive Chairman, GRT Bus Group PLC, 1989. Address: (b.) 395 King Street, Aberdeen AB24 5RP; T.-01224 650102; e-mail: moir.lockhead@firstgroup.com

Lockley, Stephen Randolph, BSc, CEng, MICE, FICT, MIHT, DipTE. Transport Consultant, since 1997; b. 19.6.43, Manchester; m., Angela; 2 d. Educ. Morecambe Grammar School; Manchester University. Highway and

Planning Engineer, Lancashire County Council, 1964-72; Transportation and Planning Engineer, Lanarkshire County Council, 1972-75; Strathclyde Regional Council: Principal Engineer (Transportation), 1975-77, Depute Director of Policy Planning, 1977-80, Principal Executive Officer, 1980-86; Director General, Strathclyde Passenger Transport Executive, 1986-97. Address: 64 Townhead Street, Strathaven, Lanarkshire ML10 6DJ; T.-01357 529395.

Lodder, Professor Christina Anne, BA, DPhil, FRSE. Professor, School of Art History, St Andrews University, since 1995; b. 21.2.48, Colchester; 1 d. Educ. York University; University of Sussex. St Andrews University: Lecturer in Art History, 1979, Reader in Art History, 1991; Trustee, National Galleries of Scotland; Member, Council, Royal Society of Edinburgh. Publications: Russian Constructivism, 1983; Constructing Modernity: The Art and Career of Naum Gabo (Co-author), 2000. Recreations: music; opera; gardening; theatre; novels. Address: (b.) School of Art History, St Andrews University, St Andrews KY16 9AD; T.-01334 462400.

Logan, Rev. Robert James Victor, MA, BD. Minister, Abdie and Dunbog linked with Newburgh, 1998-2001; Minister, Crown Church, Inverness, 1970-98; b. 8.6.38, Kilmarnock; m., Catherine Steel Young. Educ. Dundee High School; St. Andrews University; Edinburgh University. Assistant Minister, Auld Kirk of Ayr, 1962-64; Minister, Newton Parish Church, Dalkeith, 1964-70; Member, Church Boundaries' Commission, 1974-75; Clerk: Synod of Moray, 1972-75, Synod of the Southern Highlands, 1976-92, Inverness Presbytery, 1980-96; Convener, Nomination Committee, General Assembly, 1979-82; Chairman, successful group applying for franchise to operate Moray Firth Radio, 1979-81. Publication: The Lion, The Pit and the Snowy Day. Recreations: classical music; opera; bridge; reading history. Address: (h.) Lindores, 1 Murray Place, Smithton, Inverness IV2 7PX; T.-01463 790226; e-mail: rjvlogan@aol.com

Logan, Rt. Rev. Vincent, DipRE. Roman Catholic Bishop of Dunkeld, since 1981; b. 30.6.41, Bathgate. Educ. Blairs College, Aberdeen; St. Andrew's College, Drygrange. Ordained Priest, 1964; Assistant Priest, St. Margaret's, Edinburgh, 1964-66; Corpus Christi College, London, 1966-67; Chaplain, St. Joseph's Hospital, Rosewell, Midlothian, 1966-67; Adviser in Religious Education, Archdiocese of St. Andrews and Edinburgh, 1967; Parish Priest, St. Mary's, Ratho, 1977-81; Vicar Episcopal for Education, Edinburgh, 1978. Address: Bishop's House, 29 Roseangle, Dundee DD1 4LS; T.-01382 224327.

Logie, Professor Robert Howie, BSc, PhD, CPyschol, FBPsS, FRSA. Anderson Professor of Psychology, University of Aberdeen, since 1998 (Head, Department of Psychology, since 1997); b. 23.3.54, Ajmer, India; m., Elizabeth; 2 s. Educ. Aberdeen Academy; University of Aberdeen; University College, London. Researcher, MRC Applied Psychology Unit, Cambridge, 1980-86; University of Aberdeen: Lecturer in Psychology, 1987, Senior Lecturer, 1992, Personal Professor, 1995. Publications: over 120 including 12 authored or edited books, notably Visuo Spatial Working Memory, 1995. Dorothy Hodgkin Lecturer, British Association for the Advancement of Science, 1995. Recreation: choral singing. Address: William Guild Building, Old Aberdeen AB24 2UB; T.-01224 272241.

Logue, James, CEng, FIMechE, MIMgt. Business Development Manager, Scot-Train Ltd., since 1997; Personnel Director, ScotRail Railways Ltd., 1994-97; Chairman, BTPF(S); b. 13.5.39, Glasgow; m., Pamela; 1 s.; 2 d. Educ. St. Mungo's, Glasgow; Stow College, Glasgow. ScotRail: Area Engineer, 1978-89, Quality Programmes Manager, 1989-92, Retail Manager, 1992-94; Chairman, IMechE Railway Division, Scottish Branch. Recreations:

golf; DIY; car maintenance; socialising. Address: (h.) 1 Linnhe Avenue, Bishopbriggs, Glasgow G64 1HG; T.-0141-563 6598; e-mail: jim@scot-train.com

Longmore, Alexander Bryan George, MA, LLB. Deputy Lieutenant, Inverness, since 1998; Honorary Sheriff, Inverness, since 1992; General Commissioner of Inland Revenue, Inverness 1st, since 1992; b. 30.4.35, Evanton; m., Leonella Lucia; 2 s. Educ. Robert Gordon's College, Aberdeen; University of Aberdeen. Assistant Trust Officer, The National Trust Co. Ltd., Toronto, Canada, 1958-60; Teacher of English, European School, Parma, Italy, 1960-61; Solicitor, Anderson Shaw and Gilbert, Inverness (retired as Senior Partner, 1995, Consultant, since 1995). Past Chairman, Inverness Civic Trust; Past Chairman, Highland Italian Circle. Recreations: gardening; walking; theatre; reading. Address: 25 Midmills Road, Inverness IV2 3NZ; T.-01463 235236.

Lord, Geoffrey, OBE, MA, AIB, FRSA. Founder The ADAPT Trust, 1989; Council Member, National Youth Orchestras of Scotland, since 1998; Trustee and Secretary, Edinburgh Voluntary Organisations Trusts, since 1997; Trustee, PlayRight Scotland Trust, since 1998; b. 24.2.28, Rochdale; m., Jean; 1 s.; 1 d. Educ. Rochdale Grammar School; Bradford University. Midland Bank Ltd., 1946-58; Greater Manchester Probation and After-Care Service, 1958-76 (Deputy Chief Probation Officer, 1974-76); Secretary and Treasurer, Carnegie UK Trust, 1977-93; Vice-President, Selcare Trust; Chairman, Pollock Memorial Missionary Trust; Honorary Fellow, Manchester Metropolitan University, 1987; Former Trustee and Chairman, HomeStart UK; Chairman, The Unemployed Voluntary Action Fund, 1990-95; Past President, Centre for Environmental Interpretation. Publications: The Arts and Disabilities, 1981; Interpretation of the Environment, 1984. Recreations: the arts; philately; walking; enjoying life. Address: (h.) 9 Craigleith View, Edinburgh.

Lord, John, BA, FRSA. Director, Yellow Book Ltd., consultants; b. 15.4.52, Bristol; m., Wendy; 2 s.; 1 d. Educ. Australia; Woking County Grammar School; Kingston College of Further Education; Warwick University. Freelance journalist and writer; Administrative Trainee, Department of Employment; Area Manager, Training Agency, 1989-90; Chief Executive, Enterprise Ayrshire, 1990-93; Director Strategy, Scottish Enterprise, 1993-96; Director, EDAW Consultants, 1996-97; Founder, John Lord Associates, economic development consultants, 1997-2000. Publication: The Floating Harbour – A Landscape History of Bristol City Docks. Recreations: architectural history; football; the arts. Address: (b.) Studio 1010, Mile End, Abbey Mill Business Centre, Paisley PA1 1JS; e-mail: john.lord@yellowbookltd.com

Lord, Jonathan Christopher, MA. Secretary, Royal Scottish Automobile Club, since 1991; b. 29.4.53, Alverstoke; m., Angela Phillips; 1 s. Educ. Dollar Academy; St. Andrews University. Ministry of Defence (Naval), 1975-76; Royal Scottish Automobile Club, since 1976; Member, British Motor Sports Council, since 1991; MSA Rallies Committee, since 1982; FIA Observer for International Rallies; MSA Steward; Clerk of the Course, RSAC International Scottish Rally, since 1982; Secretary, RSAC (Motor Sport) Limited, since 1982; Secretary to the Vestry, St. Bride's Episcopal Church, Glasgow, since 1991. Recreations: music (especially choral singing); cricket; motor sport; following Dunfermline Athletic FC. Address: (h.) 11 Melrose Gardens, Glasgow G20 6RB; T.-0141-946 5045; e-mail: rsac_motorsport@compuserve.com

Lorimer, A. Ross, MD, FRCP, FRCPGlas, FRCPEdin. Honorary Professor, Glasgow University; Consultant Physician and Cardiologist, Glasgow Royal Infirmary, since 1970; President, Royal College of Physicians and Surgeons of Glasgow; b. 5.5.37, Bellshill; m., Fiona Marshall; 3 s.

Educ. Uddingston Grammar School; High School of Glasgow; Glasgow University. Recreations: reading; walking. Address: (b.) Royal College of Physicians and Surgeons of Glasgow, 232-242 St. Vincent Street, Glasgow.

Lorimer, Thomas Aitken (Ken), BEd, MInstAM, FIMgt, FFCS. Director and Chief Executive, Hansel Foundation, since 1998; Chief Executive, Hansel Alliance, since 1998; b. 17.5.54, Mauchline; 2 d. Educ. Belmont Academy, Ayr; Ayr Academy; Ayr College; Craigie College of Education; Strathclyde University. Joined Ayr County Council, 1971, transferred to Strathclyde Regional Council, 1975, held administrative and public relations appointments with both; Hansel Village: General Administrator,1985; General Manager, 1992. Scottish Chair, UK Council Member, Non Executive Director, Association for Residential Care; Non Executive Director, Ayrshire Council on Alcohol. Recreations: music; theatre/cinema; literature. Address: (b.) Hansel Village, Symington, Ayrshire KA1 5PU; Y.-01563 830340.

Lothian, 12th Marquess of (Peter Francis Walter Kerr), KCVO, DL; b. 8.9.22, Melbourne, near Derby; m., Antonella Newland; 2 s.; 4 d. Educ. Ampleforth College, York; Christ Church, Oxford. Parliamentary Under Secretary, Ministry of Health, 1964; Parliamentary Under Secretary, Foreign and Commonwealth Office, 1970-72; Lord in Waiting, 1972-73; Lord Warden of the Stannaries, 1977-83. Knight of Malta; Member, Queen's Bodyguard for Scotland; Chairman of Council, Scottish Branch, British Red Cross, 1973-83. Recreation: music. Address: Ferniehirst Castle, Jedburgh, Roxburghshire; T.-01835 864021/0835 862872.

Lothian, Amanda J.C., MA, LLB, DipLP. Advocate, since 1998; b. 20.9.60, Kampala; 2 s.; 1 d. Educ. Gordonstoun School; Albyn School for Girls; Aberdeen University; Edinburgh University. Recreation: shopping. Address: (h.) 28 Gayfield Square, Edinburgh EH1 3PA; T.-0131-315 4254.

Lothian, Professor Niall, BA, CA, FRSA. Professor, Graduate School of Business, Heriot-Watt University, since 1996; b. 27.2.48, Edinburgh; m., Carol Miller; 1 s.; 1 d. Educ. Daniel Stewart's College, Edinburgh; Heriot-Watt University. Lecturer, Senior Lecturer, Professor and Head, Department of Accountancy and Finance, Heriot-Watt University, 1973-96; Visiting Professor: IMEDE, Lausanne, 1979-80, INSEAD, Fontainebleau, since 1984; Consultant, United Nations Industrial Development Organisation, Vienna, since 1980; President, Institute of Chartered Accountants of Scotland, 1995-96; Chairman, Governing Council, George Watson's College, since 1999; Director, Stoddard International plc, since 1998. Publications: Accounting for Inflation: Issues and Managerial Practices, 1978; Audit Quality and Value for Money, 1983; How Companies Manage R. & D., 1984; Corporate Performance Indicators, 1987. Address: (b.) Graduate School of Business, Heriot-Watt University, PO Box 807, Riccarton, Edinburgh EH14 4AT; T.-0131-451 3090.

Loudon, Alasdair John, LLB, NP, WS. Partner, Turcan Connell WS, Edinburgh, since 2001; b. 7.4.56, Edinburgh; m., Mary V.; 1 d. Educ. Edinburgh Academy; Dundee University. Apprentice, Tods, Murray and Jamieson, WS, 1978-80; Qualified Assistant, Warner & Co., 1980-82, Partner, 1982-92; founded Loudons WS, 1992, Senior Partner, until 2001; accredited as specialist in family law; Member, Sheriff Court Rules Council for Scotland; President, Edinburgh Bar Association, 1996-98. Recreations: golf (Bruntsfield Links and Luffness New); football (Heart of Midlothian supporter). Address: (b.) Princes Exchange, 1 Earl Grey Street, Edinburgh EH3 9EE; e-mail: ajl@turcanconnell.com

Loudon, John Alexander, LLB, NP, SSC. Consultant, Dundas & Wilson CS; specialist in Liquor Licensing Law; b. 5.12.49, Edinburgh; m., Alison Jane Bruce Laird; 2 s. Educ. Edinburgh Academy; Dundee University. Apprenticeship, Tindal, Oatts and Roger, Solicitors, Glasgow. Former Member, Council, Law Society of Scotland; Secretary, Scotland Committee, British Hospitality Association; President, SSC Society; High Constable, City of Edinburgh Ward XV. Recreations: children; shooting; stalking; skiing; occasional use of a mountain bike and even more occasional golf. Address: (b.) Dundas & Wilson CS, Saltire Court, 20 Castle Terrace, Edinburgh EH1 2EN.

Loudon, John Bruce, MB, ChB, FRCPsych, DPM. Consultant Psychiatrist, Royal Edinburgh Hospital, since 1978; Principal Medical Officer (part-time, on secondment), Department of Health, Scottish Executive, since 1997; b. 12.8.43, Edinburgh; m., Susan Mary Lay; 3 s. Educ. Edinburgh Academy; Edinburgh University. Clinical Director, General Psychiatry, Royal Edinburgh Hospital, 1991-94; Head, Mental Health Service, Edinburgh Healthcare NHS Trust, 1994-96. Address: (b.) Andrew Duncan Clinic, Morningside, Edinburgh EH10 5HF; T.-0131-537 6452; e-mail: john.loudon@scotland.gsi.gov.uk

Loughrey, Ann. Director, Energy Action Scotland, since 1993. Early career in Health Service; Strathclyde Regional Council; Heatwise Dunbarton, 1986-92; EAS Senior Development Officer, 1992-93; Former member: SCVO Policy Committee; Right to Warmth; Member: NEA Executive Council; ScottishPower's Green Energy Trust; ScottishPower's Environment Forum; energywatch; National Right to Fuel; Energy Efficiency Partnerships Steering Committee; Scottish Home Energy Survey Team Steering Committee. Address: Suite 4a, Ingram House, 227 Ingram Street, Glasgow, G1 1DA; T.-0141-226 3064; e-mail: eas@eas.org.uk

Lovat, 18th Lord (Simon Fraser); b. 13.2.77. Educ. Harrow; Edinburgh University. Succeeded to title, 1995.

Love, Frances Mary. Director, Couple Counselling Scotland, since 1987; Tutor and Lecturer, Scottish Human Relations and Counselling Course, since 1986; Organisational Consultant, SIHR, since 1986; b. 2.7.38, Edinburgh; m., James Love; 1 d. Educ. Broughton Secondary School. Edinburgh Public Library Service; voluntary playleader, Edinburgh Toddlers Playcentres; Pre-School Playgroup Association: playgroup supervisor, fieldworker, Scottish Adviser; General Secretary, Pre-School Playgroups Association; Executive Officer/Company Secretary, Scottish Council for Opportunities in Play Experience (SCOPE). Member: Council, Scottish Institute of Human Relations, Management Board, COSCA, Council, Stepfamily Scotland; Convener, Counselling Working Group, Edinburgh and Lothian Council on Alcohol. Recreations: gardening; reading; theatre; dress-making; grandson. Address: (b.) 40 N. Castle Street, Edinburgh EH1 3BN; T.-0131-225 5006; e-mail: enquiries@couplecounselling.org

Love, Professor James, BA, MSc, PhD. Dean, Strathclyde Business School, since 1999; Professor of Economics, Strathclyde University, since 1995; b. 31.7.48, Dunfermline; m., Jane Lindores Scott; 2 d. Educ. Beath High School; Strathclyde University. Lecturer, Haile Sellassie 1 University, 1971-74; Lecturer, Strathclyde University, 1974-79; Lecturer, Ghana University, 1979-80; Senior Lecturer, University of Lund, 1980-81; Senior Research Fellow, Fraser of Allander Institute, 1984-86; Lecturer, Senior Lecturer, Reader, Strathclyde University, 1986-95; Head, Department of Economics, and Vice-Dean (Research), Strathclyde Business School, 1994-99. Chairman, Board of Trustees, SOLAS; Associate Adviser, British Council.

Recreations: sport; particularly the (mis)fortunes of Aberdeen FC and Cowdenbeath FC. Address: (b.) Strathclyde University, Glasgow G1 1XQ; T.-0141-548 4384.

Love, Robert Malcolm, MA (Hons), FRSAMD. Former Controller of Drama, Scottish Television; b. 9.1.37, Paisley. Educ. Paisley Grammar School; Glasgow University; Washington University, St. Louis. Actor and Director, various repertory companies, including Nottingham Playhouse, 1962-65; Producer, Thames TV, 1966-75, including Public Eye, Van Der Valk; freelance Producer, 1976-79, including Thames TV, LWT, Seacastle Film Productions, Scottish TV. Awards including: Commonwealth Film Festival, New York TV and Film Festival, Chicago Film Festival, BAFTA Scotland, nominated for International Emmy, New York, 1982; productions for Scottish include Taggart, High Road, Doctor Finlay, McCallum. Governor, RSAMD, since 1994; Member, Scottish Arts Council, 1994-99; Chair, Beckett Time Festival, 2000. Recreations: literature; music; theatre; travel.

Lovelace, 5th Earl of (Peter Axel William Locke King); b. 26.11.51; m.; succeeded to title, 1964. Address: Torridon House, Torridon, IV22 2HA.

Low, Alistair James, BSc, FFA. Director, Scottish Widows, since 1984; b. 2.8.42, Dundee; m., Shona Wallace; 2 s.; 1 d. Educ. Dundee High School; St. Andrews University. Recreations: golf; skiing; bridge. Address: (h.) Thornfield, Erskine Loan, Gullane, East Lothian.

Low, Bet, ARSA, RSW, RGI, Hon. DLitt (Glasgow). Freelance Artist; b. 27.12.24, Gourock. Educ. Greenock Academy; Glasgow School of Art; Hospitalfield College of Art. Joined Unity Theatre Company, set designing etc., 1946; exhibited in international exhibition, Warsaw, 1954; co-founder and exhibitor, first open-air exhibition on railings at Botanic Gardens, Glasgow, 1956; worked part-time as art therapist, early 60s; Co-Founder and Co-Director, New Charing Cross Gallery, Glasgow, 1963-68; major retrospective exhibition, Third Eye Centre, 1985; exhibited widely in Britain and Europe. Recreations: reading; opera; Glasgow Art Club; beach-combing; just pottering. Address: 53 Kelvinside Gardens, Glasgow G20 6BQ; T.-0141-946 1377.

Low, Cuthbert Whyte Fraser, FFA, AIA, FPMI. Chairman, Fraser Low Actuarial Consultancy Ltd., since 1997; President, Faculty of Actuaries, 1998-2000; b. 6.6.43, Glasgow; m., Jennifer Jean; 1 s.; 1 d. Educ. Merchiston Castle School, Edinburgh. Scottish Mutual Assurance Society, 1961-72; Chief Actuarial Officer, Sedgwick Group, 1972-89; Director, W.F. Corroon Ltd., 1990-96. President, Society of Pension Consultants, 1986-88; Master, Worshipful Company of Actuaries, 1995-96. Recreations: golf; tennis; swimming; dancing; bridge. Address: 4B Belford Park, Edinburgh EH4 3DP; T.-0131 332 9132.

Low, Eur Ing. Sir James (Richard) Morrison-, 3rd Bt, DL, DFH, CEng, MIEE. Director, Osborne & Hunter Ltd., Glasgow, 1956-89; b. 3.8.25; m., Ann Rawson Gordon; 1 s.; 3 d. Educ. Ardvreck; Harrow; Merchiston; Faraday House, London. Royal Corps of Signals, 1943-47 (Captain). President, Electrical Contractors Association of Scotland, 1982-84; Director, National Inspection Council of Electrical Installation Contractors, 1982-88 (Chairman, Scottish Committee, 1982-88); Chairman, Electrical Industry Liaison Committee, 1986-88; Chairman, Fife Area Scout Council, 1966-84; Chairman, Cupar Branch, East Fife Conservative Association, 1965-78; Trustee, TSB, 1960-80; President, Electrical Contractors Association of Scotland, 1982-84; DL, Fife, 1978.

Lowden, Professor Gordon Stuart, MA, LLB, CA; b. 22.5.27, Bangkok; m., Kathleen; 2 s.; 1 d. Educ. Dundee High School; Strathallan School; St. John's College, Cambridge; St. Andrews University. Trained with Moody Stuart & Robertson, CA, Dundee; became Partner, 1959; part-time Lecturer/Senior Lecturer, Dundee University, 1955-83; Honorary Professor, Department of Accountancy and Business Finance, Dundee University, since 1987; Honorary Sheriff, since 1991; former Chairman, Dundee Port Authority; Past President, Institute of Chartered Accountants of Scotland. Recreations: golf; watching rugby; bridge. Address: (h.) 169 Hamilton Street, Barnhill, Dundee DD5 2RE; T.-01382 778360.

Lowe, Professor Gordon Douglas Ogilvie, MB, ChB, MD, FRCPEdin, FRCPGlas, FRCPLond, FFPHM. Professor of Vascular Medicine, Glasgow University, since 1993; Consultant Physician, Glasgow Royal Infirmary, since 1985; Co-Director, West of Scotland Haemophilia Centre, since 1987; b. 2.1.49, London; m., Ann Harvie; 1 s.; 1 d. Educ. Dundee High School; St. Andrews University. House Officer, Royal Infirmary and Maryfield Hospital, Dundee, 1972-73; Senior House Officer, City Hospital, Nottingham, 1973-74; Registrar, Royal Infirmary, Glasgow, 1974-77; Lecturer, Glasgow University, 1978-85, Senior Lecturer, 1985-92, Reader, 1992-93. Assessor, RCPEdin.; Past President, British Society for Haemostasis and Thrombosis. Publications: editor of books and author of publications on thrombosis and bleeding disorders. Recreations: travel; railways; gardening. Address: (b.) Department of Medicine, Royal Infirmary, Glasgow G31 2ER; T.-0141-211 5412.

Lowe, Janet, BA (Hons), MBA, MIPD. Principal, Lauder College, Dunfermline, since 1996; b. 27.9.50, South Normanton; m., Donald Thomas Stewart. Educ. Swanwick Hall Grammar School; Hull University; Dundee University. Immigration Officer, Home Office, 1973-76; Personnel Assistant, Hull University, 1976-80; Administrator, Lothian Region Social Work Department, 1980-82; Napier University: Examinations Officer, Personnel Officer, Assistant Academic Registrar, 1982-88; Secretary and Registrar, Duncan of Jordanstone College of Art, 1988-93; Depute Principal, Lauder College, 1993-96. Member: Scottish Consultative Council on the Curriculum, 1995-99, Board of Management, Scottish Further Education Unit, 1993-2001, Court, Heriot-Watt University, since 1999; Member, Board, Scottish Enterprise, since 1998. Recreations: travel; literature; outdoor pursuits. Address: (b.) Lauder College, Halbeath, Dunfermline KY11 8DY; T.-01383 845002; e-mail: jlowe@lauder.ac.uk

Lowe, Martin John Brodie, BSc, PhD. Secretary to Edinburgh University, since 1989; b. 10.4.40, Dorking; m., Janet MacNaughtan; 3 s.; 1 d. Educ. Dunfermline High School; St. Andrews University. British Council Officer, with service in Tanzania and South India, 1965-69; Strathclyde University: Administrative Assistant, 1969-71, Assistant Registrar, 1971-73, Secretary to Senate, 1973-81; Secretary and Registrar, St. Andrews University, 1981-89. National Council, Voluntary Service Overseas, 1976-83; Honorary Secretary, then Chairman, Glasgow and West of Scotland VSO Committee, 1973-81; Hon. Secretary, Royal Scottish Pipers' Society, 1997-2001, Hon. Pipe Major, since 2001. Recreations: piping; hill-walking; family interests. Address: (b.) Old College, South Bridge, Edinburgh EH8 9YL; T.-0131-650 2143.

Löwenhardt, Professor John, MA, PhD. Director, Institute of Central and East European Studies, University of Glasgow, since 1997; Alexander Nove Professor, University of Glasgow, since 1997; b. 22.8.47, Almelo, Netherlands. Educ. Erasmus Lyceum, Almelo; University of Amsterdam. Lecturer then Senior Lecturer, University of Amsterdam, 1976-86; Reader, University of Leiden, 1986-97. Member, Editorial Board, Europe-Asia Studies, since

1997. Publications: The Soviet Politburo, 1982; The Reincarnation of Russia, 1995; Party Politics in Postcommunist Russia (Editor), 1998; The Army and State in Postcommunist Europe (Editor), 2001. Address: (b.) ICEES, University of Glasgow, Adam Smith Building, Room 5-602, Glasgow G12 8RT; T.-0141-330 4579; e-mail: lowenhardt@hotmail.com

Lowther, Gordon William, BSc, DipRCPath. Head of Cytogenetics, Institute of Medical Genetics, Glasgow, since 1997; b. 5.12.55, Newcastle upon Tyne. Educ. Dame Allans Boys School; Sheffield University. Clinical Cytogeneticist, Centre for Human Genetics, Sheffield, 1979-87; Principal Cytogeneticist, then Top Grade Cytogeneticist, Medical Genetics Glasgow. Member, Association of Clinical Cytogeneticists Council. Address: (b.) Institute of Medical Genetics, Yorkhill NHS Trust, Glasgow G3 8SJ; T.-0141-201 0365.

Lucas, Adrian, MHSM. Chief Executive, Scottish Ambulance Service, since 1999; b. 27.3.54, Chester; m., Susan; 2 s. Educ. Hoole Bank House School, Chester. Chief Ambulance Officer, Cheshire Ambulance Service, 1988-91; Chief Executive, Greater Manchester Ambulance Service, 1991-99. Non-Executive Director, Barronmore Industries, 1995-99. Recreations: hill-walking; windsurfing. Address: (b.) Tipperlinn Road, Edinburgh EH10 5UU; T.-0131-446 7016.

Ludlam, Professor Christopher A., BSc (Hons), MB, ChB, PhD, FRCP, FRCPath. Professor of Haematology and Coagulation Medicine, University of Edinburgh; Consultant Haematologist, Edinburgh Royal Infirmary, since 1980; Director, Edinburgh Haemophilia and Thrombosis Centre, since 1980; b. 6.6.46, Edinburgh. Educ. Edinburgh University. MRC Research Fellow, 1972-75; Senior Registrar in Haematology, University Hospital of Wales, Cardiff, 1975-78; Lecturer in Haematology, University of Wales, 1979. Address: (b.) Department of Haematology, Royal Infirmary, Edinburgh; T.-0131-536 2122; e-mail: Christopher.Ludlam@ed.ac.uk

Lueck, Christian Joseph, MA, MB, BChir, MRCP (UK), PhD, FRCP (Edin). Consultant Neurologist, Western General Hospital, Edinburgh, since 1994; b. 9.10.58, Washington DC; m., Diana Perriman; 2 d. Educ. Downside School; Cambridge University; St. Thomas' Hospital Medical School. Junior medical training, various hospitals, London and Kent, 1982-87; Wellcome Research Fellow, 1987-90; training in neurology, National Hospital for Neurology, 1990-94. Chairman, Board of Trustees, Enlighten, Action for Epilepsy, since 1999. Recreation: music. Address: (b.) Department of Clinical Neuroscience, Western General Hospital, Crewe Road, Edinburgh EH4 2XU; T.-0131-537 2452; e-mail: cl@skull.dcm.ed.ac.uk

Luke, Iain M., MP. Labour MP, Dundee East, since 2001; b. 8.10.51; m. Educ. Dundee University; Edinburgh University; Jordanhill College. Assistant Collector of Taxes, 1969-74; Lecturer, then Senior Lecturer, Dundee College of Further Education, 1983-2001. Address: (b.) House of Commons, London SW1A 0AA.

Lumsden of Cushnie, David Gordon Allen d'Aldecamb, MA (Cantab), FSA (Scot). Garioch Pursuivant of Arms, since 1986; Chairman, Castles of Scotland Preservation Trust, since 1985; President, 1745 Association and Scottish Military History Society, since 1991; b. 25.5.33, Quetta, Baluchistan, Empire of India. Educ. Allhallows, Devon; Bedford School; Jesus College, Cambridge. London Scottish TA; Executive, British American Tobacco, 1959-82; Director: Heritage Porcelain Ltd., Heritage Recordings Ltd.; Member of Lloyds, since 1985; Co-Founder, Scottish Historic Organs Trust, 1991; Member, Council, Royal Stuart Society; Convenor, Monarchist League of Scotland,

1993; Knight of Malta Honour and Devotion, 1980; Knight of Justice Sacred Military Constantinian Order of St George, 1978; Knight Order of St. Maurice and Lazarus, 1999; Patron, Aboyne Highland Games, since 1999. Recreations: shooting; polo; rowing; sailing; architectural history; Scottish history; heraldry. Address: Hamilton House, West Loan, Prestonpans EH32 9JY; T.-01875 813681.

Lumsden, Iain C., MA, FFA. Group Finance Director and Appointed Actuary, Standard Life Assurance Company, since 1990; b. 6.6.46, Perth; m., Rosemary; 1 s.; 1 d. Educ. Exeter College, Oxford University. Standard Life, since 1967. Address: (b.) 30 Lothian Road, Edinburgh EH1 2DH; T.-0131 225 2552.

Lumsden, James Alexander, MBE, TD, MA, LLB, DL. Director, Bank of Scotland, 1958-85; Director, Scottish Provident Institution, 1968-85; b. 24.1.15, Arden, Dunbartonshire; m., Sheila Cross; 3 s. Educ. Cargilfield School, Edinburgh; Rugby School; Corpus Christi College, Cambridge; Glasgow University. Territorial Army, 1937-46; Partner, Maclay Murray & Spens, Solicitors, Glasgow and Edinburgh, 1947-82; Director of certain Investment Trust companies managed by Murray Johnstone Ltd., 1967-85; Director, Burmah Oil, 1957-76; Member, Queen's Body Guard for Scotland (Royal Company of Archers), 1963; Commissioner of Income Tax, County of Dumbarton, 1964-90; Member, Committee on Company Law, 1960-62; Fellow, Law Society of Scotland. Address: (h.) Arden-Beag, 7 Station Road, Craigendoran, Helensburgh G84 7BG; T.-01436 676204.

Lumsden, Professor Keith Grant, MA, PhD, FRSE. Professor and Director, Edinburgh Business School, Heriot-Watt University; b. 7.1.35, Bathgate; m., Jean Baillie MacDonald; 1 s. Educ. Bathgate Academy; Edinburgh University; Stanford University, California. Instructor, Department of Economics, then Assistant Professor, Graduate School of Business, Stanford University, 1960-67; Research Associate, Stanford Research Institute, 1965-71; Director, Stanford University Conference: NDTE, 1966, RREE, 1968; Associate Professor, Graduate School of Business, Stanford University, 1968-75; Visiting Professor of Economics, Heriot-Watt University, 1969-70; Director: Economics Education Project, 1969-74, Behavioral Research Laboratories, 1970-72, Capital Preservation Fund Inc., 1971-75, Nielsen Engineering Research Inc., 1972-75; Member, American Economic Association Committee on Economic Education, 1978-81; Academic Director, Sea Transport Executive Programme (STEP), since 1979; Professor of Economics, Advanced Management College, Stanford University, since 1971; Affiliate Professor of Economics, INSEAD, France; Member: Economics Education 14-16 Project, Manchester University, Advisory Council, David Hume Institute, 1984-99, Board of Directors, Hewlett Packard Ltd., 1982-92; Henry Villard Award, Economics America, 1994. Publications: The Free Enterprise System, 1963; The Gross National Product, 1964; International Trade, 1965; Microeconomics: A Programmed Book, 1966; Macroeconomics: A Programmed Book, 1966; New Developments in the Teaching of Economics (Editor), 1967; Excess Demand and Excess Supply in World Tramp Shipping Markets, 1968; Recent Research in Economics Education (Editor), 1970; Basic Economics: Theory and Cases, 1973; Efficiency in Universities: The La Paz Papers (Editor), 1974; Economics Education in the United Kingdom, 1980; Economics: a distance learning study programme, 1991. Recreations: tennis; deep sea sports fishing. Address: (h.) 40 Lauder Road, Edinburgh EH9 1UE.

Lumsden, Vivien Dale Victoria, DSD, CDS. Journalist and Television and Radio Presenter, since 1984; Partner, Lumsden and Rusk Events; Restaurant Critic, Scottish Field; b. 22.11.52, Edinburgh; m., Alan Douglas (qv); 1 s.;

1 d. Educ. James Gillespie's High School for Girls, Edinburgh; RSAMD. Full-time mother, 1975-82; AA Traffic News Reporter, 1982-84; BBC Scotland: Breakfast Newsreader, 1984-85, Reporting Scotland Presenter, 1985-89, Garden Party, 1988; joined Scottish TV as Presenter, Scotland Today, 1989; also presented chat show, Telethon, BAFTA Awards, Business Game, Home Show. Recreations: cooking; writing; wine; food. Address: (b.) Broadcasting Business, 9 Lethington Road, Glasgow G46 6TA; e-mail: viv.lumsden@ntlworld.com

Lumsden, William Hepburn Russell, DSc, MD, DTM, DTH, FIBiol, FRCPEdin, FRSE. Scientific and Medical Writer; b. 27.3.14, Forfar; m., Pamela Kathleen Bartram; 2 s.; 1 d. (deceased). Educ. Queen Elizabeth's Grammar School, Darlington; Glasgow University; Liverpool University. MRC Fellow in Tropical Medicine, 1938-41; active service, Malaria Field Laboratories, RAMC, 1941-46; Yellow Fever (subsequently East African Virus) Research Institute, Entebbe, 1947-57; Director, East African Trypanosomiasis Research Organisation, Tororo, 1957-63; Lecturer, Department of Bacteriology, Edinburgh University Medical School, 1963-64; Senior Lecturer, Department of Animal Health, Royal (Dick) School of Veterinary Studies, Edinburgh University, 1964-68; Visiting Professor, Toronto University, 1968; Professor of Medical Protozoology, London School of Hygiene and Tropical Medicine, London University, 1968-79; Senior Editor, Advances in Parasitology, 1978-82; Member: Council, Royal Society of Tropical Medicine and Hygiene, 1969-73, 1974-77, Council, Royal Zoological Society of Scotland, 1967-68, Expert Advisory Panel on Parasitic Diseases (Trypanosomiasis), WHO, 1962-84, Trypanosomiasis Panel, Ministry of Overseas Development, 1973-79, International Malaria Review Teams, Bangladesh, 1978, Nepal, 1979, Sri Lanka, 1980; Editing Secretary, Berwickshire Naturalists' Club, 1988-91. Publications: Techniques with Trypanosomes, 1973; Biology of the Kinetoplastida (Editor), 1976 and 1979. Recreation: hill-walking. Address: (h.) 16A Merchiston Crescent, Edinburgh EH10 5AX; T.-0131-229 2702.

Lunan, Charles Burnett, MD, FRCOG, FRCS. Consultant Obstetrician, Princess Royal Maternity, Glasgow, since 1977; Consultant Gynaecologist, Royal Infirmary, Glasgow, since 1977; b. London; m., Helen Russell Ferrie; 2 s.; 1 d. Educ. High School of Glasgow; Glasgow University. Lecturer, Obstetrics and Gynaecology, Aberdeen University, 1973-75; Senior Lecturer, University of Nairobi, 1975-77; WHO Consultant, Family Planning Programme, Bangladesh, 1984-85. Treasurer, 1982-90, Vice-President, 1990-91, President, Royal Medico-Chirurgical Society of Glasgow, 1991-92; Secretary, Glasgow Obstetrical and Gynaecological Society, 1978-82, Vice President, since 1998.Recreations: gardening; photography; hill-walking. Address: (h.) 1 Moncrieff Avenue, Lenzie, Glasgow G66 4NL; T.-0141-776 3227.

Lunan, Michael John (Mike), MA, FFA. Convener, Rail Passengers Committee Scotland, since 2000; b. 5.3.42, Kirkcaldy; m., Peggy; 2 d. Educ. Mill Hill School; Peterhouse, Cambridge. Secretary, Isle of Arran Music Society, 1993-2000. Recreations: music; politics; omphaloscopy. Address: (h.) Achabhealaidh, Machrie, Isle of Arran, KA27 8DZ; T.-01770 840201.

Lunney, James Thomas, LLB, NP. District Chairman, The Appeals Service, since 1999; Full-time Chairman, Independent Tribunal Service, 1995-99; Director, Paisley Hammermen Society, since 1990; b. 24.7.54, Glasgow; m., Patricia Anne Lunney, BDS; 2 d. Educ. St. Mirin's Academy, Paisley; Strathclyde University. Apprentice to Pattison & Sim, Solicitors, Paisley, 1979-81; Assistant, 1981-83, Partner, 1983-95; part-time Chairman,

Independent Tribunal Service, 1992-95. Recreations: golf; reading; architecture; skiing; motor-cycling. Address: (b.) Wellington House, 134-136 Wellington Street, Glasgow G2 2XL.

Luscombe, Rt. Rev. Lawrence Edward, ChStJ, MA, MPhil, PhD, LLD, DLitt, CA, FRSA, FSA Scot. Primus of the Scottish Episcopal Church, 1985-90, and Bishop of Brechin, 1975-90; b. 10.11.24; m., Dr. Doris Morgan (deceased); 1 d. Educ. Kelham College; King's College, London; Dundee University. Indian Army, 1942-47; Major; Chartered Accountant, 1952; Partner, Galbraith Dunlop & Co. (later Watson and Galbraith), CA, 1953-63; Curate, St. Margaret's, Glasgow, 1963-66; Rector, St. Barnabas', Paisley, 1966-71; Provost, St. Paul's Cathedral, Dundee, 1971-75. Honorary Canon, Trinity Cathedral, Davenport, Iowa, since 1983; Member, Education Committee, Renfrew County Council, 1967-71; Chairman, Governing Body: Glenalmond College, 1986-94; President, Old Glenalmond Club, since 1998; Chairman, Governing Body, Edinburgh Theological College, 1985-90; Governor: Lathallan School, 1982-2000, Dundee College of Education, 1982-87; Chairman, Inter-Anglican Finance Committee, 1989-93; Member, Tayside Health Board, 1989-93; Honorary Research Fellow, Dundee University, since 1993; Member, Court of Corporation of the Sons of the Clergy, 1985-99. Address: (h.) Woodville, Kirkton of Tealing, by Dundee DD4 0RD; T.-01382 380331.

Lyall, Rev. Dr David, BSc, BD, STM, PhD. Principal, New College, Edinburgh, since 1999; Senior Lecturer, Christian Ethics and Practical Theology, Edinburgh University, since 1990; b. 15.10.36, Dunfermline; m., Margaret Wilkinson; 1 s.; 1 d. Educ. Beath High School, Cowdenbeath; Edinburgh University; Yale Divinity School. Minister, Park Parish Church, Ardrossan, 1965-71; Chaplain, Edinburgh Northern Hospitals, 1971-87; Lecturer in Practical Theology, St Andrews University, 1987-90. Secretary, International Council on Pastoral Care and Counselling, 1987-91. Publications: Helping the Helpers: Supervision and Pastoral Care; Counselling in the Pastoral and Spiritual Context. Recreations: music; football. Address: (b.) New College, Mound Place, Edinburgh EH1 2LX.

Lyall, Fiona Jane, MBE, DL, MB, ChB, DPH. Family Doctor, Laurencekirk, since 1959; Director, Grampian Television PLC, since 1980; Non-Executive Director: Aberdeen Royal Hospitals NHS Trust, since 1992, Templehill Community Council, since 1990; Deputy Lieutenant, Kincardineshire, since 1985; b. 13.4.31, Inverness; m., Dr. Alan Richards Lyall; 1 s.; 1 d. Educ. Inverness Royal Academy; Aberdeen University. Former Member, Laurencekirk Burgh Council; former Kincardine County and Grampian Regional Councillor; Member: Grampian Health Board, 1974, and Kincardine & Deeside Health Council, 1974, Children's Panel Advisory Committee, 1974, Grampian Valuation Appeals Committee, Prince's and Royal Jubilee Trust for Grampian; Treasurer, Action Research for Crippled Child; Trustee, Kincardineshire Silver Jubilee Trust, since 1985. Recreations: skiing; riding; golf. Address: Melrose Bank, Laurencekirk AB30 1FJ; T.-01561 377220; e-mail: alanlyall@aol.com

Lyall, Ian Alastair, DSC, VRD, DL, FICS; b. 16.3.17, Bangor, Co. Down; m., Eileen Patricia Bennet; 1 d. Educ. Hillhead High School, Glasgow; College of Nautical Studies, Glasgow. Chairman and Managing Director, Roxburgh Henderson & Co. Ltd., 1967-80; Director: British & Burmese Steam Navigation Co. Ltd., 1971-80, Henderson Line Ltd., 1971-80; President, Glasgow Chamber of Commerce, 1978-79; retired Lt. Commander, RNR, 1963. Recreations: sailing; fishing; shooting. Address: (h.) 21 Chapelacre, Helensburgh G84 7SH; T.-01436 673976.

Lyall, Michael Hodge, MB, ChB, ChM, FRCSEdin. Consultant Surgeon, Tayside University Hospitals NHS Trust, since 1975, Medical Director, since 2001; Honorary Senior Lecturer, Dundee University, since 1975; b. 5.12.41, Methilhill, Fife; m., Catherine B. Jarvie; 3 s. Educ. Buckhaven High School; St. Andrews University. Past President, North Fife Rotary Club; Paul Harris Fellow. Recreation: computing. Address: 1 Vernonholme, Riverside Drive, Dundee DD2 1QJ.

Lyddon, William Derek Collier, CB, DLitt, BA (Arch), DipTP, FRSGS. Vice Chairman, Edinburgh World Heritage Trust, 1999; b. 17.11.25, Loughton, Essex; m., Marian Louise Kaye Charlesworth; 2 d. Educ. Wrekin College; University College, London. Depute Chief Architect Planner, Cumbernauld Development Corporation; Chief Architect Planner, Skelmersdale Development Corporation; Chief Planner, Scottish Development Department, 1967-85. President, International Society of City and Regional Planners, 1981-84; Chairman, The Planning Exchange, 1992-95; Acting Chairman, Edinburgh Old Town Renewal Trust, 1997-99. Address: (h.) 31 Blackford Road, Edinburgh EH9 2DT; T.-0131-667 2266.

Lyell, 3rd Baron (Charles Lyell), Bt. Elected Member, House of Lords, since 1999; Parliamentary Under-Secretary of State, Northern Ireland Office, 1984-89; b. 27.3.39. Educ. Eton; Christ Church, Oxford. Scots Guards, 1957-59; CA; Opposition Whip, 1974-79; Government Whip, 1979-84; Member, Queen's Bodyguard for Scotland (Royal Company of Archers); DL, Angus, 1988. Address: (h.) Kinnordy House, Kirriemuir, Angus.

Lyle, David Angus, MA, LLB, NP, SSC, FCIS, FIMgt, FInstD, FIAM, FRSA. Consultant, Solicitor, and Chartered Company Secretary, in private practice, since 1993; b. 7.9.40; m., Dorothy Ann Clark; 1 s.; 3 d. Educ. George Watson's College, Edinburgh; Edinburgh University. Account Executive, Advertising Agencies, London; Indentured, Edinburgh Corporation; Solicitor, Lloyds and Scottish Finance Ltd., Edinburgh; Depute County Clerk, East Lothian County Council; Director of Administration and Law, Dumfries and Galloway Regional Council; Agency Secretary, Scottish Development Agency; Director/Company Secretary, Scottish Enterprise. Recreations: shooting; golf; bridge. Address: (b.) The Caledonian Suite, St Andrew House, 141 West Nile Street, Glasgow G1 2RN; T.-0141-333 1119.

Lynch, Professor Michael, MA, PhD, FRHistS, FRSE, FSAScot. Sir William Fraser Professor of Scottish History, University of Edinburgh, since 1992; Chairman, Ancient Monuments Board for Scotland, since 1996; President, Society of Antiquaries of Scotland, 1996-99; b. 15.6.46, Aberdeen. Educ. Aberdeen Grammar School; University of Aberdeen; University of London. Lecturer, Department of History, University College, Bangor, 1971-79; Department of Scottish History, University of Edinburgh: Lecturer, 1979-88, Senior Lecturer, 1988-92. Chairman, Historical Association Committee for Scotland, since 1992; Editor, The Innes Review, 1984-92. Publications: Edinburgh and the Reformation, 1981 (SAC Literary Award); The Early Modern Town in Scotland, 1986; The Scottish Medieval Town, 1987; Mary Stewart: Queen in Three Kingdoms, 1988; Scotland: A New History, 1991 (SAC Literary Award); The Reign of James VI, 2000; The Oxford Companion to Scottish History, 2001. Address: (b.) Department of Scottish History, University of Edinburgh, 17 Buccleuch Place, Edinburgh EH8 9LN; T.-0131-650 4030.

Lyon, George. MSP (Liberal Democrat), Argyll and Bute, since 1999; b. 1956, Rothesay. Educ. Rothesay Academy. Left school to help run family farming business, eventually taking over two farms; completed Nuffield scholarship, New Zealand and Australia, 1997; President, NFU of Scotland, 1997; Fellow, Royal Agricultural Societies; Honorary Associate, British Veterinary Association. Address: (b.) Constituency Office, First Floor, 7 Castle Street, Rothesay PA20 9HA; Scottish Parliament, Edinburgh EH99 1SP; T.-0131-348 5788.

Lyons, John, MP. Labour MP, Strathkelvin and Bearsden, since 2001; b. 11.7.49; 1 s.; 1 d. Educ. Woodside Secondary School; Stirling University. Mechanical engineer, 1971-88; Officer, UNISON, 1988-2001. Address: (b.) House of Commons, London SW1A 0AA.

Mac/Mc

McAllion, John, MA (Hons). MP (Labour), Dundee East, since 1987; MSP (Labour), Dundee East, since 1999; b. 13.2.48, Glasgow; m., Susan Jean; 2 s. Educ. St. Augustine's Secondary, Glasgow; St. Andrews University. Secondary, Dundee, 1973-78, Social Studies, Balgowan List D School, Dundee, 1978-82; Research Assistant to Bob McTaggart, MP, 1982-86; Regional Councillor, 1984-87; Convener, Tayside Regional Council, 1986-87. Member, Scottish Executive, Labour Party, 1986-88; Senior Vice Chairperson, Dundee Labour Party, 1986, 1987. Recreations: football; reading; music. Address: (h.) 3 Haldane Street, Dundee DD3 0HP; T.-01382 200329.

McAlpine, Joan, MA (Hons). Deputy Editor, The Herald, since 2001; Editor, Sunday Times Scotland, 2000-01; b. 28.1.64, Gourock; m., Pat Kane (qv); 2 d. Educ. St. Columba's RC Comprehensive, Greenock; James Watt Further Education College, Greenock; Glasgow University; City University, London. Reporter, Greenock Telegraph, The Scotsman; Feature Writer, Columnist, The Scotsman, 1992-95; Feature Writer and Columnist, Daily Record, 1995; Columnist and Feature Writer, then Deputy Editor, Sunday Times, 1996-2000. Journalist of the Year, Scottish Press Awards, 1999; Feature Writer of the Year, Scottish Press Awards, 1999. Publications: A Time to Rage (Co-author), 1994. Recreations: family; reading; Scotland. Address: (b.) 200 Renfield Street, Glasgow G2 3PR; T.-0141-302 7000.

McAlpine, Thomas, BSc, CEng, MIEE. Business Consultant; b. 23.9.29, Motherwell; m., Isobel Lindsay; 2 s.; 1 d. Educ. Dalziel High School, Motherwell; Strathclyde University. National Service, REME, 1952-54 (2nd Lt.); Chief Engineer, Belmos Co. Ltd., Bellshill, 1954-58; Chief Development Engineer, Mine Safety Appliances, Glasgow, 1958-62; Managing Director: Rowen Engineering Co. Ltd., Glasgow, 1962-71, Chieftain Industries PLC, Livingston, 1971-85. Former Executive Vice Chairman Administration, Scottish National Party (former Vice President, SNP); Parliamentary candidate, Clydesdale (Lanark), 1974, 1979, 1983, Dumfries, 1987; District Councillor, Clydesdale, 1988-96, now South Lanarkshire Councillor. Recreations: when young, played rugby, swimming and tennis. Address: (h.) 9 Knocklea Place, Biggar, Lanarkshire ML12 6DZ; T.-01899 220423.

McAndrew, Nicolas, CA. Chairman, Martin Currie Enhanced Income Investment Trust PLC; Chairman, Guinness Flight Extra Income Trust PLC; Chairman, Derby Trust PLC; Chairman, Scottish Asian Investment Company Ltd.; Board Member, North of Scotland Water Authority, since 1995; b. 9.12.34, London; 2 s. Educ. Winchester College. National Service (The Black Watch) commission, 1953-55; articled clerk, Peat Marwick Mitchell, 1955-61; qualified CA, 1961; S.G. Warburg & Co. Ltd., Merchant Bankers, 1962-78; became Chairman, Warburg Investment Management Ltd., and Director, Mercury Securities Ltd.; Managing Director, N.M. Rothschild & Sons Ltd., Merchant Bankers, 1979-88; Chairman, Murray Johnstone Ltd., 1992-99. Master, Worshipful Company of Grocers, 1978-79; Board Member, Highlands and Islands Enterprise, 1993-97. Recreations: fishing; shooting; golf. Address: (h.) Kilcoy Castle, Killearnan, Muir of Ord, Ross-shire IV6 7RX; T.-01463 871 393.

McArdle, Harry John, BSc (Hons), PhD, MIBiol, CBiol, FFCS. Head, Division of Growth and Function, Rowett Research Institute, since 1997; Honorary Professor, in Biomedical Sciences, University of Aberdeen, since 2000; b. 4.1.53, Glasgow; m., Karen Ann. Educ. St. Augustine School, Edinburgh; St. Andrews University. Raines Research Fellow, University of Western Australia; Senior Scientist, Murdoch Institute for Research into Birth Defects, Melbourne, Australia, 1985-90; Lecturer/Senior Lecturer, Department of Child Health, University of Dundee, 1990-96. Recreations: hillwalking; horse riding; skiing. Address: (b.) Rowett Research Institute, Bucksburn, Aberdeen AB21 9SB; T.-01224 716628; e-mail: hjm@rri.sari.ac.uk

McArthur, Archibald Roderick, CPFA. Director of Finance, Perth and Kinross Council, since 1995; b. 1.3.51, Greenock; m., Marilyn; 2 d. Educ. Greenock Academy. Trainee Accountant, Greenock Town Council, 1969; Accountant, Tayside Regional Council, 1975; Perth and Kinross District Council: Management Accountant, 1978, Depute Director of Finance, 1981, Director of Finance, 1992. Recreations: member of Blairgowrie Golf Club; supporter, St. Johnstone F.C. Address: (b.) Council Building, 2 High Street, Perth PH1 5PH; T.-01738 475501.

McArthur, Douglas B., BSc (Hons), OBE. Chief Executive, Radio Advertising Bureau, since 1992; Chairman, JICRIT Ltd.; Director: Sanctuary Group PLC, IMD PLC; b. 17.3.51, Dundee; m., Elizabeth M.A.; 3 d. Educ. Kirkton High School, Dundee; Glasgow University. Marketing management roles, Proctor and Gamble, Scottish & Newcastle, Campbell's Soups Ltd., Radio Clyde; marketing and advertising consultancy roles with Hall Advertising and Baillie Marshall Advertising. Director, Drumchapel Opportunities Ltd.; Member, Scottish Arts Council (Chairman, Drama Committee, 1989-94); Director, Balgray Communications Group Ltd. and subsidiaries, 1984-92; Fellow: Radio Academy, CAM Foundation. Recreations: swimming; music; visual arts; drama.

Macarthur, Edith. Actress; b. Ardrossan, Ayrshire. Educ. Ardrossan Academy. Began career, 1948, with Wilson Barrett Company, then Perth Repertory, Gateway Theatre Company, Citizens' Theatre, Glasgow, Bristol Old Vic, Royal Shakespeare Company, Ochtertyre Theatre, Royal Lyceum Theatre Company, West End; television work includes The Borderers, Sunset Song, Weir of Hermiston, Sutherland's Law, Take the High Road, Dr. Finlay, Hamish Macbeth; Taggart; Golden Wedding; nominated for Scottish BAFTA award in The Long Roads, 1993; recent stage appearances: solo-performance play, Marie of Scotland, Jamie the Saxt and The Thrie Estates for the Scottish Theatre Company at Edinburgh Festivals and Warsaw International Festival, 1986, Judith Bliss in Hay Fever, Royal Lyceum Theatre, 1987, Charley's Aunt, Death of a Salesman, Royal Lyceum, 1988, Daphne Laureola, Pygmalion, Pride and Prejudice, Pitlochry Festival Theatre, 1988; The Cherry Orchard, Royal Lyceum, 1989; The Cherry Orchard, The Circle, Arsenic and Old Lace, Pitlochry, 1990; Driving Miss Daisy, Perth, 1991; Cinderella, Glasgow and Edinburgh, 1990, 1991; Good, Glasgow and Edinburgh, 1992; Long Day's Journey into Night, Dundee, 1994 (TMA/Martini Best Actress nomination); The Prime of Miss Jean Brodie, London, 1994-95; The Flou'ers o' Edinburgh; On Golden Pond; Long Day's Journey into Night, Pitlochry Festival Theatre, and tour, 1996; Widows, Traverse Theatre, and tour, 1997. Recreations: music; books.

McArthur, George, OBE. Convener, Edinburgh Peace and Justice Resource Centre, since 1992; Chairman, Scottish Churches Housing Agency, 1993-2000; b. 22.7.30, Edinburgh; m., Margaret Moffat Wilson; 1 s.; 1 d. Educ. Leith Academy. Missionary (youth worker), Church of Scotland, South Africa, 1956-71; Official Correspondent for Church of Scotland's List D schools, 1972-77; involved in formation of Kirk Care Housing Association Ltd., 1973, becoming its first Director, 1978, retired, 1992. Chairman, Council, Scottish Federation of Housing Associations, 1984-86; a Vice-President, Churches National Housing

Coalition, 1995. Recreations: golf; supporting Hibernian F.C.; walking; reading. Address: (h.) 3 Craigcrook Road, Edinburgh EH4 3NQ; T.-0131-477 0312.

McArthur, John Duncan, BSc (Hons), MB, ChB (Hons), DM, FRCPGlas, MRCP, FRCPEdin. Consultant Physician and Cardiologist, Western Infirmary and Gartnavel General Hospital, Glasgow, since 1978; Honorary Clinical Senior Lecturer, Glasgow University, since 1978; b. 7.1.38, Hamilton; m., Elizabeth A. Bowie; 2 s.; 1 d. Educ. Hamilton Academy; Glasgow University. Junior doctor, Royal Infirmary, Glasgow, and in Ayrshire, 1963-67; St. Colm's College, Edinburgh, 1967-68; Missionary, Church of Scotland, working as Cardiologist at Christian Medical College Hospital, Vellore, India, 1968-73; Senior Registrar, Glasgow Teaching Hospitals, 1974-78. Elder, St. Paul's Parish Church, Milngavie. Recreations: DIY; gardening. Address: (h.) 8 Durness Avenue, Bearsden, Glasgow, G61 2AQ; T.-0141-563 9068; e-mail: jd.mcarthur@ntiworld.com

MacAskill, Kenny, LLB (Hons). MSP (SNP), Lothians, since 1999; SNP Spokesperson on Enterprise and Lifelong Learning; b. 1958, Edinburgh; m.; 2 s. Educ. Linlithgow Academy; Edinburgh University. Solicitor. Address: (b.) Scottish Parliament, Edinburgh EH99 1SP; T.-0131-348 5722; e-mail: kenny.macaskill.msp@scottish.parliament.uk

McAteer, Charles, MA, BA (Hons). Rector, Dumfries Academy, since 1995; Minutes Secretary, Headteachers' Association of Scotland; Director, Scottish Parent Teacher Council; b. 5.5.50, Glasgow; m., Anne Neil; 1 s.; 3 d. Educ. Our Lady's High School, Motherwell; Edinburgh University; Moray House College; Strathclyde University. Teacher of English, St. Augustine's High School, Edinburgh, 1972-74; Principal Teacher of English, St. Kentigern's Academy, W. Lothian, 1974-83; Depute Rector, Moffat Academy, 1983-88; Rector, Dalbeattie High School, 1988-95. Recreations: squash; indoor football; reading; walking; film; family. Address: (b.) Dumfries Academy, Academy Street, Dumfries, DG1 1DD; T.-01387 252846; e-mail: mcateerc@alg.dumgal.org.uk

Macaulay of Bragar, Rt. Hon. Lord (Donald Macaulay), QC; b. 1933. Advocate, 1963; QC (Scot), 1975; Life Peer, since 1989. Address: (b.) House of Lords, London SW1A 0PW.

Macaulay, Rev. Donald, OBE, JP. Former Minister, Park, Isle of Lewis; first Convener, Western Isles Council; b. 25.2.26, Great Bernera; m., Catherine Macleod; 3 s.; 3 d. Educ. Great Bernera School; Aberdeen University. Several years a fisherman; Member: Ross and Cromarty County Council, 1969-75, Lewis District Council, 1969-75, COSLA Policy Committee, 1975-82; Director, Western Isles Enterprise. Recreations: Gaelic; fishing; travel; local history; silviculture. Address: Garymilis, Great Bernera, Isle of Lewis; T.-01851 612341; e-mail: garymilis@talk21.com

MacAulay, Professor Emeritus Donald, MA, BA, DipGenLing. Professor of Celtic, Glasgow University, 1991-96; b. 21.5.30, Isle of Lewis; m., Ella Murray Sangster; 1 s.; 1 d. Educ. Nicolson Institute, Stornoway; Aberdeen University; Cambridge University. Lecturer in English Language, Edinburgh University, 1957-60; Lecturer in Irish and Scottish Gaelic, Trinity College, Dublin, 1960-63; Lecturer in Applied Linguistics, Edinburgh University, 1963-67; Senior Lecturer in Celtic, then Reader in Celtic, Aberdeen University, 1967-91. Publications: Seobhrach as a' Chlaich; Nua-bhardachd Ghaidhlig; The Celtic Languages. Recreations: poetry; living. Address: (b.) 5 Meggetland Terrace, Edinburgh EH14 1AN; T.-0131-443 1823.

MacAulay, Fred. Comedian; Television and Radio Presenter. Presenter, The Fred MacAulay Show, BBC Radio Scotland; television includes: Presenter, Life According to Fred; Co-host, New Year Live; Co-host, series and World Cup special, McCoist and MacAulay; Co-host, The 11 O'Clock Show; Team Captain, The Best Show in the World...Probably; Team Captain, Bring Me the Head of Light Entertainment; Team Captain, A Game of Two Halves; Presenter, Comedy Rules; Presenter, Now You See It; theatre: Bad and Crazy in a Jam.

McAveety, Frank (Francis), BA (Hons). MSP (Labour and Co-Op.), Glasgow Shettleston, since 1999; Deputy Minister for Local Government, Scottish Executive, 1999-2000; b. 27.7.62, Glasgow; m., Anita Mitchell; 1 s.; 1 d. Educ. All Saints Secondary School, Glasgow; Strathclyde University; St. Andrew's College, Bearsden. Councillor, Glasgow District Council, 1988-96; Leader, Glasgow City Council, 1997-99, Councillor, 1995-99. Member, Board, Arches Theatre Company; Chairperson, Glasgow North Co-operative Party. Recreations: labour history; record collecting; football. Address: (h.) 156 Glenbuck Avenue, Robroyston, Glasgow G33 1LW; T.-0141-558 1341.

McAvoy, Thomas McLaughlin. Government Whip, Comptroller of Her Majesty's Household, since 1997; MP (Labour and Co-operative), Glasgow Rutherglen, since 1987; b. 14.12.43, Rutherglen; m., Eleanor Kerr; 4 s. Member, Strathclyde Regional Council, 1982-87; Opposition Whip, 1990-93. Address: (b.) House of Commons, London SW1A 0AA.

MacBeth, Professor Colin, BA, MA, PhD, FRAS, FRSSA. Professor of Reservoir Geophysics, Heriot-Watt University, since 1999; b. 14.7.58, Perth; m., Fiona Mackenzie; 1 s.; 1 d. Educ. Bishop Gore Grammar School, Swansea; University College, Oxford; Edinburgh University. Teaching posts, Edinburgh; postdoctoral research, Trieste, Italy, then Utrecht, The Netherlands, 1984-88; Principal Scientific Officer, British Geological Survey, 1988-99. Member, research committees, European Association of Geoscientists and Engineers and Society of Exploration Geophysicists. Publications: Applied Seismic Anisotropy: Theory, Background and Field Studies, 2000; Multicomponent USP Analysis for Applied Seismic Anisotropy, 2002. Recreations: badminton; running; climbing. Address: (b.) Department of Petroleum Engineering, Heriot-Watt University, Edinburgh; T.-0131-451 3607; e-mail: colin.macbeth@pet.hw.ac.uk

McBeth, Douglas G., BSc, CEng, FICE, FIStructE, FIHT. Director, WSP Consulting Engineers, since 1993; Past Chairman, Institute of Civil Engineers, East of Scotland; b. 3.6.40, Dundee; m., Veronica; 1 s.; 1 d. Educ. Grove Academy, Broughty Ferry; St Andrews University; Queen's College, Dundee. Senior Structural Engineer, Kenchington Little, 1974; opened offices for the firm in Scotland, 1976; merged with Brian Ford Partnership, 1991; merged with WSP Consulting Engineers, 1993. Former Secretary and Chairman, Concrete Society Scotland; Founder and Chairman, Forth Bridges Visitor Centre Trust; first Chairman, Edinburgh Area Branch, Institution of Civil Engineers; Member, Health and Safety Board, Institution of Civil Engineers; Adjudicator, Royal Institution of Chartered Surveyors in Scotland. Publications: over 30 papers on civil and structural engineering topics. Recreations: golf; mountaineering; skiing; singing; Elder, Church of Scotland. Address: (h.) Malleny Millhouse, 31 Malleny Millgate, Balerno, Edinburgh EH14 7AY; T.-0131-449 7904.

McBryde, Professor William Wilson, LLB, PhD, LLD, FRSE. Professor of Commercial Law, Edinburgh University, since 1999; b. 6.7.45, Perth; 1 s.; 2 d. Educ. Perth Academy; Edinburgh University. Apprentice and

Assistant, Morton, Smart, Macdonald & Milligan, WS, Edinburgh, 1967-70; Court Procurator, Biggart, Lumsden & Co., Glasgow, 1970-72; Lecturer in Private Law, Glasgow University, 1972-76; Member, Scottish Law Commission Working Party on Contract Law, 1975-2000; Senior Lecturer in Private Law, Aberdeen University, 1976-87; Professor of Scots Law, Dundee University, 1987-99 (Deputy and Vice Principal, 1991-94). Specialist Parliamentary Adviser to House of Lords Select Committee on the European Communities, 1980-83; Member: Scottish Consumer Council, 1984-87, Scottish Advisory Committee on Arbitration, since 1986, Member, DTI Working Party on Rights in Security over Moveables, since 1994, Member, International Working Group on Principles of Insolvency Law, since 2000; Director, Scottish Universities' Law Institute, 1989-95; Honorary Sheriff, Tayside, Central and Fife, at Dundee; since 1991. Recreations: walking; photography. Address: (b.) Faculty of Law, University of Edinburgh, Old College, South Bridge, Edinburgh EH8 9YL.

McCabe, Thomas. MSP (Labour), Hamilton South, since 1999; Minister for Parliament, Scottish Executive, since 1999; b. 28.4.54, Hamilton. Educ. St. Martin's Secondary; Bell College of Technology. Senior Shop Steward, Hoover Ltd., 1974-93; Welfare Rights Officer, 1993-98; Leader, Hamilton District Council, 1992-96; Leader, South Lanarkshire Council, 1995-99; Vice-Convener, Strathclyde Joint Police Board, 1995-99; Member: Lanarkshire Development Agency Board, 1995-99, Executive, Scottish Labour Party, since 1991. Recreations: walking; reading; cinema. Address: (b.) Scottish Parliament, Parliament Headquarters, George IV Bridge, Edinburgh EH99 1SP; T.-0131-348 5830.

McCafferty, Rev. Allan, BSc, BD (Hons). Minister, Kirkwall East Church, since 1993; b. 19.1.67, Motherwell. Educ. Garrion Academy, Wishaw; Glasgow University; Edinburgh University. Probationer Minister, Holy Trinity Church, Bridge of Allan, 1991-93. Recreations: choral singing; hill-walking; bowling. Address: East Church Manse, Thoms Street, Kirkwall KW15 1PF; T.-01856 875469.

McCafferty, Charles, BA, AIPM. Member, Glasgow City Council (Senior Vice Chair, Development and Regeneration Services, since 1999); b. 10.6.37, Glasgow; m., Margaret McGowan; 1 s. Educ. St Gerard's Secondary; Strathclyde University. Various manual/clerical jobs, 1952-65; student, 1965-70; Further Education Lecturer, James Watt College, 1970-73; Glasgow College, Nautical Studies, 1973-91; Councillor, Glasgow City Council, since 1984; Vice-Chair, Economic Development, 1986-88; Chair, 1988-92; Deputy Leader, Glasgow City Council, 1993-94; Vice-Chair, Education, 1995-99; Member: Glasgow International Jazz Festival; Glasgow Opportunities; Scottish Enterprise Glasgow; Community Investment in Strathclyde; Citizens Theatre Board; Vice-President, Glasgow Music Festival. Recreations: listening to music; going to theatre. Address: (b.) City Chambers, George Square, Glasgow G2; T.-0141-287 5625; e-mail: charles.mccafferty@councillors.glasgow.gov.uk

McCafferty, Daniel, BA, DipEd, JP. Leader, West Dunbartonshire Council, since 2001; Board Member, NHS Greater Glasgow, since 2001; b. 15.11.49,Clydebank; m., Lynn; 1 step s.; 2 d. Educ. St Columba's Secondary School, Clydebank; Jordanhill College; Open University. Involved in voluntary community work, local politics and trade union activities since 1970; COSLA Spokesperson on education issues, 1999-2001. Recreations: reading; music; poetry of Robert Burns; travel. Address: (h.) 48 Duntocher Road, Clydebank, Glasgow G81 3LN; T.-0141-585 2988.

McCafferty, James Patrick, BSc, CEng, FICE, FIStructE, FIHT, FHKIE, MCIArb, FConsE. Director, Scott Wilson Scotland, since 1987, Managing Director, since 1995; Chairman, Institution of Civil Engineers, Glasgow and West of Scotland Association, 1998, 1999; b. 16.8.45, Kirkintilloch; m., Yvonne Muriel Landles; 3 d. Educ. St Ninian's High School, Kirkintilloch; Strathclyde University. Scott Wilson, since 1967; worked on design and construction of Glasgow's urban motorways, then on major projects in Hong Kong, 1976-82; since mid-1980s has been involved in a broad range of major infrastructure projects at home and abroad; Institution of Civil Engineers: Committee Member, since 1993, Member, Council, since 1999, Representative on Scottish Council Development and Industry Executive, since 2001; Association of Consulting Engineers: Committee Member, since 1994, Hon. Secretary, 1994-98; ACE Representative, Scottish Construction Industry Group, since 2001; Member, Adjudication Panel, Saltire Society Awards for Civil Engineering, 1993-96; Chairman, ICE Organising Committee, Glasgow City of Architecture and Design '99; Member, Advisory Group for Civil Engineering Degrees, University of Glasgow; winner of several awards; author of many technical papers. Recreations: historical engineering works; architecture; travel; gardening; flying kites. Address: (b.) Scott Wilson, 6 Park Circus, Glasgow G3 6AX; T.-0141-332 2258; e-mail: james.mccafferty@scottwilson.com

McCafferty, Margaret, MA, JP. Councillor, Glasgow City Council, since 1995 (Vice-Convener, Education, since 1999); Convener, Joint Sub-Committee, Children's Services, since 1999); Director, Centre for Independent Living in Glasgow; Director, The Co-operative Group, CWS Ltd; b. 11.9.39, Glasgow; m., Charles McCafferty; 1 s. Educ. Holyrood Senior Secondary School; Glasgow University. Scottish Gas (commercial apprentice and clerical worker); Teacher, Modern Languages, St Gerard's Secondary School, Glasgow, 1971-73; Assistant Principal Teacher of Guidance, John Bosco Secondary School, Glasgow, 1973-96. Recreations: music; theatre; choir. Address: (b.) City Chambers, George Square, Glasgow, G2; T.-0141-287 7032.

McCall, Frances, MBE. Board Member, Scottish Homes, since 1988; Member, Management Committee, Calvay Housing Co-operative, since 1984; b. 2.7.37, Glasgow; m., Thomas McCall; 2 s.; 1 d. Educ. St. Columba of Iona School; Notre Dame College. Recreations: grand-children; voluntary work. Address: (h.) 45 Calvay Road, Barlanark, Glasgow G33 4RQ; T.-0141-573 1826.

McCall, Professor James, BSc, MEd, PhD, CPsychol, AFBPsS, FRSA. Professor, Department of Educational Studies, Strathclyde University, since 1993; b. 14.7.41, Kilmarnock; m., Mary Elizabeth Stuart Maclean; 3 s. Educ. Kilmarnock Academy; Glasgow University; Aberdeen University; Jordanhill College of Education. Teacher of Science, Hillhead High School, Glasgow; Principal Teacher of Physics, Queen's Park Secondary School, Glasgow; Lecturer in Educational Psychology, Aberdeen College of Education; Jordanhill College of Education: Head, Psychology Department, Vice Principal, 1983-92, Acting Principal, 1992-93, Dean, Faculty of Education, 1993-97; Member: Board of Governors, Glasgow School of Art, 1986-98, CNAA Committee on Teacher Education, 1989-92, General Teaching Council for Scotland, 1992-97. Publications: Techniques for the Assessment of Practical Skills in Foundation Science, 1983; Techniques for Assessing Process Skills in Practical Science, 1988; Teacher Education in Europe, 1990; How to assess open-ended practical investigations in Biology, Chemistry and Physics, 1991; Partnership and Co-operation in Teacher Education, 1997. Recreations: bridge; golf. Address: (b.) Jordanhill Campus, Strathclyde University, Southbrae Drive, Glasgow G13 1PP; T.-0141-950 3366.

McCall, Kathleen Mary, DL, LRAM. Deputy Lieutenant for Borders Region, District of Tweeddale, since 1988; Patron, Borders Branch, British Red Cross Society, since 1998; b. 20.2.33, Karachi; m., J.A.G. McCall, CMG. Educ. Calder Girls' School, Seascale; Royal Scottish Academy of Music and Drama. Held various teaching posts; voluntary offices with Red Cross in Nigeria. West Linton Citizen of the Year, 2001. Recreations: music; walking; the arts. Address: (h.) Burnside, West Linton EH46 7EW; T.-01968 660488.

McCall Smith, Professor Alexander, LLB, PhD, FRSE. Professor, Faculty of Law, Edinburgh University; Author; Member, International Bioethics Commission, UNESCO; Vice Chairman, Human Genetics Commission; b. 24.8.48, Zimbabwe; m., Dr. Elizabeth Parry; 2 d. Publications: (non-fiction): Law and Medical Ethics (Co-Author); Butterworth's Medico-Legal Encyclopaedia (Co-Author); Scots Criminal Law (Co-Author); The Duty to Rescue (Co-Author); The Criminal Law of Botswana; Forensic Aspects of Sleep (Co-Author); Errors, Medicine and the Law (Co-Author); Justice and the Prosecution of Old Crimes (Co-Author); fiction: Children of Wax; Heavenly Date; The No. 1 Ladies' Detective Agency; Tears of the Giraffe; Morality for Beautiful Girls; numerous books for children. Recreation: wind instruments. Address: (h.) 16A Napier Road, Edinburgh EH10 5AY; T.-0131-229 6083.

MacCallum, Professor James Richard, BSc, PhD, DSc, CChem, FRSC, FRSE. Professor of Polymer Chemistry, St. Andrews University (Vice-Principal, 1992-96; Pro-Principal, 1997); b. 3.5.36, Kilmartin; m., Eleanor Margaret Thomson; 2 s.; 1 d. Educ. Dumfries Academy; Glasgow University. Technical Officer, ICI Fibres Division, 1961-62; ICI Research Fellow, Aberdeen University, 1962-63; Lecturer, St. Andrews University, 1964; Master, United College, 1988-92; Vice-Principal, 1992-96; Pro-Principal, 1996-97. Recreation: golf. Address: (h.) 9 Cairnsden Gardens, St. Andrews, Fife; T.-01334 473152.

MacCallum, Neil Robb. Poet, Critic and Editor; Editor, Lallans, 1996-99; Preses, Scots Language Society, 1993-95; b. 15.5.54, Edinburgh. Educ. Firrhill High School; Napier College, Edinburgh. Lothian Health Board, 1973-87; Edinburgh City Councllor, 1977-80; Assistant National Secretary, SNP, 1980-81, National Secretary, 1981-86; Arts Columnist, Scots Independent, 1991-98; Editor, Scots Glasnost, 1991-95; Committee Member, Scottish Poetry Library, 1991-95; Vice-Convener, Scots Language Resource Centre, 1993-95; his poems have been translated into Italian, Hungarian and Viennese dialect of German; Artistic Director, The Merchants o' Renoun. Publications: Report of the SNP Commission of Inquiry (Editor), 1984, Portrait of a Calvinist, 1991, Mak It New (Co-Editor), 1995, Sing Frae the Hert, (Editor), 1996, Astern's Licht, 2002; The Poems of Sydney Goodsir Smith (introduction and selection, cassette), 1999. Recreations: reading; theatre; fitness and weight-training; running. Address: (h.) 16/4 Oxgangs Drive, Edinburgh EH13 9HG; T.-0131-441 9625.

McCann, James Aloysius, MA, LLB. Solicitor and Notary Public; a founding Director, Legal Defence Union in Scotland, 1987, Chairman, since 1990; b. 14.8.39, Glasgow; m., Jane Marlow; 3 s.; 1 d. Educ. St. Mungo's Academy, Glasgow; Glasgow University. Former Member, Legal Aid Central Committee; Dean, Faculty of Dunbartonshire Solicitors, 1986-88; Convenor for Law Society PQLE Advocacy Training Courses, 1983-91; Senior Tutor (Professional Legal Practice), Glasgow University, 1981-91; Member, Law Society of Scotland Legal Aid Committee, 1987-97; Reporter, Scottish Legal Aid Board (Co-opted Member, Criminal Applications Committee, 1987-93); appointed Honorary Sheriff at Dumbarton, 1990; Temporary Sheriff, 1991-99. Recreations: sailing/ windsurfing; chess; music; golfing badly. Address: (b.) 499 Kilbowie Road, Clydebank G81 2AX.

McCann, Michael. National Officer (Scotland), Public and Commercial Services Union; Member (Labour), South Lanarkshire Council, since 1999; b. 2.1.64, Glasgow; m., Tracy Anne; 1 s.; 1 d. Educ. St. Andrew's R. C. High School, East Kilbride. Overseas Development Administration, 1982-92; Civil and Public Services Association, 1992-98. Recreations: Celtic Football Club; music; golf. Address: (b.) Suite 320-323, Baltic Chambers, 50 Wellington Street, Glasgow G2 6HJ.

McCann, Peter Toland McAree, CBE (1977), OStJ, DL, JP, BL. Solicitor and Notary Public, since 1947; b. 2.8.24, Glasgow; m., Maura Eleanor Ferris; 1 s. Educ. St. Mungo's Academy, Glasgow; Glasgow University. Councillor, Corporation of Glasgow, 1961-75; River Bailie, 1962; Magistrate, 1963-66; Police Judge, 1967-74; JP, since 1967; Lord Lieutenant, 1975-77; Lord Provost, City of Glasgow District, 1975-77; Depute Lieutenant, since 1977; Chairman, St. Thomas More Society for Lawyers, 1960; Chairman, McCann Committee for Provision of Secondary Education for Physically Disabled Children, 1968; Disabled Scot, 1973; awarded two Golden Swords from HRH Prince Fawaz of Saudi Arabia, 1977-78; awarded Silver and Golden Swords from City of Jeddah, 1975-78; awarded Medal of King Faisal of Saudi Arabia, 1976. Recreations: music; history; model railways; collecting model cars and model soldiers. Address: (h.) Craig En Ross, 31 Queen Mary Avenue, Crosshill, Glasgow G42 8DS.

McCarra, Kevin, MA, FFCS. Scottish Football Correspondent, The Times, since 1993; b. 24.1.58, Glasgow; m., Susan Stewart. Educ. Holyrood Secondary School, Glasgow; Glasgow University. Author of football books and freelance journalist, 1984-89; Football Correspondent, Scotland on Sunday, 1989-95; Scottish Football Correspondent, Sunday Times, 1995-98. Publications: author or co-author of various books including One Afternoon in Lisbon, 1988. Recreations: cinema; swimming; blethering about football. Address: (h.) 4 Belmont Street, Glasgow G12 8EY; T.-0141-338 6877; e-mail: kevin@kelvinbridge.demon.co.uk

McCarter, Ann Iestyn, SRN. Past Convener: Board of Practice and Procedure, and Business Committee, General Assembly of the Church of Scotland; Session Clerk, Newbattle Church, Dalkeith, since 1994; b. 9.5.41, Glamorgan, S. Wales; m., Iain McCarter; 1 s.; 3 d. Educ. Cheltenham Ladies' College; Western General Hospital, Edinburgh; Guy's Hospital, London. Staff Nurse/Sister, Roodlands Hospital, Haddington. Church of Scotland: Member: Board of Social Responsibility, Assembly Council, Board of National Mission; Member, Special Commission looking at Livingston ecumenical experiment; Past President, Dalkeith Branch, British Red Cross Society (awarded Badge of Honour). Recreations: choral singing; dress-making; sailing; gardening. Address: (h.) 5 Westfield Grove, Eskbank, Dalkeith EH22 3JH; T.-0131-663 3896.

McCarthy, James, BSc, FRZSS (Hon). Lecturer/ Conservation Consultant; b. 6.5.36, Dundee; m.; 2 s.; 1 d. Educ. Harris Academy, Dundee; Aberdeen University; University of East Africa, Kampala. Military Service, 1954-56 (Royal Marines, commissioned Black Watch, seconded King's African Rifles); Leverhulme Scholar, Makerere College, Kampala, 1959-61; Assistant Conservator of Forests, Tanzania, and Lecturer in Forest Ecology, Forest Training School, 1961-63; Deputy Regional Officer (North England), Nature Conservancy, 1963-69; Deputy Director (Scotland), Nature Conservancy Council, 1975-91; Member, Board, Scottish Natural Heritage. Churchill Fellow, USA, 1976; Nuffield/ Leverhulme Fellow, 1988. Recreation: cross-country skiing. Address: (h.) 6a Ettrick Road, Edinburgh; T.-0131-229 1916; e-mail: jmc36@ukonline.co.uk

McClatchie, Colin James Stewart, BSc (Econ) (Hons), MCIM. General Manager, News International Newspapers (Scotland) Ltd., since 1995; b. 1.1.49, Belfast; m., Claire McConaghy; 2 d. Educ. Coleraine Academical Institution; Queen's University, Belfast. Senior management positions, Thomson Regional Newspapers, Belfast, Newcastle, Reading, Edinburgh, 1971-84; Circulation/Marketing Director, Scottish Daily Record and Sunday Mail Ltd., 1984-94 (and Managing Director, Maxwell Free Newspapers Ltd., 1990-93); Marketing Consultant, 1995. Life Vice President, Newspaper Press Fund (Chairman, West of Scotland District, 1998-2000); Chairman, Institute of Directors, West of Scotland Branch, since 2000; Director, Scottish International Resource Programme, since 2001; Director, Scottish Enterprise Glasgow, since 2002; Chairman, Scottish Society of Epicureans, since 2002. Recreations: family; golf; theatre. Address: (b.) 124 Portman Street, Glasgow G41 1EJ; T.-0141-420 5101; e-mail: CMcClatchie@newsint.co.uk

McCleery, Professor Alison, MA, PhD, DipLang. Professor of Geography, Napier University, Edinburgh, since 1999; b. 13.10.53, Edinburgh; m., Professor Alistair McCleery (qv); 3s.; 1d. Educ. George Watson's Ladies College; Mary Erskine School; St Andrews University; Glasgow University. Research Officer/Senior Research Officer, Central Research Unit, Scottish Office, 1978-81; Senior Lecturer, Social Science, Napier University, 1981-97; Reader in Geography, 1997-99; lately Demographic Consultant, Council of Europe and Visiting Research Fellow, Institut National d'Etudes Demographiques, Paris; Member, Council, Royal Scottish Geographical Society; Secretary, International Society for Marginal Regions; Winner Royal Scottish Geographical Society President's Award, 1996; Editor, Scottish Geographical Journal, since 1998. Recreations: choral singing; amateur orchestral player (French horn). Address: (b.) Transport Research Institute, Napier University, 66 Spylaw Road, Edinburgh, EH10 5BR; T.-0131-455 5140; e-mail: sgj@napier.ac.uk

McCleery, Professor Alistair Michael, MA, MLitt, PhD. Professor of Literature and Communication, Napier University, Edinburgh, since 1995; b., 15.6.54, Londonderry; m., Professor Alison McCleery (q.v); 3s.; 1 d. Educ. Foyle College, Derry; St Andrews University; Stirling University. Tutor/Lecturer, St Andrews University; Napier University: Lecturer; Senior Lecturer; Reader; Fellow, Salzburg Seminar; Director, Scottish Centre for the Book; Editor, The Bibliotheck; Chair, UK Association for Publishing Education; Executive, International Association for Publishing Education; Advisory Panel, History of the Book in Ireland; Director, Sapphire Project; Scottish Arts Council Magazine Panel; Antiquarian Booksellers' Award, 2001; Mellon Fellow, University of Texas, 2001. Publications: Landscape and the Light: The Essays of Neil Gunn (Editor), 1987; The Ulysses Pagefinder, 1988; The Porpoise Press, 1922-39, 1988; J.M. Barrie, Farewell Miss Julie (Editor), 1989; The Ulysses Telegraph, 1990; James Joyce, Works in Progress (Editor), 1992; Charles Lamb, The Adventures of Ulysses (Editor), 1991; The History of the Book (CD-Rom), 2001. Recreations: music; film; watching rugby; Byzantine studies. Address: (b.) School of Communications, Napier University, Craighouse Campus, Edinburgh, EH10 5LG; T.-0131-455 6171; e-mail: a.mccleery@napier.ac.uk

McClellan, John Forrest, MA, Hon. FDIT. Member, Management Committee, Hanover (Scotland) Housing Association, since 1986; b. 15.8.32, Glasgow; m., Eva Maria Pressel; 3 s.; 1 d. Educ. Aberdeen Grammar School; Aberdeen University. 2nd Lt., Gordon Highlanders and Nigeria Regiment, Royal West African Frontier Force, 1954-56; entered Civil Service, 1956; Assistant Principal,

Scottish Office, 1956-59; Private Secretary to Permanent Under Secretary of State, Scottish Office, 1959-60; Principal, Scottish Office, 1960-68; Civil Service Fellow, Glasgow University, 1968-69; Assistant Secretary, Scottish Office, 1969-77; Under Secretary, Scottish Office, 1977-85; Director, Scottish International Education Trust, 1986-2001. Publication: Then A Soldier (novel), 1991. Recreations: gardening; walking. Address: (h.) 7 Cumin Place, Edinburgh EH9 2JX; T.-0131 667 8446.

McClelland, Professor John Ferguson, CBE, CIMgt, FRSA, FRSE. President, 3 Com Corporation's Business Networks Company, since 2001, Senior Vice President, Worldwide Operations, 1999-2001; Visiting Professor and Fellow, Paisley University, since 1993; b. 27.3.45, Glasgow; m., Alice; 1 d. Educ. North Kelvinside School; Glasgow College. South of Scotland Electricity Board, 1963-68; IBM Corporation, 1968-95: Controller, Greenock Manufacturing, 1977, European Director of Operations, 1980, European Manufacturing Controller, 1983, Director of Manufacturing, Greenock, 1987, Director of UK Manufacturing, 1992, Vice President, Worldwide Manufacturing, 1994; Digital Corporation, 1995-98, V.P. Worldwide Manufacturing; Global Chief Industrial Officer, Philips B.V., 1998-99. Former Chairman: Judging Panel, Quality Scotland Excellence Award, Higher Education Funding Council's Quality Assessment Committee, CBI UK Technology and Innovation Committee; Chairman, Technology Ventures Scotland; Director and Vice Chairman, Rangers Football Club PLC; Director, Haven Products Ltd. Recreations: golf; football.

McClure, Judith, MA (Oxon), DPhil, FRSA, FSAScot. Head, St. George's School, Edinburgh, since 1994; Chairman, Scottish Region, 1995-98, and Member, Council, Girls' Schools Association; b. 22.12.45, Stockton; m., Dr. Roger Collins. Educ. Newlands Grammar School, Middlesbrough; Somerville College, Oxford. Sir Maurice Powicke Research Fellow, Lady Margaret Hall, Oxford, 1976-77; Lecturer in Medieval Latin and Medieval History, Liverpool University, 1977-79; Lecturer in History, Oxford University (Jesus, Somerville and Worcester Colleges), 1979-81; Teacher and Head of Department in History and Politics, School of St. Helen & St. Katherine, Abingdon, 1981-84; Assistant Head, Kingswood School, Bath, 1984-87; Head, Royal School, Bath, 1987-93. Member: Court, University of Bath, 1989-92, General Convocation, Heriot Watt University, since 1994, Board of Governors, Clifton Hall School, 1995-99, Governing Body, Scottish Council of Independent Schools, since 1995, Management Committee, since 1998 (Chairman, Management Committee, since 2000), Board, Scottish Qualifications Authority, 1999-2000, Board, Merchiston Castle School, since 1999, Ministerial Strategy Committee on Continuing Professional Development, since 2000 (Chairman, Leadership and Management Sub-group, since 2001); Trustee, Hopetoun House, since 1998. Publication: Bede: The Ecclesiastical History (Co-author), 1994. Recreations: reading; using a computer; travelling. Address: (b.) St. George's School for Girls, Garscube Terrace, Edinburgh EH12 6BG; T.-031-332 4575.

McCluskey, Baron (John Herbert McCluskey), LLD (Dundee). Former Senator of the College of Justice in Scotland; Life Peer, since 1976; Chair, Age Concern (Scotland), since 2000; b. 12.6.29, Glasgow; m., Ruth Friedland; 2 s.; 1 d. Educ. St. Bede's Grammar School, Manchester; Holy Cross Academy, Edinburgh; Edinburgh University; MA, LLB. Admitted Faculty of Advocates, 1955; Standing Junior Counsel to Ministry of Power (Scotland), 1963; Advocate-Depute, 1964-71; QC (Scot), 1967; Chairman, Medical Appeal Tribunals for Scotland, 1972-74; Sheriff Principal of Dumfries and Galloway, 1973-74; Solicitor General for Scotland, 1974-79; Chairman, Scottish Association for Mental Health, 1985-94; Independent Chairman: Scottish Football League

Compensation Tribunal, SFA Appeals Tribunal; Reith Lecturer, BBC, 1986; LLD (Dundee), 1989; Editor, Butterworth's Scottish Criminal Law and Practice series. Publications: Law, Justice and Democracy, 1987; Criminal Appeals, 1992. Recreations: tennis; pianoforte. Address: (b.) Court of Session, Parliament House, Edinburgh EH1 1RF; T.-0131-225 2595.

McCluskey, Mary, DCE. Artistic Director (Chief Executive), Scottish Youth Theatre, since 1992; freelance Theatre Director/Drama Tutor, since 1985; b. 16.9.54, Glasgow. Educ. West Senior High School, Garden City, Michigan, USA; Hamilton College of Education; Royal Scottish Academy of Music and Drama. President, Hamilton College of Education SRC, 1975-76; Teacher, Glenlee Primary, Hamilton, 1976-79; Assistant Stage Manager, Dundee Repertory Theatre, 1980-81; YOP Supervisor, Community Projects Agency (East End), 1981-83; YTS Training Officer, Community Projects Agency (South East), 1983-85; Associate Director, Scottish Youth Theatre, 1989-91; Education Officer, Royal Shakespeare Company, 1991-92. Member, BAFTA. Adapted: Wee MacGreegor, Wee MacGreegor Enlists, Medea, Hamlet, Macbeth, The Glory. Recreations: theatre; films; books; visiting historic sites. Address: (b.) Scottish Youth Theatre, 3rd Floor, Forsyth House, 111 Union Street, Glasgow G1 3TA; e-mail: marymccluskey@scottishyouththeatre.org

McCluskie, John Cameron, LLB, CB, QC. First Scottish Parliamentary Counsel, Edinburgh, since 1999; b. 1.2.46, Glasgow; m., Janis Mary Helen McArthur; 1 s.; 1 d. Educ. Hyndland School, Glasgow; Glasgow University. Apprentice Solicitor, Boyds Glasgow, 1967-69; Assistant Town Clerk, Cumbernauld, 1969-70; Assistant Solicitor, Macdonald Jameson & Morris, Glasgow, 1970-71; Assistant Solicitor, SSEB, 1971-72; Assistant, Deputy, Scottish Parliamentary Counsel and Assistant Legal Secretary to Lord Advocate, 1972-89; First Scottish Parliamentary Counsel and Legal Secretary to Lord Advocate, 1989-99. Recreations: walking dogs; watching mogs; cutting logs. Address: (h.) Law View, Redside Steading, North Berwick; T.-01620 890296.

McCoist, Alistair (Ally) Murdoch, MBE. Footballer, Kilmarnock F.C. (formerly Glasgow Rangers); b. 24.9.62, Bellshill; m., Allison; 3 s. Educ. Hunter High School. Debut for St. Johnstone aged 16; signed for Sunderland, 1981; joined Rangers, 1983; became club's leading goal-scorer, August 1997 (421 goals); 61 caps for Scotland, since 1986; Member, Scotland squad, 1990 World Cup Finals, 1992 and 1996 European Championships; regular contributor to Question of Sport, BBC TV; ITV football pundit. Scottish Sports Personality of the Year, 1992; Scottish Sports Writers' Player of the Year, 1992. Recreations: reading autobiographies; listening to music; playing pranks on his team-mates. Address: (b.) 16 Royal Terrace, Glasgow G3 7NY.

McColgan, Elizabeth. Athlete; b. 24.5.64, Dundee; m., Peter Conor McColgan; 2 s.; 1 d. Educ. University of Alabama. Commonwealth Games Gold medallist (10,000 metres), 1986; Silver medallist, World Cross-Country Championships, 1987; Olympic Games Silver medallist (10,000 metres), 1988; Silver medallist, World Indoor Championships, 1989; Gold medallist (10,000 metres) and Bronze medallist (3,000 metres), Commonwealth Games, 1990; World 10,000 Meters Champion (Track), 1991; New York Marathon Winner, 1991; Tokyo Marathon Winner, 1992; London Marathon Winner, 1996; world records: 5,000, 10,000, half marathon on roads.

McColl, Sheriff Isabella Garden, LLB. Sheriff of Tayside Central and Fife at Dunfermline, since 2000; b. 7.11.52, Edinburgh; m., Alexander James; 1 s.; 2 d. Educ. James Gillespie's High School, Edinburgh;

Edinburgh University. Solicitor, 1975-92; Advocate, 1993-2000; Temporary Sheriff, 1999. Address: (b.) Sheriff's Chambers, Sheriff Court House, 1/6 Carnegie Drive, Dunfermline KY12 7HJ; T.-01383 724666.

McColl, James Hamilton, MBE, NDH, SDH, SHM. Freelance Horticulturalist; b. 19.9.35, Kilmarnock; m., Billie; 1 s.; 1 d. Educ. Kilmarnock Academy; West of Scotland Agricultural College. Staff Member, WSAC, Auchincruive, Ayr, 1956-59; Assistant Head Gardener, Reading University Botanic Garden, 1959-61; Horticultural Adviser/Lecturer, Shropshire Education Authority, 1961-67; Horticultural Adviser: MAFF, Leicestershire, Northants and Rutland, 1967-73, North of Scotland College of Agriculture, 1973-78; former PRO, Morrison Bowmore Distillers Ltd.; Co-Presenter, The Beechgrove Garden, BBC TV Scotland, 1978-89, since 1994. Recreations: golf; music; rugby. Address: (h.) Ayrshire House, Oldmeldrum, Aberdeenshire; T.-01651 873955.

McComb, Professor (William) David, BSc, MSc, PhD, CPhys, FInstP. Professor of Statistical Physics, Edinburgh University, since 1997; b. 31.10.40, Belfast; m., Doyleen M. McLeod; 3 d. Educ. Methodist College, Belfast; Queens University, Belfast; Manchester University. Senior Scientific Officer, Theoretical Physics Division, AERE, Harwell; Edinburgh University: Lecturer in Engineering Science, Lecturer in Physics, Reader in Physics. Publications: The Physics of Fluid Turbulence, 1990; Dynamics and Relativity, 1999. Recreations: reading; gardening; listening to music. Address: (b.) Department of Physics and Astronomy, King's Buildings, Edinburgh University, Edinburgh.

McConnachie, Brian, LLB, DipLP. Advocate; b. 20.4.59, Dundee; m., Sharon Steedman; 3 s.; 1 d. Educ. Lawside Academy; Alva Academy; University of Glasgow. A.C. Bennett and Fairweather, Edinburgh: Legal Trainee, 1981-83, Solicitor, 1983-84; Solicitor, A.C. Miller and Mackay, Perth, 1984-93; devilling, 1993-94. Recreations: family; football; Guinness. Address: Sidlaw View, Main Street, Balbeggie, Perthshire PH2 6EZ; T.-01821 640609; e-mail: bas@sidlawview.freeserve.co.uk

McConnell, Bridget Mary, MA (Hons), DIA, MEd, FRSA, FFCS. Director, Cultural and Leisure Services, Glasgow City Council, since 1998; b. 28.5.58, Lennoxtown; m., Jack Wilson McConnell (qv); 1 s.; 1 d. Educ. St. Patrick's High School, Kilsyth; Our Lady's High School, Cumbernauld; St. Andrews University; Dundee College of Commerce; Stirling University. Curator, Doorstep Gallery, Fife Regional Council, 1983-84; Arts Officer, Stirling District Council, 1984-88; Principal Arts Officer, The Arts in Fife, Fife Regional Council, 1988-96; Service Manager, Community Services, Fife Council, 1996-98. Conference Co-ordinator, Fourth International Conference in Adult Education and the Arts, St. Andrews, 1995; External Verifier, SCOTVEC Arts and Leisure Management Courses, 1990-97; Member, Board, Workshop and Artists Studio Provision Scotland (WASPS) Ltd, 1985-90; Chair, Scottish Youth Dance Festival, 1993-96 (Founder Member, 1988); Chair, Scottish Local Authority Arts Officers Group, 1993-96 (Founder Member, 1991); Vice Chair, Scottish Arts Lobby (SALVO), 1995-97; Member, Scottish Arts Council Combined Arts Committee, 1988-94; Arts Adviser to COSLA, 1997-2001; Member, Scottish Executive, National Culture Strategy Focus Group, 1999-2000; Member, Scottish Executive, Social Inclusion Task Group, 1999-2000; Board Member, RSAMD, since 2001; Awards: British/American Arts Association/University of Minnesota Fellowship, 1987. Publications: Modernising Britain: Creative Futures (Co-Author), 1997; conference papers on arts and adult education. Recreations: walking; playing piano; swimming; reading. Address: (b.) 20 Trongate, Glasgow G1 5FS; T.-0141-287 5058.

McConnell, Charles Stephen, BA (Hons), MPhil. Chief Executive, Community Learning Scotland, since 1999; Secretary General, International Association for Community Development; Chairman, UK National Training Standards Agency for Community Learning and Development; b. 20.6.51, Harrogate. Community Educator; Lecturer in Community Studies, Clydebank Technical College; Action Researcher, Community Education, Scottish Local Government Unit; Lecturer in Community Education, Dundee College of Education; Senior Policy Development Officer, National Consumer Council; Development Director, Action Resource Centre; Public and European Affairs Director, Community Development Foundation; Chief Executive, Scottish Community Education Council; former Labour Party Parliamentary candidate. Publications: Community Worker as Politiciser of the Deprived; Deprivation, Participation and Community Action; Community Education and Community Development; Post 16 — Developments in Continuing Education in Scotland; Classroom Commercials — business sponsorship of education; Consumer Action and Community Development; Community Development — the European dimension; A Citizen's Europe; Promoting Community Development in Europe; Community Development and Urban Regeneration; Community Education: The Making of an Empowering Profession. Recreations: fell-walking; reading political biography. Address: (b.) Rosebery House, 9 Haymarket Terrace, Edinburgh EH12 5EZ; T.-0131-313 2488.

McConnell, Jack Wilson, BSc, DipEd. MSP (Labour), Motherwell and Wishaw, since 1999; First Minister, since 2001 (Minister for Education, Europe and External Affairs, Scottish Executive, 2000-2001, Minister for Finance, 1999-2000); b. 30.6.60, Irvine; m., Bridget (qv); 1 s.; 1 d. Educ. Arran High School; Stirling University. Mathematics Teacher, Lornshill Academy, 1983-92; General Secretary, Scottish Labour Party, 1992-98; Chief Executive, Public Affairs Europe Limited, 1998. Member, Stirling District Council, 1984-93, Council Leader, 1990-92, Treasurer, 1988-92, Chair, Leisure and Recreation Committee, 1986-87, Equal Opportunities Committee, 1986-90; President, 1980-82, Hon. President, 1984-85 and 1991-93, Stirling University Students Association; Executive Member, Scottish Constitutional Convention, 1990-98; Deputy President, NUS Scotland, 1982-83; Chair, Board of Directors, Stirling Windows Ltd., 1988-92; Member, Labour Party Scottish Executive Committee, 1989-92; Parliamentary candidate, Perth and Kinross, 1987. Publication: Proposals for Scottish Democracy, 1989. Recreations: golf; swimming; cinema; music. Address: (b.) 265 Main Street, Wishaw ML2 7NE; T.-01698 303040; Scottish Parliament, Edinburgh EH99 1SP; T.-0131-348 5831; e-mail: jack.mcconnell.msp@scottish.parliament.uk

McConnell, Rodger Raymond, FRICS, MBA. Director of Development and Regeneration Services, Glasgow City Council, since 1998; Chairman, General Practice Division, Royal Institution of Chartered Surveyors in Scotland, 1996; b. 13.5.47, Bellshill; m., Rosalind; 3 s.; 1 d. Educ. Our Lady's High School, Motherwell; College of Estate Management; Glasgow University. Trainee Valuer, District Valuer's Office, Glasgow, 1966-71; Senior Assistant, Richard Ellis, 1971-75; Strathclyde Regional Council: Assistant Head of Estates, 1975-78, Depute Director of Estates, 1978-91; City Estates Surveyor, Glasgow District Council, 1992-95; Director of Property Services, Glasgow City Council, 1995-98; Member, Association of Chief Estates Surveyors and Property Managers in Local Government. Recreations: family activities; following sport; theatre. Address: (b.) 229 George Street, Glasgow G1 1QV; e-mail: roger.mcconnell@drs.glasgow.gov.uk

McConnell, Walter Scott, OBE, FRPharmS, PhC. Community Pharmacist, since 1962; former Vice Chairman, Ayrshire and Arran Community Health Care Trust; b.

7.4.36, Kilmarnock; m.; 1 s.; 3 d. Educ. Kilmarnock Academy; Royal Technical College, Glasgow. Former Chairman, Pharmaceutical General Council (Scotland). Recreations: curling; golf. Address: (h.) 27 Mauchline Road, Hurlford, Kilmarnock KA1 5AB; T.-01563 525393.

MacCormick, Professor Sir (Donald) Neil, Kt., QC (Hon), MEP, MA, LLD, Hon. LLD (Uppsala), Hon. LLD (Saarland), Hon. LLD (Queen's University, Ontario), Hon. LLD (Macerata), Hon. LLD (Glasgow), FRSE, FBA. Vice-Principal, 1997-1999, and Regius Professor of Public Law, Edinburgh University, since 1972 (on leave of absence, 1999-04); Member (SNP) of European Parliament for Scotland, since 1999; Vice-President, Scottish National Party, since 1999; b. 27.5.41, Glasgow; m., 1, Karen (Caroline) Rona Barr (m. diss.); 3 d.; 2, Flora Margaret Britain. Educ. High School of Glasgow; Glasgow University; Balliol College, Oxford. Lecturer in Jurisprudence, Queen's College, Dundee, 1965-67; Fellow, Balliol College, Oxford, 1967-72; Oxford University: CUF Lecturer, 1968-72, Pro-Proctor, 1970-71; Dean, Faculty of Law, Edinburgh University, 1973-76 and 1985-88; Senate Assessor, University Court, 1982-85; Provost, Faculty Group of Law and Social Sciences, 1993-97; Member, Broadcasting Council for Scotland, 1985-89; Vice President: International Association for Legal and Social Philosophy, 1991-95, Royal Society of Edinburgh, 1991-94; Member, Economic and Social Research Council, 1995-99; Member, Scottish Examination Board, 1994-97. President, Oxford Union, 1965; Scottish National Party: Executive Member, 1978-81, Council Member, 1978-84 and 1989-97; Foreign Member, Finnish Academy of Science. Publications: as author or editor, books on philosophy of law, political philosophy, etc, including Questioning Sovereignty, 1999. Address: (h.) 19 Pentland Terrace, Edinburgh EH10 6AA; T.-0131-447 7945; (b.) 6 North Charlotte Street, Edinburgh EH2 4JH; T.-0131-225 3497.

McCormick, John, MA, MEd. Controller, BBC Scotland, since 1992; b. 24.6.44; m., Jean Frances Gibbons; 1 s.; 1 d. Educ. St. Michael's Academy, Irvine; Glasgow University. Former schoolteacher; joined BBC as Education Officer, 1970; Senior Education Officer, Scotland, 1975-82; Secretary and Head of Information, BBC Scotland, 1982-87; Secretary of BBC, 1987-92. Chairman, Edinburgh International Film Festival, since 1996; Lay Member, Court, University of Strathclyde, since 1996; Board Member, Scottish Screen, since 1997; Board Member, Glasgow Science Centre, since 1998. Recreations: theatre; cinema; biography; newspapers. Address: (b.) Broadcasting House, Queen Margaret Drive, Glasgow, G12 0TT; T.-0141-339 8844.

McCormick, John St. Clair, MB ChB, FRCSEd. Medical Director, Dumfries and Galloway Royal Infirmary NHS Trust, since 1994; Consultant Surgeon, Dumfries and Galloway Royal Infirmary, since 1979; Director of Standards and Vice President, Royal College of Surgeons of Edinburgh; Member, Clinical Standards Board for Scotland, since 1999; b. 20.9.39, Sherborne; m., Fiona Helen McLean; 2 s. Educ. St. Paul's Cathedral Choir School; University of Edinburgh. Consultant Surgeon, Dunfermline and West Fife Hospital, 1974-79. Recreation: fishing. Address: Dumfries and Galloway Royal Infirmary, Bankend Road, Dumfries DG1 4AP; T.-01387 246246, Ext. 3113.

McCormick, John William Penfold, BSc, PhD. Chairman, Scottish Association for Public Transport, since 1988; Information Technology Manager, Weir Pumps Ltd., since 1979; b. 9.6.46, Renfrew; m., Linda M.L.; 1 d. Educ. Paisley Grammar School; Glasgow University. Research Fellow, Glasgow University, 1971-74; computer management, since 1975. Recreations: hill-walking; transport; music. Address: (b.) 11 Queens Crescent, Glasgow G4 9AS; T.-0141-639 3697.

McCormick, Julie Elizabeth, LLB (Hons), DipLP, NP. Solicitor; Membership Secretary, Scottish Young Lawyers Association; Member, Admissions Committee, Law Society of Scotland; b. 10.12.71, Farnborough, Kent. Educ. John Paul Academy, Glasgow; Strathclyde University. Joined Allan McDougall & Co, SSC, as trainee Solicitor, 1994; Qualified Solicitor, since 1996. Recreations: cinema; theatre; Celtic music; food and drink. Address: (b.) 3 Coates Crescent, Edinburgh EH3 7AL; T.-0131-225 2121.

McCourt, Arthur David, BSc (Hons). Chief Executive, Highland Council, since 1995; b. 11.7.47, Newburgh, Fife; m., Jan; 1 d. Educ. Bell-Baxter High School, Cupar; Edinburgh College of Art; Heriot-Watt University. Various posts with Northumberland County Council, Central Regional Council, Stirling District Council; Assistant Chief Executive, Tayside Regional Council, 1990-93. Recreation: mountaineering. Address: (b.) Glenurquhart Road, Inverness IV3 5NX; T.-01463 702838.

McCreadie, Robert Anderson, LLB, PhD, Advocate; b. 17.8.48, St. Andrews. Educ. Madras College, St. Andrews; Edinburgh University; Christ's College, Cambridge. Lecturer, Dundee University, 1974-78, Edinburgh University, 1978-93; called to Scottish Bar, 1992; Standing Junior Counsel, Department of Transport, 1994-95, Scottish Home and Health Department, 1995-99, Home Affairs and Justice Department, 1999-2000, Advocate Depute, since 2000; Member: Scottish Consumer Council, 1977-82, Social Security Appeal Tribunals, 1987-92; Labour Parliamentary Candidate, Edinburgh South, 1983; joined Scottish Liberal Party, 1985; Parliamentary Candidate: Livingston, 1987, Glasgow Central, 1989, Edinburgh South, 1992; Vice Chairman, Scottish Liberal Democrats, 1988-92; Executive Committee, Scottish Constitutional Convention, 1989-82. Publication: You and Your Rights: An A to Z Guide to the Law in Scotland, 1984 (Joint Editor). Recreations: music; Scottish history; walking. Address: (h.) 40 Marchmont Crescent, Edinburgh EH9 1HG; T.-0131-667 1383.

McCreadie, Professor Robin G., DSc, MD, FRCPsych. Director of Clinical Research, Crichton Royal Hospital, Dumfries, since 1982; Professor of Clinical Psychiatry: University of Aberdeen, University of Glasgow; b. 21.2.42, Troon; 2 d. Educ. Ayr Academy; Glasgow University. Lecturer in Psychological Medicine, Glasgow University; Consultant Psychiatrist, Gartnavel Royal Hospital, Glasgow. Recreations: hill-walking; all things Italian. Address: (b.) Crichton Royal Hospital, Dumfries; T.-01387 244000; e-mail: rgmccreadie_crh@compuserve.com

McCrone, Iain Alistair, CBE (1987), SDA. Farmer and Company Director; b. 29.3.34, Glasgow; m., Yvonne Findlay; 4 d. Educ. Glasgow Academy; Trinity College, Glenalmond; West of Scotland Agricultural College. Farming on own account, since 1956; Managing Director, McCrone Farmers Ltd., since 1958; began fish farming, 1968; Director: Highland Trout Co. (now Marine Harvest McConnell), Otter Ferry Salmon Ltd., since 1974; Member: Fife Regional Council, 1978-82; Parliamentary candidate (Conservative), Central Fife, 1979, Council, National Farmers Union of Scotland, 1977-82, Board, Glenrothes Development Corporation, 1980-96, Fife Health Board, 1983-91; Chairman, Oxford Farming Conference, 1988; Chairman, The Farmers Club, 2001; Nuffield Farming Scholar, 1966; President, Scottish Conservative and Unionist Association, 1985-87. Recreations: golf; rugby (spectator). Address: (h.) Cardsknolls, Markinch, Fife KY7 6LP; T.-01337 830267; e-mail: iain-mccrone@talk21.com

McCrone, Professor Robert Gavin Loudon, CB, MA, MSc, PhD, Hon.LLD, FRSE. Visiting Professor, Department of Business Studies, since 1994, and Hon. Fellow of the Europa Institute, since 1992, Edinburgh University; Commissioner, Parliamentary Boundary Commission for Scotland, since 1999; Director, Queen's Hall, since 1998; Trustee, Scottish Opera Endowment Trust, since 1998; b. 2.2.33, Ayr; m., 1, Alexandra Bruce Waddell (deceased); 2 s.; 1 d.; m., 2, Olive Pettigrew Moon (née McNaught); 2 step-d. Educ. St. Catharine's College, Cambridge; University of Wales; Glasgow University. Fisons Ltd., 1959-60; Lecturer in Economics, Glasgow University, 1960-65; Fellow, Brasenose College, Oxford, 1965-70; Consultant, UNESCO, 1964; Member, NEDC Working Party on Agricultural Policy, 1967-68; Adviser, House of Commons Select Committee on Scottish Affairs, 1969-70; Chief Economic Adviser, Scottish Office, 1970-92; Under Secretary, 1972-80; Secretary, Industry Department for Scotland, 1980-87; Secretary, Scottish Office Environment Department, 1987-92. Member: Economic and Social Research Council, 1986-89, Council, Royal Economic Society, 1977-82, Council, Scottish Economic Society, 1982-91, Board, Scottish Opera, 1992-98, Advisory Committee, Inquiry into Implementation of Constitutional Reform, 1995-97, National Review of Resources Allocation in the NHS in Scotland, 1998-2000; Deputy Chairman, Royal Infirmary of Edinburgh NHS Trust, 1994-99; Deputy Chairman, Lothian University Hospitals' Trust, 1999-2001; Chairman, Committee of Inquiry into Professional Conditions of Service for Teachers, 1999-2000. Publications: The Economics of Subsidising Agriculture, 1962; Scotland's Economic Progress 1951-60, 1963; Regional Policy in Britain, 1969; Scotland's Future, 1969; Housing Policy in Britain and Europe (Co-Author), 1995; European Monetary Union and Regional Development, 1997. Recreations: music; walking. Address: (b.) Department of Business Studies, Edinburgh University, 50 George Square, Edinburgh EH8 9JY; T.-0131 650 4603.

McCulloch, Andrew Grant, LLB, BSc(Soc Sci). Managing Partner, Drummond Miller WS; b. 10.2.52, Edinburgh; m.; 1 s.; 1 d. Educ. Glasgow Academy; Edinburgh University. Trained, then Assistant, Drummond & Co., 1974-79; Partner, since 1979; Member, Council, Law Society of Scotland, 1987-98, President, 1996-97; Solicitor Advocate, since 1992; Temporary Sheriff, 1992-99. President, Grange Sports Club, 1990-92. Recreations: golf; cricket; wine. Address: (b.) 31/2 Moray Place, Edinburgh; T.-0131-226 5151; e-mail: gmcculloch@drummond-miller.co.uk

McCulloch, Ian, DA, ARSA. Painter and Printmaker; b. 4.3.35, Glasgow; m., Margery Palmer; 2 s. Educ. Eastbank Academy; Glasgow School of Art. Elected Member, Society of Scottish Artists, 1964; elected Associate, Royal Scottish Academy, 1989; paintings in many private and public collections; numerous one-man and group exhibitions; 1st prize, Stirling Smith Biennial, 1985; winner, Glasgow International Concert Hall Mural Competition, 1989-90; Fine Art Fellow, Strathclyde University, since 1994. Address: (h.) 51 Victoria Road, Lenzie, Glasgow G66 5AP; T.-0141-776 1053; e-mail: ian@mccullochstudio.fsnet.co.uk

McCulloch, Professor James, BSc, PhD. Professor of Neuroscience, Glasgow University, since 1988; b. 7.4.51, Irvine; m., Mailis Christina; 2 s. Educ. Spiers School, Beith; Glasgow University. Lecturer, 1978-86, Reader, 1986-88, Glasgow University; Editor, Journal of Cerebral Blood Flow and Metabolism, since 1997. Publications: four books; 210 scientific papers. Recreations: squash; golf; skiing. Address: (b.) Glasgow University, Bearsden Road, Glasgow, G61 1QH; T.-0141-330 5828.

McCulloch, James Macdonald, BA, MRTPI. Deputy Chief Reporter, Scottish Executive, since 1997; b. 3.12.48, Dorchester; m., Jennifer Anne Hay; 3 s. Educ. Hardye's School, Dorchester; Lanchester Polytechnic, Coventry. Planning Assistant, Coventry Corporation, 1971-73; Senior Planner and Principal Planner, Scottish Development

Department, 1973-84; Reporter to Principal Reporter to Deputy Chief Reporter, since 1984. Publications include: Report of the Public Inquiry into the Scotland-Northern Ireland Interconnector. Recreations: walking; eating; amateur radio. Address: (b.) Scottish Executive Inquiry Reporters Unit, 2 Greenside Place, Edinburgh EH1 3AG; T.-0131-244 5641.

McCulloch, John David, CA, DL. Deputy Lieutenant, Midlothian, since 1992; Clerk to Church of Scotland Presbytery of Lothian, since 1994; Chartered Accountant, since 1963; b. 5.4.37, Edinburgh; m., Cicely Blackett; 2 s.; 2 d. Educ. Belhaven Hill, Dunbar; Marlborough College. Address: (h.) Auchindinny House, Penicuik EH26 8PE; T.-Penicuik 672943.

McCulloch, Margery Palmer, BA, MLitt, PhD, LRAM, FFCS. Literary scholar; m., Ian McCulloch; 2 s. Educ. Hamilton Academy; London University; Glasgow University. Publications: The Novels of Neil M. Gunn: a critical study, 1987; The Man Who Came Back: short stories and essays by Neil M. Gunn, 1991; Edwin Muir: poet, critic and novelist, 1993; many essays on writing by Scottish women. Recreation: music. Address: (h.) 51 Victoria Road, Lenzie, Glasgow G66 5AP; T.-0141-776 1053; e-mail: margery@palmermcculloch.fsnet.co.uk

McCulloch, Stuart J., BSc, MEd, DipEd. Headmaster, Belmont House School, since 1999; b. 26.12.50, Melfort; m., Anne Elizabeth (deceased); 2 s.; 1 d. Educ. Queen Mary College, London; Stirling University. Head of Geography, Stewarts Melville, Edinburgh, 1973-92; Deputy Head, Beaconhurst School, 1992-98. Recreations: most things, especially bagpipes and books. Address: (b.) Belmont House School, Newton Mearns, Glasgow G77 5DU; T.-0141-639 2922.

McCulloch, Tony, BSc, MEd, MA, FRSA. Rector, Charleston Academy, Inverness, since 1991; b. 12.12.50, Glasgow; m., Anne C.; 1 s.; 1 d. Educ. St. Pius Secondary, Glasgow; University of Ulster; Edinburgh University; Open University. Taught in Glasgow, Cumbernauld, Edinburgh, and Armadale (formerly Depute Rector, Armadale Academy, West Lothian). Recreations: traditional music; mandolin. Address: (b.) Charleston Academy, Kinmylies, Inverness; T.-01463 234324.

McCunn, Archibald Eddington, OBE, BSc (Hons), CEng, MIMechE, FIMgt; b. 27.5.27, Motherwell; m., Olive Isobel Johnston; 1 s.; 1 d. Educ. Dalziel High School; Strathclyde University. Engineering Management, Colvilles Ltd. BSC, 1952-64; Senior Consultant, Inbucon/AIC, 1964-67; Divisional Chairman, Stenhouse Industries, 1967-71; Divisional Chairman/Consultant, Grampian Holdings plc, 1971-89; Board Member, Highlands and Islands Development Board, 1985-89; Director: A.E. McCunn Consultants Ltd., 1985-95; Chairman, Craftpoint Ltd., 1986-91; Director, McConnell Salmon Ltd., 1990-94; Vice Chairman and Trustee, Argyll and Bute Countryside Trust, 1990-95; Hon. Vice-President, Scottish Salmon Growers Association, 1990-95; Board Member: State Hospital, 1992-96, Scottish Natural Heritage (South West), 1992-97; Board Member, Scottish Greenbelt Foundation, 1992-99. Recreations: painting; music; writing; cycling; gardening. Address: (h.) 2 McIntosh Way, Motherwell ML1 3BB; T.-01698 253500; e-mail: a.e.mccunn@btinternet.com

McDaid, Professor Seamus, CA, MBA. Vice Principal, University of Paisley, since 1997; Vice Chairman, Renfrewshire and Inverclyde Primary Care NHS Trust; b. 23.7.52, Glasgow; m., Alice; 2 d. Educ. St. Mungo's Academy; Glasgow University; Strathclyde University. Qualified as CA, 1974; trained with Wylie & Bisset, CA; worked for Coopers & Lybrand; joined Glasgow College as Lecturer, 1976; Senior Lecturer, 1980, Head, Department of Finance and Accounting, 1987; Dean, Faculty of Business,

Glasgow Caledonian University, 1992. Recreations: football; badminton. Address: (b.) University of Paisley, Paisley PA1 2BE; T.-0141 848 3000.

McDevitt, Professor Denis Gordon, DSc, MD, FRCP, FRCPI, FRCPEd, FFPM, FRSE. Professor of Clinical Pharmacology, Dundee University Medical School, since 1984 (Dean, Faculty of Medicine, Dentistry and Nursing, 1994-97); Honorary Consultant Physician, Tayside Universities Hospitals Trust, since 1984; Civil Consultant in Clinical Pharmacology, RAF, since 1987; Member, General Medical Council, since 1996 (Treasurer, since 2001); b. 17.11.37, Belfast; m., Anne McKee; 2 s.; 1 d. Educ. Campbell College, Belfast; Queen's University, Belfast. Assistant Professor of Medicine and Consultant Physician, Christian Medical College, Ludhiana, North India, 1968-71; Senior Lecturer in Clinical Pharmacology and Consultant Physician, Queen's University Medical School, 1971-76; Merck International Fellow in Clinical Pharmacology, Vanderbilt University, Nashville, Tennessee, 1974-75; Reader in Clinical Pharmacology, Queen's University Medical School, 1976-78; Professor of Clinical Pharmacology, Queen's University of Belfast and Consultant Physician, Belfast Teaching Hospitals, 1978-83. Chairman, Clinical Section, British Pharmacological Society, 1985-88 (Secretary, 1978-82); Member, Medicines Commission, 1986-95; President, Association of Physicians of Great Britain and Ireland, 1987-88. Recreations: golf; classical music. Address: (h.) 1 Godfrey Street, Barnhill, Dundee DD5 2QZ.

McDiarmid, Colin. Executive Editor, The Herald; b. 4.12.50, Glasgow; m., Connie; 1 s.; 1 d. Educ. Bearsden Academy; Glasgow College. Sunday Express; Glasgow Herald; East Kilbride News; Reporter/Night News Editor/Deputy News Editor/News Editor, The Herald. Recreations: golf; travel. Address: (b.) The Herald, 200 Renfield Street, Glasgow G2 3PR; T.-0141 302 7037.

Macdonald, 8th Baron, (Godfrey James Macdonald of Macdonald). Chief of the Name and Arms of Macdonald; b. 28.11.47; m., Claire Catlow; 1 s.; 3 d. Address: (h.) Kinloch Lodge, Isle of Skye.

McDonald, Hon. Lord (Robert Howat McDonald), MC (1944), MA, LLB. Senator of the College of Justice in Scotland, 1973-89; b. 15.5.16, Paisley; m., Barbara Mackenzie. Educ. John Neilson Institution, Paisley; Glasgow University. Admitted Solicitor, 1938; KOSB, 1939-46 (mentioned in Despatches); admitted, Faculty of Advocates, 1946; QC (Scot), 1957; Sheriff of Ayr and Bute, 1966-71; Member, Criminal Injuries Compensation Board, 1964-71; Chairman: Mental Welfare Commission for Scotland, 1964-83, General Nursing Council for Scotland, 1970-73. Address: (h.) 5 Doune Terrace, Edinburgh EH3 6EA.

Macdonald of Tradeston, Rt. Hon. Lord (Gus Macdonald), CBE. Minister for the Cabinet Office and Chancellor of Duchy of Lancaster, since 2001; Minister for Transport, Department of Environment, Transport and the Regions, 1999-2001; Television Journalist; b. 20.8.40, Larkhall; m., Teen; 2 d. Educ. Allan Glen's School, Glasgow. Marine engineer, Stephens, Linthouse, 1955-62; Circulation Manager, Tribune, 1963-65; Journalist, The Scotsman, 1965-67; World in Action, Granada, 1967-75; successively Head of Current Affairs, Head of Regional Programmes, Head of Features, Granada, 1975-82; C4 Viewers Ombudsman, Right to Reply, 1982-88; Scottish Television: Director of Programmes, 1986-90, Managing Director, 1990-96; Chairman, Scottish Television, subsequently Scottish Media Group plc, 1996-98; BAFTA Awards: Best Factual Series, 1973; Lifetime Achievement Award, 1997; Scottish Business Elite Awards: Business Leader of the Year, Chairman of the Year, 1997; founder Chairman, Edinburgh International Telvision Festival,

1976; Visiting Professor, Film and Media Studies, Stirling University, 1985-98; Chairman, Edinburgh International Film Festival, 1993-96; Governor, National Film and Television School, 1986-97; Member, Boards: Scottish Screen, 1997, British Film Institute, 1997-98; Chairman, Cairngorms Partnership, 1997-98; Chairman, Taylor and Francis Group plc, 1997-98; Minister for Business and Industry, Scottish Office, 1998-99. Recreations: words; music; pictures; sports; hills.

MacDonald, Alan, MA, LLB, NP. Partner, McFayden and Semple Solicitors, since 1990; b. 23.5.58, Glasgow; m., Dr Jean MacDonald. Educ. Largs High School; Ardrossan Academy; Glasgow University. Apprentice McLure Naismith Brodie and Co., 1980-82; Assistant, McLure Naismith, 1982-87; Assistant, McFayden and Semple, 1987-90. Chairman, Waverley Excursions Ltd., 1997-2001; President, Renfrewshire Chamber of Commerce; Honorary Secretary, West of Scotland Chamber Group; President, Paisley Rotary Club; Director: Paisley and Renfrew Enterprise Trust, Scottish Enterprise Renfrewshire, Incorporation of Merchants and Trades of Paisley; Member, Institute of Management. Recreations: reading; birds; growing vegetables; music. Address: (b.) 6 Gilmour Street, Paisley, PA1 1BZ; T.-01410889 9291; e-mail: law@mcfadyen-semple.co.uk

McDonald, Very Rev. Dr. Alexander, BA, DUniv (Open), CMIWS, FFCS. Moderator of the General Assembly, Church of Scotland, 1997-98; Senior Adviser in Pastoral Care, Department of Ministry, Church of Scotland, since 1988; b. 5.11.37, Bishopbriggs; m., Essdale Helen McLeod; 2 s.; 1 d. Educ. Bishopbriggs Higher Grade School; Whitehill Senior Secondary School, Glasgow; Glasgow University and Trinity College. RAF, 1954-56; Management in timber trade: 1952-54, 1956-58; motor trade, 1958-62; student, 1962-68; Minister: St. David's Bathgate, 1968-74, St. Mark's, Old Hall, Paisley, 1974-88. Trustee, Scottish Television Staff Trust; wide range of involvement with Boys' Brigade in Scotland, Scottish Spastics, mentally handicapped children, ACCORD, Christian Aid and many others; Patron, Friends of Carronvale Boys' Brigade; regular broadcaster. Recreations: reading; walking; fishing. Address: Church of Scotland, 121 George Street, Edinburgh EH2 4YN; T.-0131-225 5722.

McDonald, Alexander John. Breed Secretary, Galloway Cattle Society, since 1990; b. 12.6.39, Fochabers. Educ. Milnes High School. RAF, 1958-90. Editor and Publsher, The Galloway Journal. Recreations: country pursuits; photography. Address: (b.) 15 New Market Street, Castle Douglas DG7 1HY; T.-01556 502753.

MacDonald, Allan, MA. Managing Director: MNE Television, since 1989, Corrodale Ltd., since 1988; (first) Chairman, CRANN Ltd; (first) Chairman, Federation of TAC, REALT, CRANN and Breton TV (independent sector for film/TV/radio in Celtic countries); b. 11.6.53, Eriskay; m., Marion Margaret; 1 d. Educ. St. Vincent's College, Langbank; Blairs College, Aberdeen; Glasgow University. Senior Producer, BBC Highland, Inverness; Senior Producer/Manager, BBC Radio Nan Eilean, Stornoway; Manager, BBC Highland, Inverness; Television Producer, BBC Scotland, Glasgow; Head of Gaelic Television, Grampian TV, 1992-94. Member, Board of Management, Lews Castle College, 1992-95. Address: (h.) 39 Hughenden Gardens, Hyndland, Glasgow G12 9YH; e-mail: mne@btconnect.com

MacDonald, Angus, BSc (Hons). Head Teacher, Braidfield High School, Clydebank, since 1998; b. 15.1.53, Glasgow; m., Fiona; 3 s.; 1 d. Educ. Bellahouston Academy; Strathclyde University. Teacher, Mathematics and Navigation, Islay High School, 1976-78; Assistant Principal Teacher, Guidance, Islay High School, 1978-80; Assistant Principal Teacher,

Mathematics, Dumbarton Academy, 1980-84; Principal Teacher, Mathematics, Kilsyth Academy, 1984-90; Assistant Head Teacher, Chryston High School, 1990-95; Depute Head Teacher, Braidfield High School, 1995-98; Member, Higher Still Implementation Group. Recreations: hill-walking; climbing; mountain biking. Address: (b.) Braidfield High School, Queen Mary Avenue, Clydebank, G81 2LR; T.-0141-952 3265.

Macdonald, Angus David, MA (Hons) (Cantab), DipEd. Headmaster, Lomond School, Helensburgh, since 1986; Chairman, Clan Donald Lands Trust; b. 9.10.50, Edinburgh; m., Isabelle Marjory Ross; 2 d. Educ. Portsmouth Grammar School; Cambridge University; Edinburgh University. Assistant Teacher, Alloa Academy, 1972-73; Assistant Teacher, Edinburgh Academy, 1973-82 (Exchange Teacher, King's School, Parramatta, NSW, 1978-79); George Watson's College, Edinburgh: Principal Teacher of Geography, 1982, Deputy Principal, 1982-86. Recreations: outdoor recreation; sport; piping; gardening. Address: 8 Millig Street, Helensburgh, Argyll; T.-01436 679204.

MacDonald, Angus Donald MacKintosh, CBE, MA, LLB, CA. Joint Managing Director, MacDonald Orr Ltd, since 1981; b. 10.4.39, Glasgow; m., Louise; 2 s.; 2 d. Educ. George Watsons; Edinburgh University. Graham Smart and Annan, Chartered Accountants, 1963-67; various positions in Edinburgh, Sheffield, London and Glasgow, 3i, 1967-81; Director, MacDonald Hotels Plc, since 1990; Director, Edinburgh Fund Managers, since 1996; Chairman, Edinburgh Small Companies Trust Plc, since 1993; Vice-Chairman, City Inn Ltd.; Past President, Edinburgh Chamber of Commerce; Vice-Chairman, Scottish Enterprise Edinburgh and Lothian; Chairman, Scottish Chamber Orchestra; Director, Edinburgh Festival Society Ltd. Recreations: golf; tennis; skiing; fiddling (mainly musical!); Scottish paintings. Address: (h.) 18 Hermitage Drive, Edinburgh, EH10 6BZ; T.-0131-447 2409.

Macdonald, Angus John, BSc (Hons), PhD, FSA (Scot). Writer on architecture; Senior Lecturer, Department of Architecture, University of Edinburgh, since 1988 (Head of Department, 1996-99); Head of Environmental Studies Planning Unit, University of Edinburgh, since 1998; b. 17.1.45, Edinburgh; m., Patricia Clare Mazoura Morrow Scott. Educ. George Heriot's School, Edinburgh; University of Edinburgh. Partner, Aerographica, since 1986; Commissioner, Royal Commission on the Ancient and Historical Monuments of Scotland, since 1999. Publications: Wind Loading on Buildings, 1975; Above Edinburgh, 1989; The Highlands and Islands of Scotland, 1989; Granite and Green, 1992; Structure and Architecture, 1994; Structural Design for Architecture, 1997; Anthony Hunt, 2000. Recreations: hillwalking; music. Address: Department of Architecture, University of Edinburgh, 20 Chambers Street, Edinburgh EH1 1JZ; T.-0131-650 2323; e-mail: Angus.Macdonald@ed.ac.uk

MacDonald, Very Rev. Canon Bernard Gordon. Parish Priest, St. Mary's, Fochabers, since 1997; b. 25.12.24, Dufftown. Educ. Blairs College, Aberdeen; St. Edmund's, Herts. Curate, St. Mary's, Aberdeen, 1948-54; Parish Priest: Holy Family, Mastrick, 1954-61, St. Lawrence's, Dingwall, and St. Joseph's, Invergordon, 1961-79, St. Ninian's, Inverness, 1979-89, St. Anne's, Thurso, and St. Joachim's, Wick, 1989-97. Recreations: English literature; bowling; golf; art. Address: St Mary's, 22 South Street, Fochabers IV32 7ED; T.-01343 820 285.

MacDonald, Calum Alasdair, PhD. MP (Labour), Western Isles, since 1987; Parliamentary Under-Secretary of State, Scottish Office, 1997-99; b. 7.5.56, Stornoway. Address: (b.) House of Commons, London, SW1.

MacDonald, Professor Caroline Mary, BSc, PhD, CBiol, FIBiol. Assistant Principal, since 1997, and Professor and Head, Department of Biological Sciences, Paisley University, 1992-97; b. 4.9.51, Edinburgh; m., Alastair MacDonald; 2 d. Educ. Glasgow High School for Girls; Glasgow University. Lecturer/Senior Lecturer, Strathclyde University, 1983-92; Chairman, European Society for Animal Cell Technology, 1994-97 (Secretary and Treasurer, 1991-94); Chief Editor, Genetic Engineer and Biotechnologist, 1994-97; Member, Executive Committee, Heads of University Biological Sciences, 1992-2000 (Secretary, 1997-2000); Member, Executive Committee and Treasurer, Modern Universities Research Group. Recreations: family; gardening; travel. Address: (b.) University of Paisley, High Street, Paisley PA1 2BE; T.-0141-848 3607; e-mail: c.macdonald@paisley.ac.uk

Macdonald, Professor David Iain Macpherson, BSc, PhD, CGeol, FGS, FRGS, Polar Medal. Professor of Petroleum Geology, University of Aberdeen, since 1999; b. 31.5.53, Bridge of Allan; m., Dr. Christine Mousley; 2 d. Educ. High School of Stirling; University of Glasgow; University of Cambridge. Geologist, British Antarctic Survey, Cambridge, 1975-80; Post Doctoral Demonstrator, University of Keele, 1980-82; Geologist, BP Petroleum Development, London, 1982-84; Senior Sedimentologist, British Antarctic Survey, 1984-93; Director, Cambridge Arctic Shelf Programme, 1993-99. Publication: Sedimentation, Tectonics and Eustasy, 1991. Recreations: riding; hillwalking; reading. Address: (b.) Department of Geology and Petroleum Geology, University of Aberdeen, Meston Building, King's College, Aberdeen AB24 3UE; T.-01224 273433; e-mail: d.macdonald@abdn.ac.uk

Macdonald, David Robert, BSc (Hons), MBA. Director, Locate in Scotland; former Chief Executive, Enterprise Ayrshire; b. 10.4.51, Edinburgh; m., Mary-Anne Turner; 2 d. Educ. Daniel Stewart's College, Edinburgh; University of Stirling; University of Strathclyde. Research Assistant, University of Dundee, 1974; Economic Analyst, West Midlands County Council, 1975-77; Head of Industrial Projects, Government of Papua New Guinea, 1978-81; Senior Economist, West Midlands County Council, 1982; Industrial Economist, Project Executive and Head of Service Industries, Scottish Development Agency, 1983-85; Director, Glasgow Action, 1985-91; Director, Glasgow Development Agency, 1991-93. Recreations: cycling; skiing; hill-walking; youth church; family. Address: (b.) Locate in Scotland, 150 Broomielaw, Atlantic Quay, Glasgow G2 8LU.

MacDonald, Professor Donald Gordon, RD**, BDS, PhD, FRCPath, FDSRCPS(G). Professor of Oral Pathology, Glasgow University, since 1991; Consultant Oral Pathologist, Glasgow Dental Hospital, since 1974; b. 5.7.42, Glasgow; m., Emma Lindsay Cordiner; 2 s. Educ. Kelvinside Academy, Glasgow; Glasgow University. Assistant, then Lecturer, Glasgow University, 1964-69; Visiting Associate Professor in Oral Pathology, University of Illinois, 1969-70; Lecturer, Senior Lecturer, Reader in Oral Medicine and Pathology, Glasgow University, 1970-91; Editor, Glasgow Dental Journal, 1969-75; Honorary Consultant Forensic Odontologist, Strathclyde Police, since 1976; Vice President, Association of Head and Neck Oncologists of Great Britain, 1987-90; President, British Society for Oral Pathology, 1988-91; Dean, Dental Faculty, RCPSGlas, since 2001; Chairman, Specialty Advisory Committee for the Additional Dental Specialties, since 2000; Commodore, Royal Naval Reserves, 1995-97. Recreations: golf; curling. Address: (h.) 2 Dougalston Gardens South, Milngavie, Glasgow; T.-0141-956 2075.

MacDonald, Professor Donald Murray, MB, ChB, FRCS(Edin), Dip.Theol. Moderator, Free Church of Scotland, 1997; Professor of Apologetics and Practical Theology, Free Church College, Edinburgh, since 1997; b.

16.1.44, Kildonan, Sutherland; m., Joan; 1 s.; 3 d. Educ. Golspie Senior Secondary School; Edinburgh University. Medical and surgical training posts, Edinburgh area, 1967-73; Medical Superintendent, Lakhnadon Christian Hospital, Seoni District, India, 1973-88; divinity training, Free Church College, 1988-90; Minister Bishopbriggs Free Church of Scotland, 1990-97. Address: (b.) Free Church College, The Mound, Edinburgh EH1 2LS; T.-0131-226 5286; e-mail: dmmacdonald@freescotcoll.ac.uk

Macdonald, Rt. Rev. Finlay Angus John, MA, BD, PhD. Principal Clerk, General Assembly of the Church of Scotland; Moderator, General Assembly, Church of Scotland, 2002-03; b. 1.7.45, Watford; m., Elizabeth Mary Stuart; 2 s. Educ. Dundee High School; St. Andrews University. Assistant Minister, Bo'ness Old Kirk, 1970-71; Minister, Menstrie Parish Church, 1971-77; Junior Clerk and Treasurer, Stirling and Dunblane Presbytery, 1973-77; Minister, Jordanhill Parish Church, Glasgow, 1977-96; Convener, General Assembly Board of Practice and Procedure, 1988-92; Convener, General Assembly Business Committee, 1989-92; Depute Clerk, General Assembly, 1993-96. Recreations: music; hill-walking; reading; gardening. Address: (b.) 121 George Street, Edinburgh EH2 4YN; T.-0131-225 5722.

Macdonald, Fiona Margaret Taylor, LLB, NP. Solicitor, since 1981; Honorary Depute Procurator Fiscal, Stornoway, since 1999; b. 14.4.56, Glasgow; m., Norman Lewis Macdonald; 1 s. Educ. Hillpark Secondary School; Dundee University. Solicitor, Inverclyde District Council, 1981-83; Solicitor, Bird Semple & Crawford Heron, Stornoway, 1983-89; Solicitor, Western Isles Islands Council, 1989-98. Member, Council, Law Society of Scotland, 1992-96; Member, Western Isles Health Board, 1993-99. Address: (h.) Valasay, Goathill Crescent, Stornoway HS1 2TA; T.-01851 70 6364.

McDonald, Gerard, MA, BA (Hons), DPE. Head Teacher, Our Lady and St Patrick's High School, since, 1989; b. 26.11.39, Motherwell; m., Eileen; 2s. Educ. St Aloysius College; Glasgow University; Strathclyde University. Teacher, St Aloysius College, 1961-71; Principal Teacher, St Roch's Secondary, 1971-76; Assistant Head Teacher, St Roch's High School, 1976-80; Depute Head Teacher, St Ninian's High School, Kirkintilloch, 1980-83; Head Teacher, St Leonard's Secondary School, 1983-89. Recreations: golf; rugby; soccer. Address: (b.) Hawthornhill Road, Dumbarton, G82 5JF; T.-01389 762101.

Macdonald, Gibson Torbett. Conservative Group Leader, South Ayrshire Council; b. 21.1.33; m., Muirkirk; m., Mary Hastings Logan Lambie; 1 s.; 1 d. Educ. Kilmarnock Academy. National President, Junior Chamber Scotland; Executive Vice President, Junior Chamber International; Chairman, Ayr Branch, Ayr Conservative Association; Chairman, Ayr Conservative Constituency; Town Councillor, Royal Burgh of Ayr; District Councillor, Kyle and Carrick District (Provost, 1984-88 and 1992-96; held Convenership of Planning, Employment and Policy and Resources Committees); Chairman, Culzean Country Park Joint Committee; Member, COSLA Planning Committee. Past President, Ayr Town Twinning Association; Secretary, Franco Scottish Society (Ayrshire); President, Ayr Chamber of Commerce, 1990-92; Dean of Guildry, 1991-92; Vice-President, Ayrshire Chamber of Commerce and Industry, 1993-98. Recreations: bowling; bridge; computing; philately. Address: (h.) 14 Belmont Avenue, Ayr KA7 2JN.

Macdonald, Hugh Robert Nichol, BMus, MLitt, ARCO. Director, BBC Scottish Symphony Orchestra, since 1997; b. 11.10.48, Haddington; m., Elizabeth Jane Boase; 1 s.; 1 d. Educ. Royal High School of Edinburgh; Edinburgh University; Royal College of Music; Amsterdam University. Assistant Lecturer in Music, Hitchin College,

1971-72; Lecturer in Musicology, School of Scottish Studies, Edinburgh University, 1974-75; Assistant Lecturer in Music, Chinese University of Hong Kong, 1976-79; Lecturer in Music, Stirling University, 1979-85; Music Producer (Radio), BBC Scotland/Radio 3, 1985-88; Producer, BBC Scottish Symphony Orchestra, 1988-91; Head of Music, BBC Scotland, 1991-97. Address: (b.) BBC Scotland, Queen Margaret Drive, Glasgow G12 8DG; T.-0141-338 2606.

Macdonald, Ian Hamish, OBE, FCIBS, CIMight; b. 30.12.26, Inverness; m., Patricia Lace; 1 d. Educ. Inverness Royal Academy; Inverness Technical High School. RAFVR, 1944; Queen's Own Cameron Highlanders, 1945 (Hon. Captain, 1948); Mercantile Bank, 1948-59; The Hongkong and Shanghai Banking Corporation: Manager, 1959-72, General Manager, India, 1972-73, General Manager International, 1973-80, Executive Director, 1980-83; Chairman, Hongkong Bank of Canada, 1981-83; Chief General Manager, TSB Scotland, 1983-86, and TSB Scotland PLC, 1986-87; Director, TSB Group PLC, 1986-87; Director, Scottish Power PLC, 1987-92; Chairman, Clairmont PLC, 1987-91, First Edinburgh Homes PLC, 1988-92, EFM Dragon Trust, 1987-92, Scottish Council Foundation, 1983-92; Director, Macdonald Orr, 1987-93, TSB Northern Ireland PLC, 1987-92, Morgan Grenfell Scotland Ltd., 1987-91, AIB Group Northern Ireland PLC, 1992-96; Member, Court, Edinburgh University, 1989-92; former Chairman, Clan Donald Lands Trust. Recreations: fishing; golf; bridge. Address: (h.) Minewood Cottage, 11 Abercromby Drive, Bridge of Allan, FK9 4EA.

McDonald, Sheriff Iona Sara, MA, LLB, NP. Solicitor, since 1980; All Scotland Sheriff (floating), based at Kilmarnock, since 2000; former Partner, Mathie Morton Black and Buchanan, Ayr; former Temporary Sheriff (all Scotland jurisdiction); b. 18.11.54; m., Colin Neale McDonald; 1 s.; 1 d. Educ. Cumnock Academy; Glasgow University. Apprentice Solicitor, Cannon Orpin and Co., Glasgow, 1978-80; joined Mathie Morton Black and Buchanan, Ayr, 1980. Safeguarder; Reporter to the Court and Curator Ad Litem in adoption hearings.

McDonald, Rev. James Ian Hamilton, MA, BD, MTh, PhD, FEIS. Editor, Expository Times, since 2001; Honorary Fellow, Edinburgh University, since 1998; Reader in Christian Ethics and New Testament Studies, Edinburgh University, 1992-98; b. 7.2.33, Stonehouse; m., Jenny Paterson Fleming. Educ. Rutherglen Academy; Glasgow University; Edinburgh University. Parish Minister, Johnstone West; Baird Research Fellow in Christian Education; Lecturer in Religious Education, Moray House, Edinburgh; Lecturer in Christian Ethics and Practical Theology, then Senior Lecturer in Christian Ethics and New Testament, Edinburgh University; Associate Dean, Faculty of Divinity, 1991-94; Head, Department of Christian Ethics, 1995-97; Convener, Church of Scotland Education Committee, 1985-89; Honorary President, Scottish Church Theology Society, 1997. Recreations: gardening; reading; painting. Address: (b.) New College, Mound Place, Edinburgh EH1 2LX; T.-0131-650 7227; e-mail: j.i.h.mcdonald@div.ed.ac.uk

McDonald, Professor Janet B.I., MA, FRSE, FRSAMD, FRSA. Professor of Drama, Glasgow University, since 1979 (Head, Department of Theatre, Film and Television Studies, since 2001); b. 28.7.41, Netherlee, Renfrewshire; m., Ian James McDonald; 1 d. Educ. Hutchesons' Girls' Grammar School; Glasgow University. Member: Governing Body, Royal Scottish Academy of Music and Drama, 1979-94, Academic Council, since 1994, Board, Citizens' Theatre, 1979-82 and since 1989 (Chair, since 1991); Member, Glasgow University Court, 1991-94; Council Member, Royal Society of Edinburgh, 1994-97; Chairman: Drama and Theatre Board, Council for National Academic Awards, 1981-85, Standing Committee of University Departments of

Drama, 1982-85, Drama Committee, Scottish Arts Council, 1985-88; Chair, Creative and Performing Arts Committee, CNAA, 1989-91; Member, RAE Drama Panel, 1988, 1992; Member, Performing Arts Advisory Group, Scottish Qualifications Authority, since 1999; Member, Music and Performing Arts Research Committee, Arts and Humanities Research Board, since 2000 (Chair, since 2001). Address: (b.) Gilmorehill Centre for Theatre, Film and Television, University of Glasgow; T.-0141-330 5162.

Macdonald, Very Rev. Canon John Angus, STB, MA, MLitt. Canon, Oban Cathedral Chapter, since 2000; Treasurer, R.C. Diocese of Argyll and the Isles, since 2000; Secretary, Diocesan Finance Board, since 2000; Treasurer, Burns–Gaelic Trust, since 1997; b. 6.12.45, Askernish, South Uist. Educ. Daliburgh J.S. School; St. Mary's College, Blairs; Royal Scots College, Spain (Comillas University); Aberdeen University. Ordained, 1970; Curate, 1970-72: Rothesay, Oban, Fort William; Staff, St. Mary's College, Blairs, 1972-83, Depute Rector, 1978-83; Administrator, St. Mary's, Arisaig, 1983-85; Parish Priest: St. Mary's, Bornish, 1985, St. Peter's, Daliburgh, 1987, Fort William, 1991. School Board Member, Fort William R.C. School, since 1991; Editor, Crann, Aberdeen University Celtic Society magazine, 1974-78; Spanish language translator for Concilium, 1981-90; Member: Western Isles Islands Council Education Committee, 1985-91, Gaelic Advisory Committee, BBC, 1986-90, Western Isles Health Board, 1989-92; R.E. Adviser, Diocese of Argyll and the Isles, 1991-99; Commissioner for South Argyll, Argyll Islands and Southern Isles, Crofters Commission, 1992-98; Member, Scottish Catholic Education Commission,1993-96. Publication: The Songs of Donald Allan MacDonald (Editor), 1999. Recreations: music; reading; local and church history; hill-walking; languages; DIY. Address: (h.) St. Mary's, Belford Road, Fort William PH33 6BT; T.-01397 702174; e-mail: rcdargyllandisles@supanet.com

MacDonald, Major-General John Donald, CB, CBE, DL. Chief Executive, Earl Haig Fund Scotland; Chief Executive, Officers Association Scotland; b. 5.4.38; m., Mary Warrack; 1 s.; 2 d. Educ. George Watson's College, India; National Defence College, Latimer. Commissioned King's Own Scottish Borderers, 1958, RASC, 1963, Royal Corps of Transport, 1976-78; Commander, Armd. Division Transport Regiment, BAOR, 1978-80 (Lt.-Col.); Exchange Instructor, Australian Army Cmd. and Staff College, 1980-82; Head of Personnel and Logistics, Armd. Division, BAOR, 1983-86 (Col.); Head of Personnel and Officer for Human Resources, MoD, London, 1987-88; Distribution and Transport Director, 1 Br Corps, BAOR, 1988-91 (Brigadier); Director General, Transport and Movement (Distribution), Army, 1991-93 (Major General); Colonel Commandant, Royal Logistic Corps, 1993; Hon. Colonel, Scottish Transport Regiment, Royal Logistic Corps TA, 1996; Freeman, City of London and Liveryman, Carmen Livery Company, 1991; Queen's Commissioner, Queen Victoria School, Dunblane, 1995. FCIT; FILDM. Recreations: travel; music; art; rugby (internationalist); athletics (internationalist); golf; skiing. Address: (b.) New Haig House, Logie Green Road, Edinburgh EH7 4HR; e-mail: earlhaigfund@hotmail.com

Macdonald, Kenneth, LLB. Special Correspondent, BBC Scotland; b. 11.7.57, Paisley; m., Alyson Mitchell; 1 d. Educ. Paisley Grammar School. Reporter: St. Andrews Citizen, 1978-81, Fife Leader, 1981; Broadcaster: West Sound, 1981-82, Radio Tay, 1982; BBC Radio Scotland: Broadcaster, 1982-84, Reporter, Dundee, 1984-89, Executive Producer, 1989-93; Senior Assistant, Editorial Policy, BBC Policy and Planning Unit, London, 1991-92; Education and Science Correspondent, BBC Scotland, 1993-2000. BBC Alexander Onassis Bursary, 1988; former Honorary President, Scottish Association of Geography

Teachers. Recreations: music; history; laughter. Address: (b.) Broadcasting House, Queen Margaret Drive, Glasgow G12 8DG; T.-0141-339 8844; e-mail: ken.macdonald@bbc.co.uk

MacDonald, Margo. MSP (SNP), Lothians, since 1999; freelance journalist and broadcaster; b. Hamilton; m., Jim Sillars; 1 step s.; 2 d.; 1 step-d. Educ. Hamilton Academy; Dunfermline College. Teacher, 1963-65; barmaid and mother, 1965-73; Member of Parliament, 1973-74; Broadcaster/Writer, 1974-78; Director, Shelter, Scotland, 1978-81; Radio Forth: Broadcaster, 1981-83, Editor, Topical Programmes, 1983-85; political and current affairs broadcasting as reporter/presenter, 1985-91; former Chief Executive, Network Scotland.

Macdonald, Professor Murdo, MA, PhD, LCAD, FRSA, FSA (Scot). Professor of History of Scottish Art, University of Dundee, since 1997; b. 25.1.55, Edinburgh. Educ. Hammersmith College of Art; University of Edinburgh. Commissioning Editor, Polygon Books, 1982-94; freelance art school and university lecturing, 1986-90; freelance Art Critic (mainly for The Scotsman), 1987-92; Editor, Edinburgh Review, 1990-94; Lecturer and Adviser in Scottish Studies, Centre for Continuing Education, University of Edinburgh, 1990-97. Trustee, Sir Patrick Geddes Memorial Trust. Publications: papers on Sir Patrick Geddes; Scottish Art, 2000. Recreation: hill-walking. Address: Department of History, University of Dundee, Dundee DD1 4HN; T.-01382 344516.

MacDonald, Norman Hamilton, FRSA, FSAScot. President, Clan Donald Society of Edinburgh, since 1993; Historian to the High Council of the Chiefs of Clan Donald, since 2000; b. 4.3.33, Edinburgh; m., Morag Young McKenzie. Educ. Royal High School, Edinburgh. RAF, 1953-55; accountancy, 1955-63; S.E. Regional Hospital Board, 1963-67; Edinburgh Corporation, later Edinburgh District Council, 1967-91 (retired); Chairman, The 1745 Association, 1991-97; President, Edinburgh Gaelic Choir, 1995-97. Editor, Clan Donald Magazine. Publications: histories of MacDonalds of Glengarry and Keppoch; two cassette recordings of Gaelic and Scots songs. Address: (h.) Ceapach, 8 Ethel Terrace, Edinburgh EH10 5NB: T.-0131-447 3970.

Macdonald, Peter Cameron, DL, SDA. Farmer, 1961-96; Director, J. Dickson & Son, Gunmakers, 1968-99, Chairman, 1997-99; b. 14.12.37, Edinburgh; m., Barbara Helen Drimmie Ballantyne; 2 step-s. Educ. Loretto; East of Scotland College of Agriculture. Vice-President, Scottish Landowners' Federation, 1990-2001 (Convener, 1985-88, Council Member, 1976-2001); Council Member, Blackface Sheepbreeders Association, 1970-74; Member, Forth River Purification Board, 1979-87; Director, Royal Highland and Agricultural Society of Scotland, 1985; Deputy Lieutenant, West Lothian, since 1987. Recreations: fishing; shooting; golf. Address: Waterheads, Eddleston, Peeblesshire EH45 8QX; T.-01721 730229; e-mail: pmacdonald63@hotmail.com

Macdonald, Rhoda Mairi, MA. Head of Public Affairs, SMG Television, since 2000; b. 18.10.58, Stornoway. Educ. Nicolson Institute, Stornoway; Glasgow University; Jordanhill College. Freelance Television Presenter, 1979-88; Scottish Television: Researcher, 1988, Programme Executive, Gaelic, 1989, Head of Gaelic, 1991-99, Controller of Factual Programmes, 1998-2000. Director, Scottish Television Enterprises. Recreations: reading; cinema; cooking. Address: (b.) Scottish Television, Cowcaddens, Glasgow G2 3PR; T.-0141-300 3168.

Macdonald, Roderick, BSc(Agri), MSc. Member, Scottish Land Court, 1986-92; b. 6.2.27, Benbecula; m., Elizabeth MacLeod; 3 d. Educ. Portree High School; Aberdeen University; Michigan State University, USA. Bayer

Agriculture, 1952-54; Lands Division, Department of Agriculture and Fisheries for Scotland, 1954-67 and 1972-86, latterly as Assistant Chief; Head, Land Development Division, Highlands and Islands Development Board, 1967-72; appointed Gaelic Speaking Member, Scottish Land Court, 1986; Trustee and Surveyor, Glebes Committee, Church of Scotland, since 1994; Secretary, Highland Fund, since 1993. Recreations: golf; fiddle playing; fishing. Address: 19 Cherrytree Loan, Balerno, Edinburgh; T.-0131-449 3600.

Macdonald, Rt. Rev. Mgr. Roderick, STL. Parish Priest, Glencoe/Kinlochleven, since 1990; b. 4.11.25, Mallaig. Educ. Blairs College, Aberdeen; Gregorian University, Rome. Assistant, St. Columba's Cathedral, Oban, 1950-56, St. Peter's, Daliburgh, South Uist, 1956-58; Parish Priest: St. Mun's, Glencoe, 1958-62, St. Kieran's, Campbeltown, 1962-69, St. Mun's, Dunoon, 1969-90. Address: (b.) St. Mun's, Ballachulish, Argyll PH49 4JG; T.-01855 811203.

Macdonald, (Roderick) Lewis, MA, PhD. MSP (Labour), Aberdeen Central, since 1999; Deputy Minister for Enterprise, Transport and Lifelong Learning, since 2001; Convener, Holyrood Progress Group, 2000-01; b. 1.1.57, Stornoway; m., Sandra Inkster; 2 d. Educ. Inverurie Academy; Aberdeen University. Research and teaching posts outwith politics, 1983-87, 1992-93; Parliamentary Researcher, office of Frank Doran MP, 1987-92; Shadow Cabinet Adviser to Tom Clarke MP, 1993-97; Member, Labour Party Scottish Executive Committee, 1997-99; Parliamentary candidate, Moray, 1997; Parliamentary Researcher, office of Frank Doran MP, 1997-98. Member, Management Committee, Aberdeen Citizens' Advice Bureau, 1997-99; Member, Grampian Racial Equality Council. Recreations: history; sports and games; the countryside. Address: (b.) 25 Frederick Street Centre, Aberdeen AB24 5HY; T.-01224 647846; e-mail: Lewis.Macdonald.msp@scottish.parliament.uk

MacDonald, Professor Ronald, BA, MA, PhD. Professor of International Finance, Strathclyde University, since 1993; b. 23.4.55, Glasgow. Educ. Falkirk High School; Heriot Watt University; Manchester University. Midland Bank Fellow in Monetary Economics, Loughborough University, 1982-84; Lecturer in Economics, Aberdeen University, 1984-88; Senior Lecturer, 1988-89; Robert Fleming Professor of Finance and Investment, Dundee University, 1989-93. Visiting Professor: Queen's University, Canada, 1988, University of New South Wales, Australia, 1989, European University Institute, Florence, 1998 and 2000, University Cergy-Pontoise, 1999, Centre for Economic Studies, 1999, Reserve Bank of New Zealand, 2000; Visiting Scholar, International Monetary Fund, Washington DC, since 1991; Consultant to the European Commission. Publications: Floating Exchange Rates; International Money: theory evidence and institutions (Co-Author); five co-edited books; over 100 journal articles. Recreations: music; windsurfing; boating; cycling. Address: (b.) Department of Economics, Strathclyde University, Glasgow, G4 0LN; T.-0141-548 3861; e-mail: r.r.macdonald@strath.ac.uk

McDonald, Sheena Elizabeth, MA, DLitt. Journalist and broadcaster. Address: (b.) Curtis Brown, 28/9 Haymarket, London SW1Y 4SP.

MacDonald, Professor Simon Gavin George, MA, PhD, FInstP, FRSE; b. 5.9.23, Beauly, Inverness-shire; m., Eva Leonie Austerlitz; 1 s.; 1 d. Educ. George Heriot's, Edinburgh; Edinburgh University. Junior Scientific Officer, Royal Aircraft Establishment, Farnborough, 1943-46; Lecturer in Physics, St. Andrews University, 1948-57; Senior Lecturer in Physics: University College of the West Indies, 1957-62, St. Andrews University, 1962-67; Dundee University: Senior Lecturer in Physics, 1967-73, Professor of Physics, 1973-88, Dean of Science, 1970-73, Vice-Principal, 1974-79, Head, Department of Physics, 1979-85; Chairman, Statistics Committee, Universities Central Council on Admissions, 1989-93; Member, Scottish Universities Council on Entrance, 1969-82 (Vice-Convener, 1973-77, Convener, 1977-82); Chairman, Technical Committee, UCCA, 1979-83; Deputy Chairman, UCCA, 1983-89; Chairman, Board of Directors, Dundee Repertory Theatre, 1975-89. Publications: Problems and Solutions in General Physics; Physics for Biology and Premedical Students; Physics for the Life and Health Sciences. Recreations: bridge; golf; fiction writing. Address: (h.) 7A Windmill Road, St Andrews KY16 9JJ; T.-01334 478014.

McDonald, Thomas, MA. Headteacher, All Saints R.C. Secondary School, Glasgow, since 1998; b. 28.7.53, Helensburgh; m., Carol; 2 s. Educ. St. Patrick's High School, Dumbarton; University of Glasgow; Jordanhill College. Teacher of Modern Languages, St. Patrick's High School, Dumbarton, 1976-82; Principal Teacher of Modern Languages, St. Andrew's High School, Clydebank, 1982-89; Assistant Head Teacher, St. Mungo's Academy, Glasgow, 1989-96; Depute Head Teacher, Bellarmine R.C. Secondary School, Glasgow 1996-98. Address: (b.) 21 Scotsburn Road, Glasgow G21 3HX; T.-0141-558 1241.

McDonald, William, MBE, CA. Bursar, The Carnegie Trust for the Universities of Scotland, 1990-2001; b. 9.11.29, Perth; m., Anne Kidd Laird McDonald; 1 s.; 1 d. Educ. Perth Academy. RAF, 1952-54; Secretary, South Mills and Grampian Investment, Dundee, 1957-62; The Company of Merchants of the City of Edinburgh: Chamberlain, 1962-90, Secretary, 1971-90; Clerk and Treasurer, Incorporation of Guildry in Edinburgh, 1975-90; Joint Secretary, Scottish Council of Independent Schools, 1978-90. Scout Association: Deputy Chief Commissioner of Scotland, 1977-79, Hon. Treasurer, Scotland, 1989-93, Chairman, UK Finance Sub-Committee, 1993-98, Hon. Treasurer, European Scout Region (Geneva), 1995-2000; Chairman, Audit Committee, World Organisation Scout Movement (Geneva), since 2001; Member, High Constables of Edinburgh, since 1982; Chairman: Scottish Environmental and Outdoor Education Centres, 1987-92, Lothian Valuation Appeal Committee, 1995-2000. Recreations: Scouting; bridge. Address (h.) 1/3 Wyvern Park, Edinburgh EH9 2JY; T.-0131-662 4145; e-mail: wmcdscout@aol.com

McDonald, Very Rev. William James Gilmour, MA, BD, Hon. DD (Edinburgh); b. 3.6.24, Edinburgh; m., Patricia Watson; 1 s.; 2 d. Educ. Daniel Stewart's College; Edinburgh University; Gottingen University. Royal Artillery and Indian Artillery, 1943-46; Parish Minister, Limekilns, 1953-59; Minister, Mayfield Parish Church, Edinburgh, 1959-92; Convener, Assembly Council, 1984-87; Moderator, General Assembly of Church of Scotland, 1989-90. Chaplain, Edinburgh Merchant Company; Warrack Lecturer, 1993-95; Turnbull Trust Preacher, Melbourne, 1993-94. Address: (h.) 7 Blacket Place, Edinburgh EH9 1RN; T.-0131-667 2100.

Macdonell, Hamish Alasdair, BA (Hons). Scottish Political Editor, The Scotsman, since 2001; b. 5.1.68, Inverness; m., Louisa Mary Buller. Educ. Fettes College, Edinburgh; University of York. Reporter, Yorkshire Evening Press, 1990-94; freelance journalist, Africa and Australia, 1994-95; Press Association: Parliamentary Reporter, 1995-97, Scottish Political Editor, 1997-98; Political Editor, Scottish Daily Mail, 1998-2001. Recreations: golf; rugby; jazz. Address: 24b Albany Street, Edinburgh EH1 3QB; T.-0141-553 4600; e-mail: hmacdonell@scotsman.com

McDonnell, Michael Anthony, BD, DipCE, FIRSO. Road Safety Manager (Scotland), ROSPA, since 1990; Secretary, Scottish Accident Prevention Council, since 1990; b.

13.5.55, Bellshill; m., Rosemary Boyle; 1 s. Educ. St. Patrick's High School, Coatbridge; Hamilton College of Education; Chesters College, Glasgow. Strathclyde Regional Council, 1976-81, 1982-83, 1988-90, latterly as Assistant Road Safety Training Officer. Recreations: football; golf; cinema. Address: (b.) Slateford House, 53 Lanark Road, Edinburgh EH14 1TL; T.-0131-455 7457.

McDougall, Professor Bonnie S., BA, MA, PhD. Professor of Chinese, Edinburgh University, since 1990; b. 12.3.41, Sydney; m., A. Hansson; 1 s. Educ. University of Sydney. Lecturer in Chinese, University of Sydney; Nuffield Fellow, London University; Visiting Lecturer, Harvard University; editor, translator and teacher, Peking; Professor of Modern Chinese, University of Oslo. Recreations: reading; travelling. Address: (b.) School of Asian Studies, Edinburgh University, 8 Buccleuch Place, Edinburgh EH8 9LW; T.-0131-650 4227; e-mail: Bonnie.S.McDougall@ed.ac.uk

MacDougall, James Taylor, CBE; b. 14.5.30, Perth; m., Fiona; 1 d. Educ. Perth Academy; St. Andrews University (University College, Dundee).. Admitted as a Solicitor, 1953; National Service, commissioned Royal Armoured Corps (3 Royal Tank Regiment), 1953-55; private practice/local government, 1955-59; Procurator Fiscal Depute at Dumfries, 1959-69; Procurator Fiscal: at Elgin, 1969-76, at Dumfries, 1976-93 (including Kirkcudbright, 1987-93); Honorary Sheriff at Dumfries, since 1995. Recreations: fishing; shooting; colour photography. Address: (h.) Wheatyards, Torthorwald, Dumfries DG1 3QE; T.-01387 750683.

McDougall, John William, MP. Labour MP, Fife Central, since 2001; b. 8.12.47; m., Catherine; 1 s.; 1 d. Educ. Rosyth Dockyard College; Fife College; Glenrothes College. Leader of the Administration, Fife Council, 1987-96, Convener of the Council, 1996-2001; former Vice-Chairman, St Andrews Links Trust; former Chairman, Community Business Fife Ltd. Address: (b.) House of Commons, London SW1A 0AA.

McDougall, Professor Marilyn, MA, MEd, FCIPD. Freelance management consultant; Professor of Human Resource Development, Glasgow Caledonian University, 1998-2001; b. Glasgow; widow; 1 s.; 1 d. Educ. Hillhead High School, Glasgow; University of Glasgow; University of Sheffield. Glasgow Caledonian University: Lecturer, Senior Lecturer, Director of Projects, 1985-2001, Visiting Professor, since 2001. Member, Board of Management, Reid Kerr College, Paisley. Publications: two books, various chapters and numerous papers on human resource development and equality themes. Recreations: history of art; walking; conversation. Address: (h./b.) 341 Albert Drive, Glasgow G41 5HJ; T.-0141-424 4082; e-mail: marilyn.mcdougall@ukgateway.net

McDougall, Peter. Screenwriter; b. 1947, Greenock. Television and film work includes: Just Another Saturday, 1974 (Prix Italia); Elephant's Graveyard, 1976; Just A Boy's Game, 1979; Shoot for the Sun, 1985; Down Where The Buffalo Go, 1988; Down Among The Big Boys, 1993.

MacDougall, Robert Hugh, MB, ChB, DMRT, FRCS, FRCR, FRCPEdin. Clinical Director, Department of Clinical Oncology, Western General Hospitals, Edinburgh, and Honorary Senior Lecturer in Clinical Oncology, Edinburgh University, since 1986; Honorary Senior Lecturer, St. Andrews University; b. 9.8.49, Dundee; m., Moira Jean Gray; 1 s.; 2 d. Educ. High School of Dundee; St. Andrews University; Edinburgh University. Demonstrator in Anatomy, St. Andrews University; Registrar in Surgery, Aberdeen Royal Infirmary; Lecturer in Clinical Oncology, Edinburgh University; Consultant Radiotherapist and Oncologist, Tayside Health Board. Recreation: reading. Address: (b.) Department of Clinical Oncology, Western General Hospital, Edinburgh.

McDowall, Stuart, CBE, MA. Local Government Boundary Commissioner for Scotland, 1982-99; b. 19.4.26, Liverpool; m., Margaret B.W. Gyle; 3 s. Educ. Liverpool Institute; St. Andrews University. Royal Air Force, 1944-47; Lecturer then Senior Lecturer in Economics, St. Andrews University, 1961-91; Deputy Chairman, Central Arbitration Committee, 1976-96; Master, United College of St. Salvator and St. Leonard, St. Andrews University, 1976-80; Member: Monopolies and Mergers Commission, 1985-90, Restrictive Practices Court, 1993-96; Chairman, Fife Healthcare NHS Trust, 1994-96; Secretary, Scottish Economic Society, 1970-76. Recreations: golf; gardening; music. Address: (h.) 10 Woodburn Terrace, St. Andrews, Fife KY16 8BA; T.-01334 473247.

MacDowell, Professor Douglas Maurice, MA, DLitt, FRSE, FBA. Professor of Greek, Glasgow University, 1971-2001, now Emeritus Professor; b. 8.3.31, London. Educ. Highgate School; Balliol College, Oxford. Schoolmaster, 1954-58; Manchester University: Assistant Lecturer, 1958-61, Lecturer, 1961-68, Senior Lecturer, 1968-70, Reader, 1970-71; Visiting Fellow, Merton College, Oxford, 1969; President, Glasgow Centre, Classical Association of Scotland, 1973-75, 1977-79, 1982-84, 1988-90; Chairman, 1973-76, and Vice President, since 1976, Scottish Hellenic Society; Chairman, Council, Classical Association of Scotland, 1976-82. Publications: Andokides: On the Mysteries, 1962; Athenian Homicide Law, 1963; Aristophanes: Wasps, 1971; The Law in Classical Athens, 1978; Spartan Law, 1986; Demosthenes: Against Meidias, 1990; Aristophanes and Athens, 1995; Antiphon and Andocides (Co-author), 1998; Demosthenes: On the False Embassy, 2000. Address: 2 Grosvenor Court, 365 Byres Road, Glasgow G12 8AU.

McEachran, Colin Neil, QC, MA, LLB, JD. QC, since 1981; b. 14.1.40, Glasgow; m., Kathrine Charlotte; 2 d. Educ. Glenalmond College; Merton College, Oxford; Glasgow University; University of Chicago. Advocate, since 1968; Advocate Depute, 1974-77; QC, 1981; Member, Scottish Legal Aid Board, 1990-98; President, Pension Appeal Tribunal Scotland, since 1995; Chairman, Commonwealth Games Council for Scotland, 1995-99. Recreations: target shooting; hill-walking. Address: 13 Saxe Coburg Place, Edinburgh; T.-0131-332 6820.

McEwan, Hon. Lord (Robin Gilmour McEwan), QC, LLB, PhD. Senator of the College of Justice, since 2000; b. 12.12.43, Glasgow; m., Sheena McIntyre; 2 d. Educ. Paisley Grammar School; Glasgow University. Faulds Fellow in Law, Glasgow University, 1965-68; admitted to Faculty of Advocates, 1967; Standing Junior Counsel, Department of Energy, 1974-76; Advocate Depute, 1976-79; Chairman, Industrial Tribunals, 1981; Sheriff of Lanark, 1982-88, of Ayr, 1988-2000; Member, Scottish Legal Aid Board, 1989-96; Temporary Judge, Court of Session and High Court of Justiciary, 1991-99. Publications: Pleading in Court, 1980; A Casebook on Damages (Co-author), 1983; Contributor to Stair Memorial Encyclopaedia of the Laws of Scotland, 1986.

McEwan, Angus Maywood, BA (Hons), RSW, FFCS. Artist; Lecturer (part-time) in Art and Design, Dundee College, since 1997; b. 19.7.63, Dundee; m., Wendy Ann Bell McEwan; 2 s. Educ. Carnoustie High School; Duncan of Jordanstone College of Art. Elizabeth Greenshields Foundation Award, Canada, 1987, 1990; RSA Latimer Award, 1995; scholarship to China, 1996; RSW Prize 1999, Alexander Graham Munro Award; RSW Prize 2001, Glasgow Arts Club Fellowship; solo exhibitions: Riverside Gallery, Stonehaven, 1990, Tolquhon Gallery, Aberdeenshire, 1992, Gallery 41, Edinburgh, 1994, Royal Scottish Academy, 1996, Leith Gallery, 1997, Le Mur Vivant Fine Art, London, 1997, Leith Gallery, 2000; many mixed and group exhibitions; work in public and private collections. Recreations: art; photography; reading; walking

dog; enjoying life. Address: (h.) 7 Glenleven Drive, Wormit, Newport on Tay, Fife DD6 8NA; T.-01382 542314; e-mail: art@angusmcewan.com

McEwan, Leslie J., JP, MA, DipSA, DipSW. Director of Social Work, City of Edinburgh Council, since 1996; b. 26.2.46; m., Catherine; 2 s. Educ. St. Andrews University; Dundee University; Edinburgh University. Midlothian, East Lothian and Peebles: Child Care Officer, Children's Department, 1967-69, Social Worker, 1969-71, Senior Social Worker, 1971-74, Social Work Advisor, 1974-75; Lothian Regional Council: Divisional Director of Social Work, Midlothian, 1975-80, West Lothian, 1980-85, Depute Director of Social Work, 1985-90, Senior Depute Director of Social Work, 1990-95; Director of Social Work, 1995-96. Recreations: fly-fishing; golf; woodturning.

McEwan, M. Shirley Ramsay, MBE, FRCPEdin, MBChB. Medical Practitioner; Honorary Secretary/Medical Administrator, SHARP (Scottish Heart and Arterial Risk Prevention), since 1988; Senior Research Fellow, University Department of Medicine, Ninewells Hospital, Dundee, since 1995; b. 18.11.35, Perth. Educ. Perth Academy; St. Andrews University. House Surgeon, Dundee Royal Infirmary, 1960-61; House Physician, Kings Cross Hospital, Dundee, 1961; House Surgeon, Craigtoun Maternity Hospital, 1961-62; Trainee General Practitioner, Innerleithen, 1962-63; Assistant General Practitioner, Glasgow, 1963; Principal General Practitioner: Perth, 1963-67, Dundee, 1967-71; Senior Partner, General Practitioner, Dundee, 1971; Principal General Practitioner, Dundee, 1991-95; part-time Specialist, Lipid Clinic, Dundee Teaching Hospitals Trust, 1996-2000. President, Forfarshire Medical Association, 1998-99. Publication: Coronary Risk Factors Revisited (Co-Editor). Recreations: gardening; reading; swimming; skating; travel; music. Address: (h.) Craig Duich, 4 Golspie Terrace, Broughty Ferry, Dundee DD5 2PW; T.-01382 775510; e-mail: s.r.mcewan@dundee.ac.uk

McEwan, Roy James, BSc (Econ), DAARL, FRSA. Managing Director, Scottish Chamber Orchestra, since 1993; Member, Board, Association of British Orchestras, since 1993; b. 12.5.51, Dumfries. Educ. Dumfries High School; Carlisle Grammar School; London School of Economics; Polytechnic of Central London. House Manager, St. George's Theatre, London, 1977-78; Manager, Whitechapel Art Gallery, 1978-79; Administrator, then Director, MacRobert Arts Centre, Stirling, 1979-91; Director of Arts Development, North West Arts Board, Manchester, 1991-93. Chairman, Federation of Scottish Theatres, 1988-91; Scottish Arts Council: Member, Drama Committee, 1991, Member, Combined Arts Committee, 1993-99; Member, Board, Scottish Music Information Centre, 1994-2000. Address: (b.) 4 Royal Terrace, Edinburgh EH7 5AB.

McEwen, Professor James, MB, ChB, FRCP (Glasgow, Edinburgh, London), FFPHM, FFOM, DIH, FMedSci. Emeritus Professor and Honorary Senior Research Fellow, Glasgow University, since 2001; Professor of Public Health, Glasgow University, 1999-2001; Henry Mechan Professor of Public Health, 1989-99; Consultant in Public Health Medicine, Greater Glasgow Health Board; b. 6.2.40, Stirling; m., Elizabeth May Archibald; 1 s.; 1 d. Educ. Dollar Academy; St. Andrews University. Lecturer in Industrial Medicine, Dundee University; Senior Lecturer in Community Medicine, Nottingham University; Chief Medical Officer, The Health Education Council; Professor of Community Medicine, King's College, University of London. President, Faculty of Public Health Medicine, Royal Colleges of Physicians UK, 1998-2001. Recreations: church; gardening. Address: (b.) 1 Lilybank Gardens, Glasgow G12 8RZ. T.-0141-330 5013; e-mail: J.McEwen@adcf.gla.ac.uk

McFadden, Jean Alexandra, CBE, JP, DL, MA, LLB. Member, Glasgow City Council; Convener, Labour Group, since 1995, Convener, Policy and Resources (Regeneration Strategy) Committee, since 1999; Senior Lecturer in Law, Strathclyde University; b. 26.11.41, Glasgow; m., John (deceased). Educ. Hyndland Secondary School; Glasgow University; Strathclyde University. Principal Teacher of Classics, Strathclyde schools, 1967-86; entered local government as Member, Cowcaddens Ward, Glasgow Corporation, 1971; Glasgow District Council: Member, Scotstoun Ward, 1984, Chairman, Manpower Committee, 1974-77, Leader, Labour Group, 1977-86, and 1992-94, Leader, Council, 1980-86, and 1992-94, Treasurer, 1986-92, Convener, 1995-96, Convener, Social Strategy Committee, 1996-99; Vice Lord Lieutenant, City of Glasgow, 1980-92; President, COSLA, 1990-92; Convener, Scottish Local Government Information Unit, since 1984; Member, Board, Scottish Development Agency, 1989-91, GDA, 1992-2000; Chairman, Mayfest, 1983-97; Member, Secretary of State's Health Appointments Advisory Committee, 1994-2000; Chair, Charity Law Review Commission in Scotland, 2000; Member, Ancient Monuments Board for Scotland, since 2000. Recreations: cycling; theatre; walking; golf; West Highland terriers. Address: (h.) 16 Lansdowne Crescent, Glasgow G20 6NG; T.-0141-334 3522.

McFadyen, John Alexander Crawford, MA, LLB. Solicitor (retired); b. 11.9.36, Dunoon; m., Patricia Mary Thompson; 1 s. 2 d. Educ. Robert Gordon's College, Aberdeen; Aberdeen University. Solicitor in private practice, since 1962; Honorary Sheriff Substitute at Dumfries, since 1995. Recreation: reading. Address: (h.) Braeside, 54 Moffat Road, Dumfries DG1 1NY; T.-01387 253077.

Macfadyen, Hon. Lord (Donald James Dobbie Macfadyen), LLB, FCIArb. Senator of the College of Justice; b. 8.9.45, Glasgow; m., Christine Balfour Gourlay Hunter; 1 s.; 1 d. Educ. Hutchesons' Grammar School, Glasgow; Glasgow University. Advocate, 1969; Standing Junior Counsel, Department of Agriculture and Fisheries for Scotland, 1977-79, Scottish Home and Health Department, 1982-83; Advocate-Depute, 1979-82; QC, 1983; part-time Chairman, Medical Appeal Tribunals, 1989-95; Vice-Dean, Faculty of Advocates, 1992-95; Temporary Judge, Court of Session, 1994-95; Chairman, Council, Cockburn Association (Edinburgh Civic Trust), since 2001; Vice-Chair, Judges Forum, International Bar Association, since 2000. Address: (h.) 66 Northumberland Street, Edinburgh EH3 6JE; T.-0131-556 6043.

McFadyen, Thomas, MB, ChB. Director of Medical Services, Erskine Hospital, since 1978; b. 30.11.39, Glasgow. Educ. Allan Glen's School; Glasgow University. Appointments, Glasgow Royal Infirmary, Law Hospital, Carluke and Royal Alexandra Infirmary, Paisley. Recreation: golf. Address: (h.) 5 Elderbank, Bearsden G61 1ND; T.-0141-943 2237; (b.) Erskine Hospital, Bishopton PA7 5PU; T.-0141-814 4541.

McFall, John, BSc (Hons), BA, MBA. MP (Labour), Dumbarton, since 1987; Chairman, Treasury Committee, since 2001; Parliamentary Under Secretary of State, Northern Ireland Office, 1998-99; serves on: Information Committee, Parliamentary and Scientific Committee, Executive Committee – Parliamentary Group for Energy Studies, British/Italian Group, British/Peru Group, Retail Industry Group, Roads Study Group, Scotch Whisky Group, Parliamentary and Scientific Committee; formerly Opposition Whip with responsibility for Foreign Affairs, Defence and Trade and Industry (resigned post at time of Gulf War); former Deputy Shadow Secretary of State for Scotland; Scottish Whip, 1997-98. Recreations: jogging; reading; golf. Address: (b.) House of Commons, Westminster, London.

Macfarlane of Bearsden, Lord, (Norman (Somerville) Macfarlane), KT, Kt, DL, FRSE, HRSA, HRGI, Hon.FRIAS, Hon.FRCPSGlas, Hon. LLD (Strathclyde, 1986; Glasgow, 1988; Glasgow Caledonian, 1993; Aberdeen, 1995), DUniv (Stirling, 1992); Dr. h.c. (Edinburgh, 1992). Honorary Life President, Macfarlane Group PLC, since 1999 (Chairman, 1973-98, Managing Director, 1973-90); Honorary Life President, United Distillers (Chairman, 1987-96); b. 5.3.26; m., Marguerite Mary Campbell; 1 s.; 4 d. Educ. High School of Glasgow. Commissioned, Royal Artillery, 1945, served Palestine, 1945-47; founded N.S. Macfarlane & Co. Ltd., 1949 (became Macfarlane Group (Clansman) PLC, 1973); Underwriting Member of Lloyd's, 1978-97; Chairman: The Fine Art Society PLC, 1976-98, American Trust PLC, 1984-97 (Director, since 1980), Guinness PLC, 1987-89 (Joint Deputy Chairman, 1989-92); Deputy Chairman, Clydesdale Bank PLC, 1993-96 (Director, 1980-96); Director: General Accident Fire and Life Assurance Corporation plc, 1984-96, Edinburgh Fund Managers plc, 1980-98, Glasgow Chamber of Commerce, 1976-79; Member: Council, CBI Scotland, 1975-81, Board, Scottish Development Agency, 1979-87; Chairman, Glasgow Development Agency, 1985-92; Vice-Chairman, Scottish Ballet, 1983-87 (Director, since 1975); Director, Scottish National Orchestra, 1977-82; Lord High Commissioner, General Assembly of Church of Scotland, 1992, 1993, 1997; President, Royal Glasgow Institute of the Fine Arts, 1976-87; Member, Royal Fine Art Commission for Scotland, 1980-82; Scottish Patron, National Art Collection Fund, since 1978; Governor, Glasgow School of Art, 1976-87; Trustee: National Heritage Memorial Fund, 1984-97, National Galleries of Scotland, 1986-97; Director, Third Eye Centre, 1978-81; Member, Court, Glasgow University, 1979-87; President: Stationers' Association of GB and Ireland, 1965, Company of Stationers of Glasgow, 1968-70, Glasgow High School Club, 1970-72; Honorary President, Charles Rennie Mackintosh Society, since 1988; Regent, RCSE, since 1997; Patron, Scottish Licensed Trade Association, since 1992; Hon. Fellow, Glasgow School of Art, since 1993; knighted, 1982; created a Life Peer, 1991; created Knight of the Thistle, 1996. Recreations: golf; cricket; theatre; art. Address: (h.) 50 Manse Road, Bearsden, Glasgow G61 3PN.

MacFarlane, Professor Alistair George James, CBE, PhD, DSc, MA, ScD, FIEE, FEng, FRS, FRSE. Principal and Vice Chancellor, Heriot-Watt University, 1989-96; Chairman, Advisory Group for Scottish University for Industry, 1998-2000; Chairman, Academic Advisory Board, University of Highlands and Islands Project, since 1999 (Acting Chief Executive Officer, 2000-01); b. 1931, Edinburgh; m., Nora; 1 s. Educ. Hamilton Academy; Glasgow University. Metropolitan-Vickers Electrical Company Ltd.: Electronic Engineer, Radar and Servo Division, Group Leader, Moving Target Indication and Receiver Laboratories; Lecturer, Electrical Engineering, Queen Mary College, London University, 1959 (Reader, 1965); UMIST: Reader in Control Engineering, 1966, Professor, 1969; Cambridge University: Chair, Engineering, 1974, Head, Information Engineering Division, Fellow, Selwyn College, 1974 (Vice-Master, 1980-88); Chairman, Scottish Council for Research in Education, 1993-98; Chairman, Scottish Library and Information Council, 1994-98; Non-Executive Director, BNFL plc, 1994-2000; Member, BT Advisory Forum in Scotland, 1996-98; former Consultant Editor, International Journal of Control. Past Member: SERC Computer Board, Joint Policy Committee for National Facilities for Advanced Research Computing, Advisory Committee on Safety of Nuclear Installations; Vice-President, Royal Society, 1997-99. American Society of Mechanical Engineers Centennial Medal, 1980; Sir Harold Hartley Medal, Institute of Measurement and Control,1982; IEE Achievement Medal, 1992; IEE Faraday Medal, 1993.

Macfarlane, Rev. Alwyn James Cecil, BA, MA; b. 14.6.22, Edinburgh; m., Joan Cowell Harris; 1 s.; 1 d. Educ. Cargilfield School, Edinburgh; Rugby School; New College, Oxford; New College, Edinburgh. Captain, 6th Black Watch, North Africa, Italy and Greece, 1940-45; entered Ministry, Church of Scotland, 1951; Minister: Fodderty and Strathpeffer, 1952-59, St. Cuthbert's Church, Edinburgh (Associate), 1959-63, Portobello Old, Edinburgh, 1963-68, Newlands (South), Glasgow, 1968-85; Associate Minister, The Scots' Church, Melbourne, 1985-88. Chaplain to The Queen in Scotland; Member, The Queen's Household in Scotland. Recreations: photography; travel. Address: Flat 12, 177 Fenwick Road, Giffnock, Glasgow G46 6JD.

Macfarlane, Professor Peter Wilson, DSc, FBCS, FRCP(Glas), FESC, FRSE. Professor of Electrocardiology, Glasgow University, since 1995; b. 8.11.42, Glasgow; m., Irene Grace Muir; 2 s. Educ. Hyndland Senior Secondary School, Glasgow; Glasgow University. Glasgow University: Assistant Lecturer in Medical Cardiology, 1967, Lecturer, 1970, Senior Lecturer, 1974, Reader, 1980, Professor, 1991; President, 5th International Congress on Electrocardiology, Glasgow, 1978; Chairman, 15th and 18th Annual Conferences, International Society of Computerized Electrocardiology, 1990, 1993; Author/Editor, 14 books. Recreations: watching football; running half-marathons; playing violin. Address: (h.) 12 Barrcraig Road, Bridge of Weir PA11 3HG; T.-01505 614443; e-mail: peter.w.macfarlane@clinmed.gla.ac.uk

MacFarlane, Professor Thomas Wallace, DDS, DSc, FRSE, FRCPath, FDSRCPSGlas, FDS RCSEdin, FFCS. Professor of Oral Microbiology, Glasgow University, 1991-2001; Honorary Consultant in Oral Microbiology; Dean of the Dental School, 1995-2000; b. 12.12.42, Glasgow; m., Nancy McEwan Fyfe; 1 s. Educ. Hyndland Senior Secondary School; Glasgow University. Assistant Lecturer, Dental Histology and Pathology, 1966-69; trained in Medical Microbiology and Histopathology, Glasgow Royal Infirmary; Lecturer in Oral Medicine and Pathology, 1969-77; organised and ran the diagnostic service in Oral Microbiology, Glasgow Dental Hospital and School; Senior Lecturer in Oral Medicine and Pathology and Consultant in Oral Microbiology, 1977; Reader in Oral Medicine and Pathology, 1984-91; Head, Department of Oral Sciences, 1992-95. Recreations: music; reading; painting; walking. Address: Larchgrove, Ferntower Road, Crieff PH7 3DH; T.-01764 654952.

McFarlane, William Stewart, CA; b. 26.3.33, Glasgow; m., Sandra; 1 d. Educ. High School of Glasgow. Trained as Chartered Accountant, Wilson Stirling (now Deloitte Touche), Glasgow; Parlane McFarlane CA, 1957-58; National Service (Second Lieutenant, Royal Corps of Signals), 1959-60; Partner, McFarlane, Son & Co., CA, 1961-62, merged with Dickson, McFarlane & Robinson, CA, 1963-84, merged with Wylie & Bisset, CA, 1985-98. Member, Council, Institute of Chartered Accountants of Scotland, 1971-76, Institute's representative, directorate of Glasgow Chamber of Commerce, 1970-88; President, Glasgow Chamber of Commerce, 1990-92; Past Finance Convener, Scottish Golf Union; Past Treasurer, Scottish Squash Rackets Association; Captain, Association of Golf Club Secretaries, 1980; Past Deacon, Incorporation of Masons of Glasgow; Past President, Rotary Club of Charing Cross. Recreations: golf; curling; swimming; squash. Address: (b.) 135 Wellington Street, Glasgow G2 2XE; T.-0141-248 3904.

Macfarlane Smith, William Holmes, BSc, PhD, CBiol, MIBiol, FIMgt. Head of Scientific Liaison and Information Services, Scottish Crop Research Institute, since 1995; b. 23.4.42, Newcastle upon Tyne; m., Daphne Henderson; 3 s. Educ. Aberdeen Grammar School; Dundee High School; Aberdeen University; Reading University. Post-doctoral

research, University of Dundee, 1971-72; Rothwell Plant Breeders (Shell Nickerson): Barley Breeder, Senior Barley Breeder, Head of Barley Breeding Team, Technical Manager, 1972-78; Scottish Plant Breeding Station (subsequently Scottish Crop Research Institute): Rape and Swede Breeder, Head of Brassica Department, Leader, Commercial Brassica Breeding, 1978-95. Vice-Chairman of Board, Dundee High School; Trustee, Dundee High School Foundation; Trustee, Dundee High School Trust Fund; Past President, Dundee High School Old Boys Club; Past President, Dundee Rotary Club. Recreations: golf; hillwalking; photography. Address: (h.) 42 Holly Road, Broughty Ferry, Dundee DD5 2LZ; T.-01382 739148; e-mail: wmacfa@scri.sari.ac.uk

McGarry, Gerald William. MBChB, MD, FRCS(Glas), FRCS(Ed), FRCS(ORLHNS). Consultant Otolaryngologist, Head and Neck Surgeon, since 1995; Honorary Senior Lecturer, University of Glasgow, since 1995; b. 30.1.62, Glasgow; m., Carol; 3 s. Educ. St. Augustine Secondary School, Glasgow; Glasgow University. Senior Registrar in Otolaryngology: Glasgow Rotational Scheme, 1992, Royal Brisbane Hospital, Australia, 1993; Locum Consultant Otolaryngologist, Glasgow Royal Infirmary, 1994. Former MATTUS Tutor; former Council Member, Otorhinolaryngological Society; former Member, Medical Appeals Tribunal; Founder, Scottish Sinus Surgery Group. Publications: Picture Tests in ENT, 1999; Endoscopic Dissection of the Nose and Pacanasal Sinuses; papers on rhinology and head and neck cancer; textbook contributor. Recreations: mountaineering; aviation. Address: Department of Otolaryngology, Royal Infirmary, Glasgow G31 2ER; T.-0141-211 4330.

McGeechan, Ian. Head Coach, Scottish Rugby Union, since 2000; b. 30.10.46, Leeds. Educ. Moore Grange, Allerton Moor; Carnegie College of Physical Education. Made his debut for Yorkshire Colts, 1965, and for Yorkshire County XV, 1966; first Scotland trial, 1968; debut for Scotland as stand-off v. New Zealand at Murryfield, 1972; won 32 caps for Scotland, 20 at centre, 12 at stand-off, with nine games as captain; scored 21 points for Scotland (seven drop goals); toured with British Lions as player, South Africa, 1974, and New Zealand, 1977, playing in all eight tests; toured with British Lions as coach, Australia, 1989, New Zealand, 1993, South Africa, 1997; assistant Scotland coach to Derrick Grant, 1986-88 (including inaugural Rugby World Cup, New Zealand, 1987); Scotland coach, 1988-93, during which period Scotland completed grand slam; joined Scotland as Head Coach from Northampton Saints, having won Allied Dunbar Premiership coach of the season, 1998-99. Address: (b.) Scottish Rugby Union, Murrayfield, Edinburgh, EH12 5PJ; T.-0131-346 5000.

McGeoch, Duncan J., BSc, PhD, FRSE. Director, Medical Research Council Virology Unit, Glasgow, since 1995; Honorary Professor, Glasgow University, since 1996. Educ. Hutchesons' Grammar School; Glasgow University. Jane Coffin Childs Memorial Fund Fellow, Department of Microbiology and Molecular Genetics, Harvard Medical School, 1971-73; Researcher, Division of Virology, Department of Pathology, University of Cambridge, 1973-76; Staff Member, MRC Virology Unit, Glasgow, since 1976. Fleming Award, Society for General Microbiology, 1980; Editor, Journal of General Virology, 1984-87, Editor-in-Chief, 1988-92. Address: (b.) MRC Virology Unit, Church Street, Glasgow G11 5JR.

McGeough, Professor Joseph Anthony, FRSE, BSc, PhD, DSc, CEng, FIMechE, FIEE. Regius Professor of Engineering, Edinburgh University, since 1983; Honorary Professor, Nanjing Aeronautical and Astronautical University, China, since 1991; Visiting Professor: University Federico II of Naples, 1994, Glasgow

Caledonian University, 1997-2003; b. 29.5.40, Kilwinning; m., Brenda Nicholson; 2 s.; 1 d. Educ. St. Michael's College; Glasgow University; Aberdeen University. Research Demonstrator, Leicester University, 1966; Senior Research Fellow, Queensland University, Australia, 1967; Research Metallurgist, International Research and Development Co. Ltd., Newcastle-upon-Tyne, 1968-69; Senior Research Fellow, Strathclyde University, 1969-72; Lecturer in Engineering, Aberdeen University, 1972-77 (Senior Lecturer, 1977-80, Reader, 1980-83). Honorary Vice-President, Aberdeen University Athletic Association, since 1981; Member, Council, IMechE, since 2000; Chairman, CIRP UK, 2000-03; Editor, Journal of Processing of Advanced Materials, 1991-94; CIRP Editor, Journal of Materials Processing Technology, since 1991; Editor, Proceedings of International Conference on Computer-Aided Production Engineering, since 1986. Publications: Principles of Electrochemical Machining, 1974; Advanced Methods of Machining, 1988; Micromachining of Engineering Materials (Editor), 2001. Recreations: gardening; golf. Address: (h.) 39 Dreghorn Loan, Colinton, Edinburgh EH13 ODF; T.-0131-441 1302.

McGettrick, Professor Andrew David, BSc, PhD, FRSE, FIEE, FBCS, CEng. Professor of Computer Science, Strathclyde University, since 1984; Head, Computer and Information Sciences Department, since 2001 (Head, Computer Science Department, 1996-2001); b. 15.5.44, Glasgow; m., Sheila Margaret Girot; 5 s.; 1 d. Educ. St. Aloysius College, Glasgow; Glasgow University; Cambridge University. Lecturer, then Reader, then Professor, Strathclyde University, since 1969; Editor, Addison Wesley's International Computer Science series; Chairman, IEE Safety Critical Systems Committee; Chairman, UK Computer Science Professors Conference, 1991-93. Publications: four books as author, three books edited. Recreations: running; golf; squash. Address: (b.) Strathclyde University, Glasgow G1 1XH; T.-0141-548 3589.

McGettrick, Professor Bartholomew John, OBE, FRSAMD, KC*HS, DHLitt, FRSA, BSc (Hons), MEd (Hons), Silver Palm of Jerusalem (1996). Professor, Glasgow University; Dean, Faculty of Education; Member, General Teaching Council for Scotland, since 1986; Member, various CNAA committees; Chairman, Committee on Assessment 5-14; Chairman, Schools Commission for the Holy Land, 1999; Member, Council, International Federation of Catholic Universities; b. 16.8.45, Glasgow; m., Elizabeth Maria McLaughlin; 2 s.; 2 d. Educ. St. Aloysius' College, Glasgow; Glasgow University. Teacher and Head, Department of Geography, St. Aloysius' College, Glasgow, 1968-72; Educational Psychologist, Scottish Centre for Social Subjects, 1972-75; Assistant Principal, then Vice-Principal, Notre Dame College of Education (latterly St. Andrew's College of Education), 1975-85; Principal, St. Andrew's College of Education, 1985-99. Chairman, Catholic Education Commission for Scotland, 1981-87; Chair, "Higher Still" Task Group – Staff Development; Member, Council for Educational Technology, 1982-86; Chairman, Committee of Principals of Colleges of Education, 1990-92; President, Association Catholique Internationale des Institutions de Sciences de L'Education, 1995-2002; Chairman, Board of Governors, St. Aloysius' College, Glasgow; Chairman of Governors, Clifton Hall School, Edinburgh; Governor: Kilgraston School, Craighalbert Centre; Chairman, Governors, Craighead Institute; Member, International Committee for the Education of Teachers; Vice Chair: Educational Broadcasting Council for Scotland, 1995-99, Advisory Group on Sustainable Development; Chairman, Education for Sustainable Development Group; Chairman, Scottish Council for Independent Schools, since 1997; Chairman, Gordon Cook Foundation; Trustee, Bordesley

Institute. Recreation: sports. Address: (h.) 174 Carmunnock Road, Glasgow G44 5AJ; T.-0141-637 8112; e-mail: bjm@educ.gla.ac.uk

McGhee, Alexander. Member, Inverclyde Council; President, UK REIT Association of European Consortium, since 1999; Vice-President, REIT Europe, since 1999; b. 15.6.51, Greenock; m., Mary Kathleen; 1 s.; 2 d. Educ. St Mary's, Greenock. President, West of Scotland European Consortium, 1999; Member, COSLA European Network, since 2000; Vice-Convener, West of Scotland Strategic Planning Group, since 1995; Convener, Economic Development and Urban Regeneration; Convener, Roads and Transport Committee; Convener, Planning and Development; Chairman, Inverclyde Adoption Panel; Member, COSLA Task Force (Welfare into Work); Member, Strathclyde Passenger Transport Authority. Address: (h.) 11 Broomberry Drive, Gourock, Renfrewshire; T.-01475 634584.

McGhie, Hon. Lord (James Marshall), QC, LLB (Hons). Queen's Counsel, since 1983; Chairman, Scottish Land Court; President, Lands Tribunal for Scotland, since 1996; b. 15.10.44, Perth; m., Ann M. Cockburn; 1 s.; 1 d. Educ. Perth Academy; Edinburgh University. Advocate-Depute, 1983-86; part-time Chairman, Medical Appeal Tribunals, 1987-92; Member, Criminal Injuries Compensation Board, 1992-96. Address: (b.) 1 Grosvenor Crescent, Edinburgh; T.-0131-225 3595.

McGhie, Duncan Clark, CA. Chairman, Scottish Ballet/Scottish Opera, since 1999; b. 6.12.44, Newton Mearns, Renfrewshire; m., Una G. Carmichael; 1 s.; 1 d. Educ. George Watson's College; Institute of Chartered Accountants. CA apprenticeship, 1962-67; Financial Controller, Scottish Division, British Steel Corporation, 1967-78; Group Finance Director, Wm. Collins Publishers, 1978-84; Partner, Coopers and Lybrand (latterly Pricewaterhouse Coopers), 1984-2000; Member, Scottish Leadership Advisory Panel in review of Local Government; Vice-Convenor, Israel Centres Committee, Church of Scotland; Elder, Church of Scotland. Recreations: golf; music; walking. Address: (b.) 65 Corrour Road, Newlands, Glasgow, G43 2ED; T.-0141-632 4502.

McGillivray, Rev. (Alexander) Gordon, MA, BD, STM; b. 22.9.23, Edinburgh; m., Winifred Jean Porter; 2 s.; 2 d. Educ. George Watson's Boys' College, Edinburgh; Edinburgh University; Union Theological Seminary, New York. Royal Artillery, 1942-45; Assistant Minister, St. Cuthbert's Parish Church, Edinburgh; Minister: Waterbeck Church, 1951-58, Nairn High Church, 1958-73; Clerk, Presbytery of Edinburgh, 1973-93; Clerk, General Assembly of Church of Scotland, 1971-94, retired. Editor, Church of Scotland Yearbook, 1996-99. Recreations: golf; theatre. Address: 7 Greenfield Crescent, Balerno, Midlothian EH14 7HD; T.-0131-449 4747.

McGinlay, Alan Douglas. BSc. Head Teacher, Mearns Castle High School, since 2000; b. 14.4.50, Glasgow; m., Lynn; 1 s.; 1 d. Educ. Queen's Park Secondary; Glasgow University. Teacher, Hillpark Secondary, 1972-77; Principal Teacher, Chemistry, Williamwood/Mearns Castle, 1977-84; Assistant Head Teacher/Depute Head Teacher/Acting Head Teacher, James Hamilton Academy, 1984-91; Head Teacher, Govan High School, 1991-94; Chairman, Working Party in Information Technology, Glasgow City Council, 1997. Recreations: golf; football; badminton. Address: (b.) Mearns Castle High School, Waterfoot Road, East Renfrewshire, G77 5RU; T.-0141-577 2300; e-mail: mcginlaya@mchs.ercsch.org.uk

McGlinchey, Scott, BA, DipM, FRSA. Director, ICL Scotland, since 1998; b. 16.8.61, Edinburgh; m., Pauline; 3 s. Educ. Royal High School; Napier University. Marketing Analyst, ISTEL, 1985-87; ICL: customer and sales management, 1987-94, Client Manager, NHS, 1994-95, UK Sales and Marketing Director, IT Consultancy, 1995-98. Member, Council, CBI Scotland; Director, Young Scot; Director, Edinburgh Chamber of Commerce; Member, Scottish Executive Digital Task Force, 1999; Member, Scottish Executive Modernising Government Reference Group, 2001. Recreations: rugby; music; being dad. Address: (b.) ICL, Wallace House, 1 Lochside Avenue, Edinburgh Park, Edinburgh EH12 9DJ; T.-0131-339 0101.

McGlynn, Rt. Rev. Lord Abbot (James Aloysius) Donald, OCSO, STL, SLJ. Monk, Order of Cistercians of Strict Observance, since 1952; Abbot of Nunraw, since 1969; b. 13.8.34, Glasgow. Educ. Holyrood School, Glasgow; St. Bernardine's School, Buckinghamshire; Gregorian University, Rome. President: Scottish Council of Major Religious Superiors, 1974-77, British Isles Regional Council of Cistercian Abbeys, 1980-84; Chairman, Union of Monastic Superiors, 1985-89; Official Roman Catholic Visitor to the General Assembly, Church of Scotland, 1976 and 1985; Commandeur Ecclesiastique, Military & Hospitaller Order of St. Lazarus of Jerusalem, 1985; Patron, Cistercian Monastery, Onitsha, Nigeria; Patron, Haddington Pilgrimage of St. Mary & the Three Kings. Address: Sancta Maria Abbey, Nunraw, Garvald, Haddington EH41 4LW; T.-0162 083 0223; e-mail: domdonald@yahoo.co.uk

McGoldrick, James (Jim), BA (Hons), CCIPD, FRSA, MIMgt. Vice Principal, University of Abertay Dundee, since 1996; Chairman, Tayside University Hospital Trust, since 2000; b. 5.6.52, Glasgow; m., Diane Carthew. Educ. St. Patrick's High School, Dumbarton; Glasgow Caledonian University; Glasgow University. Recreations: football (Dumbarton); football (Dundee United); reading; cinema. Address: University of Abertay Dundee, Bell Street, Dundee DD1 H1G; T.-01382 308924.

McGougan, Donald, CPFA. Director of Finance, City of Edinburgh Council, since 1995; Director, Edinburgh Military Tattoo, since 1995; b. 26.12.50; Glasgow; m., Mandy; 1 s.; 1 d. Educ. Hermitage Academy, Helensburgh. Trainee Accountant, Midlothian County Council, 1971; Professional Assistant, City of Edinburgh District Council, 1975; Falkirk District Council: Principal Assistant, 1979, Depute Director of Finance, 1981; Depute Director of Finance, City of Edinburgh District Council, 1987. Recreations: family; golf; football. Address: (b.) Council Headquarters, Wellington Court, 10 Waterloo Place, Edinburgh EH1 3EG; T.-0131-469 3005.

McGowan, Professor David Alexander, MDS, PhD, FDSRCS, FFDRCSI, FDSRCPSG, FDSRCS (Edin). Professor of Oral Surgery, Glasgow University, 1977-99, Emeritus Professor, since 1999 (Dean of Dental Education, 1990-95); Consultant Oral Surgeon, Greater Glasgow Health Board, 1977-99; b. 18.6.39, Portadown, Co. Armagh; m., Margaret Vera Macaulay; 1 s.; 2 d. Educ. Portadown College; Queen's University, Belfast. Oral surgery training, Belfast and Aberdeen, 1961-67; Lecturer in Dental Surgery, Queen's University, Belfast, 1968; Lecturer, then Senior Lecturer and Deputy Head, Oral and Maxillofacial Surgery, London Hospital Medical College, 1968-77. Postgraduate Adviser in Dentistry, Glasgow University, 1977-90; Chairman, Dental Committee, Scottish Council for Postgraduate Medical Education, 1980-90; Dean, Dental Faculty, and Member of College Council, Royal College of Physicians and Surgeons of Glasgow, 1989-92; Member and Vice-Chairman of Executive, General Dental Council, 1989-99; Member, Court, Glasgow University, 1995-99; Chairman, National Dental Advisory Committee, 1996-99; Member, EC Advisory Committee on Training of Dental Practitioners, 1993-2001; former Council Member, British Association of Oral and Maxillofacial Surgeons. Recreations: sailing; music. Address: Rhu Lodge, Rhu, Helensburgh G84 5NF.

McGowan, Ian David, MA, PhD. Director, Centre for Publishing Studies, Stirling University, since 1988, and Senior Lecturer in English Studies, since 1992; Member, Scottish Arts Council, and Chairman, Literature Committee, 1993-97; b. Glasgow. Educ. Pembroke College, Oxford. Joined Stirling University as Lecturer in English Studies, 1973. Member and Chairman, Grants to Publishers Panel, 1985-97, Chairman, Grants to Magazines Panel, 1992-97, Scottish Arts Council; Member, Executive Committee, Book Trust Scotland, 1986-93; Trustee, Arts Trust of Scotland. Publications: The Restoration and the Eighteenth Century; Charles Dickens: Little Dorrit; Journey to the Hebrides; Principles and Practice in Book Publishing; articles and chapters. Address: (b.) Centre for Publishing Studies, Stirling University, Stirling FK9 4LA; T.-01786 473171.

McGowan, Ian Duncan, BA, FRSA. Librarian, National Library of Scotland, since 1990; b. 19.9.45, Liverpool; m., Elizabeth Ann Weir; 2 d. Educ. Liverpool Institute; Exeter College, Oxford. Assistant Keeper, National Library of Scotland, 1971-78; Keeper (Catalogues and Automation), 1978-88; Secretary of the Library, 1988-90; President, Scottish Library Association, 1998; Chairman, Britain-Russia Centre Scotland, since 1998. Address: (b.) National Library of Scotland, George IV Bridge, Edinburgh EH1 1EW; T.-0131-226 4531.

McGowan, Sheriff John, LLB. Sheriff of South Strathclyde Dumfries and Galloway at Ayr; b. 15.1.44, Kilmarnock; m., Elise Smith; 2 s. Educ. St. Joseph's Academy, Kilmarnock; Glasgow University. Admitted Solicitor, 1967; Temporary Sheriff, 1986-93; Sheriff of Glasgow and Strathkelvin, 1993-2000. Council Member, Law Society of Scotland, 1982-85. Recreations: golf; tennis; listening to music. Address: (h.) 19 Auchentrae Crescent, Ayr; T.-01292 260139; (b.) Sheriff Court House, Wellington Square, Ayr; T.-01292 268474; e-mail: Sheriff.J.McGowan@scotcourts.gov.uk

McGrath, Professor John Christie (Ian), BSc, PhD. Regius Professor of Physiology, Glasgow University, since 1991; Head of Division, Department of Neuroscience and Biomedical Systems, Institute of Biomedical and Life Sciences; b. 8.3.49, Johnstone; m., Wilma Nicol; 1 s.; 1 d. Educ. John Neilson Institution, Paisley; Glasgow University. Glasgow University: Research Fellow in Pharmacology and Anaesthesia, 1973-75, Lecturer, 1975-83, Senior Lecturer, 1983-88, Reader, 1988-89, Titular Professor, 1987-91; Co-Director, Clinical Research Initiative in Heart Failure, 1994-2000. Sandoz Prizewinner, British Pharmacological Society, 1980; Pfizer Award for Biology, 1983. Recreations: running; politics; travel. Address: (b.) West Medical Building, Glasgow University, Glasgow; T.-041-330 4483.

McGrath, Tom. Playwright and Poet; b. 1940, Rutherglen. Educ. Glasgow University. Founder Editor, International Times, 1966-67; Musical Director, Great Northern Welly Boot Show; Director, Third Eye Centre, Glasgow, 1974-77; plays include: Laurel and Hardy, 1976, The Hardman, 1977.

MacGregor, Alasdair Bruce, BA, MBChB, FRCSE. Consultant Surgeon, Royal Infirmary, Edinburgh, since 1977; Hon. Treasurer, Royal College of Surgeons of Edinburgh, since 1997; b. 11.8.38, Edinburgh; m., Elizabeth Porter; 3 s.; 1 d. Educ. Loretto School, Musselburgh; Cambridge University; Edinburgh University. House Surgeon and Physician, Royal Infirmary, Edinburgh, 1964-65; Assistant Lecturer,

Lecturer in Surgery, Edinburgh University, 1965-69; Registrar, Hammersmith Hospital, London, 1969-71; Senior Registrar, Western General Hospital, Edinburgh, 1971-76; Senior Research Fellow, University of Toronto, 1974-75. Member, Scottish Advisory Committee on Medical Workforce; Member, Council, Royal College of Surgeons of Edinburgh. Recreations: fishing; forestry; shooting; gardening. Address: (h.) 8 East Castle Road, Edinburgh EH10 5AR; T.-0131-229 4621.

McGregor, Rev. Alistair Gerald Crichton, QC, BD, BA, LLB, WS. Minister, North Leith Parish Church, Edinburgh, since 1987; Temporary Sheriff, 1984-87; b. 15.10.37, Sevenoaks, Kent; m., Margaret Dick Lees or McGregor; 2 s.; 1 d. Educ. Charterhouse; Pembroke College, Oxford; Edinburgh University. Solicitor; Advocate; QC; former Standing Junior Counsel to Queen's and Lord Treasurer's Remembrancer, to Scottish Home and Health Department and to Scottish Development Department; Past Chairman, Discipline Committee, Potato Marketing Board; former Clerk, Rules Council, Court of Session; former Tutor in Scots Law, Edinburgh University; former Chairman, Family Care; former Director, Apex (Scotland) Ltd; Governor, Loretto School; Chairman, Drug Prevention Group. Publication: Obscenity (Co-Author). Recreations: squash; tennis; swimming; travel; cinema. Address: (h.) 22 Primrose Bank Road, Edinburgh EH5; T.-0131-551 2802.

McGregor, Bill, MA, MEd. Rector, James Hamilton Academy, Kilmarnock, since 1989; b. 14.2.44, Kilmarnock; m., Elspeth Barbara Greene; 1 s.; 1 d. Educ. Kilmarnock Academy; Glasgow University. Teacher, Assistant Rector, Depute Rector, Mainholm Academy, Ayr, 1968-89. Publications: bus histories. Recreations: photography (transport); writing. Address: (h.) 25 Blackburn Drive, Ayr KA7 2XN; T.-01292 282043.

MacGregor, Professor Bryan Duncan, BSc, MSc, PhD, DipSurv, MRTPI, ARICS. MacRobert Professor of Land Economy, Aberdeen University, since 1990; b. 16.10.53, Inverness; m., Nicola; 2 twin d. Educ. Inverness Royal Academy; Edinburgh University; Heriot Watt University; Cambridge University; College of Estate Management. Lecturer, Department of Land Management, Reading University, 1981-84; Lecturer, Department of Town and Regional Planning, Glasgow University, 1984-87; Deputy, then Property Research Manager, Prudential Portfolio Managers, 1987-90. Recreations: hill-walking; football; literature; music; thinking. Address: (b.) Department of Land Economy, St. Mary's, King's College, Aberdeen University, Aberdeen AB24 3UF; T.-01224 272356.

Macgregor, Dr Donald Finlay, BSc, MBChB, FRCP(Edin), FRCPCH. Consultant Paediatrician (Hon. Senior Lecturer), Tayside University Hospoitals, Dundee, since 1996; b. 22.9.56, Bridge of Allan; m., Elspeth Mary McLeod; 1 s.; 3 d. Educ. Falkirk High School; St Andrews University; Manchester University. Senior House Officer, 1984; Registrar, 1984-88; Provincial Paediatrician, Eastern Highlands, Papua New Guinea, 1986-88; Fellow, University of British Columbia, Vancouver, 1988-90; Clinical Fellow, BC Children's Hospital, Vancouver, 1988-90; Senior Registrar, Royal Hospital for Sick Children, Edinburgh, 1990-92; Consultant Paediatrician, Lancaster and Kendal Hospitals, 1992-96. Secretary, Scottish Paediatric Society; Regional Advisor, Royal College of Paediatrics and Child Health. Recreations: family; outdoor pursuits; Third World issues. Address: (h.) Bon Accord, 2 Viewlands Road, Perth PH1 1BH; T.-01738 625796.

Macgregor, Rt. Rev. Gregor, MA, BD (Hons). Bishop of Moray, Ross and Caithness, 1994-98; b. 17.11.33, Glasgow; m., Elizabeth Jean; 1 s.; 3 d. Educ. Hutchesons' Boys Grammar School, Glasgow; St. Andrews University. Deaconed and priested, 1977; St. Michael's, Elie, 1978-81;

St. Luke's, Glenrothes, 1981-86; St. James', Dollar, 1986-90; St. Luke's, Wester Hailes, 1991-93. Recreations: hill-walking; rugby. Address: (b.) Flat 11, John Ker Court, 42 Polwarth Gardens, Edinburgh EH11 1LN; T.-0131-229 6938.

MacGregor of MacGregor, Brigadier Sir Gregor, 6th Bt. 23rd Chief of Clan Gregor; b. 22.12.25; m., Fanny Butler; 2 s. Educ. Eton. Commissioned, Scots Guards, 1944; commanding 1st Bn., Scots Guards, 1966-69; Col. Recruiting, HQ Scotland, 1971; Lt.-Col. commanding Scots Guards, 1971-74; Defence and Military Attache, British Embassy, Athens, 1975-78; Comdr., Lowlands, 1978-80; Grand Master Mason of Scotland, 1988-93; Member, Queen's Bodyguard for Scotland (Royal Company of Archers). Address: (h.) Bannatyne, Newtyle, Blairgowrie, Perthshire PH12 8TR; T.-01828 650 314.

McGregor, Iain. Honorary Secretary, SABRE (Scotland Against Being Ruled By Europe); b. 19.3.37, Stirling. Educ. Selkirk High School; Kelso High School. Army Service, REME; International Trade Exhibitions Publicist, London; Editor, BIPS International Photo-Feature Agency; Journalist, Fleet Street and provinces; Writer and Lecturer in Journalism, Asia, Europe, North America; Founding Director, Institute for Christian Media (Canada); Editor, The Patriot for Scotland; Editor and Publisher, Social Credit International; Scotland Representative, European Anti-Maastricht Alliance; Council Member, Heritage Society of Scotland. Recreations: local history; travel; music; theatre; film; books. Address: (h.) 8 Baileyfield Road, Edinburgh EH15 1DL; T.-0131-669 5275.

Macgregor, Jimmie, MBE, DA. Radio and Television Presenter; Author; Lecturer. Educ. Springburn Academy; Glasgow School of Art. Forefront of British folk revival for more than 20 years; countless radio and TV appearances, tours in Britain and abroad; more than 20 albums recorded; own daily radio programme, Macgregor's Gathering, for more than 10 years; regular TV series on long-distance walks; various books on folk song and the outdoors; has written theme music for TV and radio, illustrated books; gives regular lectures and slide shows; Life Member, RSPB, Scottish Wildlife Trust, Friends of Loch Lomond; President, Friends of River Kelvin; Vice-President, Scottish Conservation Projects and Scottish Youth Hostels Association; twice Scot of the Year; Hon. Fellow, Royal Zoological Society of Scotland. Recreations: collecting paintings, pottery, glass, furniture; the outdoors; wildlife; hill-walking; theatre; art; music; antiques; old cars; anything and everything Scottish.

McGregor, Margaret Morrice, MA, JP, DL. Director, McGregor Connexions, since 1998; Chair, Zero Tolerance Charitable Trust, since 1999; b. 22.10.42, Aberdeen; m., Michael McGregor; 2 s.; 2 step d. Educ. Aberdeen Academy; Aberdeen University. Member, Edinburgh District Council, 1987-96 (Chair, Women's Committee, 1988-96, Licensing Board, 1992-96); Chair, Equal Opportunities Committee, COSLA, 1992-96; Member, City of Edinburgh Council, 1996-99 (Chair, Women's Committee, 1996-99); Depute Lord Provost, 1996-99; Chair, Scottish Refugee Council, 1995-2000; Member, Visiting Committee, Saughton Prison. Recreations: campaigning (human rights, prison reform, animal welfare); reading; hill-walking. Address: (h.) 17 Greenpark, Liberton, Edinburgh EH17 7TA; T.-0131-664 7223; e-mail: m2mcgregor@aol.com

McGregor, Professor Peter Gregor, BA, MSc. Professor of Economics, Strathclyde University, since 1997; Head, Economics Department, since 1999; b. 7.6.51, London; m., Elaine; 2 s.; 1 d. Educ. Paisley Grammar School; Stirling University. Lecturer, Senior Lecturer, Reader, Department of Economics, Strathclyde University, 1976-97; Research Fellow, Senior Research

Fellow, Research Director, Fraser of Allander Institute, 1984-99. Editor, Regional Studies, 1991-96; Member of several editorial boards. Recreations: travel; reading; music. Address: (b.) Curran Building, 100 Cathedral Street, Glasgow G4 0LN.

McGrigor, Captain Sir Charles Edward, 5th Bt. Life Vice-President, RNLI; Member, Queen's Bodyguard for Scotland (Royal Company of Archers); a Deputy Lieutenant, Argyll and Bute; b. 5.10.22; m., Mary Bettine (eldest daughter of the late Sir Archibald Edmonstone, 6th Bt. of Duntreath); 2 s.; 2 d. Educ. Eton. Joined Army, 1941; Rifle Brigade, North Africa, Italy, Austria (mentioned in Despatches); ADC to Duke of Gloucester, 1945-47.

McGrigor, James Angus Roderick Neil. MSP (Conservative), Highlands and Islands, since 1999; b. 19.10.49, London; m.; 1 s.; 3 d. Educ. Eton; Neuchatel University, Switzerland. Traveller, shipping agent, stockbroker, fish farmer, hill farmer; Conservative candidate, Western Isles, 1997; Euro candidate, Scottish list, 1999; Chairman, Loch Awe Improvement Association; Member, Atlantic Salmon Trust Council. Recreations: music; films; fishing; literature. Address: (h.) Ardchonnel, by Dalmally, Argyll; T.-01546 603811.

McGugan, Irene. MSP (SNP), North East Scotland, since 1999; b. 1952, Angus; m.; 1 s.; 1 d. Educ. Forfar Academy; Robert Gordon's Institute of Technology, Aberdeen; Dundee University. Worked in rural India with VSO; continued voluntary work in Scotland; Childcare Manager, Angus Council. Address: (b.) Scottish Parliament, Edinburgh EH99 1SP; T.-0131-348 5711.

McGuire, Anne, MP, MA (Hons). MP (Labour), Stirling, since 1997; Lord Commissioner, HM Treasury (Government Whip), since 2001; Parliamentary Private Secretary to Secretary of State for Scotland, since 1997; Assistant Government Whip (Scotland), 1998-2001; b. 26.5.49, Glasgow; m., Len McGuire, JP, CA; 1 s.; 1 d. Educ. Our Lady and St. Francis School, Glasgow; University of Glasgow; Notre Dame College of Education. Development Officer, Community Service Volunteers, 1984-88; National Officer, CSV, 1988-93; Depute Director, Scottish Council for Voluntary Organisations, 1993-97. Address: (b.) 22 Viewfield Street, Stirling FK8 1UA; T.-01786 446515.

McGuire, Edward, ARCM, ARAM. Composer; b. 15.2.48, Glasgow. Educ. St. Augustine's Secondary School, Glasgow; Junior Department, RSAMD; Royal Academy of Music, London; State Academy of Music, Stockholm. Won National Young Composers Competition, 1969; Rant selected as test piece for 1978 Carl Flesch International Violin Competition; Proms debut, 1982, when Source performed by BBC SSO; String Quartet chosen for 40th Anniversary Concert, SPNM, Barbican, 1983; featured composer, Park Lane Group series, Purcell Room, 1993; Bath International Guitar Festival, 1996, Proms, 1997; International Viola Congress, 1998; frequent commissions and broadcasts including Euphoria (EIF/Fires of London), Songs of New Beginnings (Paragon Ensemble), Quintet II (Lontano), Peter Pan (Scottish Ballet), A Glasgow Symphony (NYOS), The Loving of Etain (Paragon Opera), Trombone Concerto (Aix-en-Provence Festival), Violin Concerto (Perth Festival, 2000), Double Bass Concerto (BBC SSO, 2002), plays flute with and writes for Whistlebinkies folk group, CDs include Timber Timbre, 1999. Address: c/o Scottish Music Information Centre, 1 Bowmont Gardens, Glasgow G12 9LR; T.-0141-334 6393.

McGurk, John C. Editorial Director, The Scotsman Publications Ltd., since 2001; b. 12.12.52, Edinburgh; m., Karen Ramsay; 1 s.; 1 d. Educ. Tynecastle Secondary School, Edinburgh. Deputy Editor, Sunday Mail, 1987-89; Editor, Sunday Sun, Newcastle-upon-Tyne, 1989-91;

Deputy Editor, Daily Record, 1991-94; Editor, Evening News, 1994-97; Editor, Scotland on Sunday, 1997-2001. Runner Up, UK Regional Editor of the Year, 1991; Scotland on Sunday, Winner UK Sunday Newspaper of the Year, 1998 and 2000, and Winner Royal Bank of Scotland Newspaper of the Year, 1999. Recreation: paying for children. Address: (b.) 108 Holyrood Road, Edinburgh EH8 8AS; T.-0131-620 8365; e-mail: jmcgurk@scotsman.com

McHaffie, Rev. Robin Dunlop, BD (Hons). Minister, Linton, Morebattle and Hownam, Yetholm, since 1991; b. 12.7.48, Glasgow; m., Hazel Wallace Lyons; 3 d. Educ. Bishopbriggs High School; Whitehill Secondary School; Glasgow University. Insurance Trainee, Management Trainee, Templeton Carpets; Publicity Manager, Philips Welding; Minister: Calton Mission, Kinning Park Church. Past Chair, Churches Together Through Garden Festival and Year of Culture. Address: (b.) The Manse, Kirk Yetholm, Kelso TD5 8PF; T.-01573 420308.

McHardy, Stuart Andrew, MA (Hons), FSAScot. Author and Storyteller; Lecturer on Scottish History and Folklore; Cultural Consultant; b. 19.4.47, Dundee; m., Sandra Davidson; 1 s. Educ. Morgan Academy, Dundee; Edinburgh University. Formerly worked in advertising and marketing and as professional musician, writer, broadcaster, journalist and poet; Director, Scots Language Resource Centre, Perth, 1993-98; Chairman, Pictish Arts Society, 1996-99. Publications: Strange Secrets of Ancient Scotland; Tales of Whisky and Smuggling; The Wild Haggis an the Greetin-Faced Nyaff; Scotland: Myth, Legend and Folklore; Edinburgh and Leith Pub Guide; Scots Poems to be Read Aloud; The Quest for Arthur; The Quest for the Nine Maidens. Recreations: music; hill-walking. Address: (h.) 52 Brunswick Street, Edinburgh EH7 5HY.

McIldowie, James Robert, MA, LLB, NP. Solicitor, since 1962; Honorary Sheriff, since 1986; b. 24.9.37, Crieff; m., Isabella Junor (June) Anderson; 2 d. Educ. Morrison's Academy, Crieff; Edinburgh University. Apprentice and Assistant in Edinburgh; joined McLean & Stewart, Dunblane and Callander, 1962; became a Partner, 1963; now Senior Partner. Accredited Expert in Agricultural Law; former Secretary and Treasurer, Highland Pony Society. Recreations: golf; music; theatre; all sports. Address: (b.) 51-53 High Street, Dunblane, Perthshire; T.-01786 823217.

McIlvanney, William. Novelist and Poet; b. 1936, Kilmarnock. Educ. Kilmarnock Academy; Glasgow University. Teacher (Assistant Rector (Curriculum), Greenwood Academy, Irvine, until 1975); Creative Writing Fellow, Strathclyde University, 1972-73; author of Remedy is None, 1966 (joint winner, Geoffrey Faber Memorial Award, 1967), A Gift from Nessus, 1968 (Scottish Arts Council Publication Award, 1969), Docherty, 1975 (Whitbread Award for Fiction, 1975), Laidlaw, 1977, The Papers of Tony Veitch, 1983, The Big Man, 1985, Strange Loyalties, 1990; three books of poetry: The Longships in Harbour, 1970, Weddings and After, 1983, In Through the Head, 1985; Surviving the Shipwreck (essays and collected journalism), 1991.

McIlwain, Alexander Edward, CBE, MA, LLB, SSC, WS, FFCS. Retired Solicitor, formerly Senior Partner, Leonards, Solicitors, Hamilton; Honorary Sheriff, South Strathclyde, Dumfries and Galloway, at Hamilton, since 1981; b. 4.7.33, Aberdeen; m., Moira Margaret Kinnaird; 3 d. Educ. Aberdeen Grammar School; Aberdeen University. Commissioned, Royal Corps of Signals, 1957-59; Burgh Prosecutor then District Prosecutor, Hamilton, 1966-76; Dean, Society of Solicitors of Hamilton, 1981-83; President, Law Society of Scotland, 1983-84; Chairman, Legal Aid Central Committee, 1985-87; Member: Central Advisory Committee for Scotland on Justices of the Peace, 1986-96; Lanarkshire Health Board, 1986-96; The Scout Council (UK), 1981-96, Cameron Committee on Shrieval

Training, 1995-97, Judicial Studies Committee, 1997-2000; Honorary Member, American Bar Association; Chairman, Lanarkshire Scout Area, 1981-91; Chairman, Hamilton Sheriff Court Project, 1990-94; Temporary Sheriff, 1984-99; President, Temporary Sheriffs Association, 1994-98; Member: Criminal Injuries Compensation Appeal Panel, Criminal Injuries Compensation Board. Publications: Time Costing and Time Recording (in collaboration); Supporting Victims in the Criminal Justice System. Recreations: gardening. Address: (h.) 7 Bothwell Road, Uddingston, Glasgow; T.-01698 813368.

McInally, Rt. Rev. Mgr. Hugh Francis, CA, PhB, STB, JP, VG. Vicar General, R.C. Diocese of Dunkeld, since 1990; Canon, 1995; Parish Priest, St. Mary's Forebank and St. Patrick's, Dundee, since 1990; b. 22.5.33, Dundee. Educ. Lawside R.C. Academy, Dundee; Séminaire St. Sulpice, Paris; L'Institut Catholiqe de Paris. C.A. apprenticeship, Alexander MacLean, C.A., Dundee, 1950-55; National Service, RAF, 1956-58; Curate: St. Columba's, Dundee, 1963-68, St. Patrick's, Dundee, 1968-72; Parish Priest: St. Fergus, Dundee, 1972-81, St. Leonard and St. Fergus, Dundee, 1981-90. Recreation: travelling. Address: St. Mary's Rectory, 22 Powrie Place, Dundee DD1 2PQ; T.-01382 226384.

Macinnes, Professor Allan Iain, MA, PhD, FRHistS, FRSA, FFCS. Burnett-Fletcher Professor of History, University of Aberdeen, since 1993; b. 26.11.49, Inverness; m., Tine Wanning. Educ. Oban High School; University of St. Andrews; University of Glasgow. University of Glasgow: Lecturer in Scottish History, 1973-89, Senior Lecturer in Scottish History, 1989-93, Director, Postgraduate School of Scottish Studies, 1992-93; Head, Department of History, Aberdeen University, 1994-97, 1998-2001. Associate Graduate Faculty, University of Guelph, since 1998; Member, Editorial Committee for the History of the Scottish Parliament, since 1991; Scottish Referee, North Carolina Colonial Records Project, 1991-94; Medieval or Later Rural Settlement Advisory Group, Historic Scotland, 1992-2001; Member, Steering Committee, History at Universities Defence Group, 1995-99; Member, Steering Committee, Irish and Scottish Academic Initiative, 1995-97 (Chair, 1995-96); Chair, Scottish Land Commission, 1996-99; Member, Advisory Panel, Scottish Parliamentary Records Project, University of St. Andrews, since 1997; Joint Founder (Chair, Steering Committee), Northern European Historical Research Network, since 1997. Fletcher Jones Fellow of the Huntington Library, San Marino, California, 1993; Frank Watson Prize in Scottish History, University of Guelph, 1997. Publications: Charles I and the Making of the Covenanting Movement, 1625-41, 1991; Clanship, Commerce and the House of Stuart, 1603-1788, 1996; published extensively on covenants, clans and clearances. Recreations: five-a-side football; supporting Hibernian; hillwalking; listening to music – especially jazz; drinking malt whisky. Address: Department of History, University of Aberdeen AB24 3FX; T.-01224 272453.

McInnes, Professor Colin Robert, BSc (Hons), PhD, CEng, FRAS, FRAeS, FRSE. Professor of Space Systems Engineering, University of Glasgow, since 1999; b. 12.2.68, Glasgow; m., Dr. Karen McInnes; 3 s. Educ. Knightswood Secondary School; University of Glasgow. Department of Aerospace Engineering, University of Glasgow: Lecturer, 1991-96, Reader, 1996-99. Royal Society of Edinburgh Bruce Preller Prize Lecture, 1998; Royal Aeronautical Society Pardoe Space Award, 2000; Philip Leverhulme Prize, 2001. Publication: Solar Sailing, 1999. Recreations: photography; hillwalking; history of science; wine. Address: Department of Aerospace Engineering, University of Glasgow, Glasgow G12 8QQ; T.-0141-330 5918/6143; e-mail: colinmc@aero.gla.ac.uk

MacInnes, Hamish, OBE, BEM, DUniv. Writer and Designer; b. 7.7.30, Gatehouse of Fleet. Educ. Gatehouse of Fleet. Mountaineer with numerous expeditions to Himalayas, Amazon and other parts of the world; Deputy Leader, 1975 Everest SW Face Expedition; film Producer/Advisor/safety expert, with Zinnemann, Connery, Eastwood, Putnam, etc.; Advisor, BBC TV live outside broadcasts on climbing; author of 20 books on travel and adventure, including two autobiographies and fiction; designed the first all-metal ice axe, Terodactyl ice climbing tools, the MacInnes stretchers; Founder, Search and Rescue Dog Association; Honorary Member, Scottish Mountaineering Club; former President, Alpine Climbing Group; world authority on mountain rescue; Doctor of Laws (Hons), Glasgow University; Hon. DSc: Heriot Watt University, Aberdeen University; Doctor of the University, University of Stirling, 1997; President, Guide Dogs Adventure Group; past Leader, Glencoe Mountain Rescue Team. Recreations: as above. Address: (h.) Glencoe, Argyll; T.-01855 811258.

McInnes, Sheriff Principal John Colin, QC, BA (Hons) (Oxon), LLB (Edin), HonLLD (St. Andrews), DL. Advocate; Sheriff Principal of South Strathclyde, Dumfries and Galloway, since 2000; Deputy Lieutenant for Fife, since 1997; b. 21.11.38, Cupar, Fife; m., Elisabeth Mabel Neilson; 1 s.; 1 d. Educ. New Park School, St. Andrews; Cargilfield School, Edinburgh; Merchiston Castle School, Edinburgh; Brasenose College, Oxford; Edinburgh University. 2nd Lt., 8th Royal Tank Regiment, 1956-58; Lt., Fife and Forfar Yeomanry, Scottish Horse, TA, 1958-64; Advocate, 1963; Director, R. Mackness & Co. Ltd., 1963-70; Chairman, Fios Group Ltd., 1970-72; Parliamentary candidate (Conservative), Aberdeen North, 1964; Tutor, Law Faculty, Edinburgh University, 1965-72; in practice, Scottish Bar, 1963-73; Sheriff of Lothian and Peebles, 1973-74; Sheriff, Tayside, Central and Fife, 1974-2000; Acting Sheriff Principal, Grampian, Highland and Islands, 2000-01. Member, St. Andrews University Court, 1983-91; Chairman, Fife Family Conciliation Service, 1988-90; Member and Vice-President: Security Service Tribunal, 1989-2001, Intelligence Services Tribunal, 1994-2001; President, The Sheriffs' Association, 1995-97; Member: Scottish Criminal Justice Forum, 1996-2000, Judicial Studies Committee, 1996-2000, Investigatory Powers Tribunal, since 2000; Chairman, Committee to Review Summary Justice in Scotland, since 2001. Publication: Divorce Law and Practice in Scotland, 1990. Recreations: fishing; shooting; hill-walking; skiing; photography. Address: (b.) Sheriff Court House, Graham Street, Airdrie ML6 6EE.

McInnes, Professor William McKenzie, MSc, PhD, CA, FRSA, ILTM. Professor of Accounting, since 1994, and Head, Department of Accounting, Finance and Law, 1995-98, Stirling University; Vice-Dean, Faculty of Management, 1996-97; b. 24.5.42, Hawick; m., Christine Mary; 1 s.; 1 d. Educ. George Watsons College, Edinburgh; Durham University; Glasgow University. Management Accountant, IBM (UK) Ltd., 1966-68; Lecturer, Kirkcaldy Technical College, 1968-70; Audit Senior, Coopers and Lybrand, Bermuda, 1970-72; Senior Lecturer, Newcastle upon Tyne Polytechnic, 1974-76; Lecturer, then Senior Lecturer, Strathclyde University, 1976-91; Director of Research, Institute of Chartered Accountants of Scotland, 1992-93; SHEFC Team Leader for Quality Assessment of Finance and Accounting, 1995-96; Elder, Cadder Parish Church. Recreations: golf; tennis; music. Address: (b.) Department of Accounting, Finance and Law, Stirling University, Stirling FK9 4LA; T.-01786 467280; e-mail: W.M.McInnes@stirling.ac.uk

Macintosh, Farquhar, CBE, MA, DipEd, DLitt, Dr. hc (Edinburgh), FEIS, FScotvec, FSQA. Chairman: Sabhal Mor Ostaig, since 1991, Education Executive Committee, Royal Blind School, since 1994, Gaelic Education Action

Group, since 1994, European Movement (Scotland), since 1996; Chairman, Forum, University of the Highlands and Islands Project, since 1999; b. 27.10.23, Isle of Skye; m., Margaret M. Inglis; 2 s.; 2 d. Educ. Portree High School; Edinburgh University; Glasgow University; Jordanhill College of Education. Taught, Greenfield Junior Secondary School, Hamilton, Glasgow Academy and Inverness Royal Academy; Headmaster: Portree High School, Oban High School; Rector, Royal High School, Edinburgh, 1972-89; Member, Highlands and Islands Development Consultative Council and Convener, Education Sub-Committee, 1965-82; Chairman: Jordanhill Board of Governors, 1970-72, BBC Secondary Programme Committee, 1972-80, Scottish Examination Board, 1977-90, School Broadcasting Council for Scotland, 1981-85; Vice-Chairman, School Broadcasting Council for UK, 1984-86; Chairman, Scottish Association for Educational Management and Administration, 1979-82; Member, Court, Edinburgh University, 1976-91; Governor, St. Margaret's School, 1989-98 (Vice-Chairman of Governors, 1996-98), Royal Blind School, Edinburgh, since 1990; President, St. Andrew Society, Edinburgh, 1996-2000; Member, Board of Governors and Foundation, UHI Millennium Institute, since 1997; Gaelic Correspondent, Weekly Scotsman, 1953-57. Recreations: hill-walking; travel; Gaelic. Address: 12 Rothesay Place, Edinburgh EH3 7SQ; T.-0131-225 4404.

McIntosh, Gordon, BSc, CAS. Corporate Director, Neighbourhood Services (Central), Aberdeen City Council; Director, Aberdeen Exhibition and Conference Centre, since 1997; b. 10.8.56; 2 s.; 1 d. Educ. Keith Grammar School; Glasgow University; Aberdeen University. KPMG (Thomson McLintock), Chartered Accountants, 1979-84; Grampian Regional Council, 1984-96; Director of Economic Development, Aberdeen City Council. Past Chairman, Scottish Local Authorities Economic Development Officers; Member, Scottish Export Forum; Past Chairman, Aberdeen and St. John Mountain Rescue Association; Past President, Junior Chamber; Trustee, The Archaeolink Trust. Recreations: mountaineering; angling; golf. Address: (b.) Aberdeen City Council, Town House, Broad Street, Aberdeen AB10 1FY; T.-01224 522000; e-mail: gmcintosh@econ.aberdeen.net.uk

McIntosh, Professor James, MA, PhD. Professor of Social Policy, Glasgow University; b. 5.12.46, Banchory; m., Jean; 2 s. Educ. Banchory Academy; Aberdeen University. MRC Medical Sociology Unit, Aberdeen, 1970-77; Glasgow University, since 1977. Publications: Communication and Awareness in a Cancer Ward; Beating the Dragon: The Recovery from Dependent Drug Use. Recreations: tennis; golf; hill-walking; music; reading; photography. Address: (b.) Department of Social Policy, Glasgow University, Lilybank House, Bute Gardens, Glasgow G12 8RT; T.-0141-330 5364.

McIntosh, Professor Jean Barbara, PhD, BSc, SRN, CMB, FRCN. Professor of Community Nursing Research, Glasgow Caledonian University, since 1993; b. 16.8.44, Fulmer; m., Professor James R.B. McIntosh; 2 s. Educ. Watford Girls' Grammar School; LSE; University College Hospital, London. Former student nurse and staff nurse; Research Fellow, Aberdeen University, 1972-76; Senior Nurse Research, Greater Glasgow Health Board, 1981-88; Reader, then Professor, Glasgow Caledonian University, since 1989. Publications: three books; numerous papers. Recreations: hill-walking; gardening; classical music. Address: (b.) Department of Nursing and Community Health, Glasgow Caledonian University, 70 Cowcaddens Road, Glasgow G4 0BA; T.-0141-331 3461; e-mail: J.McIntosh@gcal.ac.uk

Macintosh, Kenneth Donald, MA. MSP (Labour), Eastwood, since 1999; b. 15.1.62, Inverness; m., Claire Kinloch Anderson; 1 s.; 1 d. Educ. Royal High School, Edinburgh; Edinburgh University. Joined BBC, 1987; worked in News and Current Affairs, including Breakfast News, Breakfast with Frost, Nine O'Clock News; left as Senior Broadcast Journalist, 1999. Recreations: reading; music; sport – football, golf, tennis. Address: (b.) 28 Field Road, Busby G76 8SE; T.-0141-644 3330.

McIntosh, Lyndsay June, DipMgtStudies, JP. MSP (Conservative), Central Scotland, since 1999; Spokeswoman on Social Justice; Member, Equal Opportunities and Social Justice Committees; formerly: Deputy Convener, Justice 2 Committee, Law and Order Spokeswoman, Scottish Conservatives; b. 12.6.55, Glasgow; m., Gordon; 1 s.; 1 d. Educ. Duncanrig Senior Secondary School; Abertay University, Dundee. Legal secretary; civil servant; housewife/mother; company director; business consultant. Lay Inspector of Schools. Recreations: gardening; swimming; reading; horse racing; stadium concerts. Address: (b.) Scottish Parliament, Edinburgh EH99 1SP; T.-0131-348 5639; Suite 45, Fountain Business Centre, Ellis Street, Coatbridge ML5 3AA; e-mail: lyndsay.mcintosh.msp@scottish.parliament.uk

McIntosh, Sir Neil, CBE, JP, DL, FIPM, ACIS, FRSA. Convener, Scottish Council for Voluntary Organisations, since 1995; Member, UK Electoral Commission, since 2001; b. 30.1.40, Glasgow; m., Marie; 1 s.; 2 d. Educ. King's Park School, Glasgow. Industry and local government, 1957-69; Director of Personnel, Inverness County/Highland Region, 1969-85; Chief Executive: Dumfries and Galloway Region, 1985-92, Strathclyde Region, 1992-96; various public service duties, since 1996, including: Counting Officer, Scottish Parliament Referendum; Chairman, Commission on Local Government and the Scottish Parliament; Crown Agent's Adviser, Shanghai Municipal Government. Hon. Doctorate, Syracuse University, and Hon. Doctorate, Glasgow Caledonian University. Recreations: bottle collecting; dry stane dyking.

McIntosh, Robert, BSc, PhD, FICF. Chief Executive, Forest Enterprise, since 1997; b. 6.10.51, Edinburgh; m., Elizabeth Ann. Educ. Linlithgow Academy; Edinburgh University. Joined Forestry Commission, 1973: District Manager, Research Scientist, Operations Director. Recreations: shooting; farming; fishing. Address: (b.) 231 Corstorphine Road, Edinburgh EH12 7AT; T.-0131-314 6456; e-mail: carol.finlayson@forestry.gsi.gov.uk

Macintosh, Robert Macfarlan, MA, LLB. Solicitor; Chairman, Rent Assessment Committee, Glasgow, since 1966; Honorary Sheriff Substitute, Dumbarton, since 1975; b. 16.6.17, Dumbarton; m., Ann McLean Kelso; 1 s. Educ. Dumbarton Academy; George Watson's College, Edinburgh; Glasgow University. Qualified as Solicitor, 1949; Local Secretary, Dumbarton Legal Aid Committee, 1950-84; Dean, Faculty of Procurators, Dumbarton, 1973; Chairman: Dunbartonshire Rent Tribunal, 1960, Glasgow Rent Tribunal, 1974; Clerk to Commissioners of Income Tax, East and West Dunbartonshire, since 1973; President, Dumbarton Burns Club; President, Cardross Golf Club. Recreation: golf. Address: (h.) Ardmory, Peel Street, Cardross, Dunbartonshire.

McIntosh, Stewart, BA (Hons). Journalist; b. 7.5.48, Glasgow; m., Marion; 2 d. Educ. Rutherglen Academy; Strathclyde University. Assistant Secretary, STUC, 1976-79; Education Officer, GMB, 1979-83; Freelance Researcher/Reporter, BBC Scotland, 1983-87; Freelance Journalist and Writer, since 1987. UK Property Writer of the Year, 1997. Recreations: athletics; mountain biking; Rioja; Tennent's Bar; Spain. Address: (b.) 29 Cleveden Road, Glasgow G12 0PQ; T.-0141-334 8475.

McIntyre, Alasdair Duncan, CBE, BSc, DSc, FRSE, FIBiol, FRSA. Chairman, Atlantic Frontier Environmental Forum, since 1996; Chairman, Falkland Islands Exploration and Production Environmental Forum, since 1997; Emeritus Professor of Fisheries and Oceanography, Aberdeen University, since 1986; b. 17.11.26, Helensburgh; m., Catherine Helen; 1 d. Educ. Hermitage School, Helensburgh; Glasgow University. Senior Principal Scientific Officer in charge of environmental team, Marine Laboratory, Aberdeen, 1973-79; Deputy Director, Department of Agriculture and Fisheries for Scotland, Marine Laboratory, Aberdeen, 1979-83; Director of Fisheries Research for Scotland, 1983-86; Co-ordinator, UK Fisheries Research and Development, 1986; President: Estuarine and Coastal Sciences Association, 1992-95, Sir Alister Hardy Foundation for Ocean Science, 1992-99; Member, Research Board, Scottish Natural Heritage, 1992-96; Chairman: Marine Forum for Environmental Issues, 1990-98, Buckland Foundation, 1994-99; Editor, Fisheries Research. Hon. doctorate, Stirling University, 1997. Recreations: reading; food and wine; walking. Address: (h.) 63 Hamilton Place, Aberdeen AB15 5BW; T.-01224 645633; e-mail: a.d.mcintyre@abdn.ac.uk

McIntyre, Archibald Dewar, CBE, MB, ChB, DPH, FFCM, FRCPE, DIH, DTM&H; b. 18.2.28, Dunipace; m., Euphemia Hope Houston; 2 s.; 2 d. Educ. Falkirk High School; Edinburgh University. Senior Medical Officer, Overseas Civil Service, Sierra Leone; Depute Medical Officer of Health, Stirling County Council; Depute Secretary, Scottish Council for Postgraduate Medical Education; Senior Medical Officer, Scottish Home and Health Department; Principal Medical Officer, Scottish Home and Health Department, 1977-93. Recreations: gardening; photography. Address: (h.) Birchlea, 43 Falkirk Road, Linlithgow EH49 7PH; T.-01506 842063.

Macintyre, Iain Melfort Campbell, MB, ChB, MD, FRCSE, FRCPE, FSA (Scot). Consultant Surgeon, Edinburgh, since 1979; Surgeon to the Queen in Scotland, since 1997; Director of Education, Royal College of Surgeons, Edinburgh, 1997-2000; Chairman, Edinburgh Postgraduate Board for Medicine, 1995-2000; b. 23.6.44, Glasgow; m., Tessa Lorna Mary Millar; 3 d. Educ. Daniel Stewart's College, Edinburgh; Edinburgh University. Lecturer in Surgery, Edinburgh University, 1974-78; Visiting Professor, University of Natal, 1978-79; Council of Europe Travelling Fellow, 1986; Honorary Secretary, Royal College of Surgeons of Edinburgh, since 2001; Member, Council, National Medical Advisory Committee, 1992-95. Recreations: Scottish history; photography; skiing; sailing. Address: (b.) Department of Surgery, Western General Hospital, Edinburgh; T.-0131-537 1549.

McIntyre, Rev. Mgr. John, MA (Hons), STL, PhL, DipEd. Parish Priest, St. Bridget's, Baillieston, since 1995; Member, Scottish Catholic Heritage Commission, since 1981; b. 12.11.37, Airdrie. Educ. St. Aloysius College, Glasgow; Gregorian University, Rome; Glasgow University; Jordanhill College of Education. Ordained to priesthood, Rome, 1961; Assistant, St. Monica's, Coatbridge, 1962-63; student, 1963-68; staff, St. Vincent's College, Langbank, 1968-69, St. Mary's College, Blairs, Aberdeen, 1969-86 (Rector, 1985-86); Parish Priest, St. Bride's, East Kilbride, 1986-89; Rector, Scots College, Rome, 1989-95. Bradley Medal, Glasgow University, 1967. Publications: Scotland and the Holy See (Editor), 1982; The Scots College, Rome 1600–2000 (Co-Author), 2000. Recreations: English literature; bird-watching; history. Address: 15 Swinton Road, Baillieston, Glasgow G69 6DT; T.-0141-771 1058; e-mail: johnmcintyre@stbridgetsparish.fsnet.co.uk

McIntyre, Very Rev. Professor John, CVO, MA, BD, DLitt, DD, DHL, Dr hc, FRSE. Professor of Divinity, Edinburgh University, 1956-86; Honorary Chaplain to The Queen in Scotland, 1974-86 (Extraordinary Chaplain, since 1986); Dean of the Order of the Thistle, 1974-89; b. 20.5.16, Glasgow; m., Jessie Brown Buick; 2 s.; 1 d. Educ. Bathgate Academy; Edinburgh University. Ordained, 1941; Locum Tenens, Parish of Glenorchy and Inishail, 1941-43; Minister, Fenwick, Ayrshire, 1943-45; Hunter Baillie Professor of Theology, St. Andrew's College, Sydney University, 1946-56; Principal, St. Andrew's College, 1950-56, Hon. Fellow, since 1991; Principal Warden, Pollock Halls of Residence, Edinburgh University, 1960-71; Acting Principal and Vice-Chancellor, Edinburgh University, 1973-74, 1979; Principal, New College, and Dean, Faculty of Divinity, 1968-74; Moderator, General Assembly of the Church of Scotland, 1982; Convener, Board of Education, Church of Scotland, 1983-87; former Council Member (1980-86) and Vice President (1983-86), Royal Society of Edinburgh. Publications: St. Anselm and his Critics, 1954; The Christian Doctrine of History, 1957; On the Love of God, 1962; The Shape of Christology, 1966; Faith, Theology and Imagination, 1987; The Shape of Soteriology, 1992; Theology after the Storm (Editor), 1997; The Shape of Pneumatology, 1997. Address: (h.) 317 Mayfield Court, 27 West Savile Terrace, Edinburgh EH9 3DT; T.-0131-667 1203; e-mail: john.mcintyre@btinternet.com

Macintyre, Lorn, BA (Hons), PhD. Freelance Writer; b. 7.9.42, Taynuilt, Argyll; m., Mary. Educ. Stirling University; Glasgow University. Novelist and Short Story Writer; publications include Cruel in the Shadow, The Blind Bend and Empty Footsteps in Chronicles of Invernevis Series. Recreations: Scottish country dancing; nightjars; the paranormal. Address: (h.) Priormuir, by St. Andrews, Fife; T.-01334 476428.

McIntyre, Major Robert George. Salvation Army Officer, since 1967 (Divisional Commander for East Scotland Division); b. 15.10.44, Glasgow; m., Isobel Laird. Educ. Woodside Senior Secondary School; Stow College of Engineering. Commanded Salvation Army churches in Scotland, 21 years; Divisional Youth Secretary, 1984-87; Church Growth Consultant, 1991-98. Recreations: piano; brass banding; reading; computing; watching all sports. Address: 5 East Adam Street, Edinburgh EH8 9TF; T.-0131-662 3300; e-mail: robert.mcintyre@salvationarmy.org.uk

Macintyre, Professor Sally, OBE, FRSE, BA, MSc, PhD. Director, Medical Research Council Social and Public Health Sciences Unit, since 1998; Honorary Professor, Glasgow University, since 1991; b. 27.2.49, Edinburgh; m., Dr. Guy Muhlemann. Educ. Durham, London and Aberdeen Universities. Research Fellow, Aberdeen University, 1971-75; Researcher, MRC Medical Sociology Unit, Aberdeen, 1975-83; Director, MRC Medical Sociology Unit, University of Glasgow, 1983-98. Fellow, Royal Society of Medicine; Foundation Fellow, Academy of Medical Sciences. Recreations: skiing; hill-walking; climbing. Address: (b.) MRC Social and Public Health Sciences Unit, 4 Lilybank Gardens, Glasgow G12 8RZ; T.-0141-357 3949.

MacIver, Donald John Morrison, MA (Hons). Education Adviser, Western Isles Council, since 1989; b. 12.11.42, Stornoway; m., Alice Macleod; 1 s. Educ. Nicolson Institute; Aberdeen University. Teacher of Gaelic, 1968-73; Principal Teacher of Gaelic, Nicolson Institute, 1973-89. President, An Comunn Gaidhealach, 1985-90; former Director, National Gaelic Arts Project; former Member, Gaelic Books Council; former Director, Acair Publishing Co.; former Editor, Sruth (newspaper of An Comunn Gaidhealach). Publications: Gaelic Oral Composition; Gaelic Language Practice; Gaelic O-Grade Interpretation; Sgriobh Seo; Feuch Seo; Feuch Freagairt; Faic Is Freagair; Camhanaich; Eadar Peann Is Paipear; Coinneach Odhar; Grian is Uisge; Co Rinn E?; A'Chlach; Bonaidean is Breacain. Recreations: writing (prose and poetry);

computing; reading poetry; gardening; Coronation Street. Address: (h.) 32 Goathill Road, Stornoway, Isle of Lewis HS1 2NL; T.-01851 702582.

MacIver, Matthew M., MA, MEd, FRSA. Chief Executive/Registrar, General Teaching Council for Scotland, since 2001; b. 5.7.46, Isle of Lewis; m., Katrina; 1 s.; 1 d. Educ. Nicolson Institute, Stornoway; Edinburgh University; Moray House College. History Teacher, 1969-72; Principal Teacher of History, Craigmount High School, 1972-80; Assistant Rector, Royal High School, 1980-83; Depute Head Teacher, Balerno High School, 1983-86; Rector, Fortrose Academy, 1986-89; Rector, Royal High School, Edinburgh, 1989-98; Depute Registrar (Education), General Teaching Council for Scotland, 1998-2001. Chairman, Comataidh Craolaidh Gaidhlig (Gaelic Broadcasting Committee), 1996-2001; Chairman, Highlands and Islands Educational Trust; Member, Board, Comunn na Gaidhlig; Member, Scottish Council for Research in Education; Winston Churchill Travelling Fellowship, 1998. Address: (h.) 21 Durham Road, Edinburgh EH15 1NY; T.-0131-669 5029.

McKain, Bruce, LLB (Hons). Law Correspondent, The Herald, since 1978; b. 23.6.48, Dundee; m., Helen Murray Lennox, 2 s. Educ. Madras College, St. Andrews; Edinburgh University. Joined D.C. Thomson, 1970; Weekly News, Manchester and London; Peterborough Evening Telegraph; Radio Clyde; Aberdeen Evening Express. Publication: Scots Law for Journalists (Co-author). Recreations: golf (playing); almost any sport (watching); trying to avoid actions for defamation and contempt of court. Address: (b.) 10 George Street, Edinburgh; T.-0131-200 8171.

Mackay of Clashfern, Lord (James Peter Hymers), Baron (1979), PC (1979), FRSE, Hon. FRICE, FRCOG. Lord High Chancellor of Great Britain, 1987-97; Chancellor, Heriot Watt University, since 1991; b. 2.7.27, Edinburgh; m., Elizabeth Gunn Hymers; 1 s.; 2 d. Educ. George Heriot's School, Edinburgh; Edinburgh University. Lecturer in Mathematics, St. Andrews University, 1948-50; Major Scholar, Trinity College, Cambridge, in Mathematics, 1947, taken up, 1950; Senior Scholar, 1951; BA (Cantab), 1952; LLB Edinburgh (with distinction), 1955; admitted, Faculty of Advocates, 1955; QC (Scot), 1965; Standing Junior Counsel to: Queen's and Lord Treasurer's Remembrancer, Scottish Home and Health Department, Commissioners of Inland Revenue in Scotland; Sheriff Principal, Renfrew and Argyll, 1972-74; Vice-Dean, Faculty of Advocates, 1973-76; Dean, 1976-79; Lord Advocate of Scotland, 1979-84; a Senator of the College of Justice in Scotland, 1984-85; a Lord of Appeal in Ordinary, 1985-87. Part-time Member, Scottish Law Commission, 1976-79; Hon. Master of the Bench, Inner Temple, 1979; Fellow, International Academy of Trial Lawyers, 1979; Fellow, Institute of Taxation, 1981; Director, Stenhouse Holdings Ltd., 1976-77; Member, Insurance Brokers' Registration Council, 1977-79; a Commissioner of Northern Lighthouses, 1975-84; Hon. LLD: Edinburgh, 1983, Dundee, 1983, Strathclyde, 1985, Aberdeen, 1987, Cambridge, 1989, Birmingham, 1990, University of India Law School, 1994, Glasgow 1994, Bath, 1996, Leicester University, 1996, De Montfort, 1999; Hon. DCL: Newcastle, 1990, Oxford, 1998, Robert Gordon, 2000; Hon. Doctor of Laws, College of William and Mary, 1989; Hon. Fellow, Institution of Civil Engineers, 1988; Hon. Fellow, Trinity College, Cambridge, 1989; Hon. Fellow, Girton College, Cambridge, 1989; Hon. Fellow, Royal College of Surgeons, Edinburgh, 1989; Hon. Fellow, Royal College of Physicians of Edinburgh, 1990; Hon. Fellow, Royal College of Obstetricians and Gynaecologists, 1996; Fellow, American College of Trial Lawyers, 1990. Recreation: walking. Address: House of Lords, London, SW1A 0PW.

Mackay of Drumadoon, Rt. Hon. Lord (Donald Sage Mackay), PC, LLB, LLM, LLM (University of Virginia); Senator of the College of Justice in Scotland, since 2000; b. 30.1.46, Aberdeen; m., Lesley; 1 s.; 2 d. Educ. George Watson's Boys' College, Edinburgh; Edinburgh University; University of Virginia. Solicitor, 1971-76; called to Scottish Bar, 1976; QC, 1987; Advocate Depute, 1982-85; Member, Criminal Injuries Compensation Board, 1989-95; Solicitor-General for Scotland, 1995; Lord Advocate, 1995-97; Opposition Spokesman on Scotland and Constitutional Affairs, House of Lords, 1997-2000. Recreation: Isle of Arran. Address: (h.) 39 Hermitage Gardens, Edinburgh EH10 6AZ; T.-0131-447 1412.

McKay, Alexander, BSc (Hons), CertEd. Head of Education, Fife Council, since 1995; b.11.9.49, Buckie; m., Jennifer; 1 s. Educ. Fordyce Academy; Banff Academy; Aberdeen University; Aberdeen College of Education. Teacher, Perth Academy, 1972-76; Assistant Principal Teacher, Ellon Academy, 1976-78; Principal Teacher, Elgin High School, 1978-81; secondment to Scottish Curriculum Development Service as Munn-Dunning Development Officer (Mathematics) for Northern Division, 1981-83; General Adviser, Fife Regional Council, 1983-90; Chief Adviser, Fife Regional Council, 1990-93; Assistant Director of Education, Fife Regional Council, 1993-95. Recreations: walking; reading; jogging and trying to keep fit; holidays with family. Address: (b.) Fife House, North Street, Glenrothes KY7 5LT; T.-01592 414141.

MacKay, Angus, MA (Hons). MSP (Labour), Edinburgh South, since 1999; Minister for Finance and Local Government, 2000-2001; Deputy Minister for Justice, 1999-2000; b. 1964, Edinburgh. Educ. St Augustine's High School. City of Edinburgh Councillor. Address: (b.) Scottish Parliament, Edinburgh EH99 1SP; T.-0131-348 5025; e-mail: angus.mackay.msp@scottish.parliament.uk

Mackay, Angus Victor Peck, OBE, MA, BSc (Pharm), PhD (Cantab), MB, ChB, FRCPsych, FRCP (Ed), TPsych. Chairman, Health Technology Board for Scotland; Physician Superintendent and Clinical Director, Argyll and Bute Hospital, and MacKintosh Lecturer in Psychological Medicine, Glasgow University, since 1980; Member, Faculty of Neuroscience, University of Edinburgh; Chairman, Working Group on the Scottish Health Technology Assessment Centre; Member, Panel of Experts for the European Medicines Evaluation Agency; Psychiatric Representative, Committee on Safety of Medicines, DHSS, since 1983; b. 4.3.43, Edinburgh; m., Elspeth M.W. Norris; 2 s.; 2 d. Educ. George Heriot's School, Edinburgh; Edinburgh University; Churchill and Trinity Colleges, Cambridge. MRC Research Fellow, Cambridge; Member, senior clinical staff, MRC Neurochemical Pharmacology Unit, Cambridge, with appointment as Lector in Pharmacology, Trinity College (latterly, Deputy Director of Unit). Deputy Chairman, Health Services Research Committee of the Chief Scientist for Scotland; Chairman: Scottish Working Group on Mental Illness, Research and Clinical Section of Royal College of Psychiatrists (Scotland), National Mental Health Reference Group; Member: Research Committee, Mental Health Foundation, Scottish Executive, Royal College of Psychiatrists, NHS Policy Board for Scotland; Honorary Senior Lecturer, Department of Psychology, University of St. Andrews; Medical Director, Argyll and Bute NHS Trust. Recreations: rowing; sailing; rhododendrons. Address: (h.) Tigh an Rudha, Ardrishaig, Argyll; T.-01546 603272.

MacKay, Colin, CBE, BSc, MB, ChB, FRCSEng, FRCSEd, FRCSGlas. Chairman, Board of Governors, UHI Millennium Institute, since 2001; b. 8.11.36, Glasgow; m., Dr Helen MacKay; 1 s.; 2 d. Educ. Hillhead High School; Glasgow University. Surgical training, Western Infirmary, Glasgow, 1961-69; MRC

Travelling Fellowship, Boston University, 1969-70; Senior Lecturer in Surgery, Glasgow University, 1970-82; Consultant Surgeon, Western Infirmary/ Gartnavel General Hospital, Glasgow, 1982-96; Royal College of Physicians and Surgeons of Glasgow: Hon. Treasurer, 1976-86, Vice-President Surgical, 1992-94, Visitor, 1996-97, President, 1997-2000; President, Moynihan Chirurgical Club, 1995-96. Publications: Textbook of Surgical Physiology, 1978, 1988; various publications in medical journals. Recreations: travel; walking in the distinguished company of a golden retriever. Address: (h.) 73 Buchanan Drive, Bearsden, Glasgow G61 2EP; T.-0141-942 8759; and 4 Lawers Place, Aberfeldy.

McKay, Sheriff Colin Graham, MA, LLB. Sheriff of North Strathclyde at Kilmarnock, since 2001; b. 20.1.42, Bearsden; m., Sandra Anne Coli; 1 s.; 1 d. Educ. St Aloysius College; Clongowes Wood College; Glasgow University. Solicitor, 1966-90; Temporary Sheriff, 1986-90; Sheriff, since 1990. Address: (b.) Sheriff Court House, St Marnock Street, Kilmarnock KA1 1ED; T.-01563 520211.

MacKay, Colin Hinshelwood, MA (Hons), FSA Scot. Partner, Colin MacKay Associates; Broadcaster and Writer; b. 27.8.44, Glasgow; m., Olive E.B. Brownlie; 2 s. Educ. Kelvinside Academy, Glasgow; Glasgow University; Jordanhill College of Education. Reporter/Presenter: Border Television Ltd., 1967-70, Grampian Television Ltd., 1970-73; Political Editor, Scottish Television PLC, 1973-92 (Presenter, Ways and Means, 1973-86), Parliamentary Lobby Correspondent, 1985-95; recent programmes include: People and Power, Politics Tonight, and Sunday Morning with Colin MacKay (BBC Radio Scotland); Talk-In Sunday (Radio Clyde); Westminster File (Border TV); Eikon (Scottish TV); General Assembly (BBC TV/Radio); contributions to BBC World Service, Radio 4, Radio 5 Live; ITV Commentator: Papal Visit to Scotland, 1982, CBI Conference, Glasgow, 1983. Winner, Observer Mace, 1967 (British Universities Debating Championship); Member, two-man British Universities Canadian Debating Tour, 1967; Commonwealth Relations Trust Bursary to Canada, 1981; Member, Scottish Arts Council, 1988-94; BT Scottish Radio News Broadcaster of the Year, 1997. Publications: Kelvinside Academy: 1878-1978, 1978; The Scottish Dimension in Central and Eastern Canada, 1981. Recreations: music (especially opera); reading; writing.

Mackay, David James, FCIM, FILT. Chief Executive, John Menzies PLC, since 1997; b. 20.5.43, St. Andrews; m., Jane; 1 s.; 1 d. Educ. Kirkcaldy High School; Bradford University; Edinburgh University; Companion, Institute of Management, 1998; FCIT, 1993. Various posts in John Menzies PLC from Transport Manager in Northern Ireland in 1965 to Assistant Regional Director, Southern and London in 1973; returned to Edinburgh as Operations Director, 1978; Managing Director – Wholesale, 1984. Recreations: golf; walking. Address: 108 Princes Street, Edinburgh EH2 3AA; T.-0131-225 8555.

Mackay, David Johnstone, BA, ACIB. Area Manager, HSBC Bank plc, since 1998; b. 4.5.58; m., Carole; 2 s.; 1 d. Educ. Scotus Academy; Napier University. Joined Midland Bank, 1980: appointments in Manchester, Liverpool, Sheffield, London, Nottingham, Chesterfield, Glasgow; Managing Director, Griffin Credit Services Ltd., 1997-98. Recreations: golf, walking and that sort of thing. Address: (b.) 76 Hanover Street, Edinburgh EH2 1HQ; T.-0131-456 3256.

McKay, David Sutherland, OBE; b. 28.8.38, Wick; m., Catherine Margaret; 2 d. Educ. Wick High School; Robert Gordon's College. Apprenticeship in control engineering; Design Engineer, British Oxygen Co.; joined Honeywell Control Systems as Design Engineer; appointed Technical Director, 1983; Director and General Manager, JVC

Manufacturing UK Ltd., 1988-98, now retired. Director, SETG Ltd., since 1984; Member, Bell College Management Board; Visiting Professor, Strathclyde University; Honorary Fellow, Glasgow University, since 2001. Recreation: gardening; DIY. Address: (h.) Green Garth, Nethan Glen, Crossford ML8 5QU.

Mackay, Professor David William, OBE, CBiol, FIBiol, FIWEM, FBIM, MIFM. Chairman, Envirocentre PLC, since 2001; Visiting Professor, University of Strathclyde, 2001; Visiting Professor, Institute of Aquaculture, Stirling University, since 1992; Board Member, Scottish Marine Biological Association, since 1991; b. 6.4.36, Stirling; m., Maureen. Educ. High School of Stirling; Strathclyde University; Paisley College. Experimental Officer, Freshwater Fisheries Laboratory, Pitlochry; Freshwater Biologist, then Marine Survey Officer, Clyde River Purification Board; Principal Environmental Protection Officer, Government of Hong Kong; Depute Director, Clyde River Purification Board; Head of Environmental Services, Ove Arup and Partners, Hong Kong; General Manager and Clerk, North East River Purification Board, Aberdeen; Chief Officer, North East River Purification Board; Regional Director (North), Scottish Environment Protection Agency. Vice President and Secretary, Scottish Anglers National Association, 1970-89. Recreations: farming; fishing. Address: (b.) Envirocentre, Wolfson Centre, 106 Rottenrow East, Glasgow G4 0NW; T.-0141-553 4128.

Mackay, Donald George, MA PhD. Honorary Research Fellow, Aberdeen University, since 1990; b. 25.11.29; m., Elizabeth Ailsa Barr (deceased); 2 s.; 1 d. Educ. Morgan Academy, Dundee; St. Andrews University; Aberdeen University. Assistant Principal, Scottish Home Department, 1953; Assistant Secretary, Royal Commission on the Police, 1960-62; Secretary, Royal Commission on Local Government in Scotland, 1966-69; Assistant Secretary, Scottish Development and Agriculture Departments, 1969-83; Under Secretary, Scottish Agriculture and Environment Departments, 1983-88. Member, Scottish Agricultural Wages Board, 1991-97. Publication: Scotland's Rural Land Use Agencies, 1995. Recreation: hill walking; photography; music. Address: (h.) 38 Cluny Drive, Edinburgh EH10 6DX; T.-0131-447 1851.

MacKay, Professor Sir Donald Iain, MA, FRSE, FRSGS. Chairman, Grampian Holdings, since 1998; Chairman, Edinburgh Business School, since 1997; Director: Scottish Mortgage and Guarantee Trust, Edinburgh Income and Value Trust, DTZ Holdings; Honorary Professor, Heriot-Watt University, since 1982; b. 27.2.37, Kobe, Japan; m., Diana Marjory Raffan; 1 s.; 2 d. Educ. Dollar Academy; Aberdeen University. Professor of Political Economy, Aberdeen University, 1971-76; Professor of Economics, Heriot-Watt University, 1976-82; Chairman, Scottish Enterprise, 1993-97; Vice President, Scottish Association of Public Transport; Governor, National Institute of Economic and Social Research. Recreations: tennis; bridge. Address: (h.) Newfield, 14 Gamekeepers Road, Edinburgh; T.-0131-336 1936.

MacKay, Donald Stewart, BA, DipPE, AUPE. Director of Education, Midlothian, since 1996; b. 18.4.50, Edinburgh; 2 s. Educ. Firrhill Secondary, Boroughmuir Secondary, Edinburgh; Moray House College of Education; Open University. Teacher/Assistant Head Teacher/Headteacher, Fife; Curriculum Development Officer, Fife; Advisor in Primary Education, Lothian; Assistant Director of Education, Lothian. Recreations: skiing; football. Address: (b.) Fairfield House, 8 Lothian Road, Dalkeith EH22 3ZG; T.-0131-270 7500.

Mackay, Rev. Canon Douglas Brysson, FFCS. Rector, Church of the Holy Rood, Carnoustie, 1972-97; Synod Clerk, Diocese of Brechin, since 1981; Honorary Chaplain,

St. Paul's Cathedral, Dundee, since 1999; Tutor and Examiner, Communication Skills, Primary Care Medicine, University of Dundee; Chaplain, British Legion, since 2001; b. 20.3.27, Glasgow; m., Catherine Elizabeth; 2 d. Educ. Possil Senior Secondary School; Edinburgh Theological College; DipNAC, 1954. Precentor, St. Andrew's Cathedral, Inverness, 1958; Rector, Gordon Chapel, Fochabers, 1961 (also Priest-in-Charge, St. Margaret's Church, Aberlour, 1964); Canon, St. Andrew's Cathedral, Inverness, 1965; Synod Clerk, Diocese of Moray, Ross, Caithness, 1965; Honorary Canon, St. Andrew's Cathedral, Inverness, 1965; Convenor of Youth, Moray Diocese, 1965; Brechin Diocese: Convenor, Social Service Board, 1974, Convenor, Joint Board, 1974, Convenor, Administration Board, 1982, Synod Clerk, 1981; Honorary Canon, St Paul's Cathedral, Dundee, 1998; Chairman, Truth and Unity Movement, 1980-87. President: British Red Cross, Carnoustie, 1974-82, British Legion, Carnoustie, 1981; Vice-Chairman, Carnoustie Community Care, 1981; Chairman, Carnoustie Community Council, 1979-81; President, Carnoustie Rotary Club, 1976; Joint Founder and Vice Chairman, Carnoustie Community Care; Carnoustie Citizen of the Year, 1998. Recreations: golf; snooker; reading; music. Address: Balmore House, 24 Philip Street, Carnoustie DD7 6EB.

Mackay, Eileen Alison, CB, MA. Non-Executive Director, Royal Bank of Scotland Group plc, since 1996; Non-Executive Director, Edinburgh Investment Trust plc, since 1996; Council Member, Economic and Social Research Council, since 1999; b. 7.7.43, Helmsdale; m., Sir Muir Russell. Educ. Dingwall Academy; Edinburgh University. Research Officer, Department of Employment, 1965-72; various administrative assignments, Scottish Office, 1972-78; HM Treasury, 1978-80; Central Policy Review Staff, Cabinet Office, 1980-83; Assistant Secretary, Scottish Office, 1983-88; Under-Secretary, Housing, 1988-92; Principal Finance Officer, 1992-96. Member, Edinburgh University Court, since 1997; Member, Board: Scottish Enterprise Edinburgh and Lothian, since 1998, Scottish Financial Enterprise, since 2000; Member: David Hume Institute, since 1996; Carnegie Trust for the Universities of Scotland, since 2000; Member, Review Board for the Accountancy Profession, since 2000. Recreations: cinema; opera; good food and conversation.

MacKay, Professor Gilbert Ferguson, MA, DEP, PhD. Professor of Special Education, University of Strathclyde, since 2000; b. 13.12.44, Glasgow; m., Isobel Hood Spence; 1 s.; 1 d. Educ. Grantown Grammar School; Glasgow High School; Glasgow University. Teacher, Glasgow, 1967-68; Educational Psychologist, Shetland, Bury, Banff and Buchan, 1968-78; Research Psychologist, Glasgow University, 1978-82; Educational Psychologist, Renfrew, 1982-84; Special Educationalist, Jordanhill College and Strathclyde University, since 1984. Publication: Early Communication Skills (Co-Author), 1989; Teaching Children with Pragmatic Difficulties of Communication (Co-Author), 2000. Recreations: cycling; hillwalking; photography; music. Address: (h.) Okeham, 9 Glebe Lane, Newton Mearns, Renfrewshire G77 6DS; T.-0141-639 6157; g.f.mackay@strath.ac.uk

Mackay, Ian Lindsay. Chairman, H.M. Customs and Excise Scotland, and Head, Business Services and Taxes, since 1998; b. 31.8.43, Belfast; m., Carol; 1 s.; 1 d. Educ. Worthing High School. Deputy Collector, Northern Ireland, 1993; Deputy Collector, Anglia, 1996. Address: (b.) 44 York Place, Edinburgh EH1 3JW; T.-0131-469 7300.

Mackay, Ian Munro, BCom, CA. Partner, Frame, Kennedy and Forrest, Chartered Accountants, since 1999; Honorary Sheriff, Dornoch Sheriff Court, since 1985; b. 14.9.47, Brora; m., Maureen; 2 s.; 2 d. (1 d. deceased). Educ. Golspie High School; Edinburgh University. Trained

as CA in Edinburgh, qualifying in 1973; has worked in the profession since, spending three years in United Arab Emirates, returning to UK in 1979 to set up own practice, Mackay & Co., 1979-99. Auditor, Treasurer, Secretary of several local charities and sporting organisations; Secretary, Dornoch Curling Club; Past President, Sutherland Curling Province; Treasurer, Brora Ice Rink Club. Recreations: curling; local history; holidays in France or USA; garden; following most sports. Address: (h.) 4 Sutherland Road, Dornoch, Sutherland; T.-01862 810333.

Mackay, James Alexander, MA, DLitt. Author and Journalist; Numismatic and Philatelic Correspondent, Financial Times, 1972-87; President, Glasgow Philatelic Society, 2001-02; b. 21.11.36, Inverness; m., Renate Finlay-Freundlich. Educ. Hillhead High School, Glasgow; Glasgow University. Lt., RA Guided Weapons Range, Hebrides, 1959-61; Assistant Keeper, Department of Printed Books, British Museum, in charge of philatelic collections, 1961-71; returned to Scotland as a full-time Writer, 1972; Editor-in-Chief, IPC Stamp Encyclopedia, 1968-72; Columnist on antiques, Financial Times, 1967-72, philately and numismatics, 1972-85; Editor: the Burns Chronicle, 1978-91, The Burnsian, 1986-89; Consultant Editor: Coin News, since 1992, Stamp and Coin Mart, since 1995, International Stamp and Exhibition News, since 1996; Trustee, James Currie Memorial Trust, since 1987, Burns-Gaelic Trust, since 1992; Secretary, West of Scotland Numismatic Society, since 1993; Rowland Hill Awards for Authorship (1997) and Journalistic Excellence (1999). Publisher of books on philately and postal history; author of 170 books on aspects of the applied and decorative arts, numismatics, philately, postal history; Scottish books include Robert Bruce, King of Scots, 1974; Rural Crafts in Scotland, 1976; Scottish Postmarks, 1978; The Burns Federation 1885-1985, 1985; The Complete Works of Robert Burns, 1986; The Complete Letters of Robert Burns, 1987; Burnsiana, 1988; Burns-Lore of Dumfries and Galloway, 1988; Burns at Ellisland, 1989; Scottish Post Offices, 1989; Burns A-Z, 1990; Kilmarnock, 1992; Burns, a biography, 1992 (Saltire Prize); Vagabond of Verse, 1995; William Wallace Brave Heart, 1995; Land o' Burns, 1996; Allan Pinkerton, The Eye Who Never Slept, 1996; Michael Collins, 1996; Sounds out of Silence, a life of Alexander Graham Bell, 1996; Under the Gum, 1997; Little Boss: a life of Andrew Carnegie, 1997; The Man who Invented Himself: a life of Sir Thomas Lipton, 1998; I Have Not Yet Begun to Fight: a life of John Paul Jones, 1998; In my End is my Beginning: a Life of Mary Queen of Scots, 1999; Scotland's Posts, 2000. Recreations: travel; languages; music (piano-playing); photographing post offices. Address: (h.) 67 Braidpark Drive, Glasgow G46 6LY.

Mackay, John, TD, MA, FRSGS, FInstD. Chairman, Earl Haig Fund Scotland; Chairman, Scotland the Brand Judging Panel; Member, Committee, Army Benevolent Fund Scotland; Chairman, Lowland Employers Liaison Committee; b. 14.9.36, St. Andrews; m., Barbara Wallace; 1 s.; 2 d. Educ. Madras College; Dunfermline High School; Kircaldy High School; Edinburgh University. Lieutenant, 1st East Anglian Regiment, 1959-63; Territorial Army, 1964-86: Colonel, Royal Engineers (Postal and Courier); Royal Mail, 1963-96: Director, Philately, 1979-84, Chairman, Scottish Post Office Board, 1988, Operations Director, UK, 1991-92, Director and General Manager, Scotland and Northern Ireland, 1986-96. President, Lord's Taverners Scotland, 1994-98; Chairman, Scottish Premier Rugby Limited, 1996-97; Chairman, Scottish Business in the Community Executive Council, 1995-98; Chairman, Edinburgh Common Purpose, 1995-96; Board Member, Quality Scotland, 1991-98; Board Member, Scottish Business in the Community, 1993-98; Member, Quality Assessment Committee, Scottish Higher Education Funding Council, 1994-96; Founder Member, The Breakaways Golf Club. Recreations: golf; watching cricket and rugby;

reading; walking dog; convivial company. Address: (h.) Kinrymont, 8 Damside, Dean Village, Edinburgh EH4 3BB; T.-0131-226 2512.

MacKay, John, OBE, MB, ChB, FRCGP. Retired General Medical Practitioner; Member, General Medical Council; Member, Scottish National Board for Nursing, Midwifery and Health Visiting; b. 24.7.26, Glasgow; m., Matilda MacLennan Bain; 2 s.; 2 d. Educ. Govan High School; Glasgow University. Junior House Doctor, Victoria Infirmary and Southern General Hospital, Glasgow, 1949; Ship's Surgeon, 1950; Assistant in General Practice, Govan, 1951-52 (Principal, since 1953); Member, Board of Management, Glasgow South West Hospitals, prior to 1973; Tutor, University Department of General Practice, Glasgow; part-time Medical Referee, Scottish Home and Health Department; Honorary Life Manager, Govan Weavers Society; Member, Scottish General Medical Services Committee. Recreations: angling; golf; gardening. Address: (h.) Moorholm, Barr's Brae, Kilmacolm, Renfrewshire PA13 4DE; T.-Kilmacolm 3234.

Mackay, John Angus, MA. FRSA. Director, Gaelic Broadcasting Committee, since 1991; Chair Gaelic Television Trust, since 1994; Chair, International Committee of Columba Initiative, since 1998; b. 24.6.48, Shader, Isle of Lewis; m., Maria. Educ. Nicolson Institute; University of Aberdeen; Jordanhill College. Sales Rep, D.C. Thomson, Aberdeen, 1971-72; English teacher, Glasgow, 1973-77; Co-operative Development Officer, Highlands and Islands Development Board, 1977-80; Investigating Officer and Senior Development Manager, Highland and Islands Development Board, 1980-84; Chief Executive, Communn na Gaidhlig, 1985-91; Director, Gaelic Arts Agency. Recreations: books; skiing; swimming. Address: (h.) Druimard Arnol, Isle of Lewis, H52 98DB; T.-01851 710479; e-mail: johnangus@ccg.org.uk

McKay, John Henderson, CBE (1987), DL, JP, BA (Hons), PhD, Dr h.c. (Edinburgh). Chairman: Scottish Working Peoples' History Trust, 1992-2000, Edinburgh Quartet Trust, 1996-2000; Hon. Vice-President, St. Andrew Society, since 1989; Hon. President, Scottish Craftsmanship Association, since 1987; Patron, Scotland Yard Adventure Centre, since 1988; b. 12.5.29, Kirknewton; m., Catherine Watson Taylor; 1 s.; 1 d. Educ. West Calder High School; Open University. Labourer and Clerk, Pumpherston Oil Co. Ltd., 1948-50; National Service, Royal Artillery, 1950-52; Customs and Excise, 1952-85; Lord Provost of Edinburgh, 1984-88. Vice President, Royal Caledonian Horticultural Society, 1984-88 and 1993-96, Secretary and Treasurer, 1988-93; Convener, Business Committee, General Council, Edinburgh University, 1992-96; General Council Assessor, Edinburgh University Court, 1996-99; Honorary Vice President, Royal Caledonian Horticultural Society, since 1997. Recreations: gardening; reading; listening to music. Address: (h.) 2 Buckstone Way, Edinburgh EH10 6PN; T.-0131-445 2865.

McKay, Rev. Johnston Reid, MA (Glasgow), BA (Cantab). Editor, Religious Programmes, BBC Scotland, since 1999; b. 2.5.42, Glasgow. Educ. High School of Glasgow; Glasgow University; Cambridge University. Assistant Minister, St. Giles' Cathedral, 1967-71; Church Correspondent, Glasgow Herald, 1968-70; Minister, Bellahouston Steven Parish Church, 1971-78; frequent Broadcaster; Governor, Paisley College; Minister, Paisley Abbey, 1978-87; Senior Producer, Religious Programmes, BBC Scotland, 1987-99; Editor, The Bush (newspaper of Glasgow Presbytery), 1975-78; Chairman, Scottish Religious Advisory Committee, BBC, 1981-86; Stanley Mair Lecturer on Preaching, Glasgow University, 1995; Trustee, Baird Trust, since 1999; Wallace Lecturer, 2000. Publications: From Sleep and From Damnation (with James Miller), 1970; Essays in Honour of William Barclay (Joint Editor), 1976; Through Wood and Nails, 1982; This Small Pool, 1996; The Very Thing, 2001; Movements of a Curtain, 2001. Recreations: walking; gardening. Address: Upper Burnfoot, 27 Stanlane Place, Largs KA30 8DD; T.-01475 672960; e-mail: johnston.mckay@bbc.co.uk

McKay, Linda, MA (Hons). Principal and Chief Executive, Falkirk College of Further and Higher Education, since 1999; b. 27.5.51, Dunfermline. Educ. Aberdeen High School for Girls; Aberdeen University; Universite de Haute-Bretagne; Scottish School of Further Education, Jordanhill; Dundee University. Assistant Tourist Officer, Fort William Tourist Board, 1974-75; Domestic Services Manager, Craig Phadrig Hospital, Inverness, 1975-76; Lecturer and Senior Lecturer in Modern Languages and Communication, Moray College, Elgin, 1976-83; Senior Lecturer in Vocational Preparation, Dundee College of Commerce, 1983-85; Head, Department of Communication, Media and PSD, Dundee College of Further Education, 1985-90; Assistant Principal, Dundee College of Further Education, 1990-93; Depute Principal, Glenrothes College, 1993-99. Member, Police Advisory Board for Scotland; Member, Board of Governors, Scottish Police College; Member, Scottish Qualifications Authority; Member, Board, Scottish Enterprise Forth Valley. Recreations: hill-walking; gardening. Address: (b.) Grangemouth Road, Falkirk FK2 9AD; T.-01324 403203.

MacKay, Professor Norman, CBE, MD, FRCP(Glas), FRCP(Edin), FRCS(Edin), FRCGP, FCPSP, FACP(Hon), FRACP(Hon), FAMS, FAMM, FRCS(Eng), FRCS(I), FRCP(I), FCPSBangl., FCCP(Hon). Dean of Postgraduate Medicine and Professor of Postgraduate Medical Education, Glasgow University, 1989-2001; Consultant Physician, Victoria Infirmary, Glasgow, since 1974; Member, General Medical Council, since 1999; Member, Specialist Training Authority, since 1999; b. 15.9.36, Glasgow; m., Grace Violet McCaffer; 2 s.; 2 d. Educ. Govan High School; Glasgow University. Honorary Secretary: Royal College of Physicians and Surgeons of Glasgow, 1973-83, Standing Joint Committee, Scottish Royal Colleges, 1978-82, Conference of Royal Colleges and Faculties in Scotland, 1982-91; Speciality Adviser in Medicine, West of Scotland Committee of Postgraduate Medical Education, 1982-89; President, Royal Medico-Chirurgical Society of Glasgow, 1982-83; Member, Area Medical Committee, Greater Glasgow Health Board, 1987-89; President, Southern Medical Society, 1989-90; President, Royal College of Physicians and Surgeons of Glasgow, 1994-97. Address: (h.) 5 Edenhall Grove, Glasgow G77 5TS; T.-0141-616 2831.

Mackay, Peter, CB. Member, Board, Scottish Natural Heritage, since 1997; Member, Court, Napier University; Member, Competition Commission (formerly Monopolies and Mergers Commission), since 1996; Commissioner, Northern Lighthouse Board, since 1999; Director, Pacific Horizon Investment Trust, since 2001; b. 6.7.40, Arbroath; m., Sarah Holdich; 1 s.; 2 d. Educ. Glasgow High School; St. Andrews University. Teacher, New South Wales, Australia, 1962-63; Private Secretary to Secretaries of State for Scotland, 1973-75; Director for Scotland, Manpower Services Commission, 1983-85; on secondment from Scottish Office to Department of Employment, London, 1985; Under Secretary, Scottish Education Department (Further and Higher Education, Arts and Sport), 1987-89; Secretary and Chief Executive, Scottish Office Industry Department, 1990-95; Executive Director, Advanced Management Programme in Scotland, 1995-97; former Member, Board, Business Banking Division, Bank of Scotland. Recreations: Scotland; high altitudes and latitudes; dinghy sailing; sea canoeing; tennis. Address: (h.) 6 Henderland Road, Edinburgh EH12 6BB; T.-0131-337 2830.

Mackay, Rev. William Morton, MA(Hons), DipEd, ARSGS, AFAPC, MACE. Moderator, General Assembly of Free Church of Scotland, 2001; Part-time Lecturer in Church History, Free Church of Scotland College, Edinburgh; Free Church of Scotland: Clerk of Public Questions, Religion and Morals Committee, Vice-Chairman, Foreign and Overseas Mission Board; Treasurer, Edinburgh Centre, Royal Scottish Geographical Society; b. 26.3.34, Dundee; m., Catherine; 2 s.; 1 d. Educ. Morgan Academy, Dundee; Queen's College, Dundee; University of St. Andrews; Dundee College of Education; Free Church of Scotland College. Teacher, Buckhaven High School, Fife, 1959-61; ordained, 1961; Teacher, Colegio San Andres, Lima, Peru, 1961-65, Headmaster, 1966-78; Teacher, Lothian Regional Council, 1978-85; Principal, Presbyterian Ladies' College, Burwood, Victoria, Australia, 1986-97. Diploma of Honour, Government of Peru, for services to education. Publication: Thomas Chalmers: A Short Appreciation, 1980. Recreations: music; photography; cricket; rugby; reading; walking. Address: 53 Lauderdale Street, Edinburgh EH9 1DE.

McKean, Professor Charles Alexander, BA, FRSE, FRSA, FSA Scot, HonFRIBA, Hon FRIAS. Professor of Scottish Architectural History, Dundee University; Secretary, Royal Incorporation of Architects in Scotland, 1979-94; b. 16.7.46, Glasgow; m., Margaret Yeo; 2 s. Educ. Fettes College; Bristol University. RIBA: Secretary, London Region, 1968-76, Secretary, Eastern Region, 1972-79, Secretary, Community Architecture, 1976-79; Architectural Correspondent, The Times, 1977-83; Trustee, Thirlestane Castle, 1982-92; author of architectural guides to Edinburgh, Dundee, Stirling, London, Cambridge, Moray, Central Glasgow, Banff and Buchan; General Editor, RIAS/Landmark Trust Guides to Scotland. Publications: The Scottish Thirties; Edinburgh: Portrait of a City; Claim!; The Making of the Museum of Scotland; The Scottish Château. Recreations: books; glasses; gardens; stately homes. Address: (b.) Department of History, Dundee University, Perth Road, Dundee DD1 4HN; T.-01382 345738.

McKechin, Ann, LLB, DipLP. Labour MP, Glasgow Maryhill, since 2001; Solicitor; b. 22.4.61, Johnstone. Educ. Paisley Grammar School; Strathclyde University. Partner, Pacitti Jones, Solicitors, 1990-2000. Council Member, World Development Movement. Recreations: films; art history; dancing. Address: (b.) 1508 Maryhill Road, Glasgow G20 9AD; T.-0141-945 1495.

McKee, Graham Hamilton, BSc, BPhil. Chief Executive, Scottish Enterprise Tayside, since 1994; b. 11.9.51; m., Pilar; 1 s.; 2 d. Educ. Hutchesons' Grammar School, Glasgow; Glasgow University; Newcastle-upon-Tyne University. Assistant Planner, Burnley Borough Council, 1975-77; Scottish Development Agency, 1977-91, latterly as Regional Manager; Director Economic Development, Scottish Enterprise Tayside, 1991-93. Recreation: family. Address: (b.) Scottish Enterprise Tayside, Enterprise House, 45 North Lindsay Street, Dundee DD1 1HT; T.-01382 223100.

McKee, Professor (James Clark St. Clair) Sean, BSc, MA, PhD, DSc, FIMA, CMath, FRSE. Professor of Mathematics, Strathclyde University, since 1988; b. 1.7.45, Belfast. Educ. George Watson's College, Edinburgh; St. Andrews University; Dundee University; Oxford University. NCR Research Fellow, 1970-72; Lecturer in Numerical Analysis, Southampton University, 1972-75; Fellow, Hertford College, Oxford, 1975-86; Professor of Industrial Mathematics, Strathclyde University, and Consultant Mathematician, Unilever Research, 1986-88. Member, Council, ECMI; Member, IMA Programmes Committee; Founding Fellow, Institute of Contemporary Scotland. Publications: 100 papers; Industrial Numerical Analysis (Co-Editor), 1986; Vector and Parallel Computing

(Co-Editor), 1989; Artificial Intelligence in Mathematics (Co-Editor), 1994. Recreations: climbing Munros; golf; theatre; gardening. Address: (b.) Department of Mathematics, Strathclyde University, Glasgow G1 1XH; T.-0141-552 4400.

McKeganey, Professor Neil Patrick, BA, MSc (Econ), PhD. Professor of Drug Misuse Research, University of Glasgow, since 1997; Director, Centre for Drug Misuse Research, University of Glasgow, since 1994; b. 25.4.55, Sussex. Educ. Thomas Bennet School, Crawley; University of Sussex; University of London; University of Aberdeen. Member, Prevention Working Group, Advisory Council on Misuse of Drugs; Member, Executive, Society for the Study of Addiction; Member, Greater Glasgow Drug Action Team. Publications: AIDS Drugs and Sexual Risk: Lives in the Balance, 1992; Sex Work in the Streets: Prostitutes and their Clients, 1996; over 100 academic articles and articles for newspapers and magazines. Recreation: his children, Rebecca, Gabriel and Daniella-Clare; Formula One racing; ski-ing; cinema. Address: (b.) 12–15 Western Court, Glasgow G12 8SQ; T.-0141-330 3616.

McKellar, Kenneth, BSc. Singer, Composer, Writer; b. 23.6.27, Paisley. Gave first concert in local hall, aged 13; continued singing while at school, university and during his first two years working in forestry; has made numerous records of classical and popular music; numerous tours, especially in Australia and New Zealand; has appeared a number of times at the London Palladium.

McKellar, Peter Archibald, LLB (Hons). Investment Director, Standard Life, since 1999; b. 28.5.65, Glasgow; m., Kathleen Scarlett; 2 s. Educ. Daniel Stewart's and Melville College, Edinburgh; Edinburgh University. J.P. Morgan, Investment Bank, New York and London, 1986-88; EFT Group PLC, Corporate Finance Division, 1988-89; London and Edinburgh Trust plc, 1989-90; Co-Founder, Barry McKellar Ltd., 1990-95; Finance Director, Clydeport plc, 1995-98; Group Finance Director, Donside Paper Company Limited, 1998-99; Non-Executive Director, Red Lemon Studios Ltd, 1998-99. Recreations: golf; shooting; swimming. Address: (b.) 1 George Street, Edinburgh EH2 2LL; T.-0131-245 8368.

McKelvey, William Alexander Campbell, BVMS, PhD, MRCVS, CBiol, FIBiol, FRAgS. Chief Executive and Principal, Scottish Agricultural College, since 2002; b. 10.1.53, Belfast; m., Anne; 1 s.; 2 d. Educ. Regent House School; Glasgow University; Aberdeen University. Ontario Veterinary College, Canada, 1975-76; general veterinary practice, Gloucester and Peebles, 1976-83; Senior Veterinary Officer, Rowett Institute, Aberdeen, 1983-87; Senior Veterinary Officer, Macaulay Institute, Edinburgh, 1987-89; General Manager, Edinburgh Genetics, 1989-95; Assistant Director, SAC Veterinary Services, 1995-97; Director, SAC Veterinary Science Division, 1997-99; Director of Operations, SAC, 1999-2002. Member, Council, BVA Scotland. Recreations: fishing; hill-walking; conservation. Address: (b.) SAC, Central Office, Kings Buildings, West Mains Road, Edinburgh EH9 3JG; T.-0131-535 4001.

McKenna, David. Chief Executive, Victim Support Scotland, since 2001; b. 24.1.58, Glasgow. Educ. Queens Park Secondary School, Glasgow; Glasgow College of Technology. Principal Officer, Victim Support Strathclyde, 1986-93; Director of Operations, Victim Support Scotland, 1993-2000. Recreations: travel; history. Address: (b.) 23 Hardwell Close, Edinburgh EH8 9RX; T.-0131-662 5402.

McKenna, Rosemary, CBE, DCE. MP (Labour), Cumbernauld and Kilsyth; Member: Select Committee on Culture, Media and Sport, since 2001, Select Committee on

Procedure, since 2001; b. 8.5.41, Kilmacolm; m., James Stephen McKenna; 3 s.; 1 d. Educ. St. Augustine's Secondary School, Glasgow; St. Andrew's College, Bearsden. Taught in various primary schools, 1974-93; Leader of Council, Cumbernauld and Kilsyth, 1984-88, Provost 1988-92, Leader of Council, 1992-94; former Member, North Lanarkshire Council; former Policy Board Member: Local Government Management Board, Local Government International Bureau; former Member, Board, Scottish Enterprise; former Member, Executive, Scottish Constitutional Convention; Chair, Scottish Libraries and Information Council, since 1999; PPS to John Battle, MP, 1998-2000, to Brian Wilson, MP, 2000-01; President, Convention of Scottish Local Authorities, 1994-96. Recreations: reading; cooking. Address: (b.) House of Commons, London SW1A 0AA.

MacKenzie, Angus Alexander, OBE, CA. Chartered Accountant, since 1955; b. 1.3.31, Nairn; m., Catherine; 1 d. Educ. Inverness Royal Academy; Edinburgh University. National Service, RAF, 1955-57; in private practice as CA Assistant in Edinburgh, 1957-59; in private practice in Inverness, since 1959. Recreations: shooting; stalking; hill-walking; gardening. Address: (h.) Tigh an Allt, Tomatin, Inverness-shire; T.-01808 511270.

Mackenzie, Professor Ann Logan, MA. Ivy McClelland Research Professor of Spanish, Glasgow University, since 1995; General Editor, Bulletin of Spanish Studies (1923-), since 1992; b. Greenock. Educ. Greenock Academy; Glasgow University. Lecturer, Senior Lecturer, Reader, Liverpool University, 1968-95. Publications: books and articles on the theatre and liteature of 17th-century Spain and on the history of British Hispanism. Recreations: theatre; walking the dogs; house improvements. Address: (b.) 89 Gibson Street, Glasgow University, Glasgow, G12 8RS; T.-0141-330 5665; e-mail: A.Mackenzie@hispanic.arts.ac.uk

Mackenzie, Anne, MA (Hons). Broadcaster and Journalist; b. Stornoway, Isle of Lewis; m., Neil McConaghy; 1 s. Educ. Nicolson Institute, Stornoway; Glasgow University. Reporter, News Presenter, Political/Current Affairs Presenter, Grampian TV, 1981-95 (Presenter, North Tonight, Crossfire, We The Jury, etc.); Presenter, BBC Scotland, Glasgow, 1995-97 (Good Morning Scotland, Reporting Scotland, Campaign Scotland, election/devolution specials); Reporter/Presenter, Here and Now, BBC London, 1996; Presenter, Westminster Live, The World Tonight, Breakfast with Frost, BBC London, since 1998. Recreations: gardening; antiques; history; old movies.

MacKenzie, Archibald MacIntosh, DL. Vice Lord Lieutenant, Dunbartonshire, since 1990; b. 3.6.33, Inveraray; m., Margaret Young Ritchie; 1 s.; 1 d. Educ. Hermitage School, Helensburgh. Assistant Chief Constable, British Transport Police, 1982-92; Vice-President and Member, Executive Committee, Royal National Lifeboat Institution (Chairman, Dumbarton Branch); Convenor, Scottish Lifeboat Council; Chairman, Scottish Lifeboat Executive Committee, 1990-96; Member, Committee of Management, Royal National Lifeboat Institution; Director, Dunbartonshire Branch, British Red Cross, 1992-95; Chairman, Loch Lomond Rescue Committee; Non-Executive Director, Lomond Health Trust, 1995-99; Chairman, 2319 Sqd. ATC Committee; Elder, Church of Scotland; Founding Fellow, Institute of Contemporary Scotland. Recreations: sailing; golf; reading; classical music. Address: (h.) Millerston, 10 Boghead Road, Dumbarton; T.-Dumbarton 763654.

Mackenzie, Sheriff Colin Scott, DL, BL, NP. Sheriff of Grampian Highland and Islands, at Lerwick and Kirkwall, since 1992; b. 7.7.38, Stornoway; m., Christeen E.D. MacLauchlan. Educ. Nicolson Institute; Fettes College; Edinburgh University. Procurator Fiscal, Stornoway, 1969-92; Burgh Prosecutor, Stornoway, 1971-75; JP Fiscal, 1971-75; Deputy Lieutenant and Clerk to Lieutenancy of the Western Isles, 1975-92; Vice Lord Lieutenant of Islands Area, Western Isles, 1984-92; Founder President, Stornoway Flying Club, 1970; Founding Dean, Western Isles Faculty of Solicitors; elected Council Member, Law Society of Scotland, 1985-92; Convener, Criminal Law Committee, 1991-92; Elder, Church of Scotland, since 1985; Member, Board of Social Responsibility, Church of Scotland, 1990-96; Convener, Assembly Study Group on Young People and the Media, 1991-93; President, Stornoway Rotary Club, 1977; President, Lewis Pipe Band. Publications: author of article on Lieutenancy, Stair Memorial Encyclopaedia of Law of Scotland, 1987; The Last Warrior Band, 2000. Recreation: fishing. Address: (h.) Park House, Matheson Road, Stornoway, Lewis; Middlebank, Bells Road, Lerwick, Shetland.

MacKenzie, Professor Donald, BSc, PhD, FRSE. Professor of Sociology, University of Edinburgh, since 1992; b. 3.5.50, Inverness; m., Caroline Bamford; 1 d. Educ. Golspie High School; University of Edinburgh. University of Edinburgh: Lecturer in Sociology, 1975-88, Reader in Sociology, 1988-92. Visiting Professor of the History of Science, Harvard University, 1997. Co-winner, U.S. Navy Prize in Naval History, 1989; American Sociological Association Merton Award, 1993; Society for Social Studies of Science Fleck Prize, 1993. Publication: Mechanizing Proof, 2001. Recreations: cycling; walking; chess. Address: (b.) School of Social and Political Studies, George Square, Edinburgh EH8 9LL; T.-0131-650 3980.

Mackenzie, Elizabeth Alice, MA (Post-Grad), CertEd., AMBDA. Principal, Dyslexia Institute Scotland, since 1992; b. 10.9.41, Glasgow; m., Ian Mackenzie (qv); 1 s.; 1 d. Educ. St Columba's, Kilmacolm; Laurel Bank, Glasgow; St George's, Edinburgh; Froebel Educational Institute, Roehampton; Kingston University. Primary teacher in London and Scottish schools, 1963-68; Adviser on Children's Religious Programmes, ABC TV, 1965-68; research into children's books for ABC TV, 1968-70; Senior Teacher, Dyslexia Institute, Glasgow, 1989-92; Course Director, Dyslexia Institute Teacher Training Course, 1994-98. Publications: Dimensions of Dyslexia, Volume I (Contributor); Dyslexia and the Young Offender (paper). Recreations: cooking; design; watching seals. Address: (b.) 74 Victoria Crescent Road, Glasgow G12 9JN; T.-0141-334 4549; e-mail: glasgow@dyslexia-inst.org.uk

Mackenzie, Fiona I., MA (Hons), MIHM (Dip). Chief Executive, NHS Board Forth Valley, since 2001; b. 19.7.58, Edinburgh. Educ. Eastwood High School, Glasgow; University of St. Andrews. NHS Graduate Trainee, 1980-82; Hospital Administrator, West Lothian, 1982-84; Operational Manager, Royal Edinburgh Hospital, 1986-89; Assistant Unit General Manager, Mental Health Unit, Lothian Health Board, 1989-91; Acute Services Manager, Monklands Hospital, Lanarkshire Health Board; Director of Planning, Monklands and Bellshill NHS Trust, 1993-96; Chief Executive, Highland Communities NHS Trust, 1996-99; Chief Executive, Highland Primary Care NHS Trust, 1999-2001. Member, Arbuthnott Standing Committee on NHS Funding; Chairman, Scottish NHS Primary Care Modernisation Group. Recreations: sport; outdoor activities; cooking. Address: 6 Learmonth Avenue South, Edinburgh EH4 1PE; T.-0131-332 5211; e-mail: fiona.mackenzie@fvhb.scot.nhs.uk

MacKenzie, George P., BA, MLitt. Keeper of the Records of Scotland, since 2001; b. 22.9.50, Lenzie. Educ. George Watson's College; Leeds Grammar School; University of Stirling. Archivist, Scottish Record Office, 1975-84; Departmental Records Officer, General Register Office for

Scotland, 1985-86; Head of Liaison Branch, Head of Preservation Services, Scottish Record Office, 1987-94; Deputy Secretary General, International Council on Archives, Paris, 1995-96; Head of External Relations, National Archives of Scotland, 1997-2000. Recreations: travel; reading. Address: (b.) National Archives of Scotland, HM General Register House, Edinburgh EH1 3YY; T.-0131-535 1312; e-mail: george.mackenzie@nas.gov.uk

McKenzie Gordon, BSc. Country Manager, Microsoft Scotland, since 1994; Non-Executive Director, Axiomlab, since 2000; b. 5.9.59, Glasgow; m., Wilma McKenzie; 2 s. Educ. Kilmarnock Academy; Glasgow University. Britol Plc, 1981-85; IBM UK Ltd, 1985-94. Recreations: cycling. Address: (b.) 127 George Street, Edinburgh.

McKenzie, Graham. Director, Centre for Contemporary Arts, Glasgow, since 1997; b. 14.8.58, Glasgow. Educ. Renfrew High School; Heriot Watt University. Social Worker, 1978-88; freelance writer, arts critic, playwright, 1988-90; Principal Arts Officer, South East, Glasgow City Council, 1990-97. Five plays produced for stage, three for radio. Recreation: improvised music. Address: (b.) 350 Sauchiehall Street, Glasgow G2; T.-0141-332 7521.

McKenzie, Howard John Malcolm, MBSA, MCGI, MInstM, CertEd. Principal and Chief Executive, Jewel and Esk Valley College, since 2001; b. 26.7.55, Hammersmith; m., Rachel Jane Chaffey; 2 s. Educ. Ardingly College. Farm student, 1972-77; dairy farm manager, 1977-79; tenant farmer, 1979-85; Lecturer in Agriculture, 1985-88; Business Development Manager, Hertfordshire College of Agriculture, 1988-91; Director of Business Development, Oaklands College, St Albans, 1991-95; Director of Corporate Development, Motherwell College, and Managing Director, AMCOL Scotland Ltd., 1995-2001. Director, Sgeap Ltd.; Trustee, Lanarkshire Education Trust, 1995-2001. Recreations: eating; drinking; rugby; avoiding gardening. Address: (b.) 24 Milton Road East, Edinburgh EH15 2DP; T.-0131-657 7274.

MacKenzie, Hugh D., MA (Hons), FEIS, JP, FRSA. Headteacher, Craigroyston Community High School, 1972-93; Director, Craigroyston Curriculum Project, since 1980; b. 29.5.33, Edinburgh; m., Helen Joyce; 1 s.; 1 d. Educ. Royal High School; Edinburgh University; Moray House College of Education, Edinburgh. Education Officer, RAF, 1956-58; Assistant Teacher, Niddrie Marischal Junior Secondary School and Falkirk High School, 1958-62; Principal Teacher: Broxburn Academy, 1962-64, Liberton High School, 1964-70; Deputy Headteacher, Craigmount High School, 1970-72; Scottish Representative, Northern Regional Examination Board, 1973-88; Vice-Chairman, Lothian Regional Consultative Committee, 1984-87; a Director, Royal Lyceum Theatre, Edinburgh, since 1985, Scottish Community Education Council, 1985-88; President, Royal High School Rugby Club; President and Founder Member, Edinburgh Golden Oldies Rugby Club. Publication: Craigroyston Days, 1995. Recreations: rugby; squash; golf; ornithology; philately; jazz. Address: (h.) 3 Beechwood Mains, Edinburgh.

Mackenzie, Rev. Ian Murdo. Church of Scotland Minister; Writer, Broadcaster, Organist; b. 3.8.31, Fraserburgh; m., Elizabeth Alice Whitley (qv); 1 s.; 1 d. Educ. Strichen School; Fettes College; Edinburgh University. Assistant Organist, St. Giles Cathedral, 1952-58; Editor, The Student, Sooth and Breakthrough; Founder Member, Telephone Samaritans Scotland, 1960; Columnist, Edinburgh Evening Dispatch; Conductor, Calton Singers; Music Organiser, Iona Abbey; Assistant Minister, St. Giles, 1960-62; Founder, Edinburgh University CND, 1962; Scottish Secretary, Student Christian Movement, 1962-63; Assistant General Secretary, Student Christian Movement, 1963-64;

Secretary, University Teachers Group, 1963-65; Religious Adviser and Executive Producer, Religious Programmes, ABC TV, 1964-68; LWT, 1968-69; conceived and produced From Inner Space, Looking for an Answer, Don't Just Sit There, Question '68, Roundhouse; Religious Columnist, The Times, 1966-68; Minister, Peterhead Old Parish Church, 1969-73; Presenter, For Christ's Sake and What The Religious Papers Say, Grampian TV; Chairman, Scottish Religious Panel, IBA, 1970-72; Head of Religious Programmes, BBC Scotland, 1973-89; conceived Eighth Day, Voyager, Angles, Gates to Space, The Quest; Writer/Presenter, He Turned Up, Channel Four, 1990; Baird Lectures on Church Music, 1990; Presenter/Improviser of hymns and other programmes, Radio Scotland. Publications: Tunes of Glory; Vision and Belief; various papers, articles and essays. Recreations: attending concerts, cathedrals, and newsagents; driving with majestic care and attention; writing novels; wondering about God; preaching about wondering. Address: (h.) 1 Glenan Gardens, Helensburgh, Dunbartonshire, G84 8XT; T.-01436 673429.

MacKenzie, Kenneth John, CB, MA, AM. Chairman, Historic Scotland Foundation, since 2001; b. 1.5.43, Glasgow; m., Irene Mary Hogarth; 1 s.; 1 d. Educ. Birkenhead School, Cheshire; Pembroke College, Oxford; Stanford University, California. Assistant Principal, Scottish Home and Health Department, 1965-70; Private Secretary to Joint Parliamentary Under Secretary of State, Scottish Office, 1969-70; Principal: General Register Office, 1970, Regional Development Division, Scottish Office, 1970-73, Scottish Education Department, 1973-77; Civil Service Fellow: Downing College, Cambridge, 1972, Department of Politics, University of Glasgow, 1974-75; Principal Private Secretary to Secretary of State for Scotland, 1977-79; Assistant Secretary: Scottish Economic Planning Department, 1979-83, Scottish Office Finance Division, 1983-85; Principal Finance Officer, Scottish Office, 1985-88; Under Secretary, Scottish Home and Health Department, 1988-91; Scottish Office, Agriculture and Fisheries Department: Under Secretary, 1991-92, Secretary, 1992-95; Head Economic and Domestic Secretariat, Cabinet Office, 1995-97; Head, Constitution Secretariat, Cabinet Office, 1997-98; Secretary and Head of Department, Scottish Executive Development Department, 1998-2001. Member, Agriculture and Food Research Council, 1992-94; Member, Biotechnology and Biological Sciences Research Council, 1994-95. Recreations: amateur dramatics (Member, Edinburgh Civil Service Dramatic Society); church activities (Elder, St Cuthbert's Parish Church, Edinburgh). Address: (h.) 30 Regent Terrace, Edinburgh EH7 5BS; T.-0131-557 4530; e-mail: kenneth.mackenzie@ic24.net

MacKenzie, Madeleine, LLB (Hons), DipLP. Depute Scottish Parliamentary Counsel, since 1999; b. 27.8.63, Inverness. Educ. Inverness High School; Aberdeen University. Solicitor in private practice, 1986-90; Assistant Scottish Parliamentary Counsel, 1990-99. Recreations: reading; bridge; music. Address: (b.) Office of the Scottish Parliamentary Counsel, Victoria Quay, Edinburgh EH6 6QQ; T.-0131-244 1667; e-mail: madeleine.mackenzie@scotland.gsi.gov.uk

Mackenzie, Professor Robin Kenneth; BSc, MSc, PhD, CEng, FIOA, FCIOB, FCIBSE, FRSA. Head, School of the Built Environment, Napier University, since 1995; b. 28.8.44, Edinburgh; m., Georgina Fiona; 3 s. Educ. Trinity Academy; Heriot-Watt University, Edinburgh University; MIT (USA). Research Fellow, Massachusetts Institute of Technology, 1970-72; Lecturer/Senior Lecturer, Heriot-Watt University, 1973-85; Reader in Acoustics, Heriot-Watt University, 1985-90; Royal Society Industrial Fellow, 1990-93; Head, Department of Building, Sheffield Hallam University, 1993-95; Cruden Fellowship, National Science Foundation Fellowship (USA); Tyndall Medal, Institute of Acoustics, 1980; Chairman of various ISO and BSI committees on sound insulation. Publications; Auditorium Acoustics, 1974. Recreations: tennis; golf; chess; skiing. Address: (b.) Napier University, 10 Colinton Road, Edinburgh, EH10 5DT; T.-0131-455 2645; e-mail: r.mackenzie@napier.ac.uk

MacKenzie, Susan A., DipPE, CertGuid. National President, Girls' Brigade Scotland, since 1999; b. 27.6.55, Inverness. Educ. Inverness High School; Dunfermline College of Physical Education. Teacher of Physical Education, Nairn, 1976-77, Inverness Royal Academy and Drummond Special School, 1977-79, Charleston Academy, Inverness, 1979-93; Assistant Principal Teacher of Guidance, Charleston Academy, since 1993. Captain, 2nd Inverness Co. Girls' Brigade; Secretary, Girls' Brigade International Council European Fellowship; Deacon, East Church of Scotland, Inverness. Recreations: sport; music; reading; travel. Address: (h.) Cruachan, 13 Delnies Road, Inverness; T.-01463 239554; e-mail: sa.mack@virgin.net

McKenzie Smith, Ian, OBE, PRSA, PPRSW, RGI, LLD, DArt, FSA (Scot), FMA. Artist (painter); b. 3.8.35; m., Mary Rodger Fotheringham; 2 s.; 1 d. Educ. Robert Gordon's College, Aberdeen; Gray's School of Art, Aberdeen; Hospitalfield College of Art, Arbroath; Aberdeen College of Education. Teacher of Art, 1960-63; Education Officer, Council of Industrial Design, Scottish Committee, 1963-68; Director, Aberdeen Art Gallery and Museums, 1968-89; City Arts and Recreation Officer, City of Aberdeen, 1989-96. Institute of Contemporary Prints Award, 1969; RSA Guthrie Award, 1971; RSA Gillies Award, 1980; EUS Thyne Scholarship, 1980; RSW May Marshall Brown Award, 1980. Work in permanent collections: Scottish National Gallery of Modern Art, Scottish Arts Council, Arts Council of Northern Ireland, Contemporary Art Society, Aberdeen Art Gallery and Museums, Glasgow Art Gallery and Museums, Abbot Hall Art Gallery, Kendal, Hunterian Museum, Glasgow, Nuffield Foundation, Carnegie Trust, Strathclyde Education Authority, Lothian Education Authority, Royal Scottish Academy, Department of the Environment, City Art Centre, Edinburgh, Perth Art Gallery, IBM, Robert Fleming Holdings, Deutsche Bank, Grampian Hospital Art Trust; Member, Scottish Arts Council, 1970-77; Member, Scottish Museums Council, 1980-87; Member, Committee of Enquiry into the Economic Situation of the Visual Artist, Gulbenkian Foundation, 1978; Arts Advisor, COSLA, 1977-84; Member, Aberdeen University Museums Committee, 1970-96, and Music Committee, 1970-96; Honorary Member: Friends of Aberdeen Art Gallery and Museums, 2000, Peacock Printmakers, 1993; Trustee: Third Eye Centre, 1966-70, Glasgow Arts Centre, 1966-68, Alba Magazine, 1977-80, WASPS (Scotland), 1973-77, Painters Workshop (Scotland), 1975-89, John Kinross Fund, since 1990, Alexander Naysmith Fund, since 1990, Spalding Fund, since 1990, Sir William Gillies Fund, since 1990, Hospitalfield Trust, since 1990, RSA Enterprise, since 1972; Member, ICOM International Exhibitions Committee, 1986-96; Member, Advisory Council on the Export of Works of Art, since 1991; Member, Re:Source AIL Panel, since 2000; External Assessor, Glasgow School of Art, 1982-86, Duncan of Jordanstone College of Art, Dundee, 1986-90, SAC Gifting Scheme, 1997; Assessor: Ruth Davidson Memorial Trust, Morrison Portrait Award, Salvesen Art Trust, Noble Grossart Award; President, RSW, 1988-98; Deputy President, RSA, 1990-91; Treasurer, 1990, Secretary, 1991-98; Governor: Edinburgh College of Art, 1976-88, The Robert Gordon University, 1989-95; Member, Advisory Board, Robert Gordon University Heritage Unit, 1993-95; Member, Board, Scottish Sculpture Workshop, 1976-2000; Member, National Heritage Scottish Group, 1977-99; National Trust for Scotland: Member, Curatorial Committee, 1991, Member of Council, 1995-99, Member, Buildings Committee, 1998-2000; Commissioner, Museums and Galleries Commission, 1997-2000; Trustee, National Galleries of Scotland, since 1999; Vice President, NADFAS, since 2000; Fellow, Salzburg Seminar, 1981, 1984, FRSA; Hon. RA, Hon. RHA, Hon. RUA; Hon. RWA. Address: (h.) 70 Hamilton Place, Aberdeen AB15 5BA; T.-01224 644531.

McKeown, James Patrick, LLB, DipLP, NP. Solicitor; b. 17.3.59, Coatbridge; m., Pamela Mary; 2 s.; 1 d. Educ. Aberdeen University. Assistant, Esslemont & Cameron, Aberdeen, 1983-85; Company Secretary, Sysdrill Ltd., 1985-86; Assistant, C. & D. Mactaggart, 1986, appointed Partner, 1987; Chairman, Appeals Service. Vice-Chairman, Scottish Liberal Democrats, Argyll and Bute, 1990-97; former Vice President, Scottish Young Lawyers Association. Recreations: politics; travel. Address: (b.) Castlehill, Campbeltown, Argyll PA28 6AR; T.-01586 552317.

McKerrell of Hillhouse, Charles James Mure, OStJ, FSA (Scot). 15th Head of the Name; b. 23.1.41; m., May Weston Cochrane. Educ. Cranleigh. Vice-President, International Commission for Orders of Chivalry; Honorary Captain, Canadian Bush Pilots. Address: (h.) Magdalene House, Lochmaben, Dumfries DG11 1PD; T.-01387 810785.

McKerrell, Douglas Gordon, LLB. Partner: Kidstons & Co., Solicitors, Glasgow, since 1992, Maclay Murray and Spens, 1976-92; b. 18.8.44, Edinburgh; m., Elizabeth Anne (Lizanne) Brown; 3 s.; 1 d. Educ. Royal High School, Edinburgh; High School of Glasgow; Glasgow University. After training and qualifying, spent several years in private practice in London and Glasgow; Tutor/Senior Tutor, Finance and Investment, Diploma in Legal Practice, Glasgow University, 1980-89; Chairman, Rent Assessment Panel for Scotland, 1980-89; Scottish Representative, UK Committee, UNICEF, 1985-88; Chairman: Scottish Music Information Centre, 1990-93, Scottish SPCA, 1988-93; Director, Scottish International Piano Competition; Trustee, Scottish Musicians' Benevolent Fund. Publication: The Rent Acts: A Practitioner's Guide, 1985. Recreations: music; theatre; cinema; collecting records. Address: (b.) 1 Royal Bank Place, Buchanan Street, Glasgow; T.-0141-221 6551; e-mail: mail@kidstons.co.uk

McKerrow, Maureen Grant. President, Scottish Licensed Trade Association, since 2001; b. 7.12.54, Dumfries; m., Gordon McKerrow; 2 s. Educ. Dumfries Academy. Technician, 1972-78; Director, Globe Inn Ltd., 1977-79; Managing Director, Globe Inn Ltd., since 1999; Chairman, Scottish Ladies Golf Association, 1992; Member, Nicholson Committee on Licensing Reform, 2001. Recreations: curling; golf; art; Robert Burns. Address: (b.) Globe Inn Ltd., 56 High Street, Dumfries DG1 2JA; T.-01387 252335.

MacKessack-Leitch, Hilda Jane Marshall. Deputy Lieutenant, Moray, since 1993; Elgin Local Organiser, WRVS, 1976-2000; b. 4.9.40, Rothes; m., 1, Dr. Ernest V. C. Dawson (deceased); 2, David C. MacKessack-Leitch; 2 s. Educ. Elgin Academy. Past County Commissioner, The Guide Association, Moray; Past Chairman, Cancer Research Campaign Committee, Elgin and District. Recreations: cooking; walking; reading; music. Address: (h.) Inchstelly House, Alves, Elgin, Moray IV30 8UY. T.-01343 850203.

McKie, Linda, BA (Hons), MSc, PhD. Research Professor in Sociology, Glasgow Caledonian University, since 1999; Associate Director, Centre for Research on Families and Relationships, since 2001; b. 29.9.56, Belfast; m., Daniel Wybrow; 1 d. Educ. Richmond Lodge; University of Ulster; University of Bath; University of Durham. Lecturer: University of Teesside, 1986-88, University of Glasgow, 1989; Head of Intelligence Unit, Equal Opportunities

Commission, Manchester, 1990; Head of Sociology and Social Policy, Queen Margaret University College, 1991-93; Senior Lecturer, Department of General Practice and Primary Care, University of Aberdeen, 1993-99. Trustee, British Sociological Association; Trustee, Community Health UK; Trustee, Institute of Rural Health. Publications: five books and over 50 papers on gender, health and evaluation. Recreations: gym training; travel; her kind of food and wine. Address: (b.) School of Social Sciences, Glasgow Caledonian University, Glasgow G4 0BA; T.-0141-331 8627; e-mail: l.mckie@gcal.ac.uk

MacKie, Professor Rona McLeod, CBE, MD, DSc, FRCP, FRCPGlas, FRCPLond, FRCPath, FRSE, FInstBiol. Professor of Dermatology, Glasgow University, since 1978; Honorary Consultant Dermatologist, Greater Glasgow Health Board, since 1978; b. 22.5.40, Dundee; m., Sir James Black; 1 s.; 1 d. Educ. Laurelbank School, Glasgow; Glasgow University. Registrar, Department of Dermatology, Western Infirmary, Glasgow, 1970-71; Lecturer in Dermatology, Glasgow University, 1971-72; Consultant Dermatologist, Greater Glasgow Health Board, 1972-78. Publications: textbooks and papers on skin cancer. Recreations: opera; gardening; skiing. Address: Department of Dermatology, Glasgow University, Glasgow G11 6NU; T.-0141-339 8855, Ext. 4006.

McKiernan, Professor Peter, BA, MA, PhD, MIM, FBAM, FRSA. Professor of Strategic Management, St. Andrews University, since 1992; b. 28.12.53, Accrington; m., Morna; 1 s.; 1 d. Educ. Preston Catholic College; Lancaster University; Surrey University. Former M.D. of mechanical engineering company; Lecturer in Management, St. Andrews University; Senior Lecturer in Strategic Management, Warwick University. Publications: Sharpbenders; Strategies of Growth; Inside Fortress Europe; Historical Evolution of Strategic Management; Scenarios for Scotland. Recreations: soccer; sailing; cricket; poetry. Address: (b.) Department of Management, St. Andrews University KY16 9AL; T.-01334 462795.

McKillop, Professor James Hugh, BSc, MB, ChB, PhD, FRCP, FRCR. Muirhead Professor of Medicine, Glasgow University, since 1989 (Associate Dean for Medical Education, since 2000); Honorary Consultant Physician, Glasgow Royal Infirmary, since 1982; b. 20.6.48, Glasgow; m., Caroline A. Oakley; 2 d. Educ. St. Aloysius' College, Glasgow; Glasgow University. Hall Fellow in Medicine, then Lecturer in Medicine, Glasgow University, 1974-82; Postdoctoral Fellow, Stanford University Medical Center, California, 1979 and 1980; Senior Lecturer in Medicine, Glasgow University, 1982-89. Watson Prize Lecturership, Royal College of Physicians and Surgeons of Glasgow, 1979; Harkness Fellowship, Commonwealth Fund of New York, 1979-80; Robert Reid Newall Award, Stanford University, 1980; Honorary Treasurer, Scottish Society of Experimental Medicine, 1982-87; Honorary Secretary, British Nuclear Cardiology Group, 1982-87; Symposium Editor, Scottish Medical Journal, 1984-93; Council Member, British Nuclear Medicine Society, 1985-94 (Hon. Secretary, 1988-90, President, 1990-92); Editor, Nuclear Medicine Communications, 1989-98; Congress President, European Association of Nuclear Medicine, 1997, Member, Executive Committee, 1995-98, Chairman, Education Committee, 1998-2001, Member, Strategy Committee, since 1999; Chairman, Administration of Radioactive Substances Advisory Committee, Department of Health, since 1996 (Vice Chairman, 1989-95); Member, National Medical Advisory Committee, 1995-98; Specialty Adviser on Nuclear Medicine, SODOH, since 1998; Vice-President, Nuclear Medicine Section, Union Europeene Medecines Specialistes; Member, Scottish Medical and Scientific Advisory Committee, 1999-2001, Chairman, since 2001; Member, Executive Committee, Association of Physicians of Great Britain and Ireland, since 2000. Recreations: music

(especially opera); history; football. Address: (b.) University Department of Medicine, Royal Infirmary, Glasgow G31 2ER; T.-0141-211 4675.

McKinlay, Peter, CBE, MA (Hons), DrBA (Napier), FRSA. Chairman, The Wise Group, 1998-2001; Chairman, Cairngorms Housing Forum; Chairman, Next Steps Foundation (Scotland); b. 29.12.39, Campbeltown; m., Anne Thomson; 2 s.; 1 d. Educ. Campbeltown Grammar School; Glasgow University. Scottish Office, 1967-91: various posts including Principal Private Secretary to Rt. Hon. Bruce Millan, Minister of State, and Director, Scottish Prison Service; Chief Executive, Scottish Homes, 1991-99. Non-Executive Director, D.S. Crawford, 1984-86; Member, National Executive, First Division Association, 1977-80; Director, St. Mary's Cathedral Workshop, 1994-99; Board Member, The Cairngorms Partnership, 1998-99; Chairman, Tomorrow's Company in Scotland, 1998-2000. Recreations: reading; gardening; family; friends. Address: (b.) The Wise Group, 72 Charlotte Street, Glasgow G1 5DW; T.-0141-303 3131.

McKinney, Alan. Chief Executive and Secretary, Scottish Stone Liaison Committee; Secretary, Scottish Plastering and Drylining Association and Scottish Committees of the National Access and Scaffolding Confederation, National Federation of Roofing Contractors, Stone Federation GB; Secretary, National Specialist Contracts Council (Scottish Committee); First National Director, Scottish Decorators' Federation, 1990-99; Director of Organisation and Headquarters, Scottish National Party, 1977-90; b. 16.10.41, Glasgow; m., Elma; 1 s.; 1 d. Educ. Brechin High School. Time-served refrigeration engineer before entering politics full-time as National Organiser, SNP, 1977; former Election Agent, Dundee East; former elected Member, NEC. Played football for Brechin City. Recreation: golf. Address: (b.) Federation Support Services, PO Box 28011, Edinburgh EH16 6WN; T.-0131-448 0266.

McKinney, Paul Benedict, MA (Oxon). Head of News and Current Affairs, Scottish Television, since 2000; b. 21.5.64, Glasgow. Educ. St Thomas of Aquin's High School, Edinburgh; U.W.C. of the Atlantic, Wales; University College, Oxford; Moray House College of Education, Edinburgh. Researcher, Gordon Brown MP, 1988-92; Civil Servant, Scottish Office, 1992-94; Researcher, Reporter, Producer, Scottish TV News and Current Affairs, 1994-96; appointed Chief News Producer, 1996; Head of News, 1999. Recreations: theatre; opera. Address: (b.) Scottish Television, 200 Renfield Street, Glasgow G2 3PR; T.-0141-300 3000.

McKinnon, Professor Alan Campbell, MA, PhD, FILT. Professor of Logistics, School of Management, Heriot-Watt University, since 1995; b. 19.9.53, Motherwell; m., Sabine Rhode; 2 s. Educ. Perth Academy; Aberdeen University; University of British Columbia; University College, London. Lecturer, University of Leicester, 1979-87; joined staff Heriot-Watt University, 1987 as Lecturer/Senior Lecturer/Reader/Professor; Chairman, Scottish Transport Studies Group, 1989-92; Chairman, Retail Logistics Task Force (UK Government Foresight Programme), since 2000; Specialist Advisor, House of Commons Scottish Affairs Committee in its study of the future of Scotland's transport links with Europe, 1992-93; European Editor, International Journal of Physical Distribution and Logistics Management, 1990-95; Member: Scottish Office's National Transport Forum, 1998-2000; UK Government Foresight Panel on the Built Environment and Transport, since 1999. Publications: Physical Distribution Systems, 1989. Recreations: piano playing; hill walking; cycling. Address: (b.) Heriot-Watt University, Edinburgh, EH14 4AS; T.-0131-451 3850; e-mail: a.c.mckinnon@hw.ac.uk

MacKinnon, James Gordon, MA (Hons), DipTP, MRTPI. Chief Planner and Head of Planning and Building Standards Group, Scottish Executive, since 2000; b. 17.6.52, Forres; m., Gwen Moggach; 2 s. Educ. Forres Academy; Edinburgh University; Strathclyde University. Graduate planner, Burgh of Motherwell and Wishaw, 1975-79; Scottish Office: Senior Planner, 1979-86, Principal Planner, 1986-96, Assistant Chief Planner, 1996-99, Head of Planning Division, 1999-2000. Recreations: family and friends; blues; jazz; golf; squash. Address: (b.) Victoria Quay, Edinburgh EH6 6QQ; T.-0131-244 0770.

MacKinnon, Major John Farquhar, MC, DL, JP; b. 27.1.18, Melbourne; m., Sheila Pearce (deceased); 1 s.; 1 d. (deceased); 2, Mrs Anne Swann. Educ. Geelong, Australia; Corpus Christi College, Cambridge (MA). Army, Queen's Own Cameron Highlanders, 1939-46 (Major); twice wounded; Middle East, 1940-41; ADC, Governor General, Union of South Africa, 1942; Staff, UK, 1943-46 (left service due to wounds); Staff TA, 1949-54; ICI Ltd., 1949-73, Regional Manager; Secretary, British Field Sports Society, Berwickshire, 1974-80; Elder, Kirk of Lammermuir; JP, 1966; Deputy Lieutenant, Berwickshire, since 1987. Recreation: fishing. Address: (h.) Craigie Lodge, Longformacus, by Duns, Berwickshire; T.-Longformacus 890251.

Mackintosh, Hugh Robertson, OBE, MSocSc. Director, Barnardo's Scotland, since 1991; b. 10.12.47, Blair Atholl. Educ. Pitlochry High School; University of Bristol; University of Birmingham. Caldecott Community Kent (latterly as a Director), 1970-76; Assistant Director: Barnardo's, London, 1976-81, Barnardo's Scotland, 1981-91. Elder, Church of Scotland. Recreations: golf; flyfishing; curling; bowling; wine appreciation. Address: (b.) 235 Corstorphine Road, Edinburgh EH12 7AR; T.-0131-334 9893; e-mail: hugh.mackintosh@barnardos.org.uk

Mackintosh, Simon, MA, LLB, WS. Partner, Turcan Connell, WS, since 1997; Director, MacPhie of Glenbervie Ltd., since 1993; b.2.2.57, Wisbech; m., Catriona; 2 s.; 1 d. Educ. Edinburgh Academy; Glenalmond; Magdalene College, Cambridge University; Edinburgh University. W. & J. Burness: Apprentice, 1980-82, Assistant Solicitor, 1982-85; secondment, Boodle Hatfield, 1983; Partner, W. & J. Burness, 1985-97. Convener, Tax Law Committee, Law Society of Scotland; Member, International Academy of Estate and Trust Law; Member, Scottish Executive Charity Law Review Commission; Board Member, Edinburgh Book Festival, 1996-2001. Recreations: gardening; golf; rugby. Address: (b.) Princes Exchange, 1 Earl Grey Street, Edinburgh EH3 9EE; T.-0131-228 8111.

McLachlan, Alastair Stevenson, MA (Hons). Rector, Lornshill Academy, Alloa, since 1988; b. 7.8.40, Glasgow; m., Anne Rutherford; 1 s.; 1 d. Educ. High School of Glasgow; Glasgow University. Recreations: family; golf; after-dinner speaking; singing. Address: (b.) Lornshill Academy, Tullibody Road, Alloa FK10 2ES; T.-01259 214331.

Maclagan, Ian, LLB, FSAScot. Consultant, Macbeth and Maclagan, Solicitors, Rothesay; b. 21.5.43, Rothesay; m., Marjorie; 1 s. Educ. Rothesay Academy; George Watson's College; Edinburgh University. Solicitor in private practice, since 1967; Hon. Sheriff of North Strathclyde at Rothesay; Dean, Faculty of Solicitors in Bute. Trustee, Bute Museum; Past President, Buteshire Natural History Society. Publication: The Piers and Ferries of Bute. Recreations: walking; local history; archaeology; reading. Address: (b.) 34 Castle Street, Rothesay, Bute; T.-01700 503157.

McLaren, Bill. Rugby Union Commentator, BBC; b. 16.10.23. Played wing forward for Hawick; had trial for Scotland but forced to withdraw because of illness; became reporter on local newspaper; first live radio broadcast, Glasgow v. Edinburgh, 1953; former teacher of physical education.

McLaren, Iain Archibald, BA, CA. Senior Partner, KPMG Scotland, since 1999; b. 21.2.51, Edinburgh; m., Fiona; 2 s.; 2 d. Educ. Daniel Stewart's College, Edinburgh; Heriot-Watt University. CA apprentice and qualified CA, Peat Marwick Mitchell, 1971-76; Internal Audit Manager, Miller Group, 1976-78; Audit Manager, Edward Moore & Sons, 1979-81. Recreations: golf; tennis; hill-walking. Address: (b.) Saltire Court, 20 Castle Terrace, Edinburgh EH1 ZEG; T.-0131-222 2000.

MacLaren, Iain Ferguson, MB, ChB, FRCSEdin, FRCS, FRCP Edin. Consultant Surgeon, Royal Infirmary, Edinburgh, 1974-92; b. 28.9.27, Edinburgh; m., Dr. Fiona Barbara Heptonstall; 1 s.; 1 d. Educ. Edinburgh Academy; Fettes College; Edinburgh University. Captain, RAMC, Egypt, 1950-52; Surgical Registrar, Royal Hospital for Sick Children, Edinburgh, 1956-58; Senior Surgical Registrar, Royal Infirmary, 1959-63 and 1964-67; Fellow in Surgical Research, Hahnemann Medical College and Hospital, Philadelphia, 1963-64; Consultant Surgeon, Deaconess Hospital, Edinburgh, 1967-85; Vice-President, Royal College of Surgeons of Edinburgh, 1983-86 (Council Member, 1977-83 and 1987-94); Fellow, Royal Medical Society (Honorary Treasurer, 1979-85); Chairman, Royal Medical Society Trust, since 1985; Honorary Pipe-Major, Royal Scottish Pipers' Society, 1959-62; Honorary Secretary: Harveian Society of Edinburgh, 1968-87, Aesculapian Club, since 1978; Hon. Secretary, Royal College of Surgeons of Edinburgh, 1972-77; Secretary, Edinburgh University General Council, 1993-97; Chairman: Professional and Linguistic Assessments Board, General Medical Council, 1996-99, Clan MacLaren Society, 1968-91; Chieftain, Clan Labhran, 1991; President, Edinburgh University Graduates' Association, since 1999. Recreations: music; the study of military history; all aspects of Scottish culture. Address: (h.) 3 Minto Street, Edinburgh EH9 1RG; T.-0131-667 3487.

McLaren, John Harvey, RIBA, FRIAS, MRTPI. Managing Director, J. & F. Johnston Overseas Ltd., since 1984; Managing Director, J. & F. Johnston Ghana, since 1994; b. 1.7.41, Aberdeen; m., Yvette; 2 s.; 2 d. Educ. Aberdeen Grammar School; Robert Gordon's, Aberdeen; Edinburgh College of Art. Moira and Moira, 1965-69; T. Harley Haddow and Partners, 1969-71; SSHA, 1971-73; Director, J. & F. Johnston Ltd., 1973-93. Past President, Edinburgh Architectural Association; former Council Member, RIAS (Competitions Convenor and Finance Convenor); Past Chairman, Association of Consulting Architects, Scotland. Address: (h.) The Lodge, 117 Grange Loan, Edinburgh EH9 2EA.

McLatchie, Cameron, CBE, LLB. Chairman and Chief Executive, British Polythene Industries, formerly Scott & Robertson PLC, since 1988; Non-Executive Director, Royal Bank of Scotland Group PLC, since 1998; b. 18.2.47, Paisley; m., Helen Leslie Mackie; 2 s.; 1 d. Educ. Boroughmuir School, Edinburgh; Largs High School; Ardrossan Academy; Glasgow University. Whinney Murray & Co., Glasgow, 1968-70; Thomas Boag & Co. Ltd., Greenock, 1970-75; Chairman and Managing Director, Anaplast Ltd., Irvine, 1975-83; this company purchased by Scott & Robertson. Deputy Chairman, Scottish Enterprise, 1997-2000. Recreations: bridge; golf. Address: (b.) 96 Port Glasgow Road, Greenock; T.-01475 501000.

MacLaverty, Bernard. Writer; b. 14.9.42, Belfast; m., Madeline McGuckin; 1 s.; 3 d. Educ. St Malachy's College, Belfast; Queen's University, Belfast. Moved from Belfast to Scotland, 1975; has been a medical laboratory technician, a mature student, a teacher of English and, for two years in the mid-1980s, Writer-in-

Residence at Aberdeen University; has been a Guest Writer for short periods at University of Augsburg and Iowa State University; Member, Aosdana in Ireland; has published four collections of short stories and four novels; has written versions of his fiction for other media, including radio plays, television plays and screenplays. Publications: Secrets and Other Stories, 1977; Lamb, 1980; A Time to Dance and other Stories, 1982; Cal, 1983; The Great Profundo and Other Stories, 1987; Walking the Dog and Other Stories, 1994; Grace Notes, 1997; The Anatomy School, 2001.

Maclay, Baron (Joseph Paton Maclay), 3rd Baron; Bt. Deputy Lieutenant, Renfrewshire, since 1986; Director, Altnamara Shipping Plc, since 1994; Chairman, Northern Lighthouse Board, since 2001 (Commissioner, since 1996, Vice Chairman, 2000-01); Chairman, Scottish Maritime Museum, since 1998; b. 11.4.42; m., Elizabeth Anne Buchanan; 2 s.; 1 d. Educ. Winchester; Sorbonne. Managing Director: Denholm Maclay Co. Ltd., 1970-83, Denholm Maclay (Offshore) Ltd., Triport Ferries (Management) Ltd., 1975-83; Deputy Managing Director, Denholm Ship Management Ltd., 1982-83; Director: Milton Shipping Co. Ltd., 1970-83, Marine Shipping Mutual Insurance Company, 1982-83; President, Hanover Shipping Inc., 1982-83; Director: British Steamship Short Trades Association, 1978-83, North of England Protection and Indemnity Association, 1976-83; Chairman, Scottish Branch, British Sailors Society, 1979-81; Vice-President, Glasgow Shipowners & Shipbrokers Benevolent Association, 1982-83 and 1997-98; President, Glasgow Shipowners and Shipbrokers Benevolent Association, 1998-99; Director, Denholm Ship Management (Holdings) Ltd., 1991-93; Group Marketing Executive, Acomarit Group, 1993-99. Address: (h.) Duchal, Kilmacolm, Renfrewshire.

McLay, Louisa Mary, MA. Headmistress Fernhill School, since 1992; b. 14.8.45, Glasgow; m., Dr Arthur L C McLay. Educ. Notre Dame High School, Glasgow; Glasgow University. Primary teacher, Mary Immaculate Queen School, 1966-73; Fernhill School: Teacher, English/French/History, 1973-76; Principal Teacher, English, 1976-94; Deputy Head, 1978-92. Recreations: music; gardening. Address: (b.) Fernhill School, Fernbrae Avenue, Burnside, Rutherglen; T.-0141-634 2674.

MacLean, Rt. Hon. Lord (Ranald Norman Munro MacLean), BA, LLB, LLM, PC, FSA(Scot), FRSE. Senator of the College of Justice, since 1990; Queen's Counsel, since 1977; b. 18.12.38, Aberdeen; m., Pamela Ross (m. dissolved); 2 s.; 1 d. Educ. Inverness Royal Academy; Fettes College, Edinburgh; Cambridge University; Edinburgh University; Yale University. Advocate, 1964; Advocate Depute, 1972-75; Advocate Depute (Home), 1979-82; Member, Secretary of State for Scotland's Criminal Justice Forum, 1996-2000; Member, Parole Board for Scotland, 1998-2000; Chairman, Committee on Serious Violent and Sexual Offenders, 1999-2000; Chairman of Governors, Fettes College, since 1996. Recreations: hill-walking; swimming. Address: (h.) 38 Royal Terrace, Edinburgh EH7 5AH.

McLean, Angus, BL, SSC. Solicitor; Honorary Sheriff, Argyll (Dunoon); b. 26.10.12, Kilmartin, Argyll; m., Celia Jane Oliver; 1 s.; 1 d. Educ. Dunoon Grammar School; Glasgow University. Solicitor (Corrigall Ritchie & McLean, Dunoon), 1935; Royal Artillery, 1940-46; seconded Indian Army, 1942, Major (DAAG), 1945. Member, Council, Law Society of Scotland, 1950-74 (Vice President, 1964); Past President, Dunoon Business Club and Dunoon Rotary Club. Publications: History of Dunoon; Place Names of Cowal; Chronicles of Cowal, Argyll. Recreations: local history; travel; gardening. Address: (h.) 21 Ravelston Dykes, Edinburgh EH4 3JE; T.-0131-332 4774.

Maclean of Dunconnel, Sir Charles (Edward), Bt; b. 31.10.46; m.; 4 d. Educ. Eton; New College, Oxford. Publications: The Wolf Children; The Watcher; Island on the Edge of the World; Scottish Country; Romantic Scotland; The Silence. Address: (h.) Strachur House, Cairndow, Argyll PA27 8BX.

MacLean, Charles Hector, BL, AE, DL. Former Senior Partner, Montgomerie & Co., Solicitors, Glasgow; Chairman, Association for Relief of Incurables in Glasgow and West of Scotland, 1964-94; Deputy Lieutenant, County of Renfrew, 1987-99; b. 9.12.13, Glasgow; m., Rachael Malcolm Hutchesson; 3 s.; 1 d. Educ. Canford School; Glasgow University. Commissioned, 602 Squadron Auxiliary Air Force, 1936; mobilised, 1939; severely wounded, 1940, as Flt. Commander in Battle of Britain; released in rank of Wing Commander, 1945; re-commissioned as wing Commander, RAuxAF to raise and command 3602 Fighter Control Unit. Member, Committee, Earl Haig Fund Scotland, 1965-94; Vice President, Officers Association, Scottish Branch, 1983-97; Address: (h.) 71 Lochwinnoch Road, Kilmacolm, Renfrewshire.

Maclean, Christian. Manager, Floris Books, since 1976; b. 14.2.50, Edinburgh; m., Astrid; 2 s.; 1 d. Educ. Rudolf Steiner School. Treasurer, Scottish Publishers Association; Director, Scottish Book Source. Address: (b.) 15 Harrison Gardens, Edinburgh; T.-0131-337 2372.

MacLean, Colin R., BSc (Hons), DipEd, MSc. Depute Head, Schools Group (SEED), since 2000 (National Exam Co-ordinator, 2001); b. 22.5.51, Dundee; m., Ilse; 2 s.; 1 d. Educ. Forfar Academy; Edinburgh University. Teacher of Mathematics, Edinburgh, 1973-79; Education Adviser (Microelectronics/Computing), Lothian Regional Council, 1980-85; HM Inspector of Schools, 1985-96; Chief Statistician, Scottish Office, 1996-99; HM Depute Senior Chief Inspector of Schools, 1999-2000. Recreations: gardening; swimming; travel; playing computer games with my children. Address: (b.) 3-B03 Victoria Quay, Edinburgh; T.-0131-244 0859.

McLean, Colin William, MA, MBA, FFA, FSIP. Managing Director, Scottish Value Management, since 1990; b. 1.5.52. Educ. Jordanhill College School, Glasgow; Glasgow University; Deputy General Manager, FS Assurance, 1974-86; Chief Investment Officer, Scottish Provident, 1986-88; Managing Director, Templeton International, 1988-90; Vice-Chairman, Chest Heart and Stroke, Scotland; Visiting Professor, Glasgow Caledonian University, Caledonian Business School. Address: (b.) Scottish Value Management Ltd, 7 Castle Street, Edinburgh, EH2 3AH; T.-0131-226 6699.

Maclean, Sir Donald, FCOptom. Ophthalmic Optician (retired); Chairman, Ayrshire Medical Support Ltd.; b. Annan; m., Muriel Giles (deceased); 1 s.; 1 d.; m., 2, Margaret Ross. Educ. Morrison's Academy, Crieff; Heriot-Watt, Edinburgh. Ophthalmic Optician in Edinburgh, Newcastle, Perth, Ayr; Chairman, Ayrshire Local Support Committee, 1986-88; former Member, Transport Users Local Consultative Committee; Chairman, Ayr Constituency Conservative Association, 1971-75; Chairman, West of Scotland Area Council, Scottish Conservative Association, 1977-78-79; President, Scottish Conservative and Unionist Association, 1983-85; Scottish Conservative Party: Deputy Chairman, 1985-89, Vice Chairman, 1989-91; Chairman, Carrick, Cumnock and Doon Valley Conservative Association, 1998-2000; Chairman, Bell Hollingworth Ltd., 1996-99; Dean of Guildry, Ayr Guildry, 1993-95; Elder, Church of Scotland; Past President, West Highland Steamer Club; Liveryman of the Worshipful Copany of Spectacle Makers; Freeman, City of London. Recreations: photography; reading.

MacLean, Eoghainn Charles McEwen, LLB (Hons), DipLP. Advocate, since 1995; b. 17.4.66, Port of Aden; 2 s. Educ. High School of Glasgow; Glasgow University. Trainee and Solicitor, McClure Naismith, 1989-93; Solicitor, McGrigor Donald, 1993-94; devil, 1994-95; called to Scots Bar, 1995. Recreation: cross-examination. Address: (h.) 38 Dublin Street Lane North, Edinburgh EH3 6NT; T.-0131-557 1996.

Maclean, Iain Farquhar, LLB (Hons), LLM, MSc, DipLP. Advocate. Educ. Portree High School; University of Aberdeen; Emmanuel College, Cambridge; University of Edinburgh. Trainee Solicitor, Brodies WS, 1990-92; Legal Assistant to the Lord President, Court of Session, 1992-93; admitted, Faculty of Advocates, 1994. Contributor, Greens Annotated Rules of the Court of Session. Address: (b.) Advocates' Library, Parliament House, Edinburgh EH1 1RF; T.-0131-226 5071.

McLean, Jack, DA, MSIAD. Freelance Writer and Broadcaster; b. 10.8.46, Irvine. Educ. Allan Glen's School; Edinburgh College of Art; Jordanhill College. Art Teacher in Glasgow for many years; The Scotsman, 1977-81; Glasgow Herald, 1981-97; The Scotsman, 1997-98; Scotland on Sunday, 1997-99; Sports Columnist, Scottish Daily Mail, 1999-2000; Columnist, The Herald, since 2000; Radio Clyde, 1982-85; BBC Scotland Art Critic and Adviser, 1991-95; Presenter, The Jack McLean Talk Show, Scottish Television. Columnist of the Year, British Press Awards, 1985; Recipient of several Scottish Press Awards. Publications: The Bedside Urban Voltaire; More Bedside Urban Voltaire; The Sporting Urban Voltaire; City of Glasgow; Hopeless But Not Serious; Earthquake. Recreations: collecting art; dressing; cooking; public houses.

McLean, James Angus, BA, LLB, WS. Partner, Burness, since 1974; b. 25.4.47, Gosforth; m., Carol Inglis; 1 s.; 2 d. Educ. Dunoon Grammar School; Fettes College; Sidney Sussex College, Cambridge; Edinburgh University. Solicitor, 1972. Member, High Constables of Edinburgh; Member, Scottish Lawyers European Group; Member, various committees, Law Society of Scotland. Recreations: swimming; cycling; theatre. Address: (b.) 50 Lothian Road, Festival Square, Edinburgh EH3 9WJ; e-mail: jmcl@burness.co.uk

MacLean, James Gordon Bruce, MBChB, FRCS. Consultant Orthopaedic Surgeon, Perth Royal Infirmary and Ninewells Hospital, Dundee, since 1994; Honorary Lecturer, Dundee University, since 1994; b. 17.5.58, Carlisle; m., Susan Jane Roberts; 2 s.; 2 d. Educ. Merchiston Castle School, Edinburgh; Dundee University Medical School. Basic surgical training, Norfolk and Norwich Hospitals; specialist orthopaedic training, St Bartholomew's Hospital, Great Ormond Street, Stanmore; Research Fellow/Junior Consultant, University of Capetown; Regional Children's Orthopaedic Surgeon, Tayside. Recreations: hill-walking; rugby; racquet sports; boating. Address: (b.) Orthpaedic Department, Perth Royal Infirmary, Perth PH1 1NX; T.-01738 623311.

McLean, John David Ruari, CBE, DSC, Croix de Guerre. Typographer and Author; b. 10.6.17, Minnigaff; m., Antonia Maxwell Carlisle (deceased); 2 s.; 1 d. Educ. Dragon School, Oxford; Eastbourne College. Royal Navy, 1940-45; Tutor in Typography, Royal College of Art, 1948-51; Typographic Adviser, Hulton Press, 1953-60; The Observer, 1960-62; Art Editor, The Connoisseur, 1962-73; Founder-Partner, Rainbird, McLean Ltd., 1951-58; Founder Editor, Motif, 1958-67; Honorary Typographic Adviser to HM Stationery Office, 1966-80; Senior Partner, Ruari McLean Associates Ltd., 1960-81; Trustee, National Library of Scotland, 1981. Publications include: Modern Book Design, 1958; Victorian Book Design and Colour Printing, 1963; Magazine Design, 1969; Jan Tschichold, Typographer, 1975; The Thames & Hudson Manual of Typography, 1980; Benjamin Fawcett, Engraver and Colour Printer, 1988; Edward Bawden, war artist, and his letters home 1940-45 (Editor), 1989; Nicolas Bentley drew the pictures, 1990; Typographers on Type (Editor), 1995; Jan Tschichold: a life in typography, 1997; True to Type, 2000; How Typography Happens, 2000. Recreations: used to enjoy sailing and acquiring books. Address: (h.) The Studio, Sanquhar House, Sanquhar, Dumfriesshire DG4 6JL.

MacLean, Kate. MSP (Labour), Dundee West, since 1999; Convener, Equal Opportunities Committee; b. 1958, Dundee; 1 s.; 1 d. Leader of Administration, Dundee City Council, 1992-99; Vice-President, COSLA, 1996-99. Address: (b.) Scottish Parliament, Edinburgh EH99 1SP; T.-0131-348 5758.

Maclean of Duart, Major The Hon. Sir Lachlan, DL. Major, Scots Guards retired; 28th Chief of Clan Maclean; b. 25.8.42.

MacLean, Rev. Marjory Anne, LLB, BD. Depute Secretary, Board of Practice and Procedure, and Depute Clerk, General Assembly of Church of Scotland (full-time, since 1998); Minister, Stromness Parish Church, 1992-98; b. 11.6.62, Forfar. Educ. Forfar Academy; Edinburgh University. Trainee Solicitor, T.P. & J.L. Low, Kirkwall, 1985-87; Probationer then Assistant Minister, Fairmilehead Parish Church, Edinburgh, 1990-92. Company Member, St. Magnus Festival, Orkney. Recreation: chamber singing. Address: (b.) 121 George Street, Edinburgh EH2 4YN; T.-0131-240 2232.

McLean, Miller Roy, MA, LLB, NP, FCIB (Scotland). Group Director, Legal and Regulatory Affairs and Group Secretary, The Royal Bank of Scotland Group plc, since 2000; Director, Adam and Company PLC; Vice Chairman, Banco Santander, Portugal; Chairman, Whitehall and Industry Group; Director, Scottish Parliament and Business Exchange; Trustee, Industry and Parliament Trust; b. 4.12.49, Scotland; m., Anne Charlotte Gourlay; 1 s.; 1 d. Educ. Vale of Leven Academy; Glasgow University; Edinburgh University. The Royal Bank of Scotland Group plc: Assistant Secretary, 1982-83, Secretary, 1983-88; The Royal Bank of Scotland plc: Secretary, 1985-88, Group Secretary, 1988-90, Assistant Director, Legal and Administration, 1990-91, Director, Legal and Regulatory Affairs, 1991-94; Director, Group Legal and Regulatory Affairs and Group Secretary, 1994-2000. Recreations: golf; gardening; reading; music. Address: (b.) 42 St. Andrew Square, Edinburgh EH2 2YE; T.-0131-523 2223.

Maclean, Rob. Television Presenter/Commentator, BBC Scotland Sport; b. 26.11.58, Inverness; m., Pauline; 1 s.; 1 d. Educ. Invergordon Academy. Trainee Journalist, Highland News Group; Reporter, Aberdeen News and PR Services; Head of News and Sport, North Sound Radio; Television News Reporter, BBC Scotland; Sports Presenter/Reporter, Scottish Television; Sports Commentator, BBC Scotland Sport. Recreations: playing football; golf; skiing; music; movies. Address: (b.) BBC Scotland, Broadcasting House, Queen Margaret Drive, Glasgow, G12 8DG; T.-0141 338 2449.

McLean, Professor Sheila Ann Manson, LLB, MLitt, PhD, FRSE, FRCP(Edin), FRSA. International Bar Association Professor of Law and Ethics in Medicine, University of Glasgow, since 1990; Director, Institute of Law and Ethics in Medicine, since 1985; b. 20.6.51, Glasgow; m., Alan McLean (divorced). Educ. Glasgow High School for Girls; University of Glasgow. Area Reporter to Children's Panel, 1972-75; School of Law, University of Glasgow: Lecturer, 1975-85, Senior Lecturer, 1985-90. Previously: Member, Broadcasting Council for Scotland, Member, Scottish Higher Education Funding

Council, Chair, Steering Group, Review of the Professions Supplementary to Medicine Act (Department of Health appointment), Member, Scottish Office Working Group on the Confidentiality of Personal Health Information at the Interface Between Medical and Social Services, Vice-Chair, Multi-Centre Research Ethics Committee (Scotland), Secretary of State Appointee to the United Kingdom Central Council for Nursing, Midwifery and Health Visiting; currently: Chair, Scottish Criminal Cases Review Commission, Chair, Scottish Office Steering Group on Female Offenders, Member, Review Body on Doctors' and Dentists' Remuneration, has been appointed by Department of Health to review the consent provisions of the Human Fertilisation and Embryology Authority, Member, UK Xenotransplantation Interim Regulatory Authority, Member, Audit Committee, International Association of Medical Law, Member, Informal Advisory Group to the Data Protection Registrar on Biotechnology, Member, Policy Advisory Committee, Nuffield Council on Bioethics, Member, Selection Panel for the Broadcasting Council for Scotland, Member, MRC Genetics Advisory Committee, Chair, Review Group on Post Mortems (Scotland), Chair, Independent Review Group on the Removal and Retention of Organs at Post Mortem. Publications: monographs: Medicine, Morals and the Law, 1983; A Patient's Right to Know: Information Disclosure, the Doctor and the Law, 1989; The Case for Physician Assisted Suicide, 1997; Old Law, New Medicine, 1999; edited books: Legal Issues in Medicine, 1981; Human Rights: From Rhetoric to Reality, (Co-Editor), 1986; The Legal Relevance of Gender (Joint Editor), 1988; Legal Issues in Human Reproduction, 1989; Law Reform and Human Reproduction, 1992; Compensation for Personal Injury: An International Perspective, 1993; Law Reform and Medical Injury Litigation, 1995; Law and Ethics in Intensive Care, 1996; Death, Dying and the Law, 1996; Contemporary Issues in Law, Medicine and Ethics, 1996. Recreations: music; reading; playing guitar; singing. Address: School of Law, University of Glasgow, Glasgow G12 8QQ; T.-0141-330 5577.

McLean, Una. Actress; b. 1930, Strathaven. Trained, Royal Scottish Academy of Music and Drama; professional debut, Byre, St. Andrews, 1955 ; pantomime debut, Mother Goose, 1958; joined Citizens' Theatre, Glasgow, 1959; appeared in Five Past Eight revue, 1960s; many television appearances.

Maclean, Professor William James, DA, RSA, RGI, RSW, FSA Scot. Professor of Fine Art, Duncan of Jordanstone College, University of Dundee; b. 12.10.41, Inverness; m., Marian Forbes Leven; 2 s.; 1 d. Educ. Inverness Royal Academy; HMS Conway; Grays School of Art, Aberdeen. Postgraduate and Travel Scholarship, Scottish Education Trust Award, Visual Arts Bursary, Scottish Arts Council; Benno Schotz Prize; one-man exhibitions in Rome, Glasgow, Edinburgh and London; group exhibitions in Britain, Europe and North America; represented in private and public collections including Arts Council, British Museum, Scottish National Gallery of Modern Art, Fitzwilliam Museum, Cambridge, and Scottish museum collections. Hon. DLitt, St. Andrews University. Address: (h.) Bellevue, 18 Dougall Street, Tayport, Fife.

MacLeary, Alistair Ronald, MSc, DipTP, FRICS, FRTPI, FBIM, FRSA. Honorary Fellow, Commonwealth Association of Surveying and Land Economy; Member, Lands Tribunal for Scotland; MacRobert Professor of Land Economy, Aberdeen University, 1976-89 (Dean, Faculty of Law, 1982-85); b. 12.1.40, Glasgow; m., Claire Leonard; 1 s.; 1 d. Educ. Inverness Royal Academy; College of Estate Management; Heriot-Watt University; Strathclyde University. Assistant Surveyor, Gerald Eve & Co., Chartered Surveyors, 1962-65; Assistant to Director, Murrayfield Real Estate Co. Ltd., 1965-67; Assistant

Surveyor and Town Planner/Partner, Wright & Partners, 1967-76; seconded to Department of the Environment, London, 1971-73; Member: Committee of Inquiry into the Acquisition and Occupancy of Agricultural Land, 1977-79, Home Grown Timber Advisory Committee, Forestry Commission, 1981-87; Chairman, Board of Education, Commonwealth Association of Surveying and Land Economy, 1981-90; President, Planning and Development Division, Royal Institution of Chartered Surveyors, 1984-85; Editor, Land Development Studies, 1986-90; Member, Natural Environment Research Council, 1988-91. Recreations: shooting; golf. Address: (h.) St. Helen's, St. Andrew's Road, Ceres, Fife KY15 5NQ; T.-01334 828862; e-mail:armacl@lineone.net

McLeary, Bernard, MA. Director of Education Services, Inverclyde Council, since 1995; b. 29.10.51, Greenock; m., Julie; 2 d. Educ. St. Columba's High School; University of Glasgow; Notre Dame College of Education. Teacher, Principal Teacher, Assistant Head Teacher, St. Stephen's High School, 1973-84; Education Adviser, Dunbarton Division, 1984-88; Education Officer: Dunbarton Division, 1988-90, Argyll and Bute, 1990-93, Glasgow Division, 1993-95. Chairman, Working Groups on Curriculum and Special Needs; consultant to national organisations on educational matters. Recreations: collecting books on Russia; keeping fit; theatre and arts. Address: (b.) Department of Education Services, 105 Dalrymple Street, Greenock PA15 1HT; T.-01475 712824.

MacLeay, Rev. Canon John Henry James, MA. Dean of Argyll, 1987-99; Rector, St. Andrew's, Fort William, 1978-99; Canon, St. John's Cathedral, Oban, 1980-99; Honorary Canon of Oban, since 1999; b. 7.12.31, Inverness; m., Jane Speirs Cuthbert; 1 s.; 1 d. Educ. St. Edmund Hall, Oxford. Ordained Deacon, 1957; Priest, 1958; Curate: St. John's, East Dulwich, 1957-60, St. Michael's, Inverness, 1960-62; Rector, St. Michael's, Inverness, 1962-70; Priest-in-Charge, St. Columba's, Grantown-on-Spey and St. John's, Rothiemurchus, 1970-78. Recreations: fishing; reading; visiting churches and cathedrals. Address: 47 Riverside Park, Lochyside, Fort William PH33 7RB; T.-01397 700117.

McLeish, Alex, Manager, Rangers Football Club, since 2001; b. 21.1.59, Glasgow. Educ. Barrhead High School; John Neilson High School. Began professional career playing for Aberdeen Football Club, 1976; won with Aberdeen: European Cup Winners Cup medal, Super Cup medal, five Scottish Cup medals, two League Cup medals, three Championship medals; Player of the Year, Aberdeen, 1990; 77 caps for Scotland, 1980-1993; Manager: Motherwell, 1994, Hibernian, 1998. Address: Rangers Football Club, Edmiston House, 100 Edmiston Drive, Ibrox, Glasgow G51 2YX.

McLeish, Henry Baird. MP (Labour), Fife Central, since 1987; MSP (Labour), Central Fife, since 1999; First Minister, 2000-01; b. 15.6.48; m.; 1 s.; 1 step-s.; 1 d.; 1 step-d. Educ. Buckhaven High School, Methil; Heriot-Watt University. Former Research Officer and Planning Officer in local government; former Member, Kirkcaldy District Council and Fife Regional Council (Leader, 1982-87); Scottish Front Bench Spokesman for Education and Employment, 1988-89, for Employment and Training, 1989-92; Shadow Scottish Minister of State, 1992-94; Shadow Minister of Transport, 1994-95; Shadow Minister for Health, 1995-97; Minister of State, Scottish Office (Minister for Home Affairs, Local Government and Devolution), 1997-99. Recreations: reading; history; life and work of Robert Burns; malt whisky; Highlands and Islands. Address: The Scottish Parliament, Edinburgh EH99 1SP.

McLellan, Very Rev. Andrew Rankin Cowie, MA, BD, STM, DD. Minister, St. Andrew's and St. George's, Edinburgh, since 1986; Moderator, General Assembly, Church of Scotland, 2000; b. 16.6.44, Glasgow; m., Irene L. Meek; 2 s. Educ. Kilmarnock Academy; Madras College, St. Andrews; St. Andrews University; Glasgow University; Union Theological Seminary, New York. Assistant Minister, St. George's West, Edinburgh, 1969-71; Minister: Cartsburn Augustine, Greenock, 1971-80, Viewfield, Stirling, 1980-86; Member, Inverclyde District Council, 1977-80; Tutor, Glasgow University, 1978-82; Chaplain, HM Prison, Stirling, 1982-85; Convener, Church and Nation Committee, General Assembly, 1992-96; Chairman, Scottish Religious Advisory Committee, BBC, since 1996; Moderator, Church and Society Forum, Churches Together in Britain and Ireland, since 1999. Warrack Lecturer on Preaching, 2000. Publications: Preaching for these People, 1997; Gentle and Passionate, 2001. Recreations: sport; travel; books. Address: 25 Comely Bank, Edinburgh EH4 1AJ; T.-031-332 5324.

McLellan, Douglas Richard, MD, FRCPath, DipFM. Consultant Pathologist, Victoria Infirmary, Glasgow, since 1989; Honorary Senior Lecturer, Glasgow University, since 1989; b. 13.6.55, Glasgow; m., Caitriona; 3 s. Educ. High School of Glasgow; Glasgow University. Registrar in Pathology, Southern General Hospital, Glasgow, 1978-81; Honorary Senior Registrar in Neuropathology (MRC Head Injury Project), Institute of Neurological Sciences, Glasgow, 1981-84; Senior Registrar in Pathology, Western Infirmary, Glasgow, 1984-89. Recreations: bibliomania; Celtology. Address: (h.) 8 Calderwood Road, Newlands, Glasgow G43 2RP.

McLellan, James Alexander, LLB. Chief Executive, Argyll and Bute Council, since 1995 (Director of Administration, Argyll and Bute District Council, 1978-95); b. 23.12.50, Lochgilphead; m., Alexis; 2 s.; 1 d. Educ. Keil School; Glasgow University. Recreations: fishing; gardening. Address: (b.) Kilmory, Lochgilphead, Argyll PA31 8RT; T.-01546 602127.

McLellan, John Crawford, BA. Editor, Edinburgh Evening News, since 1997; b. 8.2.62, Glasgow; m., Patricia; 1 s.; 1 d. Educ. Hutchesons' Grammar School; Stirling University; Preston Polytechnic. Chester Observer, 1984-86; NW Evening Mail, 1987-90; The Journal, Newcastle, 1990-93; Edinburgh Evening News, since 1993. Recreations: rugby; football; opera; listening to country and western music. Address: (b.) 108 Holyrood Road, Edinburgh, EH8 8AS; T.-01310620 8702.

Maclennan of Rogart, Rt. Hon. Lord (Robert Adam Ross Maclennan), PC. MP (Lib. Dem.), Caithness, Sutherland and Easter Ross, 1999-2001 (MP, Caithness and Sutherland, 1966-99); Barrister-at-Law; b. 26.6.36, Glasgow; m., Helen Cutter Noyes; 2 s.; 1 d. Educ. Glasgow Academy; Balliol College, Oxford; Trinity College, Cambridge; Columbia University, New York. Parliamentary Private Secretary to Secretary of State for Commonwealth Affairs, 1967; Opposition Spokesman on Scottish Affairs and Defence, 1970; Parliamentary Under-Secretary of State, Department of Prices and Consumer Protection, 1974-79; Opposition Spokesman on Foreign Affairs, 1979; Member, Public Accounts Committee, 1979-99; Founder Member, SDP, 1981; Parliamentary Spokesman on Agriculture, 1981, Home Affairs, 1983, Economic Affairs, 1987; elected Leader, SDP, 1987; President, Liberal Democrats, 1994-98. Recreations: music; theatre; visual arts. Address: (b.) House of Lords, London SW1A 0PW; T.-020 7219 6553.

MacLennan, Professor Alexander Hope, BSc, PhD, PGCE, CChem, FRSC, FRSA. Assistant Principal and Director, University of Paisley, University Campus, Ayr, since 1999; b. 17.3.53, Glasgow; m., Alison. Educ. Bellahouston Academy; Paisley College of Technology. Research and Development Chemist, CIBA Geigy, 1979; Development Chemist, Glaxo, 1983; Paisley College: Lecturer in Organic Chemistry, 1985, CATS Co-ordinator, Credit Accumulation and Transfer Scheme, 1990, Director, CATS Unit, 1991; Director of CATS and Continuing Education, University of Paisley, 1993; Head, Department of Continuing Education, 1995; Director of Corporate Communications, 1996-99. Director, Scottish Enterprise Ayrshire, since 2001. Recreations: golf; curling; wine. Address: (b.) University of Paisley, University Campus Ayr, Beech Grove, Ayr KA8 0SR; T.-01292 886213; e-mail: a.maclennan@paisley.ac.uk

MacLennan, David Peter Hugh, LLB (Hons), WS, NP. Secretary, Edinburgh Legal Dispensary, since 1988; Member, Advisory Council on Messengers-at-Arms and Sheriff Officers, since 1993; Past President, Scottish Law Agents Society, 1998-99; b. 6.9.47, Edinburgh; m., Joan Isobel; 2 s.; 1 d. Educ. Edinburgh Academy; Edinburgh University. Apprentice Solicitor/Assistant Solicitor, 1969-73; admitted as a Solicitor, 1971; Assistant Solicitor/Partner, Balfour & Manson, Edinburgh, since 1973; Solicitor to the Society of Messengers-at-Arms and Sheriff Officers; Elder, Gorgie Parish Church, and Member, Edinburgh Presbytery; Director, Edinburgh City Mission; Member, Westray Buildings Preservation Trust; Honorary Member, Clan Gregor Society. Recreations: hill-walking; swimming; cycling; genealogy; enjoying the county of Sutherland. Address: (b.) 54-66 Frederick Street, Edinburgh EH2 1LS; T.-0131-200 1215; e-mail: davidmaclennan@balfour-manson.co.uk

MacLennan, Dolina. Actress; writer; bed and breakfast landlady; b. 1.1.38, Marvig, Isle of Lewis; 2 d. Educ. Planasker School; Nicolson Institute; Occupational Therapy College, Edinburgh. Began career as teacher of handicapped children; various projects with BBC Radio and Television; founding member, 7:84 Theatre Company, Scotland; Founder Member, The Heretics; wrote first Gaelic soap Na Moireasdanaich; devised, with Stuart Hopps, Scottish Ballet's An Clo Mov; recorded tape of short stories, Wait Till I Tell You; involved in local tourism. Recreations: preparing Scottish food; reading; laughing; enjoying good company. Address: (h.) Woodlands, St Andrews Crescent, Blair Atholl, Perthshire, PH18 5SX; T.-01796 481403.

MacLennan, Donald. President, Scottish Crofters Union, since 2000; Director, Heather Isle Meats Ltd, since 1993; Director, Lewis and Harris Auction Mart, since 1998; b. 7.4.35, Isle of Lewis; m., Joan; 2 s.; Educ. Barvas Public School; Nicolson Institute; Lewis Castle College; Inverness Technical College. Apprentice Electrician; Telegraph Technician; Hydro-Electric: District Linesman; Power Station Electrician; Electrical Engineer; Chairman, Brue Grazings Committee; President, Westside Agriculture Society; Member, Bravas and Brue 2000 Group. Recreations: angling; walking; gardening. Address: (h.) 32 Torquil Terrace, Stornoway, HS1 2HN; T.-0185170 3264; e-mail: donald.maclennan1@btinternet.com

McLennan, John Alan, DipArch (Glas), RIBA, FRIAS, FASI, MCIArb, MAPS, MAPM, ACIOB. Partner, The McLennan Partnership, since 1981; b. 29.3.50, Rutherglen; m., Jemima; 1 d. Educ. Rutherglen Academy; Glasgow University. John Drummond and Partners, Glasgow, 1977-81. Past President, Glasgow Institute of Architects; Past Deacon, Incorporation of Tailors of Rutherglen; Member, Council, RIAS. Recreations: rugby; football; squash; skiing; bowling; gardening. Address: Burnside House, Beech Avenue, High Burnside, Glasgow G73 4RJ; T.-0141-634 3322.

MacLeod, Alasdair Fraser, MA (Hons). Editor, Scottish Parliamentary Unit, BBC Scotland, since 1999; b. 11.1.64, Inverness; m., Catriona Murray; 1 s.; 2 d. Educ. Millburn Academy, Inverness; Glasgow University. BBC Scotland: trainee journalist, Radio Nan Gaidheal, 1986; Researcher, Gaelic television, 1987; Producer, Radio Nan Gaidheal, 1988; Producer, Radio Scotland, 1990; Senior Producer, Radio Scotland, 1993; Editor, weekly programmes, News and Current Affairs, 1994 (Editor, Election Night, 1997, Scotland Decides, 1997, Election '99, Election Night, 2001). Member, Scottish Parliament Advisory Committee on Broadcasting. Address: (b.) Media Centre, Scottish Parliament, Edinburgh EH99 1SP; T.-0131-248 4019.

MacLeod, Ally; b. 1931, Glasgow. Played for Third Lanark, St. Mirren, Blackburn, Hibernian, Ayr United; Manager, Ayr United, Aberdeen, Motherwell, Airdrie, Queen of the South; led Scotland to World Cup, Argentina, 1978.

MacLeod, Andrew Kenneth, BA. Head, Employment and Welfare to Work Division, Scottish Executive Enterprise and Lifelong Learning Department; b. 28.3.50, Elgin; m., Sheila Janet; 2 d. Educ. Fettes College, Edinburgh; St. John's College, Oxford. Harvard College, Oxford, 1971-74; National Economic Development Office, 1974-78; Economic Adviser, Manpower Services Commission, Office for Scotland, 1978-83; Economic Adviser/Principal, Scottish Office, 1983-90; Head, Fisheries Division III, 1990-91; Chief Executive, Scottish Fisheries Protection Agency, 1991-95. Address: (b.) Meridian Court, 5 Cadogan Street, Glasgow G2 6AT; T.-0141-242 5895; e-mail: andrew.macleod@scotland.gsi.gov.uk

MacLeod, Calum Alexander, CBE, MA, LLB, LLD. Chairman: Grampian Television, since 1993, Aberdeen Development Capital PLC, since 1986, Albyn of Stonehaven Ltd., since 1973; Deputy Chairman: Martin Currie Portfolio Investment Trust PLC, since 1999, Scottish Media Group plc, since 1997; Director, Macdonald Hotels plc, since 1995; b. 25.7.35, Stornoway; m., Elizabeth M. Davidson; 2 s.; 1 d. Educ. Nicolson Institute; Glenurquhart High School; Aberdeen University. Partner, Paull & Williamsons, Advocates, Aberdeen, 1964-80; Member, White Fish Authority, 1973-80; Member: North of Scotland Hydro-Electric Board, 1976-84, Highlands and Islands Development Board, 1984-91; Chancellor's Assessor, Aberdeen University, 1979-90; Chairman of Governors, Robert Gordon's College, 1981-94; Chairman, Scottish Council of Independent Schools, 1991-97; Chairman, Grampian Health Board, 1993-2000; Chairman, Britannia Building Society PLC, 1994-1999, North Board Member, Bank of Scotland, 1980-2000; Trustee, Carnegie Trust for the Universities of Scotland, since 1997; Governor, UHI Millennium Institute, since 2000. Recreations: golf; fishing; Hebridean coastal walking; reading; music. Address: (b.) Grampian Television, Queen's Cross, Aberdeen AB15 4XJ; T.-01224 846600.

Macleod, Rev. Professor Donald, MA. Professor of Systematic Theology, since 1978, and Principal, since 1999, Free Church College; Editor, The Monthly Record, 1977-90; Vagrant Preacher, since 1978; Chairman, Thomas Chalmers Housing Association; b. 24.11.40, Ness, Isle of Lewis; m., Mary Maclean; 3 s. Educ. Nicolson Institute, Stornoway; Glasgow University; Free Church College. Ordained Guy Fawkes Day, 1964; Minister: Kilmallie Free Church, 1964-70, Partick Highland Free Church, Glasgow, 1970-78. Recreation: paranoia.

Macleod, Donald Angus David, MB, ChB, FRCS Edin, FRCPEdin, DipSpMed, FISM. Consultant General Surgeon, since 1976; Vice President, Royal College of Surgeons of Edinburgh, 2000-03; b. 4.3.41, Selkirk; m., Lucile Janette Kirkpatrick; 1 s.; 2 d. Educ. Gordonstoun; Edinburgh University. Chairman, Lothian Health Board Basic Surgical

Training Committee, 1986-91; Director of Studies (Surgery), Edinburgh Postgraduate Board for Medicine, 1976-86; Chairman: Scottish Committee, Medical Commission for Accident Prevention, 1980-85, West Lothian Medical Staff Committee, 1986-89; Member, West Lothian Unit Management Team, 1987-89; appointed Hon. Medical Adviser, Scottish Rugby Union, 1969; appointed Member, International Rugby Football Board Medical Advisory Committee, 1978; Vice-Chairman, Medical Advisory Committee, 13th Commonwealth Games, Scotland, 1984-86; Chairman, Sports Medicine and Sports Science Consultative Group, Scottish Sports Council, 1990-93; appointed Associate Post Graduate Dean, Lister Post Graduate Institute, 1993; Chairman, Intercollegiate Board for General Surgery, UK and Ireland, 1995-98, Intercollegiate Basic Surgical Training and Examinations Committee, UK and Ireland, 1996-2000; Intercollegiate Academic Board for Sport and Exercise Medicine, UK and Ireland, 1998-2002; President, British Association of Sport and Medicine, 1996-2002; awarded Robert Atkins Award for services to sports medicine, 1992; Honorary Professor of Sports Medicine, Aberdeen University, since 1998. Recreation: orienteering. Address: (h.) Newhope, Nether Phawhope, Ettrick, Selkirkshire TD7 5JD.

MacLeod, Donald Ian Kerr, RD—, MA, LLB, WS. Partner, Shepherd & Wedderburn, WS, since 1964; b. 19.4.37, Edinburgh; m., Mary St. Clair Bridge; 1 s.; 2 d. Educ. Aberdeen Grammar School; Aberdeen University; Edinburgh University. Apprentice, MacPherson & Mackay, WS, 1957-60; Assistant, Shepherd & Wedderburn, 1960-64; Solicitor in Scotland to HM Customs and Excise and Department for Education and Employment, since 1970, and Health and Safety Executive, since 1974. Lt.-Cdr. RNR (Retd.); Member, Court of Session Rules Council; Governor, Rannoch School; Church Elder. Recreations: hockey; golf; walking. Address: (b.) Saltire Court, Castle Terrace, Edinburgh EH1 2ET; T.-0131-228 9900.

MacLeod, Duncan James, CBE; b. 1.11.34, Edinburgh; m., Joanna Bibby; 2 s.; 1 d. Educ. Eton College. Partner, Brown, Fleming and Murray, Glasgow (now Ernst and Young), 1960; Managing Partner, Ernst and Whinney, Glasgow, 1985-89; Director: Hunterston Development Co. Ltd., since 1983, Macleod Hotels Ltd., since 1960, de Jersey Co. Ltd., since 1991, Gartmore SNT Plc, since 1998, Bank of Scotland, 1973-91, Scottish Provident Institution, 1976-2001, Weir Group Plc, 1976-97, Motherwell Bridge Holdings Ltd., 1990-2001. DUniv (Stirling). Recreations: golf; shooting; fishing. Address: Monkredding House, Kilwinning; T.-01294 552336.

McLeod, Fiona Grace, MA, DipLib, ALA. MSP (SNP), West of Scotland, since 1999; b. 3.12.57, Glasgow; m., Dr A.D. Rankine; 1 s. Educ. Bearsden Academy; Edinburgh University; Glasgow University; Strathclyde University. School Librarian, Balfron High School, 1983-87; College Librarian, Glasgow North College of Nursing, 1987-90; Librarian, Huntershill Marie Curie Centre, 1995-98. Convener, Bearsden West Community Council. Recreations: visiting Scottish castles; walking. Address: (b.) Scottish Parliament, Edinburgh EH99 1SP; T.-0131-348 5669.

McLeod, Graeme, MBChB, MRCGP, FRCA. Consultant Anaesthetist, since 1995; Senior Lecturer in Anaesthesia, since 1998; b. 9.8.60, Kirkcaldy; partner, Susan Johnson; 1 s.; 2 d. Educ. Kirkcaldy High School; Edinburgh Medical School. General practice training, 1984-87; anaesthesia training, 1987-95. Publications: research papers, reviews, chapters on the use of epidurals after major surgery and in labour, and mode of action of local anaesthetics. Recreations: golf; cycling. Address: (b.) University Department of Anaesthesia, Ninewells Hospital Medical School, Dundee; T.-01382 660111, ext. 33660; e-mail: g.a.mcleod@dundee.ac.uk

MacLeod, Professor Iain Alasdair, BSc, PhD, CEng, FICE, FIStructE, FRSA. Professor of Structural Engineering, Strathclyde University, since 1981; b. 4.5.39, Glasgow; m., Barbara Jean Booth; 1 s.; 1 d. Educ. Lenzie Academy; Glasgow University. Design Engineer, Crouch and Hogg, Glasgow, 1960-62; Assistant Lecturer in Civil Engineering, Glasgow University, 1962-66; Design Engineer, H.A. Simons Ltd., Vancouver, 1966-67; Structural Engineer, Portland Cement Association, Illinois, 1968-69; Lecturer in Civil Engineering, Glasgow University, 1969-73; Professor and Head, Department of Civil Engineering, Paisley College of Technology, 1973-81; Chairman, Scottish Branch, Institution of Structural Engineers, 1985-86; Vice-President, Institution of Structural Engineers, 1989-90; Member, Standing Committee on Structural Safety, 1989-97. Recreations: climbing; sailing. Address: (b.) Department of Civil Engineering, Strathclyde University, 107 Rottenrow, Glasgow; T.-0141-548 3275.

McLeod, Ian, DA, RSW. Artist; Tutor in Drawing and Painting (part-time), Glenrothes College, since 1994; b. 27.6.39, Port Glasgow; m., Mary N. B. Rintoul; 1 s.; 1 d. Educ. Kirkcaldy High School; Burntisland Secondary School; Edinburgh College of Art; Regent Road Institute for Adult Education; Moray House Institute of Education. Welder, Burntisland Shipbuilding Co., Fife, 1954-61; Teacher of Art, Auchmuty High School, Fife, 1967-90; 10 one-man exhibitions; various Scottish Arts Council exhibitions including: Scottish Realism: Bellany, Crozier, Gillon, McLeod and Moffat, 1971, Facts and Fantasy, 1972, Expressionism in Scottish Painting, 1977; over 50 group exhibitions; work in private and public collections. Elected: SSA, 1968, GLA, 1978, RSW, 1996. Recreations: people; books; all kinds of music, especially popular 30s and 40s; left-wing politics; detesting New Labour; hoping for an independent Scotland in his lifetime; gentle hillwalking. Address: (h.) 33 Craigkennochie Terrace, Burntisland, Fife KY3 9EN; T.-01592 873440.

Macleod, Iseabail Campbell, MA. Editorial Director, Scottish National Dictionary Association Ltd., since 1986; b. 27.5.36, Glasgow. Educ. Clydebank High School; Lenzie Academy; Glasgow University. Teacher, 1958-64; Editorial Assistant, Europa Publications, 1965-66; Editor of bilingual dictionaries, Collins, Glasgow, 1966-74; Dictionaries Editor, Editorial Director, W. & R. Chambers, Edinburgh, 1974-77. Publications: Pocket Guide to Scottish Words, 1986; Pocket Scots Dictionary (Co-Editor), 1988; Scots Thesaurus (Co-Editor), 1990; Concise English-Scots Dictionary (Co-Editor), 1993; Scots School Dictionary (Co-Editor), 1996; Edinburgh Pocket Guide, 1996. Recreations: hill-walking; cooking; languages; music. Address: (h.) 11 Scotland Street, Edinburgh EH3 6PU; T.-0131-556 5683.

Macleod, Professor James Summers, LLM, CA, FTII. Professor, Faculty of Law, Edinburgh University, since 1986; Chairman: Martin Currie High Income Trust PLC, Collective Assets Trust plc; Director: Invesco Geared Opportunities Trust PLC, British Assets Trust plc; b. 3.8.41, Dumfries; m., Sheila Stromier (deceased); 2 s.; 1 d. Educ. Dumfries Academy; Glasgow University. Lecturer, Edinburgh University, 1965-68; Lecturer, Heriot Watt University, 1968-71; joined Arthur Young (now Ernst & Young), 1971; Partner, Ernst & Young, Edinburgh, 1973-98. Publications: Taxation of Insurance Business (Co-author), 4th edition, 1998; 250 papers. Recreations: bridge; music; reading. Address: (h.) 2 Bonaly Road, Edinburgh; T.-0131-441 4144.

MacLeod of MacLeod, John. 29th Chief of Clan MacLeod; b. 10.8.35; m.; 1 s.; 1 d. Educ. Eton. Address: Dunvegan Castle, Isle of Skye.

Macleod, John Alasdair Johnston, DL, FRCGP, FRCP (Glas), DCH, DObsRCOG. General Practitioner, North Uist, 1973-2000; Secretary, Western Isles Local Medical Committee (GP), 1977-91; Deputy Lieutenant, Western Isles, since 1979; Director, Taigh Chearsabhagh Trust, since 2000; Chairman, Comann na Mara, since 2001; b. 20.1.35, Stornoway; m., Lorna Jean Ferguson; 2 s.; 1 d. Educ. Nicolson Institute; Keil School; Glasgow University. National Service, Royal Navy, 1957-59; hospital posts, Glasgow and London, 1963-73; Non-Executive Director, Olscot Ltd., 1969-93; trainer in general practice, 1975-95; Visiting Professor: Department of Family Medicine, University of North Carolina, 1985, University of Western Ontario, Canada, 1998; Visiting Lecturer, Middlebury College, Vermont, USA, 1998; Honorary Life Member, World Organisation of National Colleges Academique of Family Practice, since 2001 (Member, since 1989, Member, WONCA World Group "Recruitment for Rural Practice", since 1992); Member, General Practitioner Writers Association, since 1986 (Winner, GPWA Writer, 2000). Member, Committee of North Uist Highland Gathering; Fellow, Royal Society of Medicine; Admiralty Surgeon and Agent, 1974-91; author of papers and articles, singly and jointly, on aspects of isolated practice. Recreations: boating; horticulture; photography; time-sharing. Address: (h.) Tigh-Na-Hearradh, Lochmaddy, Isle of North Uist HS6 5AE; T.-01876 500224.

Macleod, John Francis Matheson, MA, LLB, NP. Solicitor in Inverness, 1959-94; b. 24.1.32, Inverness; m., Alexandra Catherine; 1 s. Educ. Inverness Royal Academy; George Watson's College; Edinburgh University. Solicitor, Fife County Council, 1957-59; in private practice, 1959-94; Parliamentary candidate (Liberal): Moray and Nairn, 1964, Western Isles, 1966; Chairman, Highland Region, Scottish Liberal Party, until 1978; former Vice-Chairman, Broadcasting Council for Scotland; Dean, Faculty of Solicitors of the Highlands, 1988-91; Chairman, Crofters Commission, 1978-86; Member, Council, Law Society of Scotland, 1988-92; Chairman of Council, Gaelic Society of Inverness, 1996-97; Vice-Chairman, National Trust for Scotland's Culloden Advisory Committee. Address: (h.) Bona Lodge, Aldourie, Inverness; T.-01463 751327.

MacLeod, John Murray, MA (Hons). Writer at large; Columnist, The Herald, since 1991; Columnist, Stornoway Gazette, 2001; b. 15.4.66, Kilmallie, Inverness-shire. Educ. Jordanhill College School, Glasgow; James Gillespie's High School, Edinburgh; Edinburgh University. Freelance journalist and broadcaster, since 1988; Scottish Journalist of the Year, 1991; Young Scottish Journalist of the Year, 1991-92; Commended, Columnist of the Year, 1992; Commended, Feature Writer of the Year, 1996; nominated Columnist of the Year, 1999, 2001; Columnist of the Year, UK Press Gazette Regional Newspaper Awards, 1996. Publications: No Great Mischief If You Fall – The Highland Experience, 1993; Highlanders – A History of the Gaels, 1996; Dynasty – The Stuarts 1560-1807, 1999. Recreations: Dr. Who; tennis; poaching; meeting the boat; unrequited love. Address: (h.) Twin Peaks, Scott Road, Tarbert, Isle of Harris HS3 3DL; T.-01859 50 2187; e-mail: johnnyjourno@madasafish.com

MacLeod, Lorne Buchanan, BA, CA. Self-employed Chartered Accountant; b. 13.4.63, Oban. Educ. Oban High School; University of Strathclyde. Ernst and Whinney, Inverness, 1983-87; Highlands and Islands Development Board, 1987-92; Chief Executive, Skye and Lochalsh Enterprise, 1992-98; Director of Strengthening Communities, Highlands and Islands Enterprise, 1998-2000. Director, Comunn na Gaidhlig, 1998-2000; Director, Highlands and Islands Screen Services Ltd., 1998-2000; Director, Jansvans Ltd., Isle of Skye, since 2001; Board Member, Community Fund, since 2001; Council Member, Scottish Further Education Funding Council, since 2001. Winston Churchill Travelling Fellowship, 1997.

Recreations: hillwalking; sailing. Address: 9 Kilmartin Court, Shore Street, Oban, PA34 4NT; e-mail: lorne.macleod@ecosse.net

McLeod, Professor Malcolm Donald, MA, BLitt (Oxon), FRSE. Vice-Principal, External Relations and Marketing, University of Glasgow, since 1999; Director, Hunterian Museum and Art Gallery, Glasgow University, 1990-99; Chairman, Scottish Museums Council, 1996-2001; Trustee, The Hunterian Collection, London, since 1998; Curator, The Royal Society of Edinburgh; b. 19.5.41, Edinburgh; m., I.V. Barry; 2 s.; 1 d. Educ. Birkenhead School; Hertford and Exeter Colleges, Oxford. Research Assistant, Institute of Social Anthropology, Oxford, 1964-65; Lecturer, Sociology Department, University of Ghana, 1967-69; Assistant Curator, Museum of Archaeology and Ethnology, Cambridge, 1969-74; College Lecturer and Director of Studies, Magdalene and Girton Colleges, Cambridge, 1969-74; Fellow, Magdalene College, 1972-74; Keeper of Ethnography, British Museum, 1974-90; Honorary Lecturer, Department of Anthropology, UCL, 1976-81; Honorary Lecturer, Department of Archaeology, University of Glasgow, since 1992. Publications: The Asante, 1981; Treasures of African Art, 1981; Ethnic Sculpture (Co-author), 1985; Jacob Epstein Collector (Co-author), 1989. Address: (h.) Tweediemill, Sandford, Strathaven ML10 6PL.

Macleod, Mary Elizabeth, LLB (Hons), DipLP, NP. Depute Solicitor of the Church of Scotland, since 1995; b. 23.12.63, Stornoway. Educ. Nicolson Institute, Stornoway; Edinburgh University. Trainee Solicitor, Anderson, Shaw and Gilbert, Inverness, 1986-88; Assistant: Morton, Fraser and Milligan, WS, Edinburgh, 1988-90, Skene, Edwards and Garson, W. S., Edinburgh, 1990-92, Campbell Smith, Edinburgh, 1992-95. Recreations: travel; music; reading. Address: (b.) 121 George Street, Edinburgh EH2 4YN; T.-0131-225 5722.

Macleod, Murdoch, MBE, JP. Honorary Sheriff; b. 11.8.32, Shawbost, Isle of Lewis; m., Crisybil; 1 s.; 1 d. Educ. Nicolson Institute, Stornoway. Ross and Cromarty Council: Highways Department, 1955-57, Education Department, 1957-65; Stornoway Town Council: Town Clerk's Department, 1965-68, Town Clerk, 1968-75; General Manager, Secretary and Treasurer, Stornoway Pier and Harbour Commission, 1975-96. Former Deputy Chairman, Transport Users Consultative Committee for Scotland; Past Chairman, District Courts Association; Past Chairman, Western Isles Justices Committee; former Member, Council, British Ports Asssociation; former Chairman, Scottish Port Members, British Ports Association; former Deputy Chairman, British Ports Federation; former Director, Western Isles Development Fund Ltd.; Honorary President, Lewis Pipe Band; former Member, British Airways Consumer Council for Highlands and Islands; Trustee, Scottish Hydro Electric Community Trust; Past Chairman, League of Friends, Stornoway Hospitals and Homes; Chairman, Stornoway Historical Society. Recreations: reading; local history. Address: (h.) 46 Barony Square, Stornoway, Isle of Lewis; T.-01851 703024.

MacLeod, Sheriff Principal Norman Donald, QC, MA, LLB. Sheriff Principal of Glasgow and Strathkelvin, 1986-97; b. 6.3.32, Perth; m., Ursula Jane Bromley; 2 s.; 2 d. Educ. Mill Hill School; George Watson's Boys College; Edinburgh University; Hertford College, Oxford. Called to the Bar, 1956; District Officer and Crown Counsel, Colonial Service, East Africa, 1957-63; at the Bar, 1963-67; Sheriff at Glasgow, 1967-86; Commissioner, Northern Lighthouse Board, 1986-97 (Chairman, 1990-91); Honorary Sheriff, North Strathclyde. Recreation: rustic pursuits. Address: (h.) Calderbank, Lochwinnoch, Renfrewshire PA12 4DU; T.-01505 843340; e-mail: normanandjane@cs.com

MacLeod, Peter, MCIBS. Retired Banker; yachting journalist; Honorary Sheriff of North Strathclyde at Oban, since 1988; b. 9.6.33, Ruaig, Isle of Tiree; m., Jean MacDonald Buchanan; 2 s. Educ. Oban High School. Served as Captain, Royal Signals, AER; joined Royal Bank of Scotland, 1949; Bank Manager: Tobermory, Kinlochleven, Wick, Oban. Trustee and Past Commodore, Royal Highland Yacht Club; Past Chairman and Founder Treasurer, Oban Round Table; Founder Chairman, West Highland Anchorages and Moorings Association. Publication: History of Royal Highland Yacht Club, 1881-1999. Recreations: sailing; island wandering; impromptu ceilidhs; beachcombing. Address: (h.) The Wheelhouse, Ganavan, Oban, Argyll; T.-01631 563577.

MacLeod, Rev. Roderick, MA (Hons), BD, PhD (Edin), PhD (Open). Minister, Cumlodden, Lochfyneside and Lochgair, Argyll, since 1985; b. 24.6.41, Lochmaddy. Educ. Paible Secondary School; Portree High School; Edinburgh University. Minister, Berneray, North Uist, 1966-85; Member: Western Isles Islands Council, 1974-82, Western Isles Health Board, 1975-79; Clerk, Uist Presbytery, 1981-85; Mackinnon Memorial Lecturer, Cape Breton College, 1979; Visiting Scholar, Harvard Divinity School, 1981; Editor, Gaelic Supplement, Life and Work, since 1980; Depute Clerk, Presbytery of South Argyll, since 1995; President, Scottish Gaelic Texts Society, since 1996; Founder, Cruisgean (Gaelic newspaper); author of several Gaelic books; writes and broadcasts on Highland affairs in Gaelic and English. Recreations: walking; shinty. Address: Furnace, Inveraray, Argyll, PA32 8XU.

Macleod, Rev. William, BSc, ThM. Minister, Portree Free Church, since 1993; Editor, Free Church Witness; b. 2.11.51, Stornoway; m., Marion; 2 s.; 1 d. Educ. Aberdeen University; Free Church College; Westminster Seminary. Minister, Partick Free Church, Glasgow, 1976-93. Editor, Free Church Foundations, 1997-2000. Chairman, Portree High School Board. Recreations: gardening; fishing; reading. Address: (h.) Portree Free Church Manse, Staffin Road, Portree, Isle of Skye; T.-01478 612678; e-mail: w@wmacleod.freeserve.co.uk

McLernan, Sheriff Kieran Anthony, KCHS, MA, LLB. Sheriff of Grampian Highlands and Islands at Banff and Peterhead, since 1991; b. 29.4.41, Wemyss Bay; m., Joan Doherty; 1 s.; 3 d. Educ. St. Aloysius College, Glasgow; Glasgow University. Solicitor, 1965-91; Temporary Sheriff, 1986-91; Tutor, Glasgow University, 1987-91.

McLetchie, David William, LLB (Hons), WS. MSP (Conservative), Lothians, since 1999; Leader, Scottish Conservative Parliamentary Group; b. 6.8.52, Edinburgh; m., 1, Barbara Gemmell Baillie (deceased); 1 s.; 2, Sheila Elizabeth Foster. Educ. George Heriot's School; Edinburgh University. Solicitor; Partner, Tods Murray WS, since 1980. President, Scottish Conservative and Unionist Association, 1994-97. Recreations: golf; football (Heart of Midlothian); rock and pop music. Address: (b.) The Scottish Parliament, Edinburgh EH99 1SP; T.-0131-348 5659.

McMahon, Hugh Robertson, MA (Hons), FEIS. Member (Labour), European Parliament, Strathclyde West, 1984-99; Scottish Political Editor, World-Parliamentarian Magazine, since 1999; b. 17.6.38, Saltcoats; m., Helen Paterson Grant; 1 s.; 1 d. Educ. Stevenson High School; Ardrossan Academy; Glasgow University. Schoolteacher in Ayrshire (Largs High, Stevenston High, Irvine Royal Academy, Mainholm Academy); Assistant Head, Ravenspark Academy, 1971-84. Vice-Chair, EP Social Affairs, Employment and Working Environment Committee, 1992-94; Member, Social Affairs, Fisheries and Transport Committees; Chair, EP Delegation with Norway, 1989-92; currently Member, Delegation with Czechoslovakia. Recreation: golf. Address: (b.) 9 Low Road, Castlehead, Paisley PA2 6AQ.

MacMahon, Rev. Janet P.H., BD, MSc, LCST, LLCM. Chaplaincy Co-ordinator, Southern General Hospital, Glasgow, since 1992; b. 31.5.44, Glasgow; m.., Professor M.K.C. MacMahon (qv); 1 s.; 1 d. Educ. Glasgow High School for Girls; Glasgow University; Glasgow School of Speech Therapy. Senior Speech Therapist, 1965-80; Chief Speech Therapist, Greater Glasgow Health Board, 1980-82; Senior Speech Therapist, Scottish Council for Spastics, 1983-85; Assistant Minister, Cairns Church, Milngavie, and Govan Old Church, 1989-90; Research and Development Officer in special educational needs, Department of Education, Church of Scotland, 1990-92. Publications include: Walk in God's Ways, 1993. Recreations: reading crime novels; watching TV soaps. Address: (h.) 6 Jubilee Gardens, Bearsden, Glasgow G61 2RT; T.-0141-942 3671.

McMahon, Michael, BA (Hons). MSP (Labour), Hamilton North and Bellshill, since 1999; m.; 1 s.; 2 d. Educ. Our Lady's High School, Motherwell. Worked as a welder before leaving to go to university; then pursued a career in social and political research. Address: (b.) Parliamentary Advice Office, 188 Main Street, Bellshill, Lanarkshire ML4 1AE; T.-01698 304501.

MacMahon, Professor Michael Kenneth Cowan, BA, PhD, DipLing. Professor of Phonetics, Glasgow University, since 1997; b. 7.8.43, Winchester; m.., Rev. Janet P.H. MacMahon (qv); 1 s.; 1 d. Educ. Hymers College, Hull; Durham University; Göttingen University; Glasgow University; Reading University. Lecturer in Phonetics and Linguistics, Jordanhill College, Glasgow, 1966-72; Lecturer in Linguistics and Phonetics, 1972-83, Lecturer in English Language, 1983-87, Senior Lecturer in English Language, 1987-97, Glasgow University. Member, Council, International Phonetic Association; Member, Executive Committee, Henry Sweet Society; Archivist and Secretary, British Association of Academic Phoneticians. Publications numerous. Recreations: singing; flute-playing. Address: (h.) 6 Jubilee Gardens, Bearsden, Glasgow G61 2RT; T.-0141-942 3671; e-mail: m.macmahon@englang.arts.gla.ac.uk

McManus, James John, LLB, PhD. Chairman, Parole Board for Scotland, since 2000; Senior Lecturer, University of Dundee; b. 23.6.50, Cleland; m., Catherine MacKellaig; 1 s.; 4 d. Educ. Our Lady's High School, Motherwell; University of Edinburgh; University of Dundee. Tutor, University of Edinburgh, 1972-74; Lecturer, University of Wales, 1974-76; Lecturer, then Senior Lecturer, University of Dundee, 1976-94; Scottish Prisons Complaints Commissioner, 1994-99. Expert Adviser, Council of Europe, since 1993. Publication: Prisons Prisoners and the Law, 1994. Recreations: golf; cycling. Address: (b.) Government Buildings, Broomhouse Drive, Edinburgh EH11 3XA; T.-0131-244 8755; e-mail: j.j.mcmanus@dundee.ac.uk

McManus, Professor John, DSc, PhD, ARCS, DIC, FRSE, CGeol, MIEnvSci. Professor of Geology, St. Andrews University, 1993-2001, now Emeritus Professor (Reader, 1988-93); Honorary Director, Tay Estuary Research Centre, 1979-92; b. 5.6.38, Harwich; m., J. Barbara Beveridge; 2 s.; 1 d. Educ. Harwich County High School; Imperial College, London University. Assistant, then Lecturer, St. Andrews University, 1964-67; Lecturer, Senior Lecturer, Reader, Dundee University, 1967-88; UNESCO Representative, International Commission on Continental Erosion, 1980-84 and 1986; Member: Scottish Natural Heritage East Areas Board and Scientific Advisory Committee, 1992-99, Secretary of State's Committee on Waste Discharges into the Marine Environment; President, Estuarine and Brackish Water Sciences Association, 1995-98; Member, Executive, European Union for Coastal Conservation, 1997-2000; Member, Scottish Environment Protection Agency East Region Board, since 2000; Member, Eden Estuary Nature Reserve Management Committee; former Treasurer, British Sedimentological

Research Group; Consultant on Coastal Erosion and Protection to four Regional Councils; Honorary Fellow, Royal Scottish Geographical Society, since 2001; Executive Editor, Transactions of the Royal Society of Edinburgh, Earth Sciences, 1988-95; Associate Editor, Continental Shelf Research. President: Cupar Choral Association, 1968-78, Cupar Amateur Opera, 1979-91. Recreations: music; bird-watching; swimming; stamp collecting. Address: (b.) School of Geography and Geology, Purdie Building, St. Andrews University, St. Andrews, Fife KY16 9AL.

McManus, Rev. Matthew Francis. Parish Priest, Kilwinning, and St. Palladius, Dalry; b. 22.9.40, Rutherglen. Educ. Sacred Heart High School, Girvan; St. Andrew's College, Drygrange. Ordained, 1965, Assistant Priest, St. Margaret's, Ayr; Parish Priest, New Cumnock, Kirkconnel and Sanquhar, 1976-81, Kirkcudbright, 1981-88; Chairman: Dumfries and Galloway Local Health Council, 1985-87, Castle Douglas District CAB, 1984-87, Stewartry Council of Voluntary Service, 1985-88, Stewartry School Council, 1985-87; Member, Scottish Consumer Council, 1983-90; Convenor, Association of Scottish Local Health Councils, 1983-92; Complaints Reporter, Law Society of Scotland, 1985-97; Secretary, Association of Vocations Directors of Scotland, 1987-96; Member, Ayrshire and Arran Health Council, 1988-97; Non-Executive Director, Ayshire and Arran Health Board, 1997-2001; Member, North Ayrshire Education Committee; Vice Chair, Minerva Housing Association. Address: St. Winin's, St. Winning's Lane, Kilwinning KA13 6EP; T.-Kilwinning 552276.

McMaster, Brian John, CBE. Director and Chief Executive, Edinburgh International Festival, since 1991; b. 9.5.43. General Administrator, subsequently Managing Director, W.N.O., 1976-91. Address: (b.) The Hub, Castlehill, Edinburgh EH1 2NE.

McMath, Katherine Sally, MCSP. Scottish Chief Commissioner, The Guide Association Scotland, since 1997; b. 29.10.53, Edinburgh; m., Robert Patrick John McMath; 1 s.; 1 d. Educ. Lansdowne House School, Edinburgh; School of Physiotherapy, Royal Infirmary, Edinburgh. Chartered Physiotherapist. County Commissioner, West Lothian Guide Association, 1990-96; Scottish Guide Public Relations Adviser, 1987-90. Recreations: choral singing; music; badminton; tennis. Address: (b.) Scottish Guide HQ, 16 Coates Crescent, Edinburgh EH3 7AH; T.-0131-226 4511; e-mail: ksmcmath@aol.com

McMenamin, Frances Jane, QC, BA, LLB. Queen's Counsel, since 1998; b. 21.5.51, Glasgow; m., Ian McCarry. Educ. Notre Dame High School, Glasgow; Strathclyde University. Legal apprenticeship, Hughes, Dowdall & Co., Solicitors, Glasgow, 1974-76; Procurator Fiscal Depute, 1976-84; devilling at Scottish Bar, 1984-85; admitted, Faculty of Advocates, 1985; Junior Counsel practising in criminal law, 1985-98; Temporary Sheriff, 1991-97; Advocate Depute, 1997-2000; criminal defence work, since 2000; Visiting Lecturer, Scottish Police College, Tulliallan, since 1991. Member, Strathclyde University Law School Advisory Panel, since 2000. Recreations: reducing stress levels in the gym and increasing them on the golf course; reading; travelling with her husband. Address: (h.) 59 Hamilton Drive, Glasgow G12 8DP; T.-0141-339 0519; (b.) Advocates Library, Parliament House, Edinburgh EH1 1RF; T.-0131-226 5071.

McMicking, Major David John, LVO, MSc. Consultant, Human Resources/Sporting, since 1986; b. 29.4.39, Jerusalem; m., Janetta; 1 s.; 1 d. Educ. Eton; RMA, Sandhurst; Strathclyde University. Career soldier, Black Watch, rising to rank of Major; left Army, 1973; executive positions, John Menzies Holdings Ltd., 1973-86; family farming interests, since 1996. Extra Equerry, Queen

Elizabeth The Queen Mother; Chairman, Officers Association Scotland; Director, Earl Haig Fund Scotland, 1997-2000; Secretary, Friends of St. Andrew's, Jerusalem. Recreation: field sports. Address: (b.) Drumknock, Kilry, Blairgowrie PH11 8HR; T.-01575 560731.

Macmillan, Angus. Chief Executive, Western Isles Tourist Board; b. 3.12.55, Ness, Isle of Lewis; m., Isabel; 3 d. Educ. Govan High School, Glasgow. Address: (b.) 4 South Beach, Stornoway HS1 2XY; T.-01851 701818.

MacMillan of MacMillan and Knap, George Gordon, MA (Cantab). Chief of Clan MacMillan; Deputy Lieutenant, Renfrewshire; b. 20.6.30, London; m., (Cecilia) Jane Spurgin; 2 s. Educ. Aysgarth School; Eton; Trinity College, Cambridge. Schoolmaster, Wellington College, 1953-63; Lecturer, Trinity College, Toronto, 1963-64; Lecturer, Bede College, Durham, 1965-74. Resides in small historic house with gardens and woods open to the public. Address: (h.) Finlaystone, Langbank, Renfrewshire PA14 6TJ; T.-01475 540285; e-mail: chief@clanmacmillan.org

Macmillan, Very Rev. Gilleasbuig Iain, MA, BD. Minister, St. Giles', The High Kirk of Edinburgh, since 1973.

Macmillan, Gerard Patrick, MA (Hons), LLB, DipLP, NP. Partner, Macmillans, Glasgow, since 1988; President, Glasgow Bar Association, since 2000; b. 13.1.58, Glasgow. Educ. St. Aloysius College; Glasgow University; Dundee University. Assistant Solicitor, RHM, Glasgow, 1986-88; part-time Lecturer in Law of Evidence, Strathclyde University, 1990-96, Tutor in Criminal Advocacy, since 1996. Former Secretary, George McLaughlin Memorial Trust; Director, CAB, Glasgow. Recreations: running; football; rugby; reading. Address: (b.) 68 St. Vincent Terrace, Glasgow G3 8DX; T.-0141-204 1904.

MacMillan, Hector. Playwright; b. 1929, Glasgow. Plays include: The Rising, 1970; The Sash, 1973.

Macmillan, Sheriff Iain Alexander, CBE, LLD, BL. Sheriff of South Strathclyde, Dumfries and Galloway, at Hamilton, 1981-92; b. 14.11.23, Oban; m., Edith Janet McAulay; 2 s.; 1 d. Educ. Oban High School; Glasgow University; Scottish Commercial College. RAF (France, Germany, India), 1944-47; Solicitor (Sturrock & Co., Kilmarnock), 1952-81; Council Member, Law Society of Scotland, 1964-79 (President, 1976-77); Vice-President (Lay), Glasgow Art Club. Recreations: golf; music. Address: (h.) 2 Castle Drive, Kilmarnock, Ayrshire; T.-01563 525864; e-mail: mick.millan@virgin.net

McMillan, Iain Macleod, FCIB, FCIBS, FFA, FIMgt, FRSA. Director, CBI Scotland, since 1995; Member, Board, Scottish Qualifications Authority; Non-Executive Director, Scottish Ambulance Service (Chairman, Audit Committee); Director, Scottish North American Business Council; Director, Young Enterprise Scotland; Member, Advisory Committee, Scottish Economic Policy Network (scotecon); b. 25.4.51, Glasgow; m., Giuseppina; 3 s. Educ. Bearsden Academy. Trainee Banker, 1970-76; TSB Group plc: Manager, 1976-89, Senior Manager, 1989-93; Assistant Director, CBI Scotland, 1993-95. Member, Scottish Advisory Board, Equal Opportunities Commission, 1995-2001; Chairman, Higher Still Employment and Training Group, 1997-2000; Member, Scottish Executive's Committee of Review into the Careers Service, 1999-2000; Trustee, The Industrial Mission. Publications: Manufacturing Matters (Co-Author), 1994; The Challenge for Government in Scotland (principal author), 1996; Scottish Manufacturing: a shared vision (Co-Author), 1997; Business and Parliaments – Partners for Prosperity (Co-Author), 1998; Towards a Prosperous Scotland (Co-

Author), 1999. Recreations: squash; walking. Address: (b.) 16 Robertson Street, Glasgow G2 8DS; T.-0141-222 2184; e-mail: iain.mcmillan@cbi.org.uk

McMillan, Professor James Francis, MA, DPhil, FRSE. Richard Pares Professor of History, Edinburgh University, since 1999; b. 10.3.48, Glasgow; m., Donatella Fischer. Educ. St Mirin's Academy, Paisley; Glasgow University; Balliol College, Oxford. Temporary Lecturer, Glasgow University, 1972-73; Lecturer/Senior Lecturer, York University, 1973-92; Professor of European History, Strathclyde University, 1992-99. Publications: books include France and Women 1789-1914: Gender Society and Politics, 2000. Recreations: theatre; opera; concerts; travel. Address: (b.) Department of History, Edinburgh University, George Square, Edinburgh EH8 9JY.

MacMillan, James Loy, BMus, PhD. Composer and Conductor; Affiliate Composer, Scottish Chamber Orchestra, since 1990; part-time Teacher, Royal Scottish Academy of Music and Drama, since 1989; Composer/Conductor, BBC Philharmonic, since 2000; Visiting Composer, Philharmonia, since 1991; Visiting Professor, University of Strathclyde, since 1997; b. 16.7.59, Kilwinning; m., Lynne; 1 s.; 2 d. Educ. Cumnock Academy; Edinburgh University; Durham University. Principal compositions: The Confession of Isobel Gowdie, London Proms, 1990; Busqueda, Edinburgh International Festival, with Diana Rigg, 1990; featured composer, Musica Nova, 1990, Huddersfield Contemporary Music Festival, 1991; Veni, Veni, Emmanuel, percussion concerto for Evelyn Glennie, London Proms, 1992; Visitatio Sepulchri, one act opera, Mayfest, 1993; Ines de Castro, for Scottish Opera, Edinburgh International Festival, 1996; The World's Ransoming, for orchestra and cor anglaise, 1996; Cello Concerto, 1996; Symphony : Vigil, 1997; featured composer, Edinburgh International Festival, 1993; recording of Tryst and The Confession of Isobel Gowdie by BBC SSO won Gramophone Award, contemporary music category, 1993; Seven Last Words, BBC TV, 1994; Raising Sparks, 1997, for chamber ensemble; String Quartet: Why Is This Night Different?, 1988; featured composer, Raising Sparks Festival, South Bank Centre, London, 1997 (South Bank Show Award for Classical Music, 1997); Evening Standard Classical Music Award, 1997 for Outstanding Artistic Achievement for Symphony: Vigil and Raising Sparks Festival. DUniv, (Paisley); DLitt (University of Strathclyde); FRASMD; HonFRIAS.

Macmillan, Professor (John) Duncan, MA, PhD, FRSA, HRSA. Professor of the History of Scottish Art, Edinburgh University; Curator, Talbot Rice Gallery and University Collections, Edinburgh University, since 1979; Hon. Keeper of Portraits, Royal College of Surgeons, Edinburgh; Art Critic, Business a.m.; b. 7.3.39, Beaconsfield; m., Vivien Rosemary Hinkley; 2 d. Educ. Gordonstoun School; St. Andrews University; London University; Edinburgh University. Lecturer, then Senior Lecturer, then Reader, Department of Fine Art, Edinburgh University. Recreation: walking. Address: (h.) 20 Nelson Street, Edinburgh; T.-0131-556 7100.

Macmillan, John Ernest Newall, LLB, NP. Managing Partner, MacRoberts Glasgow, since 1998; b. 27.9.56, Kilmarnock; m., Caroline Elizabeth; 2 s.; 2 d. Educ. Merchiston Castle School, Edinburgh; Dundee University. Apprenticeship, Bird Semple and Crawford Herron, Glasgow, 1978-80; Solicitor, J. and J. Sturrock & Co., Kilmarnock, 1980-82; Solicitor, MacRoberts Glasgow, 1982-86, Partner (Litigation and Employment), since 1986. Vice Captain, Kilmarnock (Barassie) Golf Club; Session Clerk, Fenwick Church; Trustee, St. Aloysius College Charitable Fund. Recreations: golf; skiing; bridge; travel. Address: (b.) 152 Bath Street, Glasgow; T.-0141-332 9988; e-mail: jenm@macroberts.co.uk

MacMillan, Lt. General Sir John Richard Alexander, KCB, CBE, MA, DL. Farmer; Chairman, Erskine Hospital, 1996-2000; Commissioner, Queen Victoria School, since 1993, Chairman, since 1990; b. 8.2.32, London; m., Belinda Lumley Webb; 1 s.; 2 d. Educ. Eton; Cambridge. Army officer, 1953-91; commissioned Argyll and Sutherland Highlanders; appointed Co., 1st Bn., The Gordon Highlanders, OBE, 1972, after first Northern Ireland tour; Commander 39 Bde (Belfast), 1977; appointed CBE; appointed Colonel, The Gordon Highlanders, 1978; Eastern District, 1982; GOC Scotland, 1988-91; KCB, 1988. Formerly Chairman, Board of Governors, Blairmore School; Chairman, Scottish Conservation Projects Trust. Recreations: country; rowed (Henley 1949-53, Olympics, 1952). Address: c/o Northern Bank, 9 Donegall Square North, Belfast BT1 5GJ.

McMillan, Joyce Margaret, MA (Hons), DipEd, DLitt. h.c. (Queen Margaret Univ. College). Journalist and Arts Critic; Theatre Critic and Columnist, The Scotsman, since 1998; b. 29.8.52, Paisley. Educ. Paisley Grammar School; St. Andrews University; Edinburgh University. Theatre Reviewer, BBC Radio Scotland and The Scotsman, 1979-81; Theatre Critic, Sunday Standard, 1981-83; Radio Critic, The Herald, 1983-95; Scottish Theatre Critic, The Guardian, 1984-93; Scotland on Sunday: Social/Political Columnist, 1989-97, Theatre Critic, 1993-97; Arts/Political Columnist, The Herald, 1997-98. Chair, NUJ Freelance Branch, Edinburgh; Member, National Executive Committee, NUJ, London; Member, Consultative Steering Group on the Scottish Parliament, 1998-99; Member, Scottish National Theatre Working Group, 2000-01; Council Member, Scottish Civic Forum, 2000-02; Chair, Helsinki Citizens' Assembly, Scotland. Publications: The Traverse Story, 1963-88, 1988; Charter for the Arts in Scotland, 1992. Recreations: food; drink; films; music; talking politics. Address: 8 East London Street, Edinburgh, EH7 4BH; T.-0131-557 1726.

McMillan, Lorraine Anne, BSc (Hons), MBA. Chief Executive, Scottish Enterprise Renfrewshire, since 1999; b. 12.8.61, Johnstone; m., Ian Stuart McMillan; 1 s.; 1 d. Educ. Glasgow University; Strathclyde University. Barr and Stroud, 1982-89; Scottish Development Agency, 1989-91; Dunbartonshire Enterprise, 1991-99. Address: (b.) 27 Causeyside Street, Paisley PA1 1UL; T.-0141-848 0101.

Macmillan, Maureen, MA (Hons). MSP (Labour), Highlands and Islands, since 1999; b. 1943, Oban; m.; 2 s.; 2 d. Educ. Oban High School. Co-founder, Ross-shire Women's Aid; former teacher of English. Address: (b.) Scottish Parliament, Edinburgh EH99 1SP; T.-0131-348 5766.

McMillan, Michael Dale, BSc, LLB, NP, FFCS. Managing Partner, Burnett & Reid, Solicitors, Aberdeen; Tutor (part-time), School of Law, University of Aberdeen, since 2000; b. 15.2.44, Edinburgh; m., Isobel Ross Mackie; 2 s.; 1 d. Educ. Edinburgh Academy; Edinburgh University. Partner, Macdonalds Sergeants, Solicitors, East Kilbride and Glasgow, 1971-92; Secretary: East Kilbride Chamber of Commerce, 1971-86, East Kilbride Chamber of Trade, 1971-92; Board Member, East Kilbride Development Corporation, 1979-84; Secretary, Pilgrim Legal Users' Group, 1985-92; Captain, East Kilbride Golf Club, 1979; Chairman, Strathaven Academy School Board, 1991-92; President, East Kilbride Burns Club, 1989-91; Captain, Inchmarlo Golf Club (Banchory), 1997-99; President, Deeside Musical Society, 1998-2000; Burgess of Guild, City of Aberdeen. Recreations: golf; sailing; skiing. Address: (h.) Belnies, Strachan, Banchory, Aberdeenshire AB31 6LU; T.-01330 850249.

McMillan, Professor Thomas Murray, BSc, MAppSci, PhD, FBPsS. Professor of Clinical Neuropathology, Glasgow University, since 1999; Adviser to Greater Glasgow Health Board, since 1999; b. 7.3.54, Prestwick; m., Sarah Louise Wilson; 1 d. Educ. Prestwick High School; Ayr Academy; Aberdeen University; London University; Glasgow University. Lecturer in Clinical Psychology, Institute of Psychiatry, London; Head of Clinical Neuropsychology, St George's Healthcare, London; Professor of Clinical Psychology, Surrey University. Publications include: Handbook of Neurological Rehabilitation; Neurobehavioural Disability and Social Handicap. Recreations: cross-country running. Address: (b.) Department of Psychological Medicine, Gartnavel Royal Hospital, Glasgow, G12 0XH; T.-0141-211 2938.

McMillan, William Alister, BL. Solicitor, since 1955; b. 19.1.34, Ayr; m., Elizabeth Anne; 3 d. Educ. Strathallan; Glasgow University. Clerk of the Peace, County of Ayr, 1974-75; Honorary Sheriff, Ayr; Governor, Strathallan School. Recreations:sailing; golf; philately. Address: (h.) Afton Lodge, Mossblown, by Ayr; T.-01292 520 710.

Macmillan, Very Rev. William Boyd Robertson, MA, BD, HonLLD (Dundee), Hon. DD (Aberdeen). Minister, Dundee Parish Church (St. Mary's), 1978-93; Extra Chaplain to The Queen in Scotland, since 1997 (Chaplain in Ordinary to The Queen, 1988-97); b. 3.7.27, Keith; m., Mary Adams Bisset Murray. Educ. Royal High School, Edinburgh; Aberdeen University. Royal Navy, 1946-48; Aberdeen University, 1948-54 (President, SRC, 1953-54); Minister: St. Andrew's Church, Bo'ness, 1955-60, Fyvie Parish Church, 1960-67, Bearsden South Church, 1967-78. Convener, Board of Practice and Procedure, 1984-88, and of Business Committee, 1985-88, General Assembly, Church of Scotland; Moderator, General Assembly, 1991-92; Chaplain, City of Dundee District Council, 1978-93; Freeman of Dundee, 1991; Prelate, Order of St. John of Jerusalem (Scotland), 1993-96; Chairman of Directors, High School of Dundee, 1993-96; President, Scottish Church Society, 1993-97; Chairman, The Murray Home for Scottish Veterans, 1994-96; Trustee, Scottish National War Memorial, since 1994; Committee Member, Royal Society for the Relief of Indigent Gentlewomen of Scotland, since 1994. Recreations: golf; reading. Address: (h.) 3/5 Craigend Park, Edinburgh EH16 5XY.

Macmillan Douglas, Angus William, BA. National Director, Scottish Blood Transfusion Service, since 1997; b. 18.11.46, Edinburgh; m., Rosemary-Jane Meynell; 2 d. Educ. Blairmore School; Wellington College; Ealing Business School; INSEAD. Assistant UK Co-ordinator, British Petroleum International, 1981-84; Business Manager, BP Information Systems, 1984-85; European Developments Manager, BP Gas International, 1985-88; Managing Director, East Africa Trading, British Petroleum, 1988-91; Head of Political Affairs, British Petroleum Group, 1991-96. Representative, East African Trade Organisation, 1988-91; Member, Energy Policy Committee, CBI, 1992-96; Member, Management Committee, Industry and Parliament Trust, 1992-96; Member, Steering Committee, European Blood Alliance, since 1998; Chairman, Leah Healthcare Ltd.; Member, Royal Company of Archers (Queen's Bodyguard for Scotland). Recreations: family; tennis; walking. Address: (b.) Brigton, Douglastown, by Forfar DD8 1TP; T.-01307 820 215.

McMurdo, Ian David, BSc (Chem). Director of Education and Cultural Services, West Dunbartonshire Council, since 1995; Director, Community Learning, Scotland, since 2000; b. 28.5.49, Irvine; m., Agnes McMurdo; 1 s.; 1 d. Educ. Cumnock Academy; Strathclyde University. Teacher/Assistant Principal

Teacher, Chemistry; Principal Teacher, Chemistry; Assistant Head Teacher; PA, Chairman Education Committee, Strathclyde Regional Council; Education Officer, Dumbarton then Ayr Division, Strathclyde Regional Council; Director of Education; Member, ADES; Advisor, COSLA. Recreations: golf; hill walking; travelling; reading Burns. Address: (h.) 33 Hoyle Crescent, Cumnock, Ayrshire, KA18 1RX; T.-01290 421412; e-mail: ian.mcmurdo@west-dunbarton.gov.uk

McMurdo, Professor Marion Elizabeth Taylor, MBChB, MD, FRCPEdin, FRCPGlas, FRCPLond, CBiol, FIBiol. Professor of Ageing and Health, University of Dundee, since 1997; Honorary Consultant, Medicine for the Elderly, Dundee Healthcare Trust, since 1997; b. 16.11.55, Glasgow; m., Dr. Grant L. Hutchison. Educ. Marr College, Troon; University of Dundee. Deputy Medical Director, Drug Development (Scotland) Ltd., 1984-86; Lecturer in Geriatric Medicine, University of Dundee, 1986-88, Senior Lecturer/Reader in Ageing and Health, 1988-97. Member, Biomedical and Therapeutics Committee, Chief Scientist Office, since 1997; British Geriatrics Society Regional Training Adviser, since 1993. Recreations: golf; swimming; hill-walking; photography. Address: Department of Medicine, Ninewells Hospital and Medical School, Dundee DD1 9SY; T.-01382 632436.

McMurray, Professor John J.V., BSc (Hons), MBChB (Hons), MD, FRCP, FESC, FACC. Professor of Medical Cardiology, Glasgow University, since 1999; Consultant Cardiologist, Western Infirmary, Glasgow, since 1995; b. 17.12.58, Enniskillen, Co. Fermanagh; m., Christine; 4 s.; 1 d. Educ. St Patrick's College, Knock, Belfast; Manchester University. Consultant Cardiologist, Western General Hospital, Edinburgh, 1993-95. Publications: 200 medical and scientific papers; seven books. Recreations: reading; travelling. Address: (b.) Department of Cardiology, Western Infirmary, Glasgow G11 6NT; T.-0141-211 6311.

Macnab of Macnab, Hon. Mrs, DL. Honorary Vice President, Scotland's Gardens Scheme, since 1991 (Chairman, 1983-91); President, Central and North Fife Preservation Society; Deputy Lieutenant, Fife, since 1992; b. 6.6.36, Edinburgh; m., J.C. Macnab of Macnab (qv); 2 s.; 2 d. Member, Executive Committee, National Trust for Scotland, 1991-96; Chairman, East Fife Members' Centre, National Trust for Scotland, 1995-98. Address: (h.) Leuchars Castle Farmhouse, Leuchars, St. Andrews KY16 0EY; T.-01334 838777.

Macnab of Macnab, James Charles — The Macnab. 23rd Chief, Clan Macnab; Senior Consultant, Hill Samuel Investment Services Ltd., 1982-92, now retired; b. 14.4.26, London; m., Hon. Diana Mary Anstruther-Gray (see Hon. Mrs. Macnab of Macnab); 2 s.; 2 d. Educ. Radley College; Ashbury College, Ottawa. Served, RAF and Scots Guards, 1944-45; Lt., Seaforth Highlanders, 1945-48; Assistant Superintendant and Deputy Superintendant, Federation of Malaya Police Force, 1948-57; Captain, Seaforth Highlanders (TA), 1960-64; managed family estate and farms, 1957-82; District Councillor, Perth, 1961-64; County Councillor, Perth and Kinross Joint County Council, 1964-75; JP, 1968-86; Member: Central Regional Council, 1978-82, Queen's Bodyguard for Scotland (Royal Company of Archers). Address: (h.) Leuchars Castle Farmhouse, Leuchars, St. Andrews KY16 0EY; T.-01334 838777.

Macnair, Terence Crawford, LLB, NP. Solicitor, since 1967; Director, Argyll and the Islands Enterprise Company, since 1996; Honorary Sheriff, North Strathclyde, since 1988; b. 16.12.42, Kingston, Jamaica; m., Ishbel Ross Hunter; 1 s. Educ. High School of Glasgow; Glasgow University. Town Clerk, Lochgilphead, 1970-75; Partner, MacArthur Stewart & Orr, 1970-81; Senior Partner,

MacArthur Stewart, since 1981; Assistant Clerk, Tarbert Harbour Authority, since 1970; Clerk, Awe District Salmon Fishery Board, since 1979; President, Oban Rotary Club, 1988-89; Secretary/Treasurer, Oban and District Licensed Trade Association, since 1977; Director, North Argyll Development Agency, since 1991. Recreations: tennis; squash; golf; curling; bridge; music. Address: (b.) Boswell House, Oban; T.-01631 562215.

McNally, Rt. Rev. Anthony Joseph. Rector, Gillis College, Edinburgh, since 1987; Vicar General, Archdiocese of St. Andrews and Edinburgh, since 1985; b. 27.5.32, Edinburgh. Educ. Blairs College, Aberdeen; Seminaire St. Sulpice, Paris. Ordained Priest, 1955; Assistant Priest, Methil, Fife, 1955-63; Missioner, Calabar and Bauchi Province, Nigeria, 1963-67; Assistant Priest, Bonnybridge, 1967-72; Parish Priest, Burntisland, 1972-80, St. Peter's, Morningside, 1980-85; Parish Priest, Musselburgh, and Vicar General, Archdiocese, 1985; Parish Priest, St. Columba's, Edinburgh, since 1993. Recreations: reading; walking. Address: (b.) St. Columba's, 9 Upper Gray Street, Edinburgh EH9 1SN.

McNaught, Brian, BSc (Hons), FRSA. Rector, Garnock Academy, Kilbirnie, since 1993; b. 30.3.50, Dumfries; m., Judith Park; 3 d. Educ. Lockerbie Academy; Glasgow University. Mathematics Teacher, Annan Academy; Stranraer Academy: Principal Teacher of Mathematics, Assistant Rector; Depute Rector, Beath High School, Cowdenbeath. Recreations: angling; sea fishing; shooting. Address: (h.) 74 Greenock Road, Largs; T.-01505 682685.

McNaught, Peter Cairn, MA, MLitt, DUniv, FRSA. Principal, Craigie College of Education, Ayr, 1976-87; b. 29.5.25, Glasgow; m., Else Kristine Sandvad; 1 s.; 1 d. Educ. Hutchesons' Boys' Grammar School, Glasgow; Glasgow University. Teacher, Queen's Park and Hutchesons' Boys' Grammar Schools, Glasgow, 1952-58; Lecturer in English, Moray House College of Education, Edinburgh, 1958-60; Principal Lecturer in English, Aberdeen College of Education, 1960-61; Moray House College of Education: Senior Assistant Principal, 1961-70, Vice-Principal, 1970-75. Vice-Chairman, Scottish Council for the Validation of Courses for Teachers; Member, General Teaching Council for Scotland; Chairman, Committee of College of Education Principals, 1984-86; Vice-Chairman, West Sound; Chairman, STV Education Committee; Member, STV Staff Trust; Visiting Professor in English Studies, Strathclyde University, 1988; Director, Wider Access Programme, 1988-1992. Address: (h.) 1a Victoria Drive, Troon KA10 6EN; T.-01292 312200.

Macnaughton, Rev. (Gordon) Fraser (Hay), MA, BD, DipCPC. Parish Minister, Killermont Parish Church, Bearsden, since 1997; b. 27.3.58, Glasgow; m., Carole; 2 d. Educ. Glasgow Academy; Glasgow University; Edinburgh University. Assistant, Newlands South Church, Glasgow, 1981-85; Minister, Fenwick Parish Church, 1985-91; Chaplain, Dundee University, 1991-97. Recreations: rugby; bird-watching; conservation issues. Address: (h.) 8 Clathic Avenue, Bearsden G61 2HF; T.-0141-942 0021; e-mail: fraser.macnaughton@dial.pipex.com

McNaughton, John Ewen, OBE, JP, FRAgS. Member, Scottish Beef Council, since 1997; Chairman, Forth Valley Countryside Initiative, since 1999; b. 28.5.33, Edinburgh; m., Jananne Ogilvie Honeyman; 2 s.; 2 d. Educ. Cargilfield; Loretto. Born and bred a hill sheep farmer; after a short spell in America, began farming at Inverlochlarig with father; served on Council, NFU of Scotland; Chairman, Scotch Quality Beef & Lamb Association, 1981-97; Vice President, Royal Highland and Agricultural Society of Scotland, 1997-98; Member: British Wool Marketing Board, 1975-2000, Panel of Agricultural Arbiters, 1973-98, Red Deer Commission, 1975-92; Elder, Church of Scotland.

Recreations: yachting; stalking. Address: Inverlochlarig, Balquhidder, Lochearnhead, Perthshire FK19 8PH; T.-01877 384 232; e-mail: inverlarig@aol.com

Macnaughton, Professor Sir Malcolm Campbell, MD, LLD, FRCPGlas, FRCOG, FFFP, FRSE, FSLCOG (Hon.), FACOG (Hon.), FRCA (Hon.), FRACOG (Hon.). Vice President, Royal College of Midwives; Professor of Obstetrics and Gynaecology, Glasgow University, 1970-90; b. 4.4.25, Glasgow; m., Margaret-Ann Galt; 2 s.; 3 d. Educ. Glasgow Academy; Glasgow University. RAMC, 1949-51; Lecturer in Obstetrics and Gynaecology, Aberdeen University, 1957-61; Senior Lecturer, St. Andrews University, 1961-66; Consultant, Eastern Regional, 1966-70. Member: Chief Scientist Committee, SHHD, Biomedical Research Committee and Health Service Research Committee, SHHD, MRC Grant Committee and Cell Systems Board, MRC, Scientific Committee, Hospital Recognition Committee, RCOG; President: RCOG, 1984-87, British Fertility Society, 1993-95; Chairman: Scottish Perinatal Mortality Advisory Group, SCOTMEG Working Party on Accident and Emergency Services in Scotland. Recreations: walking; fishing; curling. Address: (h.) 15 Boclair Road, Bearsden, Glasgow G61 2AF; T.-0141-942 1909.

McNay, W. Gordon, OBE, DL, JP, BL; b. 11.12.25, Wishaw; m., Margaret C. MacKay. Educ. Wishaw High School; Glasgow University. Depute Town Clerk, Burgh of Airdrie, 1952-53; Senior Depute Town Clerk, Burgh of Motherwell and Wishaw, 1953-63; Town Clerk, Burgh of East Kilbride, 1963-75; Chief Executive, East Kilbride District Council, 1975-88. Deputy Lieutenant, Lanarkshire; Honorary Freeman, East Kilbride District. Recreations: golf; photography; philately. Address: (h.) Solbakken, 17 Kibblestane Place, Strathaven ML10 6EL; T.-01357 520889.

MacNeacail, Aonghas. Writer (poetry, journalism, scriptwriting for TV, film and radio, librettoes); b. 7.6.42, Uig, Isle of Skye; m., Gerda Stevenson (qv); 1 s. Educ. Portree High School; Glasgow University. Writing fellowships: Sabhal Mor Ostaig, 1977-79, An Comunn Gaidhealach, 1979-81, Ross and Cromarty District Council, 1988-90, Glasgow and Strathclyde Universities, 1993-95; Sabhal Mor Ostaig, 1995-98; tours to Ireland, Germany, North America, Japan, Israel, etc.; opera librettoes for Alasdair Nicolson and William Sweeney; songs for Capercaillie, Phil Cunningham; art with Simon Fraser, Kenny Munro, Diane MacLean; short-listed, Paul Hamlyn Foundation Award for Poets, 1997; Stakis Award, Scottish Writer of the Year, 1997. Publications: books: An Seachnadh, 1986; Rock-Water, 1990; Oideachadh Ceart, 1996; poems widely anthologised. Recreations: newsprint; red wine; thinking about walking.

McNee, Sir David Blackstock, Kt, QPM, FBIM, FRSA, KStJ. Non-Executive Director and Adviser to a number of public limited companies; b. 23.3.25; m., Isabella Clayton Hopkins (deceased); 1 d. Educ. Woodside Senior Secondary School, Glasgow. Joined City of Glasgow Police, 1946; Deputy Chief Constable, Dunbartonshire Constabulary, 1968; Chief Constable: City of Glasgow Police, 1971-75, Strathclyde Police, 1975-77; Commissioner, Metropolitan Police, 1977-82. Honorary Vice-President, Boys' Brigade, since 1980; Vice-President, London Federation of Boys Clubs, since 1982; Patron, Scottish Motor Neurone Association, 1982-97; President, National Bible Society of Scotland, 1983-96; Freeman, City of London, 1977; President, Glasgow City Committee, Cancer Relief, 1987-92. Recreations: fishing; golf; music.

MacNee, Professor William, MB, ChB, MD(Hons), FRCP(Glas), FRCP(Edin). Professor of Respiratory and Environmental Medicine, Edinburgh University; Visiting Professor, Department of Biological Sciences, Napier University; Honorary Consultant Physician, Lothian Health Board, since 1987; Clinical Director, Respiratory Medicine Unit, 1992-98; Patient Services Director, Respiratory Medicine, Lothian University Hospitals NHS Trust; b. 18.12.50, Glasgow; m., Edna Marina Kingsley; 1 s.; 1 d. Educ. Coatbridge High School; Glasgow University. House Physician/House Surgeon, Glasgow and Paisley, 1975-76; SHO/Registrar in Medicine, Western Infirmary/Gartnavel Hospitals, Glasgow, 1976-79; Registrar in Respiratory Medicine, City Hospital, Edinburgh, 1979-80; MRC Research Fellow/Honorary Registrar, Department of Respiratory Medicine, Royal Infirmary, Edinburgh, 1980-82; Lecturer, Department of Respiratory Medicine, City Hospital, Edinburgh, 1982-83; Senior Registrar, Respiratory Medicine/Medicine, Lothian Health Board, 1983-87; MRC Research Fellow, University of British Columbia, Vancouver, 1985-86; Senior Lecturer in Respiratory Medicine, 1987-93; Reader in Medicine, Edinburgh University, 1993-97; Head, Cardiovascular-Thoracic Service, Royal Infirmary of Edinburgh, 1998-99. Council Member, Scottish Thoracic Society, 1990-93; Hon. Secretary, British Lung Foundation (Scotland); Chairman, British Lung Foundation Scientific Committee, 1997-2000; Chairman, European Respiratory Society Scientific Programme Committee. Publications: scientific papers, reviews and books on respiratory medicine topics. Recreations: music; sport. Address: (b.) ELEGI Colt Research Laboratories, Wilkie Building, University of Edinburgh Medical School, Teviot Place, Edinburgh EH8 9AG; T.-0131-651 1435.

McNeil, Duncan. MSP (Labour), Greenock and Inverclyde, since 1999. Former shipyard worker and union organiser. Address: (b.) Scottish Parliament, Edinburgh EH99 1SP.

Macneil of Barra, Ian Roderick, BA, LLB, FSA Scot. Wigmore Professor of Law, Northwestern University, Chicago, 1980-99, Professor Emeritus, since 1999; b. 20.6.29, New York City; m., Nancy C. Wilson; 2 s.; 1 d. Educ. Scarborough School; University of Vermont; Harvard University. Lt., AUS, 1951-53; Commissioned Officer, USAR, 1950-67; practised law, 1956-59; Member, Cornell Law School Faculty, 1959-72, 1974-80; Visiting Professor, University College, Dar es Salaam, 1965-67, Duke Law School, 1971-72; Professor of Law and Member, Centre for Advanced Studies, Virginia University, 1972-74; Visiting Fellow, Centre for Socio-Legal Studies, Wolfson College, Oxford, 1979, and Edinburgh University Faculty of Law, 1979, 1987; Visiting Professor, Harvard University, 1988-89; Guggenheim Fellow, 1978-79; Fellow, American Academy of Arts and Sciences. Member, Standing Council of Scottish Chiefs; author of numerous books and articles. Recreations: walking; reading; historical studies. Seat: Kisimul Castle, Isle of Barra. Address: (h.) 95/6 Grange Loan, Edinburgh EH9 2ED; T.-0131-667 6068.

McNeil, Neil, MB, ChB, DPH, DPA, FFCM, FFPHM, MREHIS. Consultant in Public Health Medicine/Director of Community Medicine/Unit Medical Officer/District Medical Officer, Lanarkshire Health Board, 1976-92; Honorary Senior Clinical Lecturer/Honorary Clinical Lecturer, Department of Public Health, Glasgow University, 1976-92; b. 4.6.31, Glasgow; m., Florence Ward Butterworth; 2 s.; 1 d. Educ. Govan High School; Glasgow University. SHO, Senior Resident, House Physician and House Surgeon, Western Infirmary, Glasgow, 1956-58; Hall Fellow, Glasgow University, 1958-60; Registrar, Western Infirmary, Glasgow, 1960-61; Divisional Medical Officer of Health, City of Glasgow, 1962-65; Principal Lecturer in Health Education and Medical Officer, Jordanhill College, Glasgow, 1965-68; Medical Officer of Health, North-East Hampshire, and Honorary Consultant, Aldershot, 1968-69; Medical Officer, Scottish Home and Health Department, 1969-73; Honorary Lecturer, Departments of Materia Medica and Community Medicine, Glasgow University, 1973-74; Consultant Epidemiologist,

Communicable Diseases (Scotland) Unit, Ruchill Hospital, 1973-74; Senior Medical Officer, Scottish Home and Health Department, 1974-76. Dr. MacKinlay Prize in Public Health and Preventive Medicine, Glasgow University, 1962. Publications on community medicine, environmental medicine, public health, immunisation and infectious disease control. Recreations: tennis; photography; natural history; Gaelic language and culture; Scottish history and archaeology. Address: (h.) Claddach, 25 Waterfoot Road, Newton Mearns, Glasgow G77 5RU.

McNeill, Brian Ernest Brown, BA (Hons). Head of Scottish Music, RSAMD, since 2001; b. 6.4.50, Falkirk; m., Jacqueline France-McNeill. Educ. Falkirk High School; Strathclyde University. Founded Battlefield Band, 1969; professional musician and singer, since 1975; left Battlefield Band, 1990, to pursue writing career and other musical projects; various awards in traditional music; made honorary Texan, 1999, for services to Scottish music in that state. Publications: (novels) The Busker, 1989; To Answer the Peacock, 1999. Recreations: books; collecting Penguin crime novels. Address: (b.) RSAMD, 100 Renfrew Street, Glasgow, G2 3DB; T.-0141-270 8320.

Macneill, Sheriff Deirdre, LLB, QC. Sheriff, Glasgow and Strathkelvin at Glasgow, since 1999; b. 4.6.54, Aberdeen; 1 s. Educ. St. Margaret School for Girls, Aberdeen; Aberdeen University. Solicitor, 1974-80; Faculty of Advocates, 1981-99; QC, 1994. Address: 9 Wemyss Place, Edinburgh.

MacNeill, Dugald Brown, BSc, FRSC. Principal, College of Piping, since 1996; Hon. Secretary, Piobaireachd Society, since 1996; Hon. Secretary, College of Piping, since 1992; b. 17.11.30; m., Helen McKellar; 2 s.; 1 d. Educ. Ardrishaig School; Hyndland School; Glasgow University. Member/Founder Pupil, College of Piping, 1944. Recreations: bagpipe and its music; hill climbing. Address: (h.) 20 Craigleith View, Edinburgh EH4 3JZ; T.-0131-346 1155.

McNeill, James Walker, QC. Advocate, since 1978; b. 16.2.52, Dunoon; m., Katherine Lawrence McDowall; 2 s.; 1 d. Educ. Dunoon Grammar School; Sidney Sussex College, Cambridge; Edinburgh University. QC, 1991; Standing Junior Counsel, Department of Transport in Scotland, 1984-88, Inland Revenue, 1988-91. Member of Council, Scottish Universities Law Institute; Session Clerk, St. Andrew's and St. George's Parish Church, Edinburgh, since 1999. Recreations: music; hill-walking; golf; sailing; travel. Address: (b.) Advocates' Library, Parliament House, Edinburgh EH1 1RF; T.-0131-226 5071.

McNeill, Pauline, LLB. MSP (Lab), Glasgow Kelvin, since 1999; b. 12.9.62, Paisley; m., William Joseph Cahill. Educ. Our Lady's High School, Cumbernauld; Strathclyde University. President, National Union of Students (Scotland), 1986-88; Regional Organiser, GMB, 1988-99. Recreations: music; films; guitar; singing. Address: (b.) 1274 Argyle Street, Glasgow G3 8AA; T.-0141-589 7120; e-mail: pauline.mcneill.msp@scottish.parliament.uk

McNeill, Sheriff Peter Grant Brass, PhD, MA (Hons), LLB, QC. Formerly Sheriff of Lothian and Borders at Edinburgh; Chairman; Council, Scottish National Dictionary Association Ltd., since 1997; b. 3.3.29, Glasgow; m., Matilda Farquhar Rose; 1 s.; 3 d. Educ. Hillhead High School, Glasgow; Morrison's Academy, Crieff; Glasgow University. Law apprentice, Biggart Lumsden & Co., Glasgow, 1952-55; Carnegie Fellowship, 1955; Faulds Fellowship, 1956-59; Scottish Bar, 1956; Honorary Sheriff Substitute of Lanarkshire, and of Stirling, Clackmannan and Dumbarton, 1962; Standing Junior Counsel to Scottish Development Department (Highways), 1964; Advocate Depute, 1964; Sheriff of Lanarkshire,

subsequently of Glasgow and Strathkelvin, at Glasgow, 1965-82; Temporary Sheriff, 1996-98; President, Sheriffs' Association, 1982-85; Chairman: Council, Stair Society, 1990-98, Scottish Legal History Group, 1990-97, Council, Scottish National Dictionary Association Ltd., 1997-2001. Publications: Balfour's Practicks (Editor), 1962-63; An Historical Atlas of Scotland c. 400 - c. 1600 (Co-Editor), 1975; Adoption of Children in Scotland, 1982, 3rd ed., 1998; Atlas of Scottish History to 1707 (Co-Editor), 1996. Recreations: legal history; gardening; book-binding. Address: (h.) 31 Queensferry Road, Edinburgh EH4 3HB.

McNeilly, Professor Alan S., BSc, PhD, DSc, FRSE. Deputy Director, MRC Human Reproductive Sciences Unit, Edinburgh, since 1998, Acting Director, 1996-98; b. 10.2.47, Birmingham; m., Judy; 1 s.; 3 d. Educ. Handsworth Grammar School, Birmingham; Nottingham University; Reading University; Edinburgh University. Research Lecturer, Department of Reproductive Medicine, St. Bartholomew's Hospital, London, 1971-75; Visiting Professor, University of Manitoba, Canada, 1975-76; Research Scientist, MRC Reproductive Biology Unit, Edinburgh, since 1976, Deputy Director, since 1986. Member, Home Office APC, since 1998; Chairman, Society for Reproduction and Fertility, since 1999. Recreations: walking; golf; orienteering; bee-keeping; gardening. Address: (b.) 37 Chalmers Street, Edinburgh EH3 9ET; T.-0131-229 2575; e-mail: a.mcneilly@hrsu.mrc.ac.uk

Macnicol, Malcolm Fraser, MBChB, BSc (Hons), FRCS, MCh, FRCP, FRCSEd (Orth), DipSportsMed. Consultant Orthopaedic Surgeon, Children and Adults, since 1979; Senior Orthopaedic Surgeon, Edinburgh University, since 1979; b. 18.3.43; m., Anne Morag; 2 s.; 1 d. Educ. Royal High School, Edinburgh; Edinburgh University. Research Fellow, Stanford and Harvard Universities; Lecturer in Orthopaedic Surgery, Edinburgh, 1976-78; Senior Lecturer, Perth, W. Australia, 1978-79; Member, Council of Management, Journal of Bone and Joint Surgery, 1998-2000; Treasurer, Royal College of Surgeons, Edinburgh, 1987-90; President, British Orthopaedic Association, 2001-2002. Publications: six books; 120 professional papers. Recreations: painting; tennis. Address: (h.) Red House, 1 South Gillsland Road, Edinburgh EH10 5DE; T.-0131-536 0832.

McNicoll, Professor Iain Hugh, BA, PhD, FRSA. Professor of Applied Economics, Strathclyde University, since 1987; Senior Research Advisor, Fraser of Allander Institute, since 1991; b. 24.6.51, Glasgow; m. Educ. St. Mungo's Academy, Glasgow; Stirling University. Leverhulme Research Fellow, Industrial Science, Stirling University, 1974-76; Lecturer, Business Studies, Edinburgh University, 1976-79; Fellow/Senior Fellow, Director of Research, Acting Director/Director, Fraser of Allander Institute, 1979-89. Member, numerous UK government committees and advisory groups, since 1980; past visiting professorships, Toulouse Business School and University of Wittswattersrand; international assignments for World Bank, UNDP, ODA and others. Publications: two books; 18 monographs; 60 academic journal and book articles; over 200 research reports. Recreations: hi-fi; aquaria; astronomy. Address: (b.) Department of Economics, Strathclyde University, 100 Cathedral Street, Glasgow G4 0LN; T.-0141-552 4400; e-mail: iain.mcnicoll@strath.ac.uk

McNiven, Bruce, MIPD. Territorial General Manager North, Post Office Ltd., since 2001; b. 10.1.47, Kirkcaldy; m., Marilyn; 1 s.; 1 d. Educ. Kirkcaldy High School. Joined Post Office in Scotland, 1971; entered management, 1973; Assistant Head Postmaster, Newcastle upon Tyne; District Manager, Post Office Counters Ltd., North East; Deputy Director, Benefits Agency/Post Office Counters Ltd. Automation Programme. Past President, Rotary Club of Newcastle upon Tyne. Recreation: golf; Scottish rugby events; football. Address: (b.) The Athenaeum, Nelson Mandela Place, Glasgow G2 1BT; T.-0141-353 7000.

McNiven, David Martin. Songwriter, Music Director and Producer, Composer, Actor; b. 4.11.45, Glasgow; m., Angela Rew; 1 s.; 2 d. Educ. High School of Glasgow; Royal Scottish Academy of Music and Drama. Traverse Theatre Company, 1970-73; Young Lyceum, 1974-76; Mickery Theatre, 1976; Oxford and Cambridge Shakespeare Company, 1977-78; Wildcat, 1978-83; Royal Lyceum, 1987-88; various TV comedy series for ITV and BBC, since 1983, including Naked Video, Rab C. Nesbitt, The Baldy Man, etc.; Vice-Chairman, Board, Wildcat Stage Productions; three albums for Decca Records; Edinburgh Festival Fringe First Award for Hot Burlesque, 1981; Partnership, McNivensent Music. Recreations: walking to New Orleans; photography; e-mail: mcnivensent@ 1musicrow.com

Macniven, Valerie Margaret, MA (Hons). Head of Access to Justice and International Group, Scottish Executive Justice Department, since 2000; b. 14.1.51, Perth; m., Duncan Macniven (qv). Educ. Aberdeen High School for Girls; Edinburgh University. Scottish Office, 1973-82 and 1987-99; Head of Equality and Voluntary Issues Group, Scottish Executive, 1999-2000. Elder, Church of Scotland. Recreations: skiing; tennis; travel. Address: (b.) Scottish Executive Justice Department, Edinburgh EH1 3DG; T.-0131-244 8491; e-mail: valerie.macniven@ scotland.gsi.gov.uk

McNulty, Des, BA. MSP (Labour), Clydebank and Milngavie, since 1999; Member: Scottish Parliament Corporate Body, Transport and Environment Committee, Standards Committee; b. 28.7.52, Stockport; m.; 2 s. Educ. St. Bede's College Manchester; University of York; University of Glasgow. Senior Lecturer in Sociology, Glasgow Caledonian University; Director of Strategic Planning, Glasgow Caledonian University; Member, Strathclyde Regional Council, 1990-96; Member, Glasgow City Council, 1995-99; Member of Court, University of Glasgow, 1994-99; Assessor to Board, Scottish Opera, 1996-99; Chair, Glasgow Healthy City Partnership, 1995-99; Chair, Glasgow 1999 Festival of Architecture and Design, since 1996; Non Executive Director, Greater Glasgow Health Board, 1998-99; Deputy Chair, The Wise Group. Address: The Scottish Parliament, Edinburgh EH99 1SP; T.-0131-348 5918; Constituency Office, Clydebank Central Library, Dunbarton Road, Clydebank G81 1XH; T.-0141-952 7711.

McOwan, Rennie, DUniv, FSA Scot. Writer and Broadcaster, now retired; b. Stirling; m., Agnes Mooney; 3 s.; 1 d. Educ. Alva Academy. Reporter, Stirling Journal; Sub-Editor, Kemsley Newspapers, Daily Record; Public Relations, Roman Catholic Church; Sub-Editor, Features Writer, Scotsman Publications; Assistant Publicity Secretary, National Trust for Scotland; former Scottish Book Trust Lecturer under Writers in Schools and Writers in Public schemes; former Guest Lecturer, Film and Media Studies, Stirling University; Contributor to newspapers and magazines in Britain and overseas; radio and TV scripts and research; Outdoor Writers Guild Golden Eagle award for access campaigning and writing about Scottish subjects, 1997; Provost of Stirling's Civic Award (Arts and Culture), 1998; Honorary Doctorate, University of Stirling, 1996. Publications: Light on Dumyat; The White Stag Adventure; The Day the Mountain Moved; Robert Burns for Beginners; St. Andrew for Beginners; Magic Mountains; Walks in the Trossachs and the Rob Roy Country; The Green Hills; Kilchurn Castle: a history; Loch Lomond and The Trossachs; contributed to: Walking in Scotland; Poetry of the Scottish Hills; Speak to the Hills; Wild Walks; The Story of Scotland; Discover Scotland; Great Walks, Scotland; Classic Coastal Walks of Britain; On Foot Through History. Recreations: mountaineering; Scottish history and literature. Address: 7 Williamfield Avenue, Stirling FK7 9AH; T.-01786 461316.

Macphail, Sheriff Iain Duncan, QC, MA (Hons), LLB. Sheriff of Lothian and Borders at Edinburgh, since 1995; b. 24.1.38; m., Rosslyn Graham Lillias Hewitt; 1 s.; 1 d. Educ. George Watson's College; Edinburgh University; Glasgow University. Admitted Faculty of Advocates, 1963; practice, Scottish Bar, 1963-73; Faulds Fellow in Law, Glasgow University, 1963-65; Lecturer in Evidence and Procedure, Strathclyde University, 1968-69, Edinburgh University, 1969-72; Standing Junior Counsel to Scottish Home and Health Department and Department of Health and Social Security, 1971-73; Extra Advocate-Depute, 1973; Sheriff of Glasgow and Strathkelvin (formerly Lanarkshire), 1973-81; Sheriff of Tayside, Central and Fife at Dunfermline and Alloa, 1981-82; Sheriff of Lothian and Borders at Linlithgow, 1982-88, at Edinburgh, 1988-89. Member, Scottish Law Commission, 1990-94; Arthur Goodhart Professor of Legal Science, Cambridge University, 2001-02; Fellow, Selwyn College, Cambridge, 2001-02; Chairman, Scottish Association for the Study of Delinquency, 1978-81; Hon. LLD, Edinburgh, 1992. Publications: Evidence, 1987; Sheriff Court Practice, 1988. Address: (b.) Sheriff Court House, 27 Chambers Street, Edinburgh EH1 1LB; T.-0131-225 2525.

McPhee, George, MBE, BMus, FRCO, DipMusEd, RSAM, Hon. FRSCM. Visiting Professor of Organ, St. Andrews University; Chairman, Paisley International Organ Festival; Organist and Master of the Choristers, Paisley Abbey, since 1963; b. 10.11.37, Glasgow; m., Margaret Ann Scotland; 1 s.; 2 d. Educ. Woodside Senior Secondary School, Glasgow; Royal Scottish Academy of Music and Drama; Edinburgh University. Studied organ with Herrick Bunney and Fernando Germany; Assistant Organist, St. Giles' Cathedral, 1959-63; joined staff, RSAMD, 1963; Conductor, Scottish Chamber Choir, 1971-75; Conductor, Kilmarnock and District Choral Union, 1975-84; since 1971, has completed 12 recital tours of the United States and Canada; has been both Soloist and Conductor with Scottish National Orchestra; numerous recordings and broadcasts; has taken part in numerous music festivals as Soloist; Adjudicator; Examiner, Associated Board, Royal Schools of Music; Special Commissioner, Royal School of Church Music; President, Incorporated Society of Musicians, 1999-2000; Silver Medal, Worshipful Company of Musicians; Honorary Doctorate, University of Paisley. Recreations: golf; walking. Address: (h.) 17 Main Road, Castlehead, Paisley PA2 6AJ; T.-0141-889 3528; e-mail: profmcphee@netscapeonline.co.uk

Macpherson of Drumochter, Lord (James) Gordon Macpherson), 2nd Baron, JP, FRES, FRSA, FZS. Chairman and Managing Director, Macpherson, Train & Co. Ltd., since 1964; Chairman, A.J. Macpherson & Co. Ltd., since 1973; b. 22.1.24; m., 1, Dorothy Ruth Coulter (deceased); 2 d.; 1 s. deceased; 2, Catherine MacCarthy; 1 s.; 2 d. Educ. Loretto; Wells House, Malvern. RAF, 1939-45; Member, Council, London Chamber of Commerce, 1952-73; Chief, Scottish Clans Association of London, 1972-74; Chairman, Macpherson Clan Association, 1963-64; Life Managing Governor, Royal Scottish Corporation; Freeman, City of London. Address: (h.) Kyllachy, Tomatin, Inverness-shire.

McPherson, Alastair, MA, MSc, MCIT. Managing Director, ScotRail, since 1997; b. 6.7.51, Glasgow. Educ. Kings Park Secondary School, Glasgow; Glasgow University; Birmingham University. Local Government Officer, 1974-77; Tyne and Wear Passenger Transport Executive, 1977-90; National Express Group, 1990-97 (formerly Commercial Director, National Express Ltd.).

Recreation: architecture; history. Address: (b.) Caledonian Chambers, 87 Union Street, Glasgow G1 3TA; T.-0141-335 4500.

Macpherson, Archie. Sports broadcaster and journalist. Former headmaster; football commentator, BBC Scotland, until 1990; reported Olympic Games, 1984 and 1988, for BBC network; commentator, Scottish Television, since 1988; author of Action Replays, 1991; e-mail: archie@macpherson78.freeserve.co.uk

McPherson, Duncan James, CBE, MA, SDA. Farmer; formerly Convener, Highland Regional Council; b. 29.10.30, Santos, Brazil; m., Vivian Margaret; 1 s.; 1 d. Educ. Robert Gordon's College, Aberdeen; Aberdeen University. Member, Cromarty Town Council, 1964-75, Ross and Cromarty County Council, 1972-75; Chairman, Cromarty Firth Port Authority, 1986-97; Fellow, Scottish Council (Development and Industry), since 1990; former Member, Board, Scottish Natural Heritage; President, Rosemarkie Golf Club. Recreations: golf; curling; formerly rugby (Scottish trialist, 1951-56). Address: Cromarty Mains, Cromarty, Ross-shire; T.-01381 600 232.

McPherson, James Alexander Strachan, CBE, MA, BL, LLB, FSA Scot, JP. Lord Lieutenant, Banffshire, since 1987; Consultant, formerly Senior Partner, Alexander George & Co., Solicitors, Macduff; Honorary Sheriff, Grampian, Highland and Islands at Banff, since 1972; b. 20.11.27, Wormit, Fife; m., Helen Marjorie Perks, MA; 1 s.; 1 d. Educ. Banff Academy; Aberdeen University. Member, Macduff Town Council and Banff County Council, 1958-75; Provost of Macduff, 1972-75; Convener, Banff County Council, 1970-75; Member: Grampian Health Board, 1974-82, Post Office Users National Council for Scotland, 1976-80, Police Advisory Board for Scotland, 1974-86, Grampian Regional Council, 1974-90; Chairman, Public Protection Committee, 1974-86; Governor, Scottish Police College, 1974-86; President, Banffshire Society of Solicitors, 1977-80; Chairman, Banff and Buchan JP Advisory Committee, 1987-98; Chairman, Aberdeenshire JP Advisory Committee, since 1998; Member, Scottish Solicitors Discipline Tribunal, 1990-94; Vice President, Highland Territorial and Reserve Forces Association; Member, Aberdeen University Court, 1993-97. Recreations: reading; local history; sailing; swimming. Address: (h.) Dun Alastair, 126 Gellymill Street, Macduff; T.-Macduff 832377.

Macpherson, John Hannah Forbes, CBE, OStJ, CA, DUniv. Chairman of Court, University of Glasgow; former Lord Dean of Guild, Glasgow; b. 23.5.26, Glasgow; m., Margaret Graham Roxburgh; 1 s. Educ. Glasgow Academy; Merchiston Castle School, Edinburgh. Royal Naval Volunteer Reserve, 1943; Apprentice CA, Wilson Stirling & Co., 1947 (qualified, 1949); Partner, Wilson Stirling & Co. (subsequently Touche Ross & Co.), 1956-86; Chairman: Glasgow Junior Chamber of Commerce, 1965, Scottish Mutual Assurance Society, 1971, Scottish Industrial Estates Corporation, 1972, Irvine Development Corporation, 1976, TSB Scotland plc, 1984, Glasgow Development Agency, 1990; President, Glasgow Chamber of Commerce, 1980; Director: Scottish Metropolitan Property plc, 1986, TSB Group plc, 1985; Deputy Chairman, Hill Samuel Bank Ltd., 1991; Director, PCT Group plc, 1992; Governor, Merchiston Castle School, 1988; Member, Charity Appeals Committee for Prince and Princess of Wales Hospice; Director, Glasgow Native Benevolent Society. Recreations: travel; gardening; reading. Address: (h.) 16 Collylinn Road, Bearsden, Glasgow; T.-0141-942 0042.

McPherson, Malcolm Henry, LLB, WS. Solicitor; Chairman, Henderson Boyd Jackson; Chairman, Hibernian Football Club; b. 22.5.54, Edinburgh; m., Fiona Sutherland Hogg; 1 s.; 3 d. Educ. George Watson's College, Edinburgh;

Edinburgh University. Apprentice, Henderson & Jackson, WS, 1975-77; Partner, since 1978. Lay Member, Institute of Chartered Accountants of Scotland; Visiting Professor of Law, University of Sunderland. Recreations: field sports; sailing; golf. Address: (b.) 19 Ainslie Place, Edinburgh EH3 6AU; T.-0131-226 6881; e-mail: m.mcpherson@hbj.co.uk

Macpherson, Peter, FRCP, FRCR, DTCD, FLS. Emeritus Consultant Neuroradiologist, Institute of Neurological Sciences; President: British Society of Neuroradiologists, 1990-92, Botanical Society of the British Isles, 1991-93; b. 10.10.25, Inveraray; m., Agnes Cochrane Davidson; 4 d. Educ. Inveraray Grammar School; Keil School, Dumbarton; Anderson College, Glasgow. House Surgeon, Royal Infirmary, Stirling; Junior Hospital Medical Officer, Robroyston Hospital, Glasgow; Chest Physician, Argyll; Registrar/Senior Registrar, Western Infirmary, Glasgow. Commodore, Oban Sailing Club, 1958-60; President, Glasgow Natural History Society, 1979-81 and 1983-86; Honorary Secretary, Botanical Society of the British Isles, Committee for Scotland, 1977-95, Chairman, 1995-99; Plant Recorder for Lanarkshire, since 1978; Elder, Church of Scotland, since 1957. Recreations: natural history; sailing. Address: (h.) Ben Alder, 15 Lubnaig Road, Glasgow; T.-0141-632 0723.

Macpherson of Cluny (and Blairgowrie), The Honourable Sir William, KB (1983), TD, MA. 27th Hereditary Chief of the Clan Macpherson (Cluny-Macpherson); b. 1.4.26; m., Sheila McDonald Brodie; 2 s.; 1 d. Educ. Summer Fields, Oxford; Wellington College; Trinity College, Oxford (Hon. Fellow, 1991). Scots Guards, 1944-47 (Captain); 21st Special Air Service Regiment (TA), 1951-65 (Lt.-Col. Commanding, 1962-65); Honorary Colonel, 21st SAS, 1983-91. Called to the Bar, Inner Temple, 1952; Queen's Counsel, 1971-83; Recorder of the Crown Court, 1972-83; Member, Senate and Bar Council, 1979-83; Bencher, Inner Temple, 1978; Judge of the High Court of Justice (of England and Wales), Queen's Bench Division, 1983-96; Honorary Member, Northern Circuit, since 1987. Member, Queen's Bodyguard for Scotland (Royal Company of Archers), since 1976, Brigadier, 1989; Vice President, Royal Scottish Corporation; President, Highland Society of London, 1991-94; Hon. LLD, Dundee University, 1999. Recreations: golf; fishing; rugby football; archery. Address: (h.) Newton Castle, Blairgowrie, Perthshire PH10 6SU.

Macquaker, Donald Francis, CBE, MA (Oxon), LLB. Partner, T.C. Young & Son, Writers, Glasgow, 1957-93; b. 21.9.32, Stair; m., Susan Elizabeth Finlayson; 1 s.; 1 d. Educ. Winchester College; Trinity College, Oxford; Glasgow University. Greater Glasgow Health Board: Chairman, Finance and General Purposes Committee, 1974-83, Chairman, 1983-87; Chairman, Scottish Health Service Common Services Agency, 1987-91; former Member, Board of Management, Glasgow Royal Maternity Hospital and Associated Women's Hospitals (latterly Vice-Chairman); Director, Lithgows Ltd., 1987-98; Director, Prince and Princess of Wales Hospice, Glasgow, 1991-94; Chairman, Western Meeting Club (Ayr Racecourse), since 1996. Recreations: shooting; fishing; gardening. Address: (h.) Blackbyres, by Ayr; T.-01292 441088.

MacQueen, Professor Hector Lewis, LLB (Hons), PhD, FRSE. Professor of Private Law, Edinburgh University, since 1994; Dean, Faculty of Law, since 1999; b. 13.6.56, Ely; m., Frances Mary Young; 2 s.; 1 d. Educ. George Heriot's School, Edinburgh; Edinburgh University. Lecturer, Senior Lecturer, Reader, all in Law, Edinburgh University, 1979-94; Director, David Hume Institute, Edinburgh, 1991-99; Visiting Professor, Cornell University, 1991; Visiting Professor, Utrecht University, 1997; Secretary, Scottish Historical Review, 1986-99; Editor, Hume Papers on Public Policy, 1993-99; Editor, Edinburgh Law Review, since 1996; Scottish Representative, European

Contract Commission, since 1995. Publications: Common Law and Feudal Society in Medieval Scotland; Studying Scots Law; Copyright, Competition and Industrial Design; Contract Law in Scotland (Co-Author). Recreations: Scotland; cricket; walking – sometimes with golf clubs; reading. Address: (b.) Faculty of Law, Edinburgh University, Edinburgh EH8 9YL; T.-0131-650 2060; e-mail: hector.macqueen@ed.ac.uk

MacQueen, Professor Emeritus Jack (John), MA (Glasgow), MA (Cantab), Hon DLitt, FRSE. Professor Emeritus, Edinburgh University, since 1988; b. 13.2.29, Springboig; m., Winifred W. MacWalter; 3 s. Educ. Hutchesons' Boys Grammar School; Glasgow University; Christ's College, Cambridge. RAF, 1954-56 (Pilot Officer, Flying Officer); Assistant Professor of English, Washington University, St. Louis, Missouri, 1956-59; Edinburgh University: Lecturer in Medieval English and Scottish Literature, 1959-63, Masson Professor of Medieval and Renaissance Literature, 1963-72; Director, School of Scottish Studies, 1969-88; Professor of Scottish Literature and Oral Tradition, 1972-88; Endowment Fellow, 1988-92. Publications: St. Nynia, 1961, 1990; Robert Henryson, 1967; Ballattis of Luve, 1970; Allegory, 1970; Progress and Poetry, 1982; Numerology, 1985; Rise of the Historical Novel, 1989; Scotichronicon III and IV (with W. MacQueen), 1989; Scotichronicon I and II (with W. MacQueen), 1993; Scotichronicon V and VI (with W. MacQueen and D.E.R. Watt), 1995; Place-Names of West Wigtownshire, 2002; Oxford Book of Scottish Verse (with T. Scott), 1966; A Choice of Scottish Verse 1470-1570 (with W. MacQueen), 1972; Humanism in Renaissance Scotland (Co-Author), 1990. Recreations: walking; occasional archaeology; music; astronomy. Address: (h.) Slewdonan, Damnaglaur, Drummore, Stranraer DG9 9QN; e-mail: john.macqueen1@btinternet.com

McQueen, James Donaldson Wright, MA, PhD, ARSGS. Food Industry Analyst; Map Publisher; Honorary Research Fellow, Department of Geography and Topographic Science, University of Glasgow; Council Member, Royal Scottish Geographical Society; b. 14.2.37, Dumfries; m., Jean Evelyn Brown; 2 s.; 1 d. Educ. King's Park School, Glasgow; Glasgow University. Assistant Lecturer, Department of Geography, Glasgow University, 1960-61; Junior Manager, Milk Marketing Board (England and Wales), 1961-62; Scottish Milk Marketing Board, 1963-89 (Deputy Managing Director, 1985-89); Chief Executive, Scottish Dairy Trade Federation (latterly Scottish Dairy Association), 1989-95. Member: CBI Scottish Council, 1987-89, CBI National Council, 1991-94. Address: Ormlie, 53 Kingston Road, Bishopton, Renfrewshire PA7 5BA; T.-01505 862380.

McQueen, William Robert James, BSc, MA, MBA. Director of Resources, Crown Office, since 2001; b. 19.4.51, Widnes; m., Maureen Frances Hall; 2 d. Educ. Kirkham Grammar School; London University; University of California; Strathclyde University. Social Science Research Council, 1973-74; joined Scottish Office, 1974; Head, Transport Division 2, Scottish Executive (formerly Scottish Office), 1995-2001. Recreations: tennis; skiing; music. Address: (b.) Argyle House, 3 Lady Lawson Street, Edinburgh EH3 9SH; T.-0131-222 3116; e-mail: bmcqueen@copfs.gov.uk

McQuillin, Robert, BSc, MSc, FGS, FRSE. Director, Hydrocarbon Management International Ltd., since 1991; Senior Consultant, R. McQuillin & Associates, since 1990; Executive Secretary, Scottish Oil Club, since 1999; b. 28.5.35, Cumbria; m., Angela; 2 s. Educ. White House School, Brampton; Durham University; London University. British Geological Survey: Staff Geophysicist, 1957-66; set up offshore geophysical exploration of UK shelf, 1966-73; Head, Marine Geophysics Unit, 1973-85, Deputy Director, Marine Surveys, Hydrocarbons and Geothermal Energy Division, 1983-85; Britoil: Chief Geophysicist, 1985-88, Chief Scientist and Deputy Exploration Manager, 1986-88; Scientific Adviser, BP NW Europe, Exploration and Production, 1988-89; Oil Industry Consultant, 1990-91. Former Vice-President, Geological Society of London and of Geological Society of Edinburgh. Publication: An Introduction to Seismic Interpretation (principal author), 1986. Recreations: wine and food; good hotels; golf; history of art of china. Address:(b.) HMI Ltd., 94 Liberton Drive, Edinburgh EH16 6NR; T.-0131-664 2193.

McSherry, John Craig Cunningham, LLB (Hons). Advocate; part-time Sheriff, since 2000; b. 21.10.49, Irvine; m., Elaine Beattie; 2 s. Educ. Ardrossan Academy; Glasgow University. Senior Partner, McSherry Halliday, Solicitors, 1983-92. Chairman, Largs and Saltcoats Citizens Advice Bureaux, 1976-83; Council Member, Law Society of Scotland, 1982-85; part-time Immigration Appeals Adjudicator, since 2001. Recreations: country pursuits; skiing; music; bridge; golf. Address: (h.) 2 Heriot Row, Edinburgh EH3 6HU; T.-0131-556 8289; e-mail: jccmcs@hotmail.com

McSorley, George Joseph, JP, MBA, MInstM, MCIM, MInstAM. Chief Executive, Unity Enterprise Ltd., since 1991; Director, Notre Dame Centre, since 1995; b. 4.1.50, Glasgow; m., Anne Maria Leslie; 2 d. Educ. St Mary's College, Blairs, Aberdeen. Formerly: Civil Servant, Department of Employment, Personnel Manager, Community Industry, Glasgow, Area Manager, Community Industry Lower Clyde, District Manager, Social Services, Archdiocese of Glasgow. Formerly: Chair, Children's Panel Advisory Sub-Committee, Inverclyde, Vice Chair, Management Committee, Citizens Advice Bureau, Largs, Secretary, Largs Community Council, Chair, Christian Aid Largs, Chair, National Commission for Pastoral and Social Care; Member Scottish Office Beattie Committee. Recreations: family; reading; travel; ecumenical activities. Address: (h.) 34 Springkell Drive, Glasgow G41 4EZ; T.-(b.) 0141-849 0400.

McSwan, Malcolm, OBE, CA. Chairman, Adaptive Venture Managers plc, since 1995; Proprietor, Knapp Tree Farm; Director, Hearing Enhancement PLC, since 1996; Director, Ectopharma Ltd.; b. 31.8.39, Glasgow; m., Juliet Cowper-Jackson; 2 s. Educ. Royal High School, Edinburgh. Recreations: renovation; trees. Address: (h.) Latch House, Abernyte, Perthshire.

MacSween, Iain MacLean, BA (Econ), MPhil. Chief Executive, Scottish Fishermen's Organisation, since 1982; b. 20.9.49, Glasgow; m., Jean Gemmill Martin; 3 s.; 1 d. Educ. Knightswood Secondary School; Strathclyde University; Glasgow University. Fisheries Economics Research Unit, 1973-75; Department of Agriculture and Fisheries for Scotland, 1975-77; Scottish Fishermen's Organisation, since 1977; President, European Federation of Fishermen's Organisations. Address: (b.) 601 Queensferry Road, Edinburgh EH4 6EA; T.-0131-339 7972.

MacSween, Professor Sir Roddy N. M., Kt, BSc, MD, FRCPGlas, FRCPEdin, Hon. FRCP Lond, Hon. FRCSEdin, Hon. FRCSLond, Hon. FCPath S. Africa, FRCPath, FRSE, FIBiol, FMedSci. Professor of Pathology, Glasgow University, 1984-99; Honorary Consultant Pathologist, Western Infirmary, Glasgow, 1970-99; President, Royal College of Pathologists, 1996-99; Chairman, Academy of Medical Royal Colleges, 1998-2000; Member, General Medical Council, since 1999; Chairman, Unrelated Live Transplant Regulatory Authority, since 1999; b. 2.2.35, Kinloch, Lewis; m., Marjory Pentland Brown; 1 s.; 1 d. Educ. Inverness Royal Academy; Glasgow University. Honorary Fellow, South African Society of Pathologists, 1982; Otago Savings Bank Visiting Professor, Otago University, 1983; Hans Popper Lecturer in Liver Pathology, Columbia University College of Physicians and Surgeons,

New York, 1988; Henry Moon Lecturer, University of California, San Francisco, 1993; Basil Morson Lecturer, British Society of Gastroenterology, 1995; President, Royal Medico-Chirurgical Society of Glasgow, 1978-79; President, International Academy of Pathology, British Division, 1988-90; Editor, Histopathology (Journal), 1985-96. Publications: Muir's Textbook of Pathology, 13th edition (Co-Editor); Pathology of the Liver, 4th edition (Co-Editor); Recent Advances in Histopathology, Nos. 11-17; Recent Advances in Hepatology, No. 1. Former Captain, Dunaverty and Machrihanish Golf Clubs. Recreations: golf; gardening; opera; hill-walking; more golf! Address: (h.) 32 Calderwood Road, Newlands, Glasgow G43 2RU; T.-0141-637 4355; e-mail: roddymacsween@hotmail.com

MacTaggart, Kenneth Dugald, BA, PhD. Proprietor, Alba Consult; b. 15.4.53, Glasgow; m., Caroline McNicholas; 2 d. Educ. Allan Glen's School, Glasgow; Glasgow University; Paisley College; Aston University. Economic research, Aston University, 1976-80; Editor, Export Times, London, 1980-84; Editor, Property International, London and Bahrain, 1984-87; Director, Inc Publications, London, 1987-88; Senior Economist, HIDB, 1988-91; Highlands and Islands Enterprise: Director of Strategy, 1995-98, Head of Knowledge, 1998-2001. Recreations: hill-walking; piano; photography. Address: (h.) The Sutors, 28 Broadstone Park, Inverness IV2 3LA; T.-01463 233717.

McVicar, George Christie, DipMusEd, RSAM; Hon.FTSC. President, Scottish Amateur Music Association, (Chairman, 1982-95); b. 17.3.19, Dumbarton. Educ. Dumbarton Academy; Royal Scottish Academy of Music and Drama. Teacher of Music, Dunbartonshire Schools, 1946-54; Lecturer in Music, Moray House College of Education, 1954-56; Adviser in Music to Stirlingshire and subsequently Central Region, 1956-79. Former Adjudicator Member, British Federation of Music Festivals; Examiner, Trinity College of Music, 1979-91. Publications: The Saltire Scottish Song Book (formerly Oxford Scottish Song Book); Saltire Two-Part Scottish Song Book; The New Scottish Song Book; Four Burns Songs for Unaccompanied Mixed Voice Choir. Address: (h.) 22 Queen Street, Stirling FK8 1HN; T.-01786 472074.

McVicar, William, RD*, CA. Chairman of Trustees, Church of Scotland Housing and Loan Fund for Retired Ministers and Widows and Widowers of Ministers, since 1983 (Trustee, since 1976); Retired Chartered Accountant; b. 29.6.32, Rutherglen; m., Doreen Ann; 1 s.; 1 d. Educ. George Heriot's School, Edinburgh. Royal Navy, 1950-52; RNVR/RNR, 1955-86 (retired list, Commander RNR); Admitted ICAS, 1958 (T.C. Garden & Co., CA, Edinburgh); Partner, T.C. Garden & Co., CA, Edinburgh, 1962-79; Partner, Coopers and Lybrand, 1979-91. Member, Church of Scotland Board of Ministry. Recreations: travel; food and wine; gardening; golf; grand-children. Address: (h.) The Ley, Innerleithen, Peeblesshire EH44 6NL; T.-01896 830 240.

McVie, John, BL, WS, NP. Retired Solicitor; Honorary Sheriff-Substitute, Lothian and Borders; b. 7.12.19, Edinburgh; m., Lindsaye Woodburn Mair; 1 s.; 1 d. Educ. Royal High School; Edinburgh University. Captain, 7/9th Bn., The Royal Scots, 1940-46 (Signal Officer, North West Europe); mentioned in Despatches; Town Clerk, Royal Burgh of Haddington, 1951-75. Address: (h.) Ivybank, Haddington, East Lothian; T.-0162-082 3727.

MacWalter, Ronald Siller, BMSc (Hons), MB, ChB (Hons), MRCP(UK); FRCP(Edin); FRCP (Glas). Consultant Physician in General Medicine, Ninewells Hospital, Dundee, since 1997; Consultant Physician in Medicine for the Elderly, Royal Victoria Hospital, Dundee, 1986-97; Honorary Senior Lecturer in Medicine, Dundee University, Ninewells Hospital, Dundee, since 1986; Honorary Associate Professor of Medicine, Kigezi International School of Medicine, Cambridge, since 2001; b. 14.12.53, Broughty Ferry; m., Sheila Margaret Nicoll; 2 s. Educ. Harris Academy, Dundee; Dundee University; University of Florida. Registrar in Medicine and Haematology, Department of Clinical Pharmacology, Ninewells Hospital, Dundee; Senior Registrar in General Medicine and Geriatric Medicine, Nuffield Department of Medicine, John Radcliffe Hospital, Oxford. Publication: Aids to Clinical Examination; papers on stroke.

McWilliam, James, OBE, MA (Hons), DipEd. Rector, Lochaber High School, 1970-88; Chairman, Highland Health Board, 1983-91; b. 4.10.27, Portsoy, Banffshire; m., Helen C. Brodie; 3 d. Educ. Fordyce Academy, Banffshire; Glasgow University. Teacher of English, Calderhead School, Shotts, 1951; National Service (Royal Army Education Corps), 1951-53; Teacher, Coatbridge High School, 1953; Special Assistant, Beath High School, Cowdenbeath, 1958; Principal Teacher of English, Campbeltown Grammar School, 1961-70. Member, Highland Health Board, since 1978 (Chairman, Practitioners' Committee, 1981); Honorary Sheriff, Grampian, Highlands and Islands, since 1978; Past President: Lochaber Rotary Club, Lochaber EIS, Highland Secondary Headteachers Association. Recreations: music; TV; golf (occasionally). Address: (h.) 19 Seafield Street, Portsoy, Banff; T.-01261 843148.

McWilliam, Rev. Thomas Mathieson, MA, BD. Minister, Contin Parish, Ross-shire, since 1997; Clerk, Presbytery of Ross, since 2000; b. 12.11.39, Glasgow; m., Patricia Jane Godfrey; 1 s.; 1 d. Educ. Eastwood Secondary School; Glasgow University; New College, Edinburgh. Assistant Minister, Auld Kirk of Ayr, 1964-66; Minister: Dundee St. David's North, 1966-72, East Kilbride Greenhills, 1972-80, Lylesland Parish Church, Paisley, 1980-97; Convener, Youth Education Committee, General Assembly, 1980-84; Moderator, Paisley Presbytery, 1985-86; Convener, Board of Practice and Procedure, General Assembly, 1992-96. Recreations: walking; reading; gardening; bowling. Address: (h.) Contin Manse, Contin, Strathpeffer IV14 9ES; T.-01997 421380.

M

Maan, Bashir Ahmed, CBE, JP, DL, MSc, FRSA. President, Scottish Council of Voluntary Organisations, since 2001; b. 22.10.26, Maan, Pakistan; 1 s.; 3 d. Educ. D.B. High School, Quila Didar Singh; Punjab University. Involved in the struggle for creation of Pakistan as a student, 1943-47; organised rehabilitation of refugees from India in Maan and surrounding areas, 1947-48; emigrated to UK and settled in Glasgow, 1953; Founder Secretary, Glasgow Pakistan Social and Cultural Society, 1955-65 (President, 1966-69); Member, Executive Committee, Glasgow City Labour Party, 1969-70; Vice-Chairman, Glasgow Community Relations Council, 1970-75; Member, Glasgow Corporation, 1970-75 (Magistrate, City of Glasgow, 1971-74; Vice-Chairman, then Chairman, Police Committee, 1971-75); Member, National Road Safety Committee, 1971-74 and Scottish Accident Prevention Committee, 1971-75; Member, BBC Immigrant Programmes Advisory Committee, 1972-80; Convenor, Pakistan Bill Action Committee, 1973; contested East Fife Parliamentary seat, February 1974; President, Standing Conference of Pakistani Organisations in UK and Eire, 1974-77; Police Judge, City of Glasgow, 1974-75; Member: City of Glasgow District Council, 1975-84, Glasgow City Council, since 1995; Bailie, City of Glasgow, 1980-84 and 1996-99; Deputy Chairman, Commission for Racial Equality, 1977-80; Member, Scottish Gas Consumers Council, 1978-81; Member, Greater Glasgow Health Board, 1981-92; Deputy Lieutenant, Glasgow, since 1982; Hon. Research Fellow, Glasgow University, 1988-91; Founder Chairman, Scottish Pakistani Association, 1984-91, and since 1994; Judge, City of Glasgow District Courts, 1968-97; Chairman, Strathclyde Community Relations Council, 1986-93 and 1994-96; Member, BBC General Advisory Council, 1992-95; a Governor, Jordanhill College of Further Education, 1987-91; Chairman, Mosque Committee, Islamic Centre, Glasgow, 1986-91; Convener, Strathclyde Joint Police Board, since 1999; Member, Police Advisory Board Scotland, since 1999; National Council of the Muslim Council of Britain, since 1998; LLD, University of Strathclyde, 1999; DUniv, Glasgow, 2001. Publication: The New Scots. Recreations: golf; reading. Address: (h.) 8 Riverview Gardens, Glasgow G51 8EL; T.-0141-429 7689.

Machin, Professor George Ian Thom, MA, DPhil, FFCS, FRHistS. Professor of British History, Dundee University, since 1989, Head, Department of Modern History, 1992-95; b. 3.7.37, Liverpool; m., Dr. Jane Margaret Pallot; 2 s. Educ. Silcoates School, near Wakefield; Jesus College, Oxford. Research Student and Tutor, Oxford University, 1958-61; Assistant Lecturer, then Lecturer in History, Singapore University, 1961-64; Lecturer in Modern History, St. Andrews University, 1964-67; Lecturer, then Senior Lecturer, then Reader, Dundee University, 1967-89; Course Tutor, Open University in Scotland, 1971-82. Member, History Panel, Scottish Universities Council on Entrance, 1990-94; Observer, Scottish Examination Board, 1991-94; Universities' Member, History Panel, Scottish Qualifications Authority, 1997-2000 (Scottish Examination Board, 1996-97); sometime External Examiner, Universities of Cambridge, St. Andrews, Aberdeen, Hull, Leicester, Sussex, Stirling; Assessor in History, Estonian university institutions, 2001; Treasurer, Abertay Historical Society, 1966-73; Treasurer, Dundee Branch, Historical Association, 1981-92, President, 1992-95; Member, Editorial Board, Journal of Liberal Democrat History, since 2001; Founding Fellow, Institute of Contemporary Scotland, since 2000; Elder, Church of Scotland, since 1981. Publications: The Catholic Question in English Politics 1820 to 1830, 1964; Politics and the Churches in Great Britain 1832 to 1868, 1977; Politics and the Churches in Great Britain 1869 to 1921, 1987; The Liberal Governments 1905-15, 1991; Disraeli, 1995; Churches and Social Issues in Twentieth Century Britain, 1998; The Rise of Democracy in Britain, 1830-1918, 2001. Recreations: the arts; hill-walking; natural history. Address: (h.) 50 West Road, Newport-on-Tay, Fife DD6 8HP; T.-01382 543371; e-mail: g.i.t.machin@dundee.ac.uk

Mack, Professor Douglas Stuart, MA, PhD, FRSE. Professor, Stirling University, since 2000; General Editor, Association for Scottish Literary Studies, 1980-90; General Editor, Stirling/South Carolina Edition of James Hogg, since 1990; President, The James Hogg Society, since 1982; b. 30.1.43, Bellshill; m., Wilma Stewart Grant; 2 s. Educ. Uddingston Grammar School; Glasgow University; Stirling University. Research Assistant, National Library of Scotland, 1965-66; Assistant Librarian: St. Andrews University, 1966-70, Stirling University, 1970-86; Lecturer, Stirling University, 1986-94, Reader, 1994-99. Editor of various books by James Hogg and Sir Walter Scott. Recreations: watching Hamilton Accies; sailing on paddle steamers. Address: (h.) 2 Law Hill Road, Dollar FK14 7BG; T.-Dollar 742452; e-mail: d.s.mack@stir.ac.uk

Mack, Jimmy, MBE. Broadcaster and Journalist; Presenter, The Jimmy Mack Show, Radio Clyde 2, since 1990; b. 26.6.34, Greenock; m., Barbara; 1 s.; 1 d. Educ. Lenzie Academy; Bathgate Academy. Insurance Inspector, Guardian Royal Exchange Assurance Co., 1956-70; Producer and Presenter, various programmes, BBC Radio Medway, Kent, 1970-79; Presenter, Radio 1 Club, BBC Radio 1, 1967-70; Presenter, The Early Show, Night Ride, Junior Choice, BBC Radio 2, 1971-76; Producer, You and Yours, Woman's Hour, In Britain Now, BBC Radio 4, 1977-78; Presenter: The Jimmy Mack Show and Jimmy Mack's Old Gold, BBC Radio Scotland, 1979-89, Top Club and Best Years of Their Lives, Grampian TV, 1980-84, Scotland Today, Scottish TV, 1984-85, I Believe You Believe, BBC TV, 1986. Television and Radio Industries Club of Scotland Award for best live radio programme, 1986; MBE, for services to charity in Scotland, 1996. Patron, Scottish Motor Neurone Disease Association. Publication: Jimmy Mack Show Book, 1984. Recreation: photography. Address: (b.) Radio Clyde, Clydebank Business Park, Glasgow G81 2RX; T.- 0141-565 2200; e-mail: Jimmy.Mack@radioclyde.com

Mack, William, MCIBS. Chairman, Edinburgh and South East Scotland Blood Transfusion Association, since 1999; Secretary and Treasurer, Scottish National Blood Transfusion Association, since 1995; Treasurer, Scottish National Dictionary Association; b. 10.11.43, Douglas; m., Eileen Marion McFarlane; 1 s.; 1 d. Educ. Lanark Grammar School. Royal Bank of Scotland, 1960-95. Recreations: New Orleans jazz; wood-turning; walking; gardening. Address: (h.) 2 Otterburn Park, Edinburgh EH14 1JX; T.-0131-443 7636.

Mackie of Benshie, Baron (George Yull Mackie), CBE, DSO, DFC, LLD. Farmer; former Liberal Democrat Spokesman, House of Lords, on Devolution, Agriculture, Scotland, Industry; Member, Council of Europe and Western European Union, 1986-96; b. 10.7.19, Aberdeen; m., 1, Lindsay Lyall Sharp (deceased, 1985); 1 s. (deceased); 3 d.; 2, Mrs Jacqueline Lane. Educ. Aberdeen Grammar School; Aberdeen University. Bomber Command and Air Staff, 1944. Contested South Angus, 1959; Vice-Chairman (Organisation), Scottish Liberal Party, 1959-64; MP (Liberal), Caithness and Sutherland, 1964-66; Chairman, Scottish Liberal Party, 1965-70; contested Caithness and Sutherland, 1970; contested NE Scotland, European Parliamentary Election, 1979; Member, EEC Scrutiny Committee (D), House of Lords; Executive, Inter-Parliamentary Union; Chairman: Caithness Glass, 1966-84, Industrial Appeal Committee, Pitlochry Festival Theatre, 1979, Angus Committee, Salvation Army, 1976-84; Rector,

Dundee University, 1980-83; Director, Scottish Ballet, 1986-88. Address: (h.) Benshie Cottage, Oathlaw, by Forfar, Angus.

Mackie, Dugald Mabon, MA, FRSA. Secretary to University Court, University of Glasgow, since 1996; b. 26.12.52, Ayr. Educ. Ayr Academy; University of Edinburgh. Administrative Assistant: Didsbury College of Education, 1974-76, University of Aston, 1976-80; University of Strathclyde: Faculty Officer, 1980-89, Deputy Registrar, 1989-92; Secretary, Scottish Higher Education Funding Council, 1992-96; Board Member: New Opportunities Fund, since 1998, UCAS, since 1999; Member, Board of Management, Glasgow College of Building and Printing, since 2001. Recreations: mountaineering; gardening; railways. Address: (b.) University of Glasgow, Glasgow G12 8QQ; T.-0141-330 4246.

Mackie, Joyce Grant, BA (Hons), DipCE, DL. Vice-President, National Trust for Scotland, since 1988; Partner, farming business, since 1963; b. 7.5.40, Forfar; m., Bruce Stephen Mackie; 2 s.; 2 d. Educ. St. Margaret's School for Girls, Aberdeen; Moray House College of Education. Teacher, Dalmilling School, Ayr, 1961-63. National Trust for Scotland: Member, Council, 1974-79, 1985-90, Member, Executive Committee, 1976-86; former Member, Aberdeen Committee, Scottish Children's League (RSSPCC); Trustee, David Gordon Memorial Trust, since 1977; Director, Lathallan Preparatory School, Montrose, since 1979, Chairman, 1990-98; Member, Council, Glenalmond College, since 1991; Member, Church of Scotland Nomination Committee, 1985-88; former Member, Executive Committee, Aberdeen University Quincentenary Campaign. Recreations: gardening; art; Scotland. Address: (h.) Balquhindachy, Methlick, Ellon, Aberdeenshire AB41 7BY; T.-01651 806373.

Mackie, Maitland, CBE, BSc, MA, LLD. Farmer; Owner, Mackie's; Director: Farmdata, Rowett Research Services, Lloyds TSB Scotland; Chairman, Scottish Agricultural College; former Director, Rowett Research Institute; b. 21.9.37, Aberdeen; m., Dr. Halldis Mackie; 1 s.; 2 d. Educ. Aberdeen Grammar School; Aberdeen University. Former Chairman: Grampian Enterprise Ltd., Food and Animal Committees, Agricultural and Food Research Council, Farm Assured Scotch Livestock, Scottish Pig Industry Initiative; former Vice-President, National Farmers Union of Scotland. Recreations: skiing; sailing; Norway. Address: Westertown, Rothienorman, Aberdeenshire; T.-01467 671466.

Mackie, Marie Watson-Watt, MA (Hons), EdB (Dip). National Chairman, Scottish Women's Rural Institutes, 1987-93; Chairman, Borders Arts Network; Non-Executive Director, Borders Community Health NHS Trust; b. Kilmarnock; m., Alex. O. Mackie, MA (Hons), FSA Scot. Educ. Kilmarnock Academy; Glasgow University. County Federation Chairman, SWRI, Roxburghshire, 1975-81; National Vice-Chairman, SWRI, 1981-87; Member, Women's National Commission, 1987-89; former Executive Member, Scottish Institute of Adult Education; Producer, Lecturer and Adjudicator, amateur drama; Founder/Producer, Cheviot Theatre Group; Chairman, Roxburghshire Drama Association; Britain in Bloom Judge, 1975-84; SWRI Delegate to ACWW Hague conference, 1992; Member: Borders Enterprise Focus on Community Sustainability Steering Group, 1993, Council, Scottish Association of Young Farmers Clubs, 1987-94, Council, Rural Forum (Scotland), 1987-90; Chairman, Advisory Committee, Sue Ryder Home (Borders), since 1998; Member, Community Sub-Group, Borders Environmental Education Forum. Recreations: interior design; 19th-century pottery; Samoyed dogs; enjoying the countryside of Scotland; art and architecture. Address: (h.) Linton Downs, Kelso, Roxburghshire.

Macklin, Professor John, BA, PhD, Comendador de la Orden de Isabel la Catolica. Principal and Vice-Chancellor, Paisley University, since 2001; b. 9.10.47, Belfast; m., Pauline Ruben; 1 s.; 2 d. Educ. Queen's University, Belfast. Hull University: Lecturer in Hispanic Studies, 1973-85, Senior Lecturer, 1985-87, Head of Department, 1986-87; Leeds University: Cowdray Professor of Spanish, 1988-2001, Dean, Faculty of Arts, 1992-94; Dean for Research in Humanities, 1994-99; Pro Vice Chancellor, 1999-2001. Recreations: current affairs; reading; cinema; art history. Address: (b.) Paisley University, High Street, Paisley PA1 2BE; T.-0141-848 3670.

Magee, William F., LLB. Secretary, Accounts Commission for Scotland and Audit Scotland; b. 25.1.50, Glasgow; m., Helen McCann; 2 s. Educ. St. Aloysius College, Glasgow; Glasgow University. Legal work with various Scottish local authorities; Depute Director of Administration, Edinburgh District, 1984-88; Director of Administration and Legal Services, Central Region, 1988-95. Past Chairman, Society of Directors of Administration in Scotland; Governor, RSAMD. Recreations: music; literature. Address: (b.) 110 George Street, Edinburgh; T.-0131-477 1234.

Magnusson, Magnus, KBE (Hon.), MA (Oxon), FRSE, FRSA, FSA Scot. Writer and Broadcaster; Chairman, Scottish Natural Heritage, 1992-99; Patron, Institute of Contemporary Scotland; b. 12.10.29, Reykjavik, Iceland; m., Mamie Baird; 1 s.; 3 d. Educ. Edinburgh Academy; Jesus College, Oxford. Reporter, Scottish Daily Express; Features Writer, The Scotsman; Co-Presenter, Tonight, BBC TV, 1964-65; Presenter: Chronicle, Cause for Concern, Checkpoint, Mainly Magnus, BC - The Archaeology of the Bible Lands, Living Legends, Vikings!, Mastermind, 1972-97; Rector, Edinburgh University, 1975-78. Publications include: Iceland Saga; I've Started So I'll Finish; Lindisfarne - the Cradle Island; Rum - Nature's Island; The Icelandic Sagas I and II (translations); Magnus Magnusson's Quiz Book; Scotland, the Story of a Nation.

Magnusson, Sally Anne, MA (Hons). Presenter, Reporting Scotland, BBC, since 1998; Presenter, Hard Cash, BBC, since 2000; Presenter, A Family of My Own, BBC, since 2000; Presenter, Songs of Praise, BBC, since 1983; b. 11.10.55, Glasgow; m., Norman Stone; 4 s.; 1 d. Educ. Laurel Bank School; Edinburgh University. Reporter, The Scotsman, 1979-81; News/Feature Writer, Sunday Standard, 1981-83; Reporter, Current Account, BBC Scotland, 1983, Presenter, Sixty Minutes, BBC, 1983-84; Presenter, London Plus, BBC, 1984-85; Presenter, Breakfast News (formerly Breakfast Time), BBC, 1985-99. Feature Writer of the Year, Fraser Scottish Press Awards, 1982. Publications: The Flying Scotsman, 1981; Clemo-A Love Story, 1984; A Shout in the Street, 1990; Family Life, 1999. Address: (b.) c/o Curtis Brown, 28/29 Haymarket, London SW1; T.-0171-396 6600; e-mail: sally.magnusson@bbc.co.uk

Maguire, Frank, PHB, LLB. Solicitor Advocate; Thompsons, Glasgow, since 1987 (Thompsons, Edinburgh, 1981-87); b. 4.10.55, Glasgow; m., Fiona Macdonald; 3 s. Educ. St. Vincent's College, Langbank; Gregorian University, Rome; St. Mary's College, Blairs; Aberdeen University. Apprentice, McLachlan & McKenzie, Edinburgh, Robin Thompson & Partners, Edinburgh; Assistant Solicitor, Robin Thompson & Partners; Salaried Partner, Thompsons; Equity Partner, Thompsons. President, Society of Solicitor Advocates; Member, Panel of Solicitor Advocates and Personal Injury Panel, Law Society of Scotland; Member, Steering Committee, Piper Alpha Trade Union Group; Legal Adviser, STUC; Member, Royal Society of Procurators; Member, Manufacturing, Science and Finance Union. Recreations: sailing; windsurfing; running. Address: (b.) Berkeley House, 285 Bath Street, Glasgow G2 4HQ; T.-0141-221 8840.

Maguire, Sheriff John, PhL, LLB, QC. Sheriff Principal, Tayside, Central and Fife, 1990-98; b. 30.11.34, Kirkintilloch; m., Eva O'Hara; 2 s.; 2 d. Educ. St. Ninian's High School, Kirkintilloch; St. Mary's College, Blairs; Pontifical Gregorian University, Rome; Edinburgh University. Standing Junior Counsel, Ministry of Public Buildings and Works, 1962-68; Sheriff at Airdrie, 1968-73; Sheriff at Glasgow, 1973-90; Secretary, Sheriffs Association, 1982-87, President, 1988-90. Co-Founder and Chairman, PHEW, 1985-90; Chairman, Northern Lighthouse Board, 1995-97; Lieutenant for Scotland, Equestrian Order of the Holy Sepulchre of Jerusalem; Member, Parole Board for Scotland. Recreations: reading; thinking about doing the garden. Address: (h.) 3 Hatton Way, Perth PH2 7DP; T.-01738 636260.

Mahmood, Tahir Ahmed, MBBS, BSc, MD, FRCOG, FRCP(Ireland); MFFP, MBA (HCM). Consultant Obstetrician and Gynaecologist, Forth Park Hospital, Kirkcaldy, since 1990; Clinical Senior Lecturer, Obstetrics and Gynaecology, Aberdeen University, since 1990; Senior Lecturer, School of Biological and Medical Sciences, St. Andrews University, since 1995; Clinical Senior Lecturer, University of Edinburgh, since 1996; Director, Women and Children's Health Directorate, Fife Acute NHS Hospitals Trust; Member, BMA Scottish Council, since 1996; b. 7.10.53, Pakistan; m., Aasia Bashir; 2 s. Educ. King Edward Medical College, Lahore, Punjab University. Member, Scottish Hospital Staffing Review Committee, sub-speciality of obstetrics and gynaecology, 1986-88; Member, Minimal Invasive Surgery Subgroup and Clinical Resource Management — Procurement Group for Acute Unit, Fife, 1991-92; Ethicon RCOG Travelling Fellowship, 1991; Member, Senate, Aberdeen University, 1992-2000; Hon. Secretary, Northern Obstetrical and Gynaecological Society, 1993-98, Chairman, since 1999; Member, Area Medical Committee, Fife, 1993-98, Chairman, 1995-98; Member, Council, Royal College of Obstetricians and Gynaecologists, 1994-2000, and of Scottish Executive Council, 1994-2000. Recreations: reading; history; walking. Address: (b.) Forth Park Hospital, 30 Bennochy Road, Kirkcaldy, Fife; T.-01592 643355.

Main, Very Rev. Professor Alan, TD, MA, BD, STM, PhD. Professor of Practical Theology, Christ's College, Aberdeen, since 1980; Moderator, General Assembly, Church of Scotland, 1998-99; b. 31.3.36, Aberdeen; m., Anne Louise Swanson; 2 d. Educ. Robert Gordon's College, Aberdeen; University of Aberdeen; Union Theological Seminary, New York. Minister, Chapel of Garioch Parish, Aberdeenshire, 1963-70; Chaplain, University of Aberdeen, 1970-80; Chaplain, 153(H) Artillery Support Regiment, RCT(V), 1970-92; Provost, Faculty of Divinity, Aberdeen University, 1990-93; Master, Christ's College, Aberdeen, since 1992. Moderator: Garioch Presbytery, 1969-70, Aberdeen Presbytery, 1984-85; Adviser in Religious Broadcasting, Grampian Television, 1976-86; Chairman: Grampian Marriage Guidance, 1977-80, Cruse, 1981-84. Recreations: music, golf; beekeeping. Address: (h.) Kirkfield, Barthol Chapel, Inverurie AB51 8TD.

Main, Professor Brian G.M., BSc, MBA, MA, PhD. Professor of Economics, Edinburgh University, since 1991 b. 24.8.47, St. Andrews; m., June Lambert; 2 s.; 1 d. Educ. Buckhaven High School; St. Andrews University; University of California, Berkeley. Lecturer, then Reader in Economics, Edinburgh University, 1976-87; Professor of Economics and Chairman, Department of Economics, St. Andrews University, 1987-91. Recreation: fishing. Address: (b.) Management School, Edinburgh University, George Square, Edinburgh EH8 9JY; T.-0131-650 8361.

Main, Carol B.L.D., BA. Director, National Association of Youth Orchestras, since 1979; Scottish Director, Live Music Now, since 1984; Classical Music Editor, The List, since 1985; b. 21.12.58, Kirkcaldy; 1 d. Educ. Kirkcaldy High School; Edinburgh University. Freelance music critic, radio broadcaster. Board Director, Edinburgh Festival Fringe Society; Chair, Enterprise Music Scotland. Address: (b.) 14 Lennox Street, Edinburgh EH4 1QA; T.-0131 332 2110.

Main, Sir Peter (Tester), ERD, MD, LLD (Hon.), FRCPE, CIMgt; b. 21.3.25, Aberdeen; m., 1, Margaret Tweddle (deceased); 2 s.; 1 d.; 2, May Hetherington McMillan. Educ. Robert Gordon's College; Aberdeen University. House Surgeon, Aberdeen Royal Infirmary, 1948-49; Captain, RAMC, 1949-51; Medical Officer with Field Ambulance (Suez), 1956; Lt. Col., RAMC (AER), retired 1964; general practice, 1953-57; The Boots Co. PLC: joined Research Department, 1957; Director of Research, 1968; Managing Director, Industrial Division, 1979; Director, 1973-85, Vice Chairman, 1980-81, Chairman, The Boots Co. PLC, 1982-85; Director: Scottish Development Agency, 1986-91, W.A. Baxter & Sons Ltd., 1985-91. Member, National Economic Development Council, 1984-85; Chairman, Committee of Inquiry into Teachers' Pay and Conditions, Scotland, 1986; Governor, Henley Management College, 1983-86. Recreations: fishing; Scottish music. Address: Ninewells House, Chirnside, Duns, Berwickshire TD11 3XF; T.-01890 818191.

Mair, Alexander, MBE (1967). Governor, Robert Gordon's College, Aberdeen, since 1988; b. 5.11.22, Echt; m., Margaret Isobel. Educ. Skene Central School; School of Accountancy, Glasgow. Company Secretary, Grampian TV, 1961-70; appointed Director, 1967; Director and Chief Executive, 1970-87. President, Aberdeen Chamber of Commerce, 1989-91; Chairman: Aberdeen International Football Festival, 1988-91, Oil Industry Community Fund, 1993-2001, RGIT Limited, 1989-98. Recreations: golf; skiing; gardening. Address: (h.) Ravenswood, 66 Rubislaw Den South, Aberdeen AB15 4AY; T.-01224 317619.

Mair, Alistair S.F., MBE, DL, BSc, BA, FIMgt, FRSA. Managing Director, Caithness Glass Ltd., 1977-98, Chairman, 1991-98; b. 20.7.35, Drumblade; m., 1, Anne Garrow (deceased); 2, Mary Bolton; 4 s.; 1 d. Educ. Robert Gordon's College, Aberdeen; Aberdeen University. Rolls Royce, Glasgow, 1957-71: graduate apprentice, PA to General Manager, Production Control Manager, Product Centre Manager; RAF, 1960-62 (short-service commission, Technical Branch); Managing Director, Caithness Glass Ltd., 1971-75; Marketing Director, Worcester Royal Porcelain Co., 1975-76. Non-Executive Director: Grampian Television, since 1986, Crieff Hydro Ltd., since 1994 (Chairman, since 1996), Murray VCT 3 PLC, since 1997; Governor, Morrison's Academy, Crieff, since 1985 (Chairman, since 1996); Commissioner, Queen Victoria School, Dunblane, 1992-97; Member, Aberdeen University Court, since 1993, Convener, Finance and Estates Committee, since 1998, Chancellor's Assessor, Senior Lay Member, and Vice Chairman, since 2000; Chairman, Scottish Committee of University Chairmen, since 2001; Chairman, CBI Scotland, 1989-91, and Member, CBI Council, 1985-97; President, British Glass Manufacturers Confederation 1997, 1998; Chairman, Crieff Auxiliary Association (Richmond House), 1993-99; Patron, Perth and Kinross Association of Voluntary Services, since 1994; Honorary President, Duke of Edinburgh Award, Perth and Kinross, since 1993; Deputy Chairman, Cherrybank Partnership, since 2001; Chairman, Perth Conservative and Unionist Association, since 1999; Elected Member, Executive Committee, Scottish Conservative and Unionist Party, since 2001. Recreations: reading; history; O.U. student; gardening; walking; current affairs. Address: (h.) Woodend, Madderty, Crieff PH7 3PA; T.-01764 683210.

Mair, Professor Douglas. Professor, Department of Economics, Heriot-Watt University, since 1993; b. 3.6.39, Arbroath; m., Ishbel Fraser; 2 s.; 1 d. Educ. Arbroath High School; St. Andrews University. Ford Motor

Company, 1960-63; Scottish Council (Development and Industry), 1963-67; joined Heriot-Watt University, 1967. Recreation: golf. Address: (b.) Department of Economics, Heriot-Watt University, Riccarton, Edinburgh EH14 4AS; T.-0131-451 3491.

Maitland, Peter Salisbury, BSc, PhD, FRSE. Independent Consultant in Freshwater Ecology, since 1986; Visiting Professor, Glasgow University, since 1997; Founder, Scottish Freshwater Group; b. 8.12.37, Glasgow; m., Kathleen Ramsay; 1 s.; 2 d. Educ. Bearsden Academy; Glasgow University. Lecturer in Zoology, Glasgow University, 1959-67; Senior Scientific Officer, Nature Conservancy, 1967-70; Principal Scientific Officer, Institute of Terrestrial Ecology, 1970-86; Senior Lecturer in Ecology, St. Andrews University, 1978-82. Royal Society of Edinburgh Fellowship, 1980; Neill Medal, 1993; Freshwater Biological Association Fellowship, 1996; Zoological Society of London's Marsh Wildlife Award for Conservation, 1999. Publications: ten books; 200 scientific papers. Recreations: wildlife conservation; fish-keeping; gardening; walking; music. Address: (h.) Nether Sunnyside, Gladshot, Haddington EH41 4NR; T.-01620 823691.

Maitland-Carew, The Hon. Gerald Edward Ian, DL; b. 28.12.41, Dublin; m., Rosalind Averil Speke; 2 s.; 1 d. Educ. Harrow School. Army Officer, 15/19 The Kings Royal Hussars, 1960-72; looked after family estates, since 1972; Brigadier, Royal Company of Archers; Chairman, Lauderdale Hunt; Chairman, Lauderdale and Galawater Branch, Royal British Legion Scotland; Deputy Lieutenant, Ettrick and Lauderdale and Roxburgh, 1989; elected Member, Jockey Club, 1987; Member, Border Area, TA Committee; Chairman, International League for the Protection of Horses, 1999; President, Border Rifle League, 1994; Chairman, Gurkha Welfare Trust of Scotland, 1996; Racecourse Steward at Ayr, Kelso, Newcastle, Cheltenham and Newmarket. Recreations: racing; hunting; shooting. Address: (h.) Thirlestane Castle, Lauder, Berwickshire; T.-01578 722 254.

Maizels, Professor Rick, BSc, PhD. Professor of Zoology, Edinburgh University, since 1995; b. 14.5.53, London. Educ. University College London. MRC Scientific Staff, NIMR, Mill Hill, 1979-83; Lecturer, Reader and Professor, Department of Biology, Imperial College, London, 1983-95. Address: (b.) Ashworth Laboratories, Edinburgh University EH9 3JT; T.-0131-650 5511.

Malik, Bailie Hanzala, JP, BSc. Member, Glasgow City Council, since 1995; Bailie, since 1999; b. 26.11.56, Glasgow; m., Halema Sadia; 1 s.; 1 d. Educ. Paisley University. Manager, Dhool Farms Ltd, 1982-87; Financial Consultant, 1987-88; Director, Azad Video, 1988-92. Glasgow City Council: Member, Education Committee, (Senior Vice Convener), Chair of Standards and Quality Education Services, Member, Housing Committee, Member, North West Area Forum, Member, Social Work Committee; Committee Member: Queens Cross Housing Association, Charing Cross Housing Association; Director: Community Central Hall, Glasgow Anti Racist Alliance, Northwest Economic Network, Community Learning Scotland, Ethnic Minority Enterprise Centre, Queens Cross Work Space Ltd., Glasgow Careers Partnership Ltd., Glasgow Cultural Enterprises Ltd.; Chair: Justice and Minorities, Friends of Lahore (Link), Multicultural Media Forum, Woodlands Education Trust, Woodlands Advisory Committee, Ethnic Minority Respite Centre Project, West of Scotland Racial Equality Council, Ethnic Minority Family Support Association; Member, Court, Strathclyde University; Member, Advisory Council, Immigration Advisory Service. Recreations: badminton; charity work; community work; cooking; overseas travel; philately; politics; swimming. Address: (b.) Glasgow City Council, George Square, Glasgow G2 1DU; T.-0141-287 2000/7041; e-mail: hanzala.malik@councillors.glasgow.gov.uk

Mallinson, Edward John Harold, LLM, MPharm, FRPharmS, FIMgt, FRSH, HonMFPHM. Specialist in Pharmaceutical Public Health (formerly Chief Administrative Pharmaceutical Officer), Lanarkshire Health Board; b. 15.3.50, Bingley; m., Diana Gray; 2 d. Educ. Bradford Grammar School; Bradford University; Cardiff Law School. Staff Pharmacist (Ward Pharmacy Services), Bradford Royal Infirmary, 1973-78; District Pharmaceutical Officer, Perth and Kinross District, 1978-83. Secretary, Scottish Specialists in Pharmaceutical Public Health, formerly Scottish Chief Administrative Pharmaceutical Officers' Group, 1988-90, 1996, and 1999-2001 (Chairman, 1990-92, and 1997-98); Member, Scottish Executive, Royal Pharmaceutical Society of Great Britain (Hon. Secretary, Bradford & District Branch, 1978, Hon. Secretary, Dundee & Eastern Scottish Branch, 1979-83, Hon. Secretary and Treasurer, Lanarkshire Branch, since 1984); Charter Silver Medallist, 2001; Member of Council, Royal Society of Health, 1992-96, Honorary Treasurer, 1996; Vice Chairman and Secretary, Pharmaceutical Group, Royal Society of Health, 1986-89; Chairman, Strathclyde Police/Lanarkshire Health Board Drug Liaison Committee, 1985-91; Member, General Synod, Scottish Episcopal Church, 1986-95; Honorary Treasurer, Comunn Gaidhlig na h-Eaglais Easbaigich; Honorary Treasurer, Affirming Apostolic Order, 1993-98; Secretary, Lanarkshire Branch, British Institute of Management, 1989-91, Chairman, 1991-94. Recreations: genealogy; Gaelic language and culture; walking and cooking. Address: (h.) Malden, North Dean Park Avenue, Bothwell, Glasgow G71 8HH; T.-01698 852973; e-mail: ejhmallinson@bothwell54.freeserve.co.uk

Malone, Wilson, CA, MPhil. Head, Industrial Assistance Division, Scottish Executive Department of Enterprise and Lifelong Learning, (formerly Scottish Office Education and Industry Department), since 1994; b. 20.6.55, Glasgow; 1 s. Educ. Hillhead High school; Glasgow Technical College; Glasgow University. CA trainee, 1975-79; Accountant, John G. Kincaid & Co., 1980-82; Civil Servant, since 1983; Deputy Director, Locate in Scotland, 1988-94. Recreations: sailing; music. Address: (b.) Meridian Court, 5 Cadogan Street, Glasgow G2 6AT; T.-0141-242 5801.

Mann, Very Rev. Andrew Charles, STB, BA (Hons), Adv.Dip.Crim. Administrator, St. Mary's R.C. Cathedral, Aberdeen, since 2000; Parish Priest, St. Peter's Aberdeen, Sacred Heart, Aberdeen, since 1993; b. 8.6.56, Keith. Educ. St. Thomas' School, Keith; St. Vincent's School, Langbank; St. Mary's College, Blairs; Royal Scots College, Spain. Curate, St. Mary's Cathedral, Aberdeen, 1980-83; Parish Priest: St. Mary's Peterhead and Our Lady and St. John the Baptist, Ellon, 1983-89, St. Duthac's, Dornie, 1989-91; Diocesan Director of Pastoral Planning, 1991-93. Member, Joint Faiths Advisory Board on Criminal Justice. Recreations: reading; cinema; computing. Address: Cathedral House, 20 Huntly Street, Aberdeen AB10 1SH; T.-01224 640160; e-mail: andrew@acmann.freeserve.co.uk

Mann, Professor David George, BSc, PhD. Senior Principal Research Scientist, Royal Botanic Garden, Edinburgh, since 1996; Hon. Professor, Glasgow University, since 1996; b. 25.2.53, Romford, Essex; m., Lynn Barbara; 1 s.; 1 d. Educ. Brentwood School; Bristol University. Edinburgh University: Demonstrator, 1978-81, Lecturer, 1981-90, Director of Studies, 1989-90; Deputy Regius Keeper (Deputy Director), Royal Botanic Garden, Edinburgh, 1990-96. G.W. Prescott Award, 1991, 1997; Editor, Phycologia. Publications: editor/author of 80 papers and books. Recreations: classical piano; part-time degree in art. Address: (b.) Royal Botanic Garden, Inverleith Row, Edinburgh EH3 5LR; T.-0131-552 7171; e-mail: d.mann@rbge.org.uk

Mann, Gordon Laurence, DipTP, MRTPI. Managing Director, The Crichton Trust; b. 28.4.48, Dundee. Director of Planning, Shetland Islands Council, 1980-87; Director of

Physical Planning, Dumfries and Galloway Regional Council, 1987-96; Chief Planning Officer, Dumfries and Galloway Council, 1996-97. Address: (b.) Grierson House, The Crichton, Dumfries DG1 4ZE; T.-01387 247544; e-mail: gordon.mann@crichton.co.uk

Manning, Professor Aubrey William George, OBE, BSc, DPhil, FInstBiol, Dr (h c) (Toulouse), DUniv (Open), FRZSS, FRSE. Professor of Natural History, Division of Biological Sciences, Edinburgh University, 1973-97, Professor Emeritus, since 1997; b. 24.4.30, London; m.; 3 s., inc. 2 by pr. m. Educ. Strode's School, Egham; University College, London; Merton College, Oxford. Research, 1951-54; National Service, Royal Artillery, 1954-56; Lecturer, then Reader in Zoology, Edinburgh University, 1956-73; Secretary-General, International Ethological Committee, 1971-79; President: Association for the Study of Animal Behaviour, 1981-84, Biology Section, British Association for the Advancement of Science, 1993; Member: Scottish Advisory Committee, Nature Conservancy Council, 1982-89, Advisory Committee on Science, NCC, 1985-89; Chairman of Council, Scottish Wildlife Trust, 1990-96; Trustee, National Museums of Scotland, since 1997. Association for the Study of Animal Behaviour Medal, 1998; Member, Wellcome Trust Population Studies Panel, 1996-99; Dobzhansky Memorial Award, Behavioural Genetics Association, 1996; Presenter: Earth Story series, BBC2, 1998, Talking Landscapes series, BBC 2, 2001, Unearthing Mysteries series, Radio 4, 1999, 2000, 2001. Publication: An Introduction to Animal Behaviour, 5th edition, 1998; research papers in biological journals. Recreations: woodland conservation; walking; architecture. Address: (h.) The Old Hall, Ormiston, East Lothian; T.-Pencaitland 340536; e-mail: amanning@ed.ac.uk

Mansfield and Mansfield, 8th Earl of (William David Mungo James Murray), JP, DL; b. 7.7.30; m., Pamela Joan Foster; 2 s.; 1 d. Educ. Eton; Christ Church, Oxford. National Service, Malayan Campaign; called to Bar, Inner Temple, 1958; Barrister, 1958-71; Member, British Delegation to European Parliament, 1973-75; Minister of State, Scottish Office, 1979-83; Minister of State, Northern Ireland Office, 1983-84; Director: General Accident Fire and Life Assurance Corporation Ltd., 1972-79, and 1985-98; The American Trust Ltd., since 1985; Pinneys of Scotland Ltd., 1985-89; Ross Breeders Ltd., 1989-90; Hon. President, St. Andrews Society of Glasgow, 1972-92; President, Royal Scottish Country Dance Society, since 1977; Hon. Member, RICS; First Crown Estate Commissioner, 1985-95. Address: (h.) Scone Palace, Perthshire PH2 6BE.

Manson, Alexander Reid, CBE, SDA, FRAgS. Farmer; General Commissioner of Income Tax, since 1991; b. 2.9.31, Oldmeldrum; m., Ethel Mary Philip; 1 s.; 2 d. Educ. Robert Gordon's College; North of Scotland College of Agriculture. Member, Oldmeldrum Town Council, 1960-65; founder Chairman, Aberdeen Beef and Calf Ltd., 1962; Past President, Scottish Agricultural Organisation Society Ltd.; Chairman, Buchan Meat Producers Ltd., 1982-92; Member, Meat and Livestock Commission, 1986-95; Past President, Federation of Agricultural Cooperatives; Member, Williams Committee of Enquiry, 1989; Member, EU Beef Advisory Committee, 1986-96; Director, National Animal Data Centre, 1992-95; Chairman, Oldmeldrum Heritage Society, since 2000. Recreations: golf; birdwatching. Address: (h.) Kempswood, Oldmeldrum, Inverurie AB51 ODN; T.-01651 872226.

Manson, Frank, MA, MIOSH, MIIRSM. Managing Director, Registers of Scotland, since 1996; b. 18.3.50, Lerwick; m., Mary. Educ. Anderson Educational Institute, Lerwick; Edinburgh University. HM Inspector of Factories, Health and Safety Executive, 1976-80; Technical Executive, BP Detergents International, 1980-84;

Production Controller, William Muir Ltd., 1984-85; Business Development Manager, Unisys Corporation, 1985-89; Management Consultant, 1989-92; Assistant Director of Property, Tayside Region, 1992-96; Head of Central Services, Angus Council, 1995-96. Recreations: reading; walking; rugby. Address: (b.) Meadowbank House, 153 London Road, Edinburgh; T.-0131-479 3615.

Manson, Shirley. Lead singer and guitarist, Garbage, since 1995; b. 26.8.66; m., Eddie Farrell; previous bands: Goodbye Mr MacKenzie, Angelfish; albums: Garbage, 1995, Version 2.0, 1998, beautifulgarbage, 2001; performed theme song for Bond film, The World is Not Enough. Address: Mushroom Records, 1 Shorrolds Road, London SW6 7TR.

Mar and Kellie, Earl of (James Thorne Erskine). Estate Worker; Scottish Liberal Democrat Life Peer, sitting as Lord Erskine of Alloa Tower (Liberal Democrat Spokesman on Scotland, since 2001, Member, House of Lords Select Committee on the Constitution, since 2001); b. 10.3.49, Edinburgh; m., Mary Irene; 1 step s.; 4 step d. Educ. Eton; Moray House College of Education; Inverness College. Community Service Volunteer, York, 1967-68; Youth and Community Worker, Craigmillar, 1971-73; Social Worker, Sheffield, 1973-76, Grampian Region, 1976-78; Social Worker, Prison Social Worker, Community Service Supervisor, Highland Region, 1979-87; Builder, Kincardine, 1990-92; Project Worker, SACRO, Falkirk, 1992-93; Royal Auxiliary Air Force Regiment, 1979-85; Royal Naval Auxiliary Service, 1985-88; Chairman, Strathclyde Tram Inquiry, 1996; Parliamentary Commissioner, Burrell Collection (Lending) Inquiry, 1997. Recreations: canoeing; hill-walking; boat building; Alloa Tower. Address: Hilton Farm, Alloa FK10 3PS.

Maran, Professor Arnold George Dominic, MB, ChB, MD, FRCS, FACS, FRCP, FRCS (Eng), FDS (Hon). Professor of Otolaryngology, Edinburgh University, since 1988; Past President, Royal College of Surgeons; Consultant Surgeon, Royal Infirmary and City Hospital, Edinburgh, since 1974; b. 16.6.36, Edinburgh; m., Anna; 1 s.; 1 d. Educ. Daniel Stewart's College; Edinburgh University; University of Iowa. Trained in Otolaryngology in Edinburgh and America; former Consultant Otolaryngologist, Tayside Health Board, and Professor of Otolaryngology, West Virginia University. Fifteen Visiting Professorships to foreign universities; Honorary Fellowship, Royal College of Surgeons of South Africa, Royal College of Surgeons of Hong Kong, Royal College of Physicians of Edinburgh, Royal College of Surgeons of England, Royal College of Physicians and Surgeons of Glasgow. Order of Gorka Dakshina Bahu, Nepal. Publications: six books and 160 scientific papers. Recreations: golf; music; travel. Address: (h.) 27 Learmonth Terrace, Edinburgh EH4 1NZ; T.-0131-332 0055.

Marchant, Russell, MBA, BSc, CertEd. Principal and Chief Executive, Barony College, since 2001; b. 15.7.58, Windsor; divorced; partner, Amanda Niven; 1 s.; 1 d. Educ. Queen Victoria School, Dunblane; University of Edinburgh; Open University. Lecturer, Derbyshire College of Agriculture, 1981-86; Barony College: Senior Lecturer, 1986-89, Depute Principal, 1989-2001. Secretary, Scotland's Rural Colleges; Council Member, British Deer Farmers Association. Publications: Inter College Collaboration (Co-Author); An Introduction to Red Deer Farming in Britain. Recreations: rugby; golf; photography; travel; food. Address: (b.) Barony College, Parkgate, Dumfries, DG1 3NE; T.-01387 860251; e-mail: rmarchant@barony.ac.uk

Marjoribanks, John Logan, MA (Cantab), FCCA. Chairman, Local Government Boundaries Commission for Scotland, since 2000; Member, Committee of Management, Berwickshire Housing Association, since 2001; b. 21.8.44,

Nicosia, Cyprus; m., Andrea Ruth; 1 s.; 2 d. Educ. Merchiston Castle School, Edinburgh; St. John's College, Cambridge. Technical Officer, Scottish Agricultural Industries Ltd., 1965-73; Overseas Development Ministry, on secondment to Government of Zambia, Department of Agriculture, 1973-78; Commonwealth Development Corporation (now CDC Group plc): Senior Lecturer, Mananga Agricultural Management Centre, Swaziland, 1979-85, Operations Executive, Pacific Islands, CDC London Office, 1985-87, Country Manager, Zimbabwe and Mozambique, Harare, 1988-93, Director, Mananga Management Centre, Swaziland, 1993-95, Country Manager, India, New Delhi, 1995-98, Director, Public Affairs, CDC, London, 1999-2000. Recreations: heraldry; competitive cycling. Address: (h.) Eden House, Gavinton, Duns TD11 3QS; T.-01361 884523; e-mail: john@marjoribanks.com

Markland, John A., CBE, MA, PhD, ACIS. Chairman, Scottish Natural Heritage, since 1999; b. 17.5.48, Bolton; m., Muriel Harris; 4 d. Educ. Bolton School; Dundee University. Demographer, Somerset County Council, 1974-76; Senior Professional Assistant, Tayside Regional Council; Personal Assistant to Chief Executive, then Assistant Chief Executive, then Chief Executive, Fife Regional Council, 1979-95; Chief Executive, Fife Council, 1995-99. Director, Forward Scotland Ltd. (Chairman, 1996-2000); Director, Environmental Campaigns; Director, Perth Repertory Theatre Ltd.; Member, Joint Nature Conservation Committee; Member, Cairngorms Partnership Advisory Panel; Chairman, Scottish Leadership Foundation; Member, Court, University of Edinburgh. Recreations: climbing Scotland's Munros. Address: Moreland House, Cleish, Kinross KY13 0LP; T.-01577 850 278.

Marks, Frederick Charles, OBE, MA, LLB, FIMgt. Commissioner for Local Administration in Scotland (Local Government Ombudsman), 1994-2000; Local Government Adjudicator, 1994-2000; b. 3.12.34, Bellshill; m., Agnes M. Bruce; 3 s.; 1 d. Educ. Wishaw High School; Glasgow University. Depute Town Clerk, Dunfermline, 1963-68; Town Clerk, Hamilton, 1968-75; Chief Executive, Motherwell, 1974-83; General Manager, Scottish Special Housing Association, 1983-89; Deputy Chairman, Local Government Boundary Commission for Scotland, 1989-94; Vice Chairman, Fife Acute Hospitals NHS Trust, 1999-2001; Vice Chairman, Queen Margaret Hospital NHS Trust, 1994-1999. Address: (h.) Dunkeld, 33 Townhill Road, Dunfermline, Fife KY12 0JD; T.-01383 723501.

Marnoch, The Rt. Hon. Lord (Michael Stewart Rae Bruce), QC (Scot), MA, LLB, LLD (Aberdeen). Senator of the College of Justice, since 1990; b. 26.7.38; m., Alison Stewart; 2 d. Educ.; Loretto; Aberdeen University. Advocate, 1963; QC, 1975; Standing Counsel to Department of Agriculture and Fisheries for Scotland, 1973; to Highlands and Islands Development Board, 1973; Advocate-Depute, 1983-86; Member, Criminal Injuries Compensation Board, 1986-89. Chairman for Scotland, Salmon and Trout Association, 1989-94. Recreations: golf; fishing. Address: (b.) Parliament House, Edinburgh; T.-0131-225 2595.

Marquis, Alistair Forbes, BA, MEd, DipCE, FCollP. Chairman, Scotland Committee of The Boys' Brigade, 1991-2000, elected Representative, UK Brigade Executive for East Lowland Area, 1989-2000, Scottish Member, UK Management Committee, 1991-99, President, West Lothian Battalion, since 2000; Hon. Vice President, The Scout Association, The Scottish Council, 1996-2000; b. 13.1.50, Glasgow; m., Margaret Jarvie Greenlees; 1 d. Educ Queen's Park Secondary School; Jordanhill College, Glasgow; Open University; Edinburgh University. Assistant Teacher, Leithland Primary School, Glasgow, 1971-77; Assistant Head Teacher, Dedridge Primary School, West Lothian, 1977-79; Head Teacher, Bankton Primary School, West

Lothian, 1979-89; HM Inspector of Schools, 1989. Member, Scottish Committee on Special Educational Needs, 1985-88; Chairman, Lanthorn Community Complex Management Committee, 1979-82; SFA Football Referee, 1972; Church of Scotland Elder; Member, Rotary International. Recreations: gardening; reading; walking; football refereeing. Address: (h.) 39 Bankton Drive, Murieston, Livingston EH54 9EH; T.-01506 414406; e-mail: afmarquis@blueyonder.co.uk

Marr, Colin. Theatre Director, Eden Court Theatre, since 1997; b. 3.4.66, Glasgow; m., Nicky; 2 d. Educ. Hutcheson's Grammar School; University of Edinburgh; Open University. Hall Manager, Queen's Hall, Edinburgh, 1988-92; Theatre and Commercial Manager, Traverse Theatre, Edinburgh, 1992-97. Address: (b.) Bishop's Road, Inverness IV3 5SA; T.-01463 239841.

Marr, Douglas, CBE, MA, MEd. Rector, Banchory Academy, since 1995; b. 7.2.47, Aberdeen; m., Alison; 1 d. Educ. Aberdeen Grammar School; University of Aberdeen. Teacher of History, Hilton Academy, Aberdeen, 1970-71; Assistant Principal Teacher of History, Aberdeen Grammar School, 1971-76; Principal Teacher of History, Hilton Academy, Aberdeen, 1976-81; Assistant Rector, Kemnay Academy, 1981-84; Depute Rector, The Gordon Schools, Huntly, 1984-87; Headteacher: Hilton Academy, 1987-88, St. Machar Academy, Aberdeen, 1988-95. Member, Business Management Committee, University of Aberdeen, since 2001. Publication: Leisure Education and Young People's Leisure (Co-Author), 1988. Recreations: squash; suffering at the hands (and feet) of Aberdeen F. C. Address: (b.) Banchory Academy, Schoolhill, Banchory AB31 5TQ; T.-01330 823357.

Marr, Norman G., CStJ, DipArch, ARIBA, FRIAS. Consultant Architect/Planner; Director of Planning and Development, Kincardine and Deeside District Council, 1975-92; b. 19.5.37, Aberdeen. Educ. Aberdeen Grammar School; Scott Sutherland School of Architecture, Aberdeen. Architectural Assistant, Aberdeen County Council, 1961-66; Senior Research Assistant, Corporation of the City of Aberdeen, Town Planning Department, 1967-69 (Principal Development Assistant, 1970-75). Organist and Choirmaster, Denburn Parish Church, Aberdeen, since 1956; Secretary, Scottish Federation of Organists, 1970-92 (President, 1993-94); Cross Bearer, Priory of the Order of St. John in Scotland, and Member, Aberdeen Committee of the Order; Chairman, Aberdeen Civic Society; Vice-Chairman, Friends of St. Machar's Cathedral, Aberdeen, and Friends of the Kirk of St. Nicholas, Aberdeen. Recreations: organ playing/building; swimming; long-distance running; hill-walking; books; entertaining. Address: (h.) 63 Devonshire Road, Aberdeen, AB10 6XP; T.-01224 322937.

Marrian, Ian Frederic Young, MA, CA. Deputy Chief Executive and Secretary, Institute of Chartered Accountants of Scotland, since 1994 (Director of Education, since 1981); b. 15.11.43, Kilwinning; m., Moira Selina McSwan; 1 s.; 2 d. Educ. Royal Belfast Academical Institution; Queens University, Belfast; Edinburgh University. Qualified as CA, 1969; Deloitte Haskins & Sells: audit practice, Rome, 1969-72, London, 1972-73, Audit Partner, Edinburgh, 1973-78, Technical Partner, London, 1978-81. Visiting Chair, Edinburgh University. Recreations: gardening in the grand scale; wines. Address: (h.) Walled Garden, Bowerhouse, Dunbar EH42 1RE; T.-0131-347 0271.

Marsack, Robyn Louise, BA, BPhil, DPhil. Director, Scottish Poetry Library, since 2000; b. 30.1.53, Wellington, New Zealand; m., Stuart Airlie; 1 d. Educ. Wellington Girls' College; Victoria University, Wellington; Oxford University. Junior Research Fellow, Wolfson College, Oxford, 1979-82; Editor, Carcanet Press, 1982-86, Editorial Manager and Member, Board of Directors, 1986-87;

freelance editor, translator and writer, 1987-99. Member, Scottish Arts Council Literature Committee, 1994-99, Chair, Grants to Publishers Panel, 1996-99; Member, Society of Authors Committee of Management, 2001. Publications: The Cave of Making: the poetry of Louis MacNeice, 1985; Sylvia Plath, 1992; translations of several books. Recreations: reading, reading, reading. Address: (b.) Scottish Poetry Library, 5 Crichton's Close, Canongate, Edinburgh EH8 8DT; T.-0131-557 2876; e-mail: admin@spl.org.uk

Marsh, Professor John Haig, BA, MEng, PhD, CEng, FIEE, FRSA, FIEEE, FRSE, FFCS. Professor of Optoelectronic Systems, University of Glasgow, since 1996; Founder and Chief Research Officer, Intense Photonics Ltd, since 2000; b. 15.4.56, Edinburgh; m., Anabel Christine Mitchell. Educ. Glasgow Academy; Cambridge University; Liverpool University; Sheffield University. University of Sheffield: Research Fellow, 1980-83, Research Scientist, 1983-86; Department of Electronics and Electrical Engineering, University of Glasgow: Lecturer, 1986-90, Senior Lecturer, 1990-94, Reader, 1994-96. Director, NATO Advanced Study Institute, Glasgow, 1990; Member, IEE Executive Committee for Photonics Network; Founding Chair, Scottish Chapter, IEEE/LEOS, 1996-98; Vice President, LEOS, 1999-2000. Publications: Waveguide Optoelectronics (Co-editor); more than 300 papers and book chapters. Recreations: walking; cooking; music; malt whisky. Address: (b.) Intense Photonics Ltd., 4 Stanley Blvd., Hamilton International Technology Park, High Blantyre G72 0UX; e-mail: john_marsh@intensephotonics.com

Marshall, David. MP (Labour), Glasgow Shettleston, since 1979; b. 1941; m.; 2 s.; 1 d. Chairman, Select Committee on Scottish Affairs. Address: (b.) House of Commons, London, SW1A 0AA.

Marshall, Enid Ann, MA, LLB, PhD, Assoc. Hon. RICS, ACIArb, FRSA, Solicitor. Reader, Scots Law Research Unit, Stirling University, since 1994; Editor, Scottish Law Gazette, since 1983; Chairman, Social Security Appeal Tribunal, Stirling and Falkirk, since 1984; b. 10.7.32, Boyndie, Banffshire. Educ. Banff Academy; Bell-Baxter School, Cupar; St. Andrews University. Apprentice Solicitor, 1956-59; Lecturer in Law, Dundee College of Technology, 1959-72; Lecturer, then Senior Lecturer, then Reader in Business Law, Stirling University, 1972-94. Departmental Editor, Arbitration Section, Journal of Business Law, since 1976. Publications: General Principles of Scots Law; Scottish Cases on Contract; Scottish Cases on Agency; Scottish Cases on Partnerships and Companies; Scots Mercantile Law; Gill on Arbitration; Charlesworth and Morse Company Law (Scottish Editor); Notes on the Law of Property in Scotland (Editor, 3rd edition); M.C. Oliver's Company Law (10th, 11th, 12th editions). Recreations: animal welfare; veganism. Address: (h.) 24 Easter Cornton Road, Stirling FK9 5ES; T.-Stirling 472125.

Marshall, Professor Ian Howard, MA, BD, PhD (Aberdeen), BA (Cantab), DD (Asbury). Professor of New Testament Exegesis, Aberdeen University, 1979-99, Emeritus, since 1999; b. 12.1.34, Carlisle; m., Joyce Elizabeth (deceased); 1 s.; 3 d. Educ. Aberdeen Grammar School; Aberdeen University; Cambridge University; Göttingen University. Assistant Tutor, Didsbury College, Bristol; Methodist Minister, Darlington; Lecturer, then Senior Lecturer and Reader in New Testament Exegesis, Aberdeen University. Publications: Kept by the Power of God; Luke: Historian and Theologian; The Origins of New Testament Christology; New Testament Interpretation (Editor); The Gospel of Luke; I Believe in the Historical Jesus; The Epistles of John; Acts; Last Supper and Lord's Supper; Biblical Inspiration; 1 and 2 Thessalonians; Jesus the Saviour; 1 Peter; Philippians; The Acts of the Apostles;

Witness to the Gospel (Co-Editor); The Pastoral Epistles. Address: (b.) School of Divinity and Religious Studies, King's College, Aberdeen AB24 3UB; T.-01224 272388.

Marshall, Leon McGregor, CA. Senior Partner, Stevenson & Kyles, CA, Glasgow, since 1995; Convener, Church of Scotland Central Co-ordinating Committee, since 2001; Session Clerk, Kilmacolm Old Kirk, since 1997; b. 10.6.50, Glasgow; m., Barbara Anne McLean; 2 s.; 1 d. Educ. High School of Glasgow; Glasgow University (as part of CA training). Joined Stevenson & Kyles as a student, 1967; qualified CA, 1972 (joint winner, ICAS Gold Medal); made Partner, 1974. Treasurer, St Enoch's Hogganfield Church, Glasgow, 1973-80; Treasurer, Kilmacolm Old Kirk, 1984-97; Member, Board of Stewardship and Finance, General Assembly, Church of Scotland, 1990-2001 (Convener, 1997-2001); Convener, Budget and Allocation Committee, 1993-97; Reader, Church of Scotland, since 1987. Recreations: reading; travel; watching football. Address: (b.) 25 Sandyford Place, Glasgow G3 7NJ; T.-0141-248 3856; e-mail: lm@stevenson-kyles.co.uk

Marshall, Professor Mary Tara, OBE, MA, DSA, DASS. Director, Dementia Services Development Centre, Stirling University; b. 13.6.45, Darjeeling, India. Educ. Mary Erskine School for Girls; Edinburgh University; London School of Economics; Liverpool University. Child Care Officer, London Borough of Lambeth, 1967-69; Social Worker, Personal Service Society, Liverpool, 1970-74; Research Organiser, Age Concern, Liverpool, 1974-75; Lecturer in Social Studies, Liverpool University, 1975-83; Director, Age Concern Scotland, 1983-89. Governor, PPP Healthcare Medical Trust; Member: Journal of Dementia Care Advisory Board, Health and Social Care in the Community Editorial Advisory Board; former Member, Royal Commission on Long-term Care of the Elderly; Hon. DEd, Queen Margaret University College. Publications: I Can't Place This Place At All: Working with people with dementia and their carers, 1996; The State of Art in Dementia Care, 1997. Recreations: photography; bird-watching. Address: (b.) Dementia Services Development Centre, Stirling University, Stirling FK9 4LA; T.-01786 467740.

Marshall, Maud Evelyn, MA (Hons), MSc, MRTPI. Member, Scottish Arts Council (Chairperson, Lottery Capital Committee); Chairperson, The Lighthouse; Member, Court, Strathclyde University; b. 24.1.50, Glasgow. Educ. Park School, Glasgow; Edinburgh University; Swiss Federal Institute of Technology; Strathclyde University. Director of Investment and Performance, Communities Scotland. Recreations: skiing; music; travel. Address: (b.) Thistle House, 91 Haymarket Terrace, Edinburgh EH12 5HE.

Marshall, Rosalyn Adela, BSc (Hons), FCCA. Vice Principal (Strategic Planning and Development), Queen Margaret University College, since 1997; Member, Accounts Commission for Scotland, since 1997; Member, Board, Edinburgh Academy; b. 22.7.54, Dundee. Educ. High School of Dundee; Dundee University. Financial Accountant, Lothian Regional Council, 1976-79; Development Officer, Lothian Health Board, 1979-81; Edinburgh District Council: Administrative Officer, 1982-85, Principal Officer (Financial Incentives), Department of Economic Development and Estates, 1985-86; Financial Controller, Graphic Partners, Edinburgh, 1986-92; Assistant Principal, Administration and Finance, Queen Margaret College, 1992-97. Adviser, Business in the Arts. Recreations: golf; theatre; art; travel. Address: (b.) Queen Margaret University College; Edinburgh EH12 8TS; T.-0131-317 3207; e-mail: rmarshall@qmuc.ac.uk

Marshall, Professor William James, BA, M-ès-L, DPhil, MA. Professor of Modern French Studies, Glasgow University, since 2000; b. 21.2.57, Newcastle Upon Tyne. Educ. Gosforth High School; Westfield College, London; Université de Paris-X Nanterre; University of Oxford; Polytechnic of Central London. Lecteur, Université de Paris-X Nanterre, 1978- 79; Lecturer, Sunderland Polytechnic, 1982-83; Lecturer, University of Liverpool, 1983-84; Lecturer/Senior Lecturer/Reader, Southampton University, 1984-2000. Publications: Victor Serge the Uses of Dissent, 1992; Guy Hocquenghem, 1996; Quebec National Cinema, 2000; Musicals Hollywood and Beyond (co-ed.) 2000. Address: (b.) Department of French, 16 University Gardens, Glasgow, G12 8QL; T.-0141-330 4590; e-mail: b.marshall@french.arts.gla.ac.uk

Martin, David McLeod, DA, RSW, RGI. Painter; b. 30.12.22, Glasgow; m., Isobel Agnes Fowlie Smith (deceased); 4 s. Educ. Govan High School; Glasgow School of Art; Jordanhill College of Education. RAF, 1942-46. Principal Teacher, Hamilton Grammar School, 1973-83; retired early to paint full-time; exhibits regularly in Scotland; exhibited RA, 1984; numerous group shows; one man shows, Glasgow, Edinburgh, Perth, Greenock, Newcastle, Stenton, London; mixed shows: New York Art Fair, 1998, Johannesburg, 1999; former Vice President, RSW. Address: (h.) The Old Schoolhouse, 53 Gilmour Street, Eaglesham, Glasgow G76 0LG.

Martin, David Weir, BA (Econ), MA. Vice-President, European Parliament, since 1989, Member (Labour) for Lothians, 1984-99, Senior Member for Scotland, since 1999; b. 26.8.54, Edinburgh; m., Margaret Mary Cook; 1 s.; 1 d. Educ. Liberton High School; Heriot-Watt University; Leicester University. Worked as stockbroker's assistant and animal rights campaigner; became Lothian Regional Councillor, 1982; Vice-President, Mobile Projects; Director, St. Andrew Animal Fund; Rapporteur, Intergovernmental Conferences. Publications: Bringing Common Sense to the Common Market — A Left Agenda for Europe; European Union and the Democratic Deficit; Europe — An Ever Closer Union; Towards a Wider, Deeper, Federal Europe; Maastricht in a Minute; 1996 and all that; A Partnership Democracy for Europe. Recreations: soccer; reading. Address: (b.) PO Box 27030, Edinburgh EH10 7YP.

Martin, Donald, MA. Editor, Evening Express, Aberdeen, since 1997; b. 23.4.64, Glasgow. Educ. Bishopbriggs High School; Glasgow University. Assistant Editor/Deputy Editor, Wokingham Times; Launch Editor, Edinburgh and Lothians Post; Editor, Thames Valley Free Newspapers; Production Editor/Chief Sub, Reading Evening Post; Deputy Editor, Cambridge Evening News; Editor, North West Evening Mail. Recreations: golf; football; sailing. Address: (b.) Aberdeen Journals Ltd., Lang Stracht, Mastrick, Aberdeen AB15 6DP; T.-01224 690222.

Martin, Graham Dunstan, MA, BLitt, GradCertEd. Writer; Senior Lecturer, Edinburgh University, 1982-2000; b. 21.10.32, Leeds; m., 1, Ryllis Daniel; 2 s.; 1 d.; 2, Anne Crombie; 2 s. Educ. Leeds Grammar School; Oriel College and Linacre College, Oxford. Schoolteacher, 1956-65; Assistant Lecturer, then Lecturer, in French, Edinburgh University, 1965-82. Publications: (philosophy) Language, Truth and Poetry, 1975; The Architecture of Experience 1981, Shadows in the Cave, 1990; (novels) Giftwish, 1980; Catchfire, 1981; The Soul Master, 1984; Time-Slip, 1986; The Dream Wall, 1987; Half a Glass of Moonshine, 1988; poems and poetry translations. Recreations: music; jazz; walking; good food; the Celtic past. Address: 21 Mayfield Terrace, Edinburgh EH9 1RY; T.-0131-667 8160.

Martin, Iain, MA (Hons). Editor, The Scotsman; b. 2.10.71, Paisley. Educ. Castlehead High School, Paisley; Glasgow University. Assistant Editor (Politics) and Political Editor, Scotland on Sunday; Reporter, Sunday Times Scotland; Assistant Editor (Politics), The Scotsman; Deputy Editor, Scotland on Sunday. Recreation: music; wine. Address: (b.) 108 Holyrood Road, Edinburgh, EH8 8AS.

Martin, Rev. Iver, BSc, DipTheol. Minister, Bon Accord Free Church, Aberdeen, since 1997; b. 29.6.57, Grantown on Spey; m., Mairi Isabel Macdonald; 2 s.; 4 d. Educ. Camphill High School, Paisley; Robert Gordon's Institute of Technology; Free Church College. National Semiconductor (UK) Ltd.: Graduate Process Engineer, 1980, Senior Engineer, 1983; European Process Engineer, Lam Research Corporation Ltd., 1985; European Product and Sales Engineer, Silicon Glen Technology, 1987-90; own company, Solus (UK) Ltd., 1990-92; Assistant Minister, Stornoway Free Church, 1995-97. Recreations: cycling; reading; music. Address: 77 Forest Avenue, Aberdeen; T.-01224 324630; e-mail: iverm@aol.com

Martin, Rev. James, MA, BD, DD. Minister, High Carntyne, Glasgow, 1954-87; b. 21.1.21, Motherwell; m., Marion Gordon Greig; 2 d. Educ. Dalziel High School, Motherwell; Glasgow University. Minister, Newmilns West Church, 1946-54; Convener, Publications Committee, General Assembly, 1978-83 and Board of Communications, 1983-87; Bruce Lecturer, Trinity College, 1960-64. Publications: Did Jesus Rise from the Dead?; The Reliability of the Gospels; Letters of Caiaphas to Annas; Suffering Man, Loving God; The Road to the Aisle; People in the Jesus Story; A Plain Man in the Holy Land; Listening to the Bible; William Barclay: A Personal Memoir; My Friend Bobby; It's You, Minister; It's My Belief; Travels in the Holy Land; God-Collared; William Barclay in a Nutshell; You Can't Be Serious; A Parish Minister's Hats; More About Bobby; Grit for the Road of Life; Seen From My Manse Window; More Grit for Life's Road; More Views from My Manse Window; Manse Memories. Recreations: football; tennis; conversation. Address: 9 Magnolia Street, Wishaw; T.-01698 385825.

Martin, John Sharp Buchanan, BSc. Head of Transport Group, Scottish Executive, since 1998; b. 7.7.46, West Kilbride; m., Catriona Meldrum; 1 s.; 1 d. Educ. Bell-Baxter High School, Cupar; St. Andrews University. Assistant Principal, 1968-73; Private Secretary to Parliamentary Under Secretary of State, 1971-73; Principal, 1973-79; Rayner Scrutinies, 1979-80; Assistant Secretary, Highlands and Tourism Division, 1980-84; Housing Division 1, 1984-89; Transport and Local Roads Division, 1989-92; Under Secretary, School Education and Sport, 1992-98. Recreations: tennis; cricket; golf; philately. Address: (b.) Victoria Quay, Leith, Edinburgh; T.-0131-244 0629.

Martin, Michael John. Speaker of the House of Commons, since 2000 (Deputy Speaker, 1997-2000); MP (Labour), Glasgow Springburn, since 1979; Chairman, Scottish Grand Committee, since 1987; b. 3.7.45, Glasgow; m., Mary McLay; 1 s.; 1 d. Educ. St. Patrick's Boys' School, Glasgow. Member, Glasgow Corporation, 1973-74, and of Glasgow District Council, 1974-79. Member, Speaker's Panel of Chairmen, since 1987; Fellow, Parliament and Industry Trust; Member, College of Piping; Union: AEEU. Recreations: hill-walking; studying history of Forth and Clyde Canal; listening to pipe band music. Address: (h.) Speaker's House, Westminster, London SW1A 0AA.

Martin, Paul. MSP (Labour), Glasgow Springburn, since 1999; b. 1967, Glasgow; m., Fiona. Former Glasgow City Councillor. Recreations: Golf; football (in goals), playing keyboard. Address: (b.) Scottish Parliament, Edinburgh EH99 1SP; T.-0131-348 5844.

Martin, Professor Peter, PhD, CEng, FIEE, MInstP. Depute Principal, University of Abertay Dundee, since 2001; b. 19.2.47, Richmond, Yorkshire. Educ. Wimbledon College; Newcastle University; Durham University. Lecturer, Oldham College of Technology, 1971-76; Lecturer, Luton College of Higher Education, 1976-79; Senior Lecturer, Trent Polytechnic, 1979-83; Lecturer/Senior Lecturer, Dundee Institute of Technology, 1983-94; Associate Head/Head of School, University of Abertay Dundee, 1994-2001; Member, SQA Engineering Advisory Group. Recreations: travel; walking. Address: (b.) University of Abertay Dundee, Bell Street, Dundee, DD1 1HG; T.-01382 308230; e-mail: P.Martin@tay.ac.uk

Martin, Robert (Roy) Logan, QC, LLB. Advocate, since 1976; Barrister, since 1990; b. 31.7.50, Glasgow; m., Fiona Frances Neil; 1 s.; 2 d. Educ. Paisley Grammar School; Glasgow University. Solicitor, 1973-76; Member, Sheriff Courts Rules Council, 1981-84; Standing Junior Counsel, Department of Employment (Scotland), 1983-84; Advocate-Depute, 1984-87; admitted to Bar of New South Wales, 1987; Queen's Counsel, 1988; called to the Bar, Lincoln's Inn, 1990; Chairman (part-time), Industrial Tribunals, 1990-96; Chairman, Scottish Planning, Local Government and Environmental Bar Group, 1991-96; Chairman, Police Appeals Tribunal, since 1997. Affiliate, Royal Incorporation of Architects in Scotland, 1995; Honorary Secretary, The Wagering Club, 1982-91. Recreations: shooting; skiing; modern architecture; vintage motor cars. Address: (h.) Kilduff House, Athelstaneford, East Lothian EH39 5BD; T.-01620 880202.

Martin, Professor Ursula Hilda Mary, MA, PhD, CEng, FRSA. Professor, School of Mathematical and Computational Sciences, University of St Andrews, since 1992; b. 3.8.53, London. Educ. Cambridge University. Lecturer, London University, 1978-81; Visiting Professor, University of Illinois, 1981-83; Lecturer, Manchester University, 1983-87; Reader, then Professor, London University, 1987-92. Address: (b.) School of Computer Science, University of St Andrews, North Haugh, St. Andrews KY16 9SS; T.-01334 463252.

Martin, Professor William, BSc, PhD. Professor of Cardiovascular Pharmacology, Glasgow University, since 1995; External Examiner, MSc in Pharmacology, King's College, London University, since 1998; b. 12.7.55, Glasgow; m., Anne Marie McCartney; 1 s.; 1 d. Educ. Glenwood Secondary; Glasgow University. Post-doctoral Research Fellow, Babraham, Cambridge, 1980-83; Post-doctoral Research Fellow, State University of New York, 1983-85; Lecturer, Department of Cardiology, University of Wales College of Medicine, 1985-87; Member, British Pharmacological Society; Research Assessment Exercise Panel, Unit of Assessment 5-8, since 1999. Recreations: hill-walking; ballroom dancing; keeping fit. Address: (b.) Division of Neuroscience and Biomedical systems, Institute of Biomedical and Life Sciences, Glasgow University, Glasgow, G12 8QQ; T.-0141-330 4489.

Marwick, George Robert, SDA, JP. Lord Lieutenant for Orkney, 1997 (Vice Lieutenant, 1995, Deputy Lieutenant, 1976); Chairman, Swannay Farms Ltd., since 1972; Chairman, Campbeltown Creamery (Holdings) Ltd., 1974-90; Honorary Sheriff, Grampian Highlands and Islands, since 2000; b. 27.2.32, Edinburgh; m., 1, Hanne Jensen; 3 d.; 2, Norma Gerrard. Educ. Port Regis; Bryanston; Edinburgh School of Agriculture. Councillor, local government, 1968-78; Vice-Convener, Orkney County Council, 1970-74, Convener, Orkney Islands Council, 1974-78; Chairman, North of Scotland Water Board, 1970-73; Member, Scottish Agricultural Consultative Panel, 1972-98 (formerly Winter Keep Panel, 1964-72); Director, North Eastern Farmers Ltd., 1968-98;, Member:

Countryside Commission for Scotland, 1978-86, Council, National Trust for Scotland, 1979-84. Recreations: shooting; tennis; motor sport. Address: (h.) Swannay House, by Evie, Orkney; T.-01856 721365.

Marwick, Tricia. MSP (SNP), Mid-Scotland and Fife, since 1999; b. 5.11.53, Cowdenbeath; m., Frank; 1 s.; 1 d. Public Affairs Office, Shelter Scotland, 1992-99; Advisory Board Member, World Development Movement (Scotland). Recreations: reading; watching sport. Address: Scottish Parliament, Edinburgh EH99 1SP; T.-0131-348 5680; e-mail: tricia.marwick.msp@scottish.parliament.uk

Mason, Professor Sir David Kean, KB, CBE, BDS, MD, FRCS, FDS, FRCPath, FRSE, Hon. DSc, Hon. DChD, Hon. LLD, Hon. FFD, Hon. FDS, Hon. FRCS. President, General Dental Council, 1989-94; b. 5.11.28, Paisley; m., Judith Armstrong; 2 s.; 1 d. Educ. Paisley Grammar School; Glasgow Academy; St. Andrews University; Glasgow University. RAF Dental Branch, 1952-54; Registrar in Oral Surgery, Dundee, 1954-56; Senior Lecturer in Dental Surgery and Pathology, Glasgow University, 1964-67; Professor of Oral Medicine, Glasgow University, 1967-92 (Dean of Dental Education, 1980-90); Chairman, National Dental Consultative Committee, 1976-80; Member: Medicines Commission, 1976-80, Dental Committee, MRC, 1973-83, Physiological Systems Board, MRC, 1976-80, GDC, 1976-93, Dental Strategy Review Group, 1980-81, Dental Review Working Party, UGC, 1986-87, WHO Expert Committee on Oral Health, 1991-98; Convener, Dental Council, RCPSGlas, 1977-80; John Tomes Prize, RCS England, 1979; Colyer Prize RCS England, 1993; Honorary Member, British Dental Association, 1993; Honorary Member, American Dental Association, 1994. Publications: Salivary Glands in Health and Disease (Co-Author); Introduction to Oral Medicine (Co-Author); Self Assessment: Manuals I and II (Co-Editor); Oral Manifestations of Systemic Disease. Recreations: golf; tennis; gardening; enjoying the pleasure of the countryside. Address: (h.) Cherry Tree Cottage, Houston Road, Kilmacolm, Renfrewshire; T.-Kilmacolm 2001.

Mason, Douglas C., BSc. Freelance Journalist, since 1977; b. 30.9.41, Dunfermline. Educ. Bradford Grammar School; St. Andrews University. Conservative Party Organising Secretary, 1969-77; Member: Fife County Council, 1967-70, Kirkcaldy District Council, 1974-88, Scottish Housing Advisory Committee, 1978-80; Parliamentary Research Assistant, 1979-97; contested Central Fife, General Election, 1983; Convener, General Council Business Committee, St. Andrews University, 1993-2000; Member, Glenrothes Development Corporation, 1985-96; Domestic Policy Adviser, Adam Smith Institute, since 1984. Publications: Allocation and Transfer of Council Houses (Co-Author), 1980; The Qualgo Complex, 1984; Revising the Rating System, 1985; Room for Improvement, 1985; University Challenge, 1986; Time to Call Time, 1986; Ex Libris, 1986; Expounding the Arts, 1987; Licensed to Live, 1988; Pining for Profit, 1988; A Home for Enterprise, 1989; Privatizing the Posts, 1989; Wiser Councils and Shedding a Tier, 1989; Wood for the Trees, 1991; City in the Mist (Co-Editor), 1995. Recreations: books; music. Address: (h.) 84 Barnton Place, Glenrothes, Fife; T.-01592 758766; e-mail: douglasmason71@hotmail.com

Mason, John Kenneth, BA (Oxon), MPhil. Principal Private Secretary to the First Minister, Scottish Executive; b. 26.6.56, Chichester; m., Alison Margaret Cruickshanks; 1 s.; 2 d. Educ. Chichester High School; Hertford College, Oxford; University College, London. Kent County Council; Department of Environment; Scottish Office; Registers of Scotland; Head of Enterprise and Industry, Scottish Executive. Recreations: photography; gardening. Address: (b.) St. Andrew's House, Edinburgh EH1 3DG; T.-0131-244 5218.

Mason, Professor Emeritus John Kenyon French, CBE, MD, LLD, FRCPath, DMJ, FRSE. Regius Professor of Forensic Medicine, Edinburgh University, 1973-85; b. 19.12.19, Lahore; m., Elizabeth Latham (deceased); 2 s. Educ. Downside School; Cambridge University; St. Bartholomew's Hospital. Regular Officer, Medical Branch, RAF, following War Service; Consultant in charge, RAF Department of Aviation and Forensic Pathology, 1957-73. President, British Association in Forensic Medicine, 1981-83; Swiney Prize in Jurisprudence, 1978. Publication: Forensic Medicine for Lawyers, 4th Edition; Law and Medical Ethics, 5th Edition (Co-Author); Medico-legal Aspects of Reproduction and Parenthood, 2nd Edition; Human Life and Medical Practice. Address: (h.) 66 Craiglea Drive, Edinburgh EH10 5PF; T.-0131-447 2301; e-mail: Ken.Mason@ed.ac.uk

Mason, John Ringland, BAcc, CA. Leader of the Opposition, Glasgow City Council, since 1999; SNP Councillor, since 1998; b. 15.5.57, Glasgow. Educ. Hutchesons' Boys' Grammar School; Glasgow University. Qualified CA, 1980; Accountant with United Mission to Nepal, 1984-87; Scotcare Group Ltd., 1989-97; Finance Director, Gap Housing Association, 1997-2000. Member, Scottish Council, Evangelical Alliance. Recreations: Easterhouse Bapist Church; Clyde FC; hill-walking. Address: (h.) 83 Sandaig Road, Barlanark, Glasgow G33 4SZ; T.-0141-771 3260.

Massie, Allan Johnstone, BA, FRSL. Author and Journalist; b. 16.10.38, Singapore; m., Alison Langlands; 2 s.; 1 d. Educ. Drumtochty Castle; Trinity College, Glenalmond; Trinity College, Cambridge. Schoolmaster, Drumtochty Castle, 1960-71; taught EFL, 1972-75; Creative Writing Fellow, Edinburgh University, 1982-84, Glasgow and Strathclyde Universities, 1985-86; Editor, New Edinburgh Review, 1982-84; Fiction Reviewer, The Scotsman, since 1975; Television Critic, Sunday Standard, 1981-83 (Fraser of Allander Award, Critic of the Year, 1982); Sports Columnist, Glasgow Herald, 1985-88; Columnist: Daily Telegraph, Daily Mail, The Scotsman, Sunday Times. Publications: (novels): Change and Decay in all around I see; The Last Peacock; The Death of Men (Scottish Arts Council Book Award); One Night in Winter; Augustus; A Question of Loyalties; The Sins of the Father; Tiberius; The Hanging Tree; Shadows of Empire; Caesar; These Enchanted Woods; The Ragged Lion; King David; Antony; Nero's Heirs; (non-fiction): Muriel Spark; Ill Met by Gaslight; The Caesars; Portrait of Scottish Rugby; Colette; 101 Great Scots; Byron's Travels; Glasgow; Edinburgh; (as Editor): Edinburgh and the Borders in Verse; (radio play): Quintet in October; (plays): The Minstrel and the Shirra; First-Class Passengers. Recreations: reading; watching rugby, cricket, racing; walking the dogs. Address: (h.) Thirladean House, Selkirk, TD7 5LU; T.-Selkirk 20393.

Masson, Alastair H.B., BA, MB, ChB, FRCSEdin, FRCA; b. 30.1.25, Bathgate; m., Marjorie Nan Paisley-Whyte; 3 s.; 1 d. Educ. Bathgate Academy; Edinburgh University. Consultant Anaesthetist, Edinburgh Royal Infirmary (retired); Visiting Professor of Anesthesiology, South Western Medical School, Dallas, Texas, 1962-63. President: Scottish Society of Anaesthetists, 1978-79, British Society of the History of Medicine, 1989-91; Honorary Archivist, Royal College of Surgeons, Edinburgh; President, Scottish Society of the History of Medicine, 1984-87. Publications: Portraits, Paintings and Busts in the Royal College of Surgeons of Edinburgh, 1995; A College Miscellany – Some Treasured Possessions of the Royal College of Surgeons of Edinburgh, 2001. Recreations: golf; hill-walking; music; travel. Address: (h.) 28 Beechmount Park, Edinburgh.

Masterman, Eileen Mary, MA (Hons), MCIArb. Director, Royal Institution of Chartered Surveyors in Scotland, since 1992; Member, Committee of Investigation for Great Britain, since 1995; Member, Extra Parliamentary Panel, since 1996; b. Spennymoor, Co. Durham; m., Norman A. Fiddes; 2 d. Educ. St. Anthony's School for Girls, Sunderland; Dundee University. Research Assistant, Dundee University, 1976-80; Investigator and Complaints Examiner, Commissioner for Local Administration in Scotland, 1980-90; Advocates' Clerk/Business Manager, Faculty of Advocates, 1990-92. Member, Building Standards Advisory Committee, 1994-97; Director, Edinburgh Chamber of Commerce, 1994-97. Recreations: food; friends; fresh air. Address: (b.) 9 Manor Place, Edinburgh EH3 7DN; T.-0131-225 7078.

Masters, Christopher, BSc (Hons), PhD, AKC. Executive Chairman, Aggreko plc, since 1997; b. 2.5.47, Northallerton; m., Gillian Mary Hodson; 2 d. Educ. Richmond School; King's College, London; Leeds University. Shell Research BV/Shell Chemicals UK Ltd., 1971-77; joined Christian Salvesen as Business Development Manager, 1979; transferred to Christian Salvesen Inc., USA, 1982, as Director of Planning; Managing Director, Christian Salvesen Seafoods, 1983; Managing Director, Industrial Services Division, 1985; appointed a Director, Christian Salvesen PLC, 1987; Chief Executive, Christian Salvesen PLC, 1989-97; Chairman, Young Enterprise Scotland, 1994-97; Chairman, Quality Assessment Committee of Higher Education Funding Council, 1991-95; Member, Scottish Higher Education Funding Council, since 1995, Chairman, since 1998; Non-Executive Director: British Assets Trust, since 1989, Scottish Widows, 1991-2000, Scottish Chamber Orchestra Trust, since 1993; Vice Chairman, Scottish Opera, 1996-99. Recreations: wines; music. Address: (b.) Aggreko plc, 121 West Regent Street, Glasgow G2 2SD; T.-0141- 225 5900.

Mather, Professor Alexander Smith, BSc, PhD, FRSGS. Professor of Geography, University of Aberdeen, since 1995 (Head, Department of Geography, since 1998); b. 17.9.43, Aberdeenshire. Educ. Maud School; Peterhead Academy; Aberdeen Grammar School; University of Aberdeen. Editor, Scottish Geographical Magazine, 1987-94; Editor, Land Use Policy, since 1998. Publications: Land Use, 1986; Global Forest Resources, 1990; Environmental Resources (Co-author), 1995. Recreation: hill-walking. Address: (b.) Department of Geography, University of Aberdeen, Aberdeen AB24 3UF; T.-01224 272354; e-mail: a.mather@abdn.ac.uk

Matheson, Alexander (Sandy), OBE, FRPharmS, JP. Lord Lieutenant, Western Isles Area, since 2001; Chairman, Highlands and Islands Airports Ltd., since 2001; Member, Board of Governors, UHI Millennium Institute, since 2001; b. 16.11.41, Stornoway; m., Irene Mary Davidson, BSc, MSc; 2 s.; 2 d. Educ. Nicolson Institute, Stornoway; Robert Gordon's Institute of Technology, Aberdeen. Chairman, Stornoway Pier and Harbour Commission, 1991-2001 (Member, since 1968); Member, Stornoway Trust Estate, since 1967 (Chairman, 1971-81); Chairman: Stornoway Branch, RNLI, Western Isles Development Fund, 1972-98, Western Isles Health Board, 1993-2001 (Member, 1973-2001); Member, Stornoway Town Council, 1967-75; Provost of Stornoway, 1971-75; Member: Ross and Cromarty County Council, 1967-75, Western Isles Islands Council, 1974-94 (Chairman, Development Services, 1974-80, Vice-Convener, 1980-82, Convener, 1982-90); President, Islands Commission of the Conference of Peripheral Maritime Regions of Europe, 1987-91 and 1993-94; Honorary Sheriff, since 1972; Director, Harris Tweed Authority; Chairman, Roderick Smith Ltd., Stornoway. Address: (h.) 33 Newton Street, Stornoway, Isle of Lewis; T.-01851 702082.

Matheson, Allen Short, CBE, FRIBA, PPRIAS, MRTPI. Retired Partner, Matheson Gleave Partnership; b. 28.2.26, Egypt; m., Catherine Anne; 2 s. Educ. George Watson's College; Edinburgh College of Art. Past President, Royal Incorporation of Architects in Scotland; Past Chairman, Scottish Construction Industry Group; former Vice-Chairman, Board of Governors, Glasgow School of Art; former Director, Glasgow Chamber of Commerce; former Member, Royal Fine Art Commission for Scotland; Past Chairman, Joint Standing Committee of Architects, Surveyors and Building Contractors. Address: (h.) 11 Spence Street, Glasgow G20 0AW; T.-0141-946 5670.

Matheson, Ann, OBE, MA, MLitt PhD Hon. DLitt. Keeper, National Library of Scotland, 1983-2000; b. 5.7.40, Wester Ross; m., T. Russell Walker. Educ. Dingwall Academy; St Andrews University; Edinburgh University. Ferranti Ltd., 1962-64; Taught English in Finland, 1964-67; Assistant Keeper, National Library of Scotland, 1973-83; Chairman, Literature Committee, Scottish Arts Council; Chairman, Consortium of European Research Libraries; Chairman, NEWSPLAN, since 2000; Member, Professional Library Committees in the UK and Europe. Publications: Theories of Rhetoric, 1995; Gaelic Union Catalogue (co-ed.) 1984; For the Encouragement of Learning, 1989. Recreations: literature; travel; antiques. Address: (b.) Yewbank, 52 Liberton Brae, Edinburgh, EH16 6AF; T.-0131-664 2717; e-mail: a.matheson@tinyworld.co.uk

Matheson, Donald, MA, BA (Hons). Head Teacher, Hermitage Academy, Helensburgh, since 1994; b. 25.8.50, Lennoxtown; m., Katherine; 1 s.; 1 d. Educ. Albert Secondary School, Glasgow; Glasgow University. Geography Teacher, Kingswood Secondary Glasgow, 1972-76; Principal Teacher of Geography, Boclair Academy Bearsden, 1976-81; Assistant Head Teacher, Boclair Academy, 1981-85; Head Teacher, Kirkintilloch High School, 1985-94; President, Headteachers' Association of Scotland. Recreations: golf; reading; hill-walking; politics. Address: (b.) Hermitage Academy, Campbell Drive, Helensburgh, G84 7TB; T.-01436 672145.

Matheson, John Alexander, BA, MBA, CPFA. Past Chairman, Scottish Branch, Chartered Institute of Public Finance and Accountancy; Member, Board of Management, Edinburgh's Telford College, since 1998; Finance Director, Lothian Health, since 2000; b. 23.6.55, Dingwall; m., Judi; 1 s.; 1 d. Educ. Invergordon Academy; Heriot-Watt University; Edinburgh University. Finance Director, Edinburgh Healthcare NHS Trust, 1994-99. Recreation: hill-walking; golf. T.-0131-536 9086.

Matheson, Lindsay S.G., MA, MLitt. Rector, Madras College, St. Andrews, since 1997; b. 2.10.44, Edinburgh; m., Katherine R.; 2 d. Educ. Otago Boys' High School, Dunedin; George Watson's, Edinburgh; St. Andrews University; Oxford University. History Teacher, Banff Academy, 1970-72; Principal Teacher of History, Lochaber High School, 1972-80; Assistant Rector, Inverurie Academy, 1980-85; Rector, Milne's High School, Fochabers, 1985-97. Recreations: cycling; golf; bridge. Address: (h.) 52 Largo Road, St. Andrews, Fife; T.-01334 472744.

Matheson, Michael, BSc, BA, Dip. Applied Soc Sci. MSP (SNP), Central Scotland, since 1999; b. 8.9.70, Glasgow. Educ. John Bosco Secondary School; Queen Margaret College, Edinburgh; Open University. Community Occupational Therapist: Highland Regional Council, Social Work Department, 1991-93, Stirling Council, Social Work Department, 1993-99. Member, Ochils Mountain Rescue Team. Recreation: mountaineering. Address: (b.) Scottish Parliament, Edinburgh EH99 1SP; T.-0131-348 5671.

Matheson, Susan Margaret Graham, BSc (Soc Sci). Chief Executive, SACRO, since 1996; b. 6.6.49, Tarbert, Harris; 1 d. Educ. St. George's School for Girls, Edinburgh; Edinburgh University. Antique dealer, 1971-73; Research Officer, then Senior Research Officer, Scottish Office Central Research Unit, 1973-88; Director, Family Mediation Scotland, 1988-96. Honorary Member, UK College of Family Mediators. Publications: several Government research reports and other publications. Recreation: skiing. Address: (b.) 1 Broughton Market, Edinburgh EH3 6NU; T.-0131-624 7270.

Mathewson, David Carr, BSc, CA. Merchant Banker; Consultant, Andersen Corporate Finance, since 2000; b. 26.7.47, Broughty Ferry; m., Jan McIntyre; 1 s.; 1 d. Educ. Daniel Stewart's College, Edinburgh; St. Andrews University. Deloitte Haskins & Sells, Edinburgh, 1968-72; Williams Glyn & Co., London, 1972-75; Nedbank Group, South Africa, 1976-86; Noble Grossart Limited, since 1986; Director: Noble Grossart Limited, 1989-2000, Edinburgh US Tracker Trust plc, since 1998, Martin Currie High Income Trust plc, since 1998, Geared Opportunities Income Trust plc (Chairman, since 2000), Sportech plc, since 1992 (Chairman, since 2002), various private companies; Member, Council, St. Leonards School; Member, Board of Trustees, Royal Botanic Garden, Edinburgh. Recreations: family interests; golf; shooting; athletics. Address: Dalveen, 7 Barnton Park, Edinburgh EH4 6JF.

Mathewson, Sir George Ross, KT, CBE, BSc, PHD, MBA, LLD, FRSE, CEng, MIEE, CIMgt, FCIBS. Chairman, Royal Bank of Scotland Group plc, since 2001; Director: Scottish Investment Trust Ltd., since 1981, Banco Santander Central Hispano, since 2001; b. 14.5.40, Dunfermline; m., Sheila Alexandra Graham Bennett; 2 s. Educ. Perth Academy; St. Andrews University; Canisius College, Buffalo, New York. Assistant Lecturer, St. Andrews University, 1964-67; Systems Engineer (various positions), Bell Aerospace, Buffalo, New York, 1967-72; ICFC: Executive in Edinburgh Area Office, 1972-81, Area Manager, 1974-79, Director and Assistant General Manager, 1979-81; Chief Executive, Scottish Development Agency, 1981-87; Royal Bank of Scotland Group plc: joined as Director, Strategic Planning and Development, 1987, Group Chief Executive, 1992-2000, Executive Deputy Chairman, 2000-2001. Recreations: tennis; skiing; geriatric rugby; golf; business.

Mathewson, Sheila Alexandra Graham, DA. Designer; Board Member, Edinburgh College of Art, since 1997; b. 1.4.42, Aberargie, Perthshire; m., Sir George Mathewson (qv); 2 s. Educ. Dunbarney, Bridge of Earn; Perth High School; Edinburgh College of Art. Recreations: reading; art; travel; skiing.

Mathieson, Derek, MA (Hons), DipEd. Headteacher, Stewarton Academy, since 1994; b. 21.2.48, Falkirk; m., Lynne; 3 s. Educ. Graeme High School, Falkirk; Edinburgh University; Glasgow University. High School of Glasgow; Marr College, Troon; Kilwinning Academy; Belmont Academy, Ayr; Stewarton Academy. Recreations: golf; swimming. Address: (b.) Cairnduff Place, Stewarton KA3 5QF; T.-01560 482342; e-mail: derek.mathieson@east-ayrshire.co.uk

Mathieson, John George, CBE, TD, DL, BL. Retired Solicitor; Chairman, Thorntons, WS, Tayside, 1990-97; Chairman, Lloyds TSB Foundation Scotland; b. 15.6.32, Argyll; m., Shirley Bidder; 1 s.; 1 d. Educ. George Watson's College, Edinburgh; Glasgow University. Territorial Army, 1951-86: Commanding Officer The Highland Regiment RA, TA Colonel for Highlands, Honorary Colonel 105 Regiment RA(TA), Chairman, Highlands TA Association; ADC TA, the Queen, 1975-80. Scottish Director, Woolwich Building Society, 1975-96; Chairman: Independent Tribunal Service, 1992, Arbroath

Branch, Royal British Legion and Earl Haig Fund; Deputy Lieutenant, Angus, 1977; Chairman: Scottish Solicitors Discipline Tribunal, 1986-92, Royal Artillery Council for Scotland; Honorary President, Angus Bn., Boys' Brigade; Elder, Colliston Parish Church. Recreations: shooting; golf; gardening. Address: (h.) Willanyards, Colliston, Arbroath, Angus; T.-01241 890286.

Matthew, Alan Stuart, LLB. Solicitor, since 1980; b. 9.12.56, Dundee; m., Eileen; 2 d. Educ. Morgan Academy, Dundee; University of Dundee. Apprentice Solicitor, J. R. Stevenson and Marshall, Dunfermline, 1978-80; Solicitor: Thorntons & Dickies, Dundee, 1980-82, Clark Oliver, Arbroath and Forfar, 1982-84, Messrs Burns Veal and Gillan (later Burns Veal), Dundee, 1984-85; Partner: Burns Veal, 1985-98, Partner, Miller Hendry (incorporating Burns Veal), since 1998. Director, Solicitors Financial Services Ltd., 1990-2000; Member, Council, Law Society of Scotland, since 1997; Member, Council, Faculty of Solicitors and Procurators in Dundee, since 1997; Tutor, Diploma in Legal Practice, University of Dundee. Recreations: rugby; hillwalking; after dinner speaking. Address: (b.) 13 Ward Road, Dundee DD1 1LU; T.-01382 200000.

Matthews, Baird, BL. Solicitor in private practice, since 1950; Honorary Sheriff, Kirkcudbright and Stranraer; b. 19.1.25, Newton Stewart; m., Mary Thomson Hope; 2 s.; 1 d. Educ. Douglas Ewart High School; Edinburgh University. Commissioned, Royal Scots Fusiliers, 1944; demobilised as Captain, 1st Bn., 1947; Partner, A. B. & A. Matthews, Solicitors, Newton Stewart; Clerk to General Commissioners of Income Tax, Stranraer and Newton Stewart Districts, from 1952; Burgh Prosecutor, Newton Stewart, from 1968; Depute Procurator Fiscal for Wigtownshire, 1970; Chairman, Board of Local Directors, General Accident Fire and Life Assurance Corporation, 1988; Director, Newcastle Building Society (Scottish Board), 1991; Dean of Faculty of Stewartry of Kirkcudbright Solicitors, 1979; Dean of Faculty of Solicitors of the District of Wigtown, 1983; Chairman, Appeals Tribunal, 1984; President, Newton Stewart Golf Club 1996 (Centenary Year). Recreations: golf; curling. Address: (b.) Bank of Scotland Buildings, Newton Stewart, Wigtownshire; T.-01671 404100.

Matthews, Sheriff Hugh, QC, LLB (Hons). Sheriff of Glasgow and Strathkelvin, since 1997; b. 4.12.53, Port Glasgow; m., Lindsay Mary Auld Wilson. Educ. St Joseph's Academy, Kilmarnock; Glasgow Academy. Admitted to Faculty of Advocates, 1979; Standing Junior Counsel, Department of Employment, 1984-88; Advocate Depute, 1988-93; took silk, 1992; Temporary Sheriff, 1992-97. Recreations: Celtic; golf; science fiction; pub quizzes; tennis. Address: (b.) 1 Carlton Place, Glasgow G5 9DA; T.-0141-429 8888.

Matthews, Professor John Burr Lumley, MA, DPhil, FRSE, FRSA, FFCS. Honorary Professor, University of Stirling, since 1984; Honorary Fellow, Scottish Association for Marine Science; b. 23.4.35, Isleworth; m., Jane Rosemary; 1 s.; 2 d. Educ. University of Warwick; St. John's College, Oxford University. Research Scientist, Oceanographic Laboratory, Edinburgh, 1961-67; Senior Lecturer, later Professor, Department of Marine Biology, University of Bergen, Norway, 1967-84; Visiting Professor, University of British Columbia, Canada, 1977-78; Deputy Director, Dunstaffnage Marine Laboratory, 1984-88; Director, NERC Dunstaffnage Marine Laboratory and Scottish Association for Marine Science, 1988-94; Secretary, The Scottish Association for Marine Science, 1988-99. Deputy Chairman, South West Regional Board, Scottish Natural Heritage, 1994-97; Secretary, International Association for Biological Oceanography; Trustee, Oban Hospice Ltd., since 1999; Trustee, Hebridean Whale and Dolphin Trust, since 1999 (Chairman, since 2001).

Recreations: cross-country skiing; gardening (chopping and sawing). Address: (h.) Grianaig, Rockfield Road, Oban PA34 5DH; T.-01631 562734.

Maver, Professor Thomas Watt, BSc (Hons), PhD, HonFRIAS, FRSA. Professor of Computer Aided Design, Department of Architecture and Building Science, and Director of the Graduate School, Strathclyde University, since 1982 (Head of Department, 1983-85, 1988-91, Vice-Dean, Faculty of Engineering, since 1993); b. 10.3.38, Glasgow; m., Avril Elizabeth Cuthbertson; 2 d. Educ. Eastwood Secondary School; Glasgow University. Special Research Fellow, Engineering Faculty, Glasgow University, 1961-67; Strathclyde University: Research Fellow, School of Architecture, 1967-70, Director, Architecture and Building Aids Computer Unit, Strathclyde, since 1970; Visiting Professor: Technical University Eindhoven, Universiti Sains Malaysia, University of Rome (La Sapienza); Past Chairman, Design Research Society; Royal Society Esso Gold Medal, 1989; Founder, CAAD Futures and ECAADE. Recreation: experiencing Europe and beyond. Address: (h.) 8 Kew Terrace, Glasgow G12 0TD; T.-0141-339 7185.

Mavor, Professor John, BSc, PhD, DSc(Eng), Hon. DSc (Greenwich), Hon. DSc (City), FRSE, FREng, FIEEE, CEng, FIEE, CPhys, FInstP. Principal and Vice-Chancellor, Napier University, since 1994; b. 18.7.42, Kilwinning; m., Susan Christina; 2 d. Educ. Bromley Technical High School; City University; London University. AEI Research Laboratories, London, 1964-65; Texas Instruments Ltd., Bedford, 1968-70; Emihus Microcomponents Ltd., Glenrothes, 1970-71; Edinburgh University: joined 1971, first holder, Lothian Chair of Microelectronics, 1980-86, Head, Department of Electrical Engineering, 1984-89, Chairman, School of Engineering, 1987-89, Dean, Faculty of Science & Engineering, 1989-94, Chair of Electrical Enginering, 1986-94. Recreations: steam railways; hillwalking. Address: (b.) Napier University, Craiglockhart Campus, 219 Colinton Road, Edinburgh EH14 1DJ; T.-0131-455 4600.

Mavor, Ronald Henry Moray, CBE, MB, ChB, FRCP(Glas); b. 13.5.25, Glasgow; m., Sigrid Bruhn (m. diss.); 1 s.; 1 d.; 1 d. deceased. Educ. Glasgow University. In medical practice, 1948-57; Drama Critic, The Scotsman, 1957-65; Director, Scottish Arts Council, 1965-71; Professor then Head, Department of Drama, University of Saskatchewan, 1977-90; Deputy Chairman, Edinburgh Festival, 1975-81. Author of plays: The Keys of Paradise, Aurelie, Muir of Huntershill, The Partridge Dance, A Private Matter, The Quartet, A House on Temperance, The Grand Inquisitor; also Dr Mavor and Mr Bridie (biography). Address: (h.) 19 Falkland Street, Glasgow G12 9PY; T.-0141-339 3149; 250 Rue Nationale, Cahors, Lot. 46000, France; T.- 0033 (0)565 238531.

Maxton, John Alston. BA (Oxon), DipEd (Oxon). MP (Labour), Glasgow Cathcart, 1979-2001; b. 5.5.36, Oxford; m., Christine Elspeth; 3 s. Educ. Lord Williams Grammar School, Thame; University College, Oxford. Lecturer in Social Studies, Hamilton College of Education, before entering Parliament; Chairman, Association of Lecturers in Colleges of Education in Scotland, 1974-78; Member, Scottish Select Committee, 1980-83, Public Accounts Committee, 1983-84; Opposition Treasury and Scottish Whip, 1984-85; Opposition Scottish Front Bench Spokesperson on Health, Local Government and Transport, 1985-87, on Industry and Local Government Finance, 1987-92; Member: National Heritage Select Committee, Speaker's Panel of Chairmen. Recreations: listening to jazz (Director, Glasgow International Jazz Festival); running. Address: (h.) 37 Larch Grove, Hamilton ML3 8NF; T.-01698 458473.

Maxwell, Donald, MA, DMus(Hon). Professional Singer; b. 12.12.48, Perth; m., Alison Jayne Norman; 1 d. Educ. Perth Academy; Edinburgh University. Former Teacher of Geography; since 1976, professional Singer with British opera companies and orchestras; Principal Baritone, Scottish Opera, 1978-82; Principal Baritone, Welsh National Opera, 1982-85; guest appearances, BBC Proms, Edinburgh Festival, Royal Opera House, London, Vienna, Paris, Milan, Tokyo, New York, Buenos Aires – notably as Falstaff; Director, National Opera Studio, 2001; comedy – The Music Box with Linda Ormiston. Recreation: railways. Address: (b.) c/o 39 Colinhill Road, Strathaven, Lanarkshire.

Maxwell, Ingval, DA, RIBA, FRIAS, FSA Scot. Director, Technical Conservation Research and Education, Historic Scotland, since 1993; b. 28.5.44, Penpont; m., Susan Isabel Maclean; 1 s.; 1 d. Educ. Dumfries Academy; Duncan of Jordanstone College of Art, Dundee. Joined Ministry of Public Buildings and Works as Architect, 1969; Area Architect, then Principal Architect, Ancient Monuments Branch, 1972-85; Assistant Director of Works, Historic Scotland, 1985-93; RIBA Research Award, 1970-71; RIAS Thomas Ross Award, 1988; Chairman, Scottish Vernacular Buildings Working Group, 1990-94; Chairman: Scottish Conservation Forum in Training and Education, since 1994, Scottish Stone Liaison Group, since 1997; Member, RIAS Conservation Committee; Member, European Commission COST Action C5, 1996-2000; Member, Architects Accredited in Building Conservation, since 1999; Member, ICOMOS UK Executive Committee, since 1995; Member, Centre for Historic Buildings, Collections and Sites Academic Advisory Committee, since 2001; Member, UK and Ireland Blue Shield Organisation, since 2001. Publications: Building Materials of the Scottish Farmstead, 1996; Conservation of Historic Graveyards Guide for Practitioners (Co-Author), 2001. Recreations: photography; astronomy; aircraft; buildings. Address: (h.) 135 Mayfield Road, Edinburgh EH9 3AN.

Maxwell, (Thomas) Fordyce, MBE. Columnist, Rural Affairs Editor, The Scotsman; b. 21.8.45, Northumberland; m., Liz (Elizabeth Duncan); 1 s.; 1 d. Educ. Berwick Grammar School; Harper Adams Agricultural College. Farming News, 1967-69; The Scotsman: Assistant Agricultural Editor, 1969-75, Agricultural Editor, 1975-77; farming/freelance, 1977-89; rejoined The Scotsman, 1989 (former Diary Editor). Seaton Award, 1992; author of three books. Recreations: family; walking; reading. Address: (b.) 108 Holyrood Road, Edinburgh EH8 8AS; T.-0131-620 8511; e-mail: fmaxwell@scotsman.com

Maxwell, Professor Thomas Jefferson, OBE, BSc, PhD, FRSGS, FRSE, CBiol, FIBiol, FRAgS. Director, Macaulay Land Use Research Institute, 1987-2000 and Chief Executive, Macaulay Research and Consultancy Services, 1994-2000; Honorary Research Professor, Aberdeen University; Member, Agriculture and Environment Biotechnology Commission, since 2000; Council Member, National Trust for Scotland, since 2000; b. 7.10.40, Aspatria, Cumbria; m., Christine Patrick Speedie; 1 s.; 1 d. Educ. Silcoates School, Wakefield; Edinburgh University. Specialist Animal Production Adviser, East of Scotland College of Agriculture, 1967-70; Research Scientist, then Head, Animal Production Department, Hill Farming Research Organisation, 1970-87. Recreations: reading; hill-walking; gardening. Address: 12 Kingswood Crescent, Kingswells, Aberdeen AB15 8TE.

Maxwell-Irving, Alastair Michael Tivey, BSc, CEng, MIEE, MIMgt, FSAScot, FSA. Antiquarian and Archaeologist; b. 1.10.35, Witham, Essex; m., Esther Mary Hamilton, MA, LLB. Educ. Lancing College; London University; Stirling University. General Electric Company, 1957; English Electric Company, 1960; Assistant Factor, Annandale Estates, 1966; Weir Pumps Ltd., 1970-91;

founder Member and Secretary, 1975-78, Central Scotland Branch, British Institute of Management. Publications: Genealogy of the Irvings of Dumfries, 1965; The Irvings of Bonshaw, 1968; The Irvings of Dumfries, 1968; Lochwood Castle, 1968; Early Firearms and their Influence on the Military and Domestic Architecture of the Borders, 1974; Cramalt Tower: Historical Survey and Excavations, 1977-79, 1982; Borthwick Castle: Excavations 1979, 1982; Andrew Dunlop (Clockmakers' Company 1701-32), 1984; Hoddom Castle: A Reappraisal of its Architecture and Place in History, 1989; Lochwood Castle, 1990; The Castles of Buittle, 1991; Lockerbie Tower, 1992; Torthorwald Castle, 1993; Scottish Yetts and Window Grilles, 1994; The Tower-Houses of Kirtleside, 1997; Kenmure Castle, 1997; The Border Towers of Scotland: their history and architecture – The West March, 2000. Recreations: architecture and history of the Border towers of Scotland; archaeology; family history and genealogy; Florence and the art and architecture of Tuscany; horology; heraldry; photography; gardening. Address: (h.) Telford House, Blairlogie, Stirling FK9 5PX.

Maxwell-Scott, Dame Jean (Mary Monica), DCVO (1984). Lady in Waiting to Princess Alice, Duchess of Gloucester, since 1959; b. 8.6.23. VAD Red Cross Nurse, 1941-46; great-great-great grand-daughter of Sir Walter Scott. Address: (h.) Abbotsford, Melrose, Roxburghshire TD6 9BQ.

May, Christine, Dip.Inst.Mgt. Leader, Fife Council, since 1998; Vice-Chair, UK Delegation, EU Committee of Regions, since 1998; Board Member, Scottish Homes, since 1999; Board Member, Scottish Enterprise, since 1999; Chair, Objective 3 Partnership (Scotland) Ltd., since 2000; b. 23.3.48, Dublin; m., William; 1 s.; 1 d. Recreations: reading; walking; motor sports. Address: (b.) Fife Council, Fife House, North Street, Glenrothes KY7 5LT; T.-01592 416063.

May, David Jeans, MA (Hons). Rector, Craigie High School, Dundee, since 1990; b. 28.12.45, Aberdeen; m., Anne Elizabeth Raeside Eastop; 1 s.; 1 d. Educ. Robert Gordon's College, Aberdeen; Aberdeen University; Jordanhill College of Education. Teacher, St. Columba's, Gourock, 1973-74; Assistant Principal Teacher of Social Subjects, Castlehead High, Paisley, 1974-78; Principal Teacher of Modern Studies/Economics, Grange Secondary, Glasgow, 1978-84; Assistant Head Teacher, Dunoon Grammar School, 1984-87; Deputy Rector, Montrose Academy, 1987-90. Convener, SEB Modern Studies Panel; Member: Secretary of State for Scotland's Working Group on Environmental Education, Steering Committee, Scottish Office Education and Industry Department Improving School Effectiveness Project, Scottish Ethos Network National Committee. Recreations: hill-walking; golf; gardening; family. Address: (h.) Evanston, Lamondfauld Lane, Hillside, Montrose DD10 9HY; T.-0167 4830673.

May, Douglas James, LLB. Queen's Counsel, since 1989; b. 7.5.46, Edinburgh. Educ. George Heriot's; Edinburgh University. Advocate, 1971; Temporary Sheriff, 1990-99; Social Security Commissioner, Child Support Commissioner, since 1993; Parliamentary candidate (Conservative), Edinburgh East, 1974, Glasgow Cathcart, 1983. Recreations: golf (Captain: Scotland Universities Golfing Society, 1990-91, Merchants of Edinburgh Golf Club, 1997-99); photography (ARPS, 1997, President, Edinburgh Photographic Society, 1996-99); travel. Address: 23 Melville Street, Edinburgh; T.-0131-225 2201.

May, Malcolm Stuart, BA, BD, STM, CQSW. Chief Officer, Dundee Voluntary Action, since 1979; b. 9.9.40, Isle of Shapinsay, Orkney; m., Alison Wood; 1 s.; 1 d. Educ. Kilmarnock Academy; The Gordon Schools, Huntly; Hamilton Academy; Queen's University, Belfast; Glasgow University; Union Theological Seminary, New York.

Assistant Minister, The Old Kirk, West Pilton, Edinburgh, 1966-68; staff, Iona Community, Glasgow, 1968-72; social work training, 1972-73; Training Officer, Scottish Council for Voluntary Organisations, 1973-78. Member, Board of Management, Dundee College; Non-Executive Director, Tayside Health Board, 1994-98. Recreations: reading; choral singing; hill-walking. Address: (b.) Number Ten, The Centre for the Voluntary Sector, 10 Constitution Road, Dundee DD1 1LL.

Mayer, John Isaac, BCom, DipLP. Advocate, since 1992; b. 21.2.52, Glasgow; m., Elizabeth; 1 s. Educ. Westwood School; University of Edinburgh. Left school aged 14 (a year before minimum legal age), 1966 and, dodging truant officers, read surreptitiously for a year in the Mitchell Library in Glasgow, then read through a second year in 1967; engineering apprenticeship, Scottish Land Development Ltd., 1968-72; left engineering in 1974 to fulfil dream of becoming a record producer; built Phoenix Record and Filmworks, 1974-84; attended university, 1985-89; training for Scottish Bar, 1989-92; international child protection law specialist. Member, General Council, University of Edinburgh, since 2001. Publications: Nuclear Peace, 2002; various articles in legal journals; contributed to three legal textbooks. Recreations: the Delta Blues; Islay whisky; buying guitars for his son. Address: Parliament House, Edinburgh; T.-07932 623 719; e-mail: jm011a7005@blueyonder.co.uk

Mearns, Anne, MA (Hons), DipTP, MRTPI, MIMgt, AssocCIPD, FRSA. Director, The Scottish Parliament and Business Exchange, since 2001; Chairperson, Forward Scotland, since 2001; b. 20.8.47, Glasgow. Educ. Hyndland Senior Secondary School; Glasgow University; Strathclyde University. Planning assistant, Coatbridge Burgh, 1969; Planner, Lanark County Council, 1969-73; Senior Planner (Research), Glasgow Corporation, 1973-75; Supervisory Planner (Policy Analysis), 1975-78, Assistant Chief, 1978-79, Chief Planner (Policy and Intelligence), 1979-87, City of Glasgow District Council Planning Department; Chief Corporate Planner, Town Clerk's Office, 1987-89; Depute Town Clerk (Corporate Policy Development), City of Glasgow District Council, 1989-94; Chief Executive, City of Aberdeen District Council, 1994-95; Chief Executive, Highlands of Scotland Tourist Board, 1995-97; Director, Hypertour, 1995-97; business adviser, 1997-2001. Member, Glasgow University General Council Business Committee, 1987-91; Member, Editorial Board, British Urban and Regional Information Systems Association, 1988-94; Member, Council, Glasgow and West of Scotland Institute of Public Administration, 1991-94; Member, Advisory Board, Graduate School of Environmental Studies, Strathclyde University, 1993-95; Trustee, Clerk Maxwell Cancer Research Fund. Recreations: cerebral and cultural pursuits; community interests; clarsach. Address: (h.) 15 Springkell Gardens, Pollokshields, Glasgow, G41 4BP; T.-0141-424 0069.

Meek, Brian Alexander, OBE, JP. Columnist, The Herald; Chairman, Conservative Group, City of Edinburgh Council, since 1995; b. 8.2.39, Edinburgh; m., Frances C. Horsburgh; 1 s.; 1 d. Educ. Royal High School, Edinburgh; Edinburgh Secretariat College. Joined Scotsman Publications as trainee, then Sub-Editor, Features Writer; transferred to Express Newspapers as Feature Writer, Leader Writer and Rugby Correspondent; elected, Edinburgh Corporation, 1969; Leader, Conservative Group, 1970-72; elected as Bailie, 1972; Convener, Lothian Regional Council, 1982-86; Member, Edinburgh District Council, 1992-96; Vice-President, Scottish Conservative and Unionist Association, 1989-92. Address: (b.) City of Edinburgh Council, City Chambers, High Street, Edinburgh EH1 1YJ; T.-0131-529 4953; e-mail: brian.meek@edinburgh.gov.uk

Meek, David, MA, MEd. Rector, Queen Anne High School, Dunfermline, since 1997; b. 20.7.54, Bonnybridge; m., Sheena Flora Meek; 2 s. Educ. Falkirk High School; Glasgow University. Teacher, Renfrew High School; Assistant Principal Teacher, Vale of Leven Academy; Principal Teacher of English, then Assistant Head Teacher, Boclair Academy; Inspector, Quality Assurance Unit, Strathclyde; Rector, Portree High School. Address: (b.) Broomhead, Dunfermline, Fife KY12 0PQ.

Meek, Professor Donald Eachann MacDonald, MA (Cantab), MA, PhD (Glas), FRHistS. Professor of Scottish and Gaelic Studies, Edinburgh University, since 2002; b. 16.5.49, Glasgow, brought up in Tiree; m., Rachel Jane Rogers; 2 d. Educ. Oban High School; Glasgow University; Emmanuel College, Cambridge. Lecturer, Senior Lecturer and Reader in Celtic, Edinburgh University, 1979-92; Professor of Celtic, Aberdeen University, 1993-2001. Assistant Editor, Historical Dictionary of Scottish Gaelic, Glasgow University, 1973-79; Honorary Secretary, Gaelic Society of Glasgow, 1974-79; Member, Gaelic Advisory Committee to Broadcasting Council for Scotland, 1976-78 and of Gaelic Panel, National Bible Society of Scotland, since 1978; President, Edinburgh and Lothians Baptist Association, 1992-93; Clerk and Treasurer, Board of Celtic Studies (Scotland), since 1994; Chairman, Ministerial Advisory Group on Gaelic, Scottish Executive, 2001-02; Editor, Gaelic Bible, 1992 edition and later revisions; a General Editor, Dictionary of Scottish Church History and Theology, 1993; President, Scottish Church History Society, since 2001; lay preacher. Publications: books include Mairi Mhor nan Oran, 1977, second edition 1998; The Campbell Collection of Gaelic Proverbs and Proverbial Sayings, 1978; Island Harvest: A History of Tiree Baptist Church, 1988; Sunshine and Shadow: the story of the Baptists of Mull, 1991; A Mind for Mission: essays (Editor), 1992; Tuath is Tighearna: Poetry of the Clearances and the Land Agitation (Editor), 1995; The Quest for Celtic Christianity, 2000; Caran an t-Saoghail: Anthology of Nineteenth-century Gaelic Poetry, 2002; Scottish Gaelic Studies, vols. 18, 19, 20, 21 (Editor); numerous articles on Gaelic and Highland themes. Recreations: family activities; getting to know the Highlands; filling the wastepaper basket. Address: (b.) 27 George Square, Edinburgh EH8 9LD.

Mehta, Phiroze Sorabji, BSc (Hons), BSc(Eng), MSc, CEng, MIMechE, FIDiagE, FRSA. Senior Lecturer in CAD, Glasgow Caledonian University, since 1986; b. 9.10.44, Bombay; m., Margaret Jane Bowie; 2 s.; 1 d. Whessoe Ltd.: Design Engineer, 1970-75, Senior Design Engineer, 1975-78; Senior Design Engineer, Nuclear Design Department, Babcock Power Ltd., 1978-84; Senior Lecturer in Engineering Design, University of Central England, Birmingham, 1984-86. Member, Organising Committee and University Representative Member, Conference on Education and Training in Finite Element Analysis; SQA External Verifier; Institution of Mechanical Engineers: Member, Professional Interview Panel, Chairman, Glasgow Panel; Academic Liaison Officer, Institution of Incorporated Engineers; Board Member, Scottish Qualifications Authority; Member, National Qualifications Committee; Director, SPTC, 1998-2000; Secretary, Bearsden Academy PTA; Open University Tutor. Recreations: theatre; concerts; music. Address: (h.) 8 Dumgoyne Drive, Bearsden, Glasgow G61 3AP; (b.) Department of Engineering, Glasgow Caledonian University, Glasgow G4 0BA.

Meldrum, Angus Alexander, BSc, DIA. Managing Director, Tennent Caledonian Breweries Ltd., since 1992 (Director, since 1981); Director, Maclay's Brewery & Co. plc, Alloa, since 1992; Managing Director, J.G. Thomson Ltd. (Wines and Spirits Merchants), since 1992; Director, North British Trust Hotels Ltd., Edinburgh, since 1999; b. 7.11.45, Stornoway; m., Anne-Marie; 1 s. Educ. Kingussie

School; Edinburgh University; Bath University Management School. Joined Bass plc, London, 1971; Tennent Caledonian Breweries Ltd., 1978; Brands Marketing Director, Bass Brewers Ltd., Burton-on-Trent, 1990-92. Director, Bass Ireland Ltd., 1981-95; Director, Tennents Ireland Ltd. (Dublin), 1981-95; Director, Bass Export Ltd., 1990-94; President, Brewers Association of Scotland, 1992-94; Council Member, UK Brewers Society, 1992-94; Chairman, Scottish Licensed Trade Association, 1999-2000. Recreations: fishing; shooting; rugby; football; shinty; Scottish music; Gaelic culture. Address: (b.) Wellpark Brewery, 161 Duke Street, Glasgow G31 1JD; T.-0141-552 6552.

Meldrum, James, MA. Director of Administrative Services, Scottish Executive, since 1999; b. 9.8.52, Kirkintilloch. Educ. Lenzie Academy; Glasgow University. Administration Trainee/HEO (Admin), Scottish Office, 1973-79; Principal grade posts, Scottish Economic Planning Department, Scottish Development Department, Scottish Office Personnel Division, 1979-86; Deputy Director, Scottish Courts Administration, 1986-91; Head, Investment Assistance Division, Scottish Office Industry Department, 1991-94; Registrar General for Scotland, 1994-99. Address: (b.) Saughton House, Broomhouse Drive, Edinburgh EH11 3XD; T.-0131-244 4311.

Mellows, Susan Mary, BSc, PhD, DIC. Academic Registrar, Strathclyde University, since 1993; b. 20.1.44, Brackley, Northants. Educ. Brackley High School; Edinburgh University; Imperial College, London. Kodak Ltd., 1966-67; Science and Engineering Research Council, London, 1970-85; YARD Ltd., Glasgow, 1985-90 (Manager, System Dynamics and Underwater Engineering Group); joined Strathclyde University, 1990, as Deputy Registrar. Recreations: hill-walking; other outdoor activities; books; music. Address: (b.) John Anderson Campus, Strathclyde University, Glasgow G1 1XG; T.-0141-552 4400, Ext. 2002.

Melville, Ian Dunlop, MB, ChB, FRCPGlas, FRCPLond, Hon. FRCPS(Glas). Consultant Neurologist, Institute of Neurological Sciences, Glasgow, 1965-88; Honorary Clinical Lecturer, Glasgow University, 1968-88; b. 9.11.27, Glasgow; m., Eliza Duffus; 1 s.; 3 d. Educ. Shawlands Academy; Glasgow University. RAF Medical Branch; Medical Registrar, Glasgow Royal Infirmary; Academic Registrar, National Hospital for Nervous Diseases, London; Clinical Research Fellow, Medical Research Council, London; Senior Medical Registrar, Glasgow. Artist Member, Paisley Art Institute; former Editor, Bulletin of Royal College of Physicians and Surgeons, Glasgow. Recreations: golf; photography; watercolour painting. Address: (h.) 9 Mirrlees Drive, Glasgow G12 0SH; T.-0141-339 7085.

Mennie, Alastair Douglas, LLB, PhD, FSA Scot. Academic and practising lawyer; Advocate, since 1982; b. 2.10.57, Aberdeen. Educ. Aberdeen University; Edinburgh University. Part-time Lecturer in Law, 1987-92; Professor of Law: ESADE Business School, Barcelona, 1992-94, Abat Oliba University Centre, Barcelona, 1994-96, Aarhus University, 1996-99; Visiting Professor: Toulouse University, 1994, Belgrano University, Buenos Aires, 1997, University of Paris XIII, 1999, University of Paris X, 2000, Humboldt University, Berlin, 2000-01; Guest Lecturer at various Universities including Paris II, Bologna and Asuncion; Director of Studies, Hague Academy of International Law, 1997; scholarship recipient: TMC Asser Institute, The Hague, 1988, European University Institute, Florence, 1990; Cornell Law School, New York State, 1997. Publications: Domicile Flowcharts, 1991; numerous articles in British and foreign law journals. Recreations: playing the guitar; viewing modern art exhibitions;

swimming in the sea. Address: (h.) 52 Picardy Court, Rose Street, Aberdeen AB10 1UG; T.-01224 633625; e-mail: alastair_mennie@web.de

Mennie, William Patrick, BL, NP, IAC. Partner, Grigor & Young, Solicitors, Elgin and Buckie, since 1964 (Senior Partner, since 1984); b. 11.10.37, Elgin; m., Patricia Leslie Bogie; 2 s.; 1 d. Educ. Elgin Academy; Edinburgh University. Solicitor, 1960; Honorary Sheriff at Elgin, since 1993; accredited by Law Society of Scotland as a specialist in agricultural law; Secretary, Malt Distillers Association of Scotland. Recreation: game shooting. Address: (h.) Innesmill, Urquhart, Elgin; T.-01343 842643.

Menzies, The Hon. Lord (Duncan A.Y. Menzies), QC, MA (Oxon), LLB. Senator of the College of Justice, since 2001; b. 28.8.53, Edinburgh; m., Hilary Weston; 2 s. Educ. Edinburgh Academy; Cargilfield; Glenalmond; Wadham College, Oxford; Edinburgh University. Advocate, 1978; Standing Junior Counsel to The Admiralty, 1984-91; Queen's Counsel, 1991; accredited mediator, 1992; Temporary Sheriff, 1996-97; Advocate Depute, 1998-2000; Home Advocate Depute, 1998-2000; Chairman, Scottish Planning, Local Government and Environmental Bar Group, 1997-2001; Member, Faculty Council, 1997-2001; Parliamentary Candidate, Midlothian, 1983, Edinburgh Leith, 1987; founder, Scottish Wine Society, 1976. Recreations: shooting; golf; wines; planting trees. Address: (b.) Court of Session, Parliament House, Edinburgh; T.-0131-225 2595.

Menzies, George Macbeth, BA, LLB. Retired, formerly with Turcan Connell Solicitors, and Burness Solicitors; b. 18.4.43, Edinburgh; m., Patricia Mary; 1 s.; 2 d. Educ. Edinburgh Academy; Corpus Christi College, Oxford; Edinburgh University. Past Chairman, North British Steel Group (Holdings) PLC; Non-Executive Director, Cairn Petroleum Oil & Gas Ltd., 1986-88; Chairman, Fruitmarket Gallery, 1984-88; President, Edinburgh Academical Football Club, 1990-92 and 2000-01; Chairman, Endeavour Training (Scotland) Ltd., 1983-97; Director: Scottish Council for Development and Industry, 1990-99 (Fellow, since 1999), Greencastle Farming Plc, since 1995, Mercy Corps Scotland, since 2001, Scottish Community Foundation, since 2001. Recreations: walking; contemporary arts; rugby. Address: 5 Gordon Terrace, Edinburgh EH1 2ET.

Menzies, Gordon, MA (Hons), DipEd. Independent Producer (retired Head of Educational Broadcasting, BBC Scotland); b. 30.7.27, Logierait, Perthshire; m., Charlotte; 2 s.; 1 d. Educ. Breadalbane Academy, Aberfeldy; Edinburgh University. Producer/Director, Who Are the Scots?, 1971, The Scottish Nation, 1972, The Chiel Amang Us, 1974, Ballad Folk, 1975, History Is My Witness, 1976, Play Golf with Peter Alliss, 1977, Scotch and Wry, 1978-79, Two Views of Burns, 1979, Barbara Dickson in Concert, 1981-84-86, The World of Golf, 1982, The Celts, 1987, Play Better Golf with Peter Alliss, 1989, Scotch and Wry Hogmanay, 1980-93; Editor, The Afternoon Show, 1981-85; Play Snooker with Dennis Taylor, 1990; Play Bridge with Zia, 1991; In Search of Scotland, 2001. Publications: Who Are the Scots?, 1971; The Scottish Nation, 1972; History Is My Witness, 1976; Play Golf, 1977; The World of Golf, 1982; Scotch and Wry, 1986; Double Scotch and Wry, 1988; Play Better Golf, 1989; In Search of Scotland, 2001. Recreations: golf; snooker; curling; theatre. Address: (h.) 8 Ingleside, Lenzie, Glasgow G66 4GN.

Menzies, John Maxwell. Life President, John Menzies PLC (Chairman, 1952-97); b. 13.10.26; m., Patricia Eleanor Dawson; 4 d. Educ. Eton. Lt., Grenadier Guards; Member, Berwickshire County Council, 1954-57; Director: Scottish American Mortgage Co., 1959-63, Standard Life Assurance Co., 1960-63, Vidal Sassoon Inc., 1969-80, Gordon & Gotch plc, 1970-85, Atlantic Assets Trust, 1973-88, Ivory and Sime Enterprise Capital PLC (formerly Independent Investment Co. plc), 1973-96 (Chairman, 1983-96), Fairhaven International, 1980-88, Rocky Mountains Oil & Gas, 1980-85, Ivory & Sime plc, 1980-83, Personal Assets PLC, 1981-92, Bank of Scotland, 1984-94, Guardian Royal Exchange, 1985-96, Malcolm Innes & Partners Ltd., 1989-2001. Life Vice President, NewstrAid Benevolent Institution (Trustee, 1974-95, President, 1968-74, Newsvendors' Benevolent Institution); Member: Royal Company of Archers, Queen's Bodyguard for Scotland, Board of Trustees, National Library of Scotland, 1991-99. Recreations: farming; shooting; reading; travel. Address: (b.) 108 Princes Street, Edinburgh EH2 3AA; T.-0131-225 8555.

Menzies, Neil Graham Finlay, BSc, FRSA. Corporate Adviser; Scottish Adviser to Chemical Industries Association; b. 14.10.41, Meikleour; m., Lorna; 2 d. Educ. Lower School of John Lyon, Harrow; St. Andrews University. Voluntary Service Overseas, Nigeria, 1964-66; ICI, 1966-93, latterly Scottish Affairs Adviser. Non-Executive Director, Scottish Ambulance Service, 1955-99; Deputy Chairman, Scottish Water and Sewerage Customers Council, 1995-99; Member, Gas and Electricity Consumers Council, since 2000; Member, Scottish Rating and Valuation Council, 2000-01; Member, Executive, Scottish Council Development and Industry; Director, Royal Lyceum Theatre Company. Address: (b.) 13 Northumberland Street, Edinburgh EH3 6LL; T.-0131-557 4321; e-mail: Neil.Menzies@wwmail.co.uk

Mercer, Roger James, MA, FSA, FRSE, FSA Scot, MIFA. Secretary, Royal Commission for the Ancient and Historical Monuments (Scotland); b. 12.9.44, Hertfordshire; m., Susan; 1 s.; 1 d. Educ. Harrow County Grammar School; Edinburgh University. Inspector of Ancient Monuments, AM Division, Department of the Environment, London, 1969-74; Lecturer and Reader, Department of Archaeology, Edinburgh University, 1974-89. Treasurer, Society of Antiquaries of Scotland, 1977-87; Vice President: Society of Antiquaries of Scotland, 1988-91, Prehistoric Society, 1987-91, Council for British Archaeology, 1991-94; Honorary Professor of Archaeology: University of Durham, since 1995, University of Edinburgh, since 1999. Recreations: music; reading; learning. Address: (b.) RCAHMS, John Sinclair House, 16 Bernard Terrace, Edinburgh EH8 9NX.

Merchant, Bruce Alastair, OBE, LLB. Solicitor; Partner, South, Forrest, Mackintosh & Merchant, Inverness, since 1971; Deputy Chairman, Accounts Commission for Scotland; b. 17.5.45, Edinburgh; m., Joan Isobel Sinclair Hamilton; 1 s.; 2 d. Educ. Inverness Royal Academy; Aberdeen University. Council Member, Law Society of Scotland, 1982-88 (Convener, Guarantee Fund Committee, 1984-87, Convener, Finance Committee, 1987-88); Member: Highland Health Board, 1981-91, Board of Management for Inverness Hospitals, 1971-74, Inverness Local Health Council, 1975-81; Dean, Faculty of Solicitors of the Highlands, 1994-96. Address: (h.) 3 Crown Circus, Inverness; T.-01463 239980.

Merrylees, Andrew, BArch, DipTP, RSA, RIBA, FRIAS, FCSD, FRSA. Honorary Professor of Architecture, University of Dundee, since 1998; Consultant, Merrylees and Robertson, since 1997; Consultant, Hypostyle, since 2000; b. 13.10.33, Newmains; m., Maie Crawford; 2 s.; 1 d. Educ. Wishaw High School; University of Strathclyde. Sir Basil Spence, Glover and Ferguson: joined 1957, Associate, 1968, Partner, 1972; set up Andrew Merrylees Associates, 1985. Member: Advisory Council for the Arts in Scotland. RIBA Bronze Medal; Saltire Award; Civic Trust Award; Art in Architecture Award; RSA Gold Medal; SCONUL Award. Recreations: architecture; painting; cooking. Address: (b.) Quadrant, 17 Bernard Street, Edinburgh EH6 6PW; T.-0131-555 0688; e-mail: amer@hypostyle.co.uk

Meston, Professor Michael Charles, MA, LLB, JD. Professor of Scots Law, Aberdeen University, 1971-96; b. 13.12.32, Aberdeen; m., Dorothea Munro; 2 s. Educ. Robert Gordon's College, Aberdeen; Aberdeen University; Chicago University. Lecturer in Private Law, Glasgow University, 1959-64; Aberdeen University: Senior Lecturer in Comparative Law, 1964-68, Professor of Jurisprudence, 1968-71; Dean, Faculty of Law, 1970-73 and 1988-91; Honorary Sheriff, Grampian Highland and Islands, since 1972; Temporary Sheriff, 1993-99; Vice Principal, Aberdeen University, 1979-82; Trustee, National Museum of Antiquities of Scotland, 1982-85; Governor, Robert Gordon's College, Aberdeen, until 1997; Member, Grampian Health Board, 1985-91; Non-Executive Director, Aberdeen Royal Hospitals NHS Trust, 1992-97. Publications: The Succession (Scotland) Act 1964; The Matrimonial Homes (Family Protection) (Scotland) Act 1981; The Scottish Legal Tradition, 1991; The Aberdeen Stylebook 1722, 2000; Meston's Succession Opinions, 2000. Recreations: golf; photography. Address: (h.) 4 Hamilton Place, Aberdeen AB15 4BH; T.-Aberdeen 641554; e-mail: mcmeston@corgarff.demon.co.uk

Michie of Gallanach, Baroness (Janet Ray Michie). MP (Lib. Dem.), Argyll and Bute, 1987-2001; b. 4.2.34; m., Dr. Iain Michie; 2 d.; 1 d. deceased. Educ. Aberdeen High School for Girls; Lansdowne House School, Edinburgh; Edinburgh School of Speech Therapy. Area Speech Therapist, Argyll and Clyde Health Board, 1977-87. Deputy Leader, Scottish Liberal Democrats; Liberal Spokeswoman on Transport and Rural Development, 1987-88; Liberal Democrat Spokeswoman on: Scotland, 1988-97, Women's Issues, 1988-94; Member, Select Committee on Scottish Affairs, 1992-97; Vice Chairman, Scottish Liberal Party, 1976-78; Chair, Scottish Liberal Democrats, 1992-93; Vice Chairperson, Parliamentary Group on Whisky Industry, 1990-01; Vice President, Royal College of Speech and Language Therapists, 1996-2001; Honorary President, Clyde Fishermen's Association; Life Peer. Recreations: golf; swimming; gardening; watching rugby. Address: (b.) House Lords, London SW1A 0PW.

Michie, Professor David Alan Redpath, OBE, RSA, RGI, RWA, DA, FRSA, FFCS. Professor, Heriot Watt University, 1988-90; Head, School of Drawing and Painting, Edinburgh College of Art, 1982-90; b. 30.11.28, St. Raphael, France; m., Eileen Anderson Michie; 2 d. Educ. Hawick High School; Edinburgh College of Art. Travelling Scholarship, Italy, 1954-55; Lecturer, Grays School of Art, Aberdeen, 1957-61; Lecturer, Edinburgh College of Art, 1961 (Vice Principal, 1974-77). President, Society of Scottish Artists, 1961-63; Member: General Teaching Council for Scotland, 1975-80, Court, Heriot-Watt University, 1979-82, Council, British School at Rome, 1980-85, Museums and Galleries Commission, 1991-96, Royal West of England Academy, 1991-2000; Guthrie Award, RSA, 1964; David Cargill Prize, RGI, 1977; Lothian Region Award, 1977; Sir William Gillies Award, 1980; RGI Prize, 1990; Cornelissen Prize, RWA, 1992; one-man exhibitions, Mercury Gallery, London, nine times, 1966-99, Lothian Region Chambers, 1977, The Scottish Gallery, 1980, 1994, 1998, Loomshop Gallery, Lower Largo, 1981, 1987, Mercury Gallery, Edinburgh, 1986; Baarn and Amsterdam, 1991; Visiting Artist, University of the Arts, Belgrade, 1979; Visiting Professor, Faculty of Art Studio Department, UCLA, Santa Barbara, 1992. Address: (h.) 17 Gilmour Road, Edinburgh EH16 5NS.

Michie, Professor Donald, MA (Oxon), DPhil (Oxon), DSc (Oxon), Hon. DSc (NCAA), Hon. DSc (Salford), Hon. DUniv (Stirling), Hon. DSc (Aberdeen), Hon. DUniv (York). Scientific Worker, since 1949; Emeritus Professor of Machine Intelligence, since 1984; Treasurer, Human-Computer Learning Foundation, since 1995; Honorary Foreign Member, American Academy of Arts and Sciences, since 2001; b. 11.11.23, Rangoon; m., Jean Hayes; 2 s.; 2 d.

Educ. Rugby School; Oxford University. War Service, F.O., Bletchley Park, 1942-45; Research Associate, London University, 1952-58; Edinburgh University: Senior Lecturer, Reader, in Surgical Science, 1958-65, Director, Experimental Programming Unit, 1965-67, Professor of Machine Intelligence, 1967-84; Founder and first Director, Turing Institute, Glasgow, 1984-86, Chief Scientist, 1986-92. Pioneer Award, International Embryo Transfer Society (jointly), 1988; Achievement Award, Institution of Electrical Engineers, 1995; Research Excellence Award, International Joint Conference of Artificial Intelligence, 2001. Publications: The Creative Computer (Co-author), 1984; Machine Intelligence and Related Topics, 1982; On Machine Intelligence, 1986. Recreation: writing. Address: (h.) 6 Inveralmond Grove, Edinburgh EH4 6RA; T.-0131-336 3826.

Micklem, Rosalind, BA (Hons), PGCE, MPhil. Principal, Cardonald College, since 1997; b. 7.6.56, Surrey. Educ. St. Paul's Girls' School, London; Oxford University; Leicester University; London University. Lecturer, North Oxfordshire Technical College, 1979-84; Education Officer, Northants and Hounslow, 1985-89; Vice Principal, Enfield College, 1989-95; Deputy Principal, Wirral Metropolitan College, 1995-97. Address: (b.) Cardonald College, 690 Mosspark Drive, Glasgow G52 3AY; T.-0141-272 3333.

Middleton, David Fraser, MA. Head of Local Government, Europe and External Relations Group, Department of Finance and Central Services, Scottish Executive, since 1999; b. 23.6.56, Paisley; m., Diane Lamberton; 1 d. Educ. Paisley Grammar School; Glasgow University. Joined Scottish Office as Administration Trainee, 1978; Private Secretary to Minister of State, Scottish Office, 1982-84; seconded to Cabinet Office, 1984; Principal, Scottish Office Finance Group, 1984-89; Director of Strategy, Whitfield Urban Partnership, 1989-91; Assistant Secretary, Housing, 1991-96; Assistant Secretary, Roads; Head of Personnel, 1997-99. Recreation: golf (Royal Musselburgh Golf Club). Address: (b.) Scottish Executive, Victoria Quay, Edinburgh EH6 6QQ; T.-0131-244 5505.

Middleton, Robert, OBE, JP, Hon. DLitt, HonLLD. Member, Aberdeen City Council, 1995-99 (Chair of Finance, 1997-99); b. 28.7.32, Aberdeen; m., Audrey Ewen; 2 s. Educ. Aberdeen Grammar School. Started apprenticeship with Post Office Telephones, 1948; Aberdeen Town Council: elected, 1961, appointed Magistrate, 1963, Chairman of Magistrates, 1965-66, Chairman, Education Committee, 1966-69; Chairman, Labour Party in Scotland, 1986-87; contested Banffshire as Labour candidate, 1966; contested Aberdeen South, 1974 (twice) and 1983; elected, Grampian Regional Council, 1975 (Convener, 1990-95); President, North Sea Commission of the Conference of Peripheral Maritime Regions, 1992-95. Publications: North Sea Brose; Grampian Homeland; Whatever Happened to Labour (autobiography), 2001. Recreations: golf; reading; writing not very good poetry; travel; bridge; bowls. Address: (h.) 9 Stronsay Avenue, Aberdeen AB15 6HX; T.-01224 313366.

Midgley, Professor John Morton, OBE, BSc, MSc, PhD, CChem, FRSC, FRPharmS. Professor of Pharmaceutical and Medicinal Chemistry, Strathclyde University, since 1984 (Chairman and Head of Department, 1985-90); Emeritus Professor, since 1999; b. 14.7.37, York; m., Jean Mary Tillyer; 2 s. Educ. Nunthorpe Grammar School, York; Manchester University; London University. Demonstrator, Manchester University, 1959-61; Assistant Lecturer, School of Pharmacy, London University, 1962-65; Research Associate, Massachusetts Institute of Technology, 1965-66; Lecturer, then Senior Lecturer, School of Pharmacy, London University, 1965-83; Visiting Professor, Universities of: Florida, 1978-89, Panjab, 1981, Lodz, 1985, Alexandria, 1987-88; Honorary Professor, China Pharmaceutical University, Nanjing, since 1987; Member: Committee on the Review of Medicines, 1984-92, British Pharmacopoeia Commission, since 1985 (Chairman: Committee C, since 1984, Committee L, since 1991, Vice-Chairman, Committee B, since 1985), Committee on the Safety of Medicines, since 1990, European Panal of Experts on Human Medicines, since 1995, Council of Royal Pharmaceutical Society of GB, 1991-92, Science and Engineering Research Council Pharmacy Panel, 1985-90; UK Delegation to European Pharmacopoeia Commission, since 1998; Member, EPC Group of Experts, IOB, since 1999, Chairman, IOA, since 2001; Vice-Chairman, Chemistry, Pharmacy and Standards Sub-Committee, CSM, 1990-99, Chairman, since 1999; consultant to the pharmaceutical industry, USA, Japan, EU, since 1967. Recreations: fly fishing; fisheries management; training labradors; gardening; music. Address: (b.) Strathclyde University, Department of Pharmaceutical Sciences, Royal College, SIBS Building, 27 Taylor Street, Glasgow G4 0NR; T.-0141-552 4400, Ext. 2125; e-mail: prof@jmidgley.freeserve.co.uk

Milburn, Professor George Henry William, PhD, CChem, FRSC, FBIM, Dr (h.c.), FRSA. Reseach Adviser/Research Professor, Napier University, 1998-99, Head, Department of Applied Chemical and Physical Sciences, 1973-98; Adjunct Professor, University of South Florida, since 2000; Consultant, Lahti Polytechnic, Finland, since 2000; b. 25.11.34, Wallasey; m., Jean Muriel; 1 s.; 1 d. Educ. Wallasey Grammar School; Leeds University. Short service commission, Royal Corps of Signals, 1959-63; Staff Demonstrator, Leeds University, 1963-66; Research Fellow, Sydney University, 1967-68; Senior Scientific Officer, Agricultural Research Council, 1968-69; Lecturer, Plymouth Polytechnic, 1969-70; Senior Lecturer, Sheffield Polytechnic, 1970-73.Convener, Committee of Scottish University Heads of Chemistry Departments, 1994-97; Honorary Doctorate, Technical University, Budapest, 1988; Silver Star Laureate, Poland, 1996. Publications: more than 50 scientific publications including a textbook on crystal structure analysis. Recreations: golf; bridge; photography; guitar playing. Address: (h.) 9 Orchard Court, Longniddry, East Lothian; T.-01875 853228; e-mail: harry@milburnh.fsnet.co.uk

Miles, John, OBE, BSc, PhD, CBiol, FSA Scot. Ecological Adviser to the First Minister, 1999-2001; Head, Ecological Adviser's Unit, Scottish Executive (formerly Scottish Office), 1995-2001; b. 28.1.41, Rochester; m., Ann Margaret Veitch; 2 s. Educ. Sir Joseph Williamson's Mathematical School, Rochester; Reading University. Research on soil and vegetation dynamics in the Scottish uplands, Natural Environmental Research Council, 1965-92; as Senior Principal Scientific Officer, from 1988; Ecological Adviser, Ministry of Defence, 1983, for new Falkland Islands Airfield at Mount Pleasant, and during 1983-88 for decontamination of Gruinard Island; Ecological Adviser to Secretary of State for Scotland, 1987-99; Hon. Professor, Department of Environmental Science, Stirling University, since 1994. Botanical Editor, Journal of Applied Ecology, 1987-91; Member: Advisory Board, Department of Forestry, Aberdeen University, 1990-2000, Heritage Committee, Society of Antiquaries of Scotland, since 1992, Ecological Steering Group for the oilspill in Shetland, 1993-94; UK Raptor Working Group, 1995-2000; National Goose Forum, 1997-99. Publication: Vegetation Dynamics, 1979; many scientific papers. Recreations: archaeology; gardening; hill-walking; reading; wine. Address: (h.) 51 Ramsay Road, Banchory AB31 5TS; T.-01330 822727; e-mail: Johnannmiles@aol.com

Mill, Douglas Russell, LLB, BA, MBA, DUniv, WS, SSC, NP. Secretary and Chief Executive, Law Society of Scotland, since 1997; b. 3.1.57, Paisley; m., Christine; 2 s.;

1 d. Educ. Paisley Grammar School; Glasgow University. Former Depute Director, Centre for Professional Legal Studies, Strathclyde University; former Partner, MacFarlane Young & Co., Solicitors, Paisley. Publications: Successful Practice Management, 1992; Managing the Professional Partnership, 2000; Successful Law Firm Manager (Co-Author), 2000. Recreations: golf; rugby. Address: (b.) 26 Drumsheugh Gardens, Edinburgh EH3 7YR; T.-0131-226 7411.

Millan, Rt. Hon. Bruce, PC, CA. European Commissioner, 1989-95; b. 5.10.27, Dundee; m., Gwendoline May Fairey; 1 s.; 1 d. Educ. Harris Academy, Dundee. MP, Glasgow Craigton, 1959-83, Glasgow Govan, 1983-88; Parliamentary Secretary for the RAF, 1964-66; Parliamentary Secretary, Scottish Office, 1966-70; Minister of State, Scottish Office, 1974-76; Secretary of State for Scotland, 1976-79; Opposition Spokesman on Scottish Affairs, 1979-83. Address: (h.) 1 Torridon Avenue, Glasgow G41 5LA; T.-0141-427 6483.

Millan, Professor Charles Gordon, MA, PhD, FRSA. Professor of French, Strathclyde University, since 1991; b. 25.9.46, Kirkcaldy; m., Margaret Anne Robbie; 1 s.; 1 d. Educ. Kirkcaldy High; Merrywood Grammar, Bristol; Edinburgh University. Temporary Lecturer, Edinburgh University, 1970-71; Teacher, Broughton High School, 1972-76; Strathclyde University, since 1976, Director, Languages for Business Unit, since 1990 (Languages for Export Award, 1994 and 2001), Chairman, Department of Modern Languages, 1994-98 and since 2000, Vice-Dean, Faculty of Arts and Social Sciences, 1995-98; Chair, University Council of Modern Languages (ScotCom), since 2001. Publications include: Pierre Louÿs ou le Culte de l'Amitié, 1979; Stéphane Mallarmé, Poésies (jointly), 1983; A Throw of the Dice: The Life of Stéphane Mallarmé, 1994; Documents Mallarmé, new series, I, 1998, II, 2000; Situating Mallarmé, (Co-editor), 2000. Recreations: cinema; reading. Address: (b.) Livingstone Tower, Richmond Street, Glasgow G1 1XH; T.-0141-552 4400.

Millar, Professor Alan, MA, PhD. Professor of Philosophy, Stirling University, since 1994; b. 14.12.47, Edinburgh; m., Rose-Mary Marchand; 1 s. Educ. Edinburgh University; Cambridge University. Stirling University: Lecturer in Philosophy, 1971, Senior Lecturer, 1991, Head, Department of Philosophy, 1988-94. Member, Postgraduate Studentship Selection Committee, Student Awards Agency for Scotland, 1996-2000; awarded Mind Association Research Fellowship, 1996-97; Visiting Fellow, Clare Hall, Cambridge, 1997. Publications: Reasons and Experience, 1991; articles in the philosophy of mind, epistemology, philosophy of religion, history of ethics. Recreations: reading; walking; films; cooking. Address: (b.) Stirling University, Stirling FK9 4LA; T.-01786 467555.

Millar, Bob, MA, CA. Chief Executive, Scottish Homes, since 2000; b. 30.3.50, Edinburgh; m., Sandra; 1 s.; 1 d. Educ. George Heriot's School; Edinburgh University. Chartered Accountant, Touche Ross; Financial Accountant, Bredero UK Ltd., Castle Rock Housing Association; Head of Registration, Housing Corporation; Director of Strategy, Scottish Homes; Director of Miller Ventures. Address: (b.) Thistle House, 91 Haymarket Terrace, Edinburgh EH12 5HE.

Millar, Douglas Andrew Terris. Deputy Chief Executive, Glasgow Chamber of Commerce, since 1999; Non-Executive Director, Scottish Television (Regional) Ltd., since 1998; Council Member, National Youth Orchestra of Scotland, since 2000; Trustee, Scottish TV Retirement Benefit Scheme, since 2000; Trustee, Caledonian Publishing Pension Scheme, since 2000; b. 18.6.55, Dunfermline. Educ. Queen Anne High School, Dunfermline; Aberdeen College of Commerce. Civil Servant, Scottish Office, 1972-97, latterly Head of Film, Broadcasting and Gaelic Policy Branch, Education and Industry Department; Deputy Director, Scottish Chambers of Commerce, 1997-99. Elder, Dunfermline Abbey. Recreations: youth work; football. Address: (b.) 30 George Square, Glasgow G2 1EQ; T.-0141-204 8348; e-mail: douglas.millar@glasgowchamber.org

Millar, Professor Eileen Anne, MA, PhD, Cavaliere dell'Ordine al Merito della Repubblica Italiana. Stevenson Professor of Italian, University of Glasgow, since 1992; b. Glasgow. Educ. Notre Dame High School, Glasgow; University of Glasgow. University of Glasgow: Lecturer, Department of Italian, 1968, Senior Lecturer, 1982. Member, Arts and Humanities Research Board. Publications: work on the Napoleonic period in Italian literature and on Ignazio Silone. Recreations: music; travel; cooking. Address: 30 Torridon Avenue, Glasgow G41 5AU; T.-0141-427 5988; e-mail: E.Millar@italian.arts.gla.ac.uk

Millar, Graeme, BSc, FRPharmS. Chairman, Scottish Consumer Council, since 2000; Director, Dunfermline Building Society, since 2000; Chairman, Fletcher Jones Recruitment, since 2000; Chairman, Common Services Agency, NHS Scotland, since 1998; Chairman, Edinburgh Sick Kids Friends Foundation, since 1999; 21.2.55; m., Fay; 3s. Educ. Boroughmuir Senior Secondary School; Heriot-Watt University. Vice-Chairman, Lothian Health Board, 1991-93; Non Executive Member/Director, Lothian Health Board, 1984-93; Chairman, Edinburgh Sick Children's NHS Trust, 1993-99; Executive Chairman, Scottish Pharmaceutical General Council, 1998-94; Managing Director, Graeme Millar Chemists Ltd., since 1979; Chairman, Scottish NHS Trust Chairman's Group, 1996-98; Chairman, Southern Scotland Electricity Consumers Board, 1996-2000; Chairman, Royal Pharmaceutical Society of Great Britain in Scotland, 1998-2000; Member, Advisory Committee on Borderline Substances, 1998-94; Secretary, Lothian NHS Endowment Investment Advisory Committee, 1994-99; Consultant with various pharmaceutical companies; Member, Court, Merchant Company, Edinburgh; School Governor, Erskine Stewart's Melville; Director, Scottish Community Foundation. Recreations: golf at a mediocre standard; rugby; good company; good food; good wine. Address: (b.) Scottish Consumer Council, Royal Exchange House, 100 Queen Street, Glasgow, G1 3DN; T.-0141-226 5261.

Millar, Helen Jean, OBE, MA, FRSA. Deputy Lieutenant, City of Glasgow; Member, Multi Centre Research Ethics Committee for Scotland; Chairman, Consumer Congress; Member, UK Central Council for Nurses; Member, Medical Research Council Consumer Liaison Group; Member, Rail Passenger Council; Chairman, National Consumer Federation; b. 10.10.31, Glasgow; 3 s.; 2 d. Educ. Craigholme School, Glasgow; Glasgow University. Chairman, Consumers in European Community Group, 1988-91; Director, Consumer's Committee for Scotland, 1980-89; Member and Vice-Chairman, Scottish Consumer Council, 1979-87; Chairman, Strathclyde Children's Panel, 1979-81; Member, Advisory Committee on Novel Foods, 1991-98; Member, Air Users Council, 1991-98; Vice-Chairman, New Glasgow Society, 1980-87; former Lecturer in charge, Children's Panel Training, Glasgow University; Founder Member, Board, Tron Theatre Club, Glasgow. Recreations: theatre; arts in general; Glasgow; arguing. Address: (h.) 33 Aytoun Road, Glasgow G41; T.-0141-423 4152; e-mail: helen-millar@which.net

Millar, James Lauder, CBE, DBA, CA. Chairman, Clydeport PLC, since 1997; b. 4.8.30, Dundee; m., Joan Marjorie; 2 s.; 2 d. Educ. Morgan Academy, Dundee. Willliam Low & Co. PLC, 1958-94 (Finance Director/Chief Executive/Chairman); Invergordon PLC,

1988-93 (Director/Chairman); Vision Group PLC, 1994-97 (Chairman); W.E.W. PLC, 1994-97 (Chairman). Recreations: cycling; golf; reading; music; classical cars. Address: (b.) Clydeport PLC, 16 Robertson Street, Glasgow; T.-0141-221 8733.

Millar, Peter Carmichael, OBE, MA, LLB, WS. Chairman, Medical Appeal Tribunals, 1991-99, and of Pension Appeal Tribunals, 1992-99; b. 19.2.27, Glasgow; m., Kirsteen Lindsay Carnegie; 2 s.; 2 d. Educ. Aberdeen Grammar School; Glasgow University; St. Andrews University; Edinburgh University. Royal Navy, 1944-47; Partner, W. & T.P. Manuel, WS, 1954-62; Partner, Aitken Kinnear & Co., WS, 1963-87; Partner, Aitken, Nairn WS, 1987-92; Clerk, Society of Writers to HM Signet, 1964-83; Deputy Keeper of Her Majesty's Signet, 1983-91; Chairman: Church of Scotland General Trustees, 1973-85, Mental Welfare Commission for Scotland, 1983-91. Recreations: golf; hill-walking; music. Address: (h.) 25 Cramond Road North, Edinburgh EH4 6LY.

Miller, Professor Alan, BSc, PhD, CPhys, FInstP, FRSE, FIEEE (USA). Professor of Semiconductor Physics and Head, School of Physics and Astronomy, St. Andrews University, since 1993; Professor of Physics and Electrical Engineering, University of Central Florida, since 1989; b. 5.6.49, Dunfermline; m., Susan Linklater; 3 d. Educ. Gibraltar Grammar School; Edinburgh University; Bath University. Research Fellow, Heriot-Watt University, 1974-79; Visiting Assistant Professor, North Texas University, 1979-81; Senior Principal Scientific Officer, Royal Signals and Radar Establishment, Malvern, 1981-89. Editor, Optical and Quantum Electronics, and of Cambridge Studies in Modern Optics (series of monographs); Chairman, Committee of Scottish Professors of Physics; Chairman, Scottish Chapter, Lasers and Electro-Optics Society. Publications: Nonlinear Optics in Signal Processing (Editor); Nonlinear Optical Materials and Devices for Applications in Information Technology (Editor); Laser Sources and Applications (Editor); Semiconductor Quantum Optoelectronics, From Quantum Physics to Smart Devices (Editor); 150 research papers. Recreation: music. Address: (b.) Department of Physics and Astronomy, North Haugh, St. Andrews KY16 9SS; T.-01334 463122.

Miller, Alan Douglas, LLB (Hons), DipLP. Principal Reporter, Scottish Children's Reporter Administration, since 1995; b. 30.11.59, Edinburgh; m., Alison; 1 s.; 2 d. Educ. Stewart's/Melville College, Edinburgh; Edinburgh University. Assistant/Area Reporter, Strathclyde, 1985-90; Regional Reporter, Dumfries and Galloway, 1990-95; Secretary, Association of Children's Reporters, 1990-93. Associate Member, Iona Community; Non-Executive Director, Linlithgow Young People's Project Ltd. Elder, Church of Scotland. Address (b.): Ochil House, Springkerse Business Park, Stirling FK7 7XE; T.-01786 459500; e-mail: scra@dial.pipex.com

Miller, Professor Andrew, CBE, MA, BSc, PhD, FRSE, FIBiol. Principal and Vice-Chancellor, University of Stirling, 1994-2001; General Secretary, Royal Society of Edinburgh, since 2001; b. 15.2.36, Kelty, Fife; m., Rosemary S.H. Fyvie; 1 s.; 1 d. Educ. Beath High School; Edinburgh University. Assistant Lecturer in Chemistry, Edinburgh University, 1960-62; Postdoctoral Fellow, CSIRO, Melbourne, and Tutor in Chemistry, Ormond College, Melbourne University, 1962-65; Staff Scientist, MRC Laboratory of Molecular Biology, Cambridge, 1965-66; Lecturer in Molecular Biophysics, Oxford University and (from 1967) Fellow, Wolfson College, 1966-83 (Honorary Fellow, since 1995); on secondment as first Head, European Molecular Biology Laboratory, Grenoble Antenne, France, 1975-80. Committee Member: British Biophysical Society, 1972-74, SERC Synchrotron Radiation Facility Committee, 1979-82, Biological Sciences Committee, 1982-85, Neutron Beam Research Committee,

1982-85; Council Member, Institut Laue-Langevin, 1981-85; Member: MRC Joint Dental Committee, 1984-86, UGC Biological Sciences Committee, 1985-89; (part-time) Director of Research, European Synchrotron Radiation Facility, Grenoble, 1986-91; Member: Advisory Board, AFRC Food Research Institute, 1985, UFC Advisory Groups on Biological Sciences and Pre-clinical Medicine, 1989, Scientific Council, Grenoble University, 1989; Vice-Dean of Medicine, Edinburgh University, 1991-93; Professor of Biochemistry, Edinburgh University, 1984-94; Vice-Principal, Edinburgh University, 1993-94; Director, Scottish Knowledge plc, since 1997; Member, Minister of Education's Action Group on Standards in Scottish Schools, 1997-99; Member, Council, Royal Society of Edinburgh, since 1997 (Convener, International Committee, 1999-2001); Adviser to Wellcome Trust on UK–French Synchrotron, 1999-2000; Member, Scottish Executive Science Strategy Group, 1999-2000; Chairman, International Centre for Mathematical Sciences, Edinburgh, since 2001; Member, Council, Open University, since 2001. Address: Royal Society of Edinburgh, 22-26 George Street, Edinburgh EH2 2PQ.

Miller, Bill, BSc, DipTP. Member (Labour) Scotland, European Parliament, since 1999 (Glasgow, 1994-99); b. 22.7.54, Gartochan; 1 s.; 1 d. Educ. Paisley Technical College; Kingston Polytechnic. Strathclyde Regional Councillor, 1986-94. Recreations: ties; records; Kilmarnock F.C. Address: John Smith House, 145-165 West Regent Street, Glasgow G2 4RZ; T.-0141-552 2234.

Miller, Brian, BSc (Hons). Rector, Dalziel High School, Motherwell, since 1990; b. 4.1.51, Glasgow; m., Margaret; 1 s.; 1 d. Educ. High School of Glasgow; Strathclyde University. Teacher of Mathematics, 1974-77; Assistant Principal Teacher, 1977-80; Principal Teacher, 1980-84; Assistant Head Teacher, Cranhill Secondary School, Glasgow, 1984-86; Depute Head Teacher, Stonelaw High School, Glasgow, 1986-90. Recreation: bowls. Address: (b.) Crawford Street, Motherwell ML1 3AG; e-mail: bmiller@dalziel.n-lanark.sch.uk

Miller, Rev. Charles W., MA. Religious Broadcasting Director, Radio Bridge FM; Chaplain, Royal Dundee Liff Hospital, 1980-2000; b. 4.2.26, Kinross; m., Isabella Russell Stewart, MA; 3 s. Educ. St. Mary's School, Dunblane; McLaren High School, Callander; Aberdeen University; St. Andrews University. Assistant Minister, Auld Kirk of Ayr, 1953-54; Minister: Torthorwald, Dumfries, 1953-59, Munro Church, Rutherglen, 1959-65, Cruden, Aberdeenshire, 1965-72, Anstruther Parish Church, 1972-80, Fowlis Easter and Liff Parish Church, 1980-94; former Convener: Overseas Committee, Dumfries Presbytery; Church and Nation and Social Responsibility Committees, Aberdeen Presbytery; Social Responsibility Committee, St. Andrews Presbytery; Member, Scottish Churches Consultative Committee on Road Safety; Institute of Advanced Motorists: Member, Governing Council, 1962-95, elected Fellow, since 1996, Founder Member and President, Institute's Groups Association in Scotland. Recreations: caravanning; swimming; landscape painting; hospital radio broadcasting. Address: Palm Springs, Parkside, Auchterhouse, Dundee DD3 0RF; T.-01382 320407; e-mail: charlesmiller@aol.com

Miller, Sheriff Colin Brown, LLB, SSC. Sheriff for South Strathclyde, Dumfries and Galloway, since 1991; b. 4.10.46, Paisley; m., Joan Elizabeth Blyth; 3 s. Educ. Paisley Grammar School; Glasgow University. Partner, McFadyen & Semple, Solicitors, Paisley, 1971-91; Council Member, Law Society of Scotland, 1983-91 (Convener, Conveyancing Committee, 1986-89; Convener, Judicial Procedure Committee, 1989-91; Chairman, Working Party on Rights of Audience in Supreme Courts, 1990-91); Dean, Faculty of Procurators in Paisley, 1991. Recreations:

family; walking; photography; travel; railways; ships. Address: (b.) Ayr Sheriff Court, Wellington Square, Ayr; T.-01292 268474.

Miller, Sir Donald John, FREng, FRSE, BSc(Eng), DSc, DUniv, FIMechE, FIEE; b. 9.2.27, London; m., Fay G. Herriot; 1 s.; 2 d. Educ. Banchory Academy; Aberdeen University. Metropolitan-Vickers, 1947-53; British Electricity Authority, 1953-55; Preece Cardew & Rider (Consulting Engineers), 1955-66; Chief Engineer, North of Scotland Hydro-Electric Board, 1966-74; South of Scotland Electricity Board: Director of Engineering, 1974, appointed Deputy Chairman, 1979; Chairman, Scottish Power, 1982-92. Chairman, Power Division, IEE, 1977. Recreations: gardening; walking; sailing. Address: (h.) Puldohran, Gryffe Road, Kilmacolm, Renfrewshire; T.-01505 873988.

Miller, Gordon, BSc. Rector, Mearns Academy, since 1999; b. 10.10.57, Glasgow; m., Julie Elizabeth; 1 s.; 1 d. Educ. High School of Glasgow; Strathclyde University. Assistant Teacher, Lochend Secondary School, Glasgow, 1980-85; Assistant Principal Teacher and Principal Teacher of Guidance, Lochgilphead High School, 1985-92; Assistant Rector, Carluke High School, 1992-96; Depute Rector, Crieff High School, 1996-99. Recreations: golf; hill-walking. Address: (b.) Mearns Academy, Aberdeen Road, Laurencekirk AB30 1ZY; T.-01561 378817.

Miller, Hugh Craig, BSc, MB, ChB, FRCPEdin. Consultant Cardiologist, Edinburgh Royal Infirmary, since 1975; b. 7.4.42, Edinburgh; m., Isobel Margaret; 1 s.; 1 d. Educ. George Watson's College; Edinburgh University. Registrar, Edinburgh Royal Infirmary, 1969-72; Senior Registrar, Brompton Hospital, London, 1972-75; Research Fellow, Duke University, North Carolina, 1973-74; Fulbright Scholar. Recreations: skiing; sailing. Address: (h.) 12 Dick Place, Edinburgh; T.-0131-667 4235.

Miller, Ian George Tweedie, BSc, AFIMA, MBCS, CEng, FRSA. Principal, North Glasgow College, since 1990; Chairman, Skill (Scotland), since 1992; b. 5.8.42, Hamilton; m., Una; 1 s.; 1 d. Educ. George Heriot's, Edinburgh; Heriot Watt University. Research Assistant, Hatfield Polytechnic; Lecturer, Computer Science, Strathclyde University; Director, Computer Centre, Paisley College; Depute Principal, Stevenson College. Recreations: golf; bowling. Address: (b.) 110 Flemington Street, Glasgow G21 4BX; T.-0141-558 9001.

Miller, Sheriff Ian Harper Lawson, MA, LLB. Sheriff of Glasgow and Strathkelvin at Glasgow, since 2001; b. 16.1.54, Aberdeen; m., Sheila Matthews Howie; 1 s.; 3 d. Educ. Robert Gordon's College, Aberdeen; Aberdeen University. Admitted as a Solicitor, 1980; Partner, Burnett & Reid, Solicitors, Aberdeen, 1986-91; Advocate, 1992; Sheriff of Grampian, Highland and Islands at Aberdeen, 1998-2001. Recreations: reading; music. Address: (b.) Sheriff's Chambers, Sheriff Court of Glasgow and Strathkelvin, 1 Carlton Place, Glasgow G5 9DA; T.-0141-429 8888.

Miller, Rev. Ian Hunter, BA, BD. Minister, Bonhill, since 1975; b. 30.5.44, Johnstone; m., Joan Elizabeth Parr; 2 s. Educ. Johnstone High School; Glasgow University; Open University. Travel agent, latterly Branch Manager, A.T. Mays, 1962-69; Assistant Minister, Renfrew Old Kirk, 1974-75. Moderator, Dumbarton Presbytery, 1985-87; Non-executive Trustee, Argyll and Clyde Acute Hospital Trust; Chairman, Vale Project. Recreations: golf; badminton; music; drama. Address: Bonhill Manse, 1 Glebe Gardens, Bonhill, Alexandria G83 9HR; T.-01389 753039.

Miller, Ian James, OBE, MA, LLB. Chairman, Mental Welfare Commission for Scotland; Member, National Appeal Panel for Entry to Health Boards' Pharmaceutical Lists; Governor, Morrison's Academy, Crieff; Member, Business Committee, University of Edinburgh General Council; b. 21.10.38, Fraserburgh; m., Sheila Mary Hourston; 1 s.; 2 d. Educ. Fraserburgh Academy; Aberdeen University; Edinburgh University. Private legal practice, 1963-68; Senior Legal Assistant, Inverness County Council, 1968-70; Depute County Clerk, then County Clerk, Ross and Cromarty County Council, 1970-75; Chief Executive, Inverness District Council, 1975-77; Director of Law and Administration, Grampian Regional Council, 1977-84; Director, Kildonnan Investments Ltd., Aberdeen, 1984-87; Secretary and Academic Registrar, Napier University, Edinburgh, 1987-99. Recreations: golf; curling. Address: (h.) 80 Craiglockhart Road, Edinburgh EH14 1EP.

Miller, Dr Jack Elius, OBE, JP, OStJ, FRCGP; b. 7.3.18, Glasgow; m., Ida Warrens. Educ. Hillhead High School; Glasgow University. General Medical Practitioner in Glasgow (retired); Captain, Royal Army Medical Corps, 1944-46; Chairman (founder Member), Glasgow Marriage Guidance Council, 1956-61 (Hon. Vice-President, since 1961); Hon. Vice-President, Scottish Marriage Guidance Council, since 1967; Chairman: Scottish General Medical Services Committee, 1969-72, Association of Jewish Ex-Servicemen and Women of Scotland, 1952-61 and 1964-68; President, Glasgow Jewish Representative Council, 1969-72; Member, Council, BMA, 1964-81 (National Treasurer, 1972-81; Gold Medallist, 1982); Freeman, City of London; Member, Board of Deputies of British Jews, 1979-88; Vice-President, Prince and Princess of Wales Hospice, since 1981; Co-Chairman, Scottish Jewish Archives Committee, 1986-2001, President, since 2001; Chairman, Scottish Health Authorities Review of Priorities for the Eighties and Nineties, 1985-87. Publications: Glasgow Doctors' Handbook (three editions); Sharpen report. Recreations: travel; reading; communal affairs. Address: (h.) 38 Fruin Court, Fruin Avenue, Newton Mearns, Glasgow G77 6HJ; T.-0141-639 7869.

Miller, James, CBE (1986), MA, FCIOB, FCIArb, CBIM. Chairman, 1970-99, Managing Director, 1970-91, The Miller Group Ltd. (formerly James Miller & Partners); Chairman, Royal Scottish National Orchestra, since 1997; b. 1.9.34, Edinburgh; m., 1, Kathleen Dewar (deceased); 2, Iris Lloyd-Webb; 1 s.; 3 d. Educ. Edinburgh Academy; Harrow School; Balliol College, Oxford. National Service, Royal Engineers. James Miller & Partners Ltd.: joined, 1958, appointed Director, 1960; Scottish Representative, Advisory Committee to the Meteorological Services, 1980-92; Chairman, Federation of Civil Engineering Contractors, 1985-86, President, 1990-93; Director, British Linen Bank Ltd., 1983-99 (Chairman, 1997-99); Member, Scottish Advisory Board, British Petroleum, 1990-2001; Director, Bank of Scotland, 1993-2000; Deacon Convener, Incorporated Trades of Edinburgh, 1974-77; President, Edinburgh Chamber of Commerce, 1981-83; Assistant, 1982-85, Treasurer, 1990-92, Master, 1992-94, Merchant Company of Edinburgh; Chairman, Court, Heriot-Watt University, 1990-96. Recreation: shooting. Address: (h.) Alderwood, 49 Craigcrook Road, Edinburgh EH4 3PH; T.-0131-332 2222.

Miller, James David Frederick, CBE, DUniv(Stirling, Paisley), MA (Cantab), CIMgt, FIPD, FRSA. Chairman, Wolverhampton and Dudley Breweries PLC, 1992-2001; Chairman, Fairbridge Scotland, since 1998; Vice-Chairman, Forth Valley Enterprise, since 1996; Director, J. and J. Denholm Ltd., since 1997, b. 5.1.35, Wolverhampton; m., Saffrey Blackett Oxley; 3 s. (1 deceased); 1 d. Educ. Emmanuel College, Cambridge; London School of Economics. National Service, Argyll and Sutherland Highlanders (commissioned South Staffords); Council Member, Outward Bound Limited, 1985-95; Vice-Chairman, Royal National Orchestra; Director, Edinburgh Academy, 1985; Commissioner, Queen Victoria School, 1987-97; Governor, Scottish College of Textiles, 1989;

Director, Edinburgh Military Tattoo Ltd., 1990-2000; Director, Scottish Life Assurance Company, 1995-2001; Chairman, Court, Stirling University, 1992-99; Chairman, SCOTVEC, 1992-96; Chairman, Scottish Examinations Board, 1994-96; Chairman, SQA (Scottish Qualifications Authority), 1996-2000. Recreations: gardening; golf; walking. Address: (h.) Blairuskin Lodge, Kinlochard, Aberfoyle, by Stirling FK8 3TP; T.-01877 387 249; e-mail: J.D.F.M@btinternet.com

Miller, Professor James Edward, MA, PhD. Professor, Department of Theoretical and Applied Linguistics, University of Edinburgh, since 1997; b. 6.9.42, Falkirk; m., Margaret Stewart Johnstone; 3 s. Educ. Bathgate Academy; University of Edinburgh. Department of Linguistics, University of Edinburgh: Assistant Lecturer, 1967-70, Lecturer, 1970-85, Senior Lecturer, 1985-87, Reader, 1987-97. Publication: Spontaneous Spoken Language – Syntax and Discourse, 1998. Address: Department of Theoretical and Applied Linguistics, Adam Ferguson Building; 40 George Square, Edinburgh EH8 9LL; T.-0131-650 3955; e-mail: Jim.Miller@ed.ac.uk

Miller, Very Rev. John. Minister, Castlemilk East Parish, since 1971; Moderator, General Assembly, Church of Scotland, 2001-02; b. 11.11.41, Oxford; m., Mary; 3 c. Educ. Oxford University; Edinburgh University; Union Theological Seminary, New York; Teaching Certificate, Moray House College of Education. Assistant Minister, Richmond Craigmillar Church, Edinburgh, 1967-69; Chair, Management Group, Castlemilk Detached Youth-work Project, 12 years; chaired Youth Strategy Group, Castlemilk Partnership; Convener, Urban Priority Areas Sub-Committee, Department of National Mission, 1996-99; convened, Department of National Mission's Working Party on baptismal legislation. Recreation: cycling (brought in new millennium by cycling from Land's End to John O'Groats with a Roman Catholic priest). Address: (b.) 15 Castlemilk Drive, Glasgow, G45 9TL; T.-0141-631 1244.

Miller, Josephine L., BA, BMus, MLitt. Community and Education Studies Co-ordinator, Department of Scottish Music, Royal Scottish Academy of Music and Drama, since 1996; Lecturer in Scottish Music and Ethnomusicology, since 1989; freelance musician, researcher and teacher; b. 1.10.62, Carluke; m., Steven Sutcliffe; 2 s. Educ. Kirkcudbright Academy; RSAMD; Glasgow University; Edinburgh University. Provision of teaching materials and teacher support for Scottish music in schools; freelance singer and fiddler. Publications: music transcriptions for Come Gie's A Sang, 1995; The Music of Scotland (teacher support package). Recreations: gardening; walking; reading. Address: (b.) RSAMD, 100 Renfrew Street, Glasgow G2 3DB.

Miller, Keith Manson, BSc (Hons), DipMS. Chief Executive, Miller Group, since 1994; b. 19.3.49, Edinburgh. Educ. Loretto; Heriot-Watt University; Glasgow University. Managing Director: Miller Mining, 1976-90, Miller Developments, 1990-94. Director, Aberforth Smaller Companies Trust PLC. Recreations: sailing; skiing. Address: (b.) Miller Group Ltd., 18 South Groathill Avenue, Edinburgh EH4 2LW; T.-0131-315 6000; e-mail: keith.miller@miller.co.uk

Miller, Professor Kenneth, LLB, LLM, PhD. Professor of Law, Strathclyde University, since 1992 (Deputy Principal); b. 11.12.51, Paisley; m., Margaret Macleod. Educ. Paisley Grammar School; Strathclyde University; Queen's University, Canada. Lecturer in Law, then Senior Lecturer, Strathclyde University, 1975-91; Deputy General Editor, Stair Memorial Encyclopaedia of the Laws of Scotland, 1990-96; Editor, Juridical Review, since 2000; Member, Employment Law Committee and Deputy Chair, Central Arbitration Committee, Law Society of Scotland. Publications: Employment Law in Scotland (Co-Author); Property Law (Co-Author); Law of Health and Safety at Work in Scotland. Recreations: reading; golf; theatre. Address: (b.) Law School, Strathclyde University, 173 Cathedral Street, Glasgow; T.-0141-552 4400.

Miller, Sir Ronald Andrew Baird, CBE (1985), CA, DSc. former Chairman, Dawson International PLC; b. 13.5.37, Edinburgh. Non-Executive Director: Aggreko PLC, Quality Assurance Agency for Higher Education; former Chairman, Court, Napier University. Address: (b.) 7 Doune Terrace, Edinburgh EH3 6DY.

Miller, Professor William L., MA, PhD, FBA, FRSA, FRSE. Edward Caird Professor of Politics, Glasgow University, since 1985; b. 12.8.43, Glasgow; m., Fiona Thomson; 2 s.; 1 d. Educ. Aberdeen Grammar School; Royal High School, Edinburgh; Edinburgh University; Newcastle University. Formerly Lecturer, Senior Lecturer and Professor, Strathclyde University; Visiting Professor, Virginia Tech., Blacksburg, Virginia, 1983-84; also taught at Universities of Essex and Cologne; frequent Contributor to Press and TV; Member, Editorial Board: Electoral Studies. Publications: Electoral Dynamics, 1977; The End of British Politics?, 1981; The Survey Method in the Social and Political Sciences, 1983; Elections and Voters, 1987; The Quality of Local Democracy, 1988; How Voters Change, 1990; Media and Voters, 1991; Alternatives to Freedom, 1995; Political Culture in Contemporary Britain, 1996; Values and Political Change in Postcommunist Europe, 1998; Models of Local Governance, 2000; A Culture of Corruption? 2001. Address: (b.) Department of Politics, Glasgow University G12 8RT; T.-0141-330 5980.

Miller Smith, Charles, MA, Hon. LLD. Chairman, ICI Plc, since 1999; Chairman, Scottish Power, since 2000; b. 7.11.39, Glasgow; widowed; 1s.; 2d. Educ. Glasgow Academy; St Andrews University; ACCA. Unilever: Financial Director, Vinyl Products, 1970-73; Head of Planning, 1974; Finance Director, Walls Meat Company, 1976; Vice-Chairman, Hindustan Lever, 1979-81; Speciality Chemicals Group, 1981; Chief Executive, PPF International, 1983; Chief Executive, Quest International, 1986; Financial Director, Unilever Board, 1989; Executive, Unilever Foods, 1993-94; ICI: Director, since 1994; Chief Executive, 1995-99; Non-Executive Director: Midland Bank, 1994-96; HSBC Holdings Plc, since 1996. Recreations: reading; walking. Address: (b.) 9 Millbank, London, SW1P 3JF; T.-020-7834 4444.

Milligan, Rt. Hon. Lord (James George Milligan). Senator of the College of Justice, 1988-2001; b. 10.5.34. Advocate, 1959; QC, 1972; Advocate Depute, 1971-78; Chairman, Medical Appeal Tribunal (Scotland), 1979-88. Address: (b.) Parliament House, Edinburgh EH1 1RQ.

Milligan, Rt. Hon. Eric. Lord Provost and Lord Lieutenant, City of Edinburgh, since 1996; b. 27.1.51, Edinburgh; m., Janis. Educ. Tynecastle High School; Napier College of Commerce and Technology. Former printer; Member (Labour), Edinburgh District Council, 1974-78; Lothian Regional Councillor, 1978-96 (Chairman, Finance Committee, 1980-82, 1986-90, Convener, 1990-96); President, COSLA, 1988-90; City of Edinburgh Councillor, since 1995 (Convener, 1995-96); JP, Edinburgh, 1996; awarded Chevalier, Ordre National du Mérite, 1996; honorary degree: Doctor of Business Administration, Napier University, 1999; Honorary Fellow, Royal College of Surgeons of Edinburgh, 2000. Address: (b.) City Chambers, High Street, Edinburgh EH1 1YJ; T-0131 200 2000.

Mills, Harold Hernshaw, CB, BSc, PhD. Chairman, Caledonian MacBrayne Ltd.; Chairman, Edinburgh World Heritage Trust; Chairman, Land Trust; Chairman, Home in Scotland; Governor, Queen Margaret University College, Edinburgh; Trustee, Scottish Maritime Museum; b. 2.3.38, Greenock; m., Marion Elizabeth Beattie. Educ. Greenock High School; Glasgow University. Cancer Research Scientist, Roswell Park Memorial Institute, Buffalo, New York, 1962-64; Lecturer, Chemistry Department, Glasgow University, 1964-69; Principal, Scottish Home and Health Department, 1970-76; Assistant Secretary: Scottish Office, 1976-81, Privy Council Office, 1981-83, Scottish Development Department, 1983-84; Under Secretary, Scottish Development Department, 1984-88; Principal Finance Officer, Scottish Office, 1988-92; Secretary, Scottish Office Environment Department, 1992-95; Secretary and Head of Department, Scottish Office Development Department, 1995-98. Address (h.) 21 Hatton Place, Edinburgh EH9 1UB.

Mills, Ian Thomas, BSc, MPhil, MIMgt. General Manager, National Youth Choir of Scotland, since 2001; former Director of Education and Leisure Services, East Dunbartonshire Council; b. 20.5.48, Hamilton; m., Margaret; 2 d. Educ. Dalziel High School, Motherwell; Glasgow University; Strathclyde University. Chemistry Teacher, Dalziel High School, Motherwell, 1970-75; Senior Housemaster, Lanark Grammar School, 1975-78; Assistant Head Teacher, then Depute Head Teacher, Carluke High School, 1978-85; Area Education Officer, Perth and Kinross, 1985-91; Assistant Director of Education, Tayside Regional Council, 1991-95. Adviser to Scottish Arts Council; Vice Chair, Scottish Amateur Music Association. Recreations: music; family-based activities; various sports (curling, walking). Address: (b.) Mitchell Library, 201 North Street, Glasgow G3 7DN; T.-0141-287 2856.

Mills, Thomas, BEd, CBiol, MIBiol, MIM. Head Teacher, St. Patrick's High School, Coatbridge, since 1996; b. 17.2.47, Lennoxtown; m., Janice Alexis; 1 s.; 1 d. Educ. St. Mungo's Academy; St. Andrew's College; Paisley University. Teacher of Biology, John Bosco Secondary School, 1974-77; A.P.T., Biology, Lourdes Secondary School, 1977-83; Principal Teacher of Biology, Our Lady and St. Francis Secondary School, 1983-87; Assistant Head Teacher, Our Lady's High School, Motherwell, 1987-92; Depute Headteacher, John Ogilvie High School, Hamilton, 1992-96. Executive Member, Catholic Headteachers of Scotland; Commissioner, Scottish Catholic Commission for Education. Recreations: keep-fit; DIY; music; caravanning. Address: (b.) St. Patrick's High School, Muiryhall Street, Coatbridge ML5 3NN; T.-01236 426191.

Milne, Alastair David, OBE, FRSE, PhD, MSc, BSc, CEng, FIEE, SMIEEE. Managing Director, Wolfson Microelectronics Ltd., since 1984; b. 8.11.42, Edinburgh; 1 s.; 2 d. Educ. George Watson's College; Heriot-Watt University; Bristol University. Research Fellow, Bristol University, Edinburgh University; Director, Wolfson Microelectronics Institute; Non-Executive Director: Ratho Quarry Co., Edinburgh Research and Innovation Ltd., Edinburgh Research Fund; Member, Court, University of Edinburgh. Recreations: climbing; gardening; skiing. Address: (h.) 18 Napier Road, Edinburgh; T.-0131-229 2161; e-mail: david.milne@wolfsonmicro.com

Milne, Colin McLeod, LLB. President, Employment Tribunals Scotland, since 2000; b. 14.3.47, Glasgow; 1 s.; 1 d. Educ. Kilmarnock Academy; Glasgow University. Partner, Wright Johnston & Mackenzie, Solicitors, Glasgow, until 1991; appointed Chairman of Industrial Tribunals, 1991, Regional Chairman, 1994. Address: (b.) Central Office of Employment Tribunals, Eagle Building, 215 Bothwell Street, Glasgow G2 7TS; T.-0141-204 0730.

Milne, George, BSc (Hons), MEd, MBA. Headteacher, Peterhead Academy since 1991; b. 4.6.49, Aberdeen; m., Elizabeth Kerr; 2 s.; 1 d. Educ. Aberdeen Grammar School; Aberdeen University. Maths Teacher, 1972-81; Principal Teacher of Maths, Peterhead Academy, 1981-84; Assistant Head Teacher, then Depute Head, Mintlaw Academy, 1984-91. Recreations: Rotary activities; golf; reading. Address: (b.) Peterhead Academy, Prince Street, Peterhead AB42 1SY; T.-01779 472231.

Milne, James Smith, CBE, DBA. Chairman and Managing Director, Balmoral Group Ltd., since 1980; b. 26.12.40, Aberdeen; 2 d. Member, Executive Committee. SCDI; Chairman, Friends of Anchor Ari. Recreations: field sports, family. Address: (b.) Balmoral Park, Loirston, Aberdeen; T.-01224 859000.

Milne, Professor John Alexander, BA, BSc (Hons), PhD, FRSA. Deputy Director, Macaulay Land Use Research Institute; Vice-Chairman, Deer Commission for Scotland; b. 22.11.43, Edinburgh; m., Janet Erskine; 1 s. Educ. Edinburgh Academy; Edinburgh University; London University; Open University. Honorary Professor, University of Aberdeen; President, British Society of Animal Science; Deputy Editor, Grass and Forage Science. Address: (b.) Craigiebuckler, Aberdeen AB9 2QJ; e-mail: j.milne@macaulay.ac.uk

Milne, Professor John Sim, BSc (Hons), CEng, FIMechE, FRSA. Professor Emeritus, University of Abertay, Dundee, since 1996 (Professor of Mechatronics, 1993-96); b. 22.6.36, Arbroath; m., Isabella Paton; 2 s. Educ. Arbroath High School; Strathclyde University. Lecturer, then Senior Lecturer in Mechanical Engineering, Dundee Institute of Technology, 1958-93. Consultant on Mechatronics for the Scottish Qualifications Authority; co-author of two textbooks and invited contributor to two engineering reference books. Recreations: cycling; hill-walking. Address: (h.) 45 Monymusk Road, Arbroath DD11 2BZ; T.-01241 873988.

Milne, Robert Hughes, MBE, JP. Managing Director, Aberdeen Fish Curers and Merchants Association Ltd., since 1987 (Chief Executive/Secretary, 1983-87); b. 4.6.39, Pittenweem. Educ. Waid Academy, Anstruther. Assistant Chief Fisheries Advisor, then Regional Officer, Herring Industry Board, 1962-73; Development Officer/Secretary, then Secretary General, Scottish Federation of Fishermen's Co-operatives Ltd., Fishing Co-operative Trading (Scotland) Ltd. and Fishing Co-operatives (Manufacturing) Ltd., 1973-83. Served, European Community Social Problems Fisheries Committee, European Community Advisory Committee on Fisheries and Association of European Agricultural and Fisheries Co-operatives, 1973-83; Member: Isle of Man Government's Commission of Inquiry, 1982-83, various Sea Fish Industry Authority advisory committees, since 1983, SQA Food and Drink Advisory Group, since 1998; Secretary, Scottish Fish Merchants Federation Ltd., since 1984; Director/Company Secretary, Scottish Fish Merchants Group Training Association, since 1995 (Chairman, since 1996); Director, Granite City Ice Ltd., since 1998; Co-ordinator, Scottish Fish Processing Action Plan, since 2001. Burgess of Guild, City of Aberdeen. Recreations: gardening; church activities. Address: (b.) South Esplanade West, Aberdeen AB11 9FJ; T.-01224 897744.

Milton, Ian Murray, MCIM. Chairman, Milton Hotels Ltd.; Director, Nevis Range Development Company PLC; b. 25.7.45, Glasgow; m., Ann; 1 s.; 3 d. Educ. Lochaber High School; Scottish Hotel School, Glasgow. Began Milton Hotels with brother, 1965. Recreations: golf; skiing; computing. Address: (b.) Milton Hotels Ltd., 10 King Street, Stirling FK8 1BL; T.-01786 469300; e-mail: ian.milton@miltonhotels.com

Minto, 6th Earl of (Gilbert Edward George Lariston Elliot-Murray-Kynynmound), OBE (1986), JP. Lieutenant, Queen's Bodyguard for Scotland (Royal Company of Archers); President, Scottish Council on Alcohol, since 1988; Vice Lord-Lieutenant, Roxburgh, Ettrick and Lauderdale, since 1992; former Convenor, Borders Regional Council; b. 19.6.28; m., 1, Lady Caroline Child-Villiers (m. diss.); 1 s.; 1 d.; 2, Mary Elizabeth Ballantine (deceased); 3, Mrs Caroline Larlham. Educ. Eton; Sandhurst. Former Captain, Scots Guards. Address: (h.) Minto, Hawick.

Minto, Brian J. L., OBE, CA, ATII, MIMgt, FRSA. Senior Partner, Minto Finnie Parsons Turnbull, Chartered Accountants; Chairman, Scottish Fisheries Museum, Anstruther; Director, Dundee College; b. 10.8.42, Lanark; m., Margot Morris; 1 s.; 1 d. Educ. Arbroath High School. Apprentice CA, 1959-64; Scottish Malt Distillers Ltd., 1967-70. Convener, GP Committee, Institute of Chartered Accountants of Scotland, 1992-95; Member: Scottish Business Education Council, 1982-85, Scottish Vocational Education Council, 1985-97, Scottish Qualifications Authority, 1997-2000, Scottish Further Education Funding Council, 1999-2001. Recreations: golf; walking; photography. Address: (b.) 164 South Street, St. Andrews; T.-01334 472196; e-mail: bminto@mfpt.co.uk

Misra, Prem Chandra, BSc, MBBS, DPM (RCP&S, Edin and Glas), MRCPsych. Consultant Psychiatrist, Parkhead Hospital; Clinical Senior Lecturer, Glasgow University, since 1976; b. 24.7.41, Lucknow, India; m., Sandhya; 1 s.; 2 d. Educ. KK Degree College and King George's Medical College, Lucknow, India; Lucknow University. Rotating Intern, King George's Medical College Hospital, Lucknow, 1967; Demonstrator, Department of Human Physiology, Lucknow University, 1967; Resident Senior House Officer, General Medicine and Geriatrics, Wigan and Leigh Group of Hospitals, 1968-69; Resident House Surgeon, General Surgery, Wigan Royal Infirmary, 1968-69; Resident House Physician, General Medicine, Whelley Hospital, Wigan, 1969-70; Resident Senior House Officer in Psychiatry, then Resident Registrar in Psychiatry, Bolton District General Hospital, 1970-73; Senior Psychiatric Registrar (Midland Area Consultant Training Scheme), Hollymoor Hospital, Birmingham, 1973-76; Consultant Psychiatrist, Solihull Area Health Authority, 1976; appointed Consultant Psychiatrist, Glasgow Royal Infirmary and Duke Street Hospital, 1976; Consultant in Charge, Acorn Street Day Hospital, 1979; Deputy Physician Superintendent, Gartloch and Parkhead Hospitals, Glasow, 1984-92. President, Indian Association of Strathclyde, since 1981; Member, Executive Committee: Strathclyde Community Relations Council, 1981-85, Scottish Council for Racial Equality, 1982; Member: Social and Welfare Committee, CRC, for Ethnic Groups and Vietnam Refugees, 1982, Board of Directors, Scottish Refugee Council, 1994-2000; Secretary, Division of Psychiatry, Eastern District of Glasgow, 1980-94; President, British Society of Medical and Dental Hypnosis (Scotland), 1987-89; Governor, Glasgow Caledonian University; Lead Consultant of Royal College of Psychiatrists for Transcultural Psychiatry in Scotland; Member: Executive Committee, British Society of Research on Sex Education, International Scientific Committee on Sexuality and Handicap, International Advisory Board of Israel Society of Clinical and Experimental Hypnosis, International Committee of Sexologists, Society for the Advancement of Sexual Health; Executive Committee Member, European Society of Hypnosis; Justice of the Peace; awarded Ludwika Bierkoskigo Medal by Polish Medical Association for "outstanding contributions in the prevention and treatment of disabilities". Publications: Modern Trends in Hypnosis; research papers. Address: (b.) Parkhead Hospital, 81 Salamanca Street, Glasgow G31 5ES; T.-0141-211 8300.

Mitchell, Rev. Alexander Bell, DipTechEd, BD. Minister, St. Leonard's Church, Dunfermline, since 1981; b. 28.6.49, Baillieston; m., Elizabeth Brodie; 1 s.; 2 d. Educ. Uddingston Grammar School; New College, Edinburgh. Assistant Minister, Dunblane Cathedral, 1979-81. Recreations: golf; hill-walking. Address: 12 Torvean Place, Dunfermline KY11 4VY; T.-01383 721054.

Mitchell, Colin Malcolm, BSc, CBiol, MIBiol, MIMgt. Headteacher, Dumfries High School, since 1990; b. 11.6.50, Paisley; m., Pamela Margaret; 2 s. Educ. Forrester Secondary School, Edinburgh; Heriot Watt University. Teacher of Science/Biology, then Principal Teacher of Biology, Craigroyston High School, Edinburgh; Assistant Headteacher, then Depute Headteacher, Maxwelltown High School, Dumfries. Deputy team leader, Moffat Mountain Rescue Team; Chairman: Dumfries Group, Scottish Wildlife Trust, Dunscore Community Council. Recreations: mountaineering; bird-watching. Address: (b.) Dumfries High School, Marchmont, Dumfries DG1 1PX.

Mitchell, David William, CBE; b. 4.1.33, Glasgow; m., Lynda Katherine Marion Guy; 1 d. Educ. Merchiston Castle School. Cmmnd (NS), RSF, 1950; Member, Board, Western General Hospital, 1965-72; President, Timber Trades Benevolent Society of UK, 1974; Member, Scottish Council, CBI, 1979-85; Director, Mallinson-Denny (Scotland), 1977-90; Hunter Timber Scotland, 1990-92; Joint Managing Director, M. & N. Norman (Timber) Ltd., 1992-96 (Non-Executive, 1996-98); President: Scottish Timber Trade Association, 1980-82, Scottish Conservative and Unionist Association, 1981-83; Member: Scottish Council (Development and Industry), 1984-95, Board of Cumbernauld New Town, 1985-97 (Chairman, 1987-97), Board of Management, Craighalbert Centre for Children with Motor Impairment, 1992-96; Treasurer, Scottish Conservative Party, 1990-93 and since 1998. Recreations: fishing; shooting; golf. Address: Dunmullin House, Blanefield, Stirlingshire G63 9AJ; T.-01360 770885.

Mitchell, Rev. Duncan Ross, BA (Hons), BD (Hons). Minister, St. Andrews Church, West Kilbride, since 1980; b. 5.5.42, Boddam, Aberdeenshire; m., Sandra Brown; 2 s.; 1 d. Educ. Hyndland Senior Secondary School, Glasgow; Strathclyde University; Glasgow University. Worked in insurance industry, four years; Minister, Craigmailen UF Church, Bo'ness, 1972-80; Convener, Assembly Youth Committee, UF Church, 1974-79; Member: Scottish Joint Committee on Religious Education, 1974-79, Multilateral Conversation in Scotland, 1976-79, Board of Social Responsibility, Church of Scotland, 1983-86; Ardrossan Presbytery: Convener, World Mission and Unity, 1984-88, Convener, Stewardship and Finance, 1988-91, Convener, Superintendence Committee, 1994-97; Convener, General Assembly Board of World Mission and Unity's Local Involvements Committee, and Executive Member of the Board, 1987-92; Church of Scotland Delegate to Council of Churches for Britain and Ireland Assembly; Moderator, Ardrossan Presbytery, 1992-93; Member, General Assembly Ecumenical Relations Committee, and Leader of its Liaison Group. Recreations: swimming; supporting Partick Thistle; writing poetry and short stories. Address: St. Andrew's Manse, 7 Overton Drive, West Kilbride; T.-01294 823142; e-mail: ross.mitchell@virgin.net

Mitchell, George Edward, FCIBS. Treasurer and Managing Director, Bank of Scotland; b. 7.4.50, Edinburgh; m., Agnes; 3 d. Educ. Forrester High School, Edinburgh. Bank of Scotland, since 1966. Recreations: football; tennis; family. Address: (b.) Bank of Scotland, Corporate Banking, The Mound, Edinburgh EH1 1YZ; T.-0131- 243 7033.

Mitchell, Gordon K., DA, ARSA, RSW, RGI. Artist; b. 16.11.52, Edinburgh; m., Deirdre; 1 s.; 3 d. Educ. Royal High School; Edinburgh College of Art. Former Art

Teacher (Deputy Headmaster, St. Serf's School, 1986-89); elected: SSA, 1977, SAAC, 1990 (President, 1993-96), RSW, 1996, ARSA, 1998, RGI, 1998. served on council of SSA, SAAC, RSW, SABA; exhibited widely at home and abroad; work in public and private collections. Prizes and awards include: RSA Student Prize; Borders Biennial Competition; Scottish Drawing Competition; Mayfest Award; William Gillies Award; Scottish Amicable Prize; Scottish Provident Award; Whyte and Mackay Award; Dunfermline Building Society Award; RSA J. Murray Thompson Award; RSA Maude Gemmel Hutchison Award; Royal Bank of Scotland Award, RGI. Recreations: current affairs; golf. Address: 4A Randolph Cliff, Edinburgh EH3 7TZ; T.-0131-225 9550.

Mitchell, Iain Grant, QC, LLB (Hons), FSA Scot, FRSA, FFCS. Queen's Counsel, since 1992; Temporary Sheriff, 1992-97; Honorary Secretary, Scottish Conservative and Unionist Association, 1993-98, Scottish Conservative and Unionist Party, since 1998; b. 15.11.51, Edinburgh. Educ. Perth Academy; Edinburgh University. Called to Scottish Bar, 1976; Past President, Diagnostic Society of Edinburgh; former Vice-President, Edinburgh University Conservative Association; Conservative candidate, Falkirk West, General Election, 1983, Kirkcaldy, General Election, 1987, Cumbernauld and Kilsyth, General Election, 1992, Dunfermline East, General Election, 1997; Edinburgh North and Leith, General Election, 2001; Dundee East, Scottish Parliament Election, 1999; Scotland, European Election, 1999; Chairman, Trust for an International Opera Theatre of Scotland; Chairman, Scottish Baroque Ensemble Ltd., 1999-2001; Member: Executive Committee of European Movement (Scottish Council), Committee, Perth Civic Trust; Trustee, Perthshire Public Arts Trust; Chairman, Faculty of Advocates IT Group; Member, Central Advisory Committee on Justices of the Peace; Vice-Chairman, Scottish Lawyers' European Group; Vice-Chairman, Scottish Society for Computers and Law; Editor, Scottish Parliament Law Review; Joint Editor, e-law Review. Recreations: music and the arts; photography; cinema; walking; history; travel; writing; finding enough hours in the day. Address: (b.) Advocates Library, Parliament House, High Street, Edinburgh; T.-0131-226 5071.

Mitchell, Sheriff James Kenneth, LLB. Sheriff of Glasgow and Strathkelvin, since 1985; b. 30.4.49, Glasgow; m., Frances Kane; 1 s. Educ. Paisley Grammar School; Glasgow University. Solicitor, 1972-78; Partner, Ross Harper and Murphy, 1975-78; admitted Faculty of Advocates, 1979. Council Member, Sheriffs' Association, 1998-2001; Member, Glasgow Sheriff Court Standing Advisory Committee, 1997-2000; Member, National Council, Victim Support Scotland, since 2001. Recreations: family; friends; football; films; fun. Address: (b.) Sheriff's Chambers, 1 Carlton Place, Glasgow G5 9DA; T.-0141-429 8888.

Mitchell, John, BSc. Head Teacher, Kilsyth Academy, since 1985; b. 4.1.45, Kirkintilloch; m., Irene; 1 s.; 1 d. Educ. Lenzie Academy; Glasgow University; Jordanhill College. Teacher, North Kelvinside Secondary, Glasgow, 1968-70; Physics Teacher, Balfron High School, 1970-72; Bishopbriggs High School, 1972-79; Assistant Head Teacher, Kilsyth Academy, 1979-84; Depute Head Teacher, Knightswood Secondary, 1984-85; Member, Board, LT Scotland, since 2000; President, HAS, 1996; Complaints Convener, GGHB Primary Care Trust. Address: (h.) 10 Blair Drive, Milton of Campsie; T.- 01360 310477.

Mitchell, (John) Angus (Macbeth), CB, CVO, MC, LLD(Hon), (Dundee), DUniv (Stirling). b. 25.8.24, Ootacamund, India; m., Ann Williamson; 2 s.; 2 d. Educ. Marlborough College; Brasenose College, Oxford. Royal Armoured Corps (Captain), 1943-46; Scottish Office, 1949-84; Principal Private Secretary to Secretary of State for Scotland, 1958-59; Under Secretary, Social Work Services Group, 1969-74; Secretary, Scottish Education Department, 1976-84. Order of Orange-Nassau, 1946; Chairman, Scottish Marriage Guidance Council, 1965-69; Vice-Convener, Scottish Council of Voluntary Organisations, 1986-91; Member, Commission for Local Authority Accounts in Scotland, 1985-89; Chairman of Court, Stirling University, 1984-92; Chairman, Scottish Action on Dementia, 1986-94; Member, Historic Buildings Council for Scotland, 1988-94; Trustee, Dementia Services Development Trust, 1988-2000; Secretary, Greyfriars Kirkyard Trust, since 1994. Publications: Scottish Office Ministers 1885-1985; Procedures for the Reorganisation of Schools in England, 1986. Recreations: old Penguins; gravestones; family history. Address: (h.) 20 Regent Terrace, Edinburgh EH7 5BS; T.-0131-556 7671.

Mitchell, John Logan, QC, LLB (Hons). Queen's Counsel, since 1987; Advocate Depute, 1981-85; b. 23.6.47, Dumfries; m., Christine Brownlee Thomson; 1 s.; 1 d. Educ. Royal High School, Edinburgh; Edinburgh University. Called to Bar, 1974; Standing Junior Counsel to Forestry Commission; Standing Junior Counsel, Department of Agriculture and Fisheries. Past President, Royal High School F.P. Club. Recreations: running; golf. Address: (h.) 17 Braid Farm Road, Edinburgh; T.-031-447 8099.

Mitchell, Louise C., MA. Director, Glasgow Royal Concert Hall, since 1996; b. London. Educ. Lady Margaret School, London; St. Andrews University; City University, London. Assistant Manager, Scottish Baroque Ensemble, 1979-81; Concerts Manager, London Sinfonietta, 1982-87; Assistant Director, Edinburgh International Festival, 1989-91; Music Programme Manager, Barbican Centre, 1992-94; Concerts Director, London Philharmonic Orchestra, 1994-96. Member, Scottish Arts Council (Chairman, Music Committee); Member, Touring Panel, Arts Council of England. Recreations: travel; food and wine. Address: (b.) 2 Sauchiehall Street, Glasgow G2 3NY; T.-0141-353 8000.

Mitchell, Professor Emeritus Ross Galbraith, MD, FRCPEdin, FRCPCH, DCH. Professor of Child Health, Dundee University, 1973-85, now Emeritus; b. 18.11.20; m., June Phylis Butcher; 1 s.; 3 d. Educ. Kelvinside Academy, Glasgow; Edinburgh University. Surgeon Lt., Royal Naval Volunteer Reserve, 1944-47; junior medical posts, Edinburgh, Liverpool and London, 1947-52; Rockefeller Research Fellow in Physiology, Mayo Clinic, USA, 1952-53; Lecturer in Child Health, St. Andrews University, 1952-55; Consultant Paediatrician, Dundee Teaching Hospitals, 1955-63; Professor of Child Health, Aberdeen University, 1963-72. Chairman: Editorial Board, Mac Keith Press, 1980-95, Scottish Advisory Council on Child Care, 1966-68; Dean, Faculty of Medicine and Dentistry, Dundee University, 1978-81; Chairman, Aberdeen Association of Social Service, 1971-72; President: Scottish Paediatric Society, 1982-84, Harveian Society of Edinburgh, 1982-83; Member, General Medical Council, 1983-85; Vice-Chairman, Scottish Child and Family Alliance, 1985-92. Recreations: fishing; gardening; languages. Address: (h.) Craigard, Abertay Gardens, Broughty Ferry, Dundee DD5 2RR; T.-01382 776983.

Mitchison, Professor John Murdoch, ScD, FRS, FRSE. Professor Emeritus and Honorary Fellow, Edinburgh University (Professor of Zoology, 1963-88); b. 11.6.22; m., Rosalind Mary Wrong; 1 s.; 3 d. Educ. Winchester College; Trinity College, Cambridge. Army Operational Research, 1941-46; Research Scholar, then Fellow, Trinity College, Cambridge, 1946-54; Lecturer, then Reader in Zoology, Edinburgh University, 1953-62; Member, Edinburgh University Court, 1971-74, 1985-88; Dean, Faculty of Science, 1984-85; Member: Academia Europaea, Scottish Marine Biological Association, 1961-67; Executive Committee Member, International Society for Cell Biology, 1964-72; Member: Biological Committee, SRC, 1972-75,

Royal Commission on Environmental Pollution, 1974-79, Science Board, SRC, 1976-79, Working Group on Biological Manpower, DES, 1968-71, Advisory Committee on Safety of Nuclear Installations, Health and Safety Executive, 1981-84; President, British Society for Cell Biology, 1974-77. Publication: The Biology of the Cell Cycle. Address: (h.) Great Yew, Ormiston, East Lothian EH35 5NJ; T.-Pencaitland 340530.

Mitchison, Professor Emeritus Rosalind Mary, Hon DLitt, HonDUniv, FRSE, FRHistS, MA. Professor of Social History, Edinburgh University, 1981-86; b. 11.4.19, Manchester; m., J.M. Mitchison (qv); 1 s.; 3 d. Educ. Channing School, Highgate; Lady Margaret Hall, Oxford. Assistant Lecturer, Manchester University, 1943-46; Tutor, Lady Margaret Hall, Oxford, 1946-47; Assistant: Edinburgh University, 1954-57, Glasgow University, 1962-63; Lecturer, Glasgow University, 1966-67; Lecturer, then Reader, Edinburgh University, 1967-81. President, Scottish History Society, 1981-84. Publications: Agricultural Sir John, 1962; A History of Scotland, 1970; British Population Change since 1860, 1977; Life in Scotland, 1978; Lordship to Patronage: Scotland 1603-1745, 1983; Sexuality and Social Control: Scotland 1660-1780 (Co-Author), 1989; Coping with destitution: poverty and relief in Western Europe, 1991; Girls in Trouble (Co-Author), 1998; Sin in the City (Co-Author), 1998; The Old Poor Law in Scotland, 2000. Recreation: walking. Address: (h.) Great Yew, Ormiston, East Lothian EH35 5NJ; T.-Pencaitland 340530.

Mobarik, Nosheena, BA (Hons). HR/Marketing Director, M Computer Technologies, since 1997; b. 16.10.57, Mian Chunnu, Pakistan; m., Dr. Iqbal Mobarik; 1 s.; 1 d. Educ. Shawlands Academy; Strathclyde University. Brought up family, 1978-89; set up Barcodes Express, 1991; taught on social policy in healthcare, further education college, 1996-97. Director, Glasgow Caring City; Member, Council, CBI Scotland; Trustee, Save the Bosnian People Campaign, 1995. Recreations: reading (current affairs, history, literature); writing; painting. Address: (b.) M Computer Technologies, 4–12 Whitehall Street, Glasgow G3 8BN; T.-0141-243 2324; e-mail: nosheena@mcomputer.com

Moffat, Alistair Murray, MA (Hons), MPhil. Journalist; Film Maker; Chairman, STV Regional Board; b. 16.6.50, Kelso; m., Lindsay Thomas; 1 s.; 2 d. Educ. Kelso High School; St. Andrews University; Edinburgh University; London University. Ran Edinburgh Festival Fringe, 1976-81; Arts Correspondent/ Producer/Controller of Features/Director of Programmes, Scottish Television; Managing Director, Scottish Television Enterprises. Publications: The Edinburgh Fringe, 1978; Kelsae — A History of Kelso from Earliest Times, 1985; Remembering Charles Rennie Mackintosh, 1989; Arthur and the Lost Kingdom, 1999. Recreations: sleeping; supporting Kelso RFC. Address: (b.) Scottish Television, Cowcaddens, Glasgow G2 3PR.

Moffat, Douglas William John, LLB, WS. Partner, Tods Murray, WS, since 1974; b. 3.10.47, Castle Douglas; 1 s.; 1 d. Educ. The Edinburgh Academy; Edinburgh University. Scottish Secretary, British Council of Shopping Centres; Member: British Council of Offices; Member, Investment Property Forum. Recreations: cricket (SCU Committee Member); golf; squash; shooting; hillwalking. Address: (b.) 33 Bothwell Street, Glasgow G2 6NL; T.-0141-275 4771.

Moir, Dorothy Carnegie, MB, ChB, MD, FFPHM, FRCP, MBA, LFHom. Chief Administrative Medical Officer/ Director of Public Health, Lanarkshire Health Board, since 1994; Honorary Senior Clinical Lecturer in Public Health, Aberdeen University; Honorary Senior Clinical Lecturer, Department of Public Health, Glasgow University; b. 27.3.42, Aberdeen; m., Alexander D. Moir; 3 s. Educ. Albyn School for Girls, Aberdeen; Aberdeen University. Research Fellow in Therapeutics and Pharmacology, 1966-

69; Lecturer in Community Medicine, 1970-79; Community Medicine Specialist, Grampian Health Board, 1979-88; Chief Administrative Medical Officer/Director of Public Health, Forth Valley Health Board, 1988-94. Address: (b.) 14 Beckford Street, Hamilton ML3 0TA; e-mail: dorothy.moir@lanarkshirehb.scot.nhs.uk

Moir, Rev. Ian Andrew, MA, BD. Church of Scotland Adviser for Urban Priority Areas, 1991-2000; Minister, Old Kirk of Edinburgh, 1983-91; b. 9.4.35, Aberdeen; m., Elizabeth; 3 s. Educ. Aberdeen Grammar School; Aberdeen University. Sub-Warden, St. Ninian's Training Centre, Crieff, 1959-61; Superintendent, Pholela High School, Natal, 1962-73; Assistant Secretary, Church of Scotland Overseas Council, 1974-83. Recreations: walking; golf. Address: (h.) 28/6 Comely Bank Avenue, Edinburgh EH4 1EL.

Moir, Mark Duncan, LLB, DipLP. Advocate, since 2000; b. 11.9.64, Edinburgh. Educ. Boroughmuir High School; Edinburgh University. Royal Air Force Police, 1983-92; Strathclyde Police, 1992-93. Address: (h.) Park Circus, Glasgow.

Molchanov, Professor Ilya, PhD, DrRerNatHabil. Professor of Applied Probability, University of Glasgow, since 1998; b. 18.8.62, Penza, Russian Federation; 1 d. Educ. School No. 145, Kiev, Ukraine; Kiev State University. Assistant Professor, Kiev Technology Institute, 1987-92; Research Fellow: TU Bergakademie Freiberg, Germany, 1992-94, CWI Amsterdam, 1994-95; Lecturer/Reader, University of Glasgow, 1995-98. Publications: two books. Associate Editor: Metrika; Journal of Statistical Computation and Simulation; Image Analysis and Stereology. Recreations: hill-walking; badminton. Address: Department of Statistics, University of Glasgow, Glasgow G12 8QW; T.-0141-330 5141.

Mole, George Alexander (Sandy). President, National Farmers Union of Scotland, 1996-97; Chairman, Coastal Grains Ltd., since 1998; b. 7.6.43, Duns; m., Jean Mitchell; 1 s.; 2 d. Educ. St. Mary's, Melrose; Merchiston Castle. NFU of Scotland: President, Mid and East Berwick; Chairman, AFRC Cereal Consultative; Convener, Cereals Committee; Member: EEC Commission Cereals Advisory Committee, Home Grown Cereals Authority R. & D. Committee, Institute of Brewing Cereal Publicity. Recreations: golf; shooting. Address: Greenburn, Reston, Eyemouth TD14 5LP.

Mollison, Professor Denis, ScD. Professor of Applied Probability, Heriot-Watt University, since 1986; Trustee, John Muir Trust, since 1986 (Co-Founder,1983); b. 28.6.45, Carshalton; m., Jennifer Hutton; 1 s.; 3 d. Educ. Westminster School; Trinity College, Cambridge. Research Fellow, King's College, Cambridge, 1969; Lecturer in Statistics, Heriot-Watt University, 1973. Elected Member of Council, National Trust for Scotland, 1979-84, and since 1999; Chairman, Mountain Bothies Association, 1978-94. Publications: research papers on epidemics, ecology and wave energy. Address: (h.) The Laigh House, Inveresk, Musselburgh EH21 7TD; T.-0131-665 2055; e-mail: d.mollison@ma.hw.ac.uk

Molloy, Daniel Frances. Convener, Midlothian Council Social Services Committee, since 1999; Provost, 1996-99; b. 16.10.52, County Donegal; m., Mara; 1 s.; 1 d. Educ. St. Connells School, Co. Donegal. Member, Lothian Health Board, 1979-87; Convener, Midlothian District Council, 1992-96; Chairman, Midlothian Tourism Association, 1988-96; Member, Edinburgh and Lothians Tourist Board, 1996-99. Recreations: reading; walking in the countryside. Address: (h.) 57 Woodburn Bank, Dalkeith EH22 2HP; T.-0131-663 2120.

Moncreiff, 5th Baron (Harry Robert Wellwood Moncreiff), Bt; b. 4.2.15; m., Enid Marion Watson Locke (deceased); 1 s. Educ. Fettes College, Edinburgh. Lt.-Col. (Hon.), RASC (retired). Address: (h.) Tulliebole Castle, Fossoway, Kinross-shire.

Mone, Rt. Rev. John Aloysius. Bishop of Paisley, formerly Titular Bishop of Abercorn and Auxiliary Bishop of Glasgow; b. 22.6.29, Glasgow. Educ. Holyrood Secondary School; Seminaire St. Sulpice and Institut Catholique, Paris. Ordained Priest, 1952; Assistant: St. Ninian's, Knightswood, Glasgow, 1952-75, Our Lady and St. George, Glasgow, 1975-79; Parish Priest, St. Joseph's, Tollcross, Glasgow, 1979-84. Scottish President, Scottish Catholic Marriage Care; Chairman, Scottish Catholic International Aid Fund, 1975-77; President, National Justice and Peace Commission, 1987-96; President, National Social Care Commission since 1996; President/Treasurer, Scottish Catholic International Aid Fund, since 1985. Address: Diocese of Paisley, St. Laurence's, 6 Kilmacolm Road, Greenock PA15 4XP.

Mone, Michelle, Founder and Co-Owner, MJM International Ltd., inventor of the Ultimo bra. World Young Business Achiever, 2000. Address: MJM International Ltd., 7 Hollybrook Place, Glasgow G42 7HB.

Monelle, Raymond, MA, BMus, PhD, ARCM. Writer on music; Reader in Music, Edinburgh University; b. 19.8.37, Bristol; 2 d. Educ. Bristol Grammar School; Pembroke College, Oxford; Royal College of Music. Publication: Linguistics and Semiotics in Music, 1992; The Sense of Music, 2000. Address: (h.) 80 Marchmont Road, Edinburgh EH9 1HR.

Monro of Langholm, Rt. Hon The Lord (Hector), PC, AE, DL, JP, FRAgS, MP (Conservative), Dumfries, 1964-97; Under Secretary of State, Scottish Office, 1992-95; Privy Councillor, since 1995; Farmer; b. 4.10.22, Edinburgh; m., 1, Lady (Anne) Monro (deceased); 2 s., 2, Lady (Doris) Monro. Educ. Canford School; Cambridge University; Dundee School of Economics. RAF, 1941-46; Royal Auxiliary Air Force, 1946-53, Honorary Air Commodore, 1981-2000, Inspector General 1990-2000; Member, Dumfries County Council, 1952-67 (Chairman, Planning Committee and Joint Police Committee); Scottish Conservative Whip, 1967-70; Lord Commissioner, HM Treasury, 1970-71; Minister of Health and Education, Scottish Office, 1971-74; Opposition Spokesman on Scottish Affairs, 1974-75, Sport, 1974-79; Minister of Sport and Rural Affairs, 1979-81; Member: Nature Conservancy Council, 1982-91, Area Executive, NFU, 1964-97, Council, National Trust for Scotland, 1983-92; Vice-President, Scottish Rugby Union, 1975, President, 1976-77; Member, Queen's Bodyguard for Scotland (Royal Company of Archers); President: NSRA, 1987-92, ACU, 1983-90. Recreations: rugby; golf; flying; vintage cars; country sports. Address: (h.) Williamwood, Kirtlebridge, Lockerbie, Dumfriesshire; T.-01461 500213.

Montagu-Smith, Group Captain Arthur, DL, RAF (Retd); b. 17.7.15; m., Elizabeth Hood Alexander; 1 s.; 1 d. Educ. Whitgift School; RAF Staff College. Commissioned RAF, 1935; Adjutant 99 Squadron, 1938-39; served Second World War, European Theatre, North Africa and Mediterranean; Flt. Cdr., 264 Squadron, 1940, and 221 Squadron, 1941; OC 248 Squadron, 1942-43; Battle of Britain Gold Rosette, 1940; Mention-in-Despatches, 1942; Deputy Director, RAF Training, USA (Washington), 1944; OC 104 Wing, France, 1945; Hon. ADC, Governor, N.I., 1948-49; Air Adviser, New Delhi, 1949-50; RAF Representative, Chiefs of Staff Committee, UN, New York, 1951-53; HM Air Attache, Budapest, 1958-60; retired at own request, 1961; Regional Executive, Small Industries Council and Scottish Development Agency, 1962-80; Member, Elgin District Council, 1967-75; Member, Moray TAFA, 1961-68; Director, Elgin and Lossiemouth Harbour Company, 1966-90; Deputy Lieutenant, Morayshire, 1970-91; Hon. County Representative, Moray and Nairn, RAF Benevolent Fund, since 1964; Chairman, Elgin and Lossiemouth Scottish SPCA, 1971-82; Past President, Victoria League, Moray and Nairn; Past Chairman, Moray Association of Youth Clubs. Recreations: outdoor interests; travel; animal welfare. Address: (h.) Woodpark, by Lhanbryde, Elgin IV30 8LF; T.-0134 384 2220.

Monteith, Brian. MSP (Conservative), Mid-Scotland and Fife, since 1999; Conservative Spokesman on Education, Arts, Culture and Sport; m.; 2 s. Public relations consultant; former National Chairman, Scottish Young Conservatives and Federation of Conservative Students; National Co-ordinator, No, No Campaign, Scottish devolution referendum. Address: (b.) Scottish Parliament, Edinburgh EH99 1SP; T.-0131-348 5644.

Montgomery, Sir (Basil Henry) David, 9th Bt, JP, DL. Lord Lieutenant, Perth and Kinross, since 1995; Chairman, Forestry Commission, 1979-89; b. 20.3.31.

Montgomery, David Andrew, MA, CertEd. Chief Executive, East Ayrshire Council, since 1995; b. 22.10.46, Irvine; 2 s.; 1 d. Educ. Irvine Royal Academy; Glasgow University; Jordanhill College of Education. Teacher, Principal Teacher, Assistant Head Teacher, 1969-81; Strathclyde Regional Council: Principal Officer (Teacher Staffing), 1982-84; Education Officer, 1984-86; Assistant Director of Education, then Depute Director of Education, then Senior Depute, 1986-95. Recreations: photography; aviation. Address: (b.) Council Headquarters, London Road, Kilmarnock KA3 7BU; T.-01563 576002; e-mail: david.montgomery@east-ayrshire.gov.uk

Montgomery, Iona Allison Eleanor, BA (Hons), RSW. Artist; Lecturer (part-time): Edinburgh College of Art, since 1997, Grays School of Art, since 1994; b. 14.4.65, Glasgow. Educ. Boclair Academy; Glasgow School of Art; Tamarind Institute, University of New Mexico. Exhibited widely in UK, Europe, USA and Japan, since 1989; solo exhibitions in UK, Europe, USA; work in numerous public collections; Alexander Graham Munro Award, RSW, 1990; Lauder Award, 1991, Lady Artists Club Trust Award, 1992, Cross Trust Bursary, 1994, Glasgow District Council Bursary, 1995; elected, RSW, 1991. Recreations: walking; music; film; travel. Address: (h.) Flat 2/3, 171A Maryhill Road, Glasgow G20 7XL; T.-0141-332 9512.

Montrose, 8th Duke of (James Graham), OStJ. Ensign, Queen's Bodyguard for Scotland (Royal Company of Archers), Member, since 1965; Member, House of Lords, since 1995, elected Hereditary Peer, since 1999; b. 6.4.35; m., Catherine Elizabeth MacDonell; 2 s.; 1 d. Educ. Loretto. President, Royal Highland and Agricultural Society, 1997-98; Council Member, National Farmers' Union of Scotland, 1982-84, 1987-90. Address: (h.) Buchanan, Drymen, Glasgow.

Moonie, Lewis George, MB, ChB, DPM, MRCPsych, MSc, MFCM. MP (Labour), Kirkcaldy, since 1987; Under Secretary of State for Defence, since 2000; b. 25.2.47, Dundee; m., Sheila Burt; 2 s. Educ. Nicolson Institute, Stornoway; Grove Academy, Dundee; St. Andrews University. A variety of junior and senior medical posts, 1970-87, latterly Consultant in Public Health Medicine, Fife Health Board. Member: Fife Regional Council, 1982-86; former Member, Social Services Select Committee; former Member, Treasury Select Committee; Opposition Front-Bench Spokesman on Technology, 1990-92, Science and Technology, 1992-94, Industry, 1994-95, National Heritage Spokesman on Broadcasting, 1995-97; former Chair, Finance and Services Committee; former Member, House of Commons Commission. Address: (b.) 17 Tolbooth Street, Kirkcaldy, Fife KY1 1RW; T.-01592 564115.

Moore, Andrew F., BL. Director, SCIENTIA (Scottish Chapter, International Society for Business Education and Scotland's Europe House); b. 5.12.39, Leven; m., Anne MacGregor; 2 s.; 1 d. Educ. Buckhaven High School; Edinburgh University. Examiner, Estate Duty Office, Edinburgh, 1958-63; Assistant, then Depute Secretary, Scottish Council for Commercial Education, 1963-73; Depute Chief Officer, Scottish Business Education Council, 1973-80; Chief Officer, SCOTBEC, 1980-86; seconded to Stirling University, 1987-89; Director: Scottish Chambers of Commerce, 1989-95, Chinese Enterprise Management Development Programmes, 1989-94. President, International Society for Business Education, 1993-97; Chairman, Pedagogical Committee, International Society for Business Education and Member, ISBE/SIEC Executive, since 1980; Hon. Secretary, Scottish Students' Song Book Committee Ltd., 1980-93; Session Clerk, Scoonie Kirk, Leven, 1982-92; President, Leven YMCA 1972-95; Member: Leven Golfing Society Committee, 1994, RNIB Alwyn House Advisory Committee, 1994; Director: Fife Enterprise, 1994-2000, North of Scotland European Partnership, 1994-2000, Fife Careers Ltd., 1996-2000, QTAC, since 1997, Fife Business Development Ltd., since 1999, Fife Chamber of Commerce and Enterprise since 1999; Chairman, Steering Group on Health Promotion in SMEs, since 1995; Member, Disability Consulting Group, since 1999; former Member, Board of Management, Glenrothes College and Fife College of Further and Higher Education. Publication: A Century of International Co-operation in Business Education. Recreations: golf; foreign travel. Address: (h.) Annandale, Linksfield Street, Leven, Fife; T.-01333 422644; e-mail: andrewfmoore.12@btopenworld.com

Moore, George, LLB (Hons). Solicitor and Solicitor Advocate; Joint Senior Partner, Hamilton Burns Moore (now HBM Sayers), since 1973; b. 7.11.47, Kilmarnock; m., Ann Beattie; 2 s.; 1 d. Educ. High School of Glasgow; Glasgow University. Member, Glasgow and North Argyll Legal Aid Committee, 1979; Reporter to Scottish Legal Aid Board, 1986; part-time Chairman, Industrial Tribunals in Scotland, 1986; Member, Sheriff Court Rules Council, 1987. Recreations: tennis; golf; windsurfing. Address: (b.) 13 Bath Street, Glasgow G2 1HY; T.-0141-353 2121.

Moore, Graham, INSEAD, DipIntMgt. Director, BT Scotland, Northern Ireland and English Regions, since 1999; b. 24.10.48, Edinburgh; m., Doreen; 1d. General Manager, BT Asia Pacific, 1985-88; Director, BT Hong Kong, 1988; International Operations Director, BTCBP Ltd., 1988-91; Director, BT Asia Sales and Marketing, 1991-94; Managing Director, BT Northeast Asia, 1994-96; Managing Director, BT Australasia, 1996-98; BT Project Director/Chief Commercial Officer, Starhub Ltd., 1998-99; Vice Chairman, CBI Scotland; Board Member: Quality Scotland, Scottish Ballet/Opera; Member: Scottish Council Development and Industry Executive Committee; New Deal Advisory Task Force. Recreations: tennis; golf; hill walking; football; cinema. Address: (b.) Alexander Graham Bell House, 1 Lochside View, Edinburgh, EH12 9DH; T.-0131-345 1111; e-mail: graham.g.moore@bt.com

Moore, Jean, ALAM, LGSM, FRSAMD. Head of Voice, RSAMD Glasgow, since 1979; b. 21.5.43, Southport. Educ. High School for Girls, Southport; North West School of Speech and Drama. Speech and Drama Tutor, Greaves Hall Hospital, Southport, 1964-68; Voice and Speech Tutor, Sir Thomas More Approved School for Boys, Southport, 1964-68; Lecturer in Speech and Drama, Kirkby Fields College of Education, Liverpool, 1968-72; Senior Lecturer in Drama, Nene University, Northampton, 1972-78. Consultant to many corporate bodies; presented many papers at voice conferences. Recreations: voracious reader; listener to Radio 4; DIY decorator; gardener. Address: (h.) 47 Kilpatrick Gardens, Clarkston, Glasgow G76 7RF; T.-0141-638 7817.

Moore, Professor Johanna D., BS, MS, PhD. Professor, Division of Informatics, Edinburgh University, since 1998; Director, Human Communication Research Centre, since 1998; b. 16.7.57, USA; m., Dr N. Goddard; 2 s. Educ. University of California at Los Angeles (UCLA). Graduate Research Assistant, then Teaching Assistant/Teaching Fellow, UCLA; University of Pittsburgh: Research Scientist, Learning Research and Development Centre, 1990-98, Assistant Professor of Computer Science and Intelligent Systems, 1990-96, Associate Professor of Linguistics, 1996-98, Associate Professor of Computer Science and Intelligent Systems, 1996-98, Director, Intelligent Systems Program, 1996-98. Publication: Participating in Explanatory Dialogues: Interpreting and Responding to Questions in Context, 1995. Address: (b.) Division of Informatics, Edinburgh University, 2 Buccleuch Place, Edinburgh EH8 9LW; T.-0131-651 1336.

Moore, Michael, MA, CA. MP (Liberal Democrat), Tweeddale, Ettrick and Lauderdale, since 1997; UK Spokesman on Transport, since 1999, Spokesman on Scotland, since 2001; b. 3.6.65. Educ. Strathallan School; Jedburgh Grammar School; Edinburgh University. Manager, Corporate Finance practice, Coopers and Lybrand. Member, House of Commons Scottish Select Committee, 1997-99. Recreations: jazz; films; walking; rugby. Address: (b.) House of Commons, London SW1A 0AA; e-mail: michaelmoore@cix.co.uk

Moorhouse, John Edwin, DL, FRSA, FFCS. Chairman, Nobel Exhibition Trust; Director: The Piping Centre, Scottish Science Trust, CTF Training, The Gordon Cook Conversations, 2025, Adaptive Venture Managers plc; b. 7.10.41; m., Susan; 2 s.; 2 d. Educ. Bridlington School. With Shell UK, 1963-94; Chief Executive, Scottish Business in the Community, 1990-98. DL, Edinburgh; Honorary Fellow, Institute of Contemporary Scotland, since 2001. Recreations: music; theatre. Address: (h.) Monybuie House, Corsock, Castle Douglas DG7 3DY; T.-01644 440293; e-mail: john.moorhouse@btinternet.com

Moos, Khursheed Francis, OBE, MB, BS, BDS, FRCSEdin, FDS RCS (Eng, Edin), FDS RCPS (Glas). Consultant Oral and Maxillofacial Surgeon; Honorary Professor, Glasgow University; b. 1.11.34, London; m., Katharine Addison; 2 s.; 1 d. Educ. Dulwich College; Guy's Hospital, London; Westminster Hospital. National Service, RADC, Lt., 1959, Capt., 1960; Registrar in Oral Surgery, Mount Vernon Hospital, Middlesex, 1966-67; Senior Registrar, Oral Surgery, University of Wales, Cardiff, 1967-69; Consultant Oral Surgeon, S. Warwicks and Coventry Hospitals, 1969-74; Consultant Oral and Maxillofacial Surgeon, Canniesburn Hospital, Glasgow, 1974-99; Dean, Dental Faculty, Royal College of Physicians and Surgeons of Glasgow, 1992-95; Chairman, Intercollegiate Examination Board in oral and maxillofacial surgery, 1995-98; Civilian Consultant to Royal Navy, since 1976; President: Cranio-facial Society of Great Britain, 1994-95, British Association of Oral and Maxillofacial Surgeons, 1991-92; Down Surgical Prize, 1988; Colyer Medal, Royal College of Surgeons of England, 1997; Indian Medical Association (UK): Chairman, Board of Directors, since 1999, President, 1998-99. Publications include contributions to books and various papers. Recreations: music; natural history; philately; Eastern philosophy; gardening. Address: (h.) 43 Colquhoun Street, Helensburgh, Dunbartonshire G84 9JW; T.-01436 673232.

Moray, Earl of (Douglas John Moray Stuart), BA, FRICS. Chairman, Moray Estates Development Co., since 1974; b. 13.2.28, Johannesburg; m., Malvina Dorothea

Murray; 1 s.; 1 d. Educ. Hilton College, Natal; Trinity College, Cambridge. Address: (h.) Doune Park, Doune, Perthshire.

Morbey, Gillian, OBE, BA (Hons), RGN. Director, Sense Scotland, since 1989; Trustee, Family Fund, since 1996; b. 11.6.53, Glasgow; m., Jeremy Morbey; 1 s.; 1 d. Educ. Williamwood High School; Strathclyde University. Nursing career within NHS; first Development Officer, Sense Scotland, 1985. Past Chairperson, West of Scotland Branch, Scottish Association for the Deaf; Chairperson, Glasgow Council of Voluntary Services, 1994-97; Member, National Disability Council, 1998-2000. Recreations: supporter of Worldwide Fund for Nature; reading; music; walking. Address: (b.) 45 Finnieston Street, Clydeway Centre, Glasgow G3 8JU; T.-0141-564 2444.

Morgan, Alasdair, MA, BA. MSP (SNP), Galloway and Upper Nithsdale, since 1999 (Shadow Minister for Finance, Member, Finance Committee); MP (SNP), Galloway and Upper Nithsdale, 1997-2001; Vice President, Scottish National Party; b. 21.4.45, Aberfeldy; m., Anne Gilfillan; 2 d. Educ. Breadalbane Academy, Aberfeldy; Glasgow University. SNP: National Treasurer, 1983-90, Senior Vice-Convener, 1990-91, National Secretary, 1992-97. Recreation: hill-walking. Address: (h.) Nether Cottage, Crocketford, Dumfries; e-mail: Alasdair.Morgan.msp@scottish.parliament.uk

Morgan, Diane, MA, BA. Writer and publisher; b. 12.2.36; m., David I Morgan; 1 s.; 1 d. Educ. Aberdeen High School for Girls; Aberdeen University; Cambridge University. Law Lecturer, RGIT; Founding Editor/Publisher, Leopard, 1974-88. Aberdeen Civic Society Award, 1982 and 2000; Burgess of Aberdeen, since 1983. Publications: Archibald Simpson, Architect of Aberdeen (with Cuthbert Graham, 1990; Footdee (The Villages of Aberdeen series), 1993; Round About Mounthooly, 1995; The Spital, 1996; The Spital Lands: From Sunnyside to Pittodrie, 1997; Old Aberdeen, Vol. 1, 2000; A Monumental Business, 2001; Consultant, Aberdeen 1800-2000, A New History. Recreations: book collecting; travel; French Foreign Legion history. Address: (b.) Denburn Books, 49 Waverley Place, Aberdeen, AB10 1XP; T.-01224 644492; e-mail: denburn.books@virgin.net

Morgan, Edwin (George), OBE, MA, Hon. DLitt (Loughborough, Glasgow, Edinburgh, St. Andrews, Heriot-Watt), Hon.DUniv (Stirling, Waikato); Hon. MUniv (Open). Freelance Writer (Poet, Critic, Translator), since 1980; Emeritus Professor of English, Glasgow University, since 1980; Honorary Professor, University College of Wales, Aberystwyth, since 1990; b. 27.4.20, Glasgow. Educ. Rutherglen Academy; High School of Glasgow; Glasgow University. War Service, Royal Army Medical Corps, 1940-46; Glasgow University: Assistant Lecturer in English, 1947, Lecturer, 1950, Senior Lecturer, 1965, Reader, 1971, Titular Professor, 1975; Visiting Professor of English, Strathclyde University, 1987-90; appointed Poet Laureate for Glasgow, 1999; received Cholmondeley Award for Poets, 1968; Hungarian PEN Memorial Medal, 1972; Scottish Arts Council Book Awards, 1968, 1973, 1977, 1978, 1983, 1985, 1988, 1991, 1992; Saltire Society and Royal Bank Scottish Literary Award, 1983; Soros Translation Award (New York), 1985; Order of Merit, Republic of Hungary, 1997; Queen's Gold Medal for Poetry, 2000. Publications: (poetry): The Vision of Cathkin Braes, 1952, Beowulf, 1952, The Cape of Good Hope, 1955, Poems from Eugenio Montale, 1959, Sovpoems, 1961, Collins Albatross Book of Longer Poems (Editor), 1963, Starryveldt, 1965, Emergent Poems, 1967, Gnomes, 1968, The Second Life, 1968, Proverbfolder, 1969, Twelve Songs, 1970, The Horseman's Word, 1970, Scottish Poetry 1-6 (Co-Editor), 1966-72; Glasgow Sonnets, 1972, Wi the Haill Voice, 1972, The Whittrick, 1973, From Glasgow to

Saturn, 1973, Fifty Renascence Love-Poems, 1975, Rites of Passage, 1976, The New Divan, 1977, Colour Poems, 1978, Platen: Selected Poems, 1978, Star Gate, 1979, Scottish Satirical Verse (Editor), 1980, Poems of Thirty Years, 1982, Grafts/Takes, 1983, Sonnets from Scotland, 1984, Selected Poems, 1985, From the Video Box, 1986, Themes on a Variation, 1988; Tales from Limerick Zoo, 1988; Collected Poems, 1990; Hold Hands Among the Atoms, 1991; Sweeping Out the Dark, 1994; Collected Translations, 1996; Virtual and Other Realities, 1997; Demon, 1999; New Selected Poems, 2000; prose: Essays, 1974, East European Poets, 1976, Hugh MacDiarmid, 1976, Twentieth Century Scottish Classics, 1987; Nothing Not Giving Messages, 1990; Crossing the Border, 1990; Evening Will Come They Will Sew The Blue Sail, 1991; plays: The Apple-Tree, 1982; Master Peter Pathelin, 1983; Cyrano de Bergerac, 1992; Marlowe's Doctor Faustus (new version), 1999; Racine's Phaedra, 2000; AD, 2000. Address: (h.) 19 Whittingehame Court, Glasgow G12 OBG; T.-0141-339 6260.

Morgan, Professor Peter John, BSc, PhD, FIBiol, ChBiol. Director and Chief Executive, Rowett Research Institute, Aberdeen, since 1999; b. 23.2.56, Armthorpe, Yorkshire; m., Dr Denise Kelly; 1s.; 1d. Educ. Aylesbury Grammar School; Queen Mary College, London; University of Aberdeen; Imperial College, London. Recreations: music (classical and jazz); squash; swimming. Address; (b.) Rowett Research Institute, Greenburn Road, Bucksburn, Aberdeen; T.-01224 716663.

Morgan, Tom, CBE, DL, NDD, CDD; b. 24.2.14, Aberdeenshire; m., Mary Montgomery McLauchlan (deceased); 2 s. Educ. Longside School; North and West of Scotland Colleges of Agriculture. Unigate PLC, 38 years (Regional Director, Scotland); Councillor, City of Edinburgh Corporation, 1954-71, City of Edinburgh District Council, 1977-84; City Treasurer, 1968-71; Lord Provost and Lord Lieutenant, 1980-84; Chairman, Edinburgh Military Tattoo and Edinburgh International Festival, 1980-84. Recreations: golf; gardening. Address: (h.) 400 Lanark Road, Edinburgh EH13 0LX; T.-0131-441 3245.

Morison, Hugh, CBE, MA, DipEd. Chief Executive, Scotch Whisky Association, since 1994; b. 22.11.43, Bognor Regis; m.; 2 d. Educ. Chichester High School for Boys; St. Catherine's College, Oxford. Assistant Principal, Scottish Home and Health Department, 1966-69; Private Secretary to Minister of State, Scottish Office, 1969-70; Principal: Scottish Education Department, 1971-73, Scottish Economic Planning Department, 1973-79 (seconded to Offshore Supplies Office, Department of Energy, 1974-75); Assistant Secretary, Scottish Economic Planning Department, 1979-82; Gwilym Gibbon Research Fellow, Nuffield College, Oxford, 1982-83; Assistant Secretary, Scottish Development Department, 1983-84; Under Secretary, Scottish Home and Health Department, 1984-88, Scottish Office Industry Department, 1988-93; Non-Executive Director, Weir Group PLC, 1988-93; Member, Health Appointments Advisory Committee (Scotland), 1995-2000; Member, Executive Committee, Barony Housing Association, since 1996; Chairman, Scottish Business and Biodiversity Group, since 1999; President, Confédération Européenne des Producteurs de Spiritueux, since 2001; Chairman, Letterfearn Moorings Association, since 2001. Publications: The Regeneration of Local Economies, 1987; Dauphine (Co-Author), 1991. Recreations: hill-walking; archaeology; literature. Address: (b.) Scotch Whisky Association, 20 Atholl Crescent, Edinburgh, EH3 8HF; T.-0131-222 9201.

Morrice, Graeme. Leader, West Lothian Council, since 1995; Non-Executive Director, Scottish Enterprise Edinburgh and Lothian, since 1998; Non-Executive Trustee, West Lothian Healthcare NHS Trust, since

1999; b. 23.2.59, Edinburgh. Educ. Broxburn Academy; Napier University. Councillor, West Lothian, since 1987. Recreations: music; art; literature. Address: (h.) 39 Burnside Road, Uphall, Broxburn; T.-01506 853266.

Morrice, Ken, MD, DPM, FRCPsych. Poet and Writer, since 1965; Psychiatrist, since 1956; b. 14.7.24, Aberdeen; m., Norah Thompson; 1 s.; 2 d. Educ. Robert Gordon's College; Aberdeen University. Hon. Fellow, Aberdeen University Mental Health Department. Publications: Crisis Intervention; Studies in Community Care; eight volumes of poetry; numerous papers; short stories. Recreations: golf; walking; TV. Address: (h.) 30 Carnegie Crescent, Aberdeen; T.-Aberdeen 310136.

Morris, Alistair Lindsay, LLB, DipLP. Solicitor; Director, Pagan Independent Financial Advisers Ltd.; Director, Pagan Osborne Services Ltd.; Partner, Pagan Osborne; b. 30.7.58, Dunfermline; m., Sandra Willins; 2 s. Educ. Queen Anne High School, Dunfermline; Aberdeen University. Council Member, Law Society of Scotland, since 1992, Convenor, Professional Practice Committee, 1996-98, Convener, Insurance Committee, 1998-2001. Recreations: golf; motor sport; football; rugby. Address: (b.) 106 South Street, St. Andrews KY16 9QP; T.-01334 475001.

Morris, Dr Andrew David, MBChB, MSc, MD, FRCPEdin, FRCPGlas. Reader in Medicine, Dundee University, since 2000; b. 7.10.64; m., Elspeth Claire; 2 d. Educ. Robert Gordon's College, Aberdeen; Glasgow University. Undergraduate and research training, Glasgow University; since 1995, has co-ordinated the DARTS initiative (clinical network for peopole with diabetes in Tayside); Chair, Royal College of Edinburgh Diabetes Registry, since 1998; Chair, Health Technology Board for Scotland Topic Specific Group, since 2001; Chair, Scottish Diabetes Survey Monitoring Group, since 2000; Member, Modernisation Board, NHS in Scotland, since 2000. Recreations: golf; squash; family life. Address: (b.) University Department of Medicine, Ninewells Hospital and Medical School, Dundee DD1 9SY; T.-01382 632456.

Morris, Arthur MacGregor, OBE, MA, MB, BChir, FRCSEdin, FRCSEng, LRCP. Consultant Plastic Surgeon, Tayside University Hospitals Trust, since 1975; Honorary Senior Lecturer in Surgery, Dundee University, since 1975; Visiting Professor in Surgery, Knust, Kumasi, Ghana, since 2001; b. 6.5.41, Heswall; m., Victoria Margaret Whitaker; 1 s.; 1 d. Educ. Dulwich College; Cambridge University; Guy's Hospital. House Officer, 1965-66; Anatomy Demonstrator, Newcastle, 1966-67; Rotating Surgical Trainee in Surgery, Bristol, 1967-69; Research Registrar, then Casualty Registrar, Guy's Hospital, 1969-71; Plastic Surgery Registrar, Canniesburn Hospital, Glasgow, 1972; Plastic Surgery Senior Registrar, Bangour General Hospital and Royal Hospital for Sick Children, Edinburgh, 1972-75. Chairman, Scottish Council, BMA, 1995; Lead Clinician, CLEFTSiS. Publications: Complications of Plastic Surgery (book); papers. Recreations: golf; curling; photography; bee-keeping; gardening; fishing. Address: (b.) Plastic Surgery Unit, Ninewells Hospital, Dundee; T.-01382 660111.

Morris, Professor Arthur Stephen, BA, MA, PhD. Emeritus Professor, Department of Geography, Glasgow University; b. 26.12.36, Broadway, Worcestershire; m., Estela C.; 1 s.; 1 d. Educ. Chipping Campden; Exeter College, Oxford University; University of Maryland; University of Wisconsin. Instructor/Assistant Professor, Western Michigan University, 1964-67; Lecturer, Senior Lecturer, Reader, Professor, Glasgow University; Visiting Professor: Central University of Venezuela 1976-77, CEPEIGE, Quito, 1980, Colegio Mexiquense, Mexico, 1987. Publications: South America; Latin America;

Geography and Development. Recreations: gardening; music; travel. Address: (h.) The Old Manse, Shandon, near Helensburgh; T.-01436 820569.

Morris, Professor Christopher David, BA, DipEd, MIFA, FSA, FSA Scot, FRHistS, FRSA, FRSE. Professor of Archaeology, Glasgow University, since 1990, Vice-Principal, since 2000; b. 14.4.46, Preston; m., Dr. Colleen E. Batey. Educ. Queen Elizabeth's Grammar School, Blackburn; Durham University; Oxford University. Assistant Lecturer, Hockerill College of Education, Bishops Stortford, 1968-72; Lecturer, then Senior Lecturer in Archaeology, 1972-88, Reader in Viking Archaeology, 1989-90, Durham University. Member, Ancient Monuments Board for Scotland, since 1990; Royal Commissioner, Ancient and Historical Monuments of Scotland, since 2000. Recreations: classical music; opera; theatre; walking. Address: (b.) Vice-Principal's Office, Adam Smith Building, Glasgow University, Glasgow G12 8RT; T.-0141-330 3776/4690.

Morris, James Shepherd, RSA, RIBA, FRIAS, ALI. Principal, Morris and Steedman, Architects and Landscape Architects, since 1956; Member, Council, Royal Scottish Academy, since 1999 (Hon. Treasurer, 1992-99); b. 22.8.31, St. Andrews; m., Eleanor Kenner Smith; 2 s.; 1 d. Educ. Daniel Stewart's College, Edinburgh; Edinburgh School of Architecture; University of Pennsylvania. Lt., Royal Engineers, 1957-59. Member, Council: RIAS and Edinburgh Architectural Association, 1969-71, Cockburn Association, Edinburgh; Convenor, Fellowship Committee, RIAS, 1985-87; Trustee, Museum of Antiquities, 1980-86; Member, Arts Council of GB, 1973-80; Vice Chairman, Scottish Arts Council, 1976-80; Member, Management Committee, Traverse Theatre; ARSA, 1975; RSA, 1989; two RIBA awards for Scotland; British Steel Award; 10 Civic Trust awards. Recreations: painting; golf; skiing; tennis. Address: (b.) 38 Young Street, Edinburgh EH2 4JD; T.-0131-226 6563.

Morris, Jean Daveena Ogilvy, CBE, MA, MEd, LLD (Dundee and St. Andrews), OSStJ. Senior Governor, Court, University of St. Andrews, since 1998; Chairman, Parole Board for Scotland, 1980-92; b. 28.1.29, Kilmarnock; m., Rev. William J. Morris (qv); 1 s. Educ. Kilmarnock Academy; St. Andrews University. Clinical Psychologist: Royal Hospital for Sick Children, Edinburgh, St. David's Hospital, Cardiff, Church Village, Pontypridd, Quarrier's Homes, Bridge of Weir; Member, Bailie and Convener of Housing, Peterhead Town Council; Member, Aberdeen County Council; Columnist, Aberdeen Press and Journal; Chairman, Christian Action Housing Association; Member, Scottish Federation of Housing Associations; Chairman: Government Committee on Links Between Housing and Social Work (Morris Committee), Local Review Committee, Barlinnie Prison, Glasgow Abbeyfield Society; Vice Chairman, TSB Foundation; Director, Scottish Advisory Board, Abbey National; Chairman, Scotia House Development Company. Badminton Blue, St. Andrews University. Recreations: swimming; holidays in France. Address: (h.) 1 Whitehill Grove, Newton Mearns, Glasgow G77 5DH; T.-0141-639 6327.

Morris, Sheriff John C., QC, LLB. Sheriff, South Strathclyde Dumfries and Galloway, at Airdrie, since 1998; b. 11.4.52. Educ. Allan Glen's School, Glasgow; Strathclyde University. Solicitor, 1975-85; called to Scottish Bar, 1985; Advocate Depute, 1989-92; called to English Bar, 1990; Temporary Sheriff, 1993-98; took silk, Scottish Bar, 1996. Chairman, Advocates Criminal Law Group, 1996-98; Member, Temporary Sheriffs Association Committee, 1994-98. Recreations: golf; bird-watching; walking; wine. Address: (b.) Airdrie Sheriff Court, Graham Street, Airdrie ML6 6EE; T.-01236 751 121.

Morris, Philip T., BSc, FCA. Finance Director, Adam & Company Group PLC, since 1993; b. 23.10.52, Malaysia. Educ. Morrisons Academy, Crieff; St. Andrews University. Arthur Young, Chartered Accountants, London, Stavanger, Norway and Dundee Offices, 1974-87; Royal Bank of Scotland Group (Corporate Finance), 1987-93. Recreations: travel; circuit training; crosswords. Address: (b.) 22 Charlotte Square, Edinburgh EH2 4DF; T.-0131-225 8484; e-mail: Philip.Morris@Adambank.com

Morris, Professor Richard Graham Michael, MA, DPhil, FRSE, FMedSci, FRS. Chairman, Department of Neuroscience, Edinburgh University, (Professor, since 1993, Reader, 1989-93); b. 27.6.48, Worthing; m., Hilary Ann; 2 d. Educ. St. Albans, Washington DC; Marlborough College; Cambridge University; Sussex University. Addison Wheeler Fellow, Durham University, 1973-75; SSO, British Museum (Natural History), 1975-77; Researcher, BBC Television, 1977; Lecturer, St. Andrews University, 1977-86; MRC University Research Fellow, 1983-86. Member, MRC Neurosciences Grants Committee, 1981-85, MRC Neurosciences Board, 1993-98, Innovation Panel, since 1997; Hon. Secretary, Experimental Psychological Society, 1985-89; Chairman: Brain Research Association, 1990-94, Sectional Committee for Medicine and Biomedical Sciences, Royal Society of Edinburgh, 1995-97; Member, Council, European Neuroscience Association, 1994-98. Publications: academic papers and books; Learning and Memory (Co-Editor). Recreation: sailing. Address: (b.) Department of Neuroscience, Edinburgh University, 1 George Square, Edinburgh EH8 9JZ; T.-0131-650 3520/3518.

Morris, Professor Robert John, BA, DPhil. Professor of Economic and Social History, Edinburgh University, since 1993; b. 12.10.43, Sheffield; m., Barbara; 1 s.; 1 d. Educ. Acklam Hall, Middlesbrough; Keble and Nuffield Colleges, Oxford. Lecturer and Senior Lecturer in Economic and Social History, Edinburgh University, since 1968. Founding Editor, History and Computing; President, European Urban History Association. Recreation: watching vegetables grow. Address: (b.) 55 George Square, Edinburgh EH8 9JU.

Morris, Professor Robert Lyle, BSc, PhD. Professor of Parapsychology, Edinburgh University, since 1985; b. 9.7.42, Canonsburg, Pennsylvania; m., Joanna Du Barry; 2 d. Educ. Crafton High School; University of Pittsburgh; Duke University. Research Fellow, Duke University, 1969-71; Research Co-ordinator, then Research Associate, Psychical Research Foundation, 1971-74; Lecturer in Parapsychology, University of California, Santa Barbara, 1974-78; Lecturer, School of Social Sciences, University of California, Irvine, 1978-80; Research Coordinator, Communication Studies Laboratory, and Senior Research Scientist, School of Computer and Information Sciences, Syracuse University, 1980-85. Member: Council, Parapsychological Association, Council, British Society for Psychical Research; President, Psychology Section, British Association for the Advancement of Science, 1995-96. Publication: Foundations of Parapsychology: Exploring the Boundaries of Human Capability (Co-Author), 1986; Guidelines for Testing Psychic Claimants (Co-Author), 1996. Address: (b.) Psychology Department, University of Edinburgh, 7 George Square, Edinburgh EH8 9JZ; T.-0131 650 3343.

Morris, Very Rev. William James, KCVO, ChStJ, JP, BA, BD, PhD, LLD, DD, Hon. FRCP&SGlas. Minister, Glasgow Cathedral, since 1967; Chaplain in Ordinary to The Queen in Scotland, 1969-96, Extra Chaplain, since 1996; Chairman, Iona Cathedral Trust, since 1979; Dean, Chapel Royal in Scotland, 1991-96; Chaplain to The Queen's Body Guard in Scotland (Royal Company of Archers), since 1994; b. 22.8.25, Cardiff; m., Jean Daveena Ogilvy Howie (see Jean Daveena Ogilvy Morris); 1 s. Educ. Cardiff High School; University of Wales (Cardiff and Aberystwyth); Edinburgh University. Ordained, 1951; Assistant, Canongate Kirk, Edinburgh, 1949-51; Minister: Barry Island and Cadoxton Presbyterian Church of Wales, 1951-53, St. David's, Buckhaven, 1953-57, Peterhead Old Parish Church, 1957-67; Chaplain, Peterhead Prison, 1963-67; Chaplain to Lord High Commissioner, 1975-76; Moderator, Deer Presbytery, 1965-66; Chaplain: Strathclyde Police, Glasgow Academy, High School of Glasgow, Glasgow District Council, Trades House of Glasgow, West of Scotland Engineers Association, Royal Scottish Automobile Club; Member, Independent Broadcasting Authority, 1979-84 (Chairman, Scottish Advisory Committee); Member, Convocation, Strathclyde University; Honorary President, Glasgow Society of Social Service; Lord Provost's Award, 1996. Publication: A Walk Through Glasgow Cathedral, 1986; Amazing Graces, 2001. Recreation: being good, careful, and happy (not always simultaneously). Address: (h.) 1 Whitehill Grove, Newton Mearns, Glasgow G77 5DA; T.-0141 639 6327.

Morrison, Alasdair. MSP (Labour), Western Isles, since 1999; Member: Justice 2 Committee, Rural Development Committee. Former journalist, BBC in Stornoway; Editor, An Gaidheal Ur. Address: (b.) Scottish Parliament, Edinburgh EH99 1SP; T.-0131-348 5760.

Morrison, Sir Alexander Fraser, CBE, FRSA, BSc, CEng, FICE, MIHT, FScotvec, FCIOB. Director, Morrison Construction Group Plc, since 1970 (Chairman, 1984-2000); Deputy Chairman, Clydesdale Bank Plc, since 1999 (Director, since 1994); b. 20.3.48, Dingwall; m., Patricia Janice Murphy; 1 s.; 2 d. Educ. Tain Royal Academy; Edinburgh University. Morrison Construction Group, since 1970; Managing Director, 1976-84. National Federation of Civil Engineering Contractors: Chairman, 1993-94, Vice President, 1994-96; Chairman, Highlands and Islands Enterprise, 1992-98; Vice President, Royal Highland and Agricultural Society of Scotland, 1995-96; Chairman, University of the Highlands and Islands Project, 1997-2000; Director, Aberforth Split Level Trust plc; winner, 1991 Scottish Business Achievement Award; Hon. Doctor of Technology: Napier University, 1995, Glasgow Caledonian University, 1997; Honorary Doctor, Open University, 2000. Recreations: rugby; golf; skiing; opera; the countryside; theatre; art. Address: (b.) Teasses House, Ceres, Leven, Fife KY8 5PG.

Morrison, Rev. Alistair Hogarth, BTh, DipYCS. Minister, St. Mark's-Oldhall, Paisley, since 1989; b. 12.9.43, Glasgow; 1 s.; 1 d. Educ. Jordanhill College School; Aberdeen University; Jordanhill College of Education. City of Glasgow/Strathclyde Police, 1962-81 (resigned with rank of Inspector to train for Ministry); Minister, Elgin High Church, 1985-89. Strathclyde Medal for Bravery, 1976. Recreations: hill-walking; general fitness. Address: 36 Newtyle Road, Paisley PA1 3JX; T.-0141-889 4279.

Morrison, Rev. Angus, MA, BD, PhD. Minister, St. Columba's Old Parish Church, Stornoway; b. 30.8.53, Oban; m., Marion Jane Matheson; 3 s.; 1 d. Educ. Oban High School; Glasgow University; London University; Edinburgh University. Minister, Free Presbyterian Church of Scotland Oban Congregation, 1979-86, Edinburgh Congregation, 1986-89; Moderator, Southern Presbytery, Free Presbyterian Church, 1987-88; Minister, Associated Presbyterian Churches, Viewforth Congregation, Edinburgh, 1989-2000; Moderator, APC General Assembly, 1998-99. Contributor, Dictionary of Scottish Church History and Theology, 1993; Member, Gaelic Panel, Scottish Bible Society; Contributor, New Dictionary of National Biography. Recreations: reading; swimming. Address: (h.) St. Columba's Manse, Lewis Street, Stornoway, Isle of Lewis HS1 2JF.

Morrison, Charles, CA, Vice President, IBM; b. 27.8.53, Glasgow; m., Phyllis Ann Morrison. Educ. St. Columba's High School, Greenock. Reid and Mair, 1970-75; Ernst and Whinney, 1975-76; joined IBM, 1976. Recreations: golf; running. Address: Inverkip Road, Spango Valley, Greenock, PA16 0AH.

Morrison, Colin Andrew, BA, MEd, DipM, MCIM, CertEd, FCIBS. Director of Education, Chartered Institute of Bankers in Scotland, since 1991; b. 14.10.61, Ellon; m., Stella Ross Ingram. Educ. Peterhead Academy; Robert Gordon's Institute of Technology; Aberdeen College of Education; Edinburgh University. Former Outdoor Pursuits Instructor and F.E. Lecturer/Senior Lecturer; Head of Business Studies, Stevenson College, 1990-91. Recreations: dinghy sailing; skiing. Address: (b.) 38b Drumsheugh Gardens, Edinburgh EH3 7SW; T.-0131-473 7777.

Morrison, David Ralston. Writer and Painter; b. 4.8.41, Glasgow; m., Edna May Wade; 1 s.; 1 d. Educ. Glasgow High School for Boys; Hamilton Academy; Strathclyde University. Librarian: Lanark County, Edinburgh College of Art, Caithness. Founded and ran Scotia Review, Wick Folk Club, Wick Festival of Poetry, Folk and Jazz; author of numerous books of poetry; edited Essays on Neil M. Gunn, Essays on Fionn MacColla. Recreations: walking; drystanedyking; reading; music. Address: (h.) 18 MacArthur Street, Wick KW1 5AX; T.-01955 603703.

Morrison, Hamish Robertson, OBE. Chief Executive, Scottish Fishermen's Federation, since 1998; b. 24.5.44, Irvine; m., Denise Mary; 1 s.; 2 d. Educ. Kilmarnock Academy; Britannia Royal Naval College, Dartmouth. Royal Navy, 1961-70; Scottish Council Development and Industry, 1970-97 (Chief Executive, 1982-97); Chairman, PJMP Group Ltd., Architects, 1997-98. Recreations: writing and public speaking; hill-walking; gardening. Address: (b.) 14 Regent Quay, Aberdeen AB11 5AE; T.-01224 582583.

Morrison, James, RSA, RSW, DA, DUniv (Stirling). Painter in oil and watercolour; b. 11.4.32, Glasgow; m., Dorothy McCormack; 1 s.; 1 d. Educ. Hillhead High School; Glasgow School of Art. Taught part-time, 1955-58; won Torrance Memorial Prize, RGI, 1958; Visiting Artist, Hospitalfield, 1962-63; Council Member, SSA, 1964-67; staff, Duncan of Jordanstone College of Art, 1965-87; won Arts Council Travelling Scholarship to Greece, 1968; painting in various regions of France, 1976-82; numerous one-man exhibitions since 1956, in Scotland, London, Italy, West Germany, Canada; four works in private collection of Duke of Edinburgh and numerous other works in public and private collections; several group exhibitions since 1980 in UK and Europe; regular series of expeditions to paint in Canadian and Greenland High Arctic, since 1990. Publication: Aff the Squerr. Recreation: playing in a chamber music group. Address: (h.) Craigview House, Usan, Montrose, Angus; T.-Montrose 672639.

Morrison, Sheriff Nigel Murray Paton, QC. Sheriff of Lothian and Borders at Edinburgh, since 1996; b. 18.3.48, Paisley. Educ. Rannoch School. Called to the Bar of England and Wales, Inner Temple, 1972; admitted to Scottish Bar, 1975; Assistant Editor, Session Cases, 1976-82; Assistant Clerk, Rules Council, 1978-84; Clerk of Faculty, Faculty of Advocates, 1979-86; Standing Junior Counsel to Scottish Development Department (Planning), 1982-86; Temporary Sheriff, 1982-96; Chairman, Social Security Appeal Tribunals, 1982-91; Second (formerly Junior) Counsel to the Lord President of the Court of Session, 1984-89; First Counsel to the Lord President, 1989-96; Counsel to Secretary of State under Private Legislation Procedure (Scotland) Act 1936, 1986-96; QC, 1988; Chairman, Medical Appeal Tribunals, 1991-96; Trustee, National Library of Scotland, 1989-98; Director of Judicial Studies, since 2000. Publications: Green's Annotated Rules of the Court of Session (Principal Editor);

Green's Civil Practice Bulletin (Editor); Stair Memorial Encyclopaedia of the Laws of Scotland (Contributor); Sentencing Practice (Editor); Green's Litigation Styles (Assistant Editor). Recreations: music; riding; Scottish country dancing; being taken by his dog for walks. Address: 9 India Street, Edinburgh EH3 6HA; T.-0131-225 2807.

Morrison, Peter, MA, LLB. Singer; b. 14.8.40, Greenock; m., Irene; 1 s.; 1 d. Educ. Greenock Academy; Glasgow University. Private legal practice, 1968-77; own legal practice, 1977-96; Consultant, 1996-99; began professional singing career at university; first television series for BBC Scotland, 1971, continuing until 1979 and including Show of the North, Castles in the Air, Songs of Scotland, Something to Sing About (for BBC 2); other work includes Hogmanay shows, Friday Night is Music Night (radio), 1976-97, television series for Channel 4, STV and Grampian, innumerable theatre and concert performances in UK and abroad. Recreations: golf; loves cricket and rugby; loves Arran; loves the chance to work with his children when he can (not often enough); e-mail: pdamorrison@hotmail.com

Morrison, Rev. Roderick, MA, BD. Minister, Partick Gardner Street Church, Glasgow, since 1994; b. 3.7.43, Lochmaddy; m., Christina Ann MacDonald; 1 s.; 1 d. Educ. Lochportan Public School; Glasgow University and Trinity College. Assistant Minister, Drumchapel Old Parish Church, Glasgow, 1973-74; Minister: Carinish Parish Church, North Uist, 1974-81, High Church, Stornoway, Lewis, 1981-94. Recreations: sailing; fishing; shooting. Address: 148 Beechwood Drive, Broomhill, Glasgow G11 7DX; T.-0141-563 2638.

Morrison, William Garth, CBE, BA, CEng, MIEE. Lord-Lieutenant of East Lothian, since 2001; Farmer; President, Scottish Landowners Federation, since 2001; b. 8.4.43, Edinburgh; m., Gillian Cheetham; 2 s.; 1 d. Educ. Pangbourne College; Pembroke College, Cambridge. Service, Royal Navy, 1961-73, retiring with rank of Lt.; farming, since 1973; Member, Lothian Region Children's Panel, 1976-83 (Chairman, Midlothian/East Lothian Area Panel, 1978-81); Lamp of Lothian Trustee, 1978; Chairman, Lamp of Lothian Collegiate Trust, since 2001; Member: Lothian, Borders and Fife Committee, Prince's Trust, 1979, Lothian and Borders Committee, Prince's and Royal Jubilee Trusts, 1983-88, Society of High Constables of Holyroodhouse, 1979; Deputy Lieutenant, East Lothian, 1984-2001; Chief Scout, 1988-96; Member, World Scout Committee, since 1992; Chief Commissioner of Scotland, The Scout Association, 1981-88; Member, Scottish Community Education Council, 1988-95; Chairman, East and Midlothian NHS Trust, 1993-97; Chairman, Royal Infirmary of Edinburgh NHS Trust, 1997-99; Chairman, Lothian Primary Care NHS Trust, since 1999; MacRobert Trustee, 1998; SCEC Honorary Fellowship, 1995; Member, National Lottery Charities Board, 1995-99; S.E. Regional Chairman, Scottish Landowners Federation, 1996-2000; Vice President, Commonwealth Youth Exchange Council, since 1997. Recreations: golf; sailing; Scouting. Address: West Fenton, North Berwick, East Lothian; T.-01620 842154; e-mail: garthm@dial.pipex.com

Morrison, William George, MBChB, FRCPEdin, FRCA, FFAEM, MRCGP, DRCOG. Consultant in Accident and Emergency Medicine, Ninewells Hospital, Dundee, since 1993 (Associate Medical Director, Tayside University Hospitals NHS Trust); b. 18.3.56, Aberdeen; m., Audrey; 2 s.; 1 d. Educ. Mackie Academy, Stonehaven; Aberdeen University. Trained in anaesthetics, Aberdeen and Glasgow, 1980-84; trained in general practice, 1984-87; further training in accident and emergency medicine, Aberdeen, Glasgow, Southampton, Johannesburg; first consultant post, Stirling Royal Infirmary, followed by appointment as Consultant and Head of Department, Accident and

Emergency Department, Ninewells Hospital, Dundee. Recreations: rugby; skiing; gardening; classic car restoration. Address: (h.) Craigside, 1a Glamis Road, Dundee DD2 1LZ; T.-01382 644284.

Morrow, Rev. Canon Joseph John, JP, OStJ. Priest in Scottish Episcopal Church, since 1979; Advocate, since 2000; b. 12.12.54, Alloa. Educ. Edinburgh University; Dundee University. HM Commissioner, Mental Welfare Commission for Scotland. Canon, St. Paul's Cathedral, Dundee. Recreation: natural history. Address: (h.) Tigh an Uillt, Main Street, Invergowrie, Perthshire DD2 5AA; T.-01382 562802; e-mail: jjmoit@glamis.sol.co.uk

Morrow, Martin Thomas, LLB (Hons), DipLP, NP. Solicitor; b. 2.7.64, Glasgow; m., Amanda Catherine; 1 s.; 1 d. Educ. St. Aloysius College, Glasgow; University of Strathclyde. Ian McCarry Solicitors, Glasgow, 1986-88; Levy, McRae, Solicitors, Glasgow, 1988-89; Blackadder, McMonagle, Solicitors, Falkirk, 1990-92; Principal, Milligan Telford and Morrow, Solicitors, since 1992. Member, Council, Law Society of Scotland, 1997-2001. Recreations:, golf; tennis. Address: 1 Cockburn Street, Falkirk FK1 1DJ; T.-01324 633221.

Morton, Earl of (John Charles Sholto Douglas). Farmer, since 1947; property consultant, since 1985; b. 19.3.27, Lyndhurst, Hampshire; m., Sheila Mary; 2 s.; 1 d. Educ. Malmesbury. Cattle dealing and haulage work; dairy farmer; livestock farmer; estate owner. Lord of the Realm. Recreations: polo; swimming. Address: (b.) Dalmahoy Estate Office, Kirknewton, Midlothian EH27 8EB; T.-0131-333 1331.

Morton, Rev. Alasdair J., MA, BD, DipEd, DipRE, FEIS. Minister, Bowden linked with Newtown St. Boswells, 1991-2000; b. 8.6.34, Inverness; m., Gillian M. Richards; 2 s.; 2 d. Educ. Bell-Baxter School, Cupar; St. Andrews University; Hartford Theological Seminary. District Missionary/Minister, Zambia (Northern Rhodesia), 1960-65; Chaplain and Religious Education Lecturer, Malcolm Moffat Teachers' College, Serenje, Zambia, 1966-67; Principal, David Livingstone Teachers' College, Livingstone, Zambia, 1968-72; Minister, Greyfriars Parish Church, Dumfries, 1973-77; General Secretary, Department of Education, Church of Scotland, 1977-91. Recreations: choral singing; gardening. Address: 8 Ormiston Grove, Melrose TD6 9SR; T.-01896 822033; e-mail: alasgilmor@compuserve.com

Morton, Rev. Andrew Reyburn, MA, BD, DD. Honorary Fellow, Faculty of Divinity, Edinburgh University; b. 24.5.28, Kilmarnock; m., Marion Armstrong Chadwin; 2 s.; 2 d. Educ. Kilmarnock Academy; Glasgow University; Edinburgh University; Bonn University. Scottish Secretary, Student Christian Movement, 1953-56; Minister, Moncreiff Parish, East Kilbride, 1956-64; Chaplain, Edinburgh University, 1964-70; Warden, Wolfson Hall and Co-ordinating Warden, Halls of Residence, Glasgow University, 1970-74; Social Responsibility Secretary and, latterly, Secretary, Division of Community Affairs and Assistant General Secretary, British Council of Churches, 1974-81; Secretary, Inter-Church Relations Committee and Assistant Secretary, Overseas Council, subsequently Assistant Secretary, Board of World Mission and Unity, Church of Scotland, 1982-88; Deputy General Secretary, Board of World Mission and Unity, Church of Scotland, 1988-93; Associate Director, Centre for Theology and Public Issues, University of Edinburgh, 1994-2001. Recreation: walking. Address: (h.) 11 Oxford Terrace, Edinburgh, EH4 1PX; T.-0131-332 6592.

Morton, Archibald Campbell, MA, BA (Hons). Director of Education, Argyll and Bute Council, since 1995; b. 15.2.42, Kilmarnock; m., Shirley; 2 s.; 1 d. Educ. Dumfries Academy; Edinburgh University; Moray House College of Education. Teaching, 1964-83, latterly Depute Head Teacher, Cowdenknowes High School, Greenock; Education Officer, Renfrew Division, 1983-89; Senior Education Officer, Glasgow Division, 1990-93; Assistant Director of Education, Strathclyde Regional Council, 1993-95. Recreations: curling; sailing. Address: (b.) Argyll House, Alexandra Parade, Dunoon PA23 8AJ; T.-01369 704000.

Morton, Elizabeth Stewart, NP, LicIPD, FIMgt. Director of Law and Administration, Falkirk Council, since 1995; Solicitor; b. 21.8.56, Glasgow. Educ. Dalmellington High School; Ayr Academy; Glasgow University. Entered local government, 1974, as a legal apprentice; worked for Ayr County, Cunninghame District, Cumnock and Doon Valley District, Kyle and Carrick District; moved to Hamilton District as Chief Administrative Officer, 1990; returned to Ayrshire as Director of Administration and Legal Services, 1993. Address: (b.) Municipal Buildings, Falkirk FK1 5RS; T.-01324 506075.

Morton, William John Keirs, MSc, DipTP, MRTPI. Senior Director - Operations, Scottish Enterprise, since 2001; b. 14.6.49, Glasgow; m., Jan; 2 s.; 1 d. Educ. Bearsden Academy; Glasgow College of Art. Planning Assistant, Royal Burgh of Inverness, 1973-75; Project Officer, East Kilbride Development Corporation, 1975-76; SDA, 1976-87, latterly as Project Manager (Coatbridge Project); Chief Executive, Aberdeen Beyond 2000, 1987-89; Head of Urban Regeneration, SDA, 1989-90; Chief Executive, Forth Valley Enterprise, 1990-2000; Interim Chief Executive, Scottish Qualifications Authority, 2000-01. Recreations: family; travel; cycling; reading. Address: (b.) 150 Broomielaw, 5 Atlantic Quay, Glasgow G2 8LU; T.-0141- 248 2700.

Mosson, Lord Provost Alexander Francis. Lord Provost of the City of Glasgow, since 1999; Lord-Lieutenant, City of Glasgow, since 1999; b. 27.8.40, Glasgow; m., Maureen; 4 s.; 3 d. Educ. St Patrick's Primary School; St Patrick's Junior Secondary School; St Mungo's Academy. Served apprenticeship, Barclay Curles boiler shop and Alexander Stephen shipyard, Linthouse, as a plater; worked in insulating industry; then employed as an Industrial Appeals Organiser with British Red Cross Society, Scottish Branch; elected Councillor, 1984; former Deputy Lord Provost; former Vice Convener and Convener, Protective Services Committee; former Vice Convener of Personnel. Officer, Order of St. John, since 2000. Hon. LLD, Glasgow. Recreations: reading Scottish and Irish history; painting; watching football. Address: (h.) 1 Danes Drive, Glasgow G14 9HZ; T.-0141954 3360.

Mounfield, J. Hilary, MA (Hons), MICFM. Chief Executive, Epilepsy Action Scotland, since 1995; Chair, European Committee of the International Bureau for Epilepsy; Chair, Voluntary Health Scotland; b. 19.7.41, Edinburgh; 2 s.; 1 d. Educ. Boroughmuir School; Edinburgh University. Research, Scottish Development Department and Ministry of Housing, 1963-66; teaching, London, 1973-84; fund-raising for charities, 1984-91; Appeals Director, Penumbra, 1991-95. Chair: ICFM, Scotland, 1993-95, Bighearted Scotland, 1993-96, Joint Epilepsy Council, 1998-2001; Convener, ACOSVO, 1997-2000; Founding Fellow, Institute of Contemporary Scotland. Recreations: reading; art; travel. Address: (b.) 48 Govan Road, Glasgow G51 1JL; T.-0141-427 4911; e-mail: hmounfield@epilepsyscotland.org.uk

Moutinho, Professor Luiz, BA, MA, PhD, FCIM. Professor of Marketing and Director, Doctoral Programme, Glasgow University Department of Business and Management; b. 29.1.49, Lisbon. Held posts at: Cardiff Business School; University of Wales (Cardiff); Cleveland State University, Ohio; Northern

Arizona University; California State University; Director, Doctoral Programmes, Confederation of Scottish Business Schools, 1987-89; Professor of Marketing, since 1989; appointed to Foundation Chair of Marketing, Glasgow University, 1996. Publications: 17 books, most recently Contemporary Issues in Marketing, 1999; Strategic Management in Tourism, 2000. Address: (h.) Cragdarroch, Shore Road, Cove, G84 0NU; T.-01436 842851.

Mowat, Ian Robert, MA, BPhil, FLA, FRSA FRSE. Librarian, Edinburgh University, since 1997; b. 20.4.46, Dingwall; m., Margaret Louise; 1 s.; 1 d. Educ. Robert Gordon's College, Aberdeen; Aberdeen University; Sheffield University; St. Andrews University. Assistant Librarian, St. Andrews University, 1970-72, Heriot-Watt University, 1972-75; Assistant Keeper, National Library of Scotland, 1975-78; Sub-Librarian/Associate Librarian, Glasgow University, 1978-86; Librarian, Hull University, 1986-92, Newcastle University, 1992-97. Recreations: music; architectural history; walking. Address: (b.) Edinburgh University Library, George Square, Edinburgh EH8 9LJ; T.-0131-650 3378; e-mail: ian.mowat@ed.ac.uk

Mowat, Norman Ashley George, MB, ChB, MRCP (UK), FRCP, FRCP (Edin). Physician to the Queen in Scotland, since 2001; Consultant Physician and Gastroenterologist, Aberdeen Teaching Hospitals, since 1975; Clinical Senior Lecturer in Medicine, Aberdeen University, since 1975; b. 11.4.43, Cullen; m., Kathleen Mary Cowie; 1 s.; 2 d. Educ. Fordyce Academy; Aberdeen University. House Officer, then Senior House Officer, then Registrar, Aberdeen Teaching Hospitals, 1966-72; Lecturer in Medicine, Aberdeen University, 1972-73; Lecturer in Gastroenterology and Research Associate, Medical College of St. Bartholomew's, London, 1973-75. Formerly Visiting Physician to Shetland Islands; publications include Integrated Clinical Sciences: Gastroenterology (Co-Editor), 1985. Recreations: sailing; golf; soccer; reading; photography. Address: (h.) Bucholie, 13 Kings Cross Road, Aberdeen AB15 6BE; T.-01224 319223.

Muckart, Rev. Graeme Watson MacKinnon, MSc, MTheol, FSA Scot. Minister, North Church of St. Andrew, Aberdeen, since 1997; b. 11.12.43, Dunfermline; m., 1, Mary Elspeth Small; 1 s.; 1 d.; 2, Elizabeth M. Miller, PhD; 1 d. Educ. Royal Naval Schools, Malta; Willesden County Grammar School; Portsmouth Southern Grammar School; Highbury Technical College, Portsmouth; Leeds College of Art; Open University; St. Andrews University; Stirling University. Barclays Bank, 1962-64; Trainee Architect, 1964-69; architectural appointments, 1969-76; resident staff, Iona Abbey, 1976-78; divinity studies, 1978-82; Assistant Minister, Carrick Knowe, Edinburgh, 1982-83; Minister, Erskine Parish Church, Falkirk, 1983-90; Locum Minister, Carriden Parish Church, Bo'ness, 1990-92; Minister, St. Andrew's Church, Colombo, 1992-96. Chair, Falkirk Council of Churches, 1987-89; Member, Iona Community, since 1978. Recreations: painting; calligraphy; heraldry; reading; walking. Address: The Manse, 51 Osborne Place, Aberdeen AB25 2BX; T.-01224 646429.

Muggoch, Adam, ARTCS. Group Managing Director, J. W. Galloway Ltd., since 1976; b. 17.1.34, London; m., Bernice Mary; 2 s. Educ. Eastbank Academy, Glasgow; Leigh Technical College; Royal Technical College, Salford. Marks and Spencer plc: joined as Trainee, 1955, Senior Executive, 1970-76 (resigned to return to Scotland). Council Member, British Meat Manufacturers Association; Member, Research Steering Committee, Meat and Livestock Commission. Recreations: gardening; sailing. Address: (b.) Longleys, Bridge of Allan, Stirlingshire FK9 4NE; T.-01786 832911; e-mail: nancy.thomas@scotbeef.com

Muir, Alasdair R., LlB. Managing Director, Quality Meat Scotland, since 2000; b. 25.10.58, Glasgow; m., Elspeth Muir; 1 s.; 1 d. Educ. Trinity College, Glenalmond; University of Northumbria. Joined Whitbread, Long John International Whisky Division, 1982; European Manager/North American Manager, Glenmorangie, 1985; Regional Director, North and South America, Northern Europe, Morrison Bowmore Distillers, 1993-97; Vice President, Sales and Marketing, Morrison Bowmore Distillers Inc., Boston, 1997-99. Recreations: golf; rugby. Address: (b.) Quality Meat Scotland, Rural Centre, West Mains, Ingliston, Newbridge, Midlothian, EH28 8NZ; T.-0131-472 4040; e-mail: info@qmscotland.co.uk

Muir, Ian Holstein, OBE, FSQA, MIPD. Chairman, Jewel and Esk Valley College, since 1995; Board Member, Scottish Qualifications Authority, since 1997; Director, Association of Scottish Colleges, since 1996; Technology Management Consultant, since 1995; b. 14.3.37, Edinburgh; m., Pearl; 1 s. Educ. Knox Academy. Development Engineer, 1962-67; Chief Production Engineer, 1967-77; Manufacturing Manager, 1977-87; Company Systems Manager, 1987-89; Training and Education Manager, 1989-95. Chairman, Edinburgh Compact; Member, NTO Recognition Panel. Address: Mavisbank, 46 Edinburgh Road, Tranent, East Lothian EH33 1AW; T.-01875 610444; e-mail: muirih@cs.com

Muir, Robert Douglas, MA (Hons), ACIB. Chief Executive, Skye and Lochalsh Enterprise; b. 28.8.54, Irvine; m., Nanette Thomson Buchanan; 2 s. Educ. Ardrossan Academy; Glasgow University; Tubingen Universitat. Director, An Tuireann Arts Centre. Recreations: history; travel; languages; music; following the fortunes of Kilmarnock F. C. Address: (b.) King's House, The Green, Portree, Isle of Skye IV51 9BS; T.-01478 612841; e-mail: r.muir@hient.co.uk

Muir, Trevor. Chief Executive, Midlothian Council, since 1995; b. 10.7.49, Glasgow; m., Christine Ann; 1 s.; 1 d. Educ. High School of Glasgow; Langside College; Strathclyde University. Scottish Special Housing Association, 1973-77; City of Glasgow District Council, 1977-81; Director of Housing, City of Aberdeen District Council, 1981-87; Chief Executive, Midlothian District Council, 1987-96. Recreations: squash; family life. Address: (b.) Midlothian House, Buccleuch Street, Dalkeith, Midlothian EH22 1DJ.

Muldoon, Bristow, BSc, BA. MSP (Labour), Livingston, since 1999. Convener, Transport and the Environment Committee; Business analyst, Great North Eastern Railway; Member, West Lothian Council; Director, West Lothian NHS Trust. Address: (b.) Scottish Parliament, Edinburgh EH99 1SP; T.-0131-348 5760.

Mulholland, Francis, LLB (Hons), MBA, DipLP, SSC, NP. Solicitor Advocate; Assistant Procurator Fiscal, Edinburgh, since 1999; b. 18.4.59, Coatbridge; m., Marie Elizabeth. Educ. Columba High School, Coatbridge; Aberdeen University; Edinburgh University. Trainee, Bird Semple & Crawford Herron, Solicitors, Glasgow, 1982-84; Procurator Fiscal Depute: Greenock, 1984-87, Glasgow, 1987-91; Solicitor, Crown Office, Edinburgh, 1991-96; Procurator Fiscal Depute, Edinburgh, 1996; Advocate Depute, 1997-99 (first Solicitor Advocate and Member of Procurator Fiscal Service to be appointed to office of Advocate Depute). Member, Council, Society of Solicitor Advocates. Recreations: football; squash; military history. Address: (b.) Procurator Fiscal's Office, 29 Chambers Street, Edinburgh; T.-0131-226 4962.

Mullen, Ian M., BSc, MRPharmS, DL. Freelance consultant on healthcare and pharmaceutical issues; Deputy Lieutenant, Stirling and Falkirk; b. 11.5.46, Stirling; m.,

Veronica Drummond; 2 s.; 1 d. Educ. St. Modan's High School, Stirling; Heriot-Watt University. Registered MPS, 1970; self-employed community pharmacist, 1971-97; Chairman, Pharmaceutical General Council (Scotland), 1986-88; Vice-Chairman, National Pharmaceutical Consultative Committee, 1987-89; Member, UK Advisory Committee on Borderline Substances, 1986-89; Vice-Chairman, Forth Valley Health Board, 1989-91; Director, Common Services Agency of the NHS in Scotland, 1991-94, Vice-Chairman, 1993; Director, Central Scotland Chamber of Commerce, 1990-93; Chairman: St. Andrew's School Board, 1990-93, Falkirk and District Royal Infirmary NHS Trust, 1993-99; Member: Scottish Dental Practice Review Board, 1991-92, Shields Committee (NHS in Scotland), 1995-96; Chair, Scottish NHS Trust Chairmen's Group, 1998-99; Chairman: Forth Valley Acute Hospitals NHS Trust, since 1999, Scottish NHS Chairmen's Group, since 2000, Scottish Health Matters PR Agency. Recreations: walking; golf. Address: (h.) Ardenlea, 11 Arnothill, Falkirk FK1 5RZ; T.-01324 621806.

Mullen, Veronica C., BA, DipEd, FRSA. Chairman, Scottish Marriage Care, 1995-2000; b. 20.6.46, Stirling; m., Ian M. Mullen; 2 s.; 1 d. Educ. St. Modan's High School, Stirling; Craiglockhart College of Education; Heriot-Watt University. Primary school teaching, 1966-71; partner in retail pharmacy business, 1984-96; partner in healthcare consultancy, since 1990; director, holiday property company, since 1999. Recreations: tennis; travel; golf. Address: Ardenlea, 11 Arnothill, Falkirk, FK1 5RZ; T.-01324 621806.

Muller, Professor Wolfgang Helmut Wilhelm Paul, DipPhys, Dr. rer.nat.habil. Professor of Mechanical Engineering, Heriot-Watt University, since 1999; b. 13.4.59, Wiesbaden, Germany. Educ. Gymnasium an der Willmstrasse, Delmenhorst; Technical University, Berlin. Scientific Collaborator, Technical University, Berlin, 1982-86; Development Engineer, Siemens, Munich, 1986-88; Research Assistant, Hermann-Fottinger Institut, 1988-89; Visiting Scholar, Stanford University, 1990; Guest Researcher, University of California at Santa Barbara, 1990-91; Senior Engineer, Department of Mechanical Engineering, Failure Analysis Assoc., San Francisco, 1991-93; Senior Lecturer, Universitat GH Paderborn, 1993-98; Reader of Mechanical Engineering, Heriot-Watt University, 1998-99. Publications: 100 scientific papers and three books. Recreations: opera; the arts. Address: (b.) Department of Mechanical and Chemical Engineering, Heriot-Watt University, Edinburgh, EH14 4AS; T.-0131-451 3680.

Mulligan, Margaret Mary, BA (Hons). MSP (Labour), Linlithgow, since 1999; Deputy Minister for Health and Community Care; Convenor, Education, Culture and Sport Committee, 1999-2001; b. 12.2.60, Liverpool; m., John; 2 s.; 1 d. Educ. Notre Dame High School; Manchester University. Retail and personnel management, 1981-86; Councillor, Edinburgh District Council, 1988-95 (Chair of Housing, 1992-97); Councillor, City of Edinburgh Council, 1995-99. Recreations: music; theatre; sport. Address: (b.) Scottish Parliament, Edinburgh EH99 1SP; T.-0131-348 5780.

Mumford, Colin John, BMedSci, DM, FRCP(E), DIMCRCS(Ed). Consultant Neurologist, Western General Hospital, Edinburgh and Royal Infirmary of Edinburgh, since 1996; b. 24.11.59, Liverpool. Educ. St. Margaret's High School, Liverpool; Nottingham University Medical School. Senior House Officer in Medicine, Newcastle upon Tyne teaching hospitals; Registrar in Neurology, Queen's Medical Centre, Nottingham and National Hospital for Neurology, London; Research Fellow, University of Cambridge; Senior Registrar in Neurology, Edinburgh teaching hospitals. Recreations: hillwalking; motorcycling. Address: (b.) Department of Clinical Neurosciences, Western General Hospital, Edinburgh EH4 2XU; T.-0131-537 1169.

Mundell, David Gordon, LLB (Hons), MBA, NP, WS. MSP (Conservative), South of Scotland, since 1999; b. 27.5.62, Dumfries; m., Lynda Carmichael; 2 s.; 1 d. Educ. Lockerbie Academy; Edinburgh University; Strathclyde University. Trainee Solicitor, Tindal Oatts, Glasgow, 1987-87; Solicitor, Maxwell Waddell, Glasgow, 1987-89; Commercial Lawyer, Biggart Baillie, Glasgow, 1989-91; Group Legal Adviser Scotland, BT, 1991-98; Head of National Affairs, BT Scotland, 1998-99. Recreations: family pursuits; travel. Address: (b.) Scottish Parliament, Edinburgh EH99 1SP; T.-0131-348 5635; e-mail: David.Mundell.msp@scottish.parliament.uk

Mundell, John Weir. Strategic Director – Commercial, East Dunbartonshire Council; b. Edinburgh; m., Karen; 3 s. Educ. Currie High School; Heriot-Watt University. Entered local government, 1974 (City of Edinburgh Corporation, then Lothian Regional Council); Head of Central Contracts, Central Regional Council, 1994-95. Recreations: swimming; karate; gymnastics (coach); farming. Address: (b.) Tom Johnston House, Civic Way, Kirkintilloch G66 4TJ; T.-0141-578 8420.

Munn, Professor Charles William, BA, PhD, FCIBS, FRSA. Chief Executive, Chartered Institute of Bankers in Scotland; Visiting Professor, University of Paisley, since 2000; b. 26.5.48, Glasgow; m., Andrea Cuthbertson; 1 s.; 1 d. Educ. Queen's Park Secondary School, Glasgow; Langside College; Strathclyde University; Glasgow University; Jordanhill College. British Linen Bank, 1964-67; Glasgow College of Technology, Department of Finance and Accounting, 1975-78; Lecturer in Economic History, Glasgow University, 1978-86, Senior Lecturer, 1986-88. Editor, The Scottish Banker; Member: Church of Scotland Church and Nation Committee, 1990-94, Board, Scottish Qualifications Authority, since 1997. Publications: Clydesdale Bank: the First 150 Years, 1988; The Scottish Provincial Banking Companies 1747-1864, 1981. Recreation: golf. Address: (b.) Drumsheugh House, 38b Drumsheugh Gardens, Edinburgh EH3 7SW.

Munn, Sir James, OBE, MA, DEd, LLD, DUniv; b. 27.7.20, Bridge of Allan; m., Muriel Jean Millar Moles; 1 d. (deceased). Educ. Stirling High School; Glasgow University. Indian Civil Service, 1941-48; various teaching appointments, Glasgow, 1949-57; Principal Teacher of Modern Languages, Falkirk High School, 1957-66 (Depute Rector, 1962-66); Principal Examiner in Modern Languages, Scottish Examination Board, 1965-66; Rector: Rutherglen Academy, 1966-70, Cathkin High School, 1970-83; Member, University Grants Committee, 1973-82; Member, Consultative Committee on the Curriculum, 1968-80, Chairman, 1980-87; Chairman, Committee to review the Structure of the Curriculum at S3 and S4, 1975-77; Member of Court, Strathclyde University, 1983-91; Manpower Services Commission/Training Commission Chairman for Scotland, 1984-88, Chairman, GB, 1987-88; University Commissioner, 1988-95. (h.) 4 Kincath Avenue, Rutherglen, Glasgow G73 4RP; T.-0141-634 4654.

Munn, Professor Pamela, MA, MLitt, CertEd. Professor of Curriculum Research, University of Edinburgh, since 1998; b. 31.3.49, Glasgow; m., Graham Hamilton Munn. Educ. Hermitage School, Helensburgh; Aberdeen University. Teacher of History, 1972-78; Research Fellow, Stirling University, 1979-84; Lecturer in Applied Research in Education, York University, 1984-86; Senior Research Officer, then Depute Director, Scottish Council for Research in Education, 1986-94; Professor of Curriculum Research, Moray House Institute of Education, 1994-98.

Member, Scottish Consultative Council on the Curriculum; Fellowship, CIDREE, 1996; SCRE Silver Medal, 1984. Publications: The Changing Face of Education 14-16; Education in Scotland: policy and practice from pre-school to secondary, 1997; Parents and Schools: customers, managers or partners?, 1993; Alternatives to Exclusion from School, 2000. Recreations: hill-walking; gardening; reading, especially crime fiction. Address: (b.) Graduate School, Faculty of Education, University of Edinburgh, Holyrood Road, Edinburgh EH8 8AQ; T.-0131-651 6175.

Munro, Alexander, MB, ChB, ChM, FRCS. Consultant General Surgeon, Raigmore Hospital, Inverness, since 1978; Clinical Senior Lecturer in Surgery, Aberdeen University, since 1978; b. 5.6.43, Ross and Cromarty; m., Maureen E. McCreath; 2 s.; 1 d. Educ. Fortrose Academy; Aberdeen University. Training in General Surgery at Registrar and Senior Registrar level, Aberdeen Hospitals, 1971-78; specialist training, St. Mark's Hospital, 1977. Recreation: gardening. Address: (h.) 23 Eriskay Road, Inverness; T.-Inverness 223804.

Munro, Professor Colin Roy, BA, LLB. Professor of Constitutional Law, Edinburgh University, since 1990 (Dean, Faculty of Law, 1992-94); b. 17.5.49, Aberdeen; m., Ruth Elizabeth Pratt; 1 s.; 1 d. Educ. Aberdeen Grammar School; Aberdeen University. Lecturer in Law, Birmingham University, 1971-72, Durham University, 1972-80; Senior Lecturer in Law, then Reader in Law, Essex University, 1980-85; Professor of Law, Manchester University, 1985-90; Chief Examiner, London University LLB (External) Degree, 1991-97; Member, Consultative Council, British Board of Film Classification, since 2000. Publications: Television, Censorship and the Law; Studies in Constitutional Law; Devolution and the Scotland Bill (Co-Author); The Scotland Act 1998 (Co-Author). Recreations: sport; cinema and theatre; real ale. Address: (b.) Faculty of Law, Old College, South Bridge, Edinburgh EH8 9YL; T.-0131-650 2047.

Munro, David Mackenzie, BSc, PhD, FRGS, FRSA, FSAScot. Director and Secretary, Royal Scottish Geographical Society, since 1996; Member, Council, National Trust for Scotland; Chairman, Permanent Committee on Geographical Names for British Official Use; Chairman, UK Division of United Nations Group of Experts on Geographical Names; b. 28.5.50, Glasgow. Educ. Daniel Stewart's College; Edinburgh Academy; Edinburgh University. Research Associate, then Research Fellow, Edinburgh University, 1979-96; Leader/Co Leader, Edinburgh University expeditions to Central America, 1981, 1986, 1988, 1991. Chairman, Kinross-shire Civic Trust; Chairman, Michael Bruce Trust; Honorary President, Jules Verne Film Festival, Paris, 2001. Publications: Chambers World Gazetteer (Editor); Oxford Dictionary of the World (Editor); Gazetteer of the Baltic States; A World Record of Major Conflict Areas; Loch Leven and the River Leven – a Landscape Transformed; numerous articles and reports on land use in Central America. Recreations: walking; travel; exploring landscapes. Address: (b.) 40 George Street, Glasgow G1 1QE; T.-0141-552 3330.

Munro, Rev. David Peacock, MA, BD, STM. Minister, Bearsden North Church, 1967-96; Clerk, Presbytery of Dumbarton, since 1986; b. 7.9.29, Paisley; m., Jessie Scott McPherson; 3 d. Educ. Paisley Grammar School; Glasgow University; Union Theological Seminary, New York. Minister, Aberluthnott Parish Church, 1953-56, Castlehill Church, Ayr, 1956-67. Vice-Convener, General Assembly Council, 1988-90, Convener, 1990-95; Moderator, Dumbarton Presbytery, 1978-79; Chairman, General Assembly Board of Education, 1974-79; Convener, General Assembly Education Committee, 1981-85. Recreations: golf; gardening. Address: (h.) 14 Birch Road, Killearn, Glasgow G63 9SQ; T.-01360 550098.

Munro, Donnie, DA. Former Guitarist and Lead Singer, Runrig; b. Skye; m.; 3 children. Former Art Teacher, Inverness and Edinburgh; Rector, Edinburgh University, 1991-94; contested (Labour) Ross, Skye and Inverness West, 1997. Dr. HC, Edinburgh, 1994.

Munro, Graeme Neil, MA. Director and Chief Executive, Historic Scotland, since 1991; b. 28.8.44, Edinburgh; m., Nicola Susan Wells (qv); 1 s.; 1 d. Educ. Daniel Stewart's College, Edinburgh; St. Andrews University. Assistant Principal, Scottish Development Department, 1968-72; Principal, Scottish Development Department and Scottish Home and Health Department, 1972-79; Assistant Secretary, Department of Agriculture and Fisheries for Scotland, SHHD, and Central Services, 1979-90; Director, Historic Buildings and Monuments, Scottish Office Environment Department, 1990-91. Recreations: walking; reading; local history; gardening; swimming. Address: (b.) Longmore House, Salisbury Place, Edinburgh EH9 1SH; T.-0131-668 8696.

Munro of Foulis, Hector William, MRICS. 31st Chief of Clan Munro; b. 20.2.50; m., Sarah Duckworth; 1 s.; 2 d. Educ. Oratory School; Royal Agricultural College, Cirencester. Farmer and Landowner. Address: (h.) Foulis Castle, Evanton, Ross-shire.

Munro, Jack, DPE. Chief Executive, Edinburgh and Lothians Tourist Board, since 1997; b. 18.9.49, Cromarty; m., Lynn Prentice Roberts. Educ. Fortrose Academy; Jordanhill College of Education. Assistant Director of Tourism and Recreation, North East Fife District Council, 1975-82; Conference Manager, Inverness District Council, 1984-86; Director, Greater Glasgow Convention Bureau, 1986-90; Director, Edinburgh Convention Bureau, 1990-93. Chief Executive, Greater Glasgow Tourist Board, 1993-96; Chief Executive, Greater Glasgow and Clyde Valley Tourist Board, 1996-97. Chairman, British Association of Conference Towns, 1992-93; Member, Board of Directors, International Association of Convention and Visitor Bureaux (Washington, DC). Recreations: rugby; golf; Scottish history; gardening. Address: (b.) 4 Rothesay Terrace, Edinburgh EH3 7RY; T.-0131-473 3600.

Munro, Jean Mary, BA (Hons), PhD. Chairman, Council, Scottish History Society, 1989-93; b. 2.12.23; m., Robert William Munro. Educ. London University; Edinburgh University. WRNS, 1944-47; freelance historical researcher; Member, Council, National Trust for Scotland, 1964-69 and 1987-92 (Executive, 1968-80); Chairman, Council, Scottish Genealogy Society, 1983-86 (Vice-President, since 1987); Chairman, Council, Scottish Local History Forum, 1984-88. Publications (as Jean Dunlop): the British Fisheries Society; the Clan Chisholm; the Clan Mackenzie; the Clan Gordon; the Scotts; the Clan Mackintosh; (with R.W. Munro): Tain through the Centuries; The Scrimgeours; The Acts of the Lords of the Isles. Recreations: reading; walking. Address: (h.) 15a Mansionhouse Road, Edinburgh EH9 1TZ; T.-0131-667 4601.

Munro, John Farquhar. MSP (Liberal Democrat), Ross, Skye and Inverness West, since 1999; Liberal Democrat Spokesperson for Gaelic and Culture; b. 26.8.34; m. Cecilia Robertson; 1 s.; 1 d. Educ. Plockton High School; Merchant Marine College, Sharpness. Former: crofter, manager in contracting company, merchant marine officer; ran own civil engineering company; Ross County Councillor, 1966-74; Skye and Lochalsh District Councillor, 1974-96 (Convener, 1984-95); Highland Regional Councillor, 1978-82 (Chair of Gaelic); Highland Unitary Councillor, 1995-99 (Leader, Liberal Democrats Group, Chair of Roads and Transport, Chair, Rail Network Partnership); Scottish Parliament: Member, Rural Affairs Committee, 1999-2000, Equal Opportunities Committee, 1999-2000; Member, Transport Committee, since 2001, Member, Petitions

1970-79; Lord Advocate, 1974-79. Assessor, Edinburgh University Court, 1981-93 (Vice-Chairman, 1990-93). Recreations: sailing; astronomy. Address: (h.) 1 Inverleith Grove, Edinburgh EH3 5PB; T.-0131-551 5330.

Murray, Athol Laverick, PhD, MA, LLB, FRHistS, FSA Scot. Chairman, Scottish Records Association, 1997-2000; Vice-President, Society of Antiquaries of Scotland, 1989-92; Keeper of the Records of Scotland, 1985-90; b. 8.11.30, Tynemouth; m., Irene Joyce Cairns; 1 s.; 1 d. Educ. Lancaster Royal Grammar School; Jesus College, Cambridge; Edinburgh University. Research Assistant, Foreign Office, 1953; Scottish Record Office: Assistant Keeper, 1953-83, Deputy Keeper, 1983-84. Recreations: historical research; bowling. Address: (h.) 33 Inverleith Gardens, Edinburgh EH3 5PR; T.-0131-552 4465; e-mail: atholmurray@hotmail.com

Murray, (Bridget) Jane, BA (Oxon), MA, PhD. Commissioner, Royal Commission on the Ancient and Historical Monuments of Scotland, since 1999; b. 25.7.37, Tunbridge Wells; m., John Murray, QC (Lord Dervaird); 3 s. Educ. Royal Tunbridge Wells County Grammar School for Girls; St Hugh's College, Oxford; Edinburgh University. Involved in various archaeological projects and organisations. Recreations: gardening; walking; architecture. Address: (h.) 4 Moray Place, Edinburgh EH3 6DS; T.-0131-225 1881.

Murray, David Edward. Chairman, Murray International Holdings; Chairman, The Rangers Football Club plc; Founder, David Murray Foundation, 1997; b. 14.10.51, Ayr; m., Louise (deceased); 2 s. Educ. Fettes College; Broughton High School. Young Scottish Business Man of the Year, 1984; Hon. Doctorate, Heriot-Watt University, 1986; Chairman, UK 2000 (Scotland), 1987; Governor, Clifton Hall School, 1987. Recreations: sports sponsorship; collecting wine. Address: (b.) 9 Charlotte Square, Edinburgh EH2 4DR.

Murray, Elaine Kildare, BSc (Hons), PhD. MSP (Labour), Dumfries since 1999; Deputy Minister for Tourism, Culture and Sport, since 2001; b. 22.12.54, Hitchin, Herts; m., Jeff Leaver; 2 s.; 1 d. Educ. Mary Erskine School, Edinburgh; Edinburgh University; Cambridge University. Postdoctoral Research Fellow: Cavendish Laboratory, Cambridge, Royal Free Hospital, London; Senior Scientific Officer, Institute of Food Research, Reading; Associate Lecturer, Open University in Scotland. Recreations: family activities; reading; horseriding; keyboard. Address: (h.) 22 Loch Road, Dumfries; T.-01387 279205; Constituency Office, 5 Friars' Vennel, Dumfries DG1 2RQ; T.-01387 279205; e-mail: elaine.murray.msp@scottish.parliament.uk

Murray, Gordon Lindsay Kevan. Partner, Murrays WS, Solicitors; Secretary, Royal Scottish National Orchestra Society Ltd.; Director, 1990-93, Secretary and Treasurer, since 1985, Royal Scottish National Orchestra Endowment Trust; b. 23.5.53, Glasgow; m., Susan Patricia; 1 s.; 3 d. Educ. Lenzie Academy; Edinburgh University. Address: (b.) 7A Melville Crescent, Edinburgh EH3 7NA; T.-0131-625 6625; e-mail: glkm@murraysws.co.uk

Murray, Gregor Cumming, MA, MBA. Executive Director, Midlothian Enterprise Trust, since 1992; Chief Executive, Midlothian Chamber of Commerce; b. 16.4.57, Edinburgh; m., Barbara Paula Christian Parham; 1 s.; 2 d. Educ. George Watson's College, Edinburgh; Trinity College, Oxford; Edinburgh University Management School. Bank of Scotland; Investors in Industry; Leith Enterprise Trust. Recreations: fly fishing; hill-walking. Address: (b.) 25 Eskbank Road, Dalkeith EH22 1HJ; T.-0131-654 1234; e-mail: gm@met.org.uk

Murray, Iain McInnes, BSc (Hons), MEd (Hons). Head Teacher, Lanark Grammar School, since 1997; b. 1.3.46, Glasgow; m., Marilyn; 1 s. Educ. Allan Glen's High School; Glasgow University. Teacher of Physics, Paisley Grammar School, 1969-72; Assistant Principal Teacher, Science, Castlehead High School, Paisley, 1972-73; Principal Teacher of Physics, Caldervale High School, Airdrie, 1973-81; Assistant Head Teacher, Vale of Leven Academy, Alexandria, 1981-86; Depute Head Teacher, Braidfield High School, Clydebank, 1986-89; Head Teacher, Wishaw High School, 1989-92; seconded to work with school boards, 1992-94; Head Teacher, Arran High School, 1994-97. Recreations: bridge; golf. Address: (b.) Albany Drive, Lanark ML11 9AQ; T.-01555 662471; e-mail: headteacher@lanark.s-lanark.sch.uk

Murray, Rt. Rev. Ian, BA (Hons). Bishop of Argyll and The Isles, since 1999; b. 15.12.32, Lennoxtown. Educ. St. Ninian's High School, Kirkintilloch; St. Mary's College, Aberdeen; Royal Scots College, Valladolid; Open University. Ordained Priest, 1956; served: St. Mary's Cathedral, Edinburgh, St. Kenneth's Lochore, St. Columba's, Edinburgh; Vice-Rector, Royal Scots College, Valladolid, 1963-70; RC Chaplain, Stirling University, 1970-78; Parish Priest, St. Bride's Cowdenbeath, then St. Ninian's, Edinburgh; Rector, Royal Scots College, Valladolid, 1987; Parish Priest, Our Lady and St. Andrew's, Galashiels, 1994-96; appointed Parish Priest, St. Francis Xavier's, Falkirk, and Vicar-General, Archdiocese of St. Andrews and Edinburgh, 1996. Address: Bishop's House, Esplanade, Oban PA34 5AB.

Murray, Professor Isobel (Mary), MA, PhD. Writer and Critic; Professor in English, Aberdeen University; Vice President, Association of Scottish Literary Studies; Associate Editor, New Dictionary of National Biography; b. 14.2.39, Alloa; m., Bob Tait. Educ. Dollar Academy; Edinburgh University. Assistant Lecturer, Lecturer, Senior Lecturer, Reader, Department of English, Aberdeen University; books include several editions of Oscar Wilde (most recently Oscar Wilde: The Major Works, 2000), introductions to new editions of J. MacDougall Hay's Gillespie, Ian MacPherson's Shepherds' Calendar, Robin Jenkins' Guests of War, Iain Crichton Smith's Consider the Lilies, George MacKay Brown's Magnus, and Jessie Kesson's Where the Apple Ripens; edited, Beyond This Limit: Selected Shorter Fiction of Naomi Mitchison; A Girl Must Live: stories and poems by Naomi Mitchison; Ten Modern Scottish Novels (with Bob Tait), 1984; Scottish Writers Talking, 1996; Somewhere Beyond: A Jessie Kesson Companion; published Jessie Kesson: Writing Her Life, 2000 (National Library of Scotland/Saltire Society Research Book of the Year). Address: (b.) Department of English, King's College, Old Aberdeen, Aberdeen AB24 2UB; T.-Aberdeen 272644.

Murray, Professor James, BSc, ARTC, CEng, FIMechE, FIEE, FIM. Vice Principal, Napier University, 1992-95, now Emeritus Professor; b. 25.7.30, Glasgow; m., Emily Lamb Beveridge (deceased); 1 s.; 1 d. Educ. Allan Glen's School, Glasgow; Glasgow University. Development Engineer, Ferranti Ltd., Edinburgh, 1952-62; Lecturer, Department of Mechanical Engineering, Heriot-Watt University, 1962-67; Head, Department of Production Engineering, Napier College, 1967-72; Head, Department of Industrial Studies, 1972-74; Assistant Principal and Dean, Faculty of Professional Studies, 1974-82; Assistant Principal/Dean, Faculty of Technology, 1982-92. Former Member, Council: SCOTEC, EITB, IProdE; Past Chairman, IProdE, Edinburgh Section and Scotland Region; Past Chairman: CEI Scotland, CNAA Engineering Board and Research Committee; former Member, Transport Tribunal, Scotland; former Governor, Moray House College of Education; former Member of Convocation, Heriot-Watt University; Trustee, National Museums of Scotland, since 1997; Elder, Church of Scotland, since 1957; former

Chairman, Edinburgh Branch, Glasgow Graduates Association; President, Allan Glen's School Club, 1998-99. Recreations: watching rugby; visiting museums; golf; gardening; studying light rail transport systems; opera. Address: (h.) 40 Elliot Road, Edinburgh EH14 1DZ.

Murray, John, BA (Hons), DipED, MEd. Headteacher, Harlaw Academy, since 1993; b. 2.2.52, Irvine; m., Margaret McLaughlin; 2 s.; 1 d. Educ. St. Michael's Academy, Kilwinning; Strathclyde University; Glasgow University; Stirling University. Teacher, Ardrossan Academy, 1975-78; Principal Teacher, St. Mungo's, Alloa, 1978-81; Principal Teacher, Lasswade High School, 1981-86; Assistant Rector, Woodmill High School, 1986-89; Depute Rector, Kirkcaldy High School, 1989-93. Director, Instant Neighbour, Aberdeen. Recreations: family; football; golf. Address: (b.) 18 Albyn Place, Aberdeen AB10 1RG; T.-01224 589251.

Murray, Rev. John James, DipTH. Minister, Free Church of Scotland (Continuing), Edinburgh; b. 11.9.34, Dornoch; m., Cynthia MacPhee; 1 s.; 1 d. Educ. Dornoch Academy; Edinburgh University; Free Church College. Caledonian Insurance Company, 1955-59; Assistant Editor, Banner of Truth Trust, 1960-73; Minister, Free High Church, Oban, 1978-89; Minister, St. Columba's Free Church, Edinburgh, 1989-2000, Edinburgh Free Church (Continuing), since 2000. Publication: Behind a Frowning Providence. Address: (h.) 10 Esslemont Road, Edinburgh EH16 5PX; T.-0131-667 4730; e-mail: murraystcol@compuserve.com

Murray, Leonard G., KHS, KSJ, JP, BL, SSC. Retired solicitor; formerly Senior Partner, latterly Consultant, Levy & McRae, Solicitors, Glasgow; b. 16.8.33. Educ. St. Mungo's Academy, Glasgow; Glasgow University. After-dinner speaker; Wag of the Year, 2000; part-time Chairman, Employment Tribunals. Recreations: golf; gardening. Address: (h.) 23 Courthill, Bearsden, Glasgow G61 3SN.

Murray, Morris James, BSc, CEng, FIStructE, FICE. Director, Babtie Group, since 1989; Commissioner, Royal Fine Art Commission for Scotland; b. 15.2.45, Carlisle; m., Helen; 1 s.; 2 d. Educ. Annan Academy; Glasgow University. Joined Babtie after graduation, 1967; worked in various capacities in the firm, including the design of major bridge works and marine projects; appointed Managing Director of the group's Engineering Business Centre, 1998. Recreation: running. Address: (b.) 95 Bothwell Street, Glasgow G2 7HX; T.-0141-204 2511.

Murray, Professor Noreen Elizabeth, PhD, FRS, FRSE. Professor, Institute of Cell and Molecular Biology, Edinburgh University; b. 26.2.35, Burnley; m., Kenneth Murray. Educ. Lancaster Girls' Grammar School; King's College, London; Birmingham University. Research Associate, Department of Biological Sciences, Stanford University, 1960-64; Research Fellow, Botany School, Cambridge, 1964-67; Edinburgh University: Member, MRC Molecular Genetics Unit, Department of Molecular Biology, 1968-74, Lecturer, then Senior Lecturer, Department of Molecular Biology, 1974-80; Group Leader, European Molecular Biology Laboratory, Heidelberg, 1980-82; rejoined Edinburgh University as Reader, 1982. Recreation: gardening. Address: (b.) Institute of Cell and Molecular Biology, Edinburgh University, Mayfield Road, Edinburgh EH9 3JR; T.-0131-650 5374.

Murray, Norman Loch, BA, CA, FRSA. Chairman: British Linen Advisers Ltd., The AiM VCT PLC, Friends Ivory & Sime, Private Equity PLC Advisory Committee; Director: Murray tmt PLC, Penta Capital Partners Holdings Ltd., Glasgow Income Trust PLC, Cairn Energy PLC, Edinburgh Crystal Glass Company Ltd., Luxfer Holdings PLC; b. 17.3.48, Kilmarnock; m., Pamela Anne Low; 2 s. Educ. George Watson's College; Heriot-Watt University; Harvard University Graduate School of Business Administration. Scottish & Newcastle Breweries PLC, 1971-73; Arthur Young, 1973-76; Peat Marwick Mitchell & Co. (Hong Kong), 1977-80; Royal Bank of Scotland PLC, 1980-85; Director, Charterhouse Development Capital Ltd., 1985-89; Chairman, Morgan Grenfell Private Equity Ltd.; Director, Morgan Grenfell & Co. Ltd.; Director, Morgan Grenfell Asset Management Ltd., 1989-98. Former directorships (non-executive): Bristow Helicopter Group Limited, Eurodollar (Holdings) Ltd., Taunton Cider plc; Institute of Chartered Accountants of Scotland: Member of Council, 1992-98, Convener, Finance and General Purposes Committee, 1997-98; Member, Research Committee, 1986-91; Chairman, Lothian Borders and Central Area Committee, 1992-95; Chairman, British Venture Capital Association, 1997-98, of its Legal and Technical Committee, 1992-96; Deputy Chairman, Governing Council and Chairman, Finance Committee, George Watson's College; Governor, St. Columba's Hospice. Publication: Making Corporate Reports Valuable (Co-Author), 1988. Recreations: squash; golf; climbing; travel. Address: (h.) Ettrick, 8 Pentland Avenue, Edinburgh EH13 0HZ.

Murray, Robert John, MSc, MCIBS, JP. Leader, Angus Council, since 1998 (Deputy Leader, 1995-98); Board Member, NOSWA, since 1999; b. 3.2.51, Montrose; 1 s.; 1 d. Educ. Montrose Academy; University of Abertay, Dundee. Member, Tayside Regional Council, 1994-96; Convenor, Personnel and Property Committee, Angus Council, 1995-98; Vice Convenor: Tayside Valuation Joint Board, 1995-99, Tayside Contracts Joint Committee, since 1995. Recreations: cycling; walking. Address: (h.) 8 Beechgrove, Monifieth DD5 4TE.

Murray, Roderick Macpherson, BA (Hons). Director, An Lanntair, since 1985; b. 31.3.56, Coll, Isle of Lewis. Educ. Back Junior Secondary School; Nicolson Institute, Stornoway; Glasgow School of Art. Recreations: cycling; chess; arts. Address: (b.) An Lanntair, Town Hall, South Beach, Stornoway, Isle of Lewis; T.-01851 703307; e-mail: lanntair@sol.co.uk

Murray, Professor T. Stuart, MD, PhD, FRCGP, FRCPEdin, FRCPGlas. West of Scotland Director of Postgraduate General Practice Education, since 1985; Professor of General Practice, University of Glasgow, since 1992; b. 22.7.43, Muirkirk, Ayrshire; m., Anne Smith; 1 s.; 2 d. Educ. Muirkirk Junior Secondary School; Cumnock Academy; University of Glasgow. Early training in cardiology; entered general practice, 1971; Senior Lecturer in General Practice, 1977. Publication: Modified Essay Questions for the MRCGP Examination; Guide to Postgraduate Medical Education (Co-author). Recreations: travel; reading; sport. Address: (b.) 1 Horselethill Road, Glasgow G12 9LX; T.-0141-330 5276.

Murray, William James Greig, MBBS, MS, FRCS(Ed), FRCS(Eng). Consultant Surgeon, Perth Royal Infirmary, since 1990 (and Associate Medical Director, Perth Royal Infirmary); b. 19.10.51, Aberdeen; m., Pamela Jane; 2 s. 2 d. Educ. Robert Gordon's College, Aberdeen; Dulwich College Preparatory School; Westminster School; Middlesex Hospital Medical School, London University. House Surgeon, Middlesex Hospital, 1975; Registrar, Surgery/Urology, King's College Hospital, 1982-87; Senior Registrar, University College Hospital, 1987-90. Recreations: golf; gardening. Address: (b.) Perth Infirmary, Perth PH1 1NX; T.-01738 623311.

Murray-Smith, Professor David James, MSc, PhD, CEng, FIEE, MInstMC. Professor of Engineering Systems and Control, Glasgow University; b. 20.10.41, Aberdeen; m., Effie Smith; 2 s. Educ. Aberdeen Grammar School; Aberdeen University; Glasgow University. Engineer, Inertial Systems Department, Ferranti Ltd., Edinburgh, 1964-65; Glasgow University: Assistant, Department of Electrical Engineering, 1965-67, Lecturer, 1967-77, Senior

Lecturer, 1977-83, Reader, 1983-85; Dean, Faculty of Engineering, 1997-2001. Past Chairman, United Kingdom Simulation Council. Recreations: hill-walking; photography; strong interest in railways. Address: (b.) Department of Electronics and Electrical Engineering, Glasgow University, Glasgow G12 8QQ; T.-0141-330 5222.

Muscatelli, Professor Vito Antonio, MA (Hons), PhD, FRSA. Daniel Jack Professor of Political Economy, Department of Economics, Glasgow University, since 1992; Dean, Faculty of Social Sciences; b. 1.1.62, Bari, Italy; m., Elaine Flood; 1 s.; 1 d. Educ. High School of Glasgow; Glasgow University. Lecturer, Senior Lecturer, Glasgow University, 1984-92; Visiting Professor: University of Parma (Italy), 1989, Catholic University, Milan, 1991, 1997, University of Bari (Italy), since 1995; Editor, Scottish Journal of Political Economy, since 1989; Member, Council, Scottish Economic Society, since 1989; Member, Editorial Advisory Board, International Review of Economics and Business, since 1995. Hon. Fellow, Societa Italiana Degli Economisti, 1996; Member, Advisory Panel of Economic Consultants to the Secretary of State for Scotland, 1998-99. Publications: Macroeconomic Theory and Stabilisation Policy (Co-author), 1988; Economic and Political Institutions in Economic Policy (Editor of volume), 1996; articles in journals. Recreations: music; literature; football; strategic games. Address: (b.) Dean's Office, Adam Smith Building, University of Glasgow, Glasgow G12 8RT; T.-0141-330 6363/6090; e-mail: V.A.Muscatelli@socsci.gla.ac.uk

Musson, John Nicholas Whitaker, MA (Oxon). Vice Chairman, Mercy Corps Scotland, since 2000; Governor, Clifton College, Bristol, since 1989; b. 2.10.27; m., Ann Preist; 1 s.; 3 d. Educ. Clifton College; Brasenose College, Oxford. Served as Guardsman and Lt., Lancashire Fusiliers, 1945-48; HM Colonial Administrative Service (later Overseas Civil Service) 1951-59 (District Officer, N. Nigeria); British Petroleum Co., London, 1959-61; Assistant Master and Housemaster, Canford School, Dorset, 1961-72; Warden, Glenalmond College, 1972-87; Scottish Division Chairman, Headmasters' Conference, 1981-83; Scottish Director, Independent Schools Careers Organisation, 1987-93; Governor, George Watson's College, Edinburgh, 1989-98; Director and Trustee, Scottish European Aid and Mercy Corps Europe, 1996-2000; Country Director, Bosnia/Herzegovina, for Mercy Corps/Scottish European Aid, 1998-99. Recreations: travel; art; Egyptology. Address: (h.) 47 Spylaw Road, Edinburgh EH10 5BP; T.-0131-337 0089.

Myles, David Fairlie, CBE. Hill Farmer; Member, Angus District Council, 1984-96; Chairman, Dairy Produce Quota Tribunal for Scotland, since 1984; Member, Potato Marketing Board, 1988-97; b. 30.5.25, Cortachy, Kirriemuir; m., Janet I. Gall; 2 s.; 2 d. Educ. Brechin High School. Auctioneer's clerk, 1941-43; Royal Marines, 1943-46; Tenant Hill Farmer, since 1946; Director of auction company, 1963-81; Member, Transport Users Consultative Committee for Scotland, 1973-79; Council Member, NFU of Scotland, 1970-79 (Convener, Organisation and Publicity Committee, 1976-79); Member, Meat Promotion Executive, MLC, 1975-79; Chairman, North Angus and Mearns Constituency Conservative Party, 1971-74; MP (Conservative), Banff, 1979-83; Joint Secretary, Backbench Conservative Agriculture Committee, 1979-83; Secretary, Backbench Conservative European Committee, 1980-83; Member: Select Committee on Agriculture and Select Committee on European Legislation, 1979-83, North of Scotland Hydro-Electric Board, 1985-89, Angus Tourist Board, 1984-92; Dean, Guildry of Brechin, 1993-94; Lord President, Court of Deans of Scotland, 1995-96; Session Clerk, Edzell-Lethnot Parish Church, since 1996; Elder, Edzell-Lethnot Parish Church. Recreations: curling; traditional Scottish fiddle music; works of Robert Burns. Address: (h.) The Gorse, Dunlappie Road, Edzell, Brechin DD9 7UB; T.-01356 648207.

N

Nagl, Hazel Anna, DA, RSW. Artist/Painter (landscapes and still life); b. 2.11.53, Glasgow; m., James Geoffrey Keanie; 1 d. Educ. North Kelvinside Senior Secondary School; Glasgow School of Art. Exhibits on a regular basis throughout Scotland; RSW, 1988; PAI, 1995; SAAC 1994; RGI Stone Prize, 1987 and 1990; RGI Mackinlay Award, 1994; RGI Eastwood Publications Award, 1994; SAAC Prize, 1994; PAI Prize 1996 and 1998; 1st Prize, Laing Competition, 1999; RGI Prize, 2000. Address: (h.) Lawmarnock House, Troon Drive, Bridge of Weir PA11 3HF.

Nairn, Nicholas Cameron Abell. Chef/Director, Nairns Restaurant, Glasgow, since 1997; Director, Taste of Scotland; b. 12.1.59, Stirling. Educ. McLaren High School, Callander. Merchant Navy, 1976-83. Presenter: Wild Harvest, BBC2, 1996, Ready Steady Cook, BBC2, since 1996, Celebrity Ready Steady Cook, Who'll Do the Pudding, BBC1, 1996-97, Wild Harvest Two, BBC2, 1997, Island Harvest, BBC2, 1998; Chef/Director, Braeval Restaurant, Aberfoyle, 1986-96; Hon. President, Drambuie Scottish Chefs National Cookery Centre, 1997-99; Chef/Consultant, Tesco; Winner, Scottish Field/Charles Heidsieck Scottish Restaurant of the Year, 1990; Good Food Guide County Restaurant of the Year, 1991; Macallan/Decanter Scottish Restaurant of the Year, 1992; Scottish Field/Bowmore Restaurant of the Year, 1992; STB Thistle Award for Contribution to Tourism through the Media; Member, Advisory Board, Scottish Chefs Association; Lifetime Achievement Award, SCA; Hon. President, Chefs' School; Member, Masterchefs of GB. Recreations: cycling; wind-surfing; wine; eating out; travel; Scottish art; fly fishing. Address: (b.) 13 Woodside Crescent, Glasgow G3 7UP; T.-0141-353 0707; e-mail: info@nairns.co.uk

Nairn, Tom. Sociologist; b. 1932, Freuchie, Fife. Educ. Edinburgh University; Oxford University. Taught social philosophy, Birmingham University, and sociology, Hornsey College of Art; Editor, Bulletin of Scottish Politics, 1981-82; Columnist, The Scotsman. Publications: The Left Against Europe; The Break-Up of Britain?; The Enchanted Glass: Britain and its Monarchy.

Nanjiani, Shereen, MA (Hons). Journalist, Scottish Television, since 1983; b. 4.10.61, Elderslie. Educ. John Neilson High School, Paisley; Glasgow University. Joined STV as a trainee journalist, 1983; moved to reporting two years later; became presenter of Scotland Today, 1985; presented General Election programme, 1997; presented, Secret Scotland documentary series. Address: (b.) Scottish Television, Cowcaddens, Glasgow, G2 3PR.

Napier, 14th Lord, and Ettrick, 5th Baron (Francis Nigel Napier), KCVO, DL. Treasurer to Princess Margaret, Countess of Snowdon, 1998-2002 (Private Secretary, Comptroller and Equerry, 1973-98); b. 5.12.30; m.; 2 s.; 2 d. Succeeded to title, 1987.

Nash, Professor Andrew Samuel, BVMS, PhD, CBiol, FIBiol, DipECVIM, MRCVS. Professor of Small Animal Medicine, Division of Small Animal Clinical Studies, Department of Veterinary Clinical Studies, Glasgow University Veterinary School, since 1992, Director of the Veterinary Hospital, 1993-96, Vice-Dean for Student Affairs, 1995-99, Director, Student Support Services, since 1999, Senate Assessor, University Court, since 1999; Royal College of Veterinary Surgeons Recognised Specialist in Small Animal Medicine, since 1993; b. 1.8.44, Birmingham; m., Rosemary Truscott Hamilton; 1 s.; 1 d.

Educ. Judd School, Tonbridge; Glasgow University. General veterinary practice, Ilfracombe, 1967-72; House Physician, Glasgow University Veterinary School, 1973-75, then Lecturer/Senior Lecturer, 1975-92. Silver Medal in Veterinary Clinical Medicine, 1967; RSPCA Humane Award, 1970; Member, Board of Directors, Glasgow Dog and Cat Home, 1981-95; Hon. President, Scottish Cat Club, 1990-99; Member, Glasgow Presbytery, 1991-94; President, European Society of Veterinary Nephrology and Urology, 1992-94; Member, Board of Directors, Scottish Society for the Prevention of Cruelty to Animals, since 1995; author of more than 100 papers, articles, book chapters. Recreations: music; gardening; DIY; church work (church organist). Address: (b.) University of Glasgow Veterinary School, Bearsden Road, Glasgow G61 1QH; T.-0141-330 5700; e-mail: A.Nash@vet.gla.ac.uk

Nash, Professor Anthony Aubrey, BSc, MSc, PhD, FMedSci. Professor of Veterinary Pathology, Edinburgh University, since 1994; b. 6.3.49, Coalville; m., Marion Ellen Bazeley; 4 d. Educ. Nenbridge Secondary Modern School; Queen Elizabeth College, London University. Lecturer, Department of Pathology, Cambridge University, 1984; Visiting Investigator, Scripps Research Institute, La Jolla, USA, 1989; Professor and Head, Department of Veterinary Pathology, Edinburgh University, since 1994. Eleanor Roosevelt Cancer Fellowship, 1989-90. Recreations: family; gardening; football. Address: (b.) Veterinary Pathology, Summerhall, Edinburgh EH9 1QH; T.-0131-650 6164.

Nash, Victoria Jane, BSc, PhD. Chief Executive, East Dunbartonshire Council, since 1999; b. 17.6.57, Northampton; m., Robin Campbell; 2 step d. Educ. Cheadle Hulme School; Oxford Polytechnic; Stirling University. Senior Research Officer, Scottish Office Education Department, 1982-83; Project Co-ordinator, Scottish Council for Educational Technology, 1983-85; Policy Analyst, then Assistant Chief Executive, then Chief Executive, Fife Regional Council, 1985-96; Director, Scottish Water and Sewerage Customers Council, 1996-99. Recreations: singing; swimming; cats. Address: (b.) Tom Johnston House, Civic Way, Kirkintilloch, Glasgow G66 4TJ; T.-0141-578 8000; e-mail: vicki.nash@eastdunbarton.gov.uk

Naumann, Laurie M. Freelance Social Policy Adviser; Director, Scottish Council for Single Homeless, 1978-99; b. 1943, Saffron Walden; m., Barbara; 2 s.; 3 d. Educ. Edinburgh, Gloucester and Nuremberg Rudolf Steiner; Leicester University. Furniture maker, Gloucestershire; Probation and After Care Officer, Leeds; Social Worker, Edinburgh; Council of Europe Social Fellowship to Finland to study services for the drunken offender, 1976; jointly won Rosemary Delbridge Memorial Trophy for influencing Parliament to legislate, 1983; on secondment to Scottish Office Social Work Services Inspectorate, 1992-95; Board Member: Kingdom and Old Town Housing Associations, Garvald Centre, Edinburgh, Scottish Refugee Council, Refugee Survival Trust; Reviewer, Scottish Health Advisory Service; Member, Social Security Advisory Committee; Trustee, Unemployed Voluntary Action Fund; Chair: Highland Housing and Community Care Trust, Consultation and Involvement Trust Scotland. Recreations: travel; reading; walking; woodwork. Address: (h.) St. Ann's, Alexander III Street, Kinghorn, Fife KY3 9SD; T.-01592 890346.

Naylor, Brian, BSc, MPhil, FRSA. Director, Scottish Qualifications Authority, since 2001; b. 10.2.49, Altrincham; m., 1, Mary Halley (deceased); 2 s.; 2, Moira Hillen; 2 step s. Educ. Lymm Grammar School; Leicester University; Edinburgh University. Scottish Office: graduate trainee, 1976-82; Principal, 1982-89; Assistant Secretary, 1989-95; Director (Properties in Care), Historic Scotland, 1995-2001. Recreations: fishing; theatre; swimming;

walking. Address: (b.) Hanover House, 24 Douglas Street, Glasgow G2 7NQ; T.-0141-242 2055; e-mail: brian.naylor@sqa.org.uk

Naylor, (Charles) John, OBE, MA, CIMgt, FRSA. Secretary and Treasurer, Carnegie United Kingdom Trust, since 1993; b. 17.8.43, Newcastle upon Tyne; m., Margery Thomson; 2 s. Educ. Royal Grammar School, Newcastle upon Tyne; Clare College, Cambridge University. Director, YMCA National Centre, Lakeside, Cumbria, 1975-80; National Council of YMCAs: Deputy Secretary, 1980-82, National Secretary, 1982-93. Member and Chairman, YMCA European and World Committees, 1976-92; Chair, Association of Heads of Outdoor Education Centres, 1979-80; Chair, MSC and DES Working Party on Residential Experience and Unemployment, 1980-81; Member, National Advisory Council for Youth Service, 1985-88; Vice-Chairman, National Council for Voluntary Youth Services, 1985-88; Founding Convener, Scottish Grant-making Trusts' Group, 1994-97; Chairman, Brathay Exploration Group, since 1995; Group Scout Leader, 82nd Inverleith (Cramond) Scouts, since 1996; Member, Scottish Charity Law Review Commission. Publications: Guide to Scottish Grant-making Trusts; Writing Better Fund Raising Applications (Contributor); contributions to other books and periodicals. Address: (b.) Comely Park House, Dunfermline KY12 7EJ; T.-01383 721445.

Neil, Alex., MA (Hons). MSP (SNP), Central Scotland, since 1999 (Chairman, Enterprise and Lifelong Learning Committee); Economic Consultant; b. 22.8.51, Irvine; m., Isabella Kerr; 1 s. Educ. Dalmellington High School; Ayr Academy; Dundee University. Scottish Research Officer, Labour Party, 1975; General Secretary, Scottish Labour Party (SLP), 1976; Marketing Manager, 1979-83; Director: Cumnock and Doon Enterprise Trust, 1983-87, Prince's Scottish Youth Business Trust, 1987-89; Chairman, Network Scotland Ltd., 1987-93; Policy Vice-Convener, Scottish National Party, 1994-2000. Recreations: family; golf; gardening; travel. Address: (h.) 26 Overmills Road, Ayr KA7 3LQ; T.-01292 286675.

Neil, Andrew, MA (Hons). Publisher, The Scotsman, Scotland on Sunday, Edinburgh Evening News, Sunday Business, since 1996; Presenter, Despatch Box, BBC2, Late Night Live, ITV, Sunday Breakfast, BBC Radio 5; Chairman, Business Europe.com; Lord Rector, University of St. Andrews, 1997-2000; b. 21.5.49. Educ. Paisley Grammar School; Glasgow University. Conservative Research Department, 1971-72; Correspondent in Belfast, London, Washington, New York, for The Economist, 1973-82,UK Editor, London, 1982-83; Editor, Sunday Times, 1983-94; Chairman, Sky TV, 1988-90; author of Full Disclosure (autobiography). Address: (b.) The Scotsman, 108 Holyrood Road, Edinburgh EH8 8AS.

Neill, Gordon Webster McCash, DSO, SSC, NP, FInstD. Solicitor and Notary Public; Honorary Sheriff; b. Arbroath; m., Margaret Mary Lamb; 1 s.; 1 d. Educ. Edinburgh Academy. Legal apprenticeship, 1937-39; Pilot, RAF, 1939-46 (DSO, French Croix de Guerres with silver gilt star and silver star); Partner, Neill & Gibb, SSC, 1947; Chairman, Dundee Area Board, British Law Insurance Co. Ltd., 1954; Principal, Neill & Mackintosh, SSC, 1967; Consultant, Thorntons WS, 1989-96; Past Chairman, Scottish Gliding Association and Angus Gliding Club Ltd.; Past President, Chamber of Commerce, Arbroath Rotary Club and Society of Solicitors and Procurators in Angus. Recreations: golf; shooting; fishing. Address: (h.) 29 Duncan Avenue, Arbroath, Angus DD11 2DA; T.-01241 872221.

Neill, William Wilson, MA (Hons). Poet; b. 22.2.22, Prestwick; m., Doris Marie; 2 d. (by pr. m.). Educ. Ayr Academy; Edinburgh University. Served, RAF; won Sloane Verse Prize and Grierson Verse Prize while at Edinburgh University; Teacher; crowned Bard, Aviemore Mod, 1969; former Editor, Catalyst; former Editor, Lallans (Scots Language magazine); SAC Book Award, 1985; broadcasts, essays in Scotland's three tongues. Publications: Scotland's Castle, 1969; Poems, 1970; Four Points of a Saltire (Co-author), 1970; Despatches Home, 1972; Buile Shuibhne, 1974; Galloway Landscape: Poems, 1981; Cnu a Mogaill: Poems, 1983; Wild Places: Poems, 1985; Blossom, Berry, Fall: Poems 1986; Making Tracks: Poems, 1988; Straight Lines, 1992; Tales frae the Odyssey, 1992; Selected Poems, 1994; Tidsler, 1998; Stagioni, 1999; Caledonian Cramboclink, 2001; many poems in Gaelic, Scots and English magazines. Address: (h.) Burnside, Crossmichael, Castle Douglas DG7 3AP; T.-01556 670265.

Neilly, Gordon Joseph, BCom, CA. Managing Director, Intelli Corporate Finance Limited, since 1999; Director, Personal Assets Trust, since 1997; Director, Invesco Leveraged High Yield Fund, since 1999; Director, Buildstore Limited, since 1999; b. 2.7.60, Irvine; partner, Alison; 2 d. Educ. Auchenharvie Academy, Stevenston; Edinburgh University. Thomson McLintock & Co., 1981-84; Ivory & Sime plc, 1984-97, latterly as Director Business Development; Partner, RMD Group plc, 1997-99 (sold to Deloitte & Touche, 1999, and rebranded Intelli). Scottish Finance Director of the Year, 1992; Scottish Corporate Financier of the Year, 1999. Recreations: driving; travelling; all sports (in particular, football). Address: (b.) 29 Rutland Square, Edinburgh, EH1 2BW; T.-0131-222 9400.

Neilson, Margaret Marion, MA (Hons), LLB, DipLP, SSC, NP. Head of Litigation Department, Balfour & Manson; b. Falkirk; m., Raymond A. McMenamin. Educ. Mary Erskine School, Edinburgh; Edinburgh University. Balfour & Manson: Trainee, 1983, Assistant, 1985, Partner, 1987. Recreations: sport; scuba diving; travel. Address: (b.) 54-66 Frederick Street, Edinburgh EH2 1LS; T.-0131-200 1225; e-mail: maggie.neilson@balfour-manson.co.uk

Nelson, Dean Richard, BA (Hons). Scotland Editor, Sunday Times, since 2001; b. 13.6.64, Clapton, London; m., Pamela Timms; 2 s.; 1 d. Educ. King Harold Comprehensive, Waltham Abbey; University College Swansea. Researcher, Viewpoint Television, 1987; Political Editor, South China Sunday Morning Post, 1988-90; freelance Reporter, The Independent, 1991-93; The Observer: Investigations Reporter, 1993-96, Home News Editor, 1996-97, Scotland Editor, 1998-2000; Assistant Editor (Politics), The Scotsman, 2000; Deputy Editor, Sunday Times Scotland, 2000-01. Scoop of the Year, Scottish Press Awards, 2000 ("lobbygate" investigation). Recreations: family; reading; football; travel (former hippy). Address: (b.) 124 Portman Street, Kinning Park, Glasgow G41 1EJ; T.-0141 420 5261.

Nelson, (Peter) Frederick, BSc, CEng, MIEE. QA Manager, Peebles Electrical Machines Ltd.; Chairman, Scottish Outdoor Recreation Network, since 2000; b. 2.9.52, Glasgow; m., (Caroline) Ann; 3 s. Educ. John Neilson; Strathclyde University. President, Scottish Canoe Association, 1980-90; Member, Commonwealth Games Council for Scotland, since 1982; Chairman, Scottish Sports Association, 1990-96; Member, Scottish Sports Council, 1990-98; Member, Health and Safety Commission Adventure Activities Industry Advisory Committee. Elder, Davidson's Mains Parish Church. Recreations: canoeing; cycling; DIY. Address: (h.) 11 Barnton Park Place, Edinburgh EH4 6ET.

Ness, James Iain, LLB, NP. Solicitor; Member, Council, Law Society of Scotland, since 1990; Senior Partner, Austins, since 1995; b. 5.7.57, Johannesburg; m., Elaine; 1 s.; 1 d. Educ. Robert Gordon's, Aberdeen; Edinburgh University. Apprenticed, Connel & Connel, Edinburgh; Assistant, then Partner, then Senior Partner, Austins. Past

President, Rotary Club of Dalbeattie; Secretary, Cancer Relief Macmillan Fund, Dalbeattie and District. Recreation: skiing. Address: (b.) 52 High Street, Dalbeattie, DG5 4AB; T.-01556 610259; e-mail: jness@austins-solicitors.co.uk

Neumann, Jan, CBE, BSc, FREng, CEng, FIMechE, FIMarE, FIES; b. 26.6.24, Prague; m., 1, Barbara Joyce Gove (deceased); 2 s.; 2, Irene McCusker. Educ. Friends' School, Great Ayton; London University. Flight Engineer, RAF; Design Engineer, English Electric Co., Rugby; various engineering design and management positions in Yarrow Admiralty Research Department; Director: YARD Ltd., 1969-88 (Managing Director, 1978-87), Yarrow PLC, 1978-86; Board Member: SSEB, 1986-88, Scottish Nuclear, 1989-93; President, Institution of Engineers and Shipbuilders in Scotland, 1993-95; received Denny Gold Medal, IMarE, and Thomas Lowe Gray Prize, IMechE. Recreations: swimming; bowls. Address: (h.) 38 Norwood Park, Bearsden, Glasgow G61 2RZ.

Newall, Stephen Park, DL, Hon. LLD (Strathclyde). Deputy Lieutenant, Dunbartonshire, since 1985; b. 12.4.31, Bearsden, Dunbartonshire; m., Gay Sommerville Craig; 4 s.; 1 d. Educ. Loretto. Commissioned and served with Parachute Regiment, National Service, 1949-51; Sales Manager, A.P. Newall & Co., 1951-57; Managing Director, Bulten-Kanthal Stephen Newall Co. Ltd., 1957-80. Chairman: Epilepsy Association of Scotland, 1982-86, Finance Committee, University of Strathclyde, 1985-88; Council Member: Quarrier's Homes, 1983-88, Scottish Business School, 1983-85; Secretary of State for Scotland's Nominee on Court of Cranfield, 1985-92; Deacon Convener, Trades of Glasgow, 1983-84; Chairman, Court, University of Strathclyde, 1988-93. Recreations: farming; hill-walking; sailing; music. Address: (h.) Rowaleyn, Rhu, Dunbartonshire; T.-01436 820 521.

Newburgh, 12th Earl of (Don Filippo Giambattista Francesco Aldo Maria Rospigliosi); b. 4.7.42; m.; 1 d. Succeeded to title, 1986; lives in Italy.

Newell, Professor Alan F., MBE, BSc, PhD, FIEE, CEng, FBCS, FRSE, HonFCSLT. NCR Professor of Electronics and Microcomputer Systems, Dundee University, since 1980; Director, Dundee University Microcomputer Centre, since 1980; Head, Department of Applied Computing, since 1997 (Head, Applied Computer Studies Division, 1994-97; Deputy Principal, 1993-95); b. 1.3.41, Birmingham; m., Margaret; 1 s.; 2 d. Educ. St. Philip's Grammar School; Birmingham University. Research Engineer, Standard Telecommunication Laboratories; Lecturer, Department of Electronics, Southampton University. Recreations: family life; skiing; sailing. Address: (b.) Department of Applied Computing, Dundee University, Dundee, DD1 4HN; T.-01382 344144 .

Newis, Kenneth, CB, CVO, MA, FRSAMD. President, Queen's Hall (Edinburgh) Ltd.; b. 9.11.16, Crewe; m., Kathleen Barrow; 2 d. Educ. Manchester Grammar School; St. John's College, Cambridge. HM Office of Works, London, 1938-70; Under Secretary, Scottish Development Department, 1970-73; Secretary, 1973-76. Recreation: music. Address: (h.) 10/9 St. Margaret's Place, Edinburgh EH9 1AY; T.-0131-447 4138.

Newlands, Rev. Professor George McLeod, MA, BD, PhD. Professor of Divinity, Glasgow University, since 1986 (Dean, Faculty of Divinity, 1988-90); Principal, Trinity College, 1991-97; 12.7.41, Perth; m., Mary Elizabeth Wallace; 3 s. Educ. Perth Academy; Edinburgh University; Heidelberg University; Churchill College, Cambridge. Assistant Minister, Muirhouse, Edinburgh, 1969; Lecturer in Divinity, Glasgow University, 1969; University Lecturer in Divinity, Cambridge, 1973; Dean, Trinity Hall, Cambridge, 1982. Convener, Panel on Doctrine, Church of Scotland, 1995-99. Publications: Hilary of Poitiers;

Theology of the Love of God; The Church of God; Making Christian Decisions; God in Christian Perspective; Generosity and the Christian Future. Recreations: walking; music. Address: (b.) Faculty of Divinity, 4 The Square, Glasgow University, Glasgow G12 8QQ; e-mail: G.Newlands@arts.gla.ac.uk

Newton, Rosalind Ann. Director, High Blood Pressure Foundation, since 1990; b. 6.7.46, Newcastle upon Tyne. Educ. Gregg High School for Girls. Former Administrator, Edinburgh Science Festival; set up High Blood Pressure Foundation, 1990; Member, Strategy Group, Women in Business, Edinburgh Chamber of Commerce; Member, Scottish Council Development and Industry. Officer, Military and Hospitaller Order of St. Lazarus of Jerusalem. Recreations: enjoyment of the arts; swimming; travelling; entertaining. Address: (b.) Department of Medical Sciences, Western General Hospital, Edinburgh EH4 2XU; T.-0131-332 9211; e-mail: r.newton@hbpf.org.uk

Ni, Professor Xiongwei, BSc, PhD, CEng, FIChemE, Professor of Process and Reaction Engineering, Heriot-Watt University, since 1999; b. 22.2.60, Beijing, China; m., Wendy Margaret Hogg; 1s.; 1d. Educ. Yan-Ting Primary and High School, Sichuan China; Chong-Qing University, Sichuan; Leeds University. Research Fellow, Edinburgh University, 1986-89; Research Associate, Cambridge University, 1989-91; Lecturer, Teeside University, 1991-94; Strathclyde University: Lecturer, 1994-96; Senior Lecturer, 1996-97; Senior Lecturer, Heriot-Watt University, 1997-99; Foxwell Memorial Award, Institute of Energy, 1985. Recreations: tennis; badminton; golf; bridge. Address: (b.) Department of Mechanical and Chemical Engineering, Heriot-Watt University, Edinburgh, EH14 4AS; T.-0131-451 3781; e-mail: X.Ni@hw.ac.uk

Nicholls, Brian, BSc (Econ). Senior Business Consultant, Scottish Enterprise, 1991-98; Director, Scottish Opera, 1993-99; b. 21.9.28, London; m., Mary Elizabeth Harley; 1 s.; 2 d. Educ. Haberdashers' Aske's School; London University; Harvard Business School. George Wimpey Ltd., 1951-55; Constructors John Brown Ltd., 1955-75; Director, CJB Projects Ltd., 1972-75; Director, CJB Pipelines Ltd., 1974-75; Deputy Chairman, CJB Mohandessi Iran Ltd., 1974-75; Industrial Adviser to Secretary of State for Trade, 1975-78; Director: John Brown Engineering Ltd., 1978-91, John Brown Engineering Gas Turbines Ltd., 1978-91, Rugby Power Company Ltd., 1990-91; Vice President, John Brown Power Ltd., 1987-90; Member: Council, British Railway Export Group, 1976-78, British Overseas Trade Board, 1978; Vice President, Scottish Council Development and Industry, 1991-98; Fellow, Scottish Council Development and Industry, 1998. Recreations: music; reading; walking. Address: (h.) Blairlogie Park, Blairlogie, by Stirling FK9 5PY; T.-01259 761497.

Nicholson, Sheriff Principal (Charles) Gordon (Brown), QC, MA, LLB. Sheriff Principal of Lothian and Borders, since 1990; Commissioner, Scottish Law Commission, 1982-89; b. 11.9.35, Edinburgh; m., Hazel Mary Nixon; 2 s. Educ. George Watson's College, Edinburgh; Edinburgh University. Admitted to Faculty of Advocates, 1961; Advocate Depute, 1968-70; Sheriff of Dumfries and Galloway, at Dumfries, 1970-76; Sheriff of Lothian and Borders, at Edinburgh, 1976-82; Honorary President: Scottish Association for the Study of Delinquency, Victim Support Scotland; Commissioner, Northern Lighthouse Board, since 1990 (Chairman, 1994-95). Publication: The Law and Practice of Sentencing in Scotland, 1981 (2nd edition, 1992); Sheriff Court Practice (Joint Editor) (2nd edition, 1998). Recreation: music. Address: (h.) Bank O'Redfern, 24C Colinton Road, Edinburgh EH10 5EQ; T.-0131-447 4300; e-mail: gordon.nicholson2@btinternet.com

Nicholson, Liz, MA. Director, Shelter Scotland, since 1995; b. 27.9.46, Birmingham; m., Colin Nicholson; 2 s.; 1 d. Educ. Our Lady of Mercy Grammar School, Wolverhampton; Edinburgh University. Research Associate, Edinburgh University, 1988-89; Housing Campaign Worker, Shelter, 1989-92; Depute Chief Executive, Citizens Advice Scotland, 1992-95. Address: (b.) Shelter, Scotiabank House, 6 South Charlotte Street, Edinburgh EH2 4AW.

Nicholson, Peter Alexander, LLB (Hons). Managing Editor, W. Green, The Scottish Law Publisher, since 1989; General Editor, Scots Law Times, since 1985; Scottish Editor, Current Law, 1985-96; General Editor, Greens Weekly Digest, since 1986; b. 22.5.58, Stirling; m., Morag Ann Fraser; 1 s.; 3 d. Educ. St. David's RC High School, Dalkeith; Edinburgh University. Admitted as Solicitor, 1981. Lay Minister of the Eucharist. Recreations: choral singing; gardening; keeping fit. Address: (h.) 1 Frogston Gardens, Edinburgh EH10 7AF; T.-0131-445 1570.

Nickson of Renagour, Lord (David Wigley Nickson), KBE (1987), CBE (1981), DL, CBIM, FRSE. Life Peer; Chancellor, Glasgow Caledonian University, since 1993; Vice Lieutenant, Stirling and Falkirk, since 1997 (Deputy Lieutenant, 1982-97);b. 27.11.29, Eton; m., Helen Louise Cockcraft; 3 d. Educ. Eton College; Royal Military Academy, Sandhurst. Commissioned, Coldstream Guards, 1949-54; William Collins: joined, 1954, Director, 1961-85, Joint Managing Director, 1967, Vice-Chairman, 1976-83, Group Managing Director, 1979-82; Director: Scottish United Investors plc, 1970-83, General Accident plc, 1971-98 (Deputy Chairman, 1993-98), Scottish & Newcastle Breweries plc, 1981-95 (Chairman, 1983-89), Radio Clyde Ltd., 1982-85, National Australia Bank Ltd., 1991-96, National Australian Group (UK) Ltd., 1993-98, Hambros PLC, 1989-98; Chairman, Clydesdale Bank, 1991-98 (Director, 1981-98); Chairman, Pan Books, 1982-83; Chairman, Scottish Enterprise, 1990-93 (SDA, 1988-90); President, CBI, 1986-88; Chairman, CBI in Scotland, 1979-81; Chairman, Countryside Commission for Scotland, 1983-86; Member: Scottish Industrial Development Advisory Board, 1975-80, Scottish Committee, Design Council, 1978-81, Scottish Economic Council, 1980-95, National Economic Development Council, 1985-88; Chairman, Atlantic Salmon Trust, 1988-95; Chairman, Senior Salaries Review Body, 1989-95; President, Association of District Salmon Fisheries Board, since 1996; Chairman, Secretary of State for Scotland's Scottish Salmon Strategy Task Force, 1995-97; Chairman, Scottish Advisory Committee, Imperial Cancer Research Fund, 1994-2001; Trustee: Princes Youth Business Trust, 1987-90, Princess Royal's Trust for Carers, 1990-94; Director, Countryside Alliance, 1998-2000; Brigadier, Queen's Bodyguard for Scotland (Royal Company of Archers); D.Univ, Stirling, 1986; Hon. DBA Napier Polytechnic, 1990; Honorary Fellow, Paisley College, 1992; Honorary Freeman, Fishmongers Company, 1999, Honorary Freeman, City of London, 1999. Recreations: fishing; bird-watching; the countryside. Address: (h.) The River House, Doune, Perthshire FK16 6DA; T.-01786 841614.

Nicol, Rev. Douglas Alexander Oag, MA, BD (Hons). General Secretary, Church of Scotland Department of National Mission; b. 5.4.48, Dunfermline; m., Anne Wilson Gillespie; 2 s.; 1 d. Educ. Kirkcaldy High School; Edinburgh University; Glasgow University. Assistant Warden, St. Ninian's Centre, Crieff, 1972-76; Minister, Lochside, Dumfries, 1976-82; Minister, St. Columba, Kilmacolm, 1982-91. Chairman, Board of Directors, National Bible Society of Scotland, 1984-87; Convener, Board of National Mission, Church of Scotland, 1990-91. Recreations: family life and family history; travel; athletics. Address: (h.) 24 Corbiehill Avenue, Blackhall, Edinburgh EH4 5DR; T.-0131-336 1965.

Nicol, Rev. John Chalmers, MA, BD, MHSM, DipHSM. Minister, Holy Trinity Church, Bridge of Allan, since 1985; b. 6.4.39, Greenock; m., Anne Morrison MacDonald; 1 s.; 1 d. Educ. Greenock Academy; Glasgow University; Princeton Theological Seminary. Assistant Minister, Westwood Parish Church, East Kilbride, 1964-65; Minister: St. Andrew's Church, Buenos Aires, 1965-69, Bonnyrigg Parish Church, 1970-75; Secretary, Edinburgh Local Health Council, 1975-78; Principal Administrative Assistant, Argyll and Clyde Health Board, 1978-85. Recreations: fishing; Charles Rennie Mackintosh. Address: (h.) 29 Keir Street, Bridge of Allan FK9 4QJ; T.-01786 832093.

Nicoll, Eric Hamilton, CBE, FSA Scot, BSc (Hons), FICE, FCIWEM (Dip). Deputy Chief Engineer, Scottish Development Department, 1976-85; b. 15.5.25, Edinburgh; m., Helen Elizabeth Barnes; 1 s.; 1 d. Educ. George Heriot's School, Edinburgh; Edinburgh University. Engineering Assistant: Midlothian County Council Roads Department, 1945-46, Edinburgh Corporation Water Department, 1946-51; Chief Assistant County Engineer, Midlothian County Council, 1951-62; Scottish Development Department: Engineering Inspector, 1962-68, Senior Engineering Inspector, 1968-72, Assistant Chief Engineer, 1972-75. US Water Pollution Control Federation Arthur Sidney Bedell Award, 1985; Chairman, Edinburgh Recorded Music Society, 1992-95; Chairman (and Archivist), Pictish Arts Society, 1992-95; elected Professional Member, Visual Arts Scotland, 1995. Publications: Small Water Pollution Control Works: Design and Practice, 1988; A Pictish Panorama (Editor), 1995; Art Without Epoch, 1996; numerous technical and scientific papers. Recreations: wood sculpture; music; antiquities; crosswords. Address: (h.) 35 Wardie Road, Edinburgh EH5 3LJ.

Nicolson, David M., CA. Non-Executive Director: Tayburn Holdings Ltd., since 2001, InSupply, since 2001, Scottish Qualifications Authority, since 2000; Chairman, Edinburgh City Centre Management Co., since 2000; Trustee Royal Botanic Gardens, Edinburgh, since 2000; b. 22.4.42, Edinburgh; m., Elizabeth Finlay Smith; 1 s.; 1 d. Educ. Royal High School, Edinburgh. Qualified as CA with Robertson & Maxtone Graham, Edinburgh, 1964; Peat Marwick Mitchell & Co., London, 1964-67; Partner, KPMG Edinburgh, 1968-97 (Managing Partner, 1988-96); Director, KPMG Asia Pacific, 1997-99. President: Edinburgh Junior Chamber of Commerce, 1975-76, Edinburgh Chamber of Commerce and Enterprise, 1994-96; former Member of Council, Institute of Chartered Accountants of Scotland. Recreations: golf; tennis; skiing; gardening. Address: (h.) Hailes Brae, 18 Spylaw Bank Road, Edinburgh EH13 0JW; T.-0131-441 2218; e-mail: hailesbrae@aol.com

Nicolson, Professor Donald James, BA, LLB, PhD. Professor of Law, Strathclyde University, since 2001; b. 1.6.61, Cape Town. Educ. Fish Hoek High School; University of Cape Town; Cambridge University. Temporary Lecturer, University of Cape Town, 1984; Lecturer, Reading University, 1989-92; Lecturer, Bristol University, 1992-2000. Publications: Professional Legal Ethics: Critical Interrogations, 1999; Feminist Perspectives on Criminal Law, 2000. Recreations: skiing; surfing; cycling; jazz; literature. Address: (b.) School of Law, Strathclyde University, 173 Stenhouse Building, 173 Cathedral Street, Glasgow G64 0RQ; T.-0141-548 3978.

Nicolson, John Alick (Jan); b. 26.9.45, Inverness; m., Effie; 1 s. Educ. Portree High School. Board Member, Caledonian MacBrayne Ltd.; Chairman, Skye and Lochalsh Enterprise, 1991-96; Board Member, Highlands and Islands Enterprise, 1996-98; Chairman, Hi-Screen Ltd., 1997-98; Trustee, Clann Mhicneacail Lands Trust; Scottish Commissioner, Clan Nicolson of Scorrybreac; Director,

Jansvans Ltd.; Principal Partner, Jansport; Founder Member and Past Chairman, Isle of Skye Round Table. Recreations: collecting vintage vehicles; community affairs. Address: (h.) Almondbank, Viewfield Road, Portree, Isle of Skye IV51 9E4; T.-01478 612696.

Nimmo, Professor Myra A., BSc, PhD. Professor of Exercise Physiology, Strathclyde Institute of Biomedical Sciences, Strathclyde University; b. 5.1.54, Edinburgh; m., Dr. J.A. Macaskill; 2 s. Educ. Westbourne School for Girls; Glasgow University. Temporary Lecturer, Glasgow University, 1978-80; Wellcome Research Fellow, 1980-82; Lecturer in Physiology, Queen's College, Glasgow, 1982-84, Senior Lecturer in Physiotherapy and Research, 1984-87, Acting Head, Department of Physiotherapy, 1987-88; Assistant Director, Scottish Vocational Education Department, 1988-91; Assistant Principal, Jordanhill College, 1991-93; Director, Scottish Institute of Sports Medicine and Sports Science, 1993-96; Member, Scottish Sport Council, Scottish Sport World Class Advisory Group (Member, Scottish Sports Council, 1990-94); Member, UK Sport, since 1998; Olympic athlete. Recreation: general fitness. Address: (b.) Strathclyde University, Jordanhill Campus, Southbrae Drive, Glasgow G13 1PP; T.-0141-950 3722; e-mail: m.a.nimmo@strath.ac.uk

Nimmo, William, CBE, BArch, RIBA, FRIAS, FRSA. Senior Partner, William Nimmo & Partners, 1956-98, Consultant, since 1998; b. 1.4.29; m., Mae Morrison Hannah; 3 s.; 1 d. Educ. Wishaw High School; Mackintosh School of Architecture. Commissioned, Corps of Royal Engineers, 1954-55. Chairman, Braidwood Properties Ltd. Recreations: hill-walking; touring UK and Europe. Address: (h.) Auchenglen House, Braidwood, Carluke ML8 5PH; T.-01555 772021.

Nimmo Smith, Hon. Lord (William Austin Nimmo Smith), BA, LLB. Senator of the College of Justice, since 1996; b. 6.11.42, Edinburgh; m., Dr. Jennifer Nimmo Smith; 1 s.; 1 d. Educ. Eton; Balliol College, Oxford; Edinburgh University. Advocate, 1969; Standing Junior Counsel, Department of Employment, 1977-82; QC, 1982; Advocate Depute, 1983-86; Chairman, Medical Appeal Tribunals and Vaccine Damage Tribunals, 1986-91; part-time Member, Scottish Law Commission, 1988-96; Temporary Judge, Court of Session, 1995-96; Chairman of Council, Cockburn Association (Edinburgh Civic Trust), 1996-2001. Recreations: mountaineering; music. Address: (b.) Parliament House, Edinburgh EH1 1RQ.

Nisbet, James Barry Consitt, LLB, NP, JP. Stipendiary Magistrate, Glasgow, since 1984; b. 26.7.42, Forfar; m., Elizabeth McKenzie; 2 d. Educ. Forfar Academy; Edinburgh University. Legal Assistant, Warden Bruce & Co., WS, Edinburgh, 1967-68; Legal Assistant, then Junior Depute Town Clerk, then Depute Town Clerk, Perth City Council, 1968-75; Senior Depute Director of Administration, Perth and Kinross District Council, 1975-84. Head Server, St. Ninian's Episcopal Cathedral, Perth; Secretary-General, Scottish Guild of Servers. Recreations: transport, especially railways and tramways; archaeology; music; foreign travel; genealogy. Address: (b.) District Court Chambers, 21 St. Andrews Street, Glasgow G1 5PW; T.-0141-227 5424.

Nisbet, Mary Sylvia. Secretary, Edinburgh Consumer Group, since 1977; Chairman, Morningside Community Council, since 1995; b. 28.7.37, Hampstead Heath, London; m., 1, Richard Cruickshanks Paterson (deceased); 2 s.; 2, James Bruce Hay Nisbet. Educ. Hornsey High School, London. Westminster Bank Ltd., 1954-55; GPO Continental Telephone Exchange, 1955-56; Scottish Widows Fund, 1957-61; freelance market research. Member, Edinburgh CAB Executive Committee, several years; Member, Post Officers Users' Council for Scotland, 1976-82; Member, Scottish Committee, Meat and Livestock Commission, 1990-95; Member, Executive, National Federation of Consumer Groups, 1992-97.Recreations: music; walking; crosswords. Address: (h.) 4/6 Belhaven Place, Edinburgh EH10 5JN; T.-0131-447 4148; e-mail: Brucemary.Nisbet@tesco.net

Niven, Catharine, BSc, AMA, FSA(Scot). Curator, Inverness Museum and Art Gallery, since 1984; b. 23.9.52, Denbigh; m., Roger Niven. Educ. Loughton High School; Leicester University. Freelance archaeologist, working in Britain and Scandinavia; Keeper of Antiquities, Rotherham Museum, 1979-81; Assistant Curator (Archaeology), Inverness Museum and Art Gallery, 1981-84. Recreation: music. Address: (b.) Castle Wynd, Inverness IV2 3ED; T.-01463 237114.

Niven, Professor Catherine Ann (Kate), RGN, BScPsychol, PhD. Professor of Nursing and Midwifery Studies, Stirling University, since 1996; Director, NRIS, since 2000; b. 26.8.45 m.; 1 s.; 1 d. Educ. Notre Dame High School, Glasgow; Stirling University. Former staff nurse and sister; Teaching Assistant, Stirling University, 1980; Lecturer, Department of Psychology, Glasgow Polytechnic/Glasgow Caledonian University, 1983; Reader, 1993. Publications: Psychological Care for Families Before, During and After Birth (book). Recreations: gardening; having fun. Address: (b.) Stirling University, Stirling FK9 4LA; T.-01786 466341.

Niven, Stuart Matthew, BSc, DipEd, FIMgt. President Emeritus, International Vocational Education and Training Association; b. 1.3.36, Clydebank; m., Jean K. McPhee; 1 s.; 1 d. Educ. Clydebank High School; Glasgow University. Teacher of Mathematics and Physics: Clydebank High School, 1959, Stow College of Engineering, 1961; Head, Department of Mathematics and Physics, Kilmarnock College, 1964; Jordanhill College of Education: Lecturer in Mathematics, 1967, Senior Lecturer in Further Education, 1968, Principal Lecturer, 1970; Director, Scottish School of Further Education, Strathclyde University, 1983-97. Member, CNAA Further Education Board, 1978-84; Chairman, Editorial Board, Journal for Further and Higher Education in Scotland, 1976-83; Chairman, National Liaison Committee on Training of Teachers of Nursing, Midwifery and Health Visiting, 1983-88; Member, National Board for Scotland for Nursing, Midwifery and Health Visiting, 1989-93; Member, UK Central Council for Nursing, Midwifery and Health Visiting, since 1989; President, International Vocational Education and Training Association, 1994-96 (Vice President, Europe, 1990-92, President (Elect), 1992-94); Chairman, Board of Management, Clydebank College, 1996-2001; President, International Section, American Vocational Association; Member, Royal Philosophical Society of Glasgow. Publications: Vocational Further Education in Scotland, 1982; Professional Development of Further Education Lecturers in Scotland: Towards Comprehensive Provision, 1987. Publication: The First Twenty-Five Years; Changing Vocational Education and Training, 1998. Recreation: golf. Address: 5 Netherblane, Blanefield, Glasgow G63 9SW; T.-01360 770060.

Noad, Elaine, BA, MSc, DPA, DASS, CQSW. Director of Social Work, Housing and Health, South Ayrshire Council, since 1995; b. 7.7.56, London; m., Peter Noad; 2 s.; 1 d. Educ. Chorley College; Newcastle Polytechnic; Aberdeen University. Social Worker: Lothian, 1980-85, Grampian, 1985-87; Development Worker, Scottish Council on Disability, 1987-89; Principal Officer (Corporate Services), City of Edinburgh District Council, 1989-90; Social Work Manager, Tayside Regional Council, 1990-94; Assistant Director of Social Work, Grampian Regional Council, 1994-95. Recreations: swimming; hill-walking; travel; sports. Address: (b.) South Ayrshire Council, County Buildings, Wellington Square, Ayr KA7 1DR; T.-01292 612419.

Noble, Rev. Alexander Buchan, MA, BD (Hons), ThM. Minister, Fyvie with Rothienorman Parish Church, since 1999; b. 23.5.55, Fraserburgh; m., Patricia Anne West. Educ. Fraserburgh Academy; Dalziel High School, Motherwell; Glasgow University; Aberdeen University; Princeton Theological Seminary. Minister: St. Mark's Parish Church, Stirling, 1982-93, Dunbar Parish Church, 1993-99. Publication: Sunshine Through Shadows. Recreations: football; swimming; reading; writing; travel. Address: The Manse, Fyvie, Turriff AB53 8RD; T.-01651 891230.

Noble, David Hillhouse, LLB, DipMan. Chief Executive, Highlands of Scotland Tourist Board, since 1997; b. 27.4.48, Paisley; m., Hilary; 1 s.; 2 d. Educ. Greenock Academy; Glasgow University. Solicitor in private practice, Glasgow, 1970-72; Legal and Administrative Officer, Argyll County Council, 1972-73; Senior Legal and Administrative Officer, Inverness County Council, 1973-75; Chief Executive, Skye and Lochalsh District Council, 1975-96; Director, Skye and Lochalsh Enterprise, 1992-95; Area Manager, Skye and Lochalsh, The Highland Council, 1996-97. Recreations: music; running. Address: (b.) Peffery House, Strathpeffer, Ross-shire IV14 9HA; T.-01997 421160.

Noble (or Nobail), Sir Iain, Bt. of Ardkinglas and Eilean Iarmain, OBE, MA. Entrepreneur and businessman; Chairman, Sir Iain Noble & Partners Ltd., Edinburgh; b. 8.9.35, Berlin. Educ. in China, Argentina and England; University College, Oxford. Scottish Council (Development and Industry), 1964-69; Co-founder and Joint Managing Director, Noble Grossart Ltd., Edinburgh, 1969-72; Founder and Chairman: Seaforth Maritime PLC, Aberdeen, 1972-77, Noble Group Ltd (Merchant Bankers), Edinburgh, 1980-2000; Founder and Director: Adam and Company plc, 1983-94, Independent Insurance Group PLC, 1986; Director, Premium Trust PLC, since 1993, and other companies; Chairman, Skye Bridge Ltd., 1994-96; Founder and Chairman, Pràban na Linne Ltd ("The Gaelic Whiskies"), since 1979; Proprietor, Fearann Eilean Iarmain (estate management, Isle of Skye), since 1972; Member, Edinburgh University Court, 1970-73; Founder, first Chairman and Trustee, Gaelic College of Sabhal Mor Ostaig, Skye, 1975-85; Trustee: National Museums of Scotland, 1986-90, NMS Charitable Trust, since 1990; Scotsman of the Year Award, 1982 (Knights Templar); President, Saltire Society, 1993-96; Chairman, Scots Australian Council, 1990-99; Keeper of the Quaich, since 2000. Editor, Sources of Finance, 1967-69; other interests: conservation; Gaelic; heritage architecture; community development. Recreations: deasbad, comhradh, orain is ceol le deagh chompanaich. Address: An Oifig, Eilean Iarmain, An t-Eilean Sgitheanach, IV43 8QR; T.-01471 833 266; 20 Great Stuart Street, Edinburgh EH3 7TN; T.-0131-220 2400; e-mail: Sir.Iain@eilean-iarmain.co.uk

Noble, Lillias Mary, BEd, MUniv (Open). Education Adviser, Scottish Prison Service, since 1997; Board Member, Community Learning Scotland, since 1997; b. 11.9.54, Vancouver. Educ. Larkhall Academy; Hamilton College of Education; Strathclyde University. Formerly English and Guidance Teacher,Thurso High School, 1975-80; Wester Hailes Education Centre, 1980-84; Save the Children Fund, 1985-88; Director, LEAD Scotland, 1988-97; part-time Commissioner, 1992-98, and Vice Chairman, 1995-98, Mental Welfare Commission for Scotland. Recreation: climbing mountains. Address: (b.) Scottish Prison Service, Calton House, 5 Redheughs Rigg, Edinburgh EH12 9HW; T.-0131-244 8649; e-mail: l.noble@sps.gov.uk

Noble, Robin (Donald J.R.), MA, FSAScot. Honorary Chairman, Scottish Field Studies Association, since 2000; freelance environmental teacher, writer and lecturer, since 1992; b. 24.7.50, St Andrews; 1 s.; 3 d.

Educ. Trinity College, Glenalmond; Sidney Sussex College, Cambridge University. Planning Assistant, Highlands and Islands Development Board; artist/craftsman, Highland Stoneware Pottery, Lochinver; Manager/Tutor, Orkney Field Centre, Birsay; General Manager/Tutor, Aigas Field Centre; Director, Council for Scottish Archaeology. Trustee, Aigas Trust for Environmental Education; Chairman, Assynt Community Education. Publication: North and West, 2002. Recreations: hill-walking; painting; singing. Address: Glenleraig Cottage, Drumbeg, Lairg IV27 4NJ; T.-01571 833 246.

Noble, Simon John. Owner, Ardkinglas Estate, Argyll, since 1972; Chairman, Loch Fyne Oysters Ltd. (Co-Founder, 1977); Director, Noble Group Ltd., since 1977; b. 31.10.36, London. Educ. Eton; Magdalen College, Oxford. S.G. Warburg & Co., 1959-64; wine trade – French and Foreign Wines Ltd. (Founder), 1964-81; Chairman (non-Executive), Wine Importers Edinburgh Ltd., since 1975; Chairman, Loch Fyne Restaurants PLC, since 1998. Recreation: country life. Address: (b.) Loch Fyne Oysters Ltd., Cairndow, Argyll PA26 8BH; T.-01499 600264.

Noble, Sir (Thomas Alexander) Fraser, Kt (1971), MBE (1947), MA, LLD, FRSE; b. 29.4.18, Cromdale; m., Barbara A.M. Sinclair; 1 s.; 1 d. Educ. Nairn Academy; Aberdeen University. Indian Civil Service, 1940-47; Lecturer in Political Economy, Aberdeen University, 1948-57; Secretary, Carnegie Trust for Scottish Universities, 1957-62; Vice-Chancellor, Leicester University, 1962-76; Principal, Aberdeen University, 1976-81; Past Chairman of numerous public service committees, including Scottish Standing Conference of Youth Service Organisations, Home Office Advisory Committee for Probation and After Care, Television Research Committee; Chairman, UK Committee of Vice Chancellors, 1970-72; former Member of Council, Association of Commonwealth Universities. Publications: Something in India (memoir); articles, mainly on economics, education and India. Recreations: golf; listening to music. Address: (h.) Hedgerley, Victoria Street, Nairn; T.-01667 453151.

Noble, Timothy Peter, MA, MBA. Executive Chairman, Noble Group Ltd.; Chairman: Palmaris Capital plc, British Ski Academy, Darnaway Venture Capital plc; Director: Scottish Friendly Assurance Society Ltd., Murray Global Return Trust plc; b. 21.12.43; m., Elizabeth Mary Aitken; 2 s.; 1 d. Educ. University College, Oxford; Gray's Inn, London; INSEAD, Fontainebleau. Recreations: skiing; tennis; bridge; wine; astronomy; poetry. Address: (h.) Ardnahane, Barnton Avenue, Edinburgh; T.-0131-336 3565.

Noel-Paton, (Frederick) Ranald, BA, DBA (Hon). Chairman, Murray Global Return Trust plc, since 2000 (Director, since 1998); Chairman, Pacific Assets Trust plc, since 1998 (Director, since 1986); Deputy Chairman, John Menzies plc, 1997-98 (Group Managing Director, 1986-97); b. 7.11.38, Bombay; m., Patricia Anne Stirling; 4 d. Educ. Rugby School; McGill University. Investment Analyst, Greenshields Inc., 1962-63; Management Trainee, United Biscuits, 1964; various posts, British United Airways Ltd., 1965-70; various senior executive posts, British Caledonian Airways, 1970-86 (General Manager, West Africa, 1975-79, General Manager, Far East, 1980-86, Director, Caledonian Far East Airways, 1984-86); Director: General Accident plc, 1987-98, Royal Bank of Scotland Group, 1991-93, Macallan-Glenlivet plc, 1990-96. Recreations: fishing; walking; bird-watching; the arts. Address: (h.) Easter Dunbarnie, Bridge of Earn, Perth PH2 9ED.

Normand, Andrew Christie, CB, MA, LLB, LLM, SSC, FSAScot. Crown Agent for Scotland, since 1996; b. 7.2.48, Edinburgh; m., Barbara Jean Smith; 2 d. Educ. George Watson's College, Edinburgh; Edinburgh University;

Queen's University, Kingston, Ontario. Address: (b.) Crown Office, 25 Chambers Street, Edinburgh EH1 1LA; T.-0131-226 2626.

Norrie, Rev. Graham, MA, BD. Minister, Forfar: East and Old Parish Church, since 1978; b. 14.5.41, Dundee; m., Irene Seward Pearce; 2 s.; 2 d. Educ. Morgan Academy, Dundee; St. Andrews University; Edinburgh University. Assistant Minister, St. Ninian's Church, Corstorphine, 1965-67; Minister, Alloa: West Church, 1967-78. Recreations: hill-walking; football spectating. Address: (h.) The Manse, Lour Road, Forfar DD8 2BB; T.-01307 464303.

Norrie, Professor Kenneth McKenzie, LLB, DLP, PhD. Professor and Head of the Law School, University of Strathclyde; b. 23.6.59, Dundee. Educ. Kirkton High School, Dundee; University of Dundee; University of Aberdeen. Lecturer in Law: University of Dundee, 1982-83, University of Aberdeen, 1983-90; Gastprofessor, Universität Regensburg, Germany, 1990; Senior Lecturer in Law, University of Strathclyde, 1990-95; Visiting Professor, University of Sydney, Australia, 1997. Member, Children's Panel, City of Glasgow. Publications: Parent and Child; Defamation; Trusts; Children's Hearings. Recreations: philately; travel. Address: (b.) School of Law, University of Strathclyde, Stenhouse Building, 173 Cathedral Street, Glasgow G4 0RQ; T.-0141-548 3393.

North, Robert. Artistic Director, Scottish Ballet, since 1999; freelance choreographer; b. 1.6.45; m., Sheri Cook. Educ. Pierrepoint School; Central School of Art; Royal Ballet School. Dancer and choreographer, London Contemporary Dance Co., 1966-81 (Joint Artistic Director, 1980-81); Artistic Director, Ballet Rambert, 1981-86; freelance work, 1986-90; Artistic Director, Gothenburg Ballet, 1991-96; Director, Corps de Ballet, Arena di Verona, 1997-99; has choreographed ballets for companies throughout the world. Address: (b.) 261 West Princes Street, Glasgow, G4 9EE.

Northesk, 14th Earl of (David John MacRae Carnegie); b. 3.11.54; m.; 3 d.; 1 s. (deceased). Educ. Eton; UCL. Succeeded to title, 1994; elected Member, House of Lords, since 1999.

Northrop, Alasdair, BA (Hons.). Editor, Scottish Business Insider, since 2000; b. 23.5.57, Chalfont-St-Giles; partner, Irene Cook; 1 s. Educ. Leamington College for Boys; Middlesex Polytechnic. Reporter, Heart of England Newspapers, 1978-81; Sub Editor, Southern Evening Echo, Southampton, 1983-85; Deputy Editor, North Western Evening Mail, Barrow-in-Furness, 1985-89; Business Editor, Western Daily Press, Bristol, 1989-94; Business Editor, Manchester Evening News, 1994-2000. BT Business Journalist of the Year, 1996; BT North West Business Journalist of the Year, 1996. Recreations: theatre; music; walking; swimming; badminton; travelling. Address: (b.) 7 Castle Street, Edinburgh EH2 3AH; T.-0131-535 5512; e-mail: editor_sbi@insider.co.uk

Nuttall, Professor Mark Anthony, MA (Hons.), PhD. Professor of Social Anthropology, University of Aberdeen, since 2000; b. 5.7.62, Chester; m., Dr. Anita Dey-Nuttall; 1 s. Educ. Kingsway High School, Chester; University of Aberdeen, Cambridge University. Research Fellow in Social Anthropology, University of Edinburgh, 1990-92; Lecturer in Social Anthropology, Brunel University, 1992-94; Research Associate, Scott Polar Research Institute and Affiliate Assistant Professor, University of Alaska, Fairbanks, 1994-95; University of Aberdeen: Lecturer in Sociology, 1995-99, Senior Lecturer in Sociology and Anthropology, 1999-2000. Publications: Arctic Homeland, 1992; Protecting the Arctic, 1998; White Settlers, (Co-Author), 1996; Arctic Climate Impact Assessment 2000-2004 (Lead Author). Recreations: hillwalking; Arctic travel. Address: (b.) Department of Sociology and Anthropology, University of Aberdeen, Aberdeen AB24 3QY; T.-01224 272771; e-mail: m.nuttall@abdn.ac.uk

O

Oatts, Alasdair Henry James, FRICS. Regional Director, National Trust for Scotland, Argyll, Lochaber and Western Isles, since 1995; b. 22.9.53, Nairn; m., Melissa; 1 s.; 1 d. Educ. Wellington College; Royal Agricultural College, Cirencester. Employed by National Trust for Scotland, since 1979. Recreations: golf; squash; shooting. Address: (b.) Lochvoil House, Dunvaran Road, Oban PA34 4NE; T.-01631 570000; e-mail: aoatts@nts.org.uk

Ó Baoill, Professor Colm, MA, PhD. Professor of Celtic, Aberdeen University, since 1996; b. 22.9.38, Armagh, Ireland; m., Frances G. R.; 3 d. Educ. St. Patrick's College, Armagh; Queen's University of Belfast. Assistant Lecturer, Queen's University of Belfast, 1962; Aberdeen University: Lecturer, 1966, Senior Lecturer, 1980. Chief, Gaelic Society, Inverness, 1993. Address: (h.) 19 King's Crescent, Old Aberdeen AB24 3HJ; T.-01224 637064.

O'Brien, Sir Frederick William Fitzgerald, QC, MA, LLB. Sheriff Principal, Lothian and Borders, 1978-89; Convener of Sheriffs Principal, 1972-89; b. 19.7.17, Edinburgh; m., Audrey Muriel Owen; 2 s.; 1 d. Educ. Royal High School, Edinburgh; Edinburgh University. Called to Scottish Bar, 1947; QC, 1960; Commissioner, Mental Welfare Commission, 1962-65; Senior Advocate Depute, Crown Office, 1964-65; Sheriff Principal, Caithness, Sutherland, Orkney and Shetland, 1965-75; Interim Sheriff Principal, Aberdeen, Kincardine and Banff, 1969-71; Sheriff Principal, North Strathclyde, 1975-78; Interim Sheriff Principal, South Strathclyde, 1981; Member: Scottish Medical Practices Committee, 1973-76, Scottish Records Advisory Council, 1974-83; Chairman, Sheriff Court Rules Council, 1975-81; Convener, General Council Business Committee, Edinburgh University, 1980-84; Past President, Royal High School FP Club (Honorary President, 1982-91); Chairman, Edinburgh Sir Walter Scott Club, 1989-92; Commissioner, Northern Lighthouse Board, 1965-89 (Chairman, 1983-84 and 1986-87). Recreations: music; golf. Address: (h.) 22 Arboretum Road, Edinburgh EH3 5PN; T.-0131-552 1923.

O'Brien, James Paul, MA (Hons), MEd, PhD, DipEdTech, FRSA. Vice-Dean, Moray House Institute of Education, Faculty of Education, Edinburgh University; b. 23.4.50, Stirling; m., Elaine Margaret Kathleen Smith; 1 d. Educ. St. Mirin's Academy, Paisley; Glasgow University. Teacher, 1973-85; Lecturer, St. Andrew's College of Education, 1985-88, Director, 1988-93, Assistant Principal, 1992-93; Vice-Principal, Moray House Institute, 1993-98. Recreations: golf; music; reading. Address: (b.) Holyrood Campus, Holyrood Road, Edinburgh EH8 8AQ; T.-0131-651 6167.

O'Brien, Most Rev. Keith Michael Patrick, BSc, DipEd. Archbishop of St. Andrews and Edinburgh, since 1985; b. 17.3.38, Ballycastle, Northern Ireland. Educ. Saint Patrick's, Dumbarton; Holy Cross Academy, Edinburgh; Edinburgh University; St. Andrew's College, Drygrange; Moray House College of Education. Teacher, St. Columba's High School, Fife; Assistant Priest, Kilsyth, then Bathgate; Spiritual Director, St. Andrew's College, Drygrange; Rector, Blairs College, Aberdeen; ordained Archbishop by Cardinal Gray, 1985. Recreations: music; walking. Address: Saint Bennet's, 42 Greenhill Gardens, Edinburgh EH10 4BJ.

O'Brien, Susan, BA (Hons), BPhil, LLB. Queen's Counsel, since 1998; Advocate, since 1987; b. 13.8.52, Edinburgh; m., Professor Peter Ross; 2 d. Educ. St George's School for Girls, Edinburgh; York University; Edinburgh University. Admitted Solicitor, 1980;

Assistant Solicitor, Shepherd and Wedderburn, WS, 1980-86; Standing Junior Counsel to Registrar General, 1991, and to Home Office, 1992-97, and to Keeper of the Registers, 1998; Temporary Sheriff, 1995-99; part-time Chairman, Employment Tribunals, since 2000; Reporter to Scottish Legal Aid Board, since 1999. Address: (b.) Advocates' Library, Parliament Square, Edinburgh EH1 1RQ; T.-0131-226 5071.

O'Carroll, Derek, LLB (Hons), DipLP. Advocate; Member, Scottish Legal Aid Board; part-time Chairman, Social Security Appeals Tribunal; Convener, Scottish Legal Action Group; part-time Chairman, Rent Assessment Panel for Scotland; b. 20.1.60, St Albans. Educ. Cults Academy, Aberdeen; Edinburgh University. Citizens Rights Office, Edinburgh, 1982-85; Castlemilk Law Centre, Glasgow, 1985; university in Turkey, 1985-88; Transfert, Paris, 1988-90; Legal Services Agency, Glasgow, 1990-95; Govan Law Centre, Glasgow, 1995-99. Recreations: good food and wine; swimming and keep-fit; travel; doing nothing. Address: 1 Cambridge Gardens, Edinburgh EH6 5DH; e-mail: derekocarroll@blueyonder.co.uk

O'Connor, Ronald, BA (Hons), DipEd. Director of Social Work Services, Glasgow City Council, since 1999; b. 1.12.50, Glasgow; m., Marie Milne; 1 s. Educ. St Mungo's Academy, Glasgow; Stirling University. Former Teacher of Modern Languages; Assistant Head Teacher, Garnock Academy, 1983; Education Officer, Ayr Division, Strathclyde Region, 1987; Education Officer, Glasgow Division, 1990; seconded to post of Assistant Director of Education, Strathclyde, 1993; seconded to Chief Executive's office, Strathclyde, 1994; Senior Depute Director of Education Services, Glasgow City Council, 1996. Recreations: golf; football; theatre. Address: (b.) Nye Bevan House, 20 India Street, Glasgow G21 4PF; T.-0141-287 8853.

O'Donnell, Marjory Ann, MA (Hons). Director, National Asthma Campaign Scotland, since 1996; b. 8.6.49, Glasgow. Educ. Glasgow University. Teacher of Languages, 1972-76; Development Officer, Council for Voluntary Service, 1988-89; Senior Development Officer, Volunteer Development Scotland, 1989-96. Address: (b.) 2A North Charlotte Street, Edinburgh EH2 4HR; T.-0131-226 2544; e-mail: modonnell@asthma.org.uk

O'Dwyer, Professor Patrick Joseph, MCh, FRCSI, FRCSGlas. Professor of Surgery, Glasgow University, since 1998; Consultant Surgeon, Western Infirmary, Glasgow, since 1990; b. 24.7.52, Newport, Ireland; m., Marian; 3 s.; 1 d. Educ. Newport Vocational School; University College Cork. Trainee in Surgery, University Hospital, Cork, 1979-83; Research Fellow, Harvard Medical School, 1983-84; Clinical Fellow, Ohio State University, 1984-86; Lecturer in Surgery, University College Dublin, 1986-90; Senior Lecturer and Reader in Surgery, Glasgow University, 1990-98. Publications: 100 papers in journals. Recreations: music; hill-walking. Address: University Department of Surgery, Western Infirmary, Glasgow G11 6NT; T.-0141-211 2163.

O'Farrell, Rt. Rev. Mgr. Peter, BTh (Hons.). Parish Priest, St. Matthew's, Bishopbriggs, since 1998; Prelate of Honour, since 1999; b. 26.11.35, Wicklow, Ireland. Educ. CBS, Westland Row, Dublin; St. John's Seminary for the Clergy, Waterford, Ireland; Maynooth Pontifical University, Ireland. Ordained, Holy Trinity Cathedral, Waterford, Ireland; Assistant Priest: St. Aloysius, Springburn, Glasgow, 1962-73, St. Joseph's, Cumbernauld, 1973-80, St Louise, Arden, Glasgow, 1980-90; Parish Priest: Our Lady and St. Margaret's, Kinning Park, Glasgow, then St. Laurence's, Drumchapel, Glasgow, 1990-95. Tournaments

Director, Clergy Golf, 20 years. Address: St. Matthews, Bishopbriggs, 2 South Crosshill Road, Bishopbriggs, Glasgow G64 2LZ; T.-0141-772 1619.

Ogg, Derek Andrew, LLB. Queen's Counsel, since 1999; Advocate, since 1989; b. 19.9.54, Dunfermline. Educ. Dunfermline High School; Edinburgh University. Solicitor in private practice, 1980-89. Chairman, Institute of Chartered Accountants of Scotland Discipline Tribunal, since 2000; Chairman, Scottish AIDS Monitor Charitable Trust, 1983-94; Trustee, Waverly Care Trust (proprietors of Scotland's AIDS Hospice), since 1990. Recreations: hill-walking; classic cars; reading; music; occasional radio and TV commentator. Address: (h.) 18 Lanark Street, Glasgow G1 5PY; T.-0141-572 4843.

Ogilvy, Sir Francis (Gilbert Arthur), 14th Bt, ARICS. Chartered Surveyor; b. 22.4.69; m., Dorothy Margaret Stein; 2 s. Educ. Edinburgh Academy; Glenalmond College; Royal Agricultural College, Cirencester; BSc (Hons) (Reading). Address: (h.) Winton House, Pencaitland, East Lothian EH34 5AT.

O'Grady, Sheriff Michael Gerard, QC, MA, LLB. Sheriff, Glasgow and Strathkelvin at Glasgow, since 2000; b. 19.8.54, Glasgow; m., Sheena Margaret McDougall. Educ. St. Patrick's High School, Dumbarton; University of Glasgow. Solicitor, private practice (Ross Harper and Murphy, and Gordon McBain and O'Grady), 1977-88; called to the Bar, 1988; Advocate Depute, 1993-97; Standing Junior to Foreign and Commonwealth Office, 1997-98, QC, 1998. Recreations: reading; music; guitar. Address: (b.) Glasgow Sheriff Court, 1 Carlton Place, Glasgow G5 9DA; T.-0141-429 8888.

Ogston, Professor Derek, CBE, MA, MD, PhD, DSc, MLitt, FRCPEdin, FRCP, FIBiol, FRSE, FRSA. Professor of Medicine, Aberdeen University, 1983-97 (Dean, Faculty of Medicine, 1984-87; Vice-Principal, 1987-97); Member, Court, Aberdeen University, since 1998; b. 31.5.32, Aberdeen; m., Cecilia Marie; 1 s.; 2 d. Educ. King's College School, Wimbledon; Aberdeen University. Aberdeen University: Lecturer in Medicine, 1962-69, Senior Lecturer in Medicine, 1969-75, MRC Travelling Fellow, 1967-68, Reader in Medicine, 1975-76, Regius Professor of Physiology, 1977-83. Member, Grampian Health Board, 1991-97 (Vice-Chairman, 1993-97); Member, General Medical Council, 1985-94. Publications: Haemostasis: Biochemistry, Physiology and Pathology (Joint Editor), 1977; The Physiology of Hemostasis, 1983; Antifibrinolytic Drugs: Chemistry, Pharmacology and Clinical Usage, 1984; Venous Thrombosis: Causation and Prediction, 1987; Life and Works of George Smith, RSA, 2000. Recreation: history of art; gardening. Address: (h.) 64 Rubislaw Den South, Aberdeen AB15 4AY; T.-Aberdeen 316587.

O'Hagan, Professor David, BSc, PhD, DSc, MRSC, CChem. Professor and Head of Organic Chemistry, University of St. Andrews, since 2000; b. 29.9.61, Glasgow; m., Anne; 3 d. Educ. Holyrood Secondary School, Glasgow; Glasgow University; Southampton University. Postdoctoral research, Ohio State University, 1985-86; University of Durham: Demonstrator, 1986-88, Lecturer in Chemistry, 1988-99, Professor of Organic Chemistry, 1999-2000. Member, Editorial Board, Natural Product Reports, and Journal of Fluorine Chemistry. Publication: The Polyketide Metabolites, 1991. Recreations: golf; walking; gardening. Address: Millbank Park, 51 Millbank, Cupar, Fife KY15 5EA; T.-01334 650708; e-mail: dol@st-andrews.ac.uk

Ohlmeyer, Professor Jane Helen, MA, AM, PhD, FRHS. Professor in Irish History, Aberdeen University, since 2000; Head of School, History and History of Art,

since 2001; b. 28.12.62, Kitwe, N. Rhodesia; m., Alexander M.S. Green; 2 s. Educ. Methodist College, Belfast; St Andrews University; University of Illinois; Trinity College, Dublin. Lecturer in History, University of California at Santa Barbara; Visiting Professor, New York University; Lecturer in History, Aberdeen University. Trustee, National Library of Scotland, since 2000; Governor, Caledonian Research Foundation, since 2001. Publications include: Civil War and Restoration in the Three Stuart Kingdoms, 1993; Ireland from Independence to Occupation 1641-1660 (Editor), 1995; Political Thoughts in Seventeenth-Century Ireland (Editor), 2000. Address: (b.) School of History and History of Art, King's College, Aberdeen AB24 3FX; T.-01224 273886.

Oldfather, Irene, BA (Hons), MSc. MSP (Lab), Cunninghame South, since 1999; Vice Chair, Cross Party Group on Tobacco Control; b. Glasgow. Educ. Strathclyde University; University of Arizona. Researcher, Dumbarton Council on Alcohol, 1976-77; Lecturer, University of Arizona, 1977-78; Research Officer, Strathclyde Regional Council, 1978-79; various posts, Glasgow District Council Housing Department, 1979-90; Political Researcher, Alex Smith MEP, 1990-98; writer and broadcaster on European affairs, 1994-98; part-time Lecturer, Paisley University, 1996-98; Councillor, North Ayrshire, 1995-99; Member, European Committee of the Regions, 1999-2003; Chair, COSLA Task Group on EMU; Vice-Chair, West of Scotland European Consortium; Member, James Watt College Board of Management, since 1997. Address: (b.) Sovereign House, Academy Road, Irvine KA12 8RL; T.-01294 313078.

Oldham, Professor John David, BSc, PhD. Head, Animal Biology Division, SAC, since 1997; Professor of Animal Biology, SAC, since 1997; b. 20.7.49, Stockport; m., Catherine; 3 s. Educ. Cheadle Hulme School; Nottingham University. Post-doctoral Research Fellow, University of Alberta, 1973-74; Research Scientist, National Institute for Research in Dairying, 1974-84; Head, Animal Production Advisory and Development Department, Edinburgh School of Agriculture, 1984-90; Head, Genetics and Behavioural Sciences Department, SAC, 1990-97. Secretary, The Nutrition Society, 1996-99; President, EAAP Nutrition Commission; Member, Editorial Board, Animal Science; Member, RAE Agriculture Panel; former Member, Editorial Board, British Journal of Nutrition. Sir John Hammond Memorial Prize, 1990; Saltire Society/Royal Bank of Scotland Scottish Science Award, 1995. Recreations: family, home and garden; walking; theatre; reading; music; sketching. Address: Animal Biology Division, SAC, Bush Estate, Penicuik, Midlothian EH26 0QE; T.-0131-535 3201.

Oliver, Christopher William, BSc, MBBS, FRCS (Tr&Orth), FRCP, DM. Consultant Trauma and Orthopaedic Surgeon, Royal Infirmary of Edinburgh, since 1997; part-time Senior Lecturer, Orthopaedics, Edinburgh University, since 1997; b. 5.1.60, London; m., Josephine Hilton; 2 d. Educ. Romford Technical High School, London; University College Hospital, London. Basic surgical training, London and Harrow, 1985-89; Orthopaedic Registrar, York, Leeds, Harrogate, 1989-92; Research Fellow, Spinal Science, Middlesbrough, 1992-94; Senior Registrar, Oswestry and Stoke-on-Trent, 1994-96; Trauma Fellow, Harborview Hospital, Seattle, USA, 1996; Consultant Trauma Surgeon, John Radcliffe Hospital, Oxford, 1996-97. Member, national and international committees relating to medical informatics. Recreations: sailing; skiing; computers; motor-racing. Address: (b.) Edinburgh Orthopaedic Trauma Unit, Royal Infirmary of Edinburgh, Lauriston Place, Edinburgh EH3 9YW; T.-0131-536 3722; e-mail: cwoliver@rcsed.ac.uk

Oliver, Helen Marion, BCom, CA. Principal, Helen M Oliver, Chartered Accountants, since 1990; b. 19.7.57; m., Archie Bell. Educ. Lanark Grammar School; University of Edinburgh. Chiene and Tait, Chartered Accountants, Edinburgh, 1978-81; Coopers and Lybrand, Bermuda, 1981-83; Harvie and Wilson, Chartered Accountants, Wishaw, 1983-88; BBN Systems and Technologies Ltd., Edinburgh, 1988-90; part-time Lecturer, University of Edinburgh, since 1995; External Examiner, Queen Margaret University College, 1996-2000. Member, Council of Management, Couple Counselling, Lothian, 1995-2001; Committee Member: Lothian, Borders and Central Area Committee, ICAS, since 1997, Scottish Chartered Benevolent Association, since 1999, Association of Independent Accountants of Scotland, since 2001; Member, Council, Institute of Chartered Accountants of Scotland, since 2000; Treasurer, Edinburgh and Lothian Council on Alcohol, 2000-01. Recreations: hillwalking; cycling; reading; cinema. Address: (b.) 238 Queensferry Road, Edinburgh EH4 2BP; T.-0131-311 6990.

Olver, Professor Richard Edmund, BSc, MB, BS, FRCP, FRCPE, MRCPCH. James Mackenzie Professor of Child Health, Dundee; b. 26.10.41, Ayr; m.; 2 s.; 2 d. Educ. London University. House Officer and Senior House Officer posts, St. Thomas's, Addenbrookes and Brompton Hospitals, 1966-69; Lecturer, Senior Lecturer, Reader, Department of Paediatrics, University College, London, 1969-85; MRC Travelling Fellow, Cardiovascular Research Institute, San Francisco, 1973-74; Consultant Paediatrician, University College Hospital, London, 1975-85. Address: (b.) Dundee University, Dundee; e-mail: r.e.olver@dundee.ac.uk

O'Malley, Michael. Provost, Perth and Kinross Council, since 1999; Councillor, since 1984; b. 22.1.46, Alyth; m., Kate. Educ. Lawside Academy, Dundee. Engineer, British Telecom, 1962-96; Tayside Regional Councillor, 1990-96; Labour Group Leader, Perth and Kinross Council, since 1995; Chairman, Perth Common Good Fund, 1996-99; Citizen of the Year, 1994. Recreations: sport, particularly football; golf. Address: (b.) 2 High Street, Perth, PH1 15P; T.-01738 475009.

O'Neil, Brian. Director of Personnel, Historic Scotland, since 1997; b. 14.5.50, Edinburgh; m., Irene; 2 d. Educ. Gracemount Secondary School, Edinburgh. Joined Scottish Office, 1966; Head of Branch, Local Government Division, 1990-95. Recreations: golf; reading; gardening. Address: (b.) Historic Scotland, Longmore House, Salisbury Place, Edinburgh EH9 1SH; T.-0131-668 8667.

O'Neil, Danny, BSc, FFA. Deputy Chairman, Britannic Asset Management Ltd., since 2002; Group Chief Executive, Britannic plc, 2001-2002; b. 8.6.60, Glasgow; m., Patricia; 2s.; 2d. Educ. St Margaret Mary's, Glasgow University. Trainee Actuary, 1981; FS Investment Manager, 1981-87; Director, FS Investment Managers, 1987; Director, Britannia Smaller Companies Trust, 1997; Chief Executive, Britannia Asset Management Ltd., 1992-2001. Recreations: sport; golf; tennis. Correspondence address: (b.) Britannic Court, 50 Bothwell Street, Glasgow; T.-0141-222 8000; e-mail: do'neil@britannicasset.com

O'Neill, Rev. Professor John Cochrane, BA, BD, PhD, DD h.c. Professor of New Testament Language, Literature and Theology, Edinburgh University, 1985-96; b. 8.12.30, Melbourne; m., Judith Beatrice Lyall (see Judith Beatrice O'Neill); 3 d. Educ. Melbourne Church of England Grammar School; Melbourne University; Ormond College Theological Hall; University of Göttingen; Clare College, Cambridge. Senior Tutor in History, Melbourne University, 1953-55; Lecturer in New Testament Studies, Ormond College Theological Hall, Melbourne, 1960-64; Dunn Professor of New Testament Language, Literature and Theology, Westminster College, Cambridge, 1964-85. Publications: Paul's Letter to the Romans, 1975; The Bible's Authority: a portrait gallery of thinkers from Lessing to Bultmann, 1991; Who Did Jesus Think He Was?, 1995; The Point of It All: Essays on Jesus Christ, 2000. Recreations: swimming; camping. Address: (h.) 9 Lonsdale Terrace, Edinburgh EH3 9HN; T.-0131-229 6070; e-mail: joneill@ed.ac.uk

O'Neill, Judith Beatrice, MA, PGCE. Author of fiction for older children; b. 30.6.30, Melbourne; m., John Cochrane O'Neill (qv); 3 d. Educ. University of Melbourne; University of London. University Tutor, Melbourne, 1954-56; School Teacher, Cambridge, 1974-82; full-time author, since 1982. Publications: Transported to Van Diemen's Land; Jess and the River Kids; Stringybark Summer; Deepwater; The Message; So Far from Skye; Hearing Voices, 1996; Spindle River, 1998; Leaving the Island, 1998; Whirlwind, 1999. Recreations: reading; walking; music; camping; theatre. Address: (h.) 9 Lonsdale Terrace, Edinburgh EH3 9HN; T.-0131-229 6070; e-mail: joneill@ed.ac.uk

O'Neill, Martin H.M., Manager, Celtic Football Club, since 2000; b. 1.3.52, Kilrea, Northern Ireland. Played for Distillery and Derry City; Northern Ireland debut, 1971 (64 caps); joined: Nottingham Forest, 1971, Norwich, February 1981, Manchester City, June 1981, Norwich 1982, Notts County, 1983; Manager: Wycombe Wanderers, 1990, Norwich, June–December, 1995, Leicester, 1995. Address: Celtic Football Club, Celtic Park, Glasgow G40 3RE.

O'Neill, Martin (John), BA (Econ). MP (Labour), Ochil, since 1997 (Clackmannan, 1983-97, East Stirlingshire and Clackmannan, 1979-83); b. 6.1.45; m., Elaine Samuel; 2 s. Educ. Trinity Academy, Edinburgh; trades union and evening classes; Heriot-Watt University; Moray House College of Education. President, Scottish Union of Students, 1970-71; school teacher, 1974-79; Tutor, Open University, 1976-79. Member, Select Committee, Scottish Affairs, 1979-80; Opposition Spokesman, Scottish Affairs, 1980-84; Opposition Spokesman on Defence, 1984-88; Shadow Defence Secretary, 1988-92; Shadow Spokesman on Energy, 1992-95; Chair, Trade and Industry Select Committee, since 1995. Recreations: watching football; reading; listening to jazz; cinema. Address: (b.) 49 High Street, Alloa FK10 1JF; e-mail: oneillm@parliament.uk

O'Neill, Maureen Patricia, BA (Hons), DMS. Director, Age Concern Scotland, since 1993; b. 11.5.48, Uganda; m., Jonathan Clogstoun-Willmott; 1 s.; 1 d. Educ. St. Margaret's School, Hastings; Charlton Park School, Cheltenham; Birkbeck College, London University. General Secretary, Edinburgh YWCA, 1982-87; Principal Officer, Policy, Research and Development, Scottish Association for Mental Health, 1987-93; Chairperson, Edinburgh Voluntary Organisations Council. Recreations: reading; theatre; sport. Address: (b.) 113 Rose Street, Edinburgh EH2 3DT; T.-0131-220 3345.

O'Neill, Dr William M., BSc, MB, BCh, BAO, FRCGP. Scottish Secretary, British Medical Association, since 2000; b. 4.5.52, Limerick. Educ. University College and St Vincent's Hospital, Dublin. Junior medical posts, St Vincent's Hospital and Mater Hospital, Dublin; Middlesex Hospital and St Thomas's Hospital, London; principal in general practice, Kensington, London, 1993-98; Consultancy Senior Lecturer in Palliative Medicine, St Thomas's Hospital, London, 1991-93; Bristol Oncology Centre, 1993-95; Organisational Development Consultant, Primary Care Support Force, London, 1995-96; Science and Research Advisor, British Medical Association, London, 1996-2000. Address: (b.) BMA Scotland, 14 Queen Street, Edinburgh EH2 1LL; T.-0131-247 3000.

Ord, Jeff, OStJ, QFSM, GIFireE. Firemaster, Strathclyde Fire Brigade, since 1999; b. 1949, Fulwell Fire Station, Sunderland; m., Beryl; 1 s. Joined Auxiliary Fire Service, 1966; joined Sunderland Fire Brigade, 1967, following in father's footsteps; seconded to Fire Service College, 1983, seving as a College Tutor and Course Director; promoted to Kent Fire Brigade, 1986, as Commander of North Division, then Head of Operations (Assistant Chief Officer), 1987; Chief Fire Officer, Northumberland Fire and Rescue Service, 1988, becoming Director of Protective Services, Chief Fire Officer and County Emergency Planning Officer, 1992; Chief Fire Officer, South Yorkshire Fire and Rescue Service, 1996. JP, 1981; Vice President, Chief and Assistant Chief Fire Officers' Association (Member, Council, since 1990, Director of External Relations, since 1998); Assessor to Fire Services Examination Board and Fire Services Extended Interview Board. Recreations: walking; tennis; avid Sunderland FC supporter (the premier club). Address: (b.) Strathclyde Fire Brigade HQ, Bothwell Road, Hamilton ML3 0EA; e-mail: j.ord@strathclyde.fire-uk.org

O'Reilly, Denis St. John, MSc, MD, FRCP, FRCPath. Consultant Clinical Biochemist, Royal Infirmary, Glasgow, since 1984; b. 30.3.51, Cork; m., Margaret M.P. Lucey; 2 s.; 1 d. Educ. Presentation Brothers College, Cork; University College, Cork; Birmingham University. Registrar, Queen Elizabeth Medical Centre, Birmingham, 1976-78; Senior Registrar, Bristol Royal Infirmary, 1978-84; Ainsworth Scholar-Research Fellow, Norsk Hydro Institute for Cancer Research, Oslo, 1982. Recreation: hillwalking. Address: (h.) 47 Strathblane Road, Milngavie G62 8HA.

O'Reilly, Seán, BA (Hons), PhD. Director, Architectural Heritage Society of Scotland, since 1996; b. 27.8.61, Dublin; m., Dr. Deborah Mays; 1 d. Educ. Christian Brothers School, Kilcock; University College, Dublin. Lecturer, History of Art, Sligo and Dublin; Researcher and Photographer, Irish Architectural Archive, Dublin; Historic Buildings Consultant, private practice, Dublin. Editor, Journal of the Irish Georgian Society. Publications: New Lease of Life (Co-Author); Irish Houses and Gardens – from the archives of Country Life; numerous papers, articles and booklets. Address: (b.) The Glasite Meeting House, 33 Barony Street, Edinburgh EH3 6NX; T.-0131-557 0019.

Orme, Professor Joan Elizabeth, BA, DipSocStudies, DipSocStudies (App), ACSS. Professor of Social Work, Glasgow University, since 2000; b. 19.8.47, South Shields; m., Geoffrey; 1 s.; 1 d. Educ. South Shields Grammar School for Girls; Sheffield University. Probation Officer, Sheffield, 1970-72; Southampton/Hampshire, 1972-76; Lecturer, then Senior Lecturer, then Reader, Southampton University, 1976-2000. Publications: Social Work Practice, 1998; Gender and Community Care, 2001. Address: (b.) Department of Social Policy and Social Work, Lilybank House, Glasgow University, Glasgow G12 8RT; T.-0141-330 2716.

Ormiston, Linda, MA, DRSAMD, Hon. DMus (St. Andrews). Singer — Mezzo Soprano; b. 15.1.48, Motherwell. Educ. Dalziel High School, Motherwell; Glasgow University; Royal Scottish Academy of Music and Drama; London Opera Centre. Has sung all over Britain, France, Belgium, Italy, Germany, Austria, Holland and Yugoslavia; has sung regularly at Scottish Opera, Opera North, and Glyndebourne; also well-known in lighter vein and as a member of The Music Box; recordings include Noyes Fludde, HMS Pinafore and Ruddigore with New Sadlers Wells Opera and Tell Me Pretty Maiden; has appeared at New York, Vancouver, Monte Carlo, Brussels and Tokyo; debut, Frankfurt Opera, 1993; debut, Salzburg Festival, 1994; debut, English National Opera, 1995;

Presenter, BBC Radio 3 and Radio Scotland. Recreations: playing the piano; skating; golf.

Ormond, Rupert Frank Guy, BA, MA, PhD. Director, University Marine Biological Station Millport, since 1999; Senior Lecturer, London University, since 1999; Visiting Professor, Glasgow University, since 2000; b. 1.6.46, Bristol; 2 s.; 1 d. Educ. Clifton College, Bristol; Peterhouse, Cambridge. Marine Biological Station, Port Sudan, Sudan, 1972-74; Lecturer/Senior Lecturer, Biology Department, 1974-99, Director, Tropical Marine Research Unit, 1982-99, York University. District Councillor, Ryedale District Council, 1987-96; Member: North York Moors National Park Committee, 1995-96, Council, Scottish Association for Marine Science, Council, WWF Scotland, Scottish Natural Heritage Scientific Advisory Committee. Publications include: Red Sea Coral Reefs (Co-author); Marine Biodiversity (Co-author). Recreations: natural history; travel; classical music. Address: (h.) Bellevue, 16 Kames Bay, Millport, Isle of Cumbrae; T.-01475 530260.

O'Rourke, Daniel (Donny), MA. Poet, journalist, filmmaker, broadcaster, and teacher; Director, Scottish Cultural Studies, Glasgow School of Art, since 1998; Visiting Professor, Friedrich Schillen University, since 2001; Television Critic, The Scotsman; Member, Editorial Board, Edinburgh University Press, since 1999; Chair, Scottish Book Marketing Group, since 1996; Director, Scottish Book Trust, since 1998; b. 5.7.59, Port Glasgow. Educ. St. Mirin's Academy, Paisley; Glasgow University. Chairman, Scottish Youth Council, 1982-84; Producer, BBC TV and Radio Scotland, 1984-86; Reporter, Scottish Television, 1986-87, Producer, 1987-92, Head of Arts, 1992-93, Head of Arts and Documentaries, 1993-94; Executive Producer, BBC Scotland, 1994-95; Creative Writing Fellow, Glasgow University and Strathclyde University, 1995-97; Head of English and Media Studies, Department of Adult and Continuing Education, Glasgow University, 1996-98; Poet in Residence, Edinburgh International Book Festival, 1999; Columnist, Sunday Herald, 1999; Member, Manpower Services Commission Youth Training Board, 1982-84; Member, Scottish Community Education Council, 1981-84; Chairman of Judges, Scottish Writer of the Year Award, 1996, 1997; Director, Tron Theatre Company, 1993-95; Member, Editorial Board, "11/9"; Artistic Director, Reacquaintance Robert Burns in Glasgow (year-long celebration), 2000; theatre: The Kerrera Saga (with George Wyllie), 1998, On Your Nerve, A Wake for Frank O'Hara, 1996. Publications: Second City, 1991; Rooming Houses of America, 1993; Dream State, the new Scottish poets, 1994; chapter in Burns Now, 1994; Eftirs/Afters, 1996; The Waist Band and Other Poems, 1997; Across the Water, 2000 (Co-Editor); New Writing Scotland anthologies – Some Kind of Embrace, 1997, The Glory Signs, 1998, Friends and Kangaroos, 1999; Still Waiting To Be Wise (with Dave Whyte), 1999; On A Roll, 2001; poems in various anthologies and textbooks. Recreations: Italian food; playing guitar; Irish literature; Americana. Address: (h.) 63 Barrington Drive, Glasgow, G4 9ES; e-mail: donny.orourke@btinternet.com

Orr, David Campbell, MA. Director, Scottish Federation of Housing Associations, since 1990; seconded to Scottish Executive to promote community ownership of housing, 2000-01; b. 27.3.55, Kirkconnel; m., Carol; 1 s.; 2 d. Educ. Dundee University. Deputy Warden, Iona Community, Community House, 1976-77; Team Leader, then Co-ordinator, Centrepoint, Soho, 1977-86; Director, Newlon Housing Trust, 1986-90. Former Chair, Young Homelessness Group, Homeless Network, Threshold H.A.; Member: Scottish Charity Law Review Commission, 2000-01; former Member, Policy Committee and Management Board, SCVO. Recreations: watching sport — playing badly; cinema. Address: (b.) 38 York Place, Edinburgh EH1 3HU; T.-0131-556 5777; e-mail: dorr@sfha.co.uk

Orr, Sir John, OBE, OStJ, QPM, LLD (Glasgow Caledonian), DUniv (Glasgow), BA, DL. Chief Constable, Strathclyde, 1996-2001; Chairman, Kilmarnock Football Club, since 2001; Deputy Lieutenant, Dumfries, since 2001; Member: Secretary of State's Crime Prevention Council, Expert Panel on Sex Offenders, Service Authority of National Criminal Intelligence Service; Member, Nicholson Committee (Review of Liquor Licensing Laws); Trustee, Crimestoppers, since 2001; b. 3.9.45, Kilmarnock; m., Joan; 2 s.; 1 d. Educ. James Hamilton Academy, Kilmarnock; Open University; Glasgow University. Entered police as cadet, Renfrew and Bute, 1961; progressed through ranks to rank of Detective Chief Superintendent and Joint Head of Strathclyde CID; Deputy Chief Constable, Dumfries and Galloway, 1990-96; seconded 1994 to HM Inspectorate of Constabulary as Assistant Inspector of Constabulary for Scotland. Hon. President, Association of Chief Police Officers in Scotland, 1997-98; Hon. President, Glasgow Bn., Boys' Brigade; Paul Harris Fellow, Rotary International, 1997; awarded Lord Provost of Glasgow's Medal for Public Service, 1999. Recreations: reading; gardening; angling. Address: (b.) c/o Kilmarnock Football Club, Rugby Park, Kilmarnock KA1 2DP.

Orr Ewing, Major Edward Stuart, DL, JP. Lord Lieutenant, Wigtown, since 1989; b. 28.9.31, London; m., 1, F.A.B. Farquhar (m. dissolved); 2, Diana Mary Waters; 1 s.; 2 d. Educ. Sherborne; RMCS, Shrivenham. Black Watch RHR, 1950-69 (Major); Farmer and Landowner, since 1964. Recreations: country sports; skiing; sailing; painting.

Orskov, Professor Egil Robert, OBE, BSc, PhD, DSc, FRSE. Director, International Feed Resource Unit, Macaulay Institute, since 2000, previously at Rowett Research Institute, 1990-2000; International Consultant, United Nations Organization, since 1980; b. 24.5.34, Denmark; m., Joan P.; 2 s.; 1 d. Post-doctoral work, USDA, Washington, 1966-67; Rowett Research Institute: Head, Sheep Section, 1967-75, Dairy Cattle Section, 1975-85, Head, Ruminant Nutrition, 1985-90. Publications: four books; 510 papers. Recreations: music; travel; antique collector. Address: (b.) Macaulay Institute, Craigiebuckler, Aberdeen AB15 8QH; T.-01224 498243; e-mail: b.orskov@macaulay.ac.uk

Osborne, Rt. Hon. Lord (Kenneth Hilton Osborne), QC (Scot). Senator of the College of Justice, since 1990; b. 9.7.37. Advocate, 1962; QC, 1976; Chairman, Local Government Boundary Commission, 1990-2000.

Osborne, Sandra, MSc. MP (Labour), Ayr, since 1997; b. 23.2.56; m., Alastair; 2 d. Educ. Camphill Senior Secondary School, Paisley; Anniesland College; Jordanhill College; Strathclyde University. Former community worker. Address: (b.) House of Commons, London SW1A 0AA.

Osler, Douglas Alexander, MA (Hons). HM Senior Chief Inspector and Chief Executive, HM Inspectorate of Education, Scottish Executive; b. 11.10.42, Edinburgh; m., Wendy I. Cochrane; 1 s.; 1 d. Educ. Royal High School, Edinburgh; Edinburgh University; Moray House College of Education. Assistant Teacher of History/Careers Master, Liberton Secondary School, Edinburgh, 1965-68; Principal Teacher of History, Dunfermline High School, 1968-74. English Speaking Union Fellowship to USA, 1966; International Visitor Program to USA, 1989. Publications: Queen Margaret of Scotland; Sources for Modern Studies, Volumes 1 and 2. Address: (b.) Saughton House, Broomhouse Drive, Edinburgh EH11 3XD; e-mail: douglas.osler@scotland.gsi.gov.uk

O'Sullivan, Very Rev. Canon Basil, JCL. Parish Priest, Holy Family, Dunblane, since 1988; b. 1932, Fishguard. Educ. St. Finbarr's College, Cork; All Hallow's College, Dublin; Pontifical University of St. Gregory, Rome. Assistant Priest: St. Joseph's, Dundee, 1959-63, St.

Andrew's Cathedral, Dundee, 1963-70; R.C. Chaplain, Dundee University, 1964-70; Parish Priest: St. John Vianney's, Alva, 1970-74, St. Columba's, Dundee, 1974-88. Canon of Dunkeld Chapter, since 1992. Recreations: reading; gardening; walking. Address: (h.) St. Clare's, Claredon Place, Dunblane FK15 9HB; T.-01786 822146.

Oswald, Rev. John, BSc, BD, PhD. Minister, Lorne and Lowland Parish Church, since 1997; b. 10.10.47, Glasgow; m., Barbara R.; 1 s. Educ. Kelvinside Academy; Edinburgh University. Management posts, Nickerson Seed Specialists; Managing Director, David Bell Ltd., Penicuik; candidate for ministry; Assistant Minister, Eddleston linked with Peebles Old. Recreations: tennis; gardening; reading. Address: Lorne and Lowland Manse, Castlehill, Campbeltown PA28 6AN; T.-01586 552468; e-mail: revdocoz@bigfoot.com

Outram, Robert Francis, BA (Oxon). Editor, CA Magazine, since 1998; b. 8.5.61, Barnet; partner, Christina Cheong. Educ. France Hill, Camberley, Surrey; St Catherine's College, Oxford. Management trainee, Greater London Council, 1983-85; accountancy trainee, Inner London Education Authority, 1985-88; Audit trainee, KPMG, 1988-89; Journalist, Career Accountant magazine, 1989-90; Journalist, Accountancy Age, 1990-95 (appointed Editor, 1992); freelance journalist and consultant, 1995-98. Recreations: film; theatre; travel; Tottenham Hotspur FC. Address: (b.) 1A St. Bernard's Row, Stockbridge, Edinburgh EH4 1HW; T.-0131-343 7500.

Owen, Professor David Gareth, MA, BD (Hons), PhD, FICE, CEng, FRSA. Professor of Offshore Engineering, Heriot-Watt University, since 1986 (Vice Principal, since 1999); b. 6.11.40, Brecon, Wales; m., Ann Valerie Wright; 2 d. Educ. Christ College, Brecon; Downing College, Cambridge. Graduate Engineer, John Laing & Son, London; Aerospace Engineer, Marconi Space and Defence Systems, Portsmouth; Lecturer in Civil Engineering, Heriot-Watt University; Visiting Professor, University of New Hampshire; Senior Lecturer, Department of Offshore Engineering, Heriot-Watt University. Recreations: music; travelling. Address: (h.) 7 Oak Lane, Edinburgh EH12 6XH; T.-0131-339 1740.

Owens, Agnes. Author; b. 24.5.26, Milngavie; m., Patrick Owens; 2 s.; 4 d. Educ. Bearsden Academy. Worked in shops, factories and offices; came to writing by accident; author of Gentlemen of the West (Autumn Book Award, 1984), Like Birds in the Wilderness, A Working Mother, People Like That, For the Love of Willie; short stories in Lean Tales, The Seven Deadly Sins and The Seven Cardinal Virtues; wrote a play with Liz Lochhead which toured Scotland for three months. Recreations: walking; reading. Address: (h.) 21 Roy Young Avenue, Balloch, Dunbartonshire; T.-Alexandria 50921.

Oxfuird, 13th Viscount of (George Hubbard Makgill), CBE; b. 7.1.34; m.; 4 s. Succceeded to title, 1986; elected Member, House of Lords, since 1999.

P

Pacione, Professor Michael, MA, PhD. Professor of Geography, Strathclyde University, since 1990; b. 14.10.47, Dundee; m., Christine Hopper; 1 s.; 1 d. Educ. Lawside Academy, Dundee; Dundee University. Lecturer in Geography, Queens University, Belfast, 1973-75; Lecturer, Senior Lecturer, Reader, Strathclyde University, Glasgow, 1975-89; Visiting Professor, University of Guelph, 1984, and University of Vienna, 1995. Publications: 25 books and numerous academic research papers. Recreations: sport; travel; photography. Address: (b.) Department of Geography, Strathclyde University, 50 Richmond Street, Glasgow G1 1XH; T.-0141-548 3793; e-mail: michaelpacione@cs.com

Pack, Professor Donald Cecil, CBE, MA, DSc, FIMA, FEIS, FRSE. Emeritus Professor, Strathclyde University, since 1986; b. 14.4.20, Higham Ferrers; m., Constance Mary Gillam; 2 s.; 1 d. Educ. Wellingborough School; New College, Oxford. Ordnance Board, Cambridge, 1941-43; Armament Research Department, Ministry of Supply, Fort Halstead, 1943-46; Lecturer in Mathematics, St. Andrews University, 1947-52; Visiting Research Associate, Maryland University, 1951-52; Lecturer in Mathematics, Manchester University, 1952-53; Professor of Mathematics, Strathclyde University, 1953-82 (Vice-Principal, 1968-72); Honorary Professor, 1982-86; Member, various Government scientific boards and committees, 1952-84; Member, Defence Scientific Advisory Council, 1975-80; DERA Visiting Fellow, 1999; first Hon. Member, European Consortium for Mathematics in Industry, 1988; Chairman, Scottish Certificate of Education Examination Board, 1969-77; Chairman, Committee of Inquiry into Truancy and Indiscipline in Scottish Schools, 1974-77 ("Pack Report" published by HMSO, 1977); Hon. President, National Youth Orchestra of Scotland (Chairman, Steering Committee, 1978, Chairman, 1978-88); Member, Scottish Arts Council, 1980-85; Member, UK Committee for European Music Year 1985 and Chairman, Scotland Advisory Committee, 1983-86; Member: General Teaching Council for Scotland, 1966-73, Dunbartonshire Education Committee, 1960-66; Governor, Hamilton College of Education, 1976-81; Council Member, Royal Society of Edinburgh, 1960-63; Honorary Treasurer and Council Member, Institute of Mathematics and its Applications, 1964-72; Member: International Advisory Committee on Rarefied Gas Dynamics Symposia, 1976-88, British National Committee for Theoretical Mechanics, 1973-78, Council, Gesellschaft fuer angewandte Mathematik und Mechanik, 1977-83; Guest Professor: Technische Universitaet, Berlin, 1967, Bologna University and Politechnico Milan, 1980, Technische Hochschule, Darmstadt, 1981; other visiting appointments, Warsaw University, 1977, Kaiserslautern University, 1980 and 1984. Past President: Edinburgh Mathematical Society, Glasgow Mathematical Association; Honorary President, Milngavie Music Club (President, 1983-93). Recreations: music; gardening; golf. Address: (h.) 18 Buchanan Drive, Bearsden, Glasgow G61 2EW; T.-0141-942 5764.

Pagan, Graeme Henry, MBE, BL, WS. Solicitor, Hosack & Sutherland, Oban, since 1960; Honorary Sheriff of North Strathclyde at Oban, since 1988; b. 20.3.36, Cupar; m., Heather; 1 s.; 2 d. Educ. New Park, St. Andrews; Bedford School; Edinburgh University. Part-time Procurator Fiscal, Oban, 1970-79; Regional Organiser, Shelter Campaign for the Homeless, 1968-75; Chairman, Oban Housing Association, 1971-98; Founder Member, Oban Abbeyfield Society; Originator, Solicitors Will Aid; Convener, Argyll and Bute Scottish Liberal Democrats, 1991-2000.

Recreations: family; jazz; malt whisky; wandering in the Highlands on foot and bike. Address: (h.) Neaveton, Oban, Argyll; T.-01631 563737.

Page, Professor Alan Chisholm, LLB, PhD. Professor of Public Law, Dundee University, since 1985; b. 7.4.52, Broughty Ferry; m., Sheila Duffus; 1 s.; 1 d. Educ. Grove Academy; Edinburgh University. Lecturer in Law, University College, Cardiff, 1975-80; Senior Lecturer in Law, Dundee University, 1980-85; Head, Department of Law, 1980-95; Dean, Faculty of Law, 1986-89; SHEFC Lead Assessor in Law, 1995-96; Member, Tax Law Review Committee, since 1994. Publications: Legislation; Investor Protection; The Executive in the Constitution. Recreation: mountaineering. Address: (h.) Westlands, Westfield Road, Cupar, Fife KY15 5DR.

Paisley of Westerlea (Duncan Wilson), FRSA, FSA (Scot). Landowner; Company Director; 16th Head of the Name; 5th Laird of the Barony of Westerlea; Captain, Balgonie Castle; Ambassador (Overseas), Capability Scotland; Patron, Westerlea School, Edinburgh; b. 30.8.48, Woodcote; m., Valerie R. Alcantra; 3 d. Educ. Cannock House School; Westwood. Regular Army, 1966-90 (Gordon Highlanders, RAOC) General List; King's Own Scottish Borderers, 1990-95; Regional Liaison Officer, Scottish Landowners' Federation, 1992-93; since 1993: Chief Assessor (Scotland), Guild of Master Craftsmen; Chairman, Westerlea Trust; President, Scottish Tartan Society; Director, Register of all Publicly Known Tartans; Freeman of Glasgow. Recreations: hill-walking; Scottish domestic architecture; family history. Address: (h.) Glen Annan House, Moffat, Dumfriesshire DG10 9RS; T.-01683 220014 (estate); 01683 221840 (h.); e-mail: Westerlea1@aol.com

Paling, Edwin. Leader, Royal National Orchestra, since 1973; Member, The Paragon Ensemble, since 1994; Violin Teacher, Royal Scottish Academy of Music and Drama, since 1985; b. 29.12.48, Nottingham; 1 s. 2 d. Educ. Royal Academy of Music. Bournemouth Symphony Orchestra, 1970-71; City of Birmingham Symphony Orchestra, 1971-72; BBC Midland Light Orchestra, 1972. Recreation: walking. Address: 345 Kilmarnock Road, Glasgow G43 2DS; T.-0141-632 0567.

Panton, John, MBE. Professional Golfer; b. 9.10.16, Pitlochry. Won PGA Match-Play Championship, 1956 (Runner-up, 1968); PGA British Seniors', 1967-69; World Seniors', 1967 (defeated Sam Snead for title); Silver King, 1950; Daks, 1951; North British-Harrogate, 1952; Goodwin Foursomes, 1952; Yorkshire Evening News, 1954; Gleneagles-Saxone Am.-Pro. Foursomes, 1956; Woodlawn Invitation Open (West Germany), 1958-59-60; leading British player, Open Championship, 1956; Leader, PGA Order of Merit (Vardon Trophy), 1951; won Scottish Professional Championship, seven times (and joint Champion, once); Ryder Cup player, 1951-53-61; awarded Golf Writers' Trophy, 1967; Hon. Professional, Royal and Ancient Golf Club, St. Andrews.

Paolozzi, Professor Sir Eduardo, Kt, CBE, RA. Sculptor; HM Sculptor in Ordinary for Scotland, since 1986; Visiting Professor, Royal College of Art, since 1989; b. 7.3.24; 3 d. Educ. Edinburgh School of Art; Slade School. Worked in Paris, 1947-50; Instructor, Central School of Arts and Crafts, London, 1950-55; Lecturer, St Martin's School of Art, 1955-56; Professor of Ceramics, Cologne, 1977-81; Professor of Sculpture, Munich, 1981-91; numerous one-man exhibitions.

Park, Ian Michael Scott, CBE, MA, LLB. Partner, Paull & Williamsons, Advocates, Aberdeen, 1961-91, Consultant, since 1991; Member: Criminal Injuries Compensation Board, since 1983, Criminal Injuries Compensation Appeals Panel, since 1996; b. 7.4.38, Aberdeen; m., Elizabeth M.L.

Struthers; 2 s. Educ. Aberdeen Grammar School; Aberdeen University. Assistant to, subsequently Partner in, Paull & Williamsons; Member, Society of Advocates in Aberdeen, since 1962, Treasurer, 1991-92, President, 1992-93; sometime part-time Assistant, Department of Public Law, Aberdeen University; President, Law Society of Scotland, 1980-81 (Council Member, 1974-85); Chairman, Aberdeen Citizens Advice Bureau, until 1988; Secretary, Aberdeen Granite Association, 1962-84; Temporary Sheriff, 1976-84; Honorary Sheriff at Aberdeen, since 1996; part-time Chairman, Medical Appeals Tribunals, until 1996; frequent broadcaster on legal topics. Recreations: golf; gardening. Address: (h.) 46 Rubislaw Den South, Aberdeen.

Park, Neil Ferguson, BSc, MBA. Consultant, Edgewood Consultancy; Vice Chairman, Scottish Sports Association; b. 26.9.62, Gosport; m., Judith Frances; 1 s.; 1 d. Educ. Daniel Stewart's and Melville College, Edinburgh; Aberdeen University; Edinburgh University. Former Assistant Secretary, Royal Highland and Agricultural Society; former General Manager, Scottish Athletics Limited. Council Member, Royal Burgess Golfing Society of Edinburgh; Lay Member, Sports Dispute Resolution Panel. Recreations: rugby; golf; road-running. Address: (b.) 22 Craigcrook Road, Edinburgh EH4 3PG.

Parker, Anthony W. BA, MA, PhD, ILTM, FCS. Director, School of American Studies, University of Dundee, since 2000; Lecturer in History, University of Dundee, since 1996; b., 3.2.53, Little Rock, Arkansas, USA; m., Lisa Ann; 3 s. Educ. St. Andrews University; University of Georgia, Athens, Georgia, USA. Joined University of Dundee, 1996; Co-Director, Program Diploma Course for American Students, International Studies Semester Abroad Programme, since 2001. External Academic Reviewer, National Museums of Scotland, Museum of Scotland International, 2001-2002; Convener, North American Studies Group, Scottish Confederation of University and Research Libraries; Editor, Journal of Transatlantic Studies; Founding Member, Scottish Trans-Atlantic Relations Project; Council Member, Economic and Social History Society of Scotland; Fellow, Charles Warren Center for Studies in American History, Harvard University, International Seminar on the History of the Atlantic World, 1996. Publication: Scottish Highlanders in Colonial Georgia: the Recruitment, Emigration and Settlement in Darien, 1735–1748, 1997; numerous articles, book reviews, papers. Recreations: golf; more golf; rare books; antiques; photography; music; travel. Address: (b.) School of American Studies, University of Dundee, Dundee DD1 4HN; T.-01382 345465; e-mail: a.w.parker@dundee.ac.uk

Parker, Cameron Holdsworth, OBE, DL, BSc. Lord Lieutenant of Renfrewshire, since 1998; b. 14.4.32, Dundee; m., Marlyne Honeyman; 3 s. Educ. Morrison's Academy, Crieff; Glasgow University. Managing Director, latterly also Chairman, John G. Kincaid & Co. Ltd., Greenock, 1967-80; Chairman and Chief Executive, Scott Lithgow Ltd., Port Glasgow, 1980-83; Board Member, British Shipbuilders, 1977-80, 1981-83; Chief Executive, Prosper Enginering Ltd., Irvine, 1983-84; Managing Director, Lithgows Limited, 1984-92, Vice-Chairman, 1992-97. Freeman, City of London; Liveryman, Worshipful Company of Shipwrights; Member, Council, CBI Scotland, 1986-92; Member, Argyll and Clyde Health Board, 1991-95; Board Member, Scottish Homes, 1992-96; Director, Clyde Shaw Ltd., 1992-94; Honorary President, Accord Hospice, since 1998; President, SSAFA Forces Help, Renfrewshire, since 1998. Recreation: golf; gardening. Address: (h.) Heath House, Kilmacolm, Renfrewshire PA13 4PE; T.-01505 873197.

Parker, Professor Denis Michael, BA, PhD, CPsychol, FBPsS. Professor of Psychology, Glasgow Caledonian University, since 1996; Head, Department of Psychology, since 1996; b. 26. 6.43, Cork; m., Mannell Ruth; 3 s. Educ.

St. Ignatius College, London; Durham University. Addison Wheeler Research Fellow, Durham University, 1969-71; Lecturer/Senior Lecturer/Reader in Psychology, Aberdeen University, 1972-95; Visiting Professor, University of Konstanz, 1995. Recreations: hill-walking; reading; cogitating. Address: (b.) Department of Psychology, Glasgow Caledonian University, Cowcaddens Road, Glasgow G4 0BA; T.-0141-331 3120.

Parker, Timothy Robert Walter, LLB. Depute Secretary to Church of Scotland General Trustees, since 1982; b. 7.10.44, Aberdeen; m., Janet Helen Nicol; 3 d. Educ. Trinity College, Glenalmond; Aberdeen University. Private practice as Solicitor, 1969-82. Formerly: Chairman, Lothian Primary Schools Chess League, Chairman, Trinity Academy P.T.A., Secretary, Lothian Federation of P.T.A.s. Recreations: bowling; walking; watching other sports; listening to music. Address: (h.) 35 Dudley Avenue, Edinburgh EH6 4PL; T.-0131-554 2076.

Parnell, Brian K., BSc, ACGI, DipTP, FRTPI. Planning Consultant, 1965-99; Vice-Chairman and Hon. Secretary, Scottish Council for National Parks, since 1991; Visiting Professor, Centre for Planning, Strathclyde University, 1991-99; b. 18.12.22, Brighton; 2 s.; 1 d. Educ. Varndean School, Brighton; London University; Edinburgh College of Art. Captain, EME, 1943-47; Department of Planning, Midlothian County Council, 1949-57; Depute Planning Officer, Stirling County Council, 1957-64; joined Glasgow School of Art, 1964, Head, Department of Planning, 1976-87; Commissioner, Countryside Commission for Scotland, 1968-80; part-time Planning Inquiry Reporter, Scottish Office, 1982-93. Chairman, Scottish Branch, Royal Town Planning Institute, 1972-73; Executive Committee Member, National Trust for Scotland, 1973-83; Trustee, Scottish Civic Trust, since 1985; Convener, Stirling Civic Trust, since 1994. Recreations: sailing; swimming; hill-walking; travel. Address: (h.) 15 Park Terrace, Stirling FK8 2JT; T.-01786 465714.

Parr, Professor John Brian, BSc (Econ), MA, PhD, ACSS. Professor of Regional and Urban Economics, Glasgow University, since 1989; Chairman, British-Irish Section, Regional Science Association, 1981-85; b. 18.3.41, Epsom; m., Pamela Jean Harkins; 2 d. Educ. Henry Thornton School; London University; University of Washington. Instructor, University of Washington, 1966; Assistant Professor/Associate Professor, University of Pennsylvania, 1967-75; joined Glasgow University as Lecturer, 1975. Academician of the Academy of Learned Societies for the Social Sciences; Editor, Papers of the Regional Science Association, 1968-75; Associate Editor, Journal of Regional Science, since 1979; Co-Editor, European Research in Regional Science, since 1990; Member, Board of Management, Urban Studies, since 1981; Associate Editor, Annals of Regional Science, 1993-96; Member, Editorial Board, International Regional Science Review, since 1995; Member, Editorial Board, Review of Urban and Regional Development Studies, since 1995. Publications: numerous journal articles on urban and regional analysis; Christaller Central Place Structures (Co-Author); Regional Policy: Past Experience and New Directions (Co-Editor); Analysis of Regional Structure: Essays in Honour of August Lösch (Co-Editor); Market Centers and Retail Location (Co-Author). Address: (b.) Department of Urban Studies, Glasgow University, Glasgow G12 8RS; T.-0141-339 8855, Ext. 4724/5048; e-mail: J.B.Parr@socsci.gla.ac.uk

Parratt, Emeritus Professor James Roy, MSc, PhD, DSc, MD (h.c.), DSc (med), FRCPath, DipRelStudies (Cantab), FRPharmS, FESC, FISHR, FIBiol, FRSE. Professor Emeritus, Strathclyde University, since 1998; b. 19.8.33, London; m., Pamela Joan Lyndon Marels; 2 s.; 1 d. Educ. St. Clement Danes Holborn Estate Grammar School; London University. Spent nine years in Nigeria as Head of

Pharmacology, Nigerian School of Pharmacy, then in Physiology, University Medical School, Ibadan; joined Strathclyde University, 1967; appointed Reader, 1970; Personal Professor, Department of Physiology and Pharmacology, 1975-83; Professor of Cardiovascular Pharmacology, 1983-98; Research Professor, since 2001; Head, Department of Physiology and Pharmacology, 1986-90. Chairman, Cardiac Muscle Research Group, 1980-83; Vice President, European Shock Society, since 1995; Gold Medal, Szeged University, 1975; Honorary Member, Hungarian Pharmacological Society, 1983; Honorary Doctorate, Albert Szent-Gyorgi Medical University, Hungary, 1989; Gold J.E. Purkyne Honorary Medal, Academy of Sciences of Czech Republic, 1995; Sodalem honoris causa, Slovak Medical and Cardiological Societies, 1997; Honorary Member, Czech Cardiological Society, 1998; Chairman, Universities and Colleges Christian Fellowship, 1984-90; Chairman, Interserve Scotland, since 2000; former Vice-Chairman, Scripture Union; Past Chairman, SUM Fellowship; Lay Preacher, Baptist Unions of Scotland and Great Britain; Honorary President, Baptist Lay Preachers Association of Scotland, 1985-90. Recreation: music. Address: (h.) 16 Russell Drive, Bearsden, Glasgow G61 3BD; T.-0141-942 7164; (b.) Strathclyde Institute for Biomedical Sciences, 27 Taylor Street, Glasgow G4 0NR; T.-0141-548 2858; e-mail: j.r.parratt@strath.ac.uk

Pasley, Anthony du Gard, FLI, FSGD, FSA(Scot); Landscape Architect in private practice, since 1973; b. 10.8.29, Edinburgh. Educ. King's College School. Senior Associate, Sylvia Crowe and Associates, 1967-72; work has included major public projects but specialises in country gardens and estates in UK and Europe; has taught on courses at Kew Gardens, Wisley, Edinburgh and New York Botanic Gardens, Reading University, London University; Senior Lecturer/Consultant, English Gardening School; President, Paisley Family Society. Publications: Summer Flowers, 1977; The English Gardening School (Co-author), 1987. Recreations: gardening; garden and architectural history; collecting books and paintings; opera. Address: Roseburn, Haywood Road, Moffat DG10 9BU; T.-01683 220146.

Pate, James Guy Lindsay, JP, FRIAS, ARIBA, DipTP (Glas), MRTPI (retd). Retired Chartered Architect and Town Planner; Honorary Sheriff, North Strathclyde at Dunoon; b. 17.3.27, Ayr; 1st m. diss.; 2 s.; 1 d; m. 2, Christina Margaret MacKay. Educ. Ayr Academy; Glasgow School of Architecture. Royal Marines, 1946-48; Architectural Assistant, Ayr County Council and East Kilbride Development Corporation; Planning Assistant, Renfrew County Council; Founder Partner, Thomas Smith, Gibb and Pate, architects and planning consultants, 1962; Principal, J. G. Lindsay Pate and Associates, 1982-90; Arbiter, Expert Witness, Mediator and Adviser. Former Member, RIAS Practice Committee; past Member, Justices Committee, Argyll and Bute; Chairman, Argyll Conservative and Unionist Association, 1970-72; Member, Argyll County Council, 1971-75; former Member, Argyll and Bute Joint Planning Committee; served on Cowal Licensing Court; former General Commissioner for Income Tax; former Member, Local Valuation Appeal Committee for Argyll and Bute; Member, Local Board, Armed Services YMCA of the United States of America, 1968-85 (Chairman 1983-84); Steward and Member, Cowal Highland Gathering, since 1963 (Honorary Secretary, Director and Manager, 1982-95); Director, Portavadie Village Limited. Recreations: country pursuits; reading; sailing. Address: An Stabull, Ardhallow, nr Dunoon, Argyll PA23 7QL; T.-01369 704477.

Paterson, Professor Alan Alexander, LLB (Hons), DPhil (Oxon), FRSA, FRSE. Solicitor. Professor of Law, Strathclyde University, since 1984; b. 5.6.47, Edinburgh; m., Alison Jane Ross Lowdon; 2 s.; 1 d. Educ. Edinburgh Academy; Edinburgh University; Pembroke College, Oxford. Research Associate, Oxford Centre for Socio-Legal Studies, 1972-73; Lecturer, Law Faculty, Edinburgh University, 1973-84; Visiting Professor, University of New Mexico Law School, 1982, 1986. Former Chairman, Scottish Legal Action Group and British and Irish Legal Education and Technology Association; Chairman, Legal Services Group, Citizens Advice Scotland; Executive Member, Committee of Heads of University Law Schools of the UK; Vice-Chair, Joint Standing Conference on Legal Education in Scotland. Publications: The Law Lords, 1982; The Legal System of Scotland (Co-author), 1993; Paths to Justice Scotland (Co-Author), 2001. Address: (b.) Strathclyde University Law School, 173 Cathedral Street, Glasgow G4 ORQ; T.-0141-548 3341; e-mail: prof.alan.paterson@strath.ac.uk

Paterson, Calum, BA, MBA, CA. Managing Director, Scottish Equity Partners Limited, since 2000; b. 13.4.63, Edinburgh; m., Amanda McLean. Educ. Linlithgow Academy; University of Strathclyde. Ernst and Young, 1985-88; Scottish Development Agency, 1988-91; Scottish Enterprise, 1991-2000 (Director, Investment and Corporate Finance, 1996-2000). Recreations: sport; cinema; reading. Address: (b.) 17 Blythswood Square, Glasgow G2 4AD; T.-0141-273 4000.

Paterson, Professor David Maxwell, BSc, PhD. Professor in Coastal Ecology, University of St. Andrews, since 2000; b. 16.6.58, Dalry; m., Marie; 2 d. Educ. Royal High School, Edinburgh; University of Glasgow; University of Bath. Royal Society Research Fellow, University of Bristol, 1988; University of St. Andrews: Lecturer, 1993, Reader in Environmental Biology, 1996. Honorary Research Associate, Acadia University, Nova Scotia. Publications: Biostabilisation of Sediments (Joint Editor), 1994; Sedimentary Processes in the Intertidal Zone, (Joint Editor), 1998. Recreations: natural history; music; squash; family. Address: (h.) 23 Pinkerton Road, Crail, Fife KY10 3UB; T.-01333 450047; e-mail: d.paterson@st-and.ac.uk

Paterson, Douglas McCallum, MA, MEd, DMS, DipM, MIM. Chief Executive, Aberdeen City Council, since 1995; b. 20.11.49, Macduff; m., Isobel Beaton; 2 d. Educ. Banff Academy; Aberdeen University; Robert Gordon University. John Wood Group, 1971-75; Grampian Regional Council: Teacher, 1976-81, Head Teacher, 1981-86, Advisor, 1986-90, Depute Director of Education, 1990-92, Senior Depute Director, 1992-94, Director of Education, 1994-95. Recreations: local history; fishing industry; music; walking; theatre. Address: (b.) Town House, Aberdeen; T.-01224 522500.

Paterson, George Matthew, BSc (Hons), PhD. Director, Food Standards Agency Scotland, since 2000; b. 16.3.42, Edinburgh; m., Patricia; 1 s.; 2 d. Educ. George Heriot's, Edinburgh; Edinburgh University. Postdoctoral Fellow, National Research Council of Canada, 1967-69; scientific and management posts in a variety of departments of Government of Canada, 1969-99. Recreations: tennis; golf. Address: (b.) St Magnus House, 25 Guild Street, Aberdeen; T.-01224 285102.

Paterson, Gil. MSP (SNP), Central Scotland, since 1999; b. 1942, Glasgow; m.; 1 s. Educ. Possilpark Secondary School. Formerly: television mechanic, electrical repairman, automotive paint technical manager; currently owner, independent motor factor business; former Councillor, Strathclyde Regional Council; contested Glasgow Central, 1980 By-Election, 1987 General Election; Member, National Executive Committee, Scottish National Party, 1985-98 (Vice Convener Local Government, Vice Convener Administration); Scottish Parliament: Member, Procedures Committee, Equal Opportunities Committee,

Convener, Cross Party Group on Men's Violence Against Women and Children. Address: (b.) Scottish Parliament, Edinburgh EH99 1SP; T.-0131-348 5922.

Paterson, Lt. Col. Howard Cecil, TD, FSA Scot. International Tourism Consultant and Artist; b. 16.3.20, Edinburgh; m., Isabelle Mary; 1 s. Educ. Daniel Stewart's College, Edinburgh; Edinburgh College of Art. Army, 1939-49; combat duties during War; personnel selection afterwards; Territorial Army, 1949-70; serves on Lowland Reserve Forces and Cadets Association; Founder Member, Gunner Heritage Appeal; Member, City of Edinburgh Artillery Officers' Association; Member, 52nd Lowland Division Officers' Club; Assistant Personnel Manager, Jute Industries Ltd., Dundee, 1949-51; Organising Secretary, Scottish Country Industries Development Trust, 1951-66; Senior Director, Scottish Tourist Board, 1966-81. Chairman, Taste of Scotland Ltd., 1984-86; Vice-Chairman, John Buchan Society, 1990-95; Member, Scottish Committee, British Horse Society; Chairman, Trekking and Riding Society of Scotland. Publications: Tourism in Scotland; Flavour of Edinburgh (with Catherine Brown). Recreations: fishing; shooting; riding; writing; drawing and painting; natural history; history. Address: (h.) Dovewood, West Linton, Peeblesshire, EH46 7DS; T.-01968 660346.

Paterson, Rev. John Love, MA, BD, STM, FSA Scot. Minister, St. Michael's Parish Church, Linlithgow, since 1977; Chaplain to The Queen, since 1996; b. 6.5.38, Ayr; m., Lorna Begg (see Lorna Marion Paterson). Educ. Ayr Academy; Glasgow University; Edinburgh University; Union Theological Seminary, New York. Minister: Presbyterian Church of East Africa, 1964-72, St. Andrew's, Nairobi, 1968-72; Chaplain, Stirling University, 1973-77. Moderator, West Lothian Presbytery, 1985. Recreation: gardening. Address: St. Michael's Manse, Linlithgow, West Lothian; T.-01506 842195.

Paterson, Very Rev. John Munn Kirk, ACII, MA, BD, DD. Minister Emeritus, St. Paul's Church, Milngavie; b. 8.10.22, Leeds; m., Geraldine Lilian Parker; 2 s.; 1 d. Educ. Hillhead High School; Edinburgh University. Pilot, RAF, 1940-46; Insurance official, 1946-58; ordained Minister, Church of Scotland, 1964; Minister, St. John's Church, Bathgate, 1964-70; Minister, St. Paul's Church, Milngavie, 1970-87. Moderator, General Assembly, Church of Scotland, 1984-85; Life Member, Chartered Insurance Institute; Hon. Doctorate, Aberdeen University, 1986. Recreations: fishing; gardening. Address: (h.) 58 Orchard Drive, Edinburgh EH4 2DZ; T.-0131-332 5876.

Paterson, Lorna Marion, MA, Dip.Rel.Ed. General Secretary, Church of Scotland Guild, 1985-98; b. 26.1.38, Unst; m., Rev. John L. Paterson (qv). Educ. Inverurie Academy; Aberdeen University; Aberdeen College of Education. Teacher of English, History, Geography and Religious Education, 1960-62; Teacher of English, 1962-66; Administrative Assistant, Strathclyde University, 1966-68; Deputy Academic Registrar, then Education Administrator, Stirling University, 1968-79. Guider (Division Commissioner, West Lothian, 1982-85); Chairman, Linlithgow Arts Guild; Elder, St. Michael's Parish Church, Linlithgow, since 1995; Member, Women in Scotland Forum; Vice-Convener, Church of Scotland Board of Parish Education; Member, Executive Committee, Scotland's Churches' Scheme, since 1999. Recreations: singing; homemaking; church activities; reading; the arts; people. Address: (h.) St. Michael's Manse, Kirkgate, Linlithgow EH49 7AL; T.-01506 842195.

Paterson, Wilma, DRSAM, LRAM. Freelance Composer/Music Critic/Travel Writer; b. 23.4.44, Dundee; 1 s.; 1 d. Educ. Harris Academy; Royal Scottish Academy of Music. Composition study with Luigi Dallapiccola in Florence; writes chamber and incidental music; contributes to: The Scotsman, The Herald, The Lady, The Bermudian, etc.

Publications: A Country Cup; Was Byron Anorexic?; Shoestring Gourmet; Flowers and Herbs of the Bible; Lord Byron's Relish; Salmon & Women, The Feminine Angle; Songs of Scotland (with Alasdair Gray). Address: Dalvrecht Manse, Tomintoul, Ballindalloch AB37 9HN; T.-01807 580270; e-mail: wilma.paterson@virgin.net

Paterson-Brown, June, CBE, MBChB. Lord Lieutenant, Roxburgh, Ettrick and Lauderdale, since 1999; Commonwealth Chief Commissioner, Girl Guides Association, 1985-90; Vice-Chairman, Princes Trust, 1982-92; Non-Executive Director, Border Television plc, 1980-99; b. 8.2.32, Edinburgh; m., Peter Neville Paterson-Brown (qv); 1 d. Educ. Esdaile School; Edinburgh University. Medical Officer, Family Planning and Well Woman's Clinics, 1959-85; Past Chairman: County of Roxburghshire Youth Committee, Roxburgh Duke of Edinburgh Award Committee; Scottish Chief Commissioner, Girl Guides Association, 1977-82; Chairman, Borders Region Children's Panel Advisory Committee, 1982-85; Chairman, Scottish Standing Conference of Voluntary Youth Organisations, 1983-85; Trustee, MacRobert Trusts, since 1987; Trustee, Prince's Trust, 1982-94; Paul Harris Fellow, 1990; JP, since 1999. Recreations: golf; skiing; music; fishing; reading; grand-children. Address: (h.) Norwood, Hawick, Roxburghshire TD9 7HP; T.-01450 372352.

Paterson-Brown, Peter Neville, MBChB, DObst RCOG. Medical Practitioner, retired; b. 23.3.31, Hawick; m., June Garden (see June Paterson-Brown); 3 s.; 1 d. Educ. Merchiston Castle School; Edinburgh University. Medical Adviser, Red Cross Scotland, 1981-94; Member, Scottish Committee, Medical Commission on Accident Prevention, 1978-91; Director, Children's Hospice Association Scotland, 1993-2000; Vice President, React, 1991-2001. Red Cross Badge of Honour, 1995. Publication: A Matter of Life or Death. Recreations: skiing; shooting; golf; fishing. Address: (h.) Norwood, Hawick, Roxburghshire; T.-01450 372352.

Paterson-Brown, Simon, MB BS, MPhil, MS, FRCS(Ed), FRCS Eng, FCS (HK). Consultant General Surgeon, Royal Infirmary, Edinburgh, since 1994; b. 6.2.58, Edinburgh; m., Dr Sheila Finnerty; 3 d. Educ. Trinity College, Glenalmond; St. Mary's Hospital Medical School, London. Senior Lecturer in Surgery, St. Mary's Hospital, London, 1993-94. Chairman, Basic Surgical Training Programme, South East Scotland; Surgical Tutor, Royal Infirmary, Edinburgh; Member, Specialty Advisory Board (General Surgery), Royal College of Surgeons of Edinburgh. Publications: Aids to Anatomy; Guide to Practical Procedures in Medicine and Surgery; Principles and Practice of Surgical Laparoscopy (Editor); Emergency Surgery and Critical Care (Editor). Recreations: music; skiing; golf; running. Address: University Department of Surgery, Royal Infirmary, Edinburgh EH3 9YW; T.-0131-536 3819.

Paton, Hon. Lady (Ann Paton). Senator of the College of Justice, since 2000; m., Dr James Y. Paton. Educ. Laurel Bank School, Glasgow; Glasgow University (MA, LLB). Advocate, 1977; Standing Junior Counsel: Queen's and Lord Treasurer's Remembrancer, 1979, Office of Fair Trading in Scotland, 1981; QC (Scot), 1990; Advocate Depute, 1992-94. Director, Scottish Council of Law Reporting, 1995-2000; Member, Criminal Injuries Compensation Board, 1995-2000. Address: (b.) Parliament House, Edinburgh, EH1 1RQ.

Paton, Alasdair Chalmers, BSc, CEng, FICE, FCIWEM. Company Director; Chief Executive, Scottish Environment Protection Agency, 1995-2000; b. 28.11.44, Paisley; m., Zona G. Gill; 1 s.; 1 d. Educ. John Neilson Institution, Paisley; Glasgow University. Assistant Engineer, Clyde Port Authority, 1967-71; Assistant Engineer, DAFS, 1971-72; Senior Engineer, SDD, 1972-77; Engineer, Public Works Department, Hong Kong Government, 1977-80;

Senior Engineer, then Principal Engineer, SDD, 1980-87; Deputy Chief Engineer, 1987-91; Director and Chief Engineer, Engineering, Water and Waste Directorate, Scottish Office Environment Department, 1991-95. Recreations: Rotary; sailing; golf. Address: (h.) Oriel House, Academy Square, Limekilns, Fife KY11 3HN; T.-01383 872218.

Paton, Alastair George Peter, DL, MBChB, DObstRCOG. Honorary Sheriff of Lothian and Borders at Peebles, since 1991; General Commissioner of Income Tax, Peebles Division, since 1991; b. 23.5.30, Paisley; m., Ethel Jean Harris; 4 d. Educ. George Watson's College, Edinburgh; Edinburgh University Medical School. House Surgeon and House Physician, Royal Infirmary of Edinburgh, 1954-55; Surgeon Lieutenant, Royal Navy, United Kingdom and South Atlantic Station, 1955-57; House Officer, Sorrento Maternity Hospital, Birmingham, 1958; House Physician, Children's Hospital, Birmingham, 1958; General Medical Practitioner, Peebles, 1959-90. Director, Tweeddale Branch, British Red Cross, 1991-98; Non-Executive Director, Borders Health Board, 1993-99; Deputy Lieutenant, Lieutenancy of Tweeddale, since 1992; Welfare and Pensions Officer, Peebles Branch, Royal British Legion Scotland, since 1990. Recreations: gardening; music; walking. Address: (h.) Ben Ard, The Mount, Peebles EH45 9EX; T.-01721 720098.

Paton, David Romer, OBE, CStJ, DL, FRICS, FSA Scot. Chartered Surveyor; b. 5.3.35, Aberdeen; m., Juliette Burney; 2 s. Educ. Gordonstoun School; Keble College, Oxford. Chartered Surveyor in own practice; Past President, Aberdeen Chamber of Commerce; Past Chairman: Scottish Council (Development and Industry), Gordon Conservative and Unionist Association, Royal Northern & University Club, Scottish Chambers of Commerce, Aberdeen Beyond 2000, Grampian-Houston Association, Aberdeen Civic Society, Grampian Cancer Care Project; former Member: North East River Purification Board, HMG Salmon Advisory Committee, North of Scotland Water Authority, Scottish Office Scottish Salmon Strategy Task Force, Board, Association of British Chambers of Commerce; Co-Chairman, Grampian Macmillan Nurses Appeal; Chairman: NE Scotland Preservation Trust, Pitsligo Castle Trust, Don District Salmon Fishery Board, Aberdeen Harbour Board, Order and Association of St. John Aberdeen and North East; Regional Chairman, The Prince's Scottish Youth Business Trust; President: Friends of Grampian Stones, Aberdeen Civic Society; Trustee: Scottish Civic Trust, Aberdeen Tivoli Theatre Trust; Member: Committee, Architectural Heritage Society of Scotland, British Olympic Association Appeal; Grampian Initiative Ambassador; Director: Aberdeen Salmon Co Ltd, Aberdeen Chamber of Commerce, Aberdeen Harbour Services, Aberdeen Foyer Services Ltd, Macmillan Cancer Relief, Scottish Council for Development and Industry; Burgess of Guild, City of Aberdeen, 1983; Patron: Bridge of Don Community Trust, Touch of Tartan Ball, Aberdeen University 6th Century Appeal. Address: Grandhome, Danestone, Aberdeen AB22 8AR; T.-01224 722202.

Paton, George, MA, MEd, FEIS, FITD. Director, Scottish Council for Educational Technology, 1986-90; b. 5.12.31, Rutherglen; m., 1, Barbara Thomson (deceased); 2 s.; 2, J. Honor Smith. Educ. Rutherglen Academy; Glasgow University. National Service, RAEC, 1953-55; Schoolteacher, 1955-61; Lecturer in English, Jordanhill College of Education, 1961-63; Principal Lecturer in English, then Assistant Principal, Dundee College of Education, 1963-69; Principal, Hamilton College of Education, 1970-81; Depute Director, Scottish Council for Educational Technology, 1982-86. President, International Council for Educational Media, 1989-91; Member, Library Information Service Committee (Scotland), 1984-91; Executive Committee Member, Commonwealth Institute Scotland, 1985-96; Governor, David Livingstone Memorial Trust, since 1971 (Chairman, since 1994); former Convener, Education Committee, General Teaching Council for Scotland; Chairman, Strathclyde Committee, Tenovus-Scotland 1991-2000; Elder, Church of Scotland. Recreations: singing; drama; gardening. Address: (h.) 24 Low Quarry Gardens, Hamilton ML3 6RH.

Paton, Dr James Y., BSc, MBChB, MD, DCH, FRCPH, FRCP. Hon. Consultant Pediatrician, since 1989; Reader, Paediatric Respiratory Disease, Royal Hospital for Sick Children, Glasgow, since 1989; b. 8.12.51, Glasgow; m., Ann Paton. Educ. Jordanhill College School; Glasgow University. Publications; chapters and articles on Paediatric Respiratory Disease. Recreations: cycling; sailing. Address: (b.) Department of Child Health, RHSC, Yorkhill, Glasgow, G3; T.-0141-201 0238; e-mail: J.Y.Paton@clinmed.gla.ac.uk

Patrick, Bruce Robertson, BA, LLB, WS. Senior Partner, Maclay Murray & Spens, since 2000 (Partner, since 1976, Managing Partner, 1991-94); Vice-Convenor, Law Society Company Law Committee, since 1990; b. 26.11.45, London; m., Hilary Jane Sutton; 1 s.; 2 d. Educ. Glasgow Academy; Edinburgh Academy; Exeter College, Oxford University; Edinburgh University. Apprentice, Mitchells Johnston, Solicitors, Glasgow, 1971-73; Assistant, Maclay Murray and Spens, Solicitors, 1973-75; Assistant, Coward Chance, Solicitors, London, 1975-76. Management Committee Member, Castle Rock Housing Association. Recreations: sailing; golf; hillwalking. Address: (b.) 3 Glenfinlas Street, Edinburgh EH3 6AQ; T.-0131-226 5196.

Patrick, Fraser Robertson, BA, DipYCW. Director, Neighbourhood Resources and Development Department, Dundee City Council, since 1995; b. 3.7.44, Glasgow; m., Helen Grant Patrick; 2 d. Educ. King's Park Secondary, Glasgow; Open University; Jordanhill College of Education. Clubs Advisor, Glasgow Association of Youth Clubs, 1966; Assistant Youth Community Officer/Manager Fintry Community Centre, Dundee, 1967; Lecturer, Jordanhill College of Education, 1972; Area Community Education Officer, Lothian Regional Council, 1978; Community Education Training Officer, Oxfordshire City Council, 1984; Principal Community Education Officer, Tayside Regional Council, 1985; Assistant Director of Education, Tayside Regional Council, 1991; Chair, Advisory Committee, Scottish Executive Review of Community Education Training, 2000-01. Recreations: cinema; theatre; tennis; badminton; trainee grandfather. Address: (h.) 17 Collingwood Crescent, Broughty Ferry, Dundee, DD5 2SX; T.-01382 779663.

Patten, Sidney Charles, MBA, FRSA. Chief Executive, Scottish Building, since 1995; b. 30.8.50, Glasgow; m. Isabel Anne; 1 s.; 1 d. Educ. Bellahouston Academy, Glasgow; Edinburgh University; Glasgow Caledonian University. Apprentice Accountant, Renfrew County Council, 1969-73; Finance Manager, Anglo Nordic MGT Ltd., 1973-76; Principal Officer, Health Service, 1976-85; Director, Finance and Administration, ECA of Scotland, 1985-88; Secretary and Director, Marketing and Training, ECA of Scotland, 1988-92; Deputy Managing Director, ECA of Scotland, 1992-95; Director, Scottish House Builders Association, since 1995; Employers Secretary, Scottish Building Apprenticeship and Training Council, since 1995; Chairman, National Council of Industry Training Organisation; Board Member, Telford College; Visiting Lecturer, Glasgow Caledonian University. Recreations: golf; fitness training; classic cars; gardening. Address: (h.) Carron Grange, Carrongrange Avenue, Stenhousemuir, FK5 3BQ; T.-01324 555550.

Patterson, Professor Henry Desmond, BSc, MSc, DSc, CMath, FIMA, FRSE. Honorary Professor, Mathematics and Statistics Department, Edinburgh University, since 1985; b. 17.7.24, Whitby; m., Janet Mary Roffe; 1 s. Educ. Northallerton Grammar School; Pickering Grammar School; Ripon Grammar School; Leeds University. Department of Scientific and Industrial Research, 1946-47; Rothamsted Experimental Station, 1947-67; Agricultural Research Council Unit of Statistics, Edinburgh University, 1967-85. Recreations: music; mathematical and statistical programming. Address: (h.) 15 Kings Grove, Longniddry EH32 0QW; T.-01875 853012.

Patterson, Lindy Ann, LLB (Hons), WS, ACIArb. Lawyer; Partner, Head of Construction, MacRoberts; b. 12.9.58, Berwick-upon-Tweed. Educ. Eyemouth High School; Edinburgh University. UK National Vice-President, Association Internationale de Jeunes Avocats, 1991-94; Member, Commercial Court Consultative Committee; Member, Chairman's Advisory Group, RICS; Scotland's first female Solicitor Advocate (May, 1993); former Member of number of Law Society Comittees; Editor, Building Law and Development; Editor, Scottish Construction Law Review; Member, Napier University Industrial Professional and Advisory Committee. Recreations: skiing; hill-walking. Address: (b.) Excel House, 30 Semple Street, Edinburgh.

Pattison, David Arnold, BSc, PhD. Best Value Inspector, Audit Commission, since 2000; Hon. President, Scottish Youth Hostels Association; b. 9.2.41, Kilmarnock; m., Anne Ross Wilson; 2 s.; 1 d. Educ. Kilmarnock Academy; Glasgow University. Planning Assistant, Ayr County Council, 1963-64; PhD studies, Glasgow University, 1964-66; Planning Assistant, Dunbarton County Council, 1966-67; Lecturer, Strathclyde University, 1967-70; Head of Tourism, Highlands and Islands Development Board, 1970-81; Chief Executive, Scottish Tourist Board, 1981-85; Director Leisure and Tourism Consulting: Ernst & Young, 1985-89, Cobham Resource Consultants, 1989-96, Scott Wilson Resource Consultants, 1996-98; Director, David A. Pattison Associates, 1998-2000. External Examiner for postgraduate tourism courses, Strathclyde University, 1981-84; Member, Inland Waterways Amenity Advisory Council. Recreations: reading; watching soccer and rugby; golf; gardening. Address: (h.) 7 Cramond Glebe Gardens, Cramond, Edinburgh EH4 6NZ.

Pattison, Rev. Kenneth John, MA, BD, STM. Minister, Kilmuir and Logie Easter, Ross-shire, since 1996; b. 22.4.41, Glasgow; m., Susan Jennifer Brierley Jenkins; 1 s.; 2 d. Educ. Lenzie Academy; Glasgow University; Union Theological Seminary, New York. Minister, Church of Central Africa Presbyterian, Malawi, 1967-77; Minister, Park Parish Church, Ardrossan, 1977-84; Chaplain, Glasgow Royal Infirmary, 1984-90; Associate Minister, St. Andrew's and St. George's, Edinburgh, 1990-96. Convener, Chaplaincies Committee, Church of Scotland, 1993-96. Recreations: hill-walking; swimming; gardening; family history. Address: (h.) The Manse, Delny, Invergordon, IV18 0NW; T.-01862 842 280.

Patton, John. National Development Officer, Scottish League of Credit Unions, since 2000; National President, Educational Institute of Scotland, 1999-2000; b. Derry, 1942; m., Elizabeth Scott; 3 c. Taught English in Northern Ireland, 1964-71; Press Officer, civil rights movement in Derry, 1968-70; taught in West Lothian, 1971-73, Zambia, 1973-76, Central Region, since 1976; Headteacher, Banchory Primary School, Tullibody, 1985-90, Craigbank Primary School, Sauchie, 1990-2000; fluent Irish Gaelic speaker. Recreations: Scottish and Irish traditional music. Address: 50 Fir Park, Tillicoultry FK13 6PJ; T.-01259 750530; e-mail: jpatton@scottishcu.org

Pattullo, Sir (David) Bruce, Kt, CBE, BA, Hon. LLD (Aberdeen), DUniv (Stirling), Hon. DBA (Strathclyde), FRSE, FCIB (Scot). Governor, Bank of Scotland, 1991-98; Director (Non-Executive): British Linen Bank, 1977-98, Bank of Wales PLC, 1986-98, NWS Bank, 1986-98; b. 2.1.38, Edinburgh; m., Fiona Jane Nicholson; 3 s.; 1 d. Educ. Belhaven Hill School; Rugby; Hertford College, Oxford. National Service commission, Royal Scots (seconded to West Africa); joined Bank of Scotland, 1961; winner, first prize, Institute of Bankers in Scotland, 1964; Bank of Scotland: Manager, Investment Services Department, 1967-71, Deputy Manager, Bank of Scotland Finance Co. Ltd., 1971-73, Chief Executive, Group Merchant Banking Activities, 1973-78, Deputy Treasurer, 1978, Treasurer and General Manager, 1979-88, Director, 1980-98, Group Chief Executive and a Deputy Governor, Bank of Scotland, 1988-91. Chairman, Committee of Scottish Clearing Bankers, 1981–83 and 1987-89; Director, Standard Life Assurance Co., 1985-96; President, Institute of Bankers in Scotland. Recreations: tennis; hill-walking. Address: (h.) 6 Cammo Road, Edinburgh EH4 8EB.

Pawley, Professor G. Stuart, MA, PhD, FRSE, FRS. Professor of Computational Physics, Edinburgh University, since 1985; b. 22.6.37, Ilford; m., Anthea Jean Miller; 2 s.; 1 d. Educ. Bolton School; Corpus Christi College, Cambridge. Lecturer, Edinburgh University, 1964; Reader, 1970; Personal Chair, 1985; Guest Professor, Aarhus University, Denmark, 1969-70. Recreations: choral singing; mountain walking. Address: (b.) Physics Department, Kings Buildings, Edinburgh University EH9 3JZ; T.-0131-650 5300.

Paxton, Professor Roland Arthur, MBE, MSc, PhD, CEng, FICE, FRSE, AMCST. Chairman, Institution of Civil Engineers Panel for Historical Engineering Works, since 1990; Commissioner, Royal Commission on the Ancient and Historical Monuments of Scotland, since 1993; Hon. Professor, Civil and Offshore Engineering, Heriot-Watt University, since 1994; b. 29.6.32, Altrincham; m., Ann; 2 d. Educ. Altrincham Grammar School; Manchester College of Science and Technology; Heriot-Watt University. Cartographical surveyor, Ordnance Survey, 1953-55; Civil Engineer, Corporations of Sale, Manchester, Leicester, Edinburgh, and Lothian Regional Council, retiring as Senior Principal Engineer, 1959-90; Hon. Senior Research Fellow, Heriot Watt University, 1990-94. Chairman, Forth Bridges Visitor Centre Trust; Secretary and Director, Laigh Milton Viaduct Conservation Project, 1992-99; Trustee, James Clerk Maxwell Foundation; President, Edinburgh Bibliographical Society, 1992-95; Winner, Institution of Civil Engineers' Garth Watson Medal, 1999 and Carr Prize, 2001; author of books and papers on technical innovation, conservation of structures, and historical engineering. Address: (b.) Civil and Offshore Engineering, Heriot-Watt University, Edinburgh EH14 4AS; T.-0131-449 5111.

Payne, Professor Peter Lester, BA, PhD, FRHistS, FRSE. Emeritus Professor, Aberdeen University; Professor of Economic History, Aberdeen University, 1969-95; b. 31.12.29, London; m., Enid Christine Rowntree; 1 s.; 1 d. Educ. Brockley County School, London; Nottingham University. Visiting Lecturer in American Economic History, Johns Hopkins University, 1957-58; Lecturer in Economic and Social History, Nottingham University, 1958-59; Colquhoun Lecturer in Business History, Glasgow University, 1959-69; Senior Lecturer in Economic History, Glasgow University, 1964-69; Sherman Fairchild Distinguished Scholar, California Institute of Technology, Pasadena, 1977-78. Vice-President, Business Archives Council; President, Business Archives Council of Scotland; President, Aberdeen and North of Scotland Philatelic Society, 1995-97. Publications include: Rubber and Railways in the Nineteenth Century; British Entrepreneurship in the Nineteenth Century; Colvilles and the Scottish Steel Industry; The Early Scottish Limited

Companies; The Hydro; Growth and Contraction: Scottish Industry c. 1860-1990; Northern Scotland (Editor). Recreations: philately; woodwork. Address: (h.) 7 Kirkton Road, Westhill, Skene, Aberdeenshire, AB32 6LF; T.-01224 744703.

Peach, Professor Ken, BSc, PhD, FRSE. Professor of Particle Physics Experiments, Edinburgh University, since 1996; Director, Particle Physics, CLRC, Rutherford Appleton Laboratory, since 1998; b. 5.11.45, Derby; m., Elizabeth Jean. Educ. Heanor Grammar; Edinburgh University. Department of Physics, Edinburgh University: Demonstrator, 1970-75; Research Assistant, 1975-81; SERC Advanced Fellow, 1981-86; Departmental Research Officer, 1986-92; Reader, 1992-96; Deputy Leader, Particle Physics Experiemmts Division, CERN, 1996-98; Leader and Principal Investigator, Edinburgh Particle Physics experiment group, 1990-96; FInstP; Member, many scientific advisory bodies, since 1980. Publications: numerous papers and conferences. Recreations: blues; mountains. Address: (b.) CLRC, Rutherford Appleton Laboratory, Chilton, Didcot, Oxon, OX11 0QX; T.-01235 445 782.

Peacock, Professor Sir Alan Turner, Kt (1987), DSC (1945), MA, HonDUniv (Stirling), Hon. DEcon (Zurich), Hon. DScEcon (Buckingham), HonDUniv (Brunel), HonDUniv (York), HonLLD (St. Andrews), HonLLD (Dundee), HonDSc (Edinburgh), Hon. Fellow (LSE), Lib Doc (Catania), Dr.h.c. (Lisbon), Laurea (h.c.) (Turin), FBA, FRSE. Honorary Research Professor in Public Finance, Edinburgh Business School, Heriot-Watt University, since 1985; b. 26.6.22, Ryton-on-Tyne; m., Margaret Martha Astell-Burt; 2 s.; 1 d. Educ. Grove Academy; Dundee High School; St. Andrews University. Royal Navy, 1942-45; Lecturer in Economics, St. Andrews, 1947-48; Lecturer, then Reader in Economics, London School of Economics, 1948-56; Professor of Economic Science, Edinburgh University, 1956-62; Professor of Economics, York University, 1962-78 (Deputy Vice Chancellor, 1963-69); Professor of Economics, University College, Buckingham, 1978-84; Principal, then Vice Chancellor, Buckingham University, 1980-84; Chief Economic Adviser, Department of Trade and Industry (on secondment), 1973-76. Member, Royal Commission on the Constitution, 1970-73; Member, Inquiry into Retirement Provision, 1983-85; SSRC Council, 1972-73; President, International Institute of Public Finance, 1966-69 (now Honorary President); Chairman, Committee on Financing the BBC, 1985-86; Chairman, Rowntree Inquiry on Takeovers, 1989-91; Executive Director, David Hume Institute, Edinburgh, 1985-91 (Honorary Trustee, since 1991); Chairman, Scottish Arts Council, 1986-92; Chairman, Academic Advisory Council, Institute of Economic Affairs, 1991-93; Head, UN Advisory Mission to Russia on Social Protection, 1992; Non-Executive Director, Macdonald Orr Ltd., 1991-98; Chairman, Hebrides Ensemble, 1994-99; Scottish Free Enterprise Award, 1987; Keynes Lecturer, British Academy, 1994; Fellow, Accademia Nazionale dei Lincei, Rome. Publications: 30 books, over 200 articles on economic questions. Recreations: attempting to write music; hill-walking. Address: (h.) 5/24 Oswald Road, Edinburgh EH9 2HE; T.-0131-667 5677; e-mail: peacock@ebs.hw.ac.uk

Peacock, Andrew John, BSc, MPhil, MD, FRCP. Consultant Physician (Respiratory), West Glasgow Hospitals, since 1990; Director, Scottish Pulmonary Vascular Unit; b. 13.11.49, Montreal; m., Jila Pezeshgi; 1 s.; 2 d. Educ. Westminster School; St. Bartholomew's Hospital Medical College, London University; Caius College, Cambridge University. Senior House Officer, St. Bartholomew's, Addenbrookes and Queen Square Hospitals; Registrar, Brompton Hospital; Senior Registrar, Southampton Hospitals; Research Fellow, University of Colorado; Visiting Scientist, National Heart and Lung Institute, London. Physiologist, 1993 British Expedition to Everest. Publication: Pulmonary Circulation: a handbook for clinicians. Recreations: anything to do with mountains; wine; tennis; golf. Address: (b.) Scottish Pulmonary Vascular Unit, Level 8, Western Infirmary, Glasgow, G11 6NT; T.-0141-211 6327.

Peacock, Professor John Andrew, MA, PhD. Professor of Cosmology, Edinburgh University, since 1998; b. 27.3.56, Shaftesbury; m., Heather; 1 s.; 2 d. Educ. Cedars School, Leighton Buzzard; Jesus College, Cambridge. Research Astronomer, Royal Observatory, Edinburgh, 1981-92; Head of Research, Royal Observatory, Edinburgh, 1992-98; UK representative, Anglo-Australian Telescope Board, 1995-2000. Publications: Cosmological Physics, 1999. Recreations: playing classical clarinet; hill walking. Address: (b.) Institute for Astronomy, Edinburgh University, Royal Observatory, Edinburgh, EH9 3HJ; T.-0131-668 8100; e-mail: jap@roe.ac.uk

Peacock, Professor Noël A., BA, MA, Marshall Professor of French Language and Literature, University of Glasgow, since 1998; b. 28.9.45, King's Lynn; m., Sandra May Keenan; 1 s. Educ. King Edward VII Grammar School, King's Lynn; University College Cardiff. University of Glasgow: Lecturer, 1970-89, Senior Lecturer, 1989-95, Personal Professor, 1995-98; Head, Department of French, 1990-2001. Member, Scottish Examination Board: Modern Languages Panel, 1989-94, Universities Assessor of SCE/SYS French; Member, Higher Still Modern Languages Panel, 1995-97; Co-director and Co-founder, Le Nouveau Molieriste, since 1994; Member, Board of Directors, International Christian College, since 1998; Member, Comité Consultatif, French Institute, since 1999. Chevalier dans l'Ordre des Palmes Académiques, 1993. Publications: La Jalousie du Barbouille et George Dandin, 1984; L'Ecole des Femmes, 1988; Dépit Amoureux, 1989; Les Femmes Savantes, 1990; Moliere in Scotland, 1993. Recreations: sport (cricket, tennis, football, golf); theatre; gardening. Address: (b.) Department of French, University of Glasgow G12 8QL; T.-0141-330 4589.

Peacock, Peter James, CBE. MSP (Labour) Highlands and Islands, since 1999; Deputy Minister for Finance and Public Services (Deputy Minister for Children and Education, 1999-2000); b. 27.2.52, Edinburgh; 2 s. Educ. Hawick High School; Jordanhill College of Education, Glasgow. Community Worker, Orkney Islands, 1973-75; former Area Officer, Highlands, Islands, Grampian, Scottish Association of Citizens Advice Bureaux; Member, Highland Regional Council, 1982-96; former Convener, Highland Council; formerly: Member, Highlands and Islands Convention, Honorary President, Scottish Library Association, Board Member, Centre for Highlands and Islands Policy Studies, Member, Scottish Natural Heritage, Non-Executive Director, Scottish Post Office Board, Member, Highland Area Committee, SCDI, Chairman, Scottish Library and Information Council, Vice-President, COSLA; Member, European Committee of the Regions, 1993-99; former Training, Organisation and Policy Consultant; Co-author, Vice-Chairman, subsequently Chairman of successful applicant group for Independent Local Radio franchise, Moray Firth. Recreations: ornithology; golf; watching rugby union. Address: (h.) 68 Braeside Park, Balloch, Inverness; T.-01463 790371.

Peaker, Professor Malcolm, FRS, DSc, HonDSc, PhD, FZS, FLS, FIBiol, FRSE. Director, Hannah Research Institute, Ayr, since 1981; Hannah Professor, Glasgow University, since 1981; b. 21.8.43, Stapleford, Nottingham; m., Stephanie Jane Large; 3 s. Educ. Henry Mellish Grammar School, Nottingham; Sheffield University, BSc Zoology; DSc; University of Hong Kong, SRC NATO Scholar; PhD. ARC Institute of Animal Physiology, 1968-78; Head, Department of Physiology, Hannah Research

Institute, 1978-81. Chairman, London Zoo Board, 1992-93; Vice-President, Zoological Society of London, 1992-94; Member, Editorial Board: Journal of Dairy Science, 1975-78, International Zoo Yearbook, 1978-82, Journal of Endocrinology, 1981-91; Editor, British Journal of Herpetology, 1977-81; Munro Kerr Lecture, 1997; Raine Distinguished Visitor, University of Western Australia, 1998; 10th Edinburgh Centre for Rural Research/Royal Society of Edinburgh/Institute of Biology Annual Lecture, 2000; Distinguished Lecturer, University of Hong Kong, since 2000; Scientific Governor, British Nutrition Foundation, since 1997. Publications: Salt Glands in Birds and Reptiles, 1975; Avian Physiology (Editor), 1975; Comparative Aspects of Lactation (Editor), 1977; Physiological Strategies in Lactation (Co-Editor), 1984; Intercellular Signalling in the Mammary Gland (Editor), 1995; Biological Signalling and the Mammary Gland (Editor), 1997; papers. Recreations: vertebrate zoology; natural history; golf; grumbling about bureaucrats. Address: (h.) Hannah Research Institute, Ayr KA6 5HL.

Pears, John Charles, BSc (Hons). Rector, Paisley Grammar School, since 1995; b. 13.10.50, Castle Douglas; m., Margaret Blackwood; 2 s. Educ. Kirkcudbright Academy; Strathclyde University; Jordanhill College. Teacher, Kirkcudbright Academy; Principal Teacher: Braidhurst High School, Lenzie Academy; Assistant Rector, Kilmarnock Academy; Depute Rector, Johnstone High School. Elder, Church of Scotland. Recreations: sport; music; gardening. Address: (b.) Paisley Grammar School, Glasgow Road, Paisley; T.-0141-889 3484.

Pearson of Rannoch, Lord (Malcolm Everard MacLaren Pearson). Life Peer; b. 20.7.42; m.; 3 d. Chairman, PWS Holdings plc; founded Rannoch Trust, 1984.

Pearson, Francis Salmond Gillespie, MA (Oxon). Painter in oils, since 1984; b. 31.7.35, Edinburgh. Educ. Fettes College, Edinburgh; University College, Oxford; Edinburgh University. National Service, Cameron Highlanders; Assistant Master, Harrow School, 1960-61 and 1967-73; Member, Faculty of Advocates, since 1964; Headmaster, Truro Cathedral School, 1974-79; Head of Arts and Languages, Welbeck College, 1979-83. Address: (h.) 28 Douglas Crescent, Edinburgh EH12 5BA; T.-0131-225 4736.

Peat, Jeremy Alastair, BA, MSc, FRSA. Group Chief Economist, Royal Bank of Scotland, since 1993; Honorary Professor, Heriot-Watt University; Visiting Professor, Edinburgh University; Member, CBI (UK) Economic Affairs Committee; Fellow, Industry and Parliament Trust; Member, Advisory Board, Scottish Council Foundation; Council Member, Scottish Economic Society; Board Member, Scottish Higher Education Funding Council; Member, Secretary of State for Trade and Industry's Panel for Monitoring the Economy; b. 20.3.45, Haywards Heath; m., Philippa Ann; 2 d. Educ. St. Paul's School, London; Bristol University; University College London. Economic Assistant/Economic Adviser, Ministry of Overseas Development, 1969-77; Economic Adviser, Manpower Services Commission, 1978-80; Head, Employment Policy Unit, Ministry of Finance and Development Planning, Government of Botswana, 1980-84; Economic Adviser, HM Treasury, 1984-85; Senior Economic Adviser, Scottish Office, 1985-93. Hon. LLD, Aberdeen; Fellow, Chartered Institute of Bankers. Recreations: walking; reading; tennis; listening to music; golf; conservation of Rosslyn Chapel. Address: (b.) 42 St. Andrew Square, Edinburgh EH2 2YE; T.-0131-523 2277; e-mail: jeremy.peat@rbs.co.uk

Peattie, Cathy. MSP (Labour), Falkirk East, since 1999. Former Convenor, Council, Voluntary Service Scotland; former Chair, Scottish Labour Women's Committee. Address: (b.) Scottish Parliament, Edinburgh EH99 1SP; T.-0131-348 5747.

Peattie, Professor Patricia Ida, BSc, RSCN, RGN, CertEd, RNT, FRSA, MHSM. Assistant Principal. Napier University, since 1996; b. 16.1.41, Edinburgh. Educ. Hastings High School for Girls; Edinburgh University. Various clinical posts; teaching in Edinburgh and Glasgow, 1987-89; Principal, Lothian College of Nursing and Midwifery, 1989-96; Council Member, Edinburgh Medical Group, since 1990; Lothian Research Ethics Committee, since 1990; Member, Multi-Centre Research Ethics Committee for Scotland, since 1997 (Vice Chair); National Nursing and Midwifery Audit Committee, 1995-97; Governor, Moray House Institute of Education, 1997-98; Non-Executive Director, Lothian Health, since 1999; Non-Executive Trustee, Lothian Primary Care NHS Trust, since 1999; Council Member, St George's School for Girls, Edinburgh, since 2000. Recreations: reading; music; theatre; travel; friends. Address: (b.) Napier University, Sighthill Campus, Sighthill Court, Sighthill, Edinburgh EH11 4BN; T.-0131-455 3570.

Peden, Professor George Cameron, MA, DPhil, FRSE. Professor of History, Stirling University, since 1990; b. 16.2.43, Dundee; m., Alison Mary White; 3 s. Educ. Grove Academy, Broughty Ferry; Dundee University; Brasenose College, Oxford. Sub-Editor, Dundee Evening Telegraph, 1960-68; mature student, 1968-75; Tutorial Assistant, Department of Modern History, Dundee University, 1975-76; Temporary Lecturer, School of History, Leeds University, 1976-77; Lecturer in Economic and Social History, then Reader in Economic History, Bristol University, 1977-90; Visiting Fellow, All Souls College, Oxford, 1988-89. Publications: British Rearmament and the Treasury 1932-39, 1979; British Economic and Social Policy: Lloyd George to Margaret Thatcher, 1985; Keynes, The Treasury and British Economic Policy, 1988; The Treasury and British Public Policy, 1906-1959, 2000. Recreation: hill-walking. Address: (h.) Ardvurich, Leny Feus, Callander FK17 8AS; T.-01877 30488; e-mail: g.c.peden@stir.ac.uk

Peggie, Robert Galloway Emslie, CBE, DUniv, FCCA. Chairman, Board, Edinburgh College of Art, 1998-99; Chairman, Local Government Staff Commission for Scotland, 1994-97; b. 5.1.29, Bo'ness; 1 s.; 1 d. Educ. Lasswade High School. Trainee Accountant, 1946-52; Accountant in industry, 1952-57; Edinburgh Corporation, 1957-72: O. and M. Officer, Assistant City Chamberlain, Deputy City Chamberlain, Reorganisation Steering Committee; Chief Executive, Lothian Regional Council, 1974-86; Commissioner (Ombudsman) for Local Administration in Scotland, 1986-94. Former Member, Court, Heriot-Watt University (Convener, Finance Committee); Governor, Edinburgh College of Art; former Trustee, Lloyds TSB Foundation. Recreation: golf. Address: 9A Napier Road, Edinburgh EH10 5AZ; T.-0131-229 6775.

Pelham Burn, Angus Maitland, LLD, JP, DL. Director, Bank of Scotland, 1977-2000, Chairman, North of Scotland Board, since 1973; Chairman, Aberdeen Airport Consultative Committee, since 1986; Director, Dana Petroleum plc, since 1999; b. 13.12.31, London; m., Anne; 4 d. Educ. Harrow; North of Scotland College of Agriculture. Hudson's Bay Company, 1951-58; Company Director, since 1958; Chairman, Scottish Provident, 1995-98; former Chairman, Aberdeen Asset Management PLC (formerly, Aberdeen Trust PLC); Director, Abtrust Scotland Investment Company, 1989-96; Member, Kincardine County Council, 1967-75 (Vice Convener, 1973-75); Member, Grampian Regional Council, 1974-94; Member, Accounts Commission for Scotland, 1980-94 (Deputy Chairman, 1987-94); Director, Aberdeen Association for Prevention of Cruelty to Animals, 1975-95 (Chairman, 1984-89); former Chairman, Order of St. John (Aberdeen) Ltd.; Council Member, Winston Churchill Memorial Trust,

1984-94; Member, Queen's Bodyguard for Scotland (Royal Company of Archers), since 1968; Vice Lord Lieutenant, Kincardineshire, 1978-99, Deputy Lieutenant, since 1999; Governor, Lathallan School, since 2001; Honorary Degree of Doctor of Law, (Robert Gordon University), 1996. Recreations: gardening; wildlife photography. Address: The Kennels Cottage, Dess, Aboyne, Aberdeenshire AB34 5AY.

Pellew, Robin Anthony, PhD. Chief Executive, National Trust for Scotland, since 2001; b. 27.9.45, Hexham; m., Pamela; 1 s.; 1 d. Educ. Marlborough College; Edinburgh University; University College, London. Senior Research Scientist, Serengeti Research Institute, Tanzania, 1973-78; BBC Natural History Unit, 1978-79; Research Fellow, Physiology Laboratory, Cambridge, 1979-82; Senior Editor/Editorial Manager, Cambridge University Press, 1982-87; Director, Conservation Monitoring Service, IUCN, 1987-88; Director, World Conservation Monitoring Centre, 1988-93; Director and Chief Executive, WWF, 1994-99; Chief Executive, Animal Health Trust, 1999-2001. Publications: numerous scientific papers on wildlife management and conservation. Recreations: travelling to exotic places; watching wildlife. Address: (b.) Wemyss House, 28 Charlotte Square, Edinburgh EH2 4ET; T.-0131-243 9519.

Pelly, Frances, RSA. Sculptor; b. 21.7.47, Edinburgh. Educ. Morrison's Academy, Crieff; Duncan of Jordanstone College of Art, Dundee. Part-time lecturing, Dundee, 1974-78; full-time lecturing, Grays School of Art, Aberdeen, 1979-83. Recreations: riding; wildlife; gardening. Address: Quoyblackie, Rendall, Orkney KW17 2HA; T.-01856 751464.

Peltenburg, Professor Edgar, BA, PhD, FSA. Professor of Archaeology, Edinburgh University, since 1996; Director, Lemba Archaeological Research Centre, Cyprus, since 1985; b. 28.5.42, Montreal; 3 s.; 1 d. Educ. D'Arcy McGee, Montreal; Birmingham University. Lecturer in Archaeology and Resident Staff Tutor in Argyll, Glasgow University, 1969-78; Edinburgh University: Lecturer in Near Eastern Archaeology, 1978-88, Reader in Archaeology, 1988-93. Member of many committees, including UK Higher Education Funding Council's Research Assessment Panel for Archaeology. Publications include: The Burrell Collection: Western Asiatic Antiquities, 1991. Address: (b.) Department of Archaeology, Old High School, Edinburgh EH1 1LT; T.-0131-650 2379.

Pender, Sheriff David James, LLB (Hons). Sheriff of North Strathclyde, since 1995; b. 7.9.49, Glasgow; m., Elizabeth; 2 s.; 2 d. Educ. Queen's Park Senior Secondary School, Glasgow; Edinburgh University. Partner, MacArthur Stewart, Solicitors, Oban, 1977. Recreations: reading; travel; bridge. Address: (b.) Sheriff Courthouse, St. James Street, Paisley; T.-0141-887 5291.

Pender, Professor Gareth, BSc, PhD, CEng, FICE, MCIWEM. Professor of Environmental Engineering, Heriot-Watt University, since 2000; b. 24.1.60, Helensburgh; m., Isobel; 2 s.; 1 d. Educ. Vale of Leven Academy; University of Strathclyde. Civil Engineer, Crouch and Hogg, Consulting Engineers, 1984-89; Lecturer, University of Glasgow, 1989-2000. Recreations: golf; skiing. Address: (b.) Department of Civil and Offshore Engineering, Heriot-Watt University, Edinburgh EH14 4AS; T.-0131-451 3312; e-mail: g.pender@hw.ac.uk

Penman, David Roland, DA (Edin), DipTP (Edin), FRTPI, ARIAS, FSAScot. Reporter, Scottish Executive Inquiry Reporters' Unit, since 1994; b. 6.6.36, Manchester; m., Tamara Scott; 2 s.; 1 d. Educ. George Watson's Boys' College, Edinburgh; Edinburgh College of Art. Assistant Architect, private practices, 1960-67; Partner, Bamber Hall & Partners, Edinburgh, 1967-71; Depute County Planning Officer, Argyll County Council, 1971-73; County Planning Officer, Perth & Kinross Joint County Council, 1973-75; Director of Planning, Perth and Kinross District Council, 1975-94. Chairman, RTPI Scotland, 1984, Member of Council, 1978-85; President, Dundee Institute of Architects, 1988, Member of Council, 1980-90; Chairman, Scottish Urban Archaeological Trust, since 1990; formerly: Chairman, Duncan of Jordanstone College of Art, Vice-Chairman, Scottish Conservation Projects Trust, Director, Action Environment Ltd., Council Member, National Trust for Scotland. Recreations: hill-walking; art galleries; theatre; DIY; Scots history; travel. Address: (h.) 6 Arthurstone Walled Garden, by Meigle, Perthshire PH12 8QY; T.-01828 640801.

Penman, John. Editor, Business a.m., since 2000; b. 10.1.62, Glasgow; partner Lucy Patton; 1 d. Educ. St. Gregory's School, Glasgow; Greenfaulds High School, Cumbernauld; Napier College, Edinburgh. Sports Editor, Cumbernauld News, 1982-87; Chief Reporter, Evening News and Star, Carlisle, 1987-91; Assistant News Editor, Northern Echo, 1991-94; The Scotsman: Deputy News Editor, 1994-96, Political Editor, 1996-98; Assistant Editor, Daily Record, 1998; New Business Director, Daily Record and Sunday Mail, 1998-2000. Member, Advisory Group on Media for Scottish Parliament. Recreations: football; Partick Thistle FC, astronomy. Address: (b.) 40 Torphichen Street, Edinburgh; T.-0131-330 0000; e-mail: info@businessam.co.uk

Pennington, Christopher Royston, BSc (Hons), MB, ChB, MRCP, MD, FRCP, FRCPEdin. Consultant Physician (General Medicine and Gastroenterology), since 1979; Clinical Director, General Medicine, 1995-2001; Honorary Professor of Clinical Nutrition, Dundee University, since 1997; Examiner, MRCP (UK), since 1986; Chairman, British Association for Parenteral and Enteral Nutrition, since 1999; President, European Society for Parenteral and Enteral Nutrition, since 2001-02; b. 22.2.46, Chard; m., Marcia Jane Barclay; 1 d. Educ. Shebbear College; Manchester University. House Officer, Manchester Royal Infirmary, 1970-71; Registrar in Medicine, Aberdeen Royal Infirmary, 1971-74; Lecturer in Medicine, Dundee University, 1974-79. External Examiner in Medicine, Aberdeen University, 1983-86, 2000-03; Examiner, Edinburgh College of Physicians; Specialty Adviser in Gastroenterology, Medical Defence Union of Scotland. Publications: Therapeutic Nutrition: A Practical Guide, 1988; book chapters and papers on gastroenterology and clinical nutrition. Address: (h.) Balnagowan, Braehead, Invergowrie, Dundee; e-mail: Chris.R.Pennington@tuht.scot.nhs.uk

Pennington, Professor (Thomas) Hugh, MB BS, PhD, Hon. DSc (Lancaster, Strathclyde), FRCPath, FRCPEdin, FRSA, FMedSci, FRSE. Professor of Bacteriology, University of Aberdeen, since 1979; b. 19.4.38, Edgware, Middlesex; m., Carolyn Ingram Beattie; 2 d. Educ. Lancaster Royal Grammar School; St. Thomas's Hospital Medical School, London University. House appointments, St. Thomas's Hospital, 1962-63; Assistant Lecturer in Medical Microbiology, St. Thomas's Hospital Medical School, 1963-67; Postdoctoral Fellow, University of Wisconsin (Madison), 1967-68; Lecturer then Senior Lecturer in Virology, University of Glasgow, 1969-79; Dean of Medicine University of Aberdeen, 1987-92; Governor, Rowett Research Institute, 1980-88, and since 1996; Chairman, Expert Group on 1996 E.coli Outbreak in Central Scotland; Member, BBC Broadcasting Council for Scotland; Member, Scottish Food Advisory Committee of the Food Standards Agency; Caroline Walker Trust Consumer Advocate Award, 1997; Royal Institute of Public Health John Kershaw Memorial Prize, 1998. Publications: papers, articles and book chapters on viruses and bacteria, particularly their molecular epidemiology, and on food safety. Recreations: collecting books; dipterology. Address: (b.) Department of Medical Microbiology, University of Aberdeen, Aberdeen AB25 2ZD; T.-01224 681818, Ext. 52786.

Penrose, Rt. Hon. Lord (George William Penrose), QC (Scot). Senator of the College of Justice, since 1990; b. 2.6.38. Advocate, 1964; QC, 1978; Procurator to General Assembly of Church of Scotland, 1984-90.

Pentland, Brian, BSc, MB, ChB, FRCPE, FRCSLT. Consultant Neurologist in Rehabilitation Medicine, since 1982; Senior Lecturer in Rehabilitation Studies, Edinburgh University, since 1983; b. 24.6.49, Glasgow; m., Gillian Mary Duggua; 4 s. Educ. Liberton High School, Edinburgh; Edinburgh University. Junior hospital appointments in Edinburgh, Cumbria and Dundee; formerly Lecturer in Neurology in Edinburgh. Recreation: hill-walking. Address: (b.) Astley Ainslie Hospital, Grange Loan, Edinburgh EH9 2HL; T.-0131-537 9039.

Peppé, William Lawrence Tosco, OBE, JP, DL; b. 25.11.37, India; m., Deirdre Eva Preston Wakefield; 3 s. Educ. Wellington College; King's College, Cambridge. Naval Officer, 1955-91 – Commander. Recreation: country. Address: (h.) Glendrynoch Lodge, Carbost, Isle of Skye IV47 8SX; T.-01478 640218; e-mail: peppe@drynoch.demon.co.uk

Pepper, Simon Richard, OBE, BSc, MSc. Director, WWF Scotland (World Wide Fund for Nature), since 1985; b. 27.9.47, Worthing; m., Morag; 2 s.; 3 d. Educ. Aberdeen University; University College London. Quelea Project, Chad, Central Africa, 1972-73; Country Parks Officer, Essex County Council, 1973-79; Director, Cultullich Holiday Courses, Aberfeldy, 1979-85. Vice Convenor, Millennium Forest for Scotland, 1995-2001; Member, Secretary of State's Advisory Group on Sustainable Development, 1994-99. Rowing blue, Aberdeen University, Scottish Champion VIIIs, 1971; British University Champion Pairs, 1971. Recreations: enjoying the wild; managing sheep and native woodland of 42 hectare holding. Address: (h.) Upper Brae of Cultullich, Aberfeldy PH15 2EN.

Percy, Professor John Pitkeathly (Ian), CBE, LLD, CA, FRSA. Former Senior Partner, Grant Thornton, Scotland; former Chairman, The Accounts Commission; Non-Executive Director: William Wilson (Holdings) Ltd., The Weir Group PLC, Kiln PLC, Ricardo PLC; b. 16.1.42, Southport; m., Sheila; 2 d. Educ. Edinburgh Academy; Edinburgh University. Managing Partner, Grant Thornton, London, 1981-88; Honorary Professor of Accounting, Aberdeen University, 1988. Freeman, City of London; Member, British Academy of Experts; Elder, St. Cuthbert's Church of Scotland; President, Institute of Chartered Accountants of Scotland, 1990-91. Recreations: golf; fishing. Address: (b.) 1 St. Colme Street, Edinburgh EH3 6AA; T.-0131-452 8641; (h.) 30 Midmar Drive, Edinburgh; T.-0131-447 3645.

Perfect, Hugh Epton, BSc, PGCE. Associate Dean (General), Moray House Institute of Education, Faculty of Education, University of Edinburgh; b. 9.4.41, London; m., Susan; 2 d. Educ. Haberdasher's Askes' School, Hampstead; Imperial College, London. Teacher, Windsor Grammar School; Lecturer, Bulmershe College of Education, Reading; Lecturer/Senior Lecturer, Biology Department, Moray House, and Senior Assistant Principal, until 1998. Recreations: badminton; gardening; microcomputers. Address: (b.) Faculty of Education, University of Edinburgh, Holyrood Road, Edinburgh EH8 8AQ; T.-0131-651 6167.

Perman, Ray, BA, MBA. Chief Executive, Scottish Financial Enterprise, since 1999; b. 22.8.47, London; m., Fay Young; 3 s. Educ. Hemel Hempstead Grammar School; University of St. Andrews; Open University; University of Edinburgh. Journalist, 1970-83: The Times, Financial Times, Sunday Standard; Managing Director, Insider Publications, 1983-94; Development Director, Caledonian Publishing, 1994-96. Member: Scottish Council, WWF; Member, Board, Centre for Entrepreneurial Finance. Recreations: painting; forestry; playing the blues bass guitar. Address: (b.) 91 George Street, Edinburgh EH2 3ES; T.-0131-247 7700.

Perry of Walton, Rt. Hon. Lord (Walter Laing Macdonald Perry), Kt, OBE, MB, ChB, MD, DSc, FRCP, FRCPE, FRSE, FRS. President, Videotel Marine International; Life Peer, since 1979; b. 16.6.21, Dundee; m., 1, Anne Grant (m. dissolved); 3 s.; 2, Catherine Crawley; 2 s.; 1 d. Educ. Morgan Academy; Ayr Academy; Dundee High School; University College Dundee, St. Andrews University. Medical Officer, Colonial Service, 1944-46; RAF, 1946-47; Medical Research Council: member of staff, 1947-52, Director, Department of Biological Standards, 1952-58; Professor of Pharmacology, Edinburgh University, 1958-68; Vice-Chancellor, The Open University, 1968-81. Member, Editorial Board, Encyclopaedia Britannica, 1971-99; Member of Kuratorium, Fernuniversitat, Hagen, W. Germany, since 1976; Hon. Director, International Centre for Distance Learning, since 1983; Member, Academic Advisory Committee, University of E. Asia, Macau, since 1984; Member, Board, University of the World, 1987-98; Member, Select Committee of Science and Technology, House of Lords, 1997-2001. Recreations: golf; music; reading. Address: (h.) 2 Cramond Road South, Edinburgh EH4 6AD.

Perry, Professor Clive Graham, OBE, MA (Cantab), Hon. MA (Leicester), DLitt. Festival Director, Pitlochry Festival Theatre, since 1987; Professor of Theatre, Queen Margaret University College, Edinburgh, 1997-2001; (Professor and Head, Department of Drama, 1990-96); b. 17.3.36, Harrow. Educ. Wolverhampton Grammar School; Harrow County Grammar School; Cambridge University. Awarded Thames TV Scholarship to regional theatre, 1960-61; Assistant Director, Derby Playhouse; Associate Director, Castle Theatre, Farnham; Director of Productions, Phoenix Theatre, Leicester; Director, Royal Lyceum Theatre, Edinburgh, 1966-76 (Director of Theatres in Edinburgh, 1971-76); Director, Birmingham Repertory Theatre, 1976-87. DLitt, Queen Margaret University College, 2001. Recreation: theatre. Address: (b.) Pitlochry Festival Theatre, Port-Na-Craig, Pitlochry PH16 5DR; T.-01796 484600; e-mail: admin@pitlochry.org.uk

Perry, Ian, MA. Deputy Leader, Labour Group, Edinburgh City Council, since 1999; b. 13.8.51, Edinburgh; m., Jackie McFarlane; 2d. Educ. Broughton High School; Edinburgh University; Lecturer, Stevenson College, 20 years; Councillor, Edinburgh, 12 years. Address: (h.) 33 Lillyhill Terrace, Edinburgh, EH8 7DR; T.-0131-661 8359.

Perry, John Scott (Jack), BSc, CA, CPA. Office Managing Partner, Ernst and Young LLP, Glasgow, since 1995; Chairman, CBI Scotland, since 2001; b. 23.11.54, Glasgow; m., Lydia Margaret Cox; 1 s.; 2 d. Educ. Glasgow Academy; Glasgow University; Strathclyde University. Joined Ernst and Young, 1976; transferred to Ernst and Young, Dallas, Texas, 1981-83; seconded to Scottish Development Finance, 1987-88; appointed Partner, Ernst and Young, Glasgow, 1988; Head of Audit, 1994-95. Member, CBI Scotland Council, since 1995; Chairman, Craigholme School. Recreations: golf; skiing. Address: (b.) George House, 50 George Square, Glasgow G2 1RR; T.-0141-552 3456; e-mail: jperry@uk.ey.com

Perth, 17th Earl of (John David Drummond), PC (1957); b. 13.5.07; m., Nancy Seymour Fincke (deceased); 2 s. Educ. Downside; Cambridge University. Lt., Intelligence Corps, 1940; War Cabinet Offices, 1942-43; Ministry of Production, 1944-45; Minister of State for Colonial Affairs, 1957-62; First Crown Estate Commissioner, 1962-77; Member, Court, St. Andrews University, 1967-86; Trustee, National Library of Scotland, 1968-95. Hon. LLD; Hon. FRIBA; Hon. FRIAS. Address: (h.) Stobhall, by Perth PH2 6DR; T.-01821 640 332.

Petch, Professor Alison Jean, BA, MA, PhD, DipSW. Nuffield Professor of Community Care Studies, Glasgow University, since 1993; b. 5.4.50, Leeds; m., David Jarman; 2 s. Educ. Central Newcastle High School; Cambridge University. Research Planner, Livingston Development Corporation, 1973-75; Research Fellow, Strathclyde University, 1983-86; Research Fellow, then Senior Research Fellow, Social Work Research Centre, Stirling University, 1986-93. Address: (b.) Nuffield Centre for Community Care Studies, Gregory Building, Glasgow University, Glasgow G12 8QQ; T.-0141-330 5600.

Peterken, Laurence Edwin, CBE, MA. Consultant; Member, Criminal Injuries Compensation Appeal Panel, since 1997; b. 2.10.31, London; m., 1, Hanne Birgithe Von Der Recke (deceased); 1 s.; 1 d.; 2, Margaret Raynal Blair; 1 s.; 1 d. Educ. Harrow School (Scholar); Peterhouse, Cambridge (Scholar). Pilot Officer, RAF Regt., Adjt. No. 20 LAA Sqdn., 1950-52; Service Divisional Manager, Hotpoint Ltd., 1961-63; Commercial Director, then Managing Director, British Domestic Appliances Ltd., 1963-68; Director, British Printing Corporation Ltd., 1969-73; Managing Director, Fashion Multiple Division, Debenhams Ltd., 1974-76; Management Auditor, 1976-77; Controller, Operational Services, GLC, 1977-85; President, GLC Chief Officers' Guild, 1983-85; Acting Director, Royal Festival Hall, 1983-85; General Manager, Greater Glasgow Health Board, 1986-93; Director, Special Projects, NHS in Scotland, 1993-96; Chairman, Glasgow and West of Scotland Institute of Public Administration, since 1993; Member, Scottish Committee, Council for Music in Hospitals, since 1996; Trustee, The Rodolfus Choir, since 1998. Recreations: music; cycling. Address: (h.) Carlston, Kilbarchan Road, Bridge of Weir PA11 3EG.

Peterkin, Thomas William Grant, MA (Hons). Scottish Political Correspondent, Daily Telegraph, since 2001; b. 22.4.70, Edinburgh. Educ. Clifton Hall; Glenalmond College; Edinburgh University. D.C. Thomson & Co., 1993-97; Dundee Press, 1997-99; Health Correspondent, Scotland on Sunday, 1999-2001. Former Edinburgh University Yard of Ale Champion. Publication: Dundee - A Voyage of Discovery (Contributor). Recreations: piping; golf; skiing. Address: (b.) 5 Coates Crescent, Edinburgh EH3 7AL; T.-0131-473 9898.

Peterson, George Sholto, NP. Solicitor and Notary Public, since 1956; Honorary Sheriff, since 1982; b. 18.9.27, Lerwick; m., Dorothy Hilda Spence; 2 s.; 4 d. Educ. Lerwick Central Public School; Edinburgh University. Secretary, The Shetland Trust; Factor for the Marquess of Zetland; Senior Partner, Tait & Peterson, Solicitors and Estate Agents, Lerwick; Dean, Faculty of Solicitors in Shetland, 1982-98; Honorary Pastor, Ebenezer Church, Lerwick. Recreations: studying theology; reading; fishing. Address: (b.) Bank of Scotland Buildings, Lerwick, Shetland; T.-01595 693010; e-mail: info@tait-peterson.co.uk

Peterson, Stewart Neil. Editor, Greenock Telegraph, since 2000; b. 17.5.48, Gourock; m., Catherine; 3 s.; 1 d. Educ. Gourock High School; Glasgow College of Building and Printing. Compositor/Linotype operator, Gourock Times, 1965; Linotype operator, Orr, Pollock

and Co., Greenock, 1974; Greenock Telegraph: Journalist, 1976; Assistant News Editor, 1986; Deputy Editor, 1992. Past President/Hon. Member, Gourock Amateur Swimming Club; Former Member: Dunoon Housing Association; Hunter Quay Community Council. Recreations: motorcycling; poultry keeping; DIY; angling. Address: (h.) Janefield, Hunter's Quay, Argyll; T.-01369 706857.

Pethrick, Professor Richard Arthur, BSc, PhD, DSc, FRSC, FRSE. Professor in Chemistry, Strathclyde University, since 1983 (Head of Department, since 1992); b. 26.10.42; m., Joan Knowles Hume; 1 s. Educ. North Gloucestershire College, Cheltenham; London University; Salford University. Editor: British Polymer Journal, Polymer Yearbook, Polymer International, International Journal of Polymer Materials; Member, Polymer Committee, European Science Foundation; Member, Committee, MACRO Group, 1979-84; Member, SERC Polymer Materials Committee, since 1994; Elder, Merrylea Church of Scotland. Address: (b.) Department of Pure and Applied Chemistry, University of Strathclyde, Thomas Graham Building, Cathedral Street, Glasgow G1 1XL.

Petrie, Murray, FRICS, IRRV. Chairman, Tayside Primary Care NHS Trust, since 1999; Chair, Perth and Kinross Health and Social Care Co-operative, since 2000; b. 8.6.46, Keith; m., Jennifer; 3 s. Educ. High School of Dundee. Assistant/Partner/Senior Partner, Lickley Proctor, Chartered Surveyors, since 1964. Non-Executive Trustee, NHS Tayside; Director, Maggie Centre (Dundee). Recreations: rugby; golf; travelling. Address: (h.) Craigard, 6 Guthrie Terrace, Barnhill, Dundee DD5 2QY; T.-01382 776180.

Pettegree, Professor Andrew David Mark, FRHS. Professor of Modern History, St Andrews University, since 1998; b. 16.9.57, Rhyl; m., Jane Ryan; 2 d. Educ. Oundle School; Oxford University (BA Hons). Schmidt Scholarship, 1980 (MA, DPhil, 1983); research scholarship, University of Hamburg, 1982-84; Research Fellow, Peterhouse, Cambridge; became Lecturer, St Andrews University, 1986; Reader, 1994; Director, St Andrews Reformation Studies Institute, 1993; Literary Director, Royal Historical Society, 1998. Publications include: Foreign Protestant Communities in Sixteenth Century London; Emden and the Dutch Revolt. Exile and the Development of Reformed Protestantism, 1992; The Early Reformation in Europe, 1992; Calvinism in Europe, 1540-1610 (Co-Editor); The Reformation of the Parishes. The Ministry and the Reformation in Town and Country, 1993; Calvinism in Europe, 1540-1620 (Co-Editor); Marian Protestantism. Six Studies, 1996; The Reformation World, 2000. Recreations: golf; tennis. Address: (b.) Reformation Institute, 69 South Street, St Andrews KY16 9AL; T.-01334 462903.

Pfab, Professor Josef, Dip.Chem, Dr.rer.nat. Professor of Chemistry, Heriot-Watt University, Edinburgh, since 1988; b. 3.3.43, Germany; m., Frances Amy Windibank, 1s.; 1d. Educ. Max Reger Gymnasium, Amberg, Germany; Technische Universität, Munich, Germany. Heriot-Watt University: Lecturer, 1972; Reader, 1982, conducting research into photochemistry; Member, EPSRC Research Panels. Recreations: fishing; walking; cycling; music. Address: (b.) Department of Chemistry, Heriot-Watt University, Riccarton, Edinburgh, EH14 4AS; T.-0131-449 5111.

Phelps, Professor Alan David Reginald, MA, DPhil, CPhys, FInstP, FRSE. Professor, Physics and Applied Physics, Strathclyde University, since 1993 (Head of Department, 1998-2001); Chairman, Plasma Physics Group, Institute of Physics, 1995-97; b. 2.6.44, Basingstoke; m., Susan Helen Marshall; 1 d. Educ. Haverfordwest Grammar School; King's College, Cambridge; University College,

Oxford. Research Associate, National Academy of Sciences (USA), 1972-73; Research Officer, Oxford University, 1973-78; Lecturer, then Senior Lecturer, then Reader in Physics, Strathclyde University, 1978-93, Deputy Head of Department, 1993-98. Publications: 200 research papers and reports. Recreations: hill-walking; country pursuits. Address: (b.) Department of Physics and Applied Physics, John Anderson Building, Strathclyde University, Glasgow G4 0NG; T.-0141-548 3166; e-mail: a.d.r.phelps@strath.ac.uk

Philip, Hon. Lord (Alexander Morrison). Senator of the College of Justice, since 1996; b. 3.8.42, Aberdeen; m., Shona Mary Macrae; 3 s. Educ. Glasgow High School; St. Andrews University; Glasgow University. Solicitor, 1967-72; Advocate, 1973; Advocate Depute, 1982-85; QC, 1984; Chairman, Medical Appeal Tribunals, 1988-92; Chairman, Scottish Land Court, 1993-96; President, Lands Tribunal for Scotland, 1993-96. Recreations: piping; golf. Address: (b.) Parliament House, Edinburgh EH1 1RQ; T.-0131-225 2595.

Philips, Douglas John, MHSM, DipHSM. Director of Priority Services and Joint Planning, Argyll and Clyde Health Board, since 1997; b. 30.4.53, Edinburgh; m., Morag S. Hall. Educ. Dalkeith High School. Formerly General Manager, Northern Unit, Highland Health Board; Director of Community Care Development, Argyll and Clyde Health Board, 1992-97. Winston Churchill Memorial Trust Fellow, 1996; Chairman, Association of Churchill Fellows, Scottish Region. Recreations: walking the Dalmatians; creative gardening; local history; reading fiction; music; Coronation Street. Address: (h.) Windsong, Blairuskinmore, Kinlochard, Stirling FK8 3TP; T.-01877 387236; e-mail: blairuskin@aol.com

Phillips, Professor John H., MA, PhD. Professor of Biology Teaching and Vice-Provost of Medicine and Veterinary Medicine, Edinburgh University, 1996-2001; b. 19.2.41, York; m., Kerstin B. Halling; 2 d. Educ. Leighton Park School, Reading; Christ's College, Cambridge. Lecturer in Biochemistry, Makerere University, Uganda, 1967-69; scientific staff, MRC Laboratory of Molecular Biology, Cambridge, 1969-74; Department of Biochemistry, Edinburgh University, 1974-88, Director of Biology Teaching, 1988-93, Head, Department of Biochemistry, 1993-96. Recreations: natural history; Scottish mountains; visits to Sweden. Address: (h.) 46 Granby Road, Edinburgh EH16 5NW; T.-0131-667 5322.

Pia, Paul Dominic, LLB (Hons), WS, NP. Senior Partner, Burness (formerly W. & J. Burness WS), since 1974; b. 29.3.47, Edinburgh; m., Anne Christine Argent; 3 d. Educ. Holy Cross Academy, Edinburgh; Edinburgh University; University of Perugia. Law apprentice, Lindsays WS, 1968-70; admitted as Solicitor and member of Society of Writers to HM Signet, 1971; Solicitor, W. & J. Burness WS, 1971-74; Associate Member, American Bar Association; Fellow, Institute of Directors; Director, Scottish North American Business Council; Trustee, The Big Issue Scotland; Chairman, Japan Society of Scotland, 1996-2000; Chairman, Edinburgh's Japanese Garden. Publication: Care Diligence and Skill (handbook for directors). Recreations: hill-walking; travel; foreign languages. Address: (b.) 50 Lothian Road, Edinburgh; T.-0131-473 6000; (h.) Lauriston, 67 Woodford Park, Edinburgh; T.-0131-441 7051; e-mail: pdp@burness.co.uk

Pickett, Professor James, BSc (Econ), MLit. Professor Emeritus, Strathclyde University, since 1995; b. 7.6.29, Greenock; m., Janet Clelland; 1 s.; 3 d. Educ. Greenock Academy; School of Economics, Dundee; Edinburgh University; Glasgow University; University of Paris. Statistician, Dominion Bureau of Statistics, Canada; Lecturer, Senior Lecturer, Professor and Director, Livingstone Institute of Overseas Development, Strathclyde

University, 1961-95; Special Economic Adviser, UN Economic Commision for Africa; Visiting Professor, University of Saskatchewan; Economic Adviser, African Development Bank; UN Chief Economic Adviser to Ethiopian Government, 1992-95; Consultant to British, Canadian and Ghanian Governments, UN, OECD; author and editor, seven books and numerous papers; FRSA; sometime President, Scottish Union of Students. Recreations: hill-walking; listening to music; photography; computing; long-suffering support of Greenock Morton F.C. Address: (h.) 1 Divert Road, Gourock PA19 1DR; T.-01475 631046; e-mail: jamespickett@beeb.net

Picking, Anne, RMN. Labour MP, East Lothian, since 2001; b. 30.3.58, Dunfermline; m., David; 1 s. Educ. Woodmill High School. Nursing sister; NEC, Cohse and Unison; former National President, Unison; former Ashford Borough Councillor; former Chair of Organisation, Labour Party. Address: (b.) 65 High Street, Tranent, East Lothian EH33 1LN; T.-01875 614990.

Pignatelli, Frank, MA, MEd, DUniv, CIMgt, FSQA, FICPD, FScotvec, FRSA. Chief Executive Officer, SUfI Ltd., since 1999; b. 22.12.46, Glasgow; m., Rosetta Anne; 1 s.; 1 d. Educ. St. Mungo's Academy, Glasgow; University of Glasgow. Executive Director of Education, Strathclyde Regional Council, 1988-96; Group Director, Human Resources, Associated Newspapers, London, 1996-97; Chairman and Managing Director, Executive Support and Development Consultancy, since 1997; Chief Executive, Scottish Business in the Community, 1998-99. Visiting Professor, University of Glasgow: School of Education, 1993, Business School, 1997. Address: (h.) 10 Whittingehame Drive, Glasgow G12 0XX; T.-0141-285 6010.

Pike, (Kathryn) Lorna, MA (Hons). Editor, Scottish National Dictionary Association, since 2001; Research Officer, Feasibility Study, Institute for the Languages of Scotland, 2001-02; b. 8.8.56, Fort William. Educ. Lochaber High School, Fort William; Edinburgh University. Editor, Concise Scots Dictionary, 1979-83; Dictionary of the Older Scottish Tongue: Assistant Editor, 1984-86, Editor, 1986-2001. Recreations: riding; photography; handicrafts. Address: (b.) 27 George Square, Edinburgh, EH8 9LD; T.-0131-650 4149.

Pilcher, Rosamunde. Author; b. 22.9.24, Lelant, Cornwall. Began publishing short stories in Woman and Home, 1945; since then has published hundreds of short stories. Novels include Sleeping Tiger, Under Gemini, Wild Mountain Thyme, The Carousel, Voices in Summer, The Shell Seekers, September, The Blue Bedroom, Flowers in the Rain, Coming Home, Winter Solstice; play: The Dashing White Sergeant. Address: (h.) Penrowan, Longforgan, Perthshire; T.- Dundee 360393.

Pinder, Susan, MBA. Principal and Chief Executive, West Lothian College, since 2001; b. 28.12.51, Tadcaster; m., Tony; 1 s. Educ. Selby Grammar School. Twenty-five years' experience in further education, latterly as Director of Learning, Scottish University for Industry. Member, Board, ASC (Member, Objective 2 East Programme Monitoring Committee). Recreations: reading; gardening; travel. Address: West Lothian College, Almondvale Crescent, Livingston EH54 7EP; T.-01506 427802; e-mail: spinder@west-lothian.ac.uk

Piper, Professor Ronald Allen, BA, BD, PhD. Professor of Christian Origins, St. Andrews University, since 1997; b. 27.3.48, U.S.A.; m., Faith Elizabeth Woodhouse; 1 d. Educ. Pomona College, Claremont, California; London University. Lecturer in New Testament Studies, Aberdeen University, 1979-80; Lecturer in New Testament Language and Literature, St. Andrews University, 1980-92, Reader in

New Testament, 1992-97, Principal, St. Mary's College, St. Andrews University, 1992-2001, Head, School of Divinity, 1992-2001. Secretary, British New Testament Society, 1990-93; Assistant Secretary, Studiorum Novi Testamenti Societas, since 2000. Publications: Wisdom in the Q-Tradition, 1989; The Gospel Behind the Gospels, 1995; numerous journal articles. Address: (b.) St. Mary's College, St. Andrews KY16 9JU; T.-01334 462850; e-mail: rap@st-andrews.ac.uk

Pippard, Professor Martin John, BSc, MB, ChB, FRCPath, FRCP. Professor of Haematology, Dundee University, since 1989; Honorary Consultant Haematologist, Tayside University Hospitals Trust, since 1989; b. 16.1.48, London; m., Grace Elizabeth; 2 s.; 1 d. Educ. Buckhurst Hill County High School; Birmingham University. House Physician and House Surgeon, 1972-73; Senior Medical House Officer, 1973-75; Research Fellow, Nuffield Department of Clinical Medicine, Oxford, 1975-78; MRC Travelling Research Fellow, University of Washington, Seattle, 1978-80; Wellcome Trust Research Fellow and Clinical Lecturer, Nuffield Department of Clinical Medicine, 1980-83; Consultant Haematologist, MRC Clinical Research Centre and Northwick Park Hospital, 1983-88. Recreations: gardening; fell-walking. Address: (b.) Department of Molecular and Cellular Pathology, Ninewells Hospital and Medical School, Dundee DD1 9SY; T.-01382 660111; e-mail: martin.j.pippard@tuht.scot.nhs.uk

Pitcaithly, Mary, LLB, NP. Chief Executive, Falkirk Council, since 1998; b. 17.7.56, Falkirk; 1 d. Educ. Falkirk High; Edinburgh University. Depute Director, Law and Administration, Falkirk District Council, 1989-95; Assistant Chief Executive, Falkirk Council, 1995-98. Address: (b.) Municipal Buildings, Falkirk; T.-01324 506003.

Pitches, Sally Jane, LLB, NP. Executive Director, The Guide Association, since 1997; b. 5.6.57, Edinburgh. Educ. Currie High School; Strathclyde University. Solicitor, private practice, Edinburgh. Founding President, Edinburgh Breakfast Rotary Club; Senator, Junior Chamber International. Recreations: cookery; bridge; travel. Address: (b.) 16 Coates Crescent, Edinburgh; T.-0131-226 4545.

Pittock, Professor Murray G.H., MA, DPhil, FEA, FRHistS, FSAScot. Professor in Literature, Strathclyde University, since 1996 (Head, Glasgow-Strathclyde School of Scottish Studies); Co-Editor, Scottish Studies Review; b. 5.1.62; m., Anne Grace Thornton Martin; 2 d. Educ. Aberdeen Grammar School; Glasgow University; Balliol College, Oxford (Snell Exhibitioner). Lecturer, then Reader, Edinburgh University, 1989-96. Royal Society of Edinburgh BP Humanities Research Prize, 1992-94; British Academy Chatterton Lecturer in Poetry, 2002. Publications: The Invention of Scotland, 1991; Spectrum of Decadence, 1993; Poetry and Jacobite Politics in Eighteenth-Century Britain and Ireland, 1994; The Myth of the Jacobite Clans, 1995; Inventing and Resisting Britain, 1997; Jacobitism, 1998; Celtic Identity and the British Image, 1999; Scottish Nationality, 2001. Address: (b.) English Studies, Strathclyde University, Richmond Street, Glasgow, G1 1XH; T.-0141-548 4490.

Pitts, Professor Nigel Berry, BDS (Hons), PhD, FDS, RCSEng, FDS, RCSEdin, MFPHM, FFGDP (UK). Director, Dental Health Services Research Unit, since 1985; Centre Leader, Medical Research Council's Health Services Research Collaboration; Professor of Dental Health, University of Dundee, since 1991 (Dean of Dentistry, 1997-2000; b. 1954, London; m., Elizabeth Ann; 3 s. Educ. Royal Liberty School; London Hospital Medical College Dental School, London University. House Officer/Senior House Officer, The London Hospital; Lecturer, Department of Conservative Dentistry, London Hospital Medical College

Dental School; Lecturer, then Senior Lecturer, Department of Conservative Dentistry, University of Hong Kong; Vice-President, European Association for Dental Public Health; International Director, Behavioral Sciences and Health Services Research Group, International Association for Dental Research; Past President, British Association for the Study of Community Dentistry; Past President, Diagnostic Systems Group, International Association for Dental Research. Recreations: family; photography. Address: (b.) Dental School, Park Place, Dundee DD1 4HR; T.-01382 635959.

Placido, Professor Francis, BSc, PhD, FInstP, FSAS. Professor, University of Paisley, since 1999; Director, Thin Film Centre; b. 29.9.46, Dalkeith; m., Dorothy Charlotte Torrance; 2 d. Educ. Dalkeith High School; University of Edinburgh. Demonstrator, University of Edinburgh, 1972-77; Paisley College of Technology: Lecturer, 1977-89, Reader in Physics, 1989-99. John Logie Baird Award for Innovation, 1998. Recreations: food and wine; painting. Address: (b.) Thin Film Centre, University of Paisley, High Street, Paisley PA1 2BE; T.-0141-848 3610; e-mail: frank.placido@paisley.ac.uk

Platt, Joseph, LLB. Founding Partner, Philpott Platt Niblett and Wight, Solicitors, Dumbarton; Member, Council, Law Society of Scotland; b. 22.5.51, Dumbarton; m., Christina Susan; 2 s. Educ. Dumbarton Academy; Glasgow University. Qualified as Solicitor, 1974; Partner, J.W. Dunn & Co., 1976. Recreations: hill-walking; photography; reading; golf. Address: 105 Glasgow Road, Dumbarton; T.-01389 733777.

Plotkin, Professor Gordon David, BSc, PhD, FRS, FRSE. Professor in Computer Science, Edinburgh University; b. 9.9.46, Glasgow; m.; 1 s. Educ. Glasgow High School for Boys; Glasgow University; Edinburgh University. Lecturer, then Reader, Edinburgh University; Director, Laboratory for the Foundation of Computer Science; Member, Academia Europaea; Editor: Information and Computation, Mathematical Structures in Computer Science, Theoretical Computer Science, ACM Transactions on Computational Logic. Recreations: chess; hill-walking. Address: (b.) Division of Informatics, King's Buildings, Edinburgh University, Edinburgh; T.-0131-650 5158.

Pollman, Professor Karla Friedel Love, MA, MD, PhD, Drhabil. Professor of Classics, St Andrews University, since 2000; b. 21.10.63, Tuebingen. Educ. Universities of Tuebingen, Munich, Bochum; Newnham College, Cambridge. Alexander-von-Humboldt Fellow, University College London, 1993-95; Lecturer, St Andrews University, 1995; Visiting Scholar, Green College, UBC, Vancouver, 1998; Institute for Advanced Study, Princeton, 1999; Charter Fellow, Wolfson College, Oxford, 1999-2000. Publications include: books and articles on early Christian poetry, Augustine, Latin epic and satire, double standards. Recreations: singing; walking; reading. Address: (b.) School of Greek, Latin and Ancient History, St Andrews KY16 9AL.

Pollock, Sheriff Alexander, MA (Oxon), LLB. Sheriff of Grampian, Highland and Islands, at Inverness and Portree, since 2001; b. 21.7.44, Glasgow; m., Verena Francesca Gertraud Alice Ursula Critchley; 1 s.; 1 d. Educ. Rutherglen Academy; Glasgow Academy; Brasenose College, Oxford; Edinburgh University; Perugia University. Partner, Bonar Mackenzie & Kermack, WS, 1971-73; called to Scottish Bar, 1973; Conservative candidate: West Lothian, General Election, February 1974, Moray and Nairn, General Election, October 1974; MP, Moray and Nairn, 1979-83, Moray, 1983-87; Parliamentary Private Secretary to Secretary of State for Scotland, 1982-86; PPS to Secretary of State for Defence, 1986-87; Advocate Depute, 1990-91; Sheriff (Floating) of Tayside, Central and Fife, at Stirling, 1991-93; Sheriff of Grampian, Highland and Islands, at

Aberdeen and Stonehaven, 1993-2001. Member, Queen's Bodyguard for Scotland (Royal Company of Archers), since 1984. Recreations: walking; music. Address: (h.) Drumdarrach, Forres, Moray.

Pollock, Thomas Alexander Jackson, BArch, RIBA, FRIAS. Senior Partner, The Pollock Hammond Partnership, Architects; b. 7.10.48, Newbridge, Midlothian; m., Clare Gregory; 1 d. Educ. George Watson's College, Edinburgh; Middlebury College, Vermont, USA; University of Edinburgh. Michael Laird and Partners, Edinburgh, 1973-78; William A. Cadell Architects, Linlithgow, 1978-91 (Partner, 1982-91); Pollock Hammond Partnership, since 1991. Member, Conservation Committee, RIAS; Member, Cases Panel, Architectural Heritage Society of Scotland; Trustee, Clan Menzies Charitable Trust; former Chairman, Linlithgow Festival Trust. Recreations: travel; antiques; the arts. Address: (h.) Beinn Castle House, 293 High Street, Linlithgow EH49 7AT; T.-01506 844417; e-mail: mail@pollockhammondarchitects.co.uk

Ponsonby, Bernard Joseph. Political Editor, Scottish Television, since 2000, Reporter/Presenter, 1990-2000; b. Glasgow. Educ. Trinity High School, Rutherglen; Strathclyde University. Researcher to Rt. Hon. Dr Dickson Mabon, 1987; Press Officer, Scottish Liberal Democrats, 1988-89; party's first Parliamentary candidate, Glasgow Govan, 1988; PR and Media Consultant, freelance Reporter for BBC Radio Scotland, 1989-90; Principal Presenter of political, election, and by-election programmes, Scottish Television; presented Platform, since 1996, Scottish Voices, Scottish Questions, Trial by Night. Recreations: golf; Celtic Football Club. Address: (b.) Scottish Television, Cowcaddens, Glasgow G2 3PR; T.-0141-300 3000.

Ponton, Professor John Wylie, BSc, PhD, FIChemE, FEng. Professor of Chemical Engineering, Edinburgh University, since 1989; b. 2.5.43, Edinburgh; m., Katherine Jane Victoria Eachus. Educ. Melville College, Edinburgh; Edinburgh University. Recreations: engineering; amateur radio; music. Address: (b.) Department of Chemical Engineering, Edinburgh University, EH9 3JL; T.-0131-650 4860; e-mail: jack@ecosse.org

Poole, Anna I., MA. Advocate, since 1998; Singer; b. 11.8.70, Craigtoun; m., Richard J.M. Sweet. Educ. Madras College, St Andrews; Oxford University. Qualified as a Solicitor of the Supreme Court of England and Wales, 1996; then as a Scottish Solicitor with Brodies, WS, 1997; called to Scottish Bar, 1998. Director, Suffolk Life Group PLC. Recreations: music; walking; reading. Address: 5 Randolph Place, Edinburgh EH3 7TQ.

Poole, Sheriff Isobel Anne, LLB. Sheriff of Lothian and Borders; b. 9.12.41, Oxford. Educ. Oxford High School for Girls (GDST); Edinburgh University. Advocate. Recreations: country; arts; gardens; friends. Address: (b.) Sheriffs' Chambers, Sheriff Court, Edinburgh.

Poon, Professor Wilson, MA (Cantab), PhD (Cantab), FInstP, CPhys. Professor of Condensed Matter Physics, Edinburgh University, since 1999; b. 26.9.62, Hong Kong; m., Heidi Lau; 1 s.; 1 d. Educ. St Paul's Co-educational College, Hong Kong; Rugby School; Peterhouse, Cambridge. Research Fellow, St Edmund's College, Cambridge, 1986-88; Lecturer, Department of Applied Physics, Portsmouth Polytechnic, 1989; Edinburgh University: Lecturer, 1990-97; Senior Lecturer, 1997-99. Recreations: piano. Address: (b.) Department of Physics and Astronomy, Edinburgh University, Mayfield Road, Edinburgh, EH9 3JZ; T.-0131-650 5297; e-mail: w.poon@ed.ac.uk

Porteous, Brian William, BSc (Hons), MILAM, DipRM. Director of Culture, Sport and Leisure, Genesis Consulting, since 2001; b. 6.2.51, Falkirk; m., Shena; 3 s. Educ. Falkirk High School; St. Andrews University; Moray House College of Education; Loughborough University of Technology. Joined Scottish Sports Council as Development Officer, 1979, appointed Director of Operations, 1989; Depute Director, Cultural and Leisure Services and Parks and Recreation, Glasgow City Council, 1994-2001. Honorary Secretary, British Orienteering Federation, 1974-76; former Member, Board, National Coaching Foundation; President, Scottish Orienteering Association, 1996-2000. Publication: Orienteering, 1979. Recreations: golf; orienteering; amateur opera/musicals; caravanning. Address: (h.) Croft House, 2 Spoker's Loan, Balfron, Glasgow G63 0PA; T.(b.)-0845 345 3355.

Porter, Margaret Teresa, LLB, DFM. Advocate, since 1987; b. 9.8.47, Sutton Coldfield; m., Kenneth John Porter; 1 s.; 1 d. Educ. Monmouth School for Girls; Glasgow University. Glasgow University: Faulds Fellow in Law, 1982-85; Tutor in Law, 1985-94; full-time practice (criminal and civil) at Bar, 1987-91; Procurator Fiscal Depute, Glasgow, 1991-96; part-time Chairman, Social Security Appeals Tribunal, since 1996; part-time Chairman, Disability Appeals Tribunal, since 1996. Recreations: gardening; cinema; embroidery; clothes; shopping. Address: (h.) The Stables, Glenlora, by Lochwinnoch, PA12 4DN; T.-01505 843869; e-mail: J.Porter@philosophy. arts.gla.ac.uk

Potter, Christina Ann, MBA, MBCS. Principal, Elmwood College, Cupar, since 1997; b. 19.8.53, Newcastle upon Tyne; m., Tom Potter; 2 s. Educ. Glenrothes High School; Warwick University. Computer Operator, Royal Bank of Scotland, 1969-72; Computer Support Executive, ICL, 1972-83; Systems Analyst, ISTEL, 1983-84; Computer Lecturer, Tile Hill College, Coventry, 1984-95; Vice Principal, Warwickshire College, 1995-97. Recreations: walking; reading; theatre. Address: (b.) Elmwood College, Carslogie Road, Cupar KY15 4JB; T.-01334 658802.

Pottinger, Graham, LLB, CA, ACMA. Chief Executive, Scottish Mutual Assurance plc, since 1997; Managing Director, Abbey National Financial and Investment Services plc, since 1997; Director, Abbey National Life plc, since 1992; b. 14.6.49, Glasgow; m., Dorothy; 1 s.; 1 d. Educ. Jordanhill College School, Glasgow; Glasgow University. Peat Marwick Mitchell & Co., 1966-72; Partner, Deloitte Haskins & Sells, 1972-79; Controller, UK and Africa, Cargill Plc, 1980-92; Finance Director, Scottish Mutual Assurance plc, 1992-96. Member, Council, Institute of Chartered Accountants of Scotland. Recreations: swimming; gardening. Address: (b.) Abbey National House, 301 St. Vincent Street, Glasgow G2 5HN; T.-0141-275 8654.

Pounder, Professor Derrick John, MB, ChB, FRCPA, FFPathRCPI, FCAP, FRCPath, FHKCPath. Professor of Forensic Medicine, Dundee University, since 1987; b. 25.2.49, Pontypridd; m., Georgina Kelly; 1 s.; 2 d. Educ. Pontypridd Boys' Grammar; Birmingham University. Senior Lecturer (Forensic Pathology), University of Adelaide; Deputy Chief Medical Examiner, Edmonton, Alberta, and Associate Professor, Universities of Alberta and Calgary, 1985-87. Freeman of Llantrisant. Recreations: photography; medieval architecture; almost lost causes. Address: (b.) Department of Forensic Medicine, Dundee University, Dundee DD1 4HN; T.-01382 348020; e-mail: d.j.pounder@dundee.ac.uk

Powell, Robert George, MA (Hons). Business Editor, The Herald, since 1998; b. 9.4.54, Cornwall; m., Mary; 1 s.; 1 d. Educ. Frome Grammar School; Edinburgh University; University College Cardiff. Teacher, Muslim Secondary

School, Sagamu, Nigeria, 1977-78; Foreign Correspondent, Reuters, 1979-95 (Portugal, 1980-81 and 1991-95, Argentina, 1982-84, Venezuela, 1984-85, Cuba, 1986, Kenya, 1986-90, UK, 1990-91). Recreations: travel; hillwalking; wildlife observation; swimming; reading. Address: (b.) 200 Renfield Street, Glasgow G2 3PR; T.-0141-302 7000.

Powell, Shona S. DipRSA. Director, Lemon Tree, Aberdeen, since 1992; b. 10.4.56, Dundee. Educ. Kirkton High School, Dundee; Dundee College of Education; Richmond College, Sheffield. Teacher, Hayshead, Arbroath, 1977-80; Assistant to Director, Sheffield Youth Arts Festival, 1981-82; Acting Arts Co-ordinator, Sheffield Education Department, 1982-83; Administrator, Chesterfield Arts Centre, 1983-86; Co-ordinator, Town Hall Studios, Swindon, 1986-87; Director, West Wiltshire Arts Centre, 1987-90; Director, Newfest '91, Newcastle upon Tyne, 1990-91. Former Member, Scottish Arts Council Lottery Committee; former Member, SAC Combined Arts Committee; Advisory Board Member, Scottish Dance Theatre. Address: The Lemon Tree, 5 West North Street, Aberdeen AB24 5AT; T.-01224 647999.

Power, Professor Michael John, BSc, MSc, DPhil, CClinPsychol. Professor of Clinical Psychology, Edinburgh University, since 1995; b. 10.8.54, London; m., Lora Champion; 2 s.; 1 d. Educ. St Philip's Grammar School, Birmingham; University College London; Sussex University; Birmingham University. Clinical Psychologist, Guy's Hospital, London, 1982-84; Research Scientist, MRC, 1984-88; Lecturer in Clinical Psychology, Institute of Psychiatry, Maudsley Hospital, 1989-90; Senior Lecturer in Clinical Psychology, Royal Holloway, London University, 1990-94; Research Scientist, World Health Organisation, Geneva, 1994-95. Consultant Clinical Psychologist, Royal Edinburgh Hospital. Publications: Cognition and Emotion: From Order to Disorder (Co-author); Adult Psychological Problems (Co-author). Recreations: travel; literature; tennis; cinema. Address: (b.) Department of Psychiatry, Royal Edinburgh Hospital, Edinburgh, EH10 5HF; T.-0131-537 6578.

Prag, Thomas Gregory Andrew, MA, FIMgt. Radio Authority Member for Scotland; Media Consultant; b. 2.1.47, London; m., Angela; 3 s. Educ. Westminster School; Brasenose College, Oxford. Joined BBC, 1968, as Studio Manager; Producer, BBC Radio Oxford; Programme Organiser, BBC Radio Highland; first Chief Executive, Moray Firth Radio, 1981, then Managing Director, then Chairman until 1981. Trustee, Highland Community Foundation; Past President, Inverness and District Chamber of Commerce; Board Member, Highland Festival; Fellow, Radio Academy. Recreations: good intentions towards restoration of 1950 Daimler; keeping clock collection wound; family; growing vegetables; chasing deer off vegetables. Address: Windrush, Easter Muckovie, Inverness IV2 5BN; e-mail: prag@ecosse.net

Press, Professor Jeffrey Ian, BA (Hons) (Spanish), BA (Hons) (Russian), PhD. Established Professor in Russian (Comparative Linguistics), St. Andrews University, since 1995; b. 23.3.47, Oldham; m., Marie-Christine Morris; 1 s.; 1 d. Educ. Hulme Grammar School, Oldham; London University. Lecturer in Russian, Queen Mary College, London University, 1970-79, SSEES and Queen Mary College, 1979-87, Senior Lecturer, 1987-89; Professor of Slavonic and Comparative Linguistics, London University, 1990-95. Publications: books on Russian, Breton, Slavonic languages, Ukrainian and Lithuanian linguistics. Recreations: astronomy; photography; walking; learning languages. Address: (b.) St. Andrews University, St. Andrews KY16 9AL; T.-01334 463631; e-mail: jip@st-and.ac.uk

Preston, David Michael, LLB, NP. Solicitor, since 1976; b. 26.8.52, Glasgow; m., Sheila Elizabeth; 2 s. Educ. Hillhead High School; Dundee University. Part-time Depute Procurator Fiscal, 1976-79; Clerk to General Commissioners of Income Tax, since 1976; Registrar, Episcopal Diocese of Argyll and the Isles, since 1977; Partner, Hosack and Sutherland, since 1978; Member, Council, Law Society of Scotland, since 1990 (Convenor: Update Committee, 1992-96, Remuneration Committee, 1996-99, Services Committee, 1999-2000, Professional Practice, 2000-01; Vice President, 2001-02). Past Chairman and first Hon. President, Oban Round Table; Chairman, Oban Youth and Community Association, since 1980; Commodore, Oban Sailing Club, 1992-93; Secretary, Atlantis Leisure, 1991-2001. Recreations: sailing; skiing; rugby spectating; logistical supporter (travel and finance) of two sons. Address: (h.) Westbank, Duncraggan Road, Oban; T.-01631 563228.

Preston, Ian Mathieson Hamilton, CBE, BSc, PhD, FEng, MInstP, FIEE, Hon. FCIWEM. Chartered Engineer; b. 18.7.32, Bournemouth; m., Sheila Hope Pringle; 2 s. Educ. Kilmarnock Academy; Glasgow University. University Assistant Lecturer, 1957-59; joined SSEB as Assistant Reactor Physicist, 1959; various appointments until Chief Engineer, Generation Design and Construction Division, 1972; Director General, Central Electricity Generating Board, Generation Development and Construction Division, 1977-83; Deputy Chairman, South of Scotland Electricity Board, 1983-90; Chief Executive, Scottish Power, 1990-95. Non-Executive Director: Deutsche (Scotland), Hub Power Co. (Pakistan), 1995-99, Kot Addu Power Co. (Pakistan), 1996-99, Mining Scotland Ltd., 1995-98, East of Scotland Water Authority, 1995-98; Chairman, Motherwell Bridge Holdings, 1995-2001; President, Scottish Council Development and Industry, 1997-2000. Address: 10 Cameron Crescent, Carmunnock, Glasgow G76 9DX.

Price, Professor Allan, PhD, MB, BCh, FRCP(Edin), FRCR. Professor of Radiation Oncology, Edinburgh University, since 1996; b. 3.6.58, Cardiff; m., Lesley; 2 s. Educ. Yeovil School; Welsh National School of Medicine. General medical training, Swansea, Middlesborough; oncology training, Edinburgh, Hammersmith and Royal Marsden Hospitals; ICRF Clinical Research Fellow, 1988-92; Consultant Clinical Oncologist, Addenbrooke's and Papworth Hospitals, Cambridge, 1995-96. Scientific Adviser, Melville Trust; Consultant, Lilly Oncology; Member, Tenovus National Scientific Advisory Committee. Recreations: squash; skiing. Address: (b.) Department of Clinical Oncology, Western General Hospital, Edinburgh EH4 2XU; T.-0131-537 2205.

Price, Barclay. Director, Arts and Business Scotland, since 2000; b. 26.7.45, Glasgow; m., Fiona Dick. Educ. Hillhead High School. Head of Development, Crafts Council; Administrator, Hoxton Hall Community Theatre; Visual Arts Subsidy Officer, Arts Council of GB; Officer, Clydesdale Bank; Depute Director (Planning and Development), Scottish Arts Council. Address: (b.) 13 Abercromby Place, Edinburgh EH3 6LB; T.-0131-558 1277; e-mail: barclay.price@AandB.org.uk

Price, Professor Nicholas Charles, MA, DPhil (Oxon). Professor of Protein Science, Glasgow University, since 2000; b. 12.8.46, Stafford; m., Margaret Hazel Price; 1s.; 2d. Educ. King Edward VI Grammar School, Stafford; Merton College, Oxford; St John's College, Oxford. Stirling University: Lecturer, 1974-77; Senior Lecturer, 1977 -88; Reader, 1988-94; Professor of Biochemistry, 1994-2000. Publications: 3 books; 200 papers. Recreations: running; fundraising. Address: (b.) Joseph Black Building, Glasgow University, G12; T.-0141-330 2889.

Prickett, Professor (Alexander Thomas) Stephen, MA, PhD, DipEd, FAHA. Regius Professor of English Language and Literature, Glasgow University, 1990-2001, now Emeritus Professor; b. 4.6.39, Freetown, Sierra Leone; m., Patricia Roswell; 2 d. Educ. Kent College, Canterbury; Trinity Hall, Cambridge; University College, Oxford. English Teacher, Methodist College, Uzauakoli, E. Nigeria, 1962-64; Lecturer/Reader, Sussex University, 1967-82; Professor of English, Australian National University, Canberra, 1983-89. Publications: Do It Yourself Doom, 1962; Coleridge and Wordsworth: the Poetry of Growth, 1970; Romanticism and Religion, 1976; Victorian Fantasy, 1979; Words and the Word: language poetics and Biblical interpretation, 1986; England and the French Revolution, 1988; Reading the Text: Biblical criticism and literary theory, 1991; Origins of Narrative: The Romantic Appropriation of the Bible, 1996; World's Classics Bible (Editor), 1997; The Bible and Literature: A Reader, (Joint Editor), 1999; Narrative, Religion and Science: Fundamentalism versus Irony, 1700-1999, 2002. Recreations: walking; skiing; tennis; drama. Address: (b.) Department of English Literature, Glasgow University, Glasgow; T.-0141-339 4950.

Pride, Professor Stephen James, BSc, PhD, FRSE. Professor of Mathematics, Glasgow University, since 1992 (Reader in Mathematics, 1987-92); b. 8.1.49, Melbourne. Educ. Hampton High School, Melbourne; Monash University, Melbourne; Australian National University, Canberra. Research Fellow, Open University, 1974-78; Temporary Lecturer in Mathematics, King's College, London University, 1978-79; Lecturer in Mathematics, Glasgow University, 1979-87. Member, Editorial Board, London Mathematical Society, 1989-99; Member, Mathematics College, Engineering and Physical Sciences Research Council, 1997-99; Member, Commonwealth Scholarship Commission Panel of Advisers. Publications: more than 70 articles on algebra (mainly group theory and theoretical computer science). Recreations: cycling; travelling; cinema; music. Address: (h.) 54 Airlie Street, Glasgow G12 9SN; T.-0141-339 7395.

Priest, Professor Eric Ronald, BSc, MSc, PhD, FRSE. Gregory Professor of Mathematics, St. Andrews University, since 1997, formerly Professor of Theoretical Solar Physics; b. 7.11.43, Birmingham; m., Clare Wilson; 3 s.; 1 d. Educ. King Edward VI School, Birmingham; Nottingham University; Leeds University. St. Andrews University: Lecturer in Applied Mathematics, 1968, Reader, 1977; SERC Senior Fellow, 1992-97. Elected Member, Norwegian Academy of Sciences and Letters, 1994; Chair, PPARC Astronomy Committee, 1998-2001; Chair, RSE Mathematics Committee, 1996-1998; Member, HEFC Research Assessment Exercise Committee, 1992, 1996. Recreations: bridge; walking; swimming; swingnastics; children. Address: (b.) Mathematics and Statistics Department, St. Andrews University, St. Andrews KY16 9SS; T.-01334 463709.

Pritchard, Kenneth William, OBE, BL, WS. Secretary, Law Society of Scotland, 1976-97; Temporary Sheriff, 1995-99, Part-time Sheriff, since 2000; b. 14.11.33, London; Honorary Sheriff, Dundee; m., Gretta Murray; 2 s.; 1 d. Educ. Dundee High School; Fettes College; St. Andrews University. National Service, Argyll and Sutherland Highlanders, 1955-57; 2nd Lt., 1956; TA, 1957-62 (Captain); joined J. & J. Scrimgeour, Solicitors, Dundee, 1957; Senior Partner, 1970-76; Member: Sheriff Court Rules Council, 1973-76, Lord Dunpark's Committee considering Reparation upon Criminal Conviction, 1973-77; Hon. Visiting Professor, Law School, Strathclyde University; Hon. Member, Law Institute of Victoria, 1985; Hon. Member, Law Society of New Zealand, 1987; Hon. Member, Faculty of Procurators and Solicitors in Dundee; Member, University Court of Dundee, 1989-93; President,

Dundee High School Old Boys Club, 1975-76. Recreation: golf. Address: (h.) 22/4 Kinellan Road, Edinburgh EH12 6ES; T.-0131-337 4294.

Proctor, Alan. Editor, Evening Telegraph, Dundee, since 1995; b. 4.9.40, Forfar; m., Sheila Morrison Kerr; 2 d. Educ. Brechin High School. D.C. Thomson, since 1959. Recreations: walking; reading. Address: (b.) D.C. Thomson & Co. Ltd., 80 Kingsway East, Dundee DD4 8SL; T.-01382 223131.

Prosser, Rt. Hon. Lord (William David Prosser), QC, MA (Oxon), LLB, HonFRIAS, PC. Senator of the College of Justice in Scotland and Lord of Session, 1986-2001; b. 23.11.34, Edinburgh; m., Vanessa Lindsay Prosser (qv); 2 s.; 2 d. Educ. Edinburgh Academy; Corpus Christi College, Oxford; Edinburgh University. Advocate, 1962; Queen's Counsel, 1974; Vice-Dean, Faculty of Advocates, 1979-83, Dean of Faculty, 1983-86. Chairman, Royal Lyceum Theatre Company, 1987-92; Chairman, Scottish Historic Buildings Trust, 1988-98; Chairman, Royal Fine Art Commission for Scotland, 1990-95; Chairman, Scottish Architectural Education Trust; Chairman, Chamber Group of Scotland, 1993-98; Member, Franco-British Council. Address: 7 Randolph Crescent, Edinburgh EH3 7TH; T.-0131-225 2709.

Prosser, Professor James Anthony William (Tony), LLB. John Millar Professor of Law, Glasgow University, since 1992; b. 3.5.54, Ludlow. Educ. Ludlow Grammar School; Liverpool University. Research Assistant in Law, Southampton University, 1974-76; Lecturer in Law, Hull University, 1976-79; Lecturer, Senior Lecturer, Sheffield University, 1980-92; Jean Monnet Fellow, European University Institute, Florence, 1987-88. Publications: Test Cases for the Poor; Nationalised Industries and Public Control; Law and the Regulators; Privatizing Public Enterprises (Co-author); Waiving the Rules (Co-editor); Regulating the Changing Media (Co-editor). Recreations: walking; cinema; jazz. Address: (b.) School of Law, Glasgow University, Glasgow G12 8QQ; T.-0141-330 4180; e-mail: T.Prosser@law.gla.ac.uk

Prosser, (Leslie) Charles, DFA, DAEd. Secretary, Royal Fine Art Commission for Scotland, since 1976; b. 27.10.39, Harrogate; m., Coral; 1 s.; 2 d. Educ. Bath Academy of Art at Corsham Court; Slade School of Fine Art, London University. Assistant Lecturer in Fine Art, Blackpool School of Art, 1962-64; Fine Art research, Royal Academy, Stockholm, 1964-65; Lecturer in Fine Art, Leeds/Jacob Kramer College of Art, 1965-76; research in Art Education, Leeds University, 1974-75. Leverhulme European Arts Research Award, 1964; FRSA, 1997; Hon. FRIAS, 1997. Recreations: Scottish dancing and hill-walking. Address: (h.) 28 Mayfield Terrace, Edinburgh EH9 1RZ; T.-0131-668 1141.

Prosser, Vanessa Lindsay, SRCN, SCM, AMSPAR. Chairman of Council, Queen's Nursing Institute, Scotland, since 1994; b. 7.11.39, Dairsie, Fife; m., William David Prosser (qv); 2 s.; 2 d. Educ. St Leonards School, St Andrews. Medical Receptionist/Secretary, 1980; Lothian Health Council, 1984-88; Lothian Research Ethics Committee, since 1989; Scotland's Gardens Scheme, since 1996. Recreations: France. Address: (h.) 7 Randolph Crescent, Edinburgh, EH3 7TH; T.-0131-225 2709.

Proud, Professor Christopher Gregory, BSc, PhD. Chair of Biochemical Physiology, University of Dundee, since 1998 (Head, Division of Molecular Physiology); b. 29.4.53, Colchester; m., Xuemin Wang; 1 s.; 1 d. Educ. Colchester Royal Grammar School. Junior Lecturer, University of Göttingen, Germany, 1979-80; Research Fellow, University of Sussex, 1980-81; Lecturer in Biochemistry, University of Kent, Canterbury, 1982-85; Lecturer, then Reader in

Biochemistry, University of Bristol, 1985-95; Chair, University of Kent, Canterbury, 1995-97. Editor: European Journal of Biochemistry, Journal of Biological Chemistry. Address: School of Life Sciences, University of Dundee, Dundee DD1 5EH; T.-01382 344919.

Proudfoot, Edwina Valmai Windram, MA, DipEd, FSA, FSA Scot, MIFA. Archaeologist; Director, St. Andrews Heritage Services, since 1988; Honorary Research Fellow, St. Andrews University, 1985-97; b. 9.3.35, Dover; m., Professor V. Bruce Proudfoot (qv); 2 s. Educ. Invergordon Academy; Inverness Royal Academy; Edinburgh University. Lecturer (including Adult Education) in Archaeology, since 1959; director of excavations, numerous projects; Editor, Discovery and Excavation in Scotland, 1977-90; President, Council for Scottish Archaeology, 1983-89; Founder, first Chairman, Tayside and Fife Archaeological Committee, 1975-82; Member, Ancient Monuments Board for Scotland, 1986-97; Chairman, St. Andrews Preservation Trust, 1988-93; Council Member, National Trust for Scotland, 1984-89, 1993-97, and since 1999; Chairman, NTS Central, Fife and Tayside Regional Commitee, 1998-2000; Member, Executive Committee, NTS, since 1994; Chairman, E. Fife Members Centre, NTS, since 2000; Chairman, Scottish Churches Heritage Research, since 2000. Recreations: gardening; music; walking. Address: 12 Wardlaw Gardens, St. Andrews, KY16 9DW; T.-01334 473293.

Proudfoot, Professor V. Bruce, OBE, BA, PhD, FSA, FRSE, FRSGS, FSA Scot. Vice-President, Royal Scottish Geographical Society, since 1993; Emeritus Professor of Geography, St. Andrews University; b. 24.9.30, Belfast; m., Edwina Valmai Windram Field; 2 s. Educ. Royal Belfast Academical Institution; Queen's University, Belfast. Research Officer, Nuffield Quaternary Research Unit, Queen's University, Belfast, 1954-58; Lecturer in Geography: Queen's University, Belfast, 1958-59, Durham University, 1959-67; Hatfield College, Durham: Tutor, 1960-63, Librarian, 1963-65; Visiting Fellow, University of Auckland and Commonwealth Visiting Fellow, Australia, 1966; Alberta University, Edmonton: Associate Professor, 1967-70, Professor, 1970-74; Co-ordinator, Socio-Economic Opportunity Studies and Staff Consultant, Alberta Human Resources Research Council, 1971-72; Professor of Geography, St. Andrews University, 1974-93. Royal Society of Edinburgh: Convener, Earth Sciences Committee, 1983-85, Vice-President, 1985-88, Convener, Grants Committee, 1988-91, General Secretary, 1991-96; Bicentenary Medal, 1997; Chairman, Society for Landscape Studies, 1979-83; Vice-President, Society of Antiquaries of Scotland, 1982-85; President, Section H, BAAS, 1985; Chairman, Rural Geography Study Group, Institute of British Geographers, 1980-84; Chairman of Council, 1993-99, Chairman of Dundee Centre, 1993-99, Royal Scottish Geographical Society; Hon. President, Scottish Association of Geography Teachers, 1982-84; Trustee, National Museum of Antiquities of Scotland, 1982-85. Recreation: gardening. Address: (h.) Westgate, Wardlaw Gardens, St. Andrews KY16 9DW; T.-01334 473293.

Provan, James Lyal Clark. Member, South East Region, European Parliament, since 1999, Member, South Downs West, 1994-99; Vice President, European Parliament, since 1999; Chairman, EP Tourism Group; Chairman, EP Conciliation Committee with Council of Ministers; Chairman, Rowett Research Institute, Aberdeen, 1991-99 (Board Member, since 1990); Non-Executive Director, CNH Global N.V. and New Holland (Holdings), N.V.; Farmer; b. 19.12.36, Glenfarg, Perthshire; m., Roweena Adele Lewis; 2 s.; 1 d. Educ. Ardvreck School, Crieff; Oundle School, Northants; Royal Agricultural College, Cirencester. National Farmers Union of Scotland: Area President, Kinross, 1965, Fife and Kinross, 1971; Tayside Regional Councillor, 1978-81; Member, Tay River Purification Board, 1978-81; Member (Conservative), European Parliament, NE Scotland, 1979-89; European Democratic (Conservative) Spokesman on Agriculture and Fisheries, 1981-87; Questor of European Parliament, 1987-89; former Executive Director, Scottish Financial Enterprise; Chairman, McIntosh of Dyce Ltd., McIntosh Donald Ltd., 1989-94; Member, Agriculture and Food Research Council, 1990-94. Recreations: country pursuits; sailing; flying; politics; agriculture. Address: Summerfield, Glenfarg, Perthshire PH2 9QD; Middle Lodge, Barns Green, Horsham, West Sussex RH13 7NL.

Pugh, Professor John Richard, BSc, PhD, CPhys, CEng, FInstMC, MInstP. Professor, School of Engineering, Science and Design, Glasgow Caledonian University, since 2001; Member, Board of Directors, Centre for Industrial Bulk Solids Handling, since 1993; b. 16.4.52, Shrewsbury; m., Christine Haldane; 3 s. Educ. Cumbernauld High School; Whitley Bay Grammar School; Glasgow University. Research Fellow, Glasgow University, 1976-80; Physicist, Barr and Stroud Ltd., Glasgow, 1980-91; Lecturer, then Senior Lecturer, Glasgow College, 1981-90; Professor of Physics and Depute Head, Glasgow Polytechnic, 1990-92; Head of Department, 1992-2001. Tuba player, Kirkintilloch Kelvin Brass. Recreations: music; house restoration; gardening. Address: (b.) School of Engineering, Science and Design, Glasgow Caledonian University, Cowcaddens Road, Glasgow G4 0BA; T.-0141-331 3670.

Pugh, Kenneth Bryan, BSc (Hons), MAgrSc, PhD, CChem, FRSC, FCIWEM. Chemicals Management Policy Advisor, Scottish Environment Protection Agency, since 2001; b. 13.9.43, Birmingham; m., Susan; 2 s. Educ. Waverley Grammar School, Birmingham; University of Leeds; University of Reading. Scientific Officer, University College of North Wales, 1970-76; North East River Purification Board, Aberdeen: Chief Chemist, 1976-92, Assistant General Manager, 1992-96; Regional Scientist, Scottish Environment Protection Agency (North), 1996-2001. Publications: more than 40 scientific papers. Address: (b.) Greyhope House, Greyhope Road, Torry, Aberdeen AB11 9RD.

Punter, Professor David Godfrey, BA, MA, PhD, DLitt, FRSA, FSA (Scot), FEA, FFCS. Professor of English Studies, Stirling University, since 1988; b. 19.11.49, London; m., Caroline Mary Case-Punter; 1 s.; 2 d. Educ. John Lyon School, Harrow; Fitzwilliam College, Cambridge. Lecturer, University of East Anglia, 1973-84; Professor, Fudan University, Shanghai, 1983; Senior Lecturer, University of East Anglia, 1984-86; Director, Development of University English Teaching Project, 1985-86; Professor, Chinese University of Hong Kong, 1986-88. Publications: many books of literary criticism, including The Literature of Terror, The Hidden Script, and Gothic Pathologies; articles and essays on romantic and contemporary literature; four books of poetry, China and Glass, Love in the Supermarket, Asleep at the Wheel, Selected Short Stories. Recreations: child-minding; dog-minding; walking; squash. Address: (b.) Stirling University, Stirling, FK9 4LA; T.-01786 467495.

Purcell, Steven John, JP. Convener Development and Regeneration Services Committee, Glasgow City Council, since 1999; b. 19.9.72, Glasgow; m., Katrina Laidlaw Murray. Educ. St Thomas Aquinas Secondary School. Elected to Glasgow City Council, 1995; Convener, Property Services, 1998; Chair, Glasgow Townscape Heritage Initiative; Member: Greater Glasgow and Clyde Valley Tourist Board, BAFTA Scotland, Scottish Enterprise Glasgow Board. Recreations: history; music; football. Address; (b.) City Chambers, Glasgow, G2 1OU; e-mail: steven.purcell@councillors.glasgow.gov.uk

Purser, John Whitley, MA, PhD. Composer and Lecturer; Poet, Playwright, Musicologist, and Broadcaster; b. 10.2.42, Glasgow; 1 s.; 1 d. Educ. Fettes College; Glasgow University; Royal Scottish Academy of Music and Drama. Manager, Scottish Music Information Centre, 1985-87; compositions include two operas, numerous orchestral and chamber works; three books of poetry, The Counting Stick, A Share of the Wind and Amoretti; six radio plays and two radio series, A Change of Tune and Scotland's Music; music history: Is the Red Light On?, Scotland's Music; literary criticism: The Literary Works of Jack B. Yeats; awards: McVitie Scottish Writer of the Year, 1992; Glenfiddich Living Scotland Award, 1991; Giles Cooper Award, 1992; New York International Radio Festival Gold Medal, 1992; Sony Gold Medal, 1993; Oliver Brown Award, 1993; Scottish Heritage Award, 1993; Hon. Life Member, Saltire Society, 1993. Recreations: numerous. Address: (b.) 3 Drinan, Elgol, Isle of Skye IV49 9BG; T.- 01471 866262.

Purton, Patricia. Director, Royal College of Midwives, UK Board for Scotland, since 1992; b. Bristol; 2 s. Former Senior Midwife, Glasgow; former Head of Midwifery Services, Raigmore Hospital. Member of numerous professional committees and statutory bodies. Address: (b.) 37 Frederick Street, Edinburgh EH2 1EP; T.-0131-225 1633; e-mail: Patricia.Purton@ rcmscotb.org.uk

Purves, David, BSc, PhD. Editor, Lallans Magazine, 1987-95; Playwright; b. 9.4.24, Selkirk; m., Lilian Rosemary; 3 s. Educ. Galashiels Academy; Edinburgh University. Head, Trace Element Department, Edinburgh School of Agriculture, 1956-82; Supervisor, Central Analytical Department, 1982-87; author of Trace Element Contamination of the Environment, 1985; poetry collections: Thrawart Threipins, 1976, Herts Bluid, 1995; many poems in Scots published; Fringe First play, The Puddok an the Princess and rendering in Scots of Macbeth published, 1992; ten professional productions of plays in Scots; Joint Editor, Mak It New, anthology of 21 years of writing in Lallans, 1995; author of A Scots Grammar, 1997; Past Preses, Scots Language Society. Address: (h.) 8 Strathalmond Road, Edinburgh EH4 8AD; T.-0131-339 7929; e-mail: david.purves@tinyworld.co.uk

Purves, Rev. John Peter Sandison, BSc, BD. Parish Minister, Dollar, Glendevon, Muckhart, since 1990; Chaplain, Dollar Academy, since 1990; Moderator, Stirling Presbytery, 2000-01; b. 6.8.48, Edinburgh; m., Patricia Kennedy; 1 s.; 1 d. Educ. Bathgate Academy; Edinburgh University; Aberdeen University. VSO Teacher, Malawi, 1970-72; Adventure Playground Leader, Gorbals, Glasgow, 1972-74; Assistant Minister, Stonelaw Church, Rutherglen, 1977-78; Assistant Chaplain, Aberdeen University, 1978-82; Missionary, Mount Olivet, Jamaica, 1983-89. Kentucky Colonel, 1997. Recreation: cycling. Address: (h.) 2 Manse Road, Dollar FK14 7AJ; T.-01259 743432.

Purves-Hume, Ian Campbell. Director, Royal Scottish Agricultural Benevolent Institution, since 1990; b. 22.7.38, London; m., Jill Cairns Fairbairn; 2 d. Educ. Ottershaw; Royal Military Academy, Sandhurst. Army Officer, Argyll and Sutherland Highlanders, 1958-90, to rank of Brigadier. Recreations: walking; bird-watching. Address: (b.) RSABI, Ingliston, Edinburgh EH28 8NB; T.-0131-333 1023.

Purvis, John Robert, CBE, MA (Hons). Member for Scotland, European Parliament, since 1999 (Member: Industry, External Trade, Research and Energy Committee, Economic and Monetary Affairs Committee); International Business Consultant (Managing Partner, Purvis & Co.), since 1973; Director: LFGG Mason Investors European Utilities Trust PLC, since 1994; Chairman, Kingdom FM Radio Ltd., since 1997; Chairman, Belgrave Capital Management Ltd., since 1999; b. 6.7.38, St. Andrews; m.,

Louise Spears Durham; 1 s.; 2 d. Educ. Glenalmond; St. Andrews University. 2nd Lt., Scots Guards, 1956-58; First National City Bank (Citibank NA), London, New York City, Milan, 1962-69; Treasurer, Noble Grossart Ltd., Edinburgh, 1969-73; Director and Secretary, Brigton Farms Ltd., 1969-86; Managing Director, Founder, Owner, Gilmerton Management Services Ltd., 1973-92; Director: James River UK Holdings Ltd., 1984-95, Jamont NV, 1994-95; Member, European Parliament, Mid Scotland and Fife, 1979-84 (Deputy Chief Whip, Group Spokesman on Monetary Affairs, Energy, Research and Technology) Vice Chairman, European Parliament Delegation to the Gulf States; Chairman, IBA Scottish Advisory Committee, 1985-89; Member for Scotland, IBA, 1985-89; Member of Council, St. Leonards School, St. Andrews, 1981-89; Chairman, Economic Affairs Committee, Scottish Conservative and Unionist Association, 1986-97, Vice-President of Association, 1987-89; Member, Scottish Advisory Committee on Telecommunications, 1990-97; Director: Curtis Fine Papers Ltd., 1995-2001, Crown Vantage Ltd., 1995-2001. Recreations: Italy and Scotland. Address: Gilmerton House, Dunino, St. Andrews KY16 8NB; T.-01334 475830.

Pusey, Professor Peter Nicholas, MA, PhD, FRS, FRSE. Professor of Physics, Edinburgh University, since 1991; b. 30.12.42, Oxford; m., Elizabeth Nind; 2 d. Educ. St Edward's School, Oxford; Cambridge University; University of Pittsburgh, USA. Post-doctoral Fellow, IBM, New York, 1969-72; Royal Signals and Radar Establishment (now DERA), Malvern, 1972-91 (Grade 6 from 1980); Head, Department of Physics and Astronomy, Edinburgh University, 1994-97 and since 2000. Publications: numerous in scientific literature. Address: (b.) Department of Physics and Astronomy, Edinburgh University, Mayfield Road, Edinburgh, EH9 3JZ, T.-0131-650 5255; e-mail: pusey@ed.ac.uk

Pyle, Sheriff Derek Colin Wilson, LLB (Hons), NP, WS. Sheriff of Tayside Central and Fife, since 2000; b. 15.10.52, Cambridge; m., Jean Blackwood Baillie; 5 s.; 1 d. Educ. Royal High School, Edinburgh; Edinburgh University. Solicitor, since 1976; Partner, Wilson Pyle & Co., WS, 1980-89; Partner, Henderson Boyd Jackson, WS, 1989-99; Solicitor Advocate, from 1997. Formerly Fiscal to Law Society of Scotland; former Council Member, WS Society. Recreations: golf; hill-walking; painting house. Address: (b.) Sheriff's Chambers, Tay Street, Perth; T.-01738 620546.

Pyper, Mark Christopher Spring-Rice, BA. Principal, Gordonstoun Schools, since 1999 (Headmaster, Gordonstoun School, 1990-99); b. 13.8.47, Seaford; m., Jennifer L.; 1 s.; 2 d. Educ. Winchester College; Oxford University; London University. Assistant Master, Stoke Brunswick School, East Grinstead, 1966-68; Assistant Master, then Joint Headmaster, St. Wilfrid's School, Seaford, 1969-79; Registrar, Housemaster, then Deputy Headmaster, Sevenoaks School, 1979-90; Director, Sevenoaks Summer Festival, 1979-90. Address: (h.) Headmaster's House, Gordonstoun School, Elgin IV30 5RF; T.-01343 837807.

Q

Queensberry, 12th Marquess of (David Harrington Angus Douglas); b. 19.12.29. Educ. Eton. Professor of Ceramics, Royal College of Art, 1959-83; succeeded to title, 1954.

Quigley, Elizabeth, MA (Hons). Correspondent, BBC Scotland, since 1999; b. 30.10.71, Glasgow. Educ. Lenzie Academy; St Andrews University. Reporter, The Scotsman, 1995-96; Reporter, Scotland on Sunday, 1996-97; Scottish Daily Mail, from 1997: Political Reporter/Acting Features Editor/Feature Writer. Address: (b.) BBC Scotland, Queen Street, Edinburgh EH2 1JE; T.-0131-248 4215.

Quinan, Lloyd John. MSP (SNP), West of Scotland, since 1999; b. 29.4.57, Edinburgh. Educ. Queen Margaret College, Edinburgh. Actor, 1978-92; Theatre Director: Scottish Theatre Company, Traverse Theatre, Royal Lyceum, Perth Theatre, 1992-99; Television Presenter/Producer/Director: Scottish Television, ITV Network Centre, Channel 4 News, Caledonia Sterne and Wylde. Trustee, Erin Community Trust. Recreations: travel; literature; Hibernian Football Club. Address: (b.) Scottish Parliament, Edinburgh EH99 1SP; T.-0131-348 5734.

Quinault, Francis Charles, BSc, PhD. Director of Learning and Teaching Support, St. Andrews University (formerly Hebdomadar, Assistant Principal for External Affairs and Senior Lecturer in Psychology); b. 8.5.43, London; m., Wendy Ann Horton; 1 s.; 2 d. Educ. Dulwich College; St. Catharine's College, Cambridge; Bristol University. Ford Foundation Scholar, Oslo University, 1969-70. Member, National Committee for the Training of University Teachers, 1981-87. Recreations: acting; singing; hill-walking. Address: (b.) University of St. Andrews, 71 North Street, St. Andrews KY16 9AJ; T.-01334 462141; e-mail: fcq@st-and.ac.uk

Quirk, Lesley Helen, OLJ, MIMgt. Managing Partner, Quirk & Co., business and management consultancy, since 1985; b. Tarbert, Harris; m., Norman Linton Quirk (qv); 4 s. Educ. St George's School for Girls, Edinburgh. Appointed first Woman's Business Adviser in Scotland, 1988; appointed Independent Assessor for Public Appointments, 2001; Scottish Chair, Women's Network UK; Chair, Scottish Expert Advisory Group on Women's Business Issues; awarded Hon. Lady Taverner, 1985; UK Woman of Achievement, 1999; Scottish Businesswoman of the Year, 2001; Officer, Order of St Lazarus of Jerusalem, 1999. Recreations: family; DIY; gardening. Address: (h.) Glencleland House, Aberfoyle FK8 3TJ; T.-01877 387210; e-mail: lesley@quirk.co.uk

Quirk, Norman Linton, CA, MIMgt, FRSA, OLJ. Executive Director, Scottish Ballet, since 2000, Vice Chairman and Managing Director, 1998-2000; Partner, Quirk & Co., business and management consultancy, since 1991; b. 28.7.47, Glasgow; m., Lesley Helen Quirk (qv); 2 s.; 2 step-s. Educ. Dulwich College. Apprentice CA, 1965-71; Accountant/Office Manager, Thom Decorators, Coatbridge, 1971-74; Chief Accountant, Radio Clyde, Glasgow, 1974-84; Assistant Director, Institute of CAs of Scotland, 1985-87; Regional Controller, Joint Monitoring Unit, 1988-91; Managing Director, Scot FM, 1996. Chairman, Independent Radio Group of Scotland, 1996-2000; Member, Incorporation of Hammermen; Director, Scottish Society for Autism; Director, Stray Theatre Company; Lord's Taverner; Officer, Order of St Lazarus of Jerusalem. Recreations: scuba diving; working with arts organisations. Address: (h.) Glencleland House, Aberfoyle FK8 3JJ; T.-01877 387210; e-mail: norman@quirk.co.uk

Qureshi, Robina Zia. Director, Positive Action on Housing Ltd., since 1995; Actor, since 2001; b. Glasgow; 1 s. Educ. Bellahouston Academy; Bearsden Academy; Glasgow School of Art. Advice Worker, Glasgow West Advisory Service, 1986-87; Welfare Adviser, Woodlands Advice Centre, 1987-90; Project Leader, Race and Housing Project, 1990-92; Race and Housing Officer, Housing Equality Action Unit, 1992-95; Editor, Race and Housing News, 1993-96. Member: Racial Equality Advisory Forum, since 1999, Stephen Lawrence Steering Group, since 1999, Joseph Rowntree Racial Harassment in the UK Research Project, 1999-2000. Ujima Pookar Award for outstanding contribution to black community, 1996. Recreations: music; film; family; work; horse riding; minding her own business. T.-0777 332 1727; e-mail: robinaqureshi@hotmail.com

R

Racey, Professor Paul Adrian, MA, PhD, DSc, FIBiol, FRSE. Regius Professor of Natural History, Aberdeen University, since 1993 (Professor of Zoology, 1985-93); b. 7.5.44, Wisbech, Cambridgeshire; m., Anna Priscilla Notcutt; 3 s. Educ. Ratcliffe College, Leicester; Downing College, Cambridge. Rothamsted Experimental Station, Harpenden, 1965-66; Zoological Society of London, 1966-70; Unit of Reproductive Biology, Liverpool University, 1970-73; joined Department of Zoology, Aberdeen University, 1973. Recreations: riding; sailing; skiing. Address: (b.) Department of Zoology, Aberdeen University, Aberdeen AB24 2TZ; T.-01224 272858; e-mail: p.racey@abdn.ac.uk

Radcliffe, Nora. MSP (Liberal Democrat), Gordon, since 1999; b. 4.3.46, Aberdeen; m., Dr M.A. Radcliffe; 1 s.; 1 d. Educ. High School for Girls, Aberdeen; Aberdeen University. Hotel and catering industry manager, 1967-73; full-time wife and mother, 1973-88; Councillor, Gordon District Council, 1988-92; employed by Grampian Health Board, 1992-98. JP. Address: Scottish Parliament, Edinburgh EH99 1SP; T.-0131-348 5804.

Rae, Barbara Davis, CBE. Painter and Printmaker; b. 10.12.43, Falkirk; 1 s. Educ. Morrisons Academy, Crieff; Edinburgh College of Art. Travelling scholarship, France and Spain, 1966; elected RSW, 1975; President, SSA, 1983; Scottish Arts Council grant, 1985; Hunting Group prize-winner, 1991; elected RSA, 1992; elected RA, 1996; study painting, South Africa, 1996; study visit, Arizona desert, 1998; doctorate, Napier University, 1999; various solo exhibitions in London, Edinburgh and internationally; work in many public collections; Member, Royal Fine Art Commission for Scotland; Member, Board of Trustees, British School at Rome. Recreation: travel. Address: (b.) c/o Art First, 9 Cork Street, London W15 3LL; T.-020 7734 0386.

Rae, David, DipTP, MRTPI. Head of Planning, Fife Council, since 1996; b. 10.9.45; m., Ella; 2 s.; 1 d. Educ. Buckhaven High School; Edinburgh College of Art. Various planning posts, Fife, Perth, Dunbarton, 1962-75; Depute Director of Planning/Director of Planning, Kirkcaldy District Council, 1975-90; Divisional Manager, Property and Development Services, Kirkcaldy District Council, 1990-96. Past Chair, Scottish Society of Directors of Planning. Recreations: music; dogs; following East Fife F.C. Address: (b.) Fife Council, Fife House, North Street, Glenrothes KY7 5LT; T.-01592 416200; e-mail: david.rae@fife.gov.uk

Rae, Hugh Crauford. Novelist; b. 22.11.35, Glasgow; m., Elizabeth Dunn; 1 d. Educ. Knightswood School. Prolific popular novelist; author of more than 50 tiles, under a variety of pseudonyms, including Stuart Stern, James Albany and Jessica Stirling; books include (as Hugh C. Rae) Skinner, The Marksman, The Shooting Gallery, Harkfast and Privileged Strangers and (as Jessica Stirling) The Spoiled Earth, The Hiring Fair, The Dark Pasture, Treasures on Earth, Creature Comforts, Hearts of Gold, The Good Provider, The Asking Price, The Wise Child, The Welcome Light, Lantern for the Dark, The Penny Wedding, The Workhouse Girl. Recreation: golf. Address: (h.) Drumore Farm Cottage, Balfron Station, Glasgow G63 0NJ.

Rae, Sheriff Rita Emilia Anna, QC, LLB (Hons). Sheriff of Glasgow and Strathkelvin, since 1997. Educ. St. Patrick's High School, Coatbridge; Edinburgh University. Apprentice, Biggart, Lumsden & Co., Glasgow, 1972-74; Assistant Solicitor: Balfour & Manson, Edinburgh, 1974,

Biggart, Baillie & Gifford, Glasgow, 1974-76; Solicitor and Partner, Ross Harper & Murphy, Glasgow, 1976-81; Former Tutor, Advocacy and Pleading, Strathclyde University; Advocate, 1982; Queen's Counsel, 1992. Member, Sacro; Life Member, Scottish Association for the Study of Delinquency. Recreations: theatre; driving; walking; opera; music; Italy; gardening.

Rae, Scott Alexander, LLB (Hons), WS, NP, TEP. Partner, Morton Fraser WS, Edinburgh, since 1970; b. 17.12.44, Edinburgh; m., Annabel Riach; 3 s. Educ. Daniel Stewarts College, Edinburgh; Edinburgh University. Sometime Tutor and Course Leader, Edinburgh University; Law Society of Scotland Examiner in Taxation and Chairman, Board of Examiners. Member, VAT Tribunal (Scotland); Clerk, Incorporated Trades of Edinburgh; Secretary, International Academy of Estate and Trust Law; past Collector, Society of Writers to the Signet; Law Society of Scotland: Convener, Trust Law Committee, past Convener, Tax Law Committee; Director: Scottish National Dictionary Association, Harmeny Education Trust Ltd.; Trustee, John Watson's Trust. Recreations: farming; travel. Address: (b.) 30-31 Queen Street, Edinburgh EH2 1JX; T.-0131-247 1000.

Rae, Shelagh, BSc. Director of Education and Leisure, Renfrewshire Council, since 1995; b. Hamilton; m., Ian A. Rae. Educ. St. Joseph's Convent, Hartlepool; St. Andrew's High School, Kirkcaldy; Edinburgh University. Teacher of Mathematics, 1972-74; Assistant Principal Teacher, then Principal Teacher, 1974-85; Curriculum Officer, Lothian Regional Council, 1985-87; Adviser in Mathematics, then Assistant Director of Education, then Head of School Development Services, Central Regional Council, 1987-95. Recreations: reading; walking; swimming; golf. Address: (b.) Renfrewshire Council, Cotton Street, Paisley PA1 1LE; T.-0141-842 5601.

Raeburn, James B., FCIS. Director, Scottish Print Employers' Federation and Scottish Newspaper Publishers' Association, since 1984; Director, Scottish Daily Newspaper Society, since 1996; b. 18.3.47, Jedburgh; m., Rosemary Bisset; 2 d. Educ. Hawick High School. Edinburgh Corporation, 1964-69; Roxburgh County Council, 1969-71; Electrical Contractors' Association of Scotland, 1972-83 (Secretary, 1975-83). Director: Press Standards Board of Finance Ltd., since 1990, Advertising Standards Board of Finance Ltd., since 1988, National Council for the Training of Journalists, since 1993, Publishing National Training Organisation Ltd., since 2000. Recreation: golf. Address: (b.) 48 Palmerston Place, Edinburgh EH12 5DE; T.-0131-220 4353.

Raeburn, Emeritus Professor John Ross, CBE, FRSE, FIBiol, BSc, MA, PhD; b. 20.11.12, Kirkcaldy; m., Mary Roberts; 1 s.; 3 d. Educ. Manchester Grammar School; Edinburgh University; Cornell University. Professor, Agricultural Economics, Nanking University, 1936-37; Research Officer, Oxford University, 1938-39; Statistician, then Head of Agricultural Plans Branch, Ministry of Food, 1939-46; Senior Research Officer, Oxford University, 1946-49; Reader in Agricultural Economics, London University, 1949-59; Professor and Head, Department of Agriculture, Aberdeen University, 1959-78; Principal, North of Scotland College of Agriculture, 1963-78; Consultant to World Bank, 1979-88; Vice-President, International Association of Agricultural Economists, 1964-70; President, Agricultural Economics Society, 1964-65. Publications: Agriculture: Foundations, Principles and Development; The History of the International Association of Agricultural Economists (Co-author). Recreations: gardening; photography. Address: (h.) Kilravock House, Flat 15, 5 Oswald Road, Edinburgh EH9 2EA.

Raeburn, Sheriff Susan Adiel Ogilvie, LLB, QC. Sheriff of Glasgow and Strathkelvin, since 1993; b. 23.4.54, Ellon. Educ. St. Margaret's School for Girls, Aberdeen; Edinburgh University. Admitted, Faculty of Advocates, 1977; took silk, 1991; part-time Chairman, Social Security Appeal Tribunals, 1986-91; Temporary Sheriff, 1988-92; part-time Chairman, Medical Appeal Tribunals, 1992-93; Reporter to Scottish Legal Aid Board, 1990-93. Recreations: salmon fishing; the arts; travel. Address: (b.) Sheriff Court, P.O. Box 23, 1 Carlton Place, Glasgow G5 9DA; T.-0141-429 8888.

Raffan, Keith, MA (Hons). MSP (Liberal Democrat), Mid-Scotland and Fife, since 1999; b. 21.6.49. Educ. Robert Gordon's College, Aberdeen; Trinity College, Glenalmond; Corpus Christi, Cambridge University. Former TV presenter and journalist; Conservative MP, Delyn, North Wales, 1983-92; joined Liberal Democrats, 1992; introduced Controlled Drugs (Penalties) Act, 1985; National Chairman, Pressure for Economic and Social Toryism, 1970-74. Recreations: architecture; cinema; travel; hill-walking; eating; working-out. Address: (b.) Scottish Parliament, Edinburgh EH99 1SP; T.-0131-348 5800.

Raffe, Professor David James, BA, BPhil. Professor of Sociology of Education, University of Edinburgh, since 1992; b., 5.5.51, Felixstowe; m., Shirley; 1 s.; 1 d. Educ. The Leys School, Cambridge; New College and Nuffield College, Oxford University. Centre for Educational Sociology, University of Edinburgh: Research Fellow, 1975-79, Deputy Director, 1979-86, Lecturer in Education, 1979-85, Reader in Education, 1985-92. Publications: Reconstructions of Secondary Education, 1983; Fourteen to Eighteen, 1984; Education and the Youth Labour Market, 1988; British Baccalaureat, 1990; Part-time Higher Education, 1998. Address: (b.) St. John's Land, Holyrood Road, Edinburgh EH8 8AQ.

Rafferty, John, LLB (Hons), WS, MSI. Chairman, Burness, since 1997 (Partner, since 1977); b. 30.6.51, St Andrews. Educ. Edinburgh Academy; Edinburgh University. Burness: Apprentice Solicitor, 1973-75; Assistant Solicitor, 1975-77. Recreations: gardening; hill-walking; countryside. Address: (b.) 50 Lothian Road, Edinburgh EH3 9WJ; T.-0131-473 6000.

Rainey, John Bruce, BSc, MB, ChB, ChM, FRCSEdin. Consultant Surgeon, St. John's Hospital, Howden, Livingston, since 1988; Honorary Senior Lecturer in Surgery, Edinburgh University, since 1988; b. 18.5.52, Belfast; m., Dr. Linda Margaret King; 2 s.; 1 d. Educ. Royal Belfast Academical Institution; Edinburgh University. Trained in general surgery; Examiner in surgery and accident and emergency medicine for Royal College of Surgeons of Edinburgh. Aris and Gale Lecturer, Royal College of Surgeons of England, 1985. Recreations: family; sport; history and military history. Address: (h.) 23 Hatton Place, Edinburgh EH9 1UB, T.-0131-667 6216.

Rainy Brown, Edward, BSc (Forestry) (Hons). Chief Executive, NFU Scotland, since 1998; b. 6.10.49; m., Kathleen Falconer; 1 s.; 1 d. Educ. Merchiston Castle School, Edinburgh; Aberdeen University. Fontain Forestry Ltd, 1972-73; Development Officer, Scottish Agricultural Organisation Society Ltd, 1974-76; Sales Development Manager, North Eastern Farmers Ltd., 1976-82; Regional Manager, Agricultural Central Trading Ltd., 1982-84; Chief Executive, Scottish Agricultural Organisation Society Ltd, 1984-98; Chairman, Biggar High School Board, 1993-96; Member, Plunkett Foundation, 1984-98 (Vice-Chairman, 1995-98). Recreations: hill walking; cycling; rugby support; travel. Address: (h.) 8 Lodge Park, Biggar, Lanarkshire; T.-07836 329262; e-mail: ed.rainybrown@nfus.org.uk

Raistrick, Evlyn, MA. Chairman, Scottish Hockey Union, 1992-96; Tournament Director, Atlanta Olympics, 1996; Member, Rules Board, Competitions Committee, International Federation, since 1990; b. 13.8.42, Edinburgh; m., David William; 3 s. Educ. Boroughmuir School; Edinburgh University. Maths Teacher, Liberton High, 1964-72. Member, Scottish Sports Council, 1993-2001; Vice-Chairman, Executive, Scottish Sports Association, 1993-2001. Recreations: hockey; squash; golf. Address; (h.) Seton Mains House, Longniddry, East Lothian EH32 0PG.

Raj, Professor Mahendra, BSc (Eng), MBA, PhD. Director of Research, Aberdeen Business School, since 1996; Professor of International Finance, since 1996; Member, Accounts Commission for Scotland, since 2001; Editor, Studies in Economics and Finance, since 2000; Managing Editor, Journal of Business and Behavioral Sciences; b. Trivandrum, India; m., Nandini, Raj; 1d. Educ. University of Arizona; Baylor University; Kerala University. Mechanical Engineer, Fact Ltd., 1982-86; Lecturer, University of Arizona, 1989-92; Senior Lecturer, University of Waikato, New Zealand, 1993-96; Consultant, Commonwealth of Nations, 1998-99; Member of several editorial boards including: Business Journal, Journal of Global Business, Journal of Business and Behavioural Sciences, Finance India, Journal of Forensic Accounting, Journal of International Trade Law and Policy; Committee Member: American Society of Business and Behavioural Sciences; New England Business Administration Association; Association of Global Business; Academy of Linguistics, Behavioural and Social Sciences. Publications: numerous articles in over 30 publications. Recreations: magic; tennis; chess; social and cultural organisations. Address: (b.) Aberdeen Business School, Robert Gordon University, Viewfield Road, Aberdeen, AB15 7AW; T.-01224 263101.

Ralston, Professor Ian Beith McLaren, MA, PhD, FSA, FSA Scot, MIFA. Professor of Archaeology, University of Edinburgh, since 1998; Chair, CFA Archaeology Ltd., since 2000; President, Council for Scottish Archaeology, 1996-2000; b. 11.11.50, Edinburgh; m., Sandra Webb; 1 s.; 1 d. Educ. Edinburgh Academy; Edinburgh University. Aberdeen University: Research Fellow in Archaeology, 1974-77, Lecturer in Geography/ Archaeology, 1977-85; University of Edinburgh: Lecturer in Archaeology, 1985-90, Senior Lecturer in Archaeology, 1990-98. Honorary Chair, Institute of Field Archaeologists, 1991-92. Publications: Archaeological Resource Management in the United Kingdom – an introduction (Co-editor), 1993; Scotland – Environment and Archaeology 8000 BC-AD 1000 (Co-editor), 1997; The Archaeology of Britain – an Introduction from the Upper Palaeolithic to the Industrial Revolution, (Co-editor), 1999; exhibition catalogues; papers. Recreations: walking; watching St. Johnstone. Address: (b.) 12 Infirmary Street, Edinburgh EH1 1LT; T.-0131-650 2370; e-mail: ian.ralston@ed.ac.uk

Ramage, Alan W. Keeper of the Registers of Scotland, since 1994; b. 4.12.43, Edinburgh; m., Fiona Lesslie. Educ. Boroughmuir School, Edinburgh. Recreations: keeping fit; reading; working. Address: (b.) Meadowbank House, 153 London Road, Edinburgh EH8 7AU; T.-0131-659 6111.

Ramage, Professor Robert, BSc, PhD, DSc, CChem, FRSC, FRSA, FRSE, FRS. Forbes Professor of Chemistry, University of Edinburgh, 1984-2001 (Head, Department of Chemistry, 1987-90, 1997-2000); b. 4.10.35, Glasgow; m., Joan Fraser Paterson; 3 d. Educ. Whitehill Senior Secondary School; University of Glasgow. Lecturer, then Senior Lecturer, University of Liverpool, 1964-77; Professor of Organic Chemistry, then Head of Department, UMIST, 1977-84. Chairman, SERC Organic Chemistry; Member, Panel, SERC Science Board; President, Perkin Division, Royal Society of Chemistry, 1991-93; Member,

RAE Chemistry Committee, 1996; Member, Committees: Royal Society of Edinburgh, Royal Society of London; Director, Edinburgh Centre for Protein Technology, 1996-2000; Director and CSO, Albachem Ltd.; Member, international assessment committees for organic chemistry, Sweden, Switzerland, Australia, France and Denmark; Tilden Lectureship, Royal Society of Chemistry, 1986-87; Royal Society of Chemistry Award for Synthetic Organic Chemistry, 1987. Publication: Peptides (Co-editor), 1996. Recreations: sport; gardening; current affairs. Address: (b.) Department of Chemistry, University of Edinburgh, West Mains Road, Edinburgh EH9 3JJ; T.-0131-650 4721.

Ramsay, Major General Charles Alexander, CB, OBE. Landowner and Company Director; b. 12.10.36, North Berwick; m., Hon. Mary MacAndrew; 2 s.; 2 d. Educ. Eton; Sandhurst. Commissioned Royal Scots Greys, 1956; Staff College, Canada, 1967-68; Commanded Royal Scots Dragoon Guards, 1977-79; Commander 12th Armoured Brigade, 1980-82; Dep DMO MOD, 1983-84; GOC Eastern District, 1984-87; Director, General Army Organisation and Territorial Army, 1987-89; Chairman, Cockburns of Leith Ltd., 1993; Director, John Menzies Plc, Grey Horse Properties Ltd., Edinburgh Military Tattoo Ltd., Potomac Holdings Inc (USA), Morningside Holdings LLC (USA). Colonel, The Royal Scots Dragoon Guards, 1992-98; Member, Royal Company of Archers (Queen's Bodyguard for Scotland). Recreations: field sports; equitation; travel; motor-yachting; motoring. Address: (h.) Bughtrig, Coldstream, Berwickshire TD12 4JP; T.-01890 840678.

Randall, Rev. David James, MA, BD, ThM. Minister, Church of Scotland, Macduff, since 1971; b. 5.6.45, Edinburgh; m., Nan Wardlaw; 3 s.; 1 d. Educ. George Heriot's School; Edinburgh University; Princeton Theological Seminary. Recreations: jogging; reading; photography. Address: The Manse, Macduff AB45 3QL; T.-01261 832316; e-mail: djrandall@macduff.force9.co.uk

Randall, John Norman, BA, MPhil. Registrar General for Scotland, since 1999; b. 1.8.45, Bromley, Kent; 1 s.; 1 d. Educ. Bromley Grammar School; Bristol University; Glasgow University. Department of Economic Affairs; Scottish Office; Assistant Secretary, Countryside and Natural Heritage Unit, Scottish Office Agriculture, Environment and Fisheries Department, 1995-99. Recreation: hill-walking. Address: (b.) General Register Office for Scotland, Ladywell House, Edinburgh; T.-0131 314 4435.

Rankeillour, 4th Baron (Peter St. Thomas More Henry Hope). Farmer and Landowner; b. 29.5.35. Educ. Ampleforth. Address: (h.) The Achaderry Estate, Roy Bridge, Western Inverness-shire.

Rankin, Dr Andrew C., BSc, MBChB, MD, MRCP, FRCP. Senior Lecturer, Medical Cardiology, Glasgow Royal Infirmary, since 1993; b. 15.6.52, Larkhall; m., Clare Fitzsimons; 3 s. Educ. Hamilton Academy; Glasgow University. Registrar, Medical Cardiology, 1980; Lecturer, Medical Cardiology, 1984; Hon. Consultant Cardiologist, Glasgow Royal Infirmary, since 1993. Address: (b.) Department of Medical Cardiology, Glasgow Royal Infirmary, Glasgow; T.-0141-211 4833.

Rankin, Professor David W.H., MA, PhD, FRSC, CChem, FRSE. Professor of Structural Chemistry, Edinburgh University, since 1989; b. 8.6.45, Birkenhead; m., Stella M. Thomas; 3 s.; 1 d. Educ. Birkenhead School; King's College, Cambridge. Edinburgh University: ICI Research Fellow, 1969, Demonstrator, 1971, Lecturer, 1973, Reader, 1980, Professor, 1989. Publication: Structural Methods in Inorganic Chemistry. Address: (b.) Department of Chemistry, Edinburgh University, West Mains Road, Edinburgh EH9 3JJ; T.-0131-650 4728.

Rankin, Ian. Novelist; b. 1960, Fife; m.; 2 s. Educ. Edinburgh University. Has been employed as grape-picker, swine-herd, taxman, alcohol researcher, hi-fi journalist and punk musician; creator of the Inspector Rebus novels; first Rebus novel, Knots and Crosses, 1987; this series now translated into several languages; elected Hawthornden Fellow; former winner, Chandler-Fulbright Award; two CWA "Daggers"; 1997 CWA Macallan Gold Dagger for fiction for Black and Blue; 1999 Alumnus of the Year, Edinburgh University; Honorary Doctorate: University of Abertay, Dundee, University of St. Andrews.

Rankin, Shane, BA (Hons), MRTPI, PGDipBusiness. Secretary and Chief Executive, Crofters Commission, since 2000; b. 8.6.57, Antrim, N. Ireland; m., Fenella Benoist; 1s.; 1d. Educ. Banbridge Academy; Leeds Polytechnic; Strathclyde University. Planner, Gordon District Council; Senior Planner, East Lothian District Council; Economic Development Manager, East Lothian District Council; Head, Economic Development and Social Inclusion, East Lothian Council. Recreations: family; sailing; boats; cycling. Address: (b.) 4-6 Castle Wynd, Inverness, 1V2 3EQ; T.-01463 663450.

Ransford, Tessa, OBE, MA, FRSA, FFCS. Poet; b. 8.7.38, Bombay; 1 s.; 3 d. Educ. St. Leonard's School, St. Andrews; Edinburgh University; Craiglockhart College of Education. Publicity Department, Oxford University Press, 1958; in Pakistan as wife of missionary, 1960-68; Assistant to the Director, Scottish Institute of Adult Education, 1982-83; founder, Scottish Poetry Library, Director, 1984-99. Editor, Lines Review, 1988-98; books of poetry: Poetry of Persons, 1975, While It Is Yet Day, 1976, Light of the Mind, 1980, Fools and Angels, 1984; Shadows from the Greater Hill, 1987; A Dancing Innocence, 1988; Seven Valleys, 1991; Medusa Dozen and other poems, 1994; Scottish Selection, 1998; When It Works It Feels Like Play, 1998; first prize, Jubilee poetry competition, Scottish Association for the Speaking of Verse, 1974; Scottish Arts Council Book Award, 1980; Howard Sergeant Award for services to poetry, 1989; Honorary Member: The Saltire Society, 1993, Scottish Library Association, 1999; Heritage Society of Scotland Annual Award, 1996; Society of Authors Travelling Scholarship, 2001; Writing Fellow, Royal Literary Fund, since 2001; Committee Member, Scottish International PEN; Founder, School of Poets (open learning workshop for practising poets). Recreation: grandchildren. Address: (h.) 31 Royal Park Terrace, Edinburgh EH8 8JA; T.-0131-661 1277; e-mail: wisdomfield@talk21.com

Rapport, Professor Nigel Julian, BA, MA, PhD. Professor of Anthropological and Philosophical Studies, St. Andrews University, since 1996; b. 8.11.56, Cardiff; m., Elizabeth J.A. Munro; 1 s.; 1 d. Educ. Clifton College, Bristol; Cambridge University; Manchester University. Research Fellow and Associate, Institute of Social and Economic Research, Memorial University of Newfoundland, 1983-87; Lecturer, Blaustein Institute for Desert Research, Ben-Gurion University of the Negev, Israel, 1988; Lecturer, Department of Social Anthropology, Manchester University, 1989; joined St. Andrews University as Lecturer, 1993. Hon. Secretary, Association of Social Anthropologists of the UK and Commonwealth, 1994-98; President, Anthropology and Archaeology Section, British Association for the Advancement of Science, 2000-01; 1996 Royal Society of Edinburgh prize lectureship in the humanities, 1996; Royal Anthropological Institute, Curl Essay Prize, 1996. Publications: Talking Violence: an anthropological interpretation of conversation in the city, 1987; Diverse World-Views in an English Village, 1993; The Prose and the Passion: anthropology, literature and the writing of E.M. Forster, 1994; Questions of Consciousness (Co-editor), 1995; Transcendent Individual, towards a literary and liberal anthropology, 1997; Migrants of Identity: Perceptions of Home in a World of Movement

(Co-editor), 1998; Social and Cultural Anthropology: The Key Concepts, 2000. Recreations: travel; sport; literature. Address: (b.) Department of Social Anthropology, St. Andrews University, St. Andrews KY16 9AL; T.-01334 462977.

Ratter, James Alexander, BSc, PhD, FRSE, FRGS. Senior Principal Scientific Officer, Head of Tropical Biology, Royal Botanic Garden, Edinburgh, 1987-99; b. 15.2.34, Cambridge; m., Pamela Joan Allsop. Educ. Liverpool College; University of Liverpool. University Demonstrator, University of Liverpool, 1958-60; Botanist, Royal Botanic Garden, Edinburgh: Scientific Officer, 1960-64, Senior Scientific Officer, 1964-69, Principal Scientific Officer, 1969-87; Visiting Professor (Co-Founder, Ecology Department), University of Brasilia, 1976-77; Co-Leader of Biodiversity Survey, Anglo-Brazilian Maracá Rainforest Project (INPA/Royal Geographical Society/SEMA), 1987-88. Specialist Adviser, HOC Environment Committee, Climatological and Environmental Effects of Rainforest Destruction, Session 1989-90 and 1990-91; Honorary Citizen, Municipality of Nova Xavantina, Mato Grosso, Brazil, 1997; Fellow, Brazilian Academy of Sciences, 1999; awarded Grand Cross, National Order of Scientific Merit, by President of the Republic of Brazil, 2000. Recreations; field botany; Portuguese language; ornithology. Publications: Maracá: Rainforest Island (Co- Author), 1993; Maracá: The Biodiversity and Environment of an Amazonian Rainforest (Editor), 1998. Address: (b.) 20A Inverleith Row, Edinburgh EH3 5LR.

Raven, Andrew O.E., BA, DipLE, MRICS. Chairman, Deer Commission for Scotland, since 1999; Member, Board of Governors, Macaulay Land Use Research Institute, since 1997, Chairman, since 2001; b. 22.1.59, London; m., Amanda Game. Educ. Marlborough; Bristol University; Aberdeen University. Director, Ardtornish Estate Co. Ltd. and Partner, Ardtornish Farms, Morvern, Lochaber; cabinet-maker, 1980-83; Land Agent, Smiths Gore, 1985-95; Director of Land Management, John Muir Trust, 1995-98. Trustee, John Muir Trust, 1989-95; Member of Council, Rural Forum Scotland 1992-99 (Vice-Chairman, 1995-98); Member, Scottish Consumer Council, 1995-2001; Trustee, Millennium Forest for Scotland, since 1996; judge, Scottish Award for Quality in Planning; Non-Executive Forestry Commissioner, since 2000. Recreations: arts and crafts; walking. Address: (b.) Knowsley, 82 Fairfield Road, Inverness; T.-01463 231751.

Raven, Professor John Albert, MA, PhD, FRS, FRSE, Hon.PhD (Umea); FInstBiol, CBiol. Boyd Baxter Professor of Biology, University of Dundee, since 1995; b. 25.6.41, Wimbish, Essex; m., Dr. Linda Lea Handley. Educ. Friends School, Saffron Walden; St. John's College, Cambridge University. Cambridge University: Research Fellow, St. John's College, 1966-69, Demonstrator in Botany, 1968-71, Official Fellow, St. John's College, 1970-71; Department of Biological Sciences, University of Dundee: Lecturer, 1971-76, Reader, 1976-80, Personal Chair, 1980-95. Past President: Botanical Society of Scotland, British Phycological Society, Society for Experimental Biology. Publications: Energetics and Transport in Aquatic Plants, 1984; Aquatic Photosynthesis (Co-Author), 1997; numerous scientific papers. Recreations: aviation; literature; walking. Address: Division of Environmental and Applied Biology, School of Life Sciences, University of Dundee, Biological Sciences Institute, Dundee DD1 4HN; T.-01382 344281; e-mail: j.a.raven@dundee.ac.uk

Ravenhill, Professor John, BSc (Econ), MA, AM, PhD. Chair of Politics, Edinburgh University, since 2000; b. 22.8.50, Yeovil; m., Dr Maria-Stefania Wirga. Educ. Yeovil School; Hull University; University of California, Berkeley. Assistant Professor, University of Virginia, 1980-82; Lecturer/Senior Lecturer/Associate Professor, University of Sydney, 1982-90; Senior Fellow/Professor, Australian National University, 1990-2000. Publications: Apec and the Construction of Pacific Rim Regionalism; The Apian Financial Crises and the Global Financial Architecture. Recreations: opera; music. Address: (b.) School of Social and Political Studies, Adam Ferguson Building, Edinburgh University EH8 9LL; T.-0131-650 4457.

Rea, Hugh Stewart. Lieut-Colonel, Divisional Commander, West Scotland, The Salvation Army, since 1998; b. 21.10.37, Belfast; m., Christine; 2 s.; 1 d. Educ. Masonic Boys School, Dublin; William Booth Memorial College. Commissioned (ordained) as Salvation Army officer, 1963; worked in S.A. adolescent unit until 1966; served in Caribbean and Central America until 1970; three years' church leadership; returned to social work, 1974, working with homeless people in London and Birmingham; moved to middle management in Scotland, then London; Divisional Commander, London. Recreations: football supporter; reading. Address: (b.) 4 Buchanan Court, Cumbernauld Road, Stepps, Glasgow G33 6HZ; T.-0141-779 5001.

Read, Professor Andrew Fraser. BSc (Hons), DPhil. Chair of Natural History, University of Edinburgh, since 1998; b. 12.9.62, Hawera, New Zealand; m., Victoria Braithwaite; 2 s. Educ. Otago University, Dunedin, New Zealand; Oxford University. University of Oxford: Commonwealth Scholarship to Merton College, 1985-88, Junior Research Fellowship, Christ Church, 1988-92, Lecturer in Zoology, St. Catherine's College, 1989-90, Lloyd's of London Tercentenary Fellowship, 1991-92; Adjunct Professor in Evolutionary Ecology, University of Tromsø, Norway, 1992-97; BBSRC Advanced Research Fellowship, University of Edinburgh, 1993-97; BBSRC Second Advanced Research Fellowship, 1998. Recreation: hankering after mountains. Address: (b.) Institute of Cell, Animal and Population Biology, University of Edinburgh, Edinburgh EH9 3JT; T.-0131-650 5506.

Read, Professor Paul, BSc, MSc, PhD, CBiol, FIBiol, CIWEM. Associate Head, School of Life Sciences, Napier University, since 1990; b. 1.1.48, Saffron Walden; m., Jane. Educ. Palmers Grammar School, Grays; Hull University; Aston University. Research Technician, Essex Water Authority, 1969-70; Research Assistant, University of Aston, 1971-72; Research Fellow, then Lecturer, Napier College, 1972-82; Senior Lecturer, Napier Polytechnic, 1982-90. Fifty publications. Recreations: offshore sailing/cruising; gardening; hill-walking. Address: (b.) School of Life Sciences, Napier University, Colinton Road, Edinburgh EH10 5DT; T.-0131-455 2625.

Reader, Professor Keith Anthony, MA (Cantab), BPhil, DPhil (Oxon), Chevalier dans l'Ordre des Palmes Académiques. Professor of Modern French, Glasgow University, since 2000; b. 20.12.45, Tunbridge Wells. Educ. Ifield Grammar School, Crawley, Sussex; Downing College, Cambridge; St John's College, Oxford. Lecturer, Caen University, France, 1970-71; Lecturer, Ecole Normale Supérieure, Paris, 1971-73; Lecturer, Manchester Polytechnic, 1973-74; Lecturer/Reader/Professor, Kingston Polytechnic/ University, 1974-95; Professor of French, Newcastle University, 1995-2000; Member, Executive Committee, Society for French Studies, 1984-87; Editorial Board, Modern and Contemporary France, 1991-96; University Council of Modern Languages, 1996-2000. Publications include: Régis Debray, 1995; Robert Bresson, 2000. Recreations: talking; listening; agonising. Address: (b.) Modern Languages Building, Glasgow University; T.-0141-330 3660.

Reay, 14th Lord (Hugh William Mackay); b. 19.7.37; m.; 2 d.; 2 s., 1 d. by pr. m. Educ. Eton; Christ Church. Succeeded to title, 1963; Member, European Parliament, 1973-79; Parliamentary Under Secretary of State, Department of Trade and Industry, 1991-92.

Reed, Hon. Lord (Robert John Reed), LLB, DPhil. Senator of the College of Justice, since 1998; b. 7.9.56, Edinburgh; m., Jane Elizabeth Mylne; 2 d. Educ. George Watson's College, Edinburgh; Edinburgh University; Balliol College, Oxford. Standing Junior Counsel: Scottish Education Department, 1988-89, Scottish Office Home and Health Department, 1989-95; called to English Bar, 1991; QC, 1995; Advocate Depute, 1996-98; ad hoc Judge of the European Court of Human Rights, 1999. Recreations: music; visual arts. Address: (b.) Court of Session, Parliament House, Edinburgh EH1 1RQ.

Reed, Gavin Barras, BA. Chairman, John Menzies plc; b. 13.11.34, Newcastle upon Tyne; m. Muriel Joyce; 1 s.; 3 d. Educ. Eton; Trinity College, Cambridge. National Service, Fleet Air Arm; joined The Newcastle Breweries, 1958; Vice-Chairman, Scottish & Newcastle plc, 1991-94. Director: Hamilton and Inches Ltd. (Chairman), Burtonwood Brewery plc. Recreations: shooting; tennis. Address (h.) Whitehill, Aberdour, Burntisland, Fife KY3 0RW; Broadgate, West Woodburn, Northumberland NE48 2RN.

Reed, Malcolm Christopher, MA, DPhil, FCIT. Director, Strathclyde Passenger Transport Executive; b. 24.11.44, Cardigan, Wales; 2d. Educ. Royal Grammar School, Newcastle-upon-Tyne; St Catherine's College, Oxford; Nuffield College, Oxford. Assistant, Bodleian Library, Oxford; Lecturer, Glasgow University; Researcher/Associate Director, Planning Exchange, Glasgow; Planner, Chief Public Transport Co-ordinator, Greater Glasgow Passenger Transport Executive; Chief Policy Planner/Senior Executive Officer, Strathclyde Regional Council; Assistant Chief Executive; Strathclyde Regional Council. Recreations: hill walking; listening to music; travel. Address: (b.) Consort House, 12 West George Street, Glasgow, G2 1HN; T.-0141-333 3100; e-mail: director.general@spt.co.uk

Reed, Professor Peter, BA, RIBA, FRIAS, FSAScot. Emeritus Professor, Strathclyde University; b. 31.1.33, Hayes, Middlesex; m., Keow Chim Lim; 2 d. Educ. Southall Grammar School; Manchester University (State Scholar); Open University. Commissioned Officer, RAF, 1960-61; Assistant Lecturer, University of Hong Kong, 1961-64; Architect in practice, Malaysia, 1964-70; joined Strathclyde University Department of Architecture and Building Science as Lecturer, 1970; Professor of Architecture, 1986; Dean, Faculty of Engineering, 1988-90; Vice-Principal Elect, 1990-92; Vice-Principal, 1992-94. Secretary, Kilsyth Civic Trust, 1975-80; Chairman, Kilsyth Community Council, 1975-78; GIA Council, 1982-84; ARCUK Board of Education, 1985-95; Governor, Glasgow School of Art, 1982-94; Director, Glasgow West Conservation Trust, 1990-2000, Convener, 1996-2000; Chairman, Council, Charles Rennie Mackintosh Society, 1991-94. Publications include Glasgow: The Forming of the City (Editor). Recreations: opera; wine; cricket. Address: 67 Dowanside Road, Glasgow G12 9DL; T.-0141-334 1356.

Reekie, Tony. Director, Imaginate, since 1996; b. 20.12.64, Edinburgh; m., Gill Robertson; 1 s. Educ. Firrhill High School, Edinburgh. General Manager, Pen Name Theatre Co.; Administrator, 7:84 Theatre Company; Development Officer, Tag Theatre Company; General Manager, Visible Fictions Theatre Company; Director, Scottish International Children's Festival. Recreations: lamenting the state of our national game; playing with my son, Coll. Address: (b.) 45a George Street, Edinburgh EH2 2HT; T.-0131-225 8050.

Reeks, David Robin, TD, DL, BSc(Eng). Consulting Engineer, Axiom Consulting Engineers Ltd., since 1996; b. 15.6.35, Parkstone; m., Kathleen Veronica Stephens; 1 s.; 1 d. Educ. Canford School; London University. Rig Engineer, UKAEA Dounreay, 1962-67; Senior Engineer, SSEB, 1967-90; Reactor Thermal Performance Engineer, Scottish Nuclear Ltd., 1990-94. Committee Member and Volunteer Convoy Leader, Edinburgh Direct Aid to Bosnia; Deputy Lieutenant of Lanarkshire; TA Royal Engineers/Royal Corps of Transport, 1962-90. Recreations: hill-walking; Scottish country dancing. Address: 3 Cedar Place, Strathaven, Lanarkshire ML10 6DW; T.-01357 521695; e-mail: d-reeks@ukonline.co.uk

Rees, Alan Tait, MBE, MA (Cantab), CQSW; b. 4.8.31, Shanghai, China; m., Alison Margaret; 2 s.; 2 d. Educ. Kingswood School, Bath; Gonville and Caius College, Cambridge; London School of Economics; University College, Swansea. Community Development Officer, Tanzania; Lecturer in Youth and Community Studies, Moray House College; Organising Secretary, Board for Information in Youth and Community Service, Scotland; Senior Community Development Officer, Council of Social Service for Wales; Assistant Director, Edinburgh Voluntary Organisations' Council, retired 1993; Chair, Scotland Yard Adventure Centre, Edinburgh, 1986-98; Trustee, Seagull Trust; Chair, Handicabs (Lothian), 1997-2001; Secretary, Scottish Branch, International Association for the Child's Right to Play (IPA); Board Member, Scottish Alliance for Children's Rights. Recreations: gardening; painting. Address: (h.) 20 Seaforth Drive, Edinburgh EH4 2BZ; T.-0131-332 7317.

Rees, Professor Elmer Gethin, BA (Cantab), PhD (Warwick), MA (Oxon), FRSE. Professor, Department of Mathematics and Statistics, Edinburgh University, since 1979; Member, Executive Committee, International Centre for Mathematical Sciences, since 1993; Member, Scientific Steering Committee, Isaac Newton Institute, Cambridge, since 1999; b. 19.11.41, Llandybie, Wales; m., Mary Elene; 2 s. Educ. Llandeilo Grammar School; St. Catharine's College, Cambridge; Warwick University. Lecturer, Department of Pure Mathematics, Hull University, 1967-69; Member, Institute for Advanced Study, Princeton, 1969-70; Lecturer, Department of Pure Mathematics, University College of Swansea, 1970-71; Tutorial Fellow, St. Catherine's College, Oxford and Lecturer in Mathematics, Oxford University, 1971-79. Vice President, London Mathematical Society, 1994-96. Publications: Notes on Geometry; Homotopy Theory. Address: (h.) 23 Blacket Place, Edinburgh EH9 1RJ; T.-0131-667 2747; e-mail: E.G.Rees@ed.ac.uk

Rees, Jennifer Linda, BSc, PhD, FRSS, MIMgt. Director of Corporate Planning, Glasgow Caledonian University, since 1999; b. 2.7.51, Edinburgh; m., Richard; 1 s.; 1 d. Educ. Edinburgh University; Bradford University. Operational Research Analyst, then Statistical Quality Control Manager, Scottish & Newcastle Breweries Ltd.; Lecturer, Department of Business Studies, Edinburgh University; Head, Department of Management Studies, Scottish College of Textiles; Assistant Principal (Academic), Bell College of Technology. Recreations: skiing; theatre; walking. Address: (b.) Glasgow Caledonian University, Britannia Building, Cowcaddens Road, Glasgow G4 0BA.

Rees, Professor Jonathan, BMedSci, MBBS, FRCP, FRCPE, FMedSci. Grant Chair of Dermatology, University of Edinburgh, since 2000; b. 10.10.57, Cardiff; m., Anne; 2 d. Educ. St. Illtyd's College, Cardiff. Trained in internal medicine, Newcastle upon Tyne; trained in dermatology, Vienna and Newcastle-upon-Tyne; trained in molecular genetics, Newcastle-upon-Tyne and Strasborg; Professor of Dermatology, University of Newcastle, 1992-2000. President Elect, European Society for Dermatology

Research. Recreation: changing research fields. Address: (b.) Department of Dermatology, University of Edinburgh, Lauriston Building, Lauriston Place, Edinburgh EH3 9YW; T.-0131-536 2041; e-mail: jonathan.rees@ed.ac.uk

Rees, Professor Lovat Victor Charles, BSc, PhD, DSc, FRSC, CChem, FRSE. Hon. Fellow, Edinburgh University since 1993; Emeritus Professor, Imperial College, London, since 1993; b. 7.11.27, Aberdeen; m., Elizabeth Margaret; 1 s.; 2 d. Educ. Robert Gordon's College, Aberdeen; Aberdeen University. Assistant Lecturer, Aberdeen University, 1952-53; Senior Scientific Officer, AWRE, Aldermaston, 1953-57; Professor, Imperial College, London, 1958-93; Hon. Member, Federation of European Zeolite Associations, 1999. IZA Award, 2001. Publications: Zeolites (ed.), 1980-97. Recreations: golf. Address: (b.) Department of Chemistry, Edinburgh University, West Mains Road, Edinburgh, EH9 3JJ; T.-0131-650 4766; e-mail: Lovat.Rees@ed.ac.uk

Reeves, Philip Thomas Langford, RSA, PRSW, RE, RGI, ARCA. Artist; b. 7.7.31, Cheltenham; m., Christine MacLaren (deceased); 1 d. Educ. Naunton Park School, Cheltenham; Cheltenham School of Art; Royal College of Art, London. Lecturer in Graphic Design, Glasgow School of Art, 1954-70, Head of Printmaking, 1970-91. Address: (h.) 13 Hamilton Drive, Glasgow G12 8DN; T.-0141-339 0720.

Reid, Alan, MP. Liberal Democrat MP, Argyll and Bute, since 2001; b. 7.8.54. Educ. Prestwick Academy; Ayr Academy; Strathclyde University. Maths Teacher, 1976-77; Computer Programmer, 1977-85; Computer Project Manager, Glasgow University, 1985-2001. Address: (b.) House of Commons, London SW1A 0AA.

Reid, Alexander N., WS, NP, LLB. Chairman, Steedman Ramage WS, since 1993; b. 15.9.54, Aberdeen; m., Maria; 2 s. Educ. Robert Gordon's College, Aberdeen; Aberdeen University. Steedman Ramage WS: apprentice lawyer, 1975-77, Assistant, 1977-80, Partner, 1980-93. Recreations: family; sport; music. Address: (b.) 6 Alva Street, Edinburgh; T.-0131-260 6600.

Reid, Alison Hamilton, MA, DMS, FCIM, FRSA. Chief Executive, Scottish Further Education Unit, since 1995; Depute Principal, Perth College. Educ. Montrose Academy; Edinburgh University; Strathclyde University. Marketing and business development in commercial sector, 1973-81; Lecturer and Manager in Further Education, 1981-95. Address: (b.) Argyll Court, Castle Business Park, Stirling; T.-01786 892000.

Reid, Allan William, MBChB, FRCR. Consultant Radiologist: Glasgow Royal Infirmary, since 1989, Ross Hall Hospital, since 1991; Clinical Director of Imaging, Glasgow Royal Infirmary, since 1996; b. 20.6.58, Glasgow. Educ. Glasgow Academy; University of Glasgow. Recreations: photography; swimming; golf. Address: (b.) Department of Radiology, Glasgow Royal Infirmary, Glasgow G31 2ER; T.-0141-211 4783; e-mail: awr@northglasgow.scot.nhs.uk

Reid, Professor Colin Turriff, MA, LLB. Professor of Environmental Law, Dundee University, since 1995; b. 10.6.58, Aberdeen; m., M. Anne Palin; 2 d. Educ. Robert Gordon's College, Aberdeen; University College, Oxford; Gonville and Caius College, Cambridge. Lecturer in Public Law, Aberdeen University, 1980-90; Senior Lecturer in Law, Dundee University, 1991-95. Publications: Nature Conservation Law; Environmental Law in Scotland (Editor); A Guide to the Scotland Act 1998 (Co-Author). Recreations: cricket; hockey. Address: (b.) Department of Law, Dundee University, Dundee DD1 4HN; T.-01382 344461.

Reid, David C., MA, MEd. Rector, Kinross High School, since 1985; b. 4.9.43, Motherwell; m., Alison W. Ewing; 1 s.; 1 d. Educ. Wishaw High School; Glasgow University; Jordanhill College; Edinburgh University. Teacher of English, Kirkcaldy High School, 1966-71; Principal Teacher of English, Currie High School, 1971-80; Assistant Rector, Inverkeithing High School, 1980-85. Member/Chairman, English Panel, Scottish Examination Board, 1976-82; Member, IBA Educational Advisory Council (Schools Panels), 1975-86; Chairman, Channel 4 Scottish Schools Committee, 1996-98. Recreations: hill-walking; angling; conversation; reading; Scottish traditional architecture. Address: (b.) Kinross High School, Kinross, Kinross-shire KY13 8AW; T.-01577 862430; e-mail: headteacher@kinross-high.pkc.sch.uk

Reid, David Ronald, MA(Hons), LLB. Partner, Burness, since 1965; b. 23.6.37, Larbert; m., Ruth Edith; 1 d. Educ. Daniel Stewart's College, Edinburgh; Edinburgh University. Apprenticeship with W. & J. Burness, 1959-62, Assistant, 1962-65. Former Council Member, WS Society. Recreations: golf; hill-walking; music; reading. Address: (b.) 50 Lothian Road, Festival Square, Edinburgh EH3 9WJ; T.-0131-473 6000; e-mail: drr@burness.co.uk

Reid, Derek Donald, MA. Chairman, D. Macleod Ltd. (Harris Tweed); Chairman, Cherrybank Partnership; Trustee, Loch Lomond Trust; various directorships of small companies; Visiting Professor of Tourism, Abertay University, since 2000; b. 30.11.44, Aberdeen; m., Janice Anne Reid; 1 s.; 1 d. Educ. Inverurie Academy; Aberdeen University; Robert Gordon University. Cadbury-Schweppes, 1968-85 (latterly Divisional Director); founding Director/Owner, Premier Brands, 1985-90; Chief Executive, Scottish Tourist Board, 1994-96. Former Deputy Chairman, Sea Fish Industry Authority; former Deputy Chairman: Scotland The Brand; Honorary Doctorate, Business Administration, Robert Gordon University; Fellow, George Thomas Society. Recreations: golf; fishing; modern art; fine food/wine. Address: Bonhard House, Scone, Perth PH2 7PQ; T.-01738 553901.

Reid, Rev. Donald, LLB, MPhil, BD. Director, Scottish Civic Forum, since 2000; Anglican Chaplain, Universities in Glasgow, since 1995; Team Priest, St. Mary's Cathedral, Glasgow, since 1995; Chair, Jubilee 2000 Scottish Coalition, since 1997; b. 25.2.58, Bellshill. Educ. High School of Glasgow. Curate, St. John's, Greenock, 1985-88; Rector, St. John's, Ballieston, St. Serf's, Shettleston, 1988-95; Chair, East Timor Scotland Support Group; Trustee, Scottish Churches' World Exchange, 1994-2001; Convener, Scottish Churches' World Action. Recreations: cinema; photography. Address: (h.) 1/2 212 Wilton Street, Glasgow G20 6BL; T.-0141-576 5906; e-mail: DReid212@aol.com

Reid, Professor Gavin Clydesdale, MA, MSc, PhD, FRSA, FFCS. Professor in Economics, St. Andrews University, since 1991; Director, Centre for Research into Industry, Enterprise, Finance and the Firm (CRIEFF), since 1991; President, Scottish Economic Society, since 1999; b. 25.8.46, Glasgow; m., 1, Margaret Morrice or McGregor (m. diss.); 1 s.; 1 step-s.; 2, Maureen Johnson or Bagnall; 1 s.; 2 d.; 1 step.-s. Educ. Lyndhurst School; Frimley and Camberley Grammar School; Aberdeen University; Southampton University; Edinburgh University. Lecturer, Senior Lecturer, Reader in Economics, Edinburgh University, 1971-91; Visiting Associate Professor: Queen's University, Ontario, 1981-82, Denver University, Colorado, 1984; Visiting Scholar, Darwin College, Cambridge, 1987-88; Visiting Professor, University of Nice, 1998; Leverhulme Trust Research Fellowship, 1989-90; Nuffield Foundation Social Science Research Fellowship, 1997-98. Editorial Board: Scottish Journal of Political Economy, 1986-98, Small Business Economics, since 1997, Venture Capital, since 1998; Member, Council: Scottish Economic Society, since 1990, National Conference of University

Professors, since 2000; Chairman, Network of Industrial Economists, 1997-2001. Publications: The Kinked Demand Curve Analysis of Oligopoly, 1981; Theories of Industrial Organization, 1987; The Small Entrepreneurial Firm (Coauthor), 1988; Classical Economic Growth, 1989; Small Business Enterprise, 1993; Profiles in Small Business (Coauthor), 1993; Venture Capital Investment, 1998; Information System Development in the Small Firm (Coauthor), 2000. Recreations:music; reading; running; badminton. Address: (h.) 23 South Street, St. Andrews KY16 9QS; T.-01334 472932.

Reid, George, MA. MSP (SNP), Mid-Scotland and Fife, since 1999; Deputy Presiding Officer, Scottish Parliament, since 1999; Convener, Conveners' Liaison Group; b. 4.6.39, Tullibody; m., Daphne Ann; 2 d. Educ. Dollar Academy; St Andrews University. Reporter, Daily Express; Reporter, Scottish Television; Producer, Granada Television; Head of News and Current Affairs, Scottish Television; Presenter, BBC; Director of Public Affairs, International Red Cross. MP, Clackmannan and East Stirlingshire, 1974-79; Member, Parliamentary Assembly of the Council of Europe, 1975-79. Address: (b.) Scottish Parliament, Edinburgh EH99 1SP; T.-0131-348 5911.

Reid, Harry William, BA (Hons), Dr hc (Edinburgh), DUniv (Glasgow), FRSA. Writer; former Editor, The Herald; b. 23.9.47, Glasgow; m., Julie Davidson (qv); 1 d. Educ. Aberdeen Grammar School; Fettes College; Oxford University. The Scotsman: Education Correspondent, 1973-77, Features Editor, 1977-81; Sports Editor, Sunday Standard, 1981-82; Executive Editor, Glasgow Herald, 1982-83, Deputy Editor, 1983-97. Visiting Fellow, Faculty of Divinity, Edinburgh University, since 2001; commissioned by Church of Scotland to write special report on its state and prospects, 2001. Publication: Dear Country: a quest for England, 1992. Recreations: reading; walking; supporting Aberdeen Football Club. Address: 12 Comely Bank, Edinburgh EH4 1AN; T.-0131-332 6690; e-mail: harry.reid@virgin.net

Reid, Heather M.M., BSc(Hons), MSc, CPhys, MInstP, FRMS. Weather Forecaster, Met Office, since 1993; BBC Scotland Weather Forecaster, since 1994; b. 6.7.69, Paisley. Educ. Camphill High School, Paisley; Edinburgh University. Joined Met Office to work in satellite image research; became forecaster at Glasgow Weather Centre; now known as "Heather the Weather" to viewers. Past-Chair, Institute of Physics in Scotland, 1999-2001; active involvement in Edinburgh Science Festival, Techfest, and promoting the public understanding of science. Recreations: apart from lecturing and giving talks in spare time – watch cricket; hill-walking. Address: (b.) Glasgow Weather Centre, 220 St. Vincent Street, Glasgow G2 5QD; T.-0141-248 3451.

Reid, Hugh Watt, BVM&S, DipTVM, PhD, MRCVS. Head, Virology Division, Moredun Research Institute, since 1990; b. 23.6.42, Edinburgh; m., Irene Elisabeth; 1 s.; 2 d. Educ. George Watson's College, Edinburgh; Glasgow Academy; Aberdeen Grammar School; University of Edinburgh. Moredun Research Institute: Veterinary Research Officer, 1968-74, Principal Veterinary Research Officer, 1974-90. Previously officer bearer: Association of Veterinary Teachers and Research Workers, Veterinary Deer Society, Edinburgh South Liberal Party. Publications: 150 papers/book chapters. Recreations: gardening; cycling; walking. Address: Pentlands Science Park, Bush Loan, Penicuik EH26 0PZ; T.-0131-445 5111.

Reid, Professor Ian Cameron, MB, ChB, BMedBiol, PhD, MRCPsych. Professor of Psychiatry, Dundee University, since 1995; b. 13.10.60, Dunfermline; m., Isla; 1 d. Educ. Dollar Academy; Aberdeen University; Edinburgh University. Lecturer in Mental Health, Aberdeen University; Research Fellow, Department of Pharmacology, then Lecturer in Psychiatry, Edinburgh University; Senior Lecturer in Mental Health, Aberdeen University. Recreation: curry. Address: (b.) Department of Psychiatry, Ninewells Hospital and Medical School, Dundee DD1 9SY; T.-01382 632121.

Reid, Professor J.S. Grant, BSc, PhD. Professor of Plant Biochemistry, Stirling University, since 1994; b. 27.3.42, Huntly; m., Mary E. Edwards; 1 s.; 2 d. Educ. Gordon Schools, Huntly; Aberdeen University. Lecturer, University of Fribourg, Switzerland, 1970-73; Lecturer in Biochemistry, Stirling University, 1974-78; Visiting Associate Professor, University of Calgary, 1977-78; Senior Lecturer, then Reader, Stirling University, 1978-94; Visiting Professor, Unilever Research Laboratories, Netherlands, 1988. Address: (b.) Department of Biological Sciences, Stirling University, Stirling FK9 4LA; T.-01786 467762; e-mail: j.s.g.reid@stir.ac.uk

Reid, James Gordon, LLB (Hons), FCIArb. Queen's Counsel (Scotland), since 1993; Chairman (Part-time), VAT and Duties Tribunals, since 1997; Deputy Special Commissioner for Income Tax, since 1997; b. 24.7.52, Edinburgh; m., Hannah Hogg Hopkins; 3 s.; 1 d. Educ. Melville College, Edinburgh; Edinburgh University. Solicitor, 1976-80; Advocate, 1980-93; Standing Junior Counsel, Scottish Office Environment Department, 1986-93; admitted as Barrister, Inner Temple, 1991. Recreations: tennis; golf. Address: (h.) Blebo House, by St. Andrews, Fife KY15 5TZ; T.-01334 653274.

Reid, Jimmy. Journalist and Broadcaster; b. 1932. Former Engineer; prominent in campaign to save Upper Clyde Shipbuilders; former Convener of Shop Stewards, AUEW; former (Communist) Member, Clydebank Town Council; joined Labour Party and contested Dundee East, General Election, 1979; Rector, Glasgow University, 1971-74; Founder, Seven Days magazine; Columnist, The Herald, Glasgow.

Reid, Rt. Hon. John, PC, PhD. MP (Labour), Hamilton North and Bellshill, since 1997, Motherwell North, 1987-97; Secretary of State for Northern Ireland, since 2001; b. 8.5.47, Bellshill; m., Catherine McGowan (deceased); 2 s. Educ. St. Patrick's Senior Secondary School, Coatbridge; Stirling University. Scottish Research Officer, Labour Party, 1979-83; Political Adviser to Rt. Hon. Neil Kinnock, 1983-85; Scottish Organiser, Trade Unionists for Labour, 1986-87; Armed Forces Minister, 1997-98; Minister of Transport, 1998-99; Secretary of State for Scotland, 1999-2001. Recreations: crosswords; football; reading. Address: (b.) House of Commons, Westminster, London; Parliamentary Office, Montrose House, 154 Montrose Crescent, Hamilton ML3 6LL; T.-01698 454672.

Reid, Professor John Low, OBE, MA, DM, FRCP, FRSE. Regius Professor of Medicine, University of Glasgow, since 1989; Consultant Physician, Western Infirmary, Glasgow, since 1989; b. 1.10.43, Glasgow; m., Randa; 1 s.; 1 d. Educ. Kelvinside Academy; Fettes College; Magdalen College, Oxford University. Clinical and research posts, Royal Postgraduate Medical School, London and National Institutes of Health, Bethesda, USA; Regius Chair of Materia Medica, University of Glasgow, 1978-89. Publication: Lecture Notes in Clinical Pharmacology. Editor, Handbook of Hypertension. Recreations: outdoors; gardening; opera. Address: (h.) 5 Princes Terrace, Glasgow G12 9JW; T.-0141-211 2986.

Reid, Professor Kenneth Gilbert Cameron, MA, LLB, WS, FRSE. Professor of Property Law, Edinburgh University, since 1994; Law Commissioner for Scotland, since 1995; b. 25.3.54, Glasgow; m., Elspeth Christie; 2 s.; 1 d. Educ. Loretto; St. John's College, Cambridge; Edinburgh University. Admitted as a Solicitor, 1980;

Lecturer in Law, Edinburgh University, 1980. Author of numerous books and papers on the law of property. Recreation: classical music. Address: (b.) Old College, South Bridge, Edinburgh EH8 9YL; T.-0131-650 2015.

Reid, Melanie Frances, MA (Hons.). Assistant Editor and Columnist, The Herald, since 2001; b. 13.4.57, Barnet; m., David McNeil; 1 s. Educ. Ormskirk Grammar School; Edinburgh University. The Scotsman: Graduate Trainee, 1980-82, Woman's Editor, 1983-87; Sunday Mail: Woman's Editor, 1987-2000, Associate Editor, 2000; Columnist, The Express, 2000. Recreations: painting; walking; doing bad dressage. Address: (b.) The Herald, 200 Renfield Street, Glasgow G2; T.-0141-302 7160; e-mail: melanie.reid@the herald.co.uk

Reid, Sir Robert (Bob). Deputy Governor, Bank of Scotland, since 1997; Chairman, International Petroleum Exchange, since 1999; b. 1.5.34, Cupar, Fife; m., Joan; 3 s. Educ. Bell Baxter; St Andrews University. Joined Shell International Petroleum Company, 1956, much of career spent in Nigeria, Thailand, Australia; Director, Shell International Petroleum Company, 1984; Chairman/Chief Executive, Shell UK Ltd, 1985-90; Chairman, British Rail, 1990-95; Chairman, London Electricity, 1994-97; Chairman, Council of the Industrial Society, 1993-98; Chairman, British-Borneo Oil and Gas Plc, 1995-2000; Chairman Sears plc, 1995-2000; Non-Executive Director: The Merchants Trust, since 1995; Avis Europe Plc, since 1997; Sun Life Assurance Company of Canada, since 1997; Siemens Plc, since 1998; Sondex Ltd., since 1999; Chairman: Foundation for Management Education, Learning through Landscape, King's Cross Partnership; Trustee: Campaign for Learning; Civic Trust; IPE Charitable Trust; Companion, Institute of Management; Chancellor, Robert Gordon University. Recreations: golf. Address: (b.) Bank of Scotland, 38 Threadneedle Street, London EC2P 2EH; T.-020-7601 6521; e-mail: Kathleen_Murray@bankofscotland.co.uk

Reid, Robert Russell, JP. Director, Argyll Training; Member, Bute Housing Association; Honorary Sheriff; Farmer; b. 26.12.32, Campbeltown; m., Rebecca Simpson Hunter; 3 s.; 1 d. Educ. Campbeltown Grammar School; Thorpe House; Rothesay Academy. Former Chairman, Argyll and Bute NHS Trust and Argyll and Clyde Health Board. Address: (h.) Eriskay, 13 Ardmory Road, Rothesay, Bute PA20 0PG; T.-01700 50 3238.

Reid, Seona Elizabeth, BA, HonDArt, DLitt, FRSA. Director, Glasgow School of Art, since 1999; b. 21.1.50, Paisley. Educ. Park School, Glasgow; Strathclyde University; Liverpool University. Business Manager, Theatre Royal, Lincoln, 1972-73; Press Officer, Northern Dance Theatre, Manchester, 1973-76; PRO, Ballet Rambert, London, 1976-79; freelance arts consultant, 1979-81; Director, Shape, London, 1981-87; Assistant Director, Greater London Arts, 1987-90; Director, Scottish Arts Council, 1990-99. Recreations: walking; travel; the arts. Address: (b.) 167 Renfrew Street, Glasgow G3 6RQ; T.-0141-353 4500.

Reid, William James, ACII, FBIBA. Chairman, Hubert Mitchell (Insurance Brokers) Ltd.; Hon. Vice-President, Children 1st; b. 18.9.32, Edinburgh; m., Patricia; 2 s. Educ. George Heriot's School. Director, Collins Halden & Co. Ltd., 1960-68, Joint Managing Director, 1968-72, Chairman and Chief Executive, 1972-78; Director, Halden McQuaker & Co. Ltd., Glasgow, 1964-73; Director, Collins Halden & Burnett Ltd., Aberdeen, 1962-74; Director, Hogg Robinson Ltd., London, 1978-84; Chief Executive, Hogg Robinson (Scotland) Ltd., 1978-84; Chairman and Chief Executive: Collins Halden (Scotland) Ltd., 1984-90, Heath Collins Halden (Scotland) Ltd., 1990-92, C.E. Heath (Scotland)

Ltd., 1990-92; Chairman: City Business Venue (Scotland) Ltd., 1992-98, Reid Enterprise Ltd., 1992-99, Nickleby (Scotland) Ltd., 1995-98; President, Insurance Society of Edinburgh, 1978-79; Chairman, Corporation of Insurance Brokers Scotland, 1969-70; Member, National Council, Corporation of Insurance Brokers, 1968-71; Freeman of the City of London; Commander, Order of St. Lazarus. Address: (h.) 33/10 Murrayfield Road, Edinburgh EH12 6EP; T.-0131-337 1220.

Reid, Sir William Kennedy, KCB, MA, LLD (Aberdeen and Reading), FRCPEd, FRSE. Chairman, Mental Welfare Commission for Scotland, 1997-2000; Chairman, Advisory Committee on Distinction Awards, 1997-2000; Chairman of Council, St. George's School for Girls, b. 15.2.31, Aberdeen; m., Ann Campbell; 2 s.; 1 d. Educ. Robert Gordon's College; George Watson's College; Edinburgh University; Trinity College, Cambridge. Civil Servant, 1956-89, Department of Education and Science, Cabinet Office, Scottish Office; Member, Council on Tribunals and Its Scottish Committee, 1990-96; Member, Commission for Local Administration in England, 1990-96; Member, Commission for Local Administration in Wales, 1990-96. A Director, International Ombudsman Institute, 1992-96; Parliamentary Commissioner for Administration (Ombudsman), 1990-97; Health Service Commissioner for England, Scotland, Wales, 1990-97; Queen Elizabeth the Queen Mother Fellow, Nuffield Trust, 1998; Hon. D. Litt (Napier), 1998. Recreations: verse; hill-walking. Address: (h.) 11 Inverleith Terrace, Edinburgh.

Reiter, Nicholas Keith, BSc (Hons) (Econ), DipChem. Director, Deer Commission for Scotland, since 1999; m. 10.12.52, London; m., Cindie Katrina Dennong; 1 s.; 1 d. Educ. Lycee Français de Londres; London School of Economics. Department of the Environment, 1976-87; Head of Policy, Westminster City Council, 1987-89; Director, Environmental Services, Ross and Cromarty District Council, 1989-96; Head of Policy, The Highland Council, 1996-98; Chief Executive, Shetland Islands Council, 1998-99; Treasurer Lochcarron School Board. Recreations: hill walking; sea kayak; sailing; cycling; Open University. Address: (b.) Knowsley, 82 Fairfield Road, Inverness, IV3 5LH; T.-01463 231751; e-mail: Nick.Reiter@scotland.gsi.gov.uk

Reith, David Stewart, LLB, NP, WS. Partner, Lindsays WS, Solicitors, Edinburgh, since 1976; b. 15.4.51, Edinburgh; m., Elizabeth Julia Hawkins; 1 s.; 1 d. Educ. Edinburgh Academy; Fettes College; Aberdeen University. Director: Scottish Historic Buildings Trust, Cockburn Conservation Trust; Secretary: Scottish Sculpture Trust, Ponton House Trust, Cockburn Conservation Trust; Clerk, Incorporation of Cordiners; Honorary Solicitor, Architectural Heritage Society of Scotland and Fet-Lor Youth Centre. Recreations: gardening; curling; wine. Address: (h.) Chesters House, Haddington, East Lothian EH41 4LJ.

Reith, Sheriff Fiona Lennox, LLB, QC, WS, FSA Scot. Sheriff of Glasgow and Strathkelvin, since 2000; b. 17.7.55, Ipswich. Educ. Perth Academy; Aberdeen University. Solicitor, Edinburgh, 1979-82; admitted to W.S. Society, 1982; devilled, 1982-83; admitted to Faculty of Advocates, 1983; Standing Junior Counsel in Scotland to Home Office, 1989-92; Advocate-Depute, 1992-95; Standing Junior Counsel, Scottish Office Environment Department, 1995-96; QC, 1996; Sheriff of Tayside, Central and Fife, at Perth, 1999-2000. Member, Scottish Legal Aid Board Civil Legal Aid Sub-Committee and Supreme Court Reporter, 1989-92; Member, Sheriff Court Rules Council, 1989-93; External Examiner in Professional Conduct, Faculty of Advocates, since 2000. Recreations: walking; theatre; good food and wine; travel; sailing. Address: (b.)

Sheriff's Chambers, Sheriff Court of Glasgow and Strathkelvin, 1 Carlton Place, Glasgow G5 9DA; T.-0141-429 8888.

Reith, Dr William (Bill). Chairman, Royal College of General Practitioners (Scotland), since 2001; b. 17.8.50. Educ. North Berwick High School; Edinburgh University; m.; 2 d. Principal in general practice, Westburn Medical Group, Foresterhill Health Centre, Aberdeen, since 1978. Address: (b.) 25 Queen Street, Edinburgh, EH2 1JX; T.-0131-260 6800; e-mail: bill@reithw.freeserve.co.uk

Rennie, Alistair Gillies, LLB. Hon. RICS, FRSA. Deputy Keeper, Registers of Scotland, Executive Agency; b. 1.2.44, Edinburgh; m., Eleanor Sutherland; 2 d. Educ. Trinity Academy, Edinburgh; Edinburgh University. Director, East of Scotland Society for Welfare and Teaching of the Blind; Member, Deacon's Court, Royal and Ancient Burgh of Linlithgow. Recreations: reading; walking; swimming. Address: (b.) Meadowbank House, 153 London Road, Edinburgh; T.-0131-659 6111.

Rennie, Archibald Louden, CB, LLD, FDSRCS(Eng); b. 4.6.24, Guardbridge, Fife; m., Kathleen Harkess; 4 s. Educ. Madras College, St. Andrews; St. Andrews University. Experimental Officer, Minesweeping Research Division, 1944-47; joined Department of Health for Scotland, 1947; Private Secretary to Secretary of State for Scotland, 1962-63; Assistant Secretary, Scottish Home and Health Department, 1963-69; Registrar General for Scotland, 1969-73; Under Secretary, Scottish Economic Planning Department, 1973-77; Secretary, Scottish Home and Health Department, 1977-84. Vice-Chairman, Advisory Committee on Distinction Awards, 1985-94; Chancellor's Assessor, St. Andrews University, 1985-89; Member, Scottish Records Advisory Council, 1985-93; Member, Council on Tribunals, and its Scottish Committee, 1987-88; Trustee, Lockerbie Air Disaster Appeal, 1988-91; Chairman, Disciplined Services Pay Review Committee, Hong Kong, 1988; Chairman, Blacket Association, 1971-73; Commodore, Elie and Earlsferry S.C., 1992-94; Chairman, Elie Harbour Trust, 1993-99. Recreations: Firth-watching; pottering; walking; reading. Address: (h.) Well Wynd House, South Street, Elie, Fife KY9 1DN; T.-01333 330741.

Rennie, Professor Michael John, BSc, MSc, PhD, FRSE. Symers Professor of Physiology, University of Dundee, since 1983; b. 28.7.46, Wallsend on Tyne; m., Anne Macgregor Gill; 1 s.; 2 d. Educ. Newcastle Royal Grammar School; Hull University; Manchester University; Glasgow University. MRC Travelling Fellow, Washington University Medical School, St. Louis, 1974-76; Lecturer and Wellcome Senior Lecturer, Department of Medicine, University College London, 1976-83. Editor: British Journal of Intensive Care, British Journal of Homecare; Consultant to pharmaceutical industry; medical and scientific writer. Publications: 200 scientific papers. Recreations: walking; cycling; reading; cooking; eating. Address: (b.) Division of Molecular Physiology, School of Life Sciences, University of Dundee, Dundee DD1 4HN; T.-01382 344572; e-mail: m.j.rennie@dundee.ac.uk

Rennie, Professor Robert, LLB, PhD, FRSA. Partner, Harper MacLeod Solicitors, Glasgow, since 2001; Professor of Conveyancing, Glasgow University, since 1993; b. 30.6.47, Glasgow; m., Catherine Mary McGregor; 1 s.; 3 d. Educ. Lenzie Academy; Glasgow University. Apprentice then Legal Assistant, Bishop Milne Boyd & Co., Solicitors, Glasgow; joined Ballantyne & Copland as Legal Assistant, 1971, Partner, 1972-2001; Past Convener, Law Society of Scotland Conveyancing Committee; Board Member, Capability Scotland; Member, Local Interview Committee, Prince's Scottish Youth Business Trust; Director, Taggarts

(Motor Holdings) Limited. Recreation: classical music. Address: (b.) Harper MacLeod, The Ca'd'oro, 45 Gordon Street, Glasgow G1 3PE.

Rennilson, John Douglas, MA, MSc, MRTPI, ARICS, MIMgt. Director of Planning and Development, The Highland Council, since 1998 (formerly Director of Planning); b. 12.2.47, Edinburgh; m., Susan M.; 1 s.; 1 d. Educ. George Watson's College, Edinburgh; Edinburgh University; University of Wales. Lanarkshire County Council, 1970-74, latterly as Senior Planning Officer; Suffolk County Council, 1974-84, latterly as Assistant County Planning Officer (Environment); County Planning Officer, North Yorkshire County Council, 1984-96. Member, Executive, County Planning Officers Society (Chairman, Committee 3, 1989-91, and from 1995); Chairman, Scottish Society of Directors of Planning, 2000-01; Director, Highland Birchwoods; Director, Moray Firth Partnership. Recreations: golf; Scottish country dancing; branch line railways. Address: (b.) Glenurquhart Road, Inverness IV3 5NX; e-mail: john.rennilson@highland.gov.uk

Renshaw, Professor Eric, BSc, ARCS, DipStats, MPhil, PhD, CStat, FRSE. Professor of Statistics, Strathclyde University, since 1991; b. 25.7.45, Preston; m., Anne Renshaw. Educ. Arnold School, Blackpool; Imperial College, London; Manchester University; Sussex University; Edinburgh University. Lecturer, then Senior Lecturer in Statistics, Edinburgh University, 1969-91. Publication: Modelling Biological Populations in Space and Time. Recreations: skiing; golf; hill-walking; photography. Address: (b.) Department of Statistics and Modelling Science, Livingstone Tower, Strathclyde University, 26 Richmond Street, Glasgow G1 1XH; T.-0141-548 3591.

Renton, Rev. Ian Paterson, OStJ, FSA Scot, JP. Minister, St. Colm's Parish Kirk, Dalry, Edinburgh, 1966-91; b. 22.3.26, Kirkcaldy; m., Ann Gordon Mutter Macpherson; 2 s.; 1 d. Educ. Sinclairtown and Viewforth Schools, Kirkcaldy; Newbattle Abbey College; Glasgow University; St. Mary's College, St. Andrews. Shipping Clerk, Robert Wemyss & Co., Kirkcaldy, 1941-44; Sergeant, 3rd Bn., Scots Guards, 1944-47; Ministry of Labour, Kirkcaldy, 1947-48; Newbattle Abbey College, 1948-50; Youth Clubs Organiser, Roxburghshire, 1950-53; divinity studies, 1953-58; Assistant Minister, North Kirk, Aberdeen, 1958-60; Minister, St. Mark's Church, Greenwich, London, 1960-66. Member, Edinburgh City Education Committee, 1970-76; Governor: Moray House College, 1971-79, Donaldson's School, Edinburgh, 1972-75, Newbattle Abbey College, 1973-76; Member, General Assembly Committee on Education, 1973-79; Joint Chairman, Scottish Joint Committee on Religious Education, 1974-79; Member, Lothian Region Education Committee, 1977-78; Member, Edinburgh Children's Panel, 1971-74; Executive Member, Broadcasting Council, Radio Forth, 1976-79; Member, DHSS Social Security Tribunal, 1978-84; Member, Church of Scotland Board of Education, 1983-85; Member, Lothian Health Board Committee on Medical Ethics, 1984-96; Moderator, Edinburgh Presbytery, 1989-90; Chaplain to Astley Ainslie Hospital, Edinburgh, 1971-98. Recreation: tai chi. Address: 1/98 Mount Grange, Strathearn Road, Edinburgh EH9 2QY.

Renton, Stuart, MBE, RSA. Architect; Senior Partner, Reiach and Hall, 1982-92; Royal Scottish Academician, since 1997 (Associate, 1983); Chairman, Board of Governors, Edinburgh College of Art, 1992-98; Visiting Professor, Department of Architecture, Strathclyde University, 1992-98; b. 15.9.29, Edinburgh; m., Ethnie Sloan; 1 s.; 1 d. Educ. Royal High School, Edinburgh; Edinburgh College of Art (Andrew Grant Scholar, 1949-52; Civic Medalist, 1952). Military Service, RAF and RAFVR; Partner, Alan Reiach and Partners, Architects, Edinburgh, 1959; Partner, Reiach and Hall, 1965; three RIBA awards, three Civic Trust awards and commendations among successes in other national award schemes. External Examiner, several universities; Assessor for architectural awards schemes; Member, Visiting Board Panel, RIBA Education Board, 1984-95; Governor, Edinburgh College of Art, 1985-98. Recreations: skiing; game fishing; Italian hill villages. Address: Grianan, Killichonan, Rannoch, Perthshire PH17 2QW; T.-01882 633247.

Renwick, Helen Rachael (Rae), Diploma in Food and Nutrition, Cert Ed. Head Teacher, Penilee Secondary School, since 2001; b. 5.9.51, Dunfermline; m., Thomas Renwick; 1 s.; 1 d. Educ. Beath High School; Queen Margaret College. Teacher: Balwearie High School, 1972-74; Craigroyston Community High School, 1974-75; Assistant Principal Teacher, Craigroyston Community High School, 1975-79; Principal Teacher, Wester Hailes Education Centre, 1979-80; Principal Teacher, Broughton High School, 1981-90; Assistant Head, Castlebrae High, 1990-95; Depute Head, Broxburn Academy, 1995-2000. Recreations: gardening; golf; travel. Address: (b.) 47 Gilmour Road, Edinburgh, EH16 5NS; T.-0131-667 0877; e-mail: rae_renwick@yahoo.com

Renwick, Professor John Peter, MA, PhD, DLitt, FRHistS, Officier des Palmes Academiques. John Orr Professor of French, Edinburgh University, since 1980; Director, Centre de Recherches Francophones Belges, since 1995; b. 25.5.39, Gillingham; m., Claudette Gorse; 1 s.; 1 d. Educ. Gillingham Grammar School; St. Bartholomew's Grammar School, Newbury; St. Catherine's College, Oxford; Sorbonne; British Institute in Paris (Leverhulme Research Scholar). Assistant Lecturer, then Lecturer, Glasgow University, 1964-66; Fellow, Churchill College, Cambridge, 1966-72; Maitre de Conferences Associe, Departement de Francais, Universite de Clermont-Ferrand, 1970-71, 1972-74; Professor of French, New University of Ulster, 1974-80 (Pro-Vice-Chancellor, 1978-80); Member, Editorial Committee, The Complete Works of Voltaire; Member, Executive Committee, Voltaire Foundation; Médaille de la Ville de Bort. Publications: La destinee posthume de Jean-Francois Marmontel, 1972; Marmontel, Memoires, 1972; Marmontel, Voltaire and the Belisaire affair, 1974; Marmontel, Correspondence, 1974; Catalogue de la bibliotheque de Jean-Baptiste Massillon, 1977; Voltaire et Morangies, ou les Lumieres l'ont echappe belle, 1982; Chamfort devant La Posterite, 1986; Catalogue de la Bibliotheque du Comte D'Espinchal, 1988; Language and Rhetoric of the French Revolution, 1990; Voltaire, La Guerre Civile de Genève, 1990; Catalogue de la Bibliotheque du College de L'Oratoire de Riom 1619-1792, 1997; Voltaire, Brutus, 1998; Voltaire, Les Guèbres, 1999; Voltaire, Traité sur la Tolérance, 1999 and 2000; L'Invitation au Voyage (Studies in Honour of Peter France), 2000; Jean-Francois Marmontel (1723-1799): Dix études, 2000. Address: (b.) 60 George Square, Edinburgh EH8 9JU.

Reoch, Torquil, MA. Editor, News Operations, BBC Scotland, since 1997; Producer, Newsnight Scotland, since 1999; b. 17.6.54, Glasgow; m., Christine; 1 s.; 2 d. Educ. George Watson's College, Edinburgh; Edinburgh University; Glasgow University. News Trainee, BBC London, 1979; Reporter, BBC Radio Scotland, 1980; Scotland Correspondent, TV-am, 1983; News Producer, BBC Scotland, 1985; Producer, European Business Channel, Zurich, 1989; Editor, Good Morning Scotland, 1991. Recreations: family; travel; dog. Address: (b.) BBC Scotland, Queen Margaret Drive, Glasgow G12 8DG; T.-0141-338 2446.

Rettie, James Philip, CBE, TD. Farmer; Partner, Rettie Farming Co.; Director, Rettie & Co.; Director, Edinburgh and Glasgow Investment Co.; Trustee, Scottish Civic Trust, since 1982; b. 7.12.26, Dundee; m., 1, Helen Grant; 2, Diana Harvey; 2 s.; 1 d. Educ. Trinity College, Glenalmond.

Royal Engineers, 1945-48. Chairman, Sea Fish Industry Authority, 1981-87; Chairman, William Low & Co. PLC, 1980-85. Hon. Colonel, 117 and 277 FDSQNS RE (V), 1983-89. Recreations: shooting; gardening; walking. Address: (h.) Hill House, Ballindean, Inchture, Perthshire PH14 9QS; T.-01828 686337.

Reynolds, Professor Siân, BA, MA, PhD. Professor of French, Stirling University, since 1990; Translator; b. 28.7.40, Cardiff; m., Peter France; 3 d. Educ. Howell's School, Llandaff; St. Anne's College, Oxford. Lecturer and Senior Lecturer, Sussex University, 1974-89; Lecturer, Edinburgh University, 1989-90; President, UK Association for the Study of Modern and Contemporary France, 1993-99. Publications: Women, State and Revolution (Editor); Britannica's Typesetters; France Between the Wars, gender and politics; Contemporary French Cultural Studies (Joint Editor), 2000; translations include F. Braudel, The Mediterranean. Address: (b.) Stirling University, Stirling FK9 4LA; T.-01786 467530.

Rhodes, Joseph, MA. Rector, Dunoon Grammar School, since 1981; b. 9.12.45, Irvine; m., Ann Robertson; 3 s.; 3 d. Educ. Ayr Academy; Glasgow University. Teacher, History/Modern Studies, Kilmarnock Academy, 1969-71; Principal Teacher, History, Auchenharvie Academy, 1971-74; Assistant Rector, Garnock Academy, 1974 -77; Depute Rector, Oban High School, 1977-81. Address; (b.) Dunoon Grammar School, Dunoon, Argyll; T.-01369 705010.

Riach, Alan, MA (Cantab), PhD. Poet; Reader and Head, Department of Scottish Literature, University of Glasgow, since 2001; b. 1.8.57, Airdrie; m., Rae; 2 s. Educ. Gravesend School for Boys, Gravesend, Kent; Churchill College, University of Cambridge. Freelance writing and teaching, Scotland, 1985-86; Post-Doctoral Research Fellow, Lecturer, Senior Lecturer, Associate Professor of English, University of Waikato, Hamilton, New Zealand, 1986-2000; Pro-Dean, Faculty of Arts and Social Sciences, University of Waikato, Hamilton, New Zealand, 2000. Over 30 appearances on radio and television in New Zealand, Australia and Scotland. Publications: Hugh MacDiarmid's Epic Poetry, 1991; The Poetry of Hugh MacDiarmid, 1999; Hugh MacDiarmid: The Collected Works (General Editor), since 1992 (12 volumes published to 1999); The Radical Imagination: Lectures and Talks by Wilson Harris (Co-Editor); contributions to over 20 books and numerous contributions to journals; books of poetry: For What It Is (Co-Author), 1988; This Folding Map (Poems 1978-1988), 1990; An Open Return, 1991; First and Last Songs, 1995; From the Vision of Hell: An Extract of Dante, 1998, Clearances, 2001; contributor to other books of poetry. Address: (b.) Department of Scottish Literature, University of Glasgow, 6 University Gardens, Glasgow G12 8QH; T.-0141-330 6144; e-mail: A.Riach@scotlit.arts.gla.ac.uk

Rice, Professor C. Duncan, MA, PhD, FRSE, FRHistS, FRSA. Principal and Vice-Chancellor, Aberdeen University, since 1996; b. 20.10.42, Aberdeen; m., Susan Ilene; 2 s.; 1 d. Educ. Aberdeen University; Edinburgh University. Lecturer, Aberdeen University, 1966-69; Assistant Professor of History, then Associate Professor of History, Yale University, New Haven, 1970-79; Professor of History, Hamilton College, Clinton, New York, 1979-85; Professor of History, Dean of Faculty of Arts and Sciences, New York University, 1985-94 (Vice-Chancellor, 1991-96). Board Member: Scottish Opera/Ballet, National Trust for Scotland, UCEA, Socrates-UK Erasmus Council, BT Scotland, Scottish Enterprise Grampian, Rowett Research Institute. Publications: The Rise and Fall of Black Slavery; The Scots Abolitionists 1831-1961; various articles and reviews. Recreations: hill-waking; cycling. Address: (b.) Aberdeen University, King's College, Aberdeen; T.-01224 272134.

Richards, Professor Bryan Edward, BSc (Eng), DIC, PhD, CEng, FRAeSoc, AFAIAA. Mechan Professor of Aerospace Engineering, Glasgow University, since 1980; b. 30.6.38, Hornchurch; m., Margaret Owen; 2 s.; 2 d. Educ. Palmer's School, Grays; Queen Mary College, London University. Aerodynamicist, Bristol Aeroplane Company, Filton, 1960-62; Research Assistant, Imperial College, London University, 1962-66; Assistant Professor, Associate Professor, Professor, Von Karman Institute, Belgium, 1967-79; Head, Department of Aerospace Engineering, Glasgow University, 1980-90; Dean of Engineering, 1984-87. Publications: 110 articles. Recreations: sailing; hill-walking. Address: (h.) Ravenswood, 32 Suffolk Street, Helensburgh G84 9PA; T.-01436 672112.

Richards, John Deacon, CBE, AADip, DUniv, RSA, RIBA, PPRIAS. Architect; Principal, John Richards Associates, Architects, since 1986; b. 7.5.31, Shanghai; m., Margaret Brown; 1 s.; 3 d. Educ. Cranleigh School, Surrey; Architectural Association School of Architecture, London. Partner, Robert Matthew, Johnson-Marshall & Partners, 1964-86 (Chairman, Edinburgh practice, 1977-86); Member, Royal Fine Art Commission for Scotland, 1975-89; Agrement Board, 1980-83; Member, Williams Committee on National Museums and Galleries, 1981; Gold Medallist, RSA, 1972; Past President, Royal Incorporation of Architects in Scotland, 1983-85; Trustee, National Galleries of Scotland, 1986-90; Chairman, Scottish Committee, Housing Corporation, 1983-89; Board Member, Scottish Homes, 1988-93, Deputy Chairman, 1989-93; Housing Association Ombudsman for Scotland, 1993-2000. Recreations: gardening; fishing. Address: (h.) Lady's Field, Whitekirk, East Lothian; T.-01620 870206.

Richards, Professor Randolph Harvey, MA, VetMB, PhD, MRCVS, FRSM, FIBiol, ARAgS. Director, Institute of Aquaculture, University of Stirling, since 1996; Roberts Morris Bray Professor of Aquatic Veterinary Studies, since 1991; Veterinary Adviser, Scottish Quality Salmon, since 1999 (Veterinary Adviser, Scottish Salmon Growers' Association, 1986-99); b. 4.3.48, London; m., Jennifer Halley; 1 d. Educ. Grove Park Grammar School, Wrexham; Jesus College, Cambridge University; University of Stirling. University of Stirling: Deputy Director, Unit of Aquatic Pathobiology, 1976-79, Deputy Director, Institute of Aquaculture, 1979-96. Member, Veterinary Products Committee, Medicines Commission, 1992-2000. Publications: numerous papers on fish pathology in learned journals. Recreations: fine wine and food; shooting. Address: University of Stirling, Stirling FK9 4LA; T.-01786 467870; e-mail: r.h.richards@stir.ac.uk

Richardson, Professor John Stuart, MA, DPhil, FRSE. Professor of Classics, Edinburgh University, since 1987 (Dean, Faculty of Arts, and Provost, Faculty Group of Arts, Divinity and Music, 1992-97); Vice-President, Society for the Promotion of Roman Studies, since 2001, President, 1998-2001; b. 4.2.46, Ilkley; m., Patricia Helen Robotham; 2 s. Educ. Berkhamsted School; Trinity College, Oxford. Lecturer in Ancient History, Exeter College, Oxford, 1969-72, St. Andrews University, 1972-87; Priest, Scottish Episcopal Church, since 1980; Anglican Chaplain, St. Andrews University, 1980-87; Team Priest, St. Columba's, Edinburgh, since 1987; Honorary Canon, St. Mary's Cathedral, Edinburgh, since 2000. Publications: Roman Provincial Administration, 1976; Hispaniae, 1986; The Romans in Spain, 1996; Appian: The Wars of the Romans in Iberia, 2000; papers on ancient history. Recreation: choral singing. Address: (h.) 29 Merchiston Avenue, Edinburgh EH10 4PH; T.-0131-228 3094.

Richardson, Professor Neville Vincent, BA, DPhil, MRSC, MInstP, FRSE. Professor of Physical Chemistry, University of St. Andrews, since 1998; b. 25.2.50, Tadcaster; m., Jennifer Margaret; 2 step-s.; 2 d. Educ. Oglethorpe Grammar School, Tadcaster; Jesus College

University of Oxford. SRC Research Fellow, Chemistry Department, University of Birmingham, 1974-77; Research Assistant, Fritz-Haber Institute, Max Planck Society, 1974-77; University of Liverpool: Lecturer, Chemistry Department, 1979, Senior Lecturer, 1984, Professor, 1988, Director, Surface Science, IRC. Marlow Medal, Royal Society of Chemistry, 1984; British Vacuum Society Medal, 1996. Recreations: hillwalking; rock and ice climbing; skiing; squash. Address: School of Chemistry, North Haugh, University of St. Andrews, St. Andrews, Fife KY16 9ST; T.-01334 462395; e-mail: nvr@st-and.ac.uk

Riches, Christopher Gabriel, BSc. Editorial Director, Reference, HarperCollins Publishers, since 1994; b. 25.3.52, Oxford; m., Catherine Mary Gaunt; 3 s. Educ. Marlborough College; Manchester University. Copy Editor, Penguin Books, 1973-74; Oxford University Press: Science Education Editor, 1974-76, Publishing Manager, Hong Kong, 1976-81, Reference Editor, 1981-88; Publishing Manager, Collins Reference, Glasgow, 1989-94. Council Member, Scottish Publishers' Association, since 1995; Hon. Secretary, St. Mary's Episcopal Church, Aberfoyle, 1994-98; Chair, School Board, Killearn Primary School, 1997-99. Recreations: book collecting; gardening; walking. Address: (h.) Achadhu House, Main Street, Killearn G63 9RJ; T.-01360 550544.

Riches, Professor John Kenneth, MA. Professor of Divinity and Biblical Criticism, Glasgow University; b. 30.4.39, London; m., Renate Emmy Thermann; 2 s.; 1 d. Educ. Cranleigh School; Corpus Christi College, Cambridge. Assistant Curate, St. Edmund's, Costessey, Norfolk, 1965-68; Chaplain, Fellow and Director of Studies in Theology, Sidney Sussex College, Cambridge, 1968-72; Lecturer, Department of New Testament Language and Literature, Glasgow University, 1973-86; Senior Lecturer, Department of Biblical Studies, Glasgow University, 1986-91; Chairman, Balmore Trust, since 1980; Convener, Doctrine Committee, Scottish Episcopal Church, 1991-96; Convener, Provincial Overseas Committee, since 1999. Publications: Jesus and the Transformation of Judaism; The World of Jesus; A Century of New Testament Study; Matthew; The Bible: A Very Short Introduction; Conflicting Mythologies. Recreations: hill-walking; third world trading. Address: (h.) Viewfield, Balmore, Torrance, Glasgow G64 4AE; T.-01360 620254.

Richmond, Professor John, CBE, MD, FRCPE, FRCP, FRSE. President, Royal College of Physicians of Edinburgh, 1988-91; Emeritus Professor of Medicine, Sheffield University, since 1989; b. 30.5.26, Doncaster; m., Jenny Nicol; 2 s.; 1 d. Educ. Edinburgh University. RAMC, Ethiopia, Kenya, 1st Bn., KAR, N. Rhodesia, 1949-50; rural general practice, Galloway, 1950-52; Lecturer, Senior Lecturer, Reader in Medicine, Edinburgh University, 1954-73; Research Fellow, Memorial Sloan Kettering Cancer Center, New York, 1958-59; Professor of Medicine, Sheffield University, 1973-89 (Dean of Medicine, 1985-88). Senior Censor and Senior Vice-President, Royal College of Physicians of London, 1984-85; Chairman, MRCP (UK) Examining Board, 1984-89; Board of Advisors in Medicine, London University, 1984-93; External Advisor, Chinese University of Hong Kong, 1982-91; Department of Health Clinical Standards Advisory Group, 1991-94; Scottish Advisory Board, British Council, 1991-97; Member, Scottish Committee, Marie Curie Cancer Care, 1992-2001; FRCPSG, FRCPI, FACP(Hon), FFPM(Hon), FRCSE, FFPHM(Hon), FCP(SA)(Hon), FRACP(Hon). Address: (h.) 15 Church Hill, Edinburgh, EH10 4BG.

Richmond, John Kennedy, JP, DL. Chairman, Glasgow Airport Consultative Committee, since 1979; b. 23.4.37, Glasgow; m., Elizabeth Margaret; 1 s.; 1 d. Educ. King's Park Secondary School. Conservative Member, Glasgow Corporation, 1963-75; Member, Glasgow District Council,

1975-84; Deputy Lord Provost, 1977-80; Conservative Group Leader, 1975-77. Recreations: tennis; music; travel. Address: (h.) 84 Merrylee Road, Newlands, Glasgow G43 2QZ; T.-0141-637 7705; e-mail: elmari@ntlworld.com

Rickman, David Edwin, BCom (Hons). Rules Secretary, Royal and Ancient Golf Club of St. Andrews, since 1996; b. 9.10.64, St. Andrews; m., Jennifer Mary Cameron; 2 d. Educ. Madras College, St. Andrews; Edinburgh University. Joined R. & A. staff, 1987; appointed Assistant Secretary (Rules), 1990. Recreations: sport, especially golf. Address: (b.) c/o Royal and Ancient Golf Club, St. Andrews, Fife KY16 9JD; T.-01334 460000.

Rickman, Professor Geoffrey Edwin, MA, DPhil (Oxon), FBA, FRSE, FSA. Professor of Roman History, St. Andrews University, 1981-97; Master of the United College of St. Salvator and St. Leonard, 1992-96; Pro Vice Chancellor, 1996-97; b. 9.10.32, Cherat, India; m., Ann Rosemary Wilson; 1 s.; 1 d. Educ. Peter Symonds' School, Winchester; Brasenose College, Oxford. Junior Research Fellow, Queen's College, Oxford; St. Andrews University: Lecturer in Ancient History, Senior Lecturer, Professor; Visiting Fellow, Brasenose College, Oxford; Member, Institute for Advanced Study, Princeton, 1998; Council Member, Society for Promotion of Roman Studies; British School at Rome: Member, Faculty of Archaeology, History and Letters, (Chairman, 1984-87), Chairman, Council, since 1997. Publications: Roman Granaries and Storebuildings, 1971; The Corn Supply of Ancient Rome, 1980. Recreations: opera; swimming. Address: (h.) 56 Hepburn Gardens, St. Andrews, Fife; T.-St. Andrews 472063.

Riddle, Gordon Stewart, MA. Principal and Chief Ranger, Culzean Country Park, since 1976 (Property Manager, Culzean Castle and Country Park, since 2001); b. 2.10.47, Kelso; m., Rosemary Robb; 1 s.; 1 d. Educ. Kelso High School; Edinburgh University; Moray House College of Education. Biology and History Teacher, Lasswade High School, 1970-71; National Ranger Training Course, 1971-72; Ranger and Depute Principal, Culzean Country Park, 1972-75; National Park Service (USA) Training Course, 1978; Winston Churchill Travelling Fellowship, USA, 1981. Member, Royal Society for the Protection of Birds, Scottish Committee, 1995-99; Chairman, South Strathclyde Raptor Study Group, since 1994. Publications: The Kestrel; Seasons with the Kestrel. Recreations: sport; gardening; birds of prey; photography; hill-walking; music; writing. Address: (h.) Swinston, Culzean Country Park, by Maybole, Ayrshire; T.-01655 760 662.

Riddle, Philip, BA, MA, MSc. Chief Executive, VisitScotland, since 2001; b. 6.5.52, Dunfermline; m., Catherine; 3 s. Educ. Dunfermline High School; Trinity Hall, University of Cambridge; University of Edinburgh. Head, Oil and Gas Trading, Brunei Shell Petroleum, Brunei, 1982-85; Business Development Manager, Africa, Shell International Gas, London, 1985-88; Assistant Area Co-ordinator, South America, Shell International, London, 1988-91; Managing Director, Shell Namibia, Windhoek, 1991-95; Regional Development Director, Shell South Africa, Capetown, 1994-95; Vice President, Shell LPG Europe, Paris, 1995-99; Chairman, Maximedia, Leith, and organisational development consultant for various companies, 2000. Aftercare Counsellor, Prince's Scotland Youth Business Trust; Consul General for the Netherlands in Namibia, 1992-95. Recreations: skiing; diving; walking; making sense of Scotland. Address: (b.) VisitScotland, 23 Ravelston Terrace, Edinburgh EH4 3TP; T.-0131-332 2433; e-mail: philip.riddle@visitscotland.com

Riddoch, Lesley, BA (Hons). Presenter, Lesley Riddoch Programme, BBC Radio Scotland, since 1999; Associate Editor, Sunday Herald, since 1999; b. 21.2.60, Wolverhampton; m., George Gunn (divorced). Educ. High School of Glasgow; Wadham College, Oxford; University College, Cardiff. Sabbatical President, Oxford University Students Union, 1980; Reporter, BBC Radio Scotland, 1985-88; Co-Presenter, Head On, 1988-90; Presenter, Speaking Out, 1990-94; The Scotsman: Assistant Editor, 1994-96, Associate Editor, 1996-97; Speaker, The People's Parliament, Channel 4, 1994-98; Presenter, You and Yours, BBC Radio 4, 1996-98; Presenter, Midnight Hour, BBC2, 1996-98; Presenter, Channel 4's Powerhouse, 1997-98; Founder and Director, Harpies and Quines (feminist magazine). Trustee, Isle of Eigg Trust, since 1993; Director, Traverse Theatre. Norman McEwen Award, 1992; Cosmopolitan Woman of the Year (Communications), 1992; Plain English Award, 1993. Recreations: playing pool; walking. Address: (h.) Crannach Ha', Fowlis Wester, Crieff PH7 3NL.

Riemersma, Rudolph Arend, BSc, MSc, PhD, FRCPE. Assistant Director, Cardiovascular Research Unit, Edinburgh University, since 1975 (British Heart Foundation Senior Lecturer in Cardiac Biochemistry, since 1979); Professor in Medical Physiology, University of Tromso, Norway, since 1994; b. 9.5.43, Hengelo, Netherlands; m., Eva J. Nieuwenhuis; 1 s.; 1 d. Educ. Charlois Lyceum, Rotterdam; Leyden University; Edinburgh University. Biochemist, Department of Cardiology, Academic Hospital, Utrecht; postgraduate research, Royal Postgraduate Medical School, Hammersmith Hospital, London; Research Fellow, Edinburgh University, 1973. Former Vice-President, European Society of Clinical Investigation. Recreations: orienteering; skiing; hill-walking; botany. Address: (b.) Cardiovascular Research Unit, Hugh Robson Building, George Square, Edinburgh; T.-0131-650 3699.

Rifkind, Rt. Hon Sir Malcolm Leslie, KCMG, QC, LLB, MSc. Secretary of State for Foreign and Commonwealth Affairs, 1995-97; Secretary of State for Defence, 1992-95; Secretary of State for Transport, 1990-92; Secretary of State for Scotland, 1986-90; MP (Conservative), Edinburgh Pentlands, 1974-97; b. 21.6.46, Edinburgh; m., Edith Amalia Steinberg; 1 s.; 1 d. Educ. George Watson's College, Edinburgh; Edinburgh University. Assistant Lecturer, University of Rhodesia, 1967-68; called to Scottish Bar, 1970; Opposition Front-Bench Spokesman on Scottish Affairs, 1975-76; Member, Select Committee on European Secondary Legislation, 1975-76; Chairman, Scottish Conservatives' Devolution Committee, 1976; Joint Secretary, Conservative Parliamentary Foreign and Commonwealth Affairs Committee, 1977-79; Member, Select Committee on Overseas Development, 1978-79; Parliamentary Under-Secretary of State, Scottish Office, 1979-82; Parliamentary Under-Secretary of State, Foreign and Commonwealth Office, 1982-83; Minister of State, Foreign and Commonwealth Office, 1983-86; Member, Queen's Bodyguard for Scotland (Royal Company of Archers); Hon. Col., 162 Movement Control Regiment, Royal Logistic Corps.

Rigg, David, MA (Hons). University Registrar and Depute Secretary, Paisley University, since 1987; b. 15.3.48, Insch; m., Margaret Taylor Mechie; 1 s.; 1 d. Educ. Daniel Stewart's College, Edinburgh; West Calder High School; Dundee University. British Gas, 1971-73; Administrative Assistant, Strathclyde University, 1973-79; Assistant Secretary, Paisley College, 1979-87. Recreations: cutting grass; reading; theatre; supporting Hibernian Football Club. Address: (b.) Paisley University, High Street, Paisley PA1 2BE; T.-0141-848 3677.

Rigg, John Alexander, BA, MA, PhD (Cantab). Senior Economic Adviser, Scottish Executive, (formerly Scottish Office Education and Industry Department), since 1995; b. 16.11.54, Leeds; m., Angela Mary English; 1 s.; 1 d. Educ. Roundhay School, Leeds; Trinity College, Cambridge. Research Assistant, Queen Mary College, London University, 1981-82; Senior Economic Analyst, Henley Centre for Forecasting, London, 1982-85; Director, Henley

Robb, Kenneth Richard, LLB (Hons), NP. Solicitor; b. 3.9.54, Larbert; m., Susan Margaret Ringrose; 1 d. Educ. Falkirk High School; Edinburgh University. Private legal practice, 1976-2000; Member, Council, Law Society of Scotland, 1987-97; Member, Board, Scottish Child Law Centre, 1991-98; part-time Chairman: Child Support Appeal Tribunals, Disability Appeal Tribunals; Member, Scottish Solicitors Discipline Tribunal; Member, GMC PCC. Recreations: history; hill-walking; gardening. Address: (h.) 9 Brynaston Drive, Dollar, Clackmannanshire; T.-01259 743430.

Robb, Rev. Nigel James, MA, BD, ThM, MTh. Director of Educational Services, Board of Ministry, Church of Scotland, since 1998; b. 28.7.53, Glasgow. Educ. Ardrossan Academy; Glasgow University; Princeton Theological Seminary. Associate Chaplain, Edinburgh University, 1980-83; Lecturer in Pastoral Theology, Uniting Church Theological Hall, Perth, W. Australia, 1983-89; Lecturer in Christian Ethics and Practical Theology, St Mary's College, St Andrews University, 1990-97. Publications: The Preaching Triangle; A Time to Die and a Time to Live; Sermons at St Salvator's; Let All God's People Say Amen. Recreations: swimming; music; theatre. Address: (b.) 121 George Street, Edinburgh EH2 4YN; T.-0131-225 5722.

Roberton, Esther A., BA. Chair, NHS Fife; Chair, Scottish Further Education Funding Council; Non-Executive Director, Scottish Council for Development and Industry; b. 24.6.56, Kirkcaldy; m., William J. Roberton; 2 s. Educ. Buckhaven High School; Edinburgh University. Played a leading role in the campaign to secure and shape Scotland's Parliament, 1994-99. Recreations: politics; books; talking for Scotland. Address: (h.) 15 Pinewood Drive, Dalgety Bay KY11 9SP; T.-01383 824857.

Roberts, Professor Bernard, BSc, PhD, FRAS, FRSE. Professor of Solar Magnetohydrodynamics, since 1994; b. 19.2.46, Cork; m., Margaret Patricia Cartlidge; 4 s. Educ. Bletchley Secondary Modern and Bletchley Grammar Schools; Hull University; Sheffield University. Lecturer in Applied Mathematics, St. Andrews University, 1971-87, Reader, 1987-94. Chairman, UK Solar Physics Community, 1992-98; Member, Theory and Research Assessment Panel, UK Particle Physics and Astronomy Research Council, 1998-2001, Member, Solar System Science Advisory Panel, 2001-03. Recreations: hill-walking; five-a-side football; squash. Address: (b.) Mathematical Institute, St. Andrews University, St. Andrews KY16 9SS; T.-01334 463716.

Roberts, Jacqueline Claire, BA (Hons), MSc, MA (Hons), CQSW. Executive, Scottish Commission for the Regulation of Care; b. 8.1.49, Market Harborough; m.; 2 children. Educ. Loughborough High School for Girls; St. Hilda's College, Oxford University; Oxford University Department of Applied Studies. Social Worker, Oxford and Lambeth, 1971-86; Lecturer in Social Work, University of Dundee, 1986-87; Project Head, Polepark Family Counselling Centre, Tayside Regional Council Social Work Department, and Course Director, Child Protection Training, Northern College, 1987-93; management posts, social work, Dundee, 1993-97; Director of Social Work, Dundee City Council, 1997-2001. Associate Editor, Child Abuse and Neglect. 1989 Fidelio Prize. Publications: Consequences of Child Abuse (Co-Author), 1982; many papers, reports and book chapters, especially on child abuse.

Roberts, James Graeme, MA, PhD, FRSA. Vice Principal (Teaching and Learning), Aberdeen University, since 1996; b. 7.11.42, Glasgow; m., Elizabeth Watson Milo Tucker; 2 s.; 2 d. Educ. Hutchesons' Boys' Grammar School, Glasgow; St. Andrews University; Aberdeen University. Aberdeen University: Assistant Lecturer in English, 1964, Lecturer in English, 1968, Senior Lecturer, 1985, Head, Department of English, 1993; Member, University Court,

1981-89, since 1995. Trustee, Aberdeen International Football Festival; Chair, Scottish Museums Council; Elder, Ferryhill Parish Church, Aberdeen. Recreations: walking; swimming; music. Address: (b.) Aberdeen University, University Office, King's College, Aberdeen AB24 3FX; T.-01224 272017.

Roberts, Rev. Maurice Jonathon, BA, BD. Minister, Free Church of Scotland, since 1974, and of Inverness Free Church of Scotland (Continuing), since 2000; Editor, The Banner of Truth, since 1988; b. 8.3.38, Timperley; m., Alexandra Macleod; 1 d. Educ. Lymm Grammar School; Durham University; London University; Free Church College, Edinburgh. Schoolteacher. Publications: The Thought of God; Sanctification and Glorification; In Deep Valley of Truth (Korean language); The Christian's High Calling. Recreations: reading; walking. Address: 3 Abertarff Road, Inverness IV2 3NW; T.-01463 220701.

Roberts, Professor Peter Ward, BA, MA, CertEd, MRTPI, FRSA. Professor of European Strategic Planning, Dundee University, since 1995; Chair, British Urban Regeneration Association – Best Practice Committee, since 1994; Chair, Town and Country Planning Association, since 1999; b. 17.7.47, Birkenhead; m., Josephine Blythe; 1 s. Educ. Rock Ferry High School, Birkenhead; Leicester University; Manchester University; Newcastle upon Tyne University. Demonstrator, Newcastle upon Tyne University, 1969-70; Lecturer, Flintshire College of Technology, 1970-71; Senior Lecturer, Department of Town and Country Planning, Liverpool John Moores University, 1971-77; Principal Lecturer/Deputy Head of Department, Department of Urban and Regional Planning, Coventry University, 1978-86; Senior Research Manager, ECOTEC Research and Consulting, Birmingham, 1987; Professor of Urban Planning, Leeds Metropolitan University, and Joint Director, Regional Research Observatory, 1988-94. Member, Scientific Committee on the Regions of Europe; Board Member, The Planning Exchange; Deputy Chair, Urban Mines Ltd. Publications include: Environmentally Sustainable Business; Europe: A Handbook for Local Authorities (Co-author); Energy Efficiency in Housing (Co-author); Mineral Resources in Regional and Strategic Planning (Co-author); Metropolitan Planning in Britain (Co-author); Environment, Planning and Land Use (Co-author); Urban Regeneration (Co-author); Integrating Environment and Economy (Co-author). Recreations: hill-walking; collecting and reading books; canal boating; restoring classic cars; listening to opera and classical music; watching cricket. Address: (b.) Geddes Centre for Planning Research, School of Town and Regional Planning, University of Dundee, Dundee DD1 4HN.

Robertson, Hon. Lord (Ian Macdonald Robertson), TD (1946), BA, LLB, QC. Senator of the College of Justice in Scotland, 1966-87; Chairman of Governors, Merchiston Castle School, 1971-96; b. 30.10.12, Edinburgh; m., Anna Love Glen; 1 s.; 2 d. Educ. Merchiston Castle School, Edinburgh; Balliol College, Oxford; Edinburgh University. Admitted Faculty of Advocates, 1939; served War of 1939-45, 8th Bn., The Royal Scots (The Royal Regiment) - commissioned 1939; Captain/Staff Officer, 44th Lowland Infantry Brigade (15th Scottish Division); Normandy and North West Europe, 1944-45; mentioned in Despatches; Advocate Depute, 1949-51; QC, 1954; Sheriff Principal of Ayr and Bute, 1961-66; Sheriff Principal of Perth and Angus, 1966; Chairman, Medical Appeals Tribunal, 1957-63; Chairman, Scottish Joint Council for Teachers Salaries, 1965-81; Chairman, Scottish Valuation Advisory Council, 1977-86; UK Representative on Central Council, International Association of Judges, 1974-87; General Council Assessor, Edinburgh University Court, 1967-81; Chairman, Edinburgh Centre of Rural Economy and Edinburgh Centre for Tropical Veterinary Medicine, 1967-86; Governor, Merchiston Castle School, 1954-96; Captain,

Honourable Company of Edinburgh Golfers at Muirfield, 1970-72. Recreation: golf. Address: (h.) 13 Moray Place, Edinburgh EH3 6DT; T.-0131-225 6637.

Robertson of Port Ellen, Rt. Hon. Lord (George Islay MacNeill Robertson), MA, PC, FRSA. Secretary-General, NATO, since 1999; b. 12.4.46, Port Ellen, Islay; m., Sandra Wallace; 2 s.; 1 d. Educ. Dunoon Grammar School; Dundee University. Tayside Study Economics Group, 1968-69; Scottish Organiser, General, Municipal, Boilermakers Union, 1969-78; Chairman, Scottish Labour Party, 1977-78; Member, Scottish Executive, Labour Party, 1973-79, 1993-97; MP, Hamilton, 1978-97, Hamilton South, 1997-99; PPS to Secretary of State for Social Services, 1979; Opposition Spokesman on Scottish Affairs, 1979-80, on Defence, 1980-81, on Foreign and Commonwealth Affairs, 1981-93, on Scottish Affairs, 1993-97; Principal Spokesman on Europe, 1984-93; Member, Shadow Cabinet, 1993-97; Shadow Scottish Secretary, 1993-97; Secretary of State for Defence, 1997-99. Member of Board, Scottish Development Agency, 1976-78, Scottish Tourist Board, 1974-76; Board of Governors, Scottish Police College, 1975-78; Vice Chairman, British Council, 1985-93; Vice-Chairman, Westminster Foundation for Democracy, 1992-93; President, Royal Institute of International Affairs, since 2001. Hon LLD (Dundee), 2000; Hon DSc (Cranfield), 2000; Hon LLD (Bradford), 2000; Hon Doct (Baku State University, Azerbaijan), 2001; Hon. Regt. Colonel, London Scottish Regiment, 2000. Recreations: family; photography. Address: (b.) House of Lords, London SW1A.

Robertson, Professor Alastair Harry Forbes, BS, MA, PhD, FRSE. Professor of Geology, Edinburgh University, since 1996; b. 6.12.49, Edinburgh; m., Gillian Mary Robertson; 1 s.; 1 d. Educ. Edinburgh Academy; Edinburgh University; Leicester University. Demonstrator, Cambridge University, 1974-76; Lecturer in Oceanography, Edinburgh University. 1977-85; Academic Visitor, Stanford University. USA, 1985- 86; Reader, Geology, Edinburgh University, 1986-96; Member and Chairman, various national and international committees. Publications: numerous scientific papers. Recreations: outdoor activities; mountain walking; travel; music. Address: (b.) Department of Geology and Geophysics, Edinburgh University, West Mains Road, Edinburgh, EH9 3JW; T.-0131-650 8546.

Robertson, Alistair John, BMedBiol (Hons), MB, ChB, FRCPath, MIAC, FRSA, FFCS. Clinical Group Director of Clinical Support Services, Tayside University Hospitals NHS Trust; Consultant Histopathologist, Tayside Health Board, since 1982; Honorary Senior Lecturer in Pathology, Dundee University, since 1982; b. 29.6.50, Aberdeen; m., Frances Elizabeth Smith. Educ. Aberdeen Grammar School; Aberdeen University. House Physician, Ninewells Hospital, Dundee, 1975; House Surgeon, Aberdeen Royal Infirmary, 1976; Senior House Officer in Pathology, Ninewells Hospital, 1976; Lecturer in Pathology, Ninewells Hospital, 1977; Consultant in Administrative Charge, Perth and Kinross Unit Laboratories, 1982; Clinical Director in Pathology, Dundee Teaching Hospitals NHS Trust, 1993. Recreations: golf; classical music; caravanning; philately; photography; theatre. Address: (b.) Pathology Department, Ninewells Hospital and Medical School, Dundee; T.- Dundee 660111.

Robertson, Andrew (Andy) John, BSc (Hons). Chief Agricultural Officer, Scottish Executive Environment and Rural Affairs Department, since 1998; b. 12.4.55, Bristol; m., Fiona; 2 s. Educ. Glenalmond; Edinburgh University. Inspector, DAFS, Ayr, 1978-81; Senior Livestock Inspector, DAFS, Aberdeen, 1981-84; Senior Agricultural Officer, DAFS, Aberdeen, 1984-88; Principal Agricultural Officer, SOAFD, Kirkwall, 1988-94; Assistant Chief Agricultural Officer, SOAEFD,

Edinburgh, 1994-98. Recreations: most sports, including rugby, motor-cycling and curling. Address: (b.) Pentland House, 47 Robbs Loan, Edinburgh EH14 1TY; T.-0131-244 6029; e-mail: andy.robertson@scotland.gsi.gov.uk

Robertson, Andrew Ogilvie, OBE, LLB. Partner, T.C. Young & Son, Solicitors and Notaries, since 1968; Secretary, Erskine Hospital, since 1976; Secretary, Princess Royal Trust for Carers, since 1990; Chairman, Scottish Housing Association Charitable Trust, since 1991; Director, Scottish Building Society, since 1994; Chairman, Greater Glasgow Primary Care NHS Trust, since 1999; Governor, Sedbergh School, since 2000; b. 30.6.43, Glasgow; m., Sheila Sturton; 2 s. Educ Glasgow Academy; Sedbergh School; Edinburgh University. Director, Merchants House of Glasgow, since 1978; Secretary, Clydeside Federation of Community Based Housing Associations, 1978-93; Secretary, The Briggait Company Ltd., 1982-88; Director, Glasgow Chamber of Commerce, 1982-93; Chairman, Post Office Users Council for Scotland, 1988-99; Chairman, Greater Glasgow Community and Mental Health Services NHS Trust, 1994-97; Chairman, Glasgow Royal Infirmary University NHS Trust, 1997-99. Recreations: climbing; swimming; sailing; fishing. Address: (b.) 30 George Square, Glasgow, G2 1LH; T.-0141-221 5562.

Robertson, Angus, MP. SNP MP, Moray, since 2001; b. 28.9.69. Educ. Broughton High School, Edinburgh; Aberdeen University. News Editor, Austrian Broadcasting Corporation, 1991; Reporter, BBC, 1991-99; communications consultant and journalist, since 1999. Address: (b.) House of Commons, London SW1A 0AA.

Robertson, Rev. Charles, JP, MA. Minister, Canongate Kirk, since 1978; Chaplain to The Queen, since 1991; b. 22.10.40, Glasgow; m., Alison Margaret Malloch; 1 s.; 2 d. Educ. Camphill School, Paisley; Edinburgh University. Assistant Minister, North Morningside Church, Edinburgh, 1964-65; Minister, Kiltearn, Ross and Cromarty, 1965-78. Secretary, Panel on Worship, General Assembly, 1982-95, Convener, since 1995; Church of Scotland Representative on Joint Liturgical Group, since 1984, and Chairman, 1994-2000; UK Representative, English Language Liturgical Consultation, 1996-99; Secretary, Committee to Revise the Church Hymnary, since 1995; Chaplain to Lord High Commissioner, 1990, 1991 and to Her Grace The Princess Royal, 1996; Chaplain to: High Constables and Guard of Honour, since 1993, Clan Donnachaidh Society, 1981-96, Elsie Inglis Memorial Maternity Hospital, 1982-89, New Club, since 1986, Moray House, 1986-98, University of Edinburgh at Moray House, since 1998, No. 2 (City of Edinburgh) Maritime HQ Unit RAAF, since 1987, Royal Scots Club, since 1998; President, Church Service Society, 1988-91 (Hon. President, since 1991); Chairman, Board, Queensberry House Hospital, 1989-96; Chairman, Queensberry House Trust, since 1996; Governor, St. Columba's Hospice, Edinburgh, since 1986; Lecturer in Church Praise, St. Colm's College, 1980-93; Member, Broadcasting Standards Council, 1988-91 and 1992-93; Member, Historic Buildings Council for Scotland, 1990-99; Trustee, Church Hymnary Trust, since 1987; Trustee, Edinburgh Old Town Trust, 1987-91; Trustee, Edinburgh Old Town Charitable Trust, since 1994; Member, Edinburgh World Heritage Trust, 1999-2000; Co-author, By Lamplight, 2000; edited Singing the Faith, 1990, and St Margaret Queen of Scotland and Her Chapel, 1994; Secretary of Committees which compiled Hymns for a Day, 1983, Songs of God's People, 1988, Worshipping Together, 1991, Clann ag Urnaigh, 1997, Common Ground, 1998. Recreations: books; music; history; Canongate. Address: Manse of Canongate, Edinburgh EH8 8BR; T.-0131-556 3515.

Robertson, Charles Cameron, MA, DipEd, CertEd. SQH. Rector, Kelso High School, since 1999; b. 24.11.50. Luss; m., Christine; 1 s.; 1 d. Educ. Keil School, Dumbarton; Dundee University. Teacher, History/Modern Studies, Oban High School, 1974 - 79; Principal Teacher, History, Kelso High School, 1979-88; Assistant Head Teacher, Curriculum/TVEI, Berwickshire High School, 1988-96; Depute Rector, Earlston High School, 1996-99. Publications: Nationalism in Germany and Italy (Co-Author); Changing Scotland and Britain, 1830-1930 (Co-Author). Recreations: rugby; walking; gardening. Address: (b.) Kelso High School, Bowmont Street, Kelso; T.-01573 224444; e-mail: crobertson@scotborders.gov.uk

Robertson, D. Bruce, MA. Director of Education, Highland Council, since 1998; b. 7.6.51, Ellon; m., Louise Robertson; 2 d. Educ. Inverurie Academy; Aberdeen University. Teacher/Principal Teacher/Depute Rector, Grampian Regional Council, 1974-91; Education Officer/Assistant Director, Education/Depute Director, Education, Grampian Regional Council, 1991-96; Head of Education, Aberdeenshire Council, 1996-98; Co-chair, Highland Drug and Alcohol Strategy Group; Member, National Child Health Support Group; COSLA Education Advisor; Member, National SEN Advisory Forum. Recreations: golf; hill-walking. Address: (b.) Glenurquhart Road, Inverness. IV3 5NX; T.-01463 702801.

Robertson, David Andrew, MA (Hons). Minister, St. Peter's Free Church, Dundee, since 1992; Chaplain, Dundee Football Club; b. 2.5.62, Berwick-upon-Tweed; m., Annabel; 1 s.; 2 d. Educ. Tain Royal Academy, Ross-shire; University of Edinburgh; Free Church College. Minister, Clyne Free Church, Brora, 1986-92; Minister, St. Peter's Free Church, Dundee, 1992-98. Associate Chaplain: University of Dundee, University of Abertay. Recreations: football; music; chess; politics. Address: (h.) 14 Shamrock Street, Dundee; T.-01382 861401; e-mail: darobertson@blueyonder.co.uk

Robertson, Donald Buchanan, QC, BL, FSA(Scot). Advocate; Member, Criminal Injuries Compensation Board, since 1986; Temporary Judge, Court of Session, since 1991; b. 29.3.32, Ardnadam, Argyll; m., 1, Louise Charlotte Linthorst Homan, 2, Daphne Jean Black Kincaid; 1 s.; 1 d. Educ. Dunoon Grammar School; Glasgow University. Solicitor, 1954; National Service, 1954-56; Advocate, 1960; Standing Junior to Registrar of Restrictive Practices, 1970-73; Member, Sheriff Court Rules Council, 1972-75; Member, Royal Commission on Legal Services in Scotland, 1976-80; Member, Legal Aid Central Committee, 1982-85; Chairman, VAT Tribunal, 1978-85; Honorary Sheriff, Lothian and Peebles, since 1982. Recreations: shooting; Scottish history; genealogy; numismatics. Address: (h.) 11 Grosvenor Crescent, Edinburgh EH12 5EL; T.-0131-337 5544; Cranshaws Castle, by Duns, Berwickshire TD11 3SJ; T.-01361 890268.

Robertson, Professor Edmund Frederick, BSc, MSc, PhD, FRSE. Professor of Mathematics, St. Andrews University, since 1995 (Head, School of Mathematics and Statistics); b. 1.6.43, St. Andrews; m., Helena Francesca; 2 s. Educ. Madras College, St. Andrews; St. Andrews University; Warwick University. Lecturer in Pure Mathematics, then Senior Lecturer, St. Andrews University, 1968-95. Partnership Award, 1992; European Academic Software Award, 1994; American Computational Engineering and Science Award, 1995. Publications: 26 books; 100 papers. Recreations: history of mathematics; computers. Address: (b.) Mathematical Institute, North Haugh, St. Andrews KY16 9SS; T.-01334 463743.

Robertson, George F., CBE. Surveyor and Arbiter; b. 14.7.32, Edinburgh; m., Anne McGonigle; 3 d. Educ. George Heriot's School, Edinburgh; Heriot-Watt College, Edinburgh. Partner, Robertson and Dawson, Chartered Surveyors, Edinburgh, 1970-93; Lecturer (part-time), School of Architecture, Edinburgh College of Art/Heriot-Watt University, 1964-84; Chairman, Joint Standing Committee of Architects, Surveyors and Building Contractors in Scotland, 1976-78; Chairman, Board of Governors, Leith Nautical College, 1976-78; Chairman, Scottish Branch, Royal Institution of Chartered Surveyors, 1984-85; Director, Queensberry House Hospital, Edinburgh, 1983-86; Chairman, Scottish Building Contract Committee, 1983-88; Board Member, Scottish Development Agency, 1987-91; Hon. Secretary, Royal Institution of Chartered Surveyors in Scotland, 1988-90; Lay Member, Scottish Solicitors Discipline Tribunal, 1976-94; President, Rent Assessment Panel for Scotland, 1987-97. Recreations: gardening; travel; researching Scottish market crosses. Address: (h.) Gladsheil, Campbell Court, Longniddry, East Lothian EH32 0NR.

Robertson, Harry, CPFA. Chief Executive, Perth and Kinross Council, since 1995; b. 7.9.49, Dunfermline; m., Rosemary Elizabeth; 2 s. Educ. Dunfermline High School; Glasgow College of Commerce. Trainee Accountant, Burgh of Burntisland; Accountancy Assistant, Assistant Town Chamberlain, Depute Town Chamberlain, Burgh of Barrhead; Depute Director of Finance, Director of Finance, Depute Chief Executive, Chief Executive, Perth and Kinross District Council. Secretary, Perth Repertory Theatre Ltd.; Chairman, Scottish Branch, CIPFA, 1987-88; former Council Member, CIPFA; Clerk to Lord Lieutenancy, Perth and Kinross; Chief Executive and Secretary, Perth and Kinross Leisure Ltd.; Hon. Secretary, Bowerswell Memorial Homes (Perth) Ltd.; Member, Society of High Constables of the City of Perth. Recreations: golf; theatre; surfing the net; tropical fish. Address: (b.) 2 High Street, Perth PH1 5PH; T.-01738 475001; e-mail: hrobertson@pkc.gov.uk

Robertson, Iain Alasdair, CBE, LLB. Managing Director, AWG Development Group, since 2000; b. 30.10.49, Perth; m., Judith Helen Stevenson; 2 s.; 1 d. Educ. Perth Academy; Aberdeen University. Qualified as a Solicitor, 1973; service at home and abroad with British Petroleum, 1975-90, latterly as BP America's Director of Acquisitions; Chief Executive, Highlands and Islands Enterprise, 1990-2000. Board Member, Scottish Tourist Board, 1993-95; Board Member, Locate in Scotland Supervisory Board, 1992-2000; Board Member, Cairngorm Partnership, 1998-2000; Director, Quality Scotland, 1999-2000. Recreations: skiing; sailing; music. Address: (b.) 12 Atholl Crescent, Edinburgh EH3 8HA; T.-0131-228 4188; e-mail: iain.robertson@morrisonplc.com

Robertson, Ian Barr, MA, LLB. Solicitor (retired); Advocate in Aberdeen; Honorary Sheriff, Grampian, Highland and Islands, at Stonehaven; b. Aberdeen; m., Vi L. Johnston; 2 s.; 1 d. Educ. Mackie Academy; Fettes College; Aberdeen University. King's Regiment and KAR, 1939-46 (Captain); Partner, Cunningham & Robertson, Solicitors, Stonehaven, 1951-89; Joint Town Clerk, then Town Clerk, Stonehaven, 1957-75; President, Society of Town Clerks in Scotland, 1973-75; Member, Grampian Regional Council, 1974-86 (Chairman, Transportation and Roads, 1978-86); Member, Aberdeen Harbour Board, 1975-86; Member, Peterhead Bay Authority, 1978-88; Elder, Stonehaven South. Address: (h.) 15 Bath Street, Stonehaven; T.-Stonehaven 762879.

Robertson, James Downie, DA, RSA, RSW, RGI. Painter; Resident Painter, Glasgow School of Art, 1996-98; b. 2.11.31, Cowdenbeath; m., Ursula Orr Crawford (2nd marriage); 2 step-s.; 1 step-d. Educ. Hillhead High School; Glasgow School of Art. Teacher, Keith Grammar School,

Banffshire, 1957-58; Lecturer (part-time), Glasgow School of Art, 1959; elected RSW, 1962; Lecturer in Drawing and Painting, Glasgow School of Art, 1967; elected Associate, Royal Scottish Academy, 1974; Senior Lecturer, Drawing and Painting, Glasgow School of Art, 1975-96; elected, RGI, 1980; elected, RSA, 1989; Visiting Lecturer: Michaelis School of Fine Art, Cape Town University, South Africa, 1970, Grays School of Art, Aberdeen, 1986, Duncan of Jordanstone College of Art, Dundee, 1986, Newcastle-upon-Tyne Polytechnic, 1986, Millersville University, Pennsylvania, USA, 1987. Cargill Award, RGI, 1971; May Marshall Brown Award, RSW, 1976; Sir William Gillies Award, RSW, 1981; Cargill Award, RGI, 1982; Shell Expro Award, 1985; Graham Munro Award, RSW, 1987; Scottish Amicable Award, RGI, 1989; Scottish Post Office Award, RSA, 1993. Many solo and group exhibitions, UK and abroad (most recently: Roger Billcliffe Gallery, Glasgow, solo exhibiton, 2000, New Academy Gallery, London, joint exhibition, 2001, Jorgensen Fine Art Gallery, solo exhibition, 2002); work in many public, corporate and private collections; retrospective show, Glasgow School of Art, 2000. DLitt (Glasgow), 2001. Recreations: drawing; painting; reading. Address: (h.) Carruthmuir, by Kilbarchan, Renfrewshire PA10 2QA; T.-01505 613592.

Robertson, Dr James Ian Summers, FRSE, MD, FRCPLond, FRCPGlas, BSc, MB, BS, FAHA, CBiol, FIBiol. Board Member, Scottish Opera, since 1999; Board Member, Scottish Ballet, since 2000; b. 5.3.28, Welbeck; m. Maureen Patricia; 1 s.; 2 d. Educ. Queen Elizabeth's Grammar School, Mansfield; St Mary's Hospital Medical School, London University. Senior Lecturer and Hon. Consultant Physician, St Mary's Hospital, London, 1964-67; Member of staff, MRC, and Hon. Consultant Physician, Western Infirmary, Glasgow, 1967-87; Senior Consultant, Cardiovascular Medicine, Janssen Research Foundation, Belgium, 1987-94; Past President, International Society of Hypertension; former Chairman, Scientific Council on Hypertension, International Society and Federation of Cardiology; Foundation President, British Hypertension Society; former Adviser, Cardiovascular Diseases, World Health Organisation; Cheadle Gold Medal, 1954; Jodh Gold Medal, 1979. Publications: books on hypertension. Recreations: literature; opera; cricket. Address: (h.) Elmbank, Manse Road, Bowling, Glasgow G60 5AA; T.-01389 873121.

Robertson, James Roy, MBE, BSc, MBChB, FRCGP, FRCP. Principal, General Practice, Muirhouse Medical Group, since 1980; Senior Lecturer (part-time), Department of General Practice, University of Edinburgh, since 1990; Apothecary to the Royal Household at Holyrood House Palace; b. 15.3.51, Edinburgh; m., Elizabeth; 3 s. Educ. Merchiston Castle School, Edinburgh; University of Edinburgh. Member, various national governmental committees and working parties on drug abuse issues, HIV and AIDS and alcohol problems; author of papers on these subjects. Publication: Management of Drug Users in the Community (Editor), 1998. Recreations: outdoor activities; travel; family. Address: Department of Community Health Sciences, West Richmond Street, Edinburgh; e-mail: jroberts@staffmail.ed.ac.uk

Robertson, John. MP (Labour), Glasgow Anniesland, since 2000; b. 17.4.52, Glasgow; m.; 3 c. Educ. Stow College, Glasgow. Before entering Parliament, worked for 31 years with BT as telephone engineer and local customer manager. Address: (b.) House of Commons, London, SW1A 0AA.

Robertson, John Davie Manson, CBE, DL, BL, FRSE, FRSA. Chairman, Robertson Group of Companies, since 1979; Director, Stanley Services Ltd., Falkland Islands, since 1987; Member, National Health Service Tribunal, since 1990; b. 6.11.29, Golspie; m., Elizabeth Amelia Macpherson; 2 s.; 2 d. Educ. Kirkwall Grammar School; Edinburgh University. Anglo-Iranian Oil Co. and BP, UK and Middle East, 1953-58. Honorary Sheriff, Grampian, Highland and Islands, since 1977; Honorary Vice Consul for Denmark, since 1972; Honorary Consul, Federal Republic of Germany, since 1976; Chairman: Children's Panel for Orkney, 1971-76, Highlands and Islands Savings Committee, 1975-78, Children's Panel, Orkney Advisory Committee, 1977-82, Orkney Health Board, 1983-91 (Vice Chairman, 1979-83), Scottish Health Management Efficiency Group (SCOTMEG), 1985-95, Highland Health Board, 1991-97, North of Scotland Water Authority, 1995-98, Scottish Health Boards Chairmen's Group, 1995-97, Lloyds TSB Foundation for Scotland, 1997-99 (Trustee, 1989-99); Member: Board of Management, Orkney Hospitals, 1970-74, Highlands and Islands Development Consultative Council, 1989-91, Board Highlands and Islands Enterprise, 1990-95. OBE, 1978; Royal Order of Knight of Dannebrog, 1982; Officer's Cross of the Order of Merit, 1986; Deputy Lieutenant for Sutherland. Publications: Uppies and Doonies, 1967; An Orkney Anthology, 1991. Recreations: fly fishing; shooting; history. Address: (h.) Spinningdale House, Spinningdale, Sutherland IV24 3AD; T.-01862 881 240.

Robertson, John Graeme, CBiol, MIBiol, MIMgt, FLS, FRSA. Director, Habitat Scotland, since 1980; Editor, Islander Magazine, since 1995; Director, International Centre for Island Studies, since 1999; b. 15.8.54, Edinburgh; m., Anne Christie; 1 s.; 1 d. Educ. Scotus Academy, Edinburgh. Co-ordinator, Environmental Resource Centre; Co-ordinator, Friends of the Earth Scotland. Churchill Fellow, 1996; English Speaking Union William Thyne Scholar, 1999; President, Island Web Consortium. Recreations: exercising his dogs; travel to islands worldwide. Address: Hazelmount, Heron Place, Portree, Isle of Skye IV51 9EU; T.-01478 612898; e-mail: graeme@islandstudies.com

Robertson, John Shaw, MA, FFCS. Rector, Dollar Academy, since 1994; b. 7.4.50, Glasgow; m., Mary; 1 s.; 1 d. Educ. Jordanhill College School; Glasgow University. English Master, Housemaster, Assistant Headmaster, Stewart's Melville, Edinburgh, 1973-87; Deputy Rector, Dollar Academy, 1987-94; HMC Academic Policy Sub-Committee, since 1997; Council Member, SCCC; Governor, Ardvreck School; Chairman, Scottish Division, HMC, 2000. Publication: Stewart's Melville: the first Ten Years (Co-author). Recreations: cricket (Scottish); music (English); literature (international). Address: Dollar Academy, Dollar FK14 7DU; T.-01259 742511.

Robertson, Sir Lewis, CBE, FRSE, FRSA. Chairman, Carnegie Trust for the Universities of Scotland, since 1990; b. 28.11.22, Dundee; m., Elspeth Badenoch (deceased); 2 s.; 1 s. (deceased); 1 d. Educ. Trinity College, Glenalmond. Apprentice Chartered Accountant, 1939-42; RAF Intelligence, 1942-46; entered family textile business, 1946; appointed Managing Director, Robertson Industrial Textiles, 1954; first Managing Director, Scott & Robertson, 1965 (Chairman, 1968); resigned, 1970; Chief Executive, Grampian Holdings, Glasgow, 1971-76 (also Deputy Chairman, 1972-76); Non-Executive Director, Scottish & Newcastle Breweries, 1975-87; Chairman: Triplex Lloyd plc, 1982-90, Girobank Scotland, 1984-90, Borthwicks plc, 1985-89, Lilley plc, 1986-93, Havelock Europe plc, 1989-92, Stakis plc, 1991-95, Posteru Executive Group, 1991-96; Director, Whitman International, Geneva, 1987-90; Chairman, Scottish Board (and UK Council Member), British Institute of Management, 1981-83; Chairman, Eastern Regional Hospitals Board, 1960-70; Member, Committee of Enquiry into the Relationship of the Pharmaceutical Industry with the NHS, 1965-67; Member, Monopolies (later Monopolies and Mergers) Commission, 1969-76; Deputy Chairman and first Chief Executive, Scottish Development Agency, 1976-81; Member, Scottish

Economic Council, 1977-83; Member, Restrictive Practices Court, 1983-97; Member, Scottish Post Office Board, 1984-90; Member, Court, Dundee University, 1967-70 (first Finance Committee); Council Member, Scottish Business School, 1978-83; Chairman, Scottish Arts Council, and Member, Arts Council of GB, 1970-71; Chairman, Scottish Advisory Committee, British Council, 1978-87; Council Member, Scottish History Society, 1984-89; first Chairman, Policy Committee, Scottish Episcopal Church, 1974-76; Trustee, Foundation for the Study of Christianity and Society, 1983-89; Member, Advisory Board, Edinburgh Edition of the Waverley Novels, since 1986; Director, Friends of Royal Scottish Academy, 1986-95; Member, Board, British Executive Service Overseas (Chairman, Scotland), 1995-98; Royal Society of Edinburgh: Fellow, since 1978, Member, Council, 1992-2000, Treasurer, 1994-99; Chairman, Scottish Division, Imperial Society of Knights Bachelor, 1995-99; Director and Trustee, Advanced Management Programme Scotland, since 1996; Trustee and Vice-Patron, Scottish Council for Research in Education, since 1997; Trustee, Scottish Cancer Foundation, since 1999; Trustee, Foundation for Skin Research, since 1999. Hon. LLD, Dundee University, 1971; Hon. Doctorate of Business Administration, Napier University, 1992; Hon. DUniv, Stirling, 1993; Hon. LLD, Aberdeen, 1999; Hon. FRCSEdin, 1999. Recreations: work; foreign travel; computer use; music; list-making. Address: 32 Saxe Coburg Place, Edinburgh EH3 5BP; T.-0131-332 5221; e-mail: lr32scp@talk21.com

Robertson, Pamela, BA (Hons). Senior Curator, Hunterian Art Gallery, Glasgow University. Educ. St George's School for Girls, Edinburgh; University College, London. Member, Historic Buildings Council for Scotland, since 1998; Vice-Chair, C.R. Mackintosh Society, since 2001; Member, Curatorial Committee, National Trust for Scotland, since 2001; winner, Iris Foundation Award for outstanding contributions to the decorative arts, Bard University, New York, 1997. Publications include: C.R. Mackintosh: the architectural papers, 1990; C.R. Mackintosh: Art is the Flower, 1994; The Chronycle, 2001. Recreations: good food and wine; good company. Address: (b.) Hunterian Art Gallery, Glasgow University, Glasgow G12 8QQ; T.-0141-330 5431; e-mail: probert@museum.gla.ac.uk

Robertson, Professor Peter Kenneth John, BSc (Hons), DPhil, CChem, FRSC. Professor of Energy and Environmental Engineering, Robert Gordon University, since 2000; b. 5.6.64, Belfast; m., Dr Jeanette Robertson; 1s. Educ. Royal Belfast Academical Institution; University of Ulster. Research Officer, Faraday Centre, Carlow, Ireland, 1989-90; Lecturer, Carlow Regional College, Ireland, 1990-91; Higher Scientific Officer, Industrial Research and Technology Unit, 1991-95; Lecturer, School of Applied Sciences, Robert Gordon University, 1995-2000; Member, Committee, Scottish Branch Royal Society of Chemistry's Analytical Division; Chairman, North of Scotland Branch, British Association. Recreations: hill- walking; photography; golf (very badly). Address: (b.) Centre for Environmental Engineering, School of Mechanical Engineering, Robert Gordon University, Schoolhill, Aberdeen; T.-01224 262352.

Robertson, Raymond Scott, MA. Chairman, Scottish Conservative and Unionist Party, 1997-2001; b. 11.12.59, Hamilton. Educ. Garrion Academy, Wishaw; University of Glasgow; Jordanhill College of Education. Teacher of History and Modern Studies; MP, Aberdeen South, 1992-97; PPS, Northern Ireland Office, 1993-95; Minister for Education, Housing, Fisheries and Sport, Scottish Office, 1995-97. Recreations: watching football; playing squash; reading.

Robertson, Richard Ross, RSA, FRBS, DA. Sculptor; b. 10.9.14, Aberdeen; m., Kathleen May Matts; 2 d. Educ. Paisley Grammar School; Glasgow School of Art; Aberdeen Art School. Work exhibited in Aberdeen public parks and several public buildings in city and county of Aberdeen; also exhibited in several private collections in Britain, America and Holland; retired Lecturer in Sculpture, Gray's School of Art, Aberdeen. Recreations: carving; gardening; walking. Address: (h.) Creaguir, Woodlands Road, Rosemount, Blairgowrie, Perthshire; T.-01250 4970.

Robertson, Brigadier Sidney Park, MBE, TD, JP, DL, BCom. Director, S. & J.D. Robertson Group Ltd. (Chairman, 1965-79); Honorary Sheriff, Grampian, Highlands and Islands, since 1969; Vice Lord Lieutenant of Orkney, 1987-90; b. 12.3.14, Kirkwall; m., Elsa Miller Croy (deceased); 1 s.; 1 d. Educ. Kirkwall Grammar School; MIBS; Edinburgh University. Commissioned, Royal Artillery, 1940 (Despatches, NW Europe, 1945); managerial posts, Anglo-Iranian Oil Co., Middle East, 1946-51; Manager Operations/Sales, Southern Division, Shell-Mex and BP, 1951-54; founder, Robertson firm, 1954; Major Commanding 861 (Independent) Light Anti-Aircraft Battery RA (Orkney and Zetland), TA, 1956-61; Lt. Col. Commanding Lovat Scouts, 1962-65; Brigadier, CRA 51st Highland Division, 1966-67; Vice Chairman, Orkney Islands Shipping Company, 1975-79; Chairman, Orkney Hospitals Board of Management/Orkney Health Board, 1965-79; DL, 1968; Honorary Vice-President, Royal British Legion Scotland, Highlands and Islands Area, since 1975; President, Royal British Legion Scotland, Kirkwall Branch, 1957-97; Chairman, RNLI, Kirkwall Station Committee, 1972-97 (President, since 1997); Honorary Colonel, 102 (Ulster and Scottish) Light Air Defence Regiment, Royal Artillery, 1975-80; Hon. Colonel Commandant, Royal Regiment of Artillery, 1977-80; Vice President, National Artillery Association, since 1977; Chairman, Royal Artillery Council of Scotland, 1980-84; Honorary President, Orkney Bn., Boys' Brigade; Vice-President, RNLI, since 1985; President, Villars Curling Club, 1978-80, 1986-88; Honorary President: Friends of St. Magnus Cathedral, since 1994, Orkney Family History Society, since 1996; Freedom of Orkney, 1990; Honorary Fellowship, Edinburgh University, since 1996; Honorary President, Orkney Norway Friendship Association, 1999. Recreations: travel; hill-walking; angling. Address: (h.) Daisybank, Kirkwall, Orkney; T.-01856 87 2085.

Robertson, Stanley. Folklorist and Storyteller; Ballad Singer; Fish Filleter; b. 8.6.40, Aberdeen; m., Johnann; 4 s.; 2 d. Educ. Frederick Street Secondary School. Has lectured and taught in colleges and universities worldwide (including Harvard, Princeton, Utah, Idaho, New Hampshire, East Tennessee and Brandice in the USA, Napier and Edinburgh in Scotland, and schools in Britain and elsewhere); has been guest artist at storytelling festivals from Tennessee to Devon; numerous television and radio appearances in Britain, Holland and the USA. Publications: Exodus to Alford, 1988; Nyakim's Windows, 1989; Fish-Hooses, 1990; Fish-Hooses 2, 1991; Land of No Death, 1993; Ghosties and Ghoulies, 1994; plays: Scruffy Uggie, 1998, The Burkers, 1989; Jack and the Land of Dreams, 2001. Address: 9 Long Walk Place, Mastrick, Aberdeen; T.-01224 682170.

Robertson, Sue, BA, MSocSci. Director, One Parent Families Scotland, since 1988; b. 12.7.50, Carlisle; divorced; 1 s.; 2 d. Educ. Penrith Queen Elizabeth Grammar School; Oxford University; Birmingham University. Senior Economic Assistant, Scottish Economic Planning Department, 1973-78; Co-ordinator, Scottish Women's Aid, 1978-83; Training Officer, Scottish Council for Single Parents, 1983-88. Committee Member, Cairn Housing Association and PACE. Recreations: hill-walking; cycling; reading. Address: (b.) 13 Gayfield Square, Edinburgh EH1 3NX; T.-0131-556 3899.

Robertson, William Nelson, CBE, MA, FCII. Director: Morrison Construction, 1995-2001; Director, since 1996: Alliance Investment Trust, Second Alliance Investment Trust; Member, Advisory Board, Scottish Amicable, since 1997; b. 14.12.33, Berwick upon Tweed; m., Sheila Catherine; 2 d. Educ. Berwick Grammar School; Edinburgh University. Joined General Accident, 1958: Deputy Chief General Manager, 1989-90, Group Chief Executive, 1990-95, Director, 1984-95. Board Member, Association of British Insurers, 1991-95; Director: Scottish Community Foundation, 1996-99, Edinburgh New Tiger Investment Trust, 1996-2001. Member, Court, University of Abertay, Dundee, 1996-99. Recreations: hill-walking; gardening.

Robertson Sullivan, Denis, DA. Director, PS Communication Media Awareness Trainers, since 1989; Director, DRS Associates Ltd., since 2000; b. 1.3.45, Glasgow; m., Evelyn; 2 s.; 2 d. Educ. St. Augustine's Secondary School, Glasgow; Glasgow School of Art; Jordanhill College of Education. Teacher, 1969-71; Assistant Secretary, EIS, 1971-89; Director, number of PR and communication companies in the 1990s/2000; Director, Big Thinking; Scottish Board Member, Shelter, since 1999; has been Member, Executive, Scottish Liberal Democrats and precursors since 1981, former Treasurer, Scottish Lib/Dem Federal Finance, and former Executive Member. Recreations: reading; films. Address: 8 Redford Loan, Colinton, Edinburgh EH13 0AY; (h.) T.-0131-441 6054; (b.) 0131-441 3888; e-mail: denis@drs-associates.co.uk

Robins, Professor David John, BSc, PhD, DSc, CChem, FRSC, FRSE. Professor of Bio-organic Chemistry, since 1990; b. 12.8.45, Purley; m., Helen Dorothy; 1 s.; 1 d. Educ. Purley Grammar School; Exeter University. NIH Postdoctoral Fellow, University of Pittsburgh, USA, 1969-71; SRC Fellowship, University of Surrey, 1971-72; Tutorial Fellow, University of Reading, 1972-73; University of Glasgow: Lecturer, 1974-87, Senior Lecturer, 1987-88, Reader, 1988-90. Flintoff Medal and Prize, Royal Society of Chemistry, 1999. Recreations: cycling; hillwalking; gardening. Address: Department of Chemistry, University of Glasgow, Glasgow G12 8QQ; T.-0141-330 4378; e-mail: D.Robins@chem.gla.ac.uk

Robins, John F. Campaigns Consultant, Animal Concern, since 1998 (formerly Secretary); Managing Director, Ethical Promotions Ltd., since 1988; Secretary, Save Our Seals Fund, since 1996; Secretary, Animal Concern Advice Line, since 2001; b. 2.1.57, Glasgow; m., Mary E.; 1 s.; 1 d. Educ. St. Ninian's High School. Co-ordinator, Glasgow Energy Group, 1978-80; Company Secretary, Scottish Anti-Vivisection Society, 1981-88; Green Party activist and candidate, 1978-81; Delegate, Anti-Nuclear Campaign, 1978-81; Vice-Chair, Friends of the Earth (Scotland) Ltd., 1981-82; Co-ordinator, Scottish Animal Rights Network, 1983-91; Co-ordinator, Save Scotland's Seals Funds, 1988-96. Recreation: catching up on lost sleep. Address: (b.) P.O. Box 5178, Dumbarton G82 5YJ; T.-01389 841639; e-mail: animals@jfrobins.force9.co.uk

Robinson, Christopher Peter, FHCIMA. Chief Executive, Heart of Midlothian Football Club, since 1994; b. 23.3.51, Edinburgh; m., Elizabeth; 3 d. Educ. Bo'ness Academy; Napier University. Trainee Manager, Open Arms Hotel Group, 1972-78. Guest Lecturer, International Hotel Schools, Paris and Cornell; President, Hotel and Catering Institutional Management Association, 1992-93. Recreations: football; golf. Address: (b.) Tynecastle Stadium, Gorgie Road, Edinburgh EH11 2NL; T.-0131-200 7200.

Robinson, Ernest Thomson, OBE, OStJ, TD, KCLJ, CMLJ, MB, ChB, FRCGP, DRCOG. Chairman, Council, St. Andrew's Ambulance Association, since 1994; retired General Medical Practitioner; b. 18.3.34, Gartcosh; m.,

Margaret; 4 s.; 3 d. Educ. Coatbridge Secondary School; Glasgow University. Principal General Medical Practitioner, Woodside Health Centre, Glasgow (retired); former Regimental Medical Officer (rank Major), 154 Lowland Regiment RCT (TA). Publication: First Aid Book for Young People. Recreations: salmon and trout fishing. Address: (h.) 132 Prestonfield, Milngavie, Glasgow G62 7QA; T.-0141-563 7409.

Robinson, Gary Wayne. Managing Director, Moray Firth Radio, since 2000; b. 1.11.69, Halifax. Educ. Halifax Catholic High School; Glenrothes College. Commercial Producer/Presenter, Radio Tay, 1990; Senior Presenter, Tay FM, 1995; Promotions and Sponsorship Manager, Radio Tay, 1997. Director, MFR Media Trust; Board Member, Highland Food and Drink Festival; Director, Score Records. Recreations: food (cooking and eating); his dogs. Address: (b.) Moray Firth Radio, PO Box 271, Scorguie Place, Inverness IV3 8UJ; T.-01463 224433; e-mail: gary.robinson@mfr.co.uk

Robinson, Sir Ian, BSc, FREng. Chairman, Scottish Enterprise; Chairman, Amey plc; Chairman, Hilton Group plc; b. 3.5.42, Boldon, Co. Durham; m., Kay Robinson; 1 s.; 1 d. Educ. Middlesbrough High School; Leeds University. Managing Director, Parsons Corporation, 1985-86; Managing Director, John Brown Engineering and Construction, 1986-92; Chief Executive, John Brown plc, 1992-95; Director, Trafalgar House plc, 1992-95; Chief Executive, Scottish Power plc, 1995-2001. Former Non-Executive Director, RMC plc, ASDA plc. Recreations: golf; gardening. Address: (b.) 150 Broomielaw, Atlantic Quay, Glasgow G2 8LU.

Robison, Shona. MSP (SNP), North East Scotland, since 1999; Chair, Cross Party Group on Refugees and Assylum Seekers; Shadow Depute Spokesperson for Health and Community Care; b. 26.5.66, Redcar; m., Stewart Hosie. Educ. Alva Academy; Glasgow University; Jordanhill College. Home Care Organiser, 1997-99; Senior Community Worker, 1993-97; Community Worker, 1990-93; Admin Officer, 1989-90. Secretary, SNP Group, Scottish Parliament; Member, National Executive Committee, SNP. Recreation: hill-walking. Address: (b.) 8 Old Glamis Road, Dundee DD3 8HP; T.-01382 623200.

Robson, Agnes, MA. Principal Establishment Officer and Head, Corporate Services, Scottish Executive, since 2000; b. 6.10.46, Edinburgh; 1 s. Educ. Holy Cross Academy; Edinburgh University. Civil Servant, since 1968; Head, Energy Division, 1988-89; Head, Nuclear Energy Division, 1989-90; Head, Urban Policy Division, 1990-92; Director, Directorate of Primary Care, NHS Management Executive, Scottish Executive Health Department, 1992-2000. Recreations: opera; Scottish contemporary painting. Address: (b.) 16 Waterloo Place, Edinburgh.

Robson, Euan Macfarlane, BA, MSc, MICA. MSP (Liberal Democrat), Roxburgh and Berwickshire, since 1999; Deputy Minister for Parliamentary Business, since 2001; former Scottish Manager, Gas Consumers' Council; b. 17.2.54, Northumberland; m., Valerie; 2 d. Educ. Trinity College, Glenalmond; Newcastle-upon-Tyne University; Strathclyde University. Teacher, 1976-79; Deputy Secretary, Gas Consumers' Northern Council, 1981-86. Member, Northumberland County Council, 1981-89; Honorary Alderman, Northumberland CC, since 1989; Liberal/SDP Alliance candidate, Hexham, 1983, 1987; Liberal Democrat Scottish Parliamentary spokesman on: Rural Affairs, 1998-99, Justice and Home Affairs, 1999-2001. River Tweed Commissioner; author. Address: (b.) Scottish Parliament, Edinburgh EH99 1SP.

Robson, Professor Peter William Greenwell, LLB, PhD, Solicitor. Professor of Social Welfare Law, Strathclyde University, since 1992; Chairman, Shelter, since 1999; part-time Chair of Appeals Service; Director, WESLO; b. 28.3.47; m., Andrina Ann Marie Smith. Educ. Slough Grammar School; St Andrews University. Solicitor, Edinburgh, 1967-70; Lecturer, Senior Lecturer, Reader, 1970-92, at Universities of Stirling, Glasgow, Heriot Watt and Strathclyde. Publications: Residential Tenancies (2nd edition); Homeless People and the Law (3rd edition); Law and Film, 2001; Film and the Law, 2001. Recreations: football; swimming; golf; cinema. Address: (b.) Law School, Strathclyde University, 173 Cathedral Street, Glasgow G4 0RQ; T.-0141-548 3340.

Rochford, Professor Gerard, BA, BSc, FFCS. Psychotherapist; b. 17.12.32, Dorking; m., Anne Prime (dec.); 3 s.; 7 d. Educ. Worcester Royal Grammar School; Hull University; Oxford University. Medical Research Council, 1960-63; Lecturer in Psychology: Aberdeen University, 1963-67, Hong Kong University, 1967-70; Lecturer/Senior Lecturer, 1970-78, Professor of Social Work Studies, 1978-88, Aberdeen University. Member, Scottish Association of Psychoanalytical Psychotherapists. Recreations: family; friends; poetry; pottery. Address: (h.) 47 Waverley Place, Aberdeen; T.-Aberdeen 644873.

Rodger of Earlsferry, Rt. Hon. Lord (Alan Ferguson Rodger), PC, QC, MA, LLB, DCL. Lord of Appeal in Ordinary; b. 18.9.44. Educ. Kelvinside Academy, Glasgow; Glasgow University; New College, Oxford. Fellow, New College, Oxford, 1970-72; Member, Faculty of Advocates, 1974; Clerk of Faculty, 1976-79; Advocate Depute, 1985-88; Home Advocate Depute, 1986-88; Member, Mental Welfare Commission for Scotland, 1981-84; UK Delegation to CCBE, 1984-89; Maccabaean Lecturer, British Academy, 1991; Solicitor General for Scotland, 1989-92; Lord Advocate, 1992-95; Judge of the Court of Session, 1995-96; Lord President and Lord Justice General, 1996-2001. Address: (b.) House of Lords, London SW1A 0PW.

Rodger, Professor Albert Alexander, BSc (Eng), PhD, CEng, FICE, FGS. Professor of Civil Engineering, Aberdeen University, since 1997 (Dean, Faculty of Science and Engineering); b. 12.5.51, Greenock; m., Jane Helen; 2 d. Educ. Aberdeen University. Project Engineer, Cementation Research Ltd., London, 1977-79; Aberdeen University: Lecturer in Engineering, 1979-89, Senior Lecturer, 1989-95, Personal Professor, 1995-97. Winner: Award for Excellence, Aberdeen University, 1994, 1997 National John Logie Baird Award for Innovation, Halcrow Premium, Institution of Civil Engineers, 1997, Design Council Millennium Product Award, 1999, Silver Medal, Royal Academy of Engineering, 2000. Recreations: history of church architecture; photography; swimming. Address: Faculty of Science and Engineering, King's College, University of Aberdeen, Aberdeen AB24 3FX; T.-01224 272081; e-mail: a.a.rodger@abdn.ac.uk

Rodger, Willie, ARSA, RGI, DA (Glas), DUniv (Stirling). Artist in lino and woodcuts; b. 3.3.30, Kirkintilloch; m., Anne Charmian Henry; 2 s.; 2 d. Educ. Lenzie Academy; Glasgow School of Art. Visualiser, London advertising agency, 1953-54; Art Teacher, Lenzie Acacady, 1955-68; Head, Art Department, Clydebank High School, 1968-87. Artist in Residence, Sussex University, 1971; Scottish Historical Playing Cards, 1975; Saltire Awards for Art in Architecture, 1984-89; work in permanent collections in Scotland and England; commissions: Enamel Mural Exhibition Station, Glasgow; illustrations and mural, Dallas Dhu Distillery, Forres; design, Stained Glass Windows, St Mary's Parish Church, Kirkintilloch; Street Banners, 200 anniversary, Union Street, Aberdeen; edition of Lino Cut Prints, P&O Ferries; illustrations, Finding Alba, Scottish Television. Publications: Scottish Historical Playing Cards; The Field of Thistles (Illustrator); Willie Rodger, Open Eye

Gallery. Recreations: gardening; jazz. Address: Stenton, Bellevue Road, Kirkintilloch, Glasgow G66 1AP; T.-0141-776 2116.

Rodgers, Professor Eamonn Joseph, BA, MA, PhD. Professor of Spanish and Latin American Studies, University of Strathclyde, since 1990; b. 4.6.41, Belfast; m., Valerie Ann Goodman; 2 s. Educ. St. Mary's, Belfast; Queen's University, Belfast. Trinity College Dublin: Junior Lecturer in Spanish, 1964-66, Lecturer in Spanish, 1966-78, Senior Lecturer in Spanish, 1978-89. Publications: From Enlightenment to Realism: The Novels of Galdos, 1870-86, 1987; Encyclopedia of Contemporary Spanish Culture, 1999. Recreations: music; walking. Address: University of Strathclyde, 26 Richmond Street, Glasgow G1 1XH; T.-0141-548 3506; e-mail: e.rodgers@strath.ac.uk

Rodgers, Shane Andrew, BSc (Hons) Arch, Dip AAS, RIBA, FRIAS. Architect, since 1985; b. 12.2.60, Derby; m., Susan Ann; 1 s.; 1 d. Educ. Thurso High School; Robert Gordon's Institute of Technology, Aberdeen. Architect, Sinclair MacDonald and Son, Thurso, 1985-91; Partner, Leet Rodgers Practice, Thurso, 1991-98, Principal, since 1998. Aberdeen Society of Architects Silver Medal, 1984; Vice-President, Inverness Architectural Association; Member, Council, RIAS. Address: (b.) Leet Rodgers Practice, 1 West Church Street, Thurso KW14 7HY; T.-01847 893489.

Roe, Professor Nicholas Hugh, MA (Oxon), DPhil (Oxon). Professor of English Literature, St. Andrews University, since 1996; b. 14.12.55, Fareham; m., Dr. Susan Jane Stabler. Educ. Royal Grammar School, High Wycombe; Trinity College, Oxford. Lecturer in English, Queen's University of Belfast, 1982-85; St. Andrews University: Lecturer in English, 1985-94, Reader in English, 1994-96; Visiting Professor, University of Sao Paulo, 1989; Leverhulme Research Fellow, 1994-95; Director, Coleridge Conference, since 1994; Trustee, Keats-Shelley Memorial Association; Editor, Romanticism (journal). Publications: Coleridge's Imagination, 1985; Wordsworth and Coleridge, The Radical Years, 1988; The Politics of Nature, 1992; Selected Poetry of William Wordsworth, 1992; Keats and History, 1995; Selected Poems of John Keats, 1995; John Keats and the Culture of Dissent, 1997; Samuel Taylor Coleridge and the Sciences of Life, 2001. Recreations: walking; gardening; cookery; France. Address: (b.) School of English, St. Andrews University, St. Andrews KY16 9AL; T.-01334 476161.

Roe, William Deas, BSc, FRSA. Management Consultant, Rocket Science UK Ltd., since 2001; Board Member, Highlands and Islands Enterprise, since 1998; b. 9.7.47, Perth. Educ. St Modan's High School, Stirling; Edinburgh University. Director, Shelter; Director of Student Housing, Edinburgh University; Assistant Director, Scottish Council for Voluntary Organisations; Director, CEI Consultants Ltd.; Principal, William Roe Associates; Director, WorkForce One Ltd. Councillor, Edinburgh City and Lothian Region, 1978-84; Board Member, Training and Development Corporation, Maine, USA. Recreations: sailing; skiing; hill-walking; visual arts; music; travel. Address: (h.) 3 Northumberland Street, Edinburgh EH3 6LL; T.-07051 202020.

Roebuck, Michael Stuart, BSc, MEd, CertEd. Principal, Kilmarnock College, since 1996; b. 5.12.49, Huddersfield; m., Margaret Jane; 1 s.; 1 d. Educ. Marlborough Grammar School; University of Ulster; Edinburgh University. Trainee Town Planner; Lecturer/Senior Lecturer/Depute Head of Department, Stevenson College of F.E.; Assistant to the Director of Education, Lothian Region; TVEI Coordinator, Senior Adviser, Lothian Region; Principal, Lews Castle College; Director, Association of Scottish Colleges; Senior Adviser for Further Education, British Council. Recreation:

cricket (retired). Address: (b.) Kilmarnock College, Holehouse Road, Kilmarnock KA3 7AT; T.-01563 523501; e-mail: roebuckm@kilmarnock.ac.uk

Rogers, Ian Hart. Chief Executive, Scottish Decorators Federation, since 1999; b. 11.6.52, Glasgow; m., Helen; 2 s. Educ. Bearsden Academy; Clydebank College. Began career with Daily Record and Sunday Mail Ltd.; became Sales Manager/Director of roofing and housebuilding company; joined Scottish Building Employers Federation as HQ Secretary. Director, SCORE; Member, Scottish Advisory Committee, CITB. Recreations: golf; walking; reading. Address: (b.) 222 Queensferry Road, Edinburgh EH4 2BN; T.-0131-343 3300.

Rogerson, Robert William Kelly Cupples, OBE, BArch, FRIBA, FRIAS, FSA Scot, MRSH. Vice Chairman, Scottish Council on Disability, 1987-89; Chairman, Committee on Access for Scotland, 1980-89; Council Member, National Trust for Scotland, 1980-86; b. 14.5.17, Glasgow; m., Mary Clark MacNeill; 1 s.; 1 d. Educ. High School of Glasgow; Strathclyde University. Architect in private practice, 1955-56 and 1958-82 (Partner, Watson Salmond & Gray, 1956-58); Lecturer, School of Architecture, Glasgow School of Art; Past Chairman, Glasgow Building Guardian Committee; Past Chairman, RIAS Trustees of The Hill House, Helensburgh; Founder and Chairman, Glasgow Summer School; former Member, Committee on Artistic Matters, Church of Scotland. Publications: A Place at Work (Co-author); Jack Coia, His Life & Work. Recreations: gardening; travelling abroad. Address: (h.) Beinn Bhuidhe House, Glen Shira, Inveraray, Argyll PA32 8XH; T.-01499 302472.

Rolfe, Mervyn James, CBE, DL, OStJ, MEd, MSc, FRSA, FSAScot, JP. Chief Executive, Dundee and Tayside Chamber of Commerce; Depute Leader and Convener, Economic Development Committee, Dundee City Council; Lord Provost of Dundee, 1996-99; Teaching Fellow in Tourism, University of Abertay, Dundee; b. 31.7.47, Wisbech; m., Christine; 1 s. Educ. Buckhaven High School; Dundee University; University of Abertay Dundee. Civil servant, until 1983; Co-ordinator, Dundee Resources Centre for the Unemployed, 1983-87; Vice-Chair, Dundee Trades Council, 1981-82; Leader, Labour Group, Tayside Regional Council, 1994-96; Convener, Tayside Education Committee, 1986-94; Member, Executive Committee, COSLA, 1990-96; Governor, Dundee (now Northern) College of Education, 1986-94; Member, Dundee University Court, 1986-2000; Member, Scottish Community Education Council, 1986-88; Member, General Teaching Council, 1986-95; Member, Dundee Heritage Trust, 1986-99; Executive Member, Campaign for a Scottish Assembly, 1989-91; Member, Scottish Committee for Staff Development in Education, 1987-91; Board Member, Scottish Enterprise, Tayside, 1991-96, and since 1999; Member, Scottish ESF Objective 3 Monitoring Committee; Chair, East of Scotland European Consortium, since 2000; Member, East Scotland European Partnership, since 1999; Chair, City of Discovery Campaign, since 1996; Chair, Unicorn Preservation Society, since 1998; Board Member, Angus and Dundee Tourist Board, since 1999. Honorary Fellow, University of Abertay, Dundee. Recreations: reading; politics. Address: (h.) 17 Mains Terrace, Dundee; T.-01382 450073.

Rolfe, William David Ian, PhD, FRSE, FGS, FMA. Keeper of Geology, National Museums of Scotland, 1986-96; b. 24.1.36; m., Julia Mary Margaret Rayer; 2 d. Educ. Royal Liberty Grammar School, Romford; Birmingham University. Geology Curator, University Lecturer, then Senior Lecturer in Geology, Hunterian Museum, Glasgow University, 1962-81; Deputy Director, 1981-86. President, Geological Society of Glasgow, 1973-76; Editor, Scottish Journal of Geology, 1967-72; President, Edinburgh Geological Society, 1989-91; President, Palaeontological Association, 1992-94; President, Society for the History of Natural History, 1996-99. Recreations: visual arts; walking; swimming; music. Address: 4A Randolph Crescent, Edinburgh, EH3 7TH; T.-0131-226 2094.

Rolland, Lawrence Anderson Lyon, DA, PPRIBA, PPRIAS, FRSE, FRSA. Senior Partner, Hurd Rolland Partnership, 1980-97, Chairman and Consultant, since 1997; General Trustee, Church of Scotland, since 1979; Member, Court, University of Dundee, since 1993 (Chairman, since 1997, former Chairman of Audit Committee); Member, Architects Registration Board, London, and Chairman, Qualifications Advisory Group; Chairman, RIBA Education Fund Committee and Chairman of Trustees, RIBA Education Fund; b. 6.11.37, Leven; m., Mairi Melville; 2 s.; 2 d. Educ. George Watson's Boys College; Duncan of Jordanstone College of Art. Entered father's practice, 1959; joined partnership with Ian Begg bringing L. A. Rolland and Partners and Robert Hurd and Partners together as one partnership; Architect for: The Queen's Hall, Edinburgh; restoration and redesign of Bank of Scotland Head Office; much housing in Fife's royal burghs; British Golf Museum, St Andrews; General Accident Life Assurance, York; Minshull Street Crown Courts, Manchester; winner of more than 20 awards and commendations from Saltire Society, Stone Federation, Concrete Society, Civic Trust, Europa Nostra, R.I.B.A. and Times Conservation Award. President, Royal Incorporation of Architects in Scotland, 1979-81; President, Royal Institute of British Architects, 1985-87; Founder Chairman, Scottish Construction Industry Group, 1979-81; Member, Building EDC NEDC, 1982-88; Chairman, Board of Governors, Duncan of Jordanstone College of Art, 1993-94. Recreations: music; fishing. Address: (b.) Rossend Castle, Burntisland, Fife KY3 0DF; T.-01592 873535; e-mail: larryrolland@hurdrolland.co.uk

Rollo, 14th Lord (David Eric Howard Rollo); b. 1943. Succeeded to title, 1997.

Rorke, Professor John, CBE, PhD, BSc, DEng, CEng, FIMechE, FRSE. Professor Emeritus, formerly Professor of Mechanical Engineering, Heriot-Watt University, 1980-88, and Vice-Principal, 1984-88; b. 2.9.23, Dumbarton; m., Jane Craig Buchanan; 2 d. Educ. Dumbarton Academy; Royal Technical College, Glasgow. Lecturer, Strathclyde University, 1946-51; Assistant to Engineering Director, Alexander Stephen & Sons Ltd., 1951-56; Technical Manager, then General Manager and Engineering Director, William Denny & Bros. Ltd., 1956-63; Technical Director, then Sales Director, Managing Director and Chairman, Brown Bros. & Co. Ltd. and Chairman, John Hastie of Greenock Ltd., 1963-78; Managing Director, Vickers Offshore Group, 1978 (Director of Planning, Vickers PLC, 1979-80). President, Institution of Engineers and Shipbuilders in Scotland, 1985-87; Chairman, Institute of Offshore Engineering Group, 1990-94. Recreations: bridge; golf. Address: (h.) 3 Barnton Park Grove, Edinburgh; T.-0131-336 3044.

Rosborough, Linda, BSc, PhD. Head, Social Inclusion Division, Scottish Executive, since 1999. Former University Lecturer in planning and environmental studies; former advisor to Environment Committee, House of Commons; worked on university funding, Scottish Office; set up Social Inclusion Division, Scottish Executive, 1999. Address: (b.) Scottish Executive, Victoria Quay, Edinburgh; T.-0131-244 0803.

Rose, Dilys Lindsay, BA. Writer of fiction, poetry, drama, since 1980; b. 7.2.54, Glasgow; 2 d. Educ. Edinburgh University. Publications include: fiction: Our Lady of the Pickpockets, Red Tides, War Dolls, Pest Maiden; poetry: Beauty is a Dangerous Thing, Madame Doubtfire's

Dilemma. Winner, first Macallan/Scotland on Sunday short story competition, 1991; Hawthornden Fellow; RLS Memorial Award recipient, 1997; Canongate Prizewinner, 2000; e-mail: dilysrose@aol.com

Rose, Professor Richard, BA, DPhil, FBA. Director and Professor of Public Policy, Centre for the Study of Public Policy, Strathclyde University, since 1976; b. 9.4.33; m., Rosemary J.; 2 s.; 1 d. Educ. Clayton High School, Missouri, USA; Johns Hopkins University; London School of Economics; Lincoln and Nuffield Colleges, Oxford University. Political public relations, Mississippi Valley, 1954-55; Reporter, St. Louis Post-Dispatch, 1955-57; Lecturer in Government, Manchester University, 1961-66; Professor of Politics, Strathclyde University, 1966-82; Consultant Psephologist, The Times, Independent Television, Daily Telegraph, STV, UTV, etc., since 1964; Scientific Adviser, Paul Lazarsfeld Society, Vienna, since 1991; American SSRC Fellow, Stanford University, 1967; Visiting Lecturer in Political Sociology, Cambridge University, 1967; Director, ISSC European Summer School, 1973; Secretary, Committee on Political Sociology, International Sociological Association, 1970-85; Founding Member, European Consortium for Political Research, 1970; Member: US/UK Fulbright Commission, 1971-75, Eisenhower Fellowship Programme, 1971; Guggenheim Foundation Fellow, 1974; Visiting Scholar: Woodrow Wilson International Centre, Washington DC, 1974, Brookings Institute, Washington DC, 1976, American Enterprise Institute, Washington, 1980, Fiscal Affairs Department, IMF, Washington, 1984; Visiting Professor, European University Institute, Florence, 1977, 1978; Visitor, Japan Foundation, 1984; Hinkley Professor, Johns Hopkins University, 1987; Guest Professor, Wissenschaftzentrum, Berlin, 1988, 1990, Central European University, Prague, 1992-95, Max Planck Institute, Berlin, 1996; Chair, European Science Foundation Citizens in Transformation Network, since 1999; Ransone Lecturer, University of Alabama, 1990; Consultant Chairman, NI Constitutional Convention, 1976; Home Office Working Party on Electoral Register, 1975-77; Co-Founder, British Politics Group, 1974; Convenor, Work Group on UK Politics, Political Studies Association, 1976-88; Member, Council, International Political Science Association, 1976-82; Keynote Speaker, Australian Institute of Political Science, Canberra, 1978; Technical Consultant, OECD, World Bank; Director, ESRC (formerly SSRC) Research Programme, Growth of Government, 1982-86; Honorary Vice President, Political Studies Association, UK, 1986; Editor, Journal of Public Policy, since 1985 (Chairman, 1981-85); Foreign Member, Finnish Academy of Science and Letters, 1985; Member, American Academy of Arts and Sciences, 1994; Robert Marjolin AMEX Prize in International Economics, 1992; Lusswell Award for Lifetime Achievement in Public Policy, USA, 1999; Political Studies Association Award for Lifetime Achievement, 2000. Publications: The British General Election of 1959 (Co-author), 1960; Must Labour Lose? (Co-author), 1960; Politics in England, 1964; Studies in British Politics (Editor), 1966; Influencing Voters, 1967; Policy Making in Britain (Editor), 1969; People in Politics, 1970; European Politics (Joint Editor), 1971; Governing Without Consensus — An Irish Perspective, 1971; International Almanack of Electoral History (Co-author), 1974; Electoral Behaviour — A Comparative Handbook (Editor), 1974; Lessons From America (Editor), 1974; The Problem of Party Government, 1974; The Management of Urban Change in Britain and Germany (Editor), 1974; Northern Ireland — A Time of Choice, 1976; Managing Presidential Objectives, 1976; The Dynamics of Public Policy (Editor), 1976; New Trends in British Politics (Joint Editor), 1977; Comparing Public Policies (Joint Editor), 1977; What is Governing? — Purpose and Policy in Washington, 1978; Elections Without Choice (Joint Editor), 1978; Can Government Go Bankrupt? (Co-author), 1978; Britain — Progress and Decline (Joint Editor), 1980; Do Parties Make a Difference?, 1980; Challenge to Governance (Editor), 1980; Electoral Participation (Editor), 1980; Presidents and Prime Ministers (Joint Editor), 1980; Understanding the United Kingdom, 1982; United Kingdom Facts (Co-author), 1982; The Territorial Dimension in United Kingdom Politics (Joint Editor), 1982; Fiscal Stress in Cities (Joint Editor), 1982; Understanding Big Government, 1984; The Nationwide Competition for Votes (Co-author), 1984; Public Employment in Western Nations, 1985; Voters Begin to Choose (Co-author), 1986; Patterns of Parliamentary Legislation (Co-author), 1986; The Welfare State East and West (Joint Editor), 1986; Ministers and Ministries, 1987; Taxation By Political Inertia (Co-author), 1987; The Post-Modern President — The White House Meets the World, 1988; Ordinary People in Public Policy, 1989; Training Without Trainers? (Co-author), 1990; The Loyalty of Voters (Co-author), 1990; Lesson-Drawing in Public Policy, 1993; Inheritance before Choice, 1994; What Is Europe?, 1996; How Russia Votes (Co-author), 1997; Democracy and its Alternatives (Co-author), 1998; A Society Transformed: Hungary in Time-Space Perspective, (Co-author), 1999; The International Encyclopedia of Elections (Editor), 2000; Prime Minister in a Shrinking World, 2001. Recreations: architecture (historical, Britain; modern, America); music; writing. Address: (b.) CSPP, Strathclyde University, Livingstone Tower, Glasgow G1 1XH; T.-0141-548 3217.

Rosebery, 7th Earl of (Neil Archibald Primrose), DL; b. 11.2.29; m., Alison Mary Deirdre Reid; 1 s.; 4 d. Educ. Stowe; New College, Oxford. Succeeded to title, 1974. Address: (h.) Dalmeny House, South Queensferry, West Lothian.

Rosie, George. Freelance Writer and Broadcaster; b. 27.2.41, Edinburgh; m., Elizabeth Ann Burness; 2 s.; 1 d. Educ. Trinity Academy, Edinburgh; Edinburgh School of Architecture. Editor, Interior Design magazine, 1966-68; freelance magazine writer, 1968-76; Scottish Affairs Correspondent, Sunday Times, 1976-86; Reporter, Channel 4 TV series Down the Line, 1986-87, Scottish Eye, 1988; Reporter/Writer, The Englishing of Scotland, 1988, Selling Scotland, 1989; Scotching the Myth, 1990; Losing the Heid, 1991; Independence Day, 1996; Secret Scotland, 1997-98, Our Friends in the South, 1998; After Lockerbie (BAFTA Best Documentary winner, 1999); Editor, Observer Scotland, 1988-89; award winner, RSPB birds and countryside awards, 1988. Publications: British in Vietnam, 1970; Cromarty, 1975; The Ludwig Initiative, 1978; Hugh Miller, 1982; The Directory of International Terrorism, 1986; as contributor: Headlines, the Media in Scotland, 1978; Death's Enemy, the Pilgrimage of Victor Frankenstein, 2001; Scottish Government Yearbook, 1982; Scotland, Multinationals and the Third World, 1982; World Offshore Oil and Gas Industry Report, 1987; stage plays: The Blasphemer, 1990; Carlucco and the Queen of Hearts, 1991 (winner, Fringe First, The Independent Theatre Award); It Had To Be You, 1994; radio plays: The Parsi, 1992; Postcards from Shannon, 2000. Recreation: hill-walking. Address: (h.) 70 Comiston Drive, Edinburgh EH10 5QS; T.-0131-447 9660.

Ross, Rt. Hon. Lord (Donald MacArthur Ross), PC, MA, LLB. Lord Justice Clerk and President of the Second Division of the Court of Session, 1985-97; a Senator of the College of Justice, 1977-97; Chairman, Judicial Studies Committee, Scotland, since 1997; Lord High Commissioner to the General Assembly of the Church of Scotland, 1990 and 1991; b. 29.3.27, Dundee; m., Dorothy Margaret Annand; 2 d. Educ. High School of Dundee; Edinburgh University. Advocate, 1952; QC, 1964; Vice-Dean, Faculty of Advocates, 1967-73; Dean of Faculty, 1973-76; Sheriff Principal of Ayr and Bute, 1972-73; Member, Scottish Committee, Council of Tribunals, 1970-76; Member, Committee on Privacy, 1970; Deputy Chairman, Boundary Commission for Scotland, 1977-85; Member, Court, Heriot-

Watt University, 1978-90, Chairman, 1984-90; Member, Parole Board for Scotland, since 1997; Vice Chairman, Royal Society of Edinburgh, since 1999 (Member, Council, 1997-99). Hon. LLD, Edinburgh, Dundee, Abertay Dundee, Aberdeen; Hon. DUniv, Heriot-Watt; FRSE. Recreation: gardening; walking; travel. Address: (h.) 33 Lauder Road, Edinburgh EH9 2JG; T.-0131-667 5731.

Ross, Alastair Robertson, CStJ, DA, ARSA, FRBS, FSA Scot, FRSA, MBIM, Hon. FRIAS. Artist; Lecturer in Fine Art, Duncan of Jordanstone College University of Dundee, since 1994; Council Member, Royal Scottish Academy, since 1998; b. 8.8.41, Perth; m., Kathryn Margaret Greig Wilson; 1 d. Educ. St Mary's Episcopal School, Dunblane; McLaren High School, Callander; Duncan of Jordanstone College of Art, Dundee. SED Postgraduate Scholarship, 1965-66; Dickson Prize for Sculpture, 1962; Holokrome (Dundee) Sculpture Prize and Commission, 1962; SED Travelling Scholarship, 1963; Royal Scottish Academy Chalmers Bursary, 1964; Royal Scottish Academy Carnegie Travelling Scholarship, 1965; Duncan of Drumfork Scholarship, 1965; award winner, Paris Salon, 1967; Medaille de Bronze, Societe des Artistes Francais, 1968; Professional Member, Society of Scottish Artists, 1969; Lecturer in Fine Art, Duncan of Jordanstone College of Art, Dundee, 1966-94; Honorary Lecturer, Dundee University, 1969-94; Visiting Lecturer, University of Texas, Arlington, USA, 1996; Medaille D'Argent, 1970; Membre Associe, Societe des Artistes Francais, 1970; Scottish Representative and Member, Council, Royal Society of British Sculptors, 1972-92; Sir Otto Beit Medal, Royal Society of British Sculptors, 1988; Freeman, City of London, 1989; Sir William Gillies Bequest Award, Royal Scottish Academy, 1989; Council Member, Society of Scottish Artists, 1972-75; Vice President, Royal Society of British Sculptors, 1988-90; Council Member, British School at Rome, 1990-96; Hon. Fellow, Royal Incorporation of Architects in Scotland, 1992; Member, Board of Directors, Studio and Artists' Workshop Provision Scotland Ltd., since 1997; commissioned to design and sculpt Spirit of Scotland Awards, 1998-2000; exhibited work widely in UK and abroad; work in: Scottish Arts Council Collection, Perth Art Gallery and Museum, Dundee Education Authority Collection, Dundee Art Gallery and Museum, Court of the Lord Lyon HM New Register House; Rank Xerox HQ, Bucks; private collections in Austria, Switzerland, Egypt, USA, Norway, Bahamas, Canada, Portugal, India, UK; awarded Personal Civic Reception by City of Dundee, 1999; Member, Arts and Crafts in Architecture Awards Adjudication Panel, since 2001; Royal Scottish Academy representative, Trust for St. John's Kirk of Perth, since 2001. Recreations: genealogy; heraldry; travel. Address: (h.) Ravenscourt, 28 Albany Terrace, Dundee, DD3 6HS; T.-01382 224235.

Ross, Alexander (Sandy), LLB, CYCW. Managing Director, Scottish Television, since 2000; b. 17.4.48, Grangemouth; m., Alison Fraser; 2 s.; 1 d. Educ. Grangemouth High School; Edinburgh University; Moray House College. Apprentice lawyer, 1971-73; Lecturer, Paisley College, 1974-75; Producer, Granada TV, 1978-86; Controller, Arts and Entertainment, Scottish Television, 1986-95; Deputy Chief Executive, Scottish Television Enterprises, 1995-97; Controller Regional Production, Scottish Media Group, 1997-2000. Member, Edinburgh Town Council, 1971-74; Member, Edinburgh District Council, 1974-78; President, Moray House Students Union, 1976. Recreations: golf; music; reading; watching football. Address: (h.) 7 Murrayfield Avenue, Edinburgh EH12 6AU; T.-0131-539 1192; (b.) 0141-300 3000; e-mail: (h.) murrayfield7@cs.com (b.) sandy.ross@smg.plc.uk

Ross, Rev. Andrew Christian, MA, BD, STM, PhD, FRHistS, DLitt. Honorary Fellow in Ecclesiastical History, Edinburgh University; b. 10.5.31, Millerhill, Lothian; m., I. Joyce Elder; 4 s.; 1 d. (deceased). Educ. Dalkeith High School; Edinburgh University; Union Theological Seminary, New York. RAF, 1952-54; Minister, Church of Central Africa Presbyterian (Malawi), 1958-65; Senior Lecturer in Ecclesiastical History, Edinburgh University, 1966 until retirement (Principal of New College and Dean, Faculty of Divinity, 1978-84). Chairman, Lands Tribunal of Nyasaland, then Malawi Government, 1963-65; Vice Chairman, National Tenders Board, Nyasaland, then Malawi Government, 1963-65. Member, University Court, 1971-73; Convener, Student Affairs Committee, 1977-83; Kerr Lecturer, Glasgow University, 1984; Lecturer, Assembly's College, Belfast, 1985; Visiting Professor, Yale University and Dartmouth College, 1992. Publications: John Philip: Missions, Race and Politics in South Africa; Vision Betrayed: the Jesuits in China and Japan; Blantyre Mission and the Development of Malawi. Recreation: coaching and watching football. Address: (h.) 27 Colinton Road, Edinburgh; T.-0131-447 5987.

Ross, David Craib Hinshaw, LLB (Hons), NP. Partner, Biggart Baillie, Solicitors, since 1977, Chairman and Senior Partner, since 2001; Director, Glasgow Chamber of Commerce, since 1996, Deputy President, since 2001; b. 14.1.48, Glasgow; m., Elizabeth Clark; 2 s.; 1 d. Educ. Kelvinside Academy, Glasgow; Trinity College, Glenalmond; University of Glasgow. Maclay Murray and Spens: Apprenticeship, 1970-72, Assistant, 1972-75; Assistant, Biggart Baillie and Gifford, 1975-77, Head of Corporate, 1997-2001. Member, Executive, Scottish Council Development and Industry; Chairman, Euro-American Lawyers Group, since 1997; Secretary, Loganair Ltd., since 1997. Recreation: rhododendrons; windsurfing. Address: (h.) Eastfield, 10 Ledcameroch Road, Bearsden, Glasgow G61 4AB; T.-0141-942 2569.

Ross, Ernest. MP (Labour), Dundee West, since 1979; Chair, Board of Governors, Westminster Foundation for Democracy; Chair, All Party Group on Poverty; b. 27.7.42, Dundee; m., June; 2 s.; 1 d. Educ. St. John's Junior Secondary School. Apprentice Marine Fitter, Caledon Shipyard; Quality Control Inspector/Engineer, Timex. Recreations: football; cricket. Address: (b.) House of Commons, London SW1A 0AA.

Ross, Fiona, MA. Principal, International Language Academy, since 2000; Singer, Scottish traditional song (Lead Singer, Handsel); b. 16.4.65, Glasgow. Educ. Hyndland Secondary School; University of Glasgow. Taught English overseas; Marketing Manager, Basil Paterson College, 1989-92; Director of Administration and Marketing, Scripps College, California and International House, New York, 1992-95; Educational Marketing Consultant, 1995-97; Principal, Edinburgh Tutorial College, 1997-2000; Principal, Regent Edinburgh, 1997-2000. Recreations: traditional music and song; walking; good food; travel; animals. Address: (h.) 2 The Causeway, Duddingston Village, Edinburgh EH15 3PZ; T.-0131-661 8068; e-mail: FRoss90346@aol.com

Ross, George Syme, BSc (Hons). General Secretary, Headteachers' Association of Scotland, since 1998; b. 21.9.42, Glasgow; m., Nanette; 2 s. Educ. Rutherglen Academy; Strathclyde University; Jordanhill College of Education. Rutherglen Academy: Teacher, 1964-67, Special Assistant, 1967-70; Housemaster, Cathkin High School, 1970-72; Principal Teacher of Chemistry, Clydebank High School, 1972-75; Assistant Headteacher, Bannerman High School, 1975-78; Depute Headteacher, Stanley Green High School, 1978-80; Headteacher, Cowdenknowes High School, 1980-85; Headteacher, Gryffe High School, 1985-97. President, Headteachers' Association of Scotland, 1993-94; Depute Session Clerk, St. John's Church of Scotland, Largs. Recreations: hillwalking; classic cars; model railways. Address: (b.) University of Strathclyde, Jordanhill Campus, Southbrae Drive, Glasgow G13 1PP; T.-0141-950 3298/0147 674046.

Ross, Helen Elizabeth, BA, MA (Oxon), PhD (Cantab), FBPsS, CPsychol, FRSE. Honorary Reader, Stirling University, since 1994; b. 2.12.35, London. Educ. South Hampstead High School; Somerville College, Oxford; Newnham College, Cambridge. Assistant Mistress, schools in London and Oxfordshire, 1959-61; Research Assistant and student, Psychological Laboratory, Cambridge University, 1961-65; Lecturer in Psychology: Hull University, 1965-68, Stirling University, 1969-72; Senior Lecturer in Psychology, Stirling University, 1972-83; Research Fellow, DFVLR Institute for Aerospace Medicine, Bonn, 1980-81; Leverhulme Fellowship, 1983-84; Reader in Psychology, Stirling University, 1983-94; Honorary Reader, Stirling University, since 1994. Member, S.E. Regional Board, Nature Conservancy Council for Scotland, 1991-92; Fellowship Secretary, Royal Society of Edinburgh, 1994-97. Publications: Behaviour and Perception in Strange Environments, 1974; E.H. Weber: The Sense of Touch (Co-translator), 1978; E.H. Weber on the Tactile Senses (Co-translator), 1996. Recreations: skiing; curling; hill-walking; compleat Munroist, 1998; traditional music; Member, Skelpit Lug Ceilidh Band. Address: (b.) Department of Psychology, Stirling University, Stirling FK9 4LA; T.-01786 467647; e-mail: h.e.ross@stir.ac.uk

Ross, John Alexander, CBE, FRAgS. Chairman, Dumfries and Galloway NHS Board, since 2001; Chairman, Dumfries and Galloway Health Board, 1997-2000; Chairman, Dumfries and Galloway Primary Care NHS Trust, 2000-01; b. 19.2.45, Stranraer; m., Alison Jean Darling; 2 s.; 1 d. Educ. George Watson's College, Edinburgh. NFU of Scotland: Convener, Hill Farming Sub-Committee, 1984-90, Wigtown Area President, 1985-86, Convener, Livestock Committee, 1987-90, Vice-President, 1986-90, President, 1990-96. Chairman, Stranraer School Council, 1980-89; Session Clerk, Portpatrick Parish Church, 1975-80; Director, Animal Diseases Research Association; Commissioner, Meat and Livestock Commission, since 1996; Director, NFU Mutual Insurance Society, since 1996. Recreations: golf; curling. Address: Low Auchenree Farm, Portpatrick, Stranraer, Wigtownshire DG9 8TN.

Ross, Rev. Professor Kenneth Rankin, BA, BD (Hons), PhD. General Secretary, Church of Scotland Board of World Mission, since 1998; b. 31.5.58, Glasgow; m., Hester Ferguson Carmichael; 3 s. Educ. Kelvinside Academy, Glasgow; Edinburgh University. Ordained, 1982; Parish Minister, Unst, Shetland, 1982-88; Mission Partner, Board of World Mission, seconded to University of Malawi as Lecturer and latterly Professor of Theology, 1988-98; Honorary Secretary, Jubilee Scotland, since 2001. Publications: Church and Creed in Scotland, 1988; Gospel Ferment in Malawi, 1995; Here Comes Your King! Christ, Church and Nation in Malawi, 1998. Recreations: hill-walking; squash; reading; being on the island of Islay. Address: (b.) 121 George Street, Edinburgh EH2 4YN; T.-0131-225 5722; e-mail: Kross@cofscotland.org.uk

Ross, Rev. Matthew Zachary, LLB, BD, FSAScot. Minister, Ceres and Springfield Parish Church, since 1998; Convener, World Mission Committee, Presbytery of St. Andrews; b. 15.11.67, Dundee. Educ. Westminster School; Edinburgh University; Glasgow University. Research Assistant, House of Commons, 1990-91; Political Researcher, Scottish Liberal Democrats, 1992-93; Researcher, P.S. Public Affairs Consultants Ltd., Edinburgh, 1993-94; Probationer for the ministry, Duddingston Kirk, Edinburgh, 1996-98. Secretary, Scottish Church Society; Member, Board of Practice and Procedure, and of Legal Questions Committee, General Assembly of Church of Scotland; Member, Policy Committee, Centre for Theology and Public Issues, Edinburgh University, 1996-99; former Secretary, United Nations Association, Edinburgh Branch.

Recreations: history; architecture; travel (especially by rail); sharing laughter with friends. Address: (h.) The Manse, Ceres, Cupar KY15 5NQ; T.-01334 828233.

Ross, Michael David, CBE, FFA, CIMgt, FRSA. Chief Executive, Scottish Widows, since 1991; Deputy Group Chief Executive, Lloyds TSB Group, since 2000; Chairman, ABI; Chairman, Scottish Financial Enterprise; b. 9.7.46, Edinburgh; m., Pamela Marquis Speakman. Joined Scottish Widows, 1964, as Trainee Actuary: Assistant General Manager, 1986-88, Appointed Actuary, 1988, General Manager (Finance), 1988-90, Deputy Managing Director, 1990-91. Publication: Transactions of Faculty of Actuaries. Recreations: golf; curling; skiing; gardening. Address: (b.) 69 Morrison Street, Edinburgh EH3 8BW.

Ross, Neil Kilgour, MA, LLB. Partner, Grigor & Young, Solicitors, since 1989; b. 17.5.54, Sutton Coldfield; m., Kathleen Rae; 1 d. Educ. Inverurie Academy; Aberdeen University. Legal apprentice, Western Isles Islands Council, 1977-79; Legal Assistant, Angus District Council, 1979-82; Depute Director of Legal Services, Clerk of the Peace and Clerk to the Licensing Board, Western Isles Islands Council, 1982-85. Director, Moray Council on Addictions; Director, Moray Property Searchers Ltd.; contributor, Stair Memorial Encyclopedia; Member, Council, Law Society of Scotland, since 1994. Recreations: wine; gardening; cricket. Address: (b.) 1 North Street, Elgin IV30 1UA; T.-01343 544077; e-mail: neil@grigor-young.co.uk

Ross, Nicholas Julian, ARCM. Section Principal Clarinet, Orchestra of Scottish Opera, since 1992; b. 29.1.55, Orsett; divorced; 1 s.; 1 d. Educ. Oakham School; Royal Academy of Music, London. Freelance, two years; joined Scottish Opera as 2nd Clarinet, 1980. Recreation: cycling. Address: (h.) 22 Eskdale Street, Glasgow G42 8UD; T.-0141-423 1262.

Ross, Philip Wesley, TD, MD, FRCPath, FRCPE, FRCSE, FIBiol. Honorary Fellow in Medical Microbiology, University of Edinburgh; Visiting Professor, university medical schools and colleges of medicine in India and Africa; Examiner, Royal College of Surgeons of Edinburgh; Inspector, Clinical Pathology Accreditation (UK) Ltd.; b. 6.6.36, Aberdeen; m., Stella Joyce Shand; 2 s.; 1 d. Educ. Turriff Academy; Robert Gordon's College, Aberdeen; Aberdeen University (President, SRC, 1958-59). Senior Warden, Edinburgh University, 1972-83. Lt.-Col., RAMC (TA); Officer Commanding Medical Division and Edinburgh Detachment 205 Scottish General Hospital, 1975-80; Chairman: Lothian Area Division of Laboratory Medicine, 1986-89, Scottish Council, Institute of Biology, 1991-93; President and Chairman of Council, Scottish Microbiology Association, 1997-2000; former Consultant Medical Microbiologist, Royal Infirmary, Edinburgh and Reader, University of Edinburgh; Liberal Democrat Parliamentary Candidate, Monklands East, 1992; Chairman, Edinburgh East Liberal Democrats, 1996-99; Elder, Church of Scotland; Honorary Secretary, Edinburgh Society of Organists. Publications on streptococci, diseases of the mouth, throat and genital tract, infection of the newborn, antibiotics and hospital infection. Recreations: music; playing church organs (organist and choirmaster, Woodside Congregational Church, Bucksburn Parish Church, Holburn Central Church, Aberdeen, 1954-64); travel; walking; old churches; art galleries; politics. Address: (h.) The Old Yard, 38 High Street, Pittenweem, Fife KY10 2PL; T.-01333 312221.

Ross, Robert Fowler. Obituaries Editor, The Herald, since 2000; b. 9.3.40, Crossgates; m., Jeanette Miller; 1 s.; 1 d. Educ. Dunfermline High School. Trainee Reporter, Dunfermline Press; Reporter, Glasgow Herald, Scottish Daily Mail, Scotsman; The Herald: Scottish Office Correspondent, 1972-87, Edinburgh News Editor, 1987-94,

Farming Editor, since 1994. Recreations: gardening; walking. Address: (h.) 57 Oatlands Park, Linlithgow EH49 6AS; T.-01506 842892.

Ross, Thomas Leonard, LLB, DipLP. Advocate, since 2000; b. 25.10.63, Glasgow; m., Alison Mary Laurie; 2 d. Educ. Penilee Secondary, Glasgow; Strathclyde University. Admitted as Solicitor, 1985; Solicitor Advocate, 1998; admitted to Bar, 2000. President, Glasgow Bar Association, 1995; Board Member, Legal Defence Union, 1996-97; Criminal Editor, Scolag, 1994-95. Recreations: Victoria and Rachael Ross; Rangers FC; wine. Address: (h.) 7 Buchlyvie Road, Ralston, Renfrewshire PA1 3AD; T.-0141-581 9375.

Ross Stewart, David Andrew, OBE, BA (Cantab). b. 30.11.30, Edinburgh; m., Susan Olive Routh; 2 s. Educ. Rugby School; Cambridge University. Assistant General Manager, Alex. Cowan & Sons (NZ) Ltd., 1959-62; General Manager, Alex. Cowan & Sons (Stationery) Ltd., 1962-66; General Manager, Spicers (Stationery) Ltd., 1966-68; Managing Director, John Bartholomew & Son Ltd., 1968-89. Director, Quayle Munro Holdings plc; Director, Lothian Investment Fund for Enterprise Ltd.; Hon. Fellow, University of Edinburgh; Fellow, Scottish Council (Development and Industry); Convener, Finance Committee, National Trust for Scotland. Recreations: fishing; gardening. Address: (b.) 13 Blacket Place, Edinburgh EH9 1RN; T.-0131-667 3221.

Rothes, 21st Earl of (Ian Lionel Malcolm Leslie); b. 10.5.32; m.; 2 s. Educ. Eton. Succeeded to title, 1975.

Rotter, Professor John Michael, BA, MA, PhD, FICE, FIEAust. Professor of Civil Engineering, Edinburgh University, since 1989; b. 31.10.48, Chesterfield; 1 s.; 1 d. Educ. Monkton Combe School, Bath; Clare College, Cambridge University; Sydney University. Temporary Lecturer in Civil Engineering, then Lecturer, then Senior Lecturer, University of Sydney, 1975-89; Edinburgh University: Head of Department, 1989-92, Head, Planning Unit for Chemical, Civil and Environmental and Mechanical Engineering, 1992-99, inaugural Director, Division of Engineering, 1998-99. Visiting Professor, University of Washington, St. Louis, 1983-84; Visiting Research Fellow, Liverpool University, 1984; Visiting Professor: INSA, Lyon, France, 1996, 2000, T.U. Graz, Austria, 1997, Henri Poincare Université de Nancy, France, 1997, Technische Universität Wien, Austria, 2000; Convener, European Standards Committee on design of silos, tanks and pipelines, since 1994; Member, Standards Committees: American Concrete Institute, Australian Standards, European Convention for Constructional Steelwork. Publications: two books, 226 technical papers. Recreations: classical music; history; foreign places, cultures and food; hill-walking. Address: (b.) Edinburgh University, King's Buildings, Edinburgh EH9 3JN; T.-0131-650 5719.

Rowallan, Lord (John Polson Cameron), ARICS. Director, Rowallan Holdings Ltd., Rowallan Activity Centre Ltd., Rowallan Ltd.; Director, British Show Jumping Association; Chairman, Lochgoin Covenanters Trust; Chairman, Charities Shopping Day Trust; Director, Sane; b. 8.3.47, Glasgow; m., Claire Rowallan; 2 s.; 2 d; 1 steps.; 1 stepd. Educ. Eton College; Royal Agricultural College. Estate Agent, 1969-74; Farmer, since 1974; Company Director, since 1989; Commentator, since 1986; Patron, Depression Alliance. Recreations: skiing; equestrianism. Address: (h.) Meiklemosside, Fenwick, Ayrshire KA3 6AY.

Rowan-Robinson, Professor Jeremy, MA, LLM. Professor of Planning and Environmental Law, Department of Law, Aberdeen University, 1989-2001, Emeritus Professor, since 2001; Consultant in Planning and Environmental Law, Paull and Williamson, Solicitors,

Aberdeen, since 1992; b. 29.3.44, Lasswade; m., Yvonne; 2 s. Educ. University of Kent at Canterbury; Aberdeen University. Assistant Solicitor, London Borough of Redbridge, 1966; Senior Associate Solicitor, London Borough of Hillingdon, 1969; Solicitor then Deputy Clerk, Westmorland County Council, 1972; Solicitor, Lake District Special Planning Board, 1975; Lecturer, Senior Lecturer, Professor of Land Economy, Aberdeen University, 1978-89; Solicitor of the Supreme Court of England and Wales; Legal Associate, Royal Town Planning Institute. Board Member, Scottish Natural Heritage (Chairman, East Areas Board); Chairman, Access Forum for Scotland. Publications: author or co-author of eight books on planning law and related topics. Recreations: mountaineering; sailing. Address: (h.) 10 Cairnlee Crescent North, Cults, Aberdeen AB15 9TY; T.-01224 861357.

Rowley, Professor David Ian, MB, ChB, BMedBiol, MD, FRCS. Professor of Orthopaedic and Trauma Surgery, Dundee University, since 1988; b. 4.7.51, Dewsbury; m., Ingrid Ginette; 1 s.; 1 d. Educ. Wheelwright Grammar School, Dewsbury; Aberdeen University; Sheffield University. Lecturer in Orthopaedic Surgery, Sheffield University, 1981; Senior Lecturer in Orthopaedic Surgery, Manchester University, and Senior Lecturer in Orthopaedic Mechanics, Salford University, 1985-88. Orthopaedic Editor, Journal of Royal College of Surgeons of Edinburgh, 1993-98; Regional Advisor in Surgery, NE Region, Royal College of Surgeons of Edinburgh; Examiner, Royal College of Surgeons, Edinburgh; Fellow, Royal Colleges, Glasgow, England, ad eundum; Intercollegiate Board Examiner, Orthopaedics; Non-Executive Member, NHS Tayside. Recreations: gardening; reading history. Address: (h.) Marclann Cottage, Kellie Castle, Arbroath; T.-01241 876466.

Rowling, Joanne Kathleen (J.K.), OBE, BA. Writer; b. 31.7.65; m.; 1 d. Educ. Exeter University. Publications: Harry Potter and the Philosopher's Stone, 1997; Harry Potter and the Chamber of Secrets, 1998; Harry Potter and the Prisoner of Azkaban, 1999; Harry Potter and the Goblet of Fire, 2000. Address: Christopher Little Literary Agency, 10 Eel Brook Studios, 125 Moore Park Road, London SW6 4PS.

Rowlings, Professor Cherry, BA. Professor of Social Work, Stirling University, since 1991; Member, Scottish Social Services Council, since 2001; b. 10.11.44, Bristol. Educ. Duncan House School, Bristol; York University; Oxford University. Social Worker, London Borough of Croydon; Team Leader, London Borough of Lewisham; Research Officer, Oxford University; Senior Research Fellow, Keele University; Lecturer/Senior Lecturer, Bristol University. Member, CCETSW Council and Scottish Committee, 1992-2001; Non-Executive Director, Forth Valley Primary Care NHS Trust, 1998-2001. Publications: on social work and services for older people and on social work education in Europe. Address: (b.) Department of Applied Social Science, Stirling University, Stirling FK9 4LA; T.-01786 467710.

Rowlinson, Professor Peter, MA, DPhil. Professor of Mathematics, University of Stirling, since 1996; b. 23.10.44, Cambridge; m., Carolyn. Educ. Cambridgeshire High School; New College, Oxford. University of Stirling: Lecturer in Mathematics, 1969-92, Senior Lecturer in Mathematics, 1992-94, Reader in Mathematics, 1994-96. Visiting Associate Professor of Mathematics, California Institute of Technology, 1975-76. Publication: Eigenspaces of Graphs (Co-author), 1997; journal articles. Recreation: croquet. Address: Department of Computing Science and Mathematics, University of Stirling, Stirling FK9 4LA; T.-01786 467464.

Roxburghe, 10th Duke of (Guy David Innes-Ker), b. 18.11.54; m., 1, Lady Jane Meriel Grosvenor (m. diss.); 2 s.; 1 d.; 2, Virginia Mary Wynn-Williams; 1 s.; 1 d. Educ. Eton; Sandhurst; Magdalene College, Cambridge. Address: (h.) Floors Castle, Kelso.

Roy, Archibald Donald, OBE. Director of Field Operations (Scotland and North), Benefits Agency, since 2000; Director Designate, Pensions Service (Scotland), from April 2002; b. 9.1.45; m., Morag; 2 s. Educ. Woodside Secondary School, Glasgow. Management Trainee, Long John Distillers, 1963-66; Department of Social Security: various positions, Glasgow, 1966-83, Principal Inspector, London, 1983-88, Manager, Glasgow, 1988-92, Area Director, Glasgow and Paisley, 1992-97; Area Director, West of Scotland, Benefits Agency, 1997-2000. Member, Strathclyde Steering Committee, Prince's Trust Volunteers; Member, Lomond Mountain Rescue Team. Recreations: reading; music; mountaineering. Address: Argyle House, 3 Lady Lawson Street, Edinburgh EH3 9SH; T.-0131-2214520; e-mail: archie.roy@dwp.gsi.gov.uk

Roy, Frank, BA. MP (Labour), Motherwell and Wishaw, since 1997; PPS to Helen Liddell, Secretary of State for Scotland, since 2001; b. 29.8.58, Motherwell; m., Ellen Foy; 1 s.; 1 d. Educ. St Joseph's High School, Motherwell; Our Lady's High School, Motherwell; Motherwell College; Glasgow Caledonian University. Ravenscraig steelworker, 1977-91; PPS to Helen Liddell, Deputy Secretary of State for Scotland, 1998-99; PPS to Dr John Reid, MP, Secretary of State for Scotland, 1999-2001. Address: (b.) House of Commons, London SW1A 0AA; T.-0171-219 3000; e-mail: Royf@parliament.uk

Roy, Kenneth. Founder and Director, Institute of Contemporary Scotland, since 2000; Publisher, Who's Who in Scotland, since 1985; Editor, The Scottish Review, since 1994; b. 26.3.45, Falkirk; m., Margaret H. Campbell; 2 s. Educ. Denny High School. Local newspapers, 1962-1965; Glasgow Herald, 1965-67; public relations, 1967-69; founder Editor, Scottish Theatre magazine, 1969-72; news and current affairs anchorman, BBC Scotland, 1972-80; founder Managing Director, West Sound, 1980-82; founder Editor, The Journalist's Handbook, 1985-93; former weekly Columnist: Scotland on Sunday, The Herald, The Observer; former daily Columnist, The Scotsman. Critic of the Year, Scottish Press Awards, 1990, 1993; Columnist of the Year, UK Press Gazette Awards, 1994; Past President, Auchinleck Boswell Society; Winner, Oliver Brown Award, 2002. Publications: Travels in a Small Country, 1987; Conversations in a Small Country, 1989; The Closing Headlines, 1993; Scenes from a Small Country, 1994; Both Sides of the Border, 1998; Alastair Hetherington: A Man of His Word (Editor), 1998; Dictionary of Scottish Biography, Vol. I (Editor), 1999. Recreation: travel. Address: (b.) Carrick Media, 1/4 Galt House, 31 Bank Street, Irvine KA12 0LL; T.-01294 311322.

Roy, Lindsay Allan, BSc. Rector, Inverkeithing High School, since 1989; Member, Board of Management, Lauder College, since 1998, (Chairman of its Curriculum and Student Affairs Committee); Member, Council, Headteachers' Association of Scotland, since 1998; Associate Assessor, HMI Inspection of Schools, since 1997; b. 19.1.49, Perth; m., Irene Elizabeth Patterson; 2 s.; 1 d. Educ. Perth Academy; Edinburgh University. Assistant Rector, Kirkcaldy High School, 1983-86; Depute Rector, Glenwood High School, Glenrothes, 1986-89; Chairman, Modern Studies Association, 1976-79; Chairman, Modern Studies Panel, Scottish Examination Board, 1980-83; Member, Consultative Committee on the Curriculum Central Committee for Social Subjects, 1978-85; Chairman, Higher Still Group Awards Steering Committee, 1996-98. Recreation: angling. Address: (b.) Inverkeithing High School, Hillend Road, Inverkeithing, Fife; T.-01383 313400.

Royan, Professor Bruce, BA (Hons), MBA, MBCS, FIInfSc, FLA, FIMgt, FSA(Scot). Chief Executive, Scottish Cultural Resources Access Network, since 1996; Principal Consultant, Infologistix Ltd., since 1988; Visiting Professor of Publishing and Communications, Napier University, since 1997; b. 22.1.47, Luton; m., Ann Elizabeth Wilkins; 1 s.; 1 d. Educ. Dunstable Grammar School; North West Polytechnic; Glasgow University. Systems Development Manager, British Library, 1975-77; Head of Systems, National Library of Scotland, 1977-85; Director, Singapore Integrated Library Automation Service, 1985-88; Director of Information Services and University Librarian, Stirling University, 1989-96. Secretary, Working Party on Access to the National Database, 1980-83; Member, Council, Library Association of Singapore, 1987-88; Convenor, Higher Education IT Directors in Scotland, 1991-93; Executive Chairman, Bath Information and Data Services, 1991-96; Councillor, The Library Association, 1994-99; Chair, National Datasets Steering Group, 1994-96; Board Member, Croydon Libraries Internet Project, 1995-96; Chair, Scottish Collaborative On Demand Publishing Enterprise,1996-98; Councillor, Institute of Information Scientists, 1997-99; Member, Content Creation Task Group, New Opportunities Fund, 1998; Member, National Grid for Learning Scottish Steering Group, since 1998; Chair, UK Metadata for Education Group, since 2000; Chair, British Council Library and Information Advisory Committee, since 2001; Member, Culture Online Steering Committee, since 2001. Recreations: choral singing; antique maps; travel. Address: (b.) SCRAN, Abden House, 1 Marchhall Crescent, Edinburgh EH16 5HW.

Royle, Trevor Bridge, MA, FRSE. Author and Journalist; Associate Editor, Sunday Herald; b. 26.1.45, Mysore, India; m., Dr. Hannah Mary Rathbone; 3 s. Educ. Madras College, St. Andrews; Aberdeen University. Editor, William Blackwood & Sons Ltd.; Literature Director, Scottish Arts Council, 1971-79; Council Member, Scottish National Dictionary Association; Vice-Chairman, The Airborne Initiative; Scottish Arts Council Book Award, 1983. Publications: We'll Support You Evermore: The Impertinent Saga of Scottish Fitba' (Co-Editor), 1976; Jock Tamson's Bairns (Editor), 1977; Precipitous City: The Story of Literary Edinburgh, 1980; A Diary of Edinburgh, 1981; Edinburgh, 1982; Death Before Dishonour: The True Story of Fighting Mac, 1982; The Macmillan Companion to Scottish Literature, 1983; James and Jim: The Biography of James Kennaway, 1983; The Kitchener Enigma, 1985; The Best Years of their Lives: The Post-War National Service Experience, 1986; War Report: The War Correspondents' View of Battle from the Crimea to the Falklands, 1987; The Last Days of the Raj, 1989; A Dictionary of Military Quotations, 1989; Anatomy of a Regiment, 1990; In Flanders Fields: Scottish poetry and prose of the First World War, 1990; Glubb Pasha, 1992; Mainstream Companion to Scottish Literature, 1993; Orde Wingate: Irregular Soldier, 1995; Winds of Change, 1996; Scottish War Stories (Editor), 1999; Crimea – The Great Crimean War, 1854–56, 1999; radio plays: Magnificat, 1984; Old Alliances, 1985; Foreigners, 1987; Huntingtower, 1988; A Man Flourishing, 1988; The Pavilion on the Links, 1991; The Suicide Club, 1992; Tunes of Glory, 1995; stage play: Buchan of Tweedsmuir, 1991. Recreations: watching rugby football; hill-walking. Address: (h.) 6 James Street, Edinburgh EH15 2DS; T.-0131-669 2116.

Ruckley, Professor Charles Vaughan, CBE, MB, ChM, FRCSEdin, FRCPEdin. Emeritus Professor of Vascular Surgery, Edinburgh University; former Consultant Surgeon, Royal Infirmary, Edinburgh; b. 14.5.34, Wallasey; m., Valerie Anne Brooks; 1 s.; 1 d. Educ. Wallasey Grammar School; Edinburgh University. Research Fellow, University of Colorado, 1967-68. Vascular Surgical Society, Great Britain and Ireland: President, 1993-94, Secretary/Treasurer; Chairman, Venous Forum, Royal Society of Medicine, 1997-99; Member, Council, Association of

Surgeons of Great Britain and Ireland. Recreations: angling; music; skiing. Address: (b.) 1 Mayfield Terrace, Edinburgh EH9 1RU; T.-0131-667 8678.

Rumbles, Michael John, MSc (Econ), BEd. MSP (Liberal Democrat), West Aberdeenshire and Kincardine, since 1999; b. 10.6.56, South Shields; m., Pauline; 2 s. Educ. St James' School, Hebburn; Durham University; University of Wales. Army Officer, 1979-94; Team Leader, Business Management, Aberdeen College, 1995-99. Convener, Standards Committee, Scottish Parliament. Address: (b.) The Scottish Parliament, Edinburgh EH99 1SP; T.-0131-348 5798; 6 Dee Street, Banchory AB31 5ST; T.-01330 820268.

Runciman, William Chisholm, LLB. Chief Executive, Carnegie Dunfermline and Hero Fund Trusts; b. 15.11.41, Greenock; m., Eileen; 2 s. Educ. Greenock Academy; Edinburgh University. Police Officer in Edinburgh and Lothian & Borders, retiring in 1987 as Chief Superintendent; former Director, National Playing Fields Association — Scotland. Recreations: mountaineering; fishing; photography; ceramics. Address: (h.) 11 East Harbour Road, Charlestown, Fife KY11 3EA.

Rundell, David Richard, BSc, MSc, MBCS, CEng, CStat. Director of Computing Services, Heriot-Watt University, since 1990; b. 5.9.48, Plymouth; m., Nora; 3 d.; 1 step-d. Educ. Harwich County High, Harwich, Essex; St. Andrews University; Heriot-Watt University. Statistician, Medical School, Edinburgh University, 1970-76; Applications Team, Regional Computing Centre, University of Bath, 1976-79; User Services Manager, Computer Centre, Heriot-Watt University, 1979-90. Address: (b.) Computer Centre, Heriot-Watt University, Riccarton, Edinburgh EH14 4AS; T.-0131-449 5111.

Rush, Christopher, MA (Hons). Writer; b. 23.11.44, St. Monans; m., Patricia Irene Boyd (deceased); 1 s.; 1 d. Educ. Waid Academy; Aberdeen University. Former Teacher, George Watson's College, Edinburgh. Has won three Scottish Arts Council bursaries, two SAC book awards, twice been short-listed for Scottish Book of the Year Award; shortlisted for McVitie Scottish Writer of the Year, 1988; Screenwriter, Venus Peter (based on own book). Publications include: Peace Comes Dropping Slow; A Resurrection of a Kind; A Twelvemonth and A Day; Two Christmas Stories; Into the Ebb; With Sharp Compassion; Venus Peter Saves the Whale; Last Lesson of the Afternoon. Recreations: music; reading; running; the sea. Address: (h.) East Cottage, Newton of Wormiston, Crail, Fife KY10 3XH; T.-01333 451229.

Russell, Adrian Paul Grenville, PhD, BEng. Director, UK Astronomy Technology Centre, since 1998; b. 11.9.61, Sheffield; m., Lilie Anne. Educ. Newfield School, Sheffield; University of Sheffield; University of Cambridge. Joined Royal Observatory Edinburgh, 1987; posted to Hawaii as Support Scientist, James Clerk Maxwell Telescope (JCMT), 1990; Max Planck Institute, Munich, Germany, 1990; JCMT Instrumentation Programme Manager, Royal Observatory Edinburgh, 1992; UK Gemini Project Manager, 1995-2001. Address: Royal Observatory, Blackford Hill, Edinburgh EH9 3HJ; T.-0131-668 8313.

Russell, (Alastair) Muir, KCB, FRSE. Permanent Secretary, Scottish Executive, since 1999; b. 9.1.49; m., Eileen Alison Mackay. Educ. High School of Glasgow; Glasgow University. Joined Scottish Office, 1970; seconded as Secretary to Scottish Development Agency, 1975-76; Assistant Secretary, 1981; Principal Private Secretary to Secretary of State for Scotland, 1981-83; Under Secretary, 1990; seconded to Cabinet Office, 1990-92; Under Secretary (Housing), Scottish Office Environment Department, 1992-95; Deputy Secretary, Secretary and Head of Department, Scottish Office Agriculture and Fisheries Department, 1995-98; Permanent Under-Secretary of State, Scottish Office, 1998-99. Non-Executive Director, Stagecoach Holdings, 1992-95; Doctor of Laws, University of Strathclyde, 2000. Recreations: music; food; wine. Address: (b.) Scottish Executive, St Andrew's House, Regent Road, Edinburgh EH1 3DG; e-mail: muir.russell@scotland.gsi.gov.uk

Russell, Sheriff Albert Muir Galloway, CBE, QC, BA (Oxon), LLB. Sheriff, Grampian, Highland and Islands, at Aberdeen, 1971-91; b. 26.10.25, Edinburgh; m., Margaret Winifred Millar; 2 s.; 2 d. Educ. Edinburgh Academy; Wellington College; Brasenose College, Oxford; Edinburgh University. Lt., Scots Guards, 1944-47; Member, Faculty of Advocates, 1951; Standing Junior Counsel to Board of Trade, Department of Agriculture and Forestry Commission; QC (Scot), 1965; Vice Chairman, Board of Management, Southern Group of Hospitals, Edinburgh, 1966-70; Governor, Moray House College of Education, 1965-70. Recreations: golf; music. Address: (h.) Tulloch House, 1 Aultbea, Ross-shire IV22 2JB.

Russell, Professor Elizabeth Mary, CBE, MD, DipSocMed, DObstRCOG, FFCM, FRCPGlas, FRCPEdin, MRCGP, FRSE. Professor of Social Medicine, Aberdeen University; Hon. Consultant in Public Health Medicine, since 1972; b. 27.1.36, Preston. Educ. Marr College, Troon; Glasgow University. General practice until 1964; medical management and social medicine, 1964-72; academic public health and health services research, since 1972. Recreations: skiing; gardening; music. Address: (b.) Kilburn, Inchgarth Road, Pitfodels, Aberdeen AB15 9NX; T.-01224 861216; e-mail: e.m.russell@abdn.ac.uk

Russell, George Stuart, OBE, BL, CA, WS. Former Senior Partner, Strathern and Blair WS, now Anderson Strathern, WS; b. 21.1.14, Edinburgh; m., Nicholas Mary Gillespie; 1 s.; 3 d. Educ. Edinburgh Academy; Belhaven Hill; Harrow; Edinburgh University. CA, 1937; served Second World War, 1939-45 (Lt. Col.); OBE (Mil); Belgian Ordre de la Couronne; Polish Golden Cross of Merit with Swords; pursued a legal career; Fiscal, WS Society, 1973-79; Solicitor to the National Trust for Scotland, 1951-82, now Councillor Emeritus; Treasurer, Iona Community, 1947-65; President, Edinburgh Abbeyfield Society, 1978-92, now Vice-President; Vice President, UK, Abbeyfield Society, 1975-83; Trustee, Scottish Churches Architectural Heritage Trust, 1982-95; first Chairman, Lothian Building Preservation Trust, 1984-90; Member, Queen's Bodyguard for Scotland (Royal Company of Archers). Recreations: fishing; walking; erecting plaques and view indicators; history of National Trust for Scotland. Address: 59 Braid Road, Edinburgh EH10 6AR; T.-0131-447 6009.

Russell, Ian Gordon, BEd, PhD. Director, Elphinstone Institute, Aberdeen University, since 1999; b. 17.2.47, Aberdeen; m., Norma; 1 s. Educ. King's School, Ely; Nottingham High School; Sheffield City College of Education; Leeds University. Headteacher, Anston Greenlands School, Rotherham, 1986-99; fieldwork in folklore and ethnology, since 1969; broadcast, made films, lectured, in UK and USA; created archive of Village Carols; published widely on traditional singing, humour, and Christmas carols; Director, Village Carols; Director, Festival of Village Carols; Editor, Folk Music Journal, 1980-93; Director, North Atlantic Fiddle Convention. Recreations: singing and playing folk music; walking; Morris dancing; travel. Address: (b.) Elphinstone Institute, Aberdeen University, 24 High Street, Aberdeen AB24 3EB; T.-01224 272386.

Russell, Ian Simon Macgregor, BComHons. Chief Executive, Scottish Power PLC; b. 16.1.53, Edinburgh; m., Fiona; 1 s.; 1 d. Educ. George Heriot's School; Edinburgh

University. Formerly Finance Director, Scottish Power PLC. Recreations: golf; rugby. Address: (b.) 1 Atlantic Quay, Glasgow G2 8SP; T.-0141-636 4511.

Russell, Rev. John, MA. Minister, Tillicoultry Parish Church, 1978-2000; b. 29.5.33, Glasgow; m., Sheila Spence; 2 s. Educ. Cathedral School, Bombay; High School of Glasgow; Glasgow University. Licensed by Glasgow Presbytery, 1957; ordained by United Church of Canada, 1959; Assistant Minister: Trinity United Church, Kitchener, Ontario, 1958-60, South Dalziel Church, Motherwell, 1960-62; Minister: Scots Church, Rotterdam, 1963-72, Southend Parish Church, Kintyre, 1972-78; Member of various General Assembly Committees, since 1972; Convener, General Assembly's Committee on Unions and Readjustments, 1987-90; Convener, Parish Reappraisal Committee, 1990-94; Vice Convener, Board of National Mission, 1994-95; Convener, Board of National Mission, 1995-96; Moderator, Presbytery of Stirling, 1993-94; Clerk, Presbytery of Dunkeld and Meigle, 2001. Recreations: travel; reading. Address: Kilblaan, Gladstone Terrace, Birnam, Dunkeld PH8 0DP; T.-01350 728896.

Russell, John Graham, FCIT. Chairman, John G. Russell (Transport) Ltd., since 1969; Chairman, Fife Warehousing Ltd., since 1988; Director: Combined Transport Ltd., since 1991, Freight Transport Association, since 1994, Alloa Warehousing, since 1988; Chairman, The Scottish Business Crime Centre, since 1996; b. Edinburgh; m., Isobel Margaret Hogg; 2 s.; 2 d. Educ. Merchiston Castle School, Edinburgh. Address: (b.) Belgrave Street, North Industrial Estate, Bellshill ML4 3NP; T.-01698 849301; e-mail: john.russell@johngrussell.co.uk

Russell, John S., BSc. Senior Education Officer, BBC; Secretary, Educational Broadcasting Council for Scotland, since 1989; b. 14.11.46, Glasgow; m., Anne Hendry; 2 s. Educ. St. Mungo's Academy, Glasgow; University of Glasgow. Field Marketing Manager, Proctor and Gamble (UK), 1970-74; Principal Teacher, Guidance, Teacher of Geography, St. Mungo's Academy, 1974-82; Assistant Headteacher, St. Patrick's, Coatbridge, 1982-85; Education Officer, BBC, West of Scotland, 1985-89. Prison Visitor; Member, Helping Offenders Prisoners and Families. Recreations: family; work. Address: BBC, Queen Margaret Drive, Glasgow G12 8DG; T.-0141-338 3422; e-mail: john.russell@bbc.co.uk

Russell, Laurie James, BSc, MPhil. Chief Executive, Strathclyde European Partnership, since 1989; b. 8.8.51, Glasgow; m., Pam; 2 s. Educ. Glasgow University. Researcher, Planning Department, Strathclyde Regional Council, 1976-78; Area Co-ordinator, Faifley Initiative, Clydebank, 1978-84; Executive, Chief Executive's Department, Strathclyde Regional Council, 1984-87; PA to Chief Executive, Strathclyde Regional Council, 1987-89. Recreations: politics; European issues; music; golf. Address: (b.) SEP Ltd., 94 Elmbank Street, Glasgow G2 4DL; T.-0141-572 4400.

Russell, Professor Michael John, EurIng, PhD, CEng. Research Professor, Scottish Universities Research and Reactor Centre, since 1999; b. 12.3.39, Sutton, Surrey. Educ. London University; Durham University. Professor and Head, Department of Applied Geology, Strathclyde University, 1984-89; Dixon Professor of Applied Geology, Glasgow University, 1989-99; research interests: origin of life, fossilized micro-organisms on Mars. Recreation: science. Address: (h.) 27 Hamilton Drive, Glasgow G12 8DN; T.-0141-339 2711.

Russell, Michael William, MA. MSP (SNP), South of Scotland, since 1999; Shadow Minister for Children and Education; Member, Education Culture and Sport Committee; b. 9.8.53; m., Cathleen Macaskill; 1 s. Educ. Marr College, Troon; Edinburgh University. Creative

Producer, Church of Scotland, 1974-77; Director, Cinema Sgire, Western Isles, 1977-81; Founder and first Director, Celtic Film and Television Festival, 1980; Secretary General, Association for Film and Television in the Celtic Countries, 1981-83; Chief Executive, Network Scotland Ltd., 1983-91; Chief Executive, Scottish National Party, 1994-99; Director, Eala Bhan Ltd., since 1991. Parliamentary candidate (SNP), Clydesdale, 1987, Cunninghame South, Scottish Parliamentary elections, 1999; Executive Vice Convenor in charge of Publicity, SNP, 1987-91; Chairman, Save a Life in Scotland Campaign, 1986-88; Trustee, Celtic Film and TV Association, 1990-95; Board Director, Glasgow Film Theatre, 1992-96; Shadow Minister for Parliament, 1999-2000. Publications: A Poem of Remote Lives, 1997; In Waiting: travels in the shadow of Edwin Muir, 1998. Recreations: gardening; cookery. Address: The Scottish Parliament, Edinburgh EH99 1SP; T.-0131-348 5679; Constituency Office, Dalblair House, 45 Dalblair Road, Ayr KA7 1UG; T.-01292 290611; e-mail: Michael.Russell.msp@scottish.parliament.uk

Russell, Sir Robert Mark, MA (Oxon), KCMG. Chairman, C-Mist Ltd. (Centre for Maritime and Industrial Safety Technology), since 1993; b. 3.9.29, India; m., Virginia Mary Rogers; 2 s.; 2 d. Educ. Trinity College, Glenalmond; Exeter College, Oxford University. Royal Artillery, 1952-54; H.M. Diplomatic Service, 1954-89; Assistant Under Secretary of State, F.C.O., 1978-82; H.M. Ambassador to Turkey, 1983-86; Deputy Under Secretary of State, F.C.O., 1986-89. Chairman, Margaret Blackwood Housing Association, 1990-98; Chairman, Scottish International Resource Programme, 1992-2000; Chairman, Centre for Commonwealth, United Nations and International Affairs, 1996-2000. Recreations: music; travel. Address: (h.) 20 Meadow Place, Edinburgh EH9 1JR.

Russell, Robin Irvine, MD, PhD, FRCPEdin, FRCPGlas, FACN, FACP. Consultant in Charge, Department of Gastroenterology, Royal Infirmary, Glasgow, since 1970; Consultant Physician and Gastroenterologist, Royal Infirmary, Glasgow, and Glasgow University, since 1970; b. 21.12.36, Wishaw; m., Ann Tindal Wallace; 1 s.; 1 d. Educ. Glasgow University. Member, medical and scientific staff: Medical Research Council Gastroenterology Unit, London, National Institutes of Health, USA. Chairman, British Digestive Diseases Foundation (Scotland); Member: Association of Physicians, British Society of Gastroenterology, American Gastroenterological Association. Publications: Elemental Diets; Investigative Tests and Techniques in Gastroenterology; Nutrition in Gastro-Intestinal Disease; papers on mechanisms of cellular damage and protection in the gastro-intestinal tract, physiology of intestinal absorption, NSAID and Helicobacter damage in gastrointestinal tract, coeliac disease, Crohn's disease, clinical and experimental nutrition. Recreations: golf; travel; literature; music. Address: (h.) 28 Ralston Road, Bearsden, Glasgow G61 3BA; T.-0141-942 6613.

Russell, Shendl, DCE. Chairman, Scottish Official Board of Highland Dancing, since 1996; Head Teacher; b. 29.3.56, Ayr; m., Robert D. Harvey. Educ. Ayr Academy; Craigie College. Scottish Official Board of Highland Dancing: Delegate, South Africa, Australia; former Scottish champion. Recreations: dancing; football; rugby. Address: (h.) 3 Greenside Avenue, Prestwick KA9 2HB; T.-01292 478577.

Russell, Professor William Clelland, BSc, PhD, FRSE. Professor of Biochemistry, University of St. Andrews, 1984-95, now Emeritus Research Professor; b. 9.8.30, Glasgow; m. 1, Dorothy Ada Brown (deceased); 2, Margaret McDougall; 1 s.; 1 d. Educ. Allan Glens' School, Glasgow; University of Glasgow. Chemist, Royal Ordnance

Factories, 1955-56; Research Chemist, J&P Coats, Paisley, 1956-59; Research Fellow: Virology Unit, University of Glasgow, 1959-63, Ontario Cancer Institute, Toronto, Canada, 1963-64; staff member, latterly Head of Virology Division, MRC at National Institute for Medical Research, London, 1964-84. Member: MRC Grants Committee, SHHD Biomedical Committee; Chair, Scientists for Labour, since 1995. Publications: over 140 scientific papers. Recreations: walking; music. Address: (h.) 3 Osborne Terrace, Crail, Fife KY10 3RR; T.-01333 450614; e-mail: wcr@st-andrews.ac.uk

Russell-Johnston, Lord (David Russell Russell-Johnston), MA (Hons). MP (Liberal Democrat), Inverness, Nairn and Lochaber (formerly Inverness), 1964-97; b. 28.7.32, Edinburgh; m., Joan Graham Menzies; 3 s. Educ. Carbost Public School; Portree High School; Edinburgh University; Moray House College of Education. National Service: commissioned into Intelligence Corps and 2nd i/c British Intelligence Unit, Berlin, 1958-59; History Teacher, Liberton Secondary School, Edinburgh, 1961-63; Research Assistant, Scottish Liberal Party, 1963-64; Joint Parliamentary Adviser, Educational Institute of Scotland, 1964-70; Member, Royal Commission on Local Government in Scotland, 1966-69; Parliamentary Spokesman for Scottish National Federation for the Welfare of the Blind, 1967-97; Parliamentary Representative, Royal National Institute for the Blind, 1977-97; Member, Select Committee on Scottish Affairs, 1969; Parliamentary Adviser, Scottish Police Federation, 1971-75; Scottish Liberal Party: elected to Executive, 1961, and Organisation Committee, 1962, Vice Chairman, 1965, Chairman, 1970-74, Leader, 1974-88, President, 1988-94; Liberal Party Spokesman on Education, 1964-66, on Foreign Affairs, 1970-75 and 1979-85, on Scotland, 1970-73, 1975-83, 1985-88, on Devolution, 1975, on Defence, 1983-88; Member, House of Commons Committee on Privileges, 1988-92; Liberal Democrat Parliamentary Spokesman, Foreign and Commonwealth Affairs, 1988-89, European Affairs, 1988-94, East/West Relations, 1989-94, Central and Eastern Europe, 1994-97; Leader, Council of Europe Liberal Democrat and Reform Group, 1994-99; President, Council of Europe Sub Committee on Youth and Sport, 1992-94; Vice President, WEU Committee on Parliamentary and Public Relations, since 1995; Chairman, Council of Europe Committee on Culture and Education, 1996-99; President, Parliamentary Assembly of the Council of Europe, since 1999; Vice President, Liberal International, since 1994; Member, European Parliament, 1973-75 and 1976-79; Vice President, European Liberal Group and Group Spokesman on Regional Policy, 1973-75; Vice President of the Parliament's Political Committee, 1976-79; Member, Assemblies of Western European Union and Council of Europe, 1984-85, and since 1987; President, Scottish Liberal Democrats, 1988-94; Deputy Leader, Parliamentary Party, 1988-92; Vice President, ELDR, 1990-92. Created Knight Bachelor, 1985; Created Lord Russell-Johnston of Minginish in Highland, 1997. Recreations: reading; photography; shinty (Vice Chief, Camanachd Association, 1987-90). Address: House of Lords, London, SW1A OPW; T.-0171-219 5353.

Rutherford, Alan Gray, OBE, BSc, PhD, CChem, CEng, FRSC, FInstE, FInstBrew, FRSA. Chairman, Newton EH6 Ltd, since 2000; Director, Highlands and Islands Enterprise, since 1998; Hon. Professor, Heriot-Watt University, since 1998; b. 9.10.42, Cramlington; m., Roslyn Anne Moore; 1 s.; 1 d. Educ. Gosforth Grammar School, Newcastle upon Tyne; Sheffield University; Newcastle upon Tyne University. Cookson Group of companies, three years; Scottish & Newcastle Breweries, 14 years, latterly as Group Personnel Director; joined Distillers Company Ltd. as Head of Research and Development, 1984; Director, United Distillers and Vintners, UK Operations, 1988-98. Executive Member, Scottish Council Development & Industry, 1988-98; Council Member, Scotch Whisky Association, 1990-98;

President, Malt Distillers' Association of Scotland, 1991-94; Hon. Col., 15 Para (SV) and 4 Para (V), 1989-99; President, North Region, Parachute Regimental Association; Co-founder and Chairman, The Airborne Initiative (Scotland) Ltd.; Director, The Clark Pub Co. Ltd., since 1997; Member, Board of Management, International Centre for Brewing and Distilling; Liveryman, Worshipful Company of Distillers, since 1994. Recreations: TA; hillwalking; Scottish history. Address: 18 Murrayfield Gardens, Edinburgh EH12 6DF.

Rutherford, Rev. Brian Craig, PhD, BSc, BD. Minister, Mastrick Parish, Aberdeen, since 1990; Member, Aberdeen City Council, since 1999; b. 8.6.47, Glasgow; m., Jean Walker; 2 s. Educ. King's Park Secondary School, Glasgow; Glasgow University; Edinburgh University; Aberdeen University. Assistant Minister, Carrick Knowe Parish, Edinburgh, 1976-77; Minister, Strathbrock Parish, West Lothian, 1977-83; Minister, Greyfriars/St. Ann's Church, Trinidad, 1983-87; General Treasurer, Blantyre Synod, Church of Central Africa Presbyterian, Blantyre, Malawi, 1988-89. Member: Edinburgh Corporation, 1973-75, Edinburgh District Council 1974-80 (JP, 1977-80), West Lothian District Council, 1980-83, Aberdeen District Council, 1992-96. Address: (h.) 13 Beechgrove Avenue, Aberdeen AB15 5EZ; T.-01224 638011.

Rutherford, Colin, BA, CA. Chief Executive, Intelli Partners Plc/Director, Intelli Corp. Fin. Ltd., since 1999; Director: Euro Sales Finance plc, since 1998, James Donaldson & Sons Ltd., since 1994; b. 17.2.59, Edinburgh; m., Karen Elizabeth; 1 s.; 2 d. Educ. Royal High School; Heriot-Watt University. Touche Ross & Co., CAs, Edinburgh and London (Audit and Corporate Finance), 1981-85; Waverley Asset Management, Edinburgh (Unit and Investment Trust), 1985-86; founded Rutherford Manson Dowds (RMD), 1986; Chief Executive, RMD Group plc, 1997-99; Managing Partner, RMD CAs, 1986-97. Recreations: fishing; shooting; travel; wines; food. Address: (b.) 29 Rutland Square, Edinburgh EH1 2BW; T.-0131-222 9400.

Rutherford, Henry Roan, PhD, MSc, BArch, RIBA, FRIAS, MRTPI. Director, Wren Rutherford Austin Smith Lord, since 1997; b. 30.11.46, Dunfermline; m., Alison Moira Peebles; 1 s.; 1 d. Educ. Bell Baxter High School, Cupar; Heriot-Watt University; University of Edinburgh; University of Glasgow. Irvine New Town Corporation: Conservation Officer, 1972, Architect, Housing Group, 1974, Principal Architect (Housing), 1978; Partner, Wren Rutherford Architects, 1997. Awarded Joint Best Architect in Scotland, 1996; two Civic Trust Awards; four Saltire Society Awards; four RIBA Awards Scotland, four RIAS Awards. Recreations: sailing; hillwalking. Address: (b.) 202 Bath Street, Glasgow; T.-0141-331 0401.

Rutherford, William Hay, MA, LLB. Advocate in Aberdeen, since 1949; Honorary Sheriff, Grampian, Highland and Islands, since 1974; b. 9.11.16, Forres; m., Dr. Jean Aitken Steel Wilson; 1 s.; 2 d. Educ. Forres Academy; Aberdeen University. Law Apprentice, James & George Collie, Advocates, Aberdeen, 1935-39; 51st Highland Division, Royal Signals, 1939-46 (taken prisoner, St. Valery, France, 1940; held prisoner, Stalag VIIIB, Upper Silesia, 1940-45); Legal Assistant, John Angus, Advocate, Aberdeen, 1946-61; Partner, Christie, Buthlay & Rutherford, Advocates, Aberdeen, 1962-78, Raeburn Christie & Co., 1978-87. President, Society of Advocates, Aberdeen, 1985-86; Session Clerk, Kirk of St. Nicholas (City Kirk of Aberdeen), 1954-97; President, Royal Northern Agricultural Society, 1980; Chairman (part-time), Industrial Tribunals (Scotland), 1981-88; holder of British Horse Society 1994 Horse Trials Award for outstanding service to the sport. Recreations: country walking and wildlife study. Address: 38 Gladstone Place, Queen's Cross, Aberdeen AB10 6XA.

Ruthven, Ian Scott, MB, ChB, FRCP, CH, FRCPEdin, FRCPGlas, DObstRCOG. Consultant Paediatrician, Ayrshire and Arran Health Board, 1969-2001; President, Scottish Paediatric Society, 2000-01; b. 9.3.37, Glasgow; m., Louisa Mary Jolly; 1 s.; 2 d. Educ. High School of Glasgow; Glasgow University. Junior hospital appointments, various Glasgow hospitals and in New Jersey, USA; former Clinical Director, Hospital Paediatric Services in Ayrshire. Recreations: golf; angling; hill-walking. Address: (h.) Westholme, 10 Victoria Drive, Troon KA10 6EN; T.-01292 313006.

Ryan, Jack, DipComEd. Chief Executive, Crossroads (Scotland), since 1997; b. 9.6.61, Hamilton; m., Janine Barbour; 2 s. Educ. Hamilton Grammar School; Moray House, Edinburgh. Draughtsman, 1978-81; professional musician, 1981-83; Community Musician, Strathclyde Regional Council, 1983-88; Senior Development Officer, Govan Initiative Ltd., 1990-91; Project Manager, CAVOC Motherwell, 1991-92; Director, Govan Community Organisations Council, 1992-96; Lottery Officer, South Lanarkshire Council, 1997. Recreations: musician; computer programming; running/swimming. Address: (b.) 24 George Square, Glasgow; T.-0141-226 3793.

Rycroft, Philip John, MA, DPhil. Public Affairs Manager, Scottish & Newcastle, since 2000 (on secondment); Deputy Head of Policy Unit, Scottish Executive, 1999-2000; b. 22.5.61, Skipton; m., Kate Richards; 2 s. Educ. Leys School, Cambridge; Wadham College, Oxford. Scottish Office Agriculture Department, Research Division, 1989-90; Private Secretary to Scottish Office Agriculture and Fisheries Minister, 1990-91; Principal, Scottish Office Industry Department, European Central Support Unit, 1992-94; Principal, Scottish Office Fisheries Group, Fisheries Policy Branch, 1994; Cabinet of Sir Leon Brittan, European Commission, 1995-97; Head, Agricultural Policy Co-ordination and Rural Development Division and IT Support Division, Scottish Office Agriculture, Environment and Fisheries Department, 1997-98; Head, Management Group Support Staff Unit, Scottish Office, 1998-99. Recreations: hill-walking; woodwork. Address: (b.) Scottish & Newcastle, 33 Ellersly Road, Edinburgh EH12 6HX; T.-0131-528 2135; e-mail: philip.rycroft@scottish-newcastle.co.uk

S

Sadler, Professor Peter John, MA, DPhil, CChem, FRSC, FRSE. Crum Brown Professor of Chemistry, Edinburgh University, since 1996; Member, Editorial Boards, several international research journals; b. 6.4.46, Norwich; m., Tessa Elizabeth Halstead; 2 s.; 1 d. Educ. City of Norwich School; Magdalen College, Oxford. Medical Research Council Research Fellow, Cambridge University, 1971-72; National Institute for Medical Research, Mill Hill, 1972-73; Lecturer, Reader in Biological Chemistry and Professor of Chemistry, Birkbeck College, London University, 1973-96. Royal Society of Chemistry Award, 1993. Publications: 300 research publications. Recreations: gardening; music; sport. Address: (b.) Department of Chemistry, Edinburgh University, West Mains Road, Edinburgh EH9 3JJ; T.-0131-650 4729.

Salmon, Professor Trevor C., MA (Hons), MLitt, PhD, FRSA. Chair of International Relations and Jean Monnet Chair of European Integration, Aberdeen University, since 1996; Professor, College of Europe, since 1995; b. 7.9.48, Cambridge; m., June Veronica Miller; 1 d. Educ. Soham Grammar School; Aberdeen University; St. Andrews University. Lecturer, National Institute for Higher Education, Limerick, 1973-78; Lecturer in International Relations, then Senior Lecturer, St. Andrews University, 1978-90; Jean Monnet Professor of European Integration, St. Andrews University, 1990-95. Elder, Church of Scotland. Publications: Building European Union (Co-author); Understanding the European Union (Co-author); Issues in International Relations. Address: (b.) Department of Politics and International Relations, Edward Wright Building, Aberdeen University, Aberdeen AB24 3QY; T.-01224 272707; e-mail: t.c.salmon@abdn.ac.uk

Salmond, Alexander Elliot Anderson, MA (Hons). Economist; MP (SNP), Banff and Buchan, since 1987; MSP (SNP), Banff and Buchan, 1999-2001; b. 31.12.54, Linlithgow; m., Moira McGlashan. Educ. Linlithgow Academy; St. Andrews University. Vice-President: Federation of Student Nationalists, 1974-77, St. Andrews University SRC, 1977-78; Founder Member, SNP 79 Group, 1979; Assistant Agricultural and Fisheries Economist, DAFS, 1978-80; Economist, Royal Bank of Scotland, 1980-87. Hon. Vice-President, Scottish Centre for Economic and Social Research; former Member, Select Committee on Energy; National Convener, Scottish National Party, 1990-2000; Leader, SNP Westminster Group. Address: (b.) 17 Maiden Street, Peterhead, AB42 1EE; T.-01779 470444.

Salter, Professor Patrick, MSc, MCSP, CertEd, DipTP. Dean, Faculty of Health and Life Sciences, Napier University, since 1999; b. 27.3.49, Dundee; m., Shelagh MacLeod; 2 s. Educ. Lawside Academy, Dundee; Strathclyde University; Jordanhill College; Glasgow Royal School of Physiotherapy. Physiotherapist: Institute of Neurological Sciences, Southern General Hospital, Glasgow; Welland County General Hospital, Ontario, Canada; Senior Physiotherapist, Hotel Dieu Hospital, St Catherine's, Ontario, Canada; Physiotherapy Teacher, Glasgow Royal School of Physiotherapy; Senior Lecturer, Queens College, Glasgow; Professor and Head, Department of Physiotherapy, Queen Margaret University College. Recreations: golf; sports; music; reading; gardening. Address: (b.) Napier University, Canaan Lane Campus, 74 Canaan Lane, Edinburgh, EH10 4TB; T.-0131-536 5607; e-mail: p.salter@napier.ac.uk

Saltoun, Lady (Flora Marjory). Peer of the Realm, since 1979; elected Member, House of Lords, since 1999; Chief of the Name of Fraser, since 1979; b. 18.10.30, Edinburgh; 3 d. Educ. St. Mary's School, Wantage. Address: House of Lords, London, SW1A 0PW.

Salvesen, Robin Somervell, DL, FBIM, Chevalier de Dannebrog 1st Class. Director, Christian Salvesen plc; Vice-President, Association for the Protection of Rural Scotland (former Chairman); Chairman, Scottish Council, King George's Fund for Sailors; Chairman, Bells Nautical Trust; Chairman, Theodore Salvesen Trust; Trustee, Thistle Trust; Trustee, Novum Trust; b. 4.5.35, Edinburgh; m., Sari; 3 s.; 4 d. Educ. Fettes College; Oxford University. National Service commission, The Royal Scots, Queen's Own Nigeria Regiment; TA, 7/9 Bn., The Royal Scots, 8/9 Bn., The Royal Scots 52 Lowland Volunteers; retired Major; Director, shipping companies, A.F. Henry & Macgregor, Christian Salvesen plc; Lloyds Register of Shipping, 1974-87; Chamber of Shipping, 1974-88; British Shipowners Association, 1984-99; Chairman, Lights Advisory Committee, since 1987; Member, East Lothian Council, 1965-68; Royal Danish Consul, 1972-87; Vice Convenor, Daniel Stewarts and Melville College; Governor, Fettes College, 1975-85; Chairman, Leith Nautical College, 1979-88; President, Edinburgh Area Scouts, since 1991; Member, Merchant Company of the City of Edinburgh (Assistant, 1977-80); Elder, Church of Scotland; Chairman, Congregational Board, St Mary's, Haddington. Recreations: archery, shooting. Address: Eaglescairnie House, Haddington, EH41.

Samson, Brian George, DPE, DMS. Director of Sports Development, sportscotland (formerly Scottish Sports Council), since 1994; b. 9.9.47, Cupar; m., Penny; 2 s.; 1 d. Educ. Bell Baxter High School, Cupar; Jordanhill College of Education; Napier University. Principal Teacher of P.E., 1974-84; Development Officer, then Senior Development Officer, Scottish Sports Council, 1984-94. Recreations: rugby; skiing; music; ornithology. Address: (b.) South Gyle, Edinburgh EH12 9DQ; T.-0131-317 7200.

Samson, Elaine. Chief Executive, YWCA Scotland, since 2001; b. 14.11.61, Edinburgh; 1 s.; 1 d. Women's Officer (Campaigns and Promotions), Women's Unit, Edinburgh District Council, 1992-95; founding Member, Zero Tolerance Charitable Trust, and Co-Creator, Zero Tolerance Campaign Packages, 1995-97; Co-Director, Zero Tolerance Charitable Trust, 1997-2000. Address: (b.) 7B Randolph Crescent, Edinburgh EH3 7TH; T.-0131-225 7592.

Samson, George Carmichael, CompBCS, FFCS. Director of Administration, Law Society of Scotland, since 1986; b. 17.12.46, Dundee; m., Irene; 1 d. Sidlaw Industries (Organisation and Methods), 1967-77; Divisional Systems Co-ordinator, Watson & Philip PLC, 1977-86. Law Society of Scotland: Secretary, Practice Management; Member, Society for Computers and Law; Member, Centre for Law, Computers and Technology Advisory Council, University of Strathclyde Law School. Recreations: guitar; photography; golf; Mah Jong. Address: (b.) 26 Drumsheugh Gardens, Edinburgh EH3 7YR; T.-0131-476 8142.

Samuel, Agnes C., MA. Executive Director, Glasgow Opportunities, since 1988; Chairman, Linc Scotland, since 1994; b. 23.5.49, Glasgow; m., Robert M. Porter. Educ. Lanark Grammar School; Glasgow University. Language teacher, Scotland and France, 1971-74; Office Manager, SNP, Westminster, 1975-77; National Organising Secretary, SNP, 1977-79; Assistant to Secretary General, International European Construction Federation, Paris, 1979-84; Manager, Enterprise Funds for Youth, GO, 1984-87; Depute Director, GO, 1987-88. Director, Business Enterprise Scotland; Non-Executive Director, Greater Glasgow Health Board, 1996-2000;

Chair, Centre for Women's Health, GGHB, 1996-2000; Member, Merchants' House, Glasgow; SNP PPC, Argyll and Bute. Recreations: reading; swimming; photography. Address: (b.) GO, 36 North Hanover Street, Glasgow G1 2AD; T.-0141-572 8304; e-mail: agnes.samuel@go.uk.com

Sanderson of Bowden, Lord (Charles Russell Sanderson), KB. Life Peer; Chairman, Scottish Mortgage and Trust, since 1993; Chairman, Hawick Cashmere Co., since 1991; Chairman, Clydesdale Bank, since 1999; Director, Morrison Construction PLC, 1995-2001; b. 30.4.33, Melrose; m., Frances Elizabeth Macaulay; 1 s.; 1 s. deceased; 2 d. Educ. St. Mary's School, Melrose; Glenalmond College; Bradford University; Scottish College of Textiles. Commissioned, Royal Signals; Partner, Charles P. Sanderson, 1958-87; former Director, Johnston of Elgin, Illingworth Morris, Edinburgh Woollen Mills; former Chairman, Shires Investment PLC, Edinburgh Financial Trust, Scottish Pride Holdings; President, Scottish Conservative and Unionist Association, 1977-79; Chairman, National Union of Conservative and Unionist Associations Executive Committee, 1981-86; Minister of State, Scottish Office, 1987-90; Chairman, Scottish Conservative Party, 1990-93; Chairman, Scottish Peers Association, 1998-2000; Director: United Auctions Ltd., 1993-99, Watson and Philip PLC, 1993-99; Chairman, Eildon Housing Association, 1976-83; Member, Court, Napier University, 1994-2001; Chairman, Glenalmond Council, 1994-2000; Chairman, St Mary's School, Melrose, since 1998; Member, Court, Frameworker Knitters Company, since 2000; DL. Recreations: golf; amateur dramatics; photography; fishing. Address: (h.) Becketts Field, Bowden, Melrose, Roxburgh, TD6 0ST.

Sanderson, Professor Jeffrey John, BSc, PhD. Professor of Theoretical Plasma Physics, St. Andrews University, 1985-2000, Professor Emeritus, since 2001, Vice Principal, 2000, Proctor, 1997-2000; b. 25.4.37, Birmingham; m., Mirjana Adamovic; 1 s.; 1 d. Educ. George Dixon Grammar School, Birmingham; Birmingham University; Manchester University. Research Associate, Maryland University, 1961-64; Theoretical Physicist, English Electric Co., Whetstone, 1964-66; Lecturer, then Senior Lecturer, then Reader in Applied in Applied Mathematics, St. Andrews University, 1966-85; Visiting Professor, Department of Physics, College of William and Mary, USA, 1976-77. Publications: Plasma Dynamics (Co-author), 1969; Laser Plasma Interactions (Joint Editor), 1979. Recreations: chess; Scottish country dancing; five-a-side football; golf; hill-walking; choral singing. Address: (h.) 17 Spottiswoode Gardens, St. Andrews KY16 8SA; T.-01334 473862; e-mail: jjs@st-and.åc.uk

Sanderson, William. Farmer; Director, Royal Highland and Agricultural Society of Scotland, Chairman Designate, 2001-02; b. 9.3.38, Lanark; m., Netta; 4 d. Educ. Dalkeith High School. Past Chairman, South Midlothian and Lothians and Peeblesshire Young Farmers Clubs; Past Chairman, Dalkeith Agricultural Society; President, Royal Caledonian Curling Club, 1984-85; Past President, Oxenfoord and Edinburgh Curling Clubs; Scottish Curling Champion, 1971 and 1978 (2nd, World Championship 1971). Recreations: curling; exhibiting livestock. Address: (h.) Blackshiels Farm, Blackshiels, Pathhead, Midlothian; T.-01875 833288.

Sanderson, Very Rev. William Roy, MA, DD. Minister, Church of Scotland; Extra Chaplain to The Queen in Scotland, since 1977 (Chaplain-in-Ordinary, 1965-77); b. 23.9.07, Leith; m., Muriel Easton; 3 s.; 2 d. Educ. Fettes College; Oriel College, Oxford; New College, Edinburgh. Ordained, 1933; Assistant Minister, St. Giles' Cathedral, 1932-34; Minister: St. Andrew's, Lochgelly, 1935-39, The Barony of Glasgow, 1939-63, Stenton with Whittingehame, 1963-73; Moderator, Glasgow Presbytery, 1958 and Haddington and Dunbar Presbytery, 1972-74; Moderator, General Assembly, 1967; Chairman, Scottish Religious Advisory Committee, BBC, 1961-71; Member, Central Religious Advisory Committee, BBC and ITA, 1961-71; Governor, Fettes College, 1967-77; Honorary President, Church Service Society; President, New College Union, 1975. Hon. DD (Glasgow), 1959. Recreations: reading; walking. Address: (h.) 1A York Road, North Berwick, EH39 4LS; T.-01620 892780.

Sandison, Bruce Macgregor. Writer and Journalist; b. 26.9.38, Edinburgh; m., Dorothy Ann Rhodes; 2 s.; 2 d. Educ. Royal High School, Edinburgh. Commissioned into Royal Army Service Corps, 1956-60; sometime poultry farmer and agricultural contractor; full-time writing, since 1981; Columnist (environment, game fishing, hill-walking), The Herald, The Scotsman; contributor, Tales of the Loch, Sporting Gentleman's Gentleman (series), Radio Scotland, Radio 4, Landward, BBC TV. Publications: The Trout Lochs of Scotland; The Sporting Gentleman's Gentleman; Game Fishing in Scotland; The Hillwalker's Guide to Scotland; The Heather Isles; Tales of the Loch; Long Walks with Little People; Trout and Salmon Rivers and Lochs of Scotland; Walk Scotland. Recreations: hill-walking; game fishing; photography; swimming; music; reading; chess; bridge. Address: Hysbackie, Tongue, by Lairg, IV27 4XJ; T.-01847 55 274; e-mail: bruce@hysbackie.freeserve.co.uk

Sanford, Professor Anthony John, BSc, PhD, FBPsS, CPsychol. Professor of Psychology, Glasgow University, since 1982 (Head, Department of Psychology, 1983-86); b. 5.7.44, Birmingham; m., Linda Mae Moxey; 1 s.; 2 d. Educ. Waverley Grammar School; Leeds University; Cambridge University. MRC Research Scholar, Applied Psychology Unit, Cambridge; Postdoctoral Research Fellow, then Lecturer in Psychology, Dundee University; Senior Lecturer, then Reader in Psychology, Glasgow University. Gifford Lecturer in Natural Theology, Glasgow, 1983. Publications: Understanding Written Language (Co-author); Models, Mind and Man; Cognition and Cognitive Psychology; The Mind of Man; Communicating Quantities (Co-author). Recreations: hill-walking; industrial archaeology; music; cooking. Address: (b.) Department of Psychology, Glasgow University, Glasgow; T.-0141-330 4058.

Sangster, Professor Alan John, BSc (Eng), MSc, PhD, CEng, FIEE. Professor, Electromagnetic Engineering, Heriot Watt University, since 1990; b. 21.11.40, Aberdeen; m., Barbara Macleod Wilkie; 1 s.; 1 d. Educ. Aberdeen Grammar School; Aberdeen University. Research Engineer, Ferranti Ltd., Edinburgh, 1964-69; Plessey Radar Ltd., 1969-72; Lecturer, Heriot Watt University, 1972-79, Senior Lecturer, 1979-86, Reader, 1986-90. Publications: 150 papers. Recreation: golf. Address: (b.) Computing and Electrical Engineering Department, Heriot Watt University, Edinburgh; T.-0131-451 3358.

Sannella, Professor Donald Theodore, BS, MS, PhD. Professor of Computer Science, Edinburgh University, since 1998; b. 7.12.56, Boston USA; m., Monika-Jeanette Lekuse; 1 s.; 1 d. Educ. Yale University; University of California at Berkeley; Edinburgh University. Editor-in-Chief, Theoretical Computer Science, since 2000. Address: (b.) Laboratory for Foundations of Computer Science, Division of Informatics, Edinburgh University, EH9 3JZ; T.-0131-650 5184; e-mail: dts@dcs.ed.ac.uk

Sarwar, Mohammed. MP, Glasgow Govan, since 1997; b. 18.8.52; m.; 3 s.; 1 d. Educ. University of Faisalabad. Director, United Wholesalers Ltd., 1983-97; former Glasgow City Councillor. Address: House of Commons, London SW1A 1AA.

Saunders, Professor Alison Marilyn, BA, PhD. Professor of French, Aberdeen University, since 1990; b. 23.12.44, Darlington. Educ. Wimbledon High School GPDST; Durham University. Lectrice, the Sorbonne, 1968-69; Lecturer in French, Aberdeen University, 1970-85; Senior Lecturer in French, 1985-90. Recreations: swimming; gardening; DIY; cooking; antiquarian book-collecting. Address: (h.) 75 Dunbar Street, Old Aberdeen, Aberdeen AB24 3UA; T.-01224 494806.

Saunders, Ann Walker, BA, ALA, MIMgt. Director of Community and Leisure, East Renfrewshire Council, since 1995; b. 12.8.52, Glasgow; m., Christopher Saunders; 1 s.; 2 d. Educ. Hutchesons' Grammar School, Glasgow; Strathclyde University, Glasgow. Director of Arts and Libraries, then Director of Leisure Services, Renfrew District Council, 1991-95. Recreations: reading; travelling. Address: (b.) Council Offices, Eastwood Park, Giffnock, G46 6UG; T.-0141-577 3096; e-mail: ann.saunders@eastrenfrewshire.gov.uk

Saunders, Professor David Stanley, BSc, PhD, FIBiol, FRES, FRSE. Professor of Insect Physiology, Edinburgh University, 1990-99, now Emeritus Professor; b. 12.3.35, Pinner; m., Jean Margaret Comrie Doughty; 3 s. Educ. Pinner County Grammar School; King's College, London; London School of Hygiene and Tropical Medicine. Joined academic staff, Zoology Department, Edinburgh, 1958; Visiting Professor: Stanford University, California, 1971-72, North Carolina University, 1983. Publications: Insect Clocks; Introduction to Biological Rhythms. Recreations: cycling; gardening; photography. Address: (b.) Institute of Cell, Animal and Population Biology, West Mains Road, Edinburgh, EH9 3JT.

Saunders, Donald Goodbrand. Poet and Writer, since 1968; b. 16.7.49, Glasgow; m., Anne; 1 s. Educ. McLaren High School, Callander. Writer, mainly of poetry, for 30 years; published four books, as well as contributing to various Scottish and UK periodicals and anthologies; has received three Scottish Arts Council writers' bursaries. Publications include: The Glasgow Diary, 1984; Findrinny, 1990; Sour Gas and Crude, 1999. Address: (h.) 17 Jellicoe Avenue, Gartmore, FK8 3RQ; T.-0771 969 2836.

Saunders, Professor William Philip, BDS, PhD, FDSRCS(Edin), FDSRCPS(Glas), MRD. Professor of Endodontology, University of Dundee, since 2000; Dean of Dentistry, since 2000; b. 12.10.48, Carlisle; m., Elizabeth; 1 s.; 2 step s.; 1 d.; 1 step d. Educ. Maidstone Grammar School; Royal Dental Hospital of London. Dental Officer, RAF, 1970-75; general dental practice, 1975-81; Lecturer, Department of Conservative Dentistry, Dundee University, 1981-88; Senior Lecturer in Clinical Practice, Glasgow Dental Hospital and School, 1988-93; Professor in Clinical Dental Practice, Glasgow University, 1993-95, Professor of Endodontology, 1995-2000. Postgraduate Dental Hospital Tutor, Glasgow Dental Hospital, 1992-95; Editor, International Endodontic Journal, 1992-98; President, British Endodontic Society, 1997-98. Publications: numerous papers. Recreations: ornithology; natural history; Scottish art; golf; endodontics. Address: (h.) The Old Smiddy, Knapp, Inchture, PH14 9SW; T.-01828 86478.

Savage, Rev. Gordon Matthew Alexander, MA, BD. Minister, Maxwelltown West Church, Dumfries, since 1984; Clerk, Presbytery of Dumfries and Kirkcudbright, since 1987; b. 25.8.51, Old Kilpatrick; m., Mairi Janet MacKenzie; 2 s. Educ. Glasgow Academy; Edinburgh University. Assistant Minister: Dyce Parish Church, 1975-76, Dunblane Cathedral, 1976-77; Minister, Almondbank-Tibbermore with Logiealmond, 1977-84; Junior Clerk, Presbytery of Perth, 1981-84. Recreations: reading; railways; Clyde steamers; music. Address: Maxwelltown West Manse, 11 Laurieknowe, Dumfries DG2 7AH; T.-01387 252929.

Savidge, Malcolm Kemp, MP, MA (Hons), FRGU. MP (Labour), Aberdeen North, since 1997; b. 9.5.46, Redhill. Educ. Wallington County Grammar School, Surrey; University of Aberdeen; Aberdeen College of Education. Production/ Stock Control and Computer Assistant, Bryans' Electronics Ltd., 1970-71; Mathematics Teacher, Greenwood Dale Secondary School, Nottingham, 1971; Mathematics and Religious and Social Education Teacher, Peterhead Academy, 1972-73; Mathematics Teacher, Kincorth Academy, Aberdeen, 1973-97. Member, Aberdeen City Council, 1980-96: Vice-Chair, Labour Group, 1980-88, Finance Convener, Policy Vice-Convener, Deputy Leader, 1994-96; Governor, Robert Gordon's Institute of Technology, 1980-88; Governor, Aberdeen College of Education, 1980-87; JP, 1984-96; Fellow, Robert Gordon University, 1997. Recreations: exploring life; puzzles; reading; real ale; spectator sport. Address: (b.) House of Commons, London SW1A 0AA.

Saville, Alan, BA, FSA, MIFA, FSA Scot. Archaeologist; Senior Curator, National Museums of Scotland, since 1989; President, Council for Scottish Archaeology, since 2000; Member, Ancient Monuments Board for Scotland, since 2001; b. 31.12.46, London; m., Annette Carruthers. Educ. Colfe's Grammar School, London; Birmingham University. Archaeological Research Assistant, Department of the Environment, London, 1972-74; Archaeologist, Cheltenham Art Gallery and Museum, 1974-76; Field Officer, Western Archaeological Trust, Bristol, 1976-85; Archaeological Consultant, Cheltenham, 1985-89. Treasurer, Society of Antiquaries of Scotland, 1992-2000; Chairman, The Lithic Studies Society, 1983-90; Conservation Co-ordinator, The Prehistoric Society, 1989-93; Joint Editor, Transactions of the Bristol and Gloucestershire Archaeological Society, 1983-89. Recreations: book collecting; cinema. Address: (b.) Archaeology Department, National Museums of Scotland, Chambers Street, Edinburgh EH1 1JF; T.-0131-247 4054; e-mail: a.saville@nms.ac.uk

Savin, John Andrew, MA, MD (Cantab), FRCP, FRCPEdin, DIH. Consultant Dermatologist, Edinburgh Royal Infirmary (retired); former Senior Lecturer, Dermatology Department, Edinburgh University, now Honorary Fellow, Faculty of Medicine; b. 10.1.35, London; m., Patricia Margaret Steel; 2 s.; 2 d. Educ. Epsom College; Trinity Hall, Cambridge; St. Thomas's Hospital, London. Royal Naval Medical Service, 1960-64; Registrar to Skin Department, St. George's Hospital, London; Senior Registrar, St. John's Hospital for Diseases of the Skin, and St. Thomas's Hospital, London; Co-Editor, Recent Advances in Dermatology; Associate Editor, British Journal of Dermatology; former Secretary, Scottish Dermatological Society; President, British Association of Dermatologists, 1993-94; President, Section of Dermatology, Royal Society of Medicine, 1987-88. Recreations: golf; literature. Address: (h.) 86 Murrayfield Gardens, Edinburgh; T.-0131-337 7768.

Sawers, Lesley, MA, PhD, DipMktg. Director of Scottish Affairs, Consignia, since 2001; Chairman, Consignia Advisory Board for Scotland, since 2001; b. 8.1.59, Glasgow; m., William Allan McKechnie. Educ. Our Lady's High School, Cumbernauld; Glasgow University; Stirling University. Management Horizons, 1983-85; CACI Ltd., 1985-92; ScottishPower PLC, 1992-2001. Board Member, Arts and Business Scotland; Committee Member, Scottish Council Development and Industry. Recreations: golf; popular cinema; gardening. Address: (b.) Consignia PLC, 102 West Port, Edinburgh EH3 9HS; T.-0131-228 7300.

Saxon, Professor David Harold, MA, DPhil, DSc, CPhys, FInstP, FRSE. Kelvin Professor of Physics, Glasgow University, since 1990; Vice-Dean, Physical Sciences, since 2000, Head, Department of Physics and Astronomy, 1996-2001; b. 27.10.45, Stockport; m., Margaret Flitcroft; 1 s.; 1 d. Educ. Manchester Grammar School; Balliol College, Oxford; Jesus College, Oxford. Research Officer, Nuclear Physics Department, Oxford University, 1969-70; Research Associate, Columbia University, New York, 1970-73; Rutherford Appleton Laboratory, Oxon: Research Associate, 1974-75, Senior Scientific Officer, 1975-76, Principal Scientific Officer, 1976-89; Chairman, PPARC Particle Physics Committee, 1992-95; Member: Scientific Policy Committee, CERN, Geneva, 1993-98, Physics Research Committee, DESY, Hamburg, 1993-99, Research Assessment Panel (Physics), 1996; PPARC Council Member and Chairman of panel on public understanding of science, 1997-2001; Chairman, governing committee, Scottish Universities Summer Schools in Physics, since 1997; CCLRC: Council Member, 2000-01, Chairman, Particle Physics Users Advisory Committee, since 1999. Address: (b.) Department of Physics and Astronomy, Glasgow University, Glasgow, G12 8QQ; T.-0141-330 4673.

Scaltsas, Professor Theodore Constantine, BSc, MA, DPhil. Professor of Ancient Philosophy, Edinburgh University, since 1999; Founder and Director, Archelogos Projects, since 1990; b. 8.12.49, Athens; m., Patricia Ward; 1 d. Educ. Athens College; Duke University; Brandeis University; Oxford University. Philosophy Lecturer, New College, Oxford, 1980-84; Philosophy Lecturer, then Reader, Edinburgh University, 1984-99. Research Fellow, Harvard University, 1987-88; Princeton University, 1989; Academy of Athens Award in Philosophy, 1988; Henry Ford Foundation European Cultural Conservation National Award for Archelogos Projects, 1997. Publications include: The Golden Age of Virtue: Aristotle's Ethics, 1993; Substances and Universals in Aristotle's Metaphysics, 1994; Aristotle on Generation and Corruption, 1998. Recreations: wine and whisky tasting; watching films; computers. Address: (b.) Philosophy Department, David Hume Tower, George Square, Edinburgh EH8 9JX; T.-0131-650 3649; (h.) 18 Belgrave Crescent, Edinburgh EH4 3AJ; e-mail: scaltsas@ed.ac.uk

Scanlan, Michael. Solicitor; Senior Partner, Russells Gibson McCaffrey (formerly Russells) Solicitors, Glasgow, since 1982; President, Law Society of Scotland, 1999-2000; b. 6.6.46, Glasgow; m., Margaret; 1 s. Educ. St. Aloysius College, Glasgow; Glasgow University. T. F. Russell & Co.: Apprentice, 1965-70, Assistant, 1971-73, Partner, since 1973; Temporary Sheriff, 1986-96; former Member, Glasgow and North Argyll Legal Aid Committee; former Lecturer, Evidence and Procedure, Strathclyde University; former External Examiner, Glasgow University. Recreations: golf; reading. Address: (h.) Willowfield, Kirkintilloch Road, Lenzie; T.-0141-777 7677.

Scanlan, Patrick D., MA. Headteacher, St. Margaret Mary's Secondary School, Glasgow, since 1996; Secretary, Catholic Headteachers' Association of Scotland; b. 1.3.50, Johnstone; m., Patricia; 2 s. Educ. St. Mirin's Academy, Paisley; Glasgow University; Notre Dame College of Education. Assistant Teacher, St. Cuthbert's High, Johnstone, 1971-73; Principal Teacher of English, then Assistant Head Teacher, St. Brendan's High, Linwood, 1973-90; Depute Head Teacher, St. Mirin's High, Paisley, 1990-96. Recreations: sport; reading; music; travel; theatre and cinema. Address: (b.) 65 Dougrie Road, Glasgow G45 9NJ; T.-0141-634 1169; e-mail: pscanlan@hotmail.com

Scanlon, Mary Elizabeth, MA. MSP (Conservative), Highland and Islands, since 1999; b. 25.5.47, Dundee; 1 s.; 1 d. Educ. Craigo School, Montrose; Dundee University. Lecturer in Economics/Business Studies: Dundee College

of Technology, 1982-85, Perth College, 1985-88, Abertay University, 1988-94, Inverness College, 1994-99. Member, Visiting Committee, Barlinnie Prison, 1988-92. Recreation: hill-walking. Address: (b.) 37 Ardconnel Terrace, Inverness IV2 3AE; T.-01463 241004.

Schaw-Miller, Jean-Clare. Deputy Lieutenant, West Lothian, since 1980; Council Member, Guide Dogs for the Blind Association, since 1992; Chairman, Association Awards Committee, The Guide Association, since 1998; b. 22.2.37, Gloucestershire; m., Robert Grant Schaw-Miller; 1 s.; 1 d. Educ. Clifton High School for Girls, Bristol; Edinburgh College of Domestic Science. Scottish Chief Commissioner, Girl Guides Association, 1987-92. Address: (h.) Newgardens House, Dalmeny, South Queensferry, West Lothian, EH30 9TF; T.-0131-331 4612.

Scheunemann, Professor Dietrich F.G., MA, Dr.Phil. Walter H. Bruford Professor of German, University of Edinburgh, since 1990 (Head, Graduate School in Asian and Modern European Languages, since 1995); b. 16.9.39, Schlawe, Germany; m., Sieglinde; 2 s. Educ. Free University of Berlin; Yale University; University of Heidelberg. Taught: University of Heidelberg, Free University of Berlin; Sussex University: Reader in German and Comparative Literature, 1985, Chairman of German, 1987. Publications: Romankrise, 1978; Regelkram und Grenzgänge, 1988; Orality, Literacy and Modern Media, 1996; Text und Ton im Film, 1997; Europäische Kinokunst im Zeitalter des Fernsehens, 1998; European Avant-Garde – New Perspectives, 2000. Recreations: travel; theatre. Address: (b.) University of Edinburgh, David Hume Tower, George Square, Edinburgh EH8 9JX; T.-0131-650 3639.

Schlesinger, Professor Philip Ronald, BA, PhD, DrHC, ACSS, FRSA, FRSE. Professor of Film and Media Studies, Stirling University, since 1989; b. 31.8.48, Manchester; m., Sharon Joy Rose; 2 d. Educ. North Manchester Grammar School; Queen's College, Oxford; London School of Economics. University of Greenwich: Lecturer, 1974, Senior Lecturer, 1977, Principal Lecturer, 1981; Head, Division of Sociology, 1981-88, Professor of Modern Sociology, 1987-89; Social Science Research Fellow, Nuffield Foundation, 1982-83; Jean Monnet Fellow, European University Institute, Florence, 1985-86; British-Hispanic Chair of Doctoral Studies, Complutense University of Madrid, 2000-01; Chair, Research Assessment Panel for Communication, Cultural and Media Studies, 1995-96 and 1999-2001; Visiting Professor of Media and Communication, University of Oslo, since 1993; Co-Editor, Media, Culture and Society, since 1982; Media Adviser, Know How Fund, 1994-98; Board Member, Scottish Screen, since 1997; Board Member, The Research Centre, Channel 4 Television, Glasgow, since 1998; Member, Film Education Working Group reporting to Department of Culture, Media and Sport, 1998-99. Publications: Putting "Reality" Together, 1978, 1987; Televising "Terrorism", 1983; Communicating Politics, 1986; Media, Culture and Society, 1986; Los Intelectuales en la Sociedad de la Informacion, 1987; Media, State and Nation, 1991; Women Viewing Violence, 1992; Culture and Power, 1992; Reporting Crime, 1994; European Transformations, 1994; International Media Research, 1997; European Communication Council Report, 1997; Men Viewing Violence, 1998; Consenting Adults?, 2000; Open Scotland?, 2001. Recreations: the arts; walking; travel. Address: Department of Film and Media Studies, Stirling University, Stirling FK9 4LA; T.-01786 467520.

Schofield, Rev. Melville Frederick, MA. Chaplain to Western General and Associated Hospitals, Edinburgh, since 1988; b. 3.10.35, Glasgow; m., Christina Skirving Crookston. Educ. Irvine Royal Academy; Dalkeith High School; Edinburgh University and New College. Ordained Assistant, Bathgate High, 1960-61; Minister, Canal Street, Paisley, 1961-67; Minister, Laigh Kirk, Kilmarnock, 1967-

88. Former Moderator, Presbytery of Irvine and Kilmarnock; former Moderator, Synod of Ayr; radio and TV broadcaster; Past President, No. 0 Kilmarnock Burns Club. Recreations: international Burns engagements; golf; after-dinner speaking. Address: (h.) 25 Rowantree Grove, Currie, Midlothian, EH14 5AT; T.-0131-449 4745; e-mail: afterate@hotmail.com

Scobie, Rev. Andrew John, MA, BD. Minister, Cardross Parish Church, since 1965; b. 9.7.35, Windygates; m., Elizabeth Jeannette; 1 s.; 1 d. Educ. Whitehill Senior Secondary School, Glasgow; Glasgow University (Medal in Systematic Theology); Gottingen University; Tubingen University; Marburg University. Assistantship, New Kilpatrick Church, Bearsden; Moderator, Dumbarton Presbytery, 1973-74 and 1999-2000; Convener, General Assembly's Parish Education Commitee, 1978-80; Convener, General Assembly's Panel on Worship, 1986-90; Member, Joint Liturgical Group, 1987-91; Vice-Convener, General Assembly's Artistic Matters Committee, 1995-98; Ecumenical Representative, Church of England General Synod, 1995-98; Chairman or Vice-Chairman, Cardross Community Council, since inception; Executive Member, Association of Scottish Community Councils, since 1998; Publications: Studies in the Historical Jesus (Translator); contributions to New Ways to Worship, 1980, Prayers for Sunday Services, 1980, Three Orders for Holy Communion, 1986, Songs of God's People, 1988; Worshipping Together, 1991; Common Order, 1994; Common Ground, 1998. Recreations: golf; photography; wine making; visual arts. Address: The Manse, Cardross, Dumbarton G82 5LB; T.-01389 841289; e-mail: ascobie55@netscapeonline.co.uk

Scobie, William Galbraith, MB, ChB, FRCSEdin, FRCSGlas. Former Consultant Paediatric Surgeon, Lothian Health Board, now retired; part-time Senior Lecturer, Department of Clinical Surgery, Edinburgh University, 1971-92; Assistant Director, Edinburgh Postgraduate Board for Medicine, 1986-92; b. 13.10.36, Maybole; m., Elizabeth Caldwell Steel; 1 s.; 1 d. Educ. Carrick Academy, Maybole; Glasgow University. Registrar, General Surgery, Kilmarnock Infirmary; Senior Registrar, Royal Hospital for Sick Children, Glasgow; Senior Registrar, Hospital for Sick Children, London; Senior Paediatric Surgeon, Abu Dhabi, 1980-81. Recreations: fishing; golf; gardening; music. Address: (h.) 133 Caiyside, Fairmilehead, Edinburgh EH10 7HR; T.-0131-445 7404.

Scothorne, Professor Raymond John, BSc, MD, FRSE, FRCSG. Regius Professor of Anatomy, Glasgow University, 1973-90; b. 13.6.20, Nottingham; m., Audrey Gillott; 1 s.; 2 d. Educ. Royal Grammar School, Newcastle-upon-Tyne; Leeds University; Chicago University. Lecturer in Anatomy, Leeds University, 1944-50; Senior Lecturer, Glasgow University, 1950-60; Professor of Anatomy, Newcastle-upon-Tyne University, 1960-73. Anatomical Society of Gt. Britain and Ireland: Honorary Secretary, 1967-71, President, 1971-73; President, British Association of Clinical Anatomists, 1986-89; Hon. Member, American Association of Clinical Anatomists, 1995; Foundation Editor, Clinical Anatomy, 1988-2001. Recreations: the countryside; labrador dogs. Address: (b.) Southern Knowe, Friars Brae, Linlithgow, West Lothian, EH49 6BQ.

Scothorne, Richard Mark, MA, MPhil. Director, Rocket Science UK Ltd.; Director, Workforce One Ltd., since 1999; b. 17.7.53, Glasgow; m., Dr. Sarah Gledhill; 1 s. Educ. Royal Grammar School, Newcastle upon Tyne; St. Catharine's College, Cambridge; Edinburgh University. Various posts in local government, 1977-86; Scottish Director, British Shipbuilders Enterprise Ltd., 1986-87; Economic Development Manager (Depute Director of Planning), Lothian Regional Council, 1987-92; Director, Partners in Economic Development Ltd., 1992-99. Specialist Adviser to Select Committee on Education and Employment, 1997-2000. Publication: The Vital Economy:

integrating training and enterprise, 1990. Recreations: hill-walking; mountain biking; Scottish art; windsurfing. Address: (h.) 71 Murrayfield Gardens, Edinburgh, EH12 6DL; T.-0131-337 5476.

Scott, Alastair, BA. Travel writer, freelance photographer, and broadcaster; b. 19.3.54, Edinburgh; m., Sheena. Educ. Blairmore; Sedbergh; Stirling University. Travelled around the world, 1978-83; wrote three travel books, 1984-87 – Scot Free, A Scot Goes South, A Scot Returns; cycled 5,000 miles in E. Europe, 1987-88; wrote Tracks Across Alaska (800-mile sled dog journey), 1988-90; travelled Scotland, 1993-94, wrote Native Stranger; presented BBC film version of Native Stranger, 1995. Recreations: reading; running; camping; carpentry; playing concertina. Address: Arroch, Kylerhea, Isle of Skye, IV42 8NH; T.-01599 522329.

Scott, Professor Alexander, MA, MSc, PhD. Professorial Fellow, Heriot-Watt University, since 1989; b. 7.3.45, Lerwick; m., Anne Elliot; 3 d. Educ. Anderson Educational Institute; Boroughmuir Secondary; Edinburgh University. Research Assistant, Edinburgh University, 1967-70; Research Fellow, Heriot-Watt University, 1970-89; Director, The Polecon Co., 1972-89; External Examiner, CNAA, 1981-85; Member, Joint Working Party on Economics, Scottish Examination Board, 1989-90; Chairman, Southfield Housing Society, 1977-80; Executive Director, Edinburgh Business School, since 1997; Trustee, Edinburgh Quartet, since 2000. Publications: four books and numerous papers. Recreations: hill-walking; swimming; music; woodworking. Address: (b.) Edinburgh Business School, Heriot-Watt University, Edinburgh; T.-0131-451 3090.

Scott, Professor Bill, RSA. Sculptor; Professor of Sculpture, Edinburgh College of Art (Lecturer, since 1962); Elected Secretary, Royal Scottish Academy, since 1998; b. 16.8.35, Moniaive; m., Phyllis Owen Scott; 1 s.; 2 d. Educ. Dumfries Academy; Edinburgh College of Art; Ecole des Beaux Arts, Paris. One-man exhibitions: Compass Gallery, 1972, Stirling Gallery, 1974, New 57 Gallery, 1979, Lamp of Lothian, 1980, Artspace Gallery, 1980, Kirkcaldy Museum and Gallery, 1985, Talbot Rice Gallery, Edinburgh, 1995; City Gallery, Viersen, Germany, 1999; group exhibitions include: Iwate Art Festival, Japan, 1998, Sudbahnhof Gallery, Krefeld, 2000; latest commissions: Sir Alec Douglas-Home, 1998, Elizabeth Crichton Memorial, Crichton, Dumfries, 2000. Address: (h.) 45 St. Clair Crescent, Roslin, Midlothian, EH25 9NG.

Scott, Esme (Lady Scott), CBE, WS, MA, LLB, NP; b. 7.1.32, Edinburgh; m., 1, Ian Macfarlane Walker (deceased); 1 s.; 2, Kenneth Bertram Adam Scott, KCVO, CMG; 1 step-s.; 1 step-d. Educ. St. George's School for Girls, Edinburgh; Edinburgh University. Lawyer; Vice Chairman, National Consumer Council, 1984-87; Chairman, Scottish Consumer Council, 1980-85; Member, Equal Opportunities Commission, 1985-90; Past Chair, Scottish Association of Citizens Advice Bureaux; Chair, Volunteer Development Scotland, 1989-92; Chair, The Volunteer Centre UK, 1993-95; Member, Securities and Investments Board, 1991-93; Member, Court, Edinburgh University, 1989-92; Member, Scottish Committee, Council on Tribunals, 1986-92; Member, Social Security Advisory Committee, 1990-96; Member, National Council for Voluntary Organisations Board, 1993-95. Address: (h.) 13 Clinton Road, Edinburgh EH9 2AW.

Scott, Professor Hamish, MA, PhD, FRHistS. Professor of International History, St Andrews University, since 2000; b. 12.7.46, Glasgow. Educ. George Heriot's School, Edinburgh; Edinburgh University; London School of Economics. Lecturer, Birmingham University, 1970-78; joined St Andrews University as Lecturer, 1979. Publications: as author: The Rise of the Great

Powers 1648-1815, 1983; British Foreign Policy in the Age of the American Revolution, 1990; The Emergence of the Eastern Powers 1756-1775, 2001; as editor: Enlightened Absolutism, 1990; The European Nobilities in the Seventeenth and Eighteenth Centuries, 1995; Royal and Republican Sovereignty in Early Modern Europe, 1997. Recreations: classical music; hill-walking; watching sport. Address: (b.) School of History, St Andrews University, St Andrews KY16 9AL; T.-01334 462 900.

Scott, Hugh Johnstone, DA, CertEd. Writer; b. Paisley; m., Mary (Margo) Smith Craig Hamilton; 1 s.; 1 d. Educ. Paisley Grammar School; Glasgow School of Art. Various jobs, then art school; art teacher, until 1984; full-time writing since 1984, including Writing Fellow, City of Aberdeen, 1991; Lecturer in Creative Writing, Glasgow University Adult and Continuing Education Department, since 1988, Art Tutor, since 1998; Tutor in Creative Writing; winner, Woman's Realm children's short story competition, 1982; winner, children's category, Whitbread Book of the Year, 1989, for Why Weeps the Brogan?; short-listed, Mcvitie's Prize, 1990; Tutor, Arvon Foundation Ltd., 1994. Recreations: weight training; exploring England; day-dreaming; reading, of course; painting.

Scott, Ian Edward. Deputy Chief Executive and Director of Change, Scottish Court Service; m., Maureen Ferrie; 1 s.; 1 d. Educ. Bellahouston Academy. Regional Sheriff Clerk, Lothian and Borders, 1992-95; Sheriff Clerk, Edinburgh, 1992-95; Sheriff Clerk of Chancery, 1992-95; Regional Sheriff Clerk, Glasgow and Strathkelvin, 1996-98; Regional Sheriff Clerk, North Strathclyde, 1997-98; Area Director West, 1998-2001. Hon. Member, Royal Faculty of Procurators, Glasgow. Recreations: amateur astronomy; rugby; making changes. Address: (h.) Meadowbank, Annandale Avenue, Lockerbie; T.-01576 203132.

Scott, Rev. Ian Gray, BSc, BD, STM. Minister, Greenbank Parish Church, Edinburgh, since 1983; b. 31.5.41, Kirkcaldy; m., Alexandrina Angus; 1 d. Educ. Kirkcaldy High School; St. Andrews University; Union Theological Seminary, New York. Assistant Minister, St. Mungo's, Alloa, 1965-66; Minister: Holy Trinity Church, Bridge of Allan, 1966-76, Holburn Central, Aberdeen, 1976-83; Convener, Panel on Doctrine, General Assembly, 1978-82; part-time Lecturer, Faculty of Divinity, Aberdeen University, 1977-79; founder Member, Ministry and Psychotherapy Group; Convener, Board of Parish Education, Church of Scotland, 1993-97; former Member, Joint Commission on Doctrine, Church of Scotland/Roman Catholic Church. Recreations: reading; photography; caravanning; golf (so called). Address: 112 Greenbank Crescent, Edinburgh, EH10 5SZ; T.-0131-447 4032.

Scott, Ian McGregor, LLB (Hons), DipFM. Advocate, since 1990; part-time Immigration Adjudicator, since 1998; b. 4.5.51, Glasgow; m., Ann Janetta Cameron; 1 s.; 1 d. Educ. Hamilton Academy; Glasgow University. Law apprentice, 1973-75; Solicitor in private practice, Glasgow, 1975-90. Secretary, Clyde Valley Mountaineering Club. Recreations: mountaineering; military history. Address: (b.) Advocates' Library, Parliament House, Edinburgh EH1 1RF; T.-0131-226 5071.

Scott, Irene Mary, DA, BA (Hons), MA, RSW. Painter and Printmaker; b. 31.12.42, Penicuik; m., Brian Snowden Duffield; 4 s.; 1 d. Educ. Lasswade Senior Secondary School; Edinburgh College of Art; Moray House College of Education; Open University; Leeds Metropolitan University. Travelling scholarship to Holland, 1965; Art Teacher, Lothian Region, 1969-74; graphics/cartography, Tourism and Recreation Unit, University of Edinburgh, 1974-76; Assistant Principal Art Teacher, Lothian Region,

1976-89; elected Professional Member: Scottish Society of Artists, 1987, Royal Scottish Society of Painters in Watercolours, 1989; solo exhibitions, Scotland; group exhibitions, Britain and abroad; work in public and private collections, Britain and abroad; commission, Iona Abbey Inc., 1997. Member, Council: SSA, 1986-87, RSW, 1990-93; Member, Board of Directors, AXIS, 1997-2000; Member, Visual Arts Panel, Scottish Arts Council, 1998. Betty Davies Campus Award, RSW, 1990; Whyte and Mackay Purchase Prize, SSA, 1992; Art Media Prize, Highland Open, 1998; 2000 Portfolio Prize, Art.tm., Inverness. Recreations: reading; walking; gardening. Address: 1 Preston Lodge, Station Road, Prestonpans, East Lothian EH32 9EP; T.-01875 812987.

Scott, James Archibald, CB, LVO, FRSE, FScotVec, MA; b. 5.3.32, Palestine; m., Dr. Elizabeth Agnes Joyce Scott; 3 s.; 1 d. Educ. Dollar Academy; St. Andrews University; Queen's University of Ontario. RAF Pilot, 1954-56; Commonwealth Relations Office, 1956-65, serving in New Delhi and New York; Scottish Office, 1965; Private Secretary to Secretary of State for Scotland, 1969-71; Secretary, Scottish Education Department, 1984-88; Secretary, Industry Department for Scotland, 1988-91; Chief Executive, Scottish Development Agency, 1991-92; Executive Director, Scottish Financial Enterprise, 1992-95; Director, Scottish Power plc, 1993-96; Director, Dumyat Investment Trust PLC, 1995-2000; Member of Court, Heriot-Watt University, 1995-2001. Recreations: flying; golf. Address: (h.) 38 Queen's Crescent, Edinburgh EH9 2BA; T.-0131-667 8417; e-mail: jamescott@cablenet.co.uk

Scott, James Niall, LLB. Partner, McGrigor Donald, since 1979; b. 5.4.52, Glasgow; m., Judith; 2 s.; 2 d. Educ. Jordanhill College School; Aberdeen University. External Examiner, Glasgow University Law School, 1990-92; Managing Partner, McGrigor Donald, 1994-97; currently heads McGrigor Donald's Commercial Litigation Unit. Governor, Glasgow School of Art; Chairman, Mark Scott Foundation; Member, various working parties, Law Society of Scotland. Recreations: swimming; golf; hill-walking. Address: (b.) Princes Exchange, 1 Earl Grey Street, Edinburgh EH3 9HQ; T.-0131-226 7777.

Scott, James Orrock, FCCA. Board Member, Angus, East of Scotland Housing Association, since 1988; Treasurer, SHARP (Scottish Heart and Arterial Disease Risk Prevention), since 1992; b. 13.12.40, Dundee; m., Alva; 1 s. Educ. Grove Academy. Former Senior Partner, Henderson Loggie, Chartered Accountants. Past President, Scottish Branch Executive, Society of Certified Accountants; first President, Scottish Athletics Federation. Recreations: athletics; bowling. Address: (h.) 99 Monifieth Road, Broughty Ferry, Dundee DD5 2SL; T.-01382 731822.

Scott, Jane Frances. Director of Corporate Affairs, The Boots Company, Scotland, since 1999; b. 11.4.62, Oxford; partner, Christopher Wood; 1 s.; 1 d. Educ. Madras College; Napier University. Marketing Manager, Scottish and Newcastle, 1987-89; Marketing Director, The Guinea Group, 1989-97; Director of Communications, GJW Public Affairs Europe, 1997-99. Board Director, Quality Scotland; Board Director, Scottish Business in the Community; Council Member, CBI Scotland; Member, Executive, Scottish Council for Development and Industry. Address: (h.) Port Lodge, 7 High Street, Dunbar, East Lothian EH42 1EA; T.-01368 865265; e-mail: jane.scott@boots-plc.com

Scott, Professor Janine, MBBS, MD, FRCPsych. Head, Division of Psychiatry, Glasgow University, since 1999; b. 22.3.56, Nottingham. Educ. Manning Grammar School for Girls; Newcastle University. Lecturer, Senior Lecturer, then Professor in Psychiatry, Newcastle-upon-Tyne University. Trustee, Mental Health Foundation, 1994-98; Sub-Dean, Royal College of Psychiatrists, 1994-98; Professional Adviser, Manic Depression

Fellowship, since 1992; Distinguished Fellow, Academy of Cognitive Therapists. Publications: 250 in psychiatry. Recreations: playing the alto saxophone very badly; collecting Clarice Cliff pottery; scuba diving. Address: (b.) Department of Psychological Medicine, Glasgow University, Gartnavel Royal Hospital, Great Western Road, Glasgow G12 0XH.

Scott, Janys Margaret, MA (Cantab). Advocate, since 1992; b. 28.8.53, Radcliffe; m., Revd Dr Kevin F. Scott; 2 s.; 1 d. Educ. Queen Elizabeth's Girls Grammar School, Barnet; Newnham College, Cambridge. Lecturer in Iraq, 1976-78; Solicitor, Oxford, 1978-86; Solicitor, Edinburgh, 1987-91; Honorary Lecturer, Dundee University, 1989-94. Convener, Scottish Child Law Centre, 1992-97; Chairman, Stepfamily Scotland, since 1998. Address: (b.) Parliament House, Edinburgh EH1 1RF; T.-0131-226 5071.

Scott, John. MSP (Conservative), Ayr, since 2000; Member, Transport and Environment Committee; Spokesman on the Environment; m., Charity (deceased); 1 s.; 1 d. Farming at Balkissock, Ayrshire, since 1973; established fertiliser selling agency with Norsk Hydro, 1987; Founder Director, Ayrshire Country Lamb Ltd., 1988-93; partner in family catering enterprises, 1986-2000; established Ayrshire Farmers' Markets, 1999; Convener, Hill Farming Committee, National Farmers' Union of Scotland, 1993-99; Chairman, Ayrshire and Arran Farming and Wildlife Advisory Group, 1993-99; Chairman, South of Scotland Regional Wool Committee, 1996-2000; JP; Elder, Ballantrae Church; Chairman, Scottish Area Committee, UK Conservative Countryside Forum, 1998-2000. Recreations: geology; curling; bridge; rugby. Address: (b.) 1 Wellington Square, Ayr KA7 1EN.

Scott, John Andrew Ross, JP. Member, Scottish Borders Council, since 1995 (Spokesman for Transport and Environment Standards on Council Executive); News Editor, Hawick News, since 2001; b. 6.5.51, Hawick; 2 s.; 1 d. Educ. Hawick High School. Worked on father's farm, 1966-74; Journalist, Hawick News, 1977-78, Tweeddale Press Group, since 1978, Chief Reporter, Southern Reporter, 1986-2000; first SDP Member, Roxburgh District Council (1980-85) and Borders Regional Council; Chairman, Roxburgh District Licensing Board, 1984-85; first Chairman, Borders Area Party, SDP, 1981-84; Secretary, Roxburgh and Berwickshire Liberal Democrats, 1988-89, Vice Chairman, 1993-94; Chairman, Scottish Association of Direct Labour Organisations Highways Division, 1994-96; Chairman, South East Scotland Transport Partnership, since 1998; Scottish Liberal Democrat Transport Spokesman, 1998-99; Chairman, COSLA Road Safety Task Group, 1999-2001; Liberal Democrat Candidate, Dumfries, 2001. Recreations: writing; music; travel; walking. Address: (h.) 8 Union Street, Hawick, Roxburghshire; T.-01450 76324.

Scott, John Dominic, LLB, DipLP. Partner, Gilfedder and McInnes, since 1997; Chair, Scottish Human Rights Centre, since 1997; Member, Council, Edinburgh Bar Association, Secretary, since 1998; Solicitor-Advocate, since 2001; b. 20.7.64, Glasgow. Educ. Holyrood Secondary School, Glasgow; Glasgow University. Trainee and Assistant, Hughes, Dowdall & Company, Glasgow, 1985-88 (qualified Solicitor, since 1987); joined Gilfedder & McInnes, Edinburgh, 1988; Member, Executive Committee, Glasgow Bar Association, since 1997. Address: (b.) 34 Leith Walk, Edinburgh EH6 5AA; T.-0131-553 4333.

Scott, John Hamilton. Farmer; Lord-Lieutenant, Shetland; Chairman: Woolgrowers of Shetland Ltd., Shetland Trust, Belmont Trust; b. 30.11.36; m., Wendy Ronald; 1 s.; 1 d. President, Shetland NFU, 1976; Nature Conservancy Council Committee for Scotland, 1984-91; N.E. Scotland Board, Scottish Natural Heritage, 1992-97; Chairman,

Shetland Crofting, Farming and Wildlife Advisory Group, 1984-94; Chairman: Shetland Arts Trust, 1994-98, Sail Shetland Ltd., 1996-2000. Recreations: hills; music; pruning. Address: (h.) Keldabister Banks, Bressay, Shetland, ZE2 9EL; T.-01595 820281.

Scott, Rev. John Miller, MA, BD, DD, FSA (Scot). Minister, St. Andrew's Scots Memorial Church, Jerusalem, 1985-88; b. 14.8.22, Glasgow; m., Dorothy Helen Loraine Bushnell; 2 s.; 1 d. Educ. Hillhead High School; Glasgow University and Trinity College. War Service, Egypt, Italy, India, 1942-46; Assistant Minister, Barony of Glasgow, 1948-49; Minister: Baxter Park Parish, Dundee, 1949-54; High Kirk of Stevenston, 1954-63; Kirk of the Crown of Scotland (Crown Court Church, Westminster), 1963-85; Moderator, Presbytery of England, 1971, 1979; Moderator, Presbytery of Jerusalem, 1986-88; Chairman, Israel Council, 1986-88; various periods of service on General Assembly Committees; Representative, World Alliance of Reformed Churches, Ecumenical Patriarchate, Istanbul, 1988. President, Caledonian Society of London, 1983-84; instituted Kirking Service for Scottish MPs and peers, 1966; Member, UNA Religious Advisory Committee, 1983-85; Convener, St Andrews Council of Churches, 1997. Hon DD (Glasgow), 1986. Recreations: travel; historical research; reading; gardening. Address: (h.) St. Martins, 6 Trinity Place, St. Andrews KY16 8SG; T.-01334 479518; e-mail: millerscott@aol.com

Scott, Sir Kenneth Bertram Adam, KCVO, CMG. Extra Equerry to The Queen, since 1996; b. 23.1.31, Belfast; m., 1, Gay Smart; m., 2, Esme Scott (qv); 1 s.; 1 d.; 1 step. s. Educ. George Watson's College; Edinburgh University. HM Diplomatic Service, 1954-85; HM Ambassador to Yugoslavia, 1982-85; Assistant Private Secretary/Deputy Private Secretary to The Queen, 1985-96; Acting Chairman, Provisional Election Commission for Bosnia, 1996. Deputy Chairman, Hopetoun House Preservation Trust; Governor, George Watson's College; Vice-Chairman, Central Council, Royal Overseas League; Trustee, Edinburgh University Development Trust. Recreations: travel; music; golf; gardening. Address: (h.) 13 Clinton Road, Edinburgh EH9 2AW; T.-0131-447 5191.

Scott, Kirsty, MA. Scotland Correspondent, The Guardian, since 2000; b. 2.9.62, Glasgow; m., Homer Fairley; 1 s.; 1 d. Educ. High School of Dundee; Edinburgh University; Arizona State University. Reporter, United News Service, 1983-87; Reporter, Scottsdale Progress, Phoenix, Arizona, 1989-90; Writer, Columnist, The Herald, Glasgow, 1990-99. Rotary International Journalism Scholar, 1987-88. Recreations: running; photography. e-mail: kirsty.scott @guardian.co.uk

Scott, Michael M. BSc, DipEd, MIBiol, CIBiol. Deputy Chairman, Scottish Natural Heritage, since 1999; Scottish Co-ordinator, Plantlife – The Wild Plant Charity, since 1989; b. 10.5.51, Edinburgh; m., Sue Scott. Educ. George Heriot's School, Edinburgh; Madras College, St. Andrews; University of Aberdeen. Assistant Education Officer, Royal Zoological Society of Scotland, 1974-76; Scottish Field Officer, Wildlife Youth Service, World Wildlife Fund, 1976-80; self-employed natural history writer, consultant, broadcaster and conservationist, since 1980 (radio work includes: The Living World, Natural History Programme, Litmus Test, MacGregor's Gathering); Editor, Scottish Environment News, 1991-2001; Chair, Save the Cairngorms Campaign, 1990-94; Chair, Scottish Wildlife and Countryside Link, 1995-99. Publications: Young Oxford Book of Ecology, 1994; Collins' Guide to Scottish Wild Flowers, 1995. Recreations: natural history; photography; travel; Runrig concerts. Address: Strome House, North Strome, Lochcarron, Ross-shire IV54 8YJ; T.-01520 722901; e-mail: MSStrome@aol.com

Scott, Paul Henderson, CMG, MA, MLitt. Vice-President, Scottish National Party, 1991-97; President, Scottish Centre, International PEN, 1992-97; President, Saltire Society, since 1996; Convener, Advisory Council for the Arts in Scotland, 1981-97; Honorary Fellow, Glasgow University, since 1996; b. 7.11.20, Edinburgh; m., B.C. Sharpe; 1 s.; 1 d. Educ. Royal High School, Edinburgh; Edinburgh University. HM Forces, 1941-47 (Major, RA); HM Diplomatic Service in Foreign Office, Warsaw, La Paz, Havana, Montreal, Vienna, Milan, 1947-80. Rector, Dundee University, 1989-92; Convener, Scottish Centre for Economic and Social Research, 1990-95; President, Edinburgh Sir Walter Scott Club, 1996. Publications: 1707, The Union of Scotland and England, 1979; Walter Scott and Scotland, 1981; John Galt, 1985; The Age of MacDiarmid (Co-Editor), 1980; In Bed with an Elephant: The Scottish Experience, 1985; A Scottish Postbag (Co-Editor), 1986; The Thinking Nation, 1989; Towards Independence — essays on Scotland, 1991; Andrew Fletcher and the Treaty of Union, 1992; Scotland in Europe: a dialogue with a sceptical friend, 1992; Scotland: a Concise Cultural History (Editor), 1993; Defoe in Edinburgh and Other Papers, 1995; Scotland's Ruine (Co-Editor), 1995; Scotland: An Unwon Cause, 1997; Still in Bed with an Elephant, 1998; The Boasted Advantages, 1999; A Twentieth Century Life, 2002. Recreation: skiing. Address: (h.) 33 Drumsheugh Gardens, Edinburgh, EH3 7RN; T.-0131-225 1038.

Scott, Primrose Smith, CA. Head of Quality Review, Institute of Chartered Accountants of Scotland, since 1999; Senior Partner, The McCabe Partnership, 1987-99; b. 21.9.40, Gorebridge. Educ. Ayr Academy. Trained with Stewart Gilmour, Ayr; qualified as CA 1963; joined Romanes & Munro, Edinburgh, 1964; progressed through manager ranks to Partner, Deloitte Haskins & Sells, 1981-87; set up own practice, Linlithgow, 1987; moved practice to Edinburgh, 1997. Member, Accounts Commission, 1988-92; Non-Executive Director: Dunfermline Building Society, 1990, Northern Venture Trust plc, 1995; Institute of Chartered Accountants of Scotland: Member, Council, 1988-95, first Convener, GP Committee, 1990, Vice President, 1992-94, President, 1994-95; Honorary Treasurer, Hospitality Industry Trust Scotland, 1994; Fellow, SCOTVEC, 1994. Recreation: walking her three dogs. Address: (b.) CA House, 21 Haymarket Yards, Edinburgh EH12 5BH.

Scott, Sheriff Richard John Dinwoodie, MA, LLB. Sheriff of Lothian and Borders at Edinburgh, since 1986 (of Grampian, Highland and Islands, at Aberdeen and Stonehaven, 1977-86); Chairman, Scottish Association for the Study of Delinquency, since 1997; b. 28.5.39, Manchester; m., Josephine Moretta Blake; 2 d. Educ. Edinburgh Academy; Edinburgh University. Lektor, Folkuniversitet of Sweden, 1960-61; admitted to Faculty of Advocates, 1965; Standing Junior Counsel, Ministry of Defence (Air), 1969; Parliamentary candidate, 1974; Honorary Reader, Aberdeen University, 1980-86. Address: (b.) Sheriffs' Chambers, Sheriff Court House, Edinburgh, EH1 1LB; T.-031-226 7181.

Scott, Professor Roger Davidson, BSc, PhD, CPhys, FInstP, FRSE. Personal Professorship, University of Glasgow, 1994; b. 17.12.41, Lerwick; m., Marion McCluckie; 2 s.; 1 d. Educ. Anderson Institute, Lerwick; Edinburgh University. Demonstrator, Edinburgh University, 1965-68; Lecturer, then Depute Director, then Director, SURRC, 1968-98; Recreations: watching football; walking dogs; home maintenance. Address: (h.) 4 Inch Keith, East Kilbride, Glasgow G74 2JZ; T.-01355 229536.

Scott, Tavish Hamilton, BA (Hons). MSP (Liberal Democrat), Shetland, since 1999; b. 6.5.66, Inverness; m., Margaret; 1 s.; 1 d. Educ. Anderson High School, Lerwick; Napier University, Edinburgh. Research Assistant to Jim Wallace, MP, 1989-90; Press Officer,

Scottish Liberal Democrats, 1990-92; Owner/Manager, Keldabister Farm, Bressay, 1992-99; Shetland Islands Councillor, 1995-99; Chairman, Lerwick Harbour Trust, 1997-99. Recreations: football; golf; swimming; cinema; reading; current affairs. Address: (b.) Albert Building, Lerwick ZE1 0LL; T.-01595 690044.

Scott, William, BSc, MSc, MRPharmS. Chief Pharmaceutical Officer, Scottish Executive (previously Scottish Office) since 1992; b. 26.10.49, Bellshill; m., Catherine Muir Gilmour; 1 s.; 1 d. Educ. Wishaw High School; Heriot Watt University; Strathclyde University. Resident Pharmacist, Nottingham City Hospital, 1975-76; Staff Pharmacist, Eastern General Hospital, Edinburgh, 1976-79; Principal Pharmacist, Western General Hospital, Edinburgh, 1979-86; Chief Administrative Pharmaceutical Officer, Tayside Health Board, 1986-90; Deputy Chief Pharmacist, Scottish Office, 1990-92. Recreations: walking; reading; golf. Address: (b.) St. Andrews House, Edinburgh; T.-0131-244 2518.

Scott Moncrieff, John Kenneth, LLB, WS. Managing Partner, Murray Beith Murray, WS, since 2001, Partner, since 1978; b. 9.2.51, Edinburgh; m., Pilla; 1 s.; 2 d. Educ. Marlborough College; Edinburgh University. Honorary Consul to Monaco; Lecturer and Tutor, Edinburgh University. Member, Scottish Arts Council, since 1999 (Chair, Drama Committee); Board Member, Cheek by Jowl Theatre Co.; Clerk to the Abbey Court, Holyrood; Trustee, various charitable trusts and companies. Recreations: football; theatre; hillwalking. Address: (b.) 39 Castle Street, Edinburgh EH2 3BH; T.-0131-225 1200; e-mail: jscottmoncrieff@murraybeith.co.uk

Scouller, Glen, DA, RGI, RSW. Artist; b. 24.4.50, Glasgow; m., Carol Alison Marsh; 2 d. Educ. Eastbank Academy; Garthamlock Secondary; Glasgow School of Art; Hospitalfield College of Art, Arbroath. RSA Painting Award, 1972; W. O. Hutcheson Prize for Drawing, 1973; travelling scholarship, Greece, 1973; started teaching, Glasgow schools, 1974; started part-time tutoring, Glasgow School of Art, 1986; Lauder Award, Glasgow Art Club, 1987; Scottish Amicable Award, Royal Glasgow Institute of Fine Arts, 1987; Royal Glasgow Institute of Fine Arts Award, 1987; elected, RGI, 1989; painting full-time since 1989; elected, Royal Scottish Society of Painters in Watercolours, 1997; solo exhibitions: John D. Kelly Gallery, Glasgow, 1977, The Scottish Gallery, Edinburgh, 1980, Fine Art Society, Glasgow, 1985, 1988, Harbour Arts Centre, Irvine, 1986, Fine Art Society, Edinburgh, 1989, Portland Gallery, London, 1989, 1992, 1994, 1998, Macauley Gallery, Stenton, 1990, 1993, 1996, French Institute, Edinburgh, 1990, Open Eye Gallery, Edinburgh, 1992, 1994, 1997, 2000, 2002, Roger Billcliffe Fine Art, Glasgow, 1992, 1995, 1998, Everard Read Gallery, Johannesburg, 1997, 2000, 2001; Corrymella Scott Gallery, Newcastle-upon-Tyne, 1999; Lemon Street Gallery, Truro, 2002; work in public, corporate and private collections, UK and abroad. Recreations: travel; music. Address: East Loudounhill Farm, Darvel KA17 0LU; e-mail: glen@appleonline.net

Scrimgeour, John Beocher, MB, ChB, DObst, RCOG, FRCOG, FRCS(Edin), FRCP (Edin). Consultant Obstetrician and Gynaecologist, 1972-97, now retired; Honorary Senior Lecturer in Obstetrics and Gynaecology, Edinburgh University, 1972-97; Medical Director, Western General Hospitals Unit, Edinburgh, 1993-97; President, Edinburgh Obstetrical Society, 1996-97; Vice Chairman, Scottish Association of Trust Medical Directors, 1996-97; b. 22.1.39, Elgin; m., Joyce Morrin; 1 s.; 1 d. Educ. Hawick High School; Edinburgh University. General Practitioner, Edinburgh, 1963-65; Senior House Officer: Stirling Royal Infirmary, 1965, and Registrar, Eastern General Hospital, Edinburgh, 1966-69; Senior Registrar, Edinburgh Royal Infirmary, 1970-72; Senior Secretary, Edinburgh

Obstetrical Society, 1980-85; Chairman, Area Division of Obstetrics and Gynaecology, 1984-88; Member, Council, Royal College of Obstetricians and Gynaecologists, 1976-81; Member, Gynaecological Visiting Society of Great Britain and Ireland, since 1979. Publication: Towards the Prevention of Fetal Malformation, 1978. Recreations: gardening; golf; fishing. Address: (h.) Cuilaluinn, Aberfeldy, Perthshire PH15 2JW; T.-01887 820302; e-mail: j.b.scrimgeour@amserve.net

Seafield, Earl of; b. 20.3.39, London; m., Leila Refaat (2nd m.); 2 s. Educ. Eton; Cirencester Agricultural College. Recreation: countryside activities. Address: Old Cullen, Cullen, Buckie AB56 4XW; T.-01542 840221.

Seagrave, David Robert, LLB (Hons), SSC, NP. Solicitor and Notary Public; Partner, Seagrave & Co., Solicitors, Dumfries; b. 29.4.43, Berwick-on-Tweed; m., Fiona Lesley Thomson; 1 s.; 1 d. Educ. Newcastle-upon-Tyne; Glasgow University. Banking, insurance, police; Secretary, Enterprise Trust for Nithsdale, Annandale/Eskdale and the Stewartry, 1984-92; Council Member, Law Society of Scotland, 1981-87. Recreations: choral singing; shooting; fishing; golf. Address: (h.) Amulree, Islesteps, Dumfries; T.-Dumfries 264523.

Sealey, Barry Edward, CBE, BA (Hons) (Cantab), CBIM. Director: Wilson Byard PLC (Chairman), Optos plc (Chairman), The Caledonian Brewing Company Ltd., Morago Ltd., Northern 3 VCT plc, ESI Investors Ltd., Archangel Informal Investment Ltd., and other companies; Chairman, Lothian University Hospitals NHS Trust; b. 3.2.36, Bristol; m., Helen Martyn; 1 s.; 1 d. Educ. Dursley Grammar School; St. John's College, Cambridge. RAF, 1953-55. Joined Christian Salvesen as trainee, 1958; joined Board, Christian Salvesen PLC (responsible for Food Services Division), 1969; appointed Managing Director, 1981, Deputy Chairman and Managing Director, 1987; retired from Christian Salvesen, 1990. Council Member, The Industrial Society. Address: (h.) 4 Castlelaw Road, Edinburgh, EH13 0DN; e-mail: bes@morago.co.uk

Searle, Rev. David Charles, MA, DipTh. Minister of the Church of Scotland, since 1965; Warden, Rutherford House, Edinburgh, since 1993; b. 14.11.37, Swansea; m., Lorna Christine Wilson; 2 s.; 1 d. Educ. Arbroath High School; St. Andrews University; London University; Aberdeen University. Teacher, 1961-64; Assistant Minister, St. Nicholas Church, Aberdeen, 1964-65; Minister: Newhills Parish Church, 1965-75, Larbert Old, 1975-85, Hamilton Road Presbyterian Church, Bangor, Co. Down, 1985-93; Contributor, Presbyterian Herald; Editor, Rutherford Journal of Church and Ministry. Publications: Be Strong in the Lord; Truth and Love in a Sexually Disordered World; The Ten Commandments. Recreations: sail-boarding; gardening; hill-walking. Address: (b.) Rutherford House, 17 Claremont Park, Edinburgh, EH6 7PJ; T.-0131-554 1206; e-mail: searled@ rutherfordhouse.org.uk

Seaton, Professor Anthony, CBE, BA, MD (Cantab), FRCPLond, FRCPEdin, FFOM, FMedSci. Professor of Environmental and Occupational Medicine, Aberdeen University, since 1988; b. 20.8.38, London; m., Jillian Margaret Duke; 2 s. Educ. Rossall School, Fleetwood; King's College, Cambridge; Liverpool University. Assistant Professor of Medicine, West Virginia University, 1969-71; Consultant Chest Physician, Cardiff, 1971-77; Director, Institute of Occupational Medicine, Edinburgh, 1978-90. Editor, Thorax, 1977-82; Chairman, Department of Environment Expert Panel on Air Quality Standards, 1991-2002; President, British Thoracic Society, 1999; Member, Department of Health Committee on Medical Aspects of Air Pollution. Publications: books and papers on occupational and respiratory medicine. Recreations:

keeping fit; opera; painting. Address: (h.) 8 Avon Grove, Cramond, Edinburgh, EH4 6RF; T.-031-336 5113; 71 Urquhart Terrace, Aberdeen AB24 1NJ.

Seckl, Professor Jonathan Robert, BSc, MB, BS, MRCP(UK), PhD, FRCPE, FMedSci. Moncrieff-Arnott Professor of Molecular Medicine, Edinburgh University, since 1997; Professor of Endocrinology, since 1996; Head, Department of Medical Sciences, since 2001; Chairman, Molecular Medicine Centre, 1996-2001; b. 15.8.56, London; m., Molly; 1 s.; 1 d. Educ. William Ellis School, London; University College Hospital Medical School, London. Sir Jules Thorn Research Fellow in Neuroendocrinology, Charing Cross and Westminster Medical School, 1984-87; Honorary Clinical Assistant, National Hospital for Nervous Diseases, London, 1984-87; Lecturer in Medicine, Edinburgh University, 1987-89; Wellcome Trust/Royal Society of Edinburgh Senior Clinical Research Fellow, 1989-96. Address: (b.) Molecular Medicine Centre, Edinburgh University, Western General Hospital, Crewe Road, Edinburgh EH4 2XU; T.-0131-651 1035; e-mail: j.seckl@ed.ac.uk

Secombes, Professor Christopher John, BSc, PhD, DSc, FIBiol. Professor, Department of Zoology, University of Aberdeen, since 1997 (Head of Department, since 2001); Head, Scottish Fish Immunology Research Centre, University of Aberdeen, since 2001; b. 1.4.56, London; m., Karen Ruth; 2 s.; 1 d. Educ. Longdean School, Hemel Hempstead; University of Leeds; University of Hull. Research Fellow, Wageningen Agricultural University, Netherlands, 1981-82; Department of Zoology, University of Aberdeen: Research Fellow, 1982-84, Lecturer, 1984-91, Senior Lecturer, 1991-97. President-Elect, International Society for Developmental and Comparative Immunology, 2000-03; Member, NERC Marine Sciences Peer Review Committee, 2001-04; Editor, Fish and Shellfish Immunology; Member, Editorial Board: Developmental and Comparative Immunology, Veterinary Immunology and Immunopathology; Chairman, Aquatic Sciences Research Centre, Aberdeen Research Consortium, 1997-99; Member, international review panel for biology and related areas of biochemistry, Norway, 2000. Recreations: squash; hillwalking. Address: (b.) Department of Zoology, University of Aberdeen, Tillydrone Avenue, Aberdeen AB24 2TZ; T.-01224 272872; e-mail: c.secombes@abdn.ac.uk

Sefton, Allan Douglas, BSc, PhD, FIOSH. Director, Scotland, Health and Safety Executive, since 2000; Head, Offshore Safety Division, Health and Safety Executive, 1996-2000; b. 15.4.45, Glasgow; m., Jennifer; 2 s. Educ. Grammar School, Accrington; University College of North Wales, Bangor. Inspector, HM Factories Inspectorate, Glasgow; Health and Safety Executive: Principal Inspector, Hazardous Substances Division; Director, W. and N. Yorkshire, Field Operations Division; Director of Operations, Offshore Safety Division. Recreations: fly fishing; game shooting. Address: (b.) Belford House, 59 Belford Road, Edinburgh EH4 3UE; T.-0131-247 2000.

Sefton, Rev. Henry Reay, MA, BD, STM, PhD. Co-ordinator in Christian Studies, Aberdeen University, 1995-97; Consultant in Christian Studies, since 1997; Chaplain, College of St Nicholas, Aberdeen, since 1989; b. 15.1.31, Rosehearty. Educ. Brechin High School; St. Andrews University; Glasgow University; Union Theological Seminary, New York. Assistant Minister, Glasgow Cathedral, 1957-58, St. Margaret's, Knightswood, Glasgow, 1958-61; Acting Chaplain, Hope Waddell Training Institution, Nigeria, 1959; Associate Minister, St. Mark's, Wishaw, 1962; Minister, Newbattle, 1962-66; Assistant Secretary, Church of Scotland Department of Education, 1966-72; Lecturer in Church History, Aberdeen University, 1972-90, Senior Lecturer, 1991-92; Master of Christ's

College, Aberdeen, 1982-92; Alexander Robertson Lecturer, Glasgow University, 1995; Moderator, Aberdeen Presbytery, 1982-83, Synod of Grampian, 1991-92; Convener, Church of Scotland Board of Education, 1987-91; Clerk, Aberdeen Presbytery, 1993-95; Chairman, Association of University Teachers (Scotland), 1982-84. Recreations: hill-walking; church architecture; stamp and coin collecting. Address: (h.) 25 Albury Place, Aberdeen, AB11 6TQ; T.-01224 572305.

Selkirk of Douglas, Rt. Hon. Lord (James Alexander Douglas-Hamilton), QC, PC, MA, LLB. MSP (Conservative), Lothians, since 1999; MP (Conservative), Edinburgh West, 1974-97; b. 31.7.42, Strathaven; m., (Priscilla) Susan (Susie) Buchan; 4 s. Educ. Eton; Balliol College, Oxford; Edinburgh University. Officer, TA 6/7 Bn. Cameronians Scottish Rifles, 1961-66, TAVR, 1971-73, Captain 2 Bn. Lowland Volunteers; Advocate, 1968-74; Scottish Conservative Whip, 1977; a Lord Cmnr., HM Treasury, 1979-81, PPS to Malcolm Rifkind MP, at Foreign Office, later as Secretary of State for Scotland, 1983-87; Parliamentary Under Secretary of State: at the Scottish Office for Home Affairs and Environment, 1987-89; for Home Affairs and Environment, 1989-92 (with additional responsibility for local government finance 1989-90, and with additional responsibility for the arts in Scotland, 1990-92); for Education and Housing, Scottish Office, 1992-95; Minister of State for Home Affairs and Health, Scottish Office, 1995-97. Member, Scottish Select Committee Scottish Affairs 1981-83; Honorary Secretary: Conservative Parliamentary Constitutional Committee, Conservative Parliamentary Aviation Committee, since 1983; Chairman, Scottish Parliamentary All-Party Penal Affairs Committee, 1983; Honorary President, Scottish Amateur Boxing Association, 1975-98; President: Royal Commonwealth Society (Scotland), 1979-87, Scottish National Council of UN Association, 1981-87; Member, Council, National Trust for Scotland, 1977-82; Honorary Air Commodore No. 2 (City of Edinburgh) Maritime Headquarters Unit and President International Rescue Corps, 1995; Honorary Air Commodore No. 603 (City of Edinburgh) Squadron, since 2000. Oxford Boxing Blue, 1961; President, Oxford University Conservative Association, 1963; President, Oxford Union, 1964. Publications: Motive For A Mission: The Story Behind Hess's Flight to Britain, 1971; The Air Battle for Malta: The Diaries of a Fighter Pilot, 1981; Roof of the World: Man's First Flight over Everest, 1983; The Truth about Rudolf Hess, 1993. Recreations: golf; forestry; debating; history; boxing. Address: House of Lords, London; Scottish Parliament, Edinburgh EH99 1SP.

Sellers, Professor Susan Catherine, MA, DEA, PhD. Professor of English and Related Literature, St Andrews University, since 1998; b. 7.5.57, Lymington; m., Jeremy Thurlow; 1 s. Educ. British School, Brussels; Sorbonne, Paris. Senior Researcher, Ecole Normale Superieure, Paris, 1989-95; Reader, St Andrews University, 1995-98; Visiting Fellow, New Hall, Cambridge, 1994-95; Invited Fellow, St John's College, Oxford, Summer 1994. Publications: Writing Differences; Delighting the Heart; Taking Reality by Surprise; Feminist Criticism: Theory and Practice; Language and Sexual Difference; Coming To Writing (translation); Three Steps on the Ladder of Writing (translation); The Semi-Transparent Envelope: Women Writing (Co-author); The Hélène Cixous Reader; Instead of Full Stops; Hélène Cixous: Authorship, Autobiography and Love; The Cambridge Companion to Virginia Woolf (Co-author); Myth and Fairy Tale in Contemporary Women's Fiction. Recreations: film; travel; gardens; playing with her three-year-old son. Address: (b.) School of English, University of St. Andrews, Fife, KY16 9AL; T.-01334 462666.

Selway, Mark Wayne. Chief Executive, The Weir Group plc, since 2001; b. 2.6.59, Adelaide, Australia; m., Catherine; 2 s.; 1 d. Educ. Westminster School, South Australia. Britex Rainsford Pty Ltd: Marketing Manager, 1985-87, Marketing Director, 1987-88; President, Britex Rainsford Inc., 1989-95; Managing Director, Britex Rear Vision Systems, 1995-96; Executive Director and Managing Director, Automotive Components, Britex International plc, 1996-2000. Recreation: golf. Address: (b.) The Weir Group plc, 149 Newlands Road, Cathcart, Glasgow G44 4EX; T.-0141-308 3700; e-mail: m.selway@wg.weir.co.uk

Sempill, 21st Baron (James William Stuart Whitemore Sempill); b. 25.2.49; m.; 1 s.; 1 d. Educ. St Clare's Hall, Oxford. Succeeded to title, 1995; Company Director; contested (Conservative) Edinburgh North and Leith, Scottish Parliamentary election, 1999.

Semple, Colin Gordon, MA, MBChB, FRCP(Glas), FRCP(Ed), FRCP(London), MD. Consultant Physician, Southern General Hospital, Glasgow, since 1988; Honorary Clinical Senior Lecturer, Glasgow University, since 1988; b. 19.3.53, Glasgow; m., Elaine; 1 s.; 1 d. Educ. Loretto School; Brasenose College, Oxford; Glasgow University. General Physician with interest in diabetes and endocrinology and special interest in postgraduate medical education; Chairman, General Medicine Specialist Advisory Committee; Royal College of Physicians and Surgeons of Glasgow: Member, Council, 1986-90, Deputy Honorary Secretary, 1995-98, Honorary Secretary, 1998-2001. Recreations: golf; gardening; walking; curling.

Semple, David, WS, LLB, NP. Director, Core Mediation Ltd.; formerly Partner and Chairman, Semple Fraser WS; b. 29.12.43, Glasgow; m., Jet; 2 s.; 1 d. Educ. Loretto School; Glasgow University. Partner, Bird Son & Semple, 1968-73; Bird Semple and Crawford Herron, 1973-88; Bird Semple Fyfe Ireland, 1988-90. President, Glasgow Chamber of Commerce, 1996-97; Chairman, Interactive Media Alliance Scotland, 1998-99; accredited ADR Mediator, Centre for Dispute Resolution, Scotland. Recreations: golf; hill-walking; bagpipes. Address: (b.) 39 Kelvin Court, Great Western Road, Glasgow G12 0AE; T.-0141-357 4887; e-mail: david.semple@core-mediation.com

Semple, Peter d'Almaine, DL, MD, FRCPGlas, FRCPEdin, FRCPLond. Consultant Physician and Chest Specialist, Inverclyde District, since 1979; b. 30.10.45, Glasgow; m., Judith Mairi Abercromby; 2 d. Educ. Belmont House; Loretto; Glasgow University. Consultant Physician, Inverclyde Royal Hospital, 1979; former Postgraduate Medical Tutor, Inverclyde District; Honorary Clinical Senior Lecturer, Glasgow University. Past Chairman, Medical Audit Sub-Committee, Scottish Office; Past President, Greenock and District Faculty of Medicine; Past Chairman, West of Scotland Branch, British Deer Society; Past Director, Medical Audit, and Property Convenor, Royal College of Physicians and Surgeons of Glasgow; Deputy Lieutenant, Renfrewshire. Recreations: field sports; gardening. Address: (h.) High Lunderston, Inverkip, PA16 0DU; T.-01475 522342.

Semple, Walter George, BL, NP, ACI Arb. Solicitor; b. 7.5.42, Glasgow; m., Dr. Lena Ohrstrom; 3 d. Educ. Belmont House, Glasgow; Loretto School; Glasgow University. President, Glasgow Juridical Society, 1968; Tutor and Lecturer (part-time), Glasgow University, 1970-79; Council Member, Law Society of Scotland, 1976-80; Chairman, Scottish Lawyers European Group, 1978-81; Member, Commission Consultative des Barreaux Europeens, 1978-80, 1984-87; President, Association Internationale des Jeunes Avocats, 1983-84; Chairman, Scottish Branch, Institute of Arbitrators, 1989-91; Board Member, Union Internationale des Avocats, 1997-2001; Dean, Royal Faculty of Procurators in Glasgow, 1998-2001;

President, Franco Scottish Business Club, 2000-01. Recreations: golf; fishing; skiing; music. Address: (h.) 79 Lancefield Quay, Glasgow G3 8HA.

Sewel, Lord (John Buttifant Sewel), CBE. Vice-Principal, University of Aberdeen, since 1999; Parliamentary Under-Secretary of State, Scottish Office, with responsibility for Agriculture, Environment and Fisheries, 1997-99; b. 1946. Educ. Hanson Boys' Grammar School, Bradford; Durham University; University College Swansea; Aberdeen University. Councillor, Aberdeen City Council, 1974-84 (Leader of the Council, 1977-80); President, COSLA, 1982-84; Member, Accounts Commission for Scotland, 1987-96; Member, Scottish Constitutional Convention, 1994-95; successively Research Fellow, Lecturer, Senior Lecturer, Professor, Aberdeen University, from 1969; Dean, Faculty of Economic and Social Sciences, 1989-94; Vice Principal and Dean, Faculty of Social Sciences and Law, 1995-96; created Peer, 1996. Recreations: hill-walking; skiing; watching cricket. Address: Birklands, Raemoir, Banchory, Kincardineshire AB31 5QU.

Sewell, Professor John Isaac, PhD, DSc, CEng, FIEEE. Professor of Electronic Systems, Glasgow University, since 1985 (Dean, Faculty of Engineering, 1990-93, Member, Court, since 2000); b. 13.5.42, Kirkby Stephen; m., Ruth Alexandra Baxter; 1 d. Educ. Kirkby Stephen Grammar School; Durham University; Newcastle-upon-Tyne University. Lecturer, Senior Lecturer, Reader, Department of Electronic Engineering, Hull University, 1968-85. Publications: 144 papers. Recreations: swimming; climbing. Address: (h.) 16 Paterson Place, Bearsden, Glasgow, G61 4RU; T.-0141-586 5336; e-mail: Sewellmac@aol.com

Sexton, David B., BA. Head of Reserves, RSPB Scotland, since 1998; b. 12.11.60, London; m., Caroline Davies; 2 d. Educ. Haberdashers' Aske's Hatcham Boys' School, London; College of William and Mary, Williamsburg, Virginia. Warden, Sea Eagle Protection Scheme, W. Scotland, 1984-85; Field Officer, Aigas Field Centre, Inverness, 1986-87; Researcher, BBC TV Natural History Unit, Bristol, 1987-88; Assistant Reserves Manager, S. Scotland, RSPB Scotland, 1988-92; Reserves Manager, S. and W. Scotland, 1992-98. Recreations: bird-watching; hiking; travel; gardening; family. Address: (b.) RSPB Scottish HQ, Dunedin House, 25 Ravelston Terrace, Edinburgh EH4 3TP; T.-0131-311 6500.

Seymour, Professor Philip Herschel Kean, BA, MEd, PhD. Professor of Cognitive Psychology, Dundee University, since 1988; b. 9.3.38, London; m., Margaret Jean Dyson Morris; 2 s.; 2 d. Educ. Kelly College, Tavistock; Exeter College, Oxford; St. Andrews University. Dundee University: Lecturer, 1966-75, Senior Lecturer, 1975-82, Reader, 1982-88. Chairman, Scottish Dyslexia Association, 1982-85. Publications: Human Visual Cognition, 1979; Cognitive Analysis of Dyslexia, 1986. Address: (b.) Department of Psychology, Dundee University, Dundee; T.-Dundee 344614; e-mail: p.h.k.seymour@dundee.ac.uk

Shankland, Jim, FRICS, DipTP. Managing Partner, Ryden, since 1998; b. 15.3.54, Glasgow; m., Mo; 1 s.; 1 d. Speirs Parrie and Adam, 1977; Partner, Ryden since 1989 (UK, 1989-95, South Africa, 1995-98, UK, since 1998). Junior Vice Chairman, RICS in Scotland; Member: Executive Committee, SCDI, Investment Property Forum, London. Recreations: skiing; walking; golf; fishing. Address: (h.) 8 Kenmure Road, Whitecraigs, Glasgow, G46 6TU.

Shanks, Duncan Faichney, RSA, RGI, RSW. Artist; b. 30.8.37, Airdrie; m., Una Brown Gordon. Educ. Uddingston Grammar School; Glasgow School of Art. Part-time Lecturer, Glasgow School of Art, until 1979; now full-time painter; one-man shows: Stirling University, Scottish Gallery, Fine Art Society, Talbot Rice Art Gallery, Edinburgh University, Crawford Centre, Maclaurin Art Gallery, Glasgow Art Gallery, Fine Art Society, touring exhibition (Wales); taken part in shows of Scottish painting, London, 1986, Toulouse, Rio de Janeiro, 1985, Wales, 1988; Scottish Arts Council Award; Latimer and MacAulay Prizes, RSA; Torrance Award, Cargill Award, MacFarlane Charitable Trust Award, RGI; May Marshall Brown Award, RSW; The Lord Provost's Prize for painting (GOMA), 1996; tapestry commissioned by Coats Viyella, woven by Edinburgh Tapestry Company, presented to Glasgow Royal Concert Hall, 1991. Recreations: music; gardening.

Shanks, Rev. Norman James, MA, BD. Leader, Iona Community, since 1995; Member, Central Committee, World Council of Churches, since 1998; President, Scottish Churches Open College, since 2001; Member, Christian Aid Board, since 2001; b. 15.7.42, Edinburgh; m., Ruth Osborne Douglas; 2 s.; 1 d. Educ. Stirling High School; St. Andrews University; Edinburgh University. Scottish Office, 1964-79; Chaplain, Edinburgh University, 1985-88; Lecturer in Practical Theology, Glasgow University, 1988-95; Convener, Acts Commission on Justice, Peace, Social and Moral Issues, 1991-95; Chairman, Edinburgh Council of Social Service, 1985-88; Chairman, Secretary of State's Advisory Committee on Travelling People, 1985-88; Convener, Church and Nation Committee, Church of Scotland, 1988-92; Member, Broadcasting Council for Scotland, 1988-93. Recreations: armchair cricket; occasional golf. Address: (h.) 1 Marchmont Terrace, Glasgow, G12 9LT; T.-0141-339 4421.

Shanks, Thomas Henry, MA, LLB. Solicitor and Notary Public, since 1956; Honorary Sheriff, Lanark, since 1982; b. 22.10.30, Lanark; m., Marjorie A. Rendall; 1 s.; 1 d. (by pr. m.); 3 step s.; 1 step d. Educ. Lanark Grammar School; Glasgow University. Intelligence Corps (National Service), 1954-56. Depute Clerk of Peace, County of Lanark, 1961-74; Chairman, Royal Burgh of Lanark Community Council, 1977-80 and 1983-86; Captain, Lanark Golf Club, 1962 and 2001; Lanark Lord Cornet, 1968. Recreation: golf. Address: (h.) Clydesholm Braes, Lanark.

Sharp, Professor Peter Frederick, BSc, PhD, CPhys, FInstP, ARCP, FIPEM, FRSE. Professor of Medical Physics, University of Aberdeen; b. 13.8.47, Spalding; m., Elisabeth Margaret; 2 s. Educ. Spalding Grammar School; Durham University; Aberdeen University. University of Aberdeen: Lecturer in Medical Physics, 1974-83, Senior Lecturer in Medical Physics, 1983-90. Honorary Sheriff, Stonehaven. Publication: Practical Nuclear Medicine (Editor). Address: (b.) Department of Biomedical Physics and Bioengineering, Foresterhill, Aberdeen AB25 2ZD; T.-01224 552499; e-mail: p.sharp@biomed.abdn.ac.uk

Sharpe, Ian, LLB (Hons.), BA, DipLP, LLM. Advocate, since 1992; b. 23.12.55, Bellshill; m., Annette Weaver; 3 d. Educ. Scotus Academy, Edinburgh; St. David's High School, Dalkeith; Jordanhill College of Education; Open University; Strathclyde University; Edinburgh University. Assistant Manager, Milngavie Community Education Centre, 1977-79; Senior Community Education Officer, Clydebank East, 1979-82; Trainee Solicitor, Coatbridge, 1986-88; Procurator Fiscal Depute, Airdrie, 1988-92. Recreations: reading; walking. Address: (b.) Advocates' Library, Parliament House, Edinburgh EH1 1RF; e-mail: sharpe.advocate@btinternet.com

Sharratt, John, DPA, DCA, FTSI. Chief Trading Standards Officer, Scottish Borders Council (formerly Borders Regional Council), since 1988; b. 16.8.47, Manchester; m., Yvonne; 4 s. Educ. Horwich Secondary School; Bell College of Technology. Trainee, Lancashire CC, 1964-69; Senior Trading Standards Officer, Glasgow Corporation/Strathclyde RC, 1969-79; Assistant Divisional Trading Standards Officer, 1979-84, Principal TSO

(Research, Development and Training), 1984-88, Strathclyde RC. Education Secretary, Institute of Trading Standards Administration (Scottish Branch), 1985-91, Chairman, 1991-92. Recreations: squash; golf; fishing; watching rugby. Address: (b.) St. Dunstan's, High Street, Melrose, TD6 9RU; T.-0189 682 3922.

Sharwood Smith, Professor Michael Anthony, PhD, MA, DipAppLing. Professor of Languages, Heriot-Watt University, since 1999; b. 22.5.42, Cape Town, South Africa; m., Ewa Maria Wróblewska; 2 d. Educ. King's School, Canterbury; St Andrews University; Edinburgh University. English Teacher: Centre Pédagogique Regionale, Montpellier, France; British Centre, Sweden; British Council Senior Lecturer, Adam Mickiewicz University, Poznan, Poland; Senior Lecturer, Utrecht University, Netherlands. Founding Vice-President, European 2nd Language Association; set up web-based international commission on language acquisition. Publications: over 100 on English linguistics, applied linguistics and second language acquisition; books include: Second Language Learning: Theoretical Foundations, 1994. Recreations: painting and drawing; music, trumpet and guitar; flight simulation. Address: (b.) School of Languages, Heriot-Watt University, Riccarton, Edinburgh, EH14 4AS; T.-0131-449 5111, ext. 4107.

Shaw, Rev. Alistair Neil, MA (Hons), BD (Hons). Minister, Greenbank Parish Church, Clarkston, since 1999; b. 6.7.53, Kilbarchan; m., Brenda Bruce; 2 d. Educ. Paisley Grammar School; Glasgow University. Minister, Relief Parish Church, Bourtreehill, Irvine, 1982-88; Minister, Laigh Kirk, Kilmarnock, 1988-99; Moderator, Presbytery of Irvine and Kilmarnock, 1995-96. Recreations: wine-making; visiting archaeological sites; foreign travel; swimming. Address: 38 Eaglesham Road, Clarkston, Glasgow G76 7DJ; T.-0141-644 1395; e-mail: alistairn@shaw98.freeserve.co.uk

Shaw, Rev. Professor Douglas William David, MA, LLB, BD, DD, WS. Professor of Divinity, St. Andrews University, 1979-91 (Dean, Faculty of Divinity, 1983-86, Principal, St. Mary's College, 1986-92; Minister, Church of Scotland, since 1960; b. 25.6.28, Edinburgh; m., Edinburgh Academy; Loretto; Ashbury College, Ottawa; St. John's College, Cambridge; Edinburgh University. Practised law as WS (Partner, Davidson and Syme, WS, Edinburgh), 1952-57; Assistant Minister, St. George's West Church, Edinburgh, 1960-63; Official Observer, Second Vatican Council, Rome, 1962; Lecturer in Divinity, Edinburgh University, 1963-79; Principal, New College, and Dean, Faculty of Divinity, Edinburgh, 1973-78; Visiting Fellow, Fitzwilliam College, Cambridge, 1978; Visiting Lecturer, Virginia University, 1979. Publications: Who is God?, 1968; The Dissuaders, 1978, In Divers Manners (Editor), 1990; Dimensions, 1992; Theology in Scotland. Recreation: golf. Address: (h.) 4/13 Succoth Court, Edinburgh EH12 6BZ; T.-0131-337 2130; e-mail:DWilliamDShaw@aol.com

Shaw, Rev. Duncan, BD (Hons), MTh. Minister, St. John's, Bathgate, since 1978; b. 10.4.47, Blantyre; m., Margaret S. Moore; 2 s.; 1 d. Educ. St. John's Grammar School, Hamilton; Hamilton Academy; Trinity College, Glasgow University. Assistant Minister, Netherlee Parish Church, Glasgow, 1974-77. Clerk, West Lothian Presbytery, since 1982 (Moderator, 1989-90). Recreations: gardening; travel (in Scotland). Address: St. John's Parish Church Manse, Mid Street, Bathgate, EH48 1QD; T.-Bathgate 653146; e-mail: duncanshaw@dial.pipex.com

Shaw, Professor Sir John Calman, CBE, KStJ, Dr HC, LLD, BL, FRSE, CA, FCMA. Governor, Bank of Scotland, 1999-2001; b. 10.7.32, Perth; m., Shirley Botterill; 3 d. Educ. Strathallan; Edinburgh University. Qualified as Chartered Accountant, 1954; Partner, Graham, Smart &

Annan, CA, Edinburgh, latterly Deloitte Haskins & Sells, 1960-1987; President, Institute of Chartered Accountants of Scotland, 1983-84; Johnstone Smith Professor of Accountancy, Glasgow University, 1977-83; Non-Executive Director, Bank of Scotland, 1990-2001, Deputy Governor, 1991-99. Director: Scottish Mortgage and Trust PLC, 1982-2001, Scottish American Investment Company PLC, since 1986 (Chairman, 1991-2001), Templeton Emerging Markets Investment Trust PLC, Templeton Latin America Investment Trust PLC, TR European Growth Trust PLC; Chairman, Scottish Science Trust, since 1998; Lay Director, Scottish Chamber Orchestra; Chairman, David Hume Institute; Receiver General, Priory of Scotland of Most Venerable Order of St. John; Chairman, US Smaller Companies Investment Trust PLC, 1991-99; Chairman, Scottish Higher Education Funding Council, 1992-98; Board Member, Scottish Enterprise, 1990-98; Deputy Chairman, Edinburgh Festival Society, 1990-2000; Director, Scottish Metropolitan Property PLC, 1994-2000; Chairman, Scottish Financial Enterprise, 1995-99; Member, Scottish Economic Council, 1996-98; author of various texts and publications on accountancy. Recreations: listening to music; walking; travel. Address: (b.) Tayhill, Brae Street, Dunkeld PH8 0BA.

Shaw, Mark Robert, BA, MA, DPhil. Keeper of Geology and Zoology, National Museums of Scotland, since 1996; b. 11.5.45, Sutton Coldfield; m., Francesca Dennis Wilkinson; 2 d. Educ. Dartington Hall School; Oriel College, Oxford. Research Assistant (Entomology), Zoology Department, Manchester University, 1973-76; University Research Fellow, Reading University, 1977-80; Assistant Keeper, Department of Natural History, Royal Scottish Museum, 1980-83; Keeper of Natural History, National Museums of Scotland, 1983-96. Recreations: field entomology; family life. Address: (h.) 48 St. Albans Road, Edinburgh, EH9 2LU; T.-0131-667 0577.

Shaw, Neil, BSc, BA (Hons). Head Teacher, Broxburn Academy, since 1998; b. 30.12.53, Airdrie; m., Nan; 1 s.; 1 d. Educ. Airdrie Academy; University of Glasgow; Jordanhill College of Education; Open University. Mathematics Teacher, Caldervale High School, Airdrie, 1977-87; Principal Teacher of Mathematics: Crookston Castle Secondary School, Glasgow, 1987-90, Carluke High School, 1990-93; Assistant Head Teacher, Boclair Academy, Bearsden, 1993-98. Recreations: golf (eight handicap, Airdrie Golf Club); supporter of Airdrieonians F. C. Address: (b.) Cardross Road, Broxburn EH52 6AG; T.-01506 852521; e-mail: neil.shaw@westlothian.org.uk

Shaw, Richard Wright, CBE, MA, FRSA. Principal and Vice Chancellor, University of Paisley, 1992-2001; b. 22.9.41, Preston; m., Susan Angela; 2 s. Educ. Lancaster Royal Grammar School; Sidney Sussex College, Cambridge. Assistant Lecturer in Management, then Lecturer in Economics, Leeds University, 1964-69; Lecturer in Economics, then Senior Lecturer, Stirling University, 1969-84; part-time Lecturer, Glasgow University, 1978-79; Visiting Lecturer, Newcastle University, NSW, 1982; Head, Department of Economics, Stirling University, 1982-84; Professor and Head, Department of Economics and Management, Paisley College, 1984-86, Vice Principal, 1986, Principal, 1987-92. Director, Renfrewshire Enterprise, 1992-2000; Member, Scottish Economic Council, 1995-98; Director, Higher Education Careers Service Unit, 1996-2001; Member, Board of Management, Reid Kerr College, 1993-2001; Member, Scottish Business Forum, 1998-99; Convener, Committee of Scottish Higher Education Principals, 1996-98; Member, Independent Review of Higher Education Pay and Conditions, 1998-99. Fellow, Scottish Vocational Education Council, since 1995. Recreations: sketching and painting. Address: (b.) Drumbarns, 18 Old Doune Road, Dunblane FK15 9AG.

Shaw, Professor Susan Angela, MA (Cantab), FCIM. Pro Vice-Principal, Strathclyde University; Professor of Marketing, since 1991; b. 1.6.43, Bristol; m., Richard Shaw; 2 s. Educ. Kingswood Grammar School, Bristol; Girton College, Cambridge. Marketing Executive, ICI Fibres; Lecturer, Senior Lecturer, Professor, Stirling University. Council Member, Food from Britain; Member, Food Advisory Committee. Recreations: hill-walking; tennis; opera. Address: (b.) McCance Building, 16 Richmond Street, Glasgow G1 1XQ; T.-0141-552 4400.

Shaw-Stewart, Sir Houston (Mark), 11th Bt, MC (1950), TD, DL. Vice Lord Lieutenant, Strathclyde Region (Eastwood, Renfrew and Inverclyde Districts), 1980-95; b. 24.4.31; m., Lucinda Victoria Fletcher; 1 s. Educ. Eton. Coldstream Guards, 1949; 2nd Lt., Royal Ulster Rifles, Korea, 1950; Ayrshire Yeomanry, 1952; Member, Queen's Bodyguard for Scotland (Royal Company of Archers). Address: (h.) Ardgowan, Inverkip, Renfrewshire, PA16 0DW.

Shaw-Stewart, Lady (Lucinda Victoria), FRSA. National Trust for Scotland: Vice President, since 1994, Member, Executive Committee, since 1985, Convener, Curatorial Committee, since 1993; Trustee, Sir William Burrell's Trust, since 1992; b. 29.9.49, Harrogate; m., Sir Houston Shaw-Stewart Bt; 1 s. Educ. Cranborne Chase School; diploma from Study Centre for the History of the Fine and Decorative Arts. Freelance Lecturer in Fine and Decorative Arts, 1969-82; National Trust for Scotland: London Representative, 1978-82, Member, Council, 1983-88. Honorary Vice President, Ardgowan Hospice, Greenock. Address: (h.) Ardgowan, Inverkip, Renfrewshire PA16 0DW; T.-01475 521226.

Shea, Michael Sinclair MacAuslan, CVO, MA, PhD. Scottish Member, Independent Television Commission, since 1996; Chairman, Royal Lyceum Theatre, since 1998; b. 10.5.38, Carluke; m., Mona Grec Stensen; 2 d. Educ. Lenzie Academy; Gordonstoun; Edinburgh University. Entered Foreign Office, 1963; seconded to Cabinet Office; Deputy Director General, British Information Services, New York; Press Secretary to the Queen; Head of Political and Government Affairs, Hanson PLC. Former Visiting Professor, Graduate School, Strathclyde University; Trustee, National Galleries of Scotland; Governor, Gordonstoun; Board Member, Murray Johnstone companies; Non-Executive Chairman, P&A Group; Non-Executive Chairman, Nordic-Pioneer UK Ltd.; Vice-Chairman, Foundation for Skin Research; Member, Board of Directors, Edinburgh Military Tattoo; has published 25 books of fiction and non-fiction. Address: (b.) 1A Ramsay Garden, Edinburgh EH1 2NA; T.-0131-220 1456.

Shearer, David James Buchanan, BAcc, CA, FRSA. Regional Partner in charge, Scotland and Northern Ireland, Deloitte Touche, since 1999; UK Board Member, since 1999; UK Executive Group Member, since 1999; b. 24.3.59, Dumfries; partner, Virginia Braid. Educ. Eastwood High School, Glasgow; Glasgow University; Columbia University (leadership development programme). Joined Deloitte Touche (formerly Touche Ross & Co.), 1979; qualified CA, 1982; Partner, 1988; Partner in charge, Corporate Finance, 1992-99; National Corporate Finance Executive Member, 1992-99; Global Director of Corporate Finance, Deloitte Touche Tohmatsu, 1996-99. Recreations: skiing; yachting; rugby; occasional golf; art; wine. Address: (b.) Deloitte Touche, Lomond House, 9 George Square, Glasgow, G2 1QQ; T.-0141-304 5673; e-mail: david.shearer@deloitte.co.uk

Shearer, Magnus MacDonald, JP. Lord Lieutenant of Shetland, 1982-94; Honorary Consul for Sweden in Shetland and Orkney, 1958-94; Honorary Consul for Federal Republic of Germany in Shetland, 1972-87; b.

27.2.24; m., Martha Nicolson Henderson; 1 s. Educ. Anderson Educational Institute, Shetland; George Watson's College, Edinburgh. Royal Navy, Atlantic, Mediterranean and Far East, 1942-46; Royal Artillery TA, commissioned 2nd Lt., 1949; TARO, rank Captain, 1959; Honorary Secretary, Lerwick Station, RNLI, 1968-92; Chairman, Lerwick Harbour Trust, 1966-72; Member, Lerwick Town Council, 1963-69; Deputy Lieutenant of Shetland, 1973-82. Recreations: reading; bird watching; ships. Address: (h.) 4 Queens Place, Lerwick, Shetland ZE1 0BZ; T.-01595 696612.

Shedden, Alfred Charles, MA, LLB. Director: iomart Group plc, since 2000, Murray International Trust plc, since 2000, Martin Currie Japan Investment Trust plc, since 1995; Chairman: Wisdom IT Holdings Ltd., since 2000, Good Practices Ltd., since 2000, Halladale Group plc, since 2001; Member, Scottish Further Education Funding Council, since 1999; b. 30.6.44, Edinburgh; m., Irene; 1 s.; 1 d. Educ. Arbroath High School; Aberdeen University. McGrigor Donald: Partner, 1971, Managing Partner, 1985-92, Senior Partner, 1993-2000. Director, Scottish Financial Enterprise, 1989-99; Director, Standard Life Assurance Society, 1992-99; Director, Scottish Metropolitan Property PLC, 1998-2000. Address: shedden@madasafish.com

Sheed, Ronald McLean, BSc, CEng, MICE. Director of Environment, Land and Property, South Ayrshire Council, since 1995; b. 8.5.47, Glasgow; m., Beth; 1 s.; 2 d. Educ. Duncanrig Senior Secondary School, East Kilbride; Strathclyde University. Lanark County Council, 1969-75; Strathclyde Regional Council, 1975-95, latterly as Contracts Manager, Roads Direct. Recreation: sport. Address: (b.) County Buildings, Wellington Square, Ayr, KA7 1DR; T.-01292 612421; e-mail: ronnie.sheed@south-ayrshire.gov.uk

Sheehan, Sheriff Albert Vincent, MA, LLB. Sheriff of Tayside, Central and Fife, at Falkirk, since 1983; b. 23.8.36, Edinburgh; m., Edna Georgina Scott Hastings (deceased); 2 d. Educ. Bo'ness Academy; Edinburgh University. 2nd Lt., 1st Bn., Royal Scots (The Royal Regiment), 1960; Captain, Directorate of Army Legal Services, 1961; Depute Procurator Fiscal, Hamilton, 1961-71; Senior Depute Procurator Fiscal, Glasgow, 1971-74; Deputy Crown Agent for Scotland, 1974-79; Scottish Law Commission, 1979-81; Sheriff of Lothian and Borders, at Edinburgh, 1981-83. Leverhulme Fellow, 1971. Publications: Criminal Procedure in Scotland and France, 1975; Criminal Procedure, 1990. Recreations: naval history; travel. Address: (b.) Sheriff Court House, Falkirk; T.-Falkirk 620822.

Sheldon, David Henry, LLB (Hons), DipLP. Advocate, since 1998; b. 22.4.65, Dundee. Educ. High School of Dundee; Aberdeen University. Admitted as Solicitor, 1990; Lecturer in Private Law, Edinburgh University, 1990-98; Associate Dean, Faculty of Law, Edinburgh University, 1994-97; admitted to Faculty of Advocates, 1998. Former Member, Criminal Court Rules Committee. Publications: Evidence: Cases and Materials, 1996; Scots Criminal Law, 2nd edition, 1997; The Laws of Scotland: Stair Memorial Encyclopaedia (Contributor). Recreations: rock climbing; Triathlon; music; song; laughter and the love of friends. Address: (b.) Advocates' Library, Parliament House, Edinburgh EH1 1RF; T.-0131-667 2043.

Shepherd, Lt.-Col. Ian. Director of Fundraising, The Army Benevolent Fund Scotland; b. 6.4.39; m., Belinda Buchanan-Dunlop; 2 s.; 1 d. Educ. Queen's College of British Guiana; Dollar Academy; RMA Sandhurst. Commissioned into Royal Highland Fusiliers, 1960; Assistant Military Attache (Tech), Moscow, 1981-82; CO Scot Infantry Depot (Bridge of Don), 1984-86; CO, University of Aberdeen OTC, 1986-88, retired 1992. Director, Lady Haig's Poppy Factory; Member, North,

South, East Committee, The Officers' Association Scotland. Recreation: being an old soldier. Address: c/o Bank of Scotland, The Mound, Edinburgh, EH1 1YZ.

Shepherd, Professor James, BSc, MB, ChB, PhD, FRCPath, FRCP (Glas), FMedSci, FRSE. Professor in Pathological Biochemistry, Glasgow University, since 1987 (Reader, 1984-87); b. 8.4.44, Motherwell; m., Janet Bulloch Kelly; 1 s.; 1 d. Educ. Hamilton Academy; Glasgow University. Lecturer, Glasgow University: Biochemistry, 1968-72, Pathological Biochemistry, 1972-77; Assistant Professor of Medicine, Baylor College of Medicine, Houston, Texas, 1976-77; Senior Lecturer in Pathological Biochemistry, Glasgow University, 1977-84; Visiting Professor of Medicine, Geneva University, 1984; Director, West of Scotland Coronary Prevention Study; Director, Prospective Study of Pravastatin in the Elderly at Risk, since 1997; Chairman, European Atherosclerosis Society, 1993-96; author of textbooks and papers on lipoprotein metabolism and heart disease prevention. Address: (b.) Department of Biochemistry, Royal Infirmary, Glasgow, G4 OSF; T.-0141-304 4628.

Shepherd, Janet, CertEd. Secretary for Scotland, Duke of Edinburgh's Award, since 1994; b. 6.8.52, Chipping Sodbury. Educ. Rodway School; Bognor Regis College of Education. Began career with Royal Forest of Dean Grammar School; Plas Pencelli Outdoor Education Centre; Faskally Outdoor Centre; Dolcorsllwyn Hall Outdoor Education Centre, Knowsley; Howtown Outdoor Education Centre, Co. Durham; Bewerley Park Outdoor Education Centre, North Yorkshire. Recreations: travelling; ornithology; mountaineering; skiing; canoeing; embroidery; Scottish folk music. Address: (b.) 69 Dublin Street, Edinburgh EH3 6NS; T.-0131-556 9097.

Shepherd, Maurice, BSc, PhD. Managing Director, Chambers Harrap Publishers Ltd., since 1997; b. 7.8.40, Co. Tyrone; m., Marian Walker; 5 s. Educ. Royal School, Dungannon; Queen's University, Belfast. Research Fellow, UK Atomic Energy Authority, 1965; Lecturer in Chemistry, then Director of External Services, St Andrews University, 1969-91; Managing Director, W. & R. Chambers Ltd., 1991-94; Director of Electronic Publishing, Larousse PLC, 1994-97. Council Member, Scottish Publishers' Association. Recreations: music; photography; flying. Address: (h.) 8 Hallhead Road, Newington, Edinburgh EH16 5QJ; T.-0131-667 4668.

Shepherd, Robert Horne (Robbie), MBE, MUniv (Aberdeen). Freelance Broadcaster, since 1976, Presenter, Take the Floor, BBC Radio Scotland, 21 years; Journalist; b. 30.4.36, Dunecht, Aberdeen; m., Agnes Margaret (Esma); 1 s. Educ. Robert Gordon's College, Aberdeen. Left school at 15 to work in accountant's office, eventually becoming ASCA; management accountant, fish firm, 13 years; self-employed accountant; full-time on radio, since 1984. Chairman, Friends of Elphinstone Institute, University of Aberdeen. Recreations: gardening; traditional arts of Scotland, especially the use of the Doric tongue.

Sheridan, James. Labour MP, West Renfrewshire, since 2001; b. 24.11.52, Glasgow; m., Jean; 1 s.; 1 d. Educ. St Pius Secondary School. Trade union official, TGWU, 1999-2000; material handler, 1984-99; TGWU Convenor, Pilkington Optronics, 1985-99. Member, Children's Panel. Recreation: keep-fit activities. Address: (h.) 31 Park Glade, Erskine, Renfrewshire PA8 7HH.

Sheridan, Rt. Rev. Mgr. John. Prelate of Honour; Parish Priest, St. Paul's, Whiteinch, Glasgow, 1986-2000; b. 22.8.29, Clydebank. Educ. Holyrood Senior Secondary School, Glasgow; Campion House, Osterley; Royal Scots College, Valladolid, Spain. Ordained Priest, 1956; Curate in Glasgow, 1956-63; Spiritual Director, Royal Scots College,

Valladolid, Spain, 1963-69; Curate in Glasgow, 1969-84; Parish Priest, Our Lady and St. Margaret's, Kinning Park, 1984-86; Chancellor, Archdiocese of Glasgow, 1983-92. Scout Area Chaplain, Glasgow, 1960-63; Scout District Commissioner, N.E. and N.W.II Districts, Glasgow, 1970-78; National Scout Chaplain, 1978-94; Hon. Vice Chairman, Scottish Catholic Scout Advisory Council, 1995; awarded Scout Silver Acorn, 1987. Recreations: golf; painting; caravanning. Address: St. Thomas', 79 Wellwood Street, Muirkirk, East Ayrshire KA18 3QU; T.-01290 660087.

Sheridan, Tommy. MSP (Scottish Socialist), Glasgow, since 1999. Councillor; President, Anti Poll Tax Federation. Address: (b.) Scottish Parliament, Edinburgh EH99 1SP; T.-0131-348 5631.

Sherrard, Mary Stephen, MBE, BA. National President, Woman's Guild, Church of Scotland, 1993-96; Representative on Women's National Commission, 1993-98; b. 22.4.23, Renfrew; m., Rev. John A. Sherrard; 2 s.; 1 d. Educ. Girls' High School, Glasgow; Open University. Journalist; service in W.R.N.S.; playgroup work; Citizens Advice Bureau Manager; Chairman, Angus Citizens Advice Bureau; Vice-Chair, Scottish CAB. Elder, Church of Scotland. Recreations: crosswords; writing; walking on holiday. Address: (h.) Fair Havens, 19 Provost Kay Park, Victoria Manor, Kirkcaldy KY1 2RD; T.-01592 642821.

Sherratt, Professor Jonathan Adam, MA, DPhil. Professor of Mathematics, Heriot-Watt University, since 1998; Director, Centre for the Theoretical Modelling of Medicine, Heriot-Watt University, since 1999; b. 2.2.67, Nottingham. Educ. Tiffin School, Kingston-upon-Thames; Queen's College, Cambridge; Lincoln College, Oxford. Junior Research Fellow, Merton College, Oxford, 1991-93; Lecturer in Mathematics, Warwick University, 1994-97; Senior Lecturer in Mathematics, Warwick University, 1997; EPSRC, Advanced Research Fellow, 2000-2005. Address: (b.) Centre for Theoretical Modelling of Medicine, Department of Mathematics, Heriot-Watt University, Riccarton, Edinburgh, EH14 4AS; T.-0131-451 3740.

Sherriff, Robert Mark, CBE, MSI, BA, DL. Stockbroker, since 1960; Chairman, Executive Committee, Erskine Hospital, since 2000; Chairman, The MacRobert Trust Tarland, since 1994; b. 29.3.36, Kilmacolm; m., Margaret Fraser; 2 s.; 2 d. Educ. Cargilfield; Sedbergh; Trinity College, Cambridge. National Service, 1954-56; served with TA from 1956; joined R.C. Greig & Co., Stockbroker, Glasgow, 1959; became a Partner (now Director); former Vice Chairman, Greig Middleton & Co. Ltd., Glasgow; former Director, Gerrard Group PLC, London; Vice Chairman, Scottish Building Society; retired as Chairman, Highland TAVR, 1996. Recreations: tennis; golf; shooting; skiing. Address: (h.) The Old Manse, Blairdrummond, by Stirling FK9 4UX.

Sherwood, Professor John Neil, DSc, PhD, CChem, FRSC, FRSE. Burmah Professor of Physical Chemistry, Strathclyde University, since 1983; b. 8.11.33, Redruth, Cornwall; m., Margaret Enid Shaw; 2 d. Educ. Aireborough Grammar School; Bede College, Durham University. Research Fellow, Hull University, 1958-60; Lecturer, Reader and Personal Professor, Strathclyde University, 1960-83; Vice Principal, 1995-98. Recreations: hillwalking; photography; gardening. Address: (b.) Department of Pure and Applied Chemistry, Strathclyde University, Glasgow, G1 1XL; T.-041-552 4400.

Shiach, Allan G., BA. Chairman, Macallan-Glenlivet PLC, 1979-96; Chairman, Scottish Film Council, 1991-97; Chairman, Scottish Film Production Fund, 1991-96; Chairman, Scottish Screen, 1996-98; b. Elgin; m., Kathleen Breck; 2 s.; 1 d. Educ. Gordonstoun School; McGill

University, Montreal. Writer/Producer, since 1970; Writer/Co-Writer: Don't Look Now, The Girl from Petrovia, Daryl, Joseph Andrews, Castaway, The Witches, Cold Heaven, Regeneration, In Love and War, and other films; Member: Broadcasting Council for Scotland, 1988-91; Member, Council, Scotch Whisky Association, 1984-96; Chairman, Writers' Guild of G.B., 1989-91; Director, Rafford Films, since 1982; Director, Scottish Media Group plc, since 1993; Governor, British Film Institute, 1992-98; Freeman, City of London, 1988; e-mail: algscott@aol.com

Shiach, Sheriff Gordon Iain Wilson, MA, LLB, BA (Hons). Sheriff of Lothian and Borders, at Edinburgh, 1984-97, and at Peebles, 1996-97; Part-time Commissioner (Advocate), Mental Welfare Commission for Scotland, since 2001; b. 15.10.35, Elgin; m., Margaret Grant Smith; 2 d. (1 deceased). Educ. Lathallan; Gordonstoun; Edinburgh University; Open University. Admitted Advocate, 1960; practised as Advocate, 1960-72; Sheriff of Fife and Kinross, later Tayside, Central and Fife, at Dunfermline, 1972-79; Sheriff of Lothian and Borders, at Linlithgow, 1979-84; Hon. Sheriff, Elgin, since 1986; Member: Council of Sheriffs' Association, 1989-95 (President, 1993-95); Standing Committee on Criminal Procedure, 1989-93; Board, Lothian Family Conciliation Service, 1989-93; Parole Board for Scotland, 1990-99 (Vice Chairman, 1995-99); Council, Faculty of Advocates, 1993-95; Shrieval Training Group, 1994-95; Review Group on Social Work National Standards for Throughcare, 1994-95; Chairman, The Scottish Society, 1992-93, The Edinburgh Sir Walter Scott Club, 1995-98. Recreations: walking; swimming; music; art; film; theatre; e-mail: gssc23899@blueyonder.co.uk

Shields, Sir Robert, MD, DL, FRCSEd, FRCSEng, FRCPS, DSc, HonFACS, HonFRCSI, HonFRCSHK, HonFRCPEdin, FAcadMedSingap, Hon. FRACS. Senior Research Fellow, University of Glasgow, since 1999; Professor of Surgery Emeritus, Liverpool University; Consultant Surgeon, Royal Liverpool Hospital; b. 8.11.30, Paisley; m., Marianne; 1 s.; 2 d. Educ. John Neilson Institution, Paisley; Glasgow University. House Officer, Western Infirmary, Glasgow; Research Associate, Mayo Clinic, Rochester, USA; Lecturer in Surgery, Western Infirmary, Glasgow; Senior Lecturer and Reader, Welsh National School of Medicine; Honorary Consultant Surgeon, Royal Infirmary, Cardiff. Past President, James IV Association; Past President, Association of Surgeons of Great Britain and Ireland; Past President, British Society of Gastroenterology; Past President, Surgical Research Society; Past President, Royal College of Surgeons of Edinburgh, 1994-97. Recreations: walking; reading. Address: 81 Meols Drive, West Kirby, Wirral CH48 5DF; T.-0151-632 3588; Ardlarig, Tayvallich, Argyll PA31 8PJ; T.-01546 870 308; e-mail: r.shields@rcsed.ac.uk

Shields, Tom, BA. Diary Writer, The Herald, since 1979; b. 9.2.48, Glasgow; 1 s.; 1 d. Educ. Bellarmine Comprehensive; Lourdes Secondary School (no miracle); Strathclyde University. Journalist: Sunday Post, 1969-73, The Herald, since 1973. Publications: Tom Shields' Diary; Tom Shields Too; Tom Shields Free at Last; Tom Shields Goes Forth; Just the Three Weeks in Provence (Co-author). Recreation: Celtic studies. Address: (b.) 200 Renfield Street, Glasgow G2 3PR; T.-0141-302 7055 (send stories – urgent).

Shinwell, Sir (Maurice) Adrian, Kt, DL, LLB, NP, MCIArb. Solicitor; Senior Partner, Kerr Barrie, Glasgow, since 1991; Deputy Lieutenant, Renfrewshire, since 1999; b. 27.2.51; m., Lesley McLean; 2 s.; 1 d. Educ. Hutchesons' Boys' Grammar School; Glasgow University. Admitted Solicitor, 1975; joined Kerr, Barrie & Duncan, 1976; Notary Public, since 1976; Tutor (part-time), Law Faculty, Glasgow University, 1980-84; Solicitor-Mediator, since 1994; Director, St. Leonards School, Solstrale Associates

Ltd., Kerr Barrie Nominees Ltd. Scottish Conservative and Unionist Association: Member, Scottish Council, 1982-98; Chairman, Eastwood Association, 1982-85; Chairman, Cumbernauld and Kilsyth Association, 1989-91; Vice-President, 1989-92; President, 1992-94; Scottish Conservative and Unionist Party: Chairman, Candidates' Board, Member, Scottish Executive and Scottish Council, 1998-2000; Member, Central Advisory Committee on Justices of the Peace, 1996-99; Vice Chairman, Justices of the Peace Advisory Committee, East Renfrewshire, since 2000. Recreations: family; politics. Address: (h.) Sarona, South Road, Busby, Glasgow, G76 8JB; T.-0141-221 6844.

Shirran, Jane Lindsay, LLB (Hons), DipLP. Senior General Counsel, National Australia Group, Europe; b. 27.6.63, Malaysia; Educ. Albyn School; University of Aberdeen. Joined Clydesdale Bank, 1996. Recreations: African culture; travel; wildlife photography. Address: (b.) 40 St. Vincent Place, Glasgow, G1 2HL; T.-0141-223 2883.

Shirreffs, Murdoch John, MB, ChB, DObstRCOG, FRCGP, MFHom. General Medical Practitioner, Aberdeen, since 1974; Medical Hypnotherapist and Homoeopathic Specialist; Chairman, NHS Grampian Homeopathy Service; b. 25.5.47, Aberdeen; m., Jennifer McLeod. Educ. Aberdeen Grammar School; Aberdeen University. General Practice Trainer, 1977-99; Secretary, Grampian Division, British Medical Association, since 1978; former Member, BMA Scottish Council. President, North of Scotland Veterans' Hockey Club. Recreations: hockey; opera and classical music; big band jazz; DIY; gardening; food and wine; travel. Address: (h.) 72 Gray Street, Aberdeen, AB10 6JE; T.-01224 321998; e-mail: murdoch_and_jenny_shirreffs@msn.com

Short, Agnes Jean, BA (Hons), MLitt. Writer; b. Bradford, Yorkshire; m., Anthony Short (qv); 3 s.; 2 d. Educ. Bradford Girls' Grammar School; Exeter University; Aberdeen University. Various secretarial, research and teaching jobs, both in UK and abroad; took up writing, 1966; 19 novels, most of which have a Scottish setting; also short stories and radio; Constable Award, 1976. Recreations: dog-walking; whisky-tasting; good food; small hills. Address: (h.) Khantore, Crathie, by Ballater, Aberdeenshire, AB35 5TJ.

Shucksmith, Professor Mark, MA, MSc, PhD. Professor of Land Economy, University of Aberdeen, since 1993; Co-director, Arkleton Centre for Rural Development Research, University of Aberdeen, since 1995; Programme Adviser, Joseph Rowntree Foundation's Action in Rural Areas Programme, since 1997; Co-Director, Scottish Centre for Social Justice Research, since 2001; Adviser, Rural Affairs Committee, Scottish Parliament, since 2000; b. 25.8.53, London; m., Janet; 2 d. Educ. Sidney Sussex College, University of Cambridge. Department of Agricultural Economics, University of Newcastle upon Tyne, 1977-81; Lecturer then Senior Lecturer then Reader in Land Economy, University of Aberdeen, 1981-93. Former Vice-Chair, Rural Forum; Program Chair, XI World Rural Sociology Congress. Publications: several books, notably on social exclusion in rural areas, rural housing, agricultural restructuring; over 50 papers in learned journals. Recreations: music; hillwalking; reading. Address: (b.) St. Mary's, University of Aberdeen, Old Aberdeen AB24 3UF; T.-01224 273901.

Sibbald, Michael Robert, BA, MBA, MInstM. Group Human Resources Director, Argos Retail Group, since 1996; b. 30.8.48, Edinburgh; m., Margaret; 2 s.; 1 d. Educ. George Heriot's School; Heriot-Watt University; Glasgow University. Member, Advisory Board, Glasgow University Business School, since 1996; Governor, Milton Keynes College FE, since 1999. Recreations: reading; sports cars; athletics; football. Address: (h.) The Long House, Deanfoot Road, West Linton EH46 7DX; T.-01968 660569.

Sibbett, Professor Wilson, BSc, PhD. Wardlaw Professor of Natural Philosophy, St. Andrews University (Director of Research, since 1994, Chairman, Department of Physics and Astronomy, 1985-94); b. 15.3.48, Portglenone, N. Ireland; m., Barbara Anne Brown; 3 d. Educ. Ballymena Technical College; Queen's University, Belfast. Postdoctoral Research Fellow, Blackett Laboratory, Imperial College, London, 1973-76; Lecturer in Physics, then Reader, Imperial College, 1976-85. Fellow: Institute of Physics, Royal Society of Edinburgh, Royal Society (of London). Recreation: golf (to low standard). Address: (b.) Department of Physics and Astronomy, St. Andrews University, North Haugh, St. Andrews, KY16 9SS; T.-01334 463100.

Siddiqui, Mona, MA, MIL, PhD. Lecturer in Arabic and Islamic Studies, Glasgow University, since 1995; Director, Centre for the Study of Islam, Glasgow University, since 1998; b. 3.5.63, Karachi, Pakistan; m., Farhaj; 2 s. Educ. Salendine-Nook High School, Huddersfield; Leeds University; Manchester University. Lecturer in Arabic and Islamic Studies: Manchester Metropolitan University, 1989-90, Glasgow Caledonian University, 1993. Contributor, Thought for the Day, BBC Scotland and Radio 4. Recreations: interior decorating; cooking; reading. Address: (b.) 4 The Square, University of Glasgow, Glasgow G12 8QQ.

Sillars, James. Assistant Secretary-General, Arab-British Chamber of Commerce; Member, Board, Scottish Enterprise; b. 4.10.37, Ayr; m., Margo MacDonald (qv); 1 s.; 3 d. Educ. Ayr Academy. Member, Ayr Town Council and Ayr County Council Education Committee, 1960s; Member, Western Regional Hospital Board, 1965-70; Head, Organisation Department, Scottish TUC, 1968-70; MP, South Ayrshire, 1970-79; Co-Founder, Scottish Labour Party, 1976; MP, Glasgow Govan, 1988-92.

Silver, Gillian M., LLB, NP. Partner, MacNeill and Critchley, Solicitors, Inverness, since 1983; Member, Local Government Boundary Commission for Scotland, 1995-99; b. 13.5.56, Aberdeen; m., Chris. Educ. Inverness Royal Academy; Edinburgh University. Past Chairman, Highland Solicitors Property Centre Ltd.; Past Chairman, Solicitors Property Centres Scotland; Senator, Junior Chamber International. Recreations: golf; curling; choral singing; running; theatre. Address: (h.) The Garden House, Kincurdie, Rosemarkie IV10 8SJ; T.-01381 621211.

Sim, Ian Allan, BSc, CA. Secretary General, Scottish Kennel Club, since 1977; Partner, Johnston Smillie, Chartered Accountants, since 1977; b. 2.8.48, Edinburgh; 2 s. Educ. Lochaber High School; Edinburgh University. Manager, Deloittes, Chartered Accountants, 1973-76. Treasurer, St. George's West Church; Chairman/Vice Chairman, Kennel Club committees. Recreations: swimming; music. Address: (h.) 22 Craigmount Avenue, Edinburgh EH12 8HQ; T.-0131-317 7377.

Sime, Martin, MA. Director and Chief Executive, Scottish Council for Voluntary Organisations, since 1991; b. 23.9.53, Edinburgh. Educ. George Heriot's; St. Andrews University; Edinburgh University. Social and Economic History Researcher, 1976-78; Sheep Farmer, 1978-81; Freelance Researcher, 1982; Project Manager, Sprout Market Garden, 1983-85; Development/Principal Officer (Day Services), Scottish Association for Mental Health, then Director, 1985-91; Secretary, Scottish Civic Forum; Member, Scottish Advisory Task Force for the New Deal; Expert Panel on Procedures for the Scottish Parliament; Member, Lord Provost's (Edinburgh) Commission on Social Exclusion; Director, Scottish Community Foundation. Recreations: cinema; food; bridge. Address: (b.) 18/19 Claremont Crescent, Edinburgh, EH7 4QD; T.-0131-556 3882.

Simmers, Graeme Maxwell, CBE, CA. Chairman, Scottish Sports Council, 1992-99; Non-Excutive Director, Forth Valley Acute Hospitals Trust, since 1993; b. 2.5.35, Glasgow; m., Jennifer M.H. Roxburgh; 2 s.; 2 d. Educ. Glasgow Academy; Loretto School. Qualified CA, 1959; commissioned Royal Marines, 1959-61, Hon. Colonel, Royal Marines Reserve, since 2000. Former Partner, Kidsons Simmers CA; Chairman, Scottish Highland Hotels Group Ltd., 1972-92; Member, Scottish Tourist Board, 1979-86; Chairman, HCBA (Scotland), 1984-86; Past Chairman, Board of Management, Member of National Executive, BHA; Elder and Treasurer, Killearn Kirk; Governor, Queen's College, Glasgow, 1989-93; Past Chairman of Governors, Loretto School; Captain, Royal and Ancient Golf Club of St. Andrews, 2001-02 (Past Chairman, Championship Committee). OBE, 1983. Recreations: rugby; golf; skiing. Address: (h.) Kincaple, Boquhan, Balfron, near Glasgow, G63 ORW; T.-01360 440375.

Simmons, Professor John Edmund Leonard, BSc, PhD, CEng, FRSE, FIMechE, FIEE. Professor of Mechanical Engineering, Heriot Watt University, since 1992, and Dean of Engineering, since 1999 (Head, Department of Mechanical and Chemical Engineering, 1994-99); Chairman, TechniTex Faraday Partnership, since 2000; b. 24.9.47, Faversham; m., Anne; 2 s.; 2 d. Educ. Birmingham University; Cambridge University. Production Manager, Baker Perkins Chemical Machinery, Stoke on Trent, 1977-80; Design Manager, Vickers plc–Michell Bearings, Newcastle upon Tyne, 1981-84; Lecturer in Engineering, Durham University, 1984-91. Recreations: gardening; walking; travelling; cinema. Address: (b.) Heriot Watt University, Edinburgh, EH14 4AS; T.-0131-451 8014; e-mail: j.simmons@hw.ac.uk

Simpson, Alan Gordon, MA (Oxon), CEng, MICE. Partner, W. A. Fairhurst and Partners, since 1989; Chairman, National Youth Orchestra of Scotland, since 1998; b. 15.2.50, Edinburgh; m., Jan; 1 s.; 1 d. Educ. Rugby School; Magdalen College, Oxford. Brian Colquoun and Partners, 1972-78; W.A. Fairhurst and Partners, since 1979; Member, Court, Stirling University, since 1996; Member, Council, Institution of Civil Engineers, since 2000. Recreations: music; skiing; archery. Address: (h.) Duchray, Aberfoyle, Stirling; (b.) 11 Woodside Terrace, Glasgow.

Simpson, Brian Middleton, MIBiol, FRAgS. Chief Executive, Scottish Quality Salmon, since 2000; Chairman, Marketing Society in Scotland; b. 24.9.52, Perth; m., Helena; 1 s.; 2 d. Educ. Perth High School; West of Scotland Agricultural College. Agricultural Adviser, Scottish Agricultural College; Marketing Adviser, Kemira Fertilisers; Senior Project Executive, Scottish Enterprise; Chief Executive, Scotch Quality Beef and Lamb Association, 1991-2000. Recreation: hill-walking. Address: (b.) Durn, Isla Road, Perth PH2 7HG.

Simpson, David, CBE, DSc, CEng, DrEng, FIEE, FRSE, FRSA. Chairman: Simpson Research Ltd., Isocom Components Ltd., Bookham Technology Ltd., PFE Ltd., Scotish Opto Electronic Association, Lifor Ltd.; Co-Founder, Elvingston Science Centre; b. 23.11.26, Ceres; m., Janice Ann; 1 s.; 2 d. Educ. Bell Baxter School, Cupar; Dundee Technical College; Stanford University. R. & D. Engineer, Marconi, 1952-56; Managing Director, Microcell Electronics, 1956-60; General Manager, Hughes Microelectronics, 1960-62; Managing Director, Hewlett Packard Ltd., 1962-70; President, Gould Corp., Chicago, 1976-88; Chairman, various UK companies. Recreations: hill-walking; wood-carving. Address: (h.) Elvingston House, Tranent, EH33 1EH; T.-01875 852878; e-mail: xia90@dial.pipex.com

Simpson, Professor Hugh Walter, MB, ChB, MD, PhD, FRCPath, FRCP(Glas). Senior Research Fellow, University Department of Surgery, Glasgow University and Royal Infirmary; Head of Pathology, Glasgow Royal Infirmary, 1984-93; Honorary Visiting Professor, University of Minnesota, since 1970; b. 4.4.31, Ceres Fife; m., Myrtle Emslie (see Myrtle Simpson); 3 s.; 1 d. Educ. Bryanston; Edinburgh University. Leader of numerous expeditions to polar and tropical regions; awarded Polar Medal, Mungo Park and Pery Medals; Man of the Year, Greenland Radio, 1965; Gold Medal Lecture, Royal College of Surgeons of Edinburgh, 1995; Scientist of the Year Lecture, Little Rock, Arkansas, 1978. Founder Editor, International Journal of Chronobiology; Visiting Scientist, National Institute of Health, Washington, 1978-79. Publications: 160 scientific publications, especially on breast cancer. Recreation: skiing. Address: (h.) Farleiter, Kincraig PH21 1NU; T.- 01540 651288; e-mail: SimpsonHWSimpson@aol.com

Simpson, Ian Christopher, LLB. Sheriff of South Strathclyde, Dumfries and Galloway, since 1988, at Airdrie, since 1991; b. 5.7.49, Edinburgh; m., Christine Margaret Anne Strang; 2 s. Educ. Glenalmond; Edinburgh University. Admitted to Faculty of Advocates, 1974. Captain, Scottish Universities Golfing Society, 1989-90; President, All Sphere Club, 1989-90. Recreation: golf. Address: (b.) Airdrie Sheriff Court, Graham Street, Airdrie, ML6 6EE; T.-01236 751121.

Simpson, Very Rev. James Alexander, BSc (Hons), BD, STM, DD. Chaplain to the Queen in Scotland; Moderator, General Assembly of the Church of Scotland, 1994; b. 9.3.34, Glasgow; m., Helen Gray McCorquodale; 3 s.; 2 d. Educ. Eastwood Secondary School; Glasgow University; Union Seminary, New York. Minister: Grahamston Church, Falkirk, 1960-66, St. John's Renfield, Glasgow, 1966-76; Minister, Dornoch Cathedral, 1976-97. Publications: There is a time to ....; Marriage Questions Today; Doubts are not Enough; Holy Wit; Laughter Lines; The Master Mind; Dornoch Cathedral; More Holy Wit; Keywords of Faith; All About Christmas; The Laugh Shall Be First. Recreations: golf; photography; writing. Address: Dornoch, Perth Road, Bankfoot, Perthshire PH1 4ED; T.-01738 787710.

Simpson, Rev. James Hamilton, BD, LLB. Minister, The Mount Kirk, since 1965; Vice-Chairman, Church of Scotland General Trustees, since 1999; b. 29.6.36, Overtown; m., Moira W. Sellar; 2 s. Educ. Buckhaven High School; Edinburgh University; Glasgow University. Prison Chaplain, Greenock, 1971-81; Hospital Chaplain, Ravenscraig, since 1983. Recreations: sea fishing; boating; gardening; touring (especially Iberia). Address: (h.) 76 Finnart Street, Greenock; T.-01475 722338.

Simpson, J.W., BSc, MCIT, MRIN, MNI. Chief Harbour Master, Firth of Forth, and Manager, Marine Services, since 1996; Divisional Manager, Marine Services, Forth Ports PLC, 1986-96; Director, Forth Estuary Towage Ltd., since 1986; b. 30.8.44, St. Andrews; m., Barbara Hutton; 1 s.; 1 d. Educ. Grangemouth High School; Buckhaven High School; Leith Nautical College; Plymouth Polytechnic. Cadet, Furness Prince Lines, 1961-64; Navigating Officer: Shaw Savill Line, 1965-68, Overseas Containers Ltd., 1969-70; Assistant Harbour Master, then Assistant to Port Superintendent, Grangemouth, 1973-77; Port Superintendent, Leith and Granton, 1978-82; Port Manager, Grangemouth, 1982-86. Recreation: sailing. Address: (b.) Forth Ports PLC, Tower Place, Leith, EH6 7DB; T.-0131-554 6473.

Simpson, John Douglas, BSc(Hons). Headteacher, Fortrose Academy, since 1989; b. 2.3.51, Kilbirnie; m., Linda; 2 s.; 2 d. Educ. Spier's School, Beith; Glasgow University. Teacher of Biology, 1975; Principal Teacher, 1979; Assistant Headteacher, Merksworth High School,

Paisley, 1983; Depute Headteacher, Cowdenknowes High School, Greenock, 1985. Recreations: golf; snooker. Address: (b.) Fortrose Academy, Fortrose, Ross-shire; T.- 01381 620310.

Simpson, Professor Mary, MA, PhD. Professor of Classroom Learning, University of Edinburgh, since 1999; b. 4.12.42, Inverurie; m., Thomas Hardy Simpson; 1 s.; 1 d. Educ. Aberdeen Academy; Aberdeen University. Assistant Experimental Officer, Torry Research Station, Aberdeen, 1959-65; Research Officer, Dundee University, 1979-80; Researcher in Education, then Professor of Educational Research, Northern College, 1976-99. Member: Joint Working Party, Standard Grade Health Studies, 1983-85, Joint Working Party, Standard Grade Science, 1985-87, Committee on Assessment, 5–14, 1989-92, Scottish Consultative Council on the Curriculum, 1991-2000, Scottish Council for Research in Education, 1992-98, SOED Task Group on Curriculum and Assessment Higher Still Development Programme, 1994-97, Steering Committee for SOED 5–14 Evaluation Project, 1991-97, Practitioner Award Sub-committee, Scottish Council for Research in Education, 1995-98; External Examiner, St. Andrew's College, Glasgow, 1993-97; Director and Chairman, Cornerstone Community Care Ltd., 1979-2000; Director, Partnership Housing, 1988-95; Member, Langstane Housing Association, 1984-2000. Recreations: gardening; travelling; reading; learning how to be a grandmother. Address: (b.) Faculty of Education, University of Edinburgh, Holyrood Road, Edinburgh EH8 8AQ.

Simpson, Michael John Russell, BA, LLB. Head of Litigation Department, Tods Murray WS, Edinburgh (Partner, since 1970); b. 30.10.41; m., Syä; 2 s.; 1 d. Educ. Rugby School; Oxford University; Edinburgh University. Articled, Messrs Lindsays WS, Edinburgh, 1967. Member, Joint Committee of Legal Societies of Edinburgh and the Lothians; Treasurer, Society of Writers to Her Majesty's Signet. Recreations: reading; shooting; golf (The Honourable Company of Edinburgh Golfers). Address: (b.) 66 Queen Street, Edinburgh EH2 4NE; T.-0131-226 4771.

Simpson, Murray Charles Thomas, MA, PhD, ALA, LRAM. Director of Special Collections, National Library of Scotland, since 1999; b. 22.6.50, Edinburgh; m., Elizabeth S. Cumming. Educ. Dumfries Academy; Edinburgh University. Edinburgh University Library: Assistant Librarian, 1975-87; New College Librarian, 1987-95; Special Collections Librarian, 1995-99. President, Edinburgh Bibliographical Society, 2001-04. Recreations: book collecting; concert-going. Address: (b.) National Library of Scotland, George IV Bridge, Edinburgh EH1 1EW; T.-0131-226 4531.

Simpson, Myrtle Lillias, DL. Author and Lecturer; former Member, Scottish Sports Council; Past Chairman, Scottish National Ski Council; b. 5.7.31, Aldershot; m., Professor Hugh Simpson (qv); 3 s.; 1 d. Educ. 19 schools (father in Army). Writer/Explorer; author of 12 books, including travel, biography, historical and children's; first woman to ski across Greenland; attempted to ski to North Pole (most northerly point reached by a woman unsupported); numerous journeys in polar regions on ski or canoe; exploration in China and Peru; Mungo Park and Pery Medal; former Editor, Avenue (University of Glasgow magazine). Recreations: climbing; skiing; canoeing. Address: (h.) 7 Cleveden Crescent, Glasgow, G12 0PD; T.- 0141-357 1091.

Simpson, Dr Richard. MSP (Labour), Ochil, since 1999; Deputy Minister for Justice, since 2001 (Member: Finance Committee, 1999-2001, Health and Community Care Committee, 1999-2001); b. 1942, Edinburgh; m.; 2 s. Educ. Trinity College; Edinburgh University. GP and psychiatrist; former Chair, Strathcarron Hospice; Medical Adviser in

Adoption and Fostering, Scottish Medical Group, BAAF; Director, Forth Valley Primary Care Research Group. Address: (b.) Scottish Parliament, Edinburgh EH99 1SP; T.-0131-348 5740.

Simpson, Dr Sheila Anne, MBChB, DObsRCoy, DCH, BSc(Hons), MD. Clinical Geneticist; Associate Specialist, Medical Genetics, Medical School, Foresterhill, Aberdeen; b. 7.5.50, Aberdeen; m., Frazer Simpson; 2 s. Educ. Aberdeen High School for Girls; Aberdeen University. Past Chair, Scottish Medical Group, British Agencies for Adoption and Fostering; Founder Member, UK Huntington's Disease Prediction Consortium; Member, World Federation of Neurology HD Research Group; Director, Scottish Huntington's Association. Publications: Secrets in the Genes (Contributor); Truth and the Child – 10 years on. Recreations: antiquarian books; reading; walking; supporting my husband's photographic business. Address: (b.) Medical Genetics, Grampian University Hospitals, Foresterhill, Aberdeen AB25 2ZD; T.-01224 552120.

Sinclair, 17th Lord (Charles Murray Kennedy St. Clair), CVO. Lord Lieutenant, Dumfries and Galloway Region (District of Stewartry), 1982-89; Extra Equerry to the Queen Mother, since 1953; Member, Queen's Bodyguard for Scotland (Royal Company of Archers); b. 21.6.14; m., Anne Lettice Cotterell; 1 s.; 2 d. Educ. Eton; Magdalene College, Cambridge. Served Second World War (mentioned in Despatches); retired Major, Coldstream Guards. Address: (h.) Knocknalling, St. John's Town of Dalry, Castle Douglas, Kirkcudbrightshire.

Sinclair, Lady (Anne Lettice). Vice President, The National Turst for Scotland, since 1996; former Chairman, Lothian, Borders, Dumfries and Galloway Region, National Trust for Scotland, since 1995; b. 16.10.33, London; m., Lord Sinclair, CVO (qv); 1 s.; 2 d. Recreations: gardening; gundogs; botany; ornithology. Address: (h.) Knocknalling, St. John's Town of Dalry, by Castle Douglas DG7 3ST; T.-01644 430221.

Sinclair, Alan, CBE, MA, MBA, FRSA. Senior Director, Skills and Learning, Scottish Enterprise; b. 18.9.54, Bellshill; m., Michele Veldman. Educ. Our Lady's High School, Motherwell; St. Andrews University; Edinburgh University. Former Chief Executive, The Wise Group. Member, UK Advisory Group on the New Deal; Member, Scottish Task Force on the New Deal; Director, The Main Tool Company. Recreation: the great outdoor world. Address: (b.) Scottish Enterprise, 150 Broomielaw, Atlantic Quay, Glasgow G2 8LU; T.-0141-248 2700.

Sinclair, Alexander, OBE, DL, FCII. President, The Golf Foundation, 1991-96; b. 6.7.20, West Kilbride; m., Elizabeth Tennant; 2 s.; 1 d. Educ. Ardrossan Academy. Clerk, Norwich Union, 1938-40; Royal Artillery, 1940-46; joined Alexander Stenhouse Insurance Brokers, 1957 (Director, 1962); Chairman, British Insurance Brokers Association in Scotland, 1985; retired, 1985. Deputy Lieutenant, Lanarkshire, 1988; Captain, Royal & Ancient Golf Club, 1988-89; Chairman, R. & A. Selection Committee, 1969-75; President, European Golf Association, 1981-83; President, Scottish Golf Union, 1976-77; former Scottish golf internationalist and Scottish golf captain; awarded Frank Moran Award, 1979, for contribution to golf; West of Scotland Champion, 1950; semi-finalist, Scottish Amateur Championship, 1947-56; Lanarkshire Champion, three times; Scottish Senior Champion, 1979-84. Recreations: golf; curling; painting. Address: (h.) 17 Blairston Avenue, Bothwell, G71 8RZ; T.-01698 853359.

Sinclair, Rev. Colin Andrew Macalister, BA (Hons), BD (Hons). Minister, Palmerston Place Church of Scotland, since 1996; b. 16.9.53, Glasgow; m., Ruth Mary Murray; 1 s.; 3 d. Educ. Glasgow Academy; Stirling University; Edinburgh University. Training Officer, Scripture Union, Zambia, 1974-77; Assistant Minister, Palmerston Place Church of Scotland, Edinburgh, 1980-82; Church of Scotland Minister, Newton on Ayr, 1982-88; General Director, Scripture Union Scotland, 1988-96. Vice Chair, Mission Scotland; Chairman, Council of Management, Spring Harvest. Recreations: family; reading; sport. Address: (b.) Annan House, 10 Palmerston Place, Edinburgh EH12 5AA; e-mail: ColinS@globalnet.co.uk

Sinclair, Rev. David Ian, BSc, BD, PhD, DipSW. Secretary, Church and Nation Committee, Church of Scotland, since 1999; b. 23.1.55, Bridge of Allan; m., Elizabeth Mary Jones; 1 s.; 1 d. Educ. High School of Stirling; Aberdeen University; Bristol University; University College, Cardiff; Edinburgh University. President, Student Christian Movement of Britain and Ireland, 1975-76; Social Worker (Community Development), Livingston, 1980-84; Assistant Minister, Dunblane Cathedral, 1987-88; Minister, St Andrews Martyrs, 1990-99, with Boarhills and Dunino, from 1993. Recreations: photography; music; armchair sport. Address: (b.) 121 George Street, Edinburgh EH2 4YN; T.-0131-225 5722; e-mail: dsinclair@cofscotland.org.uk

Sinclair, Douglas, CBE. Chief Executive, Fife Council, since 1999; b. 28.1.46, Ellon; m., Mairi; 2 d. Educ. Inverness Royal Academy; Edinburgh University. Administrative Assistant, Midlothian CC, 1969-72; Administrative Officer, Barnardo's Scotland, 1972-75; Depute Director of Administration, then Director of Administration, Western Isles Islands Council, 1975-85; Chief Executive, Ross and Cromarty DC, 1985-90; Chief Executive, Central Regional Council, 1990-95; Chief Executive, Convention of Scottish Local Authorities (COSLA), 1995-99. Recreations: gardening; Scottish literature; walking. Address: (h.) 1 Queens Road, Stirling, FK8 2QY.

Sinclair, Eric T.A., MA, DipEd. Education Consultant, since 2000; Owner, The School Timetable Company; b. 20.9.48, Edinburgh; m., Johanna Beckley; 3 c. Educ. Bell Baxter High School, Cupar; St. Andrews University; Edinburgh University; Moray House College. Taught, Teacher Training Colleges, Cameroon, Nigeria; Head of English, English High School, Istanbul; Head of English, St Joseph's College, Dumfries; Assistant Rector, Forres Academy; Depute Rector, Bridge of Don Academy; Rector: Kirkwall Grammar School, Aboyne Academy and Deeside Community Centre, Aberdeenshire. Recreations: orienteering; squash; chess; gardening; reading. Address: (h.) Bogarn, Strachan, Banchory; T.-01330 850297; e-mail: Inganess@aol.com

Sinclair, Fiona Jane, BSc (Hons), BArch, FRIAS, MAPS. Architect in private practice, since 1982 (own practice, since 1998); Member, Historic Buildings Council for Scotland, since 1998; b. 28.8.57, Glasgow; m., David N. Page. Educ. Hyndland Senior Secondary School, Glasgow; Hermitage Academy, Helensburgh; Strathclyde University. Michael and Sue Thornley, Architects, Glasgow, 1981-98; Fiona Sinclair Architect, since 1998 (specialising in restoration of historic buildings); part-time Design Tutor, Department of Architecture, Strathclyde University, 1998-2000. Honorary Secretary, Glasgow Institute of Architects, since 1992. Publications: Scotstyle – 150 Years of Scottish Architecture, 1984; North Clyde Estuary (Co-author), 1992. Recreations: architecture – always architecture! Address: (h.) 49A William Street, Helensburgh G84 8XY; T.-(b.) 0141-552 2766.

Sinclair, Isabel Lillias, MA, BL, QC. Honorary Sheriff of Lothian and Borders, since 1979; b. Glasgow; m., J. Gordon MacDonald, BL. Educ. Shawlands Academy; Glasgow University. Newspaperwoman, 1933-46; Scottish Editor,

BBC Woman's Hour, 1948; called to Scottish Bar, 1949; appointed Queen's Counsel, 1964; Sheriff Substitute, Lanarkshire at Airdrie, 1966-68; Sheriff of Lothian and Borders at Selkirk and Peebles, then Peebles and Edinburgh, 1968-79. Address: 30 Ravelston Garden, Edinburgh, EH4 3LE; T.-0131-337 9797.

Sinclair, Martin Fraser, MA, CA. Senior Partner, Chiene & Tait, CA; Director, Albyn Trust Ltd., since 1973; Director, NESSCO Ltd., since 1982; b. 18.7.45, Greenock; m., Patricia Anne Ogilvy Smith; 1 s.; 2 d. Educ. Edinburgh Academy; Edinburgh University. Apprentice, Chiene & Tait, CA; qualified, 1970; Peat Marwick Mitchell & Co., Vancouver, 1970-73. President, Institute of Chartered Accountants Benevolent Association, 1983-84. Athletics Blue, Edinburgh University; Captain, Scottish Universities Athletics Team, 1969. Recreations: skiing; squash; orienteering. Address: (b.) 61 Dublin Street, Edinburgh EH3 6NL; T.-0131-558 5800.

Sinclair, Murray Alexander, MA (Hons) (Oxon), LLB. Divisional Solicitor, Office of the Solicitor to the Scottish Executive, since 1999; b. 29.5.61, Falkirk; m., Aileen Elizabeth Brown; 1 s.; 1 d. Educ. Dollar Academy; Christ Church, University of Oxford; Edinburgh University. Trainee Solicitor then Assistant Solicitor, Dundas and Wilson, 1985-88; joined Civil Service, 1989: advised DTI on Scots law until 1992; advised Criminal Justice Department, Scottish Office, 1993-97; Member, Constitution Group, Scottish Office, working on devolution, 1997-99; promoted to Divisional Solicitor, 1999 (Head, Development and Environment Division). Recreations: looking at the night sky; camping; watching football; reading. Address: (b.) Scottish Executive, Victoria Quay, Edinburgh; T.-0131-244 0570; e-mail: murray.sinclair@scotland.gsi.gov.uk

Sinclair, Professor Roy Stuart, BSc, MSc, PhD, FSDC, FRSC, CCol, CChem. Personal Professor, Chemistry and Chemical Engineering, 1991-97, Hon. Fellow, Paisley University, since 1998; Assistant Chief Commissioner (Scotland West), Scout Association, 1990-97; b. 21.4.33, Glasgow; m., Ellen Catherine Murray; 2 s. Educ. Allan Glen's School, Glasgow; London University (External); Paisley University; Strathclyde University. Research Assistant, J. & P. Coats, Paisley, 1950-56; Lecturer in Chemistry, Paisley College, 1956-80, Senior Lecturer, 1980-91. Immediate Past President, Paisley Philosophical Institution. Recreations: Scouting; hill-walking; occasional golf. Address: (h.) 1 Hunterhill Avenue, Paisley PA2 6SP; T.-0141-887 5488.

Sinha, Professor Brajraman Prasad, BSc, Dip. Building Science, PhD, DSc. Professor of Structural Engineering, Edinburgh University, since 1999; b. 20.12.36, Hazipur, India; m., Nageshwari Sinha; 2 s.; 1 d. Educ. Zila School, Monghyr, India; Patna University; Liverpool University; Edinburgh University. Engineering Assistant, Patina University, 1957-59; Assistant Engineer, Bihar Electricity Board, 1959-60; Assistant Engineer, Department of Public Works, Bihar, 1960-63; Design Engineer, 1968-69; Edinburgh University: Demonstrator and Researcher, 1966-68; Research Fellow to Senior Lecturer, 1969-95; Reader, 1995-99; Visiting Professor, Bihar College of Engineering, 1984; Visiting Academic, Santa Catarina Florianopolis, Brazil, since 1991; Visiting Professor, Indian Institute of Science, 2000; Executive Director, International Masonry Engineering Council for Developing Countries, since 1984. Member: Lothian Racial Equality Council, since 1984; Member, Senate, Edinburgh University, since 1984; Chairman, Hindu Temple and Cultural Centre, Edinburgh, 1985-86; President, Indian Arts Council, 1994. Publications: Structural Masonry for Developing Countries (co-ed.), 1992; Re-inforced and Pre-stressed Masonry

(contributor), 1989. Recreations: reading; overseas travel; photography; table tennis; writing. Address: (b.) Department of Civil Engineering, Edinburgh University, Kings' Buildings, Edinburgh EGH9 3JN; T.-0131-650 5726; e-mail: B.Sinha@ed.ac.uk

Sischy, Judith, BA, MA, FRSA. Director, Scottish Council of Independent Schools, since 1990; b. 20.12.47, Halifax; m., Mark Sischy. Educ. Newcastle upon Tyne Church High School; Bristol University; University of Toronto. Previously: Teacher of Modern Languages, Toronto, Canada, Edinburgh, Senior Official, Edinburgh Merchant Company. Recreations: walking; swimming; cinema. Address: (b.) 21 Melville Street, Edinburgh EH3 7PE; T.-0131-220 2106.

Siskin, Professor Clifford Haynes, MA, PhD. A.C. Bradley Professor of English Literature, Glasgow University, since 1999; b. 30.7.50, Cleveland, Ohio; m., Leslie Santee; 1 s.; 2 d. Educ. Valley Stream North High School; Stanford University; University of Virginia. Professor of English, Wayne State University, 1977-86; Visiting Scholar, Stanford University, 1986-88; Professor of English and Comparative Literature, and Head of Department, State University of Stonybrook, 1988-98. Publications: The Historicity of Romantic Discourse, 1988; The Work of Writing: Literature and Social Change in Britain 1700-1830, 1998. Address: (b.) Department of English Literature, Glasgow University, Glasgow G12 8QQ; T.-0141-330 4165.

Skene, Charles Pirie, OBE, HonDBA, FBIPP, ARPS, FRSA. Chairman, Skene Group of companies, developers and owners of first continuing care retirement community in Scotland; Visiting Professor of Entrepreneurship, Robert Gordon University; b. 30.4.35, Aberdeen; m., Alison; 1 s.; 2 d. Educ. Loretto. Past President of numerous organisations, including Aberdeen Chamber of Commerce and Association of Scottish Chambers of Commerce; Past Chairman, CBI Education and Training Committee; Chairman, CBI (Scotland) Enterprise Group, 1994-96; Member, Task Force to investigate under-achievement in schools, 1996-97; initiated Skene Young Entrepreneur's Award, Scotland, 1986; Trustee: Photographic Arts and Science Foundation, Oklahoma City, Haddo Arts Trust, Gordon Cook Foundation. Address: (b.) 23 Rubislaw Den North, Aberdeen, AB15 4AL; T.-01224 326221.

Skene, Robert Taylor, BSc, Head Teacher, Torry Academy, Aberdeen, since 1995; b. 28.12.50, Aberdeenshire; m., Jennifer; 2 s. Educ. Bankhead Academy; Robert Gordon Institute of Technology. Address: (b.) Torry Academy, Tullos Circle, Aberdeen, AB11 8HD; T.-01224 876733.

Skinner, Angus, MBA, BSc, CQSW. Chief Inspector of Social Work Services, Scotland, since 1991; b. 9.1.50, Pakistan; 1 s.; 2 d. Educ. Daniel Stewart's, Edinburgh; Edinburgh University; London University; Strathclyde University. Cheshire County Council, 1971-72; Kent County Council, 1973-75; Lothian Region Social Work Department, 1976-88; Borders Region Social Work Department, 1988-91. Address: (b.) Social Work Services Inspectorate, Area 1-C North, Victoria Quay, Edinburgh EH6 6QQ.

Skinner, Robert Gordon, LLB (Hons). Advocate, since 1987; b. 14.6.57, Glasgow; m., Eileen M.J. Paterson; 2 s. Educ. Bishopbriggs High School; Glasgow University. Law Apprentice, Hughes Dowdall & Co., Glasgow, 1978-80; Assistant and latterly Partner, Dorman Jeffrey & Co., 1980-85; McGrigor Donald, 1985-86. Part-time Chairman, Social Security Appeals Tribunal, and Disability Appeals Tribunal, 1990-99. Recreations: Whitehall, 79 Springwell Avenue, Pollokshields, Glasgow G41 4DL.

Skorupski, Professor John Maria, MA, PhD. Professor of Moral Philosophy, St. Andrews University, since 1990; b. 19.9.46, Italy; m., Barbara Mary; 2 d. Educ. St. Benedict's, Ealing; Christ's College, Cambridge. Visiting Lectureships, Nigeria and Belgium, 1971-74; University of Wales Research Fellow, University College of Swansea, 1974-76; Lecturer in Philosophy, Glasgow University, 1976-84; Professor of Philosophy, Sheffield University, 1984-90. Fellow, Royal Society of Edinburgh. Publications: Symbol and Theory, 1976; John Stuart Mill, 1989; English Language Philosophy 1750-1945, 1993; Ethical Explorations, 1999. Recreations: music; walking; skiing. Address: (h.) Cedar Lodge, Hepburn Gardens, St. Andrews, KY16 9LP; T.-01334 477590.

Slack, Rev. William G., DipTh. General Secretary, Baptist Union of Scotland, since 1995; b. 29.1.49, Edinburgh; m., Vivienne; 1 d. Educ. Trinity Academy, Edinburgh; Hamilton Academy; Baptist Theological College of Scotland. Minister, Ladywell, Livingston, 1974-82; Minister, International Baptist Church, Aberdeen, 1982-95. Recreations: philately; swimming; music. Address: (b.) 14 Aytoun Road, Glasgow, G41 5RT.

Slater, Professor Peter James Bramwell, BSc, PhD, DSc, FIBiol, FRSE. Kennedy Professor of Natural History, St. Andrews University, since 1984, Head, School of Biological and Medical Sciences, 1992-97; Dean, Faculty of Science, since 1998; b. 26.12.42, Edinburgh; m., Elisabeth Vernon Smith; 2 s. Educ. Edinburgh Academy; Glenalmond; Edinburgh University. Demonstrator in Zoology, Edinburgh University, 1966-68; Lecturer in Biology, Sussex University, 1968-84. Secretary, Association for the Study of Animal Behaviour, 1973-78, President, 1986-89, Medallist, 2000; European Editor, Animal Behaviour, 1979-82; Editor, Advances in the Study of Behavior. Recreations: walking; ornithology; music. Address: (b.) School of Biology, St. Andrews, Fife; T.-01334 463500.

Slavin, Rev. William J., MA, STL, CPsychol. Chaplain, Royal Hospital for Sick Children, Glasgow; b. 17.1.40, Bristol. Educ. Blairs College, Aberdeen; Scots College, Rome; Glasgow University. Assistant Priest, Broomhill, Glasgow, 1965-70; Educational Psychologist, Glasgow Child Guidance Service, 1970-75; Deputy Director, Jessore Training Centre, Bangladesh, 1975-80; Secretary, RC Justice and Peace Commission, 1980-85; Co-ordinator, Scottish Drugs Forum, 1986-92; Parish Priest, St. Alphonsus, The Barras, Glasgow, 1992-97. Recreation: An rud Gaidhealach. Address: (h.) 33 Partick Bridge Street, Glasgow G11 6PQ; T.-0141-338 6794; e-mail: wslavin@compuserve.com

Sleigh, Daphne Mary Walker. Leader, Conservative Group, City of Edinburgh Council, since 1995; b. 26.12.37, Lahore; m., J. Lindsay Walls; 2 s.; 1 d. Educ. Craigmount School for Girls, Hawick. Elected to Edinburgh District Council, 1982; elected to City of Edinburgh Council, 1995. Board Member, Scottish Homes, 1990-99; Member, Board, Salvation Army, since 1996; Conservative Party Scottish Spokesman for Local Government, 1997-98. Recreations: travel; walking. Address: (b.) City Chambers, High Street, Edinburgh EH1 1YJ; T.-0131-529 4282.

Sloan, Rev. Robert P., MA, BD. Minister, Braemar linked with Crathie, since 1996; Domestic Chaplain, Balmoral. Ordained, 1968. Address: Crathie, Ballater AB35 5UL.

Sloane, Professor Peter James, BA (Econ), PhD, FRSA, FRSE. Professor of Political Economy, Aberdeen University, since 1984; Vice Principal and Dean, Faculty of Social Sciences and Law, since 1996; Research Fellow, Institute for the Study of Labour (IZA), Bonn, 2001-04; b. 6.8.42, Cheadle Hulme; m., Avril Mary Urquhart; 1 s. Educ. Cheadle Hulme School; Sheffield University; Strathclyde University. Assistant Lecturer and Lecturer, Department of Political Economy, Aberdeen University, 1966-69; Lecturer in Industrial Economics, Nottingham University, 1969-75; Economic Adviser, Department of Employment Unit for Manpower Studies (on secondment), 1973-74; Professor of Economics and Management, Paisley College, 1975-84. Member, Economic and Social Research Council, 1979-85; Council Member, Scottish Economic Society, since 1983. Publications: Sex Discrimination in the Labour Market, 1976; Women and Low Pay, 1980; Sport in the Market?, 1980; Equal Employment Issues, 1981; Tackling Discrimination in the Workplace, 1982; Labour Economics, 1985; Low Pay and Earnings Mobility in Europe, 1998. Recreation: sport. Address: (b.) Department of Economics, Aberdeen University, Edward Wright Building, Dunbar Street, Old Aberdeen, Aberdeen, AB24 3QY.

Slowey, Professor Maria, BComm, DipSocSci, M.Litt. Professor and Director, Adult and Continuing Education, University of Glasgow, since 1992; Vice-Dean, Research, Faculty of Education, 1999-2001; b. 14.10.52, Dublin. Educ. Dominican Convent, Cabra; University College, Dublin; Trinity College, Dublin. Research Fellow, National Association of Adult Education of Ireland, 1976-79; Research Officer, DES National Survey of Adult Learners, 1980-82; Head, Adult Education Centre, LB of Waltham Forest, 1982-83; Lecturer in Adult Education, St Patrick's College, Maynooth, 1983-84; Senior Lecturer in Recurrent Education, subsequently Head, Centre for Continuing Education and External Relations, University of Northumbria, 1985-92. Consultant to international bodies, including OECD, Council of Europe, EC; Visiting Fellow, Centre for Policy Studies in H.E., University of California, Berkeley, Centre for Policy Studies, University of British Columbia, Vancouver, Kellog College, University of Oxford; Honorary Specialist Adviser on Continuing Education to the Committee of Scottish Higher Education Principals; Adviser, Scottish Parliament Enterprise and Lifelong Learning Committee of Inquiry on Lifelong Learning; Member, ESRC Research Priorities Board, West of Scotland Programme Monitoring Committee European Structural Funds; current and recent committee memberships include: Independent Committee of Inquiry on Student Finance in Scotland ("Cubie" Committee); Executive, Universities Association of Continuing Education; Women Returner's Network; Board of Management, Scottish Centre for Community Development; Committee on Community Education Validation and Endorsement, Scottish Community Education Council; Higher Education Policy Group, National Institute of Adult and Continuing Education; Quality Assurance Consultative Group, Higher Education Quality Council; Advisory Group on the Funding of Continuing Education, Scottish Higher Education Funding Council; Chair, Society for Research into Higher Education Continuing Education Research Group. Publications: three co-authored books and numerous official reports, papers and articles on widening access and participation in continuing and higher education. Address: (b.) Department of Adult and Continuing Education, University of Glasgow, St. Andrews Building, 1 Park Drive, Glasgow G3 6LP; e-mail: m.slowey@educ.gla.ac.uk

Smail, Peter James, MA, BM, BCh, FRCP, DCH. Group Clinical Co-ordinator, Combined Child Health Service, Grampian University Hospitals Trust, since 1999; Consultant Paediatrician, since 1980; Honorary Senior Lecturer in Child Health, Aberdeen University, since 1980; b. 10.10.43, Harrow; m., Janice Lockhart; 3 s.; 1 d. Educ. Merchant Taylors', Northwood; St. John's College, Oxford; Oxford Clinical Medical School. Lecturer in Child Health, Dundee University, 1975; Fellow in Paediatric Endocrinology, University of Manitoba, Winnipeg, 1979. Secretary, Scottish Study Group for the Care of Young Diabetics, 1984-89. Recreations: Member, Aberdeen Bach

Choir; Lay Clerk, St. Andrew's Cathedral, Aberdeen. Address: (b.) Royal Aberdeen Children's Hospital, Aberdeen, AB25 2ZG; T.-0224 681818, Ext. 53037.

Small, Christopher. Writer; b. 15.11.19, London; 3 d. Educ. Dartington Hall; Pembroke College, Oxford. Journalist and miscellaneous writer; Literary Editor and Dramatic Critic, Glasgow Herald, 1955-80. Publications:Ariel Like A Harpy: Shelley, Mary & Frankenstein; The Road to Miniluv: George Orwell, the State & God; The Printed Word. Recreation: gardening. Address: (h.) 26 Bell Place, Edinburgh, EH3 5HT; T.-0131-332 6591.

Small, Professor John Rankin, CBE, DLitt, BSc (Econ), FCCA, FCMA. Emeritus Professor, Department of Accountancy and Finance, Heriot-Watt University; b. 28.2.33, Dundee; m., Catherine Wood; 1 s.; 2 d. Educ. Harris Academy; Dundee School of Economics. Industry and commerce; Lecturer, Edinburgh University; Senior Lecturer, Glasgow University. Director of and Consultant to various organisations; President, Association of Chartered Certified Accountants, 1982-83; Vice-Principal, Heriot-Watt University, 1974-78, 1987-90, Deputy Principal, 1990-94. Chairman, Commission for Local Authority Accounts in Scotland, 1983-92; Chairman, National Appeal Panel for Entry to Pharmaceutical Lists (Scotland), 1987-95; Board Member, Scottish Homes, since 1993. Recreation: golf. Address: (b.) Heriot-Watt University, Riccarton, Edinburgh; T.-0131-451 3362.

Small, Stephen J., CQSW. Director, St Andrew's Children's Society Ltd., since 1996; b. 3.11.61, Edinburgh; m., Kay L. Anderson; 1 s.; 2 d. Educ. Holyrood RC High School, Edinburgh; Moray House College of Education. Social Worker, Humberside County Council, 1986-88; Social Worker, Lothian Regional Council (Midlothian District), 1988-95; Senior Social Worker, St Andrew's Children's Society Ltd., 1995-96. Recreations: most leisure time taken up parenting three small children, but occasionally have a game of tennis. Address: (b.) Gillis Centre, 113 Whitehouse Loan, Edinburgh EH9 1BB; T.-0131-452 8248.

Smart, Ian Stewart, LLB, NP. Convener, Legal Aid Committee, Law Society of Scotland, since 2000; Solicitor, Partner, Ian S. Smart & Co., since 1991; b. 10.9.58, Paisley. Educ. Paisley Grammar School; Glasgow University. Solicitor and then Partner, Ross Harper & Murphy, 1980-91; Council Member, Law Society of Scotland, since 1997. Chairman, Cumbernauld and Kilsyth Addiction Service; Board Member, Cumbernauld Theatre; Board Member, Cumbernauld Women's Aid. Recreations: Labour Party activist; St Mirren. Address: (b.) 3 Annan House, Cumbernauld G67 1DP; T.-01236 731027.

Smart, John Dalziel Beveridge, JP. Lord Lieutenant, Kincardineshire, since 1999; b. 12.8.32, Edinburgh; m., Valerie Blaber; 2 s. Educ. Harrow; Administrative Staff College. 2nd Lt., Black Watch (RHR), Korea, 1952; PA to Chief of Staff, 1953. J. & J. Smart (Brechin) Ltd., 1953 (Director, 1954); Director, Don Brothers, Buist & Co. Ltd., 1964 (Managing Director, 1985; retired, 1987). Chairman, British Polyolefin Textiles Association, 1986-97; Member, St. Andrews Management Institute, 1989; Chairman, Scottish American Community Relations Committee, 1990-93; Dean, Guildry of Brechin, 1991-93; DL, Kincardineshire, 1993; Member, Queen's Bodyguard for Scotland, Royal Company of Archers. Recreations: shooting; skiing. Address: (h.) Woodmyre, Edzell, Brechin DD9 7UX; T.-01356 648416.

Smethurst, Emeritus Professor Colin, BA, BLitt, MA, Officier Palmes Academiques. Marshall Professor of French, Glasgow University, 1980-98; b. 3.8.37, Bedford;

m., Claudine Rozenberg; 2 d. Educ. Slough Grammar School; Keble College, Oxford. Assistant Lecturer, Lecturer, Senior Lecturer in French, Liverpool University, 1962-80. President, Institut Francais D'Ecosse, 1989-96; Secretary, Association of University Professors of French, 1983-87; Visiting Professor, Sorbonne (Paris IV), 1998-99. Publications: Zola: Germinal; Chateaubriand: Atala, René; editions of Balzac novels. Address: (b.) Department of French, Glasgow University, Glasgow G12 8QL; T.-0141-339 8855.

Smillie, Anne. Chief Executive, Scottish Badminton Union, since 1989; Member, UK Sport, Major Events Steering Group; b. 17.8.56, Glasgow. Educ. Victoria Drive Secondary School; Anniesland College. Joined Scottish Badminton Union, 1980; Director of major badminton events, including 1992 European Championships, 1994 World Team Championships, 1997 World Team and Individual Championships. Recreations: music; reading. Address: (h.) 55 Westerton Avenue, Westerton, Glasgow; T.-0141-942 9804.

Smillie, Carol. Television Presenter. Credits include: Wheel of Fortune; The Travel Show; Holiday; The National Lottery Live; The Big Breakfast; Hearts of Gold; Get It On; Smillie's People; Changing Rooms; Midweek National Lottery Live; Holiday Memories; Holiday Heaven; Summer Holiday; Star Secrets; Holiday Swaps.

Smith of Gilmorehill, Baroness (Elizabeth Margaret Smith), MA. Peeress, House of Lords, since 1995; Deputy Lieutenant, City of Edinburgh; Non-Executive Director: Deutsche Bank (Scotland) Ltd., City Inn Ltd.; Chairman, Edinburgh Festival Fringe Society, since 1995; President, Scottish Opera; President, Birkbeck College; Member, BP Scottish Advisory Board; Council Member, Russo-British Chamber of Commerce; Trustee, Centre for European Reform; Governor, English Speaking Union; Trustee, John Smith Memorial Trust; Patron, University of Glasgow 2001 Campaign; b. 4.6.40, Ayr; m., Rt. Hon. John Smith, MP (deceased); 3 d. Educ. Hutchesons Girls Grammar School; Glasgow University. LLD, Glasgow University, 1998. Recreations: family; garden; the arts. Address: (b.) House of Lords, London, SW1A 0PW.

Smith, Professor Adam Neil, MD, DSc, FRCSE, FRCPE, FIBiol, FRSE. Formerly Wade Professor of Surgical Studies, RCSEd; formerly Consultant Surgeon, Gastro-Intestinal Unit, Edinburgh (retired); b. 27.6.26, Hamilton; m., Sibyl Mary Veitch Johnstone; 1 s.; 3 d. Educ. Lanark Grammar School; Glasgow University. Academic and Health Service appointments, since 1948; Lecturer in Surgery, Glasgow University; Medical Research Council Fellow; Reader, Edinburgh University and Western General Hospital. Vice-President and Council Member, Royal College of Surgeons of Edinburgh; awarded Medal of RCSEd, 1997; Council Member, Association of Coloproctology; Past President, British Group for Research into Pelvic Function and Disease; President, Scottish Society of Coloproctology; former Surgical Traveller, James IV Surgical Association; Commonwealth Fund Travelling Fellow in Medical Education; former Trustee, Melville Trust for Care and Cure of Cancer; Member, Council, Royal Caledonian Horticultural Society. Recreations: golf; gardening. Address: (h.) 2 Ravelston House Park, Edinburgh, EH4 3LU; T.-0131-332 4077.

Smith, Agnes Houston, BL. Honorary Sheriff, Dundee, since 1990; Non-Executive Director, Dundee Healthcare NHS Trust, 1993-99; b. 27.9.33, Prestwick; m., David Robert Smith; 3 d. Educ. Hutchesons' Girls Grammar School, Glasgow; Glasgow University. Solicitor in Paisley, Edinburgh and Dundee, 1955-92. President, Dundee Society of Glasgow University Graduates. Recreations: golf; gardening; grannying. Address: (h.) Windyridge, Kellas, by Broughty Ferry DD5 3PD; T.-01382 350475.

Smith, Sir Alan, Kt (1982), CBE (1976), DFC (1941) and Bar (1942), DL, JP. President, Dawson International plc, Kinross, since 1982; b. 14.3.17, South Shields; m., 1, Margaret Stewart Todd (deceased); 2, Alice Elizabeth Moncur; 3 s.; 2 d. Educ. Bede College, Sunderland. Self-employed, 1931-36; Unilever, 1936-39; RAF, 1939-45; Managing Director, Todd & Duncan Ltd., Kinross, 1946-60; Chairman and Chief Executive, Dawson International, Kinross, 1960-82. Chairman, Quayle Munro PLC, Edinburgh, 1982-93; Board Member, Scottish Development Agency, 1982-87; Kinross Burgh Councillor, 1952-65; Provost of Kinross, 1959-65; Tayside Regional Councillor, 1979-90; Financial Convenor, Tayside Region, 1980-86. Recreations: work; sailing. Address: (h.) Ardgairney House, Cleish, by Kinross; T.-01577 850265.

Smith, Professor Alan Gordon Rae, MA, PhD, FRAS, FRHistS, FRSE. Professor of Early Modern History, Glasgow University, since 1995; b. 22.12.36, Glasgow; m., Isabel Robertson; 1 s.; 1 d. Educ. Glasgow High School; Glasgow University; University College, London. Research Fellow, Institute of Historical Research, London University, 1961-62; Assistant in History, 1962-64, then Lecturer, Glasgow University, 1964-75; Senior Lecturer in Modern History, 1975-85; Reader, 1985-92, Professor in Modern History, 1992-95; Review Editor, History (Journal of the Historical Association), 1984-87; Member, Council, Royal Historical Society, 1990-94; Member, Governing Board, Institute of Historical Research, London University, 1994-99. Publications: The Government of Elizabethan England, 1967; The New Europe, 1969; Science and Society in the Sixteenth and Seventeenth Centuries, 1972; Servant of the Cecils: The Life of Sir Michael Hickes, 1977; The Emergence of a Nation State: The Commonwealth of England 1529-1660, 1984; The Anonymous Life of William Cecil, Lord Burghley, 1990; The Last Years of Mary Queen of Scots, 1990; Tudor Government, 1990; William Cecil, Lord Burghley, Minister of Queen Elizabeth I, 1991. Recreation: watching sport. Address: (h.) 5 Cargil Avenue, Kilmacolm, Renfrewshire; T.-Kilmacolm 3517.

Smith, Allan Keppie. CBE, DUniv, BSc, FREng, CEng, FIMechE, FWeldI. Chairman, Railcare Ltd., 1995-2001; Managing Director, Facilities Management Division, Babcock International Group PLC, Rosyth Royal Dockyard, until 1997; b. 18.5.32. Joined Army for National Service, 1953; commissioned, REME, 1954; Babcock & Wilcox: joined as Graduate Trainee, 1955; appointed: Industrial Engineering Manager, Renfrew Works, 1965, Production Director, Renfrew Works, 1974, Managing Director, Renfrew and Dumbarton Works, 1976; Managing Director, Babcock Thorn Limited and Chairman, Rosyth Royal Dockyard plc, 1986; Director, Babcock International Group PLC, 1989. Past President, Scottish Engineering; Past Chairman, Council of the Welding Institute; Honorary Doctor, University of Paisley; awarded Institute of Marketing Scottish Marketer of the Year, 1992. Address: (h.) The Forts, Hawes Brae, South Queensferry EH30 9TE; T.-0131-319 1668.

Smith, Hon. Lady (Anne Smith), QC. Senator of the College of Justice in Scotland; b. 1955; m.; 1 s.; 1 d. Educ. Edinburgh University. Admitted, Faculty of Advocates, 1980. Address: Parliament House, Parliament Square, Edinburgh EH1 1RQ.

Smith, Rt. Rev. Brian Arthur, Episcopal Bishop of Edinburgh, since 2001; b. 1943. Educ. Edinburgh University; Fitzwilliam College, Cambridge; Jesus College, Cambridge; Wescott House, Cambridge. Curate, Cuddesdon, 1972-79; Tutor, Cuddesdon College, 1972-75; Ripon College, Cuddesdon: Director of Studies, 1975-78, Senior Tutor, 1978-79; Director of Training, Diocese of Wakefield, 1979-87; Priest-in-Charge, St. John, Halifax, 1979-85; Honorary Canon, Wakefield Cathedral, 1981-87; Archdeacon of Craven, 1987-93; Bishop, 1993; Bishop

Suffragan, Tonbridge, 1993-2001. Address: Diocesan Centre, 21a Grosvenor Crescent, Edinburgh EH12 5EL; T.-0131-538 7044; e-mail: bishop@edinburgh.anglican.org

Smith, Bruce Livingstone, BSc, CEng, CArb, FIMarE, MRINA, FCMS. Hon. Secretary/Treasurer, Scottish Branch, Chartered Institute of Arbitrators, since 1997 (Past Branch Chairman); b. 29.8.45, Glasgow; m., Jacqueline McLean; 1 s.; 1 d. Educ. Glasgow University. Joined John Brown Engineering as Test Engineer on gas turbines; employed in, and bought, E.K. Wallace and Son Ltd., Marine Consultants (Chairman/Managing Director); Principal Partner, Bruce L. Smith & Associates, since 1992; Loss Adjuster and Expert in marine and aquaculture disputes. Past Chairman, Scottish Branch, Yacht Brokers, Designers, Surveyors Association; Past President, Society of Consulting Marine Engineers and Ship Surveyors. Recreations: sailing; shooting; fishing. Address: (b.) Whittinghame House, 1099 Great Western Road, Glasgow G12 0AA; T.-0141-334 7222; e-mail: brucesmith@blsa.co.uk

Smith, Caroline Anne Scott, MBChB, LLB, DipLP. Associate, Russel and Aitken WS, since 2001; b. 23.6.55, Edinburgh; 1 s.; 1 d. Educ. St Denis School, Edinburgh; Edinburgh University. Hospital doctor, 1979-82; Assistant, Warner & Co., Edinburgh, 1986-88, Morton, Fraser, Milligan, Edinburgh, 1988-93; Associate, Loudons, Edinburgh, 1993-94; Partner, Loudons, 1994-2001. Recreations: reading; walking; swimming. Address: 27 Rutland Square, Edinburgh; T.-0131-228 5500; e-mail: Caroline.Smith@russelaitken.com

Smith, David Alexander, LLB. Chairman, Shepherd and Wedderburn, WS, since 1999; Partner, since 1974; b. 17.11.47, Dundee; m., Hon. Lady Anne Smith; 1 s.; 1 d. Educ. Fettes College, Edinburgh; Edinburgh University. Joined Shepherd and Wedderburn as apprentice, 1969. Recreations: hockey; golf; skiing; walking; running; opera; classical music. Address: (h.) Bank House, Albert Terrace, Edinburgh EH10 5EA; T.-(b.) 0131-473 5292.

Smith, David Bruce Boyter, OBE, Drhc, MA, LLB, FRSA, FInstD, NP. Director and Chief Executive, Dunfermline Building Society, 1987-2001; Vice Chairman, Scottish Opera/Scottish Ballet; Past Chairman, Building Societies Association; b. 11.3.42, St. Andrews; m., Christine Anne; 1 s.; 1 d. Educ. High School, Dunfermline; Edinburgh University. Legal training, Balfour & Manson, Edinburgh; admitted Solicitor, 1968; Solicitor, Standard Life Assurance Co., 1969-73; Dunfermline Building Society: Secretary, 1974-81, General Manager (Admin.), 1981-86, Deputy Chief Executive, 1986. Past Chairman, Northern Association of Building Societies; Vice President, European Mortgage Federation; Chairman, Building Societies Trust Ltd.; Member, Council, NHBC (Scotland); Member, Scottish Conveyancing and Executry Services Board; Chairman, Institute of Directors, Scottish Division, 1994-97; Director, Scottish Fisheries Museum; Member, Building Societies Investor Protection Board; Vice Chairman of Court and Finance Convener, Edinburgh University; Life Trustee, Carnegie Trust. Recreations: golf; sailing; the arts. Address: (h.) 4 Garvock Hill, Dunfermline, Fife; T.-01383 723863.

Smith, Sheriff David Buchanan, MA, LLB, FSAScot. Sheriff of North Strathclyde at Kilmarnock, 1975-2001; b. 31.10.36, Paisley; m., Hazel Mary Sinclair; 1 s.; 1 d. Educ. Paisley Grammar School; Glasgow University; Edinburgh University. Advocate, 1961; Standing Junior Counsel to Scottish Education Department, 1968-75; Tutor, Faculty of Law, Edinburgh University, 1964-72; Trustee, Scottish Curling Museum Trust, since 1980. President, Kilmarnock and District History Group; Trustee Scottish National Dictionary Association, since 1994; President, Ayr Curling

Club, 1995-96; Treasurer, Sheriffs' Association, 1979-89, Council Member, 1998-2001; Council Member, Stair Society, since 1995, Vice Chairman of Council, since 1998; Member, Scottish Records Advisory Council, since 2000; President, Eglinton County Curling Game, since 2000. Publications: Curling: An Illustrated History, 1981; The Roaring Game: Memories of Scottish Curling, 1985; contributions to The Laws of Scotland: Stair Memorial Encyclopedia, Vol. 6; George Washington Wilson in Ayrshire, 1991; Contributor to Macphail: Sheriff Court Practice, 2nd Ed., 1998; Sport, Scotland and the Scots (Contributor), 2001. Recreations: Scotland — history and culture; curling; collecting curliana; music; architecture; grandchildren. Address: (h.) 72 South Beach, Troon, KA10 6EG; T.-01292 312130.

Smith, Sir David Cecil, Kt, MA, DPhil, FRS, FRSE. Principal and Vice-Chancellor, Edinburgh University, 1987-94; President, Wolfson College, Oxford, 1994-2000; m., Lesley Margaret Mollison Mutch; 2 s.; 1 d. Educ. St. Paul's School, London; Queen's College, Oxford. Browne Research Fellow, Queen's College, Oxford, 1956-59; Harkness Fellow, University of California, Berkeley, 1959-60; University Lecturer, Department of Agriculture, Oxford University, 1960-74; Fellow and Tutor, Wadham College, Oxford, 1964-74; Melville Wills Professor of Botany, Bristol University, 1974-80; Sibthorpian Professor of Rural Economy, Oxford University, 1980-87. President, British Lichen Society, 1972-74; President, British Mycological Society, 1980; President, Society for Experimental Biology, 1983-85; President, Scottish Association for Marine Science, 1993-2000; President, Linnean Society, since 2000. Publication: The Biology of Symbiosis (Co-author), 1987. Address: 13 Abbotsford Park, Edinburgh EH10 5DZ; T.-0131-446 0230; e-mail: david.smith@wolfson.ox.ac.uk

Smith, Professor David John, MA. Professor of Criminology, Edinburgh University, since 1994; b. 10.7.41, Egypt; m., Colette Marie Obadia; 1 s. Educ. Bootham School, York; Christ Church, Oxford. Trainee Research Executive, 1963-64; Research Officer, 1964-66; Senior Research Officer, then Board Director, Interscan Ltd., 1966-71; Senior Research Associate, Political and Economic Planning, 1972-78; Senior Fellow, Policy Studies Institute, and Head, Social Justice and Social Order Group, 1979-94. Additional Commissioner, Commission for Racial Equality, 1978-84; Specialist Adviser to Home Affairs and Employment Committees, House of Commons, 1981-82, 1986; Visiting Fellow, Lincoln College, Oxford, 1988-89. Recreations: large format photography; piano; squash. Address: (b.) Faculty of Law, Edinburgh University, Old College, South Bridge, Edinburgh, EH8 9YL; T.-0131-650 2027.

Smith, Donald Alexander, MA, PhD. Director, Netherbow Arts Centre, since 1983; Curator, John Knox House, since 1989; Director, Scottish International Storytelling Centre, since 1995; b. 15.2.56, Glasgow; m., Alison; 3 s.; 2 d. Educ. Stirling High School; Edinburgh University. Researcher, School of Scottish Studies, 1979-82. Programme Organiser, St. Margaret 900; Chairperson, Scotland 97 (anniversaries of St. Ninian and St. Columba); Organiser, Scottish Churches Millennium Programme; Chair, Scottish National Theatre Working Party (SAC/Scottish Executive), 2000-01. Publications: The Scottish Stage, 1994; Edinburgh Old Town Pilgrims' Way, 1995; John Knox House: Gateway to Edinburgh's Old Town,1996; Celtic Travellers: Scotland in the Age of the Saints, 1997; History of Scottish Theatre, 1998; Storytelling Scotland: A Nation in Narrative, 2001. Address: (b.) The Netherbow, 43-45 High Street, Edinburgh EH1 1SR; T.-0131-556 2647.

Smith, (Edward) Alistair, CBE, MA, PhD. Director, Aberdeen University International Office, since 1990; b. 16.1.39, Aberdeen. Educ. Aberdeen Grammar School; Aberdeen University. Lecturer in Geography, Aberdeen University, 1963-88; President, Scottish Conservative and Unionist Association, 1979-81; Deputy Chairman, Scottish Conservative Party, 1981-86; Member, Grampian Health Board, 1983-91; Director, Aberdeen University University Development Trust, 1982-90; Board Member, SCOTVEC, 1989-93; Member, Committee for Scotland, Nature Conservancy Council, 1989-91; Member, N.E. Regional Committee, Nature Conservancy Council, 1991-92. Publications: Europe: A Geographical Survey of the Continent (Co-author), 1979; Scotland's Future Development (Contributor), 1983. Recreations: travel; photography; music. Address: (h.) 68A Beaconsfield Place, Aberdeen, AB2 4AJ; T.-01224 642932.

Smith, Elaine A., BA (Hons), DPSM. MSP (Labour), Coatbridge and Chryston, since 1999; b. 7.5.63, Coatbridge; m., James Vann Smith; 1 s. Educ. St Patrick's School, Coatbridge; Glasgow College; St Andrew's Teacher Training College. Teacher, 1986-87; supply teacher, 1987-88; local government officer, Monklands District Council, 1988-90, Highland Regional Council, 1990-97; Volunteer Development Scotland, 1997-98; supply teacher, 1999. Recreations: family; swimming; badminton; reading. Address: (b.) Unit 65, Fountain Business Centre, Coatbridge, Lanarkshire; T.-01236 449122.

Smith, Elaine Constance. Actress; b. 2.8.58, Baillieston; m., Robert Morton; 2 d. Educ. Braidhurst High School, Motherwell; Royal Scottish Academy of Music and Drama; Moray House College of Education. Teacher of Speech and Drama, Firrhill High School, Edinburgh, 1979-82; joined 7:84 Theatre Company, 1982; moved to Wildcat Stage Productions, 1982; since 1986, worked with Borderline Theatre Co., Royal Lyceum, Dundee Rep., Tron Theatre; TV work includes City Lights and Naked Video; plays Mary Nesbitt in Rab C. Nesbitt (BBC2); original cast member, The Steamie. Board Member, Scottish Youth Theatre; Patron, Family Mediation Scotland. Recreations: swimming; aerobics; reading.

Smith, Elinor, MCIBS. Chair, South Glasgow University NHS Hospitals Trust, since 1999; Member, Standards Commission for Scotland, since 2002; b. Greenock; m., David; 1 d. Educ. Pollokshields Senior Secondary School; Glasgow Caledonian University. First woman in Bank of Scotland appointed as sole manager of branch; Associate Director of Small Business Banking, Bank of Scotland; Board Member, Scottish Enterprise Glasgow; Board Member, NHS Greater Glasgow. Recreations: sometimes placing a sacred cow in fear of its life. Address: (b.) Trust Headquarters, Southern General Hospital, 1345 Govan Road, Glasgow G51 4TF; T.-0141-201 1206.

Smith, Gregor, RSW, DA(Edin). Artist and Art Teacher; b. 15.7.44, Renton; m., Elizabeth Stevenson. Educ. Wishaw High School; Edinburgh College of Art. Andrew Grant post-graduate scholarship, 1966-67; teachers included Robin Philipson and James Cumming; exhibits at Royal Scottish Academy, RSW, Compass Gallery, etc.; Chairman, Glasgow Group; works in private and public collections. Address: Craiglilies Upper, Shore Road, Cove G84 0LY; T.-01436 842727.

Smith, Professor Hamilton, BSc, PhD, CChem, FRSC, FRCPath, FRSE. Professor of Forensic Medicine (Toxicology), Glasgow University, 1987-99; b. 27.4.34, Stirling; m., Jacqueline Ann Spittal. Educ. Kilsyth Academy; Glasgow University. Glasgow University: MRC Fellow, 1960, Special Research Fellow, 1963, Lecturer in Forensic Medicine Department, 1964, Senior Lecturer, 1973, Reader, 1984. Publication: Glaister's Medical Jurisprudence and Toxicology, 13th edition. Recreations:

golf (New Club, St. Andrews); gardening. Address: (b.) 1 Park Avenue, Kirkintilloch, Glasgow G66 1EX; T.-0141-776 2901.

Smith, Iain, BA (Hons). MSP (Scottish Liberal Democrat), North East Fife, since 1999; Deputy Minister for Parliament, 1999-2000, Liberal Democrat Local Government Spokesperson, since 2000; b. 1.5.60, Gateside, Fife. Educ. Bell Baxter High School, Cupar; Newcastle upon Tyne University. Councillor, Fife Council, 1995-99 (Leader of Opposition and Lib Dem Group, 1995-99); Councillor, Fife Regional Council, 1982-95 (Leader of Opposition and Lib Dem Group, 1986-95). Chair, Scottish Liberal Democrat General Election Campaign, 2001. Recreations: sport (mainly football and cricket); cinema; travel; reading. Address: (b.) Constituency Office, 16 Millgate, Cupar, Fife KY15 5EG; T.-01334 656361; Scottish Parliament, Edinburgh EH99 1SP; T.-0131-348 5817; e-mail: iain.smith.msp@scottish.parliament.uk

Smith, Ian, BSc, PhD, CBiol, MIBiol. Rector, Kinlochbervie High School, since 1995; b. 2.7.52, Edinburgh; m., Dianne; 2 d. Educ. Galashiels Academy; Heriot Watt University; Glasgow University. Research Biochemist, Knightswood Hospital, Glasgow, 1974-80; Teacher of Biology, Kelso High School, 1981-84; Assistant Principal Teacher of Biology, Nicolson Institute, 1984; Principal Teacher of Biology, Selkirk High School, 1984-88, Hawick High School, 1988-95. Publications: research papers on muscular dystrophy. Recreations: football; rugby; cycling; walking. Address: (b.) Kinlochbervie High School, Kinlochbervie, Sutherland IV27 4RG; T.-01971 521767; e-mail: ian.smith@highland.gov.uk

Smith, James David, OBE, MA, LLB. Retired Solicitor; b. 27.10.19, Dumbarton; m., Margaret McGregor Grant; 2 s. Educ. Dumbarton Academy; Glasgow University. Commissioned Highland Light Infantry, 1940; Town Clerk, Dumbarton, 1951-67; Chief Executive, Corporation of Greenock, 1967-75; Visiting Lecturer in Law, Paisley College of Technology, 1976-87. Address: (h.) Craigellachie, Balmaha Road, Drymen G63 0BY; T.-01360 660484.

Smith, Professor Jeremy John, BA, MPhil, PhD, AKC. Professor of English Philology, Glasgow University, since 2000; b. 18.10.55, Hampton Court; m., Dr Elaine P. Higgleton; 1 d. Educ. Kingston Grammar School, Kingston-upon-Thames; King's College, London; Jesus College, Oxford; Glasgow University. College Lecturer, Keble College, Oxford. 1978-79; Glasgow University: Lecturer, English Language, 1979-90; Senior Lecturer, 1990-96; Reader, 1996-2000. Publications: New Perspectives on Middle English Texts (ed. with S. Powell); Essentials of Early English, 1999; Historical Study of English, 1996; English of Chaucer (with M. L. Samuels), 1988. Recreations; hill walking; opera. Address: (b.) Department of English Language, Glasgow University, Glasgow, G12 8QQ; T.-0141-330 5684.

Smith, Lewis Shand, MA, BD, FRSA. Rector, St. John's Church, Dumfries, since 2000; Member, Board: Scottish Homes, Dumfries and Galloway College, Dumfries and Galloway Arts Association; b. 16.3.52, Lerwick; m., Annette; 1 s. Educ. Anderson Educational Institute, Lerwick; Aberdeen University; Edinburgh University; Edinburgh Theological College. Curate, St. Andrews, Wishaw and Holy Trinity, Motherwell, 1977-80; Rector, St. Magnus Episcopal Church, St. Colman's Church, 1980-2000. Convener, Shetland Islands Council, 1994-99; Vice-President, COSLA, 1998-99; formerly Member, Executive, Scottish Constitutional Convention. Recreations: amateur theatre; music; swimming; gardening. Address: 8 Newall Terrace, Dumfries DG1 1LW; e-mail: shand.smith@talk21.com

Smith, Professor Lorraine Nancy, BScN, MEd, PhD. Professor of Nursing, Glasgow University, since 1990 (Head of School, 1990-2001); b. 29.6.49, Ottawa; m., Christopher Murray Smith; 1 s.; 1 d. Educ. University of Ottawa; Manchester University. Member, Clinical and Biomedical Research Committee (Scotland), 1992-94; co-opted to National Board of Scotland for Nursing, Midwifery and Health Visiting; Member, Clinical Standards Advisory Group (UK), 1994-99; Convenor, Royal College of Nursing Research Society (Scotland); Member, Steering Group, Working Group of European Nurse Researchers, since 1999. Recreations: reading; bridge; sailing. Address: (b.) 5 Huntly Gardens, Glasgow G12 9AS; T.-0141-330 5498; e-mail: l.n.smith@clinmed.gla.ac.uk

Smith, Margaret, MA. MSP (Liberal Democrat), Edinburgh West; Convener, Health and Community Care Committee; b. 1961, Edinburgh; separated; 1 s.; 1 d. Educ. Broughton High School; Edinburgh University. Political organiser; Member, City of Edinburgh Council, 1995-99. Recreation: golf. Address: (b.) Scottish Parliament, Edinburgh EH99 1SP; T.-0131-348 5786.

Smith, Lord Provost Margaret Elizabeth, DipPE. Lord Provost of the City of Aberdeen, since 1999; b. 10.8.31, Oadby. Educ. Twickenham Grammar School; Southport High School for Girls; Lady Mabel College, Rotherham. PE Teacher, Fleetwood Grammar School, 1953-58; PE Teacher, Blairgowrie High School, 1958-67; Youth Officer, Chichester, West Sussex County Council, 1967-73; Neighbourhood Worker, Easterhouse, Glasgow, 1973-78; Housing Worker, Scottish Special Housing Association, Glasgow, 1978-81; Community Education Area Officer, Grampian Regional Council, 1981-91. Elected as Labour councillor, Aberdeen District Council, 1988; appointed Convenor, Women's and Equal Opportunities Committee, 1992; appointed Leader of the Administration, Aberdeen City Council, 1996. Recreations: walking; theatre/concerts; learning Russian; family and friends. Address: (b.) Town House, Aberdeen AB10 1LP; T.-01224 522637.

Smith, Matt, JP. Scottish Secretary, UNISON, since 1993; President, STUC, 1999-2000; b. 4.2.52, Irvine; m., Eileen; 1 s.; 1 d. Educ. Stevenston High School; Ardrossan Academy. NALGO employee from 1973; Senior Scottish Officer/Scottish Organiser, 1981-93; Member, STUC General Council, Treasurer, 1995-97, and since 2000; Member and Vice-Chair, Broadcasting Council for Scotland; Member: Executive, Scottish Council Development and Industry, Committee on Church and Nation of Church of Scotland, Scottish Local Government Information Unit, Centre for Scottish Public Policy, Scottish Committee of Equal Opportunities Commission, Regional Development Forum; served on: McIntosh Commission (Local Government and a Scottish Parliament), Scotland FORward, Scottish Constitutional Convention, Labour for a Scottish Parliament; Member, North Ayrshire Justice Committee; former Stevenston Burgh Councillor; parliamentary candidate, Labour, 1979. Recreations: family; travel; politics; gardening; music. Address: (b.) UNISON House, 14 West Campbell Street, Glasgow, G2 6RX; T.-0141-332 0006; e-mail: matt.smith@unison.co.uk

Smith, Nicholas Charlton, BArch, MPhil, MIOA, FRIAS, RIBA, MaPS. Partner, Charlton Smith Partnership, Carnoustie, since 1988; Teaching Fellow, Dundee University, since 1997; b. 26.8.46, Hucknall; m., Pamela Ann; 1 s.; 1 d. Educ. Southwell Minster School; Liverpool University; Nottingham University. Architectural practice, 1972-76; Lecturer, Dundee University School of Architecture, 1976-88; Creative Director, RIAS CPD Service, 1988-95; Founding Director, Association of Planning Supervisors, 1996-99.

Recreations: fly fishing; walking; music/opera; reading; travel. Address: 9 Dalhousie Street, Carnoustie DD7 6EJ; T.-01241 859495.

Smith, Nigel R. Managing Director, David Auld Valves Ltd., since 1976; b. 9.6.41, Girvan; m., Jody; 2 s.; 2 d. Educ. Dollar Academy. Lt., 4/5 Bn., Royal Scots Fusiliers (TA), 1960-67; staff and management appointments, Bowater Paper, Richard Costain, Rank Hovis McDougall. Member, Executive, Scottish Engineering Employers Association, 1985-90; Member, Broadcasting Council for Scotland, 1986-90; Member, BBC General Advisory Council, 1991-93; Member, Glasgow Development Agency, Strategy Review Panel, 1993-94; Member, Scottish Constitutional Commission, 1993-94; Chairman, Broadcasting for Scotland Campaign, 1993-97; Chairman, Scotland Forward Devolution Yes Campaign, 1997; Member, Bank of England Scottish Consultative Committee, since 1993. Recreations: hill-walking; offshore sailing; opera and choral; reading, particularly biography. Address: (b.) David Auld Valves, Cowlairs Industrial Estate, Finlas Street, Glasgow, G22 5DQ; T.-0141-557 0515.

Smith, Professor Paul Gerard, BSc, MSc, PhD, MCIWEM. Professor of Civil and Environmental Engineering, Paisley University, since 1994; b. 12.2.50, Windsor; m., Sheila Margaret Susanne Smith; 2 d. Educ. Nottingham High School; Birmingham University. Civil Engineer, Babtie Group, 1973-76; University of Strathclyde: Lecturer, Senior Lecturer; joined Paisley University, 1994; Head Department of Civil Engineering, 1996-2000; Editor-in-Chief, International Journal of Environmental Health Research, since 1990. Publications: 4 books; 70 research publications. Recreations: hill-walking; travel. Address: (h.) Ythancraig, Milton, Aberfoyle, Stirling, FK8 3TF; T.-01877 382585.

Smith, Ralph Andrew, QC, LLB, DipLP. Advocate, since 1985; QC, since 1999; b. 22.3.61, Kirkcaldy; m., Lucy Moore Inglis; 1 s.; 1 d. Educ. Edinburgh Academy; Kelvinside Academy; Aberdeen University. Solicitor, 1984; Junior Counsel to Lord President, 1989-90; Standing Junior Counsel to Department of Environment, 1992-99. Member, Faculty of Advocates committees. Recreation: field sports. Address: (h.) Castlemains, Gifford, East Lothian EH41 4PL.

Smith, Sir Robert, Bt. MP (Liberal Democrat), Aberdeenshire West and Kincardine, since 1997; b. 15.4.58; m.; 3 d. Educ. Merchant Taylors' School; Aberdeen University. Runs family estate at Crowmallie. Address: (b.) House of Commons, London SW1A 0AA.

Smith, Robert Graham, MA, DLC. Principal, Scottish National Sports Centre (Cumbrae), since 1995; b. 28.4.44, Rugby; 1 s.; 1 d. Educ. Purley Grammar School; Loughborough Colleges; Birmingham University. Address: (b.) Scottish National Sports Centre, Cumbrae, Ayrshire KA28 0HQ; T.-01475 530757.

Smith, Sir Robert Haldane, Dr.h.c., CA, FCIBS, FSA Scot. Vice Chairman, Deutshe Asset Management, since 1999; Chairman, National Museums of Scotland, since 1993; National Governor, BBC, since 1999; b. 8.8.44, Glasgow; m., Alison Marjorie Bell; 2 d. Educ. Allan Glen's School. Robb Ferguson & Co., CA, 1963-68; qualified CA, 1968; 3i, 1968-82; Royal Bank of Scotland, 1983-89; MD, Charterhouse Development Capital Ltd., 1985-89; CEO, Morgan Grenfell Development Capital Ltd., 1989-96; CEO, Morgan Grenfell Asset Management, 1996-99; Member, Deutsche Bank Group Executive Committee, since 1996; Non-Executive Director, MFI Furniture Group, 1987-2000, Bank of Scotland, 1998-2000, Financial Services

Authority, 1997-2000; Chairman, Broadcasting Council for Scotland, since 1999; Member, Financial Reporting Council, since 2001; Past President, Institute of Chartered Accountants of Scotland; President, British Association of Friends of Museums; Member, Museums and Galleries Commission, 1988-98 (Vice-Chairman, 1996-98). Publication: Managing Your Company's Finances, 1981. Address: (b.) 1 Appold Street, London EC2A 2UU; T.-0171-545 5326.

Smith, Robert Lupton, OBE, FRICS. Vice-President, Association for the Protection of Rural Scotland, since 1993 (Director, 1981-93); Chartered Surveyor in private practice, 1954-96; b. 26.4.24, Cheadle Hulme; m.; 3 d. Educ. George Watson's College; College of Estate Management; Heriot-Watt College. Chairman, Scottish Junior Branch, RICS, 1952; Member, Scottish Executive Committee, RICS, 1952-60; elected, Edinburgh Town Council, 1962-74 and Edinburgh District Council, 1974-77; Governor, Edinburgh College of Art, 1963-89; fought European Election, 1979, as Liberal; Deputy Traffic Commissioner, 1974-78; Chairman, Good Neighbours Housing Association, 1984-87; Scottish Liberal Party: Chairman, Executive Committee, 1971-74, Chairman, 1974, President, 1976-82; Council Member, Royal Scottish Geographical Society, 1957-92; Chairman, A9 Highland Hosts Group, 1995-2000; Director, Cockburn Conservation Trust Ltd., 1976-90; Chairman, Logierait Bridge Co. Ltd. Recreations: visiting Orkney; reading; looking at fine art. Address: (h.) Charleston, Dalguise, near Dunkeld, PH8 0JX; T.-01350 728968.

Smith, Roger W. Writer and Consultant; b. 28.11.38, London; 2 d. Educ. Latymer Upper School, London. Editor, The Great Outdoors, 1977-86; Editor, Environment Now, 1987-89; Editor, Scottish World, 1989-90; Past Chairman, Scottish Wild Land Group; Member, Executive Committee, National Trust for Scotland, and Convenor, NTS Countryside and Nature Conservation Comitteee. Publications include: The Winding Trail, 1981; The Great Outdoors Book of the Walking Year, 1988; Classic Walks in Scotland (Co-author), 1988; Chambers Guide to the Highlands and Islands, 1992; Catastrophes and Disasters, 1992; The Great Flood of Perth, 1993; 25 Walks: Highland Perthshire 1994; 25 Walks: Edinburgh and Lothian, 1995; Mapreading for Beginners, 1996; Insight Guide to the Scottish Highlands, 1997. Recreations: hill-walking; Scottish history. Address: (h.) 51 Benbecula, St. Leonards, East Kilbride G74 2BS; T.-01355 233394.

Smith, Ronald A., MA. General Secretary, Educational Institute of Scotland, since 1995; Member, General Council, STUC, since 1995; Member, Executive Board, European Trade Union Committee for Education, since 1995; Member, European Regional Committee, Education International; b. 9.6.51, Lerwick; m., Mae; 1 s.; 1 d. Educ. Anderson Educational Institute; Aberdeen University; Aberdeen College of Education. Teacher of Latin, then A.P.T. of Latin, then Principal Teacher of Modern Studies, Broxburn Academy, 1973-88; Assistant Secretary, EIS, 1988-95. Address: (b.) 46 Moray Place, Edinburgh, EH3 6BH; e-mail: rsmith@eis.org.uk

Smith, Sarah Elizabeth, MA. Scotland Correspondent, Channel 4 News, since 1998; Columnist, The Scotsman, since 2000; b. 22.11.68, Edinburgh. Educ. Boroughmuir High School; Glasgow University. BBC Scotland trainee, working on Good Morning Scotland, Head On, and in Northern Ireland on TV news and current affairs; Assistant Producer, BBC Youth Programmes; Researcher, Public Eye; Producer, Newsnight; Reporter, Channel 5 News. Trustee, John Smith Memorial Trust. Recreations: sleeping; shopping; eating and drinking. Address: (b.) 10 George Street, Edinburgh EH2 2DU; T.-0131-200 8195.

Smith, Shona Houston, LLB (Hons.), DipLP, NP. Solicitor, Balfour and Manson, since 1996; Chair, Family Law Association, since 1999; b. 17.11.66, Glasgow. Admitted, Solicitor, 1991; specialised in family law since 1993, initially at Gray Muirhead. Board Member, Scottish Child Law Centre, 1996-99; Committee Member, Family Law Association, 1997-99; Court Reporter and Curator ad litem. Publications: Butterworths Family Law Service (Contributor); Children's Rights in Scotland (Contributor). Recreations: travel; theatre. Address: (b.) 62 Frederick Street, Edinburgh EH2 1LS; T.-0131-200 1238; e-mail: shona.smith@balfour-manson.co.uk

Smith, Emeritus Professor Stanley Desmond, OBE, BSc, PhD, DSc, FRS, FRSE. Professor of Physics, Heriot-Watt University, 1970-96; Chairman, Edinburgh Instruments Ltd., since 1971; Chairman, Edinburgh Instruments Ltd., since 1988; b. 3.3.31, Bristol; m., Gillian Anne Parish; 1 s.; 1 d. Educ. Cotham Grammar School; Bristol University; Reading University. SSO, RAE, Farnborough, 1956-58; Research Assistant, Department of Meteorology, Imperial College, London, 1958-59; Lecturer, then Reader, Reading University, 1960-70; Head, Department of Physics, Heriot-Watt University, 1970-96. Member: Advisory Council for Applied Research and Development, 1985-87, Advisory Council on Science and Technology, 1987-88, Defence Scientific Advisory Council, 1985-91, SERC Astronomy and Planetary Science and Engineering Boards, 1985-88, Council, Institute of Physics, 1984-87; Chairman, Scottish Optoelectronics Association, 1996-98. Recreations: tennis; skiing; mountaineering; golf; raising the temperature. Address: (b.) Edinburgh Instruments Ltd., 2 Bain Square, Livingston, EH54 7DQ; T.-01506 425300.

Smith, Tommy, DUniv. Saxophonist; b. 27.4.67, Edinburgh; m., Laura. Educ. Berklee College of Music, Boston. Won best soloist and best group award, Edinburgh International Jazz Festival, aged 14; recorded his first albums as a leader, aged 15; signed to Blue Note Records, 1989; won British Jazz Award, 1989; hosted Jazz Types, BBC TV; began recording for Linn Records, 1993; founded Scottish National Jazz Orchestra, 1995; won BT British Jazz Award for Best Ensemble, ScotRail Award for most outstanding group performance, Arts Foundation/Barclays Bank jazz composition fellowship prize, 1996; has premiered three saxophone concertos; Sound of Love album reached No. 20 in American Gavin Jazz Chart; started own record company, 2000; made youngest-ever Doctor of the University, Heriot-Watt University, 1999; 16 solo albums. Recreations: cinema; cooking; camping; DIY. Address: (b.) PO Box 3743, Lanark ML11 9WD.

Smith, Professor William Ewen, BSc, DIC, PhD, DSc, FRSC, FRSE. Professor of Inorganic Chemistry, since 1987; b. 21.2.41, Glasgow; m., Frances Helen Williamson; 1 s.; 1 d. Educ. Hutchesons' Boys Grammar School; Strathclyde University. Visiting Scientist, Oak Ridge National Laboratory, 1965-67; SERC and ICI Fellow, University College, London, 1967-69; Lecturer, Reader, Professor, Strathclyde University, since 1969. Publications: 200 papers and reviews. Recreations: golf; sailing. Address: (b.) Department of Pure and Applied Chemistry, Strathclyde University, Glasgow, G1 1XL; T.-0141-552 4400.

Smith, William Leggat, CBE, MC, TD, JP, DL, BA (Oxon), LLB, LLD; b. 30.1.18, Kilmarnock; m., Yvonne Menna Williams; 1 s.; 2 d. Educ. Glasgow Academy; Queen's College, Oxford; Glasgow University. Commissioned (TA), Cameronians (Scottish Rifles), 1939; served Second World War in UK, Europe, USA; Solicitor, 1947-86; Chairman, Governors, Glasgow Academy, 1972-80; Deacon Convener, Trades of Glasgow, 1964-65; Dean, Royal Faculty of Procurators in Glasgow, 1976-79; Member, Reviewing Committee on Export of Works of Art,

1980-82; Convener, Retirement Scheme of Church of Scotland, 1976-80; Chairman, Charles Rennie Mackintosh Society, 1985-88; Chairman, Indigent Gentlewomen of Scotland Fund, 1985-93; Chairman, Glasgow School of Art, 1975-88. Recreations: gardening; salmon fishing. Address: (h.) The Cottage, Clachan of Campsie, Glasgow; T.-01360 311434.

Smith, William Wilson Campbell, MA (Cantab), LLB (Glas). Managing Partner, Biggart Baillie, Solicitors, Glasgow and Edinburgh; b. 17.5.46, Glasgow; m., Elizabeth Margaret Richards; 2 d. Educ. Glasgow Academy; St. Catharine's College, Cambridge; Glasgow University. Qualified as a Solicitor, 1972; Assistant Solicitor, Herbert Smith & Co., London, 1972-73; Partner, Biggart Baillie, since 1974. Member, various committees, Law Society of Scotland; Trustee, Glassford Sheltered Housing Trust; Member, Joint Insolvency Examination Board, 1986-95; Deacon, Incorporation of Barbers, Glasgow, 1989-90. Recreations: croquet; golf; barbershop singing. Address: (b.) Dalmore House, 310 St. Vincent Street, Glasgow, G2 5QR; T.-0141-228 8000.

Smout, Professor Thomas Christopher, CBE, MA, PhD, FRSE, FSA (Scot), FBA. HM Historiographer in Scotland; b. 19.12.33. Address: Chesterhill, Shore Road, Anstruther, Fife KY10 3DZ.

Smuga, George Muirhead Russell, MA (Hons), DipEd. Headteacher, Royal High School, Edinburgh, since 1998; b. 6.11.47, Broughty Ferry; m.; 1 s.; 1 d. Educ. Kirkcaldy High School; Edinburgh University. Principal Teacher, Modern Studies, then Assistant Headteacher, Portobello High School; Depute Headteacher, Beeslack High School; Headteacher, North Berwick High School and Manager Quality Assurance, East Lothian. Member, Higher Still National Implementation School Sector Group; co-author of four modern studies textbooks. Recreations: golf; supporting Hibernian F.C. Address: (h.) 35 Thornyhall, Dalkeith EH22 2ND; e-mail: George.Smuga@royalhigh.edin.sch.uk

Smyth, Professor John Crocket, OBE, BSc, PhD, HonDUniv (Paisley), DipEd, CBiol, FIBiol, FLS, FRSA. Emeritus Professor of Biology, Paisley University, since 1988; Honorary Professor (Division of Academic Innovation and Continuing Education), Stirling University; b. 21.3.24, Edinburgh; m., Elizabeth Wallace Learmond; 1 s.; 1 d. Educ. George Watson's College; Edinburgh University. Assistant Lecturer in Zoology, Edinburgh University; Lecturer to Head, Department of Biology, Paisley College; Chairman, Scottish Environmental Education Council, 1983-91, President, 1991-99; Commissioner, Countryside Commission for Scotland, 1990-92; Chairman, Secretary of State for Scotland's Working Group on Environmental Education, 1990-93; Vice-President, Royal Zoological Society of Scotland; Institute of Biology Charter Award for 1989; former Secretary and Chairman, Scottish Branch, Institute of Biology; Member, IUCN Commission on Education and Communication; IUCN Tree of Learning Award, 1990; Chairman, N.W. Europe Committee, 1980-85; Consultant for UNESCO-UNEP and UNCED on environmental education; Founder-Leader, Scottish Boys' Club. Address: (h.) Glenpark, Johnstone, Renfrewshire, PA5 0SP; T.-01505 320219; e-mail: jcsmyth@compuserve.com

Smyth, Professor John Fletcher, MA, MB, BChir, MD (Cantab), MSc (Lond), FRCPE, FRCP, FRCSE, FRSE, FRCR. Professor of Medical Oncology, Edinburgh University, since 1979 (Head, Division of Molecular and Clinical Medicine, since 1998, Head, Department of Clinical Oncology, 1980-98); Honorary Director, Imperial Cancer Research Fund Medical Oncology Unit, Edinburgh University, since 1980; b. 26.10.45, Dursley; m., Ann Cull; 2 d. Educ. Bryanston School; Trinity College, Cambridge.

Trained, St. Bartholomews Hospital, Royal Postgraduate Medical School and Institute of Cancer Research, London; National Cancer Institute, Bethesda; University of Chicago; Honorary Consultant Physician, Royal Marsden Hospital and Senior Lecturer, Institute of Cancer Research, London, 1976-79. President, European Society for Medical Oncology, 1992-94; Founder Member, The Monteverdi Choir; Editor-in-Chief, European Journal of Cancer, since 2001. Address: (b.) Department of Clinical Oncology, Western General Hospital, Crew Road, Edinburgh, EH4 2XU.

Solomon, Professor Sally Elizabeth, BSc (Hons), PhD. Professor of Poultry Science, Glasgow University, since 1993; President, World Poultry Science Association (UK), since 1998; Chairman, Working Group No. 4, EU Branch, World Poultry Science Association, since 1992; Secretary/Treasurer, British Poultry Science Ltd., since 1994; b. 19.4.44, Glasgow; m., Dr. Roger Tippett. Educ. Rothesay Academy; Woodside Secondary School, Glasgow; University of Glasgow. Glasgow University: Assistant Lecturer in Veterinary Histology, 1968-70, Lecturer in Veterinary Histology, 1970-86, Senior Lecturer in Veterinary Anatomy, 1986-91, Reader in Veterinary Anatomy, 1991-93. Gordon Memorial Medal, 1998; World Poultry Science Education Award, 1996. Publication: Egg and Eggshell Quality. Recreations: gardening; travel; cooking; reading. Address: Department of Veterinary Preclinical Studies, University of Glasgow, Bearsden Road, Bearsden, Glasgow G61 1QH; T.-0141-330 5717.

Somerville, David Wilkie, DipPE. Head of Community Services, Fife Council, since 1995; b. Edinburgh; m., Fiona; 1 s.; 1 d. Educ. Lasswade High School. Football: Hearts, Berwick Rangers; P.E. Teacher, Penicuik High School; Depute Director, National Sports Training Centre; Sport Development, Scottish Sports Council; Senior Assistant Director of Education, Fife Regional Council. Recreations: golf; swimming. Address: (b.) Fife Council, Fife House, North Street, Glenrothes; T.-01592 414141.

Somerville, John Kenneth, CA. Partner, French Duncan, CA, Glasgow, since 1970; Council Member, Institute of Chartered Accountants of Scotland, 1984-90; Council Member, Association of Accounting Technicians, 1989-98 (President, 1995-96); b. 1.3.42, Glasgow; m., Iris Alexa Hutchison; 3 d. Educ. Kelvinside Academy. Member, Board of Governors, Kelvinside Academy, 1976-94 (Chairman of Board, 1985-94). Recreations: golf; running. Address: (b.) 375 West George Street, Glasgow, G2 4LH; T.-0141-221 2984.

Soto-Morettini, Donna, BA, MFA, DPhil. Director of Drama, Royal Scottish Academy of Music and Drama, since 2001; b. 31.1.51, Santa Ana, California, USA. Educ. University of California, Irvine, USA; Oxford University. Professional actor, director, singer, 1968-78; Tutor in Acting: Orange Coast College, 1978-83, University of California, Irvine, 1983-84; Director of Talks, Institute for Contemporary Arts, 1988; Resident Director, Head of Acting, Central School of Speech and Drama, 1990; Head of Acting, Liverpool Institute for Performing Arts, 1994. Distinguished Alumni, University of California, Irvine, 1999. Address: 100 Renfrew Street, Glasgow G2 3DB; T.-0141-332 4101.

Souter, Brian. Chairman and Founding Partner, Stagecoach Holdings PLC; b. 1954; m.; 3 s.; 1 d. Member, Board, Scottish Enterprise. Address: (b.) 10 Dunkeld Road, Perth, PH1 5TW; T.-01738 643648.

Souter, William Alexander, MBChB(Hons), FRCSEd, FFCS. Consultant Orthopaedic Surgeon, Princess Margaret Rose Orthopaedic Hospital, Edinburgh, 1968-1997; Honorary Senior Lecturer in Orthopaedics, Edinburgh University, since 1968; Visiting Professor, Bioengineering

Department, Strathclyde University, since 1985; b. 11.5.33, Cupar; m., Kathleen Bruce Georgeson Taylor; 1 s.; 2 d. Educ. Falkirk High School; George Watson's Boys' College, Edinburgh; Medical School, Edinburgh University. Registrar in Hand Surgery, Derbyshire Royal Infirmary, 1964; Senior Registrar, Orthopaedic Department, Edinburgh, 1965-68; Instructor in Orthopaedic Surgery, University of Washington, Seattle, 1967. Member, Council, British Orthopaedic Association, 1986-88 and 1993-95; Member, Council, Royal College of Surgeons of Edinburgh, 1988-98; Inaugural President, British Elbow and Shoulder Society, 1989-90; British Society for Surgery of the Hand: Member, Council, 1977-78, 1992-94, President, 1993; Chairman, Accreditation Committee, Federation of European Societies for Surgery of the Hand, 1992-96; European Rheumatoid Arthritis Surgical Society: Member, Executive Committee, 1979-81 and 1993-2001, President, 1995-99; President, Rheumatoid Arthritis Surgical Society, 1982 and 1998-2000; Honorary Member: British Society for Surgery of the Hand, 2001, Societe Francaise Chirurgie Orthopedique et Traumatologique, 1999, Netherlands Rheumatoid Arthritis Surgical Society, 2001. Recreations: gardening; music; hill-walking; photography; golf. Address: (h.) Old Mauricewood Mains, Penicuik, Midlothian EH26 0NJ; T.-01968 672609; e-mail: WASouter@ukgateway.net

Sparks, Professor Leigh, MA, PhD, FRSA. Professor of Retail Studies, Stirling University, since 1992; Dean, Faculty of Management, 1995-2000; b. 15.2.57, Bridgend, Wales; m., Janice Lewis. Educ. Brynteg C.S.; Christ's College, Cambridge; St. David's University College, Wales. Researcher, Lecturer, Senior Lecturer, Professor, Institute for Retail Studies, Department of Marketing, Stirling University. Recreation: watching sport, especially rugby. Address: (b.) Institute for Retail Studies, Stirling University, Stirling FK9 4LA; T.-01786 467384; e-mail: Leigh.Sparks@stir.ac.uk

Spaull, Alison Mary, BSc, PhD, MBA. Director, Chief Scientist Office, Scottish Executive Health Department, since 1996; Member, Court, Glasgow University, since 2000; b. 5.8.52, Ewell. Educ. Surbiton High School; Rosebery County Grammar School; Reading University. Researcher, Rothamsted Experimental Station, 1976-85; Crop Protection Adviser, East of Scotland College of Agriculture, 1985-90; Technical Secretary, Scottish Agricultural College, 1990-93; Research and Development Manager, Scottish Agriculture College, 1993-95; Health Services Research Manager, Chief Scientist Office, Scottish Office Department of Health, 1996. English Speaking Union Thynne Scholar, 1988; Council Member, Association of Applied Biologists, 1987 and 1989-91. Recreations: gardening; walking; equestrianism; the arts. Address: (b.) St Andrew's House, Regent Road, Edinburgh.

Speakman, Professor John Roger, BSc, PhD, DSc. Professor of Zoology, Aberdeen University, since 1997; Head, Division of Appetite and Energy Balance, Rowett Research Institute, since 2000; b. 29.11.58, Leigh; m., Mary Magdelene; 1 s.; 1 d. Educ. Leigh Grammar School; Stirling University. Lecturer, 1989, Senior Lecturer, 1993, Reader, 1995, Aberdeen University; Chairman, Aberdeen Centre for Energy Regulation and Obesity, since 1998; Royal Society Leverhulme Senior Research Fellow, 2000. Publication: Body Composition Analysis: A Handbook of Non-Invasive Methods, 2001. Address: (b.) Department of Zoology, Aberdeen University, Aberdeen AB24 2TZ; T.-01224 272879.

Speirs, William MacLeod, BA (Hons), DUniv, FRSA. General Secretary, Scottish TUC; Member: Scottish Arts Council, Scottish Council Development and Industry, Central Arbitration Committee, Employment Appeal Tribunal, Scottish Enterprise Glasgow; Director: Workbase Scotland, Scottish Low Pay Unit; Chairperson, 7:84 Theatre

Company (Scotland), since 1988; b. 8.3.52, Dumbarton; 1 s.; 1 d. Educ. John Neilson High School, Paisley; Strathclyde University. Assistant Secretary, Scottish TUC, 1979-88. Chairperson, Labour Party in Scotland, 1987-88; Honorary Vice President, Scottish Friends of Palestine; Director, Scottish Trade Union Review. Recreations: reading; losing money on horses; watching St. Mirren F.C. Address: (b.) STUC, 333 Woodlands Road, Glasgow G3 6NG; T.-0141-337 8100.

Spence, Alan, MA. Writer (poet, playwright, novelist, short-story writer); b. 5.12.47, Glasgow; m., Janani (Margaret). Educ. Allan Glen's School, Glasgow; Glasgow University. Writer in Residence, Glasgow University, 1975-77, Deans Community School, 1978, Traverse Theatre, Edinburgh, 1983, City of Edinburgh, 1986-87, Edinburgh University, 1989-82, Aberdeen University, 1996-2001 (Professor in Creative Writing, since 2001); winner, People's Prize, 1991; Macallan/Scotland on Sunday Short Story competition, 1993; McVitie's Prize, 1996; TMA Drama Award, 1996. Publications: poetry: ah!; Glasgow Zen; Seasons of the Heart; short stories: Its Colours They Are Fine, Stone Garden; novels: The Magic Flute, Way to Go; plays: Sailmaker; Space Invaders; Changed Days. Recreations: meditation; running; playing flute. Address: 21 Waverley Park, Edinburgh, EH8 8ER; T.-0131-661 8403; e-mail: janaka.spence@virgin.net

Spence, Professor Alastair Andrew, CBE, MD, FRCA, FRCP (Glas & Edin), FRCS (Ed & Eng), Hon FDS, RCS Eng. Professor of Anaesthetics, Edinburgh University, 1984-98, Professor Emeritus, since 1998; President, Royal College of Anaesthetists, 1991-94; b. 18.9.36, Glasgow; m., Maureen Isobel Aitchison; 2 s. Educ. Ayr Academy; Glasgow University. Professor and Head, University Department of Anaesthesia, Western Infirmary, Glasgow, 1969-84; Editor, British Journal of Anaesthesia, 1973-83 (Chairman of the Board and Trustee, 1983-93); Hunterian Professor, Royal College of Surgeons of England, 1974; Joseph Clover Lecturer, 1990; Member, Advisory Committee on Distinction Awards, since 1992; Medical Director, Scottish Advisory Committee on Distinction Awards, 1996-2000. Recreations: golf; gardening. Address: (h.) Harewood, Kilmacolm, PA13 4HX; T.-01505 872962.

Spence, James William, KFO (Norway), RON (Netherlands), DL (Orkney), BSc, MNI, MICS. Master Mariner, since 1971; Shipbroker, since 1975; Company Director, since 1977; Honorary Sheriff, Grampian Highland and Islands (Kirkwall), since 2000; b. 19.1.45, St. Ola, Orkney; m., Margaret Paplay Stevenson (deceased); 3 s. Educ. Leith Nautical College, Edinburgh; Robert Gordon's Institute of Technology, Aberdeen; University of Wales, Cardiff. Merchant Navy, 1961-74 (Member, Nautical Institute, 1972, Member, Royal Institute of Navigation, 1971); Micoperi SpA, 1974-75 (Temporary Assistant Site Co-ordinator on Scapa Flow Project); John Jolly (Shipbrokers, Stevedores, Shipping and Forwarding Agents) since 1975 (Manager, 1975, Junior Partner, 1976-77, Proprietor and Managing Director, since 1977). Vice-Consul for Norway, 1976, Consul, 1978; Vice-Consul for the Netherlands, 1978-94; Member, Kirkwall Community Council, 1978-82; Member, Orkney Pilotage Committee, 1979-88; Chairman, Kirkwall Port Employers' Association, 1979-87 (Member, since 1975); Chairman, RNLI, Kirkwall Lifeboat Station Branch Committee, 1997 (Station Hon. Secretary, 1987-96, Deputy Launching Authority, 1976-87); Chairman, Pier Arts Centre Trust, 1989-91 (Trustee, 1980-91); Chairman, Association of Honorary Norwegian Consuls in the UK and Ireland, 1993-95. Recreations: oenology; equestrian matters; Orcadian history. Address: (h.) Alton House, Kirkwall, Orkney KW15 1NA; T.-01856 872268; e-mail: operations@johnjolly.co.uk

Spence, Professor John, ARCST, BSc, MEng, PhD, DSc, FREng, FRSE, FRSA, CEng, FIMechE. Trades House of Glasgow Professor of Mechanics of Materials, Strathclyde University, since 1982; b. 5.11.37, Chapelhall; m., Margaret Gray Hudson; 2 s. Educ. Airdrie Academy; Royal College of Science and Technology; Sheffield University. Engineering apprenticeship, Stewarts & Lloyds (now British Steel Corporation); Senior Engineer, then Head of Stress Analysis, Babcock & Wilcox Research Division; Strathclyde University: Lecturer, 1966, Senior Lecturer, Reader, Professor since 1979, Deputy Principal, Pro-Vice Principal and Vice Principal, 1994-2001. Served on many national committees: Past President, Institution of Mechanical Engineers; EPSRC; British Standards Institution; Engineering Professors Council Senate and BER; Research Assessment Exercise Panel 30; Accreditation Board, Hong Kong Institution of Engineers; Scottish Higher Education Funding Council; Royal Academy of Engineering Council. Address: (b.) Department of Mechanical Engineering, Strathclyde University, 75 Montrose Street, Glasgow, G1 1XJ; T.-0141-548 4497/2324.

Spencely, John Despenser, MA, BArch, DipTP, RIBA, PPRIAS, MRTPI, FCIArb. Chairman, Buildings Investigation Centre; b. 5.10.39, Westerham, England; m., Marilyn Anne Read; 1 d. (by pr. m.). Educ. Bryanston School; Cambridge University; Edinburgh University. Consultant Architect, Town Planner, Arbiter; former Member, Scottish Building Contract Committee; President: Edinburgh Architectural Association, 1984-86, Royal Incorporation of Architects in Scotland, 1989-91; Lay Member, Scottish Solicitors Discipline Tribunal; Board Member, Scottish Homes; Visiting Professor, Napier University; Freeman of the City of London; Liveryman, Worshipful Company of Arbitrators. Recreations: sailing; reading; collecting some unfashionable 20th century authors; making jam. Address: (b.) 6 Darnaway Street, Edinburgh EH3 6BG; T.-0131-220 6808.

Spencer, Alec P., BA (Hons), MA. Director, Rehabilitation and Care, Scottish Prison Service, since 2001; b. 12.3.46, London; m., Joan; 2 s.; 1 d. Educ. Dame Alice Owen School; Keele University. Joined Scottish Prison Service, 1972, as Assistant Governor: Polmont Borstal, Perth Prison, Glenochil; Deputy Governor, Aberdeen Prison, 1978; Prison Department HQ, 1981; Warden, Glenochil D.C., 1983; Deputy Governor, Glenochil Complex, 1987; Governor, Dungavel Prison, 1989; Governor, Peterhead Prison, 1992; Operational Adviser, PFI prison project SPS HQ, 1996; Governor, Edinburgh Prison, 1996; Governor, Glenochil Prison and Young Offenders' Institution, 2000. Chairman, Scottish Forum on Prisons and Families, 1990-2000; Butler Trust Award, 1987; Editor, ASPG Journal, 1982-90; Chairman, Governors' Committee, NUCPS, 1991-92; Hon. Senior Research Fellow, Dundee University, 1995-98; Research Associate, Centre for Law and Society, Edinburgh University; Non-Executive Director, INCLUDEM. Publication: Working with Sex Offenders in Prisons and through Release to the Community, 1999. Recreations: music; walking; writing; collecting Penguin books. Address: (b.) Scottish Prison Service HQ, Calton House, 5 Redheughs Rigg, Edinburgh EH12 9HW; T.-0131-244 8696; e-mail: alec.spencer@sps.gov.uk

Spencer, Professor Jonathan, MA, AM, DPhil. Professor of the Anthropology of South Asia, Edinburgh University, since 1999; Director, Graduate School of Social and Political Studies, Edinburgh University, since 2000; b. 23.12.54, Redhill; m., Dr Janet Carsten; 1 d. Educ. Richard Taunton College, Southampton; Edinburgh University; University of Chicago; Oxford University. Field Research, Sri Lanka, 1981-83 and 1984; Lecturer: University of Sussex, 1987; London School of Economics, 1989; Edinburgh University, 1990. Publications: A Sinhala Village in a Time of

Trouble, 1990; Sri Lanka: History and Roots of Conflict, 1990; Encyclopedia of Social and Cultural Anthropology, 1996. Recreations: food; drink; family; music. Address: (b.) Department of Social Anthropology, Edinburgh University, Edinburgh, EH8 9LL; T.-0131-650 3944.

Spencer, Very Rev. Paul Francis, CP. Rector, Saint Mungo's, Glasgow, since 1996; Catholic Chaplain, Glasgow Caledonian University, since 2001; b. 2.3.54. Educ. Saint Mungo's Academy, Glasgow; University College, Dublin; Milltown Institute, Dublin; Pontifical Gregorian University, Rome. Professed as Member of Passionist Congregation, 1977; Ordained Priest, 1980; Vicar, Saint Mungo's, Glasgow, 1981-86; Master of Novices, Cochin, India, 1986-87; post-graduate studies, Rome, 1987-89; Rector, Mission Anglophone de France, Paris, 1989-96; Provincial Consultor, Congregation of the Passion, 1992-2000; Postulator of the Cause of Canonisation of Elizabeth Prout CP, since 1994; Member, Historical Commission for the Cause of Ignatius Spencer CP, since 1993; awarded Cross Pro piis meritis, Sovereign Military Order of Malta, 1995; Chairman, Parson Street Trust, since 1999. Publications: To Heal the Broken-Hearted: The Life of Blessed Charles of Mount Argus, 1988; As a Seal upon your Heart: The Life of Saint Paul of the Cross, Founder of the Passionists, 1994. Recreation: music. Address: (h.) Saint Mungo's Retreat, 52 Parson Street, Glasgow G4 0RX; T.-0141-552 1823.

Spens, Michael Colin Barkley, MA. Headmaster, Fettes College, Edinburgh, since 1998; b. 22.9.50, Weybridge; m., Deborah Susan; 1 s.; 2 d. Educ. Marlborough College; Selwyn College, Cambridge. United Biscuits Plc, 1972-74; Radley College, Oxon, 1974-93 (Assistant Master, 1974-93, i/c Careers, 1974-84, Housemaster, 1984-93); Headmaster, Caldicott, Farnham Common, 1993-98. Recreations: golf; running; wood-turning; bridge; geology; mountaineering; electronics. Address: (h.) Headmasters' Lodge, Fettes College, Edinburgh EH4 1QX; T.-0131-311 6701.

Spiers, Rev. John McLaren, LTh, MTh. Minister, Orchardhill Church, Giffnock, since 1977; b. 12.12.43, Edinburgh; m., Janet Diane Watson; 2 d. Educ. George Watson's College, Edinburgh; Glasgow University. Probationer Assistant, Drumchapel Old Parish Church, Glasgow, 1971-72; Minister, South Church, Barrhead, 1972-77; Convener, Board of World Mission, 1996-2000; Moderator, Presbytery of Glasgow, 2001-02. Recreations: music; art; family life. Address: 23 Huntly Avenue, Giffnock, Glasgow, G46 6LW.

Spilg, Walter Gerson Spence, MB, ChB (Hons), FRCPath, FRCPG. Consultant Pathologist, Victoria Infirmary, Glasgow, 1972-99, in Administrative Charge, 1986-99; Honorary Clinical Senior Lecturer, Glasgow University, since 1973; b. 27.10.37, Glasgow; m., Vivien Anne Burns; 1 s.; 2 d. Educ. Hutchesons' Boys' Grammar School, Glasgow; Glasgow University. Registrar in Pathology, Glasgow Royal Infirmary, 1965-68; Senior Registrar in Pathology, Victoria Infirmary, Glasgow, 1968-69; Lecturer in Pathology, Glasgow University (Western Infirmary), 1969-72. Former President, Caledonian Branch, Association of Clinical Pathologists; Examiner, Royal College of Physicians and Surgeons of Glasgow. Recreation: bridge. Address: (h.) 4B Newton Court, Newton Mearns, Glasgow, G77 5QL.

Spowart, Jim, FCIBS, FCIB. Chief Executive, Intelligent Finance, since 1999; Non-Executive Director, St James's Place Capital, since 2000; b. 19.11.50, Cowdenbeath; m., Janis; 2 s. Prior to 1992, worked for 24 years in various areas of RBS; GM/Director, RoyScot Financial Services, 1992-93; MD, Direct Line Financial Services, 1993-97; MD, Direct Line Life and Direct Line Unit Trust, 1996-97; MD, Standard Life Bank, 1997-99; joined Halifax (now HBOS), 1999, to build a new bank (Intelligent Finance fully launched 2000). Recreations: golfing; reading; gardening. Address: (b.) 8 Lochside Avenue, Edinburgh Park, Edinburgh; T.-0131-658 2000.

Spratt, Col. Douglas Norman, CBE, TD. Director, Cameo of Edinburgh, since 1984; b. 18.9.20, Ramsgate; m., Margaret; 1 d (deceased). Educ. Sir Roger Manwood's Grammar School, Sandwich, Kent. Honorary Colonel 71 (Scottish) Engineer Regiment (V), 1976-90; Chairman, Lowland TAVR, 1980-84; President, Edinburgh Branch, Chartered Institute of Marketing; Chairman, Friends of the Reserve Forces Association, Scotland; Regional Chairman, Action Research in Scotland; Member, High Constables of Edinburgh; Deputy Lieutenant, City of Edinburgh; Associate Member of the Military Attaches London. Recreations: fishing; sailing. Address: (h.) 6 Fernielaw Avenue, Edinburgh, EH13 OEE; T.-0131-441 1962.

Sprent, Professor Janet I., OBE, BSc, ARCS, PhD, DSc, FRSE. Emeritus Professor of Plant Biology, Dundee University; b. 10.1.34, Slough; m., Emeritus Professor Peter Sprent. Educ. Slough High School; Imperial College, London; Tasmania University. Has spent 31 years at Dundee University; research focussed on nitrogen fixing legumes, both tree and crop species; currently involved in international collaboration, mainly in Africa and Brazil; Dean of Science and Engineering, 1987-89; Deputy Principal of the University, 1995-98. Council Member, NERC, 1991-95; Member, Scottish Higher Education Funding Council, 1992-96; Member, Joint Nature Conservation Committee, 1994-2000; Member, then Chairman, Board of Governors, Macaulay Land Use Research Institute, 1989-2001; Member, Board, Scottish Natural Heritage, since 2001. Publications: five books and over 200 chapters/papers. Recreations: research; hill-walking. Address: 32 Birkhill Avenue, Wormit, Fife DD6 8PW; T.-01382 541706; e-mail: jisprent@aol.com

Sprot of Haystoun, Lt.-Col. Aidan Mark, MC, JP. Landowner (Haystoun Estate) and Farmer, since 1965; b. 17.6.19, Lilliesleaf. Educ. Belhaven Hill; Stowe. Commissioned, Royal Scots Greys, 1940; served Palestine, 1941-42, Western Desert, 1942-43, Italy, 1943-44, NW Europe, 1944-45; continued serving with Regiment in Germany until 1952, Libya, Egypt and Jordan, 1952-55, UK, 1955-58, Germany, 1958-62; Adjutant, 1944-45; Commanding Officer, 1959-62; retired, 1962. County Councillor, Peeblesshire, 1963-75; DL (Peeblesshire), 1966-80; Lord Lieutenant, Tweeddale, 1980-94; Member, Queen's Bodyguard for Scotland (Royal Company of Archers), since 1950; County Director, Peeblesshire Branch, Red Cross, 1966-74, Patron, since 1983; Badge of Honour, British Red Cross Society, 1998; County Commissioner, Peeblesshire Scout Association, 1968-73, Chairman, 1975-80, President, 1980-94; President, Borders Area Scout Association, 1994-99; Scout Medal of Merit, 1994; Honorary Secretary, Royal Caledonian Hunt, 1964-74; President, Lowlands of Scotland TA&VRA, 1986-89; President, Lothian Federation of Boys' Clubs, 1989-96, now Hon. Vice-President; Honorary Freeman, Tweeddale District, 1994; Vice-President, Royal Highland and Agricultural Society of Scotland, 1986; Trustee, Royal Scottish Agricultural Benevolent Institution, 1989-98; Member, Church of Scotland Service Chaplains Committee, 1974-82 and 1985-92; Honorary President, Peebles Branch, Royal British Legion Scotland, since 1990; Honorary President, Tweeddale Society, since 1994. Publication: Swifter than Eagles (war memoirs). Recreations: country sports; motor cycle touring. Address: (h.) Crookston, by Peebles, EH45 9JQ; T.-Kirkton Manor 740209.

Sprott, Gavin, MA, FSAScot. Keeper, Department of Social and Technological History, National Museums of Scotland; b. 23.7.43, Dundee; m., Maureen Turnbull; 2 s.; 1 d. Educ. Edinburgh University. Research Assistant, Scottish

Country Life Section, National Museum of Antiquities of Scotland, 1972-79; Curator, Scottish Agricultural Museum, 1979-96. Recreations: cycling; walking. Address: (b.) National Museums of Scotland, Chambers Street, Edinburgh, EH1 1JF; T.-0131-247 4256.

Sproul-Cran, Robert Scott, MA (Cantab), PhD. Managing Director, Northlight Productions Ltd., since 1991; b. 14.8.50; m., Elizabeth Ann; 3 s.; 1 d. Educ. Daniel Stewart's College; Pembroke College, Cambridge; Edinburgh University. Trainee, Phillips & Drew, Stockbrokers, London, 1971-72; Announcer, then Head of Presentation, BBC Radio Scotland, 1979-85; Radio Manager, BBC Aberdeen, 1986-90; Scottish Correspondent, BBC Daytime Television, 1990-91; freelance Graphic Designer and Underwater Photographer, since 1976; Winner, Scottish Corporate Communications Award, RTS Award for video graphics; illustrated Maurice Lindsay's Glasgow; exhibited, Aberdeen Artists' annual exhibition. Publication: Thicker than Water (novel and screenplay).Recreations: oil painting; printmaking; windsurfing; sub aqua; playing bad rock guitar. Address: (b.) The Media Village, Grampian TV, Queens Cross, Aberdeen AB15 4XJ; T.-01224 646460.

Spurway, Professor Neil Connell, MA, PhD. Professor of Exercise Physiology, University of Glasgow, 1996-2001; Chair, British Association of Sport and Exercise Sciences, 2000-02; b. 22.8.36, Bradford; m., Alison Katherine Middleton; 3 s. Educ. The Grammar School, Falmouth, Cornwall; Jesus College, Cambridge University. Assistant, then Lecturer, then Senior Lecturer in Physiology, University of Glasgow, 1963-96. Chair, Physiology Section, British Association of Sports Scientists, 1991-93; Chair, Glasgow Gifford Lectureships Committee, 1994-98; Member, Exercise Physiology Steering Group, BOA, since 1991; Fellow, European College of Sports Science. Publications: Humanity, Environment and God; many papers and textbook chapters. Recreations: dinghy racing; distance running; philosophy; theatre. Address: 76 Fergus Drive, Glasgow G20 6AP; T.-0141-946 3336; e-mail: N.Spurway@bio.gla.ac.uk

Squire, Rachel Anne, BA, CQSW. MP (Labour), Dunfermline West, since 1992; b. 13.7.54, Carshalton, Surrey; m., Allan Mason. Educ. Godolphin and Latymer Girls' School; Durham University. Social Worker, Birmingham Social Services, 1975-81; National Union of Public Employees, 1981-92. Address: (b.) House of Commons, London, SW1A 0AA.

Stacey, Valerie Elizabeth, QC, LLB (Hons). Queen's Counsel, since 1999; b. 25.5.54, Lanark; m., Andrew; 2 s. Educ. Elgin Academy; Edinburgh University. Solicitor, 1978; Advocate, 1987; Advocate Depute, 1993-96; Standing Junior Counsel, Home Office in Scotland, 1996-99; Temporary Sheriff, 1997-99. Recreation: listening to music. Address: (b.) Advocates Library, Parliament House, Edinburgh EH1 1RF; T.-0131-226 5071.

Stachura, Peter Desmond, MA, PhD, DLitt, FRHistS. Reader in Modern History, Stirling University, since 1983; Director, Centre for Research in Polish History, Stirling University; b. 2.8.44, Galashiels; m., Kay Higgins; 1 s.; 1 d. Educ. St. Mirin's RC Academy, Paisley; Glasgow University; East Anglia University. Research Fellow, Institut für Europäische Geschichte, Mainz, Germany, 1970-71; Lecturer in History, Stirling University, 1971-83. Chairman (and Founder), The Polish Society, since 1996. Publications: Nazi Youth in the Weimar Republic, 1975; The Weimar Era and Hitler: a critical bibliography, 1977; The Shaping of the Nazi State (Editor), 1978; The German Youth Movement, 1900-1945, 1981; Gregor Strasser and the Rise of Nazism, 1983; The Nazi Machtergreifung (Editor), 1983; Unemployment and the Great Depression in Weimar Germany (Editor), 1986; The Weimar Republic and the Younger Proletariat: an economic and social analysis, 1989; Political Leaders in Weimar Germany: a biographical study, 1992; Themes of Modern Polish History (Editor), 1992; Poland Between the Wars, 1918-1939 (Editor), 1998; Poland in the Twentieth Century, 1999; Perspectives on Polish History (Editor), 2001. Recreations: supporting Celtic FC; discovering Poland; gardening. Address: (h.) Ashcroft House, Chalton Road, Bridge of Allan, FK9 4EF; T.-01786 832793.

Stack, Professor Margaret M., BE, MSc, PhD, EurIng, CEng, FIEI, FICorr, FIM. Professor, Mechanical Engineering, University of Strathclyde, since 2001; b. 25.10.61; m., Dr Stuart Lyon. Educ. National University of Ireland; University of Manchester, UMIST. Lecturer, UMIST, 1992-99. Recreations: literature; oil painting. Address: Hagwood, 6 Queen Street, Helensburgh; e-mail: m.m.stack@mecheng.strath.ac.uk

Stafford, William, MIWM, MREHIS. Director of Community Services, East Ayrshire Council, since 1995; b. 25.3.54, Galston; m., Margaret Ann; 1 s. Educ. Galston High School; Loudoun Academy; College of Food Technology, Glasgow. Ayr County Council, 1971-75; various posts in Environmental Health, Cumnock and Doon Valley District Council, 1975-95. Recreations: motor sport; gardening. Address: (b.) Council Headquarters, London Road, Kilmarnock; T.-01563 576023.

Stagg, Ronald Michael, BSc, MSc, PhD. Deputy Director, Fisheries Research Services, Marine Laboratory, Aberdeen, since 2001; b. 13.7.53, Llanfairfechan; m., Gillian Bishop; 1 s.; 2 d. Educ. Friars Grammar School, Bangor; University College of North Wales, Bangor; University of Aston in Birmingham; Exeter University. Post-doctoral Research Assistant, Exeter University; Lecturer in Marine Animal Physiology, Heriot-Watt University; Marine Laboratory, Aberdeen: Ecotoxicology Section Leader, UG7, 1988-97, Programme Manager, Aquaculture and Aquatic Animal Health, 1997-2001. Recreation: part-time farmer. Address: (b.) PO Box 101, Victoria Road, Aberdeen AB11 9DB; T.-01224 295540.

Stair, 14th Earl of (John David James Dalrymple); b. 4.9.61, Edinburgh. Army Officer, 1981-86; Land Owner/Manager, since 1989. Board Member, Dumfries and Galloway Enterprise; Board Member, Scottish Environment Protection Agency, West. Recreation: outdoor activities. Address: (b.) Stair Estates, Rephad, Stranraer DG9 8BX; T.-01776 702024.

Stalley, Professor Richard Frank, MA, BPhil. Professor of Ancient Philosophy, Glasgow University, since 1997; Head of Philosophy Department, since 2001; b. 26.11.42, Leamington; m., Ellen May Ladd; 1 s.; 1 d. Educ. De Aston School; Worcester College, Oxford; Harvard University. Lecturer in Moral Philosophy, Glasgow University, 1968-84; Senior Lecturer in Philosophy, 1984-97. Publications include: An Introduction to Plato's Laws, 1983; Aristotle's Politics, 1995; many articles on ancient philosophy and on Scottish philosophy. Recreations: walking; opera. Address: (b.) Philosophy Department, Glasgow University, Glasgow G12 8QQ; T.-0141-330 5045.

Stansfeld, John Raoul Wilmot, MBE, JP, DL, MA (Oxon), FIFM. Director, Joseph Johnston & Sons Ltd., since 1962; b. 15.1.35, London; m., Rosalinde Rachel Buxton; 3 s. Educ. Eton; Christ Church, Oxford. Lt., Gordon Highlanders, 1954-58; Chairman, North Esk District Salmon Fishery Board, 1967-80; Esk Fishery Board Committee, 1980-85; Vice Chairman, Association of Scottish District Salmon Fishery Boards, 1970-85; Director and Chairman, Montrose Chamber of Commerce, 1984-97; Editor, Salmon Net Magazine, 1978-85; Chairman, Scottish Fish Farmers Association, 1970-73; Secretary, Diocese of Brechin, 1968-76. Member, Royal Company of Archers

(Queen's Bodyguard for Scotland). Recreations: reading; jigsaw puzzles; trees. Address: (h.) Dunninald, Montrose, Angus, DD10 9TD; T.-01674 672666.

Stark, Edi, MA (Hons), ALA. Broadcaster and Journalist; BBC Radio Scotland: Presenter/Producer, Stark Talk, Presenter, Making the Grade; Radio 4: Presenter/Producer, The Consultants, Managing Life, Cornton Vale; b. Edinburgh; m., Gavin Stark; 1 s.; 1 d. Educ. Aberdeen University; RGIT. Community Librarian, Glasgow and Livingston; Northsound Radio: Community Co-ordinator, 1981, Senior Producer, 1982, Head of Speech Programming, 1983-89; freelance journalist, since 1990. Recreations: conversation, food and drink, travel, reading, contemporary art. Address: (b.) c/o BBC Scotland, Beechgrove Terrace, Aberdeen, AB9 2ZT; T.- 01224 384883.

Steedman, Professor Mark, BSc (Hons), PhD. Professor of Cognitive Science, Edinburgh University, since 1998; Director, Institute for Communicating Collaborative Systems, Edinburgh University, since 1998; b. 18.9.46, Middlesex; m., Professor Bonnie Webber. Educ. Watford Boys Grammar School; University of Sussex; Edinburgh University. Research Associate, School of Artificial Intelligence, Edinburgh University, 1969-72; Research Fellow, Edinburgh University, 1972-73; Research Fellow, University of Sussex. 1973-76; Lecturer, Edinburgh University, 1983-86; Reader, Edinburgh University, 1986-88; Associate Professor, Computational Linguistics, University of Pennsylvania, 1989-92; Professor of Computer and Information Science, University of Pennsylvania, 1992-98. Joint Founding Editor, Language and Cognitive Processes, 1984-92; Senior Editor, Cognitive Science, 1997-99; Advisory Editor: Cognition, since 1980; Linguistics, 1979-92; Journal of Semantics, since 1985; Language and Cognitive Processes, since 1993. Publications: Surface Structure and Interpretation, Linguistic Monograph 30, 1996; The Syntactic Process, 2000. Recreations: jazz; walking. Address: (b.) ICCS, 2 Buccleuch Place, Edinburgh, EH8 9LW; T.-0131-650 4361.

Steedman, Robert Russell, OBE, RSA, RIBA, FRSA, FRIAS, ALI, DA, MLA. Partner, Morris and Steedman, Architects and Landscape Architects; b. 3.1.29, Batu Gajah, Malaysia; m., 1, Susan Scott (m. diss.); 1 s.; 2 d.; 2, Martha Hamilton. Educ. Loretto School; School of Architecture, Edinburgh College of Art; Pennsylvania University. Governor, Edinburgh College of Art, 1974-86; Commissioner, Countryside Commission for Scotland, 1980-88; Chairman, Central Scotland Woodlands Project, 1984-88; Association for the Protection of Rural Scotland Award Panel, 1995-99; ARSA, 1973, Academician, 1979; Council Member, RSA, 1981 (Deputy President, 1982-83, 1990-2000, Secretary, 1983-91); Commissioner, Royal Fine Art Commission for Scotland, 1983-96; former Member, Council, RIAS; Member, Council, National Trust for Scotland, since 1999; nine Civic Trust Awards, 1963-78; British Steel Award, 1971; RIBA Award for Scotland, 1974; European Heritage Medal, 1975; Association for the Protection of Rural Scotland, 1977; Borders Region Award, 1984. Address: (h.) 11B Belford Mews, Edinburgh; T.-0131-225 1697.

Steel of Aikwood, Rt. Hon. Lord (David Steel), KBE, PC, DL. MSP (Liberal Democrat), Lothians, since 1999, Presiding Officer, Scottish Parliament, since 1999; MP, Tweeddale, Ettrick and Lauderdale, 1983-97 (Roxburgh, Selkirk and Peebles, 1965-83); Leader, Liberal Party, 1976-88; b. 31.3.38, Kirkcaldy; m., Judith MacGregor; 2 s.; 1 d. Educ. Prince of Wales School, Nairobi; George Watson's College, Edinburgh; Edinburgh University (MA, LLB). Assistant Secretary, Scottish Liberal Party, 1962-64; Interviewer, BBC TV Scotland, 1964-65; Presenter, weekly religious programme, STV, 1966-67, for Granada, 1969, for BBC, 1971-76; Liberal Chief Whip, 1970-75; Sponsor, Private Member's Bill to reform law on abortion, 1966-67; President, Anti-Apartheid Movement of Great Britain, 1966-69; Chairman, Shelter, Scotland, 1969-73; Member, British Council of Churches, 1971-75; Past President, Liberal International (President, 1994-96); Rector, Edinburgh University, 1982-85; Chubb Fellow, Yale, 1987; Hon. DUniv (Stirling), 1991; DLitt, University of Buckingham, 1994; Hon. Doctorate, Heriot Watt University, Edinburgh, 1996; HonLLD, Edinburgh, 1997; HonLLD, Strathclyde, 2000; HonLLD, Aberdeen 2001; awarded Freedom of Tweeddale, 1988, and Ettrick and Lauderdale, 1990; The Commander's Cross of the Order of Merit (Germany), 1992; DL, 1989; contested Central Italy seat, European elections, 1989; President, Liberal International, 1994-96; former Vice President, Countryside Alliance. Publications: Boost for the Borders, 1964; Out of Control, 1968; No Entry, 1969; The Liberal Way Forward, 1975; Militant for the Reasonable Man, 1977; High Ground of Politics, 1979; A House Divided, 1980; Border Country (with Judy Steel), 1985; The Time Has Come (with David Owen), 1987; Mary Stuart's Scotland (with Judy Steel), 1987; Against Goliath, 1989. Recreations: angling; vintage motoring. Address: (b.) Scottish Parliament, George IV Bridge, Edinburgh EH99 1SP.

Steel, Professor Christopher Michael, BSc, MB, ChB, PhD, DSc, FRCPEdin, FRCPath, FRCSEdin, FRSE, FMedSci. Professor in Medical Science, St. Andrews University, since 1994; b. 25.1.40, Buckhaven; m., Dr. Judith Margaret Spratt; 2 s.; 1 d. Educ. Prince of Wales School, Nairobi; George Watson's College, Edinburgh; Edinburgh University. House Physician/House Surgeon/ Resident/Senior House Officer, Edinburgh Teaching Hospitals; Graduate Research Fellow in Medicine, 1968; joined MRC staff, 1971; MRC Travelling Research Fellow, University of Nairobi, 1972-73; Assistant Director, MRC Human Genetics Unit, Edinburgh, 1979. Editor, Disease Markers; published over 200 scientific papers and book chapters; Member, Government Gene Therapy Advisory Committee, 1994-99. Recreations: golf; skiing; music; theatre. Address: (b.) Bute Medical Building, St. Andrews, KY16 9TS; T.-01334 476161.

Steel, Very Rev. David, MA, BD, DD, LLD. Minister Emeritus, St. Michael's, Linlithgow, since 1977; b. 5.10.10, Hamilton; m., Sheila E.N. Martin (deceased); 3 s. (eldest son: Rt. Hon. Lord Steel of Aikwood, KBE, PC, DL (qv); second eldest son: Professor C. Michael Steel (qv); 2 d. Educ. St. John's Grammar School, Hamilton; Peterhead Academy; Robert Gordon's College, Aberdeen; Aberdeen University. Minister: Denbeath, Fife, 1936-41, Bridgend, Dumbarton, 1941-46; Associate Secretary, Foreign Mission Committee, Edinburgh, 1946-49; Minister, St. Andrew's, Nairobi and East Africa, 1949-57; Locum, St. Cuthbert's, Edinburgh, 1957-58; Minister, St. Michael's, Linlithgow, 1959-76; Moderator, General Assembly of the Church of Scotland, 1974-75; Visiting Preacher and Lecturer: in America, 1953-87, St. Columba's, Pont Street, 1977, Lausanne, 1978, Tanzania, 1980; Chairman, Callendar Park College of Education, 1972-78; Vice-President: Boys' Brigade, National Bible Society of Scotland, West Lothian Historical and Amenity Society. Publications: History of St. Michael's; The Belief; Preaching through the Year. Recreations: trout fishing; travel. Address: (h.) The Elms, Whitehouse Loan, Edinburgh EH9 2EZ; T.-0131-446 6207.

Steel, David Robert, MA, DPhil. Chief Executive, Clinical Standards Board for Scotland, since 1999; b. 29.5.48, Oxford; m., Susan Elizabeth Easton; 1 s.; 1 d. Educ. Birkenhead School; Jesus and Nuffield Colleges, Oxford. Lecturer in Public Administration, Exeter University, 1972-84; Assistant Director, National Association of Health Authorities, 1984-86; Secretary, Health Board Chairmen's and General Managers' Groups and SCOTMEG, 1986-90;

NHS in Scotland: Director of Corporate Affairs, 1990-95, Head of Health Gain, 1995-99. Address: (b.) Elliott House, 8–10 Hillside Crescent, Edinburgh EH7 5EA; T.-0131-623 4298; e-mail: davids@clinicalstandards.org

Steele, Professor Robert James Campbell, BSc, MB, ChB, MD, FRCSEd, FRCSEng, FCSHK. Professor of Surgical Oncology, Dundee University, since 1996; b. 5.3.52, Edinburgh; m., Susan Margaret Cachia; 1 s.; 2 d. Educ. Daniel Stewart's College, Edinburgh; Edinburgh University. Surgical training, Edinburgh, 1977-85; Lecturer in Surgery, Chinese University of Hong Kong, 1985-86; Lecturer in Surgery, Aberdeen University, 1986-90; Senior Lecturer and Reader in Surgery, Nottingham University, 1990-96. Publications: in breast cancer, gastrointestinal surgery and colorectal cancer. Recreations: music; Scottish country dancing; country sports. Address:(b.) Department of Surgery, Ninewells Hospital, Dundee DD1 9SY; T.-01382 660111; e-mail: r.j.c.steele@dundee.ac.uk

Steele, Thomas Graham. Chairman, Radio Borders; b. 11.5.45, Lanark; m., Fiona MacAuslane; 1 s.; 1 d. Educ. Larkhall Academy, Larkhall; Skerry's College, Glasgow. Lobby Correspondent, Scottish Daily Mail; TV and Radio Presenter, BBC Glasgow; Producer, BBC Local Radio; Broadcaster, Radio Clyde; Head of News and Current Affairs, Radio Forth; Director of Programmes (Group); Managing Director, Radio Forth; Chief Executive, Today FM, Dublin. Creator, Festival City Radio; Member, Radio Academy. Recreations: sailing; reading; conversation.

Steer, Christopher Richard, BSc (Hons), MB, ChB, DCH, FRCPE, FRCPCH. Consultant Paediatrician; Clinical Tutor, Department of Child Life and Health, Edinburgh University; Hon. Senior Lecturer, Department of Biomedical Science, St. Andrews University; Lead Clinician, Paediatrics and Child Health; b. 30.5.47, Clearbrook, near Plymouth; m., Patricia Mary Lennox. Educ. St. Olaves and St. Saviours Grammar School, London; Edinburgh University. Publications: Textbook of Paediatrics (Contributor); Treatment of Neurological Disorders (Contributor). Recreation: our garden. Address: (b.) Paediatric Unit, Kirkcaldy Acute Hospitals NHS Trust, Victoria Hospital, Kirkcaldy, Fife; T.-01592 643355.

Stein, Sheriff Colin Norman Ralph, BA, LLB. Sheriff of Tayside, Central and Fife, at Arbroath, since 1991; b. 14.6.48, Glasgow; m., Dr Linda McNaught; 1 s. Educ. Glenalmond College; Durham University; Edinburgh University. Admitted Member, Faculty of Advocates, 1975; appointed Sheriff, 1991. Recreations: gardening; fishing. Address: Sheriff's Chambers, Sheriff Court, High Street, Arbroath DD11 1HL; T.-01241 876600.

Steiner, Eleanor Margaret, MB, ChB, DPH, MFCM, MRCGP, MICGP, FRSH. Formerly General Practitioner at Appin and Easdale, formerly Principal in general practice in Perthshire; Executive Member, Scottish Child Law Centre; Medical Member, Disability Appeals Tribunal; Medical Assessor, Social Security Appeal Tribunals; Aeromedical Doctor, St. John International Air Ambulance; Member, SACOT (Scottish Advisory Committee on Telecommunications); Member, DIEL (OFTEL Committee for Advice on Disabled and Elderly); Founder, National Society of Associate GPs; b. 21.5.37, Glasgow; m., Mark Rudie Steiner (qv); 1 s. Educ. Albyn School, Aberdeen; Aberdeen University. Surgical Assistant, Freiburg; worked in hospitals, Switzerland, Canada, USA; Departmental Medical Officer/Senior Medical Officer, Aberdeen City; Organiser, Family Planning Services, Aberdeen; Member, Rubella Working Party; Adviser, Aberdeen Telephone Samaritans; Assistant, Psychiatry, Murray Royal Hospital, Perth; Contributor, Scientific Congress, Institute of Advanced Medical Sciences, Moscow. Recreations: sailing;

hill-walking; international contacts. Address: (h.) Atlantic House, Ellenabeich, Isle of Seil, by Oban, Argyll, PA34 4RF; T.-Balvicar 300 593.

Steiner, Mark Rudie, LLB, NP. Legal Consultant and Defence Lawyer; Chairman, Scotland Patients Association; former part-time Chairman, Social Security Appeal Tribunal and Disability Appeal Tribunal; former Scottish Representative, Consumers in the European Community Group; Member, Potato Marketing Board Consumer Liaison Committee; Member, National Pharmaceutical Consultative Committee Working Group on Quality Assurance; m., Dr. Eleanor Steiner, DPH, MFCM, MRCGP, MICGP; 1 s. Educ. Aberdeen University. Editor, Canadian Broadcasting Corporation, Toronto and Montreal; Editor, Swiss Broadcasting Corporation, Berne; Procurator Fiscal in Scotland; Partner and Director of various firms and companies; Past Chairman, Perth Community Relations Council; Delegate, Scottish Council for Racial Equality; neutral observer at various overseas political trials; contributor to various international journals; retired Principal, Goodman Steiner & Co., Defence Lawyers and Notaries in Central Scotland; former Member, Scottish Consumer Council. Publications: travel and children's books. Recreations: sailing; developing international exchanges. Address: (h.) Atlantic House, Ellenabeich, Isle of Seil, by Oban, Argyll, PA34 4RF; T.-Balvicar 300 593.

Stell, Geoffrey Percival, BA, FSA, FSA Scot. Head of Architecture, Royal Commission on the Ancient and Historical Monuments of Scotland, since 1991; b. 21.11.44, Keighley; m., Evelyn Florence Burns; 1 s.; 1 d. Educ. Keighley Boys' Grammar School; Leeds University; Glasgow University. Historic Buildings Investigator, RCAHMS, since 1969; sometime Chairman, Scottish Vernacular Buildings Working Group; sometime Chairman, Scottish Urban Archaeological Trust; sometime Vice-President, Council for Scottish Archaeology. Publications include: Dumfries and Galloway; Monuments of Industry (Co-author); Buildings of St. Kilda (Co-author); Loads and Roads in Scotland (Co-editor); The Scottish Medieval Town (Co-editor); Galloway, Land and Lordship (Co-Editor); Materials and Traditions in Scottish Building (Co-Editor). Recreations: gardening; music; travel, particularly in Scotland and France. Address: (h.) Beechmount, Borrowstoun, Bo'ness, West Lothian, EH51 9RS; T.-01506 510366; e-mail: geoffrey@stell9.freeserve.co.uk

Stephen, Alex, FCCA. Chief Executive, Dundee City Council, since 1995; (Chief Executive, City of Dundee District Council, 1991-95); b. 17.9.48, Dundee; m., Joyce; 1 s.; 1 d. Local government since 1970. Recreation: voluntary work. Address: (b.) 21 City Square, Dundee; T.-01382 434201.

Stephen, David, FCIPD. Chief Executive, Student Awards Agency for Scotland, since 1999; b. 21.11.47, Aberdeen; m., Rosalyn Jane; 1 s.; 1 d. Educ. Aberdeen Grammar School; Aberdeen University. Various posts, Scottish Office, 1972-98; Assistant Director of Manpower, NHS Management Executive, 1988-92; Head of Personnel Policy, Scottish Office, 1992-98; Director of Operations, SAAS, 1998-99. Recreations: golf; reading; Scotch Malt Whisky Society. Address: (b.) Gyleview House, 3 Redheughs Rigg, Edinburgh EH12 9HH; T.-0131-244 5867.

Stephen, Rev. Donald Murray, TD, MA, BD, ThM. Minister, Marchmont St. Giles' Parish Church, Edinburgh, 1974-2001; Secretary, Church of Scotland Chaplains' Association, since 1991; b. 1.6.36, Dundee; m., Hilda Swan Henriksen (deceased); 2 s.; 1 d; m., 2, Marjorie Roberta Bennet. Educ. Brechin High School; Richmond Grammar School, Yorkshire; Edinburgh University; Princeton Theological Seminary. Assistant Minister, Westover Hills Presbyterian Church, Arkansas, 1962-64; Minister,

Kirkoswald, 1964-74; Chaplain, TA, 1965-85 (attached to 4/5 Bn., RSF, 205 Scottish General Hospital, 2nd Bn., 52nd Lowland Volunteers); Convener, Committee on Chaplains to Her Majesty's Forces, General Assembly, 1985-89. Recreations: golf; curling. Address: 10 Hawkhead Crescent, Edinburgh EH16 6LR; T.-0131-658 1216; e-mail: DonaldMStephen@aol.com

Stephen, Eric John. Farmer; Director, McIntosh Donald Ltd., since 1995; b. 2.1.38, Turriff; m., Norah Winifred Anderson; 1 s.; 3 d. Educ. Inverurie Academy. Former Member, Scottish Agricultural Wages Board; former Convener, Employment and Technology Committee, National Farmers Union of Scotland; Elder, Auchterless Parish Church, 35 years; Past President, Aberdeen and Kincardine Executive, NFU of Scotland; Past President, Royal Northern Agricultural Society; Past President, Aberdeen Fatstock Club; former Director: Aberdeen and Northern Marts, Aberdeen and Northern Estates; President, Turriff Show, 1992; elected Grampian Regional Councillor, 1993; Regional Member, British Wool Marketing Board, since 1993. Recreation: bowling. Address: Lower Thorneybank, Rothienorman, Inverurie, AB51 8XT; T.-018885 11233.

Stephen, Professor Kenneth William, BDS, DDSc, HDDRCPS, FDSRCS, FDSRCPS. Emeritus Professor of Dental Public Health, Glasgow University; b. 1.10.37, Glasgow; m., Anne Seymour Gardiner; 1 s.; 1 d. Educ. Hillhead High School, Glasgow; Glasgow University. General Dental Practitioner, 1960-64; House Officer, Department of Oral Surgery, Glasgow Dental Hospital, 1964-65; Lecturer, Department of Conservative Dentistry, 1965-68, Lecturer, Department of Oral Medicine and Pathology, Glasgow University, 1968-71; Visiting Lecturer, Department of Oral Physiology, Newcastle-upon-Tyne University, 1969-70; Senior Lecturer, Department of Oral Medicine and Pathology, Glasgow University, 1971-80; Reader, 1980-84. Co-President, European Organisation for Caries Research, 1978-79. Recreations: swimming; hill-walking; skiing; gardening. Address: (b.) Dental School, 378 Sauchiehall Street, Glasgow, G2 3JZ; T.-0141-211 9853; e-mail: k.stephen@dental.gla.ac.uk

Stephen, Mark, DSD. Presenter, Out of Doors, Radio Scotland, since 1997; b. 11.9.60, Aberdeen; m., Jean; 3 d. Educ. Inverurie Academy; Royal Scottish Academy of Music and Drama. Commercial Producer, Northsound ILR; Assistant Floor Manager, Researcher, Trails Producer, Senior Announcer (TV), Radio Producer, BBC Scotland. Recreations: reading; water colour painting; DIY.

Stephen, Sheriff Mhairi Margaret, BA, LLB. Sheriff of Lothian and Borders at Edinburgh, since 1997; b. 22.1.54, Falkirk. Educ. George Watson's Ladies College; Edinburgh University. Allan McDougall and Co., SSC, 1976-97 (Partner, 1981-97). Recreations: curling; golf; hill-walking; music. Address: Sheriff's Chambers, Sheriff Court, 27 Chambers Street, Edinburgh EH1 1LB; T.-0131-225 2525.

Stephen, Nicol, LLB, DipLP. MSP (Liberal Democrat), Aberdeen South, since 1999; Deputy Minister for Education, Europe and External Affairs, Scottish Executive, since 2000, formerly Deputy Minister for Enterprise and Lifelong Learning; b. 23.3.60, Aberdeen; m., Caris Doig; 1 s.; 1 d. Educ. Robert Gordon's College, Aberdeen; Aberdeen University; Edinburgh University. Trainee Solicitor, C. & P.H. Chalmers, 1981-83; Solicitor, Milne and Mackinnon, 1983-88; Senior Manager, Touche Ross Corporate Finance, 1988-91; Member, Grampian Regional Council, 1982-92 (Chair, Economic Development, 1986-91); MP, Kincardine and Deeside, 1991-92; Scottish Liberal Democrats: Parliamentary Spokesperson for Small Businesses, 1991-92, Treasurer, 1992-95, Health Spokesperson, 1995-97; Education Spokesperson, 1997-99; Director, Project

Management, management consultancy company, 1992-99; Chairman for Rail Electrification Aberdeen to Edinburgh (CREATE), 1988-92; Director, Grampian Enterprise, 1989-92. Recreation: golf. Address: (b.) 361 Holburn Street, Aberdeen AB10 7FQ; T.-01224 252728; e-mail: nicol.stephen.msp@scottish.parliament.uk

Stephenson, Professor Roger Henry, BA (Hons), PhD. William Jacks Professor of German, Glasgow University, since 1994; Head, School of Modern Languages and Cultures, Glasgow University, since 2000; Director, Centre for Intercultural Studies, Glasgow University, since 1992; b. 5.11.46, Liverpool; m., Hedy. Educ. Holt High School, Liverpool; University College London. Lecturer, German, Glasgow University, 1972; Fellow, Cornell University, NY, USA, 1979; Glasgow University: Senior Lecturer, German, 1989; Head, German Department, 1990-97; Vice President, UK and Irish Conference, University Teachers of German, 1997-98. Publications: Goethe's Wisdom Literature, 1983; Goethe's Maximem und Relexionen, 1986; Goethe's Conception of Knowledge and Science, 1995; Goethe (Co-Author), 2000. Address: (b.) Department of German, Glasgow University, Glasgow, G12 8QL; T.-0141-330 4144; e-mail: R.Stephenson@german.arts.gla.ac.uk

Stevely, Professor William Stewart, BSc, DPhil, DipEd, FIBiol. Principal and Vice Chancellor, The Robert Gordon University, since 1997; Chairman, UCAS, since 2001 (Member, Board, since 2000); Member, UCAS Board, since 2000; b. 6.4.43, West Kilbride; m., Sheila Anne Stalker; 3 s.; 2 d. Educ. Ardrossan Academy; Glasgow University; Oxford University. Lecturer and Senior Lecturer in Biochemistry, Glasgow University, 1968-88; Professor and Head, Department of Biology, Paisley College, 1988-92; Vice Principal, Paisley University, 1992-97. Member, Scottish Higher Education Funding Council, 1994-97; Member, National Board for Nursing, Midwifery and Health Visiting for Scotland, since 1993; Board Member, Quality Assurance Agency for Higher Education, since 1998; Member, Institute for Learning and Teaching, 1999-2000. Address: (b.) The Robert Gordon University, Schoolhill, Aberdeen, AB10 1FR; T.-01224 262001.

Steven, John Douglas, MB, ChB, FRCOG. Consultant Obstetrician and Gynaecologist, Stirling Royal Infirmary, since 1981; b. 20.4.46, Perth. Educ. Douglas Ewart High School, Newton Stewart; Edinburgh University. Registrar in Obstetrics and Gynaecology, Western General Hospital, Edinburgh; Senior Registrar, Obstetrics and Gynaecology, Ninewells Hospital, Dundee. Address: (b.) Stirling Royal Infirmary, Stirling, FK8 2AU; T.-01786 434000.

Stevens, Claire, BA (Hons), DipMgt (Open), MICFM (Cert), FRSA. Director–Scotland, Community Service Volunteers, since 1998; b. 26.7.58, Sudbury, Suffolk. Educ. Sudbury Girls High; Sudbury Upper School; University of Warwick. Strathclyde Regional Council, 1981-84; Basildon District Council, 1984-85; Shelter Scotland, 1985-89; Age Concern Scotland, 1989-92; Scottish Council for Single Homeless, 1992-96; The Prince's Trust, 1996-98. Member, Management Committee, Muirhouse Housing Association, 1990-99; Director, Benchtours Theatre Company, since 1999 (current Chairman). Address: (b.) Wellgate House, 200 Cowgate, Edinburgh EH1 1NQ; T.-0131-622 7766.

Stevens, Professor Paul John, BA (Cantab), MA, PhD. Professor of Petroleum Policy and Economics, Dundee University, since 1993; b. 30.4.47, Liverpool; m., Cassie Stevens; 1 s.; 1 d. Educ. Alsop High School, Liverpool; Clare College, Cambridge; London University. Assistant Professor, American University of Beirut, 1973-75; oil consultant, Beirut, 1975-77; Assistant Professor, American University of Beirut, 1977-79; Lecturer in Economics, then Senior Lecturer, University of Surrey, 1979-93.

Publications: numerous books and papers on oil and gas. Recreations: travel; food and drink; golf; carpentry. Address: (b.) CEPMLP, Dundee University, Dundee, DD1 4HN; T.-01382 344300.

Stevenson, Celia Margaret Stirton. Head of Press and Public Relations, Scottish Screen, since 1998; b. Ballantrae; m., Charles William Forbes Judge; 2 s.; 1 d. Educ. Wellington School, Ayr; Edinburgh College of Art. Interior design business, 1970-80; Reporter/Presenter, West Sound, Ayr, 1981-84; Scottish Television: Reporter/Presenter, 1984-86, Promotions trailer-maker, 1987-89, Head of Programme Planning and Film Acquisition, 1990-95; Director, Scottish Screen Locations Ltd., 1995-97; Director of Locations, Scottish Screen, 1997-98. Board Member, British Film Commission, 1997-2000; Member, Steering Group, UK Film Commission Network, 1996-98. Recreations: cooking; reading; keeping fit; gardening. Address: (b.) 249 West George Street, Glasgow G2 4QE; e-mail: celia.stevenson@scottishscreen.com

Stevenson, Professor David, BA, PhD, DLitt, FRSE. Emeritus Professor, Scottish History, St. Andrews University, since 1994; b. 30.4.42, Largs; m., Wendy B. McLeod; 2 s. Educ. Gordonstoun; Dublin University; Glasgow University. Aberdeen University: Lecturer in History, 1970-80, Senior Lecturer in History, 1980-84; Reader in Scottish History, 1984-90; St. Andrews University: Reader in Scottish History, 1990-91; Professor of Scottish History, 1991-94. Honorary Secretary, Scottish History Society, 1976-84; Fellow, Royal Historical Society. Publications: The Scottish Revolution 1637-44, 1973; Revolution and Counter-Revolution in Scotland 1644-51, 1977; Alasdair MacColla and the Highland Problem in the 17th Century, 1980; Scottish Covenanters and Irish Confederates, 1981; The Government of Scotland under the Covenanters 1637-51, 1982; Scottish Texts and Calendars (with Wendy B. Stevenson), 1987; The Origins of Freemasonry, 1988; The First Freemasons: The Early Scottish Lodges and their members, 1988; The Covenanters: the National Covenant and Scotland, 1988; King's College, Aberdeen, 1560-1641, 1990; Scotland's Last Royal Wedding, 1997; King or Covenant, 1998; Union, Revolution and Religion in 17th Century Scotland, 1998; The Beggar's Benison, 2001. Address: (h.) 5 Forgan Way, Newport on Tay, Fife DD6 8JQ.

Stevenson, Gerda. Actress, Singer, Writer, Book Illustrator, Director; b. 10.4.56, West Linton; m., Aonghas MacNeacail; 1 s. Educ. Peebles High School; Royal Academy of Dramatic Art, London (DDA, Vanbrugh Award). Has performed with 7:84 Theatre Co., Scottish Theatre Company, Royal Lyceum Theatre (Edinburgh), Traverse Theatre, Communicado, Monstrous Regiment, Victoria Theatre (Stoke on Trent), Contact Theatre (Manchester) and with Freefall at Lilian Baylis Theatre, London, and Birmingham Rep; directed Uncle Jesus for Edinburgh Festival Fringe; Assistant Director, Royal Lyceum, on Merchant of Venice and A Doll's House; Founder Member and Director, Stellar Quines Theatre Co.; TV work includes Clay, Smeddum and Greenden, Square Mile of Murder, Grey Granite, Horizon: Battered Baby, The Old Master, Taggart, Dr. Finlay, The Bill; films: The Stamp of Greatness, Tickets to the Zoo, Blue Black Permanent (BAFTA Scotland Best Film Actress Award, 1993), Braveheart; directed short film, An Iobairt, in Gaelic for BBC; extensive radio work includes title roles in Bride of Lammermoor and Catriona; freelance producer for Radio Scotland; wrote and illustrated children's book, The Candlemaker. Recreation: walking in the country.

Stevenson, (James Alexander) Stewart, MSP. SNP MSP, Banff and Buchan, since 2001; b. 15.10.46; m., Sandra Isabel Pirie. Educ. Bell Baxter School, Cupar; Aberdeen University. Director, Technology Innovation,

Bank of Scotland, 1969-99; part-time Lecturer, School of Management, Heriot-Watt University, since 2001. Address: (b.) Scottish Parliament, Edinburgh EH99 1SP.

Stevenson, Ronald, DUniv (Stirling), DMus (Aberdeen), LLD (Dundee), FRMCM, HonFRIAS. Composer and Pianist; Broadcaster; Author; b. 6.3.28, Blackburn; m., Marjorie Spedding; 1 s.; 2 d. Educ. Royal Manchester College of Music; Conservatorio Di Santa Cecilia, Rome. Senior Lecturer, Cape Town University, 1963-65; BBC Prom debut in own 2nd Piano Concerto, 1972; Aldeburgh Festival recital with Sir Peter Pears, 1973; Busoni documentary, BBC TV, 1974; BBC Radio Scotland extended series on the bagpipe, clarsach and fiddle music of Scotland, 1980-84; Artist in Residence: Melbourne University, 1980, University of W. Australia, 1982, Conservatory of Shanghai, 1985; York University, 1987; published and recorded compositions: Passacaglia for Piano, two Piano Concertos, Violin Concerto (commissioned and premiered by Menuhin), Prelude, Fugue and Fantasy for Piano, Prelude and Fugue for Organ, In Memoriam Robert Carver, St. Mary's May Songs, A Child's Garden of Verses (BBC commission), Voces Vagabundae, Salute to Nelson Mandela (march for brass band), Cello Concerto (RSNO commission), A Carlyle Suite (piano), Le Festin d'Alkan (piano). Publications: Western Music; Alan Bush - a symposium; The Paderewski Paradox; Ronald Stevenson Society. Recreations: hill-walking; reading poetry, biographies and politics. Address: (h.) Townfoot House, West Linton, Peeblesshire; T.-01968 660511.

Stevenson, Struan John Stirton. MEP for Scotland, since 1999; b. 4.4.48, Ballantrae; m., Pat Stevenson; 2 s. Educ. Strathallan School; West of Scotland Agricultural College. Conservative Councillor, Kyle and Carrick District Council, 1970-92 (Leader of the Administration, 1986-88); Conservative Group Leader, COSLA, 1986-88; European Parliament: Deputy Conservative UK Spokesman on Agriculture Committee, UK Conservative Spokesman on Fisheries Committee. Hon. Doctor of Science, State Medical Academy, Kazakhstan, 2000. Recreations: contemporary art; music; theatre; opera; poetry; hill-walking. Address: (b.) 83 Princes Street, Edinburgh EH2 2ER; T.-0131-247 6890; e-mail: sstevenson@europarl.eu.int

Stevenson, William Trevor, CBE, DL, FCIT; b. 21.3.21, Peebles; m., Alison Wilson Roy. Educ. Edinburgh Academy. Apprentice Engineer, 1937-41; Engineer, 1941-45; entered family food manufacturing business, Cottage Rusks, 1945; Managing Director, 1948-54; Chairman, 1954-59; Chief Executive, Cottage Rusks Associates, 1965-69; Regional Director, Ranks Hovis McDougall, 1969-74; Director, various companies in food, engineering, hotel and aviation industries, since 1974; Chairman, Alex. Wilkie Ltd., 1971-90; founder Chairman, Gleneagles Hotels, 1981-83; Chairman, Scottish Transport Group, 1981-86; Master, Company of Merchants of City of Edinburgh, 1978-80; Vice President, Edinburgh Chamber of Commerce, 1983-87. Recreations: flying; sailing; curling.

Stewart, A.J. (Ada F. Kay). Playwright and Author; b. 5.3.29, Tottington, Lancashire. Educ. Grammar School, Fleetwood. ATS Scottish Command; first produced play, 1951; repertory actress, 1952-54; BBC TV Staff Writer/Editor/Adaptor, Central Script Section, 1956-59; returned to Scotland, 1959, as stage and TV writer; winner, BBC New Radio Play competition, 1956; The Man from Thermopylae, presented in Festival of Contemporary Drama, Rheydt, West Germany, 1959, as part of Edinburgh International Festival, 1965, and at Masquers' Theatre, Hollywood, 1972; first recipient, Wendy Wood Memorial Grant, 1982; Polish Gold Cross for achievements in literary field. Publications: Falcon - The Autobiography of His Grace, James the 4, King of Scots, 1970; Died 1513-Born

1929 - The Autobiography of A.J. Stewart, 1978; The Man from Thermopylae, 1981. Recreation: work. Address: (h.) 33 Howe Street, Edinburgh EH3 6TF.

Stewart, Alan David, MA (Hons), MIPR. Head, Independent Television Commission (Scotland), since 2000 (Deputy Head, 1994-2000); b. 27.7.58, Falkirk; m., Christine; 2 s. Educ. Graeme High School, Falkirk; Glasgow University; Strathclyde University. Assistant Public Relations Officer, Cumbernauld Development Corporation, 1983-86; Press Officer, Strathclyde Regional Council, 1986-92; Principal Officer (Corporate Communications and Marketing), Lothian Regional Council, 1992-94. Recreations: hill-walking; cycling; supporting Falkirk FC. Address: (h.) 12 Heugh Street, Falkirk FK1 5QR; T.-01324 631997.

Stewart, Sheriff Alastair Lindsay, QC, BA (Oxon), LLB(Edin). Sheriff of Tayside, Central and Fife at Dundee, since 1990; Temporary Judge, Court of Session and High Court of Justiciary, since 1996; b. 28.11.38, Aberdeen; m., 1, Annabel Claire Stewart (m. diss.); 2 s.; 2, Sheila Anne Mackinnon. Educ. Edinburgh Academy; St. Edmund Hall, Oxford; Edinburgh University. Admitted to Faculty of Advocates, 1963; Tutor, Faculty of Law, Edinburgh University, 1963-73; Standing Junior Counsel to the Registrar of Restrictive Trading Agreements, 1968-70; Advocate Depute, 1970-73; Sheriff of Lanarkshire (later South Strathclyde, Dumfries and Galloway) at Airdrie, 1973-79; Sheriff of Grampian, Highland and Islands at Aberdeen and Stonehaven, 1979-90. Chairman, Scottish Association of Family Conciliation Services, 1986-89; Editor, Scottish Civil Law Reports, 1992-95; Member, Judicial Studies Committee, since 2000. Publications: Sheriff Court Practice (Contributor), 1988; The Scottish Criminal Courts in Action, 1990, 1997; Sheriff Court Practice (Joint General Editor and Contributor), 1998. Recreations: music; reading; walking. Address: (b.) Sheriffs' Chambers, Sheriff Court House, 6 West Bell Street, Dundee DD1 9AD; T.-01382 318218; e-mail: sheriff.astewart@scotcourts.gov.uk

Stewart, Alexander Donald, BA, LLB, WS, DL. Director, Prudential PLC; Chairman, Murray Extra Return Investment Trust PLC; b. 18.6.33, Edinburgh; m., Virginia Mary Washington; 1 s.; 5 d. Educ. Wellington College, Berkshire; Oxford University; Edinburgh University. Hon. Consul for Thailand in Scotland; DL, Perthshire. Recreations: music; field sports; winter sports. Address: (h.) Ardvorlich, Lochearnhead, Perthshire.

Stewart, Andrew Fleming, LLB (Hons.). Advocate, since 1996; b. 12.9.63, Dundee.; m., Lesley Katherine Dawson; 1 d. Educ. Perth High School; Edinburgh University. Solicitor: Clifford Chance, London, 1988-90, Tods Murray WS, Edinburgh, 1990-94; Legal Assistant to Lord President, Court of Session, 1994-95; Tutor, Law Faculty, University of Edinburgh, 1985-88 and since 1990; Lecturer (part-time), Université de Nancy 2, France, since 1994; Standing Junior Counsel, Department of Trade and Industry, since 2000; Clerk to Examiners, Faculty of Advocates, since 2001. Member, Board of Practice and Procedure, Church of Scotland, since 2001; Treasurer, Scottish Committee, Franco-British Lawyers Society, 1998-2001; Editor, Session Cases, since 2001. Recreations: golf; music. Address: Advocates Library, Parliament House, Edinburgh EH1 1RF; T.-0131-226 5071.

Stewart, Angus, QC, BA, LLB. Queen's Counsel; b. 14.12.46; m., Jennifer Margaret Stewart; 1 d. Educ. Edinburgh Academy; Balliol College, Oxford University; Edinburgh University. Called to the Scottish Bar, 1975; Keeper, Advocates' Library, since 1994; Trustee: National Library of Scotland, since 1994; Stewart Heritage Trust, since 1996, Scottish Council

of Law Reporting, since 1997; Treasurer, E Boat International Offshore Class Association, since 1994. Address: (h.) Ann Street, Edinburgh, EH4 1PJ; T.-0131-332 4083.

Stewart (nee Muir), Professor Averil M., BA, FCOT, TDip, SROT, FFCS. Head, Department of Occupational Therapy and Art Therapy, Queen Margaret University College, Edinburgh, 1986-2001; b. 7.4.43, Edinburgh; m., J. Gavin Stewart. Educ. Dunfermline High School. Member, Vice-Chairman and Chairman, Occupational Therapists Board, CPSM, 1980-92; Trustee, Dementia Services Development Centre, since 1996; Chairman, CAB Leith, 1997-2001; Convenor, Edinburgh CABx Steering Group, since 1998; Secretary, Scottish Arctic Club, since 1998. Recreations: wilderness travel; gardening. Address: (h.) 29 Highfield Crescent, Linlithgow EH49 7BG; e-mail: gaveril.stewart@virgin.net

Stewart, Brian John, CBE, MSc, CA. Chairman, Scottish & Newcastle plc, since 2000; Director (Non-Executive), Standard Life, since 1993; b. 9.4.45, Stirling; m., Shona (Seonaid); 2 s.; 1 d. Educ. Perth Academy; Edinburgh University. J. & R. Morrison, CA, Perth, 1962-67; Chief Management Accountant, Ethicon Ltd., 1969-76; joined Scottish & Newcastle plc, 1976; Corporate Development Director, 1985; Group Finance Director, 1988. Director (Non-Executive), Booker PLC, 1993-99. Recreations: skiing; golf. Address: (b.) 30 Ellersly Road, Edinburgh EH12 6HX; T.-0131-528 2000.

Stewart, David John, MP, BA (Hons). MP (Labour), Inverness East, Nairn and Lochaber, since 1997; b. 5.5.56; m., Linda; 1 s.; 1 d. Educ. Inverness High School; Paisley College; Stirling University; Open University Business School. Lecturer in Community Care, Esk Valley College, 1981; Social Worker, Dumfries and Dingwall, 1981-87; Social Work Team Manager, Highland Council, 1987-97. Patron, Shopmobility Highland. Recreations: sport; keep-fit; travel; reading. Address: (b.) Queensgate Business Centre, Fraser Street, Inverness; T.-01463 237441; e-mail: stewartd@parliament.uk

Stewart, David Roger, TD, MA, BA (Hons), FEIS. Honorary Sheriff, Selkirk, since 1983; b. 3.2.20, Glasgow; m., Gwyneth Ruth Morris; 2 s.; 1 d. Educ. Hyndland Secondary School; Glasgow High School; Glasgow University; London University. Army, 1939-46; Schoolmaster, 1947-65 (Kelvinside Academy, Galashiels Academy); Rector, Selkirk High School, 1965-81; Member: Selkirk Town Council, 1967-75, Borders Education Committee, 1975-81, Borders Regional Council, 1982-86; TA, 1939-64; Chairman, Selkirk Committee, Cancer Research Campaign. Recreations: golf; gardening; reading. Address: (h.) Cairncoed, Hillside Terrace, Selkirk TD7 4ND; T.-01750 21755.

Stewart, Douglas Fleming, MA, LLB, WS, NP, FSA Scot. Trustee Church of Scotland Trust (former Chairman); b. 22.5.27, Sydney; m., Catherine Coleman; 2 d. Educ. George Watson's College; Edinburgh University. RAF, 1945-48; Partner, J. & F. Anderson, WS, 1961-92; Solicitor, Crown Estate Scotland, 1970-91; Chairman, Commercial Union, Edinburgh Board, 1979-91, and its Scottish Advisory Committee, 1977-97. Member, Edinburgh University General Council Business Committee, 1961-69; Secretary/Treasurer, Stewart Society, 1968-87 (also Hon. Vice-President); Session Clerk, Braid Church, Edinburgh, 1979-91; President, Watsonian Club, 1989-90; Chairman, Comiston Probus Club, 1999. Publications: The Story of Braid Church (Co-Author); A Lawful Union, The annals of J & F Anderson, WS and Strathern & Blair, WS (Co-Author). Recreations: astronomy; bowling; swimming. Address: (h.) Greenhill Court, 98/5 Whitehouse Loan, Edinburgh EH9 1BD; T.-0131-447 4887.

Stewart, Ena Lamont. Playwright; b. 10.2.12, Glasgow; m., Jack Stewart (deceased); 1 s. Educ. Woodside School, Glasgow; Esdaile School, Edinburgh. Assistant, Public Library, Aberdeen, 1930-34; Medical Secretary, Radcliffe, Lancashire, 1934-37; Secretary/Receptionist, Royal Hospital for Sick Children, Glasgow, 1937-41; Baillie's Reference Library, Glasgow: Assistant Librarian, 1953-57, Librarian-in-charge, 1957-66; author of plays: Starched Aprons, Men Should Weep, The Heir to Ardmally, Business in Edinburgh, After Tomorrow (unperformed), Walkies Time, Knocking on the Wall, Towards Evening, High Places.

Stewart, George Girdwood, CB, MC, TD, BSc, FICFor, Hon. FLI; b. 12.12.19, Glasgow; m., Shelagh Jean Morven Murray; 1 s.; 1 d. Educ. Kelvinside Academy, Glasgow; Glasgow University; Edinburgh University. Royal Artillery, 1940-46 (mentioned in Despatches); Forestry Commission: District Officer, 1949-60, Assistant Conservator, 1960-67, Conservator (West Scotland), 1967-69, Commissioner, Forest and Estate Management, 1969-79. Commanding Officer, 278 (Lowland) Field Regiment RA (TA), 1956-59; President, Scottish Ski Club, 1971-75; Vice President, National Ski Federation of Great Britain and Chairman, Alpine Racing Committee, 1975-78; National Trust for Scotland: Member of Council, 1975-79, Representative, Branklyn Garden, 1980-84, Regional Representative, Central and Tayside, 1984-88; Forestry Consultant, 1989-93; Chairman, Scottish Wildlife Trust, 1981-87; Member, Countryside Commission for Scotland, 1981-88; Member, Environment Panel, British Railways Board, 1980-90; Cairngorm Estate Adviser to Highlands and Islands Enterprise, 1988-98; Associate Director, Oakwood Environmental, since 1990; Member, Cairngorm Recreation Trust, since 1986; President, Scottish National Ski Council, 1988-94, Hon. Vice-President, since 1997; Specialist Adviser to House of Lords Select Committee on EEC Forestry Policy, 1986; National Service to Sport Award, 1995; Member, British Veterans' Tennis Team, World Team Championships, 1999 and 2001; Fellow, Royal Society of Arts. Recreations: skiing; veterans' tennis; studying Scottish painting. Address: (h.) Stormont House, 11 Mansfield Road, Scone, Perth PH2 6SA; T.-01738 551815.

Stewart, Gillian Mary, BA (Hons). Head of Children and Young People's Group, Scottish Executive Education Department, since 1999, Head of Group, Scottish Office Home Department, 1992-99; b. 2.6.45, Gosforth; 2 s. Educ. Blyth Grammar School; Durham University. Joined Scottish Office, 1970, as Assistant Principal; posts held in Education, Social Work Services Group, Environment. Recreations: swimming; walking; theatre; music. Address: (b.) Victoria Quay, Edinburgh EH6 6QQ; T.-0131-244 3670.

Stewart, Professor Graham George, BSc, PhD, DSc, FIBrew, FIBiol. Director, International Centre for Brewing and Distilling, since 1994; b. 22.3.42, Cardiff; m., Olga Leonara. Educ. Cathays High School, Cardiff; University College Cardiff; Bath University. Lecturer in Biochemistry, Portsmouth College of Technology, 1967-69; various technical positions, J. Labatt Ltd., Canada, 1969-94. Recreations: rugby; music; travel. Address: (b.) Heriot-Watt University, Riccarton, Edinburgh, EH14 4AS; T.-0131-451 3184.

Stewart, James Blythe, MA, LLB, LLB, Advocate; b. 22.4.43, Methil. Educ. Buckhaven High School; University of Edinburgh. Research Assistant, Faculty of Law, University of St. Andrews, 1966-67; Heriot-Watt University: Assistant Lecturer in Law, 1967-69, Lecturer in Law, 1969-76, Senior Lecturer in Law, 1976-98; retired 1998. Associate Director, East Fife FC. Recreations: football spectating; bowls; golf. Address: (h.) 3 Comely Bank Terrace, Edinburgh EH4 1AT; T.-0131-332 8228.

Stewart, Rev. James Charles, MA, BD, STM. Minister, Kirk of St. Nicholas, Aberdeen (The City Kirk), 1980-2000; b. 29.3.33, Glasgow. Educ. Glasgow Academy; St. Andrews University; Union Theological Seminary, New York. Assistant Minister, St. John's Kirk of Perth, 1959-64; Minister: St. Andrew's Church, Drumchapel, 1964-74, East Parish Church of St. Nicholas, Aberdeen, 1974-80. Trustee, Aberdeen Endowments Trust and other trusts; Honorary President, Church Service Society; Past Chairman, Aberdeen Civic Society; Past Chairman, Third World Centre, Aberdeen. Address: 54 Murray Terrace, Aberdeen AB11 7SB; T.-01224 587071.

Stewart, John Barry Bingham, LVO, OBE, BA, CA. Past Chairman, Martin Currie Ltd.; b. 21.2.31, Edinburgh; m., Ailsa Margaret Crawford. Educ. The Leys School, Cambridge; Magdalene College, Cambridge. Accountancy training, Edinburgh; worked in London, United States and Canada; joined Martin Currie, 1960. Recreations: fishing; shooting; golf; skiing. Address: 18 Hope Terrace, Edinburgh EH9 2AR; T.-0131-447 1626.

Stewart, Sheriff John Hall, LLB. Sheriff of Strathclyde, Dumfries and Galloway, at Hamilton, since 1996, at Airdrie, 1985-96; b. 15.3.44, Bellshill; m., Marion MacCalman; 1 s.; 2 d. Educ. Airdrie Academy; St. Andrews University. Admitted Solicitor, 1971; Advocate, 1978; Past President, Uddingston RFC; Past President, Uddingston Cricket and Sports Club. Address: (b.) Sheriff Court House, Beckford Street, Hamilton, ML3 6AA.

Stewart, Rev. Norma Drummond, MA, MEd, DipTh, BD. Minister, Strathbungo Queen's Park Church, Glasgow, 1979-2000; Locum Tenens, Dennistoun Blackfriars, Glasgow, since 2000; b. 20.5.36, Glasgow. Educ. Hyndland Secondary School, Glasgow; Glasgow University; Bible Training Institute, Glasgow; University of London (External); Trinity College, Glasgow. Teacher, Garrioch Secondary School, Glasgow, 1958-62; Missionary, Overseas Missionary Fellowship, West Malaysia, 1965-74; ordained to ministry, Church of Scotland, 1977. Selection School Assessor; Convener, Education for the Ministry Committee, Glasgow Presbytery; Member, Church of Scotland Panel on Doctrine; occasional Lecturer and Tutor in Old Testament; Participant in Congress on World Evangelisation, Manila, 1989; Member, Evangelical Alliance Scotland; Pastoral Adviser, Glasgow Presbytery; Member, Council of Christians and Jews; Member, Judicial Commission, Church of Scotland. Recreation: Old Testament research; information technology. Address: 127 Nether Auldhouse Road, Glasgow G43 2YS; T.-0141 637 6956; e-mail: norma@ndstewart.fsnet.co.uk

Stewart, Norman MacLeod, BL, SSC. Consultant, Allan, Black & McCaskie, Solicitors, Elgin 1997-99, Senior Partner, 1984-97; Chairman, Elgin and Lossiemouth Harbour Board, since 1993; President, Law Society of Scotland, 1985-86; b. 2.12.34, Lossiemouth; m., Mary Slater Campbell; 4 d. Educ. Elgin Academy; Edinburgh University. Training and Legal Assistant, Alex. Morrison & Co., WS, Edinburgh, 1954-58; Legal Assistant: McLeod, Solicitor, Portsoy, 1958-59, Allan, Black & McCaskie, Solicitors, Elgin, 1959-61 (Partner, 1961-97); Council Member, Law Society of Scotland, 1976-87 (Convener, Public Relations Committee, 1979-81, and Professional Practice Committee, 1981-84). Past President, Elgin Rotary Club; Past Chairman, Moray Crime Prevention Panel; President, Edinburgh University Club of Moray, 1987-89. Recreations: walking; golf; music; Spanish culture. Address: (h.) Argyll Lodge, Lossiemouth, Moray; T.-0134381 3150.

Stewart, Patrick Loudon McIain, MBE, LLB, WS, DL. Consultant, Stewart Balfour & Sutherland, Solicitors, Campbeltown, Senior Partner, 1982-2000; Secretary, Clyde Fishermen's Association, since 1970; Honorary Sheriff at

Campbeltown; b. 25.7.45, Campbeltown; m., Mary Anne McLellan; 1 s.; 1 d. Educ. Edinburgh Academy; Edinburgh University. Partner, Stewart Balfour & Sutherland, Campbeltown, 1970; former Executive Member, Scottish Fishermen's Federation; former Director, Scottish Fishermen's Organisation Ltd.; member of many Scottish fishing industry committees; Chairman, Argyll & Bute Trust; Secretary, Campbeltown and Kintyre Enterprise Trust Ltd.; Clerk, General Commissioners of Income Tax — Islay; HQ Staff Officer Legal Affairs, Sea Cadet Corps; Honorary Legal Adviser and Trustee, Sea Cadet Association; Cadet Forces Medal. Recreations: sailing; shooting; youth work. Address: Craigadam, Campbeltown, Argyll PA28 6EP; T.-01586 552161.

Stewart, Robert Armstrong, BA, DipTP, FRTPI, MIMgt. Director of Environmental Services, The Moray Council (formerly Director, Economic Development and Planning); b. Stirling. Planning Assistant, Lanark County Council, 1968-69; Planner, Glasgow, 1969-70; Senior Assistant, then Group Leader: Development Control, West Lothian County, 1970-75; Depute Director: Planning, East Lothian District, 1975-79; Director of Planning and Development, Moray District Council. Address: (b.) Council Office, High Street, Elgin, IV30 1BX.

Stewart, Lt. Col. Robert Christie, CBE, TD; Lord Lieutenant, Clackmannanshire, since 1994; b. 3.8.26, Dollar; m., Ann Grizel Cochrane; 3 s.; 2 d. Educ. Eton; University College, Oxford. Lt., Scots Guards, 1944-49; 7th Bn., Argyll and Sutherland Highlanders TA, 1951-66; Lt.-Col., 1963-66; Hon. Col., 1/51 Highland Volunteers, 1972-75; Landowner; Lord Lieutenant, Kinross-shire, 1966-74; Member, Perth and Kinross County Council, 1953-75; Chairman, Kinross County Council, 1963-73; Chairman and President, Board of Governors, East of Scotland College of Agriculture, 1970-83. Recreations: shooting; golf; the countryside. Address: (h.) Arndean, by Dollar, FK14 7NH; T.-01259 742527.

Stewart, Susan, COT, BSc (Hons). Director, fpa Scotland (formerly The Family Planning Association), since 2000; b. 12.9.60, Glasgow; 1 s.; 1 d. Educ. Eastwood High School; Glasgow School of Occupational Therapy; Caledonian University. Occupational therapist, NHS, 1981-82; social work, 1983-87; manager, social work, 1987-92; registration and inspection officer, 1992-98; Head of Service, Sense Scotland, 1998-2000. Recreations: yoga; sewing; singing; Reiki. Address: (b.) Unit 10, Firrhill Business Centre, 74-76 Firhill Road, Glasgow G20 7BA; T.-0141-576 5015.

Stewart, Sir William, Kt, PhD, DSc, FRS, FRSE. President, Royal Society of Edinburgh, since 1999; President, British Association for the Advancement of Science, 2001; Chairman: Cyclacel Ltd., since 1998, Microbiological Research Authority, since 1999; b. 7.6.35; 1 s. Educ. Bowmore Junior Secondary School; Dunoon Grammar School; Glasgow University. Boyd Baxter Professor of Biology, 1968-94, Vice-Principal, 1985-87; Secretary and Chief Executive, AFRC, 1988-90; Chief Scientific Adviser, Cabinet Office, 1990-95, and Head of Office of Science and Technology, 1992-95. Honorary degrees from universities: Aberdeen, Abertay, Dundee, Edinburgh, Glasgow, Napier, Paisley, Stirling.

Stewartby (The Lady), Deborah Charlotte, JP. Non-Executive Director, Scottish Opera and Scottish Ballet, since 2000; Council Member, John Buchan Society (grand-daughter of John Buchan), since 2001; b. 19.10.47, London; m., Rt. Hon. Lord Stewartby; 1 s.; 2 d. Senior Researcher, 1974-92 (P.A. of Ian Stewart, MP); Director of Appeals and Public Affairs, Bryson House, Belfast, 1991-98. Governor, Princess Helena

College, 1986-99; President, Howard Cottage Society, since 1995. Recreations: performing arts; gardening; walking the dog. Address: (h.) Broughton Green, Broughton, by Biggar ML12 6HQ; T.-01899 830 362.

Stewart-Clark, Sir Jack, Bt. Member of European Parliament for East Sussex and Kent South, 1979-99; Vice President, European Parliament, 1992-97; b. 17.9.29, West Lothian; m., Lydia Loudon; 1 s.; 4 d. Educ. Eton; Balliol College, Oxford; Harvard Business School. Coldstream Guards, 1948-49; J. & P. Coats, 1952-70; Philips Industries, 1970-79 (Managing Director, Philips Electrical Ltd., 1970-74, Pye of Cambridge Ltd., 1974-79). Member, Queen's Bodyguard for Scotland, Royal Company of Archers. Publications: European Competition Law; Drugs Education, It's My Problem as Well. Recreations: golf; tennis; photography; classic cars. Address: (h.) Dundas Castle, South Queensferry, near Edinburgh, EH30 9SP; T.-0131-331 1114.

Stihler, Catherine Dalling, MA (Hons), MLitt. Member, European Parliament, since 1999; President, Public Health All-party Group; Member: Environment and Fishing Committees; b. 30.7.73, Bellshill; m., David. Educ. Coltness High School, Wishaw; St Andrews University. PA (Researcher) to Anne Begg, MP, 1997-99; Organiser for Central and Eastern European politicians' visits to Scotland, 1995-97; Member, Labour Party NEC, 1995-97, and Scottish Executive, 1993-95, 1997-99. Publication: Women and the Military (Contributor). Recreations: reading; going to the gym; singing; films; backgammon. Address: (b.) Albany Business Centre (Unit 3), Gardener Street, Dunfermline, Fife; T.-01383 731890.

Stimson, Professor William Howard, BSc, PhD, CBiol, FIBiol, FIoN, FRSE. Professor of Immunology, Strathclyde University, since 1981; Director: Immunogene Biomedical Ltd., MDC Learning Systems Ltd., Viragen (Europe) Ltd.; b. 2.11.43, Liverpool; m., Jean Scott Baird; 1 s.; 1 d. Educ. Prince of Wales School, Nairobi; St. Andrews University. Research Fellow, Department of Obstetrics and Gynaecology, Dundee University, 1970-72; Lecturer, then Senior Lecturer, Biochemistry Department, Strathclyde University, 1973-80. Holder, Glasgow Loving Cup, 1982-83; Non-Executive Director, UK and European Institute for Nanotechnology; Chairman, Biotechnology Solutions (Scottish University for Industry); Member, Editorial Boards, five scientific journals; 197 scientific publications; 11 patents. Recreations: mechanical engineering; walking; golf. Address: (b.) Department of Immunology, Strathclyde University, 31 Taylor Street, Glasgow G4 0NR; T.-0141-548 3729; e-mail: w.h.stimson@strath.ac.uk

Stirling of Garden, Col. James, CBE, TD, KStJ, BA, FRICS. Lord Lieutenant of Stirling and Falkirk, since 1983; Chartered Surveyor; Honorary Sheriff, Stirling, since 1996; b. 8.9.30; m., Fiona; 2 s.; 2 d. Educ. Rugby; Trinity College, Cambridge. Partner, Ryden and Partners, 1962-89; Director, Scottish Widows Life Assurance Society, 1974-96. Chairman, Highland TAVRA, 1981-86, President, 1990-96; Director, Woolwich Building Society, 1975-95. Prior, Order of St. John, Scotland. Address: (h.) Garden, Buchlyvie, Stirlingshire.

Stirling, Robin Colin Baillie, OBE, JP; b. 6.4.25, Bo'ness; m., Jean R. Hendrie, MA. Educ. Dalziel High School, Motherwell. Editor: Motherwell Times, 1957-85, Motherwell Times Series, 1959-85. Former Secretary, Lanarkshire Branch, NUJ; elected Life Member, NUJ, 1985; Guild of British Newspaper Editors: former Scottish Secretary, Chairman, 1967-70; NCTJ: Member, Scottish Training Committee, 1961-85, Chairman, Scottish Committee, 1978-81. Convener, Motherwell Guild of Help, since 1953; Chairman, Strathclyde Police P Division Crime Prevention Panel, 1976-84; Member: Management

Committee, Motherwell and Wishaw CAB, 1971-95 (Chairman, 1978-80), Motherwell and District Christian Aid Committee 1970-82; Honorary Vice President: Motherwell ASC, since 1986, Motherwell CC, since 1985, Lanarkshire Little Theatre; President, Motherwell Probus Club, 1987-88; Founder Chairman, Motherwell and District Music Society (Chairman, 1984-93). Recreations: gardening; music (including jazz); steam locomotives; Motherwell FC; Scottish Opera; cinema organs. Address: (h.) 37 The Loaning, Motherwell ML1 3HE; T.-63762.

Stirling of Fairburn, Roderick William Kenneth, TD, JP. Lord Lieutenant, Ross and Cromarty and Skye and Lochalsh, since 1988; Landowner and Estate Manager; President, Highlands Islands and Moray Branch, Scots Guards Association, since 1994; President, Ross/Sutherland Scout Association, since 1995; b. 17.6.32; m., Penelope Jane Wright; 4 d. Educ. Wellesley House; Harrow; Aberdeen University. National Service, Scots Guards, 1950-52 (commissioned, 1951); TA service, Seaforth and Queen's Own Highlanders, 1953-69 (retired with rank of Captain); Member, Regional Advisory Committee to Forestry Commission, 1964-85; Member, Red Deer Commission, 1964-89; Local Director, Eagle Star Insurance Co., 1966-85; Director, Moray Firth Salmon Fishing Co. Ltd., 1973-91; Member, Highland River Purification Board, 1975-90; Ross and Cromarty County Councillor, 1970-74 (Chairman of Highways, 1973-74); Member, Ross and Cromarty District Council, and its Representative on Scottish Accident Prevention Council, 1984-96; Chairman, Scottish Salmon and White Fish Co. Ltd., 1980-91; Chairman, Highland Region Valuation Appeal Committee, 1983-91. Recreations: wild life management; gardening; curling. Address: (h.) Arcan, Muir of Ord, Ross-shire IV6 7UL; T.-01997 433207.

Stirrups, Professor David Robert, MSc, BA, BDS, FDS, DOrth(RCSEng), FDS, MOrth(RCPS) Glasgow. Professor of Orthodontics, Dundee University, since 1993; b. 23.6.48, Gillingham; m., Anne; 1 s.; 1 d. Educ. Gillingham Grammar School; Sheffield University. Senior Registrar, Northern Health Authority, 1977-80; Consultant Orthodontist, Greater Glasgow Health Board, 1980-93. Member, General Dental Council, since 1999. Recreations: orienteering; mountain marathons; philately. Address: (b.) Dundee University, Dundee DD1 4HN; T.-01382 635961.

Stobie, David Johnston, FRSA, MCIBS. Non-Executive Director, Shaw Marketing & Design Ltd., since 1994; Non-Executive Chairman, Macnaughton Holdings Ltd., since 1997; Chairman, Fife Acute Hospitals NHS Trust, since 1999; Trustee: Carnegie Dunfermline and Hero Fund Trust, since 1990, Carnegie United Kingdom Trust, since 1995; b. 29.6.37, Galashiels; m., Nancy R. McIntosh; 1 s.; 1 d. Educ. George Heriot's School, Edinburgh. British Linen Bank, 1954-71; Noble Grossart Ltd., 1971-81 (Treasurer, 1976-81); British Linen Bank Ltd., 1981-96 (Business Development Director, 1986-96). Chairman, Queen Margaret NHS Trust, 1997-99; Chairman, Children 1st, 1996-2000; Recreations: family; walking; gardening. Address: (h.) Strathmore, 17 Venturefair Avenue, Dunfermline KY12 OPF; T.-01383 721396.

Stobo, James, CBE, DL, FRAgS. Farmer; Chairman, Moredun Foundation for Animal Health and Welfare, 1994-2000; Director, New Park Management Ltd.; President, Aberdeen-Angus Cattle Society, 2001-02; b. 9.12.34, Lanark; m., Pamela Elizabeth Mary Herriot; 1 s.; 2 d. Educ. Edinburgh Academy. Farming, since 1951; Past Chairman and President, Scottish Association of Young Farmers Clubs; Member, Home-Grown Cereals Authority, 1971-76; President, National Farmers' Union of Scotland, 1973-74; President, Animal Diseases Research Foundation, 1980-95; Chairman of Governors, Longridge Towers School, 1982-2000; Chairman, Scottish Seed Potato Development Council, 1988-95; Director, John Hogarth Ltd., Kelso Mills;

Vice-President, Royal Smithfield Club; Deputy Lieutenant, County of Berwick, 1987. Recreation: photography. Address: Nabdean, Berwick-upon-Tweed TD15 1SZ; T.-01289 386224.

Stockdale, Elizabeth Joan Noel, MB, ChB, DMRD, FRCR, FRCPCH, MBA. Consultant Radiologist, Royal Aberdeen Children's Hospital and Aberdeen Royal Infirmary, since 1980; Clinical Senior Lecturer, Aberdeen University, since 1980; m., Christopher Leo Stockdale; 2 s.; 1 d. Educ. Aberdeen University. House Surgeon, Aberdeen Royal Infirmary; Senior House Surgeon, Professorial Surgical Unit, Hospital for Sick Children, Great Ormond Street; Registrar, St. George's Hospital; Senior Registrar, Royal National Orthopaedic Hospital, Royal Marsden Hospital, Atkinson Morley's Hospital; Chairman, Grampian Division, BMA, 1995-97; Member, BMA Scottish Council and SCHMS, 1997-2000; Member, RCR Standing Scottish Committee, since 1997. Recreations: theatre; classical music; travel. Address: (h.) 1 Grant Road, Banchory, Kincardineshire AB31 5UW; T.-013302 823096.

Stodart of Leaston, Rt. Hon. Lord (James Anthony Stodart), PC (1974); b. 6.6.16, Exeter; m., Hazel Usher (deceased). Educ. Wellington. MP (Conservative), Edinburgh West, 1959-74; Joint Under Secretary of State, Scottish Office, 1963-64; Parliamentary Secretary, later Minister of State, Ministry of Agriculture, Fisheries and Food, 1970-74; Chairman: Agricultural Credit Corporation Ltd., 1975-87, Committee of Enquiry into Local Government in Scotland, 1980, Manpower Review of Veterinary Profession in UK, 1984-85. Publication: Land of Abundance: a study of Scottish agriculture in the 20th century. Recreations: music; preserving a sense of humour. Addresses: Lorimers, North Berwick, East Lothian.

Stoddart, Sheriff Charles Norman, LLB, LLM, PhD. Sheriff of Lothian and Borders at Edinburgh, since 1995; b. 4.4.48, Dunfermline; m., Anne Lees; 1 d. Educ. Dunfermline High School; Edinburgh University; McGill University, Montreal. Private practice as Solicitor, 1972-73; Lecturer in Scots Law, Edinburgh University, 1973-80; private practice, 1980-88; Sheriff of North Strathclyde at Paisley, 1988-95; Director of Judicial Studies in Scotland, 1997-2000. Publications: (as Co-author) The Law and Practice of Legal Aid in Scotland; Cases and Materials on Criminal Law; Cases and Materials on Criminal Procedure; (as author) Criminal Warrants; Bible John. Recreations: music; sport. Address: (b.) Sheriff's Chambers, Sheriff Court, 27 Chambers Street, Edinburgh, EH1 1LB; T.-0131-225 2525.

Stoddart, Sheila Grahame, LLB, WS, NP. Solicitor, since 1980; b. 20.11.43, Duns. Educ. Esdaile School for Girls, Edinburgh; Edinburgh University. Travel representative; beautician; BBC make-up artist; solicitor. Recreations: breeder/exhibitor/judge of Australian terriers; Member, Kennel Club; travel; reading. Address: (b.) Ayton, Berwickshire TD14 5QH; T.-018907 81209.

Stone, Professor David, MD, FRCP, FFPHM, FRCPCH. Founding Director, Paediatric Epidemiology and Community Health Unit, Department of Child Health, Glasgow University, since 1995, Professor, Glasgow University, since 2000; b. 13.5.49, Glasgow; m., Dr Susan V. Carr; 2 s.; 2 d. Educ. High School of Glasgow; Edinburgh University. Trained in general medicine and public health, Glasgow and London; Senior Lecturer in Epidemiology, Ben Gurion University of the Negev, Israel, 1981-85; Senior Lecturer, Glasgow University, since 1985. Recreations: music; dining; current affairs. Address: PEACH Unit, Yorkhill Hospital, Glasgow G3 8SJ; T.-0141-201 0178.

Stone, Professor Frederick Hope, OBE, MB, ChB, FRCP, FRCPsych, FRCPCH. Professor of Child and Adolescent Psychiatry, Glasgow University, 1977-86; Consultant Psychiatrist, Royal Hospital for Sick Children, Glasgow, since 1954; b. 11.9.21, Glasgow; m., Zelda Elston, MA; 2 s.; 1 d. Educ. Hillhead High School, Glasgow; Glasgow University. Acting Director, Lasker Mental Hygiene Clinic, Hadassah, Jerusalem, 1952-54; World Health Organisation Visiting Consultant, 1960, 1964; Member, Kilbrandon Committee, 1963-65; Secretary-General, International Association of Child Psychiatry, 1962-66; Member, Houghton Committee on Adoption, 1968-72; Chairman, Scottish Division, Royal College of Psychiatrists, 1981-84; President, Young Minds; Chairman, Strathclyde Children's Panel Advisory Committee, 1988-94. Publications: Child Psychiatry for Students (Co-author); Juvenile Justice in Scotland (Co-author). Address: (h.) Flat 3c, 2 Hutchison Court, Berryhill Road, Giffnock G46 7NN; T.-0141-638 7554.

Stone, Gordon Victor, MBChB, FFCM, MFCMI, DCM. Director of Health Improvement, Highland Health Board, since 1999; b. 4.10.45, London; m., Aileen S. Wilson; 1 s.; 1 d. Educ. Aberdeen Grammar School; Aberdeen University; Edinburgh University. Medical Officer, RAF, 1970-75; Scottish Health Service Fellow in Community Medicine, 1975-78; Specialist in Community Medicine, Grampian Health Board, 1978-89; Highland Health Board: Chief Administrative Medical Officer/Director of Public Health Medicine, 1989-94; General Manager, 1994-99. Recreations: golf; skiing. Address: (b.) Beechwood Park, Inverness, IV2 3HG; T.-01463 717123.

Stone, James Hume Walter Miéville, MA, FRSA. MSP (Liberal Democrat), Caithness, Sutherland and Easter Ross, since 1999; Liberal Democrat Spokesman for: Education and Children, 1999-2000, Highlands and Fishing, 2000-01, Equal Opportunities, since 2001; Member, Holyrood Progress Group, since 2000; freelance newspaper columnist and broadcaster, since 1991; b. 16.6.54, Edinburgh; m., Flora Kathleen Margaret Armstrong; 1 s.; 2 d. Educ. Tain Royal Academy; Gordonstoun School; St Andrews University. Cleaner, fish-gutter, stores clerk, 1977-81; Assistant Site Administrator/Site Administrator, Bechtel G.B. Ltd., 1981-84; Administration Manager, Odfjell Drilling and Consulting Co. Ltd., 1984-86; Director, Highland Fine Cheeses Ltd., 1986-94; Member, Ross and Cromarty District Council, 1986-96; Member, The Highland Council, 1995-99 (Vice-Chair, Finance). Member, Cromarty Firth Port Authority, 1998-2001; Trustee, Tain Museum Trust; Trustee, Tain Guildry Trust; Trustee, Highland Buildings Preservation Trust; Director, The Highland Festival, 1994-2000. Recreations: gardening; reading; music; butterflies and funghi. Address: (b.) Scottish Parliament, Edinburgh EH99 1SP; T.-0131-348 5789.

Stone, Sheriff Marcus, MA, LLB. Accredited Mediator, since 1993; Director, The Mediation Bureau; Hon. President, Association of Mediators; b. 22.3.21, Glasgow; m., Jacqueline Barnoin; 3 s.; 2 d. Educ. High School of Glasgow; Glasgow University. Served Second World War; admitted Solicitor, 1949; admitted Faculty of Advocates, 1965; Sheriff of North Strathclyde, at Dumbarton, 1971-76; Sheriff of Glasgow and Strathkelvin, at Glasgow, 1976-84; Sheriff of Lothian and Borders, at Linlithgow, 1984-93. Publications: Proof of Fact in Criminal Trials, 1984; Cross-examination in Criminal Trials, 1988; Fact-Finding for Magistrates, 1990; Representing Clients in Mediation, 1998. Recreations: swimming; music. Address: (b.) Advocates Library, Parliament House, Edinburgh.

Stone, Professor Trevor W., BPharm, PhD, DSc. Professor and Head of Pharmacology, Glasgow University, since 1989; b. 7.10.47, Mexborough; m., Anne Corina. Educ. Mexborough Grammar School; London University; Aberdeen University. Lecturer in Physiology, Aberdeen University, 1970-77; Senior Lecturer/Reader in Neuroscience, then Professor of Neuroscience, London University, 1977-88. Editor, British Journal of Pharmacology, 1980-86. Publications: Microiontophoresis and Pressure Ejection, 1985; Purines: Basic and Clinical Aspects, 1991; Neuropharmacology, 1995; Pills, Potions and Poisons – How Drugs Work, 2000. Recreations: photography; snooker; music; working. Address: (b.) Department of Pharmacology, West Medical Building, Glasgow University, Glasgow G12; T.-0141-330 4481.

Stott, Professor David James, MB, ChB, MD(Glas), FRCP(Glas), FRCP(Edin). Professor of Geriatric Medicine, Glasgow University, since 1994; b. 4.6.59, Rugby; m., Shiona; 1 s.; 1 d. Educ. Eastwood High School; Glasgow University. Trained in research methodology, MRC Blood Pressure Unit, 1982-84; Senior Lecturer (Honorary Consultant) in Geriatric Medicine, 1991-94. Recreations: golf; hill-walking; acoustic guitar. Address: (b.) Academic Section of Geriatric Medicine, Glasgow Royal Infirmary G4 0SF; T.-0141-211 4976.

Stove, Thomas William. Convener, Shetland Islands Council, since 1999; b. 17.7.35, Sandwick, Shetland; m., Alma; 2 d. Educ. Anderson Education Institute, Lerwick. Owner/Director, Televiradio (Shetland) Ltd., 1966-96; Member, Zetland County Council/Shetland Islands Council, 1970-78; Member, Lerwick Harbour Trust, 1980-96 (Chairman, 1983-96). Chairman, Shetland Branch, Multiple Sclerosis Society. Recreations: boating; walking; classic cars. Address: (h.) Nordaal, Sandwick, Shetland ZE2 9HP; T.-01950 431434.

Strachan, Professor Hew Francis Anthony, MA, PhD, FRHistS. Chichele Professor of the History of War and Fellow, All Souls College, University of Oxford, since 2002; Professor of Modern History, Glasgow University, 1992-2002 (Visiting Professor, since 2002); Director, Scottish Centre for War Studies, 1996-2002; Life Fellow, Corpus Christi College, Cambridge, since 1992; b. 1.9.49, Edinburgh; m., Pamela Dorothy Tennant (née Symes); 1 s.; 1 step s.; 2 d.; 1 step d. Educ. Rugby School; Corpus Christi College, Cambridge. Senior Lecturer, Department of War Studies and International Affairs, Royal Military Academy, Sandhurst, 1978-79; Research Fellow, Corpus Christi College, Cambridge, 1975-78; Fellow, Corpus Christi College, since 1979: Tutor for Admissions, 1981-88, Director of Studies in History, 1986-92, Senior Tutor, 1987 and 1989-92. Governor, Rugby School, since 1985, and Stowe School, since 1990; Member, Council, Society for Army Historical Research, 1980-95, Army Records Society, 1990-94, Council, National Army Museum, since 1994; Joint Editor, War in History; Member, Queen's Bodyguard for Scotland (Royal Company of Archers); Visiting Professor, Royal Norwegian Air Force Academy, since 2000. Publications: British Military Uniforms; History of the Cambridge University Officers Training Corps; European Armies and the Conduct of War; Wellington's Legacy: the Reform of the British Army 1830-54; From Waterloo to Balaclava: Tactics, Technology, and the British Army 1815-1854 (Templer Medal, 1986); The Politics of the British Army (Westminster Medal, 1998); Oxford Illustrated History of the First World War (Editor), 1998; The British Army, Manpower and Society into the 21st Century (Editor), 2000; The First World War Vol. I: To Arms, 2001; numerous articles and reviews. Recreations: shooting; rugby football. Address: (b.) All Souls College, University of Oxford; (h.) 5 Winton Drive, Glasgow G12 0PZ.

Strang, David James Reid, BSc, MSc. Chief Constable, Dumfries and Galloway Constabulary, since 2001; b. 9.4.58, Glasgow; m., Dr Alison B. Strang; 1 s.; 2 d. Educ. Glasgow Academy; Loretto School; St Chad's

College, Durham University; Birkbeck College, London University. Constable to Chief Superintendent, Metropolitan Police, 1980-98; Assistant Chief Constable, Lothian and Borders Police, 1998-2001. Address: (b.) Dumfries and Galloway Constabulary, Cornwall Mount, Dumfries DG1 1PZ; T.-01387 260522.

Strang, Gavin Steel, BSc (Hons), DipAgriSci, PhD. MP (Labour), East Edinburgh, since 1970; Minister for Transport, 1997-98; b. 10.7.43, Dundee; m., Bettina Smith; 1 s. Educ. Morrison's Academy, Crieff; Edinburgh University. Parliamentary Under Secretary of State, Department of Energy, February to October, 1974; Parliamentary Secretary, Ministry of Agriculture, 1974-79; Principal Labour Agriculture Spokesman, 1992-97. Recreations: golf; swimming; the countryside. Address: (b.) House of Commons, Westminster, London; T.-0171-219 3000.

Strang, William Frank Gourlay, BA (Oxon). Secretary to Forestry Commission, since 1997; b. 30.6.61, Glasgow; m., Eleanor Ann Munro-Faure; 1 d. Educ. Loretto; St. Edmund Hall, Oxford. Administration Trainee, Ministry of Agriculture Fisheries and Food, 1984; Private Secretary to Permanent Secretary, 1987-88; Private Secretary to Parliamentary Secretary, 1988-89; Agricultural Attache, British Embassy, Paris, 1990-94; Principal Private Secretary to Minister of Agriculture, 1994-97. Recreations: hillwalking; bagpipes; local church. Address: (b.) Forestry Commission, 231 Corstorphine Road, Edinburgh; T.-0131-314 6432.

Strang Steel, Sir (Fiennes) Michael, 3rd Bt; b. 22.2.43; m., Sally Russell; 2 s.; 1 d. Educ. Eton. Retired Major, 17th/21st Lancers, 1962-80. Former Forestry Commissioner; DL. Address: (h.) Philiphaugh, Selkirk, TD7 5LX.

Strang Steel, Malcolm Graham, BA (Cantab), LLB, WS. Partner, Turcan Connell, WS, since 1997; Partner, W. & J. Burness, WS, 1973-97; b. 24.11.46, Selkirk; m., Margaret Philippa Scott; 1 s.; 1 d. Educ. Eton; Trinity College, Cambridge; Edinburgh University. Sometime Chairman, Albyn Housing Society Ltd., Scottish Dyslexia Trust; Member, Council, Law Society of Scotland, 1984-90; Secretary, Scottish Agricultural Arbiters Association. Recreations: shooting; fishing; skiing; tennis; reading. Address: (b.) Princes Exchange, 1 Earl Grey Street, Edinburgh EH3 9EE; T.-0131-228 8111.

Strange, Lady (Jean Cherry), MA, FIMarE, FSAScot. Peer of the Realm, since 1986; President, War Widows Association of Great Britain, since 1990; b. 17.12.28, London; m., Humphrey Drummond of Megginch; 3 s.; 3 d. Educ. Oxenfoord Castle School; St. Andrews University; Cambridge University. Member: All Party Parliamentary Defence Group, Executive Committee, Association of Conservative Peers, 1990-93, All Party Committee for Children, Executive Committee, IPU. Publications: Love from Belinda; Lalage in Love; Creatures Great and Small; Love is Forever (poems); The Remarkable Life of Victoria Drummond, Marine Engineer. Address: (b.) Megginch Castle, Errol, Perthshire.

Strathclyde, Lord (Thomas Strathclyde), PC. Leader of the Opposition, House of Lords, since 1998; b. 22.2.60, Glasgow; m., Jane; 3 d. Educ. Wellington College; East Anglia University; University of Aix-en-Provence. Bain Clarkson, Insurance Brokers, 1982-88; Government Whip, 1988; Minister for Tourism, 1989; Minister for Agriculture and Fisheries, Scottish Office, 1990-92; Parliamentary Under Secretary of State, DoE, 1992-93; Minister of State, Department of Trade and Industry, 1993-94; Government Chief Whip, 1994-97; Opposition Chief Whip, 1997-98. Chairman, Strathclyde

Commission on Restructuring the Scottish Conservative and Unionist Party, 1997-98. Address: (b.) House of Lords, London SW1; T.-020 7219 5353.

Strathmore and Kinghorne, 18th Earl of (Michael Fergus Bowes Lyon); b. 7.6.57; m.; 3 s. President, Boys' Brigade, 1994-99; DL, Angus, since 1993. Address: Glamis Castle, Forfar, DD8 1QJ.

Straton, Timothy Duncan, TD, CA, ATII. Partner, Scott-Moncrieff, Chartered Accountants, since 1969; b. 1.10.42, Edinburgh; m., Gladys Margaret George (deceased); 1 s.; 1 d. Educ. Edinburgh Academy. Honorary Treasurer: Royal British Legion Scotland, SSAFA Forces Help (Edinburgh Mid and East Lothian Branch). Recreations: driving; photography; golf. Address: (b.) 17 Melville Street, Edinburgh EH3 7PH; T.-0131-473 3500; e-mail: tim.straton@scott-moncrieff.com

Street, Margaret Dobson; b. 18.10.20, Hawick; m., Richard Andrew Rutherford Street (deceased); 2 s. Educ. Hawick High School; Alva Academy. Civil Servant, 1938-48; Ministry of Labour and National Service, 1938-47; Ministry of National Insurance (Inspectorate), 1947-48; voluntary work since 1948, apart from freelance writing on household and conservation topics; Honorary Secretary Leith Civic Trust, until 1997, Patron, since 1998; Convener, Friends of North Carr Lightship; Member, North East Fife District Council, North Carr Management Committee; Saltire Society Representative, Council, National Trust for Scotland, 1986-95; Secretary, Mungo Park Commemoration Committee; Trustee, Robert Hurd Memorial Fund; Appeal Convener, Wallace Statue, Lanark; Member, Steering Committee, Brownsbank; Appeal Convener, Wallace Statue, Dryburgh; Vice-Chairman, Saltire Society, 1983-94, Chairman, 1995-97; Saltire Society's Andrew Fletcher of Saltoun Award for services to Scotland, 1992; Honorary Member, Saltire Society, 1997. Recreations: promotion of Scottish cultural activity; conservation; good cooking. Address: (h.) 115 Trinity Road, Edinburgh; T.-0131-552 2409.

Stretton, James, BA, FFA. Member, Court, Bank of England, since 1998; Deputy Chairman, Edinburgh International Festival; Member, Court, University of Edinburgh; b. 16.12.43, Peterborough; m., Isobel Robertson; 2 d. Educ. Laxton Grammar School, Oundle; Worcester College, Oxford. Joined Standard Life, 1965. Recreations: music; gardening; reading; golf. Address: (h.) 15 Letham Mains, Haddington EH41 4NW.

Stringer, Professor Joan Kathleen, CBE, BA, CertEd, PhD, CIMgt, FRSA, FRSE. Principal, Queen Margaret University College, Edinburgh, since 1996; Commissioner (with responsibility for Scotland), Equal Opportunities Commission, 1995-2001; Vice Convener, Committee of Scottish Higher Education Principals, since 1998; Member: Executive Committee, Scottish Council Development and Industry, since 1998, Council, World Association for Co-operative Education, since 1998, Scottish Council for Postgraduate Medical and Dental Education, since 1999, Edinburgh International Festival Council, since 1999, Scottish Health Minister's Learning Together Strategy Implementation Group, since 2000, Scottish Committee, British Council, since 2000, Scottish European Structural Funds Forum, since 2000; Department of Health's Working Group on the Modernisation of the SHO, Scottish Nursing and Midwifery Education Council Advisory Group, Universities UK (formerly CVCP) Equality Challenge Steering Group, Development Advisory Board for Scottish Opera and Scottish Ballet; Convener, Product Standards Committee, Scottish Quality Salmon; Member, Scottish Minister for Enterprise and Lifelong Learning's Careers Scotland – Shadow Ministerial Joint Supervisory Group; b. 12.5.48, Stoke on Trent; m., Roel Mali. Educ. Portland House High School, Stoke on Trent; Stoke on Trent College of Art; Keele University. Assistant Principal, Robert Gordon University, 1991-96, having joined as Lecturer, 1980; Visiting Lecturer, Aberdeen University, 1984-86; Member, Joint University Council for Social and Public Administration, 1982-91; Member, Royal Institute of Public Administration, 1984-91; Member, Management Board, North of Scotland Consortium on Wider Access, 1988-92; Auditor, Higher Education Quality Council, 1992-95; Member, Board of Management, Aberdeen College, 1992-96; Member, Grampian Health Board, 1994-96; Member, CVCP Commission on University Career Opportunities, 1995-2001; Member, Scottish Committee, National Committee of Inquiry into Higher Education (The Dearing Committee), 1996-97; Member, Human Fertilisation and Embryology Authority, 1996-99; Member, Secretary of State's Consultative Steering Group and Financial Issues Advisory Group on the Scottish Parliament, 1998-99; Chair, Northern Ireland Equality Commission Working Group, 1998-99; Commissioner, Scottish Election Commission, 1999. Address: (b.) Queen Margaret University College, Clerwood Terrace, Edinburgh, EH12 8TS; T.-01651 842430.

Strudwick, Major General Mark Jeremy, CBE. Chief Executive, The Prince's Scottish Youth Business Trust, since 2000; b. 19.4.45; m., Janet Elizabeth Coleridge Vivers; 1 s.; 1 d. Educ. St. Edmund's School, Canterbury; Royal Military Academy, Sandhurst. Commissioned, The Royal Scots (The Royal Regiment), 1966 (Colonel, 1995); served UK, BAOR, Cyprus, Canada, India, Northern Ireland (Despatches twice); Commanded, 1st Bn. The Royal Scots, 1984-87; Instructor, Staff College Camberley, 1987-88; Assistant Chief of Staff, G1/G4 HQ Northern Ireland 1988-90; Higher Command and Staff Course, 1989; Commanded, 3 Infantry Bde., 1990-91; NDC New Delhi, 1992; Deputy Military Secretary, Ministry of Defence, 1993-95; Director of Infantry, 1996-97; ADC to HM The Queen, 1996-97; General Officer Commanding, Army in Scotland, and Governor, Edinburgh Castle, 1997-2000; Colonel Commandant, The Scottish Division, 1997-2000. Member, Royal Company of Archers, Queen's Bodyguard for Scotland; Commodore Infantry Sailing Association, 1997-2000; Her Majesty's Commissioner, Queen Victoria School, Dunblane, 1997-2000; Governor: Royal School, Bath, 1993-2000, Gordonstoun School, since 1999; Chairman, Scottish Veterans' Residences. Recreations: golf; shooting; sailing. Address: c/o Regimental Headquarters, The Royal Scots (The Royal Regiment), The Castle, Edinburgh EH1 2YT; T.-0131-310 5014; e-mail: rhqroyalscots@edinburghcastle.fsnet.co.uk

Struthers, Professor Allan, BSc, MD, FRCP, FESC. Professor of Cardiovascular Medicine and Therapeutics, Dundee University, since 2000; b. 14.8.52, Glasgow; m., Julia Diggen; 1 s.; 1 d. Educ. Hutchesons' Boys' Grammar School; Glasgow University. Junior posts, Glasgow teaching hospitals, 1977-82; Senior Medical Registrar, Royal Postgraduate Medical School and Hammersmith Hospital, London, 1983-85; Wellcome Senior Lecturer, Department of Clinical Pharmacology, Ninewells Hospital, 1985-92; Professor of Clinical Pharmacology, 1992-2000. Recreations: cycling; swimming. Address: Bech-na-Mara, 5 Riverview, Newport-on-Tay DD6 8QX; T.-01382 542697.

Struthers, Professor John Joseph Mathew, MA (Hons), MPhil, FRSA. Head, Division of Economics and Enterprise, Paisley Business School, Paisley University, since 2000; b. 2.1.53, Glasgow; m., Justina Vida Offirawa; 3s. Educ. St Thomas Aquinas, Glasgow; Glasgow University. Tutor, Economics, Glasgow University, 1975-77; Lecturer, University of Ilorin, Nigeria, 1977-78; University of Paisley: Lecturer, Senior Lecturer, Professor, Dean of Faculty of Information, Social and Management Sciences, Dean of Faculty of Business;Tutor, Open University, 1979-93; Visiting Lecturer: Fourah Bay College, University of Sierra Leone, 1981; Glasgow University, 1986- 2000; Stirling University, 1990; Visiting Professor, Money and Banking, Dubai Polytechnic, 1998- 2001; led Foreign and Commonwealth Office Know-How Fund Project, Yaroslav State University, Russia, 1992-96; Paisley University Socrates-Erasmus Co-ordinator, since 1993; Director Paisley and Renfrewshire Enterprise Trust, 1993-96; Member, Association of Business Schools Undergraduate Steering Committee, since 1999; Director, Paisley Chamber of Commerce, since 1996. Publications: Money: Institutions Theory and Policy (co-author), 1986; numerous articles. Recreations: reading; walking; music; collecting things. Address: (b.) Paisley Business School, Paisley University, High Street, Paisley, PA1 2BE; T.-0141-848 3364.

Stuart, Jamie; b. 10.9.20, Glasgow; widower; 2 d. Educ. Whitehill School, Glasgow. Flying Officer/Wireless Operator/Air Gunner, RAF, 1941-46; Actor/Social Worker/Evangelist; athlete: Scottish two-miles steeplechase champion, 1948. Publications: A Glasgow Bible; Will I Be Called An Author? Address: (h.) 436 Edinburgh Road, Glasgow G33 2PW; T.-0141-778 2437.

Stuart, John Forester, MA (Cantab). Secretary General, General Synod, Scottish Episcopal Church, since 1996; b. 26.5.59, Broughty Ferry; m., Sally Ann Bell; 2 s. Educ. Dundee High School; Daniel Stewart's and Melville College; Queens' College Cambridge, College of Law, Guildford.Articled Clerk and subsequently Solicitor, MacFarlanes, London, 1982-86; Solicitor and subsequently Partner, J. & F. Anderson, Solicitors, Edinburgh (merged, 1992, to become Anderson Strathern), 1986-96. Recreations: music; walking; astronomy. Address: (b.) 21 Grosvenor Crescent, Edinburgh EH12 5EE; T.-0131-225 6357.

Stuart, Mhairi Ross, MA (Hons). Presenter, Good Morning Scotland, BBC Scotland, since 1999; b. 8.12.67, Glasgow; m., Roderick Stuart. Educ. Cleveden Secondary School, Glasgow; Glasgow University. BBC, since 1991 (News Trainee/Producer/Presenter). BT Scotland Radio News Broadcaster of the Year, 1999. Recreations: sailing; skiing. Address: (b.) News Room, BBC Scotland, Queen Margaret Drive, Glasgow G12 8DG; T.-0141-338 2676.

Stuart, Michael John, BSc (Hons). Manager, Excellence/Special Funds, Aberdeen City Council, 1999-2002; Headteacher, Kincorth Academy, 1990-99; b. 24.11.46, Fraserburgh; m., Daniele Madeleine; 2 s.; 1 d. Educ. Fraserburgh Academy; Aberdeen University. Assistant Teacher, Fraserburgh Academy, 1970-71; Kelvinside Academy, Glasgow, 1971-72; Principal Teacher, Greenwood Academy, Irvine, 1972-81; Assistant Head Teacher, Loudoun Academy, Galston, 1981-89; Depute Head Teacher, Carrick Academy, Maybole, 1989-90. Recreations: golf; angling; hill-walking. Address: (b.) Summerhill Education Centre, Stronsay Drive, Aberdeen AB15 6JA; T.-01224 346301; e-mail: mstuart@education.aberdeen.net

Stubbs, Ian Michael, LLB, CA, FTII. Partner, Maclay Murray & Spens, Solicitors, since 1973; b. 14.11.43, Birmingham; m., Joan Baird Crowther; 2 s.; 1 d. Educ. Marr College, Troon; Glasgow University. Thomson McLintock, Glasgow, 1965-68; Apprentice/Assistant, Maclay Murray & Spens, 1968-73. Council Member, Law Society of Scotland, since 1995; Council Member, Institute of Chartered Accountants of Scotland, 1986-92; Past Chairman, Board of Examiners, Law Society of Scotland; Senior Tutor, Wills Trusts and Executries, Glasgow University, 1980-86. Address: (h.) Suffolk Lodge, Methven Road, Whitecraigs, Glasgow, G46; T.-0141-639 6580.

Sturgeon, David, BL, MLitt. Registrar and Deputy Secretary, Heriot-Watt University, 1967-95; b. 10.12.35, Kilwinning; m., Nancy McDougall; 1 d.; 2 s. Educ. Dalry High School, Ayrshire (Blair Medallist, 1950); Glasgow University. National Service (RASC - War Office), 1957-59; Trainee Actuary, Scottish Widows Fund, 1959-61; Administrative Assistant, Royal College of Science and Technology (later, Strathclyde University), 1961-67. Secretary and Treasurer, Edinburgh Society of Glasgow University Graduates, since 1971; Hon. degree, Heriot-Watt University, 1996. Recreations: golf; music (particularly Scottish country dance music). Address: (h.) 10 Dalhousie Road, Eskbank, Midlothian EH22 3AS; T.-0131-663 1059; e-mail: davidsturgeon35@hotmail.com

Sturgeon, Nicola, LLB (Hons), DipLP. MSP (SNP), Glasgow, since 1999; SNP Spokesperson on Health and Community Care; b. 19.7.70, Irvine. Educ. Greenwood Academy, Irvine; University of Glasgow. Trainee Solicitor, Glasgow, 1993-95; Solicitor, Stirling, 1995-97; Solicitor, Drumchapel Law Centre, Glasgow, 1997-99. Recreations: reading; theatre; badminton. Address: (b.) Scottish Parliament, Edinburgh EH99 1SP.

Sturrock, Professor John Garrow, QC, LLB (Hons), LLM. Queen's Counsel, since 1999; Director of Training and Education, Faculty of Advocates, since 1994; Visiting Professor of Advocacy Skills and Conflict Resolution, Glasgow Graduate School of Law, since 1999; Managing Director, Core Consulting and Mediation Ltd., since 1999; b. 15.4.58, Stirling; m., Fiona Swanson; 2 s.; 1 d. Educ. Stirling High School; Waid Academy, Anstruther; Edinburgh University; University of Pennsylvania. Senior President, Edinburgh University Students' Association, 1980-81; apprentice Solicitor, 1981-83; qualified Solicitor, 1983-84; Harkness Fellow, US, 1984-85; Member, Faculty of Advocates, since 1986; Standing Junior Counsel to Department of Transport in Scotland, 1991-94; Member, Judicial Studies Committee in Scotland, since 1997; Member, Training Faculty, Centre for Dispute Resolution, since 1999; accredited Mediator, since 1996; Member, Joint Standing Committee on Legal Education, since 1988; Member, Advisory Board, Centre for Professional Legal Practice, Dundee University, since 1998; Assessor, Scottish Higher Education Funding Council, 1995-96; Elder, Mayfield-Salisbury Parish Church, since 1991. Recreations: family; golf; contemporary music; ships and the sea. Address: (h.) 22 Fountainhall Road, Edinburgh EH9 2LW; T.-0131-667 9786; e-mail: John.Sturrock@core-consulting.com

Sturrock, Professor Robert Ralph, MB, ChB, DSc, FRCSEdin. Professor of Anatomy, Dundee University, since 1992; b. 1.7.43, Dundee; m., Norma Duncan; 1 d. Educ. Dundee High School; St. Andrews University. House Surgeon, Perth Royal Infirmary, 1967-68; House Physician, Stirling Royal Infirmary, 1968; Demonstrator, then Lecturer, Anatomy Department, Dundee University, 1968-77; Visiting Associate Professor of Neuroanatomy, Iowa University, 1976; Senior Lecturer, Dundee, 1977-81; Reader in Anatomy, 1981-92. Symington Memorial Prize in Anatomy, 1978; Convener, Tayforth Universities Military Education Committee, since 1997. Address: (b.) Dundee University, Dundee, DD1 4HN.

Sturrock, Professor Roger Davidson, MB, BS, MRCS, MD, FRCPLond, FRCPGlas. McLeod/ARC Professor of Rheumatology, Glasgow University, since 1990; b. 20.10.46, Dundee; m., Helen; 3 d. Educ. Llanelli Boys' Grammar School; Queen Mary's School, Basingstoke; London University. Senior Lecturer and Hon. Consultant, Westminster Medical School, 1977-79; Senior Lecturer in Medicine and Hon. Consultant, Centre for Rheumatic Diseases, Glasgow Royal Infirmary, 1979-90; President, British Society for Rheumatology, 1996-98; Chair, Board of Trustees, Arthritis Research Campaign. Recreations: hillwalking; music; choral singing. Address: (b.) University Department of Medicine, Royal Infirmary, Glasgow G31 2ER; T.-0141-211 4687; e-mail: r.d.sturrock@clinmed.gla.ac.uk

Subak-Sharpe, Professor John Herbert, CBE, FInstBiol, BSc, PhD, FRSE. Professor Emeritus, Glasgow University and Honorary Senior Research Fellow in Virology, since 1994; Professor of Virology, Glasgow University, 1968-94; Honorary Director, MRC Virology Unit, Institute of Virology, Glasgow, 1968-94; b. 14.2.24, Vienna; m., Barbara Naomi Morris; 2 s.; 1 d. Educ. Humanistisches Gymnasium, Vienna; Birmingham University. Assistant Lecturer, Glasgow University, 1954-56; Member, ARC scientific staff, AVRI Pirbright, 1956-61; Visiting Fellow, California Institute of Technology, 1961; Member, MRC Experimental Virus Unit scientific staff, Glasgow, 1961-68; Visiting Professor, NIH, Bethesda, 1967-68. Visiting Fellow, Clare Hall, Cambridge, 1986; elected Member (Past Chairman, Course and Workshops Committee), EMBO, since 1969; Trustee (former Secretary and Vice-President), Genetical Society, 1971-99; Member, Genetic Manipulation Advisory Group, 1976-80; Chairman, MRC Training Awards Panel, 1986-89; Member, Governing Body, West of Scotland Oncological Organisation, since 1974, and Governing Body, Animal Virus Research Institute, Pirbright, 1986-88; Member, Scientific Advisory Group, Equine Virology Research Foundation, 1987-98; Member, Medical Research Council Cell Biology and Disorders Board, 1988-92; Biochemical Society CIBA Medal and Prize, 1994. Recreations: travel; bridge. Address: (h.) 63 Kelvin Court, Glasgow G12 0AG; T.-0141-339 1863.

Suckling, Professor Colin James, BSc, PhD, DSc, CChem, FRSC, FRSA, FRSE. Professor of Chemistry, Strathclyde University, since 1984 (Vice Principal, 2000-02); b. 24.3.47, Birkenhead; m., Catherine Mary Faulkner; 2 s.; 1 d. Educ. Quarry Bank High School, Liverpool; Liverpool University. Lecturer, Department of Pure and Applied Chemistry, Strathclyde University, 1972; Royal Society Smith and Nephew Senior Research Fellow, 1980; Dean, Faculty of Science, 1992-96; Deputy Principal, 1996-98; Pro-Vice Principal, 1998-2000; Convener, RSE Chemistry Committee, 1989-91; Member of Council, RSE, 1989-92; Member, General Teaching Council, 1993-95; Member, Board: Systems Level Integration Ltd., 1998-2000, Lanarkshire Technology and Innovation Centre, 1998-2000; Governor, Bell College of Technology; Chairman, West of Scotland Schools Symphony Orchestra Board. Publications: Chemistry Through Models (Co-author), 1978; Biological Chemistry (Co-author), 1980; Enzyme Chemistry, Impact and Applications (Co-author), 1984, 1989, 1998; 140 research publications. Recreations: music; horn playing. Address: (b.) Department of Pure and Applied Chemistry, Strathclyde Universtiy, 295 Cathedral Street Glasgow, G1 1XL; T.-0141-548 2271; e-mail: c.j.suckling@strath.ac.uk

Suggett, Gavin Robert, MA, MSc, FCA. Director (Managing), The Alliance Trust PLC, since 1995, The Second Alliance Trust PLC, since 1995; Director, Alliance Trust Savings Ltd., since 1986; b. 11.5.44, Sunderland; m., Louise Thomson; 1 s.; 2 d. Educ. Felsted; Christ's College Cambridge; London Business School. Deloitte Haskins & Sells; Weir Group PLC; Alliance Trust PLC: Assistant Company Secretary, Company Secretary, Director, Deputy Managing Director. Recreations: skiing; golf; gardening; keep-fit. Address: (b.) Meadow House, 64 Reform Street, Dundee DD1 1TJ; T.-01382 201700.

Sughrue, Cindy, PhD, BA (Hons). Head of Dance, Scottish Arts Council, since 2001; b. 30.3.63, Boston, USA. Educ. Sheffield University; Boston University. Freelance teacher, lecturer, performer, 1981-90; Director, Collective Gallery, 1990-94; General Manager,

Dance Base, 1994-97; Senior Performing Arts Officer, Scottish Arts Council, 1997-2001. Marshall Scholar, 1985-88; Ruth Michaelis-Jena Ratcliff Prize, special commendation, 1993. Recreations: hill-walking; attending dance/performing arts; travel. Address: (b.) Scottish Arts Council, 12 Manor Place, Edinburgh EH3 7DD; T.-0131-226 6051.

Suleiman, Professor Yasir, BA, PhD, BA, DipTFLA, FRSE. Professor of Arabic and Islamic Studies, University of Edinburgh, since 1990 (Director, Edinburgh Institute for Advanced Study of Islam and the Middle East, since 1997); b. Jerusalem (East), Palestine; m., Shahla Awad; 2 s. Educ. Amman University, Jordan; St. Andrews University; Durham University. Banker, 1973-74; Teacher of English as a Foreign Language, Kuwait, 1974-75; University of St. Andrews: Teaching Fellow in Lingusitics, 1977-80, Lecturer in Linguistics, 1980-83, Lecturer in Linguistics and Arabic, 1984-90; University of Edinburgh: Head, Department of Islamic and Middle Eastern Studies, 1990-92, Head of Asian and Modern European Languages, 1992-95, Member, Court, 1994-98. Vice-President and Chair, Council, British Society for Middle Eastern Studies, 1995-97. Publications: Arabic Sociolinguistics, 1995; Language and Identity in the Middle East and North Africa, 1996; Arabic Grammatical Tradition, 1999; Language and Society in Middle East and North Africa, 1999; Arabic Grammar and Linguistics, 1999. Recreations: squash; walking. Address: (b.) 7 Buccleuch Place, Edinburgh EH8 9LW.

Summers, John P., FREHIS, MIWM. National Director, Keep Scotland Beautiful, since 1999; b. 22.12.46, Rhynie; m., Alison; 1 s.; 1 d. Educ. Aberdeen Academy; Napier College, Edinburgh. Assistant Environmental Health Officer, Aberdeen County Council, 1972-74; Divisional Environmental Health Officer, Kincardine and Deeside District, 1974-79; Depute Director of Environmental Health, Banff and Buchan District Council, 1979-90; Moray District Council: Director of Environmental Health, 1990-94, Chief Executive, 1994-96; Director, Technical and Leisure Services, Moray Council, 1996-99. President, Royal Environmental Health Institute of Scotland, 1995-96 (Fellow, 1997). Recreations: rambling; enjoying traditional Scottish folk music and bagpipe playing; family; travelling. Address: (h.) 12 Dryburgh Crescent, Perth: T.-443148; (b.) 7 Melville Terrace, Stirling; T.-471333.

Sunter, Thomas Lacey Murray, FIMgt, FRSA, MNI. Director, Institute of Directors (Scotland), since 1997; Deputy Lieutenant, Fife; b. 14.8.41, Liverpool; m., Margaret; 3 d. Educ. Merchant Taylors School, Crosby; Royal Naval College, Dartmouth. Royal Navy, 1960-96, including command of HMS Scylla, 1984-86 and HMS Endurance, 1987-89; UN Treaty Inspector, Antarctica, 1987-89; Ministry of Defence, 1989-91; Commander, RN Forces Hong Kong, 1991-94; Naval Base Commander, Rosyth, 1994-96; Chief Executive, Business Enterprise Scotland, 1996-97. Director, Scottish Enterprise Fife; Director, Scottish Director Development Centre; Trustee, Scottish Fisheries Museum. Recreations: golf; tennis; reading. Address: (h.) Kirklands Cottage, Saline, Fife; T.-01383 723444.

Sutherland, Countess of (Elizabeth Millicent Sutherland). Chief of Clan Sutherland; b. 30.3.21; m., Charles Noel Janson; 2 s.; 1 s. (deceased); 1 d. Educ. Queen's College, London; abroad. Land Army, 1939-41; Laboratory Technician, Raigmore Hospital, Inverness, and St. Thomas's Hospital, London, 1941-45. Address: (h.) Dunrobin Castle, Sutherland; House of Tongue, Lairg, Sutherland.

Sutherland of Houndwood, Lord (Stewart Ross), FBA, FRSE, MA. Principal and Vice-Chancellor, Edinburgh University, since 1994; b. 25.2.41, Aberdeen; m., Sheena Robertson; 1 s.; 2 d. Educ. Robert Gordon's College;

Aberdeen University; Cambridge University. Assistant Lecturer, Philosophy, UCNW, 1965-68; Lecturer, Senior Lecturer, Reader, Stirling University, 1968-77; Professor, Philosophy of Religion, King's College, London, 1977-90 (Vice-Principal, 1981-85, Principal, 1985-90); Vice-Chancellor, London University, 1990-94, and HM Chief Inspector of Schools (England), 1992-94; Visiting Fellow, Australian National University, 1974; Chairman, Brit. Acad. Postgraduate Studentships, 1987-94; Member: Council for Science and Technology, 1993-2000, Hong Kong University Grants Com., since 1995, Higher Education Funding Council, England, since 1996, Iona Abbey Trust, since 1994; Editor, Religious Studies, 1984-90; Chairman: Royal Commission on the Funding of Long-Term Care of the Elderly, 1997-99, Secretary of State's Committee on Appeal Procedures, 1994-96, Royal Institute of Philosophy, since 1988, Newbattle College Trustees, since 1995; President, Society for Study of Theology, 1985, 1986. Publications: several books and papers. Recreations: jazz; theatre; rough gardening. Address: (b.) Edinburgh University, Old College, South Bridge, EH8 9YL; T.-0131-650 2150.

Sutherland, Rt. Hon. Lord (Ranald Iain Sutherland), PC, QC (Scot). Senator of the College of Justice, 1985-2001; b. 23.1.32. Advocate Depute, 1962-64, 1971-77; QC (Scot), 1969.

Sutherland, Alan D.A., MA (Hons), MBA, MA. Water Industry Commissioner for Scotland, since 1999; b. 8.4.62, Glasgow; m., Olga; 1 s.; 1 d. Educ. Eastwood High School; St Andrews University; University of Pennsylvania. Management trainee, Lloyds Bank PLC, 1984-85; Stockbroker, Savory Milln, 1985-86; Robert Fleming & Company, investment bank, 1986-91; Management Consultant, Bain & Company, 1992-97; Managing Director, Wolverine CIS Ltd., 1997-99. Recreations: theatre; restaurants; history. Address: (b.) Office of the Water Industry Commissioner for Scotland, Ochil House, Springkerse Business Park, Stirling FK7 7XE; e-mail: enquiries@watercommissioner.co.uk

Sutherland, Colin T., BSc (Hons). Head Teacher, North Berwick High School, since 1999; b. 21.11.55, Glasgow; m., Anne; 2s. Educ. Paisley Grammar School; Glasgow University. Teacher, Garnock Academy, Kilbirnie, 1978-80; Teacher, Assistant Principal Teacher, Principal Teacher (Guidance), Castlehead High School, Paisley, 1980-90; Assistant Head Teacher, Greenock High School, 1991-94; Depute Head Teacher, Port Glasgow High School, 1994-99; Church elder, since 1982; Children's Panel, 1986-90; Member, Council, Headteachers' Association of Scotland, since 1999. Recreations: family activity; reading; swimming; walking; cycling. Address: (b.) North Berwick High School, Grange Road, North Berwick, EH39 4QS; T.-01620 894661; e-mail: c_sutherland@northberwick.e-lothian.sch.uk

Sutherland, David I.M., CBE, MA, MEd, DLitt, DUniv, FCCEAM, FIMgt, FRSA. Registrar, The General Teaching Council for Scotland, 1985-2001; b. 22.1.38, Wick; m., Janet H. Webster; 2 s. Educ. Aberdeen Grammar School; Aberdeen University; University of Zurich. Teacher of Modern Languages, Aberdeen Grammar School, 1962-66; Lecturer in Education, Stranmillis College of Education, Belfast, 1966-69; Lecturer in Educational Psychology, Craigie College of Education, Ayr, 1969-72; Assistant Director of Education, Sutherland County Council, 1972-75; Divisional Education Officer (Inverness), then Depute Director of Education, Highland Regional Council, 1975-85. Recreations: golf; walking; theatre; reading. Address: Hazelwood, 5 Bonnington Road, Peebles EH45 9HF; T.-01721 722232.

Sutherland, Elizabeth (Elizabeth Margaret Marshall), FSA Scot. Writer; b. 24.8.26, Kemback, Cupar; m., Rev. John D. Marshall; 2 s.; 1 d. Educ. St. Leonard's Girls' School, St. Andrews; Edinburgh University. Social Worker for Scottish Episcopal Church, 1974-80; Curator, Groam House Museum, Rosemarkie, 1982-93; author of: Lent Term (Constable Trophy), 1973, The Seer of Kintail, 1974, Hannah Hereford (Scottish Arts Council Book Award), 1976, The Eye of God, 1977, The Weeping Tree, 1980, Ravens and Black Rain: The Story of Highland Second Sight, 1985, The Gold Key and The Green Life, 1986; In Search of the Picts, 1994; Guide to the Pictish Stones, 1997; Five Euphemias: Women in Medieval Scotland, 1999; Lydia, Wife of Hugh Miller of Cromarty, 2002. Recreations: Highland history; Gaelic language; the Picts; walking. Address: (h.) 17 Mackenzie Terrace, Rosemarkie, Ross-shire IV10 8UH; T.-Fortrose 620924.

Sutherland, George O., CA, MCT, FIMgt, FRSA. Director of Finance, Edinburgh University, since 1994; b. 5.11.44, Dundee; m., Jane; 1 s.; 3 d. Educ. Morgan Academy; St.Andrews University. TA, 1962-72. Shell International Petroleum Co. Ltd., 1969-92, serving in Libya, Hong Kong, United Arab Emirates, Norway, Brunei and Syria; set up a major World Bank power project in Pakistan, 1992-93; Member of Royal Artillery Council for Scotland Lowland Reserve Forces and Cadets Association; Joint Universities of Edinburgh Military Education Committee; Member, Advisory Board, Centre for Second World War Studies; Member, ICAS committees. Recreations: military and aviation history; organised and led expeditions in Sahara desert and Borneo jungle, the latter identifying historically significant aircraft wrecks; battlefields; flying; hill-walking; water sports; an old Morgan sports car. Address: (b.) 9–16 Chambers Street, Edinburgh EH1 1HT.

Sutherland, George William Douglas, FCMA, FRSA. Managing Director – Finance – North of Scotland Water, since 1995; b. 7.3.53, Dunoon; m., Mary; 1 s.; 2 d. Educ. Inverness High School. Dunlops; Rediffusion; Black and Decker (senior finance posts, latterly Group Financial Controller); Director of Financial Control, Grand Met; Finance Director, Express Foods Group; Finance Director, latterly Managing Director, Dairy Crest Dairies. Recreations: music; family; art. Address: (b.) North of Scotland Water, Cairngorm House, Beechwood Park, Inverness IV2 3ED; T.-01463 245400.

Sutherland, Ian, DL, DipYCS; b. 22.11.38, Edinburgh. Educ. Boroughmuir Secondary School; Moray House College of Education. Clerical, book-keeping, administrative posts, 1956-65; youth and community course, 1965-67; Youth Leader, Greenock and Kirkcaldy, 1967-71; Area Youth and Community Officer, Clackmannan County Council, 1971-73; Area Community Education Officer, Central Regional Council, 1973-93. Trustee and Hon. Secretary, Scottish Silver Jubilee and Children's Bursary Fund; Elder, St. Serf's Church of Scotland, Tullibody; Deputy Lieutenant, Clackmannanshire. Recreations: singing; gardening; hand-crafts. Address: (h.) 1 Woodside Road, Tullibody, Alloa, FK10 2QQ; T.-01259 723935.

Sutherland, Ian Douglas, FRICS, MCIArb. Managing Partner, D.M. Hall & Son, Chartered Surveyors, Partner since 1975 (joined as Trainee Surveyor, 1965); b. 23.10.45, Colombo, Ceylon; m., Kathryn Wallace (deceased); 1 s.; 1 d. Educ. St. Bees School, Cumberland. Member, Company of Merchants of the City of Edinburgh. Address: (b.) 36 Melville Street, Edinburgh EH3 7HA; T.-0131-477 6000; e-mail: douglas.sutherland@dmhall.co.uk

Sutherland, Professor Ian Wishart, BSc, PhD, DSc. Professor of Microbial Physiology, Edinburgh University, since 1991; b. 6.12.35, Perth; m., Ann Mary Barker; 1 d. Educ. Pitlochry High School; Dollar Academy; Edinburgh University. Lecturer in Bacteriology, Edinburgh University Medical School, 1961-75, Senior Lecturer, then Reader, in Microbiology, 1975-91. Member, Council, Society of General Microbiology, 1984-93; Chair, British Co-ordinating Committee for Biotechnology, 1993-96. Recreations: mountain walking; photography. Address: (b.) Institute of Cell and Molecular Biology, Edinburgh University, Edinburgh EH9 3JH; T.-0131-650 5331; e-mail: i.w.sutherland@ed.ac.uk

Sutherland, Sir William George MacKenzie, Kt. (1988), QPM. HM Chief Inspector of Constabulary for Scotland, 1996-98; Chief Constable, Lothian and Borders Police, 1983-96; b. 12.11.33, Inverness; m., Jennie Abbott; 2 d. Educ. Inverness Technical High School. Cheshire Police, 1954-73; Surrey Police, 1973-75; Hertfordshire Police, 1975-79; Chief Constable, Bedfordshire Police, 1979-83. Recreations: squash; hill-walking.

Suttie, Alan John, MIMgt. Chief Executive, Fife Society for the Blind, since 1987; b. 27.3.52, Bournemouth; m., Janet Mary; 1s. Educ. Kingsleigh School; Shoreditch College, University of London. Voluntary service overseas, India; Royal Commonwealth Society for the Blind, India; Royal National Institute for the Blind, Rehabilitation Programme Manager; Chairman, RNIB's Community Services Committee; Council Member, Sight Savers International. Recreations: hill walking; photography. Address: (b.) Fife Sensory Impairment Centre, Wilson Avenue, Kirkaldy; T.-01592 412666; e-mail: alansuttie@hotmail.com

Swainson, Charles P., MBChB, FRCPE. Consultant Renal Physician, since 1981; Medical Director, Lothian University Hospitals NHS Trust, since 1998; b. 18.5.48, Gloucester; m., Marie Irwin; 1 s. Educ. St. Edward's School, Cheltenham; Edinburgh University. Senior Lecturer, Christchurch, NZ, 1981-86; Consultant Physician, Royal Infirmary of Edinburgh, since 1986. Member, Lothian Children's Panel, 1987-95. Recreations: wine; golf; skiing. Address: (b.) Trust HQ, 1 Lauriston Place, Edinburgh EH3 9YW; T.-0131-536 3008.

Swan, Iain Ruairidh Cameron, MD, FRCS(Edin). Senior Lecturer in Otolaryngology, Glasgow University, since 1986; Consultant Otologist, MRC Institute of Hearing Research, since 1986; Honorary Consultant Otolaryngologist, Glasgow Royal Infirmary, since 1986; b. 19.5.52, Motherwell; m., Helen Buchanan; 1 s.; 1 d. Educ. Glasgow Academy; Glasgow University. SHO/Registrar, Glasgow, 1978-81; Clinical Research Fellow, MRC Institute of Hearing Research, 1981; Senior Registrar in Otolaryngology, Glasgow, 1981-86; clinical attachment, University of Tubingen, 1984-85. Examiner, Final Fellowship, Royal College of Surgeons of Edinburgh and Royal College of Physicians and Surgeons, Glasgow. Recreations: bridge; opera; mountain biking. Address: (b.) Department of Otolaryngology, Royal Infirmary, Glasgow G31 2ER; T.-0141-211 4695; e-mail: iain@ihr.gla.ac.uk

Swanson, Alexander James Grenville, MB, ChB, FRCS Edin. Consultant Orthopaedic Surgeon, 1980-2001; Honorary Senior Lecturer, University of Dundee, since 2001; b. 18.10.41, Ecclefechan; 2 s. Educ. Dingwall Academy; St. Andrews University. Postgraduate training: St. Andrews, 1967-68, Edinburgh, 1968-69, Glasgow, 1969-70, Edinburgh, 1970-74, Dunfermline, 1974-75; Lecturer, then Senior Lecturer and Honorary Consultant, Dundee University, 1975-83. Recreations: downhill skiing; cross-country skiing; travel. Address: (h.) 9 Roxburgh Terrace, Dundee DD2 1NX.

Swanson, Carol Barbara, MA, MSc, PhD, MRTPI, MIFA, FSA, FSAScot. Member, Ancient Monuments Board, since 1997; Manager, West of Scotland Archaeology Service, since 1996; b. 2.12.51, Thurso; m., Ian Johnson. Educ. Thurso High School; Edinburgh University; Strathclyde University. Planner: Lanark County Council, 1974-75, Strathclyde Regional Council, 1975-85; Regional Archaeologist, Strathclyde Regional Council, 1985-96. Address: (b.) West of Scotland Archaeology Service, 20 India Street, Glasgow G2 4PF; T.-0141-287 8334; e-mail: carol.swanson@wosas.glasgow.gov.uk

Swanson, Kenneth M., BSc, PhD, JP, DL. Farmer; Assistant Director, Technology, Dounreay Nuclear Power Development Establishment, 1986-91; Vice Lord Lieutenant, Caithness, since 1996; b. 14.2.30, Canisbay, Caithness; m., Elspeth J.W. Paton; 2 s.; 1 d. Educ. Wick High School; St. Andrews University. Flying Officer, Pilot, RAF, 1952; Lecturer in Physics, University of Wales, 1955; joined UKAEA, Dounreay, on Fast Reactors, 1958; appointed JP, 1970; DL, Caithness, 1977; Chairman, Caithness Jobs Commission, 1988-98; Director, Caithness and Sutherland Local Enterprise Company, 1990-99 (Vice-Chairman, 1994-99); Member, N.W. Board, Scottish Natural Heritage, 1992-99; author of papers and patents on the development of plutonium fuels for electricity production. Address: Knockglass, Westfield, Thurso; T.-0184 787 1201.

Swanson, Professor Philip, BA, PhD. Professor in Hispanic Studies, University of Aberdeen, since 1997; b. 26.5.59, Liverpool. Educ. St. Edward's College; University of Liverpool; University of Edinburgh. Previous posts at: University College Galway; University of Edinburgh; Queen Mary and Westfield College, University of London; State University of New York (Albany); University of Leeds. Publications: The New Novel in Latin America; Landmarks in Modern Latin American Fiction; José Donoso: The Boom and Beyond; Cómo Leer a Gabriel García Márquez. Recreations: cinema; football; walking; socialising. Address: (b.) Department of Hispanic Studies, University of Aberdeen, Aberdeen AB24 3UB; T.-01224 272549.

Swanston, Professor Michael Timothy, MA (Cantab), PhD. Professor, University of Abertay Dundee, since 1995; Depute Principal, since 2000; Head, School of Social and Health Sciences, since 1995; b. 6.6.47, Bristol; m., Georgina Mary; 1 s.; 2 d. Educ. Rugby School; Cambridge University (Pembroke College). Psychologist, Army Personnel Research Establishment, 1969-72; Lecturer in Psychology, Dundee Institute of Technology, 1972-84; Reader in Psychology, 1984-95; Honorary Research Fellow, Dundee university, since 1989. Vice-Chairman, Elmwood College Board of Management, since 2000; Director, Dundee Ice Arena, since 2000. Publications: one book; 40 papers. Recreations: golf; gardening. Address: (b.) University of Abertay Dundee, Bell Street, Dundee DD1 1HG; e-mail: m.e.swanston@abertay.ac.uk

Swapp, George David, OBE, DL, MA (Hons), DipEd. Deputy Lieutenant, Kincardineshire, since 1990; Member Aberdeenshire Council, since 1995; b. 25.5.31, Labuan; m., Eva Jane MacNab; 2 s.; 2 d. Educ. Mackie Academy, Stonehaven; Aberdeen University. RAF Staff College, graduate and directing staff, 1965-68; Ministry of Defence (Training Policy), 1971-74 and 1978-80; promoted Wing Commander, 1971; Board Chairman, RAF Officer and Aircrew Selection Centre, 1974-78; Head, RAF Officer Training Establishment, Bracknell, 1980-83; retired from RAF, 1983. Former Member, Grampian Regional Council, 1986-96; President, Stonehaven Branch, Royal British Legion; founder Member, Stonehaven Heritage Society; Vice Chairman, Dunnottar Woodland Park Association; Church Elder. Recreations: hill-walking; local history; travel; geography; protection and enhancement of amenities and woodlands. Address: (h.) 9 Urie Crescent, Stonehaven AB39 2DY; T.-Stonehaven 764124.

Sweeney, Sister Dorothea, SND, MA (Hons), BA(Soc) (Hons), PhD. Consultant and former Vice Principal, St. Andrew's College, 1985-96; b. Glasgow. Educ. Notre Dame High School, Glasgow; Glasgow University; Notre Dame College of Education; Bedford College and LSE, London University; Strathclyde University. Assistant Teacher of English, Our Lady & St. Francis Secondary School, Glasgow, 1960-63; entered Congregation of Sisters of Notre Dame, Sussex, 1963; Assistant Teacher of English, Notre Dame High School, London, 1966-67; Notre Dame College of Education: Lecturer, Department of Psychology, 1970-76, Senior Lecturer, Department of Educational Science, 1976-80, Assistant Principal, 1980-85. Member, Board of Governors, St. Andrew's College, 1980-96; Member, CNAA Inservice Education Board, 1982-87, Committee for Teacher Education, 1987-89, and Committee for Scotland, 1990-92; Member, National Inter-College Committee for Educational Research, 1982-89; Convener, School Boards, Headteacher Training, Steering Committee, 1988-89; School Boards Members Training, 1989-90; Training Consultant, National Staff Development & Appraisal Training, 1991-92; Myers-Briggs Qualified Trainer, since 1990; part-time Counsellor, since 1968; Sabbatical Semester, Weston Jesuit School of Theology, Cambridge, Massachusetts, 1998. Recreations: creative writing; dance; music; art; sport; drama; technology.

Sweeney, Patrick, MA (Hons). Head Teacher, Holy Rood High School, Edinburgh, since 1994; b. 13.4.49, Wanlockhead; m., May Grant. Educ. Blairs College, Aberdeen; Glasgow University. Taught French and Latin in various schools, 1973-85; Assistant Head Teacher, St. Augustine's High School, Edinburgh, 1985-88; on staff of Quality Assurance Division, Lothian Regional Council, 1988-94, as Co-ordinator of Lothian TVEI Project and then Regional Adviser. Recreations: travel; squash; poor golf; columnist, Times Educational Supplement Scotland ("The Sweeney"). Address: (b.) Holy Rood High School, Duddingston Road, Edinburgh, EH15 1ST.

Swinborn, Albert Victor, MA, MEd. Headteacher, Portlethen Academy, since 1997; b. 24.9.52, Aberdeen; m., Patricia. Educ. Aberdeen Grammar School; Aberdeen University. Teacher of English: Lossiemouth High School, Inverurie Academy; Principal Teacher of English, Hilton Academy; Assistant Headteacher/Depute Headteacher, Westhill Academy. Recreations: travel; Aberdeen FC; Burmese cats. Address: (b.) Portlethen Academy, Bruntland Road, Portlethen, Aberdeen AB12 4QL; T.-01224 782174.

Swinfen, Professor David Berridge, MA, DPhil, FRHistS, FRSA. Professor of Commonwealth History, Dundee University, since 1990 (Head, Department of Modern History, 1988-92, Deputy Principal, 1992-94, Vice Principal, since 1994); b. 8.11.36, Kirkcaldy; m., Ann Pettit; 2 s.; 3 d. Educ. Fettes College, Edinburgh; Hertford College, Oxford. 2/Lt., KOSB, 1956-57; Assistant Lecturer in Modern History, then Lecturer, Queen's College, Dundee, 1963-75; Director, School of American Studies, Dundee University, 1970-85; Senior Lecturer, Modern History, Dundee University, 1975-90. Chairman, Scottish Advisory Committee on Credit and Access, 1997-2001; Chairman, Scottish Credit and Qualifications Framework Development Group, 1998-2001. Publications: five books. Recreation: music. Address: (h.) 14 Cedar Road, Broughty Ferry, Dundee, DD5 3BB; T.-01382 776496; e-mail: d.b.swinfen@dundee.ac.uk

Swingler, Robert James, MD, FRCP (Edin., Lond.) Consultant Neurologist, Tayside University NHS Trust, since 1995; b. 4.7.56, London; m., Carol; 1 s.; 3 d. Educ. Wandsworth School; Guy's Hospital, University of London. Lecturer in Neurology, University of Edinburgh, 1987-90; Senior Registrar, Neurology, Dundee Royal Infirmary, 1990-95; MRC Travelling Fellow, Harvard University, 1992-93. Director, Scottish MND Association Care

Advisory Service, 1999. Recreations: running; cinema. Address: 28 Grange Road, St. Andrews KY16 8LE; T.-01382 660111; e-mail: robert.swingler@tuht.scot.nhs.uk

Swinney, John Ramsay, MA (Hons). MSP (SNP), North Tayside, since 1999; Leader, Scottish National Party, since 2000; Leader of the Opposition, Scottish Parliament, since 2000; MP (SNP), North Tayside, 1997-2001; b. 13.4.64, Edinburgh; 1 s.; 1 d. Educ. Forrester High School, Edinburgh; Edinburgh University. Research Officer, Scottish Coal Project, 1987-88; Senior Managing Consultant, Development Options Ltd., 1998-92; Strategic Planning Principal, Scottish Amicable, 1992-97. SNP Treasury Spokesman, 1995-99; Deputy Leader, Scottish National Party, 1998-2000; Shadow Minister for Enterprise and Lifelong Learning, 1999-2000. Recreation: hill-walking. Address: (b.) 35 Perth Street, Blairgowrie PH10 6DL; T.-01250 876576.

Swinton, Major General Sir John, KCVO, OBE, JP. Lord Lieutenant, Berwickshire, 1989-2000; Member, Queen's Bodyguard for Scotland (Royal Company of Archers), since 1977 (Lieutenant, since 2001); President, Borders Branch, SSAFA, since 1993; Trustee, Scottish National War Memorial, since 1988 (Chairman, since 1995); President, Berwickshire Civic Society (Chairman, 1982-96); Chairman, Berwickshire Recreation Sports Trust, since 1997; Trustee, The Scots at War Trust, since 1996; Trustee, Berwick Military Tattoo, since 1996; Patron, POWER, since 1995; b. 21.4.25, London; m., Judith Balfour Killen; 3 s.; 1 d. Educ. Harrow School. Enlisted Scots Guards, 1943; commissioned, 1944; served NW Europe (twice wounded); Malaya, 1948-51 (Despatches); ADC to Field Marshal Sir William Slim, Governor General of Australia, 1953-54; Regimental Adjutant, Scots Guards, 1960-62; Adjutant, RMA, Sandhurst, 1962-64; comd. 2nd Bn., Scots Guards, 1966-68; Lt.-Col. commanding Scots Guards, 1970-71; Commander, 4th Guards Armoured Brigade, BAOR, 1972-73; Brigadier, Lowlands and Commander, Edinburgh and Glasgow Garrisons, 1975-76; GOC London District and Major General comd. Household Division, 1976-79. Honorary Colonel, 2nd Bn., 52nd Lowland Volunteers, 1983-90; President, Lowland TA & VRA, 1992-96; National Chairman, Royal British Legion Scotland, 1986-89; Coordinator for Scotland, Duke of Edinburgh's Award 25th Anniversary Appeal, 1980 (Honorary Liaison Officer for the Borders, 1983-85); Chairman, Roxburgh and Berwickshire Conservative Association, 1983-85; Chairman, Thirlestane Castle Trust, 1984-90; Trustee, Army Museums Ogilby Trust, 1978-91; Council Member, Commonwealth Ex-Services League, 1984-98; Member, Central Advisory Committee on War Pensions, 1986-89; Chairman, St. Abbs Head National Nature Reserve Joint Management Committee, 1991-98; President, Royal Highland and Agricultural Society of Scotland, 1993-94; President, Berwickshire Naturalists Club, 1996-97; Chairman, Scottish National Motorsport Collection, 1998-2001. Address: (h.) Kimmerghame, Duns, Berwickshire; T.-01361 883277.

Sword, Ian Pollock, BSc, PhD, CChem, FRSC, FRSE, FRCP (Edin). Chairman, Inveresk Research International, since 1979; Director, Inveresk Clinical Research, since 1988; Director, SGS UK Holding Ltd., since 1989; Senior Executive Vice President, SGS Geneva, since 1994; Member, Medical Research Council, 1994-98; Scottish Higher Educational Funding Council, 1996-98; b. 6.3.42, Kilmarnock; m., Flora Collins; 2 s.; 1 d. Educ. Coatbridge High School; Glasgow University. Princeton University, New Jersey, 1967-69; Oxford University, 1969-70; Huntingdon Research Centre, 1970-73; Inveresk Research International, since 1973. Publications: editor of two books; scientific papers. Recreations: music; golf. Address: (b.) Inveresk Research International Ltd., Tranent EH33 2NE; T.-01875 614545.

Sykes, Diana Antoinette, MA (Hons). Director, Crawford Arts Centre, since 1988; b. 12.9.59, Stirling. Educ. Stirling High School; St Andrews University; Sweet Briar College, Virginia; Manchester University. Curator/Driver, Scottish Arts Council Travelling Gallery, 1983-88. Chair, Mobile Projects Association Scotland, 1986-88; Member/Chair, Scottish Arts Council Exhibitions Panel, 1995-98. Recreation: travel. Address: (b.) 93 North Street, St Andrews KY16 9AL; T.-01334 474610; e-mail: dasykes@crawfordarts.free-online.co.uk

Syme, Peter William, MA, DipAfrSts. Scottish Director, The Open University, and Vice-Chancellor's Delegate in Scotland, since 1997; b. 27.1.50, Brechin. Educ. Brechin High School; Trinity College, Glenalmond; Trinity College, Cambridge; Edinburgh University. VSO, Nigeria, 1972-74; Department of Education and Science, London, 1975-89, including Private Secretary to Sir James Hamilton, Permanent Secretary, 1979-80; seconded to Edinburgh University, 1983-85; Secretary to Review of University Grants Committee, 1985-87; Regional Director, Open University, London, 1990-97. Recreations: travel; photography; Africa. Address: (b.) The Open University in Scotland, 10 Drumsheugh Gardens, Edinburgh EH3 7QJ; T.-0131-226 3851.

Symington, Rev. Alastair Henderson, MA, BD. Minister, Old Parish Church of Troon, since 1998; Chaplain to The Queen in Scotland, since 1996; b. 15.4.47, Edinburgh; m., Eileen Margaret Jenkins; 2 d. Educ. Daniel Stewart's College, Edinburgh; Edinburgh University; Tubingen University, West Germany. Assistant Minister, Wellington Church, Glasgow, 1971-72; Chaplain, RAF, 1972-76; Minister: Craiglockhart Parish Church, Edinburgh, 1976-85, New Kilpatrick Parish Church, Bearsden, 1985-98. Convener, Committee on Chaplains to HM Forces, 1989-93; Member, Board of Practice and Procedure, since 1995; Convener, Committee on Presbytery Boundaries, since 1999; Contributor, Scottish Liturgical Review. Publications: Westminster Church Sermons, 1984; Reader's Digest Family Guide to the Bible (Co-author), 1985; For God's Sake, Ask!, 1993. Recreations: golf; rugby; music; France; wines. Address: 85 Bentinck Drive, Troon KA10 6HZ; T.-01292 313644.

T

Taggart, Professor James Hand, DMS, BSc, MA, MBA, PhD. Professor of International Business Strategy, Glasgow University, since 1999; b. 7.4.43, Galsgow; m., Dr Jennifer M. Taggart; 2 s.; 3 d. Educ. St Mungo's Academy; Glasgow University; Strathclyde University. Product Manager, Eden Vale Ltd; Project Manager, Allied Suppliers Ltd.; Director, Allied Grocery Distributors Ltd.; Director, Scotcros Foods Ltd.; Director, A. Goldberg and Sons Ltd.; Lecturer, Senior Lecturer, Strathclyde University. Publications: The World Pharmaceutical Industry, 1993; The Essence of International Business, 1993. Recreations: the great Highland bagpipe; drystane dyking. Address: (h.) Dubh Loch, Rowardennan, Stirlingshire.

Tait, A. Margaret, BSc. General Council Assessor on Court of University of Edinburgh; Member, Women in Scotland Forum and its Research Advisory Group; Member, St. Margaret's Chapel Guild, Edinburgh Castle; Vice Chairman, Lothian Healthy Volunteers and Public Health Medical Ethics Committee; Public Affairs Consultant, Scotland, British Federation of Women Graduates; b. 8.10.44, Edinburgh; m., J. Haldane Tait; 1 d. Educ. George Watson's Ladies' College, Edinburgh; Edinburgh University; Jordanhill College of Education. Former Teacher of Mathematics, Bellahouston Academy, Glasgow; former Member, Lothian Children's Panel; former Honorary Secretary, Scottish Association of Children's Panels; former Chairman, Dean House Children's Home, Edinburgh; Volunteer, Edinburgh Citizens' Advice Bureau; formerly Secretary of State's Nominee to General Teaching Council; former Member, Scottish Legal Aid Board; former Member, Lothian Health Council. Recreations: golf; speaking in Spanish and Japanese. Address: (h.) 6 Ravelston House Park, Edinburgh EH4 3LU; T.-0131-332 6795.

Tait, Rev. Thomas William, BD, RAFVR (Rtd). Parish Minister, Rattray, Blairgowrie, 1972-97; Chairman, Tayside Health Council, 1992-98; Principal Chaplain, Scotland and Northern Ireland, Air Training Corps, since 1996; b. 11.11.31, Dunfermline; m., Irene Pope; 1 s.; 2 d. Educ. Dunfermline High School; St. Colm's College, Edinburgh; Edinburgh University; Christ's College, Aberdeen; Aberdeen University. HQ Staff, Boys' Brigade, 1954-61; Missionary, Church of Scotland, South Arabia, 1962-67; ordained and inducted, 1972; Member, Assembly Council, 1984-88; Chaplain, 2519 (Strathmore) Squadron, Air Training Corps, since 1974; Chaplain, Dundee and Central Scotland Wing, ATC, 1978-96; Chairman, Blairgowrie Schools Council, 1975-89; Member, Perth and Kinross Health Council, 1980-91 (Chairman, 1984-91); Chairman, Blairgowrie and District Branch, Royal British Legion Scotland, 1992-97, and Chaplain, Angus and Perthshire Area, 1994-99; commissioned RAFVR, 1977 (retired Flt. Lt., 1988); Moderator, Dunkeld and Meigle Presbytery, 1978; Member, Secretary of State's Consultative Panel on Registration of Nursing Homes and Private Hospitals, since 1993; Member, Tayside Health Board Quality Monitoring Team, 1993-98; Member, Scottish Office Nursing Homes Standards Steering Group, 1994-97; Member, Chaplain's Committee, Air Cadet Council (UK), since 1996; Member, CRAG (Clinical Research and Audit Group), 1997-98; Member, Multi Research Ethics Committee for Scotland, 1997-2001; Convener, Scottish Association of Health Councils, 1997-98; Member, Advocacy Team, State Hospital, Carstairs. Recreations: encouraging others to work in voluntary organisations; swimming; reading; overseas travel. Address: 20 Cedar Avenue, Blairgowrie, Perthshire; T.-01250 874833.

Tallach, Rev James Ross, MB, ChB. Free Presbyterian Minister, Raasay, since 1983; occasional locum, general practitioner, Raasay; b. Tighnabruaich, Argyll; m., Mairi McCuish Martin; 2 d. Educ. Nicolson Institute, Stornoway; Aberdeen University. House jobs in surgery, medicine and obstetrics, Inverness, Aberdeen, and Bellshill, 1967-69; Medical Missionary, Mbuma, Zimbabwe, 1969-76; training for ministry, 1976-80; ordained medical missionery, Mbuma, 1980-83. Moderator of Synod, 1996; Clerk to Foreign Mission Committee of F.P. Church, since 1989; Convener, Church House, Inverness, since 2001. Recreations: gardening; walking. Address: Free Presbyterian Manse, Raasay, Kyle, Ross-shire IV40 8PB; T.-01478 660216; e-mail: jamesross@tallach.fsnet.co.uk

Tankel, Henry I., OBE, MD, FRCSEdin, FRCSGlas. Chairman, Glasgow Jewish Housing Association, 1996-2001; Surgeon, Southern General Hospital, Glasgow, 1962-91; b. 14.1.26, Glasgow; m., Judith Woolfson; 2 s.; 2 d. Educ. High School of Glasgow; Glasgow University. Fulbright Scholar, 1954-55; President, Glasgow Jewish Representative Council, 1974-77; Chairman, Glasgow Hospital Medical Services Committee, 1974-79; Board of Science and Education, 1978-81; President, United Synagogues of Scotland, 1978-85; Treasurer, Scottish Committee for Hospital Medical Services, 1978-91; Member, National Panel of Specialists, 1978-82 and 1987-91; invited to address General Assembly of Church of Scotland, 1984; Chairman, Scottish Joint Consultants Committee, 1989-92; Member, Scottish Health Service Advisory Council, 1989-93; Non-Executive Director, Southern General Hospital NHS Trust, 1993-97; Chairman, Glasgow Board of Jewish Education, 1985-90. Recreations: walking; making model boats. Address: (h.) 26 Dalziel Drive, Glasgow G41 4PU; T.-0141-423 5830.

Tannahill, Andrew James, MB, ChB, MSc, FFPHM, FRCP (Edin, Glasg). Consultant in Public Health Medicine, Argyll and Clyde NHS Board, since 2001; Honorary Clinical Senior Lecturer, Department of Public Health, Glasgow University, since 2001; b. 28.4.54, Inchinnan; m., Carol Elizabeth Fyfe. Educ. John Neilson Institution, Paisley; Glasgow University; Edinburgh University. Lecturer in Pathology, Glasgow University; Senior Registrar in Community Medicine, Lothian Health Board/Honorary Clinical Tutor, Edinburgh University; Regional Specialist in Community Medicine, East Anglian Regional Health Authority/Associate Lecturer, Cambridge University; Senior Lecturer in Public Health Medicine, Glasgow University/Honorary Consultant in Public Health Medicine, Greater Glasgow Health Board; Chief Executive, Health Education Board for Scotland/Visiting Professor, Glasgow University/Honorary Senior Lecturer, Dundee University/Honorary Fellow, Edinburgh University. Publications: Health Promotion: Models and Values (Co-author); contributor to Health Promotion: Disciplines and Diversity; papers on health education, prevention and health promotion. Recreations: countryside and bird-watching; music; theatre; photography; digital imaging; drawing and painting; reading. Address: (b.) Argyll and Clyde NHS Board, Ross House, Hawkhead Road, Paisley PA2 7BN.

Tannahill, Duncan, FIMI. Chief Executive, Glasgow Chamber of Commerce, since 2000; b. 7.5.55, Glasgow; m., Margaret; 1 s.; 1 d. Educ. Glasgow Academy; Glasgow University. Motor industry, 1976-98; self-employed, 1999-2000. Chairman, Glasgow Junior Chamber of Commerce, 1991-92; President, Glasgow Chamber of Commerce, 1997; Board Member, Glasgow Central College of Commerce, 1993-94; Member, Glasgow Employers Coalition, 1998-2000; Mentor, Business Mentoring Scotland, since 2000; Director, Glasgow City Centre Partnership, since 2000; Local Area Board Member, Young Enterprise Scotland, since 2000; Director, Glasgow Exports Ltd., since 2001; Local Area Advisory Board Member, Careers Scotland, since 2001; Chairman, Glasgow New Deal Strategic

Partnership, since 2001; Member, Glasgow Local Economic Forum, since 2001. Recreations: sailing; hillwalking; mountain biking. Address: (b.) 30 George Square, Glasgow G2 1EQ; T.-0141-572 2121; e-mail: duncan.tannahill@glasgowchamber.org

Tate, Professor Austin, BA (Hons), PhD, CEng, FBCS, FBIS, FRSE. Technical Director, AIAI (Artificial Intelligence Applications Institute), since 1985; Chair in Knowledge-Based Systems, Edinburgh University, since 1995; b. 12.5.51, Knottingley, West Yorkshire; m., Margaret. Educ. King's School, Pontefract; Lancaster University; Edinburgh University. Elected Fellow, American Association of Artificial Intelligence, since 1993. Address: (b.) AIAI, University of Edinburgh, 80 South Bridge, Edinburgh EH1 1HN; T.-0131-650 2732.

Tavener, Alan, MA, ARCO, ARCM. Director of Music, Strathclyde University, since 1980; Artistic Director, Cappella Nova, since 1982; b. 22.4.57, Weston-Super-Mare; m., Rebecca Jane Gibson. Educ. City of Bath Boys' School; Brasenose College, Oxford. Conducted several world premieres of choral works and several CDs of early and contemporary music. Recreations: architecture; exhibitions; Scottish country dancing; food and drink. Address: (b.) Strathclyde University, Livingstone Tower, Richmond Street, Glasgow G1 1XH; T.-0141-548 3444.

Tavener, Rebecca Jane. Soprano; Co-Artistic Director and Manager, Cappella Nova; b. 3.5.58, Trowbridge; m., Alan Tavener. Co-founded Cappella Nova, 1982; Concert Manager, Glasgow University, 1983-89; Founder and Director, Chorus International, 1990-94; founded Canty (medieval vocal ensemble), 1998; launched new early music consortium for Scotland, 1998; launched own recording label, ROTA, 1998. Recreations: Italophilia; retail therapy; gourmandising; reading history books. Address: (h.) 172 Hyndland Road, Glasgow G12 9HZ; T.-(b.) 0141-552 0634.

Taylor, Brian, MA (Hons). Political Editor, BBC Scotland; b. 9.1.55, Dundee; m., Pamela Moira Niven; 2 s. Educ. High School of Dundee; St. Andrews University. Reporter, Press and Journal, Aberdeen, 1977-80; Lobby Correspondent, Thomson Regional Newspapers, Westminster, 1980-85; Reporter, BBC Scotland, Glasgow, 1985-86; Co-Presenter, Left, Right and Centre, BBC Scotland, 1986-88; Political Correspondent, BBC Scotland, 1988-90. Publication: The Scottish Parliament, 1999. Recreations: golf; theatre. Address: (b.) BBC Scotland, Queen Margaret Drive, Glasgow G12 8DG.

Taylor, Charles Edwin, CBE, BSc, PhD, FRSE, CBiol, FIBiol. Director, Scottish Crop Research Institute, 1972-86; President, Association of Applied Biologists, 1989; NATO Senior Research Fellow, Istituto di Nematologia Agraria CNR, Bari, Italy; b. 11.9.23, Oystermouth; 1 d. Educ. Cardiff High School; University College, Cardiff. Pilot, RAF, 1943-46; Lecturer in Applied Zoology, Nottingham University School of Agriculture, 1949-56; Senior Entomologist, Federation of Rhodesia and Nyasaland, 1956-59; Head, Zoology Section, Scottish Horticultural Research Institute, 1959-72. President, European Society of Nematologists, 1980-84; Editor, Nematologica, 1990-96. Address: (b.) Westcroft, Longforgan, Dundee DD2 5EX; T.-01382 360 243.

Taylor, David Alexander, LLB, MSc, MBA. Chief Executive, Scottish Football Association, since 1999; Visiting Professor of Marketing, Strathclyde University, since 1999; b. 14.3.54, Forfar; m., Catherine; 2 s. Educ. Dundee High School; Edinburgh University; Strathclyde University. Solicitor, Glasgow City Council, 1979-85; Scottish Enterprise, 1985-93; Director, Europartenariat,

1993; Director, Scottish Trade International, 1994-99. Recreations: keeping fit; reading; literature. Address: (b.) Hampden Park, Glasgow G42 9AY; T.-0141-616 6004; e-mail: info@scottishfa.co.uk

Taylor, Elizabeth (Liz) Dewar, MA (Hons). Journalist and Author; b. 25.4.31, Newport, Fife; m., Adam McNeill Taylor (deceased); 1 s.; 3 d. Educ. Morgan Academy, Dundee; Galashiels Academy; King's College, Aberdeen. Reporter, Edinburgh Evening Dispatch, 1954-56; freelance stringer, Bombay, 1960-65; freelance journalist and broadcaster, since 1971. Publications include: Living with Loss; Bringing Up Children On Your Own; Living Alone; The Writing Business; 20th Century Antiques; also several books as Elisabeth McNeill. Recreations: gardening; crossword puzzles; bridge; Scrabble; cinema; horse-racing. Address: (h.) Cairnhill, Newstead, Melrose TD6 9DX; T.-0189682 2972.

Taylor, Rev. Howard, BSc (Hons), BD (Hons), MTh. Chaplain, Heriot-Watt University, since 1998; Minister, St. David's Church, Knightswood, Glasgow, 1986-98; Part-time Lecturer in Apologetics, International Christian College, since 1989; Lecturer in Moral and Social Philosophy, and Science–Religion Interface, Heriot-Watt University; b. 6.6.44, Stockport; m., Eleanor Clark; 3 s. Educ. Gravesend Technical School, Kent; Nottingham University; Edinburgh University. Maths and Physics Teacher, Malawi University; Missionary in Malawi (minister of town and rural African churches, theological teacher, teacher of African languages to missionaries); Minister, Toward and Innellan Churches, Argyll. Creator, Science–Religion Interface course, Heriot-Watt University (prize-winner for good courses in science and religion, Center for Theology and Natural Sciences, Berkeley, California). Publications: Faith Seeks Understanding, 1980; Pray Today 1982/83, 1982; In Christ All Things Hold Together; World Hope in the Middle East; The Delusion of Unbelief in a Scientific Age; Faith and Understanding; The Uniqueness of Christ in a Pluralist World, 1994; Is the New Testament the Source of Anti-Semitism?,1994. Recreations: hill walking; reading; classical music. Address: (b.) Chaplaincy Centre, Heriot-Watt University, Edinburgh EH14 4AF; T.-0131-449 5111; e-mail: H.G.Taylor@hw.ac.uk

Taylor, Rev. Ian, BSc, MA, LTh, DipEd. Lecturer on music and the arts, broadcaster, opera producer; b. 12.10.32, Dundee; m., Joy Coupar, LRAM; 2 s.; 1 d. Educ. Dundee High School; St. Andrews University; Durham University; Sheffield University; Edinburgh University. Teacher, Mathematics Department, Dundee High School; Lecturer in Mathematics, Bretton Hall College of Education; Senior Lecturer in Education, College of Ripon and York St. John; Assistant Minister, St. Giles' Cathedral, Edinburgh; Minister, Abdie & Dunbog and Newburgh, 1983-97; Moderator, Presbytery of St. Andrews, 1995-96; Secretary, History of Education Society, 1968-73; extensive work in adult education (appreciation of music and the arts); Director, Summer Schools in Music, St. Andrews University; numerous courses for St. Andrews, Edinburgh, Cambridge and Hull Universities and WEA; has played principal roles in opera and operetta; Producer, Gilbert and Sullivan Society of Edinburgh, 1979-87; Producer, Tayside Opera, 1999; compiled Theatre Music Quiz series, Radio Tay; presented own operetta, My Dear Gilbert...My Dear Sullivan, BBC; Writer of revues and documentary plays with music, including Tragic Queen (Mary Queen of Scots), St. Giles' Cathedral, Edinburgh Festival Fringe, 1982, and John Knox (Church of Scotland Video). Publications: How to Produce Concert Versions of Gilbert Sullivan; The Gilbert and Sullivan Quiz Book; The Opera Lover's Quiz Book. Address: Lundie Cottage, Arncroach, Fife KY10 2RN; T.-01333 720 222.

Taylor, Sheriff James Alastair, BSc, LLB. Sheriff of Glasgow and Strathkelvin at Glasgow; b. 21.2.51, Inverness; m., Lesley Macleod; 2 s. Educ. Nairn Academy; Aberdeen University. Apprenticed to Brander & Cruickshank, Advocates in Aberdeen, 1975-77; apprenticed to, Assistant with, Lefevre & Co., Advocates in Aberdeen, 1977-78; Assistant, later Partner, A.C. Morrison & Richards, Advocates in Aberdeen, 1978-87; Partner and latterly Head of Litigation Department, McGrigor Donald, 1988-98; attained rights of audience in Supreme Courts in Scotland, 1993; Sheriff of Lothian and Borders at Edinburgh, 1998. Convener, Rights of Audience Civil Training Course, 1995-98. Publications: International Intellectual Property Litigation (Contributor); Sentencing Practice (Contributor). Recreations: golf; music; good food and wine. Address: (b.) 1 Carlton Place, Glasgow G5 9DA; e-mail: sheriff.jtaylor@scotcourts.gov.uk

Taylor, James Bradley. Chief Executive, Northern Lighthouse Board, since 1993; Nautical Assessor to the Court of Session, since 1996; Trustee, Scotland's Lighthouse Museum, since 1995; Trustee, Bell's Nautical Trust, since 1996; b. 12.8.45, Paisley; m., Elizabeth Sherwood. Educ. George Watson's College, Edinburgh; Britannia Royal Naval College; Defence School of Languages; Royal College of Defence Studies. Royal Navy, 1963-93; commanded HM submarines: Grampus, 1974-75, Orpheus, 1975-77, Spartan, 1980-82, HM ship London, 1989-90; Chief of Staff, Submarine Flotilla, 1990-91; Royal College of Defence Studies, 1992. Community Councillor, Eddleston, Peeblesshire, since 1999; High Constable of Leith. Recreations: shooting; stalking; history; classic cars. Address: (b.) 84 George Street, Edinburgh, EH2 3DA; T.-0131-473 3100.

Taylor, Rt. Rev. John Mitchell, MA. Bishop of Glasgow and Galloway, retired 1998; now Honorary Assistant Bishop, Glasgow and Galloway b. 23.5.32, Aberdeen; m., Edna Elizabeth Maitland; 1 s.; 1 d. Educ. Banff Academy; Aberdeen University; Theological College, Edinburgh. Curate, St. Margaret's, Aberdeen; Rector: Holy Cross, Knightswood, Glasgow, St. Ninian's, Pollokshields, Glasgow, St. John the Evangelist, Dumfries; Canon, St. Mary's Cathedral, Glasgow. Recreations: angling; hill-walking; sketching; music. Address: (h.) 10 St Georges, Castle Douglas DG7 1LN.

Taylor, John Murray, MA, DipEd, MIM, FRSA. Principal, Clackmannan College, since 1987; b. 18.7.42. Educ. Banchory Academy; Aberdeen University. Teacher, Dunfermline High School, 1965-70; Principal Teacher of Classics, Kirkcudbright, Liberton, Callander, 1970-78; Assistant Director of Education, Central Region, 1978-87. Recreations: music; cycling; travel; cars; DX radio. Address: (b.) Clackmannan College of Further Education, Branshill Road, Alloa FK10 3BT; T.-01259 215121.

Taylor, Malcolm John, TD, MA (Hons), FRICS. Chartered Surveyor/Land Agent; Managing Partner, Youngs Chartered Surveyors; Member, Ancient Monuments Board for Scotland, since 1998; b. 21.11.61, Glasgow; m., Helen McKay; 2 s.; 1 d. Educ. Dumfries Academy; Aberdeen University. Trainee, C.G. Grieve & Co., Dumfries, 1985-87; joined Youngs, 1987; appointed Associate, 1991, Partner, 1998. Past Chairman, RICS Rural Practice Division. Recreations: field sports; music; natural history. Address: (b.) Youngs Chartered Surveyors, Manor Street, Forfar; T.-01307 462516.

Taylor, Margie, MSc, MBA, FDSRCSEd, FDSRCPS(Glasg), HonMFPHM. Consultant in Dental Public Health, Lanarkshire Health Board, since 1994; Honorary Senior Lecturer, Glasgow University; b. Edinburgh. Educ. James Gillespie's High School for Girls; Edinburgh University; Heriot-Watt University. Formerly Chief Administrative Dental Officer, Fife Health Board,

and Honorary Senior Lecturer, St. Andrews University. Past President, Royal Odonto-Chirurgical Society of Scotland; Board Member, Health Education Board for Scotland. Recreations: calligraphy; golfing (badly); cooking. Address: (b.) Lanarkshire Health Board, 14 Beckford Street, Hamilton ML3 0TA; T.-01698 281313.

Taylor, Martin. Guitarist/Composer, since 1972; b. 20.10.56, Harlow, Essex; m., Elizabeth Kirk; 2 s. Educ. Passmores Comprehensive School, Harlow. Self-taught guitarist (began playing aged four); became professional musician at 15, touring UK, Europe and USA; solo recording debut, 1978 (for Wave Records); toured world with Stephane Grappelli, 1979-90; recorded eight solo albums for Linn Records, 1990s, becoming biggest selling British jazz recording artist in the UK; became first British jazz artist to sign recording contract with Sony Jazz (Columbia) in over 30 years; currently tours the world as solo artist and records and composes music for television and film. Founder, Kirkmichael International Guitar Festival; Founder, Guitars for Schools Programme. Best Guitarist, British Jazz Awards, nine times; Grammy nomination, 1987; Gold Badge of Merit, British Academy of Composers and Songwriters, 1999. Publication: Kiss and Tell (autobiography), 1999. Recreations: horse racing; horse drawn gypsy wagons; collects vintage and rare American guitars and mandolins. Address: Martin Taylor (Music) Ltd., PO Box 8403, Maybole, Ayrshire KA19 7YB; T.-01655 750549; e-mail: martin@p3music.com

Taylor, Rt. Rev. Maurice, STD. Bishop of Galloway, since 1981; b. 5.5.26, Hamilton. Educ. St. Aloysius College, Glasgow; Our Lady's High School, Motherwell; Pontifical Gregorian University, Rome. Royal Army Medical Corps, UK, India, Egypt, 1944-47; Assistant Priest: St. Bartholomew's, Coatbridge, 1951-52, St. Bernadette's, Motherwell, 1954-55; Lecturer, St. Peter's College, Cardross, 1955-65; Rector, Royal Scots College, Spain, 1965-74; Parish Priest, Our Lady of Lourdes, East Kilbride, 1974-81. Episcopal Secretary, Bishops' Conference of Scotland; Vice President, Catholic Institute for International Relations; Chairman, International Commission on English in the Liturgy. Publications: The Scots College in Spain, 1971; Guatemala, A Bishop's Journey, 1991; El Salvador: Portrait of a Parish, 1992; Opening Our Lives to the Saviour (Co-author), 1995; Listening at the Foot of the Cross (Co-author), 1996. Address: 8 Corsehill Road, Ayr KA7 2ST; T.-01292 266750.

Taylor, Michael Thomas, MA, MEd. Rector, Dyce Academy, Aberdeen, since 1980; b. 17.2.47, Newcastle upon Tyne; m., Sheena Robertson; 1 s.; 2 d. Educ. Rutherford Grammar School, Newcastle upon Tyne; Trinity College, Cambridge; Aberdeen University. Teacher of Chemistry, Cannock Grammar School, 1969-75; Ellon Academy: Principal Teacher of Guidance, 1975-76, Assistant Head Teacher, 1977-78, Depute Rector, 1978-80. Secretary, Newmachar Community Council. Recreations: hill-walking; music; sailing. Address: (h.) Loch-An-Eilein, Newmachar, Aberdeenshire AB21 0UQ; T.-01651 862234.

Taylor, Peter Cranbourne, MA, CA. Chairman, Scottish National Blood Transfusion Association, since 1995; b. 11.8.38, Yeovil; m., Lois Mary; 1s.; 1d Educ. Edinburgh University. Chartered Accountant/Partner: Romanes and Munro, Edinburgh, 1964-74; Deloitte Haskins and Sells, 1974-90; Coopers and Lybrand, 1990-95. Member, Scottish Dental Practice Board, 1991-2001. Recreations: shooting; country pursuits. Address: (h.) Totleywells House, Winchburgh, West Lothian, EH52 6QJ; T.-0131-319 2155.

Taylor, Professor Samuel Sorby Brittain, BA, PhD, Officier dans l'Ordre des Palmes Academiques. Professor of French, St. Andrews University, 1977-95, now Professor Emeritus; b. 20.9.30, Dore and Totley, Derbyshire; m.,

Agnes McCreadie Ewan; 2 d. Educ. High Storrs Grammar School, Sheffield; Birmingham University; Paris University. Royal Navy, 1956-58 (Sub Lt., RNVR); Personnel Research Officer, Dunlop Rubber Co., 1958-60; Institut et Musee Voltaire, Geneva, 1960-63; St. Andrews University: Lecturer, 1963, Reader, 1972, Professor, 1977, retired 1995; Chairman, National Council for Modern Languages, 1981-85; Member, Executive Committee, Complete Works of Voltaire, 1970-85; Project Leader, Inter-University French Language Teaching Research and Development Project, 1980-88; Director, Nuffield Foundation project ("Nuffield French for science students"), 1991-99; Chairman, Scottish Joint Working Party for Standard Grade in Modern Languages, 1982-84. Publication: definitive iconography of Voltaire, 1998. Recreations: athletics timekeeping; photography; Liberal Democrats. Address: (h.) 11 Irvine Crescent, St. Andrews KY16 8LG; T.-01334 472588; e-mail: ssbt@st-andrews.ac.uk

Taylor, Dr Tom, BSc, PhD. Rector, Kingussie High School, since 1990; m., Anne; 2 d. Address: (b.) Kingussie High School, Ruthven Road, Kingussie, Invernesshire, PH21 1ES.

Taylor, William James, QC (Scotland), QC (England and Wales), MA, LLB, FRSA. Advocate, since 1971; Barrister, since 1990; b. 13.9.44, Nairn. Educ. Robert Gordon's College, Aberdeen; Aberdeen University. Standing Junior Counsel to DHSS, 1978-79, to Foreign and Commonwealth Office, 1979-86; Temporary Sheriff, 1997-99; Member, Criminal Injuries Compensation Board, 1997-2000; Member, Scottish Criminal Cases Review Commission, since 1999. Parliamentary candidate (Labour), West Edinburgh, February and October, 1974; Lothian Regional Councillor, 1973-84 (Secretary, Labour Group); Chairman, COSLA Protective Services Committee. Recreations: the arts; sailing; skiing; Scottish mountains; restoring a garden. Address: (b.) Parliament House, Parliament Square, Edinburgh EH1 1RF; T.-0131-556 0101; e-mail: qc@wjt.org.uk

Teasdale, Professor Graham Michael, MB, BS, MRCP, FRCSEdin, FRCSGlas, FMedSci, FRSE. Professor and Head, Department of Neurosurgery, Glasgow University, since 1981; Consultant Neurosurgeon, Institute of Neurological Sciences, Glasgow, since 1975; President, Society of British Neurological Surgeons, 2000-02; b. 23.9.40, Spennymoor; m.; 3 s. Educ. Johnston Grammar School, Durham; Durham University. Postgraduate clinical training, Newcastle-upon-Tyne, London and Birmingham, 1963-69; Assistant Lecturer in Anatomy, Glasgow University, 1969-71; specialist training in surgery and neurosurgery, Southern General Hospital, Glasgow, 1971-75; Senior Lecturer, then Reader in Neurosurgery, Glasgow University, 1975-81. President, International Neurotrauma Society, 1993; Chairman, European Brain Injury Consortium, 1995; President, Section of Clinical Neurosciences, Royal Society of Medicine, 1998-99. Publication: The Management of Head Injuries. Address: (b.) University Department of Neurosurgery, Institute of Neurological Sciences, Southern General Hospital, Glasgow; T.-0141-201 2019.

Tedford, Professor David John, OBE, BSc, PhD, ScD, ARCST, CEng, FIEE, SMIEEE, CPhys, FInstP, FRSE, FRSA, Order of Merit of Poland (Gold, 1986, Commander Cross, 2001), DTech (Hon. Abertay, Dundee), DSc (Hon. Robert Gordon University); DUniv (Strathclyde University). Chairman, Court, University of Abertay Dundee, since 1997; Chairman, Scottish Science Trust Scientific Advisory Committee, since 2000 (Member, since 1999); Director, Scottish Academic Consultants, since 1996; Non-Executive Director, Startech Partners Ltd., since 1997; Member, Scottish Universities' Research and Reactor Centre's Nuclear Safety Committee, since 1982; Emeritus

Professor; formerly Professor of Electrical Engineering (Foundation Chair), Strathclyde University; b. 12.7.31, Coatbridge; m., Mary White Gardner; 3 s.; 1 d. Educ. Coatbridge High School; Royal Technical College; Glasgow University. Research Engineer, Ferranti Ltd., Edinburgh, 1955-57; joined Strathclyde University as Lecturer, 1957; Deputy Principal, 1982-84, Pro-Vice Principal, 1984-86, Vice-Principal, 1986-88, Deputy Principal (International Affairs), 1988-91; Special Adviser to Principal, 1991-92. Member: Planning Committee, Hong Kong University of Science and Technology, 1986-88 (Member, Council, 1988-90); Standing Conference on University Entrance, 1989-93; Scottish Universities' Council on Entrance, 1982-94 (Chairman, 1989-94); Scottish Examination Board, 1986-93; Council, IEE, 1992-95; British National Committee and Executive Committee, CIGRE, 1985-96 (Distinguished Member, CIGRE, 1998); Council, 1989-92, and Vice President, 1992-95, Royal Society of Edinburgh, 1992-95; Education and International Relations Committees, Royal Society, 1992-95; Management Board, Bell College of Technology, Hamilton, 1989-2001 (Chairman of Council, 1990-93); Management Board, SCOTVEC, 1993-97; Chief Scientific Adviser to Secretary of State for Scotland, 1994-96; Secretary of State Scientific Adviser to Scottish Office Industry Department, 1992-94; Chairman, Technology Education Advisory Group (Scottish Consultative Council on the Curriculum), 1996-2001; Member, Steering Group, Skills Strategy for Electronics Industry, 1996-2001; Chairman, Scottish Science Trust, 1997-99; Member, Management Board, Dundee Science Trust, 1998-2001; Civil Defence Medal, 1982; IEE Achievement Medal, 1997; Fellow, Strathclyde University, 1999; President, Strathclyde University Sports Union, 1953-55. Recreations: hill-walking; music; amateur astronomy; current affairs. Address: (h.) 76 Woodlands Drive, Coatbridge, ML5 1LB; T.-01236 422016; e-mail: david.tedford@btinternet.com

Templeton, Professor Allan, MBChB, MD (Hons), FRCOG. Regius Professor of Obstetrics and Gynaecology, University of Aberdeen, since 1985; Honorary Secretary, Royal College of Obstetricians and Gynaecologists, since 1998; b. 28.6.46, Glasgow.; m., Gillian Penney; 3 s.; 1 d. Educ. Aberdeen Grammar School; University of Aberdeen. Junior hospital posts, Aberdeen Royal Infirmary; Lecturer then Senior Lecturer, University of Edinburgh. Member, Human Fertilisation and Embryology Authority. Publications: books and scientific papers on human infertility. Recreation: mountaineering. Address: (b.) Department of Obstetrics and Gynaecology, University of Aberdeen, Aberdeen Maternity Hospital, Foresterhill, Aberdeen AB25 2ZD; T.-01224 550590; e-mail: allan.templeton@abdn.ac.uk

Templeton, Ian Godfrey, MA, BA, FRSA. Warden, Glenalmond College, Perth, since 1992; b. 1.2.44, Edinburgh; m., Elisabeth Aline Robin; 1 s.; 1 d. Educ. Gordonstoun; Edinburgh University; Bedford College, London University. Assistant Master, then Housemaster, Melville College, Edinburgh, 1969-73; Housemaster, Daniel Stewart's and Melville College, Edinburgh, 1973-78; Assistant Headmaster, Robert Gordon's College, Aberdeen, 1978-85; Headmaster, Oswestry School, 1985-92. Director, Lathallan Preparatory School. Recreations: golf; skiing; choral singing. Address: Glenalmond College, Glenalmond, Perth PH1 3RY; T.-01738 880227.

Tennant, Sir Iain Mark, KT (1986). Chairman, Grampian Television PLC, 1968-89 (Vice-Chairman, 1960-68); Director, Caledonian Associated Cinemas PLC, 1950-90; Director, Clydesdale Bank PLC, 1969-89; Director, Abbey National Building Society (Chairman, Scottish Advisory Board, 1969-89); Director, Moray and Nairn Newspaper Company Ltd.; Member, Royal Company of Archers (Queen's Bodyguard in Scotland), since 1950; Crown Estate Commissioner, 1969-89; Honorary Director, Seagram

Company Ltd., Montreal; Lord Lieutenant of Morayshire, 1963-94; Lord High Commissioner to the General Assembly of the Church of Scotland, 1988, 1989; b. 11.3.19, North Berwick; m., Lady Margaret Ogilvy; 2 s.; 1 d. Educ. Eton College; Magdalene College, Cambridge. Learned about film production, Welwyn Garden City Film Studios; served in Egypt with 2nd Bn., Scots Guards, 1940-42; became Intelligence Officer, 201 Guard's Brigade; captured at the surrender of Tobruk; prisoner of war, Italy and Germany, until 1945; Founder Member, Moray Sea School, 1949; Council Member, Outward Bound Trust, 15 years; joined Board, Gordonstoun School, 1951 (Chairman, 1957-72); Member, Moray and Nairn County Council, 1956-64 (latterly Vice-Chairman, Education Committee); Member, The Times Publishing Co. Ltd., 1962-66; Member, Board, Cairngorm Sports Development Ltd., 1964-76; appointed Chairman, local Disablement Advisory Committee, 1964; Chairman, Glenlivet and Glen Grant Distilleries Ltd., 1964-70; Chairman, Glenlivet Distillers Ltd., 1970-77; Trustee, King George's Jubilee Trust, London, 1967-71; FRSA, 1971; Trustee, Churchill Trust, 1973-76; Member, Board, Courage Ltd., 1974-77; Chairman, Seagram Distillers Ltd. (in London), 1977-82; CBIM, 1983; Freeman of Moray District, 1994. Recreations: shooting; fishing. Address: (b.) Lochnabo, Lhanbryde, Moray; T.-01343 842228.

Thewliss, James, BSc (Hons). Head Teacher, Harris Academy, Dundee, since 1997; b. 24.4.53, Motherwell; m., Ann White; 1 s. Educ. Dalziel High School, Motherwell; Glasgow University. Geography Teacher, Braidhurst High School, Motherwell, 1976 -85; Principal Teacher, Geography, Perth High School, 1986-89; Assistant Rector, Perth High School, 1989-91; Assistant Head Teacher, Carluke High School, 1991-93; Depute Rector, Wallace High School, Stirling, 1993-97. Recreations: supporting Motherwell Football Club. Address: (b.) Harris Academy, Perth Road, Dundee, DD2 1NL; T.-01382 435700; headteacher@harris-academy.dundeecity.sch.uk

Thin, Andrew, BSc (Hons), MBA, DipM. Chairman, John Muir Trust, since 1997; Chairman, The Footpath Trust, since 1997; freelance management consultant, since 1995; b. 21.1.59, Edinburgh; m., Frances Elizabeth; 1 s.; 1 d. Educ. Glenalmond College; Edinburgh University. Director, James Thin Booksellers, 1985-89; Team Leader, Highlands and Islands Development Board, 1989-91; Chief Executive, Caithness and Sutherland Enterprise, 1991-95. Area Board Member, Scottish Natural Heritage; Non-Executive Director: James Thin Ltd., Ardtornish Estate Co. Ltd., ILM (Highland) Ltd. Recreations: long-distance running; canoeing; hill-walking. Address: (h.) Wester Aucherflow, by Munlochy, Ross-shire IV8 8PQ; T.-01463 811632; e-mail: andrew@thin.freeserve.co.uk

Thin, David Ainslie, BSc. Chairman, James Thin Ltd.; Chairman, Book Tokens Ltd., 1987-95; Member, Council, Executive Committee and Finance Committee, National Trust for Scotland; b. 9.7.33, Edinburgh; m., Elspeth J.M. Scott; 1 s.; 2 d. Educ. Edinburgh Academy; Loretto School; Edinburgh University. President, Booksellers Association of GB and Ireland, 1976-78. Recreations: golf; travelling; reading. Address: (h.) 60 Fountainhall Road, Edinburgh EH9 2LP; T.-0131-667 2725.

Thom, William Cameron, LLB. Criminal defence advocate, since 1991; b. 8.2.40, Falkirk; m., Alexina Helen Peebles; 1 s.; 1 d. Educ. Falkirk Technical School; Glasgow University. Police officer, 1959-74; student, 1974-79; trainee Solicitor, 1979-81; Depute Procurator Fiscal, 1981-83; Solicitor, 1983-90; Scottish Bar, since 1991. Recreations: hill-walking; Scott, Stevenson and Burns enthusiast; travelling; gardening. Address: (h.) 30 Airthrey Road, Causewayhead, Stirling FK9 5JS; T.-01786 462481.

Thomaneck, Professor Jurgen Karl Albert, JP, MEd, DrPhil, FRSA. Professor in German, Aberdeen University, 1992-2001; Aberdeen City Councillor, since 1996 (Convener, Education and Leisure Committee, since 1999); President, Aberdeen Trades Council, 1982-2001; Convenor, Grampian Joint Police Board, 1995-98; b. 12.6.41, Germany; m., Guinevere Ronald; 2 d. Educ. Universities of Kiel, Tubingen, Aberdeen. Lecturer in German, Aberdeen University, since 1968. Grampian Regional Councillor, 1984-96; Board Member, Grampian Enterprise Ltd., until 1995; President, KIMO UK, since 1996; author/editor of nine books, 15 contributions to books, 30 articles in learned journals, all in German studies. Recreation: football. Address: (h.) 17 Elm Place, Aberdeen AB25 3SN.

Thomas, Professor Michael James, OBE, OM (Poland), BSc, MBA, FRSA, FCIM. Emeritus Professor of Marketing, Strathclyde University; President, Market Research Society, since 1999; b. 15.7.33; m.; 1 s.; 1 d. Educ. University College London; Indiana University. Metal Box Co. Ltd., London, 1957-60; Syracuse University Management School, 1960-71; Lancaster University, 1972-86; appointed Professor of Marketing, Strathclyde University, 1987. Former National Chairman, Chartered Institute of Marketing. Recreation: ornithology. Address: (h.) APT.G1, Canada Court, 81 Miller Street, Glasgow G1 1EB; e-mail: michael.thomas@Mi8.com

Thomas, Professor Phillip Charles, BSc, PhD, RNutr, FIBiol, CBiol, FRAgS, FRSE. Managing Director, Artilus Ltd., since 1999; Chairman, Animal Medicines Training Regulatory Authority, since 1999; Emeritus Professor, Scottish Agricultural College, since 1999; Visiting Professor, Glasgow University, since 1999; Honorary Professor, Edinburgh University, since 1991; Chairman, Central Scotland Countryside Trust, since 2001; Member, Scottish Food Advisory Committee, since 2000; b. 17.6.42, Pontypool; m., Pamela Mary Hirst; 1 s.; 1 d. Educ. Abersychan Grammar School; University College of North Wales, Bangor. Lecturer, Department of Animal Nutrition and Physiology, Leeds University, 1966-71; Research Scientist, Hannah Research Institute, Ayr, 1971-87; Principal, West of Scotland Agricultural College, Ayr, 1987-90; Principal and Chief Executive, The Scottish Agricultural College, 1990-99; Professor of Agriculture, Glasgow University, 1987-99. Chairman, UK Advisory Committee on Animal Feedingstuffs, 1999-2001. Publications: Nutritional Physiology of Farm Animals, 1983; Silage for Milk Production, 1983. Address: (b.) Artilus Ltd., 33 Cherry Tree Park, Balerno, Midlothian EH14 5AJ.

Thompson, Professor Alan Eric, MA (Hons), PhD, FRSA, FSA(Scot). Emeritus Professor of the Economics of Government, Heriot-Watt University; b. 16.9.24; m., Mary Heather Long; 3 s.; 1 d. Educ. Edinburgh University. Edinburgh University: Assistant in Political Economy, 1952-53, Lecturer in Economics, 1953-59 and 1964-71; Professor of the Economics of Government, Heriot-Watt University, 1972-87; Parliamentary Labour candidate, Galloway, 1950, 1951; MP (Labour), Dunfermline, 1959-64; Member, Royal Fine Art Commission for Scotland, 1975-80; Chairman, Northern Offshore Maritime Resources Study, 1974-83; Governor, Newbattle Abbey College, 1975-85 (Chairman, 1980-83); Member, Local Government Boundaries Commission for Scotland, 1975-80; Member, Scottish Council for Adult Education in HM Forces, since 1973; BBC National Governor for Scotland, 1975-79; Governor, Leith Nautical College, 1981-85; Trustee, Bell's Nautical Trust, 1981-85; Parliamentary Adviser, Scottish Pharmaceutical General Council, 1984-2000. Publications: Development of Economic Doctrine (Co-author), 1980;

articles in academic journals. Recreation: writing children's stories and plays. Address: (h.) 11 Upper Gray Street, Edinburgh EH9 1SN; T.-0131-667 2140.

Thompson, Bruce Kevin, MA. Headmaster, Strathallan School, since 2000; b. 14.11.59, Bath; m., Fabienne; 2d. Educ. Newcastle High School; New College, Oxford University. Cheltenham College: Assistant Master, 1983-94; Head of Classics, 1986-94; Assistant Housemaster, 1990-94; Depute Rector, Dollar Academy, 1994-2000; Governor, Craigclowan School. Recreations: coaching rugby; rowing; weight training; music; literature. Address: (b.) Strathallan School, Forgandenny, Perth, PH2 9EG; T.-01738 815000.

Thompson, Colin, CBE, DUniv, FRSE, MA, FMA. Writer, Lecturer and Broadcaster on art and museums; b. 21.11.19, Berkhamstead; m., Jean A.J. O'Connell; 1 s.; 1 d. Educ. Sedbergh; King's College, Cambridge; Chelsea Polytechnic. Lecturer, Bath Academy of Art, Corsham, 1948-54; joined National Gallery of Scotland as Assistant Keeper, 1954; Director, National Galleries of Scotland, 1977-84. Member: Scottish Arts Council, 1976-83, Edinburgh Festival Society, since 1979, Expert Advisory Panel on Museums to Heritage Lottery Fund, 1995-98; Chairman, Scottish Museums Council, 1984-87; Chairman, Board of Governors, Edinburgh College of Art, 1989-91; Trustee, Buccleuch Heritage Trust, since 1988; Member, Scottish Mining Museum Trust, since 1987 (Chairman, 1992-96). Publications: Pictures for Scotland, 1972; Hugo Van Der Goes and the Trinity Panels in Edinburgh (Co-author), 1974; Exploring Museums: Scotland, 1990. Address: (h.) Edenkerry, Lasswade, Midlothian EH18 1LW; T.-0131-663 7927.

Thompson, Edward Henry, FCCA, FCMA. Chairman and Chief Executive, Morning Noon and Night Ltd (convenience chain), since 1991; Chairman, Scottish Retail Consortium, since 1998; b. 16.7.40, Glasgow; m., Cath; 1 s.; 1 d. Educ. Hyndland Senior Secondary School, Glasgow. Office Manager/Company Secretary, Duthie Shaw; joined Watson & Philip plc, 1963, joined Board of the company, 1976, appointed Joint Managing Director; left, 1991, to form new company. Member, Boards, Scottish Grocers Federation and British Retail Consortium; Member, Council, CBI Scotland. Recreations: Dundee United FC; 2nd home in Spain. Address: (h.) 15 Norrie Street, Broughty Ferry, Dundee DD5 2SD; T.-01382 738118.

Thompson, Francis George, IEng, FIIE, LCGI, FSA (Scot). Author of books on Highland subjects; retired Senior Lecturer, Lews Castle College, Stornoway; Secretary, Stornoway Historical Society; b. 29.3.31, Stornoway; m., Margaret Elaine Pullar; 1 s.; 3 d. Educ. Nicolson Institute, Stornoway. From 1946: supply maintenance electrician, technical writer, assistant publicity manager, lecturer; has held various offices within An Comann Gaidhealach, including editorship of Sruth, bilingual newspaper, 1967-71; books include: Harris and Lewis, 1999; Harris Tweed, 1969; Highlands and Islands, 1974; Crofting Years, 1990; Shell Guide to Northern Scotland, 1987; The Western Isles, 1988; The Supernatural Highlands, 1998. Recreation: writing! Address: Am Fasgadh, 5 Rathad na Muilne, Stornoway, Lewis; T.-01851 703812.

Thompson, Professor Paul Ian, BA (Hons), PhD. Professor of Organisational Analysis, Department of Human Resource Management, University of Strathclyde; b. 1.1.51, Wallasey; 1 d. Educ. Maghull Grammar School; Liverpool University. Lecturer in Sociology, St. Helen's College of Technology, 1974-84; appointed Senior Lecturer in Organisation Studies, Lancashire Polytechnic, 1984, going on to become Principal Lecturer and Professor in new University of Central Lancashire; appointed Professor of Management, Department of Business Studies, Edinburgh University, 1994 (Head of Department, 1998-99). Visiting Professor, Institute for Advanced Studies, Vienna, 1987, Institute of Business, Beijing, 1989; Visiting Principal Fellow, University of Wollongong, Australia, 1997; Editor, Renewal (A Journal of Labour Politics), since 1993. Recreations: music; cinema; playing and watching football, especially Everton F.C. Address: (b.) Department of Human Resource Management, The Graham Hills Building, 50 Richmond Street, Glasgow G1 1XT.

Thoms, Lisbeth Margaret, BSc, DipArch, FSAScot. Freelance archaeologist and heritage advisor; b. Kirkcaldy. Educ. Barnsley High School for Girls; Alloa Academy; Edinburgh University; St Mary's College, Durham University. Field Archaeological Officer, Dundee Art Galleries and Museums, 1972-83; Depute Curator, Dundee Art Galleries and Museums, 1983-96. Vice-Chairman, Scottish Urban Archaeological Trust; Member, Ancient Monuments Board for Scotland; Member, Advisory Panel on Treasure Trove. Recreations: golf; opera; gardening; travel. Address: 4 Portpatrick Terrace, Monifieth, Angus DD5 4TU; T.-01382 535212; e-mail: LisbethThoms@msn.com

Thomson, Craig, BA (Hons), MPhil, EdD, DipRDA, Principal, Glenrothes College, since 1999; Director, SUfI, since 2001 (Member, Advisory Council Learning and Teaching Committee, since 2001); b. 1.5.52, London; m., Carol; 1 s.; 1 d. Educ. Larbert High School; Heriot-Watt University; Bath University; Sheffield University. Teacher: Lochaber High School; Thurso High School; private training consultant with oil companies and military in Kuwait; research and educational management in Wiltshire, Somerset, Gloucester, Fife. Address: (b.) Glenrothes College, Stenton Campus, Glenrothes, Fife, KY6 2RA; T.-01592 772233.

Thomson, Professor Derick S., MA (Aberdeen), BA (Cantab), DLitt (Univ. of Wales), DLitt (Univ. of Aberdeen), FRSE, FBA. Professor of Celtic, Glasgow University, 1963-91; b. 5.8.21, Stornoway; m., Carol Galbraith; 5 s.; 1 d. Educ. Nicolson Institute, Stornoway; Aberdeen University; Cambridge University; University College of North Wales, Bangor. Taught at Edinburgh, Glasgow and Aberdeen Universities before returning to Glasgow as Professor, 1963; Chairman, Gaelic Books Council, 1968-91; Honorary President: Scottish Gaelic Texts Society, Saltire Society, Scottish Poetry Library; former Member, Scottish Arts Council; first recipient, Ossian Prize, 1974; author of numerous books and articles, including An Introduction to Gaelic Poetry, The Companion to Gaelic Scotland, European Poetry in Gaelic and collections of Gaelic poetry, including collected poems Creachadh na Clarsaich and Meall Garbh/Rugged Mountain; Editor, Gairm, since 1952. Address: (h.) 15 Struan Road, Cathcart, Glasgow G44 3AT; T.-0141-637 3704.

Thomson, Derrick. Managing Director, Grampian Television, since 1999; b. 7.3.63, Aberdeen; m., Fiona; 1 d. Educ. Kirkwall Grammar School; Golspie High School. General trainee, Cinecosse Productions, 1979; moved to Grampian, 1981, as a trainee technician; joined Central TV, 1983; became sound supervisor on a variety of high-profile productions, including worldwide documentaries; started own production business, 1989; re-joined Grampian, 1992, rising to Production Executive; moved to Scottish TV during merger, 1997, running external resources for Scottish and Grampian. Recreations: fly fishing; flying; art; photography; travel. Address: (b.) Grampian TV, Queens Cross, Aberdeen AB15 7XJ; T.-01224 846640.

Thomson, Elaine Margaret, BSc. MSP (Labour), Aberdeen North, since 1999; b. 10.8.57, Inverness; partner, Archie Flockhart. Educ. Aberdeen High School for Girls; Aberdeen University. Analyst/Programmer, ABB Vetco Gray Ltd., Aberdeen, 1982-95; IT Consultant, Absoft Ltd., Aberdeen, 1995-99. Member, SERA (Labour Environment Campaign). Recreations: reading; skiing. Address: (b.) 7A Byron Square, Northfield, Aberdeen; T.-01224 699666.

Thomson, Sir (Frederick Douglas) David, Bt, BA. Chairman, Britannia Steam Ship Insurance Association Limited, since 1986 (Director, since 1965); Chairman, Through Transport Marine Mutual Assurance Association (Bermuda) Ltd., since 1983 (Director, since 1973); Director, Danae Investment Trust Ltd., since 1979; Chairman, Jove Investment Trust PLC, since 1983; Director, Martin Currie Pacific Trust PLC, since 1985; Chairman, Ptarmigan International Capital Trust PLC, since 1990; Chairman, S.A. Meacock & Co. Ltd., since 1996; Director, Ionian Group Ltd., since 1994, Bolero International Ltd., since 1999; Chairman, Laurence J. Smith Ltd., since 1993; Chairman, Asset Management Investment Company PLC, since 2001; Director, Bolero.net, since 2000; Member, Royal Company of Archers (Queen's Bodyguard for Scotland); b. 14.2.40, Edinburgh; 2 s.; 1 d. Educ. Eton; University College, Oxford. Recreations: shooting; skiing; tennis; bonfires. Address: (h.) Holylee, Walkerburn, Peeblesshire; T.-01896 870673.

Thomson, Geddes, MA (Hons). Writer, former teacher; b. 20.9.39, Dalry; m., Lucy Faulkner; 2 s. Educ. Dalry High School; Glasgow University. Principal Teacher of English, Allan Glen's School, Glasgow, 1972-89; Shawlands Academy, Glasgow, 1989-93; Extra-Mural Lecturer, Department of Adult and Continuing Education, Glasgow University, 1985-93; WEA Tutor, 1994-98. Publications include: A Spurious Grace, 1981; Identities (Editor), 1981; The Poetry of Edwin Morgan, 1986. Recreations: supporting Partick Thistle; fishing; browsing in bookshops. Address: (h.) 48 Windyedge Crescent, Glasgow G13 1YF; T.-0141-959 5277.

Thomson, George Buchanan, FCIBS; Moderator, Dumbarton Presbytery, Church of Scotland, 2000-01; b. 10.1.24, Glasgow; m., Margaret Irene Williams. Educ. Eastwood Secondary School. Joined Union Bank of Scotland, 1940; War Service, 1942-46 with RAF (Navigator, Bomber Command); held various banking appointments, 1947-86; retired as Assistant General Manager (Branch Administration, West), Bank of Scotland; Past President, Institute of Bankers in Scotland; Director and Chairman, Association for the Relief of Incurables; Hon. Treasurer, Scottish Civic Trust; former Convener, Board of Stewardship and Finance, Church of Scotland; Director, Ian Skelly Holdings Ltd., 1986-89; Director, Clydesdale Development Company, 1988-95. Recreations: curling; bowling. Address: (h.) Kingswood, 26 Waverley Avenue, Helensburgh G84 7JU; T.-01436 672915.

Thomson, Rev. Iain Urquhart. Minister, Parish of Skene, since 1972; b. 13.12.45, Dundee; m., Christine Freeland; 1 s.; 2 d. Educ. Harris Academy, Dundee; Inverness Royal Academy; Aberdeen University; Christ's College, Aberdeen. Assistant Minister, Castlehill Church, Ayr, 1970-72. Clerk, Presbytery of Gordon, 1988-2000; Clerk and Treasurer, Synod of Grampian Trusts Committee, since 1993. Recreations: golf; theatre. Address: The Manse, Kirkton of Skene, Westhill, Aberdeenshire AB32 6LX; T.-01224 743277.

Thomson, Professor James Alick, MA, PhD. Professor of Psychology, Strathclyde University, since 2000; b. 9.12.51, Inverness; m., Dana O'Dwyer; 1 d. Educ. Inverness Royal Academy; Edinburgh University. Research Scholar, Uppsala University, Sweden, 1973; Post-doctoral Fellow, University of Paris, 1977-78; Strathclyde University: Lecturer, 1979-91, Senior Lecturer, 1992-94, Reader, 1995-99. Publications: The Facts About Child Pedestrian Accidents, 1991; Child Development and the Aims of Road Safety Education (Co-Author), 1996; Child Safety: Problem and Prevention from Pre-School to Adolescence (Co-Author), 1996; Kerbcraft: A Manual for Road Safety Professionals, 1997; Studies in Perception and Action V (Co-Editor), 1999; 60 scientific articles and government reports. Recreations: rock climbing; hillwalking; mountaineering; photography; travel; Gaelic language and literature. Address: (b.) Department of Psychology, Strathclyde University, 40 George Street, Glasgow G1 1QE; T.-0141-548 2572; e-mail: j.a.thomson@strath.ac.uk

Thomson, Sir John Adam, GCMG. b. 27.4.27, Bieldside, Aberdeen; m., 1, Elizabeth Anne McClure (deceased); 3 s.; 1 d.; 2, Judith Ogden Bullitt. Educ. Aberdeen University; Trinity College, Cambridge. Joined Foreign Office, 1950; seconded to Cabinet Office as Chief of Assessment Staff, 1968-71; Minister and Deputy Permanent Representative, NATO, 1972; Head of UK Delegation, MBFR Exploratory Talks, Vienna, 1973; Assistant Under Secretary for Defence and Disarmament, 1973-76; British High Commissioner in India, 1977-82; British Permanent Representative and Ambassador to UN, 1982-87; Principal Director, 21st Century Trust, 1987-90; Director, ANZ Grindlays, 1987-96; International Adviser, ANZ Grindlays Bank, 1996-98; Chairman, Felmings Emerging Markets Investment Trust, 1990-97; Chairman, Minority Rights Group, 1991-99; Director's Visitor, Institute for Advanced Studies, Princeton, 1995-96. Trustee, National Museums of Scotland, 1990-99; Member, Council, International Institute of Strategic Studies, 1987-96; Trustee, Aberdeen University Development Trust; Trustee, Indian National Trust for Art and Cultural Heritage; Member, Governing Body, IDS and ODI. Recreations: hill-walking; tennis.

Thomson, Professor John Aidan Francis, MA, DPhil, FRHistS. Professor Emeritus of Mediaeval History, Glasgow University, since 1999; b. 26.7.34, Edinburgh; m., Katherine J.V. Bell; 1 s.; 1 d. Educ. George Watson's Boys' College, Edinburgh; Edinburgh University; Balliol College, Oxford. Glasgow University: Assistant in Mediaeval History, 1960, Lecturer, 1961, Senior Lecturer, 1974, Reader, 1983, Titular Professor, 1994, Professor, 1995. President, Glasgow Archaeological Society, 1978-81. Publications: The Later Lollards 1414-1520, 1965; Popes and Princes 1417-1517, 1980; The Transformation of Mediaeval England 1370-1529, 1983; Towns and Townspeople in the Fifteenth Century (Editor), 1988; The Early Tudor Church and Society, 1485-1529, 1993; The Western Church in the Middle Ages, 1998. Recreations: travel and sightseeing; walking; gardening. Address: (h.) 15 Drumbeg Loan, Killearn, Stirlingshire G63 9LG; T.-01360 550712.

Thomson, John George, LLB. Advocate, since 1990; b. 4.5.58, Dundee. Educ. Morgan Academy, Dundee; Dundee University. Address: (h.) 6 Royal Circus, Edinburgh EH3 6SR; T.-0131-226 3387; e-mail: johnthomson@btinternet.com

Thomson, Professor Joseph McGeachy, LLB, FRSE, FRSA, HonFSALS. Regius Professor of Law, Glasgow University, since 1991; Commissioner, Scottish Law Commission, since 2000; b. 6.5.48, Campbeltown. Educ. Keil School, Dumbarton; Edinburgh University. Lecturer in Law, Birmingham University, 1970-74; Lecturer in Laws, King's College, London, 1974-84; Professor of Law, Strathclyde University, 1984-90. Recreations: opera; ballet; food and wine. Address: (h.) 2 Kew Terrace, Glasgow; T.-0141-334 6682.

Titterington, Professor (Donald) Michael, BSc, PhD, DipMathStat, FRSE. Professor of Statistics, Glasgow University, since 1988; b. 20.11.45, Marple, Cheshire; m., Mary Hourie Philp; 1 s. Educ. High School of Stirling; Edinburgh University; Cambridge University. Lecturer, then Senior Lecturer, then Titular Professor, Department of Statistics, Glasgow University, 1972-88; visiting appointments: Princeton University, 1978, State University of New York, 1980, Wisconsin University, 1982, Australian National University, 1982, 1994, 1995; Associate Editor, Biometrika, 1979-85, Annals of Statistics, 1983-85 and 1995-96, Journal, American Statistical Association, 1986-88 and 1991-96, and IEEE Transactions on Pattern Analysis and Machine Intelligence, 1994-96; Joint Editor, Journal of the Royal Statistical Society, Series B, 1986-89, and Statistical Science, 1992-94; Editor, Biometrika, since 1996; Council Member, Royal Statistical Society, 1987-92; elected Fellow, Institute of Mathematical Statistics, 1986; elected Member, International Statistical Institute, 1991. Publications: Statistical Analysis of Finite Mixture Distributions (Co-author); many journal articles. Recreation: being a father. Address: (b.) Department of Statistics, Glasgow University, Glasgow, G12 8QQ; T.-0141-330 5022.

Tod, Stewart, DA (Edin), RIBA, FRIAS, FSA Scot. Consultant to Stewart Tod & Partners, Architects, Edinburgh, formerly David Carr Architects; b. 30.4.27, West Wemyss; m., A. Vivienne J. Nixon; 2 s.; 2 d. Educ. Buckhaven High School; Edinburgh College of Art. RAF, 1945-48; Stratton Davis & Yates, 1952-55; Falkirk District Council, 1955-57; Carr and Matthew, 1957-60; David Carr Architects, 1960-77. General Trustee, Church of Scotland; Governor, Donaldson's College. Recreations: bee-keeping; gardening; sketching. Address: (b.) 43 Manor Place, Edinburgh; T.-0131-225 7988.

Todd, Rev. Andrew Stewart, MA, BD, DD. Minister, St. Machar's Cathedral, Old Aberdeen, 1967-93; Extra Chaplain to The Queen in Scotland, since 1996 (Chaplain-in-Ordinary, 1991-96); b. 26.5.26, Alloa; m., Janet Agnes Brown Smith; 2 s.; 2 d. Educ. High School of Stirling; Edinburgh University; Basel University. Assistant Minister, St. Cuthbert's, Edinburgh, 1951-52; Minister: Symington, Lanarkshire, 1952; North Leith, 1960; Member, Church Hymnary Revision Comittee, 1963-73; Convener, General Assembly's Committee on Public Worship and Aids to Devotion, 1974-78; Moderator, Aberdeen Presbytery, 1980-81; Convener, Panel on Doctrine, 1990-95; Member, Church Hymnary Trust; awarded Honorary Doctorate, Aberdeen University, 1982; translator of three theological books from German into English; Honorary President, Church Service Society; Honorary President, Scottish Church Society. Recreations: music; gardening. Address: (h.) Culearn, Balquhidder, Lochearnhead, Perthshire FK19 8PB; T.-01877 384662.

Todd, Professor Janet, MA, PhD. Francis Hutcheson Professor of English Literature, Glasgow University, since 2000; Honorary Fellow, Lucy Cavendish College, Cambridge, since 1999; b. 10.9.42, Llandrindod; m., Derek Hughes; 1 s.; 1 d. Educ. Dr Williams' School, Dolgellau; Newnham College, Cambridge; University of Florida. Lecturer in English, University of Cape Coast, 1964-67, University of Florida, 1969-71; Assistant Professor of English, University of Puerto Rico, 1972-74; Assistant, Associate, full Professor of English, Rutgers University, 1974-83; Fellow in English, Sidney Sussex College, 1983-90; Chair in English, University of East Anglia, 1990-2000. Publications: many books, most recently Mary Wollstonecraft: a revolutionary life, 2000. Address: (b.) Department of English Literature, Glasgow University, Glasgow G12 8QQ.

Toft, Anthony Douglas, CBE, BSc, MD, FRCPE, FRCPGlas, FRCPLond, FRCPI, FACP(Hon), FRACP(Hon), FRCSE, FRCPC(Hon), FRCGP(Hon), FFPM (Hon), FFAEM (Hon), FCPS Pakistan (Hon), FCPS Bangladesh (Hon), FAM Singapore (Hon), MAM Malaysia (Hon). Consultant Physician, Royal Infirmary, Edinburgh, since 1978; Physician to the Queen in Scotland, since 1996; Chief Medical Officer, Scottish Equitable Life Assurance, since 1987; President, British Thyroid Association, 1996-99; Chairman, Professional and Linguistic Assessment Board, since 1999; President, Royal College of Physicians of Edinburgh, 1991-94; b. 29.10.44, Perth; m., Maureen Darling; 1 s.; 1 d. Educ. Perth Academy; Edinburgh University. Chairman, Collegiate Members' Committee, Royal College of Physicians of Edinburgh, 1978; Vice-President, Royal College of Physicians, 1989-91; Chairman, Scottish Royal Colleges, 1992-94; Chairman, Joint Committee of Higher Medical Training, 1993-96; Member, Health Appointments Advisory Committee, 1994-2000. Recreations: golf; gardening. Address: (h.) 41 Hermitage Gardens, Edinburgh EH10 6AZ; T.-0131-447 2221; e-mail: toft41@hotmail.com

Tolley, David Anthony, MB, BS (Lond), FRCS, FRCSEdin. Consultant Urological Surgeon, Western General Hospital, Edinburgh, since 1980; Honorary Senior Lecturer, Department of Surgery/Urology, Edinburgh University, since 1980; Director, Scottish Lithotriptor Centre; b. 29.11.47, Warrington; m., Judith Anne Finn; 3 s.; 1 d. Educ. Manchester Grammar School; Kings College Hospital Medical School, London University. House Surgeon and Physician, Kings College Hospital; Lecturer in Human Morphology, Southampton University; Lecturer in Anatomy and Fulbright Fellow, University of Texas at Houston; Surgical Registrar, Hammersmith and Ealing Hospitals, London; Senior Surgical Registrar (Urology), Kings College Hospital, London; Senior Urological Registrar, Yorkshire Regional Training Scheme. Previously Member: MRC Working Party on Urological Cancer; MRC Working Party on Superficial Bladder Cancer; Editorial Board, British Journal of Urology; Member, Council, British Association of Urological Surgeons; Member, Standing Commitee on Postgraduate Education, Member, Council, British Association of Urological Surgeons; President, British Society for Endourology; Board, Minimal Access Therapy Training Unit Scotland; Education Committee, Royal College of Surgeons of Edinburgh; Past Chairman, Scottish Urological Oncology Group; currently: Chairman, Specialty Advisory Board in Urology, Royal College of Surgeons of Edinburgh; Member, Council, Royal College of Surgeons of Edinburgh; Chairman, Section of Endourology, British Association of Urological Surgeons; Examiner, Intercollegiate Board in Urology; Treasurer, European Society for Urotechnology; Member, Editorial Board, Journal of Endourology; Member, Editorial Board, Hungarian Endourology; Honorary Member, Romanian Society for Endourology. Recreations: golf; sailing. Address: (b.) Murrayfield Hospital, Corstorphine Road, Edinburgh; T.-0131-334 0363.

Tombs, Sebastian Martineau, BArch, DipArch (Cantab), FRIAS, ACIArb. Secretary, Royal Incorporation of Architects in Scotland, since 1995; b. 11.10.49, Sussex; m., Eva Heirman; 4 s.; 2 d. Educ. Bryanston; Cambridge University. RMJM, Edinburgh, 1975-76; Roland Wedgwood, Edinburgh, 1976-77; Fountainbridge Housing Association, Edinburgh, 1977-78; Housing Corporation, 1978-81; Edinburgh District Council Housing Department, 1982-86; Depute Secretary, RIAS, 1986-94; Founder and first Secretary, Scottish Ecological Design Association, 1991-94, Chairman, 1994-97. Founder and first Chairman, Association of Planning Supervisors, 1995-97; Scottish Liberal Democrat candidate, Edinburgh North and Leith, Scottish Parliament elections, 1999, and General Election,

2001. Recreation: choral music; doggerel; sketching. Address: (b.) 15 Rutland Square, Edinburgh, EH1 2BE; T.-0131-229 7545.

Tomkins, Patrick Lindsay, BA (Hons), RCDS. Chief Constable, Lothian and Borders Police, since 2002; b. 20.8.60, Folkestone; m., Susan; 1 s.; 1 d. Educ. Hastings Grammar School; King's College, London; Royal College of Defence Studies. Sussex Police, 1979; Chief Superintendent, Metropolitan Police, 1993; Commander, Metropolitan Police, 1997; Assistant Inspector of Constabulary, 1999. Recreations: fly fishing; cycling; reading. Address: (b.) Police Headquarters, Fettes Avenue, Edinburgh EH4 1RB; T.-0131-311 3086.

Tomlinson, Professor Alan, MSc, PhD, DSc, FCOptom, FAAO. Professor of Vision Science, Glasgow Caledonian University, since 1992; b. 18.3.44, Bolton; partner, Dr. Daphne McCulloch; 1 s. Educ. Lampton Grammar School, North London; Bradford University; Manchester University Institute of Science and Technology. Fellowship, British Optical Association, 1966; Registration, General Optical Council, 1966; Lecturer, Opthalmic Optics: Bradford University, 1967-68; UMIST, 1968-77; Director, Clinical Research, Wesley Jesson Inc, Chicago, USA, 1977-79 and 1983-86; Professor of Optometry: Indiana University, 1980-83; Southern California College of Optometry, 1986-91; Council Member, General Optical Council, since 1999; Member, British Universities Committee of Optometry, since 1992; Chair, 1997-99; Council Member, College of Optometry (UK), 1994-98; Member, Advisory Committee, American Academy of Optometry, 1993-98. Publications: Complications of Contact Lens Wear, 1992. Recreations: tennis; running; theatre; music. Address: (b.) Department of Vision Science, Glasgow Caledonian University, City Campus, Glasgow, G4 0BA; T.-0141-331 3380.

Toner, Mary Catherine, BEd (Hons), DPSE. Chief Executive, Scottish Marriage Care, since 1998; b. 14.5.46, Shotts; m., Thomas; 2 s. Educ. St. Andrew's College; Jordanhill College. Training in industry, leading to middle management and production, posts, 1967-79; Primary School Teacher, Glasgow and Lanarkshire, 1984-91; Head Teacher, St. Anthony's Primary School, West Lothian, 1991-94; Education Officer, Lothian Region and West Lothian, 1994-98. Former Counsellor, Supervisor, Tutor, Scottish Marriage Care. Recreations: travelling; learning; reading; gardening. Address: (b.) 72 Waterloo Street, Glasgow G2 7DA; T.-0141-222 2166.

Topping, Professor Barry H.V., BSc, PhD, CEng, CMath, MBCS, MICE, MIStructE, MIMechE, FIMA. Professor of Computational Mechanics, Department of Mechanical and Chemical Engineering, Heriot-Watt University, Edinburgh, since 1995; b. 14.2.52, Manchester. Educ. Bedford Modern School; City University, London. Lecturer in Civil Engineering, Edinburgh University, 1978-88; Von-Humboldt Research Fellow, Stuttgart University, 1986-87; Senior Lecturer, Heriot-Watt University, 1988-89, Reader, 1989-90, Professor of Structural Engineering, 1990-95. Co-Editor, Computers and Structures; Co-Editor, Advances in Engineering Software. Address: (b.) Department of Mechanical and Chemical Engineering, Heriot-Watt University, Riccarton, Edinburgh EH14 4AS; T.-0131-449 5111.

Torphichen, 15th Lord (James Andrew Douglas Sandilands); b. 27.8.46; m.; 4 d. Address: Calder House, Mid Calder, West Lothian.

Torrance, Rev. Professor Iain Richard, TD, MA, BD, DPhil. Dean, Faculty of Arts and Divinity, Aberdeen University, since 2001; Master, Christ's College, since 2001; a Chaplain to The Queen in Scotland, since 2001; Co-Editor, Scottish Journal of Theology, since 1982; b. 13.1.49, Aberdeen; m., Morag Ann MacHugh; 1 s.; 1 d. Educ. Edinburgh Academy; Monkton Combe School, Bath; Edinburgh University; St. Andrews University; Oriel College, Oxford University. Minister, Northmavine, Shetland, 1982-85; Lecturer in New Testament and Ethics, Queen's College, Birmingham, 1985-89; Lecturer in New Testament and Patristics, Birmingham University, 1989-93; Aberdeen University: Lecturer, 1993-97, Senior Lecturer in Divinity, 1997-99, Professor in Patristics and Christian Ethics, (Personal Chair), since 1999, Head, Department of Divinity with Religious Studies, 2000-01. Chaplain to the Moderator of the General Assembly, 1976; Member, International Dialogue between the Orthodox and the Reformed Churches, since 1992; Member, General Assembly's Panel on Doctrine, since 1993; Member, Ethics Committee, Grampian Health Board, 1996-2000; Hon. Secretary, Aberdeen A.U.T., 1995-98, Hon. President, 1998-99; Secretary, Society for the Study of Christian Ethics, 1995-98; Judge, Templeton (UK) Awards, 1994-99; TA Chaplain, 1982-97; ACF Chaplain, 1996-2000; Member, Academie Internationale des Sciences Religieuses, since 1997; Convener, General Assembly's Committee on Chaplains to HM Forces, since 1998; Senate Assessor to Aberdeen University Court, since 1999; Member, Committee of Highland TAVRA, since 1999; Member, QAA's Benchmarking Panel for Degrees in Theology and Religious Studies, 1999-2000. Publications: Christology after Chalcedon, 1988; Human Genetics: a Christian perspective (Co-author), 1995; Ethics and the Military Community, 1998; To Glorify God: Essays on Modern Reformed Liturgy (Co-Author), 1999; Bioethics for the New Millennium (Editor), 2000. Recreations: historical Scottish culture (castles, battles, literature, art). Address: (h.) Concraig Smiddy, Clinterty, Kingswells, AB15 8RN; T.-01224 790902; e-mail: i.r.torrance@abdn.ac.uk

Torrance, Rev. Professor James Bruce, MA (Hons), BD. Professor of Systematic Theology, Aberdeen University, 1977-89 (Dean, Faculty of Divinity, 1978-81); Minister, Church of Scotland, since 1950; b. 3.2.23, Chengtu, Szechwan, West China; m., Mary Heather Aitken; 1 s.; 2 d. Educ. Royal High School, Edinburgh; Edinburgh University and New College; Marburg University; Basle University; Oxford University. RAF, 1943-45; ordained, Invergowrie, Dundee, 1954; Lecturer in Divinity and Dogmatics in History of Christian Thought, 1961, and Senior Lecturer in Christian Dogmatics, 1972, New College, Edinburgh; Visiting Professor of New Testament, Union Theological Seminary, Richmond, Virginia, 1960, of Theology, Columbia Theological Seminary, 1965, and Vancouver School of Theology, 1974-75; Visiting Professor in South Africa, USA, New Zealand, Australia, Fiji, W. Samoa, Canada. Convenor, Panel on Doctrine, General Assembly, 1982-86; Joint Convener, British Council of Churches Commission on Doctrine of the Trinity, 1983-89; Joint Convenor, World Alliance of Reformed Churches, Lutheran World Federation Conversations, 1985-88; Warfield Lecturer, Princeton, 2001. Publications: Christ In Our Place (festschrift), 1989; John Duns Scotus in a Nutshell (Co-author), 1992; Worship, Community and the Triune God of Grace, 1994; Nature of Atonement (Editor), 1995; Scottish Theology, 1996; A Passion for Christ (Co-author), 1999. Recreations: bee-keeping; fishing; swimming; gardening. Address: (h.) 3 Greenbank Crescent, Edinburgh EH10 5TE; T.-0131-447 3230.

Torrance, Very Rev. Professor Thomas Forsyth, MBE, MA, BD, DrTheol, DLitt, DD, DrTeol, DTheol, DSc, FBA, FRSE. Emeritus Professor, Edinburgh University, since 1979; b. 30.8.13, Chengdu, Sichuan, China; m., Margaret Edith Spear; 2 s.; 1 d. Educ. Canadian School, Chengdu, China; Bellshill Academy, Lanarkshire; Edinburgh University; Basel University; Oriel College, Oxford. Minister: Alyth Barony Parish Church, 1940-47; served as Church of Scotland Chaplain, 1943-45; Minister,

Beechgrove Parish Church, Aberdeen, 1947-50; Edinburgh University: Professor of Church History, 1950-52, Professor of Christian Dogmatics, 1952-79; Templeton Prize, 1978; Moderator, General Assembly of the Church of Scotland, 1976-77. Cross of St. Mark, First Class, 1970; Protoprebyter of Greek Orthodox Church (Hon.), 1973; President, Academie Internationale des Sciences Religieuses, 1972-81. Publications: The Doctrine of Grace in the Apostolic Fathers, 1949; Calvin's Doctrine of Man, 1949; Royal Priesthood, 1955; Kingdom and Church, 1956; The School of Faith, 1959; Conflict and Agreement in the Church, 1959; Karl Barth: An Introduction to his Early Theology, 1962; Theology in Reconstruction, 1965; Theological Science, 1969 (Collins Prize); Space, Time and Incarnation, 1969; God and Rationality, 1971; Theology in Reconciliation, 1975; Space, Time and Resurrection, 1976; The Ground and Grammar of Theology, 1980; Christian Theology and Scientific Culture, 1980; Divine and Contingent Order, 1981; Reality and Evangelical Theology, 1982; Juridical and Physical Law, 1982; The Mediation of Christ, 1983; Transformation and Convergence in the Frame of Knowledge, 1984; Reality and Scientific Theology, 1985; The Trinitarian Faith, 1988; The Hermeneutics of John Calvin, 1988; Karl Barth: Biblical and Evangelical Theologian, 1990; Trinitarian Perspectives, 1993; Preaching Christ Today, 1993; Divine Meaning, 1995; The Christian Doctrine of God, 1995; Scottish Theology, 1996; The Person of Jesus Christ, 2000. Founding Editor of Scottish Journal of Theology. Recreations: formerly golf, squash, fishing; now walking. Address: (h.) 37 Braid Farm Road, Edinburgh EH10 6LE; T.-0131-447 3224.

Tosh, Murray, MA. MSP (Conservative), South of Scotland, since 1999 (Deputy Presiding Officer, Scottish Parliament); b. 1.9.50, Ayr; m., Christine; 2 s.; 1 d. Educ. Kilmarnock Academy; Glasgow University; Jordanhill College of Education. Principal Teacher of History, Kilwinning Academy, 1977, Belmont Academy, Ayr, 1984; Councillor, Kyle and Carrick District Council, 1987-96 (Convener of Housing, 1992-96); Chairman, Central Ayrshire Conservative and Unionist Association, 1980-83, Ayr Conservative and Unionist Association, 1985-90. Recreations: hill-walking; reading; some sports (spectator only). Address: (h.) 47a St Ninian's Road, Prestwick, Ayrshire; T.-01292 470264.

Toth, Emeritus Professor Akos George, Dr. Jur., PhD. Professor of Law, Strathclyde University, 1984-2001; Jean Monnet Chair of European Law, 1991-2001; b. 9.2.36, Mezotur, Hungary; m., Sarah Kurucz. Educ. Budapest University; Szeged University; Exeter University. Strathclyde University: Lecturer in Law, 1971-76, Senior Lecturer, 1976-82, Reader, 1982-84; British Academy Research Readership, 1993-95. Publications: Legal Protection of Individuals in the European Communities, 1978; The Oxford Encyclopaedia of European Community Law, 1990. Recreations: travel; music; opera; theatre; swimming; walking. Address: (b.) Strathclyde University, Law School, 173 Cathedral Street, Glasgow, G4 ORQ; T.-0141-548 3335; e-mail: toth@strath.ac.uk

Totten, Sheriff William John, LLB (Hons). Sheriff of Glasgow and Strathkelvin, since 1999; b. 11.9.54, Paisley; m., Shirley Ann Morrison; 1 s. Educ. John Neilson Institute, Paisley; Glasgow University. Apprentice, Tindal, Oatts and Rodger, Solicitors, 1977-79; admitted as Solicitor, 1979; Procurator Fiscal Service, 1979-83; Assistant, then Partner, Beltrami and Co., 1983-88; admitted to Faculty of Advocates, 1989; Advocate Depute, 1993-96. Recreations: cycling; skiing; swimming; travel; reading. Address: (b.) Glasgow Sheriff Court, 1 Carlton Place, Glasgow; T.-0141-429 8888.

Trainer, Professor James, MA, PhD. Professor of German, Stirling University, 1969-97 (Emeritus) (Deputy Principal, 1973-78, 1981-87, 1989-92); b. 2.3.32; m., Barbara Herta Reinhard (deceased); 2 s.; 1 d. Educ. St. Andrews University; Free University of Berlin. Lecturer in German, St. Andrews University, 1958-67; Visiting Professor, Yale University, 1964-65; Visiting Scholar, University of California at Santa Barbara, 1989; Vice-Convener, SUCE, 1987-94; Convener, SUCE Modern Languages Panel, 1979-86; Member, Inter University and Polytechnic Council, since 1983; Member, Scottish Examination Board, 1975-82; Chairman, SED Postgraduate Awards Committee, since 1989; Member, UK Fulbright Committee, 1985-93; Trustee, National Library of Scotland, 1986-91; Chairman, Scottish Conference of University Teachers of German, 1978-80; Member, National Academic Audit Unit; Member, SHEFCO Quality Assessment Committee; Member Overseas Research Students Awards Committee, CVCP; Governor, Morrison's Academy, Crieff, 1994-98. Recreations: music; cricket; translating. Address: (h.) 5 Pathfoot Avenue, Bridge of Allan FK9 4SA; T.-01786 833422; e-mail: jt4@stirling.ac.uk

Trainor, Professor Richard Hughes, BA, MA, DPhil, FRHistS, AcSS, FRSA. Vice-Chancellor and Professor of Social History, Greenwich University, since 2000; b. 31.12.48, New Jersey; m., Dr. Marguerite Wright Dupree; 1 s.; 1 d. Educ. Calvert Hall High School, Maryland; Brown University; Princeton University; Merton and Nuffield Colleges, Oxford University. Junior Research Fellow, Wolfson College, Oxford, 1977-79; Lecturer, Balliol College, Oxford, 1978-79; Glasgow University: Lecturer in Economic History, 1979-89, Senior Lecturer in Economic and Social History, 1989-95, Director, Design and Implementation of Software in History Project, 1985-89, Professor of Social History, 1995-2000, Co-Director, Computers in Teaching Initiative Centre for History, 1989-2000, Dean of Social Sciences, 1992-96, Vice-Principal, 1996-2000, Senior Vice-Principal, 1999-2000. Rhodes Scholar; Honorary Secretary, Economic History Society, since 1998; Convener, Steering Group, Learning and Teaching Support Network, since 2000; Council Member, Royal Historical Society, 1997-2001; Joint Editor, Scottish Economic and Social History, 1989-94. Publication: Black Country Elites: the exercise of authority in an industrialised area 1830-1900, 1993; University, City and State: the University of Glasgow since 1870 (Joint Author), 2000. Recreations: parenting; observing politics; tennis. Address: (h.) 45 Mitre Road, Glasgow G14 9LE; T.-0141-959 0006.

Travers, John, BA, MA. Director of Education, North Ayrshire Council, since 1995; b. 22.1.48, Catterick; m., Joy; 1 s.; 2 d. Educ. St. Patrick's High School, Dumbarton; Glasgow University. Teaching, Glasgow and Barrhead, 1977-82; Assistant Head Teacher, St. Patrick's High School, Coatbridge, 1982-84; TVEI Coordinator, James Watt College, Greenock, 1984-86; Strathclyde Regional Council: Education Officer, Renfrew Division, 1986-89, Assistant Director of Education, 1989-90, Senior Education Officer, 1990-92; Senior Depute Director of Education, Fife Regional Council, 1992-95. Address: (b.) Cunninghame House, Irvine, KA12 8EE; T.-01294 324412.

Trewavas, Professor Anthony James, BSc, PhD, FRS, FRSE, FRSA, FWIF. Professor, Institute of Cell and Molecular Biology, Edinburgh University, since 1990; b. 17.6.39, London; m., Valerie; 1 s.; 2 d. Educ. Roan Grammar School; University College, London. Lecturer/Reader, Edinburgh University; Visiting Professor, Universities of Michigan State, Calgary, California (Davis), Bonn, Illinois, North Carolina, National University of Mexico; University of Milan. Publications: 197 scientific papers; two books. Recreations: music (particularly choral); reading. Address: (h.) Old Schoolhouse, Croft Street, Penicuik EH26 9DH.

Trotter, Alexander Richard, JP, FRSA; Lord Lieutenant of Berwickshire, since 2000; President, Scottish Landowners' Federation, 1996-2001; b. 20.2.39, London; m., Julia Henrietta Greenwell; 3 s. Educ. Eton College; City of London Technical College. Royal Scots Greys, 1958-68; Member, Berwickshire County Council, 1969-75 (Chairman, Roads Committee, 1974-75); Manager, Charterhall Estate and Farm, since 1969; Chairman, Meadowhead Ltd. (formerly Mortonhall Park Ltd.), since 1974; Director, Timber Growers' GB Ltd., 1977-82; Vice Chairman, Border Grain Ltd., since 1984; Council Member, Scottish Landowners' Federation, since 1975 (Chairman, Land Use Committee, 1975-78, Convener, 1982-85); Member, Department of Agriculture Working Party on the Agricultural Holding (Scotland) Legislation, 1981-82; Member, Nature Conservancy Council, and Chairman, Scottish Committee, 1985-90; Member, UK Committee for Euro Year of the Environment, 1986-88; Member, Scottish Tourist Board Graded Holiday Parks Overseeing Committee, since 1993; Member, Queen's Bodyguard for Scotland (Royal Company of Archers). Recreations: skiing; golf; hunting; shooting. Address: Charterhall, Duns, Berwickshire, TD11 3RE; T.-01890 840210; e-mail: alex@charterhall.net

Truman, Donald Ernest Samuel, BA, PhD, FIBiol, CBiol, FRSA. Assistant Principal, University of Edinburgh, since 1998; b. 23.10.36, Leicester; m., Kathleen Ramsay; 1 s.; 1 d. Educ. Wyggeston School, Leicester; Clare College, Cambridge. NATO Research Fellow, Wenner-Gren Institute, Stockholm, 1962-63; MRC Epigenetics Research Group, Edinburgh, 1963-72; Lecturer, Department of Genetics, Edinburgh University, 1972-78; Senior Lecturer, 1978-89, Head of Department, 1984-89, Director of Biology Teaching Unit, 1985-89; Vice-Dean and Vice-Provost, Faculty of Science and Engineering, 1989-98; Aneurin Bevan Memorial Fellow, Government of India, 1978; Chairman, Edinburgh Centre for Rural Research, since 1993; Member, Council, Scottish Agricultural College, since 1995; Director, Edinburgh Technopole Company Ltd., since 1996; Member, Board of Directors, Edinburgh Lifelong Learning Partnership, since 1999. Publications: The Biochemistry of Cytodifferentiation, 1974; Differentiation in Vitro (Joint Editor), 1982; Stability and Switching in Cellular Differentiation, 1982; Coordinated Regulation of Gene Expression, 1986. Recreation: gardening; books. Address: (b.) Institute of Cell and Molecular Biology, Mayfield Road, Edinburgh EH9 3JR; T.-0131-650 7066.

Truscott, Ian, QC, LLB. Advocate, since 1988; b. 7.11.49, Perth; m., Julia; 4 s. Educ. Perth Academy; Edinburgh University; Leeds University. Solicitor, 1973-87; Advocate, since 1988; Barrister, since 1995; QC, since 1997. Address: (b.) Advocates' Library, Parliament Square, Edinburgh; T.-0131-260 5697.

Tucker, Derek Alan. Editor, Press and Journal, Aberdeen, since 1992; b. 31.10.53, Liverpool; 1 s.; 1 d. Educ. Quarry Bank High School, Liverpool; Municipal Grammar School, Wolverhampton. Reporter/Chief Reporter/News Editor/Deputy Editor, Express and Star, Wolverhampton, 1972-92. Member, Press Complaints Commission, 1995-97. Recreations: golf; travel; watching any sport not involving horses. Address: (b.) Lang Stracht, Mastrick, Aberdeen; T.-01224 690222.

Tucker, Professor John Barry, BA, MA, PhD, FRSE. Professor of Cell Biology, St. Andrews University, since 1990; b. 17.3.41, Arundel; m., Janet Stephen Murray; 2 s. Educ. Queen Elizabeth Grammar School, Atherstone; Peterhouse, Cambridge. Fulbright Travel Scholar and Research Associate, Department of Zoology, Indiana University, 1966-68; SERC Research Fellow, Department of Zoology, Cambridge, 1968-69; Lecturer in Zoology, St. Andrews University, 1969-79 (Chairman, Zoology Department, 1982-84); Reader in Zoology, 1979-90. Member: SERC Advisory Group II, 1977-80, SERC Molecular Biology and Genetics Sub-committee, 1986-89, Editorial Board of Journal of Embryology and Experimental Morphology, 1979-88. Recreations: cycling; hill-walking; tennis; reluctant gardener. Address: (b.) School of Biology, Bute Building, St. Andrews University, St. Andrews, Fife KY16 9TS; T.-01334 463560; e-mail: jbt@st-and.ac.uk

Tudhope, James Mackenzie, CB, BL; b. 11.2.27, Glasgow; m., Margaret W. Kirkwood; 2 s. Educ. Dunoon Grammar School; Glasgow University. Solicitor, 1951; private legal practice, 1951-55; Procurator Fiscal Depute, 1955; Senior Procurator Fiscal Depute, 1962; Assistant Procurator Fiscal, Glasgow, 1968-70; Procurator Fiscal: Kilmarnock 1970-73, Dumbarton, 1973-76; Regional Procurator Fiscal: South Strathclyde, Dumfries and Galloway at Hamilton, 1976-80, Glasgow and Strathkelvin, 1980-87. Member, Council, Law Society of Scotland, 1983-86; Honorary Sheriff, Kilmarnock, since 1989. Recreations (include): serendipity; worrying. Address: (h.) Point House, Dundonald Road, Kilmarnock;T.-01563 523727.

Tudor, (Fiona) Philippa, DPhil. Head, Parliamentary and Constitution Division, Scotland Office, since 2001; b. 15.2.58, Shrewsbury; m., David Beamish; 1 d. Educ. Somerville College, Oxford. Clerk, House of Lords, 1982-2001; Chief Clerk, 1993; Clerk of Private Bills and Examiner, 1997-2001. Recreation: running. Address: (b.) Dover House, Whitehall, London SW1A 2AU; T.-020 7270 6800.

Turley, Mark John, BSc (Hons), MBA, MCIOH. Director of Housing, City of Edinburgh Council, since 1996; Executive Director of Housing, City of Edinburgh District Council, since 1993; b. 25.6.60, Dudley. Educ. High Arcal Grammar School, Sedgley; Leicester University. Sheffield City Council, 1981-91; Head of Tenant Services, York City Council, 1991-93. Recreations: playing violin; reading. Address: (b.) Housing Department, 23 Waterloo Place, Edinburgh, EH1 3BH; T.-0131-529 7325.

Turmeau, Professor William Arthur, CBE, FRSE, Dr. h.c. (Edinburgh University), Doctor of Education (Napier University), BSc, PhD, CEng, FIMechE. Chairman, Scottish Environment Protection Agency, 1995-99; Principal and Vice-Chancellor, Napier University, 1982-94; b. 19.9.29, London; m., Margaret Moar Burnett; 1 d. Educ. Stromness Academy, Orkney; Edinburgh University; Moray House College of Education; Heriot-Watt University. Royal Signals, 1947-49; Research Engineer, Northern Electric Co. Ltd., Montreal, 1952-54; Mechanical Engineer, USAF, Goose Bay, Labrador, 1954-56; Contracts Manager, Godfrey Engineering Co. Ltd., Montreal, 1956-61; Lecturer, Bristo Technical Institute, Edinburgh, 1962-64; Napier College: Lecturer and Senior Lecturer, 1964-68, Head, Department of Mechanical Engineering, 1968-75, Assistant Principal and Dean, Faculty of Technology, 1975-82. Member, Foundation, University of the Highlands and Islands Project; Member, IMechE Academic Standards Committee; Trustee, Dynamic Earth Charitable Trust; Vice Chairman, ASH (Scotland). Recreations: modern jazz; Leonardo da Vinci. Address: (h.) 71 Morningside Park, Edinburgh, EH10 5EZ; T.-0131-447 4639.

Turnbull, Wilson Mark, DipArch, MLA (Penn), MBCS, RIBA, FRIAS, FLI. Principal, Mark Turnbull Landscape Architect; Chairman and Director, Turnbull Jeffrey Partnership, Landscape Architects (Principal, 1982-98); Chairman and Director, Envision, since 1999; b. 1.4.43, Edinburgh. Educ. George Watson's; Edinburgh College of Art; University of Pennsylvania. Assistant Professor of Architecture, University of Southern California, 1970-74; Partner, W.J. Cairns and Partners, Environmental Consultants, 1974-82; Partner, Design Innovations Research, 1976-81; Council Member, Cockburn

Association (Edinburgh Civic Trust), 1986-95; Commissioner, Countryside Commission for Scotland, 1988-92; Commissioner, Royal Fine Art Commission for Scotland, 1996; Chairman, Edinburgh Greenbelt Initiative, 1988-91; Director, Edinburgh Greenbelt Trust, since 1991, Vice-Chairman, since 1993. Awards: Edinburgh Corporation Medal for Civic Design; Faculty Medal, Department of Landscape Architecture, University of Pennsylvania; Fulbright Scholarship. Recreation: sailing. Address: (b.) Creag an Tuirc House, Balquhidder, Perthshire FK19 8NY; T.-01877 384 728.

Turner, John R., MA, HonMA, MusB, FRCO. Organist and Director of Music, Glasgow Cathedral, since 1965; Lecturer, Royal Scottish Academy of Music, since 1965; Organist, Strathclyde University, since 1965; b. Halifax. Educ. Rugby; Jesus College, Cambridge. Recreations: gardening; travel. Address: (h.) Binchester, 1 Cathkin Road, Rutherglen, Glasgow G73 4SE; T.-0141-634 7775.

Turner, Professor Kenneth John, BSc, PhD. Professor of Computing Science, Stirling University, since 1987; b. 21.2.49, Glasgow; m., Elizabeth Mary Christina; 2 s. Educ. Hutchesons' Boys Grammar School; Glasgow University; Edinburgh University. Data Communications Designer, International Computers Ltd., 1974-76; Senior Systems Analyst, Central Regional Council, 1976-77; Data Communications Consultant, International Computers Ltd., 1977-87. Recreations: choral singing; craft work; sailing. Address: (b.) Department of Computing Science and Mathematics, Stirling University, Stirling, FK9 4LA; T.-01786 467423.

Turner, Simon John, MA. Director, Scottish Conservative Party, since 1999; b. 18.2.63, Aberdeen; Educ. Robert Gordon College, Aberdeen; Aberdeen University; Robert Gordon University. Began career as Conservative Party agent, 1987; worked in a number of constituencies including Wokingham, Chingford, Stirling; worked for Rt. Hon. Michael Forsyth, Secretary of State for Scotland; Campaign Executive, Scottish Conservative Central Office, 1998. Recreations: film; opera; theatre. Address: (b.) 83 Princes Street, Edinburgh, EH2 2ER; T.-0131-247 6890; e-mail: stsc21163@blueyonder.co.uk

Turner Thomson, Ann Denise. Interior Designer; Council Member, Saltire Society (Chairman, Galleries Committee); Trustee, Scottish Sculpture Trust; b. 23.5.29, Molesey; m., Gordon Turner Thomson; 1 s.; 3 d. Educ. Sherborne School for Girls, Dorset; St. James's Secretarial College, London. Council Member, Scottish Arts Council, 1983-88; Council Member, National Trust for Scotland, 1990-95; Council Member, Edinburgh International Festival, 1991-97; Member, Saltire Society Galleries Committee, Art in Architecture Award Panel; Board Member, Edinburgh Printmakers Workshop, since 1999. Recreations: theatre; opera; visual arts. Address: 8 Middleby Street, Edinburgh EH9 1TD; T.-0131-667 3997.

Turok, Professor Ivan Nicholas, BSc, MSc, PhD, MRTPI. Professor of Urban Economic Development, Glasgow University, since 1996; b. 7.8.56, Cape Town; m., Elizabeth; 1 s.; 2 d. Educ. William Ellis School, London; Bristol University. Lecturer, Glasgow University, 1984-87; Senior Lecturer and Professor, Strathclyde University, 1987-96. Publications: over 60 articles and books. Recreations: hill-walking; cycling; current affairs; visiting cities. Address: (b.) 25 Bute Gardens, Glasgow G12 8RS; T.-0141-330 6274; e-mail: I.Turok@socsci.gla.ac.uk

Twaddle, Alison Mary, MA, JP. General Secretary, Church of Scotland Guild, since 1998; b. 25.1.50, Anston; m., Laurence Twaddle; 1 s.; 2 d. Educ. Broadway Grammar School, Barnsley; St Andrews University. Health Service administrator; translator;

Europe Secretary, Board of World Mission; Information Officer, Church of Scotland Guild. Address: (b.) 121 George Street, Edinburgh EH2 4YN; T.-0131-225 5722.

Tweeddale, 13th Marquis of (Edward Douglas John Hay); b. 6.8.47; succeeded to title, 1979.

Tynan, Bill. MP (Labour), Hamilton South, since 1999; Member, Scottish Select Committee; Convener, Scottish Labour Group of MPs, since 2001; Member, Executive Committee, Scottish Labour Party; m., Betty; 3 d. Scottish Divisional Officer, AEEU, 1988-1999; Member, AEEU National Policy Committee, 10 years; Treasurer, Scottish Trade Union Labour Liaison Committee; Recreations: (b.) House of Commons, London SW1A 0AA; T.-020 7219 6285; 01698 454925; e-mail: tynanb@parliament.uk

Tyre, Colin Jack, QC, LLB, DESU. Advocate, since 1987; b. 17.4.56, Dunoon; m., Elaine Patricia Carlin; 1 s.; 2 d. Educ. Dunoon Grammar School; Edinburgh University; Universite d'Aix Marseille. Lecturer in Scots Law, Edinburgh University, 1980-83; Tax Editor, CCH Editions Ltd., Bicester, 1983-86; Standing Junior Counsel to Scottish Office Environment Department in planning matters, 1995-98; Member, UK Delegation to Council of Bars and Law Societies of the EU, since 1999. Publications: CCH Inheritance Tax Reporter; contributor to Stair Memorial Encyclopaedia; Tax for Litigation Lawyers (Co-Author). Recreations: orienteering; golf; mountain walking; popular music. Address: (b.) Advocates' Library, 1 Parliament Square, Edinburgh; T.-0131-226 5071.

U

Ullrich, Kay Morrison. MSP (SNP), West of Scotland, since 1999; Scottish National Party Chief Whip; Vice President, Scottish National Party; b. 5.5.43, Prestwick; m., Grady; 1 s.; 1 d. Educ. Ayr Academy; Queen's College, Glasgow. Butlins Redcoat, 1961-64; Swimming Instructor, schools in North Ayrshire, 1973-81; Social Worker: Easterhouse (schools), 1984-86, Crosshouse Hospital (paediatric), 1986-88, Stevenston, Saltcoats, Ardrossan (child care), 1988-92; Senior Social Worker, Kilmarnock (Sheriff Court), 1992-97. Recreations: swimming; reading (politics and Scottish history); travel. Address: (h.) Tulsa, Montgomeryfield, Dreghorn, Irvine KA11 4HB; T.-01294 213331.

Upton, Professor Brian Geoffrey Johnson, BA, MA, DPhil, FRSE, FGS. Emeritus Professor of Petrology, Edinburgh University, since 1999; b. 2.3.33, London; m., Bodil Aalbaek Upton; 2 s.; 1 d. Educ. Reading School; St John's College, Oxford University. Geological Survey of Greenland, 1958-60; Fullbright Fellow, California Institute of Technology, 1961-62; Lecturer, Geology, Edinburgh University, 1962-72; Carnegie Fellow, Geophysical Laboratory, Washington, 1970-71; Edinburgh University: Reader in Geology, 1972-82; Professor of Petrology, 1982-99; Executive Editor, Journal of Petrology, 1983-94; Clough Medallist, Geological Society, Edinburgh, 2001. Recreations: painting; gardening; travel. Address: (b.) Department of Geology and Geophysics, Edinburgh University, West Mains Road, Edinburgh, EH9 3JW; T.-0131-650 4840.

U'ren, William Graham, BSc (Hons), DipTP, FRTPI. Director, Royal Town Planning Institute in Scotland; b. 28.12.46, Glasgow; m., Wendy; 2 d. Educ. Aberdeen Grammar School; Aberdeen University; Strathclyde University. Planning Assistant: Clackmannan County Council, 1970-72, Lanark County Council, 1972-75; Principal and Chief Planning Officer, Clydesdale District Council, 1975-82; Director of Planning and Technical Services, Clydesdale District Council, 1982-96; Environment Services Manager, Planning and Economic Development, South Lanarkshire Council, 1996-97. Past Chairman, Scottish Society of Directors of Planning; Convener, Historic Burghs Association of Scotland; Member, Heritage Lottery Fund Committee for Scotland; Chairman, Friends of New Lanark. Recreations: town-twinning; cricket; bird watching; philately. Address: (b.) 125 Hyndford Road, Lanark ML11 9AU.

Urquhart, Celia Margaret Lloyd, RGN, MBA, FIMgt. Chief Executive: CU Developments and associated companies, Urquhart Ltd., Coralyn Ltd.; m., George MacFarlane Sinclair. Member, Merchants House, Glasgow; Member, Association of Trades House Ladies; Past Chairman, Court, Glasgow Caledonian University; formerly: Member, Board, Scottish Enterprise, Director, Glasgow Chamber of Commerce, Member, Nursing Board for Scotland. Address: (b.) 52 St. Enoch Square, Glasgow.

Urquhart, Very Rev John. Parish Priest, St. Bernadette's, Larbert, since 1989; b. 1.7.34, Bowhill, Fife. Educ. St. Ninian's, Bowhill; St. Columba's Cowdenbeath; Blairs College, Aberdeen; Scots College, Spain; St. Andrew's College, Drygrange. Assistant: St. Joseph's, Sighthill, Edinburgh, Our Lady and St. Andrew's, Galashiels; Chaplain, St. Mary's Balnakiel; Parish Priest: St. Paul's, Muirhouse, Edinburgh, St. Margaret's, Dunfermline. Address: 323 Main Street, Larbert FK5 4EU; T.-01324 553250.

Urwin, Professor Derek William, BA, MA (Econ), PhD. Professor of Politics and International Relations, Aberdeen University, since 1990; b. 27.10.39, Consett; m., Patricia Anne Ross; 2 s. Educ. Consett Grammar School; Wolsingham Grammar School; Keele University; Manchester University. Lecturer, Strathclyde University, 1963-72; Associate Professor, University of Bergen, 1972-80; Professor, Warwick University, 1981-90. Publications: A Political History of Western Europe since 1945; The Community of Europe; From Ploughshare to Ballot Box; Politics in Western Europe Today; Centre-Periphery Structures in Europe; Dictionary of European History and Politics, since 1945; Scottish Political Behaviour. Recreations: walking; reading; marquetry. Address: (b.) Department of Politics and International Relations, Aberdeen University, Old Aberdeen, AB9 2TY; T.-01224 272716/272713.

Usher, Professor John Anthony, LLB, FRSE. Salvesen Professor of European Institutions, Edinburgh University, since 1995; Honorary Jean Monnet Professor of European Law, Edinburgh University, since 1997; Director, Europa Institute, Edinburgh University, since 1995; b. 12.8.45, Hyde; m., Jean Stewart; 2 s. Educ. Hyde County Grammar School; Newcastle upon Tyne University; Universite de Nancy. Lecturer in Law, Exeter University, 1967-74; Legal Secretary, European Court of Justice, Luxembourg, 1974-78; Lecturer in European Law, Edinburgh University, 1978-83; Reader in European Community Law, University College, London, 1983-86; Professor of European Law, Exeter University, 1986-95. Honorary Bencher, Lincolns Inn. Publications include: Law of Money and Financial Services in the EC; EC Institutions and Legislation; General Principles of EC Law; Legal Aspects of Agriculture in the EC; European Court Practice; EC Law and National Law – The Irreversible Transfer. Recreations: playing the cello; reading; travelling. Address: (b.) Europa Institute, Edinburgh University, Old College, South Bridge, Edinburgh EH8 9YL; T.-0131-650 2040.

Usher, Professor John Richard, BSc (Hons), MSc, PhD, CMATH. Professor of Mathematics, Robert Gordon University, 1998-2001; b. 12.5.44, London; m., Sheila Mary Usher McKendrick; 1 d. Educ. St. Nicholas Grammar School, London; Hull University; St Andrews University. Lecturer, Mathematics, Teeside Polytechnic, 1970-74; Senior Lecturer, Mathematics, Glasgow College of Technology, 1974-82; Head of School of Mathematics (later School of Computing and Mathematical Sciences), Robert Gordon University, 1983-92; Senior Lecturer, Mathematics, 1992-98; Scottish Branch Committee, IMA: Vice-Chairman, 1983-85, Chairman, 1985-88, Hon. Member, 1988 -89; Member, IMA Council, 1987-90; External examiner for various Universities; Examiner for SCOTEC; Moderator for SCOTVEC; Member, UCAS Scottish Higher Education Mathematical Sciences and Computing Panel; Lay Reader. Recreations: yoga; reading; walking; theatre-going; concert-going. Address: 20 St. Crispin's Road, Newtonhill, Kincardineshire AB39 3PS.

Usher, Professor Michael Barham, OBE, BSc, PhD, DUniv, CBiol, FIBiol, FRES, FRSE. Chief Scientist, Scottish Natural Heritage, 1991-2001, Leverhulme Emeritus Fellow, since 2001; b. 19.11.41, Old Colwyn; m., Kathleen Fionna Munro; 1 s.; 1 d. Educ. Portsmouth Grammar School; Edinburgh University. Lecturer, Senior Lecturer, Reader, Department of Biology, University of York, 1967-91; Adviser on termite research, British Technical Assistance to the Government of Ghana, 1971-73; research in Antarctica and Sub-Antarctica, 1980-81; joined Nature Conservancy Council for Scotland as Chief Scientific Adviser, 1991; Honorary Professor: in Zoology, University of Aberdeen, in Environmental Science, University of Stirling, in Biological Sciences, University of

Edinburgh. Member/Chairman, several Natural Environment Research Council and Economic and Social Research Council Committees. Publications: 220 scientific papers; 10 books. Recreations: walking; gardening; natural history photography; philately. Address: (b.) Department of Environmental Science, University of Stirling, Stirling, FK9 4LA.

Uttamchandani, Professor Deepak, BEng, MSc, PhD, CEng, FIEE. Professor of Optoelectronic Systems, University of Strathclyde, since 1998; b. 27.8.58, Bombay; m., Barbara. Educ. primary, secondary and tertiary levels in Nigeria; University College London. University of Strathclyde, Department of Electronic and Electrical Engineering: Lecturer, 1985, Senior Lecturer, 1991, Reader, 1995. Publications: author or co-author of nearly 200 scientific and technical publications in optoelectronic systems. Recreations: reading; travel; sport. Address: Department of Electronic and Electrical Engineering, University of Strathclyde, 204 George Street, Glasgow G1 1XW; T.-0141-548 2211; e-mail: du@eee.strath.ac.uk

V

van der Kuyl, Christiaan Richard David, BSc (Hons). President, VISentertainment plc, since 1996; b, 20.8.69, Dundee. Educ. St. Saviours High School, Dundee; Edinburgh University; Dundee University. Technology and media entrepreneur, since 1992; Chairman, Young Enterprise Scotland; Director, Schools Enterprise Scotland; Director, Sensation Science Centre, Dundee; Chairman, SGA. Recreations: playing music; golf; computer games. Address: (b.) Vis Building, Izatt Avenue, Dunfermline, Fife, KY11 3BZ; T.-01383 845300.

van Heyningen, Simon, MA, PhD, FRSC, FIBiol. Director of Quality Assurance, Edinburgh University, since 1998; Vice-Provost, Faculty Group of Medicine and Veterinary Medicine, since 1998; b. 17.12.43, London; m., Veronica Daniel; 1 s.; 1 d. Educ. Westminster School; King's College, Cambridge. Department of Chemistry, Northwestern University, Illinois, 1968-70; Department of Biochemistry, Oxford University, 1970-74; joined Department of Biochemistry, Edinburgh University, 1974. Chair, Quality Assurance Agency Benchmarking Group in Biosciences, since 2000. Address: (b.) Faculty Group Office, Medical School, Teviot Place, Edinburgh EH8 9AG; T.-0131-650 3176.

van Heyningen, Veronica, MA, MS, DPhil, FRSE, FMedSci. Section Head, MRC Human Genetics Unit, Edinburgh, since 1977; Member, Human Genetics Commission, since 2000; b. 12.11.46, Hungary; m., Dr. Simon van Heyningen; 1 s.; 1 d. Educ. Humphrey Perkins School, Leicestershire; Girton College, Cambridge; Northwestern University, Illinois; Lady Margaret Hall, Oxford. Beit Memorial Fellow, 1973-76; Howard Hughes International Research Scholar, 1993-98; Honorary Professor, Edinburgh University, 1995; Hon. Treasurer, The Genetical Society, 1994-98; Trustee, National Museums of Scotland, 1994-2000. Recreations: visiting museums; travel; talking to people. Address: (b.) MRC Human Genetics Unit, Edinburgh, EH4 2XU; T.-0131-467 8405.

Vanezis Professor Peter, OBE, MD, PhD, FRCPath, FRCP (Glas), DMJ. Regius Professor of Forensic Medicine and Science, Glasgow University, since 1993; Director, Centre for International Forensic Assistance and Human Identification Centre; Senior Civilian Consultant in Forensic Medicine to the British Army, since 1992; b. 11.12.47, Nicosia; m., Maria; 1 s.; 1 d. Educ. Wanstead High School, London; Bristol University. Lecturer/Senior Lecturer in Forensic Medicine, London Hospital Medical College, 1974-90; Reader in Forensic Medicine, Charing Cross and Westminster Medical School, 1990-93; Hon. Consultant to Cyprus Government, since 1985, Kenyons International Emergency Services, since 1993; Honorary Consultant, Medico-Legal Institute, Santiago, Chile, since 1994. Publications: Pathology of Neck Injury, 1989; Suspicious Death – Scene Investigation, 1996; various publications in forensic medicine. Recreations: golf; painting. Address: (b.) Department of Forensic Medicine and Science, Glasgow University, Glasgow G12 8QQ; T.-0141-330 4573; e-mail: p.vanezis@formed.gla.ac.uk

Vannet, Sheriff Alfred Douglas, LLB, FRSA. Sheriff of South Strathclyde, Dumfries and Galloway at Airdrie, since 2001; All-Scotland floating Sheriff, 2000-01; b. 31.7.49, Dundee; m., Pauline Margaret Renfrew; 1 s.; 1 d. Educ. High School of Dundee; Dundee University. Procurator Fiscal Depute, Dundee, 1976-77; Procurator Fiscal Depute, then Senior Procurator Fiscal Depute, Glasgow, 1977-84; Assistant Solicitor, Crown Office, 1984-90; Deputy Crown Agent, 1990-94; Regional Procurator Fiscal, Grampian, Highland and Islands at Aberdeen, 1994-97; Regional Procurator Fiscal, Glasgow and Strathkelvin, 1997-99. Honorary Member, Royal Faculty of Procurators in Glasgow, since 1997. Recreations: music; walking; curling. Address: (b.) Airdrie Sheriff Court, Graham Street, Airdrie; e-mail: sheriff.advannet@scotcourts.gov.uk

Vardy, Professor Alan Edward, BSc, PhD, DEng, EurIng, CEng, FICE, FASCE, MIAHR, MILT, FRSA. Research Professor in Civil Engineering, Dundee University, since 1995; Director, Lightweight Structures Unit, since 1998; b. 6.11.45, Sheffield; m., Susan Janet; 2 s.; 1 d. Educ. High Storrs Grammar School, Sheffield; Leeds University. Lecturer in Civil Engineering, Leeds University, 1972-75; Royal Society Warren Research Fellow, Cambridge University, 1975-79; Dundee University: Professor of Civil Engineering, 1979-95 (Deputy Principal, 1985-89, Vice-Principal, 1988-89); Director, Wolfson Bridge Research Unit, 1980-90; Royal Society/SERC Industrial Fellow, 1990-94. Address: Kirkton of Abernyte, Perthshire PH14 9SS; T.-01828 686065.

Varty, Professor E. Kenneth C., BA (Hons), PhD, DLitt, FSA, Chevalier dans l' Ordre des Palmes Academiques. Professor Emeritus and Hon. Professorial Research Fellow, Glasgow University, since 1990; Life Member, Clare Hall, Cambridge University, since 1984; b. 18.8.27, Derbyshire; m., Hedwig; 2 s. Educ. Bemrose School, Derby; Nottingham University. Assistant Researcher/Lecturer, French, University College of N. Staffs, 1953-61; Lecturer/Senior Lecturer, French, Leicester University, 1961-68; Stevenson Professor of French, Glasgow University, 1968-90; Dean, Faculty of Arts, Glasgow University, 1978-81; President, Alliance Français de Glasgow, 1982-89. Publications: Reynard, Renart, Renaert, 1999; Reynard the Fox, 2000. Recreations: travel; art galleries; museums; historic sites etc. Address: (h.) 4 Dundonald Road, Glasgow, G12 9LJ; T.-0141 339 1413.

Vas, Peter, MSc, PhD, CSc, DSc, SMIEEE, FIEE. Professor in Engineering, Department of Engineering, Aberdeen University, since 1990; b. 1.6.48, Budapest; m., S. Vasne; 2 s. Educ. Technical University of Budapest. United Electrical Machine Works, 1973-77; Newcastle University, 1977-87; Chalmers University of Technology, Lund University of Technology, 1987-90. Laureate of George Montefiore International Award, Belgium, 1990. Publications: over 180 papers; five books; several patents. Address: (b.) Department of Engineering, University of Aberdeen, Aberdeen; T.-01224 272818; e-mail: p.vas@eng.abdn.ac.uk

Veal, Sheriff Kevin Anthony, KSG, KCHS, LLB. Sheriff of Tayside Central and Fife at Forfar, since 1993; b. 16.9.46, Chesterfield; m., Monica Flynn; 2 s.; 2 d. Educ. Lawside Academy, Dundee; St. Andrews University. Partner, Burns Veal and Gillan, Dundee, 1971-93; Legal Aid Reporter, 1978-93; Temporary Sheriff, 1984-93; Tutor, Department of Law, Dundee University, 1978-85; Dean, Faculty of Procurators and Solicitors in Dundee, 1991-93. Musical Director, Cecilian Choir, Dundee, since 1975; Member, University Court, Abertay Dundee, since 1998. Recreations: organ and classical music; hill-walking. Address: (h.) Viewfield, 70 Blackness Avenue, Dundee, DD2 1JL; T.-01382 668633.

Veitch, William Hood, Honorary Sheriff, Jedburgh Sheriff Court; b. 18.5.18, Jedburgh; m., Evelyn; 2 s. Educ. Jedburgh Grammar School; Hawick High School. Trained as Inspector of Weights and Measures, 1936-39; King's Own Scottish Borderers, 1939-47; Borders Region: Inspector of Weights and Measures, 1947-69, Chief Inspector, 1969-83. Recreations: gardening; illustrated talks to voluntary organisations; Jedforest Historical Society.

Address: Inchbonny, Jedburgh; T.-01835 863539.

Vernon, Richard Geoffrey, BSc, PhD, FIBiol. Head, Science Planning and Development and Head, Molecular Homeorhesis Group, Hannah Research Intitute; Honorary Lecturer, Glasgow University; Director, Charis Food Innovation Ltd.; b. 19.2.43, Maidstone; m., Mary Christine Cunliffe; 1 s.; 1 d. Educ. Newcastle High School; Birmingham University. Research Fellow, University of Toronto, 1969-72; Senior Scientist then Head of Department, Hannah Research Institute, 1972-95; Consultant Editor, Journal of Dairy Research; Member, Editorial Board, British Journal of Nutrition, 1981-87, Domestic Animal Endocrinology (USA), 1992-95; Chairman, Scottish Section, Nutrition Society, 1989-91; Member, AFRC Animals Research Grants Board, 1991-94; Past President, Birmingham University Mountaineering Club; Chairman, Belmont Academy School Board, 1989-93. Publications: Physiological Strategies in Lactation (Co-editor); 200 scientific papers. Recreations: hill-walking; ornithology; bridge; photography. Address: (h.) 29 Knoll Park, Ayr, KA7 4RH; T.-01292 442195.

Vettese, Raymond John, DipEd, BA (Hons). Teacher and Writer; b. 1.11.50, Arbroath; m., Maureen Elizabeth. Educ. Montrose Academy; Dundee College of Education; Open University. Journalist, Montrose Review, 1968-72; student, 1972-75; barman, 1975-77; factory worker, 1977-78; clerical officer, 1978-85; teacher, since 1985 (supply teacher, 1997-2001); Library Assistant, 2001; Preses, Scots Language Society, 1991-94; William Soutar Fellowship, 1989-90; SAC Bursary, 1999. Publications: Four Scottish Poets, 1985; The Richt Noise, 1988 (Saltire Society Best First Book); A Keen New Air, 1995. Recreations: reading; music; cooking; chess. Address: (h.) 9 Tayock Avenue, Montrose, DD10 9AP; T.-01674 678943.

Vettriano, Jack. Painter. Early career in Scottish coalfields; received no formal tuition in art; first submitted works to Royal Scottish Academy, 1988; has since been exhibited in Edinburgh, London, Johannesburg and Hong Kong.

Vickerman, Professor Keith, BSc, PhD, DSc, FLS, FMedSci, FRSE, FRS. Regius Professor of Zoology, Glasgow University, 1984-98; Consultant Expert on Parasitic Diseases, World Health Organisation, 1973-98; b. 21.3.33, Huddersfield; m., Moira Dutton; 1 d. Educ. King James Grammar School, Almondbury; University College, London (Fellow, 1985). Wellcome Lecturer in Protozoology, University College, London, 1958-63; Tropical Research Fellow, Royal Society, 1963-68; Glasgow University: Reader in Zoology, 1968-74; Professor of Zoology, 1974-84, Head, Department of Zoology, 1979-85. Leeuwenhoek Lecturer, Royal Society, 1994; Linnean Society Gold Medal for contributions to science, 1996. Publications: The Protozoa (Co-author), 1967; many papers in scientific and medical journals. Recreations: drawing and painting; gardening. Address: (h.) 16 Mirrlees Drive, Glasgow G12 OSH; T.-0141-586 7794; e-mail: k.vickerman@bio.gla.ac.uk

Vincent, Catherine Lindsey, BA (Hons), MBA. Director of Corporate Strategy, sportscotland (formerly Scottish Sports Council), since 1989; b. 30.7.56, Oxford; m., Jonathan Nicholas Crook; 2 d. Educ. Rosebery Grammar School, Epsom; Newnham College, Cambridge. Research Assistant, Sheffield University, 1978; Assistant Editor, Athlone Press, 1979; Freelance Writer, 1980; Development Officer, Scottish Community Education Council, 1981; Senior Policy Analyst, Fife Regional Council, 1986. Former Chairman, Spiritual Assembly of the Baha'is of Edinburgh; former Director, Baha'i Information Scotland. Publication: Discovering Edinburgh, 1981. Recreations: reading; walking; tennis; badminton; enjoying family. Address: (b.) Caledonia House, South Gyle, Edinburgh EH12 9DQ; T.-0131-317 7200.

Vine, John. Chief Constable, Tayside Police, since 2000; m.; 2 s.; 1 d. Joined West Yorkshire Metropolitan Police, 1981; appointed Divisional Commander, Halifax; Head of Inspectorate, West Yorkshire, 1995; Assistant Chief Constable, Lancashire, 1996, latterly responsible for corporate developemnt. Recreations: running; gardening; sailing; fell-walking; reading; politics. Address: (b.) PO Box 59, West Bell Street, Dundee, DD1 9JU; T.-01382 223200; e-mail: forcedev@tayside.police.uk

Vogts, Berti. National Coach, Scottish Football Association, since 2002; b. 30.12.46, Bottgen, Germany. Joined VfB Bottgen, 1954; joined Borussia Monchengladbach, 1965; debut for West Germany, 1967 (96 caps); German Footballer of the Year, 1971; became Youth Coach, West Germany; Assistant to National Team Coach, 1986, subsequently becoming Coach of unified German team; appointed Coach, Bayer Leverkusen, 2000; Coach, Kuwait, 2001. Address: Scottish Football Association, Hampden Park, Glasgow G42 9AY.

Vowles, Kenneth Leslie, OBE, FIME, FIEE, MBIM, CEng. Executive Director, International, ScottishPower; Chairman, Manweb; Honorary Professor, Heriot-Watt University; Chairman, Eutilion; Past President, Scottish Engineering; b. 22.3.42, Newport, Gwent; m., Christine; 2 d. Educ. University of Wales. Generation Manager, National Power (Northern Group); Station Manager, Rugeley and Ironbridge Power Station. Recreation: golf. Address: (b.) 1 Atlantic Quay, Glasgow; T.-0141-636 4509; e-mail: ken.vowles@scottishpower.com

W

Waddell, Bruce. Editor, The Scottish Sun, since 1998; b. 18.3.59, Bo'ness, West Lothian; m., Catherine; 1 s. Educ. Graeme High School, Falkirk; Napier University. Reporter, Journal and Gazette, Linlithgow, 1977-87; News Sub-editor, The Scottish Sun, 1987-90; Deputy Editor, Sunday Scot, 1991; Marketing Executive, Murray International, 1991-92; Features Sub-editor, The Sun, 1992-93; Deputy Editor, The Scottish Sun, 1993-98. Recreations: golf; football; cinema; amateur drama (resting). Address: (b.) 124 Portman Street, Kinning Park, Glasgow G41 1EJ; T.-0141 420 5210.

Waddell, John MacLaren Ogilvie, LLB, WS. Corporate Finance Executive, Noble Grossart Ltd.; b. 12.4.56, Inverness; m., Alice Emily Bain; 1 s.; 1 d. Educ. Inverness Royal Academy; George Watson's College; Edinburgh University. Qualified as a Solicitor, 1980; Assistant, 1980, Partner, 1983, Steedman Ramage WS; Director of Legal Services, 1989, Member of Management Board, Christian Salvesen PLC; Head of Corporate Banking, Structured Finance, Bank of Scotland, 1999. Address: (b.) 48 Queen Street, Edinburgh EH2 3NR.

Waddell, Moray, BSc(Hons), MSc, CEng, MIEE, MIMechE, MCIBSE. Director of Engineering, Northern Lighthouse Board, since 2000; b. 22.3.64, Haddington; m., Susan Joan Tennant; 2 s. Educ. Dunbar Grammar School; Edinburgh University; Glasgow University. Trainee engineer, Property Services Agency; Engineer and Project Manager, Property Services Agency and Ministry of Defence. Recreations: sailing; motor sports. Address: (b.) 84 George Street, Edinburgh, EH2 3DA; T.-0131-473 3100.

Wade, Professor Nicholas James, BSc, PhD, FRSE. Professor of Visual Psychology, Dundee University, since 1991; b. 27.3.42, Retford, Nottinghamshire; m., Christine Whetton; 2 d. Educ. Queen Elizabeth's Grammar School, Mansfield; Edinburgh University; Monash University. Postdoctoral Research Fellow, Max-Planck Institute for Behavioural Physiology, Germany, 1969-70; Lecturer in Psychology, Dundee University, 1970-78, Reader, 1978-91. Publications: The Art and Science of Visual Illusions, 1982; Brewster and Wheatstone on Vision, 1983; Visual Allusions: Pictures of Perception, 1990; Visual Perception: an introduction, 1991; Psychologists in Word and Image, 1995; A Natural History of Vision, 1998; Purkinje's Vision: The Dawning of Neuroscience, 2001. Recreations: golf; cycling. Address: (h.) 36 Norwood, Newport-on-Tay, Fife DD6 8DW; T.-01382 543136; e-mail: n.j.wade@dundee.ac.uk

Wade, Professor Terence Leslie Brian, BA, PhD, FIL. Emeritus Professor in Russian Studies, Strathclyde University; b. 19.5.30, Southend-on-Sea; m., Mary Isobel McEwan; 2 d. Educ. Southend-on-Sea High School for Boys; Durham University; Cologne University; London University. National Service, Intelligence Corps, 1953-55; War Office Language Instructor, 1955-63; Lecturer, Scottish College of Commerce, Glasgow, 1963-64; Lecturer, Senior Lecturer, Reader, Professor, Strathclyde University, from 1964; Chairman, Department of Modern Languages, 1986-92; Professor, Research Fellow, since 1995. Convener, West of Scotland Association of Teachers of Russian; Editor, Journal of Russian Studies, 1980-86; Chairman, Association of Teachers of Russian, 1986-89; President, Association of Teachers of Russian, 1989-90; Member, Presidium, International Association of Teachers of Russian Language and Literature, since 1991; awarded Pushkin Medal for services to Russian teaching. Publications: Russian Exercises for Language Laboratories (Co-author); The Russian Preposition "do" and the Concept of Extent; Prepositions in Modern Russian; Russia Today (Co-Editor); The Gender of Soft-Sign Nouns in Russian; A Comprehensive Russian Grammar; A Russian Grammar Workbook; Russian Etymological Dictionary; The Russian Language Today (Co-Author). Address: 1 Cleveden Crescent, Glasgow, G12 OPD; T.-0141-339 3947.

Waigh, Professor Roger David, BPharm, PhD, FRPharmS, CChem, FRSC. Professor of Medicinal Chemistry, Strathclyde University, since 1991; b. 8.8.44, Loughborough; m., Sally Joy Bembridge; 1 s.; 1 d. Educ. Sir George Monoux Grammar School, Walthamstow; Bath University. Lecturer, Strathclyde University, 1970-76; Lecturer, then Senior Lecturer, Manchester University, 1976-91. Recreations: bird-watching; golf; photography. Address: (b.) Strathclyde Institute for Biomedical Sciences, 27 Taylor Street, Glasgow G4 ONR; T.-0141-548 4355.

Wake, Joseph Robert, MA, CPA. Secretary, Scotland, Education and Training Group, The British Council, since 1972; b. 16.5.42, Corbridge; 1 s.; 2 d. Educ. Royal Grammar School, Newcastle upon Tyne; Edinburgh University; Moray House College of Education. Teacher, Kirkcaldy High School, 1966-69, St. Modan's High School, Stirling, 1969-71; Principal Teacher of Modern Languages, Grangemouth High School, 1971-72. Recreations: cricket; philately; Scottish dancing. Address: (b.) 3 Bruntsfield Crescent, Edinburgh EH10 4HD; T.-0131-447 8024.

Wakeford, Air Marshal Sir Richard (Gordon), KCB (1976), LVO (1961), OBE (1958), AFC (1952). Chairman, MacRobert Trustees, 1982-94; b. 20.4.22, Torquay; m., Anne Butler; 2 s.; 1 d.; 1 d. (deceased). Educ. Montpelier School, Paignton; Kelly College, Tavistock. Entered RAF, 1941; Coastal Command, 1941-45; Transport Command, 1945-47; King's Commendation, 1946; Training Command, 1947-52; staff duties, including Director of Ops Staff, Malaya, 1952-58; CO, The Queens' Flight, 1958-61; IDC, 1969; Director, Service Intelligence, 1970-73; Commander, Anzuk Force Singapore, 1974-75; Deputy Chief of Defence Staff (Intelligence), 1975-78; retired Air Marshal, 1978. Director, RAF Benevolent Fund, Scotland, 1978-89; Commissioner, Queen Victoria School, Dunblane, 1980-90; Director, Thistle Foundation; Director, Cromar Nominess; Commander, Order of St. John, 1986. Recreation: fishing. Address: (h.) Sweethome Cottage, Inchberry Road, Fochabers, IV32 7QA; T.-01343 820 436.

Walde, Professor Thomas W., LLM, Dr.iur. Professor of International Economic, Natural Resources and Energy Law, University of Dundee, since 1991; Executive Director, Centre for Energy, Petroleum and Mineral Law and Policy; b. 1949, Germany; 1 s. Educ. Universities of Heildelberg, Frankfurt and Harvard. Institute for International Economic Law, Frankfurt, 1975-80; U.N. Natural Resources and Energy Division, 1980-85; Adviser to Governments on mineral development policies, legislation, and contract negotiations; Interregional Advisor on Petroleum and Mineral Legislation, U.N. (D.T.C.D.); EC Jean Monnet Professor of European Economic and Energy Law; Editor, Journal of Energy and Natural Resources Law; Visiting Professor, Universite de Paris II - Pantheon; Corresponding Editor, International Legal Materials; Editor, CEPMCP On-line Journal; Associate Editor: Journal of World Trade, Journal of World Investment. Address: (b.) Park Place, Dundee DD1 4HN; T.-01382 344300.

Walker, Professor Andrew Charles, BA, MSc, PhD, FInstP, FRSE, CPhys. Professor of Modern Optics, Heriot-Watt University, since 1988; Assistant Principal and Director of Postgraduate Studies; b. 24.6.48, Wembley; m., Margaret Elizabeth; 1 s.; 1 d. Educ. Kingsbury County Grammar School; Essex University. Postdoctoral Fellowship, National Research Council of Canada, 1972-74; SRC Research Fellowship, Essex University, 1974-75;

Higher/Senior Scientific Officer, UKAEA Culham Laboratory, 1975-83; Lecturer/Reader, Heriot-Watt University, 1983-88. Honorary Secretary, Quantum Electronics Group, Institute of Physics, 1982-85; Chairman, Scottish Branch, Institute of Physics, 1993-95; Member, Council, Royal Society of Edinburgh. Recreations: music; skiing; sailing. Address: (b.) Department of Physics, Heriot-Watt University, Riccarton, Edinburgh EH14 4AS; T.-0131-451 3036.

Walker, Audrey R., BA, ALA. Librarian, Signet Library, since 1994; b. 18.10.57, Glasgow. Educ. Clydebank High School; Robert Gordon University, Aberdeen. Library Assistant, 1975-80; Senior Library Assistant, Telford College, Edinburgh, 1980-84; Assistant Librarian: Scottish Office Library, 1987, Post-Graduate Medical Library, 1988-90, Advocates Library, 1990-94. Scottish Library Association: East Branch Representative to Council, Chair, Membership Services Committee; Organiser, Meadowbank National Track League. Recreations: cycling; reading; cross-stitch; cinema. Address: (b.) Signet Library, Parliament Square, Edinburgh EH1 1RF; T.-0131-225 4923.

Walker, Professor David Maxwell, CBE, QC, MA, PhD, LLD, Hon. LLD, FBA, FRSE, FRSA, FSA Scot. Regius Professor of Law, Glasgow University, 1958-90; Honorary Senior Research Fellow, since 1990; b. 9.4.20, Glasgow; m., Margaret Knox, OBE. Educ. High School of Glasgow; Glasgow University; Edinburgh University; London University. HLI and Indian Army, 1939-46; Advocate, 1948; in practice, Scottish Bar, 1948-54; Professor of Jurisprudence, Glasgow University, 1954-58; Barrister (Middle Temple), 1957; QC (Scot), 1958; Dean, Faculty of Law, Glasgow University, 1956-59; Convener, School of Law, 1984-88. Chairman, High School of Glasgow Trust. Publications: Law of Damages in Scotland; The Scottish Legal System; Law of Delict in Scotland; Law of Civil Remedies in Scotland; Law of Prescription in Scotland; Law of Contracts in Scotland; Oxford Companion to Law; Principles of Scottish Private Law (four volumes); The Scottish Jurists; Stair's Institutions (Editor); Stair Tercentenary Studies (Editor); A Legal History of Scotland, (6 Vols). Recreations: book collecting; Scottish history; motoring. Address: (h.) 1 Beaumont Gate, Glasgow G12 9EE; T.-0141-339 2802.

Walker, Professor David Morrison, OBE, DA, FSA, FSA Scot, FRSE, HFRIAS, Hon. LLD (Dundee). Honorary Professor of Art History, University of St. Andrews, since 1994; Chief Inspector of Historic Buildings, Scottish Office Environment Department, 1988-93; b. 31.1.33, Dundee; m., Averil Mary Stewart McIlwraith (deceased); 1 s. Educ. Morgan Academy, Dundee; Dundee College of Art. Voluntary work for National Buildings Record, Edinburgh, 1952-56; National Service, Royal Engineers, 1956-58; Glasgow Education Authority, 1958-59; Dundee Education Authority, 1959-61; Historic Buildings Branch, Scottish Office: Senior Investigator of Historic Buildings, 1961-76, Principal Investigator of Historic Buildings, 1976-78; Principal Inspector of Historic Buildings, 1978-88. Alice Davis Hitchcock Medallion, 1970. Publications: Dundee Nineteenth Century Mansions, 1958; Architecture of Glasgow (Co-author), 1968 (revised and enlarged edition, 1987); Buildings of Scotland: Edinburgh (Co-author), 1984; Dundee: An Illustrated Introduction (Co-author), 1984; St. Andrew's House: an Edinburgh Controversy 1912-1939, 1989; Central Glasgow: an illustrated architectural guide (Co-author), 1989. Address: (h.) 22 Inverleith Row, Edinburgh EH3 5QH.

Walker, Donald, MA (Hons). Sports Editor, The Scotsman, since 1998; b. 16.6.68, St. Andrews. Educ. Kirkcaldy High School; Edinburgh University. Trainee, DC Thomson, Dundee, 1991; Reporter, Edinburgh and Lothians Post, 1991-93; Sub-editor, Daily Mirror, London, 1993-97;

Deputy Sports Editor, The Scotsman, 1997-98. Recreations: East Fife Football Club; rugby; skiing; reading newspapers; being late. Address: (b.) 108 Holyrood Road, Edinburgh EH8 8AS.

Walker, (Edward) Michael, CBE, FRICS. Chairman, Walker Group (Scotland) Ltd., Westerwood Ltd., and associated companies, since 1986 (Founder, 1969); Chairman, Lothian and Edinburgh Ltd. (LEEL), 1996-2000 (Director, since 1991); b. 12.4.41, Aberdeen; m., Flora Margaret; 2 s.; 1 d. Educ. Aberdeen Grammar School. President, Edinburgh and District Master Builders Association, 1987 and 1996; Past President, Scottish House Builders Association; former Committee Member, NHBC (Scotland) Ltd., 1990-96; former Lord Dean of Guild, City of Edinburgh, 1992-96; Captain of Industry Award, Livingston Industrial and Commercial Association, 1987; Member, Court, Napier University. Recreations: skiing; scuba diving; walking; reading. Address: (b.) Walker Group (Scotland) Ltd., Westerwood House, Royston Road, Deans Industrial Estate, Livingston, W. Lothian; T.-01506 413101.

Walker, Ernest John Munro, CBE. Chairman, UEFA Stadia Committee; b. 20.7.28, Glasgow; m., Anne; 1 s.; 2 d. Educ. Queen's Park Secondary School. Army (Royal Horse Artillery), 1946-48; Assistant Secretary, industrial textile company, 1948-58; Assistant Secretary, Scottish Football Association, 1958-77, Secretary, 1977-90. Director, Euro-Sporting; Director, English National Stadium (Wembley); Chairman, Scottish Stadia Committee; Member, Football Work Permits Review Panel for Scotland; Vice-President, Newspaper Press Fund. Recreations: golf (past Captain, Haggs Castle GC); fishing; music; travel.

Walker, James, ARICS. Chairman, Dawn Group Ltd.; President, Scottish Building Employers Federation, 2001-02; b. 19.5.43, Glasgow; m., Sylvia Jean Weir. Educ. Bellahouston Academy, Glasgow. Apprentice Quantity Surveyor, William W. Rae, Glasgow, 1960-65; Assistant Quantity Surveyor: Armour and Partners, Paisley and Glasgow, 1965-68, Carmichael Brown Building Contractors, Glasgow, 1968-69; Chief Quantity Surveyor, Able Construction Ltd., Ayrshire, 1969-72; founding member, Dawn Group Ltd., since 1972. Recreations: sailing; golf. Address: (b.) Dawn Group Ltd., 220 West George Street, Glasgow G2 2PG; T.-0141-285 6700; e-mail: jwalker@dawn-group.co.uk

Walker, Rev. James Bernard, MA, BD, DPhil. Chaplain, St. Andrews University, since 1993; Director, Student Support Services; b. 7.5.46, Malawi; m., Sheila Mary Easton; 3 s. Educ. Hamilton Academy; Edinburgh University; Merton College, Oxford. Church of Scotland Minister: Mid Craigie linked with Wallacetown, Dundee, 1975-78, Old and St. Paul's, Galashiels, 1978-87; Principal, The Queen's College, Birmingham, 1987-93. Publication: Israel — Covenant and Land, 1988. Recreations: hill-walking; tennis; golf. Address: 3A St. Mary's Place, St. Andrews KY16 9UY; T.-01334 462865.

Walker, Michael John, LLB. Managing Partner, Maclay Murray and Spens, since 1994 (Partner, since 1981); b. 23.10.52, Glasgow; m., Elspeth Raeburn Lyle Reid; 1 s.; 1 d. Educ. Glenalmond; Dundee University. Apprenticeship, Dundas and Wilson, 1974-76; joined Maclay Murray and Spens, 1976 (secondment to Lovell White and King, 1980). Various non-executive directorships including John Menzies plc. Recreations: golf; travel. Address: 151 St. Vincent Street, Glasgow; T.-0141-248 5011.

Walker, Professor Stephen Paul, BA, PhD, CA. Professor of Accounting History, University of Edinburgh, since 1998 (Head, Department of Accounting and Business Method, 1998-2000); b. 20.6.60, King's Lynn; m., Liz; 1 s. Educ. Gaywood Park School, King's Lynn; University of Kent; University of Edinburgh. Postdoctoral Research Fellow,

University of Edinburgh, 1987-88; CA student, Ernst and Young, Chartered Accountants, Edinburgh, 1988-91; University of Edinburgh: Lecturer in Accounting, 1991-96, Senior Lecturer in Accounting, 1996-98. Academic Fellow, Institute of Chartered Accountants in England and Wales, 1994-98; Editor, The Accounting Historians' Journal, since 2000. Publications: The Society of Accountants in Edinburgh 1854–1914, 1988; Accountancy at the University of Edinburgh – The Emergence of a Viable Academic Department, 1994; Professional Reconstruction (Co-Author), 1998. Recreations: music; photography; walking. Address: William Robertson Building, 50 George Square, Edinburgh EH8 9JY; T.-0131-650 8342.

Walker, Steven, Managing Director, Scotsman Publications Ltd., since 1999; b. 7.4.61, Edinburgh; m., Elaine; 1 s. Educ. Broughton School. Sales Representative, Edinburgh Evening News, 1986-88; Group Sales Executive, Thomson Regional Newspapers, 1988-90; Highland Advertising Manager, Press and Journal, 1990-91; General Advertising Manager, Daily Record and Sunday Mail, 1991-95; Scotsman Publications Ltd: Advertising Director, 1995-98, Assistant Managing Director, 1998-99. Council Member, Scottish Daily Newspaper Society. Recreations: outdoor pursuits; watching sports. Address: (b.) 108 Holyrood Road, Edinburgh EH8 8AS; T.-0131-620 8620.

Walker, Steven Peter, LLB (Hons), DipLP, ACIArb. Advocate, since 1999; International Arbitrator and Counsel, since 2000; b. 7.4.75, Glasgow; m., Dr Yvonne Julie Walker. Educ. Christian Brothers School, Kells, Co. Meath, Ireland; University of Aberdeen. Called to the Bar 1999 (youngest Advocate in Scotland); admitted Faculty of Advocates, 2000; Member, London Court of International Arbitration; Tutor, National UK Mock Trial Competition. Recreations: skiing; chess; wine; hillwalking. Address: (b.) Advocates' Library, Parliament House, Edinburgh EH1 1RF; T.-0131-226 5071; e-mail: SPWAdvocate@aol.com

Walker, Timothy Frederick. Principal, Glenmore Lodge, Aviemore (sportscotland), since 1995; b. 11.12.48, Stannington; m., Helen; 2 d. Royal Marines (Mountain and Arctic Warfare Cadre); Outward Bound, Eskdale; Joint Services Mountain Training Centre, Scotland; Tutor, Seneca College, Ontario, Canada; Instructional Officer, Scottish Sports Council. Publications: Cross Country Skiing; Chairman, BASI Nordic; Vice Chairman, Boat of Garten Community Council; Representative, Action of Churches Together in Scotland. Recreations: all aspects of mountaineering; skiing. Address: (h.) Drumullie Steading, Boat of Garten, Inverness-shire PH24 3BX; T.-(b.) 01479 861 256; (h.) 01479 831 316.

Walker, Professor William Barclay, BSc, MSc. Professor of International Relations, St. Andrews University, since 1996; b. 7.12.46, Longforgan; m., Carolyn Scott; 1 s. Educ. Shrewsbury School; Edinburgh University. Design Engineer, Ferranti Ltd., 1970-72; Research Fellow, Science Policy Research Unit, Sussex University, 1974-78; Research Fellow, Royal Institute of International Affairs; Science Policy Research Unit, Sussex University: Senior Fellow, 1981-92, Professorial Fellow and Director of Research, 1993-96. Publications: Plutonium and Highly Enriched Uranium: World Inventories, Capabilities and Policies (Co-author), 1997; Nuclear Entrapment: THORP and the Politics of Commitment, 1999; Unchartered Waters: The UK, Nuclear Weapons and the Scottish Question (Co-Author), 2001. Recreations: piano-playing; ornithology. Address: (b.) Department of International Relations, University of St. Andrews, St. Andrews KY16 9AL; T.-01334 462934.

Wall, John. National Secretary for Scotland, MSF (Manufacturing Science and Finance); b. 31.12.46; m., Margaret; 2 s. Educ. St Augustine's, Glasgow; Glasgow College of Commerce. Admin Officer, Trade Union Officer, APEX, 1976-79; ASTMS, 1979-88; MSF, 1988-99. Recreations: five-a-side football; boxing training; reading. Address: 145-165 West Regent Street, Glasgow G2 4RZ.

Wallace, Archibald Duncan, MB, ChB. Medical Practitioner, Campbeltown, since 1950; Hon. Sheriff of North Strathclyde at Campbeltown, since 1980; b. 4.1.26, Glasgow; m., Rona B. MacLennan; 1 s.; 2 d. Educ. High School of Glasgow; Glasgow University. Sector Medical Officer, Argyll and Clyde Health Board, until 1988; Civilian MO to RAF Machrihanish, until 1988. Past Chairman, Campbeltown Branch, RNLI; Past President, Campbeltown Rotary Club; Past Captain, Machrihanish Golf Club. Recreations: golf; gardening. Address: (h.) Lilybank House, Low Askomil, Campbeltown; T.-01586 52658.

Wallace, Ben. MSP (Conservative), North East Scotland, since 1999; Conservative Deputy Spokesperson on Health and Europe; b. 1970, Farnborough. Educ. Millfield School; Royal Military Academy, Sandhurst. Army Officer, Scots Guards, 1991-98; served in Northern Ireland, Germany, Denmark, Central America; mentioned in dispatches, 1992; former ski instructor, Austrian National Ski School. Address: (b.) Scottish Parliament, Edinburgh EH99 1SP; T.-0131-348 5651.

Wallace, Dr Heather M., BSc, PhD. Senior Lecturer, Department of Medicine and Therapeutics and Biomedical Sciences, Aberdeen University, since 1991; b. 10.6.54, Edinburgh; m., Dr R. John Wallace; 1 s.; 1 d. Educ. Hamilton Academy; Glasgow University; Aberdeen University. Aberdeen University: Postdoctoral Fellow, MRC, 1979-81, CRC, 1981-83; Wellcome Lecturer, 1983; New Blood Lecturer, 1983-91, University Research Fellow, 1991-92. Recreations: golf; tennis; badminton. Address: (b.) Aberdeen University, Polwarth Building, Foresterhill, Aberdeen; T.-01224 552481.

Wallace, Rt Hon James Robert, PC, QC, MA (Cantab), LLB (Edinburgh). MSP (Liberal Democrat), Orkney, since 1999; Deputy First Minister and Minister for Justice, since 1999; MP (Liberal Democrat, formerly Liberal), Orkney and Shetland, 1983-2001; Leader, Scottish Liberal Democrats, since 1992; Advocate, 1979; QC (Scot.), 1997; b. 25.8.54, Annan; m., Rosemary Janet Fraser; 2 d. Educ. Annan Academy; Downing College, Cambridge; Edinburgh University. Called to Scottish Bar, 1979; contested Dumfries, 1979, and South of Scotland Euro Constituency, 1979; Member, Scottish Liberal Party Executive, 1976-85 (Vice-Chairman, Policy, 1982-85); Honorary President, Scottish Young Liberals, 1984-85; Liberal Democrat Spokesman on Fisheries, 1988-97, and on Scotland, since 1992; jointly awarded Andrew Fletcher Award for services to Scotland, 1998. Publication: New Deal for Rural Scotland (Co-Editor), 1983. Recreations: golf; reading; travelling (especially between London and the Northern Isles). Address: (h.) Northwood House, Tankerness, Orkney KW17 2QS; T.-01856 861383; e-mail: jim.wallace.msp@scottish.parliament.uk

Wallace, John, OBE, MA. Principal, Royal Scottish Academy of Music and Drama, since 2002; b. Fife. Educ. Buckhaven High School; King's College, Cambridge; York University; Royal Academy of Music. Principal Trumpet, Philharmonia Orchestra, 1976-94; Principal Trumpet, London Sinfonietta, from 1987; founded The Wallace Collection (brass ensemble), 1986; Artistic Director of Brass, Royal Academy of Music, 1993-2001; has premiered new works by Peter Maxwell Davies, Malcolm Arnold and James McMillan. Publication: Companion to Brass Instruments (Co-Editor), 1997.

Wallace, Rev. William Fitch, BDS, BD. Minister, Pulteneytown and Thrumster Church, since 1990; Convener, Church of Scotland Board of Social Responsibility, 1993-97; b. 6.10.39, Falkirk; m., Jean Wyness Hill; 1 s.; 3 d. Educ. Allan Glen's School; Glasgow University; Edinburgh University. Minister, Wick St. Andrew's and Thrumster Church, 1974-90; former missionary dentist. Vice-Convener, Board of Social Responsibility, 1989-92. Recreations: family; golf; gardening. Address: The Manse, Coronation Street, Wick KW1 5LS; T.-01955 603166.

Wallace, Professor William Villiers, MA, FRHistS. Director, Institute of Russian and East European Studies, Glasgow University, 1979-92, now Senior Research Fellow; Vice-President, Council for Education in World Citizenship, since 1996; b. 15.12.26, Glasgow; m., Gulli Fyfe; 2 s.; 1 d. Educ. Hutchesons' Boys' Grammar School; Glasgow University; London University. RNVR, 1944-47; appointments in History, Pittsburgh University, London University, Aberdeen University, Durham University, 1953-67; Professor of History, New University of Ulster, 1967-79. Foreign Member, Russian Academy of Technological Sciences; Visiting Professor, Sunderland University, 1995-2000. Address: (b.) Department of Russian and East European Studies, Glasgow University, Hetherington Building, Bute Gardens, Glasgow G12 8RS; T.-0141-330 5585.

Walls, Professor Andrew Finlay, OBE, MA, BLitt, DD, FSA Scot. Curator of Collections, Centre for the Study of Christianity in the Non-Western World, since 1996; Director, Scottish Institute of Missionary Studies and Honorary Professor, Research Institute of Irish and Scottish Studies, University of Aberdeen; b. 21.4.28; m., Doreen Mary Harden; 1 s.; 1 d. Librarian, Tyndale House, Cambridge, 1952-57; Lecturer in Theology, Fourah Bay College, Sierra Leone, 1957-62; Head, Department of Religion, Nigeria University, 1962-65; Aberdeen University: Lecturer in Church History, 1966-69, Senior Lecturer, 1969, first Head, Department of Religious Studies, and Riddoch Lecturer in Comparative Religion, 1970, Reader, 1975, Professor of Religious Studies, 1979-85, Emeritus Professor, 1985; Director, Centre for the Study of Christianity in the Non-Western World, 1982-96; Honorary Professor, Edinburgh University, 1987-2001; Visiting Professor of World Christianity, Yale University, 1988; Visiting Professor of Ecumenics and Mission, Princeton Theological Seminary, since 1997; Monrad Visiting Professor of World Christianity, Harvard University, 2000. Co-opted Member, Aberdeen Education Committee, 1971-74; Aberdeen City Councillor, 1974-80; Convener, Arts and Recreation, COSLA, 1978-80; Chairman, Council for Museums and Galleries in Scotland, 1978-81; Vice-Chairman, Committee of Area Museums Councils, 1980-81; Member, Williams Committee on the future of the national museums, 1979-82; Trustee, National Museum of Antiquities of Scotland, 1982-85; Member, Museums Advisory Board for Scotland, 1984-85; Trustee, National Museums of Scotland, 1985-87; Methodist Preacher; Past Chairman, Disablement Income Group, Scotland; President, British Association for the History of Religions, 1977-80; Secretary, Scottish Institute of Missionary Studies; Editor, Journal of Religion in Africa, 1967-86; Henry Martyn Lectures, Cambridge University, 1988; Margaret Harris Lectures, Dundee University, 1989; Annual Missiology Lecturer, Fuller Theological Seminary, 1996; Burns Lecturer, Otago University, New Zealand, 2000; Co-chair, Yale-Edinburgh Group on the History of the Missionary Movement. Address: (b.) Centre for the Study of Christianity in the Non-Western World, Edinburgh University, New College, Mound Place, Edinburgh EH1 2LX; T.-0131-650 8952; Scottish Institute of Missionary Studies, RIISS, University of Aberdeen, Old Aberdeen AB24 3UG; T.-01224 581920.

Walsh, Garry Michael, MSc, PhD, FIMLS. Senior Lecturer, Department of Medicine and Therapeutics, University of Aberdeen, since 1997; b. 4.8.57, London; m., Catherine. Educ. St. James' School, London; Brunel University; London University. Medical Laboratory Scientific Officer, Histocompatability Testing Laboratory, Royal Postgraduate Medical School, London; academic research, Cardiothoracic Institute, Brompton Hospital, London; Visiting Fellow, Allergy Division, National Children's Hospital, Tokyo, Japan; postdoctoral position, University of Oxford; Senior Research Fellow/Honorary Lecturer, later Honorary Senior Lecturer, Department of Medicine and Therapeutics, University of Leciester Medical School; joined Aberdeen University, 1997. Scientific Advisor, UCB Institute of Allergy, Brussels. Publications: over 80 papers and review articles in international scientific and medical journals). Recreations: hillwalking; golf; gastronome; motorcycling. Address: Department of Medicine and Therapeutics, Institute of Medical Sciences, University of Aberdeen, Foresterhill, Aberdeen AB25 2ZD; T.-01224 552786; e-mail: g.m.walsh@abdn.ac.uk

Walton, Professor Henry John, MD, PhD, FRCPE, FRCPsych, DPM, Hon.MD. Physician; Emeritus Professor of Psychiatry and of International Medical Education, Edinburgh University; b. 15.2.24, South Africa; m., Sula Wolff. Educ. University of Cape Town; London University; Columbia University, NY; Edinburgh University. Registrar in Neurology and Psychiatry, University of Cape Town, 1946-54; Head, Department of Psychiatry, 1957-60; Senior Registrar, Maudsley Hospital, London, 1955-57; Senior Lecturer in Psychiatry, then Professor of Psychiatry, Edinburgh University, 1962-85; appointed Professor of International Medical Education, 1986; Editor, Medical Education, since 1976; President, Association for Medical Education in Europe, 1972-86, Hon. Life President, since 1986; Immediate Past-President, World Federation for Medical Education (Member, Executive Council); frequent Consultant to WHO; Member, Academies of Medicine of Argentina, Belgium and Poland. Publications: as Editor: Small Group Psychotherapy, 1974; Dictionary of Psychiatry, 1985; as Co-Editor: Newer Developments in Assessing Clinical Competence, 1986; as Co-Author: Alcoholism, 1988; Report of the World Conference on Medical Education, 1988; Report on World Summit of Medical Education, 1993; International Medical Education in Graduate Prospects in a Changing World, 1998; as Contributor: Contemporary Psychiatry, 2001; International Encyclopaedia of the Social and Behavioural Sciences, 2001. Recreations: literature; visual arts, particularly Western painting and Chinese and Japanese art. Address: 38 Blacket Place, Edinburgh, EH9 1RL; T.-0131-667 7811.

Walton, Professor John Christopher, BSc, PhD, DSc, CChem, FRSC, FRSE. Professor of Reactive Chemistry, St. Andrews University, since 1997; b. 4.12.41, St. Albans; m., Jane Lehman; 1 s.; 1 d. Educ. Watford Grammar School for Boys; Sheffield University. Assistant Lecturer: Queen's College, St. Andrews, 1966-67, Dundee University, 1967-69; Lecturer in Chemistry, United College, St. Andrews, 1969-80; Senior Lecturer, 1980-86, Reader, 1986-96. Elder, Seventh-day Adventist Church. Recreations: music; philosophy. Address: (b.) School of Chemistry, St. Andrews University, St. Andrews, Fife, KY16 9ST; T.-01334 463864.

Wannop, Professor Urlan Alistair, OBE, MA, MCD, MRTPI. Emeritus Professor of Urban and Regional Planning, Strathclyde University; b. 16.4.31, Newtown St. Boswells; 1 s.; 1 d. Educ. Aberdeen Grammar School; Edinburgh University; Liverpool University. Appointments in public and private practice, 1956-68; Team Leader, Coventry-Solihull-Warwickshire Sub-Regional Planning Study, 1968-71; Director, West Central Scotland Plan, 1972-74; Senior Deputy Director of Planning, Strathclyde Regional Council, 1975-81; appointed Professor of Urban and Regional Planning, Strathclyde University, 1981. Member, Parliamentary Boundary Commission for Scotland, 1983-98. Address: (h.) 43 Lomond Street, Helensburgh G84 7ES; T.-01436 674622.

Ward, Colin, BA, CA. Chief Executive, Student Loans Company, Glasgow, since 1996; b. 23.6.47, Edinburgh; m., Marjory. Educ. Daniel Stewart's College, Edinburgh; Heriot-Watt University. Ernst and Young, 1970-74; Price Waterhouse, Glasgow, 1974-75; British Steel Corporation, 1975-77; Scottish Development Agency, 1977-90, latterly as Chief Accountant; Student Loans Company, since 1990. Recreations: sailing; gardening; classical music. Address: (b.) 100 Bothwell Street, Glasgow, G2 7JD; T.-0141-306 2010.

Ward, Professor Geoffrey Christopher, BA, MA, FRSA. Professor of English, Dundee University, since 1995; b. 18.2.54, Oldham; m., Marion Wynne-Davies; 2 s. Educ. Manchester Grammar School; Clare College, Cambridge. Lecturer, then Senior Lecturer, English Department, Liverpool University, 1978-95. Member, Editorial Board, The Cambridge Quarterly; has lectured widely. Publications: Statutes of Liberty: the New York School of Poets, 1992; Language Poetry and the American Avant-Garde, 1993; Bloomsbury Guide to Romantic Literature (Editor); The Writing of America, 2002. Recreations: poetry; music; food; beach-combing. Address: (b.) English Department, Dundee University, Dundee DD1 4HN; T.-01382 344412; e-mail: g.c.ward@dundee.ac.uk

Ward, Professor John Macqueen, CBE, CA, Companion, IEE, FRSA. Chairman, Scottish Homes; Chairman, European Assets Trust NV; Chairman, Macfarlane Group (Clansman) PLC; Chairman, Queen Margaret University College Governing Body; Director, Dunfermline Building Society; former Resident Director, Scotland and North of England, IBM United Kingdom Ltd; Professor, Heriot Watt University; b. 1.8.40, Edinburgh; m., Barbara Macintosh; 1 s.; 3 d. Educ. Edinburgh Academy; Fettes College. Joined IBM UK Ltd. at Greenock plant, 1966; worked in France and UK; appointed European Director of Information Systems, 1975, and Havant Site Director, 1981. Past Chairman: Scottish CBI, Scottish Post Office Board, Quality Scotland Foundation, Advisory Scottish Council for Education and Training Targets, Scottish Electronics Forum, Institute of Technology Management; Director, Scottish Business in the Community; Director, Greater Easterhouse Development Company, 1991-93. Honorary Doctorate, Napier University, Strathclyde University, Heriot-Watt University. Address: (b.) 102 West Port, Edinburgh EH3 9HS; T.-0131-228 7300.

Ward, Leslie Graeme, MBE. Director, Advocates for Animals, since 1989; Secretary, St.Andrew Animal Fund, since 1994; b. 12.1.51, Dunbar; m., Erika Gillian; 1 d. Educ. Dunbar Grammar School. RAF, 1969-79. Guardian, Douglas Houghton Memorial Fund; Trustee, Marchig Animal Welfare Trust; Advisory Director, World Society for the Protection of Animals; Patron, Felix Cat Rescue; Fellow, Winston Churchill Travelling Fellowship Trust. Recreations: sports; walking the dogs. Address: (b.) 10 Queensferry Street, Edinburgh. EH2 4PG; T.-0131-225 6039; e-mail: lesward@advocatesforanimals.org

Ward, Professor Mark Gordon, BA. Professor of German Language and Literature, Glasgow University, since 1997; Director of Studies, Crichton Campus, since 1999; Principal Examiner, CSYS German, since 1987; b. 4.2.51, Hemel Hempstead; m., Janet Helen; 2 s. Educ. Leeds Grammar School; King's College, London University. Tutorial Research Scholar, Bedford College, London University, 1974-75; Lecturer, then Senior Lecturer, Department of German, Glasgow University, 1975-97; Dean, Faculty of Arts, 1995-99. Publications include: Theodor Storm: Der Schimmelreiter, 1988; Laughter, Comedy and Aesthetics:

Kleist's Der Zerbrochne Krug, 1995; Perspectives on German Realism, 1998; Romantic Dreams, 1998; Theodor Storm – Erzählstrategien und Patriarchat, 1999. Recreations: music; gardening; sport. Address: (b.) Faculty of Arts, Glasgow University, Glasgow G12 8QQ; T.-0141-330 5253; e-mail: mgw@arts.gla.ac.uk

Ward, Maxwell Colin Bernard, MA. Managing Director, The Independent Investment Trust, since 2000; Director: Scottish Equitable Policyholders' Trust, since 1994, Aegon UK, since 1999, Dunedin Income Growth Investment Trust, since 2000, Foreign and Colonial Investment Trust, since 2000; b. 22.8.49, Sherborne; m., Sarah Marsham; 2 s.; 2 d. Educ. Harrow; St. Catharine's, Cambridge. Baillie Gifford & Co.: Trainee, 1971-75, Partner, 1975-2000. Director: Scottish Equitable Life Assurance Society, 1988-94, Scottish Equitable plc, 1995-99; Board Member, Capability Scotland. Recreations: tennis; squash; bridge; country pursuits. Address: (b.) 11 Charlotte Square, Edinburgh EH2 4DR; T.-0131-220 4167.

Ward Thompson, Professor Catharine J., BSc, DipLA, FLI. Professor and Director of Research, Environmental Studies, Edinburgh College of Art/Heriot Watt University, since 2000; b. 5.12.52; m., Henry Swift Thompson; 3 c. Educ. Holy Cross Convent, Chalfont St. Peter; Southampton University; Edinburgh University. Landscape Assistant/Landscape Architect/ Senior Landscape Architect, 1973-81; Lecturer and Studio Instructor, School of Landscape Architecture, Edinburgh College of Art, 1981-88; Head of School, 1989-2000. Consultant, Landscape Design and Research Unit, Heriot-Watt University, since 1989. Recreations: dance; choreography. Address: (h.) 11 Douglas Crescent, Edinburgh EH12 5BB; T.-0131-337 6818.

Wardrop, James Arneil, DL, FCIBS, FUniv, FSA (Scot), FFCS. Retired Banker; Deputy Lieutenant, Renfrewshire; Chairman, Peter Brough Bequest Fund; Vice Chairman, Accord, The Renfrewshire Hospice; Vice Chairman, Japan Society of Scotland; Secretary, Society of Friends of Paisley Abbey; b. 19.4.40, Paisley. Educ. John Neilson Institution, Paisley. Joined National Bank of Scotland, by a process of mergers absorbed into Royal Bank of Scotland, Deputy Agent, San Francisco, 1978-81; Manager, International Division, 1981-94. Member, Nominations Committee, General Assembly of Church of Scotland; Elder, Paisley Abbey; Trustee, Miss Kibble's Trust; Director, Past Chairman, Incorporated Glasgow Renfrewshire Society; Director, Kibble Education and Care Centre; Member, Committee, Scotland's Gardens Scheme, Renfrewshire and Inverclyde; Member, Master Court, Paisley Hammermen Society (Deacon, 1996-97); Lay Member of Council, Paisley Art Institute; Box Master, Old Weavers Incorporation, Paisley; Independent Member, Board Nominations Committee, Scottish Enterprise, Renfrewshire; Member, Council, Society of Friends of Glasgow Cathedral; Honorary Vice President, Ferguslie Cricket Club. Recreations: country pursuits; gardening; music. Address: (h.) Saint Kevins, Meiklerigges, Paisley, PA2 9PT; T.-0141-887 3627.

Wark, Kirsty, BA. Partner, Wark, Clements and Company, since 1990; b. 1955, Dumfries; m., Alan Clements; 1 s.; 1 d. Educ. Edinburgh University. Joined BBC as radio researcher, 1976; became radio producer, current affairs; produced and presented Seven Days, 1985; then concentrated on presenting (Reporting Scotland; Left, Right and Centre); General Election night coverage, 1987, 1992, 1997; BBC coverage, Scottish Parliamentary elections, 1999; Presenter, Breakfast Time, Edinburgh Nights, Nelson Mandela Concert; Presenter, The Late Show, 1990-93; Presenter, One Foot in the Past, 1993-99; joined Newsnight's team of presenters, 1993; Presenter, Words with Wark, Restless Nation, Building a Nation; The Kirsty Wark Show. Journalist of the Year, BAFTA Scotland,

1993; Best TV Presenter award, 1997; Scot of the Year, 1998; formed production company with husband. Recreations: family; tennis; swimming; cooking; beach-combing; reading. Address: (b.) Wark, Clements and Co. Ltd., The Tollgate, 19 Marine Crescent, Glasgow G51 1HD.

Warlow, Professor Charles Picton, BA, MB, FAcadMedSci, BChir, MD, FRCP (Lond), FRCP (Edin), FRCP (Glas). Professor of Medical Neurology, Edinburgh, since 1987; Honorary Consultant Neurologist, Western General Hospital; President, Association of British Neurologists, 2001-03; b. 29.9.43; m.; 2 s.; 1 d. Educ. Cambridge University. Lecturer in Medicine, Aberdeen University, 1971-74; Registrar and Senior Registrar in Neurology, National Hospitals for Nervous Diseases, London, and University College Hospital, London, 1974-76; Clinical Lecturer in Neurology, then Clinical Reader, Oxford University, 1976-86. Recreations: sailing; photography; mountains. Address: 5 Cumberland Street South East Lane, Edinburgh EH3 6RU.

Warner of Craigenmaddie, Gerald, OStJ, MA, FSAScot. Author; Columnist, Scotland on Sunday, since 1997; b. 22.3.45, Falkirk. Educ. St. Aloysius' College, Glasgow; Glasgow University. Vice-Chairman, Una Voce (International Latin Mass Federation), Scotland, 1965-66; Administrative Assistant, Glasgow University, 1971-74; author and broadcaster, 1974-89; Diarist (under pseudonym Henry Cockburn), Sunday Times Scotland, 1989-95; columnist, 1992-95; Special Adviser to Secretary of State for Scotland, 1995-97; Council Member, 1745 Association, 1967-70; Member, Scottish Council of Monarchist League, 1969-71; Chairman, The Monday Club - Scotland, 1973-74; Secretary, Conservative Party's Scottish Policy Committee on Education, 1976-77; Parliamentary candidate, Hamilton, October 1974. Knight of Grace and Devotion, Sovereign Military Order of Malta, 1979; Knight, Jure Sanguinis, Sacred Military Constantinian Order of St. George, 1994. Publications: Homelands of the Clans, 1980; Being of Sound Mind, 1980; Tales of the Scottish Highlands, 1982; Conquering by Degrees, 1985; The Scottish Tory Party: A History, 1988. Recreations: literature; genealogy; Brummelliana. Address: 17 Huntly Gardens, Glasgow G12 9AT.

Wasserstein, Professor Bernard Mano Julius, MA, DPhil, DLitt, FRHistS. Professor of History, Glasgow University, since 2000; President, Jewish Historical Society of England, since 2000; b. 22.1.48, London; 1 d. Educ. High School of Glasgow; Wyggeston Boys' Grammar School, Leicester; Balliol College, Oxford; Nuffield College, Oxford. Lecturer in History, Sheffield University, 1976-80; Associate Professor of History, 1980-82, and Professor, 1982-96, Brandeis University, Mass.; President, Oxford Centre for Hebrew and Jewish Studies, 1996-2000. Publications include: The British in Palestine; Britain and the Jews of Europe 1939-1945; Herbert Samuel; Vanishing Diaspora; Secret War on Shanghai; Divided Jerusalem. Recreation: walking on the island of Arran. Address: (b.) History Department, Glasgow University, Glasgow, G12 8QQ; T.-0141-357 3586.

Watchman, Karen, BA. Director, Scottish Down's Syndrome Association, since 1998; b. 9.1.65, Stockton-on-Tees; m., Mark Smith; 2 s. Educ. Ian Ramsey Comprehensive School, Stockton-on-Tees; Stockton Sixth Form College; University of Stirling; Jordanhill College of Education. NCH Action for Children: Depute Manager, Stirling Stopover, 1988-94; Depute Manager, Raploch Family Centre, 1994-96; Manager, Quality Action Group, Stirling, 1996-98; Manager, Scottish Down's Syndrome Association Central Branch Befriending Scheme. Member, School Board, Claremont Primary School, Alloa.

Recreations: family; vegetarian cooking; sport (Middlesbrough Football Club). Address: (b.) 158/160 Balgreen Road, Edinburgh EH11 3AU; T.-0131-313 4225.

Waters, Donald Henry, OBE, CA. Director, Scottish Media Group, since 1997; Deputy Chairman and Chief Executive, Grampian Television PLC, 1993-97 (Chief Executive and Director, 1987-93); b. 17.12.37, Edinburgh; m., June Leslie Hutchison; 1 s.; 2 d. Educ. George Watson's, Edinburgh; Inverness Royal Academy. Director, John M. Henderson and Co. Ltd., 1972-75; Grampian Television PLC: Company Secretary, 1975, Director of Finance, 1979; Director: Scottish Television and Grampian Sales Ltd., 1980-97, Moray Firth Radio Ltd., 1982-97, Independent Television Publications Ltd., 1987-90, Cablevision Scotland PLC, 1987-91; Chairman, Celtic Film and Television Association, 1994-96; Vice-Chairman, BAFTA Scotland; Visiting Professor of Film and Media Studies, Stirling University; Chairman, Police Dependant Trust for Grampian, 1992-96; Past Chairman, Royal Northern and University Club, Aberdeen; Chairman, Glenburnie Properties Ltd., 1993-97; Director: Central Scotland Radio Ltd. (Scot FM), 1994-96 (Chairman, 1995-96), GRT Bus Group PLC, 1994-96, British Linen Bank Ltd., 1995-99, Bank of Scotland North of Scotland Local Board, since 1999, Scottish Post Office Board, 1996-2001, Consignia Advisory Board for Scotland, since 2001; Member, ITV Council and ITV Broadcast Board; Fellow, Royal Society of Arts; Council Member, CBI Scotland, since 1994; Council Member, Cinema and Television Benevolent Fund, 1987-99; Member, Royal Television Society, since 1988; Director, Aberdeen Royal Hospital NHS Trust, 1996-99; Chairman, New Royal Aberdeen Children's Hospital Project Steering Group; Member of Council, Aberdeen Chamber of Commerce, since 1996; Governor, Aberdeen University, 1998; Governor, Robert Gordon's, Aberdeen, 1998; Member, Grampian and Islands Family Trust, since 1988; Joint Chairman, Grampian Cancer Macmillan Appeal, since 1999; Member of Council, SATRO; Burgess of Guild Assessor, since 1997. Address: (h.) Balquhidder, 141 North Deeside Road, Milltimber, Aberdeen AB13 0JS; T.-Aberdeen 867131.

Waters, Fergus Cameron. Director, Scottish Mining Museum, since 1996; b. 15.2.57, Tanzania; m., Alison Crawford. Educ. Rannoch School; Moray College of Further Education. Marketing Manager, Castlewynd Studios, 1984-88; Commercial and Marketing Manager, Ford and Etal Estates, 1988-94; General Manager, Hartlepool Historic Quay, 1994-96. Recreations: motor-biking; skiing; sailing. Address: (b.) Scottish Mining Museum, Lady Victoria Colliery, Newtongrange EH22 4QN; T.-0131-663 7519; e-mail: enquiries@scottishminingmuseum.com

Watson of Invergowrie, Lord (Michael Goodall Watson), BA (Hons). MSP (Labour), Glasgow Cathcart, since 1999; Minister for Tourism, Culture and Sport, Scottish Executive; MP (Labour), Glasgow Central, 1989-97; b. 1.5.49, Cambuslang. Educ. Dundee High School; Heriot-Watt University. Development Officer, WEA East Midlands District, 1974-77; Industrial Officer, ASTMS, 1977-79; Regional Officer, ASTMS (latterly MSF), 1979-89. Member, Scottish Executive Committee, Labour Party, 1987-90; Hon. Doctorate, University of Abertay Dundee, 1998. Publication: Rags to Riches: the official history of Dundee United FC, 1985; Year Zero: an inside view of the Scottish Parliament, 2001. Recreations: watching Dundee United FC; jogging; reading, especially political biographies. Address: (b.) Scottish Parliament, Edinburgh EH99 1SP.

Watson, Professor Alan Albert, JP, MA, BD, MB, BS, FRCP, FRCPath, DMJ, DTM&H. Emeritus Regius Professor of Forensic Medicine, Glasgow University; Honorary Consultant in Forensic Medicine, Greater

Glasgow Health Board, since 1978; Committee Member, Forensic Medicine (Scotland) Committee, since 1982; b. 20.2.29, Reading; m., Jeannette Anne Pitts; 3 s. Educ. Reading School; St. Mary's Hospital, London; Queens' College, Cambridge. Lecturer in Pathology, Glasgow University, 1964-69; University Senior Assistant Pathologist, Cambridge University, 1969-71; elected Fellow of Queen's College and Assistant Director of Studies, 1970; Consultant in Forensic Medicine, SE Asia Region, Delhi, WHO, 1977. Hon. President, Scottish Band of Hope Union. Recreations: Church activities (Baptist lay preacher). Address: (h.) 76 Arrol Drive, Ayr KA7 4AW; T.-01292 266365.

Watson, Alexander Bell, MA, MEd, FIMgt, FSA Scot, FRSA. Chief Executive, Angus Council, since 1995 (Chief Executive, Tayside Regional Council, 1995); b. 20.5.45, Airdrie; m., Jean; 3 s. Educ. Airdrie Academy; Glasgow University; Jordanhill College of Education. Teacher of Classics, Morrison's Academy, Crieff, 1968; Principal Teacher of Classics: Portree High School, 1971, McLaren High School, Callander, 1973; Assistant Director of Education: Central, 1975, Strathclyde, 1983; Senior Depute Director of Education, Central Regional Council, 1986; Director of Education, Tayside Regional Council, 1990-94. General Secretary, Association of Directors of Education in Scotland, 1993-95; Chair, National Co-ordinating Committee on Staff Development of Teachers, 1994-95; Member, Board of Management and Chair, Personnel Committee, Angus College, since 1997; Hon. Secretary, Society of Local Authority Chief Executives and Senior Managers (Scotland), since 1997; Chair, Scottish Advisory Committee, Duke of Edinburgh's Award Scheme, since 1999. Recreations: music; reading; fishing; Scottish heritage; DIY. Address: (b.) Angus Council, The Cross, Forfar DD8 1BX; T.-01307 473020.

Watson, Craig MacLean, MA (Hons). Home Affairs Correspondent, The Herald, since 2000; b. 5.3.65, Carlisle; partner, Shirley English; 1 d. Educ. Firrhill High School, Edinburgh; University of Aberdeen; Stradbroke College, Sheffield. Reporter, Nottingham Evening Post, 1992-94; joined The Herald 1994 (Reporter, then Acting Environment Correspondent). Recreations: Heart of Midlothian Football Club member and shareholder; Scottish affairs; malt whisky. Address: The Herald, 200 Renfield Street, Glasgow G2 3PR; T.-0141-302 7075; e-mail: craigwatson@onmail.co.uk

Watson, Garry Sanderson, OBE, CA. b. 31.7.40, Glasgow; m., Elizabeth Ann; 4 d. Educ. Glasgow Academy. Hill Samuel Bank, 1969-91; Scottish Legal Services Ombudsman, 1994-2000; Advisor to Standards Committee, Scottish Parliament, 2000-01; Governor, Macaulay Land Use Research Institute, since 1997; Director, Business in the Community, 1985-88; Director, Save and Invest Group, since 1993; Director, Braveheart Ventures Ltd., since 2001; Hon. Treasurer, National Association of Citizens' Advice Bureaux, 1986-91; Hon. Treasurer, Scottish Association of CAB, 1992-95; Director, Edinvar Housing Association, since 1992 (Chair, 1997-2001). Recreations: tennis; hill-walking; shooting. Address: (h.) Newlandburn House, Newlandrig, by Gorebridge, Midlothian, EH23 4NS; T.-01875 820939.

Watson, Professor George Alistair, BSc, MSc, PhD, FIMA, FRSE. Professor, Department of Mathematics, Dundee University, since 1988; b. 30.9.42, Aberfeldy; m., Hilary Mackay; 1 d. Educ. Breadalbane Academy; Edinburgh University; Australian National University. Demonstrator, Computer Unit, Edinburgh University, 1964-66; Dundee University: Research Fellow, then Lecturer, Mathematics Department, 1969-82; Senior Lecturer, Mathematical Sciences Department, 1982-84; Reader,

Department of Mathematics and Computer Science, 1984-88. Recreation: gardening. Address: (h.) 7 Albany Road, West Ferry, Dundee DD5 1NS; T.-Dundee 779473.

Watson, Professor John, BSc, ARCST, PhD, DSc. Professor in Biochemistry, Strathclyde University, since 1988 (Reader, 1985-88); Head, Department of Bioscience and Biotechnology; b. 17.6.42, Glasgow; m., Anne Brown; 2 d. Educ. Whitehill Secondary, Glasgow; Glasgow University; Strathclyde University. MRC Research Fellow, Glasgow University; Lecturer, Senior Lecturer, Reader, Professor, Strathclyde University. Recreations: golf; swimming; skiing; reading. Address: (b.) Royal College, Glasgow G1 1XW; T.-0141-548 3822.

Watson, Peter, BA, LLB, SSC. Solicitor (Levy & McRae); b. 22.1.54, Greenock; m., Claire Watson; 2 d. Educ. Eastwood High School, Glasgow; Strathclyde University; Edinburgh University; Scandinavian Maritime Law Institute, Norway; Dundee Petroleum Law Institute. Qualified, 1981; Solicitor to the Supreme Courts; Notary Public; former Temporary Sheriff, now part-time Sheriff; Past President, Society of Solicitor Advocates; Hon. Vice-President and former Chairman, Association of Mediators; Visiting Professor, Nova University, Fort Lauderdale, Florida; Member, Steering Committee, and Negotiator, Piper Alpha Disaster Group; Secretary, Braer Disaster Group; Secretary, Lockerbie Air Disaster Group; former Official Collaborator, International Labour Organisation, Geneva; Member, Criminal Rules Council; Member, Board, Sports Law Centre, Anglia University; Honorary Citizen of Nashville, Tennessee; large media practice based in Glasgow. Publications: Civil Justice System in Britain; Crimes of War – The Antony Gecas Story; The Truth Written in Blood; Dunblane -- A Predictable Tragedy; DNA and the Criminal Trial; In Pursuit of Pan Am. Recreations: working out; drinking fine wine. Address: (b.) Levy & McRae, 266 St. Vincent Street, Glasgow G2 5RL; T.-0141-307 2311.

Watson, Professor Roderick, MA, PhD, FRSE. Poet; Literary Critic and Writer; Professor for English, Stirling University; Director, Stirling Centre for Scottish Studies; b. 12.5.43, Aberdeen; m., Celia Hall Mackie; 1 s.; 1 d. Educ. Aberdeen Grammar School; Aberdeen University; Peterhouse, Cambridge. Lecturer in English, Victoria University, British Columbia, 1965-66; collections of poetry include Trio and True History on the Walls; other books include The Penguin Book of the Bicycle, The Literature of Scotland, MacDiarmid, The Poetry of Norman MacCaig and The Poetry of Scotland (Editor). Recreation: cycling; motor cycling. Address: (h.) 19 Millar Place, Stirling; T.-Stirling 475971.

Watt, Brian, MD, FRCPath, FRCP Edin, CBiol, FIBiol. Consultant Bacteriologist, City Hospital, Edinburgh, since 1982; Honorary Senior Lecturer, Department of Bacteriology, Edinburgh University, since 1974; Director, Scottish Mycobacteria Reference Laboratory; Patient Services Director, Medical Microbiology, Lothian University Hospitals NHS Trust; b. 6.12.41, Edinburgh; m., Hilary Watt; 2 d. Educ. Rudolf Steiner School; Edinburgh University. Lecturer, Department of Bacteriology, Edinburgh University, 1968-73; Consultant Microbiologist, Western General Hospital, 1973-82. Recreations: fishing; gardening; golf; tennis; singing. Address: (h.) Silverburn House, by Penicuik, Midlothian; T.-01968 672085; e-mail: BHWatt@hotmail.com

Watt, David C., DipEd, BA, DPE, CYS. Sport and Leisure Consultant and Trainer; Director: Organising Leisure, Leisure Training Consortium; Chairman, Scottish Snooker Ltd.; Board Member, Scottish Youth Dance; freelance writer. Formerly: Executive Director, Commonwealth Games Council for Scotland, President, Scottish Gymnastics Association, Scottish Partnership

Manager, New Millennium Experience Company. Address: (b.) 1 Colinton Court, Glenrothes, Fife KY6 3PE; T.-01592 743948.

Watt, Iain Alasdair, BSc (Econ). Chief Executive, Edinburgh Fund Managers; b. 30.3.45, Edinburgh; m., Lynne Neilson; 3 s.; 1 d. Educ. Edinburgh Academy; Hull University. Recreations: golf; tennis. Address: (b.) Donaldson House, 97 Haymarket Terrace, Edinburgh; T.-0131-313 1000.

Watt, Jim, MBE (1980). Boxer; b. 18.7.48, Glasgow. Turned professional, 1968; British Lightweight Champion, 1972-73, 1975-77; European Lightweight Champion, 1977-79; World Lightweight Champion, 1979-81; four successful defences of World title; Freedom of Glasgow, 1981.

Waugh, Alan, BSc (Hons), DipEd, FRSA. Head Teacher, Penicuik High School, since 1992; b. 9.2.49, Loanhead; m., Margo Watt; 1 s.; 1 d. Educ. Lasswade Senior Secondary School; Edinburgh University. Head of Chemistry, then Assistant Head Teacher, Lasswade High School Centre, 1976-86; Depute Head Teacher, James Gillespie's High School, 1986-92. Address: (b.) Penicuik High School, Carlops Road, Penicuik EH26 9EP; T.-Penicuik 674165.

Way of Plean, George Alexander, SBStJ, LLB (Hons), FSAScot, FRSA, NP, SSC, Companion of the Order of Malta. Senior Litigation Partner, Beveridge and Kellas, SSC, since 1985; b. 22.5.56, Edinburgh; m., Rosemary Calder; 1 s. Educ. Boroughmuir School; University of Edinburgh. Apprenticed to W. F. M. Whitelaw, W. S., 1978-80; Solicitor, Beveridge and Kellas, 1980-85. Secretary, Standing Council of Scottish Chiefs, since 1984; Member, Convention of the Baronage of Scotland; Vice President, Society of Solicitors in the Supreme Courts, 2000; Member, Council, Law Society of Scotland, since 2001; Freeman, City of Glasgow, 1997. Publications: Collins Clans and Family Encyclopaedia (Editor-in-Chief); Homelands of the Clans; Everyday Scots Law; Scottish Clans and Tartans. Recreations: heraldry and orders of chivalry. Address: (b.) Hope Chambers, 52 Leith Walk, Leith, Edinburgh EH6 5HW; T.-0131-554 6321.

Weatherhead, Alexander Stewart, OBE, TD, MA, LLB. Solicitor; formerly Senior Partner, Brechin Tindal Oatts (formerly Tindal Oatts), Solicitors, Glasgow (Partner, 1960-97, Consultant, 1997-98); b. 3.8.31, Edinburgh; m., Harriett Foye; 2 d. Educ. Glasgow Academy; Glasgow University. Royal Artillery, 1950-52; TA, 1952; Lt. Col. Commanding 277 (A&SH) Field Regiment, RA (TA), 1965-67, The Lowland Regiment, RA (T), 1967 and Glasgow and Strathclyde Universities OTC, 1970-73; Colonel, 1974; TAVR Colonel, Lowlands (West), 1974-76; ADC (TAVR) to The Queen, 1977-81; Honorary Colonel, Glasgow and Strathclyde Universities OTC, 1982-98; Chairman, Lowlands TAVRA, 1990-93; Member, Royal Artillery Council for Scotland, 1972-2001 (Vice Chairman, 1996-2001); Council Member, Law Society of Scotland, 1971-84 (Honorary Vice-President, 1983-84); Member, Royal Commission on Legal Services in Scotland, 1976-80; Council Member, Society for Computers and Law, 1993-96 (Chairman, 1981-84); Temporary Sheriff, 1985-92; Dean, Royal Faculty of Procurators in Glasgow, 1991-95; Director, Glasgow Chamber of Commerce, 1991-95; Member, Research Ethics Committee, Glasgow Royal Infirmary, since 1999; Member, Incorporation of Weavers of Glasgow, since 1949; Commodore, Royal Western Yacht Club, 1995-98. Recreations: tennis; sailing; reading; music. Address: (h.) 52 Partickhill Road, Glasgow, G11 5AB; T.-0141-334 6277.

Weatherhead, Very Rev. James Leslie, CBE, MA, LLB, DD. Former Principal Clerk, General Assembly of the Church of Scotland; Moderator, General Assembly, 1993; b. 29.3.31, Dundee; m., Dr Anne Elizabeth Shepherd (see

Anne E. Weatherhead); 2 s. Educ. High School of Dundee; Edinburgh University and New College, Edinburgh. Temporary Sub-Lt., RNVR (National Service), 1955-56. Licensed by Presbytery of Dundee, 1960, Presbytery of Ayr, 1960; Assistant Minister, Auld Kirk of Ayr, 1960-62; Minister: Trinity Church, Rothesay, 1962-69, Old Church, Montrose, 1969-85. Member, Broadcasting Council for Scotland, 1978-82; DD, University of Edinburgh, 1993. Address: 59 Brechin Road, Kirriemuir DD8 4DE.

Weaver, C. Giles H., FCA, MBA. Proprietor, Greywalls Hotel, Gullane, since 1976; Deputy Chairman, National Galleries of Scotland; Chairman, Historic Houses Association in Scotland; Chairman, Murray Emerging Growth and Investment Trust; b. 4.4.46; m., Rosamund B. Mayhew; 2 s.; 2 d. Educ. Eton College; London Business School. Ernst & Young, 1966-70; London Business School, 1971-73; Jessel Securities/Berry Wiggins, 1973-76; Director, Ivory & Sime plc, 1976-86; Managing Director Pensions, Prudential Portfolio Managers, 1986-90; Murray Johnstone Ltd.: CIO, 1990-93, Managing Director, 1993-99, Chairman, 1999-2000. Trustee, Lutyens Trust; Director: Aberdeen Asset Management plc, James Finlay Ltd., Charter European Trust PLC, Helical Bar PLC, Atrium Underwriting PLC. Recreations: golf; bridge; skiing; stalking. Address: (b.) Aberdeen Asset Management, 20 S. St. Andrew Street, Edinburgh EH2 2BD; T.-0131-200 3086.

Weaver, Professor Lawrence Trevelyan, MA, MB BChir, DObstRCOG, DCH, MD, FRCP, FRCPGlas, FRCPCH, FRSA. Honorary Consultant Paediatrician, Royal Hospital for Sick Children, Yorkhill, Glasgow, since 1994; Samson Gemmell Professor of Child Health, University of Glasgow, since 1996; b. 13.10.48; m., Camilla Simmons; 1 s.; 1 d. Educ. Clifton College, Bristol; Corpus Christi College, Cambridge University; St. Thomas's Hospital Medical School. General professional training Newcastle University Hospitals; MRC Training Fellow, Dunn Nutritional Laboratory and Honorary Senior Registrar, Department of Paediatrics, Addenbrooke's Hospital, Cambridge, 1984-86; Clinical Research Fellow and Fulbright Scholar, Harvard Medical School Departments of Pediatric Gastroenterology and Nutrition, Children's Hospital and Massachusetts General Hospital, Boston, 1987-88; Member, MRC Scientific Staff, Dunn Nutrition Laboratory and Honorary Consultant Paediatrician, Addenbrooke's Hospital and University of Cambridge, 1988-94; Reader in Human Nutrition, University of Glasgow, 1994-96. Member, Academic Panel, RCPCH; Member, Nutrition Committees, RCPCH and ESPGHAN. Recreations: walking; gardening. Address: (b.) Department of Child Health, Royal Hospital for Sick Children, Yorkhill, Glasgow G3 8SJ; T.-0141-201 0236.

Webb, Professor David John, MD, DSc, FRCP, FRCPE, FESC, FFPM, FMedSci. Christison Professor of Therapeutics and Clinical Pharmacology, Clinical Pharmacology Unit and Research Centre, Edinburgh University, since 1995; Head, University Department of Medical Sciences, Western General Hospital, Edinburgh, 1998-2001; Leader, Wellcome Trust Cardiovascular Research Initiative, since 1998; Head, Centre for Research in Cardiovascular Biology, Edinburgh University, since 1997; Director, Clinical Research Centre and Honorary Consultant Physician, Western General Hospital, Edinburgh, since 1990; b. 1.9.53, Greenwich; m., Dr. Margaret Jane Cullen. Educ. Dulwich College, London; London University: Royal London Hospital. Junior hospital appointments, 1977-79; Medical Registrar, Royal London rotation, 1979-82; MRC Research Fellow, MRC Blood Pressure Unit, Glasgow, and Honorary Lecturer, Glasgow University, 1982-85; Lecturer in Pharmacology and Clinical Pharmacology, St. George's Hospital Medical School, London, and Honorary Medical Senior Registrar, St. George's Hospital, London, 1985-89; Senior Lecturer in Medicine, Edinburgh University. Executive Member,

British Hypertension Society, since 1991; Member, MRC Scientific Advisory Board, since 1996; Member, Wellcome Trust Physiology and Pharmacology Panel, 1997-2000; Member, Multi-Centre Research Ethics Committee for Scotland, 1997-2000; Honorary Trustee and Joint Research Director, High Blood Pressure Foundation and Endocrine Research Trust, since 1991; Chairman, Symposium Committee, Royal College of Physicians, Edinburgh, since 1998; Chairman, Lothian Drug and Therapeutics Committee, since 1998; Chairman, Committee on Clinical Pharmacology, Royal College of Physicians, London, 1999-2000; Member, Association of Clinical Professors of Medicine and of Association of Physicians of Great Britain and Ireland; Member, Scottish Medicines Consortium, Scottish Executive Health Department; Adviser in Clinical Pharmacology and Therapeutics, Scottish Executive Health Department. Recreations: opera; bridge; summer and winter mountaineering. Address: (h.) 26 Inverleith Gardens, Edinburgh EH3 5PS; T.-0131-332 1205; e-mail: d.j.webb@ed.ac.uk

Webb, Professor Jeffrey R.L., BSc, DPhil, FRSE. Professor of Mathematics, Glasgow University, since 1997 (Reader, 1982-87); b. 19.12.45, Stourport-on-Severn; m., Angela Millard; 1 s.; 1 d. Educ. King Charles I School, Kidderminster; Sussex University. Royal Society European Programme Fellowship, 1970-71; Science Research Council Fellowship, Sussex University, 1971-73; Lecturer in Mathematics, Glasgow University, 1973-78 and 1979-82; Visiting Associate Professor, Indiana University, 1978-79; Visiting Professor, Tulane University, New Orleans, 1982. Member, Editorial Board, Glasgow Mathematical Journal; Editorial Adviser, London Mathematical Society. Recreations: chess; books; listening to music. Address: (b.) Mathematics Department, Glasgow University, Glasgow G12 8QW; T.-0141-339 8855, Ext. 5181.

Webster, Andrew George, LLB (Hons), DipLP, FRSA. Advocate, since 1992; b. 20.7.67, Wick; m., Sheila Mairead. Educ. Wick High School; University of Aberdeen. Standing Junior Counsel to: Ministry of Defence (Air Force), 1997-2000, Ministry of Defence, since 2000. Address: (b.) Advocates' Library, Parliament House, Edinburgh EH1 1RF; T.-0131-226 5071.

Webster, Ann, BSc (Hons). National Director, Girls' Brigade in Scotland since 1996; b. 16.11.43, Oxford; m., Robert Webster; 1 s.; 2 d. Educ. Stobswell Girls' Junior Secondary School, Dundee; Scottish College of Textiles, Galashiels. Analyst, WRAC, 1963-68; Assistant Domestic Services Manager, Ninewells Hospital, 1973-78. Girls' Brigade Officer, 23 years. Recreations: reading; cross-stitch; knitting; bird-watching. Address: (b.) Girls' Brigade Scotland, Boys' Brigade House, 168 Bath Street, Glasgow G2 4TQ; T.-0141-332 1765; e-mail: hq@girls-brigade-scotland.org.uk

Webster, Jack (John Barron). Author and Journalist; b. 8.7.31, Maud, Aberdeenshire; m., Eden Keith; 3 s. Educ. Maud School; Peterhead Academy; Robert Gordon's College, Aberdeen. Reporter, Turriff Advertiser; Reporter/Sub Editor, Aberdeen Press & Journal/Evening Express; Chief Sub-Editor, Scottish Sunday Express; Feature Writer, Scottish Daily Express; Feature Writer, Sunday Standard; Columnist, The Herald. Columnist of the Year, 1996; Speaker of the Year, 1996. Publications: The Dons, 1978; A Grain of Truth, 1981; Gordon Strachan, 1984; Another Grain of Truth, 1988; 'Tis Better to Travel, 1989; Alistair MacLean (biography), 1991; Famous Ships of the Clyde, 1993; The Flying Scots, 1994; The Express Years, 1994; In the Driving Seat, 1996; The Herald Years, 1996; From Dali to Burrell, 1997; Webster's World, 1997; The Reo Stakis Story, 1999; television films: The Roup, 1985; As Time Goes By, 1987; Northern Lights, 1989; Webster Goes West, 1991; John Brown: The Man Who Drew a Legend, 1994; Walking Back to Happiness, 1996;

video film: The Glory of Gothenburg, 1993. Address: (b.) 58 Netherhill Avenue, Glasgow G44 3XG; T.-0141-637 6437; e-mail: jack@jackwebster.fsnet.co.uk

Webster, Janice Helen, LLB, WS. Secretary, Scottish Law Agents' Society, since 1998; part-time Chairman, Appeals Service Tribunals, since 1998; b. 2.4.44; m., Hon. R.M. Webster (see Robin Maclean Webster); 2 d. Educ. Edinburgh University. Solicitor and Notary Public; Legal Assistant, then Senior Solicitor, Falkirk Town Council, 1967-71; in private practice, Alston Nairn & Hogg, Edinburgh, 1971-74; Deputy Secretary, Law Society of Scotland, 1974-80; Crown Counsel, then Magistrate, Government of Seychelles, 1980-82; Law Society of Scotland, 1982-90 (Deputy Secretary, Director European Affairs and Secretary, Scottish Lawyers' European Group); Director General, CCBE, 1991-93; Consultant, Bell & Scott WS, 1994-97; Member, Scottish Records Advisory Council, 1995-2000; Director, SCAN; Governor, Mary Erskine, Stewarts Melville College, since 1998; Director and Chairman, Scottish Society for Computers and Law, since 2001. Publications: Professional Ethics and Practice for Scottish Solicitors (Co-author), 1996; Human Rights and UK Practice (Editor). Recreations: singing; walking; gardening. Address: (b.) Scottish Law Agents' Society, 11 Parliament Square, Edinburgh EH1 1RF.

Webster, Michael Alan, BA, DMS, MIMgt, FRSA. Principal, Perth College, since 1991; b. 7.12.45, Manchester. Educ. Chetham's School, Manchester; Moseley Hall Grammar School; Exeter University. FE Lecturer and Head of Department, 1972-84; Education Adviser, Shropshire County Council, 1984-88, Principal Adviser, 1988-91. Recreations: hill-walking; skiing; theatre; fishing. Address: (b.) Perth College, Crieff Road, Perth, PH1 2NX; T.-01738 621171.

Webster, Professor Nigel Robert, BSc, MB, ChB, PhD, FRCA, FRCPEdin. Professor of Anaesthesia and Intensive Care, Aberdeen University, since 1994; b. 14.6.53, Walsall; m., Diana C.S. Webster; 1 s.; 2 d. Educ. Edward Shelley High School, Walsall; Leeds University. Member, scientific staff/Consultant, Clinical Research Centre, Northwick Park Hospital, Harrow; Consultant in Anaesthesia and Intensive Care, St. James's University Hospital, Leeds. Address: (b.) Institute of Medical Sciences, Foresterhill, Aberdeen AB25 2ZD; T.-01224 681818.

Webster, Professor Robin Gordon Maclennan, OBE, MA (Cantab), MA (Arch), RIBA, FRIAS, ARSA. Professor of Architecture, Scott Sutherland School of Architecture, The Robert Gordon University, Aberdeen, since 1984; Senior Partner, Robin Webster & Associates, Aberdeen, since 1984; Member, The Designers' Collaborative, since 1994; Commissioner, Royal Fine Art Commission for Scotland, 1992-98; b. 24.12.39, Glasgow; m., Katherine S. Crichton; 1 s.; 2 d. Educ. Glasgow Academy; Rugby School; St. John's College, Cambridge; University College London. Assistant, Gillespie Kidd & Coia, Architects, Glasgow, 1963-64; National Building Agency, London, 1965-67; Senior Partner, Spence and Webster, Architects, 1972-84; Lecturer, Bartlett School of Architecture, 1969-74; Visiting Lecturer, Washington University, St. Louis, 1975, Cambridge University, 1976-77, and Mackintosh School, Glasgow School of Art, 1978-84. Winner, New Parliamentary Building Competition, Westminster, 1972; 1st prize, New York Waterfront Competition, 1988; Winner, 1997 Sellic library competition for University of Edinburgh; Chairman, Association of Scottish Schools of Architecture, 1986-90; President, Aberdeen Society of Architects, 1989-91. Recreations: looking and drawing. Address: (h.) 6 Park Road, Cults, Aberdeen; T.-01224 867140.

Webster, Robin Maclean, MBE, RD, BA (Cantab), FCIArb. Employment Tribunal Chairman, Edinburgh, since 1994; b. 22.4.40; m., Janice Helen Reid (see Janice Webster); 2 d. Educ. Fettes College, Edinburgh; Christ's College, Cambridge University. Solicitor (Scotland), 1966; NP, 1970; Partner, Haddow & McLay, Solicitors, Glasgow, 1968-70; Deputy Secretary, Law Society of Scotland, 1970-76; Secretary, Scottish Lawyers' European Group, 1971-77; Office of Solicitor to Secretary of State for Scotland, 1976-88; seconded as Legal Draftsman, Seychelles Government, 1980-82; Assistant Parliamentary Draftsman, Lord Advocate's Department, 1982-83; Senior Parliamentary Counsel, Kenya Government, 1985-86; Attorney-General, Tuvalu, S. Pacific, 1986-88; Judge of the Supreme Court of Tonga, S. Pacific, 1988-91; Temporary Sheriff, 1991-96; part-time Industrial Tribunal Chairman, 1991-94; Legal Consultant, Overseas Development Administration, 1992-95. Royal Naval Reserve, 1962-90; Lt. Commander (Rtd); Chairman, Queensferry and District Unit, Sea Cadet Corps, 1994-2000; Hon. Secretary, Royal Scottish Pipers' Society, 1973-76; Elder, Palmerston Place Church of Scotland. Recreations: piping and piobaireachd; Scottish dancing; reading; dog walking. Address: (b.) Employment Tribunals, 54-56 Melville Street, Edinburgh EH3 7HF; T.-0131-226 5584.

Weeple, Edward John, MA. Head, Lifelong Learning Group, Scottish Executive Enterprise and Lifelong Learning Department, since 1999; b. 15.5.45, Glasgow; 3 s.; 1 d. Educ. St. Aloysius' College, Glasgow; Glasgow University. Entered DHSS, London, 1968; Assistant Principal, 1968-73 (Private Secretary to Minister of Health, 1971-73); Principal, 1973-78; transferred to Scottish Office, 1978; Principal (Industrial Development Division, SEPD), 1978-80; Assistant Secretary, Scottish Home and Health Department, 1980-85; Assistant Secretary, Department of Agriculture and Fisheries for Scotland, 1985-90; Head, Local Economic Development Group, Industry Department, 1990-95; Under Secretary, Lifelong Learning Group, Education and Industry Department, 1995-99. Address: (b.) Europa Building, 450 Argyle Street, Glasgow G2 8LG; T.-0141-242 0206.

Weir, Viscount (William Kenneth James Weir), BA, Hon. DEng (Glasgow), Hon. FEng. Director, The Weir Group PLC, 1966-99 (Chairman, 1983-99); Director and former Vice-Chairman, St. James' Place Capital plc; Chairman, Balfour Beatty plc, since 1996 (Deputy Chairman, 1992-96, Director, since 1977); Director, Canadian Pacific Limited; Chairman, Major British Exporters; Chairman, British Water; b. 9.11.33, Glasgow; m., 1, Diana MacDougall (m. diss.); 2, Jacqueline Mary Marr (m. diss.); 3, Marina Sevastopoulo; 2 s.; 1 d. Educ. Eton; Trinity College, Cambridge. Member, Advisory Committee, Hongkong and Shanghai Banking Corporation, 1980-92; Deputy Chairman, Charterhouse J. Rothschild PLC, 1983-85; Member, Court, Bank of England, 1972-84; Co-Chairman, RJT and Northern PLC, 1982-83; Director, 1970, Chairman, 1975-82, Great Northern Investment Trust Ltd.; Member, Scottish Economic Council, 1972-85; Director, British Steel Corporation, 1972-76; Chairman, Patrons of National Galleries of Scotland, 1984-95; Member, Queen's Bodyguard for Scotland (Royal Company of Archers). Recreations: shooting; golf; fishing. Address: (h.) Rodinghead, Mauchline, Ayrshire.

Weir, Professor Alexander Douglas, MA, MEd, FRSA. Professor of Education, Strathclyde University, since 1993; b. 2.9.42, Falkirk; m., Alison Marion Cook; 1 s.; 1 d. Educ. Falkirk High School; Edinburgh University. Lecturer, Falkirk College of Technology, 1965-67; Senior Research Officer, Scottish Council for Research in Education, 1967-74; Lecturer, Glasgow University, 1974-79; Director, Scottish Vocational Preparation Unit, 1979-85; Director, Vocational Initiatives Unit, Glasgow University, 1985-88;

Director of Research, Jordanhill College of Education, 1988-91, Assistant Principal, 1991-93; Vice Dean (Research), 1993-97, Dean, 1997-2001, Faculty of Education, Strathclyde University. Member, National Executive, Boys' Brigade, 1976-84; Chair, Strathclyde Regional Conference of Voluntary Youth Organisations, 1991-94; author of five books and 80 articles. Recreations: walking; the arts. Address: (b.) Faculty of Education, Strathclyde University, Southbrae Drive, Glasgow G13 1PP; T.-0141-950 3200.

Weir, Michael, LLB, NP. SNP MP, Angus, since 2001; b. 24.3.57, Arbroath; m., Anne; 2 d. Educ. Arbroath High School; Aberdeen University. Myers and Wills, Montrose, 1979-81; Charles Wood and Son, Kirkcaldy, 1982-83; Myers and Wills, Montrose, 1983-84; J. & D.G. Shiell, Brechin, 1984-2001. Member, Scottish Affairs Select Committee. Address: (b.) SNP Office, Community Centre, Marketgate, Arbroath DD11 1AT; T.-01241 874522.

Weir, Tom, MBE, FRSGS. Journalist and Photographer. Former Ordnance Surveyor; climbed in the Himalayas and began professional photography; author of several books on climbing and Scotland; Presenter, Weir's Way, Scottish Television.

Weller, Professor David Paul, MBBS, MPH, PHD, FRACGP, MRCGP, FAFPHM. James Mackenzie Professor of General Practice, Edinburgh University, since 2000; b. 21.7.59, Adelaide; m., Dr Belinda Weller; 1 s.; 2 d. Educ. Prince Alfred College, Adelaide; University of Adelaide. Training and working in family medicine, UK and Australia, 1984-90; PhD studies, 1991-94; Senior Lecturer, Department of General Practice, Flinders University of South Australia, 1995-99. Board Member, Lothian Primary Care Trust, Scottish Cancer Foundation. Recreations: running; hill-walking; piano. Address: (h.) 42 Craiglea Drive, Morningside, Edinburgh EH10 5PF; T.-0131-477 9385.

Welsh, Andrew Paton, MA (Hons), DipEd. MSP (SNP), Angus, since 1999 (Convener, Audit Committee); Member, Scottish Commission for Public Accounts; National Vice-President, SNP, since 1987; MP (SNP), Angus, 1997-2001 (MP, Angus East, 1987-97); b. 19.4.44, Glasgow; m., Sheena Margaret Cannon (see Sheena Margaret Welsh); 1 d. Educ. Govan High School; Glasgow University. Member, Stirling District Council, 1974; MP (SNP), South Angus, 1974-79; SNP Parliamentary Spokesman on Housing, 1974-78 and 1987-2001, Self-Employed and Small Businesses, 1975-79 and 1987-97, Agriculture, 1975-79 and 1987-97, Education, 1997-2001; Parliamentary Chief Whip, 1977-79 and 1987-99; Member, Select Committee on Members' Interests, 1989-92; Member, House of Commons Chairmen's Panel, 1997-2001; Member, Scottish Affairs Committee, 1992-2001; SNP Executive Vice Chairman for Administration, 1979-83, for Local Government, 1984-87; Parliamentary candidate, East Angus, 1983; Member, Church and Nation Committee, Church of Scotland, 1984-85; Member, Dundee University Court, 1984-87; Provost, Angus District Council, 1984-87. Recreations: music; horse riding; languages. Address: (h.) Montquhir, Carmyllie, Arbroath; T.-01241 860317; e-mail: Andrew.Welsh.msp@scottish.parliament.uk

Wemyss and March, Earl of (Francis David Charteris), KT (1966), Hon. LLD (St. Andrews), Hon. DUniv (Edinburgh), JP, BA. Lord Lieutenant, East Lothian, 1967-87; b. 19.1.12, London; m., Mavis Lynette Gordon Murray (deceased); 1 s.; 1 d. (deceased); 1 d. (deceased); 2, Shelagh Kennedy. Educ. Eton; Balliol College, Oxford. Commissioned, Lovat Scouts (TA), 1932-44; Basutoland Administrative Service, 1937-44; War Service, African Auxiliary Pioneer Corps, Middle East, 1941-44; Chairman, Council, National Trust for Scotland, 1947-67 (President,

1967-91, President Emeritus, 1991); Chairman, Scottish Churches Council, 1964-71; Chairman, Royal Commission on Ancient and Historical Monuments of Scotland, 1949-84; Vice-President, Marie Curie Memorial Foundation; President, Royal Scottish Geographical Society, 1958-62; President, National Bible Society of Scotland, 1960-83; Lieutenant, Queen's Bodyguard for Scotland (Royal Company of Archers). Recreations: countryside and conservation. Address: (h.) Gosford House, Longniddry, East Lothian EH32 0PX; T.-01875 870200.

Werritty, Professor Alan, MA(Cantab), MS, PhD, FRSE. Professor of Physical Geography, University of Dundee, since 1994 (Head, Department of Geography, since 1996); b. 19.2.45, Derby; m., Irene; 2 s. Educ. Royal Liberty School, Romford; Magdalene College, Cambridge; Pennsylvania State University. Lecturer in Geography, University of St. Andrews, 1972; Visiting Professor, State University of New York, 1977; Senior Lecturer in Geography, University of St. Andrews, 1989. Chairman, British Geomorphological Research Group, 1998 (Member, Executive Committee); Member, Council, Royal Geographical Society, since 1998 (Member, Research Committee, Vice-President from 2003); Member, Steering Committee, International Geographical Congress, Glasgow 2004; consultant on hydrology and water resources to: EC, Scottish Executive, Scottish Natural Heritage; Member, General Synod and Mission Board, Scottish Episcopal Church. Publications: over 75 articles and book chapters on physical geography, geomorphology and hydrology. Recreations: the literature, natural history and geology of Scotland; classical music; hillwalking. Address: (b.) Department of Geography, University of Dundee, Dundee DD1 4HN; T.-01382 334484; e-mail: a.werritty@dundee.ac.uk

West, Denise May, LLB (Hons), DipLP. Managing Director, Insider Group, since 2000; Director, Scottish Daily Record and Sunday Mail Ltd., since 2000; b. 1.10.59, Aberdeen. Educ. Aberdeen High School for Girls; Harlaw Academy; Edinburgh University; Aberdeen University. Sales Promotion/Marketing Manager, Aberdeen Journals Ltd., 1984-88; self-employed Consultant, 1988-91; Press Officer, Hamilton District Council, 1990-91; Sales Promotion Manager, Thomson Regional Newspapers, 1992-94; Marketing Director, Scotsman Publications Ltd., 1994-96; Marketing Director, Trinity Mirror Midlands Operation, 1996-2000. Director, Scottish Opinion Ltd. Recreation: dog walking. Address: (b.) 7 Castle Street, Edinburgh EH2 3AH; T.-0131-535 5555.

West, Peter William Alan, MA, DUniv. Secretary to the University, Strathclyde University, since 1990; President, Institutional Management in Higher Education Programme, OECD, Paris; b. 16.3.49, Edinburgh; m., Margaret Clark; 1 s.; 1 d. Educ. Edinburgh Academy; St. Andrews University. Administrator, Edinburgh University, 1972-77; Assistant Secretary, Leeds University, 1977-83; Deputy Registrar, Strathclyde University, 1983-89. Doctor (honoris causa), University of Rostov-on-Don, Russia. Recreations: reading; drinking wine; supporting Scotland's leading football team (Hibernian) through thick and thin. Address: (b.) Strathclyde University, McCance Building, 16 Richmond Street, Glasgow G1 1XQ; T.-0141-548 2001.

Whaling, Rev. Professor Frank, BA, MA, PhD, ThD, FRAS, FABI, FWLA, FIBA, FFCS. Professor of the Study of Religion, Edinburgh University; Methodist Minister; b. 5.2.34, Pontefract; m., Norma S.H.; 1 s.; 1 d. Educ. Kings School, Pontefract; Christ's College, Cambridge; Wesley House, Cambridge; Harvard University. Methodist Minister, Birmingham Central Hall, 1960-62, Faizabad and Banaras, North India, 1962-66, Eastbourne, 1966-69; Teaching Fellow, Harvard University, 1972-73; appointed Lecturer, Study of

Religion, Edinburgh University, 1973. Theyer Honor Award, Harvard, 1970-71; various Reseach Awards; Chair, Scottish Churches China Group, 1985-93; Chair, Edinburgh Inter-Faith Association, 1989-99; Director, Edinburgh Cancer Help Centre, 1987-91; Chair, Scottish Inter-Faith Symposium, 1987-94; Director, World Without Hunger (charity); Chair, Edinburgh International Centre for World Spiritualities, 1999; Chair, Scottish Council of the World Parliament of Religions, 2000. Visiting Lecturer and Professor, USA, China, South Africa, India, England. Publications: around 100 papers, over 150 reviews; books written and/or edited: An Approach to Dialogue: Hinduism and Christianity, 1966; The Rise of the Religious Significance of Rama, 1980; John and Charles Wesley, 1981; The World's Religious Traditions: Current Perspectives in Religious Studies, 1984; Contemporary Approaches to the Study of Religion: Vol. I, 1984, Vol. II, 1985; Christian Theology and World Religions, 1986; Religion in Today's World, 1987; Compassion Through Understanding, 1990; Dictionary of Beliefs and Religions, 1992; The World: How It Came Into Being and our Responsibility for It, 1994; Theory and Method in Religious Studies, 1995; A Book of Private Prayer, 2001. Recreations: music; art; sport; inter-faith activities. Address: (h.) 79 Woodfield Avenue, Edinburgh EH13 0QP; T.-0131-441 7232.

Whalley, David William McRae, BEM. Chairman, Scottish Mountain Rescue Committee, since 1998 (Member, Executive Committee, since 1990); b. 17.12.52, Ayr. Educ. Belmont Academy; Mainholm High School. Member, Scottish Mountain Rescue and RAF Mountain Rescue, since 1973; Mountain Rescue Team Leader, RAF Leuchars, 1986-89; Team Leader, RAF Kinloss, 1989-92; has attended over 800 mountain rescues and over 80 aircraft crashes over 26 years (Senior Team Leader, Lockerbie aircraft disaster); awarded two Commendations for Services to Mountain Rescue; expeditions to Alaska, Pakistan and North Ridge of Everest, 2001; Distinguished Service Award, Mountain Rescue Committee of Scotland, 2001. Recreations: mountaineering; football; golf; tennis; photography; squash. Address: (h.) 92 Forbeshill, Forres, Moray IV36 1YL; T.-01309 674181; e-mail: heavy_whalley@hotmail.com

Whatley, Professor Christopher Allan, BA, PhD, FRHistS. Bonar Professor of Modern History and Head, Department of History, Dundee University, since 1995; b. 29.5.48, Birmingham; 1 s.; 1 d. Educ. Bearsden Academy; Strathclyde University. Lecturer, Ayr College, 1975-79, Dundee University, 1979-88, St. Andrews University, 1988-92, Dundee University, 1992-94; Senior Lecturer, 1994. Editor, Scottish Economic and Social History, 1995-99; Chairman, SCCC Review Group, Scottish History in the Curriculum; Consultant Editor, Scotland's Story; Publications: The Industrial Revolution in Scotland; The Scottish Salt Industry, 1570-1850; Onwards from Osnaburgs: the rise and progress of a Scottish textile company; Bought and Sold for English Gold?: explaining the union of 1707; The Manufacture of Scottish History (Co-editor); The Life and Times of Dundee (Co-author); The Remaking of Juteopolis: Dundee 1891-1991 (Editor); John Galt (Editor); Scottish Society 1707-1830: Beyond Jacobitism, Towards Industrialisation; Victorian Dundee: Image and Realities (Co-editor). Recreations: walking; watching Dundee United FC; theatre. Address: (h.) Tayfield Cottage, Main Street, Longforgan, by Dundee DD2 5EW; T.-01382 360794; e-mail: c.a.whatley@dundee.ac.uk

Wheater, Professor Roger John, OBE, CBiol, FIBiol, FRSA, FRSGS (Hon), FRZSS (Hon), FRSE. Chairman, National Trust for Scotland, since 2000; Director, Royal Zoological Society of Scotland, 1972-98; Honorary Professor, Edinburgh University, since 1993; b. 24.11.33, Brighton; m., Jean Ord Troup; 1 s.; 1 d. Educ. Brighton,

Hove and Sussex Grammar School; Brighton Technical College. Commissioned, Royal Sussex Regiment, 1953; served Gold Coast Regiment, 1953-54; 4/5th Bn., Royal Sussex Regiment (TA), 1954-56; Colonial Police, Uganda, 1956-61; Chief Warden, Murchison Falls National Park, 1961-70; Director, Uganda National Parks, 1970-72; Member, Co-ordinating Committee, Nuffield Unit of Tropical Animal Ecology; Member, Board of Governors, Mweka College of Wildlife Management, Tanzania; Director, National Park Lodges Ltd.; Member, Uganda National Research Council; Vice Chairman, Uganda Tourist Association; Council Member, 1980, and President, 1988-91, International Union of Directors of Zoological Gardens; Chairman, Federation of Zoological Gardens of Great Britain and Ireland, 1993-96; Chairman, Anthropoid Ape Advisory Panel, 1977-91; Member, International Zoo Year Book Editorial Board, 1987-99; President, Association of British Wild Animal Keepers, 1984-99; Chairman, Membership and Licensing Committee, 1984-91; Chairman, Working Party on Zoo Licensing Act, 1981-84; Council Member, Zoological Society of London, 1991-92, 1995-99, and since 2000; Vice President, 1999; Chairman, Whipsnade Wild Animal Park, since 1999; Vice-President, World Pheasant Association, since 1994; Trustee Dian Fossey Gorilla Fund, since 1995; Chairman, European Association of Zoos and Aquaria, 1994-97; Member of Council, National Trust for Scotland, 1973-78, and since 2000, Executive Committee, 1982-87; Chairman, Cammo Estate Advisory Committee, 1980-95; ESU William Thyne Scholar, 1975 (Trustee, Thyne Scholarship, since 1997); Assessor, Council, Scottish Wildlife Trust, 1973-92; Consultant, World Tourist Organisation (United Nations), since 1980; Member, Secretary of State for Scotland's Working Group on Environmental Education, 1990-94; Board Member, Scottish Natural Heritage, 1995-99 (Deputy Chairman, 1997-99); Chairman, Access Forum, 1996-2000; Founder Patron, Dynamic Earth, Trustee, since 1999; Vice-Chairman, Edinburgh Branch, English Speaking Union, 1977-81; President, Edinburgh Special Mobile Angling Club, 1982-86; President, Cockburn Trout Angling Club, since 1997; Chairman, Tourism and Environment Forum, since 1999; Chairman, Heather Trust, since 1999; Deputy Chairman, Zoo Forum, since 1999; Vice-President, European Network of National Heritage Organisations. Recreations: country pursuits; painting; gardening. Address: (h.) 26 Dovecot Road, Edinburgh EH12 6LE; T.-0131-334 9171; e-mail: rj@wheater.fsworld.co.uk

Wheatley, Hon. Lord (John Francis Wheatley), QC, BL. Senator, College of Justice, since 2000; b. 9.5.41, Edinburgh; m., Bronwen Catherine Fraser; 2 s. Educ. Mount St. Mary's College, Derbyshire; Edinburgh University. Called to Scottish Bar, 1966; Standing Counsel to Scottish Development Department, 1968-74; Advocate Depute, 1974-78; Sheriff, Perthshire and Kinross-shire, at Perth, 1980-98; Temporary High Court Judge, 1992; Sheriff Principal of Tayside Central and Fife, 1998-2000. Recreations: music; gardening. Address: Braefoot Farmhouse, Fossoway, Kinross-shire.

Wheeler, Sir (Harry) Anthony, Kt (1988), OBE, PPRSA, Hon. RA, Hon. RHA, Hon. RGI, Hon. DDes, Hon. RBS, PPRIAS, FRIBA, FRSA, BArch, MRTPI(rtd), DipTP. Consultant, Wheeler & Sproson, Architects and Town Planners, Edinburgh and Kirkcaldy, since 1986; Hon. President, Saltire Society, since 1995; b. 7.11.19, Stranraer; m., Dorothy Jean Campbell; 1 d. Educ. Stranraer High School; Glasgow School of Architecture; Strathclyde University. War Service, Royal Artillery, 1939-46; John Keppie Scholar and Sir Rowand Anderson Studentship, RIBA Grissell Medallist, Neale Bursar; Assistant to City Architect, Oxford, to Sir Herbert Baker & Scott, London; Senior Architect, Glenrothes Development Corporation; began private practice in Fife; Senior Lecturer, Dundee School of Architecture, 1952-58; Saltire Awards and Commendations (22), Civic Trust Awards and Commendations (12); Trustee, Scottish Civic Trust, 1970-83; Member, Royal Fine Art Commission for Scotland, 1967-85; President, Royal Scottish Academy, 1983-90. Recreations: sketching and water colours; fishing; music; drama; gardens. Address: (h.) 31/6 Kinnear Road, Edinburgh EH3 5PG.

Wheeler, Professor Simon Jonathan, MA, DPhil, CEng, MICE. Cormack Professor of Civil Engineering, Glasgow University, since 1996; b. 30.4.58, Warlingham, Surrey; m., Noelle Patricia O'Rourke; 1 s.; 2 d. Educ. Whitehaven Grammar School; St. John's College, Cambridge; Balliol College, Oxford. University Lecturer in Soil Mechanics, Queen's University of Belfast, 1984-88; Lecturer in Soil Mechanics, Sheffield University, 1988-92; Lecturer in Civil Engineering, Oxford University, and Fellow of Keble College, Oxford, 1992-95. Recreation: mountaineering. Address: (b.) Department of Civil Engineering, Rankine Building, Glasgow G12 8LT; T.-0141-330 5202.

White, Iain, BSc (Hons), MEd, MIBiol, CBiol. Head Teacher, Govan High School, Glasgow, since 1994; b. 2.2.54, Greenock; m., Gail. Educ. Greenock High School; Glasgow University. Biology Teacher, then Principal Biology Teacher, Cowdenknowes High School, Greenock, 1977-87; Assistant Rector, Rothesay Academy, 1987-92; Depute Head Teacher, Port Glasgow High School, 1992-94. Past Captain, Greenock Golf Club. Recreations: golf; skiing; travel; watching football; Robert Burns; after-dinner speaking. Address: (b.) Govan High School, 12 Ardnish Street, Glasgow G51 4NB; T.-0141-445 4464; e-mail: iainwhite@ukonline.co.uk

White, Irene. Director of Administration, Scottish National Party, since 1995; b. 16.5.42, Edinburgh; m., Douglas; 2 d. Educ. Carrickvale Secondary School; Torphichen Street Further Education Commercial College. Recreations: reading; crafts; walking. Address: (h.) 6 Muirhead Place, Penicuik EH26 0LE; T.-01968 673339.

White, Sandra. MSP (SNP), Glasgow, since 1999; b. 17.8.51, Glasgow; m.; 3 c. Educ. Garthamlock Secondary School; Glasgow College; Cardonald College. Former Councillor; Press Officer, William Wallace Society. Recreations: reading; walking; meeting people. Address: (b.) Scottish Parliament, Edinburgh EH99 1SP; T.-0131-348 5689.

White, Professor Stephen Leonard, MA, PhD, DPhil, LittD. Professor of Politics, Glasgow University, since 1991; b. 1.7.45, Dublin; m., Ishbel MacPhie; 1 s. Educ. St. Andrew's College, Dublin; Trinity College, Dublin; Glasgow University; Wolfson College, Oxford. Lecturer in Politics, Glasgow University, 1971-85, Reader, 1985-91; Head of Department, 1992-98. President, British Association for Slavonic and East European Studies, 1994-97; Chief Editor, Journal of Communist Studies and Transition Politics. Publications include: Political Culture and Soviet Politics, 1979; Britain and the Bolshevik Revolution, 1980; Origins of Detente, 1986; The Bolshevik Poster, 1988; How Russia Votes (with others), 1991; After Gorbachev, 1993; Russia Goes Dry, 1996; Values and Political Change in Postcommunist Europe (with others), 1998; Russia's New Politics, 2000; The Soviet Elite from Lenin to Gorbachev (Co-author), 2000. Address: (h.) 11 Hamilton Drive, Glasgow G12 8DN; T.-0141-334 9541.

Whitefield, Gavin, CPFA, DPA. Chief Executive, North Lanarkshire Council, since 2000; b. 7.2.56; m., Grace; 2 d. Educ. Lanark Grammar School; Bell College, Hamilton. Audit Assistant, Exchequer and Audit Department, Civil Service, 1974-76; Clydesdale District Council: Assistant Auditor, 1976-84, Computer Development Officer, 1984-86, Principal Housing Officer (Finance and Administration), 1986-89; Assistant Director of Housing (Finance and

Administration), Motherwell District Council, 1989-95; Director of Housing and Property Services, North Lanarkshire Council, 1995-2000. Recreations: hillwalking; football. Address: (b.) P.O. Box 14, Civic Centre, Motherwell ML1 1TW; T.-01698 302252.

Whitefield, Karen. MSP (Labour), Airdrie and Shotts, since 1999; b. 8.1.70, Bellshill. Educ. Calderhead High School, Shotts; Glasgow Caledonian University. Civil servant, Benefits Agency, 1991-92; PA to Rachel Squire, MP, 1992-99. Congressional Intern on Capitol Hill, 1990; Member, Labour Party's National Policy Forum. Recreations: swimming; reading; travel; cake decorating. Address: (b.) 135 Station Road, Shotts ML7 4BJ; T.-01501 822200; e-mail: karen.whitefield.msp@scottish.parliament.uk

Whiten, Professor (David) Andrew, BSc, PhD, FBPS, FRSE, FBA. Professor of Evolutionary and Developmental Psychology, St. Andrews University, since 1997, Wardlaw Professor of Psychology, since 2000; b. 20.4.48, Grimsby; m., Dr. Susie Challoner; 2 d. Educ. Wintringham School, Grimsby; Sheffield University; Bristol University; Oxford University. Research Fellow, Oxford University, 1972-75; Lecturer, then Reader, St. Andrews University, 1975-97; Visiting Professor, Zurich University, 1992, Emory University, 1996. Publications: Natural Theories of Mind, 1991; Foraging Strategies of Monkeys, Apes and Humans (Co-author), 1992; Machiavellian Intelligence II, 1997. Recreations: painting; walking; wildlife; good-lifing. Address: (b.) School of Psychology, St. Andrews University, St. Andrews KY16 9JU; e-mail: a.whiten@st-and.ac.uk

Whitley, Elizabeth Young, MA. Writer; great granny and "old crone", since 1996; Hon. Vice President, Scottish Covenanters Memorials Association; b. 26.12.15, Glasgow; m., Rev. Harry Whitley (dec.); 3s. (1 dec.); 2d. Educ. Laurelbank School, Glasgow; Glasgow University; Perugia, Italy; London School of Economics. Freelance writer and voluntary social worker since schooldays; writer for BBC radio for many years, Scots Home Service, World Service; Writer: The Bulletin, Glasgow Herald, Scots Magazine; weekly radio programme, Music For You; weekly columnist, Scottish Daily Express; ran girls' clubs and mixed clubs in Port Glasgow, Partick; Chairman, Clubs' Advisory Committee, 1959-59; Member, Faversham Committee report on A.I.D.; Member, Pilkington Committee on Broadcasting; Prospective Parliamentary Candidate, SNP, against Sir Alec Douglas Home (saved deposit). Publications: Plain Mr Knox, (biography of John Knox), 1966; The Two Kingdoms, (following research into the Covenanters). Recreations: gardening; reading; listening to silence. Address: (h.) The Glebe, Southwick, Dumfries, DG2 8AR; T.-01387 780276.

Whitley, Rev. Laurence Arthur Brown, MA, BD, PhD. Minister, Montrose Old Parish, since 1985 (Busby East and West, 1975-85); b. 19.9.49, Port Glasgow; m., Catherine MacLean MacFadyen; 1 s.; 1 d. Educ. Edinburgh Academy; Edinburgh University; St. Andrews University. Assistant Minister, St. Andrews, Dundee, 1974-75. Parliamentary candidate (SNP), Dumfriesshire, February and October, 1974. Recreation: enkenotopomachetikosis. Address: (h.) 2 Rosehill Road, Montrose, Angus DD10 8ST; T.-Montrose 672447; e-mail: labwhitley@btinternet.com

Whittemore, Professor Colin Trengove, BSc, PhD, DSc, NDA, CBiol, FIBiol, FRSE. Professor of Agriculture and Rural Economy, Edinburgh University, since 1990; b. 16.7.42, Chester; m., Chris; 1 s.; 3 d. Educ. Rydal School; Newcastle-upon-Tyne University. Lecturer in Agriculture, Edinburgh University and Head, Animal Production, Advisory and Development, Edinburgh School of Agriculture; Professor of Animal Production, Head, Animal Division, Edinburgh School of Agriculture; Head, Department of Agriculture, Edinburgh University. Sir John Hammond Memorial Prize for scientific contribution to an understanding of nutrition and growth; President, British Society of Animal Science, 1998; Royal Agricultural Society of England Gold Medal for research; Mignini Oscar; David Black Award. Publications: author of over 200 research papers and five text books of animal sciences. Recreations: skiing; riding. Address: (b.) Edinburgh University, School of Agriculture, West Mains Road, Edinburgh EH9 3JG; T.-0131-667 1041.

Whitty, Niall Richard, MA, LLB. General Editor, Stair Memorial Encyclopaedia, since 2000; Visiting Professor, Edinburgh University School of Law, since 2000; b. 28.10.37, Malaya; m., Elke M.M. Gillis; 3 s.; 1 d. Educ. Morrison's Academy, Crieff; St Andrews University; Edinburgh University. Apprenticeship, 1963-65; private practice, 1965-66; Member, legal staff, Scottish Office Solicitor's office, 1967-71; legal staff, Scottish Law Commission, 1971-94; Commissioner, Scottish Law Commission, 1995-2001. Recreations: gardening; piping; legal history. Address: (h.) St Martins, Victoria Road, Haddington EH41 4DJ; T.-0162 082 2234.

Whyte, Christopher, MA (Hons), PhD. Writer and Critic; Lecturer in Scottish Literature, Glasgow University, 1990-2001, Reader, since 2001; b. 29.10.52, Glasgow. Educ. St. Aloysius College, Glasgow; Pembroke College, Cambridge. Lector, Rome University, 1977-85; Lecturer in English Literature, Edinburgh University, 1986-89. Publications: In The Face of Eternity: Eight Gaelic Poets, 1991; Uirsgeul/Myth, 1991; Euphemia MacFarrigle and the Laughing Virgin, 1995; Gendering the Nation, 1995; The Warlock of Strathearn, 1997; The Gay Decameron, 1998; The Cloud Machinery, 2000. Recreations: classical music; walking; cooking. Address: (h.) 15 Hart Street, Edinburgh EH1 3RN; T.-0131-558 3907.

Whyte, Donald, JP, FHG, FSG (Hon). Consultant Genealogist, Author and Lecturer; b. 13.3.26, Newtongrange; m., Mary Burton (deceased); 3 d. Educ. Crookston School, Musselburgh; Institute of Heraldic and Genealogical Studies, Canterbury. Agricultural and horticultural work, 1940-68; professional genealogist, 1968-76; Member, Kirkliston and Winchburgh District Council, 1964-75 (Chairman, 1970-73); Member, West Lothian County Council, 1970-75; founder Member and Vice-President, Scottish Genealogy Society; President, Association of Scottish Genealogists and Record Agents, since 1981. Publications: Kirkliston: A Short Parish History; Dictionary of Scottish Emigrants to USA (two volumes); Introducing Scottish Genealogical Research; Dictionary of Scottish Emigrants to Canada before Confederation, 2 vols; Walter MacFarlane: Clan Chief and Antiquary; Scottish Clock and Watchmakers, 1453-1900; Scottish Surnames and Families. Address: (h.) 4 Carmel Road, Kirkliston EH29 9DD; T.-0131-333 3245.

Whyte, Professor Iain Boyd, BA, MPhil, MA, PhD, FRSE, FRSA. Professor of Architectural History, Department of Architecture, Edinburgh University, since 1996; b. 6.3.47, Bexley; m., Deborah Smart; 1 s.; 1 d. Educ. St Dunstan's College; Nottingham University; Cornell University; Cambridge University; Leeds University. Lecturer, then Reader, then Professor of Architectural History, Edinburgh University; External Examiner: Courtauld Institute of Art, National University of Singapore, University College London. Getty Scholar, 1989-90; Getty Grant Ingram Senior Scholar, 1998-2000; Trustee, National Galleries of Scotland; Member, Selection Committee, 23rd Council of Europe exhibition, 1995-96; extensive publications on architectural and art history. Recreations: music; rowing. Address: (b.) Department of Architecture, 20 Chambers Street, Edinburgh EH1 1JZ; T.-0131-650 2322.

Whyte, Iain Wilson, BA, DCE, DMS. Director and General Secretary, Church of Scotland Board of Parish Education, since 1993; b. 2.12.56, Johnstone; m., Elaine; 2 d. Educ. Paisley Grammar School; Jordanhill College; Open University. Adult Education Tutor, Glasgow, 1978-82; Development Officer, Priesthill, Glasgow, 1982-84; Adult Education Officer, European Social Fund Project, Strathclyde, 1984-86; Lecturer, Cardonald College, Glasgow, 1986-90, Senior Lecturer, 1990-93. Elder, Colinton Parish Church, Edinburgh. Recreations: playing guitar, piano, organ; singing; songwriting; golf. Address: (b.) 21 Young Street, Edinburgh EH2 4HU; T.-08702 415748.

Whyte, Rev. James, BD, DipCE. Parish Minister, Broom, Newton Mearns, since 1987; b. 26.4.46, Glasgow; m., Norma Isabella West; 1 s.; 2 d. Educ. Glasgow; Jordanhill College; Glasgow University. Trained as planning engineer; studied community education (Glasgow and Boston, Mass., USA); Community Organiser with Lamp of Lothian Collegiate Trust, Haddington; Organiser of Community Education, Dumbarton, 1971-73; Assistant Principal Community Education Officer, Renfrew Division, Strathclyde Region, 1973-77; entered ministry, Church of Scotland, 1977; Assistant Minister: Barrhead Arthurlie, 1977-78, St. Marks, Oldhall, Paisley, 1978-80; Minister, Coupar Angus Abbey, 1981-87. Recreations: gardening; reading. Address: Manse of Broom, 3 Laigh Road, Newton Mearns, Glasgow G77; T.-0141-639 2916.

Whyte, Very Rev. Professor James Aitken, MA, LLD, DD, DUniv. Moderator, General Assembly of the Church of Scotland, 1988-89; Professor of Practical Theology and Christian Ethics, St. Andrews University, 1958-87; b. 28.1.20, Leith; m., 1, Elisabeth Wilson Mill (deceased); 2 s.; 1 d.; 2, Ishbel Christina Macaulay or Rathie. Educ. Daniel Stewart's College, Edinburgh; Edinburgh University. Ordained and commissioned as Chaplain to the Forces, 1945; Minister: Dunollie Road Church, Oban, 1948-54, Mayfield North Church, Edinburgh, 1954-58; Dean of Divinity, St. Andrews University, 1968-72; Principal, St. Mary's College, 1978-82; Kerr Lecturer, Glasgow University, 1969-72; Croall Lecturer, Edinburgh University, 1972-73; Hon. LLD, Dundee University, 1981; Hon.DD, St. Andrews University, 1989; Hon. DUniv., Stirling University, 1994; President, Society for the Study of Theology, 1983-84; Margaret Harris Lecturer, Dundee University, 1990. Publications: Laughter and Tears, 1993; The Dream and the Grace, 2001. Address: (h.) 13 Hope Street, St. Andrews, Fife; T.-St. Andrews 472323.

Whyte, Richard Brodie, LLB, MSc, DFM, SSC, NP. Solicitor Advocate, since 1995; Solicitor, since 1981; Part-time Legal Chairman, Appeals Service; Consultant, Adams Whyte, since 2000; b. 1.8.47, Edinburgh; m., Gail; 2 s.; 1 d. Educ. Broxburn High School; Edinburgh University; Glasgow University. Electrician, 1963-76. PhD student, Medical Faculty, Edinburgh University. Recreations: reading; watching and supporting Hibs; cinema; golf; playing poker; attending the Cheltenham Festival; wandering around art galleries. Address: (b.) Lammermuir House, Livingston EH54 6NB; T.-01506 415281.

Whyte, Robert, MB, ChB, FRCPsych, DPM. Consultant Psychotherapist, Carswell House, Glasgow, 1979-2000; b. 1.6.41, Edinburgh; m., Susan Frances Milburn; 1 s.; 1 d. Educ. George Heriot's, Edinburgh; St. Andrews University. House Officer in Surgery, Arbroath Infirmary, 1966; House Officer in Medicine, Falkirk and District Royal Infirmary, 1967; Trainee in Psychiatry, Dundee Psychiatric Services, 1967-73; Consultant Psychiatrist, Duke Street Hospital, Glasgow, 1973. Past Chairman, Scottish Association of Psychoanalytical Psychotherapists; Member, Scottish Institute of Human Relations. Address: (h.) Waverley, 70 East Kilbride Road, Busby, Glasgow G76 8HU; T.-0141-644 1659.

Wickham-Jones, Caroline R., MA, MIFA, FSA, FSA Scot, FFCS. Archaeologist; b. 25.4.55, Middlesborough; m.; 1 s. Educ. Teesside High School; Edinburgh University. Freelance archaeologist and author with research interests in early (postglacial) settlement of Scotland, stone tools, and the preservation of the cultural heritage; former Council Member, National Trust for Scotland; Council Member, Institute of Field Archaeologists, 1986-90; former Secretary, Society of Antiquaries of Scotland; former Trustee, John Muir Trust; Livery Woman of the City of London (Skinners Company); Honorary Post Doctoral Research Fellow, University of Edinburgh. Publications: Scotland's First Settlers; Arthurs Seat and Holyrood Park, a Visitor's Guide; Orkney, an Historical Guide; The Landscape of Scotland, a hidden history. Recreations: travel; wilderness walking; socialising. Address: (h.) 21 Dudley Gardens, Edinburgh EH6 4PU; e-mail: c.wickham-jones@dial.pipex.com

Wight, Robin A.F., MA, FCA, CA. Chairman, Arville Holdings, since 1995; b. 5.6.38, Edinburgh; m., Sheila; 3 s.; 1 d. Educ. Dollar Academy; Magdalene College, Cambridge. Partner, Coopers & Lybrand, 1971-96; Regional Partner, Scotland, 1977-95; Member, Executive Committee, 1978-87; Member, Governing Board, 1987-89; Member, Council, 1989-93. Recreations: skiing; golf; rugby (watching); reading; bridge; theatre. Address: (h.) 22 Regent Terrace, Edinburgh; T.-0131-556 2100; e-mail: robin.wight@btinternet.com

Wightman, John Watt, CVO, CBE, RD, MA, LLB, WS, NP. Chairman, Morton Fraser Partnership, 1988-99; Solicitor to H. M. The Queen in Scotland, 1984-99; Chairman, Craig & Rose PLC, 1993-2000; b. 20.11.33, Leith; m., Isla Macleod; 1 s.; 2 d. Educ. Daniel Stewart's College; St. Andrews University; Edinburgh University. Morton Fraser Partnership, 1960-99 (Partner, then Finance Director). Commodore, Royal Naval Reserve, 1982-85; Chairman, Lowland TAVRA, 1992-95; Elder, St. George's West Church; Trustee: Earl Haig Fund for Scotland, Douglas Haig Memorial Homes. Recreations: sailing; fishing; ornithology. Address: 10 Ann Street, Edinburgh EH4 1PJ; T.-0131-332 6463.

Wightman, Very Rev. William David, BA (Hons). Provost, St. Andrews Cathedral, Aberdeen, since 1991, also Priest-in-Charge, St. Ninian's, Aberdeen; Hon. Canon, Christchurch Cathedral, Hartford, Conn., since 1991; b. 29.1.39, Leicester; m., Karen Elizabeth Harker; 2 s.; 2 d. Educ. Alderman Newton's Grammar School, Leicester; George Dixon Grammar School, Birmingham; Birmingham University; Wells Theological College. Ordained Deacon, 1963; ordained Priest, 1964. Director, Training for Ministry (Diocese of Aberdeen and Orkney), 1989-91. Recreations: fishing; swimming; choral music. Address: (h.) 15 Morningfield Road, Aberdeen AB15 4AP; T.-01224 314765.

Wilcox, Christine Alison, BA (Hons), ALA. Librarian, S.S.C. Library, Edinburgh, since 1991; b. 18.7.63, New Zealand; m., Michael Wilcox; 2 s.; 1 d. Educ. South Wilts Grammar School, Salisbury; Manchester Polytechnic Library School. Assistant Librarian, Barlow Lyde and Barlow Gilbert, Solicitors, London, 1984-86; Librarian, Beaumont and Son, Solicitors, London, 1986-89; posting to Bahrain accompanying husband, 1989-91. Secretary, Scottish Law Librarians Group, 1993-95. Publications: Directory of Legal Libraries in Scotland; Union List of Periodical and Law Report Holdings in Scotland. Recreations: needlework; hill-walking. Address: (b.) S.S.C. Library, 11 Parliament Square, Edinburgh EH1 1RF; T.-0131-225 6268; e-mail: christine.wilcox@dial.pipex.com

Wild, John Robin, JP, BDS, DPD, FDSRCS(Edin), DGDP. Chief Dental Officer, Department of Health, 1997-2000; b. 12.9.41, Scarborough; m., Eleanor Daphne Kerr; 1

s.; 2 d. Educ. Sedbergh School; Edinburgh University; Dundee University. General Dental Practitioner, Scarborough, 1965-71; Dental Officer, East Lothian, 1971-74;Chief Administrative Dental Officer, Borders Health Board, 1974-87; Regional Dental Postgraduate Adviser, S.E. Regional Committee for Postgraduate Medical Education, 1982-87; Deputy Chief Dental Officer, 1987-93, then Chief Dental Officer and Director of Dental Services for the NHS in Scotland, 1993-97, Scottish Office Department of Health; Hon. Senior Lecturer, Dundee Dental School, since 1993; JP for District of Ettrick and Lauderdale, since 1982; Past Chairman, Scottish Council, British Dental Association; Vice President, Commonwealth Dental Association, since 1997; President, Council of European Chief Dental Officers, 1999-2000; Chairman, Scottish Borders Justices Committee, since 2000. Recreations: vintage cars (restoration and driving); music; gardening. Address: (h.) Braehead House, St. Boswells, Roxburghshire; T.-01835 823203.

Wildgoose, James Richmond, BSc, DPhil. Head of CAP Management Division, Rural Affairs Department, Scottish Executive; b. 17.4.49, Edinburgh; m., Charlotte Dorothy; 1 s.; 1 d. Educ. Melville College; Edinburgh University; Oxford University. Economic Assistant/Economic Adviser, Ministry of Agriculture, Fisheries and Food, 1976-86; Administrative Principal, MAFF Tropical Foods Division, 1986-90; Administrative Principal, Scottish Office (SDD), then Chief Agricultural Economist; Head of Food Safety and Standards Division, Scottish Office Agriculture, Environment and Fisheries Department. Address: (b.) Room 202, Pentland House, Robb's Loan, Edinburgh; T.-0131-244 6159.

Wildsmith, Professor John Anthony Winston, MD, FRCA, FRCPEd. Foundation Professor of Anaesthesia, Dundee University, since 1995; Honorary Consultant Anaesthetist, Tayside University Hospitals Trust; b. 22.2.46, Newent, Glos; m., Angela Fay Smith; 3 d. Educ. King's School, Gloucester; Edinburgh University Medical School. Spent greater part of early professional career in Edinburgh, either at University or Royal Infirmary, apart from a year at Brigham and Women's Hospital, Boston, USA; final posts in Edinburgh, Consultant/Senior Lecturer and Clinical Director for Anaesthetics, Intensive Care and Operating Theatres, Royal Infirmary, Edinburgh, 1992-95. Member, Council, Royal College of Anaesthetists; Member, Editorial Board, British Journal of Anaesthesia. Recreations: golf; wine; travel. Address: (b.) University Department of Anaesthesia, Ninewells Hospital and Medical School, Dundee DD1 9SY; T.-01382 632427; e-mail: j.a.w.wildsmith@dundee.ac.uk

Wilkes, John, BSc (Hons). Director, Equal Opportunities Commission (Scotland), since 2001; Member, Scotland Committee, Community Fund (formerly National Lotteries Charities Board), since 1999; b. 9.2.60; partner, Ian Corcoran. Educ. Keele University. Engineer, Marconi, 1981-83; Engineer, National Semiconductor, 1983-85; Sales/Marketing, BOC Group, 1985-93; Manager (West of Scotland), Scottish Aids Monitor, 1993-95; Chief Executive, Place West, 1995-99; Director Scotland, Carers UK, 1999-2001. Chair, Glasgow Gay and Lesbian Centre, 1995-98; Chair, Glasgow Council for Voluntary Sector, 1999-2001. Recreations: theatre; cinema; swimming. Address: (b.) St Stephen's House, 279 Bath Street, Glasgow G2 4JL; T.-0845 6015901.

Wilkie, Agnes, BA. Head of Features, Scottish Television; b. 6.4.56, Scotland; m., R.B. Steven; 1 d. Educ. Hamilton Academy; Strathclyde University. Editorial Assistant, D.C. Thomson, Dundee; Reporter/Women's Editor, Scottish Farmer; Features Editor, Horse and Hound; Freelance Writer/Broadcaster, Brussels; Editor, Oracle Regional Teletext; Researcher/News Producer, Scottish Television.

Recreations: keeping fit; horse riding. Address: (b.) Scottish Television, Scottish Media Group Plc, 200 Renfield Street, Glasgow, G2 3PR; T.-0141 300 3000.

Wilkie, Alex Joseph. Managing Director, Radio Forth Ltd., since 2000; b. 8.7.48, Stirling; m., Jill; 2 s. Educ. Royal High School of Stirling; Falkirk Technical College; Telford College. Sterlini Radio Ltd., 1963-69; Graham and Morton, 1969-70; Callander Park College (CCTV), 1970-74; Radio Forth Ltd., 1974-86; Managing Director, Radio Tay Ltd., 1991-2000. Board Member: Central FM, Radio Borders, Moray Firth Radio; President, Dundee and Tayside Chamber of Commerce and Industry, 2000-01; Member, School Board, Inverkeithing High School. Recreations: boating; fishing; clay pigeon shooting; youth football; reading. Address: (h.) 21 Glamis Gardens, Dalgety Bay, Fife KY11 5TD; T.-01383 823600.

Wilkie, Professor (William) Roy, MA. Emeritus Professor, Department of Human Resource Management, Strathclyde University, since 1974; b. 10.6.30, Rutherglen; m., Jill Henzell; 1 s.; 3 d. Educ. Rutherglen Academy; Aberdeen University. Lecturer and Senior Lecturer, Department of Administration, Strathclyde University, 1963-66; Director, J. & J. Denholm (Management) Ltd., 1966-70; Reader and Head, Department of Administration, Strathclyde University, 1966-73. Publications: The Concept of Organization, 1974; Managing the Police, 1986. Recreations: swimming; movies; jazz; reading. Address: (b.) Graham Hill Building, 50 Richmond Street, Glasgow; T.-0141-552 4400.

Wilkin, Andrew, BA, MA, MIL. Senior Lecturer in Italian Studies, University of Strathclyde, since 1986; b. 30.5.44, Farnborough; m., Gaynor Carole Gray; 1 s.; 1 d. (also 1 s.; 1 d. by pr. m.). Educ. Royal Naval School, Malta; University of Manchester; Open University. Assistant Lecturer, then Lecturer in Italian Studies, University of Strathclyde, 1967-86; Associate Dean, Faculty of Arts and Social Sciences, 1986-93; Course Director, BA European Studies, 1989-97. Governor, Craigie College of Education, 1985-91; Editor, Tuttitalia, 1992-97; Member, Modern Languages Panel, UCAS Scotland, 1993-2000. Publications: Harrap's Italian Verbs (Compiler), 1990; G. Verga, Little Novels of Sicily (Editor), 1973; 25 Years Emancipation? – Women in Switzerland 1971-96 (Co-Editor), 1997. Invested Cavaliere dell'Ordine al Merito della Repubblica Italiana, 1975; Elder, St. David's Memorial Park Church, Kirkintilloch. Recreations: travel; reading; Scottish History; supporting Partick Thistle F. C. Address: (b.) Department of Modern Languages, University of Strathclyde, Glasgow G1 1XH; T.-0141-548 3914; e-mail: andrew.wilkin@strath.ac.uk

Wilkins, Professor Malcolm Barrett, BSc, PhD, DSc, AKC, FRSE. Regius Professor of Botany, Glasgow University, 1970-2000, now Emeritus Professor (Dean, Faculty of Science, 1985-88; Member, University Court, 1993-97); b.27.2.33, Cardiff; m., Mary Patricia Maltby; 1 s.; 1 d. (deceased). Educ. Monkton House School, Cardiff; King's College, London University. Lecturer in Botany, King's College, London, 1958-64; Lecturer in Biology, then Professor of Biology, East Anglia University, 1964-67; Professor of Plant Physiology, Nottingham University, 1967-70. Rockefeller Foundation Fellow, Yale University, 1961-62; Corporation Research Fellow, Harvard University, 1962-63; Darwin Lecturer, British Association for the Advancement of Science, 1967; elected Corresponding (Honorary) Member, American Society of Plant Physiologists, 1984; Chairman, Life Science Working Group, European Space Agency, 1987-89; Trustee, Royal Botanic Garden, Edinburgh, 1990-99, Chairman, 1994-99; Vice President, Royal Society of Edinburgh, 1994-97; Member, Advisory Council, Scottish Agricultural College, since 1992. Recreations: fishing; model engineering. Address: (b.) IBLS, Bower Building, Glasgow University, Glasgow G12 8QQ; T.-0141-330 4450.

Wilkinson, Sheriff Alexander Birrell, QC, MA, LLB. Sheriff of Lothian and Borders at Edinburgh, 1996-2001; Sheriff of Glasgow and Strathkelvin at Glasgow, 1991-96; Temporary Judge, Court of Session, since 1993; b. 2.2.32, Perth; m., Wendy Imogen Barrett; 1 s.; 1 d. Educ. Perth Academy; St. Andrews University; Edinburgh University. Advocate, 1959; practised at Scottish Bar, 1959-69; Lecturer in Scots Law, Edinburgh University, 1965-69; Sheriff of Stirling, Dunbarton and Clackmannan, at Stirling and Alloa, 1969-72; Professor of Private Law, Dundee University, 1972-86 (Dean, Faculty of Law, 1974-76 and 1986); Sheriff of Tayside, Central and Fife at Falkirk, 1986-91; a Chairman, Industrial Tribunals (Scotland), 1972-86; Chancellor, Dioceses of Brechin, 1990-98, and of Argyll and the Isles, 1985-98, Scottish Episcopal Church; Chairman, Scottish Marriage Guidance Council, 1974-77; Chairman, Legal Services Group, Scottish Association of CAB, 1979-83; President, The Sheriffs' Association, since 1997. Publications: Gloag and Henderson's Introduction to the Law of Scotland, 8th and 9th editions (Co-editor); The Scottish Law of Evidence; The Law of Parent and Child in Scotland (Co-author); Macphail's Sheriff Court Practice, 2nd Edition (Contributor). Recreations: collecting books and pictures; reading; travel.

Wilkinson, Professor John Eric, BSc, MEd, PhD, CPsychol, FRSA. Professor of Education, Glasgow University, since 1998; Director, Higher Degrees, Glasgow University, since 1999; b. 22.5.44, Lancashire; 2 s.; 1 d. Educ. Accrington Grammar School; St Andrews University; Dundee University; Glasgow University. Assistant Master, Brockehurst Sixth Form College, 1968-70; Research Assistant, Nottingham University, 1970-72; Glasgow University: Lecturer, Education, 1973-91; Senior Lecturer, 1991-98; Head of Department, 1995-99. Publications: numerous journal articles and book chapters. Recreations: art collecting; hill walking; ballet appreciation; swimming. Address: (b.) Department of Educational Studies, Glasgow University; (h.) Flat 4, 17 Crown Terrace, Glasgow, G12 9ES.

Wilkinson, Professor Paul, MA. Professor of International Relations, St. Andrews University; Director, Centre for the Study of Terrorism and Political Violence, St. Andrews University; Writer on conflict and terrorism; b. 9.5.37, Harrow, Middlesex; m., Susan; 2 s.; 1 d. Educ. John Lyon School; University College, Swansea; University of Wales. RAF, 1959-65; Assistant Lecturer in Politics, University College, Cardiff, 1966-68; University of Wales: Lecturer, 1968-75, Senior Lecturer, 1975-77, Reader in Politics, 1978-79; Professor of International Relations, Aberdeen University, 1979-89; Editor, Terrorism and Political Violence; Member, Editorial Board, Security Handbook, Social Intelligence, Violence and Aggression, Studies in Conflict and Terrorism, Risk Management: An International Journal; Editor, Key Concepts in International Relations; Scottish Free Enterprise Award, 1982; Honorary Fellow, University College, Swansea, 1986; Special Consultant, CBS America, 1989-90, BBC, since 1989; Aviation Security Adviser to IFAPA, 1988; Safety Adviser, World Tourism and Travel Council; FRSA, 1995; Visiting Fellow, Trinity Hall, Cambridge, 1997-98; Special Adviser, House of Commons Select Committee on Defence, since 2001. Publications: Social Movement, 1971; Political Terrorism, 1974; Terrorism and the Liberal State, 1986 (revised edition); The New Fascists, 1983; Terrorism: Theory and Practice (Co-author), 1979; British Perspectives on Terrorism (Editor), 1981; Contemporary Research on Terrorism (Joint Editor), 1987; Technology and Terrorism (Editor), 1994; Terrorism: British Perspectives (Editor), 1993; Research Report for Inquiry into Legislation Against

Terrorism, Vol. II, 1996; Aviation Terrorism and Security (Joint Editor); Terrorism Versus Democracy: The Liberal State Response, 2000. Recreations: modern art; poetry; walking. Address: (b.) Department of International Relations, St. Andrews University, St. Andrews KY16 9AL; T.-01334 462900.

Wilks, Antony Hugh Francis, MBE, FNI. Chairman, Scottish Coastal Forum; Chairman, Forth Estuary Forum; Member, Board, Scottish Environment Protection Agency (East); Trustee, Scottish Coastal Heritage Trust; Direct, CoastNet; b. 29.12.36, Watford; m., Susan Chaloner Reed; 1 s.; 1 d. Educ. Oundle. Royal Navy, 1958-90, latterly Naval Base Commander, Rosyth, 1985-90. Contributor, The Naval Review; knighthood, State of Brunei. Recreation: music. Address: (b.) Easter Fossoway, Kinross-shire KY13 0PA; T.-01577 840255.

Will, David Houston, BL, NP. Vice-President, FIFA, since 1990 (Chairman, Legal Matters Committee, Member, Executive Committee and World Cup Organising Committee); b. 20.11.36, Glasgow; m., Margaret; 2 d. Educ. Brechin High School; Edinburgh University. Chairman, Brechin City FC, 1966-91; appointed to SFA Council, 1970; President, SFA, 1984-89; Vice-President, UEFA, 1986-90. Recreations: golf; curling. Address: (h.) Ingledene, 13 Latch Road, Brechin, Angus; T.-01356 622273.

Willett, Emeritus Professor Frank, CBE, MA, FRSE. Hon. Senior Research Fellow, since 1990, Director, Hunterian Museum & Art Gallery, Glasgow, 1976-90; b. 18.8.25, Bolton; m., Mary Constance Hewitt; 1 s.; 3 d. Educ. Bolton Municipal Secondary School; University College, Oxford. Keeper of Ethnology and General Archaeology, Manchester Museum, 1950-58; Government Archaeologist, Nigeria, 1958-63; Leverhulme Research Fellow, 1964; Research Fellow, Nuffield College, Oxford, 1964-66; Professor of Art History, African Studies and Interdisciplinary Studies, Northwestern University, Evanston, Illinois, 1966-76; Visiting Fellow, Clare Hall, Cambridge, 1970-71; Hon. Corresponding Member, Manchester Literary and Philosophical Society, since 1958; Vice Chairman, Scottish Museums Council, 1986-89; Fellow, Royal Anthropological Institute; Fellow, Royal Society of Edinburgh, 1979, Curator, RSE, 1992-97; Bicentenary Medal, RSE, 1999; Leadership Award, Arts Council of the African Studies Association, 1995. Publications: Ife in the History of West African Sculpture, 1967; African Art: An Introduction, 1971; Treasures of Ancient Nigeria, Co-author, 1980. Recreation: walking. Address: (b.) Hunterian Museum, University of Glasgow, Glasgow G12 8QQ; T.-0141-330 4221.

Willetts, Professor Brian Benjamin, MA, PhD, CEng, FICE, FRSE. Professor Emeritus of Engineering, Aberdeen University; b. 12.6.36, Old Hill; m., Patricia Margaret Jones; 1 s.; 1 d. Educ. King Edward VI School, Stourbridge; Emmanuel College, Cambridge. Assistant Engineer, City of Birmingham, 1959-61; Executive Engineer, Government of Northern Nigeria, 1961-63; Lecturer/Senior Lecturer, Lanchester Polytechnic, 1963-66; Aberdeen University: Lecturer/Senior Lecturer, 1967-85, Professor of Civil Engineering, 1985-2001. Address: (h.) Grove, 24 Broomlands, Kelso, Roxburghshire TD5 7PR; T.-01573 225968.

Williams, Sir Alwyn, Kt, PhD, FRS, FRSE, MRIA, FGS, Hon. FRCPS, Hon. DSc, Hon. LLD. Honorary Research Fellow, Department of Geology, Glasgow University (Principal and Vice-Chancellor, Glasgow University, 1976-88); Non-Executive Director, Scottish Daily Record and Sunday Mail Ltd., 1984-90; b. 8.6.21, Aberdare, Wales; m., Edythe Joan Bevan; 1 s.; 1 d. Educ. Aberdare Boys' Grammar School; University College of Wales, Aberystwyth. Commonwealth Fund Fellow, US National

Museum, 1948-50; Lecturer in Geology, Glasgow University, 1950-54; Professor of Geology, Queen's University, Belfast, 1954-74; Lapworth Professor of Geology, Birmingham University, 1974-76; Chairman, Scottish Hospital Endowments Research Trust, 1989-96; Member, Scottish Tertiary Education Advisory Council, 1984-86; President, Palaeontological Association, 1968-70; President, Royal Society of Edinburgh, 1985-88; Trustee and Chairman, Board of British Museum (Natural History), 1971-79; Chairman, Committee on National Museums and Galleries of Scotland, 1979-81; Honorary Fellow, Geological Society of America, since 1970; Foreign Member, Polish Academies of Science, since 1981; Hon. DSc, Universities of Wales, Queen's (Belfast) and Edinburgh; Hon. DCL, Oxford; Hon. LLD, Glasgow, Strathclyde; Hon. DUniv, Paisley; Hon. FRSAMD; Hon. FDS RCPSG; Hon. FRCPSG; Fellow, University College of Wales. Address: (h.) 25 Sutherland Avenue, Pollokshields, Glasgow G41 4HG; T.-0141-427 0589.

Williams, Colin, OBE. Director (Scotland), Princess Royal Trust for Carers, since 1991; b. 1.1.40, Aberdare; m., Margaret Ann McFarlane; 1 s.; 1 d. Educ. Aberdare Boys' Grammar School; London School of Economics; Bryn Mawr College, Philadelphia. Coal mining industry, 10 years; Scottish Office (Social Work Adviser), four years; Director, Glasgow Council for Voluntary Service, 17 years. Lay Member, Greater Glasgow Health Board, eight years; Trustee, Community Development Foundation; Chair, Scottish Community Development Centre. Recreations: gardening; music; hill-walking; cinema; reading. Address: 50 Kelvin Drive, Glasgow G20 8QN; T.-0141-946 4538.

Williams, Craig David, MA (Hons), PGDJ. Editor, Newsnight Scotland, BBC, since 2001; b. 9.8.71, Edinburgh; partner, Pauline McLean. Educ. Royal High School, Edinburgh; University of Edinburgh; Strathclyde University. Reporter: Border Telegraph, 1994-95, Radio Borders, 1995-96, Radio Forth, 1996-97; Producer, BBC Scotland News and Current Affairs, 1997-2000; Media Correspondent, Business am, 2000-01. Contributor, Scotland on Sunday (books pages). Address: (b.) BBC Scotland, Queen Margaret Drive, Glasgow G12 8DG; T.-0141-338 3440; e-mail: craig.williams@bbc.co.uk

Williams, Professor Howard Peter, MSc. Professor, Management Science Department, Strathclyde University, since 1990; Director, Network and Resource Management Centre; b. 27.2.54, St. Albans. Educ. Exeter University; Newcastle upon Tyne University. Economist, ICI Plant Protection Division, International Wool Secretariat, British Ship Research Association; Senior Research Fellow, Newcastle-upon-Tyne University. Expert Advisor, European Commission on Telecommunications Regulation. Recreations: windsurfing; opera; breadmaking. Address: (b.) Department of Management Science, Sir Graham Hills Building, Strathclyde University, Glasgow G1 1XH; T.-0141-548 3141; e-mail: Howard@mansci.strath.ac.uk

Williams, Professor Jeffrey Graham, BSc, PhD, FRSE. Professor of Developmental Biology, Dundee University, since 1998; Wellcome Trust Principal Research Fellow; b. 5.11.48, Tredegar; m., Dr Natalia Zhukovskaya; 2 s.; 2 d. Educ. Abertillery Grammar School; Kings College, London. Harkness Fellow/Postdoctoral Fellow, MIT (Boston, USA), 1973-75; Staff Scientist, ICRF, 1975-94; Jodrell Professor of Anatomy, UCL, 1994-98. Member, CRC Scientific Committee, 1992-94; Member, MRC Molecular and Cellular Medicine Board, since 1998. Recreations: squash; golf; guitar. Address: (b.) MSI/WTB Complex, Dundee University, Dow Street, Dundee DD1 5EH; T.-01382 345823.

Williams, John, QFSM, BSc, MIFireE, MCGI. Firemaster, Grampian Fire Brigade, since 1998; b. 28.2.54, Carmarthen, Wales; m., Yvette; 3 d. Educ. Gwendraeth Grammar School. Joined Dyfed Fire Brigade, 1974: Leading Firefighter, 1978, Sub Officer, 1979, Station Officer, 1983, Assistant Divisional Officer – Emergency Planning, 1987, Divisional Officer – Deputy Senior Fire Safety Officer, 1988, Divisional Officer – Senior Fire Safety Officer, 1993; Senior Divisional Officer – Area Commander, Mid and West Wales Fire Brigade, 1996; Deputy Firemaster, Grampian Fire Brigade, 1997. Chairman, Grampian Princes Trust Management Board; Member, Board of Trustees, Common Purpose, Aberdeen. Recreations: rugby football; DIY; golf; walking. Address: (h.) 15 Crombie Place, Westhill, Aberdeen AB32 6PX, T.-01224 749114; (b.) 19 North Anderson Drive, Aberdeen AB15 6DW, T.-01224 696666.

Williams, Professor Morgan Howard, BSc Hons, PhD, DSc, CEng, FBCS, FRSA. Professor of Computer Science, Heriot-Watt University, since 1980 (Head of Department, 1980-88); b. 15.12.44, Durban; 2 s. Educ. Grey High School, Port Elizabeth; Rhodes University, Grahamstown. Physicist in Antarctic Expedition, 1968-69; Rhodes University: Lecturer in Computer Science, 1970-72, Senior Lecturer, 1972-77, Professor and Head of Department, 1977-80. Address: Department of Computing and Electrical Engineering, Heriot-Watt University, Riccarton, Edinburgh EH14 4AS; T.-0131-451 3430.

Williams, Roger Bevan, PhD, BMus, FRCO, FTCL, ARCM, PGCE, FGMS. Conductor, Composer, Musician; Director of Music and Organist, University of Aberdeen, since 1991; Head, Music Department, University of Aberdeen, since 1988; b. 30.8.43, Swansea; m., Ann Therese Brennan; 1 s.; m., Katherine Ellen Smith; 2 s.; 1 d. Educ. Mirfield Grammar School, Yorkshire; Huddersfield School of Music; University College, Cardiff; Goldsmiths' College, University of London; King's College, Cambridge. Assistant Organist, Holy Trinity Church, Brompton, 1971; Lecturer, 1971, Director, 1973-75, Chiswick Music Centre; Organist, St. Patrick's Church, Soho, 1973; Musical Director, Sacred Heart Church, Wimbledon, 1975; Lecturer, West London Institute, 1975-78; Organist, Our Lady of Victories, Kensington, 1978-97; Lecturer, University of Aberdeen, 1978-88; Chorus Master, SNO Chorus, 1984-88; Harpsichordist, Aberdeen Sinfonietta, since 1988; first recording of Arne's Six Organ Concertos, 1988; Music at Castle Fraser: catalogue, 1995, CDs, 1997; numerous compositions, editions, catalogues of music holdings in North East Scotland. Recreations: board games; cooking; gardening. Address: (h.) The Old Hall, Barthol Chapel, Oldmeldrum, Inverurie AB51 8TD; T.-01651 806634.

Williamson, Professor Edwin Henry, MA, PhD. Forbes Professor of Hispanic Studies, Edinburgh University, since 1990; b. 2.10.49; m., Susan Jane Fitchie; 2 d. Educ. Edinburgh University. Lecturer in Spanish, Trinity College, Dublin, 1974-77; Lecturer in Spanish, Birkbeck College, London, 1977-90. Visiting Professor: University of Sao Paulo, Brazil, 1996, Stanford University, California, 1999. Publications: The Half-Way House of Fiction: Don Quixote and Arthurian Romance, 1984; El Quijote Y Los Libros de Caballerias, 1991; The Penguin History of Latin America, 1992; Cervantes and the Modernists, 1994. Recreations: theatre; art; film; hill-walking. Address: (b.) School of European Languages and Cultures (Hispanic Studies), Edinburgh University, David Hume Tower, George Square, Edinburgh EH8 9JX; T.-0131-650 3673.

Williamson, Raymond MacLeod, MA, LLB, FRSA, FRSAMD. Solicitor, since 1968 (Senior Partner, MacRoberts, Solicitors, Glasgow and Edinburgh); b. 24.12.42, Glasgow; m., Brenda; 1 s.; 1 d. Educ. High School of Glasgow; Glasgow University. Secretary, High School of Glasgow Educational Trust; Vice Chairman,

Royal Scottish Academy of Music and Drama; Governor, High School of Glasgow; Chairman, John Currie Singers Ltd.; Chairman, National Youth Choir of Scotland; Chairman, Scottish International Piano Competition; Chairman, Royal Scottish National Orchestra, 1985-91; Chairman, Children's Music Foundation in Scotland, 1994-2000. Recreation: music. Address: (h.) 11 Islay Drive, Newton Mearns, Glasgow G77 6UD; T.-0141-639 4133.

Wilson of Tillyorn, Baron (David Clive Wilson), KT, GCMG, MA (Oxon), PhD, FRSE. Life Peer (1992); Chairman, Scottish Committee, British Council, since 1993; Chancellor, Aberdeen University, since 1997; Member, Council, Glenalmond College, since 1994 (Chairman, since 2000); President, Bhutan Society of the UK, since 1993; President, Hong Kong Society and Hong Kong Association, since 1994; Registrar, Order of St. Michael and St. John, since 2001; Vice-President, Royal Scottish Geographical Society, since 1998; Trustee, National Museums of Scotland, since 1999; Member, Board, Martin Currie Pacific Trust; Trustee, Scotland's Churches Scheme, since 1999; Chairman, Scottish Peers Association, since 2000 (Vice-Chairman, 1998-2000); Trustee, Carnegie Trust for the Universities of Scotland, since 2000; Member, Prime Minister's Advisory Committee on Business Appointments, since 2000; b. 14.2.34, Alloa; m., Natasha Helen Mary Alexander; 2 s. Educ. Trinity College, Glenalmond; Keble College, Oxford. Entered Foreign Service, 1958; Third Secretary, Vientiane, 1959-60; language student, Hong Kong, 1960-62; Second, later First Secretary, Peking, 1963-65; FCO, 1965-68; resigned, 1968; Editor, China Quarterly, 1968-74; Visiting Scholar, Columbia University, New York, 1972; rejoined Diplomatic Service, 1974; Cabinet Office, 1974-77; Political Adviser, Hong Kong, 1977-81; Head, S. European Department, FCO, 1981-84; Assistant Under Secretary of State, FCO, 1984-87. Member, Governing Body, School of Oriental and African Studies, 1992-97; Member, Council, CBI Scotland, 1993-2000; Chairman, Scottish and Southern Energy plc (formerly Scottish Hydro Electric), 1993-2000; Hon.LLD (Aberdeen); Hon.DLitt (Sydney); Hon.DLitt (Abertay, Dundee); Hon. LLD, Chinese University, Hong Kong. KStJ. Recreations: mountaineering; reading. Address: (b.) House of Lords, London SW1A 0PW; (ho.) 64 Great King Street, Edinburgh EH3 6QY.

Wilson, Alan Oliver Arneil, MB, ChB, DPM, FRCPsych, FFCS. Former consultant in private practice, Murrayfield Hospital, Edinburgh (now retired); Member, Executive Group of Board of Directors, and Past President, World Association for Psychosocial Rehabilitation; Consultant (in Scotland), Ex-Services Mental Welfare Society; b. 4.1.30, Douglas; m., Dr. Fiona Margaret Davidson; 3 s. Educ. Biggar High School; Edinburgh University. RAMC, 1953-55; psychiatric post, Stobhill General Hospital, Glasgow, and Garlands Hospital, Carlisle, 1955-63; Consultant Psychiatrist and Deputy Physician Superintendent, St. George's Hospital, Morpeth, 1963-77; Consultant Psychiatrist, Bangour Hospitals, 1977-89; former Member, Clinical Teaching Staff, Faculty of Medicine, Edinburgh University; Clinical Lecturer, University of Newcastle upon Tyne. Chairman, Group for Study of Rehabilitation and Community Care, Scottish Division, RCPsych; Member, Ethics Committee, World Association for Social Psychiatry; Chairman, Psychosocial Rehabilitation Scotland. V.M. Bekhterev Medal awarded by Bekhterev Psychoneurological Research Institute, St. Petersburg; Gálfi Béla Award for services to Hungarian Psychosocial Rehabilitation; Co-Founder, Morpeth Northumbrian Gathering; Secretary, Edinburgh and Lothians Regional Committee, Institute of Contemporary Scotland; former Hibernian FC footballer. Recreations: golf; music; guitar; blethering. Address: (h.) 14 Cammo Hill, Edinburgh EH4 8EY; T.-0131-339 2244.

Wilson, Allan. MSP (Labour), Cunninghame North, since 1999; Deputy Minister for Environment and Rural Development; b. 1954, Glasgow; m.; 2 s. Educ. Spiers School, Beith. Former Head of Higher Education (Scotland), UNISON; Member, Independent Review of Pay and Conditions in Higher Education Institutions (Scotland); Member, Scottish Executive, Labour Party; agent, Brian Wilson, MP. Recreation: football. Address: (b.) Scottish Parliament, Edinburgh EH99 1SP; T.-0131-348 5772.

**Wilson, Andrew J., BA (Hons). MSP (SNP), Central Scotland, since 1999; Shadow Minister for Economy and Transport, since 2001; b. 27.12.70, Lanark. Educ. Coltness High School, Wishaw; Strathclyde University; St Andrews University. Economist: Forestry Commission, 1993-95, Scottish Office, 1995-96, Scottish National Party, 1996-97, Royal Bank of Scotland, Edinburgh, 1997-99. Vice President, Strathclyde University Students Association, 1991-92. Recreations: football; music; reading; cinema; swimming. Address: (b.) Scottish Parliament, Edinburgh EH99 1SP; T.-0131-348 5673.

Wilson, Brian, MA (Hons), FSA (Scot). MP (Labour), Cunninghame North, since 1987; Minister for Energy and Industry, Department of Trade and Industry, since 2001; b. 13.12.48, Dunoon; m., Joni Buchanan; 2 s.; 1 d. Educ. Dunoon Grammar School; Dundee University; University College, Cardiff. Journalist; Publisher and Founding Editor, West Highland Free Press; Contributor to The Guardian, Glasgow Herald, etc.; first winner, Nicholas Tomalin Memorial Award for Journalism; contested Ross and Cromarty, Oct., 1974, Inverness, 1979, Western Isles, 1983; front-bench spokesman on Scottish Home Affairs etc., 1988-92, Transport, 1992-94 and 1995-96, Trade and Industry, 1994-95; Minister of State, Scottish Office (Education, Industry and Highland and Islands), 1997-98; Minister for Trade, Department of Trade and Industry, 1998-99; Minister of State for Scotland, 1999-2001; Minister of State, Foreign and Commonwealth Office, 2001. Address: House of Commons, London SW1A 0AA.

Wilson, Brian, OBE, LLB. Deputy Chairman, Local Government Boundary Commission for Scotland, since 1999; b. 20.2.46, Perth; m., Isobel Esson; 3 d. Educ. Buckie High School; Aberdeen University. Management trainee, Marks and Spencer, 1966-68; apprentice, then Legal Assistant, Banff County Council, 1969-72; Senior Legal Assistant, Inverness County Council, 1972-73; Depute County Clerk, Banff County Council, 1973-75; Director of Administration and Legal Services, Banff and Buchan District Council, 1975-78; Chief Executive, Inverness District Council, 1978-95; Depute Chief Executive, The Highland Council, 1995-98. Recreations: fishing; walking; cutting hedges. Address: (h.) 11 Lochardil Place, Inverness IV2 4LN; T.-01463 231355.

Wilson, Colin Alexander Megaw, LLB (Hons). Scottish Parliamentary Counsel, since 1993; b. 4.1.52, Aberdeen; m., Mandy Esca Clay; 1 s.; 1 d. Educ. High School of Glasgow; Edinburgh University. Admitted as a Solicitor, 1975; Assistant Solicitor, then Partner, Archibald Campbell & Harley, WS, Edinburgh, 1975-79; Assistant Legal Secretary to Lord Advocate, 1979-99, and until 1993 Assistant, then Depute, Parliamentary Draftsman for Scotland. Recreations: hill-walking; cycling; choral singing; family. Address: (b.) Office of the Scottish Parliamentary Counsel, Victoria Quay, Edinburgh EH6 6QQ; T.-0131-244 1670; e-mail: colin.wilson@scotland.gsi.gov.uk

Wilson, David Steel, DipM. Chef/Proprietor, The Peat Inn, since 1972; Director, Taste of Scotland Ltd., since 1996; b. 21.1.36, Bishopbriggs; m., Patricia Ann; 1 s.; 1 d. Educ. Bishopbriggs High School; Glasgow College of Commerce. Sales/Marketing Manager in industry, 1967-71; trainee chef, 1971-72. Master Chef of G.B.; Chef Laureate; Fellow,

RSA, 1992; Hon. Doctor of Laws, Dundee University, 1997. Recreations: travel; art; sport; music; theatre. Address: (b.) The Peat Inn, by Cupar, Fife KY15 5LH; T.-0133840 206.

Wilson, Donald, BA (Hons), MSc. Member, City of Edinburgh Council, since 1999, Executive Member, Communications and Business Management, since 2001; Chairman, Edinburgh International Science Festival, since 1999; Chairman, Edinburgh Science Foundation, since 1999; b. 4.12.59, Selkirk. Educ. Galashiels Academy; University of Stirling; City University, London. Teacher of Computing, since 1984; Adult Education Tutor, since 1984; Acting Senior Teacher, ICT, 1997-99; Curriculum Development Officer, ICT, 1999-2001. Vice-Convener, Economic Development Committee, City of Edinburgh Council, 1999-2000, Convener, Children and Young People Scrutiny Panel, 2000-01; Convener, Cross Party ICT Sounding Board, 2001-02; Member, Board: International Centre for Mathematical Sciences, Edinburgh and Lothians Tourist Board. Recreations: film; opera; sci-fi; computers. Address: (h.) 20 Stenhouse Mill Lane, Edinburgh EH11 3LR; T.-0131-443 0091; e-mail: donald.wilson@edinburgh.gov.uk

Wilson, Gerald R., CB, MA, FRSE, DUniv. Chairman, Scottish Biomedical Research Trust, since 1999; Member, Board, ICL (Scotland); Special Adviser, Royal Bank of Scotland Group; b. 7.9.39, Edinburgh; m., Margaret; 1 s.; 1 d. Educ. Holy Cross Academy; Edinburgh University. Assistant Principal, Scottish Home and Health Department, 1961-65; Private Secretary, Minister of State for Scotland, 1965-66; Principal, Scottish Home and Health Department, 1966-72; Private Secretary to Lord Privy Seal, 1972-74, to Minister of State, Civil Service Department, 1974; Assistant Secretary, Scottish Economic Planning Department, 1974-77; Counsellor, Office of the UK Permanent Representative to the Economic Communities, Brussels, 1977-82; Assistant Secretary, Scottish Office, 1982-84; Under Secretary, Industry Department for Scotland, 1984-88; Secretary, Scottish Office Education and Industry Department, 1988-99, Scottish Executive Enterprise and Lifelong Learning Department, 1999; Member, Court, Strathclyde University, since 1999; Member, Board, Royal Scottish National Orchestra, since 2000; Governor, George Watson's College, Edinburgh, since 2000. Recreation: music. Address: (b.) 4 Inverleith Avenue South, Edinburgh EH3 5QA.

Wilson, Professor Gordon McAndrew, MA, PhD, FRSA. Chairman, Ayrshire and Arran Acute Hospitals NHS Trust, since 1999; b. 4.12.39, Glasgow; m., Alison Rosemary Cook; 2 s.; 1 d. Educ. Eastwood Secondary School; Glasgow University; Jordanhill College of Education. Teacher of History and Modern Studies: Eastwood Secondary School, 1963-65, Eastwood High School, 1965-67; Lecturer in Social Studies, Hamilton College of Education, 1967-73 (Head of Department, 1973-81); Principal Lecturer in Inservice Education, then Assistant Principal, Jordanhill College of Education, 1981-88; Principal, Craigie College of Education, 1988-93; Assistant Principal and Director of University Campus Ayr, Paisley University, 1993-99, now Emeritus Professor. Chairman, South Ayrshire Hospitals NHS Trust, 1997-99; Member: Board of Directors, Ayrshire Chamber of Commerce and Industry, Board of Directors, Enterprise Ayrshire, since 1994. Recreations: reading; gardening; walking; music. Address: (b.) AAANHT, Crosshouse Hospital, Kilmarnock KA2 0BE; T.-01563 572431.

Wilson, Helen Frances, DA, RSW, RGI. Artist; b. 25.7.54, Paisley; 1 d. Educ. John Neilson High School, Paisley; Glasgow School of Art. Drawings and paintings in public and private collections; awards and prizes include: Cargill Travelling Scholarship (Colonsay and Italy), 1976; First Prize, Scottish Drawing Competition, 1997; elected: RGI, 1984, RSW, 1997. Recreations: working with pre-school children; watching theatre, ballet, pantomime and people. Address: (h.) 1 Partickhill Road, Glasgow; T.-0141-339 5827.

Wilson, Ian Matthew, CB, MA. b. 12.12.26, Edinburgh; m., 1, Anne Chalmers (deceased); 3 s.; 2, Joyce Town. Educ. George Watson's College; Edinburgh University. Assistant Principal, Scottish Home Department, 1950; Private Secretary to Permanent Under Secretary of State, Scottish Office, 1953-55; Principal, Scottish Home Department, 1955; Assistant Secretary: Scottish Education Department, 1963, Scottish Home and Health Department, 1971; Assistant Under Secretary of State, Scottish Office, 1974-77; Under Secretary, Scottish Education Department, 1977-86; Secretary of Commissions for Scotland, 1987-92. Member, RSAMD Governing Body, 1992-2000; President, University of Edinburgh Graduates' Association, 1995-97; Director, Scottish International Piano Competition, since 1999. Address: (h.) 1 Bonaly Drive, Edinburgh EH13 OEJ; T.-0131-441 2541.

Wilson, James Wiseman, OBE, OStJ. Director, Barcapel Foundation, since 1970; Director, Wilson Management Ltd., since 1970; b. 31.5.33, Glasgow; m., Valerie Grant; 1 s.; 3 d. Educ. Trinity College, Glenalmond; Harvard Business School. Marketing Director, Scottish Animal Products, 1959-63; Sales Director, then Managing Director, then Chairman, Robert Wilson & Sons (1849) Ltd., 1964-85. National Trust for Scotland: Member of Council, 1977-82 and 1984-89, President, Ayrshire Members' Centre; Chairman, Management Committee, Scottish Civic Trust; Honorary President, Skelmorlie Golf Club and Irvine Pipe Band; won Aims of Industry Free Enterprise Award (Scotland), 1980. Recreations: golf; backgammon; skiing; bridge; travelling. Address: (h.) Skelmorlie Castle, Skelmorlie, Ayrshire PA17 5EY; T.-01475 521127.

Wilson, Janette Sylvia, LLB, NP. Solicitor of the Church of Scotland and Law Agent to the General Assembly, since 1995; b. 15.1.51, Inverness; m., Stuart Ronald Wilson. Educ. Inverness Royal Academy; Edinburgh University. Law Apprentice, then Assistant, Dundas & Wilson, CS, Edinburgh, 1973-77; Assistant, then Partner, Ross Harper & Murphy, Edinburgh, 1977-81; Depute Solicitor, Church of Scotland, 1981-95. Member, Scottish Charity Law Review Commission, Law Society Conveyancing Committee and In-House Lawyers Group Committee; Secretary, Scottish Churches Committee. Recreations: keeping fit; reading; gardening. Address: (b.) 121 George Street, Edinburgh; T.-0131-225 5722.

Wilson, John G., MA. Director, Scottish Law Pay Unit, since 2001; b. 28.11.56, Falkirk; m., Frances M. McGlinchey; 1 d. Educ. Camelon High School; Glasgow University. Coachbuilder, 1972-82; Project Co-ordinator, Castlemilk Housing Involvement Project, 1987-94; Director, Glasgow Council of Tenants Associations, 1994-97; The Poverty Alliance: Senior Economic Development Officer, 1998-99, Fieldwork Manager, 1999-2001. Falkirk District Councillor, 1980-82; SNP Parliamentary candidate, Hamilton South, 2001. Recreations: Tai Chi; archery; National Trust; RSPB. Address: (b.) 24 Sandyford Place, Glasgow G3 7NG; T.-0141-221 4491.

Wilson, Professor John I. B., BSc, PhD, CPhys, CEng. Professor of Materials Processing, Heriot-Watt University, since 1996; Managing Director, DILAB Ltd., since 1994; b. 4.3.47, Grimsby; m., Sheila Margaret; 2 d. Educ. Grimsby Wintringham Boys' Grammar School; Grey College, Durham University. Wolfson Fellow, St Andrews University, 1971-74; Wolfson Fellow, Heriot-Watt University, 1975-77; Research Fellow/Lecturer/Senior Lecturer/Reader, Heriot-Watt University, 1977-89; Chairman, Institute of Physics Vacuum Group Committee. Publications: one book and 150 papers; UK

Regional Editor, physica status solidi, Berlin. Recreations: walking; cycling; gardening. Address: (b.) Department of Physics, Heriot-Watt University, Riccarton, Edinburgh, EH14 4AS; T.-0131-451 3034; e-mail: j.i.b.wilson@hw.ac.uk

Wilson, Lena, BA, MBA. Senior Director, Scottish Enterprise, since 2000; b. 13.2.64, Paisley. Educ. St Andrews High School, East Kilbride; Glasgow Caledonian University; Strathclyde University. Production and quality management, electronics industry, 1985-89; Manager, Locate in Scotland, 1989-94; Deputy Chief Executive, Scottish Enterprise Forth Valley, 1994-98; Senior Advisor, World Bank, Washington DC, 1998-2000. Board Member, Scottish Leadership Foundation. Recreations: keeping fit; travel; theatre and music; socialising. Address: (b.) Scottish Enterprise, 150 Broomielaw, Atlantic Quay, Glasgow G2 8LU; T.-0141-228 2904.

Wilson, Les. Documentary Producer/Director, since 1980; Director, Caledonia, Sterne and Wyld Ltd., since 1992; b. 17.7.49, Glasgow; m., Adrienne Cochrane; 2 d. Educ. Grove Academy, Broughty Ferry. Trainee Journalist, 1969-70; hippy trail, 1970-71; Reporter, Greenock Telegraph, 1972-73; Reporter, STV, 1973-78; Editor, STV political programme, Ways and Means, 1979-80; Producer/Director, STV, 1981-92. Winner, Celtic Film Festival Award, 1991; BAFTA Scotland and British Telecom Factual/Current Affairs awards, 1997; British Telecom Factual/Current Affairs award, 1998. Member, Producers' Alliance for Cinema and Television (PACT) Scottish Committee. Publication: Scotland's War (Co-author), 1995. Recreation: Islay – the island, its people, its malts. Address: (b.) 5 Queens Crescent, Glasgow G4 9BW; T.-0141-353 3153.

Wilson, Professor Lindsay, BA, DipEd, PhD, CPyschol. Professor of Psychology, University of Stirling, since 1998 (Head, Department of Psychology, since 1995); b. 24.6.51, Aberdeen; m., Jean; 2 s. Educ. Biggar High School; University of Stirling; University of Edinburgh. Research Fellow, Max Planck Institute for Psychiatry, Munich, 1979-80; University of Stirling: Medical Research Council Training Fellow, 1980-83, Lecturer then Senior Lecturer, 1983-98. Recreations: sailing; hillwalking. Address: (b.) Department of Psychology, University of Stirling, Stirling FK9 4LA; T.-01786 467640.

Wilson, Monica Anne, BA, DipPCT. Director, CHANGE (Men Leaving to End Their Violence to Women) Ltd., since 1989; Counsellor in Primary Care, since 1997; b. 4.3.51, Arundel; m., Keith Stewart; 1 step-d. Educ. Our Lady of Sion School, Worthing; Stirling University; Edinburgh University; Strathclyde University. Research Assistant, Stirling University, 1975-78; Research Officer, Scottish Consumer Council, 1978-80; Research Fellow, Edinburgh University, 1980-82; Research and Development Officer, Forth Valley Health Board, 1985-89; Joint Co-ordinator, CHANGE Project, 1989-96. Publication: Men Who Are Violent to Women (Co-Author), 1997; Acting Chair, Respect (National Association for Perpetrator Programmes and Women's Services). Recreation: gardening; DIY; music. Address: (b.) 4-6 South Lumley Street, Grangemouth FK3 8BT; T.-01324 485595; e-mail: monica@changeweb.org.uk

Wilson, Peter Liddell, BSc, MA, FIMgt, FCIPD, FRSA. Secretary, Heriot-Watt University, since 1991; b. 8.12.42, Douglas; m., Joy Janet Gibson; 2 d. Educ. Lanark Grammar School; Glasgow University; Birkbeck College, London University. Mathematics Teacher, Lanark Grammar School, 1964-67; Royal Navy (Instructor Lieutenant), 1967-70; Army (Royal Army Educational Corps), 1970-90: Commander Education, 1st Armoured Division (Lt. Col.), 1983-85, SOI Education HQ BAOR (Lt. Col.), 1986-88, MOD (Resettlement) (Colonel), 1988-90. Chairman,

Edinburgh Conference Centre, since 1991. Recreations: golf; jogging; hill-walking; theatre. Address: (b.) Heriot-Watt University, Riccarton, Edinburgh EH14 4AS; T.-0131-451 3364.

Wilson, Peter M., QPM, LLB. Chief Constable, Fife Constabulary, since 2001; b. 24.8.53, Edinburgh; m.; 1 s.; 1 d. Educ. George Watson's College; Edinburgh University; Cambridge University (Diploma in Applied Criminology). Joined Edinburgh City Police, 1973; Lothians and Borders Police, 1975-97; Grampian Police, 1997-2001; HM Inspectorate of Constabulary, 2001. Recreation: golf. Address: (b.) Detroit Road, Glenrothes KY6 2RJ; T.-01592 418411.

Wilson, Professor Peter Northcote, CBE, BSc, MSc, Dip. Animal Genetics, PhD, DUniv, Hon.DUniv, CBiol, FBiol, FRSE. Emeritus Professor of Agriculture and Rural Economy, Edinburgh University; General Secretary, Royal Society of Edinburgh, since 1996; b. 4.4.28, Beckenham, Kent; m., Maud Ethel Bunn; 2 s.; 1 d. Educ. Whitgift School, Croydon; Wye College, London University; Edinburgh University. Lecturer in Agriculture, Makerere College, East Africa; Senior Lecturer in Agriculture, Imperial College of Tropical Agriculture, Trinidad; Professor of Tropical Agriculture, University of West Indies, Trinidad; Head of Biometrics, Unilever Research Laboratory, Bedford; Agricultural Development Director, SLF Ltd., Liverpool; Chief Agricultural Adviser, BOCM Silcock Ltd., Basingstoke. Life Fellow, Wye College, University of London; Past President, British Society of Animal Production; Past Vice President, Institute of Biology; Member, Medicines Commission, 1976-79; Chairman, Frank Parkinson Agricultural Trust, 1978-99 (Trustee, since 1992); Hon. Secretary, Institute of Biology, 1992-96; Scientific Director, Edinburgh Centre for Rural Research, 1990-96; Past President, Edinburgh Agricultural Society; Member, Council, SAC, since 1995; Vice-Convener, Business Committee, University of Edinburgh Council, 1996-2000; Member, Scottish Committee, RSPB, 1996-2000. Publications: Agriculture in the Tropics (Co-author); Improved Feeding of Cattle and Sheep (Co-author); A Tale of Two Trusts; Purchase Two Kilts. Recreations: walking; photography; philately; natural history. Address: 8 St. Thomas Road, Edinburgh EH9 2LQ.

Wilson, R. Ross, BSc, PhD, MInstP, CPhys. Managing Director, James Howden & Co. Ltd., since 1992; Director, Howden Group Technology, since 1998; Director, Scottish Enterprise Renfrewshire, since 1996; b. 13.3.47, Glasgow; m., Margaret; 2 s. Educ. Hamilton Academy; Glasgow University. Research Officer, then Vibration Group Leader, Central Electricity Research Laboratories, CEGB; Section Head, Design Analysis, Corporate Engineering Laboratory, British Steel; Design Manager, then Technical Director, James Howden Ltd. Recreations: golf; collecting Penguin books; gardening. Address: (b.) Old Govan Road, Renfrew PA4 8XJ; T.-0141-885 7300.

Wilson, Robert Gordon, BL, LLD. Solicitor; b. 16.4.38, Glasgow; m., Edith M. Hassall; 2 d. Educ. Douglas High School for Boys; Edinburgh University. National Secretary, SNP, 1963-71; MP, Dundee East, 1974-87; Scottish National Party: Chairman and National Convener, 1979-90, Vice-President, 1992-97; Rector, Dundee University, 1983-86; Member, Court, University of Abertay Dundee 1992-96; Member, Church and Nation Committee, Church of Scotland, since 2000. Recreation: reading; sailing; walking. Address: (h.) 48 Monifieth Road, Dundee DD5 2RX.

Wilson, Robert (Robin) Wight, DL, CA. Chairman, Quarriers, since 1997; b. 14.1.37, Glasgow; m., Jean; 2 s.; 1 d. Educ. Glenalmond School. Qualified as accountant, 1960; National Service, Royal Navy, 1960-61; Partner, Touche Ross and Co. (now Deloitte and Touche), 1965-94; retired, 1994; took up numerous directorships; Chairman, Ridings Sawmills Ltd., since 1989; member of various church, sport and school committees. Recreations: previously hockey and squash; now golf; skiing; travel. Address: (h.) Rossall, Gryffe Road, Kilmacolm, Renfrewshire, PA13 4AZ; T.-01505-872671.

Wilson, Roy. General Manager, Pitlochry Festival Theatre, 1961-95, Art Exhibitions Director, since 1995; b. St. Andrews. Educ. Burgh School and Madras College, St. Andrews. Proprietor, grocer's business, St. Andrews, 1953-58; Assistant Manager, Pitlochry Festival Theatre, 1958-61. Winner David K. Thomson Award, 1995, in recognition of his contribution to Pitlochry Festival Theatre. Recreations: plays and theatre in general; most forms of classical music, with particular interest in choral singing; listening to records; reading; art and antiques. Address: (h.) Kilrymont, Bruach Lane, Pitlochry, Perthshire PH16 5DG; T.-Pitlochry 472897.

Wilson, Dr Stuart Macdonald, BSc, PhD. Senior Lecturer, Tayside Institute of Child Health, since 1997; b. 12.1.57, Stockton-on-Tees. Educ. Durham School; Durham University. Research Fellowships: Glasgow University, Hong Kong University, London University; Lecturer, Institute of Biomedical and Life Sciences, Glasgow University, 1992-97. Chairman, Scottish Membrane Transport Group, since 2001. Recreations: hill-walking; cycling; angling. Address: (b.) Lung Membrane Transport Group, TICH, Ninewells Hospital and Medical School, Dundee DD1 9SY; T.-01382 632544.

Wilson, Thomas Black, OBE, BSc (Hons), CEng, MBCS, FRSA. Principal, Glasgow College of Building and Printing, since 1989; Chair, Learning + Teaching Scotland, since 2000; b. 23.12.43, Airdrie; m., Barbara Smith; 1 s.; 1 d. Educ. Cumnock Academy; Glasgow University; Jordanhill College. Principal Teacher, Prestwick Academy, 1969-74; Head, Computing Department, Ayr College, 1974-84; Depute Principal: Barmulloch College, Glasgow, 1984-86, Cardonald College, Glasgow, 1986-89. Member, Scottish Central Committee (Mathematics), 1975-82; Chair, Glasgow Telecolleges Network, 1994-2001; Member, Digital Task Force Scotland, 1999-2001; Member, National Grid for Learning Steering Group, since 1999; Chair, Scottish Council for Educational Technology, 1999-2000 (Governor, 1994-2000); Hon. Professor, Glasgow Caledonian University, since 1995. Recreations: reading; writing; music. Address: (b.) 60 North Hanover Street, Glasgow G1 2BP; T.-0141-332 9969.

Wilson, Valerie, BA, MSc, EdD. Director, Scottish Council for Research in Education, since 1999; b. Lancashire; m., 3 s. Educ. Cowley Girls' Grammar School; Hull University; Edinburgh University; Sheffield University. Teacher in various secondary schools, 1966-72; Tutor, Edinburgh University Centre for Continuing Education, 1978-85; Principal Consultant, International Training Services Ltd., 1986-90; Director, Stirling University Management Development Unit, 1991-94; Programme Manger, SCRE, 1994-97; Principal Researcher, Scottish Office Educational Research Unit, 1997-99. Publications: numerous research reports, articles and conference papers. Recreations: hill walking; gardening; reading group. Address: (b.) 15 St John Street, Edinburgh, EH8 8JR; T.-0131-557 2944; e-mail: valerie.wilson@scre.ac.uk

Wilson, William, MA. Director, Lyth Arts Centre, Wick, since 1977; b. 10.4.43, Thurso. Educ. Chelsea School of Art; Royal College of Art. Independent film-maker, London, 1968-70; Head, Film Department, Portsmouth Polytechnic, 1970-73; Lecturer in Film, Chelsea College, London University, 1968-73; jazz musician, London/Caithness, 1973-77. Recreations: jazz piano; contemporary literature. Address: (b.) Lyth Arts Centre, Lyth, Wick KW1 4UD; T.-01955 641270.

Windsor, Malcolm L., PhD, FRSC. Secretary, North Atlantic Salmon Conservation Organization, since 1984; b. 12.4.38, Bristol; m., Sally; 2 d. Educ. Cotham Grammar School, Bristol; Bristol University. Researcher, University of California, 1965-67; fisheries research, Humber Laboratory, Hull, 1967-75; Fisheries Adviser to Chief Scientist, Ministry of Agriculture and Fisheries, London, 1975-84. Secretary, Duddingston Village Conservation Society. Publication: book on fishery products. Recreations: local conservation work; jazz; walking. Address: (b.) 11 Rutland Square, Edinburgh EH1 2AS; T.-0131-228 2551; e-mail: hq@nasco.int

Windsor, Col. Rodney Francis Maurice, CBE, DL. Farmer; b. 22.2.25, Redhill; m., Deirdre Chichester (deceased); m. Angela.Stainton; 2 s.; 1 d. Educ. Tonbridge School. Enlisted Royal Armoured Corps, 1943; commissioned The Queen's Bays, 1944-52; Captain, 1949; ADC to CINC and High Commissioner Austria, 1949-50; served in North Irish Horse (TA), 1959-67; Lt. Col. Commanding, 1964-67; Colonel TA N. Ireland, 1967-71; ADC (TA) to HM The Queen, 1970-75; Member, Highland TA Association, 1971-77; Member, Banff and Buchan District Valuation Appeal Committee, 1982-96 (Chairman, 1989-96); Deputy Lieutenant:, Co. Antrim, 1967-97, Aberdeenshire, since 1989; Hon. President, Turiff Branch, Royal British Legion Scotland, since 1997; Member, Aberdeen Committee, Scottish Veterans Garden City Association, since 1993. Recreations: field sports; golf. Address: (h.) Mains of Warthill, Meikle Wartle, Inverurie, Aberdeenshire AB51 5AJ; T.-01651 821273.

Winn, Professor Philip, BA, PhD. Professor of Psychology, University of St. Andrews, since 2000; b. 31.10.54, Hull; m., Jane E. Burrows; 2 s.; 1 d. Educ. Isleworth Grammar School; University of Hull. Research Scientist, Institute of Neurology, 1979-80; Pinsent-Darwin Student in Mental Pathology, University of Cambridge, 1980-83; University of St. Andrews: Lecturer in Psychology, 1984-96, Reader in Psychology, 1996-2000. Member, National Committee, British Neuroscience Association, 1985-91. Publication: Dictionary of Biological Psychology (Editor), 2001. Recreations: football; gastronomy; literature; music. Address: (b.) School of Psychology, University of St. Andrews, St. Andrews KY16 9JU; T.-01334 462067; e-mail: pw@st-andrews.ac.uk

Winney, Robin John, MB, ChB, FRCPEdin. Consultant Renal Physician, Edinburgh Royal Infirmary, since 1978; b. 8.5.44, Dunfermline. Educ. Dunfermline High School; Edinburgh University. Recreations: badminton; curling. Address: (h.) 74 Lanark Road West, Currie, Midlothian EH14 5JZ.

Winter, Michael, BA, AKC. Artistic Director, Perth Theatre, since 1996; b. Winchelsea, Sussex. Educ. Rye Grammar School; King's College, London. Director, York Theatre Royal, 1978-84; Artistic Director, Mercury Theatre, Colchester, Essex, 1984-94. Address: (b.) 185 High Street, Perth PH1 5UW; T.-01738 472701.

Wiseman, Alan William. Director and Chairman, Robert Wiseman Dairies, since 1979; Director, Dairy Industry Federation; Director, National Dairy Council; b. 20.8.50, Giffnock. Educ. Duncanrig Senior Secondary School, East Kilbride. Left school to be one of his father's milkmen, 1967; has been a milkman ever since. President, Scottish Dairy Trade Federation, 1988-95; Scottish Businessman of the Year, 1992; Scottish Business Achievement Award, 1994; Fellow, Royal Agricultural Society. Recreations: golf; shooting. Address: (b.) Cadzow House, High Parks Farm, Hamilton.

Wishart, Colin Fraser, DA, RIBA, FRIAS. Chartered Architect; Partner, Battledown Studio, Natural Architecture, since 1996; Visiting Teaching Fellow, Duncan of Jordanstone College, University of Dundee, since 1997; architectural photographer; b. 20.8.47, Dundee; m., Sheila Buchanan; Educ. Grove Academy; Duncan of Jordanstone College of Art. Architect, Thoms and Wilkie, Chartered Architects, Dundee, 1972-73; Senior Architect, City of Dundee Corporation, 1973-90; Principal Architect, City of Dundee Council, 1990-96. Past President, Dundee Institute of Architects; Director, The Art Extraordinary Trust. Recreations: photography; fine art; music; poetry. Address: Bondfield Cottage, Carslogie Road, Cupar, Fife KY15 4HY; T.-01334 652097; e-mail: colin@bondfield34.freeserve.co.uk

Wishart, Professor Jennifer Grant, MA, PhD, CPsychol. Professor of Special Education, University of Edinburgh, since 1998; b. 9.5.48, Dundee; m., Thomas Arrol. Educ. Harris Academy, Dundee; University of Edinburgh. Research Psychologist, University of Edinburgh, 1970-96 (Research Associate, 1970-79, Research Fellow, 1979-90, Senior Research Fellow, 1990-95, Reader, 1995-96); first Scottish Chair in Special Education, Moray House Institute of Education, Heriot-Watt University, 1996-98. Advisor to Scottish UK and European Down's Syndrome Associations, International Society on Early Intervention, Partners in Advocacy, and other charities. Publications: numerous papers and chapters in psychology, education and medical journals/textbooks. Recreations: wine/food; English pointers. Address: Faculty of Education, Moray House Institute of Education, Holyrood Road, Edinburgh EH8 8AQ; T.-0131-651 6099; e-mail: J.Wishart@ed.ac.uk

Wishart, Peter, MP. SNP MP, Tayside North, since 2001; b. 9.3.62; m., Carrie; 1 s. Educ. Moray House Collee of Education. Community worker, 1984-85; musician with Runrig, 1985-2001. Address: (b.) House of Commons, London SW1A 0AA.

Wishart, Robert Charles, BSocSc, DipTP. Chief Statistician, Scottish Executive, since 1999; b. 14.8.52, Dunfermline; m., Kathy Somers; 1 s. Educ. Dunfermline High School; Birmingham University; Strathclyde University. Planning Department, Lanarkshire County Council, 1973-75; Strathclyde Regional Council, 1975-96, latterly Senior Executive Officer (Social Policy Research and Information); Depute Head of Social Policy, Glasgow City Council, 1996-99. Address: (b.) Scottish Executive, 3B02 Victoria Quay, Edinburgh EH6 6QQ; T.-0131-2443 0302.

Wishart, Ruth. Columnist, The Herald; Broadcaster, BBC Radio, since 1989; b. Glasgow; m., Rod McLeod. Educ. Eastwood Senior Secondary School. TV Editor, Daily Record, 1970-73; Woman's Editor, Daily Record, 1973-78; Assistant Editor, Sunday Mail, 1978-82; Assistant Editor, Sunday Standard, 1982-83; Freelance Writer, 1983-86; Senior Assistant Editor, The Scotsman, 1986-88.

Wiszniewski, Adrian, BA (Hons). Artist/Designer; b. 31.3.58, Glasgow; m., Diane Foley; 2 s.; 1 d. Educ. Mackintosh School of Architecture, Glasgow School of Art. Around 40 solo exhibitions throughout the world, since 1983; commissions include: two large paintings for Liverpool Anglican Cathedral 1996, Gallery of Modern Art, Glasgow, 1996, Millennium Tower, Hamilton, 1997-98; work purchased by museums worldwide including Tate Gallery, London and MOMA, New York. New York Design Award for designs of six rugs in collaboration with Edinburgh Tapestry Workshop; has created limited edition books. Recreations: looking at pictures; cinema; family.

Withers, Professor Charles William John, BSc, PhD, FRGS, FRSA, Member, Academea Europaea. Professor of Geography, Edinburgh University, since 1994; b. 6.12.54,

Edinburgh; m., Anne; 2 s.; 1 d. Educ. Daniel Stewart's College, Edinburgh; St. Andrews University; Cambridge University. Publications: author of eight books, 90 academic articles. Recreations: reading; hill-walking. Address: (b.) Department of Geography, Edinburgh University, Drummond Street, Edinburgh; T.-0131-650 2559.

Withers, John Alexander (Jack), FCIL. Writer; b. Glasgow; m., Beate (Bea) Haertel. Educ. North Kelvinside School; Jordanhill College of Education (Youth and Community Diploma). Left school at 14; worked in garage, electrical industry, labouring, National Service, unemployment, razor-blade salesman; long periods abroad, wandering, wondering, working: France, FRG, Italy, Scandinavia, Spain, North Africa; youth worker; freelance writer; ski instructor; librarian; performance poet; Scottish republican and radical; plays for radio, TV, theatre; James Kennoway Screenplay Award (shared); Scottish Arts Council Awards; short stories published in numerous journals in UK, Denmark and West Germany; Editor, Two Tongues — Two Cities; books: Glasgow Limbo, A Real Glasgow Archipelago, Balancing on a Barbed Wire Fence. Address: (h.) 16 Belmont Crescent, Glasgow; T.-0141-339 9492.

Witney, Eur. Ing. Professor Brian David, BSc, MSc, PhD, NDA, NDAgrE, CEng, FIMechE, Hon.FIAgrE, MemASAE, FFCS. Director, Land Technology Ltd., since 1995; Hon. Professor of Agricultural Engineering, Edinburgh University, since 1989; Professor of Terramechanics, Scottish Agricultural College, Edinburgh, since 1994; b. 8.6.38, Edinburgh; m., Maureen M.I. Donnelly; 1 s.; 2 d. Educ. Daniel Stewart's College, Edinburgh; Edinburgh University; Durham University; Newcastle University. Senior Research Associate, Newcastle upon Tyne University, 1962-66; Research Fellow, US Army Research Office, Duke Univ., 1966-67; Senior Scientific Officer, Military Engineering Experimental Establishment, Christchurch, 1967-70; Head, Agricultural Engineering Department, East of Scotland College of Agriculture, Edinburgh, 1970-86; Director, Scottish Centre of Agricultural Engineering, 1987-95, and Vice-Dean, Scottish Agricultural College, 1990-95. President, Institution of Agricultural Engineers, 1988-90; President, European Society of Agricultural Engineers, 1993-94; Managing Editor, Landwards, since 1996; Managing Editor, Land Technology, 1994-96; Editor and Chairman, Editorial Board, Journal of Agricultural Engineering Research, since 1998; Chairman, Douglas Bomford Trust, since 1998. EurAgEng Award for services to agricultural engineering, 2000. Publication: Choosing and Using Farm Machines. Address: (b.) Land Technology Ltd., 33 South Barnton Avenue, Edinburgh EH4 6AN; T.-0131-336 3129.

Woldman, Ethne. Chief Executive, Jewish Care Scotland, since 1996; b. 27.3.45, Glasgow; m., Harold; 1 s.; 2 d. Educ. Hutchesons' Grammar School, University of Strathclyde. Research Assistant, University of Strathclyde; Research Officer, University of Glasgow; Principal Officer, Research and Planning, Ayr County Council; Strathclyde Regional Council: Principal Officer, Principal Officer, Community Care. Trustee, Targu Mures Trust; Delegate, Glasgow Jewish Representative Council. Recreations: walking; voluntary work; theatre. Address: (b.) May Terrace, Giffnock, Glasgow G46 6LD; T.-0141-620 1800; e-mail: admin@jcarescot.org.uk

Wolf, Professor Charles Roland, BSc, PhD, FRSE, FMedSci. Director, Dundee University Biomedical Research Centre, since 1992; Honorary Director, ICRF Molecular Pharmacology Unit, Dundee, since 1992; b. 26.2.49, Sedgefield; m., Helga Losh; 1 s.; 1 d. Educ. Surrey University. Royal Society Fellow, Institute for Physiological Chemistry, University of Searland, W.

Germany 1976-77; Visiting Fellow, National Institute of Environmental Health Sciences, North Carolina, 1977-80; Visiting Scientist, ICI Central Toxicology Laboratories, Macclesfield, 1980-81; Head Scientist, Biochemistry Section, Institute of Toxicology, Mainz, W. Germany, 1981-82; Head, ICRF Molecular Pharmacology Group, Edinburgh University, 1982-92. Gerhard Zbinden Award, 2001. Publications: Molecular Genetics of Drug Resistance (Co-Editor), 1997; numerous scientific papers. Recreations: weaving; piano playing; gardening; hiking; poetry. Address: (b.) Biomedical Research Centre, Level 5, Ninewells Hospital and Medical School, Dundee DD1 9SY; T.-01382 632621.

Wolfe, William Cuthbertson, CA, JP. Member, National Council, since 1991, Member, National Executive Committee, since 1998, Scottish National Party; b. 22.2.24; 2 s.; 2 d. Educ. Bathgate Academy; George Watson's College, Edinburgh. Army Service, 1942-47, NW Europe and Far East; Air OP Pilot. Hon. Publications Treasurer, Saltire Society, 1953-60; Scout County Commissioner, West Lothian, 1960-64; Hon. President (Rector), Students' Association, Heriot-Watt University, 1966-69; contested (SNP) West Lothian, 1962, 1964, 1966, 1970, Feb. and Oct. 1974, 1979, North Edinburgh, Nov. 1973; Chairman, SNP, 1969-79, President, 1980-82; Treasurer, Scottish CND, 1982-85; Secretary, Scottish Poetry Library, 1985-91; Member, Forestry Commission's National Committee for Scotland, 1974-87. Publication: Scotland Lives.

Wolfram, Professor Julian, BSc, CEng, PhD, FRINA, MSaRS. Total Oil Marine Chair of Offshore Research and Development, Heriot-Watt University, since 1990 (Head, Department of Civil and Offshore Engineering); b. 2.8.46, London; m., Margaret Mary Lockhart; 1 s., 1 d., by pr. m. Educ. Gordonstoun; Reading University; Newcastle University. Research and Development Officer, Vickers Shipbuilders Ltd.; Lecturer (latterly Senior Lecturer) in Naval Architecture, Sunderland Polytechnic; Lecturer (latterly Senior Lecturer) in Marine Technology, Strathclyde University; Tutor, Open University; Chief Examiner, Ship Structures and Dynamics, Engineering Council; Consultant to several companies in the marine field. Publications: over 70 technical papers and reports. Recreations: sailing; squash; hill walking. Address: (b.) Heriot-Watt University, Edinburgh EH14 4AS; T.-0131-449 5111.

Wong, Professor Henry H.Y., BSc, PhD, DIC, CEng, FRAeS, DUniv. Emeritus Professor, Department of Aeronautics and Fluid Mechanics, Glasgow University; Senior Research Fellow, since 1997; Adviser to the Guangdong Higher Education Bureau, China, since 1985; Adviser to Glasgow University on Chinese Affairs, since 1986; Chair Professor, Nanjing University of Aeronautics and Astronautics, since 1987; "Concurrent" Professor, National University of Defense Technology, Changsha, since 1989; b. 23.5.22, Hong Kong; m., Joan Anstey; 2 s.; 1 d. Educ. St. Stephen College, Hong Kong; Jiao-Tong University, Shanghai; Imperial College, London; Glasgow University. Assistant Lecturer, Jiao-Tong University, 1947-48; Engineer, Armstrong Siddeley, 1949; Structural Engineer, Hunting Percival Aircraft, 1949-51; Senior Structural Engineer, de Havilland Aircraft, 1952-57; Senior Lecturer, Hatfield Polytechnic, 1957-59; Lecturer, Senior Lecturer, then Reader in Aeronautics and Fluid Mechanics, Glasgow University, from 1960; Economic and Technological Consultant to Shantou Special Economic Zone, China, since 1988. Former Treasurer and Vice-Chairman, Kilmardinny Music Circle; Chairman, Glasgow Summer School, 1979-95; City of Glasgow Lord Provost's Award, 1988. Recreations: reading; music; painting; swimming. Address: (h.) 77 Antonine Road, Bearsden, Glasgow; T.-0141-942 8346.

Wood, Alex, BA (Hons), MLitt, MEd. Principal and Head Teacher, Wester Hailes Education Centre, since 2000; b. 17.11.50, Dundee; m., Frances Kinnear; 2 d. Educ. Paisley Grammar School; New University of Ulster; Moray House College of Education; Stirling University. English Teacher, Craigroyston High School, 1973-75; Community Worker, Pilton Central Association, 1975-77; Remedial Teacher, Craigroyston High School, 1977-79; Principal Teacher, Learning Support, Craigroyston High School, 1979-90; Head of Centre, Millburn, Bathgate, 1990-96; Head Teacher, Kaimes School, 1996-99; Special Schools and Social Inclusion Manager, Edinburgh Education Department, 1999-2000; Edinburgh District Councillor, Pilton Ward, 1980-87; Parliamentary Candidate, Dumfriesshire, 1979; Parliamentary Candidate, West Edinburgh, 1984. Recreations: genealogy; horse-riding; reading. Address: (b.) 5 Murrayburn Drive, Edinburgh; T.-0131-442 2201.

Wood, Brian James, JP, BSc (Hons), FRSA. Rector, Hazlehead Academy, Aberdeen, since 1993 (Rector, Mearns Academy, 1989-93); Honorary Sheriff at Stonehaven; b. 6.12.49, Banff; m., Doreen A. Petrie; 1 s.; 1 d. Educ. Banff Academy; Aberdeen Academy; Aberdeen University; Aberdeen College of Education. Teacher of Physics, George Heriot's School, Edinburgh, 1972-75; Mackie Academy, 1975-89, latterly as Depute Rector. Chairman, Justices of the Peace for Kincardine and Deeside; Member, Chairmen of Justices Committee for Scotland; Elder, Church of Scotland. Recreations: sport; reading; music; travel; theatre; DIY. Address: (h.) 13 Edinview Gardens, Stonehaven; T.-01569 763888; e-mail: BWood@hazleheadacy.aberdeen.sch.uk

Wood, Graham Allan, MBChB, BDS, FDSRCPS, FRSC(Ed), FDSRCS(Eng). Consultant Oral and Maxillofacial Surgeon, Canniesburn Hospital, Glasgow, since 1995; Honorary Clincial Senior Lecturer, University of Glasgow, since 1995; Clinical Professor, University of Texas, USA, since 1990; b. 15.8.46, Glasgow; m., Lindsay Balfour; 1 s.; 1 d. Educ. Hillhead High School, Glasgow; University of Glasgow; University of Dundee. General dental practice, Glasgow, 1968-70; House Officer, Senior House Officer, Registrar, dental specialties, Glasgow Dental Hospital, Glasgow Victoria Infirmary and Canniesburn Hospital, 1970-72; Dental Surgeon, Grenfell Mission, Labrador, Canada, 1972-73; House Officer (plastic surgery), Dundee Royal Infirmary, 1978; Senior Registrar (oral and maxillofacial surgery), North Wales, 1979-83; Consultant, Oral and Maxillofacial Surgeon, North Wales, 1983-95. Fellow, International Association of Oral and Maxillofacial Surgeons; Fellow, British Association of Oral and Maxillofacial Surgeons. Recreations: hillwalking; golf; sailing; skiing. Address: (h.) Abbotsford, Broomknowe Road, Kilmacolm PA13 4HX; T.-01505 873954; e-mail: gawood@publiconline.co.uk

Wood, Sir Ian Clark, CBE (1982), LLD, BSc, DBA, CBIM, FCIB, FRSE. Chairman and Managing Director, John Wood Group PLC, since 1967; Chairman, J.W. Holdings, since 1982; b. 21.7.42, Aberdeen; m., Helen Macrae; 3 s. Educ. Robert Gordon's College, Aberdeen; Aberdeen University. Joined family business, John Wood & Sons, 1964; Member, PILOT; Joint Chairman, Industry Leadership Team; Chairman, Oil, Gas and Petrochemicals Supplies Office Board, 1997-2000; Chairman, Scottish Enterprise Board, 1997-2000; Fellow, Royal Society of Arts; Grampian Industrialist of the Year, 1978; Young Scottish Businessman of the Year, 1979; Scottish Free Enterprise Award, 1985; Scottish Business Achievement Award Trust — joint winner, 1992, corporate elite leadership award services category; Hon. LLD, 1984; Hon. DBA, 1998; Corporate Elite "World Player" Award, 1996; Fellow: Scottish Vocational Educational Council, Scottish

Qualifications Authority. Recreations: tennis; family; art. Address: (b.) John Wood Group PLC, John Wood House, Greenwell Road, East Tullos, Aberdeen; T.-01224 851000.

Wood, Karen Geddes, MA. Freelance arts consultant and producer; Producer, Glasgow Midsummer Carnival, since 1996; b. 13.10.59, Aberdeen. Educ. Harlaw Academy; Aberdeen University. Worked with emotionally disturbed adolescents and physically and mentally handicapped adults; began to organise professional and community dance events from Aberdeen; six-month visit to Brazil, working at Studio D Dance School; on return, set up and produced Scotland's first regional dance festival, Dance Around; since then has worked with many dance companies and arts organisations; appointed Artistic Director, Scottish Youth Dance Festival, 1994; Artistic Director, Dance Base, Edinburgh, 1991-95; Editor, Dance News Scotland; Committee Member, Dance Scotland, Scottish Dance Theatre, Scottish Carnival Arts Consortium, Plan B Collaborative Theatre. Recreations: theatre; visual art; travel; film. Address: 73 Clouston Street, Glasgow G20 8QW; T.-0141-946 1212.

Wood, Professor Robert Anderson, BSc, MB, ChB, FRCPEdin and Glas, FRCSEdin, FRCPsych. Postgraduate Medical Dean and Professor of Clinical Medicine, Aberdeen University, 1992-99; Member, Criminal Injuries Compensation Panel; b. 26.5.39, Edinburgh; m., Dr. Sheila Pirie; 1 s.; 3 d. Educ. Edinburgh Academy; Edinburgh University. Consultant Physician, Perth Royal Infirmary, 1972-92; Deputy Director of Postgraduate Medical Education, Dundee University, 1985-91; Dean, RCPE, 1992-95, Councillor, 1990-92, Treasurer, since 1999; Member, Council, MDDUS, since 1992; Member, Harveian Society (President, 1998-99). Member, Royal and Ancient, Blairgowrie, Elie and Craigie Hill golf clubs. Address: (h.) Ballomill House, Abernethy, Perthshire.

Wood, Professor Roy Christopher, BA, MPhil, PhD, PGDipHCA. Professor of Hospitality Management, Scottish Hotel School, University of Strathclyde, since 1996; Principal and Managing Director, International Hotel and Tourism Management Institutes, Luzern, Switzerland, since 2001; b. 29.7.59, Lancaster. Educ. Higham Lane School, Nuneaton; University of York; University of Bath; University of Strathclyde; Manchester Polytechnic. Lecturer in Applied Social Science, Oxford Polytechnic, 1983; Lecturer, Scottish Hotel School, University of Strathclyde, 1984-91; Senior Lecturer, Duncan of Jordanstone College of Art, 1992; Scottish Hotel School, University of Strathclyde: Senior Lecturer, 1992, Reader, 1995. Publications: author, co-author, editor or co-editor of eleven books, numerous academic papers. Recreations: music; literature; travel; art. Address: (b.) 94 Cathedral Street, Glasgow G4 0LG; T.-0141-548 3945; e-mail: r.c.wood@imi-luzern.com

Woodcock, Brian, BEd (Hons), MSc. Corporate Director, Neighbourhood Services (North), Aberdeen City Council; b. 22.4.59, St. Andrews; m., Susan; 1 s.; 1 d. Educ. Waid Academy, Anstruther; Jordanhill College. Sports Development Assistant, Central Regional Council, 1983-87; Sports Officer, Stirling District Council, 1987-89; Sport and Leisure Manager, Strathclyde District Council, 1989-90; Chief Leisure Officer, Derwentside District Council, 1990-92; Director of Leisure Services, Kilmarnock and Loudoun District Council, 1992-96. Hon. Chairman, Scottish Association of Directors of Leisure Services, 1995-98. Recreations: sport; music; theatre. Address: (b.) Aberdeen City Council, St. Nicholas House, Broad Street, Aberdeen AB10 1XJ; T.-01224 522472.

Woodroffe, Wing Commander Richard John, MBE, TQBHL. General Secretary, Royal British Legion Scotland, since 2001; b. 12.6.50, Newmarket; m., Elizabeth Clare; 3 s.

Educ. Khormaksar, Changi, Rutlish and King Alfred's (Wantage) Grammar Schools; North Berkshire College. Purser Officer, P&O Lines Ltd., 1968; joined RAF, 1971: Pilot Officer, RAF St. Athan, 1972, Deputy Officer Commanding Accounts Flight, RAF Benson, 1973-74, Officer Commanding Personnel Services Flight, RAF Saxa Vord, 1974-75, promoted to Flying Officer, 1974, Operations Wing Adjutant and No. 3 (F) Squadron Intelligence Officer, RAF Germany Harrier Force, 1976-78, promoted to Flight Lieutenant, 1978, officer Commanding Administration Flight, RAF Saxa Vord, 1979, Aide-de-Camp to Air Officer Commanding-in-Chief, Headquarters RAF Strike Command, 1980-82, Works Services and Airfield Survival Measures Project Officer, RAF Kinloss, 1982-84, promoted to Squadron Leader, 1984, College Secretariat 1 and College Press Liaison Officer, RAF College, Cranwell, 1984-86, Officer Commanding Personnel Management Squadron, RAF Bruggen, 1986-88, promoted to Wing Commander, 1988, assuming command of Administration Wing, RAF Leuchars, Fife, 1988-91, Air Member, Personnel's Management Planner and Briefer, MOD, 1991-93, Chairman of Boards, Officer and Aircrew Selection Centre, Cranwell then Deputy President, Ground Boards; posted to NATO HQ Allied Forces Central, 1996-2001. Recreations: sub-aqua; fishing; flytying; rough shooting; social golf. Address: New Haig House, Logie Green Road, Edinburgh EH7 4HR; T.-0131-557 2782; e-mail: rblshq@care4free.com

Woods, (Adrien) Charles, MA. Senior Director, Knowledge Management, Scottish Enterprise; b. 22.9.55, London. Educ. St. Andrews University. Various posts, Scottish Development Agency, 1981-91; Scottish Enterprise: Director, Policy and Planning, 1991-92, Director, Operations, 1992-94; Chief Executive, Scotland Europa, 1994-97. Recreations: golf; cycling. Address: (b.) 150 Broomielaw, Atlantic Quay, Glasgow G2 8LU; T.-0141-248 2700.

Woods, Professor Kevin James, BSc, PhD, MIHM. William R. Lindsay Professor of Health Policy and Economic Evaluation, University of Glasgow, since 2000; Chair, SAMH, since 2000; b. 9.2.53, Sale; m., Helen Denise; 3 d. Educ. Sale County Grammar School; Queen Mary College, London University. Lecturer in Health Care, Queen Mary College and London Hospital Medical College, 1979-85; Consumer and Operational Research Officer/Deputy District General Manager, North Derbyshire Health Authority, 1985-89; District General Manager, Chester Health Authority, 1990; Regional Director of Corporate Planning/Regional General Manager, Trent Regional Health Authority, 1991-94; Director of Strategy and Performance Management, NHS Management Executive, Scottish Executive, 1995-2000. Hon. Fellow, Health Services Management Unit, Manchester University, 1990-99. Recreations: running; gardening; golf; soccer. Address: (b.) Department of Public Health, University of Glasgow, Lilybank Gardens, Glasgow G12 8RZ; T.-0141-330 6822.

Woods, Professor Philip John, BSc, PhD, CPhys, FInstP. Professor of Nuclear Physics, Edinburgh University, since 2000; b. 25.6.61, Lincoln; m., Colette; 1 s.; 1 d. Educ. City Comprehensive School, Lincoln; Manchester University. Research Fellow, Birmingham University; Lecturer, then Reader, Edinburgh University, 1988-2000. Recreation: overseas travel. Address: (b.) Department of Physics and Astronomy, Edinburgh University, Edinburgh EH9 3JZ; T.-0131-650 5283.

Woolhouse, Professor Mark Edward John, MA, MSc, PhD. Chair of Veterinary Public Health and Quantitative Epidemiology, University of Edinburgh, since 1997; b. 25.4.59, Shrewsbury. Educ. Tiffin School, Kingston, Surrey; New College, University of Oxford; University of York; Queen's University, Canada. Research Fellow:

University of Zimbabwe, 1985-86, Imperial College, London, 1986-89, University of Oxford, 1989-97. Recreations: walking; fly-fishing; tennis. Address: (b.) Centre for Tropical Veterinary Medicine, University of Edinburgh, Easter Bush, Roslin, Midlothian; T.-0131-650 7347.

Woollins, Professor John Derek, BSc, PhD, FRSC, CChem. Professor (Chemistry), St Andrews University, since 1999; b. 18.8.55, Cleethorpes; m., Alexandra Martha Zoya; 3 s.; 1 d. Educ. Cleethorpes Grammar School; University of East Anglia. University of British Columbia; Michigan State University; Leeds University; Imperial College, London; Professor, Loughborough University. Publications include: (books) Non Metal Rings, Cages, Clusters; Inorganic Experiments; 250 papers. Recreations: skiing; travel. Address: (b.) Department of Chemistry, St Andrews University, St Andrews KY16 9ST; T.-01334 463861.

Woolman, Stephen, QC, LLB. Advocate, since 1987; b. 16.5.53, Edinburgh; m., Dr Helen Mackinnon; 2 d. Educ. George Heriot's School; Aberdeen University. Lecturer in Law, Edinburgh University, 1978-87; QC, 1998; Advocate Depute, 1999. Publication: Contract (3rd edition), 2001. Recreation: cinema. Address: (b.) Advocates' Library, Parliament House, Edinburgh EH1 1RF.

Wooton, Professor Ian, MA, MA, MPhil, PhD, FRSA. Bonar-Macfie Professor of Economics, Glasgow University, since 1995; Research Fellow, Centre for Economic Policy Research, London, since 1994; b. 4.4.57, Kirkcaldy; 1 s.; 1 d. Educ. Kirkcaldy High School; St. Andrews University; Columbia University, New York. Associate Professor of Economics, University of Western Ontario, London, Canada, 1982-95. Recreations: travel; architecture; calligraphy. Address: (b.) Department of Economics, Adam Smith Building, Glasgow University, Glasgow G12 8RT; T.-0141-330 4672; (h.) Flat 2B, 67 Cleveden Road, Glasgow G12 0JN; T.-0141-357 0277.

Worden, John Leonard, MA (Hons), MSc, MIPD. Dean, Napier University Business School, since 1996; b. 19.12.49, London; m., Morag; 2 s.; 2 d. Educ. Apsley Grammar; Dundee University; Leicester University. Trainee Housing Manager, Dundee Corporation, 1974; Assistant Training Officer, Tayside Regional Council, 1975; Senior Personnel Practitioner, Tayside Regional Council, 1978; Personnel Manager, Veeder Root Ltd., 1980; Lecturer, Human Resource Management, Glasgow Caledonian University, 1981; Senior Lecturer, Napier University, 1984; Associate Head/Director of Management Development Unit, Napier University, 1990; Independent Chairman, Midlothian Council Job Evaluation Appeals Committee; External examiner, Glasgow Caledonian and Robert Gordon Universities. Recreations: hill-walking; literature; football. Address: (b.) Napier University Business School, Sighthill Court, Edinburgh ; T.-0131-455 3382.

Worthington, Tony, BA, MEd. MP (Labour), Clydebank and Milngavie, since 1987; Member, International Development Select Committee; b. 11.10.41, Hertfordshire; m., Angela; 1 s.; 1 d. Educ. City School, Lincoln; London School of Economics; York University; Glasgow University. Parliamentary Under Secretary of State, Northern Ireland Office, 1997-98. Recreation: gardening. Address: (h.) 24 Cleddans Crescent, Hardgate, Clydebank; T.-01389 873195; e-mail: worthingtont@parliament.uk

Wotherspoon, (John Munro) Iain, TD, DL. Partner, MacAndrew & Jenkins, WS, since 1954; Deputy Lieutenant, Districts of Lochaber, Inverness, Badenoch and Strathspey, now Inverness, since 1982, and Clerk, since 1985; b. 19.7.24, Inverness; m., Victoria Avril Jean

Edwards; 2 s.; 2 d. Educ. Inverness Royal Academy; Loretto School; Trinity College, Oxford; Edinburgh University. Lt., Royal Signals, Europe and Burma, 1944-46; TA, 1948-78; Lt.-Col. commanding 51 (Highland) Division Signals, 1963-70; Col. Dep. Cdr. 13 Signals Gp., 1970-72; Hon. Col. 32 (Scottish) Signal Regiment, 1972-78; ADC to The Queen, 1972-76; WS, 1950; Solicitor and Land Owner. Recreations: shooting; fishing; stalking. Address: (h.) Mayfield, 62 Midmills Road, Inverness IV2 3QL; T.-(h.) 01463 233642; (b.) 01463 723501; e-mail: email@macandrewjenkins.co.uk

Wray, Professor David, MD (Hons), BDS, MB, ChB, FDSRCPS, FDSRCS (Edin), FMedSci. Professor of Oral Medicine, Glasgow University, since 1993 (Dean, Dental School, since 2000); Hon. Consultant, Greater Glasgow Health Board, since 1993; b. 3.1.51, Carshalton; m., Alyson P.M. Wray; 4 s. Educ. Uddingston Grammar School; Glasgow University. Fogarty Fellow, N.I.H. Bethesda, USA, 1979-81; Wellcome Research Fellow, Royal Dental, London, 1982; Senior Lecturer, Edinburgh University, 1983-92. Recreations: golf; curling; skiing. Address: (h.) 125 Dowanhill Street, Glasgow G12 9DN; e-mail: d.wray@dental.gla.ac.uk

Wray, James. MP (Labour), Glasgow Baillieston (formerly Glasgow Provan); b. 28.4.38; m.; 1 s.; 2 d. Former heavy goods vehicle driver; former Strathclyde Regional Councillor. Address: (b.) House of Commons, London SW1A 0AA.

Wright, Alex, ILTM, AIWSc, BSc, MA, PhD. Lecturer in Scottish Politics, University of Dundee, since 1998; Member, Scottish Consumer Council, since 1998; b. 4.1.52, Perth. Educ. Aldenham School; University of Dundee. Management posts, Meyer International plc, 1972-90; Research Fellow, University of Dundee, 1997-98; Visiting Research Fellow, Institute for Advanced Studies in the Humanities, University of Edinburgh, 2002. Member, Institute of Welsh Affairs. Publications: Scotland: The Challenge of Devolution (Editor and Contributing Author), 2000; contributions to: Region Building, 1995, EMU – An Expanding Europe and the World, 1998, Europe United, The United Kingdom Disunited, 2000. Recreations: Scottish cuisine; bird watching; walking and thinking. Address: (b.) Department of Politics, University of Dundee, Dundee DD1 4HN; T.-01382 344594; e-mail: a.wright@dundee.ac.uk

Wright, Andrew Paul Kilding, OBE, BArch, RIBA, PPRIAS, FRSA, FSA Scot. Chartered Architect and Heritage Consultant; Partner, Law & Dunbar-Nasmith, 1981-2001; b. 11.2.47, Walsall; m., Jean Patricia; 1 s.; 2 d. Educ. Queen Mary's Grammar School, Walsall; Liverpool University School of Architecture. Practising architect, since 1972; President, Inverness Architectural Association, 1986-88; External Examiner, Robert Gordon University, since 1990; Council, Royal Institute of British Architects, 1988-94 and 1995-97; President, Royal Incorporation of Architects in Scotland, 1995-97 (Member, Council, RIAS, 1985-94, 1995-99); Diocesan Architect, Diocese of Moray, Ross and Caithness, 1989-98; Consultant Architect to National Trust for Scotland for Mar Lodge Estate, 1995-99; Board Director, Glasgow 1999 Festival Company, since 1996; Member, Ancient Monuments Board for Scotland, since 1996; Commissioner, Royal Fine Art Commission for Scotland, since 1997; Hon. Adviser, Scottish Redundant Churches Trust, since 1996; Member, Church of Scotland Committee on Artistic Matters, since 1999; Trustee, Clan MacKenzie Charitable Trust, since 1998; Architectural Adviser, Holyrood Progress Group, Scottish Parliament, since 2000; Member, Award Panel for Arts and Crafts in Architecture, Saltire Society, since 2001; Conservation Adviser to Highland Buildings Preservation Trust, since 2001; Chairman, Conservation Advisory Panel to Hopetoun

House Preservation Trust, since 1992. Recreations: music; railway history; fishing. Address: (b.) 29 St. Leonards Road, Forres, IV36 1EN; T.-01309 673221.

Wright, Bill, RSW, RGI, PAI, DA. Painter; b. 1.9.31, Glasgow; m., Anne Elizabeth; 3 d. Educ. Hyndland Secondary School; Glasgow School of Art. Work in several public and private collections in Norway, USA, Germany, Switzerland, Sarajavo, Saudi Arabia, Belgium; included in exhibitions in Wales, Poland, Germany, Norway, Yugoslavia, Netherlands; elected: RSW, 1977, RGI, 1990, PAI, 1995; formerly Adviser in Art, Strathclyde Regional Council; formerly Lecturer, Scottish Arts Council; President, Scottish Artists Benevolent Society. Recreations: opera; gardening; lobster fishing. Address: (h.) Old Lagalgarve Cottage, Bellochantuy, Argyll PA28 6QE; T.-01586 820372.

Wright, Professor Crispin James Garth, MA, PhD, FBA, BPhil, DLitt, FRSE. Professor of Logic and Metaphysics, St. Andrews University, since 1978; Leverhulme Personal Research Professor, since 1998; Bishop Wardlaw Professor, since 1997; b. 21.12.42, Bagshot, Surrey; m., Catherine; 2 s. Educ. Birkenhead School; Trinity College, Cambridge. Junior Research Fellow, Trinity College, Oxford, 1967-69; Fellow/Research Fellow, All Souls College, Oxford, 1969-78. Publications: Wittgenstein on the Foundations of Mathematics, 1980; Frege's Conception of Numbers as Objects, 1983; Realism, Meaning and Truth, 1986; Truth and Objectivity, 1992. Recreations: mountaineering; gardening; travel. Address: (b.) Department of Logic and Metaphysics, St. Andrews University, St. Andrews KY16 9AL.

Wright, Professor David Frederick, MA (Cantab), DD (Edin). Professor of Patristic and Reformed Christianity, Edinburgh University, since 1999; b. 2.10.37, Hayes, Kent; m., Anne-Marie; 1 s.; 1 d. Educ. Christ's College, Cambridge; Lincoln College, Oxford. Edinburgh University: Lecturer, 1964-73, Senior Lecturer, 1973-99, Associate Dean, Faculty of Divinity, 1972-76, Dean, 1988-92, Member, University Court, 1984-87; External Examiner, Universities of Sussex, Liverpool, Durham, Cambridge, etc.; Member, Council of Management, Keston College; Chairman, Tyndale Fellowship for Biblical and Theological Research; Associate Editor, Tyndale Bulletin; Editor, Scottish Bulletin of Evangelical Theology; Secretary, of Praesidium, International Congress on Calvin Research; Chair, Scottish Evangelical Theology Society; Chair, Handsel Press; Chair, Rutherford House Trustees; recipient of Festschrift, 1997; Fellow, Royal Historical Society, 2000. Publications: Common Places of Martin Bucer, 1972; Essays in Evangelical Social Ethics (Editor), 1979; Lion Handbook History of Christianity (Consultant Editor), 1977; New Dictionary of Theology (Joint Editor), 1988; The Bible in Scottish Life and Literature (Contributor and Editor), 1988; Chosen by God: Mary in Evangelical Perspective (Contributor and Editor), 1989; Dictionary of Scottish Church History and Theology (Chief General Editor), 1993; Calvin's Old Testament Commentaries (General Editor), 1993; Martin Bucer: Reforming Church and Community (Contributor and Editor), 1994; Disruption to Diversity: Edinburgh Divinity 1846-1996 (Co-Editor and Contributor), 1996; Nelson's New Christian Dictionary (Consultant Editor and Contributor), 2001. Recreations: walking; gardening; DIY. Address: (h.) 3 East Camus Road, Edinburgh EH10 6RE; T.-0131-445 1960.

Wright, David John, MB, BS, FRCA, FRCPE. Consultant Anaesthetist, Western General Hospital, Edinburgh, since 1979; b. 13.4.44, Oswestry; m., Bronwen; 2 s.; 1 d. Educ. Bristol Grammar School; St. Bartholomew's Hospital Medical College, London. Honorary Editor, Scottish Society of the History of Medicine. Address: (h.) 20 Lennox Row, Edinburgh EH5 3JW; T.-0131-552 3439; e-mail: dr.david.wright@virgin.net

Wright, Rev. David Livingston, MA, BD, FFCS. Minister of Religion, Church of Scotland, since 1957; b. 18.5.30, Aberdeen; m., Margaret Brown; 2 s.; 1 d. Educ. Robert Gordon's College, Aberdeen; King's College, Aberdeen University. Organist and choirmaster, 1946-54; National Service, 1949-51, and TA, 1951-54; Chairman, Youth For Christ, 1952-55; Assistant, Garthdee, Aberdeen, 1955-56, West St Andrew's, 1956-57; licensed by Aberdeen Presbytery, 1957; Assistant, St Andrew's, Dundee, till December 1957; Minister: Cockenzie Chalmers Memorial, 1957-64, Forfar Lowson Memorial, 1964-71, Hawick Old, 1971-86, linked with Teviothead, 1972, Stornoway St Columba's Old Parish, 1986-98. Former Moderator, Jedburgh Presbytery and Synod of Borders; twice Moderator, Lewis Presbytery; Convener, Business, Superintendence, World Mission Committees and served on Assembly Committees; former Chairman, Scottish Reformation Society; former Chairman, National Church Association. Publications: The Meaning of the Lord's Day, 1960; Reformed Book of Common Order (Contributor), 1977; Reformed and Evangelical (Editor), 1992; The Difference Christ Makes, 1997. Recreations: golf; walking the dog; reading; occasional TV; playing piano and organ. Address: (h.) 84 Wyvis Drive, Nairn IV12 4TP; T.-01667 451613.

Wright, Professor Eric George, BSc, PhD, CBiol, MIBiol, FRCPath. Professor of Experimental Haematology, University of Dundee, since 1999; b. 11.1.49, Wolverhampton. Educ. Wolverhampton Grammar School; Sussex University, Manchester University. WHO Research Fellow, Sloan Kettering Cancer Center, New York; Research Fellow, Paterson Institute for Cancer Research, Manchester; Lecturer in Cellular Pathology, University of St. Andrews; senior scientific positions, Medical Research Council Radiation and Genome Stability Unit, Harwell; Honorary Professor, Brunel University, University of Reading. David Anderson-Berry Medal, Royal Society of Edinburgh, 1999; Member, UK Department of Health Committee on Medical Effects of Radiation in the Environment; Chairman, Radiation and Cancer Biology Committee, British Institute of Radiology; Chairman, Scientific Advisory Committee, Association for International Cancer Research. Publications: 150 scientific papers. Recreations: music; gardening; hillwalking. Address: (b.) University of Dundee, Department of Molecular and Cellular Pathology, Ninewells Hospital and Medical School, Dundee DD1 9SY; T.-01382 632169; e-mail: e.g.wright@dundee.ac.uk

Wright, Professor George, BSc, MPhil, PhD. Deputy Director and Professor of Business Administration, Strathclyde Graduate Business School, since 1991; b. 24.11.52, Louth; m., Josephine Elizabeth; 2 s. Educ. Queen Elizabeth I Grammar School; NE London Polytechnic; Brunel University. Research Assistant, Brunel University, 1974-79; Research Fellow, Huddersfield Polytechnic, 1979-81; Senior Lecturer, City of London Polytechnic, 1981-86; Reader, then Professor, Bristol Business School, 1986-91. Publications: seven books; 100 journal articles. Recreation: renovating historic houses. Address: (b.) Strathclyde Graduate Business School, 199 Cathedral Street, Glasgow G4 0QU; T.-0141-553 6000.

Wright, George Gordon. Publisher and Photographer; b. 25.6.42, Edinburgh; m., Carmen Ilie; 1 s. Educ. Darroch Secondary School; Heriot Watt College. Started publishing as a hobby, 1969; left printing trade, 1973, to develop own publishing company; founder Member, Scottish General Publishers Association; Past Chairman, Scottish Young Publishers Society; Oliver Brown Award, 1994; Secretary/Treasurer, 200 Burns Club, since 1991. Photographic Exhibitions: The Netherbow, 1979; National Library of Scotland, 2001. Publications: MacDiarmid: An Illustrated Biography, 1977; A Guide to the Royal Mile,

1979; Orkney From Old Photographs, 1981; A Guide to Holyrood Park and Arthur's Seat, 1987. Recreations: history of Edinburgh; photography; jazz. Address: (h.) 25 Mayfield Road, Edinburgh EH9 2NQ; T.-0131-667 1300.

Wright, Grahame Alan, BA (Econ), MPhil (Cantab). Depute Principal, University of Abertay Dundee; Director, Dundee Incubator Ltd., since 1997; Trustee: Dundee Heritage Trust, since 1997, Dundee North America Bursary Fund, since 1999; b. 5.8.47, Sunderland; m., Joan Margaret; 2 s.; 1 d. Educ. Mortimer County Secondary, South Shields; Open University; Newcastle Polytechnic; Clare College, Cambridge. Musical instrument retailer, 1963-77; Research Assistant, Lecturer, Senior Lecturer, Principal Lecturer, Newcastle Polytechnic, 1980-91; Head, Department of Accountancy, Economics and Law, Dundee Institute of Technology, 1991-93; appointed Assistant Principal External Relations, University of Abertay Dundee, 1993. Recreations: music; preacher, Methodist Church. Address: (h.) 12 Woodlands Park, Blairgowrie, PH10 6UW; T.-01250 875243.

Wright, John Robertson, Chairman, Edinburgh Fund Managers PLC; b. 10.9.41, London; m., Christine; 1 s.; 1 d. Educ. Daniel Stewart's College, Edinburgh. Vice President, First Interstate Bank of California, 1974-79; Assistant General Manager, Bank of Scotland, 1979-86; Director and Chief Executive Officer, Oman International Bank, 1986-93; Chief Executive and Director: Northern Bank Ltd., 1993-97, Northern Bank and National Irish Banks, 1996-97; Chief Executive and Chief General Manager, Gulf Bank KSC, Kuwait, 1997-98; Director, Clydesdale Bank PLC and Yorkshire Bank PLC, 1998-2001; President, Institute of Bankers in Ireland, 1996-97. Recreations: rugby spectating. Address: Ednam Mains House, Ednam, Kelso TD5 7QL.

Wright, Rev. Kenyon Edward, CBE, MA, BA, BSc, MTh, DLitt. Convener, Vision 21; Convener, People and Parliament; Consultant on Justice and Peace to ACTS (Action of Churches Together in Scotland); Canon Emeritus and Companion of the Order of the Cross of Nails, Coventry Cathedral; b. 31.8.32, Paisley; m., Betty Robinson; 3 d. Educ. Paisley Grammar School; Glasgow University; Cambridge University. Missionary in India, 1955-70; Director, Ecumenical Social and Industrial Institute, Durgapur, India, 1963-70; Director, Urban Ministry, Coventry Cathedral, 1970-74; Canon Residentiary and Director of International Ministry, Coventry Cathedral, 1974-81; General Secretary, Scottish Churches Council and Director, Scottish Churches House, 1981-90; former Chair, Executive, Scottish Constitutional Convention; Member, Consultative Steering Group on the Scottish Parliament. Recreations: reading; walking; travel; living life to the full. Address: 4 Katrine Crescent, Callander FK17 8JS; T.-01877 330464; e-mail: kenyonwright@aol.com

Wright, Malcolm Robert, MHSM, DipHSM. Chief Executive, Dumfries and Galloway Health Board, since 2001; Chief Executive, Dumfries and Galloway Acute and Maternity Hospitals NHS Trust, 1999-2001; b. 1.9.57, Blyth; m., Hilary; 1 s.; 1 d. Educ. Kings School, Tynemouth; Penicuik High School. Hospital Manager, Great Ormond Street, London, 1989-92; Unit General Manager, Lothian Health Board, 1992-94; Chief Executive, Edinburgh and Sick Children's NHS Trust, 1994-99. Director, Scottish Leadership Foundation. Recreations: cycling; reading; architecture. Address: (b.) Dumfries and Galloway Royal Infirmary, Bankend Road, Dumfries DG1 4AP; T.-01387 241592; e-mail: mwright@dghb.scot.nhs.uk

Wright, Philip, BSc, CEng, MICE. Head, Air, Climate and Engineering Unit, and Chief Water Engineer, Scottish Executive, Environment Group, since 1999; b. 15.4.49, Edinburgh; m., Anne Margaret; 3 d. Educ. St. Anthony's Secondary School; Tynecastle Secondary School; Heriot Watt University. Civil Engineer, Edinburgh Corporation,

1971-75, Lothian Regional Council, 1975-82; joined Scottish Office as Senior Civil Engineer, 1982; Assistant Chief Engineer, 1991; Head, European Environment and Engineering Unit, and Chief Water Engineer, 1997. Chairman, Scotland and Northern Ireland Forum for Environmental Research; Director, Foundation for Water Research. Recreations: football; racquetball; golf; walking. Address: (b.) Victoria Quay, Edinburgh EH6 6QQ; T.-0131-244 0193; e-mail: philip.wright@scotland.gsi.gov.uk

Wright, Professor Robert Edward, BA, MA, PhD, FRSA, FFCS, ILTM. Professor of Economics, University of Stirling, since 1995; b. 28.4.58, Trenton, Ontario, Canada. Educ. Trenton High School; University of Western Ontario; University of Stockholm; INED, Paris; University of Michigan. Research Fellow, Birkbeck College, London University, 1987; Lecturer/Senior Lecturer in Economics, University of Glasgow, 1991-95. Recreation: mountaineering. Address: Department of Economics, University of Stirling, Stirling FK9 4LA.

Wright, Tom, BA (Hons). Writer; b. 8.3.23, Glasgow. Educ. Coatbridge High School; Strathclyde University. Served apprenticeship in embossing and stained glass; Army, 1943-47; served in Europe and Far East, including Japan; began to publish poems and short stories after demobilisation; had first play performed, Edinburgh Festival, 1960; author of There Was A Man; began to write radio and television drama, 1963; former Creative Writing Fellow; former Script Editor, BBC Scotland Drama Department; has also been Script Editor and Story Line Editor, Take The High Road, STV; won Festival Fringe Award, 1984, for Talk of the Devil; recent work includes The Hunter and the Hill, 1994, and Forgotten Army, 1995; Past Chairman, Scottish Committee, Writers' Guild, and Scottish Society of Playwrights. Recreation: listening to music. Address: 318 Churchill Drive, Glasgow G11.

Wunsch, Nigel John, BA. Strategy and Planning Manager, Railtrack, since 2000, Business Development Manager, 1998-2000; b. 21.5.58, Bellshill; m., Linda. Educ. St. Aloysius College; Dundee College of Technology. Various local management jobs, ScotRail, 1981-91; resource planning, ScotRail, 1991-94; timetable planning, Railtrack, 1994-98. Recreations: amateur theatre. Address: (b.) Buchanan House, 58 Port Dundas Road, Glasgow; T.-0141-335 2790.

Wyke, John Anthony, MA, PhD, VetMB, FRCVS, FRSE, FMedSci. Director, Beatson Institute for Cancer Research, since 1987; Professor, Glasgow University; b. 5.4.42, Cleethorpes. Educ. Dulwich College; Cambridge University; Glasgow University; London University. Leukemia Society of America Fellow, Universities of Washington and Southern California, 1970-72; Staff Scientist, Imperial Cancer Research Fund, 1972-85; Assistant Director of Research, 1985-87. Address: (b.) Beatson Institute for Cancer Research, CRC Beatson Laboratories, Garscube Estate, Switchback Road, Bearsden, Glasgow G61 1BD; T.-0141-330 3950; e-mail: j.wyke@beatson.gla.ac.uk

Wylie, Rt. Hon. Lord (Norman Russell Wylie), PC (1970), VRD (1961), BA (Oxon), LLB (Glas). Senator of the College of Justice in Scotland, 1974- 90; b. 26.10.23, Elderslie; m., Gillian Mary Verney; 3 s. Educ. Paisley Grammar School; St. Edmund Hall, Oxford (Hon. Fellow, since 1975); Glasgow University; Edinburgh University. Fleet Air Arm, 1942-46 (subsequently RNR, Lt.-Cdr, 1954). Admitted Faculty of Advocates, 1952; Standing Junior Counsel to Air Ministry, 1956; Advocate Depute, 1958; QC, 1964; Solicitor General for Scotland, April to October, 1964; MP (Conservative), Edinburgh Pentlands, 1964-74; Lord Advocate, 1970-74. Chairman, Scottish National Committee, English Speaking Union of Commonwealth, 1978-84; Trustee, Carnegie Trust for Universities of

Scotland, 1975-95; Justice of Appeal, Republic of Botswana, 1994-96. Recreation: gardening. Address: (h.) 30 Lauder Road, Edinburgh; T.-0131-667 8377.

Wylie, Alexander Featherstonhaugh, QC, LLB, FCIArb. Lawyer; Member of the Scottish Bar, since 1978; b. 2.6.51, Perth; m., Gail Elizabeth Watson Duncan; 2 d. Educ. Edinburgh University. Qualified Solicitor in Scotland, 1976; called to Scottish Bar, 1978; Standing Junior Counsel to Accountant of Court, 1986-89; Advocate Depute, 1989-92; called to English Bar, 1990; QC (Scot), 1991. Part-time Joint Chairman, Discipline Committee, Institute of Chartered Accountants of Scotland, since 1994; Member, Scottish Legal Aid Board, since 1994; part-time Sheriff, since 2000; part-time Chairman, Police Appeals Tribunal, since 2001. Address: (b.) Advocates Library, Parliament House, Edinburgh, EH1 1RF; T.-0131-226 2881.

Wylie, Rev. William Andrew, MA; b. 17.5.27, London; m., Jennifer Barclay Mack; 4 d. by pr. m. Educ. Glasgow Academy; Glasgow University and Trinity College. Royal Navy, 1944-47; Chaplain, Clyde Division, RNVR, 1954-59; Minister: Stepps, 1953-59, Scots Kirk, Lausanne, 1959-67; General Secretary, Scottish Churches Council, 1967-71; Minister, St. Andrew's and St. George's, Edinburgh, 1972-85; Chaplain, Inverclyde Industrial Mission, 1985-86; Chaplain to the offshore oil industry, 1986-91; founded Prioritas Consultants, 1991; elected Hon. Fellow, Institute of Petroleum, 1990; elected Burgess of Aberdeen, 1990; Co-Founder and Chairman, Lausanne International School, 1962-67; Chairman of Governors, Aiglon College, Switzerland, 1984-91 (Hon. Chaplain, 1991); Governor, Fettes College, 1978-85; Hon. Citizen, Indianapolis, 1970. Recreations: gardening; writing; music; labradors; not playing golf. Address: (h.) Wellrose Cottage, Peat Inn, Fife KY15 5LH; T.-01334 840600.

Wylie, George. Artist; b. 1921, Glasgow. Installations; performances; events; best known for "paper boat" installation and exhibition, Glasgow, Liverpool, London and New York, 1989-90; Visiting Lecturer, Glasgow School of Art; Associate, Royal Scottish Academy; Hon. DLitt, Strathclyde University, Glasgow.

Wylie, Gordon Hope, DA, RSW. Painter; b. 12.2.30, Greenock; m., Helen; 2 s. Educ. Highlanders' Academy, Greenock; Greenock High School; Glasgow School of Art; Hospitalfield College of Art, Arbroath; Jordanhill College of Education. Teacher of Art and Design, Paisley Grammar School; Principal Teacher of Art and Design: St. Columba's School, Kilmacolm, Greenock Academy; former Examiner, Scottish Examination Board (Principal Examiner, Art and Design, 1980-92). Newbery Medallist, GSA, 1953, Post-diploma Award, GSA, 1953, Royal Scottish Academy Award, GSA, 1953; Alexander Graham Munro Award, RSW, 1996; Mabel McKinlay Award, RGI, 1998; paintings in collections worldwide; widely exhibited. Recreations: music (Member, Bach Choir, RSAM and RSNO Choir for many years). Address: 17 Fox Street, Greenock PA16 8BS; T.-01475 723033.

Wylie, Gordon Malcolm, SBStJ, LLB, FSA Scot, NP, TEP, FFCS, WS. Partner, Biggart Baillie, Solicitors; Clerk to the Trades House of Glasgow; Boxmaster, Convenery of Trades of Edinburgh; Preses, Grand Antiquity Society of Glasgow, 2000-01; Clerk to General Commissioners of Inland Revenue, Glasgow North and South Divisions; b. Newton Mearns. Educ. Dunoon Grammar School; Glasgow University. Honorary Treasurer, Edinburgh Summer School in Ancient Greek, 1975-99; Director, Bailford Trustees Ltd.; Chairman, Edinburgh Subscription Ball Committee; Freeman of Glasgow; Deacon, Incorporation of Hammermen of Edinburgh, 1996-99; Governor, Trades Maiden Hospital of Edinburgh; Member, Edinburgh West End Community Council; wrote Scottish contribution to International Bar Association's International Dictionary of

Succession Terms; Trustee, Britannia Panopticon Music Hall Trust. Recreations: music; history and the arts generally; country walks; foreign travel. Address: (b.) 310 St. Vincent Street, Glasgow; T.-0141-228 8000.

Wyllie, Very Rev. Hugh Rutherford, MA, Hon.DD (Aberdeen), FCIBS. Minister, Old Parish Church of Hamilton, 1981-2000; Moderator, General Assembly of the Church of Scotland, 1992-93; admitted as Hon. Freeman, District of Hamilton, 1992; b. 11.10.34, Glasgow; m., Eileen E. Cameron, MA; 2 d. Educ. Shawlands Academy; Hutchesons' Grammar School, Glasgow. Union Bank of Scotland, 1951-53; RAF, 1953-55; Glasgow University, 1956-62; Assistant Minister, Glasgow Cathedral, 1962-65; Minister, Dunbeth Church, Coatbridge, 1965-72; Minister, Cathcart South Church, Glasgow, 1972-81; Moderator, Presbytery of Hamilton, 1989-90, Convener, Business Committee, 1991-95; President, Hamilton Burns Club, 1990; founder Member, Hamilton Centre for Information for the Unemployed, 1983; introduced Dial-a-Fact on drugs and alcohol, 1986; established Hamilton Church History Project, 1984-87; Convener, General Assembly's Stewardship and Budget Committee, 1978-83; Convener, Stewardship and Finance Board, 1983-86; Convener, Assembly Council, 1987-91; Member, Board of Nomination to Church Chairs, 1985-91 and 1993-99; Member, General Assembly's Board of Practice and Procedure, 1991-95; Member, Board of Communication, since 1999; Non-Executive Director, Lanarkshire Health Care NHS Trust, 1995-99, Vice-Chairman, 1996-99; Trustee, Lanarkshire Primary Care NHS Trust, 1999-2001; Dr William Barclay Memorial Lecturer, 1994; elected Member, Council, Scout Association, 1993; Master, Hamilton Hospital, 1982-2000; Chaplain: Royal British Legion, Hamilton, since 1981, Lanarkshire Burma Star Association, since 1983, Q Division, Strathclyde Police, since 1984. Recreations: gardening; DIY; yellow labrador. Address: 18 Chantinghall Road, Hamilton ML3 8NP.

Wyllie, James Hogarth, BA, MA. Senior Lecturer in International Relations and Director, Postgraduate Strategic Studies Programme, Aberdeen University, since 1979; Member, JDM Marketing Associates, Aberdeen, since 1992; b. 7.3.51, Dumfries; m., Claire Helen Beaton; 2 s. Educ. Sanquhar Academy; Dumfries Academy; Stirling University; Lancaster University. Research Officer, Ministry of Defence, 1974-75; Tutor in Politics, Durham University, 1975-77; Lecturer in Politics, University of East Anglia, 1977-79; freelance journalism; frequent current affairs comment and analysis, BBC Radio; Commonwealth Fellow, University of Calgary, 1988; International Affairs Analyst, Grampian Television, 1989-94; Specialist Correspondent, Jane's Intelligence Review, 1992-98. Publications: Influence of British Arms; European Security in the Nuclear Age; Economist Pocket Guide to Defence (Co-author); International Politics since 1945 (Contributor); European Security in the New Political Environment. Recreations: travelling; cinema; badminton; walking. Address: (b.) Department of Politics and International Relations, Aberdeen University, Aberdeen AB24 3QY; T.-01224 272725; e-mail: j.h.wyllie@abdn.ac.uk

Wyllie, William, MBE, JP, DL, DBA. Dean of Guild, City of Aberdeen, 1981-98; Governor, Robert Gordon University, Aberdeen, since 1991; b. 5.2.32, Aberdeen; m., Mary Anne; 3 d. Educ. Robert Gordon's College, Aberdeen; Gordonstoun School, Elgin; North of Scotland College of Agriculture. W. Smith & Son, seedsmen; Hazlehead Nurseries, Aberdeen, 1952-85, retiring as Managing Director. Secretary, NE Scotland Horticultural Training Board; former Chairman, Aberdeen Airport Consultative Committee; Chairman, British Chambers of Commerce Aviation Committee. Recreations: gardening; swimming; reading. Address: (h.) 156 Kings Gate, Aberdeen, AB15 6BR; T.-01224 317811.

Y

Yadav, Professor Pradeep Kumar, BSc (Hons), MSc (Physics), MSc (Financial Studies), PhD. Professor of Finance, since 1993, Head, Department of Accounting and Finance, 1995-98, Strathclyde University; Director, Scottish Institute for Research in Investment and Finance, since 1998; b. 31.8.53, India; m., Mamta; 1 s.; 1 d. Educ. St. Xaviers School, Delhi; St. Stephen's College, University of Delhi; Strathclyde University. Member, Indian Administrative Service (formerly Indian Civil Service), 1976-86; Lecturer in Finance/Senior Lecturer in Finance, Department of Accounting and Finance, Strathclyde University, 1987-93. Publications: 25 articles in journals and books. Address: (b.) Department of Accounting and Finance, Strathclyde University, 100 Cathedral Street, Glasgow G4 0LN; T.-0141-548 3939.

Yarrow, Sir Eric Grant, MBE, DL, CEng, MRINA, FRSE. Chairman, Clydesdale Bank PLC, 1985-91 (Director, since 1962); Director, National Australia Bank Ltd., 1987-91; b. 23.4.20, Glasgow; m., 1, Rosemary Ann Young (deceased); 1 s. (deceased); 2, Annette Elizabeth Francoise Steven (m. diss.); 3 s.; 3, Joan Botting; 3 step d. Educ. Marlborough College; Glasgow University. Served engineering apprenticeship, G. & J. Weir, 1938-39; Royal Engineers, 1939-45; served Burma, 1942-45 (Major, RE, 1945); Yarrow & Co. Ltd. (later Yarrow PLC): Assistant Manager, 1946, Director, 1948, Managing Director, 1958-67, Chairman, 1962-85, President, 1985-87; Director, Standard Life Assurance Company, 1958-91; Chairman, Princess Louise Scottish Hospital, Erskine, 1980-86, Hon. President, since 1986; President, Scottish Convalescent Home for Children, 1957-70; Council Member, Royal Institution of Naval Architects, since 1957 (Vice President, 1965, Honorary Vice President, 1972); Member, General Committee, Lloyd's Register of Shipping, 1960-89; Deacon, Incorporation of Hammermen in Glasgow, 1961-62; Chairman, Yarrow (Shipbuilders) Ltd., 1962-79; Officer (Brother), Order of St. John, since 1965; Deputy Lieutenant, County of Renfrewshire, 1970-96; Prime Warden, Worshipful Company of Shipwrights, 1970-71; Council Member, Institute of Directors, 1983-90; President, Smeatonian Society of Civil Engineers, 1983-84; President, The Marlburian Club, 1984; President, Scottish Area, Burma Star Association, since 1990; Vice President, Royal Highland and Agricultural Society for Scotland, 1990. Recreation: golf. Address: (h.) Cloak, Kilmacolm, Renfrewshire PA13 4SD; T.-01505 872067; e-mail: egyarrow@aol.com

Yates, Keith, BSc (Hons), OBE. Chief Executive, Stirling Council, since 1995; b. 13.3.48, Preston; m., Aileen; 1 s.; 2 d. Educ. Preston Grammar School; Sheffield University; Liverpool University. Consultant, Peat Marwick Kates, 1971; Planning Officer, Oxfordshire County Council, 1971; Consultant, Colin Buchanan and Partners, 1972; Planning Officer, Scottish Office, 1974; Group Leader, Regional Report, Strathclyde Regional Council, 1975; senior executive posts, Strathclyde Regional Council, 1980-91; Assistant Chief Executive, Central Regional Council, 1991-95. Recreations: reading; current affairs; running; hillwalking (double Munroist). Address: (b.) Viewforth, Stirling FK8 2ET; T.-01786 443320.

Young, Alastair Duncan, BSc (Hons), CEng, MICE. Director of Land Services, Glasgow City Council, since 1995; Director, RTI Focus, since 1996; Director, Susiephone Ltd., since 1997; Past Chairman, Society of Chief Officers of Transportation in Scotland; b. 7.6.48, Glasgow; m., Janet U.H. Young; 1 s. Educ. Uddingston Grammar School; Strathclyde University. Technician, Leitch and Sharp; Strathclyde Regional Council, joining as Technician/Engineer, latterly as Regional Network Manager. Recreations: golf; cooking. Address: (b.) Richmond Exchange, 20 Cadogan Street, Glasgow, G2 7AD; T.-0141-287 9100.

Young, Professor Archie, BSc, MBChB, MD, FRCP (Glas), FRCP (Lond), FRCP (Edin). Professor of Geriatric Medicine, University of Edinburgh, since 1998; b. 19.9.46, Glasgow; 1 s. 1 d. Educ. High School of Glasgow. Training posts, Glasgow, London, Oxford; Consultant/Honorary Consultant posts: Oxford Rehabilitation Research Unit, University of Oxford, Royal Free Hospital and Medical School, London; Professor of Geriatric Medicine, Royal Free Hospital Medical School. Recreations: physical. Address: (b.) Geriatric Medicine Unit, 21 Chalmers Street, Edinburgh EH3 9EW.

Young, Chick. Football Correspondent, BBC Television and Radio, since 1988; b. 4.5.51, Glasgow. Educ. Glasgow High School; Bellahouston Academy, Glasgow. Daily Record, 1969-72; Carrick Herald, Girvan, 1972; Irvine Herald, 1972-73; Charles Buchan's Football Monthly, London, 1973-74; Editor, Scottish Football magazine, 1974-75; Scottish Daily News, 1975; Scottish Daily Express, 1976; Evening Times, Glasgow, 1977-88; Radio Clyde, 1977-95; BBC, since 1988; Sunday People, 1988-89; Scotland on Sunday, 1989-91; Columnist, Daily Star, since 1996. Fraser Award, Young Journalist of the Year, 1973; British Provincial Sports Journalist of the Year, 1987; Sony Award, British Sports Broadcaster of the Year (Bronze), 1997; Scottish Sports Journalist of the Year (Runner-up), 1997; RTS Provincial Sports Reporter of the Year, 2000. Publications: Rebirth of the Blues; Mo. Address: (b.) BBC TV Sport, Queen Margaret Drive, Glasgow G12 8DG; T.-0141-338 2622; e-mail: chick.young@bbc.co.uk

Young, Professor Daniel Greer, MB, ChB, FRCSEdin, FRCSGlas, DTM&H. Former Professor of Paediatric Surgery, Glasgow University, now Honorary Senior Research Fellow; former President, British Association of Paediatric Surgeons; b. Skipness, Argyll; m., Agnes Gilchrist Donald; 1 s.; 1 d. Educ. Wishaw High School; Glasgow University. Resident Assistant Surgeon, Hospital for Sick Children, London; Senior Lecturer, Institute of Child Health, London University; Honorary Consultant Surgeon, Hospital for Sick Children, London, and Queen Elizabeth Hospital, Hackney, London; Senior Lecturer and Head, Department of Surgical Paediatrics, Glasgow University, Honorary Consultant Surgeon (retired), Royal Hospital for Sick Children and Stobhill General Hospital, Glasgow; Honorary Senior Research Fellow, Department of Surgical Paediatrics. Honorary Secretary, Lanarkshire Division, British Medical Association; Past President, Royal Medico-Chirurgical Society of Glasgow; Honorary President, Scottish Spina Bifida Association; Member of Council, Royal College of Physicians and Surgeons; Past Chairman, Intercollegiate Board in Paediatric Surgery; Past Chairman, National Paramedic Training Board, Scottish Ambulance Service; former Member, Professional Advisory Group, Scottish Ambulance Service; Past Chairman, West of Scotland Surgical Association; Honorary Member: Hungarian Paediatric Surgical Association, South African Paediatric Surgical Association, American Surgical Paediatric Association; Trustee, Society for Research into Hydrocephalus and Spina Bifida; Denis Browne Gold Medal, 1999. Recreations: curling; fishing; gardening. Address: (b.) Department of Paediatric Surgery, Royal Hospital for Sick Children, Yorkhill, Glasgow G3 8SJ; T.-0141-201 0170.

Young, Dennis James, MA, LLB, TEP. Chairman, Blackadders, Solicitors, Dundee; b. 23.1.42, Forfar; m., Enid; 2 s. Educ. Brechin High School; St. Andrews University. Lectured part-time, Dundee University, for several years; trained, Gray Robertson & Wilkie, Dundee; joined present firm, 1967, becoming Partner, 1969; Founder

Secretary, Committee, Dundee Solicitors' Property Centre, Chairman, 1978-86; Member, Society of Trust and Estates Practitioners (Leader, Tayside and Aberdeen Regional Discussion Group); Dean, Faculty of Procurators and Solicitors in Dundee, 1993-95; Member, Council, Law Society of Scotland, 1996-97. Member, Executive Committee, Scottish Heart and Arterial Disease Risk Prevention (charity). Recreations: golf; football/rugby spectating; listening to music. Address: (b.) 30-34 Reform Street, Dundee DD1 1RJ; T.-01382 229222.

Young, Hugh Kenneth, TD, CA. Vice-Chairman, Lowland Employers Liaison Committee; Chairman, Trustees, Royal Scots Benevolent Society; Trustee, Royal Scots (War Memorial) Club; General Manager and Secretary and Member, Management Board, Bank of Scotland, 1984-96; b. 6.5.36, Galashiels; m., Marjory Bruce Wilson; 2 s.; 1 d. Educ. Edinburgh Academy. National Service, 1959-61; commissioned as 2nd Lt., Royal Scots; TA service, 1957-59, 1961-69 and 1986-92, latterly as Major; with ICFC Ltd., 1962-67; with Schroders Ltd. group, 1967-73, latterly as Manager, J. Henry Schroder Wagg & Co. Ltd.; Local Director in Edinburgh, Edward Bates & Sons Ltd., 1973-75; joined Bank of Scotland, 1975; Head of Corporate Finance, Bank of Scotland Finance Company Ltd., 1976; Director, The British Linen Bank Ltd., 1978-84 (Deputy Chief Executive, 1982-84). Recreations: squash; tennis; hill-walking. Address: (h.) 30 Braid Hills Road, Edinburgh EH10 6HY; T.-0131-447 3101.

Young, Professor Iain McEwing, BSc (Hons), PhD. Professor of Environmental Biophysics, University of Abertay Dundee, since 2000; b. 29.3.62, Paisley; m., Aileen Young; 2s. Educ. Merksworth High School, Paisley; Aberdeen University. Research Assistant, Department of Soil Science, Aberdeen University, 1984-87; Research Scientist, Scottish Crop Research Institute, 1988-2000; Member, BBSRC/NERC Soil Advisory Committee. Recreations: cinema; reading; squash; football. Address: (b.) Abertay University, Dundee, Bell Street, Dundee, DD1 1HG; T.-01382 308230; e-mail: imy@tay.ac.uk

Young, James Drummond, LLB, NP. Solicitor (Partner, McGrigor Donald, since 1985); b. 26.2.50, Broughty Ferry; m., Gillian Anne Boyd; 1 s.; 1 d. Educ. Hutchesons' Grammar School; Glasgow University. Apprentice, then Legal Assistant, McGrigor Donald & Co., 1971-75; Legal Officer, West Lothian District Council, 1975-77; Legal Assistant, then Partner, Moncrieff Warren Paterson & Co., 1977-85. Elder, Greenbank Church; Contributor, Employment Precedents and Company Policy Documents. Recreations: golf; contemporary art; cricket. Address: (b.) Princes Exchange, 1 Earl Grey Street, Edinburgh EH3 9AQ; T.-0131-226 7777; e-mail: jim.young@mcgrigors.com

Young, John Graeme Bennett, MA (Hons), PhD, DipEd. Director of Education Services, Falkirk Council, since 1995; b. 31.10.50, Bridge of Allan; m., Shena; 2 s. Educ. Striling High School; University of Glasgow; University of Edinburgh. Teacher of History and Modern Studies, Dalziel High School, Motherwell, 1976-81; Principal Teacher of History and Modern Studies, Tain Royal Academy, Ross-shire, 1981-85; Assistant Divisional Education Officer, Inverness, Highland Region, 1985-88; Assistant Director of Education/Head of Resources, Central Region, 1988-95. Recreations: reading; gardening; walking; sport (as a spectator). Address: (h.) Morven, Doune Road, Dunblane FK15 9AT; T.-01786 822305.

Young, John Henderson, OBE, JP, DL, KSJ, FIMgt. MSP (Conservative), West of Scotland, since 1999; Member, Scottish Parliament Corporate Body; Deputy Lieutenant of Glasgow, since 1981; Chairman, Association of Scottish Conservative Councillors, 1991-94; Hon. President, since 1994; Member, SPTA, 1996-99; Local Government Commissioner, Rifkind Policy Commission, 1998; Scottish Conservative Transport Spokesman, 1998; Member, Strathclyde Passenger Transport Authority; b. 21.12.30, Glasgow; m., Doris Paterson (deceased); 1 s. Educ. Hillhead High School, Glasgow; Scottish College of Commerce. RAF, 1949-51. Councillor, Glasgow Corporation, 1964-73, Glasgow District Council, 1974-96; City of Glasgow Council, 1996-99; Police Judge, 1971-72; Bailie/Magistrate of Glasgow on four occasions; Leader, Glasgow City Council, 1977-79, Leader of the Opposition, 1979-80, 1988-92, from 1996-98 (City of Glasgow Council); former Chairman/Vice-Chairman, Council committees; Parliamentary candidate (Conservative), Rutherglen, 1966, Cathcart, 1992, Eastwood, 1999; former Chairman, Cathcart Conservatives; Chairman, Glasgow Euro Constituency, 1987-91; Export Manager, Teacher's Whisky; Public Relations Consultant; former Vice-Chairman, Scottish Pakistani Association; Secretary, Scottish/South African Society, 1986-88; Governor, Hutcheson's Educational Trust, 1991-97; Member, Glasgow Sports Promotion Council; Life Member, Merchants House of Glasgow; Kentucky Colonel, 1984; Hon. Don Cossack (Russia), 1989; Lord Provost's Award, 1989. Publication: A History of Cathcart Conservative Association, 1918-93. Recreations: meeting people; history; reading; animal welfare. Address: (h.) 4 Deanwood Avenue, Netherlee, Glasgow G44 3RJ; T.-0141-637 9535.

Young, John Maclennan, OBE. Farmer, since 1949; Hon. Sheriff, Grampian, Highlands and Islands, since 1995; JP for Caithness, 1970-99; b. 6.6.33, Thurso. Educ. Thurso Miller Academy. Member, Caithness County Council, 1961-75 (Chairman, Housing Committee, 1968-73, Chairman, Planning Committee, 1973-75); Member, Highland Regional Council, 1974-90 (Chairman, Roads and Transport Committee, 1978-90); Member, The Highland Council, 1995-99; Provost of Caithness, 1995-99; Member, Caithness District Council, 1974-96 (Convener of the Council, 1974-96); President, Caithness Area Executive Commitee, NFU of Scotland, 1963 and 1964; Vice-Chairman, Scrabster Harbour Trust, since 1999; Chairman, Wick Airport Consultative Committee, since 1990. Address: (b.) Sordale, Halkirk, Caithness KW12 6XB; T.-01847 831228.

Young, Laurence Mitchell, MBE (1998). Director, Discovery Award Association, since 1995; b. 2.7.27, Dundee; m., Margaret Thomson Fawns; 1 s.; 1 d. Educ. Stobswell Junior Secondary School; Dundee Training College. Early career in building industry; military service, King's Own Scottish Borderers, 1945-48; joined Stobswell Boys' School, 1956; Technical Teacher, 1956-67, Special Assistant, 1967-73; Principal Teacher of Guidance, Craigie High School, Dundee, 1973-87; retired, 1987; involved with Duke of Edinburgh Award, since 1964: Group Scheme Leader to Stobswell Boys' School, 1964-73, Group Leader, Craigie High School, 1973-87, Duke of Edinburgh Counsellor and Advisor for Dundee, 1969-92, Secretary/Treasurer, Dundee District Award Co-ordination Committee, since 1974; Co-Founder, Tay Award, 1985-96; Founder Member, Discovery Award, since 1987: Group Leader, Pilot Group, 1987-89, Chairman, Dundee Group, 1989-93; Chairman, Association Steering Group, 1993-95; Elder, Church of Scotland, since 1968. Recreations: family; people. Address: (h.) 124 Tweed Crescent, Menzieshill, Dundee DD2 4DS; T.-01382 641800.

Young, Mark Richard, BSc, PhD, FRES, FIBiol, CBiol. Senior Lecturer, Aberdeen University, since 1989; Director, Culterty Field Station, since 1996; Member, North Board, Scottish Environment Protection Agency, since 1996; b. 27.10.48, Worcester; m., Jennifer Elizabeth Tully; 1 s.; 1 d. Educ. Kings School, Worcester; Birmingham University. Lecturer, Aberdeen University, 1973-89. Recreations: natural history; walking; ball sports; visiting Hebridean islands. Address: (b.) Culterty Field Station, Department of

Zoology, University of Aberdeen, Newburgh, Ellon, Aberdeenshire AB41 6AA; T.-01224 274420; e-mail: m.young@abdn.ac.uk

Young, Neil J., BArch, DipArch, RIBA, FIAS. Senior Partner, Young and Gault, Architects, since 1989; b. 13.8.53, Glasgow; m., May; 1 s.; 1 d. Educ. Speir's School, Beith; Glasgow University; Mackintosh School of Architecture. Founder, Young and Gault Architects, 1989. Director: British Youth for Christ, Mission Scotland, Bolivian Community Project. Recreations: church; charities; travel. Address: (b.) 28 Speirs Wharf, Glasgow G4 9TB; T.-0141-332 2225.

Young, Professor Stephen, BCom, MSc. Professor of International Business, Strathclyde University, since 1987, Head, Department of Marketing, 1992-96; b. 20.8.44, Berwick upon Tweed; 1 s.; 1 d. Educ. Berwick Grammar School; Liverpool University; Newcastle University. Economist, Government of Tanzania; Head, International Economics Department, Milk Marketing Board, 1969-73; Lecturer/Senior Lecturer, Paisley College of Technology, 1973-79; Senior Lecturer then Professor, Strathclyde Business School (Director, Strathclyde International Business Unit, from 1983). Recreations: mountaineering; cycling; running. Address: (h.) 42 Brierie Gardens, Crosslee, Johnstone PA6 7BZ; T.-01505 615554.

Young, Sheriff Principal Sir Stephen Stewart Templeton, 3rd Bt. Sheriff Principal of Grampian, Highland and Islands, since 2001; b. 24.5.47; m.; 2 s. Educ. Rugby; Trinity College, Oxford; Edinburgh University. Sheriff, Glasgow and Strathkelvin, 1984; Sheriff of North Strathclyde at Greenock, 1984-2001. Address: (b.) Sheriff Court House, Castle Street, Aberdeen AB10 1WP.

Young, William Smith Geates, LLB (Hons), NP. Managing Partner, Brechin Tindal Oatts, since 1997; b. 21.12.55, Girvan; m., Margot Glanville Jones. Educ. Girvan Academy; Glasgow University. Joined Tindal Oatts & Rodger, 1978; admitted as Solicitor, 1980; Managing Partner, Tindal Oatts, 1993. SFA Class 1 Referee List, 1990; FIFA List of International Linesmen, 1992, 1993; FIFA List of International Referees, 1994-2000. Recreations: football; golf; after-dinner speaking. Address: (b.) 48 St. Vincent Street, Glasgow G2 5HS; T.-0141-221 8012; e-mail: wsgy@bto.co.uk

Younger of Leckie, Rt. Hon. Viscount (George Kenneth Hotson Younger), KT, KCVO, TD, DL. Chairman, The Royal Bank of Scotland Group plc, 1991-2001; Lord High Commissioner to the General Assembly of the Church of Scotland, 2001-02; b. 22.9.31; m., Diana Rhona Tuck; 3 s.; 1 d. Educ. Cargilfield School, Edinburgh; Winchester College; New College, Oxford. Argyll and Sutherland Highlanders, 1950-51; 7th Bn., Argyll and Sutherland Highlanders (TA), 1951-65; Honorary Colonel, 154 (Lowland) Transport Regiment, RCT T&AVR, 1977-85; Director: George Younger & Son Ltd., 1958-68; J.G. Thomson & Co. Ltd., Leith, 1962-66; Maclachlans Ltd., 1968-70; Tennant Caledonian Breweries, 1977-79; Non Executive Director: The Royal Bank of Scotland Group plc, 1989; Murray International Trust PLC, 1989 (Chairman); Murray Global Return Trust PLC, 1989-2000 (Chairman); The Royal Yacht Britannia Trust (Chairman of Trustees); Banco Santander Central Hispano, 1991-2001; Royal Armouries Board of Trustees, 1994 (Chairman); The Fleming Mercantile Investment Trust PLC, 1994; The White Ensign Association; contested North Lanarkshire, 1959; Unionist Candidate, Kinross and West Perthshire, 1963 (stood down in favour of Sir Alec Douglas-Home); MP (Conservative), Ayr, 1964-92; Scottish Conservative Whip, 1965-67; Parliamentary Under-Secretary of State for Development, Scottish Office, 1970-74; Minister of State for Defence, 1974; Secretary of State for Scotland, 1979-86; Chairman, Conservative Party in Scotland, 1974-75

(Deputy Chairman, 1967-70); Secretary of State for Defence, 1986-89; President, National Union of Conservative and Unionist Associations, 1987-88. Brigadier, Queen's Bodyguard for Scotland (Royal Company of Archers); appointed Knight of the Most Ancient and Noble Order of the Thistle, 1995; DL, Stirlingshire, 1968. Recreations: music; tennis; sailing; golf. Address: (b.) 42 St. Andrew Square, Edinburgh EH2 2YE; T.-0131-556 8555.

Younger, John David Bingham, JP. Lord-Lieutenant of Tweeddale, since 1994; b. 20.5.39, Doune; m., Anne Rosaleen Logan; 1 s.; 2 d. Educ. Eton College; Royal Military Academy, Sandhurst. Argyll and Sutherland Highlanders, 1957-69; Scottish and Newcastle Breweries, 1969-79; Managing Director, Broughton Brewery Ltd., 1979-95; Director, Broughton Ales, 1995-96. Deputy Lieutenant, Tweeddale, 1987. Chairman, Board of Governors, Belhaven Hill School Trust, 1988; Chairman, Scottish Borders Tourist Board, 1989; Member, A&SH Regimental Trust and Committee, 1985; Member, Queen's Bodyguard for Scotland (Royal Company of Archers) since 1969, Secretary, since 1993; Vice President, RHASS, 1994. Recreation: the countryside. Address: (h.) Kirkurd House, Blyth Bridge, Peeblesshire EH46 7AH; T.-01721 752223.

Younger, Sheriff Robert Edward Gilmour, MA, LLB. Sheriff of Tayside, Central and Fife, at Stirling, since 1992 (Stirling and Alloa, 1987-92); b. 25.9.40, Stirling; m., Helen Jane Hayes; 1 s.; 1 d. Educ. Winchester; New College, Oxford; Edinburgh University; Glasgow University. Advocate, 1968-79; Sheriff of Glasgow and Strathkelvin, at Glasgow, 1979-82, and of Tayside, Central and Fife, at Stirling and Falkirk, 1982-87. Recreation:wondering. Address: (h.) Old Leckie, Gargunnock, Stirling; T.-01786 860213.

Youngson, Professor George Gray, MB, ChB, PhD, FRCSEdin. Consultant Surgeon, Royal Aberdeen Children's Hospital, since 1985; Honorary Professor of Paediatric Surgery, Aberdeen University, since 1999; b. 13.5.49, Glasgow; m., Sandra Jean Lister; 1 s.; 2 d. Educ. Buckhaven High School; Aberdeen University. House Officer to Professor George Smith, 1973; Research Fellow, 1975; Registrar in General Surgery, 1975-77; Senior Resident in Cardiac and Thoracic Surgery, University Hospital, London, Ontario, 1979; Lecturer in Clinical Surgery, Aberdeen University, 1981; Clinical Fellow, Paediatric Surgery, Hospital for Sick Children, Toronto, 1983; Lecturer in Surgical Paediatrics and Transplantation, Aberdeen University, 1984; Regional Advisor and Examiner, Royal College of Surgeons of Edinburgh. Recreations: sport (tennis, golf and squash); music (piobaireachd, guitar). Address: (h.) Birken Lodge, Bieldside, Aberdeen.

Z

Zealley, Andrew King, MB, ChB, FRCP, FRCPsych, DPM. Deputy Chairman, The State Hospitals Board for Scotland; formerly Consultant Psychiatrist, Lothian Health Board and Honorary Senior Lecturer, Edinburgh University; b. 28.10.35, Stockton-on-Tees; m., Dr. Helen Elizabeth Zealley (qv); 1 s.; 1 d. Educ. Sherborne School; Edinburgh University. Chairman, Lothian Area Medical Committee, 1978-88; Chairman, Lothian Research Ethics Committee, since 1988; Physician Superintendent, Royal Edinburgh Hospital, 1984-94; Medical Director, Edinburgh Healthcare NHS Trust, 1994-96. Publications include: Companion to Psychiatric Studies, 6th edition (Co-editor). Recreations: running; sailing; skiing. Address: (h.) Viewfield House, Tipperlinn Road, Edinburgh EH10 5ET; T.-0131-447 5545; e-mail: andrewzealley@hotmail.com

Zealley, Helen Elizabeth, OBE, QHP, MD, FRCPE, FFPHM. Chief Administrative Medical Officer and Director of Public Health, Lothian Health Board, 1988-2000; Honorary Senior Lecturer, Edinburgh University, 1988-2000; b. 10.6.40; m., Dr. Andrew Zealley (qv); 1 s.; 1 d. Educ. St. Albans High School; Edinburgh University. Former Member, Council, Royal College of Physicians, Edinburgh; former Member, Board, Faculty of Public Health Medicine; Vice President, British Association of Early Childhood Education (Hon. President, Lothian Branch); Vice President, MedAct; former Member, Court, Edinburgh University. Recreations: family and home; sailing; skiing; travel. Address: (b.) 12 Tipperlinn Road, Edinburgh EH10 5ET; T.-0131-447 5545.

Ziolkowski, Professor Anton Marjan, FRSE, MA, PhD, MSc(Econ). Professor of Petroleum Geoscience, Edinburgh University, since 1992; Guest Professor, Changchun University of Science and Technology, China, since 1997; b. 14.7.46, London; m., Kate Crowley; 2 s.; 1 d. Educ. William Ellis School, London; Chislehurst and Sidcup County Grammar School for Boys; Trinity Hall, Cambridge; London School of Economics. Staff Member, Seismic Discrimination Group, Lincoln Laboratory, Massachusetts Institute of Technology, 1971-73; Headquarters Geophysicist, National Coal Board, London, 1976-80; Independent Consultant to British National Oil Corporation, London, 1980-82; Professor of Applied Geophysics, Delft University of Technology, Netherlands, 1982-92. Publications: Deconvolution, 1984; The Vibroseis Source (Co-author), 1990. Address: (b.) Department of Geology and Geophysics, Edinburgh University, Grant Institute, King's Buildings, West Mains Road, Edinburgh EH9 3JW; T.-0131-650 8515.

von Zugbach de Sugg, Professor Reginald (Reggie) Gordon Leslie, KLJ, MA, PhD, MBIM, FMS, ACP. Emeritus Professor in Management, Paisley University, since 2000; b. 20.2.44, Derbyshire; m., Theda Claudia Susanna Stapelfeldt. Educ. City of London College; Brighton Polytechnic; London University Institute of Education; UMIST. Member, Honourable Artillery Company; Regular Army Officer (Major RAOC), 1968-86; Director of Undergraduate Studies, Glasgow Business School, Glasgow University, 1986-90; Professor in Management, Paisley University, 1990-2000; author of numerous papers; books: Power and Prestige in the British Army, 1988; The Winning Manager, 1995; Nur Einzelkampfer Siegen, 1996; Mr Downsizing, 1998; Guidon Bearer to The McKerrell of Hillhouse. Recreations: horses; dogs; real tennis; literature. Address: (h.) 7 Dowanside Road, Dowanhill, Glasgow; T.-0141-337 2228; e-mail: zugbach@ukonline.co.uk

Index to Advertisers